CROSSWORD
SOLVER

CROSSWORD
SOLVER

EDITED BY ANNE STIBBS

BLOOMSBURY

First published in 1988

Second edition published in 1995
Third edition published in 1997

This combined edition published in 2002 by
Bloomsbury Publishing Plc
38 Soho Square
London W1D 3HB

Copyright © 1988, 1995, 1997, 2000, 2002 by Bloomsbury Publishing Plc

A copy of the CIP entry for this book is available from
the British Library

ISBN 0 7475 5997 X

10 9 8 7 6 5 4 3 2 1

Compiled and typeset by Market House Books Ltd, Aylesbury
Printed in Great Britain by Clays Ltd, St Ives plc

INTRODUCTION

This book consists of a set of lists of words specifically designed to help crossword-puzzle solvers. We have included over 100,000 English words organized into words with two letters, words with three letters, four letters, etc., up to fifteen letters. Within each section, the words are arranged alphabetically.

The words chosen include proper nouns, names of people and places, as well as common two- and three-word phrases. We have also given, in many cases, plurals of nouns, comparatives and superlatives of adjectives, and inflections of verbs. In general, '–ize' endings have been used for verbs. It should be noted that '–ise' endings are also possible for these.

We hope that the book will prove useful to all who enjoy doing crossword puzzles – and, in particular, to those who enjoy completing them.

AS

May, 2000

A	D	HI	M	PE	U
AA	DA	H'M	MA	PH	UK
AB	DJ	HO	ME	PI	UM
AC	DO	HQ	MI	PM	UN
AD			MO	PR	UP
AG	**E**	**I**	MP	PS	US
AH	EH	ID	MR	PT	UU
AI	ER	IF	MS	PX	
AM	EU	IN	MY		**V**
AN	EX	IQ		**Q**	VC
AS		IT	**N**	QC	VD
AT	**F**		NO	QT	VJ
AW	FA	**J**			VS
	FE	JP	**O**	**R**	
B	FM		OF	RE	**W**
BE		**K**	OH		WC
BO	**G**	KC	ON	**S**	WE
BY	GI	KO	OP	SH	
	GO		OR	SO	**X**
C	GP	**L**	OW		XU
CB	GS	LA	OX	**T**	
CD		LO		TA	**Y**
CO	**H**	LP	**P**	TI	YE
CV	HA	LR	PA	TO	YO
	HE		PC	TV	

1

A
A
ABC
ABH
ABO
ACE
ACT
ADD
ADJ
ADO
ADS
ADV
AFT
AGE
AGM
AGO
AHA
AID
AIL
AIM
AIR
A LA
ALE
ALL
AMP
AND
ANT
ANY
AOC
APB
APE
APP
APT
ARB
ARC
ARK
ARM
ART
ASH
ASK
ASP
ASS
ATE
ATM
AUK
AWE
AWL
AXE
AYE

B
BAA
BAD
BAG
BAH
BAN
BAR
BAT
BAY
BBC
BBQ
BED
BEE
BEG
BEN
BET
BIB
BID
BIG
BIN
BIO-
BIT
BOA
BOB
BOD
BOG
BOO
BOP
BOW
BOX
BOY
BPI
BPS
BRA
BUB
BUD
BUG
BUM
BUN
BUR
BUS
BUT
BUY
BYE

C
CAB
CAD
CAM
CAN
CAP
CAR
CAT
CAW
CDS
CIA
CID
CIS
CJD
CND
CNS
COB
COD
COG
COL
CON
COO
COP
COS
COT
COW
COX
COY
CPA
CPS
CPU
CRC
CRY
CSE
CUB
CUD
CUE
CUM
CUP
CUR
CUT
CVS
CWM

D
DAB
DAD
DAM
DAY
DDI
DDR
DDT
DEB
DEF
DEM
DEN
DEP
DEW
DID
DIE
DIG
DIM
DIN
DIP
DIS
DIY
DJS
DNA
DOC
DOE
DOG
DOH
DON
DOR
DOS
DOT
DRY
D T'S
DUB
DUD
DUE
DUG
DUN
DUO
DYE

E
EAR
EAT
EBB
ECG
ECT
EEC
EEK
EEL
EFF
EGG
EGO
EKG
ELF
ELK
ELM
ELT
EMU
ENC
END
EON
EPS
ERA
ERE
ERG
ERR
ESP
ESQ
EST
ETC
EVE
EWE
EYE

F
FAB
FAD
FAG
FAN
FAR
FAT
FAX
FAY
FBI
FED
FEE
FEN
FEW
FEY
FEZ
FIB
FIE
FIG
FIN
FIR
FIT
FIX
FLU
FLY
FOB
FOE
FOG
FOP
FOR
FOX
FRO
FRY
FUG
FUN
FUR

G
GAB
GAD
GAG
GAL
GAP
GAS
GAY
GCE
GDP
GEC
GEE
GEL
GEM
GEN
GET
GIG
GIN
GI'S
GNP
GNU
GOA
GOB
GOD
GOO
GOP
GOT
GPS
GUM
GUN
GUT
GUV
GUY
GYM
GYP

H
HAD
HAE
HAG
HAH
HAM
HAN
HAP
HAS
HAT
HAW
HAY
HE'D
HEH
HEL
HEM
HEN
HEP
HER
HE'S

HET	IRE	LED	MOW	O'ER	PLY
HEW	IRK	LEE	MPS	OFF	PMS
HEX	ISM	LEG	MRI	OFT	POD
HEY	ITS	LEI	MRS	OHM	POP
HIB	ITV	LEO	MSC	OHO	POT
HIC	IUD	LET	MUD	OIK	POW
HID	IVY	LEV	MUG	OIL	POX
HIE		LIB	MUM	OLD	PPS
HIM	**J**	LID		ONE	PRE-
HIN	JAB	LIE	**N**	OOF	PRO
HIP	JAG	LIG	NAB	OPS	PRY
HIS	JAM	LIP	NAD	OPT	PTA
HIT	JAR	LIT	NAG	ORB	PTO
HOB	JAW	LOB	NAN	ORE	PUB
HOD	JAY	LOG	NAP	OTT	PUD
HOE	JET	LOO	NAV	OUR	PUG
HOG	JEW	LOP	NAY	OUT	PUN
HOM	JIB	LOT	NCO	OVA	PUP
HOO	JIG	LOW	NEC	OWE	PUS
HOP	JIT	LOX	NEE	OWL	PUT
HOT	JOB	LPS	NEG	OWN	PVC
HOW	JOG	LSD	NET		PYX
HOY	JOT	LUG	NEW	**P**	
HQS	JOY	LUV	NFL	PAD	**Q**
HRT	JPS		NHS	PAL	QCS
HSI	JUG	**M**	NIB	PAN	QUA
HUB	JUT	MAC	NIL	PAP	
HUE		MAD	NIP	PAR	**R**
HUG	**K**	MAG	NIT	PAS	RAD
HUH	KEG	MAM	NIX	PAT	RAF
HUM	KEN	MAN	NOB	PAW	RAG
HUN	KEY	MAP	NOD	PAY	RAI
HUT	KID	MAR	NON-	PCS	RAJ
	KIN	MAS	NOR	PEA	RAM
I	KIP	MAT	NOT	PEE	RAN
ICE	KIT	MAW	NOW	PEG	RAP
ICY	KOB	MAY	NRA	PEN	RAT
IDS	KOI	MEN	NSA	PEP	RAW
IFS		MET	NSU	PER	RAY
ILK	**L**	MEW	NTH	PET	REC
ILL	LAB	MIA	NUB	PEW	RED
IMP	LAD	MID	NUN	PHD	REF
INC	LAG	MIS	NUT	PHS	REP
INF	LAN	MIX		PIE	REV
INK	LAP	MOB	**O**	PIG	REX
INN	LAW	MOD	OAF	PIN	RIA
ION	LAX	MOM	OAK	PIP	RIB
IOU	LAY	MOO	OAP	PIS	RID
IPA	LCD	MOP	OAR	PIT	RIG
IQS	LCM	MOS	ODD	PIX	RIM
IRA	LEA	MOT	ODE	PLC	RIP

RNA	SEW	SUM	TOY	VET	WOO
ROB	SEX	SUN	TRY	VEX	WOP
ROC	SHE	SUP	TSK	VGA	WOT
ROD	SHY		TUB	VGC	WOW
ROE	SIC	**T**	TUC	VHF	WPC
ROM	SIN	TAB	TUG	VIA	WRY
ROT	SIP	TAG	TUT	VIE	
ROW	SIR	TAN	TVS	VIM	**Y**
RSE	SIS	TAP	TWO	VIP	YAK
RSI	SIT	TAR		VIZ	YAM
RUB	SIX	TAT	**U**	VLF	YAP
RUE	SKA	TAX	UFO	VOW	YAW
RUG	SKI	TEA	UGH	VTR	YEA
RUM	SKY	TEC	UHF		YEN
RUN	SLY	TEE	UMP	**W**	YES
RUT	SOB	TEN	UNI-	WAD	YET
RYE	SOD	THE	URN	WAG	YEW
	SOH	THY	USE	WAN	YID
S	SOL	TIA		WAR	YIN
SAC	SON	TIC	**V**	WAX	YOB
SAD	SOP	TIE	UTC	WAY	YOU
SAE	SOS	TIN	UTD	WEB	YTS
SAG	SOT	TIP	UVA	WED	
SAP	SOU	TIT	UVB	WEE	**Z**
SAT	SOW	TNT	UVC	WET	ZAP
SAW	SOX	TOD	UZI	WHO	ZED
SAY	SOY	TOE	VAC	WHY	ZEN
SDI	SPA	TOG	VAN	WIG	ZIG
SDP	SPY	TON	VAR	WIN	ZIP
SEA	STD	TOO	VAT	WIT	ZOO
SEC	STY	TOP	VCR	WOE	
SEE	SUB	TOR	VCS	WOG	
SEM	SUE	TOT	VDU	WOK	
SET	SUG	TOW	VEG	WON	

A	ALLY	AT IT	BARB	BILE	BORE
ABCS	ALMS	ATOM	BARD	BILK	BORN
ABED	ALOE	ATOP	BARE	BILL	BORT
ABET	ALPS	AUBE	BARI	BIND	BOSH
ABIA	ALSO	AUDE	BARK	BINS	BOSS
ABLE	ALTO	AUKS	BARN	BIRD	BOTH
ABLY	ALUM	AUNT	BARS	BIRL	BOUT
ABOS	AMBO	AURA	BASE	BIRO	BOWL
ABUT	AMEN	AUTO	BASH	BITE	BOWS
ACCT	AMEX	AVER	BASK	BITS	BOYS
AC/DC	AMID	AVID	BASS	BLAB	BOZO
ACER	AMIR	AVON	BAST	BLAG	BRAE
ACES	AMIS	AVOW	BATH	BLAH	BRAG
ACHE	AMOK	AWAY	BATS	BLED	BRAN
ACID	AMOY	AWED	BAUD	BLEW	BRAS
ACME	AMPS	AWLS	BAWD	BLIP	BRAT
ACNE	ANAL	AWOL	BAWL	BLOB	BRAY
ACRE	ANEW	AWRY	BAYS	BLOC	BREW
ACTS	ANKH	AXED	BEAD	BLOT	BRIM
ADAM	ANON	AXES	BEAK	BLOW	BRIT
ADEN	ANSI	AXIS	BEAM	BLUE	BRNO
ADZE	ANTE	AXLE	BEAN	BLUR	BROW
AEON	ANTI-	AYAH	BEAR	BOAR	BROZ
AERO-	ANTS	AYES	BEAT	BOAS	BUBO
AFAR	ANUS		BEAU	BOAT	BUBS
AFRO	APED	**B**	BECK	BOBS	BUCK
AGAL	APES	BAAS	BEDS	BODE	BUDS
AGED	APEX	BABE	BEEF	BODS	BUFF
AGES	APSE	BABU	BEER	BODY	BUGS
AGMS	AQUA	BABY	BEES	BOER	BULB
AGOG	ARAB	BACH	BEET	BOGS	BULK
AGRA	ARAN	BACK	BELL	BOIL	BULL
AGUE	ARCH	BADE	BELT	BOLD	BUMF
AHEM	ARCS	BAEZ	BEND	BOLE	BUMP
AHOY	ARDS	BAGS	BENS	BOLL	BUMS
AIDE	AREA	BAIL	BENT	BOLT	BUNA
AIDS	AREG	BAIT	BERK	BOMA	BUNG
AIMS	ARIA	BAJA	BERN	BOMB	BUNK
AIN'T	ARID	BAKE	BEST	BOND	BUNS
AINU	ARKS	BAKU	BETA	BONE	BUOY
AIRE	ARMS	BALD	BETS	BONN	BUPA
AIRS	ARMY	BALE	BEVY	BONY	BURB
AIRY	ARSE	BALI	BIAS	BOOB	BURK
AJAR	ARTS	BALK	BIBS	BOOK	BURN
AKIN	ARTY	BALL	BIDE	BOOM	BURP
ALAI	ASHY	BALM	BIDS	BOON	BURR
ALAR	ASIA	BAND	BIEL	BOOR	BURS
ALAS	AS IF	BANE	BIER	BOOS	BURY
ALBI	ASIR	BANG	BIFF	BOOT	BUSH
ALIT	ASPS	BANK	BIFU	BOPS	BUSK
ALKY	ASTI	BANS	BIKE	BORA	BUSS

BUST	CELL	COED	CROP	DAUB	DISS
BUSY	CENT	COGS	CROW	DAWN	DIVE
BUTE	CERT	COIF	CRUS	DAYS	DMSO
BUTS	CHAD	COIL	CRUX	DAZE	DOCK
BUTT	CHAP	COIN	CSES	D-DAY	DOCS
BUYS	CHAR	COIR	CUBA	DEAD	DODO
BUZZ	CHAT	COKE	CUBE	DEAF	DOER
BYES	CHEB	COLA	CUBS	DEAL	DOES
BYOB	CHEF	COLD	CUED	DEAN	DOFF
BYRE	CHER	COLS	CUES	DEAR	DOGE
BYTE	CHEW	COLT	CUFF	DEBS	DOGS
	CHIC	COMA	CULL	DEBT	DOHA
C	CHID	COMB	CULM	DECK	DO IT
CABS	CHIN	COME	CULT	DEED	DOLE
CADS	CHIP	COMO	CUNT	DEEM	DOLL
CAEN	CHIT	CONE	CUPS	DEEP	DOLT
CAFE	CHOP	CONK	CURB	DEER	DOME
CAGE	CHOU	CONS	CURD	DEFT	DONE
CAKE	CHOW	CONY	CURE	DEFY	DONS
CALF	CHUG	COOK	CURL	DELE	DON'T
CALI	CHUM	COOL	CURS	DELL	DOOM
CALK	CHUR	COON	CURT	DEMO	DOOR
CALL	C-IN-C	COOP	CUSP	DENS	DOPE
CALM	CINE-	COOS	CUSS	DENT	DORY
CALX	CITE	COOT	CUTE	DENY	DOSE
CAME	CITY	COPE	CUTS	DERV	DOSH
CAMP	CLAD	COPS	CYAN	DESK	DOSS
CAMS	CLAM	COPY	CYME	DEWY	DOTE
CANE	CLAN	CORD	CYST	DFEE	DOTS
CANS	CLAP	CORE	CZAR	DHAK	DOUR
CANT	CLAW	CORK		DHOW	DOVE
CAPE	CLAY	CORM	**D**	DIAL	DOWN
CAPO	CLEF	CORN	DABS	DICE	DOZE
CAPS	CLEW	COSH	DADO	DICK	DOZY
CARD	CLIP	COST	DADS	DIED	DRAB
CARE	CLOD	COSY	DAFT	DIET	DRAG
CARP	CLOG	COTS	DAGO	DIGS	DRAM
CARS	CLOP	COUP	DAIS	DIKE	DRAT
CART	CLOT	COVE	DALE	DILL	DRAW
CASE	CLOY	COWL	DAME	DIME	DRAY
CASH	CLUB	COWS	DAMN	DINE	DREW
CASK	CLUE	COXA	DAMP	DINK	DRIP
CAST	CLUJ	COZY	DAMS	DINS	DROP
CATS	COAL	CRAB	DANK	DINT	DRUB
CAUL	COAT	CRAG	DARE	DIPS	DRUG
CAVE	COAX	CRAM	DARK	DIRE	DRUM
CAVY	COBS	CRAP	DARN	DIRK	DUAL
CAWS	COCK	CRED	DART	DIRT	DUCK
CEDE	CODA	CREW	DASH	DISC	DUCT
CEDI	CODE	CRIB	DATA	DISH	DUDE
CELA	CODS	CROC	DATE	DISK	DUDS

DUEL	EGER	FAFF	FIRS	FOUL	GATE
DUES	EGGS	FAGS	FISH	FOUR	GAVE
DUET	EGOS	FAIL	FIST	FOWL	GAWD
DUFF	EIRE	FAIN	FITS	FOXY	GAWK
DUGS	ELAN	FAIR	FIVE	FRAP	GAWP
DUKE	ELBA	FAKE	FIZZ	FRAU	GAYA
DULL	ELBE	FALL	FLAB	FRAY	GAYS
DULY	ELIA	FAME	FLAG	FREE	GAZA
DUMA	ELKS	FANG	FLAK	FRET	GAZE
DUMB	ELMS	FANS	FLAN	FRIT	GCES
DUMP	ELSE	FARE	FLAP	FROE	GCSE
DUNE	EMIR	FARM	FLAT	FROG	G'DAY
DUNG	EMIT	FART	FLAW	FROM	GEAR
DUNK	EMUS	FAST	FLAX	FUCK	GEEK
DUNS	ENDS	FATE	FLAY	FUEL	GELD
DUOS	ENVY	FATS	FLEA	FUJI	GELS
DUPE	EONS	FAUN	FLED	FULL	GEMS
DUSK	EPEE	FAUX	FLEE	FUME	GENE
DUST	EPIC	FAWN	FLEW	FUMY	GENK
DUTY	ERAS	FAZE	FLEX	FUND	GENT
DWEM	ERGO	FEAR	FLIP	FUNK	GENU
DYAD	ERGS	FEAT	FLIT	FURL	GERA
DYED	ERIE	FEED	FLOE	FURS	GERM
DYER	ERNE	FEEL	FLOG	FURY	GERS
DYES	ERSE	FEES	FLOP	FUSE	GHAT
DYKE	ESPY	FEET	FLOW	FUSS	GHEE
DYNE	ET AL	FELL	FLUE	FUZZ	GIBE
	ETCH	FELT	FLUX		GIFT
E	ETON	FEND	FOAL	**G**	GIFU
EACH	EURE	FENS	FOAM	GAFF	GIGS
EARL	EURO	FERN	FOBS	GAGA	GILD
EARN	EVEN	FESS	FOCI	GAGE	GILL
EARS	EVER	FEST	FOES	GAGS	GILT
EASE	EVES	FETE	FOGS	GAIA	GIMP
EAST	EVIL	FEUD	FOGY	GAIN	GINS
EASY	EWER	FIAT	FOHN	GAIT	GIRD
EATS	EWES	FIBS	FOIL	GALA	GIRL
EBBS	EXAM	FIFE	FOLD	GALE	GIRO
ECGS	EXES	FIGS	FOLK	GALL	GIRT
ECHO	EXIT	FIJI	FOND	GALS	GISH
ECRU	EYED	FILE	FONT	GAME	GIST
EDAM	EYES	FILL	FOOD	GAMY	GIVE
EDDO	EYOT	FILM	FOOL	GANG	GIZA
EDDY	EYRE	FILO	FOOT	GAOL	GLAD
EDEN		FILS	FOPS	GAPE	GLEE
EDGE	**F**	FIND	FORA	GAPS	GLEN
EDGY	FACE	FINE	FORD	GARB	GLIB
EDIT	FACT	FINN	FORE	GARD	GLOW
EDTA	FADE	FINS	FORK	GARY	GLUE
EELS	FADO	FIRE	FORM	GASH	GLUM
EFIK	FADS	FIRM	FORT	GASP	GLUT

7

GNAT	GURU	HAST	HIND	HOVE	IDOL
GNAW	GUSH	HATE	HINT	HOWE	IFFY
GNUS	GUST	HATH	HIPS	HOWF	IGBO
GOAD	GUTS	HATS	HIRE	HOWL	IKBS
GOAL	GUVS	HAUL	HISS	HOYA	IKON
GOAT	GUYS	HAVE	HIST	HUBS	ILEX
GOBI	GYBE	HAWK	HITS	HUED	ILLS
GOBO	GYMS	HAZE	HIVE	HUES	IMAM
GOBS		HAZY	HOAD	HUFF	IMAX
GODS	**H**	HEAD	HOAR	HUGE	IMPI
GOER	HAAF	HEAL	HOAX	HUGO	IMPS
GOES	HAAR	HEAP	HOBO	HUGS	INCA
GO-GO	HABU	HEAR	HOBS	HULA	INCH
GOLD	HACK	HEAT	HOCK	HULK	INDO-
GOLF	HADE	HEBE	HODS	HULL	INDY
GONE	HADJ	HECK	HOED	HUME	INFO
GONG	HAEM	HEED	HOER	HUMP	INKS
GOOD	HAFT	HEEL	HOES	HUMS	INKY
GOOF	HAGS	HEFT	HOGG	HUNG	INNS
GOON	HA-HA	HEIR	HOGS	HUNK	INTI
GOOP	HAIG	HELA	HOKE	HUNT	INTO
GORE	HAIK	HELD	HOKI	HUON	IONS
GORY	HAIL	HELL	HOLD	HURD	IOTA
GOSH	HAIR	HELM	HOLE	HURL	IOUS
GOUT	HAJJ	HELP	HOLM	HURT	IOWA
GOWN	HAKE	HEMP	HOLP	HUSH	IPOH
GRAB	HALE	HEMS	HOLS	HUSK	IRAN
GRAF	HALF	HENS	HOLT	HUSS	IRAQ
GRAM	HALL	HENT	HOLY	HUTS	IRIS
GRAN	HALM	HERA	HOMA	HUTU	IRON
GRAY	HALO	HERB	HOME	HWAN	ISLE
GRAZ	HALT	HERD	HOMO	HWYL	ISMS
GREW	HAMA	HERE	HOMS	HYDE	ITCH
GREY	HAME	HERL	HOMY	HYMN	ITEM
GRID	HAMM	HERM	HONE	HYPE	IUDS
GRIM	HAMS	HERN	HONG	HYPO	
GRIN	HAND	HERO	HONK		
GRIP	HANG	HERR	HOOD	**I**	**J**
GRIT	HANK	HERS	HOOF	IAMB	JABS
GROG	HARD	HESS	HOOK	IBEX	JACK
GROW	HARE	HEST	HOOP	IBID	JADE
GRUB	HARK	HETH	HOOT	IBIS	JAGS
GUAM	HARL	HEWN	HOPE	ICBM	JAIL
GUFF	HARM	HICK	HOPI	ICED	JAMB
GULF	HARP	HIDE	HOPS	ICES	JAMS
GULL	HART	HIED	HORA	ICON	JAPE
GULP	HARZ	HI-FI	HORN	IDEA	JARS
GUMS	HASA	HIGH	HOSE	IDEM	JAWS
GUNN	HASH	HIKE	HOST	IDES	JAYS
GUNS	HASK	HILL	HOTS	IDLE	JAZZ
GURN	HASP	HILT	HOUR	IDLY	JEEP
					JEER

JELL	KEYS	LAID	LEWD	LOGO	MACH
JENA	KHAN	LAIN	LIAR	LOGS	MACS
JERK	KICK	LAIR	LIAS	LOGY	MADE
JEST	KIDS	LAKE	LICE	LOIN	MAFF
JETS	KIEL	LAKH	LICK	LOLL	MAGI
JEWS	KIEV	LAMA	LIDO	LONE	MAGS
JIBE	KIKE	LAMB	LIDS	LONG	MAID
JIBS	KILL	LAME	LIED	LOOK	MAIL
JIGS	KILN	LAMP	LIEF	LOOM	MAIM
JILT	KILO	LAND	LIEN	LOON	MAIN
JINN	KILT	LANE	LIES	LOOP	MAKE
JINX	KIND	LANK	LIEU	LOOS	MALE
JIVE	KINE	LAOS	LIFE	LOOT	MALI
JOBS	KING	LAPP	LIFT	LOPE	MALL
JOCK	KINK	LAPS	LIKE	LORD	MALM
JOGS	KIPS	LARD	LILO	LORE	MALT
JOHN	KIRK	LARK	LILT	LORN	MAMA
JOIN	KISS	LASH	LILY	LOSE	MAMS
JOKE	KITE	LASS	LIMA	LOSS	MANE
JOLT	KITS	LAST	LIMB	LOST	MANX
JOSH	KIVU	LATE	LIME	LOTH	MANY
JOVE	KIWI	LATH	LIMN	LOTS	MAPS
JOWL	KNAP	LAUD	LIMP	LOUD	MARE
JOYS	KNEE	LAUE	LIMY	LOUR	MARK
JUDO	KNEW	LAVA	LINE	LOUT	MARL
JUGS	KNIT	LAWN	LING	LOVE	MARS
JUJU	KNOB	LAWS	LINK	LOWS	MARY
JULY	KNOT	LAYS	LINT	LUCK	MASH
JUMP	KNOW	LAZE	LINZ	LUDO	MASK
JUNE	KOBE	LAZY	LION	LUFF	MASS
JUNK	KOFU	LEAD	LIPS	LUGO	MAST
JURA	KOGI	LEAF	LIRA	LUGS	MATE
JURY	KOHA	LEAK	LIRE	LULL	MATS
JUST	KOHL	LEAN	LISP	LUMP	MATT
JUTE	KOOK	LEAP	LIST	LUND	MAUI
	KOTA	LEAS	LITE	LUNG	MAUL
K	KRIS	LEEK	LIVE	LUNY	MAWS
KALE	KUDU	LEER	LOAD	LURE	MAYA
KANO	KURE	LEES	LOAF	LURK	MAYS
KCAL	KURU	LEFT	LOAM	LUSH	MAZE
KEEL	KYAT	LEGS	LOAN	LUST	MAZY
KEEN		LEIS	LOBE	LUTE	MEAD
KEEP	**L**	LENA	LOBS	LUVS	MEAL
KEGS	LABS	LEND	LOCH	LVIV	MEAN
KELP	LACE	LENS	LOCI	LYNX	MEAT
KENS	LACK	LENT	LOCK	LYON	MEEK
KENT	LACY	LEOS	LOCO	LYRE	MEET
KEOS	LADE	LESS	LODE		MEGA-
KEPT	LADS	LEST	LODI	**M**	MELK
KERB	LADY	LETS	LODZ	MA'AM	MELT
KERN	LAGS	LEVY	LOFT	MACE	MEMO

9

MEND	MOOD	NATO	NUBS	ONYX	PALP
MENU	MOON	NAVE	NUDE	OOPS	PALS
MEOW	MOOR	NAVY	NUKE	OOZE	PANE
MERE	MOOS	NAYS	NULL	OOZY	PANG
MESH	MOOT	NAZI	NUMB	OPAL	PANS
MESS	MOPE	NCOS	NUNN	OPEC	PANT
METE	MOPS	NEAR	NUNS	OPEN	PAPA
METZ	MORE	NEAT	NUPE	OPUS	PAPS
MEWS	MORN	NECK	NURD	ORAL	PARA-
MICA	MOSS	NEED	NUTS	ORAN	PARE
MICE	MOST	NEEM	NUUK	ORBS	PARK
MICK	MOTE	NE'ER		OREL	PARS
MIDI	MOTH	NEJD	**O**	ORES	PART
MIEN	MOTS	NEON	OAFS	ORGY	PASS
MIKE	MOVE	NERD	OAHU	ORLY	PAST
MILD	MOWN	NEST	OAKS	ORNE	PATE
MILE	MOYA	NETS	OAPS	ORSK	PATH
MILK	MRIA	NETT	OARS	ORYX	PATS
MILL	MUCH	NEWS	OATH	OSLO	PAVE
MILT	MUCK	NEWT	OATS	OSUN	PAWL
MIME	MUFF	NEXT	OBAN	OUCH	PAWN
MIND	MUGS	NIBS	OBEY	OUDH	PAWS
MINE	MULE	NICE	OBOE	OULU	PAYE
MINI	MULL	NICK	ODDS	OURS	PEAK
MINK	MUMS	NIFF	ODES	OUST	PEAL
MINT	MUON	NIGH	OGLE	OUZO	PEAR
MINX	MURK	NINE	OGRE	OVAL	PEAS
MIPS	MUSE	NIPS	OGUN	OVEN	PEAT
MIRE	MUSH	NISI	OHIO	OVER	PECK
MIRY	MUSK	NITS	OHMS	OVUM	PEED
MISO	MUSS	NIUE	OH MY	OWED	PEEK
MISS	MUST	NOBS	OH NO	OWEN	PEEL
MIST	MUTE	NODE	OILS	OWLS	PEEP
MITE	MUTI	NODS	OILY	OXEN	PEER
MITT	MUTT	NOEL	OINK	OYEZ	PEGS
MOAN	MYNA	NOES	OISE		PEGU
MOAT	MYTH	NO GO	OITA	**P**	PELT
MOBS		NONE	OKAY	PACE	PENN
MOCK	**N**	NON-U	OKRA	PACK	PENS
MODE	NAFF	NOOK	OKTA	PACT	PERK
MODS	NAGS	NOON	OMAN	PACY	PERL
MOJO	NAHA	NOPE	OMEN	PADS	PERM
MOKE	NAIL	NORD	OMIT	PAGE	PERT
MOLD	NAME	NORM	OMNI-	PAID	PERU
MOLE	NANA	NOSE	OMSK	PAIL	PESO
MOLL	NAPE	NOSH	ONCE	PAIN	PEST
MOLT	NAPS	NOSY	ONDO	PAIR	PETS
MOMS	NARA	NOTE	ONES	PAKI	PEWS
MONK	NARC	NOUN	ONLY	PALE	PHEW
MONO	NARK	NOUS	ONTO	PALL	PHON
MONS	NASA	NOVA	ONUS	PALM	PHOT

PHUT	PONY	PUNK	RATE	RIPE	RULE
PICA	POOF	PUNS	RATS	RIPS	RUMP
PICK	POOH	PUNT	RAVE	RISE	RUMS
PIED	POOL	PUNY	RAYS	RISK	RUNE
PIER	POOP	PUPA	RAZE	RITE	RUNG
PIES	POOR	PUPS	READ	RIVE	RUNS
PIGS	POPE	PURE	REAL	ROAD	RUNT
PIKE	POPS	PURI	REAM	ROAM	RUSE
PILE	PORE	PURL	REAP	ROAN	RUSH
PILL	PORI	PURR	REAR	ROAR	RUSK
PIMP	PORK	PUSH	RECK	ROBE	RUST
PINE	PORN	PUSS	REDD	ROCK	RUTS
PING	PORT	PUTT	REDO	ROCS	RYES
PINK	POSE	PUTZ	REDS	RODE	
PINS	POSH	PYRE	REED	RODS	**S**
PINT	POST		REEF	ROEG	SABA
PINY	POSY	**Q**	REEK	ROES	SACK
PION	POTS	QUAD	REEL	ROLE	SACS
PIPE	POUF	QUAY	REFS	ROLL	SAFE
PIPS	POUR	QUID	REGO	ROME	SAFI
PISA	POUT	QUIN	REIN	ROMO	SAGA
PISH	POWS	QUIP	RELY	ROMP	SAGE
PISS	PRAM	QUIT	REND	ROMS	SAGO
PITH	PRAT	QUIZ	RENO	ROOD	SAGS
PITS	PRAY	QUOD	RENT	ROOF	SAID
PITY	PREP		REPO	ROOK	SAIL
PLAN	PREY	**R**	REPS	ROOM	SAKE
PLAY	PRIG	RACE	REST	ROOT	SALE
PLEA	PRIM	RACK	REUS	ROPE	SALK
PLEB	PROB	RACY	REVS	ROPY	SALT
PLED	PROD	RAFT	RHEA	RORT	SAME
PLOD	PROF	RAGA	RIAL	ROSE	SAMP
PLOP	PROG	RAGE	RIBS	ROSY	SAN'A
PLOT	PROM	RAGS	RICE	ROTA	SAND
PLOW	PROP	RAID	RICH	ROTE	SANE
PLOY	PROS	RAIL	RICK	ROTH	SANG
PLUG	PROW	RAIN	RIDE	ROTS	SANK
PLUM	PRUT	RAKE	RIFE	ROUE	SAPS
PLUS	PSST	RAMP	RIFF	ROUT	SARD
PODS	PUBS	RAMS	RIFT	ROUX	SARI
POEM	PUCE	RAND	RIGA	ROVE	SARK
POET	PUCK	RANG	RIGS	ROWS	SASH
POKE	PUDS	RANI	RILE	RUBS	SASS
POKY	PUFF	RANK	RILL	RUBY	SATE
POLE	PUGS	RANT	RIME	RUCK	SAVE
POLL	PUKE	RAPE	RIMS	RUDE	SAWN
POLO	PULA	RAPS	RIMY	RUED	SAWS
POLY	PULL	RAPT	RIND	RUFF	SAYS
POMP	PULP	RARE	RING	RUGS	SCAB
POND	PUMA	RASH	RINK	RUHR	SCAG
PONG	PUMP	RASP	RIOT	RUIN	SCAM

SCAN	SHOP	SLOB	SOUP	SUMP	TART
SCAR	SHOT	SLOE	SOUR	SUMS	TASH
SCAT	SHOW	SLOG	SOWN	SUMY	TASK
SCOT	SHUN	SLOP	SOWS	SUNG	TA-TA
SCUD	SHUT	SLOT	SPAM	SUNK	TATS
SCUM	SIAN	SLOW	SPAN	SUNS	TAUT
SEAL	SICK	SLUB	SPAR	SUPS	TAXI
SEAM	SIDE	SLUE	SPAS	SURD	TEAK
SEAR	SIFT	SLUG	SPAT	SURE	TEAL
SEAS	SIGH	SLUM	SPAY	SURF	TEAM
SEAT	SIGN	SLUR	SPEC	SUSS	TEAR
SECS	SIKH	SLUT	SPED	SUVA	TEAS
SECT	SILK	SMOG	SPEW	SWAB	TEAT
SEED	SILL	SMUG	SPIC	SWAG	TEED
SEEK	SILO	SMUT	SPIK	SWAM	TEEM
SEEM	SILT	SNAG	SPIN	SWAN	TEES
SEEN	SIND	SNAP	SPIT	SWAP	TELE-
SEEP	SINE	SNIP	SPIV	SWAT	TELL
SEER	SING	SNOB	SPOD	SWAY	TEMA
SEES	SINH	SNOG	SPOT	SWIG	TEMP
SELF	SINK	SNOT	SPRY	SWIM	TEND
SELL	SINO-	SNOW	SPUD	SWOP	TENS
SEME	SINS	SNUB	SPUN	SWOT	TENT
SEMI	SION	SNUG	SPUR	SWUM	TERM
SEND	SIPS	SOAK	STAB	SYNC	TERN
SENT	SIRE	SOAP	STAG		TEST
SERA	SIRS	SOAR	STAR	**T**	TEXT
SERE	SITE	SOBS	STAY		THAN
SERF	SIZE	SOCA	STEM	TABS	THAT
SETA	SKEW	SOCK	STEP	TACH	THAW
SETI	SKID	SODA	STET	TACK	THEE
SETS	SKIM	SODS	STEW	TACO	THEM
SEWN	SKIN	SOFA	STIR	TACT	THEN
SEXY	SKIP	SOFT	STOL	TAGS	THEO-
SFAX	SKIS	SOIL	STOP	TAIL	THEY
SGML	SKIT	SOLD	STOW	TAKE	THIN
SHAD	SKUA	SOLE	STUB	TALC	THIS
SHAG	SKYE	SOLO	STUD	TALE	THOU
SHAH	SLAB	SOMA	STUM	TALK	THRU
SHAM	SLAG	SOME	STUN	TALL	THUD
SHAT	SLAM	SONG	STYE	TAME	THUG
SHED	SLAP	SONS	SUBS	TAMP	THUN
SHEW	SLAT	SOON	SUCH	TANG	THUS
SHIM	SLAV	SOOT	SUCK	TANH	TICK
SHIN	SLAY	SOPS	SUDS	TANK	TICS
SHIP	SLED	SORE	SUED	TANS	TIDE
SHIT	SLEW	SORT	SUER	TAPE	TIDY
SHOA	SLID	SO SO	SUET	TAPS	TIED
SHOD	SLIM	SO-SO	SUEZ	TARE	TIER
SHOE	SLIP	SOTS	SUIT	TARN	TIES
SHOO	SLIT	SOUL	SULK	TARO	TIFF
				TARS	

TILE	TOWS	UH OH	VILE	WEED	WISH
TILL	TOYS	ULNA	VINE	WEEK	WISP
TILT	TRAD	UNDO	VINO	WEEP	WITH
TIME	TRAM	UNIT	VIOL	WEFT	WITS
TINE	TRAP	UNIX	VIPS	WEIR	WOAD
TING	TRAY	UNTO	VISA	WELD	WOES
TINS	TREE	UPON	VISE	WELL	WOGS
TINT	TREK	UP TO	VOID	WELS	WOKE
TINY	TRIM	UPVC	VOLE	WELT	WOKS
TIPS	TRIO	URDU	VOLT	WEND	WOLD
TIRE	TRIP	URFA	VOTE	WENT	WOLF
TIRO	TROD	URGE	VOWS	WEPT	WOMB
TITI	TROT	URIC	VTOL	WEST	WONT
TITS	TRST	URNS		WETA	WOOD
TOAD	TRUE	USED	**W**	WETS	WOOF
TO BE	TRUG	USER	WADE	WHAM	WOOL
TO DO	TSAR	USES	WADI	WHAP	WOPS
TO-DO	TUBA	UTAH	WADS	WHAT	WORD
TODS	TUBE	UVEA	WAFT	WHEN	WORE
TOED	TUBS		WAGE	WHET	WORK
TOES	TUCK	**V**	WAGS	WHEW	WORM
TOFF	TUFT	VACS	WAIF	WHEY	WORN
TOGA	TUGS	VAIN	WAIL	WHIG	WOVE
TOGO	TULA	VALE	WAIT	WHIM	WPCS
TOGS	TUNA	VAMP	WAKE	WHIP	WRAP
TOIL	TUNE	VANE	WALK	WHIR	WREN
TOLD	TURD	VANS	WALL	WHIT	WRIT
TOLL	TURF	VARY	WAND	WHIZ	WROT
TOMB	TURN	VASE	WANE	WHOA	WUHU
TOME	TUSH	VAST	WANK	WHOM	WUSS
TONE	TUSK	VATS	WANT	WHOP	
TONS	TUTU	VAUD	WARD	WHYS	**X**
TOOK	TVEI	VDUS	WARM	WICK	XMAS
TOOL	TVER	VEAL	WARN	WIDE	X-RAY
TOOT	TWAT	VEEP	WARP	WIFE	
TOPS	TWEE	VEER	WARS	WIGS	**Y**
TORE	TWIG	VEIL	WART	WILD	YAKS
TORN	TWIN	VEIN	WARY	WILL	YAMS
TORS	TWIT	VELD	WASH	WILT	YANG
TORT	TWOS	VEND	WASP	WILY	YANK
TORY	TYPE	VENT	WATT	WIMP	YAPS
TOSA	TYRE	VERB	WAUL	WIND	YARD
TOSH	TYRO	VERY	WAVE	WINE	YARN
TOSS	TZAR	VEST	WAVY	WING	YAWL
TOTE		VETO	WAXY	WINK	YAWN
TOTO	**U**	VETS	WAYS	WINS	YAWS
TOTS	UCAS	VIAL	WEAK	WINY	YAZD
TOUL	UCCA	VICE	WEAL	WIPE	YEAH
TOUR	UELE	VIED	WEAN	WIRE	YEAR
TOUT	UFOS	VIES	WEAR	WIRY	YEAS
TOWN	UGLY	VIEW	WEBS	WISE	YELL

13

YELP	YOBS	YOUR	**Z**	ZEST	ZIZZ
YENS	YOGA	YOWL	ZANY	ZIBO	ZOND
YETI	YOGI	YOYO	ZEAL	ZINC	ZONE
YEWS	YOKE	YUAN	ZEBU	ZINE	ZOOM
YIDS	YOLK	YUCK	ZEDS	ZION	ZOOS
YIPS	YORE	YULE	ZEIN	ZIPS	ZOUK
YLEM	YORK		ZERO	ZITS	ZULU

A

A	ADIEU	AILED	ALONG	ANNEX	ARIAN
AALII	ADIOS	AIMED	ALOOF	ANNOY	ARIAS
AARAU	AD LIB	AIOLI	ALOUD	ANNUL	ARICA
ABACA	AD-LIB	AIRED	ALPHA	ANODE	ARIEL
ABACK	ADMAN	AISLE	ALTAI	ANOLE	ARIEN
ABAFT	ADMEN	AISNE	ALTAR	ANOVA	ARIES
ABASE	ADMIT	AITCH	ALTER	ANTED	ARISE
ABASH	ADMIX	AJMER	ALTOS	ANTES	ARLES
ABATE	ADOBE	AKURE	AMASS	ANTIC	ARLON
ABBEY	ADOPT	ALACK	AMAZE	ANTSY	ARMCO
ABBOT	ADORE	ALAMO	AMBER	ANVIL	ARMED
ABEAM	ADORN	ALARM	AMBIT	ANZAC	AROID
ABELE	AD REM	ALARY	AMBLE	ANZIO	AROMA
ABHOR	ADUKI	ALATE	AMBRY	AORTA	AROSE
ABIDE	ADULT	ALBEE	AMEBA	AOSTA	ARRAN
ABLED	ADUWA	ALBUM	AMEND	APACE	ARRAS
ABODE	ADZES	ALCID	AMENT	APART	ARRAY
ABOHM	AEDES	ALDAN	AMICE	APEAK	ARRIS
A-BOMB	AEGIS	ALDER	AMIDE	APERY	ARROW
ABORT	AEONS	ALDOL	AMINE	APHID	ARSES
ABOUT	AESIR	ALECK	AMINO	APHIS	ARSIS
ABOVE	AFFIX	ALERT	AMIRS	APIAN	ARSON
ABUJA	AFIRE	ALGAE	AMISS	A PIED	ARTEL
ABUSE	AFOOT	ALGAL	AMITY	APING	ARTEX
ABYSS	AFOUL	ALGID	AMMAN	APISH	ARUBA
ACCRA	AFROS	ALGIN	AMNIO	APORT	ARYAN
ACHED	AFTER	ALGOL	AMONG	APPAL	ASCII
ACHES	AGAIN	ALGOR	AMOUR	APPEL	ASCOT
ACIDS	AGAMA	ALIAS	AMPLE	APPLE	ASCUS
ACKEE	AGAPE	ALIBI	AMPLY	APPLY	ASDIC
ACORN	AGATE	ALIEN	AMUCK	APRIL	ASHEN
ACRES	AGAVE	ALIGN	AMUSE	APRON	ASHES
ACRID	AGENT	ALIKE	ANCON	APSES	ASIAN
ACTED	AGGER	A LIST	ANDES	APSIS	ASIDE
ACTIN	AGGRO	ALIVE	ANGEL	APTLY	ASKED
ACTOR	AGILE	ALKYD	ANGER	AQABA	ASKER
ACT UP	AGING	ALKYL	ANGLE	ARABS	ASKEW
ACUTE	AGISM	ALLAH	ANGLO-	ARBER	ASPEN
ADAGE	AGIST	ALLAY	ANGRY	ARBOR	ASPER
ADAMS	AGLET	ALLEN	ANGST	ARDEN	ASPIC
ADANA	AGLOW	ALLEY	ANGUS	AREAL	ASSAI
ADAPT	AGNEW	ALL IN	ANHUI	AREAS	ASSAM
ADDAX	AGONY	ALLOA	ANILE	ARECA	ASSAY
ADDED	AGORA	ALLOT	ANIMA	ARENA	ASSEN
ADDER	AGREE	ALLOW	ANION	ARETE	ASSES
ADDLE	AGUES	ALLOY	ANISE	ARGIL	ASSET
ADD-ON	AHEAD	ALLYL	ANJOU	ARGOL	ASTER
ADD UP	AHERN	ALOFT	ANKLE	ARGON	ASTIR
ADEPT	AHWAZ	ALOHA	ANNAL	ARGOS	ASTRO-
A DEUX	AIDED	ALOIN	ANNAM	ARGOT	ASWAN
AD HOC	AIDES	ALONE	ANNAN	ARGUE	AT ALL

ATHOS	BABES	BARON	BEERS	BIFID	BLINI
ATLAS	BABUL	BARRA	BEERY	BIGHT	BLINK
ATOLL	BABUS	BARRE	BEETS	BIGOT	BLIPS
ATOMS	BACCY	BARRY	BEFIT	BIG UP	BLISS
ATONE	BACKS	BARTH	BEFOG	BIHAR	B LIST
ATONY	BACON	BARYE	BEGAN	BIJOU	BLITZ
ATRIA	BADGE	BASAL	BEGAT	BIKED	BLOAT
ATRIP	BADLY	BASED	BEGET	BIKES	BLOBS
AT SEA	BAGEL	BASEL	BEGIN	BILGE	BLOCH
ATTAR	BAGGY	BASER	BEGOT	BILLS	BLOCK
ATTIC	BAHAI	BASES	BEGUM	BILLY	BLOCS
AUDIO	BAHIA	BASHO	BEGUN	BINAL	BLOIS
AUDIT	BAILS	BASIC	BEIGE	BINGE	BLOKE
AUGER	BAIRN	BASIL	BEING	BINGO	BLOND
AUGHT	BAIZE	BASIN	BEIRA	BIOME	BLOOD
AUGUR	BAKED	BASIS	BELAY	BIOTA	BLOOM
AUNTS	BAKER	BASRA	BELCH	BIPED	BLOTS
AURAL	BALAS	BASSO	BELEM	BIPOD	BLOWN
AURAS	BALDY	BASTE	BELIE	BIRCH	BLOWS
AURIC	BALED	BATCH	BELLE	BIRDS	BLOWY
AUTOS	BALER	BATED	BELLS	BIROS	BLUER
AUXIN	BALES	BATHE	BELLY	BIRTH	BLUES
AVAIL	BALKH	BATHS	BELOW	BISON	BLUFF
AVENS	BALKS	BATIK	BELTS	BITCH	BLUNT
AVERT	BALLS	BATON	BEMBA	BITES	BLURB
AVIAN	BALLY	BATTY	BENCH	BITTY	BLURT
AVOID	BALMS	BATUM	BENDS	BIYSK	BLUSH
AWAIT	BALMY	BAULK	BENIN	BIZZY	BOARD
AWAKE	BALSA	BAWDS	BENTS	BLACK	BOARS
AWARD	BALTI	BAWDY	BENUE	BLADE	BOAST
AWARE	BALTI	BAYED	BENXI	BLAIN	BOATS
AWASH	BANAL	BAYOU	BERET	BLAIR	BOBBY
AWFUL	BANDA	BEACH	BERKS	BLAME	BOCHE
AWOKE	BANDS	BEADS	BERRY	BLANC	BODED
AXIAL	BANDY	BEADY	BERTH	BLAND	BODGE
AXILE	BANES	BEAKS	BERYL	BLANK	BOERS
AXING	BANFF	BEAKY	BESET	BLARE	BOGEY
AXIOM	BANGS	BEAMS	BESOM	BLASE	BOGGY
AXLES	BANJO	BEANO	BETAS	BLAST	BOGIE
AYAHS	BANKS	BEANS	BETEL	BLAZE	BOGOR
AZIDE	BANNS	BEARD	BEVEL	BLEAK	BOGUS
AZINE	BANTU	BEARS	BEVVY	BLEAR	BOHEA
AZOIC	BARBS	BEAST	BEZEL	BLEAT	BOHOL
AZOLE	BARDS	BEATS	BHAJI	BLEED	BOILS
AZOTE	BARED	BEAUS	BHANG	BLEEP	BOISE
AZTEC	BARER	BEAUT	BIBLE	BLEND	BOLES
AZURE	BARGE	BEAUX	BICKY	BLESS	BOLLS
	BARIC	BEBOP	BIDED	BLEST	BOLTS
B	BARKS	BECKS	BIDET	BLIDA	BOLUS
	BARMY	BEECH	BIERS	BLIMP	BOMBE
BAAED	BARNS	BEEFY	BIFFS	BLIND	BOMBS
BABEL					

BONDI	BOZOS	BROWN	BURST	CALVE	CAWED
BONDS	BRACE	BROWS	BUSBY	CALYX	CD-ROM
BONED	BRACT	BRUIN	BUSED	CAMEL	CEARA
BONES	BRAES	BRUIT	BUSES	CAMEO	CEASE
BONGO	BRAGA	BRUME	BUSHY	CAMPO	CEDAR
BONNY	BRAGG	BRUNO	BUSTS	CAMPS	CEDED
BONUS	BRAID	BRUNT	BUSTY	CANAL	CEDER
BONZE	BRAIL	BRUSH	BUTCH	CANDY	CEIBA
BOOBS	BRAIN	BRUTE	BUTTE	CANEA	CELEB
BOOBY	BRAKE	B-SIDE	BUTTS	CANED	CELLA
BOOED	BRAND	BUBAL	BUTTY	CANER	CELLE
BOOKS	BRASH	BUCHU	BUTYL	CANES	CELLO
BOOMS	BRASS	BUCKS	BUXOM	CANNA	CELLS
BOONS	BRATS	BUDDY	BUYER	CANNY	CENSE
BOORS	BRAVE	BUDGE	BWANA	CANOE	CENTO
BOOST	BRAVO	BUFFS	BYATT	CANON	CENTS
BOOTH	BRAWL	BUGGY	BYLAW	CANTO	CERES
BOOTS	BRAWN	BUGLE	BYRES	CANTS	CERIC
BOOTY	BRAXY	BUILD	BYTES	CAPER	CERTS
BOOZE	BRAYS	BUILT	BYTOM	CAPES	CETUS
BOOZY	BRAZE	BULBS	BYWAY	CAPON	CEUTA
BORAX	BREAD	BULGE		CAPRI	CHAFE
BORED	BREAK	BULGY	**C**	CAPUA	CHAFF
BORER	BREAM	BULKS	CABAL	CAPUT	CHAIN
BORES	BREDA	BULKY	CABBY	CARAT	CHAIR
BORIC	BREED	BULLA	CABER	CARDS	CHALK
BORNE	BRENT	BULLS	CABIN	CARED	CHAMP
BORNO	BREST	BULLY	CABLE	CARES	CHANT
BORNU	BREVE	BUMPH	CACAO	CARET	CHAOS
BORON	BRIAR	BUMPS	CACHE	CARGO	CHAPS
BOSKY	BRIBE	BUMPY	CACTI	CARNE	CHARD
BOSOM	BRICK	BUNCH	CADDY	CAROB	CHARM
BOSON	BRIDE	BUNDU	CADET	CAROL	CHARS
BOSSY	BRIEF	BUNGS	CADGE	CARPS	CHART
BOSUN	BRIER	BUNKS	CADIZ	CARRY	CHARY
BOTCH	BRILL	BUNNY	CADRE	CARTS	CHASE
BOUGH	BRINE	BUOYS	CAFES	CARVE	CHASM
BOULE	BRING	BURGH	CAFOD	CASED	CHATS
BOUND	BRINK	BURIN	CAGED	CASES	CHEAP
BOURN	BRINY	BURKE	CAGES	CASKS	CHEAT
BOUSE	BRISK	BURKS	CAGEY	CASTE	CHECK
BOUTS	BRITS	BURLY	CAINE	CASTS	CHEEK
BOVID	BROAD	BURMA	CAIRN	CATCH	CHEEP
BOWED	BROIL	BURNS	CAIRO	CATER	CHEER
BOWEL	BROKE	BURNT	CAJUN	CATTY	CHEFS
BOWER	BROME	BURPS	CAKED	CAULK	CHEJU
BOWIE	BRONX	BURRO	CAKES	CAUSE	CHELA
BOWLS	BROOD	BURRS	CALIX	CAVAN	CHERT
BOXED	BROOK	BURRY	CALLA	CAVED	CHESS
BOXER	BROOM	BURSA	CALLS	CAVES	CHEST
BOXES	BROTH	BURSE	CALOR	CAVIL	CHEWS

CHEWY	CIRCA	CLOUT	COMMA	COVES	CRIES
CHIBA	CISCO	CLOVE	COMPO	COVET	CRIME
CHICK	CISSY	CLOWN	CONCH	COVEY	CRIMP
CHIDE	CITED	CLUBS	CONES	COVIN	CRISP
CHIEF	CITES	CLUCK	CONEY	COWED	CROAK
CHILD	CIVET	CLUES	CONGA	COWER	CROAT
CHILE	CIVIC	CLUMP	CONGE	COWES	CROCK
CHILL	CIVIL	CLUNG	CONGO	COWLS	CROFT
CHIME	CLACK	CLUNK	CONIC	COWRY	CRONE
CHINA	CLADE	CLUNY	CONKS	COXAL	CRONY
CHINE	CLAIM	CLWYD	CONTE	COXED	CROOK
CHING	CLAMP	CLYDE	CONWY	COXES	CROON
CHINK	CLAMS	COACH	COOED	COYLY	CROPS
CHINS	CLANG	COALS	COOKS	COYPU	CRORE
CHIOS	CLANK	COALY	COOLS	COZEN	CROSS
CHIPS	CLANS	COAST	COONS	CRABS	CROUP
CHIRM	CLAPS	COATS	COOPS	CRACK	CROWD
CHIRP	CLARE	COBIA	CO-OPT	CRAFT	CROWN
CHIRR	CLARO	COBRA	COOTS	CRAGS	CROWS
CHITA	CLARY	COCKS	COPAL	CRAKE	CROZE
CHITS	CLASH	COCKY	COPED	CRAMP	CRUDE
CHIVY	CLASP	COCOA	COPES	CRANE	CRUEL
CHOCK	CLASS	CODAS	COPRA	CRANK	CRUET
CHOIR	CLAVE	CODED	COPSE	CRAPE	CRUMB
CHOKE	CLAWS	CODER	CORAL	CRAPS	CRUMP
CHOKO	CLEAN	CODES	CORDS	CRASH	CRURA
CHOKY	CLEAR	CODEX	CORED	CRASS	CRUSE
CHOMP	CLEAT	CODON	CORER	CRATE	CRUSH
CHOPS	CLEEK	COEDS	CORES	CRAVE	CRUST
CHORD	CLEFS	COGON	CORFU	CRAWL	CRYPT
CHORE	CLEFT	COHSE	CORGI	CRAZE	CUBAN
CHOSE	CLERK	COIFS	CORKS	CRAZY	CUBEB
CHOUX	CLEWS	COIGN	CORMS	CREAK	CUBED
CHOWS	CLICK	COILS	CORNS	CREAM	CUBES
CHRON-	CLIFF	COINS	CORNU	CREDO	CUBIC
CHUBB	CLIMB	COKES	CORNY	CREED	CUBIT
CHUCK	CLIME	COLDS	CORPS	CREEK	CUDDY
CHUFA	CLINE	COLEY	CORSE	CREEL	CUFFS
CHUFF	CLING	COLIC	COSTA	CREEP	CUING
CHUMP	CLINK	COLON	COSTS	CREME	CULCH
CHUMS	CLINT	COLTS	COTTA	CREPE	CULET
CHUNK	CLIPS	COLZA	COUCH	CREPT	CULEX
CHURL	CLOAK	COMAL	COUDE	CRESS	CULLS
CHURN	CLOCK	COMAS	COUGH	CREST	CULPA
CHUTE	CLODS	COMBI	COULD	CRETE	CULTS
CHYLE	CLOGS	COMBO	COUNT	CREWE	CUMIN
CHYME	CLONE	COMBS	COUPE	CREWS	CUNTS
CIDER	CLOSE	COMER	COUPS	CRIBS	CUPEL
CIGAR	CLOTH	COMET	COURT	CRICK	CUPID
CIMEX	CLOTS	COMFY	COVEN	CRIED	CUPPA
CINCH	CLOUD	COMIC	COVER	CRIER	CURBS

CURCH	DARED	DELOS	DINKY	DOORS	DRESS
CURDY	DARER	DELTA	DIODE	DOOZY	DRIBS
CURED	DARES	DELVE	DIRER	DOPED	DRIED
CURES	DARKS	DEMOB	DIRGE	DOPES	DRIER
CURET	DARKY	DEMON	DIRKS	DOPEY	DRIFT
CURIA	DARNS	DEMOS	DIRTY	DORIC	DRILL
CURIE	DARTS	DEMUR	DISCO	DOSED	DRILY
CURIO	DATED	DENAR	DISCS	DOSER	DRINK
CURLS	DATER	DENIM	DISHY	DOSES	DRIPS
CURLY	DATES	DENSE	DISKS	DOTED	DRIVE
CURRY	DATUM	DENTS	DITCH	DOTER	DROIT
CURSE	DAUBS	DEPOT	DITTO	DOTTY	DROLL
CURVE	DAUBY	DEPTH	DITTY	DOUAI	DROME
CUSEC	DAUNT	DERBY	DITZY	DOUBS	DRONE
CUSHY	DAVIT	DERMA	DIVAN	DOUBT	DROOL
CUSPS	DAVOS	DERRY	DIVED	DOUGH	DROOP
CUTER	DAWNS	DESKS	DIVER	DOURO	DROPS
CUTIN	DAZED	DETER	DIVES	DOUSE	DROSS
CUT IN	DAZES	DETOX	DIVOT	DOVER	DROVE
CUTIS	DEALS	DEUCE	DIVVY	DOVES	DROWN
CUT UP	DEALT	DEVIL	DIXIE	DOWDY	DRUGS
CUZCO	DEANS	DEVON	DIZZY	DOWEL	DRUID
CYBER	DEARS	DEWAR	DJINN	DOWER	DRUMS
CYCAD	DEARY	DHAKA	DOBBY	DOWNS	DRUNK
CYCLE	DEATH	DHOLE	DOBRO	DOWNY	DRUPE
CYDER	DEBAR	DHOTI	DOCKS	DOWRY	DRUSE
CYMAR	DEBIT	DHOWS	DODGE	DOWSE	DRYAD
CYMRY	DEBTS	DIALS	DODGY	DOYEN	DRYER
CYNIC	DEBUG	DIANA	DODOS	DOZED	DRYLY
CYSTS	DEBUT	DIARY	DOERS	DOZEN	DUALA
CYTON	DECAF	DIAZO	DO FOR	DOZER	DUBAI
CZARS	DECAL	DICED	DOGES	D PHIL	DUCAL
CZECH	DECAY	DICER	DOGGO	DRABS	DUCAT
	DECKS	DICEY	DOGGY	DRAFF	DUCHY
D	DECOR	DICKS	DOGIE	DRAFT	DUCKS
DACCA	DECOY	DICKY	DOGMA	DRAGS	DUCKY
DADDY	DECRY	DICTA	DOILY	DRAIL	DUCTS
DAGGA	DEEDS	DIETS	DOING	DRAIN	DUDES
DAGOS	DEFER	DIGIT	DOLBY	DRAKE	DUELS
DAILY	DEGAS	DIJON	DOLCE	DRAMA	DUETS
DAIRY	DE-ICE	DIKES	DOLED	DRAMS	DUFFS
DAISY	DEIFY	DILDO	DOLLS	DRANK	DUKES
DAKAR	DEIGN	DIMER	DOLLY	DRAPE	DULIA
DALES	DEISM	DIMES	DOLTS	DRAWL	DULLY
DALLY	DEIST	DIMLY	DOMED	DRAWN	DULSE
DAMAN	DEITY	DINAR	DOMES	DRAWS	DUMMY
DAMES	DEKKO	DINED	DONEE	DRAYS	DUMPS
DANCE	DELAY	DINER	DONNA	DREAD	DUMPY
DANDY	DELFT	DINGO	DONOR	DREAM	DUNCE
DANIO	DELHI	DINGY	DOOMS	DREAR	DUNES
DARAF	DELLS	DINKA	DOONA	DREGS	DUNGY

DUNKS	EDUCE	ENDED	ETUDE	FALUN	FERNY
DUPED	EDUCT	ENDER	EVADE	FAMED	FERRY
DUPER	EEJIT	END ON	EVENS	FANCY	FESSE
DUPES	EERIE	ENDOW	EVENT	FANGO	FETAL
DUPLE	EFFED	ENDUE	EVERT	FANGS	FETCH
DURAS	EGEST	ENEMA	EVERY	FANNY	FETED
DUREX	EGGER	ENEMY	EVICT	FANON	FETES
DUROC	EGHAM	ENJOY	EVILS	FANTI	FETID
DURRA	EGRET	ENNIS	EVOKE	FARAD	FETOR
DURUM	EGYPT	ENNUI	EWERS	FARCE	FETUS
DUSKY	EIDER	ENROL	EXACT	FARCI	FEUDS
DUSTY	EIFEL	ENSUE	EXALT	FARCY	FEVER
DUTCH	EIGER	ENTER	EXAMS	FARED	FEZES
DUVET	EIGHT	ENTRY	EXCEL	FARER	FIATS
DWARF	EIKON	ENUGU	EXERT	FARES	FIBRE
DWEEB	EILAT	ENURE	EXILE	FARLE	FICHU
DWELL	EJECT	ENVOY	EXIST	FARMS	FICUS
DWELT	EKMAN	EOSIN	EXITS	FARTS	FIELD
DYERS	ELAND	EPACT	EXPEL	FASTS	FIEND
DYFED	ELATE	EPEES	EXTOL	FATAL	FIERY
DYING	ELBOW	EPICS	EXTRA	FATED	FIFER
DYKES	ELCHE	EPOCH	EXUDE	FATES	FIFES
DYLAN	ELDER	EPODE	EXULT	FATTY	FIFTH
DYULA	ELECT	EPOXY	EYING	FAUGH	FIFTY
	ELEGY	EPROM	EYOTS	FAULT	FIGHT
	ELEMI	EPSOM	EYRIE	FAUNA	FILAR
E	ELFIN	EQUAL		FAUNS	FILCH
	ELGIN	EQUIP	**F**	FAVUS	FILED
EAGER	ELIDE	ERASE	FABLE	FAWNS	FILER
EAGLE	ELINT	ERBIL	FACED	FAXED	FILES
EAGRE	ELITE	ERECT	FACER	FAZED	FILET
EARED	ELOPE	ERGOT	FACES	FEARS	FILLY
EARLS	ELUDE	ERNIE	FACET	FEAST	FILMS
EARLY	ELUTE	ERODE	FACIA	FEATS	FILMY
EAROM	ELVER	EROSE	FACTS	FEAZE	FILTH
EARTH	ELVES	ERRED	FADDY	FECAL	FILUM
EASED	EMBAY	ERROR	FADED	FECES	FINAL
EASEL	EMBED	ERUCT	FADER	FECIT	FINCH
EASER	EMBER	ERUPT	FAERY	FED UP	FINDS
EASTS	EMBOW	ESHER	FAILS	FEEDS	FINED
EATEN	EMCEE	ESKER	FAINT	FEIGN	FINER
EATER	EMDEN	ESPOO	FAIRS	FEINT	FINES
EAVES	EMEND	ESSAY	FAIRY	FELLS	FINGO
EBBED	EMERY	ESSEN	FAITH	FELON	FINIS
E BOAT	EMIRS	ESSEX	FAKED	FEMUR	FINNY
EBONY	EMMEN	ESTER	FAKER	FENCE	FIORD
ECLAT	EMMER	ESTOP	FAKES	FENNY	FIRED
EDEMA	EMOTE	ETHER	FAKIR	FERAL	FIRER
EDGED	EMPTY	ETHIC	FALDO	FERIA	FIRES
EDGER	ENACT	ETHOS	FALLS	FERMI	FIRMS
EDGES	ENATE	ETHYL	FALSE	FERNS	FIRRY
EDICT					
EDIFY					

FIRST	FLOPS	FORTE	FUCUS	GALLS	GENUS
FIRTH	FLORA	FORTH	FUDGE	GAMED	GEODE
FISHY	FLORY	FORTS	FUELS	GAMER	GEOID
FISTS	FLOSS	FORTY	FUGAL	GAMES	GERMS
FITCH	FLOUR	FORUM	FUGGY	GAMEY	GESSO
FITLY	FLOUT	FOSSA	FUGUE	GAMIC	GET IT
FIVER	FLOWN	FOSSE	FULLY	GAMIN	GET ON
FIVES	FLUED	FOULS	FUMED	GAMMA	GET TO
FIXED	FLUES	FOUND	FUMER	GAMMY	GETUP
FIXER	FLUFF	FOUNT	FUMES	GAMUT	GET UP
FIXES	FLUID	FOURS	FUNDS	GANDA	GHANA
FIZZY	FLUKE	FOVEA	FUNEN	GANGS	GHATS
FJELD	FLUKY	FOWEY	FUNGI	GANJA	GHENT
FJORD	FLUME	FOWLS	FUNKS	GANSU	GHOST
FLACK	FLUNG	FOXED	FUNKY	GAOLS	GHOUL
FLAGS	FLUNK	FOXES	FUNNY	GAPED	GHYLL
FLAIL	FLUOR	FOYER	FURAN	GAPER	GIANT
FLAIR	FLUSH	FRAIL	FURRY	GAPES	GIBER
FLAKE	FLUTE	FRAME	FURZE	GARDA	GIBES
FLAKY	FLUTY	FRANC	FURZY	GASES	GIDDY
FLAME	FLYBY	FRANK	FUSED	GASPS	GIFTS
FLAMY	FLYER	FRAUD	FUSEE	GASSY	GIGOT
FLANK	FOALS	FREAK	FUSEL	GATED	GIGUE
FLANS	FOAMY	FREED	FUSES	GATES	GIJON
FLAPS	FOCAL	FREER	FUSIL	GAUDY	GILET
FLARE	FOCUS	FREON	FUSSY	GAUGE	GILLS
FLASH	FOGEY	FRESH	FUSTY	GAUNT	GILTS
FLASK	FOGGY	FRETS	FUTON	GAUSS	GIPSY
FLATS	FOILS	FRIAR	FUZZY	GAUZE	GIRLS
FLAWS	FOISM	FRIED	FYLDE	GAUZY	GIRON
FLAWY	FOIST	FRIER		GAVEL	GIRTH
FLEAM	FOLDS	FRIES	**G**	GAVLE	GIVEN
FLEAS	FOLIC	FRILL	GABBA	GAWKY	GIVER
FLECK	FOLIO	FRISE	GABBY	GAYER	GIZMO
FLEER	FOLKS	FRISK	GABES	GAZED	GLACE
FLEET	FOLLY	FRITT	GABLE	GAZER	GLADE
FLESH	FONTS	FRIZZ	GABON	GCSES	GLAIR
FLEWS	FOODS	FROCK	GADID	GEARS	GLAND
FLICK	FOOLS	FROGS	GAFFE	GECKO	GLANS
FLIER	FOOTS	FROND	GAFFS	GEESE	GLARE
FLIES	FOOTY	FRONS	GAGED	GEEST	GLARY
FLING	FORAY	FRONT	GAGES	GELID	GLASS
FLINT	FORCE	FROST	GAILY	GEMMA	GLAZE
FLIPS	FORDS	FROTH	GAINS	GENES	GLEAM
FLIRT	FORGE	FROWN	GAITS	GENET	GLEAN
FLOAT	FORGO	FROZE	GALAH	GENIC	GLEBE
FLOCK	FOR IT	FRUIT	GALAS	GENIE	GLEES
FLOES	FORKS	FRUMP	GALEA	GENII	GLEET
FLONG	FORLI	FRYER	GALES	GENOA	GLENN
FLOOD	FORME	FRY-UP	GALLA	GENRE	GLENS
FLOOR	FORMS	FUCKS	GALLE	GENTS	GLIDE

GLINT	GORKI	GRITS	GYPSY	HANOI	HEAVY
GLITZ	GORSE	GROAN	GYRAL	HANSA	HEBEI
GLOAT	GOTHA	GROAT		HANSE	HEDGE
GLOBE	GOT UP	GROIN	**H**	HANTS	HEDGY
GLOGG	GOUDA	GROOM	HABER	HAPLY	HEELS
GLOOM	GOUGE	GROPE	HABIT	HAPPY	HEFEI
GLOOP	GOURD	GROSS	HACEK	HARAR	HEFTY
GLORY	GOUTY	GROUP	HACKS	HARDS	HEGEL
GLOSS	GOWER	GROUT	HADAL	HARDY	HEIRS
GLOVE	GOWNS	GROVE	HADES	HARED	HEIST
GLUED	GRABS	GROWL	HADJI	HAREM	HEJAZ
GLUER	GRACE	GROWN	HADN'T	HARES	HEKLA
GLUEY	GRADE	GRUBS	HADST	HARPS	HELEN
GLUME	GRAFT	GRUEL	HAFIZ	HARPY	HELIX
GLUTS	GRAIL	GRUFF	HAFTS	HARRY	HELLE
GLYPH	GRAIN	GRUNT	HAGAR	HARSH	HELLO
GNARL	GRAMA	GUACO	HAGEN	HARTS	HELLS
GNASH	GRAMS	GUANO	HAGUE	HASN'T	HELMS
GNATS	GRAND	GUARD	HA-HAS	HASPS	HELOT
GNOME	GRANS	GUAVA	HAIDA	HASTE	HELPS
GOADS	GRANT	GUESS	HAIFA	HASTY	HELVE
GOALS	GRAPE	GUEST	HAIKU	HATCH	HE-MAN
GOATS	GRAPH	GUIDE	HAILS	HATED	HE-MEN
GODLY	GRASP	GUILD	HAIN'T	HATES	HENAN
GOERS	GRASS	GUILE	HAIRS	HAUGH	HENCE
GOFER	GRATE	GUILT	HAIRY	HAULM	HENGE
GOGGA	GRAVE	GUISE	HAITI	HAULS	HENIE
GOIAS	GRAVY	GULAG	HAJJI	HAUNT	HENNA
GOING	GRAYS	GULAR	HAKEA	HAUSA	HENRY
GOLDS	GRAZE	GULCH	HAKES	HAVEN	HENZE
GOLEM	GREAT	GULES	HAKIM	HAVER	HERAT
GOLLY	GREBE	GULFS	HALAL	HAVES	HERBS
GOMEL	GRECO-	GULLS	HALER	HAVOC	HERBY
GONAD	GREED	GULLY	HALIC	HAVRE	HERDS
GONDI	GREEK	GULPS	HALID	HAWES	HERES
GONER	GREEN	GUMBO	HALLE	HAWKS	HERNE
GONGS	GREER	GUMMA	HALLO	HAWSE	HEROD
GONNA	GREET	GUMMY	HALLS	HAYDN	HERON
GOODS	GREYS	GUNGE	HALMA	HAZED	HERTZ
GOODY	GRIDS	GUPPY	HALOS	HAZEL	HESSE
GOOEY	GRIEF	GURUS	HALTS	HAZER	HET UP
GOOFS	GRIFT	GUSSY	HALVE	HAZES	HEWED
GOOFY	GRIKE	GUSTO	HAMAL	H-BOMB	HEWER
GOOLE	GRILL	GUSTS	HAMMY	HEADS	HEXAD
GOONS	GRIME	GUSTY	HAMZA	HEADY	HEXED
GOOSE	GRIMY	GUTSY	HANAU	HEALY	HEXER
GOOSY	GRIND	GUTTA	HANCE	HEAPS	HEXES
GORAL	GRINS	GUYED	HANDS	HEARD	HEXYL
GORED	GRIPE	GUYOT	HANDY	HEART	HICKS
GORES	GRIPS	GWENT	HANKS	HEATH	HIDER
GORGE	GRIST	GWERU	HANKY	HEAVE	HIDES

HI-FIS	HOLLO	HOVEL	IBIZA	INKED	JAMBS
HIGHS	HOLLY	HOVER	ICIER	INK IN	JAMES
HIGHT	HOLST	HOWDY	ICILY	INKLE	JAMMU
HIJAZ	HOMER	HOWLS	ICING	IN-LAW	JAMMY
HIKED	HOMES	HOYLE	ICONS	INLAY	JAPAN
HIKER	HOMEY	HSIAN	ICTIC	INLET	JAPER
HIKES	HONAN	HUBBY	ICTUS	INNER	JAPES
HILAR	HONDO	HUBEI	IDAHO	INPUT	JAUNT
HILLA	HONED	HUBLI	IDEAL	INSET	JAWED
HILLS	HONEY	HUFFY	IDEAS	INTER	JAZZY
HILLY	HONKS	HUFUF	IDIOM	INTRO	JEANS
HILTS	HONKY	HUGER	IDIOT	INUIT	JEEPS
HILUM	HONOR	HULKS	IDLED	INURE	JEERS
HILUS	HOOCH	HULLO	IDLER	INURN	JEHOL
HINDI	HOODS	HULLS	IDOLS	INVAR	JELLO
HINDS	HOOEY	HULME	IDYLL	IODIC	JELLY
HINDU	HOO-HA	HUMAN	IGLOO	IONIC	JEMMY
HINES	HOOKE	HUMIC	IKEJA	IOTAS	JENNY
HINGE	HOOKS	HUMID	IKONS	IRAQI	JEREZ
HINNY	HOOKY	HUMPH	ILEAC	IRATE	JERKS
HI NRG	HOOPS	HUMPS	ILEUM	IRBID	JERKY
HINTS	HOOTS	HUMPY	ILEUS	IRISH	JESTS
HIPPO	HOPED	HUMUS	ILIAC	IRKED	JESUS
HIPPY	HOPEH	HUNAN	ILIAD	IRONS	JETTY
HIRAM	HOPER	HUNCH	ILIUM	IRONY	JEWEL
HIRED	HOPES	HUNKS	IMAGE	ISERE	JEWRY
HIRER	HORAE	HUNTS	IMAGO	ISLAM	JIBED
HIRST	HORAL	HUPEH	IMAMS	ISLAY	JIBES
HITCH	HORDE	HURDS	IMBED	ISLES	JIDDA
HIT ON	HOREB	HURON	IMBUE	ISLET	JIFFY
HIVED	HORME	HURRY	IMIDE	ISSUE	JIHAD
HIVES	HORNS	HURST	IMINE	ISTLE	JILIN
HOARD	HORNY	HURTS	IMPEL	ITALO-	JIMMY
HOARY	HORSA	HUSKS	IMPLY	ITALY	JINAN
HOBBS	HORSE	HUSKY	IN ALL	ITCHY	JINGO
HOBBY	HORST	HUSSY	INANE	ITEMS	JINJA
HOBOS	HORSY	HUTCH	INAPT	IVIED	JINKS
HOCKS	HORUS	HYADS	INCUR	IVIES	JINNI
HOCUS	HOSEA	HYDRA	INCUS	IVORY	JIVED
HOFEI	HOSED	HYDRO	INDEX	IZMIR	JOCKS
HOFUF	HOSES	HYENA	INDIA	IZMIT	JOINS
HOGAN	HOSTA	HYING	INDIC		JOINT
HO-HUM	HOSTS	HYMEN	INDRE	**J**	JOIST
HOICK	HOTAN	HYMNS	INDUS	JABOT	JOKED
HOIST	HOTEL	HYPED	INEPT	JACKS	JOKER
HOKKU	HOTLY	HYPER	INERT	JADED	JOKES
HOKUM	HOUGH	HYPOS	INFER	JADES	JOLLY
HOLDS	HOUND		INFIX	JAFFA	JOLTS
HOLES	HOURI	**I**	IN FOR	JAILS	JONAH
HOLEY	HOURS	IAMBS	INGOT	JALAP	JORUM
HOLLA	HOUSE	I-BEAM	INION	JAMBI	JOULE

JOUST	KEENS	KNOWS	LAMED	LEARN	LIFER
JOVES	KEEPS	KNURL	LAMER	LEASE	LIFTS
JOWLS	KELLS	KOALA	LAMPS	LEASH	LIGER
JOYED	KELLY	KOCHI	LANAI	LEAST	LIGHT
JUDAS	KENNY	KOINE	LANCE	LEAVE	LIKED
JUDGE	KENYA	KONGO	LANDS	LECCE	LIKEN
JUGAL	KERBS	KONYA	LANES	LEDGE	LIKES
JUGUM	KERCH	KOOKS	LANKY	LEDGY	LILAC
JUICE	KERRY	KOOKY	LAOAG	LED ON	LILLE
JUICY	KETCH	KORAN	LAOIS	LEECH	LILOS
JUJUS	KEVEL	KOREA	LA PAZ	LEEDS	LILTS
JULEP	KEYED	KORMA	LAPEL	LEEKS	LIMBO
JUMBO	KHAKI	KRAAL	LAPSE	LEERS	LIMBS
JUMPS	KHANS	KRAFT	LAP UP	LEERY	LIMED
JUMPY	KHMER	KRAIT	LARCH	LEFTY	LIMEN
JUNCO	KIANG	KREMS	LARGE	LEGAL	LIMES
JUNES	KICKS	KRILL	LARGO	LEGER	LIMEY
JUNKS	KIKES	KRONA	LARKS	LEGGY	LIMIT
JUNTA	KILIM	KRONE	LARNE	LEGIT	LINED
JUNTO	KILLS	KROON	LAROS	LEMMA	LINEN
JURAL	KILNS	KUDOS	LARVA	LEMON	LINER
JURAT	KILOS	KUDZU	LASER	LEMUR	LINES
JUREL	KILTS	KUFIC	LASSO	LENDL	LINGO
JUROR	KINDS	KUKRI	LASTS	LENIS	LININ
JURUA	KINGS	KULAK	LATCH	LENTO	LINKS
	KININ	KURIL	LATER	LEPER	LINTY
K	KINKS	KURSK	LATEX	LET ON	LIONS
KABUL	KINKY	KUTCH	LATHE	LETUP	LIPID
KALAT	KIOSK	KWARA	LATHS	LET UP	LIRAS
KANDY	KIRIN	KWELA	LATIN	LEVEE	LISLE
KANGA	KIRKS	KYOTO	LAUGH	LEVEL	LISTS
KANSU	KIROV		LAVAL	LEVER	LITER
KAPOK	KITES	**L**	LAVER	LEVIS	LITHE
KAPUT	KITTY	LABEL	LAWKS	LEWES	LITRE
KARAT	KITWE	LACED	LAWNS	LEWIS	LIT UP
KAREN	KIWIS	LACER	LAWNY	LEXIS	LIVED
KARMA	KLONG	LACES	LAXLY	LEYTE	LIVEN
KAROO	KNACK	LADEN	LAY-BY	LHASA	LIVER
KARST	KNAVE	LADER	LAYER	LIANA	LIVES
KASAI	KNEAD	LADLE	LAY UP	LIARS	LIVID
KASHI	KNEED	LAGAN	LAZED	LIBEL	LLAMA
KAUAI	KNEEL	LAGER	LAZIO	LIBRA	LLANO
KAURI	KNEES	LAGOS	LEACH	LIBYA	LLOYD
KAYAK	KNELL	LAHTI	LEADS	LICIT	LOACH
KAZAN	KNELT	LAIRD	LEADY	LICKS	LOADS
KAZOO	KNIFE	LAIRS	LEAFY	LIDOS	LOAMY
KBYTE	KNOBS	LAITY	LEAKS	LIEGE	LOANS
KEBAB	KNOCK	LAKER	LEAKY	LIE IN	LOATH
KEDAH	KNOLL	LAKES	LEANT	LIE-IN	LOBAR
KEDGE	KNOTS	LAMAS	LEAPS	LIENS	LOBBY
KEELS	KNOWN	LAMBS	LEAPT	LIEUS	LOBED

LOBES	LOWER	MACRO	MARRY	MERGE	MINSK
LOCAL	LOWLY	MADAM	MARSH	MERIT	MINTS
LOCHS	LOYAL	MADLY	MASAI	MERRY	MINUS
LOCKS	LUCCA	MAFIA	MASAN	MERSE	MIRED
LOCUM	LUCID	MAGIC	MASER	MESIC	MIRES
LOCUS	LUCKY	MAGMA	MASKS	MESNE	MIRID
LODEN	LUCRE	MAGUS	MASON	MESON	MIRTH
LODES	LUFFA	MAIDS	MASSA	MESSY	MISER
LODGE	LUGER	MAINE	MASTS	METAL	MISSY
LOESS	LUMEN	MAINS	MATCH	METED	MISTS
LOFTS	LUMME	MAINZ	MATED	METER	MISTY
LOFTY	LUMPS	MAIZE	MATER	METHS	MITES
LOGIC	LUMPY	MAJOR	MATES	METOL	MITIS
LOG IN	LUNAR	MAKER	MATEY	ME-TOO	MITRE
LOG ON	LUNCH	MAKES	MATIN	METRE	MITTS
LOGOS	LUNGE	MALAR	MATSU	METRO	MIXED
LOINS	LUNGS	MALAY	MATTE	MEUSE	MIXER
LOIRE	LUPIN	MALES	MAUVE	MEWED	MIXES
LOLLY	LUPUS	MALLE	MAXIM	MEZZO	MIX-UP
LONER	LURCH	MALLS	MAYAN	MIAMI	MIZAR
LOOKS	LURED	MALMO	MAYBE	MIAOW	MOANS
LOOMS	LURER	MALTA	MAYN'T	MICKS	MOATS
LOONS	LURES	MALTY	MAYOR	MICRO	MOCHA
LOONY	LUREX	MAMAS	MAYST	MIDDY	MOCKS
LOOPS	LURGY	MAMBA	MAZES	MIDGE	MODAL
LOOPY	LURID	MAMBO	MBEKI	MID-ON	MODEL
LOOSE	LUSTS	MAMET	MEADS	MIDST	MODEM
LOPED	LUSTY	MAMEY	MEALS	MIENS	MODES
LOPER	LUTES	MAMMA	MEALY	MIFFY	MOERS
LORAN	LUTON	MAMMY	MEANS	MIGHT	MOGGY
LORDS	LUXOR	MANDE	MEANT	MIKES	MOGUL
LOREN	LUZON	MANED	MEATH	MILAN	MOIRE
LORIS	LYCEE	MANES	MEATY	MILCH	MOIST
LORRY	LYING	MANGE	MECCA	MILER	MOKES
LOSER	LYMPH	MANGO	MEDAL	MILES	MOKPO
LOSSY	LYNCH	MANGY	MEDAN	MILKY	MOLAL
LOTIC	LYRES	MANIA	MEDIA	MILLS	MOLAR
LOTTA	LYRIC	MANIC	MEDIC	MIMED	MOLDS
LOTUS	LYSIN	MANLY	MEDOC	MIMER	MOLDY
LOUGH	LYSIS	MANNA	MEETS	MIMES	MOLES
LOUPE	LYSOL	MANOR	MELEE	MIMIC	MOLLS
LOUSE	LYTIC	MANSE	MELON	MINCE	MOLLY
LOUSY	LYTTA	MANTA	MELOS	MINDS	MOLTO
LOUTH		MANUS	MEMOS	MINED	MOLTS
LOUTS	**M**	MAORI	MENAI	MINER	MOMMA
LOVAT	MACAO	MAPLE	MENDS	MINES	MOMMY
LOVED	MACAW	MARAE	MENUS	MINGY	MONAD
LOVER	MACES	MARCH	MEOWS	MINIM	MONAL
LOVES	MACHO	MARES	MERCA	MINIS	MONCK
LOVEY	MACLE	MARKS	MERCY	MINNA	MONEY
LOWED	MACON	MARNE	MERES	MINOR	MONKS

MONTH	MUCIN	NAILS	NEVER	NOPAL	ODIUM
MONZA	MUCKY	NAIVE	NEVIS	NO-PAR	ODOUR
MOOCH	MUCRO	NAKED	NEWEL	NORMS	OFFAL
MOODS	MUCUS	NALGO	NEWER	NORSE	OFFER
MOODY	MUDDY	NAMED	NEWLY	NORTH	OFGAS
MOOED	MUFFS	NAMES	NEWRY	NOSED	OFTEL
MOOLI	MUFTI	NAMUR	NEWSY	NOSES	OFTEN
MOONS	MUGGY	NANCY	NEWTS	NOTCH	OFWAT
MOONY	MULCH	NANNY	NEXUS	NOTED	OGIVE
MOORS	MULCT	NAPES	NICAD	NOTES	OGLED
MOOSE	MULES	NAPPA	NICAM	NOTUM	OGLER
MOPED	MULEY	NAPPE	NICER	NOUNS	OGRES
MOPER	MULGA	NAPPY	NICHE	NOVAE	OILED
MOP UP	MULLS	NARES	NICKS	NOVAS	OILER
MOP-UP	MULTI-	NARKS	NIDAL	NOVEL	OINKS
MORAL	MUMMY	NARKY	NIDUS	NO WAY	OKAPI
MORAY	MUMPS	NARVA	NIECE	NO-WIN	OKAYS
MOREL	MUMSY	NASAL	NIFFY	NOYON	OLDEN
MORES	MUNCH	NASIK	NIFTY	NUCHA	OLDER
MORNS	MUNGO	NASTY	NIGER	NUDDY	OLEUM
MORON	MURAL	NATAL	NIGHT	NUDES	OLIVE
MORPH	MUREX	NATES	NIHIL	NUDGE	OLMEC
MOSEY	MURKY	NATTY	NIKKO	NUKED	OMAGH
MOSSI	MURRE	NAURU	NIMBI	NUKUS	OMAHA
MOSSO	MUSED	NAVAL	NIMBY	NURSE	OMEGA
MOSSY	MUSER	NAVAR	NIMES	NUTTY	OMENS
MOSUL	MUSES	NAVEL	NINES	NYALA	OMUTA
MOTEL	MUSHY	NAVES	NINNY	NYLON	ON AIR
MOTES	MUSIC	NAVVY	NINON	NYMPH	ON-AIR
MOTET	MUSKY	NAXOS	NINTH		ON CUE
MOTHS	MUSTH	NAZIS	NIPPY	**O**	ONEGA
MOTHY	MUSTY	NDOLA	NISEI	OAKEN	ON ICE
MOTIF	MUTED	'NEATH	NISUS	OAKUM	ONION
MOTOR	MUTES	NECKS	NITRE	OARED	ONSET
MOTTO	MUTTS	NEEDS	NITTY	OASES	ON TAP
MOULD	MUZAK	NEEDY	NIVAL	OASIS	ON TOW
MOULT	MUZZY	NEGEV	NIXED	OATEN	OOMPH
MOUND	MWERU	NEGRO	NOBLE	OATHS	OOTID
MOUNT	MYALL	NEGUS	NOBLY	OBEAH	OOZED
MOURN	MYNAH	NEIGH	NODAL	OBESE	OPALS
MOUSE	MYOMA	NELLY	NODDY	OBOES	OP ART
MOUSY	MYOPE	NEMAN	NODES	OCCUR	OPERA
MOUTH	MYRRH	NEMEA	NODUS	OCEAN	OPINE
MOVED	MYTHS	NEPAL	NOHOW	OCHRE	OPIUM
MOVER		NEPER	NOISE	OCREA	OPTED
MOVES	**N**	NERDS	NOISY	OCTAD	OPTIC
MOVIE	NAAFI	NERVE	NOMAD	OCTAL	ORACH
MOWED	NABOB	NERVY	NONCE	OCTET	ORATE
MOWER	NACRE	NESTS	NOOKS	ODDER	ORBIT
MOXIE	NADIR	NEURO-	NO ONE	ODDLY	ORDER
MOYLE	NAIAD	NEUSS	NOOSE	ODEUM	ORGAN

ORIBI	PACES	PARRY	PENNY	PIMPS	PLICA
ORIEL	PACKS	PARSE	PENZA	PINCH	PLIED
ORION	PACTS	PARTS	PEONY	PINED	PLIER
ORIYA	PADDY	PARTY	PERAK	PINES	PLONK
ORLON	PADRE	PASAY	PERCH	PINEY	PLOTS
ORLOP	PADUA	PASHA	PERES	PINGO	PLOWS
ORMER	PAEAN	PASSE	PERIL	PINKO	PLOYS
ORRIS	PAEON	PASTA	PERKS	PINKS	PLUCK
ORURO	PAGAN	PASTE	PERKY	PINNA	PLUGS
OSAKA	PAGED	PASTO	PERRY	PINNY	PLUMB
OSCAR	PAGER	PASTS	PERSE	PINSK	PLUME
OSIER	PAGES	PASTY	PER SE	PINTA	PLUMP
OSMIC	PAILS	PATCH	PERTH	PINTO	PLUMS
OTAGO	PAINS	PATEN	PESKY	PINTS	PLUMY
OTHER	PAINT	PATER	PESOS	PINUP	PLUNK
OTTER	PAIRS	PATES	PESTO	PIOUS	PLUSH
OUGHT	PALEA	PATHS	PESTS	PIPAL	PLUTO
OUIJA	PALED	PATIO	PETAL	PIPED	PLZEN
OUJDA	PALER	PATNA	PETER	PIPER	POACH
OUNCE	PALES	PATSY	PETIT	PIPES	PO BOX
OUTDO	PALLS	PATTY	PETTY	PIPIT	PODGY
OUTER	PALLY	PAUSE	PEWEE	PIQUE	PODIA
OUTGO	PALMA	PAVED	PEWIT	PISTE	POEMS
OUTRE	PALMS	PAVIA	PHASE	PITCH	POESY
OUTRO	PALMY	PAWED	PHIAL	PITHY	POETS
OUZEL	PALSY	PAWKY	PHLOX	PITON	POGGE
OVALS	PANDA	PAWNS	PHONE	PITTA	POILU
OVARY	PANEL	PAYEE	PHONO	PIURA	POINT
OVATE	PANES	PEACE	PHOTO	PIVOT	POISE
OVENS	PANGS	PEACH	PHUTS	PIXEL	POKED
OVERS	PANIC	PEAKS	PHYLA	PIXIE	POKER
OVERT	PANNE	PEAKY	PHYLE	PIZZA	POKES
OVINE	PANSY	PEALS	PIANO	PLACE	POLAR
OVOID	PANTS	PEARL	PIAUI	PLAGE	POLED
OVOLO	PANTY	PEARS	PICKS	PLAID	POLES
OVULE	PAPAL	PEATS	PICKY	PLAIN	POLIO
OWING	PAPAS	PEATY	PICOT	PLAIT	POLJE
OWLET	PAPAW	PECAN	PIECE	PLANE	POLKA
OWNED	PAPER	PECKS	PIERS	PLANK	POLLS
OWNER	PAPPY	PEDAL	PIETA	PLANS	POLYP
OXBOW	PAPUA	PEEPS	PIETY	PLANT	POLYS
OXEYE	PARAS	PEERS	PIGGY	PLASH	POMMY
OXFAM	PARCH	PEEVE	PIGMY	PLASM	PONCE
OXIDE	PARED	PEKOE	PIING	PLATE	PONCY
OXIME	PARER	PELTS	PIKER	PLATY	PONDS
OXLIP	PARIS	PEMBA	PIKES	PLAYS	PONGS
OZONE	PARKA	PENAL	PILAF	PLAZA	PONGY
	PARKS	PENCE	PILED	PLEAD	POOCH
P	PARKY	PENIS	PILES	PLEAS	POOFS
PACED	PARMA	PENNA	PILLS	PLEAT	POOFY
PACER	PAROL	PENNE	PILOT	PLEBS	POOLE

POOLS	PRILL	PULPS	QUASH	RAGED	READY
POONA	PRIME	PULPY	QUASI-	RAGES	REALM
POOPS	PRIMO	PULSE	QUAYS	RAGGA	REAMS
POPES	PRIMP	PUMAS	QUEEN	RAIDS	REARM
POPPA	PRINK	PUMPS	QUEER	RAILS	REARS
POPPY	PRINT	PUNCH	QUELL	RAINS	REBEL
POPSY	PRION	PUNKA	QUERN	RAINY	REBUS
POP-UP	PRIOR	PUNKS	QUERY	RAISE	REBUT
PORCH	PRISE	PUNTS	QUEST	RAITA	RECAP
PORED	PRISM	PUNTY	QUEUE	RAJAH	RECON
PORES	PRIVY	PUPAE	QUICK	RAKED	RECTO
PORGY	PRIZE	PUPAL	QUIET	RAKER	RECUR
PORKY	PRO-AM	PUPAS	QUIFF	RAKES	REDAN
PORNO	PROBE	PUPIL	QUILL	RALLY	REDIA
PORTS	PRODS	PUPPY	QUILT	RAMIE	REDID
POSED	PROEM	PUREE	QUINE	RAMPS	REEDS
POSER	PROFS	PURER	QUINS	RAMUS	REEDY
POSES	PROLE	PURGE	QUINT	RANCE	REEFS
POSEY	PROMO	PURRS	QUIPS	RANCH	REEKY
POSIT	PROMS	PURSE	QUIRE	R AND B	REELS
POSSE	PRONE	PUSAN	QUIRK	R AND D	REEVE
POSTS	PRONG	PUSHY	QUIRT	RANDY	REFER
POTTO	PROOF	PUSSY	QUITE	RANEE	REFIT
POTTY	PROPS	PUT ON	QUITO	RANGE	REGAL
POUCH	PROSE	PUT-ON	QUITS	RANGY	REICH
POUFS	PROST	PUTTO	QUOIN	RANKS	REIFY
POULT	PROSY	PUTTS	QUOIT	RAPED	REIGN
POUND	PROTO-	PUTTY	QUORN	RAPES	REIKI
POUTS	PROUD	PYGMY	QUOTA	RAPHE	REIMS
POWAN	PROVE	PYLON	QUOTE	RAPID	REINS
POWER	PROWL	PYOID	QUOTH	RARER	REJIG
POWYS	PROWS	PYRAN	QUR'AN	RASHT	REKEY
POXES	PROXY	PYRES		RASPS	RELAX
PRAMS	PRUDE	PYREX	**R**	RATAL	RELAY
PRANK	PRUNE	PYXES	RABAT	RATED	RELIC
PRASE	PSALM	PYXIE	RABBI	RATEL	REMEX
PRATE	PSEUD	PYXIS	RABIC	RATES	REMIT
PRATO	PSKOV		RABID	RATIO	RENAL
PRATS	PSOAS	**Q**	RABIN	RATTY	RENEW
PRAWN	PSYCH	QATAR	RACED	RAVED	RENIN
PREEN	PUBES	QUACK	RACER	RAVEL	RENTE
PREPS	PUBIC	QUADS	RACES	RAVEN	RENTS
PRESA	PUBIS	QUAFF	RACKS	RAVER	REPAY
PRESS	PUCKS	QUAIL	RADAR	RAWER	REPEL
PRICE	PUDGY	QUAKE	RADII	RAWLY	REPLY
PRICK	PUFFS	QUAKY	RADIO	RAYON	RERAN
PRICY	PUFFY	QUALE	RADIX	RAZED	RERUN
PRIDE	PUKED	QUALM	RADOM	RAZER	RESAT
PRIED	PUKKA	QUANT	RADON	RAZOR	RESET
PRIER	PULER	QUARK	RAFTS	REACH	RESIN
PRIGS	PULLS	QUART	RAGAS	REACT	RESIT

RESTS	RIVER	ROWAN	SADLY	SAUCE	SCOUT
RETCH	RIVET	ROWDY	SAFER	SAUCY	SCOWL
RETRO	RIYAL	ROWED	SAFES	SAUNA	SCRAG
RETRO-	ROACH	ROWEL	SAGAS	SAURY	SCRAM
RETRY	ROADS	ROWER	SAGES	SAUTE	SCRAP
REUSE	ROANS	ROYAL	SAGGY	SAVED	SCREE
REVEL	ROARS	RUBLE	SAHIB	SAVER	SCREW
REVET	ROAST	RUCHE	SAIDA	SAVES	SCRIM
REVUE	ROBED	RUCKS	SAIGA	SAVIN	SCRIP
REXES	ROBES	RUDDY	SAILS	SAVOY	SCRUB
RHEAS	ROBIN	RUDER	SAINT	SAVVY	SCRUM
RHEUM	ROBLE	RUFFE	SAKAI	SAWED	SCUBA
RHINE	ROBOT	RUFFS	SAKER	SAWER	SCUFF
RHINO	ROCKS	RUGBY	SAKES	SAXON	SCULL
RHONE	ROCKY	RUING	SALAD	SAYER	SCURF
RHUMB	RODEO	RUINS	SALEM	SAY SO	SCUTE
RHYME	ROGER	RULED	SALEP	SAY-SO	SEALS
RIALS	ROGUE	RULER	SALES	SCABS	SEAMS
RICIN	ROLES	RULES	SALIC	SCADS	SEAMY
RICKS	ROLLS	RUMBA	SALLY	SCALD	SEATS
RIDER	ROMAN	RUMEN	SALOL	SCALE	SEBUM
RIDES	ROMEO	RUMMY	SALON	SCALL	SECCO
RIDGE	ROMER	RUMPS	SALOP	SCALP	SECTS
RIDGY	ROMPS	RUNES	SALPA	SCALY	SEDAN
RIFFS	RONDO	RUNGS	SALTA	SCAMP	SEDGE
RIFLE	ROODS	RUNIC	SALTS	SCAMS	SEDGY
RIFTS	ROOFS	RUN IN	SALTY	SCANS	SEDUM
RIGHT	ROOKS	RUN-IN	SALVE	SCANT	SEEDS
RIGID	ROOMS	RUNNY	SALVO	SCAPE	SEEDY
RIGOR	ROOMY	RUNTS	SAMAR	SCARE	SEERS
RILED	ROOST	RUNTY	SAMBA	SCARF	SEGNO
RILEY	ROOTS	RUN-UP	SAMEY	SCARP	SEINE
RILLS	ROPED	RUPEE	SAMOA	SCARS	SEISE
RINDS	ROPES	RURAL	SAMOS	SCART	SEISM
RINGS	ROPEY	RUSES	SANDS	SCARY	SEIZE
RINKS	ROSES	RUSHY	SANDY	SCAUP	SELBY
RINSE	ROSIN	RUSKS	SANER	SCEND	SELES
RIOJA	ROTAS	RUSSO-	SAPID	SCENE	SELVA
RIOTS	ROTOR	RUSTY	SAPPY	SCENT	SEMEN
RIPEN	ROUEN	RUTTY	SARAN	SCHWA	SEMIS
RIPER	ROUES		SARGE	SCION	SENNA
RIPON	ROUGE	**S**	SARIN	SCOFF	SENOR
RISEN	ROUGH	SABAH	SARIS	SCOLD	SENSE
RISER	ROUND	SABER	SARKY	SCONE	SENZA
RISES	ROUPY	SABIN	SAROS	SCOOP	SEOUL
RISKS	ROUSE	SABLE	SASSY	SCOOT	SEPAL
RISKY	ROUST	SABOT	SATAN	SCOPE	SEPIA
RITES	ROUTE	SABRA	SATED	SCORE	SEPOY
RITZY	ROUTS	SABRE	SATEM	SCORN	SERAC
RIVAL	ROVED	SACKS	SATIN	SCOTS	SERFS
RIVEN	ROVER	SADHU	SATYR	SCOUR	SERGE

SERIF	SHELF	SHYER	SIXTE	SLICE	SNACK
SERIN	SHELL	SHYLY	SIXTH	SLICK	SNAFU
SEROW	SHERD	SIBIU	SIXTY	SLIDE	SNAGS
SERUM	SHEWN	SIBYL	SIZAR	SLIGO	SNAIL
SERVE	SHIAH	SICKO	SIZED	SLILY	SNAKE
SERVO	SHIED	SIDED	SIZES	SLIME	SNAKY
SETAL	SHIER	SIDES	SKATE	SLIMY	SNAPS
SET ON	SHIES	SIDLE	SKEET	SLING	SNARE
SET TO	SHIFT	SIEGE	SKEIN	SLINK	SNARL
SET-TO	SHILY	SIENA	SKELP	SLIPS	SNATH
SET UP	SHINE	SIEVE	SKEWS	SLITS	SNEAK
SET-UP	SHINS	SIGHS	SKIDS	SLOBS	SNECK
SEVEN	SHINY	SIGHT	SKIED	SLOES	SNEER
SEVER	SHIPS	SIGLA	SKIEN	SLOGS	SNICK
SEWED	SHIRE	SIGMA	SKIER	SLOOP	SNIDE
SEWER	SHIRK	SIGNS	SKIES	SLOPE	SNIFF
SEXED	SHIRR	SIKHS	SKIFF	SLOPS	SNIPE
SEXES	SHIRT	SILEX	SKILL	SLOSH	SNIPS
SHABA	SHITE	SILKS	SKIMP	SLOTH	SNOBS
SHACK	SHITS	SILKY	SKINK	SLOTS	SNOEK
SHADE	SHIVE	SILLS	SKINS	SLUED	SNOGS
SHADY	SHLUH	SILLY	SKINT	SLUGS	SNOOD
SHAFT	SHOAL	SILOS	SKIPS	SLUMP	SNOOK
SHAGS	SHOAT	SILTY	SKIRL	SLUMS	SNOOP
SHAHS	SHOCK	SIMLA	SKIRT	SLUNG	SNORE
SHAKE	SHOED	SIMON	SKITS	SLUNK	SNORT
SHAKO	SHOER	SINAI	SKIVE	SLURP	SNOUT
SHAKY	SHOES	SINCE	SKUAS	SLURS	SNOWS
SHALE	SHONA	SINES	SKULK	SLUSH	SNOWY
SHALL	SHONE	SINEW	SKULL	SLUTS	SNUBS
SHALT	SHOOK	SINGE	SKUNK	SLYER	SNUFF
SHALY	SHOOT	SINKS	SLABS	SLYPE	SNUGS
SHAME	SHOPS	SINUS	SLACK	SMACK	SOAKS
SHAMS	SHORE	SIOUX	SLAGS	SMALL	SOAPS
SHANK	SHORN	SIRED	SLAIN	SMALT	SOAPY
SHAN'T	SHORT	SIREN	SLAKE	SMARM	SOBER
SHAPE	SHOTS	SIRES	SLANG	SMART	SOCHE
SHARD	SHOTT	SISAL	SLANT	SMASH	SOCHI
SHARE	SHOUT	SISSY	SLAPS	SMEAR	SOCIO-
SHARK	SHOVE	SITAR	SLASH	SMELL	SOCKS
SHARP	SHOWN	SITED	SLATE	SMELT	SOCLE
SHAVE	SHOWS	SITES	SLATS	SMILE	SODAS
SHAWL	SHOWY	SIT-IN	SLATY	SMIRK	SOFAR
SHEAF	SHRED	SITKA	SLAVE	SMITE	SOFAS
SHEAR	SHREW	SIT ON	SLAVS	SMITH	SOFIA
SHEDS	SHRUB	SIT UP	SLEDS	SMOCK	SOFTA
SHEEN	SHRUG	SIT-UP	SLEEK	SMOKE	SOFTY
SHEEP	SHUCK	SITUS	SLEEP	SMOKY	SOGGY
SHEER	SHUNT	SIVAS	SLEET	SMOLT	SOILS
SHEET	SHUSH	SIXES	SLEPT	SMOTE	SOLAR
SHEIK	SHYED	SIXMO	SLEWS	SMUTS	SOLED

SOLES	SPEND	SPUNK	STICH	STUFF	SWASH
SOL-FA	SPENT	SPURN	STICK	STULL	SWATH
SOLID	SPERM	SPURS	STIES	STUMP	SWATS
SOLOS	SPICA	SPURT	STIFF	STUNG	SWAZI
SOLTI	SPICE	SQUAB	STILE	STUNK	SWEAR
SOLUM	SPICS	SQUAD	STILL	STUNT	SWEAT
SOLVE	SPICY	SQUAT	STILT	STUPE	SWEDE
SOMME	SPIED	SQUAW	STING	STYLE	SWEEP
SONAR	SPIEL	SQUIB	STINK	SUAVE	SWEET
SONDE	SPIES	SQUID	STINT	SUCRE	SWELL
SONGS	SPIFF	STABS	STIPE	SUDAN	SWEPT
SONIC	SPIKE	STACK	STIRK	SUDOR	SWIFT
SONNY	SPIKS	STAFF	STIRS	SUDSY	SWIGS
SOOTY	SPIKY	STAGE	STOAT	SUEDE	SWILL
SOPOR	SPILE	STAGS	STOCK	SUETY	SWIMS
SOPPY	SPILL	STAGY	STOEP	SUGAR	SWINE
SORES	SPILT	STAID	STOIC	SUING	SWING
SORGO	SPINE	STAIN	STOKE	SUINT	SWIPE
SORRY	SPINS	STAIR	STOLE	SUITE	SWIRL
SORTS	SPINY	STAKE	STOMA	SUITS	SWISH
SORUS	SPIRE	STALE	STOMP	SULKS	SWISS
SOTHO	SPIRY	STALK	STONE	SULKY	SWOON
SOUGH	SPITE	STALL	STONY	SULLY	SWOOP
SOULS	SPITS	STAMP	STOOD	SUMBA	SWOPS
SOUND	SPITZ	STAND	STOOK	SUMPS	SWORD
SOUPS	SPIVS	STANK	STOOL	SUNNI	SWORE
SOUPY	SPLAT	STANS	STOOP	SUNNY	SWORN
SOUSE	SPLAY	STARE	STOPE	SUN-UP	SWOTS
SOUTH	SPLIT	STARK	STOPS	SUPER	SWUNG
SOWED	SPOCK	STARS	STORE	SUPRA	SYLPH
SOWER	SPODE	START	STORK	SURAH	SYLVA
SOYUZ	SPOIL	STASH	STORM	SURAL	SYNOD
SPACE	SPOKE	STATE	STORY	SURAT	SYRIA
SPADE	SPOOF	STAVE	STOSS	SURDS	SYRUP
SPAIN	SPOOK	STAYS	STOUP	SURER	SYSOP
SPALL	SPOOL	STEAD	STOUR	SURFY	
SPANK	SPOON	STEAK	STOUT	SURGE	**T**
SPARE	SPOOR	STEAL	STOVE	SURLY	TABBY
SPARK	SPORE	STEAM	STRAP	SUSHI	TABES
SPARS	SPORT	STEED	STRAW	SWABS	TABLE
SPASM	SPOTS	STEEL	STRAY	SWAGE	TABOO
SPATE	SPOUT	STEEP	STREW	SWAIN	TABOR
SPATS	SPRAG	STEER	STRIA	SWALE	TACET
SPAWN	SPRAT	STEIN	STRIP	SWAMI	TACIT
SPEAK	SPRAY	STELE	STROP	SWAMP	TACKS
SPEAR	SPREE	STEMS	STRUM	SWANK	TACKY
SPECK	SPRIG	STEPS	STRUT	SWANS	TACOS
SPECS	SPRIT	STERE	STUBS	SWAPS	TAEGU
SPEED	SPRUE	STERN	STUCK	SWARD	TAFFY
SPELL	SPUDS	STEWS	STUDS	SWARF	TAFIA
SPELT	SPUME	STEYR	STUDY	SWARM	TAIGA

TAILS	TAWNY	TEXTS	TIE-UP	TOLLS	TOYED
TAINO	TAXED	THANE	TIFFS	TOLYL	TOYER
TAINT	TAXER	THANK	TIGER	TOMBS	TRACE
TA'IZZ	TAXES	THAWS	TIGHT	TOMES	TRACK
TAJIK	TAXIS	THECA	TIGON	TOMMY	TRACT
TAKEN	TAXON	THEFT	TIGRE	TOMSK	TRADE
TAKER	TAYRA	THEGN	TIKKA	TONAL	TRAIL
TAKES	TAZZA	THEIR	TILDE	TONDO	TRAIN
TAKIN	T-BONE	THEME	TILED	TONED	TRAIT
TALCA	TEACH	THERA	TILER	TONER	TRAMP
TALES	TEAKS	THERE	TILES	TONES	TRAMS
TALKS	TEAMS	THERM	TILLS	TONGA	TRANS-
TALLY	TEARS	THESE	TILTH	TONGS	TRAPS
TALON	TEASE	THETA	TILTS	TONIC	TRASH
TALUS	TEATS	THEWS	TIMED	TONNE	TRASS
TAMED	TECHY	THICK	TIMER	TON UP	TRAVE
TAMER	TEENS	THIEF	TIMES	TON-UP	TRAWL
TAMMY	TEENY	THIGH	TIMID	TONUS	TRAYS
TAMPA	TEETH	THINE	TINEA	TOOLS	TREAD
TANGA	TELEX	THING	TINES	TOOTH	TREAT
TANGO	TELIC	THINK	TINGE	TOOTS	TREEN
TANGY	TELLY	THIOL	TINGS	TOPAZ	TREES
TANKS	TEMPI	THIRD	TINNY	TOPEE	TREKS
TANSY	TEMPO	THOLE	TINTS	TOPER	TREND
TANTA	TEMPS	THONG	TIPSY	TOPIC	TRESS
TANTO	TEMPT	THORN	TIP UP	TOPOS	TREWS
TAPAS	TENCH	THOSE	TIRED	TOP UP	TRIAD
TAPED	TENET	THREE	TIREE	TOQUE	TRIAL
TAPER	TENON	THREW	TIRES	TORAH	TRIBE
TAPES	TENOR	THROB	TIROS	TORCH	TRICE
TAPIR	TENSE	THROW	TITAN	TORIC	TRICK
TAPIS	TENTH	THRUM	TITHE	TORSK	TRIED
TARDY	TENTS	THUDS	TITLE	TORSO	TRIER
TARES	TEPAL	THUGS	TITRE	TORTS	TRIES
TARGA	TEPEE	THUJA	TITTY	TORUN	TRIKE
TARNS	TEPIC	THUMB	TIZZY	TORUS	TRILL
TAROS	TEPID	THUMP	TOADS	TOTAL	TRIMS
TAROT	TERMS	THUNK	TOADY	TOTED	TRINE
TARRY	TERNE	THYME	TOAST	TOTEM	TRIOL
TARSI	TERNI	TIARA	TODAY	TOTER	TRIOS
TARTS	TERNS	TIBET	TODDY	TOTES	TRIPE
TARTU	TERRA	TIBIA	TO-DOS	TOUCH	TRIPS
TASKS	TERRY	TICAL	TOE-IN	TOUGH	TRITE
TASTE	TERSE	TICKS	TOFFS	TOURS	TROLL
TASTY	TESLA	TIDAL	TOGAS	TOUTS	TRONA
TATAR	TESOL	TIDED	TOILE	TOWED	TRONK
TATRA	TESTA	TIDES	TOILS	TOWEL	TROOP
TATTY	TESTS	TIE-IN	TOKAY	TOWER	TROPE
TAUNT	TESTY	TIE-ON	TOKEN	TOWNS	TROTH
TAUPE	TETRA	TIERS	TOKYO	TOXIC	TROTS
TAWER	TEXAS	TIE UP	TOLAN	TOXIN	TROUT

TROVE	TUTOR	UNARY	UTTER	VERVE	VOIDS
TRUCE	TUTSI	UNBAR	U-TURN	VESTA	VOILE
TRUCK	TUTTI	UNCAP	UVEAL	VESTS	VOLAR
TRUER	TUTTY	UNCLE	UVULA	VETCH	VOLES
TRUES	TUTUS	UNCUS	UZBEK	VEXED	VOLTA
TRUGO	TWAIN	UNCUT		VEXER	VOLTS
TRUGS	TWANG	UNDER	**V**	VIALS	VOLVA
TRULY	TWATS	UNDID		VIAND	VOMER
TRUMP	TWEAK	UNDUE	VAASA	VIBES	VOMIT
TRUNK	TWEED	UNFIT	VADUZ	VICAR	VOTED
TRURO	'TWEEN	UNFIX	VAGAL	VICES	VOTER
TRUSS	TWEET	UNIAT	VAGUE	VICHY	VOTES
TRUST	TWERP	UNIFY	VAGUS	VIDAL	VOUCH
TRUTH	TWICE	UNION	VALES	VIDEO	VOWED
TRYMA	TWIGS	UNITE	VALET	VIEWS	VOWEL
TRY ON	TWILL	UNITS	VALID	VIGIA	VOWER
TRY-ON	TWINE	UNITY	VALSE	VIGIL	V-SIGN
TRYST	TWINS	UNLAY	VALUE	VILER	VULVA
TSARS	TWIRL	UNMAN	VALVE	VILLA	VYING
TUBAL	TWIRP	UNPEG	VAMPS	VIMEN	
TUBAS	TWIST	UNPIN	VANDA	VINCA	**W**
TUBBY	TWITE	UNRIG	VANES	VINES	WACKY
TUBER	TWITS	UNRIP	VAPID	VINIC	WADDY
TUBES	TWIXT	UNSAY	VARIA	VINYL	WADED
TUCKS	TYING	UNSET	VARIX	VIOLA	WADER
TUDOR	TYPED	UNSEX	VARNA	VIOLS	WADGE
TUFTS	TYPES	UNTIE	VARUS	VIPER	WADIS
TUFTY	TYRES	UNTIL	VARVE	VIRAL	WAFER
TULIP	TYROL	UNZIP	VASES	VIREO	WAGED
TULLE	TYROS	UP-BOW	VAULT	VIRGA	WAGER
TULSA	TYSON	UPEND	VAUNT	VIRGO	WAGES
TUMID	TZARS	UPOLU	V-CHIP	VIRTU	WAGON
TUMMY	TZU-PO	UPPER	VEDDA	VIRUS	WAHOO
TUNAS		UPSET	VEDIC	VISAS	WAIFS
TUNED	**U**	URALS	VEERY	VISBY	WAIST
TUNER	U-BOAT	URATE	VEGAN	VISES	WAIVE
TUNES	UDDER	URBAN	VEILS	VISEU	WAJDA
TUNIC	UDINE	UREAL	VEINS	VISIT	WAKED
TUNIS	UGRIC	UREDO	VEINY	VISOR	WAKEN
TUNNY	UHURU	URGED	VELAR	VISTA	WAKER
TUQUE	UIGUR	URGER	VELUM	VITAL	WAKES
TURDS	ULCER	URGES	VENAL	VITTA	WALES
TURFS	ULNAR	URINE	VENDA	VIVID	WALKS
TURFY	ULNAS	USAGE	VENIN	VIXEN	WALLS
TURIN	ULTRA-	USERS	VENOM	V-NECK	WALLY
TURKI	ULURU	USHER	VENTS	VOCAB	WALTZ
TURKU	UMBEL	USING	VENUE	VOCAL	WANDS
TURNS	UMBER	USUAL	VENUS	VODKA	WANED
TURPS	UMBRA	USURP	VERBS	VOGUE	WANES
TUSKS	UMIAK	USURY	VERGE	VOGUL	WANEY
TUTEE	UNAPT	UTERI	VERSE	VOICE	WANLY
			VERSO		

33

WANTS	WHACK	WILDS	WOOFS	XENON	YOKES
WARDS	WHALE	WILES	WOOZY	XERIC	YOLKS
WARES	WHAMS	WILLS	WORDS	XEROX	YOLKY
WARPS	WHANG	WILLY	WORDY	XHOSA	YONKS
WARTS	WHARF	WIMPS	WORKS	X-RAYS	YONNE
WARTY	WHEAL	WIMPY	WORLD	X-UNIT	YOUNG
WASHY	WHEAT	WINCE	WORMS	XYLAN	YOURS
WASPS	WHEEL	WINCH	WORMY	XYLEM	YOUSE
WASTE	WHELK	WINDS	WORRY	XYLOL	YOUTH
WATCH	WHELP	WINDY	WORSE	XYLYL	YOWLS
WATER	WHERE	WINED	WORST		YOYOS
WATTS	WHICH	WINES	WORTH	**Y**	YPRES
WAVED	WHIFF	WINEY	WOULD	YACHT	YUCCA
WAVER	WHIGS	WINGE	WOUND	YAHOO	YUCKY
WAVES	WHILE	WINGS	WOVEN	YAKUT	YUKON
WAXED	WHIMS	WINKS	WOWED	YALTA	YULAN
WAXEN	WHINE	WINZE	WRACK	YANAN	YUMAN
WAXER	WHINY	WIPED	WRAPS	YANKS	
WEALD	WHIPS	WIPER	WRATH	YAPOK	**Z**
WEALS	WHIRL	WIPES	WREAK	YAPPY	ZAIRE
WEARY	WHIRR	WIRED	WRECK	YARDS	ZAMIA
WEAVE	WHIRS	WIRER	WRENS	YARNS	ZANTE
WEBBY	WHISK	WIRES	WREST	YAWED	ZAPPY
WEBER	WHIST	WISER	WRIED	YAWLS	ZARGA
WEDGE	WHITE	WISPS	WRIER	YAWNS	ZARIA
WEDGY	WHITS	WISPY	WRING	Y-AXIS	ZARQA
WEEDS	WHIZZ	WITCH	WRIST	YEARN	Z-AXIS
WEEDY	WHOLE	WITHE	WRITE	YEARS	ZEBRA
WEEKS	WHOOP	WITHY	WRITS	YEAST	ZEIST
WEENY	WHORE	WITTY	WRONG	YELLS	ZENIC
WEEPY	WHORL	WIVES	WROTE	YELPS	ZEROS
WEIGH	WHOSE	WIZEN	WROTH	YEMEN	ZESTY
WEIRD	WICCA	WOKEN	WRUNG	YERBA	ZIBET
WEIRS	WICKS	WOLDS	WRYER	YETIS	ZILCH
WELCH	WIDEN	WOLOF	WRYLY	YIBIN	ZINGY
WELDS	WIDER	WOMAN	WUHAN	YIELD	ZIPPY
WELLS	WIDES	WOMBS	WURST	YIKES	ZLOTY
WELLY	WIDOW	WOMEN	WUSIH	YODEL	ZOMBA
WELSH	WIDTH	WONKY		YOGIC	ZONAL
WELTS	WIELD	WOODS	**X**	YOGIS	ZONED
WENCH	WIGAN	WOODY	X-AXIS	YOKED	ZONES
WESER	WIGHT	WOOED	XENIA	YOKEL	ZOOID
WETLY	WILCO	WOOER			

A	ACCORD	ADVENT	AILING	ALL OUT	AMRITA
AACHEN	ACCOST	ADVERB	AIMING	ALLOYS	AMULET
AARGAU	ACCRUE	ADVERT	AIRBED	ALLUDE	AMUSED
AARHUS	ACCUSE	ADVICE	AIRBUS	ALLURE	AMYLUM
ABACUS	ACETAL	ADVISE	AIR-DRY	ALMADA	AMYTAL
ABADAN	ACETIC	ADYGEI	AIRGUN	AL MARJ	ANABAS
ABAKAN	ACETUM	ADZHAR	AIRIER	ALMATY	ANADYR
ABASED	ACETYL	AECIUM	AIRILY	ALMOND	ANALOG
ABATED	ACHAEA	AEDILE	AIRING	ALMOST	ANCHOR
ABATIS	ACHENE	AEGEAN	AIRMAN	ALMUCE	ANCONA
ABATOR	ACHING	AERATE	AIRMEN	ALNICO	ANDEAN
ABBACY	ACIDIC	AERIAL	AIRWAY	ALPACA	ANDONG
ABBESS	ACINIC	AERIFY	AISLES	ALPHAS	ANDROS
ABBEYS	ACINUS	AEROBE	AKIMBO	ALPINE	ANEMIA
ABBOTS	ACNODE	AERUGO	AKMOLA	ALSACE	ANEMIC
ABDUCT	ACORNS	AETHER	AL-ANON	ALSIKE	ANERGY
ABELIA	ACQUIT	AFFAIR	ALARMS	ALTAIC	ANGARY
ABIDED	ACROSS	AFFECT	ALASKA	ALTAIR	ANGELS
ABIDER	ACTING	AFFINE	ALBANY	ALTARS	ANGERS
ABJECT	ACTION	AFFIRM	ALBEDO	ALTONA	ANGINA
ABJURE	ACTIVE	AFFLUX	ALBEIT	ALUDEL	ANGKOR
ABKHAZ	ACTORS	AFFORD	ALBINO	ALUMNA	ANGLED
ABLAUT	ACTS UP	AFFRAY	ALBION	ALUMNI	ANGLER
ABLAZE	ACTUAL	AFGHAN	ALBITE	ALVINE	ANGLES
ABOARD	ACUITY	AFIELD	ALBUMS	ALWAYS	ANGOLA
ABODES	ACUMEN	AFLAME	ALCOVE	AMADOU	ANGORA
ABORAL	ADAGES	AFL-CIO	ALDISS	AMATOL	ANHALT
ABOUND	ADAGIO	AFLOAT	ALDOSE	AMAZED	ANHWEI
ABRADE	ADDEND	AFRAID	ALDRIN	AMAZON	ANIMAL
ABROAD	ADDERS	AFRESH	ALECKS	AMBALA	ANIMUS
ABRUPT	ADDICT	AFRICA	ALEGAR	AMBARY	ANKARA
ABSEIL	ADDING	AFTERS	ALEPPO	AMBITS	ANKING
ABSENT	ADDLED	AGADIR	ALERTS	AMBLED	ANKLES
ABSORB	ADD-ONS	AGAMIC	A LEVEL	AMBLER	ANKLET
ABSURD	ADDUCE	AGARIC	ALGOID	AMBUSH	ANLAGE
ABULIA	ADDUCT	AGATES	AL HASA	AMEBAS	ANNABA
ABULIC	ADEPTS	AGEING	ALIBIS	AMEBIC	ANNALS
ABUSED	ADHERE	AGEISM	ALIENS	AMENDS	ANNEAL
ABUSER	ADIEUS	AGEIST	ALIGHT	AMHARA	ANNECY
ABUSES	ADIEUX	AGENCY	ALIPED	AMIDIC	ANNEXE
ABVOLT	ADJOIN	AGENDA	ALKALI	AMIDOL	ANNUAL
ABWATT	ADJURE	AGENTS	ALKANE	AMIDST	ANODES
ACACIA	ADJUST	AGE OLD	ALKENE	AMIENS	ANODIC
ACADIA	ADMIRE	AGHAST	ALKYNE	AMMINE	ANOINT
ACAJOU	ADNATE	AGNATE	ALLEGE	AMNION	ANOMIC
ACARID	ADNOUN	AGOGIC	ALLELE	AMOEBA	ANOMIE
ACARUS	ADORED	AGONIC	ALLEYS	AMORAL	ANORAK
ACCEDE	ADRIFT	AGOUTI	ALLIED	AMOUNT	ANOXIA
ACCENT	ADROIT	AGREED	ALLIER	AMOURS	ANOXIC
ACCEPT	ADSORB	AIDING	ALLIES	AMPERE	ANQING
ACCESS	ADULTS	AIKIDO	ALLIUM	AMPULE	ANSATE

ANSHAN	ARABIC	ARRIVE	ATHENS	AVENGE	BAKERS
ANSWER	ARABLE	ARROBA	AT HOME	AVENUE	BAKERY
ANTEED	ARAGON	ARROWS	AT-HOME	AVERSE	BAKING
ANTHEM	ARARAT	ARSINE	AT LAST	AVIARY	BALATA
ANTHER	ARBOUR	ARTERY	ATOLLS	AVIATE	BALBOA
ANTICS	ARCADE	ARTFUL	ATOMIC	AVIDIN	BALDLY
ANTLER	ARCANA	ARTIER	ATONAL	AVIDLY	BALEEN
ANTRIM	ARCANE	ARTIST	ATONED	AVOCET	BALING
ANTRUM	ARCHED	ARTOIS	ATONER	AVOWAL	BALKAN
ANTUNG	ARCHER	ARUNTA	ATONIC	AVOWED	BALKED
ANURAN	ARCHES	ASARUM	AT REST	AVOWER	BALKER
ANURIA	ARCHLY	ASCEND	ATRIUM	AWAKED	BALLAD
ANUSES	ARCTIC	ASCENT	ATTACH	AWAKEN	BALLET
ANVILS	ARDENT	ASCOTS	ATTACK	AWARDS	BALLOT
ANYANG	ARDOUR	ASHDOD	ATTAIN	AWEIGH	BALSAM
ANYHOW	ARENAS	ASHIER	ATTEND	AWHILE	BALSAS
ANYONE	AREOLA	ASHLAR	ATTEST	AWNING	BALTIC
ANYWAY	ARETES	ASHORE	ATTICA	AWOKEN	BAMAKO
AORIST	AREZZO	ASIANS	ATTICS	AXENIC	BAMBOO
AORTAS	ARGALI	ASIDES	ATTIRE	AXILLA	BANABA
AORTIC	ARGENT	ASKING	ATTORN	AXIOMS	BANANA
AOUDAD	ARGOSY	ASLANT	ATTRIT	AYE AYE	BANDED
AOUITA	ARGOTS	ASLEEP	ATTUNE	AYMARA	BANDIT
APACHE	ARGUED	ASMARA	ATWOOD	AZALEA	BANDOG
APATHY	ARGUER	ASPECT	AUBADE	AZORES	BANGED
APEMAN	ARGYLE	ASPIRE	AUBURN	AZOTIC	BANGER
APERCU	ARGYLL	ASSAIL	AUDILE		BANGLE
APEXES	ARIEGE	ASSAYS	AUDITS	B	BANGOR
APHIDS	ARIGHT	ASSENT	AU FAIT	BAAING	BANGUI
APHTHA	ARIOSO	ASSERT	AU FOND	BABBLE	BANISH
APIARY	ARISEN	ASSESS	AUGEND	BABIED	BANJOS
APICAL	ARISTA	ASSETS	AUGERS	BABIES	BANJUL
APICES	ARKOSE	ASSIGN	AUGITE	BABOON	BANKED
APIECE	ARMADA	ASSISI	AUGURY	BACKED	BANKER
APLITE	ARMAGH	ASSIST	AUGUST	BACKER	BANNED
APLOMB	ARMFUL	ASSIZE	AUKLET	BACK UP	BANNER
APNOEA	ARMIES	ASSORT	AU LAIT	BACKUP	BANTAM
APODAL	ARMING	ASSUME	AUMBRY	BADGER	BANTER
APOGEE	ARMLET	ASSURE	AU PAIR	BADGES	BANYAN
APOLLO	ARMOUR	ASTANA	AUREUS	BAFFLE	BAOBAB
APPEAL	ARMPIT	ASSUAN	AURORA	BAGELS	BAOTOU
APPEAR	ARMURE	ASTERN	AUROUS	BAGGED	BARBED
APPEND	ARNHEM	ASTHMA	AUSSIE	BAGUIO	BARBEL
APPLES	ARNICA	ASTRAL	AUSTIN	BAILED	BARBER
APPLET	AROMAS	ASTRAY	AUSTRO-	BAILEE	BARBET
APPOSE	AROUND	ASTUTE	AUTEUR	BAILER	BARBIE
APRILS	AROUSE	ASWARM	AUTHOR	BAILEY	BARDIC
APRONS	ARRACK	ASYLUM	AUTISM	BAILOR	BARELY
APULIA	ARRANT	ATAXIA	AUTUMN	BAIL UP	BAREST
AQUILA	ARRAYS	ATAXIC	AVATAR	BAIRNS	BARGED
ARABIA	ARREST	ATBARA	AVEIRO	BAITED	BARGEE

BARGES	BATTLE	BEHEAD	BETTED	BINGOS	BLINKS
BARING	BATTUE	BEHELD	BETTER	BINMAN	BLINTZ
BARIUM	BAUBLE	BEHEST	BEVELS	BINNED	BLITHE
BARKED	BAUCHI	BEHIND	BEVIES	BIOGAS	BLOCKS
BARKER	BAULKS	BEHOLD	BEWAIL	BIOGEN	BLOKES
BARLEY	BAWLED	BEHOVE	BEWARE	BIONIC	BLONDE
BARMAN	BAWLER	BEINGS	BEXLEY	BIOPIC	BLOODS
BARMEN	BAYEUX	BEIRUT	BEYOND	BIOPSY	BLOODY
BARNET	BAYING	BELFRY	BEZIER	BIOTIC	BLOOMS
BARNEY	BAYOUS	BELIED	BEZOAR	BIOTIN	BLOTCH
BARODA	BAZAAR	BELIEF	BHOPAL	BIPEDS	BLOTTO
BARONS	BEACON	BELIER	BHUTAN	BIRDIE	BLOUSE
BARONY	BEADED	BELIZE	BHUTTO	BIRTHS	BLOWER
BARQUE	BEADLE	BELLES	BIAFRA	BISCAY	BLOWSY
BARRED	BEAGLE	BELLOW	BIASED	BISECT	BLOW-UP
BARREL	BEAKER	BELONG	BIASES	BISHOP	BLOWZY
BARREN	BEAMED	BELSEN	BIBLES	BISKRA	BLUEST
BARROW	BEARDS	BELTED	BICEPS	BISONS	BLUFFS
BARTER	BEARER	BELTER	BICKER	BISQUE	BLUISH
BARTON	BEASTS	BELUGA	BICORN	BISSAU	BLUNGE
BARYON	BEATEN	BEMOAN	BIDDEN	BISTRE	BLURBS
BARYTE	BEATER	BEMUSE	BIDETS	BISTRO	BLURRY
BASALT	BEAUNE	BENDER	BIDING	BITCHY	B-MOVIE
BASELY	BEAUTS	BENGAL	BIFFED	BITING	BOARDS
BASEST	BEAUTY	BENGBU	BIFFIN	BITMAP	BOASTS
BASHED	BEAVER	BENIGN	BIGAMY	BITOLJ	BOATED
BASHES	BECAME	BENONI	BIG CAT	BITTEN	BOATER
BASICS	BECKET	BENUMB	BIG END	BITTER	BOATIE
BASIFY	BECKON	BENZOL	BIGGER	BLACKS	BOBBED
BASING	BECOME	BENZYL	BIGGIE	BLADES	BOBBER
BASINS	BEDAUB	BERATE	BIGHTS	BLAMED	BOBBIN
BASION	BEDBUG	BEREFT	BIGOTS	BLANCH	BOBBLE
BASKED	BEDDED	BERETS	BIG TOP	BLANKS	BOBCAT
BASKET	BEDDER	BERGEN	BIGWIG	BLARED	BOCHUM
BASQUE	BEDECK	BERING	BIHARI	BLASTS	BODEGA
BASRAH	BEDLAM	BERLEY	BIKING	BLAZED	BODICE
BASSES	BEDPAN	BERLIN	BIKINI	BLAZER	BODIES
BASSET	BEDSIT	BERTHS	BILBAO	BLAZES	BODILY
BASTED	BEEFED	BERYLS	BILGES	BLAZON	BODING
BASTIA	BEETLE	BESEEM	BILKED	BLEACH	BODKIN
BASUCO	BEFALL	BESIDE	BILKER	BLEARY	BODMIN
BATHED	BEFELL	BESOMS	BILLED	BLEATS	BOFFIN
BATHER	BEFOOL	BESTED	BILLET	BLEEPS	BOGEYS
BATHOS	BEFORE	BESTIR	BILLON	BLENCH	BOGGED
BATLEY	BEFOUL	BESTOW	BILLOW	BLENDE	BOGGLE
BATMAN	BEGGAR	BETAKE	BILLY-O	BLENDS	BOGIES
BATMEN	BEGGED	BETHEL	BINARY	BLENNY	BOGOTA
BATONS	BEGONE	BETIDE	BINATE	BLIGHT	BOILED
BATTED	BEGUMS	BETONY	BINDER	BLIMEY	BOILER
BATTEN	BEHALF	BETOOK	BINGEN	BLIMPS	BOLAND
BATTER	BEHAVE	BETRAY	BINGES	BLINDS	BOLDER

BOLDLY	BOSOMY	BRAKED	BRONZY	BUNGED	BUSSED
BOLERO	BOSSED	BRAKES	BROOCH	BUNGEE	BUSTED
BOLIDE	BOSSES	BRANCH	BROODS	BUNGLE	BUSTER
BOLSHY	BOSTON	BRANDO	BROODY	BUNION	BUSTLE
BOLSON	BOSUNS	BRANDS	BROOKS	BUNKED	BUST-UP
BOLTED	BOTANY	BRANDT	BROOMS	BUNKER	BUTANE
BOLTER	BOTCHY	BRANDY	BROWNS	BUNKUM	BUTENE
BOLTON	BOTFLY	BRASHY	BROWSE	BUNK-UP	BUTLER
BOMBAY	BOTHER	BRASOV	BRUGES	BUOYED	BUTTED
BOMBED	BOTTLE	BRASSY	BRUISE	BURBLE	BUTTER
BOMBER	BOTTOM	BRAVED	BRUMAL	BURBOT	BUTTES
BONBON	BOUAKE	BRAVER	BRUMBY	BURDEN	BUTTIE
BONDED	BOUCLE	BRAVES	BRUNCH	BUREAU	BUTTON
BONGOS	BOUGHS	BRAVOS	BRUNEI	BURGAS	BUXTON
BONIER	BOUGHT	BRAWLS	BRUTAL	BURGEE	BUYERS
BONILY	BOUGIE	BRAWNY	BRUTES	BURGER	BUYING
BONING	BOULES	BRAYED	BRUTON	BURGHS	BUYOUT
BONITO	BOULLE	BRAYER	BRYONY	BURGLE	BUZZED
BON MOT	BOUNCE	BRAZEN	BUBBLE	BURGOS	BUZZER
BONNET	BOUNCY	BRAZER	BUBBLY	BURIAL	BUZZES
BONSAI	BOUNDS	BRAZIL	BUCCAL	BURIED	BY-BLOW
BONZER	BOUNTY	BREACH	BUCKED	BURIER	BYGONE
BOOBED	BOURNS	BREAKS	BUCKET	BURLAP	BYLAWS
BOOGIE	BOURSE	BREAST	BUCKLE	BURLER	BY-LINE
BOOHOO	BOVINE	BRECON	BUDDED	BURLEY	BYPASS
BOOING	BOVVER	BREECH	BUDDHA	BURNED	BYPLAY
BOOKED	BOWELS	BREEZE	BUDDLE	BURNER	BYROAD
BOOKIE	BOWERS	BREEZY	BUDGED	BURNET	BYSSUS
BOOMED	BOWERY	BREGMA	BUDGET	BURPED	BYWAYS
BOOSTS	BOWFIN	BREMEN	BUFFED	BURPEE	BYWORD
BOOTED	BOWING	BRETON	BUFFER	BURRED	
BOOTEE-	BOWLED	BREVET	BUFFET	BURROS	**C**
BOOTHS	BOWLER	BREWER	BUGGED	BURROW	CABALS
BOOTLE	BOWMAN	BRIBER	BUGGER	BURSAL	CABANA
BOOZED	BOWMEN	BRIDAL	BUGLER	BURSAR	CABBIE
BOOZER	BOWSAW	BRIDGE	BUGLES	BURSTS	CABERS
BOPPED	BOWSER	BRIDLE	BUILDS	BURTON	CABINS
BORAGE	BOW TIE	BRIERY	BUKAVU	BURYAT	CABLED
BORANE	BOWWOW	BRIGHT	BULBAR	BUSBAR	CABLES
BORATE	BOWYER	BRITON	BULBIL	BUS BOY	CABLET
BORDER	BOXCAR	BROACH	BULBUL	BUSBOY	CABMAN
BOREAL	BOXERS	BROADS	BULGED	BUSHED	CACHES
BORERS	BOXING	BROCHE	BULGES	BUSHEL	CACHET
BORIDE	BOYISH	BROGUE	BULKED	BUSHES	CACHOU
BORING	BRACED	BROKEN	BULLET	BUSIED	CACKLE
BORNEO	BRACER	BROKER	BUMBLE	BUSIER	CACTUS
BORROW	BRACES	BROLLY	BUMMED	BUSILY	CAD/CAM
BORZOI	BRAIDS	BROMAL	BUMPED	BUSING	CADDIE
BOSKET	BRAINS	BROMIC	BUMPER	BUSKED	CADDIS
BOSNIA	BRAINY	BRONCO	BUNCHY	BUSKER	CADENT
BOSOMS	BRAISE	BRONZE	BUNDLE	BUSKIN	CADETS

CADGED	CAMPER	CARESS	CATION	CEROUS	CHEESY
CADGER	CAMPOS	CARETS	CATKIN	CERUSE	CHEQUE
CADRES	CAMPUS	CARGOS	CATNAP	CERVID	CHERRY
CAECUM	CANADA	CARHOP	CATNIP	CERVIX	CHERTY
CAELUM	CANALS	CARIES	CATSUP	CETANE	CHERUB
CAEOMA	CANAPE	CARINA	CATTLE	CETNIK	CHESTS
CAESAR	CANARD	CARING	CAUCUS	CEYLON	CHESTY
CAFTAN	CANARY	CARLOW	CAUDAD	CHA CHA	CHEWED
CAGIER	CANCAN	CARMAN	CAUDAL	CHA-CHA	CHEWER
CAGILY	CANCEL	CARMEL	CAUDEX	CHACMA	CHICHI
CAGING	CANCER	CARNAL	CAUDLE	CHAETA	CHICKS
CAHIER	CANDID	CARNES	CAUGHT	CHAFED	CHICLE
CAICOS	CANDLE	CARNET	CAUSAL	CHAFER	CHICLY
CAIQUE	CANINE	CAROBS	CAUSED	CHAFFY	CHIDED
CAIRNS	CANING	CAROLS	CAUSES	CHAINS	CHIDER
CAJOLE	CANKER	CARPAL	CAVEAT	CHAIRS	CHIEFS
CAKING	CANNED	CARPED	CAVE-IN	CHAISE	CHIGOE
CALAIS	CANNEL	CARPEL	CAVERN	CHAKRA	CHILES
CALASH	CANNES	CARPET	CAVIAR	CHALET	CHILLI
CALCAR	CANNON	CARPUS	CAVING	CHALKS	CHILLS
CALCES	CANNOT	CARREL	CAVITY	CHALKY	CHILLY
CALCIC	CANOED	CARROT	CAVORT	CHAMPS	CHIMED
CALICO	CANOES	CARSON	CAWING	CHANCE	CHIMES
CALIPH	CANONS	CARTED	CAXTON	CHANCY	CHINES
CALKED	CANOPY	CARTEL	CAYMAN	CHANGE	CHINKS
CALKIN	CANTAL	CARTER	CD-ROMS	CHANIA	CHINTZ
CALLAO	CANTED	CARTON	CEASED	CHANTS	CHIPPY
CALLED	CANTER	CARVED	CEDARS	CHANTY	CHIRAC
CALLER	CANTIC	CARVER	CEDING	CHAOAN	CHIRPS
CALL-IN	CANTLE	CASABA	CELAYA	CHAPEL	CHIRPY
CALLOW	CANTON	CASEFY	CELERY	CHARDS	CHISEL
CALL-UP	CANTOR	CASEIN	CELLAR	CHARGE	CHITIN
CALLUS	CANTOS	CASERN	CELLOS	CHARMS	CHITON
CALMED	CANTUS	CASHED	CELTIC	CHARTS	CHITTY
CALMER	CANVAS	CASHEW	CEMENT	CHASED	CHIVES
CALMLY	CANYON	CASING	CENSER	CHASER	CHOCKA
CALPAC	CAPERS	CASINO	CENSOR	CHASES	CHOCKS
CALQUE	CAPIAS	CASKET	CENSUS	CHASMS	CHOICE
CALVED	CAPONS	CASLON	CENTAL	CHASSE	CHOIRS
CALVES	CAPOTE	CASQUE	CENTER	CHASTE	CHOKED
CALVIN	CAPPED	CASSIA	CENTRE	CHATTY	CHOKER
CAMASS	CAPPER	CASSIS	CENTUM	CHAT UP	CHOKES
CAMBER	CAPSID	CASTER	CERATE	CHEATS	CHOLER
CAMDEN	CAPTOR	CASTES	CERCAL	CHECKS	CHOLLA
CAMELS	CARAFE	CASTLE	CERCIS	CHECKY	CHONJU
CAMEOS	CARATS	CASTOR	CERCUS	CHEEKS	CHOOSE
CAMERA	CARBON	CASTRO	CEREAL	CHEEKY	CHOOSY
CAMION	CARBOY	CASUAL	CEREUS	CHEEPS	CHOPPY
CAMISE	CARDED	CATCHY	CERISE	CHEERS	CHORAL
CAMLET	CAREEN	CATENA	CERIUM	CHEERY	CHORDS
CAMPED	CAREER	CATGUT	CERMET	CHEESE	CHOREA

CHORES	CLAMPS	CLOTHS	COGNAC	COMPER	CORBAN
CHORIC	CLAQUE	CLOUDS	COHEIR	COMPLY	CORBEL
CHORUS	CLARET	CLOUDY	COHERE	CONCHA	CORDED
CHOSEN	CLARKE	CLOUTS	COHORT	CONCHY	CORDON
CHOUGH	CLASPS	CLOVEN	COHOSH	CONCUR	CORERS
CHRISM	CLASSY	CLOVER	COHUNE	CONDOM	CORFAM
CHRIST	CLAUSE	CLOVES	COILED	CONDOR	CORGIS
CHROMA	CLAWED	CLOWNS	COILER	CONEYS	CORING
CHROME	CLAWER	CLOYED	COINED	CONFER	CORIUM
CHUBBY	CLAYEY	CLUBBY	COINER	CONGAS	CORKED
CHUCKS	CLEATS	CLUCKS	COIN-OP	CONGER	CORKER
CHUKAR	CLEAVE	CLUCKY	COITAL	CONGES	CORMEL
CHUKKA	CLEESE	CLUMPS	COITUS	CONGOU	CORNEA
CHUMMY	CLEFTS	CLUMPY	COLDER	CONICS	CORNEL
CHUMPS	CLENCH	CLUMSY	COLDLY	CONIES	CORNER
CHUNKS	CLEOME	CLUNKY	COLEUS	CONIUM	CORNET
CHUNKY	CLERGY	CLUTCH	COLEYS	CONKED	CORONA
CHURCH	CLERIC	COALED	COLIMA	CONKER	CORPSE
CHURLS	CLERKS	COALER	COLLAR	CONMAN	CORPUS
CHURNS	CLEVER	COARSE	COLLET	CONMEN	CORRAL
CHUTES	CLEVIS	COASTS	COLLIE	CONNED	CORSES
CICADA	CLICHE	COATED	COLMAR	CONOID	CORSET
CICERO	CLICKS	COAXED	COLONS	CONSUL	CORTEX
CIDERS	CLIENT	COAXER	COLONY	CONTRA-	CORVID
CIGARS	CLIFFS	COBALT	COLOUR	CONVEX	CORYMB
CILICE	CLIMAX	COBBER	COLUGO	CONVEY	CORYZA
CILIUM	CLIMBS	COBBLE	COLUMN	CONVOY	COSECH
CINDER	CLIMES	COBNUT	COLURE	COOING	COSHED
CINEMA	CLINAL	COBRAS	COMATE	COOKED	COSHES
CINEOL	CLINCH	COBURG	COMBAT	COOKER	COSIER
CINQUE	CLINES	COBWEB	COMBED	COOKIE	COSIES
CIPHER	CLINGY	COCCID	COMBER	COOLED	COSILY
CIRCLE	CLINIC	COCCUS	COMBOS	COOLER	COSINE
CIRCUM-	CLIP-ON	COCCYX	COMEDO	COOLIE	COSMIC
CIRCUS	CLIQUE	COCHIN	COMEDY	COOLLY	COSMOS
CIRQUE	CLITIC	COCKED	COMELY	COOLTH	COSSET
CIRRUS	CLOACA	COCKLE	COME ON	COOPED	COSTAL
CISKEI	CLOAKS	COCK-UP	COME-ON	COOPER	CO-STAR
CITIES	CLOCHE	COCOON	COMERS	COPALM	COSTLY
CITIFY	CLOCKS	CODDLE	COMETS	COPIED	COTTER
CITING	CLODDY	CODGER	COMFIT	COPIER	COTTON
CITRAL	CLOGGY	CODIFY	COMICS	COPIES	COUCAL
CITRIC	CLONAL	CODING	COMING	COPING	COUGAR
CITRIN	CLONES	COELOM	COMITY	COP-OUT	COUGHS
CITRON	CLONIC	COERCE	COMMAS	COPPED	COULEE
CITRUS	CLONUS	COEVAL	COMMIS	COPPER	COULIS
CIVETS	CLOSED	COFFEE	COMMIT	COPSES	COUNTS
CIVICS	CLOSER	COFFER	COMMON	COPTIC	COUNTY
CIVIES	CLOSES	COFFIN	COMORO	COPULA	COUPES
CLAIMS	CLOSET	COGENT	COMOSE	COQUET	COUPLE
CLAMMY	CLOTHE	COGGED	COMPEL	CORALS	COUPON

COURSE	CREAKY	CROWER	CURDLE	**D**	DAPPER
COURTS	CREAMS	CROWNS	CURFEW	DABBED	DAPPLE
COUSIN	CREAMY	CRUDER	CURIAE	DABBER	DARDIC
COVENS	CREASE	CRUETS	CURING	DABBLE	DARFUR
COVERS	CREATE	CRUISE	CURIOS	DACHAU	DARING
COVERT	CRECHE	CRUMBS	CURIUM	DACITE	DARKEN
COVEYS	CREDIT	CRUMBY	CURLED	DACOIT	DARKER
COWAGE	CREDOS	CRUMMY	CURLER	DACRON	DARKLY
COWARD	CREEDS	CRUNCH	CURLEW	DACTYL	DARNED
COWBOY	CREEKS	CRURAL	CURL UP	DADOES	DARNEL
COWING	CREELS	CRUSES	CURSED	DAEMON	DARNER
COWMAN	CREEPS	CRUSTS	CURSES	DAFTER	DARTED
COWMEN	CREEPY	CRUSTY	CURSOR	DAFTLY	DARTER
COWPAT	CRENEL	CRUTCH	CURTLY	DAGGER	DARWIN
COWPEA	CREOLE	CRUXES	CURTSY	DAGOES	DASHED
COWPOX	CRESOL	CRYING	CURVED	DAHLIA	DASHER
COWRIE	CRESTS	CRYPTS	CURVES	DAINTY	DASHES
COXING	CRETAN	CUBANE	CURVET	DAISES	DATARY
COYOTE	CRETIC	CUBBED	CUSCUS	DAKOTA	DATING
COYPUS	CRETIN	CUBING	CUSPID	DALASI	DATIVE
COZIER	CREUSE	CUBISM	CUSSED	DALIAN	DATURA
COZILY	CREWED	CUBIST	CUSSES	DALLAS	DAUBED
CRABBY	CREWEL	CUBITS	CUSTOM	DALLES	DAUBER
CRACKS	CRICKS	CUBOID	CUTELY	DALTON	DAVIES
CRACOW	CRIERS	CUCKOO	CUTEST	DAMAGE	DAVITS
CRADLE	CRIKEY	CUCUTA	CUTESY	DAMARA	DAWDLE
CRAFTS	CRIMEA	CUDDLE	CUTLER	DAMASK	DAWNED
CRAFTY	CRIMES	CUDDLY	CUTLET	DAMMAR	DAYBOY
CRAGGY	CRINGE	CUDGEL	CUTOFF	DAMMED	DAYGLO
CRAMBO	CRINUM	CUESTA	CUT OFF	DAMNED	DAYTON
CRAMPS	CRIPES	CUFFED	CUTOUT	DAMPED	DAZING
CRANED	CRISES	CUIABA	CUTTER	DAMPEN	DAZZLE
CRANES	CRISIS	CULLED	CUTUPS	DAMPER	DEACON
CRANIA	CRISPS	CULLER	CYANIC	DAMPLY	DEADEN
CRANKS	CRISPY	CULLET	CYBORG	DAMSEL	DEADLY
CRANKY	CRISTA	CULLIS	CYCLED	DAMSON	DEAFEN
CRANNY	CRITIC	CULTIC	CYCLES	DA NANG	DEALER
CRAPPY	CROAKS	CUMANA	CYCLIC	DANCED	DEARER
CRASIS	CROCKS	CUMBER	CYDERS	DANCER	DEARLY
CRATED	CROCUS	CUNEAL	CYGNET	DANCES	DEARTH
CRATER	CROFTS	CUPIDS	CYGNUS	DANDER	DEATHS
CRATES	CRONES	CUPOLA	CYMBAL	DANDLE	DEBARK
CRATON	CROOKS	CUPPAS	CYMENE	DANGER	DEBASE
CRAVAT	CRORES	CUPPED	CYMOID	DANGLE	DEBATE
CRAVED	CROSSE	CUPRIC	CYMOSE	DANIEL	DEBITS
CRAVEN	CROTCH	CUP TIE	CYMRIC	DANISH	DEBRIS
CRAWLS	CROTON	CUPULE	CYNICS	DANKER	DEBTOR
CRAYON	CROUCH	CURACY	CYPHER	DANUBE	DEBUNK
CRAZED	CROUPS	CURARE	CYPRUS	DANZIG	DEBUTS
CRAZES	CROWDS	CURATE	CYSTIC	DAPHNE	DECADE
CREAKS	CROWED	CURBED		DAPPED	DECALS

DECAMP	DELPHI	DERRIS	DIDDLE	DISEUR	DOLLAR
DECANE	DELTAS	DESCRY	DIEPPE	DISHED	DOLLED
DECANT	DELUDE	DESERT	DIESEL	DISHES	DOLLOP
DECARE	DELUGE	DESIGN	DIESIS	DISMAL	DOLMAN
DECCAN	DE LUXE	DESIRE	DIETED	DISMAY	DOLMAS
DECEIT	DELVED	DESIST	DIETER	DISOWN	DOLMEN
DECENT	DELVER	DESMAN	DIFFER	DISPEL	DOLOUR
DECIDE	DEMAND	DESMID	DIGAMY	DISTAL	DOMAIN
DECILE	DEMEAN	DESORB	DIGEST	DISTIL	DOMINO
DECKED	DEMISE	DESPOT	DIGGER	DISUSE	DONATE
DECKLE	DEMIST	DESSAU	DIGITS	DITHER	DONDER
DECOCT	DEMODE	DETACH	DIGLOT	DITTOS	DONJON
DECODE	DEMONS	DETAIL	DIK-DIK	DIVANS	DONKEY
DECOKE	DEMOTE	DETAIN	DIKTAT	DIVERS	DONNED
DECORS	DEMURE	DETECT	DILATE	DIVERT	DONORS
DECOYS	DEMURS	DETENT	DILDOS	DIVEST	DOODLE
DECREE	DENARY	DETEST	DILUTE	DIVIDE	DOO-DOO
DEDUCE	DENEST	DETOUR	DIMITY	DIVINE	DOOMED
DEDUCT	DENGUE	DE TROP	DIMMED	DIVING	DOPANT
DEEMED	DENIAL	DETTOL	DIMMER	DIWALI	DOPIER
DEEPEN	DENIED	DETUNE	DIMPLE	DJAMBI	DOPING
DEEPER	DENIER	DEUCED	DIMPLY	DJINNS	DORIAN
DEEPLY	DENIMS	DEVEIN	DIM SUM	DOABLE	DORIES
DEFACE	DE NIRO	DEVICE	DIMWIT	DOBBIN	DORMER
DEFAME	DENNED	DEVILS	DINARS	DOCENT	DORMIE
DEFEAT	DENOTE	DEVISE	DINERO	DOCILE	DORSAD
DEFECT	DENSER	DEVOID	DINERS	DOCKED	DORSAL
DEFEND	DENTAL	DEVOTE	DINGHY	DOCKER	DORSET
DEFIED	DENTED	DEVOUR	DINGLE	DOCKET	DORSUM
DEFIER	DENTEX	DEVOUT	DINING	DOCTOR	DOSAGE
DEFILE	DENTIL	DEWIER	DINKUM	DODDER	DO-SI-DO
DEFINE	DENTIN	DEWILY	DINNED	DODDLE	DOSING
DEFORM	DENUDE	DEWLAP	DINNER	DODGED	DOSSAL
DEFRAY	DENVER	DEWORM	DIOXAN	DODGEM	DOSSED
DEFTLY	DEODAR	DEXTER	DIOXIN	DODGER	DOSSER
DEFUSE	DEPART	DHARUK	DIPLEX	DODGES	DOTAGE
DEGAGE	DEPEND	DHOTIS	DIPLOE	DODOES	DOTARD
DEGREE	DEPICT	DIACID	DIPODY	DODOMA	DOTING
DEHORN	DEPLOY	DIADEM	DIPOLE	DO DUTY	DOTTED
DE-ICED	DEPORT	DIALED	DIPPED	DOFFED	DOTTER
DE-ICER	DEPOSE	DIAPER	DIPPER	DOFFER	DOTTLE
DEIFIC	DEPOTS	DIAPIR	DIRECT	DOG-EAR	DOUALA
DEISTS	DEPTHS	DIARCH	DIREST	DOGGED	DOUBLE
DEIXIS	DEPUTE	DIATOM	DIRGES	DOGGER	DOUBLY
DEJA VU	DEPUTY	DIBBED	DIRHAM	DOGIES	DOUBTS
DEJECT	DERAIL	DIBBER	DIRNDL	DOGLEG	DOUCHE
DE JURE	DERIDE	DIBBLE	DISARM	DOGMAS	DOUGHY
DELAYS	DERIVE	DICIER	DISBAR	DOG TAG	DOURLY
DELETE	DERMAL	DICING	DISBUD	DOINGS	DOUSED
DELIAN	DERMIC	DICKER	DISCOS	DOLINE	DOUSER
DELICT	DERMIS	DICTUM	DISCUS	DOLING	DOVISH

DOWNED	DRONES	DUPERY	ECLAIR	ELIDED	ENLACE
DOWNER	DRONGO	DUPING	ECTYPE	ELIXIR	ENLIST
DOWSED	DROOPY	DUPLET	ECURIE	ELOPED	ENMESH
DOWSER	DROPSY	DUPLEX	ECZEMA	ELOPER	ENMITY
DOYENS	DROSSY	DURBAN	EDDIED	EL PASO	ENNAGE
DOYLEY	DROVER	DURBAR	EDDIES	ELUDED	ENNEAD
DOZENS	DROVES	DURESS	EDGIER	ELUDER	ENOSIS
DOZIER	DROWSE	DURHAM	EDGILY	ELYSEE	ENOUGH
DOZILY	DROWSY	DURIAN	EDGING	EMBALM	ENRAGE
DOZING	DRUDGE	DURING	EDIBLE	EMBANK	ENRICH
DRABLY	DRUIDS	DUSTED	EDICTS	EMBARK	ENROBE
DRACHM	DRUNKS	DUSTER	EDIRNE	EMBERS	ENROOT
DRAFFY	DRYADS	DUSTUP	EDITED	EMBLEM	ENSIGN
DRAFTS	DRYERS	DUTIES	EDITOR	EMBODY	ENSILE
DRAFTY	DRY ICE	DUVETS	EDWARD	EMBOLY	ENSOUL
DRAGEE	DRYING	DWARFS	EERILY	EMBOSS	ENSUED
DRAGGY	DRY ROT	DYABLE	EFFACE	EMBRYO	ENSURE
DRAGON	DUBBED	DYADIC	EFFECT	EMERGE	ENTAIL
DRAINS	DUBBIN	DYEING	EFFETE	EMESIS	ENTICE
DRAKES	DUBLIN	DYNAMO	EFFIGY	EMETIC	ENTIRE
DRAMAS	DUCATS	DYNAST	EFFING	EMIGRE	ENTITY
DRAPED	DUCKED	DYNODE	EFFLUX	EMOTER	ENTOMB
DRAPER	DUCKER		EFFORT	EMPALE	ENTRAP
DRAPES	DUDEEN	**E**	EFFUSE	EMPIRE	ENTREE
DRAWEE	DUDLEY	EAGLES	EFTPOS	EMPLOY	ENVIED
DRAWER	DUELED	EAGLET	EGESTA	ENABLE	ENVIER
DRAWLS	DUELLO	EALING	EGGCUP	ENAMEL	ENVIES
DRAWLY	DUENNA	EARFUL	EGGNOG	ENATIC	ENVOYS
DREADS	DUFFEL	EARING	EGOISM	EN BLOC	ENWIND
DREAMS	DUFFER	EARNED	EGOIST	ENCAGE	ENWOMB
DREAMT	DUGONG	EARNER	EGRESS	ENCAMP	ENWRAP
DREAMY	DUGOUT	EARTHS	EGRETS	ENCASE	ENZYME
DREARY	DUIKER	EARTHY	EIGHTH	ENCASH	EOCENE
DREDGE	DULCET	EARWAX	EIGHTS	ENCODE	EOGENE
DREGGY	DULLED	EARWIG	EIGHTY	ENCORE	EOLITH
DRENCH	DULLER	EASELS	EITHER	ENCYST	EONISM
DRESSY	DULUTH	EASIER	EJECTA	ENDEAR	EOZOIC
DRIERS	DUMBER	EASILY	ELANDS	ENDING	EPARCH
DRIEST	DUMBLY	EASING	ELAPID	ENDIVE	EPIRUS
DRIFTS	DUMDUM	EASTER	ELAPSE	ENDUED	EPONYM
DRIFTY	DUMPED	EATERS	ELATED	ENDURE	EPOPEE
DRILLS	DUMPER	EATING	ELATER	ENEMAS	EPPING
DRINKS	DUNBAR	EBBING	ELBOWS	ENERGY	EQUALS
DRIPPY	DUNCES	ECARTE	ELDERS	ENFACE	EQUATE
DRIVEL	DUNDEE	ECESIS	ELDEST	ENFOLD	EQUINE
DRIVEN	DUNITE	ECHARD	ELEGIT	ENGAGE	EQUITY
DRIVER	DUNKED	ECHOED	ELEVEN	ENGINE	ERASED
DRIVES	DUNKER	ECHOES	ELEVON	ENGRAM	ERASER
DROGUE	DUNLIN	ECHOEY	ELFISH	ENGULF	ERBIUM
DROLLY	DUNNED	ECHOIC	EL GIZA	ENIGMA	ERFURT
DRONED	DUNNER	ECKERT	ELICIT	ENJOIN	ERLANG

ERMINE	EVOLVE	FABLES	FARMED	FENCED	FIJIAN
ERODED	EVZONE	FABRIC	FARMER	FENCER	FILETS
EROTIC	EXAMEN	FACADE	FAR-OFF	FENCES	FILIAL
ERRAND	EXARCH	FACETS	FAR-OUT	FENDED	FILING
ERRANT	EXCEED	FACIAL	FARROW	FENDER	FILLED
ERRATA	EXCEPT	FACIES	FARTED	FENIAN	FILLER
ERRING	EXCESS	FACILE	FASCIA	FENNEC	FILLET
ERRORS	EXCISE	FACING	FASTED	FENNEL	FILL-IN
ERSATZ	EXCITE	FACTOR	FASTEN	FENTON	FILLIP
ERYNGO	EXCUSE	FACULA	FASTER	FERBAM	FILMED
ESCAPE	EXEDRA	FADE-IN	FAT CAT	FERIAL	FILMIC
ESCARP	EXEMPT	FADING	FATHER	FERMAT	FILOSE
ESCHAR	EXETER	FAECAL	FATHOM	FERRET	FILTER
ESCHEW	EXEUNT	FAECES	FATTEN	FERRIC	FILTHY
ESCORT	EXHALE	FAENZA	FATTER	FERULA	FIMBLE
ESCROW	EXHORT	FAERIE	FAUCAL	FERULE	FINALE
ESCUDO	EXHUME	FAG END	FAUCES	FERVID	FINALS
ESKIMO	EXILED	FAGGED	FAUCET	FESCUE	FINDER
ESPIAL	EXILES	FAGGOT	FAULTS	FESTAL	FINELY
ESPIED	EXILIC	FAILED	FAULTY	FESTER	FINERY
ESPIER	EXITED	FAILLE	FAUNAL	FETIAL	FINEST
ESPRIT	EXODUS	FAINTS	FAUNAS	FETING	FINGAL
ESSAYS	EXONYM	FAIRER	FAVOUR	FETISH	FINGER
ESTATE	EXOTIC	FAIRLY	FAWNED	FETTER	FINIAL
ESTEEM	EXPAND	FAITHS	FAWNER	FETTLE	FINING
ESTRAY	EXPECT	FAJITA	FAXING	FEUDAL	FINISH
ETALON	EXPEND	FAKERS	FAZING	FEUDED	FINITE
ETCHED	EXPERT	FAKING	FEALTY	FEZZAN	FINNED
ETCHER	EXPIRE	FAKIRS	FEARED	FEZZED	FINNIC
ETHANE	EXPIRY	FALCON	FEARER	FEZZES	FIORDS
ETHENE	EXPORT	FALLAL	FEASTS	FIACRE	FIORIN
ETHICS	EXPOSE	FALLEN	FECULA	FIANCE	FIPPLE
ETHNIC	EXSERT	FALLER	FECUND	FIASCO	FIRING
ETHYNE	EXTANT	FALLOW	FEDORA	FIBBED	FIRKIN
ETYMON	EXTEND	FALSER	FEEBLE	FIBBER	FIRMED
EUBOEA	EXTENT	FALTER	FEEBLY	FIBRED	FIRMER
EUCHRE	EXTERN	FAMILY	FEEDER	FIBRES	FIRMLY
EULOGY	EXTINE	FAMINE	FEELER	FIBRIL	FIRSTS
EUNUCH	EXTORT	FAMISH	FEIJOA	FIBRIN	FIRTHS
EUREKA	EXTRAS	FAMOUS	FEINTS	FIBULA	FISCAL
EURO MP	EXUDED	FANDOM	FEISTY	FICKLE	FISHED
EUROPE	EYEFUL	FANGED	FELINE	FIDDLE	FISHER
EVADED	EYEING	FANGIO	FELLED	FIDDLY	FISHES
EVADER	EYELET	FANION	FELLER	FIDGET	FISTIC
EVENLY	EYELID	FANJET	FELLOE	FIELDS	FITFUL
EVENTS	EYRIES	FANNED	FELLOW	FIENDS	FITTED
EVILER		FANNER	FELONS	FIERCE	FITTER
EVILLY	**F**	FAN-TAN	FELONY	FIESTA	FIVERS
EVINCE	FABIAN	FARCES	FEMALE	FIFTHS	FIXATE
EVOKED	FABLED	FARINA	FEMORA	FIGHTS	FIXERS
EVOKER	FABLER	FARING	FEMURS	FIGURE	FIXING

FIXITY	FLIRTS	FOLIOS	FOULLY	FROCKS	FUNKER
FIZGIG	FLITCH	FOLIUM	FOUL-UP	FROGGY	FUNNEL
FIZZED	FLOATS	FOLKIE	FOUNTS	FROLIC	FUN RUN
FIZZER	FLOATY	FOLKSY	FOURTH	FRONDS	FURFUR
FIZZLE	FLOCKS	FOLLOW	FOVEAL	FRONTS	FURIES
FJORDS	FLOCKY	FOLSOM	FOWLER	FROSTS	FURLED
FLABBY	FLOODS	FOMENT	FOWLES	FROSTY	FURLER
FLACON	FLOORS	FONDER	FOXIER	FROTHS	FURORE
FLAGGY	FLOOZY	FONDLE	FOXILY	FROTHY	FURRED
FLAGON	FLOPPY	FONDLY	FOXING	FROWNS	FURROW
FLAILS	FLORAL	FONDUE	FOYERS	FROWZY	FUSAIN
FLAKED	FLORET	FONTAL	FRACAS	FROZEN	FUSHUN
FLAKER	FLORID	FOODIE	FRAMED	FRUGAL	FUSILE
FLAKES	FLORIN	FOOLED	FRAMER	FRUITS	FUSING
FLAMBE	FLOSSY	FOOTER	FRAMES	FRUITY	FUSION
FLAMED	FLOURY	FOOTLE	FRANCE	FRUMPS	FUSSED
FLAMER	FLOWED	FOOZLE	FRANCS	FRUMPY	FUSSER
FLAMES	FLOWER	FORAGE	FRAPPE	FRUNZE	FUSSES
FLANGE	FLUENT	FORAYS	FRATER	FRYERS	FUSTIC
FLANKS	FLUFFY	FORBAD	FRAUDS	FRYING	FUTILE
FLARED	FLUIDS	FORBID	FRAUEN	FRY-UPS	FUTONS
FLARES	FLUKES	FORCED	FRAYED	FU-CHOU	FUTURE
FLASHY	FLUKEY	FORCER	FRAZIL	FUCKED	FUZHOU
FLASKS	FLUNKY	FORCES	FREAKS	FUCKER	FUZZED
FLATLY	FLURRY	FORDED	FREAKY	FUCK-UP	
FLATUS	FLUTED	FOREGO	FREELY	FUCOID	**G**
FLAUNT	FLUTER	FOREST	FREEST	FUDDLE	GABBED
FLAVIN	FLUTES	FORFAR	FREEZE	FUDGED	GABBER
FLAWED	FLYBYS	FORGED	FRENCH	FUELED	GABBLE
FLAXEN	FLYERS	FORGER	FRENZY	FUGARD	GABBRO
FLAYED	FLYING	FORGES	FRESCO	FUGATO	GABION
FLAYER	FLYSCH	FORGET	FRESNO	FUGING	GABLED
FLECHE	FOALED	FORGOT	FRIARS	FUGUES	GABLES
FLECKS	FOAMED	FORKED	FRIARY	FUHRER	GADDED
FLEDGE	FOBBED	FORMAL	FRIDAY	FUJIAN	GADDER
FLEECE	FO'C'SLE	FORMAN	FRIDGE	FUKIEN	GADFLY
FLEECY	FODDER	FORMAT	FRIEND	FULANI	GADGET
FLEETS	FOETAL	FORMED	FRIERS	FULCRA	GADOID
FLENSE	FOETID	FORMER	FRIEZE	FULFIL	GAELIC
FLESHY	FOETOR	FORMIC	FRIGHT	FULLER	GAFFER
FLETCH	FOETUS	FORMYL	FRIGID	FULL-ON	GAFFES
FLEXED	FOGBOW	FORNIX	FRIJOL	FULMAR	GAGGED
FLEXES	FOGDOG	FORTES	FRILLS	FUMBLE	GAGGER
FLEXOR	FOGGED	FORTIS	FRILLY	FUMING	GAGGLE
FLICKS	FOGGIA	FORUMS	FRINGE	FUNDED	GAGING
FLIERS	FOGIES	FOSHAN	FRINGY	FUNDIC	GAIETY
FLIGHT	FOIBLE	FOSSIL	FRISKS	FUNDUS	GAIJIN
FLIMSY	FOILED	FOSTER	FRISKY	FUNGAL	GAINED
FLINCH	FOLDED	FOUGHT	FRIULI	FUNGIC	GAINER
FLINTS	FOLDER	FOULED	FRIVOL	FUNGUS	GAINLY
FLINTY	FOLIAR	FOULER	FRIZZY	FUNKED	GAITER

GALATA	GARRET	GENIES	GLACIS	GOBBLE	GRAECO-
GALATI	GARTER	GENIUS	GLADES	GOBIAN	GRAFTS
GALAXY	GASBAG	GENOME	GLADLY	GOBLET	GRAINS
GALENA	GASCON	GENRES	GLAIRY	GOBLIN	GRAINY
GALERE	GASHED	GENTLE	GLANCE	GODARD	GRAMME
GALIBI	GASHES	GENTLY	GLANDS	GODSON	GRANDS
GALIOT	GASIFY	GENTRY	GLARED	GODWIT	GRANGE
GALLED	GASKET	GEODIC	GLARES	GOFERS	GRANNY
GALLEY	GASKIN	GERBIL	GLARUS	GOFFER	GRANTS
GALLIC	GASMAN	GERMAN	GLASSY	GOGGLE	GRAPES
GALLON	GASMEN	GERMEN	GLAZED	GOITRE	GRAPHS
GALLOP	GASPED	GERUND	GLAZER	GO-KART	GRASSY
GALORE	GASPER	GETTER	GLAZES	GOLDEN	GRATED
GALOSH	GASSED	GETUPS	GLEAMS	GOLFER	GRATER
GALWAY	GASSER	GEYSER	GLEBES	GOLLOP	GRATES
GALYAK	GASSES	GEZIRA	GLEETY	GOMUTI	GRATIS
GAMBIA	GATEAU	GHETTO	GLIBLY	GONADS	GRAVEL
GAMBIT	GATHER	GHIBLI	GLIDED	GONDAR	GRAVEN
GAMBLE	GAUCHE	GHOSTS	GLIDER	GONERS	GRAVER
GAMBOL	GAUCHO	GHOULS	GLIDES	GONION	GRAVES
GAMELY	GAUGED	GHYLLS	GLINTS	GOODLY	GRAVID
GAMETE	GAUGER	GIANTS	GLIOMA	GOOFED	GRAYED
GAMIER	GAUGES	GIAOUR	GLITCH	GOOGLY	GRAYER
GAMINE	GAVAGE	GIBBED	GLITZY	GOOGOL	GRAZED
GAMING	GAVELS	GIBBER	GLOATS	GOOIER	GRAZER
GAMMAS	GAVIAL	GIBBET	GLOBAL	GOPHER	GRAZES
GAMMED	GAWKED	GIBBON	GLOBES	GORGED	GREASE
GAMMON	GAWKER	GIBE AT	GLOBIN	GORGER	GREASY
GANDER	GAWPED	GIBEON	GLOOMY	GORGES	GREATS
GANGED	GAYEST	GIBSON	GLORIA	GORGON	GREBES
GANGER	GAZEBO	GIDDAY	GLOSSA	GORICA	GREECE
GANGES	GAZING	GIFTED	GLOSSY	GORIER	GREEDY
GANGUE	GAZUMP	GIGGLE	GLOVED	GORILY	GREENS
GANNET	GDANSK	GIGGLY	GLOVER	GORING	GREYED
GANOID	GDYNIA	GIGOLO	GLOVES	GO-SLOW	GREYER
GANTRY	GEARED	GILDED	GLOWED	GOSPEL	GRIEVE
GAOLED	GECKOS	GILDER	GLOWER	GOSSIP	GRIFFE
GAOLER	GEDACT	GILLED	GLUING	GOTHIC	GRIGRI
GAPING	GEE-GEE	GILLIE	GLUMLY	GOUGED	GRILLE
GAPPED	GEEZER	GIMLET	GLUTEN	GOUGER	GRILLS
GARAGE	GEISHA	GIMMAL	GLYCOL	GOUGES	GRILSE
GARBED	GELADA	GINGER	GNAWED	GOURDS	GRIMLY
GARBLE	GELDED	GINKGO	GNAWER	GOVERN	GRINDS
GARCON	GELDOF	GIRDED	GNEISS	GRABEN	GRINGO
GARDEN	GELLED	GIRDER	GNOMES	GRACED	GRIPED
GARGET	GEMINI	GIRDLE	GNOMIC	GRACES	GRIPER
GARGLE	GEMMED	GIRLIE	GNOMON	GRADED	GRIPES
GARISH	GENDER	GIRTHS	GNOSIS	GRADER	GRISLY
GARLIC	GENERA	GIUSTO	GOADED	GRADES	GRISON
GARNER	GENEVA	GIVE IN	GOATEE	GRADIN	GRISTS
GARNET	GENIAL	GIVING	GOBBET	GRADUS	GRITTY

GRIVET	GUITAR	HAEMAL	HANKER	HATRED	HEBRON
GROANS	GULDEN	HAEMIC	HANKIE	HATTER	HECATE
GROATS	GULLAH	HAEMIN	HANKOW	HAULED	HECKLE
GROCER	GULLED	HAERES	HANNAH	HAULER	HECTIC
GRODNO	GULLET	HAFTER	HANSEL	HAUNCH	HECTOR
GROGGY	GULLEY	HAGBUT	HANSEN	HAUNTS	HECUBA
GROINS	GULPED	HAGGAI	HANSOM	HAVANA	HEDDLE
GROOMS	GULPER	HAGGIS	HAPPEN	HAVANT	HEDGED
GROOVE	GUMBOS	HAGGLE	HAPTEN	HAVENS	HEDGER
GROOVY	GUMMED	HAIDAN	HAPTIC	HAVEN'T	HEDGES
GROPED	GUNDOG	HAIDUK	HARALD	HAVING	HEDJAZ
GROPER	GUNG-HO	HAILED	HARARE	HAWAII	HEEDED
GROPES	GUNMAN	HAILER	HARASS	HAWHAW	HEEDER
GROTTO	GUNMEN	HAINAN	HARBIN	HAWICK	HEE-HAW
GROTTY	GUNNED	HAIRDO	HARD BY	HAWKED	HEELED
GROUCH	GUNNEL	HAIRIF	HARDEN	HAWKER	HEELER
GROUND	GUNNER	HAJJES	HARDER	HAWSER	HEENAN
GROUPS	GUNSHY	HAJJIS	HARDIE	HAYBOX	HEFTER
GROUSE	GUNTUR	HAKIMS	HARDLY	HAYMOW	HEGIRA
GROUTS	GUNYAH	HALEST	HARD-ON	HAZARD	HEIDUC
GROVEL	GURGLE	HALIDE	HARD UP	HAZELS	HEIFER
GROVES	GURJUN	HALITE	HAREEM	HAZIER	HEIGHT
GROWER	GURKHA	HALLAH	HAREMS	HAZILY	HEJIRA
GROWLS	GUSHED	HALLEL	HARING	HAZING	HEKATE
GROWTH	GUSHER	HALLEY	HARKED	H-BOMBS	HELENA
GROYNE	GUSSET	HALLOO	HARKEN	HEADED	HELIOS
GROZNY	GUSTED	HALLOS	HARLEM	HEADER	HELIUM
GRUBBY	GUTTED	HALLOW	HARLEY	HEAD-ON	HELLAS
GRUDGE	GUTTER	HALLUX	HARLOT	HEALED	HELLEN
GRUGRU	GUVNOR	HALOES	HARLOW	HEALER	HELLER
GRUMPY	GUYANA	HALOID	HARMED	HEALEY	HELLES
GRUNGE	GUYING	HALTED	HARMER	HEALTH	HELLOS
GRUNGY	GUZZLE	HALTER	HARNEY	HEANEY	HELMET
GRUNTS	GYPPED	HALTON	HAROLD	HEAPED	HELPED
GUARDS	GYPSUM	HALVAH	HARPED	HEAPER	HELPER
GUAVAS	GYRATE	HALVED	HARPER	HEARER	HELVES
GUELPH	GYROSE	HALVES	HARRAR	HEARSE	HEMMED
GUENON		HAMATE	HARRIS	HEARST	HEMMER
GUESTS	**H**	HAMELN	HARROW	HEARTH	HEMPEN
GUFFAW	HAAKON	HAMITE	HARTAL	HEARTS	HENBIT
GUIANA	HABANA	HAMLET	HARVEY	HEARTY	HENDRY
GUIDED	HABILE	HAMLYN	HASHED	HEATED	HENLEY
GUIDER	HABITS	HAMMED	HASHES	HEATER	HEPCAT
GUIDES	HACKED	HAMMER	HASLET	HEATHS	HEPTAD
GUIDON	HACKER	HAMPER	HASSAN	HEATHY	HERALD
GUILDS	HACKLE	HANDED	HASSLE	HEAUME	HERBAL
GUILIN	HADEAN	HANDEL	HASTEN	HEAVED	HERDED
GUILTY	HADITH	HANDLE	HATBOX	HEAVEN	HERDER
GUIMPE	HADJES	HANGAR	HATHOR	HEAVER	HERDIC
GUINEA	HADJIS	HANGER	HATING	HEAVES	HEREAT
GUISES	HADRON	HANG-UP	HATPIN	HEBREW	HEREBY

HEREIN	HINGER	HOLISM	HORSEY	HULLER	HYPHEN
HEREOF	HINGES	HOLLER	HOSIER	HULLOS	HYPING
HEREON	HINTED	HOLLOW	HOSING	HUMANE	
HERERO	HINTER	HOLMES	HOSTED	HUMANS	**I**
HERESY	HIPPED	HOLMIC	HOSTEL	HUMBER	IAMBIC
HERETO	HIPPER	HOLPEN	HOSTIE	HUMBLE	IAMBUS
HERIOT	HIPPIE	HOMAGE	HOT AIR	HUMBLY	IBADAN
HERMES	HIRING	HOMBRE	HOTBED	HUMBUG	IBAGUE
HERMIT	HISPID	HOMELY	HOT DOG	HUMISM	IBERIA
HERMON	HISSED	HOMIER	HOTELS	HUMMED	IBEXES
HERNIA	HISSER	HOMILY	HOTIEN	HUMMEL	IBIBIO
HEROES	HISSES	HOMING	HOT KEY	HUMMER	IBISES
HEROIC	HI-TECH	HOMINY	HOTPOT	HUMMUS	ICE AGE
HEROIN	HITHER	HONEST	HOT ROD	HUMOUR	ICEBOX
HERONS	HITLER	HONIED	HOTTER	HUMPED	ICE CAP
HERPES	HIT MAN	HONING	HOTTIE	HUMPTY	ICEMAN
HERREN	HIT MEN	HONKED	HOUDAN	HUNGER	ICEMEN
HERZOG	HITTER	HONKER	HOUNDS	HUNGRY	ICHANG
HESIOD	HIVING	HONOUR	HOURIS	HUNKER	I CHING
HESTIA	HOARDS	HONSHU	HOURLY	HUNTED	ICICLE
HETMAN	HOARSE	HOODED	HOUSED	HUNTER	ICIEST
HEWERS	HOAXED	HOODOO	HOUSEL	HUPPAH	ICONIC
HEWING	HOAXER	HOOFED	HOUSES	HURDLE	ID CARD
HEXANE	HOAXES	HOOKAH	HOVELS	HURLED	IDEALS
HEXING	HOBART	HOOKED	HOWARD	HURLER	IDEATE
HEXONE	HOBBES	HOOKER	HOWDAH	HURLEY	IDIOCY
HEXOSE	HOBBLE	HOOKUP	HOWE'ER	HURRAH	IDIOMS
HEYDAY	HOBNOB	HOOPED	HOWLED	HURRAY	IDIOTS
HIATAL	HOBOES	HOOPER	HOWLER	HURTER	IDLEST
HIATUS	HOCKED	HOOP-LA	HOWLET	HURTLE	IDLING
HICCUP	HOCKER	HOOPOE	HOWRAH	HUSAIN	IDYLLS
HICKEY	HOCKEY	HOORAH	HOYDEN	HUSHED	IGLOOS
HICKOK	HODDEN	HOORAY	HSIANG	HUSH-UP	IGNITE
HIDDEN	HODDIN	HOOTED	HUAMBO	HUSKER	IGNORE
HIDING	HODMAN	HOOTER	HUBBLE	HUSSAR	IGUACU
HIEING	HOEING	HOOVER	HUBBUB	HUSTLE	IGUANA
HIEMAL	HOGGED	HOOVES	HUBCAP	HUSTON	ILESHA
HIGGLE	HOGGER	HOPING	HUBRIS	HUXLEY	ILEXES
HIGHER	HOGGET	HOPPED	HUCKLE	HUZZAH	ILIGAN
HIGHLY	HOGNUT	HOPPER	HUDDLE	HYADES	ILKLEY
HIJACK	HOGTIE	HOPPLE	HUDSON	HYAENA	ILL-USE
HIKERS	HOHHOT	HOPPUS	HUELVA	HYALIN	ILOILO
HIKING	HOICKS	HORACE	HUESCA	HYBRID	ILORIN
HILARY	HOIDEN	HORARY	HUFFED	HYBRIS	IMAGES
HILLEL	HOISTS	HORDES	HUGELY	HYDRAS	IMBIBE
HILLER	HOLDEN	HORMIC	HUGEST	HYDRIA	IMBRUE
HIMEJI	HOLDER	HORMUZ	HUGGED	HYDRIC	IMBUED
HINDER	HOLDUP	HORNED	HUGGER	HYENAS	IMIDIC
HINDOO	HOLD UP	HORNET	HUGHES	HYMENS	IMMUNE
HINDUS	HOLIER	HORRID	HUGHIE	HYMNAL	IMMURE
HINGED	HOLILY	HORROR	HULLED	HYMNED	IMPACT

IMPAIR	INFUSE	INTROS	ITCHED	JETSAM	JOULES
IMPALA	INGEST	INTUIT	ITCHES	JET SET	JOUNCE
IMPALE	INGOTS	INUITS	ITHACA	JETTED	JOURNO
IMPART	INHALE	INULIN	ITSELF	JETTON	JOVIAL
IMPEDE	INHAUL	INURED		JEWELS	JOYFUL
IMPEND	INHERE	INVADE	**J**	JEWESS	JOYING
IMPHAL	INHUME	INVENT	JABBED	JEWISH	JOYOUS
IMPISH	INJECT	INVERT	JABBER	JHANSI	JUDAEA
IMPORT	INJURE	INVEST	JABIRU	JIBBED	JUDAIC
IMPOSE	INJURY	INVITE	JACANA	JIBBER	JUDDER
IMPOST	INK-CAP	INVOKE	JACKAL	JIBING	JUDGED
IMPROV	INKIER	INWARD	JACKED	JIGAWA	JUDGER
IMPUGN	INKING	IODATE	JACKET	JIGGED	JUDGES
IMPURE	INKPAD	IODIDE	JACKIE	JIGGER	JUDOGI
IMPUTE	INLAID	IODINE	JAFFNA	JIGGLE	JUDOKA
INARCH	INLAND	IODISM	JAGGED	JIGGLY	JUGATE
INBORN	IN-LAWS	IODIZE	JAGUAR	JIGSAW	JUGGED
INBRED	INLAYS	IODOUS	JAILED	JIHADS	JUGGLE
INCEPT	INLETS	IONIAN	JAILER	JILTED	JUICED
INCEST	INLIER	IONIZE	JAIPUR	JILTER	JUICES
INCHED	INMATE	IONONE	JALAPA	JINGLE	JUJUBE
INCHES	INMOST	IPECAC	JALOPY	JINGLY	JULEPS
INCHON	INNATE	IREFUL	JAMMED	JINXED	JULIES
INCISE	INNING	IRENIC	JAMMER	JINXES	JUMBLE
INCITE	INNUIT	IRIDIC	JANGLE	JITTER	JUMP AT
INCOME	INROAD	IRISES	JAPERY	JIVING	JUMPED
INCUBI	INRUSH	IRITIC	JAPURA	JOBBED	JUMPER
INCUSE	INSANE	IRITIS	JARGON	JOBBER	JUNEAU
INDEED	INSECT	IRKING	JARRAH	JOBBIE	JUNGLE
INDENE	INSERT	IRONED	JARRED	JOB LOT	JUNGLY
INDENT	INSETS	IRONER	JARROW	JOCKEY	JUNIOR
INDIAN	INSIDE	IRONIC	JASPER	JOCOSE	JUNKED
INDICT	INSIST	IRRUPT	JAUNTS	JOCUND	JUNKET
INDIGO	IN SITU	IRTYSH	JAUNTY	JOGGED	JUNKIE
INDITE	INSOLE	IRVINE	JAWARA	JOGGER	JUNTAS
INDIUM	INSTAR	ISATIN	JAWING	JOGGLE	JURIED
INDOLE	INSTEP	ISCHIA	JAZZED	JOHNNY	JURIES
INDOOR	INSTIL	ISLAND	JEERED	JOHORE	JURIST
INDORE	INSULA	ISLETS	JEERER	JOINED	JURORS
INDRIS	INSULT	ISOBAR	JEJUNE	JOINER	JUSTLY
INDUCE	INSURE	ISOGON	JELLED	JOINTS	JUTTED
INDUCT	INTACT	ISOHEL	JENNET	JOISTS	JUTTER
INDULT	INTAKE	ISOLEX	JERBOA	JOKERS	
INFAMY	INTEND	ISOMER	JERKED	JOKING	**K**
INFANT	INTENT	ISOPOD	JERKER	JOLTED	KABILA
INFECT	INTERN	ISRAEL	JERKIN	JORDAN	KABYLE
INFEST	INTIMA	ISSUED	JERSEY	JOSHED	KADUNA
INFIRM	INTINE	ISSUER	JESTED	JOSHES	KAFFIR
INFLOW	INTONE	ISSUES	JESTER	JOSTLE	KAFTAN
INFLUX	IN TOTO	ISTRIA	JESUIT	JOTTED	KAISER
INFORM	IN TRIM	ITALIC	JET LAG	JOTTER	KAIZEN

KAKAPO	KEYING	KNIVES	LACKED	LAPPER	LATVIA
KALISZ	KEYWAY	KNOCKS	LACKEY	LAPPET	LAUDED
KALMAR	KHALIF	KNOLLS	LACTAM	LAPSED	LAUDER
KALMIA	KHULNA	KNOTTY	LACTIC	LAPSER	LAUGHS
KALONG	KHYBER	KNOWER	LACUNA	LAPSES	LAUNCH
KALUGA	KIBOSH	KOALAS	LADDER	LAPSUS	LAUREL
KAMALA	KICKED	KODIAK	LADDIE	LAPTOP	LAVABO
KANARA	KICKER	KOHIMA	LA-DI-DA	LAP-TOP	LAVAGE
KANBAN	KICK IN	KOKAND	LADIES	LARDED	LAVISH
KANGAS	KIDDED	KOLYMA	LADING	LARDER	LAWFUL
KANPUR	KIDDER	KOPECK	LADINO	LARDON	LAWYER
KANSAS	KIDDIE	KOPPIE	LADLED	LAREDO	LAXITY
KAOLIN	KIDNAP	KOREAN	LADLER	LARGER	LAY-BYS
KARATE	KIDNEY	KORUNA	LADLES	LARGOS	LAYERS
KARATS	KIELCE	KOSHER	LADOGA	LARIAM	LAYING
KARIBA	KIGALI	KOSICE	LAGENA	LARIAT	LAYMAN
KARMIC	KIKUYU	KOVROV	LAGERS	LARINE	LAYMEN
KARPOV	KILLED	KOWTOW	LAGGED	LARISA	LAY-OFF
KASBAH	KILLER	KRAALS	LAGOON	LARKED	LAY OUT
KASSEL	KILTED	KRISES	LAHORE	LARKER	LAYOUT
KAUNAS	KILTER	KRONER	LAICAL	LARNAX	LAZIER
KAYAKS	KIMONO	KRONOR	LAID UP	LARVAE	LAZILY
KAZAKH	KINASE	KRUGER	LAIRDS	LARVAL	LAZING
KEBABS	KINDER	KUKRIS	LALANG	LARYNX	LEADEN
KEDIRI	KINDLE	KUMASI	LAMBDA	LASCAR	LEADER
KEEGAN	KINDLY	KUMISS	LAMBED	LASERS	LEAD-IN
KEELED	KINGLY	KUMMEL	LAMELY	LASHED	LEAGUE
KEENED	KIOSKS	KUNG FU	LAMENT	LASHER	LEAKED
KEENER	KIPPED	KUNLUN	LAMEST	LASHES	LEAKER
KEENLY	KIPPER	KUOPIO	LAMINA	LASHIO	LEANED
KEEPER	KIRKBY	KURGAN	LAMING	LASH-UP	LEANER
KEEP ON	KIRKUK	KUWAIT	LAMMAS	LASKET	LEAN TO
KELLER	KIRMAN	KWACHA	LAMPAS	LASSES	LEAN-TO
KELOID	KIRSCH	KWANZA	LANATE	LASSOS	LEAPED
KELPIE	KIRUNA	KYRGYZ	LANCED	LASTED	LEAPER
KELTIC	KISMET	KYUSHU	LANCER	LASTER	LEARNT
KELVIN	KISSED		LANCES	LASTLY	LEASED
KENDAL	KISSER	**L**	LANCET	LATEEN	LEASER
KENNED	KISSES		LANDAU	LATELY	LEASES
KENNEL	KISUMU	LAAGER	LANDED	LATENT	LEAVED
KENYAN	KIT BAG	LABELS	LANDES	LATEST	LEAVEN
KERALA	KITSCH	LABIAL	LANGER	LATHER	LEAVER
KERMAN	KITTED	LABILE	LANGUE	LATHES	LEAVES
KERMES	KITTEN	LABIUM	LANGUR	LATINA	LECHER
KERNEL	KLAXON	LABLAB	LANKER	LATINO	LECTIN
KERSEY	KNAVES	LABOUR	LANKLY	LATINS	LECTOR
KETENE	KNAWEL	LABRET	LANNER	LATISH	LEDGER
KETONE	KNELLS	LABRUM	LANUGO	LATIUM	LEDGES
KETOSE	KNIFED	LACHES	LAPDOG	LATRIA	LEERED
KETTLE	KNIFER	LACIER	LAPELS	LATTEN	LEEWAY
KEVLAR	KNIGHT	LACILY	LAPPED	LATTER	LEGACY

LEGATE	LIBIDO	LINKED	LOCHIA	LOPPER	LUNGER
LEGATO	LIBRAN	LINKUP	LOCKED	LOQUAT	LUNGES
LEGEND	LIBYAN	LINNET	LOCKER	LORDED	LUNULA
LEGERS	LICHEN	LINTEL	LOCKET	LORDLY	LUPINE
LEGGED	LICKED	LINTER	LOCKUP	LORICA	LUPINS
LEGION	LICKER	LIPASE	LOCULE	LOSERS	LURING
LEGIST	LIDDED	LI PENG	LOCUMS	LOSING	LURKED
LEGUAN	LIEGES	LIPIDS	LOCUST	LOSSES	LURKER
LEGUME	LIE-INS	LIPOID	LODGED	LOTION	LUSAKA
LEIDEN	LIENAL	LIPOMA	LODGER	LOTTED	LUSHES
LEKKER	LIERNE	LIQUID	LODGES	LOUDEN	LU-SHUN
LE MANS	LIFERS	LIQUOR	LOFTED	LOUDER	LUSTED
LEMNOS	LIFFEY	LISBON	LOFTER	LOUDLY	LUSTRE
LEMONS	LIFTED	LISPED	LOGGED	LOUGHS	LUTEAL
LEMONY	LIFTER	LISPER	LOGGER	LOUISE	LUVVIE
LEMURS	LIGAND	LISSOM	LOGGIA	LOUNGE	LUXATE
LENDER	LIGATE	LISTED	LOGIER	LOURED	LUXURY
LENGTH	LIGHTS	LISTEN	LOGION	LOURIE	LYCEES
LENITY	LIGNIN	LITANY	LOGJAM	LOUSED	LYCEUM
LENSES	LIGULA	LITCHI	LOGLOG	LOUVAR	LYCHEE
LENTEN	LIGULE	LITERS	LOG OUT	LOUVRE	LYNXES
LENTIC	LIKASI	LITHER	LOIRET	LOVAGE	LYRATE
LENTIL	LIKELY	LITHIA	LOITER	LOVELY	LYRICS
LEOBEN	LIKING	LITHIC	LOLLED	LOVERS	LYRIST
LEONID	LILACS	LITMUS	LOLLER	LOVEYS	LYSINE
LEPERS	LILIES	LITRES	LOLLOP	LOVING	
LEPTON	LILLEE	LITTER	LOMBOK	LOWEST	**M**
LESBOS	LIMBER	LITTLE	LOMENT	LOWING	MACACO
LESION	LIMBIC	LIVE-IN	LONDON	LOW-KEY	MACAWS
LESSEE	LIMBOS	LIVELY	LONELY	LOYANG	MACEIO
LESSEN	LIMBUS	LIVERS	LONERS	LOZERE	MACKAY
LESSER	LIMEYS	LIVERY	LONGAN	L-PLATE	MACKLE
LESSON	LIMIER	LIVING	LONGED	LUANDA	MACRON
LESSOR	LIMING	LIZARD	LONGER	LUBBER	MACULA
LETHAL	LIMITS	LLAMAS	LOOFAH	LUBECK	MADAME
LETTER	LIMNED	LOADED	LOOKED	LUBLIN	MADAMS
LETUPS	LIMNER	LOADER	LOOKER	LUCENT	MADCAP
LEVANT	LIMPED	LOAFED	LOOK-IN	LUDLOW	MADDEN
LEVEES	LIMPER	LOAFER	LOOK UP	LUFFED	MADDER
LEVELS	LIMPET	LOANED	LOOMED	LUGANO	MADE-UP
LEVERS	LIMPID	LOANER	LOONEY	LUGGED	MADMAN
LEVIED	LIMPLY	LOATHE	LOOPED	LUGGER	MADMEN
LEVIER	LINAGE	LOAVES	LOOPER	LULLED	MADRAS
LEVIES	LINDEN	LOBATE	LOOSED	LUMBAR	MADRID
LEVITY	LINEAL	LOBBED	LOOSEN	LUMBER	MADURO
LEWDLY	LINEAR	LOBITO	LOOSER	LUMMOX	MAENAD
LIABLE	LINERS	LOBOLA	LOOSES	LUMPED	MAGGOT
LIAISE	LINEUP	LOBULE	LOOTED	LUMPEN	MAGIAN
LIBBER	LINGER	LOCALE	LOOTER	LUNACY	MAGNET
LIBELS	LINGUA	LOCALS	LOPING	LUNATE	MAGNUM
LIBERO	LINING	LOCATE	LOPPED	LUNGED	MAGPIE

MAGUEY	MANILA	MASCOT	MEDICK	MESCAL	MILKED
MAGYAR	MANISA	MASERS	MEDICO	MESHED	MILKER
MAHOUT	MANLEY	MASERU	MEDICS	MESHES	MILLED
MAIDEN	MANNED	MASHED	MEDINA	MESSED	MILLER
MAIKOP	MANNER	MASHER	MEDIUM	MESSES	MILLET
MAILED	MANORS	MASHES	MEDLAR	MESS-UP	MILORD
MAILER	MANQUE	MASHIE	MEDLEY	METAGE	MILTER
MAI MAI	MANTEL	MASJID	MEEKER	METALS	MIMICS
MAIMED	MANTIC	MASKED	MEEKLY	METEOR	MIMING
MAIMER	MANTIS	MASKER	MEERUT	METERS	MIMOSA
MAINLY	MANTLE	MASONS	MEETER	METHOD	MINCED
MAJORS	MANTUA	MASQUE	MEGARA	METHYL	MINCER
MAKALU	MANUAL	MASSED	MEGILP	METIER	MINDED
MAKE DO	MANURE	MASSES	MEGOHM	METING	MINDEL
MAKE IT	MAOISM	MASSIF	MEKNES	METOPE	MINDER
MAKERS	MAOIST	MASTER	MEKONG	METRES	MINERS
MAKE UP	MAPLES	MASTIC	MELEES	METRIC	MINGLE
MAKE-UP	MAPPED	MATADI	MELLOW	METROS	MINIFY
MAKING	MAPUTO	MATING	MELODY	METTLE	MINIMA
MALABO	MAQUIS	MATINS	MELOID	MEWING	MINIMS
MALADY	MARACA	MATRIX	MELONS	MEWLER	MINING
MALAGA	MARAUD	MATRON	MELTED	MEXICO	MINION
MALANG	MARBLE	MATTED	MELTER	MEZZOS	MINIUM
MALATE	MARBLY	MATTER	MELTON	MIAOWS	MINNOW
MALAWI	MARCHE	MATURE	MEMBER	MIASMA	MINOAN
MALAYA	MARGAY	MAULED	MEMOIR	MICKEY	MINORS
MALDON	MARGIN	MAULER	MEMORY	MICMAC	MINTED
MALEIC	MARIAN	MAUNDY	MENACE	MICRON	MINTER
MALICE	MARINA	MAUSER	MENADO	MICROS	MINUET
MALIGN	MARINE	MAXIMA	MENAGE	MIDAIR	MINUTE
MALLEE	MARKED	MAXIMS	MENDED	MIDDAY	MINXES
MALLET	MARKER	MAY BUG	MENDER	MIDDEN	MIOSIS
MALLOW	MARKET	MAY DAY	MENHIR	MIDDLE	MIOTIC
MALTED	MARKKA	MAYFLY	MENIAL	MIDGES	MIRAGE
MALTHA	MARKUP	MAYHEM	MENSES	MIDGET	MIRING
MAMBAS	MARLIN	MAYORS	MENTAL	MIDGUT	MIRROR
MAMMAL	MARMOT	MAZILY	MENTON	MID-OFF	MISCUE
MAMMON	MAROON	MAZUMA	MENTOR	MIDRIB	MISERE
MANAGE	MARQUE	MCEWAN	MEOWED	MIDSTS	MISERS
MANAMA	MARRED	MEADOW	MERANO	MIDWAY	MISERY
MANANA	MARRER	MEAGRE	MERCER	MIERES	MISFIT
MANAUS	MARRON	MEALIE	MERELY	MIFFED	MISHAP
MANCHE	MARROW	MEANER	MERGED	MIGHTY	MISHIT
MANCHU	MARSHY	MEANLY	MERGER	MIKADO	MISLAY
MANEGE	MARTEN	MEASLY	MERINO	MILADY	MISLED
MANFUL	MARTIN	MEATUS	MERITS	MILDER	MISSAL
MANGER	MARTYR	MECCAS	MERLIN	MILDEW	MISSED
MANGLE	MARVEL	MEDALS	MERLON	MILDLY	MISSES
MANGOS	MARY II	MEDDLE	MERMAN	MILERS	MISSIS
MANIAC	MASCLE	MEDIAL	MERSIN	MILIEU	MISSUS
MANIAS	MASCON	MEDIAN	MERTON	MILIUM	MISTED

MISTER	MONISM	MOTTLE	MUSCID	NAGANA	NECTAR
MISUSE	MONIST	MOTTOS	MUSCLE	NAGANO	NEEDED
MITRAL	MONKEY	MOULDS	MUSCLY	NAGGED	NEEDLE
MITRES	MONTHS	MOULDY	MUSEUM	NAGGER	NEEDN'T
MITTEN	MOOING	MOULIN	MUSHES	NAGOYA	NEGATE
MIXERS	MOONED	MOULTS	MUSING	NAGPUR	NEGROS
MIXING	MOORED	MOUNDS	MUSKET	NAIADS	NEIGHS
MIX-UPS	MOOTED	MOUNTS	MUSKIE	NAILED	NEKTON
MIZZEN	MOOTER	MOUSER	MUSLIM	NAILER	NELSON
MOANED	MOPANI	MOUSEY	MUSLIN	NAKURU	NEM CON
MOANER	MOPEDS	MOUSSE	MUSSED	NAMELY	NEPALI
MOATED	MOPING	MOUTHS	MUSSEL	NAMING	NEPHEW
MOBBED	MOPOKE	MOUTON	MUSTEE	NANTES	NEREID
MOBBER	MOPPED	MOVERS	MUSTER	NAPALM	NEREIS
MOBILE	MOPPET	MOVIES	MUSTN'T	NAPIER	NERVED
MOCKED	MORALE	MOVING	MUTANT	NAPKIN	NERVES
MOCKER	MORALS	MOWERS	MUTARE	NAPLES	NESTED
MOCK UP	MORASS	MOWING	MUTATE	NAPPED	NESTER
MOCK-UP	MORBID	MOWLAM	MUTELY	NAPPER	NESTLE
MOD CON	MOREEN	MUCKED	MUTING	NARIAL	NETHER
MODELS	MORGUE	MUCKER	MUTINY	NARKED	NETTED
MODEMS	MORION	MUCOID	MUTISM	NARROW	NETTLE
MODENA	MORLEY	MUCOUS	MUTTER	NARVIK	NETTLY
MODERN	MORMON	MUDCAT	MUTTON	NASALS	NEURAL
MODEST	MORNAY	MUDDED	MUTUAL	NASIAL	NEURON
MODIFY	MORONI	MUDDLE	MUTULE	NASION	NEUTER
MODISH	MORONS	MUD PIE	MUZZLE	NASSAU	NEVADA
MODULE	MOROSE	MUESLI	MYELIN	NATANT	NEVERS
MOGULS	MORROW	MUFFED	MYNAHS	NATION	NEW AGE
MOHAIR	MORSEL	MUFFIN	MYOPIA	NATIVE	NEWARK
MOHAWK	MORTAL	MUFFLE	MYOPIC	NATRON	NEWEST
MOHOLE	MORTAR	MUFTIS	MYOSIN	NATTER	NEWHAM
MOIETY	MORULA	MUGABE	MYRIAD	NATURE	NEWISH
MOLARS	MORYAH	MUGGED	MYRICA	NAUGHT	NEWMAN
MOLDED	MOSAIC	MUGGER	MYRTLE	NAUSEA	NEWTON
MOLDER	MOSCOW	MUKLUK	MYSELF	NAUTCH	NIAMEY
MOLEST	MOSLEM	MULISH	MYSORE	NAVAHO	NIBBLE
MOLISE	MOSQUE	MULLAH	MYSTIC	NAVELS	NIBLET
MOLOCH	MOSSIE	MULLED	MYTHOS	NAVIES	NICELY
MOLOPO	MOSTLY	MULLER	MY WORD	NAZISM	NICEST
MOLTED	MOTELS	MULLET	MYXOMA	NEARBY	NICETY
MOLTEN	MOTETS	MULTAN		NEARED	NICHES
MOMENT	MOTHER	MUMBLE	**N**	NEARER	NICKED
MOMISM	MOTIFS	MUMMER	NAAFIS	NEARLY	NICKEL
MOMMAS	MOTILE	MUNICH	NABBED	NEATEN	NICKER
MONACO	MOTION	MURALS	NABLUS	NEATER	NIDIFY
MONDAY	MOTIVE	MURCIA	NABOBS	NEATLY	NIECES
MONEYS	MOTLEY	MURDER	NACHOS	NEBULA	NIELLO
MONGER	MOTMOT	MURINE	NACRED	NECKAR	NIEVRE
MONGOL	MOTORS	MURMUR	NADIRS	NECKED	NIGGER
MONIES	MOTOWN	MUSCAT	NAEVUS	NECKER	NIGGLE

NIGHTS	NOSIER	**O**	OGDOAD	OPENER	OSHAWA
NILGAI	NOSILY		OGIVAL	OPENLY	OSIERS
NIMBLE	NOSING	OAFISH	OGLING	OPERAS	OSIJEK
NIMBLY	NOSTOC	OAKHAM	OGRESS	OPERON	OSMIUM
NIMBUS	NOTARY	OAXACA	OHMAGE	OPHITE	OSMOSE
NINETY	NOTICE	OBELUS	OIDIUM	OPIATE	OSMOUS
NINGBO	NOTIFY	OBEYED	OILCAN	OPINED	OSPREY
NINGPO	NOTING	OBEYER	OILCUP	OPIOID	OSSEIN
NINTHS	NOTION	OBJECT	OILIER	OPORTO	OSSIFY
NIOBIC	NOUGAT	OBLAST	OILILY	OPPOSE	OSTEAL
NIP OUT	NOUGHT	OBLATE	OILING	OPPUGN	OSTEND
NIPPED	NOUNAL	OBLIGE	OILMAN	OPTICS	OSTIUM
NIPPER	NOVARA	OBLONG	OILMEN	OPTING	OSTLER
NIPPLE	NOVELS	OBOIST	OILRIG	OPTION	OTHERS
NIPPON	NOVENA	O'BRIEN	OIL RIG	OPUSES	OTIOSE
NITRIC	NOVICE	OBSESS	OINKED	ORACLE	OTITIS
NITWIT	NOWISE	OBTAIN	OKAYED	ORADEA	O'TOOLE
NIXING	NOZZLE	OBTECT	OLD AGE	ORALLY	OTTAVA
NO BALL	NUANCE	OBTUSE	OLD BOY	ORANGE	OTTAWA
NO-BALL	NUBBLE	OBVERT	OLDEST	ORATOR	OTTERS
NOBBLE	NUBBLY	OCCULT	OLDHAM	ORBITS	OUNCES
NOBLER	NUBILE	OCCUPY	OLD HAT	ORCEIN	OUSTED
NOBLES	NUCHAL	OCEANS	OLDISH	ORCHID	OUSTER
NOBODY	NUCLEI	OCELOT	OLD LAG	ORCHIL	OUTAGE
NODDED	NUDGED	O'CLOCK	OLD MAN	ORCHIS	OUTBID
NODDLE	NUDGER	OCTANE	OLEATE	ORDAIN	OUTCRY
NOD OFF	NUDGES	OCTANT	O LEVEL	ORDEAL	OUTDID
NODOSE	NUDISM	OCTAVE	OLIVES	ORDERS	OUTFIT
NODULE	NUDIST	OCTAVO	OMASUM	ORDURE	OUTFOX
NOESIS	NUDITY	OCTETS	OMEGAS	OREBRO	OUTGAS
NOETIC	NUGGET	OCTOPI	ONAGER	OREGON	OUTING
NOGGIN	NUKING	OCTROI	ONCOST	ORENSE	OUTLAW
NOISES	NUMBAT	OCULAR	ON EDGE	ORGANS	OUTLAY
NOMADS	NUMBED	ODDEST	ONE-OFF	ORGASM	OUTLET
NOMISM	NUMBER	ODDITY	ONE-WAY	ORGEAT	OUTMAN
NONAGE	NUMBLY	ODD JOB	ONIONS	ORGIES	OUTPUT
NONCES	NUNCIO	ODDS ON	ONLINE	ORIENT	OUTRAN
NONEGO	NURSED	ODDS-ON	ONRUSH	ORIGAN	OUTRUN
NOODLE	NURSES	ODENSE	ONSIDE	ORIGIN	OUTSET
NOOSES	NUTANT	ODESSA	ONWARD	ORIOLE	OUTWIT
NOOTKA	NUTLET	ODIOUS	OOCYTE	ORISON	OVERDO
NORDIC	NUTMEG	ODOURS	OODLES	ORISSA	OVERLY
NORITE	NUTRIA	OEDEMA	OOGAMY	ORMOLU	OVIEDO
NORMAL	NUTTED	OEUVRE	OOLITE	ORNATE	OVISAC
NORMAN	NUTTER	OFFALY	OOLOGY	ORNERY	OVOIDS
NORTHS	NUZZLE	OFFEND	OOLONG	OROIDE	OVULAR
NORWAY	NYLONS	OFFERS	OOZIER	ORPHAN	OWELTY
NOSHED	NYMPHA	OFFICE	OOZILY	ORPINE	OWERRI
NOSH-UP	NYMPHS	OFFING	OOZING	ORRERY	OWLETS
NO SIDE		OFFSET	OPAQUE	OSCARS	OWLISH
NO-SIDE		OFSTED	OPENED	OSCINE	OWNERS
		OGADEN			

OWNING	PAMPAS	PARSEE	PEACES	PENMAN	PHASIC
OXALIS	PAMPER	PARSER	PEACHY	PENNED	PHENOL
OXCART	PANADA	PARSON	PEAHEN	PENNEY	PHENOM
OXFORD	PANAMA	PARTED	PEAKED	PENNON	PHENYL
OXIDES	PANDAS	PARTLY	PEALED	PEN PAL	PHIALS
OXTAIL	PANDER	PARTON	PEANUT	PENTAD	PHILAE
OXYGEN	PANDIT	PARURE	PEARLS	PENT UP	PHIZOG
OYSTER	PANELS	PASHTO	PEARLY	PENTYL	PHLEGM
OZALID	PANICS	PASSED	PEBBLE	PENULT	PHLOEM
	PANJIM	PASSES	PEBBLY	PENURY	PHOBIA
P	PANNED	PASSIM	PECANS	PEOPLE	PHOBIC
PACIFY	PANTED	PASTED	PECKED	PEORIA	PHOBOS
PACING	PANTRY	PASTEL	PECKER	PEPLUM	PHOEBE
PACINO	PANZER	PASTES	PECTEN	PEPPED	PHONED
PACKED	PAOTOW	PASTOR	PECTIC	PEPPER	PHONES
PACKER	PAPACY	PASTRY	PECTIN	PEPSIN	PHONEY
PACKET	PAPAIN	PATCHY	PEDALS	PEPTIC	PHONIC
PADANG	PAPAYA	PATENT	PEDANT	PERFIN	PHONON
PADAUK	PAPERS	PATERS	PEDATE	PERILS	PHOOEY
PADDED	PAPERY	PATHAN	PEDDLE	PERIOD	PHOTIC
PADDLE	PAPHOS	PATHOS	PEDLAR	PERISH	PHOTON
PADRES	PAPIST	PATINA	PEDWAY	PERKED	PHOTOS
PAEANS	PAPPUS	PATIOS	PEEING	PERLIS	PHRASE
PAELLA	PAPUAN	PATMOS	PEEKED	PERMED	PHUKET
PAEONY	PAPULE	PATOIS	PEELED	PERMIT	PHYLUM
PAGANS	PAPYRI	PATRAS	PEELER	PERNIK	PHYSIC
PAGING	PARADE	PATROL	PEEPBO	PERNOD	PHYSIO
PAGODA	PARAMO	PATRON	PEEPED	PER PRO	PHYTON
PAHANG	PARANA	PATTED	PEEPER	PERRON	PIAFFE
PAID-UP	PARANG	PATTEN	PEEPUL	PERSIA	PIANOS
PAINED	PARAPH	PATTER	PEERED	PERSON	PIAZZA
PAINTS	PARCEL	PAUCAL	PEEVED	PERTLY	PICKED
PAIRED	PARDON	PAUNCH	PEEWIT	PERUKE	PICKER
PAJAMA	PARENT	PAUPER	PEGGED	PERUSE	PICKET
PALACE	PARGET	PAUSED	PEG LEG	PESADE	PICKLE
PALAIS	PARIAH	PAUSER	PEKING	PESARO	PICK-UP
PALATE	PARIAN	PAUSES	PELAGE	PESETA	PICNIC
PALELY	PARIES	PAVANE	PELITE	PESTER	PIDDLE
PALEST	PARING	PAVING	PELLET	PESTLE	PIDGIN
PALING	PARISH	PAWING	PELMET	PETALS	PIECED
PALISH	PARITY	PAWNED	PELOTA	PETARD	PIECER
PALLAS	PARKAS	PAWPAW	PELTED	PETERS	PIECES
PALLED	PARKED	PAXWAX	PELTER	PETITE	PIERCE
PALLET	PARKIN	PAYBED	PELTRY	PETREL	PIERRE
PALLID	PARLEY	PAYDAY	PELVES	PETROL	PIFFLE
PALLOR	PARODY	PAYEES	PELVIC	PETTED	PIGEON
PALMAR	PAROLE	PAYING	PELVIS	PETTER	PIGGED
PALMED	PARREL	PAYOFF	PENANG	PEWITS	PIGGIN
PALTER	PARROT	PAYOLA	PENCHI	PEWTER	PIGLET
PALTRY	PARSEC	PAYOUT	PENCIL	PHASED	PIGNUS
PAMIRS	PARSED	PCMCIA	PENGPU	PHASES	PIGNUT

PIGSTY	PISS-UP	PLEBBY	POLISH	PORTED	PREFAB
PILAFS	PISTIL	PLEDGE	POLITE	PORTER	PREFER
PILEUM	PISTOL	PLEIAD	POLITY	PORTLY	PREFIX
PILEUP	PISTON	PLENTY	POLKAS	POSERS	PREPAY
PILEUS	PITCHY	PLENUM	POLLAN	POSEUR	PREPPY
PILFER	PITHOS	PLEURA	POLLED	POSHER	PRESET
PILING	PITIED	PLEVEN	POLLEN	POSIES	PRESTO
PILLAR	PITIES	PLEXOR	POLLEX	POSING	PRETTY
PILLOW	PITMAN	PLEXUS	POLLUX	POSSES	PREWAR
PILOSE	PITMEN	PLIANT	POLONY	POSSET	PREYED
PILOTS	PITSAW	PLICAL	POL POT	POSSUM	PREYER
PILULE	PITTED	PLIERS	POLYPS	POSTAL	PRICED
PIMPED	PIVOTS	PLIGHT	POMACE	POSTED	PRICES
PIMPLE	PIXELS	PLINTH	POMADE	POSTER	PRICEY
PIMPLY	PIXIES	PLISSE	POMMEL	POSTIE	PRICKS
PINCER	PIZZAS	PLOUGH	POMPOM	POSTIL	PRIDED
PINEAL	PLACED	PLOVER	POMPON	POTAGE	PRIDES
PINENE	PLACER	PLOWED	PONCES	POTASH	PRIEST
PINERY	PLACES	PLUCKS	PONCEY	POTATO	PRIMAL
PINGED	PLACET	PLUCKY	PONCHO	POTBOY	PRIMED
PINIER	PLACID	PLUMED	PONDER	POTEEN	PRIMER
PINING	PLAGAL	PLUMES	PONDOK	POTENT	PRIMES
PINION	PLAGUE	PLUMMY	PONGED	POTFUL	PRIMLY
PINITE	PLAGUY	PLUNGE	PONGEE	POTHER	PRIMUS
PINKED	PLAICE	PLURAL	PONGID	POTION	PRINCE
PINKER	PLAIDS	PLUSES	PONIES	POTTED	PRINTS
PINKIE	PLAINS	PLUTON	PONTIC	POTTER	PRIORS
PINKOS	PLAINT	PLYING	PONTIL	POUCHY	PRIORY
PINNED	PLAITS	PNEUMA	POODLE	POUNCE	PRIPET
PINNER	PLANAR	POCKED	POOLED	POUNDS	PRISED
PINTAS	PLANED	POCKET	POOPED	POURED	PRISMS
PINTER	PLANER	PODDED	POOPER	POURER	PRISON
PINTLE	PLANES	PODIUM	POORER	POUTED	PRISSY
PINUPS	PLANET	PODZOL	POORLY	POUTER	PRIVET
PINXIT	PLANKS	POETIC	POOTLE	POWDER	PRIZED
PIPAGE	PLANTS	POETRY	POP ART	POWELL	PRIZES
PIPALS	PLAQUE	POGROM	POPERY	POWERS	PRO-AMS
PIPERS	PLASHY	POINTE	POPGUN	POWWOW	PROBED
PIPING	PLASMA	POINTS	POPISH	POZNAN	PROBER
PIPITS	PLATAN	POISED	POPLAR	PRAGUE	PROBES
PIPKIN	PLATED	POISON	POPLIN	PRAISE	PROFIT
PIPPED	PLATEN	POKERS	POPPAS	PRANCE	PROJET
PIPPIN	PLATER	POKIER	POPPED	PRANKS	PROLEG
PIQUED	PLATES	POKILY	POPPER	PRATED	PROLES
PIQUES	PLAUEN	POKING	POPPET	PRATER	PROLIX
PIQUET	PLAYED	POLAND	POPPLE	PRAWNS	PROLOG
PIRACY	PLAYER	POLDER	PORING	PRAXIS	PROMOS
PIRATE	PLAZAS	POLEYN	PORISM	PRAYED	PROMPT
PISCES	PLEACH	POLICE	PORKER	PRAYER	PRONGS
PISSED	PLEASE	POLICY	POROUS	PREACH	PRONTO
PISSES	PLEATS	POLING	PORTAL	PRECIS	PROOFS

PROPEL	PUNDIT	PUTTEE	QUINSY	RAGTAG	RARELY
PROPER	PUNIER	PUTTER	QUIRES	RAGUSA	RAREST
PROPYL	PUNISH	PUZZLE	QUIRKS	RAIDED	RARING
PROSES	PUNJAB	PYKNIC	QUIRKY	RAIDER	RARITY
PROTEA	PUNKAH	PYLONS	QUIVER	RAILED	RASCAL
PRO TEM	PUNNED	PYOSIS	QUOITS	RAILER	RASHER
PROTON	PUNNET	PYRENE	QUORUM	RAILEX	RASHES
PROVED	PUNTED	PYRITE	QUOTAS	RAINED	RASHLY
PROVEN	PUNTER	PYRONE	QUOTED	RAISED	RASPED
PROVIE	PUPATE	PYROPE	QUOTES	RAISER	RASPER
PROWLS	PUPILS	PYTHON	QWERTY	RAISES	RASTER
PROZAC	PUPPED	PYURIA		RAISIN	RATBAG
PRUDES	PUPPET		**R**	RAJAHS	RATHER
PRUNED	PUPPIS	**Q**	RABATO	RAJKOT	RATIFY
PRUNER	PURDAH	QATARI	RABAUL	RAJPUT	RATINE
PRUNES	PUREED	QINTAR	RABBIS	RAKING	RATING
PRYING	PUREES	QUACKS	RABBIT	RAKISH	RATION
PSALMS	PURELY	QUAGGA	RABBLE	RAMBLE	RATIOS
PSEUDO-	PUREST	QUAGGY	RABIES	RAMIFY	RATITE
PSEUDS	PURFLE	QUAHOG	RACEME	RAMJET	RATLAM
PSEUDY	PURGED	QUAILS	RACERS	RAMMED	RATOON
PSYCHE	PURGER	QUAINT	RACHIS	RAMMER	RATTAN
PSYCHO-	PURGES	QUAKED	RACIAL	RAMOSE	RAT-TAT
PTISAN	PURIFY	QUAKER	RACIER	RAMPUR	RATTED
PTOSIS	PURINE	QUAKES	RACILY	RAMROD	RATTER
PUBLIC	PURISM	QUALMS	RACING	RAMTIL	RATTLE
PUCKER	PURIST	QUANGO	RACISM	RANCHI	RATTLY
PUDDLE	PURITY	QUANTA	RACIST	RANCID	RAVAGE
PUDDLY	PURLED	QUARKS	RACKED	RANDAN	RAVENS
PUDSEY	PURLER	QUARRY	RACKER	RANDOM	RAVERS
PUEBLA	PURLIN	QUARTO	RACKET	RANEES	RAVE-UP
PUEBLO	PURPLE	QUARTS	RACOON	RANGED	RAVINE
PUFFED	PURRED	QUARTZ	RADDLE	RANGER	RAVING
PUFFER	PURSED	QUASAR	RADIAL	RANGES	RAVISH
PUFFIN	PURSER	QUAVER	RADIAN	RANKED	RAWEST
PUGGED	PURSES	QUAYLE	RADIOS	RANKER	RAZING
PUKING	PURSUE	QUEASY	RADISH	RANKLE	RAZORS
PULLED	PURVEY	QUEBEC	RADIUM	RANKLY	RAZZLE
PULLET	PUSHED	QUEENS	RADIUS	RANSOM	READER
PULLEY	PUSHER	QUEERS	RADOME	RANTED	REALLY
PULL-IN	PUSHES	QUEMOY	RADULA	RANTER	REALMS
PULL-ON	PUSH-UP	QUENCH	RAFFIA	RAPIDS	REAMED
PULPED	PUSSES	QUESTS	RAFFLE	RAPIER	REAMER
PULPIT	PUTLOG	QUEUED	RAFTED	RAPINE	REAPED
PULSAR	PUT OFF	QUEUES	RAFTER	RAPING	REAPER
PULSED	PUT-OFF	QUICHE	RAGBAG	RAPIST	REARED
PULSES	PUT-ONS	QUIFFS	RAGGED	RAPPED	REARER
PUMICE	PUT OUT	QUILLS	RAGING	RAPPEL	REASON
PUMMEL	PUTRID	QUILTS	RAGLAN	RAPPER	REBASE
PUMPED	PUTSCH	QUINCE	RAGMAN	RAPTOR	REBATE
PUNCHY	PUTTED	QUINOL	RAGOUT	RAREFY	REBELS

REBIND	REFLET	REMOTE	RESUME	RIBBED	RISKED
REBOOT	REFLEX	REMOVE	RETAIL	RIBBON	RISKER
REBORN	REFLUX	RENAME	RETAIN	RIBERA	RISQUE
REBUFF	REFORM	RENDER	RETAKE	RIBOSE	RITUAL
REBUKE	REFUEL	RENEGE	RETARD	RICHER	RIVALS
RECALL	REFUGE	RENNES	RETELL	RICHES	RIVERS
RECANT	REFUND	RENNET	RETENE	RICHLY	RIVETS
RECAPS	REFUSE	RENNIN	RETIAL	RICKED	RIYADH
RECAST	REFUTE	RENOWN	RETINA	RICTAL	RIYALS
RECEDE	REGAIN	RENTAL	RETIRE	RICTUS	ROAMED
RECENT	REGALE	RENTED	RETOLD	RIDDED	ROAMER
RECEPT	REGARD	RENTER	RETOOK	RIDDEN	ROARED
RECESS	REGENT	RENVOI	RETOOL	RIDDER	ROARER
RECIFE	REGGAE	REOPEN	RETORT	RIDDLE	ROASTS
RECIPE	REGIME	REPAID	RETUNE	RIDERS	ROBALO
RECITE	REGINA	REPAIR	RETURN	RIDGED	ROBAND
RECKED	REGION	REPAND	RETUSE	RIDGES	ROBBED
RECKON	REGLET	REPAST	REUSED	RIDING	ROBBER
RECODE	REGRET	REPEAL	REVAMP	RIFFLE	ROBBIN
RECOIL	REGULO	REPEAT	REVEAL	RIFLED	ROBING
RECORD	REHASH	REPENT	REVERE	RIFLER	ROBINS
RECOUP	REHEAR	REPINE	REVERS	RIFLES	ROBOTS
RECTAL	REHEAT	REPLAN	REVERT	RIGGED	ROBSON
RECTOR	REHOME	REPLAY	REVEST	RIGGER	ROBUST
RECTOS	REIGNS	REPONE	REVIEW	RIGHTS	ROCHET
RECTUM	REINED	REPORT	REVILE	RIGOUR	ROCKED
RECTUS	REJECT	REPOSE	REVISE	RIG-OUT	ROCKER
REDACT	REJIGS	REPUTE	REVIVE	RIJEKA	ROCKET
REDBUD	REJOIN	REREAD	REVOKE	RILEYS	ROCOCO
REDCAP	RELAID	RERUNS	REVOLT	RILING	RODENT
REDDEN	RELATE	RESALE	REVUES	RILLET	RODEOS
REDDER	RELAYS	RESCUE	REVVED	RIMINI	ROGERS
REDEEM	RELENT	RESEAT	REWARD	RIMMED	ROGUES
RED EYE	RELICS	RESEAU	REWIND	RIMOSE	ROLLED
REDFIN	RELICT	RESECT	REWIRE	RINGED	ROLLER
RED-HOT	RELIED	RESEDA	REWORD	RINGER	ROLL ON
REDONE	RELIEF	RESEED	REWORK	RING IN	ROLL-ON
REDOWA	RELINE	RESENT	RHEBOK	RINSED	ROMAIC
RED SEA	RELISH	RESHIP	RHESUS	RINSER	ROMANO
REDUCE	RELIVE	RESIDE	RHEUMY	RINSES	ROMANS
REECHO	RELOAD	RESIGN	RHEYDT	RIOTED	ROMANY
REEFED	REMADE	RESILE	RHINAL	RIOTER	ROMEOS
REEFER	REMAIN	RESINS	RHODES	RIPEST	ROMPED
REEKED	REMAKE	RESIST	RHODIC	RIP-OFF	RONDEL
REELED	REMAND	RESITS	RHOTIC	RIPPED	RONDOS
REELER	REMARK	RESIZE	RHYMED	RIPPER	ROOFED
REEVES	REMEDY	RESORB	RHYMES	RIPPLE	ROOKED
REFACE	REMIND	RESORT	RHYTHM	RIPPLY	ROOKIE
REFILL	REMISE	RESTED	RHYTON	RIPSAW	ROOMED
REFINE	REMISS	RESTER	RIALTO	RISERS	ROOMER
REFITS	REMORA	RESULT	RIBALD	RISING	ROOSTS

ROOTED	RUEFUL	SACRUM	SAMITE	SAWFLY	SCORES
ROOTER	RUFFLE	SADDEN	SAMOAN	SAWING	SCORIA
ROOTSY	RUFFLY	SADDER	SAMOSA	SAWYER	SCORNS
ROPIER	RUFOUS	SADDLE	SAMPAN	SAXONS	SCOTCH
ROPILY	RUGGED	SADHUS	SAMPLE	SAXONY	SCOTER
ROPING	RUGOSA	SADISM	SAMSUN	SAYING	SCOTIA
ROQUET	RUGOSE	SADIST	SANDAL	SCABBY	SCOUSE
ROSARY	RUINED	SAFARI	SANDED	SCALAR	SCOUTS
ROSIER	RUINER	SAFELY	SANDER	SCALDS	SCOWLS
ROSILY	RULERS	SAFEST	SANDHI	SCALED	SCRAPE
ROSINY	RULING	SAFETY	SANELY	SCALER	SCRAPS
ROSTER	RUMBAS	SAGELY	SANEST	SCALES	SCRAWL
ROSTOV	RUMBLE	SAGGAR	SANIES	SCALPS	SCREAM
ROSTRA	RUMBLY	SAGGED	SANITY	SCAMPI	SCREED
ROTARY	RUMMER	SAHARA	SANTER	SCAMPS	SCREEN
ROTATE	RUMOUR	SAHIBS	SANTOS	SCANTY	SCREWS
ROTGUT	RUMPLE	SAIGON	SAPELE	SCARAB	SCREWY
ROTORS	RUMPLY	SAILED	SAPOTA	SCARCE	SCRIBE
ROTTED	RUMPUS	SAILER	SAPPED	SCARED	SCRIMP
ROTTEN	RUNDLE	SAILOR	SAPPER	SCARER	SCRIPT
ROTTER	RUNNEL	SAINTS	SARGES	SCARES	SCROLL
ROTUND	RUNNER	SAIPAN	SARNIA	SCAREY	SCROOP
ROUBLE	RUN-OFF	SAITHE	SARNIE	SCARFS	SCROTA
ROUGED	RUN-UPS	SALAAM	SARONG	SCARPS	SCRUBS
ROUNDS	RUNWAY	SALADS	SARTHE	SCATTY	SCRUFF
ROUSED	RUPEES	SALAMI	SASEBO	SCENES	SCRUMP
ROUSER	RUPIAH	SALARY	SASHAY	SCENIC	SCRUMS
ROUTED	RUSHED	SALIFY	SASHES	SCENTS	SCUBAS
ROUTER	RUSHER	SALINE	SASSED	SCHEMA	SCUFFS
ROUTES	RUSHES	SALIVA	SASSES	SCHEME	SCULPT
ROVERS	RUSSET	SALLEE	SATEEN	SCHISM	SCUMMY
ROVING	RUSSIA	SALLOW	SATING	SCHIST	SCUNGY
ROWANS	RUSTED	SALMON	SATINY	SCHLEP	SCURFY
ROWERS	RUSTIC	SALONS	SATIRE	SCHOOL	SCURRY
ROWING	RUSTLE	SALOON	SATURN	SCHORL	SCURVY
ROYALS	RUTILE	SALOOP	SATYRS	SCHUSS	SCUTCH
ROZZER	RUTTED	SALTED	SAUCED	SCHWAS	SCUTUM
RUBATO	RWANDA	SALTER	SAUCER	SCHWYZ	SCUZZY
RUBBED	RYAZAN	SALTUS	SAUCES	SCILLA	SCYLLA
RUBBER		SALUKI	SAUGER	SCIONS	SCYTHE
RUBBLE	**S**	SALUTE	SAUNAS	SCLAFF	SEABED
RUBBLY		SALVED	SAVAGE	SCLERA	SEA DOG
RUBIES	SABBAT	SALVER	SAVAII	SCOFFS	SEALED
RUBLES	SABERS	SALVES	SAVANT	SCOLDS	SEALER
RUBRIC	SABLES	SALVIA	SAVERS	SCOLEX	SEAMAN
RUCKED	SABRAS	SALVOR	SAVING	SCONCE	SEAMEN
RUCKUS	SABRES	SALVOS	SAVOIE	SCONES	SEAMER
RUDDER	SACHET	SALYUT	SAVONA	SCOOPS	SEANCE
RUDDLE	SACKED	SAMARA	SAVORY	SCORCH	SEARCH
RUDELY	SACKER	SAMBAR	SAVOUR	SCORED	SEARED
RUDEST	SACRAL	SAMBAS	SAVOYS	SCORER	SEASON

SEATED	SENNIT	SEXPOT	SHERRY	SHROUD	SILVAN
SEATER	SENORA	SEXTET	SHEWED	SHRUBS	SILVER
SEAWAY	SENORS	SEXTON	SHIELD	SHRUGS	SIMIAN
SECANT	SENSED	SEXUAL	SHIEST	SHRUNK	SIMILE
SECEDE	SENSES	SHABBY	SHIFTS	SHTOOK	SIMMER
SECOND	SENSOR	SHACKS	SHIFTY	SHUCKS	SIMNEL
SECRET	SENTRY	SHADED	SHIITE	SHUFTI	SIMONY
SECTOR	SEPALS	SHADES	SHINER	SHUFTY	SIMOOM
SECUND	SEPSIS	SHADOW	SHINNY	SHUNTS	SIMPER
SECURE	SEPTAL	SHAFTS	SHINTO	SHYEST	SIMPLE
SEDANS	SEPTET	SHAGGY	SHINTY	SHYING	SIMPLY
SEDATE	SEPTIC	SHAKEN	SHIRAZ	SIALIC	SINDHI
SEDILE	SEPTUM	SHAKER	SHIRES	SIBYLS	SINEWS
SEDUCE	SEQUEL	SHAKES	SHIRTS	SICILY	SINEWY
SEEDED	SEQUIN	SHALOM	SHIRTY	SICKED	SINFUL
SEEDER	SERAPH	SHAMAN	SHITTY	SICKEN	SINGED
SEEING	SERBIA	SHAMED	SHIVER	SICKER	SINGER
SEEKER	SEREIN	SHAMMY	SHOALS	SICKIE	SINGES
SEEMED	SERENE	SHANDY	SHOALY	SICKLE	SINGLE
SEEMER	SERIAL	SHANKS	SHOCKS	SICKLY	SINGLY
SEEMLY	SERIES	SHANNY	SHODDY	SIDE-ON	SINING
SEEPED	SERIFS	SHANSI	SHOGUN	SIDING	SINKER
SEESAW	SERINE	SHANTY	SHOOED	SIDLED	SINNED
SEETHE	SERMON	SHANXI	SHOO-IN	SIDLER	SINNER
SEFTON	SEROSA	SHAPED	SHOOTS	SIECLE	SINTER
SEICHE	SEROUS	SHAPES	SHORAN	SIEGEN	SIOUAN
SEINES	SERUMS	SHARDS	SHORED	SIEGES	SIPHON
SEISER	SERVAL	SHARED	SHORES	SIENNA	SIPPED
SEISIN	SERVED	SHARER	SHORTS	SIERRA	SIPPER
SEIZED	SERVER	SHARES	SHORTY	SIESTA	SIPPET
SEIZER	SERVES	SHARIA	SHOULD	SIEVED	SIRENS
SEJANT	SERVOS	SHARKS	SHOUTS	SIEVES	SIRING
SELDOM	SESAME	SHARPS	SHOVED	SIFAKA	SIRIUS
SELECT	SESTET	SHAVED	SHOVEL	SIFTED	SIRRAH
SELLER	SET-OFF	SHAVEN	SHOVER	SIFTER	SISERA
SELVES	SETOSE	SHAVER	SHOVES	SIGHED	SISKIN
SEMEME	SETTEE	SHAVES	SHOWED	SIGHER	SISTER
SEMITE	SETTER	SHAWLS	SHOWER	SIGHTS	SITARS
SEMPRE	SETTLE	SHEARS	SHOW UP	SIGNAL	SITCOM
SEMTEX	SET-UPS	SHEATH	SHRANK	SIGNED	SITING
SENARY	SEVENS	SHEAVE	SHREDS	SIGNEE	SIT-INS
SENATE	SEVERE	SHEETS	SHREWD	SIGNER	SITTER
SENDAI	SEVRES	SHEIKH	SHREWS	SIGNET	SIT-UPS
SENDER	SEWAGE	SHEILA	SHRIEK	SIGN ON	SIXTHS
SEND UP	SEWERS	SHEKEL	SHRIFT	SIGNOR	SIZING
SEND-UP	SEWING	SHELLS	SHRIKE	SIKKIM	SIZZLE
SENECA	SEXIER	SHELVE	SHRILL	SILAGE	SKATED
SENEGA	SEXILY	SHENSI	SHRIMP	SILENT	SKATER
SENILE	SEXING	SHERDS	SHRINE	SILICA	SKATES
SENIOR	SEXISM	SHERIA	SHRINK	SILKEN	SKEINS
SENNAR	SEXIST	SHERPA	SHRIVE	SILTED	SKELLY

SKETCH	SLICKS	SMITER	SNORER	SOMBRE	SPEARS
SKEWED	SLIDES	SMITHS	SNORES	SOMITE	SPECIE
SKEWER	SLIGHT	SMITHY	SNORTS	SONANT	SPECKS
SKIBOB	SLIMLY	SMOCKS	SNOTTY	SONATA	SPEECH
SKIDOO	SLINGS	SMOGGY	SNOUTS	SONNET	SPEEDS
SKIERS	SLINKY	SMOKED	SNOWED	SONORA	SPEEDY
SKIFFS	SLIP-ON	SMOKER	SNUBBY	SONTAG	SPEISS
SKIING	SLIPPY	SMOKES	SNUFFY	SOONER	SPELLS
SKIKDA	SLIP-UP	SMOOCH	SNUGLY	SOOTHE	SPERMS
SKILLS	SLIVER	SMOOTH	SOAKED	SOPPED	SPEWED
SKIMPY	SLOGAN	SMUDGE	SOAKER	SORBET	SPEWER
SKINNY	SLOOPS	SMUDGY	SOAPED	SORBIC	SPEYER
SKIRTS	SLOPED	SMUGLY	SOARED	SORDID	SPHENE
SKIVED	SLOPER	SMUTCH	SOARER	SORELY	SPHERE
SKIVER	SLOPES	SMUTTY	SOARES	SORREL	SPHINX
SKIVVY	SLOPPY	SNACKS	SOBBED	SORROW	SPICED
SKOPJE	SLOSHY	SNAFUS	SOBBER	SORTED	SPICER
SKULLS	SLOTHS	SNAGGY	SO BE IT	SORTER	SPICES
SKUNKS	SLOUCH	SNAILS	SOCAGE	SORTIE	SPIDER
SKYCAP	SLOUGH	SNAKED	SOCCER	SOTHIC	SPIELS
SKYLAB	SLOVAK	SNAKES	SOCIAL	SOUGHS	SPIGOT
SKYROS	SLOVEN	SNAPPY	SOCKED	SOUGHT	SPIKED
SLACKS	SLOWED	SNARED	SOCKET	SOUNDS	SPIKES
SLAGGY	SLOWER	SNARER	SOCMAN	SOURCE	SPILLS
SLAKED	SLOWLY	SNARES	SODDED	SOURED	SPINAL
SLAKER	SLUDGE	SNARLS	SODDEN	SOURER	SPINEL
SLALOM	SLUDGY	SNARLY	SODIUM	SOURLY	SPINES
SLANGY	SLUICE	SNATCH	SODOMY	SOUSED	SPINET
SLANTS	SLUING	SNAZZY	SOEVER	SOUSSE	SPIRAL
SLAP-UP	SLUMMY	SNEAKS	SOFFIT	SOVIET	SPIRES
SLATED	SLUMPS	SNEAKY	SOFTEN	SOWERS	SPIRIT
SLATER	SLURRY	SNEERS	SOFTER	SOWETO	SPITAL
SLATES	SLUSHY	SNEEZE	SOFTIE	SOWING	SPITED
SLAVED	SLYEST	SNEEZY	SOFTLY	SPACED	SPLAKE
SLAVER	SMACKS	SNICKS	SOIGNE	SPACER	SPLASH
SLAVES	SMALLS	SNIDER	SOILED	SPACES	SPLEEN
SLAVIC	SMALTO	SNIFFS	SOIREE	SPADER	SPLICE
SLAYER	SMARMY	SNIFFY	SOKOTO	SPADES	SPLINE
SLEAVE	SMEARS	SNIPED	SOLACE	SPADIX	SPLINT
SLEAZE	SMEARY	SNIPER	SOLDER	SPANKS	SPLITS
SLEAZY	SMEGMA	SNIPES	SOLELY	SPARED	SPLOSH
SLEDGE	SMELLS	SNIPPY	SOLEMN	SPARER	SPOILS
SLEEPY	SMELLY	SNITCH	SOLENT	SPARES	SPOILT
SLEETY	SMELTS	SNIVEL	SOLIDI	SPARID	SPOKEN
SLEEVE	SMILAX	SNOBOL	SOLIDS	SPARKS	SPOKES
SLEIGH	SMILED	SNOOPS	SOLING	SPARRY	SPONGE
SLEUTH	SMILER	SNOOPY	SO LONG	SPARSE	SPONGY
SLEWED	SMILES	SNOOTY	SOLUTE	SPASMS	SPOOFS
SLICED	SMILEY	SNOOZE	SOLVED	SPATHE	SPOOKS
SLICER	SMIRCH	SNOOZY	SOLVER	SPAVIN	SPOOKY
SLICES	SMIRKS	SNORED	SOMALI	SPAYED	SPOOLS

SPOONS	STABLE	STEEDS	STOOLS	STRUNG	SULTAN
SPOORS	STABLY	STEELS	STOP-GO	STRUTS	SULTRY
SPORES	STACKS	STEELY	STOP IN	STUBBY	SUMACH
SPORTS	STADIA	STEERS	STORAX	STUCCO	SUMMAT
SPORTY	STAFFS	STEEVE	STORED	STUDIO	SUMMED
SPOT-ON	STAGED	STEINS	STORES	STUFFY	SUMMER
SPOTTY	STAGER	STELAR	STOREY	STUMER	SUMMIT
SPOUSE	STAGES	STENCH	STORKS	STUMPS	SUMMON
SPOUTS	STAGEY	STEPPE	STORMS	STUMPY	SUNBED
SPRAIN	STAINS	STEP UP	STORMY	STUNTS	SUNBOW
SPRANG	STAIRS	STEREO	STOUPS	STUPID	SUNDAE
SPRATS	STAKED	STERIC	STOVER	STUPOR	SUNDAY
SPRAWL	STAKES	STERNA	STOVES	STURDY	SUNDER
SPRAYS	STALAG	STERNS	STOWED	STYLAR	SUNDEW
SPREAD	STALED	STEROL	STRAFE	STYLED	SUNDRY
SPREES	STALER	STEWED	STRAIN	STYLER	SUN GOD
SPRIER	STALKS	STICKS	STRAIT	STYLES	SUNKEN
SPRIGS	STALKY	STICKY	STRAKE	STYLET	SUNLIT
SPRING	STALLS	STIFFS	STRAND	STYLUS	SUNNED
SPRINT	STAMEN	STIFLE	STRAPS	STYMIE	SUNNIS
SPRITE	STAMPS	STIGMA	STRATA	STYRAX	SUNRAY
SPROUT	STANCE	STILES	STRAWS	STYRIA	SUNSET
SPRUCE	STANCH	STILLS	STRAWY	SUABLE	SUNTAN
SPRUIT	STANDS	STILLY	STRAYS	SUAKIN	SUPERB
SPRUNG	STANZA	STILTS	STREAK	SUBBED	SUPER-G
SPRYLY	STAPES	STINGS	STREAM	SUBDUE	SUPINE
SPUNKY	STAPLE	STINGY	STREEP	SUBITO	SUPPED
SPURGE	STARCH	STINKS	STREET	SUBLET	SUPPER
SPURRY	STARED	STINTS	STRESS	SUBMIT	SUPPLE
SPURTS	STARER	STIPEL	STREWN	SUBORN	SUPPLY
SPUTUM	STARES	STIPES	STRICK	SUBSET	SURELY
SPYING	STARRY	STIRPS	STRICT	SUBTLE	SUREST
SQUABS	STARTS	STIR UP	STRIDE	SUBTLY	SURETY
SQUADS	STARVE	STITCH	STRIFE	SUBURB	SURFED
SQUALL	STASIS	STOATS	STRIKE	SUBWAY	SURFER
SQUAMA	STATED	STOCKS	STRING	SUCHOU	SURFIE
SQUARE	STATER	STOCKY	STRIPE	SUCKED	SURGED
SQUASH	STATES	STODGE	STRIPS	SUCKER	SURGER
SQUATS	STATIC	STODGY	STRIPY	SUCKLE	SURGES
SQUAWK	STATOR	STOICS	STRIVE	SUDDEN	SURREY
SQUAWS	STATUE	STOKED	STROBE	SUFFER	SURTAX
SQUEAK	STATUS	STOKER	STRODE	SUFFIX	SURVEY
SQUEAL	STAVED	STOKES	STROKE	SUGARS	SUSLIK
SQUIBS	STAVES	STOLEN	STROLL	SUGARY	SUSSED
SQUIDS	STAYED	STOLES	STROMA	SUITED	SUTTEE
SQUILL	STAYER	STOLID	STRONG	SUITES	SUTTON
SQUINT	STAY IN	STOLON	STROPS	SUITOR	SUTURE
SQUIRE	STEADS	STONED	STROUD	SULCUS	SUU KYI
SQUIRM	STEADY	STONER	STROVE	SULKED	SUZHOU
SQUIRT	STEAKS	STONES	STRUCK	SULKER	SVELTE
SQUISH	STEAMY	STOOGE	STRUMA	SULLEN	SWABIA

SWAGER	SYRUPY	TAMPON	TAUTLY	TENNIS	THEISM
SWAINS	SYSTEM	TANDEM	TAUTOG	TENONS	THEIST
SWAMIS	SYZRAN	TANGLE	TAVERN	TENORS	THEMES
SWAMPS	SYZYGY	TANGLY	TAWDRY	TENPIN	THEMIS
SWAMPY	SZEGED	TANGOS	TAXEME	TENREC	THENAR
SWANKS		TANKER	TAXIED	TENSED	THENCE
SWANKY	**T**	TANNED	TAXING	TENSER	THEORY
SWARDS	TABARD	TANNER	TAXMAN	TENSES	THERMS
SWARMS	TABBED	TANNIC	TAXMEN	TENSOR	THESES
SWATCH	TABLED	TANNIN	TAYLOR	TENTER	THESIS
SWATHE	TABLES	TANNOY	T-BONES	TENTHS	THETIC
SWATHS	TABLET	TAOISM	TEABAG	TENURE	THICKO
SWATOW	TABOOS	TAOIST	TEACUP	TENUTO	THIEVE
SWAYED	TABRIZ	TAPERS	TEAMED	TEPEES	THIGHS
SWAYER	TACKED	TAPING	TEAPOT	TEPEFY	THIMBU
SWEATS	TACKER	TAPIRS	TEAPOY	TERBIC	THINGS
SWEATY	TACKLE	TAPPED	TEARER	TERCEL	THINLY
SWEDEN	TACOMA	TAPPER	TEASED	TERCET	THIRDS
SWEDES	TACTIC	TAPPET	TEASEL	TEREDO	THIRST
SWEENY	TADJIK	TARAWA	TEASER	TERESA	THIRTY
SWEEPS	TAEJON	TARBES	TEASES	TERETE	THOLOS
SWEETS	TAG END	TARGET	TECHIE	TERGAL	THONGS
SWELLS	TAGGED	TARIFF	TECHNO	TERGUM	THORAX
SWERVE	TAHITI	TARMAC	TEDDER	TERMED	THORIC
SWIFTS	TAIHOA	TAROTS	TEDIUM	TERMLY	THORNS
SWILLS	TAILED	TARPAN	TEEING	TERMOR	THORNY
SWINES	TAILOR	TARPON	TEEMED	TERRET	THORON
SWINGE	TAINAN	TARRED	TEEPEE	TERROR	THOUGH
SWINGS	TAIPAN	TARSAL	TEETER	TERUEL	THRALL
SWIPED	TAIPEI	TARSUS	TEETHE	TESTED	THRASH
SWIPES	TAIWAN	TARTAN	TEFLON	TESTER	THREAD
SWIRLS	TAKERS	TARTAR	TEGMEN	TESTES	THREAT
SWIRLY	TAKEUP	TARTLY	TEHRAN	TESTIS	THREES
SWITCH	TAKING	TASKER	TELEDU	TETCHY	THRESH
SWIVEL	TALCUM	TASMAN	TELIAL	TETHER	THRICE
SWIVET	TALENT	TASSEL	TELIUM	TETRAD	THRIFT
SWOONS	TALION	TASTED	TELLER	TETRYL	THRILL
SWOOPS	TALKED	TASTER	TELPAL	TETTER	THRIPS
SWOOSH	TALKER	TASTES	TELSON	TETUAN	THRIVE
SWORDS	TALKIE	TATAMI	TEMPED	TEUTON	THROAT
SYDNEY	TALLER	TATARY	TEMPER	THAMES	THROBS
SYLVAN	TALLOW	TATTED	TEMPLE	THANES	THROES
SYMBOL	TALMUD	TATTER	TEMPOS	THANKS	THRONE
SYNCOM	TALONS	TATTIE	TEMUCO	THATCH	THRONG
SYNDIC	TAMBOV	TATTLE	TENACE	THAWED	THROVE
SYNODS	TAMELY	TATTOO	TENANT	THAWER	THROWN
SYNTAX	TAMERS	TAUGHT	TENDED	THECAL	THROWS
SYPHER	TAMEST	TAUNTS	TENDER	THEFTS	THRUSH
SYPHON	TAMING	TAURUS	TENDON	THEGNS	THRUST
SYRIAN	TAMPED	TAUTEN	TENETS	THEINE	THUMBS
SYRINX	TAMPER	TAUTER	TENNER	THEIRS	THUMPS

THWACK	TINGLY	TOLEDO	TOUCAN	TRENDY	TROVES
THWART	TIN GOD	TOLLED	TOUCHE	TRENTO	TROWEL
THYMIC	TIN HAT	TOLUCA	TOUCHY	TREPAN	TROYES
THYMOL	TINIER	TOLUYL	TOULON	TRESSY	TRUANT
THYMUS	TINKER	TOMATO	TOUPEE	TRIADS	TRUCES
THYRSE	TINKLE	TOMBAC	TOURED	TRIAGE	TRUCKS
TIARAS	TINKLY	TOMBOY	TOURER	TRIALS	TRUDGE
TIBIAE	TINNED	TOMCAT	TOUSLE	TRIBAL	TRUEST
TIBIAS	TIN-POT	TOM-TOM	TOUTED	TRIBES	TRUISM
TICINO	TINSEL	TONGAN	TOWAGE	TRICES	TRUMAN
TICKED	TINTED	TONGUE	TOWBAR	TRICKS	TRUMPS
TICKER	TIP-OFF	TONICS	TOWELS	TRICKY	TRUNKS
TICKET	TIPPED	TONING	TOWERS	TRICOT	TRUSTS
TICKLE	TIPPER	TONKIN	TOWHEE	TRIERS	TRUSTY
TIC TAC	TIPPET	TONNES	TOWING	TRIFID	TRUTHS
TIDBIT	TIPPLE	TONSIL	TOWNEE	TRIFLE	TRYING
TIDDLY	TIPTOE	TOOLED	TOWNIE	TRIGER	TRY-OUT
TIDIER	TIP-TOP	TOOLER	TOXINS	TRIKES	TRYSTS
TIDILY	TIRADE	TOOTED	TOXOID	TRILBY	T-SHIRT
TIDING	TIRANA	TOOTER	TOYAMA	TRILLS	TSINAN
TIDYED	TIRING	TOOTHY	TOYING	TRIMER	TSONGA
TIE-DYE	TISANE	TOOTLE	TRACED	TRIMLY	TSOTSI
TIE-INS	TISSUE	TOP DOG	TRACER	TRINAL	TSWANA
TIEPIN	TITANS	TOPEES	TRACES	TRIODE	TUAREG
TIERCE	TITBIT	TOPEKA	TRACKS	TRIOSE	TUBBED
TIE-UPS	TITCHY	TOP HAT	TRACTS	TRIPLE	TUBERS
TIFFIN	TITFER	TOPHUS	TRADED	TRIPOD	TUBING
TIFLIS	TITHER	TOPICS	TRADER	TRIPOS	TUBULE
TIGERS	TITHES	TOPPED	TRADES	TRIPPY	TUCKED
TIGHTS	TITLED	TOPPER	TRAGAL	TRITON	TUCKER
TIGRIS	TITLES	TOPPLE	TRAGIC	TRIUNE	TUCK-IN
TILDES	TITTER	TORBAY	TRAGUS	TRIVET	TUCSON
TILERS	TITTLE	TORERO	TRAILS	TRIVIA	TUFFET
TILING	TITTUP	TORIES	TRAINS	TROCAR	TUFTED
TILLED	TIVOLI	TOROID	TRAITS	TROCHE	TUFTER
TILLER	TMESIS	TOROSE	TRALEE	TROGON	TUGGED
TILTED	TOASTS	TORPID	TRAMPS	TROIKA	TUGGER
TILTER	TOBAGO	TORPOR	TRANCE	TROJAN	TULIPS
TIMARU	TOBRUK	TORQUE	TRANNY	TROLLS	TUMBLE
TIMBAL	TOCSIN	TORRID	TRASHY	TROMPE	TUMEFY
TIMBER	TO DATE	TORSOS	TRAUMA	TROOPS	TUMOUR
TIMBRE	TODDLE	TOSSED	TRAVEL	TROPES	TUMULI
TIMELY	TOE CAP	TOSSER	TRAWLS	TROPHY	TUMULT
TIMERS	TOEING	TOSSES	TREADS	TROPIC	TUNDRA
TIMING	TOFFEE	TOSS UP	TREATS	TROPPO	TUNERS
TINCAL	TOGGED	TOSS-UP	TREATY	TROTHS	TUNE-UP
TINDER	TOGGLE	TOTALS	TREBLE	TROTYL	TUNGUS
TINEAL	TOILED	TOTEMS	TREBLY	TROUGH	TUNICA
TINEID	TOILER	TOTING	TREMOR	TROUPE	TUNICS
TINGED	TOILET	TOTTED	TRENCH	TROUTS	TUNING
TINGLE	TOKENS	TOTTER	TRENDS	TROVER	TUNNEL

TUPELO	TWIRLS	UNCORK	UNPLUG	UPRISE	VACUUM
TUPPED	TWIRLY	UNCURL	UNREAD	UPROAR	VADOSE
TURBAN	TWIRPS	UNDEAD	UNREAL	UPROOT	VAGARY
TURBID	TWISTS	UNDIES	UNREST	UPSETS	VAGINA
TURBIT	TWISTY	UNDOER	UNRIPE	UPSHOT	VAINER
TURBOT	TWITCH	UNDONE	UNROLL	UPSIDE	VAINLY
TUREEN	TWO-BIT	UNDULY	UNRULY	UPTAKE	VALAIS
TURFED	TWO-PLY	UNEASE	UNSAFE	UPTICK	VALETA
TURGID	TWO-WAY	UNEASY	UNSAID	UPTILT	VALETS
TURGOR	TYCOON	UNESCO	UNSEAL	UPTIME	VALGUS
TURION	TYMPAN	UNEVEN	UNSEAM	UPTOWN	VALINE
TURKEY	TYPHUS	UNFAIR	UNSEAT	UPTURN	VALISE
TURKIC	TYPIFY	UNFOLD	UNSEEN	UPWARD	VALIUM
TURNED	TYPING	UNFREE	UNSEXY	UPWIND	VALLEY
TURNER	TYPIST	UNFURL	UNSHIP	URACIL	VALOUR
TURN IN	TYRANT	UNGUAL	UNSNAP	URALIC	VALUED
TURNIP	TYRONE	UNGUIS	UNSTEP	URANIC	VALUER
TURN ON	TYUMEN	UNGULA	UNSTOP	URANUS	VALUES
TURN-ON		UNHAIR	UNSUNG	URANYL	VALVES
TURN UP	**U**	UNHAND	UNSURE	URATIC	VANDAL
TURN-UP	UBANGI	UNHOLY	UNTIDY	URBANE	VANISH
TURRET	U-BOATS	UNHOOD	UNTIED	URCHIN	VANITY
TURTLE	UDDERS	UNHOOK	UNTOLD	UREASE	VAPOUR
TURVES	UDMURT	UNICEF	UNTRUE	UREIDE	VARDAR
TUSCAN	UGANDA	UNIONS	UNTUCK	URETER	VARESE
TUSCHE	UGLIER	UNIPOD	UNUSED	URETIC	VARIED
TUSHES	UGLIFY	UNIQUE	UNVEIL	URGENT	VARLET
TUSKER	UGRIAN	UNISEX	UNWARY	URGING	VASSAL
TUSSAH	UJJAIN	UNISON	UNWELL	URINAL	VASTLY
TUSSIS	ULCERS	UNISON	UNWEPT	UROPOD	VAULTS
TUSSLE	ULLAGE	UNITED	UNWIND	URSINE	VAUNTS
TUTORS	ULSTER	UNITER	UNWISE	URTEXT	VECTOR
TUTSAN	ULTIMA	UNJUST	UNWRAP	USABLE	VEERED
TUT-TUT	UMBRAL	UNKIND	UNYOKE	USAGES	VEGANS
TUVALU	UMBRIA	UNKNIT	UPBEAT	USANCE	VEILED
TUXEDO	UMLAUT	UNLACE	UPCAST	USED TO	VEILER
TUYERE	UMPIRE	UNLAID	UPDATE	USEFUL	VEINAL
TWANGS	UMTATA	UNLASH	UPDIKE	USHERS	VEINED
TWANGY	UNABLE	UNLEAD	UPHELD	USURER	VELARS
TWEAKS	UNAWED	UNLESS	UPHILL	UTAHAN	VELATE
TWEEDS	UNBELT	UNLIKE	UPHOLD	UTERUS	VELCRO
TWEEDY	UNBEND	UNLIVE	UPHROE	UTMOST	VELETA
TWEETS	UNBENT	UNLOAD	UPKEEP	UTOPIA	VELLUM
TWELVE	UNBIND	UNLOCK	UPLAND	U-TURNS	VELOCE
TWENTY	UNBOLT	UNMADE	UPLIFT	UVULAE	VELOUR
TWERPS	UNBORN	UNMAKE	UPLINK	UVULAR	VELSEN
TWIGGY	UNCIAL	UNMASK	UPLOAD	UVULAS	VELURE
TWILIT	UNCLAD	UNMOOR	UPPERS		VELVET
TWINED	UNCLES	UNPACK	UPPISH	**V**	VENDED
TWINER	UNCLOG	UNPAID	UPPITY	VACANT	VENDEE
TWINGE	UNCOIL	UNPICK	UPREAR	VACATE	VENDOR

VENEER	VIBORG	VOICES	WAKING	WASHIN	WESKER
VENERY	VIBRIO	VOIDED	WALKED	WASTED	WESTER
VENETO	VICARS	VOIDER	WALKER	WASTER	WETHER
VENIAL	VICTIM	VOLANT	WALK-IN	WASTES	WETTED
VENICE	VICTOR	VOLLEY	WALK-ON	WATERS	WETTER
VENIRE	VICUNA	VOLUME	WALK-UP	WATERY	WHACKS
VENOSE	VIDEOS	VOLUTE	WALLAH	WATTLE	WHALER
VENOUS	VIENNA	VOLVOX	WALLED	WATUSI	WHALES
VENTED	VIENNE	VOODOO	WALLET	WAVIER	WHAMMY
VENTER	VIEWED	VORTEX	WALLOP	WAVILY	WHARFS
VENUES	VIEWER	VOSGES	WALLOW	WAVING	WHARVE
VENULE	VIGILS	VOSTOK	WALNUT	WAXIER	WHEELS
VERBAL	VIGOUR	VOTARY	WALRUS	WAXILY	WHEEZE
VERBID	VIKING	VOTERS	WALTON	WAXING	WHEEZY
VERDIN	VILELY	VOTING	WAMPUM	WAYLAY	WHELKS
VERDUN	VILEST	VOTIVE	WANDER	WAY-OUT	WHELPS
VERGED	VILIFY	VOTYAK	WANGLE	WEAKEN	WHENCE
VERGER	VILLAS	VOWELS	WANING	WEAKER	WHERRY
VERGES	VILLUS	VOWING	WANKED	WEAKLY	WHEYEY
VERIFY	VINERY	VOX POP	WANKER	WEALTH	WHIFFS
VERILY	VINOUS	VOYAGE	WANNED	WEANED	WHIFFY
VERISM	VINYLS	VOYEUR	WANNER	WEAPON	WHILED
VERIST	VIOLAS	V-SIGNS	WANT AD	WEARER	WHILST
VERITY	VIOLET	VULGAR	WANTED	WEASEL	WHIMSY
VERMIN	VIOLIN	VULVAE	WANTER	WEAVER	WHINED
VERMIS	VIPERS	VULVAL	WANTON	WEAVES	WHINER
VERNAL	VIRAGO	VULVAS	WAPITI	WEBBED	WHINES
VERONA	VIRGIN	VYBORG	WARBLE	WEDDED	WHINGE
VERSED	VIRGOS		WAR CRY	WEDELN	WHINNY
VERSES	VIRILE	**W**	WARDED	WEDGED	WHIPPY
VERSOS	VIRTUE	WADDLE	WARDEN	WEDGES	WHIRLS
VERSUS	VISAED	WADERS	WARDER	WEEDED	WHISKS
VERTEX	VISAGE	WADGES	WARIER	WEEDER	WHISKY
VERVET	VISCID	WADING	WARILY	WEEING	WHITBY
VESICA	VISION	WAFERS	WARLEY	WEEKLY	WHITEN
VESPER	VISITS	WAFFLE	WARMED	WEEPER	WHITER
VESPID	VISORS	WAFTED	WARMER	WEEVER	WHITES
VESSEL	VISTAS	WAFTER	WARMLY	WEEVIL	WHIZZY
VESTAL	VISUAL	WAGERS	WARMTH	WEE-WEE	WHOLLY
VESTED	VITALS	WAGGED	WARM-UP	WEIGHT	WHOOPS
VESTRY	VITRIC	WAGGLE	WARNED	WEIHAI	WHOOSH
VETOED	VIVACE	WAGGLY	WARNER	WEIMAR	WHORES
VETOER	VIVIFY	WAGING	WARPED	WEIRDO	WHORLS
VETOES	VIXENS	WAGONS	WARPER	WELDED	WHYDAH
VETTED	VIZIER	WAILED	WARRED	WELDER	WICKED
VEXING	V-NECKS	WAILER	WARREN	WELDON	WICKER
VIABLE	VOCABS	WAISTS	WARSAW	WELKIN	WICKET
VIABLY	VOCALS	WAITED	WARTED	WELKOM	WIDELY
VIAGRA	VOGUES	WAITER	WASHED	WELLED	WIDEST
VIANDS	VOICED	WAIVED	WASHER	WELTER	WIDGET
VIBIST	VOICER	WAIVER	WASHES	WENDED	WIDISH

WIDNES	WINKED	WOODEN	XIAMEN	YEMENI	ZEALOT
WIDOWS	WINKER	WOOERS	XMASES	YENTAI	ZEBRAS
WIDTHS	WINKLE	WOOFER	X-RAYED	YEOMAN	ZENIST
WIELDY	WINNER	WOOING	XUZHOU	YEOMEN	ZENITH
WIFELY	WINNOW	WOOLLY	XYLENE	YES-MAN	ZEPHYR
WIGEON	WINTER	WORDED	XYLOID	YES-MEN	ZEROED
WIGGED	WINTRY	WORKED	XYLOSE	YIELDS	ZEROES
WIGGLE	WIPING	WORKER	XYSTER	YIPPEE	ZESTER
WIGGLY	WIRIER	WORLDS		YODELS	ZEUGMA
WIGHTS	WIRILY	WORMED	**Y**	YOGISM	ZIGONG
WIGWAG	WIRING	WORMER		YOGURT	ZIGZAG
WIGWAM	WIRRAL	WORSEN	YACHTS	YOKELS	ZIMMER
WILDER	WISDOM	WORTHY	YAGARA	YOKING	ZINCIC
WILDLY	WISELY	WOUNDS	YAKKED	YONDER	ZINCKY
WILFUL	WISEST	WOWING	YAMMER	YORKER	ZINNIA
WILIER	WISHED	WRAITH	YANGON	YORUBA	ZIPPED
WILLED	WISHER	WRASSE	YANKED	YOUTHS	ZIPPER
WILLER	WISHES	WREATH	YANKEE	YOWLED	ZIRCON
WILLET	WISMAR	WRECKS	YANTAI	YOWLER	ZITHER
WILLOW	WITHAL	WRENCH	YAPPED	YTTRIA	ZODIAC
WILSON	WITHER	WRETCH	YAPPER	YTTRIC	ZOMBIE
WILTED	WITHIN	WRIEST	YARDIE	YUCCAS	ZONATE
WIMBLE	WIZARD	WRIGHT	YARNED	YUNNAN	ZONING
WIMPLE	WOBBLE	WRISTS	YARROW	YUPPIE	ZONKED
WINCED	WOBBLY	WRISTY	YATTER		ZONULE
WINCER	WOEFUL	WRITER	YAUPON	**Z**	ZOOMED
WINCES	WOKING	WRITHE	YAUTIA		ZOSTER
WINCEY	WOLFED	WRONGS	YAWING	ZABRZE	ZOYSIA
WINDED	WOLVER	WRYEST	YAWNED	ZAFFER	ZURICH
WINDER	WOLVES	WRYING	YAWNER	ZAGREB	ZWOLLE
WINDOW	WOMBAT	WYVERN	YEARLY	ZAMBIA	ZYDECO
WIND UP	WONDER		YEASTY	ZANDER	ZYGOMA
WINGED	WONSAN	**X**	YELLED	ZANIER	ZYGOSE
WINGER	WONTED		YELLER	ZANILY	ZYGOTE
WINGES	WONTON	XENIAL	YELLOW	ZAPPED	ZYMASE
WINING	WOODED	XEROMA	YELPED	ZAPPER	ZYRIAN
		XHOSAN	YELPER	ZAREBA	

A	ACADIAN	ACYCLIC	AFFAIRE	AIRPORT	ALKANET
AALBORG	ACAROID	ADAGIOS	AFFAIRS	AIR RAID	ALKMAAR
ABALONE	ACAUDAL	ADAMANT	AFFIANT	AIRSHIP	ALLAYED
ABANDON	ACAUSAL	ADAMAWA	AFFIXED	AIRSICK	ALLEGED
ABASHED	ACCEDED	ADAPTED	AFFIXES	AIRWAYS	ALLEGRO
ABASING	ACCEDER	ADAPTER	AFFLICT	AITCHES	ALLELIC
ABATING	ACCENTS	ADAPTOR	AFFRAYS	AJACCIO	ALLERGY
ABAXIAL	ACCLAIM	ADAXIAL	AFFRONT	ALABAMA	ALLHEAL
ABDOMEN	ACCORDS	ADDENDA	AFGHANS	ALAGOAS	ALLONYM
ABELARD	ACCOUNT	ADDICTS	AFRICAN	A LA	ALL OVER
ABELIAN	ACCRETE	ADDRESS	AGAINST	MODE	ALLOWAY
ABERFAN	ACCRUAL	ADDUCED	AGAMETE	ALANINE	ALLOWED
ABETTED	ACCRUED	ADENINE	AGEISTS	ALARMED	ALLOYED
ABETTOR	ACCUSED	ADENOID	AGELESS	ALASKAN	ALLSEED
ABEYANT	ACCUSER	ADENOMA	AGENDAS	ALBANIA	ALL-STAR
ABFARAD	ACERATE	ADEPTLY	AGENDUM	ALBERTA	ALL-TIME
ABHENRY	ACERBIC	ADHERED	AGGRADE	ALBINIC	ALLUDED
ABIDING	ACEROSE	ADIPOSE	AGGRESS	ALBINOS	ALLURED
ABIDJAN	ACETATE	ADIVASI	AGILELY	ALBITIC	ALLURER
ABILITY	ACETIFY	ADJOINT	AGILITY	ALBUMEN	ALLUVIA
ABIOSIS	ACETONE	ADJOURN	AGITATE	ALBUMIN	ALLYING
ABJURED	ACETOUS	ADJUDGE	AGITATO	ALCAZAR	ALMA-ATA
ABJURER	ACHAEAN	ADJUNCT	AGNOMEN	ALCHEMY	ALMANAC
ABLATOR	ACHIEVE	ADJURED	AGONIES	ALCOHOL	ALMERIA
ABLEISM	ACICULA	ADJURER	AGONIST	ALCOPOP	ALMONDS
ABOLISH	ACIDIFY	ADMIRAL	AGONIZE	ALCOVES	ALMONER
ABORTED	ACIDITY	ADMIRED	AGRAFFE	AL DENTE	ALMS MAN
ABRADED	ACNODAL	ADMIRER	AGRAPHA	ALEMBIC	ALOETIC
ABRADER	ACOLYTE	ADOPTED	AGROUND	ALERTED	ALOOFLY
ABREACT	ACONITE	ADORING	AILERON	ALERTLY	ALPACAS
ABREAST	ACOUCHI	ADORNED	AILMENT	A LEVELS	ALPHORN
ABRIDGE	ACQUIRE	ADRENAL	AIMLESS	ALFALFA	ALREADY
ABRUZZI	ACREAGE	ADULATE	AIRBASE	ALGARVE	ALRIGHT
ABSCESS	ACRILAN	ADVANCE	AIRBEDS	ALGEBRA	ALSO RAN
ABSCISE	ACROBAT	ADVENTS	AIR-COOL	ALGERIA	ALSO-RAN
ABSCOND	ACROGEN	ADVERBS	AIRCREW	ALGIERS	ALTDORF
ABSENCE	ACRONYM	ADVERSE	AIRDRIE	AL HUFUF	ALTERED
ABSINTH	ACROTER	ADVICES	AIRDROP	ALIASES	ALTHAEA
ABSOLVE	ACRYLIC	ADVISED	AIRFLOW	ALI BABA	ALTHING
ABSTAIN	ACRYLYL	ADVISER	AIRGLOW	ALIDADE	ALTHORN
ABUSING	ACTABLE	AEGISES	AIRGUNS	ALIENEE	ALUMNAE
ABUSIVE	ACTINAL	AEONIAN	AIRIEST	ALIENOR	ALUMNUS
ABUTTAL	ACTINIA	AERATED	AIRINGS	ALIFORM	ALUNDUM
ABUTTED	ACTINIC	AERATOR	AIRLANE	ALIGARH	ALUNITE
ABUTTER	ACTINON	AERIALS	AIRLESS	ALIGNED	ALYSSUM
ABYSMAL	ACTIONS	AEROBIC	AIRLIFT	ALIMENT	AMADODA
ABYSSAL	ACTRESS	AEROGEL	AIRLINE	ALIMONY	AMALGAM
ABYSSES	ACTUARY	AEROSOL	AIRLOCK	ALIQUOT	AMANITA
ACACIAS	ACTUATE	AETOLIA	AIRMAIL	ALIUNDE	AMASSED
ACADEME	ACULEUS	AFFABLE	AIRMILE	ALKALIC	AMASSER
ACADEMY	ACUTELY	AFFABLY	AIRPLAY	ALKALIS	AMATEUR

AMATORY	ANATOMY	ANNUITY	APLITIC	ARCHINE	ARTISTS
AMAZING	ANCHORS	ANNULAR	APOCARP	ARCHING	ARTLESS
AMAZONS	ANCHOVY	ANNULET	APOCOPE	ARCHIVE	ARTWORK
AMBIENT	ANCHUSA	ANNULUS	APOGAMY	ARCHWAY	ARUGULA
AMBLING	ANCIENT	ANODIZE	APOGEES	ARCUATE	ARUNDEL
AMBOYNA	ANCONAL	ANODYNE	APOLOGY	ARDECHE	ASCARID
AMENDED	ANDANTE	ANOMALY	APOLUNE	ARDENCY	ASCENTS
AMENDER	ANDIRON	ANORAKS	APOMICT	ARDUOUS	ASCETIC
AMENITY	ANDORRA	ANOSMIA	APOSTIL	AREAWAY	ASCITES
AMENTIA	ANDROID	ANOTHER	APOSTLE	ARENITE	ASCITIC
AMERICA	ANEMONE	ANSWERS	APOTHEM	AREOLAR	ASCRIBE
AMHARIC	ANERGIC	ANTACID	APPAREL	ARGOLIS	ASEPSIS
AMIABLE	ANEROID	ANTEFIX	APPEALS	ARGONNE	ASEPTIC
AMIABLY	ANEURIN	ANTEING	APPEASE	ARGOTIC	ASEXUAL
AMMETER	ANGARSK	ANTENNA	APPLAUD	ARGUING	ASHAMED
AMMONAL	ANGELIC	ANTHEMS	APPLIED	ARIDITY	ASHANTI
AMMONIA	ANGELOU	ANTHERS	APPLIER	ARIETTA	ASHDOWN
AMMONIC	ANGELUS	ANT HILL	APPOINT	ARISING	ASHFORD
AMNESIA	ANGERED	ANTHILL	APPRISE	ARIZONA	ASHIEST
AMNESTY	ANGEVIN	ANT HILL	APPROVE	ARMADAS	ASHTRAY
AMNIOTE	ANGINAL	ANTHRAX	APPULSE	ARMBAND	ASIATIC
AMOEBAE	ANGIOMA	ANTIBES	APRAXIA	ARMENIA	ASININE
AMOEBAS	ANGLIAN	ANTIGEN	APRAXIC	ARMFULS	ASKANCE
AMOEBIC	ANGLIFY	ANTIGUA	APRICOT	ARMHOLE	ASOCIAL
AMORIST	ANGLING	ANTIOCH	A PRIORI	ARMIGER	ASPECTS
AMOROSO	ANGOLAN	ANTIQUE	APROPOS	ARMLESS	ASPERSE
AMOROUS	ANGORAS	ANTLERS	APSIDAL	ARMLOCK	ASPHALT
AMOUNTS	ANGRIER	ANTLION	APTERAL	ARMOIRE	ASPIRED
AMPHORA	ANGRILY	ANTONYM	APTNESS	ARMOURY	ASPIRER
AMPLIFY	ANGUINE	ANTWERP	AQUARIA	ARMPITS	ASPIRIN
AMPOULE	ANGUISH	ANUROUS	AQUATIC	ARMREST	ASSAULT
AMPULLA	ANGULAR	ANXIETY	AQUAVIT	AROUSAL	ASSAYED
AMPUTEE	ANHINGA	ANXIOUS	AQUEOUS	AROUSED	ASSAYER
AMULETS	ANILINE	ANYBODY	AQUIFER	AROUSER	ASSEGAI
AMUSING	ANILITY	ANYMORE	ARABIAN	ARRAIGN	ASSHOLE
AMYLASE	ANIMALS	ANYWAYS	ARABIST	ARRANGE	ASSIZES
AMYLENE	ANIMATE	ANYWISE	ARACAJU	ARRAYAL	ASSUAGE
AMYLOID	ANIMATO	APAGOGE	ARAL SEA	ARRAYED	ASSUMED
AMYLOSE	ANIMISM	APATITE	ARAMAIC	ARREARS	ASSUMER
ANAEMIA	ANIMIST	APELIKE	ARANEID	ARRESTS	ASSURED
ANAEMIC	ANIONIC	APETALY	ARAPAHO	ARRIVAL	ASSURER
ANAGOGE	ANISEED	APHAGIA	ARAROBA	ARRIVED	ASSYRIA
ANAGRAM	ANISOLE	APHASIA	ARBITER	ARRIVER	ASTATIC
ANAHEIM	ANKLETS	APHESIS	ARBOURS	ARROWED	ASTOUND
ANALOGY	ANNATES	APHONIA	ARBUTUS	ARSENAL	ASTRIDE
ANALYSE	ANNATTO	APHONIC	ARCADES	ARSENIC	ASTROID
ANALYST	ANNELID	APHOTIC	ARCADIA	ART DECO	ASTYLAR
ANAMBRA	ANNEXED	APHYLLY	ARCANUM	ARTICLE	ASUNDER
ANAPEST	ANNEXES	APIEZON	ARCHAIC	ARTIEST	ASYLUMS
ANARCHY	ANNOYED	APLASIA	ARCHERS	ARTISAN	ATACTIC
ANATASE	ANNUALS	APLENTY	ARCHERY	ARTISTE	ATAVISM

ATAVIST	AUXERRE	BACKERS	BALLS-UP	BARENTS	BATTENS
ATELIER	AUXESIS	BACKING	BALMIER	BARGAIN	BATTERS
AT HEART	AVAILED	BACKLOG	BALMILY	BARGEES	BATTERY
ATHEISM	AVARICE	BACK OFF	BALNEAL	BARGING	BATTIER
ATHEIST	AVATARS	BACKSAW	BALONEY	BARILLA	BATTING
ATHLETE	AVENGED	BACKUPS	BALSAMS	BARKERS	BATTLED
ATHWART	AVENGER	BACOLOD	BALTICS	BARKING	BATTLES
ATLANTA	AVENUES	BACTRIA	BALUCHI	BARMAID	BATWING
ATLASES	AVERAGE	BACULUM	BAMBARA	BARMIER	BAUBLES
ATOMISM	AVERRED	BADAJOZ	BAMBERG	BARNAUL	BAUHAUS
ATOMIST	AVERTED	BAD DEBT	BAMBINO	BARNEYS	BAULKED
ATOMIZE	AVESTAN	BAD FORM	BAMBOOS	BARONET	BAUTZEN
ATONING	AVEYRON	BADGERS	BANANAS	BAROQUE	BAUXITE
ATROPHY	AVIATOR	BADNESS	BANBURY	BAROTSE	BAVARIA
ATTACHE	AVIDITY	BAFFLED	BANDAGE	BARQUES	BAWDIER
ATTACKS	AVIGNON	BAFFLER	BANDBOX	BARRACK	BAWDILY
ATTAINT	AVIONIC	BAFFLES	BANDEAU	BARRAGE	BAWLING
ATTEMPT	AVOCADO	BAGANDA	BANDIED	BARRELS	BAYAMON
ATTIRED	AVOIDED	BAGASSE	BANDIER	BARRIER	BAYONET
ATTRACT	AVOIDER	BAGGAGE	BANDING	BARRING	BAYONNE
ATTUNED	AVOWALS	BAGGIER	BANDITS	BARROWS	BAYWOOD
AUBERGE	AVOWING	BAGGILY	BANDUNG	BARYTES	BAZAARS
AUCTION	AWAITED	BAGGING	BANEFUL	BASCULE	BAZOOKA
AUDIBLE	AWAKING	BAGHDAD	BANGERS	BASENJI	BEACHED
AUDIBLY	AWARDED	BAG LADY	BANGING	BASHFUL	BEACHES
AUDITED	AWARDEE	BAGPIPE	BANGKOK	BASHING	BEACONS
AUDITOR	AWARDER	BAGWORM	BANGLES	BASHKIR	BEADIER
AUGITIC	AWESOME	BAHAISM	BANKERS	BASILAN	BEADILY
AUGMENT	AWFULLY	BAHAIST	BANKING	BASILAR	BEADING
AUGURAL	AWKWARD	BAHAMAS	BANKSIA	BASILIC	BEADLES
AUGURED	AWLWORT	BAHRAIN	BANNERS	BASKETS	BEAGLES
AUGUSTA	AWNINGS	BAILEYS	BANNING	BASKING	BEAKERS
AU PAIRS	AXOLOTL	BAILIFF	BANNOCK	BASOTHO	BEAMING
AURALLY	AZIMUTH	BAILING	BANQUET	BAS-RHIN	BEARDED
AUREATE	AZURITE	BAIL OUT	BANSHEE	BASSEIN	BEARERS
AUREOLE	AZYGOUS	BAILOUT	BANTAMS	BASSETS	BEAR HUG
AURICLE		BAINITE	BANTOID	BASSIST	BEARING
AURORAE	**B**	BAITING	BANYANS	BASSOON	BEARISH
AURORAL	BAALBEK	BALANCE	BAODING	BASTARD	BEASTLY
AURORAS	BABASSU	BALATON	BAPTISM	BASTING	BEATERS
AUSPICE	BABBITT	BALCONY	BAPTIST	BASTION	BEATIFY
AUSSIES	BABBLED	BALDING	BAPTIZE	BATCHES	BEATING
AUSTERE	BABBLER	BALEFUL	BARBARY	BATFISH	BEATNIK
AUSTRAL	BABOONS	BALKING	BARBATE	BATHERS	BEAVERS
AUSTRIA	BABYING	BALLADE	BARBELL	BATHING	BECAUSE
AUTARKY	BABYISH	BALLADS	BARBERS	BATH MAT	BECKETT
AUTHORS	BABY-SAT	BALLARD	BARBOUR	BATHTUB	BEDBUGS
AUTOCUE	BABY-SIT	BALLAST	BARBUDA	BATHYAL	BEDDING
AUTOMAT	BACCATE	BALLETS	BARBULE	BATISTE	BEDEVIL
AUTOPSY	BACILLI	BALLOON	BARCHAN	BATSMAN	BEDEWED
AUTUMNS	BACKBAR	BALLOTS	BAR CODE	BATSMEN	BEDFORD

BEDHEAD	BEMUSED	BETTING	BILTONG	BLADDER	BLOUSES
BEDLAMS	BENARES	BETWEEN	BIMODAL	BLAMING	BLOW-DRY
BEDOUIN	BENCHER	BETWIXT	BIMORPH	BLANDER	BLOWERS
BEDPANS	BENCHES	BEVELED	BINDERS	BLANDLY	BLOWFLY
BEDPOST	BENDIGO	BEWITCH	BINDERY	BLANKET	BLOWIER
BEDRAIL	BENDING	BEXHILL	BINDING	BLANKLY	BLOWING
BEDROCK	BENEATH	BEYOGLU	BINNING	BLARING	BLOWOUT
BEDROOM	BENEFIT	BEZIQUE	BIOCIDE	BLARNEY	BLOW OUT
BEDSIDE	BENELUX	BHANGRA	BIODATA	BLASTED	BLOW-UPS
BEDSORE	BENGALI	BIASING	BIOFUEL	BLATANT	BLUBBER
BEDTIME	BENNETT	BIASSED	BIOHERM	BLATHER	BLUE GUM
BEECHES	BENTHOS	BIAXIAL	BIOLOGY	BLAUBOK	BLUEING
BEEFIER	BENZENE	BIBCOCK	BIOMASS	BLAYDON	BLUE JAY
BEEFING	BENZINE	BIBELOT	BIONICS	BLAZERS	BLUE LAW
BEEF TEA	BENZOIC	BICYCLE	BIOPICS	BLAZING	BLUE-SKY
BEEHIVE	BENZOIN	BIDDING	BIOPTIC	BLAZONS	BLUETIT
BEELINE	BENZOYL	BIEN HOA	BIOTECH	BLEAKER	BLUFFED
BEESWAX	BEOGRAD	BIFFING	BIOTITE	BLEAKLY	BLUFFER
BEETFLY	BEQUEST	BIFILAR	BIOTOPE	BLEATED	BLUFFLY
BEETLED	BERATED	BIFOCAL	BIOTYPE	BLEATER	BLUNDER
BEETLES	BERBERA	BIG CATS	BIPLANE	BLEEDER	BLUNGER
BEGGARS	BEREAVE	BIG DEAL	BIPOLAR	BLEEPED	BLUNTED
BEGGARY	BERGAMO	BIG ENDS	BIRCHED	BLEEPER	BLUNTLY
BEGGING	BERMUDA	BIGENER	BIRCHES	BLEMISH	BLURRED
BEGONIA	BERNESE	BIGFOOT	BIRD DOG	BLENDED	BLURTED
BEGUILE	BERRIES	BIG GAME	BIRDIES	BLENDER	BLUSHED
BEHAVED	BERSEEM	BIGGEST	BIRETTA	BLESBOK	BLUSHER
BEHINDS	BERSERK	BIGGIES	BISCUIT	BLESSED	BLUSHES
BEIJING	BERTHED	BIGHEAD	BISHKEK	BLETHER	BLUSTER
BEJEWEL	BESEECH	BIGHORN	BISHOPS	BLEWITS	B-MOVIES
BELARUS	BESIDES	BIG NAME	BISMUTH	BLIGHTS	BOARDED
BELATED	BESIEGE	BIGNESS	BISTORT	BLINDED	BOARDER
BELAYED	BESMEAR	BIGOTED	BISTROS	BLINDLY	BOARISH
BELCHED	BESPEAK	BIGOTRY	BITCHED	BLINKED	BOASTED
BELCHES	BESPOKE	BIG SHOT	BITCHES	BLINKER	BOASTER
BELFAST	BESTIAL	BIG TIME	BITCHIN'	BLISTER	BOATERS
BELFORT	BESTING	BIG TOPS	BIT PART	BLITZED	BOATING
BELGAUM	BEST MAN	BIGWIGS	BITTERN	BLITZES	BOATMAN
BELGIAN	BEST-OFF	BIJAPUR	BITTERS	BLOATED	BOATMEN
BELGIUM	BESTREW	BIKANER	BITTIER	BLOATER	BOBBERY
BELIEFS	BESTRID	BIKINIS	BITUMEN	BLOCKED	BOBBIES
BELIEVE	BETAINE	BILBOES	BIVALVE	BLONDER	BOBBING
BELLBOY	BETAKEN	BILIARY	BIVOUAC	BLONDES	BOBBINS
BELLEEK	BETHANY	BILIOUS	BIZARRE	BLOODED	BOBBLES
BELLIES	BETHELS	BILKING	BIZERTE	BLOOMED	BOBSLED
BELLOWS	BETHINK	BILLETS	BLABBED	BLOOMER	BOBSTAY
BELOVED	BETIDED	BILLIES	BLABBER	BLOOPER	BOBTAIL
BELTING	BETIMES	BILLING	BLACKED	BLOSSOM	BODICES
BELT MAN	BETOKEN	BILLION	BLACKEN	BLOTCHY	BODKINS
BELTWAY	BETROTH	BILLOWS	BLACKER	BLOTTED	BOFFINS
BELYING	BETTERS	BILLOWY	BLACKLY	BLOTTER	BOGARDE

BOGGIER	BOOTLEG	BOWSHOT	BRECCIA	BROODED	BUGGERY
BOGGING	BOOZERS	BOW TIES	BREEDER	BROODER	BUGGIES
BOGGLED	BOOZE UP	BOXCARS	BRENDEL	BROOKED	BUGGING
BOHEMIA	BOOZE-UP	BOXROOM	BRENNER	BROTHEL	BUGLERS
BOHRIUM	BOOZIER	BOX SEAT	BRENTON	BROTHER	BUGLOSS
BOILERS	BOOZILY	BOXWOOD	BRESCIA	BROWNED	BUILDER
BOILING	BOOZING	BOYCOTT	BREVIER	BROWNER	BUILDUP
BOK CHOY	BOPPING	BOYHOOD	BREVITY	BROWNIE	BUILD UP
BOLDEST	BORACIC	BRABANT	BREWAGE	BROWSED	BUILT-IN
BOLEROS	BORAZON	BRABHAM	BREWERY	BROWSER	BUILT-UP
BOLETUS	BORDERS	BRACING	BREWING	BRUCINE	BUKHARA
BOLIVAR	BORDURE	BRACKEN	BRIBERY	BRUISED	BULBOUS
BOLIVIA	BOREDOM	BRACKET	BRICOLE	BRUISER	BULGIER
BOLLARD	BORNEEL	BRADAWL	BRIDGET	BRUISES	BULGING
BOLOGNA	BORNITE	BRAEMAR	BRIDOON	BRUITED	BULIMIA
BOLONEY	BOROUGH	BRAGGED	BRIGADE	BRUMOUS	BULKIER
BOLSHIE	BORSCHT	BRAGGER	BRIGAND	BRUSHED	BULKILY
BOLSTER	BORSTAL	BRAHMAN	BRIMFUL	BRUSHER	BULKING
BOLTING	BORZOIS	BRAIDED	BRIMMER	BRUSHES	BULLACE
BOLZANO	BOSCAGE	BRAIDER	BRINDLE	BRUSH-UP	BULLATE
BOMBARD	BOSNIAN	BRAILLE	BRING UP	BRUSQUE	BULLDOG
BOMBAST	BOSSIER	BRAINED	BRIOCHE	BRUTISH	BULLETS
BOMBERS	BOSSILY	BRAISED	BRISKER	BRYANSK	BULLIED
BOMBING	BOSSING	BRAKING	BRISKET	BUBBLED	BULLIES
BONAIRE	BOTCHED	BRAKPAN	BRISKLY	BUBBLER	BULLION
BONANZA	BOTCHER	BRAMBLE	BRISTLE	BUBBLES	BULLISH
BONBONS	BOTCH-UP	BRAMLEY	BRISTLY	BUBONIC	BULLOCK
BONDAGE	BOTTLED	BRANAGH	BRISTOL	BUCKETS	BULRUSH
BONDING	BOTTLES	BRANDED	BRITISH	BUCKEYE	BULWARK
BONE-DRY	BOTTOMS	BRANSON	BRITONS	BUCKING	BUMBLED
BONESET	BOTTROP	BRAN TUB	BRITPOP	BUCKLED	BUMBLER
BONFIRE	BOTULIN	BRASHER	BRITTLE	BUCKLER	BUMBOAT
BONGOES	BOUCHEE	BRASHLY	BROADEN	BUCKLES	BUMMING
BONIEST	BOUDOIR	BRASSES	BROADER	BUCKRAM	BUMPERS
BONJOUR	BOULDER	BRASSIE	BROADLY	BUCKSAW	BUMPIER
BONKERS	BOUNCED	BRAVADO	BROCADE	BUCOLIC	BUMPILY
BONNETS	BOUNCER	BRAVAIS	BROCKET	BUDDIES	BUMPING
BONNIER	BOUNCES	BRAVELY	BROGLIE	BUDDING	BUMPKIN
BONUSES	BOUNDED	BRAVERY	BROGUES	BUDGETS	BUNCHED
BOOBIES	BOUNDEN	BRAVEST	BROILED	BUDGING	BUNCHES
BOOBING	BOUNDER	BRAVING	BROILER	BUFFALO	BUNDLED
BOOKEND	BOUQUET	BRAVURA	BROKERS	BUFFERS	BUNDLER
BOOKING	BOURBON	BRAWLED	BROMATE	BUFFETS	BUNDLES
BOOKISH	BOURDON	BRAWLER	BROMIDE	BUFFING	BUNGING
BOOKLET	BOURGES	BRAYING	BROMINE	BUFFOON	BUNGLED
BOOMING	BOUYANT	BRAZIER	BROMISM	BUGABOO	BUNGLER
BOORISH	BOWHEAD	BREADTH	BROMLEY	BUGANDA	BUNGLES
BOOSTED	BOWKNOT	BREAKER	BRONCHI	BUGBANE	BUNIONS
BOOSTER	BOWLERS	BREAK-IN	BRONCOS	BUGBEAR	BUNKERS
BOOTEES	BOWLINE	BREATHE	BRONZED	BUG-EYED	BUNKING
BOOTING	BOWLING	BREATHY	BRONZES	BUGGERS	BUNK OFF

BUNK-UPS	BUSKING	CADAVER	CALOTTE	CANTERS	CAREERS
BUNNIES	BUSSING	CADDIED	CALTROP	CANTHUS	CAREFUL
BUNTING	BUS STOP	CADDIES	CALUMNY	CANTING	CARFARE
BUOYAGE	BUSTARD	CADDISH	CALVARY	CANTONS	CARGOES
BUOYANT	BUSTERS	CADELLE	CALVING	CANTORS	CARHOPS
BUOYING	BUSTIER	CADENCE	CALYCES	CANVASS	CARIBOU
BURBLED	BUSTING	CADENCY	CALYCLE	CANYONS	CARIOCA
BURBLER	BUSTLED	CADENZA	CALYPSO	CANZONA	CARIOLE
BURDENS	BUSTLER	CADGERS	CALYXES	CANZONE	CARIOUS
BURDOCK	BUSTLES	CADGING	CAMBERS	CAPABLE	CARJACK
BUREAUX	BUST-UPS	CADMIUM	CAMBIAL	CAPABLY	CARLINE
BURETTE	BUSYING	CAESIUM	CAMBIST	CAP-A-	CARLING
BURGEON	BUTANOL	CAESURA	CAMBIUM	PIE	CARMINE
BURGERS	BUTCHER	CAFTANS	CAMBRAI	CAPE COD	CARNAGE
BURGESS	BUTLERS	CAGIEST	CAMBRIC	CAPELIN	CARNIFY
BURGHAL	BUTLERY	CAGOULE	CAMELOT	CAPELLA	CAROLED
BURGHER	BUTTERY	CAHOOTS	CAMERAL	CAPERED	CAROLUS
BURGLAR	BUTTIES	CAIQUES	CAMERAS	CAPITAL	CAROTID
BURGLED	BUTTING	CAISSON	CAMP BED	CAPITOL	CAROUSE
BURIALS	BUTTOCK	CAJOLED	CAMPERS	CAPORAL	CARPALE
BURLIER	BUTTONS	CAJUPUT	CAMPHOR	CAPPING	CAR PARK
BURMESE	BUTYRIC	CALABAR	CAMPING	CAPRICE	CARPETS
BURNERS	BUTYRIN	CALAMUS	CAMPION	CAPSIZE	CARPING
BURNING	BUY INTO	CALCIFY	CAM RANH	CAPSTAN	CAR POOL
BURNISH	BUYOUTS	CALCINE	CAMWOOD	CAPSULE	CARPORT
BURNLEY	BUZZARD	CALCITE	CANAPES	CAPTAIN	CARRARA
BURNOUS	BUZZERS	CALCIUM	CANARDS	CAPTION	CARRICK
BURNOUT	BUZZING	CALCULI	CANASTA	CAPTIVE	CARRIED
BURPING	BYE-BYES	CALDERA	CANCANS	CAPTORS	CARRIER
BURRING	BYELOVO	CALDRON	CANCERS	CAPTURE	CARRIES
BURRITO	BYGONES	CALENDS	CANDELA	CARABAO	CARRION
BURROWS	BY-LINES	CALGARY	CANDIED	CARABID	CARROTS
BURSARS	BYRONIC	CALIBRE	CANDIES	CARACAL	CARROTY
BURSARY	BYWORDS	CALICHE	CANDLER	CARACAS	CARRY ON
BURSTER		CALICOS	CANDLES	CARACUL	CARRY-ON
BURTHEN	**C**	CALIPEE	CANDOUR	CARAFES	CARSICK
BURTONS	CABARET	CALIPHS	CANELLA	CARAMBA	CARTAGE
BURUNDI	CABBAGE	CALKING	CANINES	CARAMEL	CARTELS
BURWEED	CABBALA	CALLAIS	CANKERS	CARAVAN	CARTERS
BURYING	CABBIES	CALLANT	CANNERY	CARAVEL	CARTING
BUSBIES	CABEZON	CALL BOX	CANNIER	CARAWAY	CARTONS
BUS BOYS	CABIMAS	CALLBOY	CANNILY	CARBENE	CARTOON
BUSHELS	CABINDA	CALLERS	CANNING	CARBIDE	CARVERS
BUSHIER	CABINET	CALLING	CANNOCK	CARBINE	CARVING
BUSHING	CABLING	CALL-INS	CANNONS	CARBONS	CASCADE
BUSHIRE	CABOOSE	CALLOUS	CANNULA	CARBOYS	CASCARA
BUSHMAN	CAB RANK	CALMEST	CANONRY	CARCASS	CASEASE
BUSHPIG	CACHETS	CALMING	CANOPUS	CARDIAC	CASEATE
BUSHTIT	CACKLED	CALOMEL	CANTALA	CARDIFF	CASEOSE
BUSIEST	CACKLER	CALORIC	CANTATA	CARDING	CASEOUS
BUSKERS	CACKLES	CALORIE	CANTEEN	CARDOON	CASERTA

CASHEWS	CATTERY	CENTURY	CHANTED	CHECK ON	CHIMNEY
CASHIER	CATTIER	CEPHEUS	CHANTER	CHECKUP	CHINESE
CASHING	CATTILY	CERAMIC	CHANTRY	CHEDDAR	CHINKED
CASINGS	CATTISH	CERATED	CHAOTIC	CHEEKED	CHINOOK
CASINOS	CATWALK	CEREALS	CHAPATI	CHEEPED	CHINTZY
CASKETS	CAUDATE	CEREBRA	CHAPEAU	CHEEPER	CHINWAG
CASPIAN	CAULINE	CERTAIN	CHAPELS	CHEERED	CHIPPED
CASQUED	CAULKED	CERTIFY	CHAPLET	CHEERIO	CHIPPER
CASQUES	CAULKER	CERUMEN	CHAPPAL	CHEESES	CHIRPED
CASSATA	CAUSING	CERVINE	CHAPPED	CHEETAH	CHIRPER
CASSAVA	CAUSTIC	CESSION	CHAPTER	CHELATE	CHIRRUP
CASSINO	CAUTERY	CESSPIT	CHARADE	CHEMISE	CHISELS
CASSOCK	CAUTION	CESTODE	CHARGED	CHEMIST	CHIVIED
CASTERS	CAVALLA	CESTOID	CHARGER	CHENGTU	CHLORAL
CASTILE	CAVALRY	CETINJE	CHARGES	CHENNAI	CHLORIC
CASTING	CAVEATS	CETOOGY	CHARIER	CHEQUER	CHOC-ICE
CASTLED	CAVE-INS	CHABLIS	CHARILY	CHEQUES	CHOCKED
CASTLES	CAVEMAN	CHABROL	CHARIOT	CHERISH	CHOCTAW
CAST OFF	CAVEMEN	CHA-CHAS	CHARITY	CHEROOT	CHOICER
CAST-OFF	CAVERNS	CHAFFED	CHARKHA	CHERUBS	CHOICES
CASTORS	CAVES IN	CHAFFER	CHARLES	CHERVIL	CHOKERS
CASUIST	CAVETTO	CHAFING	CHARLIE	CHESTED	CHOKING
CATALAN	CAVILED	CHAGRIN	CHARMED	CHESTER	CHOLERA
CATALPA	CAYENNE	CHAINED	CHARMER	CHEVIOT	CHOLINE
CATANIA	CEASING	CHAIRED	CHARNEL	CHEVRON	CHOLULA
CATARRH	CEDILLA	CHAISES	CHARPOY	CHEWIER	CHOMPED
CATBIRD	CEILING	CHALAZA	CHARQUI	CHEWING	CHOOSER
CATBOAT	CELADON	CHALCID	CHARRED	CHIANTI	CHOPPED
CATCALL	CELEBES	CHALCIS	CHARTED	CHIAPAS	CHOPPER
CATCHER	CELESTA	CHALDEA	CHARTER	CHIASMA	CHORALE
CATCHES	CELLARS	CHALETS	CHASERS	CHIBOUK	CHORDAL
CATCH IT	CELLIST	CHALICE	CHASING	CHICAGO	CHOREAL
CATCH UP	CELLNET	CHALKED	CHASMAL	CHICANE	CHORION
CATECHU	CELLULE	CHALLAH	CHASSIS	CHICANO	CHORLEY
CATERED	CELSIUS	CHALLIS	CHASTEN	CHICKEN	CHOROID
CATERER	CEMBALO	CHALONE	CHASTER	CHICORY	CHORTLE
CATFISH	CENACLE	CHAMBER	CHATEAU	CHIDDEN	CHORZOW
CATHEAD	CENSORS	CHAMFER	CHATHAM	CHIDING	CHOWDER
CATHODE	CENSUAL	CHAMOIS	CHATTED	CHIEFLY	CHROMIC
CATKINS	CENSURE	CHAMPAC	CHATTEL	CHIFFON	CHROMYL
CATLING	CENTAUR	CHAMPED	CHATTER	CHIGGER	CHRONIC
CATMINT	CENTAVO	CHANCED	CHAYOTE	CHIGNON	CHRONON
CATNAPS	CENTERS	CHANCEL	CHEAPEN	CHILEAN	CHUCKED
CAT'S-EAR	CENTIME	CHANCES	CHEAPER	CHILIAD	CHUCK IN
CAT'S EYE	CENTIMO	CHANCRE	CHEAPIE	CHILIES	CHUCKLE
CAT'S PAW	CENTNER	CHANGDE	CHEAPLY	CHILLED	CHUFFED
	CENTRAL	CHANGED	CHEATED	CHILLUM	CHUGGED
CATSUIT	CENTRED	CHANGER	CHEATER	CHILUNG	CHUKCHI
CATTALO	CENTRES	CHANGES	CHECHEN	CHIMERA	CHUKKER
	CENTRIC	CHANNEL	CHECKED	CHIMERE	CHUMMED
	CENTRUM	CHANSON	CHECK-IN	CHIMING	CHURNED

CHUTNEY	CLAPPER	CLINKER	COAXIAL	COLDISH	COMPARE
CHUVASH	CLAQUES	CLINTON	COAXING	COLDITZ	COMPASS
CHYMOUS	CLARIFY	CLIPPED	COBBERS	COLD WAR	COMPEER
CICADAS	CLARINO	CLIPPER	COBBLED	COLICKY	COMPERE
CICHLID	CLARION	CLIPPIE	COBBLER	COLITIC	COMPETE
CILIARY	CLARITY	CLIQUES	COBWEBS	COLITIS	COMPILE
CILIATE	CLARKIA	CLIQUEY	COCAINE	COLLAGE	COMPING
CIMBRIC	CLASHED	CLOACAL	COCCOID	COLLARD	COMPLEX
CINDERS	CLASHER	CLOAKED	COCCOUS	COLLARS	COMPLIN
CINDERY	CLASHES	CLOBBER	COCHLEA	COLLATE	COMPONY
CINEMAS	CLASPED	CLOCHES	COCKADE	COLLECT	COMPORT
CINERIN	CLASPER	CLOCKED	COCKIER	COLLEEN	COMPOSE
CIPHERS	CLASSED	CLOGGED	COCKING	COLLEGE	COMPOST
CIPOLIN	CLASSES	CLONMEL	COCKLES	COLLIDE	COMPOTE
CIRCLED	CLASSIC	CLOPPED	COCKNEY	COLLIER	COMPTON
CIRCLER	CLASSIS	CLOSELY	COCKPIT	COLLIES	COMPUTE
CIRCLES	CLASTIC	CLOSEST	COCK-UPS	COLLOID	COMRADE
CIRCLET	CLATTER	CLOSETS	COCONUT	COLLUDE	CONAKRY
CIRCLIP	CLAUSAL	CLOSE-UP	COCOONS	COLOBUS	CONATUS
CIRCUIT	CLAUSES	CLOSING	COCOTTE	COLOGNE	CONCAVE
CIRQUES	CLAVATE	CLOSURE	COCOYAM	COLOMBO	CONCEAL
CIRRATE	CLAVIER	CLOTHED	CODDLED	COLONEL	CONCEDE
CIRSOID	CLAVIUS	CLOTHES	CODEINE	COLONIC	CONCEIT
CISSIES	CLAWING	CLOTTED	CODFISH	COLOSSI	CONCEPT
CISSOID	CLAYPAN	CLOTURE	CODGERS	COLOURS	CONCERN
CISTERN	CLEANED	CLOUDED	CODICES	COLTISH	CONCERT
CISTRON	CLEANER	CLOUTED	CODICIL	COLUMNS	CONCHAL
CITABLE	CLEANLY	CLOWNED	CODLING	COMBATS	CONCHES
CITADEL	CLEANSE	CLOYING	COELIAC	COMBERS	CONCISE
CITHARA	CLEANUP	CLUBBED	COEQUAL	COMBINE	CONCOCT
CITIZEN	CLEAN UP	CLUBMAN	COERCED	COMBING	CONCORD
CITRATE	CLEARED	CLUCKED	COETZEE	COMB-OUT	CONCUSS
CITRINE	CLEARER	CLUMPED	COEVALS	COMBUST	CONDEMN
CITRONS	CLEARLY	CLUNIAC	COEXIST	COMECON	CONDIGN
CIVILLY	CLEAR UP	CLUPEID	COFFERS	COMEDIC	CONDOLE
CIVVIES	CLEAVED	CLUSTER	COFFINS	COMFIER	CONDOMS
CLACKED	CLEAVER	CLUTTER	COGENCY	COMFITS	CONDONE
CLADODE	CLEMENT	CLYPEAL	COGGING	COMFORT	CONDORS
CLAIMED	CLERICS	CLYPEUS	COGNACS	COMFREY	CONDUCE
CLAIMER	CLERKED	COACHED	COGNATE	COMICAL	CONDUCT
CLAMANT	CLICHED	COACHES	COGNIZE	COMINGS	CONDUIT
CLAMBER	CLICHES	COAL GAS	COHABIT	COMMAND	CONDYLE
CLAMMED	CLICKED	COALING	COHERED	COMMEND	CONFECT
CLAMOUR	CLICKER	COAL TAR	COHORTS	COMMENT	CONFESS
CLAMPED	CLIENTS	COAMING	COILING	COMMODE	CONFIDE
CLAMPER	CLIMATE	COARSEN	COIMBRA	COMMONS	CONFINE
CLANGED	CLIMBED	COARSER	COINAGE	COMMUNE	CONFIRM
CLANGER	CLIMBER	COASTAL	COINERS	COMMUTE	CONFORM
CLANGOR	CLINGER	COASTED	COINING	COMOROS	CONFUSE
CLANKED	CLINICS	COASTER	COLBERT	COMPACT	CONFUTE
CLAPPED	CLINKED	COATING	COLDEST	COMPANY	CONGEAL

CONGEST	COOLIES	CORONER	COUNTED	CRABBED	CRESSET
CONGIUS	COOLING	CORONET	COUNTER	CRACKED	CRESTED
CONICAL	COOLISH	CORPORA	COUNTRY	CRACKER	CRETINS
CONIFER	COONT.IE	CORPSES	COUPLED	CRACKLE	CREVICE
CONIINE	COOPERS	CORRADE	COUPLER	CRACK UP	CREW CUT
CONJOIN	CO-OPTED	CORRALS	COUPLES	CRACKUP	CREWING
CONJURE	COPAIBA	CORRECT	COUPLET	CRADLED	CRIBBED
CONKERS	COPEPOD	CORREZE	COUPONS	CRADLES	CRICKED
CONKING	COPIERS	CORRIDA	COURAGE	CRAFTED	CRICKET
CONNATE	COPILOT	CORRODE	COURIER	CRAIOVA	CRICOID
CONNECT	COPINGS	CORRUPT	COURSED	CRAMMED	CRIMEAN
CONNERY	COPIOUS	CORSAGE	COURSER	CRAMMER	CRIMPED
CONNING	COP-OUTS	CORSAIR	COURSES	CRAMPED	CRIMPER
CONNIVE	COPPERS	CORSETS	COURTED	CRAMPON	CRIMPLE
CONNOTE	COPPERY	CORSICA	COURTLY	CRANIAL	CRIMSON
CONQUER	COPPICE	CORTEGE	COUSINS	CRANING	CRINGED
CONSENT	COPPING	CORTONA	COUTURE	CRANIUM	CRINGLE
CONSIGN	COPULAR	CORVINE	COUVADE	CRANKED	CRINITE
CONSIST	COPYCAT	COSENZA	COVERED	CRANK UP	CRINKLE
CONSOLE	COPYING	COSHING	COVERER	CRAPPED	CRINKLY
CONSOLS	COPYIST	COSIEST	COVERTS	CRAPPIE	CRINOID
CONSORT	COQUINA	COSINES	COVER-UP	CRASHED	CRIOLLO
CONSULS	COQUITO	COSMINE	COVETED	CRASHES	CRIPPLE
CONSULT	CORACLE	COSMOID	COVETER	CRASSLY	CRISPED
CONSUME	CORBEIL	COSTARD	COWARDS	CRATERS	CRISPLY
CONTACT	CORBELS	CO-STARS	COWARDY	CRATING	CRISSAL
CONTAIN	CORDAGE	COSTATE	COWBANE	CRAVATS	CRISSUM
CONTEMN	CORDATE	COSTING	COWBELL	CRAVING	CRITICS
CONTEND	CORDIAL	COSTIVE	COWBIND	CRAWLED	CRITTER
CONTENT	CORDING	COSTNER	COWBIRD	CRAWLER	CROAKED
CONTEST	CORDITE	COSTUME	COWBOYS	CRAWLEY	CROAKER
CONTEXT	CORDOBA	COTE-	COWDREY	CRAYONS	CROATIA
CONTORT	CORDONS	D'OR	COWERED	CRAZIER	CROCEIN
CONTOUR	CORINTH	COTERIE	COWFISH	CRAZILY	CROCHET
CONTROL	CORKAGE	COTIDAL	COWGIRL	CREAKED	CROCKET
CONTUSE	CORKERS	COTINGA	COWHAND	CREAMED	CROFTER
CONVENE	CORKING	COTONOU	COWHERB	CREAMER	CRONIES
CONVENT	CORMOUS	COTTAGE	COWHERD	CREASED	CROOKED
CONVERT	CORNCOB	COTTONY	COWHIDE	CREASES	CROONED
CONVICT	CORNEAL	COUCHED	COWLICK	CREATED	CROONER
CONVOKE	CORNERS	COUCHER	COWLING	CREATOR	CROPPED
CONVOYS	CORNETS	COUCHES	COWPATS	CRECHES	CROPPER
COOKERS	CORNICE	COUGARS	COWRIES	CREDENT	CROQUET
COOKERY	CORNIER	COUGHED	COWSHED	CREDITS	CROSIER
COOKIES	CORNISH	COULDN'T	COWSLIP	CREEDAL	CROSSED
COOKING	CORNUAL	COULDST	COXCOMB	CREEPER	CROSSER
COOKOUT	CORNUTE	COULOIR	COY·NESS	CREMATE	CROSSES
COOKSON	COROLLA	COULOMB	COYOTES	CREMONA	CROSSLY
COOLANT	CORONAE	COULTER	COZENED	CRENATE	CROUTON
COOLERS	CORONAL	COUNCIL	COZENER	CREOLES	CROWBAR
COOLEST	CORONAS	COUNSEL	COZIEST	CREOSOL	CROWDED

CROWING	CULPRIT	CUSPATE	DADAIST	DASHEEN	DECADAL
CROWNED	CULTISH	CUSSING	DADDIES	DASHIKI	DECADES
CROYDON	CULTISM	CUSTARD	DADROCK	DASHING	DECAGON
CROZIER	CULTIST	CUSTODY	DAEMONS	DASYURE	DECANAL
CRUCIAL	CULTURE	CUSTOMS	DAFTEST	DATABLE	DECAPOD
CRUCIFY	CULVERT	CUTAWAY	DAGGERS	DATA BUS	DECAYED
CRUDELY	CUMBRIA	CUTBACK	DAGLOCK	DATIVAL	DECEASE
CRUDEST	CUMQUAT	CUT DOWN	DAHLIAS	DATIVES	DECEIVE
CRUDITY	CUMULET	CUTICLE	DAHOMAN	DAUBERY	DECENCY
CRUELLY	CUMULUS	CUTLASS	DAHOMEY	DAUBING	DECIARE
CRUELTY	CUNEATE	CUTLERS	DAILIES	DAUNTED	DECIBEL
CRUISED	CUNNING	CUTLERY	DAIRIES	DAUNTER	DECIDED
CRUISER	CUP CAKE	CUTLETS	DAISIES	DAUPHIN	DECIDER
CRUISES	CUPOLAS	CUTOFFS	DAKOTAN	DAWDLED	DECIDUA
CRUMBLE	CUPPING	CUTOUTS	DALLIED	DAWDLER	DECIMAL
CRUMBLY	CUPRITE	CUTTACK	DAMAGED	DAWKINS	DECKING
CRUMPET	CUPROUS	CUTTERS	DAMAGER	DAWNING	DECLAIM
CRUMPLE	CUP TIES	CUTTING	DAMAGES	DAYBOOK	DECLARE
CRUMPLY	CURABLE	CUTWORK	DAMMING	DAYBOYS	DECLASS
CRUNCHY	CURABLY	CUTWORM	DAMNIFY	DAY CARE	DECLINE
CRUNODE	CURACAO	CWMBRAN	DAMNING	DAY-CARE	DECODED
CRUPPER	CURATES	CYANATE	DAMPERS	DAYLONG	DECORUM
CRUSADE	CURATOR	CYANIDE	DAMPEST	DAYROOM	DECOYED
CRUSHED	CURBING	CYANINE	DAMPING	DAYTIME	DECOYER
CRUSHES	CURCUMA	CYANITE	DAMPISH	DAZEDLY	DECREED
CRUSTAL	CURDLED	CYBALER	DAMSELS	DAZZLED	DECREER
CRUZADO	CURE-ALL	CYCLING	DAMSONS	DEACONS	DECREES
CRYBABY	CURETTE	CYCLIST	DANCERS	DEAD END	DECRIAL
CRYOGEN	CURFEWS	CYCLOID	DANCING	DEADEYE	DECRIED
CRYPTAL	CURIOSA	CYCLONE	DANDERS	DEADPAN	DECRIER
CRYPTIC	CURIOUS	CYCLOPS	DANDIER	DEAD SET	DECUPLE
CRYSTAL	CURLERS	CYGNETS	DANDIES	DEAF-AID	DEDUCED
CTENOID	CURLEWS	CYMBALS	DANDIFY	DEALATE	DEEMING
CUBBING	CURLIER	CYNICAL	DANDLED	DEALERS	DEEPEST
CUBICAL	CURLING	CYPHERS	DANDLER	DEALING	DEEP FRY
CUBICLE	CURRANT	CYPRESS	DANGERS	DEANERY	DEFACED
CUBITAL	CURRENT	CYPRIOT	DANGLED	DEAREST	DEFACER
CUCKOLD	CURRIED	CYPSELA	DANGLER	DEARIES	DE FACTO
CUCKOOS	CURRIER	CYSTINE	DANKEST	DEATHLY	DEFAMED
CUDBEAR	CURRIES	CYSTOID	DANSEUR	DEBACLE	DEFAMER
CUDDLED	CURRISH	CYTHERA	DAPHNIA	DEBASED	DEFAULT
CUDGELS	CURSING	CZARDAS	DAPPING	DEBASER	DEFEATS
CUDLIPP	CURSIVE	CZARINA	DAPPLED	DEBATED	DEFECTS
CUDWEED	CURSORS		DAPSONE	DEBATER	DEFENCE
CUE BALL	CURSORY	**D**	DARESAY	DEBATES	DEFIANT
CUFFING	CURTAIL	DABBING	DARIOLE	DEBAUCH	DEFICIT
CUIRASS	CURTAIN	DABBLED	DARKEST	DEBITED	DEFILED
CUISINE	CURTESY	DABBLER	DARKIES	DEBORAH	DEFILER
CULCHIE	CURVING	DAB HAND	DARLING	DEBOUCH	DEFILES
CULICID	CUSHIER	DACTYLS	DARNING	DEBRIEF	DEFINED
CULLING	CUSHION	DADAISM	DARTING	DEBTORS	DEFINER

DEFLATE	DENEUVE	DESIRES	DHAHRAN	DILATED	DISCORD
DEFLECT	DENIALS	DESKTOP	DIABASE	DILATOR	DISCUSS
DEFORCE	DENIERS	DESMOID	DIABOLO	DILDOES	DISDAIN
DEFRAUD	DENIZEN	DESPAIR	DIADEMS	DILEMMA	DISEASE
DEFROCK	DENMARK	DESPISE	DIAGRAM	DILUENT	DISEUSE
DEFROST	DENNING	DESPITE	DIALECT	DILUTED	DISGUST
DEFUNCT	DENOTED	DESPOIL	DIALING	DILUTEE	DISHFUL
DEFUSED	DENSELY	DESPOND	DIALLED	DILUTER	DISHIER
DEFYING	DENSEST	DESPOTS	DIALLER	DIMETER	DISHING
DEGAUSS	DENSITY	DESSERT	DIALYSE	DIMMERS	DISJECT
DEGRADE	DENTATE	DESTINE	DIAMINE	DIMMEST	DISJOIN
DEGREES	DENTINE	DESTINY	DIAMOND	DIMMING	DISLIKE
DEHISCE	DENTING	DESTOCK	DIANOIA	DIMNESS	DISMAST
DEICIDE	DENTIST	DESTROY	DIAPERS	DIMORPH	DISMISS
DE-ICING	DENTOID	DETAILS	DIARCHY	DIMPLES	DISOBEY
DEICTIC	DENTURE	DETENTE	DIARIES	DIMWITS	DISPLAY
DEIFIED	DENUDED	DETERGE	DIARIST	DINERIC	DISPORT
DEIFIER	DENUDER	DETINUE	DIASTER	DINETTE	DISPOSE
DEIFORM	DENYING	DETOURS	DIAZINE	DINGIER	DISPUTE
DEIGNED	DEONTIC	DETRACT	DIAZOLE	DINGILY	DISRATE
DEISTIC	DEPISER	DETRAIN	DIBASIC	DINGLES	DISROBE
DEITIES	DEPLETE	DETROIT	DIBBING	DINGOES	DISRUPT
DEJECTA	DEPLORE	DETRUDE	DIBBLED	DINKIER	DISSECT
DE KLERK	DEPLUME	DEUTZIA	DIBBLER	DINNERS	DISSENT
DELAINE	DEPOSAL	DEVALUE	DIBBLES	DINNING	DISTAFF
DELAYED	DEPOSED	DEVELOP	DICIEST	DIOCESE	DISTANT
DELAYER	DEPOSER	DEVIANT	DICKENS	DIOPTRE	DISTEND
DELETED	DEPOSIT	DEVIATE	DICKIER	DIORAMA	DISTICH
DELIGHT	DEPRAVE	DEVICES	DICKIES	DIORITE	DISTORT
DELIMIT	DEPRESS	DEVILED	DICLINY	DIOXIDE	DISTURB
DELIVER	DEPRIVE	DEVILRY	DICTATE	DIPHASE	DISUSED
DELOUSE	DEPSIDE	DEVIOUS	DICTION	DIPLOID	DITCHED
DELPHIC	DEPUTED	DEVISAL	DICTUMS	DIPLOMA	DITCHER
DELTAIC	DERANGE	DEVISED	DIDDLED	DIPLONT	DITCHES
DELTOID	DERBIES	DEVISEE	DIDICOY	DIPNOAN	DITTANY
DELUDED	DERIDED	DEVISER	DIEBACK	DIPOLAR	DITTIES
DELUDER	DERIDER	DEVISOR	DIE-CAST	DIPPERS	DIURNAL
DELUGED	DERIVED	DEVIZES	DIEHARD	DIPPING	DIVERGE
DELUGES	DERIVER	DEVOICE	DIESELS	DIPSHIT	DIVERSE
DELVING	DERMOID	DEVOIRS	DIETARY	DIPTYCH	DIVIDED
DEMANDS	DERRICK	DEVOLVE	DIETING	DIREFUL	DIVIDER
DEMERGE	DERVISH	DEVOTED	DIFFUSE	DIRNDLS	DIVIDES
DEMERIT	DESCALE	DEVOTEE	DIGAMMA	DIRTIED	DIVINED
DEMESNE	DESCANT	DEWATER	DIGESTS	DIRTIER	DIVINER
DEMIGOD	DESCEND	DEWCLAW	DIGGERS	DIRTILY	DIVISOR
DEMIVEG	DESCENT	DEWDROP	DIGGING	DISABLE	DIVORCE
DEMONIC	DESERTS	DEWIEST	DIGITAL	DISAVOW	DIVULGE
DEMOTED	DESERVE	DEWLAPS	DIGNIFY	DISBAND	DIZZIER
DEMOTIC	DESIGNS	DEXTRAL	DIGNITY	DISCARD	DIZZILY
DEMOUNT	DESIRED	DEXTRAN	DIGRAPH	DISCERN	DNIEPER
DEMURER	DESIRER	DEXTRIN	DIGRESS	DISCOID	D-NOTICE

DOBRUJA	DOODLED	DRAFTED	DRONING	DUELLED	DYNAMIC
DOCKAGE	DOODLER	DRAFTEE	DRONISH	DUELLER	DYNAMOS
DOCKERS	DOODLES	DRAFTER	DROOLED	DUENNAS	DYNASTY
DOCKETS	DOOMING	DRAGGED	DROOPED	DUFFERS	DYSURIA
DOCKING	DO-OR-	DRAGGLE	DROPLET	DUGOUTS	DYSURIC
DOCTORS	DIE	DRAGNET	DROP OFF	DUKEDOM	DZONGKA
DODDERY	DOORMAN	DRAGONS	DROPOUT	DULLARD	
DODDLES	DOORMAT	DRAGOON	DROPPED	DULLEST	E
DODGEMS	DOORMEN	DRAINED	DROPPER	DULLING	EACH WAY
DODGERS	DOORWAY	DRAINER	DROSHKY	DULOSIS	EAGERLY
DODGIER	DOPIEST	DRAPERS	DROUGHT	DUMBEST	EAGLETS
DODGING	DORMANT	DRAPERY	DROVERS	DUMMIES	EARACHE
DODOISM	DORMERS	DRAPING	DROWNED	DUMPERS	EARDRUM
DOESKIN	DORMICE	DRASTIC	DROWNER	DUMPIER	EARFLAP
DOFFING	DORNICK	DRATTED	DROWSED	DUMPING	EARHOLE
DOGBANE	DOSAGES	DRAUGHT	DRUBBER	DUNDALK	EARLDOM
DOGCART	DOSSERS	DRAWBAR	DRUDGED	DUNEDIN	EARLIER
DOG DAYS	DOSSIER	DRAWERS	DRUDGER	DUNGEON	EARLOBE
DOGFISH	DOSSING	DRAWING	DRUDGES	DUNKING	EARMARK
DOGGERY	DOTAGES	DRAWLED	DRUGGED	DUNKIRK	EARMUFF
DOGGIES	DOTTIER	DRAWLER	DRUGGET	DUNNAGE	EARNERS
DOGGING	DOTTING	DRAWS IN	DRUIDIC	DUNNEST	EARNEST
DOGGONE	DOUBLED	DRAWS UP	DRUMLIN	DUNNING	EARNING
DOGLEGS	DOUBLER	DREADED	DRUMMED	DUNNITE	EARPLUG
DOG ROSE	DOUBLES	DREAMED	DRUMMER	DUODENA	EARRING
DOG TAGS	DOUBLET	DREAMER	DRUNKEN	DUOTONE	EARSHOT
DOGTROT	DOUBTED	DREDGED	DRUNKER	DUPABLE	EARTHED
DOGVANE	DOUBTER	DREDGER	DRUTHER	DURABLE	EARTHEN
DOGWOOD	DOUCHES	DRENTHE	DRYABLE	DURABLY	EARTHLY
DOILIES	DOUGHTY	DRESDEN	DRYADIC	DURANGO	EARWIGS
DOLEFUL	DOUGLAS	DRESSED	DRY DOCK	DURMAST	EASEFUL
DOLLARS	DOURINE	DRESSER	DRY-EYED	DUSKIER	EASIEST
DOLLIES	DOUSING	DRESSES	DRY LAND	DUSTBIN	EAST END
DOLLING	DOWABLE	DRESS UP	DRYNESS	DUSTERS	EASTERN
DOLLISH	DOWAGER	DRIBBLE	DRY-SALT	DUSTIER	EASTERS
DOLLOPS	DOWDIER	DRIBLET	DRY-SHOD	DUSTING	EASTING
DOLMENS	DOWDILY	DRIED UP	DRYWALL	DUSTMAN	EATABLE
DOLPHIN	DOWN-BOW	DRIFTED	DUALISM	DUSTMEN	EBB TIDE
DOLTISH	DOWNERS	DRIFTER	DUALIST	DUSTPAN	EBONITE
DOMAINS	DOWNIER	DRILLED	DUALITY	DUSTUPS	EBONIZE
DOMICAL	DOWNING	DRILLER	DUBBING	DUTIFUL	ECBOLIC
DOMINEE	DOWRIES	DRINKER	DUBIETY	DUVETYN	ECCRINE
DONATED	DOWSERS	DRIP-DRY	DUBIOUS	DVANDVA	ECDYSIS
DONATOR	DOWSING	DRIPPED	DUBNIUM	DWARFED	ECHELON
DONBASS	DOYLEYS	DRIVE IN	DUCHESS	DWARVES	ECHIDNA
DONEGAL	DOZENTH	DRIVE-IN	DUCHIES	DWELLED	ECHINUS
DONETSK	DOZIEST	DRIVERS	DUCKIES	DWELLER	ECHOING
DON JUAN	DRABBER	DRIVING	DUCKING	DWINDLE	ECHOISM
DONKEYS	DRABBLE	DRIZZLE	DUCTILE	DYARCHY	ECLAIRS
DONNING	DRACHMA	DRIZZLY	DUDGEON	DYELINE	ECLIPSE
DONNISH	DRACHMS	DROLLER	DUELING	DYEWOOD	ECLOGUE

ECOCIDE	ELATIVE	EMITTER	ENERGID	ENTRAIN	EQUATOR
ECOLOGY	ELBOWED	EMOTION	ENFEOFF	ENTRANT	EQUERRY
ECONOMY	ELDERLY	EMOTIVE	ENFIELD	ENTREAT	EQUINOX
ECORCHE	ELEATIC	EMPALER	ENFORCE	ENTREES	ERASERS
ECOTONE	ELECTED	EMPANEL	ENGAGED	ENTRIES	ERASING
ECOTYPE	ELECTOR	EMPATHY	ENGAGER	ENTROPY	ERASION
ECSTASY	ELEGANT	EMPEROR	EN GARDE	ENTRUST	ERASURE
ECTHYMA	ELEGIAC	EMPIRES	ENGINES	ENTWINE	ERECTED
ECTOPIA	ELEGIES	EMPIRIC	ENGLAND	E NUMBER	ERECTER
ECTOPIC	ELEGIST	EMPLACE	ENGLISH	ENVELOP	ERECTLY
ECTYPAL	ELEGIZE	EMPORIA	ENGORGE	ENVENOM	ERECTOR
ECUADOR	ELEMENT	EMPOWER	ENGRAFT	ENVIOUS	EREMITE
EDACITY	ELEUSIS	EMPRESS	ENGRAIL	ENVIRON	EREPSIN
EDAPHIC	ELEVATE	EMPTIED	ENGRAIN	ENVYING	ERISTIC
EDDYING	ELEVENS	EMPTIER	ENGRAVE	ENZYMES	ERITREA
EDGIEST	ELIDING	EMPTIES	ENGROSS	EOBIONT	ERMINES
EDGINGS	ELISION	EMPTILY	ENHANCE	EOSINIC	ERODENT
EDICTAL	ELITISM	EMPYEMA	ENIGMAS	EPARCHY	ERODING
EDIFICE	ELITIST	EMULATE	ENJOYED	EPAULET	EROSION
EDIFIED	ELIXIRS	EMULOUS	ENJOYER	EPEEIST	EROSIVE
EDIFIER	ELLIPSE	ENABLED	ENLARGE	EPEIRIC	EROTEMA
EDITING	EL MINYA	ENABLER	ENLIVEN	EPERGNE	EROTICA
EDITION	EL OBEID	ENACTED	EN MASSE	EPIBOLY	ERRANCY
EDITORS	ELOPING	ENACTOR	ENNOBLE	EPICARP	ERRANDS
EDUCATE	ELUDING	ENAMOUR	ENOUNCE	EPICENE	ERRATIC
EEL-LIKE	ELUSION	ENCASED	ENPLANE	EPICURE	ERRATUM
EELPOUT	ELUSIVE	ENCHAIN	ENQUIRE	EPIDOTE	ERRHINE
EELWORM	ELUVIAL	ENCHANT	ENQUIRY	EPIGEAL	ERUDITE
EFFACED	ELUVIUM	EN CLAIR	ENRAGED	EPIGENE	ERUPTED
EFFACER	ELYSIAN	ENCLAVE	ENROBER	EPIGONE	ERZURUM
EFFECTS	ELYSIUM	ENCLOSE	EN ROUTE	EPIGRAM	ESBJERG
EFFORTS	ELYTRON	ENCODED	ENSIGNS	EPIGYNY	ESCAPED
EGGCUPS	EMANATE	ENCODER	ENSLAVE	EPIMERE	ESCAPEE
EGGHEAD	EMBARGO	ENCOMIA	ENSNARE	EPISODE	ESCAPER
EGG ROLL	EMBASSY	ENCORES	ENSUING	EPISOME	ESCAPES
EGOISTS	EMBLEMS	ENCRUST	ENSURED	EPISTLE	ESCOLAR
EGOTISM	EMBOLIC	ENDARCH	ENSURER	EPITAPH	ESCORTS
EGOTIST	EMBOLUS	ENDEMIC	ENTASIA	EPITAXY	ESERINE
EGO TRIP	EMBRACE	END GAME	ENTASIS	EPITHET	ESKIMOS
EIDETIC	EMBROIL	ENDINGS	ENTEBBE	EPITOME	ESPARTO
EIDOLON	EMBRYOS	ENDIVES	ENTENTE	EPIZOIC	ESPOUSE
EIGHTHS	EMENDED	ENDLESS	ENTERED	EPIZOON	ESPYING
EIGHTVO	EMERALD	ENDMOST	ENTERER	EPOCHAL	ESQUIRE
EINKORN	EMERGED	ENDORSE	ENTERIC	EPOCHES	ESSAYED
EJECTED	EMERSED	ENDOWED	ENTERON	EPONYMY	ESSENCE
EJECTOR	EMETICS	ENDOWER	ENTHRAL	EPSILON	ESSONNE
ELAMITE	EMETINE	ENDUING	ENTHUSE	EQUABLE	ESTATES
ELAPSED	EMIGRES	ENDURED	ENTICED	EQUABLY	ESTHETE
ELASTIC	EMINENT	END USER	ENTICER	EQUALED	ESTONIA
ELASTIN	EMIRATE	ENDWAYS	ENTITLE	EQUALLY	ESTORIL
ELATION	EMITTED	ENEMIES	ENTOPIC	EQUATED	ESTREAT

ESTUARY	EXACTOR	EXPOSAL	FADEOUT	FARADAY	FEASTED
ETAGERE	EXALTED	EXPOSED	FAEROES	FARADIC	FEASTER
ETAMINE	EXALTER	EXPOSER	FAG ENDS	FARAWAY	FEATHER
ETCHERS	EXAMINE	EXPOSES	FAGGING	FARCEUR	FEATURE
ETCHING	EXAMPLE	EXPOUND	FAGGOTS	FAR EAST	FEBRILE
ETERNAL	EXARATE	EXPRESS	FAIENCE	FAR-GONE	FEDERAL
ETESIAN	EXCERPT	EXPUNGE	FAILING	FARMERS	FEDORAS
ETHANOL	EXCIMER	EXSCIND	FAILURE	FARMING	FEEBLER
ETHERIC	EXCISED	EXTENTS	FAINTED	FARNESS	FEEDBAG
ETHICAL	EXCITED	EXTINCT	FAINTER	FARRAGO	FEEDERS
ETHMOID	EXCITER	EXTRACT	FAINTLY	FARRIER	FEEDING
ETHYLIC	EXCITON	EXTREME	FAIREST	FARTHER	FEEDLOT
ETRURIA	EXCITOR	EXTRUDE	FAIRIES	FARTING	FEELERS
EUBOEAN	EXCLAIM	EXUDING	FAIRING	FARTLEK	FEELING
EUCAINE	EXCLAVE	EXULTED	FAIRISH	FASCIAL	FEIGNED
EUGENIC	EXCLUDE	EXURBIA	FAIR SEX	FASCIAS	FEIGNER
EUGENOL	EXCRETA	EXUVIAE	FAIRWAY	FASCINE	FEINTED
EUGLENA	EXCRETE	EXUVIAL	FAJITAS	FASCISM	FELAFEL
EUNUCHS	EXCUSAL	EX-WORKS	FALAFEL	FASCIST	FELINES
EUPHONY	EXCUSED	EYEBALL	FALANGE	FASHION	FELLERS
EUPHROE	EXCUSES	EYEBATH	FALASHA	FASTEST	FELLING
EUPLOID	EXECUTE	EYEBOLT	FALBALA	FASTING	FELLOWS
EUPNOEA	EXEGETE	EYEBROW	FALCATE	FATALLY	FELONRY
EURASIA	EXERGUE	EYELASH	FALCONS	FATBACK	FELSITE
EURATOM	EXERTED	EYELESS	FALKIRK	FAT CATS	FELSPAR
EURIPUS	EXHALED	EYELETS	FALLACY	FATEFUL	FELTING
EUSTASY	EXHAUST	EYELIDS	FALL GUY	FATHEAD	FELUCCA
EVACUEE	EXHIBIT	EYESHOT	FALLING	FATHERS	FELWORT
EVADING	EXHUMED	EYESORE	FALLOUT	FATHOMS	FEMALES
EVANGEL	EXHUMER	EYESPOT	FALSELY	FATIGUE	FEMORAL
EVASION	EXIGENT	EYEWASH	FALSEST	FATLING	FENCERS
EVASIVE	EXILING		FALSIES	FATNESS	FENCING
EVENING	EXISTED	**F**	FALSIFY	FATSHAN	FENDERS
EVEREST	EXITING	FABIANS	FALSITY	FATTEST	FENDING
EVERTOR	EXMOUTH	FABRICS	FALSTER	FATTIER	FENLAND
EVERTOR	EXMOUTH	FABRICS	FALSTER	FATTIER	FENLAND
EVESHAM	EXODERM	FACADES	FAMILLE	FATTIES	FERGANA
EVICTED	EXOGAMY	FACEBAR	FAMINES	FATTILY	FERMATA
EVICTED	EXOTICA	FACE-OFF	FANATIC	FATTISH	FERMENT
EVICTOR	EXPANSE	FACIALS	FAN BELT	FATTISM	FERMION
EVIDENT	EX PARTE	FACINGS	FANCIED	FATUITY	FERMIUM
EVILEST	EXPENSE	FACTFUL	FANCIER	FATUOUS	FERNERY
EVIL EYE	EXPERTS	FACTION	FANCIES	FAUCETS	FERRARA
EVILLER	EXPIATE	FACTORS	FANCILY	FAULTED	FERRATE
EVINCED	EXPIRED	FACTORY	FAN CLUB	FAUVISM	FERRETS
EVOKING	EXPIRER	FACTUAL	FANFARE	FAUVIST	FERRETY
EVOLUTE	EXPLAIN	FACULAR	FANNIES	FAUX PAS	FERRIED
EVOLVED	EXPLANT	FACULTY	FANNING	FAVOURS	FERRIES
EVOLVER	EXPLODE	FADABLE	FANTAIL	FAVRILE	FERRITE
EWE-NECK	EXPLOIT	FADDISH	FANTAST	FAWNING	FERROUS
EXACTED	EXPLORE	FADDISM	FANTASY	FEARFUL	FERRULE
EXACTLY	EXPORTS	FADDIST	FANZINE	FEARING	FERTILE

FERVENT	FILBERT	FISH-EYE	FLAWING	FLOUNCE	FOGYISH
FERVOUR	FILCHED	FISHGIG	FLAYING	FLOURED	FOIBLES
FESTIVE	FILCHER	FISHIER	FLEABAG	FLOUTED	FOILING
FESTOON	FILETED	FISHING	FLEAPIT	FLOUTER	FOISTED
FETCHED	FILIATE	FISHNET	FLECKED	FLOWAGE	FOLACIN
FETCHER	FILIBEG	FISSILE	FLEECED	FLOWERS	FOLDERS
FETLOCK	FILINGS	FISSION	FLEECES	FLOWERY	FOLDING
FETTERS	FILLETS	FISSURE	FLEEING	FLOWING	FOLDOUT
FETUSES	FILLIES	FISTULA	FLEETER	FLUENCY	FOLIAGE
FEUDING	FILLING	FITMENT	FLEMING	FLUFFED	FOLIATE
FEVERED	FILL-INS	FITNESS	FLEMISH	FLUIDAL	FOLIOSE
FEWNESS	FILLIPS	FITTERS	FLENSER	FLUIDIC	FOLKISH
FEYNESS	FILMIER	FITTEST	FLESHED	FLUMMOX	FOLLIES
FIANCES	FILMILY	FITTING	FLESHER	FLUNKED	FONDANT
FIASCOS	FILMING	FIXABLE	FLESHES	FLUNKEY	FONDEST
FIBBERS	FILMSET	FIXATED	FLESHLY	FLUORIC	FONDLED
FIBBING	FILTERS	FIXEDLY	FLEURON	FLUSHED	FONDLER
FIBROID	FIMBRIA	FIXTURE	FLEXILE	FLUSHER	FONDUES
FIBROIN	FINABLE	FIZZIER	FLEXING	FLUSHES	FOOCHOW
FIBROMA	FINAGLE	FIZZING	FLEXION	FLUSTER	FOODIES
FIBROUS	FINALES	FLACCID	FLEXURE	FLUTING	FOOLERY
FIBULAE	FINALLY	FLAG DAY	FLICKED	FLUTIST	FOOLING
FIBULAR	FINANCE	FLAGGED	FLICKER	FLUTTER	FOOLISH
FIBULAS	FINBACK	FLAGGER	FLIGHTS	FLUVIAL	FOOTAGE
FICTILE	FINCHES	FLAGMAN	FLIGHTY	FLUXION	FOOTBOY
FICTION	FINDING	FLAGONS	FLINGER	FLYABLE	FOOTING
FIDDLED	FINE ART	FLAILED	FLIPPED	FLYAWAY	FOOTMAN
FIDDLER	FINE-CUT	FLAKIER	FLIPPER	FLYBACK	FOOTMEN
FIDDLES	FINESSE	FLAKING	FLIRTED	FLYBLOW	FOOTPAD
FIDEISM	FINFOOT	FLAMING	FLIRTER	FLYBOAT	FOOTSIE
FIDEIST	FINGERS	FLANEUR	FLITTED	FLYBOOK	FOOT-TON
FIDGETS	FINICKY	FLANGER	FLITTER	FLY-FISH	FOOTWAY
FIDGETY	FININGS	FLANGES	FLIVVER	FLY HALF	FOOZLER
FIELDED	FINLAND	FLANKED	FLOATED	FLYLEAF	FOPPERY
FIELDER	FINNING	FLANKER	FLOATEL	FLYOVER	FOPPISH
FIERCER	FINNISH	FLANNEL	FLOATER	FLYPAST	FORAGED
FIERIER	FIREARM	FLAPPED	FLOCCUS	FLYTRAP	FORAGER
FIESOLE	FIREBOX	FLAPPER	FLOCKED	FOALING	FORAGES
FIESTAS	FIREBUG	FLARE-UP	FLOGGED	FOAMIER	FORAMEN
FIFTEEN	FIREDOG	FLARING	FLOGGER	FOAMING	FORAYED
FIFTIES	FIREFLY	FLASHED	FLOODED	FOBBING	FORAYER
FIGHTER	FIREMAN	FLASHER	FLOODER	FO'C'SLE	FORBADE
FIG LEAF	FIREMEN	FLASHES	FLOORED	S	FORBEAR
FIGMENT	FIREPAN	FLASKET	FLOPPED	FOCUSED	FORBORE
FIG TREE	FIRMEST	FLAT-BED	FLORIDA	FOCUSER	FORCEPS
FIGURAL	FIRMING	FLATLET	FLORINS	FOCUSES	FORCING
FIGURED	FIRSTLY	FLATTEN	FLORIST	FOGGIER	FORDING
FIGURER	FIRTREE	FLATTER	FLORUIT	FOGGILY	FOREARM
FIGURES	FISCALS	FLAUNCH	FLOSSED	FOGGING	FOREGUT
FIGWORT	FISCHER	FLAVONE	FLOTAGE	FOGHORN	FOREIGN
FILARIA	FISHERY	FLAVOUR	FLOTSAM	FOG LAMP	FORELEG

FOREMAN	FOXHOLE	FRIEDAN	FUKUOKA	FUTTOCK	GAMBLER
FOREMEN	FOXHUNT	FRIENDS	FULCRUM	FUTURES	GAMBOGE
FOREPAW	FOXIEST	FRIEZES	FULGENT	FUZZIER	GAMBOLS
FORERUN	FOXLIKE	FRIGATE	FULLEST	FUZZILY	GAMBREL
FORESAW	FOXTAIL	FRIGHTS	FULMARS	FUZZING	GAMELAN
FORESEE	FOXTROT	FRILLED	FULNESS	FYZABAD	GAMETAL
FORESTS	FRACTAL	FRINGED	FULSOME		GAMIEST
FORETOP	FRACTUS	FRINGES	FULVOUS	**G**	GANDERS
FOREVER	FRAENUM	FRISBEE	FUMARIC	GABBING	GANDZHA
FORFEIT	FRAGILE	FRISEUR	FUMBLED	GABBLED	GANGERS
FORGAVE	FRAILER	FRISIAN	FUMBLER	GABBLER	GANGING
FORGERS	FRAILTY	FRISKED	FUMBLES	GABFEST	GANGTOK
FORGERY	FRAKTUR	FRISKER	FUNCHAL	GADDING	GANGWAY
FORGING	FRAME UP	FRISKET	FUNDING	GADGETS	GANNETS
FORGIVE	FRAME-UP	FRISSON	FUNERAL	GADGETY	GANTLET
FORGOER	FRAMING	FRITTER	FUNFAIR	GADROON	GAOLERS
FORGONE	FRANCIS	FRIZZED	FUNGOID	GADWALL	GAOLING
FORKFUL	FRANKED	FRIZZER	FUNGOUS	GAFFERS	GAPPING
FORKING	FRANKER	FRIZZLE	FUNICLE	GAGAUZI	GAP YEAR
FORLORN	FRANKLY	FROEBEL	FUNKIER	GAGGING	GARAGED
FORMANT	FRANTIC	FROG-BIT	FUNKING	GAHNITE	GARAGES
FORMATE	FRAPPES	FROGMAN	FUNNELS	GAINERS	GARBAGE
FORMATS	FRAUGHT	FROGMEN	FUNNIER	GAINFUL	GARBING
FORMICA	FRAYING	FROLICS	FUNNILY	GAINING	GARBLED
FORMING	FRAZIER	FRONDED	FUN RUNS	GAINSAY	GARBLER
FORMOSA	FRAZZLE	FRONTAL	FUNSTER	GAITERS	GARCONS
FORMULA	FREAKED	FRONTED	FURBISH	GALATEA	GARDENS
FORSAKE	FRECKLE	FROSTED	FURCATE	GALEATE	GARFISH
FORSOOK	FREEBIE	FROTHED	FURCULA	GALENIC	GARGETY
FORSYTH	FREEDOM	FROWARD	FURIOSO	GALICIA	GARGLED
FORTIES	FREEING	FROWNED	FURIOUS	GALILEE	GARGLER
FORTIFY	FREEMAN	FROWNER	FURLING	GALIPOT	GARGLES
FORTUNE	FREEMEN	FROWSTY	FURLONG	GALLANT	GARLAND
FORWARD	FREESIA	FRUITED	FURNACE	GALLEON	GARMENT
FORWENT	FREEWAY	FRUITER	FURNESS	GALLERY	GARNETS
FOSSILS	FREEZER	FRUSTUM	FURNISH	GALLEYS	GARNISH
FOUETTE	FREIGHT	FUCHSIA	FURRIER	GALLFLY	GARONNE
FOULARD	FREMONT	FUCHSIN	FURRING	GALLING	GARPIKE
FOULEST	FRESCOS	FUCK ALL	FURROWS	GALLIUM	GARRETS
FOULING	FRESHEN	FUCKERS	FURROWY	GALLNUT	GARTERS
FOUL-UPS	FRESHER	FUCKING	FURTHER	GALLONS	GASBAGS
FOUNDED	FRESHET	FUCK-UPS	FURTIVE	GALLOON	GASCONY
FOUNDER	FRESHLY	FUDDLED	FUSCOUS	GALLOPS	GASEOUS
FOUNDRY	FRESNEL	FUDDLES	FUSIBLE	GALLOUS	GASHING
FOURIER	FRETFUL	FUDGING	FUSILLI	GALLOWS	GASKETS
FOURTHS	FRETSAW	FUEGIAN	FUSSIER	GALUMPH	GAS MAIN
FOUR-WAY	FRETTED	FUELING	FUSSILY	GAMBADO	GAS MASK
FOVEATE	FRIABLE	FUELLED	FUSSING	GAMBIAN	GASOHOL
FOVEOLA	FRIBBLE	FUELLER	FUSSPOT	GAMBIER	GASPING
FOWLING	FRIDAYS	FUENTES	FUSTIAN	GAMBITS	GAS PIPE
FOXFIRE	FRIDGES	FUGGIER	FUSTIER	GAMBLED	GASSIER

GASSING	GENTILE	GINSENG	GLOBOID	GODSEND	GRAINER
GASTRIC	GENUINE	GIN TRAP	GLOBOSE	GOGGLED	GRAMMAR
GASTRIN	GEODESY	GIPSIES	GLOBULE	GOGGLES	GRAMMES
GATEAUX	GEOLOGY	GIRAFFE	GLORIED	GOIANIA	GRAMPUS
GATE-LEG	GEORDIE	GIRASOL	GLORIES	GO-KARTS	GRANADA
GATEWAY	GEORGIA	GIRDERS	GLORIFY	GOLDEYE	GRANARY
GATHERS	GEORGIC	GIRDING	GLOSSAL	GOLFERS	GRANDAD
GAUCHOS	GERBILS	GIRDLED	GLOSSED	GOLFING	GRANDEE
GAUDERY	GERENUK	GIRDLER	GLOSSER	GOLIATH	GRANDER
GAUDIER	GERMANE	GIRDLES	GLOTTAL	GONADAL	GRANDLY
GAUDILY	GERMANS	GIRLISH	GLOTTIC	GONDOLA	GRANDMA
GAUGING	GERMANY	GIRONDE	GLOTTIS	GOODBYE	GRANDPA
GAUHATI	GERUNDS	GIRONNY	GLOWING	GOOD DAY	GRANGES
GAUTENG	GESTALT	GISARME	GLUCOSE	GOODIES	GRANITE
GAUZIER	GESTAPO	GITTERN	GLUE EAR	GOODISH	GRANOLA
GAVOTTE	GESTATE	GIVABLE	GLUEING	GOOFIER	GRANTED
GAWKERS	GESTURE	GIZZARD	GLUMMER	GOOFILY	GRANTEE
GAWKIER	GETABLE	GLACIAL	GLUTEAL	GOOFING	GRANTER
GAWKING	GETAWAY	GLACIER	GLUTEUS	GOOIEST	GRANTOR
GAWPING	GETTING	GLADDEN	GLUTTED	GOPHERS	GRANULE
GAYNESS	GEYSERS	GLADDER	GLUTTON	GORGING	GRAPHIC
GAZEBOS	GHASTLY	GLADDON	GLYCINE	GORGONS	GRAPNEL
GAZELLE	GHAZALI	GLAD EYE	GLYPHIC	GORIEST	GRAPPLE
GAZETTE	GHERKIN	GLAMOUR	GLYPTIC	GORILLA	GRASPED
GEARBOX	GHETTOS	GLANCED	GNARLED	GORIZIA	GRASPER
GEARING	GHILLIE	GLANCES	GNASHED	GOSHAWK	GRASSED
GECKOES	GHOSTED	GLARING	GNASHES	GOSLING	GRASSES
GEE-GEES	GHOSTLY	GLASGOW	GNATHIC	GO-SLOWS	GRASS UP
GEELONG	GIBBETS	GLASSED	GNAWING	GOSPELS	GRATERS
GEEZERS	GIBBING	GLASSES	GNOCCHI	GOSPLAN	GRATIFY
GEISHAS	GIBBONS	GLAZIER	GNOMISH	GOSPORT	GRATING
GELATIN	GIBBOUS	GLAZING	GNOSTIC	GOSSIPS	GRAUPEL
GELDING	GIBLETS	GLEAMED	GOADING	GOSSIPY	GRAVELY
GELLING	GIDDIER	GLEANED	GO-AHEAD	GOTLAND	GRAVEST
GEMMATE	GIDDILY	GLEANER	GOATEED	GOUACHE	GRAVITY
GEMMING	GIESSEN	GLEEFUL	GOATEES	GOUGING	GRAVLAX
GEMMULE	GIGGLED	GLENCOE	GOBBETS	GOULASH	GRAVURE
GEMSBOK	GIGGLER	GLENOID	GOBBLED	GOURAMI	GRAYEST
GENAPPE	GIGGLES	GLIADIN	GOBBLER	GOURMET	GRAYING
GENDERS	GIG LAMP	GLIBBER	GOBBLES	GRAB BAG	GRAZIER
GENERAL	GIGOLOS	GLIDERS	GOBELIN	GRABBED	GRAZING
GENERIC	GILBERT	GLIDING	GOBIOID	GRABBER	GREASED
GENESIS	GILDING	GLIMMER	GOBLETS	GRABBLE	GREASER
GENETIC	GILLIES	GLIMPSE	GOBLINS	GRACILE	GREATER
GENEVAN	GIMBALS	GLINTED	GODDAMN	GRACING	GREATLY
GENIPAP	GIMLETS	GLISTEN	GODDESS	GRACKLE	GREAVES
GENITAL	GIMMICK	GLITTER	GODHEAD	GRADATE	GRECIAN
GENITOR	GINGERY	GLIWICE	GODHOOD	GRADING	GREENED
GENOESE	GINGHAM	GLOATED	GODLESS	GRADUAL	GREENER
GENTEEL	GINGILI	GLOATER	GODLIER	GRAFTED	GREENIE
GENTIAN	GINGIVA	GLOBATE	GODLIKE	GRAFTER	GREETED

GREETER	GROSSES	GUISING	GYPSIES	HALIBUT	HANKIES
GREISEN	GROSSLY	GUITARS	GYRATED	HALIDOM	HANOVER
GREMIAL	GROTTOS	GUIYANG	GYRATOR	HALIFAX	HANSARD
GREMLIN	GROUCHY	GUIZHOU		HALLWAY	HANSOMS
GRENADA	GROUNDS	GUJARAT	**H**	HALOGEN	HANUMAN
GRENADE	GROUPED	GULCHES	HAARLEM	HALTERE	HANYANG
GREYEST	GROUPER	GULDENS	HABDABS	HALTERS	HA'PENNY
GREYHEN	GROUPIE	GULLETS	HABITAT	HALTING	HAPLESS
GREYING	GROUSED	GULLIES	HABITED	HALVING	HAPLITE
GREYISH	GROUSER	GULLING	HABITUE	HALYARD	HAPLOID
GREYLAG	GROUSES	GULPING	HABITUS	HAMADAN	HAP'ORTH
GRIBBLE	GROUTER	GUMBOIL	HACHURE	HAMBURG	HAPPIER
GRIDDLE	GROWERS	GUMBOOT	HACKBUT	HAMELIN	HAPPILY
GRIEVED	GROWING	GUMDROP	HACKERS	HAMHUNG	HAPTENE
GRIEVER	GROWLED	GUMMIER	HACKING	HAMITIC	HARAPPA
GRIFFIN	GROWLER	GUMMING	HACKLER	HAMLETS	HARBOUR
GRIFFON	GROWN-UP	GUMMITE	HACKLES	HAMMERS	HARDEST
GRILLED	GROWTHS	GUMSHOE	HACKNEY	HAMMING	HARDIER
GRILLER	GROYNES	GUM TREE	HACKSAW	HAMMOCK	HARDILY
GRILLES	GRUBBED	GUNBOAT	HADAWAY	HAMMOND	HARDING
GRIMACE	GRUBBER	GUNDOGS	HADDOCK	HAMPDEN	HARD NUT
GRIMIER	GRUDGED	GUNFIRE	HADRIAN	HAMPERS	HARD-ONS
GRIMMER	GRUDGER	GUNLOCK	HAEMOID	HAMPTON	HARD PAD
GRIMSBY	GRUDGES	GUNNELS	HAFNIUM	HAMSTER	HARDPAN
GRINDER	GRUFFER	GUNNERS	HAGFISH	HAMULAR	HARDTOP
GRINGOS	GRUFFLY	GUNNERY	HAGGARD	HAMULUS	HARELIP
GRINNED	GRUMBLE	GUNNING	HAGGISH	HANAPER	HARICOT
GRINNER	GRUMOUS	GUNSHOT	HAGGLED	HANCOCK	HARIJAN
GRIPERS	GRUNTED	GUNWALE	HAGGLER	HANDBAG	HARKING
GRIPING	GRUNTER	GURGLED	HAGLIKE	HANDFUL	HARLECH
GRIPPED	GRUYERE	GURNARD	HAHNIUM	HANDGUN	HARLOTS
GRIPPER	GRYPHON	GUSHERS	HAILING	HANDIER	HARMFUL
GRISTLE	G-STRING	GUSHING	HAINAUT	HANDILY	HARMING
GRISTLY	GUANACO	GUSSETS	HAIRCUT	HANDING	HARMONY
GRITTED	GUANASE	GUSTIER	HAIRDOS	HANDLED	HARNESS
GRIZZLE	GUANINE	GUSTILY	HAIRIER	HANDLER	HARPIES
GRIZZLY	GUARANI	GUSTING	HAIRNET	HANDLES	HARPING
GROANED	GUARDED	GUTLESS	HAIRPIN	HANDOUT	HARPINS
GROANER	GUARDER	GUTSIER	HAITIAN	HANDSAW	HARPIST
GROCERS	GUAYULE	GUTTATE	HAITINK	HANDSEL	HARPOON
GROCERY	GUDGEON	GUTTERS	HAKLUYT	HANDSET	HARRIED
GROGRAM	GUESSED	GUTTING	HALAKAH	HANDS-ON	HARRIER
GROLIER	GUESSER	GUVNORS	HALAKIC	HANDS UP	HARROWS
GROMMET	GUESSES	GUZZLED	HALAVAH	HANGARS	HARSHER
GROOMED	GUESTED	GUZZLER	HALBERD	HANGDOG	HARSHLY
GROOMER	GUFFAWS	GWALIOR	HALCYON	HANGERS	HARSLET
GROOVED	GUIDING	GWYNEDD	HALDANE	HANGING	HARTLEY
GROOVES	GUILDER	GWYNIAD	HALF-CUT	HANGMAN	HARVARD
GROPING	GUINEAN	GYMNAST	HALFWAY	HANGMEN	HARVEST
GROSSED	GUINEAS	GYMSLIP	HALF WIT	HANGOUT	HARWICH
GROSSER	GUIPURE	GYPPING	HALF-WIT	HANG-UPS	HARYANA

HAS BEEN	HAZIEST	HEINOUS	HERNIAS	HIPLIKE	HOGLIKE
HAS-BEEN	HAZLITT	HEIRDOM	HEROICS	HIPPEST	HOGNOSE
HASHING	HEADERS	HEIRESS	HEROINE	HIPPIES	HOGWASH
HASHISH	HEADIER	HEISTER	HEROISM	HIPSTER	HOGWEED
HASIDIC	HEADILY	HEITIKI	HERONRY	HIRABLE	HOISTED
HASIDIM	HEADING	HELICAL	HERRICK	HIRCINE	HOISTER
HASSELT	HEADMAN	HELICES	HERRING	HIRSUTE	HOKONUI
HASSIUM	HEADMEN	HELICON	HERSELF	HIRUDIN	HOKUSAI
HASSLED	HEADPIN	HELIPAD	HERTZOG	HIS NIBS	HOLDALL
HASSLES	HEADSET	HELLBOX	HESIONE	HISSING	HOLDERS
HASSOCK	HEADWAY	HELLCAT	HESSIAN	HISTOID	HOLDING
HASTATE	HEALERS	HELLENE	HESSITE	HISTONE	HOLD OUT
HASTIER	HEALING	HELLERY	HETAERA	HISTORY	HOLDUPS
HASTILY	HEALTHS	HELLION	HETAIRA	HITACHI	HOLIBUT
HATBAND	HEALTHY	HELLISH	HEXADIC	HITCHED	HOLIDAY
HATCHED	HEAPING	HELLUVA	HEXAGON	HITCHER	HOLIEST
HATCHEL	HEARING	HELMAND	HEXAPLA	HITCHES	HOLLAND
HATCHER	HEARKEN	HELMETS	HEXAPOD	HIT LIST	HOLLERS
HATCHES	HEARSAY	HELOISE	HEXOSAN	HITTING	HOLLOWS
HATCHET	HEARSES	HELOTRY	HEYDUCK	HITTITE	HOLMIUM
HATEFUL	HEARTEN	HELPFUL	HEYSHAM	HOARDED	HOLSTER
HATLESS	HEARTHS	HELPING	HEYWOOD	HOARDER	HOLY SEE
HATLIKE	HEATERS	HEMIOLA	HIALEAH	HOARIER	HOMBURG
HATPINS	HEATHEN	HEMIPOD	HIBACHI	HOARILY	HOMERIC
HATTERS	HEATHER	HEMLINE	HICCUPS	HOARSEN	HOME RUN
HAUBERK	HEATING	HEMLOCK	HICKORY	HOARSER	HOMIEST
HAUGHTY	HEAVENS	HEMMING	HIDABLE	HOATZIN	HOMINID
HAULAGE	HEAVIER	HENBANE	HIDALGO	HOAXERS	HOMOLOG
HAULIER	HEAVIES	HENCOOP	HIDEOUS	HOAXING	HOMONYM
HAULING	HEAVILY	HEN COOP	HIDINGS	HOBBEMA	HONESTY
HAUNTED	HEAVING	HENDRIX	HIELAND	HOBBIES	HONEYED
HAUNTER	HEBETIC	HENGELO	HIGHBOY	HOBBISM	HONIARA
HAURAKI	HEBRAIC	HENGIST	HIGHEST	HOBBIST	HONITON
HAUTBOY	HEBREWS	HENNERY	HIGH HAT	HOBBLED	HONKIES
HAUTEUR	HECKLED	HENPECK	HIGH TEA	HOBBLER	HONKING
HAVE-A-	HECKLER	HEPARIN	HIGHWAY	HOBLIKE	HONOURS
GO	HECTARE	HEPATIC	HIJACKS	HOBNAIL	HOODLUM
HAWKBIT	HEDGING	HEPBURN	HILBERT	HOBOISM	HOODOOS
HAWKERS	HEDONIC	HEPTANE	HILLARY	HOBOKEN	HOOGHLY
HAWKING	HEEDFUL	HEPTOSE	HILLERY	HOCKING	HOOKAHS
HAWKINS	HEEDING	HERALDS	HILLIER	HOCKNEY	HOOKERS
HAWKISH	HEELING	HERBAGE	HILLMAN	HODEIDA	HOOKIES
HAWORTH	HEELTAP	HERBALS	HILLOCK	HODGKIN	HOOKING
HAWSERS	HEERLEN	HERBERT	HIMSELF	HOEDOWN	HOOKUPS
HAYCOCK	HEFTIER	HERDING	HINDGUT	HOELIKE	HOORAYS
HAYFORK	HEFTILY	HEREDES	HINGING	HOFFMAN	HOOTERS
HAYRACK	HEGUMEN	HERETIC	HINTING	HOGARTH	HOOTING
HAYSEED	HEIFERS	HERISAU	HIONATE	HOGBACK	HOOVERS
HAYWARD	HEIFETZ	HERITOR	HIPBATH	HOGFISH	HOPEFUL
HAYWIRE	HEIGH-HO	HERMITS	HIPBONE	HOGGING	HOPHEAD
HAZARDS	HEIGHTS	HERNIAL	HIPLESS	HOGGISH	HOPKINS

HOPLITE	HOVERER	HURDLED	ICEBALL	IMPACTS	INCOMES
HOPPERS	HOWBEIT	HURDLER	ICEBERG	IMPALAS	INCROSS
HOPPING	HOWDAHS	HURDLES	ICE CAPS	IMPALED	INCUBUS
HOPPLER	HOWEVER	HURLING	ICE-COLD	IMPALER	INCURVE
HOPSACK	HOWLAND	HURRAYS	ICEFALL	IMPANEL	INDENTS
HORDEIN	HOWLERS	HURRIED	ICELAND	IMPASSE	IN DEPTH
HORDERN	HOWLING	HURTFUL	ICE PACK	IMPASTE	IN-DEPTH
HORIZON	HOYDENS	HURTING	ICE PICK	IMPASTO	INDEXED
HORMONE	HOYLAKE	HURTLED	ICE RINK	IMPEACH	INDEXER
HORNETS	HSIA-MEN	HUSBAND	ICHNITE	IMPEDED	INDEXES
HORNIER	HSINING	HUSHABY	ICICLED	IMPEDER	INDIANA
HORNILY	HSU-CHOU	HUSHING	ICICLES	IMPERIL	INDIANS
HORRIFY	HUAINAN	HUSKIER	ICINESS	IMPETUS	INDICAN
HORRORS	HUAI-NAN	HUSKIES	ICTERIC	IMPIETY	INDICIA
HORSENS	HUBBIES	HUSKILY	ICTERUS	IMPINGE	INDOORS
HORSIER	HUBCAPS	HUSSARS	ID CARDS	IMPIOUS	INDORSE
HORSILY	HUDDLED	HUSSEIN	IDEALLY	IMPLANT	INDOXYL
HOSANNA	HUDDLER	HUSSIES	IDEATUM	IMPLEAD	INDRAWN
HOSIERS	HUDDLES	HUSSISM	IDENTIC	IMPLIED	INDUCED
HOSIERY	HUFFIER	HUSSITE	IDIOTIC	IMPLODE	INDUCER
HOSPICE	HUFFILY	HUSTLED	IDOLIZE	IMPLORE	INDULGE
HOSTAGE	HUFFING	HUSTLER	IDYLLIC	IMPORTS	INEPTLY
HOSTELS	HUFFISH	HUTCHES	IGNEOUS	IMPOSED	INERTIA
HOSTESS	HUGGING	HUTCHIE	IGNITED	IMPOSER	INERTLY
HOSTILE	HUHEHOT	HUTLIKE	IGNITER	IMPOUND	INEXACT
HOSTING	HULKING	HUTMENT	IGNOBLE	IMPRESA	INFANCY
HOSTLER	HULLING	HUYGENS	IGNOBLY	IMPRESS	INFANTA
HOTBEDS	HUMANLY	HWANG HO	IGNORED	IMPREST	INFANTE
HOT DOGS	HUMBLED	HYAENAS	IGNORER	IMPRINT	INFANTS
HOTFOOT	HUMBLER	HYAENIC	IGUANAS	IMPROVE	INFARCT
HOTHEAD	HUMBUGS	HYALINE	IKEBANA	IMPULSE	INFERNO
HOTLINE	HUMDRUM	HYALITE	ILEITIS	IMPUTED	INFIDEL
HOT LINE	HUMERAL	HYALOID	ILL-BRED	IMPUTER	INFIELD
HOT LINK	HUMERUS	HYBRIDS	ILLEGAL	INANELY	INFLAME
HOTNESS	HUMIDLY	HYDATID	ILLICIT	INANITY	INFLATE
HOTPOTS	HUMIDOR	HYDRANT	ILLNESS·	INAPTLY	INFLECT
HOT RODS	HUMMING	HYDRATE	ILL WILL	IN A	INFLICT
HOT SEAT	HUMMOCK	HYDRIDE	IMAGERY	WORD	INFLOWS
HOT SPOT	HUMORAL	HYDROID	IMAGINE	INBOARD	INFRACT
HOTSPUR	HUMOURS	HYGIENE	IMAGISM	INBOUND	INFUSED
HOTTEST	HUMPING	HYMNALS	IMAGIST	INBREED	INFUSER
HOTTING	HUNCHED	HYMNING	IMAMATE	INCENSE	INGENUE
HOUDINI	HUNCHES	HYPED UP	IMBIBED	INCHING	INGESTA
HOUMOUS	HUNDRED	HYPHENS	IMBIBER	INCIPIT	INGOING
HOUNDED	HUNGARY	HYPONYM	IMBRUTE	INCISED	INGRAIN
HOUNDER	HUNGNAM		IMBUING	INCISOR	INGRATE
HOUSING	HUNKERS	**I**	IMITATE	INCITED	INGRESS
HOUSMAN	HUNLIKE		IMMENSE	INCITER	IN-GROUP
HOUSTON	HUNNISH	IAMBICS	IMMERSE	INCLINE	INGROWN
HOUTING	HUNTERS	IAPETUS	IMMORAL	INCLOSE	INHABIT
HOVERED	HUNTING	IBERIAN	IMMURED	INCLUDE	INHALED
		ICE AGES			

INHALER	INTERNS	ISOCHOR	JAMAICA	JIBBING	JOTTERS
INHERIT	INTIMAL	ISOGAMY	JAMES II	JIGGERS	JOTTING
INHIBIT	INTONED	ISOGENY	JAMMIER	JIGGING	JOURNAL
IN-HOUSE	INTONER	ISOHYET	JAMMING	JIGGLED	JOURNEY
INHUMAN	INTROIT	ISOLATE	JANGLED	JIGGLES	JOURNOS
INHUMER	INTRUDE	ISOLINE	JANGLER	JIGSAWS	JOUSTED
INITIAL	INTRUST	ISONOMY	JANITOR	JILTING	JOUSTER
INJURED	INURING	ISOTONE	JANUARY	JIM CROW	JOYLESS
INJURER	INUTILE	ISOTOPE	JARGONS	JIMJAMS	JOYRIDE
INKATHA	IN VACUO	ISOTOPY	JARRING	JIMMIES	JUBILEE
INKIEST	INVADED	ISOTRON	JASMINE	JINGLED	JUDAEAN
INKLING	INVADER	ISRAELI	JAUNTED	JINGLER	JUDAICA
INKPADS	INVALID	ISSUING	JAVELIN	JINGLES	JUDAISM
INKWELL	INVEIGH	ISTHMUS	JAWBONE	JINXING	JUDAIST
INLAYER	INVERSE	ISTRIAN	JAYWALK	JINZHOU	JUDAIZE
INMATES	INVITED	ITALIAN	JAZZIER	JITTERS	JUDASES
INNARDS	INVITER	ITALICS	JAZZILY	JITTERY	JUDGING
INNERVE	IN VITRO	ITCHIER	JAZZING	JOBBERS	JUDOIST
INNINGS	INVOICE	ITCHING	JEALOUS	JOBBERY	JUGGING
IN ORDER	INVOKED	ITEMIZE	JEERING	JOBBING	JUGGLED
INQUEST	INVOKER	ITERANT	JEHOVAH	JOBCLUB	JUGGLER
INQUIET	INVOLVE	ITERATE	JEJUNAL	JOBLESS	JUGULAR
INQUIRE	INWARDS	ITHACAN	JEJUNUM	JOB LOTS	JUICIER
INQUIRY	INWEAVE	IVANOVO	JELLABA	JOCKEYS	JUICILY
INROADS	IODIZER	IVORIAN	JELLIED	JOCULAR	JUICING
INSECTS	IONIZED	IVORIES	JELLIES	JODHPUR	JUJITSU
INSERTS	IONIZER	IZHEVSK	JELLIFY	JOGGING	JUJUBES
INSHORE	IPOMOEA		JELLING	JOGGLED	JUKEBOX
INSIDER	IPSWICH	**J**	JEMMIED	JOGGLER	JUMBLED
INSIDES	IQUIQUE	JABBING	JEMMIES	JOGGLES	JUMBLER
INSIGHT	IQUITOS	JACAMAR	JENNIES	JOG TROT	JUMBLES
INSIPID	IRANIAN	JACKALS	JERICHO	JOHN DOE	JUMPERS
INSOFAR	IRATELY	JACKASS	JERKIER	JOHNSON	JUMPIER
INSOLES	IRELAND	JACKDAW	JERKILY	JOINDER	JUMPILY
INSPECT	IRENICS	JACKETS	JERKING	JOINERS	JUMPING
INSPIRE	IRIDIUM	JACKING	JERKINS	JOINERY	JUMP-OFF
INSTALL	IRKSOME	JACKPOT	JERK OFF	JOINING	JUNDIAI
INSTANT	IRKUTSK	JACKSON	JERSEYS	JOINTED	JUNGIAN
INSTATE	IRON AGE	JACK TAR	JESTERS	JOINTER	JUNGLES
INSTEAD	IRONIES	JACOBIN	JESTING	JOINTLY	JUNIORS
INSTEPS	IRONING	JACONET	JESUITS	JOLLIED	JUNIPER
INSULAR	IRONIST	JACUZZI	JETFOIL	JOLLIER	JUNKETS
INSULIN	IRON ORE	JADEITE	JETPORT	JOLLIFY	JUNKIES
INSULTS	ISAGOGE	JAGGERY	JETTIES	JOLLILY	JUNKING
INSURED	ISCHIAL	JAGGING	JETTING	JOLLITY	JUPITER
INSURER	ISCHIUM	JAGUARS	JEWFISH	JOLTING	JURISTS
INSWING	ISFAHAN	JAILERS	JEW'S-	JONESES	JURY BOX
INTAKES	ISLAMIC	JAILING	EAR	JONQUIL	JURYMAN
INTEGER	ISLANDS	JAKARTA	JEZEBEL	JOSHING	JUSSIVE
INTENSE	ISOBARS	JALAPIC	JIANGSU	JOSTLED	JUSTICE
INTERIM	ISOBATH	JALISCO	JIANGXI	JOSTLER	JUSTIFY

JUTLAND	KERBING	KINGPIN	KOKANEE	LADDERS	LAPSING
JUTTING	KERNELS	KINKIER	KOKOBEH	LADDIES	LAPWING
	KERNITE	KINKILY	KOLDING	LADDISH	LARCENY
K	KESTREL	KINNOCK	KOLKHOZ	LADINGS	LARCHES
KABADDI	KESWICK	KINSHIP	KOLOMNA	LADLING	LARDERS
KAFFIRS	KETCHES	KINSMAN	KONGONI	LAGGARD	LARDING
KAFTANS	KETCHUP	KINSMEN	KOOKIER	LAGGING	LARGELY
KAIFENG	KETONIC	KIPPERS	KOONING	LAGOONS	LARGESS
KAINITE	KETOSIS	KIPPING	KOPECKS	LAICISM	LARGEST
KAISERS	KETTLES	KIRGHIZ	KOPEISK	LAICIZE	LARGISH
KALENDS	KEYED UP	KIRUNDI	KOUPREY	LALLANS	LARIATS
KALININ	KEYHOLE	KISSERS	KOWLOON	LAMAISM	LARKING
KALMUCK	KEYNOTE	KISSING	KREFELD	LAMAIST	LARWOOD
KAMPALA	KEY RING	KIT BAGS	KREMLIN	LAMBADA	LASAGNA
KANANGA	KHADDAR	KITCHEN	KRISHNA	LAMBAST	LASAGNE
KANNADA	KHAKASS	KITSCHY	KRYPTON	LAMBENT	LA SALLE
KANTIAN	KHALIFS	KITTENS	KUBELIK	LAMBERT	LA SCALA
KAOLACK	KHALKHA	KITTIES	KUBRICK	LAMBETH	LASCAUX
KAPITZA	KHAMSIN	KITTING	KUCHING	LAMBING	LASHING
KARACHI	KHANATE	KLAXONS	KUMAYRI	LAMELLA	LASH OUT
KARAKUL	KHARKOV	KLEENEX	KUMQUAT	LAMENTS	LASH-UPS
KARBALA	KHERSON	KNAPPER	KUNDERA	LAMINAR	LASSOED
KARELIA	KHINGAN	KNAVERY	KUNMING	LAMPERN	LASSOER
KAROSHI	KHOISAN	KNAVISH	KUNZITE	LAMPOON	LAST END
KARSTIC	KIANGSI	KNEADED	KURDISH	LAMPREY	LASTING
KASHGAR	KIANGSU	KNEADER	KUTAISI	LANCERS	LATAKIA
KASHMIR	KIBBUTZ	KNEECAP	KUWAITI	LANCETS	LATCHED
KASSALA	KICKING	KNEEING	KWANGJU	LANCHOW	LATCHES
KATANGA	KICKOFF	KNEELED	KWAZULU	LANCING	LATCHET
KATSINA	KICK OFF	KNEEPAD	KWEILIN	LANDAUS	LATENCY
KATYDID	KIDDERS	KNEES UP	KYANIZE	LANDING	LATERAL
KAYAKER	KIDDIES	KNIFING		LANDTAG	LATHERY
KAYSERI	KIDDING	KNIGHTS	**L**	LANGRES	LATIMER
KEATING	KIDNEYS	KNITTED	LABELED	LANGUID	LATRINE
KEELING	KIDSKIN	KNITTER	LABIALS	LANGUOR	LATTICE
KEELSON	KILDARE	KNOBBLY	LABIATE	LANIARY	LATVIAN
KEENEST	KILLERS	KNOCKED	LABOURS	LANKEST	LAUDING
KEENING	KILLICK	KNOCKER	LABROID	LANKIER	LAUGHED
KEEPERS	KILLING	KNOCK-ON	LACIEST	LANKILY	LAUGHER
KEEPING	KILLJOY	KNOCK-UP	LACKEYS	LANOLIN	LAUNDER
KEEPNET	KILOTON	KNOSSOS	LACKING	LANSING	LAUNDRY
KEITLOA	KILTERS	KNOTTED	LACONIC	LANTANA	LAURELS
KELVINS	KIMONOS	KNOTTER	LACQUER	LANTERN	LAWLESS
KENDREW	KINDEST	KNOW-ALL	LACTASE	LANYARD	LAW LORD
KENNEDY	KINDLED	KNOW-HOW	LACTATE	LAOTIAN	LAWSUIT
KENNELS	KINDLER	KNOWING	LACTEAL	LA PALMA	LAWYERS
KENNING	KINDRED	KNUCKLE	LACTONE	LAPDOGS	LAXNESS
KENOSIS	KINETIC	KNUCKLY	LACTOSE	LAPLACE	LAYERED
KENOTIC	KINFOLK	KOBARID	LACUNAE	LAPLAND	LAYETTE
KENTISH	KINGCUP	KOBLENZ	LACUNAR	LA PLATA	LAY-OFFS
KERATIN	KINGDOM	KOFTGAR	LACUNAS	LAPPING	LAYOUTS

LAZIEST	LEGIBLE	LEVERED	LIMPING	LIVENED	LOLLAND
L-DRIVER	LEGIBLY	LEVERET	LIMPKIN	LIVENER	LOLLARD
LEACHED	LEGIONS	LEVYING	LIMPOPO	LIVIDLY	LOLLIES
LEACHER	LEGLESS	LEXICAL	LIMULUS	LIVINGS	LOLLING
LEADERS	LEGNICA	LEXICON	LINABLE	LIVONIA	LOMBARD
LEADING	LEG-PULL	LIAISED	LINARES	LIVORNO	LONG AGO
LEAD-INS	LEGROOM	LIAISON	LINCOLN	LIZARDS	LONGBOW
LEAD OFF	LEG ROOM	LIANOID	LINCTUS	LOADING	LONGEST
LEAFAGE	LEG SIDE	LIASSIC	LINDANE	LOAFERS	LONGING
LEAFIER	LEGUMES	LIBBERS	LINDENS	LOAFING	LONGISH
LEAFLET	LEGUMIN	LIBELED	LINEAGE	LOANING	LONG TON
LEAGUED	LEGWORK	LIBERAL	LINEATE	LOATHED	LOOFAHS
LEAGUES	LE HAVRE	LIBEREC	LINEMAN	LOATHER	LOOKERS
LEAKAGE	LEIPZIG	LIBERIA	LINEMEN	LOATHLY	LOOKING
LEAKIER	LEISTER	LIBERTY	LINE-OUT	LOBBIED	LOOKOUT
LEAKING	LEISURE	LIBIDOS	LINEUPS	LOBBIES	LOOK OUT
LEANEST	LEITRIM	LIBRARY	LINGCOD	LOBBING	LOOMING
LEANING	LEMBERG	LIBRATE	LINGOES	LOBBYER	LOONIER
LEAN-TOS	LEMMING	LICENCE	LINGUAL	LOBELIA	LOONIES
LEAPING	LEMPIRA	LICENSE	LININGS	LOBSTER	LOOPING
LEARNED	LENDERS	LICKING	LINKAGE	LOBULAR	LOOSELY
LEARNER	LENDING	LIE-DOWN	LINKING	LOCALES	LOOSEST
LEASHES	LENGTHS	LIESTAL	LINKMAN	LOCALLY	LOOSING
LEASING	LENGTHY	LIFTING	LINKUPS	LOCARNO	LOOTERS
LEATHER	LENIENT	LIFTOFF	LINNETS	LOCATED	LOOTING
LEAVENS	LENTIGO	LIFT-OFF	LINOCUT	LOCATER	LOPPING
LEAVING	LENTILS	LIGHTED	LINSANG	LOCHIAL	LOQUATS
LEBANON	LEONINE	LIGHTEN	LINSEED	LOCKAGE	LORDING
LECHERS	LEOPARD	LIGHTER	LINTELS	LOCKERS	LORELEI
LECHERY	LEOTARD	LIGHTLY	LIONESS	LOCKETS	LORGNON
LECTERN	LEPANTO	LIGNIFY	LIONIZE	LOCKING	LORIENT
LECTION	LEPORID	LIGNITE	LIPETSK	LOCKJAW	LORRIES
LECTURE	LEPROSE	LIGROIN	LIP-READ	LOCKNUT	LOSABLE
LEDGERS	LEPROSY	LIGULAR	LIQUATE	LOCKOUT	LOSINGS
LEECHES	LEPROUS	LIGURIA	LIQUEFY	LOCKUPS	LOTIONS
LEERIER	LERWICK	LIKABLE	LIQUEUR	LOCOISM	LOTTERY
LEERING	LESBIAN	LIKENED	LIQUIDS	LOCULAR	LOTTING
LEE TIDE	LESIONS	LIKINGS	LISBURN	LOCUSTS	LOTUSES
LEEWARD	LESOTHO	LILTING	LISIEUX	LODGERS	LOUDEST
LEFTIES	LESSEES	LIMACON	LISPING	LODGING	LOUNGED
LEFTISM	LESSONS	LIMBATE	LISTING	LOFTIER	LOUNGER
LEFTIST	LESSORS	LIMBURG	LITCHIS	LOFTILY	LOUNGES
LEGALLY	LETDOWN	LIMEADE	LITERAL	LOFTING	LOURDES
LEGASPI	LETTERS	LIMIEST	LITHELY	LOGBOOK	LOURING
LEGATEE	LETTING	LIMINAL	LITHEST	LOGGERS	LOUSIER
LEGATES	LETTUCE	LIMITED	LITHIUM	LOGGIAS	LOUSILY
LEGATOR	LEUCINE	LIMITER	LITHOID	LOGGING	LOUSING
LEGENDS	LEUCITE	LIMNING	LITOTES	LOGICAL	LOUTISH
LEGGIER	LEUCOMA	LIMOGES	LITTERS	LOGIEST	LOUVAIN
LEGGING	LEVATOR	LIMPEST	LITURGY	LOGJAMS	LOUVRES
LEGHORN	LEVELED	LIMPETS	LIVABLE	LOGWOOD	LOVABLE

LOWBORN	LUPULIN	MAGHREB	MALVERN	MANXMAN	MARTYRS
LOWBROW	LURCHED	MAGICAL	MAMILLA	MAOISTS	MARTYRY
LOW BROW	LURCHER	MAGNATE	MAMMALS	MAPPING	MARVELS
LOW DOWN	LURCHES	MAGNETO	MAMMARY	MARABOU	MARXIAN
LOW-DOWN	LURGIES	MAGNETS	MAMMIES	MARACAS	MARXISM
LOWERED	LURIDLY	MAGNIFY	MAMMOTH	MARACAY	MARXIST
LOWLAND	LURKING	MAGNUMS	MANACLE	MARASCA	MASBATE
LOWLIER	LUSATIA	MAGPIES	MANAGED	MARATHA	MASCARA
LOW LIFE	LUSTFUL	MAHATMA	MANAGER	MARATHI	MASCOTS
LOWNESS	LUSTILY	MAHFOUZ	MANAGUA	MARBLED	MASHHAD
LOW-RISE	LUSTING	MAHICAN	MANAKIN	MARBLER	MASHING
LOW TIDE	LUSTRAL	MAH JONG	MANATEE	MARBLES	MASKING
LOYALLY	LUSTRES	MAH-JONG	MANDATE	MARBURG	MASONIC
LOYALTY	LUTEOUS	MAHONIA	MANDELA	MARCHED	MASONRY
LOZENGE	LUTHIER	MAHOUTS	MANDREL	MARCHER	MASQUES
L-PLATES	LYCHEES	MAIDENS	MANGERS	MARCHES	MASSAGE
LUALABA	LYCHNIS	MAILBAG	MANGIER	MAREMMA	MASSAWA
LUBBOCK	LYCOPOD	MAILBOX	MANGILY	MARGATE	MASSEUR
LUCERNE	LYDDITE	MAILING	MANGLED	MARGAUX	MASSIFS
LUCIDLY	LYING-IN	MAILMAN	MANGLER	MARGINS	MASSING
LUCIFER	LYNCEAN	MAILMEN	MANGLES	MARIBOR	MASSIVE
LUCKIER	LYNCHED	MAIMING	MANGOES	MARIMBA	MASTERS
LUCKILY	LYNCHER	MAINTOP	MANHOLE	MARINAS	MASTERY
LUCKNOW	LYRICAL	MAJESTY	MANHOOD	MARINER	MASTIFF
LUDDITE		MAJORCA	MANHOUR	MARINES	MASTOID
LUFFING	**M**	MAJORED	MANHUNT	MARITAL	MASURIA
LUGANDA	MACABRE	MAJORLY	MANIACS	MARKERS	MATADOR
LUGANSK	MACADAM	MAKASAR	MANIKIN	MARKETS	MATCHED
LUGGAGE	MACAQUE	MAKE OUT	MANIPUR	MARKHOR	MATCHES
LUGGERS	MACEDON	MAKES DO	MAN JACK	MARKING	MATHURA
LUGGING	MACHETE	MAKINGS	MANKIND	MARKUPS	MATINEE
LUGHOLE	MACHINE	MAKURDI	MANLIER	MARLINE	MATLOCK
LUGSAIL	MACLEAN	MALABAR	MANLIKE	MARLINS	MATRONS
LUGWORM	MACRAME	MALACCA	MAN-MADE	MARLITE	MATTERS
LULLABY	MACULAR	MALAISE	MANNERS	MARMITE	MATTING
LULLING	MADDEST	MALARIA	MANNING	MARMOTS	MATTINS
LUMBAGO	MADEIRA	MALATYA	MANNISH	MAROONS	MATTOCK
LUMENAL	MADE OUT	MALAYAN	MANNITE	MARQUEE	MATURED
LUMPIER	MADISON	MALEATE	MANNOSE	MARQUIS	MAUDLIN
LUMPILY	MADNESS	MALEFIC	MANRESA	MARRIED	MAULING
LUMPING	MADONNA	MALINES	MANROPE	MARRIER	MAUNDER
LUMPISH	MADRONA	MALINKE	MANSARD	MARRING	MAWKISH
LUMP SUM	MADURAI	MALLARD	MANSELL	MARROWS	MAXILLA
LUMUMBA	MADWORT	MALLETS	MANSION	MARSALA	MAXIMAL
LUNATIC	MAENADS	MALLEUS	MANTLED	MARSHAL	MAXIMIN
LUNCHED	MAESTRI	MALLOWS	MANTLES	MARSHES	MAXIMUM
LUNCHER	MAESTRO	MALMSEY	MANUALS	MARTENS	MAXIMUS
LUNCHES	MAFIOSO	MALTASE	MANUKAU	MARTIAL	MAXWELL
LUNETTE	MAGENTA	MALTESE	MANURED	MARTIAN	MAY DAYS
LUNGING	MAGGOTS	MALTING	MANURER	MARTINI	MAYENNE
LUOYANG	MAGGOTY	MALTOSE	MANX CAT	MARTINS	MAYFAIR

MAYORAL	MENACES	MICRONS	MINGIER	MISTERS	MOLLUSC
MAYOTTE	MENAGES	MIDDENS	MINGLED	MISTILY	MOLOKAI
MAYPOLE	MENDERS	MIDDLE C	MINIBAR	MISTIME	MOLTING
MAYWEED	MENDING	MIDGETS	MINIBUS	MISTING	MOMBASA
MAZURKA	MENDIPS	MIDIRON	MINICAB	MISTOOK	MOMENTA
MAZZARD	MENDOZA	MIDLAND	MINIMAL	MISTRAL	MOMENTS
MBABANE	MENFOLK	MIDMOST	MINIMAX	MISUSED	MOMMIES
MCENROE	MENIALS	MIDRIFF	MINIMUM	MISUSER	MONACAN
MEADOWS	MENTHOL	MIDTERM	MINIMUS	MISUSES	MONADIC
MEALIER	MENTION	MIDWEEK	MINIONS	MITCHUM	MONARCH
MEANDER	MENTORS	MIDWEST	MINIVER	MITHRAS	MONARDA
MEANEST	MEOWING	MIDWIFE	MINIVET	MITOSIS	MONCTON
MEANING	MERCIES	MIDYEAR	MINNOWS	MITOTIC	MONDAYS
MEASLES	MERCURY	MIGHTN'T	MINORCA	MITTENS	MONEYED
MEASURE	MERGERS	MIGRANT	MINSTER	MITZVAH	MONGOLS
MEATIER	MERGING	MIGRATE	MINTAGE	MIXABLE	MONGREL
MEATILY	MERITED	MIKADOS	MINTING	MIXED UP	MONITOR
MEDDLED	MERMAID	MILAZZO	MINUETS	MIXTURE	MONKEYS
MEDDLER	MERRIER	MILDEST	MINUSES	MIZORAM	MONKISH
MEDIACY	MERRILY	MILDEWY	MINUTED	MOANERS	MONOCLE
MEDIANS	MESARCH	MILEAGE	MINUTES	MOANING	MONOMER
MEDIANT	MESHING	MILIARY	MINXISH	MOBBING	MONSOON
MEDIATE	MESSAGE	MILIEUS	MIOCENE	MOBILES	MONSTER
MEDICAL	MESSIAH	MILIEUX	MIRACLE	MOBSTER	MONTAGE
MEDICOS	MESSIER	MILITIA	MIRADOR	MOCKERS	MONTANA
MEDIUMS	MESSILY	MILKERS	MIRAGES	MOCKERY	MONTANE
MEDLARS	MESSINA	MILKIER	MIRRORS	MOCKING	MONTHLY
MEDLEYS	MESSING	MILKILY	MISCALL	MOCK-UPS	MOOCHED
MEDULLA	MESS-UPS	MILKING	MISCAST	MODALLY	MOOCHER
MEEKEST	MESTIZA	MILKMAN	MISDEAL	MOD CONS	MOODIER
MEERKAT	MESTIZO	MILKMEN	MISDEED	MODELED	MOODILY
MEETING	METALED	MILK RUN	MISERLY	MODERAS	MOONEYE
MEGATON	METAMER	MILKSOP	MISFILE	MODERNS	MOONILY
MEIOSIS	METEORS	MILLDAM	MISFIRE	MODESTY	MOONING
MEIOTIC	METERED	MILLERS	MISFITS	MODICUM	MOONLIT
MEISSEN	METHANE	MILLINE	MISHAPS	MODISTE	MOONSET
MELANGE	METHODS	MILLING	MISHEAR	MODULAR	MOORAGE
MELANIC	METIERS	MILLION	MISKOLC	MODULES	MOORHEN
MELANIN	METONYM	MILLRUN	MISLAID	MODULUS	MOORING
MELILLA	METOPIC	MIMESIS	MISLEAD	MOFETTE	MOORISH
MELILOT	METRICS	MIMETIC	MISNAME	MOGADOR	MOOTING
MELISMA	METRIFY	MIMICRY	MISPLAY	MOGGIES	MOPPETS
MELODIC	METRIST	MINABLE	MISREAD	MOGILEV	MOPPING
MELTAGE	MEXICAN	MINARET	MISRULE	MOHICAN	MORAINE
MELTING	MIAOWED	MINCERS	MISSALS	MOIDORE	MORALLY
MEMBERS	MIASMAL	MINCING	MISSIES	MOISTEN	MORAVIA
MEMENTO	MIASMAS	MINDERS	MISSILE	MOISTLY	MORCEAU
MEMOIRS	MICELLE	MINDFUL	MISSING	MOLDIER	MORDANT
MEMPHIS	MICHAEL	MINDING	MISSION	MOLDING	MORDENT
MENACED	MICKEYS	MINDORO	MISSIVE	MOLDOVA	MORDVIN
MENACER	MICROBE	MINERAL	MISTAKE	MOLLIFY	MOREISH

MORELIA	MUCKILY	MURKIER	**N**	NEAREST	NEST EGG
MORELLO	MUCKING	MURKILY	NABBING	NEARING	NESTING
MORELOS	MUD BATH	MURMURS	NACELLE	NEATEST	NESTLED
MORGUES	MUDDIED	MURRAIN	NAEVOID	NEBULAE	NESTLER
MORMONS	MUDDIER	MUSCLED	NAGGERS	NEBULAR	NETBALL
MORNING	MUDDILY	MUSCLES	NAGGING	NEBULAS	NETSUKE
MOROCCO	MUDDING	MUSEFUL	NAHUATL	NECKING	NETTING
MORONIC	MUDDLED	MUSEUMS	NAIADES	NECKLET	NETTLED
MORROWS	MUDDLER	MUSHIER	NAILING	NECKTIE	NETTLES
MORSELS	MUDDLES	MUSHILY	NAIPAUL	NECROSE	NETWORK
MORTALS	MUDFISH	MUSICAL	NAIROBI	NECTARY	NEUROMA
MORTARS	MUDFLAP	MUSKETS	NAIVELY	NEEDFUL	NEURONE
MORTIFY	MUDFLAT	MUSKIER	NAIVETE	NEEDIER	NEURONE
MORTISE	MUDPACK	MUSKRAT	NAIVETY	NEEDING	NEUTRAL
MORULAR	MUD PIES	MUSLIMS	NAKEDLY	NEEDLED	NEUTRON
MOSAICS	MUEZZIN	MUSSELS	NALCHIK	NEEDLES	NEWBORN
MOSELEY	MUFFING	MUSSING	NAMABLE	NEGATED	NEW BORN
MOSELLE	MUFFINS	MUSTANG	NAME DAY	NEGATOR	NEWBURY
MOSEYED	MUFFLED	MUSTARD	NAMIBIA	NEGLECT	NEW CHUM
MOSLEMS	MUFFLER	MUSTERS	NANJING	NEGRESS	NEW DEAL
MOSOTHO	MUGGERS	MUSTIER	NANKEEN	NEGRITO	NEW MOON
MOSQUES	MUGGIER	MUSTILY	NANKING	NEGROES	NEWNESS
MOSSIER	MUGGILY	MUTABLE	NANNIES	NEGROID	NEWPORT
MOTHERS	MUGGING	MUTABLY	NANNING	NEIGHED	NEWTOWN
MOTIONS	MUGGINS	MUTAGEN	NANTONG	NEITHER	NEW TOWN
MOTIVES	MUGSHOT	MUTANTS	NANTUNG	NELLIES	NEW WAVE
MOTORED	MUGWORT	MUTTONY	NAPHTHA	NELUMBO	NEW YEAR
MOTTLED	MUGWUMP	MUZZIER	NAPKINS	NEMATIC	NEW YORK
MOTTOES	MULATTO	MUZZILY	NAPPIES	NEMESES	NEXUSES
MOUFLON	MULCHED	MUZZLED	NAPPING	NEMESIS	NIAGARA
MOUILLE	MULCTED	MUZZLER	NARKIER	NEOCENE	NIBBLED
MOULDED	MULLAHS	MUZZLES	NARKING	NEOGAEA	NIBBLER
MOULDER	MULLEIN	MYALGIA	NARRATE	NEOGENE	NIBBLES
MOULTED	MULLETS	MYALGIC	NARROWS	NEOLITH	NICKELS
MOULTER	MULLING	MYALISM	NARTHEX	NEONATE	NICKING
MOUNTED	MULLION	MYANMAR	NARWHAL	NEOTENY	NICOBAR
MOUNTER	MULLITE	MYCENAE	NASALLY	NEOTYPE	NICOSIA
MOUNTIE	MUMBLED	MYCOSIS	NASCENT	NEOZOIC	NIFTIER
MOURNED	MUMBLER	MYCOTIC	NASTIER	NEPHEWS	NIFTILY
MOURNER	MUMMERS	MYELOID	NASTILY	NEPHRON	NIGELLA
MOUSERS	MUMMERY	MYELOMA	NATIONS	NEPOTIC	NIGERIA
MOUSIER	MUMMIES	MYIASIS	NATIVES	NEPTUNE	NIGGARD
MOUSING	MUMMIFY	MYKONOS	NATTIER	NEREIDS	NIGGERS
MOUSSES	MUMMING	MYNHEER	NATTILY	NERITIC	NIGGLED
MOUTHED	MUNCHED	MYOLOGY	NATURAL	NERVATE	NIGGLER
MOUTHER	MUNCHER	MYOTOME	NATURES	NERVIER	NIGHTIE
MOVABLE	MUNDANE	MYRIADS	NAUGHTY	NERVILY	NIGHTLY
MOVABLY	MUNSTER	MYRTLES	NAURUAN	NERVINE	NIIGATA
MOVIOLA	MUNTJAC	MYSTERY	NAVARRE	NERVING	NILOTIC
MUBARAK	MURDERS	MYSTICS	NAVVIES	NERVOUS	NIMBLER
MUCKIER	MURDOCH	MYSTIFY	NAYARIT	NERVURE	NINEPIN
					NINNIES

NIOBITE	NOONDAY	NUMERAL	OBTRUDE	OINKING	OOSPORE
NIOBIUM	NO-PLACE	NUMMARY	OBVERSE	OKAYAMA	OOTHECA
NIOBOUS	NORFOLK	NUNATAK	OBVIATE	OKAYING	OOZIEST
NIPPERS	NORMANS	NUNAVUT	OBVIOUS	OKINAWA	OPACITY
NIPPIER	NORWICH	NUN BUOY	OCARINA	OLD BOYS	OPALINE
NIPPILY	NOSEBAG	NUNCIOS	OCCIPUT	OLD HAND	OPEN-AIR
NIPPING	NOSEGAY	NUNNERY	OCCLUDE	OLD LADY	OPEN DAY
NIPPLES	NOSHING	NUPTIAL	OCEANIA	OLD LAGS	OPENERS
NIRVANA	NOSIEST	NURSERY	OCEANIC	OLD MAID	OPENING
NITEROI	NOSTRIL	NURSING	OCELLAR	OLD NICK	OPERAND
NITRATE	NOSTRUM	NURTURE	OCELLUS	OLDSTER	OPERANT
NITRIDE	NOTABLE	NUTCASE	OCELOTS	OLDTIME	OPERATE
NITRIFY	NOTABLY	NUTGALL	OCHROID	OLDUVAI	OPHITIC
NITRILE	NOTCHED	NUTMEGS	OCREATE	OLEFINE	OPIATES
NITRITE	NOTCHES	NUTRIAS	OCTADIC	O LEVELS	OPINING
NITROSO	NOTELET	NUTTIER	OCTAGON	OLIVARY	OPINION
NITROUS	NOTEPAD	NUTTILY	OCTANES	OLIVINE	OPOSSUM
NITWITS	NOTHING	NUTTING	OCTAVES	OLOMOUC	OPPOSED
NIVEOUS	NOTICED	NUTWOOD	OCTOBER	OLSZTYN	OPPOSER
NO BALLS	NOTICES	NUZZLED	OCTOPOD	OLYMPIA	OPPRESS
NOBBLED	NOTIONS	NYMPHAL	OCTOPUS	OLYMPIC	OPSONIC
NOBBLER	NO TRUMP	NYMPHET	OCTUPLE	OLYMPUS	OPSONIN
NOBLEST	NO-TRUMP	NYUNGAR	OCULIST	OMENTUM	OPTICAL
NOCTUID	NOUGATS		ODDBALL	OMICRON	OPTIMAL
NOCTULE	NOUGHTS	**O**	ODDMENT	OMINOUS	OPTIMUM
NOCTURN	NOURISH		ODDNESS	OMITTED	OPTIONS
NODDING	NOUVEAU	OAKLAND	ODOROUS	OMITTER	OPULENT
NODDLES	NOVALIS	OARFISH	ODYSSEY	OMNIBUS	OPUNTIA
NODICAL	NOVELLA	OARLOCK	OEDIPAL	ON A	OQUASSA
NO DOUBT	NOVELLE	OARSMAN	OERSTED	WHIM	ORACLES
NODULAR	NOVELTY	OARSMEN	OESTRUS	ONE EYED	ORALISM
NODULES	NOVICES	OATCAKE	OFFBEAT	ONENESS	ORANGES
NO ENTRY	NOVI SAD	OATMEAL	OFFENCE	ONE-OFFS	ORATION
NOGGING	NOWHERE	OBCONIC	OFFERED	ONEROUS	ORATORS
NOGGINS	NOXIOUS	OBELISK	OFFERER	ONESELF	ORATORY
NOISIER	NOZZLES	OBELIZE	OFFHAND	ONE-STAR	ORBITAL
NOISILY	NUANCES	OBESITY	OFFICER	ONE STEP	ORBITED
NOISOME	NUCLEAR	OBEYING	OFFICES	ONE-STEP	ORCHARD
NOMADIC	NUCLEIN	OBJECTS	OFFINGS	ONETIME	ORCHIDS
NOMBRIL	NUCLEON	OBLIGED	OFF-LOAD	ON-GLIDE	ORCINOL
NOMINAL	NUCLEUS	OBLIGEE	OFF-PEAK	ONGOING	ORDEALS
NOMINEE	NUCLIDE	OBLIGER	OFFSIDE	ONITSHA	ORDERED
NONAGON	NUDGING	OBLIGOR	OGREISH	ON LEAVE	ORDERER
NON-IRON	NUDISTS	OBLIQUE	OHM'S	ONSHORE	ORDERLY
NONPLUS	NUGGETS	OBLONGS	LAW	ON SIGHT	ORDINAL
NON-PROS	NUGGETY	OBLOQUY	OBOISTS	ON STAGE	ORECTIC
NONSTOP	NULLIFY	OBOISTS	OILBIRD	ONTARIO	OREGANO
NON STOP	NULLITY	OBOVATE	OILCANS	ONWARDS	ORGANIC
NONSUIT	NULL SET	OBOVOID	OILIEST	OOLITIC	ORGANON
NON USER	NUMBERS	OBSCENE	OILRIGS	OOPHYTE	ORGANUM
NOODLES	NUMBING	OBSCURE	OILSKIN	OOSPERM	ORGANZA
		OBSERVE	OIL WELL		

ORGASMS	OUTBACK	OVATION	PACKERS	PANAMAS	PARESIS
ORIENTE	OUTCAST	OVERACT	PACKETS	PAN-ARAB	PARETIC
ORIFICE	OUTCOME	OVERAGE	PACK ICE	PANCAKE	PARFAIT
ORIGAMI	OUTCROP	OVERALL	PACKING	PANCHAX	PARIAHS
ORIGINS	OUTDATE	OVERARM	PADDIES	PANDECT	PARINGS
ORINOCO	OUTDONE	OVERAWE	PADDING	PANDITS	PARKIER
ORISONS	OUTDOOR	OVERBID	PADDLED	PANDORE	PARKING
ORIZABA	OUTFACE	OVERDID	PADDLER	PANELED	PARKWAY
ORKNEYS	OUTFALL	OVERDUE	PADDLES	PANGAEA	PARLEYS
ORLANDO	OUTFITS	OVERFLY	PADDOCK	PANICKY	PARLOUR
ORLEANS	OUTFLOW	OVERJOY	PADLOCK	PANICLE	PARLOUS
OROGENY	OUTGREW	OVERLAP	PADRONE	PANNIER	PARODIC
OROLOGY	OUTGROW	OVERLAY	PAGEANT	PANNING	PAROLED
OROTUND	OUTHAUL	OVERLIE	PAGEBOY	PANOCHA	PAROLES
ORPHANS	OUTINGS	OVERMAN	PAGINAL	PANOPLY	PARONYM
ORPHREY	OUTLAST	OVERPAY	PAGODAS	PANSIES	PAROTIC
ORTOLAN	OUTLAWS	OVERRAN	PAHSIEN	PANTHER	PAROTID
ORVIETO	OUTLAYS	OVERRUN	PAINFUL	PANTIES	PARQUET
OSCULAR	OUTLETS	OVERSAW	PAINING	PANTILE	PARRIED
OSCULUM	OUTLIER	OVERSEE	PAINTED	PANTING	PARRIES
OSHOGBO	OUTLINE	OVERSET	PAINTER	PANTOUM	PARROTS
OSMIOUS	OUTLIVE	OVERSEW	PAIRING	PANZERS	PARSEES
OSMOSIS	OUTLOOK	OVERTAX	PAIR-OAR	PAOTING	PARSERS
OSMOTIC	OUTMOST	OVERTLY	PAISLEY	PAPAYAS	PARSING
OSMUNDA	OUTPACE	OVERTOP	PAJAMAS	PAPEETE	PARSLEY
OSPREYS	OUTPLAY	OVERUSE	PALACES	PAPERED	PARSNIP
OSSEOUS	OUTPORT	OVIDUCT	PALADIN	PAPERER	PARSONS
OSSETIA	OUTPOST	OVIFORM	PALATAL	PAPILLA	PARTAKE
OSSETIC	OUTPOUR	OVULATE	PALATES	PAPISTS	PARTIAL
OSSICLE	OUTPUTS	OWN GOAL	PALAVER	PAPOOSE	PARTIED
OSSUARY	OUTRAGE	OXALATE	PALE ALE	PAPPIES	PARTIES
OSTEOID	OUTRANK	OXAZINE	PALERMO	PAPPOSE	PARTING
OSTEOMA	OUTRIDE	OXBLOOD	PALETTE	PAPRIKA	PARTITA
OSTIOLE	OUTRODE	OXCARTS	PALFREY	PAPYRUS	PARTITE
OSTLERS	OUTSELL	OXHEART	PALINGS	PARABLE	PARTNER
OSTMARK	OUTSIDE	OXIDANT	PALLETS	PARADED	PARTOOK
OSTOSIS	OUTSIZE	OXIDASE	PALLIER	PARADER	PARVENU
OSTRAVA	OUTSOLD	OXIDATE	PALLING	PARADES	PASCHAL
OSTRICH	OUTSOLE	OXIDIZE	PALLIUM	PARADOR	PASMORE
OTOCYST	OUTSTAY	OXONIAN	PALMATE	PARADOX	PASSADE
OTOLITH	OUT-TAKE	OXYACID	PALMIER	PARAGON	PASSAGE
OTOLOGY	OUTTALK	OXYSALT	PALMING	PARAIBA	PASSANT
OTRANTO	OUT-TRAY	OXYTONE	PALMIRA	PARAPET	PAS SEUL
OTTOMAN	OUTVOTE	OYSTERS	PALMIST	PARASOL	PASS FOR
OUABAIN	OUTWARD	OZONIZE	PALM OIL	PARATHA	PASSING
OUGHTN'T	OUTWASH		PALMYRA	PARBOIL	PASSION
OUR LADY	OUTWEAR	**P**	PALPATE	PARCELS	PASSIVE
OUR LORD	OUTWORK	PABULUM	PALSIED	PARCHED	PASSKEY
OURSELF	OUTWORN	PACHUCA	PAMPEAN	PARDONS	PASS OFF
OUSTERS	OVARIAN	PACIFIC	PANACEA	PAREIRA	PASS OUT
OUSTING	OVARIES	PACKAGE	PANACHE	PARENTS	PASTELS

PASTERN	PAYSLIP	PELTING	PERFUSE	PETTISH	PICKLES
PASTE UP	PEACHES	PENALLY	PERGOLA	PETUNIA	PICK-UPS
PASTE-UP	PEACOCK	PENALTY	PERHAPS	PFENNIG	PICNICS
PASTIER	PEAFOWL	PENANCE	PERIDOT	PHAETON	PICOTEE
PASTIES	PEAHENS	PENDANT	PERIGEE	PHALANX	PICRATE
PASTILY	PEAKIER	PENDENT	PERIGON	PHALLIC	PICRITE
PASTIME	PEAKING	PENDING	PERIODS	PHALLUS	PICTISH
PASTING	PEALING	PENGUIN	PERIQUE	PHANTOM	PICTURE
PASTORS	PEANUTS	PENISES	PERIWIG	PHARAOH	PIDDLED
PASTURE	PEARLER	PEN NAME	PERJURE	PHARYNX	PIDDOCK
PATCHED	PEASANT	PENNANT	PERJURY	PHASING	PIDGINS
PATCHER	PEBBLES	PENNATE	PERKIER	PHASMID	PIEBALD
PATCHES	PECCANT	PENNIES	PERKILY	PHELLEM	PIECING
PATELLA	PECCARY	PENNING	PERKING	PHILTRE	PIE-EYED
PATENCY	PECCAVI	PENNONS	PERLITE	PHIZOGS	PIERCED
PATENTS	PECKERS	PEN PALS	PERMIAN	PHLOXES	PIERCER
PATHANS	PECKING	PENRITH	PERMING	PHOBIAS	PIETIES
PATHWAY	PECKISH	PENROSE	PERMITS	PHOBICS	PIGEONS
PATIALA	PECTASE	PENSILE	PERMUTE	PHOCINE	PIGFISH
PATIENT	PECTATE	PENSION	PERPEND	PHOENIX	PIGGERY
PATRIAL	PECTIZE	PENSIVE	PERPLEX	PHONATE	PIGGIER
PATRICK	PEDALED	PENTANE	PERSEID	PHONE-IN	PIGGIES
PATRIOT	PEDANTS	PENTENE	PERSIAN	PHONEME	PIGGING
PATROLS	PEDDLED	PENTODE	PERSIST	PHONEYS	PIGGISH
PATRONS	PEDDLER	PENTOSE	PERSONA	PHONICS	PIG IRON
PATTENS	PEDICEL	PEONIES	PERSONS	PHONIER	PIG LEAD
PATTERN	PEDICLE	PEOPLED	PERSPEX	PHONING	PIGLETS
PATTERS	PEDLARS	PEOPLES	PERTAIN	PHRASAL	PIGMENT
PATTIES	PEDOCAL	PEPPERS	PERTURB	PHRASED	PIGMIES
PATTING	PEEBLES	PEPPERY	PERUGIA	PHRASES	PIGSKIN
PAUCITY	PEEKING	PEP PILL	PERUSAL	PHRATRY	PIGTAIL
PAULINE	PEELING	PEPPING	PERUSED	PHRENIC	PIGWEED
PAULIST	PEEPERS	PEP TALK	PERUSER	PHYSICS	PIKEMAN
PAUNCHY	PEEPING	PEPTIDE	PERVADE	PHYSIOS	PIKEMEN
PAUPERS	PEERAGE	PEPTIZE	PERVERT	PIANISM	PILEATE
PAUSING	PEERESS	PEPTONE	PESCARA	PIANIST	PILEOUS
PAVANES	PEERING	PERACID	PESETAS	PIANOLA	PILEUPS
PAVINGS	PEEVING	PERCALE	PESKIER	PIASTRE	PILGRIM
PAVIOUR	PEEVISH	PER CENT	PESSARY	PIAZZAS	PILLAGE
PAWKIER	PEEWITS	PERCEPT	PESTLES	PIBROCH	PILLARS
PAWKILY	PEGGING	PERCHED	PETARDS	PICADOR	PILLBOX
PAWNAGE	PEG LEGS	PERCHER	PETCOCK	PICARDY	PILLION
PAWNING	PELAGIC	PERCHES	PETIOLE	PICCOLO	PILLOCK
PAWPAWS	PELICAN	PERCOID	PET NAME	PICEOUS	PILLORY
PAYABLE	PELITIC	PERCUSS	PETRELS	PICKAXE	PILLOWS
PAYBEDS	PELLETS	PER DIEM	PETRIFY	PICKERS	PILOTED
PAY DIRT	PELMETS	PEREIRA	PETROUS	PICKETS	PILSNER
PAYLOAD	PELORIA	PERFECT	PETSAMO	PICKIER	PILULAR
PAYMENT	PELORUS	PERFIDY	PETTIER	PICKING	PIMENTO
PAYOUTS	PELOTAS	PERFORM	PETTILY	PICKLED	PIMPING
PAYROLL	PELTATE	PERFUME	PETTING	PICKLER	PIMPLED

PIMPLES	PISTOLS	PLASTID	PLUMAGE	POLYGON	PORTICO
PINBALL	PISTONS	PLATEAU	PLUMATE	POLYMER	PORTING
PINCERS	PIT A	PLATINA	PLUMBED	POLYNYA	PORTION
PINCHED	PAT	PLATING	PLUMBER	POLYPOD	PORTRAY
PINCHES	PIT-A-	PLATOON	PLUMBIC	POLYPUS	POSEURS
PINE NUT	PAT	PLATTER	PLUMING	POMMELS	POSHEST
PINETUM	PITCHED	PLAUDIT	PLUMMET	POMMIES	POSITED
PINFISH	PITCHER	PLAY-ACT	PLUMPED	POMPANO	POSITIF
PINFOLD	PITCHES	PLAYBOY	PLUMPER	POMPEII	POSSESS
PINGING	PITEOUS	PLAYERS	PLUMULE	POMPOMS	POSSETS
PINGUID	PITFALL	PLAYFUL	PLUNDER	POMPOUS	POSSUMS
PINHEAD	PITHEAD	PLAYING	PLUNGED	PONCHOS	POSTAGE
PINHOLE	PITHIER	PLAYLET	PLUNGER	PONGIER	POSTBAG
PINIEST	PITHILY	PLAY OFF	PLURALS	PONGING	POSTBOX
PINIONS	PITIFUL	PLAY-OFF	PLUSHER	PONIARD	POSTERN
PINKEST	PIT PONY	PLAYPEN	PLUVIAL	PONTIFF	POSTERS
PINKEYE	PIT PROP	PLEADED	PLYWOOD	PONTINE	POSTFIX
PINK GIN	PITTING	PLEADER	POACHED	PONTOON	POSTIES
PINKIES	PITYING	PLEASED	POACHER	POOCHES	POSTING
PINKING	PIVOTAL	PLEASER	PO BOXES	POODLES	POSTMAN
PINKISH	PIVOTED	PLEATED	POCHARD	POOFIER	POSTMEN
PINKOES	PIZZAZZ	PLEATER	POCKETS	POOH-BAH	POSTURE
PINNACE	PLACARD	PLEDGED	PODAGRA	POOLING	POSTWAR
PINNATE	PLACATE	PLEDGER	PODDING	POOPERS	POTABLE
PINNIES	PLACEBO	PLEDGES	PODESTA	POOR BOX	POTAGER
PINNING	PLACING	PLEDGET	PODGIER	POOREST	POTENCY
PINNULE	PLACKET	PLEDGOR	PODGILY	POOR LAW	POTFULS
PINTAIL	PLACOID	PLENARY	PODIUMS	POPADUM	POTHEEN
PINWORK	PLAFOND	PLEURAL	PODOLSK	POPCORN	POTHERB
PINWORM	PLAGUED	PLEURON	POETESS	POPEDOM	POTHOLE
PIONEER	PLAGUER	PLIABLE	POETICS	POP-EYED	POTHOOK
PIOUSLY	PLAGUES	PLIANCY	PO-FACED	POPGUNS	POTICHE
PIPETTE	PLAINER	PLICATE	POGONIA	POPLARS	POTIONS
PIPPING	PLAINLY	PLIGHTS	POGROMS	POPOVER	POT LUCK
PIPPINS	PLAINTS	PLINTHS	POINTED	POPPERS	POTLUCK
PIQUANT	PLAITED	PLODDED	POINTER	POPPETS	POTOMAC
PIQUING	PLANETS	PLODDER	POISING	POPPIES	POTSDAM
PIRAEUS	PLANING	PLOESTI	POISONS	POPPING	POTSHOT
PIRANHA	PLANISH	PLONKED	POKIEST	POP STAR	POTTAGE
PIRATED	PLANNED	PLOPPED	POLARIS	POPULAR	POTTERS
PIRATES	PLANNER	PLOSION	POLEAXE	PORCHES	POTTERY
PIRATIC	PLANTAR	PLOSIVE	POLECAT	PORCINE	POTTIER
PISCARY	PLANTED	PLOTTED	POLEMIC	PORIRUA	POTTIES
PISCINA	PLANTER	PLOTTER	POLICED	PORKERS	POTTING
PISCINE	PLANULA	PLOUGHS	POLITIC	PORKIER	POUCHED
PISHPEK	PLAQUES	PLOVDIV	POLLACK	PORK PIE	POUCHES
PISSING	PLASMID	PLOVERS	POLLARD	PORTAGE	POULARD
PISS-UPS	PLASMIN	PLOWING	POLLING	PORTALS	POULTRY
PISTEUR	PLASMON	PLUCKED	POLL TAX	PORTEND	POUNCED
PISTILS	PLASTER	PLUCKER	POLLUTE	PORTENT	POUNCES
PISTOIA	PLASTIC	PLUGGED	POLTAVA	PORTERS	POUNDAL

POUNDED	PRESAGE	PRIZING	PROTEGE	PUFFINS	PURSUIT
POUNDER	PRESENT	PROBANG	PROTEIN	PUGGING	PURVIEW
POURING	PRESIDE	PROBATE	PROTEST	PULLETS	PUSHERS
POUTING	PRESSED	PROBING	PROTIST	PULLEYS	PUSHIER
POVERTY	PRESSES	PROBITY	PROTIUM	PULLING	PUSHILY
POWDERS	PRESSOR	PROBLEM	PROTONS	PULL-INS	PUSHING
POWDERY	PRESS UP	PROCARP	PROTYLE	PULLMAN	PUSHKIN
POWERED	PRESS-UP	PROCEED	PROUDER	PULLOUT	PUSHROD
POWWOWS	PRESTON	PROCESS	PROUDLY	PULPIER	PUSH-UPS
PRAIRIE	PRESTOS	PROCTOR	PROVERB	PULPING	PUSSIES
PRAISED	PRESUME	PROCURE	PROVIDE	PULPITS	PUSTULE
PRAISER	PRETEEN	PRODDED	PROVING	PULSARS	PUTAMEN
PRAISES	PRETEND	PRODDER	PROVISO	PULSATE	PUT DOWN
PRALINE	PRETEST	PRODIGY	PROVOKE	PULSING	PUT-DOWN
PRANCED	PRETEXT	PRODUCE	PROVOST	PUMPING	PUT-OFFS
PRANCER	PRETZEL	PRODUCT	PROWESS	PUMPKIN	PUTREFY
PRATING	PREVAIL	PROFANE	PROWLED	PUNCHED	PUTTERS
PRATTLE	PREVENT	PROFESS	PROWLER	PUNCHER	PUTTING
PRAWNER	PREVIEW	PROFFER	PROXIES	PUNCHES	PUTTNAM
PRAYERS	PREYING	PROFILE	PROXIMA	PUNCH UP	PUT-UPON
PRAYING	PREZZIE	PROFITS	PRUDENT	PUNCH-UP	PUZZLED
PREBEND	PRICIER	PRO-FORM	PRUDERY	PUNDITS	PUZZLER
PRECAST	PRICING	PROFUSE	PRUDISH	PUNGENT	PUZZLES
PRECEDE	PRICKED	PROGENY	PRUNING	PUNIEST	PYAEMIA
PRECEPT	PRICKER	PROGRAM	PRURIGO	PUNJABI	PYAEMIC
PRECESS	PRICKET	PROJECT	PRUSSIA	PUNKAHS	PYGMIES
PRECISE	PRICKLE	PROLATE	PSALMIC	PUNNETS	PYJAMAS
PRECOOK	PRICKLY	PRO-LIFE	PSALTER	PUNNING	PYLORUS
PREDATE	PRIDING	PROLINE	PSYCHED	PUNSTER	PYNCHON
PREDICT	PRIESTS	PROLONG	PSYCHES	PUNTERS	PYRALID
PREEMPT	PRIMACY	PROMISE	PSYCHIC	PUNTING	PYRAMID
PREENED	PRIMARY	PROMMER	PSYLLID	PUPPETS	PYRETIC
PREENER	PRIMATE	PROMOTE	PTERYLA	PUPPIES	PYREXIA
PREFABS	PRIMERS	PROMPTS	PTYALIN	PUPPING	PYRITES
PREFACE	PRIMINE	PRONATE	PUBERTY	PURCELL	PYRITIC
PREFECT	PRIMING	PRONOUN	PUBLISH	PURGING	PYROGEN
PREHEAT	PRIMMER	PROOFED	PUCCOON	PURISTS	PYROSIS
PRELACY	PRIMULA	PROPANE	PUCKERS	PURITAN	PYRRHIC
PRELATE	PRINCES	PROPEND	PUCKISH	PURLIEU	PYRROLE
PRELIMS	PRINKER	PROPENE	PUDDING	PURLING	PYTHONS
PRELUDE	PRINTED	PROPHET	PUDDLED	PURLOIN	
PREMIER	PRINTER	PROPOSE	PUDDLER	PURPLES	**Q**
PREMISE	PRISING	PROPPED	PUDDLES	PURPORT	Q-FACTOR
PREMISS	PRISONS	PRO RATA	PUDENDA	PURPOSE	QINGDAO
PREMIUM	PRITHEE	PROSAIC	PUDGIER	PURPURA	QUACKED
PREPACK	PRIVACY	PROSIER	PUDGILY	PURPURE	QUADRAT
PREPAID	PRIVATE	PROSILY	PUERILE	PURRING	QUADRIC
PREPARE	PRIVIER	PROSODY	PUFFERY	PURSERS	QUAFFER
PREPONE	PRIVIES	PROSPER	PUFFIER	PURSING	QUAILED
PREPOSE	PRIVILY	PROTEAN	PUFFILY	PURSUED	QUAKERS
PREPUCE	PRIVITY	PROTECT	PUFFING	PURSUER	QUAKILY

QUAKING	QUININE	RAGBAGS	RANGING	RAVENNA	RECEDED
QUALIFY	QUINONE	RAGGING	RANGOON	RAVE-UPS	RECEIPT
QUALITY	QUINTAL	RAGOUTS	RANKERS	RAVINES	RECEIVE
QUANGOS	QUINTAN	RAGTAIL	RANKING	RAVINGS	RECIPES
QUANTAL	QUINTET	RAGTIME	RANKLED	RAVIOLI	RECITAL
QUANTIC	QUINTIC	RAGWEED	RANSACK	RAW DEAL	RECITED
QUANTUM	QUIPPED	RAG WEEK	RANSOMS	RAWHIDE	RECITER
QUARREL	QUITTED	RAGWORM	RANTERS	RAWNESS	RECKING
QUARTAN	QUITTER	RAGWORT	RANTING	RAZZLES	RECLAIM
QUARTER	QUITTOR	RAIDERS	RAPHIDE	REACHED	RECLINE
QUARTET	QUIVERS	RAIDING	RAPIDLY	REACHER	RECLUSE
QUARTIC	QUIVERY	RAILING	RAPIERS	REACHES	RECORDS
QUARTOS	QUI VIVE	RAILWAY	RAPISTS	REACTED	RECOUNT
QUASARS	QUIZZED	RAIMENT	RAPPING	REACTOR	RECOVER
QUASHED	QUIZZER	RAINBOW	RAPPORT	READERS	RECRUIT
QUASSIA	QUIZZES	RAINIER	RAPTURE	READIED	RECTIFY
QUAVERS	QUONDAM	RAINILY	RAREBIT	READIER	RECTORS
QUAVERY	QUORATE	RAINING	RASBORA	READIES	RECTORY
QUAYAGE	QUORUMS	RAINOUT	RASCALS	READILY	RECTRIX
QUECHUA	QUOTHED	RAISERS	RASHERS	READING	RECTUMS
QUEENED	QUOTING	RAISING	RASHEST	READOUT	RECURVE
QUEENLY		RAISINS	RASPING	REAGENT	RECYCLE
QUEERED	**R**	RAISINY	RATABLE	REALGAR	RED BOOK
QUEERER	RABBITS	RAKE-OFF	RATABLY	REALIGN	RED CARD
QUEERLY	RABBLER	RALEIGH	RATAFIA	REALISM	REDCOAT
QUELLED	RABBLES	RALLIED	RAT-A-	REALIST	RED DEER
QUELLER	RACCOON	RALLIER	TAT	REALITY	REDDEST
QUERIED	RACEMIC	RALLIES	RATBAGS	REALIZE	REDDISH
QUERIES	RACHIAL	RALLINE	RATCHET	REALTOR	REDFISH
QUERIST	RACIEST	RAMADAN	RATE-CAP	REAMERS	RED FLAG
QUESTED	RACISTS	RAMBLED	RATINGS	REAMING	REDFORD
QUESTER	RACKETS	RAMBLER	RATIONS	REAPERS	REDHEAD
QUETZAL	RACKETY	RAMBLES	RATLINE	REAPING	RED MEAT
QUEUING	RACKING	RAMEKIN	RATPACK	REARING	REDNECK
QUIBBLE	RACOONS	RAMMING	RAT RACE	REARMED	REDNESS
QUICHES	RACQUET	RAMMISH	RATTIER	REASONS	REDOING
QUICKEN	RADIALS	RAMPAGE	RATTILY	REBADGE	REDOUBT
QUICKER	RADIANT	RAMPANT	RATTING	REBATER	REDOUND
QUICKIE	RADIATE	RAMPART	RATTISH	REBATES	REDPOLL
QUICKLY	RADICAL	RAMPION	RATTLED	REBIRTH	REDRAFT
QUIETEN	RADICEL	RAM RAID	RATTLES	REBOUND	REDRESS
QUIETER	RADICES	RAMRODS	RAT TRAP	REBRAND	REDROOT
QUIETLY	RADICLE	RAMSONS	RAUCOUS	REBUFFS	REDSKIN
QUIETUS	RADIOED	RANCHER	RAUNCHY	REBUILD	RED SPOT
QUILMES	RADULAR	RANCHES	RAVAGED	REBUILT	RED TAPE
QUILTED	RAFFISH	RANCOUR	RAVAGER	REBUKED	REDUCED
QUILTER	RAFFLED	RANDERS	RAVAGES	REBUKER	REDUCER
QUIMPER	RAFFLER	RANDIER	RAVELED	REBUKES	REDWING
QUINARY	RAFFLES	RANDOMS	RAVELIN	REBUSES	REDWOOD
QUINATE	RAFTERS	RANGERS	RAVELLY	RECALLS	REEDIER
QUINCES	RAFTING	RANGILY	RAVENER	RECAPED	REEDING

REEFERS	REISSUE	REPASTS	RESTING	REVIVAL	RIGHTER
REEFING	REJECTS	REPEATS	RESTIVE	REVIVED	RIGHTLY
REEKING	REJOICE	REPINED	RESTOCK	REVIVER	RIGHT-ON
RE-ELECT	RELAPSE	REPLACE	RESTORE	REVOICE	RIGIDLY
REELING	RELATED	REPLAYS	RESTYLE	REVOKED	RIG-OUTS
REELMAN	RELATER	REPLETE	RESULTS	REVOKER	RIM-FIRE
RE-ENTER	RELATOR	REPLEVY	RESUMED	REVOLTS	RIMLESS
RE-ENTRY	RELATUM	REPLICA	RESUMES	REVOLVE	RIMMING
REFACED	RELAXED	REPLIED	RETABLE	REVVING	RIMROCK
REFEREE	RELAXER	REPLIER	RETAKEN	REWARDS	RINGENT
REFILLS	RELAXIN	REPLIES	RETAKER	REWIRED	RINGERS
REFINED	RELAYED	REPORTS	RETAKES	REWRITE	RINGING
REFINER	RELEASE	REPOSAL	RETCHED	REWROTE	RINGLET
REFLATE	RELIANT	REPOSED	RETHINK	REYNOSA	RINSING
REFLECT	RELIEFS	REPOSER	RETICLE	RHAETIC	RIOT ACT
REFORMS	RELIEVE	REPOSIT	RETINAE	RHATANY	RIOTERS
REFRACT	RELINED	REPRESS	RETINAL	RHENIUM	RIOTING
REFRAIN	RELIVED	REPRINT	RETINAS	RHEUMIC	RIOTOUS
REFRESH	RELYING	REPRISE	RETINOL	RHIZOID	RIPCORD
REFUGEE	REMAINS	REPROOF	RETINUE	RHIZOME	RIPENED
REFUGES	REMAKES	REPROVE	RETIRED	RHODIUM	RIPENER
REFUNDS	REMANDS	REPTANT	RETIRER	RHOMBIC	RIP-OFFS
REFUSAL	REMARKS	REPTILE	RETITLE	RHOMBUS	RIPOSTE
REFUSED	REMARRY	REPULSE	RETORTS	RHONDDA	RIPPING
REFUSER	REMATCH	REPUTED	RETOUCH	RHUBARB	RIPPLED
REFUTED	REMNANT	REQUEST	RETRACE	RHYMING	RIPPLER
REFUTER	REMODEL	REQUIEM	RETRACT	RHYTHMS	RIPPLES
REGALIA	REMORSE	REQUIRE	RETREAD	RIBBAND	RIPPLET
REGALLY	REMOTER	REQUITE	RETREAT	RIBBING	RIPSAWS
REGARDS	REMOULD	REREDOS	RETRIAL	RIBBONS	RIPTIDE
REGATTA	REMOUNT	RESCIND	RETSINA	RIB CAGE	RISIBLE
REGENCY	REMOVAL	RESCUED	RETURNS	RIBWORT	RISIBLY
REGENTS	REMOVED	RESCUER	REUNIFY	RICHARD	RISINGS
REGIMEN	REMOVER	RESCUES	REUNION	RICHEST	RISKIER
REGIMES	REMOVES	RESERVE	REUNITE	RICHLER	RISKILY
REGINAS	RENAMED	RESHAPE	REUSING	RICHTER	RISKING
REGIONS	RENDELL	RESIDED	REVALUE	RICKETS	RISOTTO
REGNANT	RENDING	RESIDER	REVELED	RICKETY	RISSOLE
REGOSOL	RENEGED	RESIDUE	REVELRY	RICKING	RITUALS
REGRATE	RENEGER	RESKILL	REVENGE	RIDDING	RIVALED
REGRESS	RENEWAL	RESNAIS	REVENUE	RIDDLED	RIVALRY
REGRETS	RENEWED	RESOLVE	REVERED	RIDDLER	RIVETED
REGROUP	RENEWER	RESORTS	REVERER	RIDDLES	RIVETER
REGULAR	RENFREW	RESOUND	REVERIE	RIDGING	RIVIERA
REGULOS	RENTALS	RESPECT	REVERSE	RIDOTTO	RIVIERE
REGULUS	RENT BOY	RESPIRE	REVIEWS	RIFFLED	RIVULET
REHOUSE	RENTERS	RESPITE	REVILED	RIFFLER	ROACHES
REIFIER	RENTIER	RESPOND	REVILER	RIFLERY	ROADBED
REIGATE	RENTING	RESTAGE	REVISAL	RIFLING	ROAD HOG
REIGNED	REORDER	RESTATE	REVISED	RIGGING	ROADMAN
REINING	REPAIRS	RESTFUL	REVISER	RIGHTED	ROAD MAP

ROADMEN	ROOMIER	ROWLOCK	RUPTURE	SALLIES	SAO LUIS
ROAD TAX	ROOMILY	ROYALLY	RUSHDIE	SALLOWS	SAPHENA
ROADWAY	ROOMING	ROYALTY	RUSHING	SALMONS	SAPIENT
ROAMERS	ROOSTED	ROZZERS	RUSSIAN	SALOONS	SAPLESS
ROAMING	ROOSTER	RUBBERS	RUSTICS	SALPINX	SAPLING
ROARING	ROOTAGE	RUBBERY	RUSTIER	SALSIFY	SAPONIN
ROASTED	ROOTING	RUBBING	RUSTILY	SALTANT	SAPPERS
ROASTER	ROOTLET	RUBBISH	RUSTING	SALTBOX	SAPPIER
ROBBERS	ROPIEST	RUBDOWN	RUSTLED	SALTERN	SAPPILY
ROBBERY	RORAIMA	RUBELLA	RUSTLER	SALTIER	SAPPING
ROBBING	RORQUAL	RUBEOLA	RUTLAND	SALTILY	SAPPORO
ROBUSTA	ROSARIO	RUBICON	RUTTILY	SALTING	SAPROBE
ROCK BUN	ROSEATE	RUBIDIC	RUTTING	SALTIRE	SAPSAGO
ROCKERS	ROSEBUD	RUBIOUS	RUTTISH	SALTPAN	SAPWOOD
ROCKERY	ROSE HIP	RUBRICS	RYBINSK	SALTPOT	SARACEN
ROCKETS	ROSELLA	RUCHING		SALUTED	SARANSK
ROCKIER	ROSEOLA	RUCKING	**S**	SALUTER	SARATOV
ROCKIES	ROSETTA	RUCTION	SABBATH	SALUTES	SARAWAK
ROCKING	ROSETTE	RUDDERS	SACATON	SALVAGE	SARCASM
ROCKOON	ROSIEST	RUDDIER	SACCATE	SALVERS	SARCOID
RODENTS	ROSINED	RUDDILY	SACCULE	SALVING	SARCOMA
RODLIKE	ROSTERS	RUDERAL	SACHETS	SALVOES	SARCOUS
ROEBUCK	ROSTOCK	RUFFIAN	SACKING	SALWEEN	SARDINE
ROE DEER	ROSTRAL	RUFFLED	SADDEST	SAMISEN	SARDIUS
ROGUERY	ROSTRUM	RUFFLER	SADDLED	SAMNIUM	SARKIER
ROGUISH	ROTATED	RUFFLES	SADDLER	SAMOSAS	SARNIES
ROISTER	ROTATOR	RUINING	SADDLES	SAMOVAR	SARONGS
ROLL BAR	ROTIFER	RUINOUS	SADIRON	SAMOYED	SARONIC
ROLLERS	ROTORUA	RULABLE	SADISTS	SAMPANS	SASSABY
ROLLICK	ROTTERS	RULINGS	SADNESS	SAMPLED	SASSARI
ROLLING	ROTTING	RUMANIA	SAFARIS	SAMPLER	SASSIER
ROLLMOP	ROTUNDA	RUMBLED	SAFFIAN	SAMPLES	SASSING
ROLL-ONS	ROUBAIX	RUMBLER	SAFFRON	SAMPRAS	SATANIC
ROLL-TOP	ROUBLES	RUMBLES	SAFROLE	SAMURAI	SATCHEL
ROLLWAY	ROUGHEN	RUMMAGE	SAGGIER	SANCTUM	SATIATE
ROMAGNA	ROUGHER	RUMMEST	SAGGING	SANCTUS	SATIETY
ROMANCE	ROUGHLY	RUMOURS	SAGUARO	SANDALS	SATINET
ROMANIA	ROUGING	RUMPLED	SAHARAN	SANDBAG	SATIRES
ROMPERS	ROULEAU	RUNAWAY	SAILING	SANDBAR	SATISFY
ROMPING	ROULERS	RUNCORN	SAILORS	SANDBOX	SATSUMA
RONDEAU	ROUNDED	RUN DOWN	SAINTED	SANDERS	SATYRIC
RONDURE	ROUNDEL	RUN-DOWN	SAINTLY	SAND FLY	SATYRID
RONTGEN	ROUNDER	RUN INTO	SALAAMS	SANDIER	SAUCERS
ROOFING	ROUNDLY	RUNNELS	SALABLE	SANDING	SAUCIER
ROOFTOP	ROUNDUP	RUNNERS	SALAMIS	SANDPIT	SAUCILY
ROOINEK	ROUND UP	RUNNIER	SALERNO	SANGRIA	SAUCING
ROOKERY	ROUSING	RUNNING	SALFORD	SANICLE	SAUNTER
ROOKIES	ROUTINE	RUN-OFFS	SALICIN	SAN JOSE	SAURIAN
ROOKING	ROUTING	RUN OVER	SALIENT	SAN JUAN	SAUSAGE
ROOMERS	ROWDIER	RUNTISH	SALLIED	SAN REMO	SAUTEED
ROOMFUL	ROWDILY	RUNWAYS	SALLIER	SANTA FE	SAVABLE

SAVAGED	SCHEMES	SCREWER	SEASIDE	SELL-OUT	SESOTHO
SAVAGES	SCHERZO	SCREW UP	SEASONS	SELTZER	SESSILE
SAVANNA	SCHISMS	SCRIBAL	SEATING	SELVAGE	SESSION
SAVANTS	SCHLUMP	SCRIBER	SEATTLE	SEMATIC	SESTINA
SAVE-ALL	SCHMUCK	SCRIBES	SEAWALL	SEMINAL	SETBACK
SAVINGS	SCHOLAR	SCRIMPY	SEAWARE	SEMINAR	SET FREE
SAVIOUR	SCHOOLS	SCRIPTS	SEAWAYS	SEMITIC	SETLINE
SAVOURY	SCIATIC	SCROLLS	SEAWEED	SENATES	SETTEES
SAWBILL	SCIENCE	SCROOGE	SECEDED	SENATOR	SETTERS
SAWDUST	SCISSOR	SCROTUM	SECEDER	SENDERS	SETTING
SAWFISH	SCOFFED	SCRUBBY	SECLUDE	SENDING	SETTLED
SAWMILL	SCOFFER	SCRUFFS	SECONDO	SEND-OFF	SETTLER
SAWN-OFF	SCOLDED	SCRUFFY	SECONDS	SEND-UPS	SETTLES
SAXHORN	SCOLDER	SCRUMPY	SECRECY	SENEGAL	SEVENTH
SAXTUBA	SCOLLOP	SCRUNCH	SECRETE	SENIORS	SEVENTY
SAYINGS	SCONCES	SCRUPLE	SECRETS	SENORAS	SEVERAL
SCABBLE	SCOOPED	SCUDDED	SECTARY	SENSATE	SEVERED
SCABIES	SCOOPER	SCUFFED	SECTILE	SENSING	SEVILLE
SCALARS	SCOOTED	SCUFFLE	SECTION	SENSORS	SEXIEST
SCALDED	SCOOTER	SCULLED	SECTORS	SENSORY	SEXISTS
SCALENE	SCOPULA	SCULLER	SECULAR	SENSUAL	SEXLESS
SCALIER	SCORERS	SCULPIN	SECURED	SEPTATE	SEXPOTS
SCALING	SCORIFY	SCUMBLE	SECURER	SEPTETS	SEXTANT
SCALLOP	SCORING	SCUMMER	SEDATED	SEPTIME	SEXTETS
SCALPED	SCORNED	SCUPPER	SEDILIA	SEQUELA	SEXTILE
SCALPEL	SCORNER	SCUTATE	SEDUCED	SEQUELS	SEXTONS
SCALPER	SCORPER	SCUTTLE	SEDUCER	SEQUENT	SFUMATO
SCAMPER	SCORPIO	SCYTHED	SEEDBED	SEQUINS	SHAANXI
SCANDAL	SCOTOMA	SCYTHES	SEED BED	SEQUOIA	SHACKED
SCANDIC	SCOURED	SEABIRD	SEEDIER	SERAPHS	SHACKLE
SCANNED	SCOURER	SEACOCK	SEEDILY	SERBIAN	SHADIER
SCANNER	SCOURGE	SEA DOGS	SEEDING	SERFDOM	SHADILY
SCAPOSE	SCOUSES	SEAFOOD	SEEKERS	SERGIPE	SHADING
SCAPULA	SCOUTED	SEAGIRT	SEEKING	SERIALS	SHADOOF
SCARABS	SCOUTER	SEA GULL	SEEMING	SERIATE	SHADOWS
SCARCER	SCOWLED	SEAGULL	SEEPAGE	SERICIN	SHADOWY
SCARIER	SCOWLER	SEA-LANE	SEEPING	SERIEMA	SHAFTED
SCARIFY	SCRAGGY	SEALANT	SEESAWS	SERINGA	SHAGGED
SCARING	SCRAPED	SEA LEGS	SEETHED	SERIOUS	SHAHDOM
SCARLET	SCRAPER	SEALERS	SEGMENT	SERMONS	SHAKERS
SCARPER	SCRAPES	SEALERY	SEGOVIA	SERPENT	SHAKE UP
SCARRED	SCRAPPY	SEALING	SEISMIC	SERPIGO	SHAKE-UP
SCARVES	SCRATCH	SEA LION	SEIZING	SERRATE	SHAKHTY
SCATTED	SCRAWLS	SEAMARK	SEIZURE	SERRIED	SHAKIER
SCATTER	SCRAWLY	SEAMIER	SEKONDI	SERUMAL	SHAKILY
SCENERY	SCRAWNY	SEA MILE	SELENIC	SERVANT	SHAKING
SCENTED	SCREAMS	SEA MIST	SELFISH	SERVERS	SHALLOP
SCEPTIC	SCREECH	SEANCES	SELLERS	SERVERY	SHALLOT
SCEPTRE	SCREEDS	SEAPORT	SELLING	SERVICE	SHALLOW
SCHEMED	SCREENS	SEARING	SELL OFF	SERVILE	SHAMANS
SCHEMER	SCREWED	SEASICK	SELL OUT	SERVING	SHAMBLE

SHAMING	SHINGLE	SHRINKS	SIGHTLY	SIPHONS	SKITTER
SHAMMED	SHINGLY	SHRIVEL	SIGMATE	SIPPING	SKITTLE
SHAMMER	SHINIER	SHRIVER	SIGMOID	SIRLOIN	SKIVERS
SHAMPOO	SHINING	SHROUDS	SIGNALS	SIROCCO	SKIVING
SHANKLY	SHINNED	SHRUBBY	SIGNETS	SIRRAHS	SKULKED
SHANNON	SHIPPED	SHUCKED	SIGNIFY	SISSIER	SKULKER
SHANTOU	SHIPPER	SHUCKER	SIGNING	SISSIES	SKY BLUE
SHAPELY	SHIPWAY	SHUDDER	SIGN OFF	SISTERS	SKY-BLUE
SHAPING	SHIRKED	SHUFFLE	SIGNORA	SITCOMS	SKYCAPS
SHARERS	SHIRKER	SHUNNED	SIGNORE	SIT-DOWN	SKYDIVE
SHARING	SHITBAG	SHUNNER	SIGNORS	SITTERS	SKY-HIGH
SHARPEN	SHITTED	SHUNTED	SILENCE	SITTING	SKYJACK
SHARPER	SHIVERS	SHUNTER	SILENTS	SITUATE	SKYLARK
SHARPLY	SHIVERY	SHUSHED	SILESIA	SIXFOLD	SKYLINE
SHATTER	SHOCKED	SHUT-EYE	SILICIC	SIX-PACK	SKYSAIL
SHAVERS	SHOCKER	SHUT-OFF	SILICLE	SIXTEEN	SKYWALK
SHAVING	SHOEING	SHUTOUT	SILICON	SIXTIES	SLACKED
SHAWNEE	SHOGUNS	SHUTTER	SILIQUA	SIZABLE	SLACKEN
SHEARED	SHOOING	SHUTTLE	SILKIER	SIZZLED	SLACKER
SHEARER	SHOOTER	SHYLOCK	SILKILY	SIZZLER	SLACKLY
SHEATHE	SHOPPED	SHYNESS	SILLIER	SKATING	SLAGGED
SHEATHS	SHOPPER	SHYSTER	SILLIES	SKATOLE	SLAKING
SHEAVES	SHORING	SIALKOT	SILTING	SKEPTIC	SLALOMS
SHEBANG	SHORTED	SIALOID	SILURID	SKETCHY	SLAMMED
SHE BEAR	SHORTEN	SIAMANG	SILVERS	SKEWERS	SLANDER
SHEBEEN	SHORTER	SIAMESE	SILVERY	SKEWING	SLANGED
SHEDDER	SHORTIE	SIBERIA	SIMIANS	SKIABLE	SLANTED
SHEERED	SHORTLY	SIBLING	SIMILAR	SKIBOBS	SLAPPED
SHEERER	SHOTGUN	SICHUAN	SIMILES	SKIDDED	SLAPPER
SHEIKHS	SHOT PUT	SICKBAY	SIMIOUS	SKIDPAN	SLASHED
SHEILAS	SHOTTEN	SICKBED	SIMPERS	SKID ROW	SLASHER
SHEKELS	SHOUTED	SICKEST	SIMPLER	SKIFFLE	SLASHES
SHELLAC	SHOUTER	SICKING	SIMPLEX	SKI JUMP	SLATING
SHELLED	SHOVELS	SICKLES	SIMULAR	SKILFUL	SLATTED
SHELTER	SHOVING	SICK PAY	SINALOA	SKI LIFT	SLAVERS
SHELVED	SHOWERS	SIDEARM	SINCERE	SKILLED	SLAVERY
SHELVER	SHOWERY	SIDECAR	SINE DIE	SKILLET	SLAVING
SHELVES	SHOWIER	SIDE CAR	SINGING	SKIMMED	SLAVISH
SHEPARD	SHOWILY	SIDINGS	SINGLED	SKIMMER	SLAYERS
SHEPPEY	SHOWING	SIDLING	SINGLES	SKIMMIA	SLAYING
SHERBET	SHOWMAN	SIEMENS	SINGLET	SKIMPED	SLEDDED
SHERIFF	SHOWMEN	SIERRAN	SINITIC	SKINFUL	SLEDDER
SHERPAS	SHOWN UP	SIERRAS	SINKERS	SKINNED	SLEDGED
SHEWING	SHOW OFF	SIESTAS	SINKING	SKINNER	SLEDGES
SHIELDS	SHOW-OFF	SIEVERT	SINLESS	SKI POLE	SLEEKED
SHIFTED	SHRIEKS	SIEVING	SINNERS	SKIPPED	SLEEKER
SHIFTER	SHRIFTS	SIFTERS	SINNING	SKIPPER	SLEEKLY
SHIITES	SHRIKES	SIFTING	SINUATE	SKIPPET	SLEEPER
SHIKOKU	SHRILLY	SIGHING	SINUIJU	SKIPTON	SLEETED
SHIMMER	SHRIMPS	SIGHTED	SINUOUS	SKIRRET	SLEEVES
SHINDIG	SHRINES	SIGHTER	SINUSES	SKIRTED	SLEIGHS

SLEIGHT	SMALL AD	SNEEZED	SOBBING	SOOTHER	SPANKED
SLENDER	SMALLER	SNEEZER	SOBERED	SOOTIER	SPANKER
SLEUTHS	SMARTED	SNEEZES	SOBERLY	SOOTILY	SPANNED
SLEWING	SMARTEN	SNICKED	SOCAGER	SOPHISM	SPANNER
SLICING	SMARTER	SNICKER	SOCIALS	SOPHIST	SPARING
SLICKED	SMARTLY	SNIDELY	SOCIETY	SOPPIER	SPARKED
SLICKER	SMASHED	SNIDEST	SOCKETS	SOPPILY	SPARKLE
SLICKLY	SMASHER	SNIFFED	SOCKEYE	SOPPING	SPARRED
SLIDING	SMASHES	SNIFFER	SOCKING	SOPRANO	SPARROW
SLIGHTS	SMASH-UP	SNIFFLE	SODDING	SORBETS	SPARSER
SLIMIER	SMATTER	SNIFTER	SOD'S	SORBOSE	SPARTAN
SLIMILY	SMEARED	SNIGGER	LAW	SORCERY	SPASTIC
SLIMMED	SMEARER	SNIGGLE	SOFA BED	SORDINO	SPATHIC
SLIMMER	SMECTIC	SNIPERS	SOFTEST	SORGHUM	SPATIAL
SLINGER	SMELLED	SNIPING	SOFTIES	SORITES	SPATTER
SLIP-ONS	SMELTED	SNIPPED	SOGGIER	SOROSIS	SPATULA
SLIPPED	SMELTER	SNIPPET	SOGGILY	SORRIER	SPAWNED
SLIPPER	SMIDGIN	SNOGGED	SOILAGE	SORRILY	SPAWNER
SLIP-UPS	SMILING	SNOOKER	SOILING	SORROWS	SPAYING
SLIPWAY	SMIRKED	SNOOPED	SOIREES	SORTIES	SPEAKER
SLITHER	SMIRKER	SNOOPER	SOJOURN	SORTING	SPEARED
SLITTED	SMITING	SNOOZED	SOLACED	SORT-OUT	SPEARER
SLITTER	SMITTEN	SNOOZER	SOLACER	SO THERE	SPECIAL
SLIVERS	SMOKERS	SNOOZES	SOLACES	SOTTISH	SPECIES
SLOBBER	SMOKIER	SNORERS	SOLANUM	SOUFFLE	SPECIFY
SLOGANS	SMOKILY	SNORING	SOLARIA	SOUGHED	SPECKLE
SLOGGED	SMOKING	SNORKEL	SOLDIER	SOUKOUS	SPECTRA
SLOGGER	SMOLDER	SNORTED	SOLICIT	SOULFUL	SPECTRE
SLOPING	SMOTHER	SNORTER	SOLIDLY	SOUNDED	SPEEDED
SLOPPED	SMUDGED	SNOWCAP	SOLIDUS	SOUNDER	SPEEDER
SLOSHED	SMUDGES	SNOWIER	SOLOIST	SOUNDLY	SPELLED
SLOTTED	SMUGGER	SNOWILY	SOLOMON	SOUPCON	SPELLER
SLOTTER	SMUGGLE	SNOWING	SOLUBLE	SOUPFIN	SPELTER
SLOUCHY	SMUTCHY	SNOWMAN	SOLVATE	SOURCES	SPENCER
SLOUGHS	SNACKED	SNOWMEN	SOLVENT	SOUREST	SPENDER
SLOUGHY	SNAFFLE	SNUBBED	SOLVERS	SOURING	SPEWING
SLOVENE	SNAGGED	SNUBBER	SOLVING	SOURSOP	SPHENIC
SLOWEST	SNAKILY	SNUFFED	SOMALIA	SOUSING	SPHERAL
SLOWING	SNAKING	SNUFFER	SOMATIC	SOUTANE	SPHERES
SLUGGED	SNAPPED	SNUFFLE	SOMEDAY	SOUTHER	SPICATE
SLUICED	SNAPPER	SNUFFLY	SOMEHOW	SOVIETS	SPICERY
SLUICES	SNARING	SNUGGLE	SOMEONE	SOVKHOZ	SPICIER
SLUMBER	SNARLED	SOAKAGE	SOMEWAY	SOWETAN	SPICILY
SLUMMED	SNARLER	SOAKING	SOMITAL	SOZZLED	SPICING
SLUMMER	SNARL UP	SO-AND-	SONANCE	SPACING	SPICULE
SLUMPED	SNARL-UP	SO	SONATAS	SPANCEL	SPIDERS
SLURPED	SNATCHY	SOAPBOX	SONDAGE	SPANDEX	SPIDERY
SLURRED	SNEAKED	SOAPIER	SONGFUL	SPANGLE	SPIELER
SLYNESS	SNEAKER	SOAPILY	SONNETS	SPANGLY	SPIGNEL
SMACKED	SNEERED	SOAPING	SOOCHOW	SPANIEL	SPIGOTS
SMACKER	SNEERER	SOARING	SOOTHED	SPANISH	SPIKIER

SPIKILY	SPORRAN	SQUELCH	STANNIC	STEERER	STIPEND
SPIKING	SPORTED	SQUIDGY	STANZAS	STELLAR	STIPPLE
SPILLED	SPORTER	SQUIFFY	STAPLED	STEMMED	STIPULE
SPILLER	SPORULE	SQUILLA	STAPLER	STEMMER	STIR-FRY
SPINACH	SPOTLIT	SQUINCH	STAPLES	STEMSON	STIRRED
SPINDLE	SPOTTED	SQUINTS	STARCHY	STENCIL	STIRRER
SPINDLY	SPOTTER	SQUINTY	STARDOM	STEN GUN	STIRRUP
SPIN-DRY	SPOUSAL	SQUIRES	STARING	STENTOR	STOCKED
SPINETS	SPOUSES	SQUIRMS	STARKER	STEPDAD	STOCKER
SPINNER	SPOUTED	SQUIRMY	STARKLY	STEPMUM	STOICAL
SPINNEY	SPOUTER	SQUIRTS	STARLET	STEPPED	STOKERS
SPIN-OFF	SPRAINS	SQUISHY	STARLIT	STEPPER	STOKING
SPINOSE	SPRAINT	STABBED	STARRED	STEPPES	STOMACH
SPINOUS	SPRAWLS	STABBER	STARTED	STEPSON	STOMPED
SPIN OUT	SPRAWLY	STABILE	STARTER	STEPS UP	STOMPER
SPINULE	SPRAYED	STABLED	STARTLE	STEREOS	STONIER
SPIRAEA	SPRAYER	STABLES	START UP	STERILE	STONILY
SPIRALS	SPREADS	STACKED	STARVED	STERLET	STONING
SPIRANT	SPRIEST	STACKER	STARVER	STERNAL	STOOD UP
SPIREME	SPRIGGY	STADDLE	STASHED	STERNER	STOOGES
SPIRITS	SPRINGE	STADIUM	STASHES	STERNLY	STOOKER
SPIROID	SPRINGS	STAFFED	STATANT	STERNUM	STOOPED
SPIRULA	SPRINGY	STAFFER	STATELY	STEROID	STOOPER
SPITING	SPRINTS	STAGGER	STATICS	STERTOR	STOPGAP
SPITTER	SPRITES	STAGILY	STATING	STETSON	STOPING
SPITTLE	SPROUTS	STAGING	STATION	STEWARD	STOPPED
SPLASHY	SPRUCED	STAIDLY	STATISM	STEWART	STOPPER
SPLAYED	SPRUCES	STAINED	STATIST	STEWING	STORAGE
SPLEENS	SPUMONE	STAINER	STATIVE	STHENIC	STOREYS
SPLENIC	SPUMOUS	STAINES	STATUED	STIBINE	STORIED
SPLICED	SPURNED	STAKING	STATUES	STICHIC	STORIES
SPLICER	SPURNER	STALEST	STATURE	STICKER	STORING
SPLICES	SPURRED	STALING	STATUTE	STICKLE	STORMED
SPLINTS	SPURTED	STALKED	STAUNCH	STICK-ON	STOUTER
SPLODGE	SPUTNIK	STALKER	STAVING	STICK UP	STOUTLY
SPLODGY	SPUTTER	STALLED	STAYERS	STICK-UP	STOWAGE
SPLURGE	SQUABBY	STAMBUL	STAYING	STIFFEN	STOWING
SPOILED	SQUACCO	STAMENS	STEALER	STIFFER	STRAFED
SPOILER	SQUALID	STAMINA	STEALTH	STIFFLY	STRAFER
SPOKANE	SQUALLS	STAMMEL	STEAMED	STIFLED	STRAINS
SPONDEE	SQUALLY	STAMMER	STEAMER	STIFLER	STRAITS
SPONGED	SQUALOR	STAMPED	STEAM UP	STIGMAS	STRANDS
SPONGER	SQUARED	STAMPER	STEARIC	STILLED	STRANGE
SPONGES	SQUARER	STANCES	STEARIN	STILLER	STRATAL
SPONGIN	SQUARES	STANDBY	STEELED	STILTED	STRATAS
SPONSON	SQUASHY	STAND BY	STEEPED	STILTON	STRATUM
SPONSOR	SQUAWKS	STANDER	STEEPEN	STIMULI	STRATUS
SPOOFER	SQUEAKS	STAND-IN	STEEPER	STINGER	STRAYED
SPOOKED	SQUEAKY	STAND UP	STEEPLE	STINKER	STRAYER
SPOONED	SQUEALS	STAND-UP	STEEPLY	STINTED	STREAKS
SPOORER	SQUEEZE	STANLEY	STEERED	STINTER	STREAKY

STREAMS	STYLIST	SUCRASE	SUNROOF	SWANSEA	SYLPHIC
STREETS	STYLIZE	SUCROSE	SUNSETS	SWAPPED	SYLPHID
STRETCH	STYLOID	SUCTION	SUNSPOT	SWAPPER	SYLVITE
STRETTA	STYLOPS	SUDANIC	SUNSTAR	SWARMED	SYMBOLS
STRETTO	STYMIED	SUDBURY	SUNTANS	SWARTHY	SYMPTOM
STREWED	STYPSIS	SUDETES	SUNTRAP	SWATHED	SYNAPSE
STREWER	STYPTIC	SUFFICE	SUNWISE	SWATTED	SYNCARP
STREWTH	STYRENE	SUFFOLK	SUPPERS	SWATTER	SYNCHRO
STRIATE	SUAVELY	SUFFUSE	SUPPING	SWAYING	SYNCOPE
STRIDES	SUAVITY	SUGARED	SUPPLER	SWEARER	SYNERGY
STRIDOR	SUBACID	SUGGEST	SUPPORT	SWEATED	SYNESIS
STRIKER	SUB-AQUA	SUICIDE	SUPPOSE	SWEATER	SYNGAMY
STRIKES	SUBARID	SUITING	SUPREME	SWEDISH	SYNODAL
STRINGS	SUBBASE	SUITORS	SUPREMO	SWEEPER	SYNODIC
STRINGY	SUBBASS	SUKHUMI	SURBASE	SWEETEN	SYNONYM
STRIPED	SUBBING	SULCATE	SURCOAT	SWEETER	SYNOVIA
STRIPER	SUBDUAL	SULKIER	SURFACE	SWEETIE	SYPHONS
STRIPES	SUBDUCT	SULKILY	SURFEIT	SWEETLY	SYRINGA
STRIPEY	SUBDUED	SULKING	SURFERS	SWELLED	SYRINGE
STRIVEN	SUBEDIT	SULLAGE	SURFING	SWELTER	SYRPHID
STRIVER	SUBERIN	SULLIED	SURGEON	SWERVED	SYSTEMS
STROBIC	SUBFUSC	SULPHUR	SURGERY	SWERVER	SYSTOLE
STROKED	SUBJECT	SULTANA	SURGING	SWERVES	SZILARD
STROKES	SUBJOIN	SULTANS	SURINAM	SWIFTER	
STROLLS	SUBLIME	SUMATRA	SURLIER	SWIFTLY	**T**
STROPHE	SUBPLOT	SUMBAWA	SURLILY	SWIGGED	TABANID
STROPPY	SUB ROSA	SUMMAND	SURMISE	SWIGGER	TABASCO
STRUDEL	SUBSETS	SUMMARY	SURNAME	SWILLED	TABBIES
STUBBED	SUBSIDE	SUMMERS	SURPASS	SWILLER	TABBING
STUBBLE	SUBSIDY	SUMMERY	SURPLUS	SWIMMER	TABLEAU
STUBBLY	SUBSIST	SUMMING	SURREAL	SWINDLE	TABLING
STUCK-UP	SUBSOIL	SUMMITS	SURREYS	SWINDON	TABLOID
STUDDED	SUBSUME	SUMMONS	SURVEYS	SWINGER	TABORET
STUDENT	SUBTEND	SUNBEAM	SURVIVE	SWINGLE	TABORIN
STUDIED	SUBTEXT	SUNBEDS	SUSPECT	SWINISH	TABULAR
STUDIES	SUBTLER	SUNBELT	SUSPEND	SWIPING	TACHYON
STUDIOS	SUBTYPE	SUNBIRD	SUSSING	SWIPPLE	TACITLY
STUFFED	SUBUNIT	SUNBURN	SUSTAIN	SWIRLED	TACKIER
STUFFER	SUBURBS	SUNDAES	SUTURAL	SWISHED	TACKIES
STUMBLE	SUBVERT	SUNDAYS	SUTURED	SWISHER	TACKILY
STUMPED	SUBWAYS	SUNDIAL	SUTURES	SWISHES	TACKING
STUMPER	SUCCEED	SUNDOWN	SWABBED	SWIVELS	TACKLED
STUNNED	SUCCESS	SUNFISH	SWABBER	SWIZZLE	TACKLER
STUNNER	SUCCOUR	SUNGLOW	SWABIAN	SWOLLEN	TACKLES
STUNTED	SUCCUBI	SUN GODS	SWADDLE	SWOONED	TACNODE
STUPEFY	SUCCUMB	SUNLAMP	SWAGGER	SWOOPED	TACTFUL
STUPORS	SUCCUSS	SUNLESS	SWAHILI	SWOPPED	TACTICS
STUTTER	SUCKERS	SUNNIER	SWALLOW	SWOTTED	TACTILE
STYGIAN	SUCKING	SUNNILY	SWAMPED	SYCOSIS	TACTUAL
STYLING	SUCKLED	SUNNING	SWANKED	SYENITE	TADPOLE
STYLISH	SUCKLER	SUNRISE	SWANNED	SYLLABI	TADZHIK

TAFFETA	TANGLER	TAUNTED	TELEXES	TERRORS	THIMBLE
TAFFIES	TANGLES	TAUNTER	TELFORD	TERSELY	THIN AIR
TAGGERS	TANGOED	TAUNTON	TELLERS	TERTIAL	THINNED
TAGGING	TANGRAM	TAUREAN	TELLIES	TERTIAN	THINNER
TAG LINE	TANKAGE	TAURINE	TELLING	TESSERA	THIONIC
TAGMEME	TANKARD	TAUTEST	TELPHER	TESTACY	THIONYL
TAIL END	TANKERS	TAVENER	TELSTAR	TESTATE	THIRSTS
TAILING	TANNAGE	TAVERNS	TEMPERA	TEST BAN	THIRSTY
TAILORS	TANNATE	TAXABLE	TEMPERS	TESTERS	THISTLE
TAINTED	TANNERS	TAX-FREE	TEMPEST	TESTIER	THISTLY
TAIYUAN	TANNERY	TAXICAB	TEMPING	TESTIFY	THITHER
TAKABLE	TANNING	TAXIING	TEMPLES	TESTILY	THORITE
TAKEOFF	TANTRUM	TAXIWAY	TEMPTED	TESTING	THORIUM
TAKE OFF	TAN-TUNG	TBILISI	TEMPTER	TETANIC	THOUGHT
TAKEOUT	TAOISTS	TBILIZI	TENABLE	TETANUS	THRALLS
TAKE OUT	TAPERED	TEABAGS	TENANCY	TETHERS	THREADS
TAKEUPS	TAPERER	TEACAKE	TENANTS	TETRODE	THREADY
TAKINGS	TAPETAL	TEA CAKE	TENCHES	TEXTILE	THREATS
TALCOSE	TAPETUM	TEACHER	TENDERS	TEXTUAL	THREE
TALENTS	TAPHOLE	TEACH-IN	TENDING	TEXTURE	R'S
TALIBAN	TAPIOCA	TEA COSY	TENDONS	THALLIC	THRIFTS
TALIPED	TAPPETS	TEACUPS	TENDRIL	THALLUS	THRIFTY
TALIPES	TAPPING	TEA GOWN	TENFOLD	THANKED	THRILLS
TALIPOT	TAPROOM	TEALEAF	TENNERS	THAWING	THRIVED
TALKERS	TAPROOT	TEAMING	TENONER	THE ARTS	THROATS
TALKIES	TARANTO	TEAPOTS	TENPINS	THEATRE	THROATY
TALKING	TARDIER	TEARFUL	TENSELY	THE BARD	THRONES
TALLAGE	TARDILY	TEAR GAS	TENSEST	THEISTS	THRONGS
TALLBOY	TARGETS	TEARING	TENSILE	THEOREM	THROUGH
TALLEST	TARIFFS	TEAROOM	TENSING	THERAPY	THROWER
TALLIED	TARMACS	TEASELS	TENSION	THEREAT	THROW IN
TALLIER	TARNISH	TEASERS	TENSIVE	THEREBY	THROW-IN
TALLIES	TARRASA	TEASHOP	TENTAGE	THEREIN	THRUSTS
TALLINN	TARRIED	TEASING	TENUITY	THEREOF	THRUWAY
TALLISH	TARRING	TEA TREE	TENUOUS	THEREON	THUDDED
TALLYHO	TARSIER	TECHILY	TEPIDLY	THERETO	THULIUM
TAMABLE	TARTANS	TECHNIC	TEQUILA	THERMAL	THUMBED
TAMARAU	TARTARS	TECTRIX	TERBIUM	THERMIC	THUMPED
TAMARIN	TASSELS	TEDIOUS	TERMING	THERMIT	THUMPER
TAMBOUR	TASTERS	TEEMING	TERMINI	THERMOS	THUNDER
TAMPERE	TASTIER	TEENAGE	TERMITE	THEROID	THURGAU
TAMPICO	TASTILY	TEEPEES	TERNARY	THEROUX	THWACKS
TAMPING	TASTING	TEGULAR	TERNATE	THEURGY	THYMINE
TAMPONS	TATOUAY	TEHERAN	TERPENE	THE WASH	THYROID
TANAGER	TATTERS	TEKTITE	TERRACE	THICKEN	THYRSUS
TANBARK	TATTIER	TELAMON	TERRAIN	THICKER	THYSELF
TANDEMS	TATTILY	TEL AVIV	TERRANE	THICKET	TIANJIN
TANGELO	TATTING	TELEOST	TERRENE	THICKIE	TIBETAN
TANGENT	TATTLED	TELERAN	TERRIER	THICKLY	TICKERS
TANGIER	TATTLER	TELESIS	TERRIFY	THIEVED	TICKETS
TANGLED	TATTOOS	TELEXED	TERRINE	THIEVES	TICKING

TICKLED	TIPPERS	TOLLING	TORREFY	TRADE IN	TRELLIS
TICKLER	TIPPETT	TOLUATE	TORRENT	TRADE-IN	TREMBLE
TICKLES	TIPPING	TOLUENE	TORREON	TRADERS	TREMBLY
TIDBITS	TIPPLER	TOMBOLA	TORSADE	TRADING	TREMOLO
TIDDLER	TIPPLES	TOMBOLO	TORSION	TRADUCE	TREMORS
TIDEWAY	TIPSIER	TOMBOYS	TORTOLA	TRAFFIC	TRENTON
TIDIEST	TIPSILY	TOMCATS	TORTONI	TRAGEDY	TREPANG
TIDINGS	TIPSTER	TOMFOOL	TORTUGA	TRAILED	TRESSES
TIDYING	TIPTOED	TOM-TOMS	TORTURE	TRAILER	TRESTLE
TIE-DIED	TIPTOES	TONEPAD	TORYISM	TRAINED	TREVISO
TIEPINS	TIRADES	TONETIC	TOSSING	TRAINEE	TRIABLE
TIFFANY	TIREDLY	TONGUES	TOSS-UPS	TRAINER	TRIACID
TIGHTEN	TISSUES	TONIGHT	TOTALED	TRAIPSE	TRIADIC
TIGHTER	TITANIA	TONNAGE	TOTALLY	TRAITOR	TRIBADE
TIGHTLY	TITANIC	TONNEAU	TOTE BAG	TRAJECT	TRIBUNE
TIGRESS	TITBITS	TONSILS	TOTEMIC	TRAMCAR	TRIBUTE
TIJUANA	TITFERS	TONSURE	TOTTERY	TRAMMEL	TRICEPS
TILAPIA	TITHING	TONTINE	TOTTING	TRAMPED	TRICKED
TILBURG	TITMICE	TOOLING	TOUCANS	TRAMPER	TRICKER
TILLAGE	TITOISM	TOOTING	TOUCHED	TRAMPLE	TRICKLE
TILLERS	TITOIST	TOOTLED	TOUCHER	TRAMWAY	TRICKLY
TILLING	TITRANT	TOOTLER	TOUCHES	TRANCES	TRICKSY
TILTING	TITRATE	TOOTLES	TOUGHEN	TRANCHE	TRICORN
TIMBALE	TITTERS	TOOTSIE	TOUGHER	TRANSIT	TRIDENT
TIMBERS	TITTIES	TOPARCH	TOUGHLY	TRANSOM	TRIDUUM
TIMBREL	TITULAR	TOPAZES	TOUPEES	TRAPANI	TRIED ON
TIMBRES	TIZZIES	TOPCOAT	TOURACO	TRAPEZE	TRIESTE
TIME LAG	TLEMCEN	TOP DOGS	TOURING	TRAPPED	TRIFLED
TIME-OUT	TOADIED	TOP HATS	TOURISM	TRAPPER	TRIFLER
TIMIDLY	TOADIES	TOPIARY	TOURIST	TRASHED	TRIFLES
TIMPANI	TOADLET	TOPICAL	TOURNAI	TRAUMAS	TRIGGER
TINAMOU	TOASTED	TOPKNOT	TOURNEY	TRAVAIL	TRILLED
TINFOIL	TOASTER	TOPLESS	TOUSLED	TRAVELS	TRILOGY
TINGING	TOASTIE	TOPMAST	TOUTING	TRAVOIS	TRIMBLE
TINGLED	TOBACCO	TOPMOST	TOWARDS	TRAWLED	TRIMMED
TINGLER	TOBOLSK	TOPONYM	TOWBOAT	TRAWLER	TRIMMER
TIN GODS	TOBY JUG	TOPPERS	TOWELED	TREACLE	TRINARY
TIN HATS	TOCCATA	TOPPING	TOWERED	TREACLY	TRINITY
TINIEST	TOCSINS	TOPPLED	TOWHEAD	TREADER	TRINKET
TINKERS	TODDIES	TOPSAIL	TOWLINE	TREADLE	TRIOLET
TINKLED	TODDLED	TOPSIDE	TOWPATH	TREAD ON	TRIPLED
TINKLES	TODDLER	TOPSOIL	TOWROPE	TREASON	TRIPLET
TINNIER	TOE CAPS	TOPSPIN	TOW ROPE	TREATED	TRIPLEX
TINNILY	TOEHOLD	TORCHES	TRABZON	TREATER	TRIPODS
TINNING	TOENAIL	TORFAEN	TRACERS	TREBLED	TRIPODY
TINTACK	TOFFEES	TORMENT	TRACERY	TREBLES	TRIPOLI
TINTING	TOGGING	TORNADO	TRACHEA	TREFOIL	TRIPPED
TINTYPE	TOGGLES	TORONTO	TRACING	TREHALA	TRIPPER
TINWARE	TOHEROA	TORPEDO	TRACKED	TREKKED	TRIPPET
TINWORK	TOILETS	TORQUAY	TRACKER	TREKKER	TRIPURA
TIP-OFFS	TOILING	TORQUES	TRACTOR	TREKKIE	TRIREME

TRISECT	TRUSTED	TURNERS	TWOSOME	UNCHAIN	UNPAGED
TRISMIC	TRUSTEE	TURNERY	TWO-STAR	UNCINUS	UNPOSED
TRISMUS	TRUSTER	TURNING	TWO-STEP	UNCIVIL	UNQUIET
TRISOME	TRYPSIN	TURNIPS	TWO-TIME	UNCLASP	UNQUOTE
TRISOMY	TRYPTIC	TURNKEY	TWO-TONE	UNCLEAN	UNRAVEL
TRITELY	TRYSAIL	TURN OFF	TYCHISM	UNCLEAR	UNREADY
TRITIUM	TRYSTER	TURN-OFF	TYCOONS	UNCLOAK	UNREEVE
TRITONE	TSARDOM	TURN-ONS	TYLOSIS	UNCLOSE	UNSCREW
TRIUMPH	TSARINA	TURN OUT	TYMPANA	UNCOUTH	UNSLING
TRIVETS	TSARIST	TURNOUT	TYMPANY	UNCOVER	UNSNARL
TRIVIAL	T-SHIRTS	TURNS UP	TYNWALD	UNCROSS	UNSOUND
TROCHAL	T-SQUARE	TURN-UPS	TYPEBAR	UNCTION	UNSTICK
TROCHEE	TSUNAMI	TURPETH	TYPESET	UNDERDO	UNSTRAP
TRODDEN	TUATARA	TURRETS	TYPHOID	UNDERGO	UNSTUCK
TROIKAS	TUBBIER	TURTLER	TYPHOON	UNDOING	UNSWEAR
TROJANS	TUBBING	TURTLES	TYPHOUS	UNDRESS	UNTHINK
TROLLED	TUBIFEX	TUSCANY	TYPICAL	UNDYING	UNTRIED
TROLLEY	TUBULAR	TUSKERS	TYPISTS	UNEARTH	UNTRUSS
TROLLOP	TUCKING	TUSSIVE	TYRANNY	UNEQUAL	UNTRUTH
TROMMEL	TUCUMAN	TUSSLED	TYRANTS	UNFROCK	UNTYING
TROOPED	TUESDAY	TUSSLES	TYRONIC	UNFUSSY	UNUSUAL
TROOPER	TUGGING	TUSSOCK	TZARINA	UNGODLY	UNVOICE
TROPHIC	TUITION	TUTORED		UNGUENT	UNWAGED
TROPICS	TUMBLED	TUTUILA	**U**	UNGULAR	UNWOUND
TROPISM	TUMBLER	TUTUOLA	UDAIPUR	UNHAPPY	UP-AND-
TROTTED	TUMBLES	TUXEDOS	UGANDAN	UNHEARD	UP
TROTTER	TUMBREL	TWADDLE	UGLIEST	UNHINGE	UPBRAID
TROUBLE	TUMMIES	TWANGED	UKRAINE	UNHORSE	UPBUILD
TROUGHS	TUMOURS	TWEAKED	UKULELE	UNICORN	UPCHUCK
TROUNCE	TUMULAR	TWEETED	ULANOVA	UNIFIED	UPDATED
TROUPER	TUMULTS	TWEETER	ULAN-UDE	UNIFIER	UPDATER
TROUPES	TUMULUS	TWELFTH	ULLAGED	UNIFORM	UPDATES
TROUSER	TUNABLE	TWELVES	ULULANT	UNITARY	UPDRAFT
TROWELS	TUNEFUL	TWIDDLE	ULULATE	UNITIES	UPENDED
TRUANCY	TUNICLE	TWIDDLY	UMBRAGE	UNITING	UPFRONT
TRUANTS	TUNISIA	TWIGGED	UMBRIAN	UNITIVE	UP FRONT
TRUCKED	TUNNELS	TWIN BED	UMBRIEL	UNKEMPT	UPGRADE
TRUCKER	TUNNIES	TWINGES	UMLAUTS	UNKNOWN	UPHEAVE
TRUCKLE	TUPPING	TWINING	UMPIRED	UNLATCH	UPLANDS
TRUDGED	TURBANS	TWINKLE	UMPIRES	UNLEARN	UPPSALA
TRUDGEN	TURBARY	TWINNED	UMPTEEN	UNLEASH	UPRAISE
TRUDGER	TURBINE	TWIN SET	UNAIDED	UNLOOSE	UPRIGHT
TRUDGES	TURBOTS	TWIRLED	UNARMED	UNLUCKY	UPRISER
TRUFFLE	TURDINE	TWIRLER	UNAWARE	UNMAKER	UPRIVER
TRUISMS	TUREENS	TWISTED	UNBONED	UNMANLY	UPSCALE
TRUMPED	TURFING	TWISTER	UNBOSOM	UNMEANT	UPSILON
TRUMPET	TURGITE	TWITTED	UNBOUND	UNMORAL	UPSKILL
TRUNDLE	TURKEYS	TWITTER	UNBOWED	UNMOVED	UPSTAGE
TRUSSED	TURKISH	TWIZZLE	UNBRACE	UNNAMED	UPSTART
TRUSSER	TURKMEN	TWOFOLD	UNCAGED	UNNERVE	UPSURGE
TRUSSES	TURMOIL	TWONESS	UNCANNY	UNOWNED	UPSWEEP

UPSWING	UTTERED	VARMINT	VERMONT	VILNIUS	VOCALLY
UPTAKES	UTTERER	VARNISH	VERNIER	VINASSE	VOCODER
UPTHROW	UTTERLY	VARSITY	VERONAL	VINEGAR	VOETSEK
UPTIGHT	UVEITIC	VARYING	VERRUCA	VINTAGE	VOICING
UP TO	UVEITIS	VASSALS	VERSACE	VINTNER	VOIDING
YOU	UVULARS	VASTITY	VERSANT	VIOLATE	VOIOTIA
UPTURNS	UXORIAL	VATICAN	VERSIFY	VIOLENT	VOLAPUK
UPWARDS		VAUDOIS	VERSION	VIOLETS	VOLCANO
URAEMIA	**V**	VAULTED	VERTIGO	VIOLINS	VOLLEYS
URAEMIC	VACANCY	VAULTER	VERVAIN	VIOLIST	VOLOGDA
URALITE	VACATED	VAUNTED	VESICAL	VIRAGOS	VOLTAGE
URANIAN	VACCINE	VAUNTER	VESICLE	VIRELAY	VOLTAIC
URANIDE	VACUITY	VECTORS	VESPERS	VIRGATE	VOLUBLE
URANITE	VACUOLE	VEDALIA	VESPINE	VIRGINS	VOLUBLY
URANIUM	VACUOUS	VEDDOID	VESSELS	VIRGOAN	VOLUMED
URANOUS	VACUUMS	VEDETTE	VESTIGE	VIRGULE	VOLUMES
URCHINS	VAGINAL	VEERING	VESTING	VIRTUAL	VOLVATE
UREDIAL	VAGINAS	VEGETAL	VESTRAL	VIRTUES	VOMITED
UREDIUM	VAGRANT	VEHICLE	VESTURE	VIRUSES	VOMITER
URETHRA	VAGUELY	VEILING	VETCHES	VISAGES	VOMITUS
URGENCY	VAINEST	VEINING	VETERAN	VISAING	VORLAGE
URIDINE	VALANCE	VEINLET	VETIVER	VIS-A-	VOTABLE
URINALS	VALENCE	VELAMEN	VETOING	VIS	VOUCHED
URINANT	VALENCY	VELIGER	VETTING	VISAYAN	VOUCHER
URINARY	VALERIC	VELLORE	VEXEDLY	VISCERA	VOX POPS
URINATE	VALIANT	VELOURS	VIADUCT	VISCOID	VOYAGED
URINOUS	VALIDLY	VELVETY	VIBRANT	VISCOSE	VOYAGER
URMSTON	VALISES	VENALLY	VIBRATE	VISCOUS	VOYAGES
URNLIKE	VALLEYS	VENATIC	VIBRATO	VISIBLE	VOYEURS
URODELE	VALONIA	VENDACE	VICENZA	VISIBLY	VULGATE
UROLITH	VALUERS	VENDING	VICEROY	VISIONS	VULPINE
UROLOGY	VALUING	VENDORS	VICINAL	VISITED	VULTURE
URUAPAN	VALVATE	VENEERS	VICIOUS	VISITOR	
URUGUAY	VALVULE	VENISON	VICOMTE	VISTAED	**W**
URUMCHI	VAMOOSE	VENTAGE	VICTIMS	VISTULA	WADABLE
USELESS	VAMPIRE	VENTING	VICTORS	VITALLY	WADDING
USHERED	VANADIC	VENTRAL	VICTORY	VITAMIN	WADDLED
USUALLY	VANDALS	VENTURE	VICTRIX	VITEBSK	WADDLER
USURERS	VANILLA	VENULAR	VICTUAL	VITIATE	WADDLES
USURPED	VANTAGE	VERANDA	VICUNAS	VITORIA	WAFFLED
USURPER	VANUATU	VERBENA	VIDEOED	VITRAIN	WAFFLES
UTENSIL	VANWARD	VERBIFY	VIDICON	VITRIFY	WAFTAGE
UTERINE	VAPIDLY	VERBOSE	VIETNAM	VITRINE	WAFTING
UTILITY	VAPOURS	VERDANT	VIEWERS	VITRIOL	WAGERED
UTILIZE	VARIANT	VERDICT	VIEWING	VITTATE	WAGERER
UT INFRA	VARIATE	VERDURE	VIKINGS	VIVIDLY	WAGGING
UTOPIAN	VARIETY	VERGERS	VILLACH	VIYELLA	WAGGISH
UTOPIAS	VARIOLA	VERGING	VILLAGE	VIZIERS	WAGGLED
UTRECHT	VARIOLE	VERGLAS	VILLAIN	V-NECKED	WAGGLES
UTRICLE	VARIOUS	VERISMO	VILLEIN	VOCABLE	WAGONER
UT SUPRA	VARLETS	VERMEIL	VILLOUS	VOCALIC	WAGTAIL

WAILFUL	WAR GAME	WAXWING	WELLING	WHIFFLE	WIGWAMS
WAILING	WARHEAD	WAXWORK	WELL-OFF	WHILING	WILDCAT
WAISTED	WARIEST	WAYBILL	WELL-SET	WHIMPER	WILD DOG
WAITERS	WARLIKE	WAYLAID	WELSHED	WHINERS	WILDEST
WAITING	WARLOCK	WAYLAIN	WELSHER	WHINGED	WILDING
WAIVERS	WARLORD	WAYSIDE	WEMBLEY	WHINING	WILIEST
WAIVING	WARMEST	WAYWARD	WENCHED	WHIPPED	WILLIES
WAKEFUL	WARMING	WEAKEST	WENCHER	WHIPPER	WILLING
WAKENED	WARM-UPS	WEALTHY	WENCHES	WHIPPET	WILLOWS
WAKENER	WARNING	WEANING	WENDING	WHIPSAW	WILLOWY
WALCOTT	WARPAGE	WEAPONS	WENDISH	WHIRLED	WILTING
WALKERS	WARPATH	WEARIED	WEST END	WHIRLER	WIMPIES
WALKIES	WARPING	WEARIER	WESTERN	WHIRRED	WIMPISH
WALKING	WARRANT	WEARILY	WESTING	WHISKED	WIMPLES
WALKMAN	WARRENS	WEARING	WET-LOOK	WHISKER	WINCHED
WALK OFF	WARRING	WEASELS	WETNESS	WHISKEY	WINCHER
WALK-ONS	WARRIOR	WEATHER	WET SUIT	WHISPER	WINCHES
WALKOUT	WARSHIP	WEAVERS	WETTEST	WHISTLE	WINCING
WALK-UPS	WARTHOG	WEAVING	WETTING	WHITEST	WINDAGE
WALLABY	WARTIME	WEBBING	WETTISH	WHITHER	WINDBAG
WALLAHS	WARWICK	WEBFOOT	WEXFORD	WHITING	WINDIER
WALLETS	WASHDAY	WEBSITE	WHACKED	WHITLOW	WINDILY
WALLEYE	WASHERS	WEB-TOED	WHACKER	WHITSUN	WINDING
WALLIES	WASHERY	WEDDING	WHALERS	WHITTLE	WINDOWS
WALLING	WASHING	WEDGING	WHALING	WHIZZED	WINDROW
WALLOON	WASHOUT	WEDLOCK	WHANGEE	WHIZZES	WINDSOR
WALLOPS	WASHTUB	WEEDIER	WHARVES	WHOEVER	WINE BAR
WALLOWS	WASPILY	WEEDILY	WHAT FOR	WHOOPED	WINGERS
WALNUTS	WASPISH	WEEDING	WHATNOT	WHOOPEE	WINGING
WALSALL	WASSAIL	WEEKDAY	WHATSIT	WHOOPER	WINGLET
WALTZED	WASTAGE	WEEKEND	WHEATEN	WHOPPED	WING NUT
WALTZER	WASTERS	WEENIER	WHEEDLE	WHOPPER	WINKERS
WALTZES	WASTING	WEEPING	WHEELED	WHORISH	WINKING
WANGLED	WASTREL	WEEVILS	WHEELER	WHORLED	WINKLED
WANGLER	WATCHED	WEEVILY	WHEELIE	WHYALLA	WINKLES
WANGLES	WATCHER	WEIGELA	WHEEZED	WICHITA	WINLESS
WANKERS	WATCHES	WEIGHED	WHEEZER	WICKETS	WINNERS
WANKING	WATERED	WEIGHER	WHEEZES	WICKING	WINNING
WANNABE	WATERER	WEIGHTS	WHEREAS	WICKLOW	WINSOME
WANNESS	WATFORD	WEIGHTY	WHEREAT	WIDE BOY	WINTERS
WANNEST	WATTAGE	WEIRDER	WHEREBY	WIDENED	WIRETAP
WANNING	WATTEAU	WEIRDIE	WHEREIN	WIDENER	WIRIEST
WANT ADS	WATTLES	WEIRDLY	WHEREOF	WIDGEON	WISBECH
WANTING	WAVELET	WEIRDOS	WHEREON	WIDOWED	WISE GUY
WAPITIS	WAVEOFF	WELCHED	WHERETO	WIDOWER	WISHFUL
WARBLED	WAVERED	WELCOME	WHERRIT	WIELDED	WISHING
WARBLER	WAVERER	WELDERS	WHETHER	WIELDER	WISPIER
WARDENS	WAVIEST	WELDING	WHETTED	WIGGING	WISPILY
WARDERS	WAXBILL	WELFARE	WHETTER	WIGGLED	WISTFUL
WARDING	WAXIEST	WELL-FED	WHICKER	WIGGLER	WITCHES
WARFARE	WAXLIKE	WELLIES	WHIFFER	WIGGLES	WITHERS

WITHOUT	WORKERS	WRESTER	XEROXES	YIELDER	ZENITHS
WITLESS	WORKING	WRESTLE	XIPHOID	YINGKOU	ZEOLITE
WITNESS	WORKMAN	WREXHAM	X-RAYING	YINGKOW	ZEPHYRS
WITTIER	WORKMEN	WRIGGLE		YODELED	ZERMATT
WITTILY	WORKOUT	WRIGGLY	**Y**	YOGHURT	ZEROING
WIZARDS	WORKSHY	WRINGER	YACHTIE	YONKERS	ZESTFUL
WIZENED	WORKSOP	WRINKLE	YAKKING	YORKIST	ZHDANOV
WOBBLED	WORKTOP	WRINKLY	YAKUTSK	YORUBAN	ZIGZAGS
WOBBLER	WORLDLY	WRITE-IN	YANGTZE	YOUNGER	ZILLION
WOBBLES	WORMIER	WRITERS	YANKEES	YOWLING	ZINCATE
WOLFING	WORMING	WRITE-UP	YANKING	YTTRIUM	ZINCITE
WOLFISH	WORN-OUT	WRITHED	YAOUNDE	YUCATAN	ZIONISM
WOLFRAM	WORRIED	WRITHER	YAPPING	YUCKIER	ZIONIST
WOMANLY	WORRIER	WRITING	YARDAGE	YUKONER	ZIP CODE
WOMBATS	WORRIES	WRITTEN	YARDARM	YULE LOG	ZIPPERS
WONDERS	WORSHIP	WROCLAW	YARD ARM	YUPPIES	ZIPPIER
WONKIER	WORSTED	WRONGED	YARNING	YUPPIFY	ZIPPING
WOODCUT	WOTCHER	WRONGER	YASHMAK		ZITHERS
WOODIER	WOULD-BE	WRONGLY	YATHRIB	**Z**	ZODIACS
WOODMAN	WOULDN'T	WROUGHT	YAWNING	ZAGAZIG	ZOISITE
WOODSIA	WOUNDED	WRYBILL	YEAR DOT	ZAIREAN	ZOMBIES
WOOFERS	WOUNDER	WRYNECK	YEARNED	ZAIRESE	ZONALLY
WOOFTER	WOUND-UP	WRYNESS	YEARNER	ZAMBEZI	ZONULAR
WOOLLEN	WRAITHS	WYCH-ELM	YELLING	ZAMBIAN	ZOOLOGY
WOOMERA	WRANGLE	WYOMING	YELLOWS	ZANIEST	ZOOMING
WOOZIER	WRAPPED	WYVERNS	YELPING	ZAPOTEC	ZOOTOMY
WOOZILY	WRAPPER		YENISEI	ZAPPIER	ZORILLA
WORDAGE	WREAKED	**X**	YEREVAN	ZAPPING	ZWICKAU
WORDIER	WREAKER	XANTHIC	YESHIVA	ZEALAND	ZYGOSIS
WORDILY	WREATHE	XANTHIN	YEW TREE	ZEALOTS	ZYGOTIC
WORDING	WREATHS	XERARCH	Y-FRONTS	ZEALOUS	ZYMOGEN
WORKBAG	WRECKED	XEROSIS	YICHANG	ZEBRINE	ZYMOSIS
WORKBOX	WRECKER	XEROTIC	YIDDISH	ZEDOARY	ZYMOTIC
WORKDAY	WRESTED	XEROXED	YIELDED	ZEELAND	ZYMURGY

A
AARDVARK
AARDWOLF
ABACUSES
ABAMPERE
ABATTOIR
ABBATIAL
ABBESSES
ABDICATE
ABDOMENS
ABDUCENT
ABDUCTED
ABELMOSK
ABEOKUTA
ABERDARE
ABERDEEN
ABERRANT
ABETTING
ABETTORS
ABEYANCE
ABHORRED
ABHORRER
ABIDANCE
ABINGDON
AB
  INITIO
ABJECTLY
ABJURING
ABKHAZIA
ABLATION
ABLATIVE
ABLUTION
ABNEGATE
ABNORMAL
ABOMASUM
ABORTING
ABORTION
ABORTIVE
ABOUNDED
ABRADANT
ABRADING
ABRASION
ABRASIVE
ABRIDGED
ABRIDGER
ABROGATE
ABRUPTLY
ABSCISSA
ABSEILED
ABSENCES
ABSENTED

ABSENTEE
ABSENTER
ABSENTLY
ABSINTHE
ABSOLUTE
ABSOLVED
ABSOLVER
ABSORBED
ABSORBER
ABSTRACT
ABSTRUSE
ABSURDLY
ABU
  DHABI
ABUNDANT
ABUTILON
ABUTMENT
ABUTTALS
ABUTTING
ACADEMIA
ACADEMIC
ACANTHUS
ACAPULCO
ACARPOUS
ACCEDING
ACCENTED
ACCENTOR
ACCEPTED
ACCEPTOR
ACCESSED
ACCESSES
ACCIDENT
ACCOLADE
ACCORDED
ACCORDER
ACCOSTED
ACCOUNTS
ACCREDIT
ACCRUING
ACCURACY
ACCURATE
ACCURSED
ACCUSERS
ACCUSING
ACCUSTOM
ACCUTRON
ACENTRIC
ACERBATE
ACERBITY
ACERVATE
ACESCENT

ACHENIAL
ACHIEVED
ACHIEVER
ACHILLES
ACHROMAT
ACHROMIC
ACICULAR
ACICULUM
ACID
  DROP
ACID-
  FAST
ACIDNESS
ACIDOSIS
ACIDOTIC
ACID
  RAIN
ACID
  TEST
ACIERATE
ACOLYTES
ACONITIC
ACOUSTIC
ACQUAINT
ACQUIRED
ACQUIRER
ACRE-
  FOOT
ACRE-
  INCH
ACRIDINE
ACRIDITY
ACRIMONY
ACROBATS
ACRODONT
ACROLEIN
ACROLITH
ACROMION
ACRONYMS
ACROSTIC
ACRYLICS
ACTINIDE
ACTINISM
ACTINIUM
ACTINOID
ACTIVATE
ACTIVELY
ACTIVISM
ACTIVIST
ACTIVITY
ACT OF
  GOD

ACTUALLY
ACTUATED
ACTUATOR
ACULEATE
ACUTANCE
ADAMS
  ALE
ADAMSITE
ADAPTERS
ADAPTING
ADAPTIVE
ADDENDUM
ADDICTED
ADDITION
ADDITIVE
ADDUCENT
ADDUCING
ADDUCTOR
ADELAIDE
ADENITIS
ADENOIDS
ADEQUACY
ADEQUATE
ADHERENT
ADHERING
ADHESION
ADHESIVE
ADJACENT
ADJOINED
ADJUDGED
ADJUNCTS
ADJURING
ADJUSTED
ADJUTANT
ADJUVANT
AD-
  LIBBED
AD-
  LIBBER
ADMIRALS
ADMIRERS
ADMIRING
ADMITTED
ADMONISH
ADOPTING
ADOPTION
ADOPTIVE
ADORABLE
ADORNING
ADRIATIC
ADROITLY

ADULARIA
ADULATOR
ADULTERY
ADUMBRAL
ADVANCED
ADVANCER
ADVANCES
ADVERTED
ADVISERS
ADVISING
ADVISORY
ADVOCAAT
ADVOCACY
ADVOCATE
ADYNAMIA
ADYNAMIC
AEGROTAT
AERATING
AERATION
AERIALLY
AEROBICS
AERODYNE
AEROFOIL
AEROGRAM
AEROLITE
AEROLOGY
AERONAUT
AEROSOLS
AEROSTAT
AESTHETE
AFEBRILE
AFFECTED
AFFERENT
AFFIANCE
AFFINITY
AFFIRMED
AFFIRMER
AFFIXING
AFFLATUS
AFFLUENT
AFFORDED
AFFOREST
AFFRONTS
AFFUSION
AFLUTTER
AFRICANS
AGARTALA
AGE
  GROUP
AGENCIES
AGENESIS

AGENETIC
AGENTIAL
AGENTIVE
AGERATUM
AGGRIEVE
AGIOTAGE
AGITATED
AGITATOR
AGITPROP
AGMINATE
AGNOSTIC
AGONIZED
AGRAPHIA
AGRARIAN
AGRESTAL
AGRIMONY
AGROLOGY
AGRONOMY
AGUEWEED
AIGRETTE
AIGUILLE
AILERONS
AILMENTS
AIRBASES
AIRBORNE
AIRBRAKE
AIRBRICK
AIRBRUSH
AIRBURST
AIRBUSES
AIRCRAFT
AIRCREWS
AIREDALE
AIRFIELD
AIRFORCE
AIR
  FORCE
AIRFRAME
AIRINESS
AIRLANES
AIRLIFTS
AIRLINER
AIRLINES
AIRLOCKS
AIR
  MILES
AIRPLANE
AIRPORTS
AIR
  RAIDS
AIRSCREW

AIRSHIPS
AIRSPACE
AIRSPEED
AIRSTRIP
AIRTIGHT
AIR-TO-
AIR
AIRWAVES
AIRWOMAN
AIRWOMEN
A LA
CARTE
ALACRITY
ALARMING
ALARMISM
ALARMIST
ALBACORE
ALBANIAN
ALBINISM
ALCATRAZ
ALCHEMIC
ALCHEVSK
ALCIDINE
ALCOHOLS
ALDEHYDE
ALDERMAN
ALDERMEN
ALDERNEY
ALDOXIME
ALEATORY
ALEHOUSE
ALERTING
ALFRESCO
ALGERIAN
ALGERINE
ALGINATE
ALGOLOGY
ALGORISM
ALHAMBRA
ALICANTE
ALIENAGE
ALIENATE
ALIENISM
ALIENIST
ALIGHTED
ALIGNING
ALIQUANT
ALIZARIN
ALKAHEST
ALKALIES
ALKALIFY

ALKALINE
ALKALIZE
ALKALOID
ALLANITE
ALLAYING
ALL
CLEAR
ALLEGING
ALLEGORY
ALLELISM
ALLELUIA
ALLEPPEY
ALLERGEN
ALLERGIC
ALLEYWAY
ALLIANCE
ALLOCATE
ALLODIAL
ALLODIUM
ALLOGAMY
ALLOPATH
ALLOTTED
ALLOTTEE
ALLOWING
ALLOYING
ALL
RIGHT
ALL
ROUND
ALL-
ROUND
ALLSPICE
ALL
THERE
ALLUDING
ALLURING
ALLUSION
ALLUSIVE
ALLUVIAL
ALLUVIUM
ALMANACS
ALMIGHTY
ALMONERS
ALOPECIA
ALPHABET
ALPHOSIS
ALPINISM
ALPINIST
ALSATIAN
ALSO-
RANS

ALTER
EGO
ALTERING
ALTHOUGH
ALTITUDE
ALTRUISM
ALTRUIST
ALUMROOT
ALVEOLAR
ALVEOLUS
AMALGAMS
AMARANTH
AMARELLE
AMARILLO
AMASSING
AMATEURS
AMAZONAS
AMBEROID
AMBIENCE
AMBITION
AMBIVERT
AMBROSIA
AMBULANT
AMBULATE
AMBUSHED
AMBUSHES
AMENABLE
AMENDING
AMERICAN
AMETHYST
AMICABLE
AMICABLY
AMITOSIS
AMITOTIC
AMMETERS
AMMONIAC
AMMONIFY
AMMONITE
AMMONIUM
AMNESIAC
AMNIOTIC
AMOEBOID
AMORETTO
AMORTIZE
AMOUNTED
AMPERAGE
AMPHIPOD
AMPHORAE
AMPHORAS
AMPOULES
AMPULLAR

AMPUTATE
AMPUTEES
AMRAVATI
AMRITSAR
AMYGDALA
AMYGDALE
ANABAENA
ANABASIS
ANABATIC
ANABLEPS
ANABOLIC
ANACONDA
ANAEROBE
ANAGLYPH
ANAGOGIC
ANAGRAMS
ANALCITE
ANALECTS
ANALEMMA
ANALOGUE
ANALYSED
ANALYSER
ANALYSES
ANALYSIS
ANALYSTS
ANALYTIC
ANAPAEST
ANAPHASE
ANAPHORA
ANARCHIC
ANASARCA
ANATHEMA
ANATOLIA
ANCESTOR
ANCESTRY
ANCHORED
ANCIENTS
ANDANTES
ANDERSON
ANDESINE
ANDESITE
ANDIRONS
ANDIZHAN
ANDORRAN
ANDROGEN
ANDROIDS
ANECDOTE
ANECHOIC
ANEMONES
ANETHOLE
ANEURYSM

ANFINSEN
ANGELENO
ANGELICA
ANGERING
ANGINOSE
ANGLESEY
ANGLICAN
ANGRIEST
ANGSTROM
ANGUILLA
ANGULATE
ANHEDRAL
ANIMATED
ANIMATOR
ANIMISTS
ANISETTE
ANKERITE
ANKYLOSE
ANNALIST
ANN
ARBOR
ANNEALED
ANNEALER
ANNEXING
ANNOTATE
ANNOUNCE
ANNOYING
ANNUALLY
ANNULATE
ANNULLED
ANNULOSE
ANODYNES
ANOINTED
ANOINTER
ANOREXIA
ANSERINE
ANSWERED
ANTABUSE
ANTEATER
ANTECEDE
ANTEDATE
ANTELOPE
ANTENNAS
ANTE-
POST
ANTERIOR
ANTEROOM
ANTEVERT
ANTHELIX
ANTHESIS
ANTHILLS

ANTIBODY
ANTIDOTE
ANTIGENS
ANTIHERO
ANTI
HERO
ANTI-
ICER
ANTILLES
ANTIMERE
ANTIMONY
ANTI-
NAZI
ANTINODE
ANTINOMY
ANTIPHON
ANTIQUES
ANTI-
RIOT
ANTITANK
ANTONINE
ANTONYMS
ANTRORSE
ANURESIS
ANYPLACE
ANYTHING
ANYWHERE
AORISTIC
APAGOGIC
APATETIC
APERIENT
APERITIF
APERTURE
APHANITE
APHELIAN
APHELION
APHORISM
APHORIST
APHORIZE
APIARIAN
APIARIES
APIARIST
APIOLOGY
APLASTIC
APOCRINE
APODOSIS
APOGAMIC
APOLOGIA
APOLOGUE
APOMIXIS
APOPHYGE
APOPLEXY

APOSPORY
APOSTASY
APOSTATE
APOSTLES
APPALLED
APPANAGE
APPARENT
APPEALED
APPEALER
APPEARED
APPEASED
APPELLEE
APPENDED
APPENDIX
APPESTAT
APPETITE
APPLAUSE
APPLE
  PIE
APPLIQUE
APPLYING
APPOSITE
APPRAISE
APPRISED
APPROACH
APPROVAL
APPROVED
APRES-
  SKI
APRICOTS
APTEROUS
APTITUDE
APYRETIC
AQUALUNG
AQUANAUT
AQUARIST
AQUARIUM
AQUARIUS
AQUATICS
AQUATINT
AQUEDUCT
AQUILINE
ARACHNID
ARAPAIMA
ARAWAKAN
ARBITERS
ARBITRAL
ARBOREAL
ARBROATH
ARCADIAN
ARCATURE

ARCHAEAN
ARCHAISM
ARCHAIST
ARCHAIZE
ARCHDUKE
ARCHIVAL
ARCHIVES
ARCHNESS
ARCHWAYS
ARC
  LIGHT
ARCTURUS
ARDENNES
ARDENTLY
AREA
  CODE
ARENITIC
AREQUIPA
ARETHUSA
ARGENTIC
ARGININE
ARGUABLE
ARGUABLY
ARGUMENT
ARIANISM
ARILLATE
ARILLODE
ARISTATE
ARKANSAS
ARMAGNAC
ARMALITE
ARMAMENT
ARMATURE
ARMBANDS
ARMCHAIR
ARMENIAN
ARMHOLES
ARMIDALE
ARMORIAL
ARMOURED
ARMOURER
ARMS
  RACE
AROMATIC
AROUSING
ARPEGGIO
ARRANGED
ARRANGER
ARRAYING
ARRESTED
ARRESTER

ARRIVALS
ARRIVING
ARROGANT
ARROGATE
ARROWING
ARSENALS
ARSENATE
ARSENIDE
ARSENITE
ARSONIST
ARTEFACT
ARTERIAL
ARTERIES
ARTESIAN
ARTFULLY
ART
  HOUSE
ARTICLED
ARTICLES
ARTIFACT
ARTIFICE
ARTINESS
ARTISANS
ARTISTES
ARTISTIC
ARTISTRY
ARYANIZE
ASBESTOS
ASCENDED
ASCENDER
ASCETICS
ASCIDIAN
ASCIDIUM
ASCOCARP
ASCORBIC
ASCRIBED
ASHTRAYS
ASNIERES
ASPERITY
ASPERSER
ASPHODEL
ASPHYXIA
ASPIRANT
ASPIRATE
ASPIRING
ASPIRINS
ASSAILED
ASSAILER
ASSAMESE
ASSASSIN
ASSAULTS

ASSAYING
ASSEGAIS
ASSEMBLE
ASSEMBLY
ASSENTED
ASSENTOR
ASSERTED
ASSERTER
ASSESSED
ASSESSOR
ASSHOLES
ASSIGNAT
ASSIGNED
ASSIGNEE
ASSIGNER
ASSIGNOR
ASSISTED
ASSISTER
ASSONANT
ASSORTED
ASSORTER
ASSUAGED
ASSUAGER
ASSUMING
ASSURING
ASSYRIAN
ASTATINE
ASTERISK
ASTERISM
ASTERNAL
ASTEROID
ASTHENIA
ASTHENIC
ASTONISH
ASTRAGAL
ASTURIAS
ASTUTELY
ASUNCION
ATARAXIA
AT
  BOTTOM
ATHEISTS
ATHENIAN
ATHEROMA
ATHLETES
ATHLETIC
ATLANTIC
ATLANTIS
AT
  LENGTH

ATOM
  BOMB
ATOMIZER
ATONABLE
ATONALLY
ATROCITY
ATROPHIC
ATROPINE
ATTACHED
ATTACHER
ATTACHES
ATTACKED
ATTACKER
ATTAINED
ATTEMPTS
ATTENDED
ATTENDEE
ATTESTED
ATTIRING
ATTITUDE
ATTORNEY
ATTUNING
ATYPICAL
AUBUSSON
AUCKLAND
AUCTIONS
AUDACITY
AUDIENCE
AUDITING
AUDITION
AUDITORS
AUDITORY
AUGSBURG
AUGURIES
AUGURING
AUGUSTLY
AUREOLES
AU
  REVOIR
AURICLES
AURICULA
AUSPICES
AUSTRIAN
AUTACOID
AUTARCHY
AUTARKIC
AUTHORED
AUTISTIC
AUTOBAHN
AUTOCRAT
AUTOCUES

AUTOGAMY
AUTOGIRO
AUTOLYSE
AUTOMATA
AUTOMATE
AUTOMATS
AUTONOMY
AUTOSOME
AUTOTOMY
AUTOTYPE
AUTOTYPY
AUTUMNAL
AUTUNITE
AUVERGNE
AVADAVAT
AVAILING
AVE
  MARIA
AVENGERS
AVENGING
AVERAGED
AVERAGES
AVERMENT
AVERRING
AVERSION
AVERSIVE
AVERTING
AVIARIES
AVIATION
AVIATORS
AVIATRIX
AVIDNESS
AVIEMORE
AVIFAUNA
AVIONICS
AVOCADOS
AVOIDING
AVOWABLE
AVULSION
AWAITING
AWAKENED
AWARDING
AWEATHER
AXILLARY
AXIOLOGY
AXLETREE
AYRSHIRE
AYURVEDA
AZIMUTHS
AZOTEMIA
AZOTEMIC

B
BABBLERS
BABBLING
BABIRUSA
BABYHOOD
BABY
  TALK
BACCARAT
BACCHIUS
BACHELOR
BACILLUS
BACKACHE
BACKBEAT
BACKBITE
BACKBONE
BACKCHAT
BACKCOMB
BACKDATE
BACK
  DOOR
BACKDROP
BACKFILL
BACKFIRE
BACKHAND
BACKINGS
BACKLASH
BACKLESS
BACKLIST
BACKLOGS
BACKPACK
BACK
  SEAT
BACKSIDE
BACKSLID
BACKSPIN
BACKSTAY
BACKSTOP
BACK
  TALK
BACKWARD
BACKWASH
BACKYARD
BACTERIA
BACTERIN
BACTRIAN
BADALONA
BAD
  BLOOD
BAD
  DEBTS
BADGERED
BADINAGE

BADLANDS
BADLY-
  OFF
BAD-
  MOUTH
BAEDEKER
BAFFLING
BAGGAGES
BAGGIEST
BAGPIPES
BAGUETTE
BAHAMIAN
BAHRAINI
BAILABLE
BAILIFFS
BAILMENT
BAILSMAN
BAKELITE
BAKERIES
BALANCED
BALANCER
BALANCES
BALDNESS
BALEARIC
BALINESE
BALLADES
BALLADRY
BALLARAT
BALLCOCK
BALL
  GAME
BALLONET
BALLOONS
BALLOTED
BALL
  PARK
BALLROOM
BALLS-
  UPS
BALLYHOO
BALMIEST
BALMORAL
BALSAMIC
BALUSTER
BANALITY
BANDAGED
BANDAGES
BANDANNA
BANDIEST
BANDITRY
BANDPASS
BANDSMAN

BANDSMEN
BANDYING
BANISHED
BANISTER
BANKABLE
BANKBOOK
BANK
  NOTE
BANK
  RATE
BANKROLL
BANKRUPT
BANNOCKS
BANQUETS
BANSHEES
BANSTEAD
BANTERED
BANTERER
BAPTISMS
BAPTISTS
BAPTIZED
BARATHEA
BARBADOS
BARBARIC
BARBECUE
BARBERRY
BARBICAN
BARBICEL
BAR
  CHART
BAR
  CODES
BAREBACK
BAREFOOT
BAREILLY
BARENESS
BARGAINS
BAR
  GRAPH
BARITONE
BARLETTA
BARMAIDS
BARMIEST
BARNACLE
BARNSLEY
BARNYARD
BAROGRAM
BARONAGE
BARONESS
BARONETS
BARONIAL
BARONIES

BAROSTAT
BAROUCHE
BARRACKS
BARRAGES
BARRATOR
BARRATRY
BARRETTE
BARRIERS
BARTERED
BARTERER
BARTIZAN
BASEBALL
BASEHEAD
BASELESS
BASELINE
BASEMENT
BASENESS
BASE
  RATE
BASICITY
BASIDIAL
BASIDIUM
BASILARY
BASILDON
BASILICA
BASILISK
BASKETRY
BASOPHIL
BASS
  CLEF
BASS
  DRUM
BASSINET
BASSISTS
BASSOONS
BASSWOOD
BASTARDS
BASTARDY
BASTILLE
BASTIONS
BASTOGNE
BATANGAS
BATHETIC
BATH
  MATS
BATHROBE
BATHROOM
BATHTUBS
BATHURST
BATSWANA
BATTENED
BATTERED

BATTERER
BATTIEST
BATTLING
BAUHINIA
BAULKING
BAVARIAN
BAWDIEST
BAYBERRY
BAYONETS
BAYREUTH
BAZOOKAS
BDELLIUM
BEACHING
BEADIEST
BEADINGS
BEAGLING
BEAM-
  ENDS
BEANPOLE
BEARABLE
BEARABLY
BEARDING
BEAR
  HUGS
BEARINGS
BEARSKIN
BEATABLE
BEATIFIC
BEATINGS
BEATNIKS
BEAT
  TIME
BEAULIEU
BEAUMONT
BEAUTIES
BEAUTIFY
BEAUVAIS
BEAVERED
BECALMED
BECHAMEL
BECKONED
BECKONER
BECOMING
BEDAUBED
BEDAZZLE
BEDECKED
BEDIMMED
BED
  LINEN
BEDOUINS
BEDPLATE
BEDPOSTS

BEDROOMS
BEDSIDES
BEDSORES
BEDSTEAD
BEDSTRAW
BEDTIMES
BEDWORTH
BEEBREAD
BEECHNUT
BEE-
  EATER
BEEFCAKE
BEEFIEST
BEEFWOOD
BEEHIVES
BEELINES
BEESWING
BEETLING
BEETROOT
BEFALLEN
BEFITTED
BEFOULER
BEFRIEND
BEGETTER
BEGGARED
BEGGARLY
BEGINING
BEGINNER
BEGOTTEN
BEGRUDGE
BEGUILED
BEGUILER
BEHAVING
BEHEADED
BEHOLDEN
BEHOLDER
BELABOUR
BELAYING
BELCHING
BELFRIES
BELGRADE
BELIEVED
BELIEVER
BELITTLE
BELLBIRD
BELLBOYS
BELLOWED
BELLOWER
BELLPULL
BELLWORT
BELLYFUL

BELMOPAN	BEVELING	BILLIONS	BISMARCK	BLAZONRY	BLOWHOLE
BELONGED	BEVELLED	BILLOWED	BISTOURY	BLEACHED	BLOWIEST
BELOVEDS	BEVERAGE	BILOBATE	BITCHIER	BLEACHER	BLOWLAMP
BELTWAYS	BEVERLEY	BIMANOUS	BITCHILY	BLEAKEST	BLOWOUTS
BEMOANED	BEWAILED	BINAURAL	BITCHING	BLEARIER	BLOWPIPE
BENADRYL	BEWAILER	BINDINGS	BITINGLY	BLEARILY	BLOW-
BEN	BEWARING	BINDWEED	BIT	BLEATING	WAVE
BELLA	BEWIGGED	BIN-	PARTS	BLEEDERS	BLOWZIER
BENEFICE	BEWILDER	LINER	BITSTOCK	BLEEDING	BLOWZILY
BENEFITS	BHATPARA	BINNACLE	BITTERLY	BLEEPERS	BLUDGEON
BENFLEET	BIANNUAL	BINOMIAL	BITTERNS	BLEEPING	BLUE
BENGHAZI	BIARRITZ	BIOASSAY	BITTIEST	BLENCHED	BABY
BENGUELA	BIASSING	BIO-	BIVALENT	BLENCHER	BLUEBELL
BENIGNLY	BIATHLON	ASSAY	BIVALVES	BLENDERS	BLUEBIRD
BENTINCK	BIBLICAL	BIOCIDAL	BIVOUACS	BLENDING	BLUE
BENTWOOD	BIBULOUS	BIOCYCLE	BIWEEKLY	BLENHEIM	BOOK
BENUMBED	BICKERED	BIODATAS	BIYEARLY	BLESSING	BLUE
BENZOATE	BICKERER	BIOLYSIS	BLABBING	BLIGHTED	CHIP
BEQUEATH	BICOLOUR	BIOLYTIC	BLACK	BLIGHTER	BLUE
BEQUESTS	BICONVEX	BIOMETRY	ART	BLIMPISH	FILM
BERATING	BICUSPID	BIONOMIC	BLACK	BLINDAGE	BLUEFISH
BERCEUSE	BICYCLED	BIOPLASM	BOX	BLINDERS	BLUE
BEREAVED	BICYCLES	BIOPSIES	BLACKCAP	BLINDING	FLAG
BEREZINA	BICYCLIC	BIOSCOPE	BLACKEST	BLINKERS	BLUEGILL
BERGAMET	BIDDABLE	BIOSCOPY	BLACK	BLINKING	BLUE
BERIBERI	BIENNIAL	BIOTITIC	EYE	BLISSFUL	GUMS
BERKELEY	BIFACIAL	BIOTYPIC	BLACKFLY	BLISTERS	BLUE
BERTHING	BIFIDITY	BIPAROUS	BLACK	BLITHELY	JAYS
BERYLINE	BIFOCALS	BIPHENYL	ICE	BLITZING	BLUE
BESANCON	BIGAMIST	BIPLANES	BLACKING	BLIZZARD	LAWS
BESIEGED	BIGAMOUS	BIRACIAL	BLACKISH	BLOATERS	BLUE
BESIEGER	BIGHEADS	BIRADIAL	BLACKLEG	BLOCKADE	MOON
BESMIRCH	BIG	BIRAMOUS	BLACKOUT	BLOCKAGE	BLUENESS
BESOTTED	NAMES	BIRCHING	BLACK	BLOCKING	BLUFFING
BESOUGHT	BIGNONIA	BIRDBATH	TIE	BLOKEISH	BLUNDERS
BESPOKEN	BIG	BIRDCAGE	BLACK-	BLONDEST	BLUNKETT
BESTIARY	SHOTS	BIRD	TIE	BLOODFIN	BLUNTING
BESTOWAL	BIG	DOGS	BLACKTOP	BLOODILY	BLURRING
BESTOWED	STICK	BIRDLIKE	BLADDERS	BLOODING	BLURTING
BESTOWER	BIG-	BIRDLIME	BLAMABLE	BLOOD	BLUSHERS
BESTREWN	TIMER	BIRDSEED	BLAMEFUL	RED	BLUSHING
BESTRIDE	BIG	BIRDS	BLANCHED	BLOOMERS	BLUSTERY
BESTRODE	WHEEL	EYE	BLANDEST	BLOOMERY	BOARDERS
BETAKING	BIJUGATE	BIRD'S-	BLANDISH	BLOOMING	BOARDING
BETATRON	BILABIAL	EYE	BLANKETS	BLOOPERS	BOARFISH
BETIDING	BILBERRY	BIRETTAS	BLASTEMA	BLOSSOMS	BOASTERS
BETRAYAL	BILINEAR	BIRTHDAY	BLASTING	BLOTCHES	BOASTFUL
BETRAYED	BILLETED	BIRTHING	BLAST-	BLOTTERS	BOASTING
BETRAYER	BILLFISH	BISCUITS	OFF	BLOTTING	BOAT
BETTERED	BILLFOLD	BISECTED	BLASTULA	BLOWFISH	HOOK
BEVATRON	BILLHOOK	BISECTOR	BLATANCY	BLOWHARD	BOATLOAD
	BILLIARD	BISEXUAL	BLAZONED		

BOA
  VISTA
BOBBINET
BOBBY
  PIN
BOBOLINK
BOBRUISK
BOBTAILS
BOBWHITE
BODILESS
BODLEIAN
BODY
  BLOW
BODYWORK
BOEHMITE
BOGEYMAN
BOGGIEST
BOGGLING
BOHEMIAN
BOILABLE
BOLDFACE
BOLDNESS
BOLIVIAN
BOLLARDS
BOLLOCKS
BOLLWORM
BOLSHIER
BOLSTERS
BOLTHOLE
BOLT
  HOLE
BOLTONIA
BOLTROPE
BOMBARDE
BOMBSITE
BOMBYCID
BONA
  FIDE
BONANZAS
BONEFISH
BONEHEAD
BONE-
  IDLE
BONELESS
BONE
  MEAL
BONFIRES
BONHOMIE
BONINESS
BONNIEST
BONS
  MOTS

BONTEBOK
BOOHOOED
BOOKABLE
BOOKCASE
BOOK
  CLUB
BOOKENDS
BOOKINGS
BOOKLETS
BOOKMARK
BOOKRACK
BOOKSHOP
BOOKWORM
BOOSTERS
BOOSTING
BOOT
  CAMP
BOOTLACE
BOOTLESS
BOOZE-
  UPS
BOOZIEST
BORA
  BORA
BORACITE
BORDEAUX
BORDELLO
BORDERED
BORDERER
BOREHOLE
BORINGLY
BORNHOLM
BOROUGHS
BORROWED
BORROWER
BORSTALS
BOSPORUS
BOSS-
  EYED
BOSSIEST
BOTANIST
BOTANIZE
BOTCHERS
BOTCHIER
BOTCHILY
BOTCHING
BOTCH-
  UPS
BOTHERED
BOTRYTIS
BOTSWANA
BOTTLING

BOTTOMRY
BOTULISM
BOUDOIRS
BOUFFANT
BOUILLON
BOULDERS
BOULLION
BOULOGNE
BOUNCERS
BOUNCIER
BOUNCILY
BOUNCING
BOUNDARY
BOUNDERS
BOUNDING
BOUNTIES
BOUQUETS
BOUTIQUE
BOUZOUKI
BOW
  BELLS
BOWSHOTS
BOWSPRIT
BOXBERRY
BOXBOARD
BOXROOMS
BOYCOTTS
BOYISHLY
BOY
  SCOUT
BRACELET
BRACHIAL
BRACHIUM
BRACKETS
BRACKISH
BRACTEAL
BRADAWLS
BRADBURY
BRADFORD
BRAGGART
BRAGGING
BRAHMANI
BRAHMANS
BRAIDING
BRAINBOX
BRAINIER
BRAINING
BRAINPAN
BRAISING
BRAMBLES
BRANCHED

BRANCHES
BRANCHIA
BRANDIES
BRANDING
BRANDISH
BRAND-
  NEW
BRASHEST
BRASILIA
BRASSARD
BRASS
  HAT
BRASSICA
BRASSIER
BRASSILY
BRATTICE
BRAUNITE
BRAWLERS
BRAWLING
BRAWNIER
BRAWNILY
BRAZENED
BRAZENLY
BRAZIERS
BRAZILIN
BREACHED
BREACHES
BREAD
  BIN
BREADNUT
BREADTHS
BREAKAGE
BREAKERS
BREAKING
BREAK-
  INS
BREATHER
BREECHES
BREEDING
BREEZILY
BRETHREN
BREVETCY
BREVIARY
BRIBABLE
BRICKBAT
BRIDGEND
BRIDGING
BRIEFING
BRIGHTEN
BRIGHTON
BRINDISI
BRIOCHES

BRISANCE
BRISBANE
BRISKEST
BRISLING
BRISTLED
BRISTLES
BRITCHES
BRITTANY
BROACHED
BROACHER
BROADEST
BROADWAY
BROCADED
BROCCOLI
BROCHURE
BROILERS
BROILING
BROKENLY
BROLLIES
BROMIDES
BRONCHIA
BRONCHOS
BRONCHUS
BRONZING
BROOCHES
BROODERS
BROODIER
BROODILY
BROODING
BROOKING
BROOKITE
BROOKLYN
BROOKNER
BROTHELS
BROTHERS
BROUGHAM
BROUHAHA
BROWBEAT
BROWNEST
BROWNIES
BROWNING
BROWNISH
BROWSING
BRUISERS
BRUISING
BRUITING
BRUNCHES
BRUNETTE
BRUSHING
BRUSH
  OFF

BRUSH-
  OFF
BRUSH-
  UPS
BRUSSELS
BRUTALLY
BRYOLOGY
BRYOZOAN
BUBALINE
BUBBLIER
BUBBLING
BUCHSHEE
BUCKAROO
BUCKBEAN
BUCKETED
BUCKHORN
BUCKLERS
BUCKLING
BUCKSHEE
BUCKSHOT
BUCKSKIN
BUDAPEST
BUDDHISM
BUDDHIST
BUDDLEIA
BUDGETED
BUFFALOS
BUFFERED
BUFFETED
BUFFETER
BUFFOONS
BUGABOOS
BUGBEARS
BUGGERED
BUILDERS
BUILDING
BUILDUPS
BUKOVINI
BULAWAYO
BULGARIA
BULGIEST
BULKHEAD
BULKIEST
BULL
  BARS
BULLDOGS
BULLDOZE
BULLETIN
BULLFROG
BULLHEAD
BULLHORN

BULLNECK
BULLOCKS
BULLRING
BULLS
  EYE
BULL'S-
  EYE
BULLSHIT
BULLYBOY
BULLYING
BULLY-
  OFF
BULWARKS
BUMBLING
BUMPIEST
BUMPKINS
BUNCHING
BUNDLING
BUNGALOW
BUNGHOLE
BUNGLERS
BUNGLING
BUNTLINE
BUOYANCY
BURAYDAH
BURBERRY
BURBLING
BURDENED
BURGHERS
BURGLARS
BURGLARY
BURGLING
BURGUNDY
BURLIEST
BURNOOSE
BURNOUTS
BURRITOS
BURROWED
BURROWER
BURSITIS
BURSTING
BURTHENS
BUSHBABY
BUSHBUCK
BUSHIEST
BUSHVELD
BUSINESS
BUS
  STOPS
BUSTIEST
BUSTLING
BUSYBODY

BUSYNESS
BUTANONE
BUTCHERS
BUTCHERY
BUTTERED
BUTTOCKS
BUTTONED
BUTTRESS
BUTYRATE
BUZZARDS
BUZZWORD
BY-
  BIDDER
BYPASSED
BYPASSES
BYRONISM

C

CABARETS
CABBAGES
CABIN
  BOY
CABINETS
CABLE
  CAR
CABLEWAY
CABOCHON
CABOODLE
CABOOSES
CABOTAGE
CAB
  RANKS
CABRILLA
CABRIOLE
CACHALOT
CACHEPOT
CACHEXIA
CACHUCHA
CACKLERS
CACKLING
CACTUSES
CADASTER
CADAVERS
CADDYING
CADENCES
CADENZAS
CADUCEUS
CADUCITY
CADUCOUS
CAERLEON
CAESURAS

CAFFEINE
CAGELING
CAGINESS
CAGLIARI
CAGOULES
CAISSONS
CAJOLERY
CAJOLING
CAKEWALK
CALABASH
CALABRIA
CALADIUM
CALAMINE
CALAMINT
CALAMITE
CALAMITY
CALATHUS
CALCIFIC
CALCITIC
CALCULUS
CALCUTTA
CALDRONS
CALENDAR
CALENDER
CALF
  LOVE
CALFSKIN
CALIBRED
CALIBRES
CALIPASH
CALIPERS
CALISAYA
CALLABLE
CALL
  GIRL
CALLINGS
CALLIOPE
CALLIPER
CALLISTO
CALLUSES
CALMNESS
CALOR
  GAS
CALORIES
CALUTRON
CALVADOS
CALVARIA
CALYCATE
CALYCINE
CALYPSOS
CALYPTRA

CAMAGUEY
CAMBODIA
CAMBOGIA
CAMBRIAN
CAMELEER
CAMELLIA
CAMEROON
CAMISOLE
CAMOMILE
CAMPAGNA
CAMPAIGN
CAMPANIA
CAMP
  BEDS
CAMPECHE
CAMPFIRE
CAMPHENE
CAMPINAS
CAMPSITE
CAMPUSES
CAMSHAFT
CANADIAN
CANAIGRE
CANAILLE
CANALIZE
CANARIES
CANBERRA
CANCELED
CANCROID
CANDIDLY
CANFIELD
CANISTER
CANNABIC
CANNABIN
CANNABIS
CANNIBAL
CANNIEST
CANNIKIN
CANNONED
CANNONRY
CANOEING
CANOEIST
CANONESS
CANONIST
CANONIZE
CANON
  LAW
CANOODLE
CANOPIES
CANTATAS
CANTEENS

CANTERED
CANT
  HOOK
CANTICLE
CANTONAL
CANVASES
CANZONET
CAPACITY
CAPERING
CAPESKIN
CAPE
  TOWN
CAPITALS
CAPITATE
CAPONIZE
CAPRICES
CAPRIFIG
CAPRIOLE
CAPSICUM
CAPSIZED
CAPSTANS
CAPSTONE
CAPSULAR
CAPSULES
CAPTAINS
CAPTIONS
CAPTIOUS
CAPTIVES
CAPTURED
CAPTURES
CAPUCHIN
CAPYBARA
CARACARA
CARACOLE
CARAMELS
CARANGID
CARAPACE
CARAVANS
CARAWAYS
CARBINES
CARBOLIC
CARBONIC
CARBONYL
CARBURET
CARDAMOM
CARDENAL
CARDIGAN
CARDINAL
CARDIOID
CARDITIS
CAREENED

CAREERED
CAREFREE
CARELESS
CARESSED
CARESSER
CARESSES
CAREWORN
CARIBOUS
CARILLON
CARINATE
CARLISLE
CARNAUBA
CARNIVAL
CAROLINA
CAROLINE
CAROLING
CAROLLED
CAROTENE
CAROUSAL
CAROUSED
CAROUSEL
CAR
  PARKS
CARPETED
CAR
  POOLS
CARPORTS
CARRERAS
CARRIAGE
CARRIERS
CARRYALL
CARRYCOT
CARRYING
CARRY
  OFF
CARRYOUT
CARRY
  OUT
CARTOONS
CARUNCLE
CARVINGS
CARYATID
CASANOVA
CASCADED
CASCADES
CASEMATE
CASEMENT
CASEWORK
CASHABLE
CASHBACK
CASH
  BACK

CASH-	CATHETER	CEMENTER	CHAIRMAN	CHARTING	CHESSMAN
BOOK	CATHEXIS	CEMENTUM	CHAIRMEN	CHARTISM	CHESTIER
CASH	CATHODES	CEMETERY	CHALAZAL	CHARTIST	CHESTILY
CARD	CATHODIC	CENOTAPH	CHALDRON	CHARTRES	CHESTNUT
CASH	CATHOLIC	CENOZOIC	CHALICES	CHASSEUR	CHEVRONS
CROP	CATIONIC	CENSORED	CHALKIER	CHASTELY	CHEWABLE
CASH	CAT'S	CENSURED	CHALKING	CHASTEST	CHEWIEST
DESK	EYES	CENSURES	CHAMBERS	CHASTISE	CHEYENNE
CASH	CAT'S-	CENSUSES	CHAMBRAY	CHASTITY	CHIASMAL
FLOW	FOOT	CENTAURS	CHAMONIX	CHASUBLE	CHIASMIC
CASHIERS	CAT'S	CENTAURY	CHAMPING	CHAT	CHIASMUS
CASHLESS	PAWS	CENTAVOS	CHAMPION	SHOW	CHIASTIC
CASHMERE	CATSUITS	CENTERED	CHANCELS	CHATTELS	CHICANER
CASSETTE	CATTIEST	CENTIARE	CHANCERY	CHATTIER	CHICANOS
CASSOCKS	CATTLEYA	CENTIMES	CHANCIER	CHATTILY	CHICKENS
CASTAWAY	CATWALKS	CENTRING	CHANCILY	CHATTING	CHICKPEA
CASTINGS	CAUCASIA	CENTRIST	CHANCING	CHAUFFER	CHICLAYO
CAST	CAUCASUS	CENTROID	CHANDLER	CHEAPEST	CHIGETAI
IRON	CAUCUSES	CEPHALAD	CHANGING	CHEATING	CHIGGERS
CAST-	CAUDALLY	CEPHALIC	CHANGSHA	CHECKERS	CHIGNONS
IRON	CAULDRON	CEPHALIN	CHANGTEH	CHECKING	CHIGWELL
CASTRATE	CAULICLE	CERAMICS	CHANNELS	CHECK-	CHILDISH
CASTRATO	CAULKING	CERAMIST	CHANTIES	INS	CHILDREN
CASTRIES	CAUSABLE	CERASTES	CHANTING	CHECKOUT	CHILIASM
CASUALLY	CAUSALLY	CERATOID	CHANUKAH	CHECKUPS	CHILIAST
CASUALTY	CAUSERIE	CERCARIA	CHAOCHOW	CHEDDITE	CHILLIER
CASUISTS	CAUSEWAY	CEREBRAL	CHAPATTI	CHEEKIER	CHILLIES
CATACOMB	CAUTIONS	CEREBRIC	CHAPBOOK	CHEEKILY	CHILLING
CATALASE	CAUTIOUS	CEREBRUM	CHAPERON	CHEEKING	CHILL
CATALYSE	CAVALIER	CEREMENT	CHAPLAIN	CHEEPING	OUT
CATALYST	CAVATINA	CEREMONY	CHAPLETS	CHEERFUL	CHILOPOD
CATAMITE	CAVEATOR	CERNUOUS	CHAPPING	CHEERIER	CHIMAERA
CATAPULT	CAVEFISH	CEROTYPE	CHAPTERS	CHEERILY	CHIMBOTE
CATARACT	CAVICORN	CERULEAN	CHARACIN	CHEERING	CHIMERAS
CATCALLS	CAVILING	CERVELAT	CHARADES	CHEETAHS	CHIMKENT
CATCH	CAVILLED	CERVICAL	CHARCOAL	CHEKIANG	CHIMNEYS
ALL	CAVILLER	CERVICES	CHARENTE	CHEMICAL	CHINAMAN
CATCH-	CAVITIES	CERVIXES	CHARGERS	CHEMISES	CHIN-
ALL	CAVORTED	CESAREAN	CHARGING	CHEMISTS	CHOU
CATCHFLY	CEDILLAS	CESSIONS	CHARIEST	CHEMNITZ	CHINDWIN
CATCHIER	CEILINGS	CESSPITS	CHARIOTS	CHEMURGY	CHINKING
CATCHILY	CELERIAC	CESSPOOL	CHARISMA	CHENILLE	CHINLESS
CATCHING	CELERITY	CETACEAN	CHARLADY	CHENOPOD	CHIPMUNK
CATECHIN	CELIBACY	CEVENNES	CHARLIES	CHEPSTOW	CHIPPIES
CATECHOL	CELIBATE	CHACONNE	CHARLOCK	CHEQUERS	CHIPPING
CATEGORY	CELLARER	CHAFFING	CHARLTON	CHEROKEE	CHIP
CATENANE	CELLARET	CHAINING	CHARMERS	CHEROOTS	SHOP
CATENARY	CELLISTS	CHAINMAN	CHARMING	CHERRIES	CHIRPIER
CATENATE	CELLULAR	CHAIN	CHARQUID	CHERTSEY	CHIRPILY
CATENOID	CELULOID	SAW	CHARRING	CHERUBIC	CHIRPING
CATERING	CEMENTED	CHAIRING	CHARTERS	CHESHIRE	CHIRRUPY
CATHEDRA					

CHISELED
CHITCHAT
CHIT
  CHAT
CHIVALRY
CHIVYING
CHLORATE
CHLORIDE
CHLORINE
CHLORITE
CHLOROUS
CHOC-
  ICES
CHOCKING
CHOICELY
CHOICEST
CHOIRBOY
CHOIRMAN
CHOISEUL
CHOLERIC
CHOMPING
CHONGJIN
CHOOSIER
CHOP
  CHOP
CHOP-
  CHOP
CHOPPERS
CHOPPIER
CHOPPILY
CHOPPING
CHOP
  SUEY
CHORALES
CHORDATE
CHORDING
CHORIAMB
CHORTLED
CHORTLES
CHORUSED
CHORUSES
CHOW-
  CHOW
CHOW
  MEIN
CHRESARD
CHRISMAL
CHRISTEN
CHROMATE
CHROMITE
CHROMIUM
CHROMOUS

CHUBBIER
CHUCKING
CHUCKLED
CHUCKLER
CHUCKLES
CHUCK
  OFF
CHUGGING
CHUKKERS
CHUMMIER
CHUMMILY
CHUMMING
CHUNKIER
CHURCHES
CHURINGA
CHURLISH
CHURNING
CHUTZPAH
CHYMOSIN
CIABATTA
CIBORIUM
CICATRIX
CICERONE
CICHLOID
CIMBRIAN
CINCHONA
CINCTURE
CINEASTE
CINERAMA
CINERARY
CINGULUM
CINNABAR
CINNAMON
CINQUAIN
CIPHERED
CIRCLETS
CIRCLING
CIRCUITS
CIRCUITY
CIRCULAR
CIRCUSES
CISLUNAR
CISTERNA
CISTERNS
CITADELS
CITATION
CITIFIED
CITIZENS
CITREOUS
CITRUSES

CITY
  HALL
CIVILIAN
CIVILITY
CIVILIZE
CIVIL
  LAW
CIVIL
  WAR
CLACKING
CLAIMANT
CLAIMING
CLAMBAKE
CLAMMIER
CLAMMILY
CLAMMING
CLAMOURS
CLAMPING
CLANGERS
CLANGING
CLANKING
CLANNISH
CLANSMAN
CLANSMEN
CLAPPERS
CLAPPING
CLAPTRAP
CLARINET
CLARIONS
CLASHING
CLASPING
CLASSICS
CLASSIER
CLASSIFY
CLASSING
CLASSISM
CLASSIST
CLATTERS
CLATTERY
CLAVICLE
CLAYLIKE
CLAYMORE
CLEAN
  CUT
CLEAN-
  CUT
CLEANERS
CLEANEST
CLEANING
CLEANSED
CLEANSER

CLEAR-
  CUT
CLEAREST
CLEARING
CLEAROUT
CLEARWAY
CLEAVAGE
CLEAVERS
CLEAVING
CLEMATIS
CLEMENCY
CLENCHED
CLENCHES
CLERICAL
CLERIHEW
CLERKDOM
CLERKING
CLEVEITE
CLEVERLY
CLICKING
CLIENTAL
CLIMATES
CLIMATIC
CLIMAXED
CLIMAXES
CLIMBERS
CLIMBING
CLINCHED
CLINCHER
CLINCHES
CLINGING
CLINICAL
CLINKERS
CLINKING
CLIPPERS
CLIPPIES
CLIPPING
CLIQUISH
CLITORAL
CLITORIS
CLOAKING
CLOCKING
CLODDISH
CLOGGING
CLOISTER
CLOPPING
CLOSE-
  SET
CLOSETED
CLOSE-
  UPS

CLOSURES
CLOTHIER
CLOTHING
CLOTTING
CLOUDIER
CLOUDILY
CLOUDING
CLOUDLET
CLOUTING
CLOWNERY
CLOWNING
CLOWNISH
CLUBBING
CLUBFEET
CLUBFOOT
CLUBHAUL
CLUCKING
CLUELESS
CLUMPING
CLUMPISH
CLUMSIER
CLUMSILY
CLUPEOID
CLUSTERS
CLUSTERY
CLUTCHED
CLUTCHES
COACHING
COACHMAN
COACHMEN
COACTION
COACTIVE
COAGULUM
COAHUILA
COALESCE
COALFACE
COALFISH
COALHOLE
COALMINE
COALPORT
COARSELY
COARSEST
COASTERS
COASTING
COATINGS
COATROOM
COAT-
  TAIL
COAUTHOR
COBALTIC
COBBLERS

COBBLING
COBWEBBY
COCA-
  COLA
COCCYGES
COCHLEAE
COCHLEAR
COCKADES
COCKATOO
COCKCROW
COCK
  CROW
COCKEREL
COCKEYED
COCKIEST
COCKNEYS
COCKPITS
COCKSPUR
COCKSURE
COCKTAIL
COCONUTS
COCOONED
CODDLING
CODICILS
CODIFIED
CODIFIER
CODOMAIN
CODPIECE
CO
  DRIVER
COENURUS
COENZYME
COEQUALS
COERCING
COERCION
COERCIVE
COEXTEND
COGENTLY
COGITATE
COGNATES
COGNOMEN
COGWHEEL
COHERENT
COHERING
COHESION
COHESIVE
COHOBATE
COIFFEUR
COIFFURE
COINAGES
COINCIDE

COINSURE
COLANDER
COLD
  CUTS
COLD
  FEET
COLD
  FISH
COLDNESS
COLD
  SNAP
COLD
  SORE
COLD-
  WELD
COLESLAW
COLISEUM
COLLAGEN
COLLAGES
COLLAPSE
COLLARED
COLLATED
COLLATOR
COLLECTS
COLLEENS
COLLEGES
COLLIDED
COLLIDER
COLLIERS
COLLIERY
COLLOGUE
COLLOQUY
COLLUDED
COLOMBES
COLOMBIA
COLONELS
COLONIAL
COLONIES
COLONIST
COLONIZE
COLOPHON
COLORADO
COLORANT
COLOSSAL
COLOSSUS
COLOTOMY
COLOURED
COLPITIS
COLUBRID
COLUMBIA
COLUMBIC
COLUMBUS

COLUMNAR
COLUMNED
COMANCHE
COMATOSE
COMBATED
COMBATER
COMBINED
COMBINER
COMBINES
COMEBACK
COMEDIAN
COMEDIES
COMEDOWN
COMELIER
COMFIEST
COMFORTS
COMITIES
COMMANDO
COMMANDS
COMMENCE
COMMENTS
COMMERCE
COMMODES
COMMONER
COMMONLY
COMMUNAL
COMMUNED
COMMUNES
COMMUTED
COMMUTER
COMPACTS
COMPADRE
COMPARED
COMPARER
COMPARES
COMPEERS
COMPERED
COMPERES
COMPETED
COMPILED
COMPILER
COMPLAIN
COMPLETE
COMPLIED
COMPLIER
COMPLINE
COMPOSED
COMPOSER
COMPOTES
COMPOUND
COMPRESS

COMPRISE
COMPUTED
COMPUTER
COMRADES
CONATION
CONATIVE
CONCEDED
CONCEITS
CONCEIVE
CONCEPTS
CONCERNS
CONCERTO
CONCERTS
CONCHOID
CONCLAVE
CONCLUDE
CONCRETE
CONDENSE
CONDOLED
CONDOLER
CONDONED
CONDONER
CONDUCED
CONDUCER
CONDUITS
CONDYLAR
CONFEREE
CONFERVA
CONFETTI
CONFIDED
CONFIDER
CONFINED
CONFINES
CONFLATE
CONFLICT
CONFOCAL
CONFOUND
CONFRERE
CONFRONT
CONFUSED
CONFUTED
CONFUTER
CONGENER
CONGRATS
CONGRESS
CONIDIAL
CONIDIUM
CONIFERS
CONJOINT
CONJUGAL
CONJUNCT

CONJURED
CONJURER
CONJUROR
CONNACHT
CONNIVED
CONNIVER
CONNOTED
CONODONT
CONOIDAL
CONQUEST
CONSERVE
CONSIDER
CONSOLED
CONSOLER
CONSOLES
CONSOMME
CONSORTS
CONSPIRE
CONSTANT
CONSTRUE
CONSULAR
CONSUMED
CONSUMER
CONTACTS
CONTANGO
CONTEMPT
CONTENTS
CONTESTS
CONTEXTS
CONTINUA
CONTINUE
CONTINUO
CONTOURS
CONTRACT
CONTRAIL
CONTRARY
CONTRAST
CONTRITE
CONTRIVE
CONTROLS
CONTUSED
CONVENED
CONVENER
CONVENTS
CONVERGE
CONVERSE
CONVERTS
CONVEXLY
CONVEYED
CONVEYER
CONVEYOR

CONVICTS
CONVINCE
CONVOKED
CONVOKER
CONVOYED
CONVULSE
COOKABLE
COOKBOOK
COOKOUTS
COOLABAR
COOLANTS
COOLIBAH
COOLNESS
COONSKIN
COOPTING
COOPTION
COPILOTS
COPLANAR
COPPERAS
COPULATE
COPYBOOK
COPYCATS
COPY-
  EDIT
COPYHOLD
COPYISTS
COQUETRY
COQUETTE
COQUILLE
CORACLES
CORACOID
CORDIALS
CORDLESS
CORDONED
CORDOVAN
CORDUROY
CORDWOOD
CORE
  TIME
CORKWOOD
CORNCOBS
CORNEOUS
CORNERED
CORNETTE
CORNICES
CORNICHE
CORNIEST
CORN
  PONE
CORNWALL
CORONARY

CORONERS
CORONETS
CORPORAL
CORRIDOR
CORRODED
CORRODER
CORSAGES
CORSAIRS
CORSELET
CORSETED
CORSETRY
CORTEGES
CORTICAL
CORTICES
CORTISOL
CORUNDUM
CORVETTE
CORYPHEE
COSECANT
COSINESS
COSMETIC
COSTLIER
COSTMARY
COST-
  PLUS
COSTUMES
COT
  DEATH
COTENANT
COTERIES
COTOPAXI
COTSWOLD
COTTAGER
COTTAGES
COTYLOID
COUCHANT
COUCHING
COUGHING
COULISSE
COUMARIC
COUMARIN
COUNCILS
COUNTERS
COUNTESS
COUNTIES
COUNTING
COUPLETS
COUPLING
COURANTE
COURLAND
COURSING

COURTESY
COURTIER
COURTING
COUSCOUS
COUSTEAU
COVALENT
COVENANT
COVENTRY
COVERAGE
COVERING
COVERLET
COVERTLY
COVER-
  UPS
COVETING
COVETOUS
COWARDLY
COWBELLS
COWBERRY
COWERING
COWHANDS
COWHERDS
COWHIDES
COWLICKS
COWLINGS
CO-
  WORKER
COWSHEDS
COWSLIPS
COXALGIA
COXALGIC
COXCOMBS
COXSWAIN
COZENAGE
COZENING
COZINESS
CRABBIER
CRABBING
CRABWISE
CRACKERS
CRACKING
CRACKLED
CRACKNEL
CRACKPOT
CRACKUPS
CRADLING
CRAFTIER
CRAFTILY
CRAFTING
CRAGGIER

CRAM-
  FULL
CRAMMERS
CRAMMING
CRAMPING
CRAMPONS
CRANE
  FLY
CRANIATE
CRANIUMS
CRANKIER
CRANKING
CRANKPIN
CRANNIED
CRANNIES
CRAPPIER
CRAPPING
CRASHING
CRASH
  PAD
CRAVENLY
CRAVINGS
CRAWFISH
CRAWLERS
CRAWLING
CRAYFISH
CRAYONED
CRAZIEST
CREAKIER
CREAKILY
CREAKING
CREAMERS
CREAMERY
CREAMIER
CREAMING
CREASING
CREATINE
CREATING
CREATION
CREATIVE
CREATORS
CREATURE
CREDENCE
CREDENZA
CREDIBLE
CREDIBLY
CREDITED
CREDITOR
CREEPERS
CREEPIER
CREEPILY

CREEPING
CREMATED
CREMATOR
CREODONT
CREOSOTE
CRESCENT
CRESTING
CRESYLIC
CRETONNE
CREVASSE
CREVICES
CREW
  CUTS
CREW
  NECK
CRIBBAGE
CRIBBING
CRICKETS
CRICKING
CRIMINAL
CRIMPING
CRIMSONS
CRINGING
CRINKLED
CRINKLES
CRIPPLED
CRIPPLES
CRISPATE
CRISPIER
CRISPING
CRISTATE
CRITERIA
CRITICAL
CRITIQUE
CRITTERS
CROAKILY
CROAKING
CROATIAN
CROCKERY
CROCOITE
CROCUSES
CROFTERS
CROMLECH
CRONYISM
CROOKING
CROONERS
CROONING
CROPPERS
CROPPING
CROSIERS
CROSSBAR

CROSSBOW
CROSSCUT
CROSS
  CUT
CROSSEST
CROSS-
  EYE
CROSSING
CROSSLET
CROSSPLY
CROSTINI
CROTCHES
CROTCHET
CROUCHED
CROUPIER
CROUPOUS
CROUTONS
CROWBARS
CROWBOOT
CROWDING
CROWFOOT
CROWNING
CROZIERS
CRUCIATE
CRUCIBLE
CRUCIFER
CRUCIFIX
CRUDITES
CRUISERS
CRUISING
CRUMBLED
CRUMBLES
CRUMHORN
CRUMMIER
CRUMPETS
CRUMPLED
CRUNCHED
CRUSADED
CRUSADER
CRUSADES
CRUSHING
CRUSTIER
CRUSTILY
CRUSTOSE
CRUTCHES
CRUZEIRO
CRY
  HAVOC
CRYOLITE
CRYONICS
CRYOSTAT

CRYOTRON
CRYSTALS
CUBATURE
CUBE
  ROOT
CUBICLES
CUBIFORM
CUBISIST
CUBISTIC
CUCKOLDS
CUCUMBER
CUCURBIT
CUDDLIER
CUDDLING
CUDGELED
CUFF
  LINK
CUL-DE-
  SAC
CULIACAN
CULINARY
CULOTTES
CULOUSLY
CULPABLE
CULPABLY
CULPRITS
CULTIGEN
CULTIVAR
CULTRATE
CULTURAL
CULTURED
CULTURES
CULVERIN
CULVERTS
CUMBERED
CUMBRIAN
CUMQUATS
CUMULOUS
CUPBOARD
CUP
  CAKES
CUP
  FINAL
CUPIDITY
CUPREOUS
CUPULATE
CURARIZE
CURASSOW
CURATIVE
CURATORS
CURCULIO
CURDLING

CURE-
  ALLS
CURITIBA
CURLICUE
CURLIEST
CURRANTS
CURRENCY
CURRENTS
CURRICLE
CURRIERY
CURRYING
CURSEDLY
CURTAINS
CURTNESS
CURTSIED
CURTSIES
CUSHIEST
CUSHIONS
CUSHIONY
CUSPIDOR
CUSSEDLY
CUSTARDS
CUSTOMER
CUSTUMAL
CUT A
  DASH
CUTAWAYS
CUTBACKS
CUTENESS
CUT
  GLASS
CUTICLES
CUTICULA
CUTINIZE
CUT-
  PRICE
CUTPURSE
CUTTINGS
CUTWATER
CUXHAVEN
CYANITIC
CYANOGEN
CYANOSIS
CYANOTIC
CYBERPET
CYCLADES
CYCLAMEN
CYCLISTS
CYCLONES
CYCLONIC
CYCLOSIS
CYLINDER

CYMATIUM
CYMOGENE
CYNICISM
CYNOSURE
CYPHERED
CYPRINID
CYRILLIC
CYSTEINE
CYSTITIS
CYTASTER
CYTIDINE
CYTOLOGY
CYTOSINE
CZARINAS

D

DABBLERS
DABBLING
DABCHICK
DAB
  HANDS
DACTYLIC
DAEMONIC
DAFFODIL
DAFTNESS
DAGESTAN
DAINTIER
DAINTIES
DAINTILY
DAIQUIRI
DAIRYMAN
DAIRYMEN
DALESMAN
DALLYING
DALMATIA
DALMATIC
DALTONIC
DAMAGING
DAMANHUR
DAMASCUS
DAMNABLE
DAMNABLY
DAMOCLES
DAMPENED
DAMPENER
DAMPNESS
DANDIEST
DANDLING
DANDRUFF
DANDYISH
DANDYISM

DANEWORT
DANGLING
DANKNESS
DANUBIAN
DARINGLY
DARK
  AGES
DARKENED
DARKENER
DARKNESS
DARKROOM
DARK
  ROOM
DARLINGS
DARTFORD
DATABASE
DATEABLE
DATELINE
DATE
  RAPE
DATOLITE
DAUGHTER
DAUNTING
DAUPHINE
DAUPHINS
DAVENTRY
DAWDLERS
DAWDLING
DAYBREAK
DAYDREAM
DAYLIGHT
DAYROOMS
DAYTIMES
DAY-TO-
  DAY
DAZZLING
DEACONRY
DEADBEAT
DEAD
  BEAT
DEAD
  DUCK
DEAD
  ENDS
DEADENED
DEADENER
DEADFALL
DEADHEAD
DEAD
  HEAT
DEADLIER
DEADLINE

DEADLOCK
DEADNESS
DEAD
  WOOD
DEAF-
  AIDS
DEAFENED
DEAF-
  MUTE
DEAFNESS
DEALFISH
DEALINGS
DEANSHIP
DEARESTS
DEARNESS
DEATHBED
DEATH
  ROW
DEBACLES
DEBARKED
DEBARRED
DEBASING
DEBATERS
DEBATING
DEBILITY
DEBITING
DEBONAIR
DEBRECEN
DEBUGGED
DEBUGGER
DEBUNKED
DEBUNKER
DEBUTANT
DECADENT
DECAMPED
DECANOIC
DECANTED
DECANTER
DECAYING
DECEASED
DECEIVED
DECEIVER
DECEMBER
DECENTLY
DECENTRE
DECIBELS
DECIDING
DECIDUAL
DECIMALS
DECIMATE
DECIPHER
DECISION

DECISIVE
DECKHAND
DECK
  HAND
DECLARED
DECLARER
DECLASSE
DECLINED
DECLINER
DECLINES
DECODING
DECOLOUR
DECORATE
DECOROUS
DECOYING
DECREASE
DECREPIT
DECRETAL
DECRYING
DECURVED
DEDICATE
DEDUCING
DEDUCTED
DEED
  POLL
DEEMSTER
DEEPENED
DEEPENER
DEEP-
  LAID
DEEPNESS
DEERSKIN
DEFACING
DEFAMING
DEFAULTS
DEFEATED
DEFEATER
DEFECATE
DEFECTED
DEFECTOR
DEFENCES
DEFENDED
DEFENDER
DEFERENT
DEFERRED
DEFERRER
DEFIANCE
DEFICITS
DEFILERS
DEFILING
DEFINING

DEFINITE
DEFLATED
DEFLATOR
DEFLEXED
DEFLOWER
DEFOREST
DEFORMED
DEFORMER
DEFRAYAL
DEFRAYED
DEFRAYER
DEFTNESS
DEFUSING
DEGASSER
DEGRADED
DEGRADER
DEICIDAL
DEIFYING
DEIGNING
DEJECTED
DELAWARE
DELAYING
DELEGACY
DELEGATE
DELETING
DELETION
DELICACY
DELICATE
DELIGHTS
DELIRIUM
DELIVERY
DELOUSED
DELPHIAN
DELUDING
DELUGING
DELUSION
DELUSIVE
DELUSORY
DEMAGOGY
DEMANDED
DEMANDER
DEMARCHE
DEMEANED
DEMENTED
DEMENTIA
DEMERARA
DEMERGER
DEMERITS
DEMERSAL
DEMESNES
DEMIGODS

DEMIJOHN
DEMILUNE
DEMISTED
DEMISTER
DEMIVOLT
DEMOBBED
DEMOCRAT
DEMOLISH
DEMONIAC
DEMONISM
DEMONIST
DEMONIZE
DEMOTING
DEMOTION
DEMOTIST
DEMPSTER
DEMURELY
DEMUREST
DEMURRAL
DEMURRED
DEMURRER
DENATURE
DENDRITE
DENDROID
DENIABLE
DENIZENS
DENOTING
DENOUNCE
DENTICLE
DENTINAL
DENTURES
DENUDATE
DENUDING
DEPARTED
DEPENDED
DEPICTED
DEPICTER
DEPILATE
DEPLETED
DEPLORED
DEPLORER
DEPLOYED
DEPONENT
DEPORTED
DEPORTEE
DEPOSING
DEPOSITS
DEPRAVED
DEPRAVER
DEPRIVED
DEPRIVER

DEPURATE
DEPUTIES
DEPUTING
DEPUTIZE
DERAILED
DERANGED
DERELICT
DERIDING
DERISION
DERISIVE
DERISORY
DERIVING
DEROGATE
DERRICKS
DESCALED
DESCANTS
DESCENTS
DESCRIBE
DESCRIED
DESCRIER
DESEEDER
DESERTED
DESERTER
DESERVED
DESERVER
DESIGNED
DESIGNER
DESINENT
DESIRING
DESIROUS
DESISTED
DESKWORK
DESOLATE
DESPATCH
DESPISED
DESPOTIC
DESSERTS
DESTINED
DESTRUCT
DETACHED
DETACHER
DETAILED
DETAINED
DETAINEE
DETAINER
DETECTED
DETECTER
DETECTOR
DETENTES
DETERRED
DETESTED

DETESTER
DETHRONE
DETONATE
DETRITAL
DETRITUS
DEUCEDLY
DEUTERON
DEVALUED
DEVIANCE
DEVIANTS
DEVIATED
DEVIATOR
DEVILING
DEVILISH
DEVILLED
DEVISING
DEVOLVED
DEVONIAN
DEVOTEES
DEVOTING
DEVOTION
DEVOURED
DEVOURER
DEVOUTER
DEVOUTLY
DEWBERRY
DEWDROPS
DEWINESS
DEWY-
  EYED
DEXTROSE
DIABASIC
DIABETES
DIABETIC
DIABOLIC
DIACIDIC
DIACONAL
DIAGNOSE
DIAGONAL
DIAGRAMS
DIAGRAPH
DIALECTS
DIALLAGE
DIALLING
DIALOGUE
DIALYSER
DIALYSIS
DIALYTIC
DIAMANTE
DIAMETER
DIAMONDS

DIANTHUS
DIAPASON
DIAPAUSE
DIAPHONE
DIAPHONY
DIARCHIC
DIARISTS
DIASCOPE
DIASPORA
DIASPORE
DIASTASE
DIASTEMA
DIASTOLE
DIASTRAL
DIASTYLE
DIATOMIC
DIATONIC
DIATRIBE
DIAZEPAM
DIBBLING
DICENTRA
DICHROIC
DICKERED
DICKIEST
DICROTIC
DICTATED
DICTATES
DICTATOR
DIDACTIC
DIDDLING
DIDYMIUM
DIDYMOUS
DIEHARDS
DIELDRIN
DIERESES
DIERESIS
DIERETIC
DIES
  IRAE
DIESTOCK
DIETETIC
DIFFERED
DIFFRACT
DIFFUSED
DIFFUSER
DIGAMIST
DIGAMOUS
DIGESTED
DIGESTER
DIGESTIF
DIGGINGS

DIGITATE
DIGITIZE
DIGITRON
DIGRAPHS
DIHEDRAL
DIHEDRON
DIHYBRID
DILATANT
DILATING
DILATION
DILATIVE
DILATORY
DILEMMAS
DILIGENT
DILUTING
DILUTION
DILUVIAL
DIMERISM
DIMERIZE
DIMEROUS
DIMETRIC
DIMINISH
DINGDONG
DINGHIES
DINGIEST
DINKIEST
DINOSAUR
DIOCESAN
DIOCESES
DIOPSIDE
DIOPTASE
DIOPTRAL
DIOPTRIC
DIORAMIC
DIORITIC
DIOXIDES
DIPHENYL
DIPLEGIA
DIPLEXER
DIPLOMAS
DIPLOMAT
DIPLOPIA
DIPLOPIC
DIPLOPOD
DIPLOSIS
DIPSTICK
DIPTERAL
DIPTERAN
DIRECTED
DIRECTLY
DIRECTOR

DIRIMENT
DIRT
  BIKE
DIRTIEST
DIRT
  ROAD
DIRTYING
DISABLED
DISABUSE
DISAGREE
DISALLOW
DISANNUL
DISARMED
DISARMER
DISARRAY
DISASTER
DISBURSE
DISCARDS
DISCIPLE
DISCLAIM
DISCLOSE
DISCORDS
DISCOUNT
DISCOVER
DISCREET
DISCRETE
DISCUSES
DISEASED
DISEASES
DISENDOW
DISGORGE
DISGRACE
DISGUISE
DISHEVEL
DISHFULS
DISHIEST
DISINTER
DISJOINT
DISJUNCT
DISKETTE
DISLIKED
DISLIKES
DISLODGE
DISLOYAL
DISMALLY
DISMAYED
DISMOUNT
DISORDER
DISOWNED
DISOWNER
DISPATCH

DISPENSE
DISPERSE
DISPIRIT
DISPLACE
DISPLAYS
DISPOSAL
DISPOSED
DISPOSER
DISPROOF
DISPROVE
DISPUTED
DISPUTER
DISPUTES
DISQUIET
DISROBED
DISROBER
DISSEISE
DISSENTS
DISSEVER
DISSOLVE
DISSUADE
DISTAFFS
DISTANCE
DISTASTE
DISTINCT
DISTRACT
DISTRAIN
DISTRAIT
DISTRESS
DISTRICT
DISTRUST
DISUNION
DISUNITE
DISUNITY
DITCHING
DITHEISM
DITHEIST
DITHERED
DITHERER
DIURESIS
DIURETIC
DIVALENT
DIVE-
  BOMB
DIVERGED
DIVERTED
DIVERTER
DIVESTED
DIVIDEND
DIVIDERS
DIVIDING

DIVI-
DIVI
DIVINELY
DIVINERS
DIVINING
DIVINITY
DIVINIZE
DIVISION
DIVISIVE
DIVISORS
DIVORCED
DIVORCEE
DIVORCER
DIVORCES
DIVULGED
DIVULGER
DIZZIEST
DJAKARTA
DJIBOUTI
DNIESTER
D-
NOTICE
S
DOCILITY
DOCKETED
DOCKLAND
DOCKSIDE
DOCKYARD
DOCTORAL
DOCTORED
DOCTRINE
DOCUMENT
DOCU-
SOAP
DODDERED
DODDERER
DODGIEST
DOGBERRY
DOGCARTS
DOG-
EARED
DOGFIGHT
DOGGEDLY
DOGGEREL
DOGGONED
DOGGY
BAG
DOGHOUSE
DOGMATIC
DO-
GOODER
DOGSBODY

DOG'S-
TAIL
DOG
TIRED
DOG-
TIRED
DOGTOOTH
DOGTROTS
DOGWATCH
DOG
WATCH
DOGWOODS
DOLDRUMS
DOLERITE
DOLOMITE
DOLOROSO
DOLOROUS
DOLPHINS
DOMELIKE
DOMESTIC
DOMICILE
DOMINANT
DOMINATE
DOMINEER
DOMINICA
DOMINION
DOMINIUM
DOMINOES
DONATING
DONATION
DONATIVE
DON
JUANS
DONLEAVY
DOODLING
DOOMSDAY
DOOMSTER
DOORBELL
DOORJAMB
DOORKNOB
DOORMATS
DOORNAIL
DOORPOST
DOORSILL
DOORSTEP
DOORSTOP
DOORWAYS
DOPAMINE
DOPINESS
DORDOGNE
DORMANCY
DORMOUSE

DORTMUND
DOSSIERS
DOTATION
DOTINGLY
DOTTEREL
DOTTIEST
DOUBLETS
DOUBLE
UP
DOUBLING
DOUBLOON
DOUBLURE
DOUBTERS
DOUBTFUL
DOUBTING
DOUGHNUT
DOUNREAY
DOURNESS
DOVECOTE
DOVETAIL
DOWAGERS
DOWDIEST
DOWNBEAT
DOWNCAST
DOWNFALL
DOWNHAUL
DOWNHILL
DOWNIEST
DOWNLOAD
DOWNPIPE
DOWNPLAY
DOWNPOUR
DOWNSIZE
DOWNSIZE
DOWNTIME
DOWNTOWN
DOWNTURN
DOWNWARD
DOWNWASH
DOWNWIND
DOXASTIC
DOXOLOGY
DOZINESS
DRABBEST
DRABNESS
DRACAENA
DRACHMAE
DRACHMAS
DRACONIC
DRAFTEES
DRAFTIER

DRAFTING
DRAGGIER
DRAGGING
DRAGGLED
DRAGLINE
DRAGNETS
DRAGOMAN
DRAGONET
DRAGOONS
DRAGROPE
DRAINAGE
DRAINING
DRAMATIC
DRAPABLE
DRATTING
DRAUGHTS
DRAUGHTY
DRAWABLE
DRAWBACK
DRAWBORE
DRAWCORD
DRAWDOWN
DRAWINGS
DRAWLING
DRAWTUBE
DREADFUL
DREADING
DREAMERS
DREAMILY
DREAMING
DREARIER
DREARILY
DREDGERS
DREDGING
DRENCHED
DRENCHER
DRESSAGE
DRESSERS
DRESSIER
DRESSILY
DRESSING
DRIBBLED
DRIBBLER
DRIBBLES
DRIBLETS
DRIFTAGE
DRIFTERS
DRIFTING
DRILLING
DRINKERS
DRINKING

DRIPPING
DRIVABLE
DRIVE-
INS
DRIVELED
DRIVEWAY
DRIZZLED
DROGHEDA
DROLLERY
DROLLEST
DROOLING
DROOPILY
DROOPING
DROP-
DEAD
DROPLETS
DROPOUTS
DROPPERS
DROPPING
DROP
SHOT
DROPSIED
DROPS
OFF
DROPWORT
DROUGHTS
DROUGHTY
DROWNING
DROWSILY
DROWSING
DRUBBING
DRUDGERY
DRUDGING
DRUGGETS
DRUGGING
DRUGGIST
DRUIDISM
DRUMBEAT
DRUMFIRE
DRUMFISH
DRUMHEAD
DRUMMERS
DRUMMING
DRUNKARD
DRUNKEST
DRUPELET
DRY-
CLEAN
DRY
DOCKS
DRY
GOODS

DRY-
STONE
DUBONNET
DUCKLING
DUCKWEED
DUCTILES
DUELLING
DUELLIST
DUE
NORTH
DUE
SOUTH
DUETTIST
DUISBURG
DUKEDOMS
DULCIANA
DULCIMER
DULLARDS
DULLNESS
DUMBBELL
DUMB-
CANE
DUMB
DOWN
DUMBNESS
DUMB
SHOW
DUMFRIES
DUMMY
RUN
DUMPIEST
DUMPLING
DUNGAREE
DUNGEONS
DUNGHILL
DUODENAL
DUODENUM
DUOLOGUE
DUPLEXES
DURATION
DURATIVE
DUSHANBE
DUSKIEST
DUSTBINS
DUSTBOWL
DUSTCART
DUSTIEST
DUSTPANS
DUTCH
CAP
DUTCHMAN
DUTIABLE

DUTY-
  FREE
DWARFING
DWARFISH
DWARFISM
DWELLING
DWINDLED
DYARCHIC
DYESTUFF
DYNAMICS
DYNAMISM
DYNAMIST
DYNAMITE
DYNASTIC
DYNATRON
DYSGENIC
DYSLEXIA
DYSLEXIC
DYSPNOEA
DYTISCID

E
EALING
EARDROPS
EARDRUMS
EARLDOMS
EARLIEST
EARLOBES
EARMUFFS
EARNINGS
EARPHONE
EARPIECE
EARPLUGS
EARRINGS
EARSHOTS
EARTHIER
EARTHILY
EARTHING
EARTHNUT
EASEMENT
EASINESS
EASTERLY
EAST
  SIDE
EASTWARD
EASTWOOD
EASY
  CARE
EASY
  MARK
EBB
  TIDES

EBBW
  VALE
ECCLESIA
ECDYSIAL
ECDYSONE
ECHELONS
ECHINATE
ECHINOID
ECLECTIC
ECLIPSED
ECLIPSER
ECLIPSES
ECLIPSIS
ECLIPTIC
ECLOGITE
ECLOSION
ECONOMIC
ECOTONAL
ECOTYPIC
ECRASEUR
ECSTATIC
ECTODERM
ECTOMERE
ECTOSARC
ECUMENIC
EDACIOUS
EDENTATE
EDGEWAYS
EDGINESS
EDIFICES
EDIFYING
EDITIONS
EDMONTON
EDUCABLE
EDUCATED
EDUCATOR
EDUCIBLE
EDUCTION
EDUCTIVE
EELGRASS
EERINESS
EFFACING
EFFECTED
EFFECTER
EFFECTOR
EFFERENT
EFFICACY
EFFIGIAL
EFFIGIES
EFFLUENT
EFFUSION

EFFUSIVE
EGESTION
EGESTIVE
EGGHEADS
EGGPLANT
EGG
  ROLLS
EGGSHELL
EGG
  TIMER
EGOISTIC
EGOMANIA
EGOTISTS
EGO
  TRIPS
EGYPTIAN
EIGHTEEN
EIGHTIES
EISENACH
EITHER-
  OR
EJECTING
EJECTION
EJECTIVE
EKISTICS
ELAPSING
ELASTANE
ELATERID
ELATERIN
ELBOWING
EL
  DORADO
ELDRITCH
ELECTING
ELECTION
ELECTIVE
ELECTORS
ELECTRET
ELECTRIC
ELECTRON
ELECTRUM
ELEGANCE
ELEMENTS
ELENCHUS
ELENCTIC
ELEPHANT
ELEVATED
ELEVATOR
ELEVENTH
EL
  FAIYUM

EL
  FERROL
ELF
  LOCKS
ELICITED
ELICITOR
ELIDIBLE
ELIGIBLE
ELISIONS
ELITISTS
ELKHOUND
ELLIPSES
ELLIPSIS
ELONGATE
ELOQUENT
ELYTROID
EMACIATE
EMANATED
EMANATOR
EMBALMED
EMBALMER
EMBARKED
EMBATTLE
EMBEDDED
EMBEZZLE
EMBITTER
EMBLAZON
EMBODIED
EMBOLDEN
EMBOLISM
EMBOSSED
EMBOSSER
EMBRACED
EMBRACER
EMBRACES
EMBRYOID
EMENDING
EMERALDS
EMERGENT
EMERGING
EMERITUS
EMERSION
EMIGRANT
EMIGRATE
EMINENCE
EMIRATES
EMISSARY
EMISSION
EMISSIVE
EMITTING
EMOTIONS

EMPATHIC
EMPERORS
EMPHASES
EMPHASIS
EMPHATIC
EMPLOYED
EMPLOYEE
EMPLOYER
EMPORIUM
EMPTIEST
EMPTYING
EMPYEMIC
EMPYREAL
EMPYREAN
EMULATED
EMULATOR
EMULSIFY
EMULSION
EMULSIVE
EMULSOID
ENABLING
ENACTING
ENACTIVE
ENACTORY
ENAMELED
ENCAENIA
ENCAMPED
ENCASING
ENCIPHER
ENCIRCLE
ENCLAVES
ENCLITIC
ENCLOSED
ENCLOSER
ENCODING
ENCOMIUM
ENCROACH
ENCUMBER
ENCYCLIC
ENDAMAGE
ENDANGER
END-
  BLOWN
ENDBRAIN
ENDEARED
ENDEMIAL
ENDEMISM
ENDERMIC
END
  GAMES
ENDOCARP

ENDODERM
ENDOGAMY
ENDOGENY
ENDORSED
ENDORSEE
ENDORSER
ENDORSOR
ENDOSOME
ENDOWING
ENDPAPER
ENDPLATE
ENDURING
END
  USERS
ENERGIZE
ENERVATE
ENFEEBLE
ENFILADE
ENFOLDED
ENFOLDER
ENFORCED
ENFORCER
ENGADINE
ENGAGING
ENGENDER
ENGINEER
ENGINERY
ENGRAVED
ENGRAVER
ENGULFED
ENHANCED
ENHANCER
ENIWETOK
ENJOINED
ENJOINER
ENJOYING
ENKINDLE
ENLARGED
ENLARGER
ENLISTED
ENLISTER
ENMESHED
ENNEADIC
ENNEAGON
ENNOBLED
ENNOBLER
ENORMITY
ENORMOUS
ENQUIRED
ENQUIRER
ENRAGING

ENRICHED	E	EQUATION	ESTANCIA	EUPHUIST	EXCEEDED
ENRICHER	NUMBER	EQUINITY	ESTEEMED	EUPNOEIC	EXCEEDER
ENROLLED	S	EQUIPAGE	ESTERASE	EURASIAN	EXCELLED
ENROLLEE	ENURESIS	EQUIPPED	ESTERIFY	EUROCRAT	EXCEPTED
ENROLLER	ENURETIC	EQUIPPER	ESTHETES	EURONOTE	EXCERPTS
ENSCHEDE	ENVELOPE	EQUITANT	ESTIMATE	EUROPEAN	EXCESSES
ENSCONCE	ENVIABLE	EQUITIES	ESTONIAN	EUROPIUM	EXCHANGE
ENSEMBLE	ENVIABLY	ERADIATE	ESTOPPEL	EUSTATIC	EXCISING
ENSHRINE	ENVIRONS	ERASABLE	ESTOVERS	EUTECTIC	EXCISION
ENSHROUD	ENVISAGE	ERASTIAN	ESTRAGON	EUXENITE	EXCITANT
ENSIFORM	ENVISION	ERASURES	ESTRANGE	EVACUANT	EXCITING
ENSILAGE	ENWREATH	ERECTILE	ESURIENT	EVACUATE	EXCLUDED
ENSLAVED	ENZOOTIC	ERECTING	ET	EVACUEES	EXCLUDER
ENSLAVER	EOLITHIC	ERECTION	CETERA	EVADABLE	EXCRETAL
ENSNARED	EPAULETS	EREMITIC	ETCHINGS	EVALUATE	EXCRETED
ENSNARER	EPHEMERA	ERETHISM	ETERNITY	EVANESCE	EXCRETER
ENSPHERE	EPIBLAST	ERGOTISM	ETERNIZE	EVANSTON	EXCURSUS
ENSURING	EPIBOLIC	ERIGERON	ETHEREAL	EVASIONS	EXCUSING
ENSWATHE	EPICALYX	ERITREAN	ETHERIFY	EVECTION	EXECRATE
ENTAILED	EPICOTYL	ERLANGEN	ETHERIZE	EVENINGS	EXECUTED
ENTAILER	EPICURES	ERRANTRY	ETHERNET	EVENNESS	EXECUTER
ENTANGLE	EPICYCLE	ERUMPENT	ETHICIST	EVENSONG	EXECUTOR
ENTELLUS	EPIDEMIC	ERUPTING	ETHICIZE	EVENTFUL	EXEGESES
ENTENDRE	EPIDOTIC	ERUPTION	ETHIOPIA	EVENTIDE	EXEGESIS
ENTENTES	EPIDURAL	ERUPTIVE	ETHIOPIC	EVENTUAL	EXEGETIC
ENTERING	EPIFOCAL	ERYTHEMA	ETHNARCH	EVERMORE	EXEMPLAR
ENTHALPY	EPIGRAMS	ESCALADE	ETHOLOGY	EVERSION	EXEMPLUM
ENTHETIC	EPIGRAPH	ESCALATE	ETHONONE	EVERYDAY	EXEMPTED
ENTHRONE	EPILEPSY	ESCALOPE	ETHOXIDE	EVERYMAN	EXEQUIES
ENTHUSED	EPILOGUE	ESCAPADE	ETHYLATE	EVERYONE	EXERCISE
ENTICING	EPINASTY	ESCAPEES	ETHYLENE	EVICTING	EXERGUAL
ENTIRELY	EPIPHANY	ESCAPING	ETIOLATE	EVICTION	EXERTING
ENTIRETY	EPIPHYTE	ESCAPISM	ETIOLOGY	EVIDENCE	EXERTION
ENTITIES	EPISCOPE	ESCAPIST	ETON	EVILDOER	EXERTIVE
ENTITLED	EPISODES	ESCHEWAL	CROP	EVILLEST	EX
ENTODERM	EPISODIC	ESCHEWED	ETRUSCAN	EVILNESS	GRATIA
ENTOMBED	EPISTLER	ESCHEWER	EUCHARIS	EVINCING	EXHALANT
ENTOZOIC	EPISTLES	ESCORTED	EUGENICS	EVINCIVE	EXHALING
ENTOZOON	EPISTYLE	ESCULENT	EULACHON	EVOCABLE	EXHAUSTS
ENTR'ACT	EPITAPHS	ESKIMOAN	EULOGIES	EVOCATOR	EXHIBITS
E	EPITASIS	ESKIMOID	EULOGIST	EVOLVING	EXHORTED
ENTRAILS	EPITHETS	ESOTERIC	EULOGIZE	EVONYMUS	EXHORTER
ENTRANCE	EPITOMIC	ESPALIER	EUONYMUS	EXACTING	EXHUMING
ENTRANTS	EPIZOISM	ESPECIAL	EUPEPSIA	EXACTION	EXIGENCY
ENTREATY	EPIZOITE	ESPOUSAL	EUPEPTIC	EXALTING	EXIGIBLE
ENTRENCH	EPONYMIC	ESPOUSED	EUPHONIC	EXAMINED	EXIGUITY
ENTREPOT	EQUALING	ESPOUSER	EUPHORIA	EXAMINEE	EXIGUOUS
ENTRESOL	EQUALITY	ESPRESSO	EUPHORIC	EXAMINER	EXISTENT
ENTRYISM	EQUALIZE	ESSAYING	EUPHOTIC	EXAMPLES	EXISTING
ENTRYWAY	EQUALLED	ESSAYIST	EUPHRASY	EXARCHAL	EXITANCE
ENTWINED	EQUATING	ESSENCES	EUPHUISM	EXCAVATE	

EX
  LIBRIS
EXOCRINE
EXOERGIC
EXORABLE
EXORCISE
EXORCISM
EXORCIST
EXORCIZE
EXORDIAL
EXORDIUM
EXOSPORE
EXOTERIC
EXOTOXIC
EXOTOXIN
EXPANDED
EXPANDER
EXPECTED
EXPEDITE
EXPELLED
EXPELLEE
EXPELLER
EXPENDED
EXPENDER
EXPENSES
EXPERTLY
EXPIABLE
EXPIATED
EXPIATOR
EXPIRING
EXPLICIT
EXPLODED
EXPLODER
EXPLOITS
EXPLORED
EXPLORER
EXPONENT
EXPORTED
EXPORTER
EXPOSING
EXPOSURE
EXPUNGED
EXPUNGER
EXTENDED
EXTENDER
EXTENSOR
EXTERIOR
EXTERNAL
EXTOLLED
EXTOLLER
EXTORTED

EXTORTER
EXTRACTS
EXTRADOS
EXTREMES
EXTRORSE
EXTRUDED
EXULTANT
EXULTING
EXUVIATE
EYEBALLS
EYEBROWS
EYEGLASS
EYELINER
EYEPATCH
EYEPIECE
EYESHADE
EYESIGHT
EYESORES
EYESTALK
EYETEETH
EYETOOTH

F

FABULIST
FABULOUS
FACEABLE
FACE
  CARD
FACE
  DOWN
FACELESS
FACE-
  LIFT
FACE
  PACK
FACETIAE
FACIALLY
FACILELY
FACILITY
FACTIONS
FACTIOUS
FACTOTUM
FADELESS
FADEOUTS
FAEROESE
FAHLBAND
FAILINGS
FAIL-
  SAFE
FAILURES
FAINEANT
FAINTEST

FAINTING
FAINTISH
FAIR
  COPY
FAIR
  GAME
FAIRINGS
FAIRLEAD
FAIRNESS
FAIRWAYS
FAITHFUL
FAIZABAD
FALCHION
FALCONER
FALCONET
FALCONRY
FALDERAL
FALKLAND
FALL
  BACK
FALLFISH
FALL
  GUYS
FALLIBLE
FALLOUTS
FALL
  OVER
FALMOUTH
FALSETTO
FALTBOAT
FALTERED
FALTERER
FAMILIAL
FAMILIAR
FAMILIES
FAMISHED
FAMOUSLY
FANAGALO
FANATICS
FAN
  BELTS
FANCIERS
FANCIEST
FANCIFUL
FANCYING
FANCY
  MAN
FANCY
  MEN
FAN
  DANCE
FANDANGO

FANFARES
FANLIGHT
FANTASIA
FANZINES
FARADISM
FARADIZE
FARCEUSE
FARCICAL
FAREWELL
FAR-
  FLUNG
FARINOSE
FARMABLE
FARMHAND
FARMLAND
FARMYARD
FARNESOL
FAROUCHE
FARRIERS
FARRIERY
FARROWED
FARTHEST
FARTHING
FASCIATE
FASCICLE
FASCISTS
FASHIONS
FASTBACK
FASTENED
FASTENER
FAST
  FOOD
FASTNESS
FATALISM
FATALIST
FATALITY
FATHEADS
FATHERED
FATHERLY
FATHOMED
FATHOMER
FATIGUED
FATIGUES
FATTENED
FATTENER
FATTIEST
FAUBOURG
FAULTIER
FAULTILY
FAULTING
FAUSTIAN

FAUTEUIL
FAVONIAN
FAVOURED
FAVOURER
FAYALITE
FEARLESS
FEARSOME
FEASIBLE
FEASIBLY
FEASTING
FEATHERS
FEATHERY
FEATURED
FEATURES
FEBRIFIC
FEBRUARY
FECKLESS
FECULENT
FEDERATE
FEEBLEST
FEEDABLE
FEEDBACK
FEEDBAGS
FEELINGS
FEIGNING
FEINTING
FELDSPAR
FELICITY
FELINITY
FELLABLE
FELLATIO
FELONIES
FELSITIC
FEMININE
FEMINISM
FEMINIST
FEMINIZE
FENDERED
FENESTRA
FERETORY
FEROCITY
FERREOUS
FERRETED
FERRETER
FERRIAGE
FERRITIN
FERRULES
FERRYING
FERRYMAN
FERRYMEN
FERVENCY

FERVIDLY
FESTERED
FESTIVAL
FESTOONS
FETATION
FETCHING
FETIALES
FETICIDE
FETISHES
FETLOCKS
FETTERED
FETTERER
FETTLING
FEVERFEW
FEVERISH
FIASCOES
FIBRILAR
FIBROSIS
FIBROTIC
FICTIONS
FIDDLING
FIDELITY
FIDGETED
FIDUCIAL
FIELD
  DAY
FIELDERS
FIELDING
FIENDISH
FIERCELY
FIERCEST
FIERIEST
FIFTIETH
FIGHTERS
FIGHTING
FIG
  LEAFS
FIGMENTS
FIGURANT
FIGURATE
FIGURINE
FIGURING
FILAGREE
FILAMENT
FILARIAL
FILATURE
FILCHING
FILECARD
FILEFISH
FILENAME
FILETING

FILICIDE
FILIFORM
FILIGREE
FILIPINO
FILLETED
FILLINGS
FILMIEST
FILM
 STAR
FILTERED
FILTHIER
FILTHILY
FILTRATE
FIMBRIAL
FINAGLER
FINALISM
FINALIST
FINALITY
FINALIZE
FINANCED
FINANCES
FINDABLE
FINDINGS
FINEABLE
FINE
 ARTS
FINE-
 DRAW
FINE
 GAEL
FINENESS
FINESPUN
FINE
 SPUN
FINE-
 TUNE
FINGERED
FINGERER
FINIALED
FINISHED
FINISHER
FINISHES
FINITELY
FINNMARK
FINOCHIO
FIREABLE
FIREARMS
FIREBACK
FIREBALL
FIREBOAT
FIREBRAT
FIREBUGS

FIRE-
 CURE
FIREDAMP
FIREDOGS
FIRE-
 PLUG
FIRESIDE
FIRETRAP
FIREWALL
FIREWEED
FIREWOOD
FIREWORK
FIRMNESS
FIRMWARE
FIRST
 AID
FIRST-
 DAY
FIRTREES
FISCALLY
FISHABLE
FISHBOLT
FISHBOWL
FISHCAKE
FISH
 FARM
FISH-
 HOOK
FISHIEST
FISHMEAL
FISHNETS
FISHSKIN
FISHTAIL
FISHWIFE
FISSIPED
FISSURES
FISTMELE
FITFULLY
FITMENTS
FITTABLE
FITTINGS
FIVEFOLD
FIVEPINS
FIVE-
 STAR
FIXATION
FIXATIVE
FIXTURES
FIZZIEST
FLABBIER
FLABBILY

FLAG
 DAYS
FLAG
 FALL
FLAGGING
FLAGPOLE
FLAGRANT
FLAGSHIP
FLAILING
FLAKIEST
FLAMBEAU
FLAMENCO
FLAMEOUT
FLAMINGO
FLANDERS
FLANERIE
FLANKING
FLANNELS
FLAPJACK
FLAPPING
FLARE-
 UPS
FLASHERS
FLASHEST
FLASHGUN
FLASH
 GUN
FLASHIER
FLASHILY
FLASHING
FLATBOAT
FLATETTE
FLAT
 FEET
FLATFISH
FLATFOOT
FLATHEAD
FLATLETS
FLATMATE
FLATNESS
FLAT
 RACE
FLAT
 SPIN
FLATTERY
FLATTEST
FLATTING
FLATTISH
FLATWARE
FLATWAYS
FLATWORM
FLAUNTED

FLAUNTER
FLAUTIST
FLAVOURS
FLAWLESS
FLAXSEED
FLEABAGS
FLEABANE
FLEABITE
FLEA
 BITE
FLEAPITS
FLEAWORT
FLECKING
FLECTION
FLEECING
FLEETEST
FLEETING
FLESHIER
FLESHING
FLESHPOT
FLETCHER
FLEXIBLE
FLEXIBLY
FLEXUOUS
FLEXURAL
FLICKERY
FLICKING
FLIMFLAM
FLIMSIER
FLIMSILY
FLINCHED
FLINCHER
FLINGING
FLINTIER
FLIP-
 FLOP
FLIPPANT
FLIPPERS
FLIPPEST
FLIPPING
FLIP
 SIDE
FLIRTING
FLITTING
FLOATAGE
FLOATERS
FLOATING
FLOCCOSE
FLOCCULE
FLOCKING
FLOGGING

FLOODING
FLOODLIT
FLOORAGE
FLOORING
FLOOZIES
FLOPPIER
FLOPPILY
FLOPPING
FLORALLY
FLORENCE
FLORIDLY
FLORIGEN
FLORISTS
FLOSSING
FLOTILLA
FLOUNCED
FLOUNCES
FLOUNDER
FLOURING
FLOURISH
FLOUTING
FLOWERED
FLOWERER
FLUE-
 CURE
FLUENTLY
FLUFFIER
FLUFFING
FLUIDICS
FLUIDITY
FLUIDIZE
FLUMMERY
FLUNKEYS
FLUNKING
FLUORENE
FLUORIDE
FLUORINE
FLURRIED
FLURRIES
FLUSHING
FLUTISTS
FLUTTERS
FLUTTERY
FLYBLOWN
FLYOVERS
FLYPAPER
FLYPASTS
FLYSHEET
FLYSPECK
FLYWHEEL
FLYWHISK

FOAMIEST
FOAMLIKE
FOB
 WATCH
FOCALIZE
FOCUSING
FOCUSSED
FOETUSES
FOGBOUND
FOGGIEST
FOGHORNS
FOG
 LAMPS
FOGLIGHT
FOIE
 GRAS
FOILABLE
FOILSMAN
FOISTING
FOLDABLE
FOLDAWAY
FOLDBOAT
FOLIATED
FOLKLORE
FOLK-
 ROCK
FOLKTALE
FOLKWAYS
FOLLICLE
FOLLOWED
FOLLOWER
FOLLOW-
 ON
FOLLOW-
 UP
FOMENTED
FOMENTER
FONDANTS
FONDLING
FONDNESS
FOOLSCAP
FOOTBALL
FOOTFALL
FOOTGEAR
FOOTHILL
FOOTHOLD
FOOTLING
FOOTMARK
FOOTNOTE
FOOTPACE
FOOTPADS
FOOTPATH

FOOTRACE
FOOTREST
FOOTROPE
FOOTSIES
FOOTSLOG
FOOTSORE
FOOTSTEP
FOOTWALL
FOOTWEAR
FOOTWELL
FOOTWORK
FOOTWORN
FORAGING
FOR A
 SONG
FORAYING
FORBEARS
FORBORNE
FORCE-
 FED
FORCEFUL
FORCIBLE
FORCIBLY
FORDABLE
FOREARMS
FOREBEAR
FOREBODE
FORECAST
FOREDECK
FOREDOOM
FOREFEET
FOREFOOT
FOREGOER
FOREGONE
FOREHAND
FOREHEAD
FOREKNOW
FORELAND
FORELEGS
FORELIMB
FORELOCK
FOREMAST
FOREMOST
FORENAME
FORENOON
FORENSIC
FOREPART
FOREPEAK
FOREPLAY
FORESAIL
FORESEEN

FORESEER
FORESIDE
FORESKIN
FORESTAL
FORESTAY
FORESTED
FORESTER
FORESTRY
FORETELL
FORETIME
FORETOLD
FOREWARN
FOREWENT
FOREWIND
FOREWING
FOREWORD
FOREYARD
FORFEITS
FORGINGS
FORGIVEN
FORGIVER
FORGOING
FORJUDGE
FORK-
 LIFT
FORMABLE
FORMALIN
FORMALLY
FORMERLY
FORMLESS
FORMULAE
FORMULAS
FORMWORK
FORNICAL
FORSAKEN
FORSAKER
FORSOOTH
FORSWEAR
FORSWORE
FORSWORN
FORTIETH
FORT
 KNOX
FORTRESS
FORTUITY
FORTUNES
FORWARDS
FORZANDO
FOSSETTE
FOSTERED
FOSTERER

FOULNESS
FOUL
 PLAY
FOUNDERS
FOUNDING
FOUNTAIN
FOUR-
 BALL
FOUR-
 DEAL
FOUR-
 EYED
FOUREYES
FOURFOLD
FOUR-
 LEAF
FOURSOME
FOUR-
 STAR
FOURTEEN
FOVEOLAR
FOWLIANG
FOWL
 PEST
FOXGLOVE
FOXHOLES
FOXHOUND
FOXHUNTS
FOXINESS
FOXTROTS
FRACTION
FRACTURE
FRAGMENT
FRAGRANT
FRAILEST
FRAMABLE
FRAME-
 UPS
FRANCIUM
FRANKEST
FRANKING
FRANKISH
FRANKLIN
FRASCATI
FRAULEIN
FRAZZLED
FREAKING
FREAKISH
FRECKLED
FRECKLES
FREE-
 BASE

FREEBIES
FREEBOOT
FREEBORN
FREEDMAN
FREE-
 FALL
FREEFONE
FREEHAND
FREEHOLD
FREE
 KICK
FREELOAD
FREE
 PASS
FREE
 PORT
FREEPOST
FREE
 REIN
FREESIAS
FREE
 TIME
FREETOWN
FREEWARE
FREEWAYS
FREE
 WILL
FREEZERS
FREEZE
 UP
FREEZE-
 UP
FREEZING
FREIBURG
FREMITUS
FRENETIC
FRENULUM
FRENZIED
FREQUENT
FRESCOES
FRESHEST
FRESHMAN
FRESHMEN
FRETLESS
FRETSAWS
FRETTING
FRETWORK
FREUDIAN
FRIARIES
FRIBBLER
FRIBOURG
FRICTION

FRIENDLY
FRIESIAN
FRIGATES
FRIGGING
FRIGHTEN
FRIGIDLY
FRILLIER
FRINGING
FRIPPERY
FRISBEES
FRISETTE
FRISKIER
FRISKILY
FRISKING
FRISSONS
FRITTATA
FRITTERS
FRIULIAN
FRIZZIER
FRIZZING
FRIZZLED
FRIZZLER
FROCKING
FROGFISH
FROMENTY
FRONDEUR
FRONTAGE
FRONTIER
FRONTING
FRONTLET
FRONT
 MAN
FRONT
 MEN
FROSTIER
FROSTILY
FROSTING
FROTHIER
FROTHILY
FROTHING
FROUFROU
FROWNING
FROWZIER
FRUCTIFY
FRUCTOSE
FRUGALLY
FRUITAGE
FRUIT
 BAT
FRUIT
 FLY
FRUITFUL

FRUITIER
FRUITING
FRUITION
FRUMENTY
FRUMPIER
FRUMPISH
FRUSTULE
FUCHSIAS
FUCOIDAL
FUDDLING
FUELLING
FUGACITY
FUGGIEST
FUGITIVE
FUGLEMAN
FULCRUMS
FULLBACK
FULL
 MOON
FULLNESS
FULL-
 PAGE
FULL
 STOP
FULL-
 TIME
FULL
 TOSS
FULMINIC
FUMAROLE
FUMATORY
FUMBLING
FUMELESS
FUMIGANT
FUMIGATE
FUMINGLY
FUMITORY
FUNCTION
FUNERALS
FUNERARY
FUNEREAL
FUNFAIRS
FUNGIBLE
FUNGUSES
FUNKIEST
FUNNELED
FUNNIEST
FURBELOW
FURCATED
FURFURAN
FURLABLE
FURLONGS

131

FURLOUGH
FURNACES
FURRIERS
FURRIERY
FURRIEST
FURROWED
FURROWER
FURTHEST
FURUNCLE
FUSELAGE
FUSIFORM
FUSILIER
FUSSIEST
FUSSPOTS
FUSTIEST
FUTILITY
FUTURISM
FUTURIST.
FUTURITY
FUZZIEST

G
GABBLING
GABBROIC
GABONESE
GABORONE
GADABOUT
GADFLIES
GADGETRY
GAFFSAIL
GAINABLE
GAINSAID
GALACTIC
GALANGAL
GALAXIES
GALBANUM
GALENISM
GALENIST
GALICIAN
GALILEAN
GALLANTS
GALLEASS
GALLEONS
GALLERIA
GALLIARD
GALLIPOT
GALLOPED
GALLOPER
GALLOWAY
GALOSHES
GALVANIC

GAMBLERS
GAMBLING
GAMBOLED
GAMECOCK
GAME
  FOWL
GAMENESS
GAMESTER
GAMINESS
GAMMA
  RAY
GAMMONER
GANDHIAN
GANG-
  BANG
GANGLAND
GANGLIAL
GANGLING
GANGLION
GANGRENE
GANGSTER
GANGWAYS
GANISTER
GANTLINE
GANTRIES
GANYMEDE
GAOLBIRD
GAOXIONG
GAPEWORM
GAPINGLY
GARAGING
GARAMOND
GARBLESS
GARBLING
GARBOARD
GARDENED
GARDENER
GARDENIA
GARGANEY
GARGLING
GARGOYLE
GARISHLY
GARLANDS
GARLICKY
GARMENTS
GARNERED
GARRISON
GARROTTE
GASIFIER
GASIFORM
GASLIGHT

GAS
  MASKS
GASOLIER
GASOLINE
GASSIEST
GASTIGHT
GASTRULA
GASWORKS
GATEFOLD
GATEPOST
GATEWAYS
GATHERED
GATHERER
GAUDIEST
GAULLISM
GAULLIST
GAUNTLET
GAUZIEST
GAVOTTES
GAWKIEST
GAZELLES
GAZETTES
GAZPACHO
GAZUMPED
GAZUMPER
GELATINE
GELATION
GELDINGS
GELIDITY
GEMINATE
GEMOLOGY
GEMSTONE
GENDARME
GENDERED
GENERALS
GENERATE
GENEROUS
GENETICS
GENIALLY
GENITALS
GENITIVE
GENIUSES
GENOCIDE
GENOTYPE
GENTIANS
GENTILES
GENTRIFY
GEODESIC
GEODETIC
GEOGNOSY
GEOMANCY

GEOMETER
GEOMETRY
GEOPHAGY
GEOPHYTE
GEOPONIC
GEORDIES
GEORGIAN
GEOTAXIS
GERANIAL
GERANIOL
GERANIUM
GERMANIC
GERM
  CELL
GERMINAL
GESTALTS
GESTAPOS
GESTURAL
GESTURED
GESTURER
GESTURES
GET
  THERE
GHANAIAN
GHERKINS
GHETTOES
GHOSTING
GHOULISH
GIANTESS
GIBBERED
GIBBSITE
GIBINGLY
GIDDIEST
GIFT-
  WRAP
GIGAFLOP
GIGANTIC
GIGGLING
GILTHEAD
GILTWOOD
GIMCRACK
GIMMICKS
GIMMICKY
GINGERED
GINGERLY
GINGIVAL
GIN
  RUMMY
GINSBERG
GIN
  SLING

GIN
  TRAPS
GIRAFFES
GIRDLING
GIRLHOOD
GISBORNE
GIVEAWAY
GIZZARDS
GLABELLA
GLABROUS
GLACIATE
GLACIERS
GLADBECK
GLADDEST
GLAD
  HAND
GLADIATE
GLADIOLI
GLADNESS
GLAD
  RAGS
GLANCING
GLANDERS
GLANDULE
GLASSIER
GLASSINE
GLASSING
GLASSMAN
GLAUCOMA
GLAUCOUS
GLAZIERS
GLAZIERY
GLEAMING
GLEANING
GLENDALE
GLIBBEST
GLIBNESS
GLIMMERS
GLIMPSED
GLIMPSER
GLIMPSES
GLINTING
GLISSADE
GLITCHES
GLITTERS
GLITTERY
GLITZIER
GLOAMING
GLOATING
GLOBALLY
GLOBULAR

GLOBULES
GLOBULIN
GLOOMFUL
GLOOMIER
GLOOMILY
GLORIOUS
GLORYING
GLOSSARY
GLOSSIER
GLOSSILY
GLOSSING
GLOWERED
GLOW-
  WORM
GLOXINIA
GLUCAGON
GLUCINUM
GLUCOSIC
GLUMMEST
GLUMNESS
GLUTELIN
GLUTTING
GLUTTONS
GLUTTONY
GLYCERIC
GLYCERIN
GLYCEROL
GLYCERYL
GLYCOGEN
GLYCOLIC
GLYPTICS
GNASHERS
GNASHING
GNATHION
GNATHITE
GNAWABLE
GNEISSIC
GNOMONIC
GOAL
  LINE
GOALPOST
GOATHERD
GOATSKIN
GOAT'S-
  RUE
GOBBLING
GOBSHITE
GOD-
  AWFUL
GODCHILD
GODLIEST
GODSENDS

GODSPEED
GODTHAAB
GOETHITE
GO-
  GETTER
GOGGLING
GOIDELIC
GOINGS
  ON
GOINGS-
  ON
GOITROUS
GOLD
  COAT
GOLD
  DUST
GOLDFISH
GOLD
  LEAF
GOLDMINE
GOLD
  RUSH
GOLF
  BALL
GOLF
  CLUB
GOLIATHS
GOLLIWOG
GOLLOPER
GOMBROON
GONDOLAS
GONIDIAL
GONIDIUM
GONOCYTE
GONOPORE
GOOD
  BOOK
GOODBYES
GOODLIER
GOODNESS
GOOD
  TURN
GOODWILL
GOODWOOD
GOOD
  WORD
GOOFIEST
GOOGLIES
GO
  PLACES
GORDIMER
GORGEDLY

GORGEOUS
GORGERIN
GORILLAS
GORINESS
GORLOVKA
GORMLESS
GOSLINGS
GOSPODIN
GOSSAMER
GOSSIPED
GOSSIPER
GOSSYPOL
GOTEBORG
GO TO
  TOWN
GOUACHES
GOURMAND
GOURMETS
GOUTWEED
GOVERNED
GOVERNOR
GRAB
  BAGS
GRABBING
GRABBLER
GRACEFUL
GRACIOUS
GRADABLE
GRADIENT
GRADUATE
GRAECISM
GRAFFITI
GRAFFITO
GRAFTERS
GRAFTING
GRAINING
GRAMPIAN
GRANDADS
GRANDEES
GRANDEST
GRANDEUR
GRAND
  MAL
GRANDMAS
GRANDPAS
GRANDSON
GRANITIC
GRANNIES
GRANTHAM
GRANTING
GRANULAR

GRANULES
GRAPHEME
GRAPHICS
GRAPHITE
GRAPNELS
GRAPPLED
GRAPPLER
GRASPING
GRASSIER
GRASSING
GRATEFUL
GRATINGS
GRATUITY
GRAVAMEN
GRAVELED
GRAVELLY
GRAVITAS
GRAVITON
GRAYLING
GREASERS
GREASIER
GREASILY
GREASING
GREATEST
GREEDIER
GREEDILY
GREENERY
GREENEST
GREENFLY
GREENING
GREENISH
GREENLET
GREENOCK
GREEN
  TEA
GREETING
GREMLINS
GRENADES
GRENOBLE
GREY
  AREA
GREYBACK
GREYNESS
GRIDDLES
GRIDIRON
GRIDLOCK
GRIEVING
GRIEVOUS
GRIFFINS
GRILLAGE
GRILLING

GRIMACED
GRIMACER
GRIMACES
GRIMIEST
GRIMMEST
GRIMNESS
GRINDERS
GRINDERY
GRINDING
GRINNING
GRIPPING
GRISEOUS
GRISETTE
GRISLIER
GRITTIER
GRITTILY
GRITTING
GRIZZLED
GRIZZLER
GROANING
GROGGIER
GROGGILY
GROMWELL
GROOMING
GROOVIER
GROSBEAK
GROSCHEN
GROSSEST
GROSSING
GROTTIER
GROTTOES
GROUCHED
GROUCHES
GROUNDED
GROUPIES
GROUPING
GROUSING
GROVELED
GROWABLE
GROWLERS
GROWLING
GROWMORE
GROWN-
  UPS
GRUBBIER
GRUBBILY
GRUBBING
GRUDGING
GRUESOME
GRUFFEST
GRUFFISH

GRUMBLED
GRUMBLER
GRUMBLES
GRUMPIER
GRUMPILY
GRUNTING
GRYPHONS
G-
  STRING
  S
GUAIACOL
GUAIACUM
GUARANTY
GUARDANT
GUARDIAN
GUARDING
GUERNSEY
GUERRERO
GUESSING
GUESTING
GUFFAWED
GUIANESE
GUIDABLE
GUIDANCE
GUILDERS
GUILEFUL
GUILTIER
GUILTILY
GUJARATI
GULFWEED
GULLIBLE
GULLIBLY
GUMBOILS
GUMBOOTS
GUMBOTIL
GUMDROPS
GUMMIEST
GUMMOSIS
GUMPTION
GUMSHOES
GUM
  TREES
GUNBOATS
GUNFLINT
GUNMETAL
GUNPAPER
GUNPOINT
GUNSHOTS
GUNSMITH
GUNSTOCK
GUNWALES

GURGLING
GURKHALI
GUSTIEST
GUTSIEST
GUTTERED
GUTTURAL
GUYANESE
GUZZLERS
GUZZLING
GYMKHANA
GYMNASTS
GYMSLIPS
GYNANDRY
GYNARCHY
GYPSEOUS
GYRATING
GYRATION
GYRATORY

H

HABAKKUK
HABANERA
HABITANT
HABITATS
HABITUAL
HABITUDE
HABITUES
HABSBURG
HACIENDA
HACKETTE
HACKNEYS
HACKSAWS
HACKWORK
HADRONIC
HAEMATIC
HAEMATIN
HAEREMAI
HA-ERH-
  PIN
HAFTARAH
HAGGADAH
HAGGADIC
HAGGLING
HAILWOOD
HAIPHONG
HAIRBALL
HAIRCUTS
HAIRGRIP
HAIRIEST
HAIRLESS
HAIRLIKE

133

HAIRLINE	HANDBELL	HARAMBEE	HARKENER	HAVELOCK	HEADWORK
HAIRNETS	HANDBILL	HARANGUE	HARLOTRY	HAVE-	HEALABLE
HAIRPINS	HANDBOOK	HARAPPAN	HARMLESS	NOTS	HEARABLE
HAIRTAIL	HANDCART	HARASSED	HARMONIC	HAVERING	HEAR
HAIRWORM	HANDCLAP	HARASSER	HARPINGS	HAVILDAR	HEAR
HAKODATE	HANDCUFF	HARBOURS	HARPISTS	HAVOCKER	HEARINGS
HALAFIAN	HANDFAST	HARD AT	HARPOONS	HAWAIIAN	HEARTIER
HALATION	HANDFEED	IT	HARRIDAN	HAWFINCH	HEARTILY
HALBERDS	HANDFULS	HARDBACK	HARRIERS	HAWKBILL	HEATEDLY
HALCYONE	HANDGRIP	HARDBAKE	HARRIMAN	HAWK-	HEATHENS
HALENESS	HANDGUNS	HARDBALL	HARRISON	EYED	HEATHERY
HALFBACK	HANDHOLD	HARD	HARROWED	HAWKLIKE	HEATLESS
HALFBEAK	HANDICAP	CASH	HARROWER	HAWKWEED	HEAT
HALF	HANDIEST	HARD	HARRUMPH	HAWTHORN	PUMP
COCK	HANDLERS	COPY	HARRYING	HAYCOCKS	HEAT
HALF-	HANDLESS	HARDCORE	HARSHEST	HAY	RASH
LIFE	HANDLIKE	HARD	HARTFORD	FEVER	HEAT
HALF-	HANDLING	CORE	HARTNELL	HAYFORKS	WAVE
MAST	HANDLOOM	HARDCORE	HARUSPEX	HAYMAKER	HEAVENLY
HALF	HANDMADE	HARD-	HARVESTS	HAYSTACK	HEAVIEST
MOON	HANDOUTS	CORE	HAS-	HAZARDED	HEAVY-
HALF	HANDOVER	HARD	BEENS	HAZELHEN	SET
NOTE	HANDRAIL	DISK	HASIDISM	HAZELNUT	HEBDOMAD
HALF	HANDS-	HARDENED	HASSLING	HAZINESS	HEBETATE
TERM	OFF	HARDENER	HASSOCKS	HEADACHE	HEBETUDE
HALF	HANDSOME	HARDHACK	HASTEFUL	HEADACHY	HEBRAISM
TIME	HANDYMAN	HARDIEST	HASTENED	HEADBAND	HEBRAIST
HALFTONE	HANDYMEN	HARD	HASTENER	HEADFAST	HEBRAIZE
HALF-	HANGBIRD	LINE	HASTIEST	HEADGEAR	HEBRIDES
WITS	HANGCHOW	HARD	HASTINGS	HEADHUNT	HECATOMB
HALF-	HANGER-	LUCK	HATBANDS	HEADIEST	HECKLERS
YEAR	ON	HARDNESS	HATCHERY	HEADINGS	HECKLING
HALIBUTS	HANGINGS	HARD	HATCHETS	HEADLAND	HECTARES
HALLIARD	HANGNAIL	NUTS	HATCHING	HEADLESS	HECTORED
HALLMARK	HANGOUTS	HARD	HATCHWAY	HEADLIKE	HEDGEHOG
HALLOWED	HANGOVER	SELL	HATEABLE	HEADLINE	HEDGEHOP
HALLOWER	HANGZHOU	HARDSHIP	HATFIELD	HEADLOCK	HEDGEROW
HALLWAYS	HANKERED	HARD	HATHAWAY	HEADLONG	HEDONICS
HALMSTAD	HANKERER	TACK	HATHORIC	HEADMOST	HEDONISM
HALO-	HANNIBAL	HARDTOPS	HATTERAS	HEADRACE	HEDONIST
LIKE	HANNOVER	HARD	HAT	HEADRAIL	HEEDLESS
HALYARDS	HANRATTY	UPON	TRICK	HEADREST	HEELBALL
HAMARTIA	HANUKKAH	HARDWARE	HAULIERS	HEADREST	HEELLESS
HAMILTON	HAPLITIC	HARDWOOD	HAUNCHED	HEADROOM	HEELPOST
HAMMERED	HAPLOSIS	HAREBELL	HAUNCHES	HEADSAIL	HEFTIEST
HAMMERER	HAPPENED	HARELIKE	HAUNTING	HEADSETS	HEGELIAN
HAMMOCKS	HAPPIEST	HARFLEUR	HAUSFRAU	HEADSHIP	HEGEMONY
HAMPERED	HAPSBURG	HARGEISA	HAUTBOIS	HEADSMAN	HEIGHTEN
HAMPERER	HAPTERON	HARICOTS	HAUTBOYS	HEADWARD	HEIMDALL
HAMSTERS	HARA-	HARIKARI	HAUT-	HEADWAYS	HEIRLESS
HANDBAGS	KIRI	HARINGEY	RHIN	HEADWIND	HEIRLOOM
HANDBALL		HARKENED		HEADWORD	HEIRSHIP

HELIACAL	HERALDRY	HIGHBORN	HIPPARCH	HOLSTERS	HONIEDLY
HELICOID	HERBLIKE	HIGHBOYS	HIPSTERS	HOLYHEAD	HONOLULU
HELIPORT	HERCULES	HIGHBROW	HIRAGANA	HOLYOAKE	HONORARY
HELLADIC	HERDSMAN	HIGHER-	HIRELING	HOLYTIDE	HONOURED
HELL-	HERDSMEN	UP	HIRI	HOLY	HONOURER
BENT	HERDWICK	HIGHJACK	MOTU	WEEK	HOODLESS
HELLCATS	HEREDITY	HIGH	HIROHITO	HOLY	HOODLIKE
HELLENES	HEREFORD	JUMP	HISPANIA	WRIT	HOODLUMS
HELLENIC	HEREINTO	HIGHLAND	HISPANIC	HOMBURGS	HOODWINK
HELLFIRE	HERESIES	HIGH	HISTOGEN	HOMEBODY	HOOFLESS
HELLHOLE	HERETICS	LIFE	HISTORIC	HOMEBRED	HOOFLIKE
HELMETED	HEREUNTO	HIGH	HITCHING	HOME	HOOKLESS
HELMINTH	HEREUPON	MASS	HITHERTO	BREW	HOOKLIKE
HELMLESS	HEREWARD	HIGHNESS	HIT	HOME	HOOKNOSE
HELMSMAN	HEREWITH	HIGH	LISTS	HELP	HOOKWORM
HELMSMEN	HERITAGE	RISE	HIVELIKE	HOMELAND	HOOLIGAN
HELOTISM	HERMETIC	HIGH-	HOACTZIN	HOMELESS	HOOPLIKE
HELPABLE	HERMITIC	RISE	HOARDING	HOMELIER	HOOSEGOW
HELPINGS	HERODIAS	HIGH	HOARIEST	HOMELIKE	HOOVERED
HELPLESS	HERPETIC	ROAD	HOARSELY	HOMEMADE	HOPEFULS
HELPMANN	HERRINGS	HIGH	HOARSEST	HOME	HOPELESS
HELPMATE	HERSCHEL	SEAS	HOBBLING	PAGE	HOPLITIC
HELPMEET	HERTFORD	HIGH	HOBBYIST	HOMERIAN	HORATIAN
HELSINKI	HERTZIAN	SPOT	HOBNAILS	HOME	HORIZONS
HELVETIA	HESIODIC	HIGHTAIL	HOCHHUTH	RULE	HORMONAL
HELVETIC	HESITANT	HIGH	HOCKTIDE	HOME	HORMONES
HELVETII	HESITATE	TECH	HOGMANAY	RUNS	HORNBEAM
HEMIOLIC	HESPERIA	HIGH	HOGSHEAD	HOMESICK	HORNBILL
HEMIPODE	HESPERUS	TIDE	HOISTING	HOMESPUN	HORNBOOK
HEMLINES	HESSIANS	HIGH	HOKKAIDO	HOMETOWN	HORNFELS
HEMLOCKS	HETAERIC	TIME	HOLDABLE	HOMEWARD	HORNIEST
HENBANES	HEXAGONS	HIGHVELD	HOLDALLS	HOMEWORK	HORNLESS
HENCHMAN	HEXAGRAM	HIGHWAYS	HOLD	HOMICIDE	HORNLIKE
HENCHMEN	HEXANOIC	HIJACKED	DEAR	HOMILIES	HORNPIPE
HENEQUEN	HEXAPLAR	HIJACKER	HOLDFAST	HOMILIST	HORNTAIL
HENGYANG	HEXAPODY	HILARITY	HOLDINGS	HOMINESS	HORNWORT
HENG-	HEZEKIAH	HILLFORT	HOLDOVER	HOMINOID	HOROLOGE
YANG	HIATUSES	HILL	HOLIDAYS	HOMODONT	HOROLOGY
HEN	HIAWATHA	FORT	HOLINESS	HOMOGAMY	HOROWITZ
HOUSE	HIBERNAL	HILLIARD	HOLISTIC	HOMOGENY	HORRIBLE
HEN	HIBERNIA	HILLIEST	HOLLANDS	HOMOGONY	HORRIBLY
PARTY	HIBISCUS	HILLOCKS	HOLLERED	HOMOLOGY	HORRIDLY
HENRYSON	HICCUPED	HILLSIDE	HOLLIDAY	HOMONYMS	HORRIFIC
HENSLOWE	HIDDENLY	HIMATION	HOLLOWED	HONDURAN	HORSEBOX
HEPATICA	HIDEAWAY	HINAYANA	HOLLOWER	HONDURAS	HORSEFLY
HEPTAGON	HIDELESS	HINCKLEY	HOLLOWLY	HONEGGER	HORSEMAN
HEPTARCH	HIDROSIS	HINDERED	HOLOCENE	HONESTLY	HORSEMEN
HEPWORTH	HIDROTIC	HINDERER	HOLOGRAM	HONEWORT	HORSIEST
HERACLEA	HIERARCH	HINDMOST	HOLOTYPE	HONEYBEE	HOSANNAS
HERACLES	HIERATIC	HINDUISM	HOLOZOIC	HONEYDEW	HOSEPIPE
HERALDED	HIGHBALL	HIPBATHS	HOLSTEIN	HONG	HOSPICES
HERALDIC		HIP		KONG	
		FLASK			

135

HOSPITAL
HOSPODAR
HOSTAGES
HOSTELRY
HOSTLERS
HOTCHPOT
HOTELIER
HOT
　FLUSH
HOTHEADS
HOTHOUSE
HOT
　LINES
HOTPLATE
HOT
　SPOTS
HOT
　STUFF
HOT
　WATER
HOUNDING
HOUNSLOW
HOUSEBOY
HOUSEFLY
HOUSEFUL
HOUSEMAN
HOUSEMEN
HOUSETOP
HOUSINGS
HOVERERS
HOVERING
HOWITZER
HRVATSKA
HSINKING
HUANG
　HUA
HUCKSTER
HUDDLING
HUFFIEST
HUGENESS
HUGGABLE
HUGUENOT
HULA
　HOOP
HULL-
　LESS
HUMANELY
HUMANISM
HUMANIST
HUMANITY
HUMANIZE
HUMANOID

HUMBLEST
HUMBLING
HUMBOLDT
HUMIDIFY
HUMIDITY
HUMILITY
HUMMOCKS
HUMMOCKY
HUMORIST
HUMOROUS
HUMOURED
HUMPBACK
HUMPHREY
HUMPLIKE
HUNCHING
HUNDREDS
HUNGERED
HUNG
　JURY
HUNGRIER
HUNGRILY
HUNTEDLY
HUNTRESS
HUNTSMAN
HUNTSMEN
HURDLERS
HURDLING
HURRYING
HURTLING
HUSBANDS
HUSH-
　HUSH
HUSKIEST
HUSKLIKE
HUSTINGS
HUSTLERS
HUSTLING
HWANG
　HAI
HYACINTH
HYDER
　ALI
HYDRACID
HYDRANTH
HYDRANTS
HYDRATED
HYDRATES
HYDRATOR
HYDROGEL
HYDROGEN
HYDROMEL
HYGIENIC

HYMENEAL
HYPERNYM
HYPNOSIS
HYPNOTIC
HYSTERIA
HYSTERIC

I

IAMBUSES
ICEBERGS
ICEBLINK
ICEBOUND
ICEBOXES
ICE
　CREAM
ICE
　LOLLY
ICE
　PACKS
ICE
　PICKS
ICE
　RINKS
ICE
　SHEET
ICE
　SKATE
ICE
　WATER
ICHTHYIC
IDEALISM
IDEALIST
IDEALITY
IDEALIZE
IDEATION
IDEATIVE
IDEE
　FIXE
IDENTIFY
IDENTITY
IDEOGRAM
IDEOLOGY
IDIOCIES
IDIOLECT
IDLENESS
IDOLATER
IDOLATRY
IDOLIZED
IDOLIZER
IDYLLIST
IGNITING
IGNITION

IGNITRON
IGNOMINY
IGNORANT
IGNORING
IGUANIAN
ILKESTON
ILLATIVE
ILL-
　FATED
ILLINOIS
ILLIQUID
ILL-
　TIMED
ILL-
　TREAT
ILLUSION
ILLUSORY
ILMENITE
IMAGINAL
IMAGINED
IMAGINER
IMBECILE
IMBEDDED
IMBIBING
IMITABLE
IMITATED
IMITATOR
IMMANENT
IMMATURE
IMMERSED
IMMINENT
IMMOBILE
IMMODEST
IMMOLATE
IMMORTAL
IMMOTILE
IMMUNITY
IMMUNIZE
IMMURING
IMPACTED
IMPAIRED
IMPAIRER
IMPALING
IMPARITY
IMPARTED
IMPARTER
IMPASSES
IMPEDING
IMPELLED
IMPELLER
IMPERIAL

IMPERIUM
IMPETIGO
IMPINGED
IMPINGER
IMPISHLY
IMPLANTS
IMPLICIT
IMPLODED
IMPLORED
IMPLORER
IMPLYING
IMPOLICY
IMPOLITE
IMPORTED
IMPORTER
IMPOSING
IMPOSTOR
IMPOTENT
IMPRINTS
IMPRISON
IMPROPER
IMPROVED
IMPROVER
IMPUDENT
IMPUGNED
IMPUGNER
IMPULSES
IMPUNITY
IMPURITY
IMPUTING
INACTION
INACTIVE
INASMUCH
IN
　CAMERA
INCENSED
INCEPTOR
INCHOATE
INCIDENT
INCISING
INCISION
INCISIVE
INCISORS
INCISURE
INCITING
INCLINED
INCLINER
INCLINES
INCLOSED
INCLUDED
INCOMING

INCREASE
INCUBATE
INCUDATE
INCURRED
INDAMINE
INDEBTED
INDECENT
INDENTED
INDENTER
INDEXERS
INDEXING
INDICANT
INDICATE
INDICIAL
INDICTED
INDICTEE
INDIGENE
INDIGENT
INDIGOID
INDIRECT
INDOCILE
INDOLENT
INDOLOGY
INDORSED
INDUCING
INDUCTED
INDUCTOR
INDULGED
INDULGER
INDULINE
INDUSIAL
INDUSIUM
INDUSTRY
INEDIBLE
INEDIBLY
INEDITED
INEQUITY
INERTIAL
INESSIVE
INEXPERT
INFAMIES
INFAMOUS
INFANTAS
INFANTRY
INFECTED
INFECTOR
INFERIOR
INFERNAL
INFERNOS
INFERRED
INFERRER

INFESTED	INLANDER	INTENTLY	INVESTOR	ISOPHONE	JAPANNED
INFESTER	INNATELY	INTERACT	INVIABLE	ISOPLETH	JAPINGLY
INFIDELS	INNER	INTERCOM	INVITING	ISOPODAN	JAPONICA
INFINITE	MAN	INTEREST	INVOICED	ISOPRENE	JAROSITE
INFINITY	INNOCENT	INTERIMS	INVOICES	ISOSTASY	JASMINES
INFIXION	IN NO	INTERIOR	INVOKING	ISOTHERE	JAUNDICE
INFLAMED	TIME	INTERLAY	INVOLUTE	ISOTHERM	JAUNTIER
INFLAMER	INNOVATE	INTERMIT	INVOLVED	ISOTONIC	JAUNTILY
INFLATED	INNUENDO	INTERMIX	INVOLVER	ISOTOPES	JAUNTING
INFLATER	INOCULUM	INTERNAL	INWARDLY	ISOTOPIC	JAVANESE
INFLEXED	INOSITOL	INTERNED	IODATION	ISOTROPY	JAVELINS
IN	INPUTTED	INTERNEE	IODOFORM	ISRAELIS	JAWBONES
FLIGHT	INQUESTS	INTERNET	IODOPSIN	ISSUABLE	JAYAPURA
IN-	INQUIRED	INTERNET	IONIZERS	ISSUANCE	JAZZIEST
FLIGHT	INQUIRER	INTERPOL	IONIZING	ISSYK-	JEALOUSY
INFLUENT	INSANELY	INTERRED	IOTACISM	KUL	JEHOVIAN
INFLUXES	INSANITY	INTERREX	IRAKLION	ISTANBUL	JEMAPPES
INFORMAL	INSCRIBE	INTERSEX	IRISHMAN	ISTHMIAN	JEMMYING
INFORMED	INSECURE	INTERVAL	IRISHMEN	ISTHMOID	JEOPARDY
INFORMER	INSERTED	INTERWAR	IRONBARK	ITALIANS	JEREMIAD
INFRA	INSERTER	IN THE	IRONCLAD	ITCHIEST	JERKIEST
DIG	INSETTED	BAG	IRON-	ITEMIZED	JEROBOAM
INFRARED	INSETTER	IN THE	GREY		JESUITIC
INFRINGE	INSIDERS	END	IRON	**J**	JET-
INFUSING	INSIGHTS	INTIMACY	HAND	JABALPUR	BLACK
INFUSION	INSIGNIA	INTIMATE	IRONWARE	JABBERED	JETFOILS
INFUSIVE	INSISTED	INTONATE	IRONWOOD	JABBERER	JETLINER
INGATHER	INSISTER	INTONING	IRONWORK	JACKBOOT	JETTISON
INGENUES	INSOLATE	INTRADOS	IROQUOIS	JACKDAWS	JEWELLED
INGESTED	INSOLENT	INTRANET	IRRIGATE	JACKFISH	JEWELLER
INGRATES	INSOMNIA	INTRENCH	IRRITANT	JACKPOTS	JEW'S
IN-	INSOMUCH	INTREPID	IRRITATE	JACKSTAY	HARP
GROUPS	INSPIRED	INTRIGUE	ISAGOGIC	JACK	JEZEBELS
INGROWTH	INSPIRER	INTRORSE	ISATINIC	TARS	JIGGERED
INGUINAL	INSPIRIT	INTRUDED	ISCHEMIC	JACOBEAN	JIGGLING
INHALANT	INSTANCE	INTRUDER	ISLAMIST	JACOBIAN	JINGLING
INHALERS	INSTANTS	INTUBATE	ISLANDER	JACOBITE	JINGOISM
INHALING	INSTINCT	INTUITED	ISMAILIA	JACQUARD	JINGOIST
INHERENT	INSTRUCT	INUNDANT	ISOBARIC	JACUZZIS	JINJIANG
INHUMANE	INSULANT	INUNDATE	ISOCHEIM	JAGGEDLY	JIPIJAPA
INIMICAL	INSULATE	INVADERS	ISOCLINE	JAILBAIT	JIUJITSU
INIQUITY	INSULTED	INVADING	ISOCRACY	JAILBIRD	JOCKEYED
INITIALS	INSULTER	INVALIDS	ISOGLOSS	JALOPIES	JOCOSELY
INITIATE	INSURERS	INVASION	ISOGONIC	JALOUSIE	JOCOSITY
INJECTED	INSURING	INVASIVE	ISOLABLE	JAMAICAN	JODHPURI
INJECTOR	INTAGLIO	INVEIGLE	ISOLATED	JAMBOREE	JODHPURS
INJURIES	INTARSIA	INVENTED	ISOLATOR	JAMMIEST	JOGGLING
INJURING	INTEGERS	INVENTOR	ISOLOGUE	JAMNAGAR	JOHN
INKBERRY	INTEGRAL	INVERTED	ISOMERIC	JANGLING	BULL
INKINESS	INTENDED	INVERTER	ISOMETRY	JANITORS	JOHNNIES
INKSTAND	INTENDER	INVESTED	ISOMORPH	JAPANESE	JOINTING

137

JOINTURE	JUVENILE	KEYPUNCH	KIRKWALL	KOWTOWED	LAMBENCY
JOKINGLY		KEY	KISHINEV	KOWTOWER	LAMBSKIN
JOLLIEST	**K**	RINGS	KISSABLE	KRAKATOA	LAME
JOLLYING	KAI	KEYSTONE	KITCHENS	KUMAMOTO	DUCK
JOSTLING	MOANA	KHARTOUM	KLAIPEDA	KUMQUATS	LAMELLAR
JOTTINGS	KAIROUAN	KHMERIAN	KLANSMAN	KUROSAWA	LAMENESS
JOURNALS	KAKEMONO	KHOIKHOI	KLONDIKE	KURTOSIS	LAMENTED
JOURNEYS	KALAHARI	KHUSKHUS	KLYSTRON	KUZNETSK	LAMENTER
JOUSTING	KAMACITE	KIAOCHOW	KNAPSACK	KWEICHOW	LAMINATE
JOVIALLY	KAMAKURA	KIBOSHES	KNAPWEED	KWEIYANG	LAMPOONS
JOYFULLY	KAMIKAZE	KICKABLE	KNEADING	KYPHOSIS	LAMPPOST
JOYOUSLY	KANARESE	KICKBACK	KNEECAPS	KYPHOTIC	LAMPREYS
JOYRIDER	KANAZAWA	KICKOFFS	KNEE		LANCELET
JOYRIDES	KANDAHAR	KICKSHAW	DEEP	**L**	LANDFALL
JOYSTICK	KANGAROO	KID-	KNEE-	LABDANUM	LANDFORM
JUBILANT	KAOLIANG	GLOVE	DEEP	LABELING	LANDINGS
JUBILATE	KAOLINIC	KIDNAPED	KNEE-	LABELLED	LANDLADY
JUBILEES	KARELIAN	KILKENNY	HIGH	LABELLER	LANDLORD
JUDAIZER	KASHMIRI	KILLDEER	KNEE-	LABELLUM	LANDMARK
JUDDERED	KATAKANA	KILLINGS	JERK	LABILITY	LANDMASS
JUDGMENT	KATMANDU	KILLJOYS	KNEELING	LABOURED	LANDMINE
JUDICIAL	KATOWICE	KILOBYTE	KNICKERS	LABOURER	LANDRACE
JUGGLERS	KATTEGAT	KILOGRAM	KNIGHTED	LABRADOR	LANDSHUT
JUGGLERY	KAUMATUA	KILOVOLT	KNIGHTLY	LABURNUM	LANDSIDE
JUGGLING	KAWASAKI	KILOWATT	KNITTERS	LACANIAN	LANDSLIP
JUGULARS	KAYAKERS	KIMONOED	KNITTING	LACERANT	LANDWARD
JUICIEST	KEDGEREE	KINABALU	KNITWEAR	LACERATE	LANGLAUF
JULIENNE	KEENNESS	KINDLIER	KNOCKERS	LACEWING	LANGUAGE
JUMBLING	KEEPSAKE	KINDLING	KNOCKING	LACEWORK	LANGUISH
JUMBO	KEESHOND	KINDNESS	KNOCKOUT	LACINESS	LANKIEST
JET	KEEWATIN	KINDREDS	KNOCK-	LA	LANKNESS
JUMPABLE	KEIGHLEY	KINETICS	UPS	CORUNA	LANNERET
JUMPED-	KELANTAN	KINGBIRD	KNOTHOLE	LACRIMAL	LANTERNS
UP	KELOIDAL	KINGBOLT	KNOTTIER	LACROSSE	LANYARDS
JUMPIEST	KEMEROVO	KINGDOMS	KNOTTILY	LACTONIC	LAPBOARD
JUMPSUIT	KENNELED	KINGFISH	KNOTTING	LACUNOSE	LAP-
JUNAGADH	KENTUCKY	KINGLIER	KNOTWEED	LADDERED	CHART
JUNCTION	KERATOID	KINGPINS	KNOWABLE	LADYBIRD	LAPELLED
JUNCTURE	KERATOSE	KINGSHIP	KNOW-	LADYLIKE	LAPIDARY
JUNGFRAU	KERCHIEF	KING-	ALLS	LADYSHIP	LAPILLUS
JUNIPERS	KERKRADE	SIZE	KNOWSLEY	LAEVULIN	LAPPETED
JUNKETER	KEROSENE	KINGSTON	KNUCKLED	LAGGARDS	LAPSABLE
JUNK	KESTEVEN	KINGWANA	KNUCKLES	LA	LAPWINGS
FOOD	KESTRELS	KINGWOOD	KOHINOOR	GUAIRA	LARBOARD
JUNK	KETAMINE	KINKAJOU	KOHLRABI	LAH-DI-	LARGESSE
MAIL	KETOXIME	KINKIEST	KOLHAPUR	DAH	LARKSOME
JUNKYARD	KEYBOARD	KINSFOLK	KOLINSKY	LAID-	LARKSPUR
JURASSIC	KEYHOLES	KINSHASA	KOMSOMOL	BACK	LARRIGAN
JURATORY	KEY	KIRIBATI	KOOKIEST	LAMASERY	LARRIKIN
JURISTIC	MONEY	KIRIGAMI	KOOTENAY	LAMBASTE	LARYNGES
JUSTICES	KEYNOTES	KIRKLEES	KORDOFAN	LAMBDOID	LARYNXES
JUSTNESS			KOSTROMA		

LASHINGS
LA
 SPEZIA
LASSOING
LAST
 POST
LAST
 WORD
LAS
 VEGAS
LATCHING
LATCHKEY
LATENESS
LATERALS
LATERITE
LATHERED
LATINATE
LATINISM
LATINIST
LATINITY
LATINIZE
LATITUDE
LATRINES
LATTERLY
LATTICES
LAUDABLE
LAUDABLY
LAUDANUM
LAUGHING
LAUGHTER
LAUNCHED
LAUNCHER
LAUNCHES
LAUREATE
LAUSANNE
LAVATION
LAVATORY
LAVENDER
LAVISHED
LAVISHER
LAVISHLY
LAWFULLY
LAWGIVER
LAWSUITS
LAXATION
LAXATIVE
LAYABOUT
LAYERING
LAYETTES
LAYSHAFT
LAYWOMAN
LAYWOMEN

LAZINESS
LAZULITE
LAZURITE
L-
 DRIVER
 S
LEACHING
LEADSMAN
LEAD
 TIME
LEADWORT
LEAFIEST
LEAF-
 LARD
LEAFLETS
LEAGUING
LEAKAGES
LEAKIEST
LEANINGS
LEANNESS
LEAPFROG
LEAP
 YEAR
LEARNERS
LEARNING
LEASABLE
LEATHERY
LEAVENED
LEAVINGS
LECITHIN
LECTERNS
LECTURED
LECTURER
LECTURES
LEEBOARD
LEERIEST
LEE
 SHORE
LEE
 TIDES
LEFT-
 HAND
LEFTISTS
LEFTOVER
LEFT
 OVER
LEFTWARD
LEFT
 WING
LEGACIES
LEGAL
 AID

LEGALESE
LEGALISM
LEGALIST
LEGALITY
LEGALIZE
LEGATEES
LEGATINE
LEGATION
LEGENDRY
LEGGIEST
LEGGINGS
LEG-
 PULLS
LEG
 SIDES
LEINSTER
LEISURED
LEMMINGS
LEMONADE
LEMUROID
LENGTHEN
LENIENCY
LENINISM
LENINIST
LENITIVE
LENTICEL
LEOPARDS
LEOTARDS
LEPIDOTE
LEPORINE
LESBIANS
LES
 CAYES
LESSENED
LETDOWNS
LETHALLY
LETHARGY
LETRASET
LETTERED
LETTERER
LETTINGS
LETTUCES
LEUCITIC
LEUKEMIA
LEVANTER
LEVELING
LEVELLED
LEVELLER
LEVERAGE
LEVERETS
LEVERING

LEVIABLE
LEVIGATE
LEVITATE
LEVKOSIA
LEWDNESS
LEWISHAM
LEWISITE
LEXICONS
LIAISING
LIAISONS
LIAONING
LIAOTUNG
LIAOYANG
LIBATION
LIBECCIO
LIBELING
LIBELLED
LIBELLEE
LIBELLER
LIBERALS
LIBERATE
LIBERIAN
LIBRETTI
LIBRETTO
LICENCES
LICENSED
LICENSEE
LICENSER
LICHENIN
LICH
 GATE
LICKINGS
LICORICE
LIE-
 DOWNS
LIENTERY
LIFE
 BELT
LIFEBOAT
LIFE
 BUOY
LIFELESS
LIFELIKE
LIFELINE
LIFELONG
LIFE
 PEER
LIFE-
 SIZE
LIFESPAN
LIFETIME

LIFE
 WORK
LIFTABLE
LIFT-
 OFFS
LIGAMENT
LIGATION
LIGATIVE
LIGATURE
LIGHT
 ALE
LIGHT
 BOX
LIGHTERS
LIGHTEST
LIGHTING
LIGNEOUS
LIGNITIC
LIGULATE
LIGULOID
LIGURIAN
LIKELIER
LIKENESS
LIKENING
LIKEWISE
LILONGWE
LIMA
 BEAN
LIMACINE
LIMASSOL
LIMAVADY
LIMBLESS
LIMEKILN
LIMERICK
LIMINESS
LIMITARY
LIMITING
LIMNETIC
LIMONENE
LIMONITE
LIMOUSIN
LIMPIDLY
LIMPNESS
LINALOOL
LINCHPIN
LINDWALL
LINEAGES
LINEALLY
LINESMAN
LINESMEN
LINGERED
LINGERER

LINGERIE
LINGUINE
LINGUIST
LINIMENT
LINKABLE
LINKAGES
LINKWORK
LINOCUTS
LINOLEUM
LINOTYPE
LINSTOCK
LIONFISH
LIONIZED
LIONIZER
LIPOGRAM
LIPOIDAL
LIPSTICK
LIQUESCE
LIQUEURS
LISSOMLY
LISTABLE
LISTENED
LISTENER
LISTEN
 IN
LISTLESS
LITANIES
LITERACY
LITERALS
LITERARY
LITERATE
LITERATI
LITHARGE
LITIGANT
LITIGATE
LITTERED
LITTORAL
LIVE
 BAIT
LIVELIER
LIVELONG
LIVENING
LIVERIED
LIVERIES
LIVERISH
LIVETRAP
LIVEWARE
LIVE
 WIRE
LIVONIAN
LIXIVIUM

LLANDAFF
LLANELLI
LOADINGS
LOADSTAR
LOANABLE
LOANWORD
LOATHING
LOBBYING
LOBBYISM
LOBBYIST
LOBELINE
LOBLOLLY
LOBOTOMY
LOBSTERS
LOCALISM
LOCALIST
LOCALITY
LOCALIZE
LOCATING
LOCATION
LOCATIVE
LOCKABLE
LOCKOUTS
LOCOWEED
LOCUTION
LODESTAR
LODGINGS
LODGMENT
LODICULE
LOESSIAL
LOFTIEST
LOGBOOKS
LOG
  CABIN
LOGICIAN
LOGICISM
LOGISTIC
LOGOGRAM
LOGOTYPE
LOGOTYPY
LOITERED
LOITERER
LOLLARDY
LOLLIPOP
LOLLOPED
LOMBARDY
LONDONER
LONDRINA
LONELIER
LONESOME

LONE
  WOLF
LONGBOAT
LONGBOWS
LONGERON
LONG
  FACE
LONGFORD
LONGHAND
LONG-
  HAUL
LONGHORN
LONGINGS
LONG
  JUMP
LONG-
  LIFE
LONGSHIP
LONG
  SHOT
LONGSPUR
LONG
  SUIT
LONG-
  TERM
LONG
  TONS
LONGUEUR
LONG
  WAVE
LONGWAYS
LOOKER-
  ON
LOOKOUTS
LOONIEST
LOONY
  BIN
LOOPHOLE
LOOSEBOX
LOOSE
  END
LOOSENED
LOOSENER
LOP-
  EARED
LOP-
  SIDED
LOQUITUR
LORDLIER
LORDOSIS
LORDOTIC
LORDSHIP
LORICATE

LORIKEET
LORRAINE
LOTHARIO
LOTHIANS
LOUDNESS
LOUNGERS
LOUNGING
LOUSIEST
LOVEBIRD
LOVELESS
LOVELIER
LOVELIES
LOVELORN
LOVESICK
LOVINGLY
LOWBROWS
LOWERING
LOWLANDS
LOWLIEST
LOW-
  LYING
LOW
  TIDES
LOW
  WATER
LOYALISM
LOYALIST
LOZENGES
LUCIDITY
LUCKIEST
LUCKLESS
LUCKY
  DIP
LUDDITES
LUDHIANA
LUGHOLES
LUGSAILS
LUGWORMS
LUKEWARM
LUMBERED
LUMBERER
LUMINARY
LUMINOUS
LUMPFISH
LUMPIEST
LUMP
  SUMS
LUNATICS
LUNATION
LUNCHEON
LUNCHING
LUNEBURG

LUNGFISH
LUNGWORM
LUNGWORT
LUNULATE
LURCHING
LURINGLY
LUSATIAN
LUSCIOUS
LUSHNESS
LUSTRATE
LUSTROUS
LUTANIST
LUTENIST
LUTEOLIN
LUTETIUM
LUTHERAN
LUXATION
LUXURIES
LYALLPUR
LYCH
  GATE
LYCHGATE
LYCH
  GATE
LYINGS-
  IN
LYMPHOID
LYMPHOMA
LYNCHING
LYNCH
  LAW
LYNCHPIN
LYONNAIS
LYREBIRD
LYRICISM
LYRICIST
LYSOSOME
LYSOZYME

M

MACADMIA
MACARONI
MACAROON
MACERATE
MACHETES
MACHINED
MACHINES
MACHISMO
MACKEREL
MACRURAL
MACRURAN

MADDENED
MADHOUSE
MADONNAS
MADRIGAL
MADURESE
MAEBASHI
MAENADIC
MAESTOSO
MAESTROS
MAFIKENG
MAGAZINE
MAGELLAN
MAGHREBI
MAGIC
  EYE
MAGICIAN
MAGNATES
MAGNESIA
MAGNETIC
MAGNETON
MAGNETOS
MAGNOLIA
MAHARAJA
MAHARANI
MAHATMAS
MAHOGANY
MAIDENLY
MAIEUTIC
MAILABLE
MAILBAGS
MAILSHOT
MAINLAND
MAIN
  LINE
MAINMAST
MAINSAIL
MAINSTAY
MAINTAIN
MAJESTIC
MAJOLICA
MAJORCAN
MAJORING
MAJORITY
MAKE
  GOOD
MAKING
  DO
MALADIES
MALAGASY
MALAISES
MALARIAL
MALARKEY

MALAYSIA
MAL DE
  MER
MALDIVES
MALENESS
MALIGNED
MALIGNER
MALIGNLY
MALINGER
MALLARDS
MALPOSED
MALTREAT
MALTSTER
MALVASIA
MAMA'S
  BOY
MAMMOTHS
MANACLED
MANACLES
MANAGERS
MANAGING
MANASSAS
MANATOID
MANCIPLE
MANDALAY
MANDAMUS
MANDARIN
MANDATED
MANDATES
MANDIBLE
MANDOLIN
MANDORLA
MANDRAKE
MANDRILL
MAN-
  EATER
MANEUVER
MANFULLY
MANGABEY
MANGANIC
MANGANIN
MANGIEST
MANGLING
MANGONEL
MANGROVE
MANHOLES
MANHOURS
MANHUNTS
MANIACAL
MANICURE
MANIFEST

MANIFOLD	MARINERS	MATADORS	MEDICALS	MENSWEAR	MEZEREON
MANIKINS	MARIPOSA	MATANZAS	MEDICARE	MENTALLY	MEZEREUM
MANITOBA	MARITIME	MATCHBOX	MEDICATE	MENTIONS	MEZIERES
MANLIEST	MARJORAM	MATCHING	MEDICINE	MEPHITIC	MIAOWING
MANNERED	MARKDOWN	MATERIAL	MEDIEVAL	MEPHITIS	MICELLAR
MANNERLY	MARKEDLY	MATERIEL	MEDIOCRE	MERCHANT	MICHIGAN
MANNHEIM	MARKETED	MATERNAL	MEDITATE	MERCIFUL	MICROBES
MANNITIC	MARKETER	MATINEES	MEDUSOID	MERCURIC	MICRODOT
MANNITOL	MARKINGS	MATRICES	MEEKNESS	MERGENCE	MIDBRAIN
MAN OF	MARKSMAN	MATRIXES	MEETINGS	MERIDIAN	MIDDLE
WAR	MARKSMEN	MATRONAL	MEGALITH	MERINGUE	CS
MAN-OF-	MARMOSET	MATRONLY	MEGATONS	MERISTEM	MIDDLING
WAR	MAROONED	MATTERED	MEGAVOLT	MERISTIC	MIDFIELD
MANORIAL	MAROQUIN	MATTRESS	MEGAWATT	MERITING	MIDLANDS
MANPOWER	MARQUEES	MATURATE	MELAMINE	MERMAIDS	MIDNIGHT
MANSARDS	MARQUESS	MATURELY	MELANGES	MERRIEST	MIDPOINT
MANSHOLT	MARQUISE	MATURING	MELANISM	MERRY	MIDRIFFS
MANSIONS	MARRIAGE	MATURITY	MELANIST	MEN	MIDWIVES
MAN-	MARRIEDS	MAUBEUGE	MELANITE	MESCALIN	MIGHTIER
SIZED	MARRYING	MAVERICK	MELANOID	MESDAMES	MIGHTILY
MANTILLA	MARSHALS	MAXILLAR	MELANOMA	MESMERIC	MIGRAINE
MANTISES	MARSH	MAXIMIZE	MELANOUS	MESOCARP	MIGRANTS
MANTISSA	GAS	MAXIMUMS	MELINITE	MESODERM	MIGRATED
MANTLING	MARTABAN	MAYORESS	MELLOWED	MESOGLEA	MIGRATOR
MAN-TO-	MARTAGON	MAYPOLES	MELLOWER	MESOZOIC	MILANESE
MAN	MARTELLO	MAZATLAN	MELLOWLY	MESQUITE	MILCH
MANUALLY	MARTIANS	MAZURKAS	MELODEON	MESSAGES	COW
MANURING	MARTINET	MEA	MELODIES	MESSENIA	MILDEWED
MANX	MARTINIS	CULPA	MELODIST	MESSIAHS	MILDNESS
CATS	MARTYRED	MEAGRELY	MELODIZE	MESSIEST	MILEAGES
MANYFOLD	MARVELED	MEALIEST	MELTABLE	MESSMATE	MILEPOST
MAPPABLE	MARXISTS	MEALWORM	MELTDOWN	MESSUAGE	MILIARIA
MAPPINGS	MARYLAND	MEANINGS	MEMBRANE	MESTIZOS	MILITANT
MAQUETTE	MARZIPAN	MEANNESS	MEMENTOS	METALING	MILITARY
MARABOUS	MASSACRE	MEANTIME	MEMORIAL	METALLED	MILITATE
MARANHAO	MASSAGED	MEASURED	MEMORIES	METALLIC	MILITIAS
MARASMIC	MASSAGER	MEASURER	MEMORIZE	METAMALE	MILKFISH
MARASMUS	MASSAGES	MEASURES	MEMSAHIB	METAMERE	MILKIEST
MARATHON	MASSEDLY	MEATBALL	MENACING	METAPHOR	MILKMAID
MARAUDER	MASSETER	MEATIEST	MENARCHE	METAZOAN	MILK
MARBLING	MASSEURS	MECHANIC	MENDABLE	METAZOIC	RUNS
MARCHERS	MASSICOT	MECHELEN	MENHADEN	METEORIC	MILKSOPS
MARCHESA	MASTERED	MECONIUM	MENIALLY	METERING	MILKWEED
MARCHESE	MASTERLY	MEDALLIC	MENINGES	METHANOL	MILKWORT
MARCHING	MASTHEAD	MEDDLERS	MENISCUS	METHYLAL	MILKY
MARGARIC	MASTIFFS	MEDDLING	MEN-OF-	METHYLIC	WAY
MARGINAL	MASTITIS	MEDELLIN	WAR	METONYMY	MILLABLE
MARIANAO	MASTODON	MEDIALLY	MENOLOGY	METRICAL	MILLIAMP
MARIGOLD	MASTOIDS	MEDIATED	MEN'S	METRITIS	MILLIARD
MARIMBAS	MASURIAN	MEDIATOR	ROOM	MEUNIERE	MILLIARY
MARINADE	MATABELE	MEDICAID	MENSURAL	MEXICALI	MILLIBAR
MARINATE					MILLIGAN

MILLINER	MISLAYER	MODIFIER	MONOCRAT	MORALISM	MOULDIER
MILLIONS	MISMATCH	MODIOLUS	MONOCYTE	MORALIST	MOULDING
MILLPOND	MISNOMER	MODISHLY	MONOGAMY	MORALITY	MOULMEIN
MILLRACE	MISOGAMY	MODULATE	MONOGENY	MORALIZE	MOULTING
MILTONIC	MISOGYNY	MOHAMMED	MONOGRAM	MORASSES	MOUNTAIN
MIMETITE	MISOLOGY	MOIETIES	MONOGYNY	MORATORY	MOUNTIES
MIMICKED	MISPLACE	MOISTURE	MONOHULL	MORAVIAN	MOUNTING
MIMICKER	MISPLEAD	MOLALITY	MONOLITH	MORBIDLY	MOURNERS
MINARETS	MISPRINT	MOLASSES	MONOLOGY	MORBIFIC	MOURNFUL
MINATORY	MISQUOTE	MOLDAVIA	MONOMIAL	MORBIHAN	MOURNING
MINCE	MISSHAPE	MOLDERED	MONOPOLE	MORDANCY	MOUSIEST
PIE	MISSILES	MOLDIEST	MONOPOLY	MOREOVER	MOUSSAKA
MINDANAO	MISSIONS	MOLDINGS	MONORAIL	MORESQUE	MOUTHFUL
MINDLESS	MISSIVES	MOLECULE	MONOSEMY	MORIBUND	MOUTHING
MIND'S	MISSOURI	MOLEHILL	MONOSOME	MORNINGS	MOVABLES
EYE	MISSPELL	MOLESKIN	MONOTONE	MOROCCAN	MOVEMENT
MINERALS	MISSPELT	MOLESTED	MONOTONY	MORONISM	MOVINGLY
MINGIEST	MISSPEND	MOLESTER	MONOTYPE	MOROSELY	MOZZETTA
MINGLING	MISSPENT	MOLLUSCS	MONOXIDE	MORPHEME	MUCHNESS
MINICABS	MISSTATE	MOLUCCAS	MONROVIA	MORPHEUS	MUCILAGE
MINIMIZE	MISTAKEN	MOLYBDIC	MONSIEUR	MORPHINE	MUCINOUS
MINIMUMS	MISTAKES	MOMENTUM	MONSOONS	MORPHING	MUCKHEAP
MINISTER	MISTIMED	MONACHAL	MONSTERS	MORRISON	MUCKIEST
MINISTRY	MISTREAT	MONADISM	MONTAGES	MORTALLY	MUCKRAKE
MINORCAN	MISTRESS	MONAGHAN	MONTEITH	MORTGAGE	MUCKWORM
MINORITY	MISTRIAL	MONANDRY	MONTEREY	MORTIMER	MUCOSITY
MINOTAUR	MISTRUST	MONARCHS	MONTREAL	MORTISER	MUD
MINSTERS	MISUSAGE	MONARCHY	MONTREUX	MORTISES	BATHS
MINSTREL	MISUSING	MONASTIC	MONUMENT	MORTMAIN	MUDDIEST
MINUTELY	MITCHELL	MONAURAL	MOOCHING	MORTUARY	MUDDLING
MINUTIAE	MITICIDE	MONAZITE	MOODIEST	MOSEYING	MUDDYING
MINUTING	MITIGATE	MONETARY	MOONBEAM	MOSQUITO	MUDFLATS
MIRACLES	MITTIMUS	MONETIZE	MOONCALF	MOSSIEST	MUDGUARD
MIREPOIX	MIXED	MONEYBOX	MOONFISH	MOTHBALL	MUDPACKS
MIRRORED	BAG	MONGOLIA	MOONLESS	MOTHERED	MUDSTONE
MIRTHFUL	MIXTURES	MONGOLIC	MOONRISE	MOTHERLY	MUENSTER
MISANDRY	MNEMONIC	MONGOOSE	MOONSEED	MOTILITY	MUEZZINS
MISAPPLY	MOBILITY	MONGRELS	MOON	MOTIONED	MUFFLERS
MISCARRY	MOBILIZE	MONISTIC	SHOT	MOTIONER	MUFFLING
MISCHIEF	MOBOCRAT	MONITION	MOONWORT	MOTIVATE	MUFULIRA
MISCIBLE	MOBSTERS	MONITORS	MOORCOCK	MOTIVITY	MUGGIEST
MISCOUNT	MOCCASIN	MONITORY	MOORHENS	MOT	MUGGINGS
MISDEEDS	MOCKABLE	MONKEYED	MOORINGS	JUSTE	MUG'S
MISERERE	MODALITY	MONKFISH	MOORLAND	MOTORBUS	GAME
MISERIES	MODELING	MON-	MOORWORT	MOTORCAR	MUGSHOTS
MISFIRED	MODELLED	KHMER	MOOSE	MOTORING	MUGWUMPS
MISFIRES	MODELLER	MONKHOOD	JAW	MOTORIST	MULATTOS
MISGUIDE	MODERATE	MONMOUTH	MOPINGLY	MOTORIZE	MULBERRY
MISHEARD	MODERATO	MONOACID	MOQUETTE	MOTORMAN	MULCHING
MISHMASH	MODESTLY	MONOCARP	MORAINAL	MOTORMEN	MULCTING
MISJUDGE	MODIFIED	MONOCLES	MORAINES	MOTORWAY	MULETEER

MULHOUSE
MULISHLY
MULLIONS
MULTIFID
MULTIPED
MULTIPLE
MULTIPLY
MUMBLING
MUNCHING
MUNIMENT
MUNITION
MURALIST
MURDERED
MURDERER
MURICATE
MURKIEST
MURMANSK
MURMURED
MURMURER
MURRAINS
MURRELET
MURRHINE
MUSCATEL
MUSCLING
MUSCULAR
MUSHIEST
MUSHROOM
MUSICALE
MUSICALS
MUSICIAN
MUSINGLY
MUSKETRY
MUSKIEST
MUSQUASH
MUSTACHE
MUSTANGS
MUSTELID
MUSTERED
MUSTIEST
MUTATION
MUTENESS
MUTICOUS
MUTILATE
MUTINEER
MUTINIED
MUTINIES
MUTINOUS
MUTTERED
MUTTERER
MUTUALLY
MUZOREWA

MUZZIEST
MUZZLING
MYCELIAL
MYCELIUM
MYCELOID
MYCETOMA
MYCOLOGY
MYELINIC
MYELITIS
MYLONITE
MYOGENIC
MYOGRAPH
MYOLOGIC
MYOSOTIS
MYOTONIA
MYOTONIC
MYRIAPOD
MYSTICAL
MYSTIQUE
MYTHICAL
MYTILENE

N

NABOBERY
NACELLES
NACREOUS
NAGALAND
NAGASAKI
NAIL
   FILE
NAILHEAD
NAINSOOK
NAISSANT
NAMANGAN
NAME
   DAYS
NAMEDROP
NAMELESS
NAMESAKE
NAMETAPE
NAMIBIAN
NANCHANG
NANTERRE
NAPHTHOL
NAPHTHYL
NAPIFORM
NARBONNE
NARCEINE
NARCISSI
NARCOSIS
NARCOTIC

NARKIEST
NARRATED
NARRATOR
NARROWED
NARROWLY
NASALITY
NASALIZE
NASCENCE
NASTIEST
NATATION
NATIONAL
NATIVISM
NATIVIST
NATIVITY
NATTERED
NATTIEST
NATURALS
NATURISM
NATURIST
NAUPLIUS
NAUSEATE
NAUSEOUS
NAUTICAL
NAUTILUS
NAVICERT
NAVIGATE
NAVY
   BLUE
NAZARENE
NAZARETH
NDJAMENA
NEAP
   TIDE
NEARCTIC
NEAR
   EAST
NEAR
   MISS
NEARNESS
NEARSIDE
NEATNESS
NEBRASKA
NEBULIZE
NEBULOUS
NECKBAND
NECKLACE
NECKLETS
NECKLINE
NECKTIES
NECROSIS
NECROTIC
NEEDIEST

NEEDLESS
NEEDLING
NEGATING
NEGATION
NEGATIVE
NEGLIGEE
NEGRILLO
NEGRITIC
NEGROISM
NEIGHING
NEKTONIC
NEMATODE
NEMBUTAL
NEOGAEAN
NEOMYCIN
NEONATAL
NEOPHYTE
NEOPLASM
NEOPRENE
NEOTERIC
NEPALESE
NEPENTHE
NEPHRITE
NEPOTISM
NEPOTIST
NERVIEST
NESCIENT
NEST
   EGGS
NESTLING
NETTLING
NETWORKS
NEURITIC
NEURITIS
NEURONIC
NEUROSES
NEUROSIS
NEUROTIC
NEUTERED
NEUTRALS
NEUTRINO
NEUTRONS
NEW
   BLOOD
NEW
   BROOM
NEWCOMER
NEW
   DEALS
NEW-
   FOUND
NEWHAVEN

NEW
   HAVEN
NEWLYWED
NEW
   MOONS
NEWSCAST
NEWSPEAK
NEWSREEL
NEWSROOM
NEW
   TOWNS
NEW
   WAVES
NEW
   WORLD
NEXT-
   DOOR
NHA
   TRANG
NIARCHOS
NIBBLING
NICENESS
NICETIES
NICHROME
NICKELED
NICKELIC
NICKNACK
NICKNAME
NICOTINE
NIELLIST
NIFTIEST
NIGERIAN
NIGGARDS
NIGGLERS
NIGGLING
NIGHTCAP
NIGHTJAR
NIGHT
   OWL
NIHILISM
NIHILIST
NIHILITY
NIJMEGEN
NIMBLEST
NIMBUSES
NINEFOLD
NINEPINS
NINETEEN
NINETIES
NIPPIEST
NIRVANAS
NIRVANIC

NITRATES
NITROGEN
NITROSYL
NIVATION
NOBBLING
NOBELIUM
NOBILITY
NOBLEMAN
NOBLEMEN
NOBODIES
NOCTURNE
NODALITY
NODOSITY
NO-GO
   AREA
NOISIEST
NOMADISM
NOMINATE
NOMINEES
NOMISTIC
NOMOLOGY
NONESUCH
NON-
   EVENT
NONJUROR
NON
   LICET
NONMETAL
NON
   RIGID
NONSENSE
NONSTICK
NONTOXIC
NONUNION
NONVOTER
NONWHITE
NOONTIME
NORMALLY
NORMANDY
NORSEMAN
NORSEMEN
NORTHERN
NORTHING
NOSEBAGS
NOSEBAND
NOSE
   BAND
NOSECONE
NOSEDIVE
NOSEGAYS
NOSINESS
NOSOLOGY

NOSTRILS
NOSTRUMS
NOTA
  BENE
NOTABLES
NOTARIAL
NOTARIES
NOTARIZE
NOTATION
NOTCHING
NOTEBOOK
NOTECASE
NOTELETS
NOTEPADS
NOTICING
NOTIFIED
NOTIFIER
NOTIONAL
NOTOGAEA
NOTORNIS
NOVATION
NOVELIST
NOVELLAS
NOVEMBER
NOVGOROD
NOWADAYS
NUBECULA
NUBILITY
NUCELLAR
NUCELLUS
NUCLEASE
NUCLEATE
NUDENESS
NUDICAUL
NUGATORY
NUISANCE
NULL
  SETS
NUMBERED
NUMBFISH
NUMBNESS
NUMERACY
NUMERALS
NUMERARY
NUMERATE
NUMEROUS
NUMINOUS
NUMMULAR
NUMSKULL
NUNEATON
NUPTIALS

NURISTAN
NURSLING
NURTURED
NURTURER
NUTATION
NUT-
  BROWN
NUTCASES
NUTHATCH
NUTHOUSE
NUTRIENT
NUTSHELL
NUTTIEST
NUZZLING
NYMPHETS
NYSTATIN

O

OAFISHLY
OAKVILLE
OARLOCKS
OATCAKES
OBDURACY
OBDURATE
OBEDIENT
OBEISANT
OBELISKS
OBERLAND
OBITUARY
OBJECTED
OBJECTOR
OBLATION
OBLATORY
OBLIGATE
OBLIGING
OBLIQUES
OBLIVION
OBSCURED
OBSERVED
OBSERVER
OBSESSED
OBSIDIAN
OBSOLETE
OBSTACLE
OBSTRUCT
OBTAINED
OBTAINER
OBTRUDED
OBTRUDER
OBTUSELY
OBVIATED

OBVOLUTE
OCARINAS
OCCASION
OCCIDENT
OCCLUSAL
OCCUPANT
OCCUPIED
OCCUPIER
OCCURRED
OCEANIAN
OCHREOUS
OCOTILLO
OCTAGONS
OCTARCHY
OCTOBERS
OCTOROON
OCULISTS
ODDBALLS
ODDITIES
ODDMENTS
ODIOUSLY
ODOMETER
ODONTOID
ODYSSEYS
OENOLOGY
OESTRIOL
OESTRONE
OESTROUS
OFF AND
  ON
OFF
  BREAK
OFFENCES
OFFENDED
OFFENDER
OFFERING
OFF-
  GLIDE
OFFICERS
OFFICIAL
OFFPRINT
OFFSHOOT
OFFSHORE
OFFSTAGE
OFF
  STAGE
OFF-
  WHITE
OFT
  TIMES
OHMMETER
OILCLOTH

OILFIELD
OIL-
  FIRED
OILINESS
OIL
  PAINT
OILSKINS
OIL
  SLICK
OILSTONE
OIL
  WELLS
OINTMENT
OKAVANGO
OKLAHOMA
OLD
  FLAME
OLD
  GUARD
OLD
  HANDS
OLD
  MAIDS
OLDSTERS
OLD-
  TIMER
OLD
  WOMAN
OLD
  WOMEN
OLD
  WORLD
OLEANDER
OLEASTER
OLEFINIC
OLIBANUM
OLIGARCH
OLIGURIA
OLIVE
  OIL
OLYMPIAD
OLYMPIAN
OMDURMAN
OMELETTE
OMISSION
OMITTING
OMNIVORE
OMPHALOS
ON AND
  OFF
ONCE-
  OVER
ONCOLOGY

ONCOMING
ONDAATJE
ONDOGRAM
ONE-
  HORSE
ONE-ON-
  ONE
ONE-
  PIECE
ONE-
  SIDED
ONE-TO-
  ONE
ONE-
  TRACK
ONLOOKER
ONRUSHES
ON-
  SCREEN
ONSTREAM
ONTOGENY
ONTOLOGY
OOGAMOUS
OOGONIAL
OOGONIUM
OOLOGIST
OOPHYTIC
OOSPHERE
OOSPORIC
OOTHECAL
OOZINESS
OPALESCE
OPAQUELY
OPENCAST
OPEN-
  EYED
OPEN
  FIRE
OPENINGS
OPENNESS
OPEN-
  PLAN
OPEN
  SHOP
OPENWORK
OPERABLE
OPERABLY
OPERATED
OPERATIC
OPERATOR
OPERETTA
OPHIDIAN

OPINICUS
OPINIONS
OPIUMISM
OPOSSUMS
OPPILATE
OPPONENT
OPPOSING
OPPOSITE
OPPUGNER
OPSONIZE
OPTATIVE
OPTICIAN
OPTIMISM
OPTIMIST
OPTIMIZE
OPTIONAL
OPULENCE
ORACULAR
ORANGERY
ORATIONS
ORATORIO
ORBITING
ORCHARDS
ORCHITIC
ORCHITIS
ORDAINED
ORDAINER
ORDERING
ORDINALS
ORDINAND
ORDINARY
ORDINATE
ORDNANCE
ORENBURG
ORGANDIE
ORGANISM
ORGANIST
ORGANIZE
ORGASMIC
ORIENTAL
ORIFICES
ORIGINAL
ORINASAL
ORNAMENT
ORNATELY
ORNITHIC
OROGENIC
OROMETER
ORPHANED
ORPIMENT
ORRERIES

ORTHODOX	OUTLINES	OVERDREW	OVERWORK	PALENCIA	·PANPIPES
ORTHOEPY	OUTLIVED	OVERFLEW	OVIDUCAL	PALENESS	PANSOPHY
OSCITANT	OUTLOOKS	OVERFLOW	OVIPOSIT	PALETTES	PANTHEON
OSCULANT	OUTLYING	OVERGROW	OVULATED	PALFREYS	PANTHERS
OSCULATE	OUTMODED	OVERHAND	OWLISHLY	PALINODE	PANTILES
OSNABURG	OUTPOINT	OVERHANG	OWN	PALISADE	PANTRIES
OSSIFIED	OUTPOSTS	OVERHAUL	GOALS	PALLADIC	PAPACIES
OSSIFIER	OUTRAGED	OVERHEAD	OXBRIDGE	PALLIATE	PAPERBOY
OSTEITIC	OUTRAGES	OVERHEAR	OXIDASIC	PALLIDLY	PAPERING
OSTEITIS	OUTREACH	OVERHEAT	OXIDIZED	PALLIEST	PAPILLON
OSTINATO	OUTRIDER	OVERHUNG	OXIDIZER	PALL	PAPISTRY
OSTIOLAR	OUTRIGHT	OVERKILL	OXPECKER	MALL	PAPOOSES
OSTRACOD	OUTRIVAL	OVERLAID	OXTONGUE	PALMETTE	PARABLES
OTIOSITY	OUTSHINE	OVERLAIN	OXYGENIC	PALMETTO	PARABOLA
OTOSCOPE	OUTSHONE	OVERLAND	OXYMORON	PALMIEST	PARADIGM
OTTOMANS	OUTSHOOT	OVERLAPS	OXYTOCIC	PALMISTS	PARADING
OUTBLUFF	OUTSIDER	OVERLAYS	OXYTOCIN	PALMITIN	PARADISE
OUTBOARD	OUTSIDES	OVERLEAF	OZONIZER	PALO	PARADROP
OUTBOUND	OUTSMART	OVERLOAD		ALTO	PARAFFIN
OUTBRAVE	OUTSTAND	OVERLONG	P	PALOMINO	PARAGOGE
OUTBREAK	OUTSTARE	OVERLOOK		PALPABLE	PARAGONS
OUTBREED	OUTSTRIP	OVERLORD	PACIFIED	PALPABLY	PARAGUAY
OUTBURST	OUTSWING	OVERMUCH	PACIFIER	PALPATED	PARAKEET
OUTCASTE	OUT-	OVERPAID	PACIFISM	PALTERER	PARALLAX
OUTCASTS	TAKES	OVERPASS	PACIFIST	PALTRIER	PARALLEL
OUTCLASS	OUTVOTED	OVERPLAY	PACKABLE	PALTRILY	PARALYSE
OUTCOMES	OUTWARDS	OVERRATE	PACKAGED	PAMPERED	PARAMENT
OUTCRIES	OUTWEIGH	OVERRIDE	PACKAGER	PAMPERER	PARAMOUR
OUTCROPS	OUTWORKS	OVERRIPE	PACKAGES	PAMPHLET	PARANOIA
OUTCROSS	OVALNESS	OVERRODE	PADDLING	PAMPLONA	PARANOID
OUTDATED	OVARITIS	OVERRULE	PADDOCKS	PANACEAN	PARAPETS
OUTDOING	OVATIONS	OVERSEAS	PADLOCKS	PANACEAS	PARAQUAT
OUTDOORS	OVENBIRD	OVERSEEN	PAEONIES	PANATELA	PARASITE
OUTFACED	OVENWARE	OVERSEER	PAGANISM	PANCAKES	PARASOLS
OUTFALLS	OVERALLS	OVERSELL	PAGANIST	PANCREAS	PARAVANE
OUTFIELD	OVERARCH	OVERSHOE	PAGANIZE	PANDA	PAR
OUTFIGHT	OVERAWED	OVERSHOT	PAGEANTS	CAR	AVION
OUTFLANK	OVERBEAR	OVERSIDE	PAGINATE	PANDANUS	PARAZOAN
OUTFLOWS	OVERBIDS	OVERSIZE	PAGO	PANDEMIC	PARCELED
OUTFLUNG	OVERBOOK	OVERSOLD	PAGO	PANDERED	PARCENER
OUTFOXED	OVERBORE	OVERSTAY	PAGURIAN	PANDERER	PARCHING
OUTGOING	OVERCALL	OVERSTEP	PAHOEHOE	PANELING	PARDONED
OUT-	OVERCAME	OVERTAKE	PAINLESS	PANELLED	PARDONER
GROUP	OVERCAST	OVERTIME	PAINTERS	PANGOLIN	PARENTAL
OUTGROWN	OVERCOAT	OVERTIRE	PAINTING	PANICKED	PARHELIC
OUT-	OVERCOME	OVERTONE	PAKISTAN	PANICLED	PARIETAL
HEROD	OVERCOOK	OVERTOOK	PALADINS	PANMIXIA	PARISHES
OUTHOUSE	OVERCROP	OVERTURE	PALATALS	PANNIERS	PARISIAN
OUTLAWED	OVERDONE	OVERTURN	PALATIAL	PANNIKIN	PARKIEST
OUTLAWRY	OVERDOSE	OVERVIEW	PALATINE	PANOPTIC	PARKLAND
OUTLINED	OVERDRAW	OVERWIND	PALAVERS	PANORAMA	PARKWAYS
			PALEFACE		

145

PARLANCE
PARLANDO
PARLEYED
PARLEYER
PARLOURS
PARMESAN
PARODIED
PARODIES
PARODIST
PAROLING
PAROTOID
PAROXYSM
PARROTED
PARRYING
PARSABLE
PARSIFAL
PARSNIPS
PARTAKEN
PARTAKER
PARTERRE
PARTHIAN
PARTIBLE
PARTICLE
PARTINGS
PARTISAN
PARTNERS
PART-
SONG
PART-
TIME
PART
WORK
PARTYING
PAR
VALUE
PARVENUS
PARZIVAL
PASADENA
PASSABLE
PASSABLY
PASSAGES
PASSBOOK
PASS
BOOK
PASSERBY
PASSIBLE
PASSIONS
PASSKEYS
PASSOVER
PASSPORT
PASSWORD
PASTERNS

PASTE-
UPS
PASTICHE
PASTIEST
PASTILLE
PASTIMES
PASTINGS
PASTORAL
PASTRAMI
PASTRIES
PASTURED
PASTURES
PATAGIUM
PATCHIER
PATCHILY
PATCHING
PATELLAR
PATELLAS
PATENTED
PATENTEE
PATENTLY
PATENTOR
PATERNAL
PATERSON
PATHETIC
PATHLESS
PATHOGEN
PATHWAYS
PATIENCE
PATIENTS
PATRIALS
PATRIOTS
PATRONAL
PATTERED
PATTERNS
PATULOUS
PAUNCHES
PAVEMENT
PAVILION
PAVLODAR
PAVONINE
PAWKIEST
PAWNSHOP
PAYCHECK
PAYLOADS
PAYMENTS
PAY
PHONE
PAYROLLS
PAYSLIPS
PEACEFUL

PEACOCKS
PEAFOWLS
PEA
GREEN
PEAKIEST
PEARLIER
PEARLITE
PEARMAIN
PEASANTS
PEBBLING
PECCABLE
PECCANCY
PECTORAL
PECULATE
PECULIAR
PEDAGOGY
PEDALFER
PEDALING
PEDALLED
PEDANTIC
PEDANTRY
PEDDLERS
PEDDLING
PEDERAST
PEDESTAL
PEDICURE
PEDIFORM
PEDIGREE
PEDIMENT
PEDIPALP
PEDOLOGY
PEDUNCLE
PEEKABOO
PEELINGS
PEEPHOLE
PEEPSHOW
PEERAGES
PEERLESS
PEGBOARD
PEIGNOIR
PEKINESE
PELICANS
PELLAGRA
PELLICLE
PELL-
MELL
PELLUCID
PELVISES
PEMBROKE
PEMMICAN
PENALIZE

PENANCES
PENCHANT
PENCILED
PENDANTS
PENDULUM
PENGUINS
PENITENT
PENKNIFE
PEN
NAMES
PENNANTS
PENNINES
PENN'ORT
H
PENOLOGY
PENSIONS
PENSTOCK
PENTACLE
PENTAGON
PENTOMIC
PENTOSAN
PENUMBRA
PENZANCE
PEOPLING
PEPPERED
PEP
PILLS
PEP
TALKS
PEPTIZER
PER
ANNUM
PERCEIVE
PERCHING
PERFORCE
PERFUMED
PERFUMER
PERFUMES
PERGOLAS
PERIANTH
PERIBLEM
PERICARP
PERIDERM
PERIDIUM
PERIGEAN
PERIGEES
PERIGYNY
PERILOUS
PERILUNE
PERINEUM
PERIODIC
PERIOTIC

PERISARC
PERISHED
PERISHER
PERIWIGS
PERJURED
PERJURER
PERKIEST
PERLITIC
PERMEANT
PERMEATE
PERMUTED
PERONEAL
PERORATE
PEROXIDE
PERSONAL
PERSONAS
PERSPIRE
PERSUADE
PERTNESS
PERUSALS
PERUSING
PERUVIAN
PERVADED
PERVADER
PERVERSE
PERVERTS
PERVIOUS
PESHAWAR
PESKIEST
PESTERED
PESTERER
PESTHOLE
PETALINE
PETALODY
PETALOID
PETECHIA
PETITION
PETIT
MAL
PET
NAMES
PETRARCH
PETROLIC
PETROSAL
PETTIEST
PETTIFOG
PETULANT
PETUNIAS
PETUNTSE
PEWTERER
PFENNIGS

PHAETONS
PHALANGE
PHANTASM
PHANTASY
PHANTOMS
PHARAOHS
PHARISEE
PHARMACY
PHASE-
OUT
PHEASANT
PHENETIC
PHENOLIC
PHILLIPS
PHILTRES
PHIMOSIS
PHONE
BOX
PHONE-
INS
PHONEMES
PHONEMIC
PHONETIC
PHONIEST
PHOSGENE
PHOSPHOR
PHOTOFIT
PHOTOMAP
PHOTOPIA
PHOTOPIC
PHOTOSET
PHRASING
PHRATRIC
PHREATIC
PHTHALIC
PHTHISIC
PHTHISIS
PHYLETIC
PHYLLITE
PHYLLODE
PHYLLOID
PHYLLOME
PHYSICAL
PHYSIQUE
PIACENZA
PIACULAR
PIANISTS
PIANOLAS
PIASSAVA
PIASTRES
PICADORS

PICCANIN
PICCOLOS
PICKABLE
PICKAXES
PICKEREL
PICKETED
PICKETER
PICKIEST
PICKINGS
PICKLING
PICKLOCK
PICK ME
UP
PICK-ME-
UP
PICOLINE
PICTURED
PICTURES
PIDDLING
PIEBALDS
PIE
CHART
PIECRUST
PIEDMONT
PIERCING
PIFFLING
PIGGIEST
PIGMENTS
PIGSKINS
PIGSTICK
PIGSTIES
PIGSWILL
PIGTAILS
PILASTER
PILCHARD
PILEWORT
PILFERED
PILFERER
PILGRIMS
PILIFORM
PILLAGED
PILLAGER
PILLIONS
PILLOCKS
PILLOWED
PILOTAGE
PILOTING
PIMENTOS
PIMIENTO
PINAFORE
PINASTER

PINCE-
NEZ
PINCHING
PINETREE
PINEWOOD
PING-
PONG
PINHEADS
PINIONED
PINK
GINS
PINKROOT
PIN
MONEY
PINNACES
PINNACLE
PINNIPED
PINOCHLE
PINPOINT
PINPRICK
PINTABLE
PINT-
SIZE
PINWHEEL
PIONEERS
PIPE
BOMB
PIPECLAY
PIPEFISH
PIPELINE
PIPE
RACK
PIPERINE
PIPETTES
PIPEWORT
PIQUANCY
PIRACIES
PIRANHAS
PIRATING
PIS
ALLER
PISIFORM
PISOLITE
PISS-
TAKE
PITCHERS
PITCHING
PITFALLS
PITHEADS
PITHIEST
PITIABLE
PITIABLY

PITILESS
PIT
PROPS
PITTANCE
PIVOTING
PIXELATE
PIZZERIA
PLACABLE
PLACARDS
PLACATED
PLACEBOS
PLACE
MAT
PLACENTA
PLACIDLY
PLAGUILY
PLAGUING
PLAINEST
PLAITING
PLANCHET
PLANFORM
PLANGENT
PLANKING
PLANKTON
PLANNERS
PLANNING
PLANOSOL
PLANTAIN
PLANTERS
PLANTING
PLANULAR
PLASTEEL
PLASTERS
PLASTICS
PLASTRAL
PLASTRON
PLATELET
PLATFORM
PLATINIC
PLATINUM
PLATONIC
PLATOONS
PLATTERS
PLATYPUS
PLAUDITS
PLAUSIVE
PLAYABLE
PLAYBACK
PLAY
BALL
PLAYBILL

PLAYBOYS
PLAYGOER
PLAYLIST
PLAYMATE
PLAY-
OFFS
PLAYPENS
PLAYROOM
PLAYSUIT
PLAYTIME
PLEADING
PLEASANT
PLEASING
PLEASURE
PLEATING
PLEBBIER
PLEBEIAN
PLECTRUM
PLEDGING
PLEIADES
PLEIN-
AIR
PLEONASM
PLETHORA
PLEURISY
PLEUSTON
PLIANTLY
PLIGHTED
PLIGHTER
PLIMSOLL
PLIOCENE
PLODDERS
PLODDING
PLONKING
PLOPPING
PLOSIVES
PLOTTING
PLOUGHED
PLOUGHER
PLUCKIER
PLUCKILY
PLUCKING
PLUGGING
PLUGHOLE
PLUMBAGO
PLUMBERS
PLUMBERY
PLUMBING
PLUMBISM
PLUMBOUS
PLUMMIER

PLUMPEST
PLUMPING
PLUNGERS
PLUNGING
PLUSHEST
PLUTONIC
PLUVIOUS
PLYMOUTH
POACEOUS
POACHERS
POACHING
POCKETED
POCKMARK
PODAGRAL
PODGIEST
PODIATRY
PODZOLIC
POETICAL
POIGNANT
POINTERS
POINTING
POISONED
POISONER
POITIERS
POKEWEED
POKINESS
POLANSKI
POLARITY
POLARIZE
POLAROID
POLEAXED
POLECATS
POLEMICS
POLE
STAR
POLICIES
POLICING
POLISHED
POLISHER
POLISHES
POLITELY
POLITICO
POLITICS
POLITIES
POLKA
DOT
POLLARDS
POLLICAL
POLLINIC
POLLSTER
POLLUTED

POLLUTER
POLO
NECK
POLONIUM
POLTROON
POLYGALA
POLYGAMY
POLYGENE
POLYGLOT
POLYGONS
POLYGYNY
POLYMATH
POLYMERS
POLYPARY
POLYPODY
POLYPOID
POLYPOUS
POLYSEMY
POLYURIA
POLYURIC
POLYZOAN
POLYZOIC
POMANDER
POMOLOGY
PONDERED
PONDERER
PONDWEED
PONGIEST
PONIARDS
PONTIFEX
PONTIFFS
PONTOONS
PONYTAIL
POOFIEST
POOH-
POOH
POOLSIDE
POOR
LAWS
POORLIER
POORNESS
POPADUMS
POPINJAY
POPOVERS
POPPADOM
POPSICLE
POPULACE
POPULATE
POPULISM
POPULIST
POPULOUS

PORKIEST
PORK
  PIES
POROSITY
PORPHYRY
PORPOISE
PORRIDGE
PORTABLE
PORTENTS
PORTHOLE
PORTICOS
PORTIERE
PORTIONS
PORTLAND
PORTLIER
PORTRAIT
PORT
  SAID
PORT
  SIDE
PORTUGAL
POSITING
POSITION
POSITIVE
POSITRON
POSOLOGY
POSSIBLE
POSSIBLY
POSTBAGS
POSTCARD
POSTCAVA
POSTCODE
POSTDATE
POST-
  FREE
POSTGRAD
POST
  HORN
POSTICHE
POSTINGS
POSTLUDE
POSTMARK
POST-
  OBIT
POSTPAID
POSTPONE
POSTURAL
POSTURED
POSTURER
POSTURES
POTASSIC
POTATION

POTATOES
POT-AU-
  FEU
POTBELLY
POTBOUND
POTENTLY
POTHOLER
POTHOLES
POTLUCKS
POT
  PLANT
POTSHERD
POTSHOTS
POTSTONE
POTTERED
POTTERER
POTTIEST
POULTICE
POUNCING
POUNDAGE
POUNDING
POWDERED
POWDERER
POWERFUL
POWERING
POZIDRIV
POZZUOLI
PRACTICE
PRACTISE
PRAEDIAL
PRAESEPE
PRAIRIES
PRAISING
PRALINES
PRANCING
PRANDIAL
PRANKISH
PRATIQUE
PRATTLED
PRATTLER
PREACHED
PREACHER
PREAMBLE
PREAXIAL
PREBENDS
PRECEDED
PRECEPTS
PRECINCT
PRECIOUS
PRECLUDE
PREDATED

PREDATOR
PREDELLA
PREENING
PREEXIST
PRE-
  EXIST
PREFACED
PREFACER
PREFACES
PREFECTS
PREFIXAL
PREFIXED
PREFIXES
PREGNANT
PREJUDGE
PRELATES
PRELATIC
PRELUDER
PRELUDES
PREMIERE
PREMIERS
PREMISES
PREMIUMS
PREMOLAR
PREMORSE
PRENATAL
PREPARED
PREPENSE
PRESAGED
PRESAGER
PRESAGES
PRESCOTT
PRESENCE
PRESENTS
PRESERVE
PRESIDED
PRESIDER
PRESIDIA
PRESIDIO
PRESS
  BOX
PRESSING
PRESSMAN
PRESSMEN
PRESS-
  UPS
PRESSURE
PRESTIGE
PRESUMED
PRESUMER
PRETENCE

PRETEXTS
PRETORIA
PRETREAT
PRETTIER
PRETTIFY
PRETTILY
PRETZELS
PREVIEWS
PREVIOUS
PREZZIES
PRIAPISM
PRICE
  TAG
PRICIEST
PRICKING
PRICKLED
PRICKLES
PRIDEFUL
PRIE-
  DIEU
PRIESTLY
PRIGGERY
PRIGGISH
PRIGGISM
PRIMATES
PRIMEVAL
PRIMMEST
PRIMNESS
PRIMROSE
PRIMULAS
PRIMUSES
PRINCELY
PRINCESS
PRINCIPE
PRINTERS
PRINTING
PRINTOUT
PRIORATE
PRIORESS
PRIORIES
PRIORITY
PRISMOID
PRISONER
PRISSIER
PRISSILY
PRISTINE
PRIVATES
PRIVIEST
PRIZE
  DAY
PROBABLE

PROBABLY
PROBATED
PROBATES
PROBLEMS
PROCAINE
PROCEEDS
PROCLAIM
PROCTORS
PROCURED
PROCURER
PRODDING
PRODIGAL
PRODROME
PRODUCED
PRODUCER
PRODUCTS
PROEMIAL
PROFANED
PROFANER
PROFILED
PROFILES
PROFITED
PROFITER
PRO
  FORMA
PROFOUND
PROGRAMS
PROGRESS
PROHIBIT
PROJECTS
PROLAPSE
PROLIFIC
PROLOGUE
PROMISED
PROMISER
PROMISES
PROMISOR
PROMOTED
PROMOTER
PROMPTED
PROMPTER
PROMPTLY
PRONATOR
PRONOUNS
PROOFING
PROPERLY
PROPERTY
PROPHAGE
PROPHASE
PROPHECY
PROPHESY

PROPHETS
PROPOLIS
PROPOSAL
PROPOSED
PROPOSER
PROPOUND
PROPPING
PROROGUE
PROSAISM
PROSIEST
PROSODIC
PROSPECT
PROSTATE
PROSTYLE
PROTASIS
PROTEGEE
PROTEGES
PROTEINS
PROTEOSE
PROTESTS
PROTOCOL
PROTOZOA
PROTRACT
PROTRUDE
PROUDEST
PROVABLE
PROVABLY
PROVENCE
PROVENLY
PROVERBS
PROVIDED
PROVIDER
PROVINCE
PROVISOS
PROVOKED
PROVOSTS
PROWL
  CAR
PROWLERS
PROWLING
PROXIMAL
PRUDENCE
PRUINOSE
PRUNABLE
PRUNELLA
PRUNELLE
PRURIENT
PRURITIC
PRURITUS
PRUSSIAN
PSALMIST

PSALMODY
PSALTERS
PSALTERY
PSEPHITE
PSORALEA
PSYCHICS
PSYCHING
PTEROPOD
PTOMAINE
PTYALISM
PUB-
  CRAWL
PUBLICAN
PUBLICLY
PUCKERED
PUDDINGS
PUDDLING
PUDENDUM
PUDGIEST
PUFFBALL
PUFFBIRD
PUFFIEST
PUGILISM
PUGILIST
PUISSANT
PULLMANS
PULLOUTS
PULLOVER
PULMONIC
PULMOTOR
PULPIEST
PULPWOOD
PULSATED
PULSATOR
PULSEJET
PULVINUS
PUMMELED
PUMPKINS
PUMP
  ROOM
PUNCHBAG
PUNCHEON
PUNCHIER
PUNCHING
PUNCH-
  UPS
PUNCTATE
PUNCTUAL
PUNCTURE
PUNGENCY
PUNINESS

PUNISHED
PUNISHER
PUNITIVE
PUNSTERS
PUPARIAL
PUPARIUM
PUPATION
PUPPETRY
PUPPY
  FAT
PUPPYISH
PURBLIND
PURCHASE
PUREBRED
PUREEING
PURENESS
PURFLING
PURIFIED
PURIFIER
PURISTIC
PURITANS
PURLIEUS
PURPLISH
PURPOSED
PURPOSES
PURPURIN
PURSLANE
PURSUANT
PURSUERS
PURSUING
PURSUITS
PURULENT
PURVEYED
PURVEYOR
PUSHBIKE
PUSHCART
PUSHIEST
PUSHOVER
PUSH-
  PULL
PUSSYCAT
PUSTULAR
PUSTULES
PUT
  ABOUT
PUTATIVE
PUT-
  DOWNS
PUTSCHES
PUTTERED
PUT TO
  SEA

PUT-UP
  JOB
PUZZLERS
PUZZLING
PYELITIC
PYELITIS
PYGIDIAL
PYGIDIUM
PYINKADO
PYODERMA
PYOGENIC
PYRAMIDS
PYRAZOLE
PYRENEAN
PYRENEES
PYRENOID
PYREXIAL
PYRIDINE
PYRIFORM
PYROSTAT
PYROXENE
PYRROLIC
PYRRUVIC
PYTHONIC
PYXIDIUM

Q

QUACKERY
QUACKING
QUAD
  BIKE
QUADRANT
QUADRATE
QUADROON
QUAGMIRE
QUAILING
QUAINTLY
QUALMISH
QUANDARY
QUANDONG
QUANTIFY
QUANTITY
QUANTIZE
QUARRELS
QUARRIED
QUARRIER
QUARRIES
QUARTERN
QUARTERS
QUARTETS
QUARTILE

QUASHING
QUATRAIN
QUAVERED
QUAVERER
QUEASIER
QUEASILY
QUECHUAN
QUEENDOM
QUEENING
QUEEREST
QUEERING
QUELLING
QUENCHED
QUENCHER
QUERCINE
QUERYING
QUESTING
QUESTION
QUIBBLED
QUIBBLER
QUIBBLES
QUIBERON
QUICKEST
QUICKIES
QUICKSET
QUIDDITY
QUIDNUNC
QUIETEST
QUIETISM
QUIETIST
QUIETUDE
QUILL
  PEN
QUILTING
QUINCUNX
QUI
  NHONG
QUINTETS
QUINTILE
QUIPPING
QUIPSTER
QUIRKIER
QUIRKILY
QUISLING
QUITTERS
QUITTING
QUIVERED
QUIVERER
QUIXOTIC
QUIZZING
QUOTABLE

QUOTHING
QUOTIENT

R
RABBITED
RABBITER
RABBITRY
RABIDITY
RACCOONS
RACEMISM
RACEMOSE
RACIALLY
RACINESS
RACK-
  RENT
RACLETTE
RACQUETS
RADIALLY
RADIANCE
RADIATED
RADIATOR
RADICALS
RADICAND
RADIOING
RADISHES
RAFFLING
RAGGEDLY
RAG
  TRADE
RAILHEAD
RAILINGS
RAILLERY
RAILROAD
RAILWAYS
RAINBAND
RAINBOWS
RAINCOAT
RAINDROP
RAINFALL
RAINIEST
RAINLESS
RAINY
  DAY
RAISABLE
RAKE-
  OFFS
RAKISHLY
RALLYING
RAMAT
  GAN
RAMBLERS
RAMBLING

RAMBUTAN
RAMEKINS
RAMENTUM
RAMIFIED
RAMOSITY
RAMPAGED
RAMPAGER
RAMPANCY
RAMPARTS
RAMSGATE
RAMULOSE
RANCAGUA
RANCHERS
RANDIEST
RANDOMLY
RANKLING
RANKNESS
RANSOMED
RANSOMER
RAPACITY
RAPESEED
RAPIDITY
RAPTNESS
RAPTURES
RARA
  AVIS
RAREFIED
RAREFIER
RARENESS
RARITIES
RASCALLY
RASHNESS
RASORIAL
RASPINGS
RAT-
  ARSED
RATCHETS
RATIFIED
RATIFIER
RATIONAL
RATIONED
RATSBANE
RATTIEST
RATTLING
RAT
  TRAPS
RAVAGING
RAVELING
RAVELLED
RAVELLER
RAVENING

RAVENOUS
RAVISHED
RAVISHER
RAW-
  BONED
RAW
  DEALS
RAWHIDES
RAZOR-
  CUT
REACHING
REACTANT
REACTING
REACTION
REACTIVE
REACTORS
READABLE
READABLY
READIEST
READINGS
READJUST
READOUTS
READYING
READY-
  MIX
REAFFIRM
REAGENTS
REALISTS
REALIZED
REALIZER
REALNESS
REAL-
  TIME
REALTORS
REAPABLE
REAPPEAR
REARMING
REARMOST
REARWARD
REASONED
REASONER
REASSURE
REAWAKEN
REBELLED
REBOUNDS
REBUFFED
REBUKING
REBUTTAL
REBUTTED
REBUTTER
RECALLED
RECANTED

RECANTER
RECAPPED
RECEDING
RECEIPTS
RECEIVED
RECEIVER
RECENTLY
RECEPTOR
RECESSED
RECESSES
RECHARGE
RECISION
RECITALS
RECITERS
RECITING
RECKLESS
RECKONED
RECKONER
RECLINED
RECLINER
RECLUSES
RECOILED
RECOILER
RECOMMIT
RECORDED
RECORDER
RECOUNTS
RECOUPED
RECOURSE
RECOVERY
RECREANT
RECREATE
RECRUITS
RECTALLY
RECURRED
RECUSANT
RECYCLED
REDACTOR
RED
  ALERT
REDBRICK
REDCOATS
RED
  CROSS
REDDENED
REDDITCH
REDEEMED
REDEEMER
REDEMAND
REDEPLOY
REDESIGN

RED
  FACED
RED-
  FACED
RED
  FLAGS
RED
  GIANT
REDGRAVE
REDHEADS
REDIRECT
RED
  LIGHT
REDNECKS
REDOLENT
REDOUBLE
REDOUBTS
REDSHANK
RED
  SHIFT
REDSKINS
REDSTART
REDUCING
REDUVIID
REDWOODS
REECHOED
REEDBUCK
REEDIEST
REEDLING
REEF
  KNOT
REELABLE
REELABLY
RE-
  EMPLOY
RE-
  EXPORT
REFACING
REFEREED
REFEREES
REFERENT
REFERRAL
REFERRED
REFERRER
REFILLED
REFINERY
REFINING
REFINISH
REFITTED
REFLATED
REFLEXES
REFOREST

REFORMED
REFORMER
REFRAINS
REFUELED
REFUGEES
REFUGIUM
REFUNDED
REFUNDER
REFUSALS
REFUSING
REFUTING
REGAINED
REGAINER
REGALITY
REGARDED
REGATTAS
REGELATE
REGENTAL
REGICIDE
REGIMENS
REGIMENT
REGIONAL
REGISTER
REGISTRY
REGRATER
REGROWTH
REGULARS
REGULATE
REGULINE
REHASHED
REHASHES
REHEARSE
REHEATER
REHOBOAM
REHOUSED
REIGNING
REIMPORT
REIMPOSE
REINDEER
REINSURE
REINVENT
REINVEST
REISSUED
REISSUER
REISSUES
REJECTED
REJECTER
REJIGGED
REJOICED
REJOICER
REJOINED

REKINDLE
RELAPSED
RELAPSER
RELAPSES
RELATING
RELATION
RELATIVE
RELAUNCH
RELAXANT
RELAXING
RELAYING
RELEASED
RELEASER
RELEASES
RELEGATE
RELENTED
RELEVANT
RELIABLE
RELIABLY
RELIANCE
RELIEVED
RELIEVER
RELIGION
RELINING
RELISHED
RELISHES
RELIVING
RELOADED
RELOCATE
REMAINED
REMAKING
REMANDED
REMARKED
REMARKER
REMARQUE
REMEDIAL
REMEDIED
REMEDIES
REMEMBER
REMIGIAL
REMINDED
REMINDER
REMITTED
REMITTER
REMNANTS
REMOTELY
REMOTEST
REMOULDS
REMOUNTS
REMOVALS
REMOVERS

REMOVING
RENAMING
RENDERED
RENDERER
RENDIBLE
RENDZINA
RENEGADE
RENEGING
RENEWALS
RENEWING
RENIFORM
RENOUNCE
RENOVATE
RENOWNED
RENTABLE
RENT
  BOYS
RENT-
  FREE
RENTIERS
RENT-
  ROLL
REOFFEND
REOPENED
REPAIRED
REPAIRER
REPARTEE
REPAYING
REPEALED
REPEALER
REPEATED
REPEATER
REPELLED
REPELLER
REPENTED
REPENTER
REPEOPLE
REPETEND
REPHRASE
REPINING
REPLACED
REPLACER
REPLAYED
REPLEVIN
REPLICAS
REPLYING
REPORTED
REPORTER
REPOSING
REPOUSSE
REPRIEVE

REPRINTS	RESORTED	REUNITED	REYNOLDS	RIJSWIJK	ROASTERS
REPRISAL	RESORTER	REUNITER	RHAETIAN	RIMOSITY	ROASTING
REPRISES	RESOURCE	REUSABLE	RHAPSODY	RINGBOLT	ROBINSON
REPROACH	RESPECTS	REVALUED	RHEOBASE	RINGBONE	ROBOTICS
REPROOFS	RESPIRED	REVAMPED	RHEOLOGY	RINGDOVE	ROBOTISM
REPROVAL	RESPITES	REVAMPER	RHEOSTAT	RING-	ROBUSTLY
REPROVED	RESPONSE	REVEALED	RHETORIC	DYKE	ROCAILLE
REPROVER	RESTATED	REVEALER	RH	RINGETTE	ROCHDALE
REPTILES	REST	REVEILLE	FACTOR	RINGHALS	ROCK
REPUBLIC	CURE	REVELING	RHINITIS	RINGLETS	BAND
REPULSED	REST	REVELLED	RHIZOMES	RING	ROCK
REPULSER	HOME	REVELLER	RHIZOPOD	ROAD	CAKE
REPULSES	RESTLESS	REVENANT	RHIZOPUS	RINGSIDE	ROCK
REQUESTS	RESTORED	REVENGED	RHODESIA	RINGWORM	DASH
REQUIEMS	RESTORER	REVENGER	RHODINAL	RINKHALS	ROCKETED
REQUIRED	RESTRAIN	REVENUED	RHOMBOID	RINSABLE	ROCKETRY
REQUIRER	RESTRICT	REVEREND	RHONCHAL	RIOT	ROCKFALL
REQUITAL	REST	REVERENT	RHONCHUS	ACTS	ROCKFISH
REQUITED	ROOM	REVERIES	RHUBARBS	RIPARIAN	ROCKFORD
REQUITER	RESUBMIT	REVERING	RHYOLITE	RIPCORDS	ROCKIEST
RESCRIPT	RESULTED	REVERSAL	RHYTHMIC	RIPENESS	ROCKLING
RESCUERS	RESUMING	REVERSED	RIBALDRY	RIPENING	ROCKROSE
RESCUING	RETAILED	REVERSER	RIB	RIPOSTED	ROCK
RESEARCH	RETAILER	REVERSES	CAGES	RIPOSTES	SALT
RESEMBLE	RETAINED	REVERTED	RIBOSOME	RIPPABLE	ROCKWEED
RESENTED	RETAINER	REVERTER	RICEBIRD	RIPPLING	ROEBUCKS
RESERVED	RETAKING	REVIEWAL	RICHMOND	RIPTIDES	ROENTGEN
RESERVER	RETARDED	REVIEWED	RICHNESS	RISKIEST	ROGATION
RESERVES	RETARDER	REVIEWER	RICKRACK	RISOTTOS	ROGATORY
RESETTER	RETCHING	REVILERS	RICKSHAW	RISSOLES	ROLE
RESETTLE	RETICENT	REVILING	RICOCHET	RITENUTO	PLAY
RESIDENT	RETICULE	REVISERS	RIDDANCE	RITUALLY	ROLLAWAY
RESIDING	RETINENE	REVISING	RIDDLING	RIVALING	ROLL
RESIDUAL	RETINITE	REVISION	RIDICULE	RIVALLED	BARS
RESIDUES	RETINUED	REVISORY	RIESLING	RIVERBED	ROLL
RESIDUUM	RETINUES	REVIVALS	RIFENESS	RIVERINE	CALL
RESIGNAL	RETIRING	REVIVIFY	RIFFLING	RIVETERS	ROLLMOPS
RESIGNED	RETORTED	REVIVING	RIFFRAFF	RIVETING	ROLL
RESIGNER	RETORTER	REVOKING	RIFLEMAN	RIVIERAS	OVER
RESINATE	RETRACED	REVOLTED	RIGADOON	RIVULETS	ROLLOVER
RESINOID	RETREADS	REVOLTER	RIGATONI	ROAD	ROLY-
RESINOUS	RETREATS	REVOLUTE	RIGHTFUL	HOGS	POLY
RESISTED	RETRENCH	REVOLVED	RIGHTING	ROAD	ROMANCED
RESISTER	RETRIALS	REVOLVER	RIGHTISM	RAGE	ROMANCES
RESISTOR	RETRIEVE	REWARDED	RIGHTIST	ROADSHOW	ROMANIES
RESOLUTE	RETROACT	REWARDER	RIGHT	ROADSIDE	ROMAN
RESOLVED	RETROFIT	REWINDER	OFF	ROAD	LAW
RESOLVER	RETRORSE	REWIRING	RIGIDITY	SIGN	ROMANSCH
RESOLVES	RETURNED	REWORDED	RIGORISM	ROADSTER	ROMANTIC
RESONANT	RETURNER	REWORKED	RIGORIST	ROAD	RONDAVEL
RESONATE	REUNIONS	REWRITES	RIGOROUS	TEST	RONDELET
				ROADWORK	RONTGENS

ROOFLESS
ROOF
  RACK
ROOFTOPS
ROOFTREE
ROOMIEST
ROOMMATE
ROOM
  MATE
ROOSTERS
ROOSTING
ROOT
  BEER
ROOT
  CROP
ROOTLESS
ROOTLIKE
ROPEWALK
ROPINESS
ROSARIAN
ROSARIES
ROSEBUSH
ROSEFISH
ROSE
  HIPS
ROSEMARY
ROSEOLAR
ROSE-
  ROOT
ROSETTES
ROSEWOOD
ROSINESS
ROSINING
ROSKILDE
ROSTRUMS
ROTARIAN
ROTATING
ROTATION
ROTATIVE
ROTATORY
ROTENONE
ROTHESAY
ROTOTILL
ROTTENLY
ROTUNDAS
ROUGHAGE
ROUGH-
  DRY
ROUGHEST
ROUGH-
  HEW
ROUGHING

ROULETTE
ROUND-
  ARM
ROUNDELS
ROUNDERS
ROUNDEST
ROUNDING
ROUNDISH
ROUNDUPS
ROUTINES
ROVE-
  OVER
ROWDIEST
ROWDYISM
ROW
  HOUSE
ROWLOCKS
ROYALISM
ROYALIST
RUBBINGS
RUBBISHY
RUBDOWNS
RUBELITE
RUBEOLAR
RUBICONS
RUBICUND
RUBIDIUM
RUBRICAL
RUCKSACK
RUCKUSES
RUDDIEST
RUDENESS
RUDIMENT
RUEFULLY
RUFFIANS
RUFFLING
RUGGEDLY
RUGOSITY
RUINABLE
RULEBOOK
RUMANIAN
RUMBLING
RUMINANT
RUMINATE
RUMMAGED
RUMMAGER
RUMMAGES
RUMOURED
RUMPLING
RUN-
  ABOUT
RUNAWAYS

RUNDOWNS
RUNNER
  UP
RUNNER-
  UP
RUNNIEST
RUPTURED
RUPTURES
RURALISM
RURALIST
RURALITY
RURALIZE
RUSH
  HOUR
RUST
  BELT
RUSTICAL
RUSTIEST
RUSTLERS
RUSTLING
RUTABAGA
RUTHENIC
RUTHLESS
RYDER
  CUP
RYE-
  BROME
RYEGRASS

S

SAARLAND
SABADELL
SABBATIC
SABOTAGE
SABOTEUR
SABULOUS
SACKLIKE
SACK
  RACE
SACREDLY
SACRISTY
SADDENED
SADDLERS
SADDLERY
SADDLING
SADISTIC
SAFENESS
SAFE
  SEAT
SAFETIES
SAGACITY
SAGGIEST

SAGITTAL
SAILABLE
SAILFISH
SAILINGS
SAILORLY
SAINFOIN
SAKHALIN
SALAAMED
SALACITY
SALARIED
SALARIES
SALEABLE
SALEABLY
SALEROOM
SALESMAN
SALESMEN
SALES
  TAX
SALIENCE
SALIENTS
SALINGER
SALINITY
SALIVARY
SALIVATE
SALLYING
SALPICON
SALTBUSH
SALTIEST
SALTILLO
SALTLICK
SALTNESS
SALTPANS
SALTWORT
SALUTARY
SALUTING
SALVABLE
SALVABLY
SALVADOR
SALVAGED
SALVAGER
SALZBURG
SAMARIUM
SAMENESS
SAMIZDAT
SAMOVARS
SAMPHIRE
SAMPLERS
SAMPLING
SAMURAIS
SANCTIFY
SANCTION

SANCTITY
SANCTUMS
SANDAKAN
SANDARAC
SANDBAGS
SANDBANK
SANDBARS
SAND-
  CAST
SAND
  DUNE
SAN
  DIEGO
SANDIEST
SANDPITS
SANDSHOE
SANDSOAP
SAND
  TRAP
SANDWELL
SANDWICH
SANDWORM
SANDWORT
SANENESS
SANGAREE
SANGUINE
SANITARY
SANITIZE
SANSKRIT
SANTA
  ANA
SANTAREM
SANTIAGO
SANTONIN
SAO
  PAULO
SAPIDITY
SAPIENCE
SAPLINGS
SAPONIFY
SAPONITE
SAPPHIRE
SAPPIEST
SAPROBIC
SAPROPEL
SARABAND
SARACENS
SARAJEVO
SARDINES
SARDINIA
SARDONIC
SARDONYX

SARGASSO
SARGODHA
SARKIEST
SARMATIA
SARRAUTE
SASHAYED
SASH
  CORD
SASSIEST
SASTRUGA
SATANISM
SATANIST
SATCHELS
SATIABLE
SATIABLY
SATIATED
SATIRIST
SATIRIZE
SATSUMAS
SATURANT
SATURATE
SATURDAY
SAUCEPAN
SAUCIEST
SAUNTERS
SAUROPOD
SAUSAGES
SAUTEING
SAVAGELY
SAVAGERY
SAVAGING
SAVANNAH
SAVANNAS
SAVIOURS
SAVORIES
SAVOROUS
SAVOURED
SAVOYARD
SAWBONES
SAWGRASS
SAWHORSE
SAWMILLS
SAWTOOTH
SCABBARD
SCABBIER
SCABBILY
SCABIOUS
SCABROUS
SCAFFOLD
SCALABLE
SCALABLY

SCALAWAG	SCHOOLIE	SCOWLING	SCURVILY	SECEDING	SELF-
SCALDING	SCHOONER	SCRABBLE	SCUTTLED	SECLUDED	MADE
SCALENUS	SCHWERIN	SCRAGGED	SCUTTLES	SECONDED	SELF-
SCALIEST	SCIAENID	SCRAGGLY	SCYTHING	SECONDER	PITY
SCALLION	SCIATICA	SCRAMBLE	SEABIRDS	SECONDLY	SELF-
SCALLOPS	SCIENCES	SCRAMMED	SEABOARD	SECRETED	RULE
SCALPELS	SCILICET	SCRANTON	SEABORNE	SECRETIN	SELFSAME
SCALPERS	SCIMITAR	SCRAPERS	SEACOAST	SECRETLY	SELF-
SCALPING	SCINCOID	SCRAPING	SEAFARER	SECTIONS	WILL
SCAMMONY	SCIRRHUS	SCRAP	SEAFRONT	SECTORAL	SELL-
SCAMPISH	SCISSILE	MAN	SEAGIRTS	SECURELY	OUTS
SCANDALS	SCISSION	SCRAPPED	SEAGOING	SECUREST	SELVAGES
SCANDIUM	SCISSORS	SCRATCHY	SEA	SECURING	SEMANTIC
SCANNERS	SCIURINE	SCRAWLED	GREEN	SECURITY	SEMARANG
SCANNING	SCIUROID	SCRAWLER	SEAGULLS	SEDATELY	SEMESTER
SCANSION	SCLAFFER	SCREAMED	SEAHORSE	SEDATING	SEMIARID
SCANTIER	SCLERITE	SCREAMER	SEALABLE	SEDATION	SEMIDOME
SCANTILY	SCLEROID	SCREECHY	SEA	SEDATIVE	SEMINARS
SCAPULAR	SCLEROMA	SCREENED	LEVEL	SEDIMENT	SEMINARY
SCAPULAS	SCLEROUS	SCREENER	SEA	SEDITION	SEMIOTIC
SCARCELY	SCOFFING	SCREWIER	LIONS	SEDUCERS	SEMITICS
SCARCEST	SCOLDING	SCREWING	SEALSKIN	SEDUCING	SEMITIST
SCARCITY	SCOLLOPS	SCREW	SEALYHAM	SEDULITY	SEMITONE
SCARGILL	SCOOPING	TOP	SEAMIEST	SEDULOUS	SEMOLINA
SCARIEST	SCOOTERS	SCRIBBLE	SEA	SEEDBEDS	SEMPLICE
SCARIOUS	SCOOTING	SCRIMPED	MILES	SEEDCASE	SENATORS
SCARRING	SCORCHED	SCRIPTED	SEA	SEEDCORN	SENDABLE
SCATHING	SCORCHER	SCROFULA	MISTS	SEEDIEST	SEND-
SCATTIER	SCORCHES	SCROLLED	SEAMLESS	SEEDLESS	OFFS
SCATTILY	SCORNFUL	SCROOGES	SEAMOUNT	SEEDLING	SENILITY
SCATTING	SCORNING	SCROTUMS	SEAPLANE	SEEDSMAN	SENORITA
SCAVENGE	SCORPION	SCROUNGE	SEAPORTS	SEEDSMEN	SENSIBLE
SCENARIO	SCORPIOS	SCRUBBED	SEA	SEESAWED	SENSIBLY
SCENTING	SCORPIUS	SCRUBBER	POWER	SEETHING	SENSUOUS
SCEPTICS	SCORSESE	SCRUMPED	SEAQUAKE	SEGMENTS	SENTENCE
SCEPTRES	SCOTCHED	SCRUNCHY	SEARCHED	SEIGNEUR	SENTIENT
SCHEDULE	SCOT	SCRUPLED	SEARCHER	SEISABLE	SENTINEL
SCHEMATA	FREE	SCRUPLES	SEARCHES	SEISMISM	SENTRIES
SCHEMERS	SCOT-	SCRUTINY	SEASCAPE	SEIZABLE	SEPALLED
SCHEMING	FREE	SCUDDING	SEASHELL	SEIZURES	SEPALOID
SCHERZOS	SCOTLAND	SCUFFING	SEASHORE	SELANGOR	SEPARATE
SCHIEDAM	SCOTOPIA	SCUFFLED	SEA	SELECTED	SEPHARDI
SCHILLER	SCOTOPIC	SCUFFLES	SNAKE	SELECTOR	SEPTUPLE
SCHIZOID	SCOTSMAN	SCULLERS	SEASONAL	SELENATE	SEQUENCE
SCHIZONT	SCOTTISH	SCULLERY	SEASONED	SELENITE	SEQUINED
SCHMALTZ	SCOURERS	SCULLING	SEASONER	SELENIUM	SEQUOIAS
SCHMUCKS	SCOURGED	SCULLION	SEAT	SELFHEAL	SERAGLIO
SCHNAPPS	SCOURGER	SCULPSIT	BELT	SELF-	SERAJEVO
SCHOLARS	SCOURGES	SCULPTOR	SEA	HELP	SERAPHIC
SCHOLIUM	SCOURING	SCUPPERS	TROUT	SELFHOOD	SERAPHIM
SCHOOLED	SCOUTING	SCURRIED	SEAWALLS	SELFLESS	SEREMBAN
			SEAWARDS		SERENADE

SERENATA	SHABBILY	SHEBEENS	SHIRTING	SHRAPNEL	SIDE DISH
SERENELY	SHACKING	SHEDABLE	SHITLESS	SHREDDED	SIDE-FOOT
SERENITY	SHACKLED	SHEDDING	SHITTIER	SHREDDER	SIDEKICK
SERGEANT	SHACKLER	SHEEPDIP	SHITTING	SHREWDER	SIDELINE
SERIALLY	SHACKLES	SHEEPDOG	SHIVERED	SHREWDLY	SIDELONG
SERIATIM	SHADDOCK	SHEEPISH	SHIVERER	SHREWISH	SIDEREAL
SERMONIC	SHADIEST	SHEEREST	SHIZUOKA	SHRIEKED	SIDERITE
SEROLOGY	SHADINGS	SHEERING	SHOCKERS	SHRIEKER	SIDE ROAD
SEROSITY	SHADOWED	SHEETING	SHOCKING	SHRIEVAL	SIDESHOW
SEROTINE	SHADOWER	SHEIKDOM	SHODDIER	SHRILLER	SIDESLIP
SERPENTS	SHAFTING	SHELDUCK	SHODDILY	SHRIMPER	SIDESMAN
SERPULID	SHAGBARK	SHELLING	SHOEBILL	SHRINKER	SIDESTEP
SERRANID	SHAGGIER	SHELTERS	SHOEHORN	SHROUDED	SIDEWALK
SERRATED	SHAGGILY	SHELVING	SHOELACE	SHRUGGED	SIDEWALL
SERVABLE	SHAGGING	SHENYANG	SHOETREE	SHRUNKEN	SIDEWAYS
SERVANTS	SHAGREEN	SHEPHERD	SHOLAPUR	SHUCKING	SIEGBAHN
SERVICED	SHAKABLE	SHERATON	SHOOTERS	SHUDDERS	SIFTINGS
SERVICES	SHAKEOUT	SHERBETS	SHOOTING	SHUDDERY	SIGHTING
SERVINGS	SHAKE-UPS	SHERIFFS	SHOOT OUT	SHUFFLED	SIGHTSEE
SERVITOR	SHAKIEST	SHETLAND	SHOOT-OUT	SHUFFLER	SIGNALED
SERVQUAL	SHALLOON	SHIELDED	SHOPGIRL	SHUFFLES	SIGNALLY
SESAMOID	SHALLOTS	SHIELDER	SHOPLIFT	SHUNNING	SIGNINGS
SESSIONS	SHALLOWS	SHIELING	SHOPPERS	SHUNTERS	SIGNORAS
SET ASIDE	SHAMABLE	SHIFTIER	SHOPPING	SHUNTING	SIGNPOST
SETBACKS	SHAMBLED	SHIFTILY	SHOPTALK	SHUSHING	SILASTIC
SETIFORM	SHAMBLES	SHIFTING	SHORTAGE	SHUTDOWN	SILENCED
SET PIECE	SHAMEFUL	SHIFT KEY	SHORT CUT	SHUTTERS	SILENCER
SET POINT	SHAMMIES	SHIITAKE	SHORT-DAY	SHUTTING	SILENCES
SET RIGHT	SHAMMING	SHILLING	SHORTEST	SHUTTLED	SILENTLY
SETSCREW	SHAMPOOS	SHILLONG	SHORTIES	SHUTTLES	SILICATE
SETTINGS	SHAMROCK	SHIMMERY	SHORTING	SHYSTERS	SILICIDE
SETTLERS	SHANDIES	SHINBONE	SHOTGUNS	SIANGTAN	SILICIFY
SETTLE UP	SHANDONG	SHINDIGS	SHOULDER	SIBERIAN	SILICONE
SETTLING	SHANGHAI	SHINGLER	SHOULDN'T	SIBILANT	SILKIEST
SEVENTHS	SHANTIES	SHINGLES	SHOUTING	SIBILATE	SILKWORM
SEVERELY	SHANTUNG	SHINIEST	SHOVELED	SIBLINGS	SILLABUB
SEVERING	SHAPABLE	SHINNIED	SHOVELER	SICILIAN	SILLIEST
SEVERITY	SHARABLE	SHINNING	SHOWBOAT	SICKBAYS	SILOXANE
SEWERAGE	SHARE-OUT	SHIPABLE	SHOWCASE	SICKBEDS	SILURIAN
SEXINESS	SHARP END	SHIPLOAD	SHOWDOWN	SICK CALL	SILVERED
SEXOLOGY	SHARPEST	SHIPMATE	SHOWERED	SICKENED	SILVERER
SEX ORGAN	SHARPISH	SHIPMENT	SHOWGIRL	SICKENER	SIMBIRSK
SEXTANTS	SHARP-SET	SHIPPERS	SHOWIEST	SICKLIER	SIMMERED
SEXTUPLE	SHAVABLE	SHIPPING	SHOWINGS	SICKNESS	SIMONIAC
SEXUALLY	SHAVINGS	SHIPWORM	SHOW-OFFS	SICKROOM	SIMONIST
SHABBIER	SHEADING	SHIPYARD	SHOWROOM	SIDEARMS	SIMPERED
	SHEARING	SHIRKERS		SIDE ARMS	SIMPERER
	SHEATHED	SHIRKING		SIDEBAND	SIMPLEST
		SHIRRING		SIDECARS	
		SHIRTIER			

SIMPLIFY	SKEPTISM	SLACKEST	SLINKIER	SLURRING	SNACKING
SIMPLISM	SKERRICK	SLACKING	SLINKILY	SLUSHIER	SNAFFLED
SIMULANT	SKETCHED	SLAGGING	SLINKING	SLUTTISH	SNAFFLES
SIMULATE	SKETCHER	SLAGHEAP	SLIPCASE	SMACKERS	SNAGGING
SINAITIC	SKETCHES	SLAG	SLIPKNOT	SMACKING	SNAPBACK
SINAPISM	SKEWBACK	HEAP	SLIP	SMALL	SNAPPERS
SINCIPUT	SKEWBALD	SLAKABLE	KNOT	ADS	SNAPPIER
SINECURE	SKEWERED	SLAMMING	SLIP	SMALLEST	SNAPPILY
SINFONIA	SKIDDING	SLANDERS	OVER	SMALL	SNAPPING
SINFULLY	SKIDPANS	SLANGILY	SLIPPAGE	FRY	SNAPPISH
SINGABLE	SKIJORER	SLANGING	SLIPPERS	SMALLISH	SNAP
SINGEING	SKI	SLANTING	SLIPPERY	SMALLPOX	SHOT
SINGLETS	JUMPS	SLAP-	SLIPPIER	SMALTITE	SNAPSHOT
SINGLING	SKI	BANG	SLIPPING	SMARMIER	SNARLING
SINGSONG	LIFTS	SLAPDASH	SLIP	SMARTEST	SNARL-
SINGULAR	SKILLETS	SLAPHEAD	ROAD	SMARTING	UPS
SINISTER	SKIMMERS	SLAPPING	SLIPSHOD	SMASHERS	SNATCHED
SINKABLE	SKIMMING	SLASHING	SLIPWAYS	SMASHING	SNATCHER
SINKHOLE	SKIMPIER	SLATTERN	SLITHERY	SMASH-	SNATCHES
SINN	SKIMPILY	SLAVERED	SLITTING	UPS	SNAZZIER
FEIN	SKIMPING	SLAVERER	SLIVERER	SMEARING	SNAZZILY
SINOLOGY	SKINCARE	SLAVONIA	SLOBBERY	SMELLIER	SNEAKERS
SINUSOID	SKIN	SLAVONIC	SLOE-	SMELLING	SNEAKIER
SIPHONAL	DEEP	SLEAZIER	EYED	SMELTERY	SNEAKILY
SIPHONED	SKIN-	SLEAZILY	SLOGGERS	SMELTING	SNEAKING
SIRENIAN	DEEP	SLEDDING	SLOGGING	SMIRCHED	SNEERING
SIRLOINS	SKIN-	SLEDGING	SLOPPIER	SMIRCHER	SNEEZING
SIROCCOS	DIVE	SLEEKEST	SLOPPILY	SMIRKING	SNICKERS
SISSIEST	SKINHEAD	SLEEKING	SLOPPING	SMITHERY	SNICKING
SISSYISH	SKINLESS	SLEEPERS	SLOPWORK	SMITHIES	SNIFFING
SISTERLY	SKINNIER	SLEEPIER	SLOSHING	SMOCKING	SNIFFLED
SISTROID	SKINNING	SLEEPILY	SLOTHFUL	SMOKABLE	SNIFFLER
SITARIST	SKIPJACK	SLEEPING	SLOTTING	SMOKIEST	SNIFFLES
SIT-	SKI	SLEETING	SLOUCHED	SMOLENSK	SNIFTERS
DOWNS	PLANE	SLEEVING	SLOUCHER	SMOOCHED	SNIGGERS
SITOLOGY	SKI	SLEIGHER	SLOUGHED	SMOOTHED	SNIGGERY
SITTINGS	POLES	SLICKERS	SLOVAKIA	SMOOTHEN	SNIGGLER
SITUATED	SKIPPERS	SLICKEST	SLOVENIA	SMOOTHER	SNIPPETS
SITZMARK	SKIPPING	SLICKING	SLOVENLY	SMOOTHIE	SNIPPILY
SIX-	SKIRMISH	SLIDABLE	SLOWDOWN	SMOOTHLY	SNIPPING
PACKS	SKIRTING	SLIGHTED	SLOW	SMOTHERY	SNITCHED
SIXPENCE	SKITTISH	SLIGHTER	DOWN	SMOULDER	SNITCHES
SIXPENNY	SKITTLES	SLIGHTLY	SLOWNESS	SMUDGILY	SNIVELED
SIXTEENS	SKIVVIED	SLIM	SLOWWORM	SMUDGING	SNIVELLY
SIXTIETH	SKIVVIES	DOWN	SLUDGIER	SMUGGEST	SNOBBERY
SIZEABLE	SKULKING	SLIMIEST	SLUGGARD	SMUGGLED	SNOBBISH
SIZZLERS	SKULLCAP	SLIMMERS	SLUGGING	SMUGGLER	SNOGGING
SIZZLING	SKYDIVER	SLIMMEST	SLUGGISH	SMUGNESS	SNOOPERS
SKELETAL	SKYLARKS	SLIMMING	SLUICING	SMUTTIER	SNOOPING
SKELETON	SKYLIGHT	SLIMNESS	SLUMMING	SMUTTILY	SNOOTIER
SKEPTICS	SKYLINES	SLINGING	SLUMPING	SNACK	SNOOTILY
	SKYWARDS		SLURPING	BAR	

SNOOZING
SNORKELS
SNORTERS
SNORTING
SNOTTIER
SNOTTILY
SNOWBALL
SNOWBIRD
SNOWDROP
SNOWFALL
SNOWIEST
SNOWLINE
SNOWSHED
SNOWSHOE
SNUBBING
SNUFFBOX
SNUFFERS
SNUFFING
SNUFFLED
SNUFFLER
SNUFFLES
SNUGGERY
SNUGGLED
SNUGNESS
SO-AND-
  SOS
SOAPBARK
SOAPIEST
SOAPLESS
SOAPSUDS
SOAPWORT
SOBERING
SOBRIETY
SOB
  STORY
SO-
  CALLED
SOCIABLE
SOCIABLY
SOCIALLY
SOCIETAL
SOCRATIC
SODALITE
SODAMIDE
SODOMITE
SODOMIZE
SOFTBALL
SOFT
  COPY
SOFTENED
SOFTENER
SOFTNESS

SOFT
  SELL
SOFT
  SOAP
SOFT
  SPOT
SOFTWARE
SOFTWOOD
SOGGIEST
SOISSONS
SOJOURNS
SOLACING
SOLANDER
SOLARIUM
SOLARIZE
SOLATIUM
SOLDERED
SOLDERER
SOLDIERS
SOLDIERY
SOLECISM
SOLECIST
SOLEMNLY
SOLENOID
SOLIDAGO
SOLIDARY
SOLIDIFY
SOLIDITY
SOLIHULL
SOLINGEN
SOLITARY
SOLITUDE
SOLOISTS
SOLONETZ
SOLSTICE
SOLUTION
SOLVABLE
SOLVENCY
SOLVENTS
SOMALIAN
SOMBRELY
SOMBRERO
SOMBROUS
SOMEBODY
SOME
  HOPE
SOMERSET
SOMETIME
SOMEWHAT
SONANTAL
SONATINA
SONGBIRD

SONGBOOK
SONGSTER
SON-IN-
  LAW
SONOBUOY
SONORANT
SONORITY
SONOROUS
SOOTHING
SOOTHSAY
SOOTIEST
SOPHISMS
SOPHISTS
SOPPIEST
SOPRANOS
SORBITOL
SORBONNE
SORCERER
SORDIDLY
SOREDIUM
SORENESS
SORICINE
SOROCABA
SORORATE
SORORITY
SORPTION
SORRENTO
SORRIEST
SORROWED
SORROWER
SORTABLE
SOUCHONG
SOUFFLES
SOUGHING
SOUL
  FOOD
SOULLESS
SOUNDBOX
SOUNDING
SOUND
  OFF
SOURDINE
SOURNESS
SOURPUSS
SOUTACHE
SOUTHERN
SOUTHING
SOUTHPAW
SOUVENIR
SOWBREAD
SOYA
  BEAN

SOY
  SAUCE
SPACE
  AGE
SPACE-
  AGE
SPACE
  BAR
SPACE-
  BAR
SPACEMAN
SPACEMEN
SPACIOUS
SPANDREL
SPANGLED
SPANGLES
SPANIARD
SPANIELS
SPANKING
SPANNERS
SPANNING
SPANSPEK
SPARABLE
SPAR
  DECK
SPARERIB
SPARE
  RIB
SPARKING
SPARKLED
SPARKLER
SPARKLES
SPARLING
SPARRING
SPARROWS
SPARSELY
SPARSEST
SPASTICS
SPATTERS
SPATULAR
SPATULAS
SPAWNING
SPEAKERS
SPEAKING
SPEARING
SPECIALS
SPECIFIC
SPECIMEN
SPECIOUS
SPECKLED
SPECKLES
SPECTATE

SPECTRAL
SPECTRES
SPECTRUM
SPECULAR
SPECULUM
SPEECHES
SPEEDIER
SPEEDILY
SPEEDING
SPEEDWAY
SPELAEAN
SPELLING
SPENDERS
SPENDING
SPERMARY
SPERMINE
SPERMOUS
SPHAGNUM
SPHENOID
SPHERICS
SPHEROID
SPHERULE
SPHINXES
SPHYGMIC
SPICCATO
SPICIEST
SPICULUM
SPIKELET
SPIKIEST
SPILLAGE
SPILLING
SPILLWAY
SPINDLES
SPINIFEX
SPINNERS
SPINNEYS
SPINNING
SPIN-
  OFFS
SPINSTER
SPIRACLE
SPIRALED
SPIRITED
SPITEFUL
SPITFIRE
SPITTING
SPITTOON
SPLASHED
SPLASHER
SPLATTED
SPLATTER

SPLAYING
SPLENDID
SPLENIAL
SPLENIUS
SPLICERS
SPLICING
SPLINTER
SPLIT
  END
SPLIT
  PEA
SPLITTER
SPLODGES
SPLOSHED
SPLOSHES
SPLURGED
SPLURGES
SPLUTTER
SPOILAGE
SPOILERS
SPOILING
SPOLIATE
SPONDAIC
SPONDEES
SPONGERS
SPONGIER
SPONGILY
SPONGING
SPONSION
SPONSORS
SPOOKIER
SPOOKILY
SPOOKING
SPOOKISH
SPOON-
  FED
SPOONFUL
SPOONING
SPORADIC
SPORRANS
SPORTFUL
SPORTIER
SPORTILY
SPORTING
SPORTIVE
SPOTLAMP
SPOTLESS
SPOTTERS
SPOTTIER
SPOTTILY
SPOTTING

SPOT-WELD	SQUAWKED	STAMPEDE	STATURES	STICKIER	STODGIER
SPOUTERS	SQUAWKER	STAMPING	STATUSES	STICKILY	STODGILY
SPOUTING	SQUEAKED	STANCHED	STATUTES	STICKING	STOICISM
SPRADDLE	SQUEAKER	STANCHER	STAYSAIL	STICKLER	STOLIDLY
SPRAINED	SQUEALED	STANDARD	STEADIED	STICKPIN	STOMACHS
SPRAWLED	SQUEALER	STANDBYS	STEADIER	STICK-UPS	STOMACHY
SPRAWLER	SQUEEGEE	STANDING	STEADILY	STIFFEST	STOMATAL
SPRAYERS	SQUEEZED	STAND-INS	STEALING	STIFLING	STOMATIC
SPRAY GUN	SQUEEZER	STANDISH	STEALTHY	STIGMATA	STOMPING
SPRAYING	SQUEEZES	STANDOFF	STEAMERS	STILBENE	STONABLE
SPREADER	SQUELCHY	STAND OUT	STEAMIER	STILBITE	STONE AGE
SPRIGGER	SQUIGGLE	STANNARY	STEAMILY	STILETTO	STONEFLY
SPRINGER	SQUIGGLY	STANNITE	STEAMING	STILLEST	STONIEST
SPRINKLE	SQUINTED	STANNOUS	STEAPSIN	STILLING	STONKING
SPRINTED	SQUINTER	STANZAIC	STEARATE	STIMULUS	STOOD OUT
SPRINTER	SQUIRMED	STAPELIA	STEATITE	STINGERS	STOOPING
SPRITELY	SQUIRMER	STAPLERS	STEELIER	STINGIER	STOPCOCK
SPROCKET	SQUIRREL	STAPLING	STEELING	STINGILY	STOPGAPS
SPROUTED	SQUIRTED	STARCHED	STEEPEST	STINGING	STOPOVER
SPRUCELY	SQUIRTER	STARCHER	STEEPING	STINGRAY	STOPPAGE
SPRUCING	SQUISHED	STARCHES	STEEPLES	STING RAY	STOPPARD
SPRYNESS	SRI LANKA	STARDUST	STEERAGE	STINKERS	STOPPERS
SPUNKIER	SRINAGAR	STARFISH	STEERING	STINKING	STOPPING
SPUNKILY	STABBERS	STARGAZE	STEINBOK	STINTING	STORABLE
SPURIOUS	STABBING	STARKERS	STELLATE	STIPENDS	STOREYED
SPURNING	STABLING	STARKEST	STELLIFY	STIPPLED	STORMIER
SPURRING	STACCATO	STARLESS	STELLITE	STIPPLER	STORMILY
SPURTING	STACKING	STARLETS	STEMHEAD	STIPULAR	STORMING
SPUTTERS	STADIUMS	STARLIKE	STEMMING	STIRLING	STORMONT
SPYGLASS	STAFFING	STARLING	STENCHES	STIRRERS	STOUTEST
SQUABBLE	STAFFMAN	STARRIER	STENCILS	STIRRING	STOWAWAY
SQUAD CAR	STAFFORD	STARRILY	STEN GUNS	STIRRUPS	STRABANE
SQUADRON	STAGGARD	STARRING	STENOSIS	STITCHED	STRADDLE
SQUALENE	STAGGERS	STARSHIP	STENOTIC	STITCHER	STRAFING
SQUALLED	STAGINGS	STAR SIGN	STEP DOWN	STITCHES	STRAGGLE
SQUALLER	STAGNANT	STARTERS	STEPPING	STITCH UP	STRAGGLY
SQUAMATE	STAGNATE	STARTING	STEPWISE	STOCKADE	STRAIGHT
SQUAMOUS	STAINING	STARTLED	STERIGMA	STOCKCAR	STRAINED
SQUANDER	STAIRWAY	STARTLER	STERLING	STOCK CAR	STRAINER
SQUARELY	STAKE OUT	STARVING	STERNEST	STOCKIER	STRAITEN
SQUAREST	STALKERS	STAR WARS	STERNSON	STOCKILY	STRANDED
SQUARING	STALKILY	STARWORT	STERNUMS	STOCKING	STRANGER
SQUARISH	STALKING	STASHING	STERNWAY	STOCKIST	STRANGLE
SQUASHED	STALLING	STATABLE	STEROIDS	STOCKMAN	STRAPPED
SQUASHER	STALLION	STATELET	STETSONS	STOCKMEN	STRAPPER
SQUASHES	STALWART	STATICAL	STEWARDS	STOCKOUT	STRATEGY
SQUATTED	STAMFORD	STATIONS	STIBNITE	STOCKPOT	STRATIFY
SQUATTER	STAMINAL	STATUARY	STICKERS	STOCKTON	STRAW MAN
	STAMMERS		STICKFUL		

STRAW	STUDBOOK	SUBORDER	SULPHATE	SUPPLIED	SWANKILY
MEN	STUDDING	SUBORNED	SULPHIDE	SUPPLIER	SWANKING
STRAYING	STUDENTS	SUBORNER	SULPHITE	SUPPLIES	SWANNERY
STREAKED	STUD	SUBOTICA	SULPHONE	SUPPORTS	SWANNING
STREAKER	FARM	SUBOXIDE	SULTANAS	SUPPOSED	SWANSKIN
STREAMED	STUDIOUS	SUBPLOTS	SULTANIC	SUPPOSER	SWANSONG
STREAMER	STUDWORK	SUBPOENA	SULTRIER	SUPPRESS	SWAN
STRENGTH	STUDYING	SUBSERVE	SULTRILY	SUPREMOS	SONG
STRESSED	STUFFIER	SUBSHRUB	SUMATRAN	SURABAYA	SWAP
STRESSES	STUFFILY	SUBSIDED	SUMMERED	SURCOATS	MEET
STRETCHY	STUFFING	SUBSIDER	SUMMITAL	SUREFIRE	SWAPPING
STREUSEL	STULTIFY	SUBSOLAR	SUMMONED	SURE	SWARMING
STREWING	STUMBLED	SUBSONIC	SUM	FIRE	SWASTIKA
STRIATED	STUMBLER	SUBSTAGE	TOTAL	SURENESS	SWATCHES
STRICKEN	STUMBLES	SUBSUMED	SUNBAKED	SURETIES	SWATHING
STRICKLE	STUMPIER	SUBTITLE	SUNBATHE	SURFABLE	SWATTERS
STRICTER	STUMPING	SUBTLEST	SUNBEAMS	SURFACED	SWATTING
STRICTLY	STUNNERS	SUBTLETY	SUNBELTS	SURFACER	SWAYABLE
STRIDDEN	STUNNING	SUBTONIC	SUNBURNT	SURFACES	SWAY-
STRIDENT	STUNTING	SUBTOTAL	SUNBURST	SURFBIRD	BACK
STRIGOSE	STUNT	SUBTRACT	SUNDERED	SURFBOAT	SWEARING
STRIKERS	MAN	SUBULATE	SUNDIALS	SURFLIKE	SWEATBOX
STRIKING	STUNT	SUBURBAN	SUNDRIES	SURGEONS	SWEATERS
STRIMMER	MEN	SUBURBIA	SUNGLASS	SURGICAL	SWEATIER
STRINGER	STUPIDER	SUCCINCT	SUNLAMPS	SURICATE	SWEATILY
STRIPIER	STUPIDLY	SUCCINIC	SUNLIGHT	SURLIEST	SWEATING
STRIPPED	STURDIER	SUCCUBUS	SUNNIEST	SURMISED	SWEEPERS
STRIPPER	STURDILY	SUCHLIKE	SUNRISES	SURMISER	SWEEPING
STROBILA	STURGEON	SUCKLING	SUNROOFS	SURMISES	SWEETEST
STROKING	STUTTERS	SUDANESE	SUNSHADE	SURMOUNT	SWEETIES
STROLLED	STYLISTS	SUDATORY	SUNSHINE	SURNAMES	SWEET
STROLLER	STYLIZED	SUDDENLY	SUNSHINY	SURPLICE	PEA
STRONGER	STYLIZER	SUFFERED	SUNSPOTS	SURPRINT	SWEETSOP
STRONGLY	STYLUSES	SUFFERER	SUNTRAPS	SURPRISE	SWELLING
STROPHES	STYMYING	SUFFICED	SUN	SURROUND	SWERVING
STROPHIC	STYPTICS	SUFFICER	VISOR	SURVEYED	SWIFTEST
STRUDELS	SUBACUTE	SUFFIXAL	SUNWARDS	SURVEYOR	SWIGGING
STRUGGLE	SUBADULT	SUFFIXES	SUPADRIV	SURVIVAL	SWILLING
STRUMMED	SUBAGENT	SUFFRAGE	SUPERBLY	SURVIVED	SWIMMERS
STRUMMER	SUBCLASS	SUFFUSED	SUPEREGO	SURVIVOR	SWIMMING
STRUMPET	SUBDUING	SUGARING	SUPERFIX	SUSPECTS	SWIMSUIT
STRUNG-	SUBERIZE	SUICIDAL	SUPERIOR	SUSPENSE	SWINDLED
UP	SUBEROSE	SUICIDES	SUPERMAN	SUTURING	SWINDLER
STRUTTED	SUBFLOOR	SUITABLE	SUPERMEN	SUZERAIN	SWINDLES
STRUTTER	SUBGENUS	SUITABLY	SUPERNAL	SVALBARD	SWINEPOX
STUBBIER	SUBGROUP	SUITCASE	SUPERSEX	SVENGALI	SWINGBIN
STUBBILY	SUBHUMAN	SULAWESI	SUPERTAX	SWABBING	SWINGERS
STUBBING	SUBJECTS	SULKIEST	SUPINATE	SWADDLED	SWINGING
STUBBLED	SUBLEASE	SULLENER	SUPINELY	SWALLOWS	SWIRLING
STUBBORN	SUBMERGE	SULLENLY	SUPPLANT	SWAMPING	SWISHEST
STUCCOED	SUBMERSE	SULLYING	SUPPLEST	SWANKIER	SWISHING
					SWITCHED

SWITCHER
SWITCHES
SWIVELED
SWOONING
SWOOPING
SWOPPING
SWOTTING
SYBARITE
SYCAMINE
SYCAMORE
SYCONIUM
SYENITIC
SYLLABIC
SYLLABLE
SYLLABUB
SYLLABUS
SYLVATIC
SYMBIONT
SYMBOLIC
SYMMETRY
SYMPATHY
SYMPHILE
SYMPHONY
SYMPOSIA
SYMPTOMS
SYNAPSIS
SYNAPTIC
SYNARCHY
SYNCARPY
SYNCLINE
SYNCOPIC
SYNDESIS
SYNDETIC
SYNDETON
SYNDICAL
SYNDROME
SYNERGIC
SYNGAMIC
SYNONYMS
SYNONYMY
SYNOPSES
SYNOPSIS
SYNOPTIC
SYNOVIAL
SYNTONIC
SYPHILIS
SYPHONED
SYRACUSE
SYRINGED
SYRINGES
SYSTEMIC

SYSTOLIC
SYZYGIAL
SZCZECIN
SZECHWAN

T

TABLEAUS
TABLEAUX
TABLEMAT
TABLOIDS
TABULATE
TACITURN
TACKIEST
TACKLING
TACONITE
TACTICAL
TACTLESS
TADPOLES
TAFFRAIL
TAGANROG
TAGMEMIC
TAHITIAN
TAICHUNG
TAILBACK
TAILCOAT
TAIL
  ENDS
TAILGATE
TAILINGS
TAILLESS
TAILORED
TAIL
  PIPE
TAILRACE
TAILSKID
TAILSPIN
TAIL
  SPIN
TAILWIND
TAIL
  WIND
TAINTING
TAJ
  MAHAL
TAKE A
  BOW
TAKEAWAY
TAKE
  CARE
TAKEOFFS
TAKEOUTS
TAKEOVER

TAKES
  OFF
TAKORADI
TALAPOIN
TALENTED
TALESMAN
TALISMAN
TALKABLE
TALK
  SHOW
TALLBOYS
TALLNESS
TALLYING
TALLYMAN
TALMUDIC
TAMANDUA
TAMARACK
TAMARIND
TAMARISK
TAMBOURS
TAMEABLE
TAMENESS
TAMESIDE
TAMPERED
TAMPERER
TAMWORTH
TANDOORI
TANGENCY
TANGENTS
TANGIBLE
TANGIBLY
TANGIEST
TANGLING
TANGOING
TANGOIST
TANGSHAN
TANKARDS
TANKED
  UP
TANTALIC
TANTALUM
TANTALUS
TANTRUMS
TANZANIA
TAP
  DANCE
TAPE
  DECK
TAPENADE
TAPERING
TAPESTRY
TAPEWORM

TAPPABLE
TAPROOTS
TARAKIHI
TARBOOSH
TARDIEST
TARGETED
TARLATAN
TARRAGON
TARRYING
TARTARIC
TARTNESS
TARTRATE
TASHKENT
TASKWORK
TASK
  WORK
TASMANIA
TASSELED
TASSELLY
TASTABLE
TASTE
  BUD
TASTEFUL
TASTIEST
TATARIAN
TATTERED
TATTIEST
TATTLERS
TATTLING
TATTOOED
TATTOOER
TAUNTING
TAURANGA
TAUTENED
TAUTNESS
TAUTOMER
TAUTONYM
TAVERNER
TAWDRILY
TAXATION
TAX
  HAVEN
TAXINGLY
TAXI
  RANK
TAXONOMY
TAXPAYER
TEABERRY
TEA
  BREAK
TEA
  CADDY

TEACAKES
TEACHERS
TEA
  CHEST
TEACHING
TEACH-
  INS
TEA
  CLOTH
TEAHOUSE
TEA-
  MAKER
TEAM-
  MATE
TEAMSTER
TEAMWORK
TEA
  PARTY
TEARABLE
TEARAWAY
TEARDROP
TEAROOMS
TEASE
  OUT
TEASPOON
TEA
  TOWEL
TECHNICS
TECTONIC
TEDDY
  BOY
TEENAGER
TEE
  SHIRT
TEESSIDE
TEETERED
TEETHING
TEETOTAL
TEGMINAL
TELECAST
TELECOMS
TELEGONY
TELEGRAM
TELEMARK
TELEPLAY
TELETEXT
TELETYPE
TELEVISE
TELEWORK
TELEXING
TELLABLE
TELLTALE

TELLURIC
TELSONIC
TEMERITY
TEMPERED
TEMPERER
TEMPESTS
TEMPLATE
TEMPORAL
TEMPTERS
TEMPTING
TENACITY
TENANTRY
TENDENCY
TENDERED
TENDERER
TENDERLY
TENDRILS
TENEFIFE
TENEMENT
TENERIFE
TENESMIC
TENESMUS
TEN
  GURUS
TENON
  SAW
TENORIST
TENORITE
TENOTOMY
TENSED
  UP
TENSIBLE
TENSIONS
TENTACLE
TENURIAL
TEOCALLI
TEOSINTE
TEPHRITE
TEPIDITY
TERAFLOP
TERATISM
TERATOID
TERATOMA
TERAWATT
TERCEIRA
TEREBENE
TERESINA
TERMINAL
TERMINUS
TERMITES
TERMITIC

TERMLESS	THATCHER	THORACES	THWARTER	TINNITUS	TOILSOME
TERNOPOL	THATCHES	THORACIC	THYROIDS	TINPLATE	TOKENISM
TERPENIC	THEARCHY	THORAXES	THYRSOID	TINSELLY	TOLERANT
TERRACES	THEATRES	THORNIER	TIAN	TINSMITH	TOLERATE
TERRAINS	THEBAINE	THORNILY	SHAN	TINTACKS	TOLIDINE
TERRAPIN	THE	THOROUGH	TIBERIAS	TIPPABLE	TOLL
TERRAZZO	BIBLE	THOUGHTS	TICKETED	TIPPLERS	CALL
TERRIBLE	THE	THOUSAND	TICKLING	TIPSIEST	TOLL-
TERRIBLY	BLUES	THRALDOM	TICKLISH	TIPSTAFF	FREE
TERRIERS	THE	THRASHED	TICK	TIPSTERS	TOLLGATE
TERRIFIC	BRINY	THRASHER	OVER	TIRELESS	TOMAHAWK
TERTIARY	THEISTIC	THREADED	TICKTACK	TIRESIAS	TOMATOES
TERYLENE	THEMATIC	THREADER	TICKTOCK	TIRESOME	TOMBAUGH
TERZETTO	THEOCRAT	THREATEN	TIDDLERS	TITANATE	TOMBLIKE
TESSERAL	THEOLOGY	THREE-D	TIDEMARK	TITANISM	TOM
TESTABLE	THEOREMS	THREE-	TIDEWAYS	TITANITE	BROWN
TESTATOR	THEORIES	PLY	TIDINESS	TITANIUM	TOMENTUM
TEST	THEORIST	THRENODY	TIE	TITANOUS	TOMMY
BANS	THEORIZE	THRESHED	BREAK	TITCHIER	GUN
TEST	THEREMIN	THRESHER	TIE-	TITHABLE	TOMMYROT
CARD	THERMALS	THRESHES	BREAK	TITIVATE	TOMMY
TEST	THERMION	THRILLED	TIE-	TITMOUSE	ROT
CASE	THERMITE	THRILLER	DYING	TITOGRAD	TOMORROW
TEST-	THEROPOD	THRIVING	TIENTSIN	TITTERED	TONALITY
CASE	THESIGER	THROBBED	TIGHTEST	TITTERER	TONE-
TESTICLE	THESPIAN	THROMBIN	TIGHTWAD	TJIREBON	DEAF
TESTIEST	THESSALY	THROMBUS	TIGRAYAN	TLAXCALA	TONELESS
TEST	THEURGIC	THRONGED	TILEFISH	TOADFISH	TONE
TUBE	THE	THROTTLE	TILLABLE	TOADFLAX	POEM
TETANIZE	WEALD	THROWING	TILLICUM	TOADYING	TONICITY
TETCHIER	THIAMINE	THROW-	TIMBRELS	TOADYISM	TONLE
TETCHILY	THIAZINE	INS	TIMBUKTU	TO AND	SAP
TETHERED	THIAZOLE	THRUMMED	TIME	FRO	TONNAGES
TETRACID	THICKEST	THRUMMER	BOMB	TO-AND-	TONSURES
TETRAPOD	THICKETS	THRUSHES	TIMECARD	FRO	TOOTHIER
TETRARCH	THICKSET	THRUSTER	TIME	TOASTERS	TOOTHILY
TEUTONIC	THIEVERY	THRUWAYS	LAGS	TOASTING	TOOTLING
TEXTBOOK	THIEVING	THUDDING	TIMELESS	TOBACCOS	TOOTSIES
TEXTILES	THIEVISH	THUGGERY	TIMELIER	TOBOGGAN	TOPARCHY
TEXTUARY	THIMBLES	THUMBING	TIMEWORK	TOBY	TOP
TEXTURAL	THIN-	THUMBNUT	TIMEWORN	JUGS	BRASS
TEXTURES	FILM	THUMPING	TIME	TOCCATAS	TOPCOATS
THAILAND	THINKING	THUNDERS	ZONE	TOCOLOGY	TOP-
THALAMIC	THINNESS	THUNDERY	TIMIDITY	TODDLERS	DRESS
THALAMUS	THINNEST	THURIBLE	TIMORESE	TODDLING	TOP-
THALLIUM	THINNING	THURIFER	TIMOROUS	TOEHOLDS	HEAVY
THALLOID	THIONINE	THURROCK	TINCTURE	TOENAILS	TOPKNOTS
THALLOUS	THIOUREA	THURSDAY	TINGLING	TOGETHER	TOP-
THANKFUL	THIRTEEN	THWACKED	TINKERED	TOGOLESE	LEVEL
THANKING	THIRTIES	THWACKER	TINKERER	TOILETRY	TOP-
THANKYOU	THISTLES	THWARTED	TINKLING	TOILETTE	NOTCH
THATCHED	THONBURI	THWARTER	TINNIEST		TOPOLOGY

TOPONYMY
TOPOTYPE
TOPPINGS
TOPPLING
TOP-
  SHELL
TORCHERE
TORCHIER
TOREADOR
TORE
  DOWN
TOREUTIC
TORMENTS
TORNADIC
TORNADOS
TOROIDAL
TORPIDLY
TORQUATE
TORRANCE
TORRENTS
TORRIDLY
TORTELLI
TORTILLA
TORTIOUS
TORTOISE
TORTUOUS
TORTURED
TORTURER
TORTURES
TOTALING
TOTALITY
TOTALIZE
TOTALLED
TOTE
  BAGS
TOTEMISM
TOTEMIST
TOTTERED
TOTTERER
TOUCHIER
TOUCHILY
TOUCHING
TOUGHEST
TOULOUSE
TOURAINE
TOURISTS
TOURISTY
TOURNEYS
TOUSLING
TOWELING
TOWELLED

TOWERING
TOWN
  HALL
TOWNSHIP
TOWNSMAN
TOWNSMEN
TOWPATHS
TOWPLANE
TOWROPES
TOXAEMIA
TOXAEMIC
TOXICANT
TOXICITY
TRACHEAL
TRACHEAS
TRACHEID
TRACHOMA
TRACHYTE
TRACINGS
TRACKING
TRACTATE
TRACTILE
TRACTION
TRACTIVE
TRACTORS
TRADABLE
TRADE
  GAP
TRADE
  OFF
TRADE-
  OFF
TRAD
  JAZZ
TRADUCED
TRADUCER
TRAFFORD
TRAGOPAN
TRAILERS
TRAILING
TRAINEES
TRAINERS
TRAINING
TRAIN
  SET
TRAIPSED
TRAITORS
TRAMLINE
TRAMMELS
TRAMPING
TRAMPLED
TRAMPLER

TRANNIES
TRANQUIL
TRANSACT
TRANSECT
TRANSEPT
TRANSFER
TRANSFIX
TRANSITS
TRANSKEI
TRANSMIT
TRANSOMS
TRANSUDE
TRAPDOOR
TRAPEZES
TRAPEZIA
TRAPPERS
TRAPPING
TRAPPIST
TRAPUNTO
TRASHCAN
TRASHIER
TRASHILY
TRASHING
TRAVELED
TRAVERSE
TRAVESTY
TRAWLERS
TRAWLING
TREADING
TREADLER
TREADLES
TREASURE
TREASURY
TREATIES
TREATING
TREATISE
TREATIZE
TREBLING
TREE
  FERN
TREELESS
TREELINE
TREENAIL
TREFOILS
TREKKING
TREMBLED
TREMBLER
TREMBLES
TREMOLOS
TRENCHER
TRENCHES

TRENDIER
TRENDIES
TRENDIFY
TRENDILY
TREPHINE
TRESPASS
TRESSURE
TRESTLES
TRIADISM
TRIAL
  RUN
TRIANGLE
TRIARCHY
TRIASSIC
TRIAXIAL
TRIAZINE
TRIAZOLE
TRIBADIC
TRIBASIC
TRIBRACH
TRIBUNAL
TRIBUNES
TRIBUTES
TRICHINA
TRICHITE
TRICHOID
TRICHOME
TRICKERY
TRICKIER
TRICKILY
TRICKING
TRICKLED
TRICTRAC
TRICYCLE
TRIDENTS
TRIFLING
TRIFOCAL
TRIGGERS
TRIGLYPH
TRIGONAL
TRIGRAPH
TRILBIES
TRILEMMA
TRILLING
TRILLION
TRILLIUM
TRIMARAN
TRIMETER
TRIMMERS
TRIMMEST
TRIMMING

TRIMNESS
TRIMORPH
TRINIDAD
TRINKETS
TRIOXIDE
TRIPLANE
TRIPLETS
TRIPLING
TRIPLOID
TRIPODAL
TRIPOSES
TRIPPERS
TRIPPING
TRIPTANE
TRIPTYCH
TRIPWIRE
TRIREMES
TRISOMIC
TRISTICH
TRITICUM
TRIUMPHS
TRIUNITY
TROCHAIC
TROCHEES
TROCHLEA
TROCHOID
TROLLEYS
TROLLING
TROLLOPS
TROMBONE
TROOPERS
TROOPING
TROPHIES
TROPICAL
TROTLINE
TROTTERS
TROTTING
TROUBLED
TROUBLER
TROUBLES
TROUNCED
TROUPERS
TROUPIAL
TROUSERS
TRUCKERS
TRUCKING
TRUCKLED
TRUDGING
TRUE-
  BLUE
TRUEBORN

TRUE-
  LIFE
TRUELOVE
TRUE
  LOVE
TRUENESS
TRUFFLES
TRUISTIC
TRUJILLO
TRUMPERY
TRUMPETS
TRUMPING
TRUNCATE
TRUNDLED
TRUNNION
TRUSSING
TRUSTEES
TRUSTFUL
TRUSTIER
TRUSTIES
TRUSTILY
TRUSTING
TRUTHFUL
TSARINAS
TSESSEBI
TSINGHAI
TSINGTAO
T-
  SQUARE
  S
TSUSHIMA
TUBBIEST
TUBELESS
TUBERCLE
TUBEROSE
TUBEROUS
TUBIFORM
TUBULATE
TUBULOUS
TUCKERED
TUCOTUCO
TUESDAYS
TUG OF
  WAR
TUG-OF-
  WAR
TUMBLERS
TUMBLING
TUMBRELS
TUMIDITY
TUMOROUS
TUMULOSE

TUNELESS
TUNGSTEN
TUNGSTIC
TUNGUSIC
TUNICATE
TUNISIAN
TUNNELED
TUNNELER
TUPPENCE
TUPPENNY
TURBANED
TURBINES
TURBOCAR
TURBOFAN
TURBOJET
TURGIDLY
TURKOMAN
TURMERIC
TURNABLE
TURNCOAT
TURNCOCK
TURN
 DOWN
TURNINGS
TURNKEYS
TURN-
 OFFS
TURNOUTS
TURNOVER
TURNPIKE
TURNSOLE
TURRETED
TUSKLIKE
TUSSLING
TUSSOCKS
TUSSOCKY
TUTELAGE
TUTELARY
TUTORAGE
TUTORIAL
TUTORING
TV
 DINNER
TWADDLER
TWANGING
TWEAKING
TWEETERS
TWEETING
TWEEZERS
TWELFTHS
TWELVEMO

TWENTIES
TWIDDLED
TWIDDLER
TWIDDLES
TWIGGING
TWILIGHT
TWIN
 BEDS
TWINKLED
TWINKLER
TWINNING
TWIN
 SETS
TWIRLERS
TWIRLING
TWISTERS
TWISTIER
TWISTING
TWITCHED
TWITCHER
TWITCHES
TWITTERS
TWITTERY
TWITTING
TWOCCING
TWO-
 EDGED
TWOFACED
TWO
 FACED
TWOPENCE
TWO
 PENCE
TWOPENNY
TWO-
 PHASE
TWO-
 PIECE
TWO-
 SIDED
TWOSOMES
TWO-
 STEPS
TWO-
 TIMED
TWO-
 TIMER
TYMPANIC
TYMPANUM
TYNESIDE
TYPECAST

TYPE
 CAST
TYPEFACE
TYPE
 FACE
TYPE-
 HIGH
TYPHONIC
TYPHOONS
TYPIFIED
TYPIFIER
TYPOLOGY
TYRAMINE
TYROLESE
TYROSINE
TZARINAS
TZATZIKI

U

UBIQUITY
UBI
 SUPRA
UGLIFIER
UGLINESS
UIGURIAN
UKULELES
ULCERATE
ULCEROUS
ULTERIOR
ULTIMATA
ULTIMATE
ULTRAISM
ULTRAIST
UMBONATE
UMBRAGES
UMBRELLA
UMPIRING
UNABATED
UNAWARES
UNBACKED
UNBARRED
UNBEATEN
UNBELIEF
UNBIASED
UNBIDDEN
UNBODIED
UNBOLTED
UNBRIDLE
UNBROKEN
UNBUCKLE
UNBURDEN

UNBUTTON
UNCAPPED
UNCHASTE
UNCHURCH
UNCIFORM
UNCINATE
UNCLENCH
UNCLE
 SAM
UNCLE
 TOM
UNCLOTHE
UNCOINED
UNCOMMON
UNCORKED
UNCOUPLE
UNCTUOUS
UNDAMPED
UNDERACT
UNDERAGE
UNDERARM
UNDERBID
UNDERBUY
UNDERCUT
UNDERDOG
UNDERFUR
UNDERLAY
UNDERLET
UNDERLIE
UNDERLIP
UNDERPAY
UNDERPIN
UNDERSEA
UNDERSET
UNDERTOW
UNDERUSE
UNDULANT
UNDULATE
UNEARNED
UNEASIER
UNEASILY
UNENDING
UNERRING
UNEVENLY
UNFAIRER
UNFAIRLY
UNFASTEN
UNFETTER
UNFILIAL
UNFOLDED
UNFOLDER

UNFORCED
UNFORMED
UNFREEZE
UNFURLED
UNGAINLY
UNGUENTS
UNGULATE
UNHANDED
UNHEALED
UNHINGED
UNHORSED
UNIATISM
UNIAXIAL
UNICORNS
UNICYCLE
UNIFORMS
UNIFYING
UNIONISM
UNIONIST
UNIONIZE
UNIPOLAR
UNIQUELY
UNITEDLY
UNIVALVE
UNIVERSE
UNIVOCAL
UNKENNEL
UNKINDER
UNKINDLY
UNKNOWNS
UNLAWFUL
UNLIKELY
UNLIMBER
UNLISTED
UNLOADED
UNLOADER
UNLOCKED
UNLOOSED
UNLOOSEN
UNLOVELY
UNMANNED
UNMARKED
UNMASKED
UNMASKER
UNMUZZLE
UNNERVED
UNOPENED
UNPACKED
UNPACKER
UNPEOPLE
UNPICKED

UNPLACED
UNPOLLED
UNPRICED
UNPROFOR
UNPROVEN
UNREASON
UNRIDDLE
UNRIFLED
UNROLLED
UNSADDLE
UNSEATED
UNSEEDED
UNSEEING
UNSEEMLY
UNSETTLE
UNSHAPEN
UNSHAVEN
UNSOCIAL
UNSPOKEN
UNSTABLE
UNSTEADY
UNSTRING
UNSUBTLE
UNSUITED
UNSWATHE
UNTANGLE
UNTAPPED
UNTAUGHT
UNTHREAD
UNTIDILY
UNTIMELY
UNTIRING
UNTITLED
UNTOWARD
UNTRENDY
UNTRUTHS
UNUSABLE
UNVALUED
UNVEILED
UNVERSED
UNVOICED
UNWALLED
UNWASHED
UNWEIGHT
UNWIELDY
UNWINDER
UNWISHED
UNWONTED
UNWORTHY
UNZIPPED

UP-	UROSCOPY	VALVULAR	VENEERED	VESUVIAN	VINOSITY
ANCHOR	UROSTYLE	VAMBRACE	VENEERER	VESUVIUS	VINTAGER
UP-AND-	URSULINE	VAMOOSED	VENERATE	VETERANS	VINTAGES
UPS	URTICATE	VAMPIRES	VENEREAL	VEXATION	VINTNERS
UPCOMING	URUSHIOL	VAMPIRIC	VENETIAN	VEXILLUM	VIOLABLE
UPDATING	USEFULLY	VANADATE	VENGEFUL	VEXINGLY	VIOLATED
UPENDING	USHERING	VANADIUM	VENOMOUS	VIADUCTS	VIOLATOR
UPGRADED	USUFRUCT	VANADOUS	VENOSITY	VIA	VIOLENCE
UPGRADER	USURIOUS	VANGUARD	VENTOLIN	MEDIA	VIPERINE
UPGROWTH	USURPERS	VANILLIC	VENTOUSE	VIATICAL	VIPEROUS
UPHEAVAL	USURPING	VANILLIN	VENTURED	VIATICUM	VIRAGOES
UPHOLDER	UTENSILS	VANISHED	VENTURER	VIBRANCY	VIRGINAL
UPLIFTED	UTERUSES	VANISHER	VENTURES	VIBRATED	VIRGINIA
UPLIFTER	UTILIZED	VANQUISH	VENUSIAN	VIBRATOR	VIRIDIAN
UP-	UTILIZER	VAPIDITY	VERACITY	VIBRATOS	VIRIDITY
MARKET	UTTERING	VAPORIZE	VERACRUZ	VIBRIOID	VIRILISM
UPPERCUT	UVULITIS	VAPOROUS	VERANDAS	VIBRISSA	VIRILITY
UPRAISER	UXORIOUS	VAPOURER	VERBALLY	VIBRONIC	VIROLOGY
UPRISING		VARACTOR	VERBATIM	VIBURNUM	VIRTUOSI
UPROOTED	**V**	VARANASI	VERBIAGE	VICARAGE	VIRTUOSO
UPROOTER	VACANTLY	VARIABLE	VERBOTEN	VICARIAL	VIRTUOUS
UPSETTER	VACATING	VARIABLY	VERCELLI	VICELIKE	VIRULENT
UPSTAGED	VACATION	VARIANCE	VERDANCY	VICENARY	VISCACHA
UPSTAIRS	VACCINAL	VARIANTS	VERDICTS	VICEROYS	VISCERAL
UPSTARTS	VACCINES	VARICOSE	VERIFIED	VICINITY	VISCOUNT
UPSTREAM	VACCINIA	VARIETAL	VERIFIER	VICTORIA	VISIONAL
UPSTROKE	VACUOLAR	VARIFORM	VERISTIC	VICTUALS	VISITANT
UPSURGES	VACUUMED	VARIOLAR	VERITIES	VIDEOFIT	VISITING
UPSWINGS	VADODARA	VARIORUM	VERJUICE	VIDEOING	VISITORS
UPTHRUST	VAGABOND	VARISTOR	VERLIGTE	VIENNESE	VISUALLY
UP TO	VAGARIES	VARITYPE	VERMOUTH	VIETCONG	VITALISM
DATE	VAGINATE	VARMINTS	VERONESE	VIETMINH	VITALIST
UP-TO-	VAGOTOMY	VASCULAR	VERONICA	VIEWLESS	VITALITY
DATE	VAGRANCY	VASCULUM	VERRUCAE	VIGILANT	VITALIZE
UPTURNED	VAGRANTS	VASELINE	VERRUCAS	VIGNETTE	VITAMINS
URALITIC	VAINNESS	VASTERAS	VERSICLE	VIGOROSO	VITELLIN
URANITIC	VALANCED	VASTNESS	VERSIONS	VIGOROUS	VITIABLE
URANYLIC	VALANCES	VAUCLUSE	VERTEBRA	VILENESS	VITIATED
URBANELY	VALDIVIA	VAULTERS	VERTEXES	VILIFIED	VITIATOR
URBANITY	VAL-	VAULTING	VERTICAL	VILIFIER	VITI
URBANIZE	D'OISE	VAUNTING	VERTICES	VILLAGER	LEVU
URETERAL	VALENCIA	VEGETATE	VERTICIL	VILLAGES	VITILIGO
URETHANE	VALERIAN	VEHEMENT	VESICANT	VILLAINS	VITREOUS
URETHRAL	VALIANCE	VEHICLES	VESICATE	VILLAINY	VITULINE
URETHRAS	VALIDATE	VEILEDLY	VESICLES	VILLATIC	VIVACITY
URGENTLY	VALIDITY	VELARIZE	VESPERAL	VILLEINS	VIVARIUM
URGINGLY	VALLETTA	VELOCITY	VESPIARY	VINCULUM	VIVA
URINATED	VALORIZE	VENALITY	VESTIGES	VINDALOO	VOCE
URNFIELD	VALOROUS	VENATION	VESTMENT	VINEGARY	VIVIFIER
UROCHORD	VALUABLE	VENDETTA	VESTRIES	VINEYARD	VIVISECT
UROPODAL	VALUATOR	VENDIBLE	VESTURAL	VINNITSA	VIXENISH

VLADIMIR	**W**	WARFARIN	WATT-	WELL	WHICKERS
VOCALESE	WADDLING	WAR	HOUR	HEAD	WHIFFIER
VOCALISE	WAFFLING	GAMES	WAVE	WELL-	WHIGGERY
VOCALISM	WAGERING	WARHEADS	BAND	HUNG	WHIGGISH
VOCALIST	WAGGLING	WARHORSE	WAVEFORM	WELL-	WHIMBREL
VOCALITY	WAGON-	WARINESS	WAVELIKE	KNIT	WHIMPERS
VOCALIZE	LIT	WARLOCKS	WAVERERS	WELL-	WHIMSIES
VOCATION	WAGTAILS	WARLORDS	WAVERING	NIGH	WHINCHAT
VOCATIVE	WAINSCOT	WARMNESS	WAVINESS	WELL	WHINGING
VOICE	WAITRESS	WARNINGS	WAXBERRY	READ	WHINNIED
BOX	WAKASHAN	WAR	WAXINESS	WELL-	WHINNIES
VOICEFUL	WAKAYAMA	PAINT	WAXPLANT	READ	WHIPCORD
VOIDABLE	WAKELESS	WARPATHS	WAXWORKS	WELL-TO-	WHIP
VOIDANCE	WAKENING	WARPLANE	WAYBILLS	DO	HAND
VOLATILE	WALKABLE	WARRANTS	WAYFARER	WELL-	WHIPLASH
VOLCANIC	WALKAWAY	WARRANTY	WAYLAYER	WORN	WHIPLIKE
VOLCANOS	WALKMANS	WARRIGAL	WEAKENED	WELSHERS	WHIPPETS
VOLITION	WALKOUTS	WARRIORS	WEAKENER	WELSHING	WHIPPING
VOLITIVE	WALKOVER	WARSHIPS	WEAKFISH	WENCHING	WHIPWORM
VOLLEYED	WALLAROO	WARTBURG	WEAKLING	WEREWOLF	WHIRLING
VOLLEYER	WALLASEY	WARTHOGS	WEAKNESS	WESLEYAN	WHIRRING
VOLPLANE	WALLEYED	WASHABLE	WEANLING	WEST	WHISKERS
VOLTAGES	WALL-	WASHBOWL	WEAPONED	BANK	WHISKERY
VOLTAISM	LIKE	WASHDAYS	WEAPONRY	WESTERLY	WHISKIES
VOLUTION	WALLOPED	WASHED-	WEARABLE	WESTERNS	WHISKING
VOLVULUS	WALLOPER	UP	WEARIEST	WESTWARD	WHISPERS
VOMERINE	WALLOWED	WASHOUTS	WEARYING	WESTWOOD	WHISTLED
VOMITING	WALLOWER	WASHROOM	WEASELED	WET	WHISTLER
VOMITIVE	WALLSEND	WASTABLE	WEASELLY	DREAM	WHISTLES
VOMITORY	WALRUSES	WASTEFUL	WEDDINGS	WET	WHITE
VONNEGUT	WALTZING	WASTRELS	WEDGWOOD	NURSE	ANT
VOORSKOT	WANDERED	WATCHDOG	WEEDIEST	WET	WHITECAP
VORACITY	WANDERER	WATCHFUL	WEEKDAYS	SUITS	WHITE-
VORONEZH	WANDEROO	WATCHING	WEEKENDS	WETTABLE	EYE
VORTEXES	WANGANUI	WATCHMAN	WEEKLIES	WETTINGS	WHITEFLY
VORTICAL	WANGLING	WATCHMEN	WEENIEST	WEYMOUTH	WHITE-
VORTICES	WANTONLY	WATERAGE	WEIGHING	WHACKING	HOT
VOTARESS	WARANGAL	WATER	WEIGHTED	WHARFAGE	WHITE
VOTARIES	WARBLERS	BAG	WEIGHTER	WHATEVER	LIE
VOTARIST	WARBLING	WATERBED	WEIRDEST	WHATNOTS	WHITENED
VOUCHERS	WAR	WATER	WELCHING	WHATSITS	WHITENER
VOUCHING	CRIES	ICE	WELCOMED	WHEATEAR	WHITEOUT
VOUSSOIR	WAR	WATERING	WELCOMER	WHEEDLED	WHITE-
VOWELIZE	CRIME	WATERLOO	WELCOMES	WHEEDLER	TIE
VOYAGERS	WAR	WATERMAN	WELDABLE	WHEELIES	WHITINGS
VOYAGING	DANCE	WATER	WELL-	WHEELING	WHITLOWS
VULGARLY	WARDENRY	RAT	BRED	WHEEZILY	WHITTLED
VULTURES	WARDRESS	WATER	WELL	WHEEZING	WHITTLER
VULVITIS	WARDROBE	SKI	DONE	WHENEVER	WHIZ-
	WARDROOM	WATER-	WELL-	WHEREVER	BANG
	WARDSHIP	SKI	DONE	WHETTING	WHIZZING
		WATERWAY	WELLHEAD	WHEYFACE	

WHIZZ
KID
WHODUNIT
WHOMEVER
WHOOPEES
WHOOPING
WHOOSHES
WHOPPERS
WHOPPING
WHOREDOM
WICKEDLY
WIDE
BOYS
WIDE-
EYED
WIDENESS
WIDENING
WIDE
OPEN
WIDE-
OPEN
WIDGEONS
WIDOWERS
WIELDERS
WIELDING
WIGGINGS
WIGGLING
WILD
BOAR
WILD
CARD
WILDCATS
WILD-
EYED
WILDFIRE
WILDFOWL
WILDLIFE
WILDNESS
WILD
OATS
WILD
WEST
WILFULLY
WILINESS
WILLABLE
WILLIWAW
WINCHING
WINDABLE
WINDBAGS
WINDBURN
WINDFALL
WINDGALL

WINDHOEK
WINDIEST
WINDLASS
WINDMILL
WINDPIPE
WINDSAIL
WINDSOCK
WINDWARD
WINE
BARS
WINESKIN
WINGLESS
WINGLIKE
WING
NUTS
WINGOVER
WINGSPAN
WINKLING
WINNABLE
WINNINGS
WINNIPEG
WINNOWED
WINNOWER
WINTERED
WINTERER
WINTRIER
WINTRILY
WIPED
OUT
WIREDRAW
WIRELESS
WIRETAPS
WIRE
WOOL
WIREWORK
WIREWORM
WIRE-
WOVE
WIRINESS
WISEACRE
WISE
GUYS
WISENESS
WISHBONE
WISPIEST
WISTERIA
WITCHERY
WITCHING
WITHDRAW
WITHDREW
WITHERED
WITHERER

WITHHELD
WITHHOLD
WITTIEST
WIZARDRY
WOBBLIER
WOBBLING
WOEFULLY
WOLFFISH
WOLFLIKE
WOMANISH
WOMANIST
WOMANIZE
WOMBLIKE
WONDERED
WONDERER
WONDROUS
WONKIEST
WOODBINE
WOODCHAT
WOODCOCK
WOODCUTS
WOODENLY
WOODIEST
WOODLAND
WOODLARK
WOODLICE
WOODNOTE
WOODPILE
WOOD
PULP
WOODRUFF
WOODRUSH
WOODSHED
WOODSMAN
WOODSMEN
WOODWIND
WOODWORK
WOODWORM
WOOLLENS
WOOLLIER
WOOLLIES
WOOLLILY
WOOLPACK
WOOLSACK
WOOZIEST
WORDBOOK
WORD-
DEAF
WORDIEST
WORDLESS
WORDPLAY

WORKABLE
WORKADAY
WORKBAGS
WORKBOOK
WORKDAYS
WORKED
UP
WORKINGS
WORKLOAD
WORKOUTS
WORKROOM
WORKSHOP
WORKTOPS
WORLD
CUP
WORM
CAST
WORM
GEAR
WORMHOLE
WORMIEST
WORMLIKE
WORMSEED
WORMWOOD
WORRIERS
WORRYING
WORSENED
WORSE-
OFF
WORSHIPS
WORSTING
WORST-
OFF
WORTHIER
WORTHIES
WORTHILY
WORTHING
WOUNDING
WRANGLED
WRANGLER
WRANGLES
WRAPOVER
WRAPPERS
WRAPPING
WRATHFUL
WREAKING
WREATHED
WRECKAGE
WRECKERS
WRECKING
WRENCHED
WRENCHES

WRESTING
WRESTLED
WRESTLER
WRETCHED
WRETCHES
WRIGGLED
WRIGGLER
WRIGGLES
WRINGERS
WRINGING
WRINKLED
WRINKLES
WRISTLET
WRITE-
INS
WRITE
OFF
WRITE-
OFF
WRITE-
UPS
WRITHING
WRITINGS
WRONGFUL
WRONGING
WURZBURG

X

XANTHATE
XANTHEIN
XANTHENE
XANTHINE
XANTHOMA
XANTHOUS
XENOGAMY
XENOLITH
XEROSERE
XEROXING
XIANGTAN
X-RAY
TUBE
XYLIDINE
XYLOCARP
XYLOTOMY

Y

YACHTING
YAHOOISM
YAKITORI
YAMMERED
YAMMERER
YARDARMS

YARN-
DYED
YASHMAKS
YEANLING
YEARBOOK
YEARLING
YEARLONG
YEARNING
YEASTILY
YELLOWED
YEOMANLY
YEOMANRY
YIELDING
YODELING
YODELLED
YODELLER
YOKELISH
YOKOHAMA
YOKOSUKA
YOUNGEST
YOUNGISH
YOURSELF
YOUTHFUL
YTTERBIA
YUCKIEST
YUGOSLAV
YULE
LOGS
YULETIDE
YVELINES

Z

ZAANSTAD
ZAIBATSU
ZANINESS
ZANZIBAR
ZAPPIEST
ZARAGOZA
ZARATITE
ZEALOTRY
ZECCHINO
ZENITHAL
ZEOLITIC
ZEPPELIN
ZERO
HOUR
ZHEJIANG
ZHITOMIR
ZIBELINE
ZILLIONS
ZIMBABWE

ZIONISTS	ZLATOUST	ZOOGLOEA	ZOONOSIS	ZOOTOXIC	ZYGOTENE
ZIP	ZODIACAL	ZOOLATER	ZOOPHILE	ZOOTOXIN	ZYMOLOGY
CODES	ZOMBIISM	ZOOLATRY	ZOOPHYTE	ZUCCHINI	
ZIPPIEST	ZONATION	ZOOMETRY	ZOOSPERM	ZUGZWANG	
ZIRCONIA	ZONETIME	ZOOM	ZOOSPORE	ZULULAND	
ZIRCONIC	ZOOCHORE	LENS	ZOOTOMIC	ZWIEBACK	

A
AARONS ROD
ABACTINAL
ABANDONED
ABASEMENT
ABASHEDLY
ABATEMENT
ABATTOIRS
ABCOULOMB
ABDICABLE
ABDICATED
ABDICATOR
ABDOMINAL
ABDUCTING
ABDUCTION
ABERRANCE
ABHORRENT
ABHORRING
ABIDINGLY
ABILITIES
A BIT
  THICK
ABJECTION
ABLUTIONS
ABNEGATOR
ABOLISHED
ABOLISHER
ABOLITION
ABOMINATE
ABORIGINE
ABORTIONS
ABOUNDING
ABOUT TURN
ABOUT-TURN
ABRASIONS
ABRASIVES
ABRIDGING
ABROGATED
ABROGATOR
ABSCESSES
ABSCONDED
ABSCONDER
ABSEILING
ABSENTEES
ABSENTING
ABSOLVING
ABSORBENT
ABSORBING
ABSTAINED
ABSTAINER
ABSTINENT

ABSTRACTS
ABSURDISM
ABSURDITY
ABUNDANCE
ABU SIMBEL
ABUSIVELY
ABUTMENTS
ABYSSINIA
ACADEMICS
ACANTHINE
ACANTHOID
ACANTHOUS
ACARIASIS
ACAROLOGY
ACCEDENCE
ACCENTING
ACCENTUAL
ACCEPTANT
ACCEPTING
ACCESSING
ACCESSION
ACCESSORY
ACCIDENCE
ACCIDENTS
ACCIPITER
ACCLAIMED
ACCLIVITY
ACCOLADES
ACCOMPANY
ACCORDANT
ACCORDING
ACCORDION
ACCOSTING
ACCOUNTED
ACCRETION
ACCRETIVE
ACCRUMENT
ACCUMBENT
ACELLULAR
ACESCENCE
ACETAMIDE
ACETIFIER
ACETYLATE
ACETYLENE
ACETYLIDE
ACHEULIAN
ACHIEVING
ACICULATE
ACID HOUSE
ACIDIFIED
ACIDIFIER

ACIDOPHIL
ACID TESTS
ACIDULATE
ACIDULOUS
ACINIFORM
ACOUSTICS
ACQUIESCE
ACQUIRING
ACQUITTAL
ACQUITTED
ACQUITTER
ACROBATIC
ACRODROME
ACROGENIC
ACRONYMIC
ACROPETAL
ACROPOLIS
ACROSPIRE
ACROSTICS
ACTINOPOD
ACTIVATED
ACTIVATOR
ACTIVISTS
ACTRESSES
ACTS OF
  GOD
ACTUALITY
ACTUALIZE
ACTUARIAL
ACTUARIES
ACTUATING
ACTUATION
ACUMINATE
ACUMINOUS
ACUTENESS
ACYCLOVIR
ADAMANTLY
ADAPTABLE
ADDICTION
ADDICTIVE
ADDITIONS
ADDITIVES
ADDRESSED
ADDRESSEE
ADDRESSER
ADDRESSES
ADDUCTION
ADEMPTION
ADENOIDAL
ADENOSINE
ADHERENCE

ADHERENTS
ADHESIONS
ADHESIVES
ADIABATIC
AD INTERIM
ADIPOCERE
ADJACENCY
ADJECTIVE
ADJOINING
ADJOURNED
ADJUDGING
ADJUSTING
ADJUTANCY
ADJUTANTS
AD-LIBBING
ADMEASURE
ADMINICLE
ADMIRABLE
ADMIRABLY
ADMIRALTY
ADMISSION
ADMISSIVE
ADMITTING
ADMIXTURE
AD NAUSEAM
ADNOMINAL
ADOPTIONS
ADORATION
ADORNMENT
ADRENALIN
ADSORBATE
ADSORBENT
ADULATION
ADULATORY
ADULTERER
ADUMBRATE
AD VALOREM
ADVANCING
ADVANTAGE
ADVECTION
ADVENTIVE
ADVENTURE
ADVERBIAL
ADVERSARY
ADVERSELY
ADVERSITY
ADVERTING
ADVERTISE
ADVISABLE
ADVISEDLY
ADVOCATED

ADVOCATES
AEOLIPILE
AEPYORNIS
AEROBATIC
AERODROME
AEROLOGIC
AEROMETER
AEROMETRY
AEROPAUSE
AEROPHONE
AEROPLANE
AEROSPACE
AESTHESIA
AESTHETES
AESTHETIC
AESTIVATE
AETHEREAL
AETIOLOGY
AFFECTING
AFFECTION
AFFECTIVE
AFFIANCED
AFFIDAVIT
AFFILIATE
AFFIRMING
AFFIXTURE
AFFLICTED
AFFLUENCE
AFFORDING
AFFRICATE
AFFRONTED
AFLATOXIN
AFORESAID
A FORTIORI
AFRIKAANS
AFRIKANER
AFRO-ASIAN
AFTERBODY
AFTERCARE
AFTERDAMP
AFTERDECK
AFTERGLOW
AFTERHEAT
AFTERLIFE
AFTERMATH
AFTERNOON
AFTERWORD
AGE GROUPS
AGGRAVATE
AGGREGATE
AGGRESSOR

AGGRIEVED	ALGEBRAIC	ALLOWEDLY	AMENDABLE	ANALEPTIC
AGITATING	ALGECIRAS	ALLUSIONS	AMENDMENT	ANALGESIA
AGITATION	ALGOMETER	ALLUVIUMS	AMENITIES	ANALGESIC
AGITATORS	ALGOMETRY	ALMA MATER	AMERASIAN	ANALOGIES
AGNOLOTTI	ALGONQUIN	ALMANDINE	AMERICANA	ANALOGIST
AGNOMINAL	ALGORITHM	ALMSHOUSE	AMERICANS	ANALOGIZE
AGNOSTICS	ALICE BAND	ALMS-HOUSE	AMERICIUM	ANALOGOUS
AGONISTIC	ALICYCLIC	ALONGSIDE	AMERINDIC	ANALOGUES
AGONIZING	ALIENABLE	ALOOFNESS	AMETHYSTS	ANALYSAND
AGREEABLE	ALIENATED	ALPENGLOW	AMETROPIA	ANALYSING
AGREEABLY	ALIENATOR	ALPHABETS	AMIANTHUS	ANALYTICS
AGREEMENT	ALIGHTING	ALSATIANS	AMIDSHIPS	ANAMNESIS
AGRIGENTO	ALIGNMENT	ALTERABLE	AMINO ACID	ANANDROUS
AGRONOMIC	ALIPHATIC	ALTERCATE	AMMOCOETE	ANANTHOUS
AGTERSKOT	ALKALOSIS	ALTER EGOS	AMMONIATE	ANAPAESTS
AHMEDABAD	ALLA BREVE	ALTERNATE	AMMONICAL	ANAPESTIC
AILANTHUS	ALLAHABAD	ALTIMETER	AMMONITIC	ANAPHORAL
AIMLESSLY	ALLANTOIC	ALTIMETRY	AMNESIACS	ANAPLASIA
AIRBRAKES	ALLANTOID	ALTIPLANO	AMNESTIES	ANAPLASTY
AIRFIELDS	ALLANTOIS	ALTISSIMO	AMOEBAEAN	ANAPTYXIS
AIRFORCES	ALL-AROUND	ALTITUDES	AMORALITY	ANARCHISM
AIR GUITAR	ALL AT	ALTRICIAL	AMOROUSLY	ANARCHIST
AIR-INTAKE	ONCE	ALTRUISTS	AMORPHISM	ANARTHRIA
AIRLETTER	ALLEGEDLY	ALUMINATE	AMORPHOUS	ANATHEMAS
AIRLIFTED	ALLELUIAS	ALUMINIUM	AMORTIZED	ANATOLIAN
AIRLINERS	ALL ENDS	ALUMINIZE	AMOUNTING	ANATOMIES
AIRPLANES	UP	ALUMINOUS	AMPERSAND	ANATOMIST
AIRPOCKET	ALLENTOWN	ALVEOLARS	AMPHIBIAN	ANATOMIZE
AIRSTREAM	ALLERGIES	ALVEOLATE	AMPHIBOLE	ANCESTORS
AIRSTRIPS	ALLERGIST	AMAGASAKI	AMPHIGORY	ANCESTRAL
AIRWORTHY	ALLETHRIN	AMARYLLIS	AMPHIOXUS	ANCHORAGE
AITCHBONE	ALLEVIATE	AMAUROSIS	AMPLIFIED	ANCHORESS
ALABAMIAN	ALLEYWAYS	AMAUROTIC	AMPLIFIER	ANCHORING
ALABASTER	ALLIANCES	AMAZEMENT	AMPLITUDE	ANCHORITE
ALARM BELL	ALLIGATOR	AMAZINGLY	AMPUTATED	ANCHOVIES
ALARMISTS	ALLOCATED	AMAZONIAN	AMSTERDAM	ANCILLARY
ALBATROSS	ALLOGRAFT	AMAZONITE	AMUSEMENT	ANCIPITAL
ALBERTITE	ALLOGRAPH	AMBERGRIS	AMUSINGLY	ANDALUSIA
ALBESCENT	ALLOMETRY	AMBERJACK	AMYGDALIN	ANDANTINO
ALCHEMIST	ALLOMORPH	AMBIENCES	AMYLOPSIN	ANDRADITE
ALCHEMIZE	ALLOPATHY	AMBIGUITY	ANABANTID	ANDROLOGY
ALCOHOLIC	ALLOPHANE	AMBIGUOUS	ANABIOSIS	ANDROMEDA
ALDEBARAN	ALLOPHONE	AMBITIONS	ANABOLISM	ANECDOTAL
ALDEBURGH	ALLOPLASM	AMBITIOUS	ANABOLITE	ANECDOTES
ALDERSHOT	ALLOTMENT	AMBLESIDE	ANACLINAL	ANECDOTIC
ALEHOUSES	ALLOTROPE	AMBLYOPIA	ANACLISIS	ANEMOLOGY
ALEMANNIC	ALLOTROPY	AMBLYOPIC	ANACLITIC	ANEUPLOID
ALEPH-NULL	ALLOTTING	AMBROSIAL	ANACONDAS	ANGEL CAKE
ALERTNESS	ALLOWABLE	AMBROTYPE	ANACRUSIS	ANGELFISH
ALFILARIA	ALLOWABLY	AMBULANCE	ANAEROBIC	ANGELICAL
ALGARROBA	ALLOWANCE	AMBUSHING	ANALECTIC	ANGIOGRAM

ANGIOLOGY	ANSWERING	APERITIFS	APPOINTER	ARCTOGAEA
ANGLE IRON	ANTALKALI	APERTURES	APPOINTOR	ARCTURIAN
ANGLESITE	ANTARCTIC	APETALOUS	APPORTION	ARCUATION
ANGLEWORM	ANTEATERS	APHERESIS	APPRAISAL	ARDUOUSLY
ANGLICANS	ANTECHOIR	APHIDIOUS	APPRAISED	AREA CODES
ANGLICISM	ANTEDATED	APHORISMS	APPRAISER	ARGENTINA
ANGLICIZE	ANTEFIXAL	APHYLLOUS	APPREHEND	ARGENTINE
ANGOSTURA	ANTELOPES	APICULATE	APPRESSED	ARGENTITE
ANGUISHED	ANTENATAL	APISHNESS	APPRISING	ARGENTOUS
ANHYDRIDE	ANTENNULE	APIVOROUS	APPROBATE	ARGILLITE
ANHYDRITE	ANTEROOMS	APLANATIC	APPROVING	ARGUMENTS
ANHYDROUS	ANTHELION	APOCOPATE	APPULSIVE	ARMADILLO
ANIMALISM	ANTHEMION	APOCRYPHA	APRIL FOOL	ARMAMENTS
ANIMALIST	ANTHODIUM	APODICTIC	APRIORITY	ARMATURES
ANIMALITY	ANTHOLOGY	APOENZYME	APTITUDES	ARMCHAIRS
ANIMALIZE	ANTHOTAXY	APOGAMOUS	AQUALUNGS	ARMISTICE
ANIMATEUR	ANTHOZOAN	APOLOGIAS	AQUAPLANE	ARMOURERS
ANIMATING	ANTHURIUM	APOLOGIES	AQUARELLE	ARMOURIES
ANIMATION	ANTICHLOR	APOLOGIST	AQUARIUMS	ARMS RACES
ANIMATISM	ANTICLINE	APOLOGIZE	AQUATINTS	AROMATIZE
ANIMISTIC	ANTIDOTES	APOPHASIS	AQUEDUCTS	ARPEGGIOS
ANIMOSITY	ANTIGENIC	APOPHYSIS	AQUILEGIA	ARRAIGNED
ANISOGAMY	ANTIKNOCK	APOPTOSIS	AQUITAINE	ARRAIGNER
ANKLEBONE	ANTIMERIC	APOSTATES	ARABESQUE	ARRANGING
ANKLE BONE	ANTIMONIC	APOSTOLIC	ARABINOSE	ARRESTING
ANKYLOSIS	ANTIMONYL	APPALLING	ARACHNOID	ARRIVISTE
ANNALISTS	ANTINODAL	APPALOOSA	ARAGONESE	ARROGANCE
ANNAPOLIS	ANTINOMIC	APPARATUS	ARAGONITE	ARROGATED
ANNAPURNA	ANTIPATHY	APPARITOR	ARAUCANIA	ARROGATOR
ANNEALING	ANTIPHONY	APPEALING	ARAUCARIA	ARROWHEAD
ANNELIDAN	ANTIPODAL	APPEARING	ARBITRAGE	ARROWROOT
ANNOTATED	ANTIPODES	APPEASING	ARBITRARY	ARROWWOOD
ANNOTATOR	ANTIQUARY	APPELLANT	ARBITRATE	ARROWWORM
ANNOUNCED	ANTIQUATE	APPELLATE	ARBITRESS	ARSENICAL
ANNOUNCER	ANTIQUITY	APPENDAGE	ARBOREOUS	ARSENIOUS
ANNOYANCE	ANTISERUM	APPENDANT	ARBORETUM	ARSONISTS
ANNUITANT	ANTITOXIC	APPENDING	ARBOVIRUS	ARTEFACTS
ANNUITIES	ANTITOXIN	APPENZELL	ARCHAISMS	ARTEMISIA
ANNULLING	ANTIVENIN	APPERTAIN	ARCHAIZER	ARTERIOLE
ANNULMENT	ANTIVIRAL	APPETENCE	ARCHANGEL	ARTERITIS
ANOESTRUS	ANTIWORLD	APPETITES	ARCHDUCAL	ARTHRITIC
ANOINTING	ANTONIONI	APPETIZER	ARCHDUCHY	ARTHRITIS
ANOMALIES	ANXIETIES	APPLAUDED	ARCHDUKES	ARTHROPOD
ANOMALOUS	ANXIOUSLY	APPLAUDER	ARCHENEMY	ARTICHOKE
ANONYMITY	ANY AMOUNT	APPLE CART	ARCHETYPE	ARTICLING
ANONYMOUS	APARTHEID	APPLEJACK	ARCHFIEND	ARTICULAR
ANOPHELES	APARTMENT	APPLE PIES	ARCHICARP	ARTIFACTS
ANORTHITE	APATHETIC	APPLIANCE	ARCHITECT	ARTIFICER
ANOSMATIC	APELDOORN	APPLICANT	ARCHIVIST	ARTIFICES
ANOXAEMIA	APENNINES	APPOINTED	ARCHIVOLT	ARTILLERY
ANOXAEMIC	APERIODIC	APPOINTEE	ARCOGRAPH	ARTLESSLY

ARYTENOID	ASSUREDLY	ATTENDING	AUTOGRAPH	BACILLARY
ASCENDANT	ASSURGENT	ATTENTION	AUTOICOUS	BACKACHES
ASCENDING	ASTERISKS	ATTENTIVE	AUTOLYSIN	BACKBENCH
ASCENSION	ASTEROIDS	ATTENUANT	AUTOLYSIS	BACKBITER
ASCERTAIN	ASTHMATIC	ATTENUATE	AUTOLYTIC	BACKBOARD
ASCOSPORE	ASTOUNDED	ATTESTANT	AUTOMATED	BACKBONES
ASCRIBING	ASTRADDLE	ATTESTING	AUTOMATIC	BACKCLOTH
ASEPALOUS	ASTRAKHAN	AT THE	AUTOMATON	BACKCROSS
ASEXUALLY	ASTROCYTE	TIME	AUTONOMIC	BACKDATED
ASHAMEDLY	ASTRODOME	ATTITUDES	AUTOPHYTE	BACK DOORS
ASHKENAZI	ASTROLABE	ATTORNEYS	AUTOPSIES	BACKDROPS
ASHKHABAD	ASTROLOGY	ATTRACTED	AUTOSOMAL	BACKFIRED
ASININITY	ASTRONAUT	ATTRACTOR	AUTOTIMER	BACKHANDS
ASPARAGUS	ASTRONOMY	ATTRIBUTE	AUTOTOMIC	BACKPACKS
ASPERSION	ASYLLABIC	ATTRITION	AUTOTOXIC	BACKPEDAL
ASPERSIVE	ASYMMETRY	ATTRITIVE	AUTOTOXIN	BACK PEDAL
ASPHALTED	ASYMPTOTE	AUBERGINE	AUTOTYPIC	BACK SEATS
ASPHALTIC	ASYNDETIC	AUBRIETIA	AUXILIARY	BACK SHIFT
ASPHALTUM	ASYNDETON	AU COURANT	AVAILABLE	BACKSIDES
ASPHYXIAL	AT A	AUCTIONED	AVAILABLY	BACKSIGHT
ASPIRANTS	GLANCE	AUCTORIAL	AVALANCHE	BACKSLIDE
ASPIRATED	ATARACTIC	AUDACIOUS	AVERAGING	BACKSPACE
ASPIRATES	ATAVISTIC	AUDIENCES	AVERSIONS	BACKSTAGE
ASPIRATOR	ATHEISTIC	AUDIO BOOK	AVERTIBLE	BACKSWEPT
ASSAILANT	ATHENAEUM	AUDIOLOGY	AVIFAUNAL	BACKTRACK
ASSAILING	ATHLETICS	AUDIPHONE	AVIRULENT	BACKWARDS
ASSASSINS	ATLANTEAN	AUDITIONS	AVOCATION	BACKWATER
ASSAULTED	ATMOLYSIS	AUGMENTED	AVOIDABLE	BACKWOODS
ASSAULTER	ATMOMETER	AUGMENTOR	AVOIDANCE	BACKYARDS
ASSAYABLE	ATMOMETRY	AU NATUREL	AVUNCULAR	BACTERIAL
ASSEMBLED	ATOM BOMBS	AUNT SALLY	AWAKENING	BACTERIUM
ASSEMBLER	ATOMICITY	AURICULAR	AWARDABLE	BACTEROID
ASSENTING	ATOMISTIC	AUSCHWITZ	AWARENESS	BADGERING
ASSERTING	ATOMIZERS	AUSTENITE	AWESTRUCK	BADMINTON
ASSERTION	ATONALISM	AUSTERELY	AWFULNESS	BAGATELLE
ASSERTIVE	ATONALITY	AUSTERITY	AWKWARDLY	BAGGINESS
ASSESSING	ATONEMENT	AUSTRALIA	AXIOMATIC	BAG LADIES
ASSESSORS	AT ONE	AUTARCHIC	AYAHUASCA	BAHUVRIHI
ASSIDUITY	TIME	AUTARKIES	AYATOLLAH	BAILIWICK
ASSIDUOUS	ATONICITY	AUTHENTIC	AYUTTHAYA	BAIN-MARIE
ASSIGNING	AT PRESENT	AUTHORESS	AZEDARACH	BAKHTARAN
ASSISTANT	ATROCIOUS	AUTHORIAL	AZEOTROPE	BALACLAVA
ASSISTING	ATROPHIED	AUTHORITY	AZIMUTHAL	BALAKLAVA
ASSOCIATE	ATTACHING	AUTHORIZE		BALALAIKA
ASSONANCE	ATTACKERS	AUTOCLAVE	**B**	BALANCING
ASSORTING	ATTACKING	AUTOCRACY		BALCONIES
ASSUAGING	ATTAINDER	AUTOCRATS	BAAGANDJI	BALEFULLY
ASSUASIVE	ATTAINING	AUTOCROSS	BABY TEETH	BALKANIZE
ASSUMABLE	ATTEMPTED	AUTOECISM	BABY TOOTH	BALLASTED
ASSURABLE	ATTEMPTER	AUTOFOCUS	BACCHANAL	BALLCOCKS
ASSURANCE	ATTENDANT	AUTOGRAFT	BACCIFORM	BALLERINA
			BACHELORS	

BALL GAMES	BARCELONA	BATTENING	BEERSHEBA	BERYLLIUM
BALLISTIC	BAR CHARTS	BATTERIES	BEESTINGS	BESEECHED
BALLOONED	BARE BONES	BATTERING	BEETLE OFF	BESETTING
BALLOTING	BAREFACED	BATTINESS	BEETROOTS	BESIEGING
BALLOTINI	BARE FACED	BATTLEAXE	BEFALLING	BESMEARED
BALLPOINT	BARGAINED	BATTLE CRY	BEFITTING	BESPATTER
BALLROOMS	BARGAINER	BAWDINESS	BEGETTING	BESTIALLY
BALLYMENA	BARGE POLE	BAYONETED	BEGGARING	BESTIRRED
BALMINESS	BAR GRAPHS	BAY WINDOW	BEGINNERS	BESTOWING
BALTHAZAR	BARITONES	BEACH BALL	BEGINNING	BESTREWED
BALTIMORE	BAR KOCHBA	BEACHHEAD	BEGRUDGED	BETE NOIRE
BAMBOOZLE	BARNACLES	BEACHSIDE	BEGUILING	BETE-NOIRE
BANBRIDGE	BARN DANCE	BEACHWEAR	BEHAVIOUR	BETHLEHEM
BANDAGING	BARNSTORM	BEADINESS	BEHEADING	BETHOUGHT
BANDANNAS	BARNYARDS	BEAN FEAST	BEHOLDERS	BETOKENED
BANDEROLE	BAROGRAPH	BEARBERRY	BEHOLDING	BETRAYALS
BANDICOOT	BAROMETER	BEARDLESS	BELATEDLY	BETRAYERS
BANDOLEER	BARONETCY	BEARISHLY	BELEAGUER	BETRAYING
BANDOLIER	BAROSCOPE	BEARNAISE	BELEMNITE	BETROTHAL
BANDSTAND	BARRACKED	BEAR'S-	BELGRAVIA	BETROTHED
BANDWAGON	BARRACUDA	FOOT	BELIEVERS	BETTERING
BANDWIDTH	BARRETTES	BEARSKINS	BELIEVING	BETTER-OFF
BANEBERRY	BARRICADE	BEASTLIER	BELITTLED	BEVELLING
BANEFULLY	BARRISTER	BEATIFIED	BELITTLER	BEVERAGES
BANGALORE	BARROW BOY	BEATITUDE	BELLATRIX	BEWAILING
BANISHING	BARTENDER	BEAUMARIS	BELLICOSE	BEWITCHED
BANISTERS	BARTERING	BEAU MONDE	BELLOWING	BHAGALPUR
BANJA LUKA	BASEBALLS	BEAUTEOUS	BELLYACHE	BHARATIYA
BANKBOOKS	BASEBOARD	BEAUTIFUL	BELLY FLOP	BHAVNAGAR
BANK DRAFT	BASELINES	BEAUX-ARTS	BELONGING	BHUTANESE
BANK NOTES	BASEMENTS	BEAVERING	BELVEDERE	BIALYSTOK
BANKROLLS	BASE METAL	BEBEERINE	BEMOANING	BIBLIOTIC
BANKRUPTS	BASE RATES	BEBINGTON	BENCHMARK	BICIPITAL
BANNISTER	BASHFULLY	BECCAFICO	BENCH MARK	BICKERING
BANQUETED	BASICALLY	BECKONING	BENEFICES	BICONCAVE
BANQUETTE	BASIFIXED	BECQUEREL	BENEFITED	BICYCLING
BANTERING	BASILICAN	BEDAUBING	BENEVENTO	BICYCLIST
BANTUSTAN	BASILICAS	BEDECKING	BENGALESE	BIDENTATE
BAPTISMAL	BASILISKS	BEDEVILED	BENGALINE	BIELEFELD
BAPTIZING	BASIPETAL	BEDFELLOW	BENIGHTED	BIFARIOUS
BARBADIAN	BAS RELIEF	BEDRAGGLE	BENIGNANT	BIFOLIATE
BARBARIAN	BAS-RELIEF	BEDRIDDEN	BENIGNITY	BIFURCATE
BARBARISM	BASS CLEFS	BED-SITTER	BENIN CITY	BIGAMISTS
BARBARITY	BASSINETS	BEDSPREAD	BENTONITE	BIGARREAU
BARBARIZE	BASTINADO	BEDSTEADS	BENZIDINE	BIG DIPPER
BARBAROUS	BATH CHAIR	BEEFEATER	BERBERINE	BIGENERIC
BARBECUED	BATHOLITH	BEEFINESS	BEREAVING	BIG-TIMERS
BARBECUES	BATHROBES	BEEFSTEAK	BEREZNIKI	BIGUANIDE
BARBICANS	BATHROOMS	BEEKEEPER	BERIOSOVA	BIG WHEELS
BARBITONE	BATHWATER	BEELZEBUB	BERKELIUM	BIJECTION
BARCAROLE	BATTALION	BEERINESS	BERKSHIRE	BIJECTIVE

BILABIALS	BITTERNUT	BLENNIOID	BLUE BLOOD	BOMBPROOF
BILABIATE	BITTINESS	BLESSEDLY	BLUE BOOKS	BOMBSHELL
BILATERAL	BIVALENCY	BLESSINGS	BLUE CHIPS	BOMBSIGHT
BILHARZIA	BIZARRELY	BLETHERED	BLUE FILMS	BOMBSITES
BILINGUAL	BLABBERED	BLIGHTERS	BLUEGRASS	BONA FIDES
BILIRUBIN	BLACKBALL	BLIGHTING	BLUE JEANS	BONEBLACK
BILLBOARD	BLACK BELT	BLIND DATE	BLUE PETER	BONE CHINA
BILLETING	BLACKBIRD	BLINDFISH	BLUEPRINT	BONEHEADS
BILLFOLDS	BLACKBUCK	BLINDFOLD	BLUESTONE	BONINGTON
BILLHOOKS	BLACKBURN	BLINDNESS	BLUFFNESS	BON VIVANT
BILLIARDS	BLACKCOCK	BLIND SPOT	BLUNDERED	BOOBY TRAP
BILLIONTH	BLACKDAMP	BLINKERED	BLUNDERER	BOOHOOING
BILLOWING	BLACKENED	BLISTERED	BLUNTNESS	BOOKCASES
BILLY GOAT	BLACK EYES	BLIZZARDS	BLURREDLY	BOOK CLUBS
BILOCULAR	BLACKFACE	BLOCKADED	BLUSTERED	BOOKMAKER
BIMONTHLY	BLACKFISH	BLOCKADER	BLUSTERER	BOOKMARKS
BIN-LINERS	BLACKHEAD	BLOCKADES	BOARDROOM	BOOKPLATE
BINOCULAR	BLACK HOLE	BLOCKAGES	BOARDWALK	BOOKSHELF
BINOMIALS	BLACK ISLE	BLOCKHEAD	BOARHOUND	BOOKSHOPS
BINTURONG	BLACKJACK	BLOCK VOTE	BOAT HOOKS	BOOKSTALL
BINUCLEAR	BLACK LEAD	BLONDNESS	BOATHOUSE	BOOKSTAND
BIOGRAPHY	BLACKLEGS	BLOOD BANK	BOATSWAIN	BOOK TOKEN
BIOHAZARD	BLACKLIST	BLOODBATH	BOAT TRAIN	BOOKWORMS
BIOLOGIST	BLACKMAIL	BLOOD FEUD	BOBBEJAAN	BOOMERANG
BIOMETRIC	BLACK MASS	BLOOD HEAT	BOBBY PINS	BOOMSLANG
BIONOMICS	BLACKNESS	BLOODLESS	BOBSLEIGH	BOONDOCKS
BIONOMIST	BLACKOUTS	BLOOD LUST	BOBTAILED	BOORISHLY
BIOSPHERE	BLACKPOLL	BLOODROOT	BOCCACCIO	BOOTBLACK
BIOSTATIC	BLACKPOOL	BLOODSHED	BODACIOUS	BOOTHROYD
BIOSTROME	BLACK SPOT	BLOODSHOT	BODY BLOWS	BOOTLACES
BIPARTITE	BLACKTAIL	BLOOD TYPE	BODYCHECK	BOOTMAKER
BIPINNATE	BLAMELESS	BLOODWORM	BODYGUARD	BOOTSTRAP
BIRDHOUSE	BLANCHING	BLOSSOMED	BOGGINESS	BOOZINESS
BIRD HOUSE	BLANDNESS	BLOTCHIER	BOHEMIANS	BORDELLOS
BIRD'S-	BLANKETED	BLOTCHILY	BOILINGLY	BORDERING
FOOT	BLANKNESS	BLOW-DRIED	BOLDFACED	BOREHOLES
BIRTHDAYS	BLASPHEME	BLOW-DRIES	BOLECTION	BORN-AGAIN
BIRTHMARK	BLASPHEMY	BLOWFLIES	BOLEGNESE	BORROWERS
BIRTHRATE	BLASTEMIC	BLOWHARDS	BOLIVIANO	BORROWING
BIRTHROOT	BLASTULAR	BLOWHOLES	BOLLINGER	BOSSA NOVA
BIRTHWORT	BLATANTLY	BLOWLAMPS	BOLLYWOOD	BOSSINESS
BISECTING	BLATHERED	BLOWPIPES	BOLOMETER	BOTANICAL
BISECTION	BLAZONING	BLOWTORCH	BOLSHEVIK	BOTANISTS
BISECTRIX	BLEACHERS	BLOWZIEST	BOLSHIEST	BOTANIZED
BISERRATE	BLEACHING	BLUBBERED	BOLSTERED	BOTCHIEST
BISEXUALS	BLEAKNESS	BLUDGEONS	BOLSTERER	BOTHERING
BISHOPRIC	BLEARIEST	BLUEBEARD	BOLTHOLES	BOTTLE-FED
BISMUTHAL	BLEMISHED	BLUEBELLS	BOMBARDED	BOTULINUS
BISMUTHIC	BLEMISHER	BLUEBERRY	BOMBARDON	BOUILLONS
BISULCATE	BLEMISHES	BLUEBIRDS	BOMBASTIC	BOULEVARD
BITCHIEST	BLENCHING	BLUE-BLACK	BOMBAZINE	BOUNCIEST

BOUNDLESS
BOUNTEOUS
BOUNTIFUL
BOURGEOIS
BOUTIQUES
BOWERBIRD
BOW LEGGED
BOW-LEGGED
BOWSPRITS
BOWSTRING
BOW WINDOW
BOX AND
  COX
BOXING DAY
BOX NUMBER
BOX OFFICE
BOYCOTTED
BOYFRIEND
BOYLES LAW
BOYLE'S
  LAW
BOY SCOUTS
BRACELETS
BRACHIATE
BRACINGLY
BRACKETED
BRACKNELL
BRACTEATE
BRACTEOLE
BRAGGARTS
BRAINIEST
BRAINLESS
BRAINSICK
BRAINWASH
BRAINWAVE
BRAIN WAVE
BRAINWAVE
BRAKE SHOE
BRAKESMAN
BRAMBLING
BRANCHIAL
BRANCHING
BRANDLING
BRAND NAME
BRANTFORD
BRASHNESS
BRASS BAND
BRASSERIE
BRASS HATS
BRASSIERE
BRASSIEST

BRAVENESS
BRAWNIEST
BRAZENING
BRAZILEIN
BRAZILIAN
BREACHING
BREAD BINS
BREADLINE
BREADROOT
BREAKABLE
BREAKAGES
BREAKAWAY
BREAKBEAT
BREAKDOWN
BREAKEVEN
BREAKFAST
BREAKNECK
BREATHILY
BREATHING
BREECHING
BRENTWOOD
BRIARROOT
BRIC A
  BRAC
BRIC-A-
  BRAC
BRICKWORK
BRICKYARD
BRICOLAGE
BRIEFCASE
BRIGADIER
BRIGHOUSE
BRILLIANT
BRIMSTONE
BRININESS
BRIOLETTE
BRIQUETTE
BRISKNESS
BRISTLING
BRITANNIA
BRITANNIC
BRITICISM
BRITISHER
BRITTONIC
BROACHING
BROADBAND
BROAD BEAN
BROADBILL
BROADCAST
BROADENED
BROAD JUMP

BROADLEAF
BROADLOOM
BROADNESS
BROADSIDE
BROADTAIL
BROCADING
BROCHETTE
BROCHURES
BROKERAGE
BROMELIAD
BROMEOSIN
BROMINATE
BROMOFORM
BRONCHIAL
BRONZE AGE
BROODIEST
BROOKABLE
BROOKLIME
BROOKWEED
BROOMCORN
BROOMRAPE
BROSCOPIC
BROTHERLY
BROUGHAMS
BROWN RICE
BRUNETTES
BRUNSWICK
BRUSH-OFFS
BRUSHWOOD
BRUSHWORK
BRUSQUELY
BRUTALITY
BRUTALIZE
BRUTISHLY
BRYLCREEM
BRYOPHYTE
BRYTHONIC
BUBBLE GUM
BUBBLIEST
BUCCANEER
BUCHAREST
BUCKBOARD
BUCKETING
BUCKHOUND
BUCKTEETH
BUCKTHORN
BUCKTOOTH
BUCKWHEAT
BUCKYBALL
BUCKYTUBE
BUDDH GAYA

BUDDHISTS
BUDGETARY
BUDGETING
BUFFALOES
BUFFERING
BUFFETING
BUGGER ALL
BUGGERING
BUGLE CALL
BUGLEWEED
BUHRSTONE
BUILDINGS
BUJUMBURA
BULGARIAN
BULGINESS
BULGINGLY
BULKHEADS
BULKINESS
BULLDOZED
BULLDOZER
BULLETINS
BULLFIGHT
BULLFINCH
BULLFROGS
BULLHORNS
BULLISHLY
BULLRINGS
BULL'S-
  EYES
BULLY BEEF
BULLYBOYS
BULLY-OFFS
BULRUSHES
BUMBLEBEE
BUMIPUTRA
BUMPINESS
BUMPTIOUS
BUNDABERG
BUNDESRAT
BUNDESTAG
BUNGALOWS
BUNGHOLES
BUNKHOUSE
BUOYANTLY
BUPRESTID
BURDENING
BURGEONED
BURGESSES
BURLESQUE
BURLINESS
BURMA ROAD

BURNINGLY
BURNISHED
BURNISHER
BURNOUSES
BURROUGHS
BURROWING
BURSARIAL
BURSARIES
BURSIFORM
BURTHENED
BUSHELLER
BUSHINESS
BUSHWHACK
BUTADIENE
BUTCHERED
BUTENANDT
BUTESHIRE
BUTHELEZI
BUTTERBUR
BUTTERCUP
BUTTERFAT
BUTTERFLY
BUTTERINE
BUTTERING
BUTTERNUT
BUTTONING
BUXOMNESS
BUZZWORDS
BYDGOSZCZ
BYPASSING
BY-PRODUCT
BYSTANDER
BY THE
  BOOK
BYZANTINE
BYZANTIUM

C

CABALLERO
CABIN BOYS
CABINETRY
CABLE CARS
CABLEGRAM
CABLE-LAID
CABOODLES
CABRIOLET
CACHECTIC
CACODEMON
CACOETHES
CACOETHIC
CACOPHONY

CACUMINAL	CANAANITE	CAPSULATE	CAROLLING	CASTILIAN
CAECILIAN	CANAL BOAT	CAPTAINCY	CAROTIDAL	CASTOR OIL
CAESAREAN	CANALIZED	CAPTAINED	CAROUSALS	CASTRATED
CAFETERIA	CANAVERAL	CAPTIVATE	CAROUSELS	CASTRATOR
CAIRNGORM	CANCELING	CAPTIVITY	CAROUSING	CASUARINA
CAITHNESS	CANCELLED	CAPTURING	CARPACCIO	CASUISTIC
CALABOOSE	CANCELLER	CARAPACES	CARPENTER	CASUISTRY
CALAMANCO	CANCEROUS	CARBAMATE	CARPENTRY	CATABASIS
CALCANEAL	CANDIDACY	CARBANION	CARPETBAG	CATABATIC
CALCANEUS	CANDIDATE	CARBAZOLE	CARPETING	CATABOLIC
CALCICOLE	CANDLEMAS	CARBINEER	CARPOLOGY	CATACLYSM
CALCIFIED	CANDLENUT	CARBOLIZE	CARRAGEEN	CATACOMBS
CALCIFUGE	CANDYTUFT	CARBONADO	CARREFOUR	CATALEPSY
CALCIMINE	CANESCENT	CARBONATE	CARRIAGES	CATALOGUE
CALCULATE	CANICULAR	CARBONIZE	CARRYALLS	CATALONIA
CALCULOUS	CANISTERS	CARBONOUS	CARRYCOTS	CATALYSER
CALENDARS	CANKEROUS	CARBON TAX	CARRY-OVER	CATALYSIS
CALENDERS	CANNELURE	CARBUNCLE	CARTAGENA	CATALYSTS
CALENDULA	CANNERIES	CARBURIZE	CARTESIAN	CATALYTIC
CALENTURE	CANNIBALS	CARCASSES	CARTHORSE	CATAMARAN
CALIBRATE	CANNINESS	CARCINOMA	CARTILAGE	CATAMENIA
CALIPHATE	CANNONADE	CARDBOARD	CARTOGRAM	CATAMOUNT
CALL A	CANNONING	CARDIGANS	CARTOUCHE	CAT-AND-
HALT	CANNULATE	CARDINALS	CARTRIDGE	DOG
CALL BOXES	CANOEISTS	CARD INDEX	CART TRACK	CATAPHYLL
CALL GIRLS	CANONICAL	CARDPHONE	CARTULARY	CATAPLASM
CALLOSITY	CANONIZED	CARD PUNCH	CARTWHEEL	CATAPLEXY
CALLOUSLY	CANOODLED	CARDPUNCH	CARYATIDS	CATAPULTS
CALMATIVE	CAN OPENER	CARDSHARP	CARYOPSIS	CATARACTS
CALORIFIC	CANTABILE	CARD SHARP	CASANOVAS	CATARRHAL
CALUMNIES	CANTALOUP	CARD TABLE	CASCADING	CATATONIA
CALVARIES	CANTERING	CAREENING	CASEATION	CATATONIC
CALVINISM	CANTICLES	CAREERING	CASEBOUND	CATCALLED
CALVINIST	CANTONESE	CAREERISM	CASE STUDY	CATCH CROP
CALVITIES	CANVASSED	CAREERIST	CASH CARDS	CATCHIEST
CAMBISTRY	CANVASSER	CAREFULLY	CASH CROPS	CATCHMENT
CAMBRIDGE	CANVASSES	CARESSING	CASH DESKS	CATCHWORD
CAMELHAIR	CAPACIOUS	CARETAKER	CASHIERED	CATECHISM
CAMELLIAS	CAPACITOR	CARIBBEAN	CASSAREEP	CATECHIST
CAMEMBERT	CAPARISON	CARIBBEES	CASSATION	CATECHIZE
CAMERAMAN	CAPE VERDE	CARILLONS	CASSEROLE	CATERWAUL
CAMERAMEN	CAPILLARY	CARINTHIA	CASSETTES	CATHARSES
CAMERA SHY	CAP IN	CARIOSITY	CASSIMERE	CATHARSIS
CAMISOLES	HAND	CARMELITE	CASSINGLE	CATHARTIC
CAMPAIGNS	CAPITULAR	CARNALIST	CASSOCKED	CATHEDRAL
CAMPANILE	CAPITULUM	CARNALITY	CASSOULET	CATHEPSIN
CAMPANULA	CAPRICCIO	CARNATION	CASSOWARY	CATHETERS
CAMPFIRES	CAPRICORN	CARNELIAN	CAST ABOUT	CATHOLICS
CAMPHORIC	CAPSAICIN	CARNIVALS	CASTANETS	CATOPTRIC
CAMPSITES	CAPSICUMS	CARNIVORE	CASTAWAYS	CATTERIES
CAMSHAFTS	CAPSIZING	CARNOTITE	CASTIGATE	CATTINESS

CATTLEMAN	CENTRISTS	CHAPERONS	CHEMPADUK	CHLORIDIC
CAUCASOID	CENTURIAL	CHAPLAINS	CHEMURGIC	CHLORITIC
CAUDATION	CENTURIES	CHAPLETED	CHENGCHOW	CHLOROSIS
CAUGHT OUT	CENTURION	CHARABANC	CHEONGSAM	CHLOROTIC
CAULDRONS	CERACEOUS	CHARACTER	CHEQUERED	CHOCK-FULL
CAUSALGIA	CERATODUS	CHARBROIL	CHERBOURG	CHOCOLATE
CAUSALITY	CERCARIAL	CHARCOALS	CHERISHED	CHOCOLATY
CAUSATION	CEREBROID	CHARINESS	CHERISHER	CHOIRBOYS
CAUSATIVE	CEREBRUMS	CHARITIES	CHERNOZEM	CHOKEABLE
CAUSEWAYS	CERECLOTH	CHARIVARI	CHERRY PIE	CHOLEROID
CAUTERANT	CERTAINLY	CHARLATAN	CHESTIEST	CHOMSKIAN
CAUTERIZE	CERTAINTY	CHARLOTTE	CHESTNUTS	CHONDRIFY
CAUTIONED	CERTIFIED	CHARMEUSE	CHEVALIER	CHONDRITE
CAVALCADE	CERTITUDE	CHARTABLE	CHEVRETTE	CHONDROMA
CAVALIERS	CERUSSITE	CHARTERED	CHICALOTE	CHONDRULE
CAVENDISH	CESAREANS	CHARWOMAN	CHICANERY	CHONGQING
CAVERNOUS	CESSATION	CHARWOMEN	CHICKADEE	CHOOSIEST
CAVILLERS	CETACEANS	CHASTENED	CHICKPEAS	CHOPHOUSE
CAVILLING	CHABAZITE	CHASTENER	CHICKWEED	CHOPLOGIC
CAVORTING	CHA-CHA-	CHASTISED	CHIEFTAIN	CHOPPIEST
CEASEFIRE	CHA	CHASUBLES	CHIHUAHUA	CHOPSTICK
CEASE-FIRE	CHAETOPOD	CHATELAIN	CHILBLAIN	CHORIONIC
CEASELESS	CHAFFINCH	CHATOYANT	CHILDHOOD	CHORISTER
CELANDINE	CHAGRINED	CHAT SHOWS	CHILDLESS	CHOROLOGY
CELEBRANT	CHAIN GANG	CHATTERED	CHILDLIKE	CHORTLING
CELEBRATE	CHAIN MAIL	CHATTERER	CHILIADAL	CHORUSING
CELEBRITY	CHAIN SAWS	CHATTIEST	CHILLIEST	CHOWKIDAR
CELESTIAL	CHAIRLIFT	CHAUFFEUR	CHINATOWN	CHRISTIAN
CELESTITE	CHAIR LIFT	CHEAPENED	CHINAWARE	CHRISTMAS
CELIBATES	CHALCOGEN	CHEAP-JACK	CHINKIANG	CHROMATIC
CELLARAGE	CHALKIEST	CHEAPNESS	CHINSTRAP	CHROMATID
CELLARMAN	CHALLENGE	CHECHENIA	CHINTZIER	CHROMATIN
CELLOIDIN	CHAMELEON	CHECKABLE	CHIPBOARD	CHROMOGEN
CELLULASE	CHAMFERER	CHECKERED	CHIPMUNKS	CHRONAXIE
CELLULOID	CHAMOMILE	CHECKLIST	CHIPOLATA	CHRONICLE
CELLULOSE	CHAMPAGNE	CHECKMATE	CHIPPINGS	CHRYSALID
CELTICIST	CHAMPAIGN	CHECKOUTS	CHIROPODY	CHRYSALIS
CEMENTING	CHAMPERTY	CHECKROOM	CHIROPTER	CHTHONIAN
CEMENTITE	CHAMPIONS	CHEEKBONE	CHIRPIEST	CHUBBIEST
CENOTAPHS	CHAMPLEVE	CHEEKIEST	CHIRRUPER	CHUCKLING
CENSORIAL	CHANCIEST	CHEERIEST	CHISELING	CHUMMIEST
CENSORING	CHANCROID	CHEERLESS	CHISELLED	CHUNGKING
CENSURING	CHANCROUS	CHELASHIP	CHISELLER	CHUNKIEST
CENTAURUS	CHANDELLE	CHELATION	CHISIMAIO	CHURCHMAN
CENTENARY	CHANDLERS	CHELICERA	CHITINOID	CHURRASCO
CENTERING	CHANDLERY	CHELIFORM	CHITINOUS	CICATRICE
CENTESIMO	CHANGCHOW	CHELONIAN	CHIVALRIC	CICATRIZE
CENTIGRAM	CHANGCHUN	CHEMICALS	CHLORACNE	CICERONES
CENTIPEDE	CHANNELED	CHEMISORB	CHLORDANE	CIGARETTE
CENTRALLY	CHANTEUSE	CHEMISTRY	CHLORELLA	CIGARILLO
CENTRIOLE	CHANTILLY	CHEMOSTAT	CHLORIDES	CILIATION

CILIOLATE
CIMMERIAN
CINCTURES
CINEMATIC
CINEPHILE
CINERARIA
CINEREOUS
CINGULATE
CIPHERING
CIRALPINE
CIRCADIAN
CIRCASSIA
CIRCINATE
CIRCUITAL
CIRCUITRY
CIRCULARS
CIRCULATE
CIRRHOSED
CIRRHOSIS
CIRRHOTIC
CIRRIPEDE
CITATIONS
CITIZENRY
CITY HALLS
CITY-STATE
CIVICALLY
CIVILIANS
CIVILIZED
CIVILIZER
CIVIL LIST
CIVIL WARS
CLADOGRAM
CLAIMABLE
CLAIMANTS
CLAMBAKES
CLAMBERED
CLAMMIEST
CLAMOROUS
CLAMOURED
CLAMPDOWN
CLAMP DOWN
CLAPBOARD
CLARENDON
CLARIFIED
CLARIFIER
CLARINETS
CLASSICAL
CLASSIEST
CLASSLESS
CLASSMATE
CLASSROOM

CLATHRATE
CLATTERED
CLAVICLES
CLAVICORN
CLAYMORES
CLAYSTONE
CLAYTONIA
CLEANABLE
CLEANNESS
CLEANSERS
CLEANSING
CLEARANCE
CLEAR-EYED
CLEARINGS
CLEARNESS
CLEARWAYS
CLEARWING
CLEAVAGES
CLEMENTLY
CLENCHING
CLERGYMAN
CLERGYMEN
CLERIHEWS
CLERKSHIP
CLEVELAND
CLIENTELE
CLIMACTIC
CLIMAXING
CLIMB DOWN
CLIMB-DOWN
CLINCHERS
CLINCHING
CLINGFILM
CLINGFISH
CLINICIAN
CLINOSTAT
CLINQUANT
CLINTONIA
CLIPBOARD
CLIP JOINT
CLIPPINGS
CLITELLUM
CLOAKROOM
CLOBBERED
CLOCKWISE
CLOCKWORK
CLOG DANCE
CLOISONNE
CLOISTERS
CLOISTRAL
CLONICITY

CLOSE CALL
CLOSEDOWN
CLOSE KNIT
CLOSE-KNIT
CLOSENESS
CLOSETING
CLOTHIERS
CLOUDBANK
CLOUDIEST
CLOUDLESS
CLOUD NINE
CLOYINGLY
CLUBBABLE
CLUBHOUSE
CLUMSIEST
CLUSTERED
CLUTCH BAG
CLUTCHING
CLUTTERED
CLYDEBANK
CNIDARIAN
COACHWORK
COADJUTOR
COADUNATE
COAGULANT
COAGULASE
COAGULATE
COALESCED
COALFACES
COALFIELD
COALHOLES
COALHOUSE
COALITION
COALMINES
COARCTATE
COARSENED
COASTLINE
COAT TAILS
COAXINGLY
COBALTITE
COBALTOUS
COCA-COLAS
COCAINISM
COCAINIZE
COCCOLITH
COCCYGEAL
COCHINEAL
COCHLEATE
COCK A
  HOOP

COCK-A-
  HOOP
COCKATIEL
COCKATOOS
COCKED HAT
COCKERELS
COCKFIGHT
COCKHORSE
COCKINESS
COCKLEBUR
COCKNEYFY
COCKROACH
COCKSCOMB
COCKSFOOT
COCKTAILS
COCOONING
CODIFYING
CODPIECES
COELOSTAT
COENOBITE
COENOCYTE
COENOSARC
COEQUALLY
COERCIBLE
COEVALITY
COEXISTED
COFFEE BAR
COFFEEPOT
COFFERDAM
COGITATED
COGITATOR
COGNATION
COGNITION
COGNITIVE
COGNIZANT
COGNOMENS
COGWHEELS
COHABITED
COHERENCE
COIFFEURS
COIFFURED
COIFFURES
COINCIDED
COINTREAU
COKULORIS
COLANDERS
COLCHICUM
COLCOTHAR
COLD CREAM
COLD-DRAWN
COLD FRAME

COLD FRONT
COLD SNAPS
COLD SORES
COLD STEEL
COLD SWEAT
COLECTOMY
COLERAINE
COLICROOT
COLICWEED
COLLAGIST
COLLAPSAR
COLLAPSED
COLLAPSES
COLLARING
COLLATING
COLLATION
COLLATIVE
COLLEAGUE
COLLECTED
COLLECTOR
COLLEGIAL
COLLEGIAN
COLLEGIUM
COLLIDING
COLLIGATE
COLLIMATE
COLLINEAR
COLLINSIA
COLLISION
COLLOCATE
COLLODION
COLLOIDAL
COLLOTYPE
COLLUDING
COLLUSION
COLLUSIVE
COLLUVIAL
COLLUVIUM
COLLYRIUM
COLOCYNTH
COLOMBIAN
COLONELCY
COLONIALS
COLONISTS
COLONIZED
COLONIZER
COLONNADE
COLORIFIC
COLOR LINE
COLOSTOMY
COLOSTRAL

COLOSTRUM	COMMODORE	CONCEALED	CONFLUENT	CONSONANT
COLOUR BAR	COMMONAGE	CONCEDING	CONFORMAL	CONSORTED
COLOUREDS	COMMONERS	CONCEITED	CONFORMED	CONSORTER
COLOURFUL	COMMON LAW	CONCEIVED	CONFORMER	CONSORTIA
COLOURING	COMMON-LAW	CONCENTRE	CONFRERES	CONSPIRED
COLOURIST	COMMOTION	CONCEPTUS	CONFUCIAN	CONSTABLE
COLOURWAY	COMMUNING	CONCERNED	CONFUSING	CONSTANCE
COLTISHLY	COMMUNION	CONCERTED	CONFUSION	CONSTANCY
COLTSFOOT	COMMUNISM	CONCERTOS	CONFUTING	CONSTANTA
COLUBRINE	COMMUNIST	CONCIERGE	CONGEALED	CONSTANTS
COLUMBIAN	COMMUNITY	CONCILIAR	CONGENIAL	CONSTRAIN
COLUMBINE	COMMUNIZE	CONCISELY	CONGER EEL	CONSTRICT
COLUMBITE	COMMUTATE	CONCISION	CONGERIES	CONSTRUCT
COLUMBIUM	COMMUTERS	CONCLAVES	CONGESTED	CONSTRUED
COLUMELLA	COMMUTING	CONCLUDED	CONGOLESE	CONSTRUER
COLUMNIST	COMPACTED	CONCOCTED	CONGRUENT	CONSULATE
COLWYN BAY	COMPACTER	CONCOCTER	CONGRUITY	CONSULTED
COMATULID	COMPACTLY	CONCORDAT	CONGRUOUS	CONSULTEE
COMBATANT	COMPANDER	CONCOURSE	CONHOIDAL	CONSULTER
COMBATING	COMPANIES	CONCRETED	CONICALLY	CONSUMERS
COMBATIVE	COMPANION	CONCUBINE	CONJOINED	CONSUMING
COMBATTED	COMPARING	CONCURRED	CONJOINER	CONTACTED
COMBINING	COMPASSES	CONCUSSED	CONJUGANT	CONTACTOR
COMBUSTOR	COMPELLED	CONDEMNED	CONJUGATE	CONTAGION
COME ABOUT	COMPELLER	CONDEMNER	CONJURERS	CONTAGIUM
COMEBACKS	COMPENDIA	CONDENSED	CONJURING	CONTAINED
COMEDIANS	COMPERING	CONDENSER	CONNECTED	CONTAINER
COMEDOWNS	COMPETENT	CONDIGNLY	CONNECTOR	CONTEMNER
COMELIEST	COMPETING	CONDIMENT	CONNEMARA	CONTENDED
COME OFF	COMPILERS	CONDITION	CONNIVENT	CONTENDER
IT	COMPILING	CONDOLING	CONNIVING	CONTENTED
COMFORTED	COMPLAINT	CONDONING	CONNOTING	CONTESTED
COMFORTER	COMPLETED	CONDUCING	CONNUBIAL	CONTESTER
COMICALLY	COMPLETER	CONDUCIVE	CONQUERED	CONTINENT
COMMANDED	COMPLEXES	CONDUCTED	CONQUEROR	CONTINUAL
COMMANDER	COMPLIANT	CONDUCTOR	CONQUESTS	CONTINUED
COMMANDOS	COMPLYING	CONDYLOID	CONSCIOUS	CONTINUER
COMMENCED	COMPONENT	CONDYLOMA	CONSCRIPT	CONTINUOS
COMMENDAM	COMPORTED	CONFERRED	CONSÉNSUS	CONTINUUM
COMMENDED	COMPOSERS	CONFERRER	CONSENTED	CONTORTED
COMMENSAL	COMPOSING	CONFERVAL	CONSENTER	CONTOURED
COMMENTED	COMPOSITE	CONFESSED	CONSERVED	CONTRACTS
COMMENTER	COMPOSTED	CONFESSOR	CONSERVER	CONTRAILS
COMMINGLE	COMPOSURE	CONFIDANT	CONSERVES	CONTRALTO
COMMINUTE	COMPOUNDS	CONFIDENT	CONSIGNED	CONTRASTS
COMMISSAR	COMPRISAL	CONFIDING	CONSIGNEE	CONTRASTY
COMMITTAL	COMPRISED	CONFINING	CONSIGNOR	CONTRIVED
COMMITTED	COMPUTERS	CONFIRMED	CONSISTED	CONTUMACY
COMMITTEE	COMPUTING	CONFITURE	CONSOCIES	CONTUMELY
COMMITTER	COMRADELY	CONFLATED	CONSOLING	CONTUSING
COMMODITY	CONCAVITY	CONFLICTS	CONSOLUTE	CONTUSION

CONTUSIVE	CORNELIAN	COTANGENT	CRACKLING	CREVASSES
CONUNDRUM	CORNERING	COT DEATHS	CRACKPOTS	CREWELIST
CONVECTOR	CORNETIST	COTE	CRACKSMAN	CREW NECKS
CONVENERS	CORNFIELD	D'AZUR	CRACKSMEN	CRIBELLUM
CONVENING	CORNFLOUR	COTENANCY	CRAFTIEST	CRICKETER
CONVERGED	CORNSTALK	COTILLION	CRAFTSMAN	CRIME WAVE
CONVERSED	COROLLARY	COTTAGERS	CRAFTSMEN	CRIMINALS
CONVERSER	CORPORALE	COTTONADE	CRAFTWORK	CRIMPLENE
CONVERTED	CORPORALS	COTTON GIN	CRAGGIEST	CRIMSONED
CONVERTER	CORPORATE	COTYLEDON	CRAIGAVON	CRINKLIER
CONVEXITY	CORPOREAL	COUCHETTE	CRANBERRY	CRINKLING
CONVEYERS	CORPOSANT	COUNSELED	CRANKCASE	CRINOLINE
CONVEYING	CORPULENT	COUNTABLE	CRANKIEST	CRIPPLING
CONVICTED	CORPUSCLE	COUNTDOWN	CRAPPIEST	CRISPIEST
CONVINCED	CORRALLED	COUNTERED	CRAPULOUS	CRISPNESS
CONVINCER	CORRASION	COUNTLESS	CRASH-DIVE	CRITERION
CONVIVIAL	CORRASIVE	COUNT NOUN	CRASH-LAND	CRITICISM
CONVOKING	CORRECTED	COUNTRIES	CRASH TEAM	CRITICIZE
CONVOLUTE	CORRECTLY	COUP	CRASSNESS	CRITIQUES
CONVOYING	CORRECTOR	D'ETAT	CRATEROUS	CROCHETED
CONVULSED	CORRELATE	COUPLINGS	CRAYONING	CROCHETER
COOKHOUSE	CORRIDORS	COURGETTE	CRAYONIST	CROCODILE
COOKSTOWN	CORRODANT	COURT CARD	CRAZINESS	CROISSANT
COOPERAGE	CORRODING	COURTELLE	CREAKIEST	CROMLECHS
COOPERATE	CORROSION	COURTEOUS	CREAMCUPS	CROOKEDLY
COORDINAL	CORROSIVE	COURTESAN	CREAMIEST	CROP-EARED
COPARTNER	CORRUGATE	COURTIERS	CREATIONS	CROQUETTE
COPESTONE	CORRUPTED	COURTLIER	CREATURAL	CROSSBARS
COPIOUSLY	CORRUPTER	COURTROOM	CREATURES	CROSSBEAM
COPOLYMER	CORRUPTLY	COURTSHIP	CREDENDUM	CROSSBILL
COPROLITE	CORSELETS	COURT SHOE	CREDITING	CROSSBOWS
COPULATED	CORTICATE	COURTYARD	CREDITORS	CROSSBRED
COPYBOOKS	CORTISONE	COUTURIER	CREDULITY	CROSS-EYED
COPYRIGHT	CORUSCATE	COVALENCY	CREDULOUS	CROSSFIRE
COQUETTES	CORVETTES	COVENANTS	CREEPIEST	CROSSHEAD
CORALLINE	CORYDALIS	COVERALLS	CREMATING	CROSSINGS
CORALLOID	CORYMBOSE	COVERINGS	CREMATION	CROSS-LINK
CORALROOT	COSEISMAL	COVERLESS	CREMATORY	CROSSNESS
CORBICULA	COSMETICS	COVERLETS	CRENATION	CROSSOVER
COR BLIMEY	COSMIC RAY	COVER NOTE	CRENULATE	CROSS TALK
CORDIALLY	COSMOGONY	COVERTURE	CREOLIZED	CROSSTREE
CORDIFORM	COSMOLOGY	COWABUNGA	CREOPHAGY	CROSSWALK
CORDONING	COSMONAUT	COWARDICE	CREOSOTED	CROSSWIND
COREOPSIS	COSMOTRON	CO-WORKERS	CREOSOTIC	CROSSWISE
CORIANDER	COSSETTED	COXCOMBRY	CREPITANT	CROSSWORD
CORKBOARD	COSTA RICA	COYOTILLO	CREPITATE	CROSSWORT
CORKSCREW	CO-STARRED	CRAB APPLE	CRESCENDO	CROTCHETS
CORMORANT	COSTLIEST	CRABBEDLY	CRESCENTS	CROTCHETY
CORN BREAD	COSTOTOMY	CRABBIEST	CRETINISM	CROUCHING
CORNBREAD	COST PRICE	CRABSTICK	CRETINOID	CROUPIERS
CORNCRAKE	COSTUMIER	CRACKDOWN	CRETINOUS	CROWBERRY

CROWN LAND
CROWNWORK
CROW'S
  FEET
CROW'S
  FOOT
CROW'S
  NEST
CRUCIALLY
CRUCIBLES
CRUCIFIED
CRUCIFIER
CRUCIFORM
CRUDITIES
CRUELTIES
CRUMBLIER
CRUMBLING
CRUMMIEST
CRUMPLING
CRUNCHIER
CRUNCHILY
CRUNCHING
CRUSADERS
CRUSADING
CRUSTIEST
CRYBABIES
CRYOMETER
CRYOMETRY
CRYOPHYTE
CRYOSCOPE
CRYOSCOPY
CRYPTOGAM
CTENIDIUM
CUBBYHOLE
CUBBY HOLE
CUBE ROOTS
CUBISISTS
CUB SCOUTS
CUCKOLDED
CUCULLATE
CUCUMBERS
CUDDLIEST
CUDGELING
CUDGELLED
CUDGELLER
CUFF LINKS
CUIRASSES
CUL-DE-
  SACS
CULLENDER
CULMINANT
CULMINATE

CULTIVATE
CULTURIST
CUMBERING
CUMBRANCE
CUNEIFORM
CUNNINGLY
CUPBEARER
CUPBOARDS
CUP FINALS
CUPOLATED
CURATIVES
CURDINESS
CURETTAGE
CURIOSITY
CURIOUSLY
CURLICUES
CURLINESS
CURLPAPER
CURRENTLY
CURRICULA
CURRYCOMB
CURSIVELY
CURSORIAL
CURSORILY
CURTAILED
CURTAINED
CURTILAGE
CURTSYING
CURVATURE
CUSHINESS
CUSHIONED
CUSPIDATE
CUSPIDORS
CUSTODIAL
CUSTODIAN
CUSTOMARY
CUSTOMERS
CUSTOMIZE
CUT A
  CAPER
CUT AND
  RUN
CUTANEOUS
CUTICULAR
CUTLASSES
CUTPURSES
CUTTHROAT
CUT-THROAT
CUTTINGLY
CYANAMIDE
CYANOTYPE

CYBERCAFE
CYBERNATE
CYBERPUNK
CYBERPUNT
CYCLAMATE
CYCLOIDAL
CYCLONITE
CYCLOPSES
CYCLORAMA
CYCLOTRON
CYLINDERS
CYMBALIST
CYMOGRAPH
CYMOPHANE
CYNICALLY
CYNOSURES
CYPHERING
CYPRESSES
CYPRINOID
CYRENAICA
CYSTEINIC
CYSTOCARP
CYSTOCELE
CYSTOLITH
CYSTOTOMY
CYTOLYSIN
CYTOLYSIS
CYTOPLASM
CYTOPLAST

D

DACHSHUND
DACTYLICS
DADAISTIC
DAFFODILS
DAILY HELP
DAINTIEST
DAIQUIRIS
DAIRY FARM
DAIRYMAID
DALAI LAMA
DALLIANCE
DALMATIAN
DALTONISM
DAMASCENE
DAMNATION
DAMNATORY
DAMNEDEST
DAMPENING
DAMP SQUIB
DAMSELFLY

DANDELION
DANDIFIED
DANGEROUS
DAREDEVIL
DARKENING
DARK HORSE
DARKROOMS
DARMSTADT
DARTBOARD
DARTMOUTH
DASHBOARD
DASHINGLY
DASTARDLY
DATABASES
DATA BUSES
DATEDNESS
DATELINES
DATE STAMP
DAUGHTERS
DAUNTLESS
DAVENPORT
DAYDREAMS
DAYDREAMY
DAYFLOWER
DAYLIGHTS
DAY SCHOOL
DEACONESS
DEADBEATS
DEAD DUCKS
DEADENING
DEAD HEART
DEAD HEATS
DEADLIEST
DEADLIGHT
DEADLINES
DEADLOCKS
DEADLY SIN
DEAD MARCH
DEAFBLIND
DEAFENING
DEAF-MUTES
DEALATION
DEAMINATE
DEANERIES
DEATHBEDS
DEATHBLOW
DEATH DUTY
DEATHLESS
DEATHLIKE
DEATH MASK
DEATH RATE

DEATH TOLL
DEATH TRAP
DEATH WISH
DEAUVILLE
DEBARKING
DEBARMENT
DEBARRING
DEBATABLE
DEBAUCHED
DEBAUCHEE
DEBAUCHER
DEBAUCHES
DEBENTURE
DEBOUCHED
DEBRIEFED
DEBUGGING
DEBUNKERS
DEBUNKING
DEBUTANTE
DECADENCE
DECAGONAL
DECALCIFY
DECALOGUE
DECAMPING
DECANTERS
DECANTING
DECAPODAL
DECASTYLE
DECATHLON
DECEITFUL
DECEIVERS
DECEIVING
DECEMBERS
DECENCIES
DECENNIAL
DECEPTION
DECEPTIVE
DECIDABLE
DECIDEDLY
DECIDUOUS
DECILLION
DECIMALLY
DECIMATED
DECIMATOR
DECIMETRE
DECISIONS
DECK CARGO
DECKCHAIR
DECKHANDS
DECKHOUSE
DECLAIMED

DECLAIMER	DEFENDING	DEMEANOUR	DEPORTING	DESPERATE
DECLARANT	DEFENSIVE	DEMIJOHNS	DEPOSABLE	DESPISING
DECLARING	DEFERENCE	DEMIMONDE	DEPOSITED	DESPOILED
DECLINATE	DEFERMENT	DEMISABLE	DEPOSITOR	DESPOILER
DECLINING	DEFERRING	DEMISTING	DEPRAVING	DESPOTISM
DECLIVITY	DEFIANTLY	DEMITASSE	DEPRAVITY	DESPUMATE
DECOCTION	DEFICIENT	DEMOBBING	DEPRECATE	DESTINIES
DECOLLATE	DEFINABLE	DEMOCRACY	DEPRESSED	DESTITUTE
DECOLLETE	DEFINIENS	DEMOCRATS	DEPRESSOR	DESTROYED
DECOMPOSE	DEFLATING	DEMOTIONS	DEPRIVING	DESTROYER
DECONTROL	DEFLATION	DEMULCENT	DEPURATOR	DESUETUDE
DECORATED	DEFLECTED	DEMULSIFY	DEPUTIZED	DESULTORY
DECORATOR	DEFLECTOR	DEMURRAGE	DERAILING	DETACHING
DECOUPAGE	DEFOLIANT	DEMURRING	DERELICTS	DETAILING
DECREASED	DEFOLIATE	DEMYSTIFY	DE RIGUEUR	DETAINEES
DECREASES	DEFORMING	DENDRITIC	DERISIBLE	DETAINING
DECREEING	DEFORMITY	DENIGRATE	DERIVABLE	DETECTING
DECREMENT	DEFRAUDED	DENITRATE	DERMATOID	DETECTION
DECRETIVE	DEFRAUDER	DENITRIFY	DERMATOME	DETECTIVE
DECRETORY	DEFRAYING	DENOTABLE	DEROGATED	DETECTORS
DECUMBENT	DEFROCKED	DENOUNCED	DERRING DO	DETENTION
DECURRENT	DEFROSTED	DENOUNCER	DERRING-DO	DETERGENT
DECUSSATE	DEFROSTER	DENSENESS	DERRINGER	DETERMENT
DEDICATED	DEGRADING	DENSITIES	DERVISHES	DETERMINE
DEDICATEE	DEGREE-DAY	DENTALIUM	DESCALING	DETERRENT
DEDICATOR	DEHISCENT	DENTATION	DESCANTER	DETERRING
DEDUCIBLE	DEHYDRATE	DENTIFORM	DESCENDED	DETERSIVE
DEDUCTING	DEJECTION	DENTISTRY	DESCENDER	DETESTING
DEDUCTION	DELEGABLE	DENTITION	DESCRIBED	DETHRONED
DEDUCTIVE	DELEGATED	DENTURIST	DESCRIBER	DETHRONER
DEED POLLS	DELEGATES	DEODORANT	DESCRYING	DETONATED
DEEDS POLL	DELETIONS	DEODORIZE	DESECRATE	DETONATOR
DEEPENING	DELICIOUS	DEOXIDIZE	DESERTERS	DETRACTED
DEEP FRIED	DELIGHTED	DEPARDIEU	DESERTING	DETRACTOR
DEEP SOUTH	DELIGHTER	DEPARTING	DESERTION	DETRAINED
DEERGRASS	DELIMITED	DEPARTURE	DESERVING	DETRIMENT
DEERHOUND	DELINEATE	DEPASTURE	DESICCANT	DETRITION
DEFALCATE	DELIRIANT	DEPENDANT	DESICCATE	DETRUSION
DEFAULTED	DELIRIOUS	DEPENDENT	DESIGNATE	DEUTERIDE
DEFAULTER	DELIRIUMS	DEPENDING	DESIGNERS	DEUTERIUM
DEFEATING	DELIVERED	DEPICTING	DESIGNING	DEVALUATE
DEFEATISM	DELIVERER	DEPICTION	DESINENCE	DEVALUING
DEFEATIST	DELOUSING	DEPICTIVE	DESIRABLE	DEVASTATE
DEFECATED	DELUSIONS	DEPICTURE	DESIRABLY	DEVELOPED
DEFECATOR	DEMAGOGIC	DEPILATOR	DESISTING	DEVELOPER
DEFECTING	DEMAGOGUE	DEPLETING	DESMIDIAN	DEVIATING
DEFECTION	DEMANDANT	DEPLETION	DES MOINES	DEVIATION
DEFECTIVE	DEMANDING	DEPLETIVE	DESOLATED	DEVIATORY
DEFECTORS	DEMANTOID	DEPLORING	DESOLATER	DEVILFISH
DEFENDANT	DEMARCATE	DEPLOYING	DESPAIRED	DEVILLING
DEFENDERS	DEMEANING	DEPORTEES	DESPERADO	DEVILMENT

DEVIOUSLY	DIATRIBES	DILATABLE	DISAVOWAL	DISH TOWEL
DEVISABLE	DIATROPIC	DILATANCY	DISAVOWED	DISHWATER
DEVITRIFY	DIAZONIUM	DILIGENCE	DISAVOWER	DISINFECT
DEVOLVING	DIAZOTIZE	DILUTIONS	DISBANDED	DISINFEST
DEVOTEDLY	DIBROMIDE	DIMENSION	DISBARRED	DISK DRIVE
DEVOTIONS	DICHASIAL	DIMIDIATE	DISBELIEF	DISKETTES
DEVOURING	DICHASIUM	DIMISSORY	DISBRANCH	DISLIKING
DEVOUTEST	DICHOGAMY	DIM-WITTED	DISBURDEN	DISLOCATE
DEXEDRINE	DICHOTOMY	DINGDONGS	DISBURSED	DISLODGED
DEXTERITY	DICHROISM	DINGINESS	DISBURSER	DISMANTLE
DEXTEROUS	DICHROITE	DINING CAR	DISCALCED	DISMASTED
DEXTRORSE	DICHROMIC	DINOCERAS	DISCARDED	DISMAYING
DIABETICS	DICKERING	DINOSAURS	DISCARDER	DISMEMBER
DIABLERIE	DICKYBIRD	DINOTHERE	DISCERNED	DISMISSAL
DIABOLISM	DICLINISM	DIOECIOUS	DISCERNER	DISMISSED
DIABOLIST	DICLINOUS	DIOESTRUS	DISCHARGE	DISOBEYED
DIABOLIZE	DICROTISM	DIPHTHONG	DISCIPLES	DISOBEYER
DIACONATE	DICTATING	DIPLOIDIC	DISCLIMAX	DISOBLIGE
DIACRITIC	DICTATION	DIPLOMACY	DISCLOSED	DISORDERS
DIACTINIC	DICTATORS	DIPLOMATE	DISCLOSER	DISOWNING
DIAERESES	DIDACTICS	DIPLOMATS	DISCOIDAL	DISPARAGE
DIAERESIS	DIETETICS	DIPLOTENE	DISCOLOUR	DISPARATE
DIAGNOSED	DIETICIAN	DIPSTICKS	DISCOMFIT	DISPARITY
DIAGNOSES	DIETITIAN	DIPSWITCH	DISCOMMON	DISPELLED
DIAGNOSIS	DIFFERENT	DIPTEROUS	DISCOUNTS	DISPELLER
DIAGONALS	DIFFERING	DIRECTING	DISCOURSE	DISPENSED
DIALECTAL	DIFFICULT	DIRECTION	DISCOVERT	DISPENSER
DIALECTIC	DIFFIDENT	DIRECTIVE	DISCOVERY	DISPERSAL
DIALOGISM	DIFFUSELY	DIRECTORS	DISCREDIT	DISPERSED
DIALOGIST	DIFFUSING	DIRECTORY	DISCUSSED	DISPERSER
DIALOGIZE	DIFFUSION	DIRECTRIX	DISDAINED	DISPLACED
DIALOGUER	DIFFUSIVE	DIRECT TAX	DISEMBARK	DISPLACER
DIALOGUES	DIGASTRIC	DIREFULLY	DISEMBODY	DISPLAYED
DIAMAGNET	DIGENESIS	DIRIGIBLE	DISENABLE	DISPLAYER
DIAMETERS	DIGENETIC	DIRT BIKES	DISENGAGE	DISPLEASE
DIAMETRAL	DIGESTANT	DIRT CHEAP	DISENTAIL	DISPORTED
DIAMETRIC	DIGESTING	DIRTINESS	DISESTEEM	DISPOSING
DIANDROUS	DIGESTION	DIRT ROADS	DISFAVOUR	DISPRAISE
DIANOETIC	DIGESTIVE	DIRT TRACK	DISFIGURE	DISPROVAL
DIAPHONIC	DIGITALIN	DIRTY WORK	DISFOREST	DISPROVED
DIAPHRAGM	DIGITALIS	DISABLING	DISGORGED	DISPUTANT
DIAPHYSIS	DIGITIZED	DISABLIST	DISGORGER	DISPUTING
DIARRHOEA	DIGITIZER	DISABUSAL	DISGRACED	DISREGARD
DIASTASIC	DIGITOXIN	DISABUSED	DISGRACER	DISRELISH
DIASTASIS	DIGLOTTIC	DISACCORD	DISGUISED	DISREPAIR
DIASTATIC	DIGNIFIED	DISAFFECT	DISGUISER	DISREPUTE
DIASTOLIC	DIGNITARY	DISAFFIRM	DISGUISES	DISROBING
DIATHERMY	DIGNITIES	DISAGREED	DISGUSTED	DISRUPTED
DIATHESIS	DIGRAPHIC	DISAPPEAR	DISHCLOTH	DISRUPTER
DIATHETIC	DIGRESSED	DISARMING	DISHONEST	DISSECTED
DIATOMITE	DIGRESSER	DISASTERS	DISHONOUR	DISSECTOR

DISSEISIN	DIVORCING	DONATIONS	DRAGGIEST	DRUGGISTS
DISSEISOR	DIVORCIVE	DONCASTER	DRAGHOUND	DRUGSTORE
DISSEMBLE	DIVULGING	DONNISHLY	DRAGOMANS	DRUMBEATS
DISSENTED	DIVULSION	DONORSHIP	DRAGONESS	DRUM MAJOR
DISSENTER	DIVULSIVE	DOODLEBUG	DRAGONFLY	DRUMSTICK
DISSIDENT	DIXIELAND	DOOHICKEY	DRAGONISH	DRUNKARDS
DISSIPATE	DIZZINESS	DOOJIGGER	DRAGOONED	DRUNKENLY
DISSOLUTE	DJAJAPURA	DOOMSAYER	DRAINABLE	DUALISTIC
DISSOLVED	DOBSONFLY	DOORBELLS	DRAINPIPE	DUBIOUSLY
DISSOLVER	DOCK BRIEF	DOORFRAME	DRAMAMINE	DUBITABLE
DISSONANT	DOCKETING	DOORKNOBS	DRAMATICS	DUBROVNIK
DISSUADED	DOCKYARDS	DOORNAILS	DRAMATIST	DUCHESSES
DISSUADER	DOCTORATE	DOORPLATE	DRAMATIZE	DUCKBOARD
DISTANCED	DOCTORING	DOORSTEPS	DRAPERIED	DUCKLINGS
DISTANCES	DOCTRINAL	DORDRECHT	DRAPERIES	DUCTILITY
DISTANTLY	DOCTRINES	DORMITORY	DRAUGHTER	DUDE RANCH
DISTEMPER	DOCUMENTS	DORMOBILE	DRAVIDIAN	DUELLISTS
DISTENDED	DODDERERS	DORONICUM	DRAWBACKS	DUFFEL BAG
DISTENDER	DODDERING	DORYPHORE	DRAWKNIFE	DULCIMERS
DISTICHAL	DODECAGON	DOSIMETER	DRAWPLATE	DUMBARTON
DISTILLED	DODGE CITY	DOSIMETRY	DREAMBOAT	DUMBBELLS
DISTILLER	DOG COLLAR	DOSSHOUSE	DREAMLAND	DUMBFOUND
DISTINGUE	DOG-EAT-	DOTTINESS	DREAMLESS	DUMB SHOWS
DISTORTED	DOG	DOUBLE BED	DREAMLIKE	DUMMY RUNS
DISTORTER	DOGFIGHTS	DOUBLED UP	DREAMTIME	DUMPINESS
DISTRAINT	DOGFISHES	DOUBLETON	DREARIEST	DUMPLINGS
DISTRICTS	DOGGY BAGS	DOUBLOONS	DRENCHING	DUNCES CAP
DISTURBED	DOGHOUSES	DOUBTABLE	DRESS CODE	DUNCE'S
DISTURBER	DOGLEGGED	DOUBTLESS	DRESS DOWN	CAP
DISUNITED	DOGMATICS	DOUGHNUTS	DRESSIEST	DUNE BUGGY
DITHERING	DOGMATISM	DOUGHTIER	DRESSINGS	DUNGANNON
DITHYRAMB	DOGMATIST	DOVECOTES	DRIBBLING	DUNGAREES
DITTANDER	DOGMATIZE	DOVETAILS	DRIFTWOOD	DUNGENESS
DIURETICS	DO-GOODERS	DOWDINESS	DRILLABLE	DUNKERQUE
DIURNALLY	DOG PADDLE	DOWITCHER	DRINKABLE	DUNSINANE
DIVALENCY	DOLEFULLY	DOWNCOMER	DRIP-DRIED	DUNSTABLE
DIVERGENT	DOLERITIC	DOWNFALLS	DRIPSTONE	DUODECIMO
DIVERGING	DOLGELLAU	DOWNGRADE	DRIVE HOME	DUODENARY
DIVERSELY	DOLLY BIRD	DOWNPOURS	DRIVELING	DUODENUMS
DIVERSIFY	DOLOMITES	DOWNRANGE	DRIVELLED	DUOLOGUES
DIVERSION	DOLOMITIC	DOWNRIGHT	DRIVELLER	DUPLEXITY
DIVERSITY	DOLTISHLY	DOWNSPOUT	DRIVE-TIME	DUPLICATE
DIVERTING	DOMESTICS	DOWNSTAGE	DRIVEWAYS	DUPLICITY
DIVERTIVE	DOMICILED	DOWNSWING	DRIZZLING	DURALUMIN
DIVESTING	DOMICILES	DOWNTHROW	DROLLNESS	DURICRUST
DIVIDABLE	DOMINANCE	DOWNTURNS	DROMEDARY	DUSKINESS
DIVIDENDS	DOMINATED	DOWNWARDS	DROPLIGHT	DUSTBOWLS
DIVINABLE	DOMINATOR	DRACONIAN	DROPPINGS	DUSTCARTS
DIVISIBLE	DOMINICAL	DRAFTIEST	DROPSICAL	DUSTSHEET
DIVISIONS	DOMINICAN	DRAFTSMAN	DROPSONDE	DUST STORM
DIVORCEES	DOMINIONS	DRAFTSMEN	DRUBBINGS	DUTCH BARN

DUTCH CAPS
DUTCH OVEN
DUTIFULLY
DUTY-FREES
DWARF STAR
DWELLINGS
DWINDLING
DYER'S-
    WEED
DYNAMETER
DYNAMITED
DYNAMITER
DYNAMITIC
DYNAMOTOR
DYNASTIES
DYSENTERY
DYSGENICS
DYSLECTIC
DYSPEPSIA
DYSPEPTIC
DYSPHAGIA
DYSPHAGIC
DYSPHASIA
DYSPHASIC
DYSPHONIA
DYSPHONIC
DYSPHORIA
DYSPHORIC
DYSPLASIA
DYSPNOEAL
DYSTHYMIA
DYSTHYMIC
DYSTROPHY
DZUNGARIA

E

EACH OTHER
EAGERNESS
EAGLE-EYED
EAGLEWOOD
EARLINESS
EARLY BIRD
EARMARKED
EARNESTLY
EARPHONES
EARPIECES
EARTHIEST
EARTHLIER
EARTHLING
EARTHRISE
EARTHSTAR

EARTHWARD
EARTHWORK
EARTHWORM
EASTBOUND
EAST ENDER
EASTER EGG
EASTERNER
EASTLEIGH
EASTWARDS
EASY CHAIR
EASYGOING
EASY GOING
EASY TERMS
EAVESDROP
EBULLIENT
ECCENTRIC
ECHOLALIA
ECHOLALIC
ECLAMPSIA
ECLAMPTIC
ECLIPSING
ECOLOGIST
ECONOMICS
ECONOMIES
ECONOMIST
ECONOMIZE
ECOSPHERE
ECOSYSTEM
ECSTASIES
ECSTATICS
ECTOBLAST
ECTOMERIC
ECTOMORPH
ECTOPHYTE
ECTOPLASM
ECTOPROCT
ECUMENISM
EDDYSTONE
EDELWEISS
EDEMATOUS
EDIBILITY
EDIFICIAL
EDINBURGH
EDITORIAL
EDUCATING
EDUCATION
EDUCATIVE
EDUCATORS
EDUCATORY
EDWARDIAN
EFFECTING

EFFECTIVE
EFFECTUAL
EFFERENCE
EFFICIENT
EFFLUENCE
EFFLUENTS
EFFLUVIAL
EFFLUVIUM
EFFORTFUL
EFFULGENT
EFFUSIONS
EGG BEATER
EGGPLANTS
EGGSHELLS
EGG TIMERS
EGLANTINE
EGOMANIAC
EGOTISTIC
EGREGIOUS
EGYPTIANS
EIDERDOWN
EIGHTFOLD
EIGHTIETH
EINDHOVEN
EIRENICON
EISEGESIS
EJACULATE
EKISTICAL
ELABORATE
EL ALAMEIN
ELAN VITAL
ELASTANCE
ELASTOMER
ELATERITE
ELATERIUM
ELBOWROOM
ELBOW ROOM
ELDERSHIP
ELECTIONS
ELECTORAL
ELECTRESS
ELECTRICS
ELECTRIFY
ELECTRODE
ELECTRONS
ELECTUARY
ELEGANTLY
ELEMENTAL
ELEOPTENE
ELEPHANTS
ELEVATING

ELEVATION
ELEVATORS
ELEVENSES
ELEVENTHS
ELICITING
ELIMINANT
ELIMINATE
ELIZABETH
ELLESMERE
ELLIPSOID
EL MANSURA
ELOCUTION
ELONGATED
ELOPEMENT
ELOQUENCE
ELSEWHERE
ELUCIDATE
ELUSIVELY
ELUTRIATE
EMACIATED
EMANATING
EMANATION
EMANATIVE
EMANATORY
EMBALMERS
EMBALMING
EMBARGOED
EMBARGOES
EMBARKING
EMBARRASS
EMBASSIES
EMBATTLED
EMBAYMENT
EMBEDDING
EMBEDMENT
EMBELLISH
EMBEZZLED
EMBEZZLER
EMBODYING
EMBOLISMS
EMBOSOMED
EMBOSSING
EMBOWMENT
EMBRACEOR
EMBRACERY
EMBRACING
EMBRASURE
EMBROCATE
EMBROIDER
EMBROILED
EMBROILER

EMBRYONIC
EMENDABLE
EMENDATOR
EMERGENCE
EMERGENCY
EMIGRANTS
EMIGRATED
EMINENCES
EMINENTLY
EMISSIONS
EMMENTHAL
EMOLLIENT
EMOLUMENT
EMOTIONAL
EMOTIVELY
EMOTIVISM
EMPANELED
EMPATHIZE
EMPENNAGE
EMPHASIZE
EMPHYSEMA
EMPIRICAL
EMPLOYEES
EMPLOYERS
EMPLOYING
EMPORIUMS
EMPOWERED
EMPRESSES
EMPTIABLE
EMPTINESS
EMPYREUMA
EMULATING
EMULATION
EMULATIVE
EMULSIONS
EMUNCTORY
ENACTMENT
ENAMELING
ENAMELLED
ENAMELLER
ENAMOURED
ENCAMPING
ENCAUSTIC
ENCHAINED
ENCHANTED
ENCHANTER
ENCHILADA
ENCHORIAL
ENCIRCLED
ENCLOSING
ENCLOSURE

ENCOMIAST	ENHANCING	ENTRANCES	EPISTASIS	ESCALATOR
ENCOMIUMS	ENHANCIVE	ENTRAPPED	EPISTATIC	ESCALOPES
ENCOMPASS	ENIGMATIC	ENTRAPPER	EPISTAXIS	ESCAPABLE
ENCOUNTER	ENJOINING	ENTREATED	EPISTEMIC	ESCAPADES
ENCOURAGE	ENJOYABLE	ENTRECHAT	EPITAPHIC	ESCAPISTS
ENCRINITE	ENJOYABLY	ENTRECOTE	EPITAXIAL	ESCHEWING
ENCRUSTED	ENJOYMENT	ENTREMETS	EPITHETIC	ESCORTING
ENDAMOEBA	ENKINDLER	ENTRE NOUS	EPITOMIST	ESKISEHIR
ENDEARING	ENLARGING	ENTRUSTED	EPITOMIZE	ESOPHAGUS
ENDEAVOUR	ENLIGHTEN	ENTRYWAYS	EPIZOOTIC	ESPERANTO
ENDLESSLY	ENLISTING	ENTWINING	EPONYMOUS	ESPIONAGE
ENDOBLAST	ENLIVENED	ENUCLEATE	EQUAL-AREA	ESPLANADE
ENDOCRINE	ENLIVENER	ENUMERATE	EQUALIZED	ESPOUSALS
ENDOERGIC	ENMESHING	ENUNCIATE	EQUALIZER	ESPOUSING
ENDOLYMPH	ENNOBLING	ENVELOPED	EQUALLING	ESPRESSOS
ENDOMORPH	EN PASSANT	ENVELOPES	EQUATABLE	ESSAOUIRA
ENDOPHYTE	ENQUIRIES	ENVIOUSLY	EQUATIONS	ESSAYISTS
ENDOPLASM	ENQUIRING	ENVISAGED	EQUERRIES	ESSENTIAL
ENDORSING	ENRAGEDLY	ENVYINGLY	EQUINOXES	ESSLINGEN
ENDOSCOPE	EN RAPPORT	ENZYMATIC	EQUIPMENT	ESTABLISH
ENDOSCOPY	ENRAPTURE	EPARCHIAL	EQUIPOISE	ESTAMINET
ENDOSPERM	ENRICHING	EPHEDRINE	EQUIPPING	ESTATE CAR
ENDOSPORE	ENROLLING	EPHEMERAL	EQUISETUM	ESTEEMING
ENDOSTEAL	ENROLMENT	EPHEMERID	EQUITABLE	ESTHETICS
ENDOSTEUM	ENSCONCED	EPHEMERIS	EQUITABLY	ESTIMABLE
ENDOTOXIC	ENSEMBLES	EPHEMERON	EQUIVOCAL	ESTIMATED
ENDOTOXIN	ENSHRINED	EPICENISM	EQUIVOQUE	ESTIMATES
ENDOWMENT	ENSLAVING	EPICENTRE	ERADICANT	ESTIMATOR
ENDURABLE	ENSNARING	EPICRISIS	ERADICATE	ESTOPPAGE
ENDURANCE	ENSTATITE	EPICRITIC	ERECTABLE	ESTRANGED
ENERGETIC	ENSUINGLY	EPICUREAN	ERECTIONS	ESTRANGER
ENERGIZED	ENTAILING	EPICURISM	ERECTNESS	ESTUARIAL
ENERGIZER	ENTAMOEBA	EPICYCLIC	EREMITISM	ESTUARIES
ENERGUMEN	ENTANGLED	EPIDEMICS	ERGOGRAPH	ESTUARINE
ENERVATED	ENTANGLER	EPIDERMAL	ERGOMETER	ESURIENCE
ENERVATOR	ENTELECHY	EPIDERMIS	ERGONOMIC	ETCETERAS
EN FAMILLE	ENTENDRES	EPIDURALS	ERISTICAL	ETERNALLY
ENFEEBLED	ENTERABLE	EPIGENOUS	EROGENOUS	ETHERIZER
ENFEEBLER	ENTERALLY	EPIGRAPHY	EROSIONAL	ETHICALLY
ENFILADED	ENTERITIS	EPIGYNOUS	EROTICISM	ETHIOPIAN
ENFILADES	ENTERTAIN	EPILEPTIC	EROTICIZE	ETHMOIDAL
ENFOLDING	ENTHRONED	EPILOGIST	ERRONEOUS	ETHNARCHY
ENFORCING	ENTHUSING	EPILOGUES	ERSTWHILE	ETHNOGENY
ENGINEERS	ENTHYMEME	EPIMYSIUM	ERUDITELY	ETHNOLOGY
ENGLACIAL	ENTITLING	EPINASTIC	ERUDITION	ETHOLOGIC
ENGRAMMIC	ENTOBLAST	EPIPHANIC	ERUPTIBLE	ETHYLENIC
ENGRAVERS	ENTOMBING	EPIPHRAGM	ERUPTIONS	ETIOLATED
ENGRAVING	ENTOPHYTE	EPIPHYSIS	ERYTHRISM	ETIQUETTE
ENGROSSED	ENTOURAGE	EPIPHYTIC	ERYTHRITE	ETRAMETER
ENGROSSER	ENTRAINED	EPIROGENY	ESCALADER	ETYMOLOGY
ENGULFING	ENTRANCED	EPISCOPAL	ESCALATED	EUCHARIST

EUCLIDEAN	EXCALIBUR	EXEMPLARY	EXPLAINER	EXTRAVERT
EUDEMONIA	EXCAUDATE	EXEMPLIFY	EXPLETIVE	EXTREMELY
EUDEMONIC	EXCAVATED	EXEMPTING	EXPLICATE	EXTREMISM
EUKARYOTE	EXCAVATOR	EXEMPTION	EXPLODING	EXTREMIST
EULOGISTS	EXCEEDING	EXEQUATUR	EXPLOITED	EXTREMITY
EULOGIZED	EXCELLENT	EXERCISED	EXPLOITER	EXTRICATE
EUPHEMISM	EXCELLING	EXERCISER	EXPLORERS	EXTRINSIC
EUPHEMIST	EXCELSIOR	EXERCISES	EXPLORING	EXTROVERT
EUPHEMIZE	EXCEPTING	EXERTIONS	EXPLOSION	EXTRUDING
EUPHONIUM	EXCEPTION	EXFOLIATE	EXPLOSIVE	EXTRUSION
EUPHONIZE	EXCEPTIVE	EXHALABLE	EXPONENTS	EXTRUSIVE
EUPHORBIA	EXCERPTER	EXHAUSTED	EXPONIBLE	EXUBERANT
EUPHRATES	EXCESSIVE	EXHAUSTER	EXPORTERS	EXUBERATE
EUPLASTIC	EXCHANGED	EXHIBITED	EXPORTING	EXUDATION
EURHYTHMY	EXCHANGER	EXHIBITOR	EXPOSABLE	EXUDATIVE
EUROCRATS	EXCHANGES	EXHORTING	EXPOSITOR	EYEBALLED
EUROPHILE	EXCHEQUER	EXISTENCE	EXPOSURES	EYEBRIGHT
EUROPOORT	EXCIPIENT	EXODONTIA	EXPOUNDED	EYELASHES
EUTHENICS	EXCISABLE	EXOENZYME	EXPOUNDER	EYELETEER
EUTHENIST	EXCISEMAN	EX OFFICIO	EXPRESSED	EYE OPENER
EUTHERIAN	EXCISIONS	EXOGAMOUS	EXPRESSER	EYE-OPENER
EUTROPHIC	EXCITABLE	EXOGENOUS	EXPRESSES	EYEPIECES
EVACUATED	EXCITEDLY	EXONERATE	EXPRESSLY	EYE SHADOW
EVACUATOR	EXCLAIMED	EXORCISER	EXPULSION	EYES RIGHT
EVADINGLY	EXCLAIMER	EXORCISMS	EXPULSIVE	EYESTRAIN
EVAGINATE	EXCLUDING	EXORCISTS	EXPUNGING	EYE STRAIN
EVALUATED	EXCLUSION	EXORCIZED	EXPURGATE	
EVALUATOR	EXCLUSIVE	EXOSMOSIS	EXQUISITE	**F**
EVAPORATE	EXCORIATE	EXOSMOTIC	EXSECTION	FABACEOUS
EVAPORITE	EXCREMENT	EXOSPHERE	EXSERTILE	FABIANISM
EVASIVELY	EXCRETING	EXOSTOSIS	EXSERTION	FABRICATE
EVENTUATE	EXCRETION	EXOTICISM	EXSICCATE	FABRIKOID
EVERGREEN	EXCRETIVE	EXPANDING	EXSTROPHY	FACE CARDS
EVERSIBLE	EXCRETORY	EXPANSILE	EXTEMPORE	FACECLOTH
EVERYBODY	EXCULPATE	EXPANSION	EXTENDING	FACE-LIFTS
EVICTIONS	EXCURRENT	EXPANSIVE	EXTENSION	FACE PACKS
EVIDENTLY	EXCURSION	EXPATIATE	EXTENSITY	FACEPLATE
EVILDOERS	EXCURSIVE	EXPECTANT	EXTENSIVE	FACE SAVER
EVILDOING	EXCUSABLE	EXPECTING	EXTENUATE	FACE-SAVER
EVINCIBLE	EXCUSABLY	EXPEDIENT	EXTERIORS	FACETIOUS
EVOCATION	EXECRABLE	EXPEDITED	EXTERNALS	FACE VALUE
EVOCATIVE	EXECRABLY	EXPEDITER	EXTIRPATE	FACSIMILE
EVOLUTION	EXECRATED	EXPELLANT	EXTOLLING	FACTIONAL
EVOLVABLE	EXECUTANT	EXPELLING	EXTOLMENT	FACTITIVE
EXACTABLE	EXECUTING	EXPENDING	EXTORTING	FACTORAGE
EXACTNESS	EXECUTION	EXPENSIVE	EXTORTION	FACTORIAL
EXALTEDLY	EXECUTIVE	EXPERTISE	EXTORTIVE	FACTORIES
EXAMINERS	EXECUTORS	EXPIATING	EXTRABOLD	FACTORING
EXAMINING	EXECUTORY	EXPIATION	EXTRACTED	FACTORIZE
EXANIMATE	EXECUTRIX	EXPIATORY	EXTRACTOR	FACTUALLY
EXANTHEMA	EXEGETICS	EXPLAINED	EXTRADITE	FACULTIES

FADDINESS	FARRAGOES	FERMENTER	FILMINESS	FIRST FOOT
FADDISHLY	FARROWING	FEROCIOUS	FILM SPEED	FIRSTHAND
FADEDNESS	FAR-SEEING	FERRETING	FILM STARS	FIRST LADY
FAGACEOUS	FARTHINGS	FERROCENE	FILM STOCK	FIRSTLING
FAGGOTING	FASCICLED	FERROTYPE	FILMSTRIP	FIRST NAME
FAINEANCE	FASCICULE	FERTILITY	FILOPLUME	FIRST-RATE
FAINTNESS	FASCIITIS	FERTILIZE	FILOSELLE	FISHCAKES
FAIRBANKS	FASCINATE	FERVENTLY	FILTERING	FISHERIES
FAIRYLAND	FASCISTIC	FESTERING	FILTER TIP	FISHERMAN
FAIRY-LIKE	FASHIONED	FESTIVALS	FILTHIEST	FISHERMEN
FAIRY RING	FASHIONER	FESTIVITY	FIMBRIATE	FISH FARMS
FAIRY-TALE	FASTENERS	FESTOONED	FINALISTS	FISHGUARD
FAITHFULS	FASTENING	FETICIDAL	FINALIZED	FISHINESS
FAITHLESS	FATALISTS	FETISHISM	FINANCIAL	FISH KNIFE
FALANGISM	FATEFULLY	FETISHIST	FINANCIER	FISHPLATE
FALANGIST	FATHEADED	FETISHIZE	FINANCING	FISH SLICE
FALCONERS	FATHERING	FETTERING	FINE-GRAIN	FISH STICK
FALCONINE	FATHOMING	FETTUCINE	FINE PRINT	FISSILITY
FALDSTOOL	FATIGABLE	FEUDALISM	FINE-TOOTH	FISTULOUS
FALLACIES	FATIGUING	FEUDALIST	FINE-TUNED	FIXATIONS
FALLALERY	FATTENING	FEUDALITY	FINGERING	FIXATIVES
FALL APART	FATTINESS	FEUDALIZE	FINGERTIP	FIXED-HEAD
FALLOPIAN	FATUITOUS	FEUDATORY	FINISHING	FIXED STAR
FALSEHOOD	FATUOUSLY	FEVERWORT	FINISTERE	FIZZINESS
FALSENESS	FAULTIEST	FIBONACCI	FIRE ALARM	FLABBIEST
FALSIFIED	FAULTLESS	FIBREFILL	FIREBALLS	FLABELLUM
FALSIFIER	FAVEOLATE	FIBRIFORM	FIREBOXES	FLACCIDLY
FALSITIES	FAVOURING	FIBRINOUS	FIREBRAND	FLAGELLAR
FALTERING	FAVOURITE	FICTIONAL	FIREBREAK	FLAGELLUM
FAMAGUSTA	FAWNINGLY	FIDEISTIC	FIREBRICK	FLAGEOLET
FAMILIARS	FEARFULLY	FIDGETING	FIRECREST	FLAGPOLES
FAMILY MAN	FEATHERED	FIDUCIARY	FIRE DRILL	FLAGRANCE
FAMILY MEN	FEATURING	FIELD ARMY	FIRE-EATER	FLAGRANCY
FANATICAL	FEBRICITY	FIELD DAYS	FIREFIGHT	FLAGSHIPS
FANCINESS	FEBRIFUGE	FIELDFARE	FIREFLIES	FLAGSTAFF
FANCY-FREE	FEBRILITY	FIELD GOAL	FIREGUARD	FLAGSTONE
FANCYWORK	FECULENCE	FIELDSMAN	FIRE IRONS	FLAG-WAVER
FANDANGLE	FECUNDATE	FIELDSMEN	FIRELIGHT	FLAKINESS
FANDANGOS	FECUNDITY	FIELD-TEST	FIREPLACE	FLAMELIKE
FANLIGHTS	FEDERATED	FIELD TRIP	FIRE-PLUGS	FLAMINGOS
FAN-TAILED	FEEDSTOCK	FIELDWORK	FIREPOWER	FLAMMABLE
FANTASIES	FEEDSTUFF	FIFTEENTH	FIREPROOF	FLANNELED
FANTASIZE	FEELINGLY	FIFTIETHS	FIRESIDES	FLAPJACKS
FANTASTIC	FEE-PAYING	FIG LEAVES	FIRESTONE	FLARE PATH
FARADIZER	FELICIFIC	FIGURE OUT	FIRESTORM	FLASHBACK
FARANDOLE	FELONIOUS	FIGURINES	FIRETHORN	FLASHBULB
FAREWELLS	FEMINISTS	FILAMENTS	FIRETRAPS	FLASHCUBE
FARMHANDS	FENESTRAL	FILIATION	FIREWATER	FLASHGUNS
FARMHOUSE	FENUGREEK	FILICIDAL	FIREWORKS	FLASHIEST
FARMSTEAD	FERMANAGH	FILLETING	FIRMAMENT	FLASHOVER
FARMYARDS	FERMENTED	FILLISTER	FIRSTBORN	FLATMATES

FLAT SPINS	FLOWCHART	FOOLHARDY	FORESHORE	FORWARDLY
FLATTENED	FLOWERAGE	FOOLISHLY	FORESIGHT	FOSSILIZE
FLATTENER	FLOWERBED	FOOLPROOF	FORESKINS	FOSSORIAL
FLATTERED	FLOWERING	FOOTBALLS	FORESTALL	FOSTERAGE
FLATTERER	FLOWERPOT	FOOTBOARD	FORESTERS	FOSTERING
FLATULENT	FLOWINGLY	FOOTFALLS	FORETASTE	FOUNDERED
FLAUNTING	FLOWMETER	FOOT FAULT	FORETOKEN	FOUNDLING
FLAUTISTS	FLUCTUANT	FOOTHILLS	FORETOOTH	FOUNDRIES
FLAVOROUS	FLUCTUATE	FOOTHOLDS	FOREWOMAN	FOUNTAINS
FLAVOURED	FLUFFIEST	FOOTLOOSE	FOREWOMEN	FOURSOMES
FLAVOURER	FLUIDIZER	FOOTNOTES	FOREWORDS	FOUR-WHEEL
FLEABITES	FLUKINESS	FOOTPATHS	FORFEITED	FOVEOLATE
FLEDGLING	FLUMMOXED	FOOTPLATE	FORFEITER	FOXGLOVES
FLEETNESS	FLUORESCE	FOOT-POUND	FORFICATE	FOXHOUNDS
FLEETWOOD	FLUOROSIS	FOOTPRINT	FORGATHER	FOXHUNTER
FLENSBURG	FLUORSPAR	FOOTRACES	FORGEABLE	FRACTIONS
FLESHIEST	FLURRYING	FOOTSTALK	FORGERIES	FRACTIOUS
FLESHINGS	FLUSTERED	FOOTSTALL	FORGETFUL	FRACTURAL
FLESHPOTS	FLUTTERED	FOOTSTEPS	FORGETTER	FRACTURED
FLEURETTE	FLUTTERER	FOOTSTOOL	FORGIVING	FRACTURES
FLEXIONAL	FLUXIONAL	FORAMINAL	FORGOTTEN	FRAGILITY
FLEXITIME	FLUXMETER	FORBEARER	FORLORNLY	FRAGMENTS
FLICKERED	FLY-FISHER	FORBIDDEN	FORMALISM	FRAGONARD
FLIGHTIER	FLY HALVES	FORBIDDER	FORMALIST	FRAGRANCE
FLIGHTILY	FLYING FOX	FORCEABLE	FORMALITY	FRAILTIES
FLIMSIEST	FLYLEAVES	FORCE FEED	FORMALIZE	FRAMBOISE
FLINCHING	FLYSHEETS	FORCE-FEED	FORMATION	FRAMEWORK
FLINTIEST	FLYWEIGHT	FORCEMEAT	FORMATIVE	FRANCHISE
FLINTLOCK	FLYWHEELS	FORCINGLY	FORMATTED	FRANCOLIN
FLIP-FLOPS	FLYWHISKS	FOREARMED	FORMICARY	FRANGIBLE
FLIPPANCY	FOAMINESS	FOREBEARS	FORMULAIC	FRANGLAIS
FLOATABLE	FOCUSABLE	FOREBODED	FORMULARY	FRANKABLE
FLOAT-FEED	FOCUSSING	FOREBODER	FORMULATE	FRANKFORT
FLOCCULUS	FOETATION	FOREBRAIN	FORMULISM	FRANKNESS
FLOGGINGS	FOETICIDE	FORECASTS	FORMULIST	FRATERNAL
FLOODABLE	FOGGINESS	FORECLOSE	FORNICATE	FRAUDSTER
FLOODGATE	FOLIATION	FORECOURT	FORSAKING	FREE AGENT
FLOOD TIDE	FOLIOLATE	FOREFRONT	FORSYTHIA	FREE-BASED
FLOOR SHOW	FOLK DANCE	FOREGOING	FORTALEZA	FREEBOARD
FLOPHOUSE	FOLKLORIC	FOREHANDS	FORTALICE	FREEHOLDS
FLOPPIEST	FOLK MUSIC	FOREHEADS	FORTHWITH	FREE HOUSE
FLOPTICAL	FOLKTALES	FOREIGNER	FORTIETHS	FREE KICKS
FLORIATED	FOLLICLES	FOREJUDGE	FORTIFIED	FREELANCE
FLORIDITY	FOLLOWERS	FORELOCKS	FORTIFIER	FREE-LIVER
FLORISTIC	FOLLOWING	FORENAMED	FORTITUDE	FREEMASON
FLOS FERRI	FOLLOW-UPS	FORENAMES	FORTNIGHT	FREEPHONE
FLOTATION	FOMENTING	FORENSICS	FORTUNATE	FREE PORTS
FLOTILLAS	FOOD CHAIN	FOREREACH	FORT WORTH	FREE-RANGE
FLOUNCING	FOOD STAMP	FORESHANK	FORTY-FIVE	FREESHEET
FLOUNDERS	FOODSTUFF	FORESHEET	FORWARDED	FREE STATE
FLOURMILL	FOOLERIES	FORESHOCK	FORWARDER	FREESTONE

FREESTYLE	FROSTIEST	FUNNY BONE	GALLSTONE	GATEPOSTS
FREE TRADE	FROSTWORK	FUNNY FARM	GALUMPHED	GATESHEAD
FREE VERSE	FROTHIEST	FURBISHED	GALVANISM	GATHERING
FREEWHEEL	FROWSTIER	FURBISHER	GALVANIZE	GAUCHERIE
FREE WORLD	FROWZIEST	FURCATION	GALWEGIAN	GAUDINESS
FREEZABLE	FRUCTUOUS	FURIOUSLY	GAMBOGIAN	GAUGEABLE
FREEZE-DRY	FRUGALITY	FURLOUGHS	GAMBOLING	GAUGEABLY
FREIGHTED	FRUIT BATS	FURNISHED	GAMECOCKS	GAULEITER
FREIGHTER	FRUITCAKE	FURNISHER	GAMMADION	GAUNTLETS
FREMANTLE	FRUITERER	FURNITURE	GAMMA RAYS	GAUNTNESS
FRENCHIFY	FRUITIEST	FURRINESS	GANDHIISM	GAUZINESS
FRENCHMAN	FRUITLESS	FURROWING	GANG-BANGS	GAWKINESS
FRENCHMEN	FRUMPIEST	FURTHERED	GANGLIONS	GAZA STRIP
FREQUENCE	FRUSTRATE	FURTHERER	GANGPLANK	GAZEHOUND
FREQUENCY	FRYING PAN	FURTIVELY	GANGSTERS	GAZETTEER
FRESHENED	FUGACIOUS	FUSELAGES	GAOLBIRDS	GAZIANTEP
FRESHENER	FUGITIVES	FUSILLADE	GARBOLOGY	GAZUMPING
FRESHNESS	FUKUSHIMA	FUSIONISM	GARDENERS	GEARBOXES
FRETBOARD	FULFILLED	FUSIONIST	GARDENIAS	GEAR LEVER
FRETFULLY	FULFILLER	FUSSINESS	GARDENING	GEAR STICK
FRETWORKS	FULGURITE	FUSTINESS	GARGOYLED	GEARWHEEL
FRIARBIRD	FULGUROUS	FUTURISTS	GARGOYLES	GEHLENITE
FRICASSEE	FULLBACKS	FUZZINESS	GARIBALDI	GELIGNITE
FRICATIVE	FULL-BLOWN		GARLANDED	GELLIGAER
FRIESIANS	FULL BOARD	**G**	GARNERING	GELSEMIUM
FRIESLAND	FULL DRESS	GABARDINE	GARNISHED	GEMMATION
FRIGHTFUL	FULLERENE	GABERDINE	GARNISHER	GEMUTLICH
FRIGIDITY	FULL-FACED	GABIONADE	GARNISHES	GENDARMES
FRILLIEST	FULL-GROWN	GADABOUTS	GARNITURE	GENEALOGY
FRISKIEST	FULL HOUSE	GADOLINIC	GARRISONS	GENE CLONE
FRITTERED	FULL MARKS	GADROONED	GARROTTED	GENERABLE
FRITTERER	FULL MONTY	GAINFULLY	GARROTTER	GENERALLY
FRIVOLITY	FULL MOONS	GAINSAYER	GARROTTES	GENERATED
FRIVOLLER	FULL-SCALE	GALACTOSE	GARRULITY	GENERATOR
FRIVOLOUS	FULL STOPS	GALANTINE	GARRULOUS	GENIALITY
FRIZZIEST	FULMINANT	GALAPAGOS	GAS FITTER	GENITALIC
FRIZZLING	FULMINATE	GALEIFORM	GAS HEATER	GENITALLY
FROCK COAT	FULSOMELY	GALENICAL	GASHOLDER	GENITIVAL
FROGMARCH	FUMAROLIC	GALINGALE	GASLIGHTS	GENITIVES
FROGMOUTH	FUMIGATED	GALLANTLY	GAS MANTLE	GENOCIDAL
FROGSPAWN	FUMIGATOR	GALLANTRY	GASOLINIC	GENOTYPIC
FROLICKED	FUNCTIONS	GALLERIED	GASOMETER	GENTEELLY
FROLICKER	FUNDAMENT	GALLERIES	GASOMETRY	GENTILITY
FRONTAGES	FUNGICIDE	GALLICISM	GASPINGLY	GENTLEMAN
FRONTALLY	FUNGIFORM	GALLICIZE	GASSINESS	GENTLEMEN
FRONT DOOR	FUNGISTAT	GALLINULE	GASTRITIC	GENTLE SEX
FRONTIERS	FUNICULAR	GALLIPOLI	GASTRITIS	GENUFLECT
FRONT LINE	FUNICULUS	GALLIVANT	GASTROPOD	GENUINELY
FRONT-PAGE	FUNNELING	GALLIWASP	GASTRULAR	GEODESIST
FRONT ROOM	FUNNELLED	GALLONAGE	GATECRASH	GEOGRAPHY
FROSTBITE	FUNNINESS	GALLOPING	GATEHOUSE	GEOLOGIST

GEOLOGIZE	GIRANDOLE	GLOWERING	GOOD TIMES	GRAPHITIC
GEOMANCER	GIRL GUIDE	GLOWINGLY	GOOD WORDS	GRAPPELLI
GEOMANTIC	GIRLISHLY	GLOW-WORMS	GOOFINESS	GRAPPLING
GEOMETRIC	GIRONDISM	GLUCOSIDE	GOOSANDER	GRASPABLE
GEOMETRID	GIRONDIST	GLUTAMINE	GOOSEFOOT	GRASSIEST
GEOPHYTIC	GIVEAWAYS	GLUTENOUS	GOOSENECK	GRASSLAND
GEOPONICS	GIVEN NAME	GLUTINOUS	GOOSESTEP	GRASSQUIT
GEORGETTE	GLABELLAR	GLYCERIDE	GOOSINESS	GRATICULE
GEOSTATIC	GLADDENED	GLYCERINE	GORAKHPUR	GRATIFIED
GEOTACTIC	GLADDENER	GLYCOSIDE	GORGEABLE	GRATIFIER
GEOTROPIC	GLADIATOR	GOAL LINES	GORGONIAN	GRATINGLY
GERANIUMS	GLADIOLUS	GOALMOUTH	GORILLIAN	GRATITUDE
GERIATRIC	GLAIREOUS	GOALPOSTS	GORILLOID	GRAVELING
GERMANDER	GLAMORGAN	GOATHERDS	GOSPELLER	GRAVELISH
GERMANISM	GLAMORIZE	GOATSKINS	GOSSIPING	GRAVELLED
GERMANITE	GLAMOROUS	GO BETWEEN	GOTHICISM	GRAVENESS
GERMANIUM	GLANDERED	GO-BETWEEN	GO THROUGH	GRAVESEND
GERMANIZE	GLANDULAR	GODESBERG	GO TO	GRAVESIDE
GERMANOUS	GLARINGLY	GODFATHER	EARTH	GRAVEYARD
GERM CELLS	GLASSIEST	GODLESSLY	GOTTINGEN	GRAVIDITY
GERMICIDE	GLASSWARE	GODLINESS	GOURMANDS	GRAVITATE
GERMINANT	GLASSWORK	GODMOTHER	GOUTINESS	GRAVY BOAT
GERMINATE	GLASSWORT	GODPARENT	GOVERNESS	GREASE GUN
GERMISTON	GLEANABLE	GO-GETTERS	GOVERNING	GREASIEST
GERUNDIAL	GLEANINGS	GOGGLE BOX	GOVERNORS	GREAT-AUNT
GERUNDIVE	GLEEFULLY	GOING-OVER	GRACELESS	GREAT BEAR
GESTATION	GLENGARRY	GOLDCREST	GRADATION	GREAT BELT
GESTATORY	GLIDINGLY	GOLDEN AGE	GRADIENTS	GREATCOAT
GESTURING	GLIMMERED	GOLDENEYE	GRADUALLY	GREAT DANE
GETTING ON	GLIMPSING	GOLDEN EYE	GRADUATED	GREATNESS
GEYSERITE	GLISSADER	GOLDENROD	GRADUATES	GREEDIEST
GHASTLIER	GLISSANDO	GOLDFIELD	GRADUATOR	GREENAWAY
GHETTOIZE	GLISTENED	GOLDFINCH	GRAMPUSES	GREENBACK
GHOSTLIER	GLITTERED	GOLD MEDAL	GRANARIES	GREEN BEAN
GHOST TOWN	GLITZIEST	GOLD-MINER	GRANDADDY	GREEN BELT
GIANT STAR	GLOBALISM	GOLDMINES	GRANDIOSE	GREEN EYED
GIBBERING	GLOBALIST	GOLD PLATE	GRANDIOSO	GREENGAGE
GIBBERISH	GLOBALIZE	GOLDSMITH	GRAND JURY	GREENHEAD
GIBRALTAR	GLOBE FISH	GOLF BALLS	GRANDNESS	GREENHORN
GIDDINESS	GLOBOSITY	GOLF CLUBS	GRAND PRIX	GREENLAND
GIFT HORSE	GLOMERATE	GOLF LINKS	GRAND SLAM	GREENLING
GIGAHERTZ	GLOMERULE	GOLLIWOGS	GRANDSONS	GREENNESS
GIGANTISM	GLOOMIEST	GOMPHOSIS	GRANITITE	GREENROOM
GILSONITE	GLORIFIED	GONDOLIER	GRANIVORE	GREEN ROOM
GILT-EDGED	GLORIFIER	GONIATITE	GRANOLITH	GREENSAND
GIMMICKRY	GLORY HOLE	GONOPHORE	GRANTABLE	GREENWICH
GINGER ALE	GLOSSIEST	GONORRHEA	GRANULATE	GREENWOOD
GINGERING	GLOSSITIC	GOODLIEST	GRANULITE	GREETINGS
GINGER NUT	GLOSSITIS	GOOD LOOKS	GRANULOMA	GREGARINE
GIN SLINGS	GLOTTIDES	GOODNIGHT	GRAPESHOT	GREGORIAN
GIPSYWORT	GLOTTISES	GOOD-SIZED	GRAPEVINE	GRENADIER

GRENADINE	GUANGDONG	GYNOECIUM	HALF DOZEN	HANDCUFFS
GREY AREAS	GUANIDINE	GYNOPHORE	HALF-DOZEN	HANDICAPS
GREYBEARD	GUANOSINE	GYRATIONS	HALF-HITCH	HANDINESS
GREYHOUND	GUARANTEE	GYRFALCON	HALF LIGHT	HANDIWORK
GREY-STATE	GUARANTOR	GYROSCOPE	HALF-LIGHT	HANDLEBAR
GREYWACKE	GUARDABLE		HALF-LIVES	HANDLOOMS
GREY WATER	GUARDEDLY	**H**	HALF MOONS	HANDOVERS
GRIDIRONS	GUARDIANS	HABERGEON	HALF NOTES	HANDRAILS
GRIEVANCE	GUARDRAIL	HABITABLE	HALFPENCE	HANDS DOWN
GRILLROOM	GUARDROOM	HABITABLY	HALFPENNY	HANDSHAKE
GRIMACING	GUARDSMAN	HABITUATE	HALF-PLATE	HANDSPIKE
GRIMALKIN	GUARDSMEN	HACIENDAS	HALFTONES	HANDSTAND
GRIMINESS	GUARD'S	HACKAMORE	HALF-TRUTH	HANGERS ON
GRINDELIA	VAN	HACKBERRY	HALITOSIS	HANGERS-ON
GRIPINGLY	GUATEMALA	HACKNEYED	HALLELUJA	HANGNAILS
GRISAILLE	GUAYAQUIL	HADROSAUR	HALLIARDS	HANGOVERS
GRISLIEST	GUERRILLA	HAECCEITY	HALL-JONES	HANKERING
GRISTLIER	GUESSABLE	HAEMATEIN	HALLMARKS	HANSEATIC
GRISTMILL	GUESSWORK	HAEMATITE	HALLOWEEN	HAPHAZARD
GRITTIEST	GUESTROOM	HAEMATOID	HALLOWE'EN	HAPHTARAH
GRIZZLING	GUFFAWING	HAEMATOMA	HALLOWING	HAPLESSLY
GROCERIES	GUIDELINE	HAEMOCOEL	HALLOWMAS	HAPLOLOGY
GROGGIEST	GUIDEPOST	HAEMOCYTE	HALLSTATT	HAPPENING
GRONINGEN	GUIDINGLY	HAEMOSTAT	HALMAHERA	HAPPINESS
GROOMSMAN	GUILDFORD	HAGBUTEER	HALOBIONT	HAPPY HOUR
GROOVIEST	GUILDHALL	HAGGADIST	HALOPHYTE	HARANGUED
GROPINGLY	GUILDSMAN	HAGGARDLY	HALOTHANE	HARANGUER
GROSGRAIN	GUILELESS	HAGGISHLY	HALTINGLY	HARANGUES
GROSSNESS	GUILLEMOT	HAGIARCHY	HAMADRYAD	HARASSING
GROTESQUE	GUILLOCHE	HAGIOLOGY	HAMADRYAS	HARBINGER
GROTTIEST	GUILTIEST	HAG-RIDDEN	HAMAMATSU	HARBOURED
GROUCHIER	GUILTLESS	HAIDAR ALI	HAMBURGER	HARBOURER
GROUCHILY	GUINEA PIG	HAILSTONE	HAMERSLEY	HARDBACKS
GROUCHING	GUITARIST	HAILSTORM	HAM-FISTED	HARDBOARD
GROUNDAGE	GULPINGLY	HAIRBRUSH	HAMMERING	HARDBOUND
GROUNDING	GUMMATOUS	HAIRCLOTH	HAMMERTOE	HARD CIDER
GROUNDNUT	GUMMINESS	HAIRGRIPS	HAMMER TOE	HARD CORES
GROUNDSEL	GUMSHIELD	HAIRINESS	HAMMURABI	HARD COURT
GROUPINGS	GUN COTTON	HAIRLINES	HAMPERING	HARDCOVER
GROUPWARE	GUNPOWDER	HAIRPIECE	HAMPSHIRE	HARD DISKS
GROVELING	GUNRUNNER	HAIR SHIRT	HAMPSTEAD	HARD DRINK
GROVELLED	GUNSMITHS	HAIR SLIDE	HAMSTRING	HARDENING
GROVELLER	GUSHINGLY	HAIRSTYLE	HAMSTRUNG	HARDHEADS
GRUBBIEST	GUSTATORY	HALEAKALA	HANDBASIN	HARDHOUSE
GRUBSTAKE	GUSTINESS	HALESOWEN	HANDBILLS	HARDIHOOD
GRUELLING	GUTTERING	HALFBACKS	HANDBOOKS	HARDINESS
GRUFFNESS	GYMKHANAS	HALF-BAKED	HANDBRAKE	HARD-LINER
GRUMBLERS	GYMNASIUM	HALF BOARD	HANDCARTS	HARD LINES
GRUMBLING	GYMNASTIC	HALF-BREED	HANDCLAPS	HARD-NOSED
GRUMPIEST	GYNAECOID	HALF-CASTE	HANDCLASP	HARDSHIPS
GUANABARA	GYNARCHIC	HALF CROWN	HANDCRAFT	HARD TIMES

HARDWOODS	HAWTHORNE	HEATHFOWL	HEMSTITCH	HEY PRESTO
HAREBELLS	HAWTHORNS	HEATHLAND	HENDIADYS	HIBERNATE
HARKENING	HAYMAKING	HEATHLIKE	HEN HOUSES	HIBERNIAN
HARLEQUIN	HAYSTACKS	HEAT PUMPS	HENPECKED	HICCUPING
HARMATTAN	HAZARDING	HEAT WAVES	HEOMANIAC	HICKORIES
HARMFULLY	HAZARDOUS	HEAVINESS	HEPATITIS	HIDDENITE
HARMONICA	HEADACHES	HEAVISIDE	HEPTAGONS	HIDEAWAYS
HARMONICS	HEADBANDS	HEAVY-DUTY	HEPTARCHY	HIDEBOUND
HARMONIES	HEADBOARD	HEBRAIZER	HERACLEAN	HIDEOUSLY
HARMONIST	HEADDRESS	HEBRIDEAN	HERALDING	HIERARCHY
HARMONIUM	HEADFIRST	HECTOGRAM	HERALDIST	HIERODULE
HARMONIZE	HEAD FIRST	HECTORING	HERBALIST	HIEROGRAM
HARMOTOME	HEADINESS	HEDGE FUND	HERBARIAL	HIEROLOGY
HARNESSED	HEADLANDS	HEDGEHOGS	HERBARIUM	HIFALUTIN
HARNESSER	HEADLIGHT	HEDGEROWS	HERBICIDE	HIGHBALLS
HARNESSES	HEADLINED	HEDONISTS	HERBIVORE	HIGHBROWS
HARPOONED	HEADLINER	HEEDFULLY	HERCULEAN	HIGH CHAIR
HARPOONER	HEADLINES	HEELPIECE	HERCYNIAN	HIGH-CLASS
HARQUEBUS	HEADPIECE	HEFTINESS	HEREAFTER	HIGH COURT
HARRIDANS	HEADREACH	HEGEMONIC	HERETICAL	HIGHER-UPS
HARROGATE	HEADRESTS	HEGUMENOS	HEREUNDER	HIGH-FLIER
HARROVIAN	HEADSCARF	HEILBRONN	HERITABLE	HIGH-FLOWN
HARROWING	HEADSHIPS	HEIMDALLR	HERITABLY	HIGH-FLYER
HARSHNESS	HEADSTALL	HEINOUSLY	HERITRESS	HIGH-GRADE
HARTBEEST	HEADSTAND	HEIRESSES	HERMITAGE	HIGH HOPES
HARTSHORN	HEAD START	HEIRLOOMS	HERMITIAN	HIGH HORSE
HARUSPICY	HEADSTOCK	HELGOLAND	HERNIATED	HIGH JINKS
HARVESTED	HEADSTONE	HELICALLY	HERODOTUS	HIGH JUMPS
HARVESTER	HEADWARDS	HELICLINE	HESELTINE	HIGHLANDS
HASDRUBAL	HEADWINDS	HELIOSTAT	HESITANCY	HIGH-LEVEL
HASHEMITE	HEADWORDS	HELIOTYPE	HESITATED	HIGHLIGHT
HASTENING	HEALINGLY	HELIOZOAN	HESITATER	HIGH POINT
HASTINESS	HEALTHFUL	HELIPORTS	HESPERIAN	HIGH-RISES
HATCHABLE	HEALTHIER	HELLDIVER	HESSONITE	HIGH ROADS
HATCHBACK	HEALTHILY	HELLEBORE	HESYCHAST	HIGH-SPEED
HATCHLING	HEARKENED	HELLENIAN	HETAERISM	HIGH SPOTS
HATCHMENT	HEARKENER	HELLENISM	HETAERIST	HIGH TABLE
HATCHWAYS	HEARTACHE	HELLENIST	HETAIRISM	HIGH TIDES
HATEFULLY	HEARTBEAT	HELLENIZE	HETERODOX	HIGH-TONED
HAT TRICKS	HEARTBURN	HELLHOUND	HETERONYM	HIGH WATER
HAUGHTIER	HEARTENED	HELLISHLY	HETEROSIS	HIJACKERS
HAUGHTILY	HEARTFELT	HELPFULLY	HEURISTIC	HIJACKING
HAVE A	HEARTHRUG	HELPMATES	HEXACHORD	HILARIOUS
BASH	HEARTIEST	HELVELLYN	HEXAGONAL	HILLBILLY
HAVENLESS	HEARTLAND	HELVETIAN	HEXAGRAMS	HILLOCKED
HAVERSACK	HEARTLESS	HELVETIUS	HEXAMETER	HILLSIDES
HAVERSIAN	HEARTSICK	HEMIALGIA	HEXAPODIC	HILVERSUM
HAVERSINE	HEARTSOME	HEMICYCLE	HEXASTICH	HIMALAYAS
HAWKSBILL	HEARTWOOD	HEMINGWAY	HEXASTYLE	HIMYARITE
HAWSEHOLE	HEARTWORM	HEMISTICH	HEXATEUCH	HINDBRAIN
HAWSEPIPE	HEATHERED	HEMITROPE	HEYERDAHL	HINDERING

HINDOOISM	HOIDENISH	HOMONYMIC	HORSESHIT	HUE AND
HINDRANCE	HOI POLLOI	HOMOPHILE	HORSESHOE	CRY
HINDSIGHT	HOLARCTIC	HOMOPHONE	HORSETAIL	HUFFINESS
HINDU KUSH	HOLDOVERS	HOMOPHONY	HORSEWEED	HUGH CAPET
HINDUSTAN	HOLD WATER	HOMOPHYLY	HORSEWHIP	HU-HO-HAO-
HINGELESS	HOLE IN	HOMOPLASY	HORSINESS	T'E
HINGELIKE	ONE	HOMOPOLAR	HORTATIVE	HUMANISTS
HIP FLASKS	HOLIDAYED	HOMOSPORY	HORTATORY	HUMANIZED
HIP POCKET	HOLINSHED	HOMOTAXIC	HOSPITALS	HUMANIZER
HIPPOCRAS	HOLLANDER	HOMOTAXIS	HOSPITIUM	HUMANKIND
HIPPOLYTA	HOLLANDIA	HONEYBEES	HOSTELLER	HUMAN-LIKE
HIPPOLYTE	HOLLERING	HONEYCOMB	HOSTESSES	HUMANNESS
HIRELINGS	HOLLOWEST	HONEYEDLY	HOSTILELY	HUMANOIDS
HIROSHIGE	HOLLOWING	HONEY-LIKE	HOSTILITY	HUMAN RACE
HIROSHIMA	HOLLYHOCK	HONEYMOON	HOTELIERS	HUMBLEBEE
HIRUNDINE	HOLLYWOOD	HONEYTRAP	HOTFOOTED	HUMBUGGER
HISPIDITY	HOLOCAINE	HONKY-TONK	HOTHEADED	HUMDINGER
HISTAMINE	HOLOCAUST	HONORARIA	HOTHOUSES	HUMECTANT
HISTIDINE	HOLOCRINE	HONORIFIC	HOTPLATES	HUMERUSES
HISTOGENY	HOLOGRAMS	HONOR ROLL	HOT POTATO	HUMIDNESS
HISTOGRAM	HOLOGRAPH	HONOURING	HOTTENTOT	HUMILIATE
HISTOLOGY	HOLOPHYTE	HOODOOISM	HOT WATERS	HUMONGOUS
HISTORIAN	HOLOTYPIC	HOOFBOUND	HOURGLASS	HUMORISTS
HISTORIES	HOLSTEINS	HOOK NOSED	HOUSEBOAT	HUMOURFUL
HIT AND	HOLSTERED	HOOK-NOSED	HOUSEBOYS	HUMOURING
RUN	HOLY GHOST	HOOKWORMS	HOUSECARL	HUMPBACKS
HIT-AND-	HOLY GRAIL	HOOLIGANS	HOUSECOAT	HUMPINESS
RUN	HOLYSTONE	HOOTNANNY	HOUSEHOLD	HUNCHBACK
HITCHCOCK	HOME ALONE	HOOVERING	HOUSELEEK	HUNDREDTH
HITCHHIKE	HOME FRONT	HOPE CHEST	HOUSELESS	HUNGARIAN
HITLERISM	HOMEGROWN	HOPEFULLY	HOUSELINE	HUNGERING
HIT-OR-	HOME GUARD	HOP GARDEN	HOUSEMAID	HUNGRIEST
MISS	HOME HELPS	HOPLOLOGY	HOUSEROOM	HUNKY DORY
HIT PARADE	HOMELANDS	HOPSCOTCH	HOUSETOPS	HUNKY-DORY
HIT WICKET	HOMELIEST	HOREHOUND	HOUSEWIFE	HUNNISHLY
HOARDINGS	HOMEMAKER	HORNBILLS	HOUSEWORK	HURRICANE
HOARFROST	HOME MOVIE	HORNINESS	HOUSTONIA	HURRIEDLY
HOARHOUND	HOMEOPATH	HORNPIPES	HOVERPORT	HURTFULLY
HOARINESS	HOMEOWNER	HORNSTONE	HOW ARE	HUSBANDED
HOATCHING	HOMESTEAD	HOROLOGIC	YOU	HUSBANDER
HOBBESIAN	HOMETOWNS	HOROSCOPE	HOWITZERS	HUSBANDRY
HOBGOBLIN	HOME TRUTH	HOROSCOPY	HOWLINGLY	HUSH MONEY
HOBNAILED	HOMEWARDS	HORRIFIED	HOWSOEVER	HUSKINESS
HOBNOBBED	HOMEYNESS	HORSEBACK	HOWTOWDIE	HYACINTHS
HO CHI	HOMICIDAL	HORSE FAIR	HOYDENISH	HYBRIDISM
MINH	HOMICIDES	HORSEHAIR	HSUAN	HYBRIDITY
HODOMETER	HOMILETIC	HORSEHIDE	T'UNG	HYBRIDIZE
HODOMETRY	HOMOGRAFT	HORSELESS	HUBRISTIC	HYBRISTIC
HODOSCOPE	HOMOGRAPH	HORSELIKE	HUCKABACK	HYDANTOIN
HOGGISHLY	HOMOLYSIS	HORSEMINT	HUCKSTERS	HYDATHODE
HOGSHEADS	HOMOLYTIC	HORSEPLAY		HYDERABAD
HOHENLOHE				

HYDRANGEA
HYDRASTIS
HYDRATION
HYDRAULIC
HYDRAZINE
HYDRAZOIC
HYDRIODIC
HYDROCELE
HYDROFOIL
HYDROLOGY
HYDROLYSE
HYDROLYTE
HYGIENIST
HYPERBOLA
HYPERBOLE
HYPERCUBE
HYPERTEXT
HYPHENATE
HYPNOTISM
HYPNOTIST
HYPNOTIZE
HYPOCRISY
HYPOCRITE
HYSTERICS

I
IBUPROFEN
ICE CREAMS
ICE HOCKEY
ICELANDER
ICELANDIC
ICE SHEETS
ICE SKATED
ICE-SKATED
ICE-SKATER
ICE SKATES
ICHNEUMON
ICHNOLOGY
ICHTHYOID
ICONOLOGY
IDEALISTS
IDEALIZED
IDEALIZER
IDENTICAL
IDENTIKIT
IDEOGRAMS
IDEOLOGUE
IDEOMOTOR
IDIOBLAST
IDIOLECTS
IDIOMATIC

IDIOPATHY
IDIOPHONE
IDOLATERS
IDOLIZING
IGNESCENT
IGNITABLE
IGNORAMUS
IGNORANCE
IGNORATIO
IGUANODON
ILEOSTOMY
ILL AT
  EASE
ILLAWARRA
ILLEGALLY
ILLEGIBLE
ILLEGIBLY
ILL GOTTEN
ILL-GOTTEN
ILLIBERAL
ILLICITLY
ILLNESSES
ILLOGICAL
ILL-OMENED
ILLUSIONS
IMAGINARY
IMAGINING
IMAGISTIC
IMBALANCE
IMBECILES
IMBEDDING
IMBRICATE
IMBROGLIO
IMIDAZOLE
IMITATING
IMITATION
IMITATIVE
IMITATORS
IMMANENCE
IMMANENCY
IMMEDIACY
IMMEDIATE
IMMENSELY
IMMENSITY
IMMERSING
IMMERSION
IMMIGRANT
IMMIGRATE
IMMINENCE
IMMINGHAM
IMMODESTY

IMMOLATED
IMMOLATOR
IMMORALLY
IMMORTALS
IMMOVABLE
IMMOVABLY
IMMUNIZED
IMMUNIZER
IMMUTABLE
IMMUTABLY
IMPACTING
IMPACTION
IMPAIRING
IMPARTIAL
IMPARTING
IMPASSION
IMPASSIVE
IMPATIENS
IMPATIENT
IMPEACHED
IMPEACHER
IMPEDANCE
IMPELLENT
IMPELLING
IMPENDING
IMPERFECT
IMPERILED
IMPERIOUS
IMPETRATE
IMPETUOUS
IMPETUSES
IMPIETIES
IMPINGING
IMPIOUSLY
IMPLANTED
IMPLANTER
IMPLEADER
IMPLEMENT
IMPLICATE
IMPLODING
IMPLORING
IMPLOSION
IMPLOSIVE
IMPOLITIC
IMPORTANT
IMPORTERS
IMPORTING
IMPORTUNE
IMPOSABLE
IMPOSTORS
IMPOSTURE

IMPOTENCE
IMPOUNDED
IMPOUNDER
IMPRECATE
IMPRECISE
IMPRESSED
IMPRESSER
IMPRESSES
IMPRINTED
IMPRINTER
IMPROBITY
IMPROMPTU
IMPROVING
IMPROVISE
IMPRUDENT
IMPUDENCE
IMPUGNING
IMPULSION
IMPULSIVE
IMPUTABLE
IN A BAD
  WAY
INABILITY
INAMORATA
INANIMATE
INANITIES
INANITION
INAPTNESS
INAUDIBLE
INAUDIBLY
INAUGURAL
IN BETWEEN
INCAPABLE
INCAPABLY
INCARNATE
INCAUTION
INCENSING
INCENTIVE
INCEPTION
INCEPTIVE
INCESSANT
INCIDENCE
INCIDENTS
INCIPIENT
INCISIONS
INCISURAL
INCLEMENT
INCLINING
INCLOSING
INCLOSURE
INCLUDING

INCLUSION
INCLUSIVE
INCOGNITO
INCOME TAX
INCOMMODE
INCORRECT
INCORRUPT
INCREASED
INCREASER
INCREASES
INCREMENT
INCRETION
INCUBATED
INCUBATOR
INCUBUSES
INCULCATE
INCULPATE
INCUMBENT
INCURABLE
INCURABLY
INCURIOUS
INCURRENT
INCURRING
INCURSION
INCURSIVE
INCURVATE
INDECENCY
INDECORUM
INDELIBLE
INDELIBLY
INDEMNIFY
INDEMNITY
INDENTING
INDENTION
INDENTURE
INDEXICAL
INDIAN INK
INDICATED
INDICATOR
INDICTING
INDIGENCE
INDIGNANT
INDIGNITY
INDIGOTIC
INDISPOSE
INDOCHINA
INDOLENCE
INDONESIA
INDORSING
INDRAUGHT
INDUCIBLE

INDUCTILE	INFUSORIA	INOTROPIC	INSWINGER	INTERVENE
INDUCTING	IN GENERAL	IN PATIENT	INTAGLIOS	INTERVIEW
INDUCTION	INGENIOUS	IN-PATIENT	INTEGRAND	INTERWOVE
INDUCTIVE	INGENUITY	INPUTTING	INTEGRANT	INTESTACY
INDULGENT	INGENUOUS	INQUILINE	INTEGRATE	INTESTATE
INDULGING	INGESTING	INQUIRIES	INTEGRITY	INTESTINE
INEBRIANT	INGESTION	INQUIRING	INTELLECT	IN THE
INEBRIATE	INGESTIVE	INQUORATE	INTENDANT	CLUB
INEBRIETY	INGLENOOK	INSCRIBED	INTENDEDS	IN THE
INEFFABLE	INGRAINED	INSCRIBER	INTENDING	DARK
INEFFABLY	INGROWING	INSECTEAN	INTENSELY	IN THE
INELASTIC	INHABITED	INSELBERG	INTENSIFY	LINE
INELEGANT	INHALANTS	INSENSATE	INTENSION	IN THE
INEPTNESS	INHALATOR	INSERTING	INTENSITY	SOUP
INERTNESS	INHAMBANE	INSERTION	INTENSIVE	IN THE
INFANTILE	INHARMONY	IN-SERVICE	INTENTION	SWIM
INFARCTED	IN HARNESS	INSETTING	INTER ALIA	INTIMATED
INFATUATE	INHERENCE	INSIDE JOB	INTERBRED	INTIMATES
INFECTING	INHERITED	INSIDE OUT	INTERCEDE	INTORSION
INFECTION	INHERITOR	INSIDIOUS	INTERCEPT	IN TRANSIT
INFECTIVE	INHIBITED	INSINCERE	INTERCITY	INTRICACY
INFERABLE	INHIBITER	INSINUATE	INTERCOMS	INTRICATE
INFERENCE	INHIBITOR	INSIPIDLY	INTERCROP	INTRIGUED
INFERIORS	INITIALED	INSISTENT	INTERDICT	INTRIGUER
INFERRING	INITIALER	INSISTING	INTERESTS	INTRIGUES
INFERTILE	INITIALLY	IN SO FAR	INTERFACE	INTRINSIC
INFESTING	INITIATED	AS	INTERFERE	INTRODUCE
INFIELDER	INITIATES	INSOLENCE	INTERFILE	INTROITAL
INFIGHTER	INITIATOR	INSOLUBLE	INTERFUSE	INTROJECT
INFIRMARY	INJECTING	INSOLVENT	INTERIORS	INTROVERT
INFIRMITY	INJECTION	INSOMNIAC	INTERJECT	INTRUDERS
INFLAMING	INJECTIVE	INSPECTED	INTERLACE	INTRUDING
INFLATING	INJURABLE	INSPECTOR	INTERLARD	INTRUSION
INFLATION	INJURIOUS	INSPIRING	INTERLEAF	INTRUSIVE
INFLECTED	INJUSTICE	INSTALLED	INTERLINE	INTRUSTED
INFLECTOR	INKSTANDS	INSTALLER	INTERLINK	INTUITING
INFLICTED	INMIGRANT	INSTANCED	INTERLOCK	INTUITION
INFLICTER	INNER CITY	INSTANCES	INTERLOPE	INTUITIVE
INFLUENCE	INNERMOST	INSTANTER	INTERLUDE	INTUMESCE
INFLUENZA	INNER TUBE	INSTANTLY	INTERMENT	INUNCTION
INFORMANT	INNERVATE	INSTIGATE	INTERNEES	INUNDATED
INFORMERS	INNKEEPER	INSTILLED	INTERNING	INUNDATOR
INFORMING	INN KEEPER	INSTILLER	INTERNIST	INUTILITY
INFRACTOR	INNOCENCE	INSTINCTS	INTERNODE	INVADABLE
INFRADIAN	INNOCUOUS	INSTITUTE	INTERPLAY	INVALIDED
INFRINGED	INNOVATED	INSULATED	INTERPOSE	INVALIDLY
INFRINGER	INNOVATOR	INSULATOR	INTERPRET	INVARIANT
INFURIATE	INNSBRUCK	INSULTING	INTERRING	INVASIONS
INFUSCATE	INNUENDOS	INSURABLE	INTERRUPT	INVECTIVE
INFUSIBLE	INOCULATE	INSURANCE	INTERSECT	INVEIGHED
INFUSIONS	INORGANIC	INSURGENT	INTERVALS	INVEIGHER
				INVEIGLED

INVEIGLER
INVENTING
INVENTION
INVENTIVE
INVENTORS
INVENTORY
INVERARAY
INVERNESS
INVERSELY
INVERSION
INVERSIVE
INVERTASE
INVERTING
INVESTING
INVIDIOUS
INVIOLACY
INVIOLATE
INVISIBLE
INVISIBLY
INVOCABLE
INVOICING
INVOLUCEL
INVOLUCRE
INVOLVING
IODOMETRY
IONOPAUSE
IPSO FACTO
IRASCIBLE
IRASCIBLY
IRIAN JAYA
IRIDOTOMY
IRISH BULL
IRISH STEW
IRONBOUND
IRON CROSS
IRON HORSE
IRONSIDES
IRONSTONE
IRONWORKS
IROQUOIAN
IRRADIANT
IRRADIATE
IRRAWADDY
IRREGULAR
IRRIGABLE
IRRIGATED
IRRIGATOR
IRRITABLE
IRRITABLY
IRRITANTS
IRRITATED

IRRITATOR
IRRUPTION
IRRUPTIVE
ISAGOGICS
ISALLOBAR
ISCHAEMIA
ISINGLASS
ISLAMABAD
ISLANDERS
ISLE OF
    MAN
ISLINGTON
ISOBARISM
ISOBATHIC
ISOCHORIC
ISOCLINAL
ISOCRATIC
ISOGAMETE
ISOGAMOUS
ISOGENOUS
ISOLATING
ISOLATION
ISOLATIVE
ISOLOGOUS
ISOMERISM
ISOMERIZE
ISOMEROUS
ISOMETRIC
ISONIAZID
ISOOCTANE
ISOPROPYL
ISOSCELES
ISOSMOTIC
ISOSTATIC
ISOSTERIC
ISOTACTIC
ISOTHERAL
ISOTHERMS
ISOTROPIC
ISRAELITE
ISTHMUSES
ITALICIZE
ITCHINESS
ITCHY FEET
ITCHY PALM
ITEMIZING
ITERATION
ITERATIVE
ITINERANT
ITINERARY
ITINERATE

ITSY BITSY
ITSY-BITSY
IVY LEAGUE

J

JABBERERS
JABBERING
JABORANDI
JACARANDA
JACKASSES
JACKBOOTS
JACK FROST
JACKFRUIT
JACK KNIFE
JACKSHAFT
JACKSMELT
JACKSNIPE
JACOBITES
JAILBIRDS
JAILBREAK
JAILHOUSE
JALANDHAR
JAMBOREES
JAM-PACKED
JANISSARY
JANSENISM
JANSENIST
JANUARIES
JAPANNING
JAPONICAS
JARGONIZE
JAUNDICED
JAUNTIEST
JAYWALKED
JAYWALKER
JEALOUSLY
JEERINGLY
JELLY BEAN
JELLYFISH
JELLY ROLL
JEREMIADS
JERKINESS
JERKINGLY
JEROBOAMS
JERUSALEM
JESTINGLY
JESUITISM
JET ENGINE
JET-SETTER
JET STREAM
JEWELFISH

JEWELLERS
JEWELLERY
JEWELLING
JEW'S
    HARPS
JIB-HEADED
JITTERBUG
JOBCENTRE
JOB CENTRE
JOBSWORTH
JOCKEYING
JOCKSTRAP
JOCULARLY
JOCUNDITY
JOE PUBLIC
JOINTRESS
JOINTWORM
JOLLINESS
JONKOPING
JORDANIAN
JOSS STICK
JOURNEYED
JOURNEYER
JOVIALITY
JOYLESSLY
JOYRIDERS
JOYRIDING
JOYSTICKS
JUBILANCE
JUDDERING
JUDGEABLE
JUDGEMENT
JUDGESHIP
JUDGINGLY
JUDGMENTS
JUDICABLE
JUDICATOR
JUDICIARY
JUDICIOUS
JUICINESS
JUKEBOXES
JULLUNDUR
JUMBO JETS
JUMPINESS
JUMP START
JUMP-START
JUMPSUITS
JUNCTIONS
JUNCTURES
JUNGLE GYM
JUNKETING

JUNOESQUE
JURIDICAL
JURY BOXES
JUSTICIAR
JUSTIFIED
JUSTIFIER
JUTLANDER
JUVENILES
JUVENILIA
JUXTAPOSE

K

KADAITCHA
KADIYEVKA
KAGOSHIMA
KAISERDOM
KALAMAZOO
KALANCHOE
KAMA SUTRA
KAMCHATKA
KAMILAROI
KAMPUCHEA
KANAMYCIN
KANGAROOS
KAOHSIUNG
KAOLINITE
KARABINER
KARAGANDA
KARAKORAM
KARAKORUM
KARLSRUHE
KARNATAKA
KARYOGAMY
KARYOSOME
KARYOTYPE
KATABATIC
KATANGESE
KATHIAWAR
KAWAGUCHI
KEEP ORDER
KEEPSAKES
KEEP STATE
KELTICISM
KELTICIST
KENNELING
KENNELLED
KENTLEDGE
KEPT WOMAN
KEPT WOMEN
KERATITIS
KERATOSIS

KERBSTONE	KNACKERED	LACERABLE	LANDWARDS	LAW SCHOOL
KERCHIEFS	KNAPSACKS	LACERATED	LANGOUSTE	LAXATIVES
KERFUFFLE	KNAVERIES	LACERTIAN	LANGUAGES	LAYABOUTS
KETONURIA	KNAVISHLY	LACHRYMAL	LANGUEDOC	LAY FIGURE
KETTERING	KNIFE EDGE	LACINIATE	LANGUIDLY	LAYPERSON
KEYBOARDS	KNIFE-EDGE	LACQUERED	LANKINESS	LAY READER
KEYHOLDER	KNIGHTING	LACQUERER	LANOLATED	LAY SISTER
KEYSTONES	KNIPHOFIA	LACTATION	LANTHANUM	LAZARETTO
KEYSTROKE	KNITTABLE	LADDERING	LAODICEAN	LAZYBONES
KIBBUTZES	KNOBBLIER	LADIES MAN	LAPLANDER	LEADERENE
KIBBUTZIM	KNOCKDOWN	LADIES'	LARCENIES	LEAD TIMES
KICKBACKS	KNOCKOUTS	MAN	LARCENIST	LEAFINESS
KICK-START	KNOTGRASS	LADIES'	LARCENOUS	LEAFLETED
KID GLOVES	KNOTTIEST	MEN	LARGENESS	LEAF MOULD
KIDNAPING	KNOWINGLY	LADYBIRDS	LARGHETTO	LEAFSTALK
KIDNAPPED	KNOWLEDGE	LADYSHIPS	LARKSPURS	LEAKINESS
KIDNAPPER	KNOXVILLE	LAEVULOSE	LARVICIDE	LEAP YEARS
KIDSTAKES	KNUCKLING	LAGOMORPH	LARYNGEAL	LEARNABLE
KIESERITE	KONIOLOGY	LALLATION	LASHINGLY	LEARNEDLY
KILLARNEY	KOOKINESS	LAMAISTIC	LAS PALMAS	LEASEBACK
KILLIFISH	KOSCIUSKO	LAMBASTED	LASSITUDE	LEASEHOLD
KILLINGLY	KOTA BHARU	LAMBSKINS	LAST-DITCH	LEASTWAYS
KILOBYTES	KOWTOWING	LAME DUCKS	LASTINGLY	LEAVENING
KILOCYCLE	KOZHIKODE	LAMENTING	LAST RITES	LECHEROUS
KILOGRAMS	KRASNODAR	LAMINABLE	LAST STRAW	LECTORATE
KILOHERTZ	KRAUTROCK	LAMINARIA	LAST THING	LECTURERS
KILOLITRE	KRIVOY ROG	LAMINATED	LATCHKEYS	LECTURING
KILOMETRE	KRONSTADT	LAMINATES	LATECOMER	LEERINGLY
KILOWATTS	KUIBYSHEV	LAMINATOR	LATERALLY	LEE SHORES
KIMBERLEY	KURDISTAN	LAMINITIS	LATERITIC	LEFTOVERS
KINDLIEST	KURRAJONG	LAMP-BLACK	LATHERING	LEFTWARDS
KINEMATIC	KWANGTUNG	LAMPOONED	LATIMERIA	LEGALIZED
KINGLIEST	KYMOGRAPH	LAMPOONER	LATINIZER	LEGATIONS
KINGMAKER		LAMPPOSTS	LATITUDES	LEGENDARY
KING'S	**L**	LAMPSHADE	LATTER-DAY	LEGGINESS
EVIL	LABELLING	LANCASTER	LAUDATION	LEGGINGED
KINGS HEAD	LABELLOID	LANCEWOOD	LAUDATORY	LEGIONARY
KING'S	LABIALISM	LANCINATE	LAUGHABLE	LEGISLATE
LYNN	LABIALITY	LAND AGENT	LAUGHABLY	LEG-WARMER
KINGSTOWN	LABIALIZE	LANDAULET	LAUNCHING	LEICESTER
KINKINESS	LABORIOUS	LANDFALLS	LAUNCH PAD	LEISURELY
KINSWOMAN	LABOUR DAY	LANDLORDS	LAUNDERED	LEITMOTIF
KIRGHIZIA	LABOURERS	LANDMARKS	LAUNDERER	LEITMOTIV
KIRKCALDY	LABOURING	LANDMINES	LAUNDRESS	LEMNISCUS
KIROVABAD	LABOURISM	LAND OF	LAUNDRIES	LEMON CURD
KISANGANI	LABOURIST	NOD	LAUREATES	LEMON SOLE
KISSINGER	LABOURITE	LANDOWNER	LAVISHING	LEND-LEASE
KITCHENER	LABRADORS	LAND ROVER	LAWGIVING	LENGTHIER
KITTENISH	LABURNUMS	LANDSCAPE	LAWLESSLY	LENGTHILY
KITTIWAKE	LABYRINTH	LANDSLIDE	LAWNMOWER	LENIENTLY
KLEENEXES	LACCOLITH	LANDSLIPS	LAWN PARTY	LENINABAD

LENINAKAN	LIFE CYCLE	LIP READER	LOBECTOMY	LOOK AFTER
LENINGRAD	LIFEGUARD	LIP-READER	LOCAL CALL	LOOK-ALIKE
LENIN PEAK	LIFELINES	LIPSTICKS	LOCALIZED	LOOK ALIVE
LEPONTINE	LIFE PEERS	LIQUATION	LOCALIZER	LOOKING UP
LEPTOSOME	LIFE-SAVER	LIQUEFIED	LOCAL TIME	LOOM-STATE
LEPTOTENE	LIFESPANS	LIQUEFIER	LOCATABLE	LOONINESS
LESSENING	LIFE STORY	LIQUIDATE	LOCATIONS	LOONY BINS
LETHALITY	LIFESTYLE	LIQUIDITY	LOCKERBIE	LOOPHOLES
LETHARGIC	LIFETIMES	LIQUIDIZE	LOCKSMITH	LOOSE ENDS
LETTERBOX	LIGAMENTS	LIQUORICE	LOCOMOTOR	LOOSE-LEAF
LETTERING	LIGATURES	LISPINGLY	LOCUTIONS	LOOSENESS
LEUCOCYTE	LIGHT BULB	LISTENERS	LODESTARS	LOOSENING
LEUCOTOMY	LIGHTENED	LISTENING	LODESTONE	LOQUACITY
LEUKAEMIA	LIGHT-FAST	LISTERISM	LODGEABLE	LORDLIEST
LEVANTINE	LIGHTNESS	LIST PRICE	LOFTINESS	LORDSHIPS
LEVELLERS	LIGHTNING	LITERALLY	LOGAOEDIC	LORGNETTE
LEVELLING	LIGHT RAIL	LITERATIM	LOGARITHM	LORRY PARK
LEVIATHAN	LIGHTSHIP	LITHENESS	LOG CABINS	LOS ALAMOS
LEVIGATOR	LIGHTS OUT	LITHIASIS	LOGICALLY	LOST CAUSE
LEVITATED	LIGHTS-OUT	LITHOLOGY	LOGICIANS	LOTTERIES
LEVITATOR	LIGHT YEAR	LITHOPONE	LOGISTICS	LOUDMOUTH
LEXICALLY	LIGNIFORM	LITHOTOMY	LOGOGRIPH	LOUISBURG
LEXINGTON	LIKELIEST	LITHUANIA	LOGOMACHY	LOUISIANA
LIABILITY	LILY-WHITE	LITIGABLE	LOINCLOTH	LOUNGE BAR
LIBATIONS	LIMA BEANS	LITIGANTS	LOITERERS	LOUSEWORT
LIBELLANT	LIME GREEN	LITIGATED	LOITERING	LOUSINESS
LIBELLING	LIMELIGHT	LITIGATOR	LOLLINGLY	LOVEBIRDS
LIBELLOUS	LIMERICKS	LITIGIOUS	LOLLIPOPS	LOVECHILD
LIBERALLY	LIMESTONE	LITTERBIN	LOLLOPING	LOVE FEAST
LIBERATED	LIMEWATER	LITTERING	LOMBARDIC	LOVELIEST
LIBERATOR	LIMITABLE	LITTORALS	LONELIEST	LOVE MATCH
LIBERTIES	LIMITLESS	LITURGICS	LONE WOLFS	LOVING CUP
LIBERTINE	LIMNOLOGY	LITURGIES	LONG BEACH	LOW COMEDY
LIBIDINAL	LIMOUSINE	LITURGISM	LONGBOATS	LOWERABLE
LIBRARIAN	LIMPIDITY	LITURGIST	LONGCLOTH	LOWER CASE
LIBRARIES	LIMPINGLY	LIVELIEST	LONG EATON	LOWERMOST
LIBRATION	LINCHPINS	LIVERPOOL	LONGEVITY	LOWESTOFT
LIBRATORY	LINEAMENT	LIVERWORT	LONGEVOUS	LOWLANDER
LIBRETTOS	LINEARITY	LIVERYMAN	LONG FACES	LOWLINESS
LIBRIFORM	LINEATION	LIVERYMEN	LONGICORN	LOW-MINDED
LICENSEES	LINEOLATE	LIVESTOCK	LONGINGLY	LOW-NECKED
LICENSING	LINGERERS	LIVE WIRES	LONGITUDE	LOW SEASON
LICHENOID	LINGERING	LIVIDNESS	LONG JOHNS	LOYALISTS
LICHENOUS	LINGUISTS	LJUBLJANA	LONG-LIVED	LOYALTIES
LIDOCAINE	LINGULATE	LLANDUDNO	LONG-RANGE	LUBRICANT
LIEGE LORD	LINKOPING	LOADSTARS	LONGSHIPS	LUBRICATE
LIENTERIC	LINOLEATE	LOADSTONE	LONGSHORE	LUBRICITY
LIFE BELTS	LINOTYPER	LOAMINESS	LONG SHOTS	LUBRICOUS
LIFEBLOOD	LIONIZING	LOAN SHARK	LONG SINCE	LUCIFERIN
LIFEBOATS	LIPOLYSIS	LOANWORDS	LONGUEUIL	LUCKINESS
LIFE BUOYS	LIPOLYTIC	LOATHSOME	LONGUEURS	LUCKY DIPS

LUCRATIVE
LUCUBRATE
LUDICROUS
LUFTWAFFE
LULLABIES
LULLINGLY
LUMBERING
LUMBERMAN
LUMBERMEN
LUMBRICAL
LUMINAIRE
LUMINANCE
LUMINESCE
LUMPINESS
LUNATICAL
LUNISOLAR
LUNITIDAL
LURIDNESS
LURKINGLY
LUSTFULLY
LUSTINESS
LUTANISTS
LUTHERISM
LUXEMBURG
LUXURIANT
LUXURIATE
LUXURIOUS
LYCHGATES
LYME REGIS
LYMINGTON
LYMPHATIC
LYONNAISE
LYOPHILIC
LYOPHOBIC
LYREBIRDS
LYRICALLY
LYRICISMS
LYRICISTS
LYSIMETER
LYSOSOMAL

M
MACARONIC
MACAROONS
MACEDOINE
MACEDONIA
MACERATED
MACERATER
MACHINATE
MACHINERY
MACHINING

MACHINIST
MACHMETER
MACKENZIE
MACKERELS
MACROCOSM
MACROCYST
MACROCYTE
MACRUROID
MACRUROUS
MADDENING
MADELEINE
MAD HATTER
MADHOUSES
MADREPORE
MADRIGALS
MAELSTROM
MAGAZINES
MAGDEBURG
MAGICALLY
MAGIC EYES
MAGICIANS
MAGIC WAND
MAGISTERY
MAGISTRAL
MAGMATISM
MAGNESIAN
MAGNESITE
MAGNESIUM
MAGNETICS
MAGNETISM
MAGNETITE
MAGNETIZE
MAGNETRON
MAGNIFICO
MAGNIFIED
MAGNIFIER
MAGNITUDE
MAGNOLIAS
MAHAJANGA
MAHARAJAH
MAHARAJAS
MAHARANIS
MAIDSTONE
MAIDUGURI
MAILBOXES
MAILCOACH
MAIL ORDER
MAILSHOTS
MAINFRAME
MAINLINED
MAIN LINES

MAINMASTS
MAINSAILS
MAINSHEET
MAINSTAYS
MAJESTICS
MAJESTIES
MAJORDOMO
MAJOR DOMO
MAJORETTE
MAJOR SUIT
MAJUSCULE
MAKE A
  MOVE
MAKE MERRY
MAKE PEACE
MAKE READY
MAKESHIFT
MAKEYEVKA
MALACHITE
MALADROIT
MALAGUENA
MALANDERS
MALATHION
MALAYALAM
MALAYSIAN
MALDIVIAN
MALFORMED
MALGRE LUI
MALIC ACID
MALICIOUS
MALIGNANT
MALIGNING
MALIGNITY
MALLEABLE
MALLEMUCK
MALLEOLAR
MALLEOLUS
MALTINESS
MALTSTERS
MALVOISIE
MAMA'S
  BOYS
MAMILLARY
MAMILLATE
MAMMALIAN
MAMMALOGY
MAMMOGRAM
MAMMONISM
MAMMONIST
MANACLING

MAN-AT-
  ARMS
MANCHURIA
MANCUNIAN
MANDARINS
MANDATARY
MANDATING
MANDATORY
MANDIBLES
MANDOLINS
MANDRAKES
MANDRILLS
MAN-EATERS
MAN-EATING
MANEUVERS
MAN FRIDAY
MANGALORE
MANGANATE
MANGANESE
MANGANITE
MANGANOUS
MANGETOUT
MANGINESS
MANGROVES
MANHANDLE
MANHATTAN
MANHUNTER
MANICURED
MANICURES
MANIFESTO
MANIFESTS
MANIFOLDS
MANIZALES
MANLINESS
MANNEQUIN
MANNERISM
MANNERIST
MANNISHLY
MANOEUVRE
MANOMETER
MANOMETRY
MANSFIELD
MANTILLAS
MANUBRIAL
MANUBRIUM
MANY-SIDED
MAPLE LEAF
MARACAIBO
MARATHONS
MARAUDERS
MARAUDING

MARCASITE
MARCH HARE
MARCH-PAST
MARCO POLO
MARDI GRAS
MARE'S
  NEST
MARGARINE
MARGARITA
MARGARITE
MARGINATE
MARIEHAMN
MARIENBAD
MARIGOLDS
MARIJUANA
MARINADES
MARINATED
MARITALLY
MARKDOWNS
MARKETEER
MARKETERS
MARKETING
MARK TWAIN
MARMALADE
MARMOREAL
MARMOSETS
MAROONING
MARQUETRY
MARQUISES
MARRAKECH
MARRIAGES
MARROWFAT
MARSEILLE
MARSHALCY
MARSHALED
MARSUPIAL
MARSUPIUM
MARTINETS
MARTINMAS
MARTYRDOM
MARTYRING
MARVELING
MARVELLED
MARZIPANS
MASCULINE
MASOCHISM
MASOCHIST
MASSACRED
MASSACRER
MASSACRES
MASSAGING

MASSIVELY	MEATBALLS	MEMORIALS	MESOPAUSE	MICROTOME
MASS MEDIA	MEATINESS	MEMORIZED	MESOPHYLL	MICROTOMY
MASTERDOM	MECHANICS	MEMORIZER	MESOPHYTE	MICROTONE
MASTERFUL	MECHANISM	MEMSAHIBS	MESSALINE	MICROWAVE
MASTERING	MECHANIST	MENADIONE	MESSENGER	MIDDLE AGE
MASTER KEY	MECHANIZE	MENAGERIE	MESSIANIC	MIDDLEMAN
MASTHEADS	MEDALLION	MEN-AT-	MESSIEURS	MIDDLEMEN
MASTICATE	MEDALLIST	ARMS	MESSINESS	MIDDLESEX
MASTODONS	MEDIAEVAL	MENDACITY	MESTRANOL	MIDDLETON
MATAMOROS	MEDIATING	MENDELIAN	METABOLIC	MIDHEAVEN
MATCHLESS	MEDIATION	MENDELISM	METALLINE	MIDNIGHTS
MATCHMARK	MEDIATIVE	MENDICANT	METALLING	MIDPOINTS
MATCH PLAY	MEDIATIZE	MENISCOID	METALLIST	MIDSTREAM
MATCHWOOD	MEDIATORS	MENOPAUSE	METALLIZE	MIDSUMMER
MATELASSE	MEDICABLE	MEN'S	METALLOID	MID-WICKET
MATERIALS	MEDICABLY	ROOMS	METALWORK	MIDWIFERY
MATERNITY	MEDICALLY	MENSTRUAL	METAMERAL	MIDWINTER
MATEYNESS	MEDICATED	MENSTRUUM	METAMERIC	MIFFINESS
MATRIARCH	MEDICINAL	MENTAL AGE	METAPHASE	MIGHTIEST
MATRICIDE	MEDICINES	MENTALISM	METAPHORS	MIGRAINES
MATRIMONY	MEDITATED	MENTALITY	METAPLASM	MIGRATING
MATRONAGE	MEDITATOR	MENTIONED	METAXYLEM	MIGRATION
MATSUMOTO	MEDULLARY	MENTIONER	METEORITE	MIGRATORY
MATSUYAMA	MEGACYCLE	MENTORIAL	METEOROID	MILCH COWS
MATTERING	MEGADEATH	MEPACRINE	METHADONE	MILESTONE
MATUTINAL	MEGAHERTZ	MERBROMIN	METHODISM	MILITANCY
MAULSTICK	MEGALITHS	MERCAPTAN	METHODIST	MILITANTS
MAUNDERED	MEGAPHONE	MERCENARY	METHODIZE	MILITARIA
MAUNDERER	MEGASPORE	MERCERIZE	METHOXIDE	MILITATED
MAURITIAN	MEGASTORE	MERCHANTS	METHYLATE	MILK FLOAT
MAURITIUS	MEGHALAYA	MERCILESS	METHYLENE	MILKINESS
MAUSOLEAN	MELANESIA	MERCURATE	METRALGIA	MILKMAIDS
MAUSOLEUM	MELANOSIS	MERCURIAL	METRICIZE	MILK SHAKE
MAVERICKS	MELATONIN	MERCUROUS	METRIC TON	MILK TOOTH
MAWKISHLY	MELBOURNE	MERGANSER	METRIFIER	MILLBOARD
MAXILLARY	MELIORATE	MERIDIANS	METROLOGY	MILLENARY
MAXIMALLY	MELIORISM	MERINGUES	METRONOME	MILLENNIA
MAXIMIZED	MELITOPOL	MERITEDLY	MEZZANINE	MILLEPEDE
MAXIMIZER	MELLOWEST	MERITLESS	MEZZOTINT	MILLEPORE
MAYFLOWER	MELLOWING	MEROCRINE	MICACEOUS	MILLERITE
MAYORALTY	MELODIOUS	MEROZOITE	MICHOACAN	MILLIBARS
MAYORSHIP	MELODIZER	MERRIMENT	MICROBIAL	MILLIGRAM
MBUJIMAYI	MELODRAMA	MERRINESS	MICROCHIP	MILLINERS
MCCARTNEY	MELTDOWNS	MERSEBURG	MICROCOPY	MILLINERY
MEANDERED	MELTINGLY	MESCALINE	MICROCOSM	MILLIONTH
MEANDERER	MELTWATER	MESENTERY	MICROCYTE	MILLIPEDE
MEANDROUS	MELUNGEON	MESICALLY	MICRODONT	MILLIVOLT
MEANS TEST	MEMBRANES	MESMERISM	MICROFILM	MILLPONDS
MEANTIMES	MEMORABLE	MESMERIST	MICROMESH	MILLSTONE
MEANWHILE	MEMORABLY	MESMERIZE	MICROPYLE	MILLWHEEL
MEASURING	MEMORANDA	MESOMORPH	MICROSOME	MILOMETER

MILWAUKEE	MISMANAGE	MOLECULAR	MONOMETER	MORTALITY
MIMICKING	MISNOMERS	MOLECULES	MONOPHAGY	MORTAL SIN
MINARETED	MISONEISM	MOLEHILLS	MONOPHONY	MORTGAGED
MINCEMEAT	MISONEIST	MOLESKINS	MONOPLANE	MORTGAGEE
MINCE PIES	MISPLACED	MOLESTERS	MONOPSONY	MORTGAGES
MINCINGLY	MISPRINTS	MOLESTING	MONORAILS	MORTGAGOR
MINEFIELD	MISQUOTED	MOLLIFIED	MONOSOMIC	MORTICIAN
MINELAYER	MISREPORT	MOLLIFIER	MONOSTICH	MORTIFIED
MINIATURE	MISSHAPEN	MOLLUSCAN	MONOSTOME	MORTIFIER
MINIBUSES	MISSILERY	MOLYBDATE	MONOTONIC	MOSAICIST
MINIDRESS	MISSIONER	MOLYBDOUS	MONOTREME	MOSCHATEL
MINIMALLY	MISSTATED	MOMENTARY	MONOTYPER	MOSQUITOS
MINIMIZED	MISTAKING	MOMENTOUS	MONOTYPIC	MOSS-GROWN
MINIMIZER	MISTIMING	MOMENTUMS	MONOXIDES	MOSSINESS
MINISCULE	MISTINESS	MONACHISM	MONSIGNOR	MOTHBALLS
MINISKIRT	MISTLETOE	MONADNOCK	MONSTROUS	MOTH EATEN
MINISTERS	MISTRIALS	MONARCHAL	MONTAUBAN	MOTH-EATEN
MINITRACK	MITICIDAL	MONASTERY	MONT BLANC	MOTHERING
MINNESOTA	MITIGABLE	MONATOMIC	MONTERREY	MOTHPROOF
MINOR SUIT	MITIGATED	MONEYBAGS	MONTHLIES	MOTIONING
MINSTRELS	MITIGATOR	MONEYLESS	MONTICULE	MOTIVATED
MINT JULEP	MITREWORT	MONEYWORT	MONTREUIL	MOTOCROSS
MINUSCULE	MNEMONICS	MONGERING	MONUMENTS	MOTORBIKE
MINUTE GUN	MOANINGLY	MONGOLIAN	MONZONITE	MOTORBOAT
MINUTE MAN	MOBILIZED	MONGOLISM	MOODINESS	MOTORCADE
MIRRORING	MOBOCRACY	MONGOLOID	MOONBEAMS	MOTORCARS
MIRTHLESS	MOCCASINS	MONGOOSES	MOON-FACED	MOTORHOME
MISADVISE	MOCKERIES	MONITORED	MOONINESS	MOTORISTS
MISBEHAVE	MOCKINGLY	MONITRESS	MOONLIGHT	MOTORIZED
MISBELIEF	MODELLING	MONKEYING	MOONRAKER	MOTORWAYS
MISCALLED	MODERATED	MONKEY NUT	MOONSCAPE	MOULDABLE
MISCHANCE	MODERATES	MONKSHOOD	MOONSHINE	MOULDERED
MISCHIEFS	MODERATOR	MONOBASIC	MOON SHOTS	MOULDIEST
MISCOUNTS	MODERATOS	MONOCHORD	MOONSTONE	MOULDINGS
MISCREANT	MODERNISM	MONOCLINE	MOOT POINT	MOUNTABLE
MISCREATE	MODERNIST	MONOCOQUE	MORACEOUS	MOUNTAINS
MISDEALER	MODERNITY	MONOCRACY	MORADABAD	MOUSETAIL
MISDIRECT	MODERNIZE	MONOCULAR	MORALISTS	MOUSETRAP
MISERABLE	MODIFIERS	MONOCYTIC	MORALIZED	MOUSINESS
MISERABLY	MODIFYING	MONODRAMA	MORALIZER	MOUSTACHE
MISFIRING	MODILLION	MONOGENIC	MORATORIA	MOUTHFULS
MISGIVING	MODULATED	MONOGRAMS	MORBIDITY	MOUTHPART
MISGOVERN	MODULATOR	MONOGRAPH	MORDACITY	MOUTHWASH
MISGUIDED	MOGADISHU	MONOLATER	MORDANTLY	MOVEABLES
MISGUIDER	MOISTENED	MONOLATRY	MORECAMBE	MOVEMENTS
MISHANDLE	MOISTENER	MONOLAYER	MORGANITE	MOVIE STAR
MISINFORM	MOISTNESS	MONOLITHS	MORMONISM	MOVIETONE
MISJUDGED	MOLDAVIAN	MONOLOGIC	MORPHEMES	MOVING VAN
MISJUDGER	MOLDAVITE	MONOLOGUE	MORPHEMIC	MUCIC ACID
MISLAYING	MOLDERING	MONOMANIA	MORPHOSIS	MUCKHEAPS
MISLEADER	MOLDINESS	MONOMERIC	MORSE CODE	MUCKINESS

MUCKRAKER	MUSTELINE	NARCOTIZE	NEMERTEAN	NEW MEXICO
MUCRONATE	MUSTERING	NARRATING	NEODYMIUM	NEW ROMNEY
MUDDINESS	MUSTINESS	NARRATION	NEOLITHIC	NEWSAGENT
MUDGUARDS	MUTAGENIC	NARRATIVE	NEOLOGISM	NEWSGROUP
MUGGINESS	MUTATIONS	NARRATORS	NEOLOGIST	NEWSHOUND
MUGGINSES	MUTILATED	NARROWING	NEOLOGIZE	NEWSINESS
MULATTOES	MUTILATOR	NASHVILLE	NEON LIGHT	NEWSPAPER
MULETEERS	MUTINEERS	NASTINESS	NEOPHYTES	NEWSPRINT
MULLINGAR	MUTINYING	NATIONALS	NEOPHYTIC	NEWSREELS
MULLIONED	MUTTERERS	NATROLITE	NEOPLASTY	NEWSROOMS
MULTICIDE	MUTTERING	NATTERING	NEOTENOUS	NEWSSHEET
MULTIFOIL	MUTUALITY	NATTINESS	NEPHELINE	NEWSSTAND
MULTIFOLD	MUTUALIZE	NATURALLY	NEPHOGRAM	NEWTONIAN
MULTIFORM	MUZZINESS	NATURISTS	NEPHOLOGY	NEW YORKER
MULTIHULL	MYCENAEAN	NAUGHTIER	NEPHRITIC	NICARAGUA
MULTIPARA	MYDRIASIS	NAUGHTILY	NEPHRITIS	NICCOLITE
MULTIPLES	MYDRIATIC	NAUSEATED	NEPHROSIS	NICHOLSON
MULTIPLET	MYOGLOBIN	NAUTILOID	NEPHROTIC	NICKELING
MULTIPLEX	MYOGRAPHY	NAVICULAR	NEPTUNIAN	NICKELLED
MULTITUDE	MYOLOGIST	NAVIGABLE	NEPTUNIUM	NICKELOUS
MUMMIFIED	MYROBALAN	NAVIGABLY	NERVE CELL	NICKNACKS
MUNDANELY	MYSTAGOGY	NAVIGATED	NERVELESS	NICKNAMED
MUNICIPAL	MYSTERIES	NAVIGATOR	NERVINESS	NICKNAMES
MUNIMENTS	MYSTICISM	NEAP TIDES	NERVOUSLY	NICOTIANA
MUNITIONS	MYSTIFIED	NEAR THING	NESCIENCE	NICOTINIC
MURDERERS	MYSTIFIER	NEBULIZER	NESTLINGS	NICTITATE
MURDERESS	MYSTIQUES	NECESSARY	NESTORIAN	NIFTINESS
MURDERING	MYTHICIZE	NECESSITY	NETANYAHU	NIGGARDLY
MURDEROUS	MYTHOLOGY	NECKBANDS	NETWORKED	NIGHTCAPS
MURKINESS	MYXOEDEMA	NECKCLOTH	NEUCHATEL	NIGHTCLUB
MURMURING	MYXOVIRUS	NECKLACES	NEURALGIA	NIGHTFALL
MUSACEOUS		NECKLINES	NEURALGIC	NIGHTGOWN
MUSCADINE	**N**	NECKPIECE	NEUROGLIA	NIGHTHAWK
MUSCARINE	NAHUATLAN	NECROLOGY	NEUROLOGY	NIGHTLIFE
MUSCATELS	NAILBRUSH	NECROTOMY	NEUROPATH	NIGHTLONG
MUSCLEMAN	NAIL FILES	NECTARIAL	NEUROTICS	NIGHTMARE
MUSCLEMEN	NAIVENESS	NECTARINE	NEUROTOMY	NIGHT OWLS
MUSCOVADO	NAIVETIES	NEEDFULLY	NEUTERING	NIGHT SOIL
MUSCOVITE	NAKEDNESS	NEEDINESS	NEUTRALLY	NIGHTTIME
MUSEOLOGY	NAMECHECK	NEFARIOUS	NEUTRETTO	NIGHTWEAR
MUSHINESS	NAMEPLATE	NEGATIONS	NEVER MIND	NIGROSINE
MUSHROOMS	NAME PLATE	NEGATIVED	NEVERMORE	NIHILISTS
MUSICALLY	NAMESAKES	NEGATIVES	NEW BROOMS	NIKOLAYEV
MUSIC HALL	NANNY GOAT	NEGLECTED	NEWCASTLE	NINETEENS
MUSICIANS	NANOMETER	NEGLECTER	NEWCOMERS	NINETIETH
MUSKETEER	NANTUCKET	NEGLIGEES	NEW FOREST	NIPPINESS
MUSKINESS	NAPHTHENE	NEGLIGENT	NEW GUINEA	NIPPONESE
MUSKMELON	NAPPINESS	NEGOTIANT	NEW JERSEY	NISI PRIUS
MUSLIMISM	NARCISSUS	NEGOTIATE	NEWLYWEDS	NISSEN HUT
MUSTACHES	NARCOTICS	NEGRITUDE	NEWLY WEDS	NITPICKER
MUSTACHIO	NARCOTISM	NEIGHBOUR	NEWMARKET	NITRAMINE

NITRATION
NITRIDING
NIVERNAIS
NO ACCOUNT
NO-ACCOUNT
NOBILIARY
NOBLENESS
NOCTILUCA
NOCTURNAL
NOCTURNES
NO-GO
    AREAS
NOISELESS
NOISINESS
NOMINALLY
NOMINATED
NOMINATOR
NOMOCRACY
NOMOGRAPH
NONAGONAL
NONEDIBLE
NONENTITY
NON-EVENTS
NON-FINITE
NONILLION
NONLINEAR
NONPAREIL
NONPAROUS
NONRACIAL
NONSMOKER
NONVERBAL
NONWHITES
NORMALITY
NORMALIZE
NORMATIVE
NORTH DOWN
NORTHEAST
NORTHERLY
NORTH POLE
NORTHWARD
NORTHWEST
NORTHWICH
NORWEGIAN
NOSEBLEED
NOSECONES
NOSEDIVED
NOSEDIVES
NOSE PIECE
NOSTALGIA
NOSTALGIC
NOSTOLOGY

NOTARIZED
NOT AT
    HOME
NOTATIONS
NOTEBOOKS
NOTEPAPER
NOTHING ON
NOTIFYING
NO-TILLAGE
NOTOCHORD
NOTOGAEAN
NOTORIETY
NOTORIOUS
NOT PROVEN
NOTRE DAME
NOURISHED
NOURISHER
NOVELETTE
NOVELISTS
NOVELTIES
NOVEMBERS
NOVITIATE
NOVOCAINE
NOXIOUSLY
NUCLEATOR
NUCLEOLAR
NUCLEOLUS
NUCLEONIC
NUEVO LEON
NUISANCES
NUKU'ALOFA
NULLIFIED
NULLIFIER
NULLIPARA
NULLIPORE
NULLITIES
NUMBERING
NUMBER ONE
NUMBER TEN
NUMBSKULL
NUMERABLE
NUMERABLY
NUMERATOR
NUMERICAL
NUMMULITE
NUMSKULLS
NUNNERIES
NUREMBERG
NURSELING
NURSEMAID
NURSERIES

NURSLINGS
NURTURING
NUTHOUSES
NUTRIENTS
NUTRIMENT
NUTRITION
NUTRITIVE
NUTSHELLS
NUTTINESS
NYASALAND
NYMPHALID
NYSTAGMIC
NYSTAGMUS

O

OAST HOUSE
OBBLIGATO
OBCORDATE
OBEDIENCE
OBEISANCE
OBELISCAL
OBFUSCATE
OBJECTIFY
OBJECTING
OBJECTION
OBJECTIVE
OBJECTORS
OBJET
    D'ART
OBJURGATE
OBLATIONS
OBLIGABLE
OBLIGATED
OBLIGATOR
OBLIQUITY
OBLIVIOUS
OBNOXIOUS
OBREPTION
OBSCENELY
OBSCENITY
OBSCURANT
OBSCURELY
OBSCURING
OBSCURITY
OBSEQUENT
OBSEQUIES
OBSERVANT
OBSERVERS
OBSERVING
OBSESSING
OBSESSION

OBSESSIVE
OBSOLESCE
OBSTACLES
OBSTETRIC
OBSTINACY
OBSTINATE
OBSTRUENT
OBTAINING
OBTRUDING
OBTRUSION
OBTRUSIVE
OBVERSION
OBVIATING
OBVIATION
OBVIOUSLY
OCCASIONS
OCCIPITAL
OCCLUDENT
OCCLUSION
OCCLUSIVE
OCCULTISM
OCCULTIST
OCCUPANCY
OCCUPANTS
OCCUPIERS
OCCUPYING
OCCURRENT
OCCURRING
OCELLATED
OCHLOCRAT
OCTAGONAL
OCTAMETER
OCTENNIAL
OCTILLION
OCTOPUSES
ODALISQUE
ODD JOBMAN
ODD-JOB
    MAN
ODD MAN
    OUT
ODD MEN
    OUT
ODOMETERS
ODOURLESS
OESTROGEN
OFF CHANCE
OFF COLOUR
OFFENBACH
OFFENDERS
OFFENDING

OFFENSIVE
OFFERINGS
OFFERTORY
OFFHANDED
OFFICE BOY
OFFICIALS
OFFICIANT
OFFICIARY
OFFICIATE
OFFICIOUS
OFF-LOADED
OFF-ROADER
OFF SEASON
OFFSHOOTS
OFFSPRING
OFF-STREET
OFF THE
    PEG
OGBOMOSHO
OILFIELDS
OIL PAINTS
OIL SLICKS
OIL TANKER
OINTMENTS
OKLAHOMAN
OLDENBURG
OLD FLAMES
OLD MASTER
OLD SCHOOL
OLD STAGER
OLD-TIMERS
OLEACEOUS
OLEANDERS
OLECRANAL
OLECRANON
OLEOGRAPH
OLEORESIN
OLFACTION
OLFACTORY
OLIGARCHY
OLIGOCENE
OLIGOPOLY
OLIVE DRAB
OLIVENITE
OLYMPIADS
OLYMPIANS
OMBUDSMAN
OMBUDSMEN
OMELETTES
OMINOUSLY
OMISSIBLE

OMISSIONS
OMNIBUSES
OMNIRANGE
OMOPHAGIA
OMOPHAGIC
ON ACCOUNT
ON A
  STRING
ONCE A
  WEEK
ONCE-OVERS
ONCOGENIC
ONDOGRAPH
ONDOMETER
ONEROUSLY
ONION DOME
ONIONSKIN
ONLOOKERS
ONLOOKING
ONOMASTIC
ONRUSHING
ONSLAUGHT
ON THE
  BEAM
ON THE
  MEND
ON THE
  NAIL
ON THE
  SPOT
ON THE
  TROT
ONTOGENIC
OOGENESIS
OOGENETIC
OOLOGICAL
OPEN-ENDED
OPEN-FACED
OPEN HOUSE
OPENING UP
OPEN ORDER
OPEN SHOPS
OPERATING
OPERATION
OPERATIVE
OPERATORS
OPERCULAR
OPERCULUM
OPERETTAS
OPHIOLOGY
OPPONENCY
OPPONENTS

OPPORTUNE
OPPOSABLE
OPPOSABLY
OPPOSITES
OPPRESSED
OPPRESSOR
OPTICALLY
OPTICIANS
OPTIMISTS
OPTIMIZED
OPTOMETER
OPTOMETRY
OPULENTLY
ORANGEADE
ORANGEISM
ORANGEMAN
ORANGE TIP
ORANG-UTAN
ORATORIES
ORATORIOS
ORBICULAR
ORCHESTRA
ORDAINING
ORDER ARMS
ORDERLIES
ORDINANCE
ORGANELLE
ORGANISMS
ORGANISTS
ORGANIZED
ORGANIZER
ORGANZINE
ORGIASTIC
ORIENTALS
ORIENTATE
ORIGINALS
ORIGINATE
ORNAMENTS
ORNITHINE
OROGRAPHY
OROLOGIST
ORPHANAGE
ORPHANING
ORRIS ROOT
ORTANIQUE
ORTHODOXY
ORTHOEPIC
ORTHOPTER
ORTHOPTIC
OSCILLATE
OSCITANCY

OSMOMETER
OSMOMETRY
OSNABRUCK
OSSICULAR
OSSIFRAGE
OSSIFYING
OSTENSIVE
OSTEOLOGY
OSTEOPATH
OSTEOTOME
OSTEOTOMY
OSTRACISM
OSTRACIZE
OSTRICHES
OTHERNESS
OTHERWISE
OTOCYSTIC
OTOLITHIC
OTOLOGIST
OTOSCOPIC
OUBLIETTE
OUR FATHER
OURSELVES
OUT AND
  OUT
OUT-AND-
  OUT
OUTBRAVED
OUTBREAKS
OUTBURSTS
OUTCASTES
OUTERMOST
OUTFACING
OUTFITTED
OUTFITTER
OUTFOUGHT
OUTFOXING
OUTGOINGS
OUTGROWTH
OUTHOUSES
OUTLASTED
OUTLAWING
OUTLAYING
OUTLINING
OUTLIVING
OUTNUMBER
OUT-OF-
  DATE
OUT OF
  STEP
OUTPLAYED
OUTRAGING

OUTRANKED
OUTRIDDEN
OUTRIDERS
OUTRIDING
OUTRIGGER
OUTRUNNER
OUTSIDERS
OUTSKIRTS
OUTSOURCE
OUTSPOKEN
OUTSPREAD
OUTSTARED
OUTSTAYED
OUTTALKED
OUTVOTING
OUTWARDLY
OUT WITH
  IT
OUTWITTED
OUTWORKER
OVATIONAL
OVEN-READY
OVERACTED
OVERAWING
OVERBLOWN
OVERBOARD
OVERBORNE
OVERBUILD
OVERCHECK
OVERCLOUD
OVERCOATS
OVERCROWD
OVERDOING
OVERDOSED
OVERDOSES
OVERDRAFT
OVERDRAWN
OVERDRESS
OVERDRIVE
OVERFLOWN
OVERFLOWS
OVERGLAZE
OVERGROWN
OVERHANGS
OVERHAULS
OVERHEADS
OVERHEARD
OVERISSUE
OVERJOYED
OVERLADEN
OVERLOADS

OVERLORDS
OVERLYING
OVERNIGHT
OVERPAINT
OVERPOWER
OVERPRICE
OVERPRINT
OVERPROOF
OVERRATED
OVERREACH
OVERREACT
OVERRIDER
OVERRULED
OVERSCORE
OVERSEERS
OVERSEXED
OVERSHOES
OVERSHOOT
OVERSIGHT
OVERSIZED
OVERSKIRT
OVERSLEEP
OVERSLEPT
OVERSPEND
OVERSPILL
OVERSTATE
OVERSTOCK
OVERTAKEN
OVERTAXED
OVERTHREW
OVERTHROW
OVERTONES
OVERTRADE
OVERTRICK
OVERTRUMP
OVERTURES
OVERVIEWS
OVERWEIGH
OVERWHELM
OVERWRITE
OVIFEROUS
OVIPAROUS
OVOTESTIS
OVULATING
OVULATION
OWNERSHIP
OXIDATION
OXIDATIVE
OXIDIZING
OXYGENATE
OXYGENIZE

OYSTER BED	PALTRIEST	PARALYSIS	PARTI PRIS	PATROL CAR
OZOCERITE	PAMPERING	PARALYTIC	PARTISANS	PATROLLED
	PAMPHLETS	PARAMATTA	PARTITION	PATROLLER
P	PANATELAS	PARAMEDIC	PARTITIVE	PATROLMAN
PACEMAKER	PANDA CARS	PARAMETER	PARTNERED	PATROLMEN
PACHYDERM	PANDEMICS	PARAMORPH	PARTRIDGE	PATRONAGE
PACHYTENE	PANDERING	PARAMOUNT	PART-SONGS	PATRONESS
PACIFIERS	PANDURATE	PARAMOURS	PART WORKS	PATRONIZE
PACIFISTS	PANEGYRIC	PARANOIAC	PARTY LINE	PATTERING
PACIFYING	PANELLING	PARAPLASM	PARTY WALL	PATTERNED
PACKAGERS	PANELLIST	PARASITES	PAS DE	PAULOWNIA
PACKAGING	PANHANDLE	PARASITIC	DEUX	PAUPERISM
PACKED-OUT	PANICKING	PARATAXIS	PASO DOBLE	PAUPERIZE
PACKHORSE	PANMUNJOM	PARATHION	PASSBOOKS	PAUSINGLY
PADERBORN	PANNIKINS	PARBOILED	PASSED OUT	PAVEMENTS
PADLOCKED	PANOPLIED	PARBUCKLE	PASSENGER	PAVILIONS
PAEDERAST	PANORAMAS	PARCELING	PASSERINE	PAWKINESS
PAEDOLOGY	PANORAMIC	PARCELLED	PASSERSBY	PAWNSHOPS
PAGANIZER	PANSOPHIC	PARCENARY	PASSIONAL	PAYCHECKS
PAGEANTRY	PANTHEISM	PARCHMENT	PASSIVELY	PAYMASTER
PAILLASSE	PANTHEIST	PARDONERS	PASSIVISM	PAY PACKET
PAILLETTE	PANTHEONS	PARDONING	PASSIVIST	PAY PHONES
PAINFULLY	PANTOMIME	PARDUBICE	PASSIVITY	PEACEABLE
PAINTBALL	PANTY HOSE	PAREGORIC	PASSOVERS	PEACEABLY
PAINTERLY	PAPARAZZI	PARENTAGE	PASSPORTS	PEACE PIPE
PAINTINGS	PAPARAZZO	PARENTING	PASSWORDS	PEACETIME
PAINTWORK	PAPERBACK	PARGETING	PASTICHES	PEARLIEST
PAKISTANI	PAPERBOYS	PARHELION	PASTILLES	PEARLITIC
PALANQUIN	PAPER CLIP	PARI PASSU	PASTINESS	PEARLIZED
PALATABLE	PAPER TAPE	PARISIANS	PASTORALE	PEARMAINS
PALATABLY	PAPERWORK	PARLEYING	PASTORALS	PEASANTRY
PALEFACES	PAPETERIE	PARLOR CAR	PASTORATE	PEA SOUPER
PALEMBANG	PAPILLARY	PARNASSUS	PASTURAGE	PECCARIES
PALESTINE	PAPILLOMA	PAROCHIAL	PASTURING	PECTINATE
PALISADES	PAPILLOTE	PARODISTS	PATAGONIA	PECULATED
PALLADIAN	PAPYRUSES	PARODYING	PATCHABLE	PECULATOR
PALLADIUM	PARABLAST	PAROICOUS	PATCHIEST	PECUNIARY
PALLADOUS	PARABOLAS	PAROLABLE	PATCHOULI	PEDAGOGIC
PALLIASSE	PARABOLIC	PARONYMIC	PATCHWORK	PEDAGOGUE
PALLIATED	PARACHUTE	PAROTITIS	PATELLATE	PEDALLING
PALLIATOR	PARADIGMS	PAROXYSMS	PATENTEES	PEDATIFID
PALMATION	PARADISAL	PARQUETRY	PATENTING	PEDERASTS
PALM BEACH	PARADISES	PARRICIDE	PATERNITY	PEDERASTY
PALMETTOS	PARADOXES	PARROTING	PATHOLOGY	PEDESTALS
PALMISTRY	PARAGOGIC	PARSIMONY	PATIENTLY	PEDICULAR
PALMITATE	PARAGRAPH	PARSONAGE	PATRIARCH	PEDICURES
PALOMINOS	PARAKEETS	PARTAKING	PATRICIAN	PEDIGREED
PALPATING	PARALLELS	PARTERRES	PATRICIDE	PEDIGREES
PALPATION	PARALYSED	PARTHENON	PATRIMONY	PEDIMENTS
PALPEBRAL	PARALYSER	PARTIALLY	PATRIOTIC	PEDUNCLED
PALPITATE	PARALYSES	PARTICLES	PATRISTIC	PEEPHOLES

PEERESSES	PEPTIDASE	PERMEANCE	PETTINESS	PHOSPHENE
PEEVISHLY	PEPTONIZE	PERMEATED	PETTISHLY	PHOSPHIDE
PEGGED OUT	PERBORATE	PERMEATOR	PETTY CASH	PHOSPHINE
PEGMATITE	PERCALINE	PER MENSEM	PETULANCE	PHOSPHITE
PEKINESES	PER CAPITA	PERMITTED	PFORZHEIM	PHOTOCELL
PEKINGESE	PERCEIVED	PERMITTER	PHAGOCYTE	PHOTOCOPY
PEKING MAN	PERCEIVER	PERMUTING	PHALANGER	PHOTOGRAM
PELLITORY	PERCHANCE	PERPETUAL	PHALANGES	PHOTONICS
PELMANISM	PERCHERON	PERPIGNAN	PHALANXES	PHOTOSTAT
PELTATION	PERCOLATE	PERPLEXED	PHALAROPE	PHOTOTUBE
PEMPHIGUS	PERCUSSOR	PERSECUTE	PHALLUSES	PHOTOTYPE
PENALIZED	PERDITION	PERSEVERE	PHANTASMS	PHRENITIC
PENALTIES	PEREGRINE	PERSIMMON	PHARISAIC	PHRENITIS
PENCHANTS	PERENNATE	PERSISTED	PHARISEES	PHTHALEIN
PENCILING	PERENNIAL	PERSISTER	PHARYNXES	PHYCOLOGY
PENCILLED	PERFECTED	PERSONAGE	PHASE-OUTS	PHYLLITIC
PENCILLER	PERFECTER	PERSONALS	PHEASANTS	PHYLLOMIC
PENDRAGON	PERFECTLY	PERSONATE	PHELLOGEN	PHYLOGENY
PENDULOUS	PERFIDIES	PERSONIFY	PHENACITE	PHYSICALS
PENDULUMS	PERFORATE	PERSONNEL	PHENAZINE	PHYSICIAN
PENEPLAIN	PERFORMED	PERSPIRED	PHENETOLE	PHYSICIST
PENETRANT	PERFORMER	PERSUADED	PHENOCOPY	PHYSIQUES
PENETRATE	PERFUMERY	PERSUADER	PHENOLATE	PHYTOTRON
PEN FRIEND	PERFUMING	PERTAINED	PHENOLOGY	PIANISTIC
PENINSULA	PERFUSION	PERTINENT	PHENOMENA	PICKETING
PENITENCE	PERFUSIVE	PERTURBED	PHENOTYPE	PICKINESS
PENITENTS	PERICLASE	PERTUSSIS	PHENOXIDE	PICK-ME-
PENKNIVES	PERICLINE	PERVADING	PHEROMONE	UPS
PENNILESS	PERICYCLE	PERVASIVE	PHILANDER	PICK PURSE
PENNINITE	PERILYMPH	PERVERTED	PHILATELY	PICNICKED
PENN'ORTHS	PERIMETER	PERVERTER	PHILIPPIC	PICNICKER
PENNY-WISE	PERIMETRY	PESSARIES	PHILOLOGY	PICOLINIC
PENNYWORT	PERIMORPH	PESSIMISM	PHLEBITIC	PICTORIAL
PEN PUSHER	PERINATAL	PESSIMIST	PHLEBITIS	PICTURING
PENSILITY	PERIODATE	PESTERING	PHLYCTENA	PIECE-DYED
PENSIONED	PERIPHERY	PESTICIDE	PHNOM PENH	PIECEMEAL
PENSIONER	PERISCOPE	PESTILENT	PHOENICIA	PIECEWORK
PENSIVELY	PERISHERS	PETAL-LIKE	PHOENIXES	PIE CHARTS
PENTAGONS	PERISHING	PETALODIC	PHONATION	PIECRUSTS
PENTAGRAM	PERISPERM	PETECHIAL	PHONATORY	PIERCABLE
PENTARCHY	PERISTOME	PETERSHAM	PHONE BOOK	PIERIDINE
PENTECOST	PERISTYLE	PETIOLATE	PHONEMICS	PIGGERIES
PENTHOUSE	PERITONEA	PETIOLULE	PHONETICS	PIGGISHLY
PENTOTHAL	PERITRACK	PETIT FOUR	PHONEY WAR	PIGGYBACK
PENTOXIDE	PERJURERS	PETITIONS	PHONINESS	PIGGYBANK
PENUMBRAL	PERJURIES	PETRI DISH	PHONOGRAM	PIGHEADED
PENUMBRAS	PERJURING	PETRIFIED	PHONOLITE	PIG-HEADED
PENURIOUS	PERKINESS	PETRIFIER	PHONOLOGY	PIGTAILED
PEPPERING	PERMALLOY	PETROLEUM	PHONOTYPE	PIKEPERCH
PEPPER POT	PERMANENT	PETROLOGY	PHONOTYPY	PIKESTAFF
PEPSINATE	PERMEABLE	PETTICOAT	PHOSPHATE	PILASTERS

PILCHARDS	PLACARDED	PLAYROOMS	PODGINESS	POLYBASIC
PILFERAGE	PLACATING	PLAYTHING	POETASTER	POLYCARPY
PILFERERS	PLACATION	PLEADABLE	POETESSES	POLYESTER
PILFERING	PLACATORY	PLEADINGS	POETICIZE	POLYGLOTS
PILLAGERS	PLACEBOES	PLEASABLE	POGO STICK	POLYGONAL
PILLAGING	PLACE CARD	PLEASANCE	POIGNANCY	POLYGONUM
PILLAR BOX	PLACE MATS	PLEASEDLY	POINCIANA	POLYGRAPH
PILLBOXES	PLACEMENT	PLEASURES	POINT DUTY	POLYMATHS
PILLORIED	PLACENTAE	PLEBBIEST	POINTEDLY	POLYMERIC
PILLORIES	PLACENTAL	PLEBEIANS	POINTLESS	POLYMORPH
PILLOWING	PLACENTAS	PLECTRUMS	POINTSMAN	POLYMYXIN
PIMPERNEL	PLACIDITY	PLENARILY	POISONERS	POLYNESIA
PINACEOUS	PLACODERM	PLENITUDE	POISON GAS	POLYPHASE
PINAFORES	PLAIN-LAID	PLENTEOUS	POISONING	POLYPHONE
PINCHBECK	PLAINNESS	PLENTIFUL	POISON IVY	POLYPHONY
PINCHCOCK	PLAINSMAN	PLEONASMS	POISONOUS	POLYPLOID
PINEAPPLE	PLAINSONG	PLEURITIC	POKEBERRY	POLYPTYCH
PINETREES	PLAINTIFF	PLEXIFORM	POKER FACE	POLYSOMIC
PINEWOODS	PLAINTIVE	PLICATION	POKERWORK	POLYTHENE
PINIONING	PLANARIAN	PLIGHTING	POLAR BEAR	POLYTONAL
PINNACLES	PLANATION	PLIMSOLLS	POLARIZED	POLYTYPIC
PINNATION	PLANETARY	PLOUGHBOY	POLARIZER	POLYVINYL
PINPOINTS	PLANETOID	PLOUGHING	POLAROIDS	POMACEOUS
PINPRICKS	PLANE TREE	PLOUGHMAN	POLEAXING	POMANDERS
PINSTRIPE	PLANGENCY	PLOUGHMEN	POLEMICAL	POMERANIA
PINTABLES	PLANISHER	PLUCKIEST	POLE VAULT	POMPADOUR
PINTADERA	PLANTABLE	PLUGBOARD	POLICE DOG	POMPOSITY
PINWHEELS	PLANTAINS	PLUGHOLES	POLICEMAN	POMPOUSLY
PIONEERED	PLASMAGEL	PLUMBABLE	POLICEMEN	PONDERING
PIOUSNESS	PLASMASOL	PLUMBEOUS	POLISHING	PONDEROUS
PIPE DREAM	PLASTERED	PLUMBICON	POLITBURO	PONDOLAND
PIPELINES	PLASTERER	PLUMB LINE	POLITESSE	PONTIANAK
PIPE RACKS	PLATELETS	PLUMMETED	POLITICAL	PONTYPOOL
PIPERONAL	PLATE RACK	PLUMMIEST	POLITICOS	PONYTAILS
PIPESTONE	PLATFORMS	PLUMPNESS	POLKA DOTS	POORHOUSE
PIPSQUEAK	PLATINIZE	PLUNDERED	POLLARDED	POORLIEST
PIQUANTLY	PLATINOID	PLUNDERER	POLLINATE	POORLY OFF
PIRATICAL	PLATINOUS	PLURALISM	POLLINIUM	POOR WHITE
PIROUETTE	PLATITUDE	PLURALIST	POLLSTERS	POPE'S
PISS-TAKES	PLAUSIBLE	PLURALITY	POLL TAXES	NOSE
PISTACHIO	PLAUSIBLY	PLURALIZE	POLLUCITE	POPINJAYS
PITCH-DARK	PLAY-ACTED	PLUS FOURS	POLLUTANT	POPLITEAL
PITCHFORK	PLAYBACKS	PLUSHNESS	POLLUTING	POPPYCOCK
PITEOUSLY	PLAY DOUGH	PLUTOCRAT	POLLUTION	POPPYHEAD
PITHINESS	PLAYED-OUT	PLUTONIUM	POLLYANNA	POPSICLES
PITOT TUBE	PLAYFULLY	PNEUMATIC	POLONAISE	POPULARLY
PIT PONIES	PLAYGOERS	PNEUMONIA	POLO NECKS	POPULATED
PITTANCES	PLAYGROUP	PNEUMONIC	POLO SHIRT	POPULISTS
PITUITARY	PLAYHOUSE	POCKETFUL	POLTROONS	PORBEAGLE
PITYINGLY	PLAYMAKER	POCKETING	POLYAMIDE	PORCELAIN
PIZZICATO	PLAYMATES	POCKMARKS	POLYANDRY	PORCUPINE

PORIFERAN	POT-BOILER	PRECISION	PRESCRIBE	PRIME COST
PORKINESS	POTENTATE	PRECLUDED	PRESCRIPT	PRIMENESS
POROMERIC	POTENTIAL	PRECOCIAL	PRESENCES	PRIME RATE
PORPHYRIN	POTHOLERS	PRECOCITY	PRESENTED	PRIME TIME
PORPOISES	POTHOLING	PRECONIZE	PRESENTEE	PRIMIPARA
PORRINGER	POTHUNTER	PRECOOKED	PRESENTER	PRIMITIVE
PORTACRIB	POT PLANTS	PRECURSOR	PRESENTLY	PRIMROSES
PORTADOWN	POTPOURRI	PREDATING	PRESERVED	PRINCEDOM
PORTATIVE	POT POURRI	PREDATION	PRESERVER	PRINCETON
PORT BLAIR	POTSHERDS	PREDATORS	PRESERVES	PRINCIPAL
PORTENDED	POTTERIES	PREDATORY	PRESETTER	PRINCIPLE
PORTERAGE	POTTERING	PREDICANT	PRESHRUNK	PRINTABLE
PORTFOLIO	POTTINESS	PREDICATE	PRESIDENT	PRINTINGS
PORTHOLES	POULTERER	PREDICTED	PRESIDING	PRINTOUTS
PORTICOES	POULTICES	PREDICTOR	PRESIDIUM	PRISMATIC
PORTIONED	POULTRIES	PREDIGEST	PRESSGANG	PRISONERS
PORTLIEST	POUNDINGS	PRE-EMPTED	PRESS GANG	PRISSIEST
PORT LOUIS	POURBOIRE	PRE-EMPTOR	PRESSINGS	PRITCHETT
PORTO NOVO	POUTINGLY	PREFACING	PRESSMARK	PRIVATEER
PORTRAITS	POVERTIES	PREFATORY	PRESSROOM	PRIVATELY
PORTRAYAL	POWDERING	PREFERRED	PRESS-STUD	PRIVATION
PORTRAYED	POWDER KEG	PREFIGURE	PRESSURED	PRIVATIVE
PORTRAYER	POWER BASE	PREFIXING	PRESSURES	PRIVATIZE
PORT SUDAN	POWERBOAT	PREFLIGHT	PRESSWORK	PRIVILEGE
PORTULACA	POWER DIVE	PREGNABLE	PRESTIGES	PRIZE DAYS
POSITIONS	POWERLESS	PREGNANCY	PRESTRESS	PROACTIVE
POSITIVES	PRACTICAL	PREHEATED	PRESTWICH	PROBABLES
POSITRONS	PRACTICES	PREJUDGED	PRESTWICK	PROBATING
POSSESSED	PRACTISED	PREJUDGER	PRESUMING	PROBATION
POSSESSOR	PRAESIDIA	PREJUDICE	PRETENCES	PROBATIVE
POSSIBLES	PRAGMATIC	PRELATISM	PRETENDED	PROBEABLE
POSTAXIAL	PRANKSTER	PRELATIST	PRETENDER	PROBINGLY
POSTCARDS	PRATINGLY	PRELATURE	PRETERITE	PROBOSCIS
POSTCODES	PRATTLERS	PRELUDIAL	PRETTIEST	PROCEDURE
POSTDATED	PRATTLING	PRELUSION	PREVAILED	PROCEEDED
POSTERIOR	PRAYERFUL	PRELUSIVE	PREVAILER	PROCEEDER
POSTERITY	PRAYER RUG	PREMATURE	PREVALENT	PROCESSED
POSTHASTE	PREACHERS	PREMIERED	PREVENTED	PROCESSES
POST HORNS	PREACHIFY	PREMIERES	PREVENTER	PROCESSOR
POSTICOUS	PREACHING	PREOCCUPY	PREVIEWED	PROCLITIC
POSTILION	PREAMBLES	PREORDAIN	PREVISION	PROCONSUL
POSTMARKS	PREBENDAL	PREPACKED	PRICELESS	PROCREANT
POSTNATAL	PRECANCEL	PREPARING	PRICE TAGS	PROCREATE
POSTPONED	PRECEDENT	PREPAYING	PRICINESS	PROCTORED
POSTPONER	PRECEDING	PREPOTENT	PRICKLIER	PROCURERS
POSTULANT	PRECENTOR	PREPUTIAL	PRICKLING	PROCURING
POSTULATE	PRECEPTOR	PRERECORD	PRIESTESS	PRODIGALS
POSTURING	PRECINCTS	PRESAGING	PRIMAEVAL	PRODIGIES
POTASSIUM	PRECIPICE	PRESBYTER	PRIMARIES	PRODROMAL
POTATIONS	PRECISELY	PRESCHOOL	PRIMARILY	PRODUCERS
POTBOILER	PRECISIAN	PRESCIENT	PRIMATIAL	PRODUCING

PROFANELY	PROPHETIC	PROXIMATE	PULVILLUS	PUTREFIED
PROFANING	PROPONENT	PROXIMITY	PULVINATE	PUTREFIER
PROFANITY	PROPOSALS	PRUDENTLY	PUMICEOUS	PUTRIDITY
PROFESSED	PROPOSERS	PRUDISHLY	PUMMELING	PUTTERING
PROFESSOR	PROPOSING	PRURIENCE	PUMMELLED	PUTTYROOT
PROFFERED	PROPRIETY	PRUSSIATE	PUMP ROOMS	PUT-UP
PROFFERER	PROPTOSIS	PRYTANEUM	PUNCHBALL	JOBS
PROFILING	PROPYLITE	PSALMISTS	PUNCH BALL	PUY DE
PROFITEER	PROROGUED	PSALMODIC	PUNCH BOWL	DOME
PROFITING	PROSCRIBE	PSEUDONYM	PUNCHIEST	PYCNIDIUM
PROFLUENT	PROSECTOR	PSORIASIS	PUNCH LINE	PYONGYANG
PROFUSELY	PROSECUTE	PSORIATIC	PUNCTILIO	PYORRHOEA
PROFUSION	PROSELYTE	PSYCHICAL	PUNCTUATE	PYRAMIDAL
PROGESTIN	PROSIMIAN	PSYCHOSES	PUNCTURED	PYRETHRIN
PROGNOSES	PROSINESS	PSYCHOSIS	PUNCTURER	PYRETHRUM
PROGNOSIS	PROSODIST	PSYCHOTIC	PUNCTURES	PYRIDOXAL
PROGRAMED	PROSPECTS	PTARMIGAN	PUNGENTLY	PYROGENIC
PROGRAMER	PROSPERED	PTERYGOID	PUNISHING	PYROLITIC
PROGRAMME	PROSTATES	PTOLEMAIC	PUPILLAGE	PYROLYSIS
PROJECTED	PROSTATIC	PUB-CRAWLS	PUPILLARY	PYROMANCY
PROJECTOR	PROSTRATE	PUBESCENT	PUPPETEER	PYROMANIA
PROLACTIN	PROTAMINE	PUBLICANS	PUPPYHOOD	PYROMETER
PROLAMINE	PROTANDRY	PUBLIC BAR	PUPPY LOVE	PYROMETRY
PROLAPSED	PROTECTED	PUBLICIST	PURCHASED	PYROXENIC
PROLAPSES	PROTECTOR	PUBLICITY	PURCHASER	PYROXYLIN
PROLEPSIS	PROTESTER	PUBLICIZE	PURCHASES	
PROLEPTIC	PROTHESIS	PUBLISHED	PUREBREDS	**Q**
PROLIXITY	PROTHETIC	PUBLISHER	PURGATION	QUADRANTS
PROLOGUES	PROTHORAX	PUCKERING	PURGATIVE	QUADRATIC
PROLONGED	PROTOCOLS	PUCKISHLY	PURGATORY	QUADRIFID
PROLONGER	PROTOGYNY	PUDGINESS	PURIFIERS	QUADRILLE
PROLUSION	PROTONEMA	PUERILISM	PURIFYING	QUADRUPED
PROLUSORY	PROTOSTAR	PUERILITY	PURLOINED	QUADRUPLE
PROMENADE	PROTOTYPE	PUERPERAL	PURLOINER	QUADRUPLY
PROMINENT	PROTOXIDE	PUFF ADDER	PURPORTED	QUAGMIRES
PROMISING	PROTOZOAN	PUFFINESS	PURPOSELY	QUAKERISM
PROMOTERS	PROTRUDED	PUGILISTS	PURPOSING	QUAKINESS
PROMOTING	PROUDNESS	PUGNACITY	PURPOSIVE	QUALIFIED
PROMOTION	PROUSTITE	PUISSANCE	PURSUANCE	QUALIFIER
PROMOTIVE	PROVENCAL	PULLOVERS	PURULENCE	QUALITIES
PROMPTING	PROVENDER	PULL ROUND	PURVEYING	QUARRELED
PRONATION	PROVIDENT	PULLULATE	PURVEYORS	QUARRYING
PRONENESS	PROVIDERS	PULMONARY	PUSHBIKES	QUARTERED
PRONGHORN	PROVIDING	PULMONATE	PUSHCARTS	QUARTERLY
PRONOUNCE	PROVINCES	PULPINESS	PUSHCHAIR	QUARTZITE
PROOFREAD	PROVISION	PULSATILE	PUSH CHAIR	QUATRAINS
PROPAGATE	PROVISORY	PULSATING	PUSHINESS	QUAVERING
PROPAGULE	PROVOKING	PULSATION	PUSHINGLY	QUEASIEST
PRO PATRIA	PROVOLONE	PULSATIVE	PUSSYFOOT	QUEBECKER
PROPELLED	PROWESSES	PULSATORY	PUSTULANT	QUEBECOIS
PROPELLER	PROWL CARS	PULVERIZE	PUSTULATE	QUEBRACHO

QUEEN-SIZE	RADIATING	RATIONING	RECEPTIVE	REDACTION
QUEERNESS	RADIATION	RATTINESS	RECESSING	RED ALERTS
QUENCHING	RADIATIVE	RATTLEBOX	RECESSION	REDBREAST
QUERCETIN	RADIATORS	RAUCOUSLY	RECESSIVE	REDBRICKS
QUERETARO	RADICALLY	RAUNCHIER	RECHARGED	REDBRIDGE
QUERULOUS	RADIOGRAM	RAUNCHILY	RECHARGER	RED CARPET
QUESTIONS	RADIOLOGY	RAUWOLFIA	RECHAUFFE	REDDENING
QUEUE-JUMP	RADIO STAR	RAVELLING	RECHERCHE	REDEEMERS
QUIBBLERS	RAFFINOSE	RAVISHING	RECIPIENT	REDEEMING
QUIBBLING	RAFFISHLY	RAZORBACK	RECITABLE	REDELIVER
QUICKENED	RAFFLESIA	RAZORBILL	RECKONING	REDEVELOP
QUICKLIME	RAIL GAUGE	RAZOR EDGE	RECLAIMED	RED GIANTS
QUICKNESS	RAILHEADS	REACHABLE	RECLINATE	RED-HANDED
QUICKSAND	RAILROADS	REACTANCE	RECLINING	RED-HEADED
QUICKSTEP	RAIN CHECK	REACTIONS	RECLUSION	RED INDIAN
QUIESCENT	RAINCOATS	READDRESS	RECLUSIVE	RED LIGHTS
QUIETENED	RAINDROPS	READINESS	RECOGNIZE	REDOLENCE
QUIETISTS	RAINFALLS	READY-MADE	RECOILING	REDOUBLED
QUIETNESS	RAIN GAUGE	REALIGNED	RECOLLECT	REDOUNDED
QUIETUSES	RAININESS	REALISTIC	RECOMMEND	RED-PENCIL
QUILLWORT	RAINMAKER	REALITIES	RECOMPOSE	RED PEPPER
QUINIDINE	RAINPROOF	REALIZING	RECONCILE	REDRESSED
QUINOLINE	RAINSTORM	REANIMATE	RECONDITE	REDRESSER
QUINONOID	RAINWATER	REAPPOINT	RECONVERT	REDUCIBLE
QUINTUPLE	RAJASTHAN	REARGUARD	RECORDERS	REDUCTASE
QUIRKIEST	RAMIFYING	REAR LIGHT	RECORDING	REDUCTION
QUISLINGS	RAMPAGING	REARRANGE	RECOUNTAL	REDUNDANT
QUITCLAIM	RAMPANTLY	REARWARDS	RECOUNTED	RE-ECHOING
QUITTANCE	RANCIDITY	REASONING	RECOUPING	REEDINESS
QUIVERFUL	RANCOROUS	REASSURED	RE-COVERED	RE-EDUCATE
QUIVERING	RANDINESS	REASSURER	RECOVERER	REEF KNOTS
QUIXOTISM	RANDOMIZE	REBATABLE	RECREANTS	REEKINGLY
QUIZZICAL	RANGINESS	REBELLING	RECREATED	RE-ELECTED
QUODLIBET	RANSACKED	REBELLION	RE-CREATOR	RE-ENFORCE
QUOTATION	RANSACKER	REBINDING	RECREMENT	RE-ENTRANT
QUOTIDIAN	RANSOMERS	REBOUNDED	RECRUITED	RE-ENTRIES
QUOTIENTS	RANSOMING	REBOUNDER	RECRUITER	RE-EXAMINE
	RANTINGLY	REBUFFING	RECTANGLE	REFECTION
R	RAPACIOUS	REBUKABLE	RECTIFIED	REFECTORY
RABBINATE	RAPID-FIRE	REBUTTALS	RECTIFIER	REFERABLE
RABBITING	RAPIDNESS	REBUTTING	RECTITUDE	REFERENCE
RABBITTED	RAPTORIAL	RECALLING	RECTOCELE	REFERENDA
RACEHORSE	RAPTUROUS	RECANTING	RECTORATE	REFERRALS
RACETRACK	RARE EARTH	RECAPPING	RECTORIAL	REFERRING
RACIALISM	RASCALITY	RECAPTION	RECTORIES	REFILLING
RACIALIST	RASPBERRY	RECAPTURE	RECUMBENT	REFINABLE
RACKETEER	RASPINGLY	RECASTING	RECURRENT	REFINANCE
RACONTEUR	RASTERIZE	RECEIVERS	RECURRING	REFITTING
RADIAL-PLY	RATEPAYER	RECEIVING	RECUSANCY	REFLATING
RADIANCES	RATIFYING	RECENSION	RECUSANTS	REFLATION
RADIANTLY	RATIONALE	RECEPTION	RECYCLING	REFLECTED

REFLECTOR	REINSURER	REMOULDED	REPRESSOR	RESIDUARY
REFLEXIVE	REISSUING	REMOUNTED	REPRIEVED	RESIGNING
REFORMERS	REITERANT	REMOVABLE	REPRIEVER	RESILIENT
REFORMING	REITERATE	REMOVABLY	REPRIEVES	RESINATED
REFORMISM	REJECTING	REMSCHEID	REPRIMAND	RESISTANT
REFORMIST	REJECTION	RENASCENT	REPRINTED	RESISTERS
REFRACTED	REJECTIVE	RENDERING	REPRINTER	RESISTING
REFRACTOR	REJIGGING	RENDITION	REPRISALS	RESISTORS
REFRAINED	REJOICING	RENEGADES	REPROBACY	RESITTING
REFRAINER	REJOINDER	RENEWABLE	REPROBATE	RESNATRON
REFRESHED	REJOINING	RENEWEDLY	REPROCESS	RESOLUBLE
REFRESHER	REKINDLED	RENOUNCED	REPRODUCE	RESOLVENT
REFUELING	RELAPSING	RENOUNCER	REPROVING	RESOLVING
REFUELLED	RELATABLE	RENOVATED	REPTILIAN	RESONANCE
REFULGENT	RELATIONS	RENOVATOR	REPTILOID	RESONATED
REFUNDING	RELATIVES	REOPENING	REPUBLICS	RESONATOR
REFURBISH	RELAXABLE	REPAIRING	REPUBLISH	RESORBENT
REFUSABLE	RELAXEDLY	REPAIRMAN	REPUDIATE	RESORTING
REFUSE BIN	RELEASING	REPARABLE	REPUGNANT	RESOUNDED
REFUSE TIP	RELEGATED	REPARABLY	REPULSING	RESOURCES
REFUTABLE	RELENTING	REPARTEES	REPULSION	RESPECTED
REGAINING	RELEVANCE	REPAYABLE	REPULSIVE	RESPECTER
REGARDANT	RELEVANCY	REPAYMENT	REPUTABLE	RESPIRING
REGARDFUL	RELIEF MAP	REPEALING	REPUTABLY	RESPONDED
REGARDING	RELIEVING	REPEATERS	REPUTEDLY	RESPONDER
REGENCIES	RELIGIONS	REPEATING	REQUESTED	RESPONSER
REGICIDAL	RELIGIOSE	REPECHAGE	REQUESTER	RESPONSES
REGICIDES	RELIGIOUS	REPELLENT	REQUIRING	RESTATING
REGIMENTS	RELIQUARY	REPELLING	REQUISITE	REST CURES
REGISTERS	RELISHING	REPENTANT	REQUITING	RESTFULLY
REGISTRAR	RELIVABLE	REPENTING	REREDOSES	REST HOMES
REGRESSED	RELOADING	REPERTORY	RERUNNING	RESTIFORM
REGRESSOR	RELOCATED	REPHRASED	RESALABLE	RESTIVELY
REGRETFUL	RELUCTANT	REPLACING	RESCINDED	RESTOCKED
REGRETTED	REMAINDER	REPLAYING	RESCINDER	RESTORERS
REGRETTER	REMAINING	REPLEADER	RESCUABLE	RESTORING
REGROUPED	REMANDING	REPLENISH	RESECTION	RESTRAINT
REGULABLE	REMANENCE	REPLETION	RESEMBLED	REST ROOMS
REGULARLY	REMARKING	REPLETIVE	RESEMBLER	RESULTANT
REGULATED	REMARRIED	REPLICATE	RESENTFUL	RESULTING
REGULATOR	REMEDYING	REPLY-PAID	RESENTING	RESUMABLE
REHASHING	REMINDERS	REPORTAGE	RESERPINE	RESURFACE
REHEARSAL	REMINDFUL	REPORTERS	RESERVING	RESURGENT
REHEARSED	REMINDING	REPORTING	RESERVIST	RESURRECT
REHEARSER	REMINISCE	REPOSEDLY	RESERVOIR	RETAILERS
REHOUSING	REMISSION	REPOSEFUL	RESETTING	RETAILING
REIMBURSE	REMISSIVE	REPOSSESS	RESETTLED	RETAINERS
REINFORCE	REMITTING	REPREHEND	RESHUFFLE	RETAINING
REINSTALL	REMODELED	REPRESENT	RESIDENCE	RETALIATE
REINSTATE	REMONTANT	REPRESSED	RESIDENCY	RETARDANT
REINSURED	REMONTOIR	REPRESSER	RESIDENTS	RETARDATE

RETARDING
RETELLING
RETENTION
RETENTIVE
RETHOUGHT
RETICENCE
RETICULES
RETICULUM
RETINITIS
RETORSION
RETORTING
RETORTION
RETOUCHED
RETOUCHER
RETRACING
RETRACTED
RETRACTOR
RETREADED
RETREATAL
RETREATED
RETRIEVAL
RETRIEVED
RETRIEVER
RETROCEDE
RETROFIRE
RETROFLEX
RETROPACK
RETROUSSE
RETURNING
REUNITING
REUTILIZE
REVALUING
REVAMPING
REVEALING
REVELATOR
REVELLING
REVELMENT
REVELROUS
REVENGING
REVERABLE
REVERENCE
REVERENDS
REVERSALS
REVERSING
REVERSION
REVERTING
REVERTIVE
REVETMENT
REVIEWERS
REVIEWING
REVISABLE

REVISIONS
REVIVABLE
REVIVABLY
REVOCABLE
REVOCABLY
REVOKABLE
REVOKABLY
REVOLTING
REVOLVERS
REVOLVING
REVULSION
REVULSIVE
REWARDING
REWIRABLE
REWORDING
REWORKING
REWRITING
REYKJAVIK
RHAPSODIC
RHEOMETER
RHEOMETRY
RHEOSTATS
RHEOTAXIS
RHEUMATIC
RH FACTORS
RHIGOLENE
RHINELAND
RHINOLOGY
RHIZOBIUM
RHIZOIDAL
RHIZOTOMY
RHODAMINE
RHODESIAN
RHODOLITE
RHODONITE
RHODOPSIN
RHOMBOIDS
RHOMBUSES
RHOTACISM
RHOTACIST
RHYMESTER
RHYOLITIC
RHYTHMICS
RIBOSOMAL
RICE PADDY
RICE PAPER
RICKSHAWS
RICOCHETS
RIDDANCES
RIDERLESS
RIDGELING

RIDGEPOLE
RIDICULED
RIDICULER
RIFLEBIRD
RIGHTEOUS
RIGHT-HAND
RIGHTISTS
RIGHTNESS
RIGHTSIZE
RIGHTWARD
RIGHT WING
RIGMAROLE
RING A
  BELL
RING ROADS
RIO BRANCO
RIO GRANDE
RIOTOUSLY
RIPOSTING
RISE ABOVE
RISKINESS
RITUALISM
RITUALIST
RITUALIZE
RIVALLING
RIVALRIES
RIVALROUS
RIVERBEDS
RIVERBOAT
RIVERHEAD
RIVERSIDE
ROADBLOCK
ROADHOUSE
ROADSHOWS
ROADSTEAD
ROADSTERS
ROAD TAXES
ROAD TESTS
ROADWORKS
ROAD WORKS
ROAST BEEF
ROASTINGS
ROBBERIES
ROBOT-LIKE
ROCHESTER
ROCKBOUND
ROCK CAKES
ROCKERIES
ROCKETEER
ROCKETING
ROCKFALLS

ROCKINESS
ROCK 'N'
  ROLL
ROCK PLANT
ROCKSHAFT
ROENTGENS
ROGUERIES
ROGUISHLY
ROISTERER
ROLE MODEL
ROLE PLAYS
ROLL CALLS
ROLLINGLY
ROMANCING
ROMAN NOSE
ROMANTICS
ROMPINGLY
ROOF RACKS
ROOKERIES
ROOMINESS
ROOMMATES
ROOT CROPS
ROOTINESS
ROOTSTOCK
ROPE TRICK
ROQUEFORT
ROSACEOUS
ROSCOMMON
ROSEWATER
ROSINWEED
ROSTELLUM
ROTAMETER
ROTARIANS
ROTATABLE
ROTATIONS
ROTAVATOR
ROTHERHAM
ROTIFERAL
ROTOVATOR
ROTTERDAM
ROTUNDITY
ROUGHCAST
ROUGH DEAL
ROUGHENED
ROUGH-HEWN
ROUGHNECK
ROUGHNESS
ROUGHSHOD
ROUNDELAY
ROUNDHEAD
ROUNDNESS

ROUNDSMAN
ROUNDSMEN
ROUND TRIP
ROUND-TRIP
ROUNDWORM
ROUTINELY
ROUTINISM
ROUTINIST
ROVING EYE
ROWAN TREE
ROWDINESS
ROW HOUSES
ROYAL BLUE
ROYALISTS
ROYALTIES
RUBBERIZE
RUBBISHED
RUBESCENT
RUBRICATE
RUBRICIAN
RUCKSACKS
RUDACEOUS
RUDBECKIA
RUDDINESS
RUDIMENTS
RUFESCENT
RUFFIANLY
RUINATION
RUINOUSLY
RULEBOOKS
RUMBLINGS
RUMINANTS
RUMINATED
RUMINATOR
RUMMAGING
RUMP STEAK
RUN-ABOUTS
RUN ACROSS
RUN-AROUND
RUNCINATE
RUNNERS-UP
RUNNER-UPS
RUNNYMEDE
RUNTINESS
RUN TO
  SEED
RUPTURING
RUSH HOURS
RUSHINESS
RUSHINGLY
RUSHLIGHT

RUSH LIGHT
RUSSETISH
RUSTICATE
RUSTICITY
RUSTINESS
RUSTPROOF
RUTABAGAS
RUTACEOUS
RUTHENIAN
RUTHENIUM
RUTILATED
RUTTINESS
RUWENZORI

S

SABADILLA
SABOTAGED
SABOTEURS
SACCHARIN
SACCULATE
SACKCLOTH
SACK RACES
SACRAMENT
SACRARIUM
SACRED COW
SACRIFICE
SACRILEGE
SACRISTAN
SADDENING
SADDLEBAG
SADDLEBOW
SAFEGUARD
SAFE HOUSE
SAFELIGHT
SAFETY NET
SAFETY PIN
SAFFLOWER
SAFRANINE
SAGACIOUS
SAGEBRUSH
SAGE DERBY
SAGE GREEN
SAGITTATE
SAILBOARD
SAILCLOTH
SAILOR HAT
SAILPLANE
SAINTE FOY
SAINT GALL
SAINTHOOD
SAINT JOHN

SAINTLILY
SAINT-OUEN
SAINT PAUL
SAINT'S
  DAY
SALAAMING
SALACIOUS
SALAD DAYS
SALAMANCA
SALARYMAN
SALERATUS
SALEROOMS
SALESGIRL
SALESROOM
SALES SLIP
SALES TALK
SALIMETER
SALIMETRY
SALISBURY
SALIVATED
SALMONOID
SALOON BAR
SALPIFORM
SALTATION
SALTINESS
SALTLICKS
SALTPETRE
SALT SPOON
SALTWATER
SALTWORKS
SALVAGING
SALVATION
SAMARITAN
SAMARKAND
SANATORIA
SANCTIONS
SANCTUARY
SANDALLED
SANDBANKS
SANDBLAST
SAND-BLIND
SANDBOXES
SAND DUNES
SAND FLIES
SANDHURST
SANDINESS
SANDPAPER
SANDPIPER
SANDSHOES
SANDSTONE
SANDSTORM

SAND TRAPS
SANFORIZE
SANGFROID
SANITARIA
SANITIZED
SAN MARINO
SANS SERIF
SANTA CRUZ
SANTANDER
SANTONICA
SAPHENOUS
SAPIENTLY
SAPODILLA
SAPPHIRES
SAPPINESS
SAPRAEMIA
SAPRAEMIC
SAPROLITE
SAPROZOIC
SAPSUCKER
SARABANDE
SARABANDS
SARACENIC
SARCASTIC
SARCOCARP
SARDINIAN
SARGASSUM
SARTORIAL
SARTORIUS
SASHAYING
SASKATOON
SASSAFRAS
SASSENACH
SATANISTS
SATELLITE
SATIATING
SATIATION
SATINWOOD
SATIRICAL
SATIRIZED
SATIRIZER
SATISFIED
SATISFIER
SATURABLE
SATURATED
SATURATER
SATURDAYS
SATURNIAN
SATURNIID
SATURNINE
SATURNISM

SAUCEPANS
SAUCINESS
SAUNTERED
SAUNTERER
SAUTERNES
SAVOURING
SAXIFRAGE
SAXOPHONE
SCABBARDS
SCABBIEST
SCABIETIC
SCAFFOLDS
SCAGLIOLA
SCALAWAGS
SCALDFISH
SCALINESS
SCALLIONS
SCALLOPED
SCALLOPER
SCALLYWAG
SCAMPERED
SCAMPERER
SCANTIEST
SCANTLING
SCANTNESS
SCAPA FLOW
SCAPEGOAT
SCAPHOPOD
SCAPOLITE
SCARABOID
SCARECROW
SCARFSKIN
SCARIFIED
SCARIFIER
SCARINGLY
SCARPERED
SCATOLOGY
SCATTERED
SCATTERER
SCATTIEST
SCAVENGED
SCAVENGER
SCENARIOS
SCENARIST
SCENTLESS
SCEPTICAL
SCHEDULAR
SCHEDULED
SCHEDULES
SCHEELITE
SCHEMATIC

SCHILLING
SCHISTOSE
SCHIZOPOD
SCHLEPPED
SCHLIEREN
SCHLIERIC
SCHMALTZY
SCHNAUZER
SCHNITZEL
SCHNORKEL
SCHOLARLY
SCHOLIAST
SCHOOLBOY
SCHOOLING
SCHOONERS
SCIENTIAL
SCIENTISM
SCIENTIST
SCIMITARS
SCINTILLA
SCIOMANCY
SCIRRHOID
SCIRRHOUS
SCLERITIC
SCLERITIS
SCLEROSAL
SCLEROSED
SCLEROSES
SCLEROSIS
SCLEROTIC
SCOLDABLE
SCOLDINGS
SCOLECITE
SCOLIOSIS
SCOLIOTIC
SCOLLOPED
SCOMBROID
SCOPOLINE
SCOPULATE
SCORBUTIC
SCORCHERS
SCORCHING
SCORECARD
SCORIFIER
SCORPIOID
SCORPIONS
SCOTCH EGG
SCOTCHING
SCOUNDREL
SCOURGING
SCOURINGS

SCRABBLED	SCRUMPING	SECTIONAL	SENESCENT	SERRIFORM
SCRABBLER	SCRUNCHED	SECTIONED	SENESCHAL	SERRULATE
SCRAGGIER	SCRUNCHIE	SECTORIAL	SENIORITY	SERVERIES
SCRAGGILY	SCRUPLING	SECUNDINE	SENORITAS	SERVICING
SCRAGGING	SCUFFLING	SECURABLE	SENSATION	SERVIETTE
SCRAMBLED	SCULLIONS	SEDATIVES	SENSELESS	SERVILELY
SCRAMBLER	SCULPTORS	SEDENTARY	SENSILLUM	SERVILITY
SCRAMBLES	SCULPTURE	SEDIMENTS	SENSITIVE	SERVITORS
SCRAMMING	SCUPPERED	SEDITIOUS	SENSITIZE	SERVITUDE
SCRAPABLE	SCURRYING	SEDUCIBLE	SENSORIUM	SESSILITY
SCRAPBOOK	SCUTATION	SEDUCTION	SENTENCED	SESSIONAL
SCRAP HEAP	SCUTCHEON	SEDUCTIVE	SENTENCES	SETACEOUS
SCRAPINGS	SCUTELLAR	SEEDINESS	SENTIENCE	SET FIRE
SCRAP IRON	SCUTELLUM	SEEDLINGS	SENTIMENT	TO
SCRAPPIER	SCUTIFORM	SEEMINGLY	SENTINELS	SET PIECES
SCRAPPILY	SCUTTLING	SEESAWING	SENTRY BOX	SET SPEECH
SCRAPPING	SEABOARDS	SEGMENTAL	SEPARABLE	SETSQUARE
SCRATCHED	SEA BREEZE	SEGMENTED	SEPARABLY	SET SQUARE
SCRATCHER	SEA CHANGE	SEGREGATE	SEPARATED	SET THEORY
SCRATCHES	SEAFARING	SEIGNEURS	SEPARATES	SETTLED IN
SCRAWLING	SEAFRONTS	SELACHIAN	SEPARATOR	SETTLINGS
SCRAWNIER	SEAHORSES	SELECTING	SEPHARDIC	SET-TOP
SCRAWNILY	SEAL-POINT	SELECTION	SEPIOLITE	BOX
SCREAMING	SEALYHAMS	SELECTIVE	SEPTARIAN	SEVENFOLD
SCREECHED	SEAMINESS	SELECTORS	SEPTARIUM	SEVENTEEN
SCREECHER	SEAPLANES	SELENIOUS	SEPTEMBER	SEVENTIES
SCREECHES	SEA POWERS	SELF-ABUSE	SEPTENARY	SEVERABLE
SCREENING	SEARCHING	SELF-DOUBT	SEPTICITY	SEVERALLY
SCREWBALL	SEASCAPES	SELF-DRIVE	SEPTUPLET	SEVERALTY
SCREWIEST	SEA SHANTY	SELFISHLY	SEPULCHRE	SEVERANCE
SCREW TOPS	SEASHELLS	SELLOTAPE	SEPULTURE	SEX APPEAL
SCREWWORM	SEASONING	SELL SHORT	SEQUACITY	SEXENNIAL
SCRIBBLED	SEAT BELTS	SEMANTICS	SEQUENCER	SEX OBJECT
SCRIBBLER	SEA URCHIN	SEMAPHORE	SEQUENCES	SEX ORGANS
SCRIBBLES	SEAWORTHY	SEMBLANCE	SEQUESTER	SEXTUPLET
SCRIMMAGE	SEBACEOUS	SEMESTERS	SERAGLIOS	SEXUALITY
SCRIMPILY	SECATEURS	SEMESTRAL	SERENADED	SFORZANDO
SCRIMPING	SECESSION	SEMI-BANTU	SERENADER	SGRAFFITO
SCRIMSHAW	SECLUDING	SEMIBREVE	SERENADES	SHABBIEST
SCRIPTURE	SECLUSION	SEMICOLON	SERGEANCY	SHACKLING
SCROLLING	SECLUSIVE	SEMIFINAL	SERGEANTS	SHADINESS
SCROUNGED	SECONDARY	SEMIFLUID	SERIALISM	SHADOW-BOX
SCROUNGER	SECONDERS	SEMILUNAR	SERIALIZE	SHADOWIER
SCRUBBERS	SECONDING	SEMIOTICS	SERICEOUS	SHADOWING
SCRUBBIER	SECRETARY	SEMIRIGID	SERIGRAPH	SHAGGIEST
SCRUBBING	SECRETING	SEMISOLID	SERIOUSLY	SHAKE A
SCRUBLAND	SECRETION	SEMISWEET	SERMONIZE	LEG
SCRUFFIER	SECRETIVE	SEMITONES	SEROLOGIC	SHAKEDOWN
SCRUMHALF	SECRETORY	SEMITONIC	SEROTINAL	SHAKEOUTS
SCRUM HALF	SECTARIAN	SEMIVOCAL	SEROTONIN	SHAKINESS
SCRUMMAGE	SECTILITY	SEMIVOWEL	SERRATION	SHALLOWED

SHALLOWER	SHININESS	SHOWPIECE	SIDEWARDS	SINGULARS
SHALLOWLY	SHINNYING	SHOW PIECE	SIGHTABLE	SINGULTUS
SHAMANISM	SHIPBOARD	SHOWPLACE	SIGHTINGS	SINHALESE
SHAMANIST	SHIPMATES	SHOWROOMS	SIGHTLESS	SINISTRAL
SHAMATEUR	SHIPMENTS	SHOW TRIAL	SIGHT-READ	SINOLOGUE
SHAMBLING	SHIPOWNER	SHREDDERS	SIGHTSEER	SINUOSITY
SHAMBOLIC	SHIPSHAPE	SHREDDING	SIGMATION	SINUOUSLY
SHAMELESS	SHIPWRECK	SHREWDEST	SIGNAL BOX	SINUSITIS
SHAMPOOED	SHIPYARDS	SHRIEKING	SIGNALING	SIPHONAGE
SHAMPOOER	SHIRTIEST	SHRILLEST	SIGNALIZE	SIPHONING
SHANGRI-LA	SHIRTTAIL	SHRINKAGE	SIGNALLED	SISYPHEAN
SHAN STATE	SHITTIEST	SHRINKING	SIGNALLER	SIT AT
SHAPELESS	SHIVERING	SHRIVELED	SIGNALMAN	HOME
SHAPELIER	SHOCKABLE	SHROUDING	SIGNALMEN	SITATUNGA
SHARECROP	SHODDIEST	SHRUBBERY	SIGNATORY	SITUATING
SHARE SHOP	SHOEHORNS	SHRUGGING	SIGNATURE	SITUATION
SHAREWARE	SHOELACES	SHUBUNKIN	SIGNBOARD	SITZKREIG
SHARKSKIN	SHOEMAKER	SHUDDERED	SIGNIFIED	SIX-FOOTER
SHARPENED	SHOESHINE	SHUFBOARD	SIGNIFIER	SIXPENCES
SHARPENER	SHOETREES	SHUFFLERS	SIGNORINA	SIXTEENMO
SHARP-EYED	SHOOT-'EM-	SHUFFLING	SIGNPOSTS	SIXTEENTH
SHARPNESS	UP	SHUNNABLE	SIKKIMESE	SIXTH FORM
SHATTERED	SHOOTINGS	SHUTDOWNS	SILENCERS	SIXTIETHS
SHATTERER	SHOOT-OUTS	SHUTTERED	SILENCING	SIZARSHIP
SHEARLING	SHOP FLOOR	SHUTTLING	SILICATES	SKAGERRAK
SHEATFISH	SHORELESS	SIBILANCE	SILICEOUS	SKEDADDLE
SHEATHING	SHORELINE	SIBILANTS	SILICOSIS	SKELETONS
SHEEPDIPS	SHORTAGES	SIBYLLINE	SILIQUOSE	SKEPTICAL
SHEEPDOGS	SHORTCAKE	SICCATIVE	SILKALINE	SKETCHERS
SHEEPFOLD	SHORT CUTS	SICKENING	SILKINESS	SKETCHIER
SHEEPSKIN	SHORTENED	SICK LEAVE	SILKWORMS	SKETCHILY
SHEEPWALK	SHORTENER	SICKLIEST	SILLABUBS	SKETCHING
SHEERLEGS	SHORTFALL	SICKROOMS	SILLINESS	SKETCHPAD
SHEERNESS	SHORTHAND	SIC PASSIM	SILTATION	SKEWBALDS
SHEFFIELD	SHORT-HAUL	SIDEBOARD	SILVERING	SKEWERING
SHEIKHDOM	SHORTHORN	SIDEBURNS	SIMAROUBA	SKEW-WHIFF
SHELDUCKS	SHORT LIST	SIDE-DRESS	SIMILARLY	SKIASCOPE
SHELF LIFE	SHORTNESS	SIDE ISSUE	SIMMERING	SKIASCOPY
SHELLFIRE	SHORT SLIP	SIDEKICKS	SIMPATICO	SKIDPROOF
SHELLFISH	SHORT-TERM	SIDELIGHT	SIMPERING	SKIJORING
SHELTERED	SHORT TIME	SIDELINED	SIMPLETON	SKILFULLY
SHELTERER	SHORT WAVE	SIDELINES	SIMULACRA	SKIMMINGS
SHEPHERDS	SHOT TOWER	SIDE ORDER	SIMULATED	SKIMPIEST
SHERBORNE	SHOULDERS	SIDERITIC	SIMULATOR	SKIN-DIVED
SHIELDING	SHOVELING	SIDEROSIS	SINCERELY	SKIN DIVER
SHIFTIEST	SHOVELLED	SIDEROTIC	SINCERITY	SKIN FLICK
SHIFT KEYS	SHOWCASES	SIDESHOWS	SINECURES	SKINFLINT
SHIFTLESS	SHOWDOWNS	SIDESLIPS	SINGAPORE	SKIN GRAFT
SHILLINGS	SHOWERING	SIDESTEPS	SINGINGLY	SKINHEADS
SHIMMERED	SHOWGIRLS	SIDESWIPE	SINGLETON	SKINNIEST
SHINBONES	SHOWINESS	SIDETRACK	SINGSONGS	SKIN-TIGHT

SKI PLANES	SLOBBERER	SNAKESKIN	SOARINGLY	SOLSTICES
SKIPPERED	SLOPINGLY	SNAKINESS	SOBBINGLY	SOLUTIONS
SKITTERED	SLOPPIEST	SNAPPABLE	SOBERNESS	SOLUTREAN
SKIVVYING	SLOUCH HAT	SNAPPIEST	SOBRIQUET	SOLVATION
SKULLCAPS	SLOUCHILY	SNAPSHOTS	SOB SISTER	SOMBREROS
SKYDIVERS	SLOUCHING	SNARE DRUM	SOCIALISM	SOMEPLACE
SKYDIVING	SLOUGHING	SNARINGLY	SOCIALIST	SOMETHING
SKYJACKED	SLOVAKIAN	SNATCHILY	SOCIALITE	SOMETIMES
SKYJACKER	SLOVENIAN	SNATCHING	SOCIALITY	SOMEWHERE
SKYLARKED	SLOWCOACH	SNAZZIEST	SOCIALIZE	SOMMELIER
SKYLARKER	SLOWDOWNS	SNEAKIEST	SOCIETIES	SOMNOLENT
SKYLIGHTS	SLOW MATCH	SNICKERED	SOCIOLOGY	SONGBIRDS
SKYROCKET	SLOWWORMS	SNIDENESS	SOCIOPATH	SONGBOOKS
SKYWRITER	SLUDGIEST	SNIFFLERS	SODA WATER	SONG CYCLE
SLACKENED	SLUGGARDS	SNIFFLING	SODOMITES	SONGOLOLO
SLACKNESS	SLUMBERED	SNIGGERED	SOFTENING	SONGSTERS
SLAGHEAPS	SLUMBERER	SNIPEFISH	SOFT FRUIT	SONIC BOOM
SLANDERED	SLUSH FUND	SNITCHING	SOFT GOODS	SONNETEER
SLANDERER	SLUSHIEST	SNIVELING	SOFT METAL	SON-OF-A-
SLANTWISE	SMALL ARMS	SNIVELLED	SOFT-PEDAL	GUN
SLAPHAPPY	SMALL BEER	SNIVELLER	SOFT SPOTS	SONS-IN-
SLAPSTICK	SMALLNESS	SNOOKERED	SOFT TOUCH	LAW
SLATINESS	SMALL TALK	SNOOTIEST	SOFTWOODS	SOOTINESS
SLATTERNS	SMALL-TIME	SNOTTIEST	SOGGINESS	SOPHISTER
SLAUGHTER	SMARMIEST	SNOWBALLS	SOI-DISANT	SOPHISTIC
SLAVERING	SMART ALEC	SNOWBERRY	SOJOURNED	SOPHISTRY
SLAVISHLY	SMART CARD	SNOW-BLIND	SOJOURNER	SOPHOMORE
SLAVONIAN	SMARTENED	SNOWBLINK	SOLAR CELL	SOPORIFIC
SLEAZIEST	SMARTNESS	SNOWBOUND	SOLARIUMS	SOPPINESS
SLEEKNESS	SMASHABLE	SNOWDONIA	SOLAR YEAR	SOPRANINO
SLEEPIEST	SMATTERER	SNOWDRIFT	SOLDERING	SORCERERS
SLEEPLESS	SMEAR TEST	SNOWDROPS	SOLDIERED	SORCERESS
SLEEPWALK	SMELLIEST	SNOWFALLS	SOLDIERLY	SORCEROUS
SLICEABLE	SMILINGLY	SNOWFIELD	SOLDIER ON	SORE POINT
SLICKNESS	SMIRCHING	SNOWFLAKE	SOLECISMS	SORITICAL
SLIDE RULE	SMOKELESS	SNOW GOOSE	SOLEMNIFY	SORRINESS
SLIGHTEST	SMOKINESS	SNOWINESS	SOLEMNITY	SORROWFUL
SLIGHTING	SMOLDERED	SNOWSHOER	SOLEMNIZE	SORROWING
SLIMINESS	SMOOCHING	SNOWSHOES	SOLENODON	SORTILEGE
SLINGSHOT	SMOOTHEST	SNOWSTORM	SOLFATARA	SORTITION
SLINKIEST	SMOOTHIES	SNOW-WHITE	SOLFEGGIO	SOSNOWIEC
SLIPCASES	SMOOTHING	SNUB-NOSED	SOLFERINO	SOSTENUTO
SLIPKNOTS	SMOTHERED	SNUFFLING	SOLICITED	SOTTO VOCE
SLIPNOOSE	SMUGGLERS	SNUGGLING	SOLICITOR	SOUBRETTE
SLIPPAGES	SMUGGLING	SOAKINGLY	SOLIDNESS	SOULFULLY
SLIPPIEST	SMUTTIEST	SOAPBERRY	SOLILOQUY	SOUL MUSIC
SLIP ROADS	SNACK BARS	SOAPBOXES	SOLIPSISM	SOUNDABLE
SLIPSHEET	SNAFFLING	SOAPINESS	SOLIPSIST	SOUNDINGS
SLITHERED	SNAIL MAIL	SOAP OPERA	SOLITAIRE	SOUNDLESS
SLIVOVITZ	SNAKEBITE	SOAPSTONE	SOLONCHAK	SOUNDNESS
SLOBBERED	SNAKEROOT	SOAPSUDSY	SOLOTHURN	SOUNDPOST

SOUND POST	SPEARWORT	SPINNERET	SPOROZOAN	SQUEAKERS
SOUP SPOON	SPECIALLY	SPINOSITY	SPORTIEST	SQUEAKIER
SOUR CREAM	SPECIALTY	SPINSTERS	SPORTS CAR	SQUEAKING
SOUTH BEND	SPECIFICS	SPINULOSE	SPORTSMAN	SQUEALERS
SOUTHDOWN	SPECIFIED	SPIRALING	SPORTSMEN	SQUEALING
SOUTHEAST	SPECIFIER	SPIRALLED	SPORULATE	SQUEAMISH
SOUTHERLY	SPECIMENS	SPIRILLAR	SPOT CHECK	SQUEEGEES
SOUTHPAWS	SPECTACLE	SPIRILLUM	SPOTLIGHT	SQUEEZERS
SOUTH POLE	SPECTATED	SPIRITING	SPOTTABLE	SQUEEZING
SOUTHPORT	SPECTATOR	SPIRITOSO	SPOTTIEST	SQUELCHED
SOUTHWARD	SPECULATE	SPIRITOUS	SPRAINING	SQUELCHER
SOUTHWARK	SPEECH DAY	SPIRITUAL	SPRAWLING	SQUIDGIER
SOUTHWEST	SPEECHIFY	SPIROGYRA	SPRAY GUNS	SQUIFFIER
SOUVENIRS	SPEEDBOAT	SPITFIRES	SPREADING	SQUIGGLER
SOU'WESTER	SPEEDIEST	SPIT IT	SPRIGHTLY	SQUIGGLES
SOVEREIGN	SPEEDSTER	OUT	SPRINGBOK	SQUINTING
SOVIETISM	SPEED TRAP	SPITTOONS	SPRINGIER	SQUIRMING
SOVIETIST	SPEEDWAYS	SPLASHIER	SPRINGILY	SQUIRRELS
SOVIETIZE	SPEEDWELL	SPLASHILY	SPRINGING	SQUIRTERS
SOYA BEANS	SPELLABLE	SPLASHING	SPRINKLED	SQUIRTING
SPACEBAND	SPELLBIND	SPLATTING	SPRINKLER	SQUISHIER
SPACED OUT	SPELLINGS	SPLAYFOOT	SPRINKLES	SQUISHING
SPACELESS	SPELUNKER	SPLEENFUL	SPRINTERS	SQUITTERS
SPACEPORT	SPENDABLE	SPLEENISH	SPRINTING	STABILITY
SPACESHIP	SPERMATIC	SPLENDOUR	SPRITSAIL	STABILIZE
SPACESUIT	SPERMATID	SPLENETIC	SPROCKETS	STABLE BOY
SPACE-TIME	SPHAGNOUS	SPLENITIS	SPROUTING	STAGE DOOR
SPACEWALK	SPHAGNUMS	SPLINTERS	SPUNKIEST	STAGEHAND
SPADEFISH	SPHENODON	SPLINTERY	SPUTTERED	STAGE HAND
SPADEWORK	SPHERICAL	SPLIT ENDS	SPUTTERER	STAGE NAME
SPAGHETTI	SPHEROIDS	SPLIT PEAS	SQUABBLED	STAGGERED
SPANGLING	SPHERULAR	SPLIT RING	SQUABBLER	STAGGERER
SPANIARDS	SPHINCTER	SPLITTING	SQUABBLES	STAGHOUND
SPANKINGS	SPHYGMOID	SPLOSHING	SQUAD CARS	STAGINESS
SPARENESS	SPICINESS	SPLURGING	SQUADRONS	STAGNANCY
SPARE PART	SPICULATE	SPLUTTERS	SQUALIDLY	STAGNATED
SPARERIBS	SPIDERMAN	SPODUMENE	SQUALLIER	STAG PARTY
SPARE TYRE	SPIDERWEB	SPOKEN FOR	SQUALLING	STAIDNESS
SPARINGLY	SPIELBERG	SPOKESMAN	SQUAMOSAL	STAINABLE
SPARKLERS	SPIKENARD	SPONGE BAG	SQUARE LEG	STAINLESS
SPARKLING	SPIKE-RUSH	SPONGIEST	SQUARE ONE	STAIRCASE
SPARK PLUG	SPIKINESS	SPONSORED	SQUARROSE	STAIRHEAD
SPARTEINE	SPILLIKIN	SPOOKIEST	SQUASHIER	STAIRWELL
SPASMODIC	SPILLWAYS	SPOONBILL	SQUASHILY	STALEMATE
SPATIALLY	SPINDLIER	SPOON-FEED	SQUASHING	STALENESS
SPATTERED	SPIN-DRIED	SPOONFULS	SQUATNESS	STALINISM
SPATULATE	SPINDRIFT	SPOONSFUL	SQUATTERS	STALINIST
SPEAKABLE	SPIN-DRYER	SPOROCARP	SQUATTEST	STALL-FEED
SPEAKEASY	SPINELESS	SPOROCYST	SQUATTING	STALLIONS
SPEARHEAD	SPININESS	SPOROCYTE	SQUAWKERS	STALWARTS
SPEARMINT	SPINNAKER	SPOROGONY	SQUAWKING	STAMINATE

STAMINODE	STEADFAST	STILLNESS	STONEWORK	STRESSFUL
STAMINODY	STEADIEST	STILL ROOM	STONEWORT	STRESSING
STAMMERED	STEADYING	STILTEDLY	STONINESS	STRETCHED
STAMMERER	STEAMBOAT	STIMULANT	STOPCOCKS	STRETCHER
STAMPEDED	STEAMED-UP	STIMULATE	STOPLIGHT	STRETCHES
STAMPEDER	STEAMIEST	STINGIEST	STOPOVERS	STRETFORD
STAMPEDES	STEAM IRON	STINGRAYS	STOPPABLE	STRIATION
STAMP MILL	STEAMROLL	STINK-BOMB	STOPPAGES	STRICTEST
STANCHING	STEAMSHIP	STINKHORN	STOPPERED	STRICTURE
STANCHION	STEATITIC	STINKWEED	STOP PRESS	STRIDENCE
STANDARDS	STEEL BAND	STINKWOOD	STOPWATCH	STRIDENCY
STAND FIRM	STEELHEAD	STIPIFORM	STOREROOM	STRIKE PAY
STAND OVER	STEELIEST	STIPITATE	STORMIEST	STRINGENT
STANDPIPE	STEEL WOOL	STIPPLING	STORNOWAY	STRINGIER
STAPEDIAL	STEELWORK	STIPULATE	STORYBOOK	STRINGILY
STAR-APPLE	STEELYARD	STIR-FRIED	STORY LINE	STRINGING
STARBOARD	STEEPENED	STIRRABLE	STORYLINE	STRIP CLUB
STARBURST	STEEPNESS	STITCHING	STOUTNESS	STRIPIEST
STARCHIER	STEERABLE	STOCKADED	STOVEPIPE	STRIPLING
STARCHILY	STEERSMAN	STOCKADES	STOWAWAYS	STRIPPERS
STARCHING	STEERSMEN	STOCKCARS	STRADDLED	STRIPPING
STARE DOWN	STELLULAR	STOCK CUBE	STRADDLER	STROBILUS
STARGAZER	STENCILED	STOCKFISH	STRAGGLED	STROLLERS
STARKNESS	STENOTYPE	STOCKHOLM	STRAGGLER	STROLLING
STARLIGHT	STENOTYPY	STOCKIEST	STRAIGHTS	STROMATIC
STARLINGS	STEPCHILD	STOCKINET	STRAINERS	STRONGARM
STARRIEST	STERADIAN	STOCKINGS	STRAINING	STRONGBOX
STAR SIGNS	STERILANT	STOCKISTS	STRALSUND	STRONGEST
STARTLING	STERILITY	STOCKPILE	STRANGELY	STRONGYLE
STATE DUMA	STERILIZE	STOCKPORT	STRANGERS	STRONTIAN
STATEHOOD	STERNMOST	STOCKPOTS	STRANGEST	STRONTIUM
STATELESS	STERNNESS	STOCKROOM	STRANGLED	STROPPIER
STATEMENT	STERNPOST	STOCK TAKE	STRANGLER	STRUCTURE
STATEROOM	STEVEDORE	STOCKYARD	STRANGLES	STRUGGLED
STATESIDE	STEVENAGE	STODGIEST	STRANGURY	STRUGGLER
STATESMAN	STICK AT	STOICALLY	STRANRAER	STRUGGLES
STATESMEN	IT	STOKEHOLD	STRAPLESS	STRUMATIC
STATIONED	STICKIEST	STOKEHOLE	STRAPPING	STRUMMING
STATIONER	STICKLERS	STOLIDITY	STRATAGEM	STRUMPETS
STATISTIC	STICKPINS	STOMACHED	STRATEGIC	STRUNG-OUT
STATOCYST	STICKSEED	STOMACHIC	STRAW POLL	STRUTTING
STATOLITH	STICKWEED	STONECHAT	STREAKERS	STRYCHNIC
STATUETTE	STICKY BUN	STONE-COLD	STREAKIER	STUBBIEST
STATUS QUO	STICKY END	STONECROP	STREAKILY	STUDBOOKS
STATUTORY	STIFFENED	STONE-DEAD	STREAKING	STUDHORSE
STAUNCHED	STIFFENER	STONE-DEAF	STREAMERS	STUFFIEST
STAUNCHER	STIFFNESS	STONEFISH	STREAMING	STUMBLING
STAUNCHLY	STIGMATIC	STONELESS	STREETCAR	STUMPIEST
STAVANGER	STILETTOS	STONE-LILY	STREISAND	STUPEFIED
STAVROPOL	STILLBORN	STONEWALL	STRENGTHS	STUPEFIER
ST BERNARD	STILL LIFE	STONEWARE	STRENUOUS	STUPIDEST

STUPIDITY	SUBMITTER	SUFFOCATE	SUPERHEAT	SUSPECTED
STUPOROUS	SUBMUCOSA	SUFFRAGAN	SUPERHERO	SUSPECTER
STURDIEST	SUBNORMAL	SUFFRAGES	SUPERIORS	SUSPENDED
STURGEONS	SUBORNING	SUFFUSING	SUPERNOVA	SUSPENDER
STUTTERED	SUBPHYLAR	SUFFUSION	SUPERPOSE	SUSPENSOR
STUTTERER	SUBPHYLUM	SUFFUSIVE	SUPERSEDE	SUSPICION
STUTTGART	SUBPOENAS	SUGAR BEET	SUPERSTAR	SUSTAINED
STYLEBOOK	SUBREGION	SUGAR CANE	SUPERVENE	SUSTAINER
STYLELESS	SUBROGATE	SUGARCANE	SUPERVISE	SUSURRANT
STYLIFORM	SUBSCRIBE	SUGGESTED	SUPINATOR	SUSURRATE
STYLISHLY	SUBSCRIPT	SUGGESTER	SUPPERADD	SUZERAINS
STYLISTIC	SUBSIDIES	SUITCASES	SUPPLIANT	SWADDLING
STYLIZING	SUBSIDING	SULCATION	SUPPLIERS	SWAGGERED
STYLOBATE	SUBSIDIZE	SULKINESS	SUPPLYING	SWAGGERER
STYLOLITE	SUBSISTED	SULLENEST	SUPPORTED	SWAHILIAN
STYLOPIZE	SUBSISTER	SULLIABLE	SUPPORTER	SWALLOWED
STYPTICAL	SUBSOCIAL	SULPHATES	SUPPOSING	SWALLOWER
STYROFOAM	SUBSOILER	SULPHIDES	SUPPURATE	SWAMPLAND
SUABILITY	SUBSTANCE	SULPHITIC	SUPREMACY	SWANKIEST
SUAVENESS	SUBSTRATA	SULPHURET	SUPREMELY	SWANS DOWN
SUBALPINE	SUBSTRATE	SULPHURYL	SUPREMITY	SWAN'S-
SUBALTERN	SUBSUMING	SULTANATE	SURAKARTA	DOWN
SUBARCTIC	SUBSYSTEM	SULTRIEST	SURCHARGE	SWANSONGS
SUBATOMIC	SUBTENANT	SUMMARIES	SURCINGLE	SWAP MEETS
SUBCLIMAX	SUBTENDED	SUMMARILY	SURCULOSE	SWARTHIER
SUBCORTEX	SUBTILIZE	SUMMARIZE	SURE THING	SWARTHILY
SUBDEACON	SUBTITLED	SUMMATION	SURFACING	SWASTIKAS
SUBDIVIDE	SUBTITLES	SUMMERING	SURFBOARD	SWATHABLE
SUBDUABLE	SUBTOTALS	SUMMING-UP	SURFEITED	SWAYINGLY
SUBDUEDLY	SUBVERTED	SUMMONING	SURFEITER	SWAZILAND
SUBEDITED	SUBVERTER	SUMMONSED	SURFPERCH	SWEARWORD
SUBEDITOR	SUBWOOFER	SUMMONSES	SURGEONCY	SWEATBAND
SUBFAMILY	SUCCEEDED	SUMPTUARY	SURGERIES	SWEATIEST
SUBJACENT	SUCCEEDER	SUMPTUOUS	SURLINESS	SWEATSHOP
SUBJECTED	SUCCENTOR	SUNBATHED	SURMISING	SWEEPBACK
SUBJOINED	SUCCESSES	SUNBATHER	SURPASSED	SWEEPINGS
SUB JUDICE	SUCCESSOR	SUNBURNED	SURPLICES	SWEET CORN
SUBJUGATE	SUCCINATE	SUNDERING	SURPLUSES	SWEETENER
SUBLEASED	SUCCOURED	SUNDOWNER	SURPRISED	SWEETMEAT
SUBLEASES	SUCCOURER	SUNDSVALL	SURPRISER	SWEETNESS
SUBLESSEE	SUCCULENT	SUNFLOWER	SURPRISES	SWEET PEAS
SUBLESSOR	SUCCUMBED	SUN LOUNGE	SURRENDER	SWEET TALK
SUBLIMATE	SUCCUMBER	SUNNINESS	SURROGACY	SWELLFISH
SUBLIMELY	SUCKLINGS	SUNSHADES	SURROGATE	SWELLINGS
SUBLIMITY	SUCTIONAL	SUNSTROKE	SURROUNDS	SWELTERED
SUBLUNARY	SUCTORIAL	SUNTANNED	SURTITLES	SWEPT-BACK
SUBMARINE	SUDORIFIC	SUN VISORS	SURVEYING	SWEPTWING
SUBMENTAL	SUFFERERS	SUPERABLE	SURVEYORS	SWERVABLE
SUBMERGED	SUFFERING	SUPERCOOL	SURVIVALS	SWIFTNESS
SUBMITTAL	SUFFICING	SUPEREGOS	SURVIVING	SWIMMABLE
SUBMITTED	SUFFIXION	SUPERFINE	SURVIVORS	SWIMMERET

SWINDLERS	SYNCOPATE	TAILGATED	TARGETING	TEDDY BEAR
SWINDLING	SYNCRETIC	TAILGATES	TARMACKED	TEDDY BOYS
SWINEHERD	SYNCYTIUM	TAILLIGHT	TARNISHED	TEDIOUSLY
SWINGEING	SYNDACTYL	TAIL-LIGHT	TARNISHER	TEENAGERS
SWING-WING	SYNDICATE	TAILORING	TARPAULIN	TEE SHIRTS
SWINISHLY	SYNDROMES	TAILPIECE	TARRAGONA	TEETERING
SWISS ROLL	SYNDROMIC	TAIL PIPES	TARTARIZE	TELECASTS
SWITCHING	SYNECTICS	TAILPLANE	TARTAROUS	TELEGENIC
SWITCH OFF	SYNERESIS	TAILSPINS	TASIMETER	TELEGONIC
SWIVELING	SYNERGISM	TAILSTOCK	TASIMETRY	TELEGRAMS
SWIVELLED	SYNERGIST	TAILWHEEL	TASK FORCE	TELEGRAPH
SWORDBILL	SYNIZESIS	TAILWINDS	TASMANIAN	TELEMETER
SWORDFISH	SYNKARYON	TAIWANESE	TASMAN SEA	TELEMETRY
SWORDPLAY	SYNOEKETE	TAKAMATSU	TASTE BUDS	TELEOLOGY
SWORDSMAN	SYNONYMIC	TAKEAWAYS	TASTELESS	TELEPATHY
SWORDSMEN	SYNOVITIC	TAKE LEAVE	TASTINESS	TELEPHONE
SWORDTAIL	SYNOVITIS	TAKE NOTES	TATTINESS	TELEPHONY
SYBARITES	SYNTACTIC	TAKEOVERS	TATTOOING	TELESCOPE
SYBARITIC	SYNTHESES	TAKE STEPS	TATTOOIST	TELESCOPY
SYCAMORES	SYNTHESIS	TAKE STOCK	TAUTENING	TELESTICH
SYCOPHANT	SYNTHETIC	TAKING OFF	TAUTOLOGY	TELEVISED
SYKTYVKAR	SYPHERING	TALIGRADE	TAUTONYMY	TELLINGLY
SYLLABARY	SYPHILOID	TALISMANS	TAXACEOUS	TELLTALES
SYLLABIFY	SYPHILOMA	TALKATIVE	TAX HAVENS	TELLURATE
SYLLABISM	SYPHONING	TALKING-TO	TAXIDERMY	TELLURIAN
SYLLABLES	SYRINGEAL	TALK SHOWS	TAXIMETER	TELLURIDE
SYLLABUBS	SYRINGING	TALL ORDER	TAXI RANKS	TELLURION
SYLLEPSIS	SYSTALTIC	TALL STORY	TAXONOMIC	TELLURITE
SYLLEPTIC		TALMUDISM	TAXPAYERS	TELLURIUM
SYLLOGISM	**T**	TALMUDIST	TEA BREAKS	TELLURIZE
SYLLOGIZE	TABESCENT	TAMARINDS	TEACHABLE	TELLUROUS
SYLPHLIKE	TABLATURE	TAMIL NADU	TEA CHESTS	TELOPHASE
SYLVANITE	TABLELAND	TAMOXIFEN	TEA CLOTHS	TELPHERIC
SYMBIOSIS	TABLEMATS	TAMPERING	TEA COSIES	TEMAZEPAM
SYMBIOTIC	TABLEWARE	TANDOORIS	TEAGARDEN	TEMPERATE
SYMBOLISM	TABLE WINE	TANGERINE	TEAHOUSES	TEMPERING
SYMBOLIST	TABULABLE	TANNERIES	TEAKETTLE	TEMPLATES
SYMBOLIZE	TABULATED	TANTALATE	TEALEAVES	TEMPORARY
SYMBOLOGY	TABULATOR	TANTALITE	TEAMSTERS	TEMPORIZE
SYMPATHIN	TACAMAHAC	TANTALIZE	TEARAWAYS	TEMPTABLE
SYMPATRIC	TACHYLYTE	TANTALOUS	TEARDROPS	TEMPTRESS
SYMPHONIC	TACITNESS	TANZANIAN	TEARFULLY	TENACIOUS
SYMPHYSIS	TACKINESS	TAP DANCER	TEARINGLY	TENACULUM
SYMPODIAL	TACTFULLY	TAP DANCES	TEASINGLY	TENANCIES
SYMPODIUM	TACTICIAN	TAPE DECKS	TEASPOONS	TENDEREST
SYMPOSIAC	TACTILITY	TAPEWORMS	TEA TASTER	TENDERING
SYMPOSIUM	TAENIASIS	TAPHONOMY	TEA TOWELS	TENDERIZE
SYNAGOGUE	TAGMEMICS	TARANTISM	TECHINESS	TENDINOUS
SYNALEPHA	TAILBACKS	TARANTULA	TECHNICAL	TENEBRISM
SYNCHRONY	TAILBOARD	TARAXACUM	TECHNIQUE	TENEBRIST
SYNCLINAL	TAILCOATS	TARDINESS	TECTONICS	TENEBROUS

TENEMENTS	TETRAPODY	THIRTIETH	TIDAL WAVE	TOADSTOOL
TENNESSEE	TETRARCHY	THITHERTO	TIDEMARKS	TOAMASINA
TENOR CLEF	TETROXIDE	THONINESS	TIDEWATER	TOAST RACK
TENSENESS	TEXTBOOKS	THORNBACK	TIED HOUSE	TOBOGGANS
TENSILITY	THALASSIC	THORNBILL	TIE-DYEING	TOCANTINS
TENSIONAL	THANJAVUR	THORNIEST	TIGER LILY	TOGLIATTI
TENSORIAL	THANKLESS	THOUSANDS	TIGHTENED	TOLERABLE
TENTACLES	THANKYOUS	THRALLDOM	TIGHTENER	TOLERABLY
TENTATION	THATCHERS	THRASHING	TIGHTEN UP	TOLERANCE
TENTATIVE	THATCHING	THREADFIN	TIGHTKNIT	TOLERATED
TENUOUSLY	THEACEOUS	THREADING	TIGHTNESS	TOLERATOR
TEPHRITIC	THEARCHIC	THREEFOLD	TIGHTROPE	TOLLBOOTH
TEREBINTH	THEATRICS	THREESOME	TIGHT SPOT	TOLLGATES
TERMAGANT	THE BROADS	THREE-STAR	TIGRESSES	TOLLHOUSE
TERMINALS	THECODONT	THREONINE	TIME BOMBS	TOLL HOUSE
TERMINATE	THE CREEPS	THRESHERS	TIME LAPSE	TOMAHAWKS
TERPINEOL	THEME PARK	THRESHING	TIME-LAPSE	TOMBOYISH
TERRAFORM	THEME SONG	THRESHOLD	TIMELIEST	TOMBSTONE
TERRAPINS	THEOCRACY	THRIFTIER	TIME LIMIT	TOMMY GUNS
TERRARIUM	THEOCRASY	THRIFTILY	TIMEPIECE	TOMORROWS
TERRIFIED	THEOMANIA	THRILLERS	TIMESAVER	TONBRIDGE
TERRIFIER	THEORISTS	THRILLING	TIME SHEET	TONE POEMS
TERRITORY	THEORIZED	THROATIER	TIMETABLE	TONKA BEAN
TERRORFUL	THEORIZER	THROATILY	TIME ZONES	TONOMETER
TERRORISM	THEOSOPHY	THROBBING	TIMISOARA	TONOMETRY
TERRORIST	THERAPIES	THRONGING	TIMOCRACY	TONSILLAR
TERRORIZE	THERAPIST	THROTTLED	TIMPANIST	TONSORIAL
TERSENESS	THERAPSID	THROTTLER	TINCTURES	TOOL-MAKER
TERVALENT	THEREFORE	THROTTLES	TINDERBOX	TOOTHACHE
TESSERACT	THEREINTO	THROWAWAY	TINGALING	TOOTHCOMB
TESSITURA	THEREUPON	THROWBACK	TINKERING	TOOTHIEST
TESTAMENT	THEREWITH	THROWSTER	TINNINESS	TOOTHLESS
TESTATORS	THERMOSES	THRUMMING	TIN OPENER	TOOTHPICK
TESTATRIX	THESAURUS	THRUSTERS	TIP AND	TOOTHSOME
TEST CARDS	THESPIANS	THRUSTING	RUN	TOOTHWORT
TEST CASES	THE STATES	THUMBNAIL	TIPPERARY	TOOWOOMBA
TESTICLES	THEURGIST	THUMBTACK	TIPSINESS	TOP DOLLAR
TESTIFIED	THICKENED	THUNDERED	TIREDNESS	TOP DRAWER
TESTIFIRE	THICKENER	THUNDERER	TITCHIEST	TOP FLIGHT
TESTIMONY	THICKHEAD	THURINGIA	TIT FOR	TOP-FLIGHT
TESTINESS	THICKLEAF	THURSDAYS	TAT	TOPIARIAN
TESTINGLY	THICKNESS	THWACKING	TITILLATE	TOPIARIST
TEST MATCH	THIGHBONE	THWARTING	TITIVATED	TOPICALLY
TEST PILOT	THINKABLE	THYLACINE	TITIVATOR	TOPMINNOW
TEST TUBES	THINK TANK	THYMIDINE	TITLE DEED	TOPOLOGIC
TETCHIEST	THINNINGS	THYRATRON	TITLE PAGE	TOPONYMIC
TETE-A-	THIO-ETHER	THYRISTOR	TITLE ROLE	TOP SECRET
TETE	THIOPHENE	THYROXINE	TITRATION	TOP-SECRET
TETHERING	THIRD-RATE	TICKETING	TITTERING	TORCHWOOD
TETRAGRAM	THIRSTIER	TIC TAC	T-JUNCTION	TOREADORS
TETRALOGY	THIRSTILY	MAN	TOADSTONE	TOREUTICS

TORMENTED	TRACEABLE	TRASHIEST	TRIBUNALS	TRIUMPHAL
TORMENTIL	TRACHYTIC	TRATTORIA	TRIBUNARY	TRIUMPHED
TORMENTOR	TRACKABLE	TRAUMATIC	TRIBUNATE	TRIUMPHER
TORNADOES	TRACKLESS	TRAVAILED	TRIBUTARY	TRIVALENT
TORPEDOED	TRACKSUIT	TRAVELING	TRICEPSES	TRIVIALLY
TORPEDOES	TRACK SUIT	TRAVELLED	TRICHITIC	TRIWEEKLY
TORPIDITY	TRACTABLE	TRAVELLER	TRICHOMIC	TROCHLEAR
TORRIDITY	TRADE GAPS	TRAVERSAL	TRICHOSIS	TROMBONES
TORSIONAL	TRADEMARK	TRAVERSED	TRICHROIC	TRONDHEIM
TORTILLAS	TRADE NAME	TRAVERSER	TRICKIEST	TROOPSHIP
TORTOISES	TRADE-OFFS	TRAVERSES	TRICKLING	TROOSTITE
TORTRICID	TRADESMAN	TREACHERY	TRICKSTER	TROPISTIC
TORTURERS	TRADESMEN	TREADMILL	TRICLINIC	TROPOLOGY
TORTURING	TRADE WIND	TREASURED	TRICOLOUR	TROSSACHS
TOTALIZER	TRADITION	TREASURER	TRICOTINE	TROUBLING
TOTALLING	TRADUCERS	TREASURES	TRICROTIC	TROUBLOUS
TOTAQUINE	TRADUCING	TREATABLE	TRICUSPID	TROUNCING
TOTEM POLE	TRAFALGAR	TREATISES	TRICYCLES	TROUSSEAU
TO THE	TRAGEDIAN	TREATMENT	TRICYCLIC	TROWELLER
FORE	TRAGEDIES	TREE FERNS	TRIDACTYL	TRPORIFIC
TOTTERING	TRAINABLE	TREENWARE	TRIENNIAL	TRUCK FARM
TOTTING UP	TRAININGS	TREE SHREW	TRIENNIUM	TRUCKLING
TOUCHABLE	TRAIN SETS	TREHALOSE	TRIFOLIUM	TRUCKLOAD
TOUCHDOWN	TRAIPSING	TREILLAGE	TRIFORIAL	TRUCK STOP
TOUCH DOWN	TRAMLINES	TRELLISES	TRIFORIUM	TRUCULENT
TOUCHIEST	TRAMMELER	TREMATODE	TRIGGERED	TRUELOVES
TOUCHLINE	TRAMPLING	TREMBLING	TRIGONOUS	TRUE NORTH
TOUCHMARK	TRANSCEND	TREMOLITE	TRIHEDRAL	TRUMP CARD
TOUCH-TYPE	TRANSEPTS	TREMOROUS	TRIHEDRON	TRUMPETED
TOUCHWOOD	TRANSEUNT	TREMULANT	TRIHYDRIC	TRUMPETER
TOUGHENED	TRANSFERS	TREMULOUS	TRILINEAR	TRUNCATED
TOUGHENER	TRANSFORM	TRENCHANT	TRILLIONS	TRUNCHEON
TOUGH LUCK	TRANSFUER	TRENCHERS	TRILOBATE	TRUNDLING
TOUGHNESS	TRANSFUSE	TRENDIEST	TRILOBITE	TRUNK CALL
TOURCOING	TRANSIENT	TRENGGANU	TRILOGIES	TRUNKFISH
TOURISTIC	TRANSLATE	TREPANNED	TRIMARANS	TRUNK ROAD
TOUT A	TRANSMUTE	TREPHINED	TRIMEROUS	TRUSTABLE
FAIT	TRANSONIC	TREPHINES	TRIMESTER	TRUST FUND
TOWELLING	TRANSPIRE	TREPONEMA	TRIMETRIC	TRUSTIEST
TOWN CLERK	TRANSPORT	TRIALLIST	TRIMMINGS	TRYING OUT
TOWN CRIER	TRANSPOSE	TRIAL RUNS	TRINITIES	TRY SQUARE
TOWN HALLS	TRANSSHIP	TRIANGLES	TRINOMIAL	TSETSE FLY
TOWN HOUSE	TRANSVAAL	TRIATHLON	TRIOELEIN	TSITSIHAR
TOWNSCAPE	TRAPDOORS	TRIATOMIC	TRIPLEXES	TUBBINESS
TOWNSHIPS	TRAPEZIAL	TRIAZOLIC	TRIPTYCHS	TUBULATOR
TOXAPHENE	TRAPEZIUM	TRIBADISM	TRIPWIRES	TUCKER BAG
TOXICALLY	TRAPEZIUS	TRIBALISM	TRISECTED	TUCKER-BAG
TOXICOSIS	TRAPEZOID	TRIBALIST	TRISECTOR	TUCKERING
TOXOPHILY	TRAPPINGS	TRIBESMAN	TRISERIAL	TUG-OF-
TRABEATED	TRAPPISTS	TRIBESMEN	TRITENESS	LOVE
TRABECULA	TRASHCANS	TRIBOLOGY	TRITURATE	

TUGS-OF-WAR	TWINKLING	UNADOPTED	UNDERGIRD	UNFLEDGED
TUILERIES	TWISTABLE	UNADVISED	UNDERGOER	UNFOLDING
TUITIONAL	TWISTEDLY	UNALLOYED	UNDERGONE	UNFOUNDED
TULIP TREE	TWISTIEST	UNANIMITY	UNDERHAND	UNFROCKED
TULIPWOOD	TWITCHING	UNANIMOUS	UNDERHUNG	UNFURLING
TULLAMORE	TWITTERED	UNAPTNESS	UNDERLAIN	UNGUARDED
TUMBLE-DRY	TWITTERER	UNASHAMED	UNDERLAYS	UNGUINOUS
TUMESCENT	TWO-BY-FOUR	UNASSUMED	UNDERLIER	UNHANDING
TUMULUSES	TWO-HANDED	UNAUDITED	UNDERLINE	UNHAPPILY
TUNEFULLY	TWOPENCES	UNBALANCE	UNDERLING	UNHARNESS
TUNGSTITE	TWO-SEATER	UNBARRING	UNDERMINE	UNHEALTHY
TUNGUSIAN	TWO-STROKE	UNBEKNOWN	UNDERMOST	UNHEARD OF
TUNING PEG	TWO-TIMERS	UNBENDING	UNDERPAID	UNHEARD-OF
TUNNELERS	TWO-TIMING	UNBINDING	UNDERPASS	UNHINGING
TUNNELING	TYMPANIST	UNBLESSED	UNDERPLAY	UNHORSING
TUNNELLED	TYMPANUMS	UNBOSOMED	UNDERPLOT	UNHURRIED
TUNNELLER	TYNEMOUTH	UNBOUNDED	UNDERPROP	UNICOLOUR
TUPPENCES	TYNESIDER	UNBRIDLED	UNDERRATE	UNIFIABLE
TURBIDITY	TYPEFACES	UNBUCKLED	UNDERSEAL	UNIFORMED
TURBINATE	TYPEWRITE	UNCANNIER	UNDERSELL	UNIFORMLY
TURBOJETS	TYPHLITIC	UNCANNILY	UNDERSHOT	UNIJUGATE
TURBOPROP	TYPHLITIS	UNCEASING	UNDERSIDE	UNINSURED
TURBULENT	TYPHOIDAL	UNCERTAIN	UNDERSOIL	UNION FLAG
TURFINESS	TYPHOIDIN	UNCHARGED	UNDERSOLD	UNIONISTS
TURGIDITY	TYPICALLY	UNCHARTED	UNDERTAKE	UNIONIZED
TURKESTAN	TYPIFYING	UNCHECKED	UNDERTINT	UNION JACK
TURNABOUT	TYRANNIES	UNCLIMBED	UNDERTONE	UNION SHOP
TURN ABOUT	TYRANNIZE	UNCONCERN	UNDERTOOK	UNIPAROUS
TURNCOATS	TYRANNOUS	UNCORKING	UNDERWEAR	UNIPLANAR
TURNCOCKS	TZETZE FLY	UNCOUNTED	UNDERWENT	UNIRAMOUS
TURNOVERS		UNCOUPLED	UNDERWING	UNISEXUAL
TURNPIKES	**U**	UNCOUTHLY	UNDESIRED	UNISONOUS
TURNROUND	UITLANDER	UNCOVERED	UNDIVIDED	UNITARIAN
TURN ROUND	UKRAINIAN	UNCREATED	UNDOUBTED	UNIT TRUST
TURNSTILE	ULAN BATOR	UNCROWDED	UNDRESSED	UNIVALENT
TURNSTONE	ULCERATED	UNCROWNED	UNDULANCE	UNIVERSAL
TURNTABLE	ULMACEOUS	UNDAUNTED	UNDULATED	UNIVERSES
TURPITUDE	ULOTRICHY	UNDECAGON	UNDULATOR	UNKINDEST
TURQUOISE	ULTIMATUM	UNDECEIVE	UNEARTHED	UNKNOWING
TUSCARORA	ULTRADIAN	UNDECIDED	UNEARTHLY	UNLEARNED
TUTIORISM	ULTRA HIGH	UNDERBODY	UNEASIEST	UNLEASHED
TUTIORIST	ULULATION	UNDERBRED	UNEATABLE	UNLIMITED
TUTORIALS	ULYANOVSK	UNDERCLAY	UNELECTED	UNLOADERS
TUT-TUTTED	UMBELLATE	UNDERCOAT	UNEQUALLY	UNLOADING
TV DINNERS	UMBELLULE	UNDERCOOK	UNETHICAL	UNLOCKING
TWAYBLADE	UMBILICAL	UNDERDOGS	UNFAILING	UNLOOSING
TWENTIETH	UMBILICUS	UNDERDONE	UNFAIREST	UNLUCKILY
TWICE-LAID	UMBRELLAS	UNDERFEED	UNFANCIED	UNMARRIED
TWICE-TOLD	UMPTEENTH	UNDERFELT	UNFEELING	UNMASKING
TWIDDLING	UNABASHED	UNDERFOOT	UNFEIGNED	UNMATCHED
		UNDERFUND	UNFITNESS	UNMEANING

UNMINDFUL	UNUSUALLY	UROPYGIAL	VANDALIZE	VENIALITY
UNMUSICAL	UNVEILING	UROPYGIUM	VANGUARDS	VENTILATE
UNNATURAL	UNWATCHED	UROSCOPIC	VANISHING	VENTRICLE
UNNERVING	UNWEARIED	URSA MAJOR	VAPIDNESS	VENTURERS
UNNOTICED	UNWEIGHED	URTICARIA	VAPORETTO	VENTURING
UNOPPOSED	UNWELCOME	URUGUAYAN	VAPORIFIC	VENUSBERG
UNPACKING	UNWILLING	USABILITY	VAPORIZED	VERACIOUS
UNPICKING	UNWINDING	USELESSLY	VAPORIZER	VERANDAED
UNPLUGGED	UNWITTING	USHERETTE	VAPOURISH	VERATRINE
UNPLUMBED	UNWORLDLY	USUALNESS	VARANGIAN	VERBALISM
UNPOLITIC	UNWRITTEN	UTILITIES	VARIABLES	VERBALIST
UNPOPULAR	UNZIPPING	UTILIZING	VARIANCES	VERBALIZE
UNPOWERED	UP AND	UTRICULAR	VARIATION	VERBASCUM
UNRAVELED	DOWN	UTTERABLE	VARICELLA	VERBOSELY
UNREALISM	UP-AND-	UTTERANCE	VARICOSIS	VERBOSITY
UNREALITY	DOWN	UTTERLESS	VARIEGATE	VERDIGRIS
UNREFINED	UPBRAIDED	UVAROVITE	VARIETIES	VERDUROUS
UNRELATED	UPBRAIDER	UXORICIDE	VARIFOCAL	VERIDICAL
UNRESERVE	UPBUILDER		VARIOLATE	VERIFYING
UNRIDDLER	UP-COUNTRY	**V**	VARIOLITE	VERITABLE
UNROLLING	UPGRADING	VACANCIES	VARIOLOID	VERITABLY
UNROUNDED	UPHEAVALS	VACATABLE	VARIOLOUS	VERMICIDE
UNRUFFLED	UPHOLDERS	VACATIONS	VARIOUSLY	VERMIFORM
UNSADDLED	UPHOLDING	VACCINATE	VARISCITE	VERMIFUGE
UNSAVOURY	UPHOLSTER	VACCINIAL	VARITYPER	VERMILION
UNSCATHED	UPLIFTING	VACILLANT	VARNISHED	VERMINOUS
UNSCREWED	UPLIGHTER	VACILLATE	VARNISHER	VERMONTER
UNSEATING	UPPER CASE	VACUOLATE	VARNISHES	VERNALIZE
UNSECURED	UPPERCUTS	VACUOUSLY	VARSITIES	VERNATION
UNSELFISH	UPPER HAND	VACUUMING	VARYINGLY	VERRUCOSE
UNSERIOUS	UPPERMOST	VAGABONDS	VASECTOMY	VERSATILE
UNSETTLED	UPRIGHTLY	VAGINITIS	VASOMOTOR	VERSIFIER
UNSHACKLE	UPRISINGS	VAGOTONIA	VASSALAGE	VERSIONAL
UNSHEATHE	UPROOTING	VAGUENESS	VASSALIZE	VERS LIBRE
UNSIGHTED	UPSETTING	VAINGLORY	VECTORIAL	VERTEBRAE
UNSIGHTLY	UPSTAGING	VALENCIES	VEERINGLY	VERTEBRAL
UNSKILFUL	UP THE	VALENTINE	VEGETABLE	VERY LIGHT
UNSKILLED	ANTE	VALIANTLY	VEGETATED	VESICULAR
UNSPARING	UP THE	VALIDATED	VEHEMENCE	VESTIBULE
UNSPOTTED	DUFF	VALIDNESS	VEHICULAR	VESTIGIAL
UNSPRAYED	UP THE	VALLATION	VEINSTONE	VESTMENTS
UNSTOPPED	POLE	VALLECULA	VELODROME	VESTRYMAN
UNSTRIPED	URANINITE	VALUABLES	VELVETEEN	VETCHLING
UNSTUDIED	URBAN MYTH	VALUATION	VENDETTAS	VEXATIONS
UNTANGLED	URCEOLATE	VALUELESS	VENDITION	VEXATIOUS
UNTENABLE	URINATING	VALVELESS	VENEERING	VEXEDNESS
UNTENURED	URINATION	VAMOOSING	VENERABLE	VEXILLARY
UNTOUCHED	URINATIVE	VAMPIRISM	VENERATED	VEXILLATE
UNTREATED	UROCHROME	VANASPATI	VENERATOR	VIABILITY
UNTUTORED	UROGENOUS	VANCOUVER	VENEZUELA	VIAREGGIO
UNTYPICAL	UROLITHIC	VANDALISM	VENGEANCE	VIBRANTLY
	UROLOGIST			

VIBRATILE	VIRGULATE	VORTICISM	WAR CLOUDS	WATERWAYS
VIBRATING	VIRTUALLY	VORTICIST	WAR CRIMES	WATERWEED
VIBRATION	VIRTUOSIC	VOUCHSAFE	WAR DANCES	WATERWORN
VIBRATIVE	VIRTUOSOS	VOYEURISM	WARDROBES	WATTMETER
VIBRATORS	VIRULENCE	VULCANIAN	WARDROOMS	WAVE BANDS
VIBRISSAL	VIRULENCY	VULCANITE	WAREHOUSE	WAVEGUIDE
VICARAGES	VISCIDITY	VULCANIZE	WARHORSES	WAVELLITE
VICARIATE	VISCOSITY	VULGARIAN	WARM FRONT	WAVEMETER
VICARIOUS	VISCOUNTS	VULGARISM	WARMONGER	WAXWORKER
VICARSHIP	VISIONARY	VULGARITY	WARRANTED	WAYFARERS
VICEGERAL	VISITABLE	VULGARIZE	WARRANTEE	WAYFARING
VICENNIAL	VISUAL AID	VULNERARY	WARRANTER	WAYLAYING
VICEREGAL	VISUALIZE	VULTURINE	WARRANTOR	WEAKENING
VICEREINE	VITACEOUS	VULTUROUS	WASHBASIN	WEAKER SEX
VICE VERSA	VITALIZER	VULVIFORM	WASHBOARD	WEAK-KNEED
VICIOUSLY	VITAMINIC		WASHCLOTH	WEAKLINGS
VICKSBURG	VITELLINE	**W**	WASHED-OUT	WEALTHIER
VICTIMIZE	VITIATING	WACKINESS	WASHINESS	WEALTHILY
VICTORIAN	VITIATION	WAD MEDANI	WASHING-UP	WEAPONEER
VICTORIES	VITRIFIED	WAFER-THIN	WASHROOMS	WEARINESS
VICTUALED	VITRIFORM	WAGE SLAVE	WASHSTAND	WEARINGLY
VIDELICET	VITRIOLIC	WAGGISHLY	WASPINESS	WEARISOME
VIDEODISC	VIVACIOUS	WAGONETTE	WASPISHLY	WEARPROOF
VIDEO GAME	VIVARIUMS	WAGONLOAD	WASSAILER	WEASELING
VIDEO TAPE	VIVA VOCES	WAILINGLY	WASTELAND	WEATHERED
VIDEOTAPE	VIVERRINE	WAINSCOTS	WATCHDOGS	WEATHERER
VIENTIANE	VIVIDNESS	WAISTBAND	WATCHWORD	WEB-FOOTED
VIEWPOINT	VOCALISTS	WAISTCOAT	WATER BIRD	WEB OFFSET
VIGESIMAL	VOCALIZER	WAISTLINE	WATERBUCK	WEDNESDAY
VIGILANCE	VOCATIONS	WAIT FOR	WATER BUTT	WEEDINESS
VIGILANTE	VOCATIVES	IT	WATER-COOL	WEEKENDED
VIGNETTES	VOICELESS	WAKEFIELD	WATERFALL	WEEKENDER
VILIFYING	VOICE MAIL	WAKEFULLY	WATERFORD	WEEKNIGHT
VILLAGERS	VOICE-OVER	WAKE ROBIN	WATERFOWL	WEEPINESS
VILLIFORM	VOJVODINA	WAKE-ROBIN	WATERHOLE	WEEPINGLY
VILLOSITY	VOL-AU-	WALBRZYCH	WATER ICES	WEIGHABLE
VIMINEOUS	VENT	WALCHEREN	WATER JUMP	WEIGH DOWN
VINACEOUS	VOLCANISM	WALKABOUT	WATERLESS	WEIGHTILY
VINCENNES	VOLCANIZE	WALKAWAYS	WATER LILY	WEIGHTING
VINDICATE	VOLCANOES	WALK ON	WATERLINE	WEIRDNESS
VINEYARDS	VOLGOGRAD	AIR	WATER MAIN	WELCOMING
VIOLATING	VOLLEYING	WALKOVERS	WATERMARK	WELL-ACTED
VIOLATION	VOLTE-FACE	WALLABIES	WATERMILL	WELL-AWARE
VIOLATIVE	VOLTMETER	WALLBOARD	WATER PIPE	WELLBEING
VIOLATORS	VOLUMETER	WALLCHART	WATER POLO	WELL-FOUND
VIOLENTLY	VOLUMETRY	WALLOPING	WATER RATE	WELL-KNOWN
VIOLINIST	VOLUNTARY	WALLOWING	WATER RATS	WELL-LINED
VIRESCENT	VOLUNTEER	WALLPAPER	WATERSHED	WELL-MEANT
VIRGINALS	VOODOOISM	WALVIS BAY	WATER-SICK	WELL OILED
VIRGINIAN	VOODOOIST	WANDERERS	WATERSIDE	WELL-OILED
VIRGINITY	VORACIOUS	WANDERING	WATER VOLE	WELL-TIMED

WELL-TRIED	WHITEFISH	WINDOW BOX	WOMENFOLK	WORTHIEST
WERNERITE	WHITE FLAG	WINDPIPES	WOMEN'S	WORTHLESS
WESLEYANS	WHITEHALL	WINDROWER	LIB	WOUNDABLE
WESTBOUND	WHITE HEAT	WINDSOCKS	WONDERFUL	WOUNDWORT
WESTERING	WHITE HOPE	WINDSTORM	WONDERING	WRANGLERS
WESTERNER	WHITE LEAD	WINDSWEPT	WOODBLOCK	WRANGLING
WESTMEATH	WHITE LIES	WINEGLASS	WOODBORER	WRAPPINGS
WESTWARDS	WHITE MEAT	WINEMAKER	WOODCHUCK	WREATHING
WET DREAMS	WHITENESS	WINEPRESS	WOODCOCKS	WRECKFISH
WET-NURSED	WHITENING	WINGSPANS	WOODCRAFT	WRENCHING
WET NURSES	WHITE ROSE	WINNEBAGO	WOODINESS	WRESTLERS
WHACKINGS	WHITEWALL	WINNOWING	WOODLOUSE	WRESTLING
WHALEBOAT	WHITEWASH	WINSOMELY	WOODPRINT	WRIGGLING
WHALEBONE	WHITEWOOD	WINTERING	WOODSCREW	WRINKLING
WHANGAREI	WHITTLERS	WINTRIEST	WOOD SCREW	WRISTBAND
WHEAT GERM	WHITTLING	WIRADHURI	WOODSHEDS	WRISTLETS
WHEATWORM	WHIZZ-BANG	WIRE-GAUGE	WOODSMOKE	WRISTLOCK
WHEEDLING	WHIZZ KIDS	WIREWORKS	WOODSTOCK	WRITE-OFFS
WHEELBASE	WHODUNITS	WIREWORMS	WOOLLIEST	WRONGDOER
WHEELWORK	WHODUNNIT	WISCONSIN	WOOZINESS	WRONGNESS
WHEREFORE	WHOLEFOOD	WISECRACK	WORCESTER	WROUGHT-UP
WHEREUPON	WHOLEMEAL	WISHBONES	WORDBREAK	WULFENITE
WHEREWITH	WHOLENESS	WISPINESS	WORDINESS	WUPPERTAL
WHERRYMAN	WHOLE NOTE	WISTFULLY	WORKBENCH	WYANDOTTE
WHETSTONE	WHOLESALE	WITCH-HUNT	WORKBOOKS	WYCH-HAZEL
WHICHEVER	WHOLESOME	WITCHLIKE	WORKFORCE	
WHICKERED	WHOSOEVER	WITH A	WORKHORSE	X
WHIFFIEST	WIDE-ANGLE	WILL	WORKHOUSE	XENOCRYST
WHIMPERED	WIDE-AWAKE	WITHDRAWN	WORKLOADS	XENOGRAFT
WHIMPERER	WIDOWHOOD	WITHERING	WORK OF	XENOPHILE
WHIMSICAL	WIDTHWISE	WITHERITE	ART	XENOPHOBE
WHININGLY	WIELDABLE	WITHSTAND	WORKPIECE	XERICALLY
WHINNYING	WIESBADEN	WITHSTOOD	WORKPLACE	XERODERMA
WHINSTONE	WIGWAGGER	WITLESSLY	WORKROOMS	XEROPHILY
WHIPPER-IN	WILD BOARS	WITNESSED	WORKSHEET	XEROPHYTE
WHIPPINGS	WILDFIRES	WITNESSER	WORKSHOPS	XYLOGRAPH
WHIP ROUND	WILLEMITE	WITNESSES	WORK-STUDY	XYLOPHONE
WHIP-ROUND	WILLINGLY	WITTICISM	WORKTABLE	
WHIPSTALL	WILLPOWER	WITTINESS	WORLD BANK	Y
WHIPSTOCK	WILTSHIRE	WOBBLIEST	WORLDLIER	YACHTINGS
WHIRLIGIG	WINCINGLY	WOEBEGONE	WORLDLING	YACHTSMAN
WHIRLPOOL	WINDBLOWN	WOKINGHAM	WORLDWIDE	YACHTSMEN
WHIRLWIND	WIND-BORNE	WOLFHOUND	WORM CASTS	YAMMERING
WHISKERED	WINDBOUND	WOLFSBANE	WORM-EATEN	YANKEEISM
WHISPERED	WINDBREAK	WOLFSBURG	WORM GEARS	YARDSTICK
WHISPERER	WINDBURNT	WOLVERINE	WORMHOLES	YAROSLAVL
WHISTLING	WINDFALLS	WOMANHOOD	WORRIEDLY	YAWNINGLY
WHITE ANTS	WIND GAUGE	WOMANIZED	WORRISOME	YEA AND
WHITEBAIT	WINDINESS	WOMANIZER	WORRYWART	NAY
WHITECAPS	WINDINGLY	WOMANKIND	WORSENING	YEARBOOKS
WHITEDAMP	WINDMILLS	WOMAN-LIKE	WORSHIPED	YEARLINGS

YEARNINGS	**Z**	ZEPPELINS –	ZOOGLOEAL	ZUCCHINIS
YELLOWFIN	ZACATECAS	ZESTFULLY	ZOOGRAPHY	ZUGSPITZE
YELLOWING	ZAMBEZIAN	ZEUGMATIC	ZOOLOGIST	ZUIDER ZEE
YELLOWISH	ZAMBOANGA	ZHANGZHOU	ZOOMETRIC	ZYGOMATIC
YESTERDAY	ZANZIBARI	ZHENGZHOU	ZOOPHILIA	ZYGOPHYTE
YIELDABLE	ZAPOTECAN	ZIGZAGGED	ZOOPHILIC	ZYGOSPORE
YODELLING	ZEALOUSLY	ZIGZAGGER	ZOOPHOBIA	ZYMOGENIC
YOHIMBINE	ZEBRA-LIKE	ZINKENITE	ZOOPHYTIC	ZYMOLOGIC
YORKSHIRE	ZEBRAWOOD	ZIONISTIC	ZOOPLASTY	ZYMOLYSIS
YOUNGSTER	ZEEBRUGGE	ZIRCALLOY	ZOOSPORIC	ZYMOLYTIC
YTTERBITE	ZEELANDER	ZIRCONIUM	ZOOSTEROL	ZYMOMETER
YTTERBIUM	ZEITGEIST	ZITHERIST	ZOOTOMIST	

A
ABANDONING
ABBREVIATE
ABDICATING
ABDICATION
ABDICATIVE
ABERRATION
ABHORRENCE
ABIOGENIST
ABIRRITANT
ABIRRITATE
ABJURATION
ABLE-
  BODIED
ABLE
  SEAMAN
ABLE
  SEAMEN
ABNEGATION
ABNEY
  LEVEL
ABNORMALLY
ABOLISHING
ABOMINABLE
ABOMINABLY
ABOMINATED
ABOMINATOR
ABORIGINAL
ABORIGINES
ABORTICIDE
ABORTIONAL
ABORTIVELY
ABOUT-
  TURNS
ABOVEBOARD
ABOVE
  BOARD
ABRASIVELY
ABREACTION
ABRIDGABLE
ABRIDGMENT
ABROGATING
ABROGATION
ABRUPTNESS
ABSCISSION
ABSCONDING
ABSOLUTELY
ABSOLUTION
ABSOLUTISM
ABSOLUTORY
ABSOLVABLE
ABSORBABLE

ABSORBANCE
ABSORBEDLY
ABSORBENCY
ABSORBENTS
ABSORPTION
ABSORPTIVE
ABSTAINERS
ABSTAINING
ABSTEMIOUS
ABSTENTION
ABSTERGENT
ABSTINENCE
ABSTRACTED
ABUNDANTLY
ABYSSINIAN
ACCELERANT
ACCELERATE
ACCENTUATE
ACCEPTABLE
ACCEPTABLY
ACCEPTANCE
ACCEPTEDLY
ACCESSIBLE
ACCESSIONS
ACCESS
  ROAD
ACCESS
  TIME
ACCIDENTAL
ACCIPITRAL
ACCLAIMING
ACCOMPLICE
ACCOMPLISH
ACCORDABLE
ACCORDANCE
ACCORDIONS
ACCOSTABLE
ACCOUNTANT
ACCOUNTING
ACCREDITED
ACCRESCENT
ACCRETIONS
ACCUMBENCY
ACCUMULATE
ACCURATELY
ACCUSATION
ACCUSATIVE
ACCUSINGLY
ACCUSTOMED
ACEPHALOUS
ACETABULUM

ACETIC
  ACID
ACETOMETER
ACETYLENIC
ACHIEVABLE
ACHONDRITE
ACHROMATIC
ACHROMATIN
ACIDIFYING
ACIDIMETER
ACIDOMETER
ACIERATION
ACOTYLEDON
ACQUAINTED
ACQUIESCED
ACQUIRABLE
ACQUITTALS
ACQUITTING
ACROBATICS
ACROMEGALY
ACRONYCHAL
ACROPHOBIA
ACROPHOBIC
ACTABILITY
ACTINIFORM
ACTINOLITE
ACTINOMERE
ACTINOZOAN
ACTIONABLE
ACTIVATING
ACTIVATION
ACTIVENESS
ACTIVITIES
ACTOMYOSIN
ACT THE
  GOAT
ADACTYLOUS
ADAMANTINE
ADAMS
  APPLE
ADAM'S
  APPLE
ADAPTATION
ADDICTIONS
ADDIS
  ABABA
ADDITIONAL
ADDRESSEES
ADDRESSING
ADDUCEABLE
ADENECTOMY
ADENOVIRUS

ADEQUATELY
ADIRONDACK
ADJECTIVAL
ADJECTIVES
ADJOURNING
ADJUDICATE
ADJUNCTIVE
ADJURATION
ADJURATORY
ADJUSTABLE
ADJUSTMENT
ADMINISTER
ADMIRATION
ADMIRINGLY
ADMISSIBLE
ADMISSIONS
ADMITTANCE
ADMITTEDLY
ADMIXTURES
ADMONISHED
ADMONISHER
ADMONITION
ADMONITORY
ADOLESCENT
ADORNMENTS
ADRENALINE
ADRENERGIC
ADROITNESS
ADSORBABLE
ADSORPTION
ADULTERANT
ADULTERATE
ADULTERERS
ADULTERESS
ADULTERINE
ADULTEROUS
ADUMBRATED
ADVANTAGES
ADVENTITIA
ADVENTURER
ADVENTURES
ADVERBIALS
ADVERTENCE
ADVERTISED
ADVERTISER
ADVOCATING
ADVOCATION
ADVOCATORY
ADZUKI
  BEAN
AECIOSPORE

AERENCHYMA
AEROBATICS
AEROBIOSIS
AEROBIOTIC
AERODROMES
AERO-
  ENGINE
AEROGRAMME
AEROGRAPHY
AEROLOGIST
AEROMETRIC
AERONAUTIC
AEROPHAGIA
AEROPHOBIA
AEROPHOBIC
AEROPLANES
AEROSPHERE
AEROSTATIC
AEROTOWING
AESTHETICS
AESTIVATOR
AFFABILITY
AFFECTEDLY
AFFECTIONS
AFFECTLESS
AFFETTUOSO
AFFIDAVITS
AFFILIATED
AFFILIATES
AFFINITIES
AFFINITIVE
AFFLICTING
AFFLICTION
AFFLICTIVE
AFFORDABLE
AFFORESTED
AFFRICATES
AFFRONTING
AFICIONADO
AFRIKANDER
AFRIKANERS
AFTERBIRTH
AFTERBRAIN
AFTERGLOWS
AFTERIMAGE
AFTERLIVES
AFTERMATHS
AFTERNOONS
AFTERPAINS
AFTERPIECE
AFTERSHAFT

227

AFTERSHAVE
AFTERSHOCK
AFTERTASTE
AFTERWARDS
AGAMICALLY
AGAPANTHUS
AGGLUTININ
AGGRANDIZE
AGGRAVATED
AGGREGATED
AGGREGATES
AGGRESSION
AGGRESSIVE
AGGRESSORS
AGITATIONS
AGREEMENTS
AGRONOMICS
AGRONOMIST
AGRYPNOTIC
AHMEDNAGAR
AIDE-DE-
  CAMP
AIR-
  HOSTESS
AIR-
  LETTERS
AIR-
  LIFTING
AIR
  MARSHAL
AIRPOCKETS
AIR
  WAYBILL
AKTYUBINSK
ALACRITOUS
ALARM
  CLOCK
ALARMINGLY
ALBESCENCE
ALBUMENIZE
ALBUMINATE
ALBUMINOID
ALBUMINOUS
ALCHEMISTS
ALCHERINGA
ALCOHOLICS
ALCOHOLISM
ALCOHOLIZE
ALDERMANIC
ALEXANDRIA
ALGEBRAIST
ALGOLAGNIA

ALGOLAGNIC
ALGONQUIAN
ALGOPHOBIA
ALGORISMIC
ALGORITHMS
ALIENATING
ALIENATION
ALIGNMENTS
ALIMENTARY
ALKALINITY
ALKYLATION
ALLARGANDO
ALLEGATION
ALLEGIANCE
ALLEGORIES
ALLEGORIST
ALLEGORIZE
ALLEGRETTO
ALLERGENIC
ALLEVIATED
ALLEVIATOR
ALLIACEOUS
ALLIGATORS
ALLITERATE
ALLOCATING
ALLOCATION
ALLOCUTION
ALLOGAMOUS
ALLOMERISM
ALLOMEROUS
ALLOMETRIC
ALLOPATHIC
ALLOPATRIC
ALLOPHONIC
ALLOTMENTS
ALLOTROPIC
ALLOWANCES
ALL-
  PURPOSE
ALL-
  ROUNDER
ALL THE
  TIME
ALLUREMENT
ALLUSIVELY
ALMA
  MATERS
ALMIGHTIER
ALMIGHTILY
ALMS-
  HOUSES
ALONGSHORE

ALPENSTOCK
ALPESTRINE
ALTARPIECE
ALTAZIMUTH
ALTERATION
ALTERATIVE
ALTERNATED
ALTERNATOR
ALTIMETERS
ALTOGETHER
ALTRINCHAM
ALTRUISTIC
AMALGAMATE
AMANUENSES
AMANUENSIS
AMATEURISH
AMATEURISM
AMBASSADOR
AMBIVALENT
AMBOCEPTOR
AMBULACRAL
AMBULACRUM
AMBULANCES
AMBULATION
AMBULATORY
AMELIORANT
AMELIORATE
AMENDMENTS
AMERINDIAN
AMIABILITY
AMIANTHINE
AMINO
  ACIDS
AMMONIACAL
AMMUNITION
AMOEBIASIS
AMOEBOCYTE
AMORTIZING
AMPELOPSIS
AMPERE-
  HOUR
AMPERE-
  TURN
AMPERSANDS
AMPHEATRIC
AMPHIASTER
AMPHIBIANS
AMPHIBIOUS
AMPHIBOLIC
AMPHIBRACH
AMPHICTYON

AMPHIGORIC
AMPHIMACER
AMPHIMIXIS
AMPHOTERIC
AMPLIFIERS
AMPLIFYING
AMPUTATING
AMPUTATION
AMUSEMENTS
AMYGDALATE
AMYGDALINE
AMYGDALOID
AMYLACEOUS
AMYLOLYSIS
ANABOLITIC
ANACHORISM
ANACOUSTIC
ANACRUSTIC
ANADROMOUS
ANAGLYPHIC
ANALGESICS
ANALOGICAL
ANALYSABLE
ANAMNESTIC
ANAMORPHIC
ANAPAESTIC
ANAPLASTIC
ANAPTYCTIC
ANARCHISTS
ANARTHROUS
ANASARCOUS
ANASTIGMAT
ANASTOMOSE
ANATOMICAL
ANATOMISTS
ANATOMIZER
ANATROPOUS
ANCESTRESS
ANCESTRIES
ANCHORAGES
ANCHORITES
ANDALUSITE
ANDERLECHT
ANDROECIAL
ANDROECIUM
ANDROGENIC
ANECDOTAGE
ANECDOTIST
ANEMICALLY
ANEMOCHORE
ANEMOGRAPH

ANEMOMETER
ANEMOMETRY
ANEMOPHILY
ANEMOSCOPE
ANESTHESIA
ANESTHETIC
ANEURYSMAL
ANGELOLOGY
ANGIOSPERM
ANGLEPOISE
ANGLICISMS
ANGLICIZED
ANGLOPHILE
ANGLOPHOBE
ANGLOPHONE
ANGLO-
  SAXON
ANGULARITY
ANGULATION
ANGWANTIBO
ANIMADVERT
ANIMALCULE
ANIMAL
  FARM
ANIMATEDLY
ANISOTROPY
ANKYLOSAUR
ANNALISTIC
ANNEXATION
ANNIHILATE
ANNO
  DOMINI
ANNOTATING
ANNOTATION
ANNOTATIVE
ANNOUNCERS
ANNOUNCING
ANNOYANCES
ANNULATION
ANNULLABLE
ANNULMENTS
ANNUNCIATE
ANOINTMENT
ANORTHITIC
ANSWERABLE
ANSWERABLY
ANTAGONISM
ANTAGONIST
ANTAGONIZE
ANTARCTICA
ANTEBELLUM

ANTECEDENT
ANTEDATING
ANTE-
  MORTEM
ANTEPENULT
ANTHOPHORE
ANTHRACENE
ANTHRACITE
ANTHRACOID
ANTHROPOID
ANTIBARYON
ANTIBIOSIS
ANTIBIOTIC
ANTIBODIES
ANTICHRIST
ANTICIPANT
ANTICIPATE
ANTICLIMAX
ANTICLINAL
ANTIDROMIC
ANTIFREEZE
ANTIFUNGAL
ANTIHEROES
ANTILEPTON
ANTILOGISM
ANTIMATTER
ANTIMERISM
ANTIMONIAL
ANTIMONOUS
ANTIPHONAL
ANTIPODEAN
ANTIPROTON
ANTIPYRINE
ANTIQUATED
ANTI-
  SEMITE
ANTISEPSIS
ANTISEPTIC
ANTISOCIAL
ANTISTATIC
ANTITHESIS
ANTITRADES
ANTITRAGUS
ANXIOLYTIC
APARTMENTS
APGAR
  SCORE
APHORISTIC
APHRODISIA
APICULTURE
APIOLOGIST

APLACENTAL
APOCALYPSE
APOCARPOUS
APOCHROMAT
APOCRYPHAL
APOLITICAL
APOLOGETIC
APOLOGISTS
APOLOGIZED
APOLOGIZER
APOPHTHEGM
APOPHYSATE
APOPHYSIAL
APOPLECTIC
APOSEMATIC
APOSTASIES
APOSTATIZE
APOSTOLATE
APOSTROPHE
APOTHECARY
APOTHECIAL
APOTHECIUM
APOTHEOSES
APOTHEOSIS
APOTROPAIC
APPALACHIA
APPARELLED
APPARENTLY
APPARITION
APPEALABLE
APPEARANCE
APPEASABLE
APPENDAGES
APPENDICES
APPENDICLE
APPENDIXES
APPERCEIVE
APPETIZERS
APPETIZING
APPLAUDING
APPLE
  CARTS
APPLIANCES
APPLICABLE
APPLICANTS
APPLICATOR
APPOINTEES
APPOINTING
APPOSITION
APPOSITIVE
APPRAISALS

APPRAISING
APPRAISIVE
APPRECIATE
APPRENTICE
APPROACHED
APPROACHES
APPROXIMAL
APRIL
  FOOLS
APTERYGIAL
AQUAMARINE
AQUAPHOBIA
AQUAPLANED
AQUAPLANES
ARABESQUES
ARACHNIDAN
ARAKAN
  YOMA
ARAUCANIAN
ARBITRABLE
ARBITRATED
ARBITRATOR
ARCHAISTIC
ARCHANGELS
ARCHBISHOP
ARCHDEACON
ARCHERFISH
ARCHESPORE
ARCHETYPAL
ARCHETYPES
ARCHIMEDES
ARCHITECTS
ARCHITRAVE
ARCHIVISTS
ARCHOPLASM
ARCTOGAEAN
ARC
  WELDING
ARENACEOUS
AREOGRAPHY
AREOLATION
ARGENTEUIL
ARGILLITIC
ARGUMENTUM
ARISTOCRAT
ARITHMETIC
ARMADILLOS
ARMAGEDDON
ARMIPOTENT
ARMISTICES
ARNHEM
  LAND

ARRAIGNING
ARRHYTHMIA
ARROGANTLY
ARROGATING
ARROGATION
ARROGATIVE
ARROWHEADS
ARTFULNESS
ARTHRALGIA
ARTHRALGIC
ARTHRITICS
ARTHROMERE
ARTICHOKES
ARTICULATE
ARTIFICERS
ARTIFICIAL
ART
  NOUVEAU
ARTY-
  CRAFTY
ASAFOETIDA
ASARABACCA
ASBESTOSIS
ASCARIASIS
ASCENDANCY
ASCENDANTS
ASCETICISM
ASCOGONIUM
ASCOMYCETE
ASCRIBABLE
ASCRIPTION
ASEXUALITY
ASPARAGINE
ASPERITIES
ASPERSIONS
AS PER
  USUAL
ASPHALTING
ASPHALTITE
ASPHYXIANT
ASPHYXIATE
ASPIDISTRA
ASPIRATING
ASPIRATION
ASPIRATORY
ASSAILABLE
ASSAILANTS
ASSAILMENT
ASSAULTING
ASSEMBLAGE
ASSEMBLIES

ASSEMBLING
ASSERTIBLE
ASSERTIONS
ASSESSABLE
ASSESSMENT
ASSET
  VALUE
ASSEVERATE
ASSIBILATE
ASSIGNABLE
ASSIGNMENT
ASSIMILATE
ASSISTANCE
ASSISTANTS
ASSOCIABLE
ASSOCIATED
ASSOCIATES
ASSONANTAL
ASSORTMENT
ASSUMPTION
ASSUMPTIVE
ASSURANCES
ASTATICISM
ASTERIATED
ASTERISKED
ASTEROIDAL
ASTHENOPIA
ASTHENOPIC
ASTHMATICS
ASTIGMATIC
ASTOMATOUS
ASTONISHED
ASTOUNDING
ASTRAGALUS
ASTRINGENT
ASTROLOGER
ASTROMETRY
ASTRONAUTS
ASTRONOMER
ASTUTENESS
ASYMMETRIC
ASYMPTOTIC
AT ALL
  TIMES
AT A
  STRETCH
ATHERMANCY
ATMOSPHERE
ATOMICALLY
ATOMIC
  BOMB

ATOMIC
  PILE
ATROCITIES
ATROPHYING
ATTACHABLE
ATTACHMENT
ATTAINABLE
ATTAINMENT
ATTEMPTING
ATTENDANCE
ATTENDANTS
ATTENTIONS
ATTENUATED
ATTENUATOR
ATTESTABLE
AT THE
  READY
ATTORNMENT
ATTRACTING
ATTRACTION
ATTRACTIVE
ATTRIBUTED
ATTRIBUTER
ATTRIBUTES
ATYPICALLY
AUBERGINES
AUCTIONEER
AUCTIONING
AUDIBILITY
AUDIOGENIC
AUDIOMETER
AUDIOMETRY
AUDITIONED
AUDITORIUM
AUGMENTING
AUREOMYCIN
AURICULATE
AURIFEROUS
AUSCULTATE
AUSFORMING
AUSPICIOUS
AUSTENITIC
AUSTERLITZ
AUSTRALIAN
AUSTRALOID
AUSTRALORP
AUTARCHIES
AUTECOLOGY
AUTHORIZED
AUTHORIZER
AUTHORSHIP

AUTOCHTHON
AUTOCRATIC
AUTOECIOUS
AUTOGAMOUS
AUTOGENOUS
AUTOGRAPHS
AUTOGRAPHY
AUTOMATICS
AUTOMATING
AUTOMATION
AUTOMATISM
AUTOMATIST
AUTOMATONS
AUTOMATOUS
AUTOMOBILE
AUTOMOTIVE
AUTONOMIST
AUTONOMOUS
AUTOPHYTIC
AUTOPLASTY
AUTOSTRADA
AUTOTOMIZE
AUTUMNALLY
AUXOCHROME
AVALANCHES
AVANT
  GARDE
AVANT-
  GARDE
AVARICIOUS
AVELLANEDA
AVENTURINE
AVICULTURE
AVOCATIONS
AVUNCULATE
AWAKENINGS
AXIOLOGIST
AYATOLLAHS
AZEOTROPIC
AZERBAIJAN
AZOBENZENE

B

BABY-
  MINDER
BABY
  SITTER
BABY-
  SITTER
BACCHANALS
BACITRACIN
BACKBITERS

BACKBITING
BACKCLOTHS
BACKCOMBED
BACKDATING
BACKFIRING
BACKGAMMON
BACKGROUND
BACKHANDED
BACKHANDER
BACKLASHES
BACK
  MATTER
BACK
  NUMBER
BACKPACKER
BACKSLIDER
BACKSPACES
BACKSTAIRS
BACKSTITCH
BACK
  STREET
BACKSTROKE
BACKWARDLY
BACKWATERS
BACULIFORM
BADEN-
  BADEN
BAD HAIR
  DAY
BAD-
  MOUTHED
BAFFLEMENT
BAGGAGE
  CAR
BAHAWALPUR
BAINBRIDGE
BALACLAVAS
BALALAIKAS
BALDERDASH
BALDHEADED
BALIKPAPAN
BALLASTING
BALLERINAS
BALLFLOWER
BALLISTICS
BALLOONING
BALLOONIST
BALLPOINTS
BALLYMONEY
BALNEOLOGY
BALUSTRADE
BAMBOOZLED

BAMBOOZLER
BANALITIES
BANANA
  SKIN
BANDERILLA
BANDLEADER
BANDMASTER
BANDOLEERS
BANDSTANDS
BANDWAGONS
BANFFSHIRE
BANGLADESH
BANISHMENT
BANK
  DRAFTS
BANKROLLED
BANKRUPTCY
BANKRUPTED
BANNERETTE
BANQUETING
BAPTISTERY
BARBARIANS
BARBARISMS
BARBARIZED
BARBECUING
BARBED
  WIRE
BARBELLATE
BAREHEADED
BARELEGGED
BARGAINING
BARGE
  POLES
BARIUM
  MEAL
BARLEYCORN
BARLEY
  WINE
BAR
  MITZVAH
BARN
  DANCES
BARNSTAPLE
BAROMETERS
BAROMETRIC
BARONESSES
BARONETAGE
BARRACKING
BARRACUDAS
BARRAMUNDA
BARRAMUNDI
BARRATROUS

BARRENNESS
BARRENWORT
BARRICADED
BARRICADER
BARRICADES
BARRISTERS
BARROW
  BOYS
BARTENDERS
BARYCENTRE
BARYSPHERE
BASALTWARE
BASE
  METALS
BASILICATA
BASKETBALL
BASKET-
  STAR
BASKETWORK
BAS-
  RELIEFS
BASSE-
  TERRE
BASSETERRE
BASS
  GUITAR
BASSOONIST
BASTARDIZE
BASUTOLAND
BATH
  CHAIRS
BATHOMETER
BATHOMETRY
BATHYMETRY
BATHYSCAPH
BATON
  ROUGE
BATTALIONS
BATTLEAXES
BATTLEDORE
BATTLEMENT
BATTLESHIP
BAYONETING
BAY
  WINDOWS
BEACH
  BALLS
BEACH
  BUGGY
BEACHCHAIR
BEACHFRONT
BEACHHEADS

BEANSPROUT
BEAR
  GARDEN
BEASTLIEST
BEATIFYING
BEATITUDES
BEAUJOLAIS
BEAUTICIAN
BEAUTIFIED
BEAUTY
  SPOT
BECOMINGLY
BECQUERELS
BEDCLOTHES
BEDEVILING
BEDEVILLED
BEDFELLOWS
BED OF
  NAILS
BED OF
  ROSES
BEDRAGGLED
BED-
  SITTERS
BEDSPREADS
BEEFEATERS
BEEF
  TOMATO
BEER
  GARDEN
BEFOREHAND
BEFOULMENT
BEFRIENDED
BEGGARWEED
BEGINNINGS
BEGRUDGING
BEHIND
  BARS
BEHINDHAND
BEHIND
  TIME
BELABOURED
BELIEVABLE
BELIEVABLY
BELITTLING
BELIZE
  CITY
BELLADONNA
BELLARMINE
BELLETRIST
BELLINZONA

BELL-
  RINGER
BELL THE
  CAT
BELLWETHER
BELL
  WETHER
BELLYACHED
BELLYACHES
BELLY
  DANCE
BELLY
  FLOPS
BELLY
  LAUGH
BELONGINGS
BELORUSSIA
BENCH
  MARKS
BENCH
  PRESS
BENEDICITE
BENEFACTOR
BENEFICENT
BENEFICIAL
BENEFITING
BENEVOLENT
BENIGNANCY
BENNINGTON
BENZOCAINE
BENZODRINE
BENZOFURAN
BEQUEATHED
BEQUEATHER
BERIBBONED
BERLIN
  WALL
BERTOLUCCI
BESEECHING
BESMEARING
BESMIRCHED
BESPEAKING
BESSARABIA
BESTIALITY
BESTIALIZE
BESTIARIES
BESTIRRING
BESTREWING
BESTRIDDEN
BESTRIDING
BEST-
  SELLER

BETELGEUSE
BETHINKING
BETOKENING
BETROTHALS
BETROTHING
BETTERMENT
BETWS-Y-
  COED
BEWILDERED
BEWITCHING
BIANNULATE
BIBLIOPOLE
BIBLIOTICS
BIBLIOTIST
BICHLORIDE
BICYCLISTS
BIENNIALLY
BIFURCATED
BIGAMOUSLY
BIG
  BROTHER
BIG
  DIPPERS
BIJOUTERIE
BILBERRIES
BILINGUALS
BILIVERDIN
BILL AND
  COO
BILLBOARDS
BILLET-
  DOUX
BILLIONTHS
BILL OF
  FARE
BILL OF
  SALE
BILLY
  GOATS
BIMESTRIAL
BIMETALLIC
BINOCULARS
BINUCLEATE
BIOCELLATE
BIODYNAMIC
BIOECOLOGY
BIOGENESIS
BIOGENETIC
BIOGRAPHER
BIOGRAPHIC
BIOLOGICAL
BIOLOGISTS

BIOMEDICAL
BIOPHYSICS
BIOPLASMIC
BIOPOIESIS
BIORHYTHMS
BIOSTATICS
BIPARIETAL
BIPARTISAN
BIPETALOUS
BIQUADRATE
BIRD OF
  PREY
BIRKENHEAD
BIRMINGHAM
BIRTHMARKS
BIRTHPLACE
BIRTH-
  RATES
BIRTHRIGHT
BIRTHSTONE
BIRTWISTLE
BISEXUALLY
BISHOPBIRD
BISHOPRICS
BISMUTHOUS
BISSEXTILE
BISULPHATE
BISULPHIDE
BISULPHITE
BISYMMETRY
BITARTRATE
BITCHINESS
BIT OF
  FLUFF
BITTERLING
BITTERNESS
BITTERWEED
BITTERWOOD
BITUMINIZE
BITUMINOUS
BIVALVULAR
BIVOUACKED
BLABBERING
BLACKAMOOR
BLACK
  BELTS
BLACKBERRY
BLACKBIRDS
BLACKBOARD
BLACK
  BOXES

BLACK
  DEATH
BLACKENING
BLACKGUARD
BLACKHEADS
BLACKHEART
BLACK
  HOLES
BLACKJACKS
BLACKLISTS
BLACK
  MAGIC
BLACK
  MARIA
BLACK
  POWER
BLACK
  SHEEP
BLACKSHIRT
BLACKSMITH
BLACKSNAKE
BLACK
  SPOTS
BLACKTHORN
BLACK
  WATCH
BLACK
  WIDOW
BLADDERNUT
BLANCMANGE
BLANKETING
BLANK
  VERSE
BLASPHEMED
BLASPHEMER
BLASTOCOEL
BLASTOCYST
BLASTODERM
BLASTOMERE
BLASTOPORE
BLATHERING
BLEACHABLE
BLEARINESS
BLEATINGLY
BLEMISHING
BLETHERING
BLIND
  ALLEY
BLIND
  DATES
BLIND
  DRUNK

BLINDFOLDS
BLIND
  SPOTS
BLISSFULLY
BLISTERING
BLITHENESS
BLITHERING
BLITHESOME
BLOCKADING
BLOCKHEADS
BLOCKHOUSE
BLOCK
  VOTES
BLONDENESS
BLOOD
  BANKS
BLOODBATHS
BLOOD
  COUNT
BLOOD
  DONOR
BLOOD
  FEUDS
BLOOD
  GROUP
BLOODHOUND
BLOODINESS
BLOOD
  LUSTS
BLOOD
  MONEY
BLOOD
  SPORT
BLOODSTAIN
BLOODSTOCK
BLOODSTONE
BLOOD
  TYPES
BLOODY
  MARY
BLOOMSBURY
BLOSSOMING
BLOTCHIEST
BLOW-BY-
  BLOW
BLOW-
  DRYING
BLOWZINESS
BLUBBERING
BLUDGEONED
BLUDGEONER
BLUE
  BABIES

BLUEBEARDS
BLUEBOTTLE
BLUE
  CHEESE
BLUE-
  COLLAR
BLUE
  DEVILS
BLUE
  MURDER
BLUE-
  PENCIL
BLUEPRINTS
BLUETHROAT
BLUE
  TONGUE
BLUNDERERS
BLUNDERING
BLUSHINGLY
BLUSTERERS
BLUSTERING
BOARDROOMS
BOARDWALKS
BOASTFULLY
BOASTINGLY
BOATHOUSES
BOATSWAINS
BOAT
  TRAINS
BOBBY
  SOCKS,
BOBSLEIGHS
BODY
  DOUBLE
BODYGUARDS
BODY
  SEARCH
BOILER
  SUIT
BOISTEROUS
BOLLOCKS-
  UP
BOLL
  WEEVIL
BOLOMETRIC
BOLSHEVIKS
BOLSHEVISM
BOLSTERING
BOMBARDIER
BOMBARDING
BOMBAY
  DUCK
BOMBSHELLS

BONDHOLDER
BONEHEADED
BONE
  MARROW
BONESHAKER
BONKBUSTER
BON
  VIVANTS
BOOBY
  PRIZE
BOOBY
  TRAPS
BOOKBINDER
BOOKKEEPER
BOOKMAKERS
BOOKMOBILE
BOOKPLATES
BOOKSELLER
BOOKSTALLS
BOOK
  TOKENS
BOOMERANGS
BOOTBLACKS
BOOTLEGGED
BOOTLEGGER
BOOTLOADER
BOOTSTRAPS
BORDERLAND
BORDERLINE
BORGERHOUT
BORROWINGS
BOTANIZING
BOTCHINESS
BOTHERSOME
BOTRYOIDAL
BOTTLE
  BANK
BOTTLE-
  FEED
BOTTLENECK
BOTTLE
  SHOP
BOTTOMLESS
BOTTOM
  LINE
BOTTOMMOST
BOULEVARDS
BOUNCINESS
BOUNDARIES
BOWDLERISM
BOWDLERIZE

BOW
  WINDOWS
BOX
  NUMBERS
BOX
  OFFICES
BOYCOTTING
BOYFRIENDS
BOYISHNESS
BRACHIOPOD
BRACHYLOGY
BRACHYURAN
BRACKETING
BRADYKININ
BRAGGINGLY
BRAHMANISM
BRAINCHILD
BRAIN
  DRAIN
BRAININESS
BRAINSTORM
BRAINWAVES
BRAKE
  SHOES
BRANCHIATE
BRANDISHED
BRANDISHER
BRAND
  NAMES
BRANDY
  SNAP
BRASHINESS
BRASS
  BANDS
BRASSBOUND
BRASSED
  OFF
BRASSERIES
BRASSIERES
BRASSINESS
BRASS
  TACKS
BRATISLAVA
BRAVISSIMO
BRAWNINESS
BRAZENNESS
BREADBOARD
BREADCRUMB
BREADFRUIT
BREADLINES
BREAKAWAYS
BREAKDOWNS

BREAKFASTS
BREAKFRONT
BREAKWATER
BREASTBONE
BREASTWORK
BREATHABLE
BRECCIATED
BREEZINESS
BRICKLAYER
BRIDEGROOM
BRIDESMAID
BRIDGEABLE
BRIDGEHEAD
BRIDGEPORT
BRIDGETOWN
BRIDGEWORK
BRIDGWATER
BRIGANTINE
BRIGHTENER
BRIGHTNESS
BRIGHTWORK
BRILLIANCE
BRILLIANCY
BRIQUETTES
BRITISHERS
BROAD
  BEANS
BROADCASTS
BROADCLOTH
BROADENING
BROAD
  GAUGE
BROADSHEET
BROADSIDES
BROADSWORD
BROCATELLE
BROKEN
  DOWN
BROKEN-
  DOWN
BROKENNESS
BROMSGROVE
BRONCHIOLE
BRONCHITIC
BRONCHITIS
BRONX
  CHEER
BROODINESS
BROOMSTICK
BROWBEATEN
BROWNED-
  OFF

BROWNFIELD
BROWNSTONE
BRUTALIZED
BRYOLOGIST
BRYOPHYTIC
BUBBLE
  WRAP
BUBONOCELE
BUCCANEERS
BUCCINATOR
BUCHENWALD
BUCKBOARDS
BUCKET
  SEAT
BUCKET
  SHOP
BUCKINGHAM
BUDGERIGAR
BUFFER
  ZONE
BUFFLEHEAD
BUFFOONERY
BULLDOZERS
BULLDOZING
BULLFIGHTS
BULLHEADED
BULLNECKED
BULLROARER
BULLY
  COURT
BUMBLEBEES
BUNCHINESS
BUNKHOUSES
BUNYA-
  BUNYA
BUON
  GIORNO
BURBERRIES
BURDENSOME
BUREAUCRAT
BURGENLAND
BURGEONING
BURGLARIES
BURGUNDIAN
BURLESQUED
BURLESQUER
BURLESQUES
BURLINGTON
BURNISHING
BURTHENING
BUSHBABIES
BUSHHAMMER

BUSHMASTER
BUSHRANGER
BUSINESSES
BUS
  STATION
BUSYBODIES
BUTCHERING
BUTTER
  BEAN
BUTTERCUPS
BUTTERFISH
BUTTERMILK
BUTTERWORT
BUTTON-
  DOWN
BUTTONHOLE
BUTTONHOOK
BUTTONWOOD
BUTTRESSED
BUTTRESSES
BY-
  ELECTION
BY-
  PRODUCTS
BYSTANDERS

C

CABANATUAN
CABIN
  CLASS
CACCIATORE
CACHINNATE
CACK-
  HANDED
CACOGENICS
CACOGRAPHY
CACOMISTLE
CACOPHONIC
CACTACEOUS
CADAVERINE
CADAVEROUS
CADET
  CORPS
CAERPHILLY
CAESAREANS
CAESPITOSE
CAFETERIAS
CALABASHES
CALABOOSES
CALAMANDER
CALAMITIES
CALAMITOUS

CALAMONDIN
CALAVERITE
CALCAREOUS
CALCEIFORM
CALCIFEROL
CALCIFUGAL
CALCIFYING
CALCITONIN
CALCSINTER
CALCULABLE
CALCULATED
CALCULATOR
CALCULUSES
CALDERDALE
CALEDONIAN
CALIBRATED
CALIBRATOR
CALIFORNIA
CALIPHATES
CALL
  CENTRE
CALL IT A
  DAY
CALLOWNESS
CALORICITY
CALUMNIATE
CALUMNIOUS
CALVINISTS
CALYPTRATE
CAMEMBERTS
CAMERAWORK
CAMERLENGO
CAMOUFLAGE
CAMPAIGNED
CAMPAIGNER
CAMPANILES
CAMPESTRAL
CAMPGROUND
CAMPHORATE
CAMPOBELLO
CANAL
  BOATS
CANALIZING
CANCELLATE
CANCELLING
CANDELABRA
CANDIDATES
CANDLEFISH
CANDLEPINS
CANDLEWICK
CANDLEWOOD

CANDYFLOSS
CANKERWORM
CANNABINOL
CANNELLONI
CANNONADES
CANNONBALL
CANONICATE
CANONICITY
CANONIZING
CANOODLING
CAN
  OPENERS
CANTABRIAN
CANTALOUPE
CANTALOUPS
CANTATRICE
CANTERBURY
CANTILEVER
CANTILLATE
CANTONMENT
CANVASBACK
CANVASSERS
CANVASSING
CAOUTCHOUC
CAPABILITY
CAPACITATE
CAPACITIES
CAPACITIVE
CAPACITORS
CAPARISONS
CAPE
  COLONY
CAP-
  HAITIEN
CAPITALISM
CAPITALIST
CAPITALIZE
CAPITATION
CAPITATIVE
CAPITULATE
CAPPUCCINO
CAPREOLATE
CAPRICIOUS
CAPRICORNS
CAPTAINING
CAPTIOUSLY
CAPTIVATED
CAPTIVATOR
CARAMELIZE
CARAVAGGIO
CARBOLATED

CARBONATED
CARBON
  COPY
CARBONIZED
CARBUNCLES
CARCINOGEN
CARDIALGIA
CARDIALGIC
CARDIOGRAM
CARDIOLOGY
CARD
  READER
CARDSHARPS
CAREERISTS
CARELESSLY
CARETAKERS
CARICATURE
CARJACKING
CARMARTHEN
CARNALLITE
CARNASSIAL
CARNATIONS
CARNELIANS
CARNIVORES
CAROLINIAN
CAROTENOID
CARPATHIAN
CARPELLARY
CARPELLATE
CARPENTERS
CARPOPHORE
CARPOSPORE
CARRIER
  BAG
CARRYING-
  ON
CARRY-
  OVERS
CARSON
  CITY
CARTHORSES
CARTHUSIAN
CARTILAGES
CARTOMANCY
CARTOONIST
CARTRIDGES
CART
  TRACKS
CARTWHEELS
CARUNCULAR
CARYATIDAL
CASABLANCA

CASCARILLA
CASE-
  HARDEN
CASEINOGEN
CASEWORKER
CASHIERING
CASSEROLES
CASSIOPEIA
CASTIGATED
CASTIGATOR
CASTING
  OFF
CASTRATING
CASTRATION
CASUALNESS
CASUALTIES
CASUS
  BELLI
CATABOLISM
CATABOLITE
CATACLINAL
CATACLYSMS
CATAFALQUE
CATALECTIC
CATALEPTIC
CATALOGUED
CATALOGUER
CATALOGUES
CATAMARANS
CATAMENIAL
CATAPLASIA
CATAPULTED
CATARRHINE
CATASTASIS
CAT
  BURGLAR
CATCALLING
CATCH A
  CRAB
CATCH
  CROPS
CATCHINESS
CATCHPENNY
CATCHWORDS
CATECHESIS
CATECHISMS
CATECHISTS
·CATECHIZED
CATEGORIES
CATEGORIZE
CATENARIAN
CATENATION

CATENULATE
CATHEDRALS
CATHOLICON
CATOPTRICS
CAT'S
  CRADLE
CATTLE
  GRID
CAULESCENT
CAUTERIZED
CAUTIONARY
CAUTIONING
CAUTIOUSLY
CAVALCADES
CAVALRYMAN
CAVALRYMEN
CAVITATION
CAVITY
  WALL
CEASE-
  FIRES
CEILOMETER
CELEBRATED
CELEBRATOR
CELLOBIOSE
CELLOPHANE
CELLULITIS
CELLULOSIC
CEMETERIES
CENOTAPHIC
CENSORABLE
CENSORIOUS
CENSORSHIP
CENSURABLE
CENTENNIAL
CENTESIMAL
CENTIGRADE
CENTIGRAMS
CENTILITRE
CENTILLION
CENTIMETRE
CENTIPEDES
CENTIPOISE
CENTRALISM
CENTRALITY
CENTRALIZE
CENTRE-
  FIRE
CENTRE-
  FOLD
CENTRE
  HALF

CENTRE
  PASS
CENTRICITY
CENTRIFUGE
CENTROMERE
CENTROSOME
CENTURIONS
CEPHALONIA
CEPHALOPOD
CEREBELLAR
CEREBELLUM
CEREBRALLY
CEREDIGION
CEREMONIAL
CEREMONIES
CEROGRAPHY
CERTIFYING
CERTIORARI
CERUMINOUS
CERVICITIS
CESSATIONS
CESSIONARY
CETOLOGIST
CHAGRINING
CHAIN
  GANGS
CHAINPLATE
CHAIN-
  REACT
CHAIN
  SMOKE
CHAIN-
  SMOKE
CHAIN
  STORE
CHAIR
  LIFTS
CHAIRWOMAN
CHAIRWOMEN
CHALCEDONY
CHALCIDICE
CHALCOCITE
CHALKBOARD
CHALKINESS
CHALLENGED
CHALLENGER
CHALLENGES
CHALYBEATE
CHAMBER
  POT
CHAMELEONS
CHAMOMILES

CHAMPIGNON
CHAMPIONED
CHANCELLOR
CHANCERIES
CHANCINESS
CHANDELIER
CHANDIGARH
CHANGEABLE
CHANGEABLY
CHANGELESS
CHANGELING
CHANGEOVER
CHANGE
  OVER
CHANNEL-
  HOP
CHANNELLED
CHANNELLER
CHAPERONED
CHAPFALLEN
CHAPLAINCY
CHARABANCS
CHARACTERS
CHARDONNAY
CHARGEABLE
CHARGE
  CARD
CHARGE
  HAND
CHARIOTEER
CHARITABLE
CHARITABLY
CHARLADIES
CHARLATANS
CHARLESTON
CHARMINGLY
CHARTERING
CHARTREUSE
CHASTENING
CHASTISING
CHATELAINE
CHATOYANCY
CHATTERBOX
CHATTERERS
CHATTERING
CHAUDFROID
CHAUFFEURS
CHAUVINISM
CHAUVINIST
CHEAPENING
CHEAPSKATE
CHEBOKSARY

CHECKLISTS
CHECKMATED
CHECKMATES
CHECKPOINT
CHECKROOMS
CHEEKBONES
CHEEKINESS
CHEEKPIECE
CHEERFULLY
CHEERINESS
CHEESECAKE
CHEESED
  OFF
CHEESINESS
CHEKHOVIAN
CHELICERAL
CHELMSFORD
CHELTENHAM
CHEMICALLY
CHEMISETTE
CHEMOTAXIS
CHEQUEBOOK
CHEQUE
  CARD
CHERISHING
CHERNOVTSY
CHERRYWOOD
CHERUBICAL
CHESAPEAKE
CHESSBOARD
CHESTINESS
CHEVALIERS
CHEVROTAIN
CHEWING
  GUM
CHEW THE
  CUD
CHEW THE
  FAT
CHEW THE
  RAG
CHICHESTER
CHICKEN
  POX
CHIEFTAINS
CHIFFCHAFF
CHIFFONIER
CHIHUAHUAS
CHILBLAINS
CHILDBIRTH
CHILDISHLY

CHILD'S PLAY
CHILIASTIC
CHILLINESS
CHIMERICAL
CHIMNEYPOT
CHIMPANZEE
CHINABERRY
CHINATOWNS
CHINCHILLA
CHINQUAPIN
CHINSTRAPS
CHINTZIEST
CHIPOLATAS
CHIROMANCY
CHIRPINESS
CHISELLERS
CHISELLING
CHITARRONE
CHITTAGONG
CHIVALROUS
CHLAMYDATE
CHLORAMINE
CHLORINATE
CHLOROFORM
CHOANOCYTE
CHOCKSTONE
CHOCOHOLIC
CHOCOLATES
CHOICENESS
CHOKEBERRY
CHONDRITIC
CHOPHOUSES
CHOPPINESS
CHOPSTICKS
CHORIAMBIC
CHORISTERS
CHRISTENED
CHRISTENER
CHRISTIANS
CHROMATICS
CHROMATIST
CHROMOMERE
CHROMONEMA
CHROMOSOME
CHRONICITY
CHRONICLED
CHRONICLER
CHRONICLES
CHRONOGRAM
CHRONOLOGY

CHRYSOLITE
CHRYSOTILE
CHUBBINESS
CHUCKER-OUT
CHUCKWALLA
CHUKKA BOOT
CHUMMINESS
CHUNKINESS
CHURCHGOER
CHURCHYARD
CHURLISHLY
CHYLACEOUS
CICATRICES
CICATRICLE
CICATRIZER
CIGARETTES
CINCHONINE
CINCHONISM
CINCHONIZE
CINCINNATI
CINDERELLA
CINERARIUM
CINNAMONIC
CINQUEFOIL
CIRCUITOUS
CIRCULATED
CIRCULATOR
CIRCUMCISE
CIRCUMFLEX
CIRCUMFUSE
CIRCUMVENT
CISMONTANE
CISTACEOUS
CISTERCIAN
CITRIC ACID
CITRONELLA
CITRULLINE
CITY FATHER
CITY-STATES
CIVILITIES
CIVILIZING
CLACTONIAN
CLADISTICS
CLADOCERAN
CLAMBERING
CLAMMINESS
CLAMOURING

CLAMPDOWNS
CLANGOROUS
CLANNISHLY
CLANSWOMAN
CLAPPED-OUT
CLARABELLA
CLARIFYING
CLASP KNIFE
CLASSIC CAR
CLASSICISM
CLASSICIST
CLASSIFIED
CLASSIFIER
CLASSMATES
CLASSROOMS
CLATTERING
CLAVICHORD
CLAVICULAR
CLAY PIGEON
CLEANSABLE
CLEAN SHEET
CLEAN SWEEP
CLEARANCES
CLEFT STICK
CLEMENTINE
CLERESTORY
CLERICALLY
CLEVER DICK
CLEVERNESS
CLIENTELES
CLINGINESS
CLINGSTONE
CLINICALLY
CLINKSTONE
CLINOMETER
CLINOMETRY
CLIPBOARDS
CLIP JOINTS
CLOAKROOMS
CLOBBERING
CLOCKMAKER
CLOCK TOWER

CLODDISHLY
CLODHOPPER
CLOGGINESS
CLOISTERED
CLOSE CALLS
CLOSED BOOK
CLOSEDOWNS
CLOSED SHOP
CLOSE SHAVE
CLOSE THING
CLOTHBOUND
CLOTHES PEG
CLOUDBANKS
CLOUDBERRY
CLOUDBURST
CLOUDINESS
CLOVE HITCH
CLOVERLEAF
CLOWNISHLY
CLOYEDNESS
CLUBFOOTED
CLUBHOUSES
CLUMSINESS
CLUSTERING
CLUTCH BAGS
CLUTTERING
CLYDESDALE
CNIDOBLAST
COACERVATE
COACTIVITY
COADJUTANT
COADJUTORS
COAGULABLE
COAGULATED
COALBUNKER
COALESCENT
COALESCING
COALFIELDS
COALHOUSES
COALITIONS
COAPTATION
COARSENESS
COARSENING
COASTGUARD

COASTLINES
COAT HANGER
COAT OF ARMS
COCHABAMBA
COCHINEALS
COCKABULLY
COCKALORUM
COCKCHAFER
COCKED HATS
COCKFIGHTS
COCKHORSES
COCKNEYISM
COCKSCOMBS
COCONUT SHY
CODSWALLOP
COELACANTH
COENOCYTIC
COEQUALITY
COERCIVELY
COERCIVITY
COEXISTENT
COEXISTING
COFFEE BARS
COFFEEPOTS
COFFEE SHOP
COFFERDAMS
COGITATING
COGITATION
COGITATIVE
COGNIZABLE
COGNIZANCE
COHABITANT
COHABITING
COHERENTLY
COHESIVELY
COIMBATORE
COINCIDENT
COINCIDING
COLATITUDE
COLCHESTER
COLCHICINE
COLD CHISEL
COLD FISHES

COLD
  FRAMES
COLD
  FRONTS
COLDSTREAM
COLD
  TURKEY
COLEMANITE
COLEOPTILE
COLEORHIZA
COLLAGENIC
COLLAPSING
COLLARBONE
COLLAR
  STUD
COLLATERAL
COLLATIONS
COLLEAGUES
COLLECTING
COLLECTION
COLLECTIVE
COLLECTORS
COLLEGIATE
COLLIERIES
COLLIMATOR
COLLISIONS
COLLOCATED
COLLOQUIAL
COLLOQUIES
COLLOQUIUM
COLLOTYPIC
COLONIZERS
COLONIZING
COLONNADED
COLONNADES
COLORATION
COLORATURA
COLOR
  LINES
COLOSSALLY
COLOSSUSES
COLOURABLE
COLOUR
  BARS
COLOURFAST
COLOUR
  FAST
COLOURINGS
COLOURLESS
COLUMBINES
COLUMELLAR
COLUMNISTS

COMANCHEAN
COMBATABLE
COMBATANTS
COMBATTING
COMBINABLE
COMBUSTION
COMEDIENNE
COME-
  HITHER
COMELINESS
COMESTIBLE
COME TO
  HAND
COME TO
  MIND
COMFORTERS
COMFORTING
COMIC
  OPERA
COMIC
  STRIP
COMMANDANT
COMMANDEER
COMMANDERS
COMMANDING
COMMEASURE
COMMENCING
COMMENDING
COMMENTARY
COMMENTATE
COMMENTING
COMMERCIAL
COMMISSARS
COMMISSARY
COMMISSION
COMMISSURE
COMMITMENT
COMMITTALS
COMMITTEES
COMMITTING
COMMODIOUS
COMMODORES
COMMONABLE
COMMONALTY
COMMONNESS
COMMON
  NOUN
COMMON
  ROOM
COMMONWEAL
COMMOTIONS
COMMUNIONS

COMMUNIQUE
COMMUNISTS
COMMUTABLE
COMMUTATOR
COMPACTING
COMPANIONS
COMPARABLE
COMPARABLY
COMPARATOR
COMPARISON
COMPASSION
COMPATIBLE
COMPATIBLY
COMPATRIOT
COMPELLING
COMPENDIUM
COMPENSATE
COMPETENCE
COMPETENCY
COMPETITOR
COMPLACENT
COMPLAINED
COMPLAINER
COMPLAINTS
COMPLEMENT
COMPLETELY
COMPLETING
COMPLETION
COMPLETIST
COMPLETIVE
COMPLEXION
COMPLEXITY
COMPLIANCE
COMPLICATE
COMPLICITY
COMPLIMENT
COMPONENTS
COMPORTING
COMPOSITES
COMPOSITOR
COMPOSTING
COMPOUNDED
COMPOUNDER
COMPREHEND
COMPRESSED
COMPRESSES
COMPRESSOR
COMPRISING
COMPROMISE
COMPULSION
COMPULSIVE

COMPULSORY
COMPUTABLE
CONCEALING
CONCEDEDLY
CONCEIVING
CONCENTRIC
CONCEPCION
CONCEPTION
CONCEPTIVE
CONCEPTUAL
CONCERNING
CONCERTINA
CONCERTINO
CONCESSION
CONCESSIVE
CONCHIOLIN
CONCHOLOGY
CONCIERGES
CONCILIATE
CONCINNITY
CONCINNOUS
CONCLAVIST
CONCLUDING
CONCLUSION
CONCLUSIVE
CONCOCTING
CONCOCTION
CONCOCTIVE
CONCORDANT
CONCORDATS
CONCOURSES
CONCRETELY
CONCRETING
CONCRETION
CONCRETIVE
CONCRETIZE
CONCUBINES
CONCURRENT
CONCURRING
CONCUSSING
CONCUSSION
CONCUSSIVE
CONDEMNING
CONDENSATE
CONDENSERS
CONDENSING
CONDESCEND
CONDIMENTS
CONDITIONS
CONDOLENCE
CONDUCIBLE

CONDUCTING
CONDUCTION
CONDUCTIVE
CONDUCTORS
CONEFLOWER
CONFECTION
CONFERENCE
CONFERMENT
CONFERRING
CONFERVOID
CONFESSING
CONFESSION
CONFESSORS
CONFIDANTS
CONFIDENCE
CONFIRMING
CONFISCATE
CONFLATING
CONFLATION
CONFLICTED
CONFLUENCE
CONFORMERS
CONFORMING
CONFORMIST
CONFORMITY
CONFOUNDED
CONFOUNDER
CONFRONTED
CONFRONTER
CONFUSABLE
CONFUSEDLY
CONGEALING
CONGENERIC
CONGENITAL
CONGER
  EELS
CONGESTION
CONGESTIVE
CONGLOBATE
CONGREGATE
CONGRESSES
CONGRUENCE
CONIFEROUS
CONJECTURE
CONJOINING
CONJOINTLY
CONJUGABLE
CONJUGATED
CONJUGATOR
CONNECTING
CONNECTION

CONNECTIVE
CONNIVANCE
CONQUERING
CONQUERORS
CONSCIENCE
CONSCRIPTS
CONSECRATE
CONSENSUAL
CONSENTING
CONSEQUENT
CONSERVING
CONSIDERED
CONSIDERER
CONSIGNEES
CONSIGNING
CONSIGNORS
CONSISTENT
CONSISTING
CONSISTORY
CONSOCIATE
CONSOLABLE
CONSONANCE
CONSONANTS
CONSORTIAL
CONSORTING
CONSORTIUM
CONSPECTUS
CONSPIRACY
CONSPIRING
CONSTABLES
CONSTANTAN
CONSTANTIA
CONSTANTLY
CONSTIPATE
CONSTITUTE
CONSTRAINT
CONSTRUCTS
CONSTRUING
CONSUETUDE
CONSULATES
CONSULSHIP
CONSULTANT
CONSULTING
CONSUMMATE
CONTACTING
CONTACTUAL
CONTAGIONS
CONTAGIOUS
CONTAINERS
CONTAINING
CONTENDERS

CONTENDING
CONTENTING
CONTENTION
CONTESTANT
CONTESTING
CONTEXTUAL
CONTEXTURE
CONTIGUITY
CONTIGUOUS
CONTINENCE
CONTINENTS
CONTINGENT
CONTINUANT
CONTINUING
CONTINUITY
CONTINUOUS
CONTINUUMS
CONTORTING
CONTORTION
CONTOURING
CONTRABAND
CONTRABASS
CONTRACTED
CONTRACTOR
CONTRADICT
CONTRAFLOW
CONTRALTOS
CONTRARIES
CONTRARILY
CONTRASTED
CONTRAVENE
CONTRIBUTE
CONTRITELY
CONTRITION
CONTRIVING
CONTROLLED
CONTROLLER
CONTROVERT
CONTUSIONS
CONUNDRUMS
CONVALESCE
CONVECTION
CONVECTIVE
CONVECTORS
CONVENABLE
CONVENANCE
CONVENIENT
CONVENTION
CONVENTUAL
CONVERGENT
CONVERGING

CONVERSANT
CONVERSELY
CONVERSING
CONVERSION
CONVERTERS
CONVERTING
CONVEYABLE
CONVEYANCE
CONVICTING
CONVICTION
CONVICTIVE
CONVINCING
CONVOCATOR
CONVOLUTED
CONVULSING
CONVULSION
CONVULSIVE
COOCH
  BEHAR
COOKHOUSES
COOL-
  HEADED
COOPERATED
COOPERATOR
COOPTATION
COOPTATIVE
COORDINATE
COPARCENER
COPENHAGEN
COPPER
  BELT
COPPERHEAD
COPROLALIA
COPROLITIC
COPROPHAGY
COPULATING
COPULATION
COPULATIVE
COPY
  EDITOR
COPYHOLDER
COPYRIGHTS
COPYWRITER
COQUELICOT
COQUETRIES
COQUETTISH
COR
  ANGLAIS
CORDIALITY
CORDIERITE
CORDILLERA

CORDON
  BLEU
CORIACEOUS
CORINTHIAN
CORKSCREWS
CORMOPHYTE
CORMORANTS
CORNACEOUS
CORNCOCKLE
CORNCRAKES
CORNED
  BEEF
CORNELIANS
CORNFLAKES
CORNFLOWER
CORNSTARCH
CORNUCOPIA
CORNWALLIS
CORONATION
CORPORATOR
CORPOREITY
CORPULENCE
CORPUSCLES
CORRALLING
CORRECTING
CORRECTION
CORRECTIVE
CORRELATED
CORRELATES
CORRESPOND
CORRIENTES
CORRIGENDA
CORRIGIBLE
CORROBOREE
CORRODIBLE
CORRUGATED
CORRUPTING
CORRUPTION
CORRUPTIVE
CORSETIERE
CORUSCATED
COS
  LETTUCE
COSMICALLY
COSMIC
  RAYS
COSMODROME
COSMOGONAL
COSMOGONIC
COSMONAUTS
COSSETTING

COSTA
  RICAN
CO-
  STARRING
COSTLINESS
COST
  PRICES
COSTUMIERS
COTANGENTS
COTILLIONS
COTTAGE
  PIE
COTTON
  GINS
COTTONSEED
COTTONTAIL
COTTONWOOD
COTTON
  WOOL
COUCHETTES
COUCH
  GRASS
COULOMETER
COUNCILLOR
COUNCILMAN
COUNCILMEN
COUNCIL
  TAX
COUNSELLED
COUNSELLOR
COUNTDOWNS
COUNTERACT
COUNTERING
COUNTERSPY
COUNTESSES
COUNT
  NOUNS
COUNTRYMAN
COUNTRYMEN
COUNTY
  TOWN
COUPS
  D'ETAT
COURAGEOUS
COURGETTES
COURSEBOOK
COURT
  CARDS
COURTESANS
COURTESIES
COURTHOUSE
COURTLIEST

COURTSHIPS
COURTYARDS
COUTURIERS
COVARIANCE
COVENANTAL
COVENANTED
COVENANTEE
COVENANTER
COVENANTOR
COVER
  NOTES
COVER
  POINT
COVETOUSLY
COWCATCHER
CRAB
  APPLES
CRACKBRAIN
CRACKDOWNS
CRADLE
  SONG
CRAFTINESS
CRANE
  FLIES
CRANESBILL
CRANIOLOGY
CRANIOTOMY
CRANKSHAFT
CRAPULENCE
CRAQUELURE
CRASH-
  DIVED
CRASH-
  DIVES
CRAVENNESS
CRAYFISHES
CREAKINESS
CREAMERIES
CREAMINESS
CREATININE
CREATIONAL
CREATIVELY
CREATIVITY
CREDITABLE
CREDITABLY
CREDIT
  CARD
CREDIT
  NOTE
CREEPINESS
CREMATIONS
CREMATORIA

CRENELLATE
CREOSOTING
CREPE
  PAPER
CRESCENDOS
CRESCENTIC
CRETACEOUS
CREWELWORK
CRIBRIFORM
CRICKETERS
CRIMINALLY
CRIMSONING
CRINKLIEST
CRINOLINES
CRISPATION
CRISPINESS
CRISSCROSS
CRITERIONS
CRITICALLY
CRITICISMS
CRITICIZED
CRITICIZER
CROAKINESS
CROCHETING
CROCODILES
CROISSANTS
CROQUETTES
CROSSBONES
CROSSBREED
CROSSCHECK
CROSSHATCH
CROSS-
  INDEX
CROSSPATCH
CROSSPIECE
CROSS-
  REFER
CROSSROADS
CROSS-
  SLIDE
CROSSTREES
CROSSWALKS
CROSSWINDS
CROSSWORDS
CROWDED
  OUT
CROWN
  COURT
CROWN
  DERBY
CROWNPIECE

CROW'S
  NESTS
CRUCIFIXES
CRUCIFYING
CRUMBLIEST
CRUNCHIEST
CRUSTACEAN
CRUSTINESS
CRYOGENICS
CRYOPHILIC
CRYOSCOPIC
CRYPTOLOGY
CRYPTOZOIC
CRYSTAL
  SET
CTENOPHORE
CUBBYHOLES
CUCKOLDING
CUCKOOPINT
CUCKOO
  PINT
CUCULIFORM
CUDDLESOME
CUDGELLING
CUERNAVACA
CULLENDERS
CULTIVABLE
CULTIVATED
CULTIVATOR
CULTURALLY
CUMBERSOME
CUMMERBUND
CUMULATION
CUMULATIVE
CUMULIFORM
CUPBEARERS
CURABILITY
CURATE'S
  EGG
CURATORIAL
CURMUDGEON
CURRENCIES
CURRICULAR
CURRICULUM
CURTAILING
CURTAINING
CURVACEOUS
CURVATURES
CUSHIONING
CUSSEDNESS
CUSTARD
  PIE

CUSTODIANS
CUSTOMIZED
CUSTOM
  MADE
CUSTOM-
  MADE
CUTTHROATS
CUTTLEBONE
CUTTLEFISH
CUT UP
  ROUGH
CYANOGENIC
CYBERNETIC
CYBERSPACE
CYCLAMATES
CYCLICALLY
CYCLOMETER
CYCLOMETRY
CYCLORAMIC
CYCLOSTOME
CYCLOSTYLE
CYLINDROID
CYMBALISTS
CYMIFEROUS
CYSTECTOMY
CYSTOSCOPE
CYSTOSCOPY
CYTOCHROME
CYTOLOGIST

D

DACHSHUNDS
DAIL
  EIRANN
DAILY
  BREAD
DAIMYO
  BOND
DAINTINESS
DAIRY
  FARMS
DAIRYMAIDS
DAISY
  WHEEL
DALAI
  LAMAS
DALMATIANS
DAMAGEABLE
DAMP
  COURSE
DAMP
  SQUIBS

DAMSELFISH
DANDELIONS
DAPPLE-
  GREY
DAREDEVILS
DARJEELING
DARK
  HORSES
DARLINGTON
DARTBOARDS
DASHBOARDS
DAUGAVPILS
DAUGHTERLY
DAYDREAMED
DAYDREAMER
DAY-
  NEUTRAL
DAY
  NURSERY
DAY
  SCHOOLS
DAY-
  TRIPPER
DEACONSHIP
DEACTIVATE
DEAD
  CENTRE
DEAD
  LETTER
DEADLINESS
DEADLY
  SINS
DEAD-
  NETTLE
DEAD
  RINGER
DEALERSHIP
DEATHBLOWS
DEATH
  MASKS
DEATH
  RATES
DEATH'S-
  HEAD
DEATH
  SQUAD
DEATH
  TOLLS
DEATH
  TRAPS
DEATHWATCH
DEBASEMENT
DEBAUCHEES

DEBAUCHERY
DEBAUCHING
DEBENTURES
DEBILITATE
DEBOUCHING
DEBRIEFING
DEBUTANTES
DECADENTLY
DECAHEDRAL
DECAHEDRON
DECAMPMENT
DECAPITATE
DECATHLONS
DECEIVABLE
DECELERATE
DECEPTIONS
DECIMALIZE
DECIMATING
DECIMATION
DECIPHERED
DECIPHERER
DECISIONAL
DECISIVELY
DECKCHAIRS
DECLAIMING
DECLARABLE
DECLASSIFY
DECLENSION
DECLINABLE
DECOCTIONS
DECOLLATOR
DECOLONIZE
DECOLORANT
DECOLORIZE
DECOMPOSED
DECOMPOSER
DECOMPOUND
DECOMPRESS
DECORATING
DECORATION
DECORATIVE
DECORATORS
DECOROUSLY
DECOUPLING
DECREASING
DECREEABLE
DECREE
  NISI
DECRESCENT
DECUMBENCE
DEDICATING

DEDICATION
DEDICATORY
DEDUCTIBLE
DEDUCTIONS
DEEP
  FREEZE
DEEP
  FRYING
DEEP-
  ROOTED
DEEP-
  SEATED
DE-
  ESCALATE
DEFACEABLE
DEFACEMENT
DEFALCATOR
DEFAMATION
DEFAMATORY
DEFAULTERS
DEFAULTING
DEFEASANCE
DEFEASIBLE
DEFEATISTS
DEFECATING
DEFECATION
DEFECTIONS
DEFENDABLE
DEFENDANTS
DEFENSIBLE
DEFENSIBLY
DEFENSIVES
DEFERMENTS
DEFERRABLE
DEFICIENCY
DEFILEMENT
DEFINITELY
DEFINITION
DEFINITIVE
DEFINITUDE
DEFLAGRATE
DEFLECTING
DEFLECTION
DEFLECTIVE
DEFLOWERED
DEFLOWERER
DEFOLIANTS
DEFOLIATED
DEFOLIATOR
DEFORESTED
DEFORESTER
DEFORMABLE

DEFRAUDING
DEFRAYABLE
DEFROCKING
DEFROSTERS
DEFROSTING
DEFUNCTIVE
DEGENERACY
DEGENERATE
DEGRADABLE
DEGRESSION
DEHISCENCE
DEHUMANIZE
DEHUMIDIFY
DEHYDRATED
DEHYDRATOR
DEJECTEDLY
DELAMINATE
DELAWAREAN
DELECTABLE
DELECTABLY
DELEGATING
DELEGATION
DELIBERATE
DELICACIES
DELICATELY
DELIGHTFUL
DELIGHTING
DELIMITING
DELINEATED
DELINEATOR
DELINQUENT
DELIQUESCE
DELIVERIES
DELIVERING
DELOCALIZE
DELPHINIUM
DELTIOLOGY
DELUSIONAL
DELUSIVELY
DEMAGOGUES
DEMANDABLE
DEMARCATED
DEMARCATOR
DEMEANOURS
DEMENTEDLY
DEMICANTON
DEMIVIERGE
DEMOBILIZE
DEMOCRATIC
DEMODULATE
DEMOGRAPHY

DEMOISELLE
DEMOLISHED
DEMOLISHER
DEMOLITION
DEMONETIZE
DEMONIACAL
DEMONOLOGY
DEMORALIZE
DEMOTIVATE
DEMURENESS
DEMURRABLE
DENATURANT
DENDRIFORM
DENDROGRAM
DENDROLOGY
DENEGATION
DENIGRATED
DENIGRATOR
DENOMINATE
DENOTATION
DENOTATIVE
DENOTEMENT
DENOUEMENT
DENOUNCING
DENSIMETER
DENSIMETRY
DENTIFRICE
DENUDATION
DENUNCIATE
DENVER
  BOOT
DEODORANTS
DEODORIZED
DEODORIZER
DEONTOLOGY
DEOXIDIZER
DEPARTMENT
DEPARTURES
DEPENDABLE
DEPENDABLY
DEPENDANTS
DEPENDENCE
DEPENDENCY
DEPICTIONS
DEPILATION
DEPILATORY
DEPLETABLE
DEPLORABLE
DEPLORABLY
DEPLOYMENT
DEPOLARIZE

DEPOPULATE
DEPORTABLE
DEPORTMENT
DEPOSITARY
DEPOSITING
DEPOSITION
DEPOSITORS
DEPOSITORY
DEPRECATED
DEPRECATOR
DEPRECIATE
DEPRESSANT
DEPRESSING
DEPRESSION
DEPRESSIVE
DEPRIVABLE
DEPURATION
DEPURATIVE
DEPUTATION
DEPUTIZING
DERACINATE
DERAILLEUR
DERAILMENT
DERBYSHIRE
DEREGULATE
DERISIVELY
DERISORILY
DERIVATION
DERIVATIVE
DERMATITIS
DERMATOGEN
DERMATOMIC
DERMATOSIS
DEROGATING
DEROGATION
DEROGATIVE
DEROGATORY
DESALINATE
DESALINIZE
DESCENDANT
DESCENDENT
DESCENDING
DESCRIBING
DESECRATED
DESECRATOR
DESERTIONS
DESERVEDLY
DESHABILLE
DESICCANTS
DESICCATED
DESICCATOR

DESIDERATA
DESIDERATE
DESIGNABLE
DESIGNATED
DESIGNATOR
DESIGNEDLY
DESISTANCE
DESOLATELY
DESOLATING
DESOLATION
DESPAIRING
DESPATCHED
DESPATCHER
DESPATCHES
DESPERADOS
DESPICABLE
DESPICABLY
DESPOILING
DESPONDENT
DESQUAMATE
DESSIATINE
DESTROYERS
DESTROYING
DESTRUCTOR
DETACHABLE
DETACHMENT
DETAINABLE
DETAINMENT
DETECTABLE
DETECTIVES
DETERGENCY
DETERGENTS
DETERMINED
DETERMINER
DETERRENCE
DETERRENTS
DETESTABLE
DETESTABLY
DETHRONING
DETONATING
DETONATION
DETONATIVE
DETONATORS
DETOXICANT
DETOXICATE
DETRACTING
DETRACTION
DETRACTIVE
DETRACTORS
DETRAINING
DETRIMENTS

DETRUNCATE
DEUTOPLASM
DEUX-
  SEVRES
DEVASTATED
DEVASTATOR
DEVELOPERS
DEVELOPING
DEVIATIONS
DEVILISHLY
DEVITALIZE
DEVOCALIZE
DEVOLUTION
DEVOTEMENT
DEVOTIONAL
DEVOUTNESS
DEXTRALITY
DIABOLICAL
DIACAUSTIC
DIACHRONIC
DIACRITICS
DIACTINISM
DIADROMOUS
DIAGENESIS
DIAGNOSING
DIAGNOSTIC
DIAGONALLY
DIAKINESIS
DIALECTICS
DIALYSABLE
DIAPASONAL
DIAPEDESIS
DIAPEDETIC
DIAPHANOUS
DIAPHRAGMS
DIAPHYSIAL
DIARRHOEAL
DIASTALSIS
DIASTALTIC
DIATHERMIC
DIATROPISM
DIBASICITY
DICHLORIDE
DICHROMATE
DICKENSIAN
DICKEY
  BIRD
DICKYBIRDS
DICTAPHONE
DICTATIONS
DICTATRESS

DICTIONARY
DICTOGRAPH
DICYNODONT
DIDYNAMOUS
DIE-
  CASTING
DIE-
  HARDISM
DIELECTRIC
DIETICIANS
DIFFERENCE
DIFFICULTY
DIFFIDENCE
DIFFRACTED
DIFFUSIBLE
DIGESTIBLE
DIGESTIONS
DIGESTIVES
DIGITALISM
DIGITALIZE
DIGITATION
DIGITIFORM
DIGITIZERS
DIGITIZING
DIGNIFYING
DIGRESSING
DIGRESSION
DIGRESSIVE
DILAPIDATE
DILATATION
DILEMMATIC
DILETTANTE
DILETTANTI
DILIGENTLY
DILLYDALLY
DIMENSIONS
DIMINISHED
DIMINUENDO
DIMINUTION
DIMINUTIVE
DIMORPHISM
DIMORPHOUS
DINERS
  CLUB
DINING
  CARS
DINING
  ROOM
DINNER
  BELL
DIPETALOUS
DIPHOSGENE

DIPHTHERIA
DIPHTHONGS
DIPHYLETIC
DIPHYLLOUS
DIPHYODONT
DIPLODOCUS
DIPLOMATIC
DIPSOMANIA
DIRECTIONS
DIRECTIVES
DIRECTNESS
DIRECTOIRE
DIRECTRESS
DIRIGIBLES
DIRT
  FARMER
DIRT
  TRACKS
DIRTY
  TRICK
DISABILITY
DISABUSING
DISALLOWED
DISAPPOINT
DISAPPROVE
DISARRANGE
DISASTROUS
DISAVOWALS
DISAVOWING
DISBANDING
DISBARMENT
DISBARRING
DISBELIEVE
DISBENEFIT
DISBURSING
DISCARDING
DISC
  BRAKES
DISCERNING
DISCHARGED
DISCHARGER
DISCHARGES
DISC
  HARROW
DISCIPLINE
DISC
  JOCKEY
DISCLAIMED
DISCLAIMER
DISCLOSING
DISCLOSURE
DISCOMFORT

DISCOMMODE
DISCOMPOSE
DISCONCERT
DISCONNECT
DISCONTENT
DISCOPHILE
DISCORDANT
DISCOUNTED
DISCOUNTER
DISCOURAGE
DISCOURSED
DISCOURSER
DISCOURSES
DISCOVERED
DISCOVERER
DISCREETLY
DISCREPANT
DISCRETELY
DISCRETION
DISCURSIVE
DISCUSSANT
DISCUSSING
DISCUSSION
DISDAINFUL
DISDAINING
DISEMBOGUE
DISEMBOWEL
DISEMBROIL
DISEMPOWER
DISENCHANT
DISENDOWER
DISENGAGED
DISENTHRAL
DISENTITLE
DISENTWINE
DISEPALOUS
DISFEATURE
DISFIGURED
DISFIGURER
DISGORGING
DISGRACING
DISGRUNTLE
DISGUISING
DISGUSTING
DISHABILLE
DISHARMONY
DISHCLOTHS
DISHEARTEN
DISHONESTY
DISH
  TOWELS

DISHWASHER
DISINCLINE
DISINHERIT
DISJOINTED
DISK
  DRIVES
DISLIKABLE
DISLOCATED
DISLODGING
DISLOYALLY
DISLOYALTY
DISMALNESS
DISMANTLED
DISMANTLER
DISMASTING
DISMISSALS
DISMISSING
DISMISSIVE
DISMOUNTED
DISOBEYING
DISOBLIGED
DISORDERED
DISORDERLY
DISOWNMENT
DISPARAGED
DISPARAGER
DISPASSION
DISPATCHED
DISPATCHES
DISPELLING
DISPENSARY
DISPENSERS
DISPENSING
DISPERMOUS
DISPERSING
DISPERSION
DISPERSIVE
DISPERSOID
DISPIRITED
DISPLACING
DISPLAYING
DISPLEASED
DISPORTING
DISPOSABLE
DISPOSSESS
DISPRAISER
DISPROVING
DISPUTABLE
DISPUTABLY
DISQUALIFY
DISQUIETED

DISRESPECT
DISRUPTING
DISRUPTION
DISRUPTIVE
DISSATISFY
DISSECTING
DISSECTION
DISSEMBLED
DISSEMBLER
DISSENSION
DISSENTERS
DISSENTING
DISSERVICE
DISSIDENCE
DISSIDENTS
DISSIMILAR
DISSIPATED
DISSIPATER
DISSOCIATE
DISSOLUBLE
DISSOLVING
DISSONANCE
DISSUADING
DISSUASION
DISSUASIVE
DISTANCING
DISTENDING
DISTENSION
DISTICHOUS
DISTILLATE
DISTILLERS
DISTILLERY
DISTILLING
DISTINCTLY
DISTORTING
DISTORTION
DISTORTIVE
DISTRACTED
DISTRACTER
DISTRAINED
DISTRAINEE
DISTRAINOR
DISTRAUGHT
DISTRESSED
DISTRIBUTE
DISTRUSTED
DISTRUSTER
DISTURBING
DISULFIRAM
DISULPHATE
DISULPHIDE

DISUNITING
DISUTILITY
DISYLLABIC
DITHEISTIC
DITHIONITE
DIVARICATE
DIVE-
  BOMBED
DIVE-
  BOMBER
DIVERGENCE
DIVERGENCY
DIVERSIONS
DIVERTEDLY
DIVERTIBLE
DIVESTIBLE
DIVESTMENT
DIVINATION
DIVINATORY
DIVING
  BELL
DIVINITIES
DIVISIONAL
DIVISIVELY
DIVULGENCE
DIYARBAKIR
DOCENTSHIP
DOC
  MARTENS
DOCTORATES
DOCTRINISM
DOCUMENTED
DODECANESE
DOG
  BISCUIT
DOGCATCHER
DOG
  COLLARS
DOGGEDNESS
DOGMATISTS
DOGMATIZER
DOGSBODIES
DOLCELATTE
DOLLARFISH
DOLL'S
  HOUSE
DOLLY
  BIRDS
DOLOROUSLY
DOMINATING
DOMINATION
DOMINATIVE

DOMINATRIX
DOMINEERED
DOMINICANS
DONER
  KEBAB
DONKEYWORK
DONNYBROOK
DOORKEEPER
DOORPLATES
DORCHESTER
DORSIGRADE
DOSIMETRIC
DOSSHOUSES
DO THE
  TRICK
DOTTED
  LINE
DOUBLE
  BASS
DOUBLE
  BEDS
DOUBLE
  BIND
DOUBLE
  CHIN
DOUBLE
  DATE
DOUBLE-
  HUNG
DOUBLE-
  PARK
DOUBLE-
  REED
DOUBLE-
  STOP
DOUBLE
  TAKE
DOUBLE-
  TALK
DOUBLE
  TIME
DOUBLETREE
DOUBTFULLY
DOUGHTIEST
DOVETAILED
DOWN-AND-
  OUT
DOWN AT
  HEEL
DOWN-AT-
  HEEL
DOWNGRADED
DOWNLOADED

DOWN-
  MARKET
DOWNPLAYED
DOWNSIZING
DOWNSPOUTS
DOWNSTAIRS
DOWNSTREAM
DRAGONHEAD
DRAGONROOT
DRAGOONAGE
DRAGOONING
DRAINPIPES
DRAMATISTS
DRAMATIZED
DRAMATIZER
DRAMATURGE
DRAMATURGY
DRAWBRIDGE
DRAWING
  PIN
DRAWSTRING
DREADFULLY
DREADLOCKS
DREAMBOATS
DREAMINESS
DREAMINGLY
DREAMLANDS
DREAM
  WORLD
DREARINESS
DRESSINESS
DRESSMAKER
DRILLSTOCK
DRIP-
  DRYING
DRIVELLERS
DRIVELLING
DROLLERIES
DROOPINESS
DROSOPHILA
DROSSINESS
DROWSINESS
DRUGSTORES
DRUM
  MAJORS
DRUMSTICKS
DRUPACEOUS
DRY
  BATTERY
DRY-
  CLEANED

DRY
  CLEANER
DUBITATION
DUCKBOARDS
DUFFEL
  BAGS
DUFFEL
  COAT
DUMBSTRUCK
DUMBWAITER
DUNCE'S
  CAPS
DUNDERHEAD
DUODECIMAL
DUODENITIS
DUPABILITY
DUPLICABLE
DUPLICATED
DUPLICATES
DUPLICATOR
DURABILITY
DURATIONAL
DUSSELDORF
DUST
  JACKET
DUSTSHEETS
DUST
  STORMS
DUTCH
  BARNS
DUTCH
  OVENS
DUTCH
  TREAT
DUTCH
  UNCLE
DYNAMISTIC
DYNAMITING
DYSENTERIC
DYSPLASTIC
DYSPROSIUM
DYSTROPHIC
DZERZHINSK

E

EAGLESTONE
EARLY
  BIRDS
EARMARKING
EARTHBOUND
EARTHINESS
EARTHLIEST

EARTHLIGHT
EARTHLINGS
EARTHQUAKE
EARTHSHINE
EARTHWARDS
EARTHWORKS
EARTHWORMS
EAR
  TRUMPET
EAST
  ANGLIA
EAST
  BERLIN
EAST
  ENDERS
EASTER
  EGGS
EASTERNERS
EASTERTIDE
EAST
  GERMAN
EAST
  INDIAN
EAST
  INDIES
EASTWARDLY
EASY
  CHAIRS
EASY DOES
  IT
EASY
  STREET
EASY
  VIRTUE
EBRACTEATE
EBULLIENCE
EBULLITION
EBURNATION
ECCENTRICS
ECCHYMOSIS
ECHINODERM
ECHOPRAXIA
ECOCENTRIC
ECOLOGICAL
ECOLOGISTS
ECONOMICAL
ECONOMISTS
ECONOMIZED
ECONOMIZER
ECOSPECIES
ECOSYSTEMS
ECOTOURISM

ECTODERMAL
ECTOENZYME
ECTOGENOUS
ECTOMORPHY
ECUADORIAN
ECUMENICAL
ECZEMATOUS
EDENTULOUS
EDIFYINGLY
EDITORIALS
EDITORSHIP
EDULCORATE
EDWARDIANS
EFFACEABLE
EFFACEMENT
EFFECTIBLE
EFFECTUATE
EFFEMINACY
EFFEMINATE
EFFERVESCE
EFFETENESS
EFFICIENCY
EFFLORESCE
EFFORTLESS
EFFRONTERY
EFFULGENCE
EFFUSIVELY
EGOCENTRIC
EGYPTOLOGY
EIDERDOWNS
EIGHTEENMO
EIGHTEENTH
EIGHTH
  NOTE
EIGHTIETHS
EISENSTADT
EISTEDDFOD
EJACULATED
EJACULATOR
ELABORATED
ELABORATOR
ELAEOPTENE
ELASTICITY
ELASTICIZE
ELATEDNESS
ELDERBERRY
ELEATICISM
ELECAMPANE
ELECTIVITY
ELECTORATE
ELECTRICAL

ELECTRODES
ELECTROJET
ELECTRONIC
ELEMENTARY
ELEVATIONS
ELEVEN-
  PLUS
ELICITABLE
ELIMINABLE
ELIMINATED
ELIMINATOR
ELLIPTICAL
ELONGATING
ELONGATION
ELONGATIVE
ELOPEMENTS
ELOQUENTLY
EL
  SALVADOR
ELUCIDATED
ELUCIDATOR
ELUTRIATOR
ELUVIATION
EMACIATION
EMANATIONS
EMANCIPATE
EMARGINATE
EMASCULATE
EMBALMMENT
EMBANKMENT
EMBARGOING
EMBARKMENT
EMBEZZLERS
EMBEZZLING
EMBITTERED
EMBITTERER
EMBLAZONED
EMBLAZONRY
EMBLEMATIC
EMBLEMENTS
EMBODIMENT
EMBOLDENED
EMBOLISMIC
EMBONPOINT
EMBOSSMENT
EMBOUCHURE
EMBRASURED
EMBRASURES
EMBRECTOMY
EMBROIDERY
EMBROILING

EMBRYOGENY
EMBRYOLOGY
EMENDATION
EMENDATORY
EMETICALLY
EMIGRATING
EMIGRATION
EMIGRATIVE
EMISSARIES
EMISSIVITY
EMMENTALER
EMMETROPIA
EMMETROPIC
EMOLLIENCE
EMOLLIENTS
EMOLUMENTS
EMPALEMENT
EMPANELING
EMPANELLED
EMPHASIZED
EMPIRICISM
EMPIRICIST
EMPLOYABLE
EMPLOYMENT
EMPOWERING
EMULSIFIED
EMULSIFIER
EMULSIONED
ENACTMENTS
ENAMELLING
ENAMELLIST
ENAMELWARE
ENAMELWORK
ENCAMPMENT
ENCASEMENT
ENCASHABLE
ENCASHMENT
ENCEPHALIC
ENCEPHALON
ENCHAINING
ENCHANTERS
ENCHANTING
ENCHILADAS
ENCIPHERER
ENCIRCLING
ENCLOSABLE
ENCLOSURES
ENCODEMENT
ENCOUNTERS
ENCOURAGED
ENCOURAGER

ENCROACHED
ENCROACHER
ENCRUSTANT
ENCUMBERED
ENCYCLICAL
ENCYSTMENT
ENDANGERED
ENDEARMENT
ENDEAVOURS
ENDOCARPAL
ENDOCRINAL
ENDOCRINIC
ENDODERMAL
ENDODERMIC
ENDODERMIS
ENDODONTIA
ENDODONTIC
ENDOENZYME
ENDOGAMOUS
ENDOGENOUS
ENDOMORPHY
ENDOPHYTIC
ENDORSABLE
ENDOSCOPIC
ENDOSMOSIS
ENDOSMOTIC
ENDOSTOSIS
ENDOWMENTS
END
  PRODUCT
ENDURINGLY
ENERGETICS
ENERGIZING
ENERVATING
ENERVATION
ENERVATIVE
ENFACEMENT
ENFEEBLING
ENFILADING
ENFLEURAGE
ENFOLDMENT
ENFORCEDLY
ENGAGEMENT
ENGAGINGLY
ENGENDERED
ENGENDERER
ENGINEERED
ENGINE
  ROOM
ENGLISHMAN
ENGLISHMEN

ENGRAVINGS
ENGROSSING
ENGULFMENT
ENHARMONIC
ENJAMBMENT
ENJOINMENT
ENJOYMENTS
ENLACEMENT
ENLISTMENT
ENLIVENING
ENORMITIES
ENORMOUSLY
ENPHYTOTIC
ENRAGEMENT
ENRAPTURED
ENRICHMENT
ENROLMENTS
ENSANGUINE
ENSCONCING
ENSHRINING
ENSHROUDED
ENSIGNSHIP
ENTAILMENT
ENTANGLING
ENTEROTOMY
ENTERPRISE
ENTHRALLED
ENTHRALLER
ENTHRONING
ENTHUSIASM
ENTHUSIAST
ENTICEMENT
ENTICINGLY
ENTIRENESS
ENTODERMAL
ENTOMBMENT
ENTOMOLOGY
ENTOPHYTIC
ENTOURAGES
ENTRAINING
ENTRANCING
ENTRAPMENT
ENTRAPPING
ENTREATIES
ENTREATING
ENTRENCHED
ENTRENCHER
ENTRUSTING
ENTRY-
  LEVEL
ENUCLEATOR

ENUMERATED
ENUMERATOR
ENUNCIABLE
ENUNCIATED
ENUNCIATOR
ENVELOPING
ENVISAGING
ENZYMOLOGY
EOSINOPHIL
EPEIROGENY
EPENTHESIS
EPENTHETIC
EPEXEGESIS
EPEXEGETIC
EPIBLASTIC
EPICANTHUS
EPICARDIAC
EPICARDIUM
EPICENTRAL
EPICENTRES
EPICUREANS
EPICYCLOID
EPIDEICTIC
EPIDEMICAL
EPIDIDYMAL
EPIDIDYMIS
EPIGASTRIC
EPIGENESIS
EPIGENETIC
EPIGLOTTAL
EPIGLOTTIS
EPIGRAPHER
EPIGRAPHIC
EPILEPTICS
EPILEPTOID
EPIMORPHIC
EPINEURIAL
EPINEURIUM
EPIPHONEMA
EPIPHYSEAL
EPIROGENIC
EPISCOPACY
EPISCOPATE
EPISIOTOMY
EPISPASTIC
EPISTERNUM
EPISTOLARY
EPITAPHIST
EPITHELIAL
EPITHELIUM
EPITOMIZED

EPITOMIZER
EPOXY
  RESIN
EPSOM
  SALTS
EQUABILITY
EQUALIZERS
EQUALIZING
EQUANIMITY
EQUANIMOUS
EQUATIONAL
EQUATORIAL
EQUESTRIAN
EQUIPOTENT
EQUITATION
EQUIVALENT
EQUIVOCATE
ERADIATION
ERADICABLE
ERADICATED
ERADICATOR
ERECTILITY
ERETHISMIC
ERGONOMICS
ERGOSTEROL
ERICACEOUS
ERINACEOUS
EROGENEITY
EROTEMATIC
EROTICALLY
EROTOGENIC
EROTOMANIA
ERRATICISM
ERUBESCENT
ERUCTATION
ERUCTATIVE
ERUPTIONAL
ERUPTIVITY
ERYSIPELAS
ERYTHRITOL
ESCADRILLE
ESCALATING
ESCALATION
ESCALATORS
ESCAPEMENT
ESCAPOLOGY
ESCARPMENT
ESCHAROTIC
ESCRITOIRE
ESCUTCHEON
ESKILSTUNA

ESPADRILLE
ESPECIALLY
ESPLANADES
ESSENTIALS
ESTATE
  CARS
ESTHETICAL
ESTIMATING
ESTIMATION
ESTIMATIVE
ESTIMATORS
ESTIPULATE
ESTRANGING
ETERNALITY
ETERNALIZE
ETERNITIES
ETHANEDIOL
ETHEREALLY
ETHNICALLY
ETHNOGENIC
ETHNOLOGIC
ETHOLOGIST
ETHYLATION
ETIOLATION
EUBACTERIA
EUCALYPTOL
EUCALYPTUS
EUCHLORINE
EUDEMONICS
EUDEMONISM
EUDIOMETER
EUDIOMETRY
EUGENICIST
EUHEMERISM
EUHEMERIST
EUHEMERIZE
EULOGISTIC
EULOGIZING
EUPATORIUM
EUPHAUSIID
EUPHEMISMS
EUPHEMIZER
EUPHONIOUS
EUPHONIUMS
EUPHORIANT
EUPHUISTIC
EURE-ET-
  LOIR
EURHYTHMIC
EUROCHEQUE
EUROCLYDON

EURODOLLAR
EUROMARKET
EURYPTERID
EURYTHMICS
EURYTROPIC
EUSTACHIAN
EUTHANASIA
EVACUATING
EVACUATION
EVACUATIVE
EVALUATING
EVALUATION
EVALUATIVE
EVANESCENT
EVANGELISM
EVANGELIST
EVANGELIZE
EVANSVILLE
EVAPORABLE
EVAPORATED
EVAPORATOR
EVECTIONAL
EVEN-
  HANDED
EVENING
  ALL
EVENING
  OUT
EVENTFULLY
EVENTUALLY
EVERGLADES
EVERGREENS
EVERY
  OTHER
EVERYTHING
EVERYWHERE
EVIDENTIAL
EVIL-
  MINDED
EVISCERATE
EVOCATIONS
EVOLVEMENT
EXACERBATE
EXACTINGLY
EXACTITUDE
EXAGGERATE
EXALTATION
EXAMINABLE
EXASPERATE
EX
  CATHEDRA
EXCAVATING

EXCAVATION
EXCAVATORS
EXCEEDABLE
EXCELLENCE
EXCELLENCY
EXCEPTABLE
EXCEPTIONS
EXCHANGING
EXCITATION
EXCITATIVE
EXCITEMENT
EXCITINGLY
EXCLAIMING
EXCLUDABLE
EXCLUSIVES
EXCOGITATE
EXCORIATED
EXCRESCENT
EXCRETIONS
EXCRUCIATE
EXCULPABLE
EXCULPATED
EXCURSIONS
EXCUSATORY
EXECRATING
EXECRATION
EXECRATIVE
EXECUTABLE
EXECUTANTS
EXECUTIONS
EXECUTIVES
EXEMPTIBLE
EXEMPTIONS
EXENTERATE
EXERCISING
EXHALATION
EXHAUSTING
EXHAUSTION
EXHAUSTIVE
EXHIBITING
EXHIBITION
EXHIBITIVE
EXHIBITORS
EXHIBITORY
EXHILARANT
EXHILARATE
EXHUMATION
EXIGENCIES
EXIGUOUSLY
EXISTENCES
EXOBIOLOGY

EXOCENTRIC
EXODONTIST
EXONERATED
EXONERATOR
EXORBITANT
EXORCIZING
EXOSPOROUS
EXOTHERMIC
EXOTICALLY
EXOTICNESS
EXPANDABLE
EXPANSIBLE
EXPANSIONS
EXPATIATED
EXPATIATOR
EXPATRIATE
EXPECTABLE
EXPECTANCY
EXPEDIENCE
EXPEDIENCY
EXPEDIENTS
EXPEDITING
EXPEDITION
EXPELLABLE
EXPENDABLE
EXPERIENCE
EXPERIMENT
EXPERTNESS
EXPIRATION
EXPIRATORY
EXPLAINING
EXPLETIVES
EXPLICABLE
EXPLICABLY
EXPLICATED
EXPLICATOR
EXPLICITLY
EXPLOITERS
EXPLOITING
EXPLOSIONS
EXPLOSIVES
EXPORTABLE
EXPOSITION
EXPOSITORY
EXPOUNDING
EXPRESSAGE
EXPRESSING
EXPRESSION
EXPRESSIVE
EXPRESSWAY
EXPULSIONS

EXPUNCTION
EXPURGATED
EXPURGATOR
EXSANGUINE
EXSICCATOR
EXTENDIBLE
EXTENSIBLE
EXTENSIONS
EXTENUATED
EXTENUATOR
EXTERNALLY
EXTINCTION
EXTINCTIVE
EXTINGUISH
EXTIRPATED
EXTIRPATOR
EXTORTIONS
EXTRACTING
EXTRACTION
EXTRACTIVE
EXTRACTORS
EXTRADITED
EXTRAMURAL
EXTRANEOUS
EXTRAVERTS
EXTRICABLE
EXTRICATED
EXTROVERTS
EXTRUSIONS
EXUBERANCE
EXULTANTLY
EXULTATION
EXULTINGLY
EXUVIATION
EYEBALLING
EYE-
  CATCHER
EYEDROPPER
EYEGLASSES
EYE-
  OPENERS
EYE
  SHADOWS
EYEWITNESS

F

FABRICATED
FABRICATOR
FABULOUSLY
FACECLOTHS

FACE-
  HARDEN
FACE
  POWDER
FACE-
  SAVERS
FACE-
  SAVING
FACE TO
  FACE
FACE-TO-
  FACE
FACE
  VALUES
FACILENESS
FACILITATE
FACILITIES
FACSIMILES
FACTITIOUS
FACT OF
  LIFE
FACTORABLE
FACTORIZED
FACTORSHIP
FACTUALISM
FACTUALIST
FAHRENHEIT
FAINTINGLY
FAIR
  COPIES
FAIR
  DINKUM
FAIRGROUND
FAIR-
  MINDED
FAIR-
  SPOKEN
FAIRYLANDS
FAIRY
  LIGHT
FAIRY
  TALES
FAISALABAD
FAITHFULLY
FALLACIOUS
FALLOW
  DEER
FALLOWNESS
FALSE
  ALARM
FALSEHOODS
FALSE
  SCENT

FALSE START
FALSE TEETH
FALSIFYING
FAMILIARLY
FAMILY NAME
FAMILY TREE
FAMISHMENT
FAMOUSNESS
FANATICISM
FANATICIZE
FANCIFULLY
FANCY DRESS
FANCY WOMAN
FANCY WOMEN
FANTASIZED
FANTOCCINI
FARCICALLY
FAR EASTERN
FARFETCHED
FARMHOUSES
FARMSTEADS
FARSIGHTED
FASCIATION
FASCICULAR
FASCICULUS
FASCINATED
FASHIONING
FASTENINGS
FASTIDIOUS
FASTIGIATE
FASTNESSES
FATALISTIC
FATALITIES
FATHERHOOD
FATHERLAND
FATHERLESS
FATHER-LIKE
FATHOMABLE
FATHOMETER
FATHOMLESS
FAT-SOLUBLE
FATTENABLE

FAULTINESS
FAVOURABLE
FAVOURABLY
FAVOURITES
FEARLESSLY
FEARNOUGHT
FEATHER BED
FEATHER BOA
FEATHERING
FEBRIFUGAL
FEBRUARIES
FECKLESSLY
FECUNDATOR
FEDERALISM
FEDERALIST
FEDERALIZE
FEDERATING
FEDERATION
FEDERATIVE
FEEBLENESS
FEET OF CLAY
FEIGNINGLY
FELICITATE
FELICITIES
FELICITOUS
FELIXSTOWE
FELLMONGER
FELLOWSHIP
FELT-TIP PEN
FEMALENESS
FEMININITY
FENESTELLA
FER-DE-LANCE
FERMENTING
FEROCITIES
FERRITE-ROD
FERTILIZED
FERTILIZER
FESTOONERY
FESTOONING
FETCHINGLY
FETIPAROUS
FETISHISTS
FETTUCCINE
FEUILLETON
FEVERISHLY

FFESTINIOG
FIANNA FAIL
FIBREBOARD
FIBREGLASS
FIBRINOGEN
FIBROBLAST
FIBROSITIS
FICKLENESS
FICTIONIST
FICTITIOUS
FIDDLEHEAD
FIDDLEWOOD
FIELD EVENT
FIELDMOUSE
FIELDSTONE
FIELD-TESTS
FIELD TRIPS
FIENDISHLY
FIERCENESS
FIFTEENTHS
FIFTY FIFTY
FIFTY-FIFTY
FIGURATION
FIGURATIVE
FIGUREHEAD
FILARIASIS
FILE SERVER
FILIALNESS
FILIBUSTER
FILMSETTER
FILMSTRIPS
FILTERABLE
FILTER TIPS
FILTHINESS
FILTRATION
FINALIZING
FINANCIERS
FINE-TUNING
FINGER BOWL
FINGERLING
FINGERNAIL
FINGERTIPS

FINISTERRE
FINNO-UGRIC
FIRE ALARMS
FIREBRANDS
FIREBREAKS
FIREBRICKS
FIRE DRILLS
FIRE-EATERS
FIRE-EATING
FIRE ENGINE
FIRE ESCAPE
FIREGUARDS
FIREPLACES
FIRE-RAISER
FIRESTORMS
FIRING LINE
FIRST CLASS
FIRST-CLASS
FIRST FLOOR
FIRST NAMES
FIRST NIGHT
FISH FINGER
FISH KNIVES
FISHMONGER
FISH SLICES
FISH STICKS
FISSIPEDAL
FISTICUFFS
FIT OF ANGER
FIT OF PIQUE
FIT THE BILL
FITZGERALD

FIVE-FINGER
FIXED-POINT
FIXED STARS
FLABBINESS
FLABELLATE
FLACCIDITY
FLAGELLANT
FLAGELLATE
FLAGITIOUS
FLAGRANTLY
FLAGSTAFFS
FLAGSTONES
FLAG-WAVING
FLAMBOYANT
FLAMEPROOF
FLAMINGOES
FLANNELING
FLANNELLED
FLARE PATHS
FLASHBACKS
FLASHBOARD
FLASHBULBS
FLASHCUBES
FLASHINESS
FLASHLIGHT
FLASH POINT
FLATFISHES
FLAT-FOOTED
FLAT RACING
FLATTENING
FLATTERERS
FLATTERING
FLATULENCE
FLAVESCENT
FLAVOURFUL
FLAVOURING
FLAWLESSLY
FLEA-BITTEN
FLEA MARKET
FLECTIONAL
FLEDGLINGS
FLEECINESS

FLEETINGLY
FLESHINESS
FLESH
  WOUND
FLETCHINGS
FLEUR-DE-
  LIS
FLEUR-DE-
  LYS
FLICKERING
FLICK
  KNIFE
FLIGHT
  DECK
FLIGHTIEST
FLIGHTLESS
FLIGHT
  PATH
FLIMSINESS
FLINTINESS
FLINTLOCKS
FLINTSHIRE
FLIPPANTLY
FLIRTATION
FLIRTINGLY
FLOATATION
FLOCCULANT
FLOCCULATE
FLOCCULENT
FLOODGATES
FLOODLIGHT
FLOOD
  TIDES
FLOORBOARD
FLOOR
  CLOTH
FLOOR
  SHOWS
FLOPHOUSES
FLOPPINESS
FLOPPY
  DISK
FLORENTINE
FLORIBUNDA
FLORISTICS
FLOTATIONS
FLOUNDERED
FLOURISHED
FLOURISHER
FLOURISHES
FLOURMILLS
FLOUTINGLY

FLOWCHARTS
FLOWERBEDS
FLOWER
  GIRL
FLOWERLESS
FLOWER-
  LIKE
FLOWERPOTS
FLUCTUATED
FLUFFINESS
FLUGELHORN
FLUID
  OUNCE
FLUMMOXING
FLUORIDATE
FLUORINATE
FLUSTERING
FLUTTERING
FLY-BY-
  NIGHT
FLYCATCHER
FLY-
  FISHING
FLYING
  BOAT
FLYING
  FISH
FLYSPECKED
FLYSWATTER
FLYWEIGHTS
FOAMFLOWER
FOAM
  RUBBER
FOB
  WATCHES
FOCAL
  POINT
FOCUS
  GROUP
FOLIACEOUS
FOLK
  DANCER
FOLK
  DANCES
FOLKESTONE
FOLKLORIST
FOLKSINESS
FOLLICULAR
FOLLICULIN
FOLLOWABLE
FOLLOWINGS
FONDLINGLY

FONTANELLE
FOOD
  STAMPS
FOODSTUFFS
FOOTBALLER
FOOTBRIDGE
FOOT-
  CANDLE
FOOT
  FAULTS
FOOTLIGHTS
FOOTPLATES
FOOTPRINTS
FOOTSTOOLS
FORBEARING
FORBIDDING
FORCEDNESS
FORCEFULLY
FORE AND
  AFT
FOREARMING
FOREBODING
FORECASTED
FORECASTER
FORECASTLE
FORECLOSED
FORECOURSE
FORECOURTS
FOREDOOMED
FOREFATHER
FOREFINGER
FOREGATHER
FOREGOINGS
FOREGROUND
FOREIGN
  AID
FOREIGNERS
FOREIGNISM
FOREMOTHER
FOREORDAIN
FORERUNNER
FORESEEING
FORESHADOW
FOREST-
  LIKE
FORETELLER
FOREWARNED
FOREWARNER
FORFEITERS
FORFEITING
FORFEITURE
FORGETTING

FORGIVABLE
FORGIVABLY
FORKEDNESS
FORMALISTS
FORMALIZED
FORMALIZER
FORMATIONS
FORMATTING
FORMIC
  ACID
FORMIDABLE
FORMIDABLY
FORMLESSLY
FORMULATED
FORMULATOR
FOR MY
  MONEY
FORNICATED
FORNICATOR
FORSTERITE
FORSWEARER
FORTE-
  PIANO
FORTHRIGHT
FORTIFIERS
FORTIFYING
FORTISSIMO
FORTNIGHTS
FORTRESSES
FORT
  SUMTER
FORTUITISM
FORTUITIST
FORTUITOUS
FORTY-
  NINER
FORTY
  WINKS
FORWARDING
FOSSILIZED
FOSTERLING
FOUDROYANT
FOUNDATION
FOUNDERING
FOUNDLINGS
FOURCHETTE
FOUR-
  COLOUR
FOUR-
  HANDED
FOURIERISM
FOURIERIST

FOUR-IN-
  HAND
FOUR-
  POSTER
FOURRAGERE
FOURSQUARE
FOUR-
  STROKE
FOURTEENTH
FOXHUNTERS
FOXHUNTING
FOX
  TERRIER
FRACTIONAL
FRACTURING
FRAGMENTAL
FRAGMENTED
FRAGRANCES
FRAGRANTLY
FRAMEWORKS
FRANCHISED
FRANCHISES
FRANCISCAN
FRANCONIAN
FRANGIPANI
FRATERNITY
FRATERNIZE
FRATRICIDE
FRAUDULENT
FRAUENFELD
FRAXINELLA
FRAY
  BENTOS
FREAKINESS
FREAKISHLY
FREDERICIA
FREE
  AGENTS
FREE-
  BASING
FREEBOARDS
FREEBOOTER
FREE
  CHURCH
FREEDWOMAN
FREE FOR
  ALL
FREE-FOR-
  ALL
FREE-
  HANDED
FREEHOLDER

FREE
  HOUSES
FREELANCED
FREELANCER
FREELANCES
FREE-
  LIVING
FREELOADED
FREELOADER
FREEMARTIN
FREEMASONS
FREE
  PARDON
FREE
  PASSES
FREE-
  SPOKEN
FREE-
  TRADER
FREIGHTAGE
FREIGHTERS
FREIGHTING
FRENCH
  BEAN
FRENCH
  HORN
FRENCH
  KISS
FRENCH
  LOAF
FRENZIEDLY
FREQUENTED
FREQUENTER
FREQUENTLY
FRESHENING
FRESHWATER
FRIABILITY
FRICANDEAU
FRICASSEES
FRICATIVES
FRICTIONAL
FRIENDLESS
FRIENDLIER
FRIENDLIES
FRIENDLILY
FRIENDSHIP
FRIGHTENED
FRIGHTENER
FRILLINESS
FRISKINESS
FRITILLARY
FRITTERING

FRIZZINESS
FROCK
  COATS
FROGHOPPER
FROLICKING
FROLICSOME
FRONTALITY
FRONTBENCH
FRONT
  DOORS
FRONT
  ROOMS
FRONTWARDS
FROSTBOUND
FROSTINESS
FROTHINESS
FROWNINGLY
FROWZINESS
FROZENNESS
FRUCTIFIED
FRUCTIFIER
FRUITCAKES
FRUITERERS
FRUIT
  FLIES
FRUITFULLY
FRUITINESS
FRUIT
  SALAD
FRUSTRATED
FRUSTRATER
FRUTESCENT
FRYING
  PANS
FUDDY-
  DUDDY
FULFILLING
FULFILMENT
FULIGINOUS
FULL-
  BODIED
FULL
  HOUSES
FULL-
  LENGTH
FULL-
  RIGGED
FULL-
  SAILED
FULLY-
  GROWN
FULMINATED

FULMINATOR
FUMATORIUM
FUMBLINGLY
FUMIGATING
FUMIGATION
FUNCTIONAL
FUNCTIONED
FUNDHOLDER
FUNEREALLY
FUNGICIDAL
FUNGICIDES
FUNICULARS
FUNICULATE
FUNNELLING
FUNNY
  BONES
FUNNY
  FARMS
FURBISHING
FURNISHING
FURTHERING
FURUNCULAR
FUSIBILITY
FUSILLADES
FUSTANELLA
FUTURISTIC
FUTUROLOGY
FUZZY
  LOGIC

G
GABARDINES
GADOLINITE
GADOLINIUM
GAFF-
  RIGGED
GAILLARDIA
GAINLINESS
GAINSAYING
GALASHIELS
GALLICIZER
GALLOGLASS
GALLSTONES
GALLUP
  POLL
GALUMPHING
GALVANIZED
GALVANIZER
GAMEKEEPER
GAMETOCYTE
GAME
  WARDEN

GANG-
  BANGED
GANG-
  BANGER
GANGLIONIC
GANGPLANKS
GANGRENOUS
GANGSTA
  RAP
GANTT
  CHART
GARAGE
  SALE
GARBAGE
  CAN
GARDEN
  CITY
GARGANTUAN
GARISHNESS
GARLANDING
GARNIERITE
GARNISHING
GARRISONED
GARROTTING
GAS
  FITTERS
GASHOLDERS
GASIFIABLE
GASOMETERS
GASOMETRIC
GAS
  STATION
GASTRALGIA
GASTRALGIC
GASTROLITH
GASTRONOME
GASTRONOMY
GASTROTOMY
GAS
  TURBINE
GATEHOUSES
GATEKEEPER
GATHERABLE
GATHERINGS
GAUCHENESS
GAULTHERIA
GAUSSMETER
GAZETTEERS
GEAR
  LEVERS
GELATINIZE
GELATINOID

GELATINOUS
GELDERLAND
GEMINATION
GEMMACEOUS
GEMOLOGIST
GENERALIST
GENERALITY
GENERALIZE
GENERATING
GENERATION
GENERATIVE
GENERATORS
GENERATRIX
GENEROSITY
GENEROUSLY
GENETICIST
GENICULATE
GENIUS
  LOCI
GENTLEFOLK
GENTLENESS
GENTRIFYED
GEOCENTRIC
GEOCHEMIST
GEODYNAMIC
GEOGNOSTIC
GEOGRAPHER
GEOLOGICAL
GEOLOGISTS
GEOMETRIZE
GEOMORPHIC
GEOPHAGIST
GEOPHAGOUS
GEOPHYSICS
GEORGETOWN
GEORGE
  TOWN
GEOSCIENCE
GEOSTATICS
GEOTHERMAL
GEOTROPISM
GERATOLOGY
GERIATRICS
GERMANIZER
GERMICIDAL
GERMICIDES
GERMINABLE
GERMINATED
GERMINATOR
GERUNDIVAL
GESTATIONS

GESUNDHEIT
GET
   HITCHED
GET-UP-
   AND-GO
GHASTLIEST
GHOSTLIEST
GHOST
   TOWNS
GHOSTWRITE
GIANT
   PANDA
GIARDIASIS
GIFTEDNESS
GIFT
   HORSES
GILLINGHAM
GINGER
   ALES
GINGER
   BEER
GINGER
   NUTS
GINGIVITIS
GIPPY
   TUMMY
GIRL
   FRIDAY
GIRLFRIEND
GIRL
   GUIDES
GIVEN
   NAMES
GIVE RISE
   TO
GLACIALIST
GLACIATION
GLACIOLOGY
GLADDENING
GLADIATORS
GLAGOLITIC
GLAIRINESS
GLAMORIZED
GLAMORIZER
GLANCINGLY
GLANDEROUS
GLASS
   FIBRE
GLASSHOUSE
GLASSINESS
GLASS-
   MAKER
GLASSWORKS

GLASWEGIAN
GLAUCONITE
GLAZING-
   BAR
GLEAMINGLY
GLENROTHES
GLIMMERING
GLIOMATOUS
GLISTENING
GLITTERATI
GLITTERING
GLOATINGLY
GLOBALISTS
GLOCHIDIUM
GLOMERULAR
GLOMERULUS
GLOOMINESS
GLORIFYING
GLORIOUSLY
GLORY
   HOLES
GLOSSARIAL
GLOSSARIES
GLOSSARIST
GLOSSINESS
GLOTTIDEAN
GLOUCESTER
GLUCOSIDAL
GLUMACEOUS
GLUTTINGLY
GLUTTONOUS
GLYCOGENIC
GLYCOLYSIS
GLYCOSIDIC
GLYCOSURIA
GLYCOSURIC
GNASHINGLY
GOALKEEPER
GOALMOUTHS
GOALSCORER
GOATSBEARD
GO-
   BETWEENS
GODFATHERS
GOD-
   FEARING
GODMOTHERS
GODPARENTS
GOGGLE-
   EYED
GOINGS-
   OVER

GOLD-
   BEATER
GOLD
   DIGGER
GOLDEN
   AGES
GOLDEN
   HOUR
GOLDEN
   MEAN
GOLDEN
   RULE
GOLDENSEAL
GOLDFIELDS
GOLDILOCKS
GOLD
   MEDALS
GOLD-
   MINING
GOLD-
   PLATED
GOLD
   RUSHES
GOLDSMITHS
GOLDTHREAD
GOLF
   COURSE
GONDOLIERS
GONGOOZLER
GONIOMETER
GONIOMETRY
GONOCOCCAL
GONOCOCCUS
GONOPHORIC
GONORRHOEA
GOOD
   FRIDAY
GOOD
   HUMOUR
GOODLINESS
GOOD
   LOOKER
GOOD
   NATURE
GOODS
   TRAIN
GOODY-
   GOODY
GOOGOLPLEX
GOOSEBERRY
GOOSEFLESH
GOOSESTEPS
GORGEOUSLY

GORGONZOLA
GORMANDIZE
GORMLESSLY
GORNO-
   ALTAI
GOTHICALLY
GO
   TOGETHER
GO TO
   GROUND
GO TO
   PIECES
GOVERNABLE
GOVERNANCE
GOVERNMENT
GRACEFULLY
GRACIOUSLY
GRADATIONS
GRADUALISM
GRADUALIST
GRADUATING
GRADUATION
GRAININESS
GRAMICIDIN
GRAMINEOUS
GRAMMARIAN
GRAMOPHONE
GRANADILLA
GRANDCHILD
GRAND
   OPERA
GRANDPAPPY
GRAND
   PIANO
GRAND
   SLAMS
GRANDS
   PRIX
GRANDSTAND
GRANGERISM
GRANGERIZE
GRANNY
   KNOT
GRANOPHYRE
GRANT-IN-
   AID
GRANULATED
GRANULATOR
GRANULITIC
GRAPEFRUIT
GRAPEVINES
GRAPHITIZE

GRAPHOLOGY
GRAPH
   PAPER
GRAPTOLITE
GRASSFINCH
GRASSINESS
GRASS
   ROOTS
GRASS
   WIDOW
GRATEFULLY
GRATIFYING
GRATUITIES
GRATUITOUS
GRAUBUNDEN
GRAVELLING
GRAVESTONE
GRAVETTIAN
GRAVEYARDS
GRAVIMETER
GRAVIMETRY
GRAVITATED
GRAVITATER
GRAVY
   BOATS
GRAVY
   TRAIN
GREASE
   GUNS
GREASEWOOD
GREASINESS
GREATCOATS
GREAT
   DANES
GREAT-
   NIECE
GREAT
   STOUR
GREAT-
   UNCLE
GREEDINESS
GREEDY-
   GUTS
GREEK
   CROSS
GREENBACKS
GREEN
   BEANS
GREEN
   BELTS
GREENBRIER
GREENFINCH
GREENFLIES

GREENGAGES
GREENHEART
GREENHORNS
GREENHOUSE
GREEN LIGHT
GREEN PAPER
GREEN POUND
GREENSBORO
GREENSHANK
GREENSTONE
GREEN THUMB
GREGARIOUS
GRENADIERS
GRENADINES
GRESSORIAL
GREYHOUNDS
GREY MARKET
GREY MATTER
GRIEVANCES
GRIEVINGLY
GRIEVOUSLY
GRIM REAPER
GRINDSTONE
GRIPPINGLY
GRISLINESS
GRISTLIEST
GRITTINESS
GROANINGLY
GROGGINESS
GROTESQUES
GROTTINESS
GROUCHIEST
GROUND BAIT
GROUND CREW
GROUNDLESS
GROUNDLING
GROUNDMASS
GROUNDNUTS
GROUND PLAN
GROUND RENT

GROUND RULE
GROUNDSMAN
GROUNDSMEN
GROUNDWORK
GROUPTHINK
GROVELLERS
GROVELLING
GRUBBINESS
GRUBSTAKES
GRUDGINGLY
GRUESOMELY
GRUMPINESS
GRUNTINGLY
GUADELOUPE
GUANAJUATO
GUANTANAMO
GUARANTEED
GUARANTEES
GUARANTIES
GUARANTORS
GUARDHOUSE
GUARDRAILS
GUARDROOMS
GUARD'S VANS
GUERRILLAS
GUESSINGLY
GUESTHOUSE
GUESTROOMS
GUIDELINES
GUILDHALLS
GUILEFULLY
GUILLEMOTS
GUILLOTINE
GUILTINESS
GUINEA FOWL
GUINEA PIGS
GUITARFISH
GUITARISTS
GUJRANWALA
GULF STREAM
GUNRUNNERS
GUNRUNNING
GURGLINGLY
GYMNASIAST
GYMNASIUMS
GYMNASTICS
GYMNOSPERM

GYNANDROUS
GYNOPHORIC
GYPSOPHILA
GYROSCOPES
GYROSCOPIC
GYROSTATIC

H

HABILIMENT
HABILITATE
HABITATION
HABITUALLY
HABITUATED
HACKBUTEER
HACKNEYISM
HADHRAMAUT
HAECKELIAN
HAEMAGOGUE
HAEMATINIC
HAEMATITIC
HAEMATOSIS
HAEMATURIA
HAEMATURIC
HAEMOLYMPH
HAEMOLYSIN
HAEMOLYSIS
HAEMOLYTIC
HAEMOPHILE
HAGIOCRACY
HAGIOLATER
HAGIOLATRY
HAGIOLOGIC
HAGIOSCOPE
HAILSTONES
HAILSTORMS
HAIRPIECES
HAIR SHIRTS
HAIR SLIDES
HAIRSPRING
HAIRSTREAK
HAIRSTYLES
HALBERDIER
HALF A CROWN
HALF-BOTTLE
HALF-BREEDS
HALF-CASTES

HALF CROWNS
HALF-LENGTH
HALF-ROTTEN
HALF-SISTER
HALF-TRUTHS
HALF VOLLEY
HALF-WITTED
HALLELUJAH
HALLMARKED
HALOGENATE
HALOGENOID
HALOGENOUS
HALOPHYTIC
HALTER-LIKE
HALTERNECK
HAMBURGERS
HAMMERFEST
HAMMERHEAD
HAMMERLESS
HAMMER-LIKE
HAMSHACKLE
HAMSTRINGS
HANDBALLER
HANDBARROW
HANDBRAKES
HANDCUFFED
HANDICRAFT
HAND IN HAND
HANDLEABLE
HANDLEBARS
HANDLELESS
HANDMAIDEN
HAND-ME-DOWN
HANDPICKED
HANDSHAKES
HANDSOMELY
HANDSPRING
HANDSTANDS
HANDSTROKE
HANKERINGS

HANKY-PANKY
HANOVERIAN
HAPLOLOGIC
HAPPENINGS
HAPPY EVENT
HAPPY HOURS
HARANGUING
HARASSMENT
HARBINGERS
HARBOURAGE
HARBOURING
HARD-BITTEN
HARD-BOILED
HARD CIDERS
HARDHEADED
HARD LABOUR
HARD-LINERS
HARD LIQUOR
HARD PALATE
HARELIPPED
HARGREAVES
HARLEQUINS
HARMLESSLY
HARMONICAS
HARMONIOUS
HARMONIUMS
HARMONIZED
HARMONIZER
HARMSWORTH
HARNESSING
HARPOONING
HARRISBURG
HARROWMENT
HARTEBEEST
HARTLEPOOL
HARUSPICAL
HARVESTERS
HARVESTING
HARVESTMAN
HASH BROWNS
HASTEFULLY

HATCHBACKS
HATCHELLER
HATCHERIES
HATCHET JOB
HATCHET MAN
HATCHET MEN
HATSHEPSUT
HATTERSLEY
HAUBERGEON
HAUGHTIEST
HAUNTINGLY
HAUSTELLUM
HAUSTORIAL
HAUSTORIUM
HAUTE-LOIRE
HAUTE-MARNE
HAVE A HEART
HAVE A POINT
HAVERSACKS
HAZARDABLE
HAZARD-FREE
HEADBOARDS
HEADCHEESE
HEADHUNTED
HEADHUNTER
HEADLIGHTS
HEADLINING
HEADMASTER
HEAD OF HAIR
HEADPHONES
HEADPIECES
HEADSPRING
HEADSQUARE
HEADSTONES
HEADSTREAM
HEADSTRONG
HEADWATERS
HEADWORKER
HEALTH FOOD
HEALTHIEST
HEARING AID

HEARKENING
HEARTBEATS
HEARTBREAK
HEARTENING
HEARTHRUGS
HEARTINESS
HEARTSEASE
HEARTTHROB
HEATEDNESS
HEATHBERRY
HEATHENDOM
HEATHENISH
HEATHENISM
HEATHENIZE
HEAT RASHES
HEAT SHIELD
HEATSTROKE
HEAT STROKE
HEAVEN-SENT
HEAVENWARD
HEAVY-LADEN
HEAVY METAL
HEAVY WATER
HEBDOMADAL
HEBETATION
HEBETATIVE
HEBRAISTIC
HECTICALLY
HECTOGRAPH
HEDONISTIC
HEEDLESSLY
HEIDELBERG
HEIGHTENED
HEIGHTENER
HEISENBERG
HELIANTHUS
HELICOPTER
HELIGOLAND
HELIOGRAPH
HELIOLATER
HELIOLATRY
HELIOMETER
HELIOMETRY
HELIOPOLIS
HELIOTAXIS

HELIOTROPE
HELIOTYPIC
HELLACIOUS
HELLBENDER
HELLENIZER
HELLESPONT
HELLRAISER
HELMET-LIKE
HELMINTHIC
HELPLESSLY
HEMELYTRAL
HEMELYTRON
HEMICYCLIC
HEMIHEDRAL
HEMIPLEGIA
HEMIPLEGIC
HEMIPTERAN
HEMIPTERON
HEMISPHERE
HEMITROPIC
HEMOGLOBIN
HEMOPHILIA
HEMORRHAGE
HEMORRHOID
HENCEFORTH
HENDECAGON
HENOTHEISM
HENOTHEIST
HEN PARTIES
HEPARINOID
HEPHAESTUS
HEPHAISTOS
HEPTAGONAL
HEPTAMETER
HEPTARCHIC
HEPTASTICH
HEPTATEUCH
HEPTATHLON
HERACLIDAN
HERACLITUS
HERBACEOUS
HERBALISTS
HERBICIDAL
HERBIVORES
HEREABOUTS
HEREDITARY
HEREDITIST
HERESIARCH
HERETOFORE

HERMITAGES
HERMOSILLO
HEROICALLY
HEROPHILUS
HESITANTLY
HESITATING
HESITATION
HESITATIVE
HESPERIDES
HESPERIDIN
HETERODONT
HETERODOXY
HETERODYNE
HETEROGAMY
HETEROGONY
HETEROLOGY
HETERONOMY
HETEROTOPY
HEULANDITE
HEURISTICS
HEXADECANE
HEXAEMERIC
HEXAEMERON
HEXAHEDRAL
HEXAHEDRON
HEXAMERISM
HEXAMEROUS
HEXAMETERS
HEXAMETRIC
HEXANGULAR
HEXAVALENT
HIBERNACLE
HIBERNATED
HIBERNATOR
HIBISCUSES
HIDDENNESS
HIERARCHAL
HIEROCRACY
HIERODULIC
HIEROGLYPH
HIEROLOGIC
HIERONYMIC
HIERONYMUS
HIEROPHANT
HIGHBINDER
HIGH CHAIRS
HIGH CHURCH
HIGH COURTS

HIGH-FLIERS
HIGH-FLYING
HIGH-HANDED
HIGH HORSES
HIGHJACKER
HIGH JUMPER
HIGHLANDER
HIGHLIGHTS
HIGH MASSES
HIGH-MINDED
HIGHNESSES
HIGH-OCTANE
HIGH POINTS
HIGH PRIEST
HIGH RELIEF
HIGH SCHOOL
HIGH SEASON
HIGH STREET
HIGH-STRUNG
HIGHWAYMAN
HIGHWAYMEN
HIJACKINGS
HILDEBRAND
HILDESHEIM
HILLINGDON
HIMYARITIC
HINAYANIST
HINDENBURG
HINDERMOST
HINDRANCES
HINDUSTANI
HINTERLAND
HIPHUGGERS
HIPPARCHUS
HIP POCKETS
HIPPOCRENE
HIPPODROME

HIPPOGRIFF
HIPPOLYTAN
HIPPOLYTUS
HIPPOMENES
HISPANIOLA
HISTAMINIC
HISTIOCYTE
HISTOGRAMS
HISTOLYSIS
HISTOLYTIC
HISTORIANS
HISTORICAL
HISTRIONIC
HIT-AND-
  MISS
HITCHHIKED
HITCHHIKER
HITHERMOST
HIT
  PARADES
HIT THE
  SACK
HOARSENESS
HOBBYHORSE
HOBGOBLINS
HOBNOBBING
HOCHHEIMER
HOCUS-
  POCUS
HODGEPODGE
HOGARTHIAN
HOITY-
  TOITY
HOKEY
  COKEY
HOKEY-
  POKEY
HOLDERSHIP
HOLES IN
  ONE
HOLIDAYING
HOLINESSES
HOLLOWNESS
HOLLYHOCKS
HOLOCAUSTS
HOLOENZYME
HOLOFERNES
HOLOGRAPHY
HOLOHEDRAL
HOLOPHYTIC-
HOLUS-
  BOLUS

HOLY
  ISLAND
HOLY
  SPIRIT
HOMEBODIES
HOME-
  BREWED
HOMECOMING
HOME
  GUARDS
HOMELINESS
HOMEMAKERS
HOMEMAKING
HOME
  MOVIES
HOME
  OFFICE
HOMEOPATHS
HOMEOPATHY
HOMEOTYPIC
HOMESTEADS
HOME
  TRUTHS
HOMEWORKER
HOMILETICS
HOMOCERCAL
HOMOCYCLIC
HOMOEOPATH
HOMOEROTIC
HOMOGAMOUS
HOMOGENATE
HOMOGENIZE
HOMOGENOUS
HOMOGONOUS
HOMOGRAPHS
HOMOLOGATE
HOMOLOGIZE
HOMOLOGOUS
HOMOLOSINE
HOMONYMITY
HOMOOUSIAN
HOMOPHONES
HOMOPHONIC
HOMOPLASTY
HOMORGANIC
HOMOSEXUAL
HOMOZYGOTE
HOMOZYGOUS
HOMUNCULAR
HOMUNCULUS
HONESTNESS
HONEYBUNCH

HONEYCOMBS
HONEYDEWED
HONEY-
  EATER
HONEYMOONS
HONORARIUM
HONORIFICS
HONOURABLE
HONOURABLY
HONOURLESS
HOODLUMISM
HOODWINKED
HOODWINKER
HOOKEDNESS
HOOTENANNY
HOPE
  CHESTS
HOPELESSLY
HOPPING
  MAD
HORIZONTAL
HORNBLENDE
HORNEDNESS
HORN-
  RIMMED
HOROLOGIST
HOROLOGIUM
HOROSCOPES
HOROSCOPIC
HORRENDOUS
HORRIDNESS
HORRIFYING
HORROR
  FILM
HORSEBOXES
HORSEFLESH
HORSEFLIES
HORSELAUGH
HORSELEECH
HORSE
  OPERA
HORSEPOWER
HORSE
  SENSE
HORSESHOES
HORSEWOMAN
HORSEWOMEN
HOSPITABLE
HOSPITABLY
HOSPITALET
HOSTELLERS
HOSTELLING

HOSTELRIES
HOT-
  BLOODED
HOTCHPOTCH
HOT
  DESKING
HOT
  FLUSHES
HOTFOOTING
HOUSEBOATS
HOUSEBOUND
HOUSECOATS
HOUSECRAFT
HOUSEFLIES
HOUSE
  GUEST
HOUSEHOLDS
HOUSEMAIDS
HOUSE OF
  GOD
HOUSE
  PARTY
HOUSEPLANT
HOUSE-
  PROUD
HOUSE-
  TRAIN
HOUSEWIVES
HOVERCRAFT
HOVERINGLY
HOVERTRAIN
HOW DO YOU
  DO
HUA KUO-
  FENG
HUCKLEBONE
HUDDLESTON
HUGUENOTIC
HULLABALOO
HUMANENESS
HUMANISTIC
HUMANITIES
HUMANIZING
HUMBERSIDE
HUMBLENESS
HUMBLINGLY
HUMBUGGERY
HUMDINGERS
HUMIDIFIED
HUMIDIFIER
HUMIDISTAT
HUMILIATED

HUMILIATOR
HUMORESQUE
HUMORISTIC
HUMOROUSLY
HUMOURLESS
HUMOURSOME
HUMPBACKED
HUNCHBACKS
HUNDREDTHS
HUNGRINESS
HUNTINGDON
HUNTRESSES
HUNTSVILLE
HURDY-
  GURDY
HURLY-
  BURLY
HURRICANES
HURRYINGLY
HUSBANDING
HUSBANDMAN
HUSBANDMEN
HYACINTHUS
HYALOPLASM
HYALURONIC
HYBRIDIZER
HYDRANGEAS
HYDRASTINE
HYDRAULICS
HYDROCORAL
HYDROFOILS
HYDROGRAPH
HYDROLOGIC
HYDROLYSER
HYDROLYSIS
HYDROLYTIC
HYDROMANCY
HYDROPONIC
HYGIENISTS
HYPERBOLAS
HYPERBOLES
HYPERBOLIC
HYPERMEDIA
HYPERSPACE
HYPHENATED
HYPNOTISTS
HYPNOTIZED
HYPOCRITES
HYPODERMIC
HYPOTENUSE
HYPOTHESES

HYPOTHESIS
HYSTERICAL

I
IAMBICALLY
IATROGENIC
ICEBREAKER
ICE
  BREAKER
ICE
  LOLLIES
ICE-
  SKATERS
ICE-
  SKATING
ICHINOMIYA
ICHTHYOSIS
ICHTHYOTIC
ICONOCLASM
ICONOCLAST
ICONOLATER
ICONOLATRY
ICONOMATIC
ICONOSCOPE
IDEALISTIC
IDEALIZING
IDEATIONAL
IDEMPOTENT
IDENTIFIED
IDENTIFIER
IDENTIKITS
IDENTITIES
IDEOGRAPHY
IDEOLOGIES
IDEOLOGIST
IDEOLOGUES
IDIOLECTAL
IDIOPATHIC
IDIOPHONIC
IDOLATRIZE
IDOLATROUS
IGNES
  FATUI
IGNOBILITY
IGNOMINIES
IJSSELMEER
ILL-
  ADVISED
ILLEGALITY
ILLEGALIZE
ILLITERACY
ILLITERATE

ILL-
  NATURED
ILLOCUTION
ILL-
  STARRED
ILL-
  TREATED
ILLUMINANT
ILLUMINATE
ILLUMINATI
ILLUMINISM
ILLUMINIST
ILLUSORILY
ILLUSTRATE
IMAGINABLE
IMBALANCES
IMBECILITY
IMBIBITION
IMBRICATED
IMBROGLIOS
IMITATIONS
IMMACULACY
IMMACULATE
IMMATERIAL
IMMATURELY
IMMATURITY
IMMEMORIAL
IMMERSIBLE
IMMIGRANTS
IMMIGRATED
IMMIGRATOR
IMMINENTLY
IMMISCIBLE
IMMOBILITY
IMMOBILIZE
IMMODERACY
IMMODERATE
IMMODESTLY
IMMOLATING
IMMOLATION
IMMORALIST
IMMORALITY
IMMORTELLE
IMMOTILITY
IMMUNIZING
IMMUNOLOGY
IMPAIRMENT
IMPALEMENT
IMPALPABLE
IMPANATION
IMPANELLED

IMPARTIBLE
IMPASSABLE
IMPATIENCE
IMPEACHING
IMPECCABLE
IMPECCABLY
IMPEDANCES
IMPEDIMENT
IMPEDINGLY
IMPENDENCE
IMPENITENT
IMPERATIVE
IMPERIALLY
IMPERILLED
IMPERSONAL
IMPERVIOUS
IMPETRATOR
IMPISHNESS
IMPLACABLE
IMPLANTING
IMPLEMENTS
IMPLICATED
IMPLICITLY
IMPLOSIONS
IMPOLITELY
IMPORTANCE
IMPORTUNED
IMPORTUNER
IMPOSINGLY
IMPOSITION
IMPOSSIBLE
IMPOSSIBLY
IMPOSTROUS
IMPOSTURES
IMPOTENTLY
IMPOUNDAGE
IMPOUNDING
IMPOVERISH
IMPREGNATE
IMPRESARIO
IMPRESSING
IMPRESSION
IMPRESSIVE
IMPRIMATUR
IMPRINTING
IMPRISONED
IMPRISONER
IMPROBABLE
IMPROBABLY
IMPROPERLY
IMPROVABLE

IMPROVISED
IMPROVISER
IMPRUDENCE
IMPUDENTLY
IMPUISSANT
IMPULSIONS
IMPUNITIES
IMPURITIES
IMPUTATION
IMPUTATIVE
IN
  ABSENTIA
INACCURACY
INACCURATE
INACTIVATE
INACTIVELY
INACTIVITY
IN
  ADDITION
INADEQUACY
INADEQUATE
INAMORATAS
IN ANY
  EVENT
INAPPOSITE
INAPTITUDE
INARTISTIC
INAUGURATE
INBREEDING
INCANDESCE
INCAPACITY
INCAPARINA
INCARNATED
INCAUTIOUS
INCENDIARY
INCENTIVES
INCEPTIONS
INCESSANCY
INCESTUOUS
INCHOATION
INCHOATIVE
INCIDENTAL
INCINERATE
INCIPIENCE
INCIPIENCY
INCISIVELY
INCITATION
INCITEMENT
INCITINGLY
INCIVILITY
INCLEMENCY

INCLINABLE
INCLOSURES
INCLUDABLE
INCLUSIONS
INCOHERENT
INCOMMODED
INCOMPLETE
INCONSTANT
INCRASSATE
INCREASING
INCREDIBLE
INCREDIBLY
INCREMENTS
INCRESCENT
INCUBATING
INCUBATION
INCUBATIVE
INCUBATORS
INCULCATED
INCULCATOR
INCULPABLE
INCULPATED
INCUMBENCY
INCUMBENTS
INCUNABULA
INCURRABLE
INCURRENCE
INCURSIONS
INDECENTLY
INDECISION
INDECISIVE
INDECOROUS
INDEFINITE
INDELICACY
INDELICATE
INDENTURED
INDENTURES
INDEXATION
INDIAN
  CORN
INDICATING
INDICATION
INDICATIVE
INDICATORS
INDICATORY
INDICTABLE
INDICTMENT
INDIGENOUS
INDIRECTLY
INDISCREET
INDISCRETE

INDISPOSED
INDISTINCT
INDIVIDUAL
INDOCILITY
INDOLENTLY
INDOLOGIST
INDONESIAN
INDOPHENOL
INDUCEMENT
INDUCTANCE
INDUCTIONS
INDULGENCE
INDUSTRIAL
INDUSTRIES
INEBRIATED
INEBRIATES
INEDUCABLE
INEDUCABLY
INEFFICACY
INELEGANCE
INELIGIBLE
INELOQUENT
INEPTITUDE
INEQUALITY
INEQUITIES
INEVITABLE
INEVITABLY
INEXISTENT
INEXORABLE
INEXORABLY
INEXPERTLY
INEXPIABLE
INEXPLICIT
IN
  EXTREMIS
INFALLIBLE
INFALLIBLY
INFARCTION
INFATUATED
INFECTIONS
INFECTIOUS
INFELICITY
INFERENCES
INFERNALLY
INFIBULATE
INFIDELITY
INFIELDERS
INFIGHTING
INFILTRATE
INFINITELY
INFINITIVE

INFINITUDE
INFLATABLE
INFLATEDLY
INFLECTING
INFLECTION
INFLECTIVE
INFLEXIBLE
INFLEXIBLY
INFLICTING
INFLICTION
INFLICTIVE
INFLUENCED
INFLUENCER
INFLUENCES
INFLUENZAL
INFORMALLY
INFORMANTS
INFORMEDLY
INFRACLASS
INFRACTION
INFRASONIC
INFREQUENT
INFRINGING
INFURIATED
INFUSORIAL
INGESTIBLE
INGLENOOKS
INGLORIOUS
INGOLSTADT
INGRATIATE
INGREDIENT
INGRESSION
INGRESSIVE
INGUSHETIA
INHABITANT
INHABITING
INHALATION
INHARMONIC
INHERENTLY
INHERITING
INHIBITING
INHIBITION
INHIBITIVE
IN HOT
  WATER
INHUMANELY
INHUMANITY
INHUMATION
INIMITABLE
INIMITABLY
INIQUITIES

INIQUITOUS
INITIALING
INITIALIZE
INITIALLED
INITIATING
INITIATION
INITIATIVE
INITIATORY
INJECTABLE
INJECTIONS
INJUNCTION
INJUNCTIVE
INJURY
  TIME
INJUSTICES
IN
  MEMORIAM
INNER
  CHILD
INNER
  TUBES
INNKEEPERS
INNOCENTLY
INNOMINATE
INNOVATING
INNOVATION
INNOVATIVE
INNOVATORS
INNUENDOES
INNUMERACY
INNUMERATE
INOCULABLE
INOCULATED
INOCULATOR
IN ONE
  PIECE
IN ONES
  CUPS
INOPERABLE
INORDINACY
INORDINATE
INOSCULATE
IN-
  PATIENTS
INQUIETUDE
INQUISITOR
INSALIVATE
INS AND
  OUTS
INSANITARY
INSATIABLE
INSATIABLY

INSCRIBING
INSECURELY
INSECURITY
INSEMINATE
INSENSIBLE
INSENSIBLY
INSENTIENT
INSERTABLE
INSERTIONS
INSIDE
  JOBS
INSIDE
  LANE
INSIGHTFUL
INSINUATED
INSINUATOR
INSIPIDITY
INSISTENCE
INSOBRIETY
INSOLATION
INSOLENTLY
INSOLVABLE
INSOLVENCY
INSOLVENTS
INSOMNIACS
INSOMNIOUS
INSOUCIANT
INSPECTING
INSPECTION
INSPECTIVE
INSPECTORS
INSPIRABLE
INSPIRITER
INSTALLING
INSTALMENT
INSTANCING
INSTIGATED
INSTIGATOR
INSTILLING
INSTILMENT
INSTITUTED
INSTITUTES
INSTITUTOR
INSTRUCTED
INSTRUCTOR
INSTRUMENT
INSUFFLATE
INSULARISM
INSULARITY
INSULATING
INSULATION

INSULATORS
INSURANCES
INSURGENCE
INSURGENCY
INSURGENTS
INTANGIBLE
INTANGIBLY
INTEGRABLE
INTEGRATED
INTEGRATOR
INTEGUMENT
INTELLECTS
INTENDANCE
INTENDANCY
INTENDMENT
INTENTIONS
INTENTNESS
INTERACTED
INTER
  ALIOS
INTERBRAIN
INTERBREED
INTERCEDED
INTERCEDER
INTERDICTS
INTERESTED
INTERFACED
INTERFACES
INTERFERED
INTERFERER
INTERFERON
INTERFLUVE
INTERGRADE
INTERGROUP
INTERLACED
INTERLAKEN
INTERLEAVE
INTERLINER
INTERLOPER
INTERLUDES
INTERLUNAR
INTERMARRY
INTERMENTS
INTERMEZZI
INTERMEZZO
INTERMODAL
INTERNALLY
INTERNMENT
INTERNODAL
INTERNSHIP
INTERPHASE

INTERPHONE
INTERPLEAD
INTERPOSAL
INTERPOSED
INTERPOSER
INTERREGNA
INTERSPACE
INTERSTATE
INTERSTICE
INTERTIDAL
INTERTWINE
INTERVENED
INTERVENER
INTERVIEWS
INTERWEAVE
INTERWOVEN
INTESTINAL
INTESTINES
IN THE
  EVENT
IN THE
  MONEY
INTIMACIES
INTIMATELY
INTIMATING
INTIMATION
INTIMIDATE
INTINCTION
INTOLERANT
INTONATION
INTOXICANT
INTOXICATE
IN
  TRAINING
INTRAMURAL
INTRENCHED
INTREPIDLY
INTRIGUING
INTRODUCED
INTRODUCER
INTROSPECT
INTROVERTS
INTRUSIONS
INTRUSTING
INTUBATION
INTUITABLE
INTUITIONS
INUNDATING
INUNDATION
INUREDNESS
INVAGINATE

INVALIDATE
INVALID
  CAR
INVALIDING
INVALIDISM
INVALIDITY
INVALUABLE
INVARIABLE
INVARIABLY
INVARIANCE
INVEIGHING
INVEIGLING
INVENTIBLE
INVENTIONS
INVERACITY
INVERCLYDE
INVERSIONS
INVERTIBLE
INVESTABLE
INVESTMENT
INVETERACY
INVETERATE
INVIGILATE
INVIGORATE
INVINCIBLE
INVINCIBLY
INVIOLABLE
INVITATION
INVITATORY
INVITINGLY
INVOCATION
INVOCATORY
INVOLUCRAL
INVOLUTION
IODIZATION
IODOMETRIC
IONIZATION
IONOSPHERE
IRENICALLY
IRIDACEOUS
IRIDECTOMY
IRIDESCENT
IRISH
  STEWS
IRISHWOMAN
IRONICALLY
IRONMONGER
IRRADIANCE
IRRADIATED
IRRADIATOR
IRRATIONAL

IRREGULARS
IRRELATIVE
IRRELEVANT
IRRELIGION
IRRESOLUTE
IRREVERENT
IRRIGATING
IRRIGATION
IRRIGATIVE
IRRITATING
IRRITATION
IRRITATIVE
IRRUPTIONS
ISENTROPIC
ISKENDERUN
ISOANTIGEN
ISOCHEIMAL
ISOCHRONAL
ISOCHROOUS
ISOCYANIDE
ISODYNAMIC
ISOGAMETIC
ISOGLOSSAL
ISOGLOTTIC
ISOLEUCINE
ISOMETRICS
ISOMORPHIC
ISOPIESTIC
ISOSEISMAL
ISOTHERMAL
ISOTROPOUS
ISRAELITES
ITALIANATE
ITALICIZED
ITCHY
  PALMS
ITINERANCY
IVORY
  TOWER

J

JACKANAPES
JACKHAMMER
JACK-
  KNIFED
JACK
  KNIVES
JACKRABBIT
JACK THE
  LAD
JACOBITISM
JAGUARONDI

JAILBREAKS
JAM
  SESSION
JAMSHEDPUR
JANITORIAL
JARDINIERE
JAUNTINESS
JAWBREAKER
JAYWALKERS
JAYWALKING
JEALOUSIES
JELLY
  BEANS
JELLY
  ROLLS
JEOPARDIZE
JERRY-
  BUILD
JERRY-
  BUILT
JERSEY
  CITY
JESUITICAL
JET
  ENGINES
JET-
  SETTERS
JETTISONED
JIANG
  ZEMIN
JIGGERMAST
JINGDEZHEN
JINGOISTIC
JITTERBUGS
JOB
  CENTRES
JOBSHARING
JOCKSTRAPS
JOCULARITY
JOGJAKARTA
JOLLY
  ROGER
JOSS
  STICKS
JOURNALESE
JOURNALISM
JOURNALIST
JOURNALIZE
JOURNEYING
JOURNEYMAN
JOURNEYMEN
JOYFULNESS

JOYOUSNESS
JUBILANTLY
JUBILATION
JUDGMENTAL
JUDICATIVE
JUDICATORY
JUDICATURE
JUDICIALLY
JUGGERNAUT
JUIZ DE
  FORA
JUMBLE
  SALE
JUMBLINGLY
JUNCACEOUS
JUNCTIONAL
JUNKETINGS
JURY-
  RIGGED
JUST AS
  WELL
JUSTICIARY
JUSTIFYING
JUST IN
  CASE
JUST-IN-
  TIME
JUVENILITY
JUXTAPOSED

K

KABARAGOYA
KALGOORLIE
KANSAS
  CITY
KANTIANISM
KAPFENBERG
KARA-
  KALPAK
KARAMANLIS
KARLSKRONA
KARYOGAMIC
KARYOLYMPH
KARYOLYSIS
KARYOLYTIC
KARYOPLASM
KARYOTYPIC
KASHMIRIAN
KAZAKHSTAN
KEEP TABS
  ON
KENILWORTH

KENNELLING
KENTUCKIAN
KERATINIZE
KERATOTOMY
KERCHIEFED
KERFUFFLES
KERMANSHAH
KERSEYMERE
KETTLEDRUM
KEYBOARDED
KEYBOARDER
KEYPUNCHED
KEYPUNCHER
KEYPUNCHES
KHABAROVSK
KIDNAPPERS
KIDNAPPING
KIDNEY
 BEAN
KIESELGUHR
KILMARNOCK
KILOLITRES
KILOMETRES
KILOMETRIC
KIMBERLITE
KINCARDINE
KINDLINESS
KINDNESSES
KINEMATICS
KINGFISHER
KINGLINESS
KINGMAKERS
KING-OF-
 ARMS
KING'S
 BENCH
KIRITIMATI
KIROVOGRAD
KISS OF
 LIFE
KITAKYUSHU
KITH AND
 KIN
KITTIWAKES
KLAGENFURT
KLANGFARBE
KNEECAPPED
KNEE-
 LENGTH
KNICK-
 KNACK

KNIFE--
 EDGES
KNIGHTHEAD
KNIGHTHOOD
KNOBBLIEST
KNOBKERRIE
KNOCKABOUT
KNOCK-
 KNEED
KOEKSISTER
KOMMUNARSK
KOMSOMOLSK
KOOKABURRA
KRAGUJEVAC
KRAMATORSK
KREMENCHUG
KRIEGSPIEL
KRISHNAISM
KRUGERRAND
KU KLUX
 KLAN
KUOMINTANG

L

LABIONASAL
LABIOVELAR
LABORATORY
LABOR
 UNION
LABOUR
 CAMP
LABOUR
 DAYS
LABOUREDLY
LABYRINTHS
LACERATING
LACERATION
LACERATIVE
LACHRYMOSE
LACKLUSTRE
LACQUERING
LACRIMATOR
LACTESCENT
LACTIC
 ACID
LACTOGENIC
LACTOMETER
LACTOSCOPE
LACUNOSITY
LACUSTRINE
LADY-
 KILLER

LADY'S-
 SMOCK
LAMARCKIAN
LAMARCKISM
LAMASERIES
LAMBASTING
LAMBDACISM
LAMBREQUIN
LAMBS
 TAILS
LAMELLATED
LAMENTABLE
LAMENTABLY
LAMINATING
LAMINATION
LAMPOONERY
LAMPOONING
LAMPSHADES
LANCASHIRE
LANCEOLATE
LAND
 AGENTS
LAND
 FORCES
LANDING
 NET
LANDLADIES
LANDLOCKED
LANDLUBBER
LANDMASSES
LAND
 ROVERS
LANDSCAPED
LANDSCAPES
LANDSLIDES
LANGLAUFER
LANGUISHED
LANGUISHER
LANGUOROUS
LANIFEROUS
LANTHANIDE
LAPAROTOMY
LAP
 DANCING
LAPIDARIAN
LAPIDARIES
LARGE-
 SCALE
LA
 ROCHELLE
LARVICIDAL
LARYNGITIC

LARYNGITIS
LASCIVIOUS
LAST
 MINUTE
LATECOMERS
LATENT
 HEAT
LATTERMOST
LAUGHINGLY
LAUNCESTON
LAUNCH
 PADS
LAUNDERING
LAUNDROMAT
LAUNDRYMAN
LAURACEOUS
LAUREATION
LAURENTIAN
LAVATIONAL
LAVATORIAL
LAVATORIES
LAVISHNESS
LAW-
 ABIDING
LAW-
 BREAKER
LAWFULNESS
LAWNMOWERS
LAWN
 TENNIS
LAWRENCIUM
LAY
 BROTHER
LAY
 FIGURES
LAYPERSONS
LAY
 READERS
LAY
 SISTERS
LEADERSHIP
LEAF-
 HOPPER
LEAFLETING
LEASEBACKS
LEAVENINGS
LEBENSRAUM
LECTIONARY
LECTORSHIP
LEEUWARDEN
LEFT-
 HANDED

LEFT-
 HANDER
LEFT-
 WINGER
LEGAL
 EAGLE
LEGALISTIC
LEGALIZING
LEGATESHIP
LEGATORIAL
LEGIBILITY
LEGISLATED
LEGISLATOR
LEGITIMACY
LEGITIMATE
LEGITIMISM
LEGITIMIST
LEGITIMIZE
LEGUMINOUS
LEG-
 WARMERS
LEISHMANIA
LEITMOTIVS
LEMNISCATE
LEMON
 GRASS
LEMON
 SOLES
LENGTHENED
LENGTHENER
LENGTHIEST
LENGTHWAYS
LENTAMENTE
LENTICULAR
LENTISSIMO
LEOPARDESS
LEPIDOLITE
LEPRECHAUN
LEPTOSOMIC
LESBIANISM
LESSEESHIP
LETCHWORTH
LETHBRIDGE
LETS FACE
 IT
LETTER
 BOMB
LETTERHEAD
LEUCOCYTES
LEUCOCYTIC
LEUCODERMA
LEUCOMAINE

LEUCOPENIA
LEUCOPENIC
LEUCOPLAST
LEVERKUSEN
LEVIATHANS
LEVIGATION
LEVITATING
LEVITATION
LEXICALITY
LEXICOLOGY
LIBATIONAL
LIBERALISM
LIBERALIST
LIBERALITY
LIBERALIZE
LIBERATING
LIBERATION
LIBERATORS
LIBERTINES
LIBIDINOUS
LIBRARIANS
LIBRETTIST
LIBREVILLE
LICENSABLE
LICENTIATE
LICENTIOUS
LIE IN
   STATE
LIEUTENANT
LIFE
   CYCLES
LIFEGUARDS
LIFE
   JACKET
LIFELESSLY
LIFE-
   SAVING
LIFESTYLES
LIGHT
   BULBS
LIGHTENING
LIGHTERAGE
LIGHTHOUSE
LIGHTNINGS
LIGHTSHIPS
LIGHT
   YEARS
LIGNOCAINE
LIKELIHOOD
LIKE-
   MINDED
LIKENESSES

LILIACEOUS
LIMICOLINE
LIMICOLOUS
LIMITARIAN
LIMITATION
LIMOUSINES
LINEAMENTS
LINECASTER
LINGUIFORM
LINGUISTIC
LINLITHGOW
LINSEED
   OIL
LIPOMATOUS
LIPOPHILIC
LIP-
   READING
LIP
   SERVICE
LIQUEFYING
LIQUESCENT
LIQUIDATED
LIQUIDATOR
LIQUIDIZED
LIQUIDIZER
LIQUORICES
LISSOMNESS
LISTENABLE
LISTLESSLY
LIST
   PRICES
LITERALISM
LITERALIST
LITERARILY
LITERATELY
LITERATION
LITERATURE
LITHOGRAPH
LITHOLOGIC
LITHOMARGE
LITHOPHYTE
LITHOTOMIC
LITHOTRITY
LITHUANIAN
LITIGATING
LITIGATION
LITTERBINS
LITTERLOUT
LITTLE
   BELT
LITTLE
   ROCK

LITURGICAL
LIVABILITY
LIVELIHOOD
LIVELINESS
LIVING
   ROOM
LIVINGSTON
LIVING
   WAGE
LIVING
   WILL
LLANGOLLEN
LOADSTONES
LOBOTOMIES
LOBSTERPOT
LOBULATION
LOCAL
   DERBY
LOCALISTIC
LOCALITIES
LOCALIZING
LOCKER
   ROOM
LOCK
   KEEPER
LOCKSMITHS
LOCKSTITCH
LOCOMOTION
LOCOMOTIVE
LOCULATION
LODESTONES
LOGANBERRY
LOGARITHMS
LOGGERHEAD
LOGICALITY
LOGISTICAL
LOGOGRAPHY
LOGOPAEDIC
LOGORRHOEA
LOGROLLING
LOINCLOTHS
LOIR-ET-
   CHER
LONELINESS
LONGBENTON
LONGHAIRED
LONG-
   HEADED
LONG
   ISLAND
LONGITUDES

LONG-
   JUMPER
LONGWINDED
LOOK-
   ALIKES
LOPHOPHORE
LOQUACIOUS
LORDLINESS
LORGNETTES
LORRY
   PARKS
LOS
   ANGELES
LOSS
   LEADER
LOST
   CAUSES
LOTUS-
   EATER
LOUDHAILER
LOUDMOUTHS
LOUISVILLE
LOUNGE
   BARS
LOUNGE
   SUIT
LOVABILITY
LOVE
   AFFAIR
LOVELINESS
LOVEMAKING
LOVING
   CUPS
LOW-
   ALCOHOL
LOWBROWISM
LOWER
   CLASS
LOWER
   HOUSE
LOWERINGLY
LOWLANDERS
LOW-
   PITCHED
LOW
   PROFILE
LOW-
   TENSION
LOXODROMIC
LUBRICANTS
LUBRICATED
LUBRICATOR
LUBRICIOUS

LUBUMBASHI
LUCUBRATOR
LUGGAGE
   VAN
LUGUBRIOUS
LULUABOURG
LUMBERJACK
LUMBER-
   ROOM
LUMBERYARD
LUMBRICOID
LUMINARIES
LUMINOSITY
LUMINOUSLY
LUMISTEROL
LUNAR
   MONTH
LURCHINGLY
LUSCIOUSLY
LUSTRATION
LUSTRATIVE
LUSTREWARE
LUSTROUSLY
LUTINE
   BELL
LUXEMBOURG
LUXURIANCE
LUXURIATED
LYCOPODIUM
LYMPHOCYTE
LYOPHILIZE

M

MAASTRICHT
MAASTRICHT
MACADAMIZE
MACEBEARER
MACEDONIAN
MACERATING
MACERATION
MACERATIVE
MACHINABLE
MACHINATOR
MACHINE
   GUN
MACHINISTS
MACH
   NUMBER
MACKINTOSH
MACROCOSMS
MACROCYTIC
MACROGRAPH

MACROPHAGE
MACROSPORE
MACULATION
MADAGASCAN
MADAGASCAR
MADCHESTER
MADREPORAL
MAELSTROMS
MAGIC
  WANDS
MAGISTRACY
MAGISTRATE
MAGNA
  CARTA
MAGNETITIC
MAGNETIZED
MAGNETIZER
MAGNIFIERS
MAGNIFYING
MAGNITUDES
MAGNUM
  OPUS
MAIDENHAIR
MAIDENHEAD
MAIDENHOOD
MAIDEN
  NAME
MAIN
  CHANCE
MAIN
  CLAUSE
MAINFRAMES
MAINLINING
MAINSPRING
MAINSTREAM
MAINTAINED
MAINTAINER
MAISONETTE
MAJOR-
  DOMOS
MAJORETTES
MAJORITIES
MAJOR
  SUITS
MAJUSCULAR
MAKE A
  POINT
MAKESHIFTS
MAKEWEIGHT
MALACOLOGY
MALADDRESS
MALAPROPOS

MALCONTENT
MALEFACTOR
MALEFICENT
MALEVOLENT
MALFEASANT
MALIGNANCY
MALINGERED
MALINGERER
MALODOROUS
MALPIGHIAN
MALTED
  MILK
MALTHUSIAN
MALTREATED
MALTREATER
MALVACEOUS
MANAGEABLE
MANAGEABLY
MANAGEMENT
MANAGERESS
MANAGERIAL
MANCHESTER
MANCHINEEL
MANCHURIAN
MANCUNIANS
MANEUVERED
MAN
  FRIDAYS
MANFULNESS
MANGOSTEEN
MANHANDLED
MANIACALLY
MANICURING
MANICURIST
MANIFESTED
MANIFESTLY
MANIFESTOS
MANIFOLDER
MANIPULATE
MANNEQUINS
MANNERISMS
MANOEUVRED
MANOEUVRER
MANOEUVRES
MAN OF
  STRAW
MANOMETERS
MANOMETRIC
MANOR
  HOUSE
MANSERVANT
MANTELTREE

MANTICALLY
MANUSCRIPT
MANZANILLA
MARASCHINO
MARCESCENT
MARCH-
  PASTS
MARCONI
  RIG
MARE'S
  NESTS
MARGARITAS
MARGINALIA
MARGINALLY
MARGUERITE
MARINATING
MARINATION
MARIONETTE
MARKEDNESS
MARKETABLE
MARKETABLY
MARKETEERS
MARKET
  TOWN
MARKSWOMAN
MARLACIOUS
MARQUISATE
MARROWBONE
MARSHALING
MARSHALLED
MARSHALLER
MARSHINESS
MARSUPIALS
MARTELLATO
MARTENSITE
MARTIAL
  ART
MARTIALISM
MARTIALIST
MARTIAL
  LAW
MARTINGALE
MARTINICAN
MARTINIQUE
MARVELLING
MARVELLOUS
MARVELMENT
MARXIANISM
MASCARPONE
MASOCHISTS
MASQUERADE
MASSACRING

MASSASAUGA
MASSETERIC
MASTECTOMY
MASTER
  CARD
MASTERHOOD
MASTER
  KEYS
MASTERMIND
MASTERSHIP
MASTERWORK
MASTICABLE
MASTICATED
MASTICATOR
MASTURBATE
MATCHBOARD
MATCHBOXES
MATCHMAKER
MATCH
  POINT
MATCHSTICK
MATERIALLY
MATERNALLY
MATO
  GROSSO
MATOZINHOS
MATRIARCHS
MATRIARCHY
MATRICIDAL
MATRICIDES
MATRILOCAL
MATTERHORN
MATTRESSES
MATURATION
MATURATIVE
MAUDLINISM
MAUNDERING
MAURITANIA
MAUSOLEUMS
MAXILLIPED
MAXIMALIST
MAXIMIZING
MAXISINGLE
MAYONNAISE
MAYORESSES
MEADOWLARK
MEAGRENESS
MEANDERING
MEANINGFUL
MEANS
  TESTS
MEASLINESS

MEASURABLE
MEASURABLY
MEASUREDLY
MECHANICAL
MECHANISMS
MECHANIZED
MECHANIZER
MECONOPSIS
MEDALLIONS
MEDALLISTS
MEDDLESOME
MEDDLINGLY
MEDICAMENT
MEDICATION
MEDICATIVE
MEDIOCRITY
MEDITATING
MEDITATION
MEDITATIVE
MEDIUM
  WAVE
MEDULLATED
MEERSCHAUM
MEFLOQUINE
MEGAGAMETE
MEGALITHIC
MEGAPHONES
MEGAPHONIC
MEGASPORIC
MEITNERIUM
MELANCHOLY
MELANESIAN
MELANISTIC
MELANOCYTE
MELANOSITY
MELBURNIAN
MELIACEOUS
MELIORABLE
MELIORATOR
MELISMATIC
MELLOPHONE
MELLOWNESS
MELODRAMAS
MELTING
  POT
MEMBERSHIP
MEMBRANOUS
MEMORANDUM
MEMORIZING
MENACINGLY
MENAGERIES

MENARCHEAL
MENDACIOUS
MENDICANCY
MENDICANTS
MENINGITIC
MENINGITIS
MEN OF
  STRAW
MENOPAUSAL
MENOPAUSIC
MENSTRUATE
MENSTRUOUS
MENSURABLE
MENTAL
  AGES
MENTAL
  NOTE
MENTIONING
MERCANTILE
MERCAPTIDE
MERCIFULLY
MERIDIONAL
MERRYMAKER
MERSEY
  BEAT
MERSEYSIDE
MESENCHYME
MESENTERIC
MESENTERON
MESITYLENE
MESMERISTS
MESMERIZED
MESMERIZER
MESOCRATIC
MESODERMAL
MESOLITHIC
MESOMORPHY
MESOPHYTIC
MESOSPHERE
MESOTHORAX
MESSENGERS
METABOLISM
METABOLITE
METABOLIZE
METACARPAL
METACARPUS
METACENTRE
METAFEMALE
METAGALAXY
METALLURGY
METAMERISM
METAPHORIC

METAPHRASE
METAPHRAST
METAPHYSIC
METAPLASIA
METASTABLE
METASTASIS
METASTATIC
METATARSUS
METATHEORY
METATHESIS
METATHETIC
METATHORAX
METEORITES
METEORITIC
METHIONINE
METHODICAL
METHODISTS
METHODIZER
METHUSELAH
METHYLATOR
METHYLDOPA
METICULOUS
METOESTRUS
METRICALLY
METRICIZED
METRIC
  TONS
METRONOMES
METRONOMIC
METRONYMIC
METROPOLIS
METTLESOME
MEXICO
  CITY
MEZZANINES
MEZZOTINTS
MIAMI
  BEACH
MICHAELMAS
MICROCHIPS
MICROCLINE
MICROCOSMS
MICROCYTIC
MICROFICHE
MICROFILMS
MICROGRAPH
MICROMETER
MICROMETRY
MICRONESIA
MICROPHONE
MICROPHYTE

MICROPRINT
MICROPYLAR
MICROSCOPE
MICROSCOPY
MICROSEISM
MICROSOMAL
MICROSPORE
MICROTOMIC
MICROTONAL
MICROWAVES
MIDAS
  TOUCH
MIDDELBURG
MIDDLE-
  AGED
MIDDLE
  AGES
MIDDLEBROW
MIDDLE
  EAST
MIDDLE
  NAME
MIDDLE
  WEST
MIDLOTHIAN
MIDSECTION
MIDSHIPMAN
MIDSHIPMEN
MIDWESTERN
MIGHTINESS
MIGNONETTE
MIGRAINOID
MIGRATIONS
MILEOMETER
MILESTONES
MILITANTLY
MILITARILY
MILITARISM
MILITARIST
MILITARIZE
MILITATING
MILITATION
MILITIAMAN
MILK
  FLOATS
MILK
  SHAKES
MILK
  TOOTHS
MILLENNIAL
MILLENNIUM
MILLEPEDES

MILLESIMAL
MILLIGRAMS
MILLILITRE
MILLIMETRE
MILLIONTHS
MILLIPEDES
MILLSTONES
MILLSTREAM
MILLWHEELS
MILLWORKER
MILLWRIGHT
MILOMETERS
MIMEOGRAPH
MINATORILY
MINDLESSLY
MIND
  READER
MINEFIELDS
MINERALIZE
MINERALOGY
MINERAL
  OIL
MINESTRONE
MINIATURES
MINIMALIST
MINIMIZING
MINISTERED
MINISTRANT
MINISTRIES
MINNESOTAN
MINORITIES
MINOR
  SUITS
MINSTRELSY
MINT
  JULEPS
MINUSCULAR
MINUTE
  HAND
MINUTENESS
MIRACIDIAL
MIRACIDIUM
MIRACULOUS
MIRTHFULLY
MISAPPLIED
MISBEHAVED
MISBEHAVER
MISCALLING
MISCARRIED
MISCASTING
MISCELLANY
MISCHANCES

MISCH
  METAL
MISCONDUCT
MISCOUNTED
MISCREANTS
MISERICORD
MISFORTUNE
MISGIVINGS
MISHANDLED
MISHEARING
MISJOINDER
MISJUDGING
MISLEADING
MISMANAGED
MISMANAGER
MISMATCHED
MISMATCHES
MISOGAMIST
MISOGYNIST
MISOGYNOUS
MISOLOGIST
MISPLACING
MISPRINTED
MISPRISION
MISQUOTING
MISREADING
MISSIONARY
MISSOURIAN
MISSPELLED
MISSTATING
MISSUPPOSE
MISTAKABLE
MISTAKABLY
MISTAKENLY
MISTRESSES
MISTRUSTED
MISTRUSTER
MITIGATING
MITIGATION
MITIGATIVE
MITTERRAND
MIXABILITY
MIXED
  GRILL
MIXOLYDIAN
MIZZENMAST
MOBILE
  HOME
MOBILIZING
MOBOCRATIC
MOCK-
  HEROIC

MODERATELY
MODERATING
MODERATION
MODERATORS
MODERNISMS
MODERNISTS
MODERNIZED
MODERNIZER
MODERNNESS
MODIFIABLE
MODISHNESS
MODULATING
MODULATION
MODULATIVE
MOGADISCIO
MOHAMMEDAN
MOISTENING
MOISTURIZE
MOLLIFYING
MOLLUSCOID
MOLYBDENUM
MONADISTIC
MONADOLOGY
MONANDROUS
MONANTHOUS
MONARCHIES
MONARCHISM
MONARCHIST
MONEGASQUE
MONETARISM
MONETARIST
MONEYBOXES
MONEYMAKER
MONEY
 ORDER
MONGRELISM
MONGRELIZE
MONILIFORM
MONITORIAL
MONITORING
MONKEY
 NUTS
MONOCARPIC
MONOCHROME
MONOCLINAL
MONOCLINIC
MONOCRATIC
MONOCYCLIC
MONOCYTOID
MONOECIOUS
MONOGAMIST

MONOGAMOUS
MONOGENOUS
MONOGRAPHS
MONOGYNIST
MONOGYNOUS
MONOHYBRID
MONOLITHIC
MONOLOGIST
MONOLOGUES
MONOMANIAC
MONOMEROUS
MONOPHOBIA
MONOPHOBIC
MONOPHONIC
MONOPLANES
MONOPLEGIA
MONOPLEGIC
MONOPODIAL
MONOPODIUM
MONOPOLIES
MONOPOLISM
MONOPOLIST
MONOPOLIZE
MONOPTEROS
MONOTHEISM
MONOTHEIST
MONOTONOUS
MONOVALENT
MONSIGNORS
MONSTRANCE
MONTE
 CARLO
MONTEGO
 BAY
MONTENEGRO
MONTEVIDEO
MONTGOMERY
MONTMARTRE
MONTPELIER
MONTSERRAT
MONUMENTAL
MONZONITIC
MOONFLOWER
MOONSCAPES
MOONSTONES
MOONSTRUCK
MOOT
 POINTS
MORALISTIC
MORALITIES
MORALIZERS

MORALIZING
MORATORIUM
MORAYSHIRE
MORBIDNESS
MORDACIOUS
MORDVINIAN
MORGANATIC
MOROSENESS
MORPHEUSES
MORPHINISM
MORPHOLOGY
MORTAL
 SINS
MORTGAGEES
MORTGAGING
MORTGAGORS
MORTICIANS
MORTIFYING
MORTUARIES
MOSQUITOES
MOSTAGANEM
MOTHERHOOD
MOTHERLESS
MOTHER'S
 BOY
MOTHER'S
 DAY
MOTHER-TO-
 BE
MOTHERWELL
MOTHERWORT
MOTIONLESS
MOTIVATING
MOTIVATION
MOTIVATIVE
MOTIVELESS
MOTONEURON
MOTORBIKES
MOTORBOATS
MOTORCADES
MOTORCYCLE
MOTORIZING
MOTOR
 LODGE
MOTS
 JUSTES
MOULDBOARD
MOULDERING
MOULDINESS
MOUNTEBANK
MOURNFULLY
MOUSETRAPS

MOUSSELINE
MOUSTACHES
MOUTH
 ORGAN
MOUTHPIECE
MOVABILITY
MOVIE
 STARS
MOVING
 VANS
MOZAMBIQUE
MOZZARELLA
MPUMALANGA
MUCKRAKERS
MUCKRAKING
MUDDLINGLY
MUDSKIPPER
MUDSLINGER
MUHAMMADAN
MUJAHEDDIN
MULBERRIES
MULIEBRITY
MULISHNESS
MULTIBIRTH
MULTIMEDIA
MULTIPLANE
MULTIPLIED
MULTIPLIER
MULTISTAGE
MULTITUDES
MUMBLINGLY
MUMBO
 JUMBO
MUMMIFYING
MUNIFICENT
MURPHY'S
 LAW
MUSCOVITES
MUSCULARLY
MUSHROOMED
MUSICAL
 BOX
MUSIC
 HALLS
MUSICOLOGY
MUSKETEERS
MUSKETRIES
MUSTACHIOS
MUSTARD
 GAS
MUTABILITY
MUTATIONAL

MUTILATING
MUTILATION
MUTILATIVE
MUTINOUSLY
MUTUAL
 FUND
MYASTHENIA
MYASTHENIC
MYCETOZOAN
MYCOLOGIST
MYCOPLASMA
MYCORRHIZA
MYCOSTATIN
MYOCARDIAL
MYOCARDIUM
MYOGRAPHIC
MYOPICALLY
MYRIAPODAN
MYRTACEOUS
MYSTAGOGIC
MYSTAGOGUE
MYSTERIOUS
MYSTICALLY
MYSTIFYING
MYTHICIZER
MYTHOMANIA
MYTHOPOEIA
MYTHOPOEIC
MYXOEDEMIC
MYXOMATOUS
MYXOMYCETE

N

NAIL-
 BITING
NAIRNSHIRE
NAMBY-
 PAMBY
NAMEPLATES
NANNY
 GOATS
NANOSECOND
NAPKIN
 RING
NAPOLEONIC
NARCISSISM
NARCISSIST
NARCOLEPSY
NARRATABLE
NARRATIONS
NARRATIVES

NARROW
 BOAT
NARROWNESS
NASTURTIUM
NATATIONAL
NATIONALLY
NATIONHOOD
NATIONWIDE
NATIVISTIC
NATIVITIES
NATTERJACK
NATURAL
 GAS
NATURALISM
NATURALIST
NATURALIZE
NATUROPATH
NAUGHTIEST
NAUSEATING
NAUSEATION
NAUSEOUSLY
NAUTICALLY
NAVIGATING
NAVIGATION
NAVIGATORS
NEAPOLITAN
NEAR
 MISSES
NEAR
 THINGS
NEBULOSITY
NEBULOUSLY
NECROLATRY
NECROMANCY
NECROPHOBE
NECROPOLIS
NEEDLEFISH
NEEDLESSLY
NEEDLEWORK
NE'ER-DO-
 WELL
NEGATIVELY
NEGATIVING
NEGATIVISM
NEGATIVIST
NEGLECTFUL
NEGLECTING
NEGLIGENCE
NEGLIGIBLE
NEGLIGIBLY
NEGOTIABLE
NEGOTIATED

NEGOTIATOR
NEIGHBOURS
NEMATOCYST
NEOLOGICAL
NEOLOGISMS
NEON
 LIGHTS
NEOPLASTIC
NEPENTHEAN
NEPHOGRAPH
NEPHOSCOPE
NEPHRALGIA
NEPHRALGIC
NEPHRIDIAL
NEPHRIDIUM
NEPHROTOMY
NEPOTISTIC
NETHERMOST
NETIQUETTE
NETTLE
 RASH
NETTLESOME
NETWORKING
NEURECTOMY
NEUROBLAST
NEUROCOELE
NEUROGENIC
NEUROLEMMA
NEUROPATHY
NEUROTOXIN
NEUTRALISM
NEUTRALIST
NEUTRALITY
NEUTRALIZE
NEUTROPHIL
NEVER-
 NEVER
NEW
 BEDFORD
NEW
 BRITAIN
NEW
 ENGLAND
NEWFANGLED
NEW
 IRELAND
NEW
 ORLEANS
NEWS
 AGENCY
NEWSAGENTS
NEWSCASTER

NEWSHOUNDS
NEWSLETTER
NEWSPAPERS
NEWSREADER
NEWSSHEETS
NEWSSTANDS
NEWSVENDOR
NEWSWORTHY
NEWTON'S
 LAW
NEW
 ZEALAND
NICARAGUAN
NICKELLING
NICKNAMING
NICOTINISM
NIDICOLOUS
NIDIFUGOUS
NIGHTCLUBS
NIGHTDRESS
NIGHTLIGHT
NIGHTMARES
NIGHTSHADE
NIGHT
 SHIFT
NIGHTSHIRT
NIGHTSTICK
NIGRESCENT
NIHILISTIC
NIMBLENESS
NINCOMPOOP
NINETEENTH
NINETIETHS
NINETY-
 NINE
NINGSIA
 HUI
NIPPLEWORT
NISSEN
 HUTS
NITPICKERS
NITPICKING
NITRIC
 ACID
NITROMETER
NO-
 ACCOUNTS
NOBEL
 PRIZE
NOBILITIES
NO-MAN'S-
 LAND

NOM DE
 PLUME
NOMINALISM
NOMINALIST
NOMINATING
NOMINATION
NOMINATIVE
NOMOGRAPHY
NOMOLOGIST
NOMOTHETIC
NONALIGNED
NONCHALANT
NONDRINKER
NONESUCHES
NONETHICAL
NONFACTUAL
NONFERROUS
NONFICTION
NONJOINDER
NONMEDICAL
NO-
 NONSENSE
NONPAREILS
NONPAYMENT
NONPLUSSED
NONSMOKERS
NONSMOKING
NONSTARTER
NONSTATIVE
NON-
 STRIKER
NONTYPICAL
NONVIOLENT
NORMALIZED
NORRKOPING
NORTHBOUND
NORTHERNER
NORTH
 POLES
NORTHWARDS
NOSEBLEEDS
NOSEDIVING
NOSOGRAPHY
NOSOLOGIST
NOSTOLOGIC
NOSY
 PARKER
NOTABILITY
NOTARIZING
NOTATIONAL
NOTEWORTHY
NOTICEABLE

NOTICEABLY
NOTIFIABLE
NOTTINGHAM
NOUAKCHOTT
NOURISHING
NOVACULITE
NOVA
 SCOTIA
NOVELETTES
NOVELISTIC
NOVITIATES
NUCLEATION
NUCLEONICS
NUCLEOSIDE
NUCLEOTIDE
NUDIBRANCH
NULLIFYING
NUMBERLESS
NUMBSKULLS
NUMERATION
NUMERATIVE
NUMERATORS
NUMEROLOGY
NUMEROUSLY
NUMISMATIC
NUMMULITIC
NUNCIATURE
NURSELINGS
NURSEMAIDS
NURSERYMAN
NURSERYMEN
NURTURABLE
NUTATIONAL
NUTCRACKER
NUTRITIOUS
NYCTALOPIA
NYCTINASTY
NYMPHOLEPT

O

OAFISHNESS
OAST
 HOUSES
OBDURATELY
OBEDIENTLY
OBEISANCES
OBELISKOID
OBERHAUSEN
OBFUSCATED
OBITUARIES
OBITUARIST

OBJECTIONS
OBJECTIVES
OBJETS DART
OBJETS D'ART
OBJURGATOR
OBLIGATING
OBLIGATION
OBLIGATIVE
OBLIGATORY
OBLIGINGLY
OBLITERATE
OBSEQUIOUS
OBSERVABLE
OBSERVABLY
OBSERVANCE
OBSESSIONS
OBSESSIVES
OBSTETRICS
OBSTRUCTED
OBSTRUCTER
OBTAINABLE
OBTAINMENT
OBTUSENESS
OBVOLUTION
OBVOLUTIVE
OCCASIONAL
OCCASIONED
OCCIDENTAL
OCCUPATION
OCCURRENCE
OCEANARIUM
OCEANGOING
OCEANOLOGY
OCELLATION
OCHLOCRACY
OCTAHEDRAL
OCTAHEDRON
OCTAMEROUS
OCTANGULAR
OCTAVALENT
OCTODECIMO
OCULOMOTOR
ODALISQUES
ODD-PINNATE
ODIOUSNESS
ODONTALGIA
ODONTALGIC
ODONTOLOGY

OEDEMATOUS
OENOLOGIST
OESOPHAGUS
OESTRADIOL
OFFENSIVES
OFFICE BOYS
OFFICIALLY
OFFICIATED
OFFICIATOR
OFF-LICENCE
OFF-LOADING
OFF-PUTTING
OFFSETTING
OFF THE CUFF
OFF THE HOOK
OFF-THE-WALL
OIL-BEARING
OIL TANKERS
OLDE WORLDE
OLD MAIDISH
OLD MASTERS
OLD SCHOOLS
OLD SCRATCH
OLEAGINOUS
OLEOGRAPHY
OLIGARCHIC
OLIGOCLASE
OLIGOPSONY
OLIGURETIC
OLIVACEOUS
OLIVE GREEN
OMMATIDIAL
OMMATIDIUM
OMNIPOTENT
OMNISCIENT
OMNIVOROUS
ONCOLOGIST

ONE ANOTHER
ONE-MAN BAND
ONE-SIDEDLY
ONOMASTICS
ONSLAUGHTS
ON THE ALERT
ON THE CARDS
ON THE ROCKS
ON THE ROPES
ON THE SPREE
OOPHORITIC
OOPHORITIS
OOPS-A-DAISY
OPALESCENT
OPAQUENESS
OPEN-HANDED
OPEN LETTER
OPEN MARKET
OPEN-MINDED
OPEN SEASON
OPEN SECRET
OPEN SESAME
OPERA BUFFA
OPERA HOUSE
OPERATIONS
OPERATIVES
OPERETTIST
OPHICLEIDE
OPHTHALMIA
OPHTHALMIC
OPPILATION
OPPOSINGLY
OPPOSITION
OPPRESSING
OPPRESSION

OPPRESSIVE
OPPRESSORS
OPPROBRIUM
OPTICAL ART
OPTIMISTIC
OPTIMIZING
OPTIONALLY
OPTOMETRIC
ORANGEWOOD
ORANGUTANG
ORATORICAL
ORCHESTRAL
ORCHESTRAS
ORDER PAPER
ORDINANCES
ORDINARILY
ORDINATION
ORDONNANCE
ORDOVICIAN
ORGANICISM
ORGANICIST
ORGANISMAL
ORGANIZERS
ORGANIZING
ORGANOLOGY
ORIENTATED
ORIGINALLY
ORIGINATED
ORIGINATOR
ORIMULSION
ORNAMENTAL
ORNAMENTED
ORNATENESS
ORNITHOPOD
ORNITHOSIS
OROGRAPHER
OROGRAPHIC
OROLOGICAL
ORPHANAGES
ORTHOCLASE
ORTHOGENIC
ORTHOGONAL
OSCILLATED
OSCILLATOR
OSCULATION
OSCULATORY
OSMIRIDIUM
OSMOMETRIC
OSSIFEROUS

OSTENSIBLE
OSTENSIBLY
OSTEOBLAST
OSTEOCLAST
OSTEOPATHS
OSTEOPATHY
OSTEOPHYTE
OSTRACIZED
OSTRACIZER
OSTRACODAN
OTOLOGICAL
OUANANICHE
OUBLIETTES
OUIJA BOARD
OUTBALANCE
OUTBIDDING
OUTBRAVING
OUTCLASSED
OUTFIELDER
OUTFITTERS
OUTFITTING
OUTFLANKED
OUTGENERAL
OUTGROWING
OUTGROWTHS
OUT-HERODED
OUTLANDISH
OUTLASTING
OUT OF COURT
OUT OF DOORS
OUT OF ORDER
OUT OF PLACE
OUT OF SIGHT
OUTPATIENT
OUTPERFORM
OUTPLAYING
OUTPOINTED
OUTPOURING
OUTRAGEOUS
OUTRANKING
OUTRIGGERS
OUTRIVALED
OUTRUNNING
OUTSELLING
OUTSHINING

OUTSMARTED
OUTSTARING
OUTSTATION
OUTSTAYING
OUTSTRETCH
OUTSWINGER
OUTTALKING
OUTWEIGHED
OUTWITTING
OUTWORKERS
OVARIOTOMY
OVERACTING
OVERACTIVE
OVERARCHED
OVERBOOKED
OVERBURDEN
OVERCHARGE
OVERCOMING
OVERDOSAGE
OVERDOSING
OVERDRAFTS
OVEREXPOSE
OVERFLIGHT
OVERFLOWED
OVERFLYING
OVERHAULED
OVERIJSSEL
OVERLAPPED
OVERLAYING
OVERLOADED
OVERLOOKED
OVERMANNED
OVERMASTER
OVERMATTER
OVERPASSES
OVERPLAYED
OVERRATING
OVERRIDDEN
OVERRIDING
OVERRULING
OVERSEEING
OVERSHADOW
OVERSIGHTS
OVERSPILLS
OVERSPREAD
OVERSTATED
OVERSTAYED
OVERSTRUNG
OVERTAXING
OVER THE
  TOP

OVERTHROWN
OVERTHROWS
OVERTHRUST
OVERTOPPED
OVERTURNED
OVERWEIGHT
OVERWORKED
OVIPOSITOR
OVULATIONS
OXIDIMETRY
OXYCEPHALY
OXYGENATED
OXYGENIZER
OXYGEN
  MASK
OXYGEN
  TENT
OYSTER
  BEDS
OZONOLYSIS

P
PACE
  BOWLER
PACEMAKERS
PACHYDERMS
PACIFIC
  RIM
PACK
  ANIMAL
PACKSADDLE
PACKTHREAD
PADDLEFISH
PADLOCKING
PAEDERASTS
PAEDERASTY
PAEDIATRIC
PAGANISTIC
PAGINATION
PAILLASSES
PAINKILLER
PAINLESSLY
PAINTBRUSH
PAKISTANIS
PALAEOCENE
PALAEOGENE
PALAEOLITH
PALAEOZOIC
PALANQUINS
PALATALIZE
PALATIALLY
PALATINATE

PALEACEOUS
PALIMPSEST
PALINDROME
PALLBEARER
PALLIASSES
PALLIATING
PALLIATION
PALLIATIVE
PALLIDNESS
PALMACEOUS
PALMETTOES
PALM
  SUNDAY
PALPATIONS
PALPEBRATE
PALPITATED
PALSY-
  WALSY
PALTRINESS
PALYNOLOGY
PANAMA
  CITY
PANAMANIAN
PAN-
  ARABISM
PANCAKE
  DAY
PANCREASES
PANCREATIC
PANCREATIN
PANEGYRICS
PANEGYRIST
PANEGYRIZE
PANELLISTS
PANGENESIS
PANGENETIC
PANHANDLED
PANHANDLER
PANHANDLES
PANICULATE
PANJANDRUM
PANTALOONS
PANTHEISTS
PANTOGRAPH
PANTOMIMES
PANTOMIMIC
PAPANDREOU
PAPAVERINE
PAPERBACKS
PAPERBOARD
PAPER
  CHASE

PAPER
  CLIPS
PAPERINESS
PAPER
  KNIFE
PAPER
  MONEY
PAPER
  TIGER
PAPISTICAL
PARABIOSIS
PARABIOTIC
PARABOLIST
PARABOLIZE
PARABOLOID
PARACHUTED
PARACHUTES
PARADIDDLE
PARAGRAPHS
PARAGUAYAN
PARALLELED
PARALOGISM
PARALOGIST
PARALYSING
PARALYTICS
PARAMARIBO
PARAMECIUM
PARAMEDICS
PARAMETERS
PARAMETRIC
PARAMNESIA
PARANOIACS
PARANORMAL
PARAPHRASE
PARAPHYSIS
PARAPLEGIA
PARAPLEGIC
PARAPODIUM
PARAPRAXIS
PARASELENE
PARASITISM
PARASITIZE
PARASITOID
PARASTICHY
PARATACTIC
PARATROOPS
PARBOILING
PARCELLING
PARCEL
  POST
PARCHMENTS
PARDONABLE

PARDONABLY
PARENCHYMA
PARENTERAL
PARENTHOOD
PARI-
  MUTUEL
PARISH-
  PUMP
PARKING
  LOT
PARK
  KEEPER
PARLIAMENT
PARLOR
  CARS
PARONYMOUS
PAROXYSMAL
PARRICIDAL
PARRICIDES
PARROTFISH
PARSONAGES
PARTIALITY
PARTICIPLE
PARTICULAR
PARTITIONS
PARTITIVES
PARTNERING
PARTRIDGES
PARTURIENT
PARTY
  LINES
PARTY
  PIECE
PARTY
  WALLS
PARVOVIRUS
PASQUINADE
PASSAGEWAY
PASSENGERS
PASSIONATE
PASTEBOARD
PASTELLIST
PASTEURISM
PASTEURIZE
PAST
  MASTER
PASTY-
  FACED
PATCHINESS
PATCHWORKS
PATENTABLE
PATERNALLY

PATHFINDER
PATHOGENIC
PATISSERIE
PATRIARCHS
PATRIARCHY
PATRICIANS
PATRICIATE
PATRICIDAL
PATRICIDES
PATRILOCAL
PATRIOTISM
PATROL
  CARS
PATROLLING
PATRONIZED
PATRONIZER
PATRONYMIC
PATTERNING
PAWNBROKER
PAYMASTERS
PAY
  PACKETS
PAY-PER-
  VIEW
PAY
  STATION
PEACE
  CORPS
PEACEFULLY
PEACEMAKER
PEACE
  PIPES
PEACHINESS
PEACH
  MELBA
PEARL
  DIVER
PEARLINESS
PEAR-
  SHAPED
PEASHOOTER
PEA
  SHOOTER
PEA
  SOUPERS
PEBBLEDASH
PECCADILLO
PECTIZABLE
PECULATING
PECULATION
PECULIARLY
PEDAGOGISM

PEDAGOGUES
PEDANTRIES
PEDERASTIC
PEDESTRIAN
PEDIATRICS
PEDICULATE
PEDICULOUS
PEDICURIST
PEDIMENTAL
PEDOLOGIST
PEEPING
  TOM
PEGMATITIC
PEJORATION
PEJORATIVE
PELLAGROUS
PELLICULAR
PELLUCIDLY
PENALIZING
PENCILLING
PENDENTIVE
PENDERECKI
PENETRABLE
PENETRALIA
PENETRANCE
PENETRATED
PENETRATOR
PEN
  FRIENDS
PENICILLIN
PENINSULAR
PENINSULAS
PENITENTLY
PENMANSHIP
PENNINE
  WAY
PENNY
  BLACK
PENNYCRESS
PENNYROYAL
PENNYWORTH
PENOLOGIST
PEN
  PUSHERS
PENSIONARY
PENSIONERS
PENSIONING
PENTAGONAL
PENTAGRAMS
PENTAMETER
PENTAQUINE
PENTASTICH

PENTATEUCH
PENTATHLON
PENTHOUSES
PENTIMENTO
PENTSTEMON
PEPPERCORN
PEPPER
  MILL
PEPPERMINT
PEPPER
  POTS
PEPPERWORT
PEPSINOGEN
PEPTIZABLE
PEPTONIZER
PERACIDITY
PERCEIVING
PERCENTAGE
PERCENTILE
PERCEPTION
PERCEPTIVE
PERCEPTUAL
PERCIPIENT
PERCOLATED
PERCOLATOR
PERCUSSION
PERCUSSIVE
PEREMPTORY
PERENNIALS
PERFECTING
PERFECTION
PERFECTIVE
PERFIDIOUS
PERFOLIATE
PERFORABLE
PERFORATED
PERFORATOR
PERFORMERS
PERFORMING
PERICLINAL
PERICYCLIC
PERIDERMAL
PERIDOTITE
PERIGYNOUS
PERIHELION
PERILOUSLY
PERIMETERS
PERIMETRIC
PERIMYSIUM
PERIODICAL
PERIOSTEUM

PERIPETEIA
PERIPHERAL
PERIPHYTON
PERIPTERAL
PERISARCAL
PERISCOPES
PERISCOPIC
PERISHABLE
PERISTOMAL
PERISTYLAR
PERISTYLES
PERITONEAL
PERITONEUM
PERITRICHA
PERIWINKLE
PERMAFROST
PERMANENCE
PERMANENCY
PERMANENTS
PERMEATING
PERMEATION
PERMEATIVE
PERMETHRIN
PERMISSION
PERMISSIVE
PERMITTING
PERNAMBUCO
PERNICIOUS
PERNICKETY
PERORATION
PEROXIDASE
PERPETRATE
PERPETUATE
PERPETUITY
PERPLEXING
PERPLEXITY
PERQUISITE
PERSECUTED
PERSECUTOR
PERSEVERED
PERSIAN
  CAT
PERSIENNES
PERSIFLAGE
PERSIMMONS
PERSISTENT
PERSISTING
PERSONABLE
PERSONABLY
PERSONAGES
PERSONALLY

PERSONALTY
PERSONATOR
PERSPIRING
PERSUADING
PERSUASION
PERSUASIVE
PERTAINING
PERTHSHIRE
PERTINENCE
PERTURBING
PERVERSELY
PERVERSION
PERVERSITY
PERVERTING
PESCADORES
PESSIMISTS
PESTICIDAL
PESTICIDES
PESTILENCE
PETERSBURG
PETIT
  FOURS
PETITIONED
PETITIONER
PETIT
  POINT
PETITS
  POIS
PETRIFYING
PETROGLYPH
PETROLATUM
PETROPOLIS
PETTICOATS
PETULANTLY
PHAGOCYTES
PHAGOCYTIC
PHAGOMANIA
PHALANGEAL
PHALANGIST
PHALLICISM
PHALLICIST
PHANEROGAM
PHANTASIES
PHANTASMAL
PHARISAISM
PHARMACIES
PHARMACIST
PHARYNGEAL
PHELLODERM
PHENACAINE
PHENACETIN

PHENFORMIN
PHENOCRYST
PHENOMENAL
PHENOMENON
PHENOTYPIC
PHILATELIC
PHILIPPICS
PHILIPPINE
PHILISTINE
PHILOSOPHY
PHLEBOTOMY
PHLEGMATIC
PHLOGISTIC
PHLOGISTON
PHLOGOPITE
PHOCOMELIA
PHOENICIAN
PHONE
  BOOKS
PHONE
  BOXES
PHONEYNESS
PHONEY
  WARS
PHONICALLY
PHONOGRAPH
PHONOLITIC
PHONOMETER
PHONOSCOPE
PHONOTYPIC
PHOSGENITE
PHOSPHATES
PHOSPHATIC
PHOSPHORIC
PHOSPHORUS
PHOTOFLOOD
PHOTOGENIC
PHOTOGRAPH
PHOTOLYSIS
PHOTOLYTIC
PHOTOMETER
PHOTOMETRY
PHOTOMURAL
PHOTONASTY
PHOTONOVEL
PHOTOPHILY
PHOTOPHORE
PHOTOSTATS
PHOTOTAXIS
PHOTOTONIC
PHOTOTONUS

PHOTOTYPIC
PHRASEBOOK
PHRENOLOGY
PHTHISICAL
PHYLACTERY
PHYLLODIAL
PHYLLOXERA
PHYLOGENIC
PHYSIATRIC
PHYSICALLY
PHYSICIANS
PHYSICISTS
PHYSIOCRAT
PHYSIOLOGY
PHYTOGENIC
PHYTOPHAGY
PHYTOTOXIN
PIANISSIMO
PIANOFORTE
PICARESQUE
PICCADILLY
PICCALILLI
PICCANINNY
PICHICIEGO
PICKPOCKET
PICNICKERS
PICNICKING
PICRIC
  ACID
PICROTOXIC
PICROTOXIN
PICTOGRAPH
PIED-A-
  TERRE
PIERCINGLY
PIGEONHOLE
PIGEON-
  TOED
PIGGYBACKS
PIGGYBANKS
PIGMENTARY
PIGSTICKER
PIKESTAFFS
PILE
  DRIVER
PILGRIMAGE
PILIFEROUS
PILLORYING
PILLOWCASE
PILLOW
  TALK

PILOT
  LIGHT
PIMPERNELS
PIMPLINESS
PINA
  COLADA
PINCERLIKE
PINCHPENNY
PINCUSHION
PINEAPPLES
PINE
  MARTEN
PINFEATHER
PINGUIDITY
PINNATIFID
PINNATIPED
PINPOINTED
PINSTRIPED
PINSTRIPES
PIONEERING
PIPED
  MUSIC
PIPE
  DREAMS
PIPERAZINE
PIPERIDINE
PIPSISSEWA
PIPSQUEAKS
PIROUETTED
PIROUETTES
PISTACHIOS
PISTILLATE
PISTON
  RING
PITCH-
  BLACK
PITCHFORKS
PITCHINESS
PITCHSTONE
PITH
  HELMET
PITILESSLY
PITOT
  TUBES
PITTSBURGH
PITYRIASIS
PLACARDING
PLACE
  CARDS
PLACEMENTS
PLAGIARISM
PLAGIARIST

PLAGIARIZE
PLAINCHANT
PLAIN
  FLOUR
PLAINTIFFS
PLANCHETTE
PLANETARIA
PLANE
  TREES
PLANGENTLY
PLANIMETER
PLANIMETRY
PLANK-
  SHEER
PLANKTONIC
PLANOMETER
PLANOMETRY
PLANTATION
PLASMAGENE
PLASMODIUM
PLASMOLYSE
PLASMOSOME
PLASTERERS
PLASTERING
PLASTIC
  ART
PLASTICINE
PLASTICITY
PLASTICIZE
PLAT DU
  JOUR
PLATE
  GLASS
PLATELAYER
PLATE
  RACKS
PLATITUDES
PLATTELAND
PLATYPUSES
PLAY-
  ACTING
PLAYFELLOW
PLAYGROUND
PLAYGROUPS
PLAYHOUSES
PLAYSCHOOL
PLAYTHINGS
PLAYWRIGHT
PLEASANTER
PLEASANTLY
PLEASANTRY
PLEASINGLY

PLEBISCITE
PLEIOTROPY
PLEONASTIC
PLESIOSAUR
PLEURODONT
PLEUROTOMY
PLEXIGLASS
PLIABILITY
PLODDINGLY
PLOUGHBOYS
PLOUGHLAND
PLUCKINESS
PLUMB
  LINES
PLUMMETING
PLUNDERERS
PLUNDERING
PLUNDEROUS
PLUPERFECT
PLURALISTS
PLURALIZER
PLUTOCRACY
PLUTOCRATS
PNEUMATICS
POCKETABLE
POCKETBOOK
POCKETFULS
POCKMARKED
PODIATRIST
POETASTERS
POETICALLY
POGO
  STICKS
POIGNANTLY
POINSETTIA
POINT-
  BLANK
POKER-
  FACED
POLAR
  BEARS
POLARITIES
POLARIZING
POLEMICIST
POLES
  APART
POLE
  VAULTS
POLITBUROS
POLITENESS
POLITICIAN
POLITICIZE

POLLARDING
POLLINATED
POLLINATOR
POLLINOSIS
POLLUTANTS
POLONAISES
POLYANTHUS
POLYATOMIC
POLYBASITE
POLYCARPIC
POLYCHAETE
POLYCHROME
POLYCHROMY
POLYCLINIC
POLYCOTTON
POLYCYCLIC
POLYDACTYL
POLYDIPSIA
POLYDIPSIC
POLYGAMIST
POLYGAMOUS
POLYGRAPHS
POLYGYNIST
POLYGYNOUS
POLYHEDRAL
POLYHEDRON
POLYMATHIC
POLYMERASE
POLYMERISM
POLYMERIZE
POLYMEROUS
POLYNESIAN
POLYNOMIAL
POLYPHAGIA
POLYPHONIC
POLYPLOIDY
POLYPODOUS
POLYRHYTHM
POLYSEMOUS
POLYTHEISM
POLYTHEIST
POLYVALENT
POMERANIAN
POMIFEROUS
POMOLOGIST
PONDERABLE
POND-
　SKATER
PONTEFRACT
PONTEVEDRA
PONTIFICAL

PONTYPRIDD
POOH-
　POOHED
POOL
　MALEBO
POORHOUSES
POOR
　WHITES
POPE'S
　NOSES
POPISHNESS
POPULARITY
POPULARIZE
POPULATING
POPULATION
PORCUPINES
PORIFEROUS
PORK
　BARREL
PORNOCRACY
POROUSNESS
PORPHYROID
PORTAMENTO
PORTCULLIS
PORTENDING
PORTENTOUS
PORTFOLIOS
PORT-
　GENTIL
PORTIONING
PORTLAOISE
PORTLINESS
PORTOBELLO
PORT OF
　CALL
PORTRAYALS
PORTRAYING
PORTSMOUTH
PORT
　TALBOT
PORTUGUESE
POSITIONAL
POSITIONED
POSITIVELY
POSITIVISM
POSITIVIST
POSSESSING
POSSESSION
POSSESSIVE
POSSESSORS
POSSESSORY

POST-
　BELLUM
POST-
　CYCLIC
POSTDATING
POSTERIORS
POSTHUMOUS
POSTILIONS
POSTLIMINY
POSTMARKED
POSTMASTER
POSTMORTEM
POST
　OFFICE
POSTPARTUM
POSTPONING
POSTSCRIPT
POSTULANCY
POSTULANTS
POSTULATED
POSTULATES
POSTULATOR
POTABILITY
POTATO
　CHIP
POTBELLIED
POTBELLIES
POTBOILERS
POTENTATES
POTENTIATE
POTENTILLA
POTENTNESS
POTHUNTERS
POTPOURRIS
POULTERERS
POULTRYMAN
POURPARLER
POWDER
　KEGS
POWDER
　PUFF
POWDER
　ROOM
POWER
　BASES
POWERBOATS
POWER
　DIVES
POWERFULLY
POWERHOUSE
POWER
　PLANT

POWER
　POINT
POZZUOLANA
PRACTICALS
PRACTISING
PRAESIDIUM
PRAGMATICS
PRAGMATISM
PRAGMATIST
PRAIRIE
　DOG
PRANCINGLY
PRANKSTERS
PRASELENIC
PRATINCOLE
PRAYER
　RUGS
PREACHMENT
PREADAMITE
PREAMBULAR
PREARRANGE
PREBENDARY
PRECARIOUS
PRECAUTION
PRECEDENCE
PRECEDENTS
PRECENTORS
PRECEPTIVE
PRECESSION
PRECIOSITY
PRECIOUSLY
PRECIPICED
PRECIPICES
PRECIPITIN
PRECISIONS
PRECLUDING
PRECLUSION
PRECLUSIVE
PRECOCIOUS
PRECONCERT
PRECOOKING
PRECURSORS
PRECURSORY
PREDACIOUS
PREDECEASE
PREDESTINE
PREDICABLE
PREDICATED
PREDICATES
PREDICTING
PREDICTION

PREDICTIVE
PREDISPOSE
PRE-
　EMINENT
PRE-
　EMPTING
PRE-
　EMPTION
PRE-
　EMPTIVE
PRE-
　EMPTORY
PREEXISTED
PREFECTURE
PREFERABLE
PREFERABLY
PREFERENCE
PREFERMENT
PREFERRING
PREFIGURED
PREFRONTAL
PREGLACIAL
PREGNANTLY
PREHEATING
PREHENSILE
PREHENSION
PREHISTORY
PREHOMINID
PREJUDGING
PREJUDICED
PREJUDICES
PRELEXICAL
PREMARITAL
PREMAXILLA
PREMEDICAL
PRENATALLY
PRENOMINAL
PREPACKAGE
PREPACKING
PREPAREDLY
PREPAYABLE
PREPAYMENT
PREPOSSESS
PREPOTENCY
PREP
　SCHOOL
PRESAGEFUL
PRESBYOPIA
PRESBYOPIC
PRESBYTERY
PRESCHOOLS
PRESCIENCE

PRESCRIBED	PRIGGISHLY	PROCTOLOGY	PROMOTIONS	PROSPECTED
PRESCRIBER	PRIMA	PROCTORIAL	PROMPTBOOK	PROSPECTOR
PRESCRIPTS	DONNA	PROCUMBENT	PROMPTNESS	PROSPECTUS
PRESENT	PRIMA	PROCURATOR	PROMULGATE	PROSPERING
DAY	FACIE	PRODIGALLY	PRONEPHRIC	PROSPERITY
PRESENT-	PRIMAQUINE	PRODIGIOUS	PRONEPHROS	PROSPEROUS
DAY	PRIME	PRODUCIBLE	PRONOMINAL	PROSTHESIS
PRESENTERS	MOVER	PRODUCTION	PRONOUNCED	PROSTHETIC
PRESENTING	PRIME	PRODUCTIVE	PRONOUNCER	PROSTITUTE
PRESERVERS	RATES	PROFESSING	PRONUCLEAR	PROSTOMIUM
PRESERVING	PRIMITIVES	PROFESSION	PRONUCLEUS	PROSTRATED
PRESETTING	PRIMORDIAL	PROFESSORS	PRO-	PROTANOPIA
PRESIDENCY	PRIMORDIUM	PROFFERING	OESTRUS	PROTANOPIC
PRESIDENTS	PRINCEDOMS	PROFICIENT	PROPAGABLE	PROTECTING
PRESIDIUMS	PRINCELING	PROFITABLE	PROPAGANDA	PROTECTION
PRESIGNIFY	PRINCESSES	PROFITABLY	PROPAGATED	PROTECTIVE
PRESS	PRINCIPALS	PROFITEERS	PROPAGATOR	PROTECTORS
AGENT	PRINCIPIUM	PROFITLESS	PROPELLANT	PROTECTORY
PRESS	PRINCIPLED	PROFLIGACY	PROPELLENT	PROTEINASE
BARON	PRINCIPLES	PROFLIGATE	PROPELLERS	PRO
PRESS	PRINTMAKER	PROFOUNDLY	PROPELLING	TEMPORE
BOXES	PRIORITIES	PROFUNDITY	PROPENSITY	PROTESTANT
PRESSGANGS	PRIORITIZE	PROGENITOR	PROPERNESS	PROTESTERS
PRESSINGLY	PRISMATOID	PROGLOTTIS	PROPER	PROTHALLIC
PRESS-	PRISMOIDAL	PROGNOSTIC	NOUN	PROTHALLUS
STUDS	PRISON	PROGRAMERS	PROPERTIED	PROTOCTIST
PRESSURING	CAMP	PROGRAMING	PROPERTIES	PROTOHUMAN
PRESSURIZE	PRISON	PROGRAMMED	PROPHECIES	PROTONEMAL
PRESUMABLE	GATE	PROGRAMMER	PROPHESIER	PROTOPATHY
PRESUMABLY	PRISSINESS	PROGRAMMES	PROPHESIED	PROTOPLASM
PRESUMEDLY	PRIVATEERS	PROGRESSED	PROPHESIES	PROTOPLAST
PRESUPPOSE	PRIVATIONS	PROGRESSES	PROPIONATE	PROTOSTELE
PRETENDERS	PRIVATIZED	PROHIBITED	PROPITIATE	PROTOTYPAL
PRETENDING	PRIVILEGED	PROHIBITER	PROPITIOUS	PROTOTYPES
PRETENSION	PRIVILEGES	PROJECTILE	PROPONENTS	PROTOXYLEM
PRETTIFIED	PRIVY	PROJECTING	PROPORTION	PROTOZOANS
PRETTINESS	PURSE	PROJECTION	PROPOSABLE	PROTRACTED
PREVAILING	PRIZEFIGHT	PROJECTIVE	PROPOSITUS	PROTRACTOR
PREVALENCE	PROCAMBIAL	PROJECTORS	PROPOUNDED	PROTRUDENT
PREVENIENT	PROCAMBIUM	PROKARYOTE	PROPOUNDER	PROTRUDING
PREVENTING	PROCEDURAL	PROLAPSING	PROPRIETOR	PROTRUSILE
PREVENTION	PROCEDURES	PROLOCUTOR	PROPULSION	PROTRUSION
PREVENTIVE	PROCEEDING	PROLONGING	PROPULSIVE	PROTRUSIVE
PREVIEWING	PROCESSING	PROMENADED	PROPYLAEUM	PROVENANCE
PREVIOUSLY	PROCESSION	PROMENADER	PROROGUING	PROVENCALE
PREVISIONS	PROCESSORS	PROMENADES	PROSCENIUM	PROVERBIAL
PREVOCALIC	PROCLAIMED	PROMETHIUM	PROSCRIBED	PROVIDENCE
PRICKLIEST	PROCLIVITY	PROMINENCE	PROSECUTED	PROVINCIAL
PRIEST-	PROCONSULS	PROMISSORY	PROSECUTOR	PROVISIONS
HOLE	PROCREATED	PROMONTORY	PROSELYTES	PROVITAMIN
PRIESTHOOD	PROCREATOR	PROMOTABLE	PROSELYTIC	PRUDENTIAL
PRIESTLIER	PROCRYPTIC			

PRURIENTLY
PSALMODIST
PSALTERIES
PSALTERIUM
PSEPHOLOGY
PSESPHITIC
PSEUDOCARP
PSEUDONYMS
PSILOCYBIN
PSITTACINE
PSITTACISM
PSYCHIATRY
PSYCHOLOGY
PSYCHOPATH
PSYCHOTICS
PTOLEMAIST
PUB-
  CRAWLED
PUBERULENT
PUBESCENCE
PUBLIC
  BARS
PUBLICISTS
PUBLICIZED
PUBLISHERS
PUBLISHING
PUERPERIUM
PUERTO
  RICO
PUGILISTIC
PUGNACIOUS
PUISSANCES
PULLULATED
PULSATIONS
PULSIMETER
PULVERABLE
PULVERIZED
PULVERIZER
PUMMELLING
PUNCH
  BALLS
PUNCHBOARD
PUNCH
  BOWLS
PUNCH-
  DRUNK
PUNCHINESS
PUNCH
  LINES
PUNCTATION
PUNCTILIOS
PUNCTUALLY

PUNCTUATED
PUNCTUATOR
PUNCTURING
PUNISHABLE
PUNISHMENT
PUNITIVELY
PUPIPAROUS
PUPPETEERS
PURCHASERS
PURCHASING
PURGATIVES
PURITANISM
PURLOINING
PURPLENESS
PURPORTING
PURPOSEFUL
PURSUANCES
PURSUIVANT
PURVEYANCE
PUSH-
  BUTTON
PUSHCHAIRS
PUT A STOP
  TO
PUTREFYING
PUTRESCENT
PUTRESCINE
PUZZLEMENT
PUZZLINGLY
PYCNOMETER
PYOGENESIS
PYORRHOEAL
PYRACANTHA
PYRETHROID
PYRIDOXINE
PYRIMIDINE
PYROGALLIC
PYROGALLOL
PYROGRAPHY
PYROLUSITE
PYROMANCER
PYROMANIAC
PYROMANTIC
PYROMETRIC
PYROPHORIC
PYROSTATIC
PYROXENITE
PYRRHOTITE
PYTHAGORAS

Q

QARAGHANDY
QUADRANGLE
QUADRANTAL
QUADRATICS
QUADRATURE
QUADRICEPS
QUADRILLES
QUADRISECT
QUADRIVIAL
QUADRUPEDS
QUADRUPLED
QUADRUPLET
QUADRUPLEX
QUAINTNESS
QUALIFIERS
QUALIFYING
QUANDARIES
QUANTIFIED
QUANTIFIER
QUANTITIES
QUARANTINE
QUARRELING
QUARRELLED
QUARRELLER
QUARTERAGE
QUARTER
  DAY
QUARTERING
QUARTERSAW
QUATERNARY
QUATERNION
QUATREFOIL
QUEASINESS
QUEENSLAND
QUENCHABLE
QUESTINGLY
QUESTIONED
QUESTIONER
QUEZON
  CITY
QUICKENING
QUICKSANDS
QUICKSTEPS
QUID PRO
  QUO
QUIESCENCE
QUIETENING
QUINTUPLET
QUIRKINESS
QUITTANCES

QUIZMASTER
QUONSET
  HUT
QUOTATIONS

R

RABBINICAL
RABBITFISH
RABBITTING
RACECOURSE
RACEHORSES
RACETRACKS
RACHMANISM
RACIALISTS
RACKETEERS
RACK-
  RENTER
RACONTEURS
RADARSCOPE
RADIATIONS
RADICALISM
RADIO
  ALARM
RADIOGENIC
RADIOGRAMS
RADIOGRAPH
RADIOLYSIS
RADIOMETER
RADIOMETRY
RADIOPAQUE
RADIOPHONY
RADIOSCOPE
RADIOSCOPY
RADIOSONDE
RADIOTOXIC
RAFSANJANI
RAGAMUFFIN
RAGGEDNESS
RAILROADED
RAIN
  CHECKS
RAIN
  FOREST
RAIN
  GAUGES
RAINMAKING
RAINSTORMS
RAISE A
  DUST
RAJYA
  SABHA
RAKISHNESS

RAMPAGEOUS
RAMSHACKLE
RANCH
  HOUSE
RANCIDNESS
RANDOMNESS
RANSACKING
RANUNCULUS
RAPPORTEUR
RARE
  EARTHS
RAREFIABLE
RATABILITY
RAT-A-TAT-
  TAT
RATE-
  CAPPED
RATIFIABLE
RATIONALES
RATIONALLY
RAT-
  RUNNING
RATTLETRAP
RAUNCHIEST
RAVAGEMENT
RAVENOUSLY
RAVISHMENT
RAWALPINDI
RAWINSONDE
RAZZMATAZZ
REACTIONAL
REACTIVATE
REACTIVELY
REACTIVITY
READERSHIP
READJUSTED
READJUSTER
READY
  MONEY
REAFFIRMED
REAFFOREST
REAL
  ESTATE
REALIGNING
REALIZABLE
REALIZABLY
REALLOCATE
REANIMATED
REAPPEARED
REAPPRAISE
REARGUARDS
REARMAMENT

267

REARRANGED
REARRANGER
REASONABLE
REASONABLY
REASSEMBLE
REASSURING
REBELLIONS
REBELLIOUS
REBIRTHING
REBOUNDING
REBUILDING
REBUKINGLY
REBUTTABLE
RECALLABLE
RECAPTURED
RECEIVABLE
RECENTNESS
RECEPTACLE
RECEPTIONS
RECESSIONS
RECHARGING
RECHRISTEN
RECIDIVISM
RECIDIVIST
RECIPIENCE
RECIPIENTS
RECIPROCAL
RECITATION
RECITATIVE
RECKLESSLY
RECKONINGS
RECLAIMANT
RECLAIMING
RECLINABLE
RECOGNIZED
RECOGNIZEE
RECOGNIZER
RECOGNIZOR
RECOILLESS
RECOMMENCE
RECOMPENSE
RECONCILED
RECONCILER
RECONSIDER
RECORDABLE
RECORDINGS
RECOUNTING
RECOUPABLE
RECOUPMENT
RECOVERIES

RE-
  COVERING
RECREATING
RECREATION
RECRUDESCE
RECRUITING
RECTANGLES
RECTIFIERS
RECTIFYING
RECUMBENCE
RECUPERATE
RECURRENCE
RED
  ADMIRAL
RED-
  BLOODED
REDBREASTS
REDCURRANT
REDECORATE
REDEDICATE
REDEEMABLE
REDEEMABLY
REDELIVERY
REDEMPTION
REDEPLOYED
RED
  HERRING
RED
  INDIANS
REDIRECTED
REDISCOUNT
REDOUBLING
REDOUNDING
RED
  PEPPERS
REDRESSING
REDUCTIONS
REDUNDANCY
RE-
  EDUCATED
RE-
  ELECTING
RE-
  ELECTION
RE-
  ENFORCER
RE-
  ENTRANCE
RE-
  EXAMINER
RE-
  EXPORTER

REFEREEING
REFERENCER
REFERENCES
REFERENDUM
REFILLABLE
REFINEMENT
REFINERIES
REFINISHER
REFLECTING
REFLECTION
REFLECTIVE
REFLECTORS
REFLEXIVES
REFORESTED
REFRACTING
REFRACTION
REFRACTIVE
REFRACTORY
REFRAINING
REFRESHFUL
REFRESHING
REFRINGENT
REFUELLING
REFUGEEISM
REFULGENCE
REFUNDABLE
REFUTATION
REGAINABLE
REGALEMENT
REGARDABLE
REGARDLESS
REGELATION
REGENERACY
REGENERATE
REGENSBURG
REGENTSHIP
REGIMENTAL
REGIMENTED
REGIONALLY
REGISTERED
REGISTERER
REGISTRANT
REGISTRARS
REGISTRIES
REGRESSING
REGRESSION
REGRESSIVE
REGRETTING
REGROUPING
REGULARITY
REGULARIZE

REGULATING
REGULATION
REGULATIVE
REGULATORS
REGULATORY
REHEARSALS
REHEARSING
REIMBURSED
REIMBURSER
REINFORCED
REINSTATED
REINSTATOR
REINSURING
REISSUABLE
REITERATED
REJECTABLE
REJECTIONS
REJOINDERS
REJUVENATE
REKINDLING
RELATIONAL
RELATIVELY
RELATIVISM
RELATIVIST
RELATIVITY
RELAXATION
RELEGATING
RELEGATION
RELENTLESS
RELEVANTLY
RELIEF
  MAPS
RELIEF
  ROAD
RELIEVABLE
RELINQUISH
RELISHABLE
RELOCATING
RELOCATION
RELUCTANCE
REMAINDERS
REMANDMENT
REMARKABLE
REMARKABLY
REMARRYING
REMEDIABLE
REMEDIABLY
REMEDIALLY
REMEDILESS
REMEMBERED
REMEMBERER

REMINISCED
REMISSIBLE
REMISSIONS
REMISSNESS
REMITTABLE
REMITTANCE
REMITTENCE
REMODELING
REMODELLED
REMODELLER
REMONETIZE
REMORSEFUL
REMOTENESS
REMOULDING
REMOUNTING
REMOVAL
  VAN
REMUNERATE
RENDERABLE
RENDERINGS
RENDEZVOUS
RENDITIONS
RENEWABLES
RENOUNCING
RENOVATING
RENOVATION
RENOVATIVE
RENOWNEDLY
RENT
  STRIKE
REORGANIZE
REPAIRABLE
REPARATION
REPARATIVE
REPATRIATE
REPAYMENTS
REPEALABLE
REPEATABLE
REPEATEDLY
REPELLENCE
REPELLENTS
REPENTANCE
REPERTOIRE
REPETITION
REPETITIVE
REPHRASING
REPLICATED
REPORTABLE
REPORTEDLY
REPOSITION
REPOSITORY

REPRESSING
REPRESSION
REPRESSIVE
REPRIEVING
REPRIMANDS
REPRINTING
REPROACHED
REPROACHER
REPROACHES
REPROBATER
REPROBATES
REPRODUCED
REPRODUCER
REPROVABLE
REPTILIANS
REPUBLICAN
REPUDIABLE
REPUDIATED
REPUDIATOR
REPUGNANCE
REPULSIONS
REPURCHASE
REPUTATION
REQUESTING
REQUIESCAT
REQUIRABLE
REQUISITES
REQUITABLE
RESCHEDULE
RESCINDING
RESCISSION
RESCISSORY
RESEARCHED
RESEARCHER
RESEARCHES
RESEMBLANT
RESEMBLING
RESENTMENT
RESERVABLE
RESERVEDLY
RESERVISTS
RESERVOIRS
RESETTLING
RESHIPMENT
RESHUFFLED
RESHUFFLES
RESIDENCES
RESIGNEDLY
RESILEMENT
RESILIENCE
RESILIENCY

RESISTANCE
RESISTIBLY
RESISTLESS
RESOLUTELY
RESOLUTION
RESOLVABLE
RESONANCES
RESONANTLY
RESONATING
RESONATION
RESONATORS
RESORCINOL
RESORPTION
RESORPTIVE
RESOUNDING
RESPECTERS
RESPECTFUL
RESPECTING
RESPECTIVE
RESPIRABLE
RESPIRATOR
RESPONDENT
RESPONDING
RESPONSIVE
RESPONSORY
RES
  PUBLICA
RESTAURANT
RESTHARROW
RESTLESSLY
RESTOCKING
RESTORABLE
RESTRAINED
RESTRAINER
RESTRAINTS
RESTRICTED
RESUMPTION
RESUMPTIVE
RESUPINATE
RESURFACED
RESURGENCE
RETAINABLE .
RETAINMENT
RETALIATED
RETALIATOR
RETHINKING
RETICENTLY
RETICULATE
RETIREMENT
RETOUCHING
RETRACTILE

RETRACTING
RETRACTION
RETRACTIVE
RETREADING
RETREATING
RETRENCHED
RETRIEVERS
RETRIEVING
RETROCHOIR
RETROGRADE
RETROGRESS
RETROSPECT
RETROVERSE
RETROVIRUS
RETURNABLE
REUNIONISM
REUNIONIST
REUNITABLE
REUTLINGEN
REVANCHISM
REVANCHIST
REVEALABLE
REVEALEDLY
REVEALMENT
REVEGETATE
REVELATION
REVENGEFUL
REVERENCED
REVERENCER
REVERENCES
REVERENTLY
REVERSIBLE
REVERTIBLE
REVETMENTS
REVIEWABLE
REVILEMENT
REVILINGLY
REVISIONAL
REVITALIZE
REVIVALISM
REVIVALIST
REVIVIFIED
REVIVINGLY
REVOCATION
REVOCATIVE
REVOKINGLY
REVOLUTION
REVOLVABLE
REVOLVABLY
REWARDABLE

REWARD
  CARD
RHAPSODIES
RHAPSODIST
RHAPSODIZE
RHEOLOGIST
RHEOMETRIC
RHEOSTATIC
RHEOTACTIC
RHEOTROPIC
RHETORICAL
RHEUMATICS
RHEUMATISM
RHEUMATOID
RHINESTONE
RHINOCEROS
RHINOSCOPY
RHIZOGENIC
RHIZOMORPH
RHIZOPODAN
RHOMBOIDAL
RHUMBATRON
RHYMESTERS
RHYTHMICAL
RIBBONFISH
RIBOFLAVIN
RICKETTSIA
RICOCHETED
RIDGEPOLES
RIDICULING
RIDICULOUS
RIEMANNIAN
RIFLE
  RANGE
RIFT
  VALLEY
RIGHTABOUT
RIGHT
  ANGLE
RIGHTFULLY
RIGHT OF
  WAY
RIGHTWARDS
RIGMAROLES
RIGORISTIC
RIGOROUSLY
RINDERPEST
RING
  BINDER
RING
  FINGER
RINGLEADER

RINGMASTER
RING-
  NECKED
RING-
  TAILED
RIPPLINGLY
RIP-
  ROARING
RISIBILITY
RISING
  DAMP
RITARDANDO
RITORNELLO
RIVER
  BASIN
ROADBLOCKS
ROADHOUSES
ROAD
  ROLLER
ROADRUNNER
ROAD-
  TESTED
ROADWORTHY
ROBUSTNESS
ROCK
  BOTTOM
ROCK
  GARDEN
ROCK
  PLANTS
ROCK
  SALMON
ROISTERERS
ROISTEROUS
ROLE
  MODELS
ROLE-
  PLAYED
ROLLED
  GOLD
ROLLICKING
ROLLING
  PIN
ROLY-
  POLIES
ROMAN
  BLIND
ROMANESQUE
ROMAN
  NOSES
ROOD
  SCREEN

ROOF
  GARDEN
ROPE
  LADDER
ROSANILINE
ROSEMALING
ROSE
  WINDOW
ROSTELLATE
ROTARY
  CLUB
ROTATIONAL
ROTISSERIE
ROTOVATORS
ROTTENNESS
ROTTWEILER
ROUGHENING
ROUGHHOUSE
ROUGH
  HOUSE
ROUGHNECKS
ROUGH
  PAPER
ROUGHRIDER
ROUGH
  STUFF
ROUNDABOUT
ROUNDHEADS
ROUNDHOUSE
ROUND
  ROBIN
ROUND-
  TABLE
ROUND
  TRIPS
ROUSEDNESS
ROUSSILLON
ROUSTABOUT
ROUTE
  MARCH
ROWING
  BOAT
ROYAL
  FLUSH
ROYALISTIC
RUB' AL
  KHALI
RUBBER
  BAND
RUBBERNECK
RUBBER
  TREE

RUBBISH
  BIN
RUBBISHING
RUBBLEWORK
RUBESCENCE
RUBIACEOUS
RUBIGINOUS
RUBRICATOR
RUDDERHEAD
RUDDERLESS
RUDDERPOST
RUEFULNESS
RUFESCENCE
RUFFIANISM
RUGBY
  UNION
RUGGEDIZED
RUGGEDNESS
RUMBLINGLY
RUMINATING
RUMINATION
RUMINATIVE
RUMPUS
  ROOM
RUNNER
  BEAN
RUN-OF-
  PAPER
RUN
  THROUGH
RUN-
  THROUGH
RUPESTRIAN
RUPTURABLE
RURITANIAN
RUSHLIGHTS
RUSSOPHILE
RUSSOPHOBE
RUSTICATED
RUSTICATOR
RUSTLINGLY
RUTHENIOUS
RUTHERFORD
RUTHLESSLY

S
SABBATICAL
SABOTAGING
SABULOSITY
SACCHARASE
SACCHARATE
SACCHARIDE

SACCHARIFY
SACCHARINE
SACCHAROID
SACCHAROSE
SACERDOTAL
SACRAMENTO
SACRAMENTS
SACRED
  COWS
SACREDNESS
SACRIFICED
SACRIFICER
SACRIFICES
SACRILEGES
SACRISTANS
SACRISTIES
SACROILIAC
SACROSANCT
SADDLEBACK
SADDLEBAGS
SADDLEBILL
SADDLERIES
SADDLE-
  SORE
SADDLETREE
SAFARI
  PARK
SAFEGUARDS
SAFE
  HOUSES
SAFETY
  BELT
SAFETY
  LAMP
SAFETY
  NETS
SAFETY
  PINS
SAHARANPUR
SAILBOARDS
SAILOR
  SUIT
SAILPLANES
SAINT-
  CLOUD
SAINT
  CROIX
SAINT-
  DENIS
SAINT
  JOHN'S
SAINT
  KILDA

SAINT
  KITTS
SAINT
  LOUIS
SAINT-
  LOUIS
SAINT
  LUCIA
SAINT'S
  DAYS
SALABILITY
SALAD
  CREAM
SALAMANDER
SALBUTAMOL
SALESCLERK
SALESGIRLS
SALES
  PITCH
SALES
  SLIPS
SALES
  TAXES
SALESWOMAN
SALESWOMEN
SALICORNIA
SALICYLATE
SALIFEROUS
SALIFIABLE
SALIMETRIC
SALIVATING
SALIVATION
SALLOWNESS
SALMANAZAR
SALMONELLA
SALMON
  LEAP
SALOON
  BARS
SALOPETTES
SALPINGIAN
SALTARELLO
SALTCELLAR
SALTIGRADE
SALT
  SHAKER
SALUBRIOUS
SALUTARILY
SALUTATION
SALUTATORY
SALVERFORM
SALZGITTER

SAMARITANS
SAMARSKITE
SAMOTHRACE
SAN
  ANTONIO
SANATORIUM
SANCTIFIED
SANCTIFIER
SANCTIMONY
SANCTIONED
SANCTIONER
SANCTITUDE
SANDALWOOD
SANDBAGGED
SANDBAGGER
SANDCASTLE
SAND
  CASTLE
SANDERLING
SANDGROUSE
SAND
  MARTIN
SANDPIPERS
SANDSTORMS
SANDWICHED
SANDWICHES
SANFORIZED
SANFORIZED
SANGUINARY
SANGUINELY
SANITARIAN
SANITARILY
SANITARIUM
SANITATION
SANITIZING
SANSKRITIC
SANTA
  CLARA
SANTA
  CLAUS
SANTA
  MARIA
SANTA
  MARTA
SAPIENTIAL
SAPONIFIER
SAPPANWOOD
SAPPHIRINE
SAPROGENIC
SAPROLITIC
SAPROPELIC
SAPROPHYTE

SAPROTROPH
SARCOPHAGI
SARMENTOSE
SARRACENIA
SASH
WINDOW
SATELLITES
SATINWOODS
SATIRIZING
SATISFYING
SATURATING
SATURATION
SATURNALIA
SATYRIASIS
SAUERKRAUT
SAUNTERING
SAUSAGE
DOG
SAVAGENESS
SAVAGERIES
SAXICOLOUS
SAXOPHONES
SAXOPHONIC
SCABBINESS
SCAFFOLDER
SCALEBOARD
SCALLOPING
SCALLYWAGS
SCALOPPINE
SCALPELLIC
SCAMPERING
SCANDALIZE
SCANDALOUS
SCANSORIAL
SCANTINESS
SCAPEGOATS
SCAPEGRACE
SCARABAEID
SCARABAEUS
SCARCEMENT
SCARCENESS
SCARCITIES
SCARECROWS
SCAREDY
CAT
SCARIFYING
SCARLATINA
SCARPERING
SCATHINGLY
SCATTER-
GUN
SCATTERING

SCATTINESS
SCAVENGERS
SCAVENGING
SCENICALLY
SCEPTICISM
SCHAERBEEK
SCHEDULING
SCHEMATISM
SCHEMATIZE
SCHEMINGLY
SCHERZANDO
SCHIPPERKE
SCHISMATIC
SCHIZOCARP
SCHIZOGONY
SCHLEPPING
SCHNITZELS
SCHOLASTIC
SCHOOLGIRL
SCHOOLMARM
SCHOOLMATE
SCHOOLWORK
SCHUMACHER
SCIENTIFIC
SCIENTISTS
SCILLONIAN
SCIOMANCER
SCIOMANTIC
SCLEROTIUM
SCLEROTOMY
SCOFFINGLY
SCOLDINGLY
SCOLLOPING
SCOREBOARD
SCORECARDS
SCORNFULLY
SCORNINGLY
SCORPAENID
SCORPIONIC
SCOTCH
EGGS
SCOTCH
MIST
SCOTCH
SNAP
SCOTCH
TAPE
SCOTTICISM
SCOUNDRELS
SCOWLINGLY
SCRABBLING
SCRAGGIEST

SCRAMBLING
SCRAPBOOKS
SCRAP
HEAPS
SCRAP
METAL
SCRAP
PAPER
SCRAPPIEST
SCRATCHIER
SCRATCHILY
SCRATCHING
SCRATCH
PAD
SCRATCHPAD
SCRAWNIEST
SCREECHING
SCREENABLE
SCREENINGS
SCREENPLAY
SCREEN
TEST
SCREWBALLS
SCRIBBLERS
SCRIBBLING
SCRIMMAGED
SCRIMMAGER
SCRIMMAGES
SCRIPTURAL
SCROFULOUS
SCROLLWORK
SCROUNGERS
SCROUNGING
SCRUBBIEST
SCRUFFIEST
SCRUMMAGED
SCRUMMAGER
SCRUMMAGES
SCRUNCHING
SCRUPULOUS
SCRUTINEER
SCRUTINIES
SCRUTINIZE
SCULLERIES
SCULPTRESS
SCULPTURAL
SCULPTURED
SCULPTURES
SCUNTHORPE
SCUPPERING
SCURRILITY
SCURRILOUS

SCURVINESS
SCUTELLATE
SCYPHIFORM
SCYPHOZOAN
SEA
ANEMONE
SEABORGIUM
SEA
BREEZES
SEA
CAPTAIN
SEA
CHANGES
SEALED-
BEAM
SEALING
WAX
SEAMANLIKE
SEAMANSHIP
SEAMSTRESS
SEARCHABLE
SEA
SERPENT
SEASONABLE
SEASONABLY
SEASONEDLY
SEASONINGS
SEA
URCHINS
SEBIFEROUS
SEBORRHOEA
SECOND
BEST
SECOND-
HAND
SECONDMENT
SECOND-
RATE
SECOND
WIND
SECRETAIRE
SECRETIONS
SECTIONING
SECULARISM
SECULARIST
SECULARIZE
SECUNDINES
SECUREMENT
SECURENESS
SECURITIES

SEDAN
CHAIR
SEDATENESS
SEDUCINGLY
SEDUCTRESS
SEDULOUSLY
SEEMLINESS
SEERSUCKER
SEETHINGLY
SEE-
THROUGH
SEGMENTARY
SEGMENTING
SEGREGABLE
SEGREGATED
SEGREGATOR
SEISMICITY
SEISMOLOGY
SELECTIONS
SELECTNESS
SELENOLOGY
SELF-
ACTING
SELF-
ACTION
SELF-
DENIAL
SELF-
ESTEEM
SELF-
FEEDER
SELFLESSLY
SELF-
REGARD
SELF-
SEEKER
SELF-
STYLED
SELF-
WILLED
SELL-BY
DATE
SELLOTAPED
SEMAPHORES
SEMAPHORIC
SEMATOLOGY
SEMIANNUAL
SEMIBREVES
SEMICIRCLE
SEMICOLONS
SEMIFINALS
SEMINALITY

SEMINARIAL
SEMINARIAN
SEMINARIES
SEMIQUAVER
SEMIVOWELS
SEMIWEEKLY
SENATORIAL
SENEGALESE
SENEGAMBIA
SENESCENCE
SENSATIONS
SENSE
 ORGAN
SENSIBILIA
SENSITIZED
SENSITIZER
SENSUALISM
SENSUALIST
SENSUALITY
SENSUOUSLY
SENTENCING
SENTENTIAL
SENTIMENTS
SEPARATELY
SEPARATING
SEPARATION
SEPARATISM
SEPARATIST
SEPARATIVE
SEPARATORS
SEPARATRIX
SEPTENNIAL
SEPTICALLY
SEPTICIDAL
SEPTIC
 TANK
SEPTILLION
SEPULCHRAL
SEPULCHRES
SEQUACIOUS
SEQUENCING
SEQUENTIAL
SEQUESTRAL
SEQUESTRUM
SERBO-
 CROAT
SERENADING
SERENENESS
SERIALIZED
SERIGRAPHY
SERIOCOMIC

SERMONICAL
SERMONIZED
SERMONIZER
SEROLOGIST
SERPENTINE
SERVICEMAN
SERVICEMEN
SERVIETTES
SERVOMOTOR
SETSQUARES
SETTING
 OUT
SETTLEABLE
SETTLEMENT
SEVASTOPOL
SEVENTIETH
SEVERANCES
SEVERENESS
SEVERITIES
SEXAGENARY
SEXAGESIMA
SEXIVALENT
SEX
 OBJECTS
SEXOLOGIST
SEXPARTITE
SEXTILLION
SEXTUPLETS
SEYCHELLES
SHABBINESS
SHADOWIEST
SHAGGED
 OUT
SHAGGINESS
SHAKEDOWNS
SHALLOWEST
SHALLOWING
SHAMANISMS
SHAMANISTS
SHAMATEURS
SHAMEFACED
SHAMEFULLY
SHAMPOOING
SHANGHAIED
SHANTYTOWN
SHAPELIEST
SHARE
 PRICE
SHARPENERS
SHARPENING
SHATTERING
SHEARWATER

SHEATHBILL
SHEATHINGS
SHEEPISHLY
SHEEP'S
 EYES
SHEEPSHANK
SHEEPSHEAD
SHEEPSKINS
SHEET
 MUSIC
SHEIKHDOMS
SHELF
 LIVES
SHELLPROOF
SHELLSHOCK
SHELTERING
SHENANIGAN
SHEPHERDED
SHERARDIZE
SHERBROOKE
SHIBBOLETH
SHIFTINESS
SHIFTINGLY
SHIFT
 STICK
SHILLELAGH
SHIMMERING
SHIPBOARDS
SHIPMASTER
SHIP-
 RIGGED
SHIPWRECKS
SHIPWRIGHT
SHIRE
 HORSE
SHIRTFRONT
SHIRTTAILS
SHISH
 KEBAB
SHOALINESS
SHOCKINGLY
SHOCKPROOF
SHODDINESS
SHOEMAKING
SHOESHINES
SHOESTRING
SHOGUN
 BOND
SHOOT A
 LINE
SHOPAHOLIC
SHOPKEEPER

SHOPLIFTED
SHOPLIFTER
SHOPSOILED
SHOPWALKER
SHOPWORKER
SHORE
 LEAVE
SHOREWARDS
SHORTBREAD
SHORTENING
SHORTFALLS
SHORT
 LISTS
SHORT-
 LIVED
SHORT-
 RANGE
SHORT
 STORY
SHOULDERED
SHOVELHEAD
SHOVELLING
SHOVELNOSE
SHOW
 JUMPER
SHOWPIECES
SHOW
 TRIALS
SHREVEPORT
SHREWDNESS
SHREWISHLY
SHREWSBURY
SHRIEVALTY
SHRILLNESS
SHRINKABLE
SHRINK-
 WRAP
SHRIVELING
SHRIVELLED
SHROPSHIRE
SHROUD-
 LAID
SHROVETIDE
SHUDDERING
SHUNT-
 WOUND
SHUTTERING
SIALAGOGIC
SIALAGOGUE
SIAMESE
 CAT
SIBILATION

SICKLEBILL
SICKLINESS
SICKNESSES
SICK
 PARADE
SIDEBOARDS
SIDE
 DISHES
SIDE
 EFFECT
SIDE
 ISSUES
SIDELIGHTS
SIDELINING
SIDE
 ORDERS
SIDEROLITE
SIDEROSTAT
SIDESADDLE
SIDE
 STREET
SIDESTROKE
SIDESWIPED
SIDESWIPER
SIDESWIPES
SIDETRACKS
SIDEWINDER
SIGHTSEERS
SIGNALIZED
SIGNALLING
SIGNATURES
SIGNIFYING
SIGNORINAS
SIGNPOSTED
SILENTNESS
SILHOUETTE
SILICULOSE
SILK
 SCREEN
SILLY
 BILLY
SILVERFISH
SILVERWARE
SILVERWEED
SIMFEROPOL
SIMILARITY
SIMILITUDE
SIMONIACAL
SIMPLE
 LIFE
SIMPLENESS
SIMPLETONS

SIMPLICITY
SIMPLIFIED
SIMPLIFIER
SIMPLISTIC
SIMULACRUM
SIMULATING
SIMULATION
SIMULATIVE
SIMULATORS
SINCIPITAL
SINECURISM
SINECURIST
SINE QUA
    NON
SINEWINESS
SINFULNESS
SINGHALESE
SINGLE
    FILE
SINGLENESS
SINGLETONS
SINGULARLY
SINHAILIEN
SINISTROUS
SINN
    FEINER
SINOLOGIST
SINUSOIDAL
SISTERHOOD
SITOSTEROL
SITUATIONS
SIX-
    FOOTERS
SIX-
    SHOOTER
SIXTEENTHS
SIXTH
    FORMS
SIXTH
    SENSE
SKATEBOARD
SKEDADDLED
SKEPTICISM
SKETCHABLE
SKETCHBOOK
SKETCHIEST
SKETCHPADS
SKIMPINESS
SKIN
    DIVERS
SKIN
    DIVING

SKIN
    FLICKS
SKINFLINTS
SKIN
    GRAFTS
SKINNINESS
SKIPPERING
SKIRMISHED
SKIRMISHER
SKIRMISHES
SKITTERING
SKITTISHLY
SKYJACKERS
SKYJACKING
SKYLARKING
SKYROCKETS
SKYSCRAPER
SKYWRITING
SLACKENING
SLANDERERS
SLANDERING
SLANDEROUS
SLANGINESS
SLANTINGLY
SLASHINGLY
SLATTERNLY
SLAVE
    TRADE
SLAVOPHILE
SLEAZINESS
SLEEPINESS
SLEEPYHEAD
SLEEVELESS
SLENDERIZE
SLIDE
    RULES
SLIGHTNESS
SLINGSHOTS
SLINKINESS
SLINKINGLY
SLIPPINESS
SLIPPINGLY
SLIPSTREAM
SLITHERING
SLOBBERING
SLOPPINESS
SLOPWORKER
SLOTHFULLY
SLOUCH
    HATS
SLOW
    MOTION

SLOW-
    WITTED
SLUGGISHLY
SLUICEGATE
SLUMBERERS
SLUMBERING
SLUMBEROUS
SLUSH
    FUNDS
SLUSHINESS
SMALL
    HOURS
SMALL
    PRINT
SMALL-
    SCALE
SMALL-
    TIMER
SMARAGDITE
SMART
    ALECK
SMARTENING
SMARTINGLY
SMATTERING
SMEARINESS
SMEAR
    TESTS
SMELLINESS
SMIRKINGLY
SMOKEHOUSE
SMOKESTACK
SMOLDERING
SMOOTHABLE
SMOOTHBORE
SMOOTHNESS
SMOTHERING
SMOULDERED
SMUDGINESS
SMUTTINESS
SNAIL'S
    PACE
SNAKEMOUTH
SNAPDRAGON
SNAPPINESS
SNAPPINGLY
SNAPPISHLY
SNARE
    DRUMS
SNARLINGLY
SNAZZINESS
SNEAKINESS
SNEAKINGLY

SNEAK
    THIEF
SNEERINGLY
SNEEZEWORT
SNICKERING
SNIFFINGLY
SNIGGERING
SNIPPINESS
SNIVELLERS
SNIVELLING
SNOBBISHLY
SNOOKERING
SNOOTINESS
SNORKELLED
SNORTINGLY
SNOTTINESS
SNOWBALLED
SNOW-
    CAPPED
SNOWDRIFTS
SNOWFIELDS
SNOWFLAKES
SNOWMAKING
SNOWMOBILE
SNOWPLOUGH
SNOWSTORMS
SNUBBINGLY
SNUFFINESS
SNUFFINGLY
SOAP
    BUBBLE
SOAP
    OPERAS
SOBERINGLY
SOBRIQUETS
SOB
    STORIES
SOCIALISTS
SOCIALITES
SOCIALIZED
SOCIALIZER
SOCIALNESS
SOCIAL
    WORK
SOCIOMETRY
SOCIOPATHY
SODDENNESS
SOFT-
    BOILED
SOFT-
    FINNED

SOFT
    FRUITS
SOFT-
    HEADED
SOFT
    OPTION
SOFT
    PALATE
SOFT-
    SOAPED
SOFT-
    SPOKEN
SOJOURNERS
SOJOURNING
SOLAR
    CELLS
SOLAR
    PANEL
SOLAR
    YEARS
SOLDERABLE
SOLDIERING
SOLECISTIC
SOLEMNIZED
SOLEMNIZER
SOLEMNNESS
SOLENOIDAL
SOLFATARIC
SOLICITING
SOLICITORS
SOLICITOUS
SOLICITUDE
SOLIDARITY
SOLIDIFIED
SOLIDIFIER
SOLID-
    STATE
SOLITAIRES
SOLITARIES
SOLITARILY
SOLSTITIAL
SOLUBILITY
SOLUBILIZE
SOLVOLYSIS
SOMALILAND
SOMATOLOGY
SOMATOTYPE
SOMBRENESS
SOMERSAULT
SOMNOLENCE
SONGSTRESS
SONGWRITER

SONIC
  BOOMS
SONIFEROUS
SONOROUSLY
SONS-OF-
  GUNS
SOOTHINGLY
SOOTHSAYER
SOPHOMORES
SORDIDNESS
SORORICIDE
SORORITIES
SOUBRIQUET
SOULLESSLY
SOUNDPROOF
SOUNDTRACK
SOUP
  SPOONS
SOUR
  GRAPES
SOURPUSSES
SOUSAPHONE
SOUTHBOUND
SOUTH
  DOWNS
SOUTHERNER
SOUTH
  KOREA
SOUTHWARDS
SOU'WESTER
  S
SOVEREIGNS
SPACECRAFT
SPACE
  PROBE
SPACESHIPS
SPACESUITS
SPACEWOMAN
SPACIOUSLY
SPADICEOUS
SPALLATION
SPARE
  PARTS
SPARE
  TYRES
SPARK
  PLUGS
SPARSENESS
SPARTANISM
SPATCHCOCK
SPATIALITY
SPATTERING

SPEARHEADS
SPECIALISM
SPECIALIST
SPECIALITY
SPECIALIZE
SPECIATION
SPECIESISM
SPECIFYING
SPECIOSITY
SPECIOUSLY
SPECTACLES
SPECTATING
SPECTATORS
SPECULATED
SPECULATOR
SPEECH
  DAYS
SPEECHLESS
SPEEDBOATS
SPEEDINESS
SPEED
  LIMIT
SPEED
  TRAPS
SPELEOLOGY
SPELLBOUND
SPELUNKING
SPEND
  LIMIT
SPERMACETI
SPERMATIUM
SPERMICIDE
SPERM
  WHALE
SPERRYLITE
SPHALERITE
SPHENOIDAL
SPHERICITY
SPHEROIDAL
SPHERULITE
SPHINCTERS
SPICEBERRY
SPIDERWEBS
SPIDERWORT
SPINAL
  CORD
SPINDLIEST
SPIN-
  DRYING
SPINESCENT
SPINNAKERS
SPIRACULAR

SPIRALLING
SPIRITEDLY
SPIRITLESS
SPIRITUALS
SPIRITUOUS
SPIROGRAPH
SPIROMETER
SPIROMETRY
SPITEFULLY
SPLANCHNIC
SPLASHBACK
SPLASH
  BACK
SPLASHDOWN
SPLASHIEST
SPLATTERED
SPLEENWORT
SPLENDIDLY
SPLINTERED
SPLIT
  HAIRS
SPLIT
  LEVEL
SPLIT-
  LEVEL
SPLIT
  RINGS
SPLUTTERED
SPLUTTERER
SPOILSPORT
SPOKESHAVE
SPOLIATION
SPONGE
  BAGS
SPONGE
  CAKE
SPONGINESS
SPONSORIAL
SPONSORING
SPOOKINESS
SPOONERISM
SPORANGIAL
SPORANGIUM
SPOROPHORE
SPOROPHYLL
SPOROPHYTE
SPOROZOITE
SPORTINESS
SPORTINGLY
SPORTIVELY
SPORTS
  CARS

SPORTSWEAR
SPOT
  CHECKS
SPOTLESSLY
SPOTLIGHTS
SPOTTINESS
SPREADABLE
SPRINGBOKS
SPRINGHAAS
SPRINGHEAD
SPRINGIEST
SPRING
  ROLL
SPRINGTAIL
SPRING
  TIDE
SPRINGTIME
SPRINGWOOD
SPRINKLERS
SPRINKLING
SPRUCENESS
SPUMESCENT
SPUNKINESS
SPURIOUSLY
SPUTTERING
SPYGLASSES
SQUABBLING
SQUALIDITY
SQUALLIEST
SQUAMATION
SQUAMULOSE
SQUANDERED
SQUANDERER
SQUARE
  DEAL
SQUARE
  KNOT
SQUARE
  MEAL
SQUARENESS
SQUARE
  ROOT
SQUASHIEST
SQUEAKIEST
SQUEEZABLE
SQUEEZEBOX
SQUELCHIER
SQUELCHING
SQUETEAGUE
SQUIDGIEST
SQUIFFIEST
SQUISHIEST

STABILATOR
STABILIZED
STABILIZER
STABLE
  BOYS
STABLEFORD
STABLENESS
STAFF
  NURSE
STAG
  BEETLE
STAGECOACH
STAGECRAFT
STAGE
  DOORS
STAGEHANDS
STAGE
  NAMES
STAGGERING
STAGNANTLY
STAGNATING
STAGNATION
STAIRCASES
STAIRWELLS
STALACTITE
STALAGMITE
STALEMATED
STALEMATES
STALKINESS
STALWARTLY
STAMMERERS
STAMMERING
STAMPEDING
STANCHABLE
STANCHIONS
STANDPIPES
STANDPOINT
STANDSTILL
STARCHIEST
STARFISHES
STARFLOWER
STARGAZERS
STARGAZING
STARRINESS
STARRY-
  EYED
STARVATION
STARVELING
STATECRAFT
STATEMENTS
STATEROOMS
STATIONARY

STATIONERS
STATIONERY
STATIONING
STATISTICS
STATOBLAST
STATOSCOPE
STATUESQUE
STATUETTES
STATUS
ZERO
STATUTABLE
STATUTE
LAW
STAUNCHEST
STAUNCHING
STAUROLITE
STAVESACRE
STAY-AT-
HOME
ST
BERNARDS
STEADINESS
STEAKHOUSE
STEALTHIER
STEALTHILY
STEAMBOATS
STEAM-
CHEST
STEAMINESS
STEAM
IRONS
STEAMSHIPS
STEAMTIGHT
STEEL
BANDS
STEELINESS
STEELWORKS
STEEPENING
STELLIFORM
STEM-
WINDER
STENCILING
STENCILLED
STENCILLER
STENOGRAPH
STENOTYPIC
STENTORIAN
STEPFAMILY
STEPFATHER
STEPLADDER
STEPMOTHER
STEPPARENT

STEPSISTER
STEREOBATE
STEREOGRAM
STEREOPSIS
STEREOTOMY
STEREOTYPE
STEREOTYPY
STERICALLY
STERILIZED
STERILIZER
STERNWARDS
STERTOROUS
STEVEDORES
STEWARDESS
STICKINESS
STICK
SHIFT
STICKTIGHT
STICKY
ENDS
STIFFENERS
STIFFENING
STIFLINGLY
STIGMATISM
STIGMATIST
STIGMATIZE
STILLBIRTH
STILL
LIFES
STIMULABLE
STIMULANTS
STIMULATED
STIMULATOR
STINGINESS
STINGINGLY
STINK-
BOMBS
STINKINGLY
STINKSTONE
STIPELLATE
STIPULABLE
STIPULATED
STIPULATOR
STIR-
FRYING
STIRRINGLY
STIRRUP
CUP
STITCHWORT
STOCHASTIC
STOCKADING

STOCK
CUBES
STOCKINESS
STOCKPILED
STOCKPILER
STOCKPILES
STOCKROOMS
STOCK-
STILL
STOCKYARDS
STODGINESS
STOKEHOLDS
STOMACHING
STOMATITIC
STOMATITIS
STOMATOPOD
STOMODAEAL
STOMODAEUM
STONE-
BLIND
STONE
FRUIT
STONEHENGE
STONEMASON
STONY
BROKE
STOOPINGLY
STOPPERING
STOREHOUSE
STOREROOMS
STORKSBILL
STORMBOUND
STORM
CLOUD
STORMINESS
STORMPROOF
STORY
LINES
STRABISMAL
STRABISMUS
STRADDLING
STRAGGLERS
STRAGGLIER
STRAGGLING
STRAIGHTEN
STRAIGHTER
STRAITENED
STRAITNESS
STRAMONIUM
STRANGLERS
STRANGLING
STRASBOURG

STRATAGEMS
STRATEGICS
STRATEGIES
STRATEGIST
STRATIFIED
STRATIFORM
STRATOCRAT
STRAWBERRY
STRAWBOARD
STRAW
POLLS
STREAKIEST
STREAMLINE
STREET
ARAB
STREETCARS
STREETWISE
STRELITZIA
STRENGTHEN
STRESS
MARK
STRETCHERS
STRETCHIER
STRETCHING
STRIATIONS
STRICTNESS
STRICTURES
STRIDENTLY
STRIDULATE
STRIDULOUS
STRIGIFORM
STRIKINGLY
STRING
BEAN
STRINGENCY
STRINGENDO
STRINGHALT
STRINGIEST
STRIPAGRAM
STRIP
CLUBS
STRIPLINGS
STRIPTEASE
STROKE
PLAY
STRONGHOLD
STRONGNESS
STRONG
ROOM
STROPPIEST
STRUCTURAL
STRUCTURED

STRUCTURES
STRUGGLING
STRUTHIOUS
STRYCHNINE
STUBBINESS
STUBBORNER
STUBBORNLY
STUDIOUSLY
STUFFINESS
STULTIFIED
STULTIFIER
STUMPINESS
STUNNINGLY
STUPEFYING
STUPENDOUS
STUPIDNESS
STURDINESS
STUTTERERS
STUTTERING
STYLISTICS
STYLOGRAPH
STYLOLITIC
STYPTICITY
SUBACETATE
SUBACIDITY
SUBALTERNS
SUBAQUATIC
SUBAQUEOUS
SUBCALIBRE
SUBCLAVIAN
SUBCOMPACT
SUBCULTURE
SUBDIVIDED
SUBDIVIDER
SUBDUCTION
SUBEDITING
SUBEDITORS
SUBGENERIC
SUBGLACIAL
SUBHEADING
SUBJACENCY
SUBJECTIFY
SUBJECTING
SUBJECTION
SUBJECTIVE
SUBJOINING
SUBJUGABLE
SUBJUGATED
SUBJUGATOR
SUBKINGDOM
SUBLEASING

SUBLETTING
SUBLIMABLE
SUBLIMATED
SUBLIMATES
SUBLIMINAL
SUBLINGUAL
SUBMARINER
SUBMARINES
SUBMEDIANT
SUBMERGING
SUBMERSION
SUBMISSION
SUBMISSIVE
SUBMITTING
SUBMONTANE
SUBOCEANIC
SUBOPTIMAL
SUBORBITAL
SUBORDINAL
SUBPOENAED
SUBPROGRAM
SUBREPTION
SUBROUTINE
SUB-
  SAHARAN
SUBSCRIBED
SUBSCRIBER
SUBSECTION
SUBSEQUENT
SUBSIDENCE
SUBSIDIARY
SUBSIDIZED
SUBSIDIZER
SUBSISTENT
SUBSISTING
SUBSPECIES
SUBSTANCES
SUBSTATION
SUBSTITUTE
SUBSTRATUM
SUBSUMABLE
SUBTANGENT
SUBTENANCY
SUBTENANTS
SUBTENDING
SUBTERFUGE
SUBTILIZER
SUBTITULAR
SUBTLENESS
SUBTLETIES
SUBTRACTED

SUBTRACTER
SUBTRAHEND
SUBTROPICS
SUBTYPICAL
SUBVENTION
SUBVERSION
SUBVERSIVE
SUBVERTING
SUCCEEDING
SUCCESSFUL
SUCCESSION
SUCCESSIVE
SUCCESSORS
SUCCINCTLY
SUCCOURING
SUCCULENCE
SUCCULENTS
SUCCUMBING
SUCCUSSION
SUCCUSSIVE
SUCKERFISH
SUCKING
  PIG
SUDDENNESS
SUFFERABLE
SUFFERANCE
SUFFERINGS
SUFFICIENT
SUFFOCATED
SUFFRAGISM
SUFFRAGIST
SUGAR
  DADDY
SUGARINESS
SUGGESTING
SUGGESTION
SUGGESTIVE
SUICIDALLY
SULLENNESS
SULPHA
  DRUG
SULPHATION
SULPHONATE
SULPHURATE
SULPHURIZE
SULPHUROUS
SULTANATES
SULTRINESS
SUMMARIZED
SUMMARIZER
SUMMATIONS

SUMMERTIME
SUMMERWOOD
SUMMINGS-
  UP
SUMMONABLE
SUMMONSING
SUNBATHERS
SUNBATHING
SUNDAY
  BEST
SUNDERLAND
SUNDOWNERS
SUNFLOWERS
SUNGLASSES
SUNLOUNGER
SUN
  LOUNGES
SUPERBNESS
SUPERCARGO
SUPERCLASS
SUPERDUPER
SUPER
  DUPER
SUPERFLUID
SUPERGIANT
SUPERGRASS
SUPERHUMAN
SUPERLUNAR
SUPERMODEL
SUPERNOVAS
SUPERORDER
SUPEROXIDE
SUPERPOWER
SUPERSEDED
SUPERSEDER
SUPERSONIC
SUPERSTARS
SUPERTONIC
SUPERVENED
SUPERVISED
SUPERVISOR
SUPINENESS
SUPPLANTED
SUPPLANTER
SUPPLEJACK
SUPPLEMENT
SUPPLENESS
SUPPLETION
SUPPLETIVE
SUPPLETORY
SUPPLIABLE
SUPPLIANCE

SUPPLIANTS
SUPPLICANT
SUPPLICATE
SUPPORTERS
SUPPORTING
SUPPORTIVE
SUPPOSABLE
SUPPOSEDLY
SUPPRESSED
SUPPRESSOR
SUPPURATED
SUPRARENAL
SURCHARGED
SURCHARGER
SURCHARGES
SUREFOOTED
SURFACTANT
SURFBOARDS
SURFCASTER
SURFEITING
SURGICALLY
SURINAMESE
SURJECTION
SURJECTIVE
SURMISABLE
SURMISEDLY
SURMOUNTED
SURMOUNTER
SURPASSING
SURPLUSAGE
SURPRISING
SURREALISM
SURREALIST
SURRENDERS
SURROGATES
SURROUNDED
SURVEYABLE
SURVIVABLE
SUSCEPTIVE
SUSPECTING
SUSPENDERS
SUSPENDING
SUSPENSION
SUSPENSIVE
SUSPENSOID
SUSPENSORY
SUSPICIONS
SUSPICIOUS
SUSTAINING
SUSTENANCE
SUSTENTION

SUTHERLAND
SUZERAINTY
SVERDLOVSK
SWAGGERERS
SWAGGERING
SWALLOWING
SWANKINESS
SWAN-
  UPPING
SWARTHIEST
SWASHINGLY
SWEARINGLY
SWEARWORDS
SWEATBANDS
SWEAT
  GLAND
SWEATINESS
SWEATSHIRT
SWEATSHOPS
SWEEPINGLY
SWEEPSTAKE
SWEETBREAD
SWEETBRIER
SWEETENERS
SWEETENING
SWEETHEART
SWEETMEATS
SWEET
  TOOTH
SWELTERING
SWERVINGLY
SWIMMINGLY
SWINEHERDS
SWINGINGLY
SWING
  SHIFT
SWIRLINGLY
SWISHINGLY
SWISS
  CHARD
SWITCHABLE
SWITCHBACK
SWITCH
  CARD
SWITCHED-
  ON
SWITCHGEAR
SWIVELLING
SWOONINGLY
SWORDCRAFT
SWORD
  DANCE

SWORDSTICK
SYCOPHANTS
SYLLABUSES
SYLLOGISMS
SYLLOGIZER
SYLPHIDINE
SYLVESTRAL
SYMBIONTIC
SYMBOLIZED
SYMMETRIZE
SYMPATHIES
SYMPATHIZE
SYMPHONIES
SYMPHONIST
SYMPHYSIAL
SYMPHYSTIC
SYMPOSIUMS
SYNAGOGUES
SYNCARPOUS
SYNCHRONIC
SYNCLASTIC
SYNCOPATED
SYNCOPATOR
SYNCRETISM
SYNCRETIST
SYNCRETIZE
SYNDICATED
SYNDICATES
SYNDICSHIP
SYNECDOCHE
SYNECOLOGY
SYNERGETIC
SYNOECIOUS
SYNONYMITY
SYNONYMIZE
SYNONYMOUS
SYNTACTICS
SYNTHESIST
SYNTHESIZE
SYNTHETISM
SYNTHETIST
SYPHILITIC
SYSTEMATIC
SYSTEMIZER

T
TABERNACLE
TABESCENCE
TABLECLOTH
TABLE
 D'HOTE

TABLELANDS
TABLE
 LINEN
TABLESPOON
TABULARIZE
TABULATING
TABULATION
TACHOGRAPH
TACHOMETER
TACHOMETRY
TACHYLYTIC
TACHYMETER
TACHYMETRY
TACITURNLY
TACTICALLY
TACTICIANS
TACTLESSLY
TAENIACIDE
TAENIAFUGE
TAGLIATELE
TAILBOARDS
TAILGATING
TAILLIGHTS
TAILORBIRD
TAILOR-
 MADE
TAILPIECES
TAJIKISTAN
TAKE IN
 HAND
TAKINGNESS
TALCAHUANO
TALEBEARER
TALISMANIC
TALKING-
 TOS
TAMABILITY
TAMAULIPAS
TAMBOURINE
TANANARIVE
TANGANYIKA
TANGENTIAL
TANGERINES
TANGLEMENT
TANTALIZED
TANTALIZER
TANTALUSES
TANTAMOUNT
TAP
 DANCERS
TAP
 DANCING

TAPERINGLY
TAPESTRIED
TAPESTRIES
TARANTELLA
TARANTULAS
TARDIGRADE
TARMACKING
TARNISHING
TARPAULINS
TASIMETRIC
TASK
 FORCES
TASKMASTER
TASTEFULLY
TATTERSALL
TATTLETALE
TATTLINGLY
TATTOOISTS
TAUNTINGLY
TAUROMACHY
TAUTOMERIC
TAUTONYMIC
TAWDRINESS
TAXABILITY
TAXATIONAL
TAXIDERMAL
TAXIMETERS
TAXONOMIST
TAX
 SHELTER
TEA
 CADDIES
TEAGARDENS
TEAM
 SPIRIT
TEA
 PARTIES
TEARJERKER
TEA
 SERVICE
TEA
 TROLLEY
TECHNETIUM
TECHNICIAN
TECHNIQUES
TECHNOCRAT
TECHNOLOGY
TECTRICIAL
TEDDY
 BEARS
TEENY
 WEENY

TELECASTER
TELEGNOSIS
TELEGRAPHS
TELEGRAPHY
TELEMETRIC
TELEPATHIC
TELEPHONED
TELEPHONER
TELEPHONES
TELESCOPED
TELESCOPES
TELESCOPIC
TELESCRIPT
TELEVISING
TELEVISION
TELEVISUAL
TELEWRITER
TELIOSPORE
TELLING-
 OFF
TELOPHASIC
TELPHERAGE
TEMPERABLE
TEMPERANCE
TEMPORIZED
TEMPORIZER
TEMPTATION
TEMPTINGLY
TENABILITY
TENDENCIES
TENDERABLE
TENDERFEET
TENDERFOOT
TENDERIZED
TENDERIZER
TENDERLOIN
TENDERNESS
TENDRILLAR
TENEMENTAL
TENGRI
 KHAN
TENNESSEAN
TENOTOMIST
TENSIMETER
TENTACULAR
TENTERHOOK
TERATOLOGY
TERENGGANU
TERMAGANCY
TERMAGANTS
TERMINABLE

TERMINALLY
TERMINATED
TERMINATOR
TERMINUSES
TERRACOTTA
TERRA
 FIRMA
TERRAMYCIN
TERREPLEIN
TERRE-
 VERTE
TERRIFYING
TERRORISTS
TERRORIZED
TERRORIZER
TERRYCLOTH
TESSELLATE
TESTACEOUS
TESTAMENTS
TESTICULAR
TESTIFYING
TEST
 PILOTS
TESTUDINAL
TETCHINESS
TETE-A-
 TETES
TETRABASIC
TETRABRACH
TETRACHORD
TETRAGONAL
TETRAPLOID
TETRAPODIC
TETRARCHIC
TETRASPORE
TETRASTICH
TETRATOMIC
TEWKESBURY
TEXTUALISM
TEXTUALIST
TEXTURALLY
THANKFULLY
THEATRICAL
THEME
 PARKS
THEME
 SONGS
THEMSELVES
THENARDITE
THEOCRATIC
THEODOLITE
THEOLOGIAN

THEOLOGIES
THEOLOGIZE
THEOPHOBIA
THEORETICS
THEORIZING
THEOSOPHIC
THERAPISTS
THEREAFTER
THEREUNDER
THERMALIZE
THERMIONIC
THERMISTOR
THERMOGRAM
THERMOPILE
THERMOSTAT
THEROPODAN
THESSALIAN
THETICALLY
THICKENERS
THICKENING
THIEVINGLY
THIEVISHLY
THIMBLEFUL
THIMEROSAL
THINK
  TANKS
THIOURACIL
THIRD
  PARTY
THIRD
  WORLD
THIRSTIEST
THIRTEENTH
THIRTIETHS
THIXOTROPY
THORIANITE
THORNINESS
THOROUGHLY
THOUGHTFUL
THOUGHT-
  OUT
THOUSANDTH
THRASH
  PUNK
THREADBARE
THREADWORM
THREATENED
THREATENER
THREEPENCE
THREE-
  PHASE

THREE-
  PIECE
THREESOMES
THRENODIES
THRESHOLDS
THRIFTIEST
THRIFTLESS
THROATIEST
THROATLASH
THROMBOGEN
THROMBOSES
THROMBOSIS
THROMBOTIC
THROTTLING
THROUGHOUT
THROUGHPUT
THROUGHWAY
THROWBACKS
THUMBNAILS
THUMBSCREW
THUMBSTALL
THUMBTACKS
THUMPINGLY
THUNDER
  BAY
THUNDERERS
THUNDERFLY
THUNDERING
THUNDEROUS
THURINGIAN
THWARTEDLY
TICKERTAPE
TICKING
  OFF
TICKLISHLY
TIDAL
  WAVES
TIEBREAKER
TIED
  HOUSES
TIEMANNITE
TIGHTENING
TIGHTROPES
TIGLIC
  ACID
TILIACEOUS
TILLANDSIA
TIMBERHEAD
TIMBERLINE
TIMBERWORK
TIMBERYARD
TIMEKEEPER

TIMELESSLY
TIME
  LIMITS
TIMELINESS
TIMEPIECES
TIMESAVING
TIME-
  SAVING
TIMESERVER
TIME
  SHEETS
TIME
  SIGNAL
TIME
  SWITCH
TIMETABLED
TIMETABLES
TIMEWORKER
TIMOROUSLY
TIMPANISTS
TINCTORIAL
TINGALINGS
TINGLINGLY
TIN
  OPENERS
TIRELESSLY
TIRESOMELY
TITANESQUE
TITILLATED
TITIVATING
TITIVATION
TITLE
  DEEDS
TITLE
  PAGES
TITLE
  ROLES
TITRATABLE
TITUBATION
T-
  JUNCTION
  S
TOADSTOOLS
TOBOGGANED
TOBOGGANER
TOCOPHEROL
TOILETRIES
TOILET
  ROLL
TOLERANTLY
TOLERATING
TOLERATION

TOLERATIVE
TOLLBOOTHS
TOLLUIDINE
TOLUIC
  ACID
TOMBSTONES
TOMFOOLERY
TOMOGRAPHY
TONALITIES
TONELESSLY
TONGUE-
  TIED
TONIC SOL-
  FA
TONIC
  WATER
TONOMETRIC
TOOL-
  MAKING
TOOTHACHES
TOOTHBRUSH
TOOTHCOMBS
TOOTHINESS
TOOTHPASTE
TOOTHPICKS
TOPAZOLITE
TOPGALLANT
TOP-
  HEAVILY
TOPICALITY
TOPOGRAPHY
TOPOLOGIST
TOPPING
  OUT
TOPSY-
  TURVY
TORBERNITE
TORCHLIGHT
TORMENTING
TORMENTORS
TORPEDOING
TORRENTIAL
TORTELLINI
TORT-
  FEASOR
TORTUOSITY
TORTUOUSLY
TORTUREDLY
TOTEMISTIC
TOTEM
  POLES
TOTIPOTENT

TOUCH-AND-
  GO
TOUCHDOWNS
TOUCHINESS
TOUCHINGLY
TOUCHLINES
TOUCHPAPER
TOUCHSTONE
TOUCH-
  TYPED
TOUGHENING
TOURMALINE
TOURNAMENT
TOURNIQUET
TOWER
  BLOCK
TOWN
  CLERKS
TOWN
  CRIERS
TOWN
  HOUSES
TOWNSCAPES
TOWNSVILLE
TOWNSWOMAN
TOXALBUMIN
TOXICOLOGY
TRABEATION
TRABECULAR
TRACHEIDAL
TRACHEITIS
TRACHYTOID
TRACK
  EVENT
TRACKLAYER
TRACKSUITS
TRACTILITY
TRACTIONAL
TRADEMARKS
TRADE
  NAMES
TRADE
  PRICE
TRADE
  ROUTE
TRADE
  UNION
TRADE
  WINDS
TRADITIONS
TRADUCIBLE

TRAFFIC JAM	TRASHINESS	TRIFLINGLY	TROMBONIST	TUBULARITY
TRAFFICKED	TRAUMATISM	TRIFOLIATE	TROOPSHIPS	TUBULATION
TRAFFICKER	TRAUMATIZE	TRIFURCATE	TROPAEOLIN	TUFFACEOUS
TRAGACANTH	TRAVAILING	TRIGEMINAL	TROPAEOLUM	TUGS-OF-LOVE
TRAGEDIANS	TRAVELLERS	TRIGGERING	TROPICALLY	TULARAEMIA
TRAGICALLY	TRAVELLING	TRIGLYPHIC	TROPICBIRD	TULARAEMIC
TRAGICOMIC	TRAVELOGUE	TRIGRAPHIC	TROPOLOGIC	TUMBLEDOWN
TRAILINGLY	TRAVELSICK	TRIHYDRATE	TROPOPAUSE	TUMBLEWEED
TRAITOROUS	TRAVERSING	TRILATERAL	TROPOPHYTE	TUMESCENCE
TRAJECTILE	TRAVERTINE	TRILINGUAL	TROTSKYISM	TUMULOSITY
TRAJECTION	TRAVESTIES	TRILITERAL	TROTSKYIST	TUMULTUOUS
TRAJECTORY	TREADMILLS	TRILLIONTH	TROTSKYITE	TUNELESSLY
TRAMONTANE	TREAD WATER	TRILOBITES	TROUBADOUR	TUNING FORK
TRAMPOLINE	TREASURERS	TRILOCULAR	TROUBLEDLY	TUNING PEGS
TRANCELIKE	TREASURIES	TRIMESTERS	TROUSSEAUS	TUNNELLING
TRANQUILLY	TREASURING	TRIMESTRAL	TROUSSEAUX	TUPPERWARE
TRANSACTED	TREATMENTS	TRIMONTHLY	TROWBRIDGE	TURBOPROPS
TRANSACTOR	TREBLE CLEF	TRIMORPHIC	TROY WEIGHT	TURBULENCE
TRANSCRIBE	TREEHOPPER	TRINOCULAR	TRUCK FARMS	TURGESCENT
TRANSCRIPT	TREMENDOUS	TRIOECIOUS	TRUCKLOADS	TURNABOUTS
TRANSDUCER	TRENCHANCY	TRIPARTITE	TRUCK STOPS	TURNAROUND
TRANSEPTAL	TRENCH COAT	TRIPHAMMER	TRUCULENCE	TURNBUCKLE
TRANSFEREE	TRENDINESS	TRIPHTHONG	TRUMP CARDS	TURNROUNDS
TRANSFEROR	TREPANNING	TRIPHYLITE	TRUMPETERS	TURNSTILES
TRANSFIXED	TREPHINING	TRIPINNATE	TRUMPETING	TURNTABLES
TRANSGRESS	TREPPANNER	TRIPLE JUMP	TRUNCATING	TURPENTINE
TRANSIENCE	TRESPASSED	TRIPLETAIL	TRUNCATION	TURQUOISES
TRANSIENCY	TRESPASSER	TRIPLICATE	TRUNCHEONS	TURTLEBACK
TRANSISTOR	TRESPASSES	TRIPLICITY	TRUNK CALLS	TURTLEDOVE
TRANSITION	TRIANGULAR	TRIPPINGLY	TRUNK ROADS	TURTLENECK
TRANSITIVE	TRIBRACHIC	TRIPTEROUS	TRUNK ROUTE	TUT-TUTTING
TRANSITORY	TRICHIASIS	TRIRADIATE	TRUSTFULLY	TWELVE-TONE
TRANSKEIAN	TRICHINIZE	TRISECTING	TRUST FUNDS	TWENTIETHS
TRANSLATED	TRICHINOUS	TRISKELION	TRUSTINESS	TWIN-BEDDED
TRANSLATOR	TRICHOCYST	TRISTICHIC	TRUTHFULLY	TWINFLOWER
TRANSLUNAR	TRICHOGYNE	TRITANOPIA	TRUTH-VALUE	TWINKLINGS
TRANSMUTED	TRICHOLOGY	TRITANOPIC	TRYINGNESS	TWISTINGLY
TRANSMUTER	TRICHOTOMY	TRITURABLE	TRYPTOPHAN	TWITTERING
TRANSPIRED	TRICHROISM	TRITURATOR	TUBERCULAR	TYMPANITES
TRANSPLANT	TRICHROMAT	TRIUMPHANT	TUBERCULIN	TYMPANITIC
TRANSPOLAR	TRICKINESS	TRIUMPHING	TUBEROSITY	TYMPANITIS
TRANSPORTS	TRICKINGLY	TRIVALENCY	TUB-THUMPER	TYPECASTER
TRANSPOSED	TRICKSTERS	TRIVANDRUM		TYPESCRIPT
TRANSPOSER	TRICOLOURS	TRIVIALITY		TYPESETTER
TRANSPUTER	TRICOSTATE	TRIVIALIZE		TYPE SETTER
TRANSUDATE	TRICROTISM	TROCHANTER		
TRANSVALUE	TRIDENTATE	TROGLODYTE		
TRANSVERSE	TRIDENTINE	TROLLEYBUS		
TRAPEZIUMS		TROLLEY BUS		
TRAPEZOIDS				

279

TYPEWRITER
TYPHLOLOGY
TYPHOGENIC
TYPING
  POOL
TYPOGRAPHY
TYPOLOGIST
TYRANNICAL
TYRANNIZED
TYRANNIZER
TYROCIDINE
TYROSINASE

U

UBIQUITOUS
ULCERATING
ULCERATION
ULCERATIVE
ULTIMATELY
ULTIMATUMS
ULTRAFICHE
ULTRAISTIC
ULTRASHORT
ULTRASONIC
ULTRASOUND
ULTRAVIRUS
UMBILICATE
UMBILIFORM
UMBRAGEOUS
UMPIRESHIP
UMPTEENTHS
UNABRIDGED
UNACCENTED
UNADJUSTED
UNAFFECTED
UN-
  AMERICAN
UNASSISTED
UNASSUMING
UNATTACHED
UNATTENDED
UNAVAILING
UNBALANCED
UNBEARABLE
UNBEARABLY
UNBEATABLE
UNBECOMING
UNBELIEVER
UNBENDABLE
UNBLINKING
UNBLUSHING

UNBOSOMING
UNBUCKLING
UNBUNDLING
UNBURDENED
UNCANNIEST
UNCARED-
  FOR
UNCARPETED
UNCIVILITY
UNCOMMONLY
UNCONFINED
UNCOUPLING
UNCOVERING
UNCREDITED
UNCRITICAL
UNCTUOSITY
UNCTUOUSLY
UNDECEIVED
UNDECEIVER
UNDEFEATED
UNDEFENDED
UNDENIABLE
UNDENIABLY
UNDERACTED
UNDERBELLY
UNDERBRUSH
UNDERCOATS
UNDERCOVER
UNDERCROFT
UNDERDRAIN
UNDERFLOOR
UNDERGLAZE
UNDERGOING
UNDERGROWN
UNDERLINED
UNDERLINGS
UNDERLYING
UNDERMINED
UNDERMINER
UNDERNAMED
UNDERNEATH
UNDERPANTS
UNDERPRICE
UNDERPROOF
UNDERQUOTE
UNDERRATED
UNDERSCORE
UNDERSEXED
UNDERSHIRT
UNDERSHOOT
UNDERSIZED

UNDERSKIRT
UNDERSLUNG
UNDERSPEND
UNDERSTAND
UNDERSTATE
UNDERSTOCK
UNDERSTOOD
UNDERSTUDY
UNDERTAKEN
UNDERTAKER
UNDERTONES
UNDERTRICK
UNDERTRUMP
UNDERVALUE
UNDERWATER
UNDERWIRED
UNDERWORLD
UNDERWRITE
UNDERWROTE
UNDETERRED
UNDIRECTED
UNDISPUTED
UNDRESSING
UNDULATING
UNDULATION
UNDULATORY
UNEARTHING
UNEASINESS
UNECONOMIC
UNEDIFYING
UNEDUCATED
UNEMPLOYED
UNENVIABLE
UNEQUALLED
UNERRINGLY
UNEVENNESS
UNEVENTFUL
UNEXAMPLED
UNEXPECTED
UNEXPLODED
UNFAIRNESS
UNFAITHFUL
UNFAMILIAR
UNFATHERED
UNFEMININE
UNFETTERED
UNFINISHED
UNFLAGGING
UNFORESEEN
UNFORGIVEN
UNFRIENDLY

UNFROCKING
UNFRUITFUL
UNGENEROUS
UNGRATEFUL
UNGRUDGING
UNGUENTARY
UNHALLOWED
UNHAMPERED
UNHANDSOME
UNHERALDED
UNHOLINESS
UNHOPED-
  FOR
UNHYGIENIC
UNICAMERAL
UNICOSTATE
UNICYCLIST
UNIFOLIATE
UNIFORMITY
UNILATERAL
UNILOCULAR
UNIMPOSING
UNIMPROVED
UNINFORMED
UNINSPIRED
UNINTENDED
UNIONISTIC
UNIONIZING
UNIQUENESS
UNISEPTATE
UNITARIANS
UNITEDNESS
UNIT
  TRUSTS
UNIVALENCY
UNIVERSITY
UNJUSTNESS
UNKINDNESS
UNKNOWABLE
UNLAWFULLY
UNLEARNING
UNLEASHING
UNLEAVENED
UNLETTERED
UNLICENSED
UNLOCKABLE
UNLOOSENED
UNMANNERED
UNMANNERLY
UNMEASURED
UNMEDIATED

UNMERCIFUL
UNMORALITY
UNNUMBERED
UNOCCUPIED
UNOFFICIAL
UNORIGINAL
UNORTHODOX
UNPATENTED
UNPLAYABLE
UNPLEASANT
UNPREPARED
UNPROMPTED
UNPROVIDED
UNPROVOKED
UNPUNCTUAL
UNPUNISHED
UNRAVELING
UNRAVELLED
UNRAVELLER
UNREACTIVE
UNREADABLE
UNREADABLY
UNRELIABLE
UNRELIEVED
UNREQUITED
UNRESERVED
UNRESOLVED
UNRIVALLED
UNRULINESS
UNSADDLING
UNSANITARY
UNSCHOOLED
UNSCRAMBLE
UNSCREENED
UNSCREWING
UNSCRIPTED
UNSEALABLE
UNSEASONED
UNSEEINGLY
UNSETTLING
UNSHAKABLE
UNSOCIABLE
UNSPEAKING
UNSPECIFIC
UNSTEADILY
UNSTINTING
UNSTOPPING
UNSTRAINED
UNSTRESSED
UNSTRIATED
UNSUITABLE

UNSURFACED
UNSWERVING
UNTANGLING
UNTHANKFUL
UNTHINKING
UNTIDINESS
UNTIRINGLY
UNTOWARDLY
UNTRUSTING
UNTRUTHFUL
UNWIELDILY
UNWINDABLE
UNWORKABLE
UNWORTHILY
UNYIELDING
UP-AND-
   UNDER
UPBRAIDING
UPBRINGING
UPHOLSTERY
UP IN THE
   AIR
UPLIFTMENT
UPON MY
   WORD
UPPER
   CLASS
UPPER
   CRUST
UPPER
   EGYPT
UPPER
   HOUSE
UPPER
   VOLTA
UPPISHNESS
UPROARIOUS
UPSETTABLE
UPSIDE
   DOWN
UPSTANDING
UP THE
   SPOUT
UP THE
   STAKE
UP THE
   STICK
UPWARDNESS
URAL-
   ALTAIC
URBANENESS
UREDOSORUS

UREDOSPORE
URETHRITIC
URETHRITIS
URINALYSIS
UROCHORDAL
UROGENITAL
UROSCOPIST
URTICARIAL
URTICATION
USEFULNESS
USHERETTES
USQUEBAUGH
USTULATION
USURPATION
USURPATIVE
USURPINGLY
UTILIZABLE
UTO-
   AZTECAN
UTOPIANISM
UTTERANCES
UXORICIDAL
UZBEKISTAN

V
VACANTNESS
VACATIONED
VACATIONER
VACCINATED
VACILLATED
VACILLATOR
VACUUM
   PUMP
VAGINISMUS
VAGOTROPIC
VAL-DE-
   MARNE
VALENTINES
VALIDATING
VALIDATION
VALIDATORY
VALLADOLID
VALLECULAR
VALPARAISO
VALUATIONS
VALVULITIS
VAMPIRE
   BAT
VANADINITE
VANDALIZED
VAN DER
   POST

VANISHMENT
VANQUISHED
VANQUISHER
VAPORIZING
VAPOURABLE
VARIATIONS
VARICELLAR
VARICOCELE
VARICOSITY
VARICOTOMY
VARIEDNESS
VARIEGATED
VARIFOCALS
ANGLO-
   SAXON
VARIOLITIC
VARIOMETER
VARITYPIST
VARNISHING
VASTNESSES
VAUDEVILLE
VAUNTINGLY
VEGETABLES
VEGETARIAN
VEGETATING
VEGETATION
VEGETATIVE
VEHEMENTLY
VELOCIPEDE
VELOCITIES
VELUTINOUS
VENATIONAL
VENDETTIST
VENERATING
VENERATION
VENEZUELAN
VENGEANCES
VENGEFULLY
VENOMOUSLY
VENOUSNESS
VENTILABLE
VENTILATED
VENTILATOR
VENTRICLES
VENTRICOSE
VERBALIZED
VERBALIZER
VERBAL
   NOUN
VERIFIABLE
VERKRAMPTE

VERMICELLI
VERMICIDAL
VERMICULAR
VERNACULAR
VERNISSAGE
VERSAILLES
VERTEBRATE
VERTICALLY
VERY
   LIGHTS
VESICATION
VESICULATE
VESPERTINE
VESTIBULAR
VESTIBULES
VESTMENTAL
VESTMENTED
VETERINARY
VIBRACULAR
VIBRACULUM
VIBRAPHONE
VIBRATIONS
VICEGERENT
VICEREINES
VICINITIES
VICOMTESSE
VICTIMIZED
VICTIMIZER
VICTIMLESS
VICTORIANA
VICTORIANS
VICTORIOUS
VICTUALING
VICTUALLED
VICTUALLER
VIDEODISCS
VIDEO
   NASTY
VIDEOPHILE
VIDEOPHONE
VIDEOTAPED
VIETNAMESE
VIEWFINDER
VIEWPOINTS
VIGILANTES
VIGILANTLY
VIGNETTING
VIGNETTIST
VIGOROUSLY
VIJAYAWADA
VILLAINOUS

VILLANELLA
VILLANELLE
VILLANOVAN
VINA DEL
   MAR
VINDICABLE
VINDICATED
VINDICATOR
VINDICTIVE
VINIFEROUS
VINYLIDENE
VIOLACEOUS
VIOLATIONS
VIOLINISTS
VIRAGINOUS
VIRESCENCE
VIROLOGIST
VIRTUALITY
VIRTUOSITY
VIRTUOUSLY
VIRULENTLY
VISCOMETER
VISCOMETRY
VISCOUNTCY
VISIBILITY
VISITATION
VISITORIAL
VISUAL
   AIDS
VISUALIZED
VISUALIZER
VITALISTIC
VITAL
   SIGNS
VITRESCENT
VITRIFYING
VITRIOLIZE
VITUPERATE
VIVIPARITY
VIVIPAROUS
VIVISECTOR
VOCABULARY
VOCAL
   CORDS
VOCATIONAL
VOCIFERANT
VOCIFERATE
VOCIFEROUS
VOETSTOETS
VOICE
   BOXES

VOICE-
OVERS
VOICEPRINT
VOLAPUKIST
VOLATILITY
VOLATILIZE
VOL-AU-
VENTS
VOLITIONAL
VOLLEYBALL
VOLT-
AMPERE
VOLTE-
FACES
VOLUBILITY
VOLUMETRIC
VOLUMINOUS
VOLUNTEERS
VOLUPTUARY
VOLUPTUOUS
VORARLBERG
VORTICELLA
VOTIVENESS
VOUCHSAFED
VULCANIZED
VULCANIZER
VULGARIZED
VULGARIZER
VULGARNESS
VULNERABLE
VULNERABLY
VULPECULAR

W

WADDLINGLY
WADING
POOL
WAGE
SLAVES
WAGGA
WAGGA
WAGGLINGLY
WAGONS-
LITS
WAINWRIGHT
WAISTBANDS
WAISTCOATS
WAISTLINES
WAITPERSON
WAKEY
WAKEY
WALKABOUTS

WALK OF
LIFE
WALLCHARTS
WALLFLOWER
WALLPAPERS
WALL
STREET
WALL-TO-
WALL
WANDERINGS
WANDERLUST
WANDSWORTH
WANTONNESS
WAREHOUSES
WARMING
PAN
WARMONGERS
WARRANTIES
WARRANTING
WARRINGTON
WASHBASINS
WASHCLOTHS
WASHING
DAY
WASHINGTON
WASHSTANDS
WASTEFULLY
WASTELANDS
WASTE
PAPER
WATCHFULLY
WATCHMAKER
WATCH
NIGHT
WATCHSTRAP
WATCHTOWER
WATCHWORDS
WATER
BIRDS
WATERBORNE
WATER
BUTTS
WATERCRAFT
WATERCRESS
WATERFALLS
WATERFOWLS
WATERFRONT
WATERHOLES
WATERINESS
WATER
JUMPS

WATER
LEVEL
WATER
MAINS
WATERMARKS
WATERMELON
WATER
METER
WATERMILLS
WATER
PIPES
WATERPOWER
WATERPROOF
WATER
RATES
WATERSCAPE
WATERSHEDS
WATER
SKIER
WATERSPOUT
WATER
TABLE
WATERTIGHT
WATER
VOLES
WATERWHEEL
WATERWINGS
WATERWORKS
WATTLEBIRD
WAVELENGTH
WAVERINGLY
WAXED
PAPER
WEAKLINESS
WEAK-
MINDED
WEAKNESSES
WEAK-
WILLED
WEALTHIEST
WEARYINGLY
WEATHERING
WEATHERMAN
WEATHERMEN
WEAVERBIRD
WEDNESDAYS
WEEDKILLER
WEEKENDERS
WEEKENDING
WEEKNIGHTS
WEIGHTLESS

WELL-
ARGUED
WELL-
CHOSEN
WELL-
EARNED
WELL-
HEELED
WELL I
NEVER
WELLINGTON
WELL-
JUDGED
WELL-
SPOKEN
WELLSPRING
WELL-
TURNED
WELL-
WISHER
WELL-
WORDED
WENTLETRAP
WEREWOLVES
WEST
BENGAL
WESTERLIES
WESTERNERS
WESTERNISM
WESTERNIZE
WEST
INDIAN
WEST
INDIES
WESTPHALIA
WEST
RIDING
WET
BLANKET
WET-
NURSING
WHARFINGER
WHATSOEVER
WHEELBASES
WHEELCHAIR
WHEELHOUSE
WHEELIE
BIN
WHEEZINESS
WHEEZINGLY
WHENSOEVER
WHEREFORES
WHETSTONES

WHICKERING
WHIMPERING
WHIPLASHES
WHIP-
ROUNDS
WHIPSTITCH
WHIRLABOUT
WHIRLIGIGS
WHIRLINGLY
WHIRLPOOLS
WHIRLWINDS
WHIRLYBIRD
WHISPERERS
WHISPERING
WHIST
DRIVE
WHITEBOARD
WHITE
DWARF
WHITE
FLAGS
WHITE
HOPES
WHITEHORSE
WHITE
HORSE
WHITE
HOUSE
WHITE
MAGIC
WHITE
METAL
WHITE
PAPER
WHITE
SAUCE
WHITESMITH
WHITE
TRASH
WHITEWATER
WHITLEY
BAY
WHITTLINGS
WHOLEFOODS
WHOLE
NOTES
WHOLESALER
WHOREHOUSE
WICKEDNESS
WICKERWORK
WICKET
GATE

WIDE-
SCREEN
WIDESPREAD
WIDOWS
MITE
WIFELINESS
WILDCATTED
WILDEBEEST
WILDERNESS
WILDFOWLER
WILFULNESS
WILLEMSTAD
WILLOWHERB
WILLY-
NILLY
WILMINGTON
WINCEYETTE
WINCHESTER
WINDBREAKS
WIND-
BROKEN
WINDEDNESS
WINDFLOWER
WINDGALLED
WIND
GAUGES
WINDJAMMER
WINDLASSES
WINDOWPANE
WINDOW-
SHOP
WINDOWSILL
WINDSCREEN
WINDSHIELD
WIND
SLEEVE
WINDSTORMS
WINDSUCKER
WIND-
SURFER

WIND
TUNNEL
WINEBIBBER
WINE
COOLER
WINEMAKING
WINTERFEED
WINTERTHUR
WINTERTIME
WINTRINESS
WIRE-
HAIRED
WIRELESSES
WIREWORKER
WISECRACKS
WISHY-
WASHY
WITCHCRAFT
WITCH-
HAZEL
WITCH-
HUNTS
WITHDRAWAL
WITHDRAWER
WITHHOLDER
WITNESS
BOX
WITNESSING
WITTENBERG
WITTICISMS
WOBBLINESS
WOEFULNESS
WOLFHOUNDS
WOLFRAMITE
WOLLONGONG
WOMANIZERS
WOMANIZING
WOMENSWEAR
WONDERLAND
WONDERMENT
WONDERWORK

WOODBLOCKS
WOODCARVER
WOODCUTTER
WOODENNESS
WOODLANDER
WOODPECKER
WOODWORKER
WOOKEY
HOLE
WOOLGROWER
WOOLLINESS
WORDLESSLY
WORKAHOLIC
WORKBASKET
WORK-
HARDEN
WORKHORSES
WORKING
DAY
WORKINGMAN
WORKPEOPLE
WORKPLACES
WORK-TO-
RULE
WORLD-
CLASS
WORLDLIEST
WORLD
POWER
WORLD-
WEARY
WORRYINGLY
WORRYWARTS
WORSHIPFUL
WORSHIPING
WORSHIPPED
WORSHIPPER
WORTHINESS
WORTHWHILE
WOUNDINGLY
WRAITHLIKE

WRATHFULLY
WRETCHEDLY
WRISTBANDS
WRISTWATCH
WRITHINGLY
WRONGDOERS
WRONGDOING
WRONGFULLY
WUNDERKIND

X

XANTHATION
XENOGAMOUS
XENOLITHIC
XENOPHOBIA
XENOPHOBIC
XEROGRAPHY
XEROPHYTIC
XIPHOSURAN
XOCHIMILCO
X-
RADIATIO
N
X-RAY
BINARY
XYLOGRAPHY
XYLOPHONES
XYLOPHONIC
XYLOTOMIST
XYLOTOMOUS

Y

YARBOROUGH
YARDSTICKS
YEASTINESS
YELLOWBARK
YELLOWBIRD
YELLOWCAKE
YELLOWLEGS
YELLOWTAIL
YELLOWWEED

YELLOWWOOD
YESTERDAYS
YESTERYEAR
YIELDINGLY
YLANG-
YLANG
YOGYAKARTA
YOSHKAR-
OLA
YOUNGBERRY
YOUNGSTERS
YOUNGSTOWN
YOURSELVES
YOUTHFULLY
YUGOSLAVIA

Z

ZAPOROZHYE
ZENER
DIODE
ZIGZAGGING
ZINCOGRAPH
ZOOGRAPHER
ZOOGRAPHIC
ZOOLATROUS
ZOOLOGICAL
ZOOLOGISTS
ZOOM
LENSES
ZOOMORPHIC
ZOOPHAGOUS
ZOOPHILISM
ZOOPHILOUS
ZOOPHOBOUS
ZOOPLASTIC
ZWITTERION
ZYGODACTYL
ZYGOMYCETE
ZYGOSPORIC
ZYMOLOGIST

A
ABANDONEDLY
ABANDONMENT
ABBEVILLIAN
ABBREVIATED
ABBREVIATOR
ABDICATIONS
ABERRATIONS
ABERYSTWYTH
ABIETIC ACID
ABIOGENESIS
ABIOGENETIC
ABLUTIONARY
ABNORMALITY
ABOLISHMENT
ABOMINATING
ABOMINATION
ABORIGINALS
ABORTIONIST
ABRACADABRA
ABRANCHIATE
ABRIDGMENTS
ABROGATIONS
ABSENTEEISM
ABSORBINGLY
ABSORPTANCE
ABSTENTIONS
ABSTENTIOUS
ABSTRACTING
ABSTRACTION
ABSTRACTIVE
ABSTRICTION
ABSURDITIES
ABUSIVENESS
ACADEMICALS
ACADEMICIAN
ACADEMICISM
ACARPELLOUS
ACATALECTIC
ACAULESCENT
ACCELERANDO
ACCELERATED
ACCELERATOR
ACCENTUATED
ACCEPTANCES
ACCEPTATION
ACCESSIONAL
ACCESSORIAL
ACCESSORIES
ACCESSORILY
ACCIPITRINE

ACCLAMATION
ACCLAMATORY
ACCLIMATIZE
ACCLIVITIES
ACCLIVITOUS
ACCOMMODATE
ACCOMPANIED
ACCOMPANIER
ACCOMPANIST
ACCOMPLICES
ACCORDANCES
ACCORDINGLY
ACCOUNTABLE
ACCOUNTANCY
ACCOUNTANTS
ACCULTURATE
ACCUMULABLE
ACCUMULATED
ACCUMULATOR
ACCUSATIONS
ACCUSATIVAL
ACCUSATIVES
ACCUSTOMING
ACETANILIDE
ACETYLATION
ACHIEVEMENT
ACHONDRITIC
ACHROMATISM
ACHROMATIZE
ACHROMATOUS
ACID-FORMING
ACIDIFIABLE
ACIDIMETRIC
ACIDOPHILIC
ACIDOPHILUS
ACIDULATION
ACINACIFORM
ACKNOWLEDGE
ACLINIC LINE
ACOUSTICIAN
ACQUAINTING
ACQUIESCENT
ACQUIESCING
ACQUIREMENT
ACQUISITION
ACQUISITIVE
ACQUITTANCE
ACRIFLAVINE
ACRIMONIOUS
ACROCARPOUS
ACROMEGALIC

ACTINICALLY
ACTINOMETER
ACTINOMETRY
ACTINOMYCIN
ACTUALITIES
ACUMINATION
ACUPRESSURE
ACUPUNCTURE
ADAM'S APPLES
ADAPTATIONS
ADIAPHORISM
ADIAPHORIST
ADIAPHOROUS
AD INFINITUM
ADIPOCEROUS
ADJOURNMENT
ADJUDICATED
ADJUDICATOR
ADJUSTMENTS
ADMIRATIONS
ADMONISHING
ADMONITIONS
ADOLESCENCE
ADOLESCENTS
ADOPTIONISM
ADOPTIONIST
ADULTERATED
ADULTERATOR
ADUMBRATING
ADUMBRATION
ADUMBRATIVE
ADVANCEMENT
ADVANCINGLY
ADVENTURERS
ADVENTURESS
ADVENTURISM
ADVENTURIST
ADVENTUROUS
ADVERBIALLY
ADVERSARIAL
ADVERSARIES
ADVERSATIVE
ADVERSITIES
ADVERTENTLY
ADVERTISERS
ADVERTISING
ADVERTORIAL
AEOLIAN HARP
AERODYNAMIC
AEROGRAMMES
AERONAUTICS

AEROSTATICS
AEROSTATION
AESTIVATION
AETIOLOGIST
AFFECTATION
AFFECTINGLY
AFFECTIONAL
AFFECTIVITY
AFFILIATING
AFFILIATION
AFFIRMATION
AFFIRMATIVE
AFFLICTIONS
AFFORESTING
AFFRANCHISE
AFFRICATIVE
AFGHANISTAN
AFICIONADOS
AFRO-ASIATIC
AFTERBIRTHS
AFTERBURNER
AFTEREFFECT
AFTERSHAVES
AFTERTASTES
AGAMOSPERMY
AGELESSNESS
AGGLOMERATE
AGGLUTINANT
AGGLUTINATE
AGGRADATION
AGGRANDIZER
AGGRAVATING
AGGRAVATION
AGGREGATING
AGGREGATION
AGGRIEVEDLY
AGNOSTICISM
AGONIZINGLY
AGONY COLUMN
AGORAPHOBIA
AGORAPHOBIC
AGRARIANISM
AGRICULTURE
AGROBIOLOGY
AGROLOGICAL
AGROSTOLOGY
AIDE-MEMOIRE
AIDES-DE-CAMP
AILUROPHILE
AILUROPHOBE
AIMLESSNESS

AIRCRAFTMAN	ALTOSTRATUS	ANALEMMATIC	ANORTHOSITE
AIRCRAFTMEN	ALUMINOSITY	ANALYSATION	ANTAGONISMS
AIRLESSNESS	ALVEOLATION	ANAMORPHISM	ANTAGONISTS
AIRSICKNESS	AMABOKOBOKO	ANAPHYLAXIS	ANTAGONIZED
AIR TERMINAL	AMALGAMATED	ANARCHISTIC	ANTALKALINE
AIX-LES-BAINS	AMARANTHINE	ANASTOMOSIS	ANTECEDENCE
ALARM CLOCKS	AMBASSADORS	ANASTOMOTIC	ANTECEDENTS
ALBATROSSES	AMBIGUGUITY	ANCIENTNESS	ANTECHAMBER
ALBUMINURIA	AMBIGUOUSLY	ANCILLARIES	ANTEPENDIUM
ALBUQUERQUE	AMBITIOUSLY	ANDROGENOUS	ANTEVERSION
ALCOHOL-FREE	AMBIVALENCE	ANDROGYNOUS	ANTHERIDIAL
ALDERMASTON	AMBLYGONITE	ANDROSPHINX	ANTHERIDIUM
ALDERPERSON	AMELIORATED	ANEMOGRAPHY	ANTHEROZOID
ALDOSTERONE	AMELIORATOR	ANEMOMETERS	ANTHOCYANIN
ALESSANDRIA	AMENABILITY	ANEMOMETRIC	ANTHOLOGIES
ALGEBRAICAL	AMENORRHOEA	ANESTHETICS	ANTHOLOGIST
ALGINIC ACID	AMERICANISM	ANESTHETIST	ANTHOLOGIZE
ALGOLAGNIST	AMERICANIZE	ANESTHETIZE	ANTHRACITIC
ALGORITHMIC	AMETHYSTINE	ANFRACTUOUS	ANTHRACNOSE
ALKALIMETER	AMICABILITY	ANGELICALLY	ANTIBIOTICS
ALKALIMETRY	AMINOPHENOL	ANGIOMATOUS	ANTICATHODE
ALKALIZABLE	AMINOPYRINE	ANGIOPLASTY	ANTICIPATED
ALL-AMERICAN	AMMONIATION	ANGLICANISM	ANTICIPATOR
ALLANTOIDAL	AMONTILLADO	ANGLICIZING	ANTICLASTIC
ALLEGATIONS	AMOROUSNESS	ANGLO-INDIAN	ANTICYCLONE
ALLEGIANCES	AMOR PATRIAE	ANGLOPHILES	ANTIFEBRILE
ALLEGORICAL	AMORPHOUSLY	ANGLOPHILIA	ANTIFOULING
ALLEVIATING	AMORTIZABLE	ANGLOPHOBES	ANTIMISSILE
ALLEVIATION	AMOUR-PROPRE	ANGLOPHOBIA	ANTIMYCOTIC
ALLEVIATIVE	AMPHETAMINE	ANGLO-SAXONS	ANTINEUTRON
ALLOCATIONS	AMPHIBIOTIC	ANIMALCULAR	ANTINUCLEAR
ALLOGRAPHIC	AMPHIBOLITE	ANIMOSITIES	ANTINUCLEON
ALLOMORPHIC	AMPHIBOLOGY	ANISEIKONIA	ANTIOXIDANT
ALLOPLASMIC	AMPHICHROIC	ANISEIKONIC	ANTIPATHIES
ALLOPURINOL	AMPHICTYONY	ANISODACTYL	ANTIPHONARY
ALL-POWERFUL	AMPHISBAENA	ANISOGAMOUS	ANTIPHRASIS
ALL-ROUNDERS	AMPHISTYLAR	ANISOMEROUS	ANTIPYRESIS
ALLUREMENTS	AMPHITRICHA	ANISOMETRIC	ANTIPYRETIC
ALMIGHTIEST	AMPLEXICAUL	ANISOTROPIC	ANTIQUARIAN
ALPHABETIZE	AMPLIFIABLE	ANNABERGITE	ANTIQUITIES
ALTARPIECES	AMPUTATIONS	ANNEXATIONS	ANTIRRHINUM
ALTERATIONS	AMYL NITRITE	ANNIHILABLE	ANTI-SEMITES
ALTERCATION	AMYLOPECTIN	ANNIHILATED	ANTI-SEMITIC
ALTERNATELY	ANACHRONISM	ANNIHILATOR	ANTISEPTICS
ALTERNATING	ANACOLUTHIA	ANNIVERSARY	ANTITUSSIVE
ALTERNATION	ANACOLUTHIC	ANNOTATIONS	ANTOFAGASTA
ALTERNATIVE	ANACOLUTHON	ANNUNCIATOR	ANTONOMASIA
ALTERNATORS	ANADIPLOSIS	ANOINTMENTS	ANXIOUSNESS
ALTITUDINAL	ANAEMICALLY	ANOMALISTIC	APATOSAURUS
ALTOCUMULUS	ANAESTHESIA	ANOMALOUSLY	APHETICALLY
ALTOGETHERS	ANAESTHETIC	ANONYMOUSLY	APHRODISIAC

APICULTURAL	AQUATICALLY	ASCETICALLY	ATOMIC PILES
APOCALYPSES	AQUICULTURE	ASKING PRICE	ATOMIZATION
APOCALYPTIC	ARABICA BEAN	ASPERGILLUS	ATRABILIOUS
APOCOPATION	ARALIACEOUS	ASPHYXIATED	ATROCIOUSLY
APOCYNTHION	ARAN ISLANDS	ASPHYXIATOR	ATTACHE CASE
APOLOGETICS	ARBITRAGEUR	ASPIDISTRAS	ATTACHMENTS
APOLOGIZING	ARBITRAMENT	ASPIRATIONS	ATTAINMENTS
APOMORPHINE	ARBITRARILY	ASSASSINATE	ATTEMPTABLE
APONEUROSIS	ARBITRATING	ASSEMBLAGES	ATTENDANCES
APONEUROTIC	ARBITRATION	ASSEMBLYMAN	ATTENTIVELY
APOPHYLLITE	ARBITRATORS	ASSEMBLYMEN	ATTENUATING
APOSIOPESIS	ARBORESCENT	ASSENTATION	ATTENUATION
APOSIOPETIC	ARCHAEOLOGY	ASSERTIVELY	ATTESTATION
A POSTERIORI	ARCHAEOZOIC	ASSESSMENTS	ATTITUDINAL
APOSTROPHES	ARCHAICALLY	ASSESSORIAL	ATTRACTABLE
APOTHEOSIZE	ARCHANGELIC	ASSEVERATED	ATTRACTIONS
APPALLINGLY	ARCHBISHOPS	ASSIDUOUSLY	ATTRIBUTING
APPARATCHIK	ARCHDEACONS	ASSIGNATION	ATTRIBUTION
APPARATUSES	ARCHDIOCESE	ASSIGNMENTS	ATTRIBUTIVE
APPARELLING	ARCHDUCHESS	ASSIMILABLE	ATTRITIONAL
APPARITIONS	ARCHEGONIUM	ASSIMILATED	AUCTIONEERS
APPEALINGLY	ARCHENEMIES	ASSOCIATING	AUDACIOUSLY
APPEARANCES	ARCHENTERIC	ASSOCIATION	AUDIOLOGIST
APPEASEMENT	ARCHENTERON	ASSOCIATIVE	AUDIOMETRIC
APPELLATION	ARCHIPELAGO	ASSORTATIVE	AUDIOTYPING
APPELLATIVE	ARDUOUSNESS	ASSORTMENTS	AUDIOTYPIST
APPERTAINED	ARENICOLOUS	ASSUAGEMENT	AUDIO-VISUAL
APPLICATION	ARGENTINEAN	ASSUMPTIONS	AUDITIONING
APPLICATIVE	ARGYLLSHIRE	ASSUREDNESS	AUDITORIUMS
APPLICATORY	ARISTOCRACY	ASSYRIOLOGY	AUGMENTABLE
APPOINTMENT	ARISTOCRATS	ASTATICALLY	AURIGNACIAN
APPORTIONED	ARMED FORCES	ASTERISKING	AUSCULTATOR
APPORTIONER	ARMIPOTENCE	ASTIGMATISM	AUSTERENESS
APPRECIABLE	ARMOURED CAR	ASTONISHING	AUSTERITIES
APPRECIABLY	ARMOUR PLATE	ASTRAPHOBIA	AUSTRALASIA
APPRECIATED	AROMATICITY	ASTRAPHOBIC	AUSTRALIANA
APPREHENDED	ARONOMASTIC	ASTRINGENCY	AUSTRALIANS
APPRENTICED	ARRAIGNMENT	ASTRINGENTS	AUSTRONESIA
APPRENTICES	ARRANGEMENT	ASTROBOTANY	AUTHORITIES
APPROACHING	ARRESTINGLY	ASTROLOGERS	AUTHORIZING
APPROBATION	ARTERIALIZE	ASTROMETRIC	AUTOCHANGER
APPROBATIVE	ARTHROMERIC	ASTRONAUTIC	AUTOCRACIES
APPROPRIATE	ARTHROSPORE	ASTRONOMERS	AUTOGENESIS
APPROVINGLY	ARTICULATED	ASTROSPHERE	AUTOGENETIC
APPROXIMATE	ARTICULATOR	ATELECTASIS	AUTOGRAPHED
APPURTENANT	ARTILLERIES	ATHEISTICAL	AUTOGRAPHIC
AQUACULTURE	ARTIODACTYL	ATHERMANOUS	AUTOKINETIC
AQUAEROBICS	ARTLESSNESS	ATHLETICISM	AUTOMOBILES
AQUAMARINES	ARYTENOIDAL	ATLANTICISM	AUTOPLASTIC
AQUAPLANING	ASCENSIONAL	ATMOSPHERES	AUTOTROPHIC
AQUARELLIST	ASCERTAINED	ATMOSPHERIC	AUXANOMETER

AUXILIARIES
AVOIRDUPOIS
AVUNCULARLY
AWESOMENESS
AWKWARDNESS
AXIOLOGICAL
AXONOMETRIC
AZERBAIJANI
AZOTOBACTER

B

BABY-MINDERS
BABY ON BOARD
BABY'S-BREATH
BABY-SITTERS
BABY-SITTING
BACCHANALIA
BACCIFEROUS
BACCIVOROUS
BACILLIFORM
BACKBENCHER
BACKBENCHES
BACKCOMBING
BACK COUNTRY
BACKGROUNDS
BACKHANDERS
BACK NUMBERS
BACKPACKERS
BACKPACKING
BACK PASSAGE
BACKPEDALED
BACKROOM BOY
BACKSLAPPER
BACKSLIDERS
BACKSLIDING
BACK STREETS
BACKSTROKES
BACK TO FRONT
BACKTRACKED
BACTERAEMIA
BACTERICIDE
BADDERLOCKS
BAD-MOUTHING
BAGGAGE CARS
BAGGAGE ROOM
BAHIA BLANCA
BAKERS DOZEN
BAKER'S DOZEN
BALANCEABLE
BALEFULNESS
BALL BEARING

BALLBREAKER
BALLETOMANE
BALLOONISTS
BALLOT PAPER
BALUCHISTAN
BALUSTRADES
BAMBOOZLING
BANANA SKINS
BANDMASTERS
BANGLADESHI
BANK ACCOUNT
BANKER'S CARD
BANK HOLIDAY
BANKROLLING
BANKRUPTING
BANNOCKBURN
BANTERINGLY
BARBARITIES
BARBARIZING
BARBAROUSLY
BARBASTELLE
BARBITURATE
BARCOO RIVER
BAREFACEDLY
BARIUM MEALS
BARLEY SUGAR
BARLEY WATER
BAR MITZVAHS
BARNSTORMED
BARNSTORMER
BAROGRAPHIC
BARONETCIES
BAROTSELAND
BARQUENTINE
BARREL ORGAN
BARRICADING
BASHFULNESS
BASINGSTOKE
BASKERVILLE
BASS GUITARS
BASSOONISTS
BASTARDIZED
BASTINADOED
BASTINADOES
BASTNAESITE
BATHING SUIT
BATHOLITHIC
BATHOMETRIC
BATHYMETRIC
BATHYSPHERE
BATSMANSHIP

BATTLE CRIES
BATTLEFIELD
BATTLEMENTS
BATTLE ROYAL
BATTLESHIPS
BATTY RIDERS
BEACHCHAIRS
BEACHCOMBER
BEAN COUNTER
BEANSPROUTS
BEARISHNESS
BEAR'S-BREECH
BEASTLINESS
BEAUHARNAIS
BEAUTEOUSLY
BEAUTICIANS
BEAUTIFULLY
BEAUTIFYING
BEAUTY QUEEN
BEAUTY SLEEP
BEAUTY SPOTS
BEAVERBOARD
BECKENBAUER
BED AND BOARD
BEDEVILLING
BEDEVILMENT
BEFITTINGLY
BEFRIENDING
BEGUILEMENT
BEGUILINGLY
BEHAVIOURAL
BELABOURING
BELARUSSIAN
BELATEDNESS
BELEAGUERED
BELL-BOTTOMS
BELLICOSITY
BELLIGERENT
BELL-RINGING
BELLYACHING
BELLY BUTTON
BELLY DANCER
BELLY DANCES
BELLY LAUGHS
BENEDICTINE
BENEDICTION
BENEDICTORY
BENEFACTION
BENEFACTORS
BENEFICENCE
BENEFICIARY

BENEVOLENCE
BENIGHTEDLY
BEQUEATHING
BEREAVEMENT
BERGSCHRUND
BESMIRCHING
BESPATTERED
BEST-SELLERS
BEST-SELLING
BETA-BLOCKER
BETES-NOIRES
BETULACEOUS
BEWILDERING
BHUBANESWAR
BIAS BINDING
BIBLIOLATRY
BIBLIOMANCY
BIBLIOMANIA
BIBLIOPHILE
BIBLIOPHISM
BIBLIOTHECA
BICARBONATE
BICENTENARY
BICEPHALOUS
BICONCAVITY
BIEDERMEIER
BIFOLIOLATE
BIFURCATING
BIFURCATION
BIG BUSINESS
BIKER JACKET
BILATERALLY
BILIOUSNESS
BILLETS-DOUX
BILLIONAIRE
BILLOWINESS
BILLS OF FARE
BILLS OF SALE
BIMETALLISM
BIMOLECULAR
BIOCATALYST
BIOCENOLOGY
BIODYNAMICS
BIOENGINEER
BIOFEEDBACK
BIOGRAPHERS
BIOGRAPHIES
BIOPHYSICAL
BIPARTITION
BIQUADRATIC
BIQUARTERLY

BIRD-BRAINED	BLINDSTOREY	BOOTLEGGING	BRITTLENESS
BIRDS OF PREY	BLOCKBUSTER	BORDERLANDS	BRITTLE-STAR
BIRD-WATCHER	BLOCKHOUSES	BORDERLINES	BROADCASTER
BIROBIDZHAN	BLOOD COUNTS	BOTANICALLY	BROAD CHURCH
BIRTHPLACES	BLOOD GROUPS	BOTHERATION	BROAD GAUGES
BIRTHRIGHTS	BLOODHOUNDS	BOTTLE BANKS	BROADMINDED
BIRTHWEIGHT	BLOODLESSLY	BOTTLEBRUSH	BROADSHEETS
BISEXUALISM	BLOOD PLASMA	BOTTLE GREEN	BROADSWORDS
BISEXUALITY	BLOOD SPORTS	BOTTLENECKS	BROMINATION
BISYMMETRIC	BLOODSTAINS	BOUNDLESSLY	BRONCHIOLAR
BIT OF FLUFFS	BLOODSTREAM	BOUNTEOUSLY	BRONTOSAURI
BITTERSWEET	BLOODSUCKER	BOURGEOISIE	BRONX CHEERS
BITTER SWEET	BLOOD VESSEL	BOURNEMOUTH	BRONZE MEDAL
BIVOUACKING	BLOOMINGTON	BOWDLERIZED	BROOMSTICKS
BLACKAMOORS	BLOTCHINESS	BOYOMA FALLS	BROTHERHOOD
BLACKBALLED	BLUDGEONING	BOYSENBERRY	BROWBEATING
BLACKBOARDS	BLUEBERRIES	BRACE AND BIT	BROWNSTONES
BLACK COMEDY	BLUE-BLOODED	BRACHIATION	BRUCELLOSIS
BLACK FOREST	BLUEBOTTLES	BRACTEOLATE	BRUSQUENESS
BLACKGUARDS	BLUE CHEESES	BRADYCARDIA	BRUTALITIES
BLACK HUMOUR	BLUE-EYED BOY	BRADYCARDIC	BRUTALIZING
BLACKLEGGED	BLUE MURDERS	BRAGGADOCIO	BRUTISHNESS
BLACKLISTED	BLUNDERBUSS	BRAHMAPUTRA	BRYOLOGICAL
BLACKMAILED	BLURREDNESS	BRAIN DRAINS	BUCARAMANGA
BLACKMAILER	BOBSLEIGHED	BRAINLESSLY	BUCKET SEATS
BLACK MARIAS	BODHISATTVA	BRAINSTORMS	BUCKET SHOPS
BLACK MARKET	BODY-CENTRED	BRAINS TRUST	BUCKLER-FERN
BLACK MASSES	BODY POLITIC	BRAINTEASER	BUCOLICALLY
BLACK MUSLIM	BOGNOR REGIS	BRAINWASHED	BUDGERIGARS
BLACK PEPPER	BOILERMAKER	BRAINWASHER	BUENOS AIRES
BLACKSHIRTS	BOILERPLATE	BRANCHIOPOD	BUFFER STATE
BLACKSMITHS	BOILER SUITS	BRANDENBURG	BUFFER STOCK
BLACK WIDOWS	BOLLOCKS-UPS	BRANDISHING	BUFFER ZONES
BLADDERWORT	BOLL WEEVILS	BRATTISHING	BULBIFEROUS
BLAMELESSLY	BOMBARDIERS	BRAZZAVILLE	BULLDOG CLIP
BLAMEWORTHY	BOMBARDMENT	BREADBASKET	BULLETPROOF
BLANCMANGES	BONDHOLDERS	BREADBOARDS	BULLFIGHTER
BLANK CHEQUE	BONE MARROWS	BREADCRUMBS	BULLFINCHES
BLASPHEMERS	BONESHAKERS	BREADFRUITS	BULLISHNESS
BLASPHEMIES	BOOBY PRIZES	BREADTHWAYS	BULLSHITTED
BLASPHEMING	BOOKBINDERS	BREADWINNER	BULL TERRIER
BLASPHEMOUS	BOOKBINDERY	BREAKFASTED	BUMPTIOUSLY
BLASTOGENIC	BOOKBINDING	BREAK THE ICE	BUNDELKHAND
BLASTOMERIC	BOOKISHNESS	BREASTPLATE	BUPIVACAINE
BLASTOPORIC	BOOKKEEPERS	BREATHALYSE	BUREAUCRACY
BLENCHINGLY	BOOKKEEPING	BREATHINESS	BUREAUCRATS
BLEPHARITIC	BOOKMOBILES	BRECONSHIRE	BURGOMASTER
BLEPHATITIS	BOOKSELLERS	BREECHBLOCK	BURKINA-FASO
BLESSEDNESS	BOOMERANGED	BREMERHAVEN	BURLESQUING
BLIND ALLEYS	BOORISHNESS	BRIDGEBOARD	BURNISHABLE
BLINDFOLDED	BOOTLEGGERS	BRISTLETAIL	BUSHWHACKER

BUSINESS END
BUSINESSMAN
BUSINESSMEN
BUS STATIONS
BUTCHERBIRD
BUTTER BEANS
BUTTERFLIES
BUTTONHOLED
BUTTONHOLES
BUTTONMOULD
BUTTRESSING
BUTYRACEOUS
BY-ELECTIONS
BYELORUSSIA

C
CABINETWORK
CABORA BASSA
CACHE MEMORY
CACOGRAPHIC
CACOPHONOUS
CALCEOLARIA
CALCICOLOUS
CALCIFEROUS
CALCIFUGOUS
CALCINATION
CALCULATING
CALCULATION
CALCULATORS
CALEFACIENT
CALEFACTION
CALEFACTORY
CALIBRATING
CALIBRATION
CALIFORNIAN
CALIFORNIUM
CALLIGRAPHY
CALLIPYGIAN
CALLOUSNESS
CALORIMETER
CALORIMETRY
CALUMNIATED
CALVINISTIC
CALYPTROGEN
CAMARADERIE
CAMERA-READY
CAMOUFLAGED
CAMOUFLAGES
CAMPAIGNERS
CAMPAIGNING
CAMPANOLOGY

CAMPANULATE
CAMPGROUNDS
CAMPO GRANDE
CANALICULAR
CANALICULUS
CANDELABRUM
CANDIDACIES
CANDLEBERRY
CANDLELIGHT
CANDLEPOWER
CANDLESTICK
CANDLEWICKS
CANINE TEETH
CANINE TOOTH
CANNIBALISM
CANNIBALIZE
CANNONBALLS
CANTHARIDES
CANTILEVERS
CAPACIOUSLY
CAPACITANCE
CAPILLARIES
CAPILLARITY
CAPITALISTS
CAPITALIZED
CAPITAL LEVY
CAPITATIONS
CAPITULATED
CAPITULATOR
CAPRICCIOSO
CAPRICORNUS
CAPSULATION
CAPTIVATING
CAPTIVATION
CARABINIERE
CARAVANNING
CARBAMIDINE
CARBONATION
CARBONIZING
CARBON PAPER
CAR-BOOT SALE
CARBORUNDUM
CARBOXYLASE
CARBOXYLATE
CARBUNCULAR
CARBURETTOR
CARBYLAMINE
CARCASSONNE
CARCINOGENS
CARDINALATE
CARD INDEXES

CARDIOGRAPH
CARDPUNCHES
CARDUACEOUS
CAREFULNESS
CARESSINGLY
CARICATURED
CARICATURES
CARMINATIVE
CARNIVOROUS
CAROLINGIAN
CARPOGONIAL
CARPOGONIUM
CARPOLOGIST
CARRAGEENAN
CARRIAGEWAY
CARRIER BAGS
CARSICKNESS
CARTOGRAPHY
CARTOONISTS
CARTWHEELED
CARUNCULATE
CARVEL-BUILT
CARVING FORK
CASE HISTORY
CASE STUDIES
CASEWORKERS
CASSITERITE
CASTELLATED
CASTER SUGAR
CASTIGATING
CASTIGATION
CASTING VOTE
CASTLEREAGH
CASTOR SUGAR
CATACAUSTIC
CATACHRESIS
CATACLASTIC
CATACLYSMIC
CATADROMOUS
CATAFALQUES
CATALOGUING
CATAPLASTIC
CATAPULTING
CATASTROPHE
CAT BURGLARS
CATCHPHRASE
CATCHWEIGHT
CATECHISMAL
CATECHISTIC
CATECHIZING
CATEGORICAL

CATEGORIZED
CATERPILLAR
CATERWAULED
CATHETERIZE
CATHOLICISM
CATHOLICITY
CATHOLICIZE
CATTLE GRIDS
CAULIFLOWER
CAUSABILITY
CAUSATIVELY
CAUSTICALLY
CAUSTICNESS
CAUTERIZING
CAVACO SILVA
CAVALIERISM
CAVERNOUSLY
CAVITY WALLS
CAVO-RELIEVO
CEASELESSLY
CELEBRATING
CELEBRATION
CELEBRATIVE
CELEBRITIES
CEMENTATION
CEMENT MIXER
CENOSPECIES
CENTENARIAN
CENTENARIES
CENTENNIALS
CENTIMETRES
CENTRALIZED
CENTREBOARD
CENTRE-FOLDS
CENTREPIECE
CENTRIFUGAL
CENTRIFUGES
CENTRIPETAL
CENTROBARIC
CENTROMERIC
CENTROSOMIC
CEPHALALGIA
CERARGYRITE
CEREBRATION
CEREBROSIDE
CEREMONIALS
CEREMONIOUS
CEROGRAPHIC
CEROPLASTIC
CERTAINTIES
CERTIFIABLE

CERTIFICATE	CHEERLEADER	CHORDOPHONE	CITIZENSHIP
CETOLOGICAL	CHEERLESSLY	CHOREODRAMA	CITRONELLAL
CHAETOGNATH	CHEESECAKES	CHOREOGRAPH	CITY FATHERS
CHAFFINCHES	CHEESECLOTH	CHOROGRAPHY	CIVIL RIGHTS
CHAFING DISH	CHEF D'OEUVRE	CHRISMATORY	CIVVY STREET
CHAIN LETTER	CHELICERATE	CHRISTENDOM	CLAIRVOYANT
CHAIN-SMOKED	CHELIFEROUS	CHRISTENING	CLAMATORIAL
CHAIN-SMOKER	CHELYABINSK	CHRISTINGLE	CLANDESTINE
CHAIN STITCH	CHEMOSMOSIS	CHRISTMASES	CLARINETIST
CHAIN STORES	CHEMOSMOTIC	CHRISTOLOGY	CLASP KNIVES
CHAIRPERSON	CHEMOSPHERE	CHROMATINIC	CLASS ACTION
CHALCANLITE	CHEMOTACTIC	CHROMINANCE	CLASSICISTS
CHALCEDONIC	CHEMOTROPIC	CHROMOGENIC	CLASSIFYING
CHALKBOARDS	CHEQUE CARDS	CHROMONEMAL	CLAVICHORDS
CHALLENGERS	CHEREMKHOVO	CHROMOPHORE	CLAY PIGEONS
CHALLENGING	CHERISHABLE	CHROMOPLASM	CLEAN-LIMBED
CHAMBERLAIN	CHESHIRE CAT	CHROMOPLAST	CLEANLINESS
CHAMBERMAID	CHESSBOARDS	CHROMOSOMAL	CLEAN-SHAVEN
CHAMBER POTS	CHEVAL GLASS	CHROMOSOMES	CLEAN SWEEPS
CHAMELEONIC	CHIAROSCURO	CHRONICALLY	CLEAR-HEADED
CHAMPERTOUS	CHIASTOLITE	CHRONICLERS	CLEAR THE AIR
CHAMPIONING	CHICANERIES	CHRONICLING	CLEETHORPES
CHANCELLERY	CHICHIHAERH	CHRONOGRAPH	CLEFT PALATE
CHANCELLORS	CHICKENFEED	CHRONOMETER	CLEFT STICKS
CHANCROIDAL	CHICKEN FEED	CHRONOMETRY	CLEISTOGAMY
CHANDELIERS	CHIFFONIERS	CHRONOSCOPE	CLERGYWOMAN
CHANGELINGS	CHILDMINDER	CHRYSALISES	CLEVER DICKS
CHANGEOVERS	CHIMNEYPOTS	CHRYSAROBIN	CLIENT STATE
CHANNELLING	CHIMPANZEES	CHRYSOBERYL	CLIFFHANGER
CHANTERELLE	CHINCHILLAS	CHRYSOLITIC	CLIMACTERIC
CHANTICLEER	CHINESE LEAF	CHRYSOPRASE	CLIMATOLOGY
CHAOTICALLY	CHINOISERIE	CHURCHGOERS	CLINANDRIUM
CHAPERONAGE	CHIPPENDALE	CHURCHGOING	CLINOMETRIC
CHAPERONING	CHIROGRAPHY	CHURCHWOMAN	CLOCK TOWERS
CHARCUTERIE	CHIROPODIST	CHURCHYARDS	CLODHOPPERS
CHARGE CARDS	CHIROPTERAN	CICATRICIAL	CLOISTERING
CHARGE HANDS	CHITCHATTED	CICATRIZANT	CLOSED SHOPS
CHARGE NURSE	CHLAMYDEOUS	CINDERELLAS	CLOSEFISTED
CHARGE SHEET	CHLORINATED	CINEMASCOPE	CLOSE-HAULED
CHAR-GRILLED	CHLORINATOR	CIRCULARITY	CLOSE SEASON
CHARIOTEERS	CHLOROPHYLL	CIRCULARIZE	CLOSE SHAVES
CHARISMATIC	CHLOROPLAST	CIRCULAR SAW	CLOSING TIME
CHASTISABLE	CHLOROPRENE	CIRCULATING	CLOSTRIDIAL
CHATELAINES	CHLOROQUINE	CIRCULATION	CLOSTRIDIUM
CHATTANOOGA	CHOANOCYTAL	CIRCULATIVE	CLOTHESLINE
CHAUFFEURED	CHOCK-A-BLOCK	CIRCULATORY	CLOTHES PEGS
CHAULMOOGRA	CHOIRMASTER	CIRCUMCISED	CLOUDBURSTS
CHAUVINISTS	CHOIR SCHOOL	CIRCUMLUNAR	CLOUD-CAPPED
CHEAPSKATES	CHOKECHERRY	CIRCUMPOLAR	CLOYINGNESS
CHECKMATING	CHOLESTEROL	CIRCUMSPECT	CLUSTER BOMB
CHECKPOINTS	CHOLINERGIC	CIRENCESTER	COADUNATION

COADUNATIVE	COLLARBONES	COMMITMENTS	COMPOSITION
COAGULATING	COLLAR STUDS	COMMODITIES	COMPOSITORS
COAGULATION	COLLECTABLE	COMMON NOUNS	COMPOUNDING
COAGULATIVE	COLLECTANEA	COMMONPLACE	COMPRESSING
COALBUNKERS	COLLECTEDLY	COMMON ROOMS	COMPRESSION
COALESCENCE	COLLECTIONS	COMMON SENSE	COMPRESSIVE
COALITIONAL	COLLECTIVES	COMMOTIONAL	COMPRESSORS
COALSCUTTLE	COLLEMBOLAN	COMMUNALISM	COMPRISABLE
COARCTATION	COLLENCHYMA	COMMUNALIST	COMPROMISED
COASTGUARDS	COLLIGATION	COMMUNALITY	COMPROMISER
COAT HANGERS	COLLIGATIVE	COMMUNALIZE	COMPROMISES
COATS OF ARMS	COLLIMATION	COMMUNICANT	COMPTOMETER
COBBLESTONE	COLLOCATING	COMMUNICATE	COMPTROLLER
COCCIDIOSIS	COLLOCATION	COMMUNIONAL	COMPULSIONS
COCCIFEROUS	COLOGARITHM	COMMUNIQUES	COMPUNCTION
COCK-A-LEEKIE	COLONIALISM	COMMUNISTIC	COMPUTATION
COCKCHAFERS	COLONIALIST	COMMUNITIES	COMPUTERATE
COCKLESHELL	COLONIZABLE	COMMUTATION	COMPUTERIZE
COCKLE SHELL	COLONOSCOPY	COMMUTATIVE	COMRADESHIP
COCKROACHES	COLORATURAS	COMMUTATORS	CONCATENATE
CODICILLARY	COLORIMETER	COMPACT DISC	CONCAVITIES
COD-LIVER OIL	COLOUR-BLIND	COMPACTEDLY	CONCEALMENT
COEDUCATION	COLOURISTIC	COMPACTNESS	CONCEITEDLY
COEFFICIENT	COLTISHNESS	COMPANY TOWN	CONCEIVABLE
COELENTERIC	COLUMBARIUM	COMPARATIVE	CONCEIVABLY
COELENTERON	COMBATIVELY	COMPARISONS	CONCENTRATE
COERCIONARY	COMBINATION	COMPARTMENT	CONCEPTACLE
COERCIONIST	COMBINATIVE	COMPASSABLE	CONCEPTIONS
COESSENTIAL	COMBUSTIBLE	COMPATRIOTS	CONCERNEDLY
COEXISTENCE	COMESTIBLES	COMPELLABLE	CONCERTANTE
COEXTENSION	COME-UPPANCE	COMPENDIOUS	CONCERTEDLY
COEXTENSIVE	COMFORTABLE	COMPENDIUMS	CONCERTGOER
COFFEE BREAK	COMFORTABLY	COMPENSATED	CONCERTINAS
COFFEE HOUSE	COMFORTLESS	COMPENSATOR	CONCESSIBLE
COFFEE SHOPS	COMIC OPERAS	COMPETENTLY	CONCESSIONS
COFFEE TABLE	COMIC STRIPS	COMPETITION	CONCILIATED
COGITATIONS	COMMANDANTS	COMPETITIVE	CONCILIATOR
COGNITIVELY	COMMANDMENT	COMPETITORS	CONCLUSIONS
COGNITIVIST	COMME IL FAUT	COMPILATION	CONCOCTIONS
COGNIZANCES	COMMEMORATE	COMPLACENCE	CONCOMITANT
COGNOSCENTI	COMMENDABLE	COMPLACENCY	CONCORDANCE
COINCIDENCE	COMMENDABLY	COMPLAINANT	CONCUBINAGE
COINSURANCE	COMMENTATED	COMPLAINERS	CONCURRENCE
COLD-BLOODED	COMMENTATOR	COMPLAINING	CONDEMNABLE
COLD CHISELS	COMMERCIALS	COMPLAISANT	CONDENSABLE
COLD COMFORT	COMMINATION	COMPLEMENTS	CONDITIONAL
COLD-HEARTED	COMMINATORY	COMPLEXIONS	CONDITIONED
COLD STORAGE	COMMINUTION	COMPLIANTLY	CONDITIONER
COLEOPTERAN	COMMISERATE	COMPLICATED	CONDOLATORY
COLLABORATE	COMMISSIONS	COMPLIMENTS	CONDOLENCES
COLLAPSIBLE	COMMISSURAL	COMPORTMENT	CONDOMINIUM

CONDONATION	CONJUGATIVE	CONSTRUCTED	CONTROVERSY
CONDUCTANCE	CONJUNCTION	CONSTRUCTOR	CONTUMELIES
CONDUCTIBLE	CONJUNCTIVA	CONSULSHIPS	CONTUSIONED
CONDUCTRESS	CONJUNCTIVE	CONSULTANCY	CONURBATION
CONFABULATE	CONJUNCTURE	CONSULTANTS	CONVALESCED
CONFECTIONS	CONJURATION	CONSUMERISM	CONVENIENCE
CONFEDERACY	CONNECTIBLE	CONSUMMATED	CONVENTICLE
CONFEDERATE	CONNECTICUT	CONSUMMATOR	CONVENTIONS
CONFERENCES	CONNECTIONS	CONSUMPTION	CONVERGENCE
CONFERMENTS	CONNOISSEUR	CONSUMPTIVE	CONVERGENCY
CONFESSEDLY	CONNOTATION	CONTACT LENS	CONVERSABLE
CONFESSIONS	CONNOTATIVE	CONTAINMENT	CONVERSANCE
CONFIDENCES	CONSCIENCES	CONTAMINANT	CONVERSIONS
CONFIDENTLY	CONSCIOUSLY	CONTAMINATE	CONVERTIBLE
CONFIDINGLY	CONSCRIPTED	CONTEMNIBLE	CONVEXITIES
CONFINEMENT	CONSECRATED	CONTEMPLATE	CONVEYANCER
CONFISCABLE	CONSECRATOR	CONTENTEDLY	CONVEYANCES
CONFISCATED	CONSECUTION	CONTENTIONS	CONVICTABLE
CONFISCATOR	CONSECUTIVE	CONTENTIOUS	CONVICTIONS
CONFLATIONS	CONSENSUSES	CONTENTMENT	CONVINCIBLE
CONFLICTING	CONSENTIENT	CONTESTANTS	CONVIVIALLY
CONFLICTION	CONSEQUENCE	CONTEXTURAL	CONVOCATION
CONFLICTIVE	CONSERVABLE	CONTINENTAL	CONVOCATIVE
CONFLUENCES	CONSERVANCY	CONTINGENCE	CONVOLUTION
CONFORMABLE	CONSERVATOR	CONTINGENCY	CONVOLVULUS
CONFORMABLY	CONSIDERATE	CONTINGENTS	CONVULSIONS
CONFORMANCE	CONSIDERING	CONTINUALLY	COOKERY BOOK
CONFORMISTS	CONSIGNABLE	CONTINUANCE	COOK ISLANDS
CONFOUNDING	CONSIGNMENT	CONTINUATOR	COOPERATING
CONFRONTING	CONSISTENCY	CONTORTIONS	COOPERATION
CONFUSINGLY	CONSOLATION	CONTRACTILE	COOPERATIVE
CONFUTATION	CONSOLATORY	CONTRACTING	COOPERATORS
CONFUTATIVE	CONSOLIDATE	CONTRACTION	COOPER CREEK
CONGEALMENT	CONSONANCES	CONTRACTIVE	COORDINATED
CONGELATION	CONSONANTAL	CONTRACTORS	COORDINATES
CONGENIALLY	CONSORTIUMS	CONTRACTUAL	COORDINATOR
CONGESTIBLE	CONSPECIFIC	CONTRACTURE	COPARCENARY
CONGREGATED	CONSPICUOUS	CONTRAFLOWS	COPING STONE
CONGREGATOR	CONSPIRATOR	CONTRAPTION	COPLANARITY
CONGRESSMAN	CONSTANTINE	CONTRARIETY	COPPERPLATE
CONGRESSMEN	CONSTELLATE	CONTRASTING	COPPERSMITH
CONGRUENTLY	CONSTERNATE	CONTRASTIVE	COPROCESSOR
CONGRUITIES	CONSTIPATED	CONTRAVENED	COPROPHILIA
CONJECTURAL	CONSTITUENT	CONTRAVENER	COPYWRITERS
CONJECTURED	CONSTITUTED	CONTRAYERVA	CORACIIFORM
CONJECTURER	CONSTITUTER	CONTRETEMPS	CORDILLERAS
CONJECTURES	CONSTRAINED	CONTRIBUTED	CORMOPHYTIC
CONJOINEDLY	CONSTRAINER	CONTRIBUTOR	CORNERSTONE
CONJUGALITY	CONSTRAINTS	CONTRIVANCE	CORNFLOWERS
CONJUGATING	CONSTRICTED	CONTROLLERS	CORNICULATE
CONJUGATION	CONSTRICTOR	CONTROLLING	CORNUCOPIAS

COROLLARIES
CORONAGRAPH
CORONATIONS
CORONERSHIP
CORPORALITY
CORPORATELY
CORPORATION
CORPORATIVE
CORPOREALLY
CORPUSCULAR
CORRECTABLE
CORRECTIONS
CORRECTIVES
CORRECTNESS
CORRELATING
CORRELATION
CORRELATIVE
CORRIGENDUM
CORROBORATE
CORROSIVELY
CORRUGATION
CORRUPTIBLE
CORRUPTIONS
CORRUPTNESS
CORS ANGLAIS
CORTICATION
CORUSCATING
CORUSCATION
COSIGNATORY
COS LETTUCES
COSMETICIAN
COSMOGONIES
COSMOGONIST
COSMOLOGIST
COSMOPOLITE
COTERMINOUS
COTES-DU-NORD
COTONEASTER
COTTAGE LOAF
COTTON CANDY
COTTONTAILS
COTYLEDONAL
COUNCIL AREA
COUNCILLORS
COUNSELLING
COUNSELLORS
COUNTENANCE
COUNTERFEIT
COUNTERFOIL
COUNTERMAND
COUNTERMINE

COUNTERMOVE
COUNTERPANE
COUNTERPART
COUNTERPLOT
COUNTERSANK
COUNTERSIGN
COUNTERSINK
COUNTERSUNK
COUNTERTYPE
COUNTERVAIL
COUNTERWORD
COUNTERWORK
COUNTRIFIED
COUNTRY CLUB
COUNTRY SEAT
COUNTRYSIDE
COUNTY COURT
COUNTY TOWNS
COUP DE GRACE
COURTEOUSLY
COURTHOUSES
COURTLINESS
COVENANTING
COVER CHARGE
COWCATCHERS
CRABBEDNESS
CRACKERJACK
CRANBERRIES
CRANIOMETER
CRANIOMETRY
CRANKSHAFTS
CRASH COURSE
CRASH-DIVING
CRASH HELMET
CRASH-LANDED
CRAZY PAVING
CREAM CHEESE
CREDENTIALS
CREDIBILITY
CREDIT CARDS
CREDIT NOTES
CREDULOUSLY
CREMATORIUM
CRENELLATED
CRENULATION
CREOPHAGOUS
CREPITATION
CREPUSCULAR
CRESTFALLEN
CRIMINALITY
CRIMINOLOGY

CRINKLEROOT
CRINKLINESS
CRITICIZING
CROCIDOLITE
CROCODILIAN
CROOKEDNESS
CROP-DUSTING
CROSSBREEDS
CROSS-GARNET
CROSS-LEGGED
CROSSPIECES
CROSS-STITCH
CROWDEDNESS
CROWN COLONY
CROWN COURTS
CROWNED HEAD
CROWN JEWELS
CROWN PRINCE
CRUCIFEROUS
CRUCIFIXION
CRUNCHINESS
CRUSTACEANS
CRUSTACEOUS
CRYOBIOLOGY
CRYOHYDRATE
CRYOSURGERY
CRYOTHERAPY
CRYPTICALLY
CRYPTOGAMIC
CRYPTOGENIC
CRYPTOGRAPH
CRYPTOZOITE
CRYSTAL BALL
CRYSTALLINE
CRYSTALLITE
CRYSTALLIZE
CRYSTALLOID
CRYSTAL SETS
CTENOPHORAN
CUCKOO CLOCK
CULMIFEROUS
CULMINATION
CULPABILITY
CULTIVATING
CULTIVATION
CULTIVATORS
CUMMERBUNDS
CUNNILINGUS
CUPELLATION
CUPRIFEROUS
CUPRONICKEL

CURATORSHIP
CURIOSITIES
CURIOUSNESS
CURMUDGEONS
CURRICULUMS
CURRY POWDER
CURTAILMENT
CURTAIN CALL
CURVILINEAR
CUSPIDATION
CUSTARD PIES
CUSTOMARILY
CUSTOM-BUILT
CUSTOMIZING
CUT-AND-DRIED
CUTTING EDGE
CYANIDATION
CYANOHYDRIN
CYBERNATION
CYBERNETICS
CYBERPHOBIA
CYCADACEOUS
CYCLOALKANE
CYCLOHEXANE
CYCLOPLEGIA
CYCLOSPORIN
CYCLOSTYLED
CYCLOTHYMIA
CYCLOTHYMIC
CYLINDRICAL
CYPERACEOUS
CYPRINODONT
CYPRIPEDIUM
CYSTICERCUS
CYSTOCARPIC
CYSTOSCOPIC
CYTOGENESIS
CYTOKINESIS
CYTOLOGICAL
CYTOLOGISTS
CYTOPLASMIC
CZESTOCHOWA

D

DACTYLOLOGY
DAGGERBOARD
DAIL EIREANN
DAIRY CATTLE
DAIRY FARMER
DAISY WHEELS
DAMAN AND DIU

DAMNABILITY	DECLAMATORY	DEHYDRATION	DENSIMETRIC
DAMP COURSES	DECLARATION	DEICTICALLY	DENTAL FLOSS
DANGER MONEY	DECLARATIVE	DEIFICATION	DENTAL PLATE
DANGEROUSLY	DECLARATORY	DELECTATION	DENTICULATE
DAPPLE-GREYS	DECLENSIONS	DELEGATIONS	DENTILABIAL
DARDANELLES	DECLINATION	DELETERIOUS	DENUMERABLE
DAREDEVILRY	DECLINATORY	DELIBERATED	DENUNCIATOR
DAR ES SALAAM	DECLIVITIES	DELIBERATOR	DEODORIZING
DATABLENESS	DECLIVITOUS	DELICIOUSLY	DEOXYGENATE
DAUNTLESSLY	DECOLLATION	DELINEATING	DEOXYRIBOSE
DAWSON CREEK	DECOLLETAGE	DELINEATION	DEPARTMENTS
DAYDREAMERS	DECOLONIZED	DELINEATIVE	DEPLORINGLY
DAYDREAMING	DECOMPOSING	DELINQUENCY	DEPLUMATION
DEACCESSION	DECORATIONS	DELINQUENTS	DEPOLARIZER
DEACTIVATOR	DECORTICATE	DELIRIOUSLY	DEPOPULATED
DEAD LETTERS	DECREPITATE	DELITESCENT	DEPORTATION
DEAD MARCHES	DECREPITUDE	DELIVERABLE	DEPOSITIONS
DEAD RINGERS	DECRESCENCE	DELIVERANCE	DEPRAVATION
DEAD SOLDIER	DECRETALIST	DELIVERYMAN	DEPRAVITIES
DEAF-AND-DUMB	DECUSSATION	DELIVERYMEN	DEPRECATING
DEALERSHIPS	DEDICATEDLY	DELPHINIUMS	DEPRECATION
DEAMINATION	DEDICATIONS	DEMAGNETIZE	DEPRECATIVE
DEATH DUTIES	DEDUCTIVELY	DEMAGOGUERY	DEPRECATORY
DEATHLESSLY	DEEP FREEZES	DEMARCATING	DEPRECIABLE
DEATHLINESS	DEERSTALKER	DEMARCATION	DEPRECIATED
DEATH RATTLE	DE-ESCALATED	DEMOCRACIES	DEPRECIATOR
DEATH'S-HEADS	DEFALCATION	DEMOCRATIZE	DEPREDATION
DEATH SQUADS	DEFECTIVELY	DEMODULATOR	DEPRESSIBLE
DEATTRIBUTE	DEFENCELESS	DEMOGRAPHER	DEPRESSIONS
DEBARKATION	DEFENSIVELY	DEMOGRAPHIC	DEPRIVATION
DEBASEDNESS	DEFERENTIAL	DEMOLISHING	DEPUTATIONS
DEBASEMENTS	DEFICIENTLY	DEMOLITIONS	DERAILMENTS
DEBILITATED	DEFINIENDUM	DEMONETIZED	DERANGEMENT
DEBOUCHMENT	DEFINITIONS	DEMONICALLY	DERECOGNIZE
DEBRIDEMENT	DEFLECTIONS	DEMONOLATER	DEREGULATED
DECALCIFIER	DEFLORATION	DEMONOLATRY	DERELICTION
DECALESCENT	DEFLOWERING	DEMONSTRATE	DERIVATIONS
DECANEDIOIC	DEFOLIATING	DEMORALIZER	DERIVATIVES
DECAPITATED	DEFOLIATION	DEMOTIVATED	DERMATOLOGY
DECAPITATOR	DEFORCEMENT	DEMOUNTABLE	DESALINATED
DECARBONIZE	DEFORESTING	DEMULSIFIER	DESCENDABLE
DECEITFULLY	DEFORMATION	DEMUTUALIZE	DESCENDANTS
DECELERATED	DEFORMITIES	DEMYSTIFIED	DESCENDIBLE
DECELERATOR	DEFRAUDMENT	DENIGRATING	DESCRIBABLE
DECEPTIVELY	DEGENERATED	DENIGRATION	DESCRIPTION
DECEREBRATE	DEGENERATES	DENITRATION	DESCRIPTIVE
DECILLIONTH	DEGLUTINATE	DENOMINABLE	DESECRATING
DECIMALIZED	DEGLUTITION	DENOMINATED	DESECRATION
DECIPHERING	DEGRADATION	DENOMINATOR	DESEGREGATE
DECKLE-EDGED	DEHUMANIZED	DENOTATIONS	DESENSITIZE
DECLAMATION	DEHYDRATING	DENOUEMENTS	DESERVINGLY

DESEXUALIZE	DIACRITICAL	DIMENSIONAL	DISBELIEVED
DESICCATING	DIADELPHOUS	DIMERCAPROL	DISBELIEVER
DESICCATION	DIAGNOSABLE	DIMIDIATION	DISBURSABLE
DESICCATIVE	DIAGNOSTICS	DIMINISHING	DISCERNIBLE
DESIDERATUM	DIALECTICAL	DIMINUENDOS	DISCERNIBLY
DESIGNATING	DIALOGISTIC	DIMINUTIONS	DISCERNMENT
DESIGNATION	DIALYSATION	DIMINUTIVES	DISCHARGING
DESIGNATIVE	DIAMAGNETIC	DINING ROOMS	DISC HARROWS
DESPATCHING	DIAMONDBACK	DINING TABLE	DISCIPLINAL
DESPERADOES	DIAPHORESIS	DINNER BELLS	DISCIPLINED
DESPERATELY	DIAPHORETIC	DINNER TABLE	DISCIPLINER
DESPERATION	DIAPOPHYSIS	DINOSAURIAN	DISCIPLINES
DESPOILMENT	DIARTHROSIS	DIOPTOMETER	DISC JOCKEYS
DESPONDENCY	DIASTROPHIC	DIOPTOMETRY	DISCLAIMERS
DESPUMATION	DIATESSARON	DIPHOSPHATE	DISCLAIMING
DESSERT WINE	DIATOMICITY	DIPHTHEROID	DISCLOSURES
DESTABILIZE	DIATONICISM	DIPHTHONGAL	DISCOGRAPHY
DESTINATION	DICEPHALISM	DIPHYCERCAL	DISCOLOURED
DESTITUTION	DICEPHALOUS	DIPLOCOCCAL	DISCOMFITED
DESTROYABLE	DICHOGAMOUS	DIPLOCOCCUS	DISCOMFITER
DESTRUCTION	DICHOTOMIES	DIPLOMATIST	DISCOMFORTS
DESTRUCTIVE	DICHOTOMIST	DIPROTODONT	DISCOMMODED
DESULTORILY	DICHOTOMIZE	DIPSOMANIAC	DISCOMPOSED
DETACHMENTS	DICHOTOMOUS	DIPSWITCHES	DISCONTINUE
DETERIORATE	DICHROMATIC	DIRECT DEBIT	DISCORDANCE
DETERMINANT	DICHROSCOPE	DIRECTIONAL	DISCOTHEQUE
DETERMINATE	DICOTYLEDON	DIRECTORATE	DISCOUNTING
DETERMINERS	DICTAPHONES	DIRECTORIAL	DISCOURAGED
DETERMINING	DICTATIONAL	DIRECTORIES	DISCOURAGER
DETERMINISM	DICTATORIAL	DIRECT TAXES	DISCOURSING
DETERMINIST	DIDACTICISM	DIRT FARMERS	DISCOURTESY
DETESTATION	DIE-CASTINGS	DIRTY OLD MAN	DISCOVERERS
DETONATIONS	DIFFERENCES	DIRTY OLD MEN	DISCOVERIES
DETRAINMENT	DIFFERENTIA	DIRTY TRICKS	DISCOVERING
DETRIBALIZE	DIFFERENTLY	DISABLEMENT	DISCREDITED
DETRIMENTAL	DIFFIDENTLY	DISACCREDIT	DISCREPANCY
DEUTERANOPE	DIFFRACTING	DISACCUSTOM	DISCUSSIBLE
DEUTEROGAMY	DIFFRACTION	DISAFFECTED	DISCUSSIONS
DEUTSCHMARK	DIFFRACTIVE	DISAFFOREST	DISEMBARKED
DEVALUATION	DIFFUSENESS	DISAGREEING	DISEMBODIED
DEVASTATING	DIFFUSIVITY	DISALLOWING	DISENCUMBER
DEVASTATION	DIGESTIONAL	DISAPPEARED	DISENGAGING
DEVASTATIVE	DIGITIGRADE	DISAPPROVAL	DISENTANGLE
DEVELOPABLE	DIGNITARIES	DISAPPROVED	DISENTHRALL
DEVELOPMENT	DIGRESSIONS	DISAPPROVER	DISFIGURING
DEVIOUSNESS	DIHYBRIDISM	DISARMAMENT	DISFORESTED
DEVITALIZED	DILAPIDATED	DISARRANGED	DISGRACEFUL
DEVOLVEMENT	DILAPIDATOR	DISASSEMBLE	DISGRUNTLED
DEVOTEDNESS	DILATOMETER	DISASSEMBLY	DISGUISABLE
DEVOURINGLY	DILATOMETRY	DISAVOWEDLY	DISGUSTEDLY
DEXTEROUSLY	DILETTANTES	DISBANDMENT	DISHEVELLED

DISHONESTLY	DISSEMINATE	DIVERSIFORM	DOUBLE-SPACE
DISHONOURED	DISSEMINULE	DIVERSIONAL	DOUBLESPEAK
DISHONOURER	DISSENSIONS	DIVERTINGLY	DOUBLE TAKES
DISHWASHERS	DISSENTIENT	DIVESTITURE	DOUBLETHINK
DISILLUSION	DISSENTIOUS	DIVINATIONS	DOUROUCOULI
DISILLUSIVE	DISSEPIMENT	DIVINE RIGHT	DOVETAILING
DISINCLINED	DISSIMILATE	DIVING BELLS	DOWN-AND-OUTS
DISINFECTED	DISSIMULATE	DIVINGBOARD	DOWNGRADING
DISINFECTOR	DISSIPATING	DIVISIONISM	DOWNHEARTED
DISINTEREST	DISSIPATION	DIVISIONIST	DOWNLOADING
DISINTERRED	DISSIPATIVE	DIVORCEABLE	DOWNPATRICK
DISJOINABLE	DISSOCIABLE	DIVORCEMENT	DOWN PAYMENT
DISJUNCTION	DISSOCIATED	DOCTRINAIRE	DOWNPLAYING
DISJUNCTIVE	DISSOLUTELY	DOCUMENTARY	DOWN-TO-EARTH
DISJUNCTURE	DISSOLUTION	DOCUMENTING	DOWNTRODDEN
DISLOCATING	DISSOLUTIVE	DODDERINGLY	DOXOLOGICAL
DISLOCATION	DISSOLVABLE	DODECAGONAL	DRAGONFLIES
DISLODGMENT	DISSONANCES	DODECAPHONY	DRAMATIZING
DISMANTLING	DISSUADABLE	DOGBERRYISM	DRAMATURGIC
DISMASTMENT	DISSYLLABIC	DOG BISCUITS	DRASTICALLY
DISMEMBERED	DISSYLLABLE	DOGCATCHERS	DRAUGHTSMAN
DISMEMBERER	DISSYMMETRY	DOLABRIFORM	DRAUGHTSMEN
DISMISSIBLE	DISTASTEFUL	DOLEFULNESS	DRAWBRIDGES
DISMOUNTING	DISTEMPERED	DOLL'S HOUSES	DRAWING PINS
DISOBEDIENT	DISTENSIBLE	DOLORIMETRY	DRAWING ROOM
DISOBLIGING	DISTILLABLE	DOMESTICATE	DRAWSTRINGS
DISORDERING	DISTINCTION	DOMESTICITY	DREADNOUGHT
DISORGANIZE	DISTINCTIVE	DOMICILIARY	DREAMLESSLY
DISPARAGING	DISTINGUISH	DOMICILIATE	DREAM TICKET
DISPARATELY	DISTORTIONS	DOMINEERING	DREAM WORLDS
DISPARITIES	DISTRACTING	DOORKEEPERS	DRESS CIRCLE
DISPATCH BOX	DISTRACTION	DOORKNOCKER	DRESSMAKERS
DISPATCHING	DISTRACTIVE	DOORSTOPPER	DRESSMAKING
DISPENSABLE	DISTRAINING	DORMITORIES	DRILLMASTER
DISPIRITING	DISTRESSFUL	DOTTED LINES	DROMEDARIES
DISPLEASING	DISTRESSING	DOUBLE AGENT	DRUNKENNESS
DISPLEASURE	DISTRIBUTED	DOUBLE BINDS	DRY CLEANERS
DISPOSITION	DISTRIBUTOR	DOUBLE-BLIND	DRY-CLEANING
DISPROVABLE	DISTRUSTFUL	DOUBLE BLUFF	DSCONTINUER
DISPUTATION	DISTRUSTING	DOUBLE-CHECK	DUAL-PURPOSE
DISQUIETING	DISTURBANCE	DOUBLE CHINS	DUBIOUSNESS
DISQUIETUDE	DISULPHURIC	DOUBLE CREAM	DUDE RANCHES
DISREGARDED	DITHYRAMBIC	DOUBLE-CROSS	DUFFEL COATS
DISREGARDER	DITTOGRAPHY	DOUBLE DATED	DUMBFOUNDED
DISRELISHED	DIVARICATOR	DOUBLE DATES	DUMBFOUNDER
DISROBEMENT	DIVE-BOMBERS	DOUBLE-DUTCH	DUMBWAITERS
DISRUPTIONS	DIVE-BOMBING	DOUBLE-EDGED	DUNDERHEADS
DISSECTIBLE	DIVERGENCES	DOUBLE-FACED	DUNE BUGGIES
DISSECTIONS	DIVERGENTLY	DOUBLE FAULT	DUNFERMLINE
DISSEMBLERS	DIVERSIFIED	DOUBLE-GLAZE	DUPLEX HOUSE
DISSEMBLING	DIVERSIFIER	DOUBLE-QUICK	DUPLICATING

DUPLICATION	EFFECTUALLY	ELIMINATION	EMPTY-HANDED
DUPLICATIVE	EFFECTUATED	ELIMINATIVE	EMPTY-HEADED
DUPLICATORS	EFFERVESCED	ELIZABETHAN	EMULOUSNESS
DUST JACKETS	EFFICACIOUS	ELLIPSOIDAL	EMULSIFYING
DUTCH TREATS	EFFICIENTLY	ELLIPTICITY	EMULSIONING
DUTCH UNCLES	EGALITARIAN	ELONGATIONS	ENARTHROSIS
DUTIABILITY	EGOCENTRISM	ELUCIDATING	ENCAMPMENTS
DUTIFULNESS	EGOMANIACAL	ELUCIDATION	ENCAPSULATE
DYNAMICALLY	EGOTISTICAL	ELUCIDATIVE	ENCEPHALOMA
DYNAMOMETER	EGREGIOUSLY	ELUCIDATORY	ENCEPHALOUS
DYNAMOMETRY	EIDETICALLY	ELUSIVENESS	ENCHAINMENT
DYSFUNCTION	EIFFEL TOWER	ELUTRIATION	ENCHANTMENT
DYSFUNCTION	EIGHTEENTHS	EMANATIONAL	ENCHANTRESS
	EINSTEINIAN	EMANCIPATED	ENCHONDROMA
E	EINSTEINIUM	EMANCIPATOR	ENCOMIASTIC
EAGER BEAVER	EISTEDDFODS	EMASCULATED	ENCOMPASSED
EARNESTNESS	EJACULATING	EMASCULATOR	ENCOUNTERED
EARTHENWARE	EJACULATION	EMBANKMENTS	ENCOUNTERER
EARTH-GRAZER	EJACULATIVE	EMBARKATION	ENCOURAGING
EARTHLINESS	EJACULATORY	EMBARRASSED	ENCROACHING
EARTHQUAKES	EJECTOR SEAT	EMBELLISHED	ENCUMBERING
EAR TRUMPETS	ELABORATELY	EMBELLISHER	ENCUMBRANCE
EASEFULNESS	ELABORATING	EMBITTERING	ENCYCLICALS
EAST ANGLIAN	ELABORATION	EMBLAZONING	ENDANGERING
EASTERN CAPE	ELABORATIVE	EMBLEMATIZE	ENDEARINGLY
EASTERNMOST	ELASTICALLY	EMBOLDENING	ENDEARMENTS
EAST GERMANY	ELASTIC BAND	EMBOLECTOMY	ENDEAVOURED
EAST LOTHIAN	ELASTOMERIC	EMBRACEABLE	ENDEAVOURER
EATING APPLE	ELASTOPLAST	EMBRACEMENT	ENDEMICALLY
EBULLIENTLY	ELBOW GREASE	EMBROCATION	ENDLESSNESS
ECCLESIARCH	ELDERFLOWER	EMBROIDERED	ENDOBLASTIC
ECCRINOLOGY	ELECTIONEER	EMBROIDERER	ENDOCARDIAL
ECHCHYMOSED	ELECTORATES	EMBROILMENT	ENDOCARDIUM
ECHOPRACTIC	ELECTORSHIP	EMBRYECTOMY	ENDOCENTRIC
ECLECTICISM	ELECTRIC EYE	EMBRYOGENIC	ENDOCRANIUM
ECOFRIENDLY	ELECTRICIAN	EMENDATIONS	ENDOCRINOUS
ECONOMETRIC	ELECTRICITY	EMERGENCIES	ENDODONTICS
ECONOMIZING	ELECTRIFIED	EMIGRATIONS	ENDODONTIST
ECOSPECIFIC	ELECTRIFIER	EMMENAGOGIC	ENDOMETRIAL
ECTOBLASTIC	ELECTROCUTE	EMMENAGOGUE	ENDOMETRIUM
ECTOGENESIS	ELECTROFORM	EMOTIONALLY	ENDOMORPHIC
ECTOMORPHIC	ELECTROLYSE	EMOTIONLESS	ENDONEURIUM
ECTOPLASMIC	ELECTROLYTE	EMOTIVENESS	ENDOPLASMIC
ECTOSARCOUS	ELECTRONICS	EMPANELLING	ENDORSEMENT
EDAPHICALLY	ELECTROTYPE	EMPANELMENT	ENDOSCOPIST
EDIFICATION	ELEGIACALLY	EMPERORSHIP	ENDOSPERMIC
EDIFICATORY	ELEPHANTINE	EMPHASIZING	ENDOSPOROUS
EDITORIALLY	ELEPHANTOID	EMPIRICALLY	ENDOTHECIAL
EDUCABILITY	ELICITATION	EMPLACEMENT	ENDOTHECIUM
EDUCATIONAL	ELIGIBILITY	EMPLOYMENTS	ENDOTHELIAL
EFFECTIVELY	ELIMINATING	EMPOWERMENT	ENDOTHELIUM

ENDOTHERMIC	ENTRUSTMENT	ERYSIPELOID	EVAPORATION
END PRODUCTS	ENTWINEMENT	ERYTHEMATIC	EVAPORATIVE
ENFORCEABLE	ENUCLEATION	ERYTHRISMAL	EVASIVENESS
ENFORCEMENT	ENUMERATING	ERYTHROCYTE	EVENING STAR
ENFRANCHISE	ENUMERATION	ESCAPEMENTS	EVENTUALITY
ENGAGEMENTS	ENUMERATIVE	ESCAPE WHEEL	EVENTUATION
ENGENDERING	ENUNCIATING	ESCARPMENTS	EVERLASTING
ENGINEERING	ENUNCIATION	ESCHATOLOGY	EVISCERATED
ENGLISH HORN	ENUNCIATIVE	ESCUTCHEONS	EVISCERATOR
ENGORGEMENT	ENVELOPMENT	ESEMPLASTIC	EXACERBATED
ENGRAILMENT	ENVIOUSNESS	ESOPHAGUSES	EXAGGERATED
ENGROSSEDLY	ENVIRONMENT	ESOTERICISM	EXAGGERATOR
ENGROSSMENT	ENZYMOLYSIS	ESSENTIALLY	EXALTEDNESS
ENHANCEMENT	ENZYMOLYTIC	ESTABLISHED	EXAMINATION
ENLARGEABLE	EPHEMERALLY	ESTABLISHER	EXANIMATION
ENLARGEMENT	EPIDERMISES	ESTATE AGENT	EXASPERATED
ENLIGHTENED	EPIDIASCOPE	ESTREMADURA	EXASPERATER
ENLIGHTENER	EPIGASTRIUM	ETHANEDIOIC	EXCAVATIONS
ENLISTED MAN	EPIGENESIST	ETHEREALITY	EXCEEDINGLY
ENLISTED MEN	EPIGRAPHIST	ETHEREALIZE	EXCELLENTLY
ENLISTMENTS	EPIPHYTOTIC	ETHICALNESS	EXCEPTIONAL
ENLIVENMENT	EPITHALAMIC	ETHNOBOTANY	EXCERPTIBLE
ENNEAHEDRAL	EPITHELIOMA	ETHNOGENIST	EXCERPTTION
ENNEAHEDRON	EPITOMIZING	ETHNOGRAPHY	EXCESSIVELY
ENNISKILLEN	EPOCH-MAKING	ETHNOLOGIST	EXCITEDNESS
ENNOBLEMENT	EQUIANGULAR	ETIOLOGICAL	EXCITEMENTS
ENNOBLINGLY	EQUIDISTANT	ETYMOLOGIES	EXCLAMATION
ENRAPTURING	EQUILATERAL	ETYMOLOGIST	EXCLAMATORY
ENSHROUDING	EQUILIBRANT	EUCHARISTIC	EXCLUSIVELY
ENSLAVEMENT	EQUILIBRATE	EUCHROMATIC	EXCOGITATOR
ENSNAREMENT	EQUILIBRIST	EUCHROMATIN	EXCORIATING
ENTABLATURE	EQUILIBRIUM	EUDIOMETRIC	EXCORIATION
ENTABLEMENT	EQUINOCTIAL	EUGENICALLY	EXCREMENTAL
ENTEROSTOMY	EQUIPOLLENT	EUPHEMISTIC	EXCRESCENCE
ENTEROVIRUS	EQUIVALENCE	EURHYTHMICS	EXCRESCENCY
ENTERPRISER	EQUIVALENCY	EUROCENTRIC	EXCULPATING
ENTERPRISES	EQUIVALENTS	EUROCHEQUES	EXCULPATION
ENTERTAINED	EQUIVOCALLY	EURODOLLARS	EXCULPATORY
ENTERTAINER	EQUIVOCATED	EUROPEANISM	EX-DIRECTORY
ENTHRALLING	ERADICATING	EUROPEANIZE	EXECRATIONS
ENTHRALMENT	ERADICATION	EURO-SCEPTIC	EXECUTIONER
ENTHUSIASMS	ERADICATIVE	EURYTHERMAL	EXECUTORIAL
ENTHUSIASTS	ERADICATORS	EVACUATIONS	EXEMPLARILY
ENTICEMENTS	ERASTIANISM	EVAGINATION	EXEMPLIFIED
ENTITLEMENT	ERGATOCRACY	EVALUATIONS	EXEMPLIFIER
ENTOBLASTIC	EROSIVENESS	EVANESCENCE	EXERCISABLE
ENTOMBMENTS	EROTOMANIAC	EVANGELICAL	EXFOLIATION
ENTOMOPHILY	ERRATICALLY	EVANGELISTS	EXFOLIATIVE
ENTRAINMENT	ERRONEOUSLY	EVANGELIZED	EXHAUSTIBLE
ENTREATMENT	ERUBESCENCE	EVANGELIZER	EXHIBITIONS
ENTRENCHING	ERUCTATIONS	EVAPORATING	EXHILARATED

EXHILARATOR
EXHORTATION
EXHORTATIVE
EXHUMATIONS
EXISTENTIAL
EXONERATING
EXONERATION
EXONERATIVE
EXORABILITY
EXORBITANCE
EXOSKELETAL
EXOSKELETON
EXOTERICISM
EXPANSIVELY
EXPATIATING
EXPATIATION
EXPATRIATED
EXPATRIATES
EXPECTANTLY
EXPECTATION
EXPECTATIVE
EXPECTORANT
EXPECTORATE
EXPEDIENTLY
EXPEDITIONS
EXPEDITIOUS
EXPENDITURE
EXPENSIVELY
EXPERIENCED
EXPERIENCES
EXPERIMENTS
EXPLAINABLE
EXPLANATION
EXPLANATORY
EXPLICATING
EXPLICATION
EXPLICATIVE
EXPLOITABLE
EXPLORATION
EXPLORATORY
EXPLOSIVELY
EXPONENTIAL
EXPORTATION
EXPOSEDNESS
EXPOSITIONS
EX POST FACTO
EXPOSTULATE
EXPRESSIBLE
EXPRESSIONS
EXPRESSWAYS
EXPROPRIATE

EXPURGATING
EXPURGATION
EXPURGATORY
EXQUISITELY
EXSICCATION
EXSICCATIVE
EXSTIPULATE
EXTEMPORIZE
EXTENSIONAL
EXTENSIVELY
EXTENUATING
EXTENUATION
EXTENUATORY
EXTERIORIZE
EXTERMINATE
EXTERNALISM
EXTERNALIST
EXTERNALITY
EXTERNALIZE
EXTIRPATING
EXTIRPATION
EXTIRPATIVE
EXTOLLINGLY
EXTRACTABLE
EXTRACTIONS
EXTRADITING
EXTRADITION
EXTRAPOLATE
EXTRAVAGANT
EXTRAVAGATE
EXTRAVASATE
EXTREMENESS
EXTREMITIES
EXTRICATING
EXTRICATION
EXTROVERTED
EXUBERANTLY
EYE-CATCHING

F

FABRICATING
FABRICATION
FABRICATIVE
FACE-CENTRED
FACETIOUSLY
FACILITATED
FACILITATOR
FACT-FINDING
FACTORIZING
FACTORY FARM
FACTS OF LIFE

FACTUALNESS
FACULTATIVE
FAIRGROUNDS
FAIR-WEATHER
FAIRY LIGHTS
FAITH HEALER
FAITHLESSLY
FALCONIFORM
FALLIBILITY
FALLING STAR
FALSE ALARMS
FALSE BOTTOM
FALSE STARTS
FALSIFIABLE
FALSTAFFIAN
FALTERINGLY
FAMILIARITY
FAMILIARIZE
FAMILY NAMES
FAMILY TREES
FANATICALLY
FANTASIZING
FARCICALITY
FARINACEOUS
FARNBOROUGH
FARRAGINOUS
FAR-REACHING
FARTHERMOST
FARTHINGALE
FASCINATING
FASCINATION
FASCINATIVE
FASHIONABLE
FAST-BREEDER
FAST-FORWARD
FATEFULNESS
FATHER-IN-LAW
FATHERLANDS
FATUOUSNESS
FAULT-FINDER
FAULTLESSLY
FAVOURINGLY
FAVOURITISM
FAWNINGNESS
FEARFULNESS
FEASIBILITY
FEATHER BEDS
FEATHER BOAS
FEATHEREDGE
FEATURE FILM
FEATURELESS

FECUNDATION
FECUNDATORY
FEDERALISTS
FEDERATIONS
FELDSPATHIC
FELICITATED
FELICITATOR
FELLOWSHIPS
FELT-TIP PENS
FEMME FATALE
FENESTRATED
FERMENTABLE
FEROCIOUSLY
FERRICYANIC
FERRIFEROUS
FERRIS WHEEL
FERROCYANIC
FERRUGINOUS
FERTILIZERS
FERTILIZING
FERULACEOUS
FERVENTNESS
FESTINATION
FESTSCHRIFT
FETISHISTIC
FEUDALISTIC
FIBRE OPTICS
FIBROMATOUS
FIBROUSNESS
FICTIONALLY
FIDGETINGLY
FIELD-EFFECT
FIELD EVENTS
FIELD HOCKEY
FIELD-HOLLER
FIELD-TESTED
FIELDWORKER
FIFTH COLUMN
FIFTH-DEGREE
FIGURED BASS
FIGUREHEADS
FILAMENTARY
FILIBUSTERS
FILL THE BILL
FILMOGRAPHY
FILMSETTING
FILTHY LUCRE
FILTRATABLE
FIMBRIATION
FINANCIALLY
FIN DE SIECLE

FINE-GRAINED	FLEET STREET	FOOT FAULTED	FORMULATION
FINES HERBES	FLESHLINESS	FOOT-LAMBERT	FORMULISTIC
FINGERBOARD	FLESH WOUNDS	FOOT-POUNDAL	FORNICATING
FINGER BOWLS	FLETCHERISM	FOOTSLOGGED	FORNICATION
FINGERNAILS	FLEURS-DE-LIS	FOPPISHNESS	FORSWEARING
FINGERPLATE	FLEXIBILITY	FORAMINIFER	FORTHCOMING
FINGERPRINT	FLICK KNIVES	FORASMUCH AS	FORTIFIABLE
FINGERSTALL	FLIGHT DECKS	FORBEARANCE	FORTNIGHTLY
FIRE BRIGADE	FLIGHTINESS	FORBIDDANCE	FORTUNATELY
FIRECRACKER	FLIGHT PATHS	FOREBODINGS	FORT WILLIAM
FIRE ENGINES	FLINCHINGLY	FORECASTERS	FORWARDNESS
FIRE ESCAPES	FLIRTATIONS	FORECASTING	FOSSILIZING
FIRE FIGHTER	FLIRTATIOUS	FORECLOSING	FOSTERINGLY
FIRE HYDRANT	FLOATATIONS	FORECLOSURE	FOUL-MOUTHED
FIRELIGHTER	FLOCCULENCE	FOREFATHERS	FOUNDATIONS
FIREPROOFED	FLOODLIGHTS	FOREFINGERS	FOUNTAIN PEN
FIRE-RAISERS	FLOORBOARDS	FOREGROUNDS	FOURDRINIER
FIRE-RAISING	FLOOR CLOTHS	FOREMANSHIP	FOUR-POSTERS
FIRE STATION	FLOORWALKER	FOREQUARTER	FOURTEENTHS
FIRING SQUAD	FLOPPY DISKS	FORERUNNERS	FOX TERRIERS
FIRMAMENTAL	FLORESCENCE	FORESEEABLE	FRACTIONARY
FIRST COUSIN	FLORILEGIUM	FORESHORTEN	FRACTIONATE
FIRST-DEGREE	FLOUNDERING	FORESIGHTED	FRACTIONIZE
FIRST-FOOTER	FLOURISHING	FORESTALLED	FRACTIOUSLY
FIRST NATION	FLOWCHARTED	FORESTALLER	FRACTURABLE
FIRST NIGHTS	FLOWER GIRLS	FORESTATION	FRAGMENTARY
FIRST PERSON	FLOWERINESS	FORETELLING	FRAGMENTING
FIRST STRIKE	FLUCTUATING	FORETHOUGHT	FRAME OF MIND
FIRST-STRING	FLUCTUATION	FORE-TOPMAST	FRANCHISING
FISHEYE LENS	FLUID OUNCES	FORE-TOPSAIL	FRANCISCANS
FISH-EYE LENS	FLUORESCEIN	FOR EVERMORE	FRANCOPHILE
FISH FARMING	FLUORESCENT	FOREWARNING	FRANCOPHOBE
FISH FINGERS	FLUORIDATED	FORFEITABLE	FRANCOPHONE
FISHMONGERS	FLUOROMETER	FORGATHERED	FRANKFURTER
FISSIONABLE	FLUOROMETRY	FORGETFULLY	FRANKLINITE
FISSIPAROUS	FLUOROSCOPE	FORGET-ME-NOT	FRANTICALLY
FLABBERGAST	FLUOROSCOPY	FORGETTABLE	FRATERNALLY
FLAGELLANTS	FLYCATCHERS	FORGIVENESS	FRATERNIZED
FLAGELLATED	FLYING BOATS	FORGIVINGLY	FRATERNIZER
FLAMBOYANCE	FLYING FOXES	FORJUDGMENT	FRATRICIDAL
FLANNELETTE	FLYING SQUAD	FORLORN HOPE	FRATRICIDES
FLANNELLING	FLYING START	FORLORNNESS	FRAUDULENCE
FLASHLIGHTS	FLYSWATTERS	FORMALISTIC	FREDERICTON
FLASH POINTS	FOCAL LENGTH	FORMALITIES	FREDRIKSTAD
FLAT-CHESTED	FOLK DANCERS	FORMALIZING	FREEBOOTERS
FLATTERABLE	FOLLICULATE	FORMATIONAL	FREE-FLOATER
FLAUNTINGLY	FOMENTATION	FORMATIVELY	FREE-FOR-ALLS
FLAVOURINGS	FOOLISHNESS	FORMICATION	FREE-HEARTED
FLAVOURLESS	FOOL'S ERRAND	FORMULAICLY	FREEHOLDERS
FLAVOURSOME	FOOTBALLERS	FORMULARIZE	FREELANCING
FLEA MARKETS	FOOTBRIDGES	FORMULATING	FREELOADERS

FREELOADING
FREEMASONIC
FREEMASONRY
FREE PARDONS
FREE-SWIMMER
FREETHINKER
FREEWHEELED
FREEZE-DRIED
FRENCH BEANS
FRENCH BREAD
FRENCH DOORS
FRENCH FRIES
FRENCH HORNS
FRENCH LEAVE
FRENCH TOAST
FRENCHWOMAN
FREQUENCIES
FREQUENTING
FRETFULNESS
FREUDIANISM
FRIENDLIEST
FRIENDSHIPS
FRIGHTENING
FRIGHTFULLY
FRINGILLINE
FRIVOLITIES
FRIVOLOUSLY
FROGMARCHED
FRONDESCENT
FRONTOLYSIS
FRONT-RUNNER
FROSTBITTEN
FRUCTIFYING
FRUGIVOROUS
FRUITLESSLY
FRUIT SALADS
FRUSTRATING
FRUSTRATION
FRUTESCENCE
FULGURATING
FULGURATION
FULL-BLOODED
FULL-FLEDGED
FULL-MOUTHED
FULMINATING
FULMINATION
FULMINATORY
FULSOMENESS
FUNAMBULIST
FUN AND GAMES
FUNCTIONARY

FUNCTIONING
FUNDAMENTAL
FUNDHOLDING
FUNGIBILITY
FUNGISTATIC
FURALDEHYDE
FURIOUSNESS
FURNISHINGS
FURTHERANCE
FURTHERMORE
FURTHERMOST
FURTIVENESS

G
GAFF-TOPSAIL
GAINFULNESS
GALLANTNESS
GALLANTRIES
GALL BLADDER
GALLINACEAN
GALLIVANTED
GALLUP POLLS
GALVANIZING
GAMEKEEPERS
GAMEKEEPING
GAMETANGIAL
GAMETANGIUM
GAMETOGENIC
GAMETOPHORE
GAMETOPHYTE
GAMOGENESIS
GAMOGENETIC
GANG-BANGING
GARAGE SALES
GARBAGE CANS
GARDEN PARTY
GARNISHMENT
GARRISONING
GARRULOUSLY
GASEOUSNESS
GAS STATIONS
GASTRECTOMY
GASTRONOMES
GASTRONOMIC
GASTROPODAN
GASTROSCOPE
GASTROSCOPY
GASTROSTOMY
GASTROTRICH
GAS TURBINES
GATECRASHED

GATECRASHER
GATEKEEPERS
GEANTICLINE
GEGENSCHEIN
GELATINIZER
GEMMIPAROUS
GEMMULATION
GEMOLOGICAL
GENDARMERIE
GENEALOGIES
GENEALOGIST
GENE LIBRARY
GENERALIZED
GENERALIZER
GENERALNESS
GENERALSHIP
GENERATIONS
GENERATION X
GENERICALLY
GENETICALLY
GENETIC CODE
GENETICISTS
GENTEELNESS
GENTIANELLA
GENTLEMANLY
GENTLEWOMAN
GENTLEWOMEN
GENTRIFYING
GENUFLECTED
GENUFLECTOR
GENUINENESS
GEOCHEMICAL
GEODYNAMICS
GEOGRAPHERS
GEOGRAPHIES
GEOMAGNETIC
GEOPHYSICAL
GEOPOLITICS
GEOSTRATEGY
GEOSTROPHIC
GEOSYNCLINE
GEOTECTONIC
GERATOLOGIC
GERMANENESS
GERMINATING
GERMINATION
GERM WARFARE
GERONTOLOGY
GERRYMANDER
GESTATIONAL
GESTICULATE

GET CRACKING
GET-TOGETHER
GHASTLINESS
GHOSTBUSTER
GHOSTLINESS
GHOSTWRITER
GIANT KILLER
GIANT PANDAS
GIBBERELLIN
GIBBOUSNESS
GIFT-WRAPPED
GIGANTESQUE
GILA MONSTER
GILLYFLOWER
GINGER BEERS
GINGERBREAD
GINGER GROUP
GIRL FRIDAYS
GIRLFRIENDS
GIRLISHNESS
GIVE-AND-TAKE
GLADIOLUSES
GLAMORIZING
GLAMOROUSLY
GLARINGNESS
GLASSBLOWER
GLASSCUTTER
GLASSHOUSES
GLASS-MAKING
GLASS-WORKER
GLASTONBURY
GLAUCONITIC
GLEEFULNESS
GLOBEFLOWER
GLOBIGERINA
GLOCHIDIATE
GLOMERATION
GLOMERULATE
GLORIFIABLE
GLOSSECTOMY
GLOSSOLALIA
GLOTTAL STOP
GLOVE PUPPET
GLOWERINGLY
GLUE-SNIFFER
GLUTATHIONE
GLYPHOGRAPH
GNATCATCHER
GOALKEEPERS
GOALKEEPING
GO BALLISTIC

GODCHILDREN
GODDAUGHTER
GODFORSAKEN
GODLESSNESS
GOLD-BEATING
GOLD DIGGERS
GOLD-DIGGING
GOLDEN EAGLE
GOLDEN SYRUP
GOLDFINCHES
GOLF COURSES
GONIOMETRIC
GONOCOCCOID
GONORRHOEAL
GOOD EVENING
GOOD LOOKERS
GOOD-LOOKING
GOOD MORNING
GOOD-NATURED
GOOD OFFICES
GORDIAN KNOT
GORMANDIZED
GORMANDIZER
GOSSIPINGLY
GO TO THE DOGS
GOURMANDISE
GOURMANDISM
GOVERNESSES
GOVERNMENTS
GRACELESSLY
GRADABILITY
GRADATIONAL
GRADE SCHOOL
GRADUALNESS
GRADUATIONS
GRAECO-ROMAN
GRAMMARIANS
GRAMMATICAL
GRAMOPHONES
GRANDADDIES
GRAND BAHAMA
GRAND CANARY
GRANDE-TERRE
GRANDFATHER
GRANDIOSITY
GRAND JURIES
GRAND MASTER
GRANDMOTHER
GRAND OPERAS
GRANDPARENT
GRAND PIANOS

GRAND RAPIDS
GRANDSTANDS
GRANGEMOUTH
GRANGERIZER
GRANITEWARE
GRANIVOROUS
GRANNY KNOTS
GRANOLITHIC
GRANOPHYRIC
GRANULARITY
GRANULATION
GRANULATIVE
GRANULOCYTE
GRAPEFRUITS
GRAPHICALLY
GRAPHOLOGIC
GRAPHOMOTOR
GRASSHOPPER
GRASS WIDOWS
GRAVESTONES
GRAVIMETRIC
GRAVITATING
GRAVITATION
GRAVITATIVE
GREASEPAINT
GREASY SPOON
GREAT CIRCLE
GREAT-NEPHEW
GREENBOTTLE
GREENGROCER
GREENHOUSES
GREENLANDER
GREENOCKITE
GREEN PAPERS
GREEN PEPPER
GRETNA GREEN
GRIDDLECAKE
GRIMACINGLY
GRINDELWALD
GRINDSTONES
GRISTLINESS
GRIZZLY BEAR
GROTESQUELY
GROTESQUERY
GROUCHINESS
GROUND CREWS
GROUND FLOOR
GROUND GLASS
GROUNDLINGS
GROUND PLANS
GROUND RENTS

GROUND RULES
GROUNDSHEET
GROUNDSPEED
GROUND STAFF
GROUNDSWELL
GROUPUSCULE
GRUELLINGLY
GRUMBLINGLY
GUADALAJARA
GUADALCANAL
GUARDEDNESS
GUARDHOUSES
GUELDER-ROSE
GUESSTIMATE
GUESTHOUSES
GUEST WORKER
GUILELESSLY
GUILLOTINED
GUILLOTINER
GUILLOTINES
GUILTLESSLY
GULLIBILITY
GUN CARRIAGE
GUNSMITHING
GURGITATION
GUTLESSNESS
GUTTA-PERCHA
GUTTER PRESS
GUTTERSNIPE
GUTTURALIZE
GYNAECOLOGY
GYPSIFEROUS
GYROCOMPASS
GYROSCOPICS
GYROSTATICS

H

HABERDASHER
HABILITATOR
HABITATIONS
HABITUATING
HABITUATION
HABITUDINAL
HADROSAURUS
HAEMACHROME
HAEMATOCELE
HAEMATOCRIT
HAEMATOLOGY
HAEMATOZOON
HAEMOCHROME
HAEMOCYANIN

HAEMOGLOBIN
HAEMOPHILIA
HAEMOPHILIC
HAEMOPTYSIS
HAEMORRHAGE
HAEMOSTASIA
HAEMOSTASIS
HAEMOSTATIC
HAGGADISTIC
HAGGARDNESS
HAGGISHNESS
HAGIOGRAPHA
HAGIOGRAPHY
HAGIOLOGIST
HAGIOSCOPIC
HAIRBREADTH
HAIRBRUSHES
HAIRDRESSER
HAIRPIN BEND
HAIR-RAISING
HAIRSPRINGS
HAIRSTYLIST
HAIR TRIGGER
HAIRWEAVING
HALBERSTADT
HALCYON DAYS
HALF-BROTHER
HALF-CENTURY
HALF-HEARTED
HALF-HOLIDAY
HALFPENNIES
HALF-SISTERS
HALF VOLLEYS
HALLMARKING
HALLUCINATE
HALOPHYTISM
HALTEMPRICE
HALTERNECKS
HALTINGNESS
HAMILTONIAN
HAMMERSMITH
HAMMERSTEIN
HAMMOCK-LIKE
HANDBREADTH
HANDCUFFING
HANDFASTING
HANDICAPPED
HANDICAPPER
HANDICRAFTS
HAND IN GLOVE
HAND LUGGAGE

HANDMAIDENS	HEALTH FOODS	HEMIHYDRATE	HEXAGONALLY
HAND-ME-DOWNS	HEALTHFULLY	HEMIMORPHIC	HEXAHYDRATE
HANDWRITING	HEALTHINESS	HEMIPTEROUS	HEXASTICHIC
HANDWRITTEN	HEARING AIDS	HEMISPHERES	HEXASTICHON
HANG GLIDING	HEART ATTACK	HEMISPHERIC	HEXATEUCHAL
HAPHAZARDLY	HEARTBROKEN	HEMITERPENE	HIBERNATING
HAPLESSNESS	HEARTHSTONE	HEMITROPISM	HIBERNATION
HAPLOGRAPHY	HEARTLESSLY	HEMOPHILIAC	HIBERNICISM
HAPPY EVENTS	HEARTSOMELY	HEMORRHAGES	HIDE-AND-SEEK
HAPPY MEDIUM	HEARTTHROBS	HEMORRHOIDS	HIDEOUSNESS
HARASSINGLY	HEATHENNESS	HEMSTITCHER	HIERARCHIES
HARBOURLESS	HEAT SHIELDS	HEPPLEWHITE	HIERARCHISM
HARD-AND-FAST	HEAVENWARDS	HEPTAHEDRAL	HIEROCRATIC
HARDECANUTE	HEAVY-HANDED	HEPTAHEDRON	HIEROGLYPHS
HARD-HEARTED	HEAVYWEIGHT	HEPTAMEROUS	HIEROLOGIST
HARD-HITTING	HEBDOMADARY	HEPTANGULAR	HIGH COMMAND
HARDICANUTE	HEBEPHRENIA	HEPTAVALENT	HIGHFALUTIN
HARD PALATES	HEBEPHRENIC	HERBIVOROUS	HIGH JUMPERS
HARD-PRESSED	HEBRAICALLY	HERCEGOVINA	HIGHLANDERS
HARDWEARING	HECKELPHONE	HERCULANEUM	HIGHLIGHTED
HARDY ANNUAL	HECTOGRAPHY	HEREDITABLE	HIGHLIGHTER
HAREBRAINED	HEDGEHOPPER	HEREDITABLY	HIGH-PITCHED
HARMFULNESS	HEEDFULNESS	HEREINAFTER	HIGH-POWERED
HARMONISTIC	HEGELIANISM	HERETICALLY	HIGH PRIESTS
HARMONIZING	HEIGHTENING	HERMENEUTIC	HIGH PROFILE
HARNESSLESS	HEINOUSNESS	HERMOUPOLIS	HIGH-RANKING
HARNESS-LIKE	HELICHRYSUM	HERO WORSHIP	HIGH SCHOOLS
HARPOON-LIKE	HELICOGRAPH	HERPESVIRUS	HIGH SHERIFF
HARPSICHORD	HELICOPTERS	HERPETOLOGY	HIGH-TENSION
HARRIS TWEED	HELIOCHROME	HERRINGBONE	HIGH TREASON
HARROWINGLY	HELIOGRAPHS	HERZEGOVINA	HIGHWAY CODE
HARTEBEESTS	HELIOGRAPHY	HESITATIONS	HIGH WYCOMBE
HARUM SCARUM	HELIOLITHIC	HESPERIDIAN	HILARIOUSLY
HARUM-SCARUM	HELIOMETRIC	HESPERIDIUM	HILLBILLIES
HARVEST HOME	HELIOSTATIC	HESYCHASTIC	HINDERINGLY
HARVESTLESS	HELIOTACTIC	HETAERISTIC	HINDQUARTER
HARVEST MOON	HELIOTROPES	HETEROCLITE	HINSHELWOOD
HATCHET JOBS	HELIOTROPIC	HETEROECISM	HIPPEASTRUM
HATCHET-LIKE	HELIOTROPIN	HETEROGRAFT	HIPPOCAMPAL
HATEFULNESS	HELLEBORINE	HETEROLYSIS	HIPPOCAMPUS
HAUGHTINESS	HELLENISTIC	HETEROLYTIC	HIPPOCRATES
HAUSTELLATE	HELLISHNESS	HETEROPHONY	HIPPOCRATIC
HAUTES-ALPES	HELMINTHOID	HETEROPHYTE	HIPPOPOTAMI
HAUTE-SAVOIE	HELPFULNESS	HETEROPOLAR	HIPPO REGIUS
HAUTE-VIENNE	HELPING HAND	HETEROSPORY	HIRSUTENESS
HAWKISHNESS	HELSINGBORG	HETEROSTYLY	HISPANICISM
HAZARDOUSLY	HEMERALOPIA	HETEROTAXIS	HISPANICIST
HEADDRESSES	HEMERALOPIC	HETEROTOPIA	HISPANICIZE
HEADHUNTERS	HEMIANOPSIA	HETEROTOPIC	HISTAMINASE
HEADHUNTING	HEMIELYTRAL	HETEROTYPIC	HISTIOCYTIC
HEADMASTERS	HEMIELYTRON	HEXADECIMAL	HISTOLOGIST

HISTORIATED	HONEYMOONED	HULLABALOOS	ICOSAHEDRON
HISTORICISM	HONEYMOONER	HUMAN RIGHTS	IDENTICALLY
HISTORICIST	HONEYSUCKER	HUMDRUMNESS	IDENTIFYING
HISTORICITY	HONEYSUCKLE	HUMIDIFIERS	IDEOLOGICAL
HISTRIONICS	HONORARIUMS	HUMIDIFYING	IDIOBLASTIC
HITCHHIKERS	HONOURS LIST	HUMILIATING	IDIOGRAPHIC
HITCHHIKING	HOODWINKING	HUMILIATION	IDIOMORPHIC
HOBBLEDEHOY	HOOLIGANISM	HUMILIATIVE	IDIOTICALLY
HOBBYHORSES	HOPEFULNESS	HUMILIATORY	IDOLATRIZER
HOGGISHNESS	HOPLOLOGIST	HUMMINGBIRD	IDOLIZATION
HOLKAR STATE	HORIZONLESS	HUNCHBACKED	IDYLLICALLY
HOLLANDAISE	HORIZONTALS	HUNGER MARCH	IGNIS FATUUS
HOLOBLASTIC	HORNBLENDIC	HUNNISHNESS	IGNOMINIOUS
HOLOCAUSTAL	HORNET'S NEST	HURRIEDNESS	IGNORAMUSES
HOLOGRAPHIC	HORNSWOGGLE	HURTFULNESS	ILE-DE-FRANCE
HOLOHEDRISM	HORROR FILMS	HUSBANDLESS	ILL-ASSORTED
HOLOMORPHIC	HORS D'OEUVRE	HYACINTHINE	ILL-FAVOURED
HOLOTHURIAN	HORSE DOCTOR	HYDNOCARPIC	ILLIBERALLY
HOMECOMINGS	HORSELAUGHS	HYDRARGYRIC	ILLIMITABLE
HOMEOPATHIC	HORSE OPERAS	HYDRARGYRUM	ILL-MANNERED
HOMEOSTASIS	HORSERADISH	HYDROCARBON	ILLOGICALLY
HOMEOSTATIC	HORTATORILY	HYDROCYANIC	ILL-TEMPERED
HOMERICALLY	HOSPITALITY	HYDROGENATE	ILL-TREATING
HOMESTEADER	HOSPITALIZE	HYDROGENIZE	ILLUMINANCE
HOME STRETCH	HOSPITALLER	HYDROGENOUS	ILLUMINATED
HOMICIDALLY	HOSTILITIES	HYDROGRAPHY	ILLUMINATOR
HOMOCENTRIC	HOT-CROSS BUN	HYDROLOGIST	ILLUSIONARY
HOMOEOPATHS	HOTHEADEDLY	HYDROLYSATE	ILLUSIONISM
HOMOEOPATHY	HOT POTATOES	HYDROMANCER	ILLUSIONIST
HOMOEROTISM	HOT-TEMPERED	HYDROMANTIC	ILLUSTRATED
HOMOGENEITY	HOURGLASSES	HYDROMEDUSA	ILLUSTRATOR
HOMOGENEOUS	HOUSE ARREST	HYDROMETEOR	ILLUSTRIOUS
HOMOGENIZED	HOUSEBROKEN	HYDROPHOBIA	ILLUVIATION
HOMOGENIZER	HOUSEFATHER	HYDROPONICS	I'M A DUTCHMAN
HOMOGRAPHIC	HOUSEHOLDER	HYPERACTIVE	IMAGINARILY
HOMOIOUSIAN	HOUSEKEEPER	HYPERMARKET	IMAGINATION
HOMOLOGICAL	HOUSE LIGHTS	HYPHENATING	IMAGINATIVE
HOMOLOGIZER	HOUSEMASTER	HYPHENATION	IMBRICATION
HOMOMORPHIC	HOUSEMOTHER	HYPNOTIZING	IMITABILITY
HOMOPHONOUS	HOUSEPARENT	HYPODERMICS	IMITATIONAL
HOMOPHYLLIC	HOUSEPLANTS	HYPOSTATIZE	IMITATIVELY
HOMOPLASTIC	HOUSEWIFELY	HYPOTHERMIA	IMMEDIATELY
HOMOPTEROUS	HOUSEWIFERY		IMMEDICABLE
HOMO SAPIENS	HOUSEWORKER	**I**	IMMIGRATING
HOMOSEXUALS	HOVERCRAFTS	ICEBREAKERS	IMMIGRATION
HOMOSPOROUS	HOW DO YOU DOS	ICHNOGRAPHY	IMMOBILIZED
HOMOTHALLIC	HSIN-HAI-LIEN	ICHTHYOLOGY	IMMOBILIZER
HOMOTHERMAL	HUCKLEBERRY	ICONOCLASTS	IMMORTALITY
HOMOZYGOSIS	HUCKSTERISM	ICONOGRAPHY	IMMORTALIZE
HOMOZYGOTIC	HUDIBRASTIC	ICONOLOGIST	IMMUNOASSAY
HONEYCOMBED	HUGUENOTISM	ICOSAHEDRAL	IMMUNOGENIC

IMMUNOLOGIC	IMPRECATION	INCOME TAXES	INDIVIDUATE
IMPANELLING	IMPRECATORY	INCOMMODING	INDIVISIBLE
IMPARTATION	IMPRECISION	INCOMPETENT	INDIVISIBLY
IMPARTIALLY	IMPREGNABLE	INCOMPLIANT	INDOCHINESE
IMPASSIONED	IMPREGNABLY	IN CONDITION	INDO-HITTITE
IMPASSIVELY	IMPREGNATED	INCONGRUITY	INDO-IRANIAN
IMPASSIVITY	IMPREGNATOR	INCONGRUOUS	INDOMITABLE
IMPASTATION	IMPRESARIOS	INCONSONANT	INDOMITABLY
IMPATIENTLY	IMPRESSIBLE	INCONSTANCY	INDO-PACIFIC
IMPEACHABLE	IMPRESSIONS	INCONTINENT	INDORSEMENT
IMPEACHMENT	IMPRESSMENT	INCORPORATE	INDUBITABLE
IMPECUNIOUS	IMPRIMATURS	INCORPOREAL	INDUBITABLY
IMPEDIMENTA	IMPRISONING	INCORRECTLY	INDUCEMENTS
IMPEDIMENTS	IMPROPRIATE	INCREASABLE	INDUCTILITY
IMPENITENCE	IMPROPRIETY	INCREASEDLY	INDUCTIONAL
IMPERATIVES	IMPROVEMENT	INCREDULITY	INDUCTIVELY
IMPERFECTLY	IMPROVIDENT	INCREDULOUS	INDULGENCES
IMPERFORATE	IMPROVINGLY	INCREMENTAL	INDULGENTLY
IMPERIALISM	IMPROVISING	INCRIMINATE	INDULGINGLY
IMPERIALIST	IMPRUDENTLY	INCULCATING	INDUPLICATE
IMPERILLING	IMPUGNATION	INCULCATION	INDUSTRIOUS
IMPERIOUSLY	IMPUISSANCE	INCULPATING	INEBRIATING
IMPERMANENT	IMPULSIVELY	INCULPATION	INEBRIATION
IMPERMEABLE	IMPUTATIONS	INCUNABULAR	INEDIBILITY
IMPERSONATE	INADVERTENT	INCURIOSITY	INEFFECTIVE
IMPERTINENT	INADVISABLE	INCURVATION	INEFFECTUAL
IMPETRATION	INALIENABLE	INCURVATURE	INEFFICIENT
IMPETRATIVE	INALTERABLE	INDECIDUOUS	INELEGANTLY
IMPETUOSITY	INATTENTION	INDEFINABLE	INELOQUENCE
IMPETUOUSLY	INATTENTIVE	INDEFINABLY	INELUCTABLE
IMPINGEMENT	INAUGURATED	INDEHISCENT	INELUCTABLY
IMPIOUSNESS	INAUGURATOR	INDEMNIFIED	INEQUITABLE
IMPLAUSIBLE	INAUTHENTIC	INDEMNIFIER	INEQUITABLY
IMPLAUSIBLY	INCALESCENT	INDEMNITIES	INERTIA REEL
IMPLEADABLE	INCANTATION	INDENTATION	INESCAPABLE
IMPLEMENTAL	INCAPSULATE	INDENTURING	INESCAPABLY
IMPLEMENTED	INCARCERATE	INDEPENDENT	INESSENTIAL
IMPLEMENTER	INCARDINATE	INDEX FINGER	INESTIMABLE
IMPLICATING	INCARNATING	INDIA RUBBER	INESTIMABLY
IMPLICATION	INCARNATION	INDICATABLE	INEXACTNESS
IMPLICATIVE	INCERTITUDE	INDICATIONS	INEXCUSABLE
IMPLORATION	INCESSANTLY	INDICATIVES	INEXCUSABLY
IMPLORATORY	INCIDENTALS	INDICTMENTS	INEXISTENCE
IMPLORINGLY	INCINERATED	INDIFFERENT	INEXPEDIENT
IMPORTANTLY	INCINERATOR	INDIGESTION	INEXPENSIVE
IMPORTATION	INCIPIENTLY	INDIGESTIVE	INFANTICIDE
IMPORTUNATE	INCLINATION	INDIGNANTLY	INFANTILISM
IMPORTUNING	INCLUSIVELY	INDIGNATION	INFANTILITY
IMPORTUNITY	INCOERCIBLE	INDIGNITIES	INFANTRYMAN
IMPOSITIONS	INCOGNIZANT	INDIRECTION	INFANTRYMEN
IMPRACTICAL	INCOHERENCE	INDIVIDUALS	INFATUATION

INFERENTIAL
INFERIORITY
INFERNALITY
INFERTILITY
INFESTATION
INFILTRATED
INFILTRATOR
INFINITIVAL
INFINITIVES
INFIRMARIES
INFIRMITIES
INFLAMINGLY
INFLAMMABLE
INFLECTIONS
INFLICTIONS
INFLUENCING
INFLUENTIAL
INFOMERCIAL
INFORMALITY
INFORMATION
INFORMATIVE
INFORMINGLY
INFRACOSTAL
INFRACTIONS
INFRANGIBLE
INFREQUENCY
INFURIATING
INFURIATION
INFUSIONISM
INFUSIONIST
INGENIOUSLY
INGENUOUSLY
INGRAINEDLY
INGRATIATED
INGRATITUDE
INGREDIENTS
INGURGITATE
INHABITABLE
INHABITANCY
INHABITANTS
INHALATIONS
INHERITABLE
INHERITANCE
INHIBITABLE
INHIBITEDLY
INHIBITIONS
INITIALLING
INITIATIONS
INITIATIVES
INITIATRESS
INJUDICIOUS

INJUNCTIONS
INJURIOUSLY
IN-LINE SKATE
INNER CITIES
INNERVATION
INNOCUOUSLY
INNOVATIONS
INNS OF COURT
INNUMERABLE
INNUTRITION
INOBSERVANT
INOCULATING
INOCULATION
INOCULATIVE
INOFFENSIVE
INOFFICIOUS
INOPERATIVE
INOPPORTUNE
IN PERPETUUM
INQUILINISM
INQUILINOUS
INQUIRINGLY
INQUISITION
INQUISITIVE
INQUISITORS
IN-RESIDENCE
INSALUBRITY
INSCRIBABLE
INSCRIPTION
INSCRIPTIVE
INSCRUTABLE
INSCRUTABLY
INSECTARIUM
INSECTICIDE
INSECTIVORE
INSEMINATED
INSEMINATOR
INSENSITIVE
INSENTIENCE
INSEPARABLE
INSEPARABLY
INSERTIONAL
INSESSORIAL
INSIDE TRACK
INSIDIOUSLY
INSINCERELY
INSINCERITY
INSINUATING
INSINUATION
INSINUATIVE
INSISTENTLY

INSOUCIANCE
INSPECTABLE
INSPECTIONS
INSPECTORAL
INSPIRATION
INSPIRATIVE
INSPIRATORY
INSPIRINGLY
INSTABILITY
INSTALMENTS
INSTATEMENT
INSTIGATING
INSTIGATION
INSTIGATIVE
INSTIGATORS
INSTINCTIVE
INSTITUTING
INSTITUTION
INSTITUTIVE
INSTRUCTING
INSTRUCTION
INSTRUCTIVE
INSTRUCTORS
INSTRUMENTS
INSUFFLATOR
INSUPERABLE
INSUPERABLY
INTAGLIATED
INTEGRATING
INTEGRATION
INTEGRATIVE
INTEGUMENTS
INTELLIGENT
INTEMPERATE
INTENSIFIED
INTENSIFIER
INTENSIONAL
INTENSIVELY
INTENTIONAL
INTERACTING
INTERACTION
INTERACTIVE
INTERATOMIC
INTERBEDDED
INTERCALARY
INTERCALATE
INTERCEDING
INTERCEPTED
INTERCEPTOR
INTERCESSOR
INTERCHANGE

INTERCOSTAL
INTERCOURSE
INTERDENTAL
INTERDICTOR
INTERESTING
INTERFACING
INTERFERING
INTERFUSION
INTERJECTED
INTERJECTOR
INTERLACING
INTERLARDED
INTERLINEAR
INTERLINGUA
INTERLINING
INTERLINKED
INTERLOCKED
INTERLOCKER
INTERLOPERS
INTERMEZZOS
INTERMINGLE
INTERMITTOR
INTERNALITY
INTERNALIZE
INTERNECINE
INTERNEURON
INTERNMENTS
INTERNSHIPS
INTERNUNCIO
INTERPOLATE
INTERPOSING
INTERPRETED
INTERPRETER
INTERRACIAL
INTERRADIAL
INTERREGNAL
INTERREGNUM
INTERRELATE
INTERROBANG
INTERROGATE
INTERRUPTED
INTERRUPTER
INTERSECTED
INTERSEXUAL
INTERSPERSE
INTERSTICES
INTERTRIBAL
INTERTWINED
INTERVENING
INTERVIEWED
INTERVIEWEE

INTERVIEWER	INVITATIONS	ITHYPHALLIC	KINDREDNESS
INTERWEAVER	INVOCATIONS	ITINERARIES	KINETICALLY
INTIMATIONS	INVOLUCRATE	ITINERATION	KINETOPLAST
INTIMIDATED	INVOLUNTARY	IVORY TOWERS	KINGFISHERS
INTIMIDATOR	INVOLVEMENT		KISS OF DEATH
INTOLERABLE	IONOSPHERIC	**J**	KITCHENETTE
INTOLERABLY	IPECACUANHA		KITCHENWARE
INTOLERANCE	IRIDESCENCE	JACKHAMMERS	KITTENISHLY
INTONATIONS	IRISH COFFEE	JACK-KNIFING	KLEPTOMANIA
INTOXICABLE	IRON CURTAIN	JACKRABBITS	KNEECAPPING
INTOXICANTS	IRONMONGERS	JACTITATION	KNICK-KNACKS
INTOXICATED	IRONMONGERY	JAM SESSIONS	KNIGHTHOODS
INTOXICATOR	IRON RATIONS	JANISSARIES	KNUCKLEBONE
INTRA-ATOMIC	IRRADIATING	JAWBREAKERS	KOOKABURRAS
INTRACOSTAL	IRRADIATION	JAYAWARDENE	KRASNOYARSK
INTRACTABLE	IRRADIATIVE	JEHOSHAPHAT	KRISTIANSEN
INTRACTABLY	IRRECUSABLE	JELLYFISHES	KRUGERRANDS
INTRADERMAL	IRREDENTISM	JEOPARDIZED	KRUGERSDORP
INTRAVENOUS	IRREDENTIST	JETTISONING	KUALA LUMPUR
INTRENCHING	IRREDUCIBLE	JOHORE BAHRU	KUMARATUNGE
INTREPIDITY	IRREDUCIBLY	JOIE DE VIVRE	KWANGCHOWAN
INTRICACIES	IRREFUTABLE	JOURNALISTS	KWASHIORKOR
INTRICATELY	IRREFUTABLY	JOURNALIZER	KYANIZATION
INTRODUCING	IRREGULARLY	JOYLESSNESS	KYMOGRAPHIC
INTROVERTED	IRRELEVANCE	JUDAIZATION	
INTRUDINGLY	IRRELIGIOUS	JUDGMENT DAY	**L**
INTRUSIONAL	IRREMOVABLE	JUDICATURES	
INTUITIONAL	IRREPARABLE	JUDICIOUSLY	LABIODENTAL
INTUITIVELY	IRREPARABLY	JUGGERNAUTS	LABORIOUSLY
INTUITIVISM	IRRESOLUBLE	JUGULAR VEIN	LABOR UNIONS
INTUITIVIST	IRRETENTIVE	JUMBLE SALES	LABOURINGLY
INTUMESCENT	IRREVERENCE	JUSTICESHIP	LABOUR PARTY
INUNDATIONS	IRREVOCABLE	JUSTICIABLE	LABRADORITE
INVAGINABLE	IRREVOCABLY	JUSTIFIABLE	LACCOLITHIC
INVALIDATED	IRRITATIONS	JUSTIFIABLY	LACERATIONS
INVALIDATOR	ISAAC NEWTON	JUVENESCENT	LACERTILIAN
INVENTIONAL	ISOCHRONIZE	JUXTAPOSING	LACINIATION
INVENTIVELY	ISODIAPHERE		LACONICALLY
INVENTORIAL	ISOELECTRIC	**K**	LACQUERWARE
INVENTORIES	ISOGEOTHERM		LACRIMATION
INVERTEBRAL	ISOLABILITY	KALASHNIKOV	LACRIMATORY
INVESTIGATE	ISOLECITHAL	KALININGRAD	LACTALBUMIN
INVESTITIVE	ISOMAGNETIC	KANCHIPURAM	LACTATIONAL
INVESTITURE	ISOMETRICAL	KARLOVY VARY	LACTESCENCE
INVESTMENTS	ISOMETROPIA	KERB CRAWLER	LACTIFEROUS
INVIABILITY	ISOMORPHISM	KETTLEDRUMS	LADY-KILLERS
INVIDIOUSLY	ISORHYTHMIC	KEYBOARDERS	LAEVOGYRATE
INVIGILATED	ISOTONICITY	KEYBOARDING	LAGOMORPHIC
INVIGILATOR	ITACOLUMITE	KEYPUNCHERS	LAICIZATION
INVIGORATED	ITALICIZING	KIDNEY BEANS	LAKE DWELLER
INVIGORATOR	ITEMIZATION	KILIMANJARO	LAKE SUCCESS
		KILLER WHALE	LAMELLATION
		KIND-HEARTED	

LAMELLICORN
LAMELLIFORM
LAMELLOSITY
LAMENTATION
LAMENTINGLY
LAMINAR FLOW
LAMMERGEIER
LAMPROPHYRE
LANARKSHIRE
LANCASTRIAN
LANCINATION
LANDHOLDING
LANDING GEAR
LANDING NETS
LANDLUBBERS
LANDSCAPING
LANDSCAPIST
LANGUISHING
LAPAROSCOPY
LAPIS LAZULI
LARGE-MINDED
LARKISHNESS
LARYNGOLOGY
LARYNGOTOMY
LATITUDINAL
LAUDABILITY
LAUGHING GAS
LAUNDERETTE
LAURUSTINUS
LAW-BREAKERS
LAWBREAKING
LAWLESSNESS
LAWN PARTIES
LAY BROTHERS
LEADING LADY
LEAF-CLIMBER
LEAPFROGGED
LEARNEDNESS
LEASEHOLDER
LEATHERBACK
LEATHERETTE
LEATHERHEAD
LEATHERWOOD
LEAVENWORTH
LEAVE TAKING
LECHEROUSLY
LECITHINASE
LECTURESHIP
LEFT-HANDERS
LEFT-WINGERS
LEGAL TENDER

LEGATIONARY
LEGERDEMAIN
LEGIONARIES
LEGIONNAIRE
LEGISLATING
LEGISLATION
LEGISLATIVE
LEGISLATORS
LEGISLATURE
LEGITIMIZED
LEMON SQUASH
LENGTHENING
LENGTHINESS
LENTIGINOUS
LEPIDOSIREN
LEPRECHAUNS
LEPROSARIUM
LEPTORRHINE
LESE-MAJESTY
LET OFF STEAM
LETTER BOMBS
LETTERBOXES
LETTERHEADS
LETTERPRESS
LEUCOCRATIC
LEUCODERMAL
LEUCORRHOEA
LEUCOTOMIES
LEVEL-HEADED
LIABILITIES
LIANYUNGANG
LIBELLOUSLY
LIBERAL ARTS
LIBERALIZED
LIBERALIZER
LIBERALNESS
LIBERATRESS
LIBERTARIAN
LIBERTICIDE
LIBERTINISM
LIBRATIONAL
LIBRETTISTS
LICENTIATES
LICKSPITTLE
LIE DETECTOR
LIEUTENANCY
LIEUTENANTS
LIFE JACKETS
LIFE OF RILEY
LIFE STORIES
LIGAMENTOUS

LIGHT-FOOTED
LIGHT-HEADED
LIGHTHOUSES
LIGHTWEIGHT
LIKABLENESS
LILLIPUTIAN
LILY-LIVERED
LIMITATIONS
LIMITLESSLY
LIMNOLOGIST
LIMP-WRISTED
LINDISFARNE
LINEAMENTAL
LINE DANCING
LINE DRAWING
LINEN BASKET
LINE OF SIGHT
LINE PRINTER
LINERTRAINS
LINGERINGLY
LINGUISTICS
LION-HEARTED
LIONIZATION
LIPOPROTEIN
LIPOSUCTION
LIQUEFIABLE
LIQUESCENCE
LIQUIDAMBAR
LIQUIDATING
LIQUIDATION
LIQUIDATORS
LIQUIDIZERS
LIQUIDIZING
LISTERIOSIS
LITERALNESS
LITERATURES
LITHOGRAPHS
LITHOGRAPHY
LITHOLOGIST
LITHOMETEOR
LITHOPHYTIC
LITHOSPHERE
LITHOTOMIST
LITTERATEUR
LITTERLOUTS
LITTLE WOMAN
LITURGISTIC
LIVABLENESS
LIVELIHOODS
LIVING ROOMS
LLOYD WEBBER

LO AND BEHOLD
LOATHSOMELY
LOBSTERPOTS
LOCAL COLOUR
LOCALIZABLE
LOCAL OPTION
LOCKER ROOMS
LOCK KEEPERS
LOCOMOTIVES
LOCUM TENENS
LOGARITHMIC
LOGGERHEADS
LOGISTICIAN
LOGOGRAPHER
LOGOGRIPHIC
LOGOMACHIST
LOGOPAEDICS
LOITERINGLY
LOLLIPOP MAN
LOLLIPOP MEN
LONDONDERRY
LONG JUMPERS
LONGSIGHTED
LONGWEARING
LOOSE CANNON
LOOSE CHANGE
LOOSESTRIFE
LOPHOBRANCH
LORD PROVOST
LORD'S PRAYER
LOSS LEADERS
LOTUS-EATERS
LOUDHAILERS
LOUDMOUTHED
LOUDSPEAKER
LOUNGE SUITS
LOUTISHNESS
LOVE AFFAIRS
LOW COMEDIES
LOWER SAXONY
LOW-PRESSURE
LOW PROFILES
LOW-SPIRITED
LOXODROMICS
LOYALTY CARD
LUBRICATING
LUBRICATION
LUBRICATIVE
LUBRICATORS
LUCRATIVELY
LUCUBRATION

LUDICROUSLY	MAGNIFICENT	MANIFESTOES	MASS-PRODUCE
LUDWIGSBURG	MAHARASHTRA	MANIPULATED	MASTER CARDS
LUGGAGE RACK	MAIDENHEADS	MANIPULATOR	MASTERCLASS
LUGGAGE VANS	MAIDEN NAMES	MANNERISTIC	MASTERFULLY
LUMBERINGLY	MAIDSERVANT	MANNISHNESS	MASTERMINDS
LUMBERJACKS	MAILING LIST	MANOEUVRING	MASTERPIECE
LUMBER-ROOMS	MAIN CLAUSES	MANOR HOUSES	MASTERWORKS
LUMBERYARDS	MAINSPRINGS	MANSERVANTS	MASTICATING
LUMBRICALIS	MAINTAINING	MANTELPIECE	MASTICATION
LUMINESCENT	MAINTENANCE	MANTELSHELF	MASTICATORY
LUNAR MONTHS	MAIN-TOPMAST	MANTOUX TEST	MASTOIDITIS
LUSTFULNESS	MAINTOPSAIL	MANUFACTORY	MASTROIANNI
LUTHERANISM	MAISONETTES	MANUFACTURE	MASTURBATED
LUXULIANITE	MAKE-BELIEVE	MANUSCRIPTS	MATCHLESSLY
LUXURIANTLY	MAKES A POINT	MARASCHINOS	MATCHMAKERS
LUXURIATING	MAKHACHKALA	MARCESCENCE	MATCHMAKING
LUXURIATION	MALADJUSTED	MARCHIONESS	MATCH POINTS
LUXURIOUSLY	MALADROITLY	MAR DEL PLATA	MATCHSTICKS
LYMPHANGIAL	MALAPROPIAN	MARE CLAUSUM	MATERIALISM
LYMPHOBLAST	MALAPROPISM	MARE LIBERUM	MATERIALIST
LYMPHOCYTIC	MALCONTENTS	MARGINALITY	MATERIALITY
LYTHRACEOUS	MALEDICTION	MARGINATION	MATERIALIZE
	MALEDICTIVE	MARICULTURE	MATERNALISM
M	MALEFACTION	MARINE CORPS	MATHEMATICS
MACADAMIZER	MALEFACTORS	MARIONETTES	MATINEE IDOL
MACHICOLATE	MALEFICENCE	MARKETPLACE	MATRIARCHAL
MACHINATION	MALEVOLENCE	MARKET PRICE	MATRICULANT
MACHINE CODE	MALFEASANCE	MARKET TOWNS	MATRICULATE
MACHINEGUNS	MALFUNCTION	MARKOV CHAIN	MATRILINEAL
MACHINE TOOL	MALICIOUSLY	MARLBOROUGH	MATRIMONIAL
MACROBIOTIC	MALIGNANTLY	MARQUESSATE	MAUDLINNESS
MACROCOSMIC	MALINGERERS	MARQUISETTE	MAUNDY MONEY
MACROGAMETE	MALINGERING	MARRAM GRASS	MAURITANIAN
MACROPHAGIC	MALOCCLUDED	MARROWBONES	MAWKISHNESS
MACROSCOPIC	MALONIC ACID	MARSHALLING	MAYONNAISES
MADDENINGLY	MALPOSITION	MARSHMALLOW	MEADOWSWEET
MADEIRA CAKE	MALPRACTICE	MARTENSITIC	MEANDERINGS
MADRIGALIAN	MALTED MILKS	MARTIAL ARTS	MEANINGLESS
MADRIGALIST	MALTREATING	MARTINETISH	MEASURELESS
MAGDALENIAN	MAMMALOGIST	MARTINETISM	MEASUREMENT
MAGGOTINESS	MAMMIFEROUS	MARTYROLOGY	MECHANICIAN
MAGHERAFELT	MAMMOGRAPHY	MASCULINIST	MECHANISTIC
MAGIC BULLET	MAMMONISTIC	MASCULINITY	MECHANIZING
MAGISTERIAL	MANAGEMENTS	MASKING TAPE	MECKLENBURG
MAGISTRALLY	MANDATORILY	MASOCHISTIC	MEDIASTINAL
MAGISTRATES	MANDOLINIST	MASONICALLY	MEDIASTINUM
MAGLEMOSIAN	MANEUVERING	MASQUERADED	MEDICAMENTS
MAGNANIMITY	MANHANDLING	MASQUERADER	MEDICATIONS
MAGNANIMOUS	MANICHAEISM	MASQUERADES	MEDICINALLY
MAGNETIZING	MANICURISTS	MASSACHUSET	MEDICINE MAN
MAGNIFIABLE	MANIFESTING	MASSIVENESS	MEDICINE MEN

MEDIEVALISM	MERRYMAKERS	MICROMETERS	MISALLIANCE
MEDIEVALIST	MERRYMAKING	MICROMETRIC	MISANTHROPE
MEDITATIONS	MESALLIANCE	MICROPHONES	MISANTHROPY
MEERSCHAUMS	MESENCHYMAL	MICROPHONIC	MISAPPLYING
MEGACEPHALY	MESMERIZING	MICROPHYTIC	MISBEGOTTEN
MEGALOBLAST	MESOBENTHOS	MICROREADER	MISBEHAVING
MEGALOMANIA	MESOCEPHALY	MICROSCOPES	MISCARRIAGE
MEGALOPOLIS	MESOGASTRIC	MICROSCOPIC	MISCARRYING
MEIOTICALLY	MESOMORPHIC	MICROSECOND	MISCELLANEA
MELANCHOLIA	MESONEPHRIC	MICROSPORIC	MISCHIEVOUS
MELANCHOLIC	MESONEPHROS	MICROTOMIST	MISCIBILITY
MELIORATION	MESOPHYLLIC	MIDDLEBROWS	MISCONCEIVE
MELIORATIVE	MESOPOTAMIA	MIDDLE CLASS	MISCONSTRUE
MELLIFEROUS	MESOSPHERIC	MIDDLE NAMES	MISCOUNTING
MELLIFLUOUS	MESOTHELIAL	MIDDLE-SIZED	MISCREATION
MELODICALLY	MESOTHELIUM	MIDNIGHT SUN	MISDESCRIBE
MELODIOUSLY	MESOTHORIUM	MIGRATIONAL	MISDIRECTED
MELTABILITY	METABOLISMS	MILITARISTS	MISE-EN-SCENE
MELTING POTS	METACENTRIC	MILITARIZED	MISERLINESS
MEMBERSHIPS	METAGENESIS	MILLEFLEURS	MISFEASANCE
MEMORABILIA	METAGENETIC	MILLENARIAN	MISFORTUNES
MEMORANDUMS	METALLOCENE	MILLILITRES	MISGOVERNOR
MEMORIALIST	METALLOIDAL	MILLIMETRES	MISGUIDANCE
MEMORIALIZE	METALLURGIC	MILLIMICRON	MISGUIDEDLY
MEMORIZABLE	METALWORKER	MILLIONAIRE	MISHANDLING
MENAQUINONE	METAMORPHIC	MILLISECOND	MISINFORMED
MENDELEVIUM	METANEPHROS	MIMEOGRAPHS	MISJUDGMENT
MENDEL'S LAWS	METAPHYSICS	MIMETICALLY	MISMANAGING
MENORRHAGIA	METAPLASMIC	MIMOSACEOUS	MISMATCHING
MENORRHAGIC	METASTASIZE	MINAS GERAIS	MISOGYNISTS
MENSTRUATED	METATHERIAN	MIND-BENDING	MISONEISTIC
MENSURATION	METATHESIZE	MIND-BLOWING	MISPRINTING
MENSURATIVE	METEMPIRICS	MINDFULNESS	MISREMEMBER
MENTALISTIC	METEOROLOGY	MIND READERS	MISREPORTED
MENTALITIES	METHODOLOGY	MIND READING	MISSING LINK
MENTAL NOTES	METHYLAMINE	MINERALIZER	MISSISSAUGA
MENTHACEOUS	METHYLATION	MINERAL OILS	MISSISSIPPI
MENTHOLATED	METONYMICAL	MINESWEEPER	MISSPELLING
MENTIONABLE	METRICATION	MINIATURIST	MISSPENDING
MEPROBAMATE	METRICIZING	MINIATURIZE	MISTRUSTFUL
MERCENARIES	METROLOGIST	MINIMUM WAGE	MISTRUSTING
MERCENARILY	MICHIGANDER	MINISTERIAL	MITHRIDATIC
MERCHANDISE	MICHIGANITE	MINISTERING	MITOTICALLY
MERCHANTMAN	MICKEY MOUSE	MINISTERIUM	MIXED GRILLS
MERCHANTMEN	MICROCOCCUS	MINISTRANTS	MOBILE HOMES
MERCILESSLY	MICROCOSMIC	MINNEAPOLIS	MOBILE PHONE
MERCURATION	MICROFICHES	MINOR PLANET	MOBILIZABLE
MERCURIALLY	MICROFILMED	MINUTE STEAK	MOCKINGBIRD
MERITOCRACY	MICROGAMETE	MIRACLE PLAY	MODERNISTIC
MERITORIOUS	MICROGRAPHY	MIRROR IMAGE	MODERNIZING
MEROBLASTIC	MICROGROOVE	MIRTHLESSLY	MODULATIONS

MOHAMMEDANS	MONSEIGNEUR	MUMS THE WORD	NARCOLEPTIC
MOISTURIZED	MONSTRANCES	MUNDANENESS	NARRATOLOGY
MOISTURIZER	MONSTROSITY	MUNICIPALLY	NARROW BOATS
MOLESTATION	MONSTROUSLY	MUNIFICENCE	NARROW GAUGE
MOLLIFIABLE	MONS VENERIS	MURDERESSES	NASOFRONTAL
MOLLYCODDLE	MONTENEGRAN	MURDEROUSLY	NASOGASTRIC
MOLYBDENITE	MONTPELLIER	MURMURINGLY	NASOPHARYNX
MOLYBDENOUS	MOONLIGHTER	MUSCLE-BOUND	NASTURTIUMS
MOMENTARILY	MORAVIANISM	MUSCOVY DUCK	NATIONALISM
MONARCHICAL	MORIBUNDITY	MUSCULARITY	NATIONALIST
MONARCHISTS	MORNING COAT	MUSCULATURE	NATIONALITY
MONASTERIAL	MORNING STAR	MUSEUM PIECE	NATIONALIZE
MONASTERIES	MORONICALLY	MUSHROOMING	NATION STATE
MONASTICISM	MORPHOLOGIC	MUSICALNESS	NATURALISTS
MONETARISTS	MORRIS DANCE	MUSIC CENTRE	NATURALIZED
MONEYLENDER	MORTALITIES	MUSKELLUNGE	NATURALNESS
MONEYMAKERS	MORTARBOARD	MUSTACHIOED	NATUROPATHS
MONEYMAKING	MORTISE LOCK	MUTAGENESIS	NATUROPATHY
MONEY ORDERS	MOSQUITO NET	MUTILATIONS	NAUGHTINESS
MONEY SUPPLY	MOTHERBOARD	MUTTERINGLY	NEANDERTHAL
MONITORSHIP	MOTHER-IN-LAW	MUTTONCHOPS	NEAR EASTERN
MONOCHASIAL	MOTHER'S BOYS	MUTUAL FUNDS	NEARSIGHTED
MONOCHASIUM	MOTHER'S RUIN	MYCOLOGICAL	NECESSARIES
MONOCHROMAT	MOTHERS-TO-BE	MYCOPROTEIN	NECESSARILY
MONOCHROMIC	MOTHPROOFED	MYCORRHIZAL	NECESSITATE
MONOCLINISM	MOTORCYCLES	MYELOMATOID	NECESSITIES
MONOCLINOUS	MOTOR LODGES	MYOCARDITIS	NECESSITOUS
MONOCULTURE	MOUNTAINEER	MYRIAPODOUS	NECKERCHIEF
MONOGENESIS	MOUNTAINOUS	MYRMECOLOGY	NECROBIOSIS
MONOGENETIC	MOUNTAINTOP	MYSTERY PLAY	NECROBIOTIC
MONOGRAMMED	MOUNTBATTEN	MYSTERY TOUR	NECROLOGIST
MONOGRAPHER	MOUNTEBANKS	MYSTIFIEDLY	NECROMANCER
MONOGRAPHIC	MOUTHORGANS	MYTHOLOGIES	NECROMANTIC
MONOHYDRATE	MOUTHPIECES	MYTHOLOGIST	NECROPHILIA
MONOHYDROXY	MOUTHWASHES	MYTHOLOGIZE	NECROPHILIC
MONOLATROUS	MOXIBUSTION	MYTHOMANIAC	NECROPHOBIA
MONOLINGUAL	MUCOPROTEIN	MYTHOPOEISM	NECROPHOBIC
MONOMANIACS	MUCRONATION	MYTHOPOEIST	NEEDFULNESS
MONOMORPHIC	MUDDLEDNESS	MYXOMATOSIS	NEEDLEPOINT
MONONUCLEAR	MUDSLINGING		NEEDLEWOMAN
MONOPHAGOUS	MUHAMMADANS	**N**	NEEDLEWOMEN
MONOPHTHONG	MULTANGULAR	NAILBRUSHES	NE'ER-DO-WELLS
MONOPOLISTS	MULTINOMIAL	NAIL VARNISH	NEFARIOUSLY
MONOPOLIZED	MULTIPARITY	NAKHICHEVAN	NEGLIGENTLY
MONOPOLIZER	MULTIPAROUS	NAMEDROPPED	NEGOTIATING
MONOSTICHIC	MULTIPLEXER	NAMEDROPPER	NEGOTIATION
MONOSTROPHE	MULTIPLYING	NAPHTHALENE	NEGOTIATORS
MONOSTYLOUS	MULTIRACIAL	NAPKIN RINGS	NEIGHBOURLY
MONOTERPENE	MULTISCREEN	NARAYANGANJ	NEOCOLONIAL
MONOTHEISTS	MULTISTOREY	NARCISSISTS	NEOLOGISTIC
MONOVALENCE	MULTIVALENT	NARCISSUSES	NEPHELINITE

NEPHOLOGIST
NEPHRECTOMY
NE PLUS ULTRA
NERVE CENTRE
NERVELESSLY
NERVOUSNESS
NETHERLANDS
NEUROFIBRIL
NEUROLOGIST
NEUROMATOUS
NEUROPATHIC
NEUROPTERAN
NEUROTICISM
NEUROTOMIST
NEUTRALIZED
NEUTRALIZER
NEUTRON BOMB
NEVER-NEVERS
NEVER SAY DIE
NEW PLYMOUTH
NEWPORT NEWS
NEW POTATOES
NEWSCASTERS
NEWSLETTERS
NEWSREADERS
NEWSVENDORS
NEW YEAR'S DAY
NEW YEAR'S EVE
NICENE CREED
NICKELODEON
NICTITATION
NIETZSCHEAN
NIGHTINGALE
NIGHTLIGHTS
NIGHTMARISH
NIGHT-PORTER
NIGHT SCHOOL
NIGHTSHADES
NIGHT SHIFTS
NIGHTSHIRTS
NIGHTSTICKS
NIGRESCENCE
NINCOMPOOPS
NINETEENTHS
NINETY-NINES
NISHINOMIYA
NITRIFIABLE
NITROGENIZE
NITROGENOUS
NITROMETRIC
NITROSAMINE

NITTY-GRITTY
NIZHNI TAGIL
NOBEL PRIZES
NOCICEPTIVE
NOCTILUCENT
NOCTURNALLY
NOISELESSLY
NOISOMENESS
NOMADICALLY
NO-MAN'S-LANDS
NOMENCLATOR
NOMINATIONS
NOMINATIVES
NOMOGRAPHER
NOMOGRAPHIC
NOMOLOGICAL
NOMS DE PLUME
NONCHALANCE
NONCREATIVE
NONDESCRIPT
NONENTITIES
NONETHELESS
NONEXISTENT
NONFEASANCE
NONHARMONIC
NONILLIONTH
NONINVASIVE
NONIRRITANT
NONMETALLIC
NONOPERABLE
NONPARTISAN
NONPLUSSING
NONRESIDENT
NONSENSICAL
NON SEQUITUR
NONSTANDARD
NONSTARTERS
NONVERBALLY
NONVIOLENCE
NORMALIZING
NORTHAMPTON
NORTH DAKOTA
NORTHEASTER
NORTHERNERS
NORTH ISLAND
NORTHUMBRIA
NORTHWESTER
NOSOGRAPHER
NOSOGRAPHIC
NOSOLOGICAL
NOSY PARKERS

NOTABLENESS
NOTHINGNESS
NOTHING TO IT
NOTICE BOARD
NOTOCHORDAL
NOTORIOUSLY
NOTOTHERIUM
NOURISHMENT
NOVOSIBIRSK
NOXIOUSNESS
NUCLEAR-FREE
NUCLEIC ACID
NUCLEOPLASM
NUEVO LAREDO
NULL AND VOID
NULLIFIDIAN
NULLIPAROUS
NUMBERPLATE
NUMERATIONS
NUMERICALLY
NUMISMATICS
NUMISMATIST
NUNCUPATIVE
NURSING HOME
NUTCRACKERS
NUTRITIONAL
NYCTINASTIC
NYCTITROPIC
NYCTOPHOBIA
NYCTOPHOBIC
NYMPHOLEPSY
NYMPHOMANIA

O

OARSMANSHIP
OBFUSCATING
OBFUSCATION
OBITER DICTA
OBJECTIVELY
OBJECTIVISM
OBJECTIVIST
OBJECTIVITY
OBJET TROUVE
OBJURGATION
OBJURGATORY
OBLIGATIONS
OBLIQUITOUS
OBLITERATED
OBLITERATOR
OBLIVIOUSLY
OBNOXIOUSLY

OBSCENITIES
OBSCURATION
OBSCURITIES
OBSERVANCES
OBSERVATION
OBSERVATORY
OBSESSIONAL
OBSOLESCENT
OBSTINATELY
OBSTIPATION
OBSTRUCTING
OBSTRUCTION
OBSTRUCTIVE
OBTRUSIVELY
OBVIOUSNESS
OCCASIONING
OCCIDENTALS
OCCULTATION
OCCUPATIONS
OCCURRENCES
OCHLOCRATIC
OCHLOPHOBIA
OCTAHEDRITE
OCTILLIONTH
ODDS AND ENDS
ODONTOBLAST
ODONTOGRAPH
ODONTOPHORE
ODORIFEROUS
ODOROUSNESS
OENOLOGICAL
OESOPHAGEAL
OESTROGENIC
OFFENSIVELY
OFFERTORIES
OFFHANDEDLY
OFFICE BLOCK
OFFICIALDOM
OFFICIALESE
OFFICIATING
OFFICIATION
OFFICIOUSLY
OFF-LICENCES
OIL PAINTING
OIL-SEED RAPE
OLD-WOMANISH
OLEOGRAPHIC
OLIGARCHIES
OLIGOCHAETE
OLIGOTROPHY
OLIVE BRANCH

OMINOUSNESS	ORIGINATION	OUTSTANDING	OXFORDSHIRE
OMMATOPHORE	ORIGINATORS	OUTSTRIPPED	OXIDATIONAL
OMNIFARIOUS	ORNAMENTING	OUTWEIGHING	OXIDIMETRIC
OMNIPOTENCE	ORNITHOLOGY	OVERACHIEVE	OXIDIZATION
OMNIPRESENT	ORNITHOPTER	OVERANXIOUS	OXYCEPHALIC
OMNISCIENCE	ORTHOCENTRE	OVERARCHING	OXYGENATING
ONAGRACEOUS	ORTHODONTIC	OVERBALANCE	OXYGENATION
ONCOLOGICAL	ORTHOGRAPHY	OVERBEARING	OXYGEN MASKS
ONE-MAN BANDS	ORTHOPAEDIC	OVERBIDDING	OXYGEN TENTS
ONEROUSNESS	ORTHOPTERAN	OVERBOOKING	OXYHYDROGEN
ONTOLOGICAL	ORTHOSCOPIC	OVERCHARGED	OXYSULPHIDE
OPALESCENCE	ORTHOSTICHY	OVERCHARGES	OZONIFEROUS
OPEN-AND-SHUT	ORTHOTROPIC	OVERCLOUDED	OZONIZATION
OPENHEARTED	OSCILLATING	OVERCROPPED	OZONOSPHERE
OPENING TIME	OSCILLATION	OVERCROWDED	
OPEN LETTERS	OSCILLATORS	OVERDEVELOP	**P**
OPEN-MOUTHED	OSCILLATORY	OVERDRAUGHT	PACE BOWLERS
OPEN SEASONS	OSCILLOGRAM	OVERDRAWING	PACIFICALLY
OPEN SECRETS	OSMOTICALLY	OVERDRESSED	PACKAGE DEAL
OPEN SESAMES	OSTENTATION	OVEREXPOSED	PACKAGE TOUR
OPEN VERDICT	OSTEOCLASIS	OVERFLOWING	PACK ANIMALS
OPERABILITY	OSTEOLOGIST	OVERGARMENT	PACKING CASE
OPERATIONAL	OSTEOPATHIC	OVERHAULING	PAEDIATRICS
OPHIOLOGIST	OSTEOPHYTIC	OVERHEARING	PAEDOLOGIST
OPHTHALMIAC	OSTEOPLASTY	OVERINDULGE	PAINFULNESS
OPINIONATED	OSTRACIZING	OVERLAPPING	PAINKILLERS
OPINION POLL	OSTRACODERM	OVERLOADING	PAINSTAKING
OPPORTUNELY	OSTRACODOUS	OVERLOOKING	PALAEARCTIC
OPPORTUNISM	OUAGADOUGOU	OVERMANNING	PALATINATES
OPPORTUNIST	OUIJA BOARDS	OVERPLAYING	PALEOGRAPHY
OPPORTUNITY	OUTBALANCED	OVERPOWERED	PALEOLITHIC
OPPOSITIONS	OUTBUILDING	OVERPRODUCE	PALESTINIAN
OPPROBRIOUS	OUTCLASSING	OVERPROTECT	PALIMPSESTS
OPTICAL DISC	OUTDISTANCE	OVERREACHED	PALINDROMES
OPTOMETRIST	OUTERCOURSE	OVERREACTED	PALINDROMIC
ORANGUTANGS	OUTFIELDERS	OVERRUNNING	PALLBEARERS
ORCHESTRATE	OUTFIGHTING	OVERSELLING	PALLIATIVES
ORDER-DRIVEN	OUTFLANKING	OVERSTAFFED	PALM SPRINGS
ORDERLINESS	OUT-HERODING	OVERSTATING	PALPABILITY
ORDER PAPERS	OUTNUMBERED	OVERSTAYING	PALPITATING
ORDINATIONS	OUT OF BOUNDS	OVERSTEPPED	PALPITATION
ORGANICALLY	OUT OF POCKET	OVERSTOCKED	PAMPAS GRASS
ORIEL WINDOW	OUT-OF-THE-WAY	OVERSTUFFED	PAMPHLETEER
ORIENTALISM	OUTPATIENTS	OVERTOPPING	PAN-AMERICAN
ORIENTALIST	OUTPOINTING	OVERTURNING	PANCAKE ROLL
ORIENTALIZE	OUTPOURINGS	OVERWEENING	PANCHEN LAMA
ORIENTATING	OUTRIVALING	OVERWHELMED	PANDEMONIAC
ORIENTATION	OUTRIVALLED	OVERWORKING	PANDEMONIUM
ORIGINALITY	OUTSMARTING	OVERWROUGHT	PANDORA'S BOX
ORIGINAL SIN	OUT SOURCING	OVIPOSITION	PANEGYRICAL
ORIGINATING	OUTSPOKENLY	OWNER-DRIVER	PANHANDLERS

PANHANDLING	PARI-MUTUELS	PATRILINEAL	PENTAMETERS
PANHELLENIC	PARIPINNATE	PATRIMONIAL	PENTANGULAR
PANIC ATTACK	PARISH CLERK	PATROL WAGON	PENTATHLONS
PANJANDRUMS	PARISHIONER	PATRONIZING	PENTAVALENT
PANTELLERIA	PARKING LOTS	PATRON SAINT	PENTECOSTAL
PANTHEISTIC	PARK KEEPERS	PATRONYMICS	PENTLANDITE
PANTOGRAPHS	PARLIAMENTS	PAUNCHINESS	PENULTIMATE
PANTOGRAPHY	PARLOUR GAME	PAVING STONE	PENURIOUSLY
PANTOMIMIST	PAROCHIALLY	PAWNBROKERS	PEOPLE MOVER
PAPER CHASES	PARONOMASIA	PAWNBROKING	PEPPERCORNS
PAPER-CUTTER	PARSON'S NOSE	PAY ENVELOPE	PEPPER MILLS
PAPERHANGER	PART COMPANY	PAY STATIONS	PEPPERMINTS
PAPER KNIVES	PARTIALNESS	PEACH MELBAS	PEPTIC ULCER
PAPER TIGERS	PARTICIPANT	PEACOCK BLUE	PEPTIZATION
PAPERWEIGHT	PARTICIPATE	PEARL DIVERS	PERAMBULATE
PAPIER-MACHE	PARTICIPIAL	PEARLY GATES	PERCEIVABLE
PAPYRACEOUS	PARTICIPLES	PEASHOOTERS	PERCENTAGES
PARABLASTIC	PARTICULARS	PECCABILITY	PERCEPTIBLE
PARACETAMOL	PARTICULATE	PECCADILLOS	PERCEPTIBLY
PARACHUTING	PARTING SHOT	PECTINATION	PERCHLORATE
PARACHUTIST	PARTITIONED	PECTIZATION	PERCHLORIDE
PARADOXICAL	PARTITIONER	PECULATIONS	PERCIPIENCE
PARAGENESIS	PARTITIVELY	PECULIARITY	PERCOLATING
PARAGENETIC	PARTNERSHIP	PECUNIARILY	PERCOLATION
PARAGLIDING	PARTURIENCY	PEDESTRIANS	PERCOLATIVE
PARAGRAPHIA	PARTURITION	PEDICULOSIS	PERCOLATORS
PARAGRAPHIC	PARTY PIECES	PEDICURISTS	PEREGRINATE
PARALDEHYDE	PARTY POOPER	PEDOLOGICAL	PERENNIALLY
PARALEIPSIS	PAS-DE-CALAIS	PEDUNCULATE	PERFECTIBLE
PARALLACTIC	PASQUINADER	PEEPING TOMS	PERFORATING
PARALLELING	PASSIBILITY	PEEVISHNESS	PERFORATION
PARALLELISM	PASSIONLESS	PELARGONIUM	PERFORATIVE
PARALLELIST	PASSION PLAY	PELLUCIDITY	PERFORMABLE
PARALLELLED	PASSIONTIDE	PELOPONNESE	PERFORMANCE
PARALYMPICS	PASSIVENESS	PENALTY AREA	PERFUNCTORY
PARAMEDICAL	PASTEBOARDS	PENDULOUSLY	PERICARDIUM
PARAMORPHIC	PASTEURIZED	PENETRALIAN	PERICARPIAL
PARAMOUNTCY	PASTEURIZER	PENETRATING	PERICLASTIC
PARAPHRASED	PAST MASTERS	PENETRATION	PERICRANIAL
PARAPHRASES	PAST PERFECT	PENETRATIVE	PERICRANIUM
PARAPLASTIC	PASTURELAND	PENICILLATE	PERIDOTITIC
PARAPLEGICS	PATCH POCKET	PENICILLIUM	PERIGORDIAN
PARASAILING	PATELLIFORM	PENITENTIAL	PERIHELIONS
PARATHYROID	PATERNALISM	PENNYWEIGHT	PERIMORPHIC
PARATROOPER	PATERNALIST	PENNYWORTHS	PERINEURIUM
PARATYPHOID	PATERNOSTER	PENOLOGICAL	PERIODICALS
PARENTHESES	PATHFINDERS	PENSIONABLE	PERIODICITY
PARENTHESIS	PATHFINDING	PENSIVENESS	PERIODONTAL
PARENTHETIC	PATHOLOGIST	PENTADACTYL	PERIODONTIC
PARESTHESIA	PATISSERIES	PENTAHEDRON	PERIOD PIECE
PARESTHETIC	PATRIARCHAL	PENTAMEROUS	PERIOSTITIC

PERIOSTITIS	PERTINENTLY	PHOTOCOPIED	PILLOWCASES
PERIPATETIC	PERTURBABLE	PHOTOCOPIER	PILLOW FIGHT
PERIPETEIAN	PERTURBABLY	PHOTOCOPIES	PILOCARPINE
PERIPHERALS	PERVASIVELY	PHOTO FINISH	PILOT LIGHTS
PERIPHERIES	PERVERSIONS	PHOTOGRAPHS	PINA COLADAS
PERIPHRASES	PERVERTEDLY	PHOTOGRAPHY	PINCUSHIONS
PERIPHRASIS	PERVERTIBLE	PHOTOMETRIC	PINEAL GLAND
PERISHABLES	PESSIMISTIC	PHOTONASTIC	PINE MARTENS
PERISHINGLY	PESTERINGLY	PHOTO-OFFSET	PINNATISECT
PERISPERMAL	PESTIFEROUS	PHOTOPERIOD	PINOCYTOSIS
PERISTALSIS	PESTILENCES	PHOTOPHOBIA	PINPOINTING
PERISTALTIC	PETITIONARY	PHOTOPHOBIC	PIPE CLEANER
PERITHECIUM	PETITIONERS	PHOTOSETTER	PIPE OF PEACE
PERITONEUMS	PETITIONING	PHOTOSPHERE	PIPERACEOUS
PERITONITIC	PETRODOLLAR	PHOTOSTATIC	PIPISTRELLE
PERITONITIS	PETROGRAPHY	PHOTOTACTIC	PIRATICALLY
PERIWINKLES	PETROLOGIST	PHOTOTROPIC	PIROUETTING
PERLOCUTION	PETTIFOGGER	PHRASAL VERB	PISCATORIAL
PERMANENTLY	PETTISHNESS	PHRASEBOOKS	PISCIVOROUS
PERMISSIBLE	PHAGOMANIAC	PHRASEOGRAM	PISTON RINGS
PERMISSIBLY	PHAGOPHOBIA	PHRASEOLOGY	PITCHBLENDE
PERMUTATION	PHAGOPHOBIC	PHTHIRIASIS	PITCHFORKED
PERORATIONS	PHALANSTERY	PHYCOLOGIST	PITCHOMETER
PERPETRATED	PHANEROZOIC	PHYCOMYCETE	PITEOUSNESS
PERPETRATOR	PHARMACISTS	PHYLLOCLADE	PITH HELMETS
PERPETUALLY	PHARYNGITIS	PHYLLOTAXIS	PITIFULNESS
PERPETUATED	PHELLOGENIC	PHYLOTACTIC	PITUITARIES
PERPLEXEDLY	PHENETIDINE	PHYSIATRICS	PLACABILITY
PERQUISITES	PHENOLOGIST	PHYSICALISM	PLAGIARISMS
PERSECUTING	PHILANDERER	PHYSICALIST	PLAGIARISTS
PERSECUTION	PHILATELIST	PHYSIOGNOMY	PLAGIARIZED
PERSECUTIVE	PHILHELLENE	PHYTOGRAPHY	PLAGIARIZER
PERSECUTORS	PHILIPPINES	PICKPOCKETS	PLAGIOCLASE
PERSEVERANT	PHILISTINES	PICKWICKIAN	PLAINSPOKEN
PERSEVERING	PHILOLOGIST	PICTORIALLY	PLAINTIVELY
PERSIAN CATS	PHILOSOPHER	PICTURE BOOK	PLANETARIUM
PERSISTENCE	PHLEBOTOMIC	PICTURE CARD	PLANETOIDAL
PERSNICKETY	PHONETICIAN	PICTURESQUE	PLANIMETRIC
PERSONALISM	PHONOGRAMIC	PIECE OF CAKE	PLANISPHERE
PERSONALIST	PHONOGRAPHS	PIECE OF WORK	PLANO-CONVEX
PERSONALITY	PHONOGRAPHY	PIEDMONTITE	PLANOGRAPHY
PERSONALIZE	PHONOLOGIST	PIEDS-A-TERRE	PLANOMETRIC
PERSONATION	PHONOMETRIC	PIEZOMETRIC	PLANTAGENET
PERSONATIVE	PHONOTYPIST	PIGEONHOLED	PLANTATIONS
PERSONIFIED	PHOSPHATASE	PIGEONHOLES	PLANTIGRADE
PERSPECTIVE	PHOSPHATIZE	PIGGISHNESS	PLASMAGENIC
PERSPICUITY	PHOSPHORATE	PIGHEADEDLY	PLASMODESMA
PERSPICUOUS	PHOSPHORISM	PIGSTICKING	PLASMOLYSIS
PERSUADABLE	PHOSPHORITE	PILE DRIVERS	PLASMOLYTIC
PERSUASIONS	PHOSPHOROUS	PILGRIMAGES	PLASTER CAST
PERTINACITY	PHOTOACTIVE	PILLAR BOXES	

PLASTICALLY	POINSETTIAS	PONTIFICATE	PRACTICABLY
PLASTIC ARTS	POINTEDNESS	POOH-POOHING	PRACTICALLY
PLASTICIZER	POINTE-NOIRE	POPULARIZED	PRAEDIALITY
PLASTOMETER	POINTILLISM	POPULARIZER	PRAESIDIUMS
PLASTOMETRY	POINTILLIST	POPULATIONS	PRAGMATISTS
PLATELAYERS	POINTLESSLY	PORK BARRELS	PRAIRIE DOGS
PLATINOTYPE	POINT OF VIEW	PORNOGRAPHY	PRATTLINGLY
PLATS DU JOUR	POISONOUSLY	PORPHYRITIC	PRAYER WHEEL
PLATYRRHINE	POLARIMETER	PORTABILITY	PREARRANGED
PLAYER PIANO	POLARIMETRY	PORTERHOUSE	PREARRANGER
PLAYFELLOWS	POLARISCOPE	PORTMANTEAU	PRECAMBRIAN
PLAYFULNESS	POLARIZABLE	PORT MORESBY	PRECAUTIONS
PLAYGROUNDS	POLEMICALLY	PORTO ALEGRE	PRECAUTIOUS
PLAYING CARD	POLE VAULTED	PORT OF CALLS	PRECESSIONS
PLAY ON WORDS	POLE VAULTER	PORT OF ENTRY	PRECIPITANT
PLAYSCHOOLS	POLICE STATE	PORT OF SPAIN	PRECIPITATE
PLAYWRIGHTS	POLICEWOMAN	PORTRAITIST	PRECIPITOUS
PLAYWRITING	POLICEWOMEN	PORTRAITURE	PRECISENESS
PLEASANTEST	POLITICALLY	PORTRAYABLE	PRECLINICAL
PLEASURABLE	POLITICIANS	POSITIONING	PRECLUDABLE
PLEASURABLY	POLITICIZED	POSITIVISTS	PRECONCEIVE
PLEASUREFUL	POLITICKING	POSITRONIUM	PRECONTRACT
PLEBEIANISM	POLLEN COUNT	POSSESSIONS	PRECRITICAL
PLEBISCITES	POLLINATING	POSSESSIVES	PREDATORILY
PLECTOGNATH	POLLINATION	POSSIBILITY	PREDECEASED
PLEISTOCENE	POLTERGEIST	POSTAL ORDER	PREDECESSOR
PLENTEOUSLY	POLYANDROUS	POSTERITIES	PREDESTINED
PLENTIFULLY	POLYCHASIUM	POSTER PAINT	PREDICAMENT
PLEOCHROISM	POLYGAMISTS	POSTGLACIAL	PREDICATING
PLEOMORPHIC	POLYGENESIS	POSTMARKING	PREDICATION
PLICATENESS	POLYGENETIC	POSTMASTERS	PREDICATIVE
PLOUGHSHARE	POLYGLOTISM	POSTMORTEMS	PREDICATORY
PLOUGHSTAFF	POLYGRAPHIC	POSTNUPTIAL	PREDICTABLE
PLUG-AND-PLAY	POLYHYDROXY	POST OFFICES	PREDICTABLY
PLUM PUDDING	POLYNUCLEAR	POSTPONABLE	PREDICTIONS
PLUNDERABLE	POLYPEPTIDE	POSTSCRIPTS	PREDIGESTED
PLURALISTIC	POLYPHONOUS	POSTULATING	PREDISPOSAL
PLURALITIES	POLYPLOIDAL	POSTULATION	PREDISPOSED
PLUTOCRATIC	POLYSTYRENE	POTATO CHIPS	PREDOMINANT
PLUVIOMETER	POLYTECHNIC	POTATO CRISP	PREDOMINATE
PLUVIOMETRY	POLYTHEISTS	POTENTIALLY	PRE-EMINENCE
PNEUMECTOMY	POLYTROPHIC	POTTING SHED	PRE-EXISTENT
PNEUMOGRAPH	POLYVALENCY	POVERTY TRAP	PRE-EXISTING
POCKETBOOKS	POLYZOARIUM	POWDER PUFFS	PREFATORILY
POCKETKNIFE	POMEGRANATE	POWDER ROOMS	PREFECTURAL
POCKET KNIFE	POMICULTURE	POWER BROKER	PREFECTURES
POCKET MONEY	POMOLOGICAL	POWERHOUSES	PREFERENCES
POCOCURANTE	POMPOUSNESS	POWERLESSLY	PREFIGURING
POCTOSCOPIC	PONDEROUSLY	POWER PLANTS	PREGNANCIES
PODIATRISTS	PONDICHERRY	POWER POINTS	PREHISTORIC
PODOPHYLLIN	PONTIFICALS	PRACTICABLE	PRE-IGNITION

PREJUDGMENT	PRETTY PENNY	PROFANENESS	PROPER NOUNS
PREJUDICIAL	PREVALENTLY	PROFANITIES	PROPHESYING
PREJUDICING	PREVARICATE	PROFESSEDLY	PROPHYLAXES
PRELIMINARY	PREVENTABLE	PROFESSIONS	PROPHYLAXIS
PRELITERACY	PREVENTABLY	PROFICIENCY	PROPINQUITY
PRELITERATE	PREVENTIVES	PROFITEERED	PROPITIABLE
PREMATURELY	PRICKLINESS	PROFITEROLE	PROPITIATED
PREMEDITATE	PRICKLY HEAT	PROFLIGATES	PROPITIATOR
PREMIERSHIP	PRICKLY PEAR	PROFUSENESS	PROPORTIONS
PREMIUM BOND	PRIESTCRAFT	PROGENITIVE	PROPOSITION
PREMONITION	PRIESTLIEST	PROGENITORS	PROPOUNDING
PREMONITORY	PRIMA DONNAS	PROGNATHISM	PROPRANOLOL
PREMUNITION	PRIMATOLOGY	PROGNATHOUS	PROPRIETARY
PREOCCUPIED	PRIME MOVERS	PROGRAMMERS	PROPRIETIES
PREORDAINED	PRIME NUMBER	PROGRAMMING	PROPRIETORS
PREPARATION	PRIMIPARITY	PROGRESSING	PROROGATION
PREPARATIVE	PRIMIPAROUS	PROGRESSION	PROSAICALLY
PREPARATORY	PRIMITIVELY	PROGRESSIVE	PROSAICNESS
PREPOSITION	PRIMITIVISM	PROHIBITING	PROS AND CONS
PREPOSITIVE	PRIMITIVIST	PROHIBITION	PROSCENIUMS
PREP SCHOOLS	PRINCIPALLY	PROHIBITIVE	PROSCRIBING
PRERECORDED	PRINTING INK	PROHIBITORY	PROSECUTING
PREROGATIVE	PRIORITIZED	PROJECTILES	PROSECUTION
PRESBYTERAL	PRISON CAMPS	PROJECTIONS	PROSECUTORS
PRESCRIBING	PRIVATIZING	PROKOPYEVSK	PROSELYTISM
PRESENTABLE	PRIZEFIGHTS	PROLATENESS	PROSELYTIZE
PRESENTABLY	PROBABILISM	PROLEGOMENA	PROSENCHYMA
PRESENT ARMS	PROBABILIST	PROLETARIAN	PROSPECTING
PRESENTIENT	PROBABILITY	PROLETARIAT	PROSPECTIVE
PRESENTMENT	PROBATIONAL	PROLIFERATE	PROSPECTORS
PRESERVABLE	PROBATIONER	PROLIFEROUS	PROSTATITIS
PRESS AGENCY	PROBLEMATIC	PROLONGMENT	PROSTHETICS
PRESS AGENTS	PROBOSCIDES	PROMENADING	PROSTITUTED
PRESS BARONS	PROBOSCISES	PROMINENCES	PROSTITUTES
PRESSGANGED	PROCEEDINGS	PROMINENTLY	PROSTITUTOR
PRESSURIZED	PROCEPHALIC	PROMISCUITY	PROSTRATING
PRESSURIZER	PROCESSIONS	PROMISCUOUS	PROSTRATION
PRESTIGIOUS	PROCHRONISM	PROMISINGLY	PROTAGONISM
PRESTISSIMO	PROCLAIMING	PROMOTIONAL	PROTAGONIST
PRESTONPANS	PROCONSULAR	PROMPTITUDE	PROTANDROUS
PRESTRESSED	PROCREATING	PROMULGATED	PROTECTIONS
PRESUMINGLY	PROCREATION	PROMULGATOR	PROTECTORAL
PRESUMPTION	PROCRUSTEAN	PROMYCELIUM	PROTECTRESS
PRESUMPTIVE	PROCTOSCOPE	PRONOUNCING	PROTEOLYSIS
PRESUPPOSED	PROCTOSCOPY	PROOFREADER	PROTEOLYTIC
PRETENDEDLY	PROCURATION	PROOF SPIRIT	PROTEROZOIC
PRETENSIONS	PROCUREMENT	PROPAGATING	PROTESTANTS
PRETENTIOUS	PRODIGALITY	PROPAGATION	PROTHROMBIN
PRETERITION	PRODUCTIONS	PROPAGATIVE	PROTOGYNOUS
PRETERITIVE	PROFANATION	PROPAGATORS	PROTOLITHIC
PRETTIFYING	PROFANATORY	PROPELLANTS	PROTOPATHIC

PROTOSTELIC	PULAU PINANG	QUADRENNIUM	RABBIT PUNCH
PROTRACTILE	PULCHRITUDE	QUADRILLION	RABELAISIAN
PROTRACTING	PULL STRINGS	QUADRUPEDAL	RACECOURSES
PROTRACTION	PULLULATING	QUADRUPLETS	RACE MEETING
PROTRACTIVE	PULLULATION	QUADRUPLING	RACQUETBALL
PROTRACTORS	PULSATILITY	QUALIFIABLE	RADIATIONAL
PROTRUDABLE	PULVERIZING	QUALITATIVE	RADICALNESS
PROTRUSIONS	PULVERULENT	QUANGOCRACY	RADIOACTIVE
PROTUBERANT	PUMPKINSEED	QUANTIFIERS	RADIO ALARMS
PROVABILITY	PUNCHED CARD	QUANTIFYING	RADIO BEACON
PROVIDENCES	PUNCTILIOUS	QUANTUM LEAP	RADIOCARBON
PROVIDENTLY	PUNCTUALITY	QUARANTINED	RADIOGRAPHY
PROVINCIALS	PUNCTUATING	QUARRELLING	RADIOLARIAN
PROVISIONAL	PUNCTUATION	QUARRELSOME	RADIOLOGIST
PROVISIONED	PUNCTURABLE	QUARTER DAYS	RADIOLUCENT
PROVISIONER	PUNISHINGLY	QUARTERDECK	RADIOMETRIC
PROVISORILY	PUNISHMENTS	QUARTER-HOUR	RADIOPACITY
PROVOCATION	PUNTA ARENAS	QUARTERLIES	RADIOPHONIC
PROVOCATIVE	PURCHASABLE	QUARTER NOTE	RADIOSCOPIC
PROVOKINGLY	PURCHASE TAX	QUAVERINGLY	RADIOTHERMY
PROXIMATELY	PUREBLOODED	QUEENLINESS	RAFFISHNESS
PROXIMATION	PURGATORIAL	QUEEN MOTHER	RAGAMUFFINS
PRUDENTNESS	PURIFICATOR	QUEEN'S BENCH	RAILROADING
PRUDISHNESS	PURITANICAL	QUERULOUSLY	RAIN FORESTS
PRUSSIC ACID	PURPLE HEART	QUESTIONARY	RAISON D'ETRE
PSEUDOMORPH	PURPOSELESS	QUESTIONERS	RALLENTANDO
PSILOMELANE	PUSHINGNESS	QUESTIONING	RAMAN EFFECT
PSITTACOSIS	PUSSYFOOTED	QUESTION TAG	RAMBOUILLET
PSYCHEDELIA	PUSSY WILLOW	QUEUE-JUMPED	RANCH HOUSES
PSYCHEDELIC	PUSTULATION	QUEUE-JUMPER	RANCOROUSLY
PSYCHIATRIC	PUTREFIABLE	QUIBBLINGLY	RANGE FINDER
PSYCHICALLY	PUTRESCENCE	QUICK-CHANGE	RANK AND FILE
PSYCHOBILLY	PYCNOMETRIC	QUICK-FREEZE	RAPACIOUSLY
PSYCHODRAMA	PYELOGRAPHY	QUICKSILVER	RAPSCALLION
PSYCHOGENIC	PYLORECTOMY	QUICK-WITTED	RAPTUROUSLY
PSYCHOGRAPH	PYRANOMETER	QUID PRO QUOS	RAREFACTION
PSYCHOMETRY	PYRARGYRITE	QUIESCENTLY	RASPBERRIES
PSYCHOMOTOR	PYROCLASTIC	QUINCUNCIAL	RASTAFARIAN
PSYCHOPATHS	PYROGALLATE	QUINDECAGON	RATE-CAPPING
PSYCHOPATHY	PYROGRAPHER	QUINTANA ROO	RATIOCINATE
PTERIDOLOGY	PYROGRAPHIC	QUINTILLION	RATIONALISM
PTERODACTYL	PYROMANIACS	QUINTUPLETS	RATIONALIST
PTOCHOCRACY	PYROTECHNIC	QUIVERINGLY	RATIONALITY
PUB-CRAWLING	PYRRHULOXIA	QUIZMASTERS	RATIONALIZE
PUBLICATION	PYRROLIDINE	QUIZZICALLY	RATTLESNAKE
PUBLIC HOUSE	PYTHAGOREAN	QUONSET HUTS	RATTLETRAPS
PUBLICIZING	PYTHONESQUE	QUOTABILITY	RAUCOUSNESS
PUBLIC WORKS		QUOTE-DRIVEN	RAUNCHINESS
PUBLISHABLE	**Q**		RAVEN-HAIRED
PUCKISHNESS	QUADRANGLES	**R**	RAVISHINGLY
PUERTO RICAN	QUADRENNIAL	RABBIT HUTCH	REACH-ME-DOWN

REACTIONARY	RECONDITION	REFRESHMENT	REMONSTRANT
REACTIONISM	RECONNOITRE	REFRIGERANT	REMONSTRATE
REACTIVATED	RECONSTRUCT	REFRIGERATE	REMORSELESS
READABILITY	RECOVERABLE	REFRINGENCY	REMOVAL VANS
READDRESSED	RECREATIONS	REFURBISHED	REMUNERABLE
READERSHIPS	RECREMENTAL	REFUTATIONS	REMUNERATED
READJUSTING	RECRIMINATE	REGENERABLE	REMUNERATOR
READ-THROUGH	RECRUITABLE	REGENERATED	RENAISSANCE
READY-TO-WEAR	RECRUITMENT	REGIMENTALS	RENEGOTIATE
READY-WITTED	RECTANGULAR	REGIMENTING	RENOVATIONS
REAFFIRMING	RECTIFIABLE	REGIONALISM	RENTABILITY
REALIGNMENT	RECTILINEAR	REGIONALIST	RENT STRIKES
REALIZATION	RECUPERATED	REGISTERING	REORGANIZED
REALPOLITIK	RECUPERATOR	REGISTRABLE	REORGANIZER
REANIMATING	RECURRENCES	REGRETFULLY	REPARATIONS
REANIMATION	RECURRENTLY	REGRETTABLE	REPARTITION
REAPPEARING	RECURRINGLY	REGRETTABLY	REPATRIATED
REAPPORTION	REDACTIONAL	REGULARIZED	REPELLINGLY
REAPPRAISAL	RED ADMIRALS	REGULATIONS	REPENTANTLY
REAPPRAISED	RED CRESCENT	REGURGITANT	REPERTOIRES
REAR ADMIRAL	REDCURRANTS	REGURGITATE	REPERTORIAL
REARRANGING	REDECORATED	REIFICATION	REPERTORIES
REASSURANCE	REDEPLOYING	REIMBURSING	REPETITIONS
REASSUREDLY	REDEVELOPED	REINCARNATE	REPETITIOUS
REBARBATIVE	REDEVELOPER	REINFORCING	REPLACEABLE
RECALESCENT	RED HERRINGS	REINSTATING	REPLACEMENT
RECANTATION	REDIFFUSION	REINSURANCE	REPLENISHED
RECAPTURING	REDIRECTING	REINTRODUCE	REPLENISHER
RECEIVABLES	REDIRECTION	REITERATING	REPLETENESS
RECEPTACLES	REDOUBTABLE	REITERATION	REPLEVIABLE
RECEPTIVELY	REDOUBTABLY	REITERATIVE	REPLICATING
RECEPTIVITY	REDRESSABLE	REJUVENATED	REPLICATION
RECESSIONAL	REDUCTIONAL	REJUVENATOR	REPLICATIVE
RECIDIVISTS	REDUNDANTLY	RELATEDNESS	REPOSSESSED
RECIPROCATE	REDUPLICATE	RELAXATIONS	REPOSSESSOR
RECIPROCITY	RE-EDUCATING	RELIABILITY	REPREHENDED
RECITATIONS	RE-EDUCATION	RELIEF ROADS	REPREHENDER
RECITATIVES	RE-ELECTIONS	RELIGIONISM	REPRESENTED
RECLAIMABLE	REFECTORIES	RELIGIOSITY	REPRESSIBLE
RECLAMATION	REFERENDUMS	RELIGIOUSLY	REPRESSIONS
RECLINATION	REFERENTIAL	RELIQUARIES	REPRIEVABLE
RECOGNITION	REFINEMENTS	RELISHINGLY	REPRIMANDED
RECOGNIZING	REFLECTANCE	RELUCTANTLY	REPRIMANDER
RECOILINGLY	REFLECTIONS	RELUCTIVITY	REPROACHFUL
RECOLLECTED	REFORESTING	REMAINDERED	REPROACHING
RECOMBINANT	REFORMATION	REMEMBERING	REPROBATION
RECOMMENDED	REFORMATIVE	REMEMBRANCE	REPROBATIVE
RECOMMENDER	REFORMATORY	REMINISCENT	REPROCESSED
RECOMPENSED	REFRACTABLE	REMINISCING	REPRODUCERS
RECOMPENSER	REFRAINMENT	REMITTANCES	REPRODUCING
RECONCILING	REFRANGIBLE	REMODELLING	REPROGRAPHY

REPROVINGLY
REPUBLICANS
REPUBLISHER
REPUDIATING
REPUDIATION
REPUDIATIVE
REPUDIATORY
REPULSIVELY
REPUTATIONS
REQUEST STOP
REQUIREMENT
REQUISITION
REQUITEMENT
RERADIATION
RESCHEDULED
RESCINDABLE
RESCINDMENT
RESCISSIBLE
RESEARCHERS
RESEARCHING
RESECTIONAL
RESEMBLANCE
RESENTFULLY
RESERVATION
RESHUFFLING
RESIDENTIAL
RESIGNATION
RESILIENTLY
RESISTANCES
RESISTENCIA
RESISTINGLY
RESISTIVITY
RESOLUTIONS
RESOURCEFUL
RESPECTABLE
RESPECTABLY
RESPIRATION
RESPIRATORS
RESPIRATORY
RESPLENDENT
RESPONDENCE
RESPONDENTS
RESPONSIBLE
RESPONSIBLY
RESPONSIONS
RESTATEMENT
RESTAURANTS
RESTFULNESS
RESTITUTION
RESTITUTIVE
RESTIVENESS

RESTORATION
RESTORATIVE
RESTRAINING
RESTRICTING
RESTRICTION
RESTRICTIVE
RESTRUCTURE
RESURFACING
RESURRECTED
RESUSCITATE
RETALIATING
RETALIATION
RETALIATIVE
RETALIATORY
RETARDATION
RETARDATIVE
RETARDINGLY
RETENTIVELY
RETENTIVITY
RETICULATED
RETINACULAR
RETINACULUM
RETINOSCOPY
RETIREMENTS
RETOUCHABLE
RETRACEABLE
RETRACEMENT
RETRACTABLE
RETRACTIONS
RETRENCHING
RETRIBUTION
RETRIBUTIVE
RETRIEVABLE
RETRIEVABLY
RETROACTION
RETROACTIVE
RETROLENTAL
RETRO-ROCKET
RETROVERTED
REUPHOLSTER
REUSABILITY
REVALUATION
REVEALINGLY
REVELATIONS
REVENGINGLY
REVERBERANT
REVERBERATE
REVERENCING
REVERENTIAL
REVERSIONER
REVISIONISM

REVISIONIST
REVITALIZED
REVIVALISTS
REVIVIFYING
REVOCATIONS
REVOLTINGLY
REVOLUTIONS
REVOLVINGLY
RHABDOMANCY
RHABDOMYOMA
RHAMNACEOUS
RHAPSODIZED
RHEOLOGICAL
RHEOTROPISM
RHETORICIAN
RHEUMATICKY
RHINESTONES
RHINOLOGIST
RHINOPLASTY
RHINOSCOPIC
RHIZOMATOUS
RHIZOPODOUS
RHIZOSPHERE
RHODE ISLAND
RHOTACISTIC
RHYTHMICITY
RICE PADDIES
RICKETINESS
RICKETTSIAL
RICOCHETING
RICOCHETTED
RIFLE RANGES
RIFT VALLEYS
RIGHT-ANGLED
RIGHT ANGLES
RIGHTEOUSLY
RIGHT-HANDED
RIGHT-HANDER
RIGHT-MINDED
RIGHTS ISSUE
RIGHTS OF WAY
RIGHT-WINGER
RIGOR MORTIS
RING BINDERS
RING FINGERS
RINGLEADERS
RINGMASTERS
RINSABILITY
RIOTOUSNESS
RITUALISTIC
RIVER BASINS

ROADHOLDING
ROAD MANAGER
ROAD PRICING
ROAD ROLLERS
ROAD TESTING
ROCK-AND-ROLL
ROCK GARDENS
ROCKHAMPTON
RODENTICIDE
RODOMONTADE
ROENTGEN RAY
ROGUISHNESS
ROLE PLAYING
ROLLERBLADE
ROLLERBLADE
ROLLER BLIND
ROLLER SKATE
ROLLER TOWEL
ROLLICKINGS
ROLLICKSOME
ROLLING MILL
ROLLING PINS
ROLLTOP DESK
ROMAN CANDLE
ROMANTICISM
ROMANTICIST
ROMANTICIZE
ROOD SCREENS
ROOF GARDENS
ROOM SERVICE
ROPE LADDERS
ROSE WINDOWS
ROTARIANISM
ROTISSERIES
ROTOGRAVURE
ROTTENSTONE
ROTUNDITIES
ROUGHCASTER
ROUGH-SPOKEN
ROUNDABOUTS
ROUNDEDNESS
ROUND ROBINS
ROUSTABOUTS
ROWING BOATS
ROYAL TENNIS
RUBBER BANDS
RUBBER PLANT
RUBBER STAMP
RUBBER TREES
RUBBISH BINS
RUBEFACIENT

RUBEFACTION
RUBICUNDITY
RUBRICATION
RUDESHEIMER
RUDIMENTARY
RUGBY LEAGUE
RULE OF THUMB
RUMBUSTIOUS
RUMINATIONS
RUMMAGE SALE
RUMPUS ROOMS
RUNNER BEANS
RUNNING JUMP
RUNNING MATE
RUN-THROUGHS
RUNTISHNESS
RUSSOPHOBIA
RUSSOPHOBIC
RUSTICATING
RUSTICATION
RUSTPROOFED
RUTTISHNESS

S
SAARBRUCKEN
SABBATARIAN
SABBATICALS
SACCULATION
SACRAMENTAL
SACRIFICIAL
SACRIFICING
SACRILEGIST
SACROILIACS
SADDENINGLY
SADDLECLOTH
SAFARI PARKS
SAFEBREAKER
SAFE-CONDUCT
SAFE-DEPOSIT
SAFEGUARDED
SAFEKEEPING
SAFETY BELTS
SAFETY CATCH
SAFETY-FIRST
SAFETY GLASS
SAFETY LAMPS
SAFETY MATCH
SAFETY RAZOR
SAFETY VALVE
SAGACIOUSLY
SAGITTARIAN

SAGITTARIUS
SAILING BOAT
SAILOR SUITS
SAINT ALBANS
SAINT-BRIEUC
SAINT GALLEN
SAINT HELENA
SAINT HELENS
SAINT HELIER
SAINTLINESS
SAINT MARTIN
SAINT MORITZ
SAINT THOMAS
SALACIOUSLY
SALAMANDERS
SALEABILITY
SALESCLERKS
SALESPEOPLE
SALESPERSON
SALICACEOUS
SALIENTNESS
SALINOMETER
SALINOMETRY
SALMONBERRY
SALMON TROUT
SALPINGITIC
SALPINGITIS
SALTATORIAL
SALTCELLARS
SALT SHAKERS
SALUTATIONS
SALVABILITY
SALVADORIAN
SALVAGEABLE
SALVATIONAL
SAL VOLATILE
SAMURAI BOND
SAN ANTONIAN
SANATORIUMS
SANCTIFYING
SANCTIONING
SANCTUARIES
SANDBAGGING
SANDBLASTED
SANDBLASTER
SAND-CASTING
SANDCASTLES
SANDPAPERED
SANDWICHING
SAN FERNANDO
SANGUINARIA

SANGUINEOUS
SANITARIUMS
SAN MARINESE
SAN SALVADOR
SANSEVIERIA
SANSKRITIST
SAPONACEOUS
SAPOTACEOUS
SAPROPHYTIC
SARCOMATOID
SARCOPHAGUS
SARDONICISM
SARGASSO SEA
SARTORIALLY
SASH WINDOWS
SATANICALLY
SATELLITIUM
SATIABILITY
SATIRICALLY
SATISFIABLE
SATURNALIAS
SAUDI ARABIA
SAURISCHIAN
SAUROPODOUS
SAUSAGE DOGS
SAUSAGE ROLL
SAVABLENESS
SAVING GRACE
SAVINGS BANK
SAVOIR-FAIRE
SAVOURINGLY
SAXOPHONIST
SCAFFOLDING
SCALARIFORM
SCAMMONIATE
SCANDALIZED
SCANDALIZER
SCANDINAVIA
SCARABAEOID
SCARBOROUGH
SCAREDY CATS
SCAREMONGER
SCARLATINAL
SCATOLOGIST
SCATTERABLE
SCENOGRAPHY
SCEPTICALLY
SCHEMATIZED
SCHISMATICS
SCHISTOSITY
SCHISTOSOME

SCHIZOPHYTE
SCHLESINGER
SCHOLARSHIP
SCHOLIASTIC
SCHOOLCHILD
SCHOOLHOUSE
SCHOOLMARMS
SCHOOLMATES
SCHWEINFURT
SCIENCE PARK
SCIENTISTIC
SCIENTOLOGY
SCINTILLATE
SCIRRHOSITY
SCLERODERMA
SCLEROMETER
SCLEROTIOID
SCOPOLAMINE
SCOREBOARDS
SCORIACEOUS
SCORPAENOID
SCOTCH BROTH
SCOTCH MISTS
SCOTCH TAPED
SCOTOMATOUS
SCOURGINGLY
SCOUTMASTER
SCRAGGINESS
SCRAPPINESS
SCRATCHCARD
SCRATCHIEST
SCRATCHINGS
SCRATCHPADS
SCRAWNINESS
SCREAMINGLY
SCREENPLAYS
SCREENSAVER
SCREEN TESTS
SCREWDRIVER
SCRIMMAGING
SCRIMPINESS
SCRIPTORIUM
SCRUBBINESS
SCRUMHALVES
SCRUMMAGING
SCRUMPTIOUS
SCRUTINEERS
SCRUTINIZED
SCRUTINIZER
SCUBA DIVING
SCULPTURING

SCYPHISTOMA	SELF-IMPOSED	SEPTICAEMIC	SHIFTLESSLY
SEA ANEMONES	SELF-INDUCED	SEPTIC TANKS	SHIFT STICKS
SEA CAPTAINS	SELFISHNESS	SEPTIFRAGAL	SHIMONOSEKI
SEARCHINGLY	SELF-LOADING	SEPTIVALENT	SHIP BISCUIT
SEARCHLIGHT	SELF-LOCKING	SEQUESTERED	SHIPBUILDER
SEARCH PARTY	SELF-PITYING	SEQUESTRANT	SHIPWRECKED
SEASICKNESS	SELF-RELIANT	SEQUESTRATE	SHIPWRIGHTS
SEBORRHOEAL	SELF-RESPECT	SERENDIPITY	SHIRE HORSES
SECESSIONAL	SELF-SEALING	SERIALIZING	SHIRTFRONTS
SECONDARILY	SELF-SEEKERS	SERICULTURE	SHIRTSLEEVE
SECOND CLASS	SELF-SEEKING	SERIES-WOUND	SHISH KEBABS
SECOND-CLASS	SELF-SERVICE	SERIOUSNESS	SHIVERINGLY
SECOND-GUESS	SELF-STARTER	SERMONIZING	SHOCKHEADED
SECOND HANDS	SELF-WINDING	SERPIGINOUS	SHOCK TROOPS
SECONDMENTS	SELL-BY DATES	SERRULATION	·SHOESTRINGS
SECOND-RATER	SELLOTAPING	SERTULARIAN	SHOPKEEPERS
SECOND SIGHT	SELL-THROUGH	SERVICEABLE	SHOPLIFTERS
SECRET AGENT	SEMANTICIST	SERVICEABLY	SHOPLIFTING
SECRETARIAL	SEMASIOLOGY	SERVICE FLAT	SHOP STEWARD
SECRETARIAT	SEMIAQUATIC	SERVICE ROAD	SHOPWALKERS
SECRETARIES	SEMIARIDITY	SERVOMOTORS	SHORT CHANGE
SECRETIVELY	SEMICIRCLES	SESQUIOXIDE	SHORT-CHANGE
SECULARIZED	SEMIDIURNAL	SETTLEMENTS	SHORTCOMING
SECULARIZER	SEMIFLUIDIC	SEVENTEENTH	SHORT CORNER
SEDAN CHAIRS	SEMIMONTHLY	SEVENTIETHS	SHORTHANDED
SEDENTARILY	SEMIOTICIAN	SEXAGESIMAL	SHORT-HANDED
SEDIMENTARY	SEMIPALMATE	SEXLESSNESS	SHORT-LISTED
SEDIMENTOUS	SEMIQUAVERS	SEXOLOGISTS	SHORT SHRIFT
SEDITIONARY	SEMISKILLED	SEXTODECIMO	SHORT-SPOKEN
SEDITIOUSLY	SEMITONALLY	SHADOW-BOXED	SHORT-WINDED
SEDUCTIVELY	SEMITRAILER	SHADOWGRAPH	SHOULDERING
SEGREGATING	SEMITROPICS	SHADOWINESS	SHOWERPROOF
SEGREGATION	SEMIVOCALIC	SHALLOWNESS	SHOW JUMPERS
SEGREGATIVE	SEMPERVIVUM	SHAMANISTIC	SHOW JUMPING
SEIGNIORAGE	SEMPITERNAL	SHAMELESSLY	SHOWMANSHIP
SEISMICALLY	SENSATIONAL	SHANGHAIING	SHOW OF HANDS
SEISMOGRAPH	SENSELESSLY	SHANKS'S PONY	SHOWSTOPPER
SEISMOLOGIC	SENSE ORGANS	SHANTYTOWNS	SHRINKINGLY
SEISMOSCOPE	SENSIBILITY	SHAPELESSLY	SHRIVELLING
SELAGINELLA	SENSITIVELY	SHAPELINESS	SHRUBBERIES
SELECTIVELY	SENSITIVITY	SHAREHOLDER	SHRUBBINESS
SELECTIVITY	SENSITIZING	SHARPBENDER	SHUFFLE PLAY
SELENOGRAPH	SENSUALISTS	SHARP-WITTED	SHUTTLECOCK
SELF-ASSURED	SENSUALNESS	SHAVING FOAM	SIAMESE CATS
SELF-CENTRED	SENTENTIOUS	SHEATH KNIFE	SIAMESE TWIN
SELF-COMMAND	SENTIMENTAL	SHEET ANCHOR	SICKENINGLY
SELF-CONCEPT	SENTRY BOXES	SHELLACKING	SIDE EFFECTS
SELF-CONTROL	SEPARATIONS	SHENANIGANS	SIDESADDLES
SELF-DEFENCE	SEPARATISTS	SHEPHERDESS	SIDESLIPPED
SELF-DENYING	SEPTAVALENT	SHEPHERDING	SIDESTEPPED
SELF-EVIDENT	SEPTICAEMIA	SHIBBOLETHS	SIDESTEPPER

SIDE STREETS	SINO-TIBETAN	SLOUCHINESS	SOLILOQUIZE
SIDESWIPING	SINUOSITIES	SLOUCHINGLY	SOLIPSISTIC
SIDETRACKED	SINUOUSNESS	SLOWCOACHES	SOLMIZATION
SIDE-WHEELER	SISTERHOODS	SLUMGULLION	SOLUBLENESS
SIENKIEWICZ	SISTER-IN-LAW	SMALL CHANGE	SOLVABILITY
SIERRA LEONE	SITTING BULL	SMALLHOLDER	SOMATICALLY
SIERRA MADRE	SITTING DUCK	SMALL-MINDED	SOMATOLOGIC
SIGHTLINESS	SITTING ROOM	SMALL SCREEN	SOMATOPLASM
SIGHT-READER	SITUATIONAL	SMALL-TIMERS	SOMERSAULTS
SIGHTSCREEN	SIX-SHOOTERS	SMART ALECKS	SOMNOLENTLY
SIGHTSEEING	SIXTH-FORMER	SMART ALECKY	SONGFULNESS
SIGNAL BOXES	SIZABLENESS	SMARTY-PANTS	SON-OF-A-BITCH
SIGNALIZING	SKATEBOARDS	SMATTERINGS	SOOTHSAYERS
SIGNATORIES	SKEDADDLING	SMILINGNESS	SOPHISTRIES
SIGNIFIABLE	SKELETONIZE	SMITHEREENS	SORORICIDAL
SIGNIFICANT	SKELETON KEY	SMITHSONITE	SORROWFULLY
SIGNPOSTING	SKEPTICALLY	SMOKESCREEN	SOTTISHNESS
SILHOUETTED	SKETCHINESS	SMOKESTACKS	SOUBRIQUETS
SILHOUETTES	SKILFULNESS	SMOOTH-FACED	SOUGHT-AFTER
SILICON CHIP	SKIMMED MILK	SMORGASBORD	SOUL BROTHER
SILLIMANITE	SKIRMISHERS	SMOULDERING	SOULFULNESS
SILLY SEASON	SKIRMISHING	SNAPDRAGONS	SOUNDLESSLY
SILVER BIRCH	SKULDUGGERY	SNIPERSCOPE	SOUNDTRACKS
SILVERINESS	SKYJACKINGS	SNORKELLING	SOUP KITCHEN
SILVER MEDAL	SKYROCKETED	SNOWBALLING	SOUSAPHONES
SILVER PAPER	SKYSCRAPERS	SNOWMOBILES	SOUTH AFRICA
SILVER PLATE	SLAUGHTERED	SNOWPLOUGHS	SOUTHAMPTON
SILVERPOINT	SLAUGHTERER	SOAP BUBBLES	SOUTH DAKOTA
SILVERSMITH	SLAVE DRIVER	SOCIABILITY	SOUTHEASTER
SIMMERINGLY	SLAVE LABOUR	SOCIALISTIC	SOUTHERNERS
SIMPERINGLY	SLAVISHNESS	SOCIALIZING	SOUTH ISLAND
SIMPLIFYING	SLEEPING BAG	SOCIOLOGIST	SOUTHWESTER
SIMPLON PASS	SLEEPING CAR	SOCIOMETRIC	SOVEREIGNTY
SIMULACRUMS	SLEEPLESSLY	SOCIOPATHIC	SOVIETISTIC
SIMULATIONS	SLEEPWALKED	SOFTHEARTED	SPACE HEATER
SINE QUA NONS	SLEEPWALKER	SOFT LANDING	SPACE PROBES
SINFONIETTA	SLEEPYHEADS	SOFT OPTIONS	SPARINGNESS
SINGAPOREAN	SLENDERIZED	SOFT PALATES	SPARROWHAWK
SINGLE-BLIND	SLENDERNESS	SOFT-PEDALED	SPASTICALLY
SINGLE-CROSS	SLEUTHHOUND	SOFT-SOAPING	SPATHACEOUS
SINGLE-PHASE	SLICED BREAD	SOFT TOUCHES	SPEAKEASIES
SINGLE-SPACE	SLICE OF LIFE	SOLANACEOUS	SPEAKERSHIP
SINGLE-TRACK	SLICKENSIDE	SOLARIMETER	SPEARHEADED
SINGULARITY	SLIDE-ACTION	SOLAR PANELS	SPECIALISMS
SINGULARIZE	SLIDING DOOR	SOLAR PLEXUS	SPECIALISTS
SINISTRORSE	SLIGHTINGLY	SOLAR SYSTEM	SPECIALIZED
SINKING FUND	SLIPPED DISC	SOLEMNITIES	SPECIALNESS
SINLESSNESS	SLIPSTREAMS	SOLEMNIZING	SPECIFIABLE
SINN FEINISM	SLOOP-RIGGED	SOLIDIFYING	SPECIFICITY
SINOLOGICAL	SLOPINGNESS	SOLILOQUIES	SPECTACULAR
SINOLOGISTS	SLOT MACHINE	SOLILOQUIST	SPECTRALITY

SPECULATING	SPONGE CAKES	STALEMATING	STEREOGRAPH
SPECULATION	SPONSORSHIP	STALLHOLDER	STEREOMETRY
SPECULATIVE	SPONTANEITY	STANDARDIZE	STEREOSCOPE
SPECULATORS	SPONTANEOUS	STANDOFFISH	STEREOSCOPY
SPEECHIFIED	SPOONERISMS	STANDPOINTS	STEREOTAXIS
SPEECHIFIER	SPOROGENOUS	STANLEY POOL	STEREOTYPED
SPEED LIMITS	SPOROGONIAL	STARA ZAGORA	STEREOTYPER
SPEEDOMETER	SPOROGONIUM	STAR CHAMBER	STEREOTYPES
SPELLBINDER	SPOROPHYTIC	STARCHINESS	STEREOTYPIC
SPENDTHRIFT	SPORTSWOMAN	STAR-CROSSED	STERILIZERS
SPERMATHECA	SPORULATION	STAR-STUDDED	STERILIZING
SPERMATOZOA	SPOT CHECKED	STARTER HOME	STERLITAMAK
SPERMICIDES	SPOTTED DICK	STARTLINGLY	STERNUTATOR
SPERMOPHILE	SPREAD-EAGLE	STARVELINGS	STETHOSCOPE
SPERM WHALES	SPREADSHEET	STATELINESS	STETHOSCOPY
SPESSARTITE	SPRINGBOARD	STATELY HOME	STEWARDSHIP
SPHEROMETER	SPRING-CLEAN	STATESWOMAN	STICHICALLY
SPHERULITIC	SPRINGFIELD	STATISTICAL	STICHOMETRY
SPHINCTERAL	SPRINGINESS	STATOLITHIC	STICKHANDLE
SPHINGOSINE	SPRING ONION	STATUTE BOOK	STICK INSECT
SPHRAGISTIC	SPRING ROLLS	STATUTORILY	STICKLEBACK
SPINA BIFIDA	SPRING TIDES	STAUNCHABLE	STICK SHIFTS
SPINAL CORDS	SPRINKLINGS	STAUNCHNESS	STIFF-NECKED
SPINELESSLY	SPUMESCENCE	STAUROLITIC	STIGMATICAL
SPINESCENCE	SQUANDERERS	STAUROSCOPE	STIGMATIZED
SPINIFEROUS	SQUANDERING	STAY-AT-HOMES	STIGMATIZER
SPINSTERISH	SQUARE DANCE	STEADFASTLY	STILLBIRTHS
SPINY-FINNED	SQUARE KNOTS	STEALTHIEST	STILTEDNESS
SPIRACULATE	SQUARE MEALS	STEAM-BOILER	STIMULATING
SPIRIFEROUS	SQUARE ROOTS	STEAM-ENGINE	STIMULATION
SPIRIT LEVEL	SQUASHINESS	STEAMROLLER	STIMULATIVE
SPIRITUALLY	SQUEAMISHLY	STEAM SHOVEL	STIPENDIARY
SPIRKETTING	SQUELCHIEST	STEAROPTENE	STIPULATING
SPIROCHAETE	SQUIGGLIEST	STEATOLYSIS	STIPULATION
SPIROMETRIC	SQUIREARCHY	STEATOPYGIA	STIPULATORY
SPITSTICKER	SQUIRMINGLY	STEATOPYGIC	STIRRUP CUPS
SPLASHBOARD	STABILIZERS	STEELWORKER	STIRRUP PUMP
SPLASHDOWNS	STABILIZING	STEEPLEJACK	STOCKBROKER
SPLASH GUARD	STADIOMETER	STEERAGEWAY	STOCKHOLDER
SPLASHINESS	STAFF NURSES	STELLARATOR	STOCKJOBBER
SPLATTERING	STAGE FRIGHT	STENCILLING	STOCK MARKET
SPLAYFOOTED	STAGE-MANAGE	STENOGRAPHY	STOCKPILING
SPLENDOROUS	STAGESTRUCK	STENOHALINE	STOCKTAKING
SPLENECTOMY	STAGGERBUSH	STENOPHAGUS	STOICALNESS
SPLENETICAL	STAGING POST	STENOTROPIC	STOMACHACHE
SPLINTERING	STAG PARTIES	STENOTYPIST	STOMACHICAL
SPLIT SECOND	STAKEHOLDER	STEPBROTHER	STOMACH PUMP
SPLUTTERING	STALACTITES	STEPHANOTIS	STOMATOLOGY
SPOILSPORTS	STALACTITIC	STEPLADDERS	STONECUTTER
SPOKESWOMAN	STALAGMITES	STEPPARENTS	STONE FRUITS
SPONDYLITIS	STALAGMITIC	STEPSISTERS	STONE-GROUND

STONEMASONS	STROBOSCOPE	SUBMERSIBLE	SUFFICIENCY
STONE'S THROW	STRONGBOXES	SUBMISSIONS	SUFFOCATING
STONEWALLED	STRONGHOLDS	SUBMITTABLE	SUFFOCATION
STONEWALLER	STRONG POINT	SUBMULTIPLE	SUFFOCATIVE
STONEWORKER	STRONG ROOMS	SUBORDINARY	SUFFRAGETTE
STOOLPIGEON	STRUCTURING	SUBORDINATE	SUFFUMIGATE
STOPWATCHES	STRUCTURIST	SUBORNATION	SUGGESTIBLE
STOREHOUSES	STRUTTINGLY	SUBORNATIVE	SUGGESTIONS
STOREKEEPER	STUBBORNEST	SUBPOENAING	SUITABILITY
STORE KEEPER	STUDENTSHIP	SUBREGIONAL	SULPHA DRUGS
STORM CLOUDS	STUDIEDNESS	SUBROGATION	SULPHUREOUS
STORYTELLER	STUDIO COUCH	SUBROUTINES	SUMMARINESS
STOURBRIDGE	STULTIFYING	SUBSCAPULAR	SUMMARIZING
STRAGGLIEST	STUMBLINGLY	SUBSCRIBERS	SUMMATIONAL
STRAIGHTEST	STUNTEDNESS	SUBSCRIBING	SUMMERHOUSE
STRAIGHT-OUT	STUPIDITIES	SUBSECTIONS	SUMMERINESS
STRAIGHTWAY	STYLISHNESS	SUBSEQUENCE	SUMPTUOUSLY
STRAININGLY	STYLIZATION	SUBSERVIENT	SUNDRENCHED
STRAITLACED	STYLOGRAPHY	SUBSIDENCES	SUNLESSNESS
STRANGENESS	STYLOPODIUM	SUBSIDIZERS	SUNNY-SIDE UP
STRANGULATE	STYLOSTIXIS	SUBSIDIZING	SUPERABOUND
STRAPHANGER	SUBASSEMBLY	SUBSISTENCE	SUPERCHARGE
STRATEGISTS	SUBAUDITION	SUBSPECIFIC	SUPERFAMILY
STRATHCLYDE	SUBAXILLARY	SUBSTANDARD	SUPERFETATE
STRATIFYING	SUBBASEMENT	SUBSTANTIAL	SUPERFICIAL
STRATOCRACY	SUBCHLORIDE	SUBSTANTIVE	SUPERFLUITY
STRATOPAUSE	SUBCOMPACTS	SUBSTATIONS	SUPERFLUOUS
STRAWFLOWER	SUBCONTRACT	SUBSTITUENT	SUPERIMPOSE
STRAWWEIGHT	SUBCONTRARY	SUBSTITUTED	SUPERINDUCE
STREAKINESS	SUBCORTICAL	SUBSTITUTES	SUPERINTEND
STREAMLINED	SUBCULTURAL	SUBSTRATIVE	SUPERIORITY
STREETLIGHT	SUBCULTURES	SUBSUMPTION	SUPERJACENT
STREET VALUE	SUBDELIRIUM	SUBSUMPTIVE	SUPERLATIVE
STRENUOSITY	SUBDIACONAL	SUBTERFUGES	SUPERLUNARY
STRENUOUSLY	SUBDIVIDING	SUBTRACTING	SUPERMARKET
STRESS MARKS	SUBDIVISION	SUBTRACTION	SUPERNATANT
STRETCHABLE	SUBDOMINANT	SUBTRACTIVE	SUPERNORMAL
STRETCHIEST	SUBDUEDNESS	SUBTROPICAL	SUPERSCRIBE
STRETCHMARK	SUBHEADINGS	SUBURBANITE	SUPERSCRIPT
STRIDULATED	SUBIRRIGATE	SUBVENTIONS	SUPERSEDEAS
STRIDULATOR	SUBJECTABLE	SUBVERSIVES	SUPERSEDING
STRIKEBOUND	SUBJUGATING	SUCCEDANEUM	SUPERSEDURE
STRING BEANS	SUBJUGATION	SUCCEEDABLE	SUPERSONICS
STRINGBOARD	SUBJUNCTION	SUCCESSIONS	SUPERSTRUCT
STRINGENTLY	SUBJUNCTIVE	SUCCESSORAL	SUPERTANKER
STRINGINESS	SUBLIMATING	SUCCOURABLE	SUPERVENING
STRINGPIECE	SUBLIMATION	SUCH AND SUCH	SUPERVISING
STRIP MINING	SUBLITTORAL	SUCKING PIGS	SUPERVISION
STRIP-SEARCH	SUBLUXATION	SUCTION PUMP	SUPERVISORS
STRIPTEASES	SUBMARGINAL	SUDETENLAND	SUPERVISORY
STROBE LIGHT	SUBMARINERS	SUFFERINGLY	SUPPLANTING

SUPPLEMENTS	SWEATSHIRTS	SYNTHESIZER	TAX SHELTERS
SUPPLICANTS	SWEEPSTAKES	SYNTHETICAL	TEARFULNESS
SUPPLICATED	SWEETBREADS	SYPHILITICS	TEARJERKERS
SUPPORTABLE	SWEETHEARTS	SYPHILOLOGY	TEA SERVICES
SUPPOSITION	SWEET PEPPER	SYSSARCOSIS	TEA TROLLEYS
SUPPOSITIVE	SWEET POTATO	SYSSARCOTIC	TECHNICALLY
SUPPOSITORY	SWEET-TALKED	SYSTEMATICS	TECHNICIANS
SUPPRESSANT	SWINDLINGLY	SYSTEMATISM	TECHNICOLOR
SUPPRESSING	SWINISHNESS	SYSTEMATIST	TECHNOCRACY
SUPPRESSION	SWISS CHARDS	SYSTEMATIZE	TECHNOCRATS
SUPPRESSIVE	SWISS CHEESE	SZOMBATHELY	TECHNOPHILE
SUPPRESSORS	SWITCHBACKS		TECHNOPHOBE
SUPPURATING	SWITCHBLADE	**T**	TEDIOUSNESS
SUPPURATION	SWITCHBOARD	TABERNACLES	TEENYBOPPER
SUPPURATIVE	SWITZERLAND	TABLECLOTHS	TEETOTALISM
SUPREMACIST	SWOLLEN HEAD	TABLESPOONS	TEETOTALLER
SUPREMATISM	SWOLLENNESS	TABLE TENNIS	TEGUCIGALPA
SUPREMATIST	SWORD DANCER	TABULATIONS	TELEBANKING
SUPREMENESS	SWORD DANCES	TACHEOMETER	TELECOMMUTE
SURBASEMENT	SWORDFISHES	TACHOGRAPHS	TELECOTTAGE
SURCHARGING	SYCOPHANTIC	TACHOMETERS	TELEGNOSTIC
SURFCASTING	SYLLABOGRAM	TACHOMETRIC	TELEGRAPHED
SURGEONFISH	SYLLOGISTIC	TACHYCARDIA	TELEGRAPHER
SURMOUNTING	SYMBOLISTIC	TACHYMETRIC	TELEGRAPHIC
SURPASSABLE	SYMBOLIZING	TACITURNITY	TELEKINESIS
SURPRISEDLY	SYMBOLOGIST	TACTFULNESS	TELEKINETIC
SURREALISTS	SYMMETRICAL	TAGLIATELLE	TELEOLOGISM
SURREBUTTAL	SYMPATHETIC	TAKE AGAINST	TELEOLOGIST
SURREBUTTER	SYMPATHIZED	TAKE-HOME PAY	TELEPATHIST
SURRENDERED	SYMPATHIZER	TALEBEARERS	TELEPHONING
SURRENDERER	SYMPETALOUS	TALENT SCOUT	TELEPHONIST
SURROGATION	SYMPHONIOUS	TALKABILITY	TELEPRINTER
SURROUNDING	SYMPTOMATIC	TALKING BOOK	TELESCOPING
SURVEILLANT	SYNAGOGICAL	TALLAHASSEE	TELESELLING
SURVIVAL KIT	SYNCHROMESH	TALL STORIES	TELEVISIONS
SUSCEPTANCE	SYNCHRONISM	TAMABLENESS	TELEWORKING
SUSCEPTIBLE	SYNCHRONIZE	TAMBOURINES	TELLING-OFFS
SUSPENDIBLE	SYNCHRONOUS	TANGIBILITY	TELUKBETUNG
SUSPENSEFUL	SYNCHROTRON	TANTALIZING	TEMERARIOUS
SUSPENSIONS	SYNCOPATING	TAPE MACHINE	TEMPERAMENT
SUSPICIONAL	SYNCOPATION	TAPE MEASURE	TEMPERATURE
SUSTAINABLE	SYNDESMOSIS	TARANTELLAS	TEMPESTUOUS
SUSTAINEDLY	SYNDESMOTIC	TARNISHABLE	TEMPORALITY
SUSTAINMENT	SYNDICALISM	TARRADIDDLE	TEMPORARILY
SUSURRATION	SYNDICALIST	TARTAR SAUCE	TEMPORIZING
SWALLOWABLE	SYNDICATING	TASKMASTERS	TEMPTATIONS
SWALLOW DIVE	SYNDICATION	TASTELESSLY	TEMPTRESSES
SWALLOWTAIL	SYNECDOCHIC	TAUTOLOGIES	TENACIOUSLY
SWALLOWWORT	SYNECOLOGIC	TAUTOLOGIZE	TENDENTIOUS
SWARTHINESS	SYNKARYONIC	TAUTOMERISM	TENDERFOOTS
SWEAT GLANDS	SYNTHESIZED	TAXIDERMIST	TENDERIZING

TENEBROSITY	THEOCENTRIC	THREADINESS	TOMBOYISHLY
TENNIS ELBOW	THEODOLITES	THREATENING	TONSILLITIS
TENORRHAPHY	THEODOLITIC	THREEPENCES	TOOTH POWDER
TENSIBILITY	THEODORAKIS	THRIFTINESS	TOPDRESSING
TENSIOMETER	THEOLOGIANS	THRILLINGLY	TOPOGRAPHER
TENTATIVELY	THEOLOGICAL	THROATINESS	TOPOGRAPHIC
TENTERHOOKS	THEOLOGIZER	THROBBINGLY	TORCHBEARER
TENUOUSNESS	THEOPHOBIAC	THROMBOCYTE	TORMENTEDLY
TEPEFACTION	THEOREMATIC	THROUGHPUTS	TORONTONIAN
TERATOGENIC	THEORETICAL	THROUGHWAYS	TORSIBILITY
TERATOLOGIC	THEOSOPHISM	THUMBSCREWS	TORTICOLLAR
TEREBIC ACID	THEOSOPHIST	THUNDERBIRD	TORTICOLLIS
TERMINATING	THERAPEUTIC	THUNDERBOLT	TORTURESOME
TERMINATION	THEREABOUTS	THUNDERCLAP	TORTURINGLY
TERMINATIVE	THEREMINIST	THYROIDITIS	TORTUROUSLY
TERMINATORY	THERETOFORE	THYROTROPIN	TOTALIZATOR
TERMINOLOGY	THERIOMORPH	THYRSANURAN	TOTEMICALLY
TERRESTRIAL	THERMIONICS	TICKINGS OFF	TOTIPALMATE
TERRICOLOUS	THERMOCLINE	TICK-TACK-TOE	TOTIPOTENCY
TERRIGENOUS	THERMOGRAPH	TIDDLYWINKS	TOUCHPAPERS
TERRITORIAL	THERMOLYSIS	TIEBREAKERS	TOUCHSTONES
TERRITORIES	THERMOLYTIC	TIED COTTAGE	TOUCH-TYPING
TERRORISTIC	THERMOMETER	TIGHTFISTED	TOUCH-TYPIST
TERRORIZING	THERMOMETRY	TIGHT-LIPPED	TOUCHY-FEELY
TERTIUM QUID	THERMOSCOPE	TIME CAPSULE	TOUR DE FORCE
TESSELLATED	THERMOSTATS	TIMEKEEPERS	TOURMALINIC
TESTABILITY	THERMOTAXIC	TIMESERVERS	TOURNAMENTS
TESTAMENTAL	THERMOTAXIS	TIMESERVING	TOURNIQUETS
TESTICULATE	THESAURUSES	TIME-SHARING	TOUT LE MONDE
TESTIMONIAL	THICKHEADED	TIME SIGNALS	TOWER BLOCKS
TESTIMONIES	THICKNESSES	TIMETABLING	TOWN PLANNER
TEST MATCHES	THICK-WITTED	TINDERBOXES	TOWNSPEOPLE
TETANICALLY	THIGMOTAXIS	TIN PAN ALLEY	TOXICOGENIC
TETRADYMITE	THIMBLEFULS	TIN-PAN ALLEY	TOXOPHILITE
TETRAHEDRAL	THIMBLEWEED	TIRUNELVELI	TOXOPLASMIC
TETRAHEDRON	THINGAMAJIG	TITANICALLY	TRACHEOTOMY
TETRAMERISM	THIN-SKINNED	TITILLATING	TRACK EVENTS
TETRAMEROUS	THIOCYANATE	TITILLATION	TRACKLAYERS
TETRAPLEGIA	THIOPENTONE	TITILLATIVE	TRACK RECORD
TETRARCHATE	THIRD DEGREE	TITLEHOLDER	TRACKSUITED
TETRASPORIC	THIRD-DEGREE	TITTERINGLY	TRADE PRICES
TETRAVALENT	THIRD PERSON	TOASTMASTER	TRADE ROUTES
THALIDOMIDE	THIRSTINESS	TOAST MASTER	TRADES UNION
THALLOPHYTE	THIRTEENTHS	TOBACCONIST	TRADESWOMAN
THANKLESSLY	THISTLEDOWN	TOBOGGANING	TRADE UNIONS
THAUMATROPE	THIXOTROPIC	TOFFEE APPLE	TRADING POST
THEATREGOER	THORACOTOMY	TOFFEE-NOSED	TRADITIONAL
THEATRICALS	THOROUGHPIN	TOILET PAPER	TRADUCEMENT
THEIRSELVES	THOUGHTLESS	TOILET ROLLS	TRADUCINGLY
THENCEFORTH	THOUSANDTHS	TOILET WATER	TRAFFICATOR
THEOBROMINE	THRASH METAL	TOLBUTAMIDE	TRAFFIC JAMS

TRAFFICKERS
TRAFFICKING
TRAGEDIENNE
TRAGICOMEDY
TRAILBLAZER
TRAINBEARER
TRAMPOLINER
TRAMPOLINES
TRANQUILITY
TRANSACTING
TRANSACTION
TRANSALPINE
TRANSCEIVER
TRANSCENDED
TRANSCRIBED
TRANSCRIBER
TRANSCRIPTS
TRANSECTION
TRANSFERASE
TRANSFERRED
TRANSFERRIN
TRANSFIGURE
TRANSFINITE
TRANSFIXING
TRANSFIXION
TRANSFORMED
TRANSFORMER
TRANSFUSION
TRANSFUSIVE
TRANSHUMANT
TRANSISTORS
TRANSITABLE
TRANSITIONS
TRANSITIVES
TRANS-JORDAN
TRANSLATING
TRANSLATION
TRANSLATORS
TRANSLOCATE
TRANSLUCENT
TRANSMITTAL
TRANSMITTED
TRANSMITTER
TRANSMUTING
TRANSPADANE
TRANSPARENT
TRANSPIERCE
TRANSPIRING
TRANSPLANTS
TRANSPONDER
TRANSPORTED

TRANSPORTER
TRANSPOSING
TRANSPUTERS
TRANSSEXUAL
TRANSURANIC
TRANSVAALER
TRANSVALUER
TRANSVERSAL
TRAPSHOOTER
TRAUMATIZED
TRAVEL AGENT
TRAVELOGUES
TRAVERSABLE
TREACHERIES
TREACHEROUS
TREACLINESS
TREASONABLE
TREASONABLY
TREASURABLE
TREBLE CLEFS
TRELLISWORK
TREMBLINGLY
TREMULOUSLY
TRENCHANTLY
TRENCH COATS
TRENCHERMAN
TRENCHERMEN
TRENDSETTER
TREPIDATION
TRESPASSING
TRESTLETREE
TRESTLEWORK
TRIABLENESS
TRIANGULATE
TRIBULATION
TRIBUTARIES
TRIBUTARILY
TRICERATOPS
TRICHINOSIS
TRICHLORIDE
TRICHOMONAD
TRICHOTOMIC
TRICKLE-DOWN
TRICKLINGLY
TRICKSINESS
TRICUSPIDAL
TRIGGERFISH
TRILLIONTHS
TRIMETROGON
TRIMORPHISM
TRINCOMALEE

TRINIDADIAN
TRIPALMITIN
TRIPLICATES
TRIQUETROUS
TRISTICHOUS
TRISULPHIDE
TRITURATION
TRIUMVIRATE
TRIVIALIZED
TROCHOPHORE
TROCORNERED
TROGLODYTES
TROGLODYTIC
TROJAN HORSE
TROMBONISTS
TROMPE L'OEIL
TROPHICALLY
TROPHOBLAST
TROPHOZOITE
TROPICALITY
TROPICALIZE
TROPISMATIC
TROPOPHYTIC
TROPOSPHERE
TROTSKYISTS
TROUBADOURS
TROUBLESOME
TROUBLE SPOT
TROUBLINGLY
TRUCULENTLY
TRUEHEARTED
TRUK ISLANDS
TRUMPETWEED
TRUNK ROUTES
TRUSTEESHIP
TRUSTWORTHY
TRYPANOSOME
TRYPSINOGEN
TSELINOGRAD
TSETSE FLIES
TUBERCULATE
TUBERCULOUS
TUB-THUMPERS
TUB-THUMPING
TUDORBETHAN
TUMBLE-DRIED
TUMBLE DRIER
TUMBLE DRYER
TUMBLE-DRYER
TUMEFACIENT
TUMEFACTION

TUNEFULNESS
TUNING FORKS
TURBINATION
TURBOCHARGE
TURBULENTLY
TURGESCENCE
TURKISH BATH
TURNAROUNDS
TURRICULATE
TURTLEDOVES
TURTLENECKS
TUTTI FRUTTI
TWELVEMONTH
TWITCHINGLY
TYNE AND WEAR
TYPECASTING
TYPESCRIPTS
TYPESETTERS
TYPE SETTING
TYPEWRITERS
TYPEWRITING
TYPEWRITTEN
TYPICALNESS
TYPING POOLS
TYPOGRAPHER
TYPOGRAPHIC
TYPOLOGICAL
TYRANNICIDE
TYRANNIZING
TYROTHRICIN
TZETZE FLIES

U

ULOTRICHOUS
ULTRAFILTER
ULTRAMARINE
ULTRAMODERN
ULTRASONICS
ULTRAVIOLET
ULVERIZABLE
UMBELLULATE
UNACCOUNTED
UNADVISEDLY
UNALTERABLE
UNAMBIGUOUS
UNAMBITIOUS
UNANIMOUSLY
UNANNOUNCED
UNAVAILABLE
UNAVOIDABLE
UNAWARENESS

UNBALANCING	UNDERSHIRTS	UNKEMPTNESS	UNTERWALDEN
UNBALLASTED	UNDERSIGNED	UNKNOWINGLY	UNTHEORIZED
UNBELIEVERS	UNDERSTAIRS	UNKNOWNNESS	UNTHINKABLE
UNBLEMISHED	UNDERSTATED	UNLOOKED-FOR	UNTOUCHABLE
UNBREAKABLE	UNDERTAKERS	UNLOOSENING	UNTRAVELLED
UNBURDENING	UNDERTAKING	UNLUCKINESS	UNUTTERABLE
UNCALLED-FOR	UNDERTHRUST	UNMANLINESS	UNUTTERABLY
UNCATCHABLE	UNDERVALUED	UNMITIGATED	UNVARNISHED
UNCERTAINLY	UNDERVALUER	UNNATURALLY	UNWARRANTED
UNCERTAINTY	UNDERWEIGHT	UNNECESSARY	UNWATCHABLE
UNCHARTERED	UNDERWRITER	UNOBTRUSIVE	UNWHOLESOME
UNCHASTENED	UNDESIGNING	UNORGANIZED	UNWILLINGLY
UNCHRISTIAN	UNDESIRABLE	UNPALATABLE	UNWITNESSED
UNCIVILIZED	UNDESIRABLY	UNPATRIOTIC	UNWITTINGLY
UNCLEANNESS	UNDEVELOPED	UNPERTURBED	UP-AND-COMING
UNCOMMITTED	UNDISCLOSED	UNPOLITICAL	UPHOLSTERED
UNCONCERNED	UNDISCUSSED	UNPRACTICAL	UPHOLSTERER
UNCONCLUDED	UNDISTORTED	UNPRACTISED	UPRIGHTNESS
UNCONFIDENT	UNDOUBTEDLY	UNPRINTABLE	UPS AND DOWNS
UNCONNECTED	UNDREAMED-OF	UNPROCESSED	UPSTRETCHED
UNCONSCIOUS	UNDRINKABLE	UNPROFESSED	URANOGRAPHY
UNCONSULTED	UNDULATIONS	UNPROMISING	URINIFEROUS
UNCONTESTED	UNEQUALNESS	UNPUBLISHED	UROCHORDATE
UNCONTRIVED	UNEQUIVOCAL	UNQUALIFIED	URTICACEOUS
UNCONVERTED	UNESSENTIAL	UNRAVELLING	USELESSNESS
UNCONVINCED	UNEXPLAINED	UNRAVELMENT	UTILITARIAN
UNCORRECTED	UNEXPRESSED	UNREALISTIC	UTILITY ROOM
UNCOUNTABLE	UNFAILINGLY	UNREASONING	UTILIZATION
UNCOUTHNESS	UNFALTERING	UNREFLECTED	UTRICULITIS
UNCRUSHABLE	UNFLAPPABLE	UNREHEARSED	
UNDECEIVING	UNFLAPPABLY	UNRELENTING	**V**
UNDECIDABLE	UNFLINCHING	UNREMITTING	VACATIONERS
UNDECIDEDLY	UNFORTUNATE	UNRIGHTEOUS	VACATIONING
UNDEMANDING	UNFULFILLED	UNSATISFIED	VACCINATING
UNDERACTING	UNGODLINESS	UNSATURATED	VACCINATION
UNDERBIDDER	UNGUICULATE	UNSAVOURILY	VACILLATING
UNDERCHARGE	UNGULIGRADE	UNSCHEDULED	VACILLATION
UNDEREXPOSE	UNHAPPINESS	UNSCRAMBLED	VACUOLATION
UNDERGROUND	UNHEALTHILY	UNSCRAMBLER	VACUOUSNESS
UNDERGROWTH	UNICELLULAR	UNSCRATCHED	VACUUM FLASK
UNDERLETTER	UNIFICATION	UNSHAKEABLE	VACUUM PUMPS
UNDERLINING	UNIFORMNESS	UNSOCIALIST	VAGABONDAGE
UNDERMANNED	UNINHABITED	UNSPARINGLY	VAGABONDISM
UNDERMINING	UNINHIBITED	UNSPEAKABLE	VAGINECTOMY
UNDERPASSES	UNINITIATED	UNSPEAKABLY	VAGRANTNESS
UNDERPAYING	UNINSPIRING	UNSPECIFIED	VALEDICTION
UNDERPINNED	UNINSULATED	UNSPONSORED	VALEDICTORY
UNDERPLAYED	UNIPERSONAL	UNSTOPPABLE	VALIDATIONS
UNDERRATING	UNIPOLARITY	UNSURPASSED	VALLE D'AOSTA
UNDERSCORED	UNIVERSALLY	UNSURPRISED	VALUATIONAL
UNDERSELLER	UNJUSTIFIED	UNSUSPECTED	VAMPIRE BATS

VANDALISTIC
VANDALIZING
VANISHINGLY
VANQUISHING
VAPORESCENT
VAPORIMETER
VAPORIZABLE
VAPOUR TRAIL
VARGAS LLOSA
VARIABILITY
VARIATIONAL
VARICELLATE
VARICELLOID
VARIEGATION
VARIOLATION
VARIOUSNESS
VASCULARITY
VASCULARIZE
VASECTOMIES
VASODILATOR
VASOPRESSIN
VATICAN CITY
VEGETARIANS
VELOCIPEDES
VENDIBILITY
VENEREOLOGY
VENESECTION
VENTILATING
VENTILATION
VENTILATIVE
VENTILATORS
VENTILATORY
VENTRICULAR
VENTRICULUS
VENTURESOME
VERACIOUSLY
VERATRIDINE
VERBALIZING
VERBAL NOUNS
VEREENIGING
VERISIMILAR
VERMICULATE
VERMICULITE
VERMINATION
VERMIVOROUS
VERNACULARS
VERRUCOSITY
VERSATILITY
VERSICOLOUR
VERTEBRATES
VERTICALITY

VERTIGINOUS
VESTIGIALLY
VETERANS DAY
VEXATIOUSLY
VEXILLOLOGY
VIBRACULOID
VIBRAPHONES
VIBRATILITY
VIBRATINGLY
VIBRATIONAL
VICARIOUSLY
VICEGERENCY
VICEROYALTY
VICEROYSHIP
VICHYSSOISE
VICIOUSNESS
VICISSITUDE
VICTIMIZING
VICTUALLING
VIDEOPHONIC
VIDEOTAPING
VIEWFINDERS
VINAIGRETTE
VINDICATING
VINDICATION
VINDICATORY
VINEDRESSER
VINEGARROON
VINEYARDIST
VINICULTURE
VINIFICATOR
VIOLABILITY
VIOLONCELLO
VIRGIN BIRTH
VIRIDESCENT
VIROLOGICAL
VISCOMETRIC
VISCOUNTESS
VISCOUSNESS
VISIBLENESS
VISIONARIES
VISITATIONS
VISUALIZING
VITICULTURE
VITRESCENCE
VITRIFIABLE
VITUPERATOR
VIVACIOUSLY
VIVISECTION
VLAARDINGEN
VLADIKAVKAZ

VLADIVOSTOK
VOCIFERANCE
VOCIFERATED
VOCIFERATOR
VOLCANICITY
VOLCANOLOGY
VOLTAMMETER
VOLUNTARIES
VOLUNTARILY
VOLUNTARISM
VOLUNTARIST
VOLUNTEERED
VOODOOISTIC
VOORTREKKER
VORACIOUSLY
VORTIGINOUS
VOUCHSAFING
VOYEURISTIC
VULCANIZING
VULGARITIES
VULGARIZING
VULGAR LATIN

W
WADING POOLS
WAGGISHNESS
WAINSCOTING
WAINSCOTTED
WAITING GAME
WAITING LIST
WAITING ROOM
WAITRESSING
WAKEFULNESS
WALKS OF LIFE
WALLFLOWERS
WALLPAPERED
WANDERINGLY
WANNE-EICKEL
WARM-BLOODED
WARM-HEARTED
WARMING PANS
WAR OF NERVES
WARRANTABLE
WASHABILITY
WASH DRAWING
WASHERWOMAN
WASHERWOMEN
WASHING DAYS
WASPISHNESS
WATCHKEEPER
WATCHMAKERS

WATCHMAKING
WATCHSTRAPS
WATCHTOWERS
WATER CANNON
WATER CLOSET
WATERCOLOUR
WATERCOURSE
WATERED-DOWN
WATERFRONTS
WATERING CAN
WATER LEVELS
WATER LILIES
WATERLOGGED
WATER MEADOW
WATERMELONS
WATERPROOFS
WATER SKIERS
WATER SKIING
WATERSPOUTS
WATER SUPPLY
WATER TABLES
WATER VAPOUR
WATERWHEELS
WATHAWURUNG
WAVELENGTHS
WAYWARDNESS
WEALTHINESS
WEARABILITY
WEAR AND TEAR
WEATHERCOCK
WEATHER SHIP
WEATHER VANE
WEATHER-WISE
WEDDING RING
WEIGHBRIDGE
WEIGHTINESS
WELCOMENESS
WELDABILITY
WELL-ADAPTED
WELL-ADVISED
WELL AND GOOD
WELLBEHAVED
WELL-DEFINED
WELL-ENDOWED
WELL-FOUNDED
WELL-GROOMED
WELLINGTONS
WELL-MEANING
WELL-ROUNDED
WELLSPRINGS
WELL-WISHERS

WELL-WISHING
WELWITSCHIA
WENSLEYDALE
WESLEYANISM
WEST COUNTRY
WESTERNIZED
WESTERNMOST
WEST GERMANY
WEST LOTHIAN
WESTMINSTER
WESTPHALIAN
WET BLANKETS
WETTABILITY
WHEEDLINGLY
WHEELBARROW
WHEELCHAIRS
WHEELHOUSES
WHEELWRIGHT
WHEREABOUTS
WHERESOEVER
WHEREWITHAL
WHIFFLETREE
WHIMSICALLY
WHIPPING BOY
WHIRLYBIRDS
WHIST DRIVES
WHITEBOARDS
WHITE-COLLAR
WHITE DWARFS
WHITE HORSES
WHITE KNIGHT
WHITE METALS
WHITE PAPERS
WHITE PEPPER
WHITE RUSSIA
WHITE-SLAVER
WHITE SPIRIT
WHITETHROAT
WHITEWASHED
WHITEWASHER
WHITEWASHES
WHITSUNTIDE
WHOLE NUMBER
WHOLESALERS

WHOREHOUSES
WICKET GATES
WILDEBEESTS
WILDFOWLING
WILLINGNESS
WINDCHEATER
WINDFALL TAX
WINDJAMMERS
WINDOW BOXES
WINDOWPANES
WINDOW SHADE
WINDOWSILLS
WINDSCREENS
WINDSHIELDS
WIND-SUCKING
WIND-SURFERS
WIND-SURFING
WIND TUNNELS
WIND TURBINE
WINEBIBBING
WINNINGNESS
WINNING POST
WINNIPEGGER
WINSOMENESS
WINTERGREEN
WIRE NETTING
WIRE-TAPPING
WISDOM TEETH
WISDOM TOOTH
WISECRACKED
WISECRACKER
WISHFULNESS
WISTFULNESS
WITCHDOCTOR
WITCH-HUNTER
WITHDRAWALS
WITHDRAWING
WITHHOLDING
WITHOUT FAIL
WITHSTANDER
WITLESSNESS
WITNESSABLE
WIZARD PRANG
WOBBLE BOARD

WOLFISHNESS
WOLF WHISTLE
WOMANLINESS
WONDERFULLY
WONDERINGLY
WONDERLANDS
WOOD ALCOHOL
WOODCARVING
WOODCUTTERS
WOODCUTTING
WOODEN SPOON
WOODPECKERS
WOODTURNING
WOODWORKING
WOOLGROWING
WORD-PERFECT
WORKABILITY
WORKAHOLICS
WORKAHOLISM
WORKBASKETS
WORKBENCHES
WORKING DAYS
WORKING WEEK
WORKMANLIKE
WORKMANSHIP
WORKSTATION
WORLD-BEATER
WORLDLINESS
WORLDLY-WISE
WORLD POWERS
WORLD SERIES
WORSHIPABLE
WORSHIPPERS
WORSHIPPING
WORTHLESSLY
WRIGGLINGLY
WRITING DESK
WRONGDOINGS
WRONGHEADED
WROUGHT IRON

X

XANTHOPHYLL
X CHROMOSOME

XENOGENESIS
XENOGENETIC
XENOGLOSSIA
XENOMORPHIC
XEROGRAPHER
XEROGRAPHIC
XEROMORPHIC
XEROPHILOUS
XEROPHYTISM
XYLOCARPOUS
XYLOGRAPHER
XYLOGRAPHIC
XYLOPHAGOUS
XYLOPHONIST

Y

YACHTSWOMAN
Y CHROMOSOME
YELLOW FEVER
YELLOWKNIFE
YELLOW PAGES
YELLOWSTONE
YEVTUSHENKO
YOUTH HOSTEL
YTTRIFEROUS
YUGOSLAVIAN
YUWAALARAAY

Z

ZANTHOXYLUM
ZEALOUSNESS
ZESTFULNESS
ZHANGJIAKOU
ZINCIFEROUS
ZINCOGRAPHY
ZOOCHEMICAL
ZOOMORPHISM
ZOOPLANKTON
ZOOTECHNICS
ZYGOMORPHIC
ZYGOTICALLY
ZYMOGENESIS
ZYMOTICALLY

A
ABBREVIATING
ABBREVIATION
ABELIAN GROUP
ABOLITIONARY
ABOLITIONISM
ABOLITIONIST
ABOMINATIONS
ABORTIONISTS
ABORTION PILL
ABRACADABRAS
ABSENT MINDED
ABSENT-MINDED
ABSOLUTENESS
ABSOLUTE ZERO
ABSORPTIVITY
ABSTEMIOUSLY
ABSTRACTEDLY
ABSTRACTIONS
ABSTRACT NOUN
ABSTRUSENESS
ACADEMICALLY
ACADEMICIANS
ACANTHACEOUS
ACCELERATING
ACCELERATION
ACCELERATIVE
ACCELERATORS
ACCENTUATING
ACCENTUATION
ACCESS COURSE
ACCIACCATURA
ACCIDENTALLY
ACCLAMATIONS
ACCLIMATIZED
ACCLIMATIZER
ACCOMMODATED
ACCOMPANISTS
ACCOMPANYING
ACCOMPLISHED
ACCOMPLISHER
ACCORDIONIST
ACCOUPLEMENT
ACCOUTREMENT
ACCUMULATING
ACCUMULATION
ACCUMULATIVE
ACCUMULATORS
ACCUSATORIAL
ACETALDEHYDE
ACHIEVEMENTS

ACHILLES' HEEL
ACHILL ISLAND
ACHLAMYDEOUS
ACHLORHYDRIA
ACKNOWLEDGED
ACKNOWLEDGER
ACOUSTICALLY
ACQUAINTANCE
ACQUIESCENCE
ACQUISITIONS
ACROSTICALLY
ACTINOMETRIC
ACTINOMYCETE
ADAPTABILITY
ADDERS TONGUE
ADDITIONALLY
ADHESIVENESS
ADJECTIVALLY
ADJOURNMENTS
ADJUDICATING
ADJUDICATION
ADJUDICATORS
ADMINISTERED
ADMINISTRATE
ADSCITITIOUS
ADULTERATING
ADULTERATION
ADUMBRATIONS
ADVANTAGEOUS
ADVENTITIOUS
ADVISABILITY
AERIFICATION
AERODONETICS
AERODYNAMICS
AEROEMBOLISM
AEROMECHANIC
AERONAUTICAL
AERONEUROSIS
AESTHETICIAN
AESTHETICISM
AETHEREALITY
AETIOLOGICAL
AFFECTATIONS
AFFECTEDNESS
AFFECTIONATE
AFFILIATIONS
AFFINITY CARD
AFFIRMATIONS
AFFIRMATIVES
AFORETHOUGHT
AFRIKANERDOM

AFRO-AMERICAN
AFTERBURNING
AFTEREFFECTS
AFTER THE FACT
AFTERTHOUGHT
AGAMOGENESIS
AGAMOGENETIC
AGARICACEOUS
AGE OF CONSENT
AGGLOMERATED
AGGLUTINABLE
AGGLUTINOGEN
AGGRAVATIONS
AGGREGATIONS
AGGRESSIVELY
AGONY COLUMNS
AGORAPHOBICS
AGRICULTURAL
AGROFORESTRY
AILUROPHILIA
AILUROPHOBIA
AIR COMMODORE
AIR-CONDITION
AIRHOSTESSES
AIR TERMINALS
ALCOHOLICITY
ALHAMBRESQUE
ALICE SPRINGS
ALIENABILITY
ALIMENTATION
ALIMENTATIVE
ALKALIMETRIC
ALL-IMPORTANT
ALL-INCLUSIVE
ALLITERATION
ALLITERATIVE
ALLOMORPHISM
ALLUSIVENESS
ALMIGHTINESS
ALPHABETICAL
ALPHABETIZER
ALPHA-BLOCKER
ALPHANUMERIC
ALSTROEMERIA
ALTERABILITY
ALTERCATIONS
ALTERNATIONS
ALTERNATIVES
ALTHORP HOUSE
ALTIMETRICAL
AMALGAMATING

AMALGAMATION
AMATEURISHLY
AMBASSADRESS
AMBIDEXTROUS
AMBITENDENCY
AMBIVALENTLY
AMELIORATING
AMELIORATION
AMELIORATIVE
AMERICANISMS
AMERICANIZED
AMERICANIZER
AMITOTICALLY
AMORTIZATION
AMORTIZEMENT
AMPHETAMINES
AMPHIBRACHIC
AMPHICOELOUS
AMPHICTYONIC
AMPHIDIPLOID
AMPHISBAENIC
AMPHITHEATRE
AMPHITHECIUM
AMPHITROPOUS
AMPULLACEOUS
AMYGDALOIDAL
ANACHRONISMS
ANAESTHETICS
ANAESTHETIST
ANAESTHETIZE
ANAGOGICALLY
ANAGRAMMATIC
ANALPHABETIC
ANALYTICALLY
ANAMORPHOSIS
ANAPHRODISIA
ANAPHYLACTIC
ANARCHICALLY
ANASTIGMATIC
ANATHEMATIZE
ANATOMICALLY
ANCHORPERSON
ANCIEN REGIME
ANDROSTERONE
ANEMOGRAPHIC
ANEMOPHILOUS
ANESTHETISTS
ANESTHETIZED
ANGLO-INDIANS
ANGLOPHILIAC
ANGUILLIFORM

ANGULARITIES
ANIMADVERTED
ANIMAL RIGHTS
ANIMATRONICS
ANNEXATIONAL
ANNIHILATING
ANNIHILATION
ANNIHILATIVE
ANNOUNCEMENT
ANNUNCIATION
ANNUNCIATIVE
ANTAGONISTIC
ANTAGONIZING
ANTANANARIVO
ANTECHAMBERS
ANTEDILUVIAN
ANTEMERIDIAN
ANTE MERIDIEM
ANTHOLOGICAL
ANTHOLOGISTS
ANTHROPOIDAL
ANTHROPOLOGY
ANTI-AIR-CRAFT
ANTICATALYST
ANTICIPATING
ANTICIPATION
ANTICIPATIVE
ANTICIPATORY
ANTICLERICAL
ANTICLIMAXES
ANTICYCLONES
ANTICYCLONIC
ANTIHALATION
ANTIMACASSAR
ANTIMAGNETIC
ANTINEUTRINO
ANTIPARALLEL
ANTIPARTICLE
ANTIPATHETIC
ANTIPERIODIC
ANTIQUARIANS
ANTIRACHITIC
ANTI-SEMITISM
ANTITHETICAL
ANTONOMASTIC
ANURADHAPURA
AORISTICALLY
APAGOGICALLY
APERIODICITY
APHRODISIACS
APICULTURIST

APLANOSPHERE
APOCHROMATIC
APOCYNACEOUS
APOGEOTROPIC
APOSTROPHIZE
APOTHECARIES
APPALACHIANS
APPARATCHIKS
APPARENTNESS
APPASSIONATO
APPEASEMENTS
APPELLATIONS
APPENDECTOMY
APPENDICITIS
APPENDICULAR
APPERCEPTION
APPERCEPTIVE
APPERTAINING
APPETIZINGLY
APPLAUDINGLY
APPLICATIONS
APPOGGIATURA
APPOINTMENTS
APPORTIONING
APPRAISINGLY
APPRECIATING
APPRECIATION
APPRECIATIVE
APPREHENDING
APPREHENSION
APPREHENSIVE
APPRENTICING
APPROACHABLE
APPROPRIABLE
APPROPRIATED
APPROXIMATED
APPURTENANCE
A PRETTY PENNY
APRON STRINGS
AQUICULTURAL
ARBITRAGEURS
ARBORESCENCE
ARBORIZATION
ARCHDEACONRY
ARCHDIOCESAN
ARCHDIOCESES
ARCHEOLOGIES
ARCHESPORIAL
ARCHETYPICAL
ARCHIPELAGIC
ARCHIPELAGOS

ARCHITECTURE
ARCHOPLASMIC
ARCTIC CIRCLE
ARGILLACEOUS
ARISTOCRATIC
ARMOURED CARS
ARMOUR-PLATED
AROMATHERAPY
AROMATICALLY
ARRAIGNMENTS
ARRANGEMENTS
ARSENOPYRITE
ARTESIAN WELL
ARTHROPODOUS
ARTHROSPORIC
ARTICULATELY
ARTICULATING
ARTICULATION
ARTICULATORY
ARTIFICIALLY
ARTILLERYMAN
ARTISTICALLY
ASCENSION DAY
ASCERTAINING
ASCOMYCETOUS
ASH WEDNESDAY
ASKING PRICES
ASPHYXIATING
ASPHYXIATION
ASSASSINATED
ASSEMBLY LINE
ASSEVERATING
ASSEVERATION
ASSIBILATION
ASSIGNATIONS
ASSIMILATING
ASSIMILATION
ASSIMILATIVE
ASSOCIATIONS
ASTONISHMENT
ASTOUNDINGLY
ASTRINGENTLY
ASTROBIOLOGY
ASTROCOMPASS
ASTROGEOLOGY
ASTROLOGICAL
ASTRONAUTICS
ASTRONOMICAL
ASTROPHYSICS
ASYMPTOMATIC
ASYNCHRONISM

ASYNCHRONOUS
ATHEROMATOUS
ATHLETE'S FOOT
ATHLETICALLY
ATHWARTSHIPS
ATLANTIC CITY
ATMOSPHERICS
ATOMIC ENERGY
ATTACHE CASES
ATTENBOROUGH
ATTESTATIONS
ATTESTED MILK
ATTITUDINIZE
ATTRACTIVELY
ATTRIBUTABLE
AUDIOLOGICAL
AUDIOMETRIST
AUGMENTATION
AUGMENTATIVE
AULD LANG SYNE
AUSCULTATION
AUSPICIOUSLY
AUSTRALASIAN
AUSTRONESIAN
AUTHENTICATE
AUTHENTICITY
AUTISTICALLY
AUTOANTIBODY
AUTOEXPOSURE
AUTOGRAPHING
AUTOHYPNOSIS
AUTOHYPNOTIC
AUTOMOBILIST
AUTONOMOUSLY
AUTOROTATION
AUTOXIDATION
AVAILABILITY
AVANT GARDISM
AVARICIOUSLY
AVICULTURIST
AVITAMINOSIS
AVOGADRO'S LAW
AWE-INSPIRING
AZATHIOPRINE

B
BABY CARRIAGE
BACCHANALIAN
BACKBENCHERS
BACKBREAKING
BACKHANDEDLY

BACK OF BEYOND
BACK PASSAGES
BACKPEDALING
BACKPEDALLED
BACKROOM BOYS
BACKSLAPPERS
BACKSLAPPING
BACKTRACKING
BACKWARDNESS
BACKWOODSMAN
BACKWOODSMEN
BACTERICIDAL
BACTERIOLOGY
BAGGAGE ROOMS
BAKING POWDER
BALANCED DIET
BALANCE SHEET
BALCONY SCENE
BALL BEARINGS
BALLOTTEMENT
BALNEOLOGIST
BALTIC STATES
BANDARANAIKE
BANDERILLERO
BANDJARMASIN
BANK ACCOUNTS
BANKER'S CARDS
BANKER'S ORDER
BANK HOLIDAYS
BANKRUPTCIES
BANTAMWEIGHT
BARBARIANISM
BARBARICALLY
BARBITURATES
BARLEY SUGARS
BARNSTORMERS
BARNSTORMING
BARORECEPTOR
BARQUISIMETO
BARRANQUILLA
BARREL ORGANS
BASIDIOSPORE
BASTARDIZING
BASTINADOING
BATAN ISLANDS
BATCH PROCESS
BATHING SUITS
BATHYSPHERES
BATTERING RAM
BATTLEFIELDS
BATTLE ROYALS

BEACH BUGGIES
BEACHCOMBERS
BEACONSFIELD
BEAT A RETREAT
BEATIFICALLY
BEAUTY QUEENS
BECHUANALAND
BEDAZZLEMENT
BEDFORDSHIRE
BEGGARLINESS
BEGRUDGINGLY
BEHAVIOURISM
BEHAVIOURIST
BELEAGUERING
BELGIAN CONGO
BELITTLEMENT
BELITTLINGLY
BELLETRISTIC
BELLIGERENCE
BELLIGERENCY
BELLIGERENTS
BELLY BUTTONS
BELLY DANCERS
BELLY-LANDING
BELOW THE BELT
BENEDICTINES
BENEDICTIONS
BENEFACTIONS
BENEFACTRESS
BENEFICENTLY
BENEFICIALLY
BENEVOLENTLY
BENZALDEHYDE
BENZOPHENONE
BENZOQUINONE
BEREAVEMENTS
BERWICKSHIRE
BESPECTACLED
BEVERLY HILLS
BEWILDERMENT
BEWITCHINGLY
BIAURICULATE
BIBLIOGRAPHY
BIBLIOMANIAC
BIBLIOPHILES
BICOLLATERAL
BIELSKO-BIALA
BIFLAGELLATE
BIFURCATIONS
BILHARZIASIS
BILINGUALISM

BILL OF HEALTH
BILL OF LADING
BILL OF RIGHTS
BIOCATALYTIC
BIOCHEMISTRY
BIODIVERSITY
BIOECOLOGIST
BIOFLAVONOID
BIOGEOGRAPHY
BIOGRAPHICAL
BIOLOGICALLY
BIOMECHANICS
BIONOMICALLY
BIOPHYSICIST
BIOSYNTHESIS
BIOSYNTHETIC
BIPROPELLANT
BIRDS-EYE VIEW
BIRD'S-EYE
  VIEW
BIRD-WATCHERS
BIREFRINGENT
BIRTH CONTROL
BISMUTHINITE
BLABBERMOUTH
BLACK AND BLUE
BLACKBALLING
BLACKBERRIES
BLACK COUNTRY
BLACKCURRANT
BLACK ECONOMY
BLACK ENGLISH
BLACKGUARDLY
BLACK-HEARTED
BLACKLEGGING
BLACKLISTING
BLACKMAILERS
BLACKMAILING
BLACK MUSLIMS
BLACK PUDDING
BLADDERWRACK
BLAENAU GWENT
BLAMEFULNESS
BLANK CHEQUES
BLARNEY STONE
BLAST FURNACE
BLASTODERMIC
BLASTOSPHERE
BLINDFOLDING
BLISSFULNESS
BLISTERINGLY

BLOCKBUSTERS
BLOCK LETTERS
BLOEMFONTEIN
BLOOD BROTHER
BLOODLETTING
BLOODSTAINED
BLOODSTREAMS
BLOODSUCKERS
BLOODTHIRSTY
BLOOD VESSELS
BLOODY-MINDED
BLUE-EYED BOYS
BLUESTOCKING
BLUNDERINGLY
BLUSTERINGLY
BOARDING CARD
BOASTFULNESS
BOBSLEIGHING
BODY LANGUAGE
BODY SNATCHER
BODY STOCKING
BOILING POINT
BOISTEROUSLY
BOLSTERINGLY
BOMBACACEOUS
BOMBARDMENTS
BOOBY-TRAPPED
BOOK-LEARNING
BOOMERANGING
BOROSILICATE
BOTTOM DRAWER
BOUGAINVILLE
BOUNCY CASTLE
BOWDLERIZING
BOWLING ALLEY
BOWLING GREEN
BRACHYLOGOUS
BRACKISHNESS
BRAINS TRUSTS
BRAIN SURGEON
BRAINTEASERS
BRAINWASHING
BREADWINNERS
BREAKFASTING
BREASTSTROKE
BREATHALYSER
BREATHALYZER
BREATHTAKING
BREECHLOADER
BREWERS YEAST
BRILLIANTINE

BRINKMANSHIP
BRISTLE-GRASS
BROADCASTERS
BROADCASTING
BRONCHOSCOPE
BRONCHOSCOPY
BRONCOBUSTER
BRONTOSAURUS
BRONZE MEDALS
BROTHERHOODS
BROTHER-IN-LAW
BROWNIE POINT
BUENAVENTURA
BUFFER STATES
BUFFER STOCKS
BULLDOG CLIPS
BULLET-HEADED
BULLFIGHTERS
BULLFIGHTING
BULLHEADEDLY
BULLSHITTING
BULL TERRIERS
BUNSEN BURNER
BUREAUCRATIC
BURGLAR ALARM
BURSERACEOUS
BUSINESSLIKE
BUSINESS SUIT
BUTTERSCOTCH
BUTTONHOLING
BUYER'S MARKET
BYELORUSSIAN

C

CABBAGE WHITE
CABIN CRUISER
CABINET-MAKER
CABLE RAILWAY
CACHINNATION
CAENOGENESIS
CAENOGENETIC
CALAMITOUSLY
CALCULATIONS
CALENDAR YEAR
CALIBRATIONS
CALISTHENICS
CALLIGRAPHER
CALLIGRAPHIC
CALLISTHENIC
CALL OF NATURE
CALORIMETRIC

CALUMNIATING
CALUMNIATION
CAMELOPARDUS
CAMI-KNICKERS
CAMOUFLAGING
CAMP FOLLOWER
CANALIZATION
CANCELLATION
CANDELABRUMS
CANDLESTICKS
CANDY-STRIPED
CANNIBALIZED
CANNON FODDER
CANONIZATION
CANTABRIGIAN
CANTANKEROUS
CAPABILITIES
CAPACITATION
CAPARISONNED
CAPE COLOURED
CAPE PROVINCE
CAPERCAILLIE
CAPILLACEOUS
CAPITAL GAINS
CAPITALIZING
CAPITULATING
CAPITULATION
CAPRICIOUSLY
CAPTIOUSNESS
CARAVANSERAI
CARBOHYDRATE
CARBONACEOUS
CARBON COPIES
CARBON DATING
CARBON PAPERS
CARBURETTORS
CARCINOGENIC
CARD-CARRYING
CARDIOGRAPHY
CARDIOLOGIST
CARDIOMEGALY
CARELESSNESS
CARIBBEAN SEA
CARICATURING
CARICATURIST
CARILLONNEUR
CARPETBAGGER
CARPET KNIGHT
CARPOLOGICAL
CARPOPHAGOUS
CARRIAGEWAYS

CARTE BLANCHE
CARTOGRAPHER
CARTOGRAPHIC
CARTWHEELING
CARVING FORKS
CARVING KNIFE
CASH AND CARRY
CASH REGISTER
CASTELLATION
CASTING VOTES
CATACHRESTIC
CATADIOPTRIC
CATASTROPHES
CATASTROPHIC
CATCHPHRASES
CATECHETICAL
CATEGORIZING
CATERPILLARS
CATERWAULING
CATS WHISKERS
CAULIFLOWERS
CAUSE CELEBRE
CAUTIOUSNESS
CAVEAT EMPTOR
CELEBRATIONS
CEMENT MIXERS
CENSORIOUSLY
CENTENARIANS
CENTRALIZING
CENTRAL KAROO
CENTREPIECES
CENTROCLINAL
CENTROSPHERE
CENTUPLICATE
CEPHALOMETER
CEPHALOMETRY
CEPHALOPODAN
CEPHALOPODIC
CEREMONIALLY
CEROGRAPHIST
CERRO DE PASCO
CERTIFICATED
CERTIFICATES
CHAIN LETTERS
CHAIN-SMOKERS
CHAIN-SMOKING
CHAIRMANSHIP
CHAIRPERSONS
CHAISE LONGUE
CHALCOGRAPHY
CHALCOPYRITE

CHAMBERLAINS
CHAMBERMAIDS
CHAMBER MUSIC
CHAMPIONSHIP
CHANGCHIAKOW
CHANGELESSLY
CHANGE OF LIFE
CHANGING ROOM
CHAPLAINCIES
CHAPTERHOUSE
CHARACTERFUL
CHARACTERIZE
CHARGE NURSES
CHARGE SHEETS
CHARLATANISM
CHARNEL HOUSE
CHASTISEMENT
CHASTITY BELT
CHATTERBOXES
CHAUFFEURING
CHAUVINISTIC
CHECKERBERRY
CHECKERBLOOM
CHEERFULNESS
CHEERLEADERS
CHEESEBURGER
CHEESEPARING
CHEESE-PARING
CHEFS D'OEUVRE
CHEMOSPHERIC
CHEMOTHERAPY
CHEMOTROPISM
CHEQUERBOARD
CHERUBICALLY
CHESHIRE CATS
CHESTERFIELD
CHIAROSCUROS
CHIEF JUSTICE
CHIEF OF STAFF
CHILDBEARING
CHILD BENEFIT
CHILDISHNESS
CHILDMINDERS
CHILDMINDING
CHILD PRODIGY
CHILPANCINGO
CHIMNEYPIECE
CHIMNEYSTACK
CHIMNEYSWEEP
CHIROGRAPHER
CHIROGRAPHIC

CHIROPODISTS	CIRCULAR SAWS	CLOSING TIMES	COLONIZATION
CHIROPRACTIC	CIRCUMCISING	CLOTHESHORSE	COLORIMETRIC
CHIROPRACTOR	CIRCUMCISION	CLOTHESLINES	COLOURLESSLY
CHITCHATTING	CIRCUMFLUOUS	CLOTHES-PRESS	COLOUR SCHEME
CHITTERLINGS	CIRCUMFUSION	CLOTTED CREAM	COLUMNIATION
CHIVALROUSLY	CIRCUMNUTATE	CLOVE HITCHES	COMBINATIONS
CHLORAMBUCIL	CIRCUMSCRIBE	CLOVERLEAVES	COMBUSTIBLES
CHLORENCHYMA	CIRCUMSTANCE	CLOWNISHNESS	COME A CROPPER
CHLORINATING	CIRCUMVENTED	CLUB SANDWICH	COME-UPPANCES
CHLORINATION	CIRCUMVENTER	CLUSTER BOMBS	COMFORTINGLY
CHLOROFORMED	CIRROCUMULUS	COACERVATION	COMMANDEERED
CHLOROHYDRIN	CIRROSTRATUS	COACHBUILDER	COMMANDMENTS
CHLOROPICRIN	CITIZENS' BAND	COACH STATION	COMMEMORATED
CHOCOLATE BOX	CITRICULTURE	COALITIONIST	COMMEMORATOR
CHOIRMASTERS	CIVIL DEFENCE	COALSCUTTLES	COMMENCEMENT
CHOIR SCHOOLS	CIVILIZATION	COBBLESTONES	COMMENDATION
CHOLERICALLY	CIVIL LIBERTY	COCKFIGHTING	COMMENDATORY
CHONDRIOSOME	CIVIL SERVANT	COCKLESHELLS	COMMENSALISM
CHOREOGRAPHS	CIVIL SERVICE	COCONUT SHIES	COMMENSURATE
CHOREOGRAPHY	CLAIRVOYANCE	COCOS ISLANDS	COMMENTARIAL
CHOROGRAPHER	CLAIRVOYANTS	CODEPENDENCY	COMMENTARIES
CHOROGRAPHIC	CLANGOROUSLY	CODIFICATION	COMMENTATING
CHRISTCHURCH	CLANNISHNESS	COEFFICIENTS	COMMENTATORS
CHRISTENINGS	CLAPPERBOARD	COELENTERATE	COMMERCIALLY
CHRISTIAN ERA	CLARINETTIST	COENESTHESIA	COMMISERATED
CHRISTIANITY	CLASS ACTIONS	COENESTHESIS	COMMISERATOR
CHRISTIANIZE	CLASSICALITY	COENESTHETIC	COMMISSARIAL
CHRISTMAS BOX	CLASSICISTIC	COERCIVENESS	COMMISSARIAT
CHRISTMAS EVE	CLASSIFIABLE	COFFEE BREAKS	COMMISSARIES
CHRIST'S-THORN	CLASSIFIED AD	COFFEE HOUSES	COMMISSIONAL
CHROMATICISM	CLAUDICATION	COFFEE KLATCH	COMMISSIONED
CHROMATICITY	CLEAR-SIGHTED	COFFEE TABLES	COMMISSIONER
CHROMATOGRAM	CLEFT PALATES	COHABITATION	COMMITTEEMAN
CHROME YELLOW	CLERESTORIED	COHESIVENESS	COMMITTEEMEN
CHROMOPHORIC	CLERESTORIES	COINCIDENCES	COMMODIOUSLY
CHROMOSPHERE	CLERK OF WORKS	COINCIDENTAL	COMMON MARKET
CHRONOGRAPHS	CLIENT STATES	COLD SHOULDER	COMMONPLACES
CHRONOLOGIES	CLIFFHANGERS	COLEOPTEROUS	COMMONWEALTH
CHRONOLOGIST	CLIFFHANGING	COLLABORATED	COMMUNICABLE
CHRONOMETERS	CLIMACTERICS	COLLABORATOR	COMMUNICABLY
CHRONOMETRIC	CLIMATICALLY	COLLECTIVELY	COMMUNICANTS
CHRONOSCOPIC	CLIMATOLOGIC	COLLECTIVISM	COMMUNICATED
CHURCHWARDEN	CLIMBING IRON	COLLECTIVIST	COMMUNICATOR
CHURLISHNESS	CLINKER-BUILT	COLLECTIVITY	COMMUNIONIST
CHURRASCARIA	CLIQUISHNESS	COLLECTIVIZE	COMMUTATIONS
CHYMOTRYPSIN	CLODDISHNESS	COLLECTORATE	COMPACT DISCS
CINCHONIDINE	CLOSE-CROPPED	COLLOCATIONS	COMPANIONATE
CINEMATHEQUE	CLOSED SEASON	COLLOIDALITY	COMPANIONWAY
CIRCUITOUSLY	CLOSE-GRAINED	COLLOQUIALLY	COMPARTMENTS
CIRCULARIZED	CLOSE SEASONS	COLLYWOBBLES	COMPASS POINT
CIRCULARIZER	CLOSING PRICE	COLONIALISTS	COMPATRIOTIC

COMPELLINGLY	CONCURRENCES	CONNOISSEURS	CONSUMMATIVE
COMPENSATING	CONCURRENTLY	CONNOTATIONS	CONSUMPTIONS
COMPENSATION	CONDEMNATION	CONNUBIALITY	CONSUMPTIVES
COMPENSATIVE	CONDEMNATORY	CONQUISTADOR	CONTAGIOUSLY
COMPENSATORY	CONDENSATION	CONSCIONABLE	CONTAINERIZE
COMPETITIONS	CONDESCENDED	CONSCRIPTING	CONTAMINANTS
COMPILATIONS	CONDITIONERS	CONSCRIPTION	CONTAMINATED
COMPLACENTLY	CONDITIONING	CONSECRATING	CONTAMINATOR
COMPLAINANTS	CONDOMINIUMS	CONSECRATION	CONTEMPLATED
COMPLAISANCE	CONDUCTIVITY	CONSECRATORY	CONTEMPLATOR
COMPLEMENTED	CONDUPLICATE	CONSENTIENCE	CONTEMPORARY
COMPLETENESS	CONFABULATED	CONSEQUENCES	CONTEMPORIZE
COMPLEXITIES	CONFABULATOR	CONSEQUENTLY	CONTEMPTIBLE
COMPLICATING	CONFECTIONER	CONSERVATION	CONTEMPTIBLY
COMPLICATION	CONFEDERATED	CONSERVATISM	CONTEMPTUOUS
COMPLIMENTED	CONFEDERATES	CONSERVATIVE	CONTENTIONAL
COMPONENTIAL	CONFERENTIAL	CONSERVATORY	CONTERMINOUS
COMPOSITIONS	CONFESSIONAL	CONSIDERABLE	CONTESTATION
COMPOS MENTIS	CONFIDENTIAL	CONSIDERABLY	CONTEXTUALLY
COMPREHENDED	CONFINEMENTS	CONSIGNATION	CONTIGUOUSLY
COMPRESSIBLE	CONFIRMATION	CONSIGNMENTS	CONTINENTALS
COMPROMISING	CONFIRMATORY	CONSISTENTLY	CONTINGENTLY
COMPTROLLERS	CONFISCATING	CONSISTORIAL	CONTINUALITY
COMPULSIVELY	CONFISCATION	CONSOCIATION	CONTINUATION
COMPULSORILY	CONFISCATORY	CONSOLATIONS	CONTINUATIVE
COMPUNCTIOUS	CONFORMATION	CONSOLIDATED	CONTINUINGLY
COMPUTATIONS	CONFOUNDEDLY	CONSOLIDATOR	CONTINUOUSLY
COMPUTERIZED	CONFRATERNAL	CONSPECTUSES	CONTORTIONAL
CONCATENATED	CONFUCIANISM	CONSPIRACIES	CONTRABASSES
CONCELEBRATE	CONFUCIANIST	CONSPIRATORS	CONTRACTIBLE
CONCENTRATED	CONFUTATIONS	CONSTABULARY	CONTRACTIONS
CONCENTRATES	CONGENIALITY	CONSTIPATION	CONTRADICTED
CONCENTRATOR	CONGENITALLY	CONSTITUENCY	CONTRADICTER
CONCEPTIONAL	CONGLOBATION	CONSTITUENTS	CONTRAPTIONS
CONCEPTUALLY	CONGLOMERATE	CONSTITUTING	CONTRAPUNTAL
CONCERTGOERS	CONGLUTINANT	CONSTITUTION	CONTRARINESS
CONCERT GRAND	CONGLUTINATE	CONSTITUTIVE	CONTRARIWISE
CONCERTINAED	CONGRATULATE	CONSTRAINING	CONTRAVENING
CONCERT PITCH	CONGREGATING	CONSTRICTING	CONTRIBUTING
CONCHIFEROUS	CONGREGATION	CONSTRICTION	CONTRIBUTION
CONCHOLOGIST	CONGREGATIVE	CONSTRICTIVE	CONTRIBUTIVE
CONCILIATING	CONIDIOPHORE	CONSTRICTORS	CONTRIBUTORS
CONCILIATION	CONJECTURING	CONSTRUCTING	CONTRIBUTORY
CONCILIATORS	CONJUGATIONS	CONSTRUCTION	CONTRIVANCES
CONCILIATORY	CONJUNCTIONS	CONSTRUCTIVE	CONTROLLABLE
CONCLUSIVELY	CONJUNCTIVAL	CONSTRUCTORS	CONTROVERTER
CONCOMITANCE	CONJUNCTIVES	CONSULTATION	CONTUMACIOUS
CONCOMITANTS	CONJUNCTURAL	CONSULTATIVE	CONTUMELIOUS
CONCORDANCES	CONJUNCTURES	CONSUMMATELY	CONURBATIONS
CONCRESCENCE	CONNECTIONAL	CONSUMMATING	CONVALESCENT
CONCUPISCENT	CONNING TOWER	CONSUMMATION	CONVALESCING

CONVECTIONAL
CONVENIENCES
CONVENIENTLY
CONVENTICLES
CONVENTIONAL
CONVERGENCES
CONVERSATION
CONVERSIONAL
CONVERTIBLES
CONVEYANCING
CONVEYER BELT
CONVINCINGLY
CONVIVIALITY
CONVOCATIONS
CONVOLUTEDLY
CONVOLUTIONS
CONVULSIVELY
COOKERY BOOKS
COOKING APPLE
COOPERATIVES
COORDINATELY
COORDINATING
COORDINATION
COPOLYMERIZE
COPROPHAGOUS
COPROPHILOUS
COPTIC CHURCH
COQUETTISHLY
CORDUROY ROAD
CORESPONDENT
CORNERSTONES
CORN EXCHANGE
CORNISH PASTY
COROLLACEOUS
CORPORALSHIP
CORPORATIONS
CORPOREALITY
CORRECTITUDE
CORRECTIVELY
CORRELATIONS
CORRELATIVES
CORRESPONDED
CORROBORATED
CORROBORATOR
CORRUGATIONS
COSMETICALLY
COSMETICIANS
COSMOLOGICAL
COSMOPOLITAN
COSTERMONGER
COST OF LIVING

COST THE EARTH
COTYLEDONARY
COTYLEDONOUS
COUNTENANCED
COUNTENANCES
COUNTERACTED
COUNTERBLAST
COUNTERCHECK
COUNTERCLAIM
COUNTERFOILS
COUNTERPANES
COUNTERPARTS
COUNTERPARTY
COUNTERPOINT
COUNTERPOISE
COUNTERPROOF
COUNTERPUNCH
COUNTERSHAFT
COUNTERSIGNS
COUNTERTENOR
COUNTRY CLUBS
COUNTRY DANCE
COUNTRY SEATS
COUNTY COURTS
COUPS DE GRACE
COURAGEOUSLY
COURT'MARTIAL
COURT-MARTIAL
COVENT GARDEN
COVER CHARGES
COVERED WAGON
COVETOUSNESS
COWARDLINESS
CRACKBRAINED
CRANIOLOGIST
CRANIOMETRIC
CRASH BARRIER
CRASH HELMETS
CRASH LANDING
CREEPY-CRAWLY
CREMATIONISM
CREMATIONIST
CREMATORIUMS
CRENELLATION
CRISSCROSSED
CRISSCROSSES
CROP-SPRAYING
CROSSBENCHER
CROSS BENCHER
CROSSBENCHES
CROSSCHECKED

CROSS-COUNTRY
CROSSCURRENT
CROSS-DRESSER
CROSS-EXAMINE
CROSS-GRAINED
CROSSPATCHES
CROSS-SECTION
CROWNED HEADS
CROWN PRINCES
CRUSH BARRIER
CRYOPLANKTON
CRYPTANALYST
CRYPTOGRAPHY
CRYPTOLOGIST
CRYSTAL BALLS
CRYSTAL CLEAR
CRYSTAL GAZER
CRYSTALLITIC
CRYSTALLIZED
CUCKOO CLOCKS
CUMULATIVELY
CUMULONIMBUS
CUPBOARD LOVE
CURARIZATION
CURATORSHIPS
CURMUDGEONLY
CURTAILMENTS
CURTAIN CALLS
CURVACEOUSLY
CUT AND THRUST
CUTTLEFISHES
CYCLOPENTANE
CYCLOSTOMATE
CYCLOSTYLING
CYSTICERCOID
CYTOCHEMICAL
CYTOGENETICS
CYTOSKELETON
CYTOTAXONOMY
CZECHOSLOVAK

D

DACTYLICALLY
DAEMONICALLY
DAIRY FARMERS
DANGER SIGNAL
DANISH PASTRY
DARBY AND JOAN
DAY NURSERIES
DEACTIVATION
DEAF-MUTENESS

DEATH FUTURES
DEATH RATTLES
DEATH WARRANT
DEBARKATIONS
DEBAUCHERIES
DEBILITATING
DEBILITATION
DEBILITATIVE
DEBT OF HONOUR
DECALCOMANIA
DECALESCENCE
DECAPITATING
DECAPITATION
DECARBONIZER
DECASYLLABIC
DECASYLLABLE
DECELERATING
DECELERATION
DECENTRALIST
DECENTRALIZE
DECIMALIZING
DECIPHERABLE
DECIPHERMENT
DECISION TREE
DECISIVENESS
DECLAMATIONS
DECLARATIONS
DECLASSIFIED
DECLENSIONAL
DECLINATIONS
DECLINOMETER
DECOLLETAGES
DECOLONIZING
DECOLORATION
DECOMMISSION
DECOMPOSABLE
DECOMPRESSED
DECONGESTANT
DECONTROLLED
DECORATIVELY
DECORTICATOR
DEDUCIBILITY
DEERSTALKERS
DE-ESCALATING
DE-ESCALATION
DEFAMATORILY
DEFICIENCIES
DEFINITENESS
DEFINITIONAL
DEFINITIVELY
DEFLAGRATION

DEFLATIONARY	DENICOTINIZE	DESPOLIATION	DICTIONARIES
DEFLATIONIST	DENOMINATING	DESPONDENTLY	DIDACTICALLY
DEFLOCCULATE	DENOMINATION	DESPOTICALLY	DIENCEPHALIC
DEFORMATIONS	DENOMINATIVE	DESQUAMATION	DIENCEPHALON
DEFORMEDNESS	DENOMINATORS	DESSERTSPOON	DIESEL ENGINE
DEFRAUDATION	DENOUNCEMENT	DESSERT WINES	DIETETICALLY
DEGENERATING	DENSITOMETER	DESTABILIZED	DIFFERENTIAL
DEGENERATION	DENSITOMETRY	DESTINATIONS	DIFFICULTIES
DEGENERATIVE	DENTAL PLATES	DESTRUCTIBLE	DIGITAL VIDEO
DEGRADATIONS	DENTILINGUAL	DESULPHURIZE	DIGITIZATION
DEHUMANIZING	DENUNCIATION	DETERIORATED	DIGRESSIONAL
DEHUMIDIFIER	DENUNCIATORY	DETERMINABLE	DILAPIDATION
DEJECTEDNESS	DEONTOLOGIST	DETERMINANTS	DILATABILITY
DELAMINATION	DEPARTMENTAL	DETHRONEMENT	DILATATIONAL
DELIBERATELY	DEPENDENCIES	DETOXICATION	DILATOMETRIC
DELIBERATING	DEPILATORIES	DETRUNCATION	DILATORINESS
DELIBERATION	DEPOLITICIZE	DETUMESCENCE	DILETTANTISH
DELIBERATIVE	DEPOPULATING	DEUTERANOPIA	DILETTANTISM
DELICATESSEN	DEPOPULATION	DEUTERANOPIC	DILLYDALLIED
DELIGHTFULLY	DEPORTATIONS	DEUTOPLASMIC	DIMINISHABLE
DELIMITATION	DEPOSITORIES	DEUTSCHE MARK	DIMINISHMENT
DELIMITATIVE	DEPRAVEDNESS	DEUTSCHMARKS	DINING TABLES
DELIQUESCENT	DEPRECIATING	DEVALUATIONS	DINNER JACKET
DELITESCENCE	DEPRECIATION	DEVELOPMENTS	DIOPTRICALLY
DELTIOLOGIST	DEPRECIATORY	DEVIATIONISM	DIPHTHERITIC
DEMAGNETIZED	DEPREDATIONS	DEVIATIONIST	DIPHTHONGIZE
DEMAGNETIZER	DEPRESSINGLY	DEVILISHNESS	DIPLOBLASTIC
DEMENTEDNESS	DEPRIVATIONS	DEVIL-MAY-CARE	DIPLOCARDIAC
DEMILITARIZE	DERACINATION	DEVITALIZING	DIPLOMATISTS
DEMIMONDAINE	DERANGEMENTS	DEXTROGYRATE	DIPROPELLANT
DEMOCRATIZED	DEREGULATING	DIABOLICALLY	DIPSOMANIACS
DEMODULATION	DEREGULATION	DIAGEOTROPIC	DIRECT DEBITS
DEMOGRAPHERS	DERELICTIONS	DIAGRAMMATIC	DIRECT OBJECT
DEMOGRAPHICS	DERESTRICTED	DIALECTICIAN	DIRECTORATES
DEMOLISHMENT	DERISIVENESS	DIALECTOLOGY	DIRECTORSHIP
DEMONETIZING	DERIVATIONAL	DIALLING CODE	DIRECT SPEECH
DEMONIACALLY	DERIVATIVELY	DIALLING TONE	DIRIGIBILITY
DEMONOLOGIST	DERMATOPHYTE	DIALYTICALLY	DISABILITIES
DEMONOPOLIZE	DEROGATORILY	DIAMAGNETISM	DISABLEMENTS
DEMONSTRABLE	DESALINATING	DIAPOPHYSIAL	DISACCHARIDE
DEMONSTRABLY	DESALINATION	DIARTHRODIAL	DISADVANTAGE
DEMONSTRATED	DESCRIPTIONS	DIASTROPHISM	DISAFFECTION
DEMONSTRATOR	DESEGREGATED	DIATHERMANCY	DISAFFILIATE
DEMOTIVATING	DESENSITIZED	DIATOMACEOUS	DISAGGREGATE
DEMOTIVATION	DESENSITIZER	DIATONICALLY	DISAGREEABLE
DEMYSTIFYING	DESERVEDNESS	DIAZOMETHANE	DISAGREEABLY
DENATURALIZE	DESIDERATION	DIBRANCHIATE	DISAGREEMENT
DENATURATION	DESIDERATIVE	DICARBOXYLIC	DISALLOWABLE
DENBIGHSHIRE	DESIGNATIONS	DICHROMATISM	DISALLOWANCE
DENDROLOGIST	DESIRABILITY	DICHROSCOPIC	DISAMBIGUATE
DENG XIAOPING	DESPAIRINGLY	DICTATORSHIP	DISANNULMENT

DISAPPEARING	DISESTABLISH	DISSEMINATED	DOMESTICABLE
DISAPPOINTED	DISFORESTING	DISSEMINATOR	DOMESTICALLY
DISAPPOINTER	DISFRANCHISE	DISSENTIENCE	DOMESTICATED
DISAPPROVING	DISGORGEMENT	DISSERTATION	DOMESTICATOR
DISARRANGING	DISGUSTINGLY	DISSEVERANCE	DOMINO EFFECT
DISASSEMBLER	DISHEVELMENT	DISSIMILARLY	DONKEY JACKET
DISASSOCIATE	DISHONOURING	DISSIMULATED	DONKEYS YEARS
DISASTROUSLY	DISINCENTIVE	DISSIMULATOR	DONKEY'S YEARS
DISBELIEVERS	DISINFECTANT	DISSOCIATING	DOORKNOCKERS
DISBELIEVING	DISINFECTING	DISSOCIATION	DOORSTEPPING
DISBURSEMENT	DISINFECTION	DISSOCIATIVE	DOORSTOPPERS
DISCIPLESHIP	DISINFLATION	DISSOLUTIONS	DORSIVENTRAL
DISCIPLINARY	DISINGENUOUS	DISSYMMETRIC	DORSOVENTRAL
DISCIPLINING	DISINHERITED	DISTEMPERING	DOUBLE-ACTING
DISCLAMATION	DISINTEGRATE	DISTILLATION	DOUBLE AGENTS
DISCOGRAPHER	DISINTERMENT	DISTILLATORY	DOUBLE BASSES
DISCOLOURING	DISINTERRING	DISTILLERIES	DOUBLE-BEDDED
DISCOMFITING	DISJOINTEDLY	DISTINCTIONS	DOUBLE BLUFFS
DISCOMFITURE	DISLOCATIONS	DISTINCTNESS	DOUBLE DAGGER
DISCOMMODING	DISLODGEMENT	DISTORTIONAL	DOUBLE-DATING
DISCOMMODITY	DISLOYALTIES	DISTRACTEDLY	DOUBLE DEALER
DISCOMPOSING	DISMEMBERING	DISTRACTIBLE	DOUBLE-DEALER
DISCOMPOSURE	DISMOUNTABLE	DISTRACTIONS	DOUBLE-DECKER
DISCONCERTED	DISOBEDIENCE	DISTRAINABLE	DOUBLE-DOTTED
DISCONNECTED	DISOPERATION	DISTRAINMENT	DOUBLE FAULTS
DISCONNECTER	DISORGANIZED	DISTRIBUTARY	DOUBLE-GLAZED
DISCONSOLATE	DISORGANIZER	DISTRIBUTING	DOUBLE-HEADER
DISCONTENTED	DISORIENTATE	DISTRIBUTION	DOUBLE-PARKED
DISCONTINUED	DISPENSARIES	DISTRIBUTIVE	DOUBLE-TALKED
DISCORDANTLY	DISPENSATION	DISTRIBUTORS	DOUBLE-TONGUE
DISCOTHEQUES	DISPENSATORY	DISTURBANCES	DOUGHNUTTING
DISCOUNTABLE	DISPIRITEDLY	DITTOGRAPHIC	DOWN PAYMENTS
DISCOURAGING	DISPLACEABLE	DIURETICALLY	DOWNSHIFTING
DISCOURTEOUS	DISPLACEMENT	DIVARICATION	DOWN SHIFTING
DISCOVERABLE	DISPOSITIONS	DIVERSIFYING	DRACONIANISM
DISCOVERTURE	DISPOSSESSED	DIVERSIONARY	DRACONICALLY
DISCREDITING	DISPOSSESSOR	DIVERTICULAR	DRAG ONES FEET
DISCREETNESS	DISPUTATIONS	DIVERTICULUM	DRAMATICALLY
DISCRETENESS	DISPUTATIOUS	DIVERTIMENTO	DRAMATIZABLE
DISCRIMINANT	DISQUALIFIED	DIVINGBOARDS	DRAUGHTBOARD
DISCRIMINATE	DISQUALIFIER	DIVINIZATION	DRAWING BOARD
DISCURSIVELY	DISQUIETEDLY	DIVISIBILITY	DRAWING ROOMS
DISCUSSIONAL	DISQUISITION	DIVISIVENESS	DREADFULNESS
DISDAINFULLY	DISREGARDFUL	DOCTRINALITY	DREADNOUGHTS
DISEMBARKING	DISREGARDING	DOCTRINARIAN	DRESS CIRCLES
DISEMBARRASS	DISRELISHING	DODECAHEDRAL	DRESSING DOWN
DISEMBOWELED	DISREPUTABLE	DODECAHEDRON	DRESSING-DOWN
DISENCHANTED	DISREPUTABLY	DODECAPHONIC	DRESSING GOWN
DISENCHANTER	DISRUPTIVELY	DOGMATICALLY	DRESSING ROOM
DISENDOWMENT	DISSATISFIED	DO-IT-YOURSELF	DRY BATTERIES
DISENTANGLED	DISSEMBLANCE	DOMESDAY BOOK	DUCKING STOOL

DUMBFOUNDING
DUMORTIERITE
DUTCH AUCTION
DUTCH COURAGE
DUTY-FREE SHOP
DWARFISHNESS
DYNAMOMETRIC
DYSTELEOLOGY

E

EAGER BEAVERS
EARSPLITTING
EARTHSHAKING
EAST AYRSHIRE
EAST BERLINER
EASTER CACTUS
EASTER ISLAND
EASTER-LEDGES
EAST FLANDERS
EAST GERMANIC
EAST KILBRIDE
EASY ON THE
  EYE
EAT HUMBLE PIE
EATING APPLES
EAT ONES WORDS
EAU DE COLOGNE
EAVESDROPPED
EAVESDROPPER
EBULLIOSCOPY
ECCENTRICITY
ECCLESIASTIC
ECCLESIOLOGY
ECHINOCOCCUS
ECHINODERMAL
ECHOLOCATION
ECLECTICALLY
ECLIPTICALLY
ECOLOGICALLY
ECONOMETRICS
ECONOMICALLY
ECOTERRORIST
ECOTYPICALLY
ECSTATICALLY
ECTOPARASITE
ECUMENICALLY
EDACIOUSNESS
EDITORIALIST
EDITORIALIZE
EDULCORATION
EFFECTUALITY

EFFECTUATING
EFFECTUATION
EFFEMINATELY
EFFERVESCENT
EFFERVESCING
EFFLORESCENT
EFFORTLESSLY
EFFUSIOMETER
EFFUSIVENESS
EGOISTICALLY
EGYPTOLOGIST
EISTEDDFODIC
EJACULATIONS
EJECTOR SEATS
ELABORATIONS
ELASMOBRANCH
ELASTICATION
ELASTIC BANDS
ELECTRICALLY
ELECTRIC EYES
ELECTRICIANS
ELECTRIFYING
ELECTROCUTED
ELECTROGRAPH
ELECTROLYSER
ELECTROLYSIS
ELECTROLYTES
ELECTROLYTIC
ELECTROMETER
ELECTROMETRY
ELECTRONVOLT
ELECTROPHONE
ELECTROPLATE
ELECTROSCOPE
ELECTROSHOCK
ELECTROTONIC
ELECTROTONUS
ELECTROTYPER
ELEEMOSYNARY
ELEPHANT'S-EAR
ELEVENTH HOUR
ELIZABETHANS
ELLIPTICALLY
ELOCUTIONARY
ELOCUTIONIST
ELOQUENTNESS
ELYSEE PALACE
EMANCIPATING
EMANCIPATION
EMANCIPATIVE
EMANCIPATORY

EMARGINATION
EMASCULATING
EMASCULATION
EMASCULATIVE
EMBARKATIONS
EMBARRASSING
EMBELLISHING
EMBEZZLEMENT
EMBITTERMENT
EMBLAZONMENT
EMBRANCHMENT
EMBROCATIONS
EMBROIDERIES
EMBROIDERING
EMBRYOLOGIST
EMIGRATIONAL
EMOTIONALISM
EMOTIONALIST
EMOTIONALITY
EMOTIONALIZE
EMPATHICALLY
EMPHATICALLY
EMPLACEMENTS
EMULSIFIABLE
ENANTIOMORPH
ENARTHRODIAL
ENCEPHALITIC
ENCEPHALITIS
ENCHANTMENTS
ENCIPHERMENT
ENCIRCLEMENT
ENCLITICALLY
ENCOMPASSING
ENCOUNTERING
ENCROACHMENT
ENCRUSTATION
ENCUMBRANCER
ENCUMBRANCES
ENCYCLOPEDIA
ENCYCLOPEDIC
ENDAMAGEMENT
ENDANGERMENT
ENDEAVOURING
ENDOCARDITIC
ENDOCARDITIS
ENDOMORPHISM
ENDOPARASITE
ENDORSEMENTS
ENDOSKELETAL
ENDOSKELETON
ENDOTHELIOID

ENDOTHELIOMA
ENDOTHERMISM
ENDURABILITY
ENERGETICIST
ENFEEBLEMENT
ENFRANCHISED
ENFRANCHISER
ENGAGINGNESS
ENGENDERMENT
ENGINE DRIVER
ENGLISH HORNS
ENGLISHWOMAN
ENGRAFTATION
ENGROSSINGLY
ENHANCEMENTS
ENLARGEMENTS
ENLIGHTENING
ENLIVENINGLY
ENORMOUSNESS
ENSHRINEMENT
ENSILABILITY
ENTANGLEMENT
ENTEROKINASE
ENTERPRISING
ENTERTAINERS
ENTERTAINING
ENTHRONEMENT
ENTHUSIASTIC
ENTHYMEMATIC
ENTICINGNESS
ENTOMOLOGIST
ENTOMOLOGIZE
ENTRANCEMENT
ENTRANCINGLY
ENTREATINGLY
ENTRENCHMENT
ENTREPRENEUR
ENUMERATIONS
ENVIABLENESS
ENVIRONMENTS
ENVISAGEMENT
ENZOOTICALLY
ENZYMOLOGIST
EOSINOPHILIC
EPENCEPHALIC
EPENCEPHALON
EPHEMERALITY
EPICUREANISM
EPICYCLOIDAL
EPIDEMIOLOGY
EPIGLOTTIDES

EPIGLOTTISES	EUPHORICALLY	EXOPHTHALMOS	EXTORTIONIST
EPIGRAMMATIC	EUSTATICALLY	EXORBITANTLY	EXTRADITABLE
EPIMORPHOSIS	EVANGELISTIC	EXOTERICALLY	EXTRADITIONS
EPISCOPALIAN	EVANGELIZING	EXPANSIONARY	EXTRAMARITAL
EPISCOPALISM	EVAPORIMETER	EXPANSIONISM	EXTRAMUNDANE
EPISODICALLY	EVENING DRESS	EXPANSIONIST	EXTRANEOUSLY
EPISTEMOLOGY	EVEN-TEMPERED	EXPATRIATING	EXTRANUCLEAR
EPITHALAMIUM	EVENTFULNESS	EXPATRIATION	EXTRAPOLATED
EQUALITARIAN	EVERY MAN JACK	EXPECTATIONS	EXTRAPOLATOR
EQUALIZATION	EVISCERATING	EXPECTORATED	EXTRASENSORY
EQUATABILITY	EVISCERATION	EXPECTORATOR	EXTRAUTERINE
EQUESTRIENNE	EVOLUTIONARY	EXPEDIENTIAL	EXTRAVAGANCE
EQUIDISTANCE	EVOLUTIONISM	EXPERIENCING	EXTRAVAGANZA
EQUILIBRATOR	EVOLUTIONIST	EXPERIENTIAL	EXTROVERSION
EQUIPOLLENCE	EXACERBATING	EXPERIMENTAL	EXTROVERSIVE
EQUIVALENTLY	EXACERBATION	EXPERIMENTED	EYEWITNESSES
EQUIVOCALITY	EXACTINGNESS	EXPERIMENTER	
EQUIVOCATING	EXAGGERATING	EXPERT SYSTEM	**F**
EQUIVOCATION	EXAGGERATION	EXPLANATIONS	FABRICATIONS
EQUIVOCATORY	EXAGGERATIVE	EXPLANTATION	FABULOUSNESS
ERGASTOPLASM	EXAMINATIONS	EXPLICITNESS	FACELESSNESS
ERYTHROBLAST	EXASPERATING	EXPLOITATION	FACILITATING
ERYTHROCYTIC	EXASPERATION	EXPLOITATIVE	FACILITATION
ERYTHROMYCIN	EXCELLENCIES	EXPLORATIONS	FACILITATIVE
ESCAPE CLAUSE	EXCHANGEABLE	EXPOSITIONAL	FACTIONALISM
ESCAPOLOGIST	EXCHANGE RATE	EXPOSITORILY	FACTIONALIST
ESCUTCHEONED	EXCITABILITY	EXPOSTULATED	FACTIOUSNESS
ESOTERICALLY	EXCLAMATIONS	EXPOSTULATOR	FACTORY FARMS
ESSENTIALISM	EXCLUSIONARY	EXPRESSIONAL	FACTUALISTIC
ESSENTIALIST	EXCOGITATION	EXPRESSIVELY	FAINT-HEARTED
ESSENTIALITY	EXCOGITATIVE	EXPRESSIVITY	FAIT ACCOMPLI
ESTABLISHING	EXCORIATIONS	EXPROPRIABLE	FAITHFULNESS
ESTATE AGENCY	EXCRESCENCES	EXPROPRIATED	FAITH HEALERS
ESTATE AGENTS	EXCRUCIATING	EXPROPRIATOR	FAITH HEALING
ESTHETICALLY	EXCRUCIATION	EXPURGATIONS	FALLACIOUSLY
ESTRANGEMENT	EXCURSIONIST	EXSANGUINITY	FALLING STARS
ETERNITY RING	EXECUTIONERS	EX-SERVICEMAN	FALSE BOTTOMS
ETERNIZATION	EXECUTORSHIP	EX-SERVICEMEN	FAMILIARIZED
ETHERIZATION	EXEGETICALLY	EXTEMPORIZED	FAMILIARIZER
ETHNOCENTRIC	EXEMPLIFYING	EXTEMPORIZER	FAMILIARNESS
ETHNOGRAPHER	EXENTERATION	EXTENDEDNESS	FAMILY CIRCLE
ETHNOGRAPHIC	EXHAUSTIVELY	EXTENSOMETER	FAMILY DOCTOR
ETHNOLOGICAL	EXHIBITIONER	EXTERMINABLE	FANCIFULNESS
ETHNOLOGISTS	EXHILARATING	EXTERMINATED	FARADIZATION
ETHOXYETHANE	EXHILARATION	EXTERMINATOR	FARSIGHTEDLY
ETHYL ALCOHOL	EXHILARATIVE	EXTERNALIZED	FASCINATEDLY
ETYMOLOGICAL	EXHORTATIONS	EXTEROCEPTOR	FASTIDIOUSLY
ETYMOLOGISTS	EXIGUOUSNESS	EXTINGUISHED	FATHER FIGURE
EUCALYPTUSES	EXOBIOLOGIST	EXTINGUISHER	FATHERLINESS
EUHEMERISTIC	EXOPEPTIDASE	EXTORTIONARY	FATHERS-IN-LAW
EUPHONICALLY	EXOPHTHALMIC	EXTORTIONATE	FATIGABILITY

FAULT-FINDING	FINALIZATION	FLYING DOCTOR	FRANKINCENSE
FAUTE DE MIEUX	FINGERBOARDS	FLYING PICKET	FRATERNALISM
FEARLESSNESS	FINGERPLATES	FLYING SAUCER	FRATERNITIES
FEARSOMENESS	FINGERPRINTS	FLYING SQUADS	FRATERNIZING
FEATHERBRAIN	FINGERSTALLS	FOCALIZATION	FRAUDULENTLY
FEATURE FILMS	FIRE BRIGADES	FOLKLORISTIC	FREAKISHNESS
FEBRIFACIENT	FIRECRACKERS	FOOL'S-PARSLEY	FREE CHURCHES
FECKLESSNESS	FIRE FIGHTERS	FOOT-AND-MOUTH	FREE-FLOATING
FEDERALISTIC	FIRE FIGHTING	FOOT FAULTING	FREESTANDING
FEEBLEMINDED	FIRE HYDRANTS	FOOTSLOGGING	FREE-SWIMMING
FEEL THE PINCH	FIRELIGHTERS	FORBEARINGLY	FREETHINKERS
FELDSPATHOSE	FIREPROOFING	FORBIDDINGLY	FREETHINKING
FELICITATING	FIRE STATIONS	FORCE-FEEDING	FREEWHEELING
FELICITATION	FIRING SQUADS	FORCEFULNESS	FREEZE-DRYING
FELICITOUSLY	FIRST COUSINS	FORCIBLENESS	FREIGHTLINER
FEMINIZATION	FIRST-FOOTING	FORE-AND-AFTER	FRENCH KISSES
FENESTRATION	FIRST-NIGHTER	FORECLOSABLE	FRENCH LOAVES
FENNELFLOWER	FIRST OFFENCE	FORECLOSURES	FRENCH POLISH
FERLINGHETTI	FIRST REFUSAL	FOREGONENESS	FRENETICALLY
FERMENTATION	FISH AND CHIPS	FOREKNOWABLE	FREQUENTABLE
FERMENTATIVE	FISH HATCHERY	FORENSICALLY	FREUDIAN SLIP
FERRICYANIDE	FISSIPALMATE	FOREORDAINED	FRIENDLINESS
FERRIS WHEELS	FISSIROSTRAL	FORESHADOWED	FRIGHTENABLE
FERROCYANIDE	FLAGELLATING	FORESHADOWER	FROGMARCHING
FERROSILICON	FLAGELLATION	FORESTALLING	FRONDESCENCE
FERTILIZABLE	FLAGELLIFORM	FORESTALMENT	FRONTBENCHER
FEVERISHNESS	FLAMBOYANTLY	FORESTAYSAIL	FRONTBENCHES
FIBRILLATION	FLAME-THROWER	FORETRIANGLE	FRONTIERSMAN
FIBRILLIFORM	FLAMMABILITY	FORGATHERING	FRONTIERSMEN
FIBRINOGENIC	FLATTERINGLY	FORGET-ME-NOTS	FRONTISPIECE
FIBRINOLYSIN	FLAVOPROTEIN	FORMALDEHYDE	FRONT-RUNNERS
FIBRINOLYSIS	FLEET ADMIRAL	FORMLESSNESS	FRUCTIFEROUS
FIBRINOLYTIC	FLICKERINGLY	FORMULARIZER	FRUITFULNESS
FIBROBLASTIC	FLITTERMOUSE	FORMULATIONS	FRUIT MACHINE
FICTIONALIZE	FLOATABILITY	FORT-DE-FRANCE	FRUMPISHNESS
FICTITIOUSLY	FLOCCULATION	FORTUITOUSLY	FRUSTRATIONS
FIDDLE-FADDLE	FLOORWALKERS	FOSSILIZABLE	FUDDY-DUDDIES
FIDDLESTICKS	FLORICULTURE	FOUNDATIONAL	FULLER'S EARTH
FIELD GLASSES	FLOWCHARTING	FOUNTAINHEAD	FULLY-FLEDGED
FIELD MARSHAL	FLUCTUATIONS	FOUNTAIN PENS	FULMINATIONS
FIELD-TESTING	FLUIDEXTRACT	FOURIERISTIC	FUNCTIONALLY
FIELDWORKERS	FLUIDIZATION	FOURTH-DEGREE	FUNDAMENTALS
FIENDISHNESS	FLUORESCENCE	FOURTH ESTATE	FURFURACEOUS
FIFTH COLUMNS	FLUORIDATING	FOURTH OF JULY	FURUNCULOSIS
FIGURATIVELY	FLUORIDATION	FRACTIONALLY	FUTILITARIAN
FIGURE-GROUND	FLUORINATION	FRACTIONATOR	FUTUROLOGIST
FIGURE SKATER	FLUOROCARBON	FRAMES OF MIND	
FILIBUSTERED	FLUOROMETRIC	FRANCHE-COMTE	**G**
FILIBUSTERER	FLUOROSCOPIC	FRANCO GERMAN	GALACTAGOGUE
FILM PREMIERE	FLUTTERINGLY	FRANGIBILITY	GALACTOMETER
FILTER-TIPPED	FLUVIOMARINE	FRANKFURTERS	GALACTOMETRY

GALL BLADDERS
GALLINACEOUS
GALLIVANTING
GALVANICALLY
GALVANOMETER
GALVANOMETRY
GALVANOSCOPE
GALVANOSCOPY
GAMESMANSHIP
GAMETOPHORIC
GAMETOPHYTIC
GAMOPETALOUS
GAMOPHYLLOUS
GAMOSEPALOUS
GARBAGE TRUCK
GARDEN CITIES
GASIFICATION
GASTIGHTNESS
GASTRONOMIST
GASTROPODOUS
GASTROSCOPIC
GASTRULATION
GATECRASHERS
GATECRASHING
GAVANIZATION
GEANTICLINAL
GENDER-BENDER
GENEALOGICAL
GENEALOGISTS
GENERALITIES
GENERALIZING
GENERAL STAFF
GENEROSITIES
GENEROUSNESS
GENICULATION
GENOTYPICITY
GENUFLECTING
GENUFLECTION
GEOCHEMISTRY
GEOGRAPHICAL
GEOLOGICALLY
GEOMAGNETISM
GEOMECHANICS
GEOPHYSICIST
GEOPOLITICAL
GEOSYNCLINAL
GERANIACEOUS
GERIATRICIAN
GERMANOPHILE
GERMANOPHOBE
GERONTOCRACY

GESTICULATED
GESTICULATOR
GET ONES CARDS
GET-TOGETHERS
GHOULISHNESS
GIANT KILLERS
GIBRALTARIAN
GIFT-WRAPPING
GIGANTICALLY
GIGANTICNESS
GINGER GROUPS
GINGERLINESS
GLABROUSNESS
GLACIOLOGIST
GLADIATORIAL
GLASSBLOWERS
GLASS-BLOWING
GLASS CEILING
GLASSCUTTERS
GLAUCOMATOUS
GLIMMERINGLY
GLISTENINGLY
GLITTERINGLY
GLOBETROTTER
GLOCKENSPIEL
GLORIOUSNESS
GLOSSOGRAPHY
GLOTTAL STOPS
GLOVE PUPPETS
GLUCOGENESIS
GLUCOGENETIC
GLUE-SNIFFERS
GLUE-SNIFFING
GLUTTONOUSLY
GLYCOGENESIS
GLYCOGENETIC
GLYCOPROTEIN
GLYPHOGRAPHY
GLYPTOGRAPHY
GNOMONICALLY
GNOTOBIOTICS
GOBBLEDEGOOK
GOBBLEDYGOOK
GOLDEN EAGLES
GOLDEN FLEECE
GOLDFISH BOWL
GOLD STANDARD
GONADOTROPIN
GOOD-HUMOURED
GOODY-GOODIES
GOOSEBERRIES

GOOSE PIMPLES
GOOSESTEPPED
GO OVER THE
TOP
GORGEOUSNESS
GORMANDIZING
GOSSIPMONGER
GOVERNMENTAL
GOVERNORSHIP
GRACEFULNESS
GRACIOUSNESS
GRADE SCHOOLS
GRADUALISTIC
GRALLATORIAL
GRAMMATOLOGY
GRAM-NEGATIVE
GRAM-POSITIVE
GRANDFATHERS
GRAND MASTERS
GRANDMOTHERS
GRANDPARENTS
GRANODIORITE
GRANULOCYTIC
GRAPHOLOGIST
GRASSHOPPERS
GRATEFULNESS
GRATIFYINGLY
GRATUITOUSLY
GREASY SPOONS
GREAT BRITAIN
GREAT CIRCLES
GREAT RED SPOT
GREEN FINGERS
GREENGROCERS
GREENGROCERY
GREEN PEPPERS
GREGARIOUSLY
GRIEVOUSNESS
GRIZZLY BEARS
GROSSULARITE
GROUND FLOORS
GROUNDLESSLY
GROUNDSHEETS
GROUND STAFFS
GROUND STROKE
GROUNDSWELLS
GROUP CAPTAIN
GROUP THERAPY
GROVELLINGLY
GROWING PAINS
GRUESOMENESS

GUADALQUIVIR
GUARANTEEING
GUARDIANSHIP
GUERRILLAISM
GUESSTIMATES
GUEST WORKERS
GUILLOTINING
GUINEA-BISSAU
GUN CARRIAGES
GUTTERSNIPES
GUTTURALNESS
GYNAECOCRACY
GYROMAGNETIC

H

HABEAS CORPUS
HABERDASHERS
HABERDASHERY
HABILITATION
HABITABILITY
HABITATIONAL
HABITUALNESS
HACKING COUGH
HAEMATEMESIS
HAEMATOBLAST
HAEMATOCRYAL
HAEMATOGENIC
HAEMATOLOGIC
HAEMATOLYSIS
HAEMATOXYLIC
HAEMATOXYLIN
HAEMATOXYLON
HAEMOPHILIAC
HAEMOPOIESIS
HAEMOPOIETIC
HAEMORRHAGIC
· HAEMORRHOIDS
HAGIOGRAPHER
HAGIOGRAPHIC
HAGIOLATROUS
HAIRDRESSERS
HAIRDRESSING
HAIRPIN BENDS
HAIR-RESTORER
HAIR'S BREADTH
HAIRSPLITTER
HAIR TRIGGERS
HALF-BROTHERS
HALF-HOLIDAYS
HALF MEASURES
HALF-TIMBERED

HALFWAY HOUSE
HALF-WITTEDLY
HALLOWEDNESS
HALLSTATTIAN
HALLUCINATED
HALLUCINATOR
HALLUCINOGEN
HALLUCINOSIS
HALOGENATION
HAMBLETONIAN
HAMMARSKJOLD
HAMMERHEADED
HAMPEREDNESS
HAMSTRINGING
HANDICAPPING
HANDKERCHIEF
HAND OVER FIST
HANDSOMENESS
HAPPENSTANCE
HAPPY-GO-LUCKY
HAPPY MEDIUMS
HAPTOTROPISM
HARD CURRENCY
HARD FEELINGS
HARD SHOULDER
HARE COURSING
HARLEQUINADE
HARLEY STREET
HARMLESSNESS
HARMONICALLY
HARMONIOUSLY
HARMONIZABLE
HARPSICHORDS
HARQUEBUSIER
HARTHACANUTE
HARVEST HOMES
HARVEST MOONS
HATCHET-FACED
HAUTE COUTURE
HAUTE CUISINE
HAUTE-GARONNE
HAUTS-DE-SEINE
HAZARD LIGHTS
HEADQUARTERS
HEADSHRINKER
HEADSTRONGLY
HEART ATTACKS
HEARTBREAKER
HEART DISEASE
HEARTENINGLY
HEART FAILURE

HEARTRENDING
HEARTSTRINGS
HEART TO HEART
HEART-TO-HEART
HEARTWARMING
HEATHENISHLY
HEAVENLINESS
HEAVYHEARTED
HEAVY PETTING
HEAVYWEIGHTS
HEBDOMADALLY
HEBETUDINOUS
HEBRAIZATION
HECTOCOTYLUS
HECTOGRAPHIC
HEDGEHOPPING
HEDGE SPARROW
HEEDLESSNESS
HEILONGJIANG
HEILUNGKIANG
HEIR APPARENT
HELICOIDALLY
HELIOCENTRIC
HELIOCHROMIC
HELIOGABALUS
HELIOGRAPHER
HELIOGRAPHIC
HELIOGRAVURE
HELIOLATROUS
HELIOTHERAPY
HELIOTROPISM
HELLENICALLY
HELLGRAMMITE
HELPING HANDS
HELPLESSNESS
HEMICHORDATE
HEMIHYDRATED
HEMIMORPHISM
HEMIMORPHITE
HEMIPARASITE
HEMISPHEROID
HEMOPHILIACS
HENDECAGONAL
HENOTHEISTIC
HERALDICALLY
HERBACEOUSLY
HERD INSTINCT
HERE AND THERE
HEREDITAMENT
HEREDITARILY
HEREINBEFORE

HERITABILITY
HERMANNSTADT
HERMENEUTICS
HERMENEUTIST
HERMETICALLY
HERMITICALLY
HERMOTENSILE
HEROD ANTIPAS
HEROICALNESS
HERPES ZOSTER
HERPETOLOGIC
HERRINGBONES
HERSTMONCEUX
HESITATINGLY
HETEROCERCAL
HETEROCYCLIC
HETERODACTYL
HETEROECIOUS
HETEROGAMETE
HETEROGAMOUS
HETEROGENOUS
HETEROGONOUS
HETEROGRAPHY
HETEROGYNOUS
HETEROLOGOUS
HETEROMEROUS
HETERONOMOUS
HETERONYMOUS
HETEROOUSIAN
HETEROPHYLLY
HETEROPLASTY
HETEROSEXISM
HETEROSEXUAL
HETEROTACTIC
HETEROZYGOTE
HETEROZYGOUS
HEXACOSANOIC
HEXAGRAMMOID
HEXAHYDRATED
HIBERNACULUM
HIBERNIANISM
HIDDEN AGENDA
HIERARCHICAL
HIERATICALLY
HIEROGLYPHIC
HIEROPHANTIC
HIGH FIDELITY
HIGH-HANDEDLY
HIGHLIGHTING
HIGHLY-STRUNG
HIGH-MINDEDLY

HIGH-PRESSURE
HIGH PROFILES
HIGH SHERIFFS
HIGH-SOUNDING
HIGH-SPIRITED
HINAYANISTIC
HINDQUARTERS
HIPPOCRENIAN
HIPPOPOTAMUS
HIRE PURCHASE
HISTOGENESIS
HISTOGENETIC
HISTOLOGICAL
HISTORICALLY
HIT A BAD
  PATCH
HOBBLEDEHOYS
HOBSON-JOBSON
HOHENZOLLERN
HOLIDAYMAKER
HOLISTICALLY
HOLOPHRASTIC
HOLOPLANKTON
HOLY OF HOLIES
HOME COUNTIES
HOME FROM HOME
HOMELESSNESS
HOMEOMORPHIC
HOMEOPATHIST
HOMESICKNESS
HOMING PIGEON
HOMOCHROMOUS
HOMOGENIZING
HOMOGONOUSLY
HOMOLOGATION
HOMOMORPHISM
HOMOPOLARITY
HOMOTAXIALLY
HOMOTHALLISM
HOMOZYGOUSLY
HONEYMOONERS
HONEYMOONING
HONEYSUCKLED
HONEYSUCKLES
HOPELESSNESS
HORIZONTALLY
HORNET'S NESTS
HORN OF PLENTY
HORRENDOUSLY
HORRIBLENESS
HORRIFICALLY

HORRIFYINGLY	HYDROCHLORIC	ILL-TREATMENT	IMPOLITENESS
HORS DE COMBAT	HYDRODYNAMIC	ILLUMINATING	IMPONDERABLE
HORS D'OEUVRES	HYDROFLUORIC	ILLUMINATION	IMPORTATIONS
HORSEMANSHIP	HYDROGENATOR	ILLUMINATIVE	IMPOVERISHED
HORSE TRADING	HYDROGEN BOMB	ILLUSIONISTS	IMPOVERISHER
HORSE-TRADING	HYDROGEOLOGY	ILLUSORINESS	IMPRECATIONS
HORSEWHIPPED	HYDROGRAPHER	ILLUSTRATING	IMPREGNATING
HORSEWHIPPER	HYDROGRAPHIC	ILLUSTRATION	IMPREGNATION
HORTICULTURE	HYDROKINETIC	ILLUSTRATIVE	IMPRESSIONAL
HORTUS SICCUS	HYDROLYSABLE	ILLUSTRATORS	IMPRESSIVELY
HOSPITALIZED	HYDROMEDUSAN	IMAGINATIONS	IMPRISONMENT
HOT-CROSS BUNS	HYDROTHERAPY	IMBECILITIES	IMPROPRIATOR
HOT-GOSPELLER	HYGIENICALLY	IMMACULATELY	IMPROVEMENTS
HOUSE ARRESTS	HYPERCORRECT	IMMEASURABLE	IMPROVIDENCE
HOUSEBREAKER	HYPERMARKETS	IMMEASURABLY	IMPUTABILITY
HOUSEFATHERS	HYPNOTHERAPY	IMMEMORIABLE	INACCESSIBLE
HOUSEHOLDERS	HYPNOTICALLY	IMMERSIONISM	INACCESSIBLY
HOUSE HUSBAND	HYPOCHONDRIA	IMMERSIONIST	INACCURACIES
HOUSEKEEPERS	HYPOCRITICAL	IMMETHODICAL	INACCURATELY
HOUSEKEEPING	HYPOTHETICAL	IMMOBILIZING	INACTIVATION
HOUSEMASTERS	HYSTERECTOMY	IMMODERATELY	INADEQUACIES
HOUSEMOTHERS	HYSTERICALLY	IMMODERATION	INADEQUATELY
HOUSE OF CARDS		IMMORALITIES	INADMISSIBLE
HOUSE OF LORDS	**I**	IMMORTALIZED	INADMISSIBLY
HOUSEPARENTS	ICE-CREAM SODA	IMMORTALIZER	INADVERTENCE
HOUSE PARTIES	ICHNEUMON FLY	IMMOVABILITY	INAPPLICABLE
HOUSE SPARROW	ICHNOGRAPHIC	IMMUNE SYSTEM	INAPPLICABLY
HOUSE-TO-HOUSE	ICHNOLOGICAL	IMMUNIZATION	INARTICULATE
HOUSE-TRAINED	ICHTHYOLOGIC	IMMUNOLOGIST	IN ATTENDANCE
HOUSEWARMING	ICHTHYOPHAGY	IMMUTABILITY	INAUDIBILITY
HOUSEY HOUSEY	ICONOCLASTIC	IMPARTIALITY	INAUGURATING
HOUSEY-HOUSEY	ICONOGRAPHER	IMPEDIMENTAL	INAUGURATION
HUBBLE-BUBBLE	ICONOGRAPHIC	IMPENETRABLE	INAUSPICIOUS
HUDDERSFIELD	ICONOLATROUS	IMPENITENTLY	INCALCULABLE
HUGGER-MUGGER	ICONOLOGICAL	IMPERATIVELY	INCALCULABLY
HUMANITARIAN	IDEALIZATION	IMPERCEPTION	INCALESCENCE
HUMANIZATION	IDENTIFIABLE	IMPERCEPTIVE	INCANDESCENT
HUMILIATIONS	IDENTITY CARD	IMPERFECTION	INCANTATIONS
HUMMINGBIRDS	IDEOLOOGICAL	IMPERFECTIVE	INCAPABILITY
HUMOROUSNESS	IDIOMORPHISM	IMPERIALISTS	INCAPACITATE
HUMPTY DUMPTY	IDIOSYNCRASY	IMPERISHABLE	INCARCERATED
HUNGER STRIKE	IDOLATROUSLY	IMPERMANENCE	INCARCERATOR
HURDY-GURDIES	IGNITABILITY	IMPERSONALLY	INCARNATIONS
HURSTMONCEUX	ILLEGAL ENTRY	IMPERSONATED	INCAUTIOUSLY
HUSEIN IBN-ALI	ILLEGALITIES	IMPERSONATOR	INCENDIARISM
HYALOPLASMIC	ILLEGIBILITY	IMPERTINENCE	INCESTUOUSLY
HYBRIDIZABLE	ILLEGITIMACY	IMPETIGINOUS	INCIDENTALLY
HYDNOCARPATE	ILLEGITIMATE	IMPLANTATION	INCINERATING
HYDRASTININE	ILLIBERALITY	IMPLEMENTING	INCINERATION
HYDROCARBONS	ILLITERATELY	IMPLICATIONS	INCINERATORS
HYDROCEPHALY	ILLOGICALITY	IMPLICITNESS	INCISIVENESS

INCIVILITIES	INDELIBILITY	INEXTIRPABLE	INSECTICIDAL
INCLINATIONS	INDELICATELY	INEXTRICABLE	INSECTICIDES
INCLINOMETER	INDEMNIFYING	INEXTRICABLY	INSECTIVORES
INCOGNIZANCE	INDENTATIONS	INFANTICIDAL	INSEMINATING
INCOHERENTLY	INDEPENDENCE	INFANTICIDES	INSEMINATION
INCOMMODIOUS	INDEPENDENCY	INFANT SCHOOL	IN SHORT ORDER
INCOMMUTABLE	INDEPENDENTS	INFATUATEDLY	INSINUATIONS
INCOMPARABLE	INDEX FINGERS	INFATUATIONS	INSOLUBILITY
INCOMPARABLY	INDEX FUTURES	INFECTIOUSLY	INSPECTINGLY
INCOMPATIBLE	INDIANAPOLIS	INFELICITOUS	INSPECTIONAL
INCOMPATIBLY	INDIAN SUMMER	INFESTATIONS	INSPECTORATE
INCOMPETENCE	INDICATIVELY	INFIBULATION	INSPIRATIONS
INCOMPETENTS	INDIFFERENCE	INFIDELITIES	INSPIRITMENT
INCOMPLETELY	INDIGENOUSLY	INFILTRATING	INSTALLATION
INCOMPLIANCE	INDIGESTIBLE	INFILTRATION	INSTILLATION
INCOMPUTABLE	INDIGESTIBLY	INFILTRATIVE	INSTITUTIONS
INCONCLUSIVE	INDIRECTNESS	INFILTRATORS	INSTRUCTIBLE
INCONFORMITY	INDISCIPLINE	INFLAMMATION	INSTRUCTIONS
INCONSEQUENT	INDISCREETLY	INFLAMMATORY	INSTRUMENTAL
INCONSISTENT	INDISCRETION	INFLATIONARY	INSUFFERABLE
INCONSOLABLE	INDISPUTABLE	INFLATIONISM	INSUFFERABLY
INCONSOLABLY	INDISPUTABLY	INFLATIONIST	INSUFFICIENT
INCONSONANCE	INDISSOLUBLE	INFLECTIONAL	INSUFFLATION
INCONSUMABLE	INDISSOLUBLY	INFLORESCENT	INSURABILITY
INCONTINENCE	INDISTINCTLY	INFOTAINMENT	INSURGENCIES
INCONVENIENT	INDIVIDUALLY	INFREQUENTLY	INSURRECTION
INCOORDINATE	INDIVIDUATOR	INFRINGEMENT	INTELLECTION
INCORPORABLE	INDOCTRINATE	INFUNDIBULAR	INTELLECTIVE
INCORPORATED	INDO-EUROPEAN	INFUNDIBULUM	INTELLECTUAL
INCORPORATOR	INDOLEACETIC	INFUSIBILITY	INTELLIGENCE
INCORPOREITY	INDOMETHACIN	INGLORIOUSLY	INTELLIGIBLE
INCORRIGIBLE	INDRE-ET-LOIRE	INGRATIATING	INTELLIGIBLY
INCORRIGIBLY	INDUSTRIALLY	INGRATIATION	INTEMPERANCE
INCRASSATION	INEFFABILITY	INHABITATION	INTENSIFIERS
INCREASINGLY	INEFFACEABLE	INHARMONIOUS	INTENSIFYING
INCRETIONARY	INEFFICIENCY	INHERITANCES	INTERACTIONS
INCRIMINATED	INELASTICITY	INHOSPITABLE	INTERCEPTING
INCRIMINATOR	INEQUALITIES	INHOSPITABLY	INTERCEPTION
INCRUSTATION	INERADICABLE	INHUMANITIES	INTERCEPTIVE
INCUBATIONAL	INERADICABLY	INIMICALNESS	INTERCEPTORS
INCUMBENCIES	INERTIA REELS	INIQUITOUSLY	INTERCESSION
INCURABILITY	INESCUTCHEON	INNOVATIONAL	INTERCESSORY
INDEBTEDNESS	INESSENTIALS	INNUTRITIOUS	INTERCHANGED
INDECISIVELY	INEXACTITUDE	INOBSERVANCE	INTERCHANGES
INDECLINABLE	INEXPEDIENCE	INOCULATIONS	INTERCONNECT
INDECOROUSLY	INEXPERIENCE	INORDINATELY	INTERCURRENT
INDEFEASIBLE	INEXPERTNESS	INOSCULATION	INTERDICTION
INDEFENSIBLE	INEXPLICABLE	INQUISITIONS	INTERDICTIVE
INDEFENSIBLY	INEXPLICABLY	INSALIVATION	INTERESTEDLY
INDEFINITELY	INEXPRESSIVE	INSALUBRIOUS	INTERFERENCE
INDEHISCENCE	INEXTENSIBLE	INSCRIPTIONS	INTERFERTILE

INTERFLUVIAL
INTERGLACIAL
INTERJECTING
INTERJECTION
INTERJECTORY
INTERLACEDLY
INTERLAMINAR
INTERLARDING
INTERLINKING
INTERLOCKING
INTERLOCUTOR
INTERMARRIED
INTERMEDIACY
INTERMEDIARY
INTERMEDIATE
INTERMINABLE
INTERMINABLY
INTERMINGLED
INTERMISSION
INTERMISSIVE
INTERMITTENT
INTERMIXABLE
INTERMIXTURE
INTERNALIZED
INTERNUNCIAL
INTEROCEPTOR
INTERPELLANT
INTERPELLATE
INTERPLEADER
INTERPOLATED
INTERPOLATER
INTERPOSABLE
INTERPRETERS
INTERPRETING
INTERPRETIVE
INTERREGNUMS
INTERROGATED
INTERROGATOR
INTERRUPTING
INTERRUPTION
INTERRUPTIVE
INTERSECTING
INTERSECTION
INTERSPATIAL
INTERSPERSED
INTERSTADIAL
INTERSTELLAR
INTERSTITIAL
INTERTEXTURE
INTERTWINING
INTERVENTION

INTERVIEWEES
INTERVIEWERS
INTERVIEWING
INTERVOCALIC
INTERWEAVING
IN THE LONG
 RUN
INTIMIDATING
INTIMIDATION
INTOLERANTLY
INTONATIONAL
INTOXICATING
INTOXICATION
INTOXICATIVE
INTRACARDIAC
INTRACRANIAL
INTRANSIGENT
INTRANSITIVE
INTRANUCLEAR
INTRAPRENEUR
INTRAUTERINE
INTRIGUINGLY
INTRODUCIBLE
INTRODUCTION
INTRODUCTORY
INTROJECTION
INTROJECTIVE
INTROVERSION
INTROVERSIVE
INTUITIONISM
INTUITIONIST
INTUMESCENCE
INTUSSUSCEPT
INVAGINATION
INVALIDATING
INVALIDATION
INVERCARGILL
INVERTEBRACY
INVERTEBRATE
INVERTED SNOB
INVESTIGABLE
INVESTIGATED
INVESTIGATOR
INVESTITURES
INVIGILATING
INVIGILATION
INVIGILATORS
INVIGORATING
INVIGORATION
INVIGORATIVE
INVISIBILITY

INVITATIONAL
INVOCATIONAL
INVOLUCELATE
INVOLUTIONAL
INVULNERABLE
INVULNERABLY
INVULTUATION
IRASCIBILITY
IRISH COFFEES
IRONING BOARD
IRRADIATIONS
IRRATIONALLY
IRREDEEMABLE
IRREDEEMABLY
IRREFRAGABLE
IRREGULARITY
IRRELEVANCES
IRRELEVANTLY
IRRELIEVABLE
IRREMEDIABLE
IRREMEDIABLY
IRREMISSIBLE
IRRESISTIBLE
IRRESISTIBLY
IRRESOLUTELY
IRRESOLUTION
IRRESOLVABLE
IRRESPECTIVE
IRRESPIRABLE
IRRESPONSIVE
IRREVERENTLY
IRREVERSIBLE
IRREVERSIBLY
IRRIGATIONAL
IRRITABILITY
ISOCHROMATIC
ISODIAMETRIC
ISOLATIONISM
ISOLATIONIST
ISOTOPICALLY
ITALIANESQUE

J

JACK-IN-THE-
 BOX
JACK O LANTERN
JACK-O'-
 LANTERN
JACK ROBINSON
JACKSONVILLE
JACOBS LADDER

JE NE SAIS
 QUOI
JEOPARDIZING
JET-PROPELLED
JIGSAW PUZZLE
JOHANNESBURG
JOURNALISTIC
JUDICATORIAL
JUGULAR VEINS
JUNIOR SCHOOL
JURISCONSULT
JURISDICTION
JURISDICTIVE
JURISPRUDENT
JUSTIFYINGLY
JUVENESCENCE

K

KALEIDOSCOPE
KARYOKINESIS
KARYOKINETIC
KARYOPLASMIC
KEEP ONES HEAD
KEEP THE PEACE
KERATOGENOUS
KERATOPLASTY
KERB CRAWLERS
KERB CRAWLING
KEYNESIANISM
KEY SIGNATURE
KILLER WHALES
KILOWATT-HOUR
KINAESTHESIA
KINAESTHETIC
KINDERGARTEN
KING'S COUNSEL
KING'S ENGLISH
KINROSS-SHIRE
KITCHENETTES
KLEPTOMANIAC
KLIPSPRINGER
KNACKER'S YARD
KNEE BREECHES
KNIGHT ERRANT
KNIGHT-ERRANT
KNOX-JOHNSTON
KOMI REPUBLIC
KOTA KINABALU
KREMLINOLOGY
KRISTIANSTAD
KYRGYZ STEPPE

L

LABORATORIES
LABOUR MARKET
LABOUR OF LOVE
LABOURSAVING
LABYRINTHINE
LACERABILITY
LACHRYMOSITY
LACTOPROTEIN
LADY'S FINGERS
LADY'S-SLIPPER
LAISSEZ-FAIRE
LAKE DISTRICT
LAMENTATIONS
LANDED GENTRY
LANDING CRAFT
LANDING FIELD
LANDING STAGE
LANDING STRIP
LANDLUBBERLY
LANGUISHMENT
LANGUOROUSLY
LANTERN-JAWED
LANTERNSLIDE
LAPIS LAZULIS
LARYNGOSCOPE
LARYNGOSCOPY
LASCIVIOUSLY
LASER PRINTER
LAST JUDGMENT
LATEENRIGGED
LATICIFEROUS
LATINIZATION
LAUNDERETTES
LAUNDRYWOMAN
LAUREATESHIP
LEADING LIGHT
LEAPFROGGING
LEASEHOLDERS
LEATHERINESS
LEAVE TAKINGS
LECTURESHIPS
LEGALIZATION
LEGIONNAIRES
LEGISLATRESS
LEGISLATURES
LEGITIMATELY
LEGITIMATION
LEGITIMATIZE
LEGITIMISTIC
LEGITIMIZING

LENTICELLATE
LEOPARD'S-BANE
LEPIDOPTERAN
LEPIDOPTERON
LETTER OPENER
LEUCOCYTOSIS
LEUCOCYTOTIC
LEUCOPOIESIS
LEUCOPOIETIC
LEUCORRHOEAL
LEVALLOISIAN
LEXICOGRAPHY
LEXICOLOGIST
LIBERALISTIC
LIBERALITIES
LIBERALIZING
LIBERAL PARTY
LIBERTARIANS
LIBERTICIDAL
LIBIDINOUSLY
LICENSE PLATE
LICENTIATION
LICENTIOUSLY
LICHTENSTEIN
LIE DETECTORS
LIFELESSNESS
LIGHT BRIGADE
LIGHT-HEARTED
LIGHTWEIGHTS
LIMNOLOGICAL
LINCOLNSHIRE
LINE DRAWINGS
LINE-ENGRAVER
LINEN BASKETS
LINE PRINTERS
LINE PRINTING
LINES OF SIGHT
LINGUA FRANCA
LIQUEFACIENT
LIQUEFACTION
LIQUEFACTIVE
LIRIODENDRON
LISTLESSNESS
LITERALISTIC
LITERARINESS
LITERATENESS
LITHOGRAPHED
LITHOGRAPHER
LITHOGRAPHIC
LITTERATEURS
LITTLE FINGER

LITTLE PEOPLE
LITURGICALLY
LIVERPUDLIAN
LIVER SAUSAGE
LIVERY STABLE
LIVING FOSSIL
LOCAL DERBIES
LOCALIZATION
LOCAL OPTIONS
LOCI CLASSICI
LOCKSMITHERY
LOCKSTITCHES
LODGING HOUSE
LOGANBERRIES
LOGANIACEOUS
LOGISTICALLY
LOLLAPALOOZA
LOMENTACEOUS
LONELY HEARTS
LONESOMENESS
LONG-DISTANCE
LONG DIVISION
LONG DRAWN OUT
LONG-DRAWN-OUT
LONGITUDINAL
LONGSHOREMAN
LONGSHOREMEN
LONG-STANDING
LONG VACATION
LONGWINDEDLY
LOOKING GLASS
LOOSE-JOINTED
LOOSE-TONGUED
LOPHOPHORATE
LOQUACIOUSLY
LOSS ADJUSTER
LOST PROPERTY
LOT-ET-GARONNE
LOUDSPEAKERS
LOUGHBOROUGH
LOVECHILDREN
LOWER AUSTRIA
LOWER CLASSES
LOW-WATER MARK
LUDWIGSHAFEN
LUGGAGE RACKS
LUGUBRIOUSLY
LUMBERJACKET
LUMINESCENCE
LUNCHEONETTE
LUSCIOUSNESS

LYMPHANGITIC
LYMPHANGITIS
LYMPHOMATOID
LYSERGIC ACID

M

MACCLESFIELD
MACHINATIONS
MACHINE CODES
MACHINE TOOLS
MACKINTOSHES
MACROCLIMATE
MACROCYTOSIS
MACROGRAPHIC
MACRONUCLEUS
MACROPHYSICS
MACROPTEROUS
MADEMOISELLE
MAGIC LANTERN
MAGISTRACIES
MAGISTRATURE
MAGNETICALLY
MAGNETIC HEAD
MAGNETIC POLE
MAGNETIC TAPE
MAGNETIZABLE
MAGNETOGRAPH
MAGNETOMETER
MAGNETOMETRY
MAGNIFICENCE
MAGNILOQUENT
MAGNITOGORSK
MAGNUM OPUSES
MAIDENLINESS
MAIDEN SPEECH
MAIDEN VOYAGE
MAID OF HONOUR
MAIDSERVANTS
MAILING LISTS
MAINE-ET-LOIRE
MAINTAINABLE
MAITRE D'HOTEL
MAJESTICALLY
MAJOR GENERAL
MAKE ENDS MEET
MALACOLOGIST
MALAPROPISMS
MALEDICTIONS
MALEFACTRESS
MALEVOLENTLY
MALFEASANCES

MALFORMATION	MASS-PRODUCED	MENAGE A TROIS	METHODICALLY
MALFUNCTIONS	MASS-PRODUCER	MENDACIOUSLY	METHOTREXATE
MALIGNANCIES	MASTECTOMIES	MEN OF LETTERS	METICULOUSLY
MALIMPRINTED	MASTER-AT-ARMS	MENSTRUATING	METONIC CYCLE
MALLEABILITY	MASTERLINESS	MENSTRUATION	METROLOGICAL
MALNOURISHED	MASTERMINDED	MEPHITICALLY	METROPOLISES
MALNUTRITION	MASTER OF ARTS	MERCANTILISM	METROPOLITAN
MALOCCLUSION	MASTERPIECES	MERCANTILIST	METRORRHAGIA
MALPRACTICES	MASTERSTROKE	MERCHANDISED	MEZZO-RELIEVO
MALTESE CROSS	MASTIGOPHORE	MERCHANDISER	MEZZO-SOPRANO
MALTREATMENT	MASTURBATING	MERCHANTABLE	MICROANALYST
MAMMALOGICAL	MASTURBATION	MERCHANT BANK	MICROBALANCE
MAN ABOUT TOWN	MATABELELAND	MERCHANT NAVY	MICROBIOLOGY
MAN-ABOUT-TOWN	MATERIALISTS	MERCIFULNESS	MICROCEPHALY
MANAGERESSES	MATERIALIZED	MERCURIALIZE	MICROCIRCUIT
MANAGERIALLY	MATERIALIZER	MERCY KILLING	MICROCLIMATE
MANDARIN DUCK	MATHEMATICAL	MERETRICIOUS	MICROFILMING
MANEUVERABLE	MATINEE IDOLS	MERISTEMATIC	MICROGRAPHER
MANGEL-WURZEL	MATRIARCHIES	MEROPLANKTON	MICROGRAPHIC
MANIFESTABLE	MATRICLINOUS	MERRY-GO-ROUND	MICROGRAVITY
MANIPULATING	MATRICULATED	MESENTERITIS	MICROHABITAT
MANIPULATION	MATRICULATOR	MESENTERONIC	MICRONUCLEUS
MANIPULATIVE	MATRONLINESS	MESMERICALLY	MICROPHYSICS
MANIPULATORY	MATTER-OF-FACT	MESOCEPHALIC	MICROSCOPIST
MANNERLINESS	MATURATIONAL	MESOGASTRIUM	MICROSECONDS
MANOEUVRABLE	MAXIMIZATION	MESOGNATHISM	MICROSEISMIC
MAN OF LETTERS	MEALY-MOUTHED	MESOGNATHOUS	MICROSTOMOUS
MANSION HOUSE	MEAN BUSINESS	MESOMORPHISM	MIDDLE COURSE
MANSLAUGHTER	MEANDERINGLY	MESOMORPHOUS	MIDDLE FINGER
MANTELPIECES	MEANINGFULLY	MESOPOTAMIAN	MIDDLE SCHOOL
MANUFACTURAL	MEASUREMENTS	MESOTHORACIC	MIDDLEWEIGHT
MANUFACTURED	MECAMYLAMINE	MESSAGE STICK	MID GLAMORGAN
MANUFACTURER	MECHANICALLY	METAGALACTIC	MIDSUMMER DAY
MARCASITICAL	MEDALLIONIST	METAGNATHISM	MIDWESTERNER
MARIE GALANTE	MEDICAMENTAL	METAGNATHOUS	MIFEPRISTONE
MARITIME ALPS	MEDICINE BALL	METALANGUAGE	MIGHT AND MAIN
MARKET FORCES	MEDIOCRITIES	METALLICALLY	MILFORD HAVEN
MARKET GARDEN	MEDITATINGLY	METALLURGIST	MILITARISTIC
MARKETPLACES	MEDITATIVELY	METALWORKERS	MILITARIZING
MARKET PRICES	MEETINGHOUSE	METALWORKING	MILLEFEUILLE
MARKSMANSHIP	MEGACEPHALIC	METAMORPHISM	MILLENARIANS
MARLINESPIKE	MEGALOCARDIA	METAMORPHOSE	MILLIONAIRES
MARRIAGEABLE	MEGALOMANIAC	METAPHORICAL	MILTON KEYNES
MARSEILLAISE	MELANCHOLIAC	METAPHRASTIC	MIMEOGRAPHED
MARSHALL PLAN	MELANCHOLILY	METAPHYSICAL	MIND-BOGGLING
MARSHMALLOWS	MELODRAMATIC	METASOMATISM	MINDLESSNESS
MARSUPIALIAN	MELTING POINT	METATHORACIC	MINE DETECTOR
MARVELLOUSLY	MEMORABILITY	METEMPIRICAL	MINERALOGIST
MASQUERADERS	MEMORIALIZER	METEORICALLY	MINERAL WATER
MASQUERADING	MEMORIZATION	METEOROGRAPH	MINESWEEPERS
MASSOTHERAPY	MEN-ABOUT-TOWN	METHACRYLATE	MINESWEEPING

MINIATURISTS	MIXED DOUBLES	MONOTRICHOUS	MULTIGRAVIDA
MINICOMPUTER	MIXED ECONOMY	MONTPARNASSE	MULTILAMINAR
MINIFICATION	MIXED FARMING	MONUMENTALLY	MULTILATERAL
MINIMIZATION	MNEMONICALLY	MOONLIGHTERS	MULTILINGUAL
MINIMUM WAGES	MOBILIZATION	MOONLIGHTING	MULTINUCLEAR
MINISTRATION	MOCKINGBIRDS	MORALITY PLAY	MULTIPARTITE
MINISTRATIVE	MODERATENESS	MORALIZATION	MULTIPLIABLE
MINOR PLANETS	MODIFICATION	MORALIZINGLY	MULTIPLICAND
MINUTE STEAKS	MODIFICATORY	MORBIFICALLY	MULTIPLICATE
MIRACLE PLAYS	MODULABILITY	MORNING COATS	MULTIPLICITY
MIRROR IMAGES	MODUS VIVENDI	MORNING DRESS	MULTIPURPOSE
MIRTHFULNESS	MOHAVE DESERT	MORNING GLORY	MULTITASKING
MISADVENTURE	MOISTURIZING	MORPHALLAXIS	MULTIVALENCY
MISALIGNMENT	MOLLIFYINGLY	MORPHOLOGIES	MULTIVARIATE
MISALLIANCES	MOLLYCODDLED	MORPHOLOGIST	MUNICIPALITY
MISANTHROPES	MONADELPHOUS	MORRIS DANCER	MUNICIPALIZE
MISANTHROPIC	MONARCHISTIC	MORRIS DANCES	MUNIFICENTLY
MISAPPREHEND	MONASTICALLY	MORTARBOARDS	MUSEUM PIECES
MISBEHAVIOUR	MONETIZATION	MORTGAGEABLE	MUSICAL BOXES
MISCALCULATE	MONEYCHANGER	MORTIFYINGLY	MUSIC CENTRES
MISCARRIAGES	MONEY-GRUBBER	MORTISE LOCKS	MUSICIANSHIP
MISCEGENETIC	MONEYLENDERS	MOSQUITO NETS	MUSICOLOGIST
MISCELLANIES	MONEYLENDING	MOTHERFUCKER	MYRMECOPHILE
MISCELLANIST	MONEY SPINNER	MOTHERLINESS	MYSTERIOUSLY
MISCONCEIVED	MONEY-SPINNER	MOTHER NATURE	MYSTERY PLAYS
MISCONCEIVER	MONISTICALLY	MOTHERS-IN-LAW	MYSTERY TOURS
MISCONDUCTED	MONKEY-PUZZLE	MOTHER TONGUE	MYSTIFYINGLY
MISCONSTRUED	MONKEY WRENCH	MOTHPROOFING	MYTHOLOGICAL
MISDEMEANANT	MONOCHLORIDE	MOTIONLESSLY	MYTHOLOGISTS
MISDEMEANOUR	MONOCHROMIST	MOTIVATIONAL	MYTHOLOGIZER
MISDIRECTING	MONODRAMATIC	MOTORCYCLIST	MYXOMYCETOUS
MISDIRECTION	MONOFILAMENT	MOTORIZATION	
MISE-EN-SCENES	MONOGAMISTIC	MOTOR SCOOTER	**N**
MISINFORMANT	MONOGAMOUSLY	MOULDABILITY	NAIL SCISSORS
MISINFORMING	MONOMANIACAL	MOUNTAINEERS	NAMBY-PAMBIES
MISINTERPRET	MONOMETALLIC	MOUNTAIN LION	NAMEDROPPERS
MISJUDGEMENT	MONOMETRICAL	MOUNTAINSIDE	NAMEDROPPING
MISJUDGMENTS	MONOMORPHISM	MOUNTAINTOPS	NANOPLANKTON
MISLEADINGLY	MONOPETALOUS	MOURNFULNESS	NANSEN BOTTLE
MISPLACEMENT	MONOPHTHONGS	MOUTHBROODER	NARCISSISTIC
MISPRONOUNCE	MONOPHYLETIC	MOUTH-TO-MOUTH	NARCOTICALLY
MISQUOTATION	MONOPHYLLOUS	MOVABLE FEAST	NARRAGANSETT
MISREPORTING	MONOPOLISTIC	MUCILAGINOUS	NARROW GAUGES
MISREPRESENT	MONOPOLIZING	MUCOPURULENT	NARROW-MINDED
MISSING LINKS	MONOSEPALOUS	MUDDLE-HEADED	NARROW SQUEAK
MISSIONARIES	MONOSPERMOUS	MULLIGATAWNY	NASALIZATION
MISSPELLINGS	MONOSTROPHIC	MULTICHANNEL	NATIONAL DEBT
MISSTATEMENT	MONOSYLLABIC	MULTIFACETED	NATIONAL HUNT
MISTREATMENT	MONOSYLLABLE	MULTIFARIOUS	NATIONALISTS
MITHRIDATISM	MONOTHEISTIC	MULTIFOLIATE	NATIONALIZED
MIXED-ABILITY	MONOTONOUSLY	MULTIFORMITY	NATIONAL PARK

NATION STATES
NATIVITY PLAY
NATURALISTIC
NATURALIZING
NATUROPATHIC
NAUSEATINGLY
NAUSEOUSNESS
NAUTICAL MILE
NAVIGABILITY
NAVIGATIONAL
NEANDERTHALS
NEBULIZATION
NEBULOUSNESS
NECESSITATED
NECKERCHIEFS
NECROLOGICAL
NECROMANCERS
NECROPHILIAC
NECROPHILISM
NECROPOLISES
NEEDLESSNESS
NEGATIVENESS
NEGATIVE POLE
NEGATIVE SIGN
NEGATIVISTIC
NEGLECTFULLY
NEGOTIATIONS
NEIGHBOURING
NEMATOCYSTIC
NEOANTHROPIC
NEOCLASSICAL
NEOLOGICALLY
NEOTERICALLY
NEPHELOMETER
NEPHOLOGICAL
NERVE CENTRES
NERVE-RACKING
NETHERLANDER
NETTLE RASHES
NEURASTHENIA
NEURASTHENIC
NEUROANATOMY
NEUROBIOLOGY
NEUROLOGICAL
NEUROLOGISTS
NEUROPTEROUS
NEUROSCIENCE
NEUROSURGEON
NEUROSURGERY
NEUROTICALLY
NEUROTOMICAL

NEUTRALIZING
NEUTRON BOMBS
NEVERTHELESS
NEW BRUNSWICK
NEW CALEDONIA
NEWFOUNDLAND
NEW HAMPSHIRE
NEWS AGENCIES
NEWSPAPERMAN
NEW TESTAMENT
NEWTOWNABBEY
NEW ZEALANDER
NIAGARA FALLS
NICOTINAMIDE
NIDIFICATION
NIETZSCHEISM
NIGHTDRESSES
NIGHTINGALES
NIMBOSTRATUS
NITROBENZENE
NITROMETHANE
NO-CLAIM BONUS
NOCTAMBULISM
NOCTAMBULIST
NOCTILUCENCE
NOCTURNALITY
NOLENS VOLENS
NOMENCLATURE
NOMINALISTIC
NONADDICTIVE
NONAGENARIAN
NONALCOHOLIC
NONALIGNMENT
NONCHALANTLY
NONCOMBATANT
NONCOMMITTAL
NONCONDUCTOR
NONCORRODING
NONE SO PRETTY
NONESSENTIAL
NONEXISTENCE
NONEXPLOSIVE
NONFICTIONAL
NONFLAMMABLE
NONIDENTICAL
NONIDIOMATIC
NONMALIGNANT
NONOPERATIVE
NONPOISONOUS
NONPOLITICAL
NONRESIDENCE

NON RESIDENCE
NONRESIDENTS
NONRESISTANT
NONSCHEDULED
NONSECTARIAN
NON SEQUITURS
NONSTRATEGIC
NONTECHNICAL
NONVIOLENTLY
NORTH AMERICA
NORTH BRABANT
NORTHEASTERN
NORTHEASTERS
NORTHERNMOST
NORTH HOLLAND
NORTHUMBRIAN
NORTHWESTERN
NOTEWORTHILY
NOTICE BOARDS
NOTIFICATION
NOURISHINGLY
NOUVEAU RICHE
NOVOKUZNETSK
NUBIAN DESERT
NUCLEOPHILIC
NUMBERPLATES
NUMEROUSNESS
NUMINOUSNESS
NUMISMATISTS
NURSERY RHYME
NURSING HOMES
NUSA TENGGARA
NUTRITIONIST
NUTRITIOUSLY
NUTS AND BOLTS
NYCTITROPISM
NYMPHOLEPTIC
NYMPHOMANIAC

O

OBERAMMERGAU
OBITER DICTUM
OBJECT LESSON
OBLANCEOLATE
OBLATE SPHERE
OBLIGATIONAL
OBLIGATORILY
OBLITERATING
OBLITERATION
OBLITERATIVE
OBSCURANTISM

OBSCURANTIST
OBSEQUIOUSLY
OBSERVATIONS
OBSOLESCENCE
OBSOLETENESS
OBSTETRICIAN
OBSTREPEROUS
OBSTRUCTIONS
OCCASIONALLY
OCCUPATIONAL
OCEANOGRAPHY
OCTOGENARIAN
OCTOSYLLABIC
OCTOSYLLABLE
ODONTOGRAPHY
ODONTOLOGIST
ODONTOPHORAL
OESOPHAGUSES
OFFICE BLOCKS
OFFICEHOLDER
OFF ONES HANDS
OFF-THE-RECORD
OIL PAINTINGS
OKLAHOMA CITY
OLD-FASHIONED
OLD MANS BEARD
OLD PRETENDER
OLD SCHOOL TIE
OLD TESTAMENT
OLD WIVES'
  TALE
OLEORESINOUS
OLIGOTROPHIC
OLYMPIC GAMES
OMNIPRESENCE
ONEIROCRITIC
ONE-SIDEDNESS
ONE-TRACK MIND
ONE-UPMANSHIP
ONOMASIOLOGY
ONOMATOPOEIA
ONOMATOPOEIC
ON THE RAMPAGE
ONYCHOPHORAN
OOPHORECTOMY
OPEN-HANDEDLY
OPENING TIMES
OPEN-MINDEDLY
OPEN QUESTION
OPEN SANDWICH
OPEN VERDICTS

OPERA GLASSES
OPERATICALLY
OPHIOLOGICAL
OPHTHALMITIS
OPINION POLLS
OPPORTUNISTS
OPPOSABILITY
OPPOSITENESS
OPPOSITIONAL
OPPRESSINGLY
OPPRESSIVELY
OPSONIZATION
OPTIMIZATION
ORANGE ROUGHY
ORATORICALLY
ORBICULARITY
ORCHESTRA PIT
ORCHESTRATED
ORCHIDACEOUS
ORDINARINESS
ORGAN GRINDER
ORGANICISTIC
ORGANIZATION
ORGANOGRAPHY
ORGANOLEPTIC
ORGANOLOGIST
ORIEL WINDOWS
ORIENTALISTS
ORIENTATIONS
ORIENTEERING
ORNAMENTALLY
OROGENICALLY
OROLOGICALLY
ORTHOCEPHALY
ORTHODONTICS
ORTHOGENESIS
ORTHOGENETIC
ORTHOGRAPHER
ORTHOGRAPHIC
ORTHOMORPHIC
ORTHOPAEDICS
ORTHOPAEDIST
ORTHOPTEROUS
ORTHORHOMBIC
ORTHOTROPISM
ORTHOTROPOUS
OSCILLATIONS
OSCILLOGRAPH
OSCILLOSCOPE
OSSIFICATION
OSTENTATIOUS

OSTEOBLASTIC
OSTEOCLASTIC
OSTEOLOGICAL
OSTEOMALACIA
OSTEOPLASTIC
OSTRACIZABLE
OTHERWORLDLY
OUTBALANCING
OUTBUILDINGS
OUTDISTANCED
OUTGENERALED
OUTLANDISHLY
OUTMANOEUVRE
OUTNUMBERING
OUTRAGEOUSLY
OUTRIVALLING
OUTSTRETCHED
OUTSTRIPPING
OVERBALANCED
OVERBURDENED
OVERCAPACITY
OVERCAUTIOUS
OVERCHARGING
OVERCLOUDING
OVERCRITICAL
OVERCROPPING
OVERCROWDING
OVERDRESSING
OVEREMPHATIC
OVERESTIMATE
OVEREXPOSING
OVERGENEROUS
OVERINDULGED
OVERMASTERED
OVERPOPULATE
OVERPOWERING
OVERREACHING
OVERREACTING
OVERREACTION
OVERSHADOWED
OVERSHOOTING
OVERSIMPLIFY
OVERSLEEPING
OVERSTEPPING
OVERSTOCKING
OVERTHROWING
OVERWHELMING
OWNER-DRIVERS
OXYACETYLENE
OXYGENIZABLE

P
PACIFICATION
PACKAGE DEALS
PACKAGE TOURS
PACKING CASES
PADDLING POOL
PAEDOGENESIS
PAEDOGENETIC
PAEDOLOGICAL
PAGANIZATION
PAINTBRUSHES
PALAEOBOTANY
PALAEOGRAPHY
PALAEOLITHIC
PALATABILITY
PALATIALNESS
PALAZZO PANTS
PALEOGRAPHER
PALEONTOLOGY
PALETTE KNIFE
PALINGENESIS
PALINGENETIC
PALPITATIONS
PALYNOLOGIST
PAMPHLETEERS
PANCAKE ROLLS
PANCHROMATIC
PANDANACEOUS
PANDEMONIUMS
PANHELLENISM
PANHELLENIST
PANOPTICALLY
PANTECHNICON
PANTISOCRACY
PANTOGRAPHER
PANTOGRAPHIC
PAPERHANGERS
PAPERHANGING
PAPERWEIGHTS
PAPULIFEROUS
PARABOLOIDAL
PARACHRONISM
PARACHUTISTS
PARADE GROUND
PARADIGMATIC
PARADISE LOST
PARADISIACAL
PARAESTHESIA
PARAESTHETIC
PARAHYDROGEN
PARALANGUAGE

PARALLEL BARS
PARALLELISMS
PARALLELLING
PARALOGISTIC
PARALYSATION
PARAMAGNETIC
PARAMILITARY
PARAMORPHISM
PARAPHRASING
PARAPHRASTIC
PARASITICIDE
PARASITOLOGY
PARATHYROIDS
PARATROOPERS
PARENTHESIZE
PARISH CLERKS
PARISHIONERS
PARISYLLABIC
PARKING LIGHT
PARKING METER
PARLOUR GAMES
PAROCHIALISM
PARSIMONIOUS
PARSON'S NOSES
PART EXCHANGE
PARTHIAN SHOT
PARTIALITIES
PARTICIPANTS
PARTICIPATED
PARTICIPATOR
PARTICULARLY
PARTING SHOTS
PARTISANSHIP
PARTITIONING
PARTNERSHIPS
PART OF SPEECH
PARTY POOPERS
PASQUEFLOWER
PASSE PARTOUT
PASSE-PARTOUT
PASSIONATELY
PASSION PLAYS
PASTEURIZING
PAST PERFECTS
PATCH POCKETS
PATERNALISTS
PATERNOSTERS
PATHETICALLY
PATHOGENESIS
PATHOGENETIC
PATHOLOGICAL

PATHOLOGISTS	PERINEURITIC	PETROLOGISTS	PHOTOCURRENT
PATRIARCHATE	PERINEURITIS	PETROZAVODSK	PHOTODYNAMIC
PATRIARCHIES	PERIODICALLY	PETTIFOGGING	PHOTOENGRAVE
PATRICLINOUS	PERIODONTICS	PETTY LARCENY	PHOTOGEOLOGY
PATROL WAGONS	PERIOD PIECES	PETTY OFFICER	PHOTOGRAPHED
PATRON SAINTS	PERIONYCHIUM	PHAGOCYTOSIS	PHOTOGRAPHER
PAVING STONES	PERIPHERALLY	PHANEROGAMIC	PHOTOGRAPHIC
PAY ENVELOPES	PERIPHRASTIC	PHANEROPHYTE	PHOTOGRAVURE
PEACEFULNESS	PERITRICHOUS	PHARMACOLOGY	PHOTOKINESIS
PEAK DISTRICT	PERMACULTURE	PHARYNGOLOGY	PHOTOKINETIC
PEANUT BUTTER	PERMANENT WAY	PHARYNGOTOMY	PHOTOMETRIST
PEARL HARBOUR	PERMANGANATE	PHELLODERMAL	PHOTOMONTAGE
PEASE PUDDING	PERMEABILITY	PHENANTHRENE	PHOTONEUTRON
PECCADILLOES	PERMISSIVELY	PHENOLOGICAL	PHOTONUCLEAR
PECKING ORDER	PERMITTIVITY	PHENOMENALLY	PHOTOPHILOUS
PEDANTICALLY	PERMUTATIONS	PHI BETA KAPPA	PHOTOPOLYMER
PEDIATRICIAN	PERNICIOUSLY	PHILADELPHIA	PHOTOREALISM
PEEBLESSHIRE	PERPETRATING	PHILADELPHUS	PHOTOSPHERIC
PEJORATIVELY	PERPETRATION	PHILANDERERS	PHOTOSTATTED
PENALIZATION	PERPETRATORS	PHILANDERING	PHOTOTHERAPY
PENALTY AREAS	PERPETUATING	PHILANTHROPY	PHOTOTHERMIC
PENDENTE LITE	PERPETUATION	PHILATELISTS	PHOTOTROPISM
PENITENTIARY	PERPETUITIES	PHILHARMONIC	PHRASAL VERBS
PENNSYLVANIA	PERPLEXITIES	PHILISTINISM	PHRASEOGRAPH
PENNULTIMATE	PERSECUTIONS	PHILODENDRON	PHRENOLOGIST
PENNY PINCHER	PERSEVERANCE	PHILOLOGICAL	PHYCOLOGICAL
PENNY WHISTLE	PERSISTENTLY	PHILOLOGISTS	PHYLETICALLY
PENTARCHICAL	PERSONA GRATA	PHILOSOPHERS	PHYSICALNESS
PEPTIC ULCERS	PERSONALIZED	PHILOSOPHIES	PHYSIOCRATIC
PERADVENTURE	PERSONIFYING	PHILOSOPHIZE	PHYSIOGNOMIC
PERAMBULATED	PERSPECTIVES	PHLEBOTOMIST	PHYSIOGRAPHY
PERAMBULATOR	PERSPICACITY	PHONEMICALLY	PHYSIOLOGIES
PERCEPTIONAL	PERSPIRATION	PHONE-TAPPING	PHYSIOLOGIST
PERCEPTIVELY	PERSPIRATORY	PHONETICALLY	PHYSOSTOMOUS
PERCEPTIVITY	PERSPIRINGLY	PHONETICIANS	PHYTOGENESIS
PERCOLATIONS	PERSUASIVELY	PHONOGRAPHER	PHYTOGENETIC
PERCUTANEOUS	PERTINACIOUS	PHONOLOGICAL	PHYTOHORMONE
PEREGRINATOR	PERTURBATION	PHONOLOGISTS	PHYTOPHAGOUS
PEREMPTORILY	PERTURBINGLY	PHONOTACTICS	PICCANINNIES
PERFECT PITCH	PERVERSENESS	PHOSPHATURIA	PICKERELWEED
PERFIDIOUSLY	PERVERSITIES	PHOSPHATURIC	PICTURE BOOKS
PERFOLIATION	PERVIOUSNESS	PHOSPHOLIPID	PICTURE CARDS
PERFORATIONS	PESTILENTIAL	PHOSPHORESCE	PIECE OF EIGHT
PERFORMANCES	PETALIFEROUS	PHOSPHORITIC	PIECES OF WORK
PERFORMATIVE	PETERBOROUGH	PHOTOACTINIC	PIGEONHOLING
PERICARDITIC	PETIT LARCENY	PHOTOCATHODE	PIGMENTATION
PERICARDITIS	PETRIFACTION	PHOTOCHEMIST	PILOT OFFICER
PERICYNTHION	PETRODOLLARS	PHOTOCHROMIC	PINEAL GLANDS
PERILOUSNESS	PETROGRAPHER	PHOTOCOMPOSE	PINK ELEPHANT
PERIMORPHISM	PETROGRAPHIC	PHOTOCOPIERS	PIPE CLEANERS
PERINEPHRIUM	PETROLOGICAL	PHOTOCOPYING	PIPES OF PEACE

PISCICULTURE
PITCHFORKING
PITIABLENESS
PITILESSNESS
PITTER-PATTER
PLACENTATION
PLACE SETTING
PLAGIARISTIC
PLAGIARIZING
PLAGIOCLIMAX
PLAIN-CLOTHES
PLAIN SAILING
PLANETARIUMS
PLANETESIMAL
PLANISPHERIC
PLANO-CONCAVE
PLANOGRAPHIC
PLASTERBOARD
PLASTER CASTS
PLASTOMETRIC
PLATONICALLY
PLAUSIBILITY
PLAYER PIANOS
PLAYING CARDS
PLAYING FIELD
PLAYS ON WORDS
PLEASANTNESS
PLEASANTRIES
PLEASINGNESS
PLEIOTROPISM
PLEOMORPHISM
PLIMSOLL LINE
PLODDINGNESS
PLOUGHSHARES
PLUMBIFEROUS
PLUM PUDDINGS
PLUTOCRACIES
PLUVIOMETRIC
PNEUMOCOCCUS
PNEUMOTHORAX
POET LAUREATE
POINTILLISTS
POINT OF ORDER
POINTS OF VIEW
POINT-TO-POINT
POLARIMETRIC
POLARIZATION
POLAROGRAPHY
POLE POSITION
POLE VAULTERS
POLE VAULTING

POLICE STATES
POLICYHOLDER
POLITICIZING
POLLEN COUNTS
POLLING BOOTH
POLTERGEISTS
POLYANTHUSES
POLYCENTRISM
POLYCHAETOUS
POLYCYTHEMIA
POLYEMBRYONY
POLYETHYLENE
POLYISOPRENE
POLYMORPHISM
POLYMORPHOUS
POLYPETALOUS
POLYPHYLETIC
POLYPHYODONT
POLYRHYTHMIC
POLYSEPALOUS
POLYSULPHIDE
POLYSYLLABIC
POLYSYLLABLE
POLYSYNDETON
POLYTECHNICS
POLYTHEISTIC
POLYTONALIST
POLYTONALITY
POLYURETHANE
POMEGRANATES
PONS ASINORUM
PONTA DELGADA
PONTIFICATED
PONTIFICATES
PONY-TREKKING
POOR RELATION
POOR-SPIRITED
POPOCATEPETL
POPULAR FRONT
POPULARIZING
POPULOUSNESS
PORNOGRAPHER
PORNOGRAPHIC
PORPHYROPSIN
PORT ADELAIDE
PORT-AU-PRINCE
PORTCULLISES
PORTE-COCHERE
PORTENTOUSLY
PORTERHOUSES
PORT HARCOURT

PORTMANTEAUS
PORTMANTEAUX
PORTS OF ENTRY
POSITIVENESS
POSITIVE POLE
POSITIVISTIC
POSSESSIVELY
POSTAGE STAMP
POSTAL ORDERS
POSTDILUVIAL
POSTDILUVIAN
POSTDOCTORAL
POSTER COLOUR
POSTER PAINTS
POSTGRADUATE
POSTHUMOUSLY
POSTMERIDIAN
POST MERIDIEM
POSTPONEMENT
POSTPOSITION
POSTPOSITIVE
POSTPRANDIAL
POTATO BEETLE
POTATO CRISPS
POTENTIALITY
POTTER'S WHEEL
POTTING SHEDS
POTTY-TRAINED
POVERTY TRAPS
POWER BROKERS
POWERFULNESS
POWER-SHARING
POWER STATION
PRACTICALITY
PRACTITIONER
PRAGMATISTIC
PRAISEWORTHY
PRASEODYMIUM
PRAYER WHEELS
PREAMPLIFIER
PREARRANGING
PREBENDARIES
PRECARIOUSLY
PRECEDENTIAL
PRECENTORIAL
PRECEPTORATE
PRECEPTORIAL
PRECESSIONAL
PRECIOUSNESS
PRECIPITANCE
PRECIPITATED

PRECIPITATES
PRECIPITATOR
PRECISIANISM
PRECISIONISM
PRECISIONIST
PRECLASSICAL
PRECOCIOUSLY
PRECOGNITION
PRECOGNITIVE
PRECONCEIVED
PRECONDITION
PRECONSCIOUS
PREDECEASING
PREDECESSORS
PREDESTINATE
PREDESTINING
PREDETERMINE
PREDICAMENTS
PREDICTIVELY
PREDIGESTING
PREDIGESTION
PREDILECTION
PREDISPOSING
PREDOMINANCE
PREDOMINATED
PREDOMINATOR
PRE-ECLAMPSIA
PRE-EMINENTLY
PRE-EMPTIVELY
PRE-EXISTENCE
PREFABRICATE
PREFECTORIAL
PREFERENTIAL
PREFORMATION
PREGNABILITY
PREJUDGEMENT
PREJUDGMENTS
PREMARITALLY
PREMAXILLARY
PREMEDITATED
PREMEDITATOR
PREMENSTRUAL
PREMIERSHIPS
PREMIUM BONDS
PREMONITIONS
PREOCCUPYING
PREORDAINING
PREPARATIONS
PREPAREDNESS
PREPONDERANT
PREPONDERATE

PREPOSITIONS
PREPOSSESSED
PREPOSTEROUS
PRERECORDING
PREREQUISITE
PREROGATIVES
PRESBYTERATE
PRESBYTERIAL
PRESBYTERIAN
PRESBYTERIES
PRESCRIPTION
PRESCRIPTIVE
PRESENTATION
PRESENTATIVE
PRESENTIMENT
PRESERVATION
PRESERVATIVE
PRESIDENCIES
PRESIDENTIAL
PRESS CUTTING
PRESS GALLERY
PRESSGANGING
PRESSINGNESS
PRESS RELEASE
PRESSURIZING
PRESUMPTIONS
PRESUMPTUOUS
PRESUPPOSING
PRETTY-PRETTY
PREVAILINGLY
PREVARICATED
PREVARICATOR
PREVENTIVELY
PREVIOUSNESS
PRICKLY PEARS
PRIDE OF PLACE
PRIESTLINESS
PRIEST-RIDDEN
PRIGGISHNESS
PRIME NUMBERS
PRIMOGENITOR
PRIMORDIALLY
PRIMULACEOUS
PRIMUM MOBILE
PRINCELINESS
PRINCE REGENT
PRINCE RUPERT
PRINCIPAL BOY
PRINCIPALITY
PRINTABILITY
PRIORITIZING

PRISMATOIDAL
PRIVATE PARTS
PRIVY COUNCIL
PRIZEFIGHTER
PROBATIONARY
PROBATIONERS
PROBLEMATIZE
PROBOSCIDEAN
PROCATHEDRAL
PROCESSIONAL
PROCLAMATION
PROCLIVITIES
PROCONSULATE
PROCTOLOGIST
PRODIGIOUSLY
PRODUCTIONAL
PRODUCTIVELY
PRODUCTIVITY
PROFANATIONS
PROFESSIONAL
PROFESSORIAL
PROFICIENTLY
PROFITEERING
PROFITLESSLY
PROFIT MARGIN
PROFOUNDNESS
PROFUNDITIES
PROGESTERONE
PROGRAMMABLE
PROGRAMMATIC
PROGRESSIONS
PROGRESSIVES
PROHIBITIONS
PROJECTIONAL
PROLEGOMENAL
PROLEGOMENON
PROLETARIANS
PROLIFERATED
PROLIFICALLY
PROLIFICNESS
PROLONGATION
PROMISED LAND
PROMONTORIES
PROMULGATING
PROMULGATION
PROMULGATORS
PRONOMINALLY
PRONOUNCEDLY
PROOFREADERS
PROOFREADING
PROPAEDEUTIC

PROPAGANDISM
PROPAGANDIST
PROPAGANDIZE
PROPENSITIES
PROPHESIABLE
PROPHYLACTIC
PROPITIATING
PROPITIATION
PROPITIATIVE
PROPITIATORY
PROPITIOUSLY
PROPORTIONAL
PROPORTIONED
PROPOSITIONS
PROROGATIONS
PROSCRIPTION
PROSCRIPTIVE
PROSECUTABLE
PROSECUTIONS
PROSELYTIZED
PROSELYTIZER
PROSOPOPOEIA
PROSPECTUSES
PROSPEROUSLY
PROSTITUTING
PROSTITUTION
PROSTRATIONS
PROTACTINIUM
PROTAGONISTS
PROTECTIVELY
PROTECTORATE
PROTESTATION
PROTESTINGLY
PROTHALAMION
PROTHONOTARY
PROTOHISTORY
PROTOMORPHIC
PROTOPLASMIC
PROTOPLASTIC
PROTOSEMITIC
PROTOTHERIAN
PROTOTROPHIC
PROTOZOOLOGY
PROTRACTEDLY
PROTUBERANCE
PROVERBIALLY
PROVIDENTIAL
PROVINCETOWN
PROVINCIALLY
PROVISIONING
PROVOCATIONS

PRUDENTIALLY
PRUSSIAN BLUE
PSEPHOLOGIST
PSEUDONYMITY
PSEUDONYMOUS
PSEUDOPODIUM
PSYCHIATRIST
PSYCHOACTIVE
PSYCHOBABBLE
PSYCHOGNOSIS
PSYCHOGRAPHY
PSYCHOLOGIES
PSYCHOLOGISM
PSYCHOLOGIST
PSYCHOLOGIZE
PSYCHOMETRIC
PSYCHOPATHIC
PSYCHOSEXUAL
PSYCHOSOCIAL
PSYCHROMETER
PTERIDOPHYTE
PTERIDOSPERM
PTERODACTYLS
PUBLICATIONS
PUBLIC HOUSES
PUBLIC SCHOOL
PUBLIC SECTOR
PUBLIC SPIRIT
PUGNACIOUSLY
PULL A FAST
 ONE
PULVERULENCE
PUMPERNICKEL
PUNCHED CARDS
PUNITIVENESS
PURIFICATION
PURIFICATORY
PURISTICALLY
PURPLE HEARTS
PURPOSE-BUILT
PURPOSEFULLY
PURSE STRINGS
PUSSYFOOTING
PUSSY WILLOWS
PUT INTO WORDS
PUT ONES OAR
 IN
PUTREFACTION
PUTREFACTIVE
PYELOGRAPHIC
PYRIDOXAMINE

PYROCATECHOL
PYROCHEMICAL
PYROELECTRIC
PYROGNOSTICS
PYROLIGNEOUS
PYROMANIACAL
PYROMORPHITE
PYROPHYLLITE
PYROSULPHATE
PYROTECHNICS

Q

QUADRAGESIMA
QUADRANGULAR
QUADRAPHONIC
QUADRILLIONS
QUADRINOMIAL
QUADRIPLEGIA
QUADRIPLEGIC
QUADRIVALENT
QUADRUMANOUS
QUALIFYINGLY
QUANTIFIABLE
QUANTITATIVE
QUANTIZATION
QUANTUM LEAPS
QUAQUAVERSAL
QUARANTINING
QUARTER-BOUND
QUARTERFINAL
QUARTERLIGHT
QUARTER NOTES
QUARTER PLATE
QUARTERSTAFF
QUEEN CONSORT
QUEEN MOTHERS
QUELQUE CHOSE
QUESTIONABLE
QUESTIONABLY
QUESTION MARK
QUESTION TAGS
QUESTION TIME
QUEUE-JUMPERS
QUEUE-JUMPING
QUINDECAPLET
QUINQUENNIAL
QUINQUENNIUM
QUINTESSENCE
QUIXOTICALLY
QUIZZICALITY

R

RABBIT WARREN
RABBLE-ROUSER
RACE MEETINGS
RACEMIZATION
RADICALISTIC
RADIO BEACONS
RADIOBIOLOGY
RADIOCHEMIST
RADIOELEMENT
RADIOGRAPHER
RADIOGRAPHIC
RADIOISOTOPE
RADIOLOGICAL
RADIOLOGISTS
RADIONUCLIDE
RADIOTHERAPY
RAISE THE ROOF
RAISON D'ETRES
RALLENTANDOS
RAMBUNCTIOUS
RAMENTACEOUS
RAMIFICATION
RANGE FINDERS
RANKINE SCALE
RAPHAELESQUE
RAPSCALLIONS
RASTAFARIANS
RATIFICATION
RATIOCINATOR
RATIONALISTS
RATIONALIZED
RATIONALIZER
RATTLESNAKES
RAVENOUSNESS
RAYLEIGH DISC
RAZZLE-DAZZLE
REACH-ME-DOWNS
REACTIVATING
REACTIVATION
REACTIVENESS
READDRESSING
READJUSTABLE
READJUSTMENT
REAFFIRMANCE
REAFFORESTED
REALIGNMENTS
REALIZATIONS
REALLOCATION
REAL PROPERTY
REAPPEARANCE

REAPPRAISALS
REAPPRAISING
REAR ADMIRALS
REASSURANCES
REASSURINGLY
REAUMUR SCALE
REBELLIOUSLY
RECALCITRANT
RECALESCENCE
RECANTATIONS
RECAPITALIZE
RECAPITULATE
RECEIVERSHIP
RECEPTIONIST
RECESSIONALS
RECIDIVISTIC
RECIPROCALLY
RECIPROCATED
RECIPROCATOR
RECKLESSNESS
RECOGNITIONS
RECOGNIZABLE
RECOGNIZABLY
RECOGNIZANCE
RECOLLECTING
RECOLLECTION
RECOLLECTIVE
RECOMMENDING
RECOMMISSION
RECOMMITMENT
RECOMPENSING
RECONCILABLE
RECONCILABLY
RECONNOITRED
RECONNOITRER
RECONSECRATE
RECONSIDERED
RECONSTITUTE
RECONVERSION
RECORD PLAYER
RECREATIONAL
RECRIMINATED
RECRIMINATOR
RECUPERATING
RECUPERATION
RECUPERATIVE
RED BLOOD CELL
REDECORATING
REDEMANDABLE
REDEMPTIONAL
REDEPLOYMENT

REDEVELOPING
REDINTEGRATE
REDISTRIBUTE
RED-LETTER DAY
REDUCIBILITY
REDUNDANCIES
REDUPLICATED
REEFER JACKET
RE-EMPLOYMENT
RE-EXAMINABLE
REFLATIONARY
REFLECTINGLY
REFLECTIONAL
REFLECTIVITY
REFORMATIONS
REFRACTIONAL
REFRACTORILY
REFRESHINGLY
REFRESHMENTS
REFRIGERANTS
REFRIGERATED
REFRIGERATOR
REFURBISHING
REFUTABILITY
REGENERATING
REGENERATION
REGENERATIVE
REGISTRATION
REGULARIZING
REGURGITATED
REHABILITATE
REIMBURSABLE
REIMPOSITION
REIMPRESSION
REINCARNATED
REINVESTMENT
REITERATIONS
REJECTIONIST
REJUVENATING
REJUVENATION
RELATIONSHIP
RELATIVISTIC
RELENTLESSLY
RELINQUISHED
RELINQUISHER
REMAINDERING
REMAINDERMAN
REMEMBRANCER
REMEMBRANCES
REMINISCENCE
REMONSTRANCE

357

REMONSTRATED
REMONSTRATOR
REMORSEFULLY
REMOVABILITY
REMUNERATING
REMUNERATION
REMUNERATIVE
RENAISSANCES
RENEGOTIABLE
RENEWABILITY
RENFREWSHIRE
RENOUNCEMENT
RENUNCIATION
RENUNCIATIVE
REORGANIZING
REPARABILITY
REPATRIATING
REPATRIATION
REPERCUSSION
REPERCUSSIVE
REPLACEMENTS
REPLENISHING
REPLICATIONS
REPOSITORIES
REPOSSESSING
REPOSSESSION
REPREHENDING
REPREHENSION
REPREHENSIVE
REPREHENSORY
REPRESENTING
REPRESSIVELY
REPRIMANDING
REPROACHABLE
REPROACHABLY
REPROCESSING
REPRODUCIBLE
REPRODUCTION
REPRODUCTIVE
REPROGRAPHIC
REPUTABILITY
REQUEST STOPS
REQUIREMENTS
REQUISITIONS
RESCHEDULING
RESEARCHABLE
RESEMBLANCES
RESERVATIONS
RESERVEDNESS
RESETTLEMENT
RESIDENTIARY

RESIDENTSHIP
RESIGNATIONS
RESIGNEDNESS
RESINIFEROUS
RESINOUSNESS
RESOLUBILITY
RESOLUTENESS
RESOLUTIONER
RESOLVEDNESS
RESOUNDINGLY
RESOURCELESS
RESPECTFULLY
RESPECTIVELY
RESPLENDENCE
RESPONSIVELY
RESPONSORIAL
RESTATEMENTS
RESTAURATEUR
RESTLESSNESS
RESTORATIONS
RESTORATIVES
RESTRAINABLE
RESTRAINEDLY
RESTRICTEDLY
RESTRICTIONS
RESTRUCTURED
RESUPINATION
RESURRECTING
RESURRECTION
RESUSCITABLE
RESUSCITATED
RESUSCITATOR
RETICULATION
RETINOSCOPIC
RETRACTILITY
RETRENCHABLE
RETRENCHMENT
RETROCESSION
RETROCESSIVE
RETROFLEXION
RETROGRESSED
RETRO-ROCKETS
RETROVERSION
REUNIONISTIC
REVALUATIONS
REVEGETATION
REVELATIONAL
REVERBERATED
REVERBERATOR
REVERENDSHIP
REVERENTNESS

REVERSIONARY
REVISABILITY
REVISIONISTS
REVITALIZING
REVIVABILITY
REVIVALISTIC
REVOCABILITY
REVOKABILITY
REVULSIONARY
RHAPSODISTIC
RHAPSODIZING
RHESUS FACTOR
RHETORICALLY
RHETORICIANS
RHINOCEROSES
RHINOCEROTIC
RHINOLOGICAL
RHINOPLASTIC
RHIZOCARPOUS
RHODODENDRON
RHOMBOHEDRAL
RHOMBOHEDRON
RHYMING SLANG
RHYTHMICALLY
RHYTHM METHOD
RIBONUCLEASE
RICHTER SCALE
RICOCHETTING
RIDICULOUSLY
RIGHTFULNESS
RIGHT-HANDERS
RIGHT-HAND MAN
RIGHT-HAND MEN
RIGHTS ISSUES
RIGHT-WINGERS
RIGOROUSNESS
RING-STREAKED
RIO DE JANEIRO
ROAD MANAGERS
ROBBEN ISLAND
ROCKING CHAIR
ROCKING HORSE
ROCKUMENTARY
ROLLER BLINDS
ROLLER SKATED
ROLLER SKATER
ROLLER-SKATER
ROLLER SKATES
ROLLER TOWELS
ROLLICKINGLY
ROLLING MILLS

ROLLING STOCK
ROLLING STONE
ROLL OF HONOUR
ROLLTOP DESKS
ROMAN CANDLES
ROMAN NUMERAL
ROMANTICALLY
ROMANTICISTS
ROMANTICIZED
ROOMING HOUSE
ROOTLESSNESS
ROSE-COLOURED
ROSTROPOVICH
ROTARY TILLER
ROUGH DIAMOND
ROUND BRACKET
ROUND THE BEND
ROUTE MARCHES
ROYAL FLUSHES
ROYAL SOCIETY
RUBBER BRIDGE
RUBBER DINGHY
RUBBERNECKED
RUBBER PLANTS
RUBBER STAMPS
RULES OF THUMB
RUMINATINGLY
RUMINATIVELY
RUMMAGE SALES
RUMOURMONGER
RUNNING JUMPS
RUNNING MATES
RUN OF THE
  MILL
RUN-OF-THE-
  MILL
RURALIZATION
RUSTPROOFING
RUTHLESSNESS

S

SABBATARIANS
SACCHARINITY
SACRILEGIOUS
SADISTICALLY
SAFE AS HOUSES
SAFEBREAKERS
SAFEGUARDING
SAFETY ISLAND
SAFETY RAZORS
SAFETY VALVES

SAILING BOATS	SAUDI ARABIAN	SCRUTINIZING	SELF-RELIANCE
SAINT ANDREWS	SAUSAGE ROLLS	SCURRILOUSLY	SELF-REPROACH
SAINT AUSTELL	SAVING GRACES	SCUTELLATION	SELF-STARTERS
SAINT-ETIENNE	SAVINGS BANKS	SEAMSTRESSES	SELKIRKSHIRE
SAINT LAURENT	SAXONY-ANHALT	SEARCH ENGINE	SELLING PLATE
SAINT LEONARD	SAXOPHONISTS	SEARCHLIGHTS	SELLING POINT
SAINT-NAZAIRE	SCALABLENESS	SEASONALNESS	SEMANTICALLY
SAINT-QUENTIN	SCANDALIZING	SEASON TICKET	SEMICIRCULAR
SAINT VINCENT	SCANDALOUSLY	SEATON VALLEY	SEMIDETACHED
SALAMANDRINE	SCANDINAVIAN	SECESSIONISM	SEMIDIAMETER
SALESMANSHIP	SCAREMONGERS	SECESSIONIST	SEMIFINALIST
SALES PITCHES	SCARIFICATOR	SECLUDEDNESS	SEMIFLUIDITY
SALIFICATION	SCARLET FEVER	SECOND COMING	SEMINIFEROUS
SALINOMETRIC	SCARLET WOMAN	SECOND COUSIN	SEMIOTICIANS
SALMON LADDER	SCARLET WOMEN	SECOND-DEGREE	SEMIPALMATED
SALMON TROUTS	SCATOLOGICAL	SECOND NATURE	SEMIPRECIOUS
SALPIGLOSSIS	SCATTERBRAIN	SECOND PERSON	SEMITROPICAL
SALT LAKE CITY	SCENESHIFTER	SECOND-STRING	SEMIVITREOUS
SALUTARINESS	SCENOGRAPHER	SECRET AGENTS	SEMPITERNITY
SALUTATORILY	SCENOGRAPHIC	SECRETARIATS	SENARMONTITE
SALVATIONISM	SCHAFFHAUSEN	SECRETIONARY	SENSIBLENESS
SALVATIONIST	SCHEMATIZING	SECRET POLICE	SENSITOMETER
SAMARITANISM	SCHIZOMYCETE	SECTARIANISM	SENSITOMETRY
SAMOA ISLANDS	SCHIZOPHYTIC	SECTIONALISM	SENSORIMOTOR
SANCTIFIABLE	SCHIZOTHYMIA	SECTIONALIST	SENSUOUSNESS
SANCTIONABLE	SCHIZOTHYMIC	SECTIONALIZE	SEPARABILITY
SANDBLASTING	SCHOLARSHIPS	SECULARISTIC	SEPARATENESS
SAND BLASTING	SCHOLASTICAL	SECULARIZING	SEPARATISTIC
SANDPAPERING	SCHOOLFELLOW	SECURITY RISK	SEPTILATERAL
SAN FRANCISCO	SCHOOLHOUSES	SEDULOUSNESS	SEPTILLIONTH
SANGUINARILY	SCHOOL-LEAVER	SEGMENTATION	SEPTUAGESIMA
SANGUINENESS	SCHOOLMASTER	SEINE-ET-MARNE	SEPTUPLICATE
SANGUINOLENT	SCHORLACEOUS	SEISMOGRAPHS	SEQUENTIALLY
SANITARINESS	SCIENCE PARKS	SEISMOGRAPHY	SEQUESTRABLE
SAN PEDRO SULA	SCINTILLATED	SEISMOLOGIST	SEQUESTRATED
SAN SEBASTIAN	SCINTILLATOR	SEISMOSCOPIC	SEQUESTRATOR
SANTALACEOUS	SCLERENCHYMA	SELENOGRAPHY	SERIAL NUMBER
SANTO DOMINGO	SCLEROMETRIC	SELENOLOGIST	SERICULTURAL
SAONE-ET-LOIRE	SCOLOPENDRID	SELF-ABSORBED	SERINGAPATAM
SAPINDACEOUS	SCORNFULNESS	SELF-ANALYSIS	SERONEGATIVE
SAPONIFIABLE	SCOTCH TAPING	SELF-ASSEMBLY	SEROPOSITIVE
SAPROPHAGOUS	SCOTCH WHISKY	SELF-CATERING	SERVICEBERRY
SARCOMATOSIS	SCOTLAND YARD	SELF-COLOURED	SERVICE FLATS
SARDONICALLY	SCOUTMASTERS	SELF-DESTRUCT	SERVICE ROADS
SARSAPARILLA	SCRATCHINESS	SELF-EDUCATED	SESQUIALTERA
SASKATCHEWAN	SCRATCH PAPER	SELF-EFFACING	SET BY THE
SATIRIZATION	SCREWDRIVERS	SELF-EMPLOYED	EARS
SATISFACTION	SCRIMSHANDER	SELF-INTEREST	SEVENTEENTHS
SATISFACTORY	SCRIPTWRITER	SELFLESSNESS	SEVENTY-EIGHT
SATISFYINGLY	SCROBICULATE	SELF PORTRAIT	SEVERANCE PAY
SATURABILITY	SCRUPULOUSLY	SELF-PORTRAIT	SEXAGENARIAN

SEXCENTENARY	SHREWISHNESS	SKITTISHNESS	SODA FOUNTAIN
SEXTILLIONTH	SHUDDERINGLY	SKYROCKETING	SOFT LANDINGS
SEXTUPLICATE	SHUFFLEBOARD	SLANDEROUSLY	SOFT-PEDALING
SHADOW-BOXING	SHUTTLECOCKS	SLAUGHTERING	SOFT-PEDALLED
SHAHJAHANPUR	SIAMESE TWINS	SLAUGHTEROUS	SOLARIZATION
SHAMATEURISM	SICK HEADACHE	SLAVE DRIVERS	SOLAR SYSTEMS
SHAMEFACEDLY	SIDEROSTATIC	SLAVONICALLY	SOLICITATION
SHAMEFULNESS	SIDESLIPPING	SLEDGEHAMMER	SOLICITOUSLY
SHARECROPPER	SIDESTEPPING	SLEEPING BAGS	SOLIDIFIABLE
SHAREHOLDERS	SIDETRACKING	SLEEPING CARS	SOLIFLUCTION
SHARPSHOOTER	SIDE-WHEELERS	SLEEPING PILL	SOLILOQUIZED
SHARP-SIGHTED	SIDE WHISKERS	SLEEPWALKERS	SOLITARINESS
SHARP-TONGUED	SIDI-BEL-ABBES	SLEEPWALKING	SOLITUDINOUS
SHATTERINGLY	SIERRA NEVADA	SLENDERIZING	SOLVENT ABUSE
SHATTERPROOF	SIGHT-READERS	SLIDING DOORS	SOMATOLOGIST
SHAVING CREAM	SIGHT-READING	SLIDING SCALE	SOMATOPLEURE
SHEATH KNIVES	SIGNIFICANCE	SLIPPERINESS	SOMERSAULTED
SHEEPISHNESS	SIGN LANGUAGE	SLIPPINGNESS	SOMNAMBULANT
SHEEPSHEARER	SILHOUETTING	SLIPSTREAMED	SOMNAMBULATE
SHEET ANCHORS	SILICIFEROUS	SLOANE RANGER	SOMNAMBULISM
SHELLACKINGS	SILICON CHIPS	SLOTHFULNESS	SOMNAMBULIST
SHELLSHOCKED	SILIQUACEOUS	SLOT MACHINES	SON ET LUMIERE
SHEPHERD'S PIE	SILVERFISHES	SLOVENLINESS	SONG AND DANCE
SHETLAND PONY	SILVER LINING	SLUGGARDNESS	SONOROUSNESS
SHIFTINGNESS	SILVER MEDALS	SLUGGISHNESS	SOOTHINGNESS
SHIJIAZHUANG	SILVERSMITHS	SLUMBERINGLY	SOPHISTICATE
SHILLY-SHALLY	SILVICULTURE	SLUTTISHNESS	SOPORIFEROUS
SHIMMERINGLY	SIMILARITIES	SMALL FORTUNE	SOUL BROTHERS
SHIPBUILDERS	SIMPLE-MINDED	SMALLHOLDERS	SOULLESSNESS
SHIPBUILDING	SIMULTANEITY	SMALLHOLDING	SOUND BARRIER
SHIPWRECKING	SIMULTANEOUS	SMASH-AND-GRAB	SOUND EFFECTS
SHIRTSLEEVES	SINANTHROPUS	SMILACACEOUS	SOUNDPROOFED
SHIRTWAISTER	SINGLE-ACTING	SMOKESCREENS	SOUP KITCHENS
SHOCKABILITY	SINGLE-ACTION	SMOOTH-SPOKEN	SOUSAPHONIST
SHOCKINGNESS	SINGLE-DECKER	SMORGASBORDS	SOUTH AMERICA
SHOCKING PINK	SINGLE-HANDED	SNAGGLETOOTH	SOUTHEASTERN
SHOOTING STAR	SINGLE-MINDED	SNAKE CHARMER	SOUTHERNMOST
SHOP STEWARDS	SINGULARNESS	SNAP FASTENER	SOUTHERNWOOD
SHORT-CHANGED	SINISTERNESS	SNAPPISHNESS	SOUTH HOLLAND
SHORT-CHANGER	SINISTRORSAL	SNEAKINGNESS	SOUTH OSSETIA
SHORT CIRCUIT	SINKING FUNDS	SNEAK PREVIEW	SOUTH SHIELDS
SHORTCOMINGS	SIPHONOPHORE	SNEAK THIEVES	SOUTHWESTERN
SHORT-LISTING	SIPHONOSTELE	SNICKERINGLY	SPACE CAPSULE
SHORTSIGHTED	SISTERLINESS	SNIGGERINGLY	SPACE HEATERS
SHORT STORIES	SISTERS-IN-LAW	SNOBBISHNESS	SPACE SHUTTLE
SHORT-WAISTED	SITTING DUCKS	SNOOPERSCOPE	SPACE STATION
SHOT IN THE	SITTING ROOMS	SOCIALIZABLE	SPACIOUSNESS
ARM	SITUATIONISM	SOCIAL WORKER	SPEAKING TUBE
SHOW BUSINESS	SKELETON KEYS	SOCIOLOGICAL	SPEARHEADING
SHOWSTOPPERS	SKELMERSDALE	SOCIOLOGISTS	SPECIALISTIC
SHOWSTOPPING	SKIPPING-ROPE	SOCIOMETRIST	SPECIALITIES

SPECIALIZING	SPORTFULNESS	STATION HOUSE	STOCKBREEDER
SPECIFICALLY	SPORTIVENESS	STATION WAGON	STOCKBROKERS
SPECIOUSNESS	SPORTSPERSON	STATISTICIAN	STOCKHOLDERS
SPECTACULARS	SPOT-CHECKING	STAYING POWER	STOCK-IN-TRADE
SPECTROGRAPH	SPOTLESSNESS	STEAK TARTARE	STOCKJOBBERS
SPECTROMETER	SPOTLIGHTING	STEAL THE SHOW	STOCKJOBBERY
SPECTROMETRY	SPOTTED DICKS	STEALTHINESS	STOCK MARKETS
SPECTROSCOPE	SPREAD-EAGLED	STEAMROLLERS	STOICHIOLOGY
SPECTROSCOPY	SPREADSHEETS	STEAM SHOVELS	STOKE-ON-TRENT
SPECULATIONS	SPRINGBOARDS	STEATOPYGOUS	STOMACHACHES
SPEECHIFYING	SPRING ONIONS	STEATORRHOEA	STOMACH PUMPS
SPEECHLESSLY	SPURIOUSNESS	STEEPLECHASE	STONECUTTING
SPEEDOMETERS	SQUAMOUSNESS	STEEPLEJACKS	STONEMASONRY
SPEEDWRITING	SQUARE DANCES	STELLIFEROUS	STONEWALLERS
SPELEOLOGIST	SQUARE-RIGGED	STENOGRAPHER	STONEWALLING
SPELLBINDERS	SQUARE-RIGGER	STENOGRAPHIC	STONY-HEARTED
SPELLBINDING	SQUEAKY-CLEAN	STENOTHERMAL	STOOLPIGEONS
SPELLCHECKER	SQUEEZEBOXES	STEPBROTHERS	STOREKEEPERS
SPENDTHRIFTS	SQUELCHINGLY	STEPCHILDREN	STOREKEEPING
SPERMATHECAL	SQUIRRELFISH	STEPDAUGHTER	STORM TROOPER
SPERMATOCYTE	STADDLESTONE	STEREOCHROME	STORMY PETREL
SPERMATOZOAL	STAFF OFFICER	STEREOCHROMY	STORYTELLERS
SPERMATOZOID	STAGECOACHES	STEREOGRAPHY	STORYTELLING
SPERMATOZOON	STAGE-MANAGED	STEREOISOMER	STOUTHEARTED
SPERMOGONIUM	STAGE MANAGER	STEREOMETRIC	STOVEPIPE HAT
SPHRAGISTICS	STAGE WHISPER	STEREOPHONIC	STRADIVARIUS
SPHYGMOGRAPH	STAGGERINGLY	STEREOPTICON	STRAGGLINGLY
SPICK AND SPAN	STAGING POSTS	STEREOSCOPIC	STRAIGHTAWAY
SPICK-AND-SPAN	STAINABILITY	STEREOTACTIC	STRAIGHTEDGE
SPIEGELEISEN	STAINED GLASS	STEREOTROPIC	STRAIGHTENED
SPINSTERHOOD	STAKEHOLDERS	STEREOTYPING	STRAIGHTENER
SPIRITEDNESS	STALACTIFORM	STEREOVISION	STRAIGHTNESS
SPIRIT LEVELS	STALLHOLDERS	STERILIZABLE	STRAINEDNESS
SPIRITUALISM	STALWARTNESS	STERNUTATION	STRAITJACKET
SPIRITUALIST	STAMMERINGLY	STERNUTATIVE	STRANGLEHOLD
SPIRITUALITY	STANDARDIZED	STERNUTATORY	STRANGULATED
SPIRITUALIZE	STANDARDIZER	STERNWHEELER	STRAPHANGERS
SPIRITUOSITY	STANDARD LAMP	STERTOROUSLY	STRAPHANGING
SPIROGRAPHIC	STANDARD TIME	STETHOSCOPES	STRATICULATE
SPITEFULNESS	STANDING ROOM	STETHOSCOPIC	STRATIGRAPHY
SPLASH GUARDS	STANDOFF HALF	STICHOMETRIC	STRATOCRATIC
SPLATTERPUNK	STAND-OFF HALF	STICK INSECTS	STRATOSPHERE
SPLENDIDNESS	STANLEY KNIFE	STICKLEBACKS	STRAWBERRIES
SPLENOMEGALY	STANNIFEROUS	STICKY WICKET	STREAMLINING
SPLIT SECONDS	STAR CHAMBERS	STIGMASTEROL	STREETS AHEAD
SPOKESPEOPLE	STAR-SPANGLED	STIGMATIZING	STREET VALUES
SPOKESPERSON	STARTING GATE	STILBOESTROL	STREETWALKER
SPONGIOBLAST	STATELY HOMES	STILETTO HEEL	STRENGTHENED
SPOON-FEEDING	STATEN ISLAND	STINKINGNESS	STRENGTHENER
SPORADICALLY	STATIONARILY	STIPULATIONS	STREPTOCOCCI
SPOROGENESIS	STATION BREAK	STIRRUP PUMPS	STREPTOMYCIN

STRETCHINESS
STRETCHMARKS
STRIDULATING
STRIDULATION
STRIDULATORY
STRIKINGNESS
STRIP CARTOON
STRIP MININGS
STROBE LIGHTS
STROBILATION
STROBOSCOPES
STROBOSCOPIC
STROMATOLITE
STRONG-MINDED
STRONG POINTS
STRONG-WILLED
STRONTIANITE
STROPHANTHIN
STROPHANTHUS
STRUCTURALLY
STRUGGLINGLY
STRYCHNINISM
STUBBORNNESS
STUDDINGSAIL
STUDIOUSNESS
STUFFED SHIRT
STUPEFACIENT
STUPEFACTION
STUPEFYINGLY
STUPENDOUSLY
STUTTERINGLY
STYLOGRAPHIC
STYRACACEOUS
SUBALTERNATE
SUBANTARCTIC
SUBAURICULAR
SUBCELESTIAL
SUBCLIMACTIC
SUBCOMMITTEE
SUBCONSCIOUS
SUBCONTINENT
SUBCUTANEOUS
SUBDEACONATE
SUBDIACONATE
SUBDIVISIONS
SUBERIZATION
SUBINFEUDATE
SUBJECTIVELY
SUBJECTIVISM
SUBJECTIVIST
SUBJECTIVITY

SUBJUNCTIVES
SUBMAXILLARY
SUBMERSIBLES
SUBMISSIVELY
SUBMITTINGLY
SUBNORMALITY
SUBORDINATED
SUBORDINATES
SUBPRINCIPAL
SUBSCRIPTION
SUBSCRIPTIVE
SUBSEQUENTLY
SUBSERVIENCE
SUBSIDIARIES
SUBSIDIARILY
SUBSIDIARITY
SUBSIDIZABLE
SUBSISTINGLY
SUBSTANTIATE
SUBSTANTIVAL
SUBSTANTIVES
SUBSTITUTING
SUBSTITUTION
SUBSTITUTIVE
SUBSTRUCTURE
SUBTEMPERATE
SUBTERRANEAN
SUBTRACTIONS
SUBURBANITES
SUBVERSIVELY
SUCCEDANEOUS
SUCCEEDINGLY
SUCCESSFULLY
SUCCESSIONAL
SUCCESSIVELY
SUCCINCTNESS
SUCTION PUMPS
SUDORIFEROUS
SUFFRAGETTES
SUFFRUTICOSE
SUGAR DADDIES
SUGGESTINGLY
SUGGESTIVELY
SUITABLENESS
SULPHONAMIDE
SULPHURATION
SUMMARIZABLE
SUMMERHOUSES
SUMMER SCHOOL
SUNDAY SCHOOL
SUPERABILITY

SUPERANNUATE
SUPERCHARGED
SUPERCHARGER
SUPERCILIARY
SUPERCILIOUS
SUPEREMINENT
SUPERFICIARY
SUPERGLACIAL
SUPERGRASSES
SUPERIMPOSED
SUPERLATIVES
SUPERMARKETS
SUPERNATURAL
SUPERPOSABLE
SUPERSEDABLE
SUPERSESSION
SUPERSTITION
SUPERSTRATUM
SUPERTANKERS
SUPERVENIENT
SUPPLEMENTAL
SUPPLEMENTED
SUPPLEMENTER
SUPPLETORILY
SUPPLICATING
SUPPLICATION
SUPPLICATORY
SUPPOSITIONS
SUPPOSITIOUS
SUPPRESSIBLE
SUPRAGLOTTAL
SUPRALIMINAL
SUPRAORBITAL
SUPRAPROTEST
SUPREMACISTS
SUPREME BEING
SUPREME COURT
SUREFOOTEDLY
SURFACE-TO-AIR
SURMOUNTABLE
SURPASSINGLY
SURPRISINGLY
SURREALISTIC
SURREJOINDER
SURRENDERING
SURROUNDEDLY
SURROUNDINGS
SURVEILLANCE
SURVEYORSHIP
SURVIVAL KITS
SUSCEPTIVITY

SUSPICIOUSLY
SUSTAININGLY
SWAGGERINGLY
SWALLOW DIVES
SWASHBUCKLER
SWEEPINGNESS
SWEET-AND-SOUR
SWEET PEPPERS
SWEET POTATOS
SWEET-TALKING
SWELTERINGLY
SWIMMING BATH
SWIMMING POOL
SWING THE LEAD
SWITCHBLADES
SWITCHBOARDS
SWIZZLE STICK
SWORD DANCERS
SYLLABICALLY
SYMBOLICALLY
SYMBOLOGICAL
SYMMETALLISM
SYMPATHIZERS
SYMPATHIZING
SYNAESTHESIA
SYNAESTHETIC
SYNAPTICALLY
SYNARTHROSIS
SYNCHROFLASH
SYNCHRONIZED
SYNCHRONIZER
SYNCHROSCOPE
SYNCLINORIUM
SYNDACTYLISM
SYNDETICALLY
SYNDICALISTS
SYNDIOTACTIC
SYNODIC MONTH
SYNONYMOUSLY
SYNOPTICALLY
SYNTHESIZERS
SYNTHESIZING
SYNTONICALLY
SYSTEMATIZED
SYSTEMATIZER
SYSTEMICALLY

T
TABERNACULAR
TABLE MANNERS
TABLE-TURNING

TACHEOMETRIC	TERATOLOGIST	THERMOSTABLE	TONSILLOTOMY
TACHYCARDIAC	TERCENTENARY	THERMOSTATIC	TOOTHBRUSHES
TACTLESSNESS	TEREBINTHINE	THERMOTROPIC	TOPDRESSINGS
TADZHIKISTAN	TERGIVERSATE	THEURGICALLY	TOP-HEAVINESS
TALCUM POWDER	TERMINATIONS	THICK-SKINNED	TOPOGRAPHERS
TALENT SCOUTS	TERRIBLENESS	THIEVISHNESS	TORMENTINGLY
TALKING POINT	TERRIFICALLY	THIGMOTACTIC	TORREFACTION
TAMBOURINIST	TERRIFYINGLY	THIGMOTROPIC	TORTUOUSNESS
TANGENTIALLY	TERRITORIALS	THINGAMAJIGS	TOTALITARIAN
TAPE MEASURES	TESSELLATION	THIOSINAMINE	TOTALIZATORS
TAPE RECORDER	TESTAMENTARY	THIOSULPHATE	TOURIST CLASS
TAPE STREAMER	TESTIMONIALS	THIRD PARTIES	TOUT ENSEMBLE
TARAMASALATA	TESTOSTERONE	THOROUGHBRED	TOWER HAMLETS
TARDENOISIAN	TEST-TUBE BABY	THOROUGHFARE	TOWER OF BABEL
TARTARIC ACID	TETANIZATION	THOROUGHNESS	TOWN PLANNERS
TASTEFULNESS	TETRACHORDAL	THOUGHTFULLY	TOWN PLANNING
TAUROMACHIAN	TETRACYCLINE	THREE QUARTER	TOXICOLOGIST
TAUTOLOGICAL	TETRAHEDRITE	THREE-QUARTER	TOXOPHILITIC
TAX COLLECTOR	TETRAPTEROUS	THREE-WHEELER	TRACEABILITY
TAXIDERMISTS	TETRASTICHIC	THROMBOCYTIC	TRACE ELEMENT
TECHNICALITY	TETRAVALENCY	THUNDERBOLTS	TRACHEOPHYTE
TECHNOBABBLE	TEUTONICALLY	THUNDERCLAPS	TRACHEOSTOMY
TECHNOGRAPHY	THALAMICALLY	THUNDERCLOUD	TRACHOMATOUS
TECHNOLOGIES	THALASSAEMIA	THUNDERFLASH	TRACING PAPER
TECHNOLOGIST	THALLOPHYTIC	THUNDERINGLY	TRACK RECORDS
TECTONICALLY	THANKFULNESS	THUNDEROUSLY	TRACTABILITY
TEENYBOPPERS	THANKSGIVING	THUNDERSTONE	TRACUCIANIST
TEETER-TOTTER	THAUMATOLOGY	THUNDERSTORM	TRADESCANTIA
TEETOTALLERS	THEANTHROPIC	THUNDER STORM	TRADESPEOPLE
TELAESTHESIA	THEATREGOERS	TICKLISHNESS	TRADING POSTS
TELAESTHETIC	THEATRICALLY	TIED COTTAGES	TRADING STAMP
TELAUTOGRAPH	THE HERMITAGE	TIME CAPSULES	TRADITIONIST
TELEGRAPHERS	THEISTICALLY	TIME EXPOSURE	TRADUCIANISM
TELEGRAPHESE	THEMATICALLY	TIME HONOURED	TRAFFICATORS
TELEGRAPHING	THEOCENTRISM	TIME-HONOURED	TRAFFIC LIGHT
TELEMEDICINE	THEOPHYLLINE	TIMELESSNESS	TRAGEDIENNES
TELEOLOGICAL	THEORETICIAN	TIME SWITCHES	TRAILBLAZING
TELEOLOGISTS	THEORIZATION	TIMOROUSNESS	TRAILER HOUSE
TELEPHONE BOX	THERAPEUTICS	TIRELESSNESS	TRAINBEARERS
TELEPHONISTS	THE REAL THING	TIRESOMENESS	TRAIN SPOTTER
TELEPRINTERS	THEREINAFTER	TITANIFEROUS	TRAINSPOTTER
TELEPROMPTER	THERMOCOUPLE	TITLEHOLDERS	TRAITOROUSLY
TELESHOPPING	THERMOGENOUS	TITTLE-TATTLE	TRAJECTORIES
TELEUTOSPORE	THERMOGRAPHY	TOASTING FORK	TRAMPISHNESS
TELEVISIONAL	THERMOLABILE	TOASTMASTERS	TRANQUILLITY
TELGENICALLY	THERMOMETERS	TOBACCONISTS	TRANQUILLIZE
TELLUROMETER	THERMOMETRIC	TOFFEE APPLES	TRANSACTIONS
TEMPERAMENTS	THERMOSCOPIC	TOGETHERNESS	TRANSCENDENT
TEMPERATURES	THERMOS FLASK	TOMFOOLERIES	TRANSCENDING
TENANT FARMER	THERMOSIPHON	TONE LANGUAGE	TRANSCRIBING
TEN-GALLON HAT	THERMOSPHERE	TONELESSNESS	TRANSCURRENT

TRANSDUCTION	TREMENDOUSLY	TUNNEL VISION	UNCINARIASIS
TRANSFERABLE	TRENDSETTERS	TURBELLARIAN	UNCLASSIFIED
TRANSFERENCE	TRENDSETTING	TURBIDIMETER	UNCOMMERCIAL
TRANSFERRING	TREPHINATION	TURBOCHARGED	UNCOMMONNESS
TRANSFIGURED	TRIBESPEOPLE	TURBOCHARGER	UNCONFORMITY
TRANSFORMERS	TRIBULATIONS	TURKISH BATHS	UNCONSENTING
TRANSFORMING	TRICHINIASIS	TURKMENISTAN	UNCONSIDERED
TRANSFORMISM	TRICHOCYSTIC	TURNING POINT	UNCONVINCING
TRANSFORMIST	TRICHOGYNIAL	TUVA REPUBLIC	UNCOVENANTED
TRANSFUSIBLE	TRICHOLOGIST	TU-WHIT TU-	UNCRITICALLY
TRANSFUSIONS	TRICHOPTERAN	WHOO	UNCTUOUSNESS
TRANSGRESSED	TRICHROMATIC	TWILIGHT ZONE	UNDECEIVABLE
TRANSGRESSOR	TRICK OR TREAT	TWISTABILITY	UNDEMOCRATIC
TRANSHUMANCE	TRIFURCATION	TWO-FACEDNESS	UNDERACHIEVE
TRANSITIONAL	TRIGGER HAPPY	TWO-WAY MIRROR	UNDERBELLIES
TRANSITORILY	TRIGGER-HAPPY	TYPIFICATION	UNDERCHARGED
TRANSLATABLE	TRIGLYCERIDE	TYPOGRAPHERS	UNDERCLOTHES
TRANSLATIONS	TRIGONOMETRY	TYRANNICALLY	UNDERCURRENT
TRANSLUCENCE	TRILINGUALLY	TYRANNICIDAL	UNDERCUTTING
TRANSLUCENCY	TRIMOLECULAR		UNDERDEVELOP
TRANSMIGRANT	TRIPARTITION	**U**	UNDERDRAWING
TRANSMIGRATE	TRIPHTHONGAL	UBIQUITOUSLY	UNDERDRESSED
TRANSMISSION	TRIPLE-TONGUE	UGLIFICATION	UNDEREXPOSED
TRANSMISSIVE	TRIPLICATION	UGLY CUSTOMER	UNDERGARMENT
TRANSMITTERS	TRIPOLITANIA	UGLY DUCKLING	UNDERGROUNDS
TRANSMITTING	TRIUMPHANTLY	ULTRAMONTANE	UNDERNOURISH
TRANSMOGRIFY	TRIUMVIRATES	ULTRAMUNDANE	UNDERPAYMENT
TRANSMUNDANE	TRIVIALITIES	UMBILICATION	UNDERPINNING
TRANSMUTABLE	TRIVIALIZING	UNACCEPTABLE	UNDERPLAYING
TRANSOCEANIC	TROCHAICALLY	UNACCUSTOMED	UNDERSCORING
TRANSPARENCY	TROCHOIDALLY	UNACQUAINTED	UNDERSELLING
TRANSPIRABLE	TROJAN HORSES	UNAFFECTEDLY	UNDERSHERIFF
TRANSPLANTED	TROLLEYBUSES	UNAFFORDABLE	UNDERSTAFFED
TRANSPLANTER	TROMBIDIASIS	UNAGGRESSIVE	UNDERSTATING
TRANSPONDERS	TROOP CARRIER	UNANSWERABLE	UNDERSTUDIED
TRANSPORTERS	TROPHALLAXIS	UNAPOLOGETIC	UNDERSTUDIES
TRANSPORTING	TROPOPHILOUS	UNAPPEALABLE	UNDERSURFACE
TRANSPORTIVE	TROUBLEMAKER	UNASSAILABLE	UNDERTAKINGS
TRANSPOSABLE	TROUBLE SPOTS	UNASSOCIATED	UNDERTRAINED
TRANSUDATORY	TROUSER PRESS	UNASSUMINGLY	UNDERUTILIZE
TRANSVAALIAN	TRUSTABILITY	UNATTAINABLE	UNDERVALUING
TRANSVERSELY	TRUSTEESHIPS	UNATTRACTIVE	UNDERWRITERS
TRANSVESTISM	TRUSTFULNESS	UNATTRIBUTED	UNDERWRITING
TRANSVESTITE	TRUTHFULNESS	UNBELIEVABLE	UNDERWRITTEN
TRANSYLVANIA	TRYPANOSOMAL	UNBELIEVABLY	UNDESIRABLES
TRAPSHOOTING	TRYPARSAMIDE	UNBIASEDNESS	UNDETERMINED
TRAUMATIZING	TUBERCULOSIS	UNCELEBRATED	UNDISCHARGED
TRAVEL AGENCY	TUMBLE-DRYERS	UNCHALLENGED	UNECONOMICAL
TRAVEL AGENTS	TUMBLE-DRYING	UNCHARITABLE	UNEMPLOYABLE
TREBLE CHANCE	TUMULTUOUSLY	UNCHARITABLY	UNEMPLOYMENT
TREELESSNESS	TUNELESSNESS	UNCHASTENESS	UNEVENTFULLY

UNEXPRESSIVE
UNEXPURGATED
UNFAITHFULLY
UNFATHOMABLE
UNFATHOMABLY
UNFAVOURABLE
UNFAVOURABLY
UNFLAGGINGLY
UNFLATTERING
UNFORGIVABLE
UNFORTUNATES
UNFREQUENTED
UNGAINLINESS
UNGOVERNABLE
UNGRATEFULLY
UNHESITATING
UNHYPHENATED
UNIDENTIFIED
UNIFOLIOLATE
UNILATERALLY
UNIMAGINABLE
UNIMPRESSIVE
UNINFLUENCED
UNINTERESTED
UNIONIZATION
UNISEXUALITY
UNITARIANISM
UNIVERSALISM
UNIVERSALIST
UNIVERSALITY
UNIVERSALIZE
UNIVERSITIES
UNKINDLINESS
UNLAWFULNESS
UNLIKELIHOOD
UNLIKELINESS
UNMANAGEABLE
UNMEASURABLE
UNMISTAKABLE
UNMISTAKABLY
UNMODERNIZED
UNOFFICIALLY
UNPARALLELED
UNPERFORATED
UNPLEASANTLY
UNPOPULARITY
UNPREJUDICED
UNPRINCIPLED
UNPRODUCTIVE
UNPROFITABLE
UNPUBLICIZED

UNQUESTIONED
UNREASONABLE
UNREASONABLY
UNRECKONABLE
UNRECOGNIZED
UNREFLECTIVE
UNREGENERACY
UNREGENERATE
UNRESERVEDLY
UNRESPONSIVE
UNRESTRAINED
UNRESTRICTED
UNSANCTIONED
UNSATURATION
UNSCIENTIFIC
UNSCRAMBLING
UNSCRUPULOUS
UNSEARCHABLE
UNSEASONABLE
UNSEASONABLY
UNSEEMLINESS
UNSEGREGATED
UNSETTLEMENT
UNSTEADINESS
UNSTRATIFIED
UNSTRUCTURED
UNSUCCESSFUL
UNSUPPORTIVE
UNSUSPECTING
UNTENABILITY
UNTHINKINGLY
UNTIMELINESS
UNTOUCHABLES
UNTOWARDNESS
UNTRAMMELLED
UNWIELDINESS
UNWORTHINESS
UNWRITTEN LAW
UPHOLSTERERS
UPHOLSTERING
UPPER AUSTRIA
UPRIGHT PIANO
UPROARIOUSLY
UP-TO-DATENESS
URANOGRAPHER
URANOGRAPHIC
URBANIZATION
URETHROSCOPE
URETHROSCOPY
URINOGENITAL
USER FRIENDLY

USER-FRIENDLY
USUFRUCTUARY
USURIOUSNESS
UTILITY ROOMS
UTTAR PRADESH
UXORIOUSNESS

V

VACCINATIONS
VACILLATIONS
VACUUM FLASKS
VACUUM-PACKED
VAINGLORIOUS
VALEDICTIONS
VALENCIENNES
VALORIZATION
VALUABLENESS
VANQUISHABLE
VANQUISHMENT
VANTAGEPOINT
VANTAGE POINT
VAPORESCENCE
VAPORIZATION
VAPOROUSNESS
VAPOUR TRAILS
VARICOLOURED
VASODILATION
VAUDEVILLIAN
VAUDEVILLIST
VEGETATIONAL
VELARIZATION
VELOCIRAPTOR
VENERABILITY
VENERATIONAL
VENGEFULNESS
VENIPUNCTURE
VENTRICOSITY
VERBENACEOUS
VERIDICALITY
VERIFICATION
VERIFICATIVE
VERTEBRATION
VERTICILLATE
VESICULATION
VESTAL VIRGIN
VIBRAPHONIST
VICE-CHAIRMAN
VICISSITUDES
VICTORIANISM
VICTORIA PLUM
VICTORIOUSLY

VIDEO NASTIES
VIGOROUSNESS
VILIFICATION
VILLAGE GREEN
VILLAHERMOSA
VILLEURBANNE
VINDICTIVELY
VINICULTURAL
VIN ORDINAIRE
VIOLONCELLOS
VIRGIN'S-BOWER
VIRIDESCENCE
VIRTUOUSNESS
VISCEROMOTOR
VISCOUNTCIES
VISITATIONAL
VISITATORIAL
VISITING CARD
VISITORS' BOOK
VITALIZATION
VITICULTURAL
VITICULTURER
VITREOUSNESS
VITUPERATION
VITUPERATIVE
VIVIFICATION
VIVISECTIONS
VIXENISHNESS
VOCABULARIES
VOCALIZATION
VOCIFERATING
VOCIFERATION
VOCIFEROUSLY
VOIDABLENESS
VOLCANICALLY
VOLTA REDONDA
VOLUMINOSITY
VOLUMINOUSLY
VOLUNTARYISM
VOLUNTARYIST
VOLUNTEERING
VOLUNTEERISM
VOLUPTUARIES
VOLUPTUOUSLY
VOMITURITION
VOTE OF THANKS
VOWELIZATION
VULCANIZABLE

W
WAGES COUNCIL

WAITING LISTS	WELL-ASSORTED	WHITE WEDDING	WORKING CLASS
WAITING ROOMS	WELL-ATTENDED	WHOLE-HEARTED	WORKING ORDER
WALKIE-TALKIE	WELL BALANCED	WHOLE NUMBERS	WORKING PARTY
WALKING STICK	WELL-BALANCED	WHORTLEBERRY	WORKING WEEKS
WALLCOVERING	WELL-DESERVED	WICKET KEEPER	WORKINGWOMAN
WALL PAINTING	WELL DISPOSED	WIDE RECEIVER	WORKSTATIONS
WALLPAPERING	WELL-DISPOSED	WIFE SWAPPING	WORLD-BEATERS
WANKEL ENGINE	WELL-EDUCATED	WIGTOWNSHIRE	WORLD-BEATING
WAREHOUSEMAN	WELL-EQUIPPED	WILDERNESSES	WORLDSHAKING
WARMONGERING	WELL-FAVOURED	WILLIAMSBURG	WORLD WIDE WEB
WARS OF NERVES	WELL-GROUNDED	WILL-O'-THE-	WORMS EYE VIEW
WARWICKSHIRE	WELL-INFORMED	WISP	WRATHFULNESS
WASH DRAWINGS	WELL-MANNERED	WINDCHEATERS	WRETCHEDNESS
WASTEFULNESS	WELL-PROVIDED	WINDING SHEET	WRISTWATCHES
WASTE PRODUCT	WELL-RECEIVED	WINDOW SHADES	WRITER'S CRAMP
WATCHFULNESS	WELL-SITUATED	WIND TURBINES	WRITING DESKS
WATER BISCUIT	WELL-TEMPERED	WINEGLASSFUL	WRITING PAPER
WATER BUFFALO	WELSH RAREBIT	WINGLESSNESS	WRONGFULNESS
WATER CANNONS	WELTERWEIGHT	WINSTON-SALEM	
WATER CLOSETS	WENSLEYDALES	WINTERBOURNE	**X**
WATERCOLOURS	WEST BROMWICH	WINTER SPORTS	
WATERCOURSES	WESTERLINESS	WISCONSINITE	X CHROMOSOMES
WATERING CANS	WESTERN ISLES	WISECRACKING	XERODERMATIC
WATERING HOLE	WESTERNIZING	WITCHDOCTORS	XIPHISTERNUM
WATERMANSHIP	WESTERN SAMOA	WITCH-HUNTING	
WATER MEADOWS	WEST FLANDERS	WITCHING HOUR	**Y**
WATERPROOFED	WEST MIDLANDS	WITHDRAWABLE	
WATTENSCHEID	WEST VIRGINIA	WITHEREDNESS	Y CHROMOSOMES
WAYS AND MEANS	WETTING AGENT	WITH OPEN ARMS	YELLOWHAMMER
WEATHERBOARD	WHEELBARROWS	WITH PLEASURE	YIELDINGNESS
WEATHER-BOUND	WHEELWRIGHTS	WITHSTANDING	YINDJIBARNDI
WEATHERCOCKS	WHENCESOEVER	WITNESS BOXES	YOUTHFULNESS
WEATHERGLASS	WHEREWITHALS	WOLF WHISTLES	YOUTH HOSTELS
WEATHERPROOF	WHIGGISHNESS	WOLLASTONITE	
WEATHER SHIPS	WHIMPERINGLY	WOMANISHNESS	**Z**
WEATHER VANES	WHIMSICALITY	WONDER-WORKER	
WEDDING RINGS	WHIPPING BOYS	WONDROUSNESS	ZINCOGRAPHER
WEIGHBRIDGES	WHIPPOORWILL	WOODENHEADED	ZINCOGRAPHIC
WEIGHTLESSLY	WHITE KNIGHTS	WOOLGATHERER	ZOOCHEMISTRY
WEIGHT LIFTER	WHITE-LIVERED	WOOLLY-HEADED	ZOOGEOGRAPHY
WELFARE STATE	WHITE SLAVERY	WORDLESSNESS	ZOOSPERMATIC
WELL-ADJUSTED	WHITEWASHING	WORD OF HONOUR	ZOOTOMICALLY
		WORKER-PRIEST	ZWITTERIONIC
			ZYGAPOPHYSIS
			ZYGOMORPHISM

A
ABBREVIATIONS
ABERDEENSHIRE
ABNORMALITIES
ABOLITIONISTS
ABORTIFACIENT
ABSORBABILITY
ACCELEROMETER
ACCENTUATIONS
ACCEPTABILITY
ACCESSIBILITY
ACCESSORINESS
ACCIDENT-PRONE
ACCLIMATIZING
ACCOMMODATING
ACCOMMODATION
ACCOMMODATIVE
ACCOMPANIMENT
ACCOMPLISHING
ACCOUTREMENTS
ACCREDITATION
ACCULTURATION
ACCUMULATIONS
ACETIFICATION
ACETYLCHOLINE
ACHILLES'
  HEELS
ACIDIFICATION
ACKNOWLEDGING
ACOTYLEDONOUS
ACQUAINTANCES
ACQUIESCENTLY
ACQUIRED TASTE
ACQUISITIVELY
ACRIMONIOUSLY
ACROBATICALLY
ACRYLONITRILE
ACTINOMORPHIC
ACTINOMYCOSIS
ACTINOMYCOTIC
ACTINOTHERAPY
ACTINOURANIUM
ACTUALIZATION
ADDITIONALITY
ADDRESSOGRAPH
ADENOIDECTOMY
ADIAPHORISTIC
ADMEASUREMENT
ADMINISTERING
ADMINISTRATOR
ADMISSIBILITY

ADMONISHINGLY
ADNYAMATHANHA
ADSORBABILITY
ADVANCED LEVEL
ADVENTURESSES
ADVENTUROUSLY
ADVERTISEMENT
AEROMECHANICS
AESTHETICALLY
AFFENPINSCHER
AFFIRMATIVELY
AFFORESTATION
AFTERTHOUGHTS
AGGIORNAMENTO
AGGLOMERATING
AGGLOMERATION
AGGLOMERATIVE
AGGLUTINATION
AGGLUTINATIVE
AGGRAVATINGLY
AGREEABLENESS
AGRICULTURIST
AGROBIOLOGIST
AIR COMMODORES
AIRCRAFTWOMAN
AIRWORTHINESS
AIX-EN-
  PROVENCE
ALBURY-WODONGA
ALCOHOLICALLY
ALCOHOLOMETER
ALDUS MANUTIUS
ALGEBRAICALLY
ALLEGORICALLY
ALLOCHTHONOUS
ALPHA AND
  OMEGA
ALTAI REPUBLIC
ALTERNATIVELY
ALUMINIFEROUS
ALUMINOTHERMY
AMALGAMATIONS
AMBASSADORIAL
AMBIDEXTERITY
AMBIGUGUITIES
AMBIGUOUSNESS
AMBITIOUSNESS
AMERICANIZING
AMERICAN SAMOA
AMNIOCENTESIS
AMORPHOUSNESS

AMPHIBLASTULA
AMPHIPROSTYLE
AMPHITHEATRES
AMPHITRICHOUS
AMPLIFICATION
AMUSEMENT PARK
ANACHRONISTIC
ANAEROBICALLY
ANAESTHETISTS
ANAESTHETIZED
ANAGRAMMATISM
ANAGRAMMATIST
ANAGRAMMATIZE
ANAL RETENTIVE
ANAPHORICALLY
ANAPHRODISIAC
ANATHEMATIZED
ANATOMIZATION
ANCHORPERSONS
ANDHRA PRADESH
ANEMOMETRICAL
ANESTHETIZING
ANFRACTUOSITY
ANGIOSPERMOUS
ANGLICIZATION
ANGLO-AMERICAN
ANGLO-CATHOLIC
ANIMADVERSION
ANIMADVERTING
ANIMALIZATION
ANISOMETROPIA
ANNEXATIONISM
ANNEXATIONIST
ANNIVERSARIES
ANNOUNCEMENTS
ANSWERABILITY
ANTAGONIZABLE
ANTHRAQUINONE
ANTHROPOMETRY
ANTHROPOPATHY
ANTHROPOPHAGI
ANTHROPOSOPHY
ANTI-APARTHEID
ANTIBACTERIAL
ANTICLIMACTIC
ANTICLINORIUM
ANTICLOCKWISE
ANTI-COMMUNIST
ANTIGENICALLY
ANTIHISTAMINE
ANTILOGARITHM

ANTIMACASSARS
ANTIMONARCHIC
ANTINOMICALLY
ANTIPERSONNEL
ANTIPRAGMATIC
ANTIPSYCHOTIC
ANTISPASMODIC
ANTISUBMARINE
APATHETICALLY
APERIODICALLY
APHELIOTROPIC
APLANATICALLY
APOCHROMATISM
APODICTICALLY
APOGEOTROPISM
APOSTROPHIZED
APPLE PIE
  ORDER
APPLICABILITY
APPORTIONABLE
APPORTIONMENT
APPRECIATIONS
APPREHENSIBLE
APPREHENSIONS
APPROPRIATELY
APPROPRIATING
APPROPRIATION
APPROXIMATELY
APPROXIMATING
APPROXIMATION
APPURTENANCES
AQUICULTURIST
ARABIAN DESERT
ARABIC NUMERAL
ARACHNOPHOBIA
ARBITRARINESS
ARBORICULTURE
ARCHAEOLOGIST
ARCHBISHOPRIC
ARCHIDIACONAL
ARCHIMANDRITE
ARCHIPELAGOES
ARCHITECTONIC
ARCHITECTURAL
ARGENTIFEROUS
ARGILLIFEROUS
ARGUMENTATION
ARGUMENTATIVE
ARGYLL AND
  BUTE
ARISTOCRACIES

ARITHMETICIAN
AROMATIZATION
ARRIERE-PENSEE
ARTERIOVENOUS
ARTESIAN WELLS
ARTICULATIONS
ARTIFICIALITY
ARTS AND
  CRAFTS
ARUNDINACEOUS
ASCERTAINABLE
ASCERTAINMENT
ASCHAFFENBURG
ASPERGILLOSIS
ASSASSINATING
ASSASSINATION
ASSAULT COURSE
ASSEMBLY LINES
ASSERTIVENESS
ASSET-STRIPPER
ASSEVERATIONS
ASSIDUOUSNESS
ASSIGNABILITY
ASSYRIOLOGIST
ASTHENOSPHERE
ASTHMATICALLY
ASTIGMATISTIC
ASTONISHINGLY
ASTRODYNAMICS
ASTROPHYSICAL
ASYNDETICALLY
ATACAMA DESERT
ATAVISTICALLY
ATHEISTICALLY
ATOMISTICALLY
ATROCIOUSNESS
ATTAINABILITY
ATTENTIVENESS
AT THE SAME
  TIME
ATTITUDINIZER
ATTRIBUTIVELY
AUBERVILLIERS
AUDACIOUSNESS
AUGMENTATIONS
AUNG SAN SUU
  KYI
AUSTRALASIANS
AUSTRO-ASIATIC
AUTECOLOGICAL
AUTHENTICALLY

AUTHENTICATED
AUTHENTICATOR
AUTHORITARIAN
AUTHORITATIVE
AUTHORIZATION
AUTOBIOGRAPHY
AUTOCATALYSIS
AUTOCHTHONISM
AUTOCHTHONOUS
AUTOMATICALLY
AUTOMATIC DOOR
AUTONOMICALLY
AUTOSTABILITY
AUXILIARY VERB
AXIOMATICALLY

B

BABY CARRIAGES
BACCALAUREATE
BACK FORMATION
BACKPEDALLING
BACKWARDATION
BACTERIOLYSIS
BACTERIOLYTIC
BACTERIOPHAGE
BALANCED DIETS
BALANCE SHEETS
BALKANIZATION
BALLISTICALLY
BALL LIGHTNING
BALNEOLOGICAL
BALSAMIFEROUS
BAMBOOZLEMENT
BANDSPREADING
BANKER'S
  ORDERS
BANTAMWEIGHTS
BARBAROUSNESS
BARBOUR JACKET
BAREFACEDNESS
BASIDIOMYCETE
BASOTHO-QWAQWA
BATTERING RAMS
BATTLE CRUISER
BATTLE-SCARRED
BEAST OF
  BURDEN
BEATIFICATION
BEAUFORT SCALE
BEAUTY PARLOUR
BEHAVIOURALLY

BEHAVIOURISTS
BELISHA BEACON
BELLES-LETTRES
BELLY-LANDINGS
BELO HORIZONTE
BENEFICIARIES
BENEFIT IN
  KIND
BERCHTESGADEN
BEWILDERINGLY
BIBLIOGRAPHER
BIBLIOGRAPHIC
BICENTENARIES
BIDIRECTIONAL
BIG BANG
  THEORY
BIGHEADEDNESS
BIGNONIACEOUS
BILLS OF
  HEALTH
BILLS OF
  LADING
BILLS OF
  RIGHTS
BIODEGRADABLE
BIOECOLOGICAL
BIOENERGETICS
BIOMETRICALLY
BIOSTATICALLY
BIOTECHNOLOGY
BIRD OF
  PASSAGE
BIRD'S-EYE
  VIEWS
BIREFRINGENCE
BLABBERMOUTHS
BLACK AND
  WHITE
BLACKBERRYING
BLACK COMEDIES
BLACKCURRANTS
BLACKGUARDISM
BLACK MOUNTAIN
BLACK PUDDINGS
BLAMELESSNESS
BLANDISHMENTS
BLANTYRE-LIMBE
BLASPHEMOUSLY
BLAST FURNACES
BLASTOGENESIS
BLIND MAN'S
  BUFF

BLOOD BROTHERS
BLOODCURDLING
BLOODLESSNESS
BLOOD PRESSURE
BLOOD RELATION
BLOTTING PAPER
BLUE MOUNTAINS
BLUE-PENCILLED
BLUESTOCKINGS
BLUNDERBUSSES
BOARDING CARDS
BOARDINGHOUSE
BOBO-DIOULASSO
BODY SNATCHERS
BODY STOCKINGS
BOILING POINTS
BOMBASTICALLY
BOOBY TRAPPING
BOON COMPANION
BORAGINACEOUS
BORDERS REGION
BOTTLE-FEEDING
BOTTOM DRAWERS
BOUGAINVILLEA
BOUILLABAISSE
BOUNDLESSNESS
BOUNTEOUSNESS
BOUNTIFULNESS
BOUSTROPHEDON
BOWLING ALLEYS
BOWLING GREENS
BRACHYCEPHALY
BRACHYPTEROUS
BRAINLESSNESS
BRAINSTORMING
BRASSICACEOUS
BRASS KNUCKLES
BROADMINDEDLY
BROKEN-HEARTED
BROMELIACEOUS
BRONCHIAL TUBE
BRONCHOSCOPIC
BROTHERLINESS
BROTHERS-IN-
  LAW
BROWNIE GUIDES
BROWNIE POINTS
BRUTALIZATION
BUBONIC PLAGUE
BUDGET DEFICIT
BUILDING BLOCK

BULLETIN BOARD
BUMPTIOUSNESS
BUNGEE JUMPING
BUNSEN BURNERS
BURDEN OF
    PROOF
BUREAUCRACIES
BUREAUCRATISM
BURGLAR ALARMS
BURNT OFFERING
BURY ST
    EDMUNDS
BUSH CARPENTER
BUSH TELEGRAPH
BUSINESS CLASS
BUSINESS SUITS
BUSINESSWOMAN
BUTCHER'S-
    BROOM
BUTTERFINGERS
BUTTER-FINGERS
BUTYRALDEHYDE

C
CABIN CRUISERS
CABINET-MAKERS
CABLE RAILWAYS
CAICOS ISLANDS
CALCARIFEROUS
CALCIFICATION
CALCULABILITY
CALENDAR MONTH
CALENDAR YEARS
CALLIGRAPHIST
CALLISTHENICS
CALORIFICALLY
CAMBRIDGE BLUE
CAMPANOLOGIST
CAMP FOLLOWERS
CAMPYLOBACTER
CANARY ISLANDS
CANCELLATIONS
CANNIBALISTIC
CANNIBALIZING
CANONIZATIONS
CAPACIOUSNESS
CAPARISONNING
CAPE COLOUREDS
CAPITAL LEVIES
CAPITULATIONS
CAPRIFICATION

CARAVANSERAIS
CARBOHYDRATES
CARBON DIOXIDE
CARBONIFEROUS
CARBONIZATION
CARBURIZATION
CARCINOMATOID
CARDIGANSHIRE
CARDINAL POINT
CARDIOGRAPHER
CARDIOGRAPHIC
CARDIOLOGICAL
CARICATURISTS
CARNIFICATION
CARPETBAGGERS
CARPET SWEEPER
CARRICKFERGUS
CARRIER PIGEON
CARTILAGINOUS
CARTOGRAPHERS
CARVING KNIVES
CASE HISTORIES
CASH DISPENSER
CASH REGISTERS
CASSEGRAINIAN
CASUISTICALLY
CATASTROPHISM
CATASTROPHIST
CATCHMENT AREA
CATECHIZATION
CATECHOLAMINE
CATEGORICALLY
CATER-CORNERED
CATHARTICALLY
CAT-O'-NINE-
    TAILS
CAUTERIZATION
CAYENNE PEPPER
CAYMAN ISLANDS
CELLULAR RADIO
CENTRAL REGION
CENTRE FORWARD
CEPHALIZATION
CEPHALOMETRIC
CEPHALOTHORAX
CEREBRAL PALSY
CEREBROSPINAL
CEREMONIALISM
CEREMONIALIST
CEREMONIOUSLY
CERTIFICATION

CERTIFICATORY
CERTIFIED MAIL
CERTIFIED MILK
CHAFING DISHES
CHAIN REACTION
CHAIN STITCHES
CHAIRMANSHIPS
CHAISE LONGUES
CHALCOGRAPHER
CHALCOGRAPHIC
CHALLENGEABLE
CHAMPIONSHIPS
CHANCELLERIES
CHANDERNAGORE
CHANDRASEKHAR
CHANGEABILITY
CHANGE OF
    HEART
CHANGE RINGING
CHANGING ROOMS
CHANNEL TUNNEL
CHANTRY CHAPEL
CHARACTERIZED
CHARACTERLESS
CHARGEABILITY
CHARGE ACCOUNT
CHARLOTTETOWN
CHARNEL HOUSES
CHARTER MEMBER
CHASTISEMENTS
CHASTITY BELTS
CHATEAUBRIAND
CHEERLESSNESS
CHEMISORPTION
CHEMORECEPTOR
CHESTERFIELDS
CHEVAL GLASSES
CHIAROSCURISM
CHIAROSCURIST
CHIEF JUSTICES
CHIEFS OF
    STAFF
CHIEFTAINSHIP
CHILDLESSNESS
CHIMNEYBREAST
CHIMNEY CORNER
CHIMNEYPIECES
CHIMNEYSTACKS
CHIMNEYSWEEPS
CHIROPRACTORS
CHLAMYDOSPORE

CHLOROBENZENE
CHLOROFORMING
CHLOROMYCETIN
CHLOROPLASTIC
CHONDRIOSOMAL
CHONDROMATOUS
CHOREOGRAPHED
CHOREOGRAPHER
CHOREOGRAPHIC
CHRISTIANIZER
CHRISTIAN NAME
CHRISTMAS CAKE
CHRISTMAS CARD
CHRISTMASTIDE
CHRISTMASTIME
CHRISTMAS TREE
CHRISTOLOGIST
CHROMATICALLY
CHROMATICNESS
CHROMATOLYSIS
CHROMATOPHORE
CHROMOPLASMIC
CHROMOPROTEIN
CHROMOSPHERIC
CHRONOBIOLOGY
CHRONOGRAPHER
CHRONOGRAPHIC
CHRONOLOGICAL
CHRYSANTHEMUM
CHURCHWARDENS
CICATRIZATION
CINEMATICALLY
CINEMATOGRAPH
CIRCULARIZING
CIRCUMAMBIENT
CIRCUMCISIONS
CIRCUMFERENCE
CIRCUMFLEXION
CIRCUMSCRIBED
CIRCUMSPECTLY
CIRCUMSTANCES
CIRCUMVALLATE
CIRCUMVENTING
CIRCUMVENTION
CIUDAD GUAYANA
CIVIL ENGINEER
CIVILIZATIONS
CIVIL SERVANTS
CLAIRAUDIENCE
CLANDESTINELY
CLAPPERBOARDS

CLARIFICATION
CLARINETTISTS
CLASSIFIED ADS
CLASSLESSNESS
CLASS STRUGGLE
CLAUSTROPHOBE
CLAVICHORDIST
CLEARANCE SALE
CLEAR-HEADEDLY
CLEARINGHOUSE
CLEISTOGAMOUS
CLERKS OF
  WORKS
CLIMACTERICAL
CLIMATOLOGIST
CLIMBING FRAME
CLIMBING IRONS
CLOSED-CIRCUIT
CLOSED SEASONS
CLOSING PRICES
CLOTHES HANGER
CLOTHESHORSES
CLUSTER-BOMBED
COACHBUILDERS
COACH STATIONS
COBELLIGERENT
COCAINIZATION
COCKER SPANIEL
COCKTAIL STICK
CODECLINATION
CODIFICATIONS
COEDUCATIONAL
COLD-BLOODEDLY
COLD-HEARTEDLY
COLLABORATING
COLLABORATION
COLLABORATIVE
COLLABORATORS
COLLATERALIZE
COLLETIVISTIC
COLLOQUIALISM
COLOUR SCHEMES
COMBAT FATIGUE
COMBINING FORM
COMMANDEERING
COMMANDERSHIP
COMMAND MODULE
COMMEMORATING
COMMEMORATION
COMMEMORATIVE
COMMENCEMENTS

COMMENDATIONS
COMMENSURABLE
COMMERCIALISM
COMMERCIALIST
COMMERCIALITY
COMMERCIALIZE
COMMISERATING
COMMISERATION
COMMISERATIVE
COMMISSARIATS
COMMISSIONERS
COMMISSIONING
COMMUNALISTIC
COMMUNAUTAIRE
COMMUNICATING
COMMUNICATION
COMMUNICATIVE
COMMUNICATORY
COMMUNITARIAN
COMMUNITY HOME
COMMUNIZATION
COMPANIONABLE
COMPANIONABLY
COMPANIONSHIP
COMPANIONWAYS
COMPARABILITY
COMPARATIVELY
COMPARTMENTAL
COMPASSIONATE
COMPASS POINTS
COMPATIBILITY
COMPATRIOTISM
COMPENDIOUSLY
COMPETITIVELY
COMPLAININGLY
COMPLAISANTLY
COMPLEMENTARY
COMPLEMENTING
COMPLICATEDLY
COMPLICATIONS
COMPLIMENTARY
COMPLIMENTING
COMPOSITIONAL
COMPREHENDING
COMPREHENSION
COMPREHENSIVE
COMPRESSIONAL
COMPUTABILITY
COMPUTATIONAL
COMPUTERIZING
CONCATENATING

CONCATENATION
CONCAVO-CONVEX
CONCENTRATING
CONCENTRATION
CONCENTRATIVE
CONCENTRICITY
CONCEPTUALISM
CONCEPTUALIST
CONCEPTUALIZE
CONCERT GRANDS
CONCERTINAING
CONCESSIONARY
CONCHOLOGICAL
CONCHOLOGISTS
CONCOMITANTLY
CONCRETE MIXER
CONCRETIONARY
CONCUPISCENCE
CONDEMNATIONS
CONDEMNED CELL
CONDENSED MILK
CONDESCENDING
CONDESCENSION
CONDITIONALLY
CONDUCIVENESS
CONDUCTOR RAIL
CONDYLOMATOUS
CONFABULATING
CONFABULATION
CONFABULATORY
CONFECTIONARY
CONFECTIONERS
CONFECTIONERY
CONFEDERACIES
CONFEDERATING
CONFEDERATION
CONFESSIONALS
CONFESSIONARY
CONFIGURATION
CONFIRMATIONS
CONFISCATIONS
CONFLAGRATION
CONFLAGRATIVE
CONFORMATIONS
CONFRATERNITY
CONFRONTATION
CONGLOMERATES
CONGLOMERATIC
CONGRATULATED
CONGRATULATOR
CONGREGATIONS

CONGRESSIONAL
CONGRESSWOMAN
CONJUGATIONAL
CONJUNCTIONAL
CONNECTING ROD
CONNING TOWERS
CONNOTATATIVE
CONQUISTADORS
CONSANGUINITY
CONSCIENTIOUS
CONSCIOUSNESS
CONSECUTIVELY
CONSEQUENTIAL
CONSERVANCIES
CONSERVATIVES
CONSERVATOIRE
CONSIDERATELY
CONSIDERATION
CONSISTENCIES
CONSOLIDATING
CONSOLIDATION
CONSPICUOUSLY
CONSPIRATRESS
CONSTELLATION
CONSTELLATORY
CONSTERNATION
CONSTITUTIONS
CONSTRAINEDLY
CONSTRICTIONS
CONSTRUCTIBLE
CONSTRUCTIONS
CONSULTANCIES
CONSULTATIONS
CONSUMMATIONS
CONTACT LENSES
CONTAINERIZED
CONTAMINATING
CONTAMINATION
CONTAMINATORS
CONTEMPLATING
CONTEMPLATION
CONTEMPLATIVE
CONTENTIOUSLY
CONTEXTUALISM
CONTEXTUALIZE
CONTINGENCIES
CONTINUATIONS
CONTORTIONIST
CONTRABANDIST
CONTRABASSIST
CONTRABASSOON

CONTRACEPTION
CONTRACEPTIVE
CONTRACTILITY
CONTRACTIONAL
CONTRACTUALLY
CONTRADICTING
CONTRADICTION
CONTRADICTIVE
CONTRADICTORY
CONTRAPUNTIST
CONTRAVENTION
CONTRIBUTIONS
CONTROVERSIAL
CONTROVERSIES
CONVALESCENCE
CONVALESCENTS
CONVERSATIONS
CONVERSAZIONE
CONVERTIPLANE
CONVEXO-CONVEX
CONVEYER BELTS
CONVOCATIONAL
CONVOLVULUSES
COOKING APPLES
COOPERATIVELY
CORDUROY ROADS
CORELIGIONIST
CO-RESPONDENCY
CO-RESPONDENTS
CORN EXCHANGES
CORPS DE
  BALLET
CORPUS CHRISTI
CORRESPONDENT
CORRESPONDING
CORRIGIBILITY
CORROBORATING
CORROBORATION
CORROBORATIVE
CORROBORATORS
CORRODIBILITY
CORROSIVENESS
CORRUPTIONIST
COSIGNATORIES
COSMOPOLITANS
COSMOPOLITISM
COST-EFFECTIVE
COSTERMONGERS
COTERMINOUSLY
COTTAGE CHEESE
COTTAGE LOAVES

COTTON-PICKING
COUNTENANCING
COUNTERACTING
COUNTERACTION
COUNTERACTIVE
COUNTERATTACK
COUNTERBLASTS
COUNTERCHARGE
COUNTERCLAIMS
COUNTERFEITED
COUNTERFEITER
COUNTERMANDED
COUNTERPOINTS
COUNTERPOISED
COUNTERPOISES
COUNTERSIGNED
COUNTERTENORS
COUNTERWEIGHT
COUNTINGHOUSE
COUNTRY COUSIN
COUNTRY DANCES
COUNTY BOROUGH
COUNTY COUNCIL
COURT CIRCULAR
COURTEOUSNESS
COURT MARTIALS
COURTS-MARTIAL
COVERED WAGONS
CRAFTSMANSHIP
CRANIOLOGICAL
CRASH BARRIERS
CRASH LANDINGS
CRASSULACEOUS
CREAM OF
  TARTAR
CREDIT ACCOUNT
CREDIT SQUEEZE
CREME DE
  MENTHE
CRIMINOLOGIST
CRISSCROSSING
CROSSBENCHERS
CROSSBREEDING
CROSSCHECKING
CROSSCURRENTS
CROSS-DRESSERS
CROSS-DRESSING
CROSS-EXAMINED
CROSS-EXAMINER
CROSS-HATCHING
CROSS-PURPOSES

CROSS-QUESTION
CROSS-REFERRED
CROSS-SECTIONS
CROSS-STITCHES
CROWN COLONIES
CROWN IMPERIAL
CROWN PRINCESS
CRUISE MISSILE
CRUISERWEIGHT
CRUSH BARRIERS
CRYOBIOLOGIST
CRYPTANALYSIS
CRYPTANALYTIC
CRYPTOCLASTIC
CRYPTOGRAPHER
CRYPTOGRAPHIC
CRYPTOZOOLOGY
CRYSTAL GAZERS
CRYSTAL GAZING
CRYSTALLINITY
CRYSTALLIZING
CUMULOSTRATUS
CURTAIN RAISER
CUSTODIANSHIP
CUT ONES
  LOSSES
CYANOBACTERIA
CYBERNETICIST
CYLINDRICALLY
CYTOCHEMISTRY
CYTOTAXONOMIC
CZECH REPUBLIC

D
DADAISTICALLY
DADDY LONGLEGS
DAGUERREOTYPE
DAGUERREOTYPY
DAMAGEABILITY
DAMNIFICATION
DANDIFICATION
DARK CONTINENT
DASTARDLINESS
DAUGHTER-IN-
  LAW
DEAD-CAT
  BOUNCE
DEAD RECKONING
DEATH WARRANTS
DEBTS OF
  HONOUR

DECAPITATIONS
DECEITFULNESS
DECENTRALIZED
DECEPTIVENESS
DECEREBRATION
DECK PASSENGER
DECLAMATORILY
DECLARATORILY
DECLASSIFYING
DECOMPOSITION
DECOMPRESSING
DECOMPRESSION
DECOMPRESSIVE
DECONGESTANTS
DECONTAMINANT
DECONTAMINATE
DECONTROLLING
DECORTICATION
DECREPITATION
DEDUCTIBILITY
DEFECTIVENESS
DEFENSIBILITY
DEFENSIVENESS
DEFERENTIALLY
DEFIBRILLATOR
DEFORESTATION
DEGLUTINATION
DEHYDROGENASE
DEHYDROGENATE
DEHYDROGENIZE
DELETERIOUSLY
DELIBERATIONS
DELICATESSENS
DELICIOUSNESS
DELINQUENCIES
DELIQUESCENCE
DELIRIOUSNESS
DEMAGNETIZING
DEMAGOGICALLY
DEMERARA SUGAR
DEMERITORIOUS
DEMILITARIZED
DEMOCRATIZING
DEMOLITIONIST
DEMONOLOGICAL
DEMONSTRATING
DEMONSTRATION
DEMONSTRATIVE
DEMONSTRATORS
DENATIONALIZE
DENDRITICALLY

DENDROLOGICAL	DIAMETRICALLY	DISCONTINUING	DISPUTABILITY
DENOMINATIONS	DIAPHRAGMATIC	DISCONTINUITY	DISQUALIFYING
DENSITOMETRIC	DIATHERMANOUS	DISCONTINUOUS	DISQUISITIONS
DENTAL SURGEON	DIATONIC SCALE	DISCOUNT STORE	DISRESPECTFUL
DENTICULATION	DIAZOTIZATION	DISCOURTESIES	DISSATISFYING
DENUNCIATIONS	DICHLAMIDEOUS	DISCREDITABLE	DISSEMINATING
DEODORIZATION	DICTATORIALLY	DISCREDITABLY	DISSEMINATION
DEONTOLOGICAL	DICTATORSHIPS	DISCREPANCIES	DISSEMINATIVE
DEOXIDIZATION	DIEFFENBACHIA	DISCRETIONARY	DISSEPIMENTAL
DEOXYGENATION	DIESEL ENGINES	DISCRIMINATED	DISSERTATIONS
DEPENDABILITY	DIFFERENTIALS	DISCRIMINATOR	DISSIMILARITY
DEPERSONALIZE	DIFFERENTIATE	DISEMBODIMENT	DISSIMILATION
DEPRECATINGLY	DIFFUSIBILITY	DISEMBOWELING	DISSIMILATIVE
DEPRECATORILY	DIGESTIBILITY	DISEMBOWELLED	DISSIMILATORY
DEPRESSOMOTOR	DIGITAL CAMERA	DISENABLEMENT	DISSIMILITUDE
DERMATOLOGIST	DILAPIDATIONS	DISENGAGEMENT	DISSIMULATING
DERMATOPHYTIC	DILLYDALLYING	DISENTAILMENT	DISSIMULATION
DERMATOPLASTY	DIMENSIONLESS	DISENTANGLING	DISSIMULATIVE
DESCRIPTIVELY	DIM-WITTEDNESS	DISFIGUREMENT	DISSOLUBILITY
DESCRIPTIVISM	DINNER JACKETS	DISFRANCHISED	DISSOLUTENESS
DESEGREGATING	DINNER SERVICE	DISGRACEFULLY	DISTASTEFULLY
DESEGREGATION	DIPHENYLAMINE	DISHARMONIOUS	DISTILLATIONS
DESENSITIZING	DIPSOMANIACAL	DISHONOURABLE	DISTINCTIVELY
DESPICABILITY	DIRECT CURRENT	DISHONOURABLY	DISTINGUISHED
DESSERTSPOONS	DIRECT OBJECTS	DISILLUSIONED	DISTINGUISHER
DESTABILIZING	DIRECTORSHIPS	DISINCENTIVES	DISTRESSINGLY
DESTRUCTIVELY	DISADVANTAGED	DISINFECTANTS	DISTRIBUTABLE
DESULTORINESS	DISADVANTAGES	DISINHERITING	DISTRIBUTIONS
DETACHABILITY	DISAFFECTEDLY	DISINTEGRABLE	DISTRUSTFULLY
DETERIORATING	DISAFFILIATED	DISINTEGRATED	DITRANSITIVES
DETERIORATION	DISAFFIRMANCE	DISINTEGRATOR	DIVERSIFIABLE
DETERIORATIVE	DISAFFORESTED	DISINTERESTED	DIVISIONALIZE
DETERMINATION	DISAGREEMENTS	DISINTERMENTS	DIVISION LOBBY
DETERMINATIVE	DISAPPEARANCE	DISINVESTMENT	DOCTRINAIRISM
DETERMINISTIC	DISAPPOINTING	DISMANTLEMENT	DOCUMENTARIES
DETESTABILITY	DISARTICULATE	DISMEMBERMENT	DOCUMENTARILY
DETRIMENTALLY	DISASSOCIATED	DISOBEDIENTLY	DOCUMENTARIST
DEUTEROGAMIST	DISBURDENMENT	DISOBLIGINGLY	DOCUMENTATION
DEVASTATINGLY	DISBURSEMENTS	DISORIENTATED	DODECAPHONISM
DEVELOPMENTAL	DISCHARGEABLE	DISPARAGEMENT	DODECAPHONIST
DEVIATIONISTS	DISCIPLINABLE	DISPARAGINGLY	DOGMATIZATION
DEVOLUTIONARY	DISCOLORATION	DISPASSIONATE	DOG'S
DEVOTIONALITY	DISCOMMODIOUS	DISPATCH BOXES	BREAKFAST
DEXTEROUSNESS	DISCOMPOSEDLY	DISPENSATIONS	DOLLARIZATION
DEXTROGLUCOSE	DISCONCERTING	DISPLACEMENTS	DOME OF THE
DIAGEOTROPISM	DISCONCERTION	DISPOSABILITY	ROCK
DIAGNOSTICIAN	DISCONFORMITY	DISPOSITIONAL	DOMESTICATING
DIALECTICIANS	DISCONNECTING	DISPOSSESSING	DOMESTICATION
DIALLING CODES	DISCONNECTION	DISPOSSESSION	DOMESTICATIVE
DIALLING TONES	DISCONNECTIVE	DISPOSSESSORY	DOMESTICITIES
DIALYSABILITY	DISCONTENTING	DISPROPORTION	DONKEY JACKETS

DOSIMETRICIAN
DOTHEBOYS HALL
DOUBLE-CHECKED
DOUBLE-CROSSED
DOUBLE-CROSSER
DOUBLE-CROSSES
DOUBLE-DEALERS
DOUBLE-DEALING
DOUBLE-DECKERS
DOUBLE FEATURE
DOUBLE FIGURES
DOUBLE-GLAZING
DOUBLE-JOINTED
DOUBLE OR
  QUITS
DOUBLE-PARKING
DOUBLE-TALKING
DOWNHEARTEDLY
DOWNING STREET
DOWN'S
  SYNDROME
DRAINING BOARD
DRAMATIC IRONY
DRAMATIZATION
DRAWING BOARDS
DRESSING GOWNS
DRESSING ROOMS
DRESSING TABLE
DRINKING WATER
DRUM MAJORETTE
DRYOPITHECINE
DUALISTICALLY
DUCKING STOOLS
DUCTLESS GLAND
DUMFRIESSHIRE
DUPLICABILITY
DUQUE DE
  CAXIAS
DUTCH AUCTIONS
DWELLING HOUSE
DYED-IN-THE-
  WOOL
DYSFUNCTIONAL
DYSMENORRHOEA

E

EAST-NORTHEAST
EAST-SOUTHEAST
EAVESDROPPERS
EAVESDROPPING
ECCENTRICALLY

ECCLESIASTICS
ECCLESIOLATER
ECCLESIOLATRY
ECONOMIZATION
ECTOPARASITIC
ECUMENICALISM
EDITORIALIZER
EDUCATED GUESS
EFFECTIVENESS
EFFERVESCENCE
EFFERVESCIBLE
EFFICACIOUSLY
EFFLORESCENCE
EGOCENTRICITY
EGOTISTICALLY
EGREGIOUSNESS
EGYPTOLOGICAL
EIGHTEEN HOLES
ELABORATENESS
ELECTIONEERER
ELECTRIC CHAIR
ELECTRIC FENCE
ELECTRIC SHOCK
ELECTRIFIABLE
ELECTROCUTING
ELECTROCUTION
ELECTROGRAPHY
ELECTROMAGNET
ELECTROMERISM
ELECTROMETRIC
ELECTROMOTIVE
ELECTROPHILIC
ELECTROPHONIC
ELECTROPHORUS
ELECTROPLATER
ELECTROSCOPIC
ELECTROSTATIC
ELECTROVALENT
ELEPHANTIASIC
ELEPHANTIASIS
ELEPHANT'S-
  FOOT
ELLESMERE PORT
EMBARRASSMENT
EMBELLISHMENT
EMBRYOLOGICAL
EMBRYONICALLY
EMILIA-ROMAGNA
EMINENCE GRISE
EMOTIONLESSLY
EMPHYSEMATOUS

EMPIRE-BUILDER
EMPIRICALNESS
EMPLOYABILITY
EMULSION PAINT
ENCAPSULATION
ENCAUSTICALLY
ENCEPHALOGRAM
ENCHANTRESSES
ENCOMPASSMENT
ENCOURAGEMENT
ENCOURAGINGLY
ENCROACHINGLY
ENCROACHMENTS
ENCULTURATION
ENCULTURATIVE
ENCUMBERINGLY
ENCYCLOPEDIAS
ENCYCLOPEDISM
ENCYCLOPEDIST
ENDOCRINOLOGY
ENDODONTOLOGY
ENDOLYMPHATIC
ENDOMETRIOSIS
ENDOPARASITIC
ENDOPEPTIDASE
ENERGETICALLY
ENFRANCHISING
ENGINE DRIVERS
ENIGMATICALLY
ENLIGHTENMENT
ENROLLED NURSE
ENTANGLEMENTS
ENTERTAINMENT
ENTHRALLINGLY
ENTHRONEMENTS
ENTOMOLOGICAL
ENTOMOLOGISTS
ENTOMOPHAGOUS
ENTOMOPHILOUS
ENTOMOSTRACAN
ENTREPRENEURS
ENUNCIABILITY
ENVIRONMENTAL
ENZYMOLOGICAL
EPIGRAMMATISM
EPIGRAMMATIST
EPIGRAMMATIZE
EPILEPTICALLY
EPIPHENOMENAL
EPIPHENOMENON
EPIPHYTICALLY

EPISCOPALIANS
EPITOMIZATION
EPIZOOTICALLY
EQUESTRIANISM
EQUILIBRATION
EQUILIBRISTIC
EQUIMOLECULAR
EQUIPONDERANT
EQUIPONDERATE
EQUIPOTENTIAL
EQUITABLENESS
EQUIVOCATIONS
ERGONOMICALLY
ERRONEOUSNESS
ERYSIPELATOUS
ESCAPOLOGISTS
ESCHATOLOGIST
ESPIRITO SANTO
ESPRIT DE
  CORPS
ESTABLISHMENT
ESTIMABLENESS
ESTRANGEMENTS
ETHNOCENTRISM
ETHNOGRAPHERS
ETHOLOGICALLY
ETIOLOGICALLY
EUROCOMMUNISM
EUSPORANGIATE
EVAPORABILITY
EVENTUALITIES
EVERLASTINGLY
EVERY WHICH
  WAY
EVOCATIVENESS
EXAGGERATEDLY
EXAGGERATIONS
EXAMINATIONAL
EXANTHEMATOUS
EXASPERATEDLY
EXCEPTIONABLE
EXCEPTIONALLY
EXCESSIVENESS
EXCHANGE RATES
EXCLAMATIONAL
EXCLAMATORILY
EXCLUDABILITY
EXCLUSIVENESS
EXCOMMUNICATE
EXCURSIVENESS
EXCUSABLENESS

EXECRABLENESS
EXEMPLARINESS
EXEMPLIFIABLE
EXEMPLI GRATIA
EXHIBITIONISM
EXHIBITIONIST
EXPANSIBILITY
EXPANSIONISTS
EXPANSIVENESS
EXPECTORATING
EXPECTORATION
EXPEDITIONARY
EXPEDITIOUSLY
EXPENDABILITY
EXPENSIVENESS
EXPERIMENTING
EXPERT SYSTEMS
EXPLANATORIES
EXPLANATORILY
EXPLOSIVENESS
EXPONENTIALLY
EXPORTABILITY
EXPOSTULATING
EXPOSTULATION
EXPOSTULATORY
EXPRESSIONISM
EXPRESSIONIST
EXPROPRIATING
EXPROPRIATION
EXPROPRIATORS
EXQUISITENESS
EXTEMPORARILY
EXTEMPORIZING
EXTENDIBILITY
EXTENSIBILITY
EXTENSIVENESS
EXTENUATINGLY
EXTERMINATING
EXTERMINATION
EXTERMINATIVE
EXTERMINATORS
EXTERNALIZING
EXTEROCEPTIVE
EXTERRITORIAL
EXTINGUISHANT
EXTINGUISHERS
EXTINGUISHING
EXTORTIONABLE
EXTORTIONISTS
EXTRACELLULAR
EXTRAGALACTIC

EXTRAJUDICIAL
EXTRAORDINARY
EXTRAPOLATING
EXTRAPOLATION
EXTRAPOLATIVE
EXTRAPOSITION
EXTRAVAGANCES
EXTRAVAGANTLY
EXTRAVAGANZAS
EXTRAVAGATION
EXTRAVASATION
EXTRAVASCULAR
EXTRINSICALLY
EYEBROW PENCIL
EYE-CATCHINGLY

F

FACETIOUSNESS
FACTORABILITY
FACTORIZATION
FAITHLESSNESS
FALLOPIAN TUBE
FALSIFICATION
FAMILIARITIES
FAMILIARIZING
FAMILY DOCTORS
FAMILY SUPPORT
FANTASTICALLY
FASCICULATION
FASCINATINGLY
FASCISTICALLY
FATHEADEDNESS
FATHER FIGURES
FAULTLESSNESS
FEATHERBEDDED
FEATHERSTITCH
FEATHER-VEINED
FEATHERWEIGHT
FEATURE-LENGTH
FEEDING BOTTLE
FELICITATIONS
FELLOW FEELING
FELONIOUSNESS
FEMMES FATALES
FEROCIOUSNESS
FERRIMAGNETIC
FERROCHROMIUM
FERROCONCRETE
FERROELECTRIC
FERROMAGNETIC
FERTILIZATION

FEUDALIZATION
FEUILLETONISM
FEUILLETONIST
FIBROVASCULAR
FICTIONALIZED
FIELD MARSHALS
FIELD OF
  VISION
FIGHTER-BOMBER
FIGURED BASSES
FIGURE OF
  EIGHT
FIGURE SKATERS
FIGURE-SKATING
FILIBUSTERING
FILING CABINET
FILM PREMIERES
FILTERABILITY
FINANCIAL YEAR
FINE-TOOTH
  COMB
FINGERPRINTED
FIRST MINISTER
FIRST OFFENDER
FISH-EYE
  LENSES
FISSION-FUSION
FLABBERGASTED
FLAGELLANTISM
FLAME-THROWERS
FLAVOPURPURIN
FLEET ADMIRALS
FLESH AND
  BLOOD
FLIGHT CAPITAL
FLIRTATIOUSLY
FLOATING-POINT
FLOATING VOTER
FLOODLIGHTING
FLORIANOPOLIS
FLORICULTURAL
FLORISTICALLY
FLOURISHINGLY
FLYING COLOURS
FLYING DOCTORS
FLYING OFFICER
FLYING PICKETS
FLYING SAUCERS
FOLLOW-THROUGH
FONTAINEBLEAU
FOOD POISONING
FOOD PROCESSOR

FOOLHARDINESS
FOOL'S
  PARADISE
FOOTBALL POOLS
FORAMINIFERAL
FORBIDDEN CITY
FOREIGN OFFICE
FOREJUDGEMENT
FOREKNOWINGLY
FOREKNOWLEDGE
FORENSICALITY
FOREORDAINING
FORESHADOWING
FORESHORTENED
FOREWARNINGLY
FORGETFULNESS
FORGIVINGNESS
FORKLIFT TRUCK
FORMALIZATION
FORMATIVENESS
FORMIDABILITY
FORTIFICATION
FORTITUDINOUS
FORTUNE HUNTER
FORTUNE-TELLER
FOSSILIFEROUS
FOSSILIZATION
FOUNDATIONARY
FRACTIONATION
FRACTIOUSNESS
FRACTOCUMULUS
FRACTOSTRATUS
FRAGMENTATION
FRANCHISEMENT
FREDERIKSBERG
FREEZING POINT
FREIGHTLINERS
FRENCH WINDOWS
FREQUENTATION
FREQUENTATIVE
FREUDIAN SLIPS
FRIDGE-FREEZER
FRIGHTENINGLY
FRIGHTFULNESS
FRINGE BENEFIT
FRIVOLOUSNESS
FRONTBENCHERS
FRONTISPIECES
FRONTOGENESIS
FRUITLESSNESS
FRUIT MACHINES

FRUMENTACEOUS
FULL-FASHIONED
FUNCTIONALISM
FUNCTIONALIST
FUNCTIONARIES
FUNDAMENTALLY
FUNNY BUSINESS
FUTURE PERFECT

G

GALLICIZATION
GALLOWS HUMOUR
GALVANOMETRIC
GALVANOSCOPIC
GALVANOTROPIC
GAMBREL-ROOFED
GAMETOGENESIS
GAMMA GLOBULIN
GARBAGE TRUCKS
GARDEN PARTIES
GARRULOUSNESS
GASTROSCOPIST
GEIGER COUNTER
GELANDESPRUNG
GELSENKIRCHEN
GENDER-BENDERS
GENERALISSIMO
GENERAL STRIKE
GENERATION GAP
GENTIANACEOUS
GENUFLECTIONS
GEOCHRONOLOGY
GEODYNAMICIST
GEOMETRICALLY
GEOMORPHOLOGY
GEOPOLITICIAN
GEOSTATIONARY
GEOTACTICALLY
GEOTROPICALLY
GERIATRICIANS
GERMANIZATION
GERMAN MEASLES
GERMANOPHILIA
GERMANOPHOBIA
GERONTOCRATIC
GERONTOLOGIST
GERRYMANDERED
GESTICULATING
GESTICULATION
GESTICULATIVE
GHETTO BLASTER

GLACIOLOGICAL
GLAMORIZATION
GLAMOROUSNESS
GLOBETROTTERS
GLOBETROTTING
GLOBULIFEROUS
GLOCKENSPIELS
GLORIFICATION
GLOSSOGRAPHER
GLUTINOUSNESS
GLYPHOGRAPHER
GLYPHOGRAPHIC
GLYPTOGRAPHER
GLYPTOGRAPHIC
GO-AS-YOU-
  PLEASE
GOING STRAIGHT
GOLDEN HAMSTER
GOLDEN JUBILEE
GOLDEN WEDDING
GOLDFISH BOWLS
GOOD AFTERNOON
GOOD-NATUREDLY
GOOD SAMARITAN
GOOSESTEPPING
GOVERNABILITY
GRACELESSNESS
GRADE CROSSING
GRAMINIVOROUS
GRAMMAR SCHOOL
GRAMMATICALLY
GRAM-MOLECULAR
GRANDCHILDREN
GRANDDAUGHTER
GRANDILOQUENT
GRANULOMATOUS
GRAPHEMICALLY
GRAPHICALNESS
GRAPHIC DESIGN
GRAPHOLOGISTS
GRAPPLING IRON
GRATIFICATION
GRAVEYARD SLOT
GRAVITATIONAL
GREAT YARMOUTH
GREEN-FINGERED
GROTESQUENESS
GROUND STROKES
GROUP CAPTAINS
GROUP PRACTICE
GUARDIAN ANGEL

GUATEMALA CITY
GUBERNATORIAL
GUIDED MISSILE
GUILELESSNESS
GUILTLESSNESS
GUNPOWDER PLOT
GYMNOSPERMISM
GYMNOSPERMOUS
GYNAECOCRATIC
GYNAECOLOGIST
GYNANDROMORPH

H

HACKING COUGHS
HAEMATOGENOUS
HAEMATOLOGIST
HAEMODIALYSIS
HAEMOPHILIOID
HAEMORRHOIDAL
HAGIOGRAPHIES
HAILE SELASSIE
HAIR-RESTORERS
HAIR-SPLITTING
HALE AND
  HEARTY
HALF-HEARTEDLY
HALFWAY HOUSES
HALICARNASSUS
HALLUCINATING
HALLUCINATION
HALLUCINATORY
HAMILCAR BARCA
HANDBRAKE TURN
HANDKERCHIEFS
HANG SENG
  INDEX
HAPHAZARDNESS
HARD-HEARTEDLY
HARD-LUCK
  STORY
HARD OF
  HEARING
HARD SHOULDERS
HARMONIZATION
HARUN AL-
  RASHID
HAVE NO TIME
  FOR
HAZARDOUSNESS
HEADSHRINKERS
HEALTHFULNESS
HEALTH VISITOR

HEARTBREAKING
HEARTBROKENLY
HEART DISEASES
HEARTLESSNESS
HEARTSICKNESS
HEARTSOMENESS
HEART-TO-
  HEARTS
HEATH ROBINSON
HEAVY HYDROGEN
HEAVY INDUSTRY
HEDGE SPARROWS
HEEBIE-JEEBIES
HEIRS APPARENT
HELLENIZATION
HELMINTHIASIS
HELMINTHOLOGY
HELTER SKELTER
HELTER-SKELTER
HEMICELLULOSE
HENDECAHEDRON
HEPTADECANOIC
HEPTAMETRICAL
HERBIVOROUSLY
HEREDITAMENTS
HEREFORDSHIRE
HERMAPHRODITE
HERNIORRHAPHY
HEROIC COUPLET
HERPES SIMPLEX
HERPETOLOGIST
HERTFORDSHIRE
HETEROGENEITY
HETEROGENEOUS
HETEROGENESIS
HETEROGENETIC
HETEROGRAPHIC
HETEROMORPHIC
HETEROPLASTIC
HETEROPTEROUS
HETEROSEXUALS
HETEROSPOROUS
HETEROSTYLOUS
HETEROTHALLIC
HETEROTROPHIC
HETEROZYGOSIS
HEURISTICALLY
HIERACOSPHINX
HIEROGLYPHICS
HIEROGLYPHIST

HIGH-AND-
 MIGHTY
HIGH CHURCHMAN
HIGHER-RATE
 TAX
HIGH EXPLOSIVE
HIGHLAND FLING
HIGH-PRESSURED
HIGH-WATER
 MARK
HILARIOUSNESS
HILDEBRANDIAN
HILDEBRANDINE
HISTOCHEMICAL
HOBSON'S
 CHOICE
HO CHI MINH
 CITY
HOIDENISHNESS
HOLE-AND-
 CORNER
HOLIDAYMAKERS
HOLIDAYMAKING
HOLY COMMUNION
HOME ECONOMICS
HOMEOMORPHISM
HOMILETICALLY
HOMOCHROMATIC
HOMOEROTICISM
HOMOGENEOUSLY
HOMOIOTHERMIC
HOMOLOGICALLY
HOMOLOGRAPHIC
HOMOOUSIANISM
HOMOSEXUALITY
HONEYDEW MELON
HONORIFICALLY
HORNS OF
 PLENTY
HORRIFICATION
HORRIPILATION
HORSE CHESTNUT
HORSEWHIPPING
HORTICULTURAL
HOSPITALIZING
HOT-GOSPELLERS
HOT-GOSPELLING
HOT-HEADEDNESS
HOUSEBREAKERS
HOUSEBREAKING
HOUSEHOLD NAME
HOUSE HUSBANDS

HOUSEMISTRESS
HOUSES OF
 CARDS
HOUSE SPARROWS
HOUSEWARMINGS
HOYDENISHNESS
HUCKLEBERRIES
HUMANITARIANS
HUMILIATINGLY
HUNDREDWEIGHT
HUNGER MARCHER
HUNGER MARCHES
HUNGER STRIKER
HUNGER STRIKES
HUNTING GROUND
HURRICANE LAMP
HYALURONIDASE
HYBRIDIZATION
HYDRAULICALLY
HYDROCEPHALIC
HYDROCEPHALUS
HYDROCHLORIDE
HYDRODYNAMICS
HYDROELECTRIC
HYDROGENATION
HYDROGEN BOMBS
HYDROKINETICS
HYDROLYSATION
HYPERCRITICAL
HYPOCHONDRIAC

I

IATROGENICITY
ICE-CREAM
 SODAS
ICHTHYOLOGIST
ICONOMATICISM
IDEALIZATIONS
IDENTICAL TWIN
IDENTITY CARDS
IDEOLOGICALLY
IDIOMATICALLY
IDIOSYNCRATIC
IGNOMINIOUSLY
ILL-CONSIDERED
ILLE-ET-
 VILAINE
ILLOCUTIONARY
ILLUMINATIONS
ILLUSIONISTIC
ILLUSTRATIONS

ILLUSTRIOUSLY
IMAGINATIVELY
IMAGISTICALLY
IMITATIVENESS
IMMATERIALISM
IMMATERIALIST
IMMATERIALITY
IMMATERIALIZE
IMMIGRATIONAL
IMMISCIBILITY
IMMORTALIZING
IMMUNIZATIONS
IMMUNOGENETIC
IMMUNOTHERAPY
IMPALPABILITY
IMPARIPINNATE
IMPARTIBILITY
IMPASSABILITY
IMPASSIONEDLY
IMPASSIVENESS
IMPECCABILITY
IMPECUNIOUSLY
IMPERCEPTIBLE
IMPERCEPTIBLY
IMPERFECTIONS
IMPERFORATION
IMPERIALISTIC
IMPERIOUSNESS
IMPERMISSIBLE
IMPERSONALITY
IMPERSONALIZE
IMPERSONATING
IMPERSONATION
IMPERSONATORS
IMPERTINENTLY
IMPERTURBABLE
IMPERTURBABLY
IMPETUOUSNESS
IMPLACABILITY
IMPONDERABLES
IMPORTUNATELY
IMPOSSIBILITY
IMPOVERISHING
IMPRACTICABLE
IMPRACTICABLY
IMPRACTICALLY
IMPRESSIONISM
IMPRESSIONIST
IMPROBABILITY
IMPROPRIATION
IMPROPRIETIES

IMPROVABILITY
IMPROVIDENTLY
IMPROVISATION
IMPULSIVENESS
INADVERTENTLY
INAPPROPRIATE
INATTENTIVELY
INAUGURATIONS
INCANDESCENCE
INCANTATIONAL
INCAPACITATED
INCAPSULATION
INCARCERATING
INCARCERATION
INCARDINATION
INCLINATIONAL
INCOMBUSTIBLE
INCOME SUPPORT
INCOMMUNICADO
INCOMPETENTLY
INCONCEIVABLE
INCONCEIVABLY
INCONDENSABLE
INCONGRUITIES
INCONGRUOUSLY
INCONSEQUENCE
INCONSIDERATE
INCONSISTENCY
INCONSPICUOUS
INCONSTANCIES
INCONTESTABLE
INCONTESTABLY
INCONVENIENCE
INCONVERTIBLE
INCONVINCIBLE
INCORPORATING
INCORPORATION
INCORPORATIVE
INCORPOREALLY
INCORRECTNESS
INCORRUPTIBLE
INCORRUPTIBLY
INCREDIBILITY
INCREDULOUSLY
INCREMENTALLY
INCRIMINATING
INCRIMINATION
INCRIMINATORY
INCRUSTATIONS
INCULPABILITY
INDEFATIGABLE

INDEFATIGABLY	INFLECTEDNESS	INSUPPORTABLE	INTERPOLATION
INDENTURESHIP	INFLEXIBILITY	INSURRECTIONS	INTERPOLATIVE
INDEPENDENTLY	INFLORESCENCE	INSUSCEPTIBLE	INTERPOSINGLY
INDESCRIBABLE	INFLUENCEABLE	INTANGIBILITY	INTERPOSITION
INDESCRIBABLY	INFLUENTIALLY	INTEGRABILITY	INTERPRETABLE
INDETERMINACY	INFORMATIONAL	INTEGUMENTARY	INTERRACIALLY
INDETERMINATE	INFORMATIVELY	INTELLECTUALS	INTERRELATION
INDETERMINISM	INFRINGEMENTS	INTELLIGENTLY	INTERROGATING
INDETERMINIST	INFURIATINGLY	INTEMPERATELY	INTERROGATION
INDIAN SUMMERS	INGENUOUSNESS	INTENTIONALLY	INTERROGATIVE
INDIFFERENTLY	INGRAINEDNESS	INTERACTIONAL	INTERROGATORS
INDISCERNIBLE	INGURGITATION	INTERACTIVELY	INTERROGATORY
INDISCRETIONS	INHOSPITALITY	INTERACTIVITY	INTERRUPTIBLE
INDISPENSABLE	INIMITABILITY	INTERBREEDING	INTERRUPTIONS
INDISPENSABLY	INJUDICIOUSLY	INTERCALARILY	INTERSECTIONS
INDISPOSITION	INLAND REVENUE	INTERCALATION	INTERSPERSING
INDISTINCTIVE	INNER MONGOLIA	INTERCALATIVE	INTERSPERSION
INDIVIDUALISM	INNOCUOUSNESS .	INTERCELLULAR	INTERSTRATIFY
INDIVIDUALIST	INNOVATIONIST	INTERCEPTIONS	INTERTROPICAL
INDIVIDUALITY	INOCULABILITY	INTERCESSIONS	INTERVENTIONS
INDIVIDUALIZE	INOFFENSIVELY	INTERCHANGING	INTRACELLULAR
INDIVIDUATION	INOPERABILITY	INTERCLAVICLE	INTRAMUSCULAR
INDOCTRINATED	INOPPORTUNELY	INTERCOLUMNAR	INTRANSIGENCE
INDOCTRINATOR	INORGANICALLY	INTERCURRENCE	INTRAPERSONAL
INDOLEBUTYRIC	INQUISITIONAL	INTEREST GROUP	INTRATELLURIC
INDUPLICATION	INQUISITIVELY	INTERESTINGLY	INTRAVASATION
INDUSTRIALISM	INQUISITORIAL	INTERFACIALLY	INTRAVENOUSLY
INDUSTRIALIST	INSATIABILITY	INTERFERINGLY	INTRINSICALLY
INDUSTRIALIZE	INSCRIPTIONAL	INTERGALACTIC	INTRODUCTIONS
INDUSTRIOUSLY	INSECTIVOROUS	INTERGRADIENT	INTROGRESSION
INEDUCABILITY	INSENSIBILITY	INTERJECTIONS	INTROSPECTION
INEFFECTIVELY	INSENSITIVELY	INTERLACEMENT	INTROSPECTIVE
INEFFECTUALLY	INSENSITIVITY	INTERLAMINATE	INTUITIVENESS
INEFFICACIOUS	INSIDIOUSNESS	INTERLOCUTION	INVARIABILITY
INEFFICIENTLY	INSIGNIFICANT	INTERLOCUTORS	INVENTIVENESS
INELIGIBILITY	INSOLVABILITY	INTERLOCUTORY	INVENTORIABLE
INEVITABILITY	INSPECTORATES	INTERLUNATION	INVERTEBRATES
INEXHAUSTIBLE	INSPECTORSHIP	INTERMARRIAGE	INVERTED COMMA
INEXHAUSTIBLY	INSPIRATIONAL	INTERMARRYING	INVERTED SNOBS
INEXORABILITY	INSPIRITINGLY	INTERMEDIATOR	INVERTIBILITY
INEXPENSIVELY	INSTABILITIES	INTERMINGLING	INVESTIGATING
INEXPERIENCED	INSTALLATIONS	INTERMISSIONS	INVESTIGATION
INEXPRESSIBLE	INSTANTANEOUS	INTERMITTENCE	INVESTIGATIVE
INEXPRESSIBLY	INSTIGATINGLY	INTERNALIZING	INVESTIGATORS
INFALLIBILITY	INSTINCTIVELY	INTERNATIONAL	INVIDIOUSNESS
INFANT PRODIGY	INSTITUTIONAL	INTEROCEPTIVE	INVINCIBILITY
INFECTIVENESS	INSTRUCTIONAL	INTEROPERABLE	INVIOLABILITY
INFERENTIALLY	INSTRUCTIVELY	INTEROSCULATE	INVOLUNTARILY
INFILTRATIONS	INSUBORDINATE	INTERPELLATOR	IONIAN ISLANDS
INFINITESIMAL	INSUBSTANTIAL	INTERPERSONAL	IRONING BOARDS
INFLAMMATIONS	INSUFFICIENCY	INTERPOLATING	IRRATIONALITY

IRRECLAIMABLE
IRRECOVERABLE
IRRECOVERABLY
IRREFRANGIBLE
IRRELIGIONIST
IRREPLACEABLE
IRREPLEVIABLE
IRREPRESSIBLE
IRREPRESSIBLY
IRRESPONSIBLE
IRRESPONSIBLY
IRRETRIEVABLE
IRRETRIEVABLY
ISOAGGLUTININ
ISODIMORPHISM
ISODIMORPHOUS
ISOELECTRONIC
ISOGEOTHERMAL
ISOLATIONISTS
ISOMERIZATION
ISOSPONDYLOUS
ITALICIZATION

J

JACK-O'-
  LANTERNS
JARGONIZATION
JEFFERSON CITY
JELLIFICATION
JET PROPULSION
JIGGERY-POKERY
JIGSAW PUZZLES
JOBS COMFORTER
JOB'S
  COMFORTER
JOLLIFICATION
JUDICIOUSNESS
JUGLANDACEOUS
JUNIOR SCHOOLS
JURISPRUDENCE
JUSTICIARSHIP
JUSTIFICATION
JUSTIFICATORY
JUXTAPOSITION

K

KALEIDOSCOPES
KALEIDOSCOPIC
KANGAROO COURT
KANGCHENJUNGA

KARL-MARX-
  STADT
KERATOPLASTIC
KETTLEDRUMMER
KEY SIGNATURES
KIDDERMINSTER
KIDNEY MACHINE
KINDERGARTENS
KIND-HEARTEDLY
KINEMATICALLY
KINETIC ENERGY
KINETONUCLEUS
KING'S
  COUNSELS
KING'S
  EVIDENCE
KIRKCUDBRIGHT
KITCHEN GARDEN
KITTY-CORNERED
KLEPTOMANIACS
KNAVE OF
  HEARTS
KNIGHTS-ERRANT
KNOWLEDGEABLE
KNOWLEDGEABLY
KNUCKLE-DUSTER
KWANGSI-CHUANG

L

LABIALIZATION
LABORIOUSNESS
LABOURS OF
  LOVE
LACKADAISICAL
LACTOBACILLUS
LADY BOUNTIFUL
LADY-IN-
  WAITING
LAEVOROTATION
LAEVOROTATORY
LAMELLIBRANCH
LANCE CORPORAL
LANDING FIELDS
LANDING STAGES
LANDING STRIPS
LANDOWNERSHIP
LANTERNSLIDES
LAPAROSCOPIES
LARYNGOLOGIST
LARYNGOSCOPIC
LASER PRINTERS
LATCHKEY CHILD

LATEROVERSION
LATIN AMERICAN
LAUGHINGSTOCK
LAUNDRY BASKET
LEADING LADIES
LEADING LIGHTS
LEAMINGTON SPA
LEATHERJACKET
LECHEROUSNESS
LEGISLATORIAL
LEISHMANIASIS
LEISURELINESS
LEPIDOPTERIST
LEPIDOPTEROUS
LEPTOCEPHALUS
LEPTOPHYLLOUS
LETHARGICALLY
LETTER OPENERS
LETTER PERFECT
LETTER-PERFECT
LETTERPRESSES
LEVEL CROSSING
LEXICOGRAPHER
LEXICOGRAPHIC
LEXICOLOGICAL
LIBRARIANSHIP
LICENSE PLATES
LICENSING LAWS
LIEBFRAUMILCH
LIECHTENSTEIN
LIFE PRESERVER
LIGHT AIRCRAFT
LIGHT-FINGERED
LIGHT-HEADEDLY
LIGNIFICATION
LIMITLESSNESS
LINE-ENGRAVING
LINGUA FRANCAS
LIPARI ISLANDS
LITHOGRAPHING
LITIGIOUSNESS
LITTLE FINGERS
LIVERY COMPANY
LIVERY STABLES
LIVING FOSSILS
LOATHSOMENESS
LODGING HOUSES
LOGOGRAMMATIC
LONDON BRIGADE
LONG HOT
  SUMMER

LONGSUFFERING
LONG VACATIONS
LONS-LE-
  SAUNIER
LOSS ADJUSTERS
LOTHIAN REGION
LOWER EAST
  SIDE
LOW-PASS
  FILTER
LOW-WATER
  MARKS
LUBRICATIONAL
LUDICROUSNESS
LUNATIC FRINGE
LUNCHEONETTES
LYMPHADENITIS
LYMPHATICALLY
LYMPHOBLASTIC
LYMPHOCYTOSIS
LYMPHOCYTOTIC
LYMPHOPOIESIS
LYMPHOPOIETIC

M

MACARONICALLY
MACHIAVELLIAN
MACHICOLATION
MACHINABILITY
MACHINEGUNNED
MACRENCEPHALY
MACROCLIMATIC
MACROECONOMIC
MACROMOLECULE
MACRONUTRIENT
MADE-TO-
  MEASURE
MADHYA PRADESH
MADRIGALESQUE
MAGIC LANTERNS
MAGISTERIALLY
MAGNANIMOUSLY
MAGNETIC FIELD
MAGNETIC HEADS
MAGNETIC NORTH
MAGNETIC POLES
MAGNETIC TAPES
MAGNETIZATION
MAGNETOMETRIC
MAGNETOMOTIVE
MAGNETOSPHERE
MAGNIFICATION

MAGNIFICENTLY
MAGNILOQUENCE
MAGNITUDINOUS
MAGNOLIACEOUS
MAIDS OF
  HONOUR
MAJOR GENERALS
MALACOLOGICAL
MALACOSTRACAN
MALADJUSTMENT
MALADMINISTER
MALADROITNESS
MALFORMATIONS
MALFUNCTIONED
MALICIOUSNESS
MALIMPRINTING
MALTHUSIANISM
MANAGEABILITY
MANDARIN DUCKS
MANGEL-WURZELS
MANIFESTATION
MANIPULATABLE
MANIPULATIONS
MANTELSHELVES
MANUFACTURERS
MANUFACTURING
MANY-SIDEDNESS
MARAGING STEEL
MARCHIONESSES
MARKETABILITY
MARKET GARDENS
MARRIAGE LINES
MARRONS GLACES
MARTYRIZATION
MARTYROLOGIST
MASSACHUSETTS
MASSIF CENTRAL
MASS-PRODUCING
MASTERFULNESS
MASTERMINDING
MASTERS-AT-
  ARMS
MASTERS OF
  ARTS
MASTERSTROKES
MASTIGOPHORAN
MASTOIDECTOMY
MATCHLESSNESS
MATERFAMILIAS
MATERIALISTIC
MATERIALIZING

MATERNALISTIC
MATHEMATICIAN
MATRICULATING
MATRICULATION
MATRILOCALITY
MATURE STUDENT
MAXILLIPEDARY
MEALS ON
  WHEELS
MEANINGLESSLY
MEASURABILITY
MECHANIZATION
MEDIATIZATION
MEDIATORIALLY
MEDIEVALISTIC
MEDITERRANEAN
MEETINGHOUSES
MEGACEPHALOUS
MEGALOBLASTIC
MEGALOMANIACS
MEGALOPOLITAN
MELODIOUSNESS
MELODRAMATIST
MELTING POINTS
MELTON MOWBRAY
MENINGOCOCCUS
MENSTRUATIONS
MENSURATIONAL
MENTAL ILLNESS
MERCENARINESS
MERCERIZATION
MERCHANDISING
MERCHANT BANKS
MERCILESSNESS
MERCURIALNESS
MERCUROCHROME
MERCY KILLINGS
MERITOCRACIES
MERITORIOUSLY
MERRY-GO-
  ROUNDS
MERTHYR TYDFIL
MESENCEPHALIC
MESENCEPHALON
MESMERIZATION
MESSIANICALLY
METABOLICALLY
METABOLIZABLE
METACHROMATIC
METALANGUAGES
METALLIFEROUS

METALLIZATION
METALLOGRAPHY
METALLURGICAL
METALLURGISTS
METAMERICALLY
METAMORPHOSED
METAMORPHOSES
METAMORPHOSIS
METAPHOSPHATE
METAPHYSICIAN
METASTABILITY
METEMPIRICIST
METENCEPHALIC
METENCEPHALON
METEOROLOGIST
METHODIZATION
METHODOLOGIES
METHODOLOGIST
METHYL ALCOHOL
METRONIDAZOLE
METROPOLITANS
MEZZO-SOPRANOS
MICROANALYSIS
MICROANALYTIC
MICROCEPHALIC
MICROCHEMICAL
MICROCLIMATIC
MICROCOMPUTER
MICRODETECTOR
MICRONUTRIENT
MICROORGANISM
MICROPARASITE
MICROPHYSICAL
MICROTONALITY
MIDDLEBROWISM
MIDDLE EASTERN
MIDDLE ENGLAND
MIDDLE FINGERS
MIDDLE PASSAGE
MIDDLESBROUGH
MIDDLE SCHOOLS
MIDDLEWEIGHTS
MIDDLE WESTERN
MID-LIFE
  CRISES
MID-LIFE
  CRISIS
MIDWAY ISLANDS
MILK CHOCOLATE
MILLENNIALIST
MILLENNIUM BUG

MILLIONAIRESS
MIMEOGRAPHING
MINE DETECTORS
MINERALOGICAL
MINERALOGISTS
MINERAL WATERS
MINICOMPUTERS
MINISTERIALLY
MIRABILE DICTU
MIRROR WRITING
MIRTHLESSNESS
MISADVENTURES
MISCALCULATED
MISCEGENATION
MISCELLANEOUS
MISCHIEVOUSLY
MISCONCEIVING
MISCONCEPTION
MISCONDUCTING
MISCONSTRUING
MISDEMEANOURS
MISERABLENESS
MISGOVERNMENT
MISJUDGEMENTS
MISMANAGEMENT
MISPROPORTION
MISQUOTATIONS
MISSISSIPPIAN
MISSTATEMENTS
MISTRUSTFULLY
MISTRUSTINGLY
MISUNDERSTAND
MISUNDERSTOOD
MITOCHONDRIAL
MITOCHONDRION
MIXED BLESSING
MIXED METAPHOR
MOBILE LIBRARY
MOBILIZATIONS
MODERNIZATION
MODIFIABILITY
MODIFICATIONS
MODUS OPERANDI
MOHAMMEDANISM
MOLLIFICATION
MOLLYCODDLING
MOMENT OF
  TRUTH
MONEYCHANGERS
MONEY-GRUBBERS
MONEY-GRUBBING

MONEY-SPINNERS
MONKEY-PUZZLES
MONMOUTHSHIRE
MONOCHROMATIC
MONOCOTYLEDON
MONOGRAMMATIC
MONOMETALLISM
MONOMETALLIST
MONOMOLECULAR
MONONUCLEOSIS
MONOPHTHONGAL
MONOPSONISTIC
MONOSYLLABISM
MONOSYLLABLES
MONOTREMATOUS
MONSTROSITIES
MONS VENERISES
MONUMENTALITY
MOONLIGHT FLIT
MORALITY PLAYS
MORAL MAJORITY
MORNING PRAYER
MORPHEMICALLY
MORPHOGENESIS
MORPHOGENETIC
MORPHOLOGICAL
MORPHOPHONEME
MORRISDANCERS
MORTIFICATION
MOTHER COUNTRY
MOTHER-OF-
   PEARL
MOTHER TONGUES
MOTION PICTURE
MOTORCYCLISTS
MOTOR SCOOTERS
MOUNTAIN LIONS
MOUNTAINSIDES
MOUNTEBANKERY
MOUTH WATERING
MOUTH-WATERING
MOVABLE FEASTS
MOVING PICTURE
MUHAMMADANISM
MULTICELLULAR
MULTICOLOURED
MULTINATIONAL
MULTIPLE STORE
MULTITUDINOUS
MULTIVIBRATOR
MUMMIFICATION

MURDEROUSNESS
MUSICAL CHAIRS
MUSICOLOGICAL
MYCOBACTERIUM
MYRMECOLOGIST
MYSTIFICATION
MYTHICIZATION

N

NARCOANALYSIS
NARCOTIZATION
NARROW SQUEAKS
NATIONAL DEBTS
NATIONALISTIC
NATIONALITIES
NATIONALIZING
NATIONAL PARKS
NATIONAL TRUST
NATIVITY PLAYS
NATURAL NUMBER
NAUTICAL MILES
NEARSIGHTEDLY
NECESSARY EVIL
NECESSITARIAN
NECESSITATING
NECESSITATION
NECESSITATIVE
NECESSITOUSLY
NECKERCHIEVES
NECROPHILIACS
NEFARIOUSNESS
NEGATIVE POLES
NEGLIGIBILITY
NEGOTIABILITY
NEGRI SEMBILAN
NEIGHBOURHOOD
NEMATHELMINTH
NEOCLASSICISM
NEOCLASSICIST
NEOPLASTICISM
NERVELESSNESS
NERVOUS SYSTEM
NEUROFIBRILAR
NEUROMUSCULAR
NEUROSURGICAL
NEUROVASCULAR
NEW PROVIDENCE
NEW SOUTH
   WALES
NEW TECHNOLOGY
NICKELIFEROUS

NIGGARDLINESS
NIGHTCLUBBING
NIGHTMARISHLY
NIGHT WATCHMAN
NITRIFICATION
NITROBACTERIA
NITROGLYCERIN
NITROPARAFFIN
NO-CLAIMS
   BONUS
NO HOLDS
   BARRED
NOISELESSNESS
NOLI-ME-
   TANGERE
NOLLE PROSEQUI
NOMENCLATURES
NOMOGRAPHICAL
NOMOLOGICALLY
NONAGENARIANS
NONAGGRESSION
NONAPPEARANCE
NONATTENDANCE
NONCOMBATANTS
NONCOMPLIANCE
NONCONCURRENT
NONCONDUCTORS
NONCONFORMISM
NONCONFORMIST
NONCONFORMITY
NONCONTAGIOUS
NONCOOPERATOR
NONFUNCTIONAL
NONINDUSTRIAL
NONINFECTIOUS
NONPRODUCTIVE
NONRETURNABLE
NONSENSICALLY
NO OIL
   PAINTING
NORADRENALINE
NORFOLK ISLAND
NORFOLK JACKET
NORMALIZATION
NORTHALLERTON
NORTH AYRSHIRE
NORTH CAROLINA
NORTHEASTERLY
NORTHEASTWARD
NORTH OSSETIAN
NORTH SOMERSET
NORTH TYNESIDE

NORTHWESTERLY
NORTHWESTWARD
NOSOLOGICALLY
NOSTALGICALLY
NOTICEABILITY
NOTIFICATIONS
NOTORIOUSNESS
NUCLEAR ENERGY
NUCLEAR FAMILY
NUCLEAR WINTER
NUCLEONICALLY
NUCLEOPLASMIC
NUCLEOPROTEIN
NUISANCE VALUE
NULLIFICATION
NUMEROLOGICAL
NUMISMATOLOGY
NURSERY RHYMES
NURSERY SCHOOL
NYMPHAEACEOUS
NYMPHOMANIACS

O

OBJECTIONABLE
OBJECTIONABLY
OBJECTIVENESS
OBJECTIVISTIC
OBJECT LESSONS
OBLATE SPHERES
OBLIVIOUSNESS
OBNOXIOUSNESS
OBSERVATIONAL
OBSERVATORIES
OBSESSIVENESS
OBSTETRICALLY
OBSTETRICIANS
OBSTRUCTIONAL
OBSTRUCTIVELY
OBTAINABILITY
OBTRUSIVENESS
OCCASIONALISM
OCCIDENTALISM
OCCIDENTALIST
OCCIDENTALIZE
OCCLUSIVENESS
OCEANOGRAPHER
OCEANOGRAPHIC
OCTOGENARIANS
ODONTOBLASTIC
ODONTOGLOSSUM
ODONTOGRAPHIC

ODONTOLOGICAL
OFFENSIVENESS
OFFHANDEDNESS
OFFICEHOLDERS
OFFICIOUSNESS
OLD AGE
  PENSION
OLD-BOY
  NETWORK
OLD SCHOOL
  TIES
OLD WIVES'
  TALES
OLIGOPOLISTIC
OLIVE BRANCHES
OMMATOPHOROUS
ONE-NIGHT
  STAND
ONE-TRACK
  MINDS
ON THE
  PREMISES
ONTOGENICALLY
ONTOLOGICALLY
OPENHEARTEDLY
OPEN THE DOOR
  TO
OPERATIONALLY
OPERATIVENESS
OPHTHALMOLOGY
OPISTHOBRANCH
OPPORTUNENESS
OPPORTUNISTIC
OPPORTUNITIES
OPPOSITIONIST
OPPROBRIOUSLY
ORANGE BLOSSOM
ORCHESTRA PITS
ORCHESTRATING
ORCHESTRATION
ORDINARY LEVEL
ORDZHONIKIDZE
ORGAN GRINDERS
ORGANIZATIONS
ORGANOGENESIS
ORGANOGENETIC
ORGANOGRAPHIC
ORGANOLOGICAL
ORGANOTHERAPY
ORIENTALISTIC
ORIENTATIONAL
ORNAMENTATION

ORNITHISCHIAN
ORNITHOLOGIST
ORTHOCEPHALIC
ORTHOEPICALLY
ORTHOGNATHISM
ORTHOGNATHOUS
ORTHOHYDROGEN
ORTHOSTICHOUS
OSCILLOGRAPHY
OSTENSIBILITY
OSTEOMALACIAL
OSTEOMYELITIS
OTHER-DIRECTED
OUTBOARD MOTOR
OUTDISTANCING
OUTGENERALING
OUTGENERALLED
OUTMANOEUVRED
OUTSPOKENNESS
OUTSTANDINGLY
OVERABUNDANCE
OVERAMBITIOUS
OVERBALANCING
OVERBEARINGLY
OVERBURDENING
OVERCONFIDENT
OVERCRITICIZE
OVERCULTIVATE
OVERDEVELOPED
OVERELABORATE
OVEREMPHASIZE
OVERESTIMATED
OVERESTIMATES
OVERINDULGING
OVERMASTERING
OVERPOPULATED
OVERREACTIONS
OVERSHADOWING
OVERSTATEMENT
OVERSUBSCRIBE
OVERWEENINGLY
OVOVIVIPAROUS
OWNER-OCCUPIED
OWNER-OCCUPIER
OYSTERCATCHER

P

PADDLE STEAMER
PADDLING POOLS
PAEDIATRICIAN
PAINSTAKINGLY

PAINTBALL GAME
PALAEOECOLOGY
PALAEOGRAPHIC
PALAEONTOLOGY
PALAEOZOOLOGY
PALEOGRAPHERS
PALETTE KNIVES
PALYNOLOGICAL
PANCHROMATISM
PANDORA'S
  BOXES
PANIC DISORDER
PANIC STATIONS
PANIC-STRICKEN
PANORAMICALLY
PANSOPHICALLY
PANTECHNICONS
PAPAVERACEOUS
PAPILLOMATOUS
PARABOLICALLY
PARADE GROUNDS
PARADOXICALLY
PARAGOGICALLY
PARALLELOGRAM
PARALYTICALLY
PARAMAGNETISM
PARANOIACALLY
PARAPHERNALIA
PARASITICALLY
PARASITICIDAL
PARASYNTHESIS
PARASYNTHETON
PARENT COMPANY
PARENTHETICAL
PAR EXCELLENCE
PARKING GARAGE
PARKING LIGHTS
PARKING METERS
PARKINSON'S
  LAW
PARLIAMENTARY
PARROT-FASHION
PART EXCHANGES
PARTHENOCARPY
PARTICIPATING
PARTICIPATION
PARTICIPIALLY
PARTI-COLOURED
PARTICULARISM
PARTICULARIST
PARTICULARITY

PARTICULARIZE
PARTS OF
  SPEECH
PASSEMENTERIE
PASSIONFLOWER
PASSIONLESSLY
PASSIVIZATION
PATENT LEATHER
PATERFAMILIAS
PATERNALISTIC
PATHOGNOMONIC
PATRIOTICALLY
PATRISTICALLY
PATRONIZINGLY
PAY-AND-
  DISPLAY
PEACEABLENESS
PEACE DIVIDEND
PEACE OFFERING
PECKING ORDERS
PECTORAL CROSS
PECULIARITIES
PEDAGOGICALLY
PEDESTRIANIZE
PEDIATRICIANS
PEDUNCULATION
PELOPONNESIAN
PELTIER EFFECT
PEMBROKESHIRE
PENALTY CORNER
PENEPLANATION
PENETRABILITY
PENETRATINGLY
PENETRATIVELY
PENICILLATION
PENITENTIALLY
PENNILESSNESS
PENNSYLVANIAN
PENNY-DREADFUL
PENNY FARTHING
PENNY-FARTHING
PENNY-PINCHERS
PENNY-PINCHING
PENNY WHISTLES
PENTANOIC ACID
PEOPLE CARRIER
PEPPER-AND-
  SALT
PEPTONIZATION
PERAMBULATING
PERAMBULATION

381

PERAMBULATORS
PERAMBULATORY
PERCUSSION CAP
PERCUSSIONIST
PEREGRINATION
PERFECTIONISM
PERFECTIONIST
PERFUNCTORILY
PERICARPOIDAL
PERICHONDRIUM
PERIODIC TABLE
PERIOPERATIVE
PERISHABILITY
PERISSODACTYL
PERMANENT WAVE
PERMANENT WAYS
PERMUTATIONAL
PERPENDICULAR
PERSEVERATION
PERSONALISTIC
PERSONALITIES
PERSONALIZING
PERSONIFIABLE
PERSPECTIVISM
PERSPICACIOUS
PERVASIVENESS
PERVERTEDNESS
PETROCHEMICAL
PETROL STATION
PETROPAVLOVSK
PETTY OFFICERS
PHALLOCENTRIC
PHARMACEUTICS
PHARMACOGNOSY
PHARMACOPOEIA
PHARYNGOSCOPE
PHARYNGOSCOPY
PHELLOGENETIC
PHENCYCLIDINE
PHENOMENALISM
PHENOMENALIST
PHENOMENOLOGY
PHENOTHIAZINE
PHENYLALANINE
PHI BETA
  KAPPAS
PHILANTHROPIC
PHILHELLENISM
PHILOSOPHICAL
PHILOSOPHIZED
PHILOSOPHIZER

PHI-PHENOMENON
PHOSPHORYLASE
PHOTOCHEMICAL
PHOTOCOMPOSER
PHOTODYNAMICS
PHOTOELECTRIC
PHOTOELECTRON
PHOTOEMISSION
PHOTOEMISSIVE
PHOTOENGRAVER
PHOTO FINISHES
PHOTOGRAPHERS
PHOTOGRAPHING
PHOTOPERIODIC
PHOTORECEPTOR
PHOTOSTATTING
PHRASEOGRAPHY
PHRASEOLOGIST
PHRENOLOGICAL
PHYCOMYCETOUS
PHYLLOQUINONE
PHYSICALISTIC
PHYSICAL JERKS
PHYSIOGNOMIES
PHYSIOGNOMIST
PHYSIOGRAPHER
PHYSIOGRAPHIC
PHYSIOLOGICAL
PHYSIOLOGISTS
PHYSIOTHERAPY
PHYSOCLISTOUS
PHYSOSTIGMINE
PHYTOPLANKTON
PICTURESQUELY
PICTURE WINDOW
PIECES OF
  EIGHT
PIEZOELECTRIC
PIGEON-CHESTED
PIGHEADEDNESS
PILOT OFFICERS
PINK ELEPHANTS
PINKING SHEARS
PISCICULTURAL
PITCHED BATTLE
PLACE SETTINGS
PLAGIOTROPISM
PLAINTIVENESS
PLASTIC BULLET
PLATINIFEROUS
PLATINIRIDIUM

PLATINIZATION
PLATINUM-BLOND
PLATITUDINIZE
PLATITUDINOUS
PLATYHELMINTH
PLAYING FIELDS
PLENTEOUSNESS
PLENTIFULNESS
PLIMSOLL LINES
PLOUGHMANSHIP
PLURALIZATION
PNEUMATICALLY
PNEUMATOLYSIS
PNEUMATOMETER
PNEUMATOMETRY
PNEUMATOPHORE
PNEUMOGASTRIC
PNEUMONECTOMY
POETIC JUSTICE
POETIC LICENCE
POETS LAUREATE
POINTLESSNESS
POINTS OF
  ORDER
POINT-TO-
  POINTS
POISONOUSNESS
POLE POSITIONS
POLICE OFFICER
POLICE STATION
POLIOMYELITIS
POLLING BOOTHS
POLLINIFEROUS
POLYADELPHOUS
POLYCHROMATIC
POLYCOTYLEDON
POLYDACTYLOUS
POLYEMBRYONIC
POLYGALACEOUS
POLYGONACEOUS
POLYPHOSPHATE
POLYPROPYLENE
POLYPROTODONT
POLYSYLLABLES
POLYSYLLOGISM
POLYSYNTHESIS
PONDERABILITY
PONDEROUSNESS
PONTIFICATING
POOR RELATIONS
PORCELLANEOUS

PORNOGRAPHERS
PORT ELIZABETH
POSITIVE POLES
POSSIBILITIES
POSTAGE STAMPS
POSTCLASSICAL
POSTER COLOURS
POSTE RESTANTE
POSTGRADUATES
POSTMAN'S
  KNOCK
POST OFFICE
  BOX
POSTOPERATIVE
POSTPONEMENTS
POTATO BEETLES
POTENTIOMETER
POTTER'S
  WHEELS
POTTY-TRAINING
POWERLESSNESS
POWER POLITICS
POWER STATIONS
POWER STEERING
PRACTICAL JOKE
PRACTITIONERS
PRAGMATICALLY
PRAYER MEETING
PRAYING MANTIS
PREADAPTATION
PREADOLESCENT
PRECAUTIONARY
PRECEPTORSHIP
PRECIOUS METAL
PRECIOUS STONE
PRECIPITATELY
PRECIPITATING
PRECIPITATION
PRECIPITATIVE
PRECIPITOUSLY
PRECONCEPTION
PRECONDITIONS
PRECONIZATION
PREDATORINESS
PREDETERMINED
PREDETERMINER
PREDICABILITY
PREDICATIVELY
PREDILECTIONS
PREDOMINANTLY
PREDOMINATING

PREDOMINATION
PREFABRICATED
PREFABRICATOR
PREFERABILITY
PREFIGURATION
PREFIGURATIVE
PREFIGUREMENT
PREJUDGEMENTS
PRELIMINARIES
PRELIMINARILY
PREMATURENESS
PREMEDICATION
PREMEDITATION
PREMEDITATIVE
PREOCCUPATION
PREORDINATION
PREPARATORILY
PREPONDERANCE
PREPONDERATED
PREPOSITIONAL
PREPOSSESSING
PREPOSSESSION
PRE-RAPHAELITE
PREREQUISITES
PRESBYTERIANS
PRESCRIPTIBLE
PRESCRIPTIONS
PRESENTATIONS
PRESENTIMENTS
PRESERVATIVES
PRESS AGENCIES
PRESS CUTTINGS
PRESS RELEASES
PRESSURE GROUP
PRESSURE POINT
PRESUMPTIVELY
PRETENTIOUSLY
PRETERNATURAL
PREVARICATING
PREVARICATION
PREVARICATORS
PRICELESSNESS
PRIMARY COLOUR
PRIMARY SCHOOL
PRIMARY STRESS
PRIME MERIDIAN
PRIME MINISTER
PRIMITIVENESS
PRIMITIVISTIC
PRIMOGENITURE
PRINCE CONSORT

PRINCIPAL BOYS
PRINTED MATTER
PRINTING PRESS
PRISONER OF
 WAR
PRISON VISITOR
PRIVATE MEMBER
PRIVATE SCHOOL
PRIVATE SECTOR
PRIVATIZATION
PRIZEFIGHTERS
PRIZEFIGHTING
PROBABILISTIC
PROBABILITIES
PROCESS-SERVER
PROCLAMATIONS
PROCONSULATES
PROCRASTINATE
PROCTOLOGICAL
PRODUCIBILITY
PROFESSIONALS
PROFESSORIATE
PROFESSORSHIP
PROFITABILITY
PROFIT MARGINS
PROFIT SHARING
PROGNOSTICATE
PROGRESSIONAL
PROGRESSIVELY
PROGRESSIVISM
PROGRESSIVIST
PROHIBITIVELY
PROJECTIONIST
PROLEPTICALLY
PROLIFERATING
PROLIFERATION
PROLIFERATIVE
PROLONGATIONS
PROMENADE DECK
PROMINENTNESS
PROMISCUOUSLY
PROMISED LANDS
PROMISINGNESS
PROMOTIVENESS
PRONOMINALIZE
PRONOUNCEABLE
PRONOUNCEMENT
PRONUNCIATION
PROPAGABILITY
PROPAGANDISTS
PROPAGANDIZED

PROPAGATIONAL
PROPAROXYTONE
PROPHETICALLY
PROPHYLACTICS
PROPITIATIOUS
PROPORTIONATE
PROPORTIONING
PROPOSITIONAL
PROPOSITIONED
PROPRIETARILY
PROPRIETORIAL
PROPRIOCEPTOR
PROSCRIPTIONS
PROSELYTIZERS
PROSELYTIZING
PROSOPOPOEIAL
PROSTAGLANDIN
PROSTATECTOMY
PROTECTIONISM
PROTECTIONIST
PROTECTORATES
PROTEINACEOUS
PROTESTANTISM
PROTESTATIONS
PROTHETICALLY
PROTOCHORDATE
PROTOHISTORIC
PROTOLANGUAGE
PROTUBERANCES
PROTUBERANTLY
PROVINCIALISM
PROVINCIALITY
PROVING GROUND
PROVISIONALLY
PROVOCATIVELY
PROXIMATENESS
PSEPHOLOGICAL
PSEPHOLOGISTS
PSEUDOMORPHIC
PSYCHIATRISTS
PSYCHOANALYSE
PSYCHOANALYST
PSYCHOANALYZE
PSYCHOBIOLOGY
PSYCHODYNAMIC
PSYCHOGENESIS
PSYCHOGENETIC
PSYCHOGNOSTIC
PSYCHOGRAPHIC
PSYCHOHISTORY
PSYCHOKINESIS

PSYCHOKINETIC
PSYCHOLOGICAL
PSYCHOLOGISTS
PSYCHOMETRICS
PSYCHOPHYSICS
PSYCHOSOMATIC
PSYCHOSURGERY
PSYCHOTHERAPY
PSYCHOTICALLY
PSYCHROPHILIC
PTERIDOLOGIST
PTERIDOPHYTIC
PUBLIC COMPANY
PUBLIC SCHOOLS
PULVERIZATION
PUNCTILIOUSLY
PUNISHABILITY
PURITANICALLY
PURPLE PASSAGE
PURPOSELESSLY
PURPOSIVENESS
PUSILLANIMITY
PUSILLANIMOUS
PUT OUT OF
 SIGHT
PYRHELIOMETER
PYROPHOSPHATE

Q

QUADRICIPITAL
QUADRILATERAL
QUADRILLIONTH
QUADRIPARTITE
QUADRISECTION
QUADRIVALENCY
QUADRUPLICATE
QUADRUPLICITY
QUALIFICATION
QUALIFICATORY
QUALITATIVELY
QUANTUM THEORY
QUARTERFINALS
QUARTERMASTER
QUARTERSTAFFS
QUARTERSTAVES
QUARTZIFEROUS
QUEENS CONSORT
QUEEN'S
 COUNSEL
QUEEN'S
 ENGLISH

QUERULOUSNESS
QUESTIONINGLY
QUESTION MARKS
QUESTIONNAIRE
QUICK-TEMPERED
QUINDECENNIAL
QUINQUAGESIMA
QUINQUEVALENT
QUINTILLIONTH
QUINTUPLICATE
QUODLIBETICAL
QUOTATION MARK

R
RABBIT HUTCHES
RABBIT PUNCHES
RABBIT WARRENS
RABBLE-ROUSING
RACK-AND-
  PINION
RADIOACTIVATE
RADIOACTIVITY
RADIOCHEMICAL
RADIOGRAPHERS
RADIOISOTOPIC
RADIOTELEGRAM
RADIOTELETYPE
RAG-AND-BONE
  MAN
RAINBOW NATION
RAMIFICATIONS
RANCOROUSNESS
RANDOMIZATION
RAPPROCHEMENT
RAPTUROUSNESS
RAREFACTIONAL
RATEABLE VALUE
RATIOCINATION
RATIONALISTIC
RATIONALIZING
RATUSHINSKAYA
REACTIONARIES
READJUSTMENTS
READ-WRITE
  HEAD
REAFFIRMATION
REAFFORESTING
REALISTICALLY
REAPPOINTMENT
REARRANGEMENT
RECALCITRANCE

RECAPITULATED
RECEPTIONISTS
RECEPTION ROOM
RECESSIVENESS
RECIPROCALITY
RECIPROCATING
RECIPROCATION
RECIPROCATIVE
RECOGNITIONAL
RECOLLECTIONS
RECOMBINATION
RECOMMENDABLE
RECOMPENSABLE
RECOMPOSITION
RECONCILEMENT
RECONCILINGLY
RECONDITENESS
RECONDITIONED
RECONDITIONER
RECONNOITRING
RECONSIDERING
RECONSTITUENT
RECONSTITUTED
RECONSTRUCTED
RECONSTRUCTOR
RECORD-CHANGER
RECORD LIBRARY
RECORD PLAYERS
RECRIMINATING
RECRIMINATION
RECRIMINATIVE
RECRIMINATORY
RECRUDESCENCE
RECRYSTALLIZE
RECTIFICATION
RED BLOOD
  CELLS
REDEEMABILITY
REDEVELOPMENT
REDISTRIBUTED
RED-LETTER
  DAYS
REDUPLICATING
REDUPLICATION
REDUPLICATIVE
REEFER JACKETS
RE-ENFORCEMENT
RE-EXAMINATION
RE-EXPORTATION
REFERENCE BOOK
REFLEXIVENESS

REFORESTATION
REFORMATIONAL
REFORMATORIES
REFRACTOMETER
REFRACTOMETRY
REFRIGERATING
REFRIGERATION
REFRIGERATIVE
REFRIGERATORS
REFURBISHMENT
REGARDFULNESS
REGIMENTATION
REGISTRARSHIP
REGISTRATIONS
REGRETFULNESS
REGURGITATING
REGURGITATION
REHABILITATED
REIGN OF
  TERROR
REIMBURSEMENT
REIMPORTATION
REINCARNATING
REINCARNATION
REINFORCEMENT
REINSTATEMENT
REJUVENESCENT
RELATIONSHIPS
RELIGIOUSNESS
RELINQUISHING
REMINISCENCES
REMISSIBILITY
REMONSTRANCES
REMONSTRATING
REMONSTRATION
REMONSTRATIVE
REMORSELESSLY
REMOTE CONTROL
RENATIONALIZE
RENEGOTIATION
RENSSELAERITE
RENUNCIATIONS
REPEATABILITY
REPELLINGNESS
REPERCUSSIONS
REPLENISHMENT
REPOSEFULNESS
REPREHENDABLE
REPREHENSIBLE
REPREHENSIBLY
REPRESENTABLE

REPROACHFULLY
REPROACHINGLY
REPRODUCTIONS
REPROGRAPHICS
REPUBLICANISM
REPUBLICANIZE
REPUBLICATION
REPUBLISHABLE
REPULSIVENESS
REQUISITIONED
REQUISITIONER
RESENTFULNESS
RESISTIBILITY
RESISTIVENESS
RESOLVABILITY
RESOURCEFULLY
RESPIRABILITY
RESPIRATIONAL
RESPLENDENTLY
RESTAURANT CAR
RESTAURATEURS
RESTRAININGLY
RESTRICTIVELY
RESTRUCTURING
RESURRECTIONS
RESUSCITATING
RESUSCITATION
RESUSCITATIVE
RETAINABILITY
RETENTIVENESS
RETICULATIONS
RETINOSCOPIST
RETROACTIVELY
RETROACTIVITY
RETROGRESSING
RETROGRESSION
RETROGRESSIVE
RETROSPECTION
RETROSPECTIVE
RETURNABILITY
REUNIFICATION
REUTILIZATION
REVEALABILITY
REVELATIONIST
REVERBERATING
REVERBERATION
REVERBERATIVE
REVERBERATORY
REVERENTIALLY
REVERSIBILITY
REVOLUTIONARY

REVOLUTIONIST
REVOLUTIONIZE
RHABDOMANTIST
RHAPSODICALLY
RHIZOCEPHALAN
RHIZOMORPHOUS
RHODOCHROSITE
RHODODENDRONS
RIBEIRAO PRETO
RIGHTEOUSNESS
RIGHT TRIANGLE
ROAD ALLOWANCE
ROCK-AND-
  ROLLER
ROCKING CHAIRS
ROCKING HORSES
ROGUES'
  GALLERY
ROLLER COASTER
ROLLER-SKATERS
ROLLER SKATING
ROLLING STONES
ROLL OF
  HONOURS
ROLL-ON ROLL-
  OFF
ROMAN CATHOLIC
ROMAN NUMERALS
ROMANTICIZING
ROOMING HOUSES
RORSCHACH TEST
ROTARY TILLERS
ROTTEN BOROUGH
ROUGH AND
  READY
ROUGH-AND-
  READY
ROUGH DIAMONDS
ROUND BRACKETS
ROUND-THE-
  CLOCK
ROXBURGHSHIRE
ROYAL HIGHNESS
RUBBERNECKING
RUBBER-STAMPED
RUMOURMONGERS
RUTHERFORDIUM
RYUKYU ISLANDS

S

SABRE-RATTLING
SACCHARIMETER

SACCHAROMETER
SACRIFICEABLE
SACRIFICIALLY
SACRIFICINGLY
SACROSANCTITY
SADOMASOCHISM
SADOMASOCHIST
SAFETY CATCHES
SAFETY CURTAIN
SAFETY ISLANDS
SAFETY MATCHES
SAGACIOUSNESS
SAINT LAWRENCE
SAKHA REPUBLIC
SALACIOUSNESS
SALAD DRESSING
SALPINGECTOMY
SALVATION ARMY
SALVATIONISTS
SAM BROWNE
  BELT
SAN BERNARDINO
SANCTIMONIOUS
SAND-BLINDNESS
SANDWICH BOARD
SAN FRANCISCAN
SANGUINOLENCY
SANITARY TOWEL
SAN LUIS
  POTOSI
SANTA CATARINA
SAPROGENICITY
SARCASTICALLY
SARCOPHAGUSES
SATANICALNESS
SATIRICALNESS
SATISFACTIONS
SATURNINENESS
SCANDALMONGER
SCARIFICATION
SCATTERBRAINS
SCENESHIFTERS
SCEPTICALNESS
SCHEMATICALLY
SCHIZOCARPOUS
SCHIZOGENESIS
SCHIZOGENETIC
SCHIZOMYCETIC
SCHIZOPHRENIA
SCHIZOPHRENIC
SCHOLARLINESS

SCHOLASTICATE
SCHOLASTICISM
SCHOOLFELLOWS
SCHOOL-LEAVERS
SCHOOLMARMISH
SCHOOLMASTERS
SCHOOLTEACHER
SCIENTOLOGIST
SCILLY ISLANDS
SCINTILLATING
SCINTILLATION
SCLEROPROTEIN
SCOLOPENDRINE
SCORCHED EARTH
SCORIFICATION
SCRIPTWRITERS
SCRIPTWRITING
SCULPTURESQUE
SEANAD EIREANN
SEA OF
  TROUBLES
SEARCH PARTIES
SEARCH WARRANT
SEASON TICKETS
SEAWORTHINESS
SECESSIONISTS
SECLUSIVENESS
SECONDARINESS
SECOND COUSINS
SECOND-GUESSED
SECOND THOUGHT
SECRETARYSHIP
SECRETIVENESS
SECRET SERVICE
SECURITY RISKS
SEDENTARINESS
SEDIMENTARILY
SEDIMENTATION
SEDIMENTOLOGY
SEDITIOUSNESS
SEDUCTIVENESS
SEGREGATIONAL
SEINE-MARITIME
SEISMOGRAPHER
SEISMOGRAPHIC
SEISMOLOGISTS
SELECTIVENESS
SELENOGRAPHER
SELENOGRAPHIC
SELF-ABASEMENT
SELF-ADDRESSED

SELF-ANNEALING
SELF-APPOINTED
SELF-ASSERTION
SELF-ASSERTIVE
SELF-ASSURANCE
SELF-CONFESSED
SELF-CONFIDENT
SELF-CONSCIOUS
SELF-CONTAINED
SELF-DECEPTION
SELF-DECEPTIVE
SELF-DEFEATING
SELF-EVIDENTLY
SELF-IMPORTANT
SELF-INDUCTION
SELF-INDUCTIVE
SELF-INDULGENT
SELF-INFLICTED
SELF-KNOWLEDGE
SELF-PITYINGLY
SELF-POSSESSED
SELF-PROPELLED
SELF-RESTRAINT
SELF-RIGHTEOUS
SELF-SACRIFICE
SELF-SATISFIED
SELLER'S
  MARKET
SELLING-PLATER
SELLING POINTS
SEMASIOLOGIST
SEMIAUTOMATIC
SEMICONDUCTOR
SEMICONSCIOUS
SEMIDETACHEDS
SEMIFINALISTS
SEMIPALATINSK
SEMIPARASITIC
SEMIPERMEABLE
SEMIPORCELAIN
SEMPER FIDELIS
SEMPER PARATUS
SENIOR CITIZEN
SENSATIONALLY
SENSELESSNESS
SENSITIVENESS
SENSITIZATION
SENTENTIOUSLY
SENTIMENTALLY
SEQUENTIALITY
SEQUESTRATING

SEQUESTRATION
SERBO-CROATIAN
SERGEANT MAJOR
SERIALIZATION
SERIAL NUMBERS
SERICULTURIST
SERJEANT AT
LAW
SERVICE CHARGE
SEVENTH HEAVEN
SEVEN-YEAR
ITCH
SEWING MACHINE
SEXAGENARIANS
SEXPLOITATION
SHAKESPEAREAN
SHAMELESSNESS
SHAPELESSNESS
SHARP PRACTICE
SHARPSHOOTERS
SHEEPSHEARING
SHEPHERDESSES
SHIFTLESSNESS
SHIP'S
CHANDLER
SHIRTWAISTERS
SHOCK ABSORBER
SHOOTING MATCH
SHOOTING STARS
SHOOTING STICK
SHOP ASSISTANT
SHORT-CHANGING
SHORT CIRCUITS
SHORT-TEMPERED
SHOULDER BLADE
SHOULDER STRAP
SHROVE TUESDAY
SICK HEADACHES
SIDESPLITTING
SIERRA LEONEAN
SIGHTLESSNESS
SIGMOIDOSCOPE
SIGMOIDOSCOPY
SIGNATURE TUNE
SIGNIFICANTLY
SIGNIFICATION
SIGNIFICATIVE
SILENT PARTNER
SILVER BIRCHES
SILVER JUBILEE
SILVER-TONGUED

SILVER WEDDING
SILVICULTURAL
SIMPLE MACHINE
SINGLE-DECKERS
SINGULARITIES
SIPHONOSTELIC
SIT ON THE
FENCE
SITTING PRETTY
SITTING TARGET
SIXTEENTH NOTE
SKEET SHOOTING
SKIRTING BOARD
SLAP AND
TICKLE
SLEDGEHAMMERS
SLEEPING PILLS
SLEEP LEARNING
SLEEPLESSNESS
SLEIGHT OF
HAND
SLIDING SCALES
SLIPSTREAMING
SMALL FORTUNES
SMALLHOLDINGS
SMELLING SALTS
SMOOTH-TONGUED
SNAKE CHARMERS
SNAP FASTENERS
SNEAK PREVIEWS
SNOW BLINDNESS
SOCIAL CHAPTER
SOCIAL CLIMBER
SOCIALIZATION
SOCIAL SCIENCE
SOCIAL SERVICE
SOCIAL WORKERS
SOCIOECONOMIC
SOCIOLINGUIST
SODA FOUNTAINS
SOFT-PEDALLING
SOLAR CONSTANT
SOLDERING IRON
SOLDIERLINESS
SOLEMNIZATION
SOLICITATIONS
SOLICITORSHIP
SOLILOQUIZING
SOLVAY PROCESS
SOMATOPLASTIC
SOMATOPLEURAL

SOMERSAULTING
SOMNAMBULANCE
SOMNAMBULATOR
SOMNAMBULISTS
SONS-OF-
BITCHES
SOPHISTICALLY
SOPHISTICATED
SOPHISTICATES
SOPHISTICATOR
SOPORIFICALLY
SORROWFULNESS
SOUL-SEARCHING
SOUNDING BOARD
SOUNDLESSNESS
SOUNDPROOFING
SOUTH CAROLINA
SOUTHEAST ASIA
SOUTHEASTERLY
SOUTHEASTWARD
SOUTHEND-ON-
SEA
SOUTHERLINESS
SOUTHERN OCEAN
SOUTH TYNESIDE
SOUTHWESTERLY
SOUTHWESTWARD
SOVIETIZATION
SPACE INVADERS
SPACE SHUTTLES
SPACE STATIONS
SPASMODICALLY
SPEAKING TUBES
SPECIAL BRANCH
SPECIAL SCHOOL
SPECIFICATION
SPECIFICATIVE
SPECTACULARLY
SPECTROGRAPHY
SPECTROMETRIC
SPECTROSCOPES
SPECTROSCOPIC
SPECULATIVELY
SPEECH THERAPY
SPELEOLOGICAL
SPELEOLOGISTS
SPENDING MONEY
SPERMATICALLY
SPERMATOPHORE
SPERMATOPHYTE
SPHERICALNESS

SPHEROIDICITY
SPHINGOMYELIN
SPHYGMOGRAPHY
SPINE-CHILLING
SPINELESSNESS
SPINNING JENNY
SPINNING WHEEL
SPIRITUALISTS
SPIRITUALIZER
SPIT AND
POLISH
SPITTING IMAGE
SPLAYFOOTEDLY
SPLENDIFEROUS
SPLINTER GROUP
SPONTANEOUSLY
SPORTSMANLIKE
SPORTSMANSHIP
SPREAD BETTING
SPREAD-EAGLING
SPRIGHTLINESS
SPRING CHICKEN
SPRING-CLEANED
SQUANDERINGLY
SQUARE-BASHING
SQUARE BRACKET
SQUEAMISHNESS
SQUIREARCHIES
STABILIZATION
STAFF OFFICERS
STAFFORDSHIRE
STAFF SERGEANT
STAGE MANAGERS
STAGE-MANAGING
STAGE WHISPERS
STALKING-HORSE
STAMINIFEROUS
STANDARDIZING
STANDARD LAMPS
STANDING ORDER
STANDOFFISHLY
STAPHYLOCOCCI
STARCH-REDUCED
STARTING BLOCK
STARTING GATES
STARTING PRICE
STATELESSNESS
STATE-OF-THE-
ART
STATESMANLIKE
STATESMANSHIP

STATION BREAKS
STATION HOUSES
STATIONMASTER
STATION WAGONS
STATISTICALLY
STATISTICIANS
STEADFASTNESS
STEAMROLLERED
STEEPLECHASER
STEEPLECHASES
STEERING WHEEL
STENOGRAPHERS
STENOPETALOUS
STENOPHYLLOUS
STEPPING-STONE
STERCORACEOUS
STEREOGRAPHIC
STEREOSCOPIST
STEREOTROPISM
STEREOTYPICAL
STERILIZATION
STICKING POINT
STICK IN THE
  MUD
STICK-IN-THE-
  MUD
STIFF UPPER
  LIP
STILETTO HEELS
STIMULATINGLY
STIPENDIARIES
STIRLINGSHIRE
STOCKBREEDERS
STOCKBREEDING
STOCK EXCHANGE
STOICHIOMETRY
STOLONIFEROUS
STOMATOPLASTY
STOP AT
  NOTHING
STORM TROOPERS
STORMY PETRELS
STOVEPIPE HATS
STRAIGHTEDGES
STRAIGHTENING
STRAIGHT-FACED
STRAIGHT FIGHT
STRAIGHT RAZOR
STRAITJACKETS
STRANGLEHOLDS
STRANGULATING
STRANGULATION

STRATEGICALLY
STRATIGRAPHER
STRATIGRAPHIC
STRATOCUMULUS
STRATOSPHERIC
STRAW-COLOURED
STREETWALKERS
STRENGTHENING
STRENUOUSNESS
STREPTOCARPUS
STREPTOCOCCAL
STREPTOCOCCUS
STREPTOKINASE
STRIKEBREAKER
STRIP CARTOONS
STRIP LIGHTING
STROBILACEOUS
STROMATOLITIC
STRUCTURALISM
STRUCTURALIST
STUDENTS'
  UNION
STUDIO COUCHES
STUFFED SHIRTS
STYLISTICALLY
SUBCOMMITTEES
SUBCONTINENTS
SUBCONTRACTED
SUBCONTRACTOR
SUBDIVISIONAL
SUBEQUATORIAL
SUBIRRIGATION
SUBJECT MATTER
SUBLIEUTENANT
SUBMACHINE GUN
SUBORDINATING
SUBORDINATION
SUBORDINATIVE
SUBPOPULATION
SUBREPTITIOUS
SUBSCRIPTIONS
SUBSERVIENTLY
SUBSIDIZATION
SUBSTANTIALLY
SUBSTANTIATED
SUBSTANTIATOR
SUBSTANTIVELY
SUBSTANTIVIZE
SUBSTITUTABLE
SUBSTITUTIONS
SUBSTRUCTURAL

SUBSTRUCTURES
SUBTILIZATION
SUBVENTIONARY
SUFFICIENCIES
SUFFOCATINGLY
SUFFRAGANSHIP
SUFFRAGETTISM
SUFFUMIGATION
SULPHADIAZINE
SULPHURIC ACID
SUMMARIZATION
SUMMER SCHOOLS
SUMPTUOUSNESS
SUNDAY SCHOOLS
SUPERABUNDANT
SUPERADDITION
SUPERANNUATED
SUPERCALENDER
SUPERCHARGERS
SUPERCHARGING
SUPERCOLUMNAR
SUPERCRITICAL
SUPEREMINENCE
SUPERFETATION
SUPERFICIALLY
SUPERFLUIDITY
SUPERFLUOUSLY
SUPERHUMANITY
SUPERIMPOSING
SUPERINTENDED
SUPERLATIVELY
SUPERNATATION
SUPERNUMERARY
SUPERORDINATE
SUPERPHYSICAL
SUPERPOSITION
SUPERSENSIBLE
SUPERSTITIONS
SUPERSTITIOUS
SUPERVENIENCE
SUPPLANTATION
SUPPLEMENTARY
SUPPLEMENTING
SUPPLICATIONS
SUPPLY TEACHER
SUPPOSITIONAL
SUPPOSITORIES
SUPRANATIONAL
SURFACE-ACTIVE
SURREPTITIOUS
SURROGATESHIP

SURVIVABILITY
SUSTENTACULAR
SWASHBUCKLING
SWEET NOTHINGS
SWIMMING BATHS
SWIMMING POOLS
SWIZZLE STICKS
SWOLLEN HEADED
SWORDSMANSHIP
SYBARITICALLY
SYLLABOGRAPHY
SYLLEPTICALLY
SYLLOGISTICAL
SYLLOGIZATION
SYMBOLIZATION
SYMMETRICALLY
SYMPATHECTOMY
SYMPATHOLYTIC
SYMPATRICALLY
SYMPHONICALLY
SYMPHYSICALLY
SYNARTHRODIAL
SYNCHRONISTIC
SYNCHRONIZING
SYNDICALISTIC
SYNTACTICALLY
SYNTHETICALLY
SYPHILOLOGIST
SYRINGOMYELIA
SYRINGOMYELIC
SYSTEMATIZING
SYSTEMATOLOGY
SYSTEMIZATION
SYZYGETICALLY

T

TACHISTOSCOPE
TACHYPHYLAXIS
TAKE A BACK
  SEAT
TAKE THE
  PLEDGE
TALKATIVENESS
TALKING POINTS
TANGENTIALITY
TANTALIZATION
TANTALIZINGLY
TAPE RECORDERS
TAR AND
  FEATHER

TARN-ET-GARONNE
TARTARIZATION
TASTELESSNESS
TATAR REPUBLIC
TAX-DEDUCTIBLE
TAXONOMICALLY
TAYSIDE REGION
TEAR A STRIP OFF
TECHNOLOGICAL
TECHNOLOGISTS
TEETER-TOTTERS
TELAUTOGRAPHY
TELECOMMUTING
TELEGRAPH POLE
TELEMARKETING
TELENCEPHALIC
TELENCEPHALON
TELEPHOTO LENS
TELEPROMPTERS
TELEUTOSPORIC
TELEVISIONARY
TEMPERABILITY
TEMPERAMENTAL
TEMPERATENESS
TEMPESTUOUSLY
TEMPORARINESS
TEMPORIZATION
TEMPORIZINGLY
TENACIOUSNESS
TENANT FARMERS
TENDENTIOUSLY
TENDERHEARTED
TENDERIZATION
TEN-GALLON HATS
TENPIN BOWLING
TENTATIVENESS
TERGIVERSATOR
TERMINABILITY
TERMINATIONAL
TERMINOLOGIES
TERMINOLOGIST
TERPSICHOREAN
TERRACED HOUSE
TERRESTRIALLY
TERRORIZATION
TESTIFICATION
TETARTOHEDRAL
TETRABASICITY

TETRACHLORIDE
TETRADYNAMOUS
TETRASTICHOUS
TETRASYLLABIC
TETRASYLLABLE
THALASSOCRACY
THANKLESSNESS
THANKSGIVINGS
THEANTHROPISM
THEANTHROPIST
THEATRICALITY
THE CUT OF A CARD
THE GONDOLIERS
THE LIONS SHARE
THE MAGIC FLUTE
THENCEFORWARD
THEOLOGICALLY
THEORETICALLY
THERIOMORPHIC
THERMOCHEMIST
THERMODYNAMIC
THERMOGENESIS
THERMOGRAPHER
THERMOGRAPHIC
THERMONUCLEAR
THERMOPLASTIC
THERMOSETTING
THERMOS FLASKS
THERMOSTATICS
THERMOTHERAPY
THERMOTROPISM
THETFORD MINES
THIGMOTROPISM
THORACOPLASTY
THOROUGHBREDS
THOROUGHFARES
THOROUGHGOING
THOROUGHPACED
THOUGHTLESSLY
THOUGHT POLICE
THREATENINGLY
THREE-CORNERED
THREE-DAY EVENT
THREE LINE WHIP
THREE-LINE WHIP
THREMMATOLOGY

THUNDERCLOUDS
THUNDERSHOWER
THUNDERSTORMS
THUNDERSTRUCK
THYROIDECTOMY
TIME AFTER TIME
TIME-AND-MOTION
TIME-CONSUMING
TIME EXPOSURES
TIME SIGNATURE
TINTINNABULAR
TINTINNABULUM
TITILLATINGLY
TITTLE-TATTLED
TITTLE-TATTLER
TOAD-IN-THE-HOLE
TOASTING FORKS
TOILET-TRAINED
TOLERABLENESS
TOLERATIONISM
TOLERATIONIST
TONE LANGUAGES
TONGUE TWISTER
TONSILLECTOMY
TOOTHSOMENESS
TOPOGRAPHICAL
TOPOLOGICALLY
TORRE DEL GRECO
TORTOISESHELL
TOTIPALMATION
TOXICOLOGICAL
TOXICOLOGISTS
TOXOPLASMOSIS
TRACE ELEMENTS
TRACHEOTOMIST
TRADE UNIONISM
TRADE UNIONIST
TRADING ESTATE
TRADING STAMPS
TRADITIONALLY
TRAFFIC CIRCLE
TRAFFIC ISLAND
TRAFFIC LIGHTS
TRAFFIC WARDEN
TRAGICOMEDIES
TRAILER HOUSES
TRANQUILLIZED
TRANQUILLIZER

TRANSACTINIDE
TRANSACTIONAL
TRANSATLANTIC
TRANSCAUCASIA
TRANSCENDENCE
TRANSCENDENCY
TRANSCRIBABLE
TRANSCRIPTION
TRANSFIGURING
TRANSFORMABLE
TRANSGRESSING
TRANSGRESSION
TRANSGRESSIVE
TRANSGRESSORS
TRANSISTORIZE
TRANSLATIONAL
TRANSLATORIAL
TRANSLITERATE
TRANSLOCATION
TRANSMIGRATOR
TRANSMISSIBLE
TRANSMISSIONS
TRANSMITTANCE
TRANSMITTANCY
TRANSMUTATION
TRANSPARENTLY
TRANSPIRATION
TRANSPIRATORY
TRANSPLANTING
TRANSPORTABLE
TRANSPORT CAFE
TRANSPORTEDLY
TRANSPOSITION
TRANSSHIPMENT
TRANSVESTITES
TRANSYLVANIAN
TRAPEZOHEDRAL
TRAPEZOHEDRON
TRAUMATICALLY
TREACHEROUSLY
TREASURERSHIP
TREASURE TROVE
TREASURE-TROVE
TREASURY NOTES
TREMULOUSNESS
TREPONEMATOUS
TRIANGULARITY
TRIANGULATION
TRIATOMICALLY
TRIBOELECTRIC
TRICENTENNIAL

TRICHOLOGISTS
TRICHOMONADAL
TRICHROMATISM
TRIGONOMETRIC
TRILATERATION
TRILINGUALISM
TRIMETHADIONE
TRIPLOBLASTIC
TRIPOLITANIAN
TRISACCHARIDE
TROOP CARRIERS
TROPHALLACTIC
TROPHOBLASTIC
TROUBLEMAKERS
TRUCIAL STATES
TRUSTWORTHILY
TRUTH-FUNCTION
TUBERCULATION
TUBUAI ISLANDS
TUBULIFLOROUS
TURBOCHARGERS
TURBOCHARGING
TURBO-ELECTRIC
TURING MACHINE
TURNING CIRCLE
TURNING POINTS
TWO-WAY
  MIRRORS
TYPOGRAPHICAL
TYRANNIZINGLY
TYRANNOSAURUS
TYRANNOUSNESS

U

UGLY DUCKLINGS
ULTRANATIONAL
UMBELLIFEROUS
UMBILICAL CORD
UNACCOMPANIED
UNACCOUNTABLE
UNACCOUNTABLY
UNADULTERATED
UNADVENTUROUS
UNADVISEDNESS
UNASHAMEDNESS
UNBELIEVINGLY
UNBENDINGNESS
UNBLESSEDNESS
UNCEASINGNESS
UNCEREMONIOUS
UNCERTAINNESS

UNCHALLENGING
UNCHARISMATIC
UNCIRCUMCISED
UNCLEANLINESS
UNCOMFORTABLE
UNCOMFORTABLY
UNCOMPENSATED
UNCOMPETITIVE
UNCOMPLAINING
UNCOMPLICATED
UNCONCERNEDLY
UNCONDITIONAL
UNCONDITIONED
UNCONFORMABLE
UNCONSCIOUSLY
UNCONSTRAINED
UNCONSUMMATED
UNCONTENTIOUS
UNCOORDINATED
UNCROWNED KING
UNDECIDEDNESS
UNDERACHIEVED
UNDERACHIEVER
UNDERBREEDING
UNDERCARRIAGE
UNDERCHARGING
UNDERCURRENTS
UNDERDRAINAGE
UNDEREDUCATED
UNDEREMPLOYED
UNDERESTIMATE
UNDEREXPOSING
UNDEREXPOSURE
UNDERGARMENTS
UNDERGRADUATE
UNDERHANDEDLY
UNDER MILK
  WOOD
UNDERMININGLY
UNDERPAINTING
UNDERPINNINGS
UNDERSTANDING
UNDERSTRENGTH
UNDERSTUDYING
UNDISCIPLINED
UNDISTRIBUTED
UNEARTHLINESS
UNEMBARRASSED
UNENFORCEABLE
UNENLIGHTENED
UNEQUIVOCALLY

UNEXCEPTIONAL
UNEXPERIENCED
UNFALTERINGLY
UNFAMILIARITY
UNFASHIONABLE
UNFEELINGNESS
UNFLINCHINGLY
UNFORESEEABLE
UNFORGETTABLE
UNFORGETTABLY
UNFORTUNATELY
UNFOUNDEDNESS
UNGUARDEDNESS
UNHEALTHINESS
UNICAMERALISM
UNICAMERALIST
UNILATERALISM
UNILLUSTRATED
UNIMPEACHABLE
UNIMPEACHABLY
UNINHABITABLE
UNINHIBITEDLY
UNINTELLIGENT
UNINTENTIONAL
UNINTERRUPTED
UNITED KINGDOM
UNITED NATIONS
UNIVERSALNESS
UNIVERSAL TIME
UNMENTIONABLE
UNMUSICALNESS
UNNATURALNESS
UNNECESSARILY
UNOBTRUSIVELY
UNPATRONIZING
UNPRECEDENTED
UNPREDICTABLE
UNPRESSURIZED
UNPRETENTIOUS
UNQUALIFIABLE
UNQUESTIONING
UNREADABILITY
UNRELENTINGLY
UNRELIABILITY
UNREMITTINGLY
UNREPRESENTED
UNRUFFLEDNESS
UNSAVOURINESS
UNSELFISHNESS
UNSERVICEABLE
UNSIGHTLINESS

UNSOCIABILITY
UNSUBSTANTIAL
UNSUITABILITY
UNSUSTAINABLE
UNTHREATENING
UNTRADITIONAL
UNTRANSFORMED
UNWARRANTABLE
UNWILLINGNESS
UNWRITTEN LAWS
UPRIGHT PIANOS
UP TO THE
  MINUTE
UP-TO-THE-
  MINUTE
URETHROSCOPIC
UTI POSSIDETIS
UTTERABLENESS

V

VACILLATINGLY
VACUUM CLEANER
VALUE-ADDED
  TAX
VALUE JUDGMENT
VALUELESSNESS
VANTAGE POINTS
VAPOURABILITY
VAPOURISHNESS
VARICOSE VEINS
VARIOLIZATION
VASOINHIBITOR
VAULTING HORSE
VEGETARIANISM
VENEREOLOGIST
VENETIAN BLIND
VENTRILOQUIAL
VENTRILOQUISM
VENTRILOQUIST
VENTRILOQUIZE
VERACIOUSNESS
VERBALIZATION
VERBIFICATION
VERITABLENESS
VERMICULATION
VERMINOUSNESS
VERNACULARISM
VERNALIZATION
VERSIFICATION
VESTAL VIRGINS
VESTMANAEYJAR

VEXATIOUSNESS
VEXED QUESTION
VEXILLOLOGIST
VICARIOUSNESS
VICE PRESIDENT
VICIOUS CIRCLE
VICTIMIZATION
VICTORIA CROSS
VICTORIA PLUMS
VILIFICATIONS
VINDICABILITY
VINICULTURIST
VIOLONCELLIST
VIRGINIA BEACH
VIRGIN ISLANDS
VISCOUNTESSES
VISIONARINESS
VISITING CARDS
VISITORS'
  BOOKS
VISUALIZATION
VITRIFICATION
VITRIOLICALLY
VIVACIOUSNESS
VIVISECTIONAL
VOCIFERATIONS
VOICELESSNESS
VOLATILIZABLE
VOLCANIZATION
VOLCANOLOGIST
VOLUNTARINESS
VOLUNTARISTIC
VOTE OF
  CENSURE
VOTES OF
  THANKS
VOUCHSAFEMENT

VRAISEMBLANCE
VULCANIZATION
VULGARIZATION
VULNERABILITY

W

WALKIE-TALKIES
WALKING PAPERS
WALKING STICKS
WALL PAINTINGS
WALTHAM FOREST
WARM-HEARTEDLY
WASHINGTONIAN
WASTE PRODUCTS
WATCH THE
  CLOCK
WATER BISCUITS
WATER BUFFALOS
WATERING HOLES
WATERING PLACE
WATERPROOFING
WATER SOFTENER
WATER SUPPLIES
WATTLE AND
  DAUB
WEARISOMENESS
WEATHER-BEATEN
WEATHERBOARDS
WEIGHT LIFTERS
WEIGHT LIFTING
WELFARE STATES
WELL-APPOINTED
WELL-CONNECTED
WELL-DEVELOPED
WELL-PRESERVED
WELL-QUALIFIED
WELL-SUPPORTED

WELL-THOUGHT-
  OF
WELSH RAREBITS
WELTERWEIGHTS
WEST BERKSHIRE
WESTERN SAHARA
WEST GLAMORGAN
WEST-NORTHWEST
WEST-SOUTHWEST
WEST YORKSHIRE
WETTING AGENTS
WHEELER DEALER
WHEELER-DEALER
WHIMSICALNESS
WHIPPOORWILLS
WHITE ELEPHANT
WHITE WEDDINGS
WHOLESOMENESS
WHOOPING COUGH
WICKET KEEPERS
WIDE-AWAKENESS
WILDCAT STRIKE
WILHELMSHAVEN
WILL-O'-THE-
  WISPS
WILLOW PATTERN
WINDING SHEETS
WINDOW-DRESSER
WINDOW-SHOPPED
WINDOW-SHOPPER
WING COMMANDER
WITHDRAWNNESS
WITHERINGNESS
WITWATERSRAND
WOLVERHAMPTON
WOMEN'S
  STUDIES

WONDERFULNESS
WONDER-WORKING
WOODCRAFTSMAN
WOOLGATHERING
WORD BLINDNESS
WORD PROCESSOR
WORK-HARDENING
WORSHIPPINGLY
WORTHLESSNESS
WRONGHEADEDLY

X

XANTHOCHROISM
XEROPHTHALMIA
XEROPHTHALMIC
XINJIANG UYGUR

Y

YACHTSMANSHIP
YEOMAN SERVICE
YOUNG MARRIEDS

Z

ZEBRA CROSSING
ZEUGMATICALLY
ZIGZAGGEDNESS
ZINJANTHROPUS
ZOOGEOGRAPHER
ZOOGEOGRAPHIC
ZOOSPORANGIAL
ZOOSPORANGIUM
ZYGAPOPHYSEAL
ZYGODACTYLISM
ZYGODACTYLOUS

A

ABOVE-MENTIONED
ABSENT-MINDEDLY
ABSORBEFACIENT
ABSTEMIOUSNESS
ABSTRACTEDNESS
ABSTRACTIONISM
ACCLIMATIZABLE
ACCOMMODATIONS
ACCOMPANIMENTS
ACCOMPLISHABLE
ACCOMPLISHMENT
ACCOUNTABILITY
ACCUMULATIVELY
ACHONDROPLASIA
ACHROMATICALLY
ACKNOWLEDGMENT
ACQUIRED TASTES
ACROSS THE BOARD
ACROSS-THE-BOARD
ACTION STATIONS
ADENOCARCINOMA
ADMINISTRATION
ADMINISTRATIVE
ADMINISTRATORS
ADMINISTRATRIX
ADULT EDUCATION
ADVANCED LEVELS
ADVANTAGEOUSLY
AEROBALLISTICS
AEROMECHANICAL
AFFECTIONATELY
AFOREMENTIONED
AGGLOMERATIONS
AGGRANDIZEMENT
AGGRESSIVENESS
AGRICULTURISTS
AGROBIOLOGICAL
AGUASCALIENTES
AIR-CONDITIONED
AIR VICE-MARSHAL
ALCOHOLIZATION

ALLEGORIZATION
ALL-IN WRESTLING
ALLITERATIVELY
ALLOPATHICALLY
ALLOPATRICALLY
ALLOTROPICALLY
ALL OVER THE SHOP
ALPES MARITIMES
ALPHABETICALLY
ALSACE-LORRAINE
ALTRUISTICALLY
AMARANTHACEOUS
AMATEURISHNESS
AMBASSADORSHIP
AMBASSADRESSES
AMBIDEXTROUSLY
AMERICAN INDIAN
AMMONIFICATION
AMPHIARTHROSIS
AMPHIBOLOGICAL
AMPHIPROSTYLAR
AMUSEMENT PARKS
ANACARDIACEOUS
ANAESTHETIZING
ANAMNESTICALLY
ANAMORPHOSCOPE
ANATHEMATIZING
ANCIENT MARINER
ANDORRA LA VELLA
ANGINA PECTORIS
ANGLO-AMERICANS
ANGLO-CATHOLICS
ANIMADVERSIONS
ANISODACTYLOUS
ANTAGONIZATION
ANTHROPOLOGIST
ANTHROPOMETRIC
ANTHROPOPATHIC
ANTHROPOSOPHIC
ANTICHLORISTIC
ANTICIPATORILY

ANTIDEPRESSANT
ANTIHISTAMINES
ANTILOGARITHMS
ANTIMONARCHIST
ANTIPERSPIRANT
ANTIPHLOGISTIC
ANTIPRAGMATISM
ANTIQUATEDNESS
ANTIREPUBLICAN
ANTISEPTICALLY
ANTITHETICALLY
APARTMENT HOUSE
APOLOGETICALLY
APOPLECTICALLY
APOSTROPHIZING
APPENDECTOMIES
APPENDICECTOMY
APPLES AND PEARS
APPORTIONMENTS
APPRECIATIVELY
APPREHENSIVELY
APPRENTICESHIP
APPROPRIATIONS
APPROVED SCHOOL
APPROXIMATIONS
ARABIC NUMERALS
ARCHAEOLOGICAL
ARCHAEOLOGISTS
ARCHBISHOPRICS
ARCHETYPICALLY
ARCHIDIACONATE
ARCHIEPISCOPAL
ARCHIMANDRITES
ARCHITECTONICS
ARITHMETICALLY
ARITHMETICIANS
ARRONDISSEMENT
ARTICULATENESS
ARTIODACTYLOUS
AS CLEAR AS A BELL
AS DRUNK AS A LORD
AS SAFE AS HOUSES
ASSASSINATIONS
ASSAULT COURSES

ASSET-STRIPPING
ASSOCIATIONISM
AS THE CASE MAY BE
ASTIGMATICALLY
ASTROLOGICALLY
ASTRONAVIGATOR
ASTRONOMICALLY
ASTROPHYSICIST
ASYMMETRICALLY
ASYMPTOTICALLY
AT DAGGERS DRAWN
ATTRACTIVENESS
AUF WIEDERSEHEN
AUSPICIOUSNESS
AUTHENTICATING
AUTHENTICATION
AUTHENTICITIES
AUTHORITARIANS
AUTHORIZATIONS
AUTOBIOGRAPHER
AUTOBIOGRAPHIC
AUTOCRATICALLY
AUTOIONIZATION
AUTOMATIC PILOT
AUTOPHYTICALLY
AUTORADIOGRAPH
AUTOSUGGESTION
AUTOSUGGESTIVE
AUXILIARY VERBS
AWE-INSPIRINGLY

B

BACCALAUREATES
BACHELOR OF ARTS
BACK FORMATIONS
BACKHANDEDNESS
BACK-SEAT DRIVER
BACTERIOLOGIST
BACTERIOPHAGIC
BACTERIOSTASIS
BACTERIOSTATIC

BALANCE OF
POWER
BALANCE OF
TRADE
BALSAMINACEOUS
BANANA
REPUBLIC
BANNER
HEADLINE
BAROMETRICALLY
BASIDIOSPOROUS
BASTARDIZATION
BATCH
PROCESSED
BATHING
MACHINE
BATTLE
CRUISERS
BE-ALL AND
END-ALL
BEASTS OF
BURDEN
BEATIFICATIONS
BEAUTIFICATION
BEAUTY
PARLOURS
BEHIND THE
TIMES
BELISHA
BEACONS
BERBERIDACEOUS
BERKSHIRE
DOWNS
BESIDE THE
POINT
BEST BEFORE
DATE
BIBLIOGRAPHERS
BIBLIOGRAPHIES
BIG GAME
HUNTING
BIOCLIMATOLOGY
BIODEGRADABLES
BIOENGINEERING
BIOGENETICALLY
BIOGRAPHICALLY
BIOLUMINESCENT
BIPARTISANSHIP
BIRD OF
PARADISE
BIRDS OF
PASSAGE
BITUMINIZATION

BLACK
MARKETEER
BLANK
CARTRIDGE
BLOCK AND
TACKLE
BLOOD
POISONING
BLOOD
PRESSURES
BLOOD
RELATIONS
BLOOD
SACRIFICE
BLOODTHIRSTILY
BLUE-
PENCILLING
BOARDINGHOUSES
BOARDING
SCHOOL
BOIS DE
BOULOGNE
BOISTEROUSNESS
BOLOMETRICALLY
BOON
COMPANIONS
BOUCHES-DU-
RHONE
BOUGAINVILLEAS
BOUILLABAISSES
BOULEVERSEMENT
BOWDLERIZATION
BRACHYCEPHALIC
BRACHYDACTYLIA
BRACHYDACTYLIC
BREAD-AND-
BUTTER
BREAKFAST
TABLE
BREATHLESSNESS
BREMSSTRAHLUNG
BRIGHT AND
EARLY
BRONCHIAL
TUBES
BRONCHIECTASIS
BRONCHOSCOPIST
BRUSSELS
SPROUT
BUILDING
BLOCKS
BULLETIN
BOARDS

BULLHEADEDNESS
BUREAU DE
CHANGE
BURNT
OFFERINGS
BUSMAN'S
HOLIDAY

C

CADAVEROUSNESS
CALAMINE
LOTION
CALENDAR
MONTHS
CALLIGRAPHISTS
CAMPANOLOGISTS
CAMPANULACEOUS
CANTANKEROUSLY
CAPITALIZATION
CAPITAL
LETTERS
CAPPARIDACEOUS
CAPRICIOUSNESS
CARBON
MONOXIDE
CARCINOMATOSIS
CARDINAL
POINTS
CARDIOVASCULAR
CARPET
SWEEPERS
CARRIER
PIGEONS
CARRYING
CHARGE
CARTOGRAPHICAL
CARTRIDGE
PAPER
CASEMENT
WINDOW
CASH AND
CARRIES
CASH
DISPENSERS
CATCHMENT
AREAS
CATECHETICALLY
CATEGORIZATION
CATHEDRAL
CLOSE
CATHERINE
WHEEL

CATHODE RAY
TUBE
CAUGHT
UNAWARES
CAUSES
CELEBRES
CENSORIOUSNESS
CENTRAL
HEATING
CENTRALIZATION
CENTRE
FORWARDS
CENTRIFUGATION
CERCOPITHECOID
CHAIN
REACTIONS
CHAISES
LONGUES
CHANGEABLENESS
CHANTRY
CHAPELS
CHARACTER
ACTOR
CHARACTERISTIC
CHARACTERIZING
CHARGE
ACCOUNTS
CHARITABLENESS
CHARLATANISTIC
CHARTER
MEMBERS
CHECHENO-
INGUSH
CHEMOSYNTHESIS
CHEMOSYNTHETIC
CHEMOTHERAPIST
CHEST OF
DRAWERS
CHICKENHEARTED
CHIEF
CONSTABLE
CHIEF
EXECUTIVE
CHIEF
INSPECTOR
CHIEFTAINSHIPS
CHILD
PRODIGIES
CHIMNEYBREASTS
CHIMNEY
CORNERS
CHINCHERINCHEE

CHINESE LANTERN
CHINLESS WONDER
CHLOROPHYLLOID
CHLOROPHYLLOUS
CHLOROTHIAZIDE
CHLORPROMAZINE
CHLORPROPAMIDE
CHOLINESTERASE
CHOREOGRAPHERS
CHOREOGRAPHING
CHRISTIAN NAMES
CHRISTMAS BOXES
CHRISTMAS CAKES
CHRISTMAS CARDS
CHRISTMAS TREES
CHRISTOLOGICAL
CHROMATOGRAPHY
CHROMATOPHORIC
CHRYSANTHEMUMS
CIGARETTE PAPER
CINCHONIZATION
CINEMATOGRAPHY
CIRCUIT BREAKER
CIRCULAR LETTER
CIRCUMAMBIENCE
CIRCUMAMBULATE
CIRCUMFERENCES
CIRCUMLOCUTION
CIRCUMLOCUTORY
CIRCUMNAVIGATE
CIRCUMNUTATION
CIRCUMSCISSILE
CIRCUMSCRIBING
CIRCUMSPECTION
CIRCUMSTANTIAL
CIRCUMVOLUTION
CIRCUMVOLUTORY
CIVIL ENGINEERS
CLARIFICATIONS
CLASS-CONSCIOUS

CLASSIFICATION
CLASSIFICATORY
CLAUSTROPHOBIA
CLAUSTROPHOBIC
CLEARANCE SALES
CLEARINGHOUSES
CLEAR-SIGHTEDLY
CLIMBING FRAMES
CLOAK-AND-DAGGER
CLOTHES HANGERS
CLUB SANDWICHES
CLUSTER BOMBING
COCK-A-DOODLE-DOO
COCKER SPANIELS
COCKTAIL LOUNGE
COCKTAIL STICKS
COESSENTIALITY
COFFEE KLATCHES
COINCIDENTALLY
COLD SHOULDERED
COLLAPSIBILITY
COLLECTIVE FARM
COLLECTIVE NOUN
COLLECTOR'S ITEM
COLLOQUIALISMS
COLORADO BEETLE
COLOURFASTNESS
COLOURLESSNESS
COMBINING FORMS
COMBUSTIBILITY
COMFORTABLY OFF
COMFORT STATION

COMMAND MODULES
COMMENSURATION
COMMERCIALIZED
COMMISERATIONS
COMMISSIONAIRE
COMMITTEE STAGE
COMMON FRACTION
COMMON-OR-GARDEN
COMMUNICATIONS
COMMUNITY CHEST
COMMUNITY HOMES
COMPLEMENTIZER
COMPREHENSIBLE
COMPREHENSIBLY
COMPREHENSIONS
COMPREHENSIVES
COMPULSIVENESS
CONCATENATIONS
CONCAVO-CONCAVE
CONCELEBRATION
CONCENTRATIONS
CONCEPTUALIZED
CONCESSIONAIRE
CONCRETE JUNGLE
CONCRETE MIXERS
CONCRETE POETRY
CONCRETIZATION
CONDEMNED CELLS
CONDENSABILITY
CONDITIONALITY
CONDUCTOR RAILS
CONDUPLICATION
CONFABULATIONS
CONFEDERATIONS
CONFIDENTIALLY
CONFIGURATIONS
CONFLAGRATIONS
CONFORMABILITY
CONFRONTATIONS
CONGLOMERATION

CONGLUTINATIVE
CONGRATULATING
CONGRATULATION
CONGRATULATORY
CONGREGATIONAL
CONJUNCTIVITIS
CONNECTING RODS
CONQUISTADORES
CONRAIL, CONRAIL
CONSANGUINEOUS
CONSCRIPTIONAL
CONSERVATIONAL
CONSERVATIVELY
CONSERVATOIRES
CONSERVATORIES
CONSIDERATIONS
CONSOLIDATIONS
CONSPIRATORIAL
CONSTABULARIES
CONSTANTINOPLE
CONSTELLATIONS
CONSTITUENCIES
CONSTITUTIONAL
CONSTRUCTIONAL
CONSTRUCTIVELY
CONSTRUCTIVISM
CONSTRUCTIVIST
CONSUETUDINARY
CONTAGIOUSNESS
CONTAINERIZING
CONTEMPORARIES
CONTEMPORARILY
CONTEMPTUOUSLY
CONTINENTALISM
CONTINENTALIST
CONTINENTALITY
CONTORTIONISTS
CONTRACEPTIVES
CONTRACT BRIDGE
CONTRADICTIONS
CONTRAINDICANT
CONTRAINDICATE
CONTRAPOSITION
CONTRAPUNTALLY
CONTRAVENTIONS
CONTRIBUTORIAL
CONTROVERTIBLE
CONTUMACIOUSLY

CONTUMELIOUSLY
CONVENTIONALLY
CONVERSATIONAL
CONVERSAZIOONI
CONVERTIBILITY
CONVEXO-
 CONCAVE
COPPER-
 BOTTOMED
CORELIGIONISTS
CORNISH
 PASTIES
CORPORATION
 TAX
CORRESPONDENCE
CORRESPONDENTS
CORRUPTIBILITY
CORTICOSTEROID
CORTICOSTERONE
CORTICOTROPHIN
COUNTERACTIONS
COUNTERATTACKS
COUNTERBALANCE
COUNTERFEITERS
COUNTERFEITING
COUNTERMANDING
COUNTERMEASURE
COUNTERMENSURE
COUNTERPOISING
COUNTERSHADING
COUNTERSIGNING
COUNTERSINKING
COUNTERVAILING
COUNTINGHOUSES
COUNTRY
 COUSINS
COUNTY
 COUNCILS
COURAGEOUSNESS
COURT-
 MARTIALED
COURT OF
 INQUIRY
COVERING
 LETTER
CRADLE
 SNATCHER
CRAMP ONES
 STYLE
CREDIBILITY
 GAP
CREDITABLENESS

394

CREDIT
 ACCOUNTS
CREDIT
 SQUEEZES
CREEPY-
 CRAWLIES
CRIMINAL
 RECORD
CRIMINOLOGICAL
CRIMINOLOGISTS
CROCODILE
 TEARS
CROSS-
 COUNTRIES
CROSS-
 EXAMINERS
CROSS-
 EXAMINING
CROSS-
 FERTILIZE
CROSS-
 POLLINATE
CROSS
 REFERENCE
CROSS-
 REFERENCE
CROSS-
 REFERRING
CROSS-
 SECTIONAL
CROWN AND
 ANCHOR
CRUISE
 MISSILES
CRYPTAESTHESIA
CRYPTOGRAPHERS
CSECHOSLOVAKIA
CUCURBITACEOUS
CURRENT
 ACCOUNT
CURRICULA
 VITAE
CURRUGATED
 IRON
CURTAIN
 RAISERS
CURVILINEARITY
CYANOCOBALAMIN
CYBERNETICALLY
CYTOTAXONOMIST

D

DAGUERREOTYPER

DAGUERREOTYPES
DANISH
 PASTRIES
DATA
 PROCESSING
DAUGHTERLINESS
DAUGHTERS-IN-
 LAW
DAY OF
 RECKONING
DEAD MANS
 HANDLE
DEAD TO THE
 WORLD
DECEIVABLENESS
DECENTRALIZING
DECIMALIZATION
DECLASSIFIABLE
DECLENSIONALLY
DECLINE AND
 FALL
DECOLONIZATION
DECOLORIZATION
DECONTAMINATED
DECONTAMINATOR
DEFENESTRATION
DEFLOCCULATION
DEGENERATENESS
DEHUMANIZATION
DELECTABLENESS
DELIBERATENESS
DELIGHTFULNESS
DELOCALIZATION
DEMILITARIZING
DEMISEMIQUAVER
DEMOBILIZATION
DEMOCRATICALLY
DEMONETIZATION
DEMONSTRATIONS
DEMORALIZATION
DENATIONALIZED
DENOMINATIONAL
DENTAL
 SURGEONS
DEPLORABLENESS
DEPOLARIZATION
DEPOSIT
 ACCOUNT
DERMATOLOGICAL
DERMATOLOGISTS
DERMATOPLASTIC
DEROGATORINESS

DESTRUCTIONIST
DETERMINEDNESS
DEVIL'S
 ADVOCATE
DEVITALIZATION
DEXTROROTATION
DEXTROROTATORY
DIABOLICALNESS
DIAGNOSTICALLY
DIALECTOLOGIST
DIAMOND
 JUBILEE
DIAMOND
 WEDDING
DIAPHANOUSNESS
DIAPHOTOTROPIC
DICHROMATICISM
DICOTYLEDONOUS
DIELECTRICALLY
DIESEL-
 ELECTRIC
DIEU ET MON
 DROIT
DIFFERENTIABLE
DIFFERENTIATED
DIFFERENTIATOR
DIFFRACTOMETER
DIGITALIZATION
DIG ONES HEELS
 IN
DIMENHYDRINATE
DIMENSIONALITY
DINITROBENZENE
DINNER
 SERVICES
DINOFLAGELLATE
DIPLOMATICALLY
DIPLOSTEMONOUS
DIRECTIONALITY
DIRECT
 TAXATION
DISAFFILIATING
DISAFFILIATION
DISAFFORESTING
DISAPPEARANCES
DISAPPOINTEDLY
DISAPPOINTMENT
DISAPPROBATION
DISAPPROVINGLY
DISARRANGEMENT
DISARTICULATOR
DISASSOCIATING

DISASSOCIATION
DISBELIEVINGLY
DISCIPLINARIAN
DISCOLORATIONS
DISCOMPOSINGLY
DISCONNECTEDLY
DISCONNECTIONS
DISCONSOLATELY
DISCONSOLATION
DISCONTENTEDLY
DISCONTENTMENT
DISCONTINUANCE
DISCOUNTENANCE
DISCOUNT
  STORES
DISCOURAGEMENT
DISCOURAGINGLY
DISCOURTEOUSLY
DISCRIMINATING
DISCRIMINATION
DISCRIMINATORY
DISCURSIVENESS
DISEMBARKATION
DISEMBOGUEMENT
DISEMBOWELLING
DISEMBOWELMENT
DISENCHANTMENT
DISENFRANCHISE
DISENTHRALMENT
DISEQUILIBRIUM
DISESTABLISHED
DISFEATUREMENT
DISFIGUREMENTS
DISFORESTATION
DISFRANCHISING
DISGRUNTLEMENT
DISHEARTENMENT
DISILLUSIONING
DISINCLINATION
DISINFESTATION
DISINGENUOUSLY
DISINHERITANCE
DISINTEGRATING
DISINTEGRATION
DISINTEGRATIVE
DISJOINTEDNESS
DISORDERLINESS
DISORIENTATING
DISORIENTATION
DISPARAGEMENTS
DISPENSABILITY

DISPENSATIONAL
DISPUTATIOUSLY
DISQUALIFIABLE
DISQUIETEDNESS
DISRESPECTABLE
DISSERTATIONAL
DISSERVICEABLE
DISSIMULATIONS
DISSOCIABILITY
DISSOLVABILITY
DISSUASIVENESS
DISTENSIBILITY
DISTINGUISHING
DISTRIBUTIONAL
DISTRIBUTIVELY
DIURETICALNESS
DIVERTICULITIS
DIVERTICULOSIS
DIVERTISSEMENT
DNEPROPETROVSK
DOG IN THE
  MANGER
DO-IT-
  YOURSELFER
DOMESTIC
  ANIMAL
DOUBLE
  BREASTED
DOUBLE-
  BREASTED
DOUBLE-
  CHECKING
DOUBLE-
  CROSSERS
DOUBLE-
  CROSSING
DOUBLE
  ENTENDRE
DOUBLE
  FEATURES
DOUBTING
  THOMAS
DOWN IN THE
  DUMPS
DRAINING
  BOARDS
DRAMATIZATIONS
DRESSING
  TABLES
DRESS
  REHEARSAL
DRIVING
  LICENCE

DROP IN THE
  OCEAN
DRUM
  MAJORETTES
DUCKS AND
  DRAKES
DUCTLESS
  GLANDS
DWELLING
  HOUSES
DYER'S-
  GREENWEED
DYNAMOELECTRIC
DYSMENORRHOEAL

E
ECCENTRICITIES
ECCLESIASTICAL
ECCLESIOLOGIST
ECONOMETRICIAN
EDITIO
  PRINCEPS
EDUCATIONALIST
EFFERVESCENTLY
EFFERVESCINGLY
EFFORTLESSNESS
EGALITARIANISM
EGOCENTRICALLY
ELDER
  STATESMAN
ELDER
  STATESMEN
ELECTIONEERING
ELECTRA
  COMPLEX
ELECTROCHEMIST
ELECTROCUTIONS
ELECTRODEPOSIT
ELECTRODYNAMIC
ELECTROGRAPHIC
ELECTROKINETIC
ELECTRONICALLY
ELECTRONIC
  MAIL
ELECTROSTATICS
ELECTROSURGERY
ELECTROTHERMAL
ELECTROVALENCY
ELEMENTARINESS
ELLIPTICALNESS
EMBARRASSINGLY
EMBARRASSMENTS

EMBELLISHMENTS
EMBLEMATICALLY
EMOTIONALISTIC
EMPHATICALNESS
EMULSIFICATION
EMULSION
  PAINTS
ENANTIOMORPHIC
ENCAPSULATIONS
ENCEPHALOGRAPH
ENCOURAGEMENTS
ENDOCRINE
  GLAND
ENDOCRINOLOGIC
ENDOPHYTICALLY
ENDOSMOTICALLY
ENFANT
  TERRIBLE
ENFORCEABILITY
ENGAGEMENT
  RING
ENHARMONICALLY
ENLIGHTENINGLY
ENROLLED
  NURSES
ENTEROGASTRONE
ENTERPRISINGLY
ENTERTAININGLY
ENTERTAINMENTS
ENTOMOSTRACOUS
EPEXEGETICALLY
EPICONTINENTAL
EPIDEMIOLOGIST
EPIGENETICALLY
EPIGRAPHICALLY
EPISTEMOLOGIST
EQUIPONDERANCE
EQUIVOCATINGLY
ERYTHROBLASTIC
ERYTHROPOIESIS
ERYTHROPOIETIC
ESCAPE
  VELOCITY
ESCHATOLOGICAL
ESTABLISHMENTS
ESTATE
  AGENCIES
ESTERIFICATION
ETERNALIZATION
ETHERIFICATION
ETHNOCENTRISMS
ETHNOLOGICALLY

ETYMOLOGICALLY
EULOGISTICALLY
EUPHONICALNESS
EUPHORBIACEOUS
EUPHUISTICALLY
EUSTACHIAN
TUBE
EUTROPHICATION
EVANGELICALISM
EVANGELIZATION
EVAPORATED
MILK
EVEN-
HANDEDNESS
EVENING
DRESSES
EVIL-
MINDEDNESS
EVOLUTIONISTIC
EXACERBATINGLY
EXAGGERATINGLY
EXASPERATINGLY
EXCEPTIONALITY
EXCLAUSTRATION
EXCOMMUNICABLE
EXCOMMUNICATED
EXCOMMUNICATOR
EXCRUCIATINGLY
EXHAUSTIBILITY
EXHAUSTIVENESS
EXHIBITIONISTS
EXHILARATINGLY
EXISTENTIALISM
EXISTENTIALIST
EXOTHERMICALLY
EXPANSIONISTIC
EXPENSE
ACCOUNT
EXPERIMENTALLY
EXPOSTULATIONS
EXPRESSIONISTS
EXPRESSIONLESS
EXPRESSIVENESS
EXPROPRIATIONS
EXTEMPORANEOUS
EXTENDED
FAMILY
EXTENSIONALITY
EXTINGUISHABLE
EXTINGUISHMENT
EXTORTIONATELY
EXTRACANONICAL

EXTRACTABILITY
EXTRANEOUSNESS
EXTRAVEHICULAR
EYEBROW
PENCILS

F

FACTITIOUSNESS
FACTORY
FARMING
FAINT-
HEARTEDLY
FAIR-
MINDEDNESS
FAIRY
GODMOTHER
FAITS
ACCOMPLIS
FALLACIOUSNESS
FALLOPIAN
TUBES
FALSE
PRETENCES
FALSIFICATIONS
FAMILY
PLANNING
FARSIGHTEDNESS
FASTIDIOUSNESS
FATALISTICALLY
FATHERS AND
SONS
FAVOURABLENESS
FEATHERBEDDING
FEATHERBRAINED
FEATHERWEIGHTS
FEDERALIZATION
FEEDING
BOTTLES
FEEL THE
DRAUGHT
FELICITOUSNESS
FEMININE
ENDING
FEMME DE
CHAMBRE
FERMENTABILITY
FERRIMAGNETISM
FERROMAGNESIAN
FERROMAGNETISM
FERROMANGANESE
FICTIONALIZING
FICTITIOUSNESS
FIDEICOMMISSUM

FIELDS OF
VISION
FIELD
TELEGRAPH
FIFTH
COLUMNIST
FIGHTING
CHANCE
FIGURATIVENESS
FIGURE OF
SPEECH
FIGURES OF
EIGHT
FILING
CABINETS
FILLING
STATION
FINANCIAL
YEARS
FINE-TOOTH
COMBS
FINGER
PAINTING
FINGERPRINTING
FINSTERAARHORN
FIRST
OFFENDERS
FISSIONABILITY
FLABBERGASTING
FLIGHT-
RECORDER
FLIGHT
SERGEANT
FLOATING
VOTERS
FLOG A DEAD
HORSE
FLORICULTURIST
FLOWER-OF-AN-
HOUR
FLYING
BUTTRESS
FLYING
DUTCHMAN
FLYING
OFFICERS
FOLLOW MY
LEADER
FOLLOW-MY-
LEADER
FOLLOW-
THROUGHS
FOOD
PROCESSORS

FORBIDDEN
FRUIT
FORBIDDINGNESS
FOREIGN
AFFAIRS
FOREORDAINMENT
FORESHORTENING
FORETHOUGHTFUL
FORE-
TOPGALLANT
FORKLIFT
TRUCKS
FORTHRIGHTNESS
FORTIFICATIONS
FORTUITOUSNESS
FORTUNE
HUNTERS
FORTUNE-
TELLERS
FORWARD-
LOOKING
FOUNDING
FATHER
FOUR-LETTER
WORD
FRATERNIZATION
FREE
ENTERPRISE
FREEZING
POINTS
FRENCH
DRESSING
FRENCH
POLISHED
FRIDGE-
FREEZERS
FRIENDLESSNESS
FRINGE
BENEFITS
FROZEN
SHOULDER
FRUCTIFICATION
FULLY-
FASHIONED
FUNCTIONALISTS
FUNDAMENTALISM
FUNDAMENTALIST
FUNDAMENTALITY
FUNERAL
PARLOUR
FURFURALDEHYDE
FUTURISTICALLY

G

GALACTOPOIESIS
GALACTOPOIETIC
GALVANOTROPISM
GASTROVASCULAR
GAVE UP THE
  GHOST
GEIGER
  COUNTERS
GELATINIZATION
GENEALOGICALLY
GENERALISSIMOS
GENERALIZATION
GENERAL
  STRIKES
GENTRIFICATION
GEOCENTRICALLY
GEOGRAPHICALLY
GERMAN
  SHEPHERD
GERONTOLOGICAL
GERRYMANDERING
GESTICULATIONS
GET ONES OWN
  BACK
GHETTO
  BLASTERS
GLANDULAR
  FEVER
GLOBE
  ARTICHOKE
GLOBETROTTINGS
GLORIFICATIONS
GLORY-OF-THE-
  SNOW
GLOSSY
  MAGAZINE
GLUCOCORTICORD
GOLDEN
  JUBILEES
GOLDEN
  WEDDINGS
GOLD-OF-
  PLEASURE
GOOD-FOR-
  NOTHING
GOOD-
  HUMOUREDLY
GOOD
  SAMARITANS
GRACE-AND-
  FAVOUR

GRADE
  CROSSINGS
GRAMMAR
  SCHOOLS
GRAMMATICALITY
GRAMMATOLOGIST
GRANDDAUGHTERS
GRANDILOQUENCE
GRANGERIZATION
GRAPHITIZATION
GRAPPLING
  IRONS
GRASP THE
  NETTLE
GRATIFICATIONS
GRATUITOUSNESS
GREGARIOUSNESS
GREGORIAN
  CHANT
GROUNDLESSNESS
GROUP
  PRACTICES
GUARDIAN
  ANGELS
GUIDED
  MISSILES
GUY FAWKES
  NIGHT
GYNAECOLOGICAL
GYNAECOLOGISTS
GYROSTABILIZER

H

HABERDASHERIES
HAEMACYTOMETER
HAEMAGGLUTININ
HAEMATOBLASTIC
HAEMATOGENESIS
HAEMATOPOIESIS
HAEMATOPOIETIC
HAEMATOTHERMAL
HAEMOCYTOMETER
HALFPENNYWORTH
HALFWITTEDNESS
HALICARNASSIAN
HALLUCINATIONS
HALLUCINOGENIC
HANDICRAFTSMAN
HANDSOME
  SALARY
HANGING
  GARDENS

HAPAX
  LEGOMENON
HARD
  CURRENCIES
HARD-
  HEADEDNESS
HARMONIOUSNESS
HARPSICHORDIST
HEAD LIKE A
  SIEVE
HEADMASTERSHIP
HEADSTRONGNESS
HEARTRENDINGLY
HEARTWARMINGLY
HEATHENISHNESS
HEBRAISTICALLY
HEGIRA
  CALENDAR
HELL FOR
  LEATHER
HELTER-
  SKELTERS
HEMEL
  HEMPSTEAD
HEMISPHEROIDAL
HENRIETTA
  MARIA
HEREDITABILITY
HEREDITARINESS
HERMAPHRODITES
HERMAPHRODITIC
HERMAPHRODITUS
HEROIC
  COUPLETS
HERO
  WORSHIPPED
HERPES
  LABIALIS
HETEROCHROMOUS
HETEROGONOUSLY
HETEROLECITHAL
HETEROMORPHISM
HETERONOMOUSLY
HETERONYMOUSLY
HETEROPHYLLOUS
HETEROPOLARITY
HETEROSEXUALLY
HIERARCHICALLY
HIGH
  COMMISSION
HIGH COURT
  JUDGE

HIGH
  EXPLOSIVES
HIGH-
  HANDEDNESS
HIGHLAND
  FLINGS
HIGH-
  MINDEDNESS
HIGH-
  PRESSURING
HIGH-
  PRINCIPLED
HIGH SPEED
  TRAIN
HIGH
  TECHNOLOGY
HIGH WATER
  MARKS
HIPPOPOTAMUSES
HISTOCHEMISTRY
HISTOLOGICALLY
HISTOLYTICALLY
HISTOPATHOLOGY
HISTOPLASMOSIS
HISTORICALNESS
HISTORIOGRAPHY
HISTRIONICALLY
HOEK VAN
  HOLLAND
HOLDING
  COMPANY
HOLD NO BRIEF
  FOR
HOLIER-THAN-
  THOU
HOMOCHROMATISM
HOMOGENIZATION
HOMOIOUSIANISM
HOMOPHONICALLY
HONEYDEW
  MELONS
HONOURABLENESS
HORATIUS
  COCLES
HORIZONTALNESS
HORRENDOUSNESS
HORROR-
  STRICKEN
HORSE
  CHESTNUTS
HORSE
  LATITUDES
HORTICULTURIST

HOSPITABLENESS
HOT WATER
  BOTTLE
HOT-WATER
  BOTTLE
HOUSEHOLD
  NAMES
HOUSEMAID'S
  KNEE
HOUSE OF
  COMMONS
HOUSING
  PROJECT
HUMIDIFICATION
HUMOURLESSNESS
HUNGER
  MARCHERS
HUNGER
  STRIKERS
HUNTING
  GROUNDS
HURRICANE
  LAMPS
HYDROCELLULOSE
HYDROCORTISONE
HYDROGENOLYSIS
HYDROLOGICALLY
HYDROMAGNETICS
HYDROMECHANICS
HYPERBOLICALLY
HYPERSENSITIVE
HYPOCHONDRIACS
HYPOCRITICALLY
HYPODERMICALLY
HYPOTHETICALLY
HYSTERECTOMIES

I

ICEBERG
  LETTUCE
ICHNEUMON
  FLIES
ICHTHYOPHAGOUS
IDEALISTICALLY
IDENTICAL
  TWINS
IDENTIFICATION
IDEOLOOGICALLY
IDIOSYNCRASIES
ILLEGALIZATION
ILLEGITIMATELY
ILLIMITABILITY

ILLUSTRATIONAL
ILLUSTRATIVELY
IMMETHODICALLY
IMMOBILIZATION
IMMUNOGENETICS
IMMUNOGLOBULIN
IMMUNOREACTION
IMPARISYLLABIC
IMPEACHABILITY
IMPERCEPTIVITY
IMPERMEABILITY
IMPERSONATIONS
IMPERTURBATION
IMPLAUSIBILITY
IMPLEMENTATION
IMPOLITENESSES
IMPRACTICALITY
IMPREGNABILITY
IMPRESSIONABLE
IMPRESSIONABLY
IMPRESSIONALLY
IMPRESSIONISTS
IMPRESSIVENESS
IMPROVISATIONS
INADVISABILITY
INALIENABILITY
INALTERABILITY
INAPPRECIATIVE
INAPPREHENSIVE
INAPPROACHABLE
INARTICULATELY
INARTISTICALLY
INAUSPICIOUSLY
INCANDESCENTLY
INCAPACITATING
INCAPACITATION
INCAUTIOUSNESS
INCESTUOUSNESS
INCOMMENSURATE
INCOMMODIOUSLY
INCOMMUNICABLE
INCOMPLETENESS
INCOMPRESSIBLE
INCONCLUSIVELY
INCONSIDERABLE
INCONSISTENTLY
INCONVENIENCED
INCONVENIENCES
INCONVENIENTLY
INCOORDINATION
INDECIPHERABLE

INDECIPHERABLY
INDECOROUSNESS
INDEFINITENESS
INDESTRUCTIBLE
INDESTRUCTIBLY
INDETERMINABLE
INDETERMINABLY
INDIAN
  ELEPHANT
INDIFFERENTISM
INDIFFERENTIST
INDIGENOUSNESS
INDIRECT
  OBJECT
INDIRECT
  SPEECH
INDISCRIMINATE
INDISPOSITIONS
INDISTINCTNESS
INDIVIDUALISTS
INDIVIDUALIZED
INDIVIDUALIZER
INDIVISIBILITY
INDOCTRINATING
INDOCTRINATION
INDOMITABILITY
INDUBITABILITY
INDUSTRIALISTS
INDUSTRIALIZED
INEFFECTUALITY
INELUCTABILITY
INERTIA
  SELLING
INESSENTIALITY
INESTIMABILITY
INEXCUSABILITY
INFECTIOUSNESS
INFLAMMABILITY
INFLAMMATORILY
INFRALAPSARIAN
INFRANGIBILITY
INFRASTRUCTURE
INGRATIATINGLY
INHABITABILITY
INHARMONIOUSLY
INHERITABILITY
INITIALIZATION
IN LOCO
  PARENTIS
INNUMERABILITY
INQUISITIONIST
INSANITARINESS

INSCRUTABILITY
INSEPARABILITY
INSIDER
  DEALING
INSIGNIFICANCE
INSTITUTIONARY
INSTRUCTORSHIP
INSUFFICIENTLY
INSUPERABILITY
INSUPPRESSIBLE
INSURMOUNTABLE
INSURRECTIONAL
INTEGRATIONIST
INTELLECTUALLY
INTELLIGENTSIA
INTENTIONALITY
INTERCESSIONAL
INTERCOMMUNION
INTERDEPENDENT
INTEREST
  GROUPS
INTERFERENTIAL
INTERFEROMETER
INTERFEROMETRY
INTERFERTILITY
INTERGRADATION
INTERJECTIONAL
INTERLOCUTRESS
INTERMEDIARIES
INTERMIGRATION
INTERMITTENTLY
INTERMITTINGLY
INTERMOLECULAR
INTERNAL
  MARKET
INTERNATIONALE
INTERNATIONALS
INTERPELLATION
INTERPENETRANT
INTERPENETRATE
INTERPLANETARY
INTERPOLATIONS
INTERPOSITIONS
INTERPRETATION
INTERPRETATIVE
INTERRELATIONS
INTERROGATIONS
INTERROGATIVES
INTERSECTIONAL
INTERSEXUALITY
INTERSPERSEDLY

INTERTWININGLY
INTERVENTIONAL
INTOLERABILITY
INTO THE
  BARGAIN
INTOXICATINGLY
INTRACTABILITY
INTRACUTANEOUS
INTRAMOLECULAR
INTRANSIGENTLY
INTRANSITIVELY
INTRODUCTORILY
INVERTED
  COMMAS
INVESTIGATIONS
INVIGORATINGLY
IODOMETRICALLY
IRRECONCILABLE
IRRECONCILABLY
IRREDUCIBILITY
IRREFUTABILITY
IRREGULARITIES
IRREMOVABILITY
IRREPARABILITY
IRREPROACHABLE
IRREPROACHABLY
IRRESOLUBILITY
IRREVOCABILITY
ISOPIESTICALLY

J

JACK-IN-THE-
  BOXES
JOB'S
  COMFORTERS
JOLLIFICATIONS
JOURNALIZATION
JURISDICTIONAL
JUSTICIABILITY
JUSTIFIABILITY

K

KAISERSLAUTERN
KAMENSK-
  URALSKI
KANGAROO
  COURTS
KEEP ONES CHIN
  UP
KEEP ONES HAND
  IN
KERATINIZATION

KEYHOLE
  SURGURY
KIDNEY
  MACHINES
KINDERGARTENER
KITCHEN
  GARDENS
KNICKERBOCKERS
KNIGHT-
  ERRANTRY
KNOCK ON THE
  HEAD
KNUCKLE-
  DUSTERS
KOSOVO-
  METOHIJA

L

LABOUR
  EXCHANGE
LAMELLIROSTRAL
LANCE
  CORPORALS
LAND ON ONES
  FEET
LARGE
  INTESTINE
LARGER THAN
  LIFE
LARYNGOLOGICAL
LARYNGOSCOPIST
LASCIVIOUSNESS
LATITUDINARIAN
LAUGHINGSTOCKS
LAUNDRY
  BASKETS
LAW OF THE
  JUNGLE
LEADING
  ARTICLE
LEADING
  STRINGS
LEAVE OF
  ABSENCE
LEFT-
  HANDEDNESS
LEFT IN THE
  LURCH
LEGALISTICALLY
LEGERDEMAINIST
LEGION OF
  HONOUR
LEGITIMIZATION

LENDING
  LIBRARY
LETS CALL IT A
  DAY
LETTER OF
  CREDIT
LEVEL
  CROSSINGS
LEXICOGRAPHERS
LIBERALIZATION
LIBERAL
  STUDIES
LIBERTARIANISM
LIBIDINOUSNESS
LICENTIATESHIP
LICENTIOUSNESS
LIFE
  EXPECTANCY
LIFE
  PRESERVERS
LIGHT
  AIRCRAFTS
LIGNOCELLULOSE
LIKE-
  MINDEDNESS
LINE ONES
  POCKET
LINGUISTICALLY
LISTEN TO
  REASON
LITHOLOGICALLY
LITTLE BY
  LITTLE
LITTLE GREEN
  MEN
LOCAL
  AUTHORITY
LOCUS
  CLASSICUS
LONGITUDINALLY
LONG-
  SUFFERANCE
LONGWINDEDNESS
LOOKING
  GLASSES
LOVING
  KINDNESS
LOXODROMICALLY
LUGUBRIOUSNESS

M

MACADAMIZATION
MACHINEGUNNING

MACROECONOMICS
MACROEVOLUTION
MACROMOLECULAR
MAGNETIC
  FIELDS
MAGNIFICATIONS
MAHALLA EL
  KUBRA
MAKE
  ALLOWANCES
MAKE THE
  RUNNING
MAKE UP ONES
  MIND
MALACOPHYLLOUS
MALACOSTRACOUS
MALE
  CHAUVINIST
MALFUNCTIONING
MALPIGHIACEOUS
MALTESE
  CROSSES
MANIFESTATIONS
MAN IN THE
  STREET
MANIPULABILITY
MANNERLESSNESS
MANOMETRICALLY
MANUFACTURABLE
MARCHING
  ORDERS
MARKET
  GARDENER
MARKET
  RESEARCH
MARTYROLOGICAL
MASON-DIXON
  LINE
MASSAGE
  PARLOUR
MASSOTHERAPIST
MASS
  PRODUCTION
MATERNITY
  LEAVE
MATHEMATICALLY
MATHEMATICIANS
MATTER OF
  COURSE
MATTER-OF-
  FACTLY
MATURE
  STUDENTS

MAUNDY
THURSDAY
MEANINGFULNESS
MECHANOTHERAPY
MEDDLESOMENESS
MEDITATIVENESS
MEGALOCEPHALIC
MEGALOMANIACAL
MEGAPHONICALLY
MEGASPOROPHYLL
MELANCHOLINESS
MENDACIOUSNESS
MENTAL
HOSPITAL
MEPHISTOPHELES
MERCAPTOPURINE
MERCHANT
NAVIES
MERETRICIOUSLY
MESDEMOISELLES
METACHROMATISM
METALLOGRAPHER
METALLOGRAPHIC
METAMORPHOSING
METAPHORICALLY
METAPHYSICALLY
METAPSYCHOLOGY
METASTATICALLY
METEMPSYCHOSIS
METEOROGRAPHIC
METEOROLOGICAL
METEOROLOGISTS
METHAEMOGLOBIN
METHODICALNESS
METHODOLOGICAL
METICULOUSNESS
MICROBAROGRAPH
MICROBIOLOGIST
MICROCEPHALOUS
MICROCHEMISTRY
MICROCIRCUITRY
MICROCOMPUTERS
MICROECONOMICS
MICROMETEORITE
MICROORGANISMS
MICROPARASITIC
MICROPROCESSOR
MICROPYROMETER
MICROSTOMATOUS
MICROSTRUCTURE
MIDDLE-
DISTANCE

MIGHT-HAVE-
BEENS
MILITARIZATION
MILITARY
POLICE
MILLENARIANISM
MINERALIZATION
MISAPPLICATION
MISAPPREHENDED
MISAPPROPRIATE
MISCALCULATING
MISCALCULATION
MISCONCEPTIONS
MISINFORMATION
MISINTERPRETED
MISINTERPRETER
MISREPRESENTED
MISREPRESENTER
MIXED
ECONOMIES
MIXED
METAPHORS
MOCK-
HEROICALLY
MOCK TURTLE
SOUP
MODERNIZATIONS
MOMENTS OF
TRUTH
MONGRELIZATION
MONKEY
BUSINESS
MONKEY
WRENCHES
MONOCARPELLARY
MONOCHROMATISM
MONOLITHICALLY
MONOPOLIZATION
MONOPROPELLANT
MONOSACCHARIDE
MOONLIGHT
FLITS
MORALISTICALLY
MORGANATICALLY
MORNING
GLORIES
MORPHOPHONEMIC
MOTHER
SUPERIOR
MOTIONLESSNESS
MOTION
PICTURES

MOTIVELESSNESS
MOUNTAINEERING
MOVING
PAVEMENT
MOVING
PICTURES
MUCOMEMBRANOUS
MUCOUS
MEMBRANE
MULTIFACTORIAL
MULTIFARIOUSLY
MULTILATERALLY
MULTINATIONALS
MULTIPLE
STORES
MULTIPLICATION
MULTIPLICATIVE
MUNICIPALITIES
MUSTARD
PLASTER
MYELENCEPHALIC
MYELENCEPHALON
MYOCARDIOGRAPH
MYOGRAPHICALLY
MYRMECOLOGICAL
MYRMECOPHAGOUS
MYRMECOPHILOUS
MYSTAGOGICALLY
MYSTERIOUSNESS

N
NANSEN
PASSPORT
NARCOSYNTHESIS
NARRATIVE
VERSE
NASOPHARYNGEAL
NASTY BIT OF
WORK
NATIONAL
ANTHEM
NATIVE
AMERICAN
NATURAL
HISTORY
NATURALIZATION
NATURAL
SCIENCE
NEANDERTHAL
MAN
NEBUCHADNEZZAR
NEGLECTFULNESS

NEIGHBOURHOODS
NEOCOLONIALISM
NEOCOLONIALIST
NERVOUS
SYSTEMS
NEUROPATHOLOGY
NEUTRALIZATION
NEWFOUNDLANDER
NEWS
CONFERENCE
NEWSWORTHINESS
NIGHT
BLINDNESS
NIGHT
WATCHMANS
NIL
DESPERANDUM
NINE DAYS'
WONDER
NITROCELLULOSE
NITROGLYCERINE
NOBLESSE
OBLIGE
NO-CLAIM
BONUSES
NOLO
CONTENDERE
NONATTRIBUTIVE
NONCOMMITTALLY
NONCONFORMISTS
NONCOOPERATION
NONCOOPERATIVE
NONDISJUNCTION
NONEQUIVALENCE
NONINFLAMMABLE
NONPROGRESSIVE
NON
PROSEQUITUR
NONRESIDENTIAL
NONRESTRICTIVE
NONSTIMULATING
NORFOLK
JACKETS
NORTHERN
LIGHTS
NORTH-
NORTHEAST
NORTH-
NORTHWEST
NORTHUMBERLAND
NOTEWORTHINESS
NOUVEAUX
RICHES

NO-WIN
   SITUATION
NUCLEAR
   REACTOR
NUCLEAR
   WINTERS
NURSERY
   SCHOOLS
NUTRITIOUSNESS
NYCTAGINACEOUS
NYMPHOMANIACAL

O

OBSEQUIOUSNESS
OBSERVABLENESS
OBSTREPEROUSLY
OBSTRUCTIONISM
OBSTRUCTIONIST
OCCUPATIONALLY
OCEAN
   GRAYHOUND
OCEANOGRAPHERS
OEDIPUS
   COMPLEX
OLD MAN OF THE
   SEA
OLD PEOPLE'S
   HOME
OLD TIME
   DANCING
OLIGARCHICALLY
OLIGOPSONISTIC
ONE-ARMED
   BANDIT
ONEIROCRITICAL
ONE-NIGHT
   STANDS
ON ONES BEAM
   ENDS
ON THE OTHER
   HAND
ON THE
   THRESHOLD
OPEN-
   HANDEDNESS
OPEN-
   MINDEDNESS
OPEN
   SANDWICHES
OPEN
   UNIVERSITY
OPERATING
   TABLE

OPERATIONALISM
OPHTHALMOSCOPE
OPHTHALMOSCOPY
OPPOSITE
   NUMBER
OPPRESSIVENESS
OPTIMISTICALLY
ORCHESTRATIONS
ORDINARY
   LEVELS
ORDINARY
   SEAMAN
ORDNANCE
   SURVEY
ORGANIZATIONAL
ORGANIZED
   CRIME
ORGANOGRAPHIST
ORGANOMETALLIC
ORNITHOLOGICAL
ORNITHOLOGISTS
OROBANCHACEOUS
OROGRAPHICALLY
ORTHOCHROMATIC
ORTHODOX
   CHURCH
ORTHOGENICALLY
ORTHOGRAPHICAL
ORTHOPHOSPHATE
OSCILLOGRAPHIC
OSMOMETRICALLY
OSTENTATIOUSLY
OSTEOARTHRITIC
OSTEOARTHRITIS
OSTEOLOGICALLY
OTOLARYNGOLOGY
OUTBOARD
   MOTORS
OUTGENERALLING
OUTLANDISHNESS
OUTMANOEUVRING
OUTRAGEOUSNESS
OVERCAPITALIZE
OVERCOMPENSATE
OVERDEVELOPING
OVERENTHUSIASM
OVERESTIMATING
OVERESTIMATION
OVERINDULGENCE
OVERPOPULATION
OVERPOWERINGLY
OVERPRODUCTION

OVERPROTECTION
OVERSIMPLIFIED
OVERSTATEMENTS
OVERSUBSCRIBED
OVER-THE-
   COUNTER
OVERWHELMINGLY
OWNER-
   OCCUPIERS
OXYHAEMOGLOBIN
OYSTERCATCHERS

P

PACHYDERMATOUS
PACKAGE
   HOLIDAY
PADDLE
   STEAMERS
PAEDIATRICIANS
PAEDOMORPHOSIS
PAGANISTICALLY
PALAEANTHROPIC
PALAEETHNOLOGY
PALAEOBOTANIST
PALATALIZATION
PALEONTOLOGIST
PAN-
   AMERICANISM
PANCAKE
   LANDING
PANGENETICALLY
PANHELLENISTIC
PAPILLOMATOSIS
PARABOLIZATION
PARALLELEPIPED
PARALLELOGRAMS
PARAPHERNALIAS
PARAPSYCHOLOGY
PARASITOLOGIST
PARATACTICALLY
PARENCHYMATOUS
PARKING
   GARAGES
PARSIMONIOUSLY
PARTHENOCARPIC
PARTICULARIZED
PARTICULARIZER
PARTURIFACIENT
PASSENGER
   TRAIN
PASSING THE
   BUCK

PASSIONATENESS
PASSIONFLOWERS
PASSIVE
   SMOKING
PASTEURIZATION
PAST
   PARTICIPLE
PATE DE FOIE
   GRAS
PATENT
   MEDICINE
PATHOLOGICALLY
PAVEMENT
   ARTIST
PEACE
   OFFERINGS
PENITENTIARIES
PENNY
   DREADFULS
PENNY-
   FARTHINGS
PENNY-
   HALFPENNY
PEPPERCORN
   RENT
PERAMBULATIONS
PERCEIVABILITY
PERCEPTIBILITY
PERCUSSION
   CAPS
PERCUSSIONISTS
PEREGRINATIONS
PEREMPTORINESS
PERFECT
   BINDING
PERFECTIBILITY
PERFECTIONISTS
PERFIDIOUSNESS
PERIMETRICALLY
PERISCOPICALLY
PERLOCUTIONARY
PERMANENT
   WAVES
PERMISSIBILITY
PERMISSIVENESS
PERNICIOUSNESS
PERNICKETINESS
PEROXIDE
   BLONDE
PERPENDICULARS
PERSONABLENESS
PERSONAL
   COLUMN

PERSONAL
  ESTATE
PERSONAL
  STEREO
PERSON-TO-
  PERSON
PERSUADABILITY
PERSUASIVENESS
PERTINACIOUSLY
PETIT
  BOURGEOIS
PETIT
  LARCENIST
PETROCHEMICALS
PETROCHEMISTRY
PETROLEUM
  JELLY
PETROL
  STATIONS
PETTY
  BOURGEOIS
PETTY
  LARCENIES
PHANTASMAGORIA
PHANTASMAGORIC
PHARMACEUTICAL
PHARMACOLOGIST
PHARMACOPOEIAL
PHARMACOPOEIAS
PHARMACOPOEIST
PHARYNGOLOGIST
PHARYNGOSCOPIC
PHENOBARBITONE
PHENOTYPICALLY
PHILANTHROPIST
PHILATELICALLY
PHILOLOGICALLY
PHILOSOPHIZING
PHLEGMATICALLY
PHONOLOGICALLY
PHOSPHOPROTEIN
PHOSPHORESCENT
PHOSPHOROSCOPE
PHOTOCHEMISTRY
PHOTOCONDUCTOR
PHOTOENGRAVING
PHOTOGENICALLY
PHOTOGRAMMETRY
PHOTOPERIODISM
PHOTOSENSITIVE
PHOTOSENSITIZE
PHOTOSYNTHESIS

PHOTOSYNTHETIC
PHOTOTYPICALLY
PHRASEOGRAPHIC
PHRASEOLOGICAL
PHTHALOCYANINE
PHYTOGEOGRAPHY
PHYTOPATHOLOGY
PHYTOSOCIOLOGY
PICTURE
  WINDOWS
PIEZOCHEMISTRY
PILGRIM
  FATHERS
PINCER
  MOVEMENT
PINNATIPARTITE
PINS AND
  NEEDLES
PISCICULTURIST
PITCH-
  BLACKNESS
PITCHED
  BATTLES
PLAIN
  CHOCOLATE
PLANCK
  CONSTANT
PLASTER OF
  PARIS
PLASTIC
  BULLETS
PLASTICIZATION
PLASTIC
  SURGEON
PLASTIC
  SURGERY
PLATINOCYANIDE
PLATINUM
  BLONDE
PLATITUDINIZER
PLEA
  BARGAINING
PLEONASTICALLY
PLETHYSMOGRAPH
PLUMBER'S
  FRIEND
PNEUMATIC
  DRILL
PNEUMOBACILLUS
PNEUMOCONIOSIS
PNEUMODYNAMICS
POIKILOTHERMAL
POLEMONIACEOUS

POLICE
  OFFICERS
POLICE
  STATIONS
POLITICIZATION
POLLING
  STATION
POLYCARPELLARY
POLYCHROMATISM
POLYMERIZATION
POLYNUCLEOTIDE
POLYPHONICALLY
POLYSACCHARIDE
POLYSYNTHESISM
PONTOON
  BRIDGES
POOR-
  SPIRITEDLY
POPULARIZATION
PORPHYROGENITE
PORTENTOUSNESS
PORTULACACEOUS
POSSESSIVENESS
POSTMILLENNIAL
POSTPOSITIONAL
POTENTIALITIES
PRACTICABILITY
PRACTICALITIES
PRACTICAL
  JOKER
PRACTICAL
  JOKES
PRAISEWORTHILY
PRAYER
  MEETINGS
PREADOLESCENCE
PREARRANGEMENT
PRECARIOUSNESS
PRECIOUS
  METALS
PRECIOUS
  STONES
PRECIPITATIONS
PRECOCIOUSNESS
PRECONCEPTIONS
PREDACIOUSNESS
PREDESTINARIAN
PREDESTINATION
PREDETERMINATE
PREDETERMINERS
PREDETERMINING
PREDICTABILITY

PREDISPOSITION
PREFABRICATING
PREFABRICATION
PREFERENTIALLY
PREFIGURATIONS
PREMEDITATEDLY
PREOCCUPATIONS
PREORDINATIONS
PREPONDERANTLY ·
PREPONDERATING
PREPONDERATION
PREPOSSESSIONS
PREPOSTEROUSLY
PRE-
  RAPHAELITES
PRESCRIPTIVELY
PRESCRIPTIVISM
PRESCRIPTIVIST
PRESENCE OF
  MIND
PRESENTATIONAL
PRESENT
  PERFECT
PRESERVABILITY
PRESIDENT
  ELECT
PRESIDENT-
  ELECT
PRESS
  GALLERIES
PRESSURE
  COOKER
PRESSURE
  GROUPS
PRESSURE
  POINTS
PRESSURIZATION
PRESUMPTUOUSLY
PRESUPPOSITION
PREVARICATIONS
PREVENTIVENESS
PRIMA
  BALLERINA
PRIMARY
  COLOURS
PRIMARY
  SCHOOLS
PRIME
  MINISTERS
PRINCE
  CHARMING
PRINCES
  CONSORT

PRINCIPALITIES
PRINCIPAL
  PARTS
PRINTED
  CIRCUIT
PRISONERS OF
  WAR
PRISON
  VISITORS
PRIVATE
  MEMBERS
PRIVATE
  SCHOOLS
PRIVATE
  SOLDIER
PRO BONO
  PUBLICO
PROCRASTINATED
PROCRASTINATOR
PROCRYPTICALLY
PRODIGIOUSNESS
PRODUCTION
  LINE
PRODUCTIVENESS
PROFESSIONALLY
PROFESSORIALLY
PROFESSORSHIPS
PROGESTATIONAL
PROGNOSTICATED
PROGNOSTICATOR
PROGRAMME
  MUSIC
PROHIBITIONARY
PROHIBITIONISM
PROHIBITIONIST
PROJECTIONISTS
PROLETARIANISM
PROLIFERATIONS
PROMENADE
  DECKS
PRONOUNCEMENTS
PRONUNCIATIONS
PROPAEDEUTICAL
PROPAGANDIZING
PROPER
  FRACTION
PROPITIOUSNESS
PROPORTIONALLY
PROPORTIONMENT
PROPOSITIONING
PROPRIETORALLY
PROPRIOCEPTIVE

PROSENCEPHALON
PROSPEROUSNESS
PROSTHETICALLY
PROSTHODONTICS
PROSTHODONTIST
PROTECTIONISTS
PROTECTIVENESS
PROTHONOTARIAL
PROTOZOOLOGIST
PROTRACTEDNESS
PROTRUSIVENESS
PROVENTRICULAR
PROVENTRICULUS
PROVIDENTIALLY
PROVINCIALISMS
PROVING
  GROUNDS
PSEUDOMORPHISM
PSYCHOANALYSED
PSYCHOANALYSIS
PSYCHOANALYSTS
PSYCHOANALYTIC
PSYCHOANALYZER
PSYCHOCHEMICAL
PSYCHODRAMATIC
PSYCHODYNAMICS
PSYCHOLINGUIST
PSYCHOLOGISTIC
PSYCHONEUROSIS
PSYCHONEUROTIC
PSYCHOPHYSICAL
PSYCHOSOMATICS
PSYCHOSURGICAL
PSYCHOTECHNICS
PTERIDOLOGICAL
PUBLIC
  NUISANCE
PUBLIC
  SPIRITED
PUBLIC-
  SPIRITED
PUGILISTICALLY
PUGNACIOUSNESS
PURCHASABILITY
PURPLE
  PASSAGES
PURPOSEFULNESS
PURSE
  STRINGSES
PUT THE SCREWS
  ON
PYELONEPHRITIS

PYRAMID
  SELLING
PYRHELIOMETRIC
PYROMETALLURGY
PYROMETRICALLY
PYROPHOTOMETER
PYROPHOTOMETRY
PYROTECHNICSES
PYRRHIC
  VICTORY

Q

QUADRAGENARIAN
QUADRILATERALS
QUALIFICATIONS
QUANTIFICATION
QUANTITATIVELY
QUARTERMASTERS
QUEEN'S
  COUNSELS
QUEEN'S
  EVIDENCE
QUESTION
  MASTER
QUESTIONNAIRES
QUICK ON THE
  DRAW
QUINQUEFOLIATE
QUINQUEPARTITE
QUINQUEVALENCY
QUINTESSENTIAL
QUOTATION
  MARKS

R

RADIOBIOLOGIST
RADIOCHEMISTRY
RADIO
  FREQUENCY
RADIOSENSITIVE
RADIOTELEGRAPH
RADIOTELEMETRY
RADIOTELEPHONE
RADIOTELEPHONY
RADIO
  TELESCOPE
RADIOTHERAPIST
RAILWAY
  STATION
RAMBUNCTIOUSLY
RAMPAGEOUSNESS
RANUNCULACEOUS

RAPPROCHEMENTS
RASTAFARIANISM
RATEABLE
  VALUES
RATE OF
  EXCHANGE
READY FOR
  ACTION
REAFFIRMATIONS
REAL-TIME
  SYSTEM
REARRANGEMENTS
REAR VIEW
  MIRROR
REASONABLENESS
REBELLIOUSNESS
RECAPITULATING
RECAPITULATION
RECAPITULATIVE
RECEPTION
  ROOMS
RECKLINGHAUSEN
RECOMMENCEMENT
RECOMMENDATION
RECOMMENDATORY
RECONCILIATION
RECONCILIATORY
RECONDITIONING
RECONNAISSANCE
RECONSTITUTING
RECONSTITUTION
RECONSTRUCTING
RECONSTRUCTION
RECONSTRUCTIVE
RECORD-
  BREAKING
RECOVERABILITY
RECREATION
  ROOM
RECRIMINATIONS
RECRUDESCENCES
RECTANGULARITY
RECTIFICATIONS
REDEVELOPMENTS
REDINTEGRATION
REDINTEGRATIVE
REDISTRIBUTING
REDISTRIBUTION
REFERENCE
  BOOKS
REFLECTIVENESS
REFRACTIVENESS

REFRACTOMETRIC
REFRACTORINESS
REFRANGIBILITY
REGARDLESSNESS
REGISTERED
POST
REGISTER
OFFICE
REGISTRATIONAL
REGISTRY
OFFICE
REGRESSIVENESS
REGULARIZATION
REHABILITATING
REHABILITATION
REHABILITATIVE
REIGNS OF
TERROR
REIMBURSEMENTS
REINCARNATIONS
REINFORCEMENTS
REINSTALLATION
REINSTATEMENTS
REINTRODUCTION
REJUVENESCENCE
RELATIVE
CLAUSE
RELENTLESSNESS
RELINQUISHMENT
REMARKABLENESS
REMEMBRANCE
DAY
REMONETIZATION
REMORSEFULNESS
REMUNERABILITY
REMUNERATIVELY
REORGANIZATION
REPETITIVENESS
REPLACEABILITY
REPORTED
SPEECH
REPRESENTATION
REPRESENTATIVE
REPRESSIVENESS
REPRIMANDINGLY
REQUISITIONARY
REQUISITIONING
RESPECTABILITY
RESPECTFULNESS
RESPONSIBILITY
RESPONSIVENESS

RESTAURANT
CARS
RESTRICTEDNESS
RESTRICTIONIST
RESURRECTIONAL
RETRACTABILITY
RETRIEVABILITY
RETROGRADATION
RETROGRADATORY
RETRO-
OPERATIVE
RETROSPECTIVES
REVERBERATIONS
REVEREND
MOTHER
REVISED
VERSION
REVITALIZATION
REVIVIFICATION
REVOLUTIONIZED
REVOLUTIONIZER
RHEUMATIC
FEVER
RHINENCEPHALIC
RHINENCEPHALON
RHIZOCEPHALOUS
RHYTHM AND
BLUES
RICINOLEIC
ACID
RIDICULOUSNESS
RIGHT
TRIANGLES
RIO GRANDE DO
SUL
ROADWORTHINESS
ROARING
FORTIES
ROCKET-
LAUNCHER
ROCKY
MOUNTAINS
ROENTGENOPAQUE
ROLLER
COASTERS
ROMAINE
LETTUCE
ROMAN
CATHOLICS
RORSCHACH
TESTS
ROTTEN
BOROUGHS

ROUGH-AND-
TUMBLE
RUBBER
DINGHIES
RUBBER-
STAMPING
RUBBING
ALCOHOL
RUDIMENTARILLY
RUNNING
REPAIRS
RUN THE
GAUNTLET
RUSH ONES
FENCES

S

SACRAMENTALISM
SACRAMENTALIST
SACRAMENTALITY
SACRAMENTARIAN
SACRILEGIOUSLY
SADOMASOCHISTS
SAFE-DEPOSIT
BOX
SAFETY
CURTAINS
SALAD
DRESSINGS
SALUBRIOUSNESS
SANCTIFICATION
SANDWICH
BOARDS
SANDWICH
COURSE
SANGUINARINESS
SANITARY
TOWELS
SANTIAGO DE
CUBA
SAPONIFICATION
SATELLITE
STATE
SATISFACTIONAL
SATISFACTORILY
SAVE ONES
BREATH
SAVINGS
ACCOUNT
SAWN-OFF
SHOTGUN
SAXIFRAGACEOUS
SCANDALIZATION

SCANDALMONGERS
SCANDALOUSNESS
SCATTERBRAINED
SCHEMATIZATION
SCHISMATICALLY
SCHIZOMYCETOUS
SCHIZOPHRENICS
SCHIZOPHYCEOUS
SCHOOLCHILDREN
SCHOOLMISTRESS
SCHOOLTEACHERS
SCIENCE
FICTION
SCIENTIFICALLY
SCINTILLOMETER
SCOTCH
WHISKIES
SCREEN
PRINTING
SCRUBBING
BRUSH
SCRUPULOUSNESS
SCRUTINIZINGLY
SCURRILOUSNESS
SEARCH
WARRANTS
SEASONABLENESS
SECOND-
GUESSING
SECOND
THOUGHTS
SECULARIZATION
SEGREGATIONIST
SELF-
ABNEGATION
SELF-
ABSORPTION
SELF-
ANALYTICAL
SELF-
CONFIDENCE
SELF-
CONTROLLED
SELF-
DESTRUCTED
SELF-
DISCIPLINE
SELF-
EFFACEMENT
SELF-
EMPLOYMENT
SELF-
GOVERNMENT

SELF-IMPORTANCE
SELF-INDUCTANCE
SELF-INDULGENCE
SELF-INFLICTION
SELF-INTERESTED
SELF-JUSTIFYING
SELF-POSSESSION
SELF-PROTECTION
SELF-RESPECTFUL
SELF-RESPECTING
SELF-SUFFICIENT
SELF-SUPPORTING
SEMAPHORICALLY
SEMASIOLOGICAL
SEMICENTENNIAL
SEMICONDUCTION
SEMICONDUCTORS
SEMIELLIPTICAL
SEMIPARASITISM
SENIOR CITIZENS
SENSATIONALISM
SENSATIONALIST
SENTIMENTALISM
SENTIMENTALIST
SENTIMENTALITY
SENTIMENTALIZE
SEPARATE TABLES
SEPARATIVENESS
SEPTUAGENARIAN
SEQUESTRATIONS
SERGEANT-AT-ARMS
SERGEANT MAJORS
SERIALIZATIONS
SERIOCOMICALLY
SERJEANT-AT-ARMS
SERVICEABILITY

SERVICE CHARGES
SERVICE STATION
SERVOMECHANISM
SESQUIPEDALIAN
SEWING MACHINES
SHAGGY-DOG STORY
SHAMEFACEDNESS
SHEET LIGHTNING
SHEPHERD'S-PURSE
SHERARDIZATION
SHETLAND PONIES
SHIHCHIACHUANG
SHILLY-SHALLIED
SHILLYSHALLIER
SHIP'S CHANDLERS
SHOCK ABSORBERS
SHOCK TREATMENT
SHOOTING STICKS
SHOP ASSISTANTS
SHOPPING CENTRE
SHORT-CIRCUITED
SHORTSIGHTEDLY
SHOTGUN WEDDING
SHOULDER BLADES
SHOULDER STRAPS
SIDEWALK ARTIST
SIGMOIDOSCOPIC
SIGNATURE TUNES
SIGNIFICATIONS
SILENT PARTNERS
SILICIFICATION

SILVER JUBILEES
SILVER WEDDINGS
SILVICULTURIST
SIMAROUBACEOUS
SIMPLE FRACTURE
SIMPLE INTEREST
SIMPLE MACHINES
SIMPLIFICATION
SIMPLIFICATIVE
SIMPLISTICALLY
SIMULTANEOUSLY
SINGLE-BREASTED
SINGLE-MINDEDLY
SINKIANG-UIGHUR
SINKING FEELING
SIPHONOPHOROUS
SITTING TARGETS
SIXTEENTH NOTES
SKATE ON THIN ICE
SKIRTING BOARDS
SLANDEROUSNESS
SLAP ON THE WRIST
SLATTERNLINESS
SLAUGHTERHOUSE
SLIPSHODDINESS
SLOTTED SPATULA
SLUGGARDLINESS
SLUMBEROUSNESS
SMALL INTESTINE
SOCIAL CLIMBERS
SOCIAL SCIENCES
SOCIAL SECURITY
SOCIAL SERVICES

SOCIOLOGICALLY
SOCIOPOLITICAL
SODIUM CHLORIDE
SOLDERING IRONS
SOLICITOUSNESS
SOLIDIFICATION
SOMNAMBULATION
SOMNAMBULISTIC
SOPHISTICATION
SOUL-DESTROYING
SOUNDING BOARDS
SOUTHEASTWARDS
SOUTHERN LIGHTS
SOUTH-SOUTHEAST
SOUTH-SOUTHWEST
SOUTHWESTWARDS
SPATIOTEMPORAL
SPEAKERS CORNER
SPECIALIZATION
SPECIAL LICENCE
SPECIAL SCHOOLS
SPECIFICATIONS
SPECTROGRAPHIC
SPECTROSCOPIST
SPEECHLESSNESS
SPERMATOGONIAL
SPERMATOGONIUM
SPERMATOPHORAL
SPERMATOPHYTIC
SPERMATORRHOEA
SPERMIOGENESIS
SPERMIOGENETIC
SPHEROIDICALLY
SPHYGMOGRAPHIC
SPINNING WHEELS
SPINTHARISCOPE
SPIRITLESSNESS
SPIRITUALISTIC
SPIROCHAETOSIS
SPIRONOLACTONE

SPITTING IMAGES
SPLINTER GROUPS
SPONGIOBLASTIC
SPORADICALNESS
SPRECHSTIMMUNG
SPRING CHICKENS
SPRING-CLEANING
SQUADRON LEADER
SQUARE BRACKETS
STAFF SERGEANTS
STAGE DIRECTION
STAMPING GROUND
STANDARD-BEARER
STANDING ORDERS
STANDOFF HALVES
ST ANDREWS CROSS
STAPHYLOCOCCAL
STAPHYLOCOCCUS
STAPHYLOPLASTY
STARTING BLOCKS
STARTING PISTOL
STARTING PRICES
START SOMETHING
STATE'S EVIDENCE
STATIONARINESS
STATIONMASTERS
STATUESQUENESS
STEAMROLLERING
STEAMTIGHTNESS
STEERING WHEELS
STEPPING-STONES
STERCORICOLOUS
STERCULIACEOUS

STEREOMETRICAL
STEREOSPECIFIC
STERTOROUSNESS
STICKING POINTS
STIGMATIZATION
STINGING NETTLE
STIPPLING BRUSH
STIR ONES STUMPS
STOCHASTICALLY
STOCKBROKERAGE
STOCK EXCHANGES
STOCKING-FILLER
STOICHIOMETRIC
STOLEN PROPERTY
STOPS AT NOTHING
STORE DETECTIVE
STORM IN A TEACUP
STRAIGHT FIGHTS
STRAIGHTJACKET
STRAIGHT JACKET
STRATICULATION
STRATIFICATION
STRAWBERRY MARK
STREET-CREDIBLE
STREPTOTHRICIN
STRETCHABILITY
STRETCHER PARTY
STRIDULOUSNESS
STRIKEBREAKERS
STRIKEBREAKING
STRONG LANGUAGE
STRONG-MINDEDLY
STUDENTS' UNIONS
STULTIFICATION

STUMBLING BLOCK
STUPENDOUSNESS
SUBALTERNATION
SUBCONSCIOUSLY
SUBCONTINENTAL
SUBCONTRACTING
SUBCONTRACTORS
SUBCUTANEOUSLY
SUBINFEUDATION
SUBINFEUDATORY
SUBJECTABILITY
SUBJECTIVISTIC
SUBJECT-RAISING
SUBLIEUTENANCY
SUBLIEUTENANTS
SUBMACHINE GUNS
SUBMERSIBILITY
SUBMICROSCOPIC
SUBMISSIVENESS
SUBSIDIARINESS
SUBSTANTIALISM
SUBSTANTIALIST
SUBSTANTIALITY
SUBSTANTIATING
SUBSTANTIATION
SUBSTANTIATIVE
SUBTERRESTRIAL
SUBVERSIVENESS
SUCCESSFULNESS
SUCCESSIVENESS
SUGGESTIBILITY
SUGGESTIVENESS
SULPHANILAMIDE
SULPHATHIAZOLE
SULPHISOXAZOLE
SULPHONMETHANE
SULPHURIZATION
SULPHUROUSNESS
SUPERABUNDANCE
SUPERANNUATION
SUPERCILIOUSLY
SUPERCONDUCTOR
SUPERELEVATION
SUPERFICIALITY
SUPERINCUMBENT
SUPERINDUCTION
SUPERINTENDENT
SUPERINTENDING

SUPERNATURALLY
SUPERNORMALITY
SUPERPHOSPHATE
SUPERSATURATED
SUPERSCRIPTION
SUPERSONICALLY
SUPERSTRUCTURE
SUPPLY TEACHERS
SUPPORTABILITY
SUPPORTING PART
SUPRAMOLECULAR
SUPRASEGMENTAL
SUREFOOTEDNESS
SURGICAL SPIRIT
SURPASSINGNESS
SURPRISINGNESS
SUSCEPTIBILITY
SUSPENDIBILITY
SUSPENSIVENESS
SUSPICIOUSNESS
SWIMMING TRUNKS
SWORD-SWALLOWER
SYMBIONTICALLY
SYMBOLICALNESS
SYMMETRIZATION
SYMPATHIZINGLY
SYMPTOMATOLOGY
SYNCHRONICALLY
SYNCRETIZATION
SYNERGETICALLY
SYNONYMOUSNESS
SYNTHESIZATION
SYNTHETIZATION
SYPHILITICALLY
SYSTEMATICALLY
SYSTEMS ANALYST

T

TACHISTOSCOPIC
TAKE IN GOOD PART
TALK OF THE DEVIL
TARTAN TROUSERS
TAUTOLOGICALLY

TECHNICALITIES
TELANGIECTASIS
TELANGIECTATIC
TELAUTOGRAPHIC
TELEGRAPH
  POLES
TELEMETRICALLY
TELEOLOGICALLY
TELEPATHICALLY
TELEPHONE
  BOXES
TELESCOPICALLY
TELETYPESETTER
TERCENTENARIES
TERGIVERSATION
TERGIVERSATORY
TERMINOLOGICAL
TERRACED
  HOUSES
TERRITORIALISM
TERRITORIALIST
TERRITORIALITY
TERRITORIALIZE
TERROR-
  STRICKEN
TEST-TUBE
  BABIES
TETRAETHYL
  LEAD
THAUMATROPICAL
THE
  AMBASSADORS
THE FOUR
  SEASONS
THE LIFE OF
  RILEY
THEOCENTRICITY
THEOCRATICALLY
THEOLOGIZATION
THEOSOPHICALLY
THERIANTHROPIC
THERMAESTHESIA
THERMOCHEMICAL
THERMODYNAMICS
THERMOELECTRIC
THERMOELECTRON
THERMOJUNCTION
THERMOMAGNETIC
THERMOPLASTICS
THIOCYANIC
  ACID
THOUGHTFULNESS

THREE-DAY
  EVENTS
THREE-
  HALFPENCE
THREE-LINE
  WHIPS
THREE-POINT
  TURN
THRIFTLESSNESS
THROMBOPLASTIC
THROMBOPLASTIN
THYMELAEACEOUS
THYROTOXICOSIS
TICKLED TO
  DEATH
TIERRA DEL
  FUEGO
TIME
  IMMEMORIAL
TIME
  SIGNATURES
TITTLE-
  TATTLING
TOAD OF TOAD
  HALL
TOILET
  TRAINING
TO-ING AND
  FRO-ING
TONGUE
  TWISTERS
TORTOISESHELLS
TRACTION
  ENGINE
TRADE
  UNIONISTS
TRADING
  ESTATES
TRADITIONALISM
TRADITIONALIST
TRADUCIANISTIC
TRAFFIC
  CALMING
TRAFFIC
  CIRCLES
TRAFFIC
  ISLANDS
TRAFFIC
  WARDENS
TRAGICOMICALLY
TRAITOROUSNESS
TRANQUILLIZERS
TRANQUILLIZING

TRANSCAUCASIAN
TRANSCENDENTAL
TRANSCENDENTLY
TRANSCENDINGLY
TRANSCRIPTIONS
TRANSFERENTIAL
TRANSFORMATION
TRANSFORMATIVE
TRANSGRESSIBLE
TRANSGRESSIONS
TRANSISTORIZED
TRANSITIONALLY
TRANSITIVENESS
TRANSITORINESS
TRANS-
  JORDANIAN
TRANSLITERATED
TRANSLITERATOR
TRANSMIGRATION
TRANSMIGRATIVE
TRANSMIGRATORY
TRANSMISSIVITY
TRANSMOGRIFIED
TRANSMUTATIONS
TRANSPARENCIES
TRANSPLANTABLE
TRANSPORTATION
TRANSPORT
  CAFES
TRANSPOSITIONS
TRANSVALUATION
TRANSVERSENESS
TRAUMATIZATION
TRAVEL
  AGENCIES
TRAVELLERS
  TALE
TRAVELSICKNESS
TREAD THE
  BOARDS
TREASURE
  ISLAND
TREASURE
  TROVES
TREMENDOUSNESS
TRICHINIZATION
TRICHOMONIASIS
TRICHOTOMOUSLY
TRICK OR
  TREATED
TRIDIMENSIONAL
TRINITROCRESOL

TRINITROPHENOL
TRISOCTAHEDRAL
TRISOCTAHEDRON
TRISTAN DA
  CUNHA
TRIVIALIZATION
TROPIC OF
  CANCER
TROUBLESHOOTER
TROUSER
  PRESSES
TUMULTUOUSNESS
TUNBRIDGE
  WELLS
TURBOGENERATOR
TURF
  ACCOUNTANT
TURKISH
  DELIGHT
TURN A DEAF
  EAR TO
TURNING
  CIRCLES
TWO-
  DIMENSIONAL
TYRANNICALNESS

U

UBIQUITOUSNESS
ULTIMOGENITURE
ULTRAMODERNISM
ULTRAMODERNIST
ULTRAMONTANISM
ULTRAMONTANIST
ULTRASONICALLY
ULTRASTRUCTURE
UMBILICAL
  CORDS
UNACCOMMODATED
UNACCOMPLISHED
UNACCOUNTED
  FOR
UNACCOUNTED-
  FOR
UNAPPRECIATIVE
UNAPPROACHABLE
UNAPPROPRIATED
UNAVOIDABILITY
UNBEARABLENESS
UNBECOMINGNESS
UNCOMPROMISING
UNCONSCIONABLE

UNCONSCIONABLY
UNCONTAMINATED
UNCONTROLLABLE
UNCONVENTIONAL
UNCONVINCINGLY
UNCORROBORATED
UNDERACHIEVERS
UNDERACHIEVING
UNDERCARRIAGES
UNDERESTIMATED
UNDERESTIMATES
UNDERGRADUATES
UNDERMENTIONED
UNDERNOURISHED
UNDERSECRETARY
UNDERSTANDABLE
UNDERSTANDABLY
UNDERSTANDINGS
UNDERSTATEMENT
UNDERVALUATION
UNDESIRABILITY
UNECONOMICALLY
UNENTHUSIASTIC
UNEVENTFULNESS
UNEXPECTEDNESS
UNFAITHFULNESS
UNFLAPPABILITY
UNFRIENDLINESS
UNFRUITFULNESS
UNGRATEFULNESS
UNHANDSOMENESS
UNHOLY
  ALLIANCE
UNICELLULARITY
UNIDENTIFIABLE
UNIDIRECTIONAL
UNIFORMITARIAN
UNINCORPORATED
UNINTELLIGENCE
UNINTELLIGIBLE
UNIPERSONALITY
UNIVERSALISTIC
UNIVERSAL
  JOINT
UNKNOWABLENESS
UNMENTIONABLES
UNPLEASANTNESS
UNPRACTICALITY
UNPREMEDITATED
UNPREPAREDNESS
UNPROFESSIONAL

UNQUESTIONABLE
UNQUESTIONABLY
UNRECOGNIZABLE
UNRESERVEDNESS
UNRESTRAINEDLY
UNSATISFACTORY
UNSCRUPULOUSLY
UNTHANKFULNESS
UNTHINKABILITY
UNTOUCHABILITY
UPSIDE-
  DOWNNESS
UPSTANDINGNESS
UPWARDLY-
  MOBILE
UST-
  KAMENOGORSK
UTILITARIANISM

V
VACUUM
  CLEANERS
VALERIANACEOUS
VALETUDINARIAN
VALUE
  JUDGMENTS
VASOINHIBITORY
VAULTING
  HORSES
VEGETABLE
  KNIFE
VEGETATIVENESS
VENDING
  MACHINE
VENETIAN
  BLINDS
VENTRILOQUISTS
VENTURE
  CAPITAL
VERISIMILITUDE
VERTICILLASTER
VERTICILLATION
VESPERTILIONID
VESTED
  INTEREST
VEXED
  QUESTIONS
VICE-
  CHANCELLOR
VICE-
  PRESIDENCY
VICIOUS
  CIRCLES

VICTORIOUSNESS
VIEW ON THE
  STOUR
VILLAINOUSNESS
VINDICTIVENESS
VISHAKHAPATNAM
VITRIFIABILITY
VITRIOLIZATION
VITUPERATIVELY
VIVISECTIONIST
VOCIFEROUSNESS
VOLATILIZATION
VOLCANOLOGICAL
VOLUMETRICALLY
VOLUMINOUSNESS
VOLUPTUOUSNESS
VOROSHILOVGRAD
VOTES OF
  CENSURE
VULGAR
  FRACTION
VULGARIZATIONS
VULVOVAGINITIS

W
WARRANTABILITY
WARRANT
  OFFICER
WASHING
  MACHINE
WATERCOLOURIST
WATERING
  PLACES
WATERPROOFNESS
WATER-
  REPELLENT
WATER-
  RESISTANT
WATER
  SOFTENERS
WATERTIGHTNESS
WEAK-
  MINDEDNESS
WEATHERABILITY
WEATHERPROOFED
WEATHER
  STATION
WEIGHTLESSNESS
WE LIVE AND
  LEARN
WELL-
  ACCUSTOMED

WELL-
  ACQUAINTED
WELL-
  DOCUMENTED
WESTERNIZATION
WET ONES
  WHISTLE
WHEELER-
  DEALERS
WHEELER-
  DEALING
WHIMSICALITIES
WHIPPERSNAPPER
WHITE BLOOD
  CELL
WHITE
  ELEPHANTS
WHOLE-
  HEARTEDLY
WHORTLEBERRIES
WILDCAT
  STRIKES
WILD GOOSE
  CHASE
WILD-GOOSE
  CHASE
WILLIAM AND
  MARY
WIND
  INSTRUMENT
WINDOW
  DRESSING
WINDOW-
  SHOPPERS
WINDOW
  SHOPPING
WINDOW-
  SHOPPING
WIND-
  POLLINATED
WING
  COMMANDERS
WOMEN'S
  MOVEMENT
WORCESTER
  SAUCE
WORD
  PROCESSING
WORD
  PROCESSORS
WORKING
  PARTIES
WORLD-
  WEARINESS

WORMWOOD
  SCRUBS
WORSHIPFULNESS
WORTHWHILENESS

X

XANTHOPHYLLOUS
XEROPHYTICALLY

Y

YOUTH
  HOSTELLER

Z

ZEBRA
  CROSSINGS
ZINGIBERACEOUS

A

A BUNDLE OF NERVES
ACANTHOCEPHALAN
ACCLIMATIZATION
ACCOMMODATINGLY
ACCOMPLISHMENTS
ACHONDROPLASTIC
ACHROMATIZATION
ACIDIMETRICALLY
ACKNOWLEDGEABLE
ACKNOWLEDGMENTS
ACOUSTIC COUPLER
ACQUISITIVENESS
ADMINISTRATIONS
A DROP IN THE OCEAN
AERODYNAMICALLY
AFFRANCHISEMENT
AGAINST THE GRAIN
AGGLUTINABILITY
AGRANULOCYTOSIS
AIR CHIEF MARSHAL
AIR-CONDITIONING
AIRCRAFT CARRIER
AIR VICE-MARSHALS
ALGORITHMICALLY
ALIMENTARY CANAL
ALIVE AND KICKING
ALPHABETIZATION
ALUMINOSILICATE
AMARYLLIDACEOUS
AMBASSADORSHIPS
AMERICAN INDIANS
AMERICANIZATION
A MONTH OF SUNDAYS
AMUSEMENT ARCADE
ANABOLIC STEROID
ANARCHISTICALLY
ANCYLOSTOMIASIS
ANIMAL HUSBANDRY
ANIMATED CARTOON
ANOMALISTICALLY
ANTARCTIC CIRCLE
ANTEPENULTIMATE
ANTHROPOCENTRIC
ANTHROPOGENESIS
ANTHROPOGENETIC
ANTHROPOLOGICAL
ANTHROPOLOGISTS
ANTHROPOMETRIST
ANTHROPOMORPHIC
ANTICHOLINERGIC

ANTICLERICALISM
ANTI-IMPERIALISM
ANTI-IMPERIALIST
ANTILOGARITHMIC
ANTINATIONALIST
ANTIPERISTALSIS
ANTIPERSPIRANTS
APARTMENT HOUSES
APOCALYPTICALLY
APPRENTICESHIPS
APPROACHABILITY
APPROPRIATENESS
APPROVED SCHOOLS
ARCHIEPISCOPATE
ARCHITECTURALLY
ARGUMENTATIVELY
ARTERIALIZATION
ASCLEPIADACEOUS
ASSIMILATIONIST
ASSOCIATE DEGREE
ASTRONAUTICALLY
ASTRONAVIGATION
ASTROPHYSICISTS
ATHEROSCLEROSIS
ATHEROSCLEROTIC
ATMOSPHERICALLY
AT THE DROP OF A
  HAT
ATTORNEY GENERAL
AUDIOMETRICALLY
AUTHORITATIVELY
AUTOBIOGRAPHIES
AUTOCORRELATION
AUTOGRAPHICALLY
AUTOMATIC PILOTS
AUTORADIOGRAPHY
AUTOTRANSFORMER
AVERSION THERAPY

B

BACHELOR'S DEGREE
BACK-SEAT DRIVERS
BACTERIOLOGICAL
BACTERIOLOGISTS
BACTERIOPHAGOUS
BALLROOM DANCING
BANANA REPUBLICS
BANNER HEADLINES
BANQUETING HOUSE
BASIDIOMYCETOUS
BATCH PROCESSING

BATHING MACHINES
BATHOMETRICALLY
BATHYMETRICALLY
BEATEN AT THE POST
BED AND BREAKFAST
BENEFIT OF CLERGY
BIBLIOGRAPHICAL
BIBLIOPHILISTIC
BINOCULAR VISION
BIOASTRONAUTICS
BIOGEOGRAPHICAL
BIOLUMINESCENCE
BIOTECHNOLOGIST
BIRDS OF A FEATHER
BIRDS OF PARADISE
BISYMMETRICALLY
BLACK MARKETEERS
BLACKWATER FEVER
BLAMEWORTHINESS
BLANK CARTRIDGES
BLOCK AND TACKLES
BLOOD-AND-THUNDER
BOARDING SCHOOLS
BONDED WAREHOUSE
BOW STREET RUNNER
BRAKE HORSE POWER
BREAKING THE NEWS
BRING AND BUY SALE
BROADMINDEDNESS
BROKEN-HEARTEDLY
BRUSSELS SPROUTS
BUBBLE AND SQUEAK
BUILDING SOCIETY
BUREAU DE CHANGES
BUSMAN'S HOLIDAYS
BUTTERFLY STROKE

C

CABLE TELEVISION
CANNIBALIZATION
CAPRIFOLIACEOUS
CARDIOPULMONARY
CARPOMETACARPUS
CARRYING CHARGES
CASEMENT WINDOWS
CATEGORIZATIONS
CATHERINE WHEELS
CATHETERIZATION
CATHODE RAY TUBES
CATHOLICIZATION
CENTRE OF GRAVITY

CEPHALOCHORDATE
CEPHALOTHORACIC
CEREBROVASCULAR
CEREMONIOUSNESS
CHAPTER AND VERSE
CHARACTERISTICS
CHARENT-MARITIME
CHARGE D'AFFAIRES
CHECKING ACCOUNT
CHEMICAL WARFARE
CHEMOTACTICALLY
CHEMOTROPICALLY
CHENOPODIACEOUS
CHESTS OF DRAWERS
CHIEF CONSTABLES
CHIEF INSPECTORS
CHINESE CHEQUERS
CHINESE LANTERNS
CHINLESS WONDERS
CHLORAMPHENICOL
CHOLECALCIFEROL
CHOLECYSTECTOMY
CHONDRIFICATION
CHROMATOGRAPHER
CHROMATOGRAPHIC
CHROMATOPHOROUS
CHRONOGRAMMATIC
CHRONOLOGICALLY
CHUCK-WILL'S-WIDOW
CHURCH OF ENGLAND
CIGARETTE HOLDER
CIGARETTE PAPERS
CINEMATOGRAPHER
CINEMATOGRAPHIC
CIRCUIT BREAKERS
CIRCULARIZATION
CIRCUMAMBULATOR
CIRCUMFERENTIAL
CIRCUMLOCUTIONS
CIRCUMNAVIGABLE
CIRCUMNAVIGATED
CIRCUMNAVIGATOR
CIRCUMSCRIPTION
CIRCUMSTANTIATE
CIRCUMVALLATION
CLANDESTINENESS
CLASSIFICATIONS
CLAUSTROPHOBICS
CLEAR-HEADEDNESS
CLERMONT-FERRAND
CLOUD CUCKOO LAND

CLOUD-CUCKOO-LAND
COCK-A-DOODLE-DOOS
COCKNEYFICATION
COCKTAIL LOUNGES
COFFEE-TABLE BOOK
COLD-BLOODEDNESS
COLD-HEARTEDNESS
COLD-SHOULDERING
COLLECTIVE FARMS
COLLECTIVE NOUNS
COLLECTOR'S ITEMS
COLLISION COURSE
COLORADO BEETLES
COLOUR BLINDNESS
COMBINATION LOCK
COMEDY OF MANNERS
COME INTO ONES OWN
COMFORT STATIONS
COMITY OF NATIONS
COMMERCIALISTIC
COMMERCIALIZING
COMMISSIONAIRES
COMMITTEE STAGES
COMMODIFICATION
COMMON FRACTIONS
COMMUNALIZATION
COMMUNICABILITY
COMMUNITY CENTRE
COMMUNITY CHESTS
COMPASSIONATELY
COMPETITIVENESS
COMPLICATEDNESS
COMPREHENSIVELY
COMPRESSIBILITY
COMPUTERIZATION
CONCEPTUALISTIC
CONCEPTUALIZING
CONCESSIONAIRES
CONCRETE JUNGLES
CONFECTIONERIES
CONFIDENCE TRICK
CONFIDENTIALITY
CONFIGURATIONAL
CONFRATERNITIES
CONGLOMERATIONS
CONGRATULATIONS
CONSCIENCE MONEY
CONSCIENTIOUSLY
CONSCRIPTIONIST
CONSENTING ADULT
CONSERVATIONISM

CONSERVATIONIST
CONSIDERATENESS
CONSPICUOUSNESS
CONSTITUTIONALS
CONSUMER DURABLE
CONTEMPORANEITY
CONTEMPORANEOUS
CONTEMPTIBILITY
CONTENTIOUSNESS
CONTORTIONISTIC
CONTRACTIBILITY
CONTRAINDICATED
CONTROVERSIALLY
CONVENIENCE FOOD
CONVENTIONALISM
CONVENTIONALIST
CONVENTIONALITY
CONVENTIONALIZE
CONVOLVULACEOUS
CORRELATIVENESS
CORRESPONDINGLY
COSMOPOLITANISM
COST-EFFECTIVELY
COTTAGE HOSPITAL
COTTAGE INDUSTRY
COUNTERATTACKED
COUNTERATTACKER
COUNTERBALANCED
COUNTERBALANCES
COUNTERCLAIMANT
COUNTERIRRITANT
COUNTER IRRITANT
COUNTERMEASURES
COUNTERPROPOSAL
COURT-MARTIALING
COURT-MARTIALLED
COURTS OF INQUIRY
COVERING LETTERS
CREASE RESISTANT
CREATIVE WRITING
CREDIBILITY GAPS
CRICKET PAVILION
CRIMINAL CLASSES
CROSS-FERTILIZED
CROSSOPTERYGION
CROSS-QUESTIONED
CROSS-QUESTIONER
CROSS-REFERENCES
CROSSWORD EDITORS
CROWN PRINCESSES
CRYSTALLIZATION

CRYSTALLOGRAPHY
CUCKOO IN THE NEST
CURRENT ACCOUNTS
CURRICULUM VITAE
CUT AND COME AGAIN
CYTOMEGALOVIRUS

D
DAYLIGHT ROBBERY
DAYS OF RECKONING
DECALCIFICATION
DECARBONIZATION
DECARBOXYLATION
DECIPHERABILITY
DECOMPOSABILITY
DECONTAMINATING
DECONTAMINATION
DECONTAMINATIVE
DECONTEXTUALIZE
DEFINITE ARTICLE
DEHYDROGENATION
DELIRIUM TREMENS
DELIVER THE GOODS
DEMAGNETIZATION
DEMOCRATIZATION
DEMONSTRABILITY
DEMONSTRATIONAL
DEMONSTRATIVELY
DEMULSIFICATION
DEMYSTIFICATION
DENATIONALIZING
DENITRIFICATION
DEPARTMENTALISM
DEPARTMENTALIZE
DEPARTMENT STORE
DEPARTURE LOUNGE
DEPENDENT CLAUSE
DEPOSIT ACCOUNTS
DERMATOGLYPHICS
DERMATOPHYTOSIS
DESCRIPTIVENESS
DESENSITIZATION
DESEXUALIZATION
DESTABILIZATION
DESTRUCTIBILITY
DESTRUCTIVENESS
DETRIBALIZATION
DEVELOPMENT AREA
DEVIL'S ADVOCATES
DEVITRIFICATION
DIALECTOLOGICAL

DIAMAGNETICALLY
DIAMOND JUBILEES
DIAMOND WEDDINGS
DIAPHOTOTROPISM
DICHOTOMIZATION
DIESEL-HYDRAULIC
DIFFERENTIATING
DIFFERENTIATION
DIGITAL COMPUTER
DIRECTION FINDER
DISADVANTAGEOUS
DISAPPOINTINGLY
DISAPPOINTMENTS
DISARTICULATION
DISCIPLINARIANS
DISCONCERTINGLY
DISCONTINUATION
DISCONTINUITIES
DISCONTINUOUSLY
DISCOUNTENANCED
DISCOURAGEMENTS
DISCRETIONARILY
DISENCUMBERMENT
DISENTANGLEMENT
DISESTABLISHING
DISHEARTENINGLY
DISHEARTENMENTS
DISILLUSIONMENT
DISINCLINATIONS
DISINFLATIONARY
DISINTERESTEDLY
DISORDERLY HOUSE
DISORGANIZATION
DISPASSIONATELY
DISREPUTABILITY
DISRESPECTFULLY
DISSATISFACTION
DISSATISFACTORY
DISSERTATIONIST
DISSIMILARITIES
DISTASTEFULNESS
DISTINCTIVENESS
DISTINGUISHABLE
DISTRACTIBILITY
DISTRUSTFULNESS
DITHYRAMBICALLY
DIVERSIFICATION
DIVISION LOBBIES
DO-IT-YOURSELFERS
DOLICHOCEPHALIC
DOMESTIC ANIMALS

DOMESTIC SCIENCE
DOMESTIC SERVICE
DORSIVENTRALITY
DOUBLE-BARRELLED
DOUBLE ENTENDRES
DOUBLE STANDARDS
DOUBLE WHITE LINE
DRAUGHTSMANSHIP
DRESSING STATION
DRESS REHEARSALS
DRIVE-BY SHOOTING
DRIVING LICENCES
DRUIDICAL CIRCLE
DUAL CARRIAGEWAY
DUAL CITIZENSHIP
DUTCH ELM DISEASE

E
EARTHSHATTERING
EAT ONES HEART OUT
ECCLESIASTICISM
ECCLESIOLOGICAL
EDUCATED GUESSES
EDUCATIONALISTS
ELECTRIC BLANKET
ELECTRIFICATION
ELECTROACOUSTIC
ELECTROANALYSIS
ELECTROANALYTIC
ELECTROCHEMICAL
ELECTRODIALYSIS
ELECTRODYNAMICS
ELECTROKINETICS
ELECTROLYSATION
ELECTROMAGNETIC
ELECTRONEGATIVE
ELECTROPHORESIS
ELECTROPHORETIC
ELECTROPOSITIVE
ELECTROSURGICAL
ELEVATED RAILWAY
EMANCIPATIONIST
EMINENCES GRISES
ENANTIOMORPHISM
ENCEPHALOGRAPHY
ENCHONDROMATOUS
ENCOMIASTICALLY
ENDOCRINE GLANDS
ENDOCRINOLOGIST
ENDOTHERMICALLY
ENDOWMENT POLICY

ENFRANCHISEMENT
ENGAGEMENT RINGS
ENTENTE CORDIALE
ENTREPRENEURIAL
ENVIRONMENTALLY
EPIDEMIOLOGICAL
EPISCOPALIANISM
EPISTEMOLOGICAL
EPITHELIOMATOUS
EQUALITARIANISM
ETERNAL TRIANGLE
ETHEREALIZATION
ETHNIC CLEANSING
ETHNOCENTRICITY
EUCHARISTICALLY
EUDIOMETRICALLY
EUPHEMISTICALLY
EUROPEANIZATION
EUSTACHIAN TUBES
EVERLASTINGNESS
EXCEPTIONALNESS
EXCHANGEABILITY
EXCLAMATION MARK
EXCOMMUNICATING
EXCOMMUNICATION
EXCOMMUNICATIVE
EXEMPLIFICATION
EXEMPLIFICATIVE
EXHIBITIONISTIC
EXPEDITIOUSNESS
EXPENSE ACCOUNTS
EXPERIMENTALISM
EXPERIMENTALIST
EXPERIMENTATION
EXPOSTULATINGLY
EXPRESSIONISTIC
EXTEMPORARINESS
EXTEMPORIZATION
EXTERIORIZATION
EXTERNALIZATION
EXTRACURRICULAR
EXTRALINGUISTIC
EXTRAORDINARILY

F

FAIRY GODMOTHERS
FAMILIARIZATION
FAMILY ALLOWANCE
FASHIONABLENESS
FATHER CHRISTMAS
FEATURELESSNESS

FELLOW TRAVELLER
FEUILLETONISTIC
FIDEICOMMISSARY
FIFTH COLUMNISTS
FIGURES OF SPEECH
FILLING STATIONS
FINISHING SCHOOL
FIRST LIEUTENANT
FLIBBERTIGIBBET
FLIGHT SERGEANTS
FLIRTATIOUSNESS
FOLDING ONES ARMS
FOOT-POUND-SECOND
FOREIGN EXCHANGE
FORESIGHTEDNESS
FORKED LIGHTNING
FORMULARIZATION
FOUNDATION STONE
FOUNDING FATHERS
FOUR-DIMENSIONAL
FOUR-LETTER WORDS
FOURTH DIMENSION
FRACTIONIZATION
FRAGMENTARINESS
FRANKFURT AM MAIN
FREE ASSOCIATION
FRENCH POLISHING
FRIENDLY SOCIETY
FROM STEM TO STERN
FULL-BLOODEDNESS
FUNDAMENTALISTS
FUNERAL DIRECTOR
FUNERAL PARLOURS
FUTILITARIANISM

G

GAME SET AND MATCH
GASTROENTERITIC
GASTROENTERITIS
GASTRONOMICALLY
GENERAL DELIVERY
GENERAL ELECTION
GENERALIZATIONS
GENERAL PRACTICE
GENTLEMAN-AT-ARMS
GENTLEMAN FARMER
GENTLEMANLINESS
GENTLEMEN-AT-ARMS
GERMAN SHEPHERDS
GET ONES SKATES ON
GIVE ONESELF AWAY

GIVE THE GAME AWAY
GLOBE ARTICHOKES
GLOSSY MAGAZINES
GLOUCESTERSHIRE
GLUCONEOGENESIS
GNOTOBIOTICALLY
GOLDEN HANDSHAKE
GOLDEN RETRIEVER
GOOD-FOR-NOTHINGS
GOOD-NATUREDNESS
GO OFF THE DEEP END
GORNO-BADAKHSHAN
GOVERNOR-GENERAL
GRAPHIC DESIGNER
GREGORIAN CHANTS
GUTTURALIZATION
GYNANDROMORPHIC

H

HACKNEY CARRIAGE
HAEMAGGLUTINATE
HAEMOFLAGELLATE
HAEMOGLOBINURIA
HALF-HEARTEDNESS
HALL OF RESIDENCE
HALLUCINATIONAL
HAMAMELIDACEOUS
HAMMER AND SICKLE
HARD-HEARTEDNESS
HARD LUCK STORIES
HARMONISTICALLY
HARVEST FESTIVAL
HAVE A BONE TO PICK
HEARTBREAK HOUSE
HEARTBREAKINGLY
HEARTBROKENNESS
HEAVY-HANDEDNESS
HEIR PRESUMPTIVE
HELIOCENTRICITY
HELIOMETRICALLY
HELIOTROPICALLY
HELLENISTICALLY
HELMINTHOLOGIST
HENDECASYLLABIC
HENDECASYLLABLE
HERBIVOROUSNESS
HEREDITARIANISM
HERMAPHRODITISM
HERMENEUTICALLY
HERO-WORSHIPPING
HETEROCHROMATIC

HETEROCHROMATIN
HETEROGENEOUSLY
HETEROSEXUALITY
HEXACHLOROPHENE
HEXYLRESORCINOL
HIGH COMMISSIONS
HIGHER EDUCATION
HIMACHAL PRADESH
HIPPOCRATIC OATH
HISPANICIZATION
HISTORIC PRESENT
HISTORIOGRAPHER
HISTORIOGRAPHIC
HOLOBLASTICALLY
HOLOGRAPHICALLY
HOLY ROMAN EMPIRE
HOMEOPATHICALLY
HOMOCENTRICALLY
HOMOGENEOUSNESS
HOMOPLASTICALLY
HOPE AGAINST HOPE
HORTICULTURALLY
HOSPITALIZATION
HOT-WATER BOTTLES
HOUSEHOLDERSHIP
HOUSEHOLD TROOPS
HOUSEWIFELINESS
HOUSING PROJECTS
HUMANITARIANISM
HUMANITARIANIST
HUNTINGDONSHIRE
HYDROBROMIC ACID
HYDROGENIZATION
HYDROMECHANICAL
HYDROMETALLURGY
HYPERCRITICALLY

I

ICEBERG LETTUCES
IDIOMORPHICALLY
IMMEASURABILITY
IMMERSION HEATER
IMMORTALIZATION
IMMUNOCHEMISTRY
IMMUNOGENICALLY
IMMUNOLOGICALLY
IMPECUNIOUSNESS
IMPENETRABILITY
IMPERISHABILITY
IMPONDERABILITY
IMPRESCRIPTIBLE

IMPRESSIONISTIC
IMPROBABILITIES
IMPROVISATIONAL
INACCESSIBILITY
INADMISSIBILITY
INAPPLICABILITY
INAPPROPRIATELY
INATTENTIVENESS
IN BLACK AND WHITE
INCALCULABILITY
INCIDENTAL MUSIC
INCOMMENSURABLE
INCOMMUNICATIVE
INCOMMUTABILITY
INCOMPARABILITY
INCOMPATIBILITY
INCOMPREHENSION
INCOMPREHENSIVE
INCOMPUTABILITY
INCONGRUOUSNESS
INCONSEQUENTIAL
INCONSIDERATELY
INCONSIDERATION
INCONSISTENCIES
INCONSOLABILITY
INCONSPICUOUSLY
INCONVENIENCING
INCORRIGIBILITY
INCREDULOUSNESS
INDECENT ASSAULT
INDEFEASIBILITY
INDEFENSIBILITY
INDEMNIFICATION
INDETERMINISTIC
INDIAN ROPE-TRICK
INDIGESTIBILITY
INDIRECT OBJECTS
INDISCRETIONARY
INDISPUTABILITY
INDISSOLUBILITY
INDIVIDUALISTIC
INDIVIDUALIZING
INDUSTRIALIZING
INDUSTRIOUSNESS
INEFFACEABILITY
INEFFECTIVENESS
INEXPENSIVENESS
INEXPLICABILITY
INEXTENSIBILITY
INEXTRICABILITY
INFANT PRODIGIES

INFINITESIMALLY
INFRASTRUCTURES
INFUNDIBULIFORM
INJUDICIOUSNESS
INOFFENSIVENESS
INOPPORTUNENESS
INQUISITIVENESS
INQUISITORIALLY
INSENSIBILITIES
INSIGNIFICANTLY
INSTALLMENT PLAN
INSTANTANEOUSLY
INSTRUMENTALISM
INSTRUMENTALIST
INSTRUMENTALITY
INSTRUMENTATION
INSUBORDINATELY
INSUBORDINATION
INSURANCE POLICY
INSURRECTIONARY
INSURRECTIONISM
INSURRECTIONIST
INTELLECTUALISE
INTELLECTUALISM
INTELLECTUALIST
INTELLECTUALITY
INTELLECTUALIZE
INTELLIGIBILITY
INTENSIFICATION
INTERCHANGEABLE
INTERCHANGEABLY
INTERCLAVICULAR
INTERCOLLEGIATE
INTERCONNECTION
INTERDEPENDENCE
INTERFEROMETRIC
INTERLAMINATION
INTERLOCUTORILY
INTERNALIZATION
INTERNAL REVENUE
INTERNATIONALES
INTERNATIONALLY
INTEROSCULATION
INTERPENETRABLE
INTERPRETATIONS
INTERROGATINGLY
INTERROGATIONAL
INTERROGATIVELY
INTERROGATORIES
INTERROGATORILY
INTERSCHOLASTIC

INTERVENTIONISM
INTERVENTIONIST
IN THE LAST RESORT
INTRANSIGENTIST
INTROSPECTIONAL
INTROSPECTIVELY
INTUSSUSCEPTION
INTUSSUSCEPTIVE
INVESTIGATIONAL
INVOLUNTARINESS
INVOLUNTATARILY
INVULNERABILITY
IRREDEEMABILITY
IRREFRAGABILITY
IRREMISSIBILITY
IRRESISTIBILITY
IRRESOLVABILITY
IRREVERSIBILITY

J
JACK-OF-ALL-TRADES
JAPANESE LANTERN
JEHOVAH'S WITNESS
JUMPING-OFF PLACE
JURISPRUDENTIAL
JUXTAPOSITIONAL

K
KABARDINO-BALKAR
KEEPS ONES HAND IN
KIND-HEARTEDNESS

L
LABOUR EXCHANGES
LABOUR INTENSIVE
LABOUR-INTENSIVE
LABYRINTHICALLY
LACKADAISICALLY
LADIES-IN-WAITING
LAISSEZ-FAIREISM
LARGE INTESTINES
LATERAL THINKING
LAUGHING JACKASS
LEADING ARTICLES
LEADING QUESTION
LET ONES HAIR DOWN
LETTERS OF CREDIT
LEVEL-HEADEDNESS
LIGHT-HEADEDNESS
LIGHT MACHINE GUN
LIGHTNING STRIKE

LIKE THE CLAPPERS
LILY OF THE VALLEY
LIVERY COMPANIES
LOCAL GOVERNMENT
LOGARITHMICALLY
LOIRE-ATLANTIQUE
LOPHOBRANCHIATE
LOURENCO MARQUES

M
MACHINE-READABLE
MACROCOSMICALLY
MACROSCOPICALLY
MACROSPORANGIUM
MAD AS A MARCH HARE
MAGNANIMOUSNESS
MAGNETOCHEMICAL
MAGNETOELECTRIC
MAGNETO ELECTRIC
MAGNIFYING GLASS
MALACOPTERYGIAN
MALASSIMILATION
MALE CHAUVINISTS
MALPRACTITIONER
MANIC-DEPRESSIVE
MANIFESTATIONAL
MANNERISTICALLY
MANOEUVRABILITY
MARKET GARDENERS
MARKET GARDENING
MARRIAGEABILITY
MARSHALLING YARD
MARXISM-LENINISM
MARXIST-LENINIST
MASSAGE PARLOURS
MASTER CRAFTSMAN
MASTER OF SCIENCE
MATERIALIZATION
MEANINGLESSNESS
MECHANISTICALLY
MEGALOCEPHALOUS
MELANCHOLICALLY
MELLIFLUOUSNESS
MEMORIALIZATION
MENDING ONES WAYS
MENISPERMACEOUS
MENSTRUAL PERIOD
MENTAL DEFECTIVE
MENTAL HOSPITALS
MENTALISTICALLY
MEPHISTOPHELEAN

MEROBLASTICALLY
METACINNABARITE
METAGENETICALLY
METALINGUISTICS
METALLURGICALLY
METAMATHEMATICS
METHODISTICALLY
METROPOLITANISM
MICROBIOLOGICAL
MICROBIOLOGISTS
MICROELECTRONIC
MICROPHOTOGRAPH
MICROPROCESSORS
MICROSCOPICALLY
MICROSPORANGIUM
MICROSPOROPHYLL
MIDDLE OF NOWHERE
MIDDLE-OF-THE-ROAD
MINIATURIZATION
MISAPPLICATIONS
MISAPPREHENDING
MISAPPREHENSION
MISAPPREHENSIVE
MISAPPROPRIATED
MISCALCULATIONS
MISCELLANEOUSLY
MISCHIEVOUSNESS
MISCONSTRUCTION
MISINTERPRETING
MISREPRESENTING
MISTRUSTFULNESS
MOBILE LIBRARIES
MODERNISTICALLY
MOLOTOV COCKTAIL
MONCHEN-GLADBACH
MONEY FOR OLD ROPE
MONOGRAPHICALLY
MONOUNSATURATED
MONTE CARLO RALLY
MONTMORILLONITE
MOOG SYNTHESIZER
MOONLIGHT SONATA
MORNING SICKNESS
MORPHOLOGICALLY
MORPHOPHONEMICS
MOTHER COUNTRIES
MOTHER SUPERIORS
MOVING STAIRCASE
MULTITUDINOUSLY
MUSCULOSKELETAL
MUSTARD AND CRESS

MUSTARD PLASTERS
MUTATIS MUTANDIS
MYTHOLOGIZATION

N

NAGORNO-KARABAKH
NATIONAL ANTHEMS
NATIONAL GALLERY
NATIONALIZATION
NATIONAL SERVICE
NATURAL SCIENCES
NEARSIGHTEDNESS
NEEDLE AND THREAD
NEGATIVE-RAISING
NEIGHBOURLINESS
NEOARSPHENAMINE
NEOLOGISTICALLY
NEUROHYPOPHYSIS
NEUROPATHICALLY
NEUROPHYSIOLOGY
NEUROPSYCHIATRY
NEUROPSYCHOLOGY
NEUROSURGICALLY
NEWS CONFERENCES
NIGHTMARISHNESS
NINE DAYS' WONDERS
NITROCHLOROFORM
NITROGENIZATION
NOMOGRAPHICALLY
NON COMPOS MENTIS
NONCONTRIBUTING
NONCONTRIBUTORY
NONINTERVENTION
NON INTERVENTION
NONINTOXICATING
NONPRODUCTIVITY
NON-PROFIT-MAKING
NONSENSICALNESS
NONSTANDARDIZED
NORTH COUNTRYMAN
NOTWITHSTANDING
NOUVELLE CUISINE
NO-WIN SITUATIONS
NUCLEAR FAMILIES
NUCLEAR REACTORS
NUCLEOSYNTHESIS
NUMBER-CRUNCHING

O

OBJECTIFICATION
OBSERVATION POST

OBSTRUCTIONISTS
OBSTRUCTIVENESS
OESTROGENICALLY
OLD AGE PENSIONER
OLD PEOPLE'S HOMES
OLIGOSACCHARIDE
OMNIDIRECTIONAL
ONCE IN A BLUE MOON
ONE-ARMED BANDITS
ONES HEART BLEEDS
ON THE BACK BURNER
OPEN-AND-SHUT CASE
OPENHEARTEDNESS
OPERATING SYSTEM
OPHTHALMOLOGIST
OPHTHALMOSCOPIC
OPINIONATEDNESS
OPISTHOGNATHISM
OPISTHOGNATHOUS
OPPOSITE NUMBERS
OPTICAL ILLUSION
OPTOELECTRONICS
ORIENTALIZATION
ORNITHORHYNCHUS
ORTHOCHROMATISM
ORTHOPSYCHIATRY
OSTEOPATHICALLY
OUT OF THE PICTURE
OVERCAPITALIZED
OVERCOMPENSATED
OVERDEVELOPMENT
OVERSIMPLIFYING
OXYTETRACYCLINE

P

PAINSTAKINGNESS
PALAEOBOTANICAL
PALAEOGRAPHICAL
PALAEONTOGRAPHY
PALAEONTOLOGIST
PALAEOZOOLOGIST
PALEONTOLOGISTS
PANCAKE LANDINGS
PANTHEISTICALLY
PARAGENETICALLY
PARAGRAPHICALLY
PARALLACTICALLY
PARASITOLOGICAL
PARASYMPATHETIC
PARENT COMPANIES
PARENTHETICALLY

PARLIAMENTARIAN
PARTHENOGENESIS
PARTHENOGENETIC
PARTICULARISTIC
PARTICULARITIES
PARTICULARIZING
PASSIFLORACEOUS
PASSIONLESSNESS
PAST PARTICIPLES
PATENT MEDICINES
PATHETIC FALLACY
PAVEMENT ARTISTS
PAYING IN ADVANCE
PELICAN CROSSING
PENTATONIC SCALE
PENTOTHAL SODIUM
PEPPERCORN RENTS
PEREGRINE FALCON
PERFUNCTORINESS
PERIODONTICALLY
PERIPATETICALLY
PERISTALTICALLY
PEROXIDE BLONDES
PERPENDICULARLY
PERPETUAL MOTION
PERSONAL COLUMNS
PERSONALITY CULT
PERSONALIZATION
PERSONAL PRONOUN
PERSONAL STEREOS
PERSONA NON GRATA
PERSONIFICATION
PERSPICACIOUSLY
PERSPICUOUSNESS
PESSIMISTICALLY
PHANTASMAGORIAS
PHARMACODYNAMIC
PHARMACOGNOSIST
PHARMACOGNOSTIC
PHARMACOLOGICAL
PHARMACOLOGISTS
PHARYNGOLOGICAL
PHENOLPHTHALEIN
PHENYLKETONURIA
PHILANTHROPISTS
PHILOSOPHICALLY
PHLEBOSCLEROSIS
PHOSPHATIZATION
PHOSPHOCREATINE
PHOSPHORESCENCE
PHOTOCONDUCTION

PHOTODEGRADABLE
PHOTOELASTICITY
PHOTOGRAMMETRIC
PHOTOJOURNALISM
PHOTOJOURNALIST
PHOTOLITHOGRAPH
PHOTOMECHANICAL
PHOTOMETRICALLY
PHOTOMICROGRAPH
PHOTOMULTIPLIER
PHOTOSENSITIZED
PHOTOTELEGRAPHY
PHOTOTOPOGRAPHY
PHOTOTRANSISTOR
PHOTOTYPESETTER
PHOTOTYPOGRAPHY
PHOTOZINCOGRAPH
PHYSICOCHEMICAL
PHYSIOTHERAPIST
PHYTOGEOGRAPHER
PHYTOPLANKTONIC
PICTURE-POSTCARD
PICTURESQUENESS
PIEZOMETRICALLY
PINCER MOVEMENTS
PITHECANTHROPUS
PLASMOLYTICALLY
PLASTIC SURGEONS
PLATINUM BLONDES
PLATYHELMINTHIC
PLEASURABLENESS
PLENIPOTENTIARY
PLEUROPNEUMONIA
PLIGHT ONES TROTH
PLOUGHMAN'S LUNCH
PLUMBAGINACEOUS
PLUMBER'S FRIENDS
PLUTOCRATICALLY
PNEUMATIC DRILLS
POIKILOTHERMISM
POISON-PEN LETTER
POLICE CONSTABLE
POLITICAL ASYLUM
POLLING STATIONS
POLYGENETICALLY
POLYGRAPHICALLY
POLYUNSATURATED
PORTMANTEAU WORD
POST OFFICE BOXES
POVERTY-STRICKEN
POWER OF ATTORNEY

PRAYING MANTISES
PREACHIFICATION
PRECANCELLATION
PRECIPITOUSNESS
PREDISPOSITIONS
PREFERENTIALITY
PREHISTORICALLY
PREPOSITIONALLY
PRESBYTERIANISM
PRESCRIPTIVISTS
PRESENCE CHAMBER
PRESENTABLENESS
PRESENTATIONISM
PRESENTATIONIST
PRESS CONFERENCE
PRESSURE COOKERS
PRESTIDIGITATOR
PRESTIGIOUSNESS
PRESUMPTIVENESS
PRESUPPOSITIONS
PRETENTIOUSNESS
PRETERNATURALLY
PRIMA BALLERINAS
PRIMARY STRESSES
PRINCE CHARMINGS
PRINTED CIRCUITS
PRINTING PRESSES
PRIVATE PROPERTY
PRIVATE SOLDIERS
PRIVY COUNCILLOR
PROBLEMATICALLY
PROCRASTINATING
PROCRASTINATION
PRODUCTION LINES
PROFESSIONALISM
PROFESSIONALIST
PROGENITIVENESS
PROGNOSTICATING
PROGNOSTICATION
PROGNOSTICATIVE
PROGNOSTICATORS
PROGRESSIVENESS
PROHIBITIONISTS
PROHIBITIVENESS
PROLETARIANNESS
PROMISCUOUSNESS
PROPER FRACTIONS
PROPORTIONALITY
PROPORTIONATELY
PROPYLENE GLYCOL
PROSELYTIZATION

PROSENCHYMATOUS
PROTOZOOLOGICAL
PROVOCATIVENESS
PSEPHOLOGICALLY
PSEUDOMUTUALITY
PSYCHEDELICALLY
PSYCHIATRICALLY
PSYCHOACOUSTICS
PSYCHOANALYSING
PSYCHOBIOLOGIST
PSYCHOGENICALLY
PSYCHOLOGICALLY
PSYCHOMETRICIAN
PSYCHOPATHOLOGY
PSYCHOSEXUALITY
PSYCHOTECHNICAL
PSYCHOTHERAPIST
PSYCHOTOMIMETIC
PTOLEMAIC SYSTEM
PUBLIC COMPANIES
PUBLIC NUISANCES
PUBLIC OWNERSHIP
PUBLIC RELATIONS
PULCHRITUDINOUS
PUNCTILIOUSNESS
PUNCTUATION MARK
PURITANICALNESS
PURPOSELESSNESS
PUSILLANIMOUSLY
PUT ONES FOOT DOWN
PUT OUT MORE FLAGS
PYROELECTRICITY

Q

QUADRUPLICATION
QUARRELSOMENESS
QUARTER SESSIONS
QUATERCENTENARY
QUEEN'S EVIDENCES
QUESTION MASTERS
QUICK-WITTEDNESS
QUINQUAGENARIAN
QUINTUPLICATION
QUODLIBETICALLY

R

RADIOACTIVATION
RADIOBIOLOGICAL
RADIOLOCATIONAL
RADIOMICROMETER
RADIOPHONICALLY

417

RADIOSCOPICALLY
RADIOTELEGRAPHY
RADIOTELEPHONIC
RADIO TELESCOPES
RADIOTHERAPISTS
RAILWAY STATIONS
RASTAFARIANISMS
RATE OF EXCHANGES
RATIONALIZATION
REAFFORESTATION
REAL-ESTATE AGENT
REARGUARD ACTION
RECAPITULATIONS
RECOGNIZABILITY
RECOMMENDATIONS
RECONCILABILITY
RECONNAISSANCES
RECONSIDERATION
RECONSTRUCTIBLE
RECONSTRUCTIONS
RECORD LIBRARIES
RECREATION ROOMS
REDOUBTABLENESS
REFRESHER COURSE
REGISTERED NURSE
REGISTER OFFICES
REGISTRY OFFICES
REGIUS PROFESSOR
REINDUSTRIALIZE
RELATIVE CLAUSES
RELATIVE PRONOUN
REMORSELESSNESS
REPETITIOUSNESS
REPRESENTATIONS
REPRESENTATIVES
REPROACHFULNESS
REPRODUCIBILITY
RESOURCEFULNESS
RESPECTABLENESS
RESPONSIBLENESS
RESTRICTIVENESS
RESURRECTIONARY
RESURRECTIONISM
RESURRECTIONIST
RESURRECTION MEN
RETROGRESSIVELY
RETROSPECTIVELY
REVEREND MOTHERS
REVOLUTIONARIES
REVOLUTIONARILY
REVOLUTIONIZING

RHOMBENCEPHALON
RIBONUCLEIC ACID
RIGHT-HANDEDNESS
RIGHT-MINDEDNESS
RITUALISTICALLY
ROBIN GOODFELLOW
ROGUES' GALLERIES
ROMANTICIZATION
ROUGH-AND-TUMBLES
ROUND-SHOULDERED
ROYAL HIGHNESSES
RUMBUSTIOUSNESS
RUSSIAN ROULETTE

S

SADOMASOCHISTIC
SALES RESISTANCE
SANCTIMONIOUSLY
SANDWICH COURSES
SAPROPHYTICALLY
SARRACENIACEOUS
SATURATION POINT
SAVINGS ACCOUNTS
SAWN-OFF SHOTGUNS
SCARBOROUGH FAIR
SCHISTOSOMIASIS
SCHOOL OF THOUGHT
SCINTILLATINGLY
SCLERODERMATOUS
SCRUMPTIOUSNESS
SEA ISLAND COTTON
SECONDARY MODERN
SECONDARY STRESS
SECOND CHILDHOOD
SECOND IN COMMAND
SECOND-IN-COMMAND
SECURITY COUNCIL
SEINE-SAINT-DENIS
SELECT COMMITTEE
SELF-CENTREDNESS
SELF-CONFIDENTLY
SELF-CONSCIOUSLY
SELF-DESTRUCTING
SELF-DESTRUCTION
SELF-DISCIPLINED
SELF-EXAMINATION
SELF-EXPLANATORY
SELF-IMPORTANTLY
SELF-IMPROVEMENT
SELF-INDULGENTLY
SELF-LIQUIDATING

SELF-POLLINATION
SELF-POSSESSEDLY
SELF-REPROACHFUL
SELF-RIGHTEOUSLY
SELF-SACRIFICING
SELF-SUFFICIENCY
SENSATIONALISTS
SENSE OF OCCASION
SENTENTIOUSNESS
SENTIMENTALISTS
SENTIMENTALIZED
SEPTUAGENARIANS
SERGEANTS-AT-ARMS
SERVICE STATIONS
SERVOMECHANICAL
SERVOMECHANISMS
SESQUICARBONATE
SHARP-WITTEDNESS
SHILLY SHALLYING
SHILLY-SHALLYING
SHOOTING GALLERY
SHOOTING MATCHES
SHOPPING CENTRES
SHORT-CIRCUITING
SHORT-HANDEDNESS
SHORTHAND TYPIST
SHOTGUN WEDDINGS
SHOWING ONES HAND
SHRINKING VIOLET
SHRINK RESISTANT
SICKNESS BENEFIT
SIDEWALK ARTISTS
SIESMOLOGICALLY
SIMPLE FRACTURES
SIMPLICIDENTATE
SIMPLIFICATIONS
SINGULARIZATION
SINISTRODEXTRAL
SITUATION COMEDY
SITUATION ETHICS
SLAUGHTERHOUSES
SLEEPING PARTNER
SLOTTED SPATULAS
SLOUGH OF DESPOND
SLOW ON THE UPTAKE
SMALL INTESTINES
SMALL-MINDEDNESS
SMELLS OF THE LAMP
SOCIAL DEMOCRATS
SOCIALISTICALLY
SOCIOLINGUISTIC

SOFT FURNISHINGS
SOFTHEARTEDNESS
SOLEMNIFICATION
SOUNDED THE ALARM
SOW DRAGONS TEETH
SPANISH-AMERICAN
SPANISH OMELETTE
SPECIALIZATIONS
SPECIAL LICENCES
SPECIAL PLEADING
SPECIFIC GRAVITY
SPECULATIVENESS
SPEECHIFICATION
SPEECH THERAPIST
SPERMATOGENESIS
SPERMATOGENETIC
SPINNING JENNIES
SPLIT INFINITIVE
SPONTANEOUSNESS
SPUR-OF-THE-MOMENT
SQUADRON LEADERS
SQUARE THE CIRCLE
STAGE DIRECTIONS
STAMPING GROUNDS
STANDARD-BEARERS
STANDARDIZATION
STANDOFFISHNESS
STAND ONES GROUND
STAPHYLOPLASTIC
STAPHYLORRHAPHY
STAR-OF-BETHLEHEM
STARS AND STRIPES
STARVATION WAGES
STATE DEPARTMENT
STEREOCHEMISTRY
STEREOISOMERISM
STEREOISOMETRIC
STICKING PLASTER
STINGING NETTLES
STOCKBROKER BELT
STOCKING-FILLERS
STOICHIOLOGICAL
STORE DETECTIVES
STRAIGHTFORWARD
STRAIGHTJACKETS
STRATIFICATIONS
STRAWBERRY MARKS
STRETCHER-BEARER
STUMBLING BLOCKS
SUBORDINATENESS
SUBSISTENCE CROP

SUBSPECIFICALLY
SUBSTANTIVENESS
SUGGESTIBLENESS
SULPHUREOUSNESS
SUNRISE INDUSTRY
SUPERADDITIONAL
SUPERCONDUCTION
SUPERCONDUCTIVE
SUPERCONDUCTORS
SUPERFLUOUSNESS
SUPERIMPOSITION
SUPERINCUMBENCE
SUPERINDUCEMENT
SUPERINTENDENCE
SUPERINTENDENCY
SUPERINTENDENTS
SUPERLATIVENESS
SUPERNATURALISM
SUPERNATURALIST
SUPERNUMERARIES
SUPERSTITIOUSLY
SUPERSTRUCTURAL
SUPERSTRUCTURES
SUPPLEMENTARILY
SUPPLEMENTATION
SUPPLY AND DEMAND
SUPPORTING PARTS
SURREPTITIOUSLY
SUSCEPTIBLENESS
SWIMMING COSTUME
SWIM WITH THE TIDE
SWORD OF DAMOCLES
SYCOPHANTICALLY
SYLLABIFICATION
SYMBOL-FORMATION
SYMBOLISTICALLY
SYMMETRICALNESS
SYMPATHETICALLY
SYMPATHOMIMETIC
SYMPTOMATICALLY
SYNCHRONIZATION
SYNCHRONOUSNESS
SYNECDOCHICALLY
SYNECOLOGICALLY
SYNOPTIC GOSPELS
SYSTEMATIZATION
SYSTEMS ANALYSTS

T

TACHOMETRICALLY
TACHYMETRICALLY

TAKEN FOR GRANTED
TAKE TO ONES HEELS
TARSOMETATARSAL
TARSOMETATARSUS
TECHNOLOGICALLY
TECHNOSTRUCTURE
TELEGRAPHICALLY
TELEPHONE NUMBER
TELEPHOTOGRAPHY
TELEPHOTO LENSES
TELESTEREOSCOPE
TELETYPESETTING
TEMPERAMENTALLY
TEMPESTUOUSNESS
TEN COMMANDMENTS
TENDENTIOUSNESS
TENDERHEARTEDLY
TERMINOLOOGICAL
TERRITORIAL ARMY
TETRABRANCHIATE
THALASSOTHERAPY
THATS MORE LIKE IT
THE BACK OF BEYOND
THE COAST IS CLEAR
THEOREMATICALLY
THE POWERS THAT BE
THERAPEUTICALLY
THERIANTHROPISM
THERMIONIC VALVE
THERMOBAROGRAPH
THERMOCHEMISTRY
THERMOSTABILITY
THICKHEADEDNESS
THICK-WITTEDNESS
THOUGHTLESSNESS
THREE-LEGGED RACE
THREE-POINT TURNS
THROMBOEMBOLISM
THYROCALCITONIN
TIGHTFISTEDNESS
TIGHTROPE WALKER
TIMES IMMEMORIAL
TOOK SOME BEATING
TOPOGRAPHICALLY
TOTALITARIANISM
TO THE MANNER BORN
TOWER OF STRENGTH
TRACTION ENGINES
TRADITIONALISTS
TRAINING COLLEGE
TRANSCRIPTIONAL

TRANSFERABILITY
TRANSFIGURATION
TRANSFIGUREMENT
TRANSFORMATIONS
TRANSGRESSINGLY
TRANSILLUMINATE
TRANSISTORIZING
TRANSLATABILITY
TRANSLITERATING
TRANSLITERATION
TRANSMOGRIFYING
TRANSMUTATIONAL
TRANSPARENTNESS
TRANSPLANTATION
TRANSPOSABILITY
TRANSPOSITIONAL
TRANSUBSTANTIAL
TREACHEROUSNESS
TREASONABLENESS
TRIBROMOETHANOL
TRICHLOROETHANE
TRICK OR TREATING
TRINITROBENZENE
TRINITROTOLUENE
TROPICALIZATION
TROUBLESHOOTERS
TROUBLESOMENESS
TRUSTWORTHINESS
TRYPANOSOMIASIS
TURF ACCOUNTANTS
TYPOGRAPHICALLY
TYRANNOSAURUSES

U
ULTRACENTRIFUGE
ULTRAFILTRATION
ULTRAMICROMETER
ULTRAMICROSCOPE
ULTRAMICROSCOPY
ULTRASTRUCTURAL
UNBELIEVABILITY
UNCEREMONIOUSLY
UNCHALLENGEABLE
UNCOMMUNICATIVE
UNCOMPLIMENTARY
UNCONCERNEDNESS
UNCONDITIONALLY
UNCONNECTEDNESS

UNCONSCIOUSNESS
UNDEMONSTRATIVE
UNDERCAPITALIZE
UNDEREMPLOYMENT
UNDERESTIMATING
UNDERESTIMATION
UNDERHANDEDNESS
UNDERPRIVILEGED
UNDERPRODUCTION
UNDERSTATEMENTS
UNDER-THE-COUNTER
UNDISTINGUISHED
UNEMPLOYABILITY
UNEQUIVOCALNESS
UNEXCEPTIONABLE
UNEXCEPTIONABLY
UNFLINCHINGNESS
UNFORTUNATENESS
UNHOLY ALLIANCES
UNINTERRUPTEDLY
UNIVERSAL JOINTS
UNKNOWN QUANTITY
UNOBTRUSIVENESS
UNPARLIAMENTARY
UNPRECEDENTEDLY
UNPREMEDITATION
UNPRETENTIOUSLY
UNPROFITABILITY
UNPRONOUNCEABLE
UNSOPHISTICATED
UNWHOLESOMENESS

V
VALETUDINARIANS
VALUE-ADDED TAXES
VASCULARIZATION
VASOCONSTRICTOR
VEGETABLE KNIVES
VEGETABLE MARROW
VENDING MACHINES
VENEREAL DISEASE
VENTRILOQUISTIC
VENTURESOMENESS
VERTIGINOUSNESS
VESPERTILIONINE
VESTED INTERESTS
VICE-CHANCELLORS
VICISSITUDINARY

VICTORIA CROSSES
VIDEOCONFERENCE
VIRGINIA CREEPER
VITAL STATISTICS
VIVISECTIONISTS
VOYEURISTICALLY
VULGAR FRACTIONS

W
WALRUS MOUSTACHE
WARM-BLOODEDNESS
WARM-HEARTEDNESS
WAR OF JENKINS EAR
WARRANT OFFICERS
WASHING MACHINES
WEATHERBOARDING
WEATHER BOARDING
WEATHER FORECAST
WEATHERPROOFING
WEATHER STATIONS
WELL-CONSTRUCTED
WELL-ESTABLISHED
WELL-INTENTIONED
WHIPPERSNAPPERS
WHISTLE-STOP TOUR
WHITE BLOOD CELLS
WHITED SEPULCHRE
WHITE MANS BURDEN
WILD-GOOSE CHASES
WIND INSTRUMENTS
WIND-POLLINATION
WINDSCREEN WIPER
WISHFUL THINKING
WRONGHEADEDNESS

X
XENOMORPHICALLY
XEROGRAPHICALLY

Y
YOURS FAITHFULLY
YOUTH HOSTELLERS
YOUTH HOSTELLING

Z
ZYGOPHYLLACEOUS

Words that contain letter Q not followed by U

Anqing City in China

Aqaba Port in Jordan, on the Gulf of Aqaba

Aqmola Former name of Astana, capital of Kazakhstan

Basotho-Qwaqwa Former Bantu Homeland in South Africa

Chongqing City in China

Dimashq Arabic name for Damascus, capital of Syria

faqir Muslim or Hindu holy man

inqilab Urdu word for revolution

Iqbal Sir Mohammed Iqbal, Indian Muslim poet, philosopher, and political leader

Iraq Country in the Middle East

Iraqi **1** Inhabitant of Iraq **2** Relating to Iraq

Jiang Qing Chinese communist politician, widow of Mao Tse-Tung

Lailat-ul-Qadr Annual night of prayer and study for Muslims

Masqat Arabic name for Muscat, capital of Oman

mbaqanga Style of Black popular music in South Africa

Qabis Arabic name for Gabés, port in Tunisia

Qabis bin Said Sultan of Oman

Qaddafi Moamar al-Qaddafi, leader of Libya

Qaddish Jewish prayer, especially for the dead

qadi Muslim judge

Qairwan Holy city in Tunisia

QANTAS Australian national airline (Queensland and Northern Territory Aerial Services)

qat Type of bush found in Ethiopia

Qatar Country in Arabia

Qattara Depression Depression in the Sahara

qawwali Muslim religious song

Qeshm Iranian island

Qian Long Chinese emperor

qibla The direction of Mecca

Qingdao Port in China

Qinghai Province of China

qintar Albanian coin

Qiqihar City in China

Qishm Iranian island

Qom Holy city in Iran

qoph Hebrew letter Q

qorma Indian dish of meat and vegetables

Qu Qiu Bai Chinese communist leader and writer

Qwaqwa Former Bantu Homeland in South Africa

qwerty Standard layout of English typewriter/computer keyboard

Sercq French name for Sark in the Channel Islands

Si-ma Qian Ancient Chinese historian

Zaqaziq City in Egypt

Zarqa City in Jordan

Words that start with letter X

xanthate Salt or ester of xanthic acid

xanthein Yellow pigment found in flowers

xanthene Crystalline compound used in dyes

xanthic Relating to xanthic acid

xanthin Orange-yellow pigment found in plants

xanthine Crystalline compound found in urine

Xanthippe The wife of Socrates; any nagging or quarrelsome woman

xanthism Abnormal yellowness of skin, fur, etc.

xanthochroid Relating to races having light hair and pale skin

xanthochroism Excessive yellowness in goldfish, etc.

xanthoma Yellow-brown patch or nodule on the skin

xanthophyll Yellow pigment found in plants

xanthous Relating to races having light hair and pale skin

Xanthus The chief city of ancient Lycia in Asia Minor

Xavier St Francis Xavier, Spanish Jesuit missionary

xebec Small three-masted ship

xenia 1 Gift or offering **2** Influence of pollen upon the developed fruit

Xenocrates Greek philosopher

xenocryst Crystal of different origin found in igneous rock

xenogamy Cross-fertilization

xenogeneic Derived from an individual of a different species

xenogenesis Production of offspring unlike either parent

xenoglossia Ability to speak a language one has never learned

xenograft Graft of tissue from an individual of a different species

xenolith Rock fragment of different origin found in igneous rock

xenomorphic (Of a mineral) having a different form from the surrounding rock

xenon Gaseous chemical element

Xenophanes Greek philosopher and poet

xenophile Person who likes foreign people or things

xenophobe Person who dislikes foreign people or things

xenophobia Fear or hatred of foreign people and things

Xenophon Greek general and historian

xeranthemum Several Mediterranean plants, especially the immortelle

xerarch (Of plant successions) originating in a dry habitat

Xeres Former name of Jerez in Spain

xeric (Of plants) growing in dry conditions

xeroderma Abonormal dryness of the skin

xerography Photocopying process

xeromorphic (Of plants) having protection against excessive water loss

xerophilous Adapted to a dry habitat

xerophthalmia Dryness in the eye

xerophyte Plant that is adapted to dry conditions

xerosere Plant succession originating in a dry habitat

xerosis Abnormal dryness of skin or other tissues

xerostomia Abnormal dryness of the mouth

Xerox Tradename for a photocopying process

Xhosa Bantu people and language of South Africa

xi Greek letter X

Xia Gui Chinese landscape painter

Xi An City in China

Xiang River in China

Ximenes Ximenes de Cisneros, Spanish cardinal and statesman

Xingú River in Brazil

Xining City in China

Xinjiang Uygur Administrative division of China

xiphisternum The lowest part of the breast bone

xiphoid (Of bodily parts) sword-shaped

xiphosuran Horseshoe crab

Xizang Chinese name for Tibet

Xmas Christmas

xoanon Carved image of a god

Xochimilco Town and lake in Mexico

x-ray Electromagnetic radiation of very short wavelength, used in medical diagnosis etc.

Xuthus Son of Hellen in Greek mythology

Xuzhou City in China

xylan Yellow carbohydrate found in wood and straw

xylem Plant tissue that conducts water and nutrients

xylene Liquid hydrocarbon used as a solvent.

xylidine Xylene derivative used in dyes.

xylocarp Fruit with a hard woody shell

xylogenous (Of insects etc.) living in or on wood

xylograph Engraved wooden block or print made from one

xylography Art of printing from wooden blocks

xyloid Relating to or like wood

xylophagous (Of insects etc.) feeding on wood

xylophone Tuned wooden percussion instrument

xylorimba Large xylophone

xylose Sugar found in wood and straw, used in food for diabetics

xylotomous (Of insects etc.) boring into wood

xylotomy Preparation of wood sections for microscope examination

xylyl Derived from xylene

xyst 1 (In ancient Greece) covered portico used for athletics **2** (In ancient Rome) treelined garden walk

xyster Surgical file for scraping bone

Other titles published by Bloomsbury

Crossword Lists

Anne Stibbs, 2000, £8.99
ISBN 0 7475 5070 0

An essential reference book for all crossword and word-game lovers.
More than 100,000 words are listed by length under numerous
categories, including hobbies, birds, animals, Greek and Roman gods,
countries, capitals, prime ministers, Nobel Prize winners, trees,
flowers, books of the Bible, gemstones and many more. While most of
the lists are collections of things, there are also lists of types of
words – abbreviations, acronyms, palindromes, homophones and
common two-word phrases – as well as well-known foreign words and
phrases.

Anagram Finder

John Daintith, 2000, £9.99
ISBN 0 7475 5080 8

A companion to the *Crossword Solver* and *Crossword Lists*, the
Anagram Finder contains over 100,000 entries arranged in length
order from two to sixteen letters, including plural forms and many
proper names and common phrases. Each word or phrase is accompanied by an anagram key, composed by arranging the letters in alphabetical order. Palindromes and backwords are also included. The most
comprehensive anagram solver available.

To order Bloomsbury books, simply fill in the form below and return it to the following address:

Bloomsbury Mail Order
PO Box 29
Douglas
Isle of Man
IM99 1BQ
UK

or phone: 01624 836 000 quoting title, author and credit card number
or fax: 01624 837 033 quoting title, author and credit card number
overseas code: +441624
e-mail bookshop @enterprise.net
www.bookpost.co.uk

Please send me the following Bloomsbury books
   Quantity   Title/Author
....
....
....
....
....

I enclose a cheque/postal order made payable to Book Post
Please charge my Visa/MasterCard/American Express/Switch/Delta
card (details as follows)

Card no...
Expiry date..
Signature...
Name...
Address...
....

Please allow 28 days for delivery.
Free postage and packing in the UK (please include £1 postage and packing for each paperback outside the UK)

For a full list of all the titles published by Bloomsbury Publishing Plc, Publisher of the Year 1999, telephone 020 7494 2111.
www.bloomsbury.com

CROSSWORD
LISTS

EDITED BY ANNE STIBBS

BLOOMSBURY

First published in 1989

This combined edition published in 2002 by
Bloomsbury Publishing Plc
38 Soho Square
London W1D 3HB

A copy of the CIP entry for this book is available from
the British Library

ISBN 0 7475 5997 X

10 9 8 7 6 5 4 3 2

Compiled and typeset by Market House Books Ltd, Aylesbury
Printed in Great Britain by Clays Ltd, St Ives plc

INTRODUCTION

This book is one of a series of reference books for crossword puzzles, including the *Crossword Solver* and the *Anagram Finder*, both published by Bloomsbury. In this volume we have listed words under categories – people, places, birds, animals, fish, breeds of dog, Greek gods, names of drinks, and so on, in the hope that the user can quickly find the required answer to a clue. We have chosen the contents for their usefulness and have tried to concentrate on words that actually appear in crosswords. We have also presented the information in the most helpful way. Usually, this means listing the words in length order – 3-letter, 4-letter, 5-letter words, etc., and then in alphabetical order within each section. In some cases we have used simple alphabetical or logical order and some information is presented in tabular form.

We have also included additional information in many of the lists; for example, the birth and death dates of people or the colours of gemstones. This is partly to help the reader to find the correct word, but we also hope that owners of the book will find it a useful reference source in its own right.

While most of the lists are collections of things, there are also lists of types of words – for example, palindromes, back words, homophones (words that sound like others), abbreviations and acronyms, and common two-word phrases. The book also contains a short section of familiar quotations, as well as well-known foreign words and phrases. To help the reader find his or her way about, there is a Contents page that lists all the tables and lists in the order in which they appear in the book. In addition, there is an index in the back of the book. This gives the tables and lists in alphabetical order, but also includes cross references. For instance, a reader interested in 'jewels' will be directed to the list of *gemstones*, 'girl' might indicate a girl's first name, listed under *first names*, and so on. The index also contains hints on solving cryptic clues. There are many conventions used by setters of crosswords – 'love' often indicates the letter O, 'cardinal' might be a compass point, N, S, E, or W, twisted could suggest an anagram, etc. A selection of these has been included in the index.

In using the book, the reader should also be aware of the inflection of words. The most common, for the purpose of crosswords, is the use of plurals, and it is usually apparent from the wording of the clue whether the answer is a singular or plural. When nouns have regular plurals, only the singular forms have been included. Another point is that verbs are invariably shown with -*ize* endings. The alternative -*ise* ending may have been used in the puzzle. The same principle applies to nouns with -*ization*.

Since the original publication of the book in 1989, a large number of useful comments and suggestions for additional lists have been received from readers. These have been incorporated into both the 1997 and this new and expanded third edition. The editor would like to thank these correspondents and also thank all the people who have been involved in the production of the book. Their names are listed under Acknowledgments.

Anne Stibbs
Aylesbury 2000

ACKNOWLEDGMENTS

Fran Alexander
Peter Blair
Beth Bonham
Eve Daintith
John Daintith
Joan Gallagher
Robert Kerr
Jonathan Law
Sandra McQueen
David Pickering
Kathy Rooney
Mark Salad
Jessica Scholes
Gwen Shaw
Kate Smith
Brenda Tomkins
Linda Wells
Edmund Wright

CONTENTS

v

viii

GEOGRAPHY

COUNTRIES OF THE WORLD

AFGHANISTAN
  Capital: Kabul
  Currency: afghani [pul, *pl.* puli (*or* puls)]
ALBANIA
  Capital: Tirana (*or* Tiranë)
  Currency: lek, *pl.* lekë (*or* leks) [qindar (*or* qintar *or* qindarka)]
ALGERIA
  Capital: Algiers
  Currency: dinar [centime]
ANDORRA
  Capital: Andorra la Vella
  Currency: French franc [centime] and Spanish peseta [céntimo]
ANGOLA
  Capital: Luanda
  Currency: kwanza [lwei]
ANTIGUA AND BARBUDA
  Capital: Saint John's
  Currency: East Caribbean dollar [cent]
ARGENTINA
  Capital: Buenos Aires
  Currency: peso [austral]
ARMENIA
  Capital: Yerevan
  Currency: dram [louma]
AUSTRALIA
  Capital: Canberra
  Currency: dollar [cent]
AUSTRIA
  Capital: Vienna
  Currency: schilling [groschen]
AZERBAIJAN
  Capital: Baku
  Currency: manat [gopik]
THE BAHAMAS
  Capital: Nassau
  Currency: dollar [cent]
BAHRAIN
  Capital: Manama
  Currency: dinar [fils]
BANGLADESH
  Capital: Dhaka
  Currency: taka [poisha]
BARBADOS
  Capital: Bridgetown
  Currency: dollar [cent]
BELARUS
  Capital: Minsk
  Currency: rouble [copeck (*or* kopek)]

BELAU
  Capital: Koror
  Currency: US dollar [cent]
BELGIUM
  Capital: Brussels
  Currency: franc [centime]
BELIZE
  Capital: Belmopan
  Currency: dollar [cent]
BENIN
  Capital: Porto-Novo
  Currency: CFA franc [centime]
BHUTAN
  Capital: Thimphu
  Currency: ngultrum, *pl.* ngultrum [chetrum]
BOLIVIA
  Capital: La Paz
  Currency: boliviano [centavo]
BOSNIA-HERCEGOVINA (*or* BOSNIA AND HERZEGOVINA)
  Capital: Sarajevo
  Currency: marka
BOTSWANA
  Capital: Gaborone
  Currency: pula [thebe]
BRAZIL
  Capital: Brasília
  Currency: real [centavo]
BRUNEI
  Capital: Bandar Seri Begawan
  Currency: dollar [sen]
BULGARIA
  Capital: Sofia
  Currency: lev, *pl.* leva (*or* levs) [stotinka, *pl.* stotinki]
BURKINA FASO
  Capital: Ouagadougou
  Currency: CFA franc [centime]
BURMA
  See MYANMAR
BURUNDI
  Capital: Bujumbura
  Currency: franc [centime]
CAMBODIA
  Capital: Phnom Penh
  Currency: riel [sen]
CAMEROON
  Capital: Yaoundé
  Currency: CFA franc [centime]

CANADA
Capital: Ottawa
Currency: dollar [cent]
CAPE VERDE
Capital: Praia
Currency: escudo [centavo]
CENTRAL AFRICAN REPUBLIC
Capital: Bangui
Currency: CFA franc [centime]
CHAD
Capital: N'Djaména
Currency: CFA franc [centime]
CHILE
Capital: Santiago
Currency: peso [centavo]
CHINA
Capital: Beijing (*or* Peking)
Currency: renminbi yuan [fen]
COLOMBIA
Capital: Bogotá
Currency: peso [centavo]
COMOROS
Capital: Moroni
Currency: franc [centime]
CONGO, DEMOCRATIC REPUBLIC OF
Capital: Kinshasa
Currency: franc [centime]
CONGO-BRAZZAVILLE, REPUBLIC OF
Capital: Brazzaville
Currency: CFA franc [centime]
COSTA RICA
Capital: San José
Currency: colón, *pl.* colónes (*or* colóns)
[céntimo]
CÔTE D'IVOIRE
Capital: Yamoussoukro
Currency: CFA franc [centime]
CROATIA
Capital: Zagreb
Currency: kuna, *pl.* kune (*or* kuna) [lipa]
CUBA
Capital: Havana
Currency: peso [centavo]
CYPRUS
Capital: Nicosia (*or* Lefkosia)
Currency: pound [cent]
CZECH REPUBLIC
Capital: Prague
Currency: koruna [haler, *pl.* haleru (*or* haler *or*
halura)]
DENMARK
Capital: Copenhagen
Currency: krone, *pl.* kroner (*or* kronen) [øre]
DJIBOUTI
Capital: Djibouti
Currency: franc [centime]
DOMINICA
Capital: Roseau
Currency: East Caribbean dollar [cent]
DOMINICAN REPUBLIC
Capital: Santo Domingo
Currency: peso [centavo]

ECUADOR
Capital: Quito
Currency: sucre [centavo]
EGYPT
Capital: Cairo
Currency: pound [piastre]
EL SALVADOR
Capital: San Salvador
Currency: colón, *pl.* colones (*or* colons)
[centavo]
EQUATORIAL GUINEA
Capital: Malabo
Currency: CFA franc [centime]
ERITREA
Capital: Asmara
Currency: nakfa
ESTONIA
Capital: Tallinn
Currency: kroon, *pl.* krooni (*or* kroons) [sent
(*or* cent), *pl.* senti]
ETHIOPIA
Capital: Addis Adaba
Currency: birr [cent]
FIJI
Capital: Suva
Currency: dollar [cent]
FINLAND
Capital: Helsinki
Currency: markka [penni, *pl.* penniä (*or*
penni)]
FRANCE
Capital: Paris
Currency: franc [centime]
GABON
Capital: Libreville
Currency: CFA franc [centime]
THE GAMBIA
Capital: Banjul
Currency: dalasi [butut]
GEORGIA
Capital: Tbilisi
Currency: lari [tetri]
GERMANY
Capital: Berlin
Currency: Deutschmark (*or* Deutsche Mark)
[pfennig, *pl.* pfennige (*or* pfennigs)]
GHANA
Capital: Accra
Currency: cedi [pesewa]
GREECE
Capital: Athens
Currency: drachma, *pl.* drachmae (*or*
drachmas) [lepton, *pl.* lepta (*or* leptons)]
GRENADA
Capital: St George's
Currency: East Caribbean dollar [cent]
GUATEMALA
Capital: Guatemala City
Currency: quetzal, *pl.* quetzales [centavo]
GUINEA
Capital: Conakry
Currency: franc [cauris (*or* centime)]

GUINEA-BISSAU
Capital: Bissau
Currency: CFA franc
GUYANA
Capital: Georgetown
Currency: dollar [cent]
HAITI
Capital: Port-au-Prince
Currency: gourde [centime]
HONDURAS
Capital: Tegucigalpa
Currency: lempira [centavo]
HUNGARY
Capital: Budapest
Currency: forint [fillér]
ICELAND
Capital: Reykjavik
Currency: króna, *pl.* krónur [eyrir, *pl.* aurar]
INDIA
Capital: New Delhi
Currency: rupee [paisa, *pl.* paise (*or* paisa)]
INDONESIA
Capital: Jakarta
Currency: rupiah [sen]
IRAN
Capital: Tehrān
Currency: rial
IRAQ
Capital: Baghdad
Currency: dinar [fils]
IRELAND, REPUBLIC OF
Capital: Dublin
Currency: punt [penny, *pl.* pence (*or* pennies)]
ISRAEL
Capital: Jerusalem
Currency: shekel (*or* sheqel) [agora, *pl.* agorot]
ITALY
Capital: Rome
Currency: lira, *pl.* lire (*or* liras) [centesimo, *pl.* centesimi]
JAMAICA
Capital: Kingston
Currency: dollar [cent]
JAPAN
Capital: Tokyo
Currency: yen [sen]
JORDAN
Capital: Amman
Currency: dinar [fils]
KAZAKHSTAN
Capital: Astana (*or* Akmola)
Currency: tenge
KENYA
Capital: Nairobi
Currency: shilling [cent]
KIRIBATI
Capital: Tarawa
Currency: Australian dollar [cent]

KOREA, DEMOCRATIC PEOPLE'S REPUBLIC OF (North Korea)
Capital: P'yŏngyang
Currency: won [chon (*or* jun)]
KOREA, REPUBLIC OF (South Korea)
Capital: Seoul
Currency: won [chon (*or* chun *or* jeon)]
KUWAIT
Capital: Kuwait City
Currency: dinar [fils]
KYRGYZSTAN
Capital: Bishkek
Currency: som [tyin]
LAOS
Capital: Vientiane
Currency: kip [at]
LATVIA
Capital: Riga
Currency: lat, *pl.* lati (*or* lats) [santimi]
LEBANON
Capital: Beirut
Currency: pound [piastre]
LESOTHO
Capital: Maseru
Currency: loti [sente, *pl.* lisente]
LIBERIA
Capital: Monrovia
Currency: dollar [cent]
LIBYA
Capital: Tripoli
Currency: dinar [dirham (*or* dirhem)]
LIECHTENSTEIN
Capital: Vaduz
Currency: Swiss franc [centime]
LITHUANIA
Capital: Vilnius
Currency: litas, *pl.* litai (*or* lits *or* litu) [centas, *pl.* centai (*or* centas)]
LUXEMBOURG
Capital: Luxembourg
Currency: franc [centime]
MACEDONIA
Capital: Skopje
Currency: dinar [para]
MADAGASCAR
Capital: Antananarivo
Currency: Malagasy franc [centime]
MALAWI
Capital: Lilongwe
Currency: kwacha [tambala]
MALAYSIA
Capital: Kuala Lumpur
Currency: ringgit (*or* dollar) [sen (*or* cent)]
MALDIVES
Capital: Malé
Currency: rufiyaa [laari (*or* lari *or* laree)]
MALI
Capital: Bamako
Currency: CFA franc [centime]
MALTA
Capital: Valletta
Currency: lira, *pl.* lire (*or* liras) [cent]

MARSHALL ISLANDS
Capital: Dalap-Uliga-Darrit
Currency: US dollar [cent]
MAURITANIA
Capital: Nouakchott
Currency: ouguiya (*or* ougiya) [khoum]
MAURITIUS
Capital: Port Louis
Currency: rupee [cent]
MEXICO
Capital: Mexico City
Currency: peso [centavo]
MICRONESIA, FEDERATED STATES OF
Capital: Palikir
Currency: US dollar [cent]
MOLDOVA
Capital: Kishinev (*or* Chişinău)
Currency: leu, *pl.* lei [ban, *pl.* bani]
MONACO
Capital: Monaco-Ville
Currency: French franc [centime]
MONGOLIA
Capital: Ulaanbaatar (*or* Ulan Bator)
Currency: tugrik [möngö]
MOROCCO
Capital: Rabat
Currency: dirham (*or* dirhem) [centime]
MOZAMBIQUE
Capital: Maputo
Currency: metical [centavo]
MYANMAR (BURMA)
Capital: Yangôn (Rangoon)
Currency: kyat [pya]
NAMIBIA
Capital: Windhoek
Currency: dollar [cent]
NAURU
Capital: Yaren
Currency: Australian dollar [cent]
NEPAL
Capital: Kathmandu
Currency: rupee [paisa, *pl.* paise (*or* paisa)]
NETHERLANDS
Capital: Amsterdam
Currency: guilder [cent]
NEW ZEALAND
Capital: Wellington
Currency: dollar [cent]
NICARAGUA
Capital: Managua
Currency: córdoba [centavo]
NIGER
Capital: Niamey
Currency: CFA franc [centime]
NIGERIA
Capital: Abuja
Currency: naira [kobo]
NORWAY
Capital: Oslo
Currency: krone, *pl.* kroner (*or* kronen) [øre]

OMAN
Capital: Muscat
Currency: rial [baiza]
PAKISTAN
Capital: Islamabad
Currency: rupee [paisa, *pl.* paise (*or* paisa)]
PANAMA
Capital: Panama City
Currency: balboa [centésimo (*or* cent)]
PAPUA NEW GUINEA
Capital: Port Moresby
Currency: kina [toea]
PARAGUAY
Capital: Asunción
Currency: guaraní [céntimo]
PAULA *See* BELAU
PERU
Capital: Lima
Currency: sol, *pl.* soles [cént]
PHILIPPINES
Capital: Manila
Currency: peso [centavo]
POLAND
Capital: Warsaw
Currency: złoty [grosz, *pl.* groszy]
PORTUGAL
Capital: Lisbon
Currency: escudo [centavo]
QATAR
Capital: Doha
Currency: riyal [dirham (*or* dirhem)]
ROMANIA
Capital: Bucharest
Currency: leu, *pl.* lei [ban, *pl.* bani]
RUSSIA
Capital: Moscow
Currency: rouble [kopeck (*or* copeck)]
RWANDA
Capital: Kigali
Currency: franc [centime]
SAINT KITTS (*or* CHRISTOPHER) AND NEVIS
Capital: Basseterre
Currency: East Caribbean dollar [cent]
SAINT LUCIA
Capital: Castries
Currency: East Caribbean dollar [cent]
SAINT VINCENT AND THE GRENADINES
Capital: Kingstown
Currency: East Caribbean dollar [cent]
SAMOA
Capital: Apia
Currency: tala [sene]
SAN MARINO
Capital: San Marino
Currency: Italian lira, *pl.* lire (*or* liras)
[centesimo, *pl.* centesimi]
SÃO TOMÉ AND PRÍNCIPE
Capital: São Tomé
Currency: dobra [cêntimo]
SAUDI ARABIA
Capital: Riyadh
Currency: riyal [halala, *pl.* halala (*or* halalah
or halalas)]

SENEGAL
Capital: Dakar
Currency: CFA franc [centime]
SEYCHELLES
Capital: Victoria
Currency: rupee [cent]
SIERRA LEONE
Capital: Freetown
Currency: leone [cent]
SINGAPORE
Capital: Singapore
Currency: dollar [cent]
SLOVAKIA
Capital: Bratislava
Currency: koruna [haler (*or* halier), *pl.* haleru
    (*or* halierov *or* halura)]
SLOVENIA
Capital: Ljubljana
Currency: tolar, *pl.* tolarji (*or* tolars)
    [stotin]
SOLOMON ISLANDS
Capital: Honiara
Currency: dollar [cent]
SOMALIA
Capital: Mogadishu
Currency: shilling [cent]
SOUTH AFRICA
Capital: Pretoria
Currency: rand [cent]
SPAIN
Capital: Madrid
Currency: peseta [céntimo]
SRI LANKA
Capital: Colombo
Currency: rupee [cent]
SUDAN
Capital: Khartoum
Currency: dinar
SURINAME
Capital: Paramaribo
Currency: guilder [cent]
SWAZILAND
Capital: Mbabane
Currency: Lilangeni [cent]
SWEDEN
Capital: Stockholm
Currency: krona, *pl.* kronor [öre]
SWITZERLAND
Capital: Bern
Currency: franc [centime]
SYRIA
Capital: Damascus
Currency: pound [piastre]
TAIWAN
Capital: Taipei
Currency: dollar [cent]
TAJIKISTAN
Capital: Dushanbe
Currency: rouble [tanga]
TANZANIA
Capital: Dodoma
Currency: shilling [cent]

THAILAND
Capital: Bangkok
Currency: baht [satang, *pl.* satang (*or* stangs
    or satangs)]
TOGO
Capital: Lomé
Currency: CFA franc [centime]
TONGA
Capital: Nuku'alofa
Currency: pa'anga [seniti]
TRINIDAD AND TOBAGO
Capital: Port of Spain
Currency: dollar [cent]
TUNISIA
Capital: Tunis
Currency: dinar [millime]
TURKEY
Capital: Ankara
Currency: lira, *pl.* lire [kurus]
TURKMENISTAN
Capital: Ashkhabad (*or* Ashgabat)
Currency: manat [tenge]
TUVALU
Capital: Fongafale
Currency: dollar [cent]
UGANDA
Capital: Kampala
Currency: shilling [cent]
UKRAINE
Capital: Kiev
Currency: hryvnya (*or* hryvna) [kopiyka]
UNITED ARAB EMIRATES
Capital: Abu Dhabi
Currency: dirham [fils]
UNITED KINGDOM
Capital: London
Currency: pound [penny, *pl.* pence]
UNITED STATES OF AMERICA
Capital: Washington, DC
Currency: dollar [cent]
URUGUAY
Capital: Montevideo
Currency: peso [centésimo]
UZBEKISTAN
Capital: Tashkent
Currency: sum, *pl.* sum (*or* sumy)
    [teen]
VANUATU
Capital: Port Vila
Currency: vatu [centime]
VATICAN CITY STATE
Capital: Vatican City
Currency: Italian lira, *pl.* lire
    [centesimo]
VENEZUELA
Capital: Caracas
Currency: bolívar [céntimo]
VIETNAM
Capital: Hanoi
Currency: dong [xu]

YEMEN
Capital: Sana'a
Currency: riyal [fils]
YUGOSLAVIA
Capital: Belgrade
Currency: dinar [para]
ZAÏRE *See* CONGO, DEMOCRATIC REPUBLIC
OF

ZAMBIA
Capital: Lusaka
Currency: kwacha [ngwee]
ZIMBABWE
Capital: Harare
Currency: dollar [cent]

DEPENDENCIES

AUSTRALIA
ASHMORE AND CARTIER ISLANDS
THE AUSTRALIAN ANTARCTIC TERRITORY
CHRISTMAS ISLAND
Principal Settlement: Flying Fish Cove
COCOS (KEELING) ISLANDS
Principal Settlement: West Island
CORAL SEA ISLANDS TERRITORY
HEARD ISLAND AND MCDONALD ISLAND
NORFOLK ISLAND
Capital: Kingstown

DENMARK
FAROE ISLANDS
Capital: Tórshavn
GREENLAND
Capital: Nuuk (Godthåb)

FRANCE
FRENCH GUIANA
Capital: Cayenne
FRENCH POLYNESIA
Capital: Papeete
GUADELOUPE
Capital: Basse-Terre
MARTINIQUE
Capital: Fort-de-France
MAYOTTE
Capital: Dzaoudzi
NEW CALEDONIA
Capital: Nouméa
RÉUNION
Capital: Saint-Denis
SAINT PIERRE AND MIQUELON
Capital: Saint-Pierre
WALLIS AND FUTUNA
Capital: Mata-Utu

THE NETHERLANDS
ARUBA
Capital: Oranjestad
NETHERLANDS ANTILLES
Capital: Willemstad

NEW ZEALAND
COOK ISLANDS
Capital: Avarua
NIUE
Capital: Alofi
THE ROSS DEPENDENCY
TOKELAU

NORWAY
BOUVET ISLAND
JAN MAYEN
PETER THE FIRST ISLAND
PRINCESS RAGNHILD LAND
QUEEN MAUD LAND
SVALBARD
Principal Settlement: Longyearbyen

PORTUGAL
MACAU
Capital: Macau

UNITED KINGDOM
ANGUILLA
Capital: The Valley
BERMUDA
Capital: Hamilton
BRITISH ANTARCTIC TERRITORY
BRITISH INDIAN OCEAN TERRITORY
BRITISH VIRGIN ISLANDS
Capital: Road Town
CAYMAN ISLANDS
Capital: George Town
FALKLAND ISLANDS
Capital: Stanley
GIBRALTAR
Capital: Gibraltar
GUERNSEY
Capital: St Peter Port
ISLE OF MAN
Capital: Douglas
JERSEY
Capital: St Helier

MONTSERRAT
  Capital: Plymouth
PITCAIRN ISLANDS
  Sole town: Adamstown
SAINT HELENA
  Capital: Jamestown
SOUTH GEORGIA AND THE SOUTH
  SANDWICH ISLANDS
TURKS AND CAICOS ISLANDS
  Capital: Cockburn Town

UNITED STATES
  AMERICAN SAMOA
    Capital: Pago Pago
  GUAM
    Capital: Agaña
  NORTHERN MARIANA ISLANDS
    Principal Settlement: Saipan
  PUERTO RICO
    Capital: San Juan
  UNITED STATES VIRGIN ISLANDS
    Capital: Charlotte Amalie

CAPITALS

CAPITAL	COUNTRY
ABU DHABI	UNITED ARAB EMIRATES
ABUJA	NIGERIA
ACCRA	GHANA
ADDIS ABABA	ETHIOPIA
ALGIERS	ALGERIA
AMMAN	JORDAN
AMSTERDAM	NETHERLANDS
ANDORRA LA VELLA	ANDORRA
ANKARA	TURKEY
ANTANANARIVO	MADAGASCAR
APIA	SAMOA
ASHKHABAD (OR ASHGABAT)	TURKMENISTAN
ASMARA	ERITREA
ASTANA	KAZAKHSTAN
ASUNCIÓN	PARAGUAY
ATHENS	GREECE
BAGHDAD	IRAQ
BAKU	AZERBAIJAN
BAMAKO	MALI
BANDAR SERI BEGAWAN	BRUNEI
BANGKOK	THAILAND
BANGUI	CENTRAL AFRICAN REPUBLIC
BANJUL	THE GAMBIA
BASSETERRE	SAINT KITTS AND NEVIS
BEIJING	CHINA
BEIRUT	LEBANON
BELGRADE	YUGOSLAVIA
BELMOPAN	BELIZE
BERLIN	GERMANY
BERN	SWITZERLAND
BISHKEK	KYRGYZSTAN
BISSAU	GUINEA-BISSAU
BOGOTÁ	COLOMBIA
BRASÍLIA	BRAZIL
BRATISLAVA	SLOVAKIA

CAPITAL	COUNTRY
BRAZZAVILLE	CONGO-BRAZZAVILLE
BRIDGETOWN	BARBADOS
BRUSSELS	BELGIUM
BUCHAREST	ROMANIA
BUDAPEST	HUNGARY
BUENOS AIRES	ARGENTINA
BUJUMBURA	BURUNDI
CAIRO	EGYPT
CANBERRA	AUSTRALIA
CARACAS	VENEZUELA
CASTRIES	SAINT LUCIA
CHIŞINĂU	MOLDOVA
COLOMBO	SRI LANKA
CONAKRY	GUINEA
COPENHAGEN	DENMARK
DAKAR	SENEGAL
DALAP-ULIGA-DARRIT	MARSHALL ISLANDS
DAMASCUS	SYRIA
DHAKA	BANGLADESH
DJIBOUTI	DJIBOUTI
DODOMA	TANZANIA
DOHA	QATAR
DUBLIN	IRELAND, REPUBLIC OF
DUSHANBE	TAJIKSTAN
FONGAFALE	TUVALU
FREETOWN	SIERRA LEONE
GABORONE	BOTSWANA
GEORGETOWN	GUYANA
GUATEMALA CITY	GUATEMALA
HANOI	VIETNAM
HARARE	ZIMBABWE
HAVANA	CUBA
HELSINKI	FINLAND
HONIARA	SOLOMON ISLANDS
ISLAMABAD	PAKISTAN
JAKARTA	INDONESIA
JERUSALEM	ISRAEL
KABUL	AFGHANISTAN

7

CAPITALS

CAPITAL	COUNTRY	CAPITAL	COUNTRY
KAMPALA	UGANDA	PHNOM PENH	CAMBODIA
KATHMANDU	NEPAL	PORT-AU-PRINCE	HAITI
KHARTOUM	SUDAN	PORT VILA	VANUATU
KIEV	UKRAINE	PORT LOUIS	MAURITIUS
KIGALI	RWANDA	PORT MORESBY	PAPUA NEW GUINEA
KINGSTON	JAMAICA	PORT OF SPAIN	TRINIDAD AND
KINGSTOWN	SAINT VINCENT AND		TOBAGO
	THE GRENADINES	PORTO-NOVO	BENIN
KINSHASA	CONGO, DEMOCRATIC	PRAGUE	CZECH REPUBLIC
	REPUBLIC OF	PRAIA	CAPE VERDE
KISHINEV	MOLDOVA	PRETORIA	SOUTH AFRICA
KOROR	BELAU	P'YONGYANG	NORTH KOREA
KUALA LUMPUR	MALAYSIA	QUITO	ECUADOR
KUWAIT CITY	KUWAIT	RABAT	MOROCCO
LA PAZ	BOLIVIA	RANGOON	BURMA
LEFKOSIA	CYPRUS	REYKJAVIK	ICELAND
LIBREVILLE	GABON	RIGA	LATVIA
LILONGWE	MALAWI	RIYADH	SAUDI ARABIA
LIMA	PERU	ROME	ITALY
LISBON	PORTUGAL	ROSEAU	DOMINICA
LJUBLJANA	SLOVENIA	ST GEORGE'S	GRENADA
LOME	TOGO	SAINT JOHN'S	ANTIGUA AND
LONDON	UNITED KINGDOM		BARBUDA
LUANDA	ANGOLA	SANA'A	YEMEN
LUSAKA	ZAMBIA	SAN JOSÉ	COSTA RICA
LUXEMBOURG	LUXEMBOURG	SAN MARINO	SAN MARINO
MADRID	SPAIN	SAN SALVADOR	EL SALVADOR
MALABO	EQUATORIAL GUINEA	SANTIAGO	CHILE
MALÉ	MALDIVES	SANTO DOMINGO	DOMINICAN
MANAGUA	NICARAGUA		REPUBLIC
MANAMA	BAHRAIN	SÃO TOMÉ	SÃO TOMÉ AND
MANILA	PHILIPPINES		PRÍNCIPE
MAPUTO	MOZAMBIQUE	SARAJEVO	BOSNIA AND
MASERU	LESOTHO		HERCEGOVINA
MBANE	SWAZILAND	SEOUL	SOUTH KOREA
MEXICO CITY	MEXICO	SINGAPORE	SINGAPORE
MINSK	BELARUS	SKOPJE	MACEDONIA
MOGADISHU	SOMALIA	SOFIA	BULGARIA
MONACO-VILLE	MONACO	STOCKHOLM	SWEDEN
MONROVIA	LIBERIA	SUVA	FIJI
MONTEVIDEO	URUGUAY	TAIPEI	TAIWAN
MORONI	COMOROS	TALLINN	ESTONIA
MOSCOW	RUSSIA	TARAWA	KIRIBATI
MUSCAT	OMAN	TASHKENT	UZBEKISTAN
NAIROBI	KENYA	T'BILISI	GEORGIA
NASSAU	THE BAHAMAS	TEGUCIGALPA	HONDURAS
N'DJAMENA	CHAD	TEHRAN	IRAN
NEW DELHI	INDIA	THIMPHU	BHUTAN
NIAMEY	NIGER	TIRANA (OR TIRANË)	ALBANIA
NICOSIA	CYPRUS	TOKYO	JAPAN
NOUAKCHOTT	MAURITANIA	TRIPOLI	LIBYA
NUKU'ALOFA	TONGA	TUNIS	TUNISIA
OSLO	NORWAY	ULAANBAATAR	MONGOLIA
OTTAWA	CANADA	(OR ULAN BATOR)	
OUAGADOUGOU	BURKINA FASO	VADUZ	LIECHTENSTEIN
PALIKIR	MICRONESIA	VALLETTA	MALTA
PANAMA CITY	PANAMA	VATICAN CITY	VATICAN CITY STATE
PARAMARIBO	SURINAME	VICTORIA	SEYCHELLES
PARIS	FRANCE	VIENNA	AUSTRIA
PEKING	CHINA	VIENTIANE	LAOS

CAPITAL	COUNTRY	CAPITAL	COUNTRY
VILNIUS	LITHUANIA	YAMOUSSOUKRO	CÔTE D'IVOIRE
WARSAW	POLAND	YANGÔN	MYANMAR
WASHINGTON, DC	UNITED STATES OF AMERICA	YAOUNDÉ	CAMEROON
		YAREN	NAURU
WELLINGTON	NEW ZEALAND	YEREVAN	ARMENIA
WINDHOEK	NAMIBIA	ZAGREB	CROATIA

CURRENCIES

CURRENCY — COUNTRIES

AFGHANI — AFGHANISTAN
AGORA — ISRAEL
AGOROT — ISRAEL
AGOROTH — ISRAEL
AT — LAOS
AURAR — ICELAND
AUSTRAL — ARGENTINA
AUSTRALIAN DOLLAR — KIRIBATI, NAURU
BAHT — THAILAND
BAIZA — OMAN
BALBOA — PANAMA
BAN — MOLDOVA, ROMANIA
BANI — MOLDOVA, ROMANIA
BIRR — ETHIOPIA
BOLÍVAR — VENEZUELA
BOLIVIANO — BOLIVIA
BUTUT — THE GAMBIA
CAURIS — GUINEA
CEDI — GHANA
CENT — ANTIGUA AND BARBUDA, AUSTRALIA, THE BAHAMAS, BARBADOS, BELAU, BELIZE, CANADA, CYPRUS, DOMINICA, ERITREA, ESTONIA, ETHIOPIA, FIJI, GRENADA, GUYANA, JAMAICA, KENYA, KIRIBATI, LIBERIA, MALAYSIA, MALTA, MARSHALL ISLANDS, MAURITIUS, MICRONESIA, NAMIBIA, NAURU, NETHERLANDS, NEW ZEALAND, PANAMA, SAINT KITTS AND NEVIS, SAINT LUCIA, SAINT VINCENT AND THE GRENADINES, SEYCHELLES, SIERRA LEONE, SINGAPORE, SOLOMON ISLANDS, SOMALIA, SOUTH AFRICA, SRI LANKA, SURINAME, SWAZILAND, TAIWAN, TANZANIA, TRINIDAD AND TOBAGO, TUVALU, UGANDA, UNITED STATES OF AMERICA, ZIMBABWE
CÉNT — PERU
CENTAI — LITHUANIA
CENTAS — LITHUANIA
CENTAVO — BOLIVIA, BRAZIL, CAPE VERDE, CHILE, COLOMBIA, CUBA, DOMINICAN REPUBLIC, ECUADOR, EL SALVADOR, GUATEMALA, HONDURAS, MEXICO, MOZAMBIQUE, NICARAGUA, PHILIPPINES, PORTUGAL
CENTESIMI — ITALY, SAN MARINO, VATICAN CITY
CENTESIMO — ITALY, SAN MARINO, VATICAN CITY
CENTÉSIMO — PANAMA, URUGUAY
CENTIME — ALGERIA, ANDORRA, BELGIUM, BENIN, BURKINA FASO, BURUNDI, CAMEROON, CENTRAL AFRICAN REPUBLIC, CHAD, COMOROS, CONGO, CÔTE D'IVOIRE, DJIBOUTI, EQUATORIAL GUINEA, FRANCE, GABON, GUINEA, HAITI, LIECHTENSTEIN, LUXEMBOURG, MADAGASCAR, MALI, MONACO, MOROCCO, NIGER, RWANDA, SENEGAL, SWITZERLAND, TOGO, VANUATU
CÉNTIMO — ANDORRA, COSTA RICA, PARAGUAY, SPAIN, VENEZUELA
CÊNTIMO — SÃO TOMÉ AND PRÍNCIPE
CFA FRANC — BENIN, BURKINA FASO, CAMEROON, CENTRAL AFRICAN REPUBLIC, CHAD, COMOROS, CONGO, CÔTE D'IVOIRE, EQUATORIAL GUINEA, GABON, GUINEA-BISSAU, MALI, NIGER, SENEGAL, TOGO
CHETRUM — BHUTAN
CHON — SOUTH KOREA
CHUN — SOUTH KOREA
COLON — COSTA RICA
COLÓN — EL SALVADOR
COLONES — COSTA RICA, EL SALVADOR
COLONS — COSTA RICA, EL SALVADOR
COPECK — BELARUS, RUSSIA
COPEK — BELARUS, RUSSIA, TAJIKSTAN
CÓRDOBA — NICARAGUA
DALASI — THE GAMBIA
DEUTSCHE MARK — GERMANY
DEUTSCHMARK — GERMANY
DINAR — BAHRAIN, IRAQ, JORDAN, KUWAIT, LIBYA, MACEDONIA, SUDAN, TUNISIA, YUGOSLAVIA
DIRHAM (DIRHEM) — LIBYA, MOROCCO, QATAR, UNITED ARAB EMIRATES

DOBRA — SÃO TOMÉ AND PRÍNCIPE
DOLLAR — AUSTRALIA, THE BAHAMAS,
  BARBADOS, BELIZE, BRUNEI, CANADA, FIJI,
  GUYANA, JAMAICA, LIBERIA, MALAYSIA,
  NAMIBIA, NEW ZEALAND, SINGAPORE,
  SOLOMON ISLANDS, TAIWAN, TRINIDAD
  AND TOBAGO, TUVALU, UNITED STATES OF
  AMERICA, ZIMBABWE
DONG — VIETNAM
DRACHMA — GREECE
DRACHMAE — GREECE
DRACHMAS — GREECE
DRAM — ARMENIA
EAST CARIBBEAN DOLLAR — ANTIGUA AND
  BARBUDA, DOMINICA, GRENADA, SAINT
  KITTS AND NEVIS, SAINT LUCIA, SAINT
  VINCENT AND THE GRENADINES
ESCUDO — CAPE VERDE, PORTUGAL
EYRIR — ICELAND
FEN — CHINA
FILLÉR — HUNGARY
FILS — BAHRAIN, IRAQ, JORDAN, KUWAIT,
  UNITED ARAB EMIRATES, YEMEN, YEMEN
FORINT — HUNGARY
FRANC — BELGIUM, BURUNDI, CONGO,
  DJIBOUTI, FRANCE, GUINEA,
  LUXEMBOURG, RWANDA, SWITZERLAND
GOPIK — AZERBAIJAN
GOURDE — HAITI
GROSCHEN — AUSTRIA
GROSZ — POLAND
GROSZY — POLAND
GUARANÍ — PARAGUAY
GUILDER — NETHERLANDS, SURINAME
HALALA — SAUDI ARABIA
HALER — CZECH REPUBLIC, SLOVAKIA
HALERU — CZECH REPUBLIC, SLOVAKIA
HALIER — SLOVAKIA
HALIEROV — SLOVAKIA
HALURA — CZECH REPUBLIC
HRYVNA — UKRAINE
HRYVNYA — UKRAINE
ITALIAN LIRA — SAN MARINO, VATICAN CITY
JEON — SOUTH KOREA
JUN — NORTH KOREA
KHOUM — MAURITANIA
KINA — PAPUA NEW GUINEA
KIP — LAOS
KOBO — NIGERIA
KOPECK — BELARUS, RUSSIA, TAJIKSTAN
KOPEK — BELARUS, RUSSIA, TAJIKSTAN
KOPIYKA — UKRAINE
KORUNA — CZECH REPUBLIC, SLOVAKIA
KRONA — SWEDEN
KRÓNA — ICELAND
KRONE — DENMARK, NORWAY
KRONEN — DENMARK, NORWAY

KRONER — DENMARK, NORWAY
KRONOR — SWEDEN
KRÓNUR — ICELAND
KROON — ESTONIA
KROONI — ESTONIA
KROONS — ESTONIA
KUNA — CROATIA
KUNE — CROATIA
KURUS — TURKEY
KURUSH — TURKEY
KWACHA — MALAWI, ZAMBIA
KWANZA — ANGOLA
KYAT — MYANMAR (BURMA)
LAARI — MALDIVES
LAREE — MALDIVES
LARI — GEORGIA, MALDIVES
LAT — LATVIA
LATI — LATVIA
LATS — LATVIA
LEI — MOLDOVA, ROMANIA
LEK — ALBANIA
LEKË — ALBANIA
LEKS — ALBANIA
LEMPIRA — HONDURAS
LEONE — SIERRA LEONE
LEPTA — GREECE
LEPTON — GREECE
LEU — MOLDOVA, ROMANIA
LEV — BULGARIA
LEVA — BULGARIA
LEVS — BULGARIA
LILANGENI — SWAZILAND
LIPA — CROATIA
LIRA — ITALY, MALTA, TURKEY
LIRAS — ITALY, MALTA, SAN MARINO,
  TURKEY, VATICAN CITY
LIRE — ITALY, MALTA, SAN MARINO, TURKEY,
  VATICAN CITY
LISENTE — LESOTHO
LITAI — LITHUANIA
LITAS — LITHUANIA
LITS — LITHUANIA
LITU — LITHUANIA
LOTI — LESOTHO
LOUMA — ARMENIA
LWEI — ANGOLA
MANAT — AZERBAIJAN, TURKMENISTAN
MARKA — BOSNIA-HERCEGOVINA
MARKKA — FINLAND
METICAL — MOZAMBIQUE
MILLIME — TUNISIA
MÖNGÖ — MONGOLIA
NAKFA — ERITREA
NAIRA — NIGERIA
NGULTRUM — BHUTAN
NGWEE — ZAMBIA
ØRE — DENMARK, NORWAY

ÖRE — SWEDEN
OUGIYA — MAURITANIA
OUGUIYA — MAURITANIA
PA'ANGA — TONGA
PAISA — INDIA, NEPAL, PAKISTAN
PAISE — INDIA, NEPAL, PAKISTAN
PARA — MACEDONIA, YUGOSLAVIA
PENCE — IRELAND, REPUBLIC OF, UNITED
  KINGDOM
PENNI — FINLAND
PENNIÄ — FINLAND
PENNIES — IRELAND, REPUBLIC OF, UNITED
  KINGDOM
PENNY — IRELAND, REPUBLIC OF, UNITED
  KINGDOM
PESETA — SPAIN
PESEWA — GHANA
PESO — ARGENTINA, CHILE, COLOMBIA,
  CUBA, DOMINICAN REPUBLIC, MEXICO,
  PHILIPPINES, URUGUAY
PFENNIG — GERMANY
PFENNIGE — GERMANY
PFENNIGS — GERMANY
PIASTRE — EGYPT, LEBANON, SYRIA
POISHA — BANGLADESH
POUND — CYPRUS, EGYPT, LEBANON,
  SYRIA, UNITED KINGDOM
PUL — AFGHANISTAN
PULA — BOTSWANA
PULI — AFGHANISTAN
PULS — AFGHANISTAN
PUNT — IRELAND, REPUBLIC OF
PYA — MYANMAR (BURMA)
QINDAR — ALBANIA
QINDARKA — ALBANIA
QINTAR — ALBANIA
QUETZAL — GUATEMALA
QUETZALES — GUATEMALA
RAND — SOUTH AFRICA
REAL — BRAZIL
RENMINBI — CHINA
RIAL — IRAN, OMAN
RIYAL — YEMEN
RIEL — CAMBODIA
RINGGIT — MALAYSIA
RIYAL — QATAR, SAUDI ARABIA
ROUBLE — BELARUS, RUSSIA, TAJIKSTAN
RUFIYAA — MALDIVES
RUPEE — INDIA, MAURITIUS, NEPAL,
  PAKISTAN, SEYCHELLES, SRI LANKA

RUPIAH — INDONESIA
SANTIMI — LATVIA
SATANG — THAILAND
SATANGS — THAILAND
SCHILLING — AUSTRIA
SEN — BRUNEI, CAMBODIA, INDONESIA,
  JAPAN, MALAYSIA
SENE — SAMOA
SENITI — TONGA
SENT — ESTONIA
SENTE — LESOTHO
SENTI — ESTONIA
SHEKEL — ISRAEL
SHEQEL — ISRAEL
SHILLING — KENYA, SOMALIA, TANZANIA,
  UGANDA
SOL — PERU
SOLES — PERU
SOM — KYRGYZSTAN
SPANISH PESETA — ANDORRA
STANGS — THAILAND
STOTIN — SLOVENIA
STOTINKA — BULGARIA
STOTINKI — BULGARIA
SUCRE — ECUADOR
SUM — UZBEKISTAN
SUMY — UZBEKISTAN
SWISS FRANC — LIECHTENSTEIN
TAKA — BANGLADESH
TALA — SAMOA
TAMBALA — MALAWI
TANGA — KAJIKSTAN
TEEN — UZBEKISTAN
TENGE — KAZAKHSTAN, TURKMENISTAN
TETRI — GEORGIA
THEBE — BOTSWANA
TOEA — PAPUA NEW GUINEA
TOLAR — SLOVENIA
TOLARJI — SLOVENIA
TOLARS — SLOVENIA
TUGRIK — MONGOLIA
TYIN — KYRGYZSTAN
US DOLLAR — BELAU, MARSHALL ISLANDS,
  MICRONESIA
VATU — VANUATU
WON — NORTH KOREA, SOUTH KOREA
XU — VIETNAM
YEN — JAPAN
YUAN — CHINA
ZLOTY — POLAND

11

OLD NAMES OF CAPITAL AND MAJOR CITIES

CURRENT NAME	OLD NAME(S) (MOST RECENT FIRST)	CURRENT NAME	OLD NAME(S) (MOST RECENT FIRST)
ALMATY	ALMA-ATA; VERNY	KIROV	VYATKA
ANTANANARIVO	TANANARIVE	KOROR	CORRORA
ASTANA	AKMOLA	LUANDA	SÃO PAULO DE
BANDAR SERI	BRUNEI TOWN		LOANDA
BEGAWAN		MALABO	SANTA ISABEL
BANJUL	BATHURST	MAPUTO	LOURENÇO MARQUES
BEIJING	PEI-P'ING (OR	MEXICO CITY	TENOCHTITLÁN
(OR PEKING)	BEIBING); TA-TU	MONTREAL	VILLE-MARIE
BISHKEK	FRUNZE	MUMBAI	BOMBAY
(OR PISHPEK)		NABEREZHNYE	BREZHNEV; CHELNY
BOGOTÁ	BACATÁ	CHELNY	
BUJUMBURA	USUMBURA	NAPLES	NEAPOLIS
CAIRO	EL QAHIRA;	N'DJAMENA	FORT LAMY
	EL FUSTAT	NIZHNY	GORKY (OR GORKI)
CARACAS	SANTIAGO DE LEÓN	NOVGOROD	
DE CARACAS		NOUMÉA	PORT-DE-FRANCE
CHARLOTTE	SAINT THOMAS	NUUK	GODTHAÅB
AMALIE		OTTAWA	BYTOWN
CONSTANTINE	CIRTA	OSLO	KRISTIANIA
DHAKA	DACCA	PAGO PAGO	PANGO PANGO
DNEPROPETROVSK	EKATERINOSLAV	PALIKIR	KOLONIA
DONETSK	STALINO; YUZOVKA	PERM	MOLOTOV
DÚN LAOGHAIRE	KINGSTOWN;	SAMARA	KUYBYSHEV
	DUNLEARY	SANTO DOMINGO	CIUDAD TRUJILLO
DUSHANBE	STALINABAD;	SOFIA	SERDICA
	DYUSHAMBE	ST PETERSBURG	LENINGRAD;
EKATERINBURG	SVERDLOVSK		PETROGRAD
EAST LONDON	PORT REX	T'BILISI	TIFLIS
FAISALABAD	LYALLPUR	THESSALONÍKI	SALONIKA;
FORT-DE-FRANCE	FORT ROYAL		THESSALONICA
GABERONE	GABERONES	TOKYO	EDO
HARARE	SALISBURY	TRIPOLI	OEA
HO CHI MINH CITY	SAIGON	UJANG PANDANG	MACASSAR (OR
ISTANBUL	CONSTANTINOPLE;		MAKASAR)
	BYZANTIUM	ULAANBAATAR	URGA
IZMIR	SMYRNA	VADODARA	BARODA
JAKARTA	BATAVIA	VOLGOGRAD	STALINGRAD;
KANPUR	CAWNPORE		TSARITSYN
KINSHASA	LÉOPOLDVILLE		

OLD NAMES OF COUNTRIES

CURRENT NAME	OLD NAME(S) (MOST RECENT FIRST)	CURRENT NAME	OLD NAME(S) (MOST RECENT FIRST)
BANGLADESH	EAST PAKISTAN	MALDIVES	MALDIVE ISLANDS
BELAU	PALAU (*OR* PELEW)	MALI	FRENCH SUDAN
BELIZE	BRITISH HONDURAS	MONGOLIA	MONGOLIAN PEOPLE'S
BENIN	DAHOMEY		REPUBLIC; OUTER
BOLIVIA	UPPER PERU		MONGOLIA
BOTSWANA	BECHUANALAND	MYANMAR	BURMA
BURKINA FASO	UPPER VOLTA	NAMIBIA	SOUTH WEST AFRICA
CAYMAN ISLANDS	LAS TORTUGAS	NAURU	PLEASANT ISLAND
CONGO,	ZAÏRE; CONGO;	NEW ZEALAND	STATEN LAND
DEMOCRATIC	BELGIAN CONGO;	NIUE	SAVAGE ISLAND
REPUBLIC OF	CONGO FREE STATE	OMAN	MUSCAT AND OMAN
ETHIOPIA	ABYSSINIA	PUERTO RICO	PORTO RICO
GHANA	GOLD COAST	SINGAPORE	TUMASIK
GUINEA	FRENCH GUINEA;		(*OR* TEMASEK)
	RIVIÈRES DU SUD	SRI LANKA	CEYLON
GUINEA-BISSAU	PORTUGUESE GUINEA	SURINAME	DUTCH GUIANA
GUYANA	BRITISH GUIANA	TAIWAN	FORMOSA
HAITI	SAINT-DOMINIQUE	TANZANIA	TANGANYIKA
INDONESIA	DUTCH EAST INDIES	THAILAND	SIAM
IRAN	PERSIA	TOGO	FRENCH TOGOLAND
IRAQ	MESOPOTAMIA	TUNISIA	CARTHAGE
IRELAND,	EIRE; IRISH FREE	TURKEY	OTTOMAN EMPIRE
REPUBLIC OF	STATE	TUVALU	ELLICE ISLANDS
JORDAN	TRANSJORDAN	UNITED ARAB	TRUCIAL STATES
KENYA	EAST AFRICA	EMIRATES	
	PROTECTORATE	VANUATU	NEW HEBRIDES
KIRIBATI	GILBERT ISLANDS	ZAMBIA	NORTHERN RHODESIA
LESOTHO	BASUTOLAND	ZIMBABWE	RHODESIA; SOUTHERN
MADAGASCAR	MALAGASY REPUBLIC		RHODESIA
MALAWI	NYASALAND		

ENGLISH COUNTIES AND SELECTED LOCAL AUTHORITIES

AUTHORITY (Administrative Centre)

*AVON (Bristol)
BATH AND NORTH-EAST SOMERSET (Bath)
BEDFORD(SHIRE) (Bedford)
BERKSHIRE (Reading)
BUCKINGHAM(SHIRE) (Aylesbury)
CALDERDALE (Halifax)
CAMBRIDGE(SHIRE) (Cambridge)
CHESHIRE (Chester)
*CLEVELAND (Middlesborough)
CORNWALL (Truro)
*CUMBERLAND (Carlisle)
CUMBRIA (Carlisle)
DERBY(SHIRE) (Matlock)
DEVON (Exeter)
DORSET (Dorchester)
DURHAM (Durham)
EAST RIDING (OF YORKSHIRE) (Beverley)
EAST SUSSEX (Lewes)
ESSEX (Chelmsford)
GLOUCESTER(SHIRE) (Gloucester)
†GREATER LONDON (London)
†GREATER MANCHESTER (Manchester)
HALTON (Runcorn)
HAMPSHIRE (Winchester)
*HEREFORD AND WORCESTER (Worcester)
HEREFORD(SHIRE) (Hereford)
HERTFORD(SHIRE) (Hertford)
*HUMBERSIDE (Beverley)
*HUNTINGDON(SHIRE) (Huntingdon)
ISLE OF WIGHT (Newport, IOW)
KENT (Maidstone)
KIRKLEES (Huddersfield)
LANCASHIRE (Preston)
LEICESTER(SHIRE) (Leicester)
LINCOLN(SHIRE) (Lincoln)
MEDWAY (Gillingham)
†MERSEYSIDE (Liverpool)
NORFOLK (Norwich)

13

NORTHAMPTON(SHIRE) (Northampton)
NORTH-EAST LINCOLNSHIRE (Grimsby)
NORTH LINCOLNSHIRE (Scunthorpe)
NORTH SOMERSET (Weston-super-Mare)
*NORTH RIDING (OF YORK-SHIRE) (Middlesbrough)
NORTH TYNESIDE (Wallsend)
NORTHUMBERLAND (Morpeth)
NORTH YORKSHIRE (Northallerton)
NOTTINGHAM(SHIRE) (Nottingham)
OXFORD(SHIRE) (Oxford)
REDCAR AND CLEVELAND (Redcar)

RUTLAND (Oakham)
SALOP (name for Shropshire between 1974 and 1980)
SHROPSHIRE (Shrewsbury)
SOMERSET (Taunton)
SOUTH GLOUCESTERSHIRE (Thornbury)
SOUTH TYNESIDE (South Shields)
†SOUTH YORKSHIRE (Barnsley)
STAFFORD(SHIRE) (Stafford)
SUFFOLK (Ipswich)
SURREY (Guildford)
SUSSEX (Lewes)
TELFORD AND WREKIN (Telford)
†TYNE AND WEAR (Newcastle-Upon-Tyne)
WARWICK(SHIRE) (Warwick)

WEST BERKSHIRE (Newbury)
†WEST MIDLANDS (Birmingham)
*WESTMORLAND (Kendal)
*WEST RIDING (OF YORKSHIRE) (Wakefield)
WEST SUSSEX (Chichester)
†WEST YORKSHIRE (Wakefield)
WILTSHIRE (Trowbridge)
WIRRAL (Birkenhead)
*WORCESTER(SHIRE) (Worcester)

*indicates a former county
†metropolitan county

WELSH COUNTIES AND SELECTED LOCAL AUTHORITIES

AUTHORITY (Administrative Centre)

*ANGLESEY (Llangefni)
BLAENAU GWENT (Ebbw Vale)
*BRECON(SHIRE) (Brecon)
*CAERNARFON(SHIRE) (Caernarfon)
*CARDIGAN(SHIRE) (Aberystwyth)
CARMARTHEN(SHIRE) (Carmarthen)
CEREDIGION (Aberaeron)
*CLWYD (Mold)
CONWY (Bodlondeb)

DENBIGH(SHIRE) (Ruthin)
*DYFED (Carmarthen)
FLINTSHIRE (Mold)
*GLAMORGAN (Cardiff)
*GWENT (Cwmbran)
GWYNEDD (Caernarfon)
*MERIONETH (Dolgellan)
*MID GLAMORGAN (Cardiff)
MONMOUTH(SHIRE) (Cwmbran)
*MONTGOMERY(SHIRE) (Welshpool)
NEATH PORT TALBOT (Port Talbot)
PEMBROKE(SHIRE) (Haverfordwest)

POWYS (Llandrindod Wells)
*RADNOR(SHIRE) (Llandrindod Wells)
RHONDDA CYNON TAFF (Clydach Vale)
*SOUTH GLAMORGAN (Cardiff)
SWANSEA (Swansea)
TORFAEN (Pontypool)
VALE OF GLAMORGAN (Barry)
*WEST GLAMORGAN (Swansea)
WREXHAM (Wrexham)

*indicates a former county

SCOTTISH REGIONS, COUNTIES, AND SELECTED LOCAL AUTHORITIES

AUTHORITY (Administrative Centre)

ABERDEEN(SHIRE) (Aberdeen)
ANGUS (Forfar)
ARGYLL AND BUTE (Lochgilphead)
*ARGYLL (Lochgilphead)
*AYR(SHIRE) (Ayr)
*BANFF (Banff)
*BERWICK (Duns)

*BORDERS
*BUTE (Rothesay)
*CAITHNESS (Wick)
*CENTRAL (Stirling)
CLACKMANNAN(SHIRE) (Alloa)
DUMFRIES AND GALLOWAY (Dumfries)
*DUMFRIES (Dumfries)
*DUNBARTONSHIRE (Dumbarton)

EAST AYRSHIRE (Kilmarnock)
EAST DUNBARTONSHIRE (Kirkintilloch)
EAST LOTHIAN (Haddington)
EAST RENFREWSHIRE (Giffnock)
FIFE (Glenrothes)
*GRAMPIAN (Aberdeen)
HIGHLAND (Inverness)
INVERCLYDE (Greenock)

*INVERNESS(-SHIRE)
  (Inverness)
*KINCARDINE(SHIRE)
  (Stonehaven)
*KINROSS (Kinross)
*KIRKCUDBRIGHT
  (Kirkcudbright)
*LANARK(SHIRE) (Hamilton)
*LOTHIAN (Edinburgh)
MIDLOTHIAN (Dalkeith)
MORAY (Elgin)
*NAIRN (Nairn)
NORTH AYRSHIRE (Irvine)
NORTH LANARKSHIRE
  (Motherwell)
ORKNEY (Kirkwall)

*PEEBLES (Peebles)
PERTH AND KINROSS (Perth)
*PERTH(SHIRE) (Perth)
RENFREW(SHIRE) (Paisley)
*ROSS AND CROMARTY
  (Dingwall)
*ROXBURGH (Newtown St.
  Boswells)
SCOTTISH BORDERS
  (Newton St. Boswells)
*SELKIRK (Selkirk)
SHETLAND (Lerwick)
SOUTH AYRSHIRE (Ayr)
SOUTH LANARKSHIRE
  (Hamilton)
STIRLING (Stirling)

*STRATHCLYDE (Glasgow)
*SUTHERLAND (Golspie)
*TAYSIDE (Dundee)
WEST DUNBARTONSHIRE
  (Dumbarton)
WESTERN ISLES (Lewis)
WEST LOTHIAN (Livingston)
*WIGTOWN(SHIRE)
  (Stranraer)
ZETLAND (former name for
  Shetland)

*indicates a former region or
county

PROVINCES AND COUNTIES OF IRELAND

PROVINCE
COUNTY (County Town)

CONNACHT
MAYO (Castlebar)
SLIGO (Sligo)
GALWAY (Galway)
LEITRIM (Carrick-on-Shannon)
ROSCOMMON (Roscommon)

LEINSTER
LOUTH (Dundalk)
MEATH (Trim)
CARLOW (Carlow)
DUBLIN (Dublin)
OFFALY (Tullamore)

KILDARE (Naas)
WEXFORD (Wexford)
WICKLOW (Wicklow)
KILKENNY (Kilkenny)
LAOIGHIS [or LAOIS or LEIX]
  (Portlaoighise or Portlaoise)
LONGFORD (Longford)
WESTMEATH (Mullingar)

MUNSTER
CORK (Cork)
CLARE (Ennis)
KERRY (Tralee)
LIMERICK (Limerick)
TIPPERARY (Clonmel)
WATERFORD (Waterford)

ULSTER
*DOWN (Downpatrick)
CAVAN (Cavan)
*ARMAGH (Armagh)
*ANTRIM (Belfast)
*TYRONE (Omagh)
DONEGAL (Lifford)
MONAGHAN (Monaghan)
*FERMANAGH (Enniskillen)
*LONDONDERRY
  (Londonderry)

*indicates counties of N
Ireland

AMERICAN STATES

STATE	ABBREVIATION	NICKNAME	CAPITAL
ALABAMA	ALA	COTTON	MONTGOMERY
ALASKA	ALAS	LAST FRONTIER	JUNEAU
ARIZONA	ARIZ	GRAND CANYON	PHOENIX
ARKANSAS	ARK	LAND OF OPPORTUNITY	LITTLE ROCK
CALIFORNIA	CAL	GOLDEN	SACRAMENTO
COLORADO	COLO	CENTENNIAL	DENVER
CONNECTICUT	CONN	CONSTITUTION	HARTFORD
DELAWARE	DEL	FIRST	DOVER
FLORIDA	FLA	SUNSHINE	TALLAHASSEE
GEORGIA	GA	EMPIRE STATE OF THE SOUTH	ATLANTA
HAWAII	HA	ALOHA	HONOLULU
IDAHO	IDA	GEM	BOISE
ILLINOIS	ILL	LAND OF LINCOLN	SPRINGFIELD
INDIANA	IND	HOOSIER	INDIANAPOLIS

STATE	ABBREVIATION	NICKNAME	CAPITAL
IOWA	IA	HAWKEYE	DES MOINES
KANSAS	KAN	SUNFLOWER	TOPEKA
KENTUCKY	KY	BLUEGRASS	FRANKFORT
LOUISIANA	LA	PELICAN	BATON ROUGE
MAINE	ME	PINE TREE	AUGUSTA
MARYLAND	MD	OLD LINE	ANNAPOLIS
MASSACHUSETTS	MASS	BAY	BOSTON
MICHIGAN	MICH	WOLVERINE	LANSING
MINNESOTA	MINN	GOPHER	ST. PAUL
MISSISSIPPI	MISS	MAGNOLIA	JACKSON
MISSOURI	MO	SHOW ME	JEFFERSON CITY
MONTANA	MONT	TREASURE	HELENA
NEBRASKA	NEBR	CORNHUSKER	LINCOLN
NEVADA	NEV	SILVER	CARSON CITY
NEW HAMPSHIRE	NH	GRANITE	CONCORD
NEW JERSEY	NJ	GARDEN	TRENTON
NEW MEXICO	N MEX	LAND OF ENCHANTMENT	SANTA FÉ
NEW YORK	NY	EMPIRE	ALBANY
NORTH CAROLINA	NC	TARHEEL	RALEIGH
NORTH DAKOTA	N DAK	FLICKERTAIL	BISMARCK
OHIO	OH	BUCKEYE	COLUMBUS
OKLAHOMA	OKLA	SOONER	OKLAHOMA CITY
OREGON	OREG	BEAVER	SALEM
PENNSYLVANIA	PA	KEYSTONE	HARRISBURG
RHODE ISLAND	RI	OCEAN	PROVIDENCE
SOUTH CAROLINA	SC	PALMETTO	COLUMBIA
SOUTH DAKOTA	S DAK	SUNSHINE	PIERRE
TENNESSEE	TENN	VOLUNTEER	NASHVILLE
TEXAS	TEX	LONE STAR	AUSTIN
UTAH	UT	BEEHIVE	SALT LAKE CITY
VERMONT	VT	GREEN MOUNTAIN	MONTPELIER
VIRGINIA	VA	OLD DOMINION	RICHMOND
WASHINGTON	WASH	EVERGREEN	OLYMPIA
WEST VIRGINIA	W VA	MOUNTAIN	CHARLESTON
WISCONSIN	WIS	BADGER	MADISON
WYOMING	WYO	EQUALITY	CHEYENNE

AUSTRALIAN STATES AND TERRITORIES

AUSTRALIAN CAPITAL TERRITORY
NEW SOUTH WALES
NORTHERN TERRITORY
QUEENSLAND
SOUTH AUSTRALIA
TASMANIA
VICTORIA
WESTERN AUSTRALIA

CANADIAN PROVINCES OR TERRITORIES

PROVINCE/TERRITORY	ABBREVIATION
ALBERTA	AB
BRITISH COLUMBIA	BC
MANITOBA	MB
NEW BRUNSWICK	NB
NEWFOUNDLAND AND LABRADOR	NF
NORTHWEST TERRITORIES	NT
NOVA SCOTIA	NS
NUNAVUT	(not assigned)
ONTARIO	ON
PRINCE EDWARD ISLAND	PE
QUEBEC	QC
SASKATCHEWAN	SK
YUKON TERRITORY	YT

NEW ZEALAND ISLANDS AND TERRITORIES

COOK ISLANDS
NIUE
NORTH ISLAND
ROSS DEPENDENCY
SOUTH ISLAND
TOKELAU

THE EUROPEAN UNION

STATE	ACCESSION YEAR
AUSTRIA	1995
BELGIUM	1958
DENMARK	1973
FINLAND	1995
FRANCE	1958
GERMANY	1958
GREECE	1981
IRELAND	1973
ITALY	1958
LUXEMBOURG	1958
NETHERLANDS	1958
PORTUGAL	1986
SPAIN	1986
SWEDEN	1995
UK	1973

TOWNS AND CITIES

AFGHANISTAN

5
HERAT
KABUL

8
KANDAHAR

ALBANIA

6
TIRANA
TIRANE

ALGERIA

4
ORAN

7
ALGIERS

ANGOLA

6
HUAMBO
LOBITO
LUANDA

ARGENTINA

7
CORDOBA
LA PLATA
ROSARIO

9
LA MATANZA

11
BAHIA BLANCA
BUENOS AIRES

AUSTRALIA

5
PERTH

6
DARWIN
HOBART
SYDNEY

8
ADELAIDE
BRISBANE
CANBERRA

9
MELBOURNE

9—continued
NEWCASTLE

12
ALICE SPRINGS

AUSTRIA

6
VIENNA

8
SALZBURG

9
INNSBRUCK

AZERBAIJAN

4
BAKU

BANGLADESH

5
DHAKA

10
CHITTAGONG

BELARUS

5
BREST
MINSK

BELGIUM

5
GHENT
LIÈGE
NAMUR
YPRES

6
BRUGES
DINANT
OSTEND

7
ANTWERP
MALINES

8
BRUSSELS

**BOSNIA AND
HERCEGOVINA**

5
TUZLA

6
MOSTAR

8
SARAJEVO

9
BANJA LUKA

BRAZIL

5
BELEM
MANAUS

6
RECIFE

8
BRASILIA
SALVADOR
SAO PAULO

11
PORTO ALEGRE

12
RIO DE JANEIRO

13
BELO HORIZONTE

BULGARIA

5
SOFIA
VARNA

BURMA
SEE MYANMAR

CANADA

6
OTTAWA
QUEBEC
REGINA

7
CALGARY
HALIFAX
ST JOHN'S
TORONTO

8
EDMONTON
HAMILTON
KINGSTON
MONTREAL
VICTORIA
WINNIPEG

9
VANCOUVER
SASKATOON

10
THUNDER BAY

11
FREDERICTON

12
NIAGARA FALLS

13
CHARLOTTETOWN

CHILE

8
SANTIAGO

10
VALPARAISO

CHINA

4
LUTA
SIAN

5
WUHAN

6
ANSHAN
CANTON
DAIREN
FUSHUN
HARBIN
MUKDEN
PEKING
TSINAN

7
BEIJING
KUNMING
LANCHOW
NANKING
TAIYUAN

8
SHANGHAI
SHENYANG
TIENTSIN

9
CHANGCHUN
CHUNGKING

10
PORT ARTHUR

COLOMBIA

4
CALI

6
BOGOTÁ

8
MEDELLÍN

9
CARTAGENA

12
BARRANQUILLA

15
SANTA FÉ DE
 BOGOTÁ

CONGO, DEMOCRA-
TIC REPUBLIC OF

6
BOKAVU

8
KINSHASA

10
LUBUMBASHI

CROATIA

5
SPLIT

6
ZAGREB

CUBA

6
HAVANA

14
SANTIAGO DE CUBA

CZECH REPUBLIC

4
BRNO

6
PRAGUE

DENMARK

5
ARHUS

6
ODENSE

10
COPENHAGEN

ECUADOR

5
QUITO

9
GUAYAQUIL

EGYPT

4
GIZA
SUEZ

5
ASWAN
CAIRO
LUXOR
TANTA

6
THEBES

7
MANSURA
MEMPHIS
ZAGAZIG

8
ISMAILIA
PORT SAID

10
ALEXANDRIA

ENGLAND

3
ELY
EYE
RYE
WEM

4
BATH
BRAY
BUDE
BURY
CLUN
DEAL
DISS
ETON
HOLT
HOVE
HULL
HYDE
INCE
LEEK
LOOE
LYDD
ROSS
RYDE
SHAP
WARE
WARK
YARM

4—continued
YORK

5
ACTON
ALTON
BACUP
BLYTH
BOURN
CALNE
CHARD
CHEAM
COLNE
COWES
CREWE
DERBY
DOVER
EGHAM
EPSOM
FILEY
FOWEY
FROME
GOOLE
HAWES
HEDON
HURST
HYTHE
LEEDS
LEIGH
LEWES
LOUTH
LUTON
MARCH
OLNEY
OTLEY
POOLE
REETH
RIPON
RISCA
RUGBY
SARUM
SELBY
STOKE
STONE
TEBAY
THAME
TRING
TRURO
WELLS
WIGAN

6
ALFORD
ALSTON
ASHTON
BARNET
BARROW
BARTON
BATLEY
BATTLE
BAWTRY
BEDALE
BELPER

6—continued
BODMIN
BOGNOR
BOLTON
BOOTLE
BOSTON
BRUTON
BUNGAY
BURTON
BUXTON
CASTOR
COBHAM
CROMER
DARWEN
DUDLEY
DURHAM
EALING
ECCLES
EPPING
EXETER
GORING
HANLEY
HARLOW
HARROW
HAVANT
HENLEY
HEXHAM
HOWDEN
ILFORD
ILKLEY
ILSLEY
JARROW
KENDAL
LEYTON
LONDON
LUDLOW
LYNTON
LYTHAM
MALDON
MALTON
MARLOW
MASHAM
MORLEY
NASEBY
NELSON
NESTON
NEWARK
NEWENT
NEWLYN
NEWTON
NORHAM
OAKHAM
OLDHAM
ORMSBY
OSSETT
OUNDLE
OXFORD
PENRYN
PEWSEY
PINNER
PUDSEY
PUTNEY

19

6—continued

RAMSEY
REDCAR
RIPLEY
ROMNEY
ROMSEY
RUGELY
SEAHAM
SEATON
SELSEY
SETTLE
SNAITH
ST IVES
STROOD
STROUD
SUTTON
THIRSK
THORNE
TOTNES
WALTON
WATTON
WESTON
WHITBY
WIDNES
WIGTON
WILTON
WITHAM
WITNEY
WOOLER
YEOVIL

7

ALNWICK
ANDOVER
APPLEBY
ARUNDEL
ASHFORD
AYLSHAM
BAMPTON
BANBURY
BARKING
BECCLES
BEDFORD
BELFORD
BERWICK
BEWDLEY
BEXHILL
BICKLEY
BILSTON
BOURTON
BOWFELL
BRANDON
BRISTOL
BRIXHAM
BROMLEY
BURNHAM
BURNLEY
BURSLEM
CAISTOR
CATFORD
CAWSTON
CHARING

7—continued

CHATHAM
CHEADLE
CHEDDAR
CHESHAM
CHESTER
CHORLEY
CLACTON
CLIFTON
CRAWLEY
CROYDON
DARSLEY
DATCHET
DAWLISH
DEVIZES
DORKING
DOUGLAS
DUNSTER
ELSTREE
ENFIELD
EVERTON
EVESHAM
EXMOUTH
FAREHAM
FARNHAM
FELTHAM
GLOSSOP
GOSPORT
GRIMSBY
HALIFAX
HAMPTON
HARWICH
HAWORTH
HELSTON
HEYWOOD
HITCHIN
HONITON
HORNSEA
HORNSEY
HORSHAM
IPSWICH
IXWORTH
KESWICK
KINGTON
LANCING
LANGTON
LEDBURY
LEYBURN
LINCOLN
MALVERN
MARGATE
MATLOCK
MOLESEY
MORETON
MORPETH
MOSSLEY
NEWBURY
NEWPORT
NORWICH
OLDBURY
OVERTON
PADSTOW

7—continued

PENRITH
POULTON
PRESCOT
PRESTON
RAINHAM
READING
REDHILL
REDRUTH
REIGATE
RETFORD
ROMFORD
ROSSALL
ROYSTON
RUNCORN
SALFORD
SALTASH
SANDOWN
SAXELBY
SEAFORD
SHIFNAL
SHIPLEY
SHIPTON
SILLOTH
SKIPTON
SPILSBY
STAINES
STILTON
ST NEOTS
SUDBURY
SUNBURY
SWANAGE
SWINDON
SWINTON
TAUNTON
TELFORD
TENBURY
TETBURY
THAXTED
TILBURY
TORQUAY
TWYFORD
VENTNOR
WALSALL
WALTHAM
WANTAGE
WAREHAM
WARWICK
WATCHET
WATFORD
WEOBLEY
WICKWAR
WINDSOR
WINSLOW
WINSTER
WISBECK
WORKSOP

8

ABINGDON
ALFRETON
ALNMOUTH

8—continued

AMESBURY
AMPTHILL
AXBRIDGE
AYCLIFFE
BAKEWELL
BARNSLEY
BERKELEY
BEVERLEY
BICESTER
BIDEFORD
BOLSOVER
BRACKLEY
BRADFORD
BRAMPTON
BRIDPORT
BRIGHTON
BROMYARD
BROSELEY
CAMBORNE
CARLISLE
CATERHAM
CHERTSEY
CLEVEDON
CLOVELLY
COVENTRY
CREDITON
DAVENTRY
DEBENHAM
DEDWORTH
DEPTFORD
DEWSBURY
EGREMONT
EVERSLEY
FAKENHAM
FALMOUTH
FOULNESS
GRANTHAM
GRANTOWN
HADLEIGH
HAILSHAM
HALSTEAD
HASTINGS
HATFIELD
HELMSLEY
HEREFORD
HERNE BAY
HERTFORD
HINCKLEY
HOLBEACH
HUNMANBY
ILKESTON
KEIGHLEY
KINGSTON
LAVENHAM
LECHLADE
LISKEARD
LONGTOWN
LYNMOUTH
MARYPORT
MIDHURST
MINEHEAD

8—continued

NANTWICH
NEWHAVEN
NUNEATON
ORMSKIRK
OSWESTRY
PENZANCE
PERSHORE
PETERLEE
PETWORTH
PEVENSEY
PLAISTOW
PLYMOUTH
RAMSGATE
REDDITCH
RICHMOND
RINGWOOD
ROCHDALE
ROTHBURY
SALTBURN
SANDGATE
SANDWICH
SEDBERGH
SHANKLIN
SHELFORD
SHIPSTON
SIDMOUTH
SKEGNESS
SLEAFORD
SOUTHEND
SPALDING
STAFFORD
ST ALBANS
STAMFORD
STANHOPE
STANWELL
ST HELENS
STOCKTON
STRATTON
SURBITON
SWAFFHAM
TAMWORTH
THETFORD
THORNABY
TIVERTON
TUNSTALL
UCKFIELD
UXBRIDGE
WALLASEY
WALLSEND
WANSTEAD
WESTBURY
WETHERAL
WETHERBY
WEYMOUTH
WOODFORD
WOOLWICH
WORTHING
YARMOUTH

9

ALDEBURGH

9—continued

ALDERSHOT
ALLENDALE
ALRESFORD
AMBLESIDE
ASHBOURNE
ASHBURTON
AVONMOUTH
AYLESBURY
BLACKBURN
BLACKPOOL
BLANDFORD
BLISWORTH
BRACKNELL
BRAINTREE
BRENTFORD
BRENTWOOD
BRIGHOUSE
BROUGHTON
CAMBRIDGE
CARNFORTH
CASTLETON
CHESILTON
CHINGFORD
CLITHEROE
CONGLETON
CRANBORNE
CRANBROOK
CREWKERNE
CRICKLADE
CUCKFIELD
DARTMOUTH
DEVONPORT
DONCASTER
DONINGTON
DROITWICH
DRONFIELD
DUNGENESS
DUNSTABLE
ELLESMERE
FAVERSHAM
FLEETWOOD
GATESHEAD
GODALMING
GRAVESEND
GREENWICH
GRINSTEAD
GUILDFORD
HARROGATE
HASLEMERE
HAVERHILL
HAWKHURST
HOLMFIRTH
ILCHESTER
IMMINGHAM
KETTERING
KING'S LYNN
KINGSWEAR
LAMBOURNE
LANCASTER
LEICESTER
LICHFIELD

9—continued

LIVERPOOL
LONGRIDGE
LOWESTOFT
LYME REGIS
LYMINGTON
MAIDSTONE
MANSFIELD
MIDDLETON
NEWCASTLE
NEWMARKET
NEW ROMNEY
NORTHWICH
OTTERBURN
PEMBRIDGE
PENISTONE
PENKRIDGE
PENYGHENT
PICKERING
ROCHESTER
ROTHERHAM
SALISBURY
SALTFLEET
SEVENOAKS
SHEERNESS
SHEFFIELD
SHERBORNE
SMETHWICK
SOUTHGATE
SOUTHPORT
SOUTHWELL
SOUTHWOLD
STARCROSS
ST AUSTELL
STEVENAGE
STOCKPORT
STOKESLEY
STOURPORT
STRATFORD
TARPORLEY
TAVISTOCK
TENTERDEN
TONBRIDGE
TOWCESTER
TYNEMOUTH
ULVERSTON
UPMINSTER
UPPINGHAM
UTTOXETER
WAINFLEET
WAKEFIELD
WARKWORTH
WEYBRIDGE
WHERNSIDE
WHITHAVEN
WIMBLEDON
WINCANTON
WOKINGHAM
WOODSTOCK
WORCESTER
WYMONDHAM

10

ACCRINGTON
ALDBOROUGH
ALTRINCHAM
BARNSTAPLE
BEDLINGTON
BELLINGHAM
BILLERICAY
BIRKENHEAD
BIRMINGHAM
BRIDGNORTH
BRIDGWATER
BROMSGROVE
BROXBOURNE
BUCKINGHAM
CANTERBURY
CARSHALTON
CHELMSFORD
CHELTENHAM
CHICHESTER
CHIPPENHAM
CHULMLEIGH
COGGESHALL
COLCHESTER
CULLOMPTON
DARLINGTON
DORCHESTER
DUKINFIELD
EASTBOURNE
ECCLESHALL
FARNINGHAM
FOLKESTONE
FRESHWATER
GILLINGHAM
GLOUCESTER
HALESWORTH
HARTLEPOOL
HASLINGDON
HEATHFIELD
HORNCASTLE
HORNCHURCH
HUNGERFORD
HUNSTANTON
HUNTINGDON
ILFRACOMBE
KENILWORTH
KINGSCLERE
KIRKOSWALD
LAUNCESTON
LEAMINGTON
LEOMINSTER
LITTLEPORT
MAIDENHEAD
MALMESBURY
MANCHESTER
MEXBOROUGH
MICHELDEAN
MIDDLEWICH
MILDENHALL
NAILSWORTH
NOTTINGHAM
OKEHAMPTON

10–continued
ORFORDNESS
PANGBOURNE
PATRINGTON
PEACEHAVEN
PONTEFRACT
PORTISHEAD
PORTSMOUTH
POTTER'S BAR
RAVENGLASS
ROCKINGHAM
SAXMUNDHAM
SHEPPERTON
SHERINGHAM
SHREWSBURY
STALBRIDGE
ST LEONARDS
STOWMARKET
SUNDERLAND
TEDDINGTON
TEIGNMOUTH
TEWKESBURY
THAMESMEAD
TORRINGTON
TROWBRIDGE
TWICKENHAM
WALSINGHAM
WARMINSTER
WARRINGTON
WASHINGTON
WEDNESBURY
WELLINGTON
WESTWARD HO
WHITCHURCH
WHITSTABLE
WHITTLESEY
WILLENHALL
WINCHELSEA
WINCHESTER
WINDERMERE
WINDLESHAM
WIRKSWORTH
WITHERNSEA
WOODBRIDGE
WORKINGTON

11
BASINGSTOKE
BEARMINSTER
BOGNOR REGIS
BOURNEMOUTH
BRIDLINGTON
BUNTINGFORD
CLEETHORPES
COCKERMOUTH
EAST RETFORD
GLASTONBURY
GREAT MARLOW
GUISBOROUGH
HALTWHISTLE
HAMPTON WICK
HATHERLEIGH

11–continued
HIGH WYCOMBE
INGATESTONE
LEYTONSTONE
LITTLESTONE
LUDGERSHALL
LUTTERWORTH
MABLETHORPE
MANNINGTREE
MARKET RASEN
MARLBOROUGH
MUCH WENLOCK
NEW BRIGHTON
NEWTON ABBOT
NORTHAMPTON
PETERSFIELD
POCKLINGTON
RAWTENSTALL
SCARBOROUGH
SHAFTESBURY
SOUTHAMPTON
SOUTH MOLTON
STALYBRIDGE
ST MARGARET'S
STOURBRIDGE
TATTERSHALL
WALLINGFORD
WALTHAMSTOW
WESTMINSTER
WHITECHURCH
WOODHALL SPA

12
ATTLEBOROUGH
BEXHILL-ON-SEA
CASTLE RISING
CHESTERFIELD
CHRISTCHURCH
GAINSBOROUGH
GREAT GRIMSBY
GREAT MALVERN
HUDDERSFIELD
INGLEBOROUGH
LONG STRATTON
LOUGHBOROUGH
MACCLESFIELD
MILTON KEYNES
MORECAMBE BAY
NORTH BERWICK
NORTH SHIELDS
NORTH WALSHAM
PETERBOROUGH
SHOEBURYNESS
SHOTTESBROOK
SOUTH SHIELDS
STOKE-ON-TRENT

13
BARNARD CASTLE
BERKHAMPSTEAD
BISHOP'S CASTLE
BOROUGHBRIDGE
BRIGHTLINGSEA

13–continued
BURTON-ON-TRENT
BURY ST EDMUNDS
CHIPPING ONGAR
FINCHAMPSTEAD
GODMANCHESTER
GREAT YARMOUTH
HIGHAM FERRERS
KIDDERMINSTER
KIRKBY STEPHEN
KNARESBOROUGH
LITTLEHAMPTON
LYTHAM ST ANNES
MARKET DEEPING
MARKET DRAYTON
MELCOMBE REGIS
MELTON MOWBRAY
MIDDLESBROUGH
NORTHALLERTON
SAFFRON WALDEN
SHEPTON MALLET
WOLVERHAMPTON
WOOTTON BASSET

14
BERWICK-ON-
 TWEED
BISHOP AUCKLAND
BISHOPS WALTHAM
CHIPPING BARNET
CHIPPING NORTON
HEMEL HEMPSTEAD
KIRKBY LONSDALE
MARKET
 BOSWORTH
MORTIMER'S CROSS
STOCKTON-ON-
 TEES
STONY STRATFORD
SUTTON COURTNEY
TUNBRIDGE WELLS
WELLINGBOROUGH
WEST HARTLEPOOL

15+
ASHTON-UNDER-
 LYNE
BARROW-IN-
 FURNESS
BISHOP'S
 STORTFORD
BURNHAM-ON-
 CROUCH
CASTLE
 DONINGTON
LEIGHTON
 BUZZARD
NEWCASTLE-ON-
 TYNE
ST LEONARDS-ON-
 SEA

15+–continued
STRATFORD-ON-
 AVON
SUTTON COLDFIELD
WELWYN GARDEN
 CITY
WESTON-SUPER-
 MARE

ERITREA

6
ASMARA
ASMERA

ESTONIA

7
TALLINN

FRANCE

3
AIX
PAU

4
ALBI
CAEN
LYON
METZ
NICE

5
ARLES
ARRAS
BREST
DIJON
EVIAN
LILLE
LYONS
MACON
NANCY
NIMES
PARIS
REIMS
ROUEN
TOURS
TULLE

6
AMIENS
BAYEUX
CALAIS
CANNES
DIEPPE
LE MANS
NANTES
RHEIMS
ST MALO
TOULON
VERDUN

7
AJACCIO
ALENÇON
AVIGNON
BAYONNE
DUNKIRK
LE HAVRE
LIMOGES
LOURDES
ORLÉANS

8
BESANÇON
BIARRITZ
BORDEAUX
BOULOGNE
CHARTRES
GRENOBLE
SOISSONS
ST TROPEZ
TOULOUSE

9
ABBEVILLE
CHERBOURG
DUNKERQUE
MARSEILLE
MONTAUBAN
PERPIGNAN
ST ETIENNE

10
MARSEILLES
MONTELIMAR
STRASBOURG
VERSAILLES

11
ARMENTIÈRES
MONTPELLIER

15
CLERMONT-
FERRAND

GERMANY

4
BONN
GERA
KIEL
KÖLN
SUHL

5
ESSEN
HALLE
MAINZ
TRIER
WORMS

6
AACHEN
BERLIN
BOCHUM

6–continued
BREMEN
CASSEL
ERFURT
KASSEL
LÜBECK
MUNICH
TRÈVES

7
COBLENZ
COLOGNE
COTTBUS
DRESDEN
HAMBURG
HANOVER
HOMBURG
KOBLENZ
LEIPZIG
MÜNCHEN
POTSDAM
ROSTOCK
SPANDAU

8
AUGSBURG
DORTMUND
HANNOVER
MANNHEIM
NÜRNBERG
SCHWERIN

9
BRUNSWICK
DARMSTADT
FRANKFURT
MAGDEBURG
NUREMBERG
STUTTGART
WIESBADEN
WUPPERTAL

10
BADEN BADEN
BAD HOMBURG
DÜSSELDORF
HEIDELBERG

11
BRANDENBURG
SAARBRÜCKEN

13
AIX-LA-CHAPELLE
KARL-MARX-STADT

GREECE

6
ATHENS
SPARTA
THEBES

7
CORINTH

7–continued
MYCENAE
PIRAEUS

11
THESSALONIKI

HUNGARY

4
PÉCS
PUNE

8
BUDAPEST

INDIA

4
AGRA

5
AJMER
ALWAR
DELHI
KOTAH
PATNA
POONA
SIMLA
SURAT

6
BHOPAL
BOMBAY
HOWRAH
IMPHAL
INDORE
JAIPUR
JHANSI
KALYAN
KANPUR
KOHIMA
MADRAS
MEERUT
MUMBAI
MYSORE
NAGPUR
RAMPUR

7
BENARES
GWALIOR
JODHPUR
LUCKNOW

8
AGARTALA
AMRITSAR
CALCUTTA
CAWNPORE
JAMALPUR
LUDHIANA
SHILLONG
SRINAGAR
VADODARA

8–continued
VARANASI

9
AHMADABAD
ALLAHABAD
BANGALORE
HYDERABAD

10
CHANDIGARH
DARJEELING
JAMSHEDPUR
TRIVANDRUM

11
BHUBANESWAR

INDONESIA

5
MEDAN

7
BANDUNG
JAKARTA

8
SEMARANG
SURABAJA

9
PALEMBANG

IRAN

6
ABADAN
SHIRAZ
TABRIZ
TEHRAN

7
ISFAHAN
MASHHAD

IRAQ

5
BASRA
MOSUL

6
KIRKUK

7
BAGHDAD
KARBALA

**IRELAND, REPUBLIC
OF**

4
BRAY
COBH
CORK

4—continued
MUFF
NAAS
TRIM
TUAM

5
BALLA
BOYLE
CAVAN
CLARE
ENNIS
KELLS
SLIGO

6
ARKLOW
BANTRY
CALLAN
CARLOW
CARNEY
CASHEL
DUBLIN
GALWAY
SHRULE
TRALEE

7
ATHLONE
BLARNEY
CARRICK
CLONMEL
DONEGAL
DUNDALK
DUNMORE
KILDARE
LIFFORD
SHANNON
WEXFORD
WICKLOW
YOUGHAL

8
BALLYBAY
BUNCRANA
CLONTARF
DROGHEDA
KILKENNY
LIMERICK
LISTOWEL
LONGFORD
MAYNOOTH
MONAGHAN
RATHDRUM

9
CASTLEBAR
CONNEMARA
KILLARNEY
MULLINGAR
ROSCOMMON
TIPPERARY
TULLAMORE
WATERFORD

10
CASTLEFINN
KILCONNELL
SHILLELAGH
SKIBBEREEN
STRANORLAR

11
LETTERKENNY

12
DUN LAOGHAIRE

13
CASTLEBLAYNEY
INNISHTRAHULL
PORTLAOIGHISE

16
CARRICK-ON-
  SHANNON

ISRAEL

4
GAZA

5
HAIFA
JAFFA

7
TEL AVIV

9
BEERSHEBA
JERUSALEM

ITALY

4
BARI
PISA
ROME

5
GENOA
MILAN
OSTIA
PADUA
PARMA
SIENA
TURIN

6
MODENA
NAPLES
REGGIO
TRENTO
VENICE
VERONA

7
BOLOGNA
BERGAMO
BRESCIA
CATANIA

7—continued
FERRARA
MESSINA
PALERMO
PERUGIA
PESCARA
POMPEII
RAVENNA
SALERNO
SAN REMO
TRIESTE
VATICAN

8
CAGLIARI
FLORENCE
SYRACUSE

9
AGRIGENTO

JAPAN

4
FUGI
KOBE

5
KYOTO
OSAKA
TOKYO

6
NAGOYA
TOYOTA

7
FUKUOKA
HITACHI
SAPPORO

8
KAWASAKI
NAGASAKI
YOKOHAMA

9
HIROSHIMA

10
KITAKYUSHU

KAZAKHSTAN

6
ALMATY

9
KARAGANDA

KENYA

4
LAMU

7
MOMBASA

7—continued
NAIROBI

KOREA, SOUTH

5
SEOUL

9
PANMUNJON

KYRGYZSTAN

7
BISHPEK
PISHPEK

LATVIA

4
RIGA

LEBANON

4
TYRE

5
SIDON

6
BEIRUT

7
TRIPOLI

LIBYA

4
HOMS

6
TOBRUK

7
TRIPOLI

LITHUANIA

7
VILNIUS

MACEDONIA

6
SKOPJE

MALI

6
BAMAKO

8
TIMBUKTU

MEXICO

6
JUAREZ
PUEBLA

8
ACAPULCO
VERACRUZ

9
MONTERREY

11
GUADALAJARA

MOLDOVA

8
CHIŞINĂ
KISHINEV

MOROCCO

3
FEZ

5
RÀBAT

6
AGADIR
MEKNES

7
TANGIER

8
TANGIERS

9
MARRAKECH
MARRAKESH

10
CASABLANCA

MYANMAR

3
AVA

6
YANGON

7
RANGOON

8
MANDALAY

NETHERLANDS

5
BREDA
HAGUE

6
ARNHEM

6–continued
LEIDEN
LEYDEN

7
UTRECHT

8
THE HAGUE

9
AMSTERDAM
DORDRECHT
EINDHOVEN
ROTTERDAM

10
MAASTRICHT

NEW ZEALAND

6
NAPIER
NELSON

7
DUNEDIN

8
AUCKLAND

10
WELLINGTON

12
CHRISTCHURCH

NIGERIA

4
KANO

5
ABUJA
ENUGU
LAGOS

6
IBADAN

NORTHERN IRELAND

5
DOAGH
GLYNN
KEADY
LARNE
NEWRY
OMAGH
TOOME

6
ANTRIM
ARMAGH
AUGHER
BANGOR

6–continued
BELCOO
BERAGH
COMBER
LURGAN
RAPHOE

7
BELFAST
BELLEEK
CALEDON
CLOGHER
CRUMLIN
DERVOCK
DROMORE
FINAGHY
FINTONA
GILFORD
GLENARM
KILKEEL
LISBURN
POMEROY

8
AHOGHILL
ANNALONG
DUNGIVEN
HILLTOWN
HOLYWOOD
LIMAVADY
PORTRUSH
STRABANE
TRILLICK

9
BALLINTRA
BALLYMENA
BALLYMORE
BALLYNURE
BANBRIDGE
BUSHMILLS
CARNLOUGH
COLERAINE
COOKSTOWN
CRAIGAVON
CUSHENDUN
DUNGANNON
LISNASKEA
MONEYMORE
NEWCASTLE
PORTADOWN
RASHARKIN
ROSTREVOR
TANDRAGEE
TOVERMORE

10
ALDERGROVE
AUGHNACLOY
BALLYCLARE
BALLYGOWAN
BALLYMONEY
BALLYRONEY
CASTLEDERG

10–continued
COALISLAND
CUSHENDALL
DONAGHADEE
MARKETHILL
PORTAFERRY
SAINTFIELD
STRANGFORD
TANDERAGEE

11
BALLYCASTLE
BALLYGAWLEY
CARRICKMORE
CROSSMAGLEN
DOWNPATRICK
DRAPERSTOWN
ENNISKILLEN
LONDONDERRY
MAGHERAFELT
NEWTOWNARDS
PORTGLENONE
PORTSTEWART
RANDALSTOWN
RATHFRILAND
WARRENPOINT

12
BALLYHALBERT
BALLYNAHINCH
CASTLE DAWSON
CASTLEWELLAN
FIVEMILETOWN
HILLSBOROUGH
STEWARTSTOWN

13
BROOKE-BOROUGH
CARRICKFERGUS
CRAWFORDSBURN
DERRYGONNELLY

14
NEWTOWN
 STEWART

NORWAY

4
OSLO

6
BERGEN

9
TRONDHEIM

PAKISTAN

6
LAHORE
MULTAN
QUETTA

7
KARACHI

8
PESHAWAR

9
HYDERABAD
ISLAMABAD

10
FAISALABAD
GUJRANWALA
RAWALPINDI

PERU

4
LIMA

5
CUZCO

PHILIPPINES

6
MANILA

10
QUEZON CITY

POLAND

4
LODZ

5
POSEN

6
DANZIG
GDANSK
KRAKOW
LUBLIN
WARSAW

7
BRESLAU

8
PRZEMYSL

PORTUGAL

6
LISBON
OPORTO

RUSSIA

3&4
UFA
OMSK
PERM
TVER

5
KAZAN
PSKOV

6
MOSCOW
SAMARA

7
IRKUTSK
YAKUTSK

8
NOVGOROD
SMOLENSK

9
ASTRAKHAN
KALINGRAD
VOLGOGRAD

11
CHELYABINSK
NOVOSIBIRSK
VLADIVOSTOK

12
EKATERINBURG
ROSTOV-NA-DONU
ST PETERSBURG

14
NIZHNY NOVGOROD

SAUDI ARABIA

5
MECCA

6
JEDDAH
MEDINA
RIYADH

SCOTLAND

3
AYR
UIG

4
ALVA
BARR
DUNS
ELIE
KIRN
LUSS
NIGG
OBAN
REAY
RONA
STOW
WICK

5
ALLOA
ANNAN

5—continued
APPIN
AVOCH
AYTON
BANFF
BEITH
BRORA
BUNAW
BUSBY
CERES
CLOVA
CLUNE
CRAIL
CUPAR
DENNY
DOWNE
ELGIN
ELLON
ERROL
FYVIE
GOVAN
INSCH
ISLAY
KEISS
KEITH
KELSO
LAIRG
LARGO
LEITH
NAIRN
PERTH
SALEN
TROON

6
ABOYNE
ALFORD
BARVAS
BEAULY
BERVIE
BIGGAR
BO'NESS
BUCKIE
CARRON
CAWDOR
COMRIE
CRIEFF
CULLEN
CULTER
DOLLAR
DRYMEN
DUNBAR
DUNDEE
DUNLOP
DUNNET
DUNOON
DYSART
EDZELL
FINDON
FORFAR
FORRES
GIRVAN

6—continued
GLAMIS
HAWICK
HUNTLY
IRVINE
KILLIN
KILMUN
LANARK
LAUDER
LESLIE
LINTON
LOCHEE
MEIGLE
MOFFAT
PLADDA
RESTON
RHYNIE
ROSYTH
ROTHES
SHOTTS
THURSO
TONGUE
WISHAW
YARROW

7
AIRDRIE
BALFRON
BALLOCH
BANAVIE
BOWMORE
BRAEMAR
BRECHIN
BRODICK
CANOBIE
CANTYRE
CARBOST
CARGILL
CARLUKE
CRATHIE
CULROSS
CUMNOCK
DENHOLM
DOUGLAS
DUNKELD
DUNNING
EVANTON
FAIRLIE
FALKIRK
GALSTON
GIFFORD
GLASGOW
GLENCOE
GOLSPIE
GOUROCK
GRANTON
GUTHRIE
HALKIRK
KENMORE
KESSOCK
KILMORY
KILSYTH

7—continued

KINROSS
KINTORE
LAMLASH
LARBERT
LYBSTER
MACDUFF
MAYBOLE
MELDRUM
MELROSE
MELVICH
METHVEN
MILMUIR
MONIKIE
MUTHILL
NEWPORT
PAISLEY
PEEBLES
POLMONT
POOLEWE
PORTREE
PORTSOY
RENFREW
SADDELL
SARCLET
SCOURIE
SELKIRK
STANLEY
STRATHY
TARBERT
TARLAND
TAYPORT
TRANENT
TUNDRUM
TURRIFF
ULLSTER
YETHOLM

8

ABERDEEN
ABERLADY
ABINGTON
ARBROATH
ARMADALE
ARROCHAR
AULDEARN
BALLATER
BANCHORY
BARRHILL
BEATTOCK
BLANTYRE
BURGHEAD
CANISBAY
CARNWATH
CREETOWN
CROMARTY
DALKEITH
DALMALLY
DINGWALL
DIRLETON
DUFFTOWN
DUMFRIES

8—continued

DUNBEATH
DUNBLANE
DUNSCORE
EARLSTON
EYEMOUTH
FINDHORN
FORTROSE
GIFFNOCK
GLENLUCE
GREENLAW
GREENOCK
HAMILTON
INVERARY
INVERURY
JEANTOWN
JEDBURGH
KILBRIDE
KILNIVER
KILRENNY
KINGHORN
KIRKWALL
LANGHOLM
LATHERON
LEUCHARS
LOANHEAD
MARKINCH
MARYKIRK
MONIAIVE
MONTROSE
MONYMUSK
MUIRKIRK
NEILSTON
NEWBURGH
NEWMILNS
PENICUIK
PITSLIGO
POOLTIEL
QUIRAING
ROTHESAY
ST FERGUS
STIRLING
STRICHEN
TALISKER
TARANSAY
TRAQUAIR
ULLAPOOL
WHITHORN
WOODSIDE

9

ABERFELDY
ABERFOYLE
ARDROSSAN
BERRIDALE
BETTYHILL
BLACKLARG
BRACADALE
BRAERIACH
BROADFORD
BROUGHTON
BUCKHAVEN

9—continued

CAIRNTOUL
CALLANDER
CARSTAIRS
DUMBARTON
EDINBURGH
FERINTOSH
FOCHABERS
INCHKEITH
INVERARAY
INVERNESS
JOHNSTONE
KILDRUMMY
KINGUSSIE
KIRKCALDY
LEADHILLS
LOCHGELLY
LOCHINVAR
LOCHNAGAR
LOCKERBIE
LOGIERAIT
MAUCHLINE
MILNGAVIE
PETERHEAD
PITLOCHRY
PORT ELLEN
PRESTWICK
RICCARTON
RONALDSAY
ROTHIEMAY
SALTCOATS
SHIELDAIG
SLAMANNAN
ST ANDREWS
STEWARTON
ST FILLANS
STRANRAER
STRATHDON
STRONTIAN
THORNHILL
TOBERMORY
TOMINTOUL

10

ABBOTSFORD
ACHNASHEEN
ANSTRUTHER
APPLECROSS
ARDRISHAIG
AUCHINLECK
BALLANTRAE
BLACKADDER
CARNOUSTIE
CARSPHAIRN
CASTLETOWN
COATBRIDGE
COLDINGHAM
COLDSTREAM
DALBEATTIE
DRUMLITHIE
EAST LINTON
GALASHIELS

10—continued

GLENROTHES
JOHNSHAVEN
KILCREGGAN
KILLENAULE
KILMAINHAM
KILMALCOLM
KILMARNOCK
KILWINNING
KINCARDINE
KINGSBARNS
KIRKMAIDEN
KIRKOSWALD
KIRRIEMUIR
LENNOXTOWN
LESMAHAGOW
LINLITHGOW
LIVINGSTON
MILNATHORT
MOTHERWELL
PITTENWEEM
PORTOBELLO
RUTHERGLEN
STONEHAVEN
STONEHOUSE
STONEYKIRK
STRATHAVEN
STRATHEARN
STRATHMORE
TWEEDMOUTH
WEST CALDER
WILSONTOWN

11

ABERCHIRDER
BALQUHIDDER
BANNOCKBURN
BLAIR ATHOLL
BLAIRGOWRIE
CAMPBELTOWN
CHARLESTOWN
CUMBERNAULD
DRUMMELZIER
DUNFERMLINE
ECCLEFECHAN
FETTERCAIRN
FORT WILLIAM
FRASERBURGH
HELENSBURGH
INVERGORDON
KIRKMICHAEL
LOSSIEMOUTH
LOSTWITHIEL
MAXWELLTOWN
MUSSELBURGH
PORT GLASGOW
PORT PATRICK
PRESTONPANS
PULTNEYTOWN
STRATHBLANE

12

AUCHTERARDER

27

12–continued
BALLACHULISH
EAST KILBRIDE
FORT AUGUSTUS
GARELOCHHEAD
INNERLEITHEN
KINLOCHLEVEN
LAWRENCEKIRK
LOCHGILPHEAD
PORTMAHOMACK
STRATHPEFFER
TILLICOULTRY

13
AUCHTERMUCHTY
CASTLE DOUGLAS
COCKBURNSPATH
DALMELLINGTON
INVERKEITHING
INVERKEITHNIE
KIRKCUDBRIGHT
KIRKINTILLOCH
NEWTON STEWART
ROTHIEMURCHUS

SLOVAKIA

10
BRATISLAVA

SLOVENIA

9
LJUBLJANA

SOUTH AFRICA

6
DURBAN
SOWETO

8
CAPE TOWN
MAFEKING
PRETORIA

9
KIMBERLEY
LADYSMITH

10
ALEXANDRIA
EAST LONDON
SIMONSTOWN

11
GRAHAMSTOWN
SHARPEVILLE

12
BLOEMFONTEIN
JOHANNESBURG

13
PORT ELIZABETH

16
PIETERMARITZ-
  BURG

SPAIN

4
VIGO

5
CADIZ

6
BILBAO
MADRID
MALAGA

7
BADAJOZ
CORDOBA
GRANADA
SEVILLE

8
ALICANTE
PAMPLONA
VALENCIA
ZARAGOZA

9
BARCELONA
CARTAGENA
LAS PALMAS
SANTANDER
SARAGOSSA

12
SAN SEBASTIAN

SRI LANKA

5
GALLE
KANDY

7
COLOMBO

11
TRINCOMALEE

SUDAN

6
BERBER

7
DONGOLA

8
KHARTOUM
OMDURMAN

SWEDEN

5
MALMÖ

7
UPPSALA

8
GÖTEBORG

9
STOCKHOLM

10
GOTHENBURG

11
HELSINGBORG

SWITZERLAND

4
BÂLE
BERN

5
BASEL
BASLE

6
GENEVA
ZURICH

7
LUCERNE

8
LAUSANNE

SYRIA

4
HOMS

6
ALEPPO

7
PALMYRA

8
DAMASCUS

TAIWAN

6
TAIBEI
TAIPEI

9
KAO-HSIUNG

TAJIKISTAN

8
DUSHANBE

TANZANIA

6
DODOMA

8
ZANZIBAR

11
DAR ES SALAAM

TURKEY

5
ADANA
IZMIR

6
ANKARA
SMYRNA

7
ERZERUM

8
ISTANBUL

9
BYZANTIUM

14
CONSTANTINOPLE

TURKMENISTAN

9
ASHKHABAD

UKRAINE

4
KIEV
LVOV

5
YALTA

6
ODESSA

7
DONETSK

USA

4
GARY
LIMA
RENO
TROY
WACO
YORK

5
AKRON
BOISE
BRONX
BUTTE
FLINT
MIAMI
OMAHA
OZARK

5—continued
SALEM
SELMA
TULSA
UTICA

6
ALBANY
AUSTIN
BANGOR
BILOXI
BOSTON
CAMDEN
CANTON
DALLAS
DAYTON
DENVER
DULUTH
EL PASO
EUGENE
FRESNO
LOWELL
MOBILE
NASSAU
NEWARK
OXNARD
PEORIA
ST PAUL
TACOMA
TOLEDO
TOPEKA
TUCSON
URBANA

7
ABILENE
ANAHEIM
ATLANTA
BOULDER
BUFFALO
CHICAGO
CONCORD
DETROIT
HAMPTON
HOBOKEN
HOUSTON
JACKSON
KEY WEST
LINCOLN
MADISON
MEMPHIS
MODESTO
NEW YORK
NORFOLK
OAKLAND
ORLANDO
PHOENIX
RALEIGH
READING
ROANOKE
SAGINAW
SAN JOSÉ
SEATTLE

7—continued
SPOKANE
ST LOUIS
WICHITA
YONKERS

8
BERKELEY
BROOKLYN
COLUMBUS
DEARBORN
GREEN BAY
HANNIBAL
HARTFORD
HONOLULU
LAKELAND
LAS VEGAS
NEW HAVEN
OAK RIDGE
PALO ALTO
PASADENA
PORTLAND
RICHMOND
SAN DIEGO
SANTA ANA
SAVANNAH
STAMFORD
STOCKTON
SYRACUSE
WHEELING

9
ANCHORAGE
ANNAPOLIS
ARLINGTON
BALTIMORE
BETHLEHEM
CAMBRIDGE
CHAMPAIGN
CHARLOTTE
CLEVELAND
DES MOINES
FAIRBANKS
FORT WAYNE
FORT WORTH
GALVESTON
HOLLYWOOD
JOHNSTOWN
KALAMAZOO
LANCASTER
LEXINGTON
LONG BEACH
MANHATTAN
MILWAUKEE
NASHVILLE
NEW LONDON
NORTHEAST
PRINCETON
RIVERSIDE
ROCHESTER
WATERBURY
WORCESTER
YPSILANTI

10
ATOMIC CITY
BATON ROUGE
BIRMINGHAM
CHARLESTON
CINCINATTI
EVANSVILLE
GREENSBORO
GREENVILLE
HARRISBURG
HUNTSVILLE
JERSEY CITY
KANSAS CITY
LITTLE ROCK
LONG BRANCH
LOS ANGELES
LOUISVILLE
MIAMI BEACH
MONTGOMERY
NEW BEDFORD
NEW ORLEANS
PITTSBURGH
PROVIDENCE
SACRAMENTO
SAINT LOUIS
SAN ANTONIO
WASHINGTON
YOUNGSTOWN

11
ALBUQUERQUE
CEDAR RAPIDS
CHATTANOOGA
GRAND RAPIDS
MINNEAPOLIS
NEWPORT NEWS
PALM SPRINGS
SCHENECTADY
SPRINGFIELD

12
ATLANTIC CITY
BEVERLY HILLS
FAYETTEVILLE
INDEPENDENCE
INDIANAPOLIS
JACKSONVILLE
NEW BRUNSWICK
NIAGARA FALLS
OKLAHOMA CITY
PHILADELPHIA
POUGHKEEPSIE
SALT LAKE CITY
SAN FRANCISCO
SANTA BARBARA

13
CORPUS CHRISTI
ST PETERSBURGH

14
FORT LAUDERDALE

15
COLORADO
  SPRINGS

UZBEKISTAN

8
TASHKENT

9
SAMARKAND

VENEZUELA

7
CARACAS

9
MARACAIBO

WALES

3
USK

4
BALA
HOLT
MOLD
PYLE
RHYL

5
BARRY
CHIRK
FLINT
NEATH
NEVIN
TENBY
TOWYN

6
AMLWCH
BANGOR
BRECON
BUILTH
CONWAY
MARGAM
RUABON
RUTHIN

7
CARBURY
CARDIFF
CWMBRAN
DENBIGH
MAESTEG
NEWPORT
NEWTOWN
ST ASAPH
SWANSEA
WREXHAM

8
ABERAVON

29

8—continued
ABERDARE
ABERGELE
BARMOUTH
BRIDGEND
CAERLEON
CARDIGAN
CHEPSTOW
DOLGELLY
EBBW VALE
HAWARDEN
HOLYHEAD
HOLYWELL
KIDWELLY
KNIGHTON
LAMPETER
LLANELLI
LLANELLY
LLANRWST
MONMOUTH
PEMBROKE
RHAYADER
SKERRIES
SKIFNESS
TALGARTH
TREDEGAR
TREGARON

9
ABERAERON

9—continued
ABERDOVEY
ABERFFRAW
BEAUMARIS
BODLONDEB
CARNARVON
CRICCIETH
FESTINIOG
FISHGUARD
LLANBERIS
LLANDUDNO
NEW RADNOR
PONTYPOOL
PORTHCAWL
PORTMADOC
PWHLLHELI
WELSHPOOL

10
CADER IDRIS
CAERNARFON
CAERNARVON
CAPEL CURIG
CARMARTHEN
CRICKHOWEL
FFESTINIOG
LLANDOVERY
LLANFYLLIN
LLANGADOCK
LLANGOLLEN

10—continued
LLANIDLOES
MONTGOMERY
PLINLIMMON
PONTYPRIDD
PORTH NIGEL
PORT TALBOT
PRESTEIGNE

11
ABERGAVENNY
ABERYSTWYTH
CLYDACH VALE
MACHYNLLETH
OYSTERMOUTH

12
LLANDILOFAWR
LLANTRISSANT
YSTRAD MYNACH

13
HAVERFORDWEST
MERTHYR TYDFIL

YEMEN

4
ADEN
SAN'A

5
SANA'A

YUGOSLAVIA

3
NÍŠ

9
PODGORICA

7
NOVI SAD

8
BELGRADE

ZIMBABWE

6
HARARE

8
BULAWAYO

PORTS

ALGERIA

4
ORAN

6
SKIKDA

7
ALGIERS

9
PORT ARZEW

ANGOLA

6
LOBITO
LUANDA

ARGENTINA

7
LA PLATA

11
BUENOS AIRES

AUSTRALIA

6
SYDNEY

7
DAMPIER
GEELONG

8
ADELAIDE
BRISBANE

9
MELBOURNE

9—continued
NEWCASTLE

10
FREEMANTLE

11
PORT JACKSON

12
PORT ADELAIDE

BELGIUM

6
OSTEND

7
ANTWERP

9
ZEEBRUGGE

BENIN

7
COTONOU

9
PORTO NOVO

BRAZIL

4
PARA

5
BELEM

6
RECIFE
SANTOS

7
TOBARAO

10
PERNAMBUCO

12
RIO DE JANEIRO

BULGARIA

5
VARNA

BURMA

5
AKYAB

6
SITTWE

7
RANGOON

8
MOULMEIN

CAMEROON

6
DOUALA

CANADA

7
HALIFAX
KITIMAT

8
MONTREAL

9
CHURCHILL
ESQUIMALT
OWEN SOUND
VANCOUVER

11
THREE RIVERS

CHANNEL ISLANDS

8
ST HELIER

11
SAINT HELIER
ST PETER PORT

CHILE

5
ARICA

8
COQUIMBO

10
VALPARAISO

CHINA

4
AMOY

6
CHEFOO
HANKOW
SWATOW
WEIHAI

7
FOOCHOW
YINGKOW

8
SHANGHAI
TIENTSIN

10
PORT ARTHUR

COLUMBIA

9
CARTAGENA

12
BARRANQUILLA
BUENAVENTURA

**CONGO,
DEMOCRATIC
REPUBLIC OF**

6
MATADI

9
MBUJI-MAYI

CORSICA

6
BASTIA

7
AJACCIO

CUBA

6
HAVANA

14
SANTIAGO DE CUBA

CYPRUS

7
LARNACA

8
LIMASSOL

DENMARK

6
ODENSE

7
AALBORG
HORSENS

8
ELSINORE

9
HELSINGÖR

10
COPENHAGEN

13
FREDERIKSHAVN

ECUADOR

9
GUAYAQUIL

EGYPT

4
SUEZ

8
DAMIETTA
PORT SAID

10
ALEXANDRIA

ENGLAND

4
HULL

5
DOVER

6
LONDON

7
CHATHAM
GRIMSBY
HARWICH
TILBURY

8
FALMOUTH
NEWHAVEN
PENZANCE
PLYMOUTH
PORTLAND
SANDWICH
WEYMOUTH

9
AVONMOUTH
DEVONPORT
GRAVESEND

9–continued
KING'S LYNN
LIVERPOOL
NEWCASTLE
SHEERNESS

10
BARNSTAPLE
COLCHESTER
FELIXSTOWE
FOLKESTONE
HARTLEPOOL
PORTSMOUTH
SUNDERLAND
TEIGNMOUTH
WHITSTABLE

11
CINQUE PORTS
SOUTHAMPTON

12
NORTH SHIELDS
PORT SUNLIGHT

13
MIDDLESBROUGH

FINLAND

8
HELSINKI

FRANCE

5
BREST

6
CALAIS
CANNES
DIEPPE
TOULON

7
DUNKIRK
LE HAVRE

8
BORDEAUX
BOULOGNE
HONFLEUR

9
CHERBOURG
FOS-SUR-MER
MARSEILLE

10
LA ROCHELLE
MARSEILLES

FRENCH GUIANA

7
CAYENNE

PORTS

GERMANY

4
KIEL

5
EMDEN

6
BREMEN
WISMAR

7
HAMBURG
ROSTOCK

8
CUXHAVEN

9
FLENSBURG

10
TRAVEMÜNDE

11
BREMERHAVEN

13
WILHELMS-HAVEN

GHANA

4
TEMA

8
TAKORADI

GREECE

5
CANEA
CORFU

6
PATRAS
RHODES

7
PIRAEUS

8
NAVARINO

10
HERMOPOLIS

11
HERMOUPOLIS

HAWAII

8
HONOLULU

11
PEARL HARBOR

HUNGARY

8
BUDAPEST

INDIA

6
BOMBAY
COCHIN
HALDIA
KANDLA
MADRAS

8
CALCUTTA
COCANADA
KAKINADA

11
MASULIPATAM
PONDICHERRY

12
MASULIPATNAM

INDONESIA

6
PADANG

7
JAKARTA

8
MACASSAR
PARADEEP

IRAN

6
ABADAN

7
BUSHIRE

IRAQ

5
BASRA

IRELAND

4
COBH
CORK

7
DONEGAL
DUNDALK
YOUGHAL

12
DUN LAOGHAIRE

ISRAEL

4
ACRE
AKKO
ELAT

5
EILAT
HAIFA

6
ASHDOD

ITALY

4
BARI

5
GAETA
GENOA
OSTIA
TRANI

6
ANCONA
NAPLES
VENICE

7
LEGHORN
MARSALA
MESSINA
PALERMO
SALERNO
TRAPANI
TRIESTE

8
BRINDISI

IVORY COAST

7
ABIDJAN

JAMAICA

8
KINGSTON

9
PORT ROYAL

10
MONTEGO BAY

JAPAN

4
KOBE

5
KOCHI
OSAKA

8
HAKODATE
NAGASAKI
YOKOHAMA

9
HIROSHIMA
KAGOSHIMA

11
SHIMONOSEKI

KENYA

7
MOMBASA

KUWAIT

12
MINA AL-AHMADI

LEBANON

6
BEIRUT

LIBYA

7
TRIPOLI

8
BENGHAZI

MADAGASCAR

8
TAMATAVE

MALAYSIA

6
PENANG

9
PORT KLANG

10
GEORGE TOWN

12
KOTAKINABALU

MAURITANIA

10
NOUAKCHOTT

MAURITIUS

9
PORT LOUIS

MEXICO

7
GUAYMAS

8
VERACRUZ

MOROCCO

4
SAFI

5
CEUTA
RABAT

6
AGADIR
TETUÁN

7
MELILLA
MOGADOR
TANGIER

9
ESSAOUIRA

10
CASABLANCA

14
MINA HASSAN TANI

MOZAMBIQUE

5
BEIRA

6
MAPUTO

NETHERLANDS

5
DELFT

8
FLUSHING

9
AMSTERDAM
EUROPOORT
ROTTERDAM

10
VLISSINGEN

NEW ZEALAND

6
NELSON

8
AUCKLAND
GISBORNE

9
LYTTELTON

NIGERIA

5
LAGOS

12
PORT HARCOURT

**NORTHERN
IRELAND**

5
LARNE

7
BELFAST

NORWAY

4
OSLO

6
BERGEN
LARVIK
NARVIK
TROMSØ

9
STAVANGER
TRONDHEIM

10
HAMMERFEST
KRISTIANIA

12
KRISTIANSAND

PAKISTAN

6
CHALNA

7
KARACHI

PANAMA

5
COLON

6
BALBOA

9
CRISTOBAL

PAPUA NEW GUINEA

11
PORT MORESBY

PERU

3
ILO

6
CALLAO

8
MATARINI

10
SAN JUAN BAY

PHILIPPINES

4
CEBU

6
MANILA

POLAND

6
DANZIG
GDANSK
GDYNIA

7
STETTIN

8
SZCZECIN

9
KOLOBRZEG

PORTUGAL

6
LISBON
OPORTO

PUERTO RICO

7
SAN JUAN

ROMANIA

10
CONSTANTSA

RUSSIA

8
PECHENGA
TAGANROG

9
ARCHANGEL

11
VLADIVOSTOK

12
ST PETERSBURG

SAUDI ARABIA

6
JEDDAH

SCOTLAND

4
TAIN
WICK

5
LEITH
SCAPA

6
DUNBAR
DUNDEE

8
GREENOCK

9
ARDROSSAN
SCAPA FLOW
STORNAWAY

11
GRANGEMOUTH
PORT GLASGOW

SENEGAL

5
DAKAR

SIERRA LEONE

8
FREETOWN

SOUTH AFRICA

6
DURBAN

8
CAPE TOWN

9
MOSSEL BAY
PORT NATAL

10
EAST LONDON
SIMONSTOWN

11
RICHARD'S BAY

13
PORT ELIZABETH

SOUTH KOREA

5
PUSAN

SPAIN

5
PALMA
PALOS

6
BILBAO
FERROL
MALAGA

7
CORUNNA
FUNCHAL

8
ALICANTE
ARRECIFE
LA CORUÑA

9
ALGECIRAS
BARCELONA
CARTAGENA
LAS PALMAS
PORT MAHON

SRI LANKA

5
GALLE

7
COLOMBO

SUDAN

6
SUAKIN

9
PORT SUDAN

SWEDEN

5
LULEA

5–continued

MALMÖ
WISBY
YSTAD

6
KÄLMAR

8
GÖTEBORG
HALMSTAD
NYKÖPING

9
STOCKHOLM

10
GOTHENBURG

11
HELSINGBORG

TAIWAN

6
TAINAN

7
KEELUNG

9
KAO-HSIUNG

TANZANIA

6
MTWARA

11
DAR ES SALAAM

TRINIDAD AND TOBAGO

11
PORT-OF-SPAIN

TURKEY

5
IZMIR

6
SMYRNA

8
ISTANBUL

14
CONSTANTINOPLE

URUGUAY

10
MONTEVIDEO

USA

4
ERIE

7
DETROIT
HOUSTON
NEW YORK
NORFOLK
SEATTLE

8
NEW HAVEN

9
BALTIMORE
GALVESTON
NANTUCKET
PENSACOLA

10
BRIDGEPORT
CHARLESTON
JERSEY CITY
LOS ANGELES
NEW BEDFORD
NEW ORLEANS
PERTH AMBOY
PORTSMOUTH

11
ROCK HARBOUR

12
SAN FRANCISCO

VENEZUELA

8
LA GUIARA

12
PUERTO HIERRO

13
PUERTO CABELLO

WALES

7
CARDIFF
SWANSEA

8
HOLYHEAD
LLANELLI
PEMBROKE

9
PORTMADOC

12
MILFORD HAVEN

YEMEN

4
ADEN

5
MOCHA

6
AHMEDI

7
HODEIDA

YUGOSLAVIA

3
BAR

5
KOTOR

7
CATTARO

ISLANDS

3
RUM

4
ARAN
BALI
CEBU
CUBA
EDGE
EIGG
GUAM
JAVA
JURA
MULL
OAHU
SARK
SKYE

5
ARRAN
BANKS
CERAM
CORFU
CRETE
DEVON
HAITI
ISLAY
LEWIS
LEYTE
LUZON
MALTA
PANAY
SAMAR
TIMOR

6
BAFFIN
BORNEO
CYPRUS
FLORES
HAINAN

6–continued
HARRIS
HAWAII
HONSHU
JERSEY
KODIAK
KYUSHU
MADURA
NEGROS
ORKNEY
PENANG
RHODES
SICILY
TAHITI
TAIWAN

7
BAHRAIN
BARENTS
BERMUDA
CELEBES
CORSICA
CURAÇAO
GOTLAND
GRENADA
ICELAND
IRELAND
JAMAICA
MADEIRA
MAJORCA
MINDORO
OKINAWA
PALAWAN
RATHLIN
SHIKOKU
ST LUCIA
SUMATRA
WRANGEL

8
ALDERNEY

8–continued
BARBADOS
DOMINICA
GUERNSEY
HOKKAIDO
HONG KONG
MALAGASY
MELVILLE
MINDANAO
SAKHALIN
SARDINIA
SHETLAND
SOMERSET
SRI LANKA
SULAWESI
TASMANIA
TENERIFE
TRINIDAD
UNALASKA
VICTORIA
VITI LEVU
ZANZIBAR

9
ANTICOSTI
AUSTRALIA
ELLESMERE
GREENLAND
HALMAHERA
ISLE OF MAN
MANHATTAN
MAURITIUS
NANTUCKET
NEW GUINEA
SINGAPORE
ST VINCENT
VANCOUVER

10
CAPE BRETON
GUADELOUPE

10–continued
HISPANIOLA
LONG ISLAND
MADAGASCAR
MARTINIQUE
NEW BRITAIN
NEW IRELAND
NEW ZEALAND
PUERTO RICO

11
AXEL HEIBERG
GUADALCANAL
ISLE OF PINES
ISLE OF WIGHT

12
BOUGAINVILLE
GREAT BRITAIN
NEW CALEDONIA
NEWFOUNDLAND
NOVAYA ZEMLYA

13
NORTH EAST LAND
PRINCE OF WALES
PRINCE PATRICK
SANTA CATALINA

14
TIERRA DEL FUEGO

15
MARTHA'S
  VINEYARD
WEST SPITS-
  BERGEN

18
PRINCE EDWARD
  ISLAND

OCEANS AND SEAS

3&4
ARAL (SEA)
AZOV (SEA OF)
DEAD (SEA)
JAVA (SEA)
KARA (SEA)
RED (SEA)
ROSS (SEA)
SAVA (SEA)

5
BANDA (SEA)
BLACK (SEA)
CHINA (SEA)
CORAL (SEA)
IRISH (SEA)
JAPAN (SEA OF)
NORTH (SEA)
TIMOR (SEA)

5–continued
WHITE (SEA)

6
AEGEAN (SEA)
ARCTIC (OCEAN)
BALTIC (SEA)
BERING (SEA)
CELTIC (SEA)
INDIAN (OCEAN)
INLAND (SEA)
IONIAN (SEA)
LAPTEV (SEA)
NANHAI (SEA)
TASMAN (SEA)
YELLOW (SEA)

7
ANDAMAN (SEA)
ARABIAN (SEA)

7–continued
ARAFURA (SEA)
BARENTS (SEA)
BEHRING (SEA)
CASPIAN (SEA)
DONG HAI (SEA)
GALILEE (SEA OF)
MARMARA (SEA OF)
OKHOTSK (SEA OF)
PACIFIC (OCEAN)
WEDDELL (SEA)

8
ADRIATIC (SEA)
AMUNDSEN (SEA)
ATLANTIC (OCEAN)
BEAUFORT (SEA)
HUANG HAI (SEA)
LIGURIAN (SEA)

8–continued
SARGASSO (SEA)
TIBERIAS (SEA OF)

9
ANTARCTIC (OCEAN)
CARIBBEAN (SEA)
EAST CHINA (SEA)
GREENLAND (SEA)

10+
BELLINGSHAUSEN
  (SEA)
MEDITERRANEAN
  (SEA)
PHILIPPINE (SEA)
SETO-NAIKAI (SEA)
SOUTH CHINA (SEA)

BAYS

3
ISE (Japan)
MAL (Republic of
  Ireland)
TOR (England)

4
ACRE (Israel)
CLEW (Republic of
  Ireland)
LUCE (Scotland)
LYME (England)
PIGS (Cuba)
VIGO (Spain)
WICK (Scotland)

5
ALGOA (South Africa)
CÁDIZ (Spain)
CASCO (USA)
DVINA (Russia)
FUNDY (Canada)
HAWKE (New
  Zealand)
JAMES (Canada)
MILNE (New Guinea)
OMURA (Japan)
OSAKA (Japan)
SLIGO (Republic of
  Ireland)
TABLE (South Africa)
TAMPA (USA)
TOKYO (Japan)
URADO (Japan)
VLORË (Albania)

6
ABUKIR (Egypt)
ALASKA (USA)
ARIAKE (Japan)
BAFFIN (Baffin Island,
  Greenland)
BANTRY (Republic of
  Ireland)
BENGAL (India,
  Bangladesh,
  Myanmar)
BISCAY (France,
  Spain)
BOTANY (Australia)
CALLOA (Peru)
COLWYN (Wales)
DINGLE (Republic of
  Ireland)
DUBLIN (Republic of
  Ireland)
GALWAY (Republic of
  Ireland)
GDANSK (Poland)
HUDSON (Canada)
JERVIS (Australia)
LOBITO (Angola)
MANILA (Philippines)
MOBILE (USA)
NAPLES (Italy)
NEWARK (USA)
PLENTY (New
  Zealand)
RAMSEY (Isle of Man)

6–continued
TASMAN (New
  Zealand)
TOYAMA (Japan)
TRALEE (Republic of
  Ireland)
UNGAVA (Canada)
VYBORG (Finland)
WALVIS (Namibia)
WIGTON (Scotland)

7
ABOUKIR (Egypt)
BRITTAS (Republic of
  Ireland)
CAPE COD (USA)
DELAGOA
  (Mozambique)
DUNDALK (Republic
  of Ireland)
FLORIDA (USA)
KAVÁLLA (Greece)
KILLALA (Republic of
  Ireland)
MONTEGO (Jamaica)
MORETON (Australia)
NEW YORK (USA)
POVERTY (New
  Zealand)
SETÚBAL (Portugal)
SWANSEA (Wales)
THUNDER (Canada)
TRINITY (Canada)
WALFISH (Namibia)

7–continued
WEXFORD (Republic
  of Ireland)
YOUGHAL (Republic
  of Ireland)

8
BIDEFORD (England)
BISCAYNE (USA)
BUZZARDS (USA)
CAMPECHE (Mexico)
CARDIGAN (Wales)
DELAWARE (USA)
DUNMANUS
  (Republic of Ireland)
FALSE BAY (South
  Africa)
GEORGIAN (Canada)
GWEEBARA
  (Republic of Ireland)
HANGZHOU (China)
JIANZHOU (China)
PLYMOUTH (USA)
QUIBERON (France)
SAN PEDRO (USA)
SANTIAGO (Cuba)
ST BRIDES (Wales)
ST MICHEL (France)
TREMADOG (Wales)

9
BOMBETOKA
  (Madagascar)
DISCOVERY
  (Australia)

9–continued
ENCOUNTER
  (Australia)
FAMAGUSTA (Cyprus)
FROBISHER
  (Canada)
GIBRALTAR (Gibraltar,
  Spain)
GUANABARA(Brazil)
INHAMBANE
  (Mozambique)
LIVERPOOL
  (England)
MAGDALENA
  (Mexico)
MORECAMBE
  (England)

9–continued
PLACENTIA(Canada)
ST AUSTELL
  (England)
WHITE PARK
  (Northern Ireland)

10
BALLYHEIGE
  (Republic of Ireland)
BALLYTEIGE
  (Republic of Ireland)
BARNSTAPLE
  (England)
BRIDGWATER
  (England)
CAERNARFON
  (Wales)

10–continued
CAERNARVON
  (Wales)
CARMARTHEN
  (Wales)
CHESAPEAKE (USA)
CIENFUEGOS (Cuba)
GUANTÁNAMO
  (Cuba)

11
BRIDLINGTON
  (England)
LÜTZOW-HOLME
  (Antarctica)
PORT PHILLIP
  (Australia)

11–continued
TRINCOMALEE (Sri
  Lanka)

12+
CORPUS CHRISTI
  (USA)
ESPÍRITO SANTO
  (Brazil)
MASSACHUSETTS
  (USA)
NARRAGANSETT
  (USA)
PASSAMAQUODDY
  (Canada, USA)
SAN FRANCISCO
  (USA)

STRAITS

4
BASS (Australia,
  Tasmania)
COOK (New Zealand)
PALK (India, Sri
  Lanka)

5
CANSO (Canada)
DAVIS (Canada,
  Greenland)
DOVER (England,
  France)
KERCH (Ukraine,
  Russia)
KOREA (South Korea,
  Japan)
MENAI (Wales)
SUMBA (Indonesia:
  Sumba, Flores)
SUNDA (Indonesia:
  Sumatra, Java)
TATAR (Russia)
TIRAN (Egypt, Saudi
  Arabia)

6
BANGKA (Indonesia:
  Bangka, Sumatra)
BERING (Alaska,
  Russia)
HAINAN (China)
HORMUZ (Iran,
  Oman)
HUDSON (Canada)
JOHORE (Malaysia,
  Singapore)
LOMBOK (Indonesia:
  Bali, Lombok)
SOEMBA (Indonesia:
  Sumba, Flores)
TAIWAN (Taiwan,
  China)
TORRES (Australia,
  New Guinea)

7
BASILAN (Philippines:
  Basilan, Mindanao)
DENMARK
  (Greenland, Iceland)

7–continued
FLORIDA (USA,
  Cuba)
FORMOSA (Taiwan,
  China)
GEORGIA (Canada)
MAKASAR (Borneo,
  Sulawesi)
MALACCA (Peninsular
  Malaysia, Sumatra)
MESSINA (Sicily, Italy)
OTRANTO (Italy,
  Albania)
SOENDRA (Indonesia:
  Sumba, Java)
TSUGARU (Japan)

8
CLARENCE
  (Australia)
MACASSAR (Borneo,
  Sulawesi)
MACKINAC (Straits of;
  USA)

8–continued
MAGELLAN (Chile,
  Tierra del Fuego)
MAKASSAR (Borneo,
  Sulawesi)
SURABAYA (Indo-
  nesia: Java, Madura)

9
BELLE ISLE (Canada)
GIBRALTAR (Gibraltar,
  Spain, Morocco)
LA PÉROUSE (Japan,
  Russia)
SOERABAJA (Indo-
  nesia: Java, Madura)

10+
GOLDEN GATE (USA)
JUAN DE FUCA
  (Canada, USA)
SAN BERNARDINO
  (Philippines: Luzon,
  Samar)

LAKES, LOCHS, AND LOUGHS

3&4
ARAL (Kazahkstan,
  Uzbekistan)
AWE (Scotland)
BALA (Wales)
CHAD (West Africa)

3&4–continued
COMO (Italy)
ERIE (Canada, USA)
EYRE (Australia)
KIVU (Congo,
  Rwanda)

3&4–continued
NEMI (Italy)
NESS (Scotland)
TANA (Ethiopia)
VAN (Turkey)

5
FOYLE (Ireland)
GARDA (Italy)
GREAT (Australia)
GREAT (USA,
  Canada)

5—continued
HURON (USA, Canada)
KIOGA (Uganda)
KYOGA (Uganda)
LÉMAN (Switzerland, France)
LEVEN (Scotland)
LOCHY (Scotland)
MAREE (Scotland)
NEAGH (Northern Ireland)
NYASA (Malawi, Tanzania, Mozambique)
ONEGA (Russia)
TAUPO (New Zealand)
URMIA (Iran)

6
ALBERT (Congo, Democratic Republic of, Uganda)
BAIKAL (Russia)
EDWARD (Congo, Democratic Republic of, Uganda)
GENEVA (Switzerland, France)
KARIBA (Zambia, Zimbabwe)
LADOGA (Russia)
LOMOND (Scotland)
LOP NOR (China)
MALAWI (Malawi, Tanzania, Mozambique)
MOBUTU (Congo, Democratic Republic of, Uganda)
NASSER (Egypt)
NATRON (Tanzania)
PEIPUS (Estonia, Russia)
POYANG (China)

6—continued
RUDOLF (Kenya, Ethiopia)
SAIMAA (Finland)
VÄNERN (Sweden)

7
BALATON (Hungary)
BELFAST (Northern Ireland)
DERWENT (England)
KATRINE (Scotland)
KOKO NOR (China)
LUCERNE (Switzerland)
NU JIANG (China, Burma)
ONTARIO (Canada, USA)
QINGHAI (China)
ST CLAIR (USA, Canada)
TORRENS (Australia)
TURKANA (Kenya, Ethiopia)

8
BALKHASH (Kazakhstan)
CHIEMSEE (Germany)
CONISTON (England)
DONGTING (China)
GRASMERE (England)
ISSYK KUL (Kyrgyzstan)
MAGGIORE (Italy, Switzerland)
MAZURIAN (Poland)
MENINDEE (Australia)
MICHIGAN (USA)
NEUSIEDL (Austria, Hungary)
SUPERIOR (USA, Canada)
TITICACA (Peru, Bolivia)
TONLE SAP (Cambodia)
TUNG-T'ING (China)

8—continued
VICTORIA (Uganda, Tanzania, Kenya)
WINNIPEG (Canada)

9
ATHABASCA (Canada)
BANGWEULU (Zambia)
CHAMPLAIN (USA)
CONSTANCE (Germany)
ENNERDALE (England)
GREAT BEAR (Canada)
GREAT SALT (USA)
MARACAIBO (Venezuela)
THIRLMERE (England)
TRASIMENO (Italy)
ULLSWATER (England)
WAST WATER (England)

10+
BUTTERMERE (England)
GREAT SLAVE (Canada)
IJSSELMEER (Netherlands)
KARA-BOGAZ-GOL (Turkmenistan)
OKEECHOBEE (USA)
STRANGFORD (Northern Ireland)
TANGANYIKA (Burundi, Congo, Democratic Republic of, Tanzania, Zambia)
VIERWALDSTÄTTERSEE (Switzerland)
WINDERMERE (England)

RIVERS

2&3
AIN (France)
ALN (England)
BUG (Ukraine, Poland, Germany)
CAM (England)
DEE (Scotland, Wales, England)
DON (Russia, Scotland, England, France, Australia)
EMS (Germany, Netherlands)
ESK (Australia)
EXE (England)
FAL (England)
FLY (Papua New Guinea)
HAN (China)
KWA (Congo, Democratic Republic of)
LEA (England)

2&3—continued
LEE (Republic of Ireland)
LOT (France)
OB (Russia)
PO (Italy)
RED (USA)
RUR (Germany)
RYE (England)
TAY (Scotland)
URE (England)
USK (Wales, England)
WEY (England)
WYE (Wales, England)
YEO (England)

4
ADDA (Italy)
ADUR (England)
AIRE (England, France)

4—continued
AMUR (Mongolia, Russia, China)
ARNO (Italy)
ARUN (Nepal)
AUBE (France)
AVON (England)
BANN (Northern Ireland)
BEAS (India)
BURE (England)
CHER (France)
COLN (England)
DART (England)
DOON (Scotland)
DOVE (England)
EBRO (Spain)
EDEN (England, Scotland)
ELBE (Germany, Czech Republic)
EMBA (Kazakhstan)

4—continued
ISIS (England)
JUBA (E. Africa)
KAMA (Russia)
KURA (Turkey, Georgia, Azerbaijan)
LAHN (Germany)
LECH (Germany, Austria)
LENA (Russia)
LUNE (England)
LÜNE (Germany)
MAAS (Netherlands)
MAIN (Germany, Northern Ireland)
MIÑO (Spain)
MOLE (England)
NILE (Sudan, Egypt)
ODER (Germany, Czech Republic, Poland)
OHIO (USA)

4—continued

OISE (France)
OUSE (England)
OXUS (Turkmenistan, Uzbekistan)
PEEL (Australia, USA)
RAVI (India, Pakistan)
REDE (England)
RUHR (Germany)
SAAR (Germany, France)
SPEY (Scotland)
TAFF (Wales)
TAJO (Spain)
TARN (France)
TAWE (Wales)
TAWI (India)
TEES (England)
TEJO (Brazil)
TEST (England)
TYNE (Scotland, England)
URAL (Russia, Kazakhstan)
VAAL (South Africa)
WEAR (England)
YARE (England)

5

ADIGE (Italy)
AISNE (France)
ALLAN (Scotland, Syria)
ALLER (Spain, Germany)
ANNAN (Scotland)
BENUE (Nigeria)
BRENT (England)
CAMEL (England)
CHARI (Cameroon, Chad)
CLYDE (Scotland, Canada)
COLNE (England)
CONGO (Congo, Democratic Republic of)
DNEPR (Russia, Belarus, Ukraine)
DOUBS (France, Switzerland)
DOURO (Spain, Portugal)
DOVEY (Wales)
DRAVA (Italy, Austria, Yugoslavia, Hungary)
DUERO (Spain)
DVINA (Russia)
FORTH (Scotland)
FOYLE (Northern Ireland)

5—continued

FROME (Australia)
INDUS (India, Pakistan, China)
JAMES (USA, Australia)
JUMNA (India)
JURUÁ (Brazil)
KAFUE (Zambia)
KASAI (Angola, Congo, Democratic Republic of)
KUBAN (Russia)
LAGAN (Northern Ireland)
LIPPE (Germany)
LOIRE (France)
MARNE (France)
MAROS (Indonesia)
MEUSE (France, Belgium)
MINHO (Spain, Portugal)
MUREŞ (Romania, Hungary)
NEGRO (Spain, Brazil, Argentina, Bolivia, Paraguay, Uruguay, Venezuela)
NEMAN (Belarus, Lithuania)
NIGER (Nigeria, Mali, Guinea)
OTTER (England)
PEACE (Canada, USA)
PEARL (USA, China)
PECOS (USA)
PIAVE (Italy)
PURUS (Brazil)
RANCE (France)
RHINE (Switzerland, Germany, Netherlands)
SAALE (Germany)
SAÔNE (France)
SEINE (France)
SLAVE (Canada)
SNAKE (USA)
SOMME (France)
STOUR (England)
SWALE (England)
TAGUS (Portugal, Spain)
TAMAR (England)
TIBER (Italy)
TRENT (England)
TWEED (England, Scotland)
VOLGA (Russia, USA)
VOLTA (Ghana)

5—continued

WESER (Germany)
XINGU (Brazil)
ZAÏRE (Congo, Democratic Republic of)

6

ALLIER (France)
AMAZON (Peru, Brazil)
ANGARA (Russia)
BÍO-BÍO (Chile)
CHENAB (Pakistan)
CLUTHA (New Zealand)
COOPER (Australia)
COQUET (England)
CROUCH (England)
DANUBE (Germany, Austria, Romania, Hungary, Slovakia, Bulgaria)
DNESTR (Ukraine, Moldova)
ESCAUT (Belgium, France)
FRASER (Canada)
GAMBIA (The Gambia, Senegal)
GANGES (India)
GLOMMA (Norway)
HUDSON (USA)
HUNTER (Australia)
IRTYSH (China, Kazakhstan, Russia)
ITCHEN (England)
JAPURÁ (Brazil)
JORDAN (Israel, Jordan)
KOLYMA (Russia)
LIFFEY (Republic of Ireland)
LODDON (Australia, England)
MAMORÉ (Brazil, Bolivia)
MEDINA (USA)
MEDWAY (England)
MEKONG (Laos, China)
MERSEY (England)
MONNOW (England, Wales)
MURRAY (Australia, Canada)
NECKAR (Germany)
NEISSE (Poland, Germany)
OGOOUÉ (Gabon)
ORANGE (South Africa)
ORWELL (England)

6—continued

PARANÁ (Brazil)
PLATTE (USA)
RIBBLE (England)
ST JOHN (Liberia, USA)
SALADO (Argentina, Cuba, Mexico)
SEVERN (England)
SUTLEJ (Pakistan, India, China)
THAMES (England)
TICINO (Italy, Switzerland)
TIGRIS (Iraq, Turkey)
TUGELA (South Africa)
USSURI (China, USSR)
VIENNE (France)
VLTAVA (Czech Republic)
WABASH (USA)
WEAVER (England)
YELLOW (China, USA, Papua New Guinea)

7

BERMEJO (Argentina)
CAUVERY (India)
DAMODAR (India)
DARLING (Australia)
DERWENT (England)
DURANCE (France)
GARONNE (France)
GIRONDE (France)
HELMAND (Afghanistan)
HOOGHLY (India)
HUANG HO (China)
LACHLAN (Australia)
LIMPOPO (South Africa, Zimbabwe, Mozambique)
LUALABA (Congo, Democratic Republic of)
MADEIRA (Brazil)
MARAÑÓN (Brazil, Peru)
MARITSA (Bulgaria)
MOSELLE (Germany)
ORONTES (Syria)
PECHORA (Russia)
POTOMAC (USA)
SALWEEN (Myanmar, China)
SCHELDT (Belgium)
SENEGAL (Senegal)
SHANNON (Republic of Ireland)

7–continued
SONGHUA (Vietnam, China)
SUNGARI (China)
SUWANNEE (USA)
URUGUAY (Uruguay, Brazil)
VISTULA (Poland)
WAIKATO (New Zealand)
XI JIANG (China)
YANGTZE (China)
YENISEI (Russia)
ZAMBEZI (Zambia, Angola, Zimbabwe, Mozambique)

8
AMU DARYA (Turkmenistan, Uzbekistan)
ARAGUAIA (Brazil)
ARKANSAS (USA)
CANADIAN (USA)
CHARENTE (France)
COLORADO (USA)
COLUMBIA (USA)

8–continued
DEMERARA (Guyana)
DORDOGNE (France)
GODAVARI (India)
MANAWATU (New Zealand)
MENDERES (Turkey)
MISSOURI (USA)
PARAGUAY (Paraguay)
PUTUMAYO (Ecuador)
RÍO BRAVO (Mexico)
SAGUENAY (Canada)
SYR DARYA (Uzbekistan, Kazakhstan)
TORRIDGE (England)
TUNGUSKA (Russia)
VOLTURNO (Italy)
WANSBECK (England)
WINDRUSH (England)

9
ATHABASCA (Canada)
CHURCHILL (Canada)

9–continued
ESSEQUIBO (Guyana)
EUPHRATES (Iraq)
GREAT OUSE (England)
HSI CHIANG (China)
IRRAWADDY (Burma)
MACKENZIE (Australia)
MAGDALENA (Colombia)
RIO GRANDE (Jamaica)
TENNESSEE (USA)

10
CHANG JIANG (China)
CHAO PHRAYA (Thailand)
COPPERMINE (Canada)
HAWKESBURY (Australia)
SHENANDOAH (USA)
ST LAWRENCE (USA)

11
ASSINIBOINE (Canada)
BRAHMAPUTRA (China, India)
MISSISSIPPI (USA)
SUSQUEHANNA (USA)
YELLOWSTONE (USA)

12
GUADALQUIVIR (Spain)
MURRUMBIDGEE (Australia)
RÍO DE LA PLATA (Argentina, Uruguay)
SASKATCHEWAN (Canada)

MOUNTAINS AND HILLS

3
ASO (MT) (Japan)
IDA (MT) (Turkey)

4
ALPS (France, Switzerland, Italy, Austria)
BLUE (MTS) (Australia)
COOK (MT) (New Zealand)
ETNA (MT) (Sicily)
HARZ (MTS) (Germany)
JAYA (MT) (Indonesia)
JURA (MTS) (France, Switzerland)
OSSA (MT) (Australia)
RIGI (Switzerland)
URAL (MTS) (Russia)

5
ALTAI (MTS) (Russia, China, Mongolia)
ANDES (South America)

5–continued
ATHOS (MT) (Greece)
ATLAS (MTS) (Morocco, Algeria)
BLACK (MTS) (Wales)
COAST (MTS) (Canada)
EIGER (Switzerland)
ELGON (MT) (Uganda, Kenya)
GHATS (India)
KAMET (MT) (India)
KENYA (MT) (Kenya)
LENIN (PEAK) (Russia)
LOGAN (MT) (Canada)
PELÉE (MT) (Martinique)
ROCKY (MTS) (USA, Canada)
SAYAN (MTS) (Russia)
SNOWY (MTS) (Australia)
TATRA (MTS) (Poland, Slovakia)

5–continued
WEALD (THE) (England)

6
ANTRIM (HILLS) (Northern Ireland)
ARARAT (MT) (Turkey)
BALKAN (MTS) (Bulgaria)
CARMEL (MT) (Israel)
EGMONT (MT) (New Zealand)
ELBERT (MT) (USA)
ELBRUS (MT) (Russia, Georgia)
ELBURZ (MTS) (Iran)
EREBUS (MT) (Antartica)
HERMON (MT) (Syria, Lebanon)
HOGGAR (MTS) (Algeria)
KUNLUN (MTS) (China)
LADAKH (RANGE) (India)
MATOPO (HILLS) (Zimbabwe)

6–continued
MENDIP (HILLS) (England)
MOURNE (MTS) (Northern Ireland)
OLIVES (MT OF) (Israel)
PAMIRS (Tajikistan, China, Afghanistan)
PINDUS (MTS) (Greece, Albania)
TAURUS (MTS) (Turkey)
VOSGES (France)
ZAGROS (MTS) (Iran)

7
AHAGGAR (MTS) (Algeria)
BERNINA (Switzerland)
BROCKEN (Germany)
CHEVIOT (HILLS) (United Kingdom)
CHIANTI (Italy)
EVEREST (MT) (Nepal, China)
OLYMPUS (MT) (Greece)

7—continued
PALOMAR (MT) (USA)
RAINIER (MT) (USA)
RORAIMA (MT)
(Brazil, Guyana,
Venezuela)
RUAPEHU (MT) (New
Zealand)
SKIDDAW (England)
SLEMISH (Northern
Ireland)
SNOWDON (Wales)
SPERRIN (MTS)
(Northern Ireland)
ST ELIAS (MTS)
(Alaska, Yukon)
TIBESTI (MTS) (Chad,
Libya)
WICKLOW (MTS)
(Republic of Ireland)

8
ARDENNES
(Luxembourg,
Belgium, France)
BEN NEVIS (Scotland)
CAMBRIAN (MTS)
(Wales)
CAUCASUS (MTS)
(Georgia, Azerbaijan,
Armenia)
CÉVENNES (France)
CHILTERN (HILLS)
(England)
COTOPAXI (Ecuador)
COTSWOLD (HILLS)
(England)
FLINDERS (RANGE)
(Australia)
FUJIYAMA (Japan)
HYMETTUS (MT)
(Greece)
JUNGFRAU
(Switzerland)
KAIKOURA
(RANGES) (New
Zealand)
MUSGRAVE
(RANGES)
(Australia)
PENNINES (England)
PYRENEES (France,
Spain)
STANOVOI (RANGE)
(Russia)

8—continued
TIAN SHAN
(Tajikistan, China,
Mongolia)
VESUVIUS (Italy)

9
ACONCAGUA (MT)
(Argentina)
ALLEGHENY (MTS)
(USA)
ANNAPURNA (MT)
(Nepal)
APENNINES (Italy)
CAIRNGORM (MTS)
(Scotland)
DOLOMITES (Italy)
DUNSINANE
(Scotland)
GRAMPIANS
(Scotland)
HAMERSLEY
(RANGE) (Australia)
HELVELLYN(England)
HIMALAYAS (S. Asia)
HINDU KUSH (Central
Asia)
HUASCARÁN (Peru)
KARAKORAM
(RANGE) (China,
Pakistan, India)
KOSCIUSKO (MT)
(Australia)
MONT BLANC
(France, Italy)
NANDA DEVI (MT)
(India)
PACARAIMA (MTS)
(Brazil, Venezuela,
Guyana)
PARNASSUS (MT)
(Greece)
RUWENZORI (MTS)
(Congo, Democratic
Republic of, Uganda)
TIRICH MIR (MT)
(Pakistan)
ZUGSPITZE
(Germany)

10
ADIRONDACK (MTS)
(USA)
CADER IDRIS (Wales)
CANTABRIAN (MTS)
(Spain)

10—continued
CARPATHIAN (MTS)
(Slovakia, Poland,
Romania, Hungary,
Ukraine, Moldova)
CHIMBORAZO (MT)
(India)
DHAULAGIRI (MT)
(Nepal)
ERZGEBIRGE (Czech
Republic, Germany)
KEBNEKAISE
(Sweden)
LAMMERMUIR
(HILLS) (Scotland)
MACDONNELL
(RANGES)
(Australia)
MAJUBA HILL (South
Africa)
MATTERHORN
(Switzerland, Italy)
MIDDLEBACK
(RANGE) (Australia)
MONTSERRAT
(Spain)
MOUNT LOFTY
(RANGES)
(Australia)

11
ANTI-LEBANON
(MTS) (Lebanon,
Syria)
APPALACHIAN (MTS)
(USA)
DRAKENSBERG
(MTS) (South Africa)
JOTUNHEIMEN
(Norway)
KILIMANJARO (MT)
(Tanzania)
MONADHLIATH (MTS)
(Scotland)
NANGA PARBAT (MT)
(Pakistan)
SCAFELL PIKE
(England)
SIERRA MADRE
(Mexico)

12
CITLALTÉPETL
(Mexico)
GODWIN AUSTEN
(MT) (Pakistan)

12—continued
GOLAN HEIGHTS
(Syria)
GRAN PARADISO
(Italy)
INGLEBOROUGH
(England)
KANCHENJUNGA
(MT) (Nepal)
PEAK DISTRICT
(England)
POPOCATÉPETL
(MT) (Mexico)
SIDING SPRING (MT)
(Australia)
SIERRA MORENA
(Spain)
SIERRA NEVADA
(Spain, USA)
SLIEVE DONARD
(Northern Ireland)
WARRUMBUNGLE
(RANGE) (Australia)

13
CARRANTUOHILL
(Republic of Ireland)
COMMUNISM PEAK
(Tajikistan)
GROSSGLOCKNER
(Austria)
KANGCHENJUNGA
(MT) (Nepal)
KOMMUNIZMA PIK
(Tajikistan)
OJOS DEL SALADO
(Argentina, Chile)
SIERRA MAESTRA
(Cuba)

14+
BERNESE
OBERLAND
(Switzerland)
FICHTELGEBIRGE
(Germany)
FINSTERAARHORN
(Switzerland)
MACGILLICUDDY'S
REEKS (Republic of
Ireland)
SHIRÉ HIGHLANDS
(Malawi)

VOLCANOES

3
ASO (Japan)
AWU (Indonesia)

4
ETNA (Sicily)
FOGO (Cape Verde
Islands)
GEDE (Indonesia)
KABA (Indonesia)
LAKI (Iceland)
NILA (Indonesia)
POAS (Costa Rica)
SIAU (Indonesia)
TAAL (Philippines)

5
AGUNG (Indonesia)
ASAMA (Japan)
ASKJA (Iceland)
DEMPO (Indonesia)
FUEGO (Guatemala)
HEKLA (Iceland)
KATLA (Iceland)
MANAM (Papua New
Guinea)
MAYON (Philippines)
NOYOE (Iceland)
OKMOK (USA)
PALOE (Indonesia)
PELÉE (Martinique)
SPURR (USA)

6
ALCEDO (Galapagos
Islands)
AMBRIM (Vanuatu)
BIG BEN (Heard
Island)
BULENG (Indonesia)
COLIMA (Mexico)
DUKONO (Indonesia)
IZALCO (El Salvador)
KATMAI (USA)
LASCAR (Chile)
LASSEN (USA)
LLAIMA (Chile)
LOPEVI (Vanuatu)
MARAPI (Indonesia)

6–continued
MARTIN (USA)
MEAKAN (Japan)
MERAPI (Indonesia)
MIHARA (Japan)
O'SHIMA (Japan)
OSORNO (Chile)
PACAYA
(Guatemala)
PAVLOF (USA)
PURACÉ (Colombia)
SANGAY (Ecuador)
SEMERU
(Indonesia)
SLAMAT (Indonesia)
TACANA
(Guatemala)
UNAUNA (Indonesia)

7
ATITLAN
(Guatemala)
BÁRCENA (Mexico)
BULUSAN
(Philippines)
DIDICAS (Philippines)
EL MISTI (Peru)
GALERAS (Colombia)
JORULLO (Mexico)
KILAUEA (USA)
OMETEPE
(Nicaragua)
PUYEHUE (Chile)
RUAPEHU (New
Zealand)
SABRINA (Azores)
SOPUTAN (Indonesia)
SURTSEY (Iceland)
TERNATE (Indonesia)
TJAREME (Indonesia)
TOKACHI (Japan)
TORBERT (USA)
TRIDENT (USA)
VULCANO (Italy)

8
BOGOSLOF (USA)

8–continued
CAMEROON
(Cameroon)
COTOPAXI (Ecuador)
DEMAVEND (Iran)
FONUALEI (Tonga
Islands)
FUJIYAMA (Japan)
HUALALAI (USA)
KERINTJI (Indonesia)
KRAKATAU
(Indonesia)
KRAKATOA
(Indonesia)
MAUNA LOA (USA)
NIUAFO'OU (Tonga)
RINDJANI (Indonesia)
SANGEANG
(Indonesia)
TARAWERA (New
Zealand)
VESUVIUS (Italy)
YAKEDAKE (Japan)

9
AMBUROMBU
(Indonesia)
BANDAI-SAN (Japan)
CLEVELAND (USA)
COSEGUINA
(Nicaragua)
COTACACHI
(Ecuador)
GAMKONORA
(Indonesia)
GRIMSVÖTN
(Iceland)
MOMOTOMBO
(Nicaragua)
MYOZIN-SYO (Japan)
NGAURUHOE (New
Zealand)
PARICUTIN (Mexico)
RININAHUE (Chile)
SANTORINI (Greece)
STROMBOLI (Italy)
TONGARIRO (New
Zealand)

10
ACATENANGO
(Guatemala)
CAPELINHOS
(Azores)
CERRO NEGRO
(Nicaragua)
GUALLATIRI (Chile)
HIBOK HIBOK
(Philippines)
LONG ISLAND (Papua
New Guinea)
MIYAKEJIMA (Japan)
NYAMIAGIRA (Congo,
Democratic Republic
of)
NYIRAGONGO
(Congo, Democratic
Republic of)
SANTA MARIA
(Guatemala)
SHISHALDIN (USA)
TUNGURAHUA
(Ecuador)
VILLARRICA (Chile)

11
GREAT SITKIN (USA)
KILIMANJARO
(Tanzania)
LA SOUFRIÈRE
(Saint Vincent and
the Grenadines)
TUPUNGATITO
(Chile)
WHITE ISLAND (New
Zealand)

12
HUAINAPUTINA
(Peru)
POPOCATÉPETL
(Mexico)

DESERTS

4
GILA
GOBI
THAR

5
NAMIB
NEFUD
NEGEV
OLMOS
ORDOS
SINAI
STURT

6
ARUNTA
GIBSON
MOJAVE

6–continued
NUBIAN
SAHARA
SYRIAN
UST'-URT

7
ALASHAN
ARABIAN
ATACAMA
KARA KUM
MORROPE
PAINTED
SECHURA
SIMPSON

8
COLORADO

8–continued
KALAHARI
KYZYL KUM
MUYUNKUM
VIZCAINO

9
BLACK ROCK
DASHT-I-LUT
DZUNGARIA

10
AUSTRALIAN
BET-PAK-DALA
GREAT SANDY
PATAGONIAN
RUB'AL KHALI

11
DASHT-I-KAVIR
DASHT-I-MARGO
DEATH VALLEY

13
GREAT SALT LAKE
GREAT VICTORIA

14
BOLSON DE MAPIMI

16
TURFAN
  DEPRESSION

NATIONAL PARKS

PARK	LOCATION	SPECIAL FEATURE
Abisko	Sweden	
Abruzzo	Italy	
Altos de Campana	Panama	
Amazônia	Brazil	
Angkor	Kampuchea	Khmer civilization remains
Arusha	Tanzania	
Atitlán	Guatemala	
Awāsh	Ethiopia	
Babiogórski	Poland	
Banff	Alberta, Canada	hot springs at Sulphur Mountain
Bayarischer Wald	Bavaria, West Germany	
Belovezhskaya	Belorussia	
Białowieski	Poland	
Cabo de Hornos	Chile	automatically operated lighthouse
Canaima	Venezuela	Salto Angel
Cañon del Rio Blanco	Mexico	
Canyonlands	Utah, United States	landforms carved in the red sandstone
Carlsbad Caverns	New Mexico	largest area of caverns in the world
Carnarvon	Queensland	
Chobe	Botswana	
Corbett	Uttar Pradesh, India	
Cradle Mountain–Lake Saint Clair	Tasmania, Australia	
Daisetsuzan	Japan	
Denali	Alaska, United States	Mt. McKinley
Djung-kulon	Indonesia	
Etosha	Namibia	
Everglades	Florida, United States	
Fiordland	New Zealand	
Franklin D. Roosevelt	Uruguay	
Fray Jorge	Chile	
Fuji-Hakone-Izu	Japan	

NATIONAL PARKS

PARK	LOCATION	SPECIAL FEATURE
Fundy	New Brunswick, Canada	
Galápagos	Ecuador	giant iguanas and giant tortoises
Gemsbok	Botswana	
Gir Lion	Gujarāt, India	
Glacier	Montana, United States	
Gorongosa	Mozambique	
Grand Canyon	Arizona, United States	
Gran Paradiso	Italy	
Great Smoky Mountains	North Carolina & Tennessee, United States	
Hawaii Volcanoes	Hawaii, United States	
Henri Pittier	Venezuela	
Hohe Tauern	Austria	Krimmler Waterfall
Hortobágyi	Hungary	
Huascarán	Peru	Nevado Huascarán
Iguaçu	Brazil	Iguaçu Falls
Iguazú	Argentina	Iguazú River cliffs; Iguazú Falls
Isle Royale	Michigan, United States	
Ixtacihuatl-Popocatépetl	Mexico	
Jasper	Alberta, Canada	Columbia Icefield
Kabalega	Uganda	Kabalega Falls
Kafue	Zambia	
Kaieteur	Guyana	Kaieteur Falls
Kalahari Gemsbok	Cape of Good Hope, South Africa	
Karatepe-Asiantaş	Turkey	Hittite, Roman, and Phoenician civilizations ruins
Katmai	Alaska, United States	
Kaziranga	Assam, India	
Khao Yai	Thailand	
Kilimanjaro	Tanzania	
Komoé	Ivory Coast	
Kosciusko	New South Wales, Australia	Mt. Kosciusko
Kruger	Transvaal, South Africa	
Lake District	England	Lake Windermere
Los Glaciares	Argentina	glacial landforms
Manovo-Gounda-Saint Floris	Central African Republic	
Manu	Peru	
Mayon Volcano	Phillippines	Mayon Volcano
Mesa Verde	Colorado, United States	remains of cliff dwellings of pre-Columbian Indians
Moçâmedes Reserva	Angola	
Mount Apo	Phillippines	
Mount Aspiring	New Zealand	Mt. Aspiring
Mount Carmel	Israel	
Mount Cook	New Zealand	Mt. Cook; Tasman Glacier
Nahuel Huapi	Argentina	Mt. Tronador
Nairobi	Kenya	
Namib Desert	Namibia	
Odzala	Congo	
Olympic	Washington, United States	
Olympus	Greece	
Pellas-Ounastunturi	Finland	
Pembrokeshire Coast	Wales	
Petrified Forest	Arizona, United States	forests of petrified trees
Pfälzerwald	Rheinland-Pfalz, West Germany	
Pico de Orizaba	Mexico	Citlaltépetl volcano

PARK	LOCATION	SPECIAL FEATURE
Plitvička, Jezera	Croatia	
Puracé	Columbia	
Pyrénées Occidentales	France	
Rapa Nui	Chile	sites of an ancient civilization
Redwood	California, United States	
Retezat	Romania	
Rocky Mountain	Colorado, United States	
Rondane	Norway	
Ruwenzori	Uganda	
Sarek	Sweden	
Schweizerische	Switzerland	
Serengeti	Tanzania	
Setto-Naikai	Japan	
Sierra Nevada de Mérida	Venezuela	
Skaftafell Thingvellir	Iceland	
Snowdonia	Wales	Snowdon Peak
Stirling Range	Western Australia, Australia	
Stolby Zapovednik	Russia	
Tatransky Národni	Slovakia	
Tatrzański	Poland	
Teberdinsky Zapovednik	Russia	
Tikal	Guatemala	ruins of Mayan city
Tortuguero	Costa Rica	green sea turtles
Toubkal	Morocco	
Triglavski Narodni	Slovenia	Kanjavec Peak; Savica Waterfalls
Tsavo	Kenya	
Uluru	Northern Territory, Australia	Mt. Olga; Ayers Rock
Valle de Ordesa	Spain	
Vanoise	France	
Veluwezoom, Het	Netherlands	
Victoria Falls	Zimbabwe & Zambia	Victoria Falls
Virunga	Zaire	
Volcanoes	Rwanda	
Wankie	Zimbabwe	
Waterton Lakes	Alberta, Canada	
Waza	Cameroon	
Wood Buffalo	Alberta & Northwest Territories, Canada	reserve for bison herds
W. Parc	Benin, Niger, & Burkina Faso	
Yellowstone	Wyoming, Montana, & Idaho, United States	Old Faithful
Yoho	British Columbia, Canada	Takakkaw Falls
Yorkshire Dales	England	
Yosemite	California, United States	Yosemite Falls
Zion	Utah, United States	

ANIMALS AND PLANTS

ANIMALS

7–continued
GRAMPUS
GUANACO
GYMNURE
HAMSTER
LEMMING
LEOPARD
LINSANG
MACAQUE
MAMMOTH
MANATEE
MARKHOR
MEERKAT
MOLE RAT
MOON RAT
MOUFLON
MUSKRAT
NARWHAL
NOCTULE
OPOSSUM
PACK RAT
PANTHER
PECCARY
POLECAT
PRIMATE
RACCOON
RED DEER
ROE DEER
RORQUAL
SEALION
SIAMANG
SOUSLIK
SUN BEAR
TAMARIN
TAMAROU
TARSIER
WALLABY
WARTHOG
WILDCAT
ZORILLA

8
AARDVARK
AARDWOLF
ANTEATER
ANTELOPE
AXIS DEER
BABIRUSA
BONTEBOK
BUSHBABY
BUSHBUCK
CACHALOT
CAPYBARA
CHIPMUNK
DORMOUSE
ELEPHANT
ENTELLUS
FRUIT BAT
HEDGEHOG
IRISH ELK
KANGAROO

8–continued
KINKAJOU
MANDRILL
MANGABEY
MARMOSET
MONGOOSE
MUSK DEER
MUSQUASH
PANGOLIN
PLATYPUS
PORPOISE
REEDBUCK
REINDEER
RUMINANT
SEA OTTER
SEI WHALE
SQUIRREL
STEINBOK
TALAPOIN
TAMANDUA
VISCACHA
WALLAROO
WATER RAT
WILD BOAR

9
ARCTIC FOX
ARMADILLO
BANDICOOT
BINTURONG
BLACK BEAR
BLACKBUCK
BLUE WHALE
BROWN BEAR
DEER MOUSE
DESERT RAT
DROMEDARY
FLYING FOX
GOLDEN CAT
GROUNDHOG
GUINEA PIG
HAMADRYAS
MONOTREME
MOUSE DEER
ORANG-UTAN
PACHYDERM
PALM CIVET
PAMPAS CAT
PHALANGER
POLAR BEAR
PORCUPINE
PRONGHORN
PROSIMIAN
SILVER FOX
SITATUNGA
SLOTH BEAR
SOLENODON
SPRINGBOK
THYLACINE
TREE SHREW
WATERBUCK

9–continued
WATER VOLE
WOLVERINE
WOODCHUCK

10
ANGWANTIBO
BARBARY APE
BOTTLENOSE
CACOMISTLE
CHEVROTAIN
CHIMPANZEE
CHINCHILLA
CHIROPTERA
FALLOW DEER
FIELDMOUSE
GOLDEN MOLE
HARTEBEEST
HONEY MOUSE
HOODED SEAL
JAGUARUNDI
KODIAK BEAR
MONA MONKEY
OTTER SHREW
PALLAS'S CAT
PILOT WHALE
PINE MARTEN
POUCHED RAT
PRAIRIE DOG
RACCOON DOG
RHINOCEROS
RIGHT WHALE
SPERM WHALE
SPRINGHAAS
TIMBER WOLF
VAMPIRE BAT
WATER SHREW
WHITE WHALE
WILDEBEEST

11
BARBASTELLE
BARKING DEER
DOUROUCOULI
FLYING LEMUR
GRASS MONKEY
GRIZZLY BEAR
HARBOUR SEAL
HONEY BADGER
KANGAROO RAT
KILLER WHALE
LEOPARD SEAL
PATAS MONKEY
PIPISTRELLE
PRAIRIE WOLF
RAT KANGAROO
RED SQUIRREL
SEROTINE BAT
SNOW LEOPARD

12
ELEPHANT SEAL

12–continued
HARVEST MOUSE
HIPPOPOTAMUS
HORSESHOE BAT
HOWLER MONKEY
JUMPING MOUSE
KLIPSPRINGER
MOUNTAIN LION
POCKET GOPHER
RHESUS MONKEY
ROAN ANTELOPE
SNOWSHOE HARE
SPIDER MONKEY
TREE KANGAROO
WATER BUFFALO
WOOLLY MONKEY

13
ANTHROPOID APE
CRABEATER SEAL
DORCAS GAZELLE
HUMPBACK WHALE
MARSUPIAL MOLE
ROYAL ANTELOPE
SABLE ANTELOPE
TASMANIAN WOLF

14
CAPUCHIN MONKEY
CLOUDED LEOPARD
FLYING SQUIRREL
GROUND SQUIRREL
MOUNTAIN BEAVER
NEW WORLD
  MONKEY
OLD WORLD
  MONKEY
PÈRE DAVID'S DEER
SPECTACLED BEAR
SQUIRREL MONKEY
TASMANIAN DEVIL

15+
CHINESE WATER
  DEER
DUCK-BILLED
  PLATYPUS
FLYING PHALANGER
PROBOSCIS
  MONKEY
PYGMY HIPPO-
  POTAMUS
SCALY-TAILED
  SQUIRREL
WHITE RHINO-
  CEROS
WOOLLY RHINO-
  CEROS
WOOLLY SPIDER
  MONKEY

ANIMALS AND THEIR GENDER

ANIMAL	MALE	FEMALE	ANIMAL	MALE	FEMALE
ANTELOPE	BUCK	DOE	HARE	BUCK	DOE
ASS	JACKASS	JENNYASS	HARTEBEAST	BULL	COW
BADGER	BOAR	SOW	HORSE	STALLION	MARE
BEAR	BOAR	SOW	IMPALA	RAM	EWE
BOBCAT	TOM	LIONESS	JACKRABBIT	BUCK	DOE
BUFFALO	BULL	COW	KANGAROO	BUCK	DOE
CAMEL	BULL	COW	LEOPARD	LEOPARD	LEOPARDESS
CARIBOU	STAG	DOE	LION	LION	LIONESS
CAT	TOM	QUEEN	MOOSE	BULL	COW
CATTLE	BULL	COW	OX	BULLOCK	COW
CHICKEN	COCK	HEN	PEACOCK	PEACOCK	PEAHEN
COUGAR	TOM	LIONESS	PHEASANT	COCK	HEN
COYOTE	DOG	BITCH	PIG	BOAR	SOW
DEER	STAG	DOE	RHINOCEROS	BULL	COW
DOG	DOG	BITCH	ROEDEER	ROEBUCK	DOEDEER
DONKEY	JACKASS	JENNYASS	SEAL	BULL	COW
DUCK	DRAKE	DUCK	SHEEP	RAM	EWE
ELAND	BULL	COW	SWAN	COB	PEN
ELEPHANT	BULL	COW	TIGER	TIGER	TIGRESS
FERRET	JACK	JILL	WALRUS	BULL	COW
FISH	COCK	HEN	WEASEL	BOAR	COW
FOX	FOX	VIXEN	WHALE	BULL	COW
GIRAFFE	BULL	COW	WOLF	DOG	BITCH
GOAT	BILLYGOAT	NANNYGOAT	ZEBRA	STALLION	MARE
GOOSE	GANDER	GOOSE			

ADJECTIVES

CREATURE	ADJECTIVE	CREATURE	ADJECTIVE
BEAR	URSINE	FROG	BATRACHIAN
BEE	APIAN	GOAT	CAPRINE; HIRCINE
BULL	TAURINE	GOOSE	ANSERINE
CAT	FELINE	HARE	LEPORINE
CHIPMUNK	SCIURINE	HORSE	EQUINE
CIVET	VIVERRINE	LION	LEONINE
COW	BOVINE	LIZARD	SAURIAN
CRAB	CRUSTACEAN or CRUSTACEOUS	LOBSTER	CRUSTACEAN or CRUSTACEOUS
DEER	CERVID or CERVINE	MONGOOSE	VIVERRINE
DOG	CANINE	MONKEY	SIMIAN
DOLPHIN	CETACEAN or CETACEOUS	MOUSE	MURINE
DONKEY	ASININE	PIG	PORCINE
EEL	ANGUILLIFORM	PORPOISE	CETACEAN or CETACEOUS
ELEPHANT	ELEPHANTINE	RAT	MURINE
FERRET	MUSTELINE	SEAL	OTARID; PHOCINE
FISH	PISCINE	SEA LION	OTARID
FOWL	GALLINACEOUS	SHEEP	OVINE
FOX	VULPINE		

CREATURE	ADJECTIVE	CREATURE	ADJECTIVE
SHRIMP	CRUSTACEAN or CRUSTACEOUS	TOAD	BATRACHIAN
SKUNK	MUSTELINE	TORTOISE	CHELONIAN
SNAKE	ANGUINE; COLUBRINE; OPHIDIAN; SERPENTINE	TURTLE	CHELONIAN
		VIPER	VIPERINE or VIPEROUS
SPIDER	ARACHNOID	WEASEL	MUSTELINE
SQUIRREL	SCIURINE	WHALE	CETACEAN or CETACEOUS
TERRAPIN	CHELONIAN	WOLF	LUPINE
		WORM	VERMIFORM

ANIMALS AND THEIR YOUNG

ANIMAL	YOUNG	ANIMAL	YOUNG
ANTELOPE	KID	HARE	LEVERET
BADGER	CUB	HARTEBEAST	CALF
BEAR	CUB	HAWK	CHICK
BEAVER	KITTEN	HORSE	FOAL
BOBCAT	KITTEN	JACKRABBIT	KITTEN
BUFFALO	CALF	KANGAROO	JOEY
CAMEL	CALF	LEOPARD	CUB
CARIBOU	FAWN	LION	CUB
CAT	KITTEN	MONKEY	INFANT
CATTLE	CALF	OX	STOT
CHICKEN	CHICK	PHEASANT	CHICK
COUGAR	KITTEN	PIG	PIGLET
COYOTE	PUPPY	RHINOCEROS	CALF
DEER	FAWN	ROEDEER	KID
DOG	PUPPY	SEAL	CALF
DUCK	DUCKLING	SHEEP	LAMB
ELAND	CALF	SKUNK	KITTEN
ELEPHANT	CALF	SWAN	CYGNET
ELK	CALF	TIGER	CUB
FISH	FRY	TOAD	TADPOLE
FROG	TADPOLE	WALRUS	CUB
FOX	CUB	WEASEL	KIT
GIRAFFE	CALF	WHALE	CALF
GOAT	KID	WOLF	CUB
GOOSE	GOSLING	ZEBRA	FOAL

COLLECTIVE TERMS

ANIMAL	COLLECTIVE TERM	ANIMAL	COLLECTIVE TERM
ANTELOPE	HERD	GOOSE	GAGGLE
APE	SHREWDNESS	HARE	HUSKE
ASS	DROVE	HARTEBEAST	HERD
BADGER	CETE	HAWK	CAST
BEAR	SLEUTH	HORSE	HERD
BEAVER	COLONY	IMPALA	COUPLE
BLOODHOUND	SUTE	JACKRABBIT	HUSK
BOAR	SOUNDER	KANGAROO	TROOP
BUFFALO	HERD	KINE	DROVE
CAMEL	TRAIN	LEOPARD	LEAP
CARIBOU	HERD	LION	PRIDE
CAT	CLUSTER	MOLE	LABOUR
CATTLE	HERD	MONKEY	TROOP
CHAMOIS	HERD	MOOSE	HERD
CHICKEN	FLOCK	MOUSE	NEST
CHOUGH	CHATTERING	OX	TEAM
COLT	RAG	PEACOCK	PRIDE
COOT	FLEET	PHEASANT	BROOD
COYOTE	PACK	PIG	TRIP
DEER	HERD	RHINOCEROS	CRASH
DOG	PACK	ROEDEER	BEVY
DONKEY	DROVE	ROOK	BUILDING
DUCK	PADDLING	SEAL	POD
ELAND	HERD	SHEEP	FLOCK
ELEPHANT	HERD	SNAKE	KNOT
ELK	GANG	TOAD	NEST
FERRET	BUSINESS	WALRUS	POD
FISH	SCHOOL	WEASEL	PACK
FOX	TROOP	WHALE	SCHOOL
GELDING	BRACE	WOLF	PACK
GIRAFFE	HERD	ZEBRA	HERD
GOAT	FLOCK		

BREEDS OF CATS

3
REX

4
MANX

5
CREAM
SMOKE
TABBY

6
BIRMAN
HAVANA

7
BURMESE

7–continued
PERSIAN
RED SELF
SIAMESE
SPOTTED
TURKISH

8
DEVON REX
RED TABBY

9
BLUE CREAM

10
ABYSSINIAN
BROWN TABBY

10–continued
CHINCHILLA
CORNISH REX

11
BLUE BURMESE
BRITISH BLUE
COLOURPOINT
RUSSIAN BLUE
SILVER TABBY

12
BROWN BURMESE

13
CHESTNUT BROWN
RED ABYSSINIAN

13—continued
TORTOISESHELL

14
LONG HAIRED BLUE
TORTIE AND WHITE

15
RED-POINT SIAMESE

18
BLUE-POINTED SIAMESE
SEAL-POINTED SIAMESE
TORTIE-POINT SIAMESE

19
LILAC-POINTED SIAMESE
TABBY-POINTED SIAMESE

20+
CHOCOLATE-POINTED
 SIAMESE

BREEDS OF DOGS

3
PUG

4
PULI

5
BOXER
CORGI
HUSKY
SPITZ

6
BEAGLE
BORZOI
BRIARD
COLLIE
KELPIE
POODLE
SALUKI
SETTER

7
BASENJI
BULLDOG
GRIFFON
HARRIER
LOWCHEN
LURCHER
MALTESE
MASTIFF
POINTER
SAMOYED
SHELTIE
SHIH TZU
SPANIEL
TERRIER
WHIPPET

8
ALSATIAN
CHOW CHOW
ELKHOUND
FOXHOUND
KEESHOND
PAPILLON
SHEEPDOG

9
CHIHUAHUA
DACHSHUND
DALMATIAN
DEERHOUND
GREAT DANE
GREYHOUND
LHASA APSO
PEKINGESE
RETRIEVER
SCHNAUZER
STAGHOUND
ST BERNARD

10
BLOODHOUND
FOX TERRIER
OTTERHOUND
POMERANIAN
ROTTWEILER
SCHIPPERKE
WEIMARANER
WEIMERANER
WELSH CORGI

11
AFGHAN HOUND
BASSET HOUND
BULL MASTIFF
BULL TERRIER
IBIZAN HOUND
IRISH SETTER
SKYE TERRIER

12
CAIRN TERRIER
FINNISH SPITZ
IRISH TERRIER
JAPANESE CHIN
NEWFOUNDLAND
PHARAOH HOUND
SILKY TERRIER
WELSH TERRIER

13
AFFENPINSCHER
BORDER TERRIER

13—continued
BOSTON TERRIER
COCKER SPANIEL
ENGLISH SETTER
HUNGARIAN PULI

14
GERMAN SHEPHERD
IRISH WOLFHOUND

15
AIREDALE TERRIER
ALASKAN MALAMUTE
GOLDEN RETRIEVER
HUNGARIAN VIZSLA
LAKELAND TERRIER
SCOTTISH TERRIER
SEALYHAM TERRIER
SPRINGER SPANIEL

16
KERRY BLUE TERRIER
PYRENEAN MOUNTAIN
SHETLAND SHEEPDOG
YORKSHIRE TERRIER

17
BEDLINGTON TERRIER
DOBERMANN PINSCHER
LABRADOR RETRIEVER

18
JACK RUSSELL TERRIER
KING CHARLES SPANIEL
LARGE MUNSTERLANDER
OLD ENGLISH SHEEPDOG
RHODESIAN RIDGEBACK

20+
DANDIE DINMONT TERRIER
STAFFORDSHIRE BULL
 TERRIER
WEST HIGHLAND WHITE
 TERRIER
WIREHAIRED POINTING
 GRIFFON

BREEDS OF HORSES AND PONIES

3
COB
DON

4
ARAB
BARB
FELL
POLO
RUSS

5
DALES
FJORD
HUCUL
KONIK
LOKAI
ORLOV
PINTO
SHIRE
TERSK
TIMOR
WELSH

6
ALBINO
BASUTO
EXMOOR
MERENS
MORGAN
TARPAN
VIATKA

7
CASPIAN
COMTOIS
CRIOLLO
FURIOSA
HACKNEY
JUTLAND
LLANERO
MUSTANG
NORIKER
QUARTER
SORRAIA

8
BUDEONNY

8–continued
CAMARGUE
DARTMOOR
GALICEÑO
HIGHLAND
HOLSTEIN
KABARDIN
KARABAIR
KARABAKH
LUSITANO
PALOMINO
SHETLAND

9
AKHAL-TEKE
ALTER-REAL
APPALOOSA
CONNEMARA
FALABELLA
HAFLINGER
KNABSTRUP
NEW FOREST
OLDENBURG
PERCHERON

9–continued
SCHLESWIG

10
ANDALUSIAN
AVELIGNESE
CLYDESDALE
GELDERLAND
HANOVERIAN
IRISH DRAFT
LIPIZZANER

11
NOVOKIRGHIZ

12
CLEVELAND BAY
SUFFOLK PUNCH
THOROUGHBRED

13
WELSH MOUNTAIN

16
TENNESSEE
  WALKING

BREEDS OF CATTLE

3
GIR

5
DEVON
KERRY
LUING

6
DEXTER
JERSEY
SUSSEX

7
BEEFALO
BRANGUS

8
AYRSHIRE
FRIESIAN
GALLOWAY
GUERNSEY
HEREFORD
HIGHLAND

8–continued
LIMOUSIN

9
CHAROLAIS
SHORTHORN
SIMMENTAL

10
BROWN SWISS
LINCOLN RED
MURRAY GREY

10–continued
WELSH BLACK

11
JAMAICA HOPE
MARCHIGIANA

13
ABERDEEN ANGUS
DROUGHTMASTER
TEXAS LONGHORN

BREEDS OF PIGS

5
DUROC
WELSH

8
PIETRAIN

8–continued
TAMWORTH

9
BERKSHIRE
HAMPSHIRE

10
LARGE WHITE

15
SWEDISH
  LANDRACE

17
BRITISH SADDLE-
  BACK
GLOUCESTER OLD
  SPOT

BREEDS OF SHEEP

4
LONK
MULE
SOAY

5
CARDY
CHIOS
JACOB
LLEYN
MORFE
TEXEL

6
AWASSI
MASHAM

6–continued
MERINO
ROMNEY

7
CHEVIOT
GOTLAND
KARAKUL
LACAUNE
SUFFOLK

8
HERDWICK
LONGMYND
POLWARTH
PORTLAND

8–continued
SHETLAND

9
HEBRIDEAN
LONGWOOLS
OLDENBERG
ROUGH FELL
SWALEDALE
TEESWATER

10
CORRIEDALE
DORSET HORN
EXMOOR HORN
POLL DORSET

11
MANX LOGHTAN
WENSLEYDALE

13
WELSH MOUNTAIN
WILTSHIRE HORN

15
FRIES MELKSCHAAP

17
SCOTTISH BLACK-
FACE

18
WHITEFACED
WOODLAND

BREEDS OF POULTRY

4
BUFF (goose)

5
MARAN (chicken)
PEARL (guinea fowl)
PEKIN (duck)
ROMAN (goose)
ROUEN (duck)
WHITE (guinea fowl)

6
ANCONA (chicken)
CAYUGA (duck)
EMBDEN (goose)
SILKIE (chicken)

7
AFRICAN (goose)
CHINESE (goose)
CRESTED (duck)
DORKING (chicken)
LEGHORN (chicken)

7–continued
MUSCOVY (duck)
PILGRIM (goose)

8
LAVENDER (guinea
fowl)
TOULOUSE (goose)

9
AYLESBURY (duck)
WELSUMMER
(chicken)

10
BARNVELDER
(chicken)
BELTSVILLE (turkey)
BOURBON RED
(turkey)
INDIAN GAME
(chicken)

10–continued
ROSS RANGER
(chicken)
SEBASTOPOL
(goose)

11
CUCKOO MARAN
(chicken)
LIGHT SUSSEX
(chicken)

12
BLACK NORFOLK
(turkey)
INDIAN RUNNER
(duck)
NARRAGANSETT
(turkey)
PLYMOUTH ROCK
(chicken)
WHITE HOLLAND
(turkey)

13
BUFF ORPINGTON
(duck)
KHAKI CAMPBELL
(duck)
MAMMOTH BRONZE
(turkey)
WHITE AUSTRIAN
(turkey)

14
BLACK EAST INDIE
(duck)
RHODE ISLAND RED
(chicken)
WELSH HARLEQUIN
(duck)
WHITE WYANDOTTE
(chicken)

15
CAMBRIDGE
BRONZE (turkey)

POINTS OF A HORSE

CANNON BONE
CHEEK
CHEST
CHESTNUT
CHIN GROOVE
COFFIN BONE
CORONET
CREST
CROUP
DOCK
ELBOW
ERGOT
FEATHERS
FETLOCK
FETLOCK JOINT

FLANK
FOREARM
FORELOCK
FROG
GASKIN
GULLET
HEEL
HIND QUARTERS
HOCK
HOOF
KNEE
LOIN
MANE
NAVICULAR BONE
PASTERN

PEDAL BONE
POINT OF HIP
POINT OF SHOULDER
POLL
RIBS
SHANK
SHEATH
SHOULDER
SPLINT BONE
STIFLE
TAIL
TENDON
WINDPIPE
WITHERS

BIRDS

3
AUK
EMU
JAY
MOA
OWL
TIT
TUI

4
CHAT
COLY
COOT
CROW
DODO
DOVE
DUCK
GULL
HAWK
HUIA
IBIS
KAGU
KITE
KIWI
KNOT
LARK
LORY
RAIL
RHEA
ROOK
RUFF
SHAG
SKUA
SMEW
SWAN

4—continued
TEAL
TERN
WREN

5
BOOBY
CRAKE
CRANE
DIVER
EAGLE
EGRET
EIDER
FINCH
GOOSE
GREBE
HERON
HOBBY
MACAW
MYNAH
NODDY
OUZEL
PIPIT
PRION
QUAIL
RAVEN
ROBIN
SCAUP
SERIN
SNIPE
STILT
STORK

6
AVOCET

6—continued
BARBET
BULBUL
CANARY
CHOUGH
CONDOR
CUCKOO
CURLEW
DARTER
DIPPER
DRONGO
DUNLIN
FALCON
FULMAR
GANNET
GODWIT
HOOPOE
JABIRU
JACANA
KAKAPO
LINNET
MAGPIE
MARTIN
MERLIN
MOTMOT
ORIOLE
OSPREY
PARROT
PEEWIT
PETREL
PIGEON
PLOVER
PUFFIN
QUELEA

6—continued
RATITE
ROLLER
SHRIKE
SISKIN
TAKAHE
THRUSH
TOUCAN
TROGON
TURACO
TURKEY
WHIDAH
WHYDAH
WIGEON

7
ANTBIRD
BABBLER
BARN OWL
BITTERN
BLUETIT
BUNTING
BUSTARD
BUZZARD
COAL TIT
COURSER
DUNNOCK
EMU WREN
FANTAIL
FINFOOT
FISH OWL
GADWALL
GOSHAWK
GRACKLE
HARRIER

7–continued

HAWK OWL
HOATZIN
JACAMAR
JACKDAW
KESTREL
LAPWING
MALLARD
MANAKIN
MARABOU
MINIVET
MOORHEN
OILBIRD
ORTOLAN
OSTRICH
PEACOCK
PEAFOWL
PELICAN
PENGUIN
PINTAIL
POCHARD
QUETZAL
REDPOLL
REDWING
ROSELLA
SEAGULL
SERIEMA
SKIMMER
SKYLARK
SPARROW
SUNBIRD
SWALLOW
TANAGER
TINAMOU
TOURACO
VULTURE
WAGTAIL
WARBLER
WAXBILL
WAXWING
WRYBILL
WRYNECK

8

ACCENTOR
AVADAVAT
BATELEUR
BEE-EATER
BLACKCAP
BLUEBIRD
BOATBILL
BOBOLINK
CARACARA
CARDINAL
COCKATOO
CURASSOW
DABCHICK
DOTTEREL
EAGLE OWL
FISH HAWK
FLAMINGO
GAMEBIRD

8–continued

GARGANEY
GREAT TIT
GROSBEAK
HAWFINCH
HORNBILL
LOVEBIRD
LYREBIRD
MANNIKIN
MEGAPODE
MUTE SWAN
NIGHTJAR
NUTHATCH
OVENBIRD
OXPECKER
PARAKEET
PHEASANT
PYGMY OWL
REDSHANK
REDSTART
REEDLING
RIFLEMAN
ROCK DOVE
SCOPS OWL
SCREAMER
SEA EAGLE
SHELDUCK
SHOEBILL
SNOWY OWL
SONGBIRD
STARLING
SWIFTLET
TAWNY OWL
TITMOUSE
TRAGOPAN
WHEATEAR
WHIMBREL
WHINCHAT
WHIPBIRD
WHITE-EYE
WILDFOWL
WOODCHAT
WOODCOCK

9

ALBATROSS
BALD EAGLE
BLACKBIRD
BLACK SWAN
BOWERBIRD
BRAMBLING
BROADBILL
BULLFINCH
CASSOWARY
CHAFFINCH
COCKATIEL
CORMORANT
CORNCRAKE
CROSSBILL
CURRAWONG
FIELDFARE
FIRECREST

9–continued

FRANCOLIN
FRIARBIRD
FROGMOUTH
GALLINULE
GOLDCREST
GOLDENEYE
GOLDFINCH
GUILLEMOT
GYRFALCON
HILL MYNAH
KITTIWAKE
LITTLE OWL
MERGANSER
MOUSEBIRD
PARTRIDGE
PHALAROPE
PTARMIGAN
RAZORBILL
RED GROUSE
RIFLEBIRD
RING OUZEL
SANDPIPER
SCRUB BIRD
SNAKEBIRD
SNOW GOOSE
SPOONBILL
STONECHAT
THICKHEAD
THORNBILL
TRUMPETER
TURNSTONE

10

ARCTIC TERN
BEARDED TIT
BRENT GOOSE
BUDGERIGAR
CHIFFCHAFF
CRESTED TIT
DEMOISELLE
DIVING DUCK
FLYCATCHER
GRASSFINCH
GREENFINCH
GREENSHANK
GUINEA FOWL
HAMMERHEAD
HARPY EAGLE
HONEYEATER
HONEY GUIDE
HOODED CROW
JUNGLE FOWL
KINGFISHER
KOOKABURRA
MALLEE FOWL
MUTTONBIRD
NIGHT HERON
NUTCRACKER
PRATINCOLE
SACRED IBIS
SADDLEBACK

10–continued

SAGE GROUSE
SANDERLING
SANDGROUSE
SCREECH OWL
SHEARWATER
SHEATHBILL
SONG THRUSH
SUN BITTERN
TAILORBIRD
TROPIC BIRD
TURTLE DOVE
WEAVERBIRD
WOODPECKER
WOOD PIGEON
ZEBRA FINCH

11

BLACK GROUSE
BRUSH TURKEY
BUTCHERBIRD
BUTTON QUAIL
CANADA GOOSE
CARRION CROW
DIAMONDBIRD
FRIGATE BIRD
GNATCATCHER
GOLDEN EAGLE
HERRING GULL
HUMMINGBIRD
LAMMERGEIER
LAUGHING OWL
MOCKINGBIRD
MUSCOVY DUCK
NIGHTINGALE
REED WARBLER
SNOW BUNTING
SPARROWHAWK
STONE CURLEW
STORM PETREL
TREECREEPER
WALLCREEPER
WEAVERFINCH
WHITETHROAT
WOODCREEPER
WREN BABBLER

12

BURROWING OWL
CAPERCAILLIE
CUCKOO-SHRIKE
DABBLING DUCK
FAIRY PENGUIN
FLOWERPECKER
GREYLAG GOOSE
HEDGE SPARROW
HONEYCREEPER
HOUSE SPARROW
LANNER FALCON
MANDARIN DUCK
MARSH HARRIER
MISTLE THRUSH
MOURNING DOVE

ADJECTIVES

12–continued
PERCHING DUCK
SHOVELER DUCK
STANDARDWING
UMBRELLA BIRD
WHIPPOORWILL
YELLOWHAMMER

13
ADJUTANT STORK
AMERICAN EAGLE
BARNACLE GOOSE
CROCODILE BIRD

13–continued
ELEPHANT BIRDS
FAIRY BLUEBIRD
HARLEQUIN DUCK
HAWAIIAN GOOSE
LONG-TAILED TIT
OYSTERCATCHER
PASSERINE BIRD
SECRETARY BIRD
WHISTLING DUCK
WHOOPING CRANE

14
BEARDED VULTURE
BIRD OF PARADISE
DARWIN'S FINCHES
EMPEROR PENGUIN
GOLDEN PHEASANT
GRIFFON VULTURE
OWLET FROG-
  MOUTH
PLAINS-WANDERER

15+
BALTIMORE ORIOLE

15+–continued
GREAT CRESTED
  GREBE
IVORY-BILLED
  WOODPECKER
LAUGHING JACKASS
PASSENGER
  PIGEON
PEREGRINE FALCON
PHILIPPINE EAGLE
TYRANT FLY-
  CATCHER

ADJECTIVES

BIRD	ADJECTIVE	BIRD	ADJECTIVE
BIRD	AVIAN	PARROT	PSITTACINE
CROW	CORVINE	SONGBIRD	OSCINE
DOVE	COLUMBINE	SPARROW	PASSERINE
EAGLE	AQUILINE	SWALLOW	HIRUNDINE
FOWL	GALLINACEOUS	THRUSH	TURDINE

FISH

3
COD
DAB
EEL
GAR
IDE
RAY

4
BASS
CARP
CHAR
CHUB
DACE
DORY
FISH
GOBY
HAKE
LING
OPAH
ORFE
PIKE
RUDD
SHAD
SOLE

4–continued
TOPE
TUNA

5
BLEAK
BREAM
BRILL
DANIO
GRUNT
GUPPY
LOACH
MOLLY
PERCH
PORGY
ROACH
SAURY
SHARK
SKATE
SMELT
SPRAT
TENCH
TETRA
TROUT
TUNNY

6
BARBEL
BELUGA
BLENNY
BONITO
BOWFIN
BURBOT
GUNNEL
KIPPER
MARLIN
MINNOW
MULLET
PLAICE
PUFFER
REMORA
SAITHE
SALMON
TARPON
TURBOT
WEEVER
WRASSE

7
ALEWIFE
ANCHOVY

7–continued
BATFISH
CATFISH
CICHLID
CROAKER
DOGFISH
EELPOUT
GARFISH
GARPIKE
GOURAMI
GROUPER
GUDGEON
GURNARD
HADDOCK
HAGFISH
HALIBUT
HERRING
HOGFISH
ICEFISH
LAMPREY
MUDFISH
OARFISH
PIRANHA
POLLACK

7–continued
POMPANO
RATFISH
SARDINE
SAWFISH
SCULPIN
SEA BASS
SNAPPER
SUNFISH
TELEOST
TORPEDO
WHITING

8
ALBACORE
BLUEFISH
BRISLING
BROTULID
BULLHEAD
CAVE FISH
CHARACIN
CHIMAERA
DEVIL RAY
DRAGONET
DRUMFISH
FILEFISH
FLATFISH
FLATHEAD
FLOUNDER
FROGFISH
GOLDFISH
GRAYLING
JOHN DORY
LUNGFISH
MACKEREL
MANTA RAY
MONKFISH

8–continued
MOONFISH
MORAY EEL
PILCHARD
PIPEFISH
SAILFISH
SEA BREAM
SEA HORSE
SEA PERCH
SEA ROBIN
SKIPJACK
STINGRAY
STURGEON
SWAMP EEL
TOADFISH
WOLF FISH

9
ANGELFISH
BARRACUDA
BLUE SHARK
CLINGFISH
CONGER EEL
GLASSFISH
GLOBEFISH
GOOSEFISH
GRENADIER
KILLIFISH
LATIMERIA
LEMON SOLE
MURRAY COD
PEARLFISH
PIKEPERCH
PILOT FISH
PLACODERM
PORBEAGLE
RED MULLET

9–continued
RED SALMON
STARGAZER
STONE BASS
STONEFISH
SWORDFISH
SWORDTAIL
THREADFIN
TIGERFISH
TOP MINNOW
TRUNKFISH
WHITEBAIT
WHITEFISH
WRECKFISH
ZEBRA FISH

10
ANGLERFISH
ARCHER FISH
BOMBAY DUCK
COELACANTH
CORNETFISH
CYCLOSTOME
DAMSELFISH
DRAGONFISH
FLYING FISH
GHOST SHARK
GUITAR FISH
LUMPSUCKER
MIDSHIPMAN
MUDSKIPPER
NEEDLEFISH
NURSE SHARK
PADDLEFISH
PARROT FISH
PINK SALMON
PLACODERMI

10–continued
RIBBONFISH
SHIELD FERN
SILVERSIDE
TIGER SHARK
WHALE SHARK
WHITE SHARK

11
ELECTRIC EEL
ELECTRIC RAY
GOBLIN SHARK
HATCHETFISH
LANTERN FISH
MOORISH IDOL
STICKLEBACK
SURGEONFISH
TRIGGERFISH

12+
BASKING SHARK
CLIMBING PERCH
FIGHTING FISH
FOUR-EYED FISH
GREENLAND SHARK
HAMMERHEAD
  SHARK
LABYRINTH FISH
MACKEREL SHARK
MILLER'S THUMB
MOUTHBROODER
PORCUPINE FISH
REQUIEM SHARK
SCORPION FISH
SOCKEYE SALMON
THRESHER SHARK
YELLOWFIN TUNA

SEASHELLS

3
SUN
4
HARP
5
TULIP
6
NUTMEG
7
JUNONIA
SUNDIAL
8
DYE MUREX
LION'S PAW

8–continued
NOBLE PEN
PHEASANT
TURK'S CUP
9
ANGEL WING
BAT VOLUTE
BURSA FROG
GIANT CLAM
PINK CONCH
ROTA MUREX
SPINY VASE
TELESCOPE
TENT OLIVE
WEDGE CLAM

10
BLUE MUSSEL
CAMEO HELMT
COAT-OF-MAIL
CROWN CONCH
DELPHINULA
DRUPE SNAIL
EYED COWRIE
PAPERY RAPA
QUAHOG CLAM
SCALED WORM
WINGED FROG
11
BEAR PAW CLAM
CLIONE SNAIL
FRONS OYSTER

11–continued
GREEN TURBAN
HEART COCKLE
MUSIC VOLUTE
ONYX SLIPPER
OSTRICH FOOT
PAPER BUBBLE
PEARL OYSTER
SACRED CHANK
TEXTILE CONE
TIGER COWRIE
12
AMORIA VOLUTE
ATLANTIC CONE
FLORIDA MITER
GAUDY ASAPHIS

12–continued
GOLDEN COWRIE
GOLDEN TELLIN
LIMA FILE CLAM
MONEY COWRIES
PACIFIC AUGER
PARTRIDGE TUN
PELICAN'S FOOT
SCOTCH BONNET
SPIKED LIMPET
SPINDLE TIBIA

13
ANGULAR VOLUTE
BABLYON TURRID
BLEEDING TOOTH
CARDINAL MITER
COMMERCIAL TOP
COSTATE COCKLE
FIGHTING CONCH
GEOGRAPHY CONE
JACKKNIFE CLAM
JAPANESE CONES
PAPER NAUTILUS
PRICKLY HELMET
RIDGED ABALONE
SPIRAL BABYLON
SUNRISE TELLIN
TURKEY WING ARK
VENUS COMB CLAM

14
CHANNELED WHELK
DISTAFF SPINDLE
ELEGANT FIMBRIA
EPISCOPAL MITER
IMPERIAL VOLUTE

14–continued
INDONESIAN CLAM
LEUCODON COWRIE
LEWIS' MOON SNAIL
LIGHTNING WHELK
PANAMANIAN CONE
PHILIPPINE CONE
POLYNESIAN CONE
TAPESTRY TURBAN
TRITON'S TRUMPET
VENUS COMB
  MUREX

15
BITTERSWEET CLAM
BULL-MOUTH
  HELMET
JAPANESE CARRIER
NEW ENGLAND
  WHELK
PANAMANIAN
  AUGER
PILGRIM'S SCALLOP
SUNBURST
  CARRIER
TURRITELLA SNAIL
WATERING POT
  CLAM
WEST INDIAN
  CHANK
WEST AFRICAN
  CONE

16
ASIAN MOON
  SCALLOP

16–continued
ATLANTIC SURF
  CLAM
DONKEY EAR
  ABALONE
EDIBLE BAY
  SCALLOP
FRILLED
  DOGWINKLE
GLORY-OF-INDIA
  CONE
ORANGE-MOUTH
  OLIVE
PAGODA
  PERIWINKLE
PERPLICATE
  VOLUTE
PINK-MOUTHED
  MUREX
ROOSTERTAIL
  CONCH
WEDDING CAKE
  VENUS

17
AUSTRALIAN
  TRUMPET
CHAMBERED
  NAUTILUS
FLORIDA HORSE
  CONCH
PACIFIC WING
  OYSTER
SANTA CRUZ
  LATIAXIS
VIOLET SPIDER
  CONCH

18
ATLANTIC DEER
  COWRIE
GIANT KNOBBED
  CERITH
GLORY-OF-THE-
  SEAS CONE
GREAT KEYHOLE
  LIMPET
PACIFIC GRINNING
  TUN
PRECIOUS WENTLE-
  TRAP
WHITE-SPOTTED
  MARGIN

19
TANKERVILLE'S
  ANCILLA

20+
ARTHRITIC SPIDER
  CONCH
ATLANTIC THORNY
  OYSTER
COLOURFUL
  ATLANTIC MOON
ELEPHANT'S SNOUT
  VOLUTE
IMBRICATE CUP-
  AND-SAUCER
MIRACULOUS
  THATCHERIA

REPTILES AND AMPHIBIANS

3
ASP
BOA
OLM

4
FROG
NEWT
TOAD

5
ADDER
AGAMA
COBRA
GECKO
KRAIT
MAMBA

5–continued
SIREN
SKINK
SNAKE
TOKAY
VIPER

6
CAYMAN
GAVIAL
IGUANA
LIZARD
MOLOCH
MUGGER
PYTHON
TAIPAN
TURTLE

6–continued
ZALTYS

7
AXOLOTL
GHARIAL
REPTILE
TUATARA

8
ANACONDA
BASILISK
BULLFROG
CONGO EEL
MATAMATA
MOCCASIN
MUDPUPPY

8–continued
PIT VIPER
RINGHALS
SEA SNAKE
SLOWWORM
TERRAPIN
TORTOISE
TREE FROG

9
ALLIGATOR
BLINDWORM
BOOMSLANG
BOX TURTLE
CAECILIAN
CHAMELEON
CROCODILE

9–continued
HAIRY FROG
PUFF ADDER
TREE SNAKE
VINE SNAKE
WART SNAKE
WHIP SNAKE

10
BLACK SNAKE
BUSHMASTER
CHUCKWALLA
CLAWED FROG
COPPERHEAD
CORAL SNAKE
FER-DE-LANCE
GLASS SNAKE

10–continued
GRASS SNAKE
HELLBENDER
HORNED TOAD
NATTERJACK
POND TURTLE
SALAMANDER
SAND LIZARD
SIDEWINDER
WATER SNAKE
WORM LIZARD

11
AMPHISBAENA
CONSTRICTOR
COTTONMOUTH
DIAMONDBACK

11–continued
FLYING SNAKE
GABOON VIPER
GILA MONSTER
GOLIATH FROG
GREEN TURTLE
HORNED VIPER
MIDWIFE TOAD
RATTLESNAKE
SMOOTH SNAKE

12
FLYING LIZARD
HORNED LIZARD
KOMODO DRAGON

13
BEARDED LIZARD

FRILLED LIZARD
GIANT TORTOISE
MANGROVE SNAKE
MONITOR LIZARD
RUSSELL'S VIPER
SPADEFOOT TOAD
WATER MOCCASIN

14+
FIRE SALAMANDER
HAWKSBILL TURTLE
LEATHERBACK
  TURTLE
SNAKE-NECKED
  TURTLE
SOFT-SHELLED
  TURTLE

INSECTS

3
ANT
BEE
BUG
FLY

4
FLEA
GNAT
WASP

5
APHID
DRONE
LOUSE
MIDGE

6
BEDBUG
BEETLE
BOT FLY
CAPSID
CHAFER
CHIGOE
CICADA
EARWIG
GAD FLY
HORNET
LOCUST
LOOPER
MAGGOT
MANTIS
MAYFLY
SAWFLY
THRIPS
WEEVIL

7
ANTLION
ARMY ANT
BLOWFLY
CRICKET
CUTWORM
DIPTERA
FIRE ANT
FIREFLY
KATYDID
PROTURA
SANDFLY
STYLOPS
TERMITE

8
ALDERFLY
ARMY WORM
BLACKFLY
BOOKWORM
CRANEFLY
FIREBRAT
FRUIT FLY
GALL WASP
GLOWWORM
GREENFLY
HONEY ANT
HONEYBEE
HORNTAIL
HORSE FLY
HOUSEFLY
HOVERFLY
LACEWING
LADYBIRD
MASON BEE
MEALWORM
MEALYBUG

8–continued
MOSQUITO
PHASMIDA
PLANT BUG
SHEEP KED
SILKWORM
SNAKEFLY
STINK BUG
STONEFLY
WATER BUG
WHITE FLY
WIREWORM
WOODWASP
WOODWORM

9
AMAZON ANT
ANOPHELES
BLOODWORM
BOOKLOUSE
BUMBLEBEE
CADDIS FLY
CHINCH BUG
COCKROACH
CORN BORER
DAMSELFLY
DOBSONFLY
DOR BEETLE
DRAGONFLY
DRIVER ANT
GALL MIDGE
GROUND BUG
ICHNEUMON
LAC INSECT
OIL BEETLE
ROBBER FLY
SCREWWORM

9–continued
SHIELD BUG
TSETSE FLY
WARBLE FLY
WHIRLIGIG

10
BARK BEETLE
BLUEBOTTLE
BOLL WEEVIL
COCKCHAFER
COLEOPTERA
DIGGER WASP
DROSOPHILA
DUNG BEETLE
FROGHOPPER
JUNE BEETLE
LEAF BEETLE
LEAF HOPPER
LEAF INSECT
PHYLLOXERA
POND SKATER
POTTER WASP
ROVE BEETLE
SILVERFISH
SPANISH FLY
SPIDER WASP
SPITTLEBUG
SPRINGTAIL
STAG BEETLE
TREEHOPPER
WEBSPINNER
WOOLLY BEAR

11
ASSASSIN BUG
BACKSWIMMER

11–continued
BLACK BEETLE
BRISTLETAIL
BUFFALO GNAT
BUSH CRICKET
CANTHARIDIN
CATERPILLAR
CLICK BEETLE
GRASSHOPPER
MOLE CRICKET
PLANT HOPPER
SCALE INSECT
SCORPION FLY
STICK INSECT
TIGER BEETLE

11–continued
WATER BEETLE

12
CACTOBLASTIS
CARPENTER BEE
CARPET BEETLE
DIVING BEETLE
GROUND BEETLE
HERCULES MOTH
SCARAB BEETLE
SEXTON BEETLE
WATER BOATMAN
WATER STRIDER

13
BLISTER BEETLE
BURYING BEETLE
COTTON STAINER
DADDY LONGLEGS
ELM BARK BEETLE
GIANT WATER BUG
GOLIATH BEETLE
LEAFCUTTER ANT
LEAFCUTTER BEE
SOLDIER BEETLE
WATER SCORPION

14+
AMBROSIA BEETLE

14+–continued
BOMBARDIER
  BEETLE
CABBAGE ROOT FLY
COLORADO BEETLE
CUCKOO-SPIT
  INSECT
DARKLING BEETLE
DEATHWATCH
  BEETLE
DEVIL'S COACH
  HORSE
HERCULES BEETLE
SLAVE-MAKING ANT
TORTOISE BEETLE

BUTTERFLIES

3&4
OWL
BLUE
LEAF
MONK

5
ARGUS
BROWN
DRYAD
FRIAR
HEATH
JOKER
NYMPH
SATYR
SNOUT
WHITE
ZEBRA

6
ACRAEA
APOLLO
COPPER
DIADEM
GLIDER
HERMIT
MORPHO

7
ADMIRAL
FESTOON

7–continued
LEOPARD
MONARCH
RINGLET
SKIPPER
SULPHUR

8
BIRDWING
BLACK EYE
BLACK-TIP
CARDINAL
CHARAXES
CYMOTHOE
GRAYLING
MILKWEED

9
ATLAS BLUE
BATH WHITE
BRIMSTONE
CLEOPATRA
COMMODORE
GOLDEN TIP
HACKBERRY
METALMARK
ORANGE TIP
SWORDTAIL
WALL BROWN
WOOD WHITE

10
ADONIS BLUE
ARCTIC BLUE
ARRAN BROWN
BLACK SATYR
BUSH BEAUTY
CRIMSON TIP
FRITILLARY
GATEKEEPER
GRASS JEWEL
HAIRSTREAK
LARGE WHITE
PLAIN TIGER
RED ADMIRAL
SILVER-LINE
SMALL WHITE

11
AMANDA'S BLUE
FOREST QUEEN
GRASS YELLOW
MEADOW BROWN
PAINTED LADY
PARNASSIANS
SWALLOWTAIL

12
DOTTED BORDER
MAP BUTTERFLY
MARBLED WHITE

12–continued
SPECKLED WOOD
WHITE ADMIRAL

13
CLOUDED YELLOW
CHALK-HILL BLUE
PEARL CRESCENT
PURPLE EMPEROR
TORTOISESHELL
WOODLAND BROWN

14
AFRICAN MIGRANT
COMMA BUTTERFLY
LEMON TRAVELLER
MOUNTAIN BEAUTY
PAINTED EMPRESS

15+
CAMBERWELL
  BEAUTY
GREAT SOOTY
  SATYR
MOTHER-OF-PEARL
  BLUE
NETTLE-TREE
  BUTTERFLY
PEACOCK
  BUTTERFLY
TWO-TAILED PASHA

MOTHS

2&3
IO
OWL

4
GOAT
HAWK
PUSS

5
ATLAS
EGGAR
FAIRY
GHOST
GYPSY
OWLET
REGAL

5—continued
SWIFT
TIGER
YUCCA

6
BURNET
CALICO
ERMINE
LAPPET

7
BAGWORM
CLOTHES
EMPEROR
FLANNEL
PYRALID

7—continued
TUSSOCK
URANIAS

8
CINNABAR
FORESTER
SILKWORM

9
AILANTHUS
BRAHMAEID
CARPENTER
CLEARWING
GEOMETRID
SALT MARSH
SATURNIID
UNDERWING

10
BLACK WITCH
LEAF ROLLER

11
HUMMINGBIRD
OLETHREUTID
PYROMORPHID

13
BLINDED SPHINX
GIANT SILKWORM

14
DEATH'S HEAD
  HAWK
PANDORA'S SPHINX

PLANTS AND FLOWERS

3
ABE
HOP
IVY
RYE

4
DOCK
FERN
FLAG (*Iris*)
FLAX
HEMP
IRIS (flag, sweet flag,
  gladdon)
JUTE
LILY
PINK (carnation)
RAPE
REED
RICE
ROSE
RUSH
TARE
UPAS
WOAD

5
AGAVE
ASTER (Michaelmas
  daisy)
AVENS
BRIAR
CANNA

5—continued
CYCAD
DAISY
HENNA
JALAP
KUDZU
LOTUS
LUPIN
OXLIP (*Primula*)
PANSY (*Viola*)
PEONY
PHLOX
POPPY
SEDGE
SENNA
SISAL
TULIP
VIOLA (pansy, violet)

6
ALLIUM
ALSIKE (clover)
BALSAM
BLUETS
BRYONY
CACTUS
CLOVER (trefoil)
COLEUS
COTTON
COWPEA
CROCUS
DAHLIA

6—continued
DARNEL
FESCUE
HYSSOP
MADDER
MEDICK
MILLET
NETTLE (*Urtica*)
ORCHID
PETREA
PEYOTE (cactus)
RATTAN
SALVIA
SPURGE
SQUILL (*Scilla*)
SUNDEW
TEASEL
THRIFT
TWITCH (couch
  grass)
VIOLET (*Viola*)
YARROW
ZINNIA

7
ACONITE
  (monkshood)
ALFALFA
ALKANET
ANEMONE
ASTILBE
BEGONIA

7—continued
BISTORT (snakeroot)
BRACKEN (fern)
BUGLOSS
BULRUSH (reed
  mace)
BURDOCK
CAMPION
CATMINT
CLARKIA
COWSLIP (*Primula*)
DAY LILY
DOGBANE
DOG ROSE
FIGWORT
FREESIA
FROG-BIT
GENTIAN
GLADDON (*Iris*)
GUARANA
HEMLOCK
HENBANE
HONESTY (*Lunaria*)
JONQUIL (*Narcissus*)
KINGCUP (marsh
  marigold)
LOBELIA
MILFOIL (yarrow)
MULLEIN (Aaron's
  rod)
OPUNTIA (prickly
  pear)

7–continued
PAPYRUS
PETUNIA
PIGWEED
PRIMULA (cowslip, primrose)
RAGWORT
ROSELLE
SAGUARO
SANICLE
SPURREY
THISTLE
TIMOTHY
TOBACCO
TREFOIL (clover)
VERBENA (vervain)
VERVAIN (*Verbena*)

8
ACANTHUS
AGRIMONY
ARUM LILY (cuckoo-pint, lords-and-ladies)
ASPHODEL
AURICULA
BEDSTRAW
BERGENIA
BINDWEED (*Convolvulus*)
BLUEBELL
CATBRIER
CAT'S TAIL (reed-mace)
CHARLOCK
CLEAVERS (goose-grass)
CLEMATIS (old man's beard, traveller's joy)
CROWFOOT
CYLCAMEN
DAFFODIL
DIANTHUS
EELGRASS
EUCHARIS (amazon lily)
FLEABANE
FLEAWORT
FOXGLOVE (*Digitalis*)
FUMITORY
GERANIUM (*Pelargonium*)
GLOXINIA
GOUTWEED (ground elder)
HAREBELL
HAWKWEED
HENEQUEN
HIBISCUS (rose of China, rose of Sharon)
HORNWORT
HYACINTH

8–continued
ICE PLANT
KNAPWEED
LADY FERN
LARKSPUR
LUNGWORT
MARIGOLD
MILKWEED
MILKWORT
MOSS PINK (*Phlox*)
PLANTAIN
PLUMBAGO
POLYPODY
PRIMROSE (*Primula*)
REEDMACE (bulrush, cat's-tail)
ROCK ROSE
SAINFOIN
SALTWORT
SAMPHIRE
SCABIOUS
SEED FERN
SELF HEAL
SHAMROCK (clover, medick, wood sorrel)
SNOWDROP
SOAPWORT
SWEET PEA
TOAD LILY (fritillary)
TUBEROSE
VALERIAN
VERONICA (speedwell)
WAXPLANT
WOODBINE (virginia creeper)
WOODRUSH
WORMWOOD

9
AARON'S ROD (mullein)
AMARYLLIS (belladonna lily)
ANTHURIUM
AQUILEGIA (columbine)
ARROWROOT
BLUEGRASS
BROOMRAPE
BRYOPHYTE
BUCKWHEAT
BUTTERCUP
CAMPANULA (Canterbury bell)
CANDYTUFT
CARNATION (pink)
CELANDINE
CHICKWEED
CINERARIA
COCKLEBUR

9–continued
COCKSFOOT (orchard grass)
COLTSFOOT
COLUMBINE (*Aquilegia*)
CORDGRASS
CORN POPPY
CORYDALIS
CYMBIDIUM (orchid)
DANDELION
DEVIL'S FIG (prickly poppy)
DOG VIOLET
EDELWEISS
EGLANTINE (sweet briar)
EYEBRIGHT
GERMANDER
GLADIOLUS
GLASSWORT
GOLDENROD (*Solidago*)
GOOSEFOOT (pigweed)
GRASS TREE
GROUND IVY
GROUNDSEL
HELLEBORE (Christmas rose)
HERB PARIS
HOLLYHOCK
HORSETAIL
HOUSELEEK
IMPATIENS (touch-me-not, busy Lizzie)
JABORANDI
MARE'S TAIL
MONEYWORT (creeping jenny)
MONKSHOOD (aconite)
MOSCHATEL (town-hall clock)
NARCISSUS (jonquil)
PATCHOULI
PIMPERNEL
PYRETHRUM
QUILLWORT
ROYAL FERN
SAFFLOWER
SAXIFRAGE (London pride)
SNAKEROOT (bistort)
SPEEDWELL (*Veronica*)
SPIKENARD
STONECROP
SUNFLOWER
SWEET FLAG (*Iris*)
TORMENTIL
WATER LILY

9–continued
WITCHWEED
WOUNDWORT

10
AGAPANTHUS
AMARANTHUS (love-lies-bleeding)
AMAZON LILY
ASPIDISTRA
BELLADONNA (deadly nightshade)
BUSY LIZZIE
BUTTERWORT
CHARMOMILE
CINQUEFOIL
CITRONELLA
CLIFFBREAK (fern)
CORNCOCKLE
CORNFLOWER
COUCH GRASS (twitch, quack grass)
COW PARSLEY
CRANESBILL
CUCKOOPINT (arum lily)
DAMASK ROSE
DRAGONROOT
DYER'S BROOM
FRITILLARY (snake's head, leopard lily, toad lily)
GAILLARDIA (blanket flowers)
GOATSBEARD
GOOSEGRASS (cleavers)
GRANADILLA (passionflower)
GREENBRIER (catbrier)
HELIOTROPE
HERB ROBERT
JIMSONWEED (thorn apple)
LADY'S SMOCK
MARGUERITE (oxeye daisy)
MIGNONETTE
MONTBRETIA
MOONFLOWER (morning glory)
NASTURTIUM
OPIUM POPPY
OXEYE DAISY (marguerite)
PENNYROYAL
PERIWINKLE
POLYANTHUS (*Primula*)
QUACK GRASS (couch grass)

10–continued
SHIELD FERN
SNAKE'S HEAD
SNAPDRAGON
 (*Antirrhinum*)
SOW THISTLE
SPIDERWORT
SPLEENWORT
STITCHWORT
SWEET BRIAR
 (eglantine)
THORN APPLE
 (jimsonweed)
TOUCH-ME-NOT
WALLFLOWER
WATERCRESS
WELSH POPPY
WILLOWHERB
WOOD SORREL

11
ANTIRRHINUM (snap-
 dragon)
BISHOP'S WEED
 (ground elder)
BITTERSWEET
 (woody nightshade)
BLADDERWORT
CALCEOLARIA
CANARY GRASS
CONVOLVULUS
 (bindweed)
FIG MARIGOLD
FORGET-ME-NOT
GILLYFLOWER
 (gilliflower, pink,
 carnation)
GLOBE FLOWER
GROUND ELDER
 (goutweed, bishop's
 weed)
HELLEBORINE
 (orchid)
HONEYSUCKLE
IPECACUANHA

11–continued
KANGAROO PAW
LEOPARD LILY (fritil-
 lary, blackberry lily)
LONDON PRIDE
 (saxifrage)
LOVE-IN-A-MIST
MARRAM GRASS
MARSH MALLOW
MEADOWSWEET
PAMPAS GRASS
PONTENTILLA
 (cinquefoil)
PRICKLY PEAR
 (cactus)
RAGGED ROBIN
RED-HOT POKER
ROSE OF CHINA
 (*Hibiscus*)
RUBBER PLANT
SEA LAVENDER
SHRIMP PLANT
SPIDER PLANT
ST JOHN'S WORT
STRAWFLOWER
WELWITSCHIA
WINTERGREEN

12
AUTUMN CROCUS
 (meadow saffron)
CENTURY PLANT
COMPASS PLANT
 (turpentine plant)
GLOBE THISTLE
LADY'S SLIPPER
MONKEYFLOWER
MORNING GLORY
 (moonflower)
OLD MAN CACTUS
OLD MAN'S BEARD
 (*Clematis*)
ORCHARD GRASS
 (cocksfoot)

12–continued
PITCHER PLANT
PRICKLY POPPY
 (devil's fig)
QUAKING GRASS
ROSE OF SHARON
 (*Hibiscus*)
SOLOMON'S SEAL
SWEET WILLIAM
VENUS FLYTRAP

13
AFRICAN VIOLET
BIRD'S NEST FERN
BLEEDING HEART
CALYPSO ORCHID
CARRION FLOWER
CHRISTMAS ROSE
 (hellebore)
CHRYSANTHEMUM
CREEPING JENNY
 (moneywort)
ELEPHANT GRASS
GARLIC MUSTARD
 (jack-by-the-hedge)
GRAPE HYACINTH
MARSH MARIGOLD
 (kingcup)
MEADOW SAFFRON
 (autumn crocus)
PASSIONFLOWER
 (granadilla)
RANUNCULACEAE
ROSE OF JERICHO
SLIPPER ORCHID
TOWNHALL CLOCK
 (moschatel)
TRAVELLER'S JOY
 (*Clematis*)
WINTER ACONITE

14
BELLADONNA LILY
 (*Amaryllis*)
BLACKBERRY LILY
 (leopard lily)

14–continued
BLANKET FLOWERS
CANTERBURY BELL
 (*Campanula*)
CASTOR-OIL PLANT
HEDGEHOG CACTUS
JACK-BY-THE-
 HEDGE (garlic mus-
 tard)
LORDS-AND-LADIES
 (arum lily)
MAIDENHAIR FERN
TRUMPET CREEPER

15+
BIRD-OF-PARADISE
 FLOWER
BIRD'S NEST
 ORCHID
BLACK NIGHTSHADE
DEADLY NIGHT-
 SHADE (belladonna)
DOG'S TOOTH
 VIOLET
ENCHANTER'S
 NIGHTSHADE
GRASS OF
 PARNASSUS
LILY-OF-THE-VALLEY
LOVE-LIES-BLEED-
 ING (*Amaranthus*)
MICHAELMAS DAISY
 (*Aster*)
ORGAN-PIPE
 CACTUS
SNOW-ON-THE-
 MOUNTAIN
SQUIRTING
 CUCUMBER
STAR OF
 BETHLEHEM
TURPENTINE PLANT
 (compass plant)
WOODY NIGHT-
 SHADE (bittersweet)

TREES AND SHRUBS

3
ASH
BOX
ELM
FIG
FIR
MAY (hawthorn)
OAK

3–continued
TEA
YEW

4
ANIL
COCA
DATE (palm)
KAVA

4–continued
KOLA (cola)
NIPA (palm)
PALM
PINE
TEAK

5
ALDER

5–continued
ASPEN
BALSA
BEECH (*Fagus*)
BIRCH
BROOM
CACAO
CAPER

TREES AND SHRUBS

5–continued
CEDAR
EBONY
ELDER
ERICA (heath, heather)
FURZE (gorse)
GORSE (furze)
HAZEL
HEATH (*Erica*)
HOLLY
KARRI
LARCH
LILAC
MAPLE
OSIER (willow)
PECAN (hickory)
ROWAN (mountain ash)
SAVIN (juniper)
YUCCA

6
ACACIA
AZALEA
BAMBOO
BANYAN
BAOBAB
BONSAI
BO TREE
CASSIA
DAPHNE
DATURA
DEODAR (cedar)
DERRIS
DURIAN
GINKGO (maidenhair tree)
GOMUTI (sugar palm)
JARRAH
JINBUL (coolabar)
JUJUBE
LAUREL
LOCUST (carob tree, St John's bread)
MIMOSA
MOOLAR (coolabar)
MYRTLE
NUTMEG
ORACHE
POPLAR
PRIVET
PROTEA
REDBUD (judas tree)
RED GUM (*Eucalyptus*)
SALLOW (willow)
SALVIA
SAPPAN
SPRUCE
WILLOW

7
AMBOYNA
ARBUTUS
BEBEERU (green-heart)
BLUE GUM (*Eucalyptus*)
CORK OAK
CYPRESS
DOGWOOD
DURMAST (oak)
FUCHSIA
GUM TREE (*Eucalyptus*)
HEATHER (*Erica*, ling)
HEMLOCK
HICKORY (pecan)
HOLM OAK (holly oak)
JASMINE
JUNIPER
MUGWORT (wormwood)
OIL PALM
PALMYRA
REDWOOD
ROSEBAY (oleander)
SEQUOIA (redwood, wellingtonia, big tree)
SOURSOP
SPIRAEA
SYRINGA (lilac, mock orange)

8
BARBERRY (*Berberis*)
BASSWOOD
BAYBERRY
BERBERIS (barberry)
BERGAMOT
BLACKBOX (coolabar)
BOX ELDER (maple)
CALABASH
CAMELLIA
CINCHONA
COOLABAR (jinbul, moolar, blackbox, dwarf box)
CORKWOOD (balsa)
DWARF BOX (coolabar)
EUONYMUS (spindle tree)
GARDENIA
GUAIACUM
HAWTHORN (may)
HORNBEAM
IRONWOOD
JAPONICA
LABURNUM (golden chain, golden rain)
LAVENDER

8–continued
MAGNOLIA (umbrella tree)
OLEANDER (rosebay)
QUANDONG
RAMBUTAN
ROSEWOOD
SAGO PALM
SALTBUSH
SILKY OAK
SWEET GUM
SWEETSOP
SYCAMORE (maple)
TAMARISK
TOLU TREE
VIBURNUM (snowball tree)
WISTERIA
WOODBINE (virginia creeper)
WORMWOOD (mugwort)

9
ARAUCARIA (monkey puzzle tree)
BEARBERRY
BUCKTHORN
CAROB TREE (locust)
CORAL TREE
EUPHORBIA (crown of thorns, poinsettia, snow-on-the-mountain)
FIRETHORN (pyracantha)
FLAME TREE (flamboyant)
FORSYTHIA (golden bell)
JACARANDA
JUDAS TREE (redbud)
KALANCHOE
KAURI PINE
MANGROVES
MISTLETOE
PLANE TREE
POINCIANA
POISON IVY
SASSAFRAS
SATINWOOD
SCREW PINE
STINKWOOD
STONE PINE
SWEETWOOD (greenheart)
TULIP TREE
WHITEBEAM

10
ARBOR VITAE
BIRD CHERRY

10–continued
BRAZILWOOD
COFFEE TREE
COTTONWOOD
DOUGLAS FIR
DRAGON TREE
EUCALYPTUS (blue gum, red gum)
FRANGIPANI (pagoda tree, temple flower)
GOLDEN BELL (forsythia)
GOLDEN RAIN - (laburnum)
GREENHEART (sweetwood, bebeeru)
JOSHUA TREE
MANGOSTEEN
MOCK ORANGE
PAGODA TREE (frangipani)
POINSETTIA
PYRACANTHA
RAFFIA PALM
RUBBER TREE
WITCH HAZEL
YELLOWWOOD

11
BOTTLEBRUSH
CABBAGE PALM
CAMPHOR TREE
CHAULMOOGRA
COTONEASTER
CYPRESS PINE
DAWN REDWOOD
GOLDEN CHAIN (laburnum)
GUELDER ROSE
HONEY LOCUST
JUMPING BEAN
MOUNTAIN ASH (rowan)
PENCIL CEDAR (juniper)
PHYLLANTHUS
SERVICE TREE
SLIPPERY ELM
SPINDLE TREE
STEPHANOTIS
TALIPOT PALM

12
CHERRY LAUREL
CREOSOTE BUSH
CUCUMBER TREE
CUSTARD APPLE (soursop, sweetsop)
INCENSE CEDAR
MONKEY PUZZLE
SNOWBALL TREE

64

12–continued
ST JOHN'S BREAD (locust)
SWAMP CYPRESS
TEMPLE FLOWER (frangipani)
TREE OF HEAVEN
UMBRELLA TREE (*Magnolia*)

13
BOUGAINVILLEA
BUTCHER'S BROOM
CROWN OF THORNS
HORSE CHESTNUT

13–continued
JAPANESE CEDAR
JAPANESE MAPLE
PAPER MULBERRY
PEACOCK FLOWER
 (flamboyant)
WAYFARING TREE

14+
FLAMBOYANT TREE (flame
tree, peacock flower)
FLOWERING CURRANT

14+–continued
JERUSALEM CHERRY
MAIDENHAIR TREE
 (ginkgo)
STRAWBERRY TREE
TRAVELLER'S TREE
TURPENTINE TREE
VIRGINIA CREEPER
 (woodbine)

FRUIT, VEGETABLES, AND PULSES

3
FIG
PEA
YAM

4
BEET
EDDO (taro)
KALE
KIWI
LEEK
LIME (linden)
OKRA (lady's
 fingers, gumbo)
PEAR
PLUM
SLOE
TARO (eddo,
 dasheen,
 elephant's ear)

5
APPLE
CAROB
CHARD (swiss
 chard)
CRESS
GRAPE
GUAVA
GUMBO (okra)
LEMON
MANGO
MAIZE
MELON (musk,
 honeydew, can-
 teloupe, water)
OLIVE
ONION (spring
 onion, scallion)
PEACH
SWEDE

6
ALMOND
BANANA
CARROT
CASHEW
CELERY
CHERRY
CITRON
COB NUT
DAMSON
ENDIVE
GARLIC
LENTIL
LICHEE
LINDEN (lime)
LITCHI
LOQUAT
LYCHEE (litchi,
 lichee)
MANIOC
 (cassava)
MARROW
MEDLAR
ORANGE
PAWPAW
PEANUT
 (groundnut)
POTATO
PRUNUS (plum,
 almond, apri-
 cot, cherry)
QUINCE
RADISH
SORREL
SQUASH
TOMATO
TURNIP
WALNUT

7
ALFALFA
APRICOT

7–continued
AVOCADO
BRAMBLE
 (blackberry)
BULLACE (plum)
CABBAGE
CASSAVA
 (manioc)
CHICORY
CURRANT
DASHEEN (taro)
FILBERT
GENIPAP
GHERKIN
KUMQUAT
LETTUCE
PARSNIP
PUMPKIN
RHUBARB
SALSIFY
SATSUMA
 (tangerine)
SHALLOT
SPINACH

8
BEETROOT
BILBERRY
 (blaeberry,
 huckleberry,
 whortleberry)
BRASSICA
 (broccoli,
 cabbage)
BROCCOLI
CAPSICUM
 (sweet pepper,
 chilli, paprika)
CELERIAC (knob
 celery)
CHESTNUT
CHICK PEA

8–continued
CUCUMBER
DEWBERRY
EARTHNUT
 (groundnut)
EGGPLANT
 (aubergine)
KOHLRABI
 (cabbage)
MANDARIN
 (tangerine)
MULBERRY
MUNG BEAN
 (green gram)
MUSHROOM
OLEASTER
 (russian olive,
 trebizond date)
SCALLION
SUGAR PEA
SOYA BEAN
TAMARIND
ZUCCHINI
 (courgette)

9
ARTICHOKE
ASPARAGUS
AUBERGINE
 (eggplant)
BLAEBERRY
 (bilberry)
BROAD BEAN
CALABRESE
COCODEMER
COURGETTE
 (marrow,
 zucchini)
CRAB APPLE
CRANBERRY
CROWBERRY
DWARF BEAN

9–continued
GREENGAGE
GROUNDNUT
 (peanut, earth-
 nut)
MANGETOUT
NECTARINE
PERSIMMON
PETIT POIS
PINEAPPLE
PISTACHIO
RADICCHIO
RASPBERRY
SAPODILLA
STAR APPLE
SWEET CORN
TANGERINE

10
ADZUKI BEAN
BEAN SPROUT
BLACKBERRY
 (bramble)
BUTTER BEAN
CLEMENTINE
ELDERBERRY
FRENCH BEAN
 (kidney bean)
GOOSEBERRY
GRAPEFRUIT
 (*Citrus
 Paradisi*)
KIDNEY BEAN
LOGANBERRY
RED CABBAGE
REDCURRANT
RUNNER BEAN
SALAD ONION
SNAKE GOURD
STRAWBERRY
STRING BEAN
SWISS CHARD

FUNGI

11
CAULIFLOWER
COCONUT PALM
HORSERADISH
HUCKLEBERRY
  (bilberry)
POMEGRANATE

11–continued
SPRING ONION
SWEET POTATO

12+
BLACKCURRANT
BRUSSELS SPROUT

12+–continued
ELEPHANT'S EAR
  (taro)
JERUSALEM
  ARTICHOKE
LADY'S FINGERS
  (okra)

12+–continued
MANGEL-WURZEL
  (beet)
SAVOY CABBAGE
WATER CHESTNUT
WHORTLEBERRY
  (bilberry)

FUNGI

4
CÈPE

5
MOREL
YEAST

6
AGARIC
INK CAP

7
AMANITA
BLEWITS
BOLETUS
CANDIDA
TRUFFLE

8
DEATH CAP
MUSHROOM
PUFFBALL

9
CUP FUNGUS
EARTHSTAR
FLY AGARIC
PSILOCYBE
RUST FUNGI
STINKHORN
TOADSTOOL

10
BREAD MOULD

10–continued
CHAMPIGNON

11
ASCOMYCETES
ASPERGILLUS
CHANTERELLE
HONEY
  FUNGUS
PENICILLIUM
SLIME MOULDS

13
BRACKET
  FUNGUS

14
BASID-
  IOMYCETES

15
PARASOL
  MUSHROOM

FERNS

4
TREE

5
ROYAL

7
BRACKEN
OSMUNDA

8
LADY FERN

8–continued
POLYPODY
STAGHORN

9
BIRD'S NEST

10
CLIFFBRAKE
DRYOPTERIS
MAIDENHAIR
SPLEENWORT

11
HART'S
  TONGUE

GRASSES, SEDGES, AND RUSHES

3
FOG
OAT
RYE
TEF

4
BENT
CORN
REED
RICE
RUSH

5
BROME
DURRA
MAIZE
PADDY
PANIC
SEDGE
SPELT
WHEAT

6
BAMBOO

6–continued
BARLEY
DARNEL
FESCUE
FIORIN
MELICK
MILLET
QUITCH
REDTOP
ZOYSIA

7
BULRUSH
ESPARTO
FOXTAIL
PAPYRUS
SORGHUM
WILD OAT

8
CUTGRASS
DOG'S-TAIL
OAT-GRASS

8–continued
REED MACE
RYEGRASS
SPARTINA
SPINIFEX
TEOSINTE
WILD RICE
WOODRUSH

9
BLUEGRASS
BROOMCORN

9–continued
COCKSFOOT
CORDGRASS
CRABGRASS
GAMA GRASS
HAIR-GRASS
LYME GRASS
REED GRASS
STAR GRASS
SUGAR CANE
WIRE GRASS

10
BEACH GRASS

10–continued
BEARD GRASS
BUNCH GRASS
CHINA GRASS
COUCH GRASS
HERD'S-GRASS
INDIAN CORN
INDIAN RICE
LEMON GRASS
QUACK GRASS
SPEAR GRASS
SWORD GRASS

11
CANARY GRASS

11–continued
COTTON GRASS
FINGER GRASS
MARRAM GRASS
MEADOW GRASS
PAMPAS GRASS
SWITCH GRASS
TWITCH GRASS
VERNAL GRASS

12
BERMUDA GRASS
BRISTLE GRASS
BUFFALO GRASS
FEATHER GRASS

12–continued
ORCHARD GRASS
QUAKING GRASS
TIMOTHY GRASS
TUSSOCK GRASS
YORKSHIRE FOG

13+
ELEPHANT GRASS
KENTUCKY BLUE-
  GRASS
SQUIRREL-TAIL
  GRASS

PEOPLE

WORLD LEADERS

3

FOX, Charles James
(1749–1806; British Whig
politician)
LIE, Trygve (Halvdan)
(1896–1968; Norwegian
Labour politician)

4

BENN, Anthony Neil
Wedgwood (1925– ; British
Labour politician)
BLUM, Léon (1872–1950;
French socialist)
BOSE, Subhas Chandra (c.
1897–c. 1945; Indian
nationalist leader)
COOK, Sir Joseph (1860–1947;
Australian statesman)
DÍAZ, Porfirio (1830–1915;
Mexican soldier)
FOOT, Michael (Mackintosh)
(1913– ; British Labour
politician)
GORE, Al(bert) H., Jr
(1948– ; US politician)
HOLT, Harold Edward
(1908–67; Australian
statesman)
HOWE, Sir Richard Edward
Geoffrey (1926– ; British
Conservative politician)
HULL, Cordell (1871–1955; US
Democratic politician)
KING, Jr, Martin Luther
(1929–68; US Black civil-
rights leader)
KING, William Lyon Mackenzie
(1874– 1950; Canadian
statesman)
KIRK, Norman Eric (1923–74;
New Zealand statesman)
KOHL, Helmut (1930– ;
German statesman)
MEIR, Golda (1898–1978;
Israeli stateswoman)
NAGY, Imre (1896– 1958;
Hungarian statesman)

4–continued

OWEN, Dr David (1938– ;
British politician)
RHEE, Syngman (1875–1965;
Korean statesman)
RUSK, David Dean (1909–94;
US statesman)
TOJO (Hideki) (1884–1948;
Japanese general)
TONE, Theobald Wolfe
(1763–98; Irish nationalist)
TUTU, Desmond (1931– ;
South African clergyman)
WARD, Sir Joseph George
(1856–1930; New Zealand
statesman)

5

AGNEW, Spiro Theodore
(1918–96; US Republican
politician)
AHERN, Bertie (1951– ; Irish
statesman)
ASTOR, Nancy Witcher,
Viscountess (1879–1964;
British politician)
BANDA, Hastings Kamuzu
(1905–97; Malawi statesman)
BARAK, Ehud (1942–; Israeli
politician)
BEGIN, Menachem (1913–92;
Israeli statesman)
BERIA, Lavrenti Pavlovich
(1899–1953; Soviet politician)
BEVAN, Aneurin (1897–1960;
British Labour politician)
BEVIN, Ernest (1881–1951;
British politician)
BLAIR, Tony (1953– ; British
politician)
BOTHA, Louis (1862–1919;
South African statesman)
BOTHA, Pieter Willem
(1916– ; South African
statesman)
CLARK, Charles Joseph
(1939– ; Canadian
statesman)

5–continued

CLARK, Helen (1950– ; New
Zealand politician)
DAYAN, Moshe (1915–81;
Israeli general)
DEBRÉ, Michel (1912–96;
French statesman)
DESAI, Shri Morarji Ranchhodji
(1896–95; Indian statesman)
DE WET, Christian Rudolf
(1854–1922; Afrikaner
politician and soldier)
EBERT, Friedrich (1871–1925;
German statesman)
EMMET, Robert (1778–1803;
Irish nationalist)
FLOOD, Henry (1732–91; Irish
politician)
LAVAL, Pierre (1883–1945;
French statesman)
LENIN, Vladimir Ilich
(V I Ulyanov, 1870–1924;
Russian revolutionary)
LODGE, Henry Cabot
(1850–1924; US Republican
politician)
LYNCH, Jack (1917–99; Irish
statesman)
LYONS, Joseph Aloysius
(1879–1939; Australian
statesman)
MAJOR, John (1943– ; British
politician)
MANIN, Daniele (1804–57;
Italian patriot)
MBEKI, Thabo (1942– ;
South African politician)
MBOYA, Tom (1930–69;
Kenyan politician)
MENON, Krishna (Vengalil
Krishnan Krishna Menon,
1896–1974; Indian diplomat)
NEHRU, Jawaharlal
(1889–1964; Indian
statesman)
NKOMO, Joshua (1917–99;
Zimbabwean politician)

5–continued

OBOTE, Apollo Milton
(1925– ; Ugandan
statesman)
PERÓN, Juan Domingo
(1895–1974; Argentine
statesman)
PUTIN, Vladimir (1952– ;
Russian politician)
RABIN, Yitshak (1922–95;
Israeli statesman)
SADAT, Anwar (1918–81;
Egyptian statesman)
SMITH, Ian Douglas (1919– ;
Rhodesian politician)
SMUTS, Jan Christiaan
(1870–1950; South African
statesman and general)
SPAAK, Paul Henri
(1899–1972; Belgian
statesman)
STEEL, David Martin Scott
(1938– ; British politician)
VANCE, Cyrus (1917– ; US
statesman)
VILLA, Pancho (Francesco V,
(1878–1923; Mexican
revolutionary)

6

ARAFAT, Yassir (1929– ;
Palestinian leader)
BARTON, Sir Edmund
(1849–1920; Australian
statesman)
BHUTTO, Benazir (1953– ;
Pakistani politician)
BHUTTO, Zulfikar Ali (1928–79;
Pakistani statesman)
BORDEN, Sir Robert Laird
(1854–1937; Canadian
statesman)
BRANDT, Willy (1913–92; West
German statesman)
BRIGHT, John (1811–89;
British radical politician)
BRUTON, John Gerard
(1947– ; Irish statesman)
BUTLER, Richard Austen,
Baron (1902–82; British
Conservative politician)
CHIRAC, Jacques (1932– ;
French statesman)
COATES, Joseph Gordon
(1878–1943; New Zealand
statesman)
COBDEN, Richard (1804–65;
British politician and
economist)
CRIPPS, Sir Richard Stafford
(1889–1952; British Labour
politician)

6–continued

CURTIN, John Joseph
(1885–1945; Australian
statesman)
CURZON, George Nathaniel,
1st Marquess (1859–1925;
British politician)
DAVITT, Michael (1846–1906;
Irish nationalist)
DEAKIN, Alfred (1856–1919;
Australian statesman)
DJILAS, Milovan (1911–95;
Yugoslav politician)
DUBČEK, Alexander (1921–92;
Czechoslovak statesman)
DULLES, John Foster
(1888–1959; US Republican
politician and diplomat)
ERHARD, Ludwig (1897–1977;
German statesman)
FADDEN, Sir Arthur William
(1895–1973; Australian
statesman)
FISHER, Andrew (1862–1928;
Australian statesman)
FLEURY, André Hercule de,
Cardinal (1653–1743; French
statesman)
FORBES, George William
(1869–1947; New Zealand
statesman)
FRANCO, Francisco
(1892–1975; Spanish general
and statesman)
FRASER, John Malcolm
(1930– ; Australian
statesman)
FRASER, Peter (1884–1950;
New Zealand statesman)
GANDHI, Indira (1917–84;
Indian stateswoman)
GANDHI, Mohandas
Karamchand (1869–1948;
Indian nationalist leader)
GÖRING, Hermann Wilhelm
(1893–1946; German Nazi
politician)
GORTON, John Grey
(1911– ; Australian
statesman)
GRIVAS, Georgios
(1898–1974; Greek general)
HEALEY, Denis Winston
(1917– ; British politician)
HOWARD, John (1939– ;
Australian politician)
HUGHES, William Morris
(1864–1952; Australian
statesman)
JUÁREZ, Benito Pablo
(1806–72; Mexican
statesman)

6–continued

KAUNDA, Kenneth David
(1924– ; Zambian
statesman)
KRUGER, Stephanus
Johannes Paulus
(1825–1904; Afrikaner
statesman)
MARCOS, Ferdinand Edralin
(1917–89; Philippine
statesman)
MASSEY, William Ferguson
(1856–1925; New Zealand
statesman)
MOBUTU, Sese Seko (Joseph
Désiré M, (1930–97; Zaïrese
statesman)
MOSLEY, Sir Oswald Ernald
(1896–1980; British fascist)
NASSER, Gamal Abdel
(1918–70; Egyptian
statesman)
O'BRIEN, Conor Cruise
(1917– ; Irish diplomat)
O'NEILL, Terence, Baron
(1914–90; Northern Irish
statesman)
PÉTAIN, Henri Philippe
(1856–1951; French general
and statesman)
POWELL, John Enoch
(1912–98; British politician)
QUAYLE, Dan (1947– ; US
politician)
REVERE, Paul (1735–1818;
American revolutionary)
RHODES, Cecil John
(1853–1902; South African
financier and statesman)
SAVAGE, Michael Joseph
(1872–1940; New Zealand
statesman)
SEDDON, Richard John
(1845–1906; New Zealand
statesman)
STALIN, Joseph (1879–1953;
Soviet statesman)
SUÁREZ, Adolfo, Duke of
(1932– ; Spanish
statesman)
THORPE, John Jeremy
(1929– ; British Liberal
politician)
WATSON, John Christian
(1867–1941; Australian
statesman)
WILKES, John (1725–97;
British journalist and
politician)
ZAPATA, Emiliano
(?1877–1919; Mexican
revolutionary)

7

ACHESON, Dean Gooderham (1893–1971; US lawyer and statesman)

ASHDOWN, Paddy (1941– ; Social and Liberal Democrat politician)

ATATÜRK, Kemal (Mustafa Kemal, 1881–1938; Turkish statesman)

BATISTA (y Zaldívar), Fulgencio (1901–73; Cuban statesman)

BENNETT, Richard Bedford, Viscount (1870–1947; Canadian statesman)

BOLÍVAR, Simón (1783–1830; South American statesman)

BORMANN, Martin (1900–45; German Nazi leader)

CLINTON, Bill (1946– ; US statesman)

CLINTON, de Witt (1769–1828; US statesman)

COLLINS, Michael (1890–1922; Irish nationalist)

GADDAFI, Moammar Al- (or Qaddafi, 1942– ; Libyan colonel and statesman)

GRATTAN, Henry (1746–1820; Irish politician)

GRIMOND, Joseph (1913–93; British politician)

GROMYKO, Andrei (1909–89; Soviet statesman)

HIMMLER, Heinrich (1900–45; German Nazi politician)

HOLLAND, Sir Sidney George (1893–1961; New Zealand statesman)

HUSSEIN (ibn Talal (1935–99; King of Jordan)

HUSSEIN, Saddam (1937– ; Iraqi politician)

KEATING, Paul John (1944– ; Australian statesman)

JENKINS, Roy Harris (1920– ; British politician and historian)

KINNOCK, Neil (1942– ; Labour politician)

KOSYGIN, Aleksei Nikolaevich (1904–80; Soviet statesman)

LUMUMBA, Patrice Hemery (1925–61; Congolese statesman)

MACLEOD, Iain Norman (1913–70; British Conservative politician)

MANDELA, Nelson (Rolihlahla) (1918– ; South African lawyer and politician)

7–continued

MAZZINI, Giuseppe (1805–72; Italian patriot)

MCMAHON, William (1908–80; Australian statesman)

MENZIES, Sir Robert Gordon (1894–1978; Australian statesman)

MINTOFF, Dominic (1916– ; Maltese statesman)

MOLOTOV, Vyacheslav Mikhailovich (1890–1986; Soviet statesman)

NYERERE, Julius Kambarage (1922–99; Tanzanian statesman)

PAISLEY, Ian (1926– ; Northern Irish politician)

PARNELL, Charles Stewart (1846–91; Irish politician)

PEARSON, Lester Bowles (1897–1972; Canadian statesman)

RAFFLES, Sir Thomas Stamford (1781–1826; British colonial administrator)

SALAZAR, António de Oliveira (1889–1970; Portuguese dictator)

SCHMIDT, Helmut (1918– ; German statesman)

SCULLIN, James Henry (1876–1953; Australian statesman)

SHASTRI, Shri Lal Bahadur (1904–66; Indian statesman)

SUHARTO (1921– ; Indonesian statesman and general)

TROTSKY, Leon (1879–1940; Russian revolutionary)

TRUDEAU, Pierre Elliott (1919– ; Canadian statesman)

VORSTER, Balthazar Johannes (1915–83; South African statesman)

WHITLAM, Edward Gough (1916– ; Australian statesman)

YELTSIN, Boris (1931– ; Russian statesman)

8

ADENAUER, Konrad (1876–1967; German statesman)

AMIN DADA, Idi (c. 1925– ; Ugandan politician and president)

ARISTIDE, Jean-Bertrand (1953– ; Haitian statesman)

8–continued

AYUB KHAN, Mohammad (1907–74; Pakistani statesman)

BEN BELLA, Ahmed (1916– ; Algerian statesman)

BISMARCK, Otto Eduard Leopold, Prince Von (1815–98; Prussian statesman)

BOUCHARD, Lucien (1938– ; Canadian politician)

BREZHNEV, Leonid Ilich (1906–82; Soviet statesman)

BUKHARIN, Nikolai Ivanovich (1888–1938; Soviet politician)

BULGANIN, Nikolai Aleksandrovich (1895–1975; Soviet statesman)

CHRÉTIEN, Jean (1934– ; Canadian statesman)

COSGRAVE, William Thomas (1880–1965; Irish statesman)

CROSSMAN, Richard Howard Stafford (1907–74; British Labour politician)

DALADIER, Édouard (1884–1970; French statesman)

DE GAULLE, Charles André Joseph Marie (1890–1970; French general and statesman)

DE VALERA, Eamon (1882–1975; Irish statesman)

DOLLFUSS, Engelbert (1892–1934; Austrian statesman)

DUVALIER, François (1907–71; Haitian politician)

EICHMANN, Adolf (1906–62; German Nazi politician)

FRANKLIN, Benjamin (1706–90; US diplomat)

GOEBBELS, Paul Joseph (1897–1945; German Nazi politician)

GRIFFITH, Arthur (1872–1922; Irish journalist and nationalist)

HARRIMAN, William Averell (1891–1986; US diplomat)

HASTINGS, Warren (1732–1818; British colonial administrator)

HIROHITO (1901–89; Emperor of Japan)

HOLYOAKE, Sir Keith Jacka (1904–83; New Zealand statesman)

HONECKER, Erich (1912–94; East German statesman)

8–continued

HUMPHREY, Hubert Horatio (1911–1978; US Democratic politician)

IBARRURI, Dolores (1895–1989; Spanish politician)

KENYATTA, Jomo (*c.* 1891–1978; Kenyan statesman)

KHOMEINI, Ayatollah Ruholla (1900–89; Iranian Shiite Muslim leader)

MALENKOV, Georgi Maksimilianovich (1902–88; Soviet statesman)

MCALEESE, Mary (1951– ; Irish politician)

MCCARTHY, Joseph Raymond (1908–57; US Republican senator)

MORRISON, Herbert Stanley, Baron (1888–1965; British Labour politician)

MUZOREWA, Bishop Abel Tendekayi (1925– ; Zimbabwean statesman)

O'CONNELL, Daniel (1775–1847; Irish politician)

O'HIGGINS, Bernardo (?1778–1842; Chilean national hero)

PINOCHET, Augusto (1915– ; Chilean general)

PODGORNY, Nikolai (1903–83; Soviet statesman)

POINCARÉ, Raymond (1860–1934; French statesman)

POMPIDOU, Georges Jean Raymond (1911–74; French statesman)

QUISLING, Vidkun Abraham Lauritz Jonsson (1887–1945; Norwegian army officer and Nazi collaborator)

RASPUTIN, Grigori Yefimovich (*c.* 1872–1916; Russian mystic)

SCHRÖDER, Gerhard (1944– ; German politician)

SIHANOUK, Norodim, Prince (1923– ; King of Cambodia)

SIKORSKI, Władysław (1881–1943; Polish general and statesman)

THATCHER, Margaret (1925– ; British stateswoman)

ULBRICHT, Walter (1893–1973; East German statesman)

8–continued

VERWOERD, Hendrik Frensch (1901–66; South African statesman)

WALDHEIM, Kurt (1918– ; Austrian diplomat and statesman)

WEIZMANN, Chaim Azriel (1874–1952; Israeli statesman)

WELENSKY, Sir Roy (1907–92; Rhodesian statesman)

WILLIAMS, Shirley Vivien Teresa Brittain (1930– ; British politician)

9

AGA KHAN IV (1936– ; Imam of the Ismaili sect of Muslims)

ANDREOTTI, Giulio (1919– ; Italian politician)

BEN-GURION, David (1886–1973; Israeli statesman)

CASTRO RUZ, Fidel (1926– ; Cuban statesman)

CHOU EN-LAI (*or* Zhou En Lai, 1898–1976; Chinese communist statesman)

CHURCHILL, Lord Randolph Henry Spencer (1849–95; British Conservative politician)

GAITSKELL, Hugh (1906–63; British politician)

GARIBALDI, Giuseppe (1807–82; Italian soldier)

GORBACHOV, Mikhail Sergeevich (1931– ; Soviet statesman)

HENDERSON, Arthur (1863–1935; British Labour politician)

HO CHI MINH (Nguyen That Thanh, 1890–1969; Vietnamese statesman)

KISSINGER, Henry Alfred (1923– ; US diplomat and political scientist)

LA GUARDIA, Fiorello Henry (1882–1947; US politician

LUXEMBURG, Rosa (1871–1919; German revolutionary)

MACDONALD, James Ramsay (1866–1937; British statesman)

MACDONALD, Sir John Alexander (1815–91; Canadian statesman)

MILOŠEVIĆ, Slobodan (1941– ; Serbian politician)

9–continued

MUSSOLINI, Benito Amilcare Andrea (1883–1945; Italian fascist dictator)

PANKHURST, Emmeline (1858–1928; British suffragette)

STEVENSON, Adlai Ewing (1900–65; US Democratic politician)

10

ABDULLAH II (1962– ; King of Jordan)

BERNADOTTE, Jean Baptiste Jules (*c.* 1763–1844; French marshal)

CARRINGTON, Peter Alexander Rupert, 6th Baron (1919– ; British Conservative politician)

CLEMENCEAU, Georges (1841–1929; French statesman)

KHRUSHCHEV, Nikita Sergeevich (1894–1971; Soviet statesman)

LEE KUAN YEW (1923– ; Singaporean statesman)

MAO TSE-TUNG (*or* Mao Ze Dong, 1893–1976; Chinese communist statesman)

MITTERRAND, François Maurice (1916–96; French statesman)

RIBBENTROP, Joachim von (1893–1946; German Nazi politician)

VOROSHILOV, Kliment Yefremovich (1881–1969; Soviet marshal and statesman)

11

ABDUL RAHMAN, Tunku (1903–73; Malaysian statesman)

CASTLEREAGH, Robert Stewart, Viscount (1769–1822; British statesman)

DIEFENBAKER, John George (1895–1979; Canadian statesman)

HORE-BELISHA, Isaac Leslie, 1st Baron (1893–1957; British politician)

IZETBEGOVIĆ, Alija (1925– ; Bosnian politician)

MAKARIOS III, Mikhail Khristodolou Mouskos (1913–77; Cypriot churchman and statesman)

11–continued

MOUNTBATTEN (of Burma), Louis, 1st Earl (1900–79; British admiral and colonial administrator)

SELWYN LLOYD, John, Baron (1904–78; British Conservative politician)

WILBERFORCE, William (1759–1833; British philanthropist)

12

BANDARANAIKE, Solomon (1899–1959; Sri Lankan statesman)

FREI MONTALVA, Eduardo (1911–82; Chilean statesman)

12–continued

HAMMARSKJÖLD, Dag (1905–61; Swedish international civil servant)

MENDÈS-FRANCE, Pierre (1907–82; French statesman)

PAPADOPOULOS, George (1919– ; Greek colonel)

SHEVARDNADZE, Eduard Amvrosiyevich (1928– ; Georgian statesman)

13

CHIANG KAI-SHEK (or Jiang Jie Shi, 1887–1975; Nationalist Chinese soldier and statesman)

14

ALLENDE GOSSENS, Salvador (1908–73; Chilean statesman)

CLIVE OF PLASSEY, Robert, Baron (1725–74; British soldier and colonial administrator)

15

GISCARD D'ESTAING, Valéry (1926– ; French statesman)

20+

AYATOLLAH RUHOLLA KHOMEINI. See KHOMEINI, Ayatollah Ruholla.

HAILSHAM OF ST MARY-LEBONE, Baron (Quintin McGarel Hogg; 1907–)

MILITARY LEADERS

3

LEE, Robert E (1807–70; US Confederate commander)

NEY, Michel, Prince of Moscow (1769–1815; French marshal)

4

ALBA, Fernando Alvarez de Toledo, Duke of (1507–83; Spanish general)

BART, Jean (1650–1702; French admiral)

BYNG, George, Viscount Torrington (1663–1733; English admiral)

DIAZ, Porfirio (1830–1915; Mexican soldier)

FOCH, Ferdinand (1851–1929; French marshal)

HAIG, Douglas, 1st Earl (1861–1928; British field marshal)

HOOD, Samuel, 1st Viscount (1724–1816; British admiral)

HOWE, Richard, Earl (1726–99; British admiral)

JODL, Alfred (1890–1946; German general)

RAIS, Gilles de (or G de Retz 1404–40; French marshal)

RÖHM, Ernst (1887–1934; German soldier)

ROON, Albrecht, Graf von (1803–79; Prussian general)

4–continued

SAXE, Maurice, Comte de (1696–1750; Marshal of France)

SLIM, William Joseph, 1st Viscount (1891–1970; British field marshal)

TOGO (Heihachiro) (1847–1934; Japanese admiral)

5

ANDRÉ, John (1751–80; British soldier)

ANSON, George Anson, Baron (1697–1762; British admiral)

BLAKE, Robert (1599–1657; English admiral)

BLIGH, William (1754–1817; British admiral)

CIMON (d. c. 450 BC; Athenian general and politician)

DEWEY, George (1837–1917; US admiral)

DRAKE, Sir Francis (1540–96; English navigator and admiral)

EL CID (Rodrigo Diáz de Vivar, c. 1040–99; Spanish warrior)

GATES, Horatio (?1728–1806; American general)

HAWKE, Edward, 1st Baron (1705–81; British admiral)

JONES, John Paul (1747–92; American naval commander)

5–continued

LALLY, Thomas, Comte de (1702–66; French general)

LEVEN, Alexander Leslie, 1st Earl of (1580–1661; Scottish general)

MOORE, Sir John (1761–1809; British general)

MURAT, Joachim (1767–1815; French marshal)

PERRY, Matthew C (1794–1858; US naval officer)

PRIDE, Thomas (d. 1658; English parliamentary soldier)

SULLA, Lucius Cornelius (c. 138–78 BC; Roman dictator)

TILLY, Johan Tserclaes, Graf von (1559–1632; Bavarian general)

TROMP, Maarten (1598–1653; Dutch admiral)

WOLFE, James (1727–59; British soldier)

6

AETIUS, Flavius (d. 454 AD; Roman general)

ARNOLD, Benedict (1741–1801; American general)

BAYARD, Pierre Terrail, Seigneur de (c. 1473–1524; French soldier)

BEATTY, David, 1st Earl (1871–1936; British admiral)

6–continued

BENBOW, John (1653–1702; English naval officer)

CRONJE, Piet Arnoldus (c. 1840–1911; South African general)

CUSTER, George Armstrong (1839–76; US cavalry general)

DARLAN, Jean (Louis Xavier) François (1881–1942; French admiral)

DÖNITZ, Karl (1891–1981; German admiral)

DUNDEE, John Graham of Claverhouse, 1st Viscount (c. 1649–89; Scottish soldier)

DUNOIS, Jean d'Orléans, Comte de (1403–68; French general)

FISHER, John Arbuthnot, 1st Baron (1841–1920; British admiral)

FRENCH, John, 1st Earl of Ypres (1852–1925; British field marshal)

FULLER, J F C (1878–1966; British soldier)

GINKEL, Godert de, 1st Earl of Athlone (1644–1703; Dutch general)

GORDON, Charles George (1833–85; British general)

GRANBY, John Manners, Marquess of (1721–70; British soldier)

GREENE, Nathaneal (1742–86; American general)

HALSEY, William F (1882–1959; US admiral)

JOFFRE, Joseph Jacques Césaire (1852–1931; French marshal)

KEITEL, Wilhelm (1882–1946; German field marshal)

KLÉBER, Jean Baptiste (1753–1800; French general)

KONIEV, Ivan Stepanovich (1897–1973; Soviet marshal)

MARIUS, Gaius (c. 157–86 BC; Roman general)

MOLTKE, Helmuth, Graf von (1800–91; Prussian field marshal)

MOREAU, Jean Victor (1763–1813; French general)

NAPIER (of Magdala), Robert Cornelis, 1st Baron (1810–90; British field marshal)

NAPIER, Sir Charles James (1782–1853; British general)

6–continued

NARSES (c. 480–574 AD; Byzantine general)

NELSON, Horatio, Viscount (1758–1805; British admiral)

NIMITZ, Chester W (1885–1966; US admiral)

OUTRAM, Sir James (1803–63; British soldier)

PATTON, George S (1885–1945; US general)

PAULUS, Friedrich (1890–1957; German field marshal)

PÉTAIN, (Henri) Philippe (1856–1951; French general and statesman)

RAEDER, Erich (1876–1960; German admiral)

RAGLAN, Fitzroy James Henry Somerset, 1st Baron (1788–1855; British field marshal)

RODNEY, George Brydges, 1st Baron (1719–92; British admiral)

ROMMEL, Erwin (1891–1944; German general)

RUPERT, Prince (1619–82; Cavalry officer)

RUYTER, Michiel Adriaanszoon de (1607–76; Dutch admiral)

TEDDER, Arthur William, 1st Baron (1890–1967; British air marshal)

VERNON, Edward (1684–1757; British admiral)

WAVELL, Archibald Percival, 1st Earl (1883–1950; British field marshal)

WILSON, Henry Maitland, 1st Baron (1881–1964; British field marshal)

WILSON, Sir Henry Hughes (1864–1922; British field marshal)

ZHUKOV, Georgi Konstantinovich (1896–1974; Soviet marshal)

7

AGRIPPA, Marcus Vipsanius (?63–12 BC; Roman general)

ALLENBY, Edmund Henry Hynman, 1st Viscount (1861–1936; British field marshal)

ARTIGAS, José Gervasio (1764–1850; national hero of Uruguay)

7–continued

ATHLONE, Alexander Cambridge, 1st Earl of (1874–1957; British soldier)

BAZAINE, Achille François (1811–88; French marshal)

BERWICK, James Fitzjames, Duke of (1670–1734; Marshal of France)

BLÜCHER, Gebhard Leberecht von, Prince of Wahlstatt (1742–1819; Prussian general)

BRADLEY, Omar Nelson (1893–1981; US general)

DECATUR, Stephen (1779–1820; US naval officer)

DENIKIN, Anton Ivanovich (1872–1947; Russian general)

DOWDING, Hugh Caswall Tremenheere, 1st Baron (1882–1970; British air chief marshal)

FAIRFAX, Thomas, 3rd Baron (1612–71; English general)

JACKSON, Andrew (1767–1845; US statesman and general)

JACKSON, Stonewall (Thomas Jonathan J, 1824–63; US Confederate general)

KOLCHAK, Alexander Vasilievich (1874–1920; Russian admiral)

LAMBERT, John (1619–83; English parliamentary general)

LYAUTEY, Louis Hubert Gonzalve (1854–1934; French marshal)

MASSÉNA, André (?1756–1817; French marshal)

METAXAS, Ioannis (1871–1941; Greek general)

MORTIER, Édouard Adolphe Casimir Joseph, Duc de Trévise (1768–1835; French marshal)

PHILLIP, Arthur (1738–1814; British admiral)

REGULUS, Marcus Attilus (d. c. 251 BC; Roman general)

ROBERTS, Frederick Sleigh, 1st Earl (1832–1914; British field marshal)

SHERMAN, William Tecumseh (1820–91; US Federal general)

SHOVELL, Sir Cloudesley (1650–1707; English admiral)

7—continued

SUVOROV, Aleksandr Vasilievich, Count (1729–1800; Russian field marshal)

TANCRED (c. 1078–1112; Norman Crusader)

TIRPITZ, Alfred von (1849–1930; German admiral)

TURENNE, Henri de la Tour d'Auvergne, Vicomte de (1611–75; French marshal)

VENDÔME, Louis Joseph, Duc de (1654–1712; French marshal)

VILLARS, Claude Louis Hector, Duc de (1653–1734; French marshal)

WALLACE, Lew (1827–1905; US soldier)

WINGATE, Orde Charles (1903–44; British soldier)

WRANGEL, Peter Nikolaievich, Baron (1878–1928; Russian general)

8

AGRICOLA, Gnaeus Julius (40–93 AD; Roman governor)

ANGLESEY, Henry William Paget, 1st Marquess of (1768– 1854; British field marshal)

AUGEREAU, Pierre François Charles, Duc de Castiglione (1757–1816; French marshal)

BADOGLIO, Pietro (1871–1956; Italian general)

BERTRAND, Henri Gratien, Comte (1773–1844; French marshal)

BOURMONT, Louis Auguste Victor de Ghaisnes, Comte de (1773–1846; French marshal)

BURGOYNE, John (1722–92; British general)

CAMPBELL, Colin, Baron Clyde (1792–1863; British field marshal)

CARDIGAN, James Thomas Brudenell, 7th Earl of (1797–1868; British cavalry officer)

CARRANZA, Venustiano (1859–1920; Mexican statesman and soldier)

COCHRANE, Thomas, 10th Earl of Dundonald (1775–1860; British admiral)

CROMWELL, Oliver (1599–1658; English soldier and statesman)

8—continued

GUESCLIN, Bertrand du (c. 1320–80; French commander)

HANNIBAL (247–c. 183 BC; Carthaginian general)

IRONSIDE, William Edmund, 1st Baron (1880–1959; British field marshal)

JELLICOE, John Rushworth, 1st Earl (1859–1935; British admiral)

KORNILOV, Lavrentia Georgievich (1870–1918; Russian general)

LUCULLUS, Lucius Licinius (d. c. 57 BC; Roman general)

LYSANDER (d. 395 BC; Spartan general)

MARSHALL, George C (1880–1959; US general)

MONTCALM, Louis Joseph de Montcalm-Grozon, Marquis de (1712–59; French general)

O'HIGGINS, Bernardo (?1778–1842; Chilean national hero)

PERSHING, John J (1860–1948; US general)

SANDWICH, John Montagu, 4th Earl of (1718–92; first lord of the admiralty)

SHERIDAN, Philip H (1831–88; US Federal general)

STILICHO, Flavius (d. 408 AD; Roman general)

STILWELL, Joseph W (1883–1946; US general)

WOLSELEY, Garnet Joseph, 1st Viscount (1833–1913; British field marshal)

9

ANGOULÊME, Charles de Valois, Duc d' (1573–1650; French soldier)

ANTIPATER (397–319 BC; Macedonian general)

ANTONESCU, Ion (1882–1946; Romanian general)

ARISTIDES (the Just) (c. 520–c. 468 BC; Athenian statesman)

BONAPARTE, Napoleon (1769–1821; French emperor)

DUMOURIEZ, Charles François Du Périer (1739–1823; French general)

GNEISENAU, August, Graf Neithardt von (1760–1831; Prussian field marshal)

9—continued

GRENVILLE, Sir Richard (?1541–91; British sailor)

HASDRUBAL (d. 207 BC; Carthaginian general)

KITCHENER (of Khartoum), Horatio Herbert, 1st Earl (1850–1916; British field marshal)

LAFAYETTE, Marie Joseph Gilbert Motier, Marquis de (1757–1834; French general and politician)

MACARTHUR, Douglas (1880–1964; US general)

MARCELLUS, Marcus Claudius (d. 208 BC; Roman general)

MCCLELLAN, George B (1826–85; Federal general)

MILTIADES (c. 550–489 BC; Athenian general)

NEWCASTLE, William Cavendish, Duke of (1592–1676; English soldier)

OLDCASTLE, Sir John (c. 1378–1417; English soldier)

PRETORIUS, Andries (1799–1853; Afrikaner leader)

RUNDSTEDT, Gerd von (1875–1953; German field marshal)

SANTA ANNA, Antonio López de (1794–1876; Mexican soldier)

TRENCHARD, Hugh Montague, 1st Viscount (1873–1956; The first British air marshal)

10

ABERCROMBY, Sir Ralph (1734–1801; British general)

ALANBROOKE, Alan Francis Brooke, 1st Viscount (1883–1963; British field marshal)

ALCIBIADES (c. 450–404 BC; Athenian general and politician)

ANTIGONUS I (c. 382–301 BC; Macedonian general)

AUCHINLECK, Sir Claude (1884–1981; British field marshal)

BELISARIUS (c. 505–65 AD; Byzantine general)

BERNADOTTE, Jean Baptiste Jules (1763–1844)

CORNWALLIS, Charles, 1st Marquess (1738–1805; British general)

10–continued

CUMBERLAND, William Augustus, Duke of (1721–65; British general)

ENVER PASHA (1881–1922; Turkish soldier)

FLAMININUS, Titus Quinctius (*c.* 230–*c.* 174 BC; Roman general)

HINDENBURG, Paul von Beneckendorff und von (1847–1934; German general)

KESSELRING, Albert (1885–1960; German general)

KUBLAI KHAN (1215–94; Mongol conqueror of China)

MANNERHEIM, Carl Gustaf Emil, Baron von (1867–1951; Finnish general)

MONTGOMERY (of Alamein), Bernard Law, 1st Viscount (1887–1976; British field marshal)

OGLETHORPE, James Edward (1696–1785; English general)

RICHTHOFEN, Manfred, Freiherr von (1892–1918; German air ace)

SCHLIEFFEN, Alfred, Graf von (1833–1913; German general)

TIMOSHENKO, Semyon Konstantinovich (1895–1970; Soviet marshal)

VILLENEUVE, Pierre (1763–1806; French admiral)

10–continued

WELLINGTON, Arthur Wellesley, Duke of (1769–1852; British general)

11

ALBUQUERQUE, Alfonso de (1453–1515; Portuguese governor in India)

BADEN-POWELL, Robert Stephenson Smyth, 1st Baron (1857–1941; British general)

BEAUHARNAIS, Alexandre, Vicomte de (1760–94; French general)

BRAUCHITSCH, Walther von (1881–1948; German general)

COLLINGWOOD, Cuthbert, 1st Baron (1750–1810; British admiral)

EPAMINONDAS (*c.* 418–362 BC; Theban general)

LIDDELL HART, Sir Basil Henry (1895–1970; British soldier)

MARLBOROUGH, John Churchill, 1st Duke of (1650–1722; British general)

MÜNCHHAUSEN, Karl Friedrich, Freiherr von (1720–97; German soldier)

PONIATOWSKI, Józef (1763–1813; Marshal of France)

WALLENSTEIN, Albrecht Wenzel von (1583–1634; Bohemian-born general)

12

IBRAHIM PASHA (1789–1848; Ottoman general)

13

EUGÈNE OF SAVOY, Prince (1663–1736; Austrian general)

FABIUS MAXIMUS, Quintus (d. 203 BC; Roman general)

HAMILCAR BARCA (d. *c.* 229 BC; Carthaginian general)

14

BARCLAY DE TOLLY, Mikhail Bogdanovich, Prince (1761–1818; Russian field marshal)

CLIVE OF PLASSEY, Robert, Baron (1725–74; British soldier and colonial administrator)

15

CASSIUS LONGINUS, Gaius (d. 42 BC; Roman general)

SCIPIO AFRICANUS (236–183 BC; Roman general)

16

ALEXANDER OF TUNIS, Harold, 1st Earl (1891–1969; British field marshal)

17

HOWARD OF EFFINGHAM, Charles, 2nd Baron (1536–1624; English Lord High Admiral)

20+

BERNHARD OF SAXE-WEIMAR, Duke (1604–39; German general)

SCIPIO AEMILIANUS AFRICANUS (*c.* 185–129 BC; Roman general)

PRIME MINISTERS OF GREAT BRITAIN (FROM 1721)

NAME	(TERM)	NAME	(TERM)
ROBERT WALPOLE	(1721–42)	JOHN STUART, EARL OF BUTE	(1762–63)
SPENCER COMPTON, EARL OF WILMINGTON	(1742–43)	GEORGE GRENVILLE	(1763–65)
HENRY PELHAM	(1743–54)	CHARLES WATSON-WENTWORTH, MARQUIS OF ROCKINGHAM	(1765–66)
THOMAS PELHAM-HOLLES, DUKE OF NEWCASTLE	(1754–56)	WILLIAM PITT, EARL OF CHATHAM	(1766–68)
WILLIAM CAVENDISH, DUKE OF DEVONSHIRE	(1756–57)	AUGUSTUS HENRY FITZROY, DUKE OF GRAFTON	(1768–70)
THOMAS PELHAM-HOLLES, DUKE OF NEWCASTLE	(1757–62)	FREDERICK NORTH	(1770–82)

NAME	(TERM)	NAME	(TERM)
CHARLES WATSON-WENTWORTH, MARQUIS OF ROCKINGHAM	(1782)	JOHN RUSSELL, EARL RUSSELL	(1865–66)
WILLIAM PETTY, EARL OF SHELBURNE	(1782–83)	EDWARD STANLEY, EARL OF DERBY	(1866–68)
WILLIAM HENRY CAVENDISH BENTINCK, DUKE OF PORTLAND	(1783)	BENJAMIN DISRAELI	(1868)
		WILLIAM EWART GLADSTONE	(1868–74)
WILLIAM PITT (SON OF EARL OF CHATHAM)	(1783–1801)	BENJAMIN DISRAELI, EARL OF BEACONSFIELD	(1874–80)
HENRY ADDINGTON	(1801–04)	WILLIAM EWART GLADSTONE	(1880–85)
WILLIAM PITT	(1804–06)	ROBERT GASCOYNE-CECIL, MARQUIS OF SALISBURY	(1885–86)
WILLIAM WYNDHAM GRENVILLE, BARON GRENVILLE	(1806–07)	WILLIAM EWART GLADSTONE	(1886)
WILLIAM BENTINCK, DUKE OF PORTLAND	(1807–09)	ROBERT GASCOYNE-CECIL, MARQUIS OF SALISBURY	(1886–92)
SPENCER PERCEVAL	(1809–12)	WILLIAM EWART GLADSTONE	(1892–94)
ROBERT BANKS JENKINSON, EARL OF LIVERPOOL	(1812–27)	ARCHIBALD PHILIP PRIMROSE, EARL OF ROSEBERY	(1894–95)
GEORGE CANNING	(1827)	ROBERT GASCOYNE-CECIL, MARQUIS OF SALISBURY	(1895–1902)
FREDERICK JOHN ROBINSON, VISCOUNT GODERICH	(1827–28)	ARTHUR JAMES BALFOUR	(1902–05)
ARTHUR WELLESLEY, DUKE OF WELLINGTON	(1828–30)	HENRY CAMPBELL-BANNERMAN	(1905–08)
CHARLES GREY, EARL GREY	(1830–34)	HERBERT HENRY ASQUITH	(1908–16)
WILLIAM LAMB, VISCOUNT MELBOURNE	(1834)	DAVID LLOYD GEORGE	(1916–22)
ROBERT PEEL	(1834–35)	ANDREW BONAR LAW	(1922–23)
WILLIAM LAMB, VISCOUNT MELBOURNE	(1835–41)	STANLEY BALDWIN	(1923–24)
ROBERT PEEL	(1841–46)	JAMES RAMSAY MACDONALD	(1924)
JOHN RUSSELL	(1846–52)	STANLEY BALDWIN	(1924–29)
EDWARD GEORGE GEOFFREY SMITH STANLEY, EARL OF DERBY	(1852)	JAMES RAMSAY MACDONALD	(1929–35)
GEORGE HAMILTON GORDON, EARL OF ABERDEEN	(1852–55)	STANLEY BALDWIN	(1935–37)
HENRY JOHN TEMPLE, VISCOUNT PALMERSTON	(1855–58)	NEVILLE CHAMBERLAIN	(1937–40)
		WINSTON CHURCHILL	(1940–45)
EDWARD STANLEY, EARL OF DERBY	(1858–59)	CLEMENT RICHARD ATTLEE	(1945–51)
		WINSTON CHURCHILL	(1951–55)
HENRY TEMPLE, VISCOUNT PALMERSTON	(1859–65)	ANTHONY EDEN	(1955–57)
		HAROLD MACMILLAN	(1957–63)
		ALEC DOUGLAS-HOME	(1963–64)
		HAROLD WILSON	(1964–70)
		EDWARD HEATH	(1970–74)
		HAROLD WILSON	(1974–76)
		JAMES CALLAGHAN	(1976–79)
		MARGARET THATCHER	(1979–90)
		JOHN MAJOR	(1990–97)
		TONY BLAIR	(1997–)

THE PRESIDENTS OF THE UNITED STATES OF AMERICA

NAME	(TERM)	NAME	(TERM)
GEORGE WASHINGTON	(1789–97)	GROVER CLEVELAND	(1885–89)
JOHN ADAMS	(1797–1801)	BENJAMIN HARRISON	(1889–93)
THOMAS JEFFERSON	(1801–09)	GROVER CLEVELAND	(1893–97)
JAMES MADISON	(1809–17)	WILLIAM MCKINLEY	(1897–1901)
JAMES MONROE	(1817–25)	THEODORE ROOSEVELT	(1901–09)
JOHN QUINCY ADAMS	(1825–29)	WILLIAM HOWARD TAFT	(1909–13)
ANDREW JACKSON	(1829–37)	WOODROW WILSON	(1913–21)
MARTIN VAN BUREN	(1837–41)	WARREN GAMALIEL HARDING	(1921–23)
WILLIAM HENRY HARRISON	(1841)	CALVIN COOLIDGE	(1923–29)
JOHN TYLER	(1841–45)	HERBERT CLARK HOOVER	(1929–33)
JAMES KNOX POLK	(1845–49)	FRANKLIN DELANO ROOSEVELT	(1933–45)
ZACHARY TAYLOR	(1849–50)	HARRY S. TRUMAN	(1945–53)
MILLARD FILLMORE	(1850–53)	DWIGHT DAVID EISENHOWER	(1953–61)
FRANKLIN PIERCE	(1853–57)	JOHN FITZGERALD KENNEDY	(1961–63)
JAMES BUCHANAN	(1857–61)	LYNDON BAINES JOHNSON	(1963–69)
ABRAHAM LINCOLN	(1861–65)	RICHARD MILHOUS NIXON	(1969–74)
ANDREW JOHNSON	(1865–69)	GERALD RUDOLPH FORD	(1974–77)
ULYSSES SIMPSON GRANT	(1869–77)	JAMES EARL CARTER	(1977–81)
RUTHERFORD BIRCHARD HAYES	(1877–81)	RONALD WILSON REAGAN	(1981–89)
JAMES ABRAM GARFIELD	(1881)	GEORGE HERBERT WALKER BUSH	(1989–93)
CHESTER ALAN ARTHUR	(1881–85)	WILLIAM JEFFERSON CLINTON	(1993–)

RULERS OF ENGLAND

KINGS OF KENT

HENGEST	(c. 455–488)
GERIC surnamed OISC	(488–?512)
OCTA	(?512–?)
EORMENRIC	(*N560)
ETHELBERT I	(560–616)
EADBALD	(616–640)
EARCONBERT	(640–664)
EGBERT I	(664–673)
HLOTHERE*	(673–685)
EADRIC*	(685–686)
SUAEBHARD*	(676–692)
OSWINI*	(?688–?690)
WIHTRED*	(690–725)
ETHELBERT II*	(725–762)
EADBERT*	(?725–?762)
ALRIC*	(c. 750s)
EARDWULF*	(747–762)
SIGERED*	(?762)
EANMUND*	(c. 759–765)
HEABERHT*	(764–765)
EGBERT II	(c. 765–780)
EALHMUND	(784–786)
EADBERT (PRAEN)	(796–798)
EADWALD	(?798 or 807)

CUTHRED	(798–807)
BALDRED	(?–825)

KINGS OF DEIRA

AELLI	(c. 560–590)
EDWIN	(?590–592)
ETHELFRITH	(592–616)
EDWIN	(616–632)
OSRIC	(632–633)
OSWALD (ST.)	(633–641)
OSWINE	(644–651)
ETHELWALD	(651–654)

KINGS OF NORTHUMBRIA

ETHELFRITH	(592–616)
EDWIN	(616–632)
OSWALD (ST.)	(633–641)
OSWIU	(654–670)
EGFRITH	(670–685)
ALDFRITH	(685–704)
OSRED I	(704–716)
COENRED	(716–718)
OSRIC	(718–729)
CEOLWULF	(729–737)

77

KINGS OF NORTHUMBRIA (cont.)

EADBERT	(737–758)
OSWULF	(c. 758)
ETHELWALD MOLL	(758–765)
ALCHRED	(765–774)
ETHELRED I	(774–778)
ELFWALD I	(778–788)
OSRED II	(788–790)
ETHELRED I	(790–796)
OSBALD	(796)
EARDWULF	(796–806)
ELFWALD II	(806–808)
EARDWULF	(?808)
EANRED	(808–840)
ETHELRED II	(840–844)
REDWULF	(844)
ETHELRED II	(844–849)
OSBERT	(849–862)
AELLE	(862–867)
EGBERT I	(867–873)
RICSIG	(873–876)
EGBERT II	(876–?878)

KINGS OF MERCIA

CEARL	(c. 600)
PENDA	(632–654)
WULFHERE	(657–674)
ETHELRED	(674–704)
COENRED	(704–709)
CEOLRED	(709–716)
ETHELBALD	(716–?757)
BEORNRED	(757)
OFFA	(757–796)
EGFRITH	(796)
COENWULF	(796–?821)
CEOLWULF I	(821–823)
BEORNWULF	(823–825)
LUDECAN	(825–827)
WIGLAF	(827–840)
BEORHTWULF	(840–852)
BURGRED	(852–874)
CEOLWULF II	(874–?883)

KINGS OF THE WEST SAXONS

CERDIC	(519–534)
CYNRIC	(534–560)
CEAWLIN	(560–591)
CEOL	(591–597)
CEOLWULF	(597–611)
CYNEGILS	(611–643)
CENWALH	(643–672)
SEAXBURH (Queen)	(?672–?674)
AESCWINE	(674–676)
CENTWINE	(676–685)
CAEDWALLA	(685–688)
INI	(688–726)
AETHELHEARD	(726–?740)
CUTHRED	(740–756)
SIGEBERHT	(756–757)

CYNEWULF	(757–786)
BEORHTRIC	(786–802)
EGBERT	(802–839)
ETHELWULF	(839–855)
ETHELBALD	(855–860)
ETHELBERT	(860–866)
ETHELRED	(866–871)
ALFRED	(871–899)
EDWARD THE ELDER	(899–925)
ATHELSTAN	(925–939)
EDMUND	(939–946)
EDRED	(946–955)

RULERS OF ENGLAND

EDWY	(955–959)
EDGAR	(959–975)
EDWARD THE MARTYR	(975–979)
ETHELRED	(979–1013)
SWEGN FORKBEARD	(1013–14)
ETHELRED	(1014–16)
EDMUND IRONSIDE	(1016)
CANUTE	(1016–35)
HAROLD HAREFOOT	(1035–40)
HARTACNUT	(1040–42)
EDWARD THE CONFESSOR	(1042–66)
HAROLD GODWINSON	(1066)
EDGAR ETHELING	(1066)
WILLIAM I (THE CONQUEROR)	(1066–87)
WILLIAM II (RUFUS)	(1087–1100)
HENRY I	(1100–35)
STEPHEN	(1135–54)
HENRY II	(1154–89)
RICHARD I	(1189–99)
JOHN	(1199–1216)
HENRY III	(1216–72)
EDWARD I	(1272–1307)
EDWARD II	(1307–27)
EDWARD III	(1327–77)
RICHARD II	(1377–99)
HENRY IV	(1399–1413)
HENRY V	(1413–22)
HENRY VI	(1422–61; 1470–71)
EDWARD IV	(1461–83)
EDWARD V	(1483)
RICHARD III	(1483–85)
HENRY VII	(1485–1509)
HENRY VIII	(1509–47)
EDWARD VI	(1547–53)
JANE (LADY JANE GREY)	(1553)
MARY	(1553–58)
PHILIP*	(1554–58)
ELIZABETH I	(1558–1603)
JAMES I	(1603–25)
CHARLES I	(1625–49)
THE COMMONWEALTH	(1649–60)
[OLIVER CROMWELL	(1653–58)
RICHARD CROMWELL	(1658–59)]
CHARLES II	(1660–85)
JAMES II	(1685–88)
WILLIAM AND MARY	(1689–1694)
WILLIAM III	(1694–1702)

ANNE	(1702–14)	EDWARD VII	(1901–10)
GEORGE I	(1714–27)	GEORGE V	(1910–36)
GEORGE II	(1727–60)	EDWARD VIII (DUKE OF	
GEORGE III	(1760–1820)	WINDSOR)	(1936)
GEORGE IV	(1820–30)	GEORGE VI	(1936–52)
WILLIAM IV	(1830–37)	ELIZABETH II	(1952–)
VICTORIA	(1837–1901)	* Joint rulers	

SCOTTISH RULERS

KENNETH I (MACALPIN)	(843–58)	EDGAR	(1097–1107)
DONALD I	(858–62)	ALEXANDER I	(1107–24)
CONSTANTINE I	(862–77)	DAVID I	(1124–53)
AEDH	(877–78)	MALCOLM IV	(1153–65)
GIRAC	(878–89)	WILLIAM THE LION	(1165–1214)
EOCHA	(878–89)	ALEXANDER II	(1214–49)
DONALD II	(889–900)	ALEXANDER III	(1249–86)
CONSTANTINE II	(900–43)	MARGARET, MAID OF NORWAY	(1286–90)
MALCOLM I	(943–54)	JOHN BALLIOL	(1292–96)
INDULPHUS	(954–62)	ROBERT I (BRUCE)	(1306–29)
DUFF	(962–66)	DAVID II	(1329–71)
COLIN	(966–71)	ROBERT II	(1371–90)
KENNETH II	(971–95)	ROBERT III	(1390–1406)
CONSTANTINE III	(995–97)	JAMES I	(1406–37)
KENNETH III	(997–1005)	JAMES II	(1437–60)
MALCOLM II	(1005–34)	JAMES III	(1460–88)
DUNCAN I	(1034–40)	JAMES IV	(1488–1513)
MACBETH	(1040–57)	JAMES V	(1513–42)
MALCOLM III	(1058–93)	MARY STUART,	
DONALD III (BANE)	(1093–94, 1094–97)	QUEEN OF SCOTS	(1542–67)
DUNCAN II	(1094)	JAMES VI OF SCOTLAND	(1567–1625)

ROMAN RULERS

NAME	(DATE OF OFFICE)	NERVA	(96–98)
(Usurpers in italics)		TRAJAN	(98–117)
		HADRIAN	(117–138)
AUGUSTUS	(27 BC–AD 14)	ANTONINUS PIUS	(138–161)
TIBERIUS	(14–37)	MARCUS AURELIUS	(161–180)
CALIGULA	(37–41)	LUCIUS VERUS	(161–169)
CLAUDIUS	(41–54)	COMMODUS	(180–192)
NERO	(54–68)	PERTINAX	(193)
GALBA	(68–69)	DIDUS JULIANUS	(193)
OTHO	(69)	NIGER	(193)
VITELLIUS	(69)	SEPTIMUS SEVERUS	(193–211)
VESPASIAN	(69–79)	CARACALLA	(211–217)
TITUS	(79–81)	GETA	(209–212)
DOMITIAN	(81–96)	MACRINUS	(217–218)

ROMAN RULERS (continued)

ELAGABALUS	(218–222)
ALEXANDER SEVERUS	(222–235)
MAXIMIN I	(235–238)
GORDIAN I	(238)
GORDIAN II	(238)
BALBINUS	(238)
MAXIMUS	(238)
GORDIAN III	(238–244)
PHILIP	(244–249)
DECIUS	(249–251)
HOSTILIAN	(251)
GALLUS	(251–253)
AEMILIAN	(253)
VALERIAN	(253–260)
GALLIENUS	(253–268)
CLAUDIUS II	(268–269)
QUINTILLUS	(269–270)
AURELIAN	(270–275)
TACITUS	(275–276)
FLORIAN	(276)
PROBUS	(276–282)
CARUS	(282–283)
CARINUS	(283–285)
NUMERIAN	(283–284)
†DIOCLETIAN	(284–305; abdicated)
*MAXIMIAN	(286–305; 306–308)
*CONSTANTIUS I	(305–306)
†GALERIUS	(305–311)
*SEVERUS	(306–307)
†LICINIUS	(308–324)
MAXIMIN	(310–313)
*MAXENTIUS	(306–312)
CONSTANTINE I (THE GREAT)	(312–337)
CONSTANTINE II	(337–340)
CONSTANS	(337–350)

CONSTANTIUS II	(337–361)
MAGNENTIUS	(350–351)
JULIAN	(360–363)
JOVIAN	(363–364)
*VALENTINIAN I	(364–375)
†VALENS	(364–378)
†PROCOPIUS	(365–366)
*GRATIAN	(375–383)
*VALENTINIAN II	(375–392)
THEODOSIUS I	(379–395)
†ARCADIUS	(395–408)
*HONORIUS	(395–423)
CONSTANTINE III	(407–411)
†THEODOSIUS II	(408–450)
*CONSTANTIUS III	(421–423)
VALENTINIAN III	(423–455)
†MARCIAN	(450–457)
PETRONIUS MAXIMUS	(455)
*AVITUS	(455–456)
†LEO I	(457–474)
*MAJORIAN	(457–461)
*LIBIUS SEVERUS	(461–467)
*ANTHEMIUS	(467–472)
OLYBRIUS	(472–473)
GLYCERIUS	(473)
*JULIUS NEPOS	(474–475)
†LEO II	(474)
†ZENO	(474–491)
ROMULUS AUGUSTULUS	(475–476)

*Emperors of the Western Roman Empire only

†Emperors of the Eastern Roman Empire (at Constantinople) before the fall of Rome (476). (For Eastern emperors after 476, *see* BYZANTINE RULERS.)

BYZANTINE RULERS

Name	(Date of office)
(Usurpers in italics)	
ZENO	(474–491)
BASILICUS	(475–76)
ANASTASIUS I	(491–518)
JUSTIN I	(518–527)
JUSTINIAN I	(527–565)
JUSTIN II	(565–578)
TIBERIUS II CONSTANTINE	(578–582)
MAURICE TIBERIUS	(582–602)
PHOCAS	(602–610)
HERACLIUS	(610–641)
HERACLIUS CONSTANTINE	(641)
HERACLONAS	(641)
CONSTANS II	(641–668)
CONSTANTINE IV	(668–685)

JUSTINIAN II RHINOTMETUS	(685–695, 705–711)
LEONTIUS	(695–698)
TIBERIUS III	(698–705)
PHILIPPICUS	(711–713)
ANASTASIUS II	(713–716)
THEODOSIUS III	(716–717)
LEO III	(717–741)
CONSTANTINE V COPRONYMUS	(741–775)
LEO IV	(775–780)
CONSTANTINE VI	(780–797)
IRENE	(797–802)
NICEPHORUS I	(802–811)
STAURACIUS	(811)
MICHAEL I RHANGABE	(811–813)
LEO V	(813–820)

MICHAEL II BALBUS	(820–829)
THEOPHILUS	(829–842)
MICHAEL III	(842–867)
BASIL I	(867–886)
LEO VI	(886–912)
ALEXANDER	(912–913)
CONSTANTINE VII PORPHYROGENITUS	(913–959)
ROMANUS I LECAPENUS	(920–944)
ROMANUS II	(959–963)
NICEPHOROUS II PHOCAS	(963–969)
JOHN I TZIMISCES	(969–976)
BASIL II BULGAROCTONUS	(976–1025)
CONSTANTINE VIII	(1025–28)
ROMANUS III ARGYRUS	(1028–34)
MICHAEL IV	(1034–41)
MICHAEL V CALAPHATES	(1041–42)
ZOE	(1042–56)
CONSTANTINE IX MONOMACHUS	(1042–55)
THEODORA	(1055–56)
MICHAEL VI STRATIOTICUS	(1056–57)
ISAAC I COMNENUS	(1057–59)
CONSTANTINE X DUCAS	1059–67)
ROMANUS IV DIOGENES	(1067–71)
MICHAEL VII DUCAS	(1071–78)
NICEPHORUS III BOTANIATES	(1078–81)
ALEXIUS I COMNENUS	(1081–1118)
JOHN II COMNENUS	(1118–43)
MANUEL I COMNENUS	(1143–80)
ALEXIUS II COMNENUS	(1180–83)
ANDRONICUS I COMNENUS	(1183–85)

ISAAC II ANGELUS	(1185–95, 1203–04)
ALEXIUS III ANGELUS	(1195–1203)
ALEXIUS V DUCAS MURTZUPHLUS	(1204)
*BALDWIN I	(1204–06)
*HENRY	(1206–16)
*PETER	(1217)
*YOLANDE	(1217–19)
*ROBERT	(1219–28)
*BALDWIN II	(1228–61)
*JOHN	(1231–37)
†CONSTANTINE (XI) LASCARIS	(1204–05?)
†THEODORE I LASCARIS	(1205*N22)
†JOHN III DUCAS VATATZES	(1222–54)
†THEODORE II LASCARIS	(1254–58)
†JOHN IV LASCARIS	(1258–61)
MICHAEL VIII PALAEOLOGUS	(1261–82)
ANDRONICUS II PALAEOLOGUS	(1282–1328)
ANDRONICUS III PALAEOLOGUS	(1328–41)
JOHN V PALAEOLOGUS	(1341–76, 1379–90, 1390–91)
JOHN VI CANTACUZENUS	(1347–54)
ANDRONICUS IV PALAEOLOGUS	(1376–77)
JOHN VII PALAEOLOGUS	(1390)
MANUEL II PALAEOLOGUS	(1391–1425)
JOHN VIII PALAEOLOGUS	(1421–48)
CONSTANTINE XI PALAEOLOGUS	(1448–53)

*Latin emperors

†Nicaean emperors

ANCIENT EGYPTIAN RULERS

DYNASTIES
(all dates are BC):

Earliest dynasties
I 3200–3000
II 3000–2780

Old Kingdom

III	2780–2720
IV	2720–2560
V	2560–2420
VI	2420–2270

First Intermediate Period

VII–VIII	2270–2240
IX–X	2240–2100

Middle Kingdom

XI	2100–2000
XII	2000–1788

Second Intermediate Period

XIII–XVI	1788–1600
XVII	1600–1555

The Empire

XVIII	1555–1350
XIX	1350–1200
XX	1200–1090
XXI	1090–945
XXII	945–c. 745
XXIII	c. 745–718
XXIV	718–712

Late Period

XXV	712–663
XXVI	663–525
XXVII	525–332
XXVIII	405–399
XXIX	399–379
XXX	379–341
Ptolemaic	323–30

ANCIENT EGYPTIAN RULERS (continued)

NARMER	
MENES	
AHA	
DEN	
HETEPSEKHEMWY	
RENEB	
NYNETJER	
PERIBSEN	
KHASEKHEM	
KHASEKHEMWY	
SANAKHTE	
DJOSER	
NETJERYKHET	
SEKHEMKHET	
KHABA	
HUNI	
SNEFRU	
KHUFU	
CHEOPS	
REDJEDEF	
SHEPSESKAF	
KHAFRE	
USERKAF	
SAHURE	
NEFERIAKARE	
RENEFEREF	
NUSERRE	
MENKAUHOR	
DJEDKARE IZEZI	
UNAS	
TETI	
PEPI I	
MERENRE	
PEPI II	
IBI	
NEFERKARE	
KHETY	
MERIKARE	
INYOTEF I	(2081–2065 BC)
INYOTEF II	(2065–2016 BC)
INYOTEF III	(2016–2008 BC)
MENTUHOTEP I	(2008–1957 BC)
MENTUHOTEP II	(1957–1945 BC)
MENTUHOTEP III	(1945–1938 BC)
AMENEMHET I	(1938–1908 BC)
SESOSTRIS I	(1918–1875 BC)
AMENEMHET II	(1876–1842 BC)
SESOSTRIS II	(1844–1837 BC)
SESOSTRIS III	(1836–1818 BC)
AMENEMHET III	(1818–1770 BC)
AMENEMHET IV	(1770–1760 BC)
SEBEKNEFRU	(1760–1756 BC)
APOPIS	
KAMOSE	
AHMOSE	(c. 1539–1514 BC)
AMENHOTEP I	(c. 1514–1493 BC)
THUTMOSE I	(1493–c. 1482 BC)
THUTMOSE II	(c. 1482–1479 BC)
THUTMOSE III	(1479–1426 BC)
HATSHEPSUT	(c. 1481–c. 1458 BC)

AMENHOTEP II	(c. 1426–1400 BC)
THUTMOSE IV	(1400–1390 BC)
AMENHOTEP III	(1390–1353 BC)
AMENHOTEP IV	(1353–1336 BC)
AKHENATON	(1353–1336 BC)
SMENKHKARE	(1335–1332 BC)
TUTANKHATEN	(1352– c. 1323 BC)
TUTANKHAMEN	(1352–c. 1323 BC)
AY	(1323–1319 BC)
HOREMHEB	(1319–c. 1292 BC)
RAMSES I	(1292–1290 BC)
SETI I	(1290–1279 BC)
RAMSES II	(1279–1213 BC)
MARNEPTAH	(1213–1204 BC)
SETI II	(1204–1198 BC)
SIPTAH	(1198–1193 BC)
TAUSERT	(1193–1190 BC)
SETNAKHT	(1190–1187 BC)
RAMSES III	(1187–1156 BC)
RAMSES IV	(1156–1150 BC)
RAMSES V	(1150–1145 BC)
RAMSES VI	(1145–1137 BC)
RAMSES VII	(1137–c. 1132 BC)
RAMSES VIII	(c. 1132–1126 BC)
RAMSES IX	(1126–1108 BC)
RAMSES X	(1108–1104 BC)
RAMSES XI	(1104–c. 1075 BC)
SMENDES	(c. 1075 BC)
PINUDJEM I	
PSUSENNES I	(c. 1045–c. 997 BC)
AMENEMOPE	(c. 998–c. 989 BC)
OSORKON I	(c. 979–c. 973 BC)
PSUSENNES II	(c. 964–c. 950 BC)
SHESHONK	(c. 950–929 BC)
OSORKON II	(c. 929–c. 914 BC)
OSORKON III	c. 888–c. 860 BC)
OSORKON IV	(c. 777–c. 750 BC)
KASHTA	
SHEPENWEPE I	
AMONIRDIS I	
BOCCHORIS	(c. 722–c. 715 BC)
SHABAKA	(c. 719–703 BC)
SHEBITKU	(703–690 BC)
TAHARQA	(690–664 BC)
TANUTAMON	(664 BC)
PSAMTIK I	(664–610 BC)
PSAMMETICHUS I	(664–610 BC)
NECHO II	(610–595 BC)
PSAMTIK II	(595–589 BC)
APRIES	(589–570 BC)
AMASIS II	(570–526 BC)
AHMOSE II	(570–526 BC)
CAMBYSES II	(526–522 BC)
DARIUS I	(522–486 BC)
ARTAXERXES I	(465–424 BC)
DARIUS II	(424–404 BC)
AMYRTAEUS	(404–399 BC)
ACHORIS	(393–380 BC)
NEPHERITES II	(380 BC)
NECTANEBO I	(380–362 BC)
TACHOS	(c. 365–360)
NECTANEBO II	(360–343 BC)

PTOLEMY I SOTER	(305–282 BC)	PTOLEMY VIII	(145–116 BC)
PTOLEMY II PHILADELPHUS	(285–246 BC)	EURGETES II	
PTOLEMY III EVERGETES	(246–222 BC)	PHYSCON	
PTOLEMY IV PHILOPATOR	(222–205 BC)	PTOLEMY XII AULETES	(80–51 BC)
PTOLEMY V EPIPHANES	(205–180 BC)	PTOLEMY XIII	(51–47 BC)
PTOLEMY VI PHILOMETOR	(180–145 BC)	CLEOPATRA VII	(51–30 BC)

ARTISTS, SCULPTORS, AND ARCHITECTS

3

ARP, Jean (1887–1966; French sculptor and poet)

DOU, Gerrit (1613–75; Dutch painter)

FRY, Roger (1866–1934; British painter and art critic)

LIN, Maya (1959– ; US sculptor and architect)

LOW, Sir David (1871–1963; New Zealand-born cartoonist)

4

ADAM, Robert (1728–92; British architect and interior designer)

CAPP, Al (Alfred Caplin, 1909–79; US cartoonist)

CUYP, Aelbert Jacobsz (1620–91; Dutch landscape painter)

DADD, Richard (1817–86; British painter)

DALI, Salvador (1904–89; Spanish surrealist painter)

DIOR, Christian (1905–57; French fashion designer)

DORÉ, Gustave (1832–83; French illustrator, painter, and sculptor)

DUFY, Raoul (1877–1953; French painter)

ERTÉ (Romain de Tirtoff, 1892–1990; French fashion illustrator and designer, born in Russia)

ETTY, William (1787–1849; British painter)

GABO, Naum (Naum Neemia Pevsner, 1890–1977; Russian sculptor)

GOES, Hugo van der (c. 1440–82; Flemish painter)

GOYA, Francesco de (1746–1828; Spanish painter)

4—continued

GRIS, Juan (José Victoriano González, 1887–1927; Spanish-born cubist painter)

GROS, Antoine Jean, Baron (1771–1835; French painter)

HALS, Frans (c. 1581–1666; Dutch painter)

HILL, David Octavius (1802–70; Scottish painter and photographer)

HUNT, William Holman (1827–1910; British painter)

JOHN, Augustus (1878–1961; British painter)

KAHN, Louis Isadore (1901–74; US architect)

KENT, William (1685–1748; English architect, landscape gardener, and interior designer)

KLEE, Paul (1879–1940; Swiss painter and etcher)

LAMB, Henry (1885–1960; Australian-born British painter)

LELY, Sir Peter (Pieter van der Faes, 1618–80; English portrait painter of Dutch descent)

LOOS, Adolph (1870–1933; Austrian architect)

MAES, Nicolas (or N Maas, 1634–93; Dutch painter)

MARC, Franz (1880–1916; German expressionist painter)

MIRÓ, Joan (1893–1983; Spanish painter)

NASH, John (1752–1835; British architect)

NASH, Paul (1889–1946; British painter)

NEER, Aert van der (c. 1603–77; Dutch landscape painter)

OPIE, John (1761–1807; British portrait and history painter)

4—continued

RENI, Guido (1575–1642; Italian painter)

ROSA, Salvator (1615–73; Italian painter and etcher)

SHAW, Norman (1831–1912; British architect)

WARD, Sir Leslie (1851–1922; British caricaturist)

WEST, Benjamin (1738–1820; British painter of American birth)

WOOD, Christopher (1901–30; English painter)

WOOD, Grant (1892–1942; US painter)

WOOD, John, of Bath (1704–54; English architect)

WREN, Sir Christopher (1632–1723; English architect and scientist)

ZORN, Anders (1860–1920; Swedish artist)

5

AALTO, Alvar (1898–1976; Finnish architect)

ATGET, Eugène (1856–1927; French photographer)

BACON, Francis (1909–92; British painter, born in Dublin)

BACON, John (1740–99; British neoclassical sculptor)

BAKST, Léon (Lev Samoilovich Rosenberg, 1866–1924; Russian artist)

BALLA, Giacomo (1871–1958; Italian futurist painter)

BARRY, Sir Charles (1795–1860; British architect)

BLAKE, Peter (1932– ; British painter)

BOSCH, Hieronymus (Jerome van Aeken, c. 1450–c. 1516; Dutch painter)

BOUTS, Dierick (c. 1400–75; Netherlandish painter)

5—continued

BROWN, Capability (Lancelot B, 1716–83; British landscape gardener)

BROWN, Ford Madox (1821–93; British painter, born in Calais)

BURRA, Edward (1905–76; British painter)

CAMPI, Giulio (1502–72; Italian Renaissance architect)

COROT, Jean Baptiste Camille (1796–1875; French landscape painter)

CRANE, Walter (1845–1915; British illustrator, painter, and designer of textiles and wallpaper)

CROME, John (1768–1821; British landscape painter and etcher)

DAGLY, Gerhard (c. 1653–?1714; Belgian artist)

DANBY, Francis (1793–1861; Irish painter)

DANCE, George (c. 1700–68; British architect)

DAVID, Gerard (c. 1460–1523; Netherlandish painter)

DAVID, Jacques Louis (1748–1825; French neoclassical painter)

DEGAS, Edgar (1834–1917; French painter and sculptor)

DENIS, Maurice (1870–1943; French painter, designer, and art theorist)

DÜRER, Albrecht (1471–1528; German painter)

ENSOR, James Sydney, Baron (1860–1949; Belgian painter)

ERNST, Max (1891–1976; German artist)

FOLEY, John Henry (1818–74; British sculptor)

FREUD, Lucian (1922– ; German-born British painter)

GADDI, Taddeo (c. 1300–?1366; Florentine painter)

GIBBS, James (1682–1754; British architect)

GILES, Carl Ronald (1916–95; British cartoonist)

GORKY, Arshile (Vosdanig Adoian, 1905–48; US painter, born in Armenia)

GOYEN, Jan Josephszoon van (1596–1656; Dutch landscape painter and etcher)

5—continued

GRANT, Duncan James Corrowr (1885–1978; British painter and designer)

GROSZ, George (1893–1959; German painter and draughtsman)

HIRST, Damien (1965– ; British artist and sculptor)

HOMER, Winslow (1836–1910; US painter)

HOOCH, Pieter de (1629–c. 1684; Dutch painter)

HORTA, Victor (1861–1947; Belgian architect)

JOHNS, Jasper (1930– ; US artist)

JONES, Inigo (1573–1652; English classical architect)

KEENE, Charles Samuel (1823–91; British artist and illustrator)

KLIMT, Gustav (1862–1918; Viennese Art Nouveau artist)

KLINT, Kaare (1888–1954; Danish furniture designer)

LEACH, Bernard (1887–1979; British potter, born in Hong Kong)

LEECH, John (1817–64; British caricaturist)

LÉGER, Fernand (1881–1955; French painter)

LE VAU, Louis (1612–70; French baroque architect)

LIPPI, Fra Filippo (c. 1406–69; Florentine painter)

LOTTO, Lorenzo (c. 1480–1556; Venetian painter)

LOWRY, L S (1887–1976; British painter)

MACKE, August (1887–1914; German painter)

MANET, Edouard (1832–83; French painter)

MENGS, Anton Raphael (1728–79; German painter)

METSU, Gabriel (1629–67; Dutch painter)

MONET, Claude (1840–1926; French impressionist painter)

MOORE, Henry (1898–1986; British sculptor)

MOSES, Grandma (Anna Mary Robertson M, 1860–1961; US primitive painter)

MUNCH, Edvard (1863–1944; Norwegian painter and printmaker)

MYRON (5th century BC; Athenian sculptor)

5—continued

NADAR (Gaspard Felix Tournachon, 1820–1910; French photographer and caricaturist)

NERVI, Pier Luigi (1891–1979; Italian architect)

NOLAN, Sir Sidney (1917–92; Australian painter)

NOLDE, Emil (E Hansen, 1867–1956; German expressionist painter and printmaker)

OUDRY, Jean-Baptiste (1686–1755; French rococo painter and tapestry designer)

PHYFE, Duncan (or Fife, 1768–1854; US cabinetmaker and furniture designer, born in Scotland)

PIPER, John (1903–92; British painter and writer)

PUGIN, Augustus Welby Northmore (1812–52; British architect and theorist)

QUANT, Mary (1934– ; British fashion designer)

REDON, Odilon (1840–1916; French symbolist painter and lithographer)

RICCI, Sebastiano (1659–1734; Venetian painter)

RILEY, Bridget Louise (1931– ; British painter)

RODIN, Auguste (1840–1917; French sculptor)

SCOTT, Sir George Gilbert (1811–78; British architect)

SHAHN, Ben (1898–1969; Lithuanian-born US artist)

SOANE, Sir John (1753–1837; British architect)

STEEN, Jan (c. 1626–79; Dutch painter)

STOSS, Veit (c. 1445–1533; German gothic sculptor and woodcarver)

TOBEY, Mark (1890–1976; US painter)

VICKY (Victor Weisz, 1913–66; British cartoonist, born in Berlin)

WATTS, George Frederick (1817–1904; British artist)

WYATT, James (1747–1813; British architect)

6

ALBERS, Josef (1888–1976; German abstract painter)

6–continued

ARCHER, Thomas (1668–1743; English baroque architect)

BEATON, Sir Cecil (1904–80; British photographer)

BEHZAD (c. 1455–c. 1536; Persian painter)

BENTON, Thomas Hart (1889–1975; US painter)

BEWICK, Thomas (1753–1828; British wood engraver)

BOUDIN, Eugène (1824–98; French painter)

BOULLE, André Charles (or Buhl, 1642–1732; French cabinetmaker)

BRANDT, Bill (1905–83; British photographer)

BRAQUE, Georges (1882–1963; French painter)

BRATBY, John (1928–92; British painter and writer)

BREUER, Marcel Lajos (1902–81; US architect, born in Hungary)

BUFFET, Bernard (1928–99; French painter)

BUTLER, Reg Cotterell (1913–81; British sculptor)

CALDER, Alexander (1898–1976; US sculptor)

CALLOT, Jacques (c. 1592–1635; French graphic artist)

CANOVA, Antonio (1757–1822; Italian sculptor)

CARDIN, Pierre (1922– ; French fashion designer)

CASSON, Sir Hugh (1910–99; British architect)

CHANEL, Coco (Gabrielle C, 1883–1971; French fashion designer)

CLOUET, Jean (c. 1485–1540; French portrait painter)

COOPER, Samuel (1609–72; British miniaturist)

COSWAY, Richard (1742–1821; British portrait miniaturist)

COTMAN, John Sell (1782–1842; British landscape watercolourist and etcher)

DERAIN, André (1880–1954; French postimpressionist painter)

DE WINT, Peter (1784–1849; British landscape painter)

EAKINS, Thomas (1844–1916; US painter)

6–continued

FLORIS, Cornelis (1514–75; Flemish artist)

FLORIS, Frans (c. 1516–70; Flemish artist)

FOSTER, Norman (1935– ; British architect)

FULLER, Richard Buckminster (1895–1983; US inventor and architect)

FUSELI, Henry (Johann Heinrich Füssli, 1741–1825; British painter of Swiss birth)

GÉRARD, François, Baron (1770–1837; French painter)

GIOTTO (Giotto di Bondone, c. 1266–1337; Italian painter and architect)

GIRTIN, Thomas (1775–1802; British landscape painter)

GOUJON, Jean (c. 1510–68; French Renaissance sculptor)

GREUZE, Jean-Baptiste (1725–1805; French painter)

GUARDI, Francesco (1712–93; Venetian painter)

HOLLAR, Wenceslaus (1607–77; Bohemian etcher)

HOUDON, Jean Antoine (1741–1828; French sculptor)

INGRES, Jean-Auguste-Dominique (1780–1867; French painter)

ISABEY, Jean Baptiste (1767–1855; French portrait painter and miniaturist)

JOCHHO (d. 1057; Japanese sculptor)

KNIGHT, Dame Laura (1877–1970; British painter)

LASDUN, Sir Denys (1914– ; British architect)

LA TOUR, Georges de (1593–1652; French painter)

LA TOUR, Maurice-Quentin de (1704–88; French portrait pastellist)

LE BRUN, Charles (1619–90; French history and portrait painter and designer)

LE NAIN, Antoine (c. 1588–1648; French painter)

LE NAIN, Louis (c. 1593–1648; French painter)

LE NAIN, Mathieu (c. 1607–77; French painter)

LESCOT, Pierre (c. 1510–78; French architect)

LONGHI, Pietro (Pietro Falca, 1702–85; Venetian painter)

LURÇAT, Jean (1892–1966; French painter)

6–continued

MARINI, Marino (1901–80; Italian sculptor and painter)

MARTIN, John (1789–1854; British painter)

MASSYS, Quentin (or Matsys, Messys, Metsys, c. 1466–1530; Flemish painter)

MILLET, Jean François (1814–75; French painter)

MOREAU, Gustave (1826–98; French symbolist painter)

MORONI, Giovanni Battista (c. 1525–78; Italian painter)

MORRIS, William (1834–96; British designer and artist)

OLIVER, Isaac (?1556–1617; English portrait miniaturist, born in France)

OROZCO, José (1883–1949; Mexican mural painter)

OSTADE, Adrian van (1610–85; Dutch painter and etcher)

PALMER, Samuel (1805–81; British landscape painter and etcher)

PAXTON, Sir Joseph (1801–65; British architect)

PISANO, Andrea (Andrea de Pontedera, c. 1290–1348; Italian sculptor)

PISANO, Nicola (c. 1220–c. 1278; Italian sculptor)

RENOIR, Pierre Auguste (1841–1919; French impressionist painter)

RIBERA, José de (or Jusepe R, 1591– 1652; Spanish-born painter and etcher)

RIVERA, Diego (1886–1957; Mexican mural painter)

ROMNEY, George (1734–1802; British portrait painter)

ROTHKO, Mark (Marcus Rothkovitch, 1903–70; Russian-born US painter)

RUBENS, Peter Paul (1577–1640; Flemish painter)

SCARFE, Gerald (1936– ; British cartoonist)

SEARLE, Ronald William Fordham (1920– ; British cartoonist)

SESSHU (Sesshu Toyo, 1420–1506; Japanese landscape painter)

SEURAT, Georges (1859–91; French painter)

SIGNAC, Paul (1863–1935; French painter and art theorist)

6—continued

SISLEY, Alfred (1839–99; Impressionist painter)

SLUTER, Claus (c. 1345–1406; Dutch sculptor)

SPENCE, Sir Basil (1907–76; British architect)

STUBBS, George (1724–1806; British animal painter)

TANGUY, Yves (1900–55; French surrealist painter)

TISSOT, James Joseph Jacques (1836–1902; French painter and etcher)

TITIAN (Tiziano Vecellio, c. 1488–1576; Venetian painter)

TURNER, Joseph Mallord William (1775–1851; British landscape and marine painter)

VASARI, Giorgio (1511–74; Italian painter, architect, and writer)

VOYSEY, Charles Francis Annesley (1857–1941; British architect and designer)

WARHOL, Andy (Andrew Warhola, 1926–87; US pop artist)

WEYDEN, Rogier van der (c. 1400–64; Flemish painter)

WILKIE, Sir David (1785–1841; Scottish painter)

WILSON, Richard (1714–82; British landscape painter)

WRIGHT, Frank Lloyd (1869–1959; US architect)

XIA GUI (or Hsia Knei, c. 1180–c. 1230; Chinese landscape painter)

ZEUXIS (late 5th century BC; Greek painter)

7

ALBERTI, Leon Battista (1404–72; Italian Renaissance architect)

ALLSTON, Washington (1779–1843; US Romantic painter)

ANTENOR (late 6th century BC; Athenian sculptor)

APELLES (4th century BC; Greek painter)

ASTBURY, John (1688–1743; English potter)

BARLACH, Ernst (1870–1938; German expressionist sculptor and playwright)

BASSANO, Jacopo (Jacopo or Giacomo da Ponte, c. 1517–92; Italian painter)

7—continued

BEHRENS, Peter (1868–1940; German architect)

BELLINI, Jacopo (c. 1400–c. 1470; Venetian painter)

BERNINI, Gian Lorenzo (1598–1680; Italian sculptor and architect)

BONNARD, Pierre (1867–1947; French painter)

BORGLUM, Gutzon (1867–1941; US sculptor)

BOUCHER, François (1703–70; French rococo painter)

BROUWER, Adriaen (c. 1605–38; Flemish painter)

CAMERON, Julia Margaret (1815–79; British photographer, born in Calcutta)

CASSATT, Mary (1844–1926; US painter)

CELLINI, Benvenuto (1500–71; Florentine goldsmith and sculptor)

CENNINI, Cennino (c. 1370–c. 1440; Florentine painter)

CÉZANNE, Paul (1839–1906; French postimpressionist painter)

CHAGALL, Marc (1887–1985; Russian-born painter and printmaker)

CHARDIN, Jean-Baptiste-Siméon (1699–1779; French painter)

CHIRICO, Giorgio de (1888–1978; Italian painter, born in Greece)

CHRISTO (1935–　; Bulgarian-born artist)

CIMABUE, Giovanni (Cenni de Peppi, c. 1240–c. 1302; Florentine painter)

CLODION (Claude Michel, 1738–1814; French rococo sculptor)

COURBET, Gustave (1819–77; French painter)

DAUMIER, Honoré (1808–79; French caricaturist, painter, and sculptor)

DELORME, Philibert (?1510–70; French Renaissance architect)

DELVAUX, Paul (1897–94; Belgian painter)

DUCHAMP, Marcel (1887–1968; French artist)

EL GRECO (Domenikos Theotokopoulos, 1541–1614; Painter of Greek parentage, born in Crete)

7—continued

EPSTEIN, Sir Jacob (1880–1959; British sculptor of US birth)

EXEKIAS (6th century BC; Athenian potter and vase painter)

FABERGÉ, Peter Carl (1846–1920; Russian goldsmith and jeweller)

FLAXMAN, John Henry (1755–1826; British sculptor and book illustrator)

FONTANA, Domenico (1543–1607; Italian architect)

FOUQUET, Jean (c. 1420–81; French painter and manuscript illuminator)

GAUGUIN, Paul (1848–1903; French postimpressionist painter)

GIBBONS, Grinling (1648–1721; English wood carver and sculptor)

GILLRAY, James (1756–1815; British caricaturist)

GOZZOLI, Benozzo (Benozzo di Lese, 1420–97; Florentine painter)

GROPIUS, Walter (1883–1969; German architect)

GUARINI, Guarino (1624–83; Italian baroque architect)

HASSALL, John (1868–1948; British artist)

HERRERA, Juan de (1530–97; Spanish architect)

HOBBEMA, Meindert (1638–1709; Dutch landscape painter)

HOCKNEY, David (1937–　; British painter, draughtsman, and printmaker)

HOGARTH, William (1697–1764; British painter and engraver)

HOKUSAI (Katsushika H, 1760–1849; Japanese painter and book illustrator)

HOLLAND, Henry (1745–1806; British architect)

HOPPNER, John (1758–1810; British portrait painter)

ICTINUS (5th century BC; Greek architect)

JOHNSON, Cornelius (Janssen van Ceulen, 1593–1661; English portrait painter)

KNELLER, Sir Godfrey (1646–1723; English portrait painter of German birth)

7–continued

LALIQUE, René (1860–1945; French Art Nouveau jeweller and glassmaker)

LAMERIE, Paul de (1688–1751; English silversmith)

L'ENFANT, Pierre-Charles (1754–1825; US architect and town planner of French birth)

LE NÔTRE, André (1613–1700; French landscape gardener)

LIMBURG, Pol de (active *c.* 1400–*c.* 1416; French manuscript illuminator)

LIMOSIN, Léonard (*or* Limousin, *c.* 1505–*c.* 1577; French artist)

LOCHNER, Stefan (*c.* 1400–51; German painter)

LUTYENS, Sir Edwin Landseer (1869–1944; British architect)

MACLISE, Daniel (1806–70; Irish portrait and history painter)

MADERNA, Carlo (1556–1629; Roman architect)

MAILLOL, Aristide (1861–1944; French sculptor)

MANSART, François (*or* Mansard, 1596–1666; French classical architect)

MARTINI, Simone (*c.* 1284–1344; Italian painter)

MATISSE, Henri (1869–1954; French painter and sculptor)

MEMLING, Hans (*or* Memlinc, *c.* 1430–1494; German painter)

MILLAIS, Sir John Everett (1829–96; British painter)

MORANDI, Giorgio (1890–1964; Italian still-life painter and etcher)

MORISOT, Berthe (1841–95; French painter)

MORLAND, George (1763–1804; British painter)

MURILLO, Bartolomé Esteban (1617–82; Spanish painter)

NEUMANN, Balthasar (1687–1753; German architect)

O'KEEFFE, Georgia (1887–1986; US painter)

ORCAGNA, Andrea (Andrea di Cione, *c.* 1308–*c.* 1368; Florentine artist)

PALISSY, Bernard (1510–89; French potter)

PASMORE, Victor (1908–98; British artist)

7–continued

PATINIR, Joachim (*or* Patenier, *c.* 1485–1524; Flemish painter)

PEVSNER, Antoine (1886–1962; Russian sculptor and painter)

PHIDIAS (*c.* 490–*c.* 417 BC; Athenian sculptor)

PICABIA, Francis (1879–1953; French painter and writer)

PICASSO, Pablo (1881–1973; Spanish artist)

POLLOCK, Jackson (1912–56; US painter)

POUSSIN, Nicolas (1594–1665; French painter)

PRUD'HON, Pierre Paul (1758–1823; French painter and draughtsman)

RACKHAM, Arthur (1867–1939; British watercolourist and book illustrator)

RAEBURN, Sir Henry (1756–1823; Scottish portrait painter)

RAPHAEL (Raffaello Sanzio, 1483–1520; Italian Renaissance painter and architect)

REDOUTÉ, Pierre Joseph (1759–1841; French flower painter)

ROBERTS, Tom (1856–1931; Australian painter, born in Britain)

ROUAULT, Georges (1871–1958; French artist)

RUBLYOV, Andrey (*or* A Rublev, *c.* 1370–1430; Russian icon painter)

SARGENT, John Singer (1856–1925; US portrait painter, born in Florence)

SCHIELE, Egon (1890–1918; Austrian expressionist painter)

SEGHERS, Hercules Pieterzoon (*c.* 1589–*c.* 1638; Dutch landscape painter and etcher)

SHEPARD, Ernest Howard (1879–1976; British artist)

SICKERT, Walter Richard (1860–1942; British impressionist, born in Munich)

SNOWDON, Antony Armstrong-Jones, Earl of (1930– ; British photographer)

SNYDERS, Frans (1579–1657; Flemish animal painter)

7–continued

SOUTINE, Chaim (1893–1943; Lithuanian-born painter, who emigrated to Paris)

SPENCER, Sir Stanley (1891–1959; British painter)

TENNIEL, Sir John (1820–1914; British cartoonist and book illustrator)

TIBALDI, Pellegrino (1527–96; Italian architect and painter)

TIEPOLO, Giovanni Battista (1696–1770; Venetian rococo painter)

UCCELLO, Paolo (P di Dono, 1397–1475; Florentine painter and craftsman)

UTRILLO, Maurice (1883–1955; French painter)

VAN DYCK, Sir Anthony (*or* Vandyke, 1599–1641; Flemish baroque painter)

VAN EYCK, Jan (*c.* 1390–1441; Flemish painter)

VAN GOGH, Vincent (1853–90; Dutch postimpressionist painter)

VERMEER, Jan (1632–75; Dutch painter)

VIGNOLA, Giacomo da (1507–73; Roman mannerist architect)

WATTEAU, Antoine (1684–1721; French rococo painter)

ZADKINE, Ossip (1890–1967; French sculptor of Russian birth)

ZOFFANY, Johann (*c.* 1733–1810; German-born English painter)

ZUCCARO, Federico (1543–1609; Italian painter)

ZUCCARO, Taddeo (1529–66; Italian painter)

8

AALTONEN, Wäinö (1894–1966; Finnish sculptor)

AMMANATI, Bartolommeo (1511–92; Florentine architect and sculptor)

ANGELICO, Fra (Guido di Pietro, *c.* 1400–55; Italian painter)

ANNIGONI, Pietro (1910–88; Italian painter)

ANTELAMI, Benedetto (active 1177–1233; Italian sculptor)

BECKMANN, Max (1884–1950; German expressionist painter)

8—continued

BOCCIONI, Umberto
(1882–1916; Italian futurist
painter and sculptor)

BRAMANTE, Donato
(1444–1514; Italian
Renaissance architect)

BRANCUSI, Constantin
(1876–1957; Romanian
sculptor)

BRONZINO, Il (Agnolo di
Cosimo, 1503–72; Florentine
mannerist painter)

CARRACCI, Annibale
(1560–1609; Italian painter)

CASTAGNO, Andrea del (Andrea di Bartolo de Simone, c.
1421–57; Italian painter)

CHAMBERS, Sir William
(1723–96; British architect
and interior designer)

CRESSENT, Charles
(1685–1768; French
cabinetmaker)

CRIVELLI, Carlo (c. 1430–95;
Venetian painter)

DAUBIGNY, Charles-François
(1817–78; French landscape
painter)

DELAUNAY, Robert
(1885–1941; French painter)

DRYSDALE, Sir Russell
(1912–81; Australian painter,
born in England)

DUBUFFET, Jean (1901–85;
French painter and sculptor)

FILARETE (Antonio Averlino, c.
1400–c. 1469; Italian
Renaissance architect)

FRAMPTON, Sir George
James (1860–1928; British
sculptor)

GHIBERTI, Lorenzo (c.
1378–1455; Florentine
Renaissance sculptor)

GIORDANO, Luca (1632–1705;
Neapolitan painter,
nicknamed LUCA FA
PRESTO)

GOSSAERT, Jan (c. 1478–c.
1532; Flemish painter)

GUERCINO (Giovanni
Francesco Barbieri,
1591–1666; Italian painter)

HEPWORTH, Dame Barbara
(1903–75; British sculptor)

HILLIARD, Nicholas
(1547–1619; English portrait
miniaturist)

JACOBSEN, Arne (1902–71;
Danish architect and designer
of furniture and wallpaper)

8—continued

JONGKIND, Johan Barthold
(1819–91; Dutch landscape
painter and etcher)

JORDAENS, Jakob
(1593–1678; Flemish painter)

KIRCHNER, Ernst Ludwig
(1880–1938; German
expressionist painter and
printmaker)

LANDSEER, Sir Edwin Henry
(1802–73; British artist)

LAWRENCE, Sir Thomas
(1769–1830; British painter)

LIPCHITZ, Jacques
(1891–1973; Lithuanian
cubist sculptor)

LOMBARDO, Pietro
(c. 1438–1515; Italian
sculptor and architect)

LYSIPPUS (4th century BC;
Court sculptor of Alexander
the Great)

MAGRITTE, René (1898–1967;
Belgian surrealist painter)

MALEVICH, Kazimir
(1878–1935; Russian painter
and art theorist)

MANTEGNA, Andrea (c.
1431–1506; Italian Renaissance painter and engraver)

MASACCIO (Tommaso di
Giovanni di Simone Guidi,
1401–28; Florentine painter)

MASOLINO (Tommaso di
Cristoforo Fini, 1383–?1447;
Italian painter)

MEEGEREN, Hans van
(1889–1947; Dutch painter)

MONDRIAN, Piet (Pieter
Cornelis Mondriaan,
1872–1944; Dutch painter)

MULREADY, William
(1786–1863; British painter)

MUNNINGS, Sir Alfred
(1878–1959; British painter)

NIEMEYER, Oscar (1907– ;
Brazilian architect)

PALLADIO, Andrea (1508–80;
Italian architect)

PIRANESI, Giambattista
(1720–78; Italian etcher)

PISSARRO, Camille
(1830–1903; French
impressionist painter, born in
the West Indies)

PONTORMO, Jacopo da (J
Carrucci, 1494–1557; Italian
mannerist painter)

REYNOLDS, Sir Joshua
(1723–92; British portrait
painter)

8—continued

ROBINSON, William Heath
(1872–1944; British cartoonist
and book illustrator)

ROUSSEAU, Henri
(1844–1910; French painter)

ROUSSEAU, Théodore
(1812–67; French Romantic
painter)

RUISDAEL, Jacob van
(?1628–82; Dutch landscape
painter)

SAARINEN, Eero (1910–61;
US architect, born in Finland)

SASSETTA (Stefano di
Giovanni, c. 1392–c. 1450;
Italian painter)

SEVERINI, Gino (1883–1966;
Italian painter)

SHERATON, Thomas
(1751–1806; British furniture
designer)

SOUFFLOT, Jacques Germain
(1713–80; French architect)

SULLIVAN, Louis Henry
(1856–1924; US architect)

TERBORCH, Gerard (1617–81;
Dutch painter)

VANBRUGH, Sir John
(1664–1726; English
architect)

VASARELY, Victor (1908–97;
Hungarian-born painter)

VERONESE, Paolo (P Caliari,
1528–88; Italian painter)

VLAMINCK, Maurice de (1876-
1958; French painter)

VUILLARD, Édouard
(1868–1940; French artist)

WEDGWOOD, Josiah
(1730–95; British potter,
industrialist, and writer)

WHISTLER, James McNeill
(1834–1903; US painter)

WHISTLER, Rex (1905–44;
British artist)

WOOLLETT, William (1735–85;
British engraver)

ZURBARÁN, Francisco de
(1598–1664; Spanish painter)

9

ALTDORFER, Albrecht (c.
1480–1538; German artist)

BARTHOLDI, Frédéric August
(1834–1904; French sculptor)

BEARDSLEY, Aubrey Vincent
(1872–98; British illustrator)

BONINGTON, Richard Parkes
(1801–28; British painter)

9–continued

BORROMINI, Francesco (1599–1667; Italian baroque architect)

BOURDELLE, Émile (1861–1929; French sculptor)

CANALETTO (Antonio Canal, 1697–1768; Venetian painter)

CARPACCIO, Vittore (c. 1460–c. 1525; Venetian painter)

CAVALLINI, Pietro (c. 1250–c. 1330; Italian painter)

COCKERELL, Charles Robert (1788–1863; British architect)

CONSTABLE, John (1776–1837; British landscape painter)

CORNELIUS, Peter von (1783–1867; German painter)

CORREGGIO (Antonio Allegri, c. 1494–1534; Italian Renaissance painter)

COURRÈGES, André (1923– ; French fashion designer)

DE KOONING, Willem (1904–89; US painter of Dutch birth)

DELACROIX, Eugène (1798–1863; French Romantic painter)

DELAROCHE, Paul (1797–1859; French history and portrait painter)

DONATELLO (Donato de Nicolo di Betti Bardi, c. 1386–1466; Florentine sculptor)

FABRITIUS, Carel (1622–54; Dutch painter)

FEININGER, Lyonel (1871–1956; US painter and illustrator)

FRAGONARD, Jean Honoré (1732–1806; French rococo painter)

FRIEDRICH, Caspar David (1774–1840; German Romantic landscape painter)

GÉRICAULT, Théodore (1791–1824; French painter)

GIORGIONE (c. 1477–1510; Italian painter)

GREENAWAY, Kate (1846–1901; British artist and book illustrator)

GREENOUGH, Horatio (1805–52; US neoclassical sculptor)

9–continued

GRÜNEWALD, Matthias (Mathis Gothardt, d. 1528; German painter)

HAWKSMOOR, Nicholas (1661–1736; English baroque architect)

HIROSHIGE (Ando Tokitaro, 1797–1858; Japanese colour-print artist)

HONTHORST, Gerrit von (1590–1656; Dutch painter)

JAWLENSKY, Alexey von (1864–1941; Russian expressionist painter)

KANDINSKY, Wassily (1866–1944; Russian expressionist painter and art theorist)

KAUFFMANN, Angelica (1741–1807; Swiss painter)

KOKOSCHKA, Oskar (1886–1980; Austrian expressionist painter and writer)

LISSITZKY, El (Eliezer L, 1890–1941; Russian painter and architect)

MEŠTROVIĆ, Ivan (1883–1962; US sculptor, born in Yugoslavia)

MUYBRIDGE, Eadweard (Edward James Muggeridge, 1830–1904; US photographer, born in Britain)

NICHOLSON, Ben (1894–1982; British artist)

NOLLEKENS, Joseph (1737–1823; British neoclassical sculptor)

OLDENBURG, Claes; (1929– ; US sculptor, born in Sweden)

PISANELLO (Antonio Pisano, c. 1395–c. 1455; Italian international gothic painter, draughtsman, and medallist)

ROUBILLAC, Louis François (or L F Roubiliac, 1695–1762; French sculptor)

SIQUEIROS, David Alfaro (1896–1974; Mexican painter)

STIEGLITZ, Alfred (1864–1946; US photographer)

THORNHILL, Sir James (1675–1734; English baroque decorative painter)

VELÁZQUEZ, Diego Rodriguez de Silva (1599–1660; Spanish painter)

VITRUVIUS (Marcus Vitruvius Pollio, 1st century BC; Roman architect)

9–continued

WOUWERMAN, Philips (1619–68; Dutch painter)

10

ALMA-TADEMA, Sir Lawrence (1836–1912; Dutch painter)

ALTICHIERO (c. 1330–c. 1390; Italian painter)

ARCHIPENKO, Alexander (1887–?1964; Russian-born sculptor and painter)

ARCIMBOLDO, Giuseppe (1527–93; Mannerist painter)

BERRUGUETE, Alonso (c. 1488–1561; Castillian painter)

BERRUGUETE, Pedro (c. 1450–c. 1504; Castillian painter)

BOTTICELLI, Sandro (Alessandro di Mariano Filipepi, c. 1445–1510; Florentine Renaissance painter)

BURLINGTON, Richard Boyle, 3rd Earl of (1694–1753; English architect)

BURNE-JONES, Sir Edward Coley (1833–98; Pre-Raphaelite painter)

CARAVAGGIO (Michelangelo Merisi, 1573–1610; Italian painter)

CHAMPAIGNE, Philippe de (1602–74; French portrait painter)

CRUIKSHANK, George (1792–1872; British caricaturist, painter, and illustrator)

EUPHRONIOS (late 6th–early 5th centuries BC; Athenian potter and vase painter)

GIACOMETTI, Alberto (1901–66; Swiss sculptor and painter)

LORENZETTI, Ambrogio (c. 1290–?1348; Italian painter)

MACKINTOSH, Charles Rennie (1868–1928; Scottish architect and designer)

MEISSONIER, Jean-Louis-Ernest (1815–91; French painter)

MODIGLIANI, Amedeo (1884–1920; Italian painter and sculptor)

MOHOLY-NAGY, László (1895–1946; Hungarian artist)

MOTHERWELL, Robert (1915–91; US abstract painter)

10—continued

POLLAIUOLO, Antonio (c. 1432–98; Florentine Renaissance artist)

POLYCLITUS (5th century BC; Greek sculptor)

PRAXITELES (mid-4th century BC; Athenian sculptor)

RICHARDSON, Henry Hobson (1838–86; US architect)

ROWLANDSON, Thomas (1756–1827; British caricaturist)

SCHWITTERS, Kurt (1887–1958; German artist and poet)

SENEFELDER, Aloys (1771–1834; German playwright and engraver)

SIGNORELLI, Luca (c. 1441–1523; Italian Renaissance painter)

SUTHERLAND, Graham Vivian (1903–80; British artist)

TANGE KENZO (1913– ; Japanese architect)

TINTORETTO (Jacopo Robusti, 1518–94; Venetian painter)

VAN DE VELDE, Henry (1863–1957; Belgian Art Nouveau architect, interior designer, and painter)

VERROCCHIO, Andrea del (Andrea del Cione, c. 1435–88; Italian sculptor, painter, and goldsmith)

WATERHOUSE, Alfred (1830–1905; British architect)

ZUCCARELLI, Francesco (1702–88; Italian painter)

11

ABERCROMBIE, Sir Patrick (1879–1957; British architect)

BARTOLOMMEO, Fra (Baccio della Porta, 1472–1517; Florentine Renaissance painter)

BUTTERFIELD, William (1814–1900; British architect)

CALLICRATES (5th century BC; Athenian architect)

CALLIMACHUS (late 5th century BC; Greek sculptor)

CHIPPENDALE, Thomas (1718–79; British cabinetmaker)

CHODOWIECKI, Daniel Nikolaus (1726–1801; German painter and engraver)

11—continued

DELLA ROBBIA, Luca (1400–82; Florentine Renaissance sculptor)

DOMENICHINO (Domenico Zampieri, 1581–1641; Italian painter)

GHIRLANDAIO, Domenico (Domenico di Tommaso Bigordi, 1449–94; Florentine painter)

GIAMBOLOGNA (Giovanni da Bologna or Jean de Boulogne, 1529–1608; Italian mannerist sculptor)

GISLEBERTUS (early 12th century; French romanesque sculptor)

HEPPLEWHITE, George (d. 1786; British furniture designer and cabinetmaker)

LE CORBUSIER (Charles-Édouard Jeanneret, 1887–1965; French architect, born in Switzerland)

TERBRUGGHEN, Hendrik (1588–1629; Dutch painter)

THORVALDSEN, Bertel (or B Thorwaldsen, 1768–1844; Danish sculptor)

12

BRUNELLESCHI, Filippo (1377–1446; Italian architect)

FANTIN-LATOUR, Henri (1836–1904; French painter)

GAINSBOROUGH, Thomas (1727–88; British portrait and landscape painter)

GAUDÍ Y CORNET, Antonio (1852–1926; Spanish architect)

GIULIO ROMANO (Giulio Pippi, c. 1499–1546; Italian mannerist painter and architect)

LICHTENSTEIN, Roy (1923–97; US painter)

LUCA FA PRESTO (Nickname of Luca Giordano)

PALMA VECCHIO, Jacopo (J Negretti, c. 1480–1528; Italian painter)

PARMIGIANINO (Girolamo Francesco Maria Mazzola, 1503–40; Italian painter)

PINTURICCHIO (Bernardino di Betto, c. 1454–1513; Italian Renaissance painter)

RAUSCHENBERG, Robert (1925– ; US artist)

12—continued

SAINT-LAURENT, Yves (1936– ; French fashion designer)

SCHIAPARELLI, Elsa (1896–1973; Italian-born fashion designer)

VIOLLET-LE-DUC, Eugène Emmanuel (1814–79; French architect and author)

WINTERHALTER, Franz Xavier (1806–73; German painter and lithographer)

13

LORENZO MONACO (Piero di Giovanni, c. 1370–1425; Italian painter)

PIERO DI COSIMO (P di Lorenzo, 1462–1521; Florentine Renaissance painter)

WILLIAMS-ELLIS, Sir Clough (1883–1978; Welsh architect)

14

ANDREA DEL SARTO (Andrea d'Agnolo, 1486–1530; Italian painter)

BÉRAIN THE ELDER, Jean (1637–1711; French designer, engraver, and painter)

CARTIER-BRESSON, Henri (1908– ; French photographer)

CLAUDE LORRAINE (Claude Gellée, 1600–82; French landscape painter)

COUSIN THE ELDER, Jean (1490–1560; French artist and craftsman)

GAUDIER-BRZESKA, Henri (1891–1915; French sculptor)

LUCAS VAN LEYDEN (Lucas Hugensz or Jacobsz, c. 1494–1533; Dutch artist)

MIES VAN DER ROHE, Ludwig (1886–1969; German architect)

15

CRANACH THE ELDER, Lucas (Lucas Müller, 1472–1553; German artist)

HARDOUIN-MANSART, Jules (1646–1708; French baroque architect)

KITAGAWA UTAMARO (1753–1806; Japanese artist)

LEONARDO DA VINCI (1452–1519; Italian artistic and scientific genius of the Renaissance)

15–continued
TOULOUSE-LAUTREC, Henri de (1864–1901; French artist)

16
BRUEGHEL THE ELDER, Pieter (*or* Bruegel, 1525–69; Flemish painter)
FISCHER VON ERLACH, Johann Bernhard (1656–1723; Austrian architect)
PUVIS DE CHAVANNES, Pierre (1824–98; French painter)
REMBRANDT VAN RIJN (1606–69; Dutch painter and etcher)
UTAGAWA KUNIYOSHI (Igusa Magosaburo, 1797–1861; Japanese painter and printmaker)

17
DOMENICO VENEZIANO (active *c.* 1438–1461; Italian painter)

17–continued
GENTILE DA FABRIANO (Niccolo di Giovanni di Massio, *c.* 1370–1427; Florentine painter)
HERRERA THE YOUNGER, Francisco de (1622–85; Spanish baroque painter and architect)
HOLBEIN THE YOUNGER, Hans (*c.* 1497–1543; German painter)
TENIERS THE YOUNGER, David (1610–90; Flemish painter)

18
ANTONELLO DA MESSINA (*c.* 1430–*c.* 1479; Italian painter)
JACOPO DELLA QUERCIA (*c.* 1374–1438; Italian Renaissance sculptor)
LEIGHTON OF STRETTON, Frederic, Baron (1830–96; British painter and sculptor)

19
DUCCIO DI BUONINSEGNA (*c.* 1255–*c.* 1318; Italian painter)
PIERO DELLA FRANCESCA (*c.* 1420–92; Italian Renaissance painter)

20
DESIDERIO DA SETTIGNANO (*c.* 1430–64; Italian Renaissance sculptor)
MICHELANGELO BUONARROTI (1475–1564; Italian sculptor, painter, and architect)
MICHELOZZO DI BARTOLOMMEO (1396–1472; Florentine Renaissance sculptor and architect)

WRITERS, PLAYWRIGHTS, AND POETS

2
FO, Dario (1926– ; Italian playwright)

3
ECO, Umberto (1932– ; Italian writer)
FRY, Christopher (C Harris, 1907– ; British dramatist)
GAY, John (1685–1732; British poet and dramatist)
KYD, Thomas (1558–94; English dramatist)
PAZ, Octavio (1914–98; Mexican poet)
SUE, Eugène (Joseph Marie S, 1804–57; French novelist)

4
AGEE, James (1909–55; US poet and novelist)
AMIS, Kingsley (1922–95; British novelist and poet)
ASCH, Sholem (1880–1957; Jewish novelist)
BANA (7th century AD; Sanskrit writer)
BAUM, L Frank (1856–1919; US novelist)

4–continued
BENN, Gottfried (1886–1956; German poet)
BLOK, Aleksandr Aleksandrovich (1880–1921; Russian symbolist poet)
BÖLL, Heinrich (1917–85; German novelist)
BOLT, Robert Oxton (1924–95; British dramatist)
BOND, Edward (1934– ; British dramatist)
BUCK, Pearl S (1892–1973; US novelist)
CARY, Joyce (1888–1957; British novelist)
CRUZ, Sor Juana Inéz de la (1651–95; Mexican poet)
DAHL, Roald (1916–90; British author)
DEUS, João de (1830–96; Portuguese poet)
DU FU (*or* Tu Fu; 712–70 AD; Chinese poet)
FORD, Ford Madox (Ford Hermann Hueffer, 1873–1939; British novelist)

4–continued
FORD, John (1586–*c.* 1640; English dramatist)
FOXE, John (1516–87; English religious writer)
GALT, John (1779–1839; Scottish novelist)
GIDE, André (1869–1951; French novelist and critic)
GRAY, Thomas (1716–71; British poet)
GUNN, Thomson W (1929– ; British poet)
HARE, Sir David (1947– ; British playwright)
HART, Moss (1904–61; US dramatist)
HILL, Geoffrey (1932– ; British poet)
HOGG, James (1770–1835; Scottish poet and writer)
HOOD, Thomas (1799–1845; British poet)
HOPE, Anthony (Sir Anthony Hope Hawkins; 1863–1933; British novelist)

4–continued

HUGO, Victor (1802–85; French poet, dramatist, and novelist)

HUNT, Leigh (1784–1859; British poet and journalist)

KIVI, Alexis (A Stenvall, 1834–72; Finnish poet, dramatist, and novelist)

LAMB, Charles (1775–1834; British essayist and critic)

LEAR, Edward (1812–88; British artist and poet)

LIVY (Titus Livius, 59 BC–17 AD; Roman writer)

LOTI, Pierre (Julien Viaud; 1850–1923; French novelist)

LYLY, John (c. 1554–1606; English dramatist and writer)

MANN, Thomas (1875–1955; German novelist)

MUIR, Edwin (1887–1959; Scottish poet)

NASH, Ogden (1902–71; US humorous writer)

NEXØ, Martin Andersen (1869–1954; Danish novelist)

OVID (Publius Ovidius Naso 43 BC–17 AD; Roman poet)

OWEN, Wilfred (1893–1918; British poet)

POPE, Alexander (1688–1744; British poet)

READ, Sir Herbert (1893–1968; British poet)

RHYS, Jean (1894–1979; British novelist)

ROTH, Philip (1933–   ; US novelist)

ROWE, Nicholas (1674–1718; British dramatist)

RUIZ, Juan (c. 1283–c. 1350; Spanish poet)

SADE, Donatien Alphonse François, Marquis de (1740–1814; French novelist)

SA'DI (Mosleh al-Din S, c. 1215–92; Persian poet)

SAKI (H H Munro, 1870–1916; British humorous short-story writer)

SAND, George (Aurore Dupin, Baronne Dudevant, 1804–76; French novelist)

SETH, Vikram (1952–   ; Indian-born novelist)

SHAW, George Bernard (1856–1950; Irish dramatist)

SNOW, C P, Baron (1905–80; British novelist)

TATE, Allen (1899–1979; US poet and critic)

4–continued

TATE, Nahum (1652–1715; British poet)

URFÉ, Honoré d' (1568–1625; French novelist)

VEGA, Lope Félix de (1562–1635; Spanish poet and dramatist)

WAIN, John (1925–94; British novelist and poet)

WARD, Artemus (Charles Farrar Browne, 1834–67; US humorous writer)

WARD, Mrs Humphry (1851–1920; British novelist)

WEBB, Mary (1881–1927; British novelist)

WEST, Dame Rebecca (Cicely Isabel Fairfield, 1892–1983; British novelist and journalist)

WEST, Nathanael (Nathan Weinstein, 1903–40; US novelist)

WOOD, Mrs Henry (1814–87; British novelist)

WREN, P C (1885–1941; British novelist)

WYSS, Johann Rudolph (1782–1830; Swiss writer)

ZOLA, Émile (1840–1902; French novelist)

5

ADAMS, Henry (1838–1918; US historian)

ADAMS, Richard (1920–   ; British novelist)

AGNON, Shmuel Yosef (Samuel Josef Czaczkes, 1888–1970; Jewish novelist)

ALBEE, Edward (1928–   ; US dramatist)

ARANY, János (1817–82; Hungarian poet)

AUDEN, W H (1907–73; British poet)

BABEL, Isaac Emmanuilovich (1894–1941; Russian short-story writer)

BARTH, John (1930–   ; US novelist)

BATES, H E (1905–74; British writer)

BEHAN, Brendan (1923–64; Irish playwright)

BELLO, Andrés (1781–1865; Venezuelan scholar and poet)

BELYI, Andrei (Boris Nikolaevich Bugaev, 1880–1934; Russian poet)

BEMBO, Pietro (1470–1547; Italian scholar)

5–continued

BENDA, Julien (1867–1956; French novelist and philosopher)

BENÉT, Stephen Vincent (1898–1943; US poet and novelist)

BETTI, Ugo (1892–1953; Italian dramatist)

BOWEN, Elizabeth (1899–1973; British novelist, born in Dublin)

BRANT, Sebastian (?1458–1521; German poet)

BROCH, Hermann (1886–1951; Austrian novelist)

BUNIN, Ivan Alekseevich (1879–1953; Russian poet and novelist)

BURNS, Robert (1759–96; Scottish poet)

BUTOR, Michel (1926–   ; French experimental novelist and critic)

BYATT, A S (1936–   ; British writer)

BYRON, George Gordon, Lord (1788–1824; British poet)

CAMUS, Albert (1913–60; French novelist)

CAREW, Thomas (c. 1595–1640; British poet)

CLARE, John (1793–1864; British poet)

COLUM, Padraic (Patrick Colm; 1881–1972; Irish poet)

CRAIK, Dinah Maria Mulock (1826–87; British novelist)

CRANE, Hart (1899–1932; US poet)

CRANE, Stephen (1871–1900; US novelist)

DARÍO, Rubén (Félix García Sarmiento; 1867–1916; Nicaraguan poet)

DEFOE, Daniel (1660–1731; British novelist)

DONNE, John (1572–1631; English poet)

DOYLE, Sir Arthur Conan (1859–1930; British author)

DOYLE, Roddy (1958–   ; Irish novelist)

DUMAS, Alexandre (1802–70; French novelist and dramatist)

DURAS, Marguerite (1914– ; French novelist)

ELIOT, George (Mary Ann Evans, 1819–80; British novelist)

5–continued

ELIOT, T S (1888–1965; Anglo-American poet, critic, and dramatist)

ELYOT, Sir Thomas (c. 1490–1546; English scholar)

EWALD, Johannes (1743–81; Danish poet and playwright)

FRIEL, Brian (1929– ; Irish playwright)

FROST, Robert Lee (1874–1963; US poet)

GENET, Jean (1910–86; French novelist and dramatist)

GOGOL, Nikolai Vasilievich (1809–52; Russian novelist and dramatist)

GORKI, Maksim (Aleksei Maksimovich Peshkov; 1868–1936; Russian novelist)

GOSSE, Sir Edmund (1849–1928; British critic)

GOWER, John (c. 1330–1408; English poet)

GRASS, Günter (1927– ; German novelist and poet)

GREEN, Henry (Henry Vincent Yorke; 1905–73; British novelist)

HAFIZ, Shams al-Din Muhammad (?1326–90; Persian lyric poet)

HALLE, Adam de la (c. 1240–90; French poet and musician)

HARDY, Thomas (1840–1928; British novelist and poet)

HARTE, Brett (1836–1902; US short-story writer)

HAŠEK, Jaroslav (1883–1923; Czech novelist)

HEINE, Heinrich (1797–1856; German Jewish poet and writer)

HENRY, O (William Sidney Porter, 1862–1910; US short-story writer)

HESSE, Hermann (1877–1962; German novelist and poet)

HOMER (8th century BC; Greek epic poet)

HOOFT, Pieter Corneliszoon (1581–1647; Dutch poet)

IBSEN, Henrik (1828–1906; Norwegian playwright and poet)

JAMES, Henry (1843–1916; US novelist and critic)

JAMES, P D (1920– ; British novelist)

JARRY, Alfred (1873–1907; French dramatist)

5–continued

JONES, David (1895–1974; Anglo-Welsh writer)

JONES, LeRoi (1934– ; US dramatist and poet)

JOYCE, James (1882–1941; Irish novelist and poet)

KAFKA, Franz (1883–1924; Czech writer)

KEATS, John (1795–1821; British poet)

KEMAL, Namik (1840–88; Turkish poet, novelist, and dramatist)

KESEY, Ken (1935– ; US novelist)

LEWIS, C S (1898–1963; British writer)

LEWIS, Matthew Gregory (1775–1818; British novelist)

LEWIS, Sinclair (1885–1951; US novelist)

LEWIS, Wyndham (1882–1957; British novelist)

LODGE, David (1935– ; British novelist)

LODGE, Thomas (1558–1625; English poet, dramatist, and writer)

LOWRY, Malcolm (1909–57; British novelist)

LUCAN (Marcus Annaeus Lucanus, 39–65 AD; Roman poet)

MAMET, David (1947– ; US playwright)

MAROT, Clément (1496–1544; French poet)

MARSH, Dame Ngaio (1899–1981; New Zealand detective-story writer)

MARTÍ, José Julián (1853–95; Cuban poet)

MASON, A E W (1865–1948; British novelist)

MILNE, A A (1882–1956; British novelist and dramatist)

MOORE, Marianne (1887–1972; US poet)

MOORE, Thomas (1779–1852; Irish poet)

MURRY, John Middleton (1889–1957; British literary critic)

MUSIL, Robert (1880–1942; Austrian novelist)

MYERS, F W H (1843–1901; British essayist and poet)

NASHE, Thomas (1567–c. 1601; British dramatist)

NOYES, Alfred (1880–1958; British poet)

5–continued

ODETS, Clifford (1906–63; US dramatist)

O'HARA, John (1905–70; US novelist)

OPITZ, Martin (1597–1639; German poet)

ORCZY, Baroness Emmusca (1865–1947; British novelist)

OTWAY, Thomas (1652–85; British dramatist)

OUIDA (Marie Louise de la Ramée, 1839–1908; British novelist)

PAN GU (or P'an Ku; 32–92 AD; Chinese historian)

PATON, Alan (1903–88; South African novelist)

PEAKE, Mervyn (1911–68; British novelist)

PEELE, George (1556–96; English dramatist)

PÉGUY, Charles (1873–1914; French poet and essayist)

PERSE, Saint-John (Alexis Saint-Léger, 1887–1975; French poet)

PLATH, Sylvia (1932–63; US poet and writer)

POUND, Ezra (1885–1972; US poet and critic)

POWYS, John Cowper (1872–1963; British novelist)

PRIOR, Matthew (1664–1721; British poet)

PULCI, Luigi (1432–84; Italian poet)

RAINE, Kathleen (1908– ; British poet)

READE, Charles (1814–84; British novelist)

RILKE, Rainer Maria (1875–1926; Austrian poet)

ROLFE, Frederick William (1860–1913; British novelist)

SACHS, Hans (1494–1576; German poet and folk dramatist)

SACHS, Nelly (1891–1970; German Jewish poet and dramatist)

SAGAN, Françoise (Françoise Quoirez, 1935– ; French writer)

SCOTT, Sir Walter (1771–1832; Scottish novelist)

SETON, Ernest Thompson (1860–1946; US writer)

SHUTE, Nevil (Nevil Shute Norway, 1899–1960; British novelist)

5—continued

SIMMS, William Gilmore (1806–70; US novelist)

SMART, Christopher (1722–71; British poet)

SMITH, Stevie (Florence Margaret S, 1902–71; British poet)

SPARK, Muriel (1918–   ; British novelist)

STAËL, Anne Louise Germaine Necker, Madame de (1766–1817; French writer)

STEIN, Gertrude (1874–1946; US writer)

STORM, Theodor Woldsen (1817–1888; German writer)

STOWE, Harriet Beecher (1811–96; US novelist)

SVEVO, Italo (Ettore Schmitz, 1861–1928; Italian novelist)

SWIFT, Graham (1946–   ; British novelist)

SWIFT, Jonathan (1667–1745; Anglo-Irish poet and satirist)

SYNGE, John Millington (1871–1909; Anglo-Irish dramatist)

TASSO, Torquato (1544–95; Italian poet)

TIECK, Ludwig (1773–1853; German writer)

TWAIN, Mark (Samuel Langhorne Clemens, 1835–1910; US novelist)

UDALL, Nicholas (1505–56; English dramatist)

VARRO, Marcus Terentius (116–27 BC; Roman poet)

VERNE, Jules (1828–1905; French writer)

VIDAL, Gore (1925–   ; US novelist and essayist)

VIGNY, Alfred de (1797–1863; French poet, novelist, and dramatist)

WALEY, Arthur (1889–1966; British translator and poet)

WAUGH, Evelyn (1903–66; British novelist)

WEISS, Peter (1916–82; German dramatist and novelist)

WELLS, H G (1866–1946; British novelist)

WHITE, Patrick (1912–90; Australian novelist)

WHITE, T H (1906–64; British novelist)

WILDE, Oscar (O Fingal O'Flahertie Wills W, 1854–1900; British dramatist and poet)

5—continued

WOLFE, Charles (1791–1823; Irish poet)

WOLFE, Thomas (1900–38; US novelist)

WOOLF, Virginia (1882–1941; British novelist)

WYATT, Sir Thomas (1503–42; English poet)

YEATS, William Butler (1865–1939; Irish poet and dramatist)

YONGE, Charlotte (1823–1901; British novelist)

ZWEIG, Arnold (1887–1968; East German-Jewish novelist)

ZWEIG, Stefan (1881–1942; Austrian Jewish writer)

6

ACCIUS, Lucius (170–c. 85 BC; Roman tragic dramatist)

ADAMOV, Arthur (1908–70; French dramatist)

ALCOTT, Louisa May (1832–88; US novelist)

ALDISS, Brian W (1925–   ; British novelist)

ALEMÁN, Mateo (1547–?1614; Spanish writer)

ALGREN, Nelson (1909–81; US novelist)

AMBLER, Eric (1909–   ; British novelist)

ANDRIĆ, Ivo (1892–1975; Serbian writer)

ARAGON, Louis (1897–1982; French poet, novelist, and journalist)

ASCHAM, Roger (1515–68; English scholar and writer)

ASIMOV, Isaac (1920–92; US science fiction writer, born in Russia)

AUBREY, John (1626–97; English antiquary)

AUSTEN, Jane (1775–1817; British novelist)

AZORÍN (José Martínéz Ruíz, 1874–1967; Spanish novelist, essayist, and critic)

AZUELA, Mariano (1873–1952; Mexican novelist)

BALZAC, Honoré de (1799–1850; French novelist)

BARHAM, Richard Harris (1788–1845; British humorous writer)

BARKER, George (1913–91; British poet)

BARNES, William (1801–86; British poet)

6—continued

BAROJA, Pío (1872–1956; Spanish novelist)

BARRÈS, Maurice (1862–1923; French writer)

BARRIE, Sir James (1860–1937; British dramatist and novelist)

BELLAY, Joachim de (1522–60; French poet)

BELLOC, Hilaire (1870–1953; British poet and essayist)

BELLOW, Saul (1915–   ; Canadian-born US novelist)

BESANT, Sir Walter (1836–1901; British novelist)

BIALIK, Chaim Nachman (1873–1934; Jewish poet and translator)

BIERCE, Ambrose Gwinnett (1842–?1914; US writer)

BINYON, Laurence (1869–1943; British poet)

BLYTON, Enid (1897–1968; British writer of children's books)

BORGES, Jorge Luis (1899–1986; Argentinian writer)

BORROW, George Henry (1803–81; British writer)

BRECHT, Bertolt (1898–1956; German dramatist and poet)

BRETON, André (1896–1966; French poet)

BRIDIE, James (Osborne Henry Mavor; 1888–1951; British dramatist)

BRONTË, Anne (1820–49; British novelist)

BRONTË, Charlotte (1816–55; British novelist)

BRONTË, Emily (1818–48; British novelist)

BROOKE, Rupert (1887–1915; British poet)

BROWNE, Sir Thomas (1605–82; English writer)

BRYANT, William Cullen (1794–1878; US poet, journalist, and critic)

BUCHAN, John, 1st Baron Tweedsmuir (1875–1940; British novelist)

BUNYAN, John (1628–88; English writer)

BÜRGER, Gottfried (1747–94; German poet)

BURNEY, Fanny (Mrs Frances Burney D'Arblay; 1752–1840; British novelist)

6–continued

BUTLER, Samuel (1612–80; British satirical poet)

BUTLER, Samuel (1835–1902; British novelist)

CAMÕES, Luís de (c. 1524–80; Portuguese poet)

CAPOTE, Truman (1924–84; US novelist)

CARSON, Rachel Louise (1907–64; US science writer)

CAVAFY, Constantine (C Kavafis, 1863–1933; Greek poet)

CÉLINE, Louis Ferdinand (L F Destouches, 1884–1961; French novelist)

CIBBER, Colley (1671–1757; British dramatist)

CLARKE, Marcus (1846–81; Australian novelist, born in London)

COLMAN, George (1732–94; British dramatist)

CONRAD, Joseph (Teodor Josef Konrad Watęcz Korzeniowski, 1857–1924; Polish-born British novelist)

COOPER, James Fenimore (1789–1851; US novelist)

COWLEY, Abraham (1618–67; English poet)

COWPER, William (1731–1800; British poet)

CRABBE, George (1754–1832; British poet)

CRONIN, A J (1896–1981; British novelist)

DANIEL, Samuel (?1562–1619; English poet, dramatist, and critic)

DAUDET, Alphonse (1840–97; French novelist)

DAVIES, W H (1871–1940; British poet)

DEKKER, Thomas (c. 1572–1632; British dramatist and pamphleteer)

DOWSON, Ernest (1867–1900; British poet)

DRYDEN, John (1631–1700; British poet)

DUNBAR, William (c. 1460–c. 1530; Scots poet)

ÉLUARD, Paul (Eugène Grindel, 1895–1952; French poet)

EMPSON, Sir William (1906–84; British poet and critic)

ENNIUS, Quintus (238–169 BC; Roman poet)

6–continued

EVELYN, John (1620–1706; English diarist)

FOUQUÉ, Friedrich Heinrich Karl, Baron de la Motte (1777–1843; German novelist and dramatist)

FOWLES, John (1926– ; British novelist)

FRANCE, Anatole (Jacques Anatole François Thibault 1844–1924; French novelist)

FRISCH, Max (1911–91; Swiss dramatist and novelist)

FUGARD, Athol (1932– ; South African dramatist)

FULLER, Roy (1912–91; British poet and novelist)

FULLER, Thomas (1608–61; British historian)

GEORGE, Stefan (1868–1933; German poet)

GIBBON, Edward (1737–94; British historian)

GIBRAN, Khalil (1883–1931; Lebanese mystic and poet)

GOETHE, Johann Wolfgang von (1749–1832; German poet)

GRAVES, Robert (1895–1985; British poet, critic, and novelist)

GREENE, Graham (1904–91; British novelist)

GREENE, Robert (c. 1558–92; English dramatist)

HAMSUN, Knut (1859–1952; Norwegian novelist)

HARRIS, Joel Chandler (1848–1908; US novelist and short-story writer)

HEANEY, Seamus (1939– ; Irish poet)

HEBBEL, Friedrich (1813–63; German dramatist)

HELLER, Joseph (1923– ; US novelist)

HESIOD (8th century BC; Greek poet)

HILTON, James (1900–54; British novelist)

HOLMES, Oliver Wendell (1809–94; US essayist and poet)

HORACE (Quintus Horatius Flaccus; 65–8 BC; Roman poet)

HUDSON, W H (1841–1922; British naturalist and writer)

HUGHES, Richard (1900–76; British novelist)

6–continued

HUGHES, Ted (1930–98; British poet)

HUGHES, Thomas (1822–96; British writer)

IRVING, Washington (1783–1859; US short-story writer)

ISAACS, Jorge (1837–95; Colombian novelist)

JENSEN, Johannes (1873–1950; Danish novelist and poet)

JONSON, Ben (1572–1637; English dramatist and poet)

KAISER, Georg (1878–1945; German dramatist)

KELLER, Gottfried (1819–90; German-Swiss poet and novelist)

KLEIST, Heinrich von (1777–1811; German dramatist)

LACLOS, Pierre Choderlos de (1741–1803; French novelist)

LANDOR, Walter Savage (1775–1864; British poet and prose writer)

LANIER, Sidney (1842–81; US poet)

LARKIN, Philip (1922–85; British poet)

LAWLER, Ray (1921– ; Australian dramatist)

LE FANU, Sheridan (1814–73; Irish novelist)

LEONOV, Leonid (1899–1994; Soviet novelist and playwright)

LESAGE, Alain-René (1668–1747; French novelist)

LIVELY, Penelope (1933– ; British novelist)

LONDON, Jack (1876–1916; US novelist)

LOWELL, Amy (1874–1925; US poet)

LOWELL, James Russell (1819–91; US poet)

LOWELL, Robert (1917–77; US poet)

LU HSÜN (or Chou Shu-jen 1881–1936; Chinese writer)

MACHEN, Arthur (1863–1947; Welsh novelist)

MAILER, Norman (1923– ; US novelist and journalist)

MALORY, Sir Thomas (?1400–71; English writer)

MCEWAN, Ian (1948– ; British novelist)

95

6–continued

MERCER, David (1928–80; British dramatist)

MILLAY, Edna St Vincent (1892–1950; US poet)

MILLER, Arthur (1915– ; US dramatist)

MILLER, Henry (1891–1980; US novelist)

MILTON, John (1608–74; English poet)

MOLNÁR, Ferenc (1878–1952; Hungarian dramatist)

MORGAN, Charles (1894–1958; British novelist and dramatist)

MÖRIKE, Eduard Friedrich (1804–75; German poet and novelist)

MOTION, Andrew (1952– ; British poet and writer)

MUNTHE, Axel (1857–1949; Swedish author)

MUSSET, Alfred de (1810–57; French poet and dramatist)

NERUDA, Pablo (Neftalí Ricardo Reyes 1904–73; Chilean poet)

NERVAL, Gérard de (Gérard Labrunie 1808–55; French poet)

NESBIT, Edith (1858–1924; British children's writer)

O'BRIEN, Flann (Brian O'Nolan 1911–66; Irish novelist and journalist)

O'CASEY, Sean (1880–1964; Irish dramatist)

O'NEILL, Eugene (1888–1953; US dramatist)

ORWELL, George (Eric Blair; 1903–50; British novelist, born in India)

PARKER, Dorothy Rothschild (1893–1967; US humorous writer)

PAVESE, Cesare (1908–50; Italian novelist and poet)

PETÖFI, Sándor (1823–49; Hungarian poet)

PINDAR (518–438 BC; Greek poet)

PINERO, Sir Arthur Wing (1855–1934; British dramatist)

PINTER, Harold (1930– ; British dramatist)

PIOZZI, Hester Lynch (1741–1821; British writer)

PLOMER, William (1903–73; South African poet and novelist)

6–continued

PORTER, Katherine Anne (1890–1980; US short-story writer and novelist)

PORTER, Peter (1929– ; British poet)

POTTER, Beatrix (1866–1943; British children's writer)

POTTER, Stephen (1900–70; British writer)

POWELL, Anthony (1905– ; British novelist)

PROUST, Marcel (1871–1922; French novelist)

RACINE, Jean (1639–99; French dramatist)

RAMSAY, Allan (?1685–1758; Scottish poet)

RANSOM, John Crowe (1888–1974; US poet)

RUNYON, Damon (1884–1946; US humorous writer)

SAPPER (H C McNeile, 1888–1937; British novelist)

SAPPHO (c. 612–c. 580 BC; Greek poet)

SARDOU, Victorien (1831–1908; French dramatist)

SARTRE, Jean-Paul (1905–80; French philosopher, novelist, dramatist, and critic)

SAVAGE, Richard (c. 1696–1743; British poet)

SAYERS, Dorothy L (1893–1957; British writer)

SIDNEY, Sir Philip (1554–86; English poet)

SILONE, Ignazio (Secondo Tranquilli, 1900–78; Italian novelist)

SINGER, Isaac Bashevis (1904–91; US novelist and short-story writer)

SMILES, Samuel (1812–1904; British writer)

STEELE, Sir Richard (1672–1729; British essayist and dramatist)

STERNE, Laurence (1713–68; British novelist)

STOKER, Bram (Abraham S, 1847–1912; Irish novelist)

STOREY, David (1933– ; British novelist and dramatist)

SURREY, Henry Howard, Earl of (1517–47; English poet)

SYMONS, Arthur (1865–1945; British poet and critic)

TAGORE, Rabindranath (1861–1941; Indian poet)

6–continued

THOMAS, Dylan (1914–53; Welsh poet)

THOMAS, Edward (1878–1917; British poet)

TOLLER, Ernst (1893–1939; German playwright and poet)

TRAVEN, B (Berick Traven Torsvan, 1890–1969; US novelist)

UHLAND, Ludwig (1787–1862; German poet)

UNDSET, Sigrid (1882–1949; Norwegian novelist)

UPDIKE, John (1932– ; US novelist and short-story writer)

VALÉRY, Paul (1871–1945; French poet, essayist, and critic)

VILLON, François (1431–?1463; French poet)

VIRGIL (Publius Vergilius Maro, 70–19 BC; Roman poet)

VONDEL, Joost van den (1587–1679; Dutch dramatist and poet)

WALLER, Edmund (1606–87; British poet)

WALTON, Izaak (1593–1683; English writer)

WARTON, Joseph (1722–1800; British poet and critic)

WELDON, Fay (1931– ; British writer)

WERFEL, Franz (1890–1945; Austrian Jewish poet, dramatist, and novelist)

WESKER, Arnold (1932– ; British dramatist)

WILDER, Thornton (1897–1975; US novelist and dramatist)

WILSON, Colin (1931– ; British critic and novelist)

WILSON, Edmund (1895–1972; US critic and essayist)

WILSON, Sir Angus (1913–91; British novelist)

WOTTON, Sir Henry (1568–1639; English poet)

WRIGHT, Judith (1915– ; Australian poet)

WRIGHT, Richard (1908–60; US novelist and critic)

7

ADDISON, Joseph (1672–1719; British essayist and poet)

AELFRIC (c. 955–c. 1020; Anglo-Saxon prose writer)

7–continued

ALARCÓN, Pedro Antonio de (1833–91; Spanish novelist)

ALBERTI, Raphael (1902–99; Spanish poet)

ALCAEUS (6th century BC; Greek lyric poet)

ALDANOV, Mark (M Aleksandrovich Landau, 1886–1957; Russian novelist)

ALDRICH, Thomas Bailey (1836–1907; US short- story writer and poet)

ALEGRÍA, Ciro (1909–61; Peruvian novelist)

ALFIERI, Vittorio, Count (1749–1803; Italian poet and dramatist)

ALLENDE, Isabel (1942– ; Peruvian novelist)

ANEIRIN (6th century AD; Welsh poet)

ARETINO, Pietro (1492–1556; Italian satirist)

ARIOSTO, Ludovico (1474–1533; Italian poet)

ARRABAL, Fernando (1932– ; Spanish playwright and novelist)

BALCHIN, Nigel (1908–70; British novelist)

BALDWIN, James Arthur (1924–87; US novelist, essayist, and dramatist)

BARBOUR, John (1316–95; Scottish poet)

BECKETT, Samuel (1906–89; Irish novelist, dramatist, and poet)

BEDDOES, Thomas Lovell (1803–49; British poet)

BENNETT, Arnold (1837–1931; British novelist)

BENTLEY, Edmund Clerihew (1875–1956; British writer)

BERGMAN, Hjalmar (1883–1931; Swedish novelist and dramatist)

BLUNDEN, Edmund Charles (1896–1974; British poet and critic)

BOIARDO, Matteo Maria, Conte di Scandiano (1441–94; Italian poet)

BOILEAU(-Despréaux), Nicolas (1636–1711; French poet and critic)

BOSWELL, James (1740–95; Scottish writer)

BO ZHU YI (or Po Chü-i; 772–846; Chinese poet)

7–continued

BRADLEY, Andrew Cecil (1851–1935; British literary critic)

BRIDGES, Robert Seymour (1844–1930; British poet)

BÜCHNER, Georg (1813–37; German dramatist)

BURGESS, Anthony (John Burgess Wilson; 1917–93; British novelist and critic)

BURNETT, Frances Eliza Hodgson (1849–1924; British novelist)

CAEDMON (d. c. 680 AD; English poet)

CAO CHAN (or Zao Zhan; ?1715–63; Chinese novelist)

CAROSSA, Hans (1878–1956; German novelist)

CARROLL, Lewis (Charles Lutwidge Dodgson; 1832–98; British writer)

CHAPMAN, George (c. 1560–1634; British poet and dramatist)

CHAUCER, Geoffrey (c. 1342–1400; English poet)

CHEKHOV, Anton Pavlovich (1860–1904; Russian dramatist and short-story writer)

CHÉNIER, André de (1762–94; French poet, born in Istanbul)

CHU YUAN (c. 343 BC–c. 289 BC; Chinese poet)

CLAUDEL, Paul (1868–1955; French dramatist and poet)

CLELAND, John (1709–89; English novelist)

COCTEAU, Jean (1889–1963; French poet and artist)

COETZEE, J M (1940– ; South African novelist)

COLETTE (Sidonie-Gabrielle C, 1873–1954; French novelist)

COLLINS, William (1721–59; British poet)

COLLINS, William Wilkie (1824–89; British novelist)

CORELLI, Marie (1854–1924; British novelist)

CRASHAW, Richard (c. 1613–49; British poet)

CREELEY, Robert (1926– ; US poet)

DA PONTE, Lorenzo (1749–1838; Italian author)

DELEDDA, Grazia (1871–1936; Italian novelist)

DICKENS, Charles (1812–70; British novelist)

7–continued

DINESEN, Isak (Karen Blixen, Baroness Blixen-Finecke, 1885–1962; Danish author)

DOUGLAS, Gavin (?1474–1522; Scottish poet)

DOUGLAS, Norman (1868–1952; British novelist)

DRABBLE, Margaret (1939– ; British novelist)

DRAYTON, Michael (1563–1631; English poet)

DREISER, Theodore (1871–1945; US novelist)

DUHAMEL, Georges (1884–1966; French novelist)

DUNSANY, Edward John Moreton Drax Plunkett, 18th Baron (1878–1957; Irish author)

DURRELL, Lawrence George (1912–90; British novelist and poet, born in India)

EMERSON, Ralph Waldo (1803–82; US essayist and poet)

ERCILLA, Alonso de (1533–94; Spanish poet)

EUPOLIS (late 5th century BC; Greek dramatist)

FERRIER, Susan Edmonstone (1782–1854; Scottish novelist)

FEYDEAU, Georges (1862–1921; French playwright)

FIRBANK, Ronald (1886–1926; British novelist)

FLECKER, James Elroy (1884–1915; British poet)

FLEMING, Ian (1908–64; British author)

FLEMING, Paul (1609–40; German poet)

FONTANE, Theodor (1819–98; German novelist)

FORSTER, E M (1879–1970; British novelist)

FOSCOLO, Ugo (1778–1827; Italian poet)

FRENEAU, Philip (1752–1832; US poet)

FRÖDING, Gustaf (1860–1911; Swedish lyric poet)

GAARDER, Jostein (1952– ; Norwegian novelist)

GASKELL, Elizabeth Cleghorn (1810–65; British novelist)

GAUTIER, Théophile (1811–72; French poet)

GILBERT, Sir William Schwenk (1836–1911; British comic dramatist)

7–continued

GISSING, George Robert (1857–1903; British novelist)

GOLDING, William (1911–93; British novelist)

GOLDONI, Carlo (1707–93; Italian comic playwright)

GRAHAME, Kenneth (1859–1932; British children's writer)

GRISHAM, John (1955– ; US novelist)

GUARINI, Giovanni Battista (1538–1612; Italian poet)

HAGGARD, Sir H Rider (1856–1925; British novelist)

HAMMETT, Dashiell (1894–1961; US novelist)

HARTLEY, L P (1895–1972; British novelist)

HELLMAN, Lillian (1905–84; US dramatist)

HERBERT, George (1593–1633; English poet)

HERRICK, Robert (1591–1674; English poet)

HEYWOOD, Thomas (c. 1574–1641; English dramatist)

HOLBERG, Ludvig, Baron (1684–1754; Danish playwright and poet)

HOPKINS, Gerard Manley (1844–89; British poet)

HOUSMAN, A E (1859–1936; British poet and scholar)

IBN EZRA, Abraham Ben Meir (1093–1167; Hebrew poet and scholar)

IONESCO, Eugène (1912–94; French dramatist)

JEFFERS, Robinson (1887–1962; US poet)

JIMÉNEZ, Juan Ramón (1881–1958; Spanish poet)

JUVENAL (Decimus Junius Juvenalis, c. 60–c. 130 AD; Roman satirist)

KÄSTNER, Erich (1899–1974; German novelist and poet)

KAUFMAN, George S (1889–1961; US dramatist)

KENDALL, Henry (1841–82; Australian poet)

KEROUAC, Jack (1922–69; US novelist)

KIPLING, Rudyard (1865–1936; British writer and poet)

KLINGER, Friedrich Maximilian von (1752–1831; German dramatist)

7–continued

LABICHE, Eugène (1815–88; French dramatist)

LARDNER, Ring (1885–1933; US short-story writer)

LAXNESS, Halldór (1902–98; Icelandic novelist and essayist)

LAYAMON (early 13th century; English poet)

LEACOCK, Stephen (1869–1944; English-born Canadian humorist)

LE CARRÉ, John (David Cornwell, 1931– ; British novelist)

LESSING, Doris (1919– ; British novelist)

LESSING, Gotthold Ephraim (1729–81; German dramatist and writer)

LINDSAY, Vachel (1879–1931; US poet)

LYDGATE, John (c. 1370–c. 1450; English poet)

MACHAUT, Guillaume de (c. 1300–77; French poet)

MALAMUD, Bernard (1914–86; US novelist)

MALRAUX, André (1901–76; French novelist and essayist)

MANZONI, Alessandro (1785–1873; Italian poet and novelist)

MARLOWE, Christopher (1564–93; English dramatist and poet)

MARRYAT, Captain Frederick (1792–1848; British novelist)

MARSTON, John (1576–1634; English dramatist)

MARTIAL (Marcus Valerius Martialis, c. 40–c. 104 AD; Roman poet)

MARVELL, Andrew (1621–78; English poet)

MASTERS, Edgar Lee (1868–1950; US poet)

MAUGHAM, W Somerset (1874–1965; British novelist and dramatist)

MAURIAC, François (1885–1970; French novelist)

MAUROIS, André (Émile Herzog; 1885–1967; French biographer, novelist, and critic)

MÉRIMÉE, Prosper (1803–70; French novelist)

MISHIMA, Yukio (Kimitake Hiraoka; 1925–70; Japanese novelist and playwright)

7–continued

MISTRAL, Frédéric (1830–1914; French poet)

MISTRAL, Gabriela (Lucila Godoy Alcayaga, 1889–1957; Chilean poet)

MOLIÈRE (Jean-Baptiste Poquelin, 1622–73; French dramatist)

MONTAGU, Lady Mary Wortley (1689–1762; English writer)

MONTALE, Eugenio (1896–1981; Italian poet)

MORAVIA, Alberto (Alberto Pincherle, 1907–90; Italian novelist)

MURDOCH, Dame Iris (1919–99; British novelist)

NABOKOV, Vladimir (1899–1977; US novelist)

NAEVIUS, Gnaeus (c. 270–c. 200 BC; Roman poet)

NAIPAUL, V S (1932– ; West Indian novelist)

NOVALIS (Friedrich Leopold, Freiherr von Hardenberg; 1772–1801; German poet and writer)

O'CONNOR, Frank (Michael O'Donovan; 1903–66; Irish short-story writer)

OSBORNE, John (1929–94; British dramatist)

PATMORE, Coventry (1823–96; British poet)

PEACOCK, Thomas Love (1785–1866; British satirical novelist)

PLAUTUS, Titus Maccius (c. 254–184 BC; Roman dramatist)

PRÉVERT, Jacques (1900–77; French poet)

PUSHKIN, Aleksandr (1799–1837; Russian poet, novelist, and dramatist)

PYNCHON, Thomas (1937– ; US novelist)

QUENEAU, Raymond (1903–79; French novelist and poet)

RANSOME, Arthur Mitchell (1884–1967; British journalist and children's writer)

REGNIER, Henri François Joseph de (1864–1936; French poet)

RICHLER, Mordecai (1931– ; Canadian novelist)

RIMBAUD, Arthur (1854–91; French poet)

7–continued

ROLLAND, Romain
(1866–1944; French novelist,
dramatist, and essayist)

ROMAINS, Jules (Louis
Farigoule; 1885–1972; French
poet, novelist, and dramatist)

RONSARD, Pierre de
(1524–85; French poet)

ROSTAND, Edmond
(1868–1918; French
dramatist)

ROUSSEL, Raymond
(1877–1933; French writer
and dramatist)

ROWLING, J K (?1964– ;
British children's writer)

RUSHDIE, Salman (1947– ;
British novelist)

SAROYAN, William (1908–81;
US dramatist and fiction
writer)

SASSOON, Siegfried
(1886–1967; British poet and
writer)

SCARRON, Paul (1610–60;
French poet, dramatist, and
satirist)

SEFERIS, George (Georgios
Seferiadis, 1900–71; Greek
poet)

SHAFFER, Peter (1926– ;
British dramatist)

SHELLEY, Percy Bysshe
(1792–1822; British poet)

SIMENON, Georges (1903–89;
Belgian novelist)

SIMONOV, Konstantin
(1915–79; Soviet novelist,
playwright, poet, and
journalist)

SITWELL, Edith (1887–1964;
British poet and writer)

SKELTON, John (c.
1460–1529; English poet)

SOUTHEY, Robert
(1774–1843; British poet and
writer)

SOYINKA, Wole (1934– ;
Nigerian dramatist and poet)

SPENDER, Sir Stephen
(1909–95; British poet and
critic)

SPENSER, Edmund (c.
1552–99; English poet)

STEVENS, Wallace
(1879–1955; US poet)

SURTEES, Robert Smith
(1803–64; British novelist)

TERENCE (Publius Terentius
Afer, c. 185–c. 159 BC;
Roman dramatist)

7–continued

THESPIS (6th century BC;
Greek poet)

THOMSON, James (1700–48;
British poet)

THURBER, James
(1894–1961; US humorous
writer and cartoonist)

TOLKIEN, J R R (1892–1973;
British scholar and writer)

TOLSTOY, Leo, Count
(1828–1910; Russian writer)

TRAVERS, Ben (1886–1980;
British dramatist)

TUTUOLA, Amos (1920–97;
Nigerian writer)

VAN DUYN, Mona (1921– ;
US poet)

VAUGHAN, Henry (c. 1622–95;
English poet)

VICENTE, Gil (c. 1465–1536;
Portuguese dramatist)

WALLACE, Edgar (1875–1932;
British novelist)

WALPOLE, Sir Hugh
(1884–1941; British novelist)

WEBSTER, John (c. 1580–c.
1625; English dramatist)

WHARTON, Edith (1862–1937;
US novelist)

WHITMAN, Walt (1819–92; US
poet)

WIELAND, Christoph Martin
(1733–1813; German novelist
and poet)

YESENIN, Sergei
Aleksandrovich (1895–1925;
Russian poet)

8

ABU NUWAS (c. 762–c. 813
AD; Arab poet)

ANACREON (6th century BC;
Greek lyric poet)

ANCHIETA, José de (1534–97;
Portuguese poet)

ANDERSEN, Hans Christian
(1805–75; Danish author)

ANDERSON, Sherwood
(1876–1941; US author)

APULEIUS, Lucius (2nd
century AD; Roman writer and
rhetorician)

ASTURIAS, Miguel Ángel
(1899–1974; Guatemalan
novelist and poet)

BANDEIRA, Manuel Carneiró
de Sousa (1886–1968;
Brazilian poet)

BANVILLE, Théodore Faullain
de (1823–89; French poet)

8–continued

BARBUSSE, Henri
(1873–1935; French novelist)

BEAUMONT, Francis
(1584–1616; British
dramatist)

BEAUVOIR, Simone de
(1908–86; French novelist
and essayist)

BECKFORD, William
(?1760–1844; British writer)

BEERBOHM, Sir Max
(1872–1956; British
caricaturist and writer)

BELINSKY, Vissarion
(1811–48; Russian literary
critic)

BENCHLEY, Robert Charles
(1889–1945; US humorist)

BERANGER, Pierre Jean de
(1780–1857; French poet and
songwriter)

BERNANOS, Georges
(1888–1948; French novelist)

BETJEMAN, Sir John
(1906–84; British poet)

BJØRNSON, Bjørnstjerne
(1832–1910; Norwegian
novelist, poet, and playwright)

BRADBURY, Ray (1920– ; US
science-fiction writer)

BRENTANO, Clemens
(1778–1842; German writer)

BROOKNER, Anita (1928– ;
British writer and art historian)

BROWNING, Robert (1812–89;
British poet)

CAMPBELL, Roy (1901–57;
South African poet)

CAMPBELL, Thomas
(1777–1844; British poet)

CARDUCCI, Giosuè
(1835–1907; Italian poet and
critic)

CASTILHO, Antonio Feliciano
de (1800–75; Portuguese
poet)

CATULLUS, Valerius (c. 84–c.
54 BC; Roman poet)

CHANDLER, Raymond
(1888–1959; US novelist)

CHARTIER, Alain (c. 1385–c.
1440; French poet and prose
writer)

CHRISTIE, Dame Agatha
(1891–1976; British author of
detective fiction and
playwright)

CLAUDIAN (c. 370–404 AD;
Roman poet)

8—continued

CONGREVE, William (1670–1729; British dramatist)

CONSTANT, Benjamin (1767–1830; French novelist)

CROMPTON, Richmal (Richmal Crompton Lamburn, 1890–1969; British children's author)

CUMMINGS, e e (1894–1962; US poet)

CYNEWULF (early 9th century AD; Anglo-Saxon religious poet)

DAVENANT, Sir William (1606–68; English dramatist and poet)

DAY LEWIS, C (1904–72; British poet and critic)

DE LA MARE, Walter (1873–1956; British poet, novelist, and anthologist)

DONLEAVY, J P (1926– ; Irish-American novelist)

ETHEREGE, Sir George (c. 1635–c. 1692; English dramatist)

FARQUHAR, George (1678–1707; Irish dramatist)

FAULKNER, William (1897–1962; US novelist)

FIELDING, Henry (1707–54; British novelist and dramatist)

FIRDAUSI (Abul Qasim Mansur; c. 935–c. 1020; Persian poet)

FLAUBERT, Gustave (1821–80; French novelist)

FLETCHER, John (1579–1625; English dramatist)

FORESTER, C S (1899–1966; British novelist)

GINSBERG, Allen (1926–97; US poet)

GONCOURT, Edmond de (1822–96; French writer)

HENRYSON, Robert (15th century; Scottish poet)

HOCHHUTH, Rolf (1933– ; Swiss dramatist)

HUYSMANS, Joris Karl (1848–1907; French novelist)

JEAN PAUL (Johann Paul Friedrich Richter, 1763–1825; German novelist)

KALIDASA (5th century AD; Indian poet)

KENEALLY, Thomas (1935– ; Australian writer)

KINGSLEY, Charles (1819–79; British writer)

8—continued

KOESTLER, Arthur (1905–83; British writer)

KOTZEBUE, August von (1761–1819; German dramatist and novelist)

LAFORGUE, Jules (1860–87; French poet)

LAGERLÖF, Selma Ottiliana Lovisa (1858–1940; Swedish novelist)

LANGLAND, William (c. 1330–c. 1400; English poet)

LAS CASES, Emmanuel, Comte de (1776–1842; French writer)

LAWRENCE, D H (1885–1930; British novelist, poet, and painter)

LEOPARDI, Giacomo (1798–1837; Italian poet)

LOCKHART, John Gibson (1794–1854; Scottish biographer and journalist)

LONGINUS (1st century AD; Greek rhetorician)

LOVELACE, Richard (1618–57; English Cavalier poet)

MACAULAY, Dame Rose (1881–1958; British novelist)

MACLEISH, Archibald (1892–1982; US poet)

MACNEICE, Louis (1907–63; Irish-born British poet)

MALHERBE, François de (1555–1628; French poet and critic)

MALLARMÉ, Stéphane (1842–98; French poet)

MARIVAUX, Pierre Carlet de Chamblain de (1688–1763; French dramatist)

MARQUAND, J P (1893–1960; US novelist)

MCCARTHY, Mary (1912–89; US novelist)

MELVILLE, Herman (1819–91; US novelist)

MENANDER (c. 341–c. 290 BC; Greek dramatist)

MEREDITH, George (1828–1909; British poet and novelist)

MICHELET, Jules (1798–1874; French historian)

MITCHELL, Margaret (1909–49; US novelist)

MORRISON, Toni (1931– ; US writer)

NEKRASOV, Nikolai Alekseevich (1821–78; Russian poet)

8—continued

NICOLSON, Sir Harold (1886–1968; British literary critic)

ONDAATJE, Michael (1943– ; Canadian writer)

PALGRAVE, Francis Turner (1824–97; British poet and anthologist)

PERELMAN, S J (1904–79; US humorous writer)

PERRAULT, Charles (1628–1703; French poet and fairytale writer)

PETRARCH (Francesco Petrarca, 1304–74; Italian poet)

PHAEDRUS (1st century AD; Roman writer)

PHILEMON (c. 368–c. 264 BC; Greek dramatist)

PLUTARCH (c. 46–c. 120 AD; Greek biographer and essayist)

RABELAIS, François (1483–1553; French satirist)

RADIGUET, Raymond (1903–23; French novelist)

RATTIGAN, Sir Terence (1911–77; British dramatist)

REMARQUE, Erich Maria (1898–1970; German novelist)

RICHARDS, Frank (Charles Hamilton, 1876–1961; British children's writer)

RUNEBERG, Johan Ludvig (1804–77; Finnish poet)

SALINGER, J D (1919– ; US novelist)

SANDBURG, Carl (1878–1967; US poet)

SARAMAGO, José (1922– ; Portuguese writer)

SARRAUTE, Nathalie (1900–99; French novelist, born in Russia)

SCALIGER, Julius Caesar (1484–1558; Italian humanist scholar)

SCHILLER, Friedrich (1759–1805; German dramatist, poet, and writer)

SHADWELL, Thomas (c. 1642–92; British dramatist)

SHERIDAN, Richard Brinsley (1751–1816; Anglo-Irish dramatist)

SILLITOE, Alan (1928– ; British novelist)

SINCLAIR, Upton (1878–1968; US novelist)

8–continued

SMOLLETT, Tobias (1721–71; British novelist)

SPILLANE, Mickey (Frank Morrison S, 1918– ; US detective-story writer)

STENDHAL (Henri Beyle, 1783–1842; French novelist)

STOPPARD, Sir Tom (1937– ; British dramatist)

SUCKLING, Sir John (1609–42; English poet and dramatist)

SU DONG PO (or Su Tung-p'o, 1036–1101; Chinese poet)

TALIESIN (6th century AD; Welsh poet)

TENNYSON, Alfred, Lord (1809–92; British poet)

THOMPSON, Francis (1859–1907; British poet and critic)

TIBULLUS, Albius (c. 55–c. 19 BC; Roman poet)

TOURNEUR, Cyril (c. 1575–1626; English dramatist)

TRAHERNE, Thomas (c. 1637–74; English poet)

TRILLING, Lionel (1905–75; US literary critic)

TROLLOPE, Anthony (1815–82; British novelist)

TULSIDAS (c. 1532–1623; Indian poet)

TURGENEV, Ivan (1818–83; Russian novelist)

VERLAINE, Paul (1844–96; French poet)

VOLTAIRE (François-Marie Arouet, 1694–1778; French writer)

VONNEGUT, Kurt (1922– ; US novelist)

WEDEKIND, Frank (1864–1918; German dramatist)

WHITTIER, John Greenleaf (1807–92; US poet)

WILLIAMS, Tennessee (1911–83; US dramatist)

WILLIAMS, William Carlos (1883–1963; US poet)

ZAMYATIN, Yevgenii Ivanovich (1884–1937; Russian novelist)

9

AESCHYLUS (c. 525–456 BC; Greek tragic dramatist)

AINSWORTH, W Harrison (1805–82; British historical novelist)

9–continued

AKHMATOVA, Anna (Anna Andreevna Gorenko, 1889–1966; Russian poet)

ALDINGTON, Richard (1892–1962; British poet, novelist, and biographer)

ALLINGHAM, Margery (1904–66; British detective-story writer)

ARBUTHNOT, John (1667–1735; Scottish writer)

AYCKBOURN, Alan (1939– ; British dramatist)

BLACKMORE, R D (1825–1900; British historical novelist)

BLACKWOOD, Algernon Henry (1869–1951; British novelist and short-story writer)

BOCCACCIO, Giovanni (1313–75; Italian writer and poet)

BURROUGHS, Edgar Rice (1875–1950; US novelist)

BURROUGHS, William (1914–97; US novelist)

CERVANTES, Miguel de (1547–1616; Spanish novelist)

CHARTERIS, Leslie (L Charles Bowyer Yin, 1907–93; British novelist)

CHURCHILL, Charles (1731–64; British poet)

COLERIDGE, Samuel Taylor (1772–1834; British poet)

CORNEILLE, Pierre (1606–84; French dramatist)

D'ANNUNZIO, Gabriele (1863–1938; Italian poet, novelist, and dramatist)

DE LA ROCHE, Mazo (1885–1961; Canadian novelist)

DE QUINCEY, Thomas (1785–1859; British essayist and critic)

DICKINSON, Emily (1830–86; US poet)

DOOLITTLE, Hilda (1886–1961; US poet)

DOS PASSOS, John (1896–1970; US novelist)

DU MAURIER, George (1834–96; British caricaturist and novelist)

ECKERMANN, Johann Peter (1792–1854; German writer)

EDGEWORTH, Maria (1767–1849; Anglo-Irish writer)

9–continued

EHRENBERG, Iliya Grigorievich (1891–1967; Soviet author)

EURIPIDES (c. 480–406 BC; Greek dramatist)

FROISSART, Jean (1337–c. 1400; French chronicler and poet)

GIRAUDOUX, Jean (1882–1944; French dramatist and novelist)

GOLDSMITH, Oliver (1730–74; Anglo-Irish writer)

GONCHAROV, Ivan Aleksandrovich (1812–91; Russian novelist)

GOTTSCHED, Johann Christoph (1700–66; German critic)

GREENWOOD, Walter (1903–74; British novelist)

HAUPTMANN, Gerhart (1862–1946; German dramatist)

HAWTHORNE, Nathaniel (1804–64; US novelist and short-story writer)

HEMINGWAY, Ernest (1899–1961; US novelist)

HIGHSMITH, Patricia (1921–95; US author of crime fiction)

HÖLDERLIN, Friedrich (1770–1843; German poet)

ISHERWOOD, Christopher (1904–86; British novelist)

JEFFERIES, Richard (1848–87; British novelist and naturalist)

KLOPSTOCK, Friedrich Gottlieb (1724–1803; German poet)

LA BRUYÈRE, Jean de (1645–96; French satirist)

LA FAYETTE, Mme de (Marie Madeleine, Comtesse de L F, 1634–93; French novelist)

LAMARTINE, Alphonse de (1790–1869; French poet)

LAMPEDUSA, Giuseppe Tomasi di (1896–1957; Italian novelist)

LERMONTOV, Mikhail (1814–41; Russian poet and novelist)

LINKLATER, Eric (1889–1974; Scottish novelist)

LLEWELLYN, Richard (R D V L Lloyd, 1907–83; Welsh novelist)

9–continued

LOMONOSOV, Mikhail Vasilievich (1711–65; Russian poet)

LOVECRAFT, H P (1890–1937; US novelist and short-story writer)

LUCRETIUS (Titus Lucretius Carus, c. 95–c. 55 BC; Roman philosopher and poet)

MACKENZIE, Sir Compton (1883–1972; British novelist)

MALAPARTE, Curzio (Kurt Erich Suckert; 1898–1957; Italian novelist and dramatist)

MANSFIELD, Katherine (Kathleen Mansfield Beauchamp, 1888–1923; New Zealand short-story writer)

MARINETTI, Filippo Tommaso (1876–1944; Italian poet and novelist)

MARTINEAU, Harriet (1802–76; British writer)

MASEFIELD, John (1878–1967; British poet)

MASSINGER, Philip (1583–1640; English dramatist)

MCCULLERS, Carson (1917–67; US novelist and playwright)

MIDDLETON, Thomas (1580–1627; English dramatist)

MONSARRAT, Nicholas (John Turney, 1910–79; British novelist)

MONTAIGNE, Michel de (1533–92; French essayist)

MUTANABBI, Abu At-Tayyib Ahmad Ibn Husayn al- (915–65 AD; Arab poet)

O'FLAHERTY, Liam (1897–1984; Irish novelist)

PARKINSON, Northcote (1909–93; British author)

PASTERNAK, Boris (1890–1960; Russian poet and novelist)

POLIZIANO (or Politian; 1454–94; Italian poet and scholar)

PRITCHETT, V S (1900–97; British short-story writer and critic)

RADCLIFFE, Ann (1764–1823; British novelist)

ROCHESTER, John Wilmot, 2nd Earl of (1647–80; British poet)

9–continued

SACKVILLE, Thomas, 1st Earl of Dorset (1536–1608; British poet and dramatist)

SCHREINER, Olive (1855–1920; South African novelist)

SHENSTONE, William (1714–63; British poet)

SHOLOKHOV, Mikhail (1905–84; Soviet novelist)

SOPHOCLES (c. 496–406 BC; Greek dramatist)

STEINBECK, John (1902–68; US novelist)

STEVENSON, Robert Louis (1850–94; British novelist)

STURLUSON, Snorri (1178–1241; Icelandic poet)

SWINBURNE, Algernon Charles (1837–1909; British poet)

THACKERAY, William Makepeace (1811–63; British novelist)

TSVETAEVA, Marina (1892–1941; Russian poet)

UNGARETTI, Giuseppe (1888–1970; Italian poet)

VERHAEREN, Émile (1844–96; Belgian poet)

VITTORINI, Elio (1908–66; Italian novelist)

WERGELAND, Henrik Arnold (1808–45; Norwegian poet)

WODEHOUSE, Sir P G (1881–1975; US humorous writer)

WYCHERLEY, William (1640–1716; English dramatist)

10

BAINBRIDGE, Beryl (1934– ; British novelist and playwright)

BAUDELAIRE, Charles (1821–67; French poet)

BILDERDIJK, Willem (1756–1831; Dutch poet and dramatist)

CAVALCANTI, Guido (c. 1255–1300; Italian poet)

CHATTERJEE, Bankim Chandra (1838–94; Indian novelist)

CHATTERTON, Thomas (1752–70; British poet)

CHESTERTON, G K (1874–1936; British essayist, novelist, and poet)

CONSCIENCE, Hendrik (1812–83; Flemish novelist)

10–continued

DAZAI OSAMU (Tsushima Shuji; 1909–48; Japanese novelist)

DIO CASSIUS (c. 150–235 AD; Roman historian)

DRINKWATER, John (1882–1937; British poet and dramatist)

DÜRRENMATT, Friedrich (1921–90; Swiss dramatist and novelist)

FITZGERALD, Edward (1809–83; British poet)

FITZGERALD, F Scott (1896–1940; US novelist)

GALSWORTHY, John (1867–1933; British novelist and dramatist)

JEAN DE MEUN (c. 1240–c. 1305; French poet)

KHLEBNIKOV, Velimir (Victor K, 1885–1922; Russian poet)

LA FONTAINE, Jean de (1621–95; French poet)

LAGERKVIST, Pär (1891–1974; Swedish novelist, poet, and dramatist)

LONGFELLOW, Henry Wadsworth (1807–82; US poet)

MACDIARMID, Hugh (Christopher Murray Grieve, 1892–1978; Scottish poet)

MANDELSTAM, Osip (1891–?1938; Russian poet)

MAUPASSANT, Guy de (1850–93; French short-story writer and novelist)

MCGONAGALL, William (1830–1902; Scottish poet)

MICKIEWICZ, Adam (1798–1855; Polish poet)

OSTROVSKII, Aleksandr Nikolaevich (1823–86; Russian dramatist)

PIRANDELLO, Luigi (1867–1936; Italian dramatist and novelist)

PROPERTIUS, Sextus (c. 50–c. 16 BC; Roman poet)

RICHARDSON, Henry Handel (Ethel Florence R, 1870–1946; Australian novelist)

RICHARDSON, Samuel (1689–1761; British novelist)

RUTHERFORD, Mark (William Hale White, 1831–1913; British novelist)

10—continued

SCHNITZLER, Arthur (1862–1931; Austrian Jewish dramatist and novelist)

STRINDBERG, August (1849–1912; Swedish dramatist and writer)

TANNHÄUSER (c. 1200–c. 1270; German poet)

THEOCRITUS (c. 310–250 BC; Greek poet)

VAN DER POST, Sir Laurens (1906–96; South African novelist)

WILLIAMSON, Henry (1895–1977; British novelist)

WORDSWORTH, William (1770–1850; British poet)

XENOPHANES (6th century BC; Greek poet)

11

ANZENGRUBER, Ludwig (1839–89; Austrian dramatist and novelist)

APOLLINAIRE, Guillaume (Wilhelm de Kostrowitzky, 1880–1918; French poet)

ARCHILOCHUS (c. 680–c. 640 BC; Greek poet)

BACCHYLIDES (c. 516–c. 450 BC; Greek lyric poet)

BLESSINGTON, Marguerite, Countess of (1789–1849; Irish author)

CALLIMACHUS (c. 305–c. 240 BC; Greek poet)

CASTIGLIONE, Baldassare (1478–1529; Italian writer)

DOSTOIEVSKI, Fedor Mikhailovich (1821–81; Russian novelist)

EICHENDORFF, Josef, Freiherr von (1788–1857; German writer)

GARCÍA LORCA, Federico (1898–1936; Spanish poet and dramatist)

GRILLPARZER, Franz (1791–1872; Austrian dramatist)

KAZANTZAKIS, Nikos (1885–1957; Greek novelist and poet)

LAUTRÉAMONT, Comte de (Isidore Ducasse, 1846–70; French writer)

MAETERLINCK, Maurice (1862–1949; Belgian poet and dramatist)

11—continued

MATSUO BASHO (Matsuo Munefusa, 1644–94; Japanese poet)

MAYAKOVSKII, Vladimir (1893–1930; Russian poet)

MONTHERLANT, Henry de (1896–1972; French novelist and dramatist)

'OMAR KHAYYAM (?1048–?1122; Persian poet)

PÉREZ GALDÓS, Benito (1843–1920; Spanish novelist)

SHAKESPEARE, William (1564–1616; English dramatist)

SIENKIEWICZ, Henryk (1846–1916; Polish novelist)

STIERNHIELM, Georg Olofson (1598–1672; Swedish poet)

YEVTUSHENKO, Yevgenii (1933– ; Soviet poet)

12

ARISTOPHANES (c. 450–c. 385 BC; Greek comic dramatist)

BEAUMARCHAIS, Pierre-Augustin Caron de (1732–99; French dramatist)

BLASCO IBÁÑEZ, Vicente (1867–1928; Spanish novelist)

FERLINGHETTI, Lawrence (1919– ; US poet)

FEUCHTWANGER, Lion (1884–1958; German novelist and dramatist)

HOFMANNSTHAL, Hugo von (1874–1929; Austrian poet and dramatist)

LÓPEZ DE AYALA, Pero (c. 1332–c. 1407; Spanish poet and chronicler)

MARTIN DU GARD, Roger (1881–1958; French novelist)

MATTHEW PARIS (c. 1200–59; English chronicler)

ROBBE-GRILLET, Alain (1922– ; French novelist)

SAINT-EXUPÉRY, Antoine de (1900–44; French novelist)

SOLZHENITSYN, Aleksandr (1918– ; Russian novelist)

VOZNESENSKII, Andrei (1933– ; Soviet poet)

13

BERTRAN DE BORN (?1140–?1215; French troubadour poet)

13—continued

CASTELO BRANCO, Camilo (1825–95; Portuguese novelist)

CHATEAUBRIAND, Vicomte de (1768–1848; French writer)

CSOKONAI VITÉZ, Mihaly (1773–1805; Hungarian poet)

GARCÍA MÁRQUEZ, Gabriel (1928– ; Colombian novelist)

HARISHCHANDRA (1850–85; Hindi poet, dramatist, and essayist, also known as Bharatendu)

MARIE DE FRANCE (12th century AD; French poet)

TIRSO DE MOLINA (Gabriel Téllez, c. 1584–1648; Spanish dramatist)

ZEAMI MOTOKIYO (1363–c. 1443; Japanese playwright)

14

BRILLAT-SAVARIN, Anthelme (1755–1826; French writer)

COMPTON-BURNETT, Dame Ivy (1892–1969; British novelist)

DAFYDD AP GWILYM (c. 1320–c. 1380; Welsh poet)

DANTE ALIGHIERI (1265–1321; Italian poet)

DROSTE-HÜLSHOFF, Annette von (1797–1848; German poet and novelist)

GÓNGORA Y ARGOTE, Luis de (1561–1627; Spanish poet)

GRIMMELSHAUSEN, Hans Jacob Christoph von (c. 1625–76; German novelist)

JACOPONE DA TODI (c. 1236–1306; Italian religious poet)

LECONTE DE LISLE, Charles Marie René (1818–94; French poet)

OEHLENSCHLÄGER, Adam (1779–1850; Danish poet and playwright)

PRÉVOST D'EXILES, Antoine François, Abbé (1697–1763; French novelist)

SULLY-PRUDHOMME, René François Armand (1839–1907; French poet)

WOLLSTONECRAFT, Mary (1759–97; British writer)

ZORRILLA Y MORAL, José (1817–93; Spanish poet and dramatist)

15

ALARCÓN Y MENDOZA, Juan Ruiz de (1581–1639; Spanish dramatist)

DIODORUS SICULUS (1st century BC; Greek historian)

PLINY THE YOUNGER (Gaius Plinius Caecilius Secundus, c. 61–c. 113 AD; Roman writer)

16

CHRÉTIEN DE TROYES (12th century AD; French poet)

CYRANO DE BERGERAC, Savinien (1619–55; French writer and dramatist)

KAWABATA YASUNARI (1899–1972; Japanese novelist)

PETRONIUS ARBITER (1st century AD; Roman satirist)

17

CALDERÓN DE LA BARCA, Pedro (1600–81; Spanish dramatist)

17–continued

GUILLAUME DE LORRIS (13th century; French poet and author)

TANIZAKI JUN-ICHIRO (1886–1965; Japanese novelist)

18

APOLLONIUS OF RHODES (3rd century BC; Greek epic poet)

KAKINOMOTO HITOMARO (c. 680–710; Japanese poet)

THOMAS OF ERCELDOUNE (13th century; English poet and prophet)

19

BENOIT DE SAINTE-MAURE (12th century AD; French poet)

CHIKAMATSU MONZAEMON (Sugimori Nobumori; 1653–1724; Japanese dramatist)

VILLIERS DE L'ISLE-ADAM, Philippe Auguste, Comte de (1838–89; French poet, novelist, and dramatist)

20+

BERNARDIN DE SAINT-PIERRE, Jacques Henri (1737–1814; French naturalist and writer)

DIONYSIUS OF HALICARNASSUS (1st century BC; Greek historian)

DRUMMOND OF HAWTHORNDEN, William (1585–1649; Scots poet)

ECHEGARAY Y EIZAGUIRRE, José (1832–1916; Spanish dramatist)

GOTTFRIED VON STRASSBURG (13th century; German poet)

WALTHER VON DER VOGELWEIDE (c. 1170–c. 1230; German poet)

WOLFRAM VON ESCHENBACH (c. 1170–c. 1220; German poet)

PHILOSOPHERS

4

AYER, Sir Alfred (Jules) (1910–89; British philosopher)

HUME, David (1711–76; Scottish philosopher and historian)

KANT, Immanuel (1724–1804; German philosopher)

MACH, Ernst (1838–1916; Austrian physicist and philosopher)

MARX, Karl (Heinrich) (1818–83; German philosopher)

MILL, James (1773–1836; Scottish writer and philosopher)

MORE, Henry (1614–87; English philosopher)

MOZI (or Motzu; ?470–?391 BC; Chinese philosopher)

RAZI, ar (or Rhazes; c. 865–c. 928 AD; Persian physician and philosopher)

REID, Thomas (1710–96; Scottish philosopher)

RYLE, Gilbert (1900–76; British philosopher)

4–continued

VICO, Giambattista (or Giovanni Battista Vico; 1668–1744; Italian historical philosopher)

WEIL, Simone (1909–43; French mystic and philosopher)

5

AMIEL, Henri Frédéric (1821–81; Swiss philosopher and writer)

BACON, Francis, 1st Baron Verulam, Viscount St Albans (1561–1626; English lawyer and philosopher)

BENDA, Julien (1867–1956; French novelist and philosopher)

BODIN, Jean (1530–96; French philosopher and jurist)

BRUNO, Giordano (1548–1600; Italian philosopher)

BUBER, Martin (1878–1965; Austrian-born Jewish religious philosopher)

5–continued

BURKE, Edmund (1729–97; British political philosopher and politician)

CHU XI (or Chu Hsi; 1130–1200; Chinese philosopher)

COMTE, Auguste (1798–1857; French philosopher)

CROCE, Benedetto (1866–1952; Italian philosopher)

DEWEY, John (1859–1952; US philosopher and educationalist)

FLUDD, Robert (1574–1637; English physician and philosopher)

FROMM, Erich (1900–80; US psychologist and philosopher)

HEGEL, Georg Wilhelm Friedrich (1770–1831; German philosopher)

IQBAL, Sir Mohammed (?1875–1938; Indian Muslim poet and philosopher)

5–continued

LACAN, Jacques (Marie Emile) (1901–81; French psycho-analyst and philosopher)

LOCKE, John (1632–1704; English philosopher)

MOORE, G(eorge); E(dward) (1873–1958; British philosopher)

PLATO (429–347 BC; Greek philosopher)

QUINE, Willard van Orman (1908–; US philosopher)

RAMUS, Petrus (Pierre de la Ramée; 1515–72; French humanist philosopher and logician)

RENAN, (Joseph; Ernest (1823–92; French philosopher and theologian)

SMITH, Adam (1723–90; Scottish moral philosopher and political economist)

SOREL, Georges (1847–1922; French social philosopher)

6

ADORNO, Theodor (Wiesengrund) (1903–64; German philosopher)

AGNESI, Maria Gaetana (1718–99; Italian mathematician and philosopher)

ARENDT, Hannah (1906–75; German-born US political philosopher)

AUSTIN, John Langshaw (1911–60; British philosopher)

BERLIN, Sir Isaiah (1909–97; Latvian-born British philosopher and historian)

CARNAP, Rudolf (1891–1970; German-born logical positivist philosopher)

COUSIN, Victor (1792–1867; French philosopher)

FICHTE, Johann Gottlieb (1762–1814; German philosopher)

GODWIN, William (1756–1836; British political philosopher and novelist)

HERDER, Johann Gottfried (1744–1803; German philosopher and poet)

HERZEN, Aleksandr (Ivanovich) (1812–70; Russian political philosopher)

HOBBES, Thomas (1588–1679; English political philosopher)

6–continued

KRIPKE, Saul (1940– ; US philosopher)

LUKACS, Giorgi (1885–1971; Hungarian Marxist philosopher)

ORESME, Nicole d' (c. 1320–82; French philosopher and churchman)

PEIRCE, Charles Sanders (1839–1914; US philosopher and logician)

POPPER, Sir Karl Raimund (1902–94; Austrian-born philosopher)

SARTRE, Jean-Paul (1905–80; French philosopher, novelist, dramatist, and critic)

TAGORE, Rabindranath (1861–1941; Indian poet, philosopher, and teacher)

7

ABELARD, Peter (1079–1142; French philosopher)

ALKINDI, Abu Yusuf Ya'qub ibn Ishaq (died c. 870; Muslim Arab philosopher)

AQUINAS, St Thomas (c. 1225–74; Italian Dominican theologian, scholastic philosopher, and Doctor of the Church)

ARNAULD, Antoine (1612–94; French theologian, philosopher, and logician)

BENTHAM, Jeremy (1748–1832; British philosopher)

BERGSON, Henri (1859–1941; French philosopher and psychologist)

BLONDEL, Maurice (1861–1949; French philosopher)

BRADLEY, Francis Herbert (1846–1924; British philosopher)

BURIDAN, Jean (c. 1297–c. 1358; French scholastic philosopher)

CHARRON, Pierre (1541–1603; French theologian and philosopher)

DERRIDA, Jacques (1930– ; French philosopher)

DESTUTT, Antoine Louis Claude, Comte de Tracy (1754–1836; French philosopher and politician)

7–continued

DIDEROT, Denis (1713–84; French philosopher and writer)

EDWARDS, Jonathan (1703–58; American theologian and philosopher)

ERIGENA, John Scotus (c. 800–c. 877; Irish-born medieval philosopher)

GENTILE, Giovanni (1875–1944; Italian philosopher)

GUARINI, Guarino (1624–83; Italian baroque architect, philosopher, and mathematician)

HUSSERL, Edmund (1859–1938; German philosopher)

HYPATIA (d. 415 AD; Neoplatonist philosopher and mathematician)

JASPERS, Karl (Theodor) (1883–1969; German philosopher)

LEIBNIZ, Gottfried Wilhelm (1646–1716; German philosopher and mathematician)

MENCIUS (Mengzi or Mengtzu; 371–289 BC; Chinese moral philosopher)

MUMFORD, Lewis (1895–1990; US social philosopher)

MURDOCH, Dame Iris (1919–99; British novelist and philosopher)

PROCLUS (410–85 AD; Neoplatonist philosopher)

PYRRHON (or Pyrrho; c. 360–c. 270 BC; Greek philosopher)

RUSSELL, Bertrand Arthur William, 3rd Earl (1872–1970; British philosopher)

SANKARA (or Shankara; 8th century AD; Hindu philosopher)

SCHLICK, Moritz (1882–1936; German philosopher)

SCRUTON, Roger (Vernon) (1944–; British philosopher and cultural historian)

SPENCER, Herbert (1820–1903; British philosopher)

SPINOZA, Benedict (or Baruch de S.; 1632–77; Dutch philosopher, theologian, and scientist)

8

ALFARABI, Mohammed ibn Tarkhan (d. 950; Muslim philosopher, physician, mathematician, and musician)

AVERROES (Ibn Rushd; 1126–98; Muslim philosopher)

AVICENNA (980–1037; Persian philosopher and physician)

BERDYAEV, Nikolai (1874–1948; Russian mystical philosopher)

BERKELEY, George (1685–1753; Irish bishop and idealist philosopher)

BOETHIUS, Anicius Manlius Severinus (c. 480–524 AD; Roman statesman and philosopher)

BRENTANO, Franz (1838–1916; German psychologist and philosopher)

CASSIRER, Ernst (1874–1945; German philosopher and historian)

EPICURUS (341–270 BC; Greek philosopher)

FOUCAULT, Michel (1926–84; French philosopher)

GASSENDI, Pierre (1592–1655; French physicist and philosopher)

GEULINCX, Arnold (1624–69; Belgian-born philosopher)

HAN FEI ZI (d. 233 BC; Chinese diplomat and philosopher of law)

HARTMANN, Eduard von (1842–1906; German philosopher)

HARTMANN, Nicolai (1882–1950; Russian-born German philosopher)

KROCHMAL, Nachman (1785–1840; Jewish philosopher)

PLOTINUS (205–70 AD; Greek philosopher)

PORPHYRY (232–305 AD; Syrian-born philosopher)

RAMANUJA (11th century AD; Indian-born Hindu philosopher and theologian)

ROSCELIN (died c. 1125; French scholastic philosopher)

ROUSSEAU, Jean Jacques (1712–78; French philosopher and writer)

8–continued

SIDGWICK, Henry (1838–1900; British moral philosopher)

SOCRATES (c. 469–399 BC; Athenian philosopher)

SOLOVIOV, Vladimir Sergevich (1853–1900; Russian philosopher and poet)

SPENGLER, Oswald (1880–1936; German philosopher)

STRAWSON, Sir Peter Frederick (1919–; British philosopher)

VOLTAIRE (FrançoisMarie Arouet; 1694–1778; French philosopher)

ZHUANGZI (or Chuangtzu; c. 369–286 BC; Chinese philosopher)

9

ALTHUSSER, Louis (1918–90; Algerian-born French philosopher)

ARISTOTLE (384–322 BC; Greek philosopher and scientist)

BOSANQUET, Bernard (1848–1923; British philosopher)

CLEANTHES (c. 310–230 BC; Greek philosopher)

CONDILLAC, Étienne Bonnot de (1715–80; French philosopher and psychologist)

CONDORCET, Marie Jean Antoine de Caritat, Marquis de (1743–94; French philosopher and politician)

CONFUCIUS (Kong Zi or K'ungfutzu; c. 551–479 BC; Chinese philosopher)

DESCARTES, René (1596–1650; French philosopher)

EPICTETUS (c. 60–110 AD; Stoic philosopher)

FEUERBACH, Ludwig Andreas (1804–72; German philosopher)

HEIDEGGER, Martin (1889–1976; German philosopher)

HELVÉTIUS, Claude Adrien (1715–71; French philosopher)

HUTCHESON, Francis (1694–1746; Scottish philosopher)

9–continued

LEUCIPPUS (5th century BC; Greek philosopher)

LUCRETIUS (Titus Lucretius Carus; c. 95–c. 55 BC; Roman philosopher and poet)

NAGARJUNA (c. 150–c. 250 AD; Indian Buddhist monk and philosopher)

NIETZSCHE, Friedrich (1844–1900; German philosopher)

PLEKHANOV, Georgi Valentinovich (1857–1918; Russian revolutionary and Marxist philosopher)

PUFENDORF, Samuel von (1632–94; German philosopher)

SANTAYANA, George (1863–1952; Spanish-born US philosopher and poet)

SCHELLING, Friedrich (1775–1854; German philosopher)

WHITEHEAD, A(lfred); N(orth) (1861–1947; British philosopher and mathematician)

10

ANAXAGORAS (c. 500–428 BC; Greek philosopher)

ANAXIMENES (died c. 528 BC; Greek philosopher)

ARISTIPPUS (c. 435–c. 356 BC; Greek philosopher)

BAUMGARTEN, Alexander Gottlieb (1714–62; German philosopher)

CAMPANELLA, Tommaso (1568–1639; Italian philosopher and Dominican friar)

CUMBERLAND, Richard (1631–1718; English moral philosopher)

DEMOCRITUS (c. 460–370 BC; Greek philosopher and scientist)

DUNS SCOTUS, John (c. 1260–1308; Scottish-born Franciscan philosopher)

EMPEDOCLES (c. 490–430 BC; Sicilian Greek philosopher)

FONTENELLE, Bernard le Bovier de (1657–1757; French philosopher)

HERACLITUS (c. 535–c. 475 BC; Greek philosopher)

IBN GABIROL, Solomon (c. 1021–c. 1058; Spanish-born Jewish philosopher and poet)

10–continued

IBN KHALDUN (1332–1406; Arab historian and philosopher)

MAIMONIDES, Moses (1135–1204; Jewish philosopher and physician)

PARMENIDES (c. 510–c. 450 BC; Greek philosopher)

PYTHAGORAS (6th century BC; Greek philosopher and religious leader)

SWEDENBORG, Emanuel (1688–1772; Swedish scientist, mystic, and philosopher)

ZENO OF ELEA (born c. 490 BC; Greek philosopher)

11

BOLINGBROKE, Henry St John, 1st Viscount (1678–1751; English statesman and philosopher)

COLLINGWOOD, R(obin); G(eorge) (1889–1943; British philosopher)

JUDAH HALEVI (or Halevy; c. 1075–1141; Jewish poet and philosopher)

KIERKEGAARD, Søren (1813–55; Danish philosopher)

MALEBRANCHE, Nicolas (1638–1715; French philosopher and theologian)

MENDELSSOHN, Moses (1729–86; German Jewish philosopher)

11–continued

MONTESQUIEU, Charles Louis de Secondat, Baron de (1689–1755; French historical philosopher and writer)

VIVEKANANDA, Swami (1862–1902; Hindu philosopher)

ANAXIMANDER (c. 610–c. 546 BC; Greek philosopher)

ANTISTHENES (c. 445–c. 360 BC; Greek philosopher)

12

MERLEAUPONTY, Maurice (1908–61; French philosopher)

PHILO JUDAEUS (c. 30 BC–45 AD; Jewish philosopher)

SCHOPENHAUER, Arthur (1788–1860; German philosopher)

THEOPHRASTUS (c. 370–286 BC; Greek philosopher and scientist)

UNAMUNO Y JUGO, Miguel de (1864–1936; Spanish writer and philosopher)

WITTGENSTEIN, Ludwig (1889–1951; Austrian philosopher)

ZENO OF CITIUM (c. 335–262 BC; Greek philosopher)

13

DIO CHRYSOSTOM (2nd century AD; Greek philosopher and orator)

13–continued

ORTEGA Y GASSET, José (1883–1955; Spanish philosopher and writer)

14

ALBERTUS MAGNUS, St (c. 1200–80; German bishop, philosopher, and Doctor of the Church)

WOLLSTONECRAFT, Mary (1759–97; British writer)

15

JOHN OF SALISBURY (c. 1115–80; English philosopher)

WILLIAM OF OCKHAM (c. 1285–1349; English scholastic philosopher)

16

ALEXANDER OF HALES (c. 1170–1245; English scholastic philosopher)

17

APOLLONIUS OF TYANA (1st century AD; Pythagorean philosopher)

BERNARD OF CHARTRES (died c. 1130; French scholastic philosopher)

18

PICO DELLA MIRANDOLA, Giovanni, Conte (1463–94; Italian Renaissance philosopher)

MUSICIANS AND COMPOSERS

3

BAX, Sir Arnold Edward Trevor (1883–1953; British composer)

4

ADAM, Adolphe-Charles (1803–56; French composer)

ARNE, Thomas Augustine (1710–78; British composer)

BACH, Johann Sebastian (1685–1750; German composer and keyboard player)

BERG, Alban (1885–1935; Austrian composer)

4–continued

BING, Sir Rudolf (1902– ; British opera administrator)

BLOW, John (1649–1708; English composer)

BÖHM, Karl (1894–1981; Austrian conductor)

BULL, John (c. 1562–1628; English composer and organist)

BUSH, Alan Dudley (1900– ; British composer)

BUTT, Dame Clara (1873–1936; British contralto singer)

4–continued

BYRD, William (?1543–1623; English composer)

CAGE, John (1912–92; US composer)

HESS, Dame Myra (1890–1965; British pianist)

IVES, Charles (1874–1954; US composer)

LALO, Édouard (1823–92; French composer)

LILL, John (1944– ; British pianist)

LIND, Jenny (1820–87; Swedish soprano)

4–continued

NONO, Luigi (1924–90; Italian composer)

ORFF, Carl (1895–1982; German composer and conductor)

PÄRT, Arvo (1935– ; Estonian composer)

WOLF, Hugo (1860–1903; Austrian composer)

WOOD, Sir Henry (1869–1944; British conductor)

5

ALKAN, Charles Henri Valentin (C H V Morhange, 1813–88; French pianist and composer)

ARRAU, Claudio (1903–91; Chilean pianist)

AUBER, Daniel François Esprit (1782–1871; French composer)

AURIC, Georges (1899–1983; French composer)

BAKER, Dame Janet (1933– ; British mezzo-soprano)

BERIO, Luciano (1925– ; Italian composer)

BIZET, Georges (Alexandre César Léopold B, 1838–75; French composer)

BLISS, Sir Arthur Edward Drummond (1891–1975; British composer)

BLOCH, Ernest (1880–1959; Swiss-born composer)

BOEHM, Theobald (1794–1881; German flautist)

BOULT, Sir Adrian (1889–1983; British conductor)

BOYCE, William (c. 1710–79; British composer)

BREAM, Julian Alexander (1933– ; British guitarist and lutenist)

BRIAN, Havergal (1876–1972; British composer)

BRUCH, Max (1838–1920; German composer)

BÜLOW, Hans Guido, Freiherr von (1830–94; German pianist and conductor)

DAVIS, Sir Colin (1927– ; British conductor)

D'INDY, Vincent (1851–1931; French composer)

DUFAY, Guillaume (c. 1400–74; Burgundian composer)

DUKAS, Paul (1865–1935; French composer)

5–continued

DUPRÉ, Marcel (1886–1971; French organist and composer)

ELGAR, Sir Edward (1857–1934; British composer)

EVANS, Sir Geraint (1922–92; Welsh baritone)

FALLA, Manuel de (1876–1946; Spanish composer)

FAURÉ, Gabriel (1845–1924; French composer and organist)

FIELD, John (1782–1837; Irish pianist and composer)

FRIML, Rudolph (1879–1972; Czech-born composer and pianist)

GIGLI, Beniamino (1890–1957; Italian tenor)

GLASS, Philip (1937– ; US composer)

GLUCK, Christoph Willibald (1714–87; German composer)

GOBBI, Tito (1915–84; Italian baritone)

GOEHR, Alexander (1932– ; British composer)

GRIEG, Edvard Hagerup (1843–1907; Norwegian composer)

GROVE, Sir George (1820–1900; British musicologist)

HALLÉ, Sir Charles (Karl Hallé, 1819–1895; German conductor and pianist)

HAYDN, Franz Joseph (1732–1809; Austrian composer)

HENZE, Hans Werner (1926– ; German composer)

HOLST, Gustav (1874–1934; British composer and teacher)

IBERT, Jacques (1890–1962; French composer)

LEHÁR, Franz (Ferencz L, 1870–1948; Hungarian composer)

LISZT, Franz (Ferencz L, 1811–86; Hungarian pianist and composer)

LOCKE, Matthew (c. 1622–77; English composer)

LULLY, Jean Baptiste (Giovanni Battista Lulli, 1632–87; French composer)

MELBA, Dame Nellie (Helen Porter Armstrong, 1861–1931; Australian soprano)

5–continued

MOORE, Gerald (1899–1987; British pianist)

MUNCH, Charles (1892–1968; French conductor)

OGDON, John (1937–89; British pianist)

PARRY, Sir Hubert (1848–1918; British composer)

PATTI, Adelina (Adela Juana Maria, 1843–1919; Italian-born operatic soprano)

PEARS, Sir Peter (1910–86; British tenor)

RAVEL, Maurice (1875–1937; French composer)

REGER, Max (1873–1916; German composer, organist, and teacher)

SATIE, Erik (1866–1925; French composer)

SHARP, Cecil (1859–1924; British musician)

SOLTI, Sir Georg (1912–97; Hungarian-born British conductor)

SOUSA, John Philip (1854–1933; US composer and bandmaster)

SPOHR, Louis (Ludwig S, 1784–1859; German violinist and composer)

STERN, Isaac (1920– ; Russian-born US violinist)

SZELL, George (1897–1970; Hungarian conductor)

TEYTE, Dame Maggie (1888–1976; British soprano)

VERDI, Giuseppe (1813–1901; Italian composer)

WEBER, Carl Maria von (1786–1826; German composer)

WEILL, Kurt (1900–50; German composer)

WIDOR, Charles Marie (1844–1937; French organist and composer)

6

ARNOLD, Malcolm (1921– ; British composer)

BARBER, Samuel (1910–81; US composer)

BARTÓK, Béla (1881–1945; Hungarian composer)

BATTLE, Kathleen (1948– ; US soprano)

BISHOP, Sir Henry Rowley (1786–1855; British composer and conductor)

6–continued

BOULEZ, Pierre (1925– ; French composer and conductor)

BRAHMS, Johannes (1833–97; German composer)

BRIDGE, Frank (1879–1941; British composer)

BURNEY, Charles (1726–1814; British musicologist, organist, and composer)

BUSONI, Ferruccio (1866–1924; Italian virtuoso pianist and composer)

CALLAS, Maria (Maria Anna Kalageropoulos, 1923–77; US-born soprano)

CARTER, Elliott (1908– ; US composer)

CARUSO, Enrico (1873–1921; Italian tenor)

CASALS, Pablo (Pau C, 1876–1973; Spanish cellist, conductor, and composer)

CHOPIN, Frédéric (François, 1810–49; Polish composer)

CLARKE, Jeremiah (?1673–1707; English composer and organist)

CORTOT, Alfred (1877–1962; French pianist and conductor)

COWELL, Henry (1897–1965; US composer)

CURWEN, John (1816–80; British teacher who perfected the Tonic Sol-fa system)

CURZON, Sir Clifford (1907–82; British pianist)

DAVIES, Sir Peter Maxwell (1934– ; British composer)

DELIUS, Frederick (1862–1934; British composer)

DIBDIN, Charles (1745–1814; British composer, actor, and singer)

DUPARC, Henri (Marie Eugène Henri Foucques D, 1848–1933; French composer)

DVOŘÁK, Antonín (1841–1904; Czech composer)

ENESCO, Georges (G Enescu, 1881–1955; Romanian violinist and composer)

FLOTOW, Friedrich von (1812–83; German composer)

FRANCK, César Auguste (1822–90; Belgian composer, organist, and teacher)

6–continued

GALWAY, James (1939– ; Irish flautist)

GLINKA, Mikhail Ivanovich (1804–57; Russian composer)

GOUNOD, Charles François (1818–93; French composer)

GRÉTRY, André Ernest Modeste (1741–1813; Belgian composer)

GROVES, Sir Charles (1915–92; British conductor)

HALÉVY, Jacques François (Fromental Elias Levy, 1799–1862; French composer)

HANDEL, George Frederick (1685–1759; German composer)

HARRIS, Roy (1898–1979; US composer)

HOTTER, Hans (1909– ; German baritone)

HUMMEL, Johann Nepomuk (1778–1837; Hungarian pianist and composer)

JOCHUM, Eugen (1902–87; German conductor)

KODÁLY, Zoltan (1882–1967; Hungarian composer)

KRENEK, Ernst (1900–91; Austrian composer)

LASSUS, Roland de (c. 1532–94; Flemish composer)

LIGETI, György (1923– ; Hungarian composer)

MAAZEL, Lorin (1930– ; US conductor)

MAHLER, Gustav (1860–1911; Austrian composer and conductor)

MORLEY, Thomas (1557–1603; English composer, music printer and organist)

MOZART, Wolfgang Amadeus (1756–91; Austrian composer)

PREVIN, André (Andreas Ludwig Priwin, 1929– ; German-born conductor, pianist, and composer)

RAMEAU, Jean Philippe (1683–1764; French composer)

RATTLE, Sir Simon (1955– ; British conductor)

RUBBRA, Edmund (1901–86; British composer)

SCHÜTZ, Heinrich (1585–1672; German composer)

6–continued

TALLIS, Thomas (c. 1505–85; English composer)

VARÈSE, Edgard (1883–1965; French composer)

WAGNER, Richard (1813–83; German composer)

WALTER, Bruno (B W Schlesinger, 1876–1962; German conductor)

WALTON, Sir William (1902–83; British composer)

WEBERN, Anton von (1883–1945; Austrian composer)

7

ALBÉNIZ, Isaac Manuel Francisco (1860–1909; Spanish composer and pianist)

ALLEGRI, Gregorio (1582–1652; Italian composer)

ANTHEIL, George (1900–59; US composer)

BABBITT, Milton (1916– ; US composer)

BEECHAM, Sir Thomas (1879–1961; British conductor)

BELLINI, Vincenzo (1801–35; Italian opera composer)

BENNETT, Richard Rodney (1936– ; British composer)

BENNETT, Sir William Sterndale (1816–75; British pianist)

BERLIOZ, Hector (1803–69; French composer and conductor)

BORODIN, Aleksandr Porfirevich (1833–87; Russian composer)

BRENDEL, Alfred (1931– ; Austrian pianist)

BRAXTON, Anthony (1945– ; US composer)

BRITTEN, Benjamin, Baron (1913–76; British composer and pianist)

CABALLÉ, Montserrat (1933– ; Spanish soprano)

CACCINI, Giulio (c. 1545–c. 1618; Italian singer and composer)

CAMPION, Thomas (or Campian, 1567–1620; English composer)

CAVALLI, Francesco (1602–76; Italian composer)

COPLAND, Aaron (1900–90; US composer)

7–continued

CORELLI, Arcangelo (1653–1713; Italian violinist and composer)

DEBUSSY, Claude (1862–1918; French composer)

DELIBES, Leo (1836–91; French composer)

DOMINGO, Placido (1941– ; Spanish tenor)

DOWLAND, John (1563–1626; English composer and lutenist)

FARNABY, Giles (c. 1565–1640; English composer)

FERRIER, Kathleen (1912–53; British contralto)

GALUPPI, Baldassare (1706–85; Venetian composer)

GIBBONS, Orlando (1583–1625; English composer, organist, and virginalist)

GIULINI, Carlo Maria (1914– ; Italian conductor)

GORECKI, Henryk (1933– ; Polish composer)

HAMMOND, Dame Joan (1912–96; British soprano)

HOFMANN, Joseph Casimir (1876–1957; Polish-born pianist)

IRELAND, John Nicholson (1879–1962; British composer)

JANÁČEK, Leoš (1854–1928; Czech composer)

JOACHIM, Joseph (1831–1907; Hungarian violinist and composer)

KARAJAN, Herbert von (1908–89; Austrian conductor)

KUBELIK, Rafael (1914–96; Czech conductor)

LAMBERT, Constant (1905–51; British composer and conductor)

LEHMANN, Lilli (1848–1929; German soprano)

LEHMANN, Lotte (1885–1976; German soprano)

MALCOLM, George John (1917– ; British harpsichordist)

MARTINŮ, Bohuslav (1890–1959; Czech composer)

MENOTTI, Gian Carlo (1911– ; Italian-born US composer)

7–continued

MENUHIN, Sir Yehudi (1916–99; British violinist)

MILHAUD, Darius (1892–1974; French composer)

MONTEUX, Pierre (1875–1964; French conductor)

NICOLAI, Otto Ehrenfried (1810–49; German conductor and composer)

NIELSEN, Carl (1865–1931; Danish composer and conductor)

NIKISCH, Arthur (1855–1922; Hungarian conductor)

NILSSON, Birgit Marta (1918– ; Swedish soprano)

OKEGHEM, Jean d' (c. 1425–c. 1495; Flemish composer)

ORMANDY, Eugene (E Blau, 1899–1985; Hungarian-born US conductor)

PÉROTIN (Latin name: Perotinus Magnus, c. 1155–c. 1202; French composer)

POULENC, Francis (1899–1963; French composer)

PUCCINI, Giacomo (1858–1924; Italian opera composer)

PURCELL, Henry (1659–95; English composer and organist)

RICHTER, Hans (1843–1916; Hungarian conductor)

RICHTER, Sviatoslav (1915–97; Ukrainian pianist)

RODRIGO, Joaquín (1902– ; Spanish composer)

ROSSINI, Gioacchino Antonio (1792–1868; Italian composer)

ROUSSEL, Albert (1869–1937; French composer)

RUGGLES, Carl (1876–1971; US composer)

SALIERI, Antonio (1750–1825; Italian composer and conductor)

SARGENT, Sir Malcolm (1895–1967; British conductor)

SCHUMAN, William (1910–91; US composer)

SMETANA, Bedřich (1824–84; Bohemian composer)

SOLOMON (S Cutner, 1902– ; British pianist)

STAINER, Sir John (1840–1901; British composer and organist)

7–continued

STAMITZ, Johann (Jan Stamic, 1717–57; Bohemian composer)

STRAUSS, Richard (1864–1949; German composer and conductor)

THIBAUD, Jacques (1880–1953; French violinist)

THOMSON, Virgil (1896–1989; US composer and conductor)

TIPPETT, Sir Michael (1905–98; British composer)

VIVALDI, Antonio (1678–1741; Italian composer and violinist)

WARLOCK, Peter (Philip Heseltine, 1894–1930; British composer and music scholar)

WEELKES, Thomas (c. 1575–1623; English composer and organist)

WELLESZ, Egon (1885–1974; Austrian composer)

XENAKIS, Yannis (1922– ; Greek composer)

8

ALBINONI, Tomaso (1671–1750; Italian composer)

ANSERMET, Ernest (1883–1969; Swiss conductor)

BERKELEY, Sir Lennox Randal Francis (1903–89; British composer)

BRUCKNER, Anton (1824–96; Austrian composer and organist)

CHABRIER, Emmanuel (1841–94; French composer)

CHAUSSON, Ernest (1855–99; French composer)

CIMAROSA, Domenico (1749–1801; Italian composer)

CLEMENTI, Muzio (1752–1832; Italian pianist and composer)

COUPERIN, François (1668–1733; French composer)

DOHNÁNYI, Ernö (Ernst von D, 1877–1960; Hungarian composer and pianist)

FLAGSTAD, Kirsten Malfrid (1895–1962; Norwegian soprano)

GARDINER, Sir John Eliot (1943– ; British conductor)

GERSHWIN, George (Jacob Gershvin, 1898–1937; US composer)

8—continued

GESUALDO, Carlo, Prince of Venosa (*c.* 1560–1631; Italian composer)

GLAZUNOV, Aleksandr Konstantinovich (1865–1936; Russian composer)

GOOSSENS, Sir Eugene (1893–1962; British conductor and composer)

GRAINGER, Percy Aldridge (1882–1961; Australian composer and pianist)

GRANADOS, Enrique (1867–1916; Spanish composer and pianist)

HONEGGER, Arthur (1892–1955; French composer)

HOROWITZ, Vladimir (1904–89; Russian pianist)

KREISLER, Fritz (1875–1962; Austrian violinist)

MACONCHY, Dame Elizabeth (1907–94; British composer)

MARENZIO, Luca (1553–99; Italian composer)

MASCAGNI, Pietro (1863–1945; Italian composer)

MASSENET, Jules (1842–1912; French composer)

MELCHIOR, Lauritz (1890–1973; Danish tenor)

MESSAGER, André (1853–1929; French composer and conductor)

MESSIAEN, Olivier (1908–92; French composer, organist, and teacher)

MILSTEIN, Nathan (1904–92; US violinist)

MUSGRAVE, Thea (1928– ; Scottish composer)

OISTRAKH, David (1908–75; Russian violinist)

PAGANINI, Niccolò (1782–1840; Italian violinist)

PHILIDOR, André Danican (d. 1730; French musician)

RESPIGHI, Ottorino (1879–1936; Italian composer)

SCHNABEL, Artur (1882–1951; Austrian pianist)

SCHUBERT, Franz (1797–1828; Austrian composer)

SCHULLER, Gunther (1925– ; US composer)

SCHUMANN, Elisabeth (1885–1952; German-born soprano)

8—continued

SCHUMANN, Robert (1810–56; German composer)

SCRIABIN, Alexander (1872–1915; Russian composer and pianist)

SESSIONS, Roger (1896–1985; US composer)

SIBELIUS, Jean (Johan Julius Christian S, 1865–1957; Finnish composer)

STANFORD, Sir Charles (1852–1924; Irish composer)

SULLIVAN, Sir Arthur (1842–1900; British composer)

TAVERNER, John (*c.* 1495–1545; English composer)

TE KANAWA, Dame Kiri (1944– ; New Zealand soprano)

TELEMANN, Georg Philipp (1681–1767; German composer)

VICTORIA, Tomás Luis de (*c.* 1548–1611; Spanish composer)

WILLIAMS, John (1941– ; Australian guitarist)

ZABALETA, Nicanor (1907–93; Spanish harpist)

9

ADDINSELL, Richard (1904–77; British composer)

ASHKENAZY, Vladimir (1937– ; Russian pianist and conductor)

BALAKIREV, Mili Alekseevich (1837–1910; Russian composer)

BARENBOIM, Daniel (1942– ; Israeli pianist and composer)

BEETHOVEN, Ludwig van (1770–1827; German composer)

BERNSTEIN, Leonard (1918–90; US conductor, composer, and pianist)

BOULANGER, Nadia (1887–1979; French composer, teacher, and conductor)

BUXTEHUDE, Dietrich (1637–1707; Danish organist and composer)

CHALIAPIN, Feodor Ivanovich (1873–1938; Russian bass)

CHERUBINI, Maria Luigi (1760–1842; Italian composer)

9—continued

CHRISTOFF, Boris (1919–93; Bulgarian singer)

DOLMETSCH, Arnold (1858–1940; British musician and instrument maker)

DONIZETTI, Gaetano (1797–1848; Italian composer)

DUNSTABLE, John (d. 1453; English composer)

HINDEMITH, Paul (1895–1963; German composer and viola player)

HODDINOTT, Alun (1929– ; Welsh composer)

KLEMPERER, Otto (1885–1973; German conductor)

LANDOWSKA, Wanda (1877–1959; Polish-born harpsichordist)

MACKERRAS, Sir Charles (1925– ; US-born Australian conductor)

MALIPIERO, Gian Francesco (1882–1973; Italian composer and teacher)

MEYERBEER, Giacomo (Jacob Liebmann Beer, 1791–1864; German composer and pianist)

OFFENBACH, Jacques (J Eberst, 1819–80; French composer)

PAVAROTTI, Luciano (1935– ; Italian tenor)

PERGOLESI, Giovanni (1710–36; Italian composer)

SCARLATTI, Domenico (1685–1757; Italian composer, harpsichordist, and organist)

STOKOWSKI, Leopold (1882–1977; British-born conductor)

TORTELIER, Paul (1914–90; French cellist)

TOSCANINI, Arturo (1867–1957; Italian conductor)

10

BARBIROLLI, Sir John (1899–1970; British conductor)

BIRTWISTLE, Harrison (1934– ; British composer)

BOCCHERINI, Luigi (1743–1805; Italian violoncellist and composer)

GALLI-CURCI, Amelita (1882–1963; Italian soprano)

MUSICIANS AND COMPOSERS

10–continued

LOS ANGELES, Victoria de
(1923– ; Spanish soprano)
MENGELBERG, William
(1871–1951; Dutch
conductor)
MONTEVERDI, Claudio
(1567–1643; Italian
composer)
MUSSORGSKI, Modest
Petrovich (1839–81; Russian
composer)
PADEREWSKI, Ignacy
(1860–1941; Polish pianist
and composer)
PALESTRINA, Giovanni
Pierluigi da (?1525–94; Italian
composer)
PENDERECKI, Krzysztof
(1933– ; Polish composer)
PRAETORIUS, Michael (M
Schultheiss, 1571–1621;
German composer)
RAWSTHORNE, Alan
(1905–71; British composer)
RUBINSTEIN, Anton (1829–94;
Russian pianist and
composer)
RUBINSTEIN, Artur
(1888–1982; Polish-born
pianist)
SAINT-SAËNS, Camille
(1835–1921; French
composer, conductor, pianist,
and organist)
SCHOENBERG, Arnold
(1874–1951; Austrian-born
composer)
SKALKOTTAS, Nikos
(1904–49; Greek composer)
STRADIVARI, Antonio
(?1644–1737; Italian violin
maker)
STRAVINSKY, Igor
(1882–1971; Russian-born
composer)
SUTHERLAND, Dame Joan
(1926– ; Australian
soprano)

10–continued

TETRAZZINI, Luisa
(1871–1940; Italian soprano)
VILLA-LOBOS, Heitor
(1887–1959; Brazilian
composer)

11

CHARPENTIER, Gustave
(1860–1956; French
composer)
FURTWÄNGLER, Wilhelm
(1886–1954; German
conductor)
HUMPERDINCK, Engelbert
(1854–1921; German
composer)
LEONCAVALLO, Ruggiero
(1858–1919; Italian
composer)
LESCHETIZKY, Theodor
(1830–1915; Polish pianist
and piano teacher)
LLOYD WEBBER, Andrew
(1948– ; British composer)
LLOYD WEBBER, Julian
(1951– ; British cellist)
LUTOSLAWSKI, Witold
(1913–94; Polish composer)
MENDELSSOHN, Felix (Jacob
Ludwig Felix Mendelssohn-
Bartholdy, 1809–47; German
composer)
RACHMANINOV, Sergei
(1873–1943; Russian com-
poser, pianist, and conductor)
SCHWARZKOPF, Elisabeth
(1915– ; German soprano)
STOCKHAUSEN, Karlheinz
(1928– ; German
composer)
SZYMANOWSKI, Karol (1882–
1937; Polish composer)
TCHAIKOVSKY, Peter Ilich
(1840–93; Russian
composer)
WOLF-FERRARI, Ermanno
(1876–1948; Italian
composer)

12

DALLAPICCOLA, Luigi
(1904–1975; Italian composer
and pianist)
GUIDO D'AREZZO (c. 990–c.
1050; Italian monk and
musical theorist)
KHACHATURIAN, Aram Ilich
(1903–78; Soviet composer,
born in Armenia)
KOUSSEVITSKY, Sergei
(1874–1951; Russian
composer)

13

ROUGET DE L'ISLE, Claude
Joseph (1760–1836; French
composer)

14

FISCHER-DIESKAU, Dietrich
(1925– ; German baritone)
JAQUES-DALCROZE, Émile
(1865–1950; Swiss
composer)
JOSQUIN DES PREZ (c.
1450–1521; Flemish
composer)
RIMSKY-KORSAKOV, Nikolai
(1844–1908; Russian
composer)

15

COLERIDGE-TAYLOR, Samuel
(1875–1912; British
composer)
VAUGHAN WILLIAMS, Ralph
(1872–1958; British
composer)

17

STRAUSS THE YOUNGER,
Johann (1825–99; Austrian
violinist, conductor, and
composer)

STAGE AND SCREEN PERSONALITIES

3

BOW, Clara (US film actress)
COX, Robert (English comic actor)
FOY, Eddie (US actor)
HAY, Will (British comedian)
LEE, Gypsy Rose (US entertainer)
RAY, Satyajit (Indian film director)
RIX, Sir Brian (British actor)
SIM, Alastair (Scottish actor)

4

ARNE, Susanna Maria (British actress)
BIRD, Theophilus (English actor)
BOND, Edward (British dramatist)
CANE, Andrew (English actor)
CHAN, Jackie (Hong Kong actor-director)
COBB, Lee J (US actor)
COOK, Peter (British comedy actor)
DALY, Augustin (US theatre manager)
DEAN, James (US film actor)
DUFF, Mrs (US actress)
DUSE, Eleonora (Italian actress)
FORD, John (US film director)
FORD, Harrison (US film actor)
GISH, Lillian (US actress)
GOLD, Jimmy (British comedian)
GRAY, Dulcie (British actress)
GRAY, 'Monsewer' Eddie (British comedian)
HALL, Sir Peter (British theatre director)
HOPE, Bob (US comedian, born in Britain)
KEAN, Edmund (British actor)
KNOX, Teddy (British comedian)
LAHR, Bert (US actor)
LANG, Fritz (German film director)
LEAN, Sir David (British film director)
LUNT, Alfred (US actor)
NUNN, Trevor (British theatre director)
OWEN, Alun Davies (British dramatist)
PAGE, Geraldine (US actress)

4–continued

PIAF, Edith (French cabaret and music-hall performer)
RANK, J Arthur (British industrialist and film executive)
REED, Sir Carol (British film director)
REID, Beryl (British actress)
RIGG, Diana (British actress)
SHER, Anthony (British actor)
TATE, Harry (British music-hall comedian)
TREE, Sir Herbert Beerbohm (British actor and theatre manager)
WEST, Mae (US actress)

5

ALLEN, Chesney (British comedian)
ALLEN, Woody (US film actor and director)
ARMIN, Robert (British actor)
ASTON, Anthony (Irish actor)
BADEL, Alan (British actor)
BARON, André (French actor)
BARON, Michel (French actor)
BARRY, Elizabeth (English actress)
BARRY, Spranger (Irish actor)
BATES, Alan (British actor)
BETTY, William Henry West (British boy actor)
BLOOM, Claire (British actress)
BOOTH, Barton (British actor)
BOOTH, Edwin Thomas (US actor)
BOOTH, Junius Brutus (US actor)
BOYER, Charles (French film actor)
BRICE, Fanny (US actress)
BROOK, Peter (British theatre director)
BROWN, Pamela (British actor)
BRYAN, Dora (British actress)
CAINE, Sir Michael (British film actor)
CAPRA, Frank (US film director, born in Italy)
CAREY, Joyce (British actress)
CARNÉ, Marcel (French film director)
CLAIR, René (French film director)
CLIVE, Kitty (British actress)
CLOSE, Glenn (uS actress)
CONTI, Italia (British actress)

5–continued

DAVIS, Bette (US film actress)
DENCH, Dame Judi (British actress)
EDWIN, John (British actor)
EKHOF, Konrad (German actor and director)
EVANS, Dame Edith (British actress)
FLYNN, Errol (Australian actor, born in Tasmania)
FONDA, Henry (US film actor and director)
GABIN, Jean (French film actor)
GABLE, Clark (US film actor)
GARBO, Greta (Swedish actress)
GOZZI, Carlo (Italian dramatist)
GRANT, Cary (US film actor, born in England)
GWYNN, Nell (English actress)
HAIGH, Kenneth (British actor)
HANDL, Dame Irene (British actress)
HANKS, Tom (US actor)
HAWKS, Howard (US film director)
HICKS, Sir Seymour (British actor-manager)
IRONS, Jeremy (British actor)
KAZAN, Elia (US stage and film director and novelist)
KELLY, Grace (US film actress)
KORDA, Sir Alexander (British film producer and director)
LA RUE, Danny (British female impersonator)
LEIGH, Vivien (British actress)
LENYA, Lotte (German actress and singer)
LIFAR, Serge (Russian ballet dancer and choreographer)
LLOYD, Harold (US film comedian)
LLOYD, Marie (British music-hall entertainer)
LOREN, Sophia (Italian film actress)
LOSEY, Joseph (US film director)
LUCAS, George (US film director)
MAYER, Louis B (US film producer, born in Russia)
MILES, Bernard (British theatre director and actor)
MILLS, Sir John (British actor)

5–continued

MOORE, Dudley (British actor and songwriter)
NERVO, Jimmy (British comedian)
NIVEN, David (British film actor)
PAIGE, Elaine (British actress and singer)
PASCO, Richard (British actor)
PETIT, Roland (French ballet dancer and choreographer)
POLUS (Greek tragic actor)
POPOV, Oleg Konstantinovich (Russian clown)
POWER, Tyrone (US actor)
PRYCE, Jonathan (British actor)
ROBEY, Sir George Edward (British music-hall comedian)
SMITH, Maggie Natalie (British actress)
TERRY, Dame Ellen Alice (British actress)
TOPOL, Chaim (Israeli actor)
TRACY, Spencer (US film actor)
TUTIN, Dorothy (British actress)
WAJDA, Andrzej (Polish film director)
WAYNE, John (US film actor)

6

ADRIAN, Max (British actor)
AINLEY, Henry (British actor)
AITKEN, Maria (British actress)
ALIZON (French actor)
ALLEYN, Edward (English actor)
ALTMAN, Robert (US film director)
ARNAUD, Yvonne Germaine (French actress)
ARTAUD, Antonin (French actor, poet, producer, and theoretician of the theatre)
ASHTON, Sir Frederick (British ballet dancer and choreographer, born in Ecuador)
ATKINS, Eileen (British actress)
BACALL, Lauren (US film actress)
BALCON, Sir Michael (British film producer)
BARDOT, Brigitte (French film actress)
BARNUM, Phineas Taylor (US showman)
BAYLIS, Lilian (British theatre manager)
BÉJART, Joseph (French actor)

6–continued

BÉJART, Maurice (French ballet dancer and choreographer)
BENSON, Sir Frank (British actor-manager)
BLASIS, Carlo (Italian dance teacher)
BOCAGE (French actor)
BOGART, Humphrey (US film actor)
BRANDO, Marlon (US actor)
BRIERS, Richard (British actor)
BROOKE, Gustavus Vaughan (British actor)
BROUGH, Lionel (British actor)
BROWNE, Robert (English actor)
BRYANT, Michael (British actor)
BUÑUEL, Luis (Spanish film director)
BURTON, Richard Walter (British actor, born in Wales)
CAGNEY, James (US actor)
CALLOW, Simon (British actor)
CANTOR, Eddie (US singer and actor)
CASSON, Sir Lewis (British actor and director)
CIBBER, Colley (British actor-manager)
COLMAN, Ronald (British actor)
CONWAY, William Augustus (British actor)
COOPER, Dame Gladys (British actress)
COOPER, Gary (US film actor)
COWARD, Sir Noël (British dramatist, composer, and actor)
COWELL, Joe Leathley (British actor)
CRANKO, John (British choreographer, born in South Africa)
CROSBY, Bing (US popular singer and film actor)
CURTIS, Tony (US film actor)
DE NIRO, Robert (US film actor)
DE SICA, Vittorio (Italian film director)
DEVINE, George Alexander Cassady (British theatre manager, director, and actor)
DIGGES, Dudley (British actor)
DISNEY, Walt (US film producer and animator)
DRAPER, Ruth (US actress)
DREYER, Carl Theodor (Danish film director)
DUNCAN, Isadora (US dancer)

6–continued

FIELDS, Gracie (British popular entertainer)
FIELDS, W C (US actor)
FINLAY, Frank (British actor)
FINNEY, Albert (British actor)
FLEURY (French actor)
FOKINE, Michel (Russian ballet dancer and choreographer)
FORMAN, Miloš (Czech film director)
FORMBY, George (British music hall singer)
FOSTER, Jodie (US actress)
GIBSON, Mel (Australian film actor and director)
GODARD, Jean-Luc (French film director)
GONG LI (Chinese actress)
GORING, Marius (British actor)
GRAHAM, Martha (US ballet dancer and choreographer)
GUITRY, Sacha (French actor and dramatist)
HARLOW, Jean (US film actress)
HERZOG, Werner (German film director)
HILLER, Dame Wendy (British actress)
HOWARD, Leslie (British actor of Hungarian descent)
HUSTON, John (US film director)
IRVING, Sir Henry (British actor and manager)
JACOBI, Derek (British actor)
JOLSON, Al (US actor and singer)
JORDAN, Dorothy (British actress)
JOUVET, Louis (French actor and theatre director)
KEATON, Buster (US comedian of silent films)
KEMBLE, John Philip (British actor and manager)
KENDAL, Felicity (British actress)
LANDEN, Dinsdale (British actor)
LAUDER, Sir Harry (Scottish singer and music-hall comedian)
LEMMON, Jack (US actor)
LESSER, Anton (British actor)
LILLIE, Beatrice Gladys (British actress, born in Canada)
LIPMAN, Maureen (British actress)
MARTIN, Mary (US actress)
MASSEY, Daniel (British actor)

6–continued

MASSEY, Raymond Hart (Canadian actor)
MCEWAN, Geraldine (British actress)
MCKERN, Leo (Australian actor)
MERMAN, Ethel (US actress)
MONROE, Marilyn (US film actress)
MORLEY, Robert (British actor)
NEWMAN, Paul (US film actor)
O'TOOLE, Peter (British actor)
PACINO, Al (US actor)
PETIPA, Marius (French dancer and choreographer)
PORTER, Eric (British actor)
QUAYLE, Sir Anthony (British actor)
RACHEL (French actress)
RÉJANE (French actress)
ROBSON, Dame Flora (British actress)
ROGERS, Ginger (US actress and singer)
ROWLEY, Thomas (English dramatist and actor)
SHUTER, Ned (British actor)
SINDEN, Donald (British actor)
SNIPES, Wesley (US actor)
STEELE, Tommy (British singer and actor)
STREEP, Meryl (US actress)
SUZMAN, Janet (British actress)
TAYLOR, Elizabeth (US film actress, born in England)
TEARLE, Godfrey Seymour (British actor)
TEMPLE, Shirley (US film actress)
TILLEY, Vesta (British music-hall entertainer)
WARREN, William (US actor, born in Britain)
WELLES, Orson (US film actor and director)
WILDER, Billy (US film director, born in Austria)
WOLFIT, Sir Donald (British actor and manager)

7

ACHURCH, Janet (British actress)
ACKLAND, Joss (British actor)
AESOPUS, Claudius (Roman tragic actor)
ALLGOOD, Sara (Irish actress)
ANTOINE, André (French actor, director, and theatre manager)

7–continued

BEAUVAL (French actor)
BELLAMY, George Anne (British actress)
BENNETT, Hywel (British actor, born in Wales)
BENNETT, Jill (British actress)
BERGMAN, Ingmar (Swedish film and stage director)
BERGMAN, Ingrid (Swedish actress)
BERGNER, Elisabeth (Austrian actress)
BLAKELY, Colin (British actor)
BOGARDE, Dirk (British film actor of Dutch descent)
BRANAGH, Kenneth (British actor)
BRESSON, Robert (French film director)
BURBAGE, Richard (English actor)
CALVERT, Louis (British actor)
CAMERON, James (Canadian film director)
CAMPION, Jane (New Zealand film director)
CASARÉS, Maria (French actress)
CELESTE, Céline (French actress)
CHABROL, Claude (French film director)
CHAPLIN, Charlie (US film actor, born in Britain)
COLBERT, Claudette (US film actress, born in France)
COLLIER, Constance (British actress)
COMPTON, Fay (British actress)
CONDELL, Henry (English actor)
CONNERY, Sir Sean (Scottish film actor)
COPPOLA, Francis Ford (US film director)
CORALLI, Jean (Italian ballet dancer and choreographer)
CORNELL, Katharine (US actress)
COSTNER, Kevin (US film actor and director)
DEBURAU, Jean-Gaspard (French pantomimist, born in Bohemia)
DÉJAZET, Pauline-Virginie (French actress)
DELYSIA, Alice (French actress and singer)
DE MILLE, Cecil B (US film producer and director)

7–continued

DENEUVE, Catherine (French film actress)
DENISON, Michael (British actor)
DOGGETT, Thomas (British actor)
DOTRICE, Roy (British actor)
DOUGLAS, Kirk (US film actor)
DURANTE, Jimmy (US actor and singer, known as 'Schnozzle')
ELLIOTT, Denholm (British actor)
FELLINI, Federico (Italian film director)
FONTEYN, Dame Margot (British ballet dancer)
GARLAND, Judy (US singer and film actress)
GARRICK, David (English actor)
GIELGUD, Sir John (British actor)
GINGOLD, Hermione (British actress)
GOLDWYN, Samuel (US film producer)
GREGORY, Lady Augusta (Irish theatre patron and dramatist)
GUTHRIE, Tyrone (British theatre director)
HANCOCK, Sheila (British actress)
HANCOCK, Tony (British comedian)
HAWTREY, Sir Charles (British actor-manager)
HEPBURN, Audrey (British actress)
HEPBURN, Katharine (US actress)
HOFFMAN, Dustin (US film actor)
HOPKINS, Sir Anthony (British actor)
HORDERN, Sir Michael (British actor)
HOUDINI, Harry (US magician)
IFFLAND, August Wilhelm (German actor)
JACKSON, Glenda (British actress)
JOHNSON, Dame Celia (British actress)
KARLOFF, Boris (British character actor)
KUBRICK, Stanley (US film writer, director, and producer)
LACKAYE, Wilton (US actor)

7–continued

LANGTRY, Lillie (British actress, known as the 'Jersey Lily')

LAROQUE (French actor)

LÉOTARD, Jules (French acrobat and music-hall performer)

MADONNA (US pop singer and film actress)

MARCEAU, Marcel (French mime)

MARKOVA, Dame Alicia (British ballet dancer)

MASSINE, Léonide (Russian ballet dancer and choreographer)

MCKENNA, Siobhán (Irish actress)

MCQUEEN, Steve (US film actor)

MICHELL, Keith (Australian actor)

NUREYEV, Rudolf (Russian ballet dancer)

OLIVIER, Laurence Kerr, Lord (British actor)

OXBERRY, William (British actor)

PAVLOVA, Anna (Russian ballet dancer)

PAXINOU, Katina (Greek actress)

PLUMMER, Christopher (Canadian actor)

PORTMAN, Eric (British actor)

QUILLEY, Denis (British actor)

RAMBERT, Dame Marie (British ballet dancer and choreographer)

REDFORD, Robert (US film actor)

RISTORI, Adelaide (Italian actress)

ROBARDS, Jason (US actor)

ROBBINS, Jerome (US ballet dancer and choreographer)

ROBESON, Paul Bustil (US Black actor)

RUSSELL, Ken (British film director)

SALVINI, Tommaso (Italian actor)

SELLERS, Peter (British comic actor)

SIDDONS, Sarah (English actress)

STEWART, James (US film actor)

STRITCH, Elaine (US actress)

TEMPEST, Dame Marie (British actress)

7–continued

ULANOVA, Galina (Russian ballet dancer)

USTINOV, Peter Alexander (British actor, director, and dramatist)

VESTRIS, Madame (British actress)

WITHERS, Googie (British actress)

8

ABINGTON, Frances (British actress)

ALDRIDGE, Ira Frederick (US actor)

ANDERSON, Dame Judith (Australian actress)

ANDREINI, Francesco (Italian actor-manager and playwright)

ANDREINI, Giovann Battista (Italian actor)

ANDREINI, Isabella (Italian actress)

ASHCROFT, Dame Peggy (British actress)

BADDELEY, Hermione (British actress)

BANCROFT, Anne (US actress)

BANKHEAD, Tallulah (US actress)

BARRAULT, Jean-Louis (French actor and director)

BERKELEY, Busby (US dance director)

BRASSEUR, Pierre (French actor)

BUCHANAN, Jack (Scottish actor-manager)

CALDWELL, Zoë (Australian actress)

CAMPBELL, Mrs Patrick (British actress)

CHANNING, Carol (US actress and singer)

CLEMENTS, Sir John (British actor-manager)

CRAWFORD, Joan (US film actress)

CRAWFORD, Michael (British actor)

DANCOURT, Florent (French actor and playwright)

DE LA TOUR, Frances (British actress)

DE VALOIS, Dame Ninette (British ballet dancer and choreographer, born in Ireland)

DEVRIENT, Ludwig (German actor)

8–continued

DIETRICH, Marlene (German film actress and singer)

DUFRESNE (French actor)

EASTWOOD, Clint (US film actor and director)

ESTCOURT, Richard (English actor)

FLAHERTY, Robert (US film director)

FLANAGAN, Bud (British comedian)

FLORENCE, William Jermyn (US actor)

FLORIDOR (French actor)

GRENFELL, Joyce (British actress)

GRIERSON, John (British film director)

GRIMALDI, Joseph (British clown)

GUINNESS, Sir Alec (British actor)

HARRISON, Rex (British actor)

HELPMANN, Sir Robert Murray (Australian ballet dancer, choreographer, and actor)

KUROSAWA, Akira (Japanese film director)

KYNASTON, Ned (English actor)

LANSBURY, Angela (US actress)

LAUGHTON, Charles (British actor)

LAWRENCE, Gertrude (British actress)

LEIGHTON, Margaret (British actress)

MACLAINE, Shirley (US actress)

MACREADY, William Charles (British actor and theatre manager)

MATTHEWS, Jessie (British actress)

MCKELLEN, Ian (British actor)

MERCOURI, Melina (Greek actress and politician)

NAUGHTON, Charlie (British comedian)

NAZIMOVA, Alla (Russian actress)

NIJINSKY, Vaslav (Russian ballet dancer)

PFEIFFER, Michelle (US actress)

PICKFORD, Mary (Canadian-born US film actress)

POLANSKI, Roman (Polish film director, born in Paris)

8–continued

REDGRAVE, Corin (British actor)

REDGRAVE, Lynn (British actress)

REDGRAVE, Sir Michael (British actor)

REDGRAVE, Vanessa (British actress)

ROBINSON, Edward G (US film actor, born in Romania)

SCOFIELD, Paul (British actor)

SCORSESE, Martin (US film director)

SELZNICK, David O (US film producer)

STROHEIM, Erich von (US film director and actor)

THOMPSON, Emma (British actress)

VISCONTI, Luchino (Italian film director)

WHITELAW, Billie (British actress)

WILLIAMS, Kenneth (British comic actor)

WILLIAMS, Michael (British actor)

ZIEGFELD, Florenz (US theatrical producer)

9

ALMODÓVAR, Pedro (Spanish film director)

ANTONIONI, Michelangelo (Italian film maker)

BARKWORTH, Peter (British actor)

BARRYMORE, Ethel (US actress)

BARRYMORE, John (US actor)

BARRYMORE, Lionel (US actor)

BARRYMORE, Maurice (British actor)

BELLECOUR (French actor)

BELLEROSE (French actor-manager)

BERIOSOVA, Svetlana (Russian ballet dancer)

BERNHARDT, Sarah (French actress)

BETTERTON, Thomas (English actor)

CHEN KAIGE (Chinese film director)

CHEVALIER, Maurice (French singer and actor)

COURTENAY, Tom (British actor)

DEPARDIEU, Gérard (French film actor)

9–continued

DIAGHILEV, Sergei (Russian ballet impresario)

DU MAURIER, Sir Gerald (British actor-manager)

FAIRBANKS, Douglas (US film actor)

FAVERSHAM, William (US actor)

FERNANDEL (French comedian)

FEUILLÈRE, Edwige (French actress)

FISHBURNE, Larry (US actor)

GRAMATICA, Irma (Italian actress)

GROSSMITH, George (British actor)

GRÜNDGENS, Gustav (German actor)

LAPOTAIRE, Jane (British actress)

MACMILLAN, Sir Kenneth (British ballet dancer and choreographer)

MONCRIEFF, Gladys (Australian actress)

NICHOLSON, Jack (US film actor)

PECKINPAH, Sam (US film director)

PLEASENCE, Donald (British actor)

PLOWRIGHT, Joan Anne (British actress)

PREMINGER, Otto (US film director, born in Austria)

REINHARDT, Max (Austrian theatre director)

SPIELBERG, Steven (US film director)

STERNBERG, Josef von (US film director, born in Austria)

STREISAND, Barbra (US singer and actress)

THORNDIKE, Dame Sybil (British actress)

VALENTINO, Rudolf (US film actor, born in Italy)

10

BALANCHINE, George (US ballet dancer and choreographer, born in Russia)

BASSERMANN, Albert (German actor)

BELLEROCHE (French actor)

BERTOLUCCI, Bernardo (Italian film director)

BOUCICAULT, 'Dot' (British actor-manager)

10–continued

BOUCICAULT, Nina (British actress)

CARTWRIGHT, William (English actor)

CUNNINGHAM, Merce (US dancer and choreographer)

D'OYLY CARTE, Richard (British theatre impresario and manager)

EISENSTEIN, Sergei (Russian film director)

FASSBINDER, Rainer Werner (German film director)

LITTLE TICH (British music-hall comedian)

LITTLEWOOD, Joan (British theatre director)

MONTFLEURY (French actor)

RICHARDSON, Ian (British actor)

RICHARDSON, Sir Ralph (British actor)

ROSSELLINI, Roberto (Italian film director)

RUTHERFORD, Dame Margaret (British actress)

WOFFINGTON, Peg (Irish actress)

ZEFFIRELLI, G Franco (Italian director and stage designer)

11

BEAUCHÂTEAU (French actor)

BIANCOLELLI, Giuseppe Domenico (French actor)

BRACEGIRDLE, Anne (English actress)

BRAITHWAITE, Dame Lilian (British actress)

COURTNEIDGE, Dame Cicely (British actress)

DAUVILLIERS (French actor)

MACLIAMMÓIR, Micheál (Irish actor and dramatist)

MASTROIANNI, Marcello (Italian actor)

MISTINGUETT (French singer and comedienne)

SCHLESINGER, John (British film and theatre director)

12

BRUSCAMBILLE (French actor)

MARX BROTHERS (US family of comic film actors)

STANISLAVSKY, Konstantin (Russian actor and theatre director)

13
ROSCIUS GALLUS, Quintus
(Roman comic actor)

14
MIZOGUCHI KENJI (Japanese
film director)

15
FFRANGCON-DAVIES, Gwen
(British actress)
FORBES-ROBERTSON, Sir
Johnston (British actor-
manager)

15—continued
GRANVILLE-BARKER, Harley
(British theatre director)
KOBAYASHI MASAKI
(Japanese film director)

SCIENTISTS AND INVENTORS

3
DAM, Carl Peter Henrik
(1895–1976; Danish
biochemist)
KAY, John (1704–c. 1764;
British inventor)
LEE, Tsung-Dao (1926–   ; US
physicist)
OHM, Georg Simon (1787–
1854; German physicist)
RAY, John (1627–1705; English
naturalist)

4
ABEL, Niels Henrik (1802–29;
Norwegian mathematician)
ABEL, Sir Frederick Augustus
(1827–1902; British chemist)
ADER, Clément (1841–1926;
French engineer and inventor)
AIRY, Sir George Biddell
(1801–92; British astronomer)
BAER, Karl Ernest von
(1792–1876; Russian
embryologist)
BELL, Alexander Graham
(1847–1922; Scottish scientist
and inventor)
BENZ, Karl (1844–1929;
German engineer)
BIRÓ, Laszlo (1900–85;
Hungarian inventor)
BOHR, Niels Henrik David
(1885–1962; Danish
physicist)
BORN, Max (1882–1970;
British physicist)
BOSE, Sir Jagadis Chandra
(1858–1937; Indian plant
physiologist and physicist)
COHN, Ferdinand Julius
(1839–1884; German
botanist)
COKE, Thomas William, of
Holkham, Earl of Leicester
(1752–1842; British
agriculturalist)

4—continued
CORT, Henry (1740–1800;
British inventor)
DAVY, Sir Humphry
(1778–1829; British chemist
and inventor)
EADS, John Buchanan
(1820–87; US civil engineer)
FUST, Johann (1400–66;
German printer)
GOLD, Thomas (1920–   ;
Austrian-born astronomer)
GRAY, Asa (1810–88; US
botanist)
HAHN, Otto (1879–1968;
German chemist and
physicist)
HESS, Victor Francis
(1883–1964; US physicist)
HOWE, Elias (1819–67; US
inventor)
KOCH, Robert (1843–1910;
German bacteriologist)
LAND, Edwin Herbert
(1909–91; US inventor)
LAUE, Max Theodor Felix Von
(1879–1960; German
physicist)
LOEB, Jacques (1859–1924;
US zoologist)
MACH, Ernst (1838–1916;
Austrian physicist)
MAYO (family of US medical
researchers)
OTIS, Elisha Graves (1811–61;
US inventor)
OTTO, Nikolaus August
(1832–91; German engineer)
RABI, Isidor Isaac (1898–88;
US physicist)
RYLE, Sir Martin (1918–84;
British astronomer)
SWAN, Sir Joseph Wilson
(1828–1914; British physicist)
TODD, Alexander Robertus,
Baron (1907–97; British
biochemist)

4—continued
TULL, Jethro (1674–1741;
English agriculturalist and
inventor of the seed drill)
UREY, Harold Clayton
(1893–1981; US physicist)
WATT, James (1736–1819;
British engineer)
YANG, Chen Ning (1922–   ;
US physicist)

5
ADAMS, John Couch
(1819–92; English
astronomer)
AIKEN, Howard Hathaway
(1900–73; US mathematician)
AMICI, Giovanni Battista
(1786–1863; Italian
astronomer, microscopist, and
optical instrument maker)
ASTON, Francis William
(1877–1945; British chemist)
AVERY, Oswald Theodore
(1877–1955; Canadian
bacteriologist)
BACON, Roger (c. 1214–c.
1292; English scientist)
BAILY, Francis (1774–1844;
British amateur astronomer)
BAIRD, John Logie
(1888–1946; British electrical
engineer)
BAKER, Sir Benjamin
(1840–1907; British civil
engineer)
BANKS, Sir Joseph
(1743–1820; British botanist
and explorer)
BATES, Henry Walter
(1825–92; British naturalist
and explorer)
BEEBE, Charles William
(1877–1962; US explorer and
naturalist)
BETHE, Hans Albrecht
(1906–   ; US physicist)

5—continued

BLACK, Joseph (1728–99; Scottish physician and chemist)

BLOCH, Felix (1905–83; US physicist)

BONDI, Sir Hermann (1919– ; British cosmologist and mathematician)

BOOLE, George (1815–64; British mathematician)

BOSCH, Carl (1874–1940; German chemist)

BOTHE, Walther Wilhelm Georg Franz (1891–1957; German experimental physicist)

BOVET, Daniel (1907–92; Swiss pharmacologist)

BOWEN, Norman Levi (1887–1956; Canadian experimental petrologist)

BOWER, Frederick Orpen (1855–1948; British botanist)

BOYLE, Robert (1627–91; British physicist and chemist)

BRAGG, Sir William Henry (1862–1942; British physicist)

BRAHE, Tycho (1546–1601; Danish astronomer)

BROWN, Robert (1773–1858; Scottish botanist)

BÜRGE, Joost (1552–1632; Swiss mathematician)

CHAIN, Sir Ernst Boris (1906–79; British biochemist)

CREED, Frederick (1871–1957; Canadian inventor)

CRICK, Francis Harry Compton (1916– ; British biophysicist)

CURIE, Marie (1867–1934; Polish chemist)

CURIE, Pierre (1859–1906; French physicist)

DEBYE, Peter Joseph Wilhelm (1884–1966; Dutch physicist and chemist)

DIELS, Otto Paul Hermann (1876–1954; German chemist)

DIRAC, Paul Adrien Maurice (1902–84; British physicist)

ELTON, Charles (1900–91; British zoologist)

EULER, Leonhard (1707–83; Swiss mathematician)

EVANS, Oliver (1755–1819; American engineer)

FABRE, Jean Henri (1823–1915; French entomologist)

5—continued

FABRY, Charles (1867–1945; French physicist)

FERMI, Enrico (1901–54; US physicist)

FREGE, Gottlob (1848–1925; German mathematician and logician)

GABOR, Dennis (1900–79; British electrical engineer)

GALLE, Johann Gottfried (1812–1910; German astronomer)

GAUSS, Karl Friedrich (1777–1855; German mathematician)

GEBER (14th century; Spanish alchemist)

GIBBS, Josiah Willard (1839–1903; US physicist)

GÖDEL, Kurt (1906–78; US mathematician)

HABER, Fritz (1868–1934; German chemist and inventor)

HARDY, Godfrey Harold (1877–1947; British mathematician)

HENRY, Joseph (1797–1878; US physicist)

HERTZ, Heinrich Rudolf (1857–94; German physicist)

HOOKE, Robert (1635–1703; British physicist)

HOYLE, Sir Fred (1915– ; British astronomer)

JEANS, Sir James Hopwood (1877–1946; British mathematician and astronomer)

JOULE, James Prescott (1818–89; British physicist)

KOLBE, Hermann (1818–84; German chemist)

KREBS, Sir Hans Adolf (1900–81; British biochemist)

KROTO, Sir Harold (1939– ; British chemist)

LAWES, Sir John Bennet (1814–1900; British agriculturalist)

LIBBY, Willard Frank (1908–80; US chemist)

LODGE, Sir Oliver Joseph (1851–1940; British physicist)

LYELL, Sir Charles (1797–1875; British geologist)

MAXIM, Sir Hiram Stevens (1840–1916; British inventor)

MAYER, Julius Robert Von (1814–78; German physicist)

MONGE, Gaspard (1746–1818; French mathematician)

5—continued

MONOD, Jacques-Lucien (1910–76; French biochemist)

MORSE, Samuel Finley Breese (1791–1872; US inventor)

NOBEL, Alfred Bernhard (1833–96; Swedish chemist)

NOBLE, Sir Andrew (1831–1915; British physicist)

PAULI, Wolfgang (1900–58; US physicist)

POPOV, Aleksandr Stepanovich (1859–1905; Russian physicist)

PROUT, William (1785–1850; British chemist and physiologist)

RAMAN, Sir Chandrasekhara Venkata (1888–1970; Indian physicist)

REBER, Grote (1911– ; US astronomer)

RHINE, Joseph Banks (1895–1980; US psychologist)

ROSSE, William Parsons, 3rd Earl Of (1800–67; Irish astronomer)

SEGRÈ, Emilio (1905–89; US physicist)

SMITH, Sir Keith Macpherson (1890–1955; Australian aviator)

SODDY, Frederick (1877–1956; British chemist)

STAHL, Georg Ernst (1660–1734; German physician and chemist)

TATUM, Edward Lawrie (1909–75; US geneticist)

TESLA, Nikola (1856–1943; US electrical engineer)

VOLTA, Alessandro Giuseppe Antonio Anastasio, Count (1745–1827; Italian physicist)

WEBER, Ernst Heinrich (1795–1878; German physiologist)

WHITE, Gilbert (1720–93; English naturalist)

YOUNG, Thomas (1773–1829; British physician and physicist)

6

ACHARD, Franz Karl (1753–1821; German chemist)

ADRIAN, Edgar Douglas, 1st Baron (1889–1977; British physiologist)

AGNESI, Maria Gaetana (1718–99; Italian mathematician)

6—continued

ALFVÉN, Hannes Olof Gösta (1908–95; Swedish astrophysicist)

AMPÈRE, André Marie (1775–1836; French physicist)

APPERT, Nicolas (1750–1841; French inventor)

ARCHER, Frederick Scott (1813–57; British inventor and sculptor)

BAEYER, Adolf Von (1835–1917; German chemist)

BEADLE, George Wells (1903–89; US geneticist)

BODONI, Giambattista (1740–1813; Italian printer)

BOLYAI, János (1802–60; Hungarian mathematician)

BONNET, Charles (1720–93; Swiss naturalist)

BORDET, Jules Jean Baptiste Vincent (1870–1961; Belgian bacteriologist)

BOVERI, Theodor Heinrich (1862–1915; German cell biologist)

BRAMAH, Joseph (1748–1814; British engineer and inventor)

BRIGGS, Henry (1561–1630; English mathematician)

BRUNEL, Isambard Kingdom (1806–59; British engineer)

BUFFON, Georges Louis Leclerc, Comte de (1707–88; French naturalist)

BUNSEN, Robert Wilhelm (1811–99; German chemist)

CALVIN, Melvin (1911–97; US biochemist)

CANTOR, Georg (1845–1918; Russian mathematician)

CARNOT, Sadi (1796–1832; French scientist and soldier)

CARREL, Alexis (1873–1944; French surgeon)

CARVER, George Washington (1864–1943; US agriculturalist)

CAUCHY, Augustin Louis, Baron (1789–1857; French mathematician)

CAXTON, William (c. 1422–91; The first English printer)

CAYLEY, Arthur (1821–95; British mathematician)

CAYLEY, Sir George (1773–1857; British engineer and pioneer designer of flying machines)

6—continued

CUVIER, Georges, Baron (1769–1832; French zoologist)

DALTON, John (1766–1844; British chemist)

DARWIN, Charles Robert (1809–1882; British naturalist)

DE BARY, Heinrich Anton (1831–88; German botanist)

DE DUVE, Christian (1917– ; Belgian biochemist)

DREYER, Johan Ludvig Emil (1852–1926; Danish astronomer)

DU MONT, Allen Balcom (1901–65; US engineer)

DUNLOP, John Boyd (1840–1921; Scottish inventor)

ECKERT, John Presper (1919–95; US electronics engineer)

EDISON, Thomas Alva (1847–1931; US inventor)

ENDERS, John Franklin (1897–1985; US microbiologist)

ENGLER, Gustav Heinrich Adolf (1844–1930; German botanist)

EUCLID (c. 300 BC; Greek mathematician)

FERMAT, Pierre de (1601–65; French mathematician)

FINSEN, Niels Ryberg (1860–1904; Danish physician)

FOKKER, Anthony Hermann Gerard (1890–1939; Dutch aircraft manufacturer)

FRANCK, James (1882–1964; US physicist)

FRISCH, Karl Von (1886–1982; Austrian zoologist)

FRISCH, Otto Robert (1904–79; Austrian-born physicist)

FULTON, Robert (1765–1815; American inventor)

GALOIS, Évariste (1811–32; French mathematician)

GALTON, Sir Francis (1822–1911; British scientist)

GEIGER, Hans (1882–1945; German physicist)

GESNER, Conrad (1516–65; Swiss physician)

GRAHAM, Thomas (1805–69; British physicist)

HALLEY, Edmund (1656–1742; British astronomer)

6—continued

HEVESY, George Charles Von (1885–1966; Hungarian-born chemist)

HOOKER, Sir William Jackson (1785–1865; British botanist)

HUBBLE, Edwin Powell (1889–1953; US astronomer)

HUTTON, James (1726–97; Scottish physician)

HUXLEY, Thomas Henry (1825–95; British biologist)

JANSKY, Karl Guthe (1905–50; US radio engineer)

JENSON, Nicolas (c. 1420–80; French printer)

JOLIOT, Frédéric (1900–59; French physicist)

KELVIN, William Thomson, 1st Baron (1824–1907; Scottish physicist)

KEPLER, Johannes (1571–1630; German astronomer)

KINSEY, Alfred (1894–1956; US zoologist and sociologist)

LANDAU, Lev Davidovich (1908–68; Soviet physicist)

LARTET, Édouard Armand Isidore Hippolyte (1801–71; French archaeologist)

LIEBIG, Justus, Baron Von (1803–73; German chemist)

LORENZ, Konrad (1903–89; Austrian zoologist)

LOVELL, Sir Bernard (1913– ; British astronomer)

LOWELL, Percival (1855–1916; US astronomer)

MARKOV, Andrei Andreevich (1856–1922; Russian mathematician)

MARTIN, Archer John Porter (1910– ; British biochemist)

MARTIN, Pierre-Émile (1824–1915; French engineer)

MCADAM, John Loudon (1756–1836; British inventor)

MENDEL, Gregor Johann (1822–84; Austrian botanist)

MORGAN, Thomas Hunt (1866–1945; US geneticist)

MORLEY, Edward Williams (1838–1923; US chemist)

MORRIS, Desmond John (1928– ; British zoologist)

MULLER, Hermann Joseph (1890–1967; US geneticist)

MÜLLER, Paul Hermann (1899–1965; Swiss chemist)

NAPIER, John (1550–1617; Scottish mathematician)

6–continued

NERNST, Walther Hermann (1864–1941; German physical chemist)

NEWTON, Sir Isaac (1642–1727; British physicist and mathematician)

OLBERS, Heinrich Wilhelm Matthäus (1758–1840; German astronomer)

PASCAL, Blaise (1623–62; French mathematician and physicist)

PENNEY, William George, Baron (1909–91; British mathematician)

PERKIN, Sir William Henry (1838–1907; British chemist)

PERRIN, Jean-Baptiste (1870–1942; French physicist)

PLANCK, Max Karl Ernst Ludwig (1858–1947; German physicist)

POWELL, Cecil Frank (1903–69; British physicist)

PROUST, Joseph-Louis (1754–1826; French chemist)

RAMSAY, Sir William (1852–1916; Scottish chemist)

RENNIE, John (1761–1821; British civil engineer)

SANGER, Frederick (1918– ; British biochemist)

SAVERY, Thomas (c. 1650–1715; English engineer)

SHOLES, Christopher Latham (1819–90; US inventor)

SINGER, Isaac Merrit (1811–75; US inventor)

SLOANE, Sir Hans (1660–1753; British physician and naturalist)

STOKES, Sir George Gabriel (1819–1903; British physicist and mathematician)

STRUVE, Otto (1897–1963; US astronomer)

SUTTON, Walter Stanborough (1877–1916; US geneticist)

TALBOT, William Henry Fox (1800–77; British botanist and physicist)

TAYLOR, Brook (1685–1737; English mathematician)

TAYLOR, Frederick Winslow (1856–1915; US engineer)

TELLER, Edward (1908– ; US physicist)

TOWNES, Charles Hard (1915– ; US physicist)

6–continued

VAUBAN, Sébastian Le Prestre de (1633–1707; French military engineer)

WALLIS, Sir Barnes (1887–1979; British aeronautical engineer)

WALTON, Ernest Thomas Sinton (1903–95; Irish physicist)

WATSON, James Dewey (1928– ; US geneticist)

WIENER, Norbert (1894–1964; US mathematician)

WIGNER, Eugene Paul (1902–95; US physicist)

WILSON, Charles Thomson Rees (1869–1959; British physicist)

WILSON, Edmund Beecher (1856–1939; US biologist)

WÖHLER, Friedrich (1800–82; German chemist)

WRIGHT, Orville (1871–1948; US aviator)

YUKAWA, Hideki (1907–81; Japanese physicist)

ZEEMAN, Pieter (1865–1943; Dutch physicist)

7

AGASSIZ, Jean Louis Rodolphe (1807–73; Swiss natural historian)

ALVAREZ, Luis Walter (1911–88; US physicist)

AUDUBON, John James (1785–1851; US naturalist)

BABBAGE, Charles (1792–1871; British mathematician and inventor)

BARDEEN, John (1908–91; US physicist)

BARNARD, Edward Emerson (1857–1923; US astronomer)

BATESON, William (1861–1926; British biologist)

BATTANI, Al- (c. 858–929; Islamic astronomer)

BERGIUS, Friedrich (1884–1949; German chemist)

BORLAUG, Norman (1914– ; US plant breeder)

BRAILLE, Louis (1809–52; French inventor of system of writing and printing for the blind)

BROUWER, Luitzen Egbertus Jan (1881–1966; Dutch mathematician)

BURBANK, Luther (1849–1926; US plant breeder)

7–continued

CANDELA, Felix (1910– ; Mexican engineer)

CARDANO, Girolamo (1501–76; Italian mathematician)

COMPTON, Arthur Holly (1892–1962; US physicist)

CORRENS, Carl Erich (1864–1933; German botanist and geneticist)

COULOMB, Charles Augustin de (1736–1806; French physicist)

CROOKES, Sir William (1832–1919; British physicist)

CURTISS, Glenn (1878–1930; US aviator and aeronautical engineer)

DAIMLER, Gottlieb (1834–1900; German inventor)

DANIELL, John Frederic (1790–1845; British chemist)

DE LA RUE, Warren (1815–89; British astronomer)

DE VRIES, Hugo Marie (1848–1935; Dutch botanist)

DOPPLER, Christian Johann (1803–53; Austrian physicist)

DRIESCH, Hans Adolf Eduard (1867–1941; German zoologist)

EICHLER, August Wilhelm (1839–87; German botanist)

FARADAY, Michael (1791–1867; British chemist and physicist)

FEYNMAN, Richard Phillips (1918–88; US physicist)

FISCHER, Emil Hermann (1852–1919; German chemist)

FLEMING, Sir John Ambrose (1849–1945; British electrical engineer)

FOURIER, Jean Baptiste Joseph, Baron (1768–1830; French mathematician and physicist)

FRESNEL, Augustin Jean (1788–1827; French physicist)

GAGARIN, Yuri Alekseevich (1934–68; Soviet cosmonaut)

GALVANI, Luigi (1737–98; Italian physician)

GILBERT, William (1544–1603; English physicist)

GODDARD, Robert Hutchings (1882–1945; US physicist)

GREGORY, James (1638–75; Scottish mathematician and astronomer)

7–continued

HAECKEL, Ernst Heinrich (1834–1919; German zoologist)

HAWORTH, Sir Walter Norman (1883–1950; British biochemist)

HELMONT, Jan Baptist van (1580–1644; Belgian alchemist and physician)

HERMITE, Charles (1822–1901; French mathematician)

HILBERT, David (1862–1943; German mathematician)

HODGKIN, Alan Lloyd (1914– ; British physiologist)

HODGKIN, Dorothy Mary Crowfoot (1910–95; British biochemist)

HOPKINS, Sir Frederick Gowland (1861–1947; British biochemist)

HUGGINS, Sir William (1824–1910; British astronomer)

HUYGENS, Christiaan (1629–95; Dutch astronomer and physicist)

JUSSIEU (French family of botanists)

KAPITZA, Peter Leonidovich (1894–1984; Soviet physicist)

KENDALL, Edward Calvin (1886–1972; US biochemist)

KENDREW, Sir John Cowdery (1917–97; British biochemist)

KHORANA, Har Gobind (1922– ; US biochemist)

KIDINNU (4th century BC; Babylonian mathematician and astronomer)

KOZIREV, Nikolai Aleksandrovich (1908– ; Russian astronomer)

LALANDE, Joseph-Jérôme le Français de (1732–1807; French astronomer)

LAMARCK, Jean-Baptiste de Monet, Chevalier de (1744–1829; French naturalist)

LAMBERT, Johann Heinrich (1728–77; German mathematician and astronomer)

LANGLEY, Samuel Pierpont (1834–1906; US astronomer)

LAPLACE, Pierre Simon, Marquis de (1749–1827; French mathematician and astronomer)

7–continued

LESSEPS, Ferdinand de (1805–94; French diplomat)

LOCKYER, Sir Joseph Norman (1836–1920; British astronomer)

LORENTZ, Hendrick Antoon (1853–1928; Dutch physicist)

LUMIÈRE, Auguste (1862–1954; French photographer and inventor)

LYSENKO, Trofim Denisovich (1898–1976; Soviet biologist)

MARCONI, Guglielmo (1874–1937; Italian electrical engineer)

MAXWELL, James Clerk (1831–79; Scottish physicist)

MEITNER, Lise (1878–1968; Austrian physicist)

MESSIER, Charles (1730–1817; French astronomer)

MOSELEY, Henry Gwyn Jeffries (1887–1915; British physicist)

NEUMANN, John Von (1903–57; US mathematician)

OERSTED, Hans Christian (1777–1851; Danish physicist)

ONSAGER, Lars (1903–76; US chemist)

OSTWALD, Wilhelm (1853–1932; German chemist)

PARSONS, Sir Charles Algernon (1854–1931; British engineer)

PASTEUR, Louis (1822–95; French chemist and microbiologist)

PAULING, Linus Carl (1901–94; US chemist)

PICCARD (family of Swiss scientists)

POISSON, Siméon Dénis (1781–1840; French mathematician)

PRANDTL, Ludwig (1875–1953; German physicist)

PTOLEMY (or Claudius Ptolemaeus, 2nd century AD; Egyptian mathematician, astronomer, and geographer)

PURCELL, Edward Mills (1912–97; US physicist)

RÉAUMUR, René-Antoine Ferchault de (1683–1757; French physicist)

RIEMANN, Georg Friedrich Bernhard (1826–66; German mathematician)

7–continued

RUMFORD, Benjamin Thompson, Count (1753–1814; American-born scientist)

SANDAGE, Allan Rex (1926– ; US astronomer)

SCHEELE, Carl Wilhelm (1742–86; Swedish chemist)

SCHWANN, Theodor (1810–82; German physiologist)

SEABORG, Glenn Theodore (1912– ; US physicist)

SHEPARD, Jr, Allan Bartlett (1923– ; US astronaut)

SIEMENS, Ernst Werner von (1816–92; German electrical engineer)

SIMPSON, George Gaylord (1902– ; US palaeontologist)

SZILARD, Leo (1898–1964; US physicist)

TELFORD, Thomas (1757–1834; British civil engineer)

THENARD, Louis-Jacques (1777–1857; French chemist)

THOMSON, Sir Joseph John (1856–1940; British physicist)

TUPOLEV, Andrei Niklaievich (1888–1972; Soviet designer)

TYNDALL, John (1820–93; Irish physicist)

VAVILOV, Nikolai Ivanovich (1887–1943; Soviet plant geneticist)

WAKSMAN, Selman Abraham (1888–1973; US microbiologist)

WALLACE, Alfred Russel (1823–1913; British naturalist)

WEGENER, Alfred Lothar (1880–1930; German geologist)

WHITNEY, Eli (1765–1825; American inventor)

WHITTLE, Sir Frank (1907–96; British aeronautical engineer)

WILKINS, Maurice Hugh Frederick (1916– ; New Zealand physicist)

ZIEGLER, Karl (1898–1973; German chemist)

8

AGRICOLA, Georgius (1494–1555; German physician and mineralogist)

ANDERSON, Carl David (1905–91; US physicist)

ÅNGSTRÖM, Anders Jonas (1814–74; Swedish physicist and astronomer)

8—continued

AVOGADRO, Amedeo, Conte di Quaregna e Ceretto (1776–1856; Italian physicist)

BAKEWELL, Robert (1725–95; British agriculturalist)

BESSEMER, Sir Henry (1813–98; British engineer and inventor)

BIRKHOFF, George David (1864–1944; US mathematician)

BJERKNES, Vilhelm Friman Koren (1862–1951; Norwegian meteorologist and physicist)

BLACKETT, Patrick Maynard Stuart, Baron (1897–1974; British physicist)

BRATTAIN, Walter Houser (1902–87; US physicist)

BREWSTER, Sir David (1781–1868; Scottish physicist)

BRIDGMAN, Percy Williams (1882–1961; US physicist)

BRINDLEY, James (1716–72; British canal builder)

BUSHNELL, David (1742–1824; US inventor; built the first submarine)

CALMETTE, Albert Léon Charles (1863–1933; French bacteriologist)

CHADWICK, Sir James (1891–1974; British physicist)

CLAUSIUS, Rudolf Julius Emanuel (1822–88; German physicist)

CROMPTON, Samuel (1753–1827; British inventor)

CULPEPER, Nicholas (1616–54; English physician)

DAGUERRE, Louis-Jacques-Mandé (1789–1851; French inventor)

DEDEKIND, Richard (1831–1916; German mathematician)

DE FOREST, Lee (1873–1961; US electrical engineer)

DE MORGAN, Augustus (1806–71; British mathematician and logician)

EINSTEIN, Albert (1879–1955; German physicist)

ERICSSON, John (1803–89; US naval engineer and inventor)

FOUCAULT, Jean Bernard Léon (1819–68; French physicist)

8—continued

GASSENDI, Pierre (1592–1655; French physicist)

GELL-MANN, Murray (1929– ; US physicist)

GUERICKE, Otto Von (1602–86; German physicist)

HAMILTON, Sir William Rowan (1805–65; Irish mathematician)

HERSCHEL, Sir William (1738–1822; British astronomer)

ILYUSHIN, Sergei Vladimirovich (1894–1977; Soviet aircraft designer)

IPATIEFF, Vladimir Nikolaievich (1867–1952; US physicist)

JACQUARD, Joseph-Marie (1752–1834; French inventor)

KENNELLY, Arthur Edwin (1861–1939; US electrical engineer)

KLAPROTH, Martin Heinrich (1743–1817; German chemist)

KOROLIOV, Sergei Pavlovich (1906–66; Soviet aeronautical engineer)

LAGRANGE, Joseph Louis, Comte de (1736–1813; French mathematician and astronomer)

LANGMUIR, Irving (1881–1957; US chemist)

LAWRENCE, Ernest Orlando (1901–58; US physicist)

LEGENDRE, Adrien Marie (1752–1833; French mathematician)

LEMAÎTRE, Georges Édouard, Abbé (1894–1966; Belgian priest and astronomer)

LEUCKART, Karl Georg Friedrich Rudolph (1822–98; German zoologist)

LINNAEUS, Carolus (Carl Linné; 1707–78; Swedish botanist)

LIPSCOMB, William Nunn (1919– ; US chemist)

LONSDALE, Dame Kathleen (1903–71; Irish physicist)

MAUDSLAY, Henry (1771–1831; British engineer)

MCMILLAN, Edwin Mattison (1907–91; US physicist)

MERCATOR, Gerardus (1512–94; Flemish geographer)

8—continued

MEYERHOF, Otto Fritz (1884–1951; US biochemist)

MILLIKAN, Robert Andrews (1868–1953; US physicist)

MILSTEIN, César (1927– ; British molecular biologist)

MITCHELL, Reginald Joseph (1895–1937; British aeronautical engineer)

MULLIKEN, Robert Sanderson (1896–1986; US chemist and physicist)

NEWCOMEN, Thomas (1663–1729; English blacksmith and inventor of steam engine)

OLIPHANT, Sir Mark Laurence Elwin (1901– ; Australian physicist)

POINCARÉ, Jules Henri (1854–1912; French mathematician)

RAYLEIGH, John William Strutt, 3rd Baron (1842–1919; British physicist)

RHETICUS (1514–76; German mathematician)

ROBINSON, Sir Robert (1886–1975; British chemist)

ROEBLING, John Augustus (1806–69; US engineer)

ROENTGEN, Wilhelm Konrad (1845–1923; German physicist)

SABATIER, Paul (1854–1941; French chemist)

SAKHAROV, Andrei Dimitrievich (1921–89; Soviet physicist)

SHOCKLEY, William Bradfield (1910–89; US physicist)

SHRAPNEL, Henry (1761–1842; British army officer, who invented the shrapnel shell)

SIKORSKY, Igor Ivan (1889–1972; US aeronautical engineer)

STIRLING, James (1692–1770; Scottish mathematician)

VAN ALLEN, James Alfred (1914– ; US physicist)

VAN'T HOFF, Jacobus Henricus (1852–1911; Dutch chemist)

WEISMANN, August Friedrich Leopold (1834–1914; German biologist)

WOODWARD, Robert Burns (1917–79; US chemist)

8—continued

ZERNICKE, Frits (1888–1966; Dutch physicist)

ZWORYKIN, Vladimir Kosma (1889–1982; US physicist)

9

ABU AL-WAFA (940–98 AD; Persian mathematician and astronomer)

ARKWRIGHT, Sir Richard (1732–92; British inventor)

ARMSTRONG, Edwin Howard (1890–1954; US electrical engineer)

ARMSTRONG, William George, Baron (1810–1900; British engineer)

ARRHENIUS, Svante August (1859–1927; Swedish physicist and chemist)

BECQUEREL, Henri (1852–1908; French physicist)

BERNOULLI (family of Swiss mathematicians and physicists)

BERTHELOT, Marcelin (1827–1907; French chemist)

BERZELIUS, Jöns Jakob, Baron (1779–1848; Swedish chemist)

BOLTZMANN, Ludwig Eduard (1844–1906; Austrian physicist)

BRONOWSKI, Jacob (1908–74; British mathematician)

CAVENDISH, Henry (1731–1810; British physicist)

CHEBISHEV, Pafnuti Lvovich (1821–94; Russian mathematician)

CHERENKOV, Pavel Alekseievich (1904–90; Russian physicist)

COCKCROFT, Sir John Douglas (1897–1967; British physicist)

CORNFORTH, Sir John Warcup (1917–   ; Australian chemist)

D'ALEMBERT, Jean Le Rond (1717–83; French mathematician)

DAUBENTON, Louis Jean Marie (1716–1800; French naturalist)

DAVENPORT, Charles Benedict (1866–1944; US zoologist)

EDDINGTON, Sir Arthur Stanley (1882–1944; British theoretical astronomer)

9—continued

ENDLICHER, Stephan Ladislaus (1804–49; Hungarian botanist)

FIBONACCI, Leonardo (c. 1170–c. 1230; Italian mathematician)

FLAMSTEED, John (1646–1719; English astronomer)

GAY-LUSSAC, Joseph Louis (1778–1850; French chemist and physicist)

GUTENBERG, Johann (c. 1400–c. 1468; German printer)

HEAVISIDE, Oliver (1850–1925; British physicist)

HELMHOLTZ, Hermann Ludwig Ferdinand Von (1821–94; German physicist and physiologist)

HOPKINSON, John (1849–98; British physicist and electrical engineer)

JOHANNSEN, Wilhelm Ludvig (1857–1927; Danish geneticist)

JOSEPHSON, Brian David (1940–   ; British physicist)

KIRCHHOFF, Gustav Robert (1824–87; German physicist)

KURCHATOV, Igor Vasilievich (1903–60; Soviet physicist)

LANKESTER, Sir Edwin Ray (1847–1929; British zoologist)

LAVOISIER, Antoine Laurent (1743–94; French chemist)

LEDERBERG, Joshua (1925–   ; US geneticist)

LEVERRIER, Urbain Jean Joseph (1811–77; French astronomer)

LIOUVILLE, Joseph (1809–82; French mathematician)

MACINTOSH, Charles (1766–1843; Scottish chemist)

MACMILLAN, Kirkpatrick (d. 1878; Scottish inventor)

MICHELSON, Albert Abraham (1852–1931; US physicist)

NICHOLSON, William (1753–1815; British chemist)

NIRENBERG, Marshall Warren (1927–   ; US biochemist)

PELLETIER, Pierre Joseph (1788–1842; French chemist)

PRIESTLEY, Joseph (1733–1804; British chemist)

REMINGTON, Eliphalet (1793–1863; US inventor)

SCHLEIDEN, Matthias Jakob (1804–81; German botanist)

9—continued

STEINMETZ, Charles Proteus (1865–1923; US electrical engineer)

TINBERGEN, Nikolaas (1907–94; Dutch zoologist and pioneer ethologist)

ZSIGMONDY, Richard Adolph (1865–1929; Austrian chemist)

ZUCKERMAN, Solly, Baron (1904–93; British anatomist)

10

ARCHIMEDES (c. 287–c. 212 BC; Greek mathematician and inventor)

ARROWSMITH, Aaron (1750–1823; British cartographer)

BARKHAUSEN, Heinrich (1881–1956; German physicist)

BERTHOLLET, Claude Louis, Comte (1748–1822; French chemist and physician)

BLENKINSOP, John (1783–1831; British engineer)

CANNIZZARO, Stanislao (1826–1910; Italian chemist)

CARTWRIGHT, Edmund (1743–1823; British inventor)

COPERNICUS, Nicolaus (1473–1543; Polish astronomer)

DOBZHANSKY, Theodosius (1900–75; US geneticist)

FITZGERALD, George Francis (1851–1901; Irish physicist)

FOURNEYRON, Benoît (1802–67; French engineer)

FRAUNHOFER, Joseph Von (1787–1826; German physicist)

HARGREAVES, James (d. 1778; English inventor)

HEISENBERG, Werner Karl (1901–76; German physicist)

HIPPARCHUS (c. 190–c. 120 BC; Greek astronomer)

HOFMEISTER, Wilhelm Friedrich Benedict (1824–77; German botanist)

INGENHOUSZ, Jan (1730–99; Dutch physician and plant physiologist)

KOLMOGOROV, Andrei Nikolaevich (1903–87; Soviet mathematician)

LILIENTHAL, Otto (1848–96; German aeronautical engineer)

10–continued

LIPPERSHEY, Hans (d. c. 1619; Dutch lens grinder)

MAUPERTUIS, Pierre Louis Moreau de (1698–1759; French mathematician)

MENDELEYEV, Dimitrii Ivanovich (1834–1907; Russian chemist)

METCHNIKOV, Ilya Ilich (1845–1916; Russian zoologist)

RUTHERFORD, Ernest, 1st Baron (1871–1937; English physicist)

SOMMERFELD, Arnold Johannes Wilhelm (1868–1951; German physicist)

STAUDINGER, Hermann (1881–1965; German chemist)

STEPHENSON, George (1781–1848; British engineer)

SWAMMERDAM, Jan (1637–80; Dutch naturalist and microscopist)

TORRICELLI, Evangelista (1608–47; Italian physicist)

TOURNEFORT, Joseph Pitton de (1656–1708; French botanist)

TREVITHICK, Richard (1771–1833; British engineer)

WATSON-WATT, Sir Robert Alexander (1892–1973; Scottish physicist)

WHEATSTONE, Sir Charles (1802–75; British physicist)

11

AL-KHWARIZMI, Muhammed Ibn Musa (c. 780–c. 850 AD; Arabic mathematician)

BASKERVILLE, John (1706–75; British printer)

BHOSKHARA II (1114–c. 1185; Indian mathematician)

CHAMBERLAIN, Owen (1920– ; US physicist)

GOLDSCHMIDT, Richard Benedict (1878–1958; US geneticist)

11–continued

HINSHELWOOD, Sir Cyril Norman (1897–1967; British chemist)

JOLIOT-CURIE, Irène (1896–1956; French physicist)

LE CHÂTELIER, Henri-Louis (1850–1936; French chemist)

LEEUWENHOEK, Antonie van (1632–1723; Dutch scientist)

LOBACHEVSKI, Nikolai Ivanovich (1793–1856; Russian mathematician)

MONTGOLFIER, Jacques-Étienne (1745–99; French balloonist and inventor)

NOSTRADAMUS (1503–66; French physician and astrologer)

OPPENHEIMER, J Robert (1904–67; US physicist)

SCHRÖDINGER, Erwin (1887–1961; Austrian physicist)

SHERRINGTON, Sir Charles Scott (1857–1952; British physiologist)

SPALLANZANI, Lazzaro (1729–99; Italian physiologist)

TSIOLKOVSKI, Konstantin Eduardovich (1857–1935; Russian aeronautical engineer)

VAN DER WAALS, Johannes Diderik (1837–1923; Dutch physicist)

12

AMBARTSUMIAN, Viktor Amazaspovich (1908–96 Armenian astrophysicist)

SZENT-GYÖRGYI, Albert (1893–1986; US biochemist)

13

ARAGO FRANÇOIS (1786–1853; French astronomer and physicist)

CHANDRASEKHAR, Subrahmanyan (1910–95; US astronomer)

REGIOMONTANUS (1436-76; German astronomer and mathematician)

14

GALILEO GALILEI (1564–1642; Italian mathematician, physicist, and astronomer)

15

EUDOXUS OF CNIDUS (c. 408–c. 355 BC; Greek astronomer and mathematician)

16

HERO OF ALEXANDRIA (mid-1st century AD; Greek engineer and mathematician)

17

APOLLONIUS OF PERGA (c. 261–c. 190 BC; Greek mathematician)

18

ARISTARCHUS OF SAMOS (c. 310–230 BC; Greek astronomer)

LECOQ DE BOISBAUDRAN, Paul-Émile (1838–1912; French chemist)

PAPPUS OF ALEXANDRIA (3rd century BC; Greek mathematician)

19

DIOSCORIDES PEDANIUS (c. 40–c. 90 AD; Greek physician)

KEKULÉ VON STRADONITZ, Friedrich August (1829–96; German chemist)

20+

IOPHANTUS OF ALEXANDRIA (mid-3rd century AD; Greek mathematician)

ERATOSTHENES OF CYRENE (c. 276–c. 194 BC; Greek astronomer)

GEOFFROY SAINT-HILAIRE, Étienne (1772–1844; French naturalist)

SOSIGENES OF ALEXANDRIA (1st century BC; Greek astronomer)

ECONOMISTS

4

LIST, Friedrich (1789–1846; German economist)

MARX, Karl (Heinrich; (1818–83; German philosopher, economist, and revolutionary)

WARD, Barbara, Baroness Jackson (1914–81; British economist and conservationist)

WEBB, Sidney (James;, Baron Passfield (1859–1947; British economist and socialist)

5

DEFOE, Daniel (1660–1731; British novelist, economist, and journalist)

FOGEL, Robert William (1926– ; US historian and economist)

HAYEK, Friedrich August von (1899–1992; British economist)

MEADE, James Edward (1907–95; British economist)

PASSY, Frédéric (1822–1912; French economist and politician)

PIGOU, Arthur Cecil (1877–1954; British economist)

SMITH, Adam (1723–90; Scottish moral philosopher and political economist)

TOBIN, James (1918– ; US economist)

6

ANGELL, Sir Norman (1874–1967; British author, economist, and Labour politician)

6–continued

BARUCH, Bernard (1870–1965; US economist)

COBDEN, Richard (1804–65; British politician and economist)

DELORS, Jacques (Lucien Jean; (1925– ; French politician and economist)

ERHARD, Ludwig (1897–1977; German statesman and economist)

FRISCH, Ragnar (1895–1973; Norwegian economist)

JEVONS, William Stanley (1835–1882; British economist, logician, and statistician)

KEYNES, John Maynard, 1st Baron (1883–1946; British economist)

MONNET, Jean (1888–1979; French economist)

MYRDAL, Gunnar (1898–1987; Swedish sociologist and economist)

PARETO, Vilfredo (1848–1932; Italian economist and sociologist)

TURGOT, Anne Robert Jacques, Baron de l'Aulne (1727–81; French economist)

7

BAGEHOT, Walter (1826–77; British economist, political theorist, literary critic, and journalist)

KUZNETS, Simon (1901–85; US economist)

7–continued

MALTHUS, Thomas Robert (1766–1834; British clergyman and economist)

QUESNAY, François (1694–1774; French economist)

RICARDO, David (1772–1823; British political economist)

TOYNBEE, Arnold (1852–83; British economist and philanthropist)

WOOTTON, Barbara, Baroness (1897–1988; British educationalist and economist)

8

BECCARIA, Cesare Bonesana, Marchese de (1738–94; Italian legal theorist and political economist)

FRIEDMAN, Milton (1912– ; US economist)

MANSHOLT, Sicco (1908–95; Dutch politician and economist)

PHILLIPS, A W (1914–75; British economist)

9

BEVERIDGE, William Henry Beveridge, 1st Baron (1879–1963; British economist, writer, and academic)

GALBRAITH, John Kenneth (1908– ; US economist)

TINBERGEN, Jan (1903–94; Dutch economist)

NOBEL PRIZE WINNERS

PHYSICS

1901	W RÖNTGEN (GER)
1902	H ANTOON LORENTZ (NETH)
	P ZEEMAN (NETH)
1903	A BECQUEREL (FR)
	P CURIE (FR)
	M CURIE (FR)
1904	LORD RAYLEIGH (GB)
1905	P LENARD (GER)
1906	SIR J J THOMSON (GB)
1907	A A MICHELSON (US)
1908	G LIPPMANN (FR)
1909	G MARCONI (ITALY)
	K BRAUN (GER)
1910	J VAN DER WAALS (NETH)
1911	W WIEN (GER)
1912	N G DALÉN (SWED)

1913	H KAMERLINGH ONNES (NETH)		R MÖSSBAUER (GER)
1914	M VON LAUE (GER)	1962	L D LANDAU (USSR)
1915	SIR W BRAGG (GB)	1963	J H D JENSEN (GER)
	SIR L BRAGG (GB)		M G MAYER (US)
1916	(NO AWARD)		E P WIGNER (US)
1917	C BARKLA (GB)	1964	C H TOWNES (US)
1918	M PLANCK (GER)		N G BASOV (USSR)
1919	J STARK (GER)		A M PROKHOROV (USSR)
1920	C GUILLAUME (SWITZ)	1965	J S SCHWINGER (US)
1921	A EINSTEIN (SWITZ)		R P FEYNMAN (US)
1922	N BOHR (DEN)		S TOMONAGA (JAPAN)
1923	R MILLIKAN (US)	1966	A KASTLER (FR)
1924	K SIEGBAHN (SWED)	1967	H A BETHE (US)
1925	J FRANCK (GER)	1968	L W ALVAREZ (US)
	G HERTZ (GER)	1969	M GELL-MANN (US)
1926	J PERRIN (FR)	1970	H ALVÉN (SWED)
1927	A H COMPTON (US)		L NÉEL (FR)
	C WILSON (GB)	1971	D GABOR (GB)
1928	SIR O RICHARDSON (GB)	1972	J BARDEEN (US)
1929	PRINCE L DE BROGLIE (FR)		L N COOPER (US)
1930	SIR C RAMAN (INDIA)		J R SCHRIEFFER (US)
1931	(NO AWARD)	1973	L ESAKI (JAPAN)
1932	W HEISENBERG (GER)		I GIAEVER (US)
1933	P A M DIRAC (GB)		B JOSEPHSON (GB)
	E SCHRÖDINGER (AUSTRIA)	1974	SIR M RYLE (GB)
1934	(NO AWARD)		A HEWISH (GB)
1935	SIR J CHADWICK (GB)	1975	J RAINWATER (US)
1936	V HESS (AUSTRIA)		A BOHR (DEN)
	C ANDERSON (US)		B MOTTELSON (DEN)
1937	C DAVISSON (US)	1976	B RICHTER (US)
	SIR G P THOMSON (GB)		S TING (US)
1938	E FERMI (ITALY)	1977	P W ANDERSON (US)
1939	E LAWRENCE (US)		SIR N F MOTT (GB)
1943	O STERN (US)		J H VAN VLECK (US)
1944	I RABI (US)	1978	P L KAPITSA (USSR)
1945	W PAULI (AUSTRIA)		A A PENZIAS (US)
1946	P BRIDGMAN (US)		R W WILSON (US)
1947	SIR E APPLETON (GB)	1979	S L GLASHOW (US)
1948	P BLACKETT (GB)		A SALAM (PAK)
1949	H YUKAWA (JAPAN)		S WEINBERG (US)
1950	C POWELL (GB)	1980	J CRONIN (US)
1951	SIR J COCKCROFT (GB)		V FITCH (US)
	E WALTON (IRE)	1981	K SIEGBAHN (SWED)
1952	F BLOCH (US)		N BLOEMBERGEN (US)
	E PURCELL (US)		A SCHAWLOW (US)
1953	F ZERNIKE (NETH)	1982	K G WILSON (US)
1954	M BORN (GB)	1983	S CHANDRASEKHAR (US)
	W BOTHE (GER)		W FOWLER (US)
1955	W LAMB, JR (US)	1984	C RUBBIA (ITALY)
	P KUSCH (US)		S VAN DER MEER (NETH)
1956	W SHOCKLEY (US)	1985	K VON KLITZING (GER)
	J BARDEEN (US)	1986	E RUSKA (GER)
	W BRATTAIN (US)		G BINNIG (GER)
1957	TSUNG-DAO LEE (CHINA)		H ROHRER (SWITZ)
	C N YANG (CHINA)	1987	A MÜLLER (SWITZ)
1958	P A CHERENKOV (USSR)		G BEDNORZ (GER)
	I M FRANK (USSR)	1988	L M LEDERMAN (US)
	I Y TAMM (USSR)		M SCHWARTZ (US)
1959	E SEGRÈ (US)		J STEINBERGER (GER)
	O CHAMBERLAIN (US)	1989	H DEHMELT (US)
1960	D GLASER (US)		W PAULM (GER)
1961	R HOFSTADTER (US)		N RAMSEY (US)

1990	J FRIEDMAN (US)	1936	P DEBYE (NETH)
	H KENDALL (US)	1937	SIR W HAWORTH (GB)
	R TAYLOR (CAN)		P KARRER (SWITZ)
1991	P De GENNES (FR)	1938	R KUHN (GER)
1992	G CHARPAK (FR)	1939	A BUTENANDT (GER)
1993	R HULSE (US)		L RUZICKA (SWITZ)
	J TAYLOR (US)	1943	G DE HEVESY (HUNG)
1994	B BROCKHOUE (CAN)	1944	O HAHN (GER)
	C SHULL (US)	1945	A VIRTANEN (FIN)
1995	M PERL (US)	1946	J SUMNER (US)
	F REINES (US)		J NORTHROP (US)
1996	D M LEE (US)		W STANLEY (US)
	D D OSCHEROF (US)	1947	SIR R ROBINSON (GB)
	R C RICHARDSON (US)	1948	A TISELIUS (SWED)
1997	S CHU (US)	1949	W GIAUQUE (US)
1998	R B LAUGHLIN (US)	1950	O DIELS (GER)
	H L STÖRMER (GER)		K ALDER (GER)
	D C TSUI (US)	1951	E MCMILLAN (US)
1999	G 't HOOFT (NETH)		G SEABORG (US)
	M J G VELTMAN (NETH)	1952	A MARTIN (GB)
			R SYNGE (GB)

CHEMISTRY

		1953	H STAUDINGER (GER)
		1954	L C PAULING (US)
1901	J V HOFF (NETH)	1955	V DU VIGNEAUD (US)
1902	E FISCHER (GER)	1956	N SEMYONOV (USSR)
1903	S ARRHENIUS (SWED)		SIR C HINSHELWOOD (GB)
1904	SIR W RAMSAY (GB)	1957	SIR A TODD (GB)
1905	A VON BAEYER (GER)	1958	F SANGER (GB)
1906	H MOISSAN (FR)	1959	J HEYROVSKY (CZECH)
1907	E BUCHNER (GER)	1960	W LIBBY (US)
1908	LORD RUTHERFORD (GB)	1961	M CALVIN (US)
1909	W OSTWALD (GER)	1962	J C KENDREW (GB)
1910	O WALLACH (GER)		M F PERUTZ (GB)
1911	M CURIE (FR)	1963	G NATTA (ITALY)
1912	V GRIGNARD (FR)		K ZIEGLER (GER)
	P SABATIER (FR)	1964	D M C HODGKIN (GB)
1913	A WERNER (SWITZ)	1965	R B WOODWARD (US)
1914	T RICHARDS (US)	1966	R S MULLIKEN (US)
1915	R WILLSTÄTTER (GER)	1967	M EIGEN (GER)
1916	(NO AWARD)		R G W NORRISH (GB)
1917	(NO AWARD)		G PORTER (GB)
1918	F HABER (GER)	1968	L ONSAGER (US)
1919	(NO AWARD)	1969	D H R BARTON (GB)
1920	W NERNST (GER)		O HASSEL (NOR)
1921	F SODDY (GB)	1970	L F LELOIR (ARG)
1922	F ASTON (GB)	1971	G HERZBERG (CAN)
1923	F PREGL (AUSTRIA)	1972	C B ANFINSEN (US)
1924	(NO AWARD)		S MOORE (US)
1925	R ZSIGMONDY (AUSTRIA)		W H STEIN (US)
1926	T SVEDBERG (SWED)	1973	E FISCHER (GER)
1927	H WIELAND (GER)		G WILKINSON (GB)
1928	A WINDAUS (GER)	1974	P J FLORY (US)
1929	SIR A HARDEN (GB)	1975	J W CORNFORT (AUSTR)
	H VON EULER-CHELPIN (SWED)		V PRELOG (SWITZ)
1930	H FISCHER (GER)	1976	W M LIPSCOMB (US)
1931	K BOSCH (GER)	1977	I PRIGOGINE (BELGIUM)
	F BERGIUS (GER)	1978	P MITCHELL (GB)
1932	I LANGMUIR (US)	1979	H C BROWN (US)
1933	(NO AWARD)		G WITTIG (GER)
1934	H UREY (US)	1980	P BERG (US)
1935	F JOLIOT-CURIE (FR)		W GILBERT (US)
	I JOLIOT-CURIE (FR)		F SANGER (GB)

1981	K FUKUI (JAPAN)
	R HOFFMANN (POL)
1982	A KLUG (GB)
1983	H TAUBE (US)
1984	R B MERRIFIELD (US)
1985	H HAUPTMAN (US)
	J KARLE (US)
1986	D HERSCHBACH (US)
	Y TSEH LEE (US)
	J POLANYI (CAN)
1987	D CRAM (US)
	J LEHN (FR)
	C PEDERSEN (US)
1988	J DIESENHOFER (GER)
	R HUBER (GER)
	H MICHEL (GER)
1989	S ALTMAN (US)
	T CECH (US)
1990	E CORY (US)
1991	R ERNST (SWITZ)
1992	R MARCUS (CAN)
1993	K MULLIS (US)
	M SMITH (US)
1994	G OLAH (US)
1995	P CRUTZEN (NETH)
	M MOLINA (MEX)
	F ROWLAND (US)
1996	SIR H KROTO (GB)
	R CURL (US)
	R SMALLEY (US)
1997	P D BOYER (US)
	J C SKOU (DEN)
	J E WALKER (GB)
1998	W KOHN (US)
	J A POPE (GB)
1999	A H ZEWAIL (EGYPT & US)

PHYSIOLOGY OR MEDICINE

1901	E VON BEHRING (GER)
1902	SIR R ROSS (GB)
1903	N R FINSEN (DEN)
1904	I PAVLOV (RUSS)
1905	R KOCH (GER)
1906	C GOLGI (ITALY)
	S RAMÓN Y CAJAL (SPAIN)
1907	A LAVERAN (FR)
1908	P EHRLICH (GER)
	I MECHNIKOV (RUSS)
1909	E KOCHER (SWITZ)
1910	A KOSSEL (GER)
1911	A GULLSTRAND (SWED)
1912	A CARREL (FR)
1913	C RICHET (FR)
1914	R BÁRÁNY (AUSTRIA)
1915	(NO AWARD)
1916	(NO AWARD)
1917	(NO AWARD)
1919	J BORDET (BELG)
1920	A KROGH (DEN)
1921	(NO AWARD)
1922	A V HILL (GB)

	O MEYERHOF (GER)
1923	SIR F G BANTING (CAN)
	J J R MACLEOD (GB)
1924	W EINTHOVEN (NETH)
1925	(NO AWARD)
1926	J FIBIGER (DEN)
1927	J WAGNER VON JAUREGG
	(AUSTRIA)
1928	C NICOLLE (FR)
1929	C EIJKMAN (NETH)
	SIR F HOPKINS (GB)
1930	K LANDSTEINER (US)
1931	O WARBURG (GER)
1932	E D ADRIAN (GB)
	SIR C SHERRINGTON (GB)
1933	T H MORGAN (US)
1934	G R MINOT (US)
	W P MURPHY (US)
	G H WHIPPLE (US)
1935	H SPEMANN (GER)
1936	SIR H H DALE (GB)
	O LOEWI (GER)
1937	A SZENT-GYÖRGYI (HUNG)
1938	C HEYMANS (BELG)
1939	G DOMAGK (GER)
1943	H DAM (DEN)
	E A DOISY (US)
1944	J ERLANGER (US)
	H S GASSER (US)
1945	SIR A FLEMING (GB)
	E B CHAIN (GB)
	LORD FLOREY (AUSTR)
1946	H J MULLER (US)
1947	C F CORI (US)
	G T CORI (US)
	B HOUSSAY (ARG)
1948	P MÜLLER (SWITZ)
1949	W R HESS (SWITZ)
	A E MONIZ (PORT)
1950	P S HENCH (US)
	E C KENDALL (US)
	T REICHSTEIN (SWITZ)
1951	M THEILER (S AF)
1952	S A WAKSMAN (US)
1953	F A LIPMANN (US)
	SIR H A KREBS (GB)
1954	J F ENDERS (US)
	T H WELLER (US)
	F ROBBINS (US)
1955	A H THEORELL (SWED)
1956	W FORSSMANN (GER)
	D RICHARDS (US)
	A F COURNAND (US)
1957	D BOVET (ITALY)
1958	G W BEADLE (US)
	E L TATUM (US)
	J LEDERBERG (US)
1959	S OCHOA (US)
	A KORNBERG (US)
1960	SIR F MACFARLANE BURNET
	(AUSTR)
	P B MEDAWAR (GB)

1961	G VON BÉKÉSY (US)			M BROWN (US)
1962	F H C CRICK (GB)	1986	S COHEN (US)
	J D WATSON (US)		R LEVI-MONTALCINI (ITALY)
	M WILKINS (GB)	1987	S TONEGAWA (JAPAN)
1963	SIR J C ECCLES (AUSTR)	1988	J W BLACK (GB)
	A L HODGKIN (GB)		G B ELION (US)
	A F HUXLEY (GB)		G H HITCHINGS (US)
1964	K BLOCH (US)	1989	M BISHOP (US)
	F LYNEN (GER)		H VARMUS (US)
1965	F JACOB (FR)	1990	J MURRAY (US)
	A LWOFF (FR)		E THOMAS (US)
	J MONOD (FR)	1991	E NEHER (GER)
1966	C B HUGGINS (US)		B SAKMANN (GER)
	F P ROUS (US)	1992	E FISCHER (US)
1967	H K HARTLINE (US)		E KREBS (US)
	G WALD (US)	1993	R ROBERTS (US)
	R A GRANIT (SWED)		P SHARP (US)
1968	R W HOLLEY (US)	1994	A GILMAN (US)
	H G KHORANA (US)		M RODBELL (US)
	M W NIRENBERG (US)	1995	E LEWIS (US)
1969	M DELBRÜCK (US)		C NÜESSLEIN-VOLHARD (GER)
	A D HERSHEY (US)		E WIESCHAUS (US)
	S E LURIA (US)	1996	P DOHERTY (AUSTR)
1970	J AXELROD (US)		R ZINKERNAGEL (SWITZ)
	SIR B KATZ (GB)	1997	S B PRUSINER (US)
	U VON EULER (SWED)	1998	R F FURCHGOTT (US)
1971	E W SUTHERLAND, JR (US)		L J IGNARRO (US)
1972	G M EDELMAN (US)		F MURAD (US)
	R R PORTER (GB)	1999	G BLOBEL (US)
1973	K VON FRISCH (GER)		

1973 K VON FRISCH (GER)
    K LORENZ (GER)
    N TINBERGEN (NETH)

LITERATURE

1974	A CLAUDE (US)
1901	S PRUDHOMME (FR)

1974 A CLAUDE (US)
    C DE DUVE (BELG)
    G E PALADE (BELG)

1901 S PRUDHOMME (FR)
1902 T MOMMSEN (GER)
1903 B BJØRNSON (NOR)
1904 F MISTRAL (FR)
    J ECHEGARAY Y EIZAGUIRRE
     (SPAIN)

1975 D BALTIMORE (US)
    R DULBECCO (US)
    H M TEMIN (US)
1976 B S BLUMBERG (US)
    D G GAJDUSEK (US)
1977 R S YALOW (US)
    R GUILLEMIN (US)
    A V SCHALLY (US)
1978 W ARBER (SWITZ)
    D NATHANS (US)
    H SMITH (US)
1979 A M CORMACK (US)
    G N HOUNSFIELD (GB)
1980 G SNELL (US)
    J DAUSSET (FR)
    B BENACERRAF (US)
1981 R SPERRY (US)
    D HUBEL (US)
    T WIESEL (SWED)
1982 S K BERGSTROM (SWED)
    B I SAMUELSON (SWED)
    J R VANE (GB)
1983 B MCCLINTOCK (US)
1984 N K JERNE (DEN)
    G J F KÖHLER (GER)
    C MILSTEIN (GB)
1985 J GOLDSTEIN (US)

1905 H SIENKIEWICZ (POL)
1906 G CARDUCCI (ITALY)
1907 R KIPLING (GB)
1908 R EUCKEN (GER)
1909 S LAGERLÖF (SWED)
1910 P VON HEYSE (GER)
1911 M MAETERLINCK (BELG)
1912 G HAUPTMANN (GER)
1913 SIR R TAGORE (INDIA)
1914 (NO AWARD)
1915 R ROLLAND (FR)
1916 V VON HEIDENSTAM (SWED)
1917 K GJELLERUP (DEN)
    H PONTOPPIDAN (DEN)
1919 C SPITTELER (SWITZ)
1920 K HAMSUN (NOR)
1921 A FRANCE (FR)
1922 J BENAVENTE Y MARTINEZ
    (SPAIN)
1923 W B YEATS (IRE)
1924 W S REYMONT (POL)
1925 G B SHAW (IRE)
1926 G DELEDDA (ITALY)
1927 H BERGSON (FR)

1928	S UNDSET (NOR)	1986	W SOYINKA (NIGERIA)
1929	T MANN (GER)	1987	J BRODSKY (US)
1930	S LEWIS (US)	1988	N MAHFOUZ (EGYPT)
1931	E A KARLFELDT (SWED)	1989	C J CELA (SPAIN)
1932	J GALSWORTHY (GB)	1990	O PAZ (MEX)
1933	I BUNIN (USSR)	1991	N GORDIMER (S AF)
1934	L PIRANDELLO (ITALY)	1992	D WALCOTT (ST LUCIA)
1935	(NO AWARD)	1993	T MORRISON (US)
1936	E O'NEILL (US)	1994	KENSABURO OË (JAPAN)
1937	R M DU GARD (FR)	1995	S HEANEY (IRE)
1938	P BUCK (US)	1996	W SZYMBORSKA (POL)
1939	F E SILLANPÄÄ (FIN)	1997	D FO (ITALY)
1940	(NO AWARD)	1998	J SARAMAGO (PORT)
1941	(NO AWARD)	1999	G GRASS (GER)
1942	(NO AWARD)		
1943	(NO AWARD)	**PEACE**	
1944	J V JENSEN (DEN)		
1945	G MISTRAL (CHILE)	1901	J H DUNANT (SWITZ)
1946	H HESSE (SWITZ)		F PASSY (FR)
1947	A GIDE (FR)	1902	E DUCOMMUN (SWITZ)
1948	T S ELIOT (GB)		C A GOBAT (SWITZ)
1949	W FAULKNER (US)	1903	SIR W CREMER (GB)
1950	B RUSSELL (GB)	1904	INSTITUTE OF INTERNATIONAL
1951	P F LAGERKVIST (SWED)		LAW (FOUNDED, 1873)
1952	F MAURIAC (FR)	1905	BARONESS VON SUTTNER
1953	SIR WINSTON CHURCHILL (GB)		(AUSTRIA)
1954	E HEMINGWAY (US)	1906	T ROOSEVELT (US)
1955	H K LAXNESS (ICE)	1907	E TEODORO MONETA (ITALY)
1956	J R JIMÉNEZ (SPAIN)		L RENAULT (FR)
1957	A CAMUS (FR)	1908	K P ARNOLDSON (SWED)
1958	B L PASTERNAK (DECLINED	1909	BARON D'ESTOURNELLES DE
	AWARD) (USSR)		CONSTANT (FR)
1959	S QUASIMODO (ITALY)		A BEERNAERT (BELG)
1960	S J PERSE (FR)	1910	INTERNATIONAL PEACE BUREAU
1961	I ANDRIĆ (YUGOS)		(FOUNDED, 1891)
1962	J STEINBECK (US)	1911	T ASSER (NETH)
1963	G SEFERIS (GR)		A FRIED (AUSTRIA)
1964	J-P SARTRE (DECLINED AWARD)	1912	E ROOT (US)
	(FR)	1913	H LAFONTAINE (BELG)
1965	M SHOLOKHOV (USSR)	1914	(NO AWARD)
1966	S Y AGNON (ISR)	1915	(NO AWARD)
	N SACHS (SWED)	1916	(NO AWARD)
1967	M A ASTURIAS (GUAT)	1917	INTERNATIONAL RED CROSS
1968	K YASUNARI (JAPAN)		COMMITTEE (FOUNDED, 1863)
1969	S BECKETT (IRE)	1918	(NO AWARD)
1970	A I SOLZHENITSYN (USSR)	1919	W WILSON (US)
1971	P NERUDA (CHILE)	1920	L BOURGEOIS (FR)
1972	H BÖLL (GER)	1921	K BRANTING (SWED)
1973	P WHITE (AUSTR)		C L LANGE (NOR)
1974	E JOHNSON (SWED)	1922	F NANSEN (NOR)
	H MARTINSON (SWED)	1923	(NO AWARD)
1975	E MONTALE (ITALY)	1924	(NO AWARD)
1976	S BELLOW (US)	1925	SIR A CHAMBERLAIN (GB)
1977	S ALEIXANDRE (SPAIN)		C G DAWES (US)
1978	I B SINGER (US)	1926	A BRIAND (FR)
1979	O ELYTIS (GREECE)		G STRESEMANN (GER)
1980	C MILOSZ (US)	1927	F BUISSON (FR)
1981	E CANETTI (BULG)		L QUIDDE (GER)
1982	G GARCIA MARQUEZ (COLOMBIA)	1928	(NO AWARD)
1983	W GOLDING (GB)	1929	F B KELLOGG (US)
1984	J SEIFERT (CZECH)	1930	N SÖDERBLOM (SWED)
1985	C SIMON (FR)	1931	J ADDAMS (US)

N M BUTLER (US)

1932	(NO AWARD)
1933	SIR N ANGELL (GB)
1934	A HENDERSON (GB)
1935	C VON OSSIETZKY (GER)
1936	C S LAMAS (ARG)
1937	VISCOUNT CECIL OF CHELWOOD (GB)
1938	NANSEN INTERNATIONAL OFFICE FOR REFUGEES (FOUNDED, 1931)
1939	(NO AWARD)
1940	(NO AWARD)
1941	(NO AWARD)
1942	(NO AWARD)
1943	(NO AWARD)
1944	INTERNATIONAL RED CROSS COMMITTEE (FOUNDED, 1863)
1945	C HULL (US)
1946	E G BALCH (US)
	J R MOTT (US)
1947	AMERICAN FRIENDS' SERVICE COMMITTEE (US)
	FRIENDS' SERVICE COUNCIL (LONDON)
1948	(NO AWARD)
1949	LORD BOYD-ORR (GB)
1950	R BUNCHE (US)
1951	L JOUHAUX (FR)
1952	A SCHWEITZER (FR)
1953	G C MARSHALL (US)
1954	OFFICE OF THE UNITED NATIONS HIGH COMMISSIONER FOR REFUGEES (FOUNDED, 1951)
1955	(NO AWARD)
1956	(NO AWARD)
1957	L B PEARSON (CAN)
1958	D G PIRE (BELG)
1959	P J NOEL-BAKER (GB)
1960	A J LUTHULI (S AF)
1961	D HAMMARSKJÖLD (SWED)
1962	L C PAULING (US)
1963	INTERNATIONAL RED CROSS COMMITTEE (FOUNDED, 1863)
	LEAGUE OF RED CROSS SOCIETIES (GENEVA)
1964	M LUTHER KING, JR (US)
1965	UNITED NATIONS CHILDREN'S FUND (FOUNDED, 1946)
1966	(NO AWARD)
1967	(NO AWARD)
1968	R CASSIN (FR)
1969	INTERNATIONAL LABOUR ORGANISATION (FOUNDED, 1919)
1970	N E BORLAUG (US)
1971	W BRANDT (GER)
1972	(NO AWARD)
1973	H KISSINGER (US)
	LE DUC THO (DECLINED AWARD) (N VIET)
1974	S MACBRIDE (IRE)

	E SATO (JAPAN)
1975	A S SAKHAROV (USSR)
1976	MRS B WILLIAMS (N IRE)
	MISS M CORRIGAN (N IRE)
1977	AMNESTY INTERNATIONAL (FOUNDED IN UK, 1961)
1978	A SADAT (EGYPT)
	M BEGIN (ISR)
1979	MOTHER TERESA (YUGOS)
1980	A P ESQUIVEL (ARG)
1981	OFFICE OF THE U N HIGH COMMISSION FOR REFUGEES (FOUNDED, 1951)
1982	A GARCIA ROBLES (MEX)
	MRS A MYRDAL (SWED)
1983	L WALESA (POL)
1984	BISHOP D TUTU (S AF)
1985	INTERNATIONAL PHYSICIANS FOR THE PREVENTION OF NUCLEAR WAR (FOUNDED, 1980)
1986	E WIESEL (US)
1987	OSCAR ARIAS SÁNCHEZ (COSTA RICA)
1988	THE UNITED NATIONS PEACE-KEEPING FORCES
1989	DALAI LAMA (TIBET)
1990	M GORBACHOV (RUSS)
1991	A SAN SUU KYI (BURMESE)
1992	R MENCHU
1993	F W DE KLERK (S AF)
	N MANDELA (S AF)
1994	Y ARAFAT (PALESTINE)
	S PERES (ISR)
	Y RABIN (ISR)
1995	J ROTBLAT (GB)
1996	J RAMOS-HORTA (E TIMOR)
	C BELO (E TIMOR)
1997	THE INTERNATIONAL CAMPAIGN TO BAN LANDMINES
1998	J HUME (N IRE)
	D TRIMBLE (N IRE)
1999	MÉDICINS SANS FRONTIÈRES

ECONOMICS

1969	R FRISCH (NOR)
	J TINBERGEN (NETH)
1970	P A SAMUELSON (US)
1971	S KUZNETS (US)
1972	R HICKS (GB)
	K J ARROW (US)
1973	W LEONTIEF (US)
1974	G MYRDAL (SWED)
	F A VON HAYEK (GB)
1975	L KANTOROVICH (USSR)
	T C KOOPMANS (US)
1976	M FRIEDMAN (US)
1977	B OHLIN (SWED)
	J E MEADE (GB)
1978	H A SIMON (US)
1979	T W SCHULTZ (US)
	A LEWIS (GB)

1980	L R KLEIN (US)	1992	G S BECKER (US)
1981	J TOBIN (US)	1993	R FOGEL (US)
1982	G J STIGLER (US)		D NORTH (US)
1983	G DEBREU (US)	1994	J HARSANYI (US)
1984	R STONE (GB)		J NASH (US)
1985	F MODIGLIANI (US)		R SELTON (GER)
1986	J M BUCHANAN, JR (US)	1995	R LUCAS (US)
1987	R M SOLOW (US)	1996	J MIRRLEES (GB)
1988	M ALLAIS (FR)		W VICKREY (CAN)
1989	T HAAVELMO (NOR)	1997	R C MERTON (US)
1990	H MARKOWITZ (US)		M S SCHOLES (US)
	W F SHARPE (US)	1998	A SEN (INDIA)
	M MILLER (US)	1999	R A MUNDELL (CAN)
1991	R H COASE (GB)		

EXPLORERS, PIONEERS, AND ADVENTURERS

4

BYRD, Richard E (1888–1957; US explorer)

CANO, Juan Sebastián del (*c.* 1460–1526; Spanish navigator)

COOK, Captain James (1728–79; British navigator)

DIAS, Bartolomeu (*c.* 1450–*c.* 1500; Portuguese navigator)

EYRE, Edward John (1815–1901; British explorer)

GAMA, Vasco da (*c.* 1469–1524; Portuguese navigator)

HUME, Hamilton (1797–1873; Australian explorer)

HUNT, John, Baron (1910– ; British mountaineer)

KIDD, William (*c.* 1645–1701; Scottish sailor)

PARK, Mungo (1771–*c.* 1806; Scottish explorer)

POLO, Marco (*c.* 1254–1324; Venetian traveller)

ROSS, Sir James Clark (1800–62; British explorer)

SOTO, Hernando de (?1496–1542; Spanish explorer)

5

BAKER, Sir Samuel White (1821–93; British explorer)

BARTH, Heinrich (1821–65; German explorer and geographer)

BOONE, Daniel (1734–1820; American pioneer)

BRUCE, James (1730–94; British explorer)

5—continued

BURKE, Robert O'Hara (1820–61; Irish explorer)

CABOT, John (Giovanni Caboto, *c.* 1450–*c.* 1499; Italian explorer)

DAVIS, John (*or* J Davys *c.* 1550–1605; English navigator)

FUCHS, Sir Vivian (1908–99; British explorer)

LAIRD, Macgregor (1808–61; Scottish explorer)

OATES, Lawrence Edward Grace (1880–1912; British explorer)

OÑATE, Juan de (d. 1630; Spanish conquistador)

PARRY, Sir William Edward (1790–1855; British navigator)

PEARY, Robert Edwin (1856–1920; US explorer)

SCOTT, Robert Falcon (1868–1912; British explorer)

SMITH, Dick (1944– ; Australian adventurer)

SPEKE, John Hanning (1827–64; British explorer)

STURT, Charles (1795–1869; British explorer)

TEACH, Edward (d. 1718; British pirate)

6

ALCOCK, Sir John (1892–1919; British aviator)

BAFFIN, William (*c.* 1584–1622; English navigator)

BALBOA, Vasco Núñez de (*c.* 1475–1517; Spanish explorer)

6—continued

BERING, Vitus Jonassen (1681–1741; Danish navigator)

BRAZZA, Pierre Paul François Camille Savorgnan de (1852–1905; French explorer)

BROOKE, Sir James (1803–68; British explorer)

BURTON, Sir Richard (1821–90; British explorer)

CABRAL, Pedro Álvares (?1467–1520; Portuguese navigator)

CARSON, Kit (Christopher C, 1809–68; US frontiersman)

CORTÉS, Hernán (1485–1547; Spanish conquistador)

HUDSON, Henry (d. 1611; English navigator)

MORGAN, Sir Henry (*c.* 1635–88; Welsh buccaneer)

NANSEN, Fridtjof (1861–1930; Norwegian explorer)

NOBILE, Umberto (1885–1978; Italian aviator)

STUART, John McDouall (1815–66; Scottish explorer)

TASMAN, Abel Janszoon (*c.* 1603–*c.* 1659; Dutch navigator)

7

BARENTS, Willem (*c.* 1550–97; Dutch navigator)

BLÉRIOT, Louis (1872–1936; French aviator)

BRANSON, Richard (1950– ; British entrepreneur and adventurer)

7–continued

CARPINI, Giovanni da Pian del (*c.* 1180–*c.* 1252; Italian traveller)

CARTIER, Jacques (1491–1557; French navigator)

CÓRDOBA, Francisco Fernández de (d. 1518; Spanish explorer)

COVILHÃ, Pêro da (*c.* 1460–*c.* 1526; Portuguese explorer)

DAMPIER, William (*c.* 1652–1715; English explorer)

EARHART, Amelia (1898–1937; US aviator)

FIENNES, Sir Ranulph (1944– ; British explorer)

FRÉMONT, John C (1813–90; US explorer)

GILBERT, Sir Humphrey (*c.* 1539–83; English navigator)

HAWKINS, Sir John (1532–95; English navigator)

HILLARY, Sir Edmund (1919– ; New Zealand mountaineer and explorer)

HINKLER, Herbert John Lewis (1892–1933; Australian aviator)

LA SALLE, Robert Cavelier, Sieur de (1643–87; French explorer)

MCCLURE, Sir Robert John Le Mesurier (1807–73; Irish explorer)

PIZARRO, Francisco (*c.* 1475–1541; Spanish conquistador)

PYTHEAS (4th century BC; Greek navigator)

RALEIGH, Sir Walter (1554–1618; British explorer)

SELKIRK, Alexander (1676–1721; Scottish sailor)

STANLEY, Sir Henry Morton (1841–1904; British explorer)

WILKINS, Sir George Hubert (1888–1958; British explorer)

7–continued

WRANGEL, Ferdinand Petrovich, Baron von (1794–1870; Russian explorer)

8

AMUNDSEN, Roald (1872–1928; Norwegian explorer)

COLUMBUS, Christopher (1451–1506; Italian navigator)

COUSTEAU, Jacques Yves (1910–97; French underwater explorer)

FLINDERS, Matthew (1774–1814; British navigator and hydrographer)

FRANKLIN, Sir John (1786–1847; British explorer)

MAGELLAN, Ferdinand (*c.* 1480–1521; Portuguese explorer)

MARCHAND, Jean Baptiste (1863–1934; French explorer)

VESPUCCI, Amerigo (1454–1512; Italian navigator)

9

BLANCHARD, Jean Pierre François (1753–1809; French balloonist)

CHAMPLAIN, Samuel de (1567–1635; French explorer)

FROBISHER, Sir Martin (*c.* 1535–94; English navigator)

HEYERDAHL, Thor (1914– ; Norwegian ethnologist)

IBERVILLE, Pierre Le Moyne, Sieur d' (1661–1706; French-Canadian explorer)

LEICHARDT, Ludwig (1813–48; German explorer)

LINDBERGH, Charles A (1902–74; US aviator)

MARQUETTE, Jacques (1637–75; French explorer)

PAUSANIAS (2nd century AD; Greek traveller)

RASMUSSEN, Knud Johan Victor (1879–1933; Danish explorer)

9–continued

VANCOUVER, George (*c.* 1758–98; British navigator)

VELÁSQUEZ, Diego (?1465–1522; Spanish explorer)

10

BARBAROSSA (Khayr ad-Din, d. 1546; Turkish pirate)

ERIC THE RED (late 10th century; Norwegian explorer)

SHACKLETON, Sir Ernest Henry (1874–1922; British explorer)

11

IBN BATTUTAH (1304–?1368; Arab traveller)

LA CONDAMINE, Charles Marie de (1701–74; French geographer)

LIVINGSTONE, David (1813–73; Scottish missionary and explorer)

PONCE DE LEON, Juan (1460–1521; Spanish explorer)

12

BOUGAINVILLE, Louis Antoine de (1729–1811; French navigator)

LEIF ERIKSSON (11th century; Icelandic explorer)

NORDENSKJÖLD, Nils Adolf Erik, Baron (1832–1901; Swedish navigator)

14

BELLINGSHAUSEN, Fabian Gottlieb, Baron von (1778–1852; Russian explorer)

DUMONT D'URVILLE, Jules Sébastien César (1790–1842; French navigator)

17

HENRY THE NAVIGATOR (1394–1460; Portuguese navigator and patron of explorers)

SPORTSMEN

3

ALI, Muhammad (Cassius Marcellus Clay, 1942– ; US boxer)

COE, Sebastian (1956– ; British middle-distance runner)

LEE, Bruce (1940–73; US kungfu expert)

4

ASHE, Arthur (1943–93; US tennis player)

BORG, Bjorn (1956– ; Swedish tennis player)

CLAY, Cassius. *See* Ali, Muhammad

CRAM, Steve (1960– ; British middle-distance runner)

DUKE, Geoffrey E (1923– ; British racing motorcyclist)

GRAF, Steffi (1969– ; German tennis player)

HILL, Damon (1960– ; British motor-racing driver)

HILL, Graham (1929–75; British motor-racing driver)

HOAD, Lewis Alan (1934–94; Australian tennis player)

HUNT, James (1947–93; British motor-racing driver)

JOHN, Barry (1945– ; Welsh Rugby Union footballer)

KHAN, Imran (1952– ; Pakistani cricketer)

KING, Billie Jean (*born* Moffitt, 1943– ; US tennis player)

LARA, Brian (1969– ; West Indian cricketer)

LOMU, Jonah (1975– ; New Zealand Rugby Union footballer)

MILO (late 6th century BC; Greek wrestler)

MOSS, Stirling (1929– ; British motor-racing driver)

OWEN, Michael (1979– ; British Association footballer)

PELÉ (1940– ; Brazilian Association footballer)

WADE, Virginia (1945– ; British tennis player)

5

BLAKE, Peter (1948– ; New Zealand yachtsman)

BLYTH, Chay (1940– ; British yachtsman)

5–continued

BRUNO, Frank (1961– ; British heavyweight boxer)

BUDGE, Don (1916–2000; US tennis player)

BUENO, Maria (1939– ; Brazilian tennis player)

BUSBY, Matt (1909–94; British Association footballer)

CLARK, Jim (1937–68; British motor-racing driver)

COURT, Margaret (*born* Smith, 1942– ; Australian tennis player)

CURRY, John Anthony (1949–94; British ice skater)

EVERT, Christine (1954– ; US tennis player)

FALDO, Nick (1957– ; British golfer)

GRACE, William Gilbert (1848–1915; British cricketer)

GREIG, Tony (1946– ; Rhodesian-born cricketer)

HAGEN, Walter Charles (1892–1969; US professional golfer)

HOBBS, Jack (1882–1963; British cricketer)

HOGAN, Ben (1912– ; US professional golfer)

HOYLE, Edmond (1672–1769; British authority on card games)

JEEPS, Dickie (1931– ; British Rugby Union footballer)

JONES, Bobby (1902–71; US amateur golfer)

LAUDA, Niki (1949– ; Austrian motor-racing driver)

LAVER, Rod (1938– ; Australian tennis player)

LEWIS, Carl (1961– ; US athlete)

LEWIS, Lennox (1965– ; British boxer)

LLOYD, Clive (1944– ; West Indian cricketer)

LOUIS, Joe (1914–81; US boxer)

MEADE, Richard (1938– ; British three-day-event horse rider)

MEADS, Colin Earl (1935– ; New Zealand Rugby Union footballer)

5–continued

MOORE, Bobby (1941–93; British Association footballer)

NURMI, Paavo Johannes (1897–1973; Finnish middle-distance and long-distance runner)

OVETT, Steve (1955– ; British middle-distance runner)

OWENS, Jesse (1913–80; US sprinter, long jumper, and hurdler)

PERRY, Fred (1909–95; British tennis and table-tennis player)

SELES, Monica (1973– ; US tennis player)

SMITH, Harvey (1938– ; British showjumper and equestrian)

SPITZ, Mark Andrew (1950– ; US swimmer)

TYSON, Mike (1966– ; US boxer)

VIREN, Lasse Artturi (1949– ; Finnish middle-distance and long-distance runner)

WOODS, Tiger (1975– ; US golfer)

6

AGASSI, Andre (1970– ; US tennis player)

BORDER, Allan (1955– ; Australian cricketer)

BOTHAM, Ian (1955– ; British cricketer)

BROOME, David (1940– ; British showjumper)

BROUGH, Louise (1923– ; US tennis player)

CAWLING, Evonne (*born* Goolagong, 1951– ; Australian tennis player)

CRUYFF, Johann (1947– ; Dutch Association footballer)

D'INZEO, Colonel Piero (1923– ; Italian show jumper and equestrian)

EDBERG, Stefan (1966– ; Swedish tennis player)

FANGIO, Juan Manuel (1911–95; Argentinian motor-racing driver)

HADLEE, Sir Richard (1951– ; New Zealand cricketer)

6–continued

HENDRY, Stephen (1969– ; British snooker player)

HENMAN, Tim (1974– ; British tennis player)

HINGIS, Martina (1980– ; Swiss tennis player)

HUTTON, Len (1916–90; British cricketer)

KARPOV, Anatoly (1951– ; Russian chess player)

KEEGAN, Kevin (1951– ; British footballer)

LASKER, Emanuel (1868–1941; German chess player)

MORPHY, Paul Charles (1837–84; US chess player)

PALMER, Arnold (1929– ; US golfer)

RAMSEY, Alf (1922–99; British Association footballer)

RHODES, Wilfred (1877–1973; British cricketer)

SHEENE, Barry (1950– ; British racing motorcyclist)

SMYTHE, Pat (1928– ; British showjumper and equestrian)

SOBERS, Gary (1936– ; West Indian cricketer)

TUNNEY, Gene (1897–1978; US boxer)

7

BRABHAM, Jack (1926– ; Australian motor-racing driver)

BRADMAN, Donald George (1908– ; Australian cricketer)

CANTONA, Eric (1966– ; French footballer)

CARNERA, Primo (1906–67; Italian boxer)

COMPTON, Denis (1918–97; British cricketer)

CONNORS, Jimmy (1952– ; US tennis player)

COWDREY, Colin (1932– ; British cricketer)

DEMPSEY, Jack (1895–1983; US boxer)

FISCHER, Bobby (1943– ; US chess player)

FRAZIER, Joe (1944– ; US boxer)

GUNNELL, Sally (1966– ; British athlete)

HAMMOND, Wally (1903–65; British cricketer)

JOHNSON, Michael (1967– ; US sprinter)

7–continued

LENGLEN, Suzanne (1899–1938; French tennis player)

LINEKER, Gary (1960– ; British footballer)

MCBRIDE, Willie John (1939– ; Irish Rugby Union footballer)

MCENROE, John (1959– ; US tennis player)

MANSELL, Nigel (1953– ; British motor-racing driver)

SAMPRAS, Pete (1971– ; US tennis player)

SPASSKY, Boris (1937– ; Russian chess player)

STEWART, Jackie (1939– ; British motor-racing driver)

SURTEES, John (1934– ; British racing motorcyclist and motor-racing driver)

TREVINO, Lee (1939– ; US golfer)

TRUEMAN, Fred (1931– ; British cricketer)

WHYMPER, Edward (1840–1911; British mountaineer)

WINKLER, Hans Günter (1926– ; German showjumper)

ZÁTOPEK, Emil (1922– ; Czech long-distance runner)

8

AGOSTINI, Giacomo (1944– ; Italian racing motorcyclist)

ALEKHINE, Alexander (1892–1946; French chess player)

ATHERTON, Michael (1968– ; British cricketer)

CAMPBELL, Sir Malcolm (1885–1949; British land- and water-speed racing driver)

CHARLTON, Bobby (1937– ; British Association footballer)

CHRISTIE, Linford (1960– ; British sprinter)

COMANECI, Nadia (1961– ; Romanian gymnast)

HAILWOOD, Mike (1940–81; British racing motorcyclist)

HAKKINEN, Mika (1968– ; Finnish motor-racing driver)

HAWTHORN, Mike (1929–58; British motor-racing driver)

JOSELITO (1895–1920; Spanish matador)

KAPIL DEV, (1959– ; Indian cricketer)

8–continued

KORCHNOI, Victor (1931– ; Soviet-born chess player)

LINDWALL, Raymond Russell (1921–96; Australian cricketer)

MATTHEWS, Stanley (1915–2000; British Association footballer)

NEWCOMBE, John (1944– ; Australian tennis player)

NICKLAUS, Jack William (1940– ; US golfer)

RICHARDS, Sir Gordon (1904–86; British jockey)

RICHARDS, Viv (1952– ; West Indian cricketer)

ROBINSON, Sugar Ray (1920–89; US boxer)

ROSEWALL, Ken (1934– ; Australian tennis player)

RUSEDSKI, Greg (1973– ; Canadian-born British tennis player)

SULLIVAN, John Lawrence (1858–1918; US boxer)

THOMPSON, Daley (1958– ; British decathlete)

WILLIAMS, J P R (1949– ; Welsh Rugby Union footballer)

WILLIAMS, SERENA (1981– ; US tennis player)

WILLIAMS, VENUS (1980– ; US tennis player)

9

BANNISTER, Roger (1929– ; British middle-distance runner)

BONINGTON, Chris (1934– ; British mountaineer)

BOTVINNIK, Mikhail Moiseivich (1911–95; Russian chess player)

COULTHARD, David (1971– ; British motor-racing driver)

DAVENPORT, Lindsay (1976– ; US tennis player)

D'OLIVIERA, Basil Lewis (1931– ; South African-born cricketer)

GASCOIGNE, Paul (1967– ; British footballer)

GOOLAGONG, Evonne. See Cawley, Evonne

LLEWELLYN, Harry (1911– ; British showjumper and equestrian)

PETROSIAN, Tigran Vartanovich (1929–84; Soviet chess player)

9–continued
SCHMELING, Max (1905– ;
German boxer)
SUTCLIFFE, Herbert
(1894–1978; British cricketer)
SZEWINSKA, Irena (1946– ;
Polish athlete)

10
CARPENTIER, Georges
(1894–1975; French boxer)
CULBERTSON, Ely
(1891–1955; US bridge
authority)
IMRAN KHAN (1952– ;
Pakistani cricketer)
JUANTORENA, Alberto
(1951– ; Cuban middle-
distance runner)

10–continued
SCHUMACHER, Michael
(1969– ; German motor-
racing driver)
WILLS MOODY, Helen
(1905–98; US tennis player)

11
BALLESTEROS, Severiano
(1957– ; Spanish golfer)
CONSTANTINE, Learie
Nicholas, Baron (1902–71;
West Indian cricketer)
FITZSIMMONS, Bob
(1862–1917; New Zealand
boxer)
NAVRATILOVA, Martina
(1956– ; Czech-born US
tennis player)

11–continued
WEISSMULLER, Johnny
(1904–84; US swimmer)

12
KNOX-JOHNSTON, Sir Robin
(1939– ; British yachtsman)

19
CAPABLANCA Y GRAUPERA,
José Raúl (1888–1942;
Cuban chess player)
RANJITSINHJI VIBHAJI,
Kumar Shri, Maharajah Jam
Sahib of Nawanagar
(1872–1933; Indian cricketer)

MURDERERS

MURDERER	YEAR	DETAILS
ALLEN, Peter and WELBY, John	1964	Murdered John West. Last two men to be hanged in Britain.
BENTLEY, Derek and CRAIG, ChristoperMiles.	1952	Both men were convicted of the murder of PC Miles Bentley was hanged, although he did not fire a shot, on the grounds that he had incited his younger partner to murder. Craig, who was too young for the death sentence, was im-prisoned until 1963. This case caused considerable public disquiet and was used in the abolition-of-hanging debate.

BORDEN, Lizzie	1892	Accused of the murder of her father and stepmother in Fall River, Massachusetts, but was acquitted. Public opinion was that she was guilty.
		     Lizzie Borden took an axe
		     And gave her mother forty whacks.
		     When she saw what she had done,
		     She gave her father forty-one.

BRADY, Ian and HINDLEY, Myra	1966	Sentenced to life imprisonment for the brutal murder of five children. They were known as the Moors murders as at least three children were killed and buried on the Lan-cashire moors; some of the bodies were never recovered.
BURKE, William and HARE, William	1827–28	Burke was sentenced to death for the murder of Mary Patterson, James Wilson, and Margaret Docherty; Hare was granted immunity from prosecution by offering to turn King's Evidence. Burke and Hare, with the help of their partners, lured victims to their lodging house, murdered them and sold their bodies to an Edinburgh anatomist, Dr Knox. They are known to have murdered 16 people over a period of nine months, although the exact total is unknown.
BUSH, Edwin	1961	Hanged for the murder of Mrs Elsie Batten. He was identified from an indentikit portrait – the first use of the system in Britain.

MURDERERS

CHRISTIE, John	1943–53	Hanged for the murder of his wife, Ethel Christie, whose body was found under the floorboards of 10 Rillington Place, London. The bodies of five other women were found behind the kitchen wall and buried in the garden.
CORDER, William	1827	Sentenced to death for the murder of Maria Marten. Although her family had been led to believe that she was happily married and living on the Isle of Wight, her mother had a dream that she had been murdered and buried in the Red Barn on Corder's father's farm. Her body was found there.
COTTON, Mary Ann	1872	Hanged for the murder of her stepson Charles Cotton. She was estimated to have killed 14 victims who were diagnosed as having died of gastric fever. She was arrested following the discovery of arsenic in the body of her stepson and the bodies of her husband, baby, and two stepchildren were exhumed. They were also found to have died of arsenical poisoning.
CRIPPEN, Dr Hawley Harvey	1910	US doctor who poisoned his actress wife Cora (called Belle Elmore) in London. He attempted to escape to America with his mistress Ethel LeNeve on the *SS Montrose*, but was arrested on board following one of the first uses of ship-to-shore radio.
ELLIS, Ruth	1955	Convicted of the murder of her boyfried David Blakely. Last woman to be hanged in Britain.
HAIGH, John	1949	Hanged for the murder of Olivia Durand-Deacon. Haigh thought he could not be tried for murder as he had destroyed the body in an acid bath. However, the discovery of gallstones, bone fragments, and false teeth meanth that the remains could be identified.
HALLIWELL, Kenneth	1967	Murdered his lover, the British dramatist Joe Orton (1933–67).
HANRATTY, James	1961	Hanged for the murder of Michael Gregsten, after a trial lasting 21 days. Controversy surrounded the verdict. Much of the evidence was based on the identification of Hanratty by Valerie Storie (Gregsten's lover, who was present at the murder). Hanratty's alibi that he had been in Rhyl when the murder was committed was disbelieved. The uncertainty relating to the verdict added fuel to the campaign against hanging.
JACK THE RIPPER	1888	Brutally murdered at least five prostitutes in the Whitechapel area. There has been great controversy about the identity of the murderer.
KENT, Constance	1860	Sentenced to death, commuted to life imprisonment, for the murder of her half-brother, Francis. In 1885 she was released and went to Australia, where she trained as a nurse under the name of Ruth Kaye. She successfully rebuilt her life and died in 1944, at the age of 100.
NEILSON, Donald	1974–75	Sentenced to life imprisonment for the murder of four men. He was know as 'The Black Panther'.
NILSEN, Denis	1979–83	Convicted of the murder of six men after the discovery of human remains in a manhole at the side of the flats where he lived. He boasted of killing over 15 men in total.

PEACE, Charles	1876	Hanged for the murder of Arthur Dyson. Peace was a burglar who carried the 'tools of his trade' in a violin case. His activities were spread over a 25 year period, during which he became notorious.
ROBINSON, John	1927	Suffocated Minnie Alice Bonati. He dismembered her body and hid it in a trunk which he handed to the left-luggage office at Charing Cross station.
SMITH, George (*alias* Oliver Love, George Rose, Henry Williams, Oliver James, John Lloyd)	1912	Hanged for the murder of Bessie Mundy. The story became known as 'The Brides in the Bath' when it was revealed that Smith bigamously married his victims and, in three instances, killed them in their baths. In each inquest a verdict of accidental drowning was brought in, and Smith claimed the possessions or life insurance of his 'wife'.
STRATTON, Alfred and Albert	1905	Convicted of the murders of Mr and Mrs Farrow. The case made legal history because the jury was convinced of the guilt of the two brothers after a fingerprint found at the scene of the crime was found to match that of Alfred Stratton.
SUTCLIFFE, Peter	1975–80	Sentenced to life imprisonment following the murder of 13 women. Known as the 'Yorkshire Ripper', Sutcliffe claimed he had a mission from God to kill prostitutes (although several of his victims were not prostitutes).
TURPIN, Dick	1735	Hanged at York for the murder of Thomas Morris. Notorious for highway robberies, a reward of £200 was placed on his head.
WEST, Frederick and Rosemary	?1970–94	Frederick West committed suicide before his trial for the murder of 12 young women. Rosemary West was sentenced to life imprisonment for the murder of 10 young women.

THE ARTS

ART TERMS

2
OP

3
FEC
INC
OIL
POP

4
BODY
BUST
CAST
DADA
HERM
KORE
SIZE
SWAG
TERM
WASH

5
BRUSH
BURIN
CHALK
EASEL
FECIT
GESSO
GLAZE
MODEL
NAIVE
PIETÀ
PUTTO
SALON
SCULP
SECCO
SEPIA
STYLE
TONDO

6
ASHCAN
BISTRE
CANVAS
CUBISM
FRESCO
GOTHIC
GROUND
KIT-CAT

6—continued
KITSCH
KOUROS
LIMNER
MAESTÀ
MEDIUM
MOBILE
MOSAIC
PASTEL
PATINA
PENCIL
PURISM
RELIEF
ROCOCO
SCHOOL
SKETCH
STUCCO
STYLUS
TUSCAN
VEDUTA
VERISM

7
ACADEMY
ARCHAIC
ATELIER
BAROQUE
BAUHAUS
BITUMEN
BODEGÓN
CABINET
CAMAÏEU
CARTOON
COLLAGE
COSMATI
DIPTYCH
DRAWING
ECORCHÉ
ETCHING
GOUACHE
IMPASTO
INCIDIT
LINOCUT
LOST WAX
MODELLO
MONTAGE
PALETTE

7—continued
PIGMENT
POCHADE
REALISM
SCUMBLE
SFUMATO
SINOPIA
TEMPERA
VANITAS
VARNISH
WOODCUT

8
ABSTRACT
AIR-BRUSH
ALLEGORY
ANCIENTS
AQUATINT
ARMATURE
ARRICCIO
BARBIZON
BOZZETTO
CARYATID
CHARCOAL
DRÔLERIE
DRYPOINT
EMULSION
FIXATIVE
FROTTAGE
FUTURISM
GRAFFITI
HATCHING
INTAGLIO
INTONACO
MANDORLA
MAQUETTE
PASTICHE
PLEURANT
POUNCING
PREDELLA
REPOUSSÉ
SCULPSIT
STAFFAGE
TACHISME
TESSERAE
TRECENTO
TRIPTYCH

8—continued
VENETIAN

9
ALLA PRIMA
ANTI-CERNE
AQUARELLE
AUTOGRAPH
BRUSHWORK
BYZANTINE
CAPRICCIO
COLOURIST
DISTEMPER
ENGRAVING
GRISAILLE
GROTESQUE
INTIMISME
LANDSCAPE
MAHLSTICK
MAULSTICK
MEZZOTINT
MINIATURE
POLYPTYCH
PRIMITIVE
SCULPTURE
STILL LIFE
STIPPLING
SYMBOLISM
TENEBRISM
VORTICISM

10
ARRICCIATO
ART NOUVEAU
ASSEMBLAGE
AUTOMATISM
AVANTGARDE
BIOMORPHIC
CARICATURE
CIRE-PERDUE
CRAQUELURE
FLORENTINE
METALPOINT
MONOCHROME
MORBIDEZZA
NATURALISM
PENTIMENTO
PROVENANCE

10—continued
QUADRATURA
REPOUSSOIR
ROMANESQUE
SURREALISM
SYNTHETISM
TURPENTINE
XYLOGRAPHY

11
BAMBOCCANTI
BIEDERMEIER
CAROLINGIAN
CHIAROSCURO

11—continued
CONTÉ CRAYON
DIVISIONISM
ECLECTICISM
ILLUSIONISM
IMPRIMATURA
LITHOGRAPHY
MASTERPIECE
PERSPECTIVE
PICTURESQUE
POINTILLISM
PORTRAITURE
RENAISSANCE

11—continued
RETROUSSAGE
STYLIZATION
SUPREMATISM
TROMPE L'OEIL
WATERCOLOUR

12
ACRYLIC PAINT
ANAMORPHOSIS
CLOISONNISME
CONTRAPPOSTO
COUNTERPROOF
ILLUMINATION

12—continued
PRECISIONISM
QUATTROCENTO
SUPERREALISM

13
ARCHITECTONIC
EXPRESSIONISM
FÊTE CHAMPÊTRE
IMPRESSIONISM
PAPIERS COLLÉS

14
CONSTRUCTIVISM

ARCHITECTURAL TERMS

3
BAY
CAP
DIE
EYE
KEY

4
AMBO
ANTA
APSE
ARCH
BAND
BEAD
BELL
BOSS
DADO
DAIS
DOME
FRET
FROG
FUST
NAVE
PELE
STOA

5
AISLE
AMBRY
ARRIS
ATTIC
CONGÉ
CROWN
CRYPT
DORIC
FOILS
GABLE
GLYPH
HELIX
INLAY

5—continued
IONIC
LOBBY
NEWEL
ROMAN
SCAPE
SHAFT
SHANK
TALON
TENIA
TUDOR
VERGE

6
ABACUS
ACCESS
ALCOVE
ARCADE
ATRIUM
ATTICK
AUMBRY
BELFRY
BONNET
BROACH
CANOPY
CHEVET
COLUMN
CORONA
CRENEL
CUPOLA
DAGGER
DENTIL
DIAPER
FAÇADE
FILLET
FINIAL
FLÈCHE
FRESCO
FRIEZE
GABLET

6—continued
GAZEBO
GOTHIC
GUTTAE
HEROIC
LESENE
LINTEL
LINTOL
LOGGIA
LOUVRE
MANTEL
MERLON
METOPE
MUTULE
NORMAN
OCULUS
PAGODA
PATERA
PLINTH
PULPIT
QUADRA
REGULA
ROCOCO
SCAPUS
SCROLL
SEDILE
SOFFIT
TROPHY
URELLA
VESTRY
VOLUTE
WREATH
XYSTUS
ZIG-ZAG

7
ANNULET
ARCH RIB
ASTYLAR
BALCONY

7—continued
BAROQUE
BASTION
BOULTIN
BUTMENT
CAPITAL
CAVETTO
CHANCEL
CHEVRON
CORNICE
CROCHET
CROCKET
DISTYLE
ECHINUS
ENCARPA
ENTASIS
EUSTYLE
FESTOON
FLEURON
FLUTING
GADROON
GALILEE
GALLERY
LACUNAR
LANTERN
LATTICE
LEQUEAR
LUNETTE
NARTHEX
NULLING
OBELISK
ORATORY
PARVISE
PORTAIL
PORTICO
POSTERN
PTEROMA
REEDING
REGENCY

7–continued
REREDOS
ROSETTE
ROTUNDA
ROUNDEL
SCALLOP
SPANISH
SYSTYLE
TESSARA
TONDINO
TRACERY
TRUMEAU

8
ABUTMENT
ACANTHUS
AEDICULA
APOPHYGE
ASTRAGAL
ATLANTES
BALUSTER
BARTIZAN
BASILICA
BEAK HEAD
CARYATID
CIMBORIO
CINCTURE
CRENELLE
CRESTING
CYMATIUM
DIASTYLE
DIPTERAL
DOG-TOOTH
EDGE ROLL
EXTRADOS
FORMERET
GARGOYLE
INTRADOS
KEEL ARCH
KEYSTONE

8–continued
LICH GATE
LYCH GATE
MISERERE
PAVILION
PEDESTAL
PEDIMENT
PILASTER
PREDELLA
PULPITUM
ROCAILLE
SPANDREL
SPANDRIL
TORCHING
TRANSEPT
TRIGLYPH
TYMPANUM
VERANDAH
VIGNETTE
WAINSCOT

9
ACROPOLIS
ANTEFIXAE
ANTHEMION
APEX STONE
ARABESQUE
ARCH BRICK
ARCHIVOLT
ATTIC BASE
BIRD'S BEAK
BYZANTINE
CAMPANILE
CANEPHORA
CARTOUCHÈ
CAULICOLI
CLOISTERS
COLONNADE
COMPOSITE
DRIPSTONE

9–continued
FOLIATION
GROTESQUE
HEXASTYLE
HYPOCAUST
HYPOSTYLE
INGLE NOOK
LABEL STOP
LACUNARIA
LINENFOLD
MEZZANINE
MOULDINGS
OCTASTYLE
PALLADIAN
REFECTORY
SGRAFFITO
STRAPWORK
STYLOBATE
TRABEATED
TRIFORIUM
TRILITHON
VESTIBULE
ZOOPHORUS

10
ACROTERION
AMBULATORY
ARAEOSTYLE
ARCHITRAVE
BALDACHINO
BALL FLOWER
BALUSTRADE
BATTLEMENT
CINQUEFOIL
COLONNETTE
CORINTHIAN
EGG AND DART
ENRICHMENT
HAGIOSCOPE
LADY CHAPEL

10–continued
LANCET ARCH
MISERICORD
MODILLIONS
PIETRA DURA
PRESBYTERY
PYCNOSTYLE
QUATREFOIL
ROMANESQUE
ROOD SCREEN
ROSE WINDOW
SEXPARTITE
TETRASTYLE
TRACHELION

11
CASTELLATED
ENTABLATURE
FAN VAULTING
HARELIP ARCH
LEADED LIGHT
MANTELPIECE
MANTELSHELF
ORIEL WINDOW
RENAISSANCE
RETICULATED

12
AMPHITHEATRE
BLIND TRACERY
COCKLE STAIRS
EGG AND TONGUE
LANCET WINDOW
PORTE-COCHÈRE

13
AMPHI-PROSTYLE

14
ANGULAR CAPITAL
FLYING BUTTRESS
HYPOTRACHELION

ANTIQUE-TRADE TERMS

3
WAF

4
COST
KITE
LUMP
RING

5
AGGRO
FOLKY
FRESH
LYLE'S

5–continued
MOODY
REPRO
RIGHT
ROUGH
RUN UP
TOUCH
TRADE
VICKY

6
LOOKER
MADE-UP

6–continued
PERIOD
PUNTER
RUNNER
SMALLS
TOTTER

7
BREAKER
CALL-OUT
CUT DOWN
KNOCKER
MILLER'S

8
AS BOUGHT
BENT GEAR
BOUGHT IN
CHAIRMAN
DOWN TO ME
ESTIMATE
FOLLOWER
MARRIAGE
SCLENTER

9
CLEARANCE

9–continued
INNER RING
SIX AND TWO

10
COMMERCIAL
FOUR AND TWO

10–continued
OFF THE WALL
OLD FRIENDS

11
EIGHT AND TWO
HAMMER PRICE

11–continued
OUT OF THE AIR
SIGHT UNSEEN

12+
COLLECTOR'S ITEM
KNOCKING DOWN

FURNITURE

3
COT

4
CRIB
DESK
SOFA

5
BENCH
BERTH
CHEST
COUCH
DIVAN
FUTON
STALL
STOOL
Z-BED

6
BUREAU
CRADLE
DAY BED
LOWBOY
SETTEE
SETTLE

7
BUNK BED
CABINET
CAMP BED
CASSONE
COMMODE
DRESSER
HAMMOCK
HIGHBOY
LECTERN
SHELVES
SOFA BED
TALLBOY
TWIN BED
WHATNOT

8
ARMCHAIR
BAR STOOL
BOOKCASE
BOX CHAIR
END TABLE
LOVE SEAT
RECLINER
TEA TABLE
WARDROBE
WATER BED

9
BOOKSHELF
CAMP CHAIR
CANE CHAIR
CARD TABLE
CLUB CHAIR
DAVENPORT
DECK CHAIR
DOUBLE BED
EASY CHAIR
EMPIRE BED
HIGH CHAIR
HOPE CHEST
PIER TABLE
SIDEBOARD
SIDE CHAIR
SIDE TABLE
SINGLE BED
WING CHAIR
WORK TABLE

10
BUCKET SEAT
CANTERBURY
CHOIR STALL
ESCRITOIRE
FEATHER BED
SECRETAIRE
TRUCKLE BED

11
BARREL CHAIR
CANOPIED BED
CARVER CHAIR
COFFEE TABLE
COLONIAL BED
DINING CHAIR
DINING TABLE
FOLDAWAY BED
GAMING TABLE
KING-SIZE BED
LOUNGE CHAIR
MORRIS CHAIR
PANELLED BED
READING DESK
ROLL-TOP DESK
SHAKER CHAIR
STUDIO COUCH
SWIVEL CHAIR
WOODEN CHAIR
WRITING DESK

12
BEDSIDE TABLE
BOSTON ROCKER
BOTTOM DRAWER
CHAISE LONGUE
CHESTERFIELD
CHINA CABINET
CONSOLE TABLE
FOLDING CHAIR
GATE-LEG TABLE
GRECIAN COUCH
KITCHEN TABLE
KNEE-HOLE DESK
LEATHER CHAIR
LIBRARY TABLE
MILKING STOOL
NURSING CHAIR
QUEEN-SIZE BED
ROCKING CHAIR

12–continued
SLANT-TOP DESK
SLOPE-TOP DESK
WELSH DRESSER
WINDSOR CHAIR
WRITING TABLE

13
BENTWOOD CHAIR
CAPTAIN'S CHAIR
DOUBLE DRESSER
DRESSING TABLE
DRINKS CABINET
DROP-LEAF TABLE
FOUR-POSTER BED
LIQUOR CABINET
MIRROR CABINET
PEDESTAL TABLE
PEMBROKE TABLE
SHERATON CHAIR
STRAIGHT CHAIR

14
CHEST OF
  DRAWERS
CORNER
  CUPBOARD
PANEL-BACK CHAIR
QUEEN-ANNE CHAIR
RECLINING CHAIR
WHEEL-BACK CHAIR

15+
COCKTAIL CABINET
CONVERTIBLE SOFA
LADDER-BACK
  CHAIR
UPHOLSTERED
  CHAIR

143

FURNITURE TERMS

3
EAR

4
BAIL
BULB
HUSK
OGEE
SWAG

5
APRON
BEVEL
BOMBÉ
CLEAT
DOWEL
FRETS
GESSO
INLAY
LOPER
OVOLO
SHELL
SKIRT
SPLAT
SQUAB
STILE

6
DIAPER
FIGURE
FILLET
FINIAL
FLY-LEG
FRIEZE
LINING
MUNTIN
ORMOLU
PATERA
PATINA
PLINTH

6–continued
REBATE
RUNNER
SCROLL
VENEER
VOLUTE

7
AMORINI
BANDING
BEADING
BLISTER
BUN FOOT
CARCASE
CASTORS
CHAMFER
CORNICE
EN SUITE
FLUTING
GALLERY
HIPPING
LOZENGE
LUNETTE
PAD FOOT
PAW FOOT
REEDING
ROUNDEL
SALTIRE
TAMBOUR
TURNING

8
ACANTHUS
ARCADING
ASTRAGAL
BALUSTER
BOW FRONT
CABOCHON
DOVETAIL

8–continued
HOOP BACK
LION MASK
MOULDING
PEDIMENT
PIE CRUST
PILASTER
RAM'S HEAD
SABRE LEG
SUNBURST
SWAN-NECK
TERMINAL
WAINSCOT

9
ANTHEMION
ARABESQUE
BLIND FRET
CAMEO BACK
CARTOUCHE
DROP FRONT
FALL FRONT
GUILLOCHE
LINENFOLD
MARQUETRY
MEDALLION
PARQUETRY
RULE JOINT
SHOE-PIECE
SPADE FOOT
SPOON BACK
STRAPWORK
STRETCHER
STRIATION
STRINGING

10
BOULLE WORK
BREAK-FRONT

10–continued
EGG-AND-DART
ESCUTCHEON
GADROONING
KEY PATTERN
LADDER BACK
MITRE JOINT
MONOPODIUM
QUARTERING
SERPENTINE
SHIELD-BACK
UNDER-BRACE

11
BALL-AND-CLAW
BALLOON BACK
BRACKET FOOT
CABRIOLE LEG
CHIP-CARVING
COCKBEADING
COUNTERSINK
CUP-AND-COVER
LATTICEWORK
SPIRAL TWIST

12
CRESTING RAIL
DISHED CORNER
FIELDED PANEL
OYSTER VENEER

13+
BARLEY-SUGAR
 TWIST
BOBBIN TURNING
BROKEN PEDIMENT
CHANNEL MOULDING
COLUMN TURNING
MORTISE-AND-
 TENON

POTTERY AND PORCELAIN

3&4
AULT
BOW
MING
TANG

5
DELFT
DERBY
IMARI
SPODE

6
BISQUE
BRETBY
CANTON
MINTON
PARIAN
RUSKIN
SEVRES

7
BELLEEK

7–continued
BISCUIT
BRISTOL
CHELSEA
DOULTON
FAIENCE
ITALIAN
MEISSEN
MOULDED
NEW HALL

7–continued
REDWARE
SATSUMA
TOBY JUG

8
CANEWARE
CAUGHLEY
CHAFFERS
COALPORT
FAIRINGS

8–continued
MAIOLICA
MAJOLICA
NANTGARW
PLYMOUTH
SALOPIAN
SLIPWARE
WEDGWOOD

9
AGATE WARE
CHINA CLAY
CRACKLING
CREAMWARE
DAVENPORT

9–continued
HARD PASTE
LINTHORPE
LIVERPOOL
LOWESTOFT
MOORCROFT
PEARLWARE
PRATTWARE
SOFT PASTE
STONEWARE
STONEWARE
WORCESTER

10
CANTON WARE

10–continued
CHINA STONE
LUSTREWARE
MARTINWARE
PILKINGTON
POLYCHROME
ROCKINGHAM
SALT-GLAZED
STONE CHINA
TERRACOTTA

11
BLACK BASALT
CAPODIMONTE
EARTHENWARE

11–continued
FAMILLE ROSE
FAMILLE VERT
LONGTON HALL
PATE-SUR-PATE

12+
ASIATIC PHEASANT
BLUE AND WHITE
CAMBRIAN POTTERY
MASON'S
  IRONSTONE CHINA
NAGASAKI WARE
STAFFORDSHIRE
WILLOW PATTERN

LITERARY TERMS

3
ODE
WIT

4
EPIC
FOOT
IAMB
MYTH

5
ELEGY
FABLE
GENRE
ICTUS
IRONY
LYRIC
METRE
NOVEL
OCTET
PROSE
RHYME
STYLE
THEME
VERSE

6
BALLAD
BATHOS
CESURA
CLICHÉ
DACTYL
HUBRIS
LAMENT
MONODY
OCTAVE
PARODY
PATHOS
SATIRE
SCHOOL
SEPTET
SESTET

6–continued
SIMILE
SONNET
STANZA
STRESS
SYMBOL

7
CAESURA
CONCEIT
COUPLET
DICTION
ELISION
EPIGRAM
EPISTLE
EPITAPH
EUPHONY
FABLIAU
HUMOURS
IMAGERY
NEMESIS
PARADOX
PROSODY
PYRRHIC
REALISM
SPONDEE
SUBPLOT
TRAGEDY
TROCHEE

8
ALLEGORY
ANAPAEST
AUGUSTAN
DIDACTIC
ELEMENTS
EXEMPLUM
EYE RHYME
METAPHOR
OXYMORON
PASTORAL
QUATRAIN

8–continued
RHETORIC
SCANSION
SYLLABLE
TRIMETER

9
AMBIGUITY
ASSONANCE
BURLESQUE
CATHARSIS
CLASSICAL
EUPHEMISM
FREE VERSE
HALF RHYME
HEXAMETER
HYPERBOLE
MONOMETER
OCTAMETER
PARARHYME

10
BLANK VERSE
CARICATURE
DENOUEMENT
EPIC SIMILE
HEPTAMETER
MOCK HEROIC
NATURALISM
PENTAMETER
PICARESQUE
SPOONERISM
SUBJECTIVE
TETRAMETER

11
ANACHRONISM
COURTLY LOVE
END STOPPING
ENJAMBEMENT
GOTHIC NOVEL
HORATIAN ODE

11–continued
MALAPROPISM
NOBLE SAVAGE
OBJECTIVITY
TRAGICOMEDY

12
ALLITERATION
ONOMATOPOEIA

13
ANTHROPOMORPH
HEROIC COUPLET
INTERNAL RHYME

14
EXISTENTIALISM
FEMININE ENDING
MILTONIC SONNET
ROMANTIC POETRY
SENTIMENTALITY

15
MASCULINE ENDING
PATHETIC FALLACY
PERSONIFICATION

16
PETRARCHAN
  SONNET

18
METAPHYSICAL
  POETRY
NEGATIVE
  CAPABILITY
OMNISCIENT
  NARRATOR

20+
STREAM OF
  CONSCIOUSNESS

MUSICAL TERMS

TERM – definition

1 & 2
F – loud
FF - very loud
MF – half loud
P – soft
PP – very soft
SF – strongly accented

3
BIS – repeat
DIM – becoming softer
PED – abbr. for pedal
PIÙ – more
PIZ – plucked
RFZ – accentuated
RIT – slowing down, holding back
SFZ – strongly accented
TEN – held
VIF – lively (Fr.)

4
CODA – final part of a movement
MOTO – motion
RALL – slowing down
SINO – up to; until
TIEF – deep; low (Ger.)

5
AD LIB – at will
ASSAI – very
BUFFO – comic
DOLCE – sweet
FORTE – loud
LARGO – very slow
LENTO – slowly
MESTO – sad, mournful
MEZZO – half
MOLTO – very much
MOSSO – moving, fast
PIANO – soft
QUASI – almost, as if
SEGNO – sign
SENZA – without
SOAVE – sweet; gentle
STARK – strong, loud (Ger.)
TACET – instrument is silent
TANTO – so much
TEMPO – the speed of a composition
TUTTI – all
ZOPPA – in syncopated rhythm

6
ADAGIO – slow
AL FINE – to the end

6–continued
CHIUSO – stopped (of a note); closed
DA CAPO – from the beginning
DEHORS – outside; prominent
DIVISI – divided
DOPPIO – double
FACILE – easy, fluent
LEGATO – bound, tied (of notes), smoothly
MARCIA – march
NIENTE – nothing
NOBILE – noble
RETENU – held back
SEMPRE – always, still
SUBITO – immediately
TENUTO – held

7
AGITATO – agitated; rapid tempo
ALLEGRO – lively, brisk
AL SEGNO – as far as the sign
AMOROSO – loving, emotional
ANIMATO – spirited
ATTACCA – attack; continue without a pause
CALANDO – ebbing; lessening of tempo
CODETTA – small coda; to conclude a passage
CON BRIO – with vigour
DOLENTE – sorrowful
ESTINTO – extremely softly, almost without tone
GIOCOSO – merry; playful
MARCATO – accented
MORBIDO – soft, delicate
PESANTE – heavily, firmly
SCHNELL – fast (Ger.)
SFOGATO – effortless; in a free manner
SORDINO – mute
STRETTO – accelerating or intensifying; overlapping of entries of fugue

8
A BATTUTA – return to strict time
A PIACERE – as you please
BRILLANT – brilliant
COL CANTO – accompaniment to follow solo line
COL LEGNO – to strike strings with stick of the bow
CON FUOCO – fiery; vigorous
DAL SEGNO – from the sign
IN MODO DI – in the manner of

8–continued
MAESTOSO – majestic
MODERATO – moderately
PORTANDO – carrying one note into the next
RITENUTO – slowing down, holding back
SOURDINE – mute (Fr.)
STACCATO – detached
VIVEMENT – lively (Fr.)

9
ADAGIETTO – quite slow
CANTABILE – in a singing fashion
CANTILENA – lyrical, flowing
CRESCENDO – becoming louder
FIORITURA – decoration of a melody
GLISSANDO – sliding scale played on instrument
MENO MOSSO – slower pace
MEZZA VOCE – at half power
OBBLIGATO – not to be omitted
PIUTTOSTO – somewhat
PIZZICATO – plucked
SCHNELLER – faster (Ger.)
SFORZANDO – strongly accented
SIN'AL FINE – up to the end
SLENTANDO – slowing down
SOSTENUTO – sustained
SOTTO VOCE – quiet subdued tone

10
AFFETTUOSO – tender
ALLA CACCIA – in hunting style
ALLARGANDO – broadening; more dignified
ALLEGRETTO – quite lively, brisk
DIMINUENDO – becoming softer
FORTISSIMO – very loud
MEZZOFORTE – half loud
NOBILMENTE – nobly
PERDENDOSI – dying away gradually
PIANISSIMO – very soft
PORTAMENTO – carrying one note into the next
RAVVIVANDO – quickening
RITARDANDO – slowing down, holding back

10–continued
SCHERZANDO – joking;
 playing
SCHLEPPEND – dragging;
 deviating from correct speed
 (Ger.)
SCORREVOLE – gliding; fluent
STRINGENDO – tightening;
 intensification

11
ACCELERANDO – accelerating
AFFRETTANDO – hurrying
MINACCIANDO – menacing
RALLENTANDO – slowing
 down
RINFORZANDO – accentuated

12
ALLA CAPPELLA – in church
 style
LEGGERAMENTE – lightly
13
LEGGIERAMENTE – lightly

TONIC SOL-FA

DOH   RAY   ME   FAH   SOH   LAH   TE

MUSICAL INSTRUMENTS

2
UD (lute)
YÜ (scraper)

3
BIN (vina)
KIT (fiddle)
LUR (horn)
OUD (ud)
SAZ (lute)
SHŌ (mouth
 organ)
TAR (drum; lute)
UTI (lute)

4
BATA (drum)
BIWA (lute)
CH'IN (zither)
DRUM
FIFE
FUYE (flute)
GONG
HARP
HORN
KENA (quena)
KHEN (mouth
 organ)
KOTO (zither)
LIRA (fiddle)
LUTE
LYRA (lyre)
LYRE
MU YÜ (drum)
MVET (zither)

4–continued
OBOE
OUTI (lute)
P'I P'A (lute)
PIPE
ROTE (lyre)
RUAN (lute)
SONA (shawm)
TRO-U (fiddle)
URUA (clarinet)
VINA (stringed
 instrument
 related to sitar)
VIOL
WHIP
 (percussion)
ZOBO (mirliton)

5
AULOI (shawm)
BANJO
BELLS
BHAYA
 (kettledrum)
BUGLE
BUMPA (clarinet)
CELLO
CHANG
 (dulcimer)
CHIME
CLAVE
COBZA (lute)
CORNU
 (trumpet)
CRWTH (lyre)

5–continued
DAULI (drum)
DHOLA (drum)
DOBRO (guitar)
ERH-HU (fiddle)
FIDEL (fiddle)
FIDLA (zither)
FLUTE
GAITA (bagpipe)
GAJDY (bagpipe)
GUSLE (fiddle)
HURUK (drum)
KAKKO (drum)
KANUN (qanun)
KAZOO (mirliton)
KERAR (lyre)
KO-KIU (fiddle)
MBILA
 (xylophone)
NGOMA (drum)
NGURU (flute)
OKEDO (drum)
ORGAN
PIANO
PI NAI (shawm)
PU-ILU
 (clappers)
QANUN (zither)
QUENA (flute)
RASPA (scraper)
REBAB (fiddle)
REBEC (fiddle)
SARON
 (metallophone)

5–continued
SHAWM
SHENG (mouth
 organ)
SITAR (lute)
TABLA (drum)
TABOR (drum)
TAIKO (drum)
TIBIA (shawm)
TIPLE (shawm)
TI-TZU (flute)
TUDUM (drum)
TUMYR (drum)
TUPAN (drum)
VIOLA
YUN LO (gong)
ZURLA (shawm)
ZURNA (shawm)

6
ALBOKA
 (hornpipe)
ARGHUL
 (clarinet)
BAGANA (lyre)
BINIOU
 (bagpipe)
CARNYX
 (trumpet)
CHAKAY (zither)
CHA PEI (lute)
CORNET
CURTAL (double
 reed)
DARBUK (drum)

6–continued
FANDUR (fiddle)
FIDDLE
FUJARA (flute)
GEKKIN (lute)
GENDER
 (metallophone)
GONGUE
 (percussion)
GUITAR
HU CH'IN (fiddle)
HUMMEL (zither)
KENONG (gong)
KISSAR (lyre)
KOBORO (drum)
LIRICA (fiddle)
LIRONE (fiddle)
LITUUS
 (trumpet)
LONTAR
 (clappers)
MAYURI (lute)
MOROPI (drum)
NAKERS (drums)
NAQARA
 (drums)
NTENGA (drum)
O-DAIKO (drum)
OMBGWE (flute)
P'AI PAN
 (clappers)
POMMER
 (shawm)

147

6—continued

RACKET (double reed)
RAMKIE (lute)
RATTLE
SANTIR (dulcimer)
SHAING (horn)
SHAKER
SHANAI (shawm)
SHIELD (percussion)
SHOFAR (horn)
SOPILE (shawm)
SPINET
SPOONS (clappers)
SRALAY (shawm)
SURNAJ (shawm)
SWITCH (percussion)
SYRINX (panpipe)
TAM-TAM (gong)
TOM-TOM (drum)
TXISTU (flute)
VALIHA (zither)
VIELLE (fiddle)
VIOLIN
YANGUM (dulcimer)
ZITHER

7

ADENKUM (stamping tube)
ALPHORN (trumpet)
ANKLUNG (rattle)
ATUMPAN (kettledrum)
BAGPIPE
BARYTON (viol)
BASSOON
BODHRAN (drum)
BONNANG (gong)
BOW HARP
BOX LYRE
BUCCINA (trumpet)
BUISINE (trumpet)
BUMBASS
CELESTE
CHANGKO (drum)
CITTERN
CORNETT
COWBELL
CROTALS (percussion)
CYMBALS
DA-DAIKO (drum)
DIPLICE (clarinet)
DUGDUGI (drum)
ENZENSE (zither)
FITHELE (fiddle)
GADULKA (fiddle)
GITTERN
GLING-BU (flute)
HULA IPU (percussion)

7—continued

INGUNGU (drum)
ISIGUBU (drum)
KACHAPI (zither)
KALUNGU (talking drum)
KAMANJE (fiddle)
KANTELE (zither)
KEMANAK (clappers)
KITHARA (lyre)
KOMUNGO (zither)
MACHETE (lute)
MANDOLA (lute)
MARACAS (percussion)
MASENQO (fiddle)
MIGYAUN (zither)
MOKUGYO (drum)
MURUMBU (drum)
MUSETTE (bagpipe)
MUSETTE (shawm)
OBUKANO (lyre)
OCARINA (flute)
OCTAVIN (wind)
ORPHICA (piano)
PANDORA (cittern)
PANPIPE
PIANINO
PIBCORN (hornpipe)
PICCOLO
PIFFARO (shawm)
QUINTON (viol)
RESHOTO (drum)
RINCHIK (cymbals)
SACKBUT (trombone)
SALPINX (trumpet)
SAMISEN (lute)
SANTOOR (dulcimer)
SARANGI (fiddle)
SARINDA (fiddle)
SAW-THAI (fiddle)
SAXHORN
SAXTUBA
SERPENT
SHIWAYA (flute)
SISTRUM (rattle)
SORDINE (kit)
SORDONE (double reed)
SPAGANE (clappers)
TAM ÂM LA (gong)
TAMBURA (lute)
TERBANG (drum)
THEORBO (lute)
TIKTIRI (clarinet)
TIMPANI
TRUMPET
TSUZUMI (drum)
UJUSINI (flute)
UKULELE
VIHUELA (guitar)
VIOLONE (viol)

7—continued

WHISTLE
YUN NGAO (gong)
ZUMMARA (clarinet)

8

ALGHAITA (shawm)
ALTOHORN
AUTOHARP
BANDOURA (lute)
BASS DRUM
BASS HORN
BOMBARDE (shawm)
BOUZOUKI (lute)
BOWL LYRE
BUZZ DISK
CALLIOPE (mechanical organ)
CARILLON
CHIME BAR
CIMBALOM (dulcimer)
CIPACTLI (flute)
CLAPPERS
CLARINET
CLAVICOR (brass family)
CLAW BELL
COURTAUT (double reed)
CRECELLE (cog rattle)
CRUMHORN (double reed)
DULCIMER
DVOYNICE (flute)
GONG DRUM
HANDBELL
HAND HORN
HAWKBELL
JEW'S HARP
KAYAKEUM (zither)
KHUMBGWE (flute)
LANGLEIK (zither)
LANGSPIL (zither)
LAP ORGAN (melodeon)
MANDOLIN (lute)
MELODEON
MELODICA
MIRLITON (kazoo)
MRIDANGA (drum)
OLIPHANT (horn)
O-TSUZUMI (drum)
OTTAVINO (virginal)
P'AI HSIAO (panpipe)
PENORCON (cittern)
POCHETTE (kit)
PSALTERY (zither)
PUTORINO (trumpet)
RECORDER
RKAN-DUNG (trumpet)

8—continued

RKAN-LING (horn)
RONÉAT-EK (xylophone)
SAN HSIEN (lute)
SIDE DRUM
SLIT DRUM
SONAJERO (rattle)
SRINGARA (fiddle)
SURBAHAR (lute)
TALAMBAS (drum)
TARABUKA (drum)
TAROGATO (clarinet; shawm)
TIMBALES (drum)
TRIANGLE
TRO-KHMER (fiddle)
TROMBONE
VIOLETTA (viol)
VIRGINAL
YANGCHIN (dulcimer)
YUEH CH'IN (lute)
ZAMPOGNA (bagpipe)

9

ACCORDION
ANGLE HARP
ARPANETTA (zither)
BALALAIKA (lute)
BANDURRIA (lute)
BANJOLELE
BASSONORE (bassoon)
BOMBARDON (tuba)
CASTANETS
CHALUMEAU (clarinet)
COG RATTLE
COMPONIUM (mechanical organ)
CORNEMUSE (bagpipe)
CORNOPEAN (brass family)
CROOK HORN
DAIBYOSHI (drum)
DARABUKKE (drum)
DJUNADJAN (zither)
DUDELSACK (bagpipes)
DVOJACHKA (flute)
EUPHONIUM (brass family)
FLAGEOLET (flute)
FLEXATONE (percussion)
GONG AGENG
HACKBRETT (dulcimer)
HARMONICA
HARMONIUM

9—continued

HYDRAULIS (organ)
KELONTONG (drum)
KÖNIGHORN (brass
family)
LAUNEDDAS (clarinet)
MANDOBASS (lute)
MANDOLONE (lute)
MORIN-CHUR (fiddle)
ORPHARION (cittern)
PICCO PIPE (flute)
PIEN CH'ING
(lithophone)
ROMMELPOT (drum)
SAXOPHONE
TALLHARPA (lyre)
TOTOMBITO (zither)
TUBA-DUPRÉ
WOOD BLOCK
WURLITZER
XYLOPHONE
XYLORIMBA
(xylophone)

10

BANANA DRUM
BARREL DRUM
BASSANELLO (double
reed)
BASSET HORN
BIBLE REGAL (organ)
BICITRABIN (vina)
BIRD SCARER
BONGO DRUMS
BULL-ROARER
CHENGCHENG
(cymbals)
CHITARRONE (lute)
CLAVICHORD
CLAVIORGAN
COLASCIONE (lute)
CONTRABASS
(double bass)
COR ANGLAIS
DIDGERIDOO
(trumpet)
DOUBLE BASS
FLUGELHORN

10—continued

FRENCH HORN
GEIGENWERK
(mechanical
harpsichord)
GONG CHIMES
GRAND PIANO
HANDLE DRUM
HURDY GURDY
KETTLEDRUM
LITHOPHONE
(percussion)
MANDOCELLO (lute)
MELLOPHONE (horn)
MOSHUPIANE (drum)
MOUTH ORGAN
OPHICLEIDE (brass
family)
RANASRINGA (horn)
SAXOTROMBA
SHAKUHACHI (flute)
SOUSAPHONE
SPITZHARFE (zither)
SYMPHONIUM
(mouth organ)
TAMBOURINE (drum)
TEPONAZTLI (drum)
THUMB PIANO (jew's
harp)
TIN WHISTLE
TLAPIZTALI (flute)
TSURI DAIKO (drum)

11

AEOLIAN HARP
ANGEL CHIMES
BARREL ORGAN
BELL CITTERN
BIVALVE BELL
BLADDER PIPE
BOARD ZITHER
CLAPPER BELL
FIPPLE FLUTE
GAMBANG KAYA
(xylophone)
GUITAR-BANJO
HAND TRUMPET
HARPSICHORD

11—continued

HECKELPHONE
(oboe)
NYCKELHARPA
PAIMENSARVI (horn)
PANHUÉHUETL
(drum)
SARON DEMONG
(metallophone)
SLEIGH BELLS
SPIKE FIDDLE
THEORBO-LUTE
UCHIWA DAIKO
(drum)
VIOLA D'AMORE
(viol)
VIOLONCELLO

12

DIPLO-KITHARA
(zither)
GANSA GAMBANG
(metallophone)
GANSA JONGKOK
(metallophone)
GLOCKENSPIEL
(metallophone)
GUITAR-VIOLIN
HI-HAT CYMBALS
KANTELEHARPE
(lyre)
MANDOLINETTO
(ukulele)
PEACOCK SITAR
(lute)
RAUSCHPFEIFE
(double reed)
SARRUSOPHONE
(brass)
SHOULDER HARP
STOCK-AND-HORN
(hornpipe)
TIPPOO'S TIGER
(organ)
TUBULAR BELLS
VIOLA DA GAMBA
(viol)
WHISTLE FLUTE

13

COCKTAIL DRUMS
CONTRABASSOON
DOUBLE BASSOON
(contrabassoon)
HARDANGERFELE
(fiddle)
HECKELCLARINA
(clarinet)
SAVERNAKE HORN
SCHRILLPFEIFE
(flute)
SLIDE TROMBONE
VIOLA BASTARDA
(viol)

14

CLARINET D'AMORE
CLAVICYTHERIUM
(harpsichord)
CYTHARA ANGLICA
(harp)
JINGLING JOHNNY
TLAPANHUÉHUETL
(drum)
TRICCABALLACCA
(clappers)

15

CLASSICAL GUITAR
MOOG
SYNTHESIZER
TURKISH CRESCENT
(jingling johnny)

16

CHINESE WOOD
BLOCK
CHITARRA
BATTENTE (guitar)
CYLINDRICAL
DRUMS
DEUTSCHE
SCHALMEI (double
reed)
STRUMENTO DI
PORCO (zither)

THEATRICAL TERMS

2

OP
SM

3

ACT
ARC
ASM

3—continued

GEL
HAM
LEG
PIT
RUN
SET

4

BLUE
BOOK
BOOM
DROP
EXIT
FLAT

4—continued

GAFF
GOBO
GODS
GRID
IRIS
LEKO

4—continued

MASK
OLIO
PIPE
PROP
RAIL
RAKE

4—continued
SOCK
TABS
TAIL
WING

5
ABOVE
ACTOR
AD LIB
AGENT
APRON
ARENA
ASIDE
BELOW
BRACE
CLOTH
CLOUD
FLIES
FLOAT
FOYER
GAUZE
GLORY
HALLS
HEAVY
HOIST
INSET
LYRIC
MANET
ODEUM
PERCH
SCENE
SCRIM
SKENE
SLIPS
SLOTE
SOUND
STAGE
STALL
STILE
TRAPS
TRUCK
VISOR

6
BARREL
BATTEN
BOARDS
BORDER
BOX SET
BRIDGE
BUSKER
CELLAR
CENTRE
CIRCLE
CRITIC
DIMMER
GEGGIE
GROOVE
MAKE-UP
NEUMES
OLD MAN
POSTER

6—continued
UPPET
RETURN
RUNWAY
SCRUTO
SEA ROW
TEASER
TELARI
TOGGLE
WALK-ON

7
ACT DROP
ACTRESS
AULAEUM
BALCONY
BENEFIT
CALL BOY
CATWALK
CIRCUIT
CURTAIN
DIORAMA
FLIPPER
GALLERY
JORNADA
MANAGER
MATINÉE
ON STAGE
PINSPOT
RAIN BOX
ROLL-OUT
ROSTRUM
ROYALTY
SCENERY
SKY DOME
SPOT BAR
TABLEAU
TOP DROP
TRILOGY
TUMBLER
TWO-FOLD
UPSTAGE
VALANCE

8
AUDITION
BLACKOUT
BOOK FLAT
BOOK WING
CALL DOOR
CHAIRMAN
CUT-CLOTH
DESIGNER
DIRECTOR
DUMB SHOW
ELEVATOR
EPILOGUE
FAUTEUIL
FOX WEDGE
JUVENILE
LASHLINE
LIBRETTO
LIGHTING

8—continued
OFF STAGE
OLD WOMAN
PANORAMA
PARADISO
PARALLEL
PASS DOOR
PLATFORM
PLAYBILL
PRODUCER
PROLOGUE
PROMPTER
SCENARIO
SET PIECE
SILL IRON
SIPARIUM
SKY CLOTH
STAR TRAP
VAMP TRAP
WARDROBE

9
ACOUSTICS
BACKCLOTH
BACKSTAGE
BOAT TRUCK
BOX OFFICE
CALL BOARD
CARPET CUT
CYCLORAMA
DOWNSTAGE
FAN EFFECT
FOOTLIGHT
GRAVE TRAP
GREEN ROOM
GROUNDROW
HAND-PROPS
HEMP HOUSE
LIGHT PIPE
LIMELIGHT
LOFT BLOCK
NOISES OFF
OPEN STAGE
ORCHESTRA
PENNY GAFF
PERIAKTOI
PROJECTOR
PROMENADE
PROVINCES
REFLECTOR
REHEARSAL
REPERTORY
ROD-PUPPET
ROPE HOUSE
SAND-CLOTH
SCENE DOCK
SET WATERS
SIGHT LINE
SKY BORDER
SLAPSTICK
SLIP STAGE
SOUBRETTE

9—continued
SPOTLIGHT
STAGE CREW
STAGE DOOR
STAGE PROP
STAGE RAKE
THREE-FOLD
THROWLINE
THYRISTOR
TORMENTOR
TRAVELLER
TRICKWORK
WATER ROWS

10
ANTI-MASQUE
AUDITORIUM
AVANT-GARDE
BUILT STUFF
CORNER TRAP
CURTAIN SET
DRAG ARTIST
FLOODLIGHT
FOLLOW SPOT
GHOST GLIDE
HALL KEEPER
HOUSE LIGHT
IMPRESARIO
INNER STAGE
LYCOPODIUM
MARIONETTE
PIPE BATTEN
PROMPT SIDE
SADDLE-IRON
SCIOPTICON
SHOW PORTAL
SPECTATORY
STAGE CLOTH
STRIP LIGHT
THUNDER RUN
TREE BORDER
UNDERSTUDY

11
BACKING FLAT
BOOK CEILING
BORDER LIGHT
BRISTLE TRAP
CURTAIN CALL
DRESS CIRCLE
FALLING FLAP
FORMAL STAGE
FRESNEL SPOT
LIGHT BATTEN
LOW COMEDIAN
OFF-BROADWAY
PROFILE SPOT
RISE-AND-SINK
ROLL CEILING
SCENE RELIEF
SPIELTREPPE
STAGE-KEEPER
STROBE LIGHT

11—continued
SWITCHBOARD
TRITAGONIST
UPPER CIRCLE
WAGGON STAGE
WIND MACHINE

12
ACTOR-MANAGER
AMPHITHEATRE
AUTHOR'S NIGHT
CAULDRON TRAP
CEILING-CLOTH
CHOREOGRAPHY
CONCERT PARTY
CORSICAN TRAP
COSTUME DRAMA
CURTAIN-MUSIC
FLYING EFFECT
FRONT OF HOUSE
LIGHT CONSOLE
LOBSTERSCOPE
MASKING PIECE
PEPPER'S GHOST
PROFILE BOARD
REVERBERATOR
RUNDHORIZONT
SCISSOR CROSS
SOUND EFFECTS
STAGE MANAGER
STAGE SETTING
STEREOPTICON
STICHOMYTHIA
STOCK COMPANY
THUNDERSHEET
TRANSPARENCY
TWOPENNY GAFF

13
DETAIL SCENERY
DEUS EX MACHINA
IMPROVISATION
LATERNA MAGICA
MAZARINE FLOOR
PLATFORM STAGE
PORTAL OPENING
SAFETY CURTAIN
STAGE LIGHTING
SUPERNUMERARY
WORD REHEARSAL

14
CONTOUR CURTAIN
COURTROOM
 DRAMA
DRAPERY SETTING
DRESS REHEARSAL
FOOTLIGHTS TRAP
GENERAL UTILITY
JACKKNIFE STAGE
KUPPELHORIZONT
MEZZANINE FLOOR
OFF-OFF-
 BROADWAY
PAGEANT LANTERN
PRIVATE THEATRE
PROSCENIUM ARCH
REVOLVING STAGE
STAGE DIRECTION

15
BARN DOOR
 SHUTTER
FLEXIBLE STAGING

15—continued
HAND WORKED
 HOUSE
INCIDENTAL MUSIC
MULTIPLE SETTING
PROSCENIUM
 DOORS
QUICK-CHANGE
 ROOM
STAGE-DOOR
 KEEPER
TRAVERSE CURTAIN

16
ALIENATION EFFECT
ASPHALEIAN
 SYSTEM
COMPOSITE
 SETTING
DRAMATIS
 PERSONAE
DRAWING-ROOM
 DRAMA
PROSCENIUM
 BORDER
TOURING
 COMPANIES

17
CUP-AND-SAUCER
 DRAMA

18
BESPEAK
 PERFORMANCE
CARBON ARC
 SPOTLIGHT

18—continued
DRUM-AND-SHAFT
 SYSTEM
FEMALE
 IMPERSONATOR
GRAND MASTER
 CONTROL
LINSENSCHEINWER
 FER
TECHNICAL
 REHEARSAL

19
COUNTERWEIGHT
 SYSTEM
SIMULTANEOUS
 SETTING
TRANSFORMATION
 SCENE

20+
ADVERTISEMENT
 CURTAIN
ASSISTANT STAGE
 MANAGER
CARRIAGE-AND-
 FRAME SYSTEM
CHARIOT-AND-POLE
 SYSTEM
PROMENADE
 PRODUCTIONS
SILICON
 CONTROLLED
 RECTIFIER
SYNCHRONOUS
 WINCH SYSTEM

BALLET TERMS

4
BRAS
DEMI
JETÉ
PLIÉ
POSÉ
SAUT
TUTU
VOLÉ

5
ARQUÉ
BARRE
BATTU
BEATS
BRISÉ
COLLÉ

5—continued
COUPÉ
DÉCOR
ÉLÈVE
FONDU
LIGNE
PASSÉ
PIQUÉ
PIVOT
PORTÉ
ROSIN
SAUTÉ
SERRÉ
TOMBÉ

6
APLOMB

6—continued
À TERRE
ATTACK
BAISSÉ
BALLON
CAMBRÉ
CHAINÉ
CHANGÉ
CHASSÉ
CROISÉ
DÉGAGÉ
DÉTIRÉ
DEVANT
ÉCARTÉ
ÉFFACÉ
ÉLANCÉ
ENTRÉE

6—continued
ÉPAULÉ
ÉTENDU
ÉTOILE
FAILLI
JARRET
MONTER
PENCHÉ
POINTE
RELEVÉ
RETIRÉ
VOYAGÉ

7
ALLONGÉ
ARRONDI
ATTAQUE

151

7—continued
BALANCÉ
DANSEUR
DÉBOITÉ
ÉCHAPPÉ
EMBOITÉ
ÉTENDRE
FOUETTÉ
JARRETÉ
LEOTARD
MAILLOT
MARQUER
POISSON
RAMASSÉ
RETOMBÉ
SISSONE
SOUTENU
TAQUETÉ

8
ASSEMBLÉ
ATTITUDE
BACK BEND

8—continued
BALLONNÉ
BALLOTTÉ
BATTERIE
CABRIOLE
CAGNEAUX
CORYPHÉE
DANSEUSE
DÉBOULÉS
DERRIÈRE
DÉTOURNÉ
GLISSADE
PISTOLET
RENVERSÉ
SERPETTE
SPOTTING
STULCHIK
TONNELET

9
ARABESQUE
BALLABILE
COU DE PIED

9—continued
DÉVELOPPÉ
ÉLÉVATION
ENTRECHAT
ENVELOPPÉ
ÉQUILIBRE
HORTENSIA
JUPONNAGE
LIMBERING
MARCHEUSE
PAS DE DEUX
PIROUETTE
RACCOURCI
RÉVÉRENCE
REVOLTADE

10
BATTEMENTS
ENLÈVEMENT
ÉPAULEMENT
SOUBRESAUT
TAQUETERIE

11
CONTRETEMPS
PAS DE BASQUE

12
CHOREOGRAPHY
ENCHAÎNEMENT
GARGOUILLADE

13
CHOREOGRAPHER
CORPS DE BALLET

14
CLOSED POSITION
DIVERTISSEMENT
PRIMA BALLERINA

15
AUTOUR DE LA
  SALLE

17
RÉGISSEUR-
  GÉNÉRALE

NOVEL TITLES

NOVEL (Author)

3
SHE (H Rider Haggard)

4
DR NO (Ian Fleming)
EMMA (Jane Austen)
GIGI (Colette)
NANA (Émile Zola)

5
CHÉRI (Colette)
KIPPS (H G Wells)
SCOOP (Evelyn Waugh)
SYBIL (Benjamin Disraeli)
ZADIG (Voltaire)

6
AMELIA (Henry Fielding)
BEN HUR (Lew Wallace)
CHOCKY (John Wyndham)
LOLITA (Vladimir Nabokov)
PAMELA (Henry Fielding)
ROB ROY (Walter Scott)

7
CAMILLA (Fanny Burney)
CANDIDE (Voltaire)
CECILIA (Fanny Burney)
DRACULA (Bram Stoker)
EREWHON (Samuel Butler)

7—continued
EVELINA (Fanny Burney)
IVANHOE (Walter Scott)
REBECCA (Daphne Du
  Maurier)
SHIRLEY (Charlotte Brontë)
THE FALL (Albert Camus)
ULYSSES (James Joyce)

8
ADAM BEDE (George Eliot)
CRANFORD (Mrs Gaskell)
JANE EYRE (Charlotte Brontë)
LUCKY JIM (Kingsley Amis)
SWAN SONG (John
  Galsworthy)
THE IDIOT (Fyodor
  Mikhailovich Dostoevsky)
THE MAGUS (John Fowles)
THE REBEL (Albert Camus)
TOM JONES (Henry Fielding)
VILLETTE (Charlotte Brontë)
WAVERLEY (Walter Scott)

9
AGNES GREY (Anne Brontë)
BILLY LIAR (Keith Waterhouse)
CONINGSBY (Benjamin
  Disraeli)
DUBLINERS (James Joyce)

9—continued
GLENARVON (Lady Caroline
  Lamb)
HARD TIMES (Charles
  Dickens)
I CLAUDIUS (Robert Graves)
KIDNAPPED (R L Stevenson)
LOVE STORY (Erich Segal)
ROGUE MALE (Geoffrey
  Household)
THE CHIMES (Charles
  Dickens)
THE DEVILS (Fyodor
  Mikhailovich Dostoevsky)
THE HEROES (Charles
  Kingsley)
THE HOBBIT (J R R Tolkien)
THE PLAGUE (Albert Camus)
VICE VERSA (F Anstey)

10
ANIMAL FARM (George
  Orwell)
BLEAK HOUSE (Charles
  Dickens)
CANCER WARD (Alexander
  Solzhenitsyn)
CLAYHANGER (Arnold
  Bennett)
DON QUIXOTE (Cervantes)
GOLDFINGER (Ian Fleming)

10—continued
IN CHANCERY (John Galsworthy)
KENILWORTH (Walter Scott)
LORNA DOONE (R D Blackmore)
PERSUASION (Jane Austen)
THE RAINBOW (D H Lawrence)
TITUS ALONE (Mervyn Peake)
TITUS GROAN (Mervyn Peake)
VANITY FAIR (William Makepeace Thackeray)

11
BLACK BEAUTY (Anna Sewell)
BURMESE DAYS (George Orwell)
CAKES AND ALE (W Somerset Maugham)
COUSIN BETTE (Honoré de Balzac)
DAISY MILLER (Henry James)
GORMENGHAST (Mervyn Peake)
LITTLE WOMEN (Louisa M Alcott)
LOST HORIZON (James Hilton)
MIDDLEMARCH (George Eliot)
MRS DALLOWAY (Virginia Woolf)
OLIVER TWIST (Charles Dickens)
SILAS MARNER (George Eliot)
THE BIG SLEEP (Raymond Chandler)
THE OUTSIDER (Albert Camus)
WAR AND PEACE (Leo Tolstoy)
WOMEN IN LOVE (D H Lawrence)

12
ANNA KARENINA (Leo Tolstoy)
A SEVERED HEAD (Iris Murdoch)
BARNABY RUDGE (Charles Dickens)
BRIGHTON ROCK (Graham Greene)
CASINO ROYALE (Ian Fleming)
DOMBEY AND SON (Charles Dickens)
FRANKENSTEIN (Mary Shelley)
GUY MANNERING (Walter Scott)
HEADLONG HALL (Thomas Love Peacock)
LITTLE DORRIT (Charles Dickens)
MADAME BOVARY (Gustave Flaubert)
MOLL FLANDERS (Daniel Defoe)
OF MICE AND MEN (John Steinbeck)
ROGUE JUSTICE (Geoffrey Household)
ROOM AT THE TOP (John Braine)
THE DECAMERON (Boccaccio)
THE GO-BETWEEN (L P Hartley)
THE LOST WORLD (Arthur Conan Doyle)
THE MOONSTONE (Wilkie Collins)
THE PROFESSOR (Charlotte Brontë)

13
A KIND OF LOVING (Stan Barstow)
A MODERN COMEDY (John Galsworthy)
BRAVE NEW WORLD (Aldous Huxley)
DANIEL DERONDA (George Eliot)
DOCTOR ZHIVAGO (Boris Pasternak)
FANNY AND ZOOEY (J D Salinger)
JACOB FAITHFUL (Captain Marryat)
JUST-SO STORIES (Rudyard Kipling)
LES MISÉRABLES (Victor Hugo)
LIVE AND LET DIE (Ian Fleming)
LIZA OF LAMBETH (W Somerset Maugham)
MANSFIELD PARK (Jane Austen)

13—continued
NORTH AND SOUTH (Mrs Gaskell)
PINCHER MARTIN (William Golding)
SKETCHES BY BOZ (Charles Dickens)
SMILEY'S PEOPLE (John Le Carré)
SONS AND LOVERS (D H Lawrence)
TARKA THE OTTER (Henry Williamson)
THE BLUE LAGOON (H de Vere Stacpoole)
THE CHRYSALIDS (John Wyndham)
THE GOLDEN BOWL (Henry James)
THE HISTORY MAN (Malcolm Bradbury)
THE LAST TYCOON (F Scott Fitzgerald)
THÉRÈSE RAQUIN (Émile Zola)
ZULEIKA DOBSON (Max Beerbohm)

14
A MAN OF PROPERTY (John Galsworthy)
A ROOM OF ONE'S OWN (Virginia Woolf)
A ROOM WITH A VIEW (E M Forster)
A TOWN LIKE ALICE (Neville Shute)
CHANGING PLACES (David Lodge)
CIDER WITH ROSIE (Laurie Lee)
CROTCHET CASTLE (Thomas Love Peacock)
DEATH ON THE NILE (Agatha Christie)
DECLINE AND FALL (Evelyn Waugh)
GOODBYE, MR CHIPS (James Hilton)
JUDE THE OBSCURE (Thomas Hardy)
LORD OF THE FLIES (William Golding)
NIGHTMARE ABBEY (Thomas Love Peacock)
OUR MAN IN HAVANA (Graham Greene)
PICKWICK PAPERS (Charles Dickens)
RITES OF PASSAGE (William Golding)
ROBINSON CRUSOE (Daniel Defoe)
THE AMBASSADORS (Henry James)
THE CORAL ISLAND (R M Ballantyne)
THE FIRST CIRCLE (Alexander Solzhenitsyn)
THE FORSYTE SAGA (John Galsworthy)
THE GREAT GATSBY (F Scott Fitzgerald)
THE KRAKEN WAKES (John Wyndham)
THE LONG GOODBYE (Raymond Chandler)
THE SECRET AGENT (Joseph Conrad)
THE SILVER SPOON (John Galsworthy)
THE TIME MACHINE (H G Wells)
THE WATER-BABIES (Charles Kingsley)
THE WHITE MONKEY (John Galsworthy)
THE WOODLANDERS (Thomas Hardy)
TREASURE ISLAND (R L Stevenson)
TRISTRAM SHANDY (Laurence Sterne)
WHAT MAISIE KNEW (Henry James)

15
A CHRISTMAS CAROL (Charles Dickens)
A FAREWELL TO ARMS (Ernest Hemingway)
A PASSAGE TO INDIA (E M Forster)
COLD COMFORT FARM (Stella Gibbons)
EUSTACE AND HILDA (L P Hartley)
GONE WITH THE WIND (Margaret Mitchell)
GOODBYE TO BERLIN (Christopher Isherwood)
NORTHANGER ABBEY (Jane Austen)
OUR MUTUAL FRIEND (Charles Dickens)
PORTRAIT OF A LADY (Henry James)
PORTRAIT OF CLARE (Francis Brett Young)
STRAIT IS THE GATE (André Gide)

15–continued

THE COUNTRY GIRLS (Edna O'Brien)
THE INVISIBLE MAN (H G Wells)
THE SECRET GARDEN (Frances Hodgson Burnett)
THE SILMARILLION (J R R Tolkien)
THE TRUMPET MAJOR (Thomas Hardy)
THE WHITE COMPANY (Arthur Conan Doyle)
THE WOMAN IN WHITE (Wilkie Collins)
THREE MEN IN A BOAT (Jerome K Jerome)

16

A CLOCKWORK ORANGE (Anthony Burgess)
A TALE OF TWO CITIES (Charles Dickens)
DAVID COPPERFIELD (Charles Dickens)
GULLIVER'S TRAVELS (Jonathan Swift)
MARTIN CHUZZLEWIT (Charles Dickens)
MR MIDSHIPMAN EASY (Captain Marryat)
NICHOLAS NICKLEBY (Charles Dickens)
TENDER IS THE NIGHT (F Scott Fitzgerald)
TEN LITTLE NIGGERS (Agatha Christie)
THE GRAPES OF WRATH (John Steinbeck)
THE PLUMED SERPENT (D H Lawrence)
THE SCARLET LETTER (Nathaniel Hawthorne)
WUTHERING HEIGHTS (Emily Brontë)

17

ALICE IN WONDERLAND (Lewis Carroll)
DR JEKYLL AND MR HYDE (R L Stevenson)
GREAT EXPECTATIONS (Charles Dickens)
KING SOLOMON'S MINES (H Rider Haggard)
MY BROTHER JONATHAN (Francis Brett Young)
POINT COUNTER POINT (Aldous Huxley)
PRIDE AND PREJUDICE (Jane Austen)
THE DEVILS OF LOUDUN (Aldous Huxley)
THE DIARY OF A NOBODY (G and W Grossmith)
THE LORD OF THE RINGS (J R R Tolkien)
THE MIDWICH CUCKOOS (John Wyndham)
THE MILL ON THE FLOSS (George Eliot)
THE WAR OF THE WORLDS (H G Wells)
THE WINGS OF THE DOVE (Henry James)
WIVES AND DAUGHTERS (Mrs Gaskell)

18

A HIGH WIND IN JAMAICA (Richard Hughes)
ANNA OF THE FIVE TOWNS (Arnold Bennett)
CRIME AND PUNISHMENT (Fyodor Dostoevsky)
NINETEEN EIGHTY-FOUR (George Orwell)
SWALLOWS AND AMAZONS (Arthur Ransome)
THE CATCHER IN THE RYE (J D Salinger)
THE MOON AND SIXPENCE (W Somerset Maugham)
THE OLD MAN AND THE SEA (Ernest Hemingway)
THE PRISONER OF ZENDA (Anthony Hope)
THE THIRTY-NINE STEPS (John Buchan)
THE THREE MUSKETEERS (Alexandre Dumas)

19

BRIDESHEAD REVISITED (Evelyn Waugh)
FOR WHOM THE BELL TOLLS (Ernest Hemingway)

19–continued

SENSE AND SENSIBILITY (Jane Austen)
THE DAY OF THE TRIFFIDS (John Wyndham)
THE GULAG ARCHIPELAGO (Alexander Solzhenitsyn)
THE HISTORY OF MR POLLY (H G Wells)
THE MAN IN THE IRON MASK (Alexandre Dumas)
THE OLD CURIOSITY SHOP (Charles Dickens)
THE PILGRIM'S PROGRESS (John Bunyan)
THE RIDDLE OF THE SANDS (Erskine Childers)
THE SCARLET PIMPERNEL (Baroness Orczy)
THE SCREWTAPE LETTERS (C S Lewis)
THE VICAR OF WAKEFIELD (Oliver Goldsmith)
THE WIND IN THE WILLOWS (Kenneth Grahame)
TOM BROWN'S SCHOOLDAYS (Thomas Hughes)

20+

A CONNECTICUT YANKEE IN KING ARTHUR'S COURT (Mark Twain)
A DANCE TO THE MUSIC OF TIME (Anthony Powell)
AS I WALKED OUT ONE MIDSUMMER MORNING (Laurie Lee)
CHILDREN OF THE NEW FOREST (Captain Marryat)
FAR FROM THE MADDING CROWD (Thomas Hardy)
JOHN HALIFAX, GENTLEMAN (Mrs Craik)
KEEP THE ASPIDISTRA FLYING (George Orwell)
LADY CHATTERLEY'S LOVER (D H Lawrence)
LARK RISE TO CANDLEFORD (Flora Thompson)
LITTLE LORD FAUNTLEROY (Frances Hodgson Burnett)
MURDER ON THE ORIENT EXPRESS (Agatha Christie)
OUT OF THE SILENT PLANET (C S Lewis)
AROUND THE WORLD IN EIGHTY DAYS (Jules Verne)
TESS OF THE D'URBERVILLES (Thomas Hardy)
THE ADVENTURES OF HUCKLEBERRY FINN (Mark Twain)
THE ADVENTURES OF TOM SAWYER (Mark Twain)
THE BEAUTIFUL AND DAMNED (F Scott Fitzgerald)
THE BRIDE OF LAMMERMOOR (Walter Scott)
THE BROTHERS KARAMAZOV (Fyodor Mikhailovich Dostoevsky)
THE CRICKET ON THE HEARTH (Charles Dickens)
THE FRENCH LIEUTENANT'S WOMAN (John Fowles)
THE HEART OF MIDLOTHIAN (Walter Scott)
THE HISTORY OF HENRY ESMOND (William Makepeace Thackeray)

20+—continued

THE HONOURABLE SCHOOLBOY (John Le Carré)

THE INNOCENCE OF FATHER BROWN (G K Chesterton)

THE ISLAND OF DOCTOR MOREAU (H G Wells)

THE LAST OF THE MOHICANS (James Fenimore Cooper)

THE MEMOIRS OF SHERLOCK HOLMES (Arthur Conan Doyle)

THE MYSTERIES OF UDOLPHO (Mrs Radcliffe)

THE MYSTERIOUS AFFAIR AT STYLES (Agatha Christie)

THE MYSTERY OF EDWIN DROOD (Charles Dickens)

THE PICTURE OF DORIAN GRAY (Oscar Wilde)

20+—continued

THE PRIME OF MISS JEAN BRODIE (Muriel Spark)

THE RED BADGE OF COURAGE (Stephen Crane)

THE RETURN OF THE NATIVE (Thomas Hardy)

THE TENANT OF WILDFELL HALL (Anne Brontë)

TINKER, TAILOR, SOLDIER, SPY (John Le Carré)

TWENTY THOUSAND LEAGUES UNDER THE SEA (Jules Verne)

TWO YEARS BEFORE THE MAST (Richard Henry Dana)

UNDER THE GREENWOOD TREE (Thomas Hardy)

PLAY TITLES

TITLE (Playwright)

4
LOOT (Joe Orton)
ROSS (Terence Rattigan)

5
CASTE (T W Robertson)
FAUST (Goethe)
MEDEA (Euripides)
ROOTS (Arnold Wesker)

6
GHOSTS (Henrik Ibsen)
HAMLET (William Shakespeare)
HENRY V (William Shakespeare)
PHÈDRE (Jean Racine)
PLENTY (David Hare)
STRIFE (John Galsworthy)

7
AMADEUS (Peter Shaffer)
ATHALIE (Jean Racine)
CANDIDA (G B Shaw)
ELECTRA (Sophocles)
GALILEO (Bertolt Brecht)
HENRY IV (William Shakespeare)
HENRY VI (William Shakespeare)
JUMPERS (Tom Stoppard)
MACBETH (William Shakespeare)
OTHELLO (William Shakespeare)

7—continued
THE LARK (Jean Anouilh)
THE ROOM (Harold Pinter)
VOLPONE (Ben Jonson)

8
ANTIGONE (Sophocles)
HAY FEVER (Noël Coward)
KING JOHN (William Shakespeare)
KING LEAR (William Shakespeare)
PERICLES (William Shakespeare)
PETER PAN (J M Barrie)
TARTUFFE (Molière)
THE BIRDS (Aristophanes)
THE FROGS (Aristophanes)
THE MISER (Molière)

9
ALL MY SONS (Arthur Miller)
BILLY LIAR (Willis Hall and Keith Waterhouse)
CAVALCADE (Noël Coward)
CYMBELINE (William Shakespeare)
DR FAUSTUS (Christopher Marlowe)
FLARE PATH (Terence Rattigan)
GOLDEN BOY (Clifford Odets)
HAPPY DAYS (Samuel Beckett)
HENRY VIII (William Shakespeare)
PYGMALION (G B Shaw)

9—continued
RICHARD II (William Shakespeare)
SAINT JOAN (G B Shaw)
THE CIRCLE (W Somerset Maugham)
THE CRITIC (Sheridan)
THE DEVILS (John Whiting)
THE RIVALS (Sheridan)

10
ALL FOR LOVE (John Dryden)
ANDROMAQUE (Jean Racine)
AURENG-ZEBE (John Dryden)
CORIOLANUS (William Shakespeare)
I AM A CAMERA (John Van Druten)
OEDIPUS REX (Sophocles)
RICHARD III (William Shakespeare)
THE BACCHAE (Euripides)
THE BALCONY (Jean Genet)
THE HOSTAGE (Brendan Behan)
THE SEAGULL (Anton Chekhov)
THE TEMPEST (William Shakespeare)
UNCLE VANYA (Anton Chekhov)

11
A DOLL'S HOUSE (Henrik Ibsen)
AS YOU LIKE IT (William Shakespeare)

11—continued
JOURNEY'S END (R C Sherriff)
LOVE FOR LOVE (William Congreve)
PANDORA'S BOX (Frank Wedekind)
ROOKERY NOOK (Ben Travers)
THE BANKRUPT (Alexander Ostrovsky)
THE CONTRAST (Royall Tyler)
THE CRUCIBLE (Arthur Miller)
THE WILD DUCK (Henrik Ibsen)

12
AFTER THE FALL (Arthur Miller)
ANNA CHRISTIE (Eugene O'Neill)
BEDROOM FARCE (Alan Ayckbourn)
BLITHE SPIRIT (Noël Coward)
BLOOD WEDDING (García Lorca)
CHARLEY'S AUNT (Brandon Thomas)
DUEL OF ANGELS (Jean Giraudoux)
JULIUS CAESAR (William Shakespeare)
MAJOR BARBARA (G B Shaw)
PRIVATE LIVES (Noël Coward)
THE ALCHEMIST (Ben Jonson)
THE ANATOMIST (James Bridie)
THE APPLE CART (G B Shaw)
THE BROKEN JUG (Heinrich von Kleist)
THE CARETAKER (Harold Pinter)
THE MOUSETRAP (Agatha Christie)
THREE SISTERS (Anton Chekhov)
TWELFTH NIGHT (William Shakespeare)

13
ARMS AND THE MAN (G B Shaw)
A TASTE OF HONEY (Shelagh Delaney)
HOBSON'S CHOICE (Harold Brighouse)
LE MISANTHROPE (Molière)
QUALITY STREET (J M Barrie)
THE ACHARNIANS (Aristophanes)
THE DUMB WAITER (Harold Pinter)
THE JEW OF MALTA (Christopher Marlowe)
THE LINDEN TREE (J B Priestley)
THE MAGISTRATE (Pinero)
THE MATCHMAKER (Thornton Wilder)
THE WHITE DEVIL (John Webster)
THE WINSLOW BOY (Terence Rattigan)
TIMON OF ATHENS (William Shakespeare)
UNDER MILK WOOD (Dylan Thomas)

14
AN IDEAL HUSBAND (Oscar Wilde)
MAN AND SUPERMAN (G B Shaw)
ROMEO AND JULIET (William Shakespeare)
SEPARATE TABLES (Terence Rattigan)
THE CORN IS GREEN (Emlyn Williams)
THE COUNTRY GIRL (Clifford Odets)
THE DEEP BLUE SEA (Terence Rattigan)
THE FIRE-RAISERS (Max Frisch)
THE GHOST SONATA (August Strindberg)
THE OLD BACHELOR (William Congreve)
THE PHILANDERER (G B Shaw)
THE TROJAN WOMEN (Euripides)
THE WINTER'S TALE (William Shakespeare)
THIS HAPPY BREED (Noël Coward)

15
BARTHOLOMEW FAIR (Ben Jonson)
DANGEROUS CORNER (J B Priestley)
DESIGN FOR LIVING (Noël Coward)
HEARTBREAK HOUSE (G B Shaw)
LOOK BACK IN ANGER (John Osborne)
MARRIAGE À LA MODE (John Dryden)
PRESENT LAUGHTER (Noël Coward)
THE CONSTANT WIFE (W Somerset Maugham)
THE ICEMAN COMETH (Eugene O'Neill)
TITUS ANDRONICUS (William Shakespeare)
TWO NOBLE KINSMEN (William Shakespeare)
VENICE PRESERVED (Thomas Otway)
WAITING FOR GODOT (Samuel Beckett)

16
A CUCKOO IN THE NEST (Ben Travers)
AN INSPECTOR CALLS (J B Priestley)
CAT ON A HOT TIN ROOF (Tennessee Williams)
DEATH OF A SALESMAN (Arthur Miller)
LOVE'S LABOUR'S LOST (William
    Shakespeare)
PILLARS OF SOCIETY (Henrik Ibsen)
RING ROUND THE MOON (Jean Anouilh)
THE ADDING MACHINE (Elmer Rice)
THE AMERICAN DREAM (Edward Albee)
THE BIRTHDAY PARTY (Harold Pinter)
THE CHERRY ORCHARD (Anton Chekhov)
THE COCKTAIL PARTY (T S Eliot)
THE FAMILY REUNION (T S Eliot)
THE MASTER BUILDER (Henrik Ibsen)
WHAT THE BUTLER SAW (Joe Orton)

17
A MAN FOR ALL SEASONS (Robert Bolt)
AN ITALIAN STRAW HAT (Eugène Labiche)
ARSENIC AND OLD LACE (Joseph Kesselring)
BAREFOOT IN THE PARK (Neil Simon)
JUNO AND THE PAYCOCK (Sean O'Casey)
MEASURE FOR MEASURE (William
    Shakespeare)
ROMANOFF AND JULIET (Peter Ustinov)
THE BEAUX' STRATAGEM (George Farquhar)
THE COMEDY OF ERRORS (William
    Shakespeare)
THE DEVIL'S DISCIPLE (G B Shaw)
THE DOCTOR'S DILEMMA (G B Shaw)
THE DUCHESS OF MALFI (John Webster)
THE GLASS MENAGERIE (Tennessee Williams)
THE GOOD-NATURED MAN (Oliver Goldsmith)
THE SCHOOL FOR WIVES (Molière)
THE SUPPLIANT WOMEN (Aeschylus)
'TIS PITY SHE'S A WHORE (John Ford)

18
AN ENEMY OF THE PEOPLE (Henrik Ibsen)
ANTONY AND CLEOPATRA (William
    Shakespeare)
CAESAR AND CLEOPATRA (G B Shaw)
FIVE FINGER EXERCISE (Peter Shaffer)
FRENCH WITHOUT TEARS (Terence Rattigan)
LADY WINDERMERE'S FAN (Oscar Wilde)
SHE STOOPS TO CONQUER (Oliver Goldsmith)

18—continued

SUDDENLY LAST SUMMER (Tennessee Williams)
THE BROWNING VERSION (Terence Rattigan)
THE ROMANS IN BRITAIN (Howard Brenton)
TROILUS AND CRESSIDA (William Shakespeare)

19

ANDROCLES AND THE LION (G B Shaw)
CHIPS WITH EVERYTHING (Arnold Wesker)
MUCH ADO ABOUT NOTHING (William Shakespeare)
TAMBURLAINE THE GREAT (Christopher Marlowe)
THE MERCHANT OF VENICE (William Shakespeare)
THE SCHOOL FOR SCANDAL (Sheridan)
THE TAMING OF THE SHREW (William Shakespeare)
WHAT EVERY WOMAN KNOWS (J M Barrie)

20+

ACCIDENTAL DEATH OF AN ANARCHIST (Dario Fo)
ALL GOD'S CHILLUN GOT WINGS (Eugene O'Neill)
ALL'S WELL THAT ENDS WELL (William Shakespeare)
A MIDSUMMER NIGHT'S DREAM (William Shakespeare)

20+—continued

A STREETCAR NAMED DESIRE (Tennessee Williams)
A WOMAN OF NO IMPORTANCE (Oscar Wilde)
CAPTAIN BRASSBOUND'S CONVERSION (G B Shaw)
ENTERTAINING MR SLOANE (Joe Orton)
INADMISSIBLE EVIDENCE (John Osborne)
MOURNING BECOMES ELECTRA (Eugene O'Neill)
MURDER IN THE CATHEDRAL (T S Eliot)
ROSENCRANTZ AND GUILDENSTERN ARE DEAD (Tom Stoppard)
THE ADMIRABLE CRICHTON (J M Barrie)
THE BARRETTS OF WIMPOLE STREET (Rudolf Besier)
THE CAUCASIAN CHALK CIRCLE (Bertolt Brecht)
THE GOVERNMENT INSPECTOR (Nikolai Gogol)
THE IMPORTANCE OF BEING EARNEST (Oscar Wilde)
THE LADY'S NOT FOR BURNING (Christopher Fry)
THE MERRY WIVES OF WINDSOR (William Shakespeare)
THE SECOND MRS TANQUERAY (Pinero)
THE TWO GENTLEMEN OF VERONA (William Shakespeare)
WHO'S AFRAID OF VIRGINIA WOOLF? (Edward Albee)

FICTIONAL CHARACTERS

CHARACTER (*Title*, Author)

3

FOX, Brer (*Uncle Remus*, J. C. Harris)
GOG (*The Tower of London*, W. H. Ainsworth)
HUR, Judah (*Ben Hur*, L. Wallace)
JIM, 'Lord' (*Lord Jim*, J. Conrad)
KIM (*Kim*, Rudyard Kipling)
LEE, General Robert E. (*Abraham Lincoln*, J. Drinkwater)
LEE, Lorelei (*Gentlemen Prefer Blondes*, Anita Loos)
OWL (*Winnie the Pooh*, A. A. Milne)
ROO (*Winnie the Pooh*, A. A. Milne)
TOM (*The Water Babies*, C. Kingsley)
TOM, 'Uncle' (*Uncle Tom's Cabin*, Harriet B. Stowe)

4

ABEL (*Middlemarch*, George Eliot)
CASS, Eppie (*Silas Marner*, George Eliot)

4—continued

CASY, Rev. Jim (*The Grapes of Wrath*, J. Steinbeck)
CUFF, Sergeant (*The Moonstone*, W. Collins)
DEAN, Ellen (*Wuthering Heights*, Emily Brontë)
EAST (*Tom Brown's Schooldays*, T. Hughes)
EASY, John (*Mr Midshipman Easy*, Captain Marryat)
EYRE, Jane (*Jane Eyre*, Charlotte Brontë)
FAWN, Lord Frederic (*Phineas Finn*, A. Trollope)
FELL, Dr Gideon (*The Black Spectacles*, J. Dickson Carr)
FINN, Huckleberry (*Huckleberry Finn*, Tom Sawyer*, M. Twain)
FINN, Phineas (*Phineas Finn*, A. Trollope)
GRAY, Dorian (*The Picture of Dorian Gray*, Oscar Wilde)
GRAY, Nelly (*Faithless Nelly Gray*, T. Hood)
GUNN, Ben (*Treasure Island*, R. L. Stevenson)
HOOK, Captain James (*Peter Pan*, J. M. Barrie)
HYDE, Edward (*Dr Jekyll and Mr Hyde*, R. L. Stevenson)

4—continued

JUDY (*Wee Willie Winkie*, R. Kipling)

LAMB, Leonard (*Middlemarch*, George Eliot)

MOLE, Mr (*The Wind in the Willows*, K. Grahame)

NANA (*Peter Pan*, J. M. Barrie)

NASH, Richard (Beau) (*Monsieur Beaucaire*, Booth Tarkington)

PUCK (Robin Goodfellow) (*Puck of Pook's Hill*, R. Kipling)

RAMA (Tiger Tiger) (*The Jungle Book*, R. Kipling)

REED, Mrs (*Jane Eyre*, Charlotte Brontë)

RIDD, John (*Lorna Doone*, R. D. Blackmore)

SEAL, Basil (*Put Out More Flags*, E. Waugh)

SMEE (*Peter Pan*, J. M. Barrie)

TOAD, Mr (*The Wind in the Willows*, K. Grahame)

TROY, Sergeant Francis (*Far from the Madding Crowd*, T. Hardy)

VANE, Harriet (*Strong Poison*, Dorothy L. Sayers)

VANE, Lady Isabel (*East Lynne*, Mrs Henry Wood)

WOLF, 'Brer' (*Uncle Remus*, J. C. Harris)

5

ADLER, Irene (*The Adventures of Sherlock Holmes*, A. Conan Doyle)

AKELA (*The Jungle Book*, R. Kipling)

ALIBI, Tom (*Waverley*, W. Scott)

ATHOS (*The Three Musketeers*, Alexandre Dumas)

BALOO (*The Jungle Book*, R. Kipling)

BLAKE, Franklin (*The Moonstone*, W. Collins)

BONES, Captain Billy (*Treasure Island*, R. L. Stevenson)

BOOBY, Sir Thomas (*Joseph Andrews*, H. Fielding)

BRUFF (*The Moonstone*, W. Collins)

BULBO, Prince (*The Rose and the Ring*, W. M. Thackeray)

CHANT, Mercy (*Tess of the D'Urbervilles*, T. Hardy)

CLACK, Drusilla (*The Moonstone*, W. Collins)

CLARE, Angel (*Tess of the D'Urbervilles*, T. Hardy)

DARCY, Fitzwilliam (*Pride and Prejudice*, Jane Austen)

DEANS, Effie/Jeanie (*The Heart of Midlothian*, W. Scott)

DIXON, James (*Lucky Jim*, K. Amis)

DOONE, Lorna (*Lorna Doone*, R. D. Blackmore)

EAGER, Rev. Cuthbert (*Room with a View*, E. M. Forster)

FANNY (*Fanny's First Play*, G. B. Shaw)

FLYNN, Father James (*The Dubliners*, J. Joyce)

GESTE, Beau (*Beau Geste*, P. C. Wren)

GWYNN, Nell (*Simon Dale*, A. Hope)

HANDS, Israel (*Treasure Island*, R. L. Stevenson)

HATCH, Bennet (*The Black Arrow*, R. L. Stevenson)

JONES, Tom (*Tom Jones*, H. Fielding)

KANGA (*Winnie the Pooh*, A. A. Milne)

KIPPS, Arthur (*Kipps*, H. G. Wells)

5—continued

LEIGH, Captain Sir Amyas (*Westward Ho!*, C. Kingsley)

MAGOG (*The Tower of London*, W. H. Ainsworth)

MARCH, Amy/Beth/Josephine (Jo)/Meg (*Little Women*, etc., Louisa M. Alcott)

MERCY (*Pilgrim's Progress*, J. Bunyan)

MITTY, Walter (*The Secret Life of Walter Mitty*, J. Thurber)

MOORE, Mrs (*A Passage to India*, E. M. Forster)

O'HARA, Kimball (*Kim*, Rudyard Kipling)

O'HARA, Scarlett (*Gone with the Wind*, Margaret Mitchell)

OTTER, Mr (*The Wind in the Willows*, K. Grahame)

PAGET, Jean (*A Town like Alice*, N. Shute)

POLLY, Alfred (*The History of Mr Polly*, H. G. Wells)

POOLE, Grace (*Jane Eyre*, Charlotte Brontë)

PORGY (*Porgy*, Du Bose Heyward)

PRISM, Miss Laetitia (*The Importance of Being Earnest*, Oscar Wilde)

PUNCH (*Wee Willie Winkie*, R. Kipling)

READY, Masterman (*Masterman Ready*, F. Marryat)

REMUS, Uncle (*Uncle Remus* series, J. C. Harris)

RYDER, Charles (*Brideshead Revisited*, E. Waugh)

SALLY (*Sally in Our Alley*, H. Carey)

SAMBO (*Just So Stories*, R. Kipling)

SHARP, Rebecca (Becky) (*Vanity Fair*, W. M. Thackeray)

SLOPE, Rev. Obadiah (*Barchester Towers*, A. Trollope)

SLOTH (*Pilgrim's Progress*, J. Bunyan)

SMITH, Winston (*1984*, G. Orwell)

SNOWE, Lucy (*Villette*, Charlotte Brontë)

TARKA (*Tarka the Otter*, H. Williamson)

THUMB, Tom (*The Tale of Two Bad Mice*, Beatrix Potter)

TOPSY (*Uncle Tom's Cabin*, Harriet B. Stowe)

UNCAS (*The Last of the Mohicans*, J. Fennimore Cooper)

6

AITKEN (*Prester John*, J. Buchan)

ARAMIS (*The Three Musketeers*, Alexandre Dumas)

AYESHA (*She*, H. Rider Haggard)

BENNET, Catherine/Elizabeth/Jane/Lydia/Mary (*Pride and Prejudice*, Jane Austen)

BESSIE (*Jane Eyre*, Charlotte Brontë)

BINKIE, Lady Grizzel (*Vanity Fair*, W. M. Thackeray)

BOVARY, Emma (*Madame Bovary*, G. Flaubert)

BUTLER, Rhett (*Gone with the Wind*, Margaret Mitchell)

CACKLE (*Vanity Fair*, W. M. Thackeray)

CARDEW, Cecily (*The Importance of Being Earnest*, Oscar Wilde)

6–continued

CRUSOE, Robinson (*Robinson Crusoe*, D. Defoe)

DANGLE (*The Critic*, R. B. Sheridan)

EEYORE (*Winnie the Pooh*, A. A. Milne)

ELAINE (*Idylls of the King*, Lord Tennyson)

'FRIDAY' (*Robinson Crusoe*, D. Defoe)

FRITHA (*The Snow Goose*, P. Gallico)

GARTER, Polly (*Under Milk Wood*, D. Thomas)

GATSBY, Major Jay (*The Great Gatsby*, F. Scott Fitzgerald)

GEORGE (*Three Men in a Boat*, J. K. Jerome)

GERARD, Etienne (*The Exploits of Brigadier Gerard*, A. Conan Doyle)

GILPIN, John (*John Gilpin*, W. Cowper)

GLOVER, Catherine (*The Fair Maid of Perth*, W. Scott)

GORDON, Squire (*Black Beauty*, A. Sewell)

GRIMES (*The Water Babies*, C. Kingsley)

HANNAY, Richard (*The Thirty-Nine Steps*, J. Buchan)

HARKER, Jonathan/Minna (*Dracula*, Bram Stoker)

HARMAN, Joe (*A Town like Alice*, N. Shute)

HAROLD, Childe (*Childe Harold's Pilgrimage*, Lord Byron)

HEARTS, King of/Knave of/Queen of (*Alice in Wonderland*, L. Carroll)

HOLMES, Mycroft (*The Return of Sherlock Holmes*, A. Conan Doyle)

HOLMES, Sherlock (*A Study in Scarlet, The Sign of Four, The Hound of the Baskervilles*, etc., A. Conan Doyle)

HOOPER, Fanny (*Fanny by Gaslight*, M. Sadleir)

JEEVES (*Thank you, Jeeves*, P. G. Wodehouse)

JEKYLL, Henry (*Dr Jekyll and Mr Hyde*, R. L. Stevenson)

LAURIE (*Little Women*, Louisa M. Alcott)

LAURIE, Annie (*Annie Laurie*, Douglass)

LEGREE, Simon (*Uncle Tom's Cabin*, Harriet B. Stowe)

LINTON, Edgar (*Wuthering Heights*, Emily Brontë)

MANGAN, Boss (*Heartbreak House*, G. B. Shaw)

MANSON, Dr Andrew (*The Citadel*, A. J. Cronin)

MARPLE, Jane (*A Pocket Full of Rye*, Agatha Christie)

MERLIN (*Idylls of the King*, Lord Tennyson)

MODRED, Sir (*Idylls of the King*, Lord Tennyson)

MOREAU, André-Louis (*Scaramouche*, R. Sabatini)

MOREAU, Dr (*The Island of Dr Moreau*, H. G. Wells)

MORGAN, Angharad/Huw (*How Green Was My Valley*, R. Llewellyn)

MORGAN, Organ (*Under Milk Wood*, D. Thomas)

MOWGLI (*The Jungle Book*, R. Kipling)

NUTKIN, Squirrel, (*The Tale of Squirrel Nutkin*, Beatrix Potter)

OMNIUM, Duke of (Family name Palliser) (*The Barsetshire series*, Angela Thirkell)

PICKLE, Peregrine (*Peregrine Pickle*, T. Smollett)

6–continued

PIGLET, Henry Pootel (*Winnie the Pooh*, A. A. Milne)

POIROT, Hercule (*The Mysterious Affair at Styles*, Agatha Christie)

RABBIT (*Winnie the Pooh*, A. A. Milne)

RABBIT, 'Brer' (*Uncle Remus*, J. C. Harris)

RABBIT, The White (*Alice in Wonderland*, L. Carroll)

RIVERS, St John (*Jane Eyre*, Charlotte Brontë)

RUSTUM (*Sohrab and Rustum*, M. Arnold)

SAWYER, Tom (*The Adventures of Tom Sawyer*, M. Twain)

SHANDY, Tristram (*Tristram Shandy*, L. Sterne)

SILVER, Long John (*Treasure Island*, R. L. Stevenson)

SIMNEL, Lambert (*Perkin Warbeck*, John Ford)

SOHRAB (*Sohrab and Rustum*, M. Arnold)

TEMPLE, Miss (*Jane Eyre*, Charlotte Brontë)

THORNE, Dr Thomas (*Doctor Thorne*, A. Trollope)

THORPE, Isabella (*Northanger Abbey*, Jane Austen)

TILNEY, Henry (*Northanger Abbey*, Jane Austen)

TURNER, Jim (Captain Flint) (*Swallows and Amazons*, A. Ransome)

UMPOPA (*King Solomon's Mines*, H. Rider Haggard)

WALKER, John/Roger/Susan/Titty/Vicky (*Swallows and Amazons*, A. Ransome)

WESTON, Mrs (*Emma*, Jane Austen)

WILKES, Ashley/India (*Gone with the Wind*, Margaret Mitchell)

WIMSEY, Lord Peter Death Bredon (*Whose Body?*, Dorothy L. Sayers)

7

AISGILL, Alice (*Room at the Top*, J. Braine)

BAGSTER (*Middlemarch*, George Eliot)

BEESLEY (*Lucky Jim*, Kingsley Amis)

BINGLEY, Charles (*Pride and Prejudice*, Jane Austen)

BRANDON, Colonel (*Sense and Sensibility*, Jane Austen)

CANDOUR, Mrs (*The School for Scandal*, R. B. Sheridan)

CHESNEY, Jack (*Charley's Aunt*, Brandon Thomas)

COLLINS, Rev. William (*Pride and Prejudice*, Jane Austen)

CYPRESS, Mr (*Nightmare Abbey*, T. L. Peacock)

DANVERS, Mrs (*Rebecca*, Daphne du Maurier)

DESPAIR, Giant (*Pilgrim's Progress*, J. Bunyan)

DRACULA, Count (*Dracula*, Bram Stoker)

EPICENE (*Epicene*, B. Jonson)

FAIRFAX, Gwendolen (*The Importance of Being Earnest*, Oscar Wilde)

FAIRFAX, Jane (*Emma*, J. Austen)

FAIRFAX, Mrs (*Jane Eyre*, Charlotte Brontë)

FAIRLIE, Frederick (*Woman in White*, W. Collins)

FAUSTUS (*The History of Dr Faustus*, C. Marlowe)

7—continued

FORSYTE, Fleur/Irene/Jolyon/Jon/Soames (*The Forsyte Saga*, J. Galsworthy)

GALAHAD (*Idylls of the King*, Lord Tennyson)

GERAINT (*Idylls of the King*, Lord Tennyson)

GRANTLY, Bishop of Barchester (*The Warden, Barchester Towers*, A. Trollope)

HAWKINS, Jim (*Treasure Island*, R. L. Stevenson)

HENTZAU, Rupert of (*The Prisoner of Zenda*, A. Hope)

HERRIES, Francis (*Rogue Herries*, H. Walpole)

HIGGINS, Henry (*Pygmalion*, G. B. Shaw)

IVANHOE, Wilfred, Knight of (*Ivanhoe*, W. Scott)

JENKINS, Rev. Eli (*Under Milk Wood*, D. Thomas)

KEELDAR, Shirley (*Shirley*, Charlotte Brontë)

LAMPTON, Joe (*Room at the Top*, J. Braine)

LATIMER, Darsie (*Redgauntlet*, W. Scott)

LAWLESS (*The Black Arrow*, R. L. Stevenson)

LINCOLN, Abraham (*Abraham Lincoln*, J. Drinkwater)

LUCIFER (*Faustus*, C. Marlowe)

MARKHAM, Gilbert (*The Tenant of Wildfell Hall*, Anne Brontë)

MESSALA (*Ben Hur*, L. Wallace)

MICHAEL, Duke of Strelsau (*The Prisoner of Zenda*, A. Hope)

MINIVER, Mrs Caroline (*Mrs Miniver*, Jan Struther)

MORLAND, Catherine (*Northanger Abbey*, Jane Austen)

NOKOMIS (*Song of Hiawatha*, H. W. Longfellow)

PORTHOS (*The Three Musketeers*, Alexandre Dumas)

PROUDIE, Dr/Mrs (*Framley Parsonage*, A. Trollope)

RAFFLES, A. J. (*Raffles* series, E. W. Hornung)

RANDALL, Rebecca (*Rebecca of Sunnybrook Farm*, Kate D. Wiggin)

RATTLER, Martin (*Martin Rattler*, R. M. Ballantyne)

REBECCA (*Rebecca*, Daphne du Maurier)

REBECCA (*Rebecca of Sunnybrook Farm*, Kate D. Wiggin)

RED KING (*Alice Through the Looking Glass*, L. Carroll)

ROBSART, Amy (*Kenilworth*, W. Scott)

SANDERS (Sandi) (*Sanders of the River*, E. Wallace)

SHELTON, Richard (*The Black Arrow*, R. L. Stevenson)

SHIPTON, Mother (*The Luck of Roaring Camp*, Bret Harte)

SMOLLET, Captain (*Treasure Island*, R. L. Stevenson)

SORRELL, Christopher (Kit) (*Sorrell and Son*, W. Deeping)

ST CLARE, Evangeline (Little Eva) (*Uncle Tom's Cabin*, Harriet B. Stowe)

TIDDLER, Tom (*Adam's Opera*, Clemence Dane)

WARBECK, Perkin (*Perkin Warbeck*, John Ford)

7—continued

WESTERN, Mrs/Sophia/Squire, (*Tom Jones*, H. Fielding)

WILLIAM (*Just William*, Richmal Crompton)

WINSLOW, Ronnie (*The Winslow Boy*, T. Rattigan)

WOOSTER, Bertie (*Thank You, Jeeves*, P. G. Wodehouse)

8

ABSOLUTE, Sir Anthony (*The Rivals*, R. B. Sheridan)

ANGELICA (*The Rose and the Ring*, W. M. Thackeray)

APOLLYON (*Pilgrim's Progress*, J. Bunyan)

ARMITAGE, Jacob (*The Children of the New Forest*, Captain Marryat)

BACKBITE, Sir Benjamin (*The School for Scandal*, R. B. Sheridan)

BAGHEERA (*The Jungle Book*, R. Kipling)

BLACK DOG (*Treasure Island*, R. L. Stevenson)

CARRAWAY, Nick (*The Great Gatsby*, F. Scott Fitzgerald)

CASAUBON, Rev. Edward, (*Middlemarch*, George Eliot)

CRAWFURD, David (*Prester John*, J. Buchan)

CRICHTON, Bill (*The Admirable Crichton*, J. M. Barrie)

DASHWOOD, Henry (*Sense and Sensibility*, Jane Austen)

DE BOURGH, Lady Catherine (*Pride and Prejudice*, Jane Austen)

DE WINTER, Maximilian (*Rebecca*, Daphne du Maurier)

EARNSHAW, Catherine (*Wuthering Heights*, Emily Brontë)

EVERDENE, Bathsheba (*Far from the Madding Crowd*, T. Hardy)

FFOULKES, Sir Andrew (*The Scarlet Pimpernel*, Baroness Orczy)

FLANDERS, Moll (*Moll Flanders*, D. Defoe)

FLASHMAN (*Tom Brown's Schooldays*, T. Hughes)

GLORIANA (*The Faërie Queen*, E. Spenser)

GOLLANTZ, Emmanuel (*Young Emmanuel*, N. Jacob)

GULLIVER, Lemuel (*Gulliver's Travels*, J. Swift)

GUNGA DIN (*Barrack-room Ballads*, R. Kipling)

HIAWATHA (*The Song of Hiawatha*, H. W. Longfellow)

KNIGHTLY, George (*Emma*, J. Austen)

LANCELOT, Sir (*Idylls of the King*, Lord Tennyson)

LANGUISH, Lydia (*The Rivals*, R. B. Sheridan)

LAURENCE, Theodore (*Little Women*, Louisa M. Alcott)

LESSWAYS, Hilda (*The Clayhanger Trilogy*, Arnold Bennett)

LESTRADE, of Scotland Yard (*A Study in Scarlet*, A. Conan Doyle)

LOCKWOOD (*Wuthering Heights*, Emily Brontë)

8–continued

MACAVITY (*Old Possum's Book of Practical Cats*, T. S. Eliot)

MALAPROP, Mrs (*The Rivals*, R. B. Sheridan)

MARY JANE (*When We Were Very Young*, A. A. Milne)

MORIARTY, Professor James (*Memoirs of Sherlock Holmes*, A. Conan Doyle)

O'FERRALL, Trilby (*Trilby*, George du Maurier)

OLIFAUNT, Nigel (*The Fortunes of Nigel*, W. Scott)

O'TRIGGER, Sir Lucius (*The Rivals*, R. B. Sheridan)

PALLISER, Lady Glencora/Plantagenet (*Phineas Finn*, A. Trollope)

PRIMROSE, Dr Charles (*The Vicar of Wakefield*, O. Goldsmith)

QUANTOCK, Mrs Daisy (*Queen Lucia*, E. F. Benson)

RED QUEEN (*Alice Through the Looking Glass*, L. Carroll)

SHOTOVER, Captain (*Heartbreak House*, G. B. Shaw)

ST BUNGAY, Duke of (*Phineas Finn*, A. Trollope)

SVENGALI (*Trilby*, George du Maurier)

THATCHER, Becky (*The Adventures of Tom Sawyer*, M. Twain)

TRISTRAM (*Idylls of the King*, Lord Tennyson)

TULLIVER, Maggie/Tom (*The Mill on the Floss*, George Eliot)

VERINDER, Lady Julia (*The Moonstone*, W. Collins)

WATER RAT (Ratty) (*The Wind in the Willows*, K. Grahame)

WAVERLEY, Edward (*Waverley*, W. Scott)

WHITEOAK (family) (*The Whiteoak Chronicles*, Mazo de la Roche)

WHITE-TIP (*Tarka the Otter*, Henry Williamson)

WHITTIER, Pollyanna (*Pollyanna*, Eleanor H. Porter)

WILLIAMS, Percival William (*Wee Willie Winkie*, R. Kipling)

WORTHING, John (*The Importance of Being Earnest*, Oscar Wilde)

9

ABBEVILLE, Horace (*Cannery Row*, J. Steinbeck)

ABLEWHITE, Godfrey (*The Moonstone*, W. Collins)

ALLWORTHY, Squire (*Tom Jones*, H. Fielding)

BABBERLEY, Lord Fancourt (*Charley's Aunt*, Brandon Thomas)

BARRYMORE (*The Hound of the Baskervilles*, A. Conan Doyle)

BRACKNELL, Lady (*The Importance of Being Earnest*, Oscar Wilde)

BULSTRODE, Nicholas (*Middlemarch*, George Eliot)

CHAINMAIL (*Crotchet Castle*, T. L. Peacock)

CHRISTIAN (*Pilgrim's Progress*, J. Bunyan)

CHURCHILL, Frank (*Emma*, Jane Austen)

9–continued

D'ARTAGNAN (*The Three Musketeers*, Alexandre Dumas)

DOOLITTLE, Eliza (*Pygmalion*, G. B. Shaw)

GREYSTOKE, Lord (*Tarzan* series, E. R. Burroughs)

GUINEVERE (*Idylls of the King*, Lord Tennyson)

INDIAN JOE (*The Adventures of Tom Sawyer*, M. Twain)

LEICESTER, Earl of (*Kenilworth*, W. Scott)

MACGREGOR, Robin (*Rob Roy*, W. Scott)

MARCH HARE, The (*Alice in Wonderland*, L. Carroll)

MARCHMAIN, Lady Cordelia/Lady Julia/Lord Sebastian/ Marquis of/Teresa/The Earl of Brideshead (*Brideshead Revisited*, E. Waugh)

MEHITABEL, the cat (*Archy and Mehitabel*, D. Marquis)

MERRILIES, Meg (*Guy Mannering*, W. Scott)

MINNEHAHA (*The Song of Hiawatha*, H. W. Longfellow)

MONCRIEFF, Algernon (*The Importance of Being Earnest*, Oscar Wilde)

PENDENNIS, Arthur (Pen) (*Pendennis*, W. M. Thackeray)

PERCIVALE (*Idylls of the King*, Lord Tennyson)

RED KNIGHT (*Alice Through the Looking Glass*, L. Carroll)

ROCHESTER, Bertha/Edward Fairfax (*Jane Eyre*, Charlotte Brontë)

SHERE KHAN (Lungri) (*The Jungle Book*, R. Kipling)

SOUTHDOWN, Earl of (*Vanity Fair*, W. M. Thackeray)

TAMERLANE (*Tamerlane*, N. Rowe)

TANQUERAY, Aubrey (*The Second Mrs Tanqueray*, A. W. Pinero)

TIGER LILY (*Peter Pan*, J. M. Barrie)

TRELAWNEY, Rose (*Trelawney of the Wells*, A. W. Pinero)

TRELAWNEY, Squire (*Treasure Island*, R. L. Stevenson)

TWITCHETT, Mrs Tabitha (*The Tale of Tom Kitten*, Beatrix Potter)

VIRGINIAN, The (*The Virginian*, O. Wister)

WAYNFLETE, Lady Cicely (*Captain Brassbound's Conversion*, G. B. Shaw)

WOODHOUSE, Emma/Isabella (*Emma*, Jane Austen)

10

ABRAMS MOSS (*Pendennis*, W. M. Thackeray)

ALLAN-A-DALE (*Ivanhoe*, W. Scott)

ARROWPOINT (*Daniel Deronda*, George Eliot)

BELLADONNA (*Vanity Fair*, W. M. Thackeray)

CHALLENGER, Professor (*The Lost World*, A. Conan Doyle)

CRIMSWORTH, William (*The Professor*, Charlotte Brontë)

EVANGELINE (*Evangeline*, H. W. Longfellow)

FAUNTLEROY, Lord Cedric Errol (*Little Lord Fauntleroy*, F. H. Burnett)

10–continued

GOODFELLOW, Robin (*St Ronan's Well*, W. Scott)

HEATHCLIFF (*Wuthering Heights*, Emily Brontë)

HORNBLOWER, Horatio (The *Hornblower* series, C. S. Forester)

HUNCA MUNCA (*The Tale of Two Bad Mice*, Beatrix Potter)

HUNTER-DUNN, Joan (*A Subaltern's Love Song*, J. Betjeman)

JACKANAPES (*Jackanapes*, Juliana H. Ewing)

LETHBRIDGE, Daphne (*The Dark Tide*, Vera Brittain)

MAN IN BLACK (*A Citizen of the World*, O. Goldsmith)

MAULEVERER, Lord (*Cranford*, Mrs Gaskell)

MOCK TURTLE, THE (*Alice in Wonderland*, L. Carroll)

PUDDLEDUCK, Jemima (*The Tale of Jemima Puddleduck*, Beatrix Potter)

QUATERMAIN, Allan (*King Solomon's Mines*, H. Rider Haggard)

RASSENDYLL, Rudolf (*The Prisoner of Zenda*, A. Hope)

STARKADDER, Judith/Old Mrs (*Cold Comfort Farm*, Stella Gibbons)

TINKER BELL (*Peter Pan*, J. M. Barrie)

TWEEDLEDEE (*Alice Through the Looking-Glass*, L. Carroll)

TWEEDLEDUM (*Alice Through the Looking-Glass*, L. Carroll)

UNDERSHAFT, Barbara (*Major Barbara*, G. B. Shaw)

WILLOUGHBY, John (*Sense and Sensibility*, Jane Austen)

WINDERMERE, Lord Arthur/Margaret (*Lady Windermere's Fan*, Oscar Wilde)

11

ADDENBROOKE, Bennett (*Raffles*, E. W. Hornung)

DURBEYFIELD, Tess (*Tess of the D'Urbervilles*, T. Hardy)

JABBERWOCKY (*Alice Through the Looking-Glass*, L. Carroll)

11–continued

MACCROTCHET (*Crotchet Castle*, T. L. Peacock)

MONTMORENCY, the dog (*Three Men in a Boat*, J. K. Jerome)

REDGAUNTLET, Sir Arthur Darsie (*Redgauntlet*, W. Scott)

TAMBURLAINE (*Tamburlaine*, C. Marlowe)

TAM O'SHANTER (*Tam O'Shanter*, R. Burns)

TIGGY-WINKLE, Mrs (*The Tale of Mrs Tiggy-Winkle*, Beatrix Potter)

TITTLEMOUSE, Mrs Thomasina (*The Tale of Mrs Tittlemouse*, Beatrix Potter)

TRUMPINGTON, Lady (*The Virginians*, W. M. Thackeray)

12

BROCKLEHURST (*Jane Eyre*, Charlotte Brontë)

CAPTAIN FLINT (*Swallows and Amazons*, A. Ransome)

FRANKENSTEIN, Victor (*Frankenstein*, M. W. Shelley)

HUMPTY-DUMPTY (*Alice Through the Looking-Glass*, L. Carroll)

PENNYFEATHER, Paul (*Decline and Fall*, E. Waugh)

13

WINNIE-THE-POOH (Edward Bear) (*Winnie-the-Pooh*, A. A. Milne)

14

MEPHISTOPHELES (*Doctor Faustus*, C. Marlowe)

RIKKI-TIKKI-TAVI (*The Jungle Book*, R. Kipling)

SAMUEL WHISKERS (*The Tale of Samuel Whiskers*, Beatrix Potter)

WORLDLY-WISEMAN (*Pilgrim's Progress*, J. Bunyan)

15

OGMORE-PRITCHARD, Mrs (*Under Milk Wood*, D. Thomas)

VALIANT-FOR-TRUTH (*Pilgrim's Progress*, J. Bunyan)

VIOLET ELIZABETH (*Just William*, Richmal Crompton)

DICKENSIAN CHARACTERS

CHARACTER (Novel)

2

JO (*Bleak House*)

3

AMY (*Oliver Twist*)

BET, Betsy (*Oliver Twist*)

3–continued

BUD, Rosa (*Edwin Drood*)

CLY (*A Tale of Two Cities*)

GAY, Walter (*Dombey and Son*)

JOE (*Pickwick Papers*)

TOX, Miss (*Dombey and Son*)

4

ANNE (*Dombey and Son*)

4–continued

BAPS (*Dombey and Son*)

BEGS, Mrs Ridger (*David Copperfield*)

BRAY, Madeline (*Nicholas Nickleby*)

BRAY, Walter (*Nicholas Nickleby*)

4—continued

DICK, Mr (*Oliver Twist*)
DUFF (*Oliver Twist*)
FIPS, Mr (*Martin Chuzzlewit*)
FOGG (*Pickwick Papers*)
GAMP, Mrs Sarah (*Martin Chuzzlewit*)
GRIP (*Barnaby Rudge*)
HAWK, Sir Mulberry (*Nicholas Nickleby*)
HEEP, Uriah (*David Copperfield*)
HUGH (*Barnaby Rudge*)
JOWL, Mat (*The Old Curiosity Shop*)
JUPE, Cecilia (*Hard Times*)
KAGS (*Oliver Twist*)
KNAG, Miss (*Nicholas Nickleby*)
LIST, Isaac (*The Old Curiosity Shop*)
MANN, Mrs (*Oliver Twist*)
MARY (*Pickwick Papers*)
MELL, Charles (*David Copperfield*)
MIFF, Mrs (*Dombey and Son*)
OMER (*David Copperfield*)
PEAK (*Barnaby Rudge*)
PELL, Solomon (*Pickwick Papers*)
PEPS, Dr Parker (*Dombey and Son*)
POTT, Minverva (*Pickwick Papers*)
'RIAH (*Our Mutual Friend*)
RUGG, Anastasia (*Little Dorrit*)
TIGG, Montague (*Martin Chuzzlewit*)
WADE, Miss (*Little Dorrit*)
WEGG, Silas (*Our Mutual Friend*)

5

ADAMS, Jack (*Dombey and Son*)
ALLEN, Arabella/Benjamin (*Pickwick Papers*)
BATES, Charley (*Oliver Twist*)
BETSY (*Pickwick Papers*)
BRASS, Sally/Sampson (*The Old Curiosity Shop*)
BRICK, Jefferson (*Martin Chuzzlewit*)
BROWN, Alice/Mrs (*Dombey and Son*)
BUZUZ, Sergeant (*Pickwick Papers*)
CASBY, Christopher (*Little Dorrit*)
CHICK, John/Louisa (*Dombey and Son*)
CLARE, Ada (*Bleak House*)

5—continued

CLARK (*Dombey and Son*)
CLIVE (*Little Dorrit*)
CROWL (*Nicholas Nickleby*)
CRUPP, Mrs (*David Copperfield*)
DAISY, Solomon (*Barnaby Rudge*)
DAVID (*Nicholas Nickleby*)
DAWES, Mary (*Dombey and Son*)
DINGO, Professor (*Bleak House*)
DIVER, Colonel (*Martin Chuzzlewit*)
DONNY, Mrs (*Bleak House*)
DOYCE, Daniel (*Little Dorrit*)
DROOD, Edwin (*Edwin Drood*)
DUMPS, Nicodemus (*Pickwick Papers*)
FAGIN (*Oliver Twist*)
FLITE, Miss (*Bleak House*)
GILES (*Oliver Twist*)
GILLS, Solomon (*Dombey and Son*)
GOWAN, Harry (*Little Dorrit*)
GREEN, Tom (*Barnaby Rudge*)
GRIDE, Arthur (*Nicholas Nickleby*)
GUPPY, William (*Bleak House*)
HEXAM, Charlie/Jesse/Lizzie (*Our Mutual Friend*)
JANET (*David Copperfield*)
JONES, Mary (*Barnaby Rudge*)
KROOK (*Bleak House*)
LOBBS, Maria/'Old' (*Pickwick Papers*)
LORRY, Jarvis (*A Tale of Two Cities*)
LUCAS, Solomon (*Pickwick Papers*)
LUPIN, Mrs (*Martin Chuzzlewit*)
MEALY (*David Copperfield*)
'MELIA (*Dombey and Son*)
MIGGS, Miss (*Barnaby Rudge*)
MILLS, Julia (*David Copperfield*)
MOLLY (*Great Expectations*)
MOULD (*Martin Chuzzlewit*)
NANCY (*Oliver Twist*)
NANDY, John Edward (*Little Dorrit*)
NOGGS, Newman (*Nicholas Nickleby*)
PERCH (*Dombey and Son*)
PINCH, Ruth/Tom (*Martin Chuzzlewit*)
PRICE, 'Tilda (*Nicholas Nickleby*)
PROSS, Miss/Solomon (*A Tale of Two Cities*)
QUALE (*Bleak House*)

5—continued

QUILP, Daniel (*The Old Curiosity Shop*)
RUDGE, Barnaby/Mary (*Barnaby Rudge*)
SALLY, Old (*Oliver Twist*)
SCOTT, Tom (*The Old Curiosity Shop*)
SHARP (*David Copperfield*)
SIKES, Bill (*Oliver Twist*)
SLURK (*Pickwick Papers*)
SLYME, Chevy (*Martin Chuzzlewit*)
SMIKE (*Nicholas Nickleby*)
SNOBB, The Hon (*Nicholas Nickleby*)
SQUOD, Phil (*Bleak House*)
STAGG (*Barnaby Rudge*)
TOOTS, Mr P (*Dombey and Son*)
TRABB (*Great Expectations*)
TRENT, Frederick/Nellie (*The Old Curiosity Shop*)
TWIST, Oliver (*Oliver Twist*)
VENUS, Mr (*Our Mutual Friend*)
WATTY (*Pickwick Papers*)

6

BADGER, Dr Bayham/Laura/Malta/Matthew/Quebec/Woolwich (*Bleak House*)
BAILEY, Benjamin (*Martin Chuzzlewit*)
BAILEY, Captain (*David Copperfield*)
BAMBER, Jack (*Pickwick Papers*)
BANTAM, Angelo Cyrus (*Pickwick Papers*)
BARKER, Phil (*Oliver Twist*)
BARKIS (*David Copperfield*)
BARLEY, Clara (*Great Expectations*)
BARNEY (*Oliver Twist*)
BEDWIN, Mrs (*Oliver Twist*)
BETSEY, Jane (*Dombey and Son*)
BITZER (*Hard Times*)
BOFFIN, Henrietta/Nicodemus (*Our Mutual Friend*)
BONNEY (*Nicholas Nickleby*)
BRIGGS (*Dombey and Son*)
BUMBLE (*Oliver Twist*)
BUNSBY, Captain (*Dombey and Son*)
CARKER, Harriet/James/John (*Dombey and Son*)
CARTON, Sydney (*A Tale of Two Cities*)
CHEGGS, Alick (*The Old Curiosity Shop*)

6–continued

CLARKE (*Pickwick Papers*)
CODGER, Mrs (*Martin Chuzzlewit*)
CODLIN, Thomas (*The Old Curiosity Shop*)
CONWAY, General (*Barnaby Rudge*)
CORNEY, Mrs (*Oliver Twist*)
CURDLE (*Nicholas Nickleby*)
CUTLER, Mr/Mrs (*Nicholas Nickleby*)
CUTTLE, Captain Ned (*Dombey and Son*)
DARNAY, Charles (*A Tale of Two Cities*)
DARTLE, Rosa (*David Copperfield*)
DENNIS, Ned (*Barnaby Rudge*)
DIBABS, Mrs (*Nicholas Nickleby*)
DODSON (*Pickwick Papers*)
DOMBEY, Fanny/Florence/Louisa/Paul (*Dombey and Son*)
DORKER (*Nicholas Nickleby*)
DORRIT, Amy/Edward/Fanny/Frederick/William (*Little Dorrit*)
DOWLER, Captain (*Pickwick Papers*)
FEEDER (*Dombey and Son*)
FEENIX (*Dombey and Son*)
FIZKIN, Horatio (*Pickwick Papers*)
FOLIAR (*Nicholas Nickleby*)
GEORGE (*The Old Curiosity Shop*)
GEORGE (*Pickwick Papers*)
GEORGE, Mr (*Bleak House*)
GORDON, Lord George (*Barnaby Rudge*)
GRAHAM, Mary (*Martin Chuzzlewit*)
GROVES, 'Honest' James (*The Old Curiosity Shop*)
GUNTER (*Pickwick Papers*)
HARMON, John (*Our Mutual Friend*)
HARRIS, Mrs (*Martin Chuzzlewit*)
HAWDON, Captain (*Bleak House*)
HIGDEN, Betty (*Our Mutual Friend*)
HOMINY, Major (*Martin Chuzzlewit*)
HOWLER, Rev M (*Dombey and Son*)
JARLEY, Mrs (*The Old Curiosity Shop*)
JASPER, Jack (*Edwin Drood*)
JINGLE, Alfred (*Pickwick Papers*)
KETTLE, La Fayette (*Martin Chuzzlewit*)
LAMMLE, Alfred (*Our Mutual Friend*)
LOBLEY (*Edwin Drood*)
LUMLEY, Dr (*Nicholas Nickleby*)
MAGNUS, Peter (*Pickwick Papers*)
MALDEN, Jack (*David Copperfield*)
MARLEY, Jacob (*A Christmas Carol*)
MARTON (*The Old Curiosity Shop*)
MAYLIE, Harrie/Mrs/Rose (*Oliver Twist*)
MERDLE, Mr (*Little Dorrit*)
MILVEY, Rev Frank (*Our Mutual Friend*)
MIVINS (*Pickwick Papers*)
MODDLE, Augustus (*Martin Chuzzlewit*)
MORFIN (*Dombey and Son*)
MULLET, Professor (*Martin Chuzzlewit*)
NIPPER, Susan (*Dombey and Son*)
PANCKS (*Little Dorrit*)
PERKER (*Pickwick Papers*)
PHUNKY (*Pickwick Papers*)
PIPKIN, Nathaniel (*Pickwick Papers*)
PIRRIP, Philip (*Great Expectations*)

6–continued

POCKET, Herbert/Matthew/Sarah (*Great Expectations*)
POGRAM, Elijah (*Martin Chuzzlewit*)
RADDLE, Mr and Mrs (*Pickwick Papers*)
RIGAUD, Monsieur (*Little Dorrit*)
SAPSEA, Thomas (*Edwin Drood*)
SAWYER, Bob (*Pickwick Papers*)
SCALEY (*Nicholas Nickleby*)
SLEARY, Josephine (*Hard Times*)
'SLOPPY' (*Our Mutual Friend*)
SOWNDS (*Dombey and Son*)
STRONG, Dr (*David Copperfield*)
TACKER (*Martin Chuzzlewit*)
TAPLEY, Mark (*Martin Chuzzlewit*)
TARTAR (*Edwin Drood*)
TIPPIN, Lady (*Our Mutual Friend*)
TISHER, Mrs (*Edwin Drood*)
TOODLE (*Dombey and Son*)
TUPMAN, Tracy (*Pickwick Papers*)
VARDEN, Dolly/Gabriel (*Barnaby Rudge*)
VHOLES (*Bleak House*)
VUFFIN (*The Old Curiosity Shop*)
WALKER, Mick (*David Copperfield*)
WARDLE, Emily/Isabella/Mr/Rachel (*Pickwick Papers*)
WELLER, Sam/Tony (*Pickwick Papers*)
WILFER, Bella/Lavinia/Reginald (*Our Mutual Friend*)
WILLET, Joe/John (*Barnaby Rudge*)
WINKLE, Nathaniel (*Pickwick Papers*)
WOPSLE (*Great Expectations*)

7

BAILLIE, Gabriel (*Pickwick Papers*)
BANGHAM, Mrs (*Little Dorrit*)
BARBARA (*The Old Curiosity Shop*)
BARBARY, Miss (*Bleak House*)
BARDELL, Mrs Martha/Tommy (*Pickwick Papers*)
BAZZARD (*Edwin Drood*)
BELLING, Master (*Nicholas Nickleby*)
BLIMBER, Dr (*Dombey and Son*)
BLOTTON (*Pickwick Papers*)
BOBSTER, Cecilia/Mr (*Nicholas Nickleby*)
BOLDWIG, Captain (*Pickwick Papers*)
BROGLEY (*Dombey and Son*)
BROOKER (*Nicholas Nickleby*)
BROWDIE, John (*Nicholas Nickleby*)
BULLAMY (*Martin Chuzzlewit*)
CHARLEY (*David Copperfield*)
CHESTER, Edward/Sir John (*Barnaby Rudge*)
CHILLIP, Dr (*David Copperfield*)
CHIVERY, John (*Little Dorrit*)
CHOLLOP, Hannibal (*Martin Chuzzlewit*)
CHUFFEY (*Martin Chuzzlewit*)
CLEAVER, Fanny (*Our Mutual Friend*)
CLENNAM, Arthur (*Little Dorrit*)
CLUBBER, Sir Thomas (*Pickwick Papers*)
CRACKIT, Toby (*Oliver Twist*)
CRAWLEY, Young Mr (*Pickwick Papers*)
CREAKLE (*David Copperfield*)

7–continued

CREWLER, Mrs/Rev Horace/Sophy (*David Copperfield*)
CRIMPLE, David (*Martin Chuzzlewit*)
CROOKEY (*Pickwick Papers*)
DAWKINS, Jack (*Oliver Twist*)
DEDLOCK, Sir Leicester/Volumnia (*Bleak House*)
DEFARGE, Madame (*A Tale of Two Cities*)
DOLLOBY (*David Copperfield*)
DRUMMLE, Bentley (*Great Expectations*)
DUBBLEY (*Pickwick Papers*)
DURDLES (*Edwin Drood*)
EDMUNDS, John (*Pickwick Papers*)
ESTELLA (*Great Expectations*)
FLEMING, Agnes (*Oliver Twist*)
GABELLE, Theophile (*A Tale of Two Cities*)
GARGERY, Biddy/Joe/Pip (*Great Expectations*)
GARLAND, Abel/Mrs/Mr (*The Old Curiosity Shop*)
GASPARD (*A Tale of Two Cities*)
GAZINGI, Miss (*Nicholas Nickleby*)
GENERAL, Mrs (*Little Dorrit*)
GILBERT, Mark (*Barnaby Rudge*)
GRANGER, Edith (*Dombey and Son*)
GRIDLEY (*Bleak House*)
GRIMWIG (*Oliver Twist*)
GRUDDEN, Mrs (*Nicholas Nickleby*)
HAGGAGE, Dr (*Little Dorrit*)
HEYLING, George (*Pickwick Papers*)
JAGGERS (*Great Expectations*)
JELLYBY, Caddy/Mrs/Peepy (*Bleak House*)
JINKINS (*Martin Chuzzlewit*)
JOBLING, Dr John (*Martin Chuzzlewit*)
JOBLING, Tony (*Bleak House*)
JOHNSON, Mr (*Nicholas Nickleby*)
JORKINS (*David Copperfield*)
KEDGICK, Captain (*Martin Chuzzlewit*)
KENWIGS, Morleena (*Nicholas Nickleby*)
LARKINS, Mr (*David Copperfield*)
LEEFORD, Edward (*Oliver Twist*)
LEWSOME (*Martin Chuzzlewit*)
MALLARD (*Pickwick Papers*)
MANETTE, Dr/Lucie (*A Tale of Two Cities*)
MEAGLES (*Little Dorrit*)
MINERVA (*Pickwick Papers*)
MOWCHER, Miss (*David Copperfield*)
NADGETT (*Martin Chuzzlewit*)
NECKETT, Charlotte/Emma/Tom (*Bleak House*)
NUBBLES, Christopher (*The Old Curiosity Shop*)
NUPKINS, George (*Pickwick Papers*)
PAWKINS, Major (*Martin Chuzzlewit*)
PILKINS, Dr (*Dombey and Son*)
PIPCHIN, Mrs (*Dombey and Son*)
PODSNAP, Georgiana/Mr (*Our Mutual Friend*)
QUINION (*David Copperfield*)
SAMPSON, George (*Our Mutual Friend*)
SCADDER, Zephaniah (*Martin Chuzzlewit*)
SCROOGE, Ebenezer (*A Christmas Carol*)
SIMMONS, William (*Martin Chuzzlewit*)
SKEWTON, Hon Mrs (*Dombey and Son*)
SKYLARK, Mr (*David Copperfield*)
SLAMMER, Dr (*Pickwick Papers*)

7–continued

SLUMKEY, Hon Samuel (*Pickwick Papers*)
SNAGSBY (*Bleak House*)
SNAWLEY (*Nicholas Nickleby*)
SNUBBIN, Sergeant (*Pickwick Papers*)
SPARSIT, Mrs (*Hard Times*)
SPENLOW, Dora (*David Copperfield*)
SQUEERS, Fanny/Wackford (*Nicholas Nickleby*)
STARTOP (*Great Expectations*)
STRYVER, C J (*A Tale of Two Cities*)
TAMAROO, Miss (*Martin Chuzzlewit*)
TODGERS, Mrs (*Martin Chuzzlewit*)
TROTTER, Job (*Pickwick Papers*)
TRUNDLE (*Pickwick Papers*)
WACKLES, Jane/Melissa/Sophie (*The Old Curiosity Shop*)
WATKINS (*Nicholas Nickleby*)
WEMMICK (*Great Expectations*)
WICKHAM, Mrs (*Dombey and Son*)
WITHERS (*Dombey and Son*)

8

AKERSHEM, Sophronia (*Our Mutual Friend*)
BAGSTOCK, Major (*Dombey and Son*)
BARNWELL, B B (*Martin Chuzzlewit*)
BILLIKIN, Mrs (*Edwin Drood*)
BLATHERS (*Oliver Twist*)
BOYTHORN, Lawrence (*Bleak House*)
BRAVASSA, Miss (*Nicholas Nickleby*)
BROWNLOW, Mr (*Oliver Twist*)
CLAYPOLE, Noah (*Oliver Twist*)
CLUPPINS (*Pickwick Papers*)
CRADDOCK, Mrs (*Pickwick Papers*)
CRATCHIT, Belinda/Bob/Tiny Tim (*A Christmas Carol*)
CRIPPLES, Mr (*Little Dorrit*)
CRUMMLES, Ninetta/Vincent (*Nicholas Nickleby*)
CRUNCHER, Jeremiah/Jerry (*A Tale of Two Cities*)
CRUSHTON, Hon Mr (*Pickwick Papers*)
DATCHERY, Dick (*Edwin Drood*)
D'AULNAIS (*A Tale of Two Cities*)
FINCHING, Mrs Flora (*Little Dorrit*)
FLEDGEBY, Old/Young (*Our Mutual Friend*)
GASHFORD (*Barnaby Rudge*)
HAREDALE, Emma/Geoffrey/Reuben (*Barnaby Rudge*)
HAVISHAM, Miss (*Great Expectations*)
HORTENSE (*Bleak House*)
JARNDYCE, John (*Bleak House*)
LA CREEVY, Miss (*Nicholas Nickleby*)
LANDLESS, Helena/Neville (*Edwin Drood*)
LANGDALE (*Barnaby Rudge*)
LENVILLE (*Nicholas Nickleby*)
LITTIMER (*David Copperfield*)
LOSBERNE (*Oliver Twist*)
MAGWITCH, Abel (*Great Expectations*)
MARY ANNE (*David Copperfield*)
MATTHEWS (*Nicholas Nickleby*)
MICAWBER, Wilkins (*David Copperfield*)
MUTANHED, Lord (*Pickwick Papers*)

DICKENSIAN CHARACTERS

8—continued

NICKLEBY, Godfrey/Kate/Nicholas/Ralph (*Nicholas Nickleby*)
PEGGOTTY, Clara/Daniel/Ham/Little Em'ly (*David Copperfield*)
PICKWICK, Samuel (*Pickwick Papers*)
PLORNISH, Thomas (*Little Dorrit*)
POTATOES (*David Copperfield*)
SCADGERS, Lady (*Pickwick Papers*)
SKIFFINS, Miss (*Great Expectations*)
SKIMPOLE, Arethusa/Harold/Kitty/Laura (*Bleak House*)
SKITTLES, Sir Barnet (*Dombey and Son*)
SMIGGERS, Joseph (*Pickwick Papers*)
SPARKLER, Edmund (*Little Dorrit*)
STIGGINS (*Pickwick Papers*)
TRADDLES, Tom (*David Copperfield*)
TROTWOOD, Betsey (*David Copperfield*)
WESTLOCK, John (*Martin Chuzzlewit*)
WRAYBURN, Eugene (*Our Mutual Friend*)

9

BELVAWNEY, Miss (*Nicholas Nickleby*)
BERINTHIA (*Dombey and Son*)
BLACKPOOL, Stephen (*Hard Times*)
BOUNDERBY, Josiah (*Hard Times*)
CHARLOTTE (*Oliver Twist*)
CHEERYBLE, Charles/Frank/Ned (*Nicholas Nickleby*)
CHICKWEED, Conkey (*Oliver Twist*)
CHUCKSTER (*The Old Curiosity Shop*)
COMPEYSON (*Great Expectations*)
FIBBITSON, Mrs (*David Copperfield*)
GRADGRIND, Louisa/Thomas (*Hard Times*)
GREGSBURY (*Nicholas Nickleby*)
GREWGIOUS (*Edwin Drood*)
HARTHOUSE, James (*Hard Times*)
HEADSTONE, Bradley (*Our Mutual Friend*)
LIGHTWOOD, Mortimer (*Our Mutual Friend*)
LILLYVICK (*Nicholas Nickleby*)
MANTALINI, Mr (*Nicholas Nickleby*)
MURDSTONE, Edward/Jane (*David Copperfield*)
OLD BARLEY (*Great Expectations*)
PARDIGGLE, Francis/O A (*Bleak House*)
PECKSNIFF, Charity/Mercy/Seth (*Martin Chuzzlewit*)
PRISCILLA (*Bleak House*)
RIDERHOOD, Pleasant/Roger (*Our Mutual Friend*)
SMALLWEED, Bartholomew/Joshua/Judy (*Bleak House*)
SMORLTORK, Count (*Pickwick Papers*)

9—continued

SNODGRASS, Augustus (*Pickwick Papers*)
SUMMERSON, Esther (*Bleak House*)
SWIVELLER, Richard (*The Old Curiosity Shop*)
TAPPERTIT, Simon (*Barnaby Rudge*)
VENEERING, Anastasia/Hamilton (*Our Mutual Friend*)
VERISOPHT, Lord Frederick (*Nicholas Nickleby*)
WICKFIELD, Agnes/Mr (*David Copperfield*)
WITHERDEN, Mr (*The Old Curiosity Shop*)
WOODCOURT, Allan (*Bleak House*)

10

AYRESLEIGH, Mr (*Pickwick Papers*)
CHUZZLEWIT, Anthony/Diggory/George/Jonas/Martin/Mrs Ned/Toby (*Martin Chuzzlewit*)
CRISPARKLE, Rev Septimus (*Edwin Drood*)
FLINTWINCH, Affery/Ephraim/Jeremiah (*Little Dorrit*)
MACSTINGER, Mrs (*Dombey and Son*)
ROUNCEWELL, Mrs (*Bleak House*)
SNEVELLICI, Miss (*Nicholas Nickleby*)
SOWERBERRY (*Oliver Twist*)
STARELEIGH, Justice (*Pickwick Papers*)
STEERFORTH, James (*David Copperfield*)
TATTYCORAM (*Little Dorrit*)
TURVEYDROP, Prince (*Bleak House*)
TWINKLETON, Miss (*Edwin Drood*)
WATERBROOK (*David Copperfield*)
WITITTERLY, Julia (*Nicholas Nickleby*)

11

COPPERFIELD, Clara/David (*David Copperfield*)
'DISMAL JIMMY' (*Pickwick Papers*)
'GAME CHICKEN', The (*Dombey and Son*)
MARCHIONESS, The (*The Old Curiosity Shop*)
PUMBLECHOOK (*Great Expectations*)
SPOTTLETOES, Mrs (*Martin Chuzzlewit*)
ST EVREMONDE, Marquis de/Marquise de (*A Tale of Two Cities*)
SWEEDLEPIPE, Paul (*Martin Chuzzlewit*)
TULKINGHORN (*Bleak House*)

12

HONEYTHUNDER, Luke (*Edwin Drood*)
'SHINY WILLIAM' (*Pickwick Papers*)
SWEET WILLIAM (*The Old Curiosity Shop*)
TITE-BARNACLE, Clarence/Ferdinand/Junior/Lord Decimus/Mr (*Little Dorrit*)

15

VON KOELDWETHOUT (*Nicholas Nickleby*)

SHAKESPEAREAN CHARACTERS

CHARACTER (*Play*)

3
HAL (*1 Henry IV*)
NYM (*Henry V, The Merry Wives of Windsor*)

4
ADAM (*As You Like It*)
AJAX (*Troilus and Cressida*)
EROS (*Antony and Cleopatra*)
FORD, Mistress (*The Merry Wives of Windsor*)
GREY (*Henry V*)
HERO (*Much Ado About Nothing*)
IAGO (*Othello*)
IRAS (*Antony and Cleopatra*)
LEAR (*King Lear*)
PAGE, Mistress (*The Merry Wives of Windsor*)
PETO (*2 Henry IV*)
PUCK (*A Midsummer Night's Dream*)
SNUG (*A Midsummer Night's Dream*)

5
AARON (*Titus Andronicus*)
ARIEL (*The Tempest*)
BELCH, Sir Toby (*Twelfth Night*)
BLUNT (*2 Henry IV*)
CAIUS, Doctor (*The Merry Wives of Windsor*)
CELIA (*As You Like It*)
CLEON (*Pericles*)
CORIN (*As You Like It*)
DIANA (*All's Well that Ends Well*)
EDGAR (*King Lear*)
ELBOW (*Measure for Measure*)
FESTE (*Twelfth Night*)
FLUTE (*A Midsummer Night's Dream*)
FROTH (*Measure for Measure*)
GOBBO, Launcelot (*The Merchant of Venice*)
JULIA (*The Two Gentlemen of Verona*)
LAFEW (*All's Well That Ends Well*)
MARIA (*Love's Labour's Lost, Twelfth Night*)
PARIS (*Troilus and Cressida*)
PERCY (*1 Henry IV*)
PHEBE (*As You Like It*)
PINCH (*The Comedy of Errors*)

5–continued
POINS (*1 Henry IV, 2 Henry IV*)
PRIAM (*Troilus and Cressida*)
REGAN (*King Lear*)
ROMEO (*Romeo and Juliet*)
SNOUT (*A Midsummer Night's Dream*)
TIMON (*Timon of Athens*)
TITUS (*Titus Andronicus*)
VIOLA (*Twelfth Night*)

6
AEGEON (*The Comedy of Errors*)
ALONSO (*The Tempest*)
ANGELO (*Measure for Measure*)
ANTONY (*Antony and Cleopatra*)
ARCITE (*The Two Noble Kinsmen*)
ARMADO (*Love's Labour's Lost*)
AUDREY (*As You Like It*)
BANQUO (*Macbeth*)
BIANCA (*The Taming of the Shrew, Othello*)
BOTTOM (*A Midsummer Night's Dream*)
BRUTUS (*Coriolanus, Julius Caesar*)
CASSIO (*Othello*)
CHIRON (*Titus Andronicus*)
CLOTEN (*Cymbeline*)
DENNIS (*As You Like It*)
DROMIO (*The Comedy of Errors*)
DUMAIN (*Love's Labour's Lost*)
DUNCAN (*Macbeth*)
EDMUND (*King Lear*)
EMILIA (*Othello, The Two Noble Kinsmen*)
FABIAN (*Twelfth Night*)
FENTON (*The Merry Wives of Windsor*)
FULVIA (*Antony and Cleopatra*)
HAMLET (*Hamlet*)
HECATE (*Macbeth*)
HECTOR (*Troilus and Cressida*)
HELENA (*A Midsummer Night's Dream, All's Well That Ends Well*)
HERMIA (*A Midsummer Night's Dream*)
IMOGEN (*Cymbeline*)
JULIET (*Romeo and Juliet, Measure for Measure*)

6–continued
LUCIUS (*Titus Andronicus*)
MARINA (*Pericles*)
MUTIUS (*Titus Andronicus*)
OBERON (*A Midsummer Night's Dream*)
OLIVER (*As You Like It*)
OLIVIA (*Twelfth Night*)
ORSINO (*Twelfth Night*)
OSWALD (*King Lear*)
PISTOL (*2 Henry IV, Henry V, The Merry Wives of Windsor*)
POMPEY (*Measure for Measure, Antony and Cleopatra*)
PORTIA (*The Merchant of Venice*)
QUINCE (*A Midsummer Night's Dream*)
RUMOUR (*2 Henry IV*)
SCROOP (*Henry V*)
SILVIA (*The Two Gentlemen of Verona*)
TAMORA (*Titus Andronicus*)
THASIA (*Pericles*)
THURIO (*The Two Gentlemen of Verona*)
TYBALT (*Romeo and Juliet*)
VERGES (*Much Ado About Nothing*)

7
ADRIANA (*The Comedy of Errors*)
AEMILIA (*The Comedy of Errors*)
AGRIPPA (*Antony and Cleopatra*)
ALARBUS (*Titus Andronicus*)
ANTONIO (*The Merchant of Venice, The Tempest*)
BEROWNE (*Love's Labour's Lost*)
BERTRAM (*All's Well That Ends Well*)
CALCHAS (*Troilus and Cressida*)
CALIBAN (*The Tempest*)
CAPULET (*Romeo and Juliet*)
CESARIO (*Twelfth Night*)
CLAUDIO (*Much Ado About Nothing, Measure for Measure*)
COSTARD (*Love's Labour's Lost*)
DIONYZA (*Pericles*)
DOUGLAS (*1 Henry IV*)
ESCALUS (*Measure for Measure*)

7–continued

FLAVIUS (*Timon of Athens*)
FLEANCE (*Macbeth*)
GONERIL (*King Lear*)
GONZALO (*The Tempest*)
HORATIO (*Hamlet*)
HOTSPUR (*1 Henry IV*)
IACHIMO (*Cymbeline*)
JACQUES (*As You Like It*)
JESSICA (*The Merchant of Venice*)
LAERTES (*Hamlet*)
LAVINIA (*Titus Andronicus*)
LEONTES (*The Winter's Tale*)
LORENZO (*The Merchant of Venice*)
LUCIANA (*The Comedy of Errors*)
MACBETH (*Macbeth*)
MACDUFF (*Macbeth*)
MALCOLM (*Macbeth*)
MARIANA (*Measure for Measure, All's Well That Ends Well*)
MARTIUS (*Titus Andronicus*)
MIRANDA (*The Tempest*)
NERISSA (*The Merchant of Venice*)
OCTAVIA (*Antony and Cleopatra*)
OPHELIA (*Hamlet*)
ORLANDO (*As You Like It*)
OTHELLO (*Othello*)
PALAMON (*The Two Noble Kinsmen*)
PAULINA (*The Winter's Tale*)
PERDITA (*The Winter's Tale*)
PISANIO (*Cymbeline*)
PROTEUS (*The Two Gentlemen of Verona*)
QUICKLY, Mistress (*1 Henry IV, 2 Henry IV, The Merry Wives of Windsor*)
QUINTUS (*Titus Andronicus*)
SHALLOW, Justice (*2 Henry IV, The Merry Wives of Windsor*)
SHYLOCK (*The Merchant of Venice*)
SILENCE (*2 Henry IV*)
SILVIUS (*As You Like It*)
SLENDER (*The Merry Wives of Windsor*)
SOLINUS (*The Comedy of Errors*)
THESEUS (*A Midsummer Night's Dream, The Two Noble Kinsmen*)
TITANIA (*A Midsummer Night's Dream*)
TROILUS (*Troilus and Cressida*)

7–continued

ULYSSES (*Troilus and Cressida*)
WILLIAM (*As You Like It*)

8

ACHILLES (*Troilus and Cressida*)
AUFIDIUS (*Coriolanus*)
BAPTISTA (*The Taming of the Shrew*)
BARDOLPH (*Henry IV, Henry V, The Merry Wives of Windsor*)
BASSANIO (*The Merchant of Venice*)
BEATRICE (*Much Ado About Nothing*)
BELARIUS (*Cymbeline*)
BENEDICK (*Much Ado About Nothing*)
BENVOLIO (*Romeo and Juliet*)
CHARMIAN (*Antony and Cleopatra*)
CLAUDIUS (*Hamlet*)
COMINIUS (*Coriolanus*)
CORDELIA (*King Lear*)
CRESSIDA (*Troilus and Cressida*)
DIOMEDES (*Antony and Cleopatra, Troilus and Cressida*)
DOGBERRY (*Much Ado About Nothing*)
DON PEDRO (*Much Ado About Nothing*)
FALSTAFF (*The Merry Wives of Windsor, Henry IV*)
FLORIZEL (*The Winter's Tale*)
GERTRUDE (*Hamlet*)
GRATIANO (*The Merchant of Venice*)
HERMIONE (*The Winter's Tale*)
ISABELLA (*Measure for Measure*)
LUCENTIO (*The Taming of the Shrew*)
LYSANDER (*A Midsummer Night's Dream*)
MALVOLIO (*Twelfth Night*)
MENENIUS (*Coriolanus*)
MERCUTIO (*Romeo and Juliet*)
MONTAGUE (*Romeo and Juliet*)
MORTIMER (*1 Henry IV*)
OCTAVIUS (*Antony and Cleopatra*)
PANDARUS (*Troilus and Cressida*)
PAROLLES (*All's Well That Ends Well*)
PERICLES (*Pericles*)

8–continued

PHILOTEN (*Pericles*)
POLONIUS (*Hamlet*)
PROSPERO (*The Tempest*)
RODERIGO (*Othello*)
ROSALIND (*As You Like It*)
ROSALINE (*Love's Labour's Lost*)
SICINIUS (*Coriolanus*)
STEPHANO (*The Tempest*)
TRINCULO (*The Tempest*)
VIOLENTA (*All's Well That Ends Well*)
VOLUMNIA (*Coriolanus*)

9

AGUECHEEK, Sir Andrew (*Twelfth Night*)
ANTIOCHUS (*Pericles*)
ARVIRAGUS (*Cymbeline*)
BASSIANUS (*Titus Andronicus*)
BRABANTIO (*Othello*)
CAMBRIDGE (*Henry V*)
CLEOPATRA (*Antony and Cleopatra*)
CYMBELINE (*Cymbeline*)
DEMETRIUS (*A Midsummer Night's Dream, Antony and Cleopatra, Titus Andronicus*)
DESDEMONA (*Othello*)
ENOBARBUS (*Antony and Cleopatra*)
FERDINAND (*Loves Labours Lost, The Tempest*)
FREDERICK (*As You Like It*)
GLENDOWER, Owen (*1 Henry IV*)
GUIDERIUS (*Cymbeline*)
HELICANUS (*Pericles*)
HIPPOLYTA (*A Midsummer Night's Dream, The Two Noble Kinsmen*)
HORTENSIO (*The Taming of the Shrew*)
KATHERINA (*The Taming of the Shrew*)
KATHERINE (*Henry V, Love's Labour's Lost*)
MAMILLIUS (*The Winter's Tale*)
PATROCLUS (*Troilus and Cressida*)
PETRUCHIO (*The Taming of the Shrew*)
POLIXENES (*The Winter's Tale*)
SEBASTIAN (*The Tempest, Twelfth Night*)
TEARSHEET, Doll (*2 Henry IV*)
VALENTINE (*The Two Gentlemen of Verona*)

9–continued
VINCENTIO (*Measure for Measure, The Taming of the Shrew*)

10
ALCIBIADES (*Timon of Athens*)
ANTIPHOLUS (*The Comedy of Errors*)
CORIOLANUS (*Coriolanus*)
FORTINBRAS (*Hamlet*)
JAQUENETTA (*Love's Labour's Lost*)
LONGAVILLE (*Love's Labour's Lost*)
LYSIMACHUS (*Pericles*)

10–continued
POSTHUMOUS (*Cymbeline*)
SATURNINUS (*Titus Andronicus*)
TOUCHSTONE (*As You Like It*)

11
ROSENCRANTZ (*Hamlet*)

12
GUILDENSTERN (*Hamlet*)

14
CHRISTOPHER SLY (*The Taming of the Shrew*)

CHARACTERS FROM JANE AUSTEN

CHARACTER (Novel)

ALLEN, Mr/Mrs (*Northanger Abbey*)
BATES, Mrs (*Emma*)
BENNET, Jane/Elizabeth/Catherine/Mary/Lydia (*Pride and Prejudice*)
BENWICK, Captain (*Persuasion*)
BERTRAM, Lady Maria/Sir Thomas/ Rev Edmund/Maria/Julia (*Mansfield Park*)
BINGLEY, Charles/Caroline/Louisa (*Pride and Prejudice*)
BRANDON, Colonel (*Sense and Sensibility*)
CAMPBELL, Colonel/Jane (*Emma*)
CHURCHILL, Frank (*Emma*)
CLAY, Mrs (*Persuasion*)
COLLINS, Rev William (*Pride and Prejudice*)
CRAWFORD, Henry/Mary/Admiral (*Mansfield Park*)
CROFT, Admiral (*Persuasion*)
DARCY, Fitzwilliam/Lady Anne/Georgiana (*Pride and Prejudice*)
DASHWOOD, Henry/John/Fanny/Elinor/Marianne/Margaret (*Sense and Sensibility*)
DE BOURGH, Lady Catherine (*Pride and Prejudice*)
DIXON, Mr (*Emma*)
ELTON (*Emma*)
FAIRFAX, Jane (*Emma*)
FERRARS, Edward/Robert (*Sense and Sensibility*)
FITZWILLIAM, Colonel (*Pride and Prejudice*)
FORSTER, Colonel/Harriet (*Pride and Prejudice*)
GARDINER, Edward (*Pride and Prejudice*)
GODDARD, Mrs (*Emma*)
GRANT, Rev Dr (*Mansfield Park*)
HARVILLE, Captain (*Persuasion*)
HAYTER, Mrs (*Persuasion*)

HURST, Louisa (*Pride and Prejudice*)
JENNINGS, Mrs (*Sense and Sensibility*)
KNIGHTLEY, George/John/Isabella (*Emma*)
LUCAS, Sir William/Charlotte/Marie (*Pride and Prejudice*)
MARTIN, Robert (*Emma*)
MIDDLETON, Sir John (*Sense and Sensibility*)
MORLAND, Catherine/James/Sarah/George/Harriet (*Northanger Abbey*)
MUSGROVE, Mary/Richard/Charles/Henrietta/Laura (*Persuasion*)
NORRIS, Mrs/Rev Mr (*Mansfield Park*)
PALMER, Mrs Charlotte (*Sense and Sensibility*)
PERRY (*Emma*)
PHILLIPS, Mrs (*Pride and Prejudice*)
PRICE, Mrs Frances/Lieutenant/Fanny/William/Susan (*Mansfield Park*)
RUSHWORTH, Maria/James (*Mansfield Park*)
RUSSELL, Lady (*Persuasion*)
SHEPHERD, John (*Persuasion*)
SMITH, Harriet (*Emma*)
SMITH, Mrs (*Persuasion*)
SMITH, Mrs (*Sense and Sensibility*)
STEELE, Anne/Lucy (*Sense and Sensibility*)
THORPE, Mrs/Isabella/John/Edward/William (*Northanger Abbey*)
TILNEY, Henry/Eleanor/General/Captain Fred (*Northanger Abbey*)
WENTWORTH, Captain Frederick (*Persuasion*)
WESTON, Mrs (*Emma*)
WICKHAM, George (*Pride and Prejudice*)
WILLIAMS, Eliza (*Sense and Sensibility*)
WILLOUGHBY, John (*Sense and Sensibility*)
WOODHOUSE, Emma/Isabella (*Emma*)
YATES, Hon John (*Mansfield Park*)

LOVERS OF FACT AND FICTION

ANNA KARENINA AND LEON VRONSKI
ANTONY AND CLEOPATRA
AUCASSIN AND NICOLETTE
BEATRICE AND BENEDICK
BONNIE AND CLYDE
BYRON AND LADY CAROLINE LAMB
CHARLES II AND NELL GWYN
CHARLES PARNELL AND KITTY O'SHEA
CHOPIN AND GEORGE SAND
DANTE AND BEATRICE
DAPHNIS AND CHLOE
DARBY AND JOAN
DAVID AND BATHSHEBA
DIDO AND AENEAS
EDWARD VII AND LILLIE LANGTRY
EDWARD VIII AND WALLIS SIMPSON
ELIZABETH BARRETT AND ROBERT
  BROWNING
ELIZABETH BENNETT AND FITZWILLIAM
  DARCY
EROS AND PSYCHE
GEORGE IV AND MARIA FITZHERBERT
GERTRUDE STEIN AND ALICE B. TOKLAS
HARLEQUIN AND COLUMBINE
HEATHCLIFF AND CATHY
HELOISE AND ABELARD
HERO AND LEANDER
HORATIO NELSON AND LADY EMMA
  HAMILTON

HUMPHREY BOGART AND LAUREN BACALL
JANE EYRE AND EDWARD ROCHESTER
JOHN OF GAUNT AND KATHERINE
  SWYNFORD
LADY CHATTERLEY AND MELLORS
LANCELOT AND GUINEVERE
NAPOLEON AND JOSEPHINE
ODYSSEUS AND PENELOPE
OSCAR WILDE AND LORD ALFRED DOUGLAS
PAOLO AND FRANCESCA
PARIS AND HELEN
PETRARCH AND LAURA
PORGY AND BESS
PYGMALION AND GALATEA
PYRAMUS AND THISBE
RICHARD BURTON AND ELIZABETH TAYLOR
RIMBAUD AND VERLAINE
ROBIN HOOD AND MAID MARIAN
ROMEO AND JULIET
ROSALIND AND ORLANDO
SAMSON AND DELILAH
SCARLETT O'HARA AND RHETT BUTLER
SPENCER TRACEY AND KATHARINE
  HEPBURN
TRISTAN AND ISOLDE
TROILUS AND CRESSIDA
VIRGINIA WOOLF AND VITA SACKVILLE-
  WEST
W. B. YEATS AND MAUD GONNE

FICTIONAL DETECTIVES

CHARACTER	(Creator)
MARTIN AINSWORTH	(Michael Underwood)
SUPERINTENDENT RODERICK ALLEYN	(Ngaio Marsh)
INSPECTOR ENRIQUE ALVAREZ	(Roderic Jeffries)
SIR JOHN APPLEBY	(Michael Innes)
SERGEANT NICK ATTWELL	(Michael Underwood)
INSPECTOR BILL AVEYARD	(James Fraser)
PROFESSOR ANDREW BASNETT	(E. X. Ferrars)
SUPERINTENDENT BATTLE	(Agatha Christie)
SERGEANT WILLIAM BEEF	(Leo Bruce)
TOMMY AND TUPPENCE BERESFORD	(Agatha Christie)
COLONEL PETER BLAIR	(J. R. L. Anderson)
INSPECTOR BLAND	(Julian Symons)
DR. WILLIAM BLOW	(Kenneth Hopkins)
INSPECTOR SALVADOR BORGES	(John and Emery Bonett)
DAME BEATRICE BRADLEY	(Gladys Mitchell)
CONSTABLE JOHN BRAGG	(Henry Wade)
MILES BREDON	(Ronald A. Knox)
ERNST BRENDEL	(J. C. Masterman)

FICTIONAL DETECTIVES

SID HALLEY	(Dick Francis)
SUPERINTENDENT HANNASYDE	(Georgette Heyer)
PAUL HARRIS	(Gavin Black)
JIMMIE HASWELL	(Herbert Adams)
INSPECTOR HAZLERIGG	(Michael Gilbert)
INSPECTOR HEMINGWAY	(Georgette Heyer)
SHERLOCK HOLMES	(Arthur Conan Doyle)
CHARLES HONEYBATH	(Michael Innes)
TAMARA HOYLAND	(Jessica Mann)
INSPECTOR HARRY JAMES	(Kenneth Giles)
INSPECTOR BENJAMIN JURNET	(S. T. Haymon)
SUPERINTENDENT RICHARD JURY	(Martha Grimes)
INSPECTOR KELSEY	(Emma Page)
INSPECTOR MIKE KENNY	(Eilís Dillon)
SUPERINTENDENT SIMON KENWORTHY	(John Buxton Hilton)
INSPECTOR DON KERRY	(Jeffrey Ashford)
INSPECTOR KYLE	(Roy Vickers)
GERALD LEE	(Kenneth Hopkins)
CORPORAL JUAN LLORCA	(Delano Ames)
INSPECTOR HENRY LOTT	(Henry Wade)
LOVEJOY	(Jonathan Gash)
ADAM LUDLOW	(Simon Nash)
SUPERINTENDENT MACDONALD	(E. C. R. Lorac)
MAIGRET	(Georges Simenon)
ANTONY MAITLAND	(Sara Woods)
DAN MALLETT	(Frank Parrish)
INSPECTOR MALLETT	(Cyril Hare)
PROFESSOR GIDEON MANCIPLE	(Kenneth Hopkins)
PROFESSOR MANDRAKE	(John and Emery Bonett)
SUPERINTENDENT SIMON MANTON	(Michael Underwood)
MISS JANE MARPLE	(Agatha Christie)
INSPECTOR GEORGE MARTIN	(Francis Beeding)
PERRY MASON	(Erle Stanley Gardner)
SUPERINTENDENT GEORGE MASTERS	(Douglas Clark)
KINSEY MILLHOUSE	(Sue Grafton)
SUPERINTENDENT STEVEN MITCHELL	(Josephine Bell)
INSPECTOR MONTERO	(Simon Nash)
INSPECTOR MORSE	(Colin Dexter)
ARIADNE OLIVER	(Agatha Christie)
DAI OWEN	(Henry Calvin)
CHARLES PARIS	(Simon Brett)
INSPECTOR PETER PASCOE	(Reginal Hill)
AMELIA PEABODY	(Elizabeth Peters)
DOUGLAS PERKINS	(Marian Babson)
SERGEANT PATRICK PETRELLA	(Michael Gilbert)
MIKAEL PETROS	(James Anderson)
FRANCIS PETTIGREW	(Cyril Hare)
SUPERINTENDENT JAMES PIBBLE	(Peter Dickinson)
SUPERINTENDENT ARNOLD PIKE	(Philip MacDonald)
MISS MELINDA PINK	(Gwen Moffat)
INSPECTOR THOMAS AND CHARLOTTE E. PITT	(Anne Perry)
INSPECTOR POINTER	(A. Fielding)
HERCULE POIROT	(Agatha Christie)
SUPERINTENDENT TOM POLLARD	(Elizabeth Lemarchand)
INSPECTOR JOHN POOL	(Henry Wade)
THOMAS PRESTON	(Francis Beeding)
DR. LANCELOT PRIESTLEY	(John Rhode)
INSPECTOR WALTER PURBRIGHT	(Colin Watson)
DR. HENRY PYM	(W. J. Burley)
INSPECTOR DOUGLAS QUANTRILL	(Sheila Radley)
ELLERY QUEEN	(Ellery Queen)

COLONEL RACE	(Agatha Christie)
SUPERINTENDENT GEORGE ROGERS	(Jonathan Ross)
INSPECTOR RUDD (FINCH)	(June Thomson)
ALAN RUSSELL	(Nigel FitzGerald)
DR. KAY SCARPETTA	(Patricia Cornwell)
ROGER SHERINGHAM	(Anthony Berkeley)
JEMIMA SHORE	(Antonia Fraser)
MAUD SILVER	(Patricia Wentworth)
INSPECTOR C. D. SLOAN	(Catherine Aird)
SUPERINTENDENT BEN SPENCE	(Michael Allen)
MATTHEW STOCK	(Leonard Tourney)
NIGEL STRANGEWAYS	(Nicholas Blake)
JEREMY STURROCK	(Jeremy Sturrock)
PROFESSOR HILARY TAMAR	(Sarah Caudwell)
INSPECTOR LUKE THANET	(Dorothy Simpson)
KATE THEOBALD	(Lionel Black)
LIZZIE THOMAS	(Anthony Oliver)
DR. JOHN THORNDYKE	(R. Austin Freeman)
SUPERINTENDENT GEORGE THORNE	(John Penn)
SUPERINTENDENT HENRY AND EMILY TIBBETT	(Patricia Moyes)
MARK TREASURE	(David Williams)
PHILIP TRENT	(E. C. Bentley)
SUPERINTENDENT PERRY TRETHOWAN	(Robert Barnard)
MISS AMY TUPPER	(Josephine Bell)
V. I. WARSHAWSKI	(Sara Paretsky)
MALCOLM WARREN	(C. H. B. Kitchin)
CLAUD WARRINGTON-REEVE	(Josephine Bell)
JOHN WEBBER	(Anthony Oliver)
INSPECTOR REGINALD WEXFORD	(Ruth Rendell)
INSPECTOR WILKINS	(James Anderson)
INSPECTOR WILKINS	(Francis Beeding)
LORD PETER WIMSEY	(Dorothy L. Sayers)
DR. DAVID WINTRINGHAM	(Josephine Bell)
NERO WOLFE	(Rex Stout)
SUPERINTENDENT CHARLES WYCLIFFE	(W. J. Burley)

GILBERT AND SULLIVAN

OPERAS

Alternative title

THESPIS	(The Gods Grown Old)
TRIAL BY JURY	
THE SORCERER	
HMS PINAFORE	(The Lass that Loved a Sailor)
THE PIRATES OF PENZANCE	(The Slave of Duty)
PATIENCE	(Bunthorne's Bride)
IOLANTHE	(The Peer and the Peri)
PRINCESS IDA	(Castle Adamant)
THE MIKADO	(The Town of Titipu)
RUDDIGORE	(The Witch's Curse)
THE YEOMEN OF THE GUARD	(The Merryman and his Maid)
THE GONDOLIERS	(The King of Barataria)
UTOPIA, LIMITED	(The Flowers of Progress)
THE GRAND DUKE	(The Statutory Duel)

CHARACTERS (*Operas*)

4
ADAM (*Ruddigore*)
ELLA (*Patience*)
GAMA (*Princess Ida*)
INEZ (*The Gondoliers*)
JANE (*Patience*)
KATE (*The Pirates of Penzance*)
KO-KO (*The Mikado*)
LUIZ (*The Gondoliers*)
RUTH (*The Pirates of Penzance*)

5
ALINE (*The Sorcerer*)
CELIA (*Iolanthe*)
CYRIL (*Princess Ida*)
EDITH (*The Pirates of Penzance*)
EDWIN (*Trial by Jury*)
FLETA (*Iolanthe*)
LEILA (*Iolanthe*)
MABEL (*The Pirates of Penzance*)
TESSA (*The Gondoliers*)

6
ALEXIS (*The Sorcerer*)
ANGELA (*Patience*)
ISABEL (*The Pirates of Penzance*)
PEEP-BO (*The Mikado*)
SAPHIR (*Patience*)
YUM-YUM (*The Mikado*)

7
CASILDA (*The Gondoliers*)
FLORIAN (*Princess Ida*)
KATISHA (*The Mikado*)
LEONARD (*The Yeomen of the Guard*)
MELISSA (*Princess Ida*)
PHYLLIS (*Iolanthe*)
POOH-BAH (*The Mikado*)

8
ANGELINA (*Trial by Jury*)
FREDERIC (*The Pirates of Penzance*)
GIANETTA (*The Gondoliers*)
HILARION (*Princess Ida*)
IOLANTHE (*Iolanthe*)
NANKI-POO (*The Mikado*)
PATIENCE (*Patience*)
PISH-TUSH (*The Mikado*)
SERGEANT (*The Pirates of Penzance*)
STREPHON (*Iolanthe*)

9
BUNTHORNE (*Patience*)
JACK POINT (*The Yeomen of the Guard*)
JOSEPHINE (*HMS Pinafore*)
PITTI-SING (*The Mikado*)

10
DAME HANNAH (*Ruddigore*)
HILDEBRAND (*Princess Ida*)
LADY PSYCHE (*Princess Ida*)
PIRATE KING (*The Pirates of Penzance*)
ROSE MAYBUD (*Ruddigore*)
SIR RODERIC (*Ruddigore*)

11
DICK DEADEYE (*HMS Pinafore*)
LADY BLANCHE (*Princess Ida*)
MAD MARGARET (*Ruddigore*)
MOUNTARARAT (*Iolanthe*)
PRINCESS IDA (*Princess Ida*)

12
ELSIE MAYNARD (*The Yeomen of the Guard*)
PHOEBE MERYLL (*The Yeomen of the Guard*)
SIR MARMADUKE (*The Sorcerer*)

13
LADY SANGAZURE (*The Sorcerer*)
MARCO PALMIERI (*The Gondoliers*)
ROBIN OAKAPPLE (*Ruddigore*)

14
COLONEL FAIRFAX (*The Yeomen of the Guard*)
DAME CARRUTHERS (*The Yeomen of the Guard*)
RALPH RACKSTRAW (*HMS Pinafore*)

15
CAPTAIN CORCORAN (*HMS Pinafore*)
DUKE OF DUNSTABLE (*Patience*)
DUKE OF PLAZA TORO (*The Gondoliers*)
EARL OF TOLLOLLER (*Iolanthe*)
LITTLE BUTTERCUP (*HMS Pinafore*)
SIR JOSEPH PORTER (*HMS Pinafore*)
WILFRED SHADBOLT (*The Yeomen of the Guard*)

16
COLONEL CALVERLEY (*Patience*)
GIUSEPPE PALMIERI (*The Gondoliers*)
RICHARD DAUNTLESS (*Ruddigore*)

18
ARCHIBALD GROSVENOR (*Patience*)

19
JOHN WELLINGTON WELLS (*The Sorcerer*)
MAJOR-GENERAL STANLEY (*The Pirates of Penzance*)

20
SIR DESPARD MURGATROYD (*Ruddigore*)
SIR RICHARD CHOLMONDELEY (*The Yeomen of the Guard*)

CHARACTERS FROM OPERA

CHARACTER (*Opera*, Composer)

3
LIU (*Turandot*, Puccini)

4
AIDA (*Aida*, Verdi)
ELSA (*Lohengrin*, Wagner)
ERDA (*Das Rheingold*, *Götterdämmerung*, *Siegfried*, Wagner)
ERIK (*The Flying Dutchman*, Wagner)
FROH (*Das Rheingold*, Wagner)
GORO (*Madame Butterfly*, Puccini)
KATE (*Madame Butterfly*, Puccini)
LOGE (*Das Rheingold*, Wagner)
LUNA, THE COUNT OF (*Il Trovatore*, Verdi)
MARY (*The Flying Dutchman*, Wagner)
MIME (*Das Rheingold*, *Götterdämmerung*, *Siegfried*, Wagner)
MIMI (*La Bohême*, Puccini)
OCHS, BARON (*Der Rosenkavalier*, Strauss)
PANG (*Turandot*, Puccini)
PING (*Turandot*, Puccini)
PONG (*Turandot*, Puccini)

5
BERTA (*The Barber of Seville*, Rossini)
BONZE, THE (*Madame Butterfly*, Puccini)
CALAF (*Turandot*, Puccini)
EDGAR; EDGARDO (*Lucy of Lammermoor*, Donizetti)
FREIA (*Das Rheingold*, Wagner)
GILDA (*Rigoletto*, Verdi)
HAGEN (*Götterdämmerung*, Wagner)
LUCIA See LUCY ASHTON
PETER (*Hansel and Gretel*, Humperdinck)
SENTA (*The Flying Dutchman*, Wagner)
TIMUR (*Turandot*, Puccini)
WITCH (*Hansel and Gretel*, Humperdinck)
WOTAN, THE WANDERER (*Das Rheingold*, *Die Walküre*, *Götterdämmerung*, *Siegfried*, Wagner)

6
AILSIE; ALISA (*Lucy of Lammermoor*, Donizetti)
ALTOUM, THE EMPEROR (*Turandot*, Puccini)
ANNINA (*Der Rosenkavalier*, Strauss; (*La Traviata*, Verdi)
ARTURO See ARTHUR BUCKLAW
BENOIT (*La Bohême*, Puccini)
CARMEN (*Carmen*, Bizet)
DALAN D (*The Flying Dutchman*, Wagner)
DONNER (*Das Rheingold*, Wagner)
FAFNER (*Das Rheingold*, *Götterdämmerung*, *Siegfried*, Wagner)
FASOLT (*Das Rheingold*, Wagner)
FIGARO (*The Barber of Seville*, Rossini; The *Marriage of Figaro*, Mozart)
FRICKA (*Das Rheingold*, *Die Walküre*, *Götterdämmerung*, Wagner)

6–continued
GRETEL (*Hansel and Gretel*, Humperdinck)
HANSEL (*Hansel and Gretel*, Humperdinck)
MANTUA,THE DUKE OF (*Rigoletto*, Verdi)
NORINA (*Don Pasquale*, Donizetti)
NORMAN; NORMANNO (*Lucy of Lammermoor*, Donizetti)
ORTRUD (*Lohengrin*, Wagner)
PAMINA (*The Magic Flute*, Mozart)
RAMFIS; RAMPHIS (*Aida*, Verdi)
ROSINA (*The Barber of Seville*, Rossini)
SOPHIE (*Der Rosenkavalier*, Strauss)
SUZUKI (*Madame Butterfly*, Puccini)
TAMINO (*The Magic Flute*, Mozart)
ZUNIGA (*Carmen*, Bizet)

7
AMNERIS (*Aida*, Verdi)
ANTONIO (*The Marriage of Figaro*, Mozart)
AZUCENA (*Il Trovatore*, Verdi)
BARTOLA, DR (*The Marriage of Figaro*, Mozart)
BARTOLO, DR (*The Barber of Seville*, Rossini)
COLLINE (*La Bohême*, Puccini)
DESPINA (*Cosi Fan Tutte*, Mozart)
DON JOSÉ (*Carmen*, Bizet)
EDGARDO See EDGAR
ERNESTO (*Don Pasquale*, Donizetti)
FANINAL (*Der Rosenkavalier*, Strauss)
GERTRUD (*Hansel and Gretel*, Humperdinck)
GETRUNE (*Götterdämmerung*, Wagner)
GRENVIL, DR (*La Traviata*, Verdi)
GUNTHER (*Götterdämmerung*, Wagner)
HUNDING (*Die Walküre*, Wagner)
LEONORA (*Il Trovatore*, Verdi)
MANRICO (*Il Trovatore*, Verdi)
MASETTO (*Don Giovanni*, Mozart)
MICAELA (*Carmen*, Bizet)
MUSETTA (*La Bohême*, Puccini)
RADAMES (*Aida*, Verdi)
RAMPHIS See RAMFIS
RODOLFO (*La Bohême*, Puccini)
SANDMAN (*Hansel and Gretel*, Humperdinck)
SCARPIA, BARON (*Tosca*, Puccini)
SUSANNA (*The Marriage of Figaro*, Mozart)
ZERLINA (*Don Giovanni*, Mozart)

8
ALBERICH (*Das Rheingold*, *Götterdämmerung*, *Siegfried*, Wagner)
ALMAVIVA, COUNTESS (*The Marriage of Figaro*, Mozart)
ALMAVIVA, COUNT (*The Barber of Seville*, Rossini; The *Marriage of Figaro*, Mozart)
AMONASRO (*Aida*, Verdi)
DEW FAIRY (*Hansel and Gretel*, Humperdinck)
FERRANDO (*Cosi Fan Tutte*, Mozart; *Il Trovatore*, Verdi)
FIORELLO (*The Barber of Seville*, Rossini)
GERHILDE (*Die Walküre*, Wagner)

8—continued

HELMWIGE (*Die Walküre*, Wagner)
MARCELLO (*La Bohême*, Puccini)
MARIANNE (*Der Rosenkavalier*, Strauss)
NORMANNO *See* NORMAN
OCTAVIAN (*Der Rosenkavalier*, Strauss)
ORTLINDE (*Die Walküre*, Wagner)
PAPAGENA (*The Magic Flute*, Mozart)
PAPAGENO (*The Magic Flute*, Mozart)
RAIMONDO *See* BIDE-THE-BENT
SARASTRO (*The Magic Flute*, Mozart)
SIEGMUND (*Die Walküre*, Wagner)
SIEGRUNE (*Die Walküre*, Wagner)
SPOLETTA (*Tosca*, Puccini)
TURANDOT, PRINCESS (*Turandot*, Puccini)
WOGLINDE (*Das Rheingold*, *Götterdämmerung*, Wagner)
YAMADORI, PRINCE (*Madame Butterfly*, Puccini)

9

ANGELOTTI (*Tosca*, Puccini)
BARBARINA (*The Marriage of Figaro*, Mozart)
CHERUBINO (*The Marriage of Figaro*, Mozart)
DON CURZIO (*The Marriage of Figaro*, Mozart)
DONNA ANNA (*Don Giovanni*, Mozart)
DORABELLA (*Cosi Fan Tutte*, Mozart)
ESCAMILLO (*Carmen*, Bizet)
GRIMGERDE (*Die Walküre*, Wagner)
GUGLIELMO (*Cosi Fan Tutte*, Mozart)
LEPORELLO (*Don Giovanni*, Mozart)
LOHENGRIN (*Lohengrin*, Wagner)
MADDALENA (*Rigoletto*, Verdi)
MALATESTA, DR (*Don Pasquale*, Donizetti)
PINKERTON, LIEUTENANT B F (*Madame Butterfly*, Puccini)
ROSSWEISS (*Die Walküre*, Wagner)
SCHAUNARD (*La Bohême*, Puccini)
SHARPLESS (*Madame Butterfly*, Puccini)
SIEGFRIED (*Götterdämmerung*, *Siegfried*, Wagner)
SIEGLINDE (*Die Walküre*, Wagner)
VALZACCHI (*Der Rosenkavalier*, Strauss)
WALTRAUTE (*Die Walküre*, *Götterdämmerung*, Wagner)
WELLGUNDE (*Das Rheingold*, *Götterdämmerung*, Wagner)

10

BRÜNNHILDE (*Die Walküre*, *Götterdämmerung*, *Siegfried*, Wagner)
DON ALFONSO (*Cosi Fan Tutte*, Mozart)
DON BASILIO (*The Barber of Seville*, Rossini; *The Marriage of Figaro*, Mozart)
DON OTTAVIO (*Don Giovanni*, Mozart)
FIORDILIGI (*Cosi Fan Tutte*, Mozart)
FLOSSHILDE (*Das Rheingold*, *Götterdämmerung*, Wagner)
LUCY ASHTON; LUCIA (*Lucy of Lammermoor*, Donizetti)
MARCELLINA (*The Marriage of Figaro*, Mozart)
MONOSTATOS (*The Magic Flute*, Mozart)

11

BIDE-THE-BENT; RAIMONDO (*Lucy of Lammermoor*, Donizetti)
DON GIOVANNI (*Don Giovanni*, Mozart)
DONNA ELVIRA (*Don Giovanni*, Mozart)
DON PASQUALE (*Don Pasquale*, Donizetti)
FLORIO TOSCA (*Tosca*, Puccini)
HENRY ASHTON; ENRICO (*Lucy of Lammermoor*, Donizetti)
MARSCHALLIN (*Der Rosenkavalier*, Strauss)
SPARAFUCILE (*Rigoletto*, Verdi)

12

COMMENDATORE, THE (*Don Giovanni*, Mozart)
FLORA BERVOIX (*La Traviata*, Verdi)
SCHWERTLEITE (*Die Walküre*, Wagner)

13

ARTHUR BUCKLAW; ARTURO (*Lucy of Lammermoor*, Donizetti)

14+

ALFREDO GERMONT (*La Traviata*, Verdi)
FRIEDRICH VON TELRAMUND (*Lohengrin*, Wagner)
GIORGIO GERMONT (*La Traviata*, Verdi)
HENRY I OF GERMANY (*Lohengrin*, Wagner)
MADAME BUTTERFLY (*Madame Butterfly*, Puccini)
MARIO CAVARADOSSI (*Tosca*, Puccini)
VIOLETTA VALERY (*La Traviata*, Verdi)

SCIENCE AND TECHNOLOGY

WEIGHTS AND MEASURES

2
CM
DR
FT
GR
HL
IN
KG
KM
LB
MG
ML
MM
OZ
YD

3
AMP
ARE
BAR
BEL
BIT
CWT
DWT
ELL
ERG
LUX
MHO
MIL
MIM
NIT
OHM
RAD
REM
ROD
TON
TUN

4
ACRE
BALE
BARN
BOLT
BYTE
CASK
CORD
CRAN
DRAM

4—continued
DYNE
FOOT
GILL
GRAM
HAND
HIDE
HOUR
INCH
KILO
KNOT
LINE
LINK
MILE
MOLE
NAIL
PECK
PHON
PHOT
PICA
PINT
PIPE
POLE
REAM
ROOD
SLUG
SPAN
TORR
TROY
VOLT
WATT
YARD

5
CABLE
CARAT
CHAIN
CRITH
CUBIT
CURIE
CUSEC
CYCLE
DEBYE
FARAD
FERMI
GAUGE
GAUSS
GRAIN

5—continued
HENRY
HERTZ
JOULE
LITRE
LUMEN
METRE
MINIM
NEPER
OUNCE
PERCH
POINT
POISE
POUND
QUART
QUIRE
STADE
STERE
STILB
STOKE
STONE
TESLA
THERM
TOISE
TONNE
WEBER

6
AMPERE
BARREL
BUSHEL
CANDLE
CENTAL
DEGREE
DENIER
DRACHM
FATHOM
FIRKIN
GALLON
GRAMME
KELVIN
LEAGUE
MEGOHM
MICRON
MINUTE
NEWTON
PARSEC
PASCAL

6—continued
RADIAN
RÉAMUR
SECOND
STOKES

7
CALORIE
CANDELA
CENTNER
COULOMB
DECIBEL
DIOPTER
FARADAY
FURLONG
GILBERT
HECTARE
KILOBAR
KILOTON
LAMBERT
MAXWELL
MEGATON
OERSTED
POUNDAL
QUARTER
QUINTAL
RÖNTGEN
SCRUPLE
SIEMENS

8
ÅNGSTROM
CHALDRON
HOGSHEAD
KILOGRAM
KILOWATT
QUADRANT
MEGAWATT
MICROOHM
WATT-HOUR

9
BOARD-FOOT
CENTIGRAM
CUBIC FOOT
CUBIC INCH
CUBIC YARD
DECALITRE
DECAMETRE

9–continued
DECILITRE
DECIMETRE
FOOT-POUND
HECTOGRAM
KILOCYCLE
KILOHERTZ
KILOLITRE
KILOMETRE
LIGHT-YEAR
MEGACYCLE
MEGAFARAD
MEGAHERTZ

9–continued
METRIC TON
MICROGRAM
MICROWATT
MILLIGRAM
NANOMETRE
SCANTLING
STERADIAN

10+
BARLEYCORN
CENTILITRE
CENTIMETRE

10+–continued
CUBIC METRE
DECAGRAMME
DECIGRAMME
FLUID OUNCE
HECTOLITRE
HORSEPOWER
HUNDREDWEIGHT
KILOGRAMME
MICROFARAD
MILLILITRE
MILLIMETRE
NANOSECOND

10+–continued
PENNYWEIGHT
RUTHERFORD
SQUARE
  CENTIMETRE
SQUARE INCH
SQUARE
  KILOMETRE
SQUARE MILE
SQUARE YARD

PAPER MEASURES

4
BALE
COPY
DEMY
POST
POTT
REAM

5
ATLAS
BRIEF
CROWN
DRAFT
QUIRE

5–continued
ROYAL

6
BAG CAP
BUNDLE
CASING
MEDIUM

7
EMPEROR
KENT CAP

8
ELEPHANT

8–continued
FOOLSCAP
HAVEN CAP
IMPERIAL

9
CARTRIDGE
COLOMBIER
LARGE POST
MUSIC DEMY

10
DOUBLE DEMY
DOUBLE POST
GRAND EAGLE

10–continued
SUPER ROYAL

11
ANTIQUARIAN
IMPERIAL CAP
PINCHED POST

14
DOUBLE ELEPHANT

15
DOUBLE LARGE
  POST

ELEMENTARY PARTICLES

2
XI

3
ETA
PHI
PSI

4
KAON
MUON
PION

5
BOSON
GLUON
MESON
OMEGA
QUARK
SIGMA

6
BARYON
HADRON
LAMBDA
LEPTON

6–continued
PHOTON
PROTON

7
FERMION
HYPERON
NEUTRON
TACHYON

8
DEUTERON
ELECTRON

8–continued
GRAVITON
NEUTRINO
POSITRON

9
NEUTRETTO

12
ANTIPARTICLE
BETA PARTICLE

13
ALPHA PARTICLE

THE CHEMICAL ELEMENTS

NAME	(SYMBOL)

NAME	(SYMBOL)	NAME	(SYMBOL)	NAME	(SYMBOL)	NAME	(SYMBOL)
		DUBNIUM	(DB)	MANGANESE	(MN)	RUBIDIUM	(RB)
		DYSPROSIUM	(DY)	MEITNERIUM	(MT)	RUTHENIUM	(RU)
ACTINIUM	(AC)	EINSTEINIUM	(ES)	MENDELEVIUM	(MD)	SAMARIUM	(SM)
ALUMINIUM	(AL)	ERBIUM	(ER)	MERCURY	(HG)	SCANDIUM	(SC)
AMERICIUM	(AM)	EUROPIUM	(EU)	MOLYBDENUM	(MO)	SELENIUM	(SE)
ANTIMONY	(SB)	FERMIUM	(FM)	NEODYMIUM	(ND)	SILICON	(SI)
ARGON	(AR)	FLUORINE	(F)	NEON	(NE)	SILVER	(AG)
ARSENIC	(AS)	FRANCIUM	(FR)	NEPTUNIUM	(NP)	SODIUM	(NA)
ASTATINE	(AT)	GADOLINIUM	(GD)	NICKEL	(NI)	STRONTIUM	(SR)
BARIUM	(BA)	GALLIUM	(GA)	NIOBIUM	(NB)	SULPHUR	(S)
BERKELIUM	(BK)	GERMANIUM	(GE)	NITROGEN	(N)	TANTALUM	(TA)
BERYLLIUM	(BE)	GOLD	(AU)	NOBELIUM	(NO)	TECHNETIUM	(TC)
BISMUTH	(BI)	HAFNIUM	(HF)	OSMIUM	(OS)	TELLURIUM	(TE)
BOHRIUM	(BH)	HASSIUM	(HS)	OXYGEN	(O)	TERBIUM	(TB)
BORON	(B)	HELIUM	(HE)	PALLADIUM	(PD)	THALLIUM	(TL)
BROMINE	(BR)	HOLMIUM	(HO)	PHOSPHORUS	(P)	THORIUM	(TH)
CADMIUM	(CD)	HYDROGEN	(H)	PLATINUM	(PT)	THULIUM	(TM)
CAESIUM	(CS)	INDIUM	(IN)	PLUTONIUM	(PU)	TIN	(SN)
CALCIUM	(CA)	IODINE	(I)	POLONIUM	(PO)	TITANIUM	(TI)
CALIFORNIUM	(CF)	IRIDIUM	(IR)	POTASSIUM	(K)	TUNGSTEN	(W)
CARBON	(C)	IRON	(FE)	PRASEODYMIUM		URANIUM	(U)
CERIUM	(CE)	KRYPTON	(KR)		(PR)	VANADIUM	(V)
CHLORINE	(CL)	LANTHANUM	(LA)	PROMETHIUM	(PM)	WOLFRAM	(W)
CHROMIUM	(CR)	LAWRENCIUM	(LR)	PROTACTINIUM	(PA)	XENON	(XE)
COBALT	(CO)	LEAD	(PB)	RADIUM	(RA)	YTTERBIUM	(YB)
COLUMBIUM	(CB)	LITHIUM	(LI)	RADON	(RN)	YTTRIUM	(Y)
COPPER	(CU)	LUTETIUM	(LU)	RHENIUM	(RE)	ZINC	(ZN)
CURIUM	(CM)	MAGNESIUM	(MG)	RHODIUM	(RH)	ZIRCONIUM	(ZR)

COMMON CHEMICALS

4	6–continued	7–continued	8–continued	10
ALUM	PHENOL	QUINONE	PEROXIDE	CAPRIC ACID
LIME	POTASH	REALGAR	PHOSGENE	CYANIC ACID
UREA	QUINOL	RED LEAD	PLUMBAGO	FORMIC ACID
	SILICA	SODA ASH	PROPANOL	LACTIC ACID
5	XYLENE	STYRENE	SODA LIME	LAURIC ACID
BORAX		TOLUENE	SODAMIDE	MUSTARD GAS
ETHER	**7**		STRONTIA	NITRIC ACID
FREON	ACETATE	**8**		OXALIC ACID
FURAN	ALUMINA	BERYLLIA	**9**	PICRIC ACID
HALON	AMMONIA	CATECHOL	ACETYLENE	SLAKED LIME
	ANILINE	CHLORIDE	AQUA REGIA	TANNIC ACID
6	BENZENE	CINNABAR	BLANC FIXE	WATER GLASS
BARYTA	BORAZON	CORUNDUM	BORIC ACID	ZINC BLENDE
CETANE	BROMIDE	CYANOGEN	BROMOFORM	
CRESOL	CALOMEL	FLUORIDE	FERROCENE	**11**
DIOXAN	CAMPHOR	FLUORITE	IODIC ACID	ACRYLIC ACID
ETHANE	CHLORAL	FORMALIN	LIMEWATER	BENZOIC ACID
HEXANE	CYANIDE	MAGNESIA	PHOSPHINE	BUTYRIC ACID
IODIDE	ETHANOL	MELAMINE	PROPYLENE	CAPROIC ACID
LITHIA	HEPTANE	METHANOL	QUICKLIME	CAUSTIC SODA
LITMUS	PENTANE	NEOPRENE	SALTPETRE	DIPHOSPHINE

ALLOYS

11–continued
FUMARIC ACID
IODOMETHANE
LAUGHING GAS
MALONIC ACID
NITRIC OXIDE
NITROUS ACID
PRUSSIC ACID
SAL AMMONIAC
STEARIC ACID
SUGAR OF LEAD
WASHING SODA

12
ACETALDEHYDE
BENZALDEHYDE
BENZOQUINONE
CAPRYLIC ACID
CARBOLIC ACID
CARBONIC ACID
DECANOIC ACID
ETHYL ALCOHOL
FLUOROCARBON
FORMALDEHYDE
FULMINIC ACID
GREEN VITRIOL
HYDROQUINONE
NITROBENZENE
NITROUS OXIDE
OIL OF VITRIOL
PERMANGANATE

12–continued
PHTHALIC ACID
TARTARIC ACID

13
ISOCYANIC ACID
METHANOIC ACID
METHYL ALCOHOL
PROPANOIC ACID
SILVER NITRATE
SODIUM CYANIDE
SULPHURIC ACID
VINYL CHLORIDE

14
CALCIUM CARBIDE
CARBON MONOXIDE
CHLORAL HYDRATE
COPPER SULPHATE
HYDROIODIC ACID
METHYL CHLORIDE
NITROCELLULOSE
PHOSPHORIC ACID
SODIUM CHLORIDE
SODIUM SULPHATE
SULPHUR DIOXIDE
TETRAETHYL LEAD

15
ABSOLUTE
  ALCOHOL

15–continued
BLEACHING
  POWDER
HYDROBROMIC ACID
HYDROCYANIC ACID
HYDROGEN
  CYANIDE
NITROGEN DIOXIDE
PHOSPHOROUS
  ACID
SODIUM HYDROXIDE
SULPHUR TRIOXIDE
TETRAHYDRO-
  FURAN

16
CALCIUM
  CARBONATE
CALCIUM
  HYDROXIDE
HYDROCHLORIC
  ACID
HYDROFLUORIC
  ACID
HYDROGEN
  FLUORIDE
HYDROGEN
  PEROXIDE
HYPOCHLOROUS
  ACID

16–continued
NITROGEN
  MONOXIDE

17
BICARBONATE OF
  SODA
MAGNESIUM
  CHLORIDE
POTASSIUM
  CHLORIDE
SODIUM
  BICARBONATE
VANADIUM
  PENTOXIDE

18
CHLOROFLUORO-
  CARBON
DIMETHYL
  SULPHOXIDE
MAGNESIUM
  CARBONATE

19+
BUCKMINSTER-
  FULLERENE
CARBON TETRA-
  CHLORIDE
POTASSIUM
  BICARBONATE
POTASSIUM
  PERMANGANATE

ALLOYS

ALLOY – main components

4
ALNI – iron, nickel, aluminium,
  copper
BETA – titanium, aluminium,
  vanadium, chromium

5
ALPHA – titanium, aluminium,
  tin, copper, zirconium, nio-
  bium, molybdenum
BRASS – copper, zinc
INVAR – iron, nickel
MAZAC – zinc, aluminium,
  magnesium, copper
MONEL – nickel, cobalt, iron
STEEL – iron, carbon

6
ALNICO – aluminium, nickel,
  cobalt

6–continued
BABBIT – tin, lead, antimony,
  copper
BRONZE – copper, tin
CUNICO – iron, cobalt, copper,
  nickel
CUNIFE – iron, cobalt, nickel
FEROBA – iron, barium oxide,
  iron oxide
PEWTER – tin, lead
SOLDER – lead, tin (soft), cop-
  per, zinc (brazing)

7
ALCOMAX – aluminium, cobalt,
  nickel, copper, lead, niobium
ALUMNEL – aluminium,
  chromium
AMALGAM – mercury, various
CHROMEL – nickel, chromium

7–continued
COLUMAN – iron, chromium,
  nickel, aluminium, nobium,
  copper
ELINVAR – iron, nickel,
  chromium, tungsten
INCONEL – nickel, chromium,
  iron
KANTHAL – chromium, alu-
  minium, iron
MUMETAL – iron, nickel, copper, chromium
NIMONIC – nickel, chromium,
  iron, titanium, aluminium,
  manganese, silicon

8
CAST IRON – carbon, iron
DOWMETAL – magnesium,
  aluminium, zinc, manganese
GUNMETAL – copper, tin, zinc
HIPERNIK – nickel, iron

8–continued

KIRKSITE – zinc, aluminium, copper
MANGANIN – copper, manganese, nickel
NICHROME – nickel, iron, chromium
VICALLOY – iron, cobalt, vanadium
ZIRCALOY – zirconium, tin, iron, nickel, chromium

9

DURALUMIN – aluminium, copper, silicon, magnesium, manganese, zinc
HASTELLOY – nickel, molybdenum, iron, chromium, cobalt, tungsten
PERMALLOY – nickel, iron
PERMINVAR – nickel, iron, cobalt
TYPE METAL – lead, tin, antimony

10

CONSTANTAN – copper, nickel
MISCH METAL – cerium, various
MUNTZ METAL – copper, zinc
ROSE'S METAL – bismuth, lead, tin
SUPERALLOY – type of stainless steel
WOOD'S METAL – lead, tin, bismuth, cadmium

11

CUPRONICKEL – copper, nickel
ELECTROTYPE – lead, tin, antimony
SUPERMALLOY – iron, nickel
SUPERMENDUR – iron, cobalt

12

FERROSILICON – iron, silicon
GERMAN SILVER – copper, nickel, zinc, lead, tin
SILVER SOLDER – copper, silver, zinc

13

FERROCHROMIUM – iron, chromium
FERROTUNGSTEN – iron, tungsten
FERROVANADIUM – iron, vanadium

14

ADMIRALTY METAL – copper, zinc
BRITANNIA METAL – tin, antimony, copper
FERROMANGANESE – iron, manganese
PHOSPHOR BRONZE – copper, tin, phosphorus
STAINLESS STEEL – iron, chromium, vanadium

MATHEMATICAL TERMS

3
SET
SUM

4
BASE
CUBE
MEAN
NODE
RING
ROOT
SINE
SURD

5
ARRAY
DIGIT
FIELD
GROUP
LIMIT
LOCUS
POWER
PROOF
RATIO
UNITY

6
COSINE
FACTOR
GOOGOL
MATRIX
MEDIAN

6–continued
ORIGIN
SCALAR
SECANT
SERIES
SQUARE
SUBSET
TENSOR
VECTOR

7
ALGEBRA
DIVISOR
FORMULA
FRACTAL
INTEGER
INVERSE
MODULUS
PRODUCT
TANGENT
UNKNOWN

8
ABSCISSA
ADDITION
ANALYSIS
BINOMIAL
CALCULUS
COSECANT
CUBE ROOT
DIVISION

8–continued
EQUATION
EXPONENT
FRACTION
FUNCTION
FUZZY SET
GRADIENT
IDENTITY
JULIA SET
LIE GROUP
MULTIPLE
OPERATOR
QUOTIENT
SOLUTION
VARIABLE

9
ALGORITHM
ASYMPTOTE
CANTOR SET
CONJUGATE
COTANGENT
EXPANSION
FACTORIAL
INTEGRAND
INTERCEPT
ITERATION
LOGARITHM
NUMERATOR
PARAMETER
RECURSION

9–continued
REMAINDER
SET THEORY
SUB-GROUP
TRANSFORM

10
DERIVATIVE
DIFFERENCE
EIGENVALUE
FRACTAL SET
GAME THEORY
GOOGOLPLEX
INEQUALITY
MULTIPLIER
PERCENTILE
POLYNOMIAL
QUATERNION
REAL NUMBER
RECIPROCAL
SQUARE ROOT

11
ALIQUOT PART
BANACH SPACE
CHAOS THEORY
COEFFICIENT
DENOMINATOR
DETERMINANT
EIGENVECTOR
GALOIS GROUP

11—continued
GROUP THEORY
INTEGRATION
KLEIN BOTTLE
MAGIC SQUARE
MARKOV CHAIN
MÖBIUS STRIP
PERMUTATION
POWER SERIES
PRIME NUMBER
SUBTRACTION
VENN DIAGRAM
WHOLE NUMBER

12
BAYES' THEOREM
DECIMAL POINT
GÖDEL NUMBERS
HILBERT SPACE
LONG DIVISION
MULTIPLICAND
NEWTON METHOD
NUMBER THEORY
SIMPSON'S RULE
SQUARE NUMBER
SUBSTITUTION
TAYLOR SERIES

13
ANTILOGARITHM
ARGAND DIAGRAM
COMPLEX NUMBER
EIGENFUNCTION
EUCLID'S AXIOMS
EULER'S FORMULA
EXTRAPOLATION
FOURIER SERIES
GAUSS'S THEOREM
GEOMETRIC MEAN
GREEN'S THEOREM
INTERPOLATION
L'HÔPITAL'S RULE
MANDELBROT SET
ORDINAL NUMBER
PERFECT NUMBER
PERFECT SQUARE
QUEUING THEORY
STOKES' THEOREM

14
ARITHMETIC MEAN
ASSOCIATIVE LAW

14—continued
BOOLEAN ALGEBRA
CARDINAL NUMBER
CAUCHY SEQUENCE
COMMUTATIVE LAW
EULER'S CONSTANT
HYPERBOLIC SINE
LINEAR EQUATION
MULTIPLICATION
NATURAL NUMBERS
NULL HYPOTHESIS
PROPER FRACTION
RATIONAL NUMBER
ROOT-MEAN-SQUARE
VULGAR FRACTION

15
BESSEL FUNCTIONS
BINOMIAL THEOREM
DIFFERENTIATION
DIRICHLET SERIES
DISTRIBUTIVE LAW
FOURIER ANALYSIS
HERMITIAN MATRIX
IMAGINARY NUMBER
LAPLACE OPERATOR
LEIBNIZ'S THEOREM
MACLAURIN SERIES
MERSENNE NUMBERS
MIDPOINT THEOREM
PASCAL'S TRIANGLE
RUSSELL'S PARADOX
STATIONARY POINT

16
BERNOULLI NUMBERS
DEFINITE INTEGRAL
DE MOIVRE'S FORMULA
FIBONACCI NUMBERS
HILBERT'S PROBLEMS
HYPERBOLIC COSINE
IMPROPER FRACTION
INTEGRAL CALCULUS
IRRATIONAL NUMBER
LAGRANGE'S THEOREM
MONTE CARLO METHOD
NATURAL LOGARITHM
POLAR COORDINATES
RECURRING DECIMAL
REMAINDER THEOREM
REPEATING DECIMAL

17
APOLLONIUS' THEOREM
CATASTROPHE THEORY
COMMON DENOMINATOR
EUCLIDEAN GEOMETRY
HYPERBOLIC TANGENT
PARTIAL DERIVATIVE
POINT OF INFLECTION
SIGNIFICANT FIGURE
TRANSFINITE NUMBER

18
COORDINATE GEOMETRY
FERMAT'S LAST THEOREM
FOUR-COLOUR THEOREM
INDEFINITE INTEGRAL
LEAST SQUARES METHOD
NAPIERIAN LOGARITHM
PYTHAGORAS' THEOREM
RIEMANNIAN GEOMETRY

19
BRIGGSIAN LOGARITHMS
DIOPHANTINE EQUATION
EXPONENTIAL FUNCTION
HARMONIC PROGRESSION
HIGHEST COMMON FACTOR
LEGENDRE POLYNOMIALS
POISSON DISTRIBUTION

20+
ARITHMETIC PROGRESSION
CARTESIAN COORDINATES
CHINESE REMAINDER
   THEOREM
DIFFERENTIAL CALCULUS
DIFFERENTIAL EQUATION
GAUSSIAN DISTRIBUTION
GEOMETRIC PROGRESSION
INFINITESIMAL CALCULUS
LOBACHEVSKIAN
   GEOMETRY
LOWEST COMMON
   DENOMINATOR
LOWEST COMMON
   MULTIPLE
SIMULTANEOUS EQUATIONS
STIRLING'S APPROXIMATION
TRIGONOMETRIC FUNCTION
TRANSCENDENTAL
   FUNCTION

GEOMETRIC FIGURES AND CURVES

3
ARC

4
CONE
CUBE
KITE
LINE
LOOP
LUNE
OVAL
ROSE
ZONE

5
CHORD
CONIC
HELIX
LOCUS
NAPPE
OGIVE
PLANE
PRISM
RHOMB
SHEET
SOLID
TORUS
WEDGE
WITCH

6
CIRCLE
CONOID
FOLIUM
LAMINA
NORMAL
OCTANT
PENCIL
RADIUS
SECTOR
SPHERE
SPIRAL
SPLINE
SQUARE

7
ANNULUS
CISSOID
CYCLOID
DECAGON
ELLIPSE
EVOLUTE
FRACTAL
HEXAGON
LIMAÇON
OCTAGON
PERIGON
POLYGON
PYRAMID
RHOMBUS
SEGMENT
SURFACE
TANGENT
TREFOIL
TRIDENT

8
CARDIOID
CATENARY
CATENOID
CONCHOID
CONICOID
CYLINDER
ENVELOPE
EPICYCLE
EXCIRCLE
FRUSTRUM
GEODESIC
HEPTAGON
INCIRCLE
INVOLUTE
PARABOLA
PENTAGON
PRISMOID
QUADRANT
RHOMBOID
ROULETTE
SPHEROID
TRACTRIX

8—continued
TRIANGLE
TROCHOID

9
ANTIPRISM
CRUCIFORM
DIRECTRIX
DODECAGON
ELLIPSOID
HYPERBOLA
ISOCHRONE
KOCH CURVE
LOXODROME
MULTIFOIL
PENTAGRAM
PENTANGLE
RHUMB LINE
SINE CURVE
STROPHOID
TRAPEZIUM
TRAPEZOID

10
ACUTE ANGLE
ANCHOR RING
CYLINDROID
EPICYCLOID
HEMISPHERE
HEXAHEDRON
KAPPA CURVE
LEMNISCATE
OCTAHEDRON
PARABOLOID
PEANO CURVE
POLYHEDRON
PRISMATOID
QUADRANGLE
QUADREFOIL
RIGHT ANGLE
SEMICIRCLE
SERPENTINE
TRISECTRIX

11
CORNU SPIRAL
EPITROCHOID
HEPTAHEDRON
HYPERBOLOID
HYPOCYCLOID
ICOSAHEDRON
KLEIN BOTTLE
LATUS RECTUM
MÖBIUS STRIP
OBTUSE ANGLE
PENTAHEDRON
REFLEX ANGLE
TAUTOCHRONE
TETRAHEDRON

12
HYPOTROCHOID
PSEUDOSPHERE
RHOMBOHEDRON
SIGMOID CURVE

13
CIRCUMFERENCE
CUBOCTAHEDRON
PARALLELOGRAM
PARALLELOTOPE
PEDAL TRIANGLE
PERPENDICULAR
QUADRILATERAL

14
SNOWFLAKE CURVE

15
BRACHISTOCHRONE
SCALENE TRIANGLE

17
ICOSIDODECA-
HEDRON
ISOSCELES
TRIANGLE

19
EQUILATERAL
TRIANGLE

ELECTRONIC COMPONENTS

3
FET
LED
RCD

4
CHIP
FUSE

4—continued
GATE

5
CHOKE
DIODE
IGFET
RELAY

5—continued
SHUNT
VALVE

6
BRIDGE
DYNAMO
FILTER

6—continued
JUGFET
MOSFET
SWITCH
TRIODE

7
AMMETER

7—continued
BATTERY
COUNTER
MAGNETO
PENTODE
SPEAKER
TETRODE

COMPUTER TERMS

8
ARMATURE
BISTABLE
FLIP-FLOP
INDUCTOR
RESISTOR
RHEOSTAT
SOLENOID
VARACTOR
WINDINGS

9
AMPLIFIER
CAPACITOR
GUNN DIODE
MICROCHIP
RECTIFIER
THYRISTOR

9—continued
VOLTMETER
WAVEGUIDE

10
ALTERNATOR
ATTENUATOR
MICROPHONE
OSCILLATOR
OSCILLATOR
TRANSDUCER
TRANSISTOR
ZENER DIODE

11
ELECTRON GUN
LOUDSPEAKER
SILICON CHIP
TRANSFORMER

12
ELECTRON LENS
ELECTRON TUBE
GALVANOMETER
LOGIC CIRCUIT
OSCILLOSCOPE
PHOTOCATHODE

13
SEMICONDUCTOR

14
CIRCUIT BREAKER
PRINTED CIRCUIT

15+
ELECTRON
  MULTIPLIER

15+—continued
FIELD-EFFECT
  TRANSISTOR
INTEGRATED
  CIRCUIT
LIGHT-EMITTING
  DIODE
N-TYPE SEMI-
  CONDUCTOR
PHOTOMULTIPLIER
P-TYPE SEMI-
  CONDUCTOR
THERMIONIC
  CATHODE
WHEATSTONE
  BRIDGE

COMPUTER TERMS

1&2
K
AI
BS
CD
CR
DP
LF
MB
NL
PC
UI

3
BIT
BUG
BUS
CAD
CAL
CAM
CBL
CPU
DTP
DVD
GIG
GUI
ICR
ISP
JOB
KEY
MEG
NET
OCR
RAM
ROM
RUN

3—continued
URL
VDA
VDU
WAN
WEB
WWW

4
BAUD
BOOT
BYTE
CHIP
COPY
DATA
DISK
DUMP
EDIT
FILE
FLOP
GOTO
ICON
LOOP
MENU
NODE
PROM
SAVE
WAND

5
ABORT
BLOCK
CACHE
CD-ROM
CRASH
DEBUG

5—continued
E-MAIL
EPROM
ERASE
FIELD
INPUT
LOGIN
LOGON
MACRO
MODEM
MOUSE
OCTAL
PATCH
PIXEL
QUEUE
SPOOL
VIRUS
WRITE

6
ACCESS
BACKUP
BINARY
BITMAP
BITNET
BOOT UP
BRANCH
BRIDGE
CLIENT
CURSOR
DAEMON
DECODE
DELETE
ESCAPE
FILTER
FORMAT

6—continued
GOPHER
HEADER
KEYPAD
LAPTOP
LOGOFF
LOGOUT
MEMORY
NYBBLE
ON-LINE
OUTPUT
PACKET
PARITY
PARSER
RASTER
RECORD
ROUTER
SCROLL
SECTOR
SPIDER
SPRITE
USENET
VECTOR

7
ADDRESS
ARCHIVE
ARPANET
BROWSER
CHANNEL
COMMAND
COMPILE
COUNTER
CRACKER
DECIMAL
DISPLAY

7—continued
EURONET
FIDONET
HASHING
HOT SPOT
MAILBOX
MONITOR
NESTING
NETWORK
NEWLINE
OFF-LINE
PALMTOP
PARSING
PLOTTER
PRINTER
PROGRAM
SCANNER
SORTING
STORAGE
TOOLBOX
UPGRADE
WYSIWYG

8
ANALYZER
BETA TEST
CHAT ROOM
COMPILER
DISKETTE
DOWNLOAD
DOWNTIME
ETHERNET
GIGABYTE
GRAPHICS
HALFWORD
HARD DISK

8–continued
HARDWIRE
HOME PAGE
INTERNET
INTRANET
JOYSTICK
KEYBOARD
KILOBYTE
LANGUAGE
LIGHT PEN
LINEFEED
MEGABYTE
NOTEBOOK
PASSWORD
QUADWORD
REAL TIME
REGISTER
REPEATER
ROBOTICS

9
ALGORITHM
BACKSPACE
BANDWIDTH
BENCHMARK
BOOTSTRAP
CHARACTER
CLOCK RATE
DATA ENTRY
DECOMPILE
DIGITIZER
DIRECTORY
DOWNGRADE
E-COMMERCE
FIXED DISK
HANDSHAKE
HASH TABLE
HEARTBEAT
HYPERTEXT
INTERFACE
MAINFRAME
PROCESSOR
SOUND CARD
THESAURUS
TRACKBALL

10
CLOCK CYCLE
CYBERSPACE
DATA TABLET
DIAGNOSTIC
ENCRYPTION
FILE SERVER
FLOPPY DISK
MULTIMEDIA
PERIPHERAL
PREPROCESS
PROGRAMMER
SERIAL PORT
SOURCE CODE
TEXT EDITOR
TRANSISTOR
VACUUM TUBE

11
ACCUMULATOR
BAND PRINTER
BELT PRINTER
COMPACT DISK
COMPRESSION
COPROCESSOR
CYBERNETICS
DRUM PRINTER
INTERPRETER
LINE PRINTER
MOTHERBOARD
MULTIPLEXER
OPTICAL DISK
PROGRAMMING
SCREEN SAVER
SEMANTIC NET
STAR NETWORK
TIME SHARING
TRANSCEIVER
TROJAN HORSE
WORKSTATION

12
ALPHANUMERIC
ASSEMBLY CODE
BUBBLE MEMORY
CHAIN PRINTER
CHARACTER SET
COLOR PRINTER
DEVICE DRIVER
DIRECT ACCESS
ENCRYPTION
EXPERT SYSTEM
LASER PRINTER
MINICOMPUTER
MULTITASKING
PARALLEL PORT
PROGRAM SUITE
SEARCH ENGINE
USER-FRIENDLY
WORLDWIDE WEB

13
AUTHORING TOOL
BAR-CODE READER
BARREL PRINTER
BULLETIN BOARD
COMPATIBILITY
CYBERCOMMERCE
DATA STRUCTURE
DOT COM COMPANY
DYNAMIC MEMORY
FLOPTICAL DISK
HYPERTEXT LINK
IMPACT PRINTER
INK-JET PRINTER
MICROCOMPUTER
NEURAL NETWORK
PRIMARY MEMORY
SUPERCOMPUTER
USER INTERFACE
WINDOW MANAGER

13–continued
WORD PROCESSOR

14
CARRIAGE RETURN
DATA PROCESSING
ELECTRONIC MAIL
FLAT-BED PLOTTER
PAPER-TAPE PUNCH
READ-ONLY MEMORY
SYSTEM SOFTWARE
THEOREM PROVING
UTILITY PROGRAM
VOLATILE MEMORY

15
ACOUSTIC COUPLER
BATCH PROCESSING
CONTROL SEQUENCE
CRYOGENIC MEMORY
DATABASE PROGRAM
ELECTRONIC BRAIN
OPERATING SYSTEM
PAPER-TAPE READER
RULE-BASED SYSTEM
SPELLING CHECKER
TERMINAL DISPLAY
WIDE-AREA
  NETWORK

16
BUBBLE-JET
  PRINTER
COMPILED LAN-
  GUAGE
DOT-MATRIX
  PRINTER
PERSONAL
  COMPUTER
SOLID-STATE
  MEMORY
TOKEN RING
  NETWORK
TURNKEY
  OPERATION
VIDEO DISPLAY UNIT

17
DAISYWHEEL
  PRINTER
DESKTOP
  PUBLISHING
HIGH-LEVEL
  LANGUAGE
PARALLEL
  PROCESSOR
PERSONAL
  ORGANIZER

18
IONOGRAPHIC
  PRINTER
PRINTABLE
  CHARACTER

18–continued
RANDOM-ACCESS
  MEMORY
RELATIONAL
  DATABASE
SPREADSHEET
  PROGRAM

19
COMPUTER-AIDED
  DESIGN
PERCEPTUAL
  COMPUTING
PROGRAMMING
  LANGUAGE
SEMICONDUCTOR
  MEMORY
TOUCHSCREEN
  SOFTWARE

20+
APPLICATIONS
  SOFTWARE
ARTIFICIAL
  INTELLIGENCE
CENTRAL
  PROCESSING UNIT
COMPUTER-AIDED
  MANUFACTURE
COMPUTER-AS-
  SISTED LEARNING
COMPUTER-BASED
  LEARNING
ERASABLE PRO-
  GRAMMABLE READ-
  ONLY MEMORY
FLOATING-POINT
  OPERATION
GRAPHICAL USER
  INTERFACE
HEXADECIMAL
  CHARACTER
HIERARCHICAL
  DATABASE
INTELLIGENT
  CHARACTER
  RECOGNITION
INTERNET SERVICE
  PROVIDER
MODULATOR-
  DEMODULATOR
NATURAL-LANGUAGE
  PROCESSING
OPTICAL CHARAC-
  TER RECOGNITION
PROGRAMMABLE
  READ-ONLY MEM-
  ORY
TOUCHSCREEN
  HARDCOPY DEVICE
WHAT YOU SEE IS
  WHAT YOU GET

COMPUTER LANGUAGES

4GL
ADA
ALGOL
APL
ASSEMBLER
ASSEMBLY
  LANGUAGE
AUTOCODE
C
C++
COBOL

COMAL
COMMON LISP
CORAL
CPL
CSL
EULISP
FORTH
FORTRAN
IPL
JAVA
JOVIAL

LISP
LOGO
MACLISP
PASCAL
PILOT
PL/1
PL/360
POP-11
POP-2
POSTSCRIPT
PROLOG

QUICKBASIC
RPG
SGML
SNOBOL
UCSD PASCAL
VBA
VISUAL BASIC
VISUAL BASIC FOR
  APPLICATIONS
VISUAL C++
WORD BASIC

PLANETS AND SATELLITES

MAIN PLANETS (NAMED SATELLITES)

MERCURY
VENUS
EARTH (MOON)
MARS (PHOBOS, DEIMOS)
JUPITER (METIS, ADRASTEA, AMALTHEA,
  THEBE, IO, EUROPA, GANYMEDE, CAL-
  LISTO, LEDA, HIMALIA, LYSITHEA, ELARA,
  ANANKE, CARME, PASIPHAE, SINOPE)
SATURN (MIMAS, ENCELADUS, TETHYS,
  TELESTO, CALYPSO, DIONE, RHEA,
  HELENE, TITAN, HYPERION, IAPETUS,
  PHOEBE, JANUS, PAN, ATLAS,
  PROMETHEUS, PANDORA, EPIMETHEUS)
URANUS (MIRANDA, ARIEL, UMBRIEL,
  TITANIA, OBERON, CORDELIA, OPHELIA,
  BIANCA, CRESSIDA, DESDEMONA, JOLIET,
  PORTIA, ROSALIND, BELINDA, PUCK,
  CALIBAN, SYCORAX)
NEPTUNE (TRITON, NEREID, NAIAD,
  THALASSA, DESPINA, GALATEA, PROTEUS,
  LARISSA)
PLUTO (CHARON)

MINOR PLANETS

ACHILLES
ADONIS
AGAMEMNON
AMOR
APOLLO
ASTRAEA
ATEN
CERES
CHIRON
DACTYL
DAVIDA
EROS
EUNOMIA
EUPHROSYNE
EUROPA
GASPRA
HEBE
HEPHAISTOS
HERMES
HIDALGO
HYGIEA
ICARUS
IDA

IRIS
JUNO
MATHILDE
PALLAS
VESTA

COMETS

4	5–continued	6–continued	7–continued	8–continued
FAYE	KOPFF	TUTTLE	VÄISÄLÄ	DAYLIGHT
			WHIPPLE	HALE-BOPP
5	6	7		KOHOUTEK
BIELA	HALLEY	BENNETT	8	WESTPHAL
ENCKE	OLBERS	D'ARREST	BORRELLY	

9
COMAS SOLÀ
CROMMELIN
HYAKUTAKE

10
PONS-BROOKS

10—continued
SCHAUMASSE

11
AREND-ROLAND
SWIFT-TUTTLE

12
PONS-WINNECKE

13
SHOEMAKER-LEVY
STEPHAN-OTERMA

14
BRONSEN-METCALF

15
GIACOBINI-ZINNER
GRIGG-SKJELLERUP

NAMED NEAREST AND BRIGHTEST STARS

4
ROSS
VEGA
WOLF

5
CYGNI
DENEB
RIGEL
SIRUS
SPICA

6
ADHARA

6—continued
ALTAIR
CASTOR
CRUCIS
KRUGER
LUYTEN
POLLUX
SHAULA
SIRIUS

7
ANTARES
CANOPUS

7—continued
CAPELLA
LALANDE
PROCYON
REGULUS
TAU CETI

8
ACHERNAR
ARCTURUS
BARNARD'S
CENTAURI
KAPTEYN'S

9
ALDEBARAN
BELLATRIX
FOMALHAUT

10+
BETELGEUSE
EPSILON INDI
ALPHA CENTAURI
EPSILON ERIDANI
PROXIMA CENTAURI

THE CONSTELLATIONS

3
ARA
LEO

4
APUS
CRUX
GRUS
LYNX
LYRA
PAVO
VELA

5
ARIES
CETUS
DRACO
HYDRA
INDUS
LEPUS
LIBRA
LUPUS
MENSA
MUSCA

5—continued
NORMA
ORION
PYXIS
VIRGO

6
ANTLIA
AQUILA
AURIGA
BOÖTES
CAELUM
CANCER
CARINA
CORVUS
CRATER
CYGNUS
DORADO
FORNAX
GEMINI
HYDRUS
OCTANS
PICTOR

6—continued
PISCES
PUPPIS
SCUTUM
TAURUS
TUCANA
VOLANS

7
CEPHEUS
COLUMBA
LACERTA
PEGASUS
PERSEUS
PHOENIX
SAGITTA
SERPENS
SEXTANS

8
AQUARIUS
CIRCINUS
EQUULEUS
ERIDANUS

8—continued
HERCULES
LEO MINOR
SCORPIUS
SCULPTOR

9
ANDROMEDA
CENTAURUS
CHAMELEON
DELPHINUS
MONOCEROS
OPHIUCHUS
RETICULUM
URSA MAJOR
URSA MINOR
VULPECULA

10
CANIS MAJOR
CANIS MINOR
CASSIOPEIA
HOROLOGIUM
TRIANGULUM

11
CAPRICORNUS
SAGITTARIUS
TELESCOPIUM

12+
CAMELOPAR-
  DALIS
CANES
  VENATICI
COMA
  BERENICES
CORONA AUS-
  TRALIS
CORONA
  BOREALIS
MICRO-
  SCOPIUM
PISCIS
  AUSTRINUS
TRIANGULUM
  AUSTRALE

METEOR SHOWERS

6	7–continued	8–continued	11
LYRIDS	TAURIDS	PERSEIDS	QUADRANTIDS
URSIDS			
	8	10	12
7	CEPHEIDS	AUSTRALIDS	CAPRICORNIDS
CYGNIDS	GEMINIDS	OPHIUCHIDS	
LEONIDS	ORIONIDS	PHOENICIDS	

ASTRONOMERS ROYAL

JOHN FLAMSTEED (1675–1719)
EDMUND HALLEY (1720–42)
JAMES BRADLEY (1742–62)
NATHANIEL BLISS (1762–64)
NEVIL MASKELYNE (1765–1811)
JOHN POND (1811–35)
SIR GEORGE BIDDELL AIRY (1835–81)
SIR WILLIAM H. M. CHRISTIE (1881–1910)

SIR FRANK WATSON DYSON (1910–33)
SIR HAROLD SPENCER JONES (1933–55)
SIR RICHARD WOOLLEY (1955–71)
SIR MARTIN RYLE (1972–82)
SIR FRANCIS GRAHAM-SMITH (1982–91)
SIR ARNOLD WOLFENDALE (1991–95)
SIR MARTIN REES (1995–)

GEOLOGICAL TIME SCALE

ERA	PERIOD	EPOCH
CENOZOIC	QUATERNARY	HOLOCENE
		PLEISTOCENE
	TERTIARY	PLIOCENE
		IOCENE
		OLIGOCENE
		EOCENE
		PALAEOCENE
MESOZOIC	CRETACEOUS	
	JURASSIC	
	TRIASSIC	
PALAEOZOIC	PERMIAN	
	CARBONIFEROUS	
	DEVONIAN	
	SILURIAN	
	ORDOVICIAN	
	CAMBRIAN	
PRECAMBRIAN	PRECAMBRIAN	

CLOUDS

ALTOCUMULUS	CIRROSTRATUS	CUMULUS	STRATOCUMULUS
ALTOSTRATUS	CIRRUS	NIMBOSTRATUS	STRATUS
CIRROCUMULUS	CUMULONIMBUS		

NOTABLE WINDS

4
BERG
BISE
BORA
FÖHN

5
BURAN
FOEHN
GIBLI
ZONDA

6
AUSTRU
GHIBLI
HABOOB
KAMSIN
SANIEL
SIMOOM
SOLANO

7
CHINOOK
ETESIAN

7–continued
GREGALE
KHAMSIN
MELTEMI
MISTRAL
MONSOON
PAMPERO
SIROCCO

8
LEVANTER
LIBECCIO

8–continued
PAPAGAYO
SANTA ANA
WILLIWAW

9
HARMATTAN
LIBECCHIO
SNOW EATER

10
CAPE DOCTOR
EUROCLYDON

10–continued
TRAMONTANA
TRAMONTANE
WET CHINOOK
WILLY-WILLY

11
TEHUANTEPEC

12+
BRICKFIELDER
SOUTHERLY
  BUSTER

PREHISTORIC ANIMALS

8
EOHIPPUS
RUTIODON
SMILODON

9
IGUANODON
TRACHODON

10
ALLOSAURUS
ALTISPINAX
BAROSAURUS
DIPLODOCUS
DRYOSAURUS
EUPARKERIA
MESOHIPPUS
ORTHOMERUS
PLIOHIPPUS
PTERANODON
STEGOCERAS

11
ANATOSAURUS
ANCHISAURUS
APATOSAURUS
APHANERAMMA
CETIOSAURUS

11–continued
COELOPHYSIS
DEINONYCHUS
KRITOSAURUS
MANDASUCHUS
MERYCHIPPUS
MONOCLONIUS
POLACANTHUS
PTERODACTYL
RIOJASAURUS
SAUROLOPHUS
SCOLOSAURUS
SPINOSAURUS
STEGOSAURUS
TARBOSAURUS
TRICERATOPS

12
ANKYLOSAURUS
BRONTOSAURUS
CAMPTOSAURUS
CERATOSAURUS
CHASMOSAURUS
DEINOCHEIRUS
HYLAEOSAURUS
KENTROSAURUS
LAMBEOSAURUS

12–continued
MEGALOSAURUS
ORNITHOMIMUS
OURANOSAURUS
PLATEOSAURUS
TICINOSUCHUS

13
BRACHIOSAURUS
COMPSOGNATHUS
CORYTHOSAURUS
DESMATOSUCHUS
DILOPHOSAURUS
EDMONTOSAURUS
ERYTHROSUCHUS
HYPSELOSAURUS
HYPSILOPHODON
LESOTHOSAURUS
PANOPLOSAURUS
PENTACERATOPS
PROTOCERATOPS
PTERODACTYLUS
SCELIDOSAURUS
SCLEROMOCHLUS
STYRACOSAURUS
TENONTOSAURUS
TYRANNOSAURUS

14
BALUCHITHERIUM
CETIOSAURISCUS
CHASMATOSAURUS
EUOPLOCEPHALUS
MASSOSPONDYLUS
PSITTACOSAURUS
THESCELOSAURUS

15
PARASAUROLOPHUS
PROCHENEOSAURUS

16
PACHYRHI-
  NOSAURUS
PROCOMPSOG-
  NATHUS

17
HETERO-
  DONTOSAURUS

18
PACHY-
  CEPHALOSAURUS

189

ROCKS AND MINERALS

4
GOLD
MICA
OPAL
RUBY
TALC

5
AGATE
BERYL
BORAX
EMERY
FLINT
SHALE
SHARD
SKARN
TOPAZ
TRONA

6
ACMITE
ALBITE
ARKOSE
AUGITE
BARITE
BASALT
COPPER
DACITE
DUNITE
GABBRO
GALENA
GARNET
GNEISS
GYPSUM
HALITE
HAÜYNE
HUMITE
ILLITE
LEVYNE
MINIUM
NORITE
NOSEAN
PELITE
PYRITE
PYROPE
QUARTZ
RUTILE
SALITE
SCHIST
SCHORL
SILICA
SILVER
SPHENE
SPINEL
URTITE
ZIRCON

7
ALNOITE

7–continued
ALTAITE
ALUNITE
ANATASE
APATITE
ARSENIC
AXINITE
AZURITE
BARYTES
BAUXITE
BIOTITE
BISMUTH
BORNITE
BRECCIA
BRUCITE
CALCITE
CALOMEL
CELSIAN
CITRINE
COESITE
CUPRITE
DIAMOND
DIORITE
EMERALD
EPIDOTE
FELSITE
FOYAITE
GAHNITE
GEDRITE
GRANITE
GUMMITE
HELVITE
HESSITE
HOPEITE
HUNTITE
IJOLITE
JADEITE
KAINITE
KERNITE
KYANITE
LEUCITE
LIGNITE
MELLITE
MULLITE
OLIVINE
ORTHITE
RASPITE
REALGAR
SPARITE
SYENITE
SYLVITE
THORITE
THULITE
ZEOLITE
ZINCITE
ZOISITE

8
AEGIRINE
ALLANITE
ALUNOGEN
ANALCIME
ANALCITE
ANDESINE
ANDORITE
ANKERITE
ANTIMONY
ARCANITE
AUGELITE
AUTUNITE
BASANITE
BIXBYITE
BLOEDITE
BLUE JOHN
BOEHMITE
BORACITE
BRAGGITE
BRAUNITE
BRAVOITE
BRONZITE
BROOKITE
CALAMINE
CHIOLITE
CHLORITE
CHROMITE
CINNABAR
CORUNDUM
CROCOITE
CRYOLITE
CUBANITE
DATOLITE
DIALLAGE
DIASPORE
DIGENITE
DIOPSIDE
DIOPTASE
DOLERITE
DOLOMITE
ECLOGITE
ENARGITE
EPSOMITE
ESSEXITE
EULYTITE
EUXENITE
FAYALITE
FELDSPAR
FLUORITE
GIBBSITE
GOETHITE
GRAPHITE
HANKSITE
HAWAIITE
HEMATITE
HYACINTH
IDOCRASE

8–continued
ILMENITE
IODYRITE
JAROSITE
LAZURITE
LIMONITE
LITHARGE
MARSHITE
MEIONITE
MELANITE
MELILITE
MESOLITE
MIERSITE
MIMETITE
MONAZITE
MONETITE
MYLONITE
NEPHRITE
ORPIMENT
PARISITE
PERIDOTE
PERTHITE
PETALITE
PLATINUM
PORPHYRY
PREHNITE
PSAMMITE
PYRIBOLE
PYROXENE
RHYOLITE
ROCKSALT
SANIDINE
SAPPHIRE
SELLAITE
SIDERITE
SMECTITE
SODALITE
STANNITE
STEATITE
STIBNITE
STILBITE
STOLSITE
STRUVITE
TITANITE
TONALITE
TRACHYTE
VARISITE
VATERITE
WEHRLITE
WURTZITE
XENOTIME

9
ACANTHITE
ALMANDINE
ALUMINITE
AMPHIBOLE
ANDRADITE

9–continued
ANGLESITE
ANHYDRITE
ANORTHITE
ARAGONITE
ARGENTITE
ATACAMITE
BENITOITE
BRIMSTONE
BROMYRITE
BUNSENITE
BYTOWNITE
CARNALITE
CARNOTITE
CELESTITE
CERUSSITE
CHABAZITE
CHINACLAY
COBALTITE
COLUMBITE
COPIAPITE
COTUNNITE
COVELLITE
DANBURITE
DERBYLITE
DIATOMITE
ENSTATITE
ERYTHRITE
EUCAIRITE
EUCLASITE
EUDIALITE
FERBERITE
FIBROLITE
FLUORSPAR
GEHLENITE
GMELINITE
GOSLARITE
GRANULITE
GREYWACKE
GROSSULAR
GRUNERITE
HARMOTOME
HERCYNITE
HERDERITE
HORNSTONE
KAOLINITE
KIESERITE
LANARKITE
LAWSONITE
LEUCITITE
LIMESTONE
LODESTONE
MAGNESITE
MAGNETITE
MALACHITE
MALIGNITE
MANGANITE
MARCASITE

9—continued

MARGARITE
MARIALITE
MENDIPITE
MICROLITE
MIGMATITE
MILLERITE
MISPICKEL
MONZONITE
MORDENITE
MUGEARITE
MUSCOVITE
NANTOKITE
NATROLITE
NEPHELINE
NICCOLITE
OLDHAMITE
OLIVENITE
PECTOLITE
PENNINITE
PERCYLITE
PERICLASE
PHENAKITE
PHONOLITE
PIGEONITE
PISTACITE
POLLUCITE
POWELLITE
PROUSTITE
PULASKITE
QUARTZITE
RHODONITE
SANDSTONE
SCAPOLITE
SCHEELITE
SCOLECITE
SCORODITE
SMALLTITE
SOAPSTONE
SPODUMENE
STRENGITE
SYLVANITE
TACHYLITE
TANTALITE
TAPIOLITE
THERALITE
THOLEIITE
TREMOLITE
TRIDYMITE
TURQUOISE
URANINITE
VIVIANITE
WAGNERITE
WAVELLITE
WILLEMITE
WITHERITE
WULFENITE
ZEUNERITE

10

ACTINOLITE
ÅKERMANITE

10—continued

ALABANDITE
ANDALUSITE
ANKARAMITE
ARSENOLITE
BOROLONITE
BOURNONITE
BRONZITITE
CACOXENITE
CALEDONITE
CANCRINITE
CERVANTITE
CHALCEDONY
CHALCOCITE
CHLORITOID
CHRYSOLITE
CLAUDETITE
CLINTONITE
COLEMANITE
CONNELLITE
COQUIMBITE
CORDIERITE
DOUGLASITE
DYSCRASITE
EMPLECTITE
EMPRESSITE
EPIDIORITE
FORSTERITE
GANOMALITE
GARNIERITE
GAYLUSSITE
GEIKIELITE
GLAUBERITE
GLAUCONITE
GREENSTONE
HAMBERGITE
HEULANDITE
HORNBLENDE
HUEBNERITE
IGNIMBRITE
JAMESONITE
KIMBERLITE
LANTHANITE
LAUMONTITE
LAURIONITE
LEPIDOLITE
LHERZOLITE
LIMBURGITE
MASCAGNITE
MATLOCKITE
MEERSCHAUM
MELILITITE
MELTEIGITE
MICROCLINE
MIRABILITE
MOISSANITE
NEWBERYITE
OLIGOCLASE
ORTHOCLASE
PARAGONITE
PEKOVSKITE
PERIDOTITE

10—continued

PERTHOSITE
PHLOGOPITE
PHOSGENITE
PIEMONTITE
POLYBASITE
PYRALSPITE
PYROCHLORE
PYROLUSITE
PYRRHOTITE
RHYODACITE
RICHTERITE
RIEBECKITE
SAFFLORITE
SAMARSKITE
SAPPHIRINE
SERPENTINE
SHONKINITE
SPERRYLITE
SPHALERITE
STAUROLITE
STERCORITE
STISHOVITE
TESCHENITE
THENARDITE
THOMSONITE
THORIANITE
TORBERNITE
TOURMALINE
TRAVERTINE
TROEGERITE
ULLMANNITE
ULVÖSPINEL
VANADINITE
VITROPHYRE
WEBSTERITE
WHEWELLITE
WOLFRAMITE
ZINCBLENDE

11

ALLEMONTITE
AMBLYGONITE
ANORTHOSITE
APOPHYLLITE
BADDELEYITE
BERTRANDITE
BERYLLONITE
BROCHANTITE
CALCARENITE
CALCILUTITE
CALCIRUDITE
CARBONATITE
CARBORUNDUM
CASSITERITE
CERARGYRITE
CHARNOCKITE
CHIASTOLITE
CHLOANTHITE
CHONDRODITE
CHRYSOBERYL
CHRYSOCOLLA

11—continued

CLINOCHLORE
COBALTBLOOM
DAUBREELITE
EGLESTONITE
FERROAUGITE
FRANKLINITE
GLAUBER SALT
GLAUCOPHANE
GREENOCKITE
HARZBURGITE
HASTINGSITE
HAUSMANNITE
HYPERSTHENE
ICELAND SPAR
KATOPHORITE
LAPIS LAZULI
LEADHILLITE
LOELLINGITE
MANGANOSITE
MELANTERITE
MOLYBDENITE
MONTROYDITE
NEPHELINITE
NORDMARKITE
PENFIELDITE
PENTLANDITE
PHILLIPSITE
PITCHBLENDE
PLAGIOCLASE
PSILOMELANE
PUMPELLYITE
PYRARGYRITE
PYROCHROITE
RADIOLARITE
ROCK CRYSTAL
SILLIMANITE
SMITHSONITE
SPESSARTITE
TITANAUGITE
TRIPHYLLITE
VALENTINITE
VERMICULITE
VESUVIANITE
VILLIAUMITE
ZINNWALDITE

12

ANORTHOCLASE
ARSENOPYRITE
BISMUTHINITE
BOULANGERITE
CALCISILTITE
CHALCANTHITE
CHALCOPYRITE
CLAY MINERALS
CLINOPTOLITE
CLINOZOISITE
CRISTOBALITE
EDDINGTONITE
FELDSPATHOID
FERGUSSONITE

12–continued
FLUORAPATITE
GROSSULARITE
HEDENBERGITE
HEMIMORPHITE
LUXULLIANITE
METACINNABAR
MONTICELLITE
PYROMORPHITE
PYROPHYLLITE
RHODOCROSITE
SENARMONTITE
SKUTTERUDITE
STRONTIANITE
SYENODIORITE
TERLINGUAITE

12–continued
TETRAHEDRITE
THOMSENOLITE
TRACHYBASALT
WOLLASTONITE

13
ANTHOPHYLLITE
BREITHAUPTITE
CLINOPYROXENE
CUMMINGTONITE
JACUPIRANGITE
KALIOPHYLLITE
LEPIDOCROCITE
LITCHFIELDITE
ORTHOPYROXENE
QUARTZARENITE

13–continued
RHODOCHROSITE
STILPNOMELANE
THERMONATRITE
UNCOMPAHGRITE

14
CRYOLITHIONITE
HYDROMAGNESITE
LECHATELIERITE
LITHIOPHYLLITE
ORTHOQUARTZITE
PSEUDOBROOKITE
RAMMELSBERGITE
TRACHYANDESITE
XANTHOPHYLLITE

15
MONTMORILLONITE
PSEUDOTACHYLITE
STIBIOTANTALITE

16
GALENABISMUTHITE
ORTHOFERROSILITE
PHARMA-
  COSIDERITE

17
HYDRO-
  GROSSULARITE
TELLURO-
  BISMUTHITE

ORES

ELEMENT – ore(s)

3
TIN – cassiterite

4
IRON – haematite, magnetite
LEAD – galena
ZINC – sphalerite, smithsonite,
  calamine

5
BORON – kernite

6
BARIUM – barite, witherite
CERIUM – monazite,
  bastnaesite
COBALT – cobaltite, smaltite,
  erythrite
COPPER – malachite, azurite,
  chalcopyrite, bornite, cuprite
ERBIUM – monazite,
  bastnaesite
INDIUM – sphalerite,
  smithsonite, calamine
NICKEL – pentlandite,
  pyrrhotite
OSMIUM – iridosime
RADIUM – pitchblende,
  carnotite
SILVER – argentite, horn silver
SODIUM – salt

7
ARSENIC – realgar, orpiment,
  arsenopyrite
CADMIUM – greenockite
CAESIUM – lepidolite, pollucite
CALCIUM – limestone,
  gypsum, fluorite

7–continued
GALLIUM
HAFNIUM – zircon
HOLMIUM – monazite
IRIDIUM
LITHIUM – lepidolite,
  spodumene
MERCURY – cinnabar
NIOBIUM – columbite-tantalite,
  pyrochlore, euxenite
RHENIUM – molybdenite
RHODIUM
SILICON – silica
THORIUM – monazite
THULIUM – monazite
URANIUM – pitchblende,
  uraninite, carnotite
YTTRIUM – monazite

8
ANTIMONY – stibnite
CHROMIUM – chromite
LUTETIUM – monazite
PLATINUM – sperrylite
RUBIDIUM – lepidolite
SAMARIUM – monazite,
  bastnaesite
SCANDIUM – thortveitite,
  davidite
SELENIUM – pyrites
TANTALUM – columbite-
  tantalite
THALLIUM – pyrites
TITANIUM – rutile, ilmenite,
  sphere
TUNGSTEN – wolframite,
  scheelite
VANADIUM – carnotite,
  roscoelite, vanadinite

9
ALUMINIUM – bauxite
BERYLLIUM – beryl
GERMANIUM – germanite,
  argyrodite
LANTHANUM – monazite,
  bastnaesite
MAGNESIUM – magnesite,
  dolomite
MANGANESE – pyrolusite,
  rhodochrosite
NEODYMIUM – monazite,
  bastnaesite
PALLADIUM
POTASSIUM – sylvite,
  carnallite, polyhalite
RUTHENIUM – pentlandite,
  pyroxinite
STRONTIUM – celestite,
  strontianite
TELLURIUM
YTTERBIUM – monazite

10
DYSPROSIUM – monazite,
  bastnaesite
GADOLINIUM – monazite,
  bastnaesite
MOLYBDENUM – molybdenite,
  wulfenite
PHOSPHORUS – apatite

12
PRASEODYMIUM – monazite,
  bastnaesite
PROTACTINIUM – pitchblende

GEMSTONES

STONE (colour)

4
JADE (green, mauve, brown)
ONYX (various colours, banded)
OPAL (white, milky blue, or black with rainbow-coloured reflections)
RUBY (red)

5
AGATE (brown, red, blue, green, yellow)
BERYL (green, blue, pink)

5–continued
TOPAZ (usually yellow or colourless)

6
GARNET (red)
ZIRCON (all colours)

7
CITRINE (yellow)
DIAMOND (colourless)
EMERALD (green)

8
AMETHYST (purple)
SAPPHIRE (blue and other colours except red)

8–continued
SUNSTONE (whitish-red-brown flecked with gold)

9
MALACHITE (dark green banded)
MOONSTONE (white with bluish tinge)
SOAPSTONE (white or greenish)
TURQUOISE (greenish-blue)

10
AQUAMARINE (turquoise, greenish-blue)

10–continued
BLOODSTONE (green with red spots)
CHALCEDONY (red, brown, grey, or black)
SERPENTINE (usually green or white)
TOURMALINE (all colours)

11
LAPIS LAZULI (deep blue)

ECONOMIC TERMS AND THEORIES

3
GDP
GNP

4
FIFO

5
SLUMP

7
DUOPOLY
MARXISM
NEW DEAL
SLAVERY
STATICS
SURPLUS

8
FUNGIBLE
LENINISM
MONOPOLY
PROPERTY

9
BOOM CYCLE
BUST CYCLE
FREE TRADE
INELASTIC
LIQUIDITY
OLIGOPOLY
PUT OPTION

9–continued
RECESSION

10
ADDED VALUE
BEAR MARKET
BROAD MONEY
BULL MARKET
CAPITALISM
DEPRESSION
FISCAL DRAG
FREE MARKET
INVESTMENT
MONETARISM
PROTECTION
TRADE CYCLE
TROTSKYISM
VALUE ADDED

11
COLONIALISM
COMPETITION
CONSUMERISM
DEMAND CURVE
IMPERIALISM
MARGINALISM
MATERIALISM
NARROW MONEY
PHYSIOCRACY
REVISIONISM
STAGFLATION

11–continued
SYNDICALISM

12
ECONOMETRICS
ECONOMIC RENT
FISCAL POLICY
FIVE-YEAR PLAN
GOLD STANDARD
KEYNESIANISM
MARKET FORCES
MERCANTILISM
MIXED ECONOMY
NEW ECONOMICS
PRODUCTIVITY
PUBLIC SECTOR
SURPLUS VALUE
TRADE BARRIER

13
DEMAND ECONOMY
EXCHANGE VALUE
FUTURES MARKET
NEO-CLASSICISM
OPTIONS MARKET
PRIVATE SECTOR

14
BALANCED BUDGET
COMMAND ECONOMY

14–continued
CORPORATE STATE
ECONOMIC GROWTH
ECONOMIC POLICY
MACROECONOMICS
MICROECONOMICS
MONETARY POLICY
NATIONAL INCOME
WINDFALL PROFIT

15
AGGREGATE DEMAND
INFLATIONARY GAP
POSITIONAL GOODS
SUPPLY AND DEMAND
TOTALITARIANISM
VELOCITY OF MONEY
WAGE-PRICE SPIRAL

16
COST OF PRODUCTION
DEFICIT FINANCING
DIVISION OF LABOUR
ECONOMIES OF SCALE

16—continued
INSTITUTIONALISM
RETAIL PRICE INDEX
WELFARE ECONOMICS

17
MEANS OF PRODUCTION

18
DIMINISHING RETURNS
ECONOMIC CLASSICISM

18—continued
ELASTICITY OF DEMAND
PERFECT COMPETITION

19+
DIALECTICAL MATERIALISM
ECONOMIC EQUILIBRIUM
GROSS DOMESTIC
 PRODUCT
GROSS NATIONAL PRODUCT
LAISSEZ-FAIRE ECONOMICS

19+—continued
PRICES AND INCOMES
 POLICY
SUPPLY-SIDE ECONOMICS

MEDICINE AND HEALTH

MEDICAL FIELDS AND SPECIALTIES

7
ANATOMY
MYOLOGY
OTOLOGY
UROLOGY

8
CYTOLOGY
EUGENICS
NOSOLOGY
ONCOLOGY
SEROLOGY

9
AETIOLOGY
ANDROLOGY
AUDIOLOGY
HISTOLOGY
NECROLOGY
NEUROLOGY
ORTHOTICS
OSTEOLOGY
PATHOLOGY
PLEOPTICS
RADIOLOGY
RHINOLOGY

10
CARDIOLOGY
EMBRYOLOGY
GERIATRICS
IMMUNOLOGY
MORPHOLOGY
NEPHROLOGY
OBSTETRICS
ORTHOPTICS
PROCTOLOGY
PSYCHOLOGY
SEMEIOLOGY
TERATOLOGY

11
DERMATOLOGY
GERONTOLOGY
GYNAECOLOGY
HAEMATOLOGY
LARYNGOLOGY
LOGOPAEDICS
PAEDIATRICS
RADIOGRAPHY
STOMATOLOGY

12
CYTOGENETICS
EPHEBIATRICS
EPIDEMIOLOGY
ORTHOPAEDICS
PHARMACOLOGY
RADIOBIOLOGY
RHEUMATOLOGY
SYNDESMOLOGY
THERAPEUTICS
TRAUMATOLOGY

13
ENDOCRINOLOGY
OPHTHALMOLOGY
PSYCHOMETRICS

14
OTOLARYNGOLOGY
SYMPTOMATOLOGY

15
DERMATOGLYPHICS
NEUROPHYSIOLOGY
PSYCHOPATHOLOGY

16
GASTRO-
  ENTEROLOGY
PSYCHO-
  GERIATRICS
PSYCHO-
  PHYSIOLOGY

17+
COGNITIVE
  PSYCHOLOGY
INTERVENTIONAL
  RADIOLOGY
NUCLEAR
  CARDIOLOGY
OTORHINO-
  LARYNGOLOGY
PSYCHO-
  LINGUISTICS
PSYCHO-
  PHARMACOLOGY

COMPLEMENTARY/ALTERNATIVE THERAPIES

ACUPUNCTURE
AROMATHERAPY
ART THERAPY
AVERSION THERAPY
BALNEOTHERAPY
BEHAVIOUR THERAPY
CHIROPRACTIC
COGNITIVE THERAPY
COLOUR THERAPY
CONFRONTATION THERAPY
CRYSTAL THERAPY
DRAMA THERAPY
ELECTROCONVULSIVE
  THERAPY
ELECTROSHOCK THERAPY
ELECTROTHERAPY
FAMILY THERAPY

GERSON CURE
GESTALT THERAPY
GROUP THERAPY
HOMEOPATHY
HUMANISTIC THERAPY
HYDROTHERAPY
HYPNOTHERAPY
INSULIN SHOCK THERAPY
MECHANOTHERAPY
MEGAVITAMIN THERAPY
METRAZOL SHOCK
  THERAPY
MUSIC THERAPY
NARCOTHERAPY
NATUROPATHY
OCCUPATIONAL THERAPY
OSTEOPATHY

PLAY THERAPY
PRIMAL THERAPY
PSYCHOTHERAPY
RATIONAL–EMOTIVE
  THERAPY
RECREATIONAL THERAPY
REFLEXOLOGY
REGRESSION THERAPY
RELAXATION THERAPY
RELEASE THERAPY
ROGERIAN THERAPY
SEX THERAPY
SHIATSU
SHOCK THERAPY
SLEEP THERAPY
SOUND THERAPY

BONES

3
RIB

4
ULNA

5
ANVIL
COSTA
FEMUR
ILIUM
INCUS
PUBIS
SKULL
SPINE
TALUS
TIBIA
VOMER

6
CARPAL
CARPUS
COCCYX
CUBOID
FIBULA
HALLUX
HAMMER
PELVIS

6–continued
RACHIS
RADIUS
SACRUM
STAPES
TARSAL
TARSUS

7
CRANIUM
HIPBONE
HUMERUS
ISCHIUM
JAWBONE
KNEECAP
KNEEPAN
MALLEUS
MASTOID
MAXILLA
PATELLA
PHALANX
SCAPULA
STERNUM
STIRRUP

8
BACKBONE

8–continued
CLAVICLE
HEEL BONE
MANDIBLE
SCAPHOID
SHINBONE
SPHENOID
VERTEBRA

9
ANKLEBONE
CALCANCUS
CHEEKBONE
FUNNY BONE
HYOID BONE
MAXILLARY
NASAL BONE
PHALANGES
THIGHBONE
WRISTBONE

10
ASTRAGALUS
BREASTBONE
CANNON BONE
COLLARBONE
HAUNCH BONE

10–continued
METACARPAL
METACARPUS
METATARSAL
METATARSUS

11
ETHMOID BONE
FLOATING RIB
FRONTAL BONE

12
PARIETAL BONE
SPINAL COLUMN
TEMPORAL BONE

13
OCCIPITAL BONE
SESAMOID BONES
SHOULDER BLADE
ZYGOMATIC BONE

14+
INNOMINATE BONE
VERTEBRAL
  COLUMN

MAJOR ARTERIES

AORTA
BRACHIAL
CAROTID
FEMORAL

HEPATIC
ILIAC
INNOMINATE
MESENTERIC

PULMONARY
RADIAL
RENAL
SUBCLAVIAN

THORACIC
TIBIAL
ULNAR

MAJOR VEINS

BASILIC
BRACHIAL
CEPHALIC
FEMORAL
HEPATIC

HEPATIC PORTAL
ILIAC
INFERIOR VENA
  CAVA
JUGULAR

PULMONARY
RENAL
SAPHENOUS
SUBCLAVIAN

SUPERIOR VENA
  CAVA
SUPRARENAL
TIBIAL

THE EAR

ANVIL
AUDITORY NERVE
BASILAR
 MEMBRANE
COCHLEA
EARDRUM
EUSTACHIAN TUBE
FENESTRA OVALIS
FENESTRA
 ROTUNDA

HAMMER
INCUS
INNER EAR
LABYRINTH
MALLEUS
MEMBRANE OF
 REISSNER
MIDDLE EAR
ORGAN OF CORTI
OSSICLES

OVAL WINDOW
PINNA
RECEPTOR CELLS
ROUND WINDOW
SACCULE
SCALA MEDIA
SCALA TYMPANI
SCALA VESTIBULI
SEMICIRCULAR
 CANAL

STAPES
STIRRUP
TECTORIAL
 MEMBRANE
TUNNEL OF CORTI
TYMPANIC
 MEMBRANE
UTRICLE
VESTIBULAR NERVE

THE EYE

AQUEOUS HUMOUR
BLIND SPOT
CHOROID
CILIARY BODY
CONE
CONJUNCTIVA
CORNEA

EYELASH
FOVEA
HYALOID CANAL
IRIS
LACRIMAL GLAND
LENS
MEIBOMIAN GLAND

OPTIC NERVE
PUPIL
RETINA
ROD
SCLERA
VITREOUS HUMOUR
YELLOW SPOT

MUSCLES

4
PSOAS

5
TERES

6
BICEPS
RECTUS
SOLEUS
VASTUS

7
DELTOID
GLUTEUS
ILIACUS
TRICEPS

8
ANCONEUS
MASSETER
OPPONENS
PECTORAL
PERONEUS
PLATYSMA
POSTURAL
RHOMBOID
SCALENUS
SERRATUS
SKELETAL
TIBIALIS

9
DEPRESSOR
ILIOPSOAS

9–continued
MYLOHYOID
OBTURATOR
POPLITEUS
QUADRATUS
SARTORIUS
SPHINCTER
SUPINATOR
TRAPEZIUS
VOLUNTARY

10
BRACHIALIS
BUCCINATOR
EPICRANIUS
HYOGLOSSUS
QUADRICEPS

10–continued
STYLOHYOID
TEMPORALIS

11
ORBICULARIS
STERNOHYOID

12
STYLOGLOSSUS

13+
GASTROCNEMIUS
STERNOMASTOID
STERNOCLEIDO-
 MASTOID

GLANDS

5
LIVER
SWEAT

6
BUCCAL
PINEAL
TARSAL
THYMUS

7
ADRENAL
COWPER'S

7–continued
GASTRIC
MAMMARY
PAROTID
THYROID

8
BRUNNER'S
DUCTLESS
EXOCRINE
PANCREAS
PROSTATE

8–continued
SALIVARY

9
ENDOCRINE
MEIBOMIAN
PITUITARY
PREPUTIAL
SEBACEOUS

10
BARTHOLIN'S
SUBLINGUAL

10–continued
SUPRARENAL
VESTIBULAR

11
LIEBERKÜHN'S
PARATHYROID

12
SUBMAXILLARY

13
BULBOURETHRAL
SUBMANDIBULAR

SURGICAL OPERATIONS

7
MYOTOMY – MUSCLE
LOBOTOMY – NERVE FIBRES FROM FRONTAL LOBE OF BRAIN

8
MYECTOMY – MUSCLE
TENOTOMY – TENDON
VAGOTOMY – VAGUS NERVE
VASOTOMY – SPERM DUCT

9
AMNIOTOMY – AMNIOTIC MEMBRANES
COLECTOMY – COLON
COLOSTOMY – COLON
COLPOTOMY – VAGINA
CORDOTOMY – PART OF SPINAL CORD
CYSTOTOMY – BLADDER
GONIOTOMY – DUCT IN EYE
ILEECTOMY – ILEUM
ILEOSTOMY – ILEUM
IRIDOTOMY – IRIS
LEUCOTOMY – NERVE FIBRES IN BRAIN
LITHOTOMY – KIDNEY STONE
LOBECTOMY – LOBE OF AN ORGAN
MYOPLASTY – MUSCLE
NEUROTOMY – NERVE
OSTECTOMY – BONE
OSTEOTOMY – BONE
OTOPLASTY – EAR
PUBIOTOMY – PUBIC BONE

9–continued
PYELOTOMY – PELVIS OF KIDNEY
RHIZOTOMY – NERVE ROOTS
THYROTOMY – THYROID GLAND
TOPECTOMY – PART OF BRAIN
VALVOTOMY –HEART VALVE
VASECTOMY – SPERM DUCT

10
ANTRECTOMY – PART OF STOMACH
ANTROSTOMY – BONE CAVITY
APICECTOMY – ROOT OF TOOTH
ARTHROTOMY – JOINT CAPSULE
CAECOSTOMY – CAECUM
CORDECTOMY – VOCAL CORD
CRANIOTOMY – SKULL
CYSTECTOMY – BLADDER
CYSTOSTOMY – BLADDER
EMBRYOTOMY – FETUS
ENTEROTOMY – INTESTINE
EPISIOTOMY – VAGINAL OPENING
GASTROTOMY – STOMACH
HYMENOTOMY – HYMEN
IRIDECTOMY – IRIS
JEJUNOTOMY – JEJUNUM
KERATOTOMY – CORNEA
LAPAROTOMY – ABDOMEN

10–continued
LUMPECTOMY – BREAST TUMOUR
MASTECTOMY – BREAST
MYOMECTOMY – FIBROIDS
NEPHROTOMY – KIDNEY
NEURECTOMY – NERVE
ORBITOTOMY – BONE AROUND EYE
OVARIOTOMY – OVARY
PHLEBOTOMY – VEIN
PLEUROTOMY – PLEURAL MEMBRANE
PROCTOTOMY – RECTUM OR ANUS
RACHIOTOMY – BACKBONE
SCLEROTOMY – WHITE OF EYE
SCROTOTOMY – SCROTUM
STERNOTOMY – BREAST-BONE
TARSECTOMY – ANKLE BONES OR EYELID TISSUE
TENOPLASTY – TENDON
THYMECTOMY – THYMUS GLAND
UVULECTOMY – UVULA
VARICOTOMY – VARICOSE VEIN
VITRECTOMY – VITREUS HUMOUR
VULVECTOMY – VULVA

11
ANGIOPLASTY – BLOOD VESSEL
ARTERIOTOMY – ARTERY

11–continued
ARTHRECTOMY – JOINT
CAPSULOTOMY – LENS CAPSULE OF EYE
COLPOPLASTY – VAGINA
CYSTOPLASTY – BLADDER
EMBOLECTOMY – EMBOLUS, BLOOD CLOT
ENTERECTOMY – INTESTINE
ENTEROSTOMY – SMALL INTESTINE
FRAENECTOMY – TISSUE BENEATH TONGUE
GASTRECTOMY – STOMACH
GASTROSTOMY – STOMACH
GENIOPLASTY – CHIN
GLOSSECTOMY – TONGUE
HELCOPLASTY – SKIN ULCERS
HEPATECTOMY – LIVER
HYSTEROTOMY – WOMB
INCUDECTOMY – MIDDLE EAR OSSIDE
JEJUNECTOMY – JEJUNUM
JEJUNOSTOMY – JEJUNUM
KERATECTOMY – CORNEA
LABIOPLASTY –LIPS
LARYNGOTOMY – LARYNX
MAMMOPLASTY – BREAST
MYRINGOTOMY – EARDRUM
NEPHRECTOMY – KIDNEY
NEPHROSTOMY – KIDNEY
OMENTECTOMY – PERI-TONEUM OF STOMACH
ORCHIDOTOMY – TESTIS
OVARIECTOMY – OVARY
PAPILLOTOMY – PART OF BILE DUCT
PHLEBECTOMY – VEIN
PLEURECTOMY – PLEURAL MEMBRANE
POLYPECTOMY – POLYP
PROCTECTOMY – RECTUM
PYELOPLASTY – PELVIS OF KIDNEY
PYLORECTOMY – PART OF STOMACH
RHINOPLASTY – NOSE
SCLERECTOMY – WHITE OF EYE
SPLENECTOMY – SPLEEN
SYNOVECTOMY – MEM-BRANE AROUND JOINT
TARSOPLASTY – EYELID
THALAMOTOMY – PART OF BRAIN
THORACOTOMY – CHEST CAVITY
TRACHEOTOMY – WINDPIPE
TYMPANOTOMY – EARDRUM
URETEROTOMY – URETER
URETHROTOMY – URETHRA

11–continued
VALVULOTOMY – HEART VALVE
VARICECTOMY – VARICOSE VEINS
VESICOSTOMY – BLADDER

12
ARTERIECTOMY – ARTERY
ARTHROPLASTY – JOINT
CHEILOPLASTY – LIPS
CINGULECTOMY – PART OF BRAIN
DUODENOSTOMY – DUODENUM
GASTROPLASTY – STOMACH
GINGIVECTOMY – GUM TISSUE
HERNIOPLASTY – HERNIA
HYSTERECTOMY – WOMB
KERATOPLASTY – CORNEA
LARYNGECTOMY – LARYNX
MASTOIDOTOMY – MASTOID BONE
MENISCECTOMY – KNEE CARTILAGE
OOPHORECTOMY –OVARY
ORCHIDECTOMY – TESTIS
PALATOPLASTY – CLEFT PALATE
PALLIDECTOMY – PART OF BRAIN
PHALLOPLASTY – PENIS
PYLOROPLASTY – STOMACH OUTLET
STAPEDECTOMY – THIRD EAR OSSICLE
THORACECTOMY – RIB
THROMBECTOMY – BLOOD CLOT
TONSILLOTOMY – TONSIL
TRACHEOSTOMY – WIND PIPE
TURBINECTOMY – BONE IN NOSE
URETERECTOMY – URETER
URETEROSTOMY – URETER
URETHROSTOMY – URETHRA
VAGINOPLASTY – VAGINA

13
ADENOIDECTOMY – ADENOIDS
ARTERIOPLASTY – ARTERY
CARDIOMYOTOMY – STOMACH OPENING
DERMATOPLASTY – SKIN
HEMICOLECTOMY – PART OF COLON
HEPATICOSTOMY – LIVER
ILEOCOLOSTOMY – ILEUM AND COLON

13–continued
MASTOIDECTOMY – MASTOID
MYRINGOPLASTY – EARDRUM
NEURONOPLASTY – NERVES
OESOPHAGOTOMY – GULLET
OPHTHALMOTOMY – EYE
PANCREATOTOMY – PANCREAS
PERINEOPLASTY – VAGINAL OPENING
PHALANGECTOMY – FINGER OR TOE BONES
PHARYNGECTOMY – PHARYNX
PHRENICECTOMY – PHRENIC NERVE
PNEUMONECTOMY – LUNG
PROSTATECTOMY – PROSTATE GLAND
PYLOROMYOTOMY – STOMACH OUTLET
SALPINGECTOMY – FALLOPIAN TUBE
SALPINGOSTOMY – FALLOPIAN TUBE
SIGMOIDECTOMY – PART OF COLON
STAPHYLECTOMY – UVULA
SYMPATHECTOMY – SYMPATHETIC NERVE
SYMPHYSIOTOMY – FRONT OF PELVIS
THORACOPLASTY – CHEST CAVITY
THYROIDECTOMY – THYROID GLAND
TONSILLECTOMY – TONSILS
TRABECULOTOMY – DUCT IN EYE
MYRINGOTOMY, TYMPAN-OTOMY – EARDRUM
TYMPANOPLASTY – EARDRUM
URETEROPLASTY – URETER
URETHROPLASTY – URETHRA
VASOVASOSTOMY – REJOIN-ING OF SEVERED SPERM DUCT
VESICULECTOMY – SEMINAL VESICLE

14
APPENDICOSTOMY – APPENDIX
BLEPHAROPLASTY –EYELID
CHOLECYSTOTOMY – GALL BLADDER

14–continued

CHOLEDOCHOTOMY – BILE DUCT
CLITORIDECTOMY – CLITORIS
ENDARTERECTOMY – INNER WALL OF
  ARTERY
EPIDIDYMECTOMY – SPERM DUCT
HYPOPHYSECTOMY – PITUITARY GLAND
OESOPHAGOSTOMY – GULLET
OPHTHALMECTOMY – EYE
PANCREATECTOMY – PANCREAS
SEQUESTRECTOMY – DEAD BONE
SPHINCTEROTOMY – SPHINCTER MUSCLE
TRABECULECTOMY – PART OF EYE

15

CHOLECYSTECTOMY – GALL BLADDER
ILEOPROCTOSTOMY – ILEUM AND RECTUM
JEJUNOILEOSTOMY – JEJUNUM AND ILEUM
LITHONEPHROTOMY – KIDNEY STONE
LYMPHADENECTOMY – LYMPH NODE
NEPHROLITHOTOMY – KIDNEY STONE
PYELOLITHOTOMY – KIDNEY STONE

16

PERICARDIOSTOMY – MEMBRANE AROUND
  HEART
PROCTOCOLECTOMY – RECTUM AND
  COLON
SPHINCTERECTOMY – SPHINCTER MUSCLE
STRICTUROPLASTY – STRICTURE
VENTRICULOSTOMY – CAVITY OF BRAIN

17

GASTROENTEROSTOMY – STOMACH AND
  SMALL INTESTINE

17–continued

GASTROJEJUNOSTOMY – STOMACH AND
  JEJUNUM
HAEMORRHOIDECTOMY – HAEMORRHOIDS
PARATHYROIDECTOMY – PARATHYROID
  GLAND

18

COLPOPERINEOPLASTY – VAGINAL
  OPENING
EPIDIDYMOVASOSTOMY – SPERM DUCTS
GASTRODUODENOSTOMY – STOMACH AND
  DUODENUM
URETEROENTEROSTOMY – URETER AND
  BOWEL
VASO-EPIDIDYMOSTOMY – SPERM DUCTS

19

CHOLECYSTENTEROSTOMY – GALL
  BLADDER AND SMALL INTESTINE
URETERONEOCYSTOSTOMY – URETER AND
  BLADDER
URETEROSIGMOIDOSTOMY – URETER AND
  PART OF BOWEL

20+

CHOLECYSTODUODENOSTOMY – GALL
  BLADDER AND DUODENUM
CHOLECYSTOGASTROSTOMY – GALL
  BLADDER AND STOMACH
DACRYOCYSTORHINOSTOMY – TEAR SAC
  AND NOSE
GASTRO-OESOPHAGOSTOMY – STOMACH
  AND GULLET
TRANSURETERO-URETEROSTOMY – ONE
  URETER TO THE OTHER

MEDICATION

4	7–continued	8	8–continued	9–continued
DOPA	CHLORAL	ANTABUSE	SUBTILIN	CARBACHOL
	CODEINE	BARBITAL	URETHANE	CARBROMAL
5	DAPSONE	COLCYNTH	VIOMYCIN	CASTOR OIL
ALOES	DIGOXIN	COLISTIN	WARFARIN	CLEMIZOLE
JALAP	DOXEPIN	DIAZEPAM		CLONIDINE
L-DOPA	EMETINE	ETHOTOIN	**9**	CLOPAMIDE
OPIUM	HEPARIN	FRADICIN	ALOXIPRIN	CORTISONE
SENNA	HIRUDIN	GLUCAGON	AMILORIDE	CYCLIZINE
	INSULIN	HYOSCINE	AZAPETINE	DIGITALIS
6	MENTHOL	LAETRILE	BARBITONE	DIGITOXIN
HEROIN	METHOIN	LEVODOPA	BECLAMIDE	DITHRANOL
OUBAIN	MOGADON	MANNITOL	BENZHEXOL	EPSOM SALT
	MUSTINE	MAZINDOL	BIPERIDEN	ETOGLUCID
7	PULVULE	MORPHINE	BISACODYL	FRUSEMIDE
ACONITE	QUININE	NAPROXEN	BISULPHAN	GALLAMINE
ASPIRIN	SOTALOL	NEOMYCIN	BLEOMYCIN	GLYMIDINE
BROMIDE	SURAMIN	OXAZEPAM	BUCLIZINE	IPRINDOLE
CALOMEL	TYLOCIN	PIMOZIDE	BUPHENINE	ISONIAZID
CASCARA				

9–continued

KANAMYCIN
LORAZEPAM
MECLOZINE
MEGESTROL
MELPHALAN
MEPACRINE
MESTRANOL
METFORMIN
METHADONE
MIANSERIN
MYCOMYCIN
NADROLONE
NIALAMIDE
NICOTINYL
NIFURATEL
NUX VOMICA
OESTROGEN
OXACILLIN
PETHIDINE
PHENAZONE
PHENETOIN
POLYMIXIN
PRIMIDONE
PROMAZINE
PROQUANIL
PYOCYANIN
QUINIDINE
RIFAMYCIN
RIMITEROL
STANOLONE
SULTHIAME
TRICLOFOS
TROXIDONE
VANOMYCIN

10

ALPRENOLOL
AMANTADINE
AMPICILLIN
ANTAZOLINE
BASITRACIN
BENORYLATE
CANDICIDIN
CARBOMYCIN
CEPHALEXIN
CLOFIBRATE
CLONAZEPAM
CLORINDOLE
COLCHICINE
CROTAMITON
CYTARABINE
DICOUMAROL
DIPENZEPIN
DIPIPANONE
DISULFIRAM
ERYTHRITOL
ETHAMBUTOL
ETHINAMATE
ETHYNODIOL
FENOPROFEN
FLURAZEPAM

10–continued

FRAMYCETIN
GENTAMYCIN
ICHTHAMMOL
IMIPRAMINE
IPRONIAZID
ISOXUPRINE
KETOPROFEN
LINCOMYCIN
MEPERIDINE
MEPHENESIN
MEPYRAMINE
METHYLDOPA
METOLAZONE
METOPROLOL
NITRAZAPAM
NOVOBIOCIN
OXPRENADOL
OXYPERTINE
PAPAVERINE
PENICILLIN
PHENACETIN
PHENELZINE
PHOLCODINE
PICROTOXIN
PIPERAZINE
PREDNISONE
PRIMAQUINE
PROBENECID
PROPANOLOL
PYOCYANASE
RESORCINOL
RIFAMPICIN
SALBUTAMOL
STRYCHNINE
TOLAZAMIDE
TOLAZOLINE
TROMETAMOL
URAMUSTINE

11

ACETANILIDE
ACTINOMYCIN
ALKA SELTZER
ALLOPURINOL
AMOBARBITAL
AMODIAQUINE
AMPHETAMINE
AMYL NITRITE
ANILERIDINE
APOMORPHINE
BETHANIDINE
CAPREOMYCIN
CARBIMAZOLE
CARISPRODOL
CLINDAMYCIN
CLOREXOLONE
CYCLOSERINE
CYPROTERONE
DESERPIDINE
DESIPRAMINE
DIAMORPHINE

11–continued

DIENOESTROL
DOXORUBICIN
DOXYCYCLINE
ETHEBENECID
ETHIONAMIDE
ETHISTERONE
HALOPERIDOL
HYDROXYUREA
HYDROXYZINE
HYOSCYAMINE
IDOXURIDINE
IPECACUANHA
LEVORPHANOL
MAPROTILINE
MATHIMAZOLE
MEPROBAMATE
METHENOLONE
METHICILLIN
METHOXAMINE
MITHRAMYCIN
NAPHAZOLINE
NIKETHAMIDE
PAPAVERETUM
PARACETAMOL
PARALDEHYDE
PAROMOMYCIN
PENTAZOCINE
PHENAZOCINE
PHENETURIDE
PHENINDIONE
PHENIRAMINE
PHENTERMINE
PRENYLAMINE
PROGESTOGEN
TERBUTALINE
THEOBROMINE
THIOGUANINE
THIOPENTONE
THYMOXAMINE
TRIAMTERENE
TRIAZIQUONE
TYROTHRYCIN
VASOPRESSIN
VINBLASTINE
VINCRISTINE

12

AMPHOTERICIN
AZATHIOPRINE
BROMO SELTZER
CHLORAMBUCIL
CHLORBUTANOL
CHLORDANTOIN
CHLORHEXADOL
CLOMIPRAMINE
CYCLANDELATE
DEBRISOQUINE
DICHLOROPHEN
DISOPYRAMIDE
DROSTANOLONE
ERYTHROMYCIN

12–continued

ETHOSUXIMIDE
FENFLURIDINE
FLUOXURIDINE
FLUPHENAZINE
FLUSPIRILENE
GLAUBER'S SALT
GRISEOFULVIN
GUAIPHENESIN
GUANETHIDINE
HYDRALLAZINE
HYDRARGAPHEN
INDOMETHACIN
ISOPRENALINE
LIOTHYRONINE
LYNOESTRENOL
MANNOMUSTINE
MECAMYLAMINE
METHANDRIONE
METHAQUALONE
METHOTREXATE
METHYPRYLONE
METHYSERGIDE
OLEANDOMYCIN
ORPHENADRINE
OXOLINIC ACID
OXYMESTERONE
PERPHENAZINE
PHENSUXIMIDE
PHENTOLAMINE
PHILOCARPINE
PIPERIDOLATE
PODOPHYLLINE
PREDNISOLONE
PROCARBAZINE
PROCYCLIDINE
PROMETHAZINE
PROTHIPENDYL
PYRAZINAMIDE
ROCHELLE SALT
SALICYLAMIDE
SELTZER WATER
STILBOESTROL
STREPTOMYCIN
SULPHADOXINE
TETRACYCLINE
THEOPHYLLINE
THIACETAZONE
THIORIDAZINE
TRIMEPRAZINE
TRIMIPRAMINE
TRYPARSAMIDE
VALPROIC ACID

13

ACETAZOLAMIDE
ACETOHEXAMIDE
ALLYLESTRENOL
AMINOPHYLLINE
AMITRIPTYLINE
BETAMETHASONE
BUTOBARBITONE

13–continued
CARBAMAZEPINE
CARBENICILLIN
CARBINOXAMINE
CEPHALOGLYCIN
CEPHALORIDINE
CEPHALOSPORIN
CHLORMEZANONE
CO-TRIMOXAZOLE
DEXAMETHASONE
DIATHIAZININE
DIHYDRALAZINE
DIPHENOXYLATE
DIPROPHYLLINE
GLIBENCLAMIDE
HEXOBARBITONE
MEFANAMIC ACID
METHANDERIONE
METHAPYRILENE
METHYLENE BLUE
MITROBRONITOL
NALIDIXIC ACID
NORTRYPTYLINE
ORCIPRENALINE
PENICILLAMINE
PHENMETRAZINE
PHENOTHIAZINE
PHENYLEPHRINE
PHYSOSTIGMINE
PROPANTHELINE
PROTHIONAMIDE
PROTRIPTYLINE
SALICYLIC ACID
SPECTINOMYCIN
SULPHADIAZINE
THIOPROPAZATE
TRIAMCINOLONE

14
ACETYLCYSTEINE
AMYLOBARBITONE
BECLOMETHASONE
BENDROFLUAZIDE
BENZODIAZEPINE
CHLORAL HYDRATE
CHLORCYCLIZINE
CHLOROPYRILENE
CHLOROTHIAZIDE
CHLORPROMAZINE
CHLORPROPAMIDE
CHLORTHALIDONE
CROMOLYN SODIUM
CYCLOBARBITONE
CYCLOPENTAMINE
CYCLOPENTOLATE
CYPROHEPTADINE
DEXAMPHETAMINE
DEXTROMORAMIDE

14–continued
DIETHYLPROPION
DIHYDROCODEINE
DIMENHYDRINATE
DIMETHISTERONE
DYDROGESTERONE
ETHACRYNIC ACID
ETHYLOESTRENOL
FLUFENAMIC ACID
GLUTETHIMIDINE
HEPTABARBITONE
HYDROCORTISONE
LIQUID PARAFFIN
MERCAPTOPURINE
METHOSERPIDINE
MILK OF MAGNESIA
NITROFURANTOIN
NORETHISTERONE
PARAMETHADIONE
PENTOBARBITONE
PHENETHICILLIN
PHENYLBUTAZONE
SEIDLITZ POWDER
SODIUM SULPHATE
SULPHACETAMIDE
SULPHADIDIMINE
SULPHAFURAZOLE
SULPHISOXAZOLE
XYLOMETAZOLINE

15
CHLORAMPHENICOL
CHLORMETHIAZOLE
CHLORPROTHIXENE
DEXTROTHYROXINE
DIMETHOTHIAZINE
DIPHENHYDRAMINE
FLUDROCORTISONE
METHYLCELLULOSE
NITROGEN MUSTARD
NORETHANDROLONE
OXYPHENBUTAZONE
OXYTETRACYCLINE
PENTAERYTHRITOL
PHENAZOPYRIDINE
PHENOLPHTHALEIN
SULPHAMETHIZOLE
SULPHAQUANIDINE
SULPHINPYRAZOLE
THYROCALCITONIN
TRANYLCYPROMINE
TRIFLUOPERAZINE

16
BENZYL PENICILLIN
BROMOPHENIRAMINE
CHLORDIAZEPOXIDE
CHLOROTRIANISENE
CHLORPHENIRAMINE

16–continued
CHLORPHENOXAMINE
CHLORPHENTERMINE
CYCLOPENTHIAZIDE
CYCLOPHOSPHAMIDE
DEXTROMETHORPHAN
LITHIUM CARBONATE
METHOXYPHENAMINE
PARAFORMALDEHYDE
PHENOXYBENZAMINE
PROCHLORPERAZINE
TETRAHYDROZOLINE

17
BICARBONATE OF SODA
CEPHALOTHIN SODIUM
CHLORTETRACYCLINE
CHOLINE SALICYLATE
CLOXACILLIN SODIUM
DICHLOROPHENAMIDE
DIHYDROERGOTAMINE
ETHINYLOESTRADIOL
MAGNESIUM SULPHATE
METHOTRIMEPRAZINE
METHYLAMPHETAMINE
SODIUM BICARBONATE
SULPHAMETHOXAZOLE

18
DEXTROPROPOXYPHENE
DICHLORALPHENAZONE
DIMETHYLSULPHOXIDE
HYDROXYAMPHETAMINE
MAGNESIUM CARBONATE
MAGNESIUM HYDROXIDE
METHYLTESTOSTERONE
PROCAINE PENICILLIN

19
DIETHYLSTILBESTEROL
DIHYDROSTREPTOMYCIN
ETHYL BISCOUMACETATE
GLYCERINE TRINITRATE
HYDROCHLOROTHIAZIDE
HYDROXYPROGESTERONE
HYDROXYSTILBAMIDINE
MEDROXYPROGESTERONE
PHENYLPROPANOLAMINE

20+
BENTHAZINE PENICILLIN
BROMODIPHENYLHYDRAINE
CHLORAZEPATE POTASSIUM
CHOLINE THEOPHYLLINATE
DIMETHYLCHLORTETRACY-
  CLINE
PARA-AMINOSALICYLIC ACID
PHENOXYMETHYLPENI-
  CILLIN
PHTHALYLSULPHATHIAZOLE

PSYCHOLOGY TERMS

2&3
ID
IQ
ADD
DSM
ECT
EGO
PVS
REM

4
AMOK
FEAR
KORO
MIND
PICA
PTSD
SADS
SANE
SKEW

5
ANIMA
BINGE
FUGUE
FUROR
HABIT
IMAGO
LATAH
MANIA

6
ABULIA
AFFECT
ANIMUS
ANOMIA
AUTISM
CENSOR
DÉJÀ VU
ENGRAM
EONISM
FADING
LIBIDO
MENCAP
MUTISM
PHOBIA
PSYCHE
SADISM
SCHISM
SODOMY
STRESS
TRANCE

7
AMENTIA
AMNESIA
ANXIETY
AROUSAL
BONDING
BULIMIA

7—continued
COMPLEX
COUVADE
DEREISM
ECSTASY
EIDETIC
ELATION
EMOTION
EMPATHY
FANTASY
IMAGERY
INSIGHT
LERESIS
OPERANT
PARADOX
PSYCHIC
SHAPING
T-GROUP
WINDIGO
ZOOPSIA

8
ANALYSIS
ANOREXIA
APHRENIA
ASTHENIC
ATARAXIA
AVOIDANT
BISEXUAL
BLOCKING
CHAINING
CONATION
CONFLICT
DELUSION
DEMENTIA
DOPAMINE
DYSBULIA
DYSLOGIA
EUPHORIA
EXPOSURE
FREUDIAN
FROTTAGE
GENOGRAM
HEBETUDE
HYSTERIA
IDEATION
ILLUSION
INSANITY
INSTINCT
LOBOTOMY
NEUROSIS
ONEIRISM
PARANOIA
PARANOID
PSELLISM
REACTIVE
SUPEREGO

9
ADDICTION
AEROPHAGY
AGROMANIA
AKATHISIA
ANALYSAND
ANHEDONIA
ARCHETYPE
ASYNDESIS
AUTOSCOPY
BABY BLUES
CATALEPSY
CATATONIA
COCAINISM
COGNITION
DYSPHEMIA
DYSSOCIAL
ECHOLALIA
EROTICISM
EXTROVERT
FETISHISM
FLASHBACK
FRIGIDITY
GEOPHAGIA
HYPOBULIA
HYPOMANIA
IDEOMOTOR
IMITATION
IMPLOSION
INTROVERT
LALLATION
LEUCOTOMY
MASOCHISM
MENTAL AGE
MODELLING
MONOMANIA
NEOLOGISM
OBSESSION
OBSESSIVE
PALILALIA
PRECOCITY
PROMPTING
PSYCHOSIS
PYROMANIA
SCULPTING
SPLITTING
SURROGATE
SYMBOLISM
VOYEURISM
ZOOPHOBIA

10
ABREACTION
ALIENATION
ANANKASTIC
APOTREPTIC
ATTACHMENT
BELL AND PAD

10—continued
BORDERLINE
CHILD ABUSE
CITALOPRAM
CLUTTERING
COMPULSION
CONVERSION
COPROLALIA
DEPENDENCE
DEPRESSION
DIPSOMANIA
DIVAGATION
DROMOMANIA
ECHOPRAXIA
EROTOMANIA
EXALTATION
EXTINCTION
FOLIE À DEUX
GESTALTISM
HANDEDNESS
HYPNAGOGIC
HYPOTHYMIA
HYSTERICAL
IMPRINTING
LESBIANISM
LOGORRHOEA
MONOPHOBIA
NARCISSISM
NECROMANIA
NEGATIVISM
OLANZAPINE
PAEDERASTY
PARAMNESIA
PAREIDOLIA
PAROXETINE
PERCEPTION
PITHIATISM
POLYPHAGIA
PROJECTION
PSYCHIATRY
PSYCHOLOGY
PSYCHOPATH
REGRESSION
REPRESSION
RUMINATION
SAMARITANS
SATYRIASIS
SERTINDOLE
SERTRALINE
STAMMERING
STEREOTYPY
STUTTERING
SUGGESTION
WITHDRAWAL
XENOPHOBIA
ZOOPHILISM

11
AGORAPHOBIA
ALEXITHYMIA
AMBIVALENCE
BIOFEEDBACK
COUNSELLING
CYCLOTHYMIA
DOUBLE-BIND
DYSPAREUNIA
ECHOKINESIS
GANSER STATE
GLOSSOLALIA
HEBEPHRENIA
HYPERPRAXIA
HYPNOPOMPIC
IDIOT SAVANT
KLEPTOMANIA
LYCANTHROPY
MEGALOMANIA
MELANCHOLIA
NEUROTICISM
NYCTOPHILIA
NYCTOPHOBIA
NYCTOPHONIA
NYMPHOMANIA
ORIENTATION
PAEDOPHILIA
PALIPHRASIA
PARAGRAPHIA
PARAPHRENIA
PARASUICIDE
PERSONALITY
PSYCHODRAMA
PSYCHOGENIC
RETARDATION
RETROGRAPHY
RISPERIDONE
ROLE PLAYING
SAD SYNDROME
SCHIZOTYPAL
SEXUAL ABUSE
SUBLIMATION
THALAMOTOMY
UNCONSCIOUS

12
BEHAVIOURISM
CANCER PHOBIA
CINGULECTOMY
CONDITIONING
DISPLACEMENT
DISSOCIATION
EXTRAVERSION
EXTROVERSION
FEINGOLD DIET
FLAGELLATION
GROUP THERAPY
HALFWAY HOUSE
HYPERGRAPHIA
HYPERKINESIA
HYPOCHONDRIA
INTRAVERSION

12–continued
INTROJECTION
INTROVERSION
NECROPHILISM
NEURASTHENIA
ONOMATOMANIA
PALINGRAPHIA
PHANEROMANIA
PREPAREDNESS
PSEUDOPLEGIA
PSYCHIATRIST
PSYCHOLOGIST
PSYCHOTICISM
SOMNAMBULISM
SUBCONSCIOUS
SUBSTITUTION
TIME SAMPLING
TRANSFERENCE
TRANSVESTISM

13
ANTIPSYCHOTIC
CONFABULATION
CROSS-DRESSING
DEREALIZATION
EVENT SAMPLING
EXHIBITIONISM
FAMILY THERAPY
HALLUCINATION
HOMOSEXUALITY
MENTAL ILLNESS
NORMALIZATION
PANIC DISORDER
PERSEVERATION
PHARMACOMANIA
PSYCHOKINESIS
PSYCHOMETRICS
PSYCHOSOMATIC
PSYCHOSURGERY
PSYCHOTHERAPY
REINFORCEMENT
RORSCHACH TEST
SCHIZOPHRENIA
SLEEP-WALKING
SOMNILOQUENCE
TWILIGHT STATE
VERBIGERATION

14
AUTOSUGGESTION
CLAUSTROPHOBIA
DISORIENTATION
DRUG DEPENDENCE
EFFORT SYNDROME
ENCOUNTER
  GROUP
IDENTIFICATION
MENTAL HANDICAP
NOCTAMBULATION
OEDIPUS COMPLEX
ONOMATOPOIESIS
PARAPSYCHOLOGY
PROJECTIVE TEST

14–continued
PSYCHOANALYSIS
PSYCHONEUROSIS
RETT'S SYNDROME
SECURITY OBJECT
SENILE DEMENTIA
TRANSSEXUALISM
WECHSLER SCALES

15
ANOREXIA
  NERVOSA
AVERSION THERAPY
BIPOLAR DISORDER
CAPGRAS'
  SYNDROME
CONDUCT
  DISORDER
DYSMORPHOPHO-
  BIA
ELECTRONARCOSIS
FREE ASSOCIATION
HELLER'S
  SYNDROME
HETEROSEXUALITY
NEUROPSYCHIATRY
PSEUDOMUTUALITY
PSYCHOPATHOLOGY
RATIONALIZATION
RETENTION DEFECT
SEXUAL DEVIATION
THOUGHT
  STOPPING

16
BEHAVIOUR
  THERAPY
BRIQUET'S
  SYNDROME
COGNITIVE
  THERAPY
CORE-AND-
  CLUSTER
DEFENCE
  MECHANISM
EXPRESSED
  EMOTION
FRAGILE-X
  SYNDROME
GLOBUS
  HYSTERICUS
INTELLIGENCE TEST
LOCKED-IN
  SYNDROME
MENTAL
  DEFICIENCY
MENTAL HEALTH
  ACTS
MENTAL
  IMPAIRMENT
NERVOUS
  BREAKDOWN

16–continued
OVERCOMPENSA-
  TION
PSYCHOGERI-
  ATRICS
PSYCHOPHYSIOL-
  OGY
SPECIAL HOSPITALS
TRICHOTILLOMANIA

17
AFFECTIVE
  DISORDER
ASPERGER'S
  SYNDROME
BELLE
  INDIFFERENCE
CIRCUMSTANTIAL-
  ITY
DEPERSONALIZA-
  TION
DYSMNESIC
  SYNDROME
DYSTHYMIC
  DISORDER
FLEXIBILITAS CEREA
MENTAL
  RETARDATION
PSYCHOLINGUIS-
  TICS
REACTION
  FORMATION
RELAXATION
  THERAPY
SEPARATION
  ANXIETY
TOURETTE'S
  SYNDROME

18
ASSOCIATION OF
  IDEAS
ATTACHMENT
  DISORDER
CONVERSION
  DISORDER
DOPAMINE
  HYPOTHESIS
GRADED SELF-
  EXPOSURE
INFERIORITY
  COMPLEX
KNIGHT'S-MOVE
  THOUGHT
KORSAKOFF'S
  SYNDROME
LEARNING
  DISABILITY
RESPONSE
  PREVENTION
SENSORY
  DEPRIVATION

PHOBIAS

ACAROPHOBIA - ITCHING
ACAROPHOBIA - MITES
ACERBOPHOBIA - SOURNESS
ACEROPHOBIA - SOURNESS
ACHLUOPHOBIA - DARKNESS
ACOUSTICOPHOBIA - SOUND
ACROPHOBIA - HIGH PLACES
ACROPHOBIA - SHARPNESS
AEROPHOBIA - DRAUGHTS
AGORAPHOBIA - CROWDS
AGORAPHOBIA - OPEN PLACES
AGYROPHOBIA - STREETS (CROSSING)
AILUROPHOBIA - CATS
ALGOPHOBIA - PAIN
ALTOPHOBIA - HIGH PLACES
AMATHOPHOBIA - DUST
ANAEMOPHOBIA - ANAEMIA
ANCRAOPHOBIA - WIND
ANDROPHOBIA - MEN
ANGINOPHOBIA - NARROWNESS
ANGLOPHOBIA - ENGLISH
ANTHOPHOBIA - FLOWERS
ANTHROPOPHOBIA - PEOPLE
ANTLOPHOBIA - FLOODS
APEIROPHOBIA - INFINITY
APIPHOBIA - BEES
ARACHNEPHOBIA - SPIDERS
ASTHENOPHOBIA - WEAKNESS
ASTRAPHOBIA - LIGHTNING
ASTRAPOPHOBIA - LIGHTNING
ATELOPHOBIA - IMPERFECTION
ATEPHOBIA - RUIN
AULOPHOBIA - FLUTES
AUROPHOBIA - GOLD
AUTOPHOBIA - LONELINESS
BACILLOPHOBIA - MICROBES
BACTERIOPHOBIA - BACTERIA
BALLISTOPHOBIA - BULLETS
BAROPHOBIA - GRAVITY
BATHOPHOBIA - DEPTH
BATOPHOBIA - HIGH BUILDINGS
BATOPHOBIA - HIGH PLACES
BATRACHOPHOBIA - REPTILES

BELONEPHOBIA - NEEDLES
BLENNOPHOBIA - SLIME
BROMIDROSIPHOBIA - BODY ODOUR
BRONTOPHOBIA - THUNDER
CANCEROPHOBIA - CANCER
CANCERPHOBIA - CANCER
CARCINOPHOBIA - CANCER
CARDIOPHOBIA - HEART DISEASE
CHAETOPHOBIA - HAIR
CHEIMAPHOBIA - COLD
CHEIMATOPHOBIA - COLD
CHIONOPHOBIA - SNOW
CHLOEROPHOBIA - CHOLERA
CHROMETOPHOBIA - MONEY
CHROMOPHOBIA - COLOUR
CHRONOPHOBIA - TIME (DURATION)
CIBOPHOBIA - FOOD
CLAUSTROPHOBIA - ENCLOSED PLACES
CLINOPHOBIA - BED (GOING TO BED)
CNIDOPHOBIA - INSECT STINGS
COITOPHOBIA - COITUS
COMETOPHOBIA - COMETS
COPROPHOBIA - FAECES
COPROSTASOPHOBIA - CONSTIPATION
CREMNOPHOBIA - PRECIPICES
CRYOPHOBIA - ICE, FROST
CRYSTALLOPHOBIA - CRYSTALS
CYMOPHOBIA - WAVES
CYNOPHOBIA - DOGS
DEMONOPHOBIA - DEMONS
DEMOPHOBIA - CROWDS
DERMATOPATHOPHOBIA - SKIN DISEASE
DERMATOSIOPHOBIA - SKIN
DIABETOPHOBIA - DIABETES
DIKEPHOBIA - JUSTICE
DORAPHOBIA - FUR
DROMOPHOBIA - MOTION
ECCLESIOPHOBIA - CHURCH
ECOPHOBIA - HOME
EISOPTROPHOBIA - MIRRORS
ELECTROPHOBIA - ELECTRICITY
ELEUTHEROPHOBIA - FREEDOM
EMETOPHOBIA - VOMITING
ENETOPHOBIA - PINS

ENTOMOPHOBIA - INSECTS
EOSOPHOBIA - DAWN
ERGOPHOBIA - WORK
ERMITOPHOBIA - LONELINESS
EROTOPHOBIA - SEX
ERYTHROPHOBIA - BLUSHING
FEBRIPHOBIA - FEVER
FRANCOPHOBIA - FRENCH
GALLOPHOBIA - FRENCH
GAMETOPHOBIA - MARRIAGE
GENOPHOBIA - SEX
GEPHYROPHOBIA - BRIDGES (CROSSING)
GERMANOPHOBIA - GERMANS
GEUMATOPHOBIA - TASTE
GLOSSOPHOBIA - SPEECH
GRAPHOPHOBIA - WRITING
GYNEPHOBIA - WOMEN
HADEPHOBIA - HELL
HAGIOPHOBIA - SAINTS
HAMARTOPHOBIA - SIN
HAPHOPHOBIA - TOUCH
HAPTOPHOBIA - TOUCH
HARPAXOPHOBIA - ROBBERS
HEDONOPHOBIA - PLEASURE
HELIOPHOBIA - SUN
HELMINTHOPHOBIA - WORMS
HEMAPHOBIA - BLOOD
HEMATOPHOBIA - BLOOD
HEMOPHOBIA - BLOOD
HERPETOPHOBIA - REPTILES
HIEROPHOBIA - PRIESTS
HIPPOPHOBIA - HORSES
HODOPHOBIA - TRAVEL
HOMICHLOPHOBIA - FOG
HORMEPHOBIA - SHOCK
HYDROPHOBIA - WATER
HYDROPHOBOPHOBIA - RABIES
HYGROPHOBIA - DAMPNESS
HYPEGIAPHOBIA - RESPONSIBILITY
HYPNOPHOBIA - SLEEP
HYPSOPHOBIA - HIGH PLACES
ICHTHYOPHOBIA - FISH
IDEOPHOBIA - IDEAS
JAPANOPHOBIA - JAPANESE
JUDEOPHOBIA - JEWS

KAKORRAPHIAPHOBIA - FAILURE
KATAGELOPHOBIA - RIDICULE
KENOPHOBIA - VOID
KERAUNOPHOBIA - THUNDER
KINETOPHOBIA - MOTION
KLEPTOPHOBIA - STEALING
KONIOPHOBIA -DUST
KOPOPHOBIA - FATIGUE
LALIOPHOBIA - SPEECH
LALOPHOBIA - SPEECH
LIMNOPHOBIA - LAKES
LINONOPHOBIA - STRING
LOGOPHOBIA - WORDS
LYSSOPHOBIA - INSANITY
MANIPHOBIA - INSANITY
MASTIGOPHOBIA - BEATING
MECHANOPHOBIA - MACHINERY
MENINGITOPHOBIA - MENINGITIS
METALLOPHOBIA - METAL
MICROBIOPHOBIA - MICROBES
MICROPHOBIA - SMALL THINGS
MONOPHOBIA - LONELINESS
MUSICOPHOBIA - MUSIC
MUSOPHOBIA - MICE
MYSOPHOBIA - DIRT
MYXOPHOBIA - SLIME
NECROPHOBIA -CORPSES
NEGROPHOBIA - NEGROES
NEOPHOBIA - NEW THINGS
NEPHOPHOBIA - CLOUDS
NEPHOPHOBIA - DISEASE
NYCTOPHOBIA - NIGHT
OCHLOPHOBIA - MOBS
OCHOPHOBIA - VEHICLES
ODONTOPHOBIA - TEETH
OECOPHOBIA - HOME
OECOPHOBIA - HOME
OIKOPHOBIA - HOME
OIKOPHOBIA - HOME
OLFACTOPHOBIA - SMELL
OMMETAPHOBIA - EYES
ONOMATOPHOBIA - NAMES
OPHICIOPHOBIA SNAKES
OPHIOPHOBIA - SNAKES
OPHRESIOPHOBIA - SMELL
ORNITHOPHOBIA - BIRDS

OSMOPHOBIA - SMELL
OURANOPHOBIA - HEAVEN
OURANOPHOBIA - HEAVEN
PAEDOPHOBIA - CHILDREN
PANPHOBIA - EVERYTHING
PANTOPHOBIA - EVERYTHING
PAPAPHOBIA - POPE
PARASITOPHOBIA - PARASITES
PARTHENOPHOBIA - YOUNG GIRLS
PATHOPHOBIA - DISEASE
PATROIOPHOBIA - HEREDITY
PECCATIPHOBIA - SIN
PEDICULOPHOBIA - LICE
PENIAPHOBIA - POVERTY
PHAGOPHOBIA - SWALLOWING
PHARMACOPHOBIA - DRUGS
PHASMOPHOBIA - GHOSTS
PHILOSOPHOBIA - PHILOSOPHY
PHOBOPHOBIA - FEAR
PHONOPHOBIA - SPEECH
PHOTOPHOBIA - LIGHT
PHRONEMOPHOBIA - THINKING
PHTHISIOPHOBIA - TUBERCULOSIS
PNEUMATOPHOBIA - SPIRITS
PNIGEROPHOBIA - SMOTHERING
PNIGOPHOBIA - SMOTHERING
POGONOPHOBIA - BEARDS
POINEPHOBIA - PUNISHMENT
POLITICOPHOBIA - POLITICS
POTAMOPHOBIA - RIVERS
POTOPHOBIA - DRINK
PTERONOPHOBIA - FEATHERS
PYROPHOBIA - FIRE
RECTOPHOBIA - RECTUM
RHABDOPHOBIA - MAGIC
RUSSOPHOBIA - RUSSIANS
RYPOPHOBIA - SOILING
SATANOPHOBIA - SATAN
SCABIOPHOBIA - SCABIES
SCIOPHOBIA - SHADOWS
SCOTOPHOBIA - DARKNESS
SIDEROPHOBIA - STARS

SINOPHOBIA - CHINESE
SITOPHOBIA - FOOD
SNAKEPHOBIA - SNAKES
SPERMATOPHOBIA - GERMS
SPERMOPHOBIA - GERMS
STASOPHOBIA - STANDING
STYGIOPHOBIA - HELL
SYMMETROPHOBIA - SYMMETRY
SYPHILOPHOBIA - SYPHILIS
TACHOPHOBIA - SPEED
TELEPHONOPHOBIA - TELEPHONE
TERATROPHOBIA - MONSTERS
TEUTONOPHOBIA - GERMANS
THAASOPHOBIA - IDLENESS
THALASSOPHOBIA - SEA
THANATOPHOBIA - DEATH
THEOPHOBIA - GOD
THERMOPHOBIA - HEAT
THIXOPHOBIA - TOUCH
TOCOPHOBIA - CHILDBIRTH
TONITROPHOBIA - THUNDER
TOPOPHOBIA - PLACES
TOXICOPHOBIA - POISON
TOXIPHOBIA - POISON
TOXOPHOBIA - POISON
TRAUMATOPHOBIA - INJURY
TREMOPHOBIA - TREMBLING
TRICHOPATHOPHOBIA - HAIR DISEASE
TRICHOPHOBIA - HAIR
TRICINOPHOBIA - TRICHINOSIS
TRISKAIDEKAPHOBIA - THIRTEEN
TRYPANOPHOBIA - INOCULATION
TUBERCULOPHOBIA - TUBERCULOSIS
TYRANNOPHOBIA - TYRANTS
URANOPHOBIA - HEAVEN
UROPHOBIA - URINE
VACCINOPHOBIA - INOCULATION
VENEROPHOBIA - VENEREAL DISEASE
VERMIPHOBIA - WORMS
XENOPHOBIA - FOREIGNERS
ZELOPHOBIA - JEALOUSY

RELIGION AND MYTHOLOGY

BOOKS OF THE BIBLE

OLD TESTAMENT

GENESIS
EXODUS
LEVITICUS
NUMBERS
DEUTERONOMY
JOSHUA
JUDGES
RUTH
1 SAMUEL
2 SAMUEL
1 KINGS
2 KINGS
1 CHRONICLES
2 CHRONICLES
EZRA
NEHEMIAH
ESTHER
JOB
PSALMS
PROVERBS
ECCLESIASTES
SONG OF SOLOMON

ISAIAH
JEREMIAH
LAMENTATIONS
EZEKIEL
DANIEL
HOSEA
JOEL
AMOS
OBADIAH
JONAH
MICAH
NAHUM
HABAKKUK
ZEPHANIAH
HAGGAI
ZECHARIAH
MALACHI

NEW TESTAMENT

MATTHEW
MARK
LUKE
JOHN

THE ACTS
ROMANS
1 CORINTHIANS
2 CORINTHIANS
GALATIANS
EPHESIANS
PHILIPPIANS
COLOSSIANS
1 THESSALONIANS
2 THESSALONIANS
1 TIMOTHY
2 TIMOTHY
TITUS
PHILEMON
HEBREWS
JAMES
1 PETER
2 PETER
1 JOHN
2 JOHN
3 JOHN
JUDE
REVELATION

APOCRYPHA

I ESDRAS
II ESDRAS
TOBIT
JUDITH
THE REST OF
  ESTHER
WISDOM
ECCLESIASTICUS
BARUCH, WITH
  EPISTLE OF
  JEREMIAH
SONG OF THE
  THREE CHILDREN
SUSANNA
BEL AND THE
  DRAGON
PRAYER OF
  MANASSES
I MACCABEES
II MACCABEES

BIBLICAL CHARACTERS

OLD TESTAMENT

AARON – elder brother of Moses; 1st high priest of Hebrews

ABEL – second son of Adam and Eve; murdered by brother Cain

ABRAHAM – father of Hebrew nation

ABSALOM – David's spoilt third son; killed after plotting against his father

ADAM – the first man created; husband of Eve

BAAL – fertility god of Canaanites and Phoenicians

BATHSHEBA – mother of Solomon

BELSHAZZAR – last king of Babylon, son of Nebuchadnezzar; Daniel interpreted his vision of writing on the wall as foretelling the downfall of his kingdom

BENJAMIN – youngest son of Jacob and Rachel. His descendants formed one of the 12 tribes of Israel

CAIN – first son of Adam and Eve; murdered his brother Abel

DANIEL – prophet at the court of Nebuchadnezzar with a gift for interpreting dreams

DAVID – slayed the giant Goliath

DELILAH – a Philistine seducer and betrayer of Samson

ELIJAH – Hebrew prophet, taken into heaven in a fiery chariot

ELISHA – prophet and disciple of Elijah

ENOCH – father of Methuselah

EPHRAIM – son of Joseph; founded one of the 12 tribes of Israel

ESAU – elder of Isaac's twin sons; tricked out of his birthright by his younger brother Jacob

ESTHER – beautiful Israelite woman; heroically protected her people

EVE – first woman; created as companion for Adam in Garden of Eden

EZEKIEL – prophet of Israel captured by Babylonians

GIDEON – Israelite hero and judge

GOLIATH – Philistine giant killed by David

HEZEKIAH – king of Judah (c 715–686 BC)

ISAAC – son of Abraham and Sarah, conceived in their old age; father of Jacob and Esau

ISAIAH – the greatest old testament prophet

ISHMAEL – Abraham's son by Hagar, handmaiden to his wife, Sarah; rival of Isaac

ISRAEL – new name given to Jacob after his reconciliation with Esau

JACOB – second son of Isaac and Rebekah, younger twin of Esau whom he tricked out of his inheritance. The 12 tribes of Israel were named after his sons and grandsons

JEREMIAH – one of the great prophets; foretold destruction of Jerusalem

JEZEBEL – cruel and lustful wife of Ahab, king of Israel

JOB – long-suffering and pious inhabitant of Uz

JONAH – after ignoring God's commands he was swallowed by a whale

JONATHAN – eldest son of Saul and close friend of David

JOSEPH – favourite son of Jacob and Rachel with his "coat of many colours"; sold into slavery by his jealous brothers

JOSHUA – succeeded Moses and led Israelites against Canaan. He defeated Jericho where the walls fell down

JUDAH – son of Jacob and Leah; founded tribe of Judah

LOT – nephew of Abraham; he escaped the destruction of Sodom, but his wife was turned into a pillar of salt for looking back

METHUSELAH – son of Enoch, the oldest person ever (969 years)

MIRIAM – sister of Aaron and Moses whom she looked after as a baby; prophetess and leader of Israelites

MOSES – Israel's great leader and lawgiver, he led the Israelites out of captivity in Egypt to the promised land of Canaan. Received ten commandments from Jehovah on Mt Sinai

NATHAN – Hebrew prophet at courts of David and Solomon

NEBUCHADNEZZAR – king of Babylon

NOAH – grandson of Methuselah, father of Shem, Ham, and Japheth; built ark to save his family and all animal species from the great flood

REBEKAH – wife of Isaac, mother of Jacob and Esau

RUTH – Moabite who accompanied her mother-in-law Naomi to Bethlehem. Remembered for her loyalty

SAMSON – Israelite judge of great physical strength; seduced and betrayed by Delilah

SAMUEL – prophet and judge of Israel

SARAH – wife of Abraham, mother of Isaac

SAUL – first king of Israel

SOLOMON – son of David and Bathsheba; remembered for his great wisdom and wealth

NEW TESTAMENT

ANDREW – fisherman and brother of Peter; one of 12 Apostles

BARABAS – Cypriot missionary; introduced Paul to the Church

BARABBAS – robber and murderer; in prison with Jesus and released instead of him

BARTHOLOMEW – possibly same person as Nathaniel, one of the 12 Apostles

CAIAPHAS – high priest of the Jews; Jesus brought to him after arrest

GABRIEL – angel who announced birth of Jesus to Mary; and of John the Baptist to Zechariah

HEROD – 1. the Great, ruled when Jesus was born 2. Antipas, son of Herod the Great, ruled when John the Baptist was murdered 3. Agrippa, killed James (brother of John) 4. Agrippa II, before whom Paul was tried

JAMES – 1. the Greater, one of 12 Apostles, brother of John 2. the Less, one of 12 Apostles 3. leader of the Church in Jerusalem and author of the New Testament epistle

JESUS – founder of Christianity

JOHN – youngest of 12 Apostles

JOHN THE BAPTIST – announced coming of Jesus, and baptized him

JOSEPH – 1. husband of Mary the mother of Jesus 2. of Arimathea, a secret disciple of Jesus

JUDAS ISCARIOT – the disciple who betrayed Jesus

LAZARUS – brother of Mary and Martha, raised from the dead by Jesus

LUKE – companion of Paul, author of Luke and Acts

MARK – author of the gospel; companion of Paul, Barnabas, and Peter

MARTHA – sister of Mary and Lazarus, friend of Jesus

MARY – 1. mother of Jesus 2. sister of Martha and Lazarus 3. Magdalene, cured by Jesus and the first to see him after the resurrection

MATTHEW – one of 12 Apostles, author of the gospel

MATTHIAS – chosen to replace the apostle Judas

MICHAEL – a chief archangel

NATHANIEL – see Bartholomew

NICODEMUS – a Pharisee who had a secret meeting with Jesus

PAUL – formerly Saul of Tarsus, persecutor of Christians; renamed after his conversion. Apostle to the Gentiles and author of epistles

PETER – Simon, one of 12 Apostles; denied Jesus before the crucifixion but later became leader of the Church

PHILIP – one of 12 Apostles

PILATE – Roman procurator of Judea; allowed Jesus to be crucified

SALOME – 1. wife of Zebedee, mother of James and John 2. daughter of Herodias; danced before Herod for the head of John the Baptist

SAUL – *see* Paul

SIMON – 1. Simon Peter *see* Peter 2. the Canaanite, one of 12 Apostles 3. one of Jesus' four brothers 4. the leper, in whose house Jesus was anointed 5. of Cyrene, carried the cross of Jesus 6. the tanner, in whose house Peter had his vision

STEPHEN – Christian martyr, stoned to death

THOMAS – one of 12 Apostles, named 'Doubting' because he doubted the resurrection

TIMOTHY – Paul's fellow missionary; two of Paul's epistles are to him

TITUS – convert and companion of Paul, who wrote him one epistle

PATRON SAINTS

NAME (Patron of)

AGATHA (bell-founders)

ALBERT THE GREAT (students of natural sciences)

ANDREW (Scotland)

BARBARA (gunners and miners)

BERNARD OF MONTJOUX (mountaineers)

CAMILLUS (nurses)

CASIMIR (Poland)

CECILIA (musicians)

CHRISTOPHER (wayfarers)

CRISPIN (shoemakers)

DAVID (Wales)

DIONYSIUS (DENIS) OF PARIS (France)

DUNSTAN (goldsmiths, jewellers, and locksmiths)

DYMPNA (insane)

ELIGIUS *or* ELOI (metalworkers)

ERASMUS (sailors)

FIACRE (gardeners)

FRANCES CABRINI (emigrants)

FRANCES OF ROME (motorists)

FRANCIS DE SALES (writers)

FRANCIS XAVIER (foreign missions)

FRIDESWIDE (Oxford)

GEORGE (England)

GILES (cripples)

HUBERT (huntsmen)

JEROME EMILIANI (orphans and abandoned children)

JOHN OF GOD (hospitals and booksellers)

JUDE (hopeless causes)

JULIAN (innkeepers, boatmen, travellers)

KATHERINE OF ALEXANDRIA (students, philosophers, and craftsmen)

LUKE (physicians and surgeons)

MARTHA (housewives)

NICHOLAS (children, sailors, unmarried girls, merchants, pawnbrokers, apothecaries, and perfumeries)

PATRICK (Ireland)

PETER NOLASCO (midwives)

SAVA (Serbian people)

VALENTINE (lovers)

VITUS (epilepsy and nervous diseases)

WENCESLAS (Czechoslovakia)

ZITA (domestic servants)

RELIGIOUS ORDERS

AUGUSTINIAN

BARNABITE

BENEDICTINE

BRIGITTINE

CAMALDOLESE

CAPUCHINS

CARMELITE

CARTHUSIAN

CISTERCIAN

DOMINICAN

FRANCISCAN

HOSPITALLERS

JERONYMITE

MINIMS

POOR CLARES

PREMONSTRATEN-SIAN

SALESIAN

SERVITE

SYLVESTRINE

TEMPLARS

THEATINE

TRAPPIST

TRINITARIAN

URSULINE

VISITANDINE, VISITATION

RELIGIOUS MOVEMENTS

3
BON
I AM
ZEN

4
AINU

5
BOSCI
ISLAM
KEGON
THAGS
THUGS

6
BABISM
PARSIS
SHINTO
TAOISM
VOODOO

7
AJIVIKA
BAHAISM
GIDEONS
JAINISM
JUDAISM
JUMPERS
LAMAISM
MORMONS

7–continued
PARSEES
QUAKERS
SHAKERS
SIKHISM
WAHABIS
ZIONISM

8
ABELIANS
ABELITES
ACOEMETI
ADAMITES
ADMADIYA
AHMADIYA
AMARITES
BAPTISTS
BUDDHISM
HINDUISM
HUMANISM
MAR THOMA
NICHIREN
NOSAIRIS
STUDITES

9
CALVINISM
CHUNTOKYO
FRANKISTS
HICKSITES

9–continued
HUGUENOTS
JANSENISM
METHODIST
PANTHEISM

10
ABSTINENTS
ADVENTISTS
AGONIZANTS
AMBROSIANS
BUCHANITES
CALIXTINES
PURATINISM

11
ABODE OF LOVE
ABRAHAMITES
ANABAPTISTS
ANGLICANISM
ARMINIANISM
BASILIDEANS
BERNARDINES
CATHOLICISM
COVENANTERS

12
ABECEDARIANS
BENEDICTINES
CHRISTIANITY

12–continued
SPIRITUALISM
UNITARIANISM

13
MOHAMMEDANISM
PROTESTANTISM
REDEMPTORISTS
SALVATION ARMY

14
CONGREGATIONAL
FUNDAMENTALISM

15
PRESBYTERIANISM

16
CHRISTIAN SCIENCE
PLYMOUTH
  BRETHREN
ROMAN
  CATHOLICISM

17
ANTIPAEDO-
  BAPTISTS
CONGREGATIONAL-
  ISM
JEHOVAH'S
  WITNESSES

CLERGY

ARCHBISHOP
ARCHDEACON
BISHOP
CANON

CARDINAL
CHAPLAIN
CURATE
DEACON

DEAN
ELDER
MINISTER

PARSON
POPE
PRIEST

RECTOR
VICAR
VICAR-FORANE

POPES

POPE (DATE OF ACCESSION)

ST PETER (42)
ST LINUS (67)
ST ANACLETUS (Cletus) (76)
ST CLEMENT I (88)
ST EVARISTUS (97)

ST ALEXANDER I (105)
ST SIXTUS I (115)
ST TELESPHORUS (125)
ST HYGINUS (136)
ST PIUS I (140)
ST ANICETUS (155)
ST SOTERUS (166)

ST ELEUTHERIUS (175)
ST VICTOR I (189)
ST ZEPHYRINUS (199)
ST CALLISTUS I (217)
ST URBAN I (222)
ST PONTIAN (230)
ST ANTERUS (235)

ST FABIAN (236)
ST CORNELIUS (251)
ST LUCIUS I (253)
ST STEPHEN I (254)
ST SIXTUS II (257)
ST DIONYSIUS (259)
ST FELIX I (269)
ST EUTYCHIAN (275)
ST CAIUS (283)
ST MARCELLINUS (296)
ST MARCELLUS I (308)
ST EUSEBIUS (309)
ST MELCHIADES (311)
ST SYLVESTER I (314)
ST MARCUS (336)
ST JULIUS I (337)
LIBERIUS (352)
ST DAMASUS I (366)
ST SIRICIUS (384)
ST ANASTASIUS I (399)
ST INNOCENT I (401)
ST ZOSIMUS (417)
ST BONIFACE I (418)
ST CELESTINE I (422)
ST SIXTUS III (432)
ST LEO I (the Great) (440)
ST HILARY (461)
ST SIMPLICIUS (468)
ST FELIX III (483)
ST GELASIUS I (492)
ANASTASIUS II (496)
ST SYMMACHUS (498)
ST HORMISDAS (514)
ST JOHN I (523)
ST FELIX IV (526)
BONIFACE II (530)
JOHN II (533)
ST AGAPETUS I (535)
ST SILVERIUS (536)
VIGILIUS (537)
PELAGIUS I (556)
JOHN III (561)
BENEDICT I (575)
PELAGIUS II (579)
ST GREGORY I (the Great)
   (590)
SABINIANUS (604)
BONIFACE III (607)
ST BONIFACE IV (608)
ST DEUSDEDIT (Adeodatus I)
   (615)
BONIFACE V (619)
HONORIUS I (625)
SEVERINUS (640)
JOHN IV (640)
THEODORE I (642)
ST MARTIN I (649)
ST EUGENE I (654)
ST VITALIAN (657)
ADEODATUS II (672)
DONUS (676)
ST AGATHO (678)

ST LEO II (682)
ST BENEDICT II (684)
JOHN V (685)
CONON (686)
ST SERGIUS I (687)
JOHN VI (701)
JOHN VII (705)
SISINNIUS (708)
CONSTANTINE (708)
ST GREGORY II (715)
ST GREGORY III (731)
ST ZACHARY (741)
STEPHEN II (III)* (752)
ST PAUL I (757)
STEPHEN III (IV) (768)
ADRIAN I (772)
ST LEO III (795)
STEPHEN IV (V) (816)
ST PASCHAL I (817)
EUGENE II (824)
VALENTINE (827)
GREGORY IV (827)
SERGIUS II (844)
ST LEO IV (847)
BENEDICT III (855)
ST NICHOLAS I (858)
ADRIAN II (867)
JOHN VIII (872)
MARINUS I (882)
ST ADRIAN III (884)
STEPHEN V (VI) (885)
FORMOSUS (891)
BONIFACE VI (896)
STEPHEN VI (VII) (896)
ROMANUS (897)
THEODORE II (897)
JOHN IX (898)
BENEDICT IV (900)
LEO V (903)
SERGIUS III (904)
ANASTASIUS III (911)
LANDUS (913)
JOHN X (914)
LEO VI (928)
STEPHEN VII (VIII) (928)
JOHN XI (931)
LEO VII (936)
STEPHEN VIII (IX) (939)
MARINUS II (942)
AGAPETUS II (946)
JOHN XII (955)
LEO VIII (963)
BENEDICT V (964)
JOHN XIII (965)
BENEDICT VI (973)
BENEDICT VII (974)
JOHN XIV (983)
JOHN XV (985)
GREGORY V (996)
SYLVESTER II (999)
JOHN XVII (1003)
JOHN XVIII (1004)

SERGIUS IV (1009)
BENEDICT VIII (1012)
JOHN XIX (1024)
BENEDICT IX (1032)
GREGORY VI (1045)
CLEMENT II (1046)
BENEDICT IX (1047)
DAMASUS II (1048)
ST LEO IX (1049)
VICTOR II (1055)
STEPHEN IX (X) (1057)
NICHOLAS II (1059)
ALEXANDER II (1061)
ST GREGORY VII (1073)
VICTOR III (1086)
URBAN II (1088)
PASCHAL II (1099)
GELASIUS II (1118)
CALLISTUS II (1119)
HONORIUS II (1124)
INNOCENT II (1130)
CELESTINE II (1143)
LUCIUS II (1144)
EUGENE III (1145)
ANASTASIUS IV (1153)
ADRIAN IV (1154)
ALEXANDER III (1159)
LUCIUS III (1181)
URBAN III (1185)
GREGORY VIII (1187)
CLEMENT III (1187)
CELESTINE III (1191)
INNOCENT III (1198)
HONORIUS III (1216)
GREGORY IX (1227)
CELESTINE IV (1241)
INNOCENT IV (1243)
ALEXANDER IV (1254)
URBAN IV (1261)
CLEMENT IV (1265)
GREGORY X (1271)
INNOCENT V (1276)
ADRIAN V (1276)
JOHN XXI (1276)
NICHOLAS III (1277)
MARTIN IV (1281)
HONORIUS IV (1285)
NICHOLAS IV (1288)
ST CELESTINE V (1294)
BONIFACE VIII (1294)
BENEDICT XI (1303)
CLEMENT V (1305)
JOHN XXII (1316)
BENEDICT XII (1334)
CLEMENT VI (1342)
INNOCENT VI (1352)
URBAN V (1362)
GREGORY XI (1370)
URBAN VI (1378)
BONIFACE IX (1389)
INNOCENT VII (1404)
GREGORY XII (1406)

211

MARTIN V (1417)
EUGENE IV (1431)
NICHOLAS V (1447)
CALLISTUS III (1455)
PIUS II (1458)
PAUL II (1464)
SIXTUS IV (1471)
INNOCENT VIII (1484)
ALEXANDER VI (1492)
PIUS III (1503)
JULIUS II (1503)
LEO X (1513)
ADRIAN VI (1522)
CLEMENT VII (1523)
PAUL III (1534)
JULIUS III (1550)
MARCELLUS II (1555)
PAUL IV (1555)
PIUS IV (1559)
ST PIUS V (1566)
GREGORY XIII (1572)
SIXTUS V (1585)

URBAN VII (1590)
GREGORY XIV (1590)
INNOCENT IX (1591)
CLEMENT VIII (1592)
LEO XI (1605)
PAUL V (1605)
GREGORY XV (1621)
URBAN VIII (1623)
INNOCENT X (1644)
ALEXANDER VII (1655)
CLEMENT IX (1667)
CLEMENT X (1670)
INNOCENT XI (1676)
ALEXANDER VIII (1689)
INNOCENT XII (1691)
CLEMENT XI (1700)
INNOCENT XIII (1721)
BENEDICT XIII (1724)
CLEMENT XII (1730)
BENEDICT XIV (1740)
CLEMENT XIII (1758)
CLEMENT XIV (1769)

PIUS VI (1775)
PIUS VII (1800)
LEO XII (1823)
PIUS VIII (1829)
GREGORY XVI (1831)
PIUS IX (1846)
LEO XIII (1878)
ST PIUS X (1903)
BENEDICT XV (1914)
PIUS XI (1922)
PIUS XII (1939)
JOHN XXIII (1958)
PAUL VI (1963)
JOHN PAUL I (1978)
JOHN PAUL II (1978)
*Stephen II died before conse-
cration and was dropped from
the list of popes in 1961;
Stephen III became
Stephen II

ARCHBISHOPS OF CANTERBURY

**ARCHBISHOP
(DATE OF ACCESSION)**

AUGUSTINE (597)
LAURENTIUS (604)
MELLITUS (619)
JUSTUS (624)
HONORIUS (627)
DEUSDEDIT (655)
THEODORUS (668)
BEORHTWEALD (693)
TATWINE (731)
NOTHELM (735)
CUTHBEORHT (740)
BREGUWINE (761)
JAENBEORHT (765)
ÆTHELHEARD (793)
WULFRED (805)
FEOLOGILD (832)
CEOLNOTH (833)
ÆTHELRED (870)
PLEGMUND (890)
ÆTHELHELM (914)
WULFHELM (923)
ODA (942)
ÆLFSIGE (959)
BEORHTHELM (959)
DUNSTAN (960)
ÆTHELGAR (988)
SIGERIC SERIO (990)
ÆLFRIC (995)

ÆLFHEAH (1005)
LYFING (1013)
ÆTHELNOTH (1020)
EADSIGE (1038)
ROBERT OF JUMIÈGES
  (1051)
STIGAND (1052)
LANFRANC (1070)
ANSELM (1093)
RALPH D'ESCURES (1114)
WILLIAM OF CORBEIL (1123)
THEOBALD OF BEC (1139)
THOMAS BECKET (1162)
RICHARD OF DOVER (1174)
BALDWIN (1184)
REGINALD FITZJOCELIN
  (1191)
HUBERT WALTER (1193)
REGINALD (1205)
JOHN DE GRAY (1205)
STEPHEN LANGTON (1213)
WALTER OF EVESHAM (1128)
RICHARD GRANT
  (Wethershed) (1229)
RALPH NEVILL (1231)
JOHN OF SITTINGBOURNE
  (1232)
JOHN BLUND (1232)
EDMUND RICH (1234)
BONIFACE OF SAVOY (1245)

ADAM OF CHILLENDEN
  (1270)
ROBERT KILWARDBY (1273)
ROBERT BURNELL (1278)
JOHN PECHAM (1279)
ROBERT WINCHELSEY
  (1295)
THOMAS COBHAM (1313)
WALTER REYNOLDS (1314)
SIMON MEPHAM (1328)
JOHN STRATFORD (1334)
JOHN OFFORD (1348)
THOMAS BRADWARDINE
  (1349)
SIMON ISLIP (1349)
SIMON LANGHAM (1366)
WILLIAM WHITTLESEY (1369)
SIMON SUDBURY (1375)
WILLIAM COURTENAY (1381)
THOMAS ARUNDEL (1397)
ROGER WALDEN (1398)
THOMAS ARUNDEL (1399)
HENRY CHICHELE (1414)
JOHN STAFFORD (1443)
JOHN KEMPE (1452)
THOMAS BOURGCHIER
  (1454)
JOHN MORTON (1486)
HENRY DEANE (1501)
WILLIAM WARHAM (1504)
THOMAS CRANMER (1533)

REGINALD POLE (1556)
MATTHEW PARKER (1559)
EDMUND GRINDAL (1576)
JOHN WHITGIFT (1583)
RICHARD BANCROFT (1604)
GEORGE ABBOT (1611)
WILLIAM LAUD (1633)
WILLIAM JUXON (1660)
GILBERT SHELDON (1663)
WILLIAM SANCROFT (1678)
JOHN TILLOTSON (1691)
THOMAS TENISON (1695)
WILLIAM WAKE (1716)
JOHN POTTER (1737)
THOMAS HERRING (1747)

MATTHEW HUTTON (1757)
THOMAS SECKER (1758)
FREDERICK CORNWALLIS
  (1768)
JOHN MOORE (1783)
CHARLES MANNERS
  SUTTON (1805)
WILLIAM HOWLEY (1828)
JOHN BIRD SUMNER (1848)
CHARLES THOMAS
  LONGLEY (1862)
ARCHIBALD CAMPBELL TAIT
  (1868)
EDWARD WHITE BENSON
  (1883)

FREDERICK TEMPLE (1896)
RANDALL THOMAS
  DAVIDSON (1903)
COSMO GORDON LANG
  (1928)
GEOFFREY FRANCIS FISHER
  (1945)
ARTHUR MICHAEL RAMSEY
  (1961)
FREDERICK DONALD
  COGGAN (1974)
ROBERT ALEXANDER
  KENNEDY RUNCIE (1980)
GEORGE LEONARD CAREY
  (1991)

RELIGIOUS TERMS

2
BA
HO
OM

3
ALB
ARA
AUM
HAJ
PEW
PIX
PYX
YAD

4
AMBO
APSE
AZAN
BEMA
BUJI
BULL
COPE
COWL
FONT
HADJ
HAJJ
HALO
HELL
HOOD
HOST
HYMN
JUBE
KAMA
KNOP
LENT
MACE
MASS
NAOS
NAVE

4–continued
OLAH
RAMA
SOMA
TIEN
VOID
WAKE
YOGA

5
ABBOT
ABYSS
AGATI
AISLE
ALLEY
ALTAR
AMBRY
AMICE
ANGEL
APRON
ARMOR
BANNS
BASON
BEADS
BIBLE
BIMAH
BODHI
BRIEF
BUGIA
BURSE
COTTA
CREED
CROSS
CRUET
DIKKA
EMETH
EPHOD
FALDA
GOHEI
HYLIC

5–continued
IHRAM
KALPA
KARMA
LAVER
LIMBO
MOTZI
NICHE
PASCH
PESAH
PESHA
PSALM
ROSHI
SHIVA
STOUP
SYNOD
TOTEM
USHER
VEDAS
WAFER

6
ABBACY
ABODAH
ADVENT
AGUNAH
AHIMSA
AKASHA
AKEDAH
AL CHET
ANOINT
ANTHEM
AUMBRY
AVODAH
BARSOM
BAT KOL
BEADLE
BELFRY
CANTOR
CHOHAN

6–continued
CHOVAH
CHRISM
CLERGY
DHARMA
DHYANA
DITTHI
DOSSAL
DUCHAN
EASTER
FLECHE
FRATER
GLORIA
HEAVEN
HEKHAL
HESPED
KAIROS
KIBLAH
KISMET
KITTEL
LITANY
MANTRA
MATINS
MISSAL
NIGGUN
NIMBUS
ORATIO
ORISON
PARVIS
PESACH
PRAYER
PULPIT
ROCHET
ROSARY
SANGHA
SERMON
SERVER
SHARI'A
SHRIVE

6–continued
SPIRIT
SUTRAS
TAUHID
TIPPET
VERGER
VESTRY

7
ACCIDIA
ACCIDIE
ACOLYTE
AGRAPHA
AMPULLA
ANGELUS
APOSTIL
APOSTLE
APPAREL
ASHAMNU
ATHEISM
AUREOLE
BADCHAN
BANKERS
BAPTISM
BATHING
BELL COT
BERAKAH
BIRETTA
CASSOCK
CHALICE
CHAMETZ
CHANCEL
CHANTRY
CHAPTER
CHAZZAN
CHRISOM
COLLECT
COMPLIN
CORNICE
CROSIER

213

7–continued

CROZIER
DHARANI
DIOCESE
DIPTYCH
EILETON
FISTULA
GAYATRI
GELILAH
GEULLAH
GRADINE
GREMIAL
HASSOCK
HEATHEN
HEKDESH
INTROIT
KHEREBU
LECTERN
LOCULUS
MANIPLE
MINARET
MOZETTA
NARTHEX
NIRVANA
NOCTURN
PALLIUM
PENANCE
PILGRIM
PURUSHA
REQUIEM
REREDOS
SAMSARA
STHIBEL
TALLITH
TONSURE
TRINITY
TZADDIK
VESPERS
WORSHIP

8

ABLUTION
ABSTEMII
A CAPELLA
AFFLATUS

8–continued

AFFUSION
AFIKOMEN
AGNUS DEI
ANTIPHON
ARMORIUM
AUTO DA FE
AVE MARIA
BEADROLL
BELL COTE
BEMIDBAR
BENEFICE
BREVIARY
BUTSUDEN
CANCELLI
CANTICLE
CIBORIUM
CINCTURE
COMPLINE
CONCLAVE
CORPORAL
CRUCIFIX
DALMATIC
DIKERION
DISCIPLE
DOXOLOGY
EPIPHANY
EVENSONG
FRONTLET
HABDALAH
MANIPULE
NATIVITY
NER TAMID
NIVARANA
OBLATION
PAROKHET
PASSOVER
PREDELLA
RESPONSE
SACRISTY
SURPLICE
TASHLICH
TRIPTYCH
VESTMENT

9

ADIAPHORA
ANAMNESIS
APOCRYPHA
ARBA KOSOT
ARCHANGEL
ASPERSION
CANDLEMAS
CARTOUCHE
CATACOMBS
CATECHISM
CERECLOTH
CHALITZAH
CHRISTMAS
COLLATION
COMMUNION
EPHPHETHA
EUCHARIST
FALDSTOOL
FLABELLUM
FORMULARY
MUNDATORY
OFFERTORY
PACE-AISLE
PURGATORY
SANCTUARY
YOM KIPPUR

10

ABSOLUTION
AGATHOLOGY
ALLOCUTION
AMBULATORY
ANTECHAPEL
APOCALYPSE
BALDACHINO
BAR MITZVAH
BAS MITZVAH
BAT MITZVAH
BENEDICTUS
CATAFALQUE
CLERESTORY
CUTTY STOOL
HAGIOSCOPE
INDULGENCE

10–continued

INTINCTION
INVOCATION
LADY CHAPEL
PRESBYTERY
SEXAGESIMA

11

ABBREVIATOR
ABOMINATION
AGNOSTICISM
ALITURGICAL
ANTEPENDIUM
ANTIMINSION
ASPERGILLUM
BENEDICTION
CHRISTENING
HUMERAL VEIL
INQUISITION
INVESTITURE
SCRIPTORIUM

12

ANTILEGOMENA
ARON HA-KODESH
ASH WEDNESDAY
CONFIRMATION
CONGREGATION
SEPTUAGESIMA

13

BEATIFICATION
BIRKAT HA-MAZON
EPITRACHELION

14

FOLDED CHASUBLE
MAUNDY THURSDAY

17

CONSUBSTANTIA-
TION

RELIGIOUS BUILDINGS

3

WAT

4

CELL
KIRK

5

ABBEY
BET AM
CELLA

5–continued

DUOMO
HONDO
JINGU
JINJA

6

CHAPEL
CHURCH
MOSQUE
PAGODA

6–continued

PRIORY

7

CHANTRY
CONVENT
DEANERY
MINSTER

8

BASILICA

8–continued

CLOISTER
HOUNFORT
LAMASERY

9

BADRINATH
CATHEDRAL
MONASTERY
SYNAGOGUE

12

BET HA-
 KNESSET
BET HA-
 MIDRASH
CHAPTER HOUSE
MEETINGHOUSE

13

ANGELUS
 TEMPLE

RELIGIOUS FESTIVALS

Date	Festival	Religion
Jan	Epiphany	Christian
Jan	Imbolc	Pagan
Jan, Feb	New Year	Chinese
Feb, Mar	Shrove Tuesday	Christian
Feb, Mar	Ash Wednesday	Christian
Feb, Mar	Purim	Jewish
Feb, Mar	Mahashivaratri	Hindu
Feb, Mar	Holi	Hindu
Mar, Apr	Easter	Christian
Mar, Apr	Passover	Jewish
Mar, Apr	Holi Mohalla	Sikh
Mar, Apr	Rama Naumi	Hindu
Mar, Apr	Ching Ming	Chinese
Apr	Baisakhi	Sikh
Apr	Beltane	Pagan
Apr, May	Lailat ul-Isra wal Mi'raj	islamic
Apr, May	Lailat ul-Bara'h	Islamic
Apr, May	Vesak	Buddhist
May, June	Shavuoth	Jewish
May, June	Lailat ul-Qadr	Islamic
May, June	Eid ul-Fitr	Islamic
May, June	Martyrdom of Guru Arjan	Sikh
June	Dragon Boat Festival	Chinese
June	Summer Solstice	Pagan
July	Dhammacakka	Buddhist
July	Eid ul-Adha	Islamic
Aug	Raksha Bandhan	Hindu
Aug	Lammas	Pagan
Aug, Sept	Janmashtami	Hindu
Sept	Moon Festival	Chinese
Sept, Oct	Rosh Hashana	Jewish
Sept, Oct	Yom Kippur	Jewish
Sept, Oct	Succoth	Jewish
Oct	Dusshera	Hindu
Oct	Samhain	Pagan
Oct, Nov	Diwali	Hindu, Sikh
Nov	Guru Nanak's Birthday	Sikh
Nov	Bodhi Day	Buddhist
Dec	Christmas	Christian
Dec	Hanukkah	Jewish
Dec	Winter Festival	Chinese
Dec	Winter Solstice	Pagan
Dec, Jan	Birthday of Guru Gobind Singh	Sikh
Dec, Jan	Martyrdom of Guru Tegh Bahadur	Sikh

HINDU DEITIES

ADITI - goddess of heaven; mother of the gods
AGNI - god of fire
AHI or IHI - the Sistrum Player
AMARAVATI - city of the gods
AMRITA - water of life
BALI - demon who became king of heaven and earth
BRAHMA - the Creator
DEVI - a mother goddess
DITI - mother of the demons
GANDHARVAS - celestial musicians
GANESHA - god of literature, wisdom, and prosperity
GARUDA - the devourer, identified with fire and the sun
HANUMAN - a monkey chief
INDRA - king of the gods; god of war and storm
JYESTHA - goddess of misfortune

KAMA - god of desire
KARTTIKEYA - war-god; god of bravery
KUBERA - god of wealth; guardian of the north
LAKSHMI - goddess of fortune
MANASA - sacred mountain and lake
PRITHIVI - earth-goddess; goddess of fertility
SARANYU - goddess of the clouds
SARASVATI - goddess of speech
SHITALA - goddess of smallpox
SHIVA - the Destroyer
SOMA - ambrosial offering to the gods
SUGRIVA - monkey king
SURYA - the sun-god
VAYU - god of the wind
VISVAKARMA - architect for the gods
VISHNU - the Preserver
YAMA - king of the dead
VARUNA - god of water

GREEK AND ROMAN MYTHOLOGY

MYTHOLOGICAL CHARACTERS

ACHILLES – Greek hero; invulnerable except for his heel

ADONIS – renowned for his beauty

AGAMEMNON – king of Mycenae

AJAX – Greek warrior

ATLAS – bore heaven on his shoulders

BELLEROPHON – Corinthian hero who rode winged horse Pegasus

BOREAS – the north wind

CERBERUS – three-headed dog, guarded Hades

CHARON – boatman who rowed dead across river Styx

CHARYBDIS – violent whirlpool

CIRCE – sorceress who had the power to turn men into beasts

CYCLOPS – one of a race of one-eyed giants (cyclopes)

DAEDALUS – craftsman; designed and built the labyrinth in Crete

GORGONS – three sisters (Stheno, Euryale, and Medusa) who had snakes for hair and whose appearance turned people to stone

HADES – the Underworld

HELEN OF TROY – famed for her beauty; cause of Trojan war

HERACLES – famed for his courage and strength; performed the twelve labours

HERCULES – Roman name for HERACLES

HYDRA – many-headed snake

JASON – led the Argonauts in search of the Golden Fleece

LETHE – river in Hades whose water caused forgetfulness

MIDAS – King of Phrygia whose touch turned everything to gold

MINOTAUR – monster with the head of a bull and the body of a man. It was kept in the Cretan labyrinth and fed with human flesh

NARCISSUS – beautiful youth who fell in love with his own reflection

ODYSSEUS – Greek hero of the Trojan war

OEDIPUS – king of Thebes; married his mother

OLYMPUS – a mountain; the home of the gods

ORPHEUS – skilled musician

PANDORA – the first woman; opened the box that released all varieties of evil

PERSEUS – Greek hero who killed the Gorgon Medusa

POLYPHEMUS – leader of the Cyclopes

ROMULUS – founder of Rome

SATYRS – hoofed spirits of forests, fields, and streams

SCYLLA – six-headed sea monster

SIBYL – a prophetess

SIRENS – creatures depicted as half women, half birds, who lured sailors to their deaths

STYX – main river of Hades, across which Charon ferried the souls of the dead

THESEUS – Greek hero who killed the Cretan Minotaur

ULYSSES – Roman name for ODYSSEUS

GREEK GODS (ROMAN EQUIVALENT)

APHRODITE – goddess of beauty and love (VENUS)

APOLLO – god of poetry, music, and prophecy (APOLLO)

ARES – god of war (MARS)

ARTEMIS – goddess of the moon (DIANA)

ASCLEPIUS – god of medical art (AESCULAPIUS)

ATHENE – goddess of wisdom (MINERVA)

CHARITES – 3 daughters of Zeus: Euphrosyne, Aglaia, and Thalia; personified grace, beauty, and charm (GRACES)

CRONOS – god of agriculture (SATURN)

DEMETER – goddess of agriculture (CERES)

DIONYSUS – god of wine and fertility (BACCHUS)

EOS – goddess of dawn (AURORA)

EROS – god of love (CUPID)

FATES – 3 goddesses who determine man's destiny: Clotho, Lachesis, and Atropos

HEBE – goddess of youth (JUVENTAS)

HECATE – goddess of witchcraft (HECATE)

HELIOS – god of the sun (SOL)

HEPHAESTUS – god of destructive fire (VULCAN)

HERA – queen of heaven, goddess of women and marriage (JUNO)

HERMES – messenger of gods (MERCURY)

HESTIA – goddess of the hearth (VESTA)

HYPNOS – god of sleep (SOMNUS)

NEMESIS – goddess of retribution

PAN – god of woods and fields (FAUNUS)

PERSEPHONE – goddess of the Underworld (PROSERPINE)

PLUTO – god of the Underworld (PLUTO)

PLUTUS – god of wealth

POSEIDON – god of the sea (NEPTUNE)

RHEA – goddess of nature (CYBELE)

SELENE – goddess of the moon (LUNA)

THANATOS – god of death (MORS)

ZEUS – supreme god; god of sky and weather (JUPITER)

ROMAN GODS (GREEK EQUIVALENT)

AESCULAPIUS (ASCLEPIUS)
APOLLO (APOLLO)
AURORA (EOS)
BACCHUS (DIONYSUS)
CERES (DEMETER)
CUPID (EROS)
CYBELE (RHEA)
DIANA (ARTEMIS)
FAUNUS (PAN)
GRACES (CHARITES)
HECATE (HECATE)
JUNO (HERA)
JUPITER (ZEUS)
JUVENTAS (HEBE)

LUNA (SELENE)
MARS (ARES)
MERCURY (HERMES)
MINERVA (ATHENE)
MORS (THANATOS)
NEPTUNE (POSEIDON)
PLUTO (PLUTO)
PROSERPINE (PERSEPHONE)
SATURN (CRONOS)
SOL (HELIOS)
SOMNUS (HYPNOS)
VENUS (APHRODITE)
VESTA (HESTIA)
VULCAN (HEPHAESTUS)

THE TWELVE LABOURS OF HERCULES

THE NEMEAN LION
THE LERNAEAN HYDRA
THE WILD BOAR OF ERYMANTHUS
THE STYMPHALIAN BIRDS
THE CERYNEIAN HIND
THE AUGEAN STABLES
THE CRETAN BULL
THE MARES OF DIOMEDES
THE GIRDLE OF HIPPOLYTE
THE CATTLE OF GERYON
THE GOLDEN APPLES OF THE HESPERIDES
THE CAPTURE OF CERBERUS

THE NINE MUSES

CALLIOPE (EPIC POETRY)
CLIO (HISTORY)
ERATO (LOVE POETRY)
EUTERPE (LYRIC POETRY)
MELPOMENE (TRAGEDY)
POLYHYMNIA (SACRED SONG)
TERPSICHORE (DANCING)
THALIA (COMEDY)
URANIA (ASTRONOMY)

NORSE MYTHOLOGY

AEGIR – god of the sea
ALFHEIM – part of Asgard inhabited by the light elves
ASGARD – the home of the gods
ASK – name of the first man, created from a fallen tree
BALDER – god of the summer sun
BRAGI – god of poetry
EIR – goddess of healing
EMBLA – name of first woman, created from a fallen tree
FORSETI – god of justice
FREY – god of fertility and crops
FREYJA – goddess of love and night
FRIGG – Odin's wife; supreme goddess
GUNGNIR – Odin's magic spear
HEIMDAL – guardian of Asgard
HEL – goddess of the dead
HÖDUR – god of night
IDUN – wife of Bragi; guardian of the golden apples of youth

LOKI – god of evil
MIDGARD – the world of men
NORNS – three goddesses of destiny: Urd (Fate), Skuld (Being), and Verdandi (Necessity)
ODIN – supreme god; god of battle, inspiration, and death
RAGNAROK – final battle between gods and giants, in which virtually all life is destroyed
SIF – wife of Thor; her golden hair was cut off by Loki
SLEIPNIR – Odin's eight-legged horse
THOR – god of thunder
TYR – god of war
VALHALLA – hall in Asgard where Odin welcomed the souls of heroes killed in battle
VALKYRIES – nine handmaidens of Odin who chose men doomed to die in battle
YGGDRASILL – the World Tree, an ash linking all the worlds
YMIR – giant from whose body the world was formed

EGYPTIAN MYTHOLOGY

AMON-RA – supreme god
ANUBIS – jackel-headed son of Osiris; god of the dead
BES – god of marriage
GEB – earth-god
HATHOR – cow-headed goddess of love
HORUS – hawk-headed god of light
ISIS – goddess of fertility
MAAT – goddess of law, truth, and justice
MIN – god of virility
MONT – god of war
MUT – wife of Amon-Ra
NEHEH – god of eternity

NUN or NU – the primordial Ocean
NUT – goddess of the sky
OSIRIS – ruler of the afterlife
PTAH – god of the arts
RA – the sun god
RENPET – goddess of youth
SEKHMET – goddess of war
SET or SETH – god of evil
SHU – god of air
TEFNUT – goddess of dew and rain
THOTH – god of wisdom
UPUAUT – warrior-god; god of the dead

NORTH AMERICAN MYTHOLOGY

ADLIVUN – Eskimo land of the unhappy dead
AGLOOKIK – Eskimo spirit of hunters
AHSONNUTLI – chief god of the Navaho Indians
AKYCHA – the Sun
ANGAKOO – Eskimo shaman
ANGUTA – Eskimo ruler of the underworld
ANINGAN – the Moon
BIG OWL – cannibalistic monster of the Apache Indians
COYOTE – trickster god
DZOAVITS – Shoshone ogre
GLOOSKAP – agent of good; made the sky, earth, creatures, and mankind
HIAWATHA – legendary sage of the Iroquois Indians who founded the League of Five Nations
HINO – Iroquois god of thunder
HINUN – thunder spirit of the Iroquois Indians
ICTINIKE – trickster god of the Sioux Indians
MALSUM – agent of evil; made the mountains, valleys, snakes

NANA BOZHO (MANA BOZHO) – trickster god of the Algonquins
NANOOK – the Bear (the Pleiades)
NAPI – chief god of the Blackfoot
NATOS – sun god of the Blackfoot Indians
NAYENEZGANI – hero of Navaho legend; name means 'slayer of evil gods'
NEGAFOK – cold weather spirit
SEDNA – the great Sea Mother; Eskimo goddess of the underworld and sea
SPIDER WOMAN – benevolent creature who helped Nayenezgani defeat the powers of evil
TIRAWA – chief god of the Pawnee, who created the world and set the course of the sun, moon, and stars
TORNAQ – familiar of a shaman
TSOHANOAI – Navaho sun god, who carries the sun on his back across the sky
WAKONDA – great god of the Sioux Indians whose name means 'great power above'
WONOMI – sky god of the Maidu Indians who was abandoned in favour of Coyote

CENTRAL AND SOUTH AMERICAN MYTHOLOGY

AH PUCH – Maya god of death
BACHUE – mother goddess and protector of crops
BOCHICA – Colombian founder hero; appears as an old bearded man
CHAC – Maya rain god

CINTEOTL – Aztec god of maize
COATLICUE – Aztec earth goddess; a devouring goddess who was only satisfied by human flesh and blood
CUPAY (SUPAY) – Inca god of death

EHECATL – Aztec god of the winds who introduced sexual love to mankind

GUINECHEN – chief deity of Araucanian Indians, associated with fertility

HUITZILOPOCHTLI – chief god of the Aztecs

INTI – sun god from whom Inca dynasty traced its descent

ITZAMNA – chief god of the Maya

IXCHEL – Maya moon goddess

IXTAB – Maya goddess of suicide

IXTLILTON – Aztec god of medicine

KUAT – sun god of the Mamaiurans

MIXCOATL – Aztec god of the chase

MONTEZUMA – Aztec god whose name was taken from the last emperor

PACHAMAMA – Earth goddess of the Incas

PILLAN – thunder god of Araucanian Indians

QUETZALCOATL – a priest-king of Central America; the snake-bird god or plumed serpent

TEZCATLIPOCA – Aztec god of summer sun; bringer of harvests as well as drought

TLALOC – rain god of Central America, worshipped by the Toltecs and Aztecs

TUPAN – thunder god of the Guarani Indians

VAICA – magician and medicine-man of the Jurunas

VIRACOCHA – creator god of the Incas

XIPETOTEC – Aztec god of agriculture and self-torture; his name means 'flayed lord'

XOCHIQUETZAL – Aztec goddess of flowers and fruits

AUSTRALIAN MYTHOLOGY

AKURRA – serpent god

ALCHERA – 'Dreamtime', primeval time when the ancestors sang the world into existence

ARUNKULTA – Aranda spirit of evil

BAGADJIMBIRI – ancestral creator of gods

BIAME – god of creation

BIRRAHGNOOLOO – chief wife of Biame

BOLUNG – serpent god; giver of life

BOOMERANG – symbolizes the rainbow and the connection of opposites (e.g. heaven and earth)

BRALGU – island of the dead

BUNJIL – god of creation

BUNYIP – monster and giver of mystic healing rites

DILGA – earth goddess

DJANBUN – many who turned into a platypus after blowing too hard on a fire-stick

KAPOO – ancestral kangaroo who gave cats their spots

MANGAR-KUNGER-KUNJA – great lizard ancestor of the Aranda

MARINDI – ancestral dog whose blood turned the rocks red

PUNDJEL – creator god who made the first human being

WATI-KUTJARA – two lizard men of Central Australia

YURLUNYUR – ancestor of the Murngin of the northern Australia, known as the great copper python or the rainbow serpent

AFRICAN MYTHOLOGY

ABASSI – sky god of the Efik

ADROA – creator god of the Lugbara

ADU OGYINAE – first man of the Ashanti

ALA – mother goddess of the Ibo, eastern Nigeria

AMMA – an egg; seed of the cosmos; god of creation

ANANSI – W African trickster god

ASA – supreme god of the Akamba

BUMBA – creator god of the Bushongo of the Democratic Republic of Congo

CHINAWEJI – serpent; founder of the universe

CHUKU – supreme god of the Ibo, eastern Nigeria

DXUI – first god of creation

ESHU – messenger between High God and humans

ESHU – trickster god of the Yoruba who carried messages from the gods to mankind

EVENING STAR – wife of MWETSI, bearer of animals and people

FARO – maker of the sky

GU – heavenly blacksmith

IFA – god of medicine and prophecy

IMANA – supreme god of the Banyarwanda, Rwanda

JOK – creator god of the Alur

KAANG – creator god of the southwest African Bushmen
LEZA – supreme god of the Bantu
MAWU-LISA – twin creator gods
MBOOM – god of creation
MINIA – serpent; founder of the universe
MORNING STAR – wife of MWETSI, bearer of grass, shrubs, etc.
MOYNA – hero who invented the bull-roarer
MULUNGU – all-knowing sky god of the Nyamwezi
MWARI – High God
MWETSI – the first man

NANA – earth goddess of the Yoruba
NGAAN – god of creation
NGEWO – sky god of the Miende
NOMMO – a creator god
NTORO – the soul, in the beliefs of the Ashanti
NYAME – mother goddess
OGUN – war god of the Yoruba
PEMBA – maker of the earth
RUHANGA – high god of the Bangoro
UNKULUNKULU – supreme god of the Zulus
WELE – chief god of the Abaluyia of Kenya
WOOD – name of all the nine children of MBOOM

ARTHURIAN LEGEND

AGRAVAIN – younger brother of Gawain, helped expose Lancelot's and Guinevere's adultery to Arthur
AMFORTAS – Fisher King who looked after the Grail
ARTHUR – legendary British leader of the Knights of the Round Table
AVALON – wonderful island where Arthur was taken to be healed of this wounds
BORS – only knight to achieve the quest of the Holy Grail, and to survive and return to Arthur's court
CAMELOT – capital of Arthur's kingdom
ECTOR – foster father of Arthur, father of Kay
EXCALIBUR – Arthur's magic sword
GALAHAD – son of Lancelot; purest of the Knights of the Round Table; succeeded in the quest of the Grail
GAWAIN – nephew of Arthur, son of Morgan Le Fay; searched for the Grail
GRAIL (SANGREAL, THE HOLY GRAIL) – said to be the vessel of the Last Supper; in the custody of the Fisher King

GUINEVERE – wife of Arthur, lover of Lancelot
IGRAINE – wife of Uther Pendragon; mother of Arthur and Morgan le Fay
KAY – foster brother of Arthur
LADY OF THE LAKE – enchantress who raised Lancelot and gave Arthur Excalibur
LANCELOT or LAUNCELOT – knight and lover of Queen Guinevere
LUCAN – most trusted of Arthur's friends
MERLIN – magician and bard who prepared Arthur for kingship
MORDRED or MODRED – son of Arthur and his half-sister Morgause
MORGAN LE FAY – sorceress and healer; half-sister of Arthur
MORGAUSE – half-sister of Arthur; mother of Mordred, Gawain, Gareth, and Agravain
NIMUE – enchantress with whom Merlin fell in love
PERCIVAL or PERCEVAL – knight who vowed to seek the Grail
UTHER PENDRAGON – father of Arthur
VIVIANE – the Lady of the Lake

CELTIC MYTHOLOGY

ANGUS – Irish god of love
ANNWN – the Underworld in Welsh mythology
ANU – earth goddess, mother of the gods of Ireland
ARAWN – Welsh king of the Underworld (Annwn)
BALOR – Irish one-eyed god of death
BANSHEE – English name for Bean Sidhe, the Irish fairy, whose wailing foretells the approach of death

BECUMA – Irish goddess, who was banished to earth
BELINUS – god of the sun
BELTAIN – first day of summer – 1st May
BRANWEN – daughter of Llyr
BRIGIT, BRIGHID – bringer of the spring – became St Bride
CERNUNNOS – god of wild beasts
CIAN – Irish father of the sun god Lugh

COCIDIUS – god of hunting
CONN – high king of Ireland
COVENTINA – goddess of water
CU CHULAINN – Irish hero, foster-son of King
Conchobhar
DAGHDHA, THE – The Good God (of Ireland)
DANA – Irish mother goddess
DIAN-CECHT – Irish god of medicine
DIERDRE – daughter of the Ulster lord Felim
Mac Dall who was forced to marry Conchobhar,
and never smiled again
DONN – Irish god of the dead
EPONA – goddess of horsemen and animals
FINN MAC COOL (FINGAL) – legendary Irish
hero who obtained wisdom from the salmon of
knowledge (Fintan)
FLIDHAIS – goddess of the moon and hunting
GREEN MAN – fertility god
GWYDION – Welsh priest-king and magician
GWYNN – Welsh god of the Underworld
HERNE – the hunter

LUGH – Irish sun god
MABON – god of youth
MANANNAN – Irish sea god
MEDB – legendary Queen of Connacht –
possibly prototype of Mab, British Queen of the
fairies
MORRIGAN – Irish goddess of war
NUADA – high king of Ireland
OENGHUS – god of love
OSSIAN – Irish hero
PRYDERI – son of Pwyll and Rhiannon, who
eventually succeeded his father as lord of Dyfed
PWYLL – Chief of Annwn (Prince of Dyfed)
RHIANNON – wife of Pwyll who was falsely
accused of killing her son
SAMHAIN – first day of winter – 1st November
SHEELA-NA-GIG – goddess of fertility
SIDHE – Irish fairies of the Otherworld
TALIESIN – Welsh wizard who knew the secrets
of the past, present, and future
TARANIS – the thunderer

MYTHOLOGICAL AND IMAGINARY BEINGS

3
ELF
NIX
ORC
ROC

4
FAUN
JINN
OGRE
PUCK
YETI

5
DEMON
DWARF
FAIRY
FIEND
GENIE
GHOST
GHOUL
GIANT
GNOME
GOLEM
HARPY
JOTUN
LAMIA
NYMPH

5–continued
PIXIE
PRETA
SATYR
SYLPH
TROLL

6
AFREET
AZAZEL
BUNYIP
DAEMON
DRAGON
DYBBUK
FAFNIR
FURIES
GOBLIN
HOBBIT
KELPIE
KOBOLD
KRAKEN
RAVANA
SINBAD
SPHINX
SPRITE
UNDINE
ZOMBIE

7
AMAZONS
BANSHEE
BROWNIE
CENTAUR
CHIMERA
GREMLIN
GRENDEL
GRIFFIN
INCUBUS
LORELEI
MERMAID
PHOENIX
SILENUS
UNICORN
VAMPIRE

8
BABA YAGA
BARGHEST
BASILISK
BEHEMOTH
QUEEN MAB
SUCCUBUS
WEREWOLF

9
GILGAMESH

9–continued
HOBGOBLIN
MANTICORE
NIBELUNGS
PIED PIPER
ROBIN HOOD

10
HIPPOGRIFF
LEPRECHAUN
SALAMANDER
SANTA CLAUS

11
AMPHISBAENA
HIPPOCAMPUS
POLTERGEIST
RIP VAN WINKLE
SCHEHEREZADE

12+
ABOMINABLE
SNOWMAN
FATHER CHRISTMAS
LOCH NESS
MONSTER
ROBIN
GOODFELLOW

WORK

PROFESSIONS, TRADES, AND OCCUPATIONS

2	5	5–continued	6–continued	6–continued
GP	ACTOR	PIPER	BOOKIE	FARMER
MD	AD-MAN	PLYER	BOWMAN	FELLER
MO	AGENT	PUPIL	BREWER	FICTOR
PM	BAKER	QUACK	BROKER	FISHER
	BONZE	QUILL	BUGLER	FITTER
3	BOOTS	RABBI	BURLER	FLAYER
DOC	BOSUN	RATER	BURSAR	FORGER
DON	CADDY	REEVE	BUSKER	FOWLER
GYP	CLERK	RUNER	BUTLER	FRAMER
PRO	CLOWN	SCOUT	CABBIE	FULLER
REP	COACH	SEWER	CABMAN	GAFFER
SPY	COMIC	SHOER	CALKER	GANGER
VET	CRIER	SLAVE	CANNER	GAOLER
	CRIMP	SMITH	CARTER	GAUCHO
4	CURER	SOWER	CARVER	GAUGER
AMAH	DAILY	STAFF	CASUAL	GIGOLO
AYAH	ENVOY	SWEEP	CENSOR	GILDER
BABU	EXTRA	TAMER	CLERGY	GILLIE
BARD	FAKIR	TAWER	CLERIC	GLAZER
BOSS	FENCE	TAXER	CODIST	GLOVER
CHAR	FIFER	TILER	COINER	GRAVER
CHEF	FILER	TUNER	COMBER	GROCER
COOK	FINER	TUTOR	CONDER	GUIDER
CREW	FLIER	TYLER	COOLIE	GUIDON
DIVA	GIPSY	USHER	COOPER	GUNMAN
DYER	GLUER	VALET	COPPER	GUNNER
GANG	GROOM	VINER	CO-STAR	HARPER
GRIP	GUARD		COSTER	HATTER
HACK	GUIDE	**6**	COWBOY	HAWKER
HAND	GUILD	AIRMAN	COWMAN	HEALER
HEAD	HAKIM	ARCHER	CRITIC	HEAVER
HERD	HARPY	ARTIST	CUTLER	HODMAN
HIND	HELOT	AURIST	CUTTER	HOOPER
MAGI	HIRER	AUTHOR	DANCER	HORNER
MAID	HIVER	BAGMAN	DEALER	HOSIER
MATE	HOPPO	BAILER	DIGGER	HUNTER
MIME	LEECH	BAILOR	DOCKER	INTERN
PAGE	LUTER	BALKER	DOCTOR	ISSUER
PEON	MASON	BANKER	DOWSER	JAILER
POET	MEDIC	BARBER	DRAPER	JAILOR
SEER	MINER	BARGEE	DRAWER	JOBBER
SERF	NAVVY	BARKER	DRIVER	JOCKEY
SYCE	NURSE	BARMAN	DROVER	JOINER
TOUT	OILER	BATMAN	EDITOR	JOWTER
WARD	OWLER	BEARER	FABLER	JURIST
WHIP	PILOT	BINDER	FACTOR	KEELER
		BOFFIN		

6–continued	6–continued	6–continued	7–continued	7–continued
KEEPER	RECTOR	TUBMAN	BOATMAN	FLESHER
KILLER	REGENT	TURNER	BONDMAN	FLORIST
LACKEY	RELIEF	TYCOON	BOOKMAN	FLUNKEY
LANDER	RENTER	TYPIST	BOTTLER	FLUTIST
LASCAR	RIGGER	USURER	BRIGAND	FOOTBOY
LAWYER	RINGER	VACHER	BUILDER	FOOTMAN
LECTOR	ROBBER	VALUER	BURGLAR	FOOTPAD
LENDER	ROOFER	VAMPER	BUTCHER	FOREMAN
LOADER	ROOTER	VANMAN	BUTTONS	FOUNDER
LOGMAN	SACKER	VASSAL	CALLBOY	FRISEUR
LUMPER	SAILOR	VENDER	CAMBIST	FROGMAN
MARKER	SALTER	VENDOR	CARRIER	FUELLER
MATRON	SALVOR	VERGER	CASEMAN	FURRIER
MEDICO	SAPPER	VERSER	CASHIER	GATEMAN
MENDER	SARTOR	VIEWER	CATERER	GIRDLER
MENIAL	SAWYER	WAITER	CAULKER	GLAZIER
MENTOR	SCRIBE	WALLER	CELLIST	GLEANER
MERCER	SEA-DOG	WARDEN	CHANTER	GLEEMAN
MILKER	SEALER	WARDER	CHAPMAN	GLOSSER
MILLER	SEAMAN	WARPER	CHEMIST	GRAFFER
MINTER	SEINER	WASHER	CHORIST	GRAFTER
MONGER	SEIZOR	WEAVER	CLEANER	GRAINER
MORISK	SELLER	WEEDER	CLICKER	GRANGER
MUMMER	SERVER	WELDER	CLIPPIE	GRANTEE
MUMPER	SETTER	WHALER	COALMAN	GRANTOR
MYSTIC	SEXTON	WORKER	COBBLER	GRAZIER
NAILER	SHROFF	WRIGHT	COCKLER	GRINDER
NOTARY	SINGER	WRITER	COLLIER	GYMNAST
NURSER	SIRCAR		CO-PILOT	HACKLER
OBOIST	SKIVVY	**7**	COPYIST	HARPIST
OILMAN	SLATER	ABACIST	CORONER	HAULIER
ORATOR	SLAVER	ABIGAIL	CORSAIR	HELOTRY
OSTLER	SLAVEY	ACOLYTE	COUNSEL	HERBIST
PACKER	SLEUTH	ACOLYTH	COURIER	HERDMAN
PARSON	SNARER	ACROBAT	COWHERD	HERITOR
PASTOR	SOCMAN	ACTRESS	COWPOKE	HIGGLER
PAVIER	SORTER	ACTUARY	CROFTER	HOGHERD
PAVIOR	SOUTER	ALEWIFE	CROPPER	HOSTLER
PEDANT	SPICER	ALMONER	CURATOR	INDEXER
PEDLAR	SQUIRE	ANALYST	CURRIER	INLAYER
PENMAN	STAGER	APPOSER	CUSTODE	IRONIST
PICKER	STOKER	ARABIST	DANSEUR	JANITOR
PIEMAN	STORER	ARBITER	DENTIST	JUGGLER
PIRATE	SUTLER	ARTISAN	DIALIST	JUNKMAN
PITMAN	TABLER	ARTISTE	DIETIST	JURYMAN
PLATER	TAILOR	ASSAYER	DITCHER	KEELMAN
PLAYER	TAMPER	ASSIZER	DOMINIE	KNACKER
PORTER	TANNER	ASSURED	DOORMAN	KNITTER
POTBOY	TASKER	ASSURER	DRAGMAN	LACEMAN
POTTER	TASTER	AUDITOR	DRAPIER	LINKBOY
PRIEST	TELLER	AVIATOR	DRAWBOY	LINKMAN
PRUNER	TERMER	AWARDER	DRAYMAN	LOCKMAN
PURSER	TESTER	BAILIFF	DREDGER	LOMBARD
QUERRY	TILLER	BANDMAN	DRESSER	MALTMAN
RABBIN	TINKER	BARMAID	DROGMAN	MANAGER
RAGMAN	TINMAN	BELLBOY	DRUMMER	MANGLER
RANGER	TINNER	BELLHOP	DUSTMAN	MARBLER
RATTER	TOLLER	BEST BOY	FARRIER	MARCHER
READER	TOUTER	BIRDMAN	FASCIST	MARINER
REAPER	TRACER	BLASTER	FIDDLER	MARSHAL
REAVER	TRADER	BLENDER	FIREMAN	MATADOR

223

7–continued	7–continued	8–continued	8–continued	8–continued
MATELOT	SNIPPER	BANDSMAN	FABULIST	LINESMAN
MEALMAN	SOCAGER	BARGEMAN	FACTOTUM	LUMBERER
MEATMAN	SOLDIER	BEARHERD	FALCONER	MAGICIAN
MIDWIFE	SOLOIST	BEDESMAN	FAMULIST	MAGISTER
MILKMAN	SPENCER	BEDMAKER	FARMHAND	MALTSTER
MODISTE	SPINNER	BIT-MAKER	FERRYMAN	MASSEUSE
MONEYER	SPOTTER	BLEACHER	FIGURANT	MEASURER
MONITOR	STAINER	BOATSMAN	FILMSTAR	MECHANIC
MOOTMAN	STAMPER	BONDMAID	FINISHER	MEDALIST
MOULDER	STAPLER	BONDSMAN	FISHWIFE	MELODIST
NEWSBOY	STATIST	BOTANIST	FLATFOOT	MERCATOR
OCULIST	STEERER	BOWMAKER	FLAUTIST	MERCHANT
OFFICER	STEWARD	BOXMAKER	FLETCHER	METAL-MAN
ORDERER	SURGEON	BREWSTER	FODDERER	MILKMAID
ORDERLY	SWABBER	BROACHER	FORESTER	MILLHAND
PACKMAN	SWEEPER	CABIN BOY	FORGEMAN	MILLINER
PAGEBOY	TABORER	CELLARER	FUGLEMAN	MINISTER
PAINTER	TALLIER	CERAMIST	GANGSTER	MINSTREL
PALMIST	TAPSTER	CHANDLER	GARDENER	MODELLER
PANTLER	TAXI-MAN	CHOIRBOY	GAVELMAN	MULETEER
PEDDLER	TEACHER	CIDERIST	GENDARME	MURALIST
PIANIST	TIPSTER	CLAQUEUR	GLASSMAN	MUSICIAN
PICADOR	TRACKER	CLOTHIER	GOATHERD	NEWSHAWK
PLANNER	TRAINER	COACHMAN	GOVERNOR	NOVELIST
PLANTER	TRAPPER	CO-AUTHOR	GUARDIAN	ONION-MAN
PLEADER	TRAWLER	CODIFIER	GUNSMITH	OPERATOR
PLUMBER	TRIMMER	COISTRIL	HAMMERER	OPTICIAN
POACHER	TRUCKER	COLLATOR	HANDMAID	ORDAINER
POSTBOY	TRUSTEE	COMEDIAN	HANDYMAN	ORDINAND
POSTMAN	TUMBLER	COMPILER	HATMAKER	ORGANIST
PRESSER	TURNKEY	COMPOSER	HAYMAKER	OUTRIDER
PRESTOR	VINTNER	CONJURER	HEAD COOK	OVERSEER
PRINTER	VIOLIST	CONVEYOR	HEADSMAN	PARGETER
PUDDLER	WAGONER	COURTIER	HELMSMAN	PARODIST
RANCHER	WARRIOR	COW-LEECH	HENCHMAN	PENMAKER
REALTOR	WEBSTER	COXSWAIN	HERDSMAN	PERFUMER
REFINER	WEIGHER	CROUPIER	HIRELING	PETERMAN
RIVETER	WHEELER	CUTPURSE	HISTRION	PEWTERER
ROADMAN	WHETTER	DAIRYMAN	HOME HELP	PICAROON
ROASTER	WIREMAN	DANSEUSE	HOTELIER	PLOUGHER
RUSTLER	WOODMAN	DECKHAND	HOUSEBOY	POLISHER
SACRIST	WOOLMAN	DEFENDER	HUCKSTER	PORTRESS
SADDLER	WORKMAN	DESIGNER	HUNTSMAN	POSTILER
SAMPLER	WRAPPER	DIRECTOR	IMPORTER	POTMAKER
SAMURAI		DOG-LEECH	IMPROVER	PREACHER
SCOURER	**8**	DOMESTIC	INKMAKER	PREFACER
SCRAPER	ADSCRIPT	DOUGHBOY	INVENTOR	PRELUDER
SERVANT	AERONAUT	DRAGOMAN	JAPANNER	PRESSMAN
SETTLER	ALGERINE	DRUGGIST	JET PILOT	PROBATOR
SHARPER	ANALYSER	EDUCATOR	JEWELLER	PROCURER
SHEARER	APHORIST	EMBALMER	JONGLEUR	PROMOTER
SHIPPER	APIARIST	EMISSARY	KIPPERER	PROMPTER
SHOPBOY	APRON-MAN	ENGINEER	LABOURER	PROSAIST
SHOWMAN	ARBORIST	ENGRAVER	LANDGIRL	PROVIDER
SHUNTER	ARMORIST	ENROLLER	LANDLADY	PSALMIST
SILKMAN	ARMOURER	EPIC POET	LANDLORD	PUBLICAN
SIMPLER	ARRESTOR	ESSAYIST	LAPIDARY	PUGILIST
SKINNER	ASSESSOR	ESSOINER	LARCENER	PURVEYOR
SKIPPER	ATTORNEY	EXORCIST	LARDERER	QUARRIER
SLIPPER	BAGMAKER	EXPLORER	LEADSMAN	RAFTSMAN
SMELTER	BAGPIPER	EXPORTER	LECTURER	RANCHERO

8—continued
RAPPEREE
RECEIVER
REGRATER
RELESSEE
RELESSOR
REPAIRER
REPORTER
RESETTER
RESTORER
RETAILER
RETAINER
REVIEWER
REWRITER
RIVETTER
ROMANCER
RUGMAKER
RUMOURER
SALESMAN
SATIRIST
SAWBONES
SCULLION
SCULPTOR
SEAMSTER
SEA-ROVER
SEASONER
SEEDSMAN
SEMPSTER
SERVITOR
SHEARMAN
SHEPHERD
SHIPMATE
SHIP'S BOY
SHOPGIRL
SHOWGIRL
SIDESMAN
SIMPLIST
SKETCHER
SMUGGLER
SPACEMAN
SPEARMAN
SPEEDCOP
SPURRIER
STARCHER
STITCHER
STOCKMAN
STOREMAN
STRIPPER
STRUMMER
STUNTMAN
SUPPLIER
SURVEYOR
SWINDLER
TABOURER
TALLYMAN
TAVERNER
TEAMSTER
THATCHER
THESPIAN
THRESHER
TIN MINER
TINSMITH

8—continued
TORTURER
TOYMAKER
TRIPEMAN
TRUCKMAN
TURNCOCK
TURNSPIT
TUTORESS
UNIONIST
VALUATOR
VINTAGER
VIRTUOSO
VOCALIST
VOLUMIST
WAITRESS
WALKER-ON
WARDRESS
WARRENER
WATCHMAN
WATERMAN
WET NURSE
WHALEMAN
WHITENER
WHITSTER
WIGMAKER
WINNOWER
WOOL-DYER
WRESTLER

9
ALCHEMIST
ALLUMINOR
ANATOMIST
ANNOTATOR
ANNOUNCER
ARBORATOR
ARCHERESS
ARCHITECT
ARCHIVIST
ART CRITIC
ART DEALER
ARTIFICER
ASTRONAUT
ATTENDANT
AUTHORESS
BALLADIST
BALLERINA
BANK AGENT
BARRISTER
BARROW BOY
BEEFEATER
BEEKEEPER
BIOLOGIST
BOATSWAIN
BODYGUARD
BOILERMAN
BONDSLAVE
BONDWOMAN
BOOKMAKER
BOOTBLACK
BOOTMAKER
BUCCANEER

9—continued
BURNISHER
BUS DRIVER
CAB DRIVER
CAFÉ OWNER
CAMERAMAN
CAR DRIVER
CARETAKER
CARPENTER
CARVANEER
CASEMAKER
CATECHIST
CELLARMAN
CHARWOMAN
CHAUFFEUR
CHEAPJACK
CHORISTER
CLARIFIER
CLERGYMAN
CLINICIAN
CLOGMAKER
COALMINER
COALOWNER
COLLECTOR
COLOURIST
COLUMNIST
COMPRADOR
CONCIERGE
CONDUCTOR
CONSERVER
COSMONAUT
COST CLERK
COSTUMIER
COURTESAN
COUTURIER
COWFEEDER
COWKEEPER
CRACKSMAN
CRAFTSMAN
CRAYONIST
CYMBALIST
DAILY HELP
DAIRYMAID
DECORATOR
DECRETIST
DESK CLERK
DETECTIVE
DICE-MAKER
DIE-SINKER
DIETETIST
DIETITIAN
DIRECTRIX
DISPENSER
DISSECTOR
DISTILLER
DOCTORESS
DRAFTSMAN
DRAMATIST
DRAWLATCH
DRUM-MAKER
DRYSALTER
ECOLOGIST

9—continued
EMBEZZLER
ENAMELLER
ENGINEMAN
ENGROSSER
EPITOMIST
ERRAND BOY
ESTIMATOR
EXAMINANT
EXCAVATOR
EXCERPTOR
EXCHANGER
EXCISEMAN
EXECUTIVE
EXERCITOR
EXORCISER
FABRICANT
FASHIONER
FELT-MAKER
FIGURANTE
FILM ACTOR
FILM EXTRA
FILM-MAKER
FINANCIER
FIRE-EATER
FISH-CURER
FISHERMAN
FISH-WOMAN
FLAG-MAKER
FLAX-WENCH
FLYFISHER
FREELANCE
FREIGHTER
FRIPPERER
FRUITERER
FURBISHER
FURNISHER
GALVANIST
GASFITTER
GAZETTEER
GEM-CUTTER
GEOLOGIST
GLADIATOR
GLUEMAKER
GOLDSMITH
GONDOLIER
GOSPELLER
GOVERNESS
GROUNDMAN
GUARDSMAN
GUERRILLA
GUITARIST
GUN-RUNNER
HARLEQUIN
HARMONIST
HARPOONER
HARVESTER
HELLENIST
HERBALIST
HERBARIAN
HERBORIST
HERB-WOMAN

9—continued

HIRED HAND
HIRED HELP
HISTORIAN
HOG-RINGER
HOMEOPATH
HOP-PICKER
HOSTELLER
HOUSEMAID
HOUSEWIFE
HYGIENIST
HYPNOTIST
INCUMBENT
INGRAFTER
INNHOLDER
INNKEEPER
INSCRIBER
INSPECTOR
INTENDANT
IRONSMITH
ITINERANT
JACK-SMITH
JOB-MASTER
KENNEL-MAN
LACEMAKER
LACQUERER
LADY'S MAID
LAND AGENT
LANDREEVE
LARCENIST
LAUNDERER
LAUNDRESS
LEGIONARY
LIBRARIAN
LINOTYPER
LIONTAMER
LIVERYMAN
LOAN AGENT
LOCKMAKER
LOCKSMITH
LOG-ROLLER
LUMBERMAN
MACHINIST
MAGNETIST
MAJORDOMO
MALE MODEL
MALE NURSE
MAN-AT-ARMS
MANNEQUIN
MECHANIST
MEDALLIST
MEMOIRIST
MERCENARY
MESMERIST
MESSENGER
METALLIST
METRICIAN
MILL-OWNER
MODELGIRL
MORTICIAN
MUFFIN-MAN
MUSKETEER

9—continued

MUSKETOON
MYOLOGIST
NAVIGATOR
NEGOTIANT
NEOLOGIAN
NEOLOGIST
NEWSAGENT
NURSEMAID
ODD JOB MAN
OFFICE BOY
OPERATIVE
ORDINATOR
OSTEOPATH
OTOLOGIST
OUTFITTER
PASQUILER
PAYMASTER
PEDAGOGUE
PERFORMER
PHYSICIAN
PHYSICIST
PINKMAKER
PITSAWYER
PLANISHER
PLASTERER
PLOUGHBOY
PLOUGHMAN
PLURALIST
POETASTER
POINTSMAN
POLICEMAN
POP ARTIST
PORTERESS
PORTRAYER
PORTREEVE
POSTILION
POSTWOMAN
POULTERER
PRACTISER
PRECENTOR
PRECEPTOR
PREDICANT
PRELECTOR
PRIESTESS
PRIVATEER
PROFESSOR
PROFILIST
PROVEDORE
PUBLICIST
PUBLISHER
PULPITEER
PUPPETEER
PYTHONESS
QUALIFIER
QUARRYMAN
RACKETEER
RAILMAKER
RECRUITER
REFORMIST
REHEARSER
RIBBONMAN

9—continued

ROADMAKER
ROPEMAKER
ROUNDSMAN
RUM-RUNNER
SACRISTAN
SAFEMAKER
SAILMAKER
SCARIFIER
SCAVENGER
SCENARIST
SCHOLIAST
SCHOOLMAN
SCIENTIST
SCRIVENER
SCYTHEMAN
SEA-ROBBER
SECRETARY
SHIPOWNER
SHIP'S MATE
SHOEBLACK
SHOEMAKER
SIGHTSMAN
SIGNALMAN
SINOLOGUE
SOAPMAKER
SOLICITOR
SONNETEER
SORCERESS
STABLEBOY
STABLEMAN
STAGEHAND
STATIONER
STAY-MAKER
STEERSMAN
STEVEDORE
SUBEDITOR
SUCCENTOR
SUR-MASTER
SWAN-UPPER
SWINEHERD
SWITCHMAN
SWORDSMAN
SYNDICATE
SYNOPTIST
TABLEMAID
TACTICIAN
TAILORESS
TEATASTER
TENTMAKER
TEST PILOT
THERAPIST
THEURGIST
THROWSTER
TIMBERMAN
TIREWOMAN
TOOLSMITH
TOWN CLERK
TOWNCRIER
TRADESMAN
TRAGEDIAN
TRAVELLER

9—continued

TREASURER
TREPANNER
TRIBUTARY
TRUMPETER
TYMPANIST
USHERETTE
VARNISHER
VERSIFIER
VETTURINO
VEXILLARY
VIOLINIST
VOLCANIST
VOLTIGEUR
WADSETTER
WARRANTEE
WARRANTER
WASHERMAN
WAXWORKER
WHITESTER
WINEMAKER
WOOD-REEVE
WORKWOMAN
ZOOKEEPER
ZOOLOGIST
ZOOTOMIST

10

ABLE SEAMAN
ACCOMPTANT
ACCOUCHEUR
ACCOUNTANT
ACOLOTHIST
ADVERTISER
AEROLOGIST
AGROLOGIST
AGRONOMIST
AIR HOSTESS
AIR STEWARD
ALGEBRAIST
AMANUENSIS
APOTHECARY
APPRENTICE
ARBALISTER
ARBITRATOR
ASTROLOGER
ASTRONOMER
ATMOLOGIST
AUCTIONEER
AUDIT CLERK
BALLOONIST
BALLPLAYER
BANDMASTER
BASEBALLER
BASSOONIST
BEADSWOMAN
BEAUTICIAN
BELL-HANGER
BELL-RINGER
BIOCHEMIST
BIOGRAPHER
BLACKSMITH

10–continued

BLADESMITH
BLOCKMAKER
BLUEJACKET
BOMBARDIER
BONDSWOMAN
BONESETTER
BOOKBINDER
BOOKHOLDER
BOOKKEEPER
BOOKSELLER
BOOTLEGGER
BRICKLAYER
BRICKMAKER
BRUSHMAKER
BUREAUCRAT
BUTTERWIFE
CARTOONIST
CARTWRIGHT
CASH-KEEPER
CAT BREEDER
CAT BURGLAR
CERAMICIST
CHAIR-MAKER
CHARGEHAND
CHARIOTEER
CHIRURGEON
CHORUS GIRL
CHRONICLER
CIRCUITEER
CLAIM AGENT
CLAPPER BOY
CLOCKMAKER
CLOG DANCER
CLOTH MAKER
COACHMAKER
COAL-BACKER
COAL-FITTER
COALHEAVER
COAL-MASTER
CO-ASSESSOR
COASTGUARD
COLLOCUTOR
COLLOQUIST
COLPORTEUR
COMEDIENNE
COMPOSITOR
COMPOUNDER
CONCORDIST
CONTRACTOR
CONTROLLER
COPYHOLDER
COPYWRITER
CORDWAINER
COUNSELLOR
CULTIVATOR
CUSTOMS MAN
CYTOLOGIST
DELINEATOR
DIRECTRESS
DISC JOCKEY
DISCOUNTER

10–continued

DISCOVERER
DISHWASHER
DISPATCHER
DISTRAINER
DISTRAINOR
DOCKMASTER
DOG BREEDER
DOG-FANCIER
DOORKEEPER
DRAMATURGE
DRESSMAKER
DRUMMER-BOY
DRY CLEANER
EMBLAZONER
EMBOWELLER
ENAMELLIST
EPHEMERIST
EPITAPHIST
EPITOMIZER
EVANGELIST
EXAMINATOR
EXPLORATOR
EYE-SERVANT
FELL-MONGER
FILE-CUTTER
FILIBUSTER
FILM EDITOR
FIREMASTER
FIRE-WORKER
FISHMONGER
FLIGHT CREW
FLOWERGIRL
FLUVIALIST
FOLK-DANCER
FOLK-SINGER
FORECASTER
FRAME-MAKER
FREEBOOTER
FUND RAISER
GAMEKEEPER
GAME WARDEN
GEAR-CUTTER
GEISHA GIRL
GENETICIST
GEOGRAPHER
GLEE-SINGER
GLOSSARIST
GLUE-BOILER
GOLD-BEATER
GOLD-DIGGER
GOLD-WASHER
GOVERNANTE
GRAMMARIAN
GUNSLINGER
HACKNEY-MAN
HALL PORTER
HANDMAIDEN
HARVESTMAN
HATCHELLER
HEAD PORTER
HEAD WAITER

10–continued

HIEROPHANT
HIGHWAYMAN
HORN PLAYER
HOROLOGIST
HORSECOPER
HORSE-LEECH
HOUSE AGENT
HUCKSTRESS
HUSBANDMAN
INOCULATOR
INSTITUTOR
INSTRUCTOR
INTERAGENT
IRONMONGER
IRONWORKER
JOURNALIST
JOURNEYMAN
KENNELMAID
KEYBOARDER
LAUNDRYMAN
LAW OFFICER
LEGISLATOR
LIBRETTIST
LIGHTERMAN
LIME-BURNER
LINOTYPIST
LIQUIDATOR
LOBSTERMAN
LOCK-KEEPER
LUMBERJACK
MAGISTRATE
MANAGERESS
MANICURIST
MANSERVANT
MATCHMAKER
MEAT-HAWKER
MEDICAL MAN
MILITIAMAN
MILLWRIGHT
MINERALIST
MINISTRESS
MINTMASTER
MISSIONARY
MOONSHINER
NATURALIST
NAUTCH GIRL
NEGOTIATOR
NEWSCASTER
NEWS EDITOR
NEWSVENDOR
NEWSWRITER
NIGHT NURSE
NOSOLOGIST
NURSERYMAN
OBITUARIST
OIL PAINTER
ORCHARDIST
OSTEOLOGER
OVERLOOKER
PANEGYRIST
PANTRYMAID

10–continued

PARK-KEEPER
PARK-RANGER
PASQUILANT
PASTRY-COOK
PATHFINDER
PAWNBROKER
PEARL-DIVER
PEDIATRIST
PEDICURIST
PELTMONGER
PENOLOGIST
PERRUQUIER
PHARMACIST
PHILOLOGER
PIANO TUNER
PICKPOCKET
PLATELAYER
PLAYWRIGHT
POLITICIAN
PORTIONIST
POSTILLION
POSTMASTER
PRESCRIBER
PRIMA DONNA
PRIVATE EYE
PROCURATOR
PROGRAMMER
PRONOUNCER
PROPRIETOR
PROSPECTOR
PROTRACTOR
PROVEDITOR
PUNCTURIST
PYROLOGIST
QUIZ-MASTER
RAILWAYMAN
RAT-CATCHER
RECITALIST
RESEARCHER
RINGMASTER
ROADMENDER
ROPEDANCER
ROUGHRIDER
SAFEBLOWER
SALES FORCE
SALESWOMAN
SCHOOLMARM
SCRUTINEER
SCULPTRESS
SEA-CAPTAIN
SEAMSTRESS
SECOND MATE
SEMINARIST
SERVING-MAN
SEXOLOGIST
SHIP-BROKER
SHIP-HOLDER
SHIPMASTER
SHIPWRIGHT
SHOPFITTER
SHOPKEEPER

10—continued

SHOPWALKER
SIGNWRITER
SILENTIARY
SILK-MERCER
SILK-WEAVER
SINOLOGIST
SKIRMISHER
SLOP SELLER
SNEAK THIEF
SOAP-BOILER
SPECIALIST
STAFF NURSE
STEERSMATE
STEWARDESS
STIPULATOR
STOCKTAKER
STONE-BORER
STONEMASON
STRATEGIST
STREET-WARD
SUPERCARGO
SUPERVISER
SURCHARGER
SURFACE-MAN
SWAN-KEEPER
SYMPHONIST
TALLY CLERK
TASKMASTER
TAXI-DRIVER
TEA-BLENDER
TEA PLANTER
TECHNICIAN
TECHNOCRAT
THEOGONIST
THEOLOGIAN
THEOLOGIST
THRENODIST
TIMEKEEPER
TRACTARIAN
TRADE UNION
TRAFFIC COP
TRAFFICKER
TRAM-DRIVER
TRANSACTOR
TRANSLATOR
TRAWLERMAN
TREASURESS
TROUBADOUR
TYPESETTER
UNDERTAKER
VETERINARY
VICTUALLER
VIVANDIÈRE
VOCABULIST
WAINWRIGHT
WARRIORESS
WATCHMAKER
WATERGUARD
WHARFINGER
WHITESMITH
WHOLESALER

10—continued

WINEGROWER
WINE-WAITER
WIREWORKER
WOODCARVER
WOODCUTTER
WOOD-MONGER
WOODWORKER
WOOL-CARDER
WOOL-COMBER
WOOL-DRIVER
WOOL-GROWER
WOOL-SORTER
WOOL-TRADER
WOOL-WINDER
YARDMASTER
ZINC-WORKER
ZOOGRAPHER
ZYMOLOGIST

11

ACCOMPANIST
ACCOUCHEUSE
ACOUSTICIAN
ADJUDICATOR
ALLOPATHIST
ANNUNCIATOR
ANTIQUARIAN
APPLE-GROWER
ARBITRATRIX
ARMY OFFICER
ARQUEBUSIER
ARTILLERIST
AUDIO TYPIST
AUSCULTATOR
BANK CASHIER
BANK MANAGER
BARGEMASTER
BASKETMAKER
BATTI-WALLAH
BATTOLOGIST
BEACHCOMBER
BELL-FOUNDER
BILL-STICKER
BIRD-CATCHER
BIRD-FANCIER
BIRD-WATCHER
BOATBUILDER
BODY SERVANT
BOILERSMITH
BONDSERVANT
BROADCASTER
BULLFIGHTER
CANDLEMAKER
CAR SALESMAN
CAT'S-MEAT-MAN
CHAIR-MENDER
CHALK-CUTTER
CHAMBERMAID
CHIFFONNIER
CHIROLOGIST
CHIROMANCER

11—continued

CHIROPODIST
CHOIRMASTER
CHRONOLOGER
CINDER-WENCH
CLOCK-SETTER
CLOTH-WORKER
COAL-WHIPPER
COFFIN-MAKER
COLLAR-MAKER
CONDISCIPLE
CONDOTTIERE
CONDUCTRESS
CONFEDERATE
CONGRESSMAN
CONSECRATOR
CONSERVATOR
CONVEYANCER
COPPERSMITH
COSMOGONIST
COSMOLOGIST
CRANE DRIVER
CRIMEWRITER
CUB REPORTER
CYPHER CLERK
DELIVERY MAN
DEMOGRAPHER
DISPENSATOR
DRAUGHTSMAN
DUTY OFFICER
ELECTRICIAN
EMBLEMATIST
EMBROIDERER
ENTERTAINER
ESTATE AGENT
ETHNOLOGIST
ETYMOLOGIST
EXECUTIONER
EXTORTIONER
FACE-PAINTER
FACTORY HAND
FAITH HEALER
FANCY-MONGER
FIELD WORKER
FIGURE-MAKER
FILING CLERK
FINESTILLER
FIRE INSURER
FLAX-DRESSER
FLESH-MONGER
FOURBISSEUR
FRINGE-MAKER
FRUIT PICKER
FUNAMBULIST
GALLEY-SLAVE
GENEALOGIST
GHOSTWRITER
GLASS-BENDER
GLASS-BLOWER
GLASS-CUTTER
GLASS-WORKER
GRAVE-DIGGER

11—continued

GREENGROCER
HABERDASHER
HAGIOLOGIST
HAIRDRESSER
HAIR STYLIST
HARDWAREMAN
HEDGE-PRIEST
HEDGE-WRITER
HIEROLOGIST
HISTOLOGIST
HORSE DOCTOR
HORSE TRADER
HOSPITALLER
HOTEL-KEEPER
HOUSEMASTER
HOUSEMOTHER
HYMNOLOGIST
ILLUMINATOR
ILLUSIONIST
ILLUSTRATOR
INFANTRYMAN
INSTITUTIST
INTERPRETER
INTERVIEWER
IRON-FOUNDER
IVORY-CARVER
IVORY-TURNER
IVORY-WORKER
KITCHENMAID
LAMPLIGHTER
LAND STEWARD
LAUNDRYMAID
LEADING LADY
LEDGER CLERK
LIFEBOATMAN
LIGHTKEEPER
LINEN DRAPER
LITHOLOGIST
LITHOTOMIST
LORRY DRIVER
MADRIGALIST
MAIDSERVANT
MAMMALOGIST
MASTER BAKER
MECHANICIAN
MEDICINE MAN
MEMORIALIST
MERCHANTMAN
METAL WORKER
MINIATURIST
MONEY-BROKER
MONEY-LENDER
MONOGRAPHER
MULE-SPINNER
MUSIC CRITIC
MUSIC MASTER
MYOGRAPHIST
MYSTERIARCH
MYTHOLOGIST
NECROLOGIST
NECROMANCER

11–continued	11–continued	12–continued	12–continued
NEEDLEWOMAN	SHIP'S MASTER	BANTAMWEIGHT	GLASS-GRINDER
NEUROLOGIST	SHOPSTEWARD	BELLOWS-MAKER	GLOSSOLOGIST
NEUROTOMIST	SILK-THROWER	BIBLIOLOGIST	GREASEMONKEY
NIGHT PORTER	SILVERSMITH	BIBLIOPEGIST	GUILD BROTHER
NIGHTWORKER	SLAUGHTERER	BIBLIOPOLIST	GYMNOSOPHIST
NOMENCLATOR	SLAVE-DRIVER	BOOKING CLERK	GYNECOLOGIST
NUMISMATIST	SLAVE-HOLDER	BUS CONDUCTOR	HAGIOGRAPHER
OFFICE STAFF	SMALLHOLDER	CABINET-MAKER	HALIOGRAPHER
ONION-SELLER	SOCIOLOGIST	CALLIGRAPHER	HARNESS-MAKER
OPERA SINGER	STAGE-DRIVER	CARICATURIST	HEAD GARDENER
OPHIOLOGIST	STEEPLEJACK	CARPET-FITTER	HOMEOPATHIST
ORIENTALIST	STOCKBROKER	CARTOGRAPHER	HORSE-BREAKER
ORTHOPEDIST	STOCKJOBBER	CATACLYSMIST	HORSE-COURSER
OSTEOLOGIST	STONECUTTER	CEROGRAPHIST	HORSE-KNACKER
PAMPHLETEER	STOREKEEPER	CHEESEMONGER	HOTEL MANAGER
PANEL-BEATER	SUNDRIESMAN	CHIEF CASHIER	HOUSEBREAKER
PANTOMIMIST	SYSTEM-MAKER	CHIMNEY-SWEEP	HOUSEPAINTER
PAPERHANGER	TAXIDERMIST	CHIROPRACTOR	HOUSE STEWARD
PARLOURMAID	TELEGRAPHER	CHRONOLOGIST	HOUSE SURGEON
PATHOLOGIST	TELEPHONIST	CHURCHWARDEN	HYDROGRAPHER
PATTENMAKER	TICKET AGENT	CIRCUIT RIDER	HYDROPATHIST
PEARLFISHER	TOASTMASTER	CIVIL SERVANT	HYPOTHECATOR
PETROLOGIST	TOBACCONIST	CLARINETTIST	IMMUNOLOGIST
PETTIFOGGER	TOOTH-DRAWER	CLERK OF WORKS	IMPROPRIATOR
PHILATELIST	TOPOGRAPHER	CLOTH-SHEARER	INSTRUCTRESS
PHILOLOGIST	TORCH-BEARER	COACH-BUILDER	INVOICE CLERK
PHONOLOGIST	TOWN PLANNER	COLEOPTERIST	JERRY-BUILDER
PHYTOLOGIST	TOXOPHILITE	COMMISSIONER	JOINT-TRUSTEE
POLYPHONIST	TRAIN-BEARER	CONCHOLOGIST	JURISCONSULT
PORK BUTCHER	TRANSCRIBER	CONFECTIONER	JUVENILE LEAD
PORTRAITIST	TRANSPORTER	CORN CHANDLER	KING'S COUNSEL
PRECEPTRESS	TRAVEL AGENT	COSMOGRAPHER	KNIFE-GRINDER
PRINT-SELLER	TYPE-FOUNDER	COSTERMONGER	KNIFE-THROWER
PROBATIONER	TYPOGRAPHER	CRAFTS-MASTER	LABOURING MAN
PROMULGATOR	UNDERBEARER	CRANIOLOGIST	LAND SURVEYOR
PROOFREADER	UNDERLETTER	CRYPTOGAMIST	LATH-SPLITTER
PROPERTY MAN	UNDERWRITER	DANCE HOSTESS	LEADER-WRITER
PROPRIETRIX	UPHOLSTERER	DEEP-SEA DIVER	LEXICOLOGIST
QUESTIONARY	VERSEMONGER	DEMONOLOGIST	LITHOGRAPHER
RADIOLOGIST	VINE-DRESSER	DEMONSTRATOR	LONGSHOREMAN
RAG MERCHANT	WASHERWOMAN	DENDROLOGIST	LOSS ADJUSTER
REPRESENTER	WATCHKEEPER	DRAMATURGIST	LUMBER-DEALER
REPUBLISHER	WAX-CHANDLER	ECCLESIASTIC	MAITRE D'HOTEL
RHETORICIAN	WHEEL-CUTTER	EGYPTOLOGIST	MAKE-UP ARTIST
ROADSWEEPER	WHEELWRIGHT	ELECUTIONIST	MALACOLOGIST
SAFEBREAKER	WHITEWASHER	ENGINE-DRIVER	MANUAL WORKER
SANDWICH MAN	WITCH-DOCTOR	ENTOMOLOGIST	MANUFACTURER
SANSCRITIST	WOOL-STAPLER	ENTOMOTOMIST	MASS PRODUCER
SAXOPHONIST	XYLOPHONIST	ENTREPRENEUR	MEAT-SALESMAN
SCOUTMASTER	ZOOGRAPHIST	ESCAPOLOGIST	METALLURGIST
SCRAPDEALER		ETHNOGRAPHER	MEZZO SOPRANO
SCRIP-HOLDER	12	EXPERIMENTER	MICROSCOPIST
SECRET AGENT	ACCORDIONIST	FAMILY DOCTOR	MINERALOGIST
SEDITIONARY	ACTOR MANAGER	FARM LABOURER	MISCELLANIST
SERVANT GIRL	AMBULANCE MAN	FILM DIRECTOR	MONEY-CHANGER
SERVING-MAID	ANAESTHETIST	FILM PRODUCER	MONOGRAPHIST
SHARE-BROKER	ANIMALCULIST	FIRST OFFICER	MORRIS-DANCER
SHEEPFARMER	ARCHEOLOGIST	FLYING DOCTOR	MOSAIC-ARTIST
SHEPHERDESS	ARTILLERYMAN	FOOTPLATEMAN	MOSAIC-WORKER
SHIPBREAKER	BALLET DANCER	GEOMETRICIAN	MYTHOGRAPHER
SHIPBUILDER	BALLET MASTER	GERIATRICIAN	NEWSPAPERMAN

12—continued

NUTRITIONIST
OBSTETRICIAN
OFFICE JUNIOR
ONEIROCRITIC
ORCHESTRATOR
ORGAN-BUILDER
ORGAN-GRINDER
ORTHODONTIST
ORTHOGRAPHER
OVARIOTOMIST
PAPER-STAINER
PATTERN-MAKER
PEDIATRICIAN
PHONOGRAPHER
PHOTOGRAPHER
PHRENOLOGIST
PHYSIOLOGIST
PLANT MANAGER
PLOUGHWRIGHT
PLUMBER'S MATE
PLYER-FOR-HIRE
POSTMISTRESS
PRACTITIONER
PRESS OFFICER
PRESTIGIATOR
PRISON WARDER
PRIZE-FIGHTER
PROFESSIONAL
PROPAGANDIST
PROPRIETRESS
PSYCHIATRIST
PSYCHOLOGIST
PUBLICITY MAN
PUPIL-TEACHER
PUPPET-PLAYER
QUARRY MASTER
RACING DRIVER
RADIOGRAPHER
RECEPTIONIST
REMEMBRANCER
RESTAURATEUR
RIDING-MASTER
RIGHT-HAND MAN
RUBBER-GRADER
SALES MANAGER
SCENE-PAINTER
SCENE-SHIFTER
SCHOOLMASTER
SCREENWRITER
SCRIPTWRITER
SCULLERY-MAID
SEED-MERCHANT
SEISMOLOGIST
SHARECROPPER
SHARPSHOOTER
SHIP CHANDLER
SHIP'S HUSBAND
SHOE-REPAIRER
SILVER-BEATER
SLAUGHTERMAN
SNAKE-CHARMER

12—continued

SOCIAL WORKER
SOIL MECHANIC
SPECIAL AGENT
SPEECHWRITER
SPICE-BLENDER
SPORTSCASTER
SPORTSWRITER
STAGE MANAGER
STATISTICIAN
STENOGRAPHER
STONEBREAKER
STONEDRESSER
STONESQUARER
STREET-TRADER
STREET-WALKER
SUGAR-REFINER
TAX-COLLECTOR
TECHNOLOGIST
TELEGRAPH BOY
TELEGRAPHIST
TEST ENGINEER
THERAPEUTIST
THIEF-CATCHER
TICKET-PORTER
TIMBER TRADER
TOLL-GATHERER
TOURIST AGENT
TOXICOLOGIST
TRADESPEOPLE
TRANSPLANTER
TRICHOLOGIST
UNDERMANAGER
UNDERSERVANT
VETERINARIAN
WAITING-WOMAN
WAREHOUSEMAN
WATER DIVINER
WINE MERCHANT
WOOD-ENGRAVER
WORKS MANAGER
ZINCOGRAPHER

13

ADMINISTRATOR
AGRICULTURIST
ANTIQUE DEALER
ARACHNOLOGIST
ARCHAEOLOGIST
ARITHMETICIAN
ARTICLED CLERK
ASSYRIOLOGIST
BARBER-SURGEON
BIBLIOGRAPHER
CALICO-PRINTER
CAMPANOLOGIST
CARTOGRAPHIST
CHARTOGRAPHER
CHICKEN-FARMER
CHIROGRAPHIST
CHOREOGRAPHER
CHRONOGRAPHER

13—continued

CIVIL ENGINEER
CLEARSTARCHER
COFFEE-PLANTER
COMETOGRAPHER
CONTORTIONIST
CONTRABANDIST
COTTON-SPINNER
COUNTER-CASTER
COUNTERFEITER
CRANIOSCOPIST
CRYPTOGRAPHER
DANCING MASTER
DEIPNOSOPHIST
DERMATOLOGIST
DIAGNOSTICIAN
DIAMOND-CUTTER
DRAUGHTSWOMAN
DRAWING-MASTER
DRESS DESIGNER
DRILL SERGEANT
ELECTROPLATER
ELECTROTYPIST
EMIGRATIONIST
ENCYCLOPEDIST
ENTOZOOLOGIST
EPIGRAMMATIST
ESTATE MANAGER
FENCING-MASTER
FORTUNE-TELLER
FREIGHT-BROKER
GALVANOLOGIST
GASTRILOQUIST
GLOSSOGRAPHER
GLYPHOGRAPHER
GROUND-BAILIFF
GYNAECOLOGIST
HARBOUR MASTER
HIEROGLYPHIST
HORSE-MILLINER
HOSPITAL NURSE
ICHTHYOLOGIST
INDUSTRIALIST
INTELLIGENCER
JOINT-EXECUTOR
LETTER-CARRIER
LETTER-FOUNDER
LEXICOGRAPHER
LIGHTHOUSE-MAN
MAID-OF-ALL-WORK
MASTER-BUILDER
MASTER MARINER
MATHEMATICIAN
MELODRAMATIST
METAPHYSICIAN
METEOROLOGIST
METOPOSCOPIST
MUSIC MISTRESS
NIGHT-WATCHMAN
OLD-CLOTHES-MAN
ORNITHOLOGIST
ORTHOGRAPHIST

13—continued

PARK ATTENDANT
PERIODICALIST
PHARMACEUTIST
PHYSIOGNOMIST
PHYSIOGRAPHER
POSTURE-MASTER
POULTRY FARMER
PRIVATEERSMAN
PROCESS-SERVER
PSALMOGRAPHER
PSYCHOANALYST
PTERIDOLOGIST
PUBLIC SPEAKER
QUEEN'S COUNSEL
RACING-TIPSTER
REVOLUTIONARY
REVOLUTIONIST
RUBBER-PLANTER
SAILING MASTER
SCHOOLTEACHER
SCIENCE MASTER
SHOP ASSISTANT
SILK-THROWSTER
SINGING-MASTER
STATION-MASTER
STENOGRAPHIST
STEREOSCOPIST
STETHOSCOPIST
STREET-SWEEPER
SUB-CONTRACTOR
SUPERINTENDER
SUPERNUMERARY
THAUMATURGIST
THIMBLE-RIGGER
TOLL COLLECTOR
TRADE UNIONIST
TRAMCAR-DRIVER
TRAM CONDUCTOR
VENTRILOQUIST
VIOLONCELLIST
WINDOW-CLEANER
WINDOW-DRESSER
WOOLLEN-DRAPER
WRITING-MASTER

14

ADMINISTRATRIX
ANTHROPOLOGIST
AUTOBIOGRAPHER
BACTERIOLOGIST
BALLET MISTRESS
BILLIARD-MARKER
BILLIARD-PLAYER
CHAMBER-COUNSEL
CHIMNEY-SWEEPER
CITIZEN-SOLDIER
CLASSICS MASTER
COLOUR SERGEANT
COMMISSIONAIRE
DANCING PARTNER
DISCOUNT-BROKER

14–continued
ECCLESIOLOGIST
EDUCATIONALIST
ENCYCLOPAEDIST
EXCHANGE-BROKER
GRAMMATICASTER
HANDICRAFTSMAN
HERESIOGRAPHER
HORTICULTURIST
HOUSE DECORATOR
HOUSE FURNISHER
LANGUAGE MASTER
LEATHER-DRESSER
MANUAL LABOURER
MARKET-GARDENER
MEDICAL OFFICER
MERCHANT-TAILOR
MISCELLANARIAN
MONEY-SCRIVENER
MOTHER-SUPERIOR
MUSIC PUBLISHER

14–continued
NAVAL PENSIONER
OPTHALMOLOGIST
PAINTER-STAINER
PHARMACOLOGIST
PNEUMATOLOGIST
PSALMOGRAPHIST
RECEPTION CLERK
REPRESENTATIVE
SCHOOLMISTRESS
SHIP'S-CARPENTER
SIDEROGRAPHIST
SPECTACLE-MAKER
SPECTROSCOPIST
SUPERINTENDENT
SYSTEMS ANALYST
TALLOW CHANDLER
WATER-COLOURIST
WEATHER PROPHET

15
ARBORICULTURIST

15–continued
ASSISTANT MASTER
BOW STREET
 RUNNER
CROSSING-
 SWEEPER
CRUSTACEOLOGIST
DANCING MISTRESS
DIAMOND
 MERCHANT
DOMESTIC SERVANT
FORWARDING
 AGENT
GENTLEMAN-
 FARMER
HACKNEY
 COACHMAN
HEART SPECIALIST
HELMINTHOLOGIST
HIEROGRAMMATIST
HISTORIOGRAPHER

15–continued
INSTRUMENTALIST
INSURANCE BROKER
MUSICAL DIRECTOR
NUMISMATOLOGIST
PALAEONTOLOGIST
PLATFORM-
 SPEAKER
PORTRAIT-PAINTER
PROGRAMME
 SELLER
PROVISION DEALER
RAILWAY ENGINEER
RESURRECTIONIST
SCRIPTURE-
 READER
SLEEPING PARTNER
STRETCHER-
 BEARER
TICKET COLLECTOR
TIGHTROPE
 WALKER

TOOLS

3
AWL
AXE
BIT
DIE
FAN
GAD
GIN
HOD
HOE
JIG
LOY
SAW
ZAX

4
ADZE
BILL
BORE
BROG
BURR
CART
CELT
CRAB
FILE
FORK
FROW
GAGE
HINK
HOOK
JACK

4–continued
LAST
LOOM
MALL
MAUL
MULE
NAIL
PICK
PIKE
PLOW
RAKE
RASP
RULE
SOCK
SPUD
TRUG
VICE
WHIM

5
ANVIL
AUGER
BEELE
BENCH
BESOM
BETTY
BEVEL
BLADE
BORER
BRACE
BURIN

5–continued
CHUCK
CHURN
CLAMP
CLAMS
CLASP
CLEAT
CRAMP
CRANE
CROOM
CROZE
CUPEL
DOLLY
DRILL
FLAIL
FLANG
FORGE
GAUGE
GAVEL
GOUGE
HOIST
INCUS
JACKS
JEMMY
JIMMY
KNIFE
LATHE
LEVEL
LEVER
MOWER
PARER

5–continued
PLANE
PLUMB
PREEN
PRISE
PRONG
PUNCH
QUERN
QUOIN
RATCH
RAZOR
SARSE
SCREW
SPADE
SPIKE
SPILE
SPILL
SWAGE
TEMSE
TOMMY
TONGS
TROMP
TRONE
WEDGE
WINCH

6
BARROW
BENDER
BLOWER
BODKIN

6–continued

BORCER
BOW-SAW
BRAYER
BROACH
BURTON
CHASER
CHISEL
COLTER
CREVET
CRUSET
DIBBER
DIBBLE
DOFFER
DREDGE
DRIVER
FANNER
FAUCET
FERRET
FOLDER
GIMLET
GRAVER
HACKLE
HAMMER
HARROW
JAGGER
JIGGER
JIG SAW
LADDER
MALLET
MORTAR
MULLER
OLIVER
PALLET
PENCIL
PESTLE
PITSAW
PLANER
PLIERS
PLOUGH
PONTEE
POOLER
RAMMER
RASPER
REAPER
RIDDLE
RIPSAW
RUBBER
SANDER
SAW-SET
SCREEN
SCYTHE
SEGGER
SHEARS
SHOVEL
SICKLE
SIFTER
SKEWER
SLEDGE
SLICER
SQUARE
STIDDY

6–continued

STITHY
STRIKE
TACKLE
TENTER
TREPAN
TROWEL
TUBBER
TURREL
WIMBLE
WRENCH

7

BOASTER
BRADAWL
CAPSTAN
CATLING
CAUTERY
CHAMFER
CHIP-AXE
CHOPPER
CLEAVER
COULOIR
COULTER
CRAMPON
CRISPER
CROWBAR
CUVETTE
DERRICK
DIAMOND
DOG-BELT
DRUDGER
FISTUCA
FORCEPS
FRETSAW
FRUGGIN
GRADINE
GRAINER
GRAPNEL
GRUB AXE
HACKSAW
HANDSAW
HATCHET
HAY FORK
JOINTER
MANDREL
MATTOCK
NIPPERS
NUT HOOK
PICKAXE
PIERCER
PINCERS
PLUMMET
POLE AXE
POUNDER
PRICKER
SALT-PAN
SCALPEL
SCAUPER
SCRAPER
SCREWER
SCRIBER

7–continued

SEED LOP
SPADDLE
SPANNER
SPITTLE
SPRAYER
STROCAL
TENONER
THIMBLE
TRESTLE
TRIBLET
T-SQUARE
TWIBILL
TWISTER
WHIP-SAW
WHITTLE
WOOLDER

8

BARK MILL
BAR SHEAR
BEAKIRON
BENCH PEG
BILL HOOK
BISTOURY
BLOOMARY
BLOWLAMP
BLOWPIPE
BOATHOOK
BOWDRILL
BULL NOSE
BUTTERIS
CALIPERS
CANTHOOK
CROW MILL
CRUCIBLE
DIE STOCK
DOWEL BIT
DRILL BOW
EDGE TOOL
FILATORY
FIRE KILN
FLAME GUN
FLAX COMB
GAVELOCK
GEE CRAMP
HANDLOOM
HANDMILL
HAND VICE
HAY KNIFE
HORSE HOE
LAPSTONE
LEAD MILL
MITRE BOX
MOLEGRIP
MUCK RAKE
NUT SCREW
OILSTONE
PAINT PAD
PANEL SAW
PICKLOCK
PINCHERS

8–continued

PLUMB BOB
POLISHER
POWER SAW
PRONG-HOE
PUNCHEON
REAP HOOK
SAW WREST
SCISSORS
SCUFFLER
SLATE AXE
STILETTO
STRICKLE
TENON SAW
THROSTLE
TOOTH KEY
TWEEZERS
TWIST BIT
WATERCAN
WATER RAM
WEED HOOK
WINDLASS
WINDMILL

9

BELT PUNCH
BENCH HOOK
BOLT AUGER
BOOT CRIMP
CANKER BIT
CANNIPERS
CAN OPENER
CENTRE BIT
COMPASSES
CORKSCREW
COTTON GIN
CRAMP IRON
CURRY COMB
CUTTER BAR
DOG CLUTCH
DRAW KNIFE
DRAW-PLATE
EXCAVATOR
EYELETEER
FILLISTER
FINING POT
FORK CHUCK
GAS PLIERS
HAMMER AXE
HANDBRACE
HANDSCREW
HANDSPIKE
HOLING AXE
HUMMELLER
IMPLEMENT
JACKKNIFE
JACKPLANE
JACKSCREW
LACE FRAME
LAWNMOWER
NAIL PUNCH
NUT WRENCH

9–continued
PITCH FORK
PLANE IRON
PLANISHER
PLUMBLINE
PLUMBRULE
SCREWJACK
SCRIBE AWL
SHEARLEGS
SHEEP HOOK
STEELYARD
SUGAR MILL
TIN OPENER
TRY SQUARE
TURF SPADE
TURN BENCH
TURNSCREW
WATERMILL

10
BUSH HARROW
CLASPKNIFE
CLAWHAMMER
COLD CHISEL
CRANE'S BILL
CULTIVATOR
DRAY PLOUGH
DRIFT BOLTS
DRILLPRESS
DRILLSTOCK
EMERY WHEEL
FIRING IRON
GRINDSTONE
INSTRUMENT
MASONRY BIT
MASTICATOR
MITRE BLOCK
MOTOR MOWER
MOULD BOARD
PAINTBRUSH
PERFORATOR
PIPE WRENCH
POINTED AWL
SCREW PRESS
SLEEK STONE
SNOWPLOUGH
SPOKESHAVE
STEAM PRESS
STEPLADDER

10–continued
TENTERHOOK
THUMBSCREW
THUMBSTALL
TILT HAMMER
TRIP HAMMER
TURF CUTTER
TURNBUCKLE
WATERCRANE
WATERGAUGE
WATERLEVEL
WHEEL BRACE

11
BRACE-AND-BIT
BREAST DRILL
CHAFF CUTTER
CHAIN BLOCKS
CHAIN WRENCH
CHEESE PRESS
COUNTERSINK
CRAZING MILL
CRISPING PIN
CROSSCUT SAW
DRILL BARROW
DRILL HARROW
DRILL PLOUGH
FANNING MILL
GRUBBING HOE
HELVEHAMMER
JAGGING IRON
MACHINE TOOL
MONKEY BLOCK
PAINT ROLLER
PLOUGHSHARE
PRUNING HOOK
RABBET PLANE
REAPING-HOOK
SAWING STOOL
SCREWDRIVER
SINGLE-EDGED
SKIM COULTER
SNATCH BLOCK
SPIRIT LEVEL
SQUARING ROD
STEAM HAMMER
STONE HAMMER
STRAW CUTTER
STRIKE BLOCK

11–continued
STUBBLE RAKE
SWARD CUTTER
SWINGPLOUGH
TAPEMEASURE
TURFING IRON
TWO-FOOT RULE
WARPING HOOK
WARPING POST
WEEDING FORK
WEEDING HOOK
WEEDING RHIM
WHEELBARROW

12
BARKING IRONS
BELT ADJUSTER
BRANDING IRON
BREASTPLOUGH
CAULKING TOOL
COUNTER GAUGE
CRADEL SCYTHE
CRAMPING IRON
CRIMPING IRON
CRISPING IRON
CURLING TONGS
DRILL GRUBBER
DRIVING SHAFT
DRIVING WHEEL
EMERY GRINDER
FLOUR DRESSER
GLASS FURNACE
HYDRAULIC RAM
MANDREL LATHE
MARLINE SPIKE
MONKEY WRENCH
PRUNING KNIFE
PULLEY BLOCKS
RUNNING BLOCK
SCRIBING IRON
SLEDGE HAMMER
SLIDING BEVEL
SOCKET CHISEL
STONE BREAKER
STRAIGHTEDGE
SWINGLE KNIFE
TOUCH NEEDLES
TRENCH PLOUGH
TURFING SPADE

12–continued
TURNING LATHE
WATER BELLOWS
WEEDING TONGS

13
CHOPPING BLOCK
CHOPPING KNIFE
CYLINDER PRESS
ELECTRIC DRILL
GRAPPLING-IRON
HYDRAULIC JACK
PACKING NEEDLE
SCRIBING BLOCK
SEWING MACHINE
SOLDERING BOLT
SOLDERING IRON
SOWING MACHINE
SPINNING JENNY
SPINNING WHEEL
STOCKING FRAME
SUBSOIL PLOUGH
TWO-HOLE PLIERS
WEEDING CHISEL

14
BLOWING MACHINE
CARDING MACHINE
DRAINING ENGINE
DRAINING PLOUGH
PENUMATIC DRILL
REAPING MACHINE
SMOOTHING PLANE
SWINGLING KNIFE
THRUSTING SCREW
WEEDING FORCEPS

15
CARPENTER'S
  BENCH
CRIMPING MACHINE
DREDGING MACHINE
DRILLING MACHINE
ENTRENCHING
  TOOL
PESTLE AND
  MORTAR
PUMP SCREW-
  DRIVER
WEIGHING MACHINE

MILITARY TERMS

TITLES

ROYAL AIR FORCE RANKS

MARSHAL OF THE ROYAL
  AIR FORCE
AIR CHIEF MARSHAL
AIR MARSHAL
AIR VICE-MARSHAL
AIR COMMODORE
GROUP CAPTAIN
WING COMMANDER
SQUADRON LEADER
FLIGHT LIEUTENANT
FLYING OFFICER
PILOT OFFICER
MASTER AIR LOADMASTER
MASTER AIR ELECTRONIC
  OPERATOR
MASTER ENGINEER
MASTER NAVIGATOR
MASTER SIGNALLER
MASTER PILOT
WARRANT OFFICER
CHIEF TECHNICIAN
FLIGHT SERGEANT
SERGEANT
CORPORAL
JUNIOR TECHNICIAN
SENIOR AIRCRAFTMAN
LEADING AIRCRAFTMAN
AIRCRAFTMAN 1ST CLASS
AIRCRAFTMAN 2ND CLASS

ARMY RANKS

FIELD MARSHAL
GENERAL
LIEUTENANT-GENERAL
MAJOR-GENERAL
BRIGADIER
COLONEL
LIEUTENANT-COLONEL
MAJOR
CAPTAIN
LIEUTENANT
SECOND-LIEUTENANT
SERGEANT-MAJOR
QUARTERMASTER-
  SERGEANT
SERGEANT
CORPORAL
LANCE-CORPORAL
BOMBARDIER
PRIVATE

ROYAL NAVY RANKS

ADMIRAL OF THE FLEET
ADMIRAL
VICE-ADMIRAL
REAR-ADMIRAL
COMMODORE
CAPTAIN
COMMANDER
LIEUTENANT-COMMANDER
LIEUTENANT
SUB-LIEUTENANT
CHIEF PETTY OFFICER
PETTY OFFICER
LEADING SEAMAN
ABLE SEAMAN
ORDINARY SEAMAN
JUNIOR SEAMAN

DECORATIONS AND MEDALS

AIR FORCE CROSS (AFC)
AIR FORCE MEDAL (AFM)
ALBERT MEDAL (AM)
CONSPICUOUS GALLANTRY MEDAL (CGM)
DISTINGUISHED FLYING CROSS (DFC)
DISTINGUISHED FLYING MEDAL (DFM)
DISTINGUISHED SERVICE CROSS (DSC)
DISTINGUISHED SERVICE MEDAL (DSM)

GEORGE CROSS (GC)
GEORGE MEDAL (GM)
MEDAL FOR DISTINGUISHED CONDUCT IN
  THE FIELD (DCM)
MILITARY CROSS (MC)
MILITARY MEDAL (MM)
THE DISTINGUISHED SERVICE ORDER (DSO)
VICTORIA CROSS (VC)

BATTLES

2
RÉ, ÎLE DE (1627, Anglo-French Wars)

3
ACS (1849, Hungarian Rising)
AIX, ÎLE D' (1758, Seven Years' War)
DEE, BRIG OF (1639, Bishops' War)
GOA (1511, 1570, Portuguese Conquest)
HUÉ (1968, Vietnam War)
ULM (1805, Napoleonic Wars)

4
ACRE (1189–1191, Third Crusade; 1291,
    Crusader-Turkish Wars; 1799, French
    Revolutionary Wars; 1840, Egyptian Revolt)
AGRA (1803, Second British-Maratha War; 1857,
    Indian Mutiny)
ALMA (1854, Crimean War)
AONG (1857, Indian Mutiny)
ARAS (1775, First British-Maratha War)
AVUS (198 BC, Second Macedonian War)
BAZA (1489, Spanish-Muslim Wars)
BEDR (623, Islamic Wars)
BEGA (1696, Ottoman Wars)
CUBA (1953, Castro Revolt)
DEEG (1780, First British-Maratha War; 1804,
    Second British-Maratha War)
GAZA (332 BC, Alexander's Asiatic Campaigns;
    312 BC, Wars of Alexander's Successors; 1917,
    World War I)
GELT, THE (1570, Anglo-Scottish Wars)
GUAM (1944, World War II)
JENA (1806, Napoleonic Wars)
KARS (1855, Crimean War)
KIEV (1941, World War II)
KULM (1813, Napoleonic Wars)
LAON (1814, Napoleonic Wars)
LECK, THE (1632, Thirty Years' War)
LENS (1648, Thirty Years' War)
LÓDŹ (1914, World War I)
MAIN, THE (9 BC, Germanic War)
MAYA, COLDE (1813, Peninsular War)
METZ (1870, Franco-Prussian War)
NEON (354 BC, Sacred War)
NILE (1798, French Revolutionary Wars)
NIVE (1813, Peninsular War)
NOVI (1799, French Revolutionary Wars)
ONAO (1857, Indian Mutiny)
ORAN (1509, Spanish Invasion of Morocco;
    1940, World War II)
OREL (1943, World War II)
RAAB (1809, Napoleonic Wars)
ROME (387 BC, First Invasion of the Gauls; 408,
    Wars of the Western Roman Empire; 472,
    Ricimer's Rebellion; 537, 546, Wars of the
    Byzantine Empire; 1082, Norman Seizure;
    1527, Wars of Charles V; 1849, Italian Wars of
    Independence)

4—continued
SCIO (1769, Ottoman Wars)
SOHR (1745, War of the Austrian Succession)
ST LÔ (1944, World War II)
TOBA (1868, Japanese Revolution)
TROY (1100 BC)
TRUK (1944, World War II)
VEII (405 BC, Rise of Rome)
ZELA (67 BC, Third Mithridatic War; 47 BC, Wars
    of the First Triumvirate)

5
ACCRA (1824, 1825, First British-Ashanti War)
ADUWA (1896, Italian Invasion of Ethiopia)
ALAMO, STORMING OF THE (1836, Texan
    Rising)
ALLIA, THE (390 BC, The First Invasion of the
    Gauls)
ALSEN (1864, Schleswig-Holstein War)
ANZIO (1944, World War II)
ARGOS (195 BC, Roman Invasion of Greece)
ARIUS (214 BC, The Wars of the Hellenistic
    Monarchies)
ARRAH (1857, Indian Mutiny)
ARRAS (1654, Wars of Louis XIV; 1917, World
    War I)
A SHAU (1966, Vietnam War)
AURAY (1364, Hundred Years' War)
BAHUR (1752, Seven Years' War)
BANDA (1858, Indian Mutiny)
BANDS, THE (961, Danish Invasion of Scotland)
BEREA (1852, Kaffir Wars)
BETWA (1858, Indian Mutiny)
BOYNE, THE (1690, War of the Grand Alliance)
BREST (1512, War of the Holy League)
BRILL (1572, Netherlands War of Independence)
BURMA (1942, 1943, World War II)
BUXAR (1764, British Conquest of Bengal)
CADIZ (1587, Anglo-Spanish War)
CAIRO (1517, Ottoman Wars)
CARPI (1701, War of the Spanish Succession)
CEŞME (1770, Ottoman Wars)
CRÉCY (1346, Hundred Years' War)
CRETE (1941, World War II)
DAK TO (1967, Vietnam War)
DELHI (1297, First Tatar Invasion of India; 1398,
    Second Tatar Invasion; 1803, Second British-
    Maratha War; 1804, Second British-Maratha
    War; 1857, Indian Mutiny)
DOUAI (1710, War of the Spanish Succession)
DOURO (1809, Peninsular War)
DOVER (1652, Anglo-Dutch Wars)
DOWNS, THE (1666, Anglo-Dutch Wars)
ELENA (1877, Russo-Turkish War)
EL TEB (1884, British-Sudan Campaigns)
EMESA (272, Wars of the Roman Empire)
ENGEN (1800, French Revolutionary Wars)

5–continued

EYLAU (1807, Napoleonic Wars)
GENOA (1746, Patriotic Rising; 1795, 1800, French Revolutionary Wars)
GOITS (1848, Italian Wars of Independence)
GUBAT (1885, British Sudan Campaigns)
HANAU (1813, Napoleonic Wars)
HIPPO (430, Wars of the Western Roman Empire)
IMOLA (1797, French Revoutionary Wars)
ISSUS (333 BC, Alexander's Asiatic Campaigns; 1488, Ottoman Wars)
JASSY (1620, Ottoman Wars)
KAGUL (1770, Ottoman Wars)
KALPI (1858, Indian Mutiny)
KAREE (1900, Second Boer War)
KAZAN (1774, Cossack Rising)
KOLIN (1757, Seven Years' War)
KOTAH (1858, Indian Mutiny)
LAGOS (1693, War of the Grand Alliance)
LA PAZ (1865, Bolivian Civil War)
LARGS (1263, Norse Invasion of Scotland)
LEWES (1264, Barons' Wars)
LEYTE (1944, World War II)
LIÈGE (1914, World War I)
LIGNY (1815, Napoleonic Wars)
LILLE (1708, War of the Spanish Succession)
LISSA (1866, Seven Weeks' War)
LUZON (1945, World War II)
LYONS (197, Civil Wars of the Roman Empire)
MAIDA (1806, Napoleonic Wars)
MALTA (1565, Ottoman Wars; 1798, French Revolutionary Wars; 1942, World War II)
MARNE (1914, 1918, World War I)
MAXEN (1759, Seven Years' War)
MUDKI (1845, First British-Sikh War)
MUNDA (45 BC, Civil War of Caesar and Pompey)
MURSA (351, Civil Wars of the Roman Empire)
MYLEX (36 BC, Wars of the Second Triumvirate)
NAMUR (1914, World War I)
PARIS (1814, Napoleonic Wars; 1870, Franco-Prussian War)
PATAY (1429, Hundred Years' War)
PODOL (1866, Seven Weeks' War)
PRUTH, THE (1770, Ottoman Wars)
RAMLA (1177, Crusader-Turkish Wars)
REDAN, THE GREAT (1855, Crimean War)
REIMS (1814, Napoleonic Wars)
ROUEN (1418, Hundred Years' War)
SEDAN (1870, Franco-Prussian War)
SELBY (1644, English Civil War)
SEOUL (1950, Korean War)
SLUYS (1340, Hundred Years' War)
SOMME (1916, 1918, World War I)
SPIRA (1703, War of the Spanish Succession)
SPURS (1302, Flemish War; 1513, Anglo-French Wars)
STOKE (1487, Lambert Simnel's Rebellion)
TAMAI (1884, British Sudan Campaigns)
TEXEL (1653, Anglo-Dutch Wars)
TOURS (732, Muslim Invasion of France)

5–continued

TUNIS (255 BC, First Punic War; 1270, Eighth Crusade)
TURIN (312, Civil Wars of the Roman Empire; 1706, War of the Spanish Succession)
UTICA (49 BC, Civil War of Caesar and Pompey; 694, Muslim Conquest of Africa)
VALMY (1792, French Revolutionary Wars)
VARNA (1444, Anti-Turkish Crusade; 1828, Ottoman Wars)
VARUS, DEFEAT OF (AD 9, Wars of the Roman Empire)
VASAQ (1442, Ottoman Wars)
WAVRE (1815, Napoleonic Wars)
WÖRTH (1870, Franco-Prussian War)
YPRES (1914, 1915, 1917, World War I)
ZENTA (1679, Ottoman Wars)
ZNAIM (1809, Napoleonic Wars)

6

AACHEN (1944, World War II)
ABUKIR (1799, 1801, French Revolutionary Wars)
ABU KRU (1885, British Sudan Campaigns)
ACTIUM (31 BC, Wars of the Second Triumvirate)
ALEPPO (638, Muslim Invasion of Syria; 1400, Tatar Invasion of Syria; 1516, Ottoman Wars)
ALFORD (1645, English Civil War)
ALIWAL (1846, First British-Sikh War)
AMIENS (1870, Franco-Prussian War)
ANGORA (1402, Tatar Invasion of Asia Minor)
ARBELA (331 BC, Alexander's Asiatic Campaigns)
ARCOLA (1796, French Revolutionary Wars)
ARGAON (1803, Second British-Maratha War)
ARKLOW (1798, Irish Rebellion)
ARNHEM (1944, World War II)
ARSOUF (1191, Third Crusade)
ARTOIS (1915, World War I)
ASHTEE (1818, Third British-Maratha War)
ASIAGO (1916, World War I)
ASPERN (1809, Napoleonic Wars)
ASSAYE (1803, Second British-Maratha War)
ATBARA (1898, British Sudan Campaigns)
AZORES (1591, Anglo-Spanish War)
BARDIA (1941, World War II)
BARNET (1471, Wars of the Roses)
BASING (871, Danish Invasion of Britain)
BAYLEN (1808, Peninsular War)
BEAUGÉ (1421, Hundred Years' War)
BENDER (1768, Ottoman Wars)
BERGEN (1759, Seven Years' War)
BEYLAN (1831, Egyptian Revolt)
BILBAO (1937, Spanish Civil War)
BUSACO (1810, Peninsular War)
CALAIS (1346, Hundred Years' War; 1558, Anglo-French Wars)
CAMDEN (1780, American Revolutionary War)
CAMPEN (1759, Seven Years' War)
CHANDA (1818, Third British-Maratha War)
CHIARI (1701, War of the Spanish Succession)
CHIZAI (1372, Hundred Years' War)

6–continued

DANZIG (1627, Thirty Years' War; 1807, 1813, Napoleonic Wars)
DARGAI (1897, British Northwest Frontier Campaign)
DELPHI (355 BC, Sacred War)
DENAIN (1712, War of the Spanish Succession)
DESSAU (1626, Thirty Years' War)
DIEPPE (1942, World War II)
DJERBA (1560, Ottoman Wars)
DOLLAR (875, Danish Invasions of Scotland)
DUNBAR (1296, 1339, Wars of Scottish Independence; 1650, Cromwell's Scottish Campaign)
DUNDEE (1899, Second Boer War)
DÜPPEL (1864, Schleswig-Holstein War)
ERBACH (1800, French Revolutionary Wars)
FERKEH (1896, British Sudan Campaigns)
GAZALA (1942, World War II)
GEBORA (1811, Peninsular War)
GERONA (1809, Peninsular War)
GHAZNI (1839, First British-Afghan War)
GISORS (1197, Anglo-French Wars)
GROZKA (1739, Ottoman Wars)
HALLUE (1870, Franco-Prussian War)
HARLAW (1411, Scottish Civil War)
HASHIN (1885, British Sudan Campaigns)
HAVANA (1748, War of the Austrian Succession; 1762, Seven Years' War)
HEXHAM (1464, Wars of the Roses)
HÖCHST (1622, Thirty Years' War)
INCHON (1950, Korean War)
INGOGO (1881, First Boer War)
ISMAIL (1790, Ottoman Wars)
ISONZO (1915, World War I)
JERSEY (1550, Anglo-French Wars)
JHANSI (1857, Indian Mutiny)
KHELAT (1839, First British-Afghan War)
KIRKEE (1817, Third British-Maratha War)
KOKEIN (1824, First Burma War)
KOTZIN (1622, 1673, Ottoman Wars)
KRONIA (1738, Ottoman Wars)
LANDAU (1702, War of the Spanish Succession)
LANDEN (1693, War of the Grand Alliance)
LAWARI (1803, Second British-Maratha War)
LE MANS (1871, Franco-Prussian War)
LERIDA (1642, 1647, Thirty Years' War)
LONATO (1796, French Revolutionary Wars)
LUTTER (1626, Thirty Years' War)
LÜTZEN (1632, Thirty Years' War; 1813, Napoleonic Wars)
MADRAS (1746, War of the Austrian Succession; 1758, Seven Years' War)
MADRID (1936, Spanish Civil War)
MAIDAN (1842, First British-Afghan War)
MAJUBA (1881, First Boer War)
MALAGA (1487, Spanish-Muslim Wars; 1704, War of the Spanish Succession)
MALAYA (1941, World War II)
MALDON (991, Danish Invasions of Britain)
MANILA (1898, Spanish-American War)
MANTUA (1797, French Revolutionary Wars)
MARGUS (285, Civil Wars of the Roman Empire)

6–continued

MEDOLA (1796, French Revolutionary Wars)
MERTON (871, Danish Invasions of Britain)
MEXICO (1520, Conquest of Mexico)
MINDEN (1759, Seven Years' War)
MOHACZ (1526, 1687, Ottoman Wars)
MORAWA (1443, Ottoman Wars)
MOSCOW (1941, World War II)
MUKDEN (1905, Russo-Japanese War; 1948, Chinese Civil War)
MULTAN (1848, Second British-Sikh War)
MUTINA (43 BC, Roman Civil Wars)
MYTTON (1319, Wars of Scottish Independence)
NACHOD (1866, Seven Weeks' War)
NÁJARA (1367, Hundred Years' War)
NASEBY (1645, English Civil War)
NICAEA (1097, First Crusade)
NORWAY (1940, World War II)
OCKLEY (851, Danish Invasions of Britain)
OLMÜTZ (1758, Seven Years' War)
OPORTO (1809, Peninsular War)
ORTHEZ (1814, Peninsular War)
OSTEND (1601, Netherlands War of Independence)
OSWEGO (1756, Seven Years' War)
OTUMBA (1520, Spanish Conquest of Mexico)
PEKING (1214, Tatar Invasion of China)
PLEI ME (1965, Vietnam War)
PLEVNA (1877, Russo-Turkish War)
POLAND (1939, World War II)
PONANI (1780, First British-Mysore War)
PRAGUE (1620, Thirty Years' War; 1757, Seven Years' War)
QUEBEC (1759, 1760, Seven Years' War)
RABAUL (1943, World War II)
RAPHIA (217 BC, Wars of the Hellenistic Monarchies)
RASZYN (1809, Napoleonic Wars)
RHODES (1480, Ottoman Wars)
RIVOLI (1797, French Revolutionary Wars)
ROCROI (1643, Thirty Years' War)
ROLICA (1808, Peninsular War)
RUMANI (1915, World War I)
SACILE (1809, Napoleonic Wars)
SADOWA (1866, Seven Weeks' War)
SAIGON (1968, Vietnam War)
SAINTS, THE (1782, American Revolutionary War)
SANGRO (1943, World War II)
SHILOH (1862, American Civil War)
SICILY (1943, World War II)
SINOPE (1853, Crimean War)
SORATA (1780, Inca Rising)
STE FOY (1760, Seven Years' War)
ST KITS (1667, Anglo-Dutch Wars)
TAURIS (47 BC, Civil War of Caesar and Pompey)
THURII (282 BC, Roman Civil Wars)
TOBRUK (1941, 1942, World War II)
TOFREK (1885, British-Sudan Campaigns)
TORGAU (1760, Seven Years' War)
TOULON (1707, War of the Spanish Succession; 1744, War of the Austrian Succession; 1793, French Revolutionary Wars)

6–continued

TOWTON (1461, Wars of the Roses)
TSINAN (1948, Chinese Civil War)
TUDELA (1808, Peninsular War)
ULUNDI (1879, Zulu-British War)
USHANT (1794, French Revolutionary Wars)
VENICE (1848, Italian Wars of Independence)
VERDUN (1916, World War I)
VERONA (312, Civil Wars of the Roman Empire)
VIENNA (1529, 1683, Ottoman Wars)
WAGRAM (1809, Napoleonic Wars)
WARSAW (1831, Second Polish Rising; 1914, World War I; 1918, Russo-Polish War; 1939, 1944, World War II)
WERBEN (1631, Thirty Years' War)
WIAZMA (1812, Napoleonic Wars)
ZÜRICH (1799, French Revolutionary Wars)

7

ABRAHAM, PLAINS OF (1759, Seven Years' War)
ABU KLEA (1885, British Sudan Campaigns)
ALBUERA (1811, Peninsular War)
ALGIERS (1775, Spanish-Algerian War; 1816, Bombardment of)
ALIGARH (1803, First British-Maratha War)
ALKMAAR (1573, Netherlands War of Independence; 1799, French Revolutionary Wars)
ALMORAH (1815, British-Gurkha War)
ALNWICK (1093, Anglo-Scottish Wars)
AMOAFUL (1874, Second British-Ashanti War)
ANTIOCH (1097, First Crusade)
ANTWERP (1576, Netherlands War of Independence; 1832, Liberation of Belgium; 1914, World War I)
ARIKERA (1791, Second British-Mysore War)
ASCALON (1099, First Crusade)
ASHDOWN (871, Danish Invasion of Britain)
ATHENRY (1316, Conquest of Ireland)
AUGHRIM (1691, War of the English Succession)
BAGHDAD (1401, Mongul Invasion of Mesopotamia)
BALKANS (1940, 1944, World War II)
BAROSSA (1811, Peninsular War)
BASSANO (1796, French Revolutionary Wars)
BASSEIN (1780, First British-Maratha War)
BATAVIA (1811, Napoleonic Wars)
BAUTZEN (1813, Napoleonic Wars)
BELMONT (1899, Second Boer War)
BENBURB (1646, Great Irish Rebellion)
BÉTHUNE (1707, War of the Spanish Succession)
BIBERAC (1796, French Revolutionary Wars)
BOURBON (1810, Napleonic Wars)
BRESLAU (1757, Seven Years' War)
BRIENNE (1814, Napoleonic Wars)
BULL RUN (1861, 1862, American Civil War)
CADSAND (1357, Hundred Years' War)
CALAFAT (1854, Crimean War)
CALICUT (1790, Second British-Mysore War)
CARIGAT (1791, Second British-Mysore War)
CASSINO (1944, World War II)

7–continued

CHETATÉ (1854, Crimean War)
COLENSO (1899, Second Boer War)
COLOMBO (1796, French Revolutionary Wars)
CORINTH (394 BC, Corinthian War; 1862, American Civil War)
CORONEL (1914, World War I)
CORUMBA (1877, Paraguayan War)
CORUNNA (1809, Peninsular War)
CRAONNE (1814, Napoleonic Wars)
CRAVANT (1423, Hundred Years' War)
CREFELD (1758, Seven Years' War)
CROTOYE (1347, Hundred Years' War)
CURICTA (49 BC, Civil War of Caesar and Pompey)
DEORHAM (577, Wessex against the Welsh)
DODOWAH (1826, First British-Ashanti War)
DRESDEN (1813, Napleonic Wars)
DUNDALK (1318, Scottish Invasion of Ireland)
DUNKELD (1689, Jacobite Rising)
DUNKIRK (1940, World War II)
DUPPLIN (1332, Baliol's Rising)
ECKMÜHL (1809, Napoleonic Wars)
ELK HORN (1862, American Civil War)
ESSLING (1809, Napoleonic Wars)
EVESHAM (1265, Barons' War)
FALKIRK (1298, Wars of Scottish Independence; 1746, The Forty-five Rebellion)
FERRARA (1815, Napoleon's Hundred Days)
FLEURUS (1622, Thirty Years' War; 1690, War of the Grand Alliance; 1794, French Revolutionary Wars)
FLODDEN (1513, Anglo-Scottish Wars)
FRANLIN (1864, American Civil War)
FULFORD (1066, Norse Invasion of England)
GALICIA (1914, World War I)
GATE PAH (1864, Maori-British War)
GHERAIN (1763, British Conquest of Bengal)
GHOAINE (1842, First British-Afghan War)
GORARIA (1857, Indian Mutiny)
GORLICE (1915, World War I)
GRASPAN (1899, Second Boer War)
GRENADA (1779, American Revolutionary War; 1983, American Invasion)
GUJERAT (1849, Second British-Sikh War)
GWALIOR (1780, First British-Maratha War; 1858, Indian Mutiny)
HAARLEM (1572, Netherlands War of Independence)
HASLACH (1805, Napoleonic Wars)
HOOGHLY, THE (1759, Anglo-Dutch Wars in India)
IWO-JIMA (1945, World War II)
JAMAICA (1655, Anglo-Spanish Wars)
JAVA SEA (1942, World War II)
JITGURH (1815, British Gurkha War)
JUTLAND (1916, World War I)
KALUNGA (1814, British-Gurkha War)
KAMBULA (1879, Zulu War)
KASHGAL (1883, British Sudan Campaigns)
KHARKOV (1942, 1943, World War II)
KHE SANH (1968, Vietnam War)

7—continued
KILSYTH (1645, English Civil War)
KINEYRI (1848, Second British-Sikh War)
KINLOSS (1009, Danish Invasion of Scotland)
KINSALE (1601, O'Neill's Rebellion)
KRASNOI (1812, Napoleonic Wars)
LA HOGUE (1692, War of the Grand Alliance)
L'ECLUSE (1340, Hundred Years' War)
LEGHORN (1653, Anglo-Dutch Wars)
LEIPZIG (1631, Thirty Years' War; 1813, Napoleonic Wars)
LEUTHEN (1757, Seven Years' War)
LINCOLN, FAIR OF (1217, First Barons' War)
LINDLEY (1900, Second Boer War)
LOCNINH (1967, Vietnam War)
LUCKNOW (1857, Indian Mutiny)
MAIWAND (1880, Second British-Afghan War)
MALAKOV (1855, Crimean War)
MANSÛRA (1250, Seventh Crusade)
MARENGO (1800, French Revolutionary Wars)
MARGATE (1387, Hundred Years' War)
MAROSCH, THE (101, Roman Empire Wars)
MATAPAN, CAPE (1941, World War II)
MEMPHIS (1862, American Civil War)
METHVEN (1306, Wars of Scottish Independence)
MINORCA (1756, Seven Years' War; 1762, American Revolutionary War)
MOGILEV (1812, Napoleonic Wars)
MOSKOWA (1812, Napoleonic Wars)
NAM DONG (1964, Vietnam War)
NANKING (1949, Chinese Civil War)
NEUWIED (1797, French Revolutionary Wars)
NEWBURN (1640, Anglo-Scottish Wars)
NEWBURY (1643, 1644, English Civil War)
NEW ROSS (1798, Irish Rebellion)
NIAGARA (1759, Seven Years' War)
NIVELLE (1813, Peninsular War)
OKINAWA (1945, World War II)
OOSCATA (1768, First British-Mysore War)
OPEQUAN (1864, American Civil War)
ORLÉANS (1428, Hundred Years' War)
PARKANY (1663, Ottoman Wars)
PLASSEY (1757, Seven Years' War)
POLOTSK (1812, Napoleonic Wars)
PRESTON (1648, English Civil War; 1715, The Fifteen Rebellion)
PULTUSK (1806, Napoleonic Wars)
RASTADT (1796, French Revolutionary Wars)
READING (871, Danish Invasions of Britain)
RIO SECO (1808, Peninsular War)
RUMANIA (1916, World War I)
RUSPINA (46 BC, Civil War of Caesar and Pompey)
SABUGAL (1811, Peninsular War)
SAGUNTO (1811, Peninsular War)
SALERNO (1943, World War II)
SAN JUAN (1898, Spanish-American War)
SCUTARI (1474, Ottoman Wars)
SEALION, OPERATION (1940, World War II)
SENEKAL (1900, Second Boer War)
SHARQAT (1918, World War I)

7—continued
SINUIJU (1951, Korean War)
SKALITZ (1866, Seven Weeks' War)
SOBRAON (1846, First British-Sikh War)
ST DENIS (1567, French Religious Wars; 1837, French-Canadian Rising)
ST LUCIA (1794, French Revolutionary Wars)
SURINAM (1804, Napoleonic Wars)
TALNEER (1818, Third British-Maratha War)
TANJORE (1758, Seven Years' War; 1773, First British-Mysore War)
TARANTO (1940, World War II)
THAPSUS (46 BC, Civil War of Caesar and Pompey)
TREBBIA (1799, French Revolutionary Wars)
TRIPOLI (643, Muslim Conquest of Africa)
TUNISIA (1942, World War II)
UKRAINE (1943, World War II)
VIMEIRO (1808, Peninsular War)
VINAROZ (1938, Spanish Civil War)
VITORIA (1813, Peninsular War)
WARBURG (1760, Seven Years' War)
WARGAOM (1779, First British-Maratha War)
WEPENER (1900, Second Boer War)
WIMPFEN (1622, Thirty Years' War)
WINKOVO (1812, Napoleonic Wars)

8
ABERDEEN (1644, English Civil War)
ABU HAMED (1897, British Sudan Campaigns)
ACAPULCO (1855, Mexican Liberal Rising)
ALICANTE (1706, War of the Spanish Succession)
AMALINDE (1818, Kaffir Wars)
ANTIETAM (1862, American Civil War)
ASIRGHAR (1819, Third British-Maratha War)
ASSUNDUN (1016, Danish Invasions of Britain)
ATLANTIC (1917, World War I)
AULDEARN (1645, English Civil War)
AZIMGHUR (1858, Indian Mutiny)
BAGRADAS (49 BC, Wars of the First Triumvirate)
BASTOGNE (1944, World War II)
BEDA FOMM (1941, World War II)
BELGRADE (1456, 1717, 1789, Ottoman Wars)
BEREZINA (1812, Napoleonic War)
BEYMAROO (1841, First British-Afghan War)
BISMARCK (1941, World War II)
BLENHEIM (1704, War of the Spanish Succession)
BLUEBERG (1806, Napoleonic Wars)
BORODINO (1812, Napoleonic Wars)
BOULOGNE (1544, Anglo-French Wars)
BOUVINES (1214, Anglo-French Wars)
BROOKLYN (1776, American Revolutionary War)
CALCUTTA (1756, Seven Years' War)
CALDIERO (1796, French Revolutionary Wars; 1805, Napoleonic Wars)
CARLISLE (1745, The Forty-five Rebellion)
CARRICAL (1758, Seven Years' War)
CARTHAGE (533, Byzantine Empire Wars)
CASTELLA (1813, Peninsular War)

8—continued

CAWNPORE (1857, Indian Mutiny)
CHERITON (1644, English Civil War)
CLONTARF (1014, Norse Invasion of Ireland)
COCHEREL (1364, Hundred Years' War)
CORAL SEA (1942, World War II)
CULLODEN (1746, The Forty-five Rebellion)
CZARNOVO (1806, Napoleonic Wars)
DAMASCUS (1918, World War I)
DOMINICA (1782, American Revolutionary War)
DROGHEDA (1641, Great Irish Rebellion; 1649, Cromwell's Campaign in Ireland)
DRUMCLOG (1679, Covenanters' Rising)
EDGEHILL (1642, English Civil War)
ESPINOSA (1808, Peninsular War)
ETHANDUN (878, Danish Invasions of Britain)
FAIR OAKS (1862, American Civil War)
FLANDERS (1940, World War II)
FLORENCE (406, Wars of the Western Roman Empire)
FLUSHING (1809, Napoleonic Wars)
FORMIGNY (1450, Hundred Years' War)
FREIBURG (1644, Thirty Years' War)
FRETEVAL (1194, Anglo-French Wars)
GAULAULI (1858, Indian Mutiny)
GITSCHIN (1866, Seven Weeks' War)
GOODWINS, THE (1666, Anglo-Dutch Wars)
GRAF SPEE (1939, World War II)
GÜNZBURG (1805, Napoleonic Wars)
HASTINGS (1066, Norman Conquest)
HERACLEA (280 BC, Pyrrhus' Invasion of Italy; 313, Roman Civil Wars)
HERRINGS, THE (1429, Hundred Years' War)
HONG KONG (1941, World War II)
INKERMAN (1854, Crimean War)
JEMAPPES (1792, French Revolutionary Wars)
KANDAHAR (1648, Perso-Afghan Wars; 1834, Afghan Tribal Wars; 1880, Second British-Afghan War)
KATZBACH (1813, Napoleonic Wars)
KHARTOUM (1884, British-Sudan Campaigns)
KIRBEKAN (1885, British Sudan Campaigns)
KORYGAOM (1818, Third British-Maratha War)
KUMANOVO (1912, 1st Balkan War)
LANGPORT (1645, English Civil War)
LANGSIDE (1568, Scottish Civil War)
LE CATEAU (1914, World War I)
LEITSKAU (1813, Napoleonic Wars)
LIEGNITZ (1760, Seven Years' War)
LOBOSITZ (1756, Seven Years' War)
LUNCARTY (980, Danish Invasions of Scotland)
LYS RIVER (1918, World War I)
MAFEKING (1899, Second Boer War)
MAHIDPUR (1817, Third British-Maratha War)
MARATHON (490 BC, Persian-Greek Wars)
MEDELLIN (1809, Peninsular War)
MEDENINE (1943, World War II)
MESSINES (1917, World War I)
MONTREAL (1760, Seven Years' War)
MORTLACK (1010, Danish Invasions of Scotland)
MORTMANT (1814, Napoleonic Wars)

8—continued

MÖSKIRCH (1800, French Revolutionary Wars)
MOUSCRON (1794, French Revolutionary Wars)
MÜHLBERG (1547, German Reformation Wars)
MUSA BAGH (1858, Indian Mutiny)
NAVARINO (1827, Greek War of Independence)
OMDURMAN (1898, British-Sudan Campaigns)
ONESSANT (1778, American Revolutionary War)
OSTROWNO (1812, Napoleonic Wars)
OVERLORD, OPERATION (1944, World War II)
PALO ALTO (1846, American-Mexican War)
PEA RIDGE (1862, American Civil War)
PESHAWAR (1001, Afghan Invasion of India)
PHILIPPI (42 BC, Roman Civil Wars)
POITIERS (507, Gothic Invasion of France; 1356, Hundred Years' War)
PORTLAND (1653, Anglo-Dutch Wars)
PYRAMIDS (1798, French Revolutionary Wars)
PYRENEES (1813, Peninsular War)
RICHMOND (1862, American Civil War)
ROSSBACH (1757, Seven Years' War)
ROVEREDO (1796, French Revolutionary Wars)
SAALFELD (1806, Napoleonic Wars)
SAPIENZA (1490, Ottoman Wars)
SARATOGA (1777, American Revolutionary War)
SHOLAPUR (1818, Third British-Maratha War)
SIDASSIR (1799, Third British-Mysore War)
SILISTRA (1854, Crimean War)
SMOLENSK (1708, Great Northern War; 1812, Napoleonic Wars; 1941, World War II)
SORAUREN (1813, Peninsular War)
SPION KOP (1900, Second Boer War)
ST ALBANS (1455, 1461, Wars of the Roses)
STANDARD, THE (1138, Anglo-Scottish Wars)
STE CROIX (1807, Napoleonic Wars)
ST GEORGE (1500, Ottoman Wars)
ST MIHIEL (1918, World War I)
STOCKACH (1799, French Revolutionary Wars)
ST PRIVAT (1870, Franco-Prussian War)
STRATTON (1643, English Civil War)
ST THOMAS (1807, Napoleonic Wars)
TALAVERA (1809, Peninsular War)
THETFORD (870, Danish Invasions of England)
TIBERIAS (1187, Crusader-Saracen Wars)
TOULOUSE (1814, Napoleonic Wars)
TRINIDAD (1797, French Revolutionary Wars)
TSINGTAO (1914, World War I)
VALLETTA (1798, French Revolutionary Wars)
VALUTINO (1812, Napoleonic Wars)
VERNEUIL (1424, Hundred Years' War)
VILLIERS (1870, Franco-Prussian War)
WATERLOO (1815, Napoleonic Wars)
WIESLOCH (1622, Thirty Years' War)
YORKTOWN (1781, American Revolutionary War; 1862, American Civil War)
ZORNDORF (1758, Seven Years' War)

9

ABENSBERG (1809, Napoleonic Wars)
AGINCOURT (1415, Hundred Years' War)
AHMADABAD (1780, First British-Maratha War)

9—continued

AHMED KHEL (1880, Second British-Afghan War)
AIGUILLON (1347, Hundred Years' War)
ALCÁNTARA (1580, Spanish Conquest of Portugal; 1706, War of the Spanish Succession)
ALRESFORD (1644, English Civil War)
ALTENDORF (1632, Thirty Years' War)
AMSTETTEN (1805, Napoleonic Wars)
ANGOSTURA (1847, American-Mexican War; 1868, Paraguayan War)
ASKULTSIK (1828, Ottoman Wars)
AUERSTADT (1806, Napoleonic Wars)
AYLESFORD (456, Jutish Invasion of Britain)
BALACLAVA (1854, Crimean War)
BALLYMORE (1798, Irish Rebellion)
BANGALORE (1791, Second British-Mysore War)
BARCELONA (1705, War of the Spanish Succession; 1938, Spanish Civil War)
BERGFRIED (1807, Napleonic Wars)
BHURTPORE (1805, Second British-Maratha War; 1827, Second Siege of)
BLUFF COVE (1982, Falkland Isles)
BOIS-LE-DUC (1794, French Revolutionary Wars)
BORGHETTO (1796, French Revolutionary Wars)
BRENTFORD (1642, English Civil War)
BRIG OF DEE (1639, Bishops' Wars)
BUCHAREST (1771, Ottoman Wars)
BURNS HILL (1847, Kaffir Wars)
BYZANTIUM (318 BC, Wars of Alexander's Successors; 323, Civil Wars of the Roman Empire)
CAPE HENRY (1781, American Revolutionary War)
CAPORETTO (1917, World War I)
CASILINUM (554, Byzantine Empire Wars)
CASTILLON (1453, Hundred Years' War)
CHAMPAGNE (1915, World War I)
CHARASIAB (1879, Second British-Afghan War)
CROSSKEYS (1862, American Civil War)
CUDDALORE (1783, American Revolutionary War)
DENNEWITZ (1813, Napoleonic Wars)
DORYLAEUM (1097, First Crusade)
DUNSINANE (1054, Anglo-Scottish Wars)
EBRO RIVER (1938, Spanish Civil War)
EDERSBERG (1809, Napoleonic Wars)
EDGEWORTH (1469, Wars of the Roses)
EL ALAMEIN (1942, World War II)
ELCHINGEN (1805, Napoleonic Wars)
ELLANDUNE (825, Wessex versus Mercia)
EMPINGHAM (1470, Wars of the Roses)
FIVE FORKS (1865, American Civil War)
FRIEDLAND (1807, Napoleonic Wars)
FRONTIERS, BATTLE OF THE (1914, World War I)
GALLIPOLI (1915, World War I)
GIBRALTAR (1704, War of the Spanish Succession; 1779, American Revolutionary War)
GLADSMUIR (1745, The Forty-five Rebellion)

9—continued

GLEN FRUIN (1604, Scottish Civil Wars)
GLENLIVET (1594, Huntly's Rebellion)
GRAMPIANS, THE (Roman Invasion of Scotland)
GUINEGATE (1513, Anglo-French Wars)
GUMBINNEN (1914, World War I)
HEILSBERG (1807, Napoleonic Wars)
HOCHKIRCH (1758, Seven Years' War)
HÖCHSTÄDT (1800, French Revolutionary Wars)
JERUSALEM (70 AD, Jewish Wars of Roman Empire; 637, Muslim Invasion of Syria; 1099, First Crusade; 1187, Crusader-Turkish Wars; 1917, World War I; 1948, Israeli-Arab Wars)
JUGDULLUK (1842, First British-Afghan War)
KASSASSIN (1882, Egyptian Revolt)
KIMBERLEY (1899, Second Boer War)
KISSINGEN (1866, Seven Weeks' War)
LADYSMITH (1899, Second Boer War)
LANG'S NECK (1881, First Boer War)
LANSDOWNE (1643, English Civil Wars)
LENINGRAD (1944, World War II)
LEXINGTON (1775, American Revolutionary War; 1861, American Civil War)
LEYTE GULF (1944, World War II)
LÖWENBERG (1813, Napoleonic Wars)
MAGDEBURG (1631, Thirty Years' War)
MALAVILLY (1799, Third British-Mysore War)
MANGALORE (1783, First British-Mysore War)
MANSFIELD (1864, American Civil War)
MARIA ZELL (1805, Napoleonic Wars)
MARSAGLIA (1693, War of the Grand Alliance)
MILLESIMO (1796, French Revolutionary Wars)
MOHRUNGEN (1807, Napoleonic Wars)
MONTEREAU (1814, Napoleonic Wars)
MONTERREY (1846, Amercian-Mexican War)
MUKWANPUR (1816, British-Gurkha War)
NASHVILLE (1863, American Civil War)
NAULOCHUS (36 BC, Wars of the Second Triumvirate)
NAVARRETE (1367, Hundred Years' War)
NEGAPATAM (1746, War of the Austrian Succession; 1781, Second British Mysore War; 1782, American Revolutionary War)
NEW GUINEA (1942, World War II)
NEW MARKET (1864, American Civil War)
NICOPOLIS (1396, Ottoman Wars; 1877, Russo-Turkish War)
NUJUFGHUR (1857, Indian Mutiny)
OCEAN POND (1864, American Civil War)
OLTENITZA (1853, Crimean War)
OTTERBURN (1388, Wars of Scottish Independence)
OUDENARDE (1708, War of the Spanish Succession)
PHARSALUS (48 BC, Civil War of Caesar and Pompey; 1897, Greco-Turkish Wars)
POLLICORE (1781, First British-Mysore War)
PORTO NOVO (1781, First British-Mysore War)
PRIMOLANÓ (1796, French Revolutionary Wars)
PRINCETON (1777, American Revolutionary War)

9—continued

RAMILLIES (1706, War of the Spanish
Succession)
RAMNUGGUR (1849, Second British-Sikh War)
RATHMINES (1649, Cromwell's Campaign in
Ireland)
RHINELAND, THE (1945, World War II)
ROSEBURGH (1460, Anglo-Scottish Wars)
SADULAPUR (1848, Second British-Sikh War)
SALAMANCA (1812, Peninsular War; 1858,
Mexican Liberal Rising)
SANTANDER (1937, Spanish Civil War)
SARAGOSSA (1700, War of the Spanish
Succession; 1808, Peninsular War)
SEDGEMOOR (1685, Monmouth's Rebellion)
SEVENOAKS (1450, Cade's Rebellion)
SHEERNESS (1667, Anglo-Dutch Wars)
SHERSTONE (1016, Danish Invasion of
England)
SHOLINGUR (1781, First British-Mysore War)
SINGAPORE (1942, World War II)
SITABALDI (1817, Third British-Maratha War)
SOUTHWARK (1450, Cade's Rebellion)
STADTLOHN (1623, Thirty Years' War)
STAFFARDA (1690, War of the Grand Alliance)
STORMBERG (1899, Second Boer War)
ST QUENTIN (1557, Franco-Spanish Wars;
1871, Franco-Prussian War)
STRALSUND (1628, Thirty Years' War; 1715,
Great Northern War)
SUDDASAIN (1848, Second British-Sikh War)
TARRAGONA (1811, Peninsular War)
TCHERNAYA (1855, Crimean War)
TOLENTINO (1815, Napoleonic Wars)
TOU MORONG (1966, Vietnam War)
TOURCOING (1794, French Revolutionary Wars)
TRAFALGAR (1805, Napoleonic Wars)
TRAUTENAU (1866, Seven Weeks' War)
TREBIZOND (1461, Ottoman Wars)
TRINKITAT (1884, British-Sudan Campaigns)
VAALKRANZ (1900, Second Boer War)
VAUCHAMPS (1814, Napoleonic Wars)
VICKSBURG (1862, American Civil War)
VIMY RIDGE (1917, World War I)
WAKEFIELD (1460, Wars of the Roses)
WANDIWASH (1760, Seven Years' War; 1780,
First British-Mysore War)
WORCESTER (1651, English Civil War)
WÜRTZBURG (1796, French Revolutionary
Wars)

10

ADRIANOPLE (1205, Fourth Crusade; 1913,
First Balkan War)
ALEXANDRIA (642, Muslim Invasion of Egypt;
1801, British Invasion of Egypt; 1881, Egyptian
Revolt)
ANCRUM MOOR (1545, Anglo-Scottish Wars)
ARTOIS-LOOS (1915, World War I)
AUSTERLITZ (1805, Napoleonic Wars)
BALL'S BLUFF (1861, American Civil War)

10—continued

BEACHY HEAD (1690, War of the Grand
Alliance)
BEAUSÉJOUR (1755, Seven Year's War)
BENNINGTON (1777, American Revolutionary
War)
BLACKWATER (1598, O'Neill's Rebellion)
BLORE HEATH (1459, Wars of the Roses)
BRANDYWINE (1777, American Revolutionary
War)
BRUNANBURH (937, Danish Invasion)
BUENA VISTA (1846, American-Mexican War)
CAMPERDOWN (1797, French Revolutionary
Wars)
CEDAR CREEK (1864, American Civil War)
CHARLESTON (1863, American Civil War)
CHEVY CHASE (1388, Wars of Scottish
Independence)
CHIPPENHAM (878, Danish Invasions of Britain)
COPENHAGEN (1801, French Revolutionary
Wars; 1807, Napoleonic Wars)
DALMANUTHA (1900, Second Boer War)
DOGGER BANK (1781, American Revolutionary
War; 1915, World War I)
DUNGANHILL (1647, Great Irish Rebellion)
DYRRACHIUM (48 BC, Civil War of Caesar and
Pompey)
ENGLEFIELD (871, Danish Invasion of Britain)
FEROZESHAH (1845, First British-Sikh War)
FETHANLEAG (584, Saxon Conquests)
FUTTEYPORE (1857, Indian Mutiny)
GAINES' MILL (1862, American Civil War)
GERMANTOWN (1777, American Revolutionary
War)
GETTYSBURG (1863, American Civil War)
GLEN MALONE (1580, Colonization of Ireland)
GORODECZNO (1812, Napoleonic Wars)
GOTHIC LINE (1944, World War II)
GRANT'S HILL (1758, Seven Years' War)
GRAVELINES (1558, Franco-Spanish Wars)
GRAVELOTTE (1870, Franco-Prussian War)
GUADELOUPE (1794, French Revolutionary
Wars)
HABBANIYAH (1941, World War II)
HASTENBECK (1757, Seven Years' War)
HEATHFIELD (633, Mercia against Northumbria)
HELIGOLAND (1807, Napoleonic Wars)
HELIOPOLIS (1800, French Revolutionary Wars)
HELLESPONT (323, War of the Two Empires)
HOLLABRUNN (1805, Napleonic Wars)
INVERLOCHY (1645, English Civil War)
JELLALABAD (1842, First British-Afghan War)
KHOJAH PASS (1842, First British-Afghan War)
KÖNIGGRÄTZ (1866, Seven Weeks' War)
KORNSPRUIT (1900, Second Boer War)
KUNERSDORF (1759, Seven Years' War)
KUT-EL-AMARA (1915, World War I)
LA FAVORITA (1797, French Revolutionary Wars)
LAKE GEORGE (1755, Seven Years' War)
LA ROCHELLE (1372, Hundred Years' War;
1627, French Religious Wars)
LA ROTHIÈRE (1814, Napoleonic Wars)

10–continued

LOUDON HILL (1307, Wars of Scottish Independence)
LOUISBOURG (1745, War of the Austrian Succession; 1758, Seven Years' War)
LÜLEBÜRGAZ (1912, Balkan Wars)
LUNDY'S LANE (1814, War of 1812)
MAASTRICHT (1579, Netherlands War of Independence)
MAHARAJPUR (1843, Gwalior Campaign; 1857, Indian Mutiny)
MARETH LINE (1943, World War II)
MARIENDAHL (1645, Thirty Years' War)
MARTINIQUE (1794, French Revolutionary Wars; 1809, Napoleonic Wars)
MASERFIELD (642, Northumbria against Mercia)
MICHELBERG (1805, Napoleonic Wars)
MONTEBELLO (1800, French Revolutionary Wars; 1859, Italian Wars of Independence)
MONTENOTTE (1796, French Revolutionary Wars)
MONTEVIDEO (1807, Napoleonic Wars; 1843, 1851, 1863, Uruguayan Civil War)
MONTFAUCON (886, Norman Invasion of France)
MONTMIRAIL (1814, Napoleonic Wars)
MOUNT TABOR (1799, French Revolutionary Wars)
NAROCH LAKE (1916, World War I)
NEERWINDEN (1693, War of the Grand Alliance; 1793, French Revolutionary Wars)
NEW ORLEANS (1814, War of 1812; 1862, American Civil War)
NÖRDLINGEN (1634, 1645, Thirty Year's War)
OSTROLENKA (1853, Crimean War)
PAARDEBERG (1900, Second Boer War)
PANDU NADDI (1857, Indian Mutiny)
PEN SELWOOD (1016, Danish Invasions of Britain)
PEREMBACUM (1780, First British-Mysore War)
PERRYVILLE (1862, American Civil War)
PERSEPOLIS (316 BC, Wars of Alexander's Successors)
PETERSBURG (1864, American Civil War)
PIAVE RIVER (1918, World War I)
PONT VALAIN (1370, Hundred Years' War)
PORT ARTHUR (1894, Sino-Japanese War; 1904, Russo-Japanese War)
PORT HUDSON (1863, American Civil War)
QUATRE BRAS (1815, Napoleonic Wars)
RAKERSBERG (1416, Ottoman Wars)
RUHR POCKET (1945, World War II)
SANNA'S POST (1900, Second Boer War)
SANTA LUCIA (1842, Rio Grande Rising)
SAVANDROOG (1791, Second British-Mysore War)
SEINE MOUTH (1416, Hundred Years' War)
SEVASTOPOL (1854, Crimean War)
SEVEN PINES (1862, American Civil War)
SHREWSBURY (1403, Percy's Rebellion)
SHROPSHIRE (AD 50, Roman Conquest of Britain)

10–continued

SIDI REZEGH (1941, World War II)
SOLWAY MOSS (1542, Anglo-Scottish Wars)
STALINGRAD (1942, World War II)
STEENKERKE (1692, War of the Grand Alliance)
STILLWATER (1777, American Revolutionary War)
STONE RIVER (1862, American Civil War)
TALANA HILL (1899, Second Boer War)
TANNENBERG (1914, World War I)
TEL-EL-KEBIR (1882, Egyptian Revolt)
TETTENHALL (910, Danish Invasions of England)
TEWKESBURY (1471, Wars of the Roses)
TIPPERMUIR (1644, English Civil War)
TRAVANCORE (1789, Second British-Mysore War)
WARTEMBERG (1813, Napoleonic Wars)
WATTIGNIES (1793, French Revolutionary Wars)
WILDERNESS, THE (1864, American Civil War)
WINCHESTER (1863, American Civil War)

11

ALAM EL HALFA (1942, World War II)
ALESSANDRIA (1799, French Revolutionary Wars)
AN LAO VALLEY (1966, Vietnam War)
BANNOCKBURN (1314, Wars of Scottish Independence)
BELLEAU WOOD (1918, World War I)
BISMARCK SEA (1943, World War II)
BLANQUEFORT (1450, Hundred Years' War)
BRAMHAM MOOR (1408, Northumberland's Rebellion)
BREITENFELD (1642, Thirty Years' War)
BRENNEVILLE (1119, Anglo-French Wars)
BUENOS AIRES (1806, 1807, Napoleonic Wars; 1874, Mitre's Rebellion)
BUNKER'S HILL (1775, American Revolutionary War)
CAMELODUNUM (43, Roman Invasion of Britain)
CARBIESDALE (1650, English Civil War)
CARENAGE BAY (1778, American Revolutionary War)
CASTIGLIONE (1706, War of the Spanish Succession; 1796, French Revolutionary Wars)
CHAMPAUBERT (1814, Napoleonic Wars)
CHATTANOOGA (1863, American Civil War)
CHICKAMAUGA (1863, American Civil War)
CHILIANWALA (1849, Second British-Sikh War)
CHRYSOPOLIS (324, War of the Two Empires)
COLDHARBOUR (1864, American Civil War)
DIAMOND HILL (1900, Second Boer War)
DINGAAN'S DAY (1838, Afrikaner-Zulu War)
DRIEFONTEIN (1900, Second Boer War)
DÜRRENSTEIN (1805, Napoleonic Wars)
ELANDS RIVER (1900, Second Boer War)
FARRUKHABAD (1804, Second British-Maratha War)
FERRYBRIDGE (1461, Wars of the Roses)
FISHER'S HILL (1864, American Civil War)

11–continued

FORT ST DAVID (1758, Seven Years' War)
GIBBEL RUTTS (1798, Irish Rebellion)
GROSS-BEEREN (1813, Napoleonic Wars)
GUADALAJARA (1937, Spanish Civil War)
GUADALCANAL (1942, World War II)
HADRIANOPLE (323, War of the Two Empires; 378, Second Gothic Invasion of the East)
HALIDON HILL (1333, Wars of Scottish Independence)
HEAVENFIELD (634, Northumbria against the British)
HOHENLINDEN (1800, French Revolutionary Wars)
HONDSCHOOTE (1793, French Revolutionary Wars)
ÎLE DE FRANCE (1810, Napoleonic Wars)
ISANDHLWANA (1879, Zulu-British War)
LANGENSALZA (1866, Seven Weeks' War)
LONDONDERRY (1689, War of the Grand Alliance)
LOSTWITHIEL (1644, English Civil War)
MALVERN HILL (1862, American Civil War)
MARSTON MOOR (1644, English Civil War)
MASULIPATAM (1759, Seven Years' War)
MERSA MATRÛH (1942, World War II)
MILL SPRINGS (1862, American Civil War)
MODDER RIVER (1899, Second Boer War)
MONTE LEZINO (1796, French Revolutionary Wars)
MONTMORENCI (1759, Seven Years' War)
MORSHEDABAD (1763, British Conquest of Bengal)
NOISSEVILLE (1870, Franco-Prussian War)
NORTHAMPTON (1460, Wars of the Roses)
PEARL HARBOR (1941, World War II)
PEIWAR KOTAL (1878, Second British-Afghan War)
PHILIPHAUGH (1645, English Civil War)
PIETER'S HILL (1900, Second Boer War)
PONDICHERRY (1748, War of the Austrian Succession; 1760, Seven Years' War; 1778, 1783, American Revolutionary War)
PRESTONPANS (1745, The Forty-five Rebellion)
QUIBERON BAY (1759, Seven Years' War)
RAJAHMUNDRY (1758, Seven Years' War)
REDDERSBERG (1900, Second Boer War)
RHEINFELDEN (1638, Thirty Years' War)
RIETFONTEIN (1899, Second Boer War)
RORKE'S DRIFT (1879, Zulu-British War)
ROWTON HEATH (1645, English Civil War)
SALDANHA BAY (1796, French Revolutionary Wars)
SAN GIOVANNI (1799, French Revolutionary Wars)
SAUCHIE BURN (1488, Rebellion of the Scottish Barons)
SHERIFFMUIR (1715, The Fifteen Rebellion)
SIDI BARRÂNI (1940, World War II)
TAILLEBOURG (1242, Anglo-French Wars)
TARAWA-MAKIN (1943, World War II)
TEL-EL-MAHUTA (1882, Egyptian Revolt)

11–continued

TELLICHERRY (1780, First British-Mysore War)
TEUTTLINGEN (1643, Thirty Years' War)
TICONDEROGA (1758, Seven Years' War; 1777, American Revolutionary War)
TRINCOMALEE (1759, Seven Years' War; 1767, First British-Mysore War; 1782, American Revolutionary War)
VINEGAR HILL (1798, Irish Rebellion)
WALTERSDORF (1807, Napoleonic Wars)
WEDNESFIELD (911, Danish Invasions of England)
WEISSENBURG (1870, Franco-Prussian War)
WHITE RUSSIA (1943, World War II)

12

ADWALTON MOOR (1643, English Civil War)
ALGEÇIRAS BAY (1801, French Revolutionary Wars)
ARCIS-SUR-AUBE (1814, Napoleonic Wars)
ATHERTON MOOR (1643, English Civil War)
BANDA ISLANDS (1796, French Revolutionary Wars)
BERGEN-OP-ZOOM (1747, War of the Austrian Succession; 1799, French Revolutionary Wars)
BLOEMFONTEIN (1900, Second Boer War)
BRADDOCK DOWN (1643, English Civil War)
CHICKAHOMINY (1864, American Civil War)
ELANDSLAAGTE (1899, Second Boer War)
EUTAW SPRINGS (1781, American Revolutionary War)
FORT DONELSON (1862, American Civil War)
HAMPTON ROADS (1862, American Civil War)
HARPER'S FERRY (1862, American Civil War)
HEDGELEY MOOR (1464, Wars of the Roses)
HENGESTESDUN (837, Danish Invasions of Britain)
HOMILDON HILL (1402, Anglo-Scottish Wars)
KIRCH-DENKERN (1761, Seven Years' War)
KÖNIGSWARTHA (1813, Napoleonic Wars)
KURSK SALIENT (1943, World War II)
LYNN HAVEN BAY (1781, American Revolutionary War)
MIDWAY ISLAND (1942, World War II)
MÜNCHENGRÄTZ (1866, Seven Weeks' War)
MURFREESBORO (1862, American Civil War)
NECHTAN'S MERE (685, Northumbrian Invasion of Scotland)
OONDWA NULLAH (1763, British Conquest of Bengal)
PENOBSCOT BAY (1779, American Revolutionary War)
PETERWARDEIN (1716, Ottoman Wars)
PINKIE CLEUGH (1547, Anglo-Scottish Wars)
PORT REPUBLIC (1862, American Civil War)
PRAIRIE GROVE (1862, American Civil War)
RICH MOUNTAIN (1861, American Civil War)
RONCESVALLES (1813, Peninsular War)
ROUNDWAY DOWN (1643, English Civil War)
RULLION GREEN (1666, Covenanters' Rising)
SAN SEBASTIAN (1813, Peninsular War; 1836, First Carlist War)

12–continued

SECUNDERBAGH (1857, Indian Mutiny)
SERINGAPATAM (1792, Second British-Mysore War; 1799, Third British-Mysore War)
SOUTHWOLD BAY (1672, Anglo-Dutch Wars)
SPOTSYLVANIA (1864, American Civil War)
TET OFFENSIVE, THE (1968, Vietnam War)
WILLIAMSBURG (1862, American Civil War)
WILSON'S CREEK (1861, American Civil War)
WROTHAM HEATH (1554, Wyatt's Insurrection)

13

AIX-LA-CHAPELLE (1795, French Revolutionary Wars)
BADULI-KI-SERAI (1857, Indian Mutiny)
BELLE-ÎLE-EN-MER (1759, 1761, Seven Years' War; 1795, French Revolutionary Wars)
BOROUGHBRIDGE (1322, Rebellion of the Marches)
BOSWORTH FIELD (1485, Wars of the Roses)
CAPE ST VINCENT (1797, French Revolutionary Wars)
CEDAR MOUNTAIN (1862, American Civil War)
CHANDERNAGORE (1757, Seven Years' War)
CIUDAD RODRIGO (1812, Peninsular War)
FALKLAND ISLES (1914, World War I; 1982, Falklands War)
FARQUHAR'S FARM (1899, Second Boer War)
FORT FRONTENAC (1758, Seven Years' War)
FRANKENHAUSEN (1525, Peasants' War)
GLENMARRESTON (683, Angles' Invasion of Britain)
HORNS OF HATTIN (1187, Crusader-Saracen Wars)
INVERKEITHING (1317, Anglo-Scottish Wars)
KASSERINE PASS (1943, World War II)
KILLIECRANKIE (1689, Jacobite Rising)
LITTLE BIG HORN (1876, Sioux Rising)
MAGERSFONTEIN (1899, Second Boer War)
MASURIAN LAKES (1914, 1915, World War I)
MOLINOS DEL REY (1808, Peninsular War)
MOUNT SELEUCUS (353, Civil Wars of the Roman Empire)
NEVILLE'S CROSS (1346, Anglo-Scottish Wars)
NEWTOWN BUTLER (1689, War of the Grand Alliance)
NORTHALLERTON (1138, Anglo-Scottish Wars)
NORTH FORELAND (1666, Anglo-Dutch Wars)
PASSCHENDAELE (1917, World War I)
PELELIU-ANGAUR (1944, World War II)
PHILIPPINE SEA (1944, World War II)
PORTO PRAIA BAY (1781, American Revolutionary War)
ROANOKE ISLAND (1862, American Civil War)
SOUTH MOUNTAIN (1862, American Civil War)
SPANISH ARMADA (1588, Anglo-Spanish War)
SUDLEY SPRINGS (1862, American Civil War)
WHITE OAK SWAMP (1862, American Civil War)
YOUGHIOGHENNY (1754, Seven Years' War)
ZUSMARSHAUSEN (1647, Thirty Years' War)

14

BERWICK-ON-TWEED (1296, Wars of Scottish Independence)
BOTHWELL BRIDGE (1679, Covenanters' Rising)
BRISTOE STATION (1863, American Civil War)
CAPE FINISTERRE (1747, War of the Austrian Succession; 1805, Napoleonic Wars)
CHALGROVE FIELD (1643, English Civil War)
CHÂTEAU-THIERRY (1814, Napoleonic Wars)
CONSTANTINOPLE (668, Muslim Invasion of Europe; 1203–04, Fourth Crusade; 1261, Reconquest by Byzantines; 1422, Ottoman Invasion of Europe; 1453, Turkish Conquest)
CROPREDY BRIDGE (1644, English Civil War)
DRUMMOSSIE MOOR (1746, The Forty-five Rebellion)
FREDERICKSBURG (1862, American Civil War)
FUENTES DE OÑORO (1811, Peninsular War)
KOVEL-STANISLAV (1916, World War I)
LA BELLE FAMILLE (1759, Seven Years' War)
LOOSECOAT FIELD (1470, Wars of the Roses)
MARIANA ISLANDS (1944, World War II)
MORTIMER'S CROSS (1461, Wars of the Roses)
NICHOLSON'S NECK (1899, Second Boer War)
PEACH TREE CREEK (1864, American Civil War)
PUSAN PERIMETER (1950, Korean War)
ROUVRAY-ST-DENIS (1429, Hundred Years' War)
SANTIAGO DE CUBA (1898, Spanish-American War)
SAVAGE'S STATION (1862, American Civil War)
SECESSIONVILLE (1862, American Civil War)
SINAI PENINSULA (1956, Israeli-Arab War)
SOLOMON ISLANDS (1942, World War II)
STAMFORD BRIDGE (1066, Norse Invasion of Britain; 1453, Wars of the Roses)
STIRLING BRIDGE (1297, Wars of Scottish Independence)
VITTORIO VENETO (1918, World War I)

15

ALEUTIAN ISLANDS (1943, World War II)
AMATOLA MOUNTAIN (1846, Kaffir Wars)
APPOMATTOX RIVER (1865, American Civil War)
BATTLE OF BRITAIN (1940, World War II)
BEAVER'S DAM CREEK (1862, American Civil War)
FRANKFURT-ON-ODER (1631, Thirty Years' War)
GROSS-JÄGERSDORF (1757, Seven Years' War)
HELIGOLAND BIGHT (1914, World War I)
KHOORD KABUL PASS (1842, First British-Afghan War)
MALOYAROSLAVETS (1812, Napoleonic Wars)
MISSIONARY RIDGE (1863, American Civil War)
PLAINS OF ABRAHAM (1759, Seven Years' War)
SEVEN DAYS' BATTLE (1862, American Civil War)
SPANISH GALLEONS (1702, War of the Spanish Succession)

16
BATAAN-CORREGIDOR (1941, World War II)
BRONKHORST SPRUIT (1880, First Boer War)
CAMBRAI-ST QUENTIN (1918, World War I)
CHANCELLORSVILLE (1863, American Civil
    War)
FORT WILLIAM HENRY (1757, Seven Years'
    War)
KINNESAW MOUNTAIN (1864, American Civil
    War)
MONONGAHELA RIVER (1755, Seven Years'
    War)
SALUM-HALFAYA PASS (1941, World War II)

17
BURLINGTON HEIGHTS (1813, War of 1812)
DODECANESE ISLANDS (1943, World War II)
GUSTAV-CASSINO LINE (1943, World War II)
INHLOBANE MOUNTAIN (1879, Zulu War)
KWAJALEIN-ENIWETOK (1944, World War II)
LA FÈRE CHAMPENOISE (1814, Napoleonic
    Wars)

17–continued
PITTSBURGH LANDING (1862, American Civil
    War)
POLAND-EAST PRUSSIA (1944, World War II)
VAN TUONG PENINSULA (1965, Vietnam War)

18
GUILFORD COURTHOUSE (1781, American
    Revolutionary War)
MEUSE-ARGONNE FOREST (1918, World War I)

19
CHU PONG-IA DRANG RIVER (1965, Vietnam
    War)
'GLORIOUS FIRST OF JUNE' (1794, French
    Revolutionary Wars)

20+
RHINE AND THE RUHR POCKET, THE (1945,
    World War II)
SHANNON AND CHESAPEAKE (1813, War of
    1812)
THIRTY-EIGHTH PARALLEL (1951, Korean War)

ARMOUR

4
JACK
MAIL

5
ARMET
BACYN
BUFFE
CREST
CULET
GIPON
IMBER
JUPEL
JUPON
LAMES
SALET
VISOR

6
ALETES
BASNET
BHANJU
BRACER
BRIDLE
BRUGNE
CALOTE
CAMAIL
CASQUE
CASSIS
CELATE
CHEEKS

6–continued
CRENEL
CRINET
CUELLO
GORGET
GUSSET
HEAUME
HELMET
MASCLE
MESAIL
MORIAN
MORION
SALADE
SHIELD
TABARD
UMBRIL

7
AILETES
BACINET
BALDRIC
BARBUTE
BASINET
BUCKLER
CHAUCES
CORSLET
CRUPPER
CUIRASS
CUISSES
CULESET
FENDACE

7–continued
FRONTAL
GAUCHET
GOUCHET
GREAVES
HAUBERK
HOGUINE
LANIERS
MURSAIL
PANACHE
PLACARD
POITRAL
SURCOAT
VISIERE

8
ALLECRET
BARDINGS
BASCINET
BAUDRICK
BRASSARD
BRAYETTE
BUFF COAT
BURGINOT
BURGONET
CABASSET
CHAMPONS
CHANFRON
CHAUCHES
CHAUSSES
COD PIECE

8–continued
COLLERET
COLLETIN
CORSELET
CRINIERE
GAUNTLET
HALECRET
JAMBEAUX
JAZERANT
PAULDRON
PECTORAL
PLASTRON
SABATONS
SOLARETS
SOLERETS
TESTIERE

9
BAINBERGS
BEINBERGS
CHAIN MAIL
CHAMPFRON
CHAUSSONS
EPAULETTE
HAUSSE-COL
JACK BOOTS
POURPOINT
REREBRACE
SABATYNES

10
AVENTAILLE
BANDED MAIL
BARREL HELM
BRICHETTES
BRIGANDINE
CROISSANTS
ECREVISSES
EMBOITMENT
FLANCHARDS
LAMBREQUIN

11
BREASTPLATE
BREASTSTRAP
BRIGANDYRON
BRIGANTAYLE
CHAPEL DE
    FER
ESPALLIERES
PLATE ARMOUR

13
ARMING
    DOUBLET

15
IMBRICATE
    ARMOUR

WEAPONS

2
NU
V1
V2

3
AXE
BOW
DAG
DAS
GUN
GYN
TNT

4
ADZE
BARB
BILL
BOLO
BOLT
BOMB
CLUB
DIRK
FANG
FOIL
KORA
KRIS
MACE
MINE
PIKE
SHOT
TANK
TOCK
TUCK

5
A-BOMB
ANCUS
ANKUS
ANLAS
ARROW
ASWAR
BATON
BIDAG
BILBO
BOLAS
BOSON
BRAND
ESTOC
FLAIL
FUSEE
FUSIL
GUPTI
H-BOMB
KERIS
KHORA
KILIG
KILIJ

5—continued
KNIFE
KUKRI
KYLIE
LANCE
LATCH
PILUM
PRODD
RIFLE
SABRE
SHELL
SLING
SPEAR
STAKE
STAVE
SWORD
TACHI
WADDY

6
AMUKTA
ARMLET
BARKAL
BARONG
BASTON
BODKIN
BULLET
CANNON
CARCAS
CEMTEX
CUDGEL
DAGGER
DAISHO
DRAGON
DUM-DUM
DUSACK
EXOCET
KATANA
KERRIE
KHANDA
KIKUKI
KODOGU
MASSUE
MAZULE
MORTAR
MUSKET
NAPALM
PARANG
PETARD
PISTOL
POP GUN
QILLIJ
QUIVER
RAMROD
RAPIER
ROCKET
SCYTHE

6—continued
SEMTEX
SUMPIT
TALWAR
VGO GUN

7
ASSEGAI
AWL-PIKE
BALASAN
BALISTA
BAYONET
BELFREY
BILIONG
BOMBARD
BOURDON
BREN GUN
CALIVER
CALTRAP
CARABEN
CARBINE
CARREAU
CHAKRAM
CHALCOS
CHOPPER
CURRIER
CUTLASS
DUDGEON
DUSSACK
FAUCHON
FIRE-POT
GRENADE
HALBARD
HALBART
HALBERD
HAND GUN
HARPOON
KASTANE
KINDJAL
LONG BOW
MISSILE
MUSQUET
PONIARD
PUNT GUN
QUARREL
SHASHQA
SHINKEN
STEN GUN
TORPEDO
TRIDENT

8
AMUSETTE
ARBALEST
ARBALETE
ARQUEBUS
ATOM BOMB
AXE-KNIFE

8—continued
BASELARD
BASILARD
BLOWPIPE
CALTHORP
CANISTER
CARABINE
CATAPULT
CHACHEKA
CLADIBAS
CLAYMORE
CROSSBOW
DERINGER
DESTRIER
FALCHION
FALCONET
FAUCHARD
FIRELOCK
HACKBUTT
HAIL SHOT
HAQUEBUT
HASSEGAI
HOWITZER
PETRONEL
POIGNARD
QUERQUER
REPEATER
REVOLVER
SCIMITAR
SHAMSHIR
SHRAPNEL
SPONTOON
SUMPITAN
TOMAHAWK
TOMMY GUN

9
ACK-ACK GUN
ARTILLERY
BADELAIRE
BANDELEER
BANDOLIER
BANNEROLE
BATTLE-AXE
BIG BERTHA
BOOMERANG
CARRONADE
CARTOUCHE
CARTRIDGE
CHAIN SHOT
DETONATOR
DOODLE-BUG
FALCASTRA
FLAGELLUM
FLAMBERGE
FLINTLOCK
GELIGNITE

WEAPONS

9—continued
GRAPESHOT
GUNPOWDER
HARQUEBUS
KNOBSTICK
MATCHLOCK
MAZZUELLE
MILLS BOMB
MUSKETOON
POM-POM GUN
SLUNG SHOT
TRUNCHEON

10
ARTILLATOR
BANDEROLLE
BRANDESTOC
BROAD ARROW
BROADSWORD
CANNON BALL

10—continued
FIRE-STICKS
FLICK KNIFE
GATLING GUN
KNOBKERRIE
LETTER BOMB
LIMPET MINE
MACHINE GUN
PEA-SHOOTER
POWDERHORN
SIDEWINDER
SMALL SWORD
SWORD STICK

11
ANTI-TANK GUN
ARMOURED CAR
BLUNDERBUSS
HAND GRENADE
KHYBER KNIFE

11—continued
MISERICORDE
NEUTRON BOMB

12
BATTERING RAM
BREECH LOADER
BRIDLE CUTTER
FIRE CARRIAGE
FLAME-THROWER
HYDROGEN BOMB

13
BRASS KNUCKLES
DUELLING SWORD
GUIDED MISSILE
KNUCKLE DUSTER
THROWING KNIFE

14
DUELLING PISTOL

14—continued
INCENDIARY BOMB
NUCLEAR WEAPONS
ROCKET LAUNCHER
SAWN-OFF
  SHOTGUN

15
ANTI-AIRCRAFT GUN

16
BALLISTIC MISSILE

18
HEAT-SEEKING
  MISSILE

20+
DOUBLE-
  BARRELLED
  SHOTGUN

TRANSPORT

VEHICLES

3
BMX
BUS
CAB
CAR
FLY
GIG
VAN

4
AUTO
BIKE
CART
DRAG
DRAY
EKKA
HACK
JEEP
LUGE
SHAY
SLED
TAXI
TRAM
TRAP
TUBE
WAIN

5
ARABA
BRAKE
BUGGY
COACH
COUPÉ
CRATE
CYCLE
DANDY
DOOLY
LORRY
METRO
MOPED
MOTOR
PALKI
SEDAN
SULKY
TONGA
TRAIN
TRUCK
WAGON

6
BERLIN
CLASH
CHAISE
DIESEL
FIACRE
GO-CART
HANSOM
HEARSE
HOTROD
HURDLE
JALOPY
JITNEY
LANDAU
LIMBER
LITTER
MAGLEV
MODEL-T
ROCKET
SALOON
SLEDGE
SLEIGH
SNOCAT
SURREY
TANDEM
TANKER
TOURER
TRICAR
WEASEL

7
AUTOBUS
AUTOCAR
BICYCLE
BOB-SLED
BRITZKA
BROWSER
CALÈCHE
CARAVAN
CAROCHE
CHARIOT
COASTER
DOG-CART
DROSHKY
FLIVVER
GROWLER
HACKERY
HARD-TOP

7—continued
OFF-ROAD
OMNIBUS
OPEN-CAR
PHÆTON
PULLMAN
SCOOTER
SHUNTER
SIDE-CAR
TALLY-HO
TAXI-CAB
TILBURY
TRACTOR
TRAILER
TROLLEY
TUMBRIL
TWO-DOOR
UNICORN
VIS-À-VIS
WHISKEY

8
BAROUCHE
BRANCARD
BROUGHAM
CABLE-CAR
CAPE-CART
CARRIAGE
CARRIOLE
CLARENCE
CURRICLE
DEAD-CART
DORMEUSE
FOUR-DOOR
HORSE-BUS
HORSE-CAB
HORSE-VAN
ICE-YACHT
KIBITZKA
MONORAIL
MOTOR-CAR
MOTOR-VAN
OLD CROCK
PONY-CART
PUSH-BIKE
QUADRIGA
RICKSHAW
ROADSTER

8—continued
RUNABOUT
SOCIABLE
STAFF CAR
STEAM-CAR
TOBOGGAN
TRICYCLE
UNICYCLE
VICTORIA

9
AMBULANCE
BOAT-TRAIN
BOB-SLEIGH
BUBBLECAR
BUCKBOARD
CABRIOLET
CHAR-À-BANC
DILIGENCE
ESTATE-CAR
FUNICULAR
HORSE-CART
LIMOUSINE
MAIL-COACH
MILKFLOAT
MILK TRAIN
MONOCYCLE
MOTOR-BIKE
PALANKEEN
PALANQUIN
RACING CAR
SPORTS CAR
STREET-CAR
STRETCHER
TARANTASS
TIN LIZZIE
TWO-SEATER
WAGONETTE

10
AUTOMOBILE
BAIL GHARRY
BEACHWAGON
BLACK MARIA
FIRE-ENGINE
FOUR-IN-HAND
GOODS TRAIN
JINRICKSHA

249

10—continued
LOCAL TRAIN
LOCOMOTIVE
MOTOR-COACH
MOTOR-CYCLE
NIGHT TRAIN
OUTSIDE CAR
PADDYWAGON
PEDAL-CYCLE
PONY-ENGINE
POST-CHAISE
RATTLETRAP
SEDAN-CHAIR
SHANDRYDAN
SINCLAIR C5
SNOWPLOUGH
STAGE-COACH
STAGE-WAGON
STATE COACH
TROLLEY-BUS
TROLLEY-CAR
TWO-WHEELER
VELOCIPEDE

11
BONE-BREAKER
BULLOCK-CART
CONVERTIBLE
DIESEL TRAIN
FOUR-WHEELER
GUN-CARRIAGE
JAUNTING-CAR
JINRICKSHAW
LANDAULETTE
MAIL-PHÆTON
QUADRICYCLE
SIT-UP-AND-BEG
SOUPED-UP CAR
STEAM-ENGINE
STEAM-ROLLER
THIKA-GHARRY
WHITECHAPEL

12
COACH AND FOUR
DÉSOBLIGEANT
DOUBLE-DECKER

12—continued
EXPRESS TRAIN
FREIGHT TRAIN
HORSE-AND-CART
LUGGAGE TRAIN
PANTECHNICON
PUFFING BILLY
RAILWAY TRAIN
SINGLE-DECKER
STATION-WAGON
STEAM-OMNIBUS
THROUGH TRAIN

13
CYCLE-RICKSHAW
ELECTRIC TRAIN
GOVERNESS-CART
HORSE-CARRIAGE
PENNYFARTHING
PEOPLE CARRIER
RACING CHARIOT
SHOOTING-BRAKE

14
FOUR-WHEEL DRIVE
PASSENGER TRAIN
RIDING-CARRIAGE
TRACTION ENGINE

15
HACKNEY-CARRIAGE
PRAIRIE-SCHOONER

16
MOTORIZED
  BICYCLE
UNDERGROUND
  TRAIN

17
HORSELESS
  CARRIAGE

18
TRAVELLING
  CARRIAGE

SHIPS AND BOATS

3
ARK
COG
HOY
TUG

4
ARGO
BARK
BOAT
BRIG
BUSS
DHOW
DORY
GRAB
JUNK
PROA
PUNT
RAFT
SAIC
SNOW
TROW
YAWL

5
BARGE
CANOE
COBLE
DANDY
FERRY
FUNNY

5—continued
KAYAK
KETCH
LINER
NOBBY
PRAHU
SHELL
SKIFF
SLOOP
SMACK
TRAMP
U-BOAT
UMIAK
XEBEC
YACHT

6
BARQUE
BAWLEY
BIREME
CAIQUE
CARVEL
CUTTER
DINGHY
DOGGER
DUG-OUT
GALLEY
HOOKER
HOPPER
LAUNCH
LORCHA

6—continued
LUGGER
PACKET
RANDAN
SAMPAN
SEALER
SLAVER
TANKER
TENDER
WHALER

7
BUMBOAT
CARAVEL
CARRACK
CLIPPER
COASTER
COLLIER
CORACLE
CORSAIR
CURRACH
DREDGER
DRIFTER
DROMOND
FELUCCA
FLY-BOAT
FRIGATE
GABBARD
GALLEON
GONDOLA
JANGADA

7—continued
PINNACE
PIRAGUA
POLACCA
POLACRE
ROWBOAT
SCULLER
STEAMER
TARTANE
TOWBOAT
TRAWLER
TRIREME
WAR SHIP

8
BILANDER
BUDGEROW
COCKBOAT
CORVETTE
CRUMSTER
DAHABIYA
FIRESHIP
FOLDBOAT
GALLIVAT
LIFEBOAT
LONG-BOAT
MAIL-SHIP
NOAH'S ARK
OUTBOARD
SAILBOAT
SCHOONER

8–continued
SHOWBOAT

9
BUCENTAUR
CARGO-BOAT
CATAMARAN
CRIS-CRAFT
FREIGHTER
HOUSE BOAT
JOLLY-BOAT
LIGHTSHIP
MOTORBOAT
MOTORSHIP
MUD-HOPPER
OUTRIGGER
RIVER-BOAT
ROTOR SHIP
SHIP'S BOAT

9–continued
SLAVE-SHIP
SPEEDBOAT
STEAMBOAT
STEAMSHIP
STORESHIP
SUBMARINE

10
BANANA-BOAT
BRIGANTINE
PADDLE-BOAT
PICKET BOAT
PIRATE-SHIP
PRISON-SHIP
QUADRIREME
ROWING BOAT
TEA-CLIPPER
TRAIN-FERRY

10–continued
VIKING-SHIP
WIND-JAMMER

11
BARQUENTINE
CHASSE-MARÉE
COCKLE-SHELL
DOUBLE-CANOE
FISHING-BOAT
HOPPER-BARGE
MAIL-STEAMER
PENTECONTER
PILOT VESSEL
QUINQUEREME
SAILING-SHIP
THREE-MASTER

12
CABIN-CRUISER

12–continued
ESCORT VESSEL
FISHING SMACK
HOSPITAL SHIP
MERCHANT SHIP
PLEASURE BOAT
SAILING BARGE
STERN-WHEELER

13
HERRING-FISHER
PASSENGER SHIP
TRANSPORT SHIP

14
CHANNEL STEAMER
COASTING VESSEL
FLOATING PALACE
OCEAN
  GREYHOUND

AIRCRAFT

3
JET

4
KITE

5
PLANE

6
AIR CAR
BOMBER
GLIDER

7
AIRSHIP
BALLOON
BIPLANE

7–continued
CLIPPER
FIGHTER
JUMP-JET
SHUTTLE

8
AEROSTAT
AIRPLANE
AUTOGIRO
CONCORDE
JUMBO-JET
ROTODYNE
SEA-PLANE
TRIPLANE
TURBO-JET
WARPLANE

8–continued
ZEPPELIN

9
AEROPLANE
DIRIGIBLE
MAIL-PLANE
MONOPLANE
SAILPLANE
TURBO-PROP

10
FLYING-BOAT
GAS-BALLOON
HELICOPTER
HOVERCRAFT
HYDROPLANE

11
FIRE-BALLOON

12
FREIGHT-PLANE

13
STRATOCRUISER

14
FLYING BEDSTEAD
PASSENGER PLANE

18
MONTGOLFIER
  BALLOON

INTERNATIONAL AIRPORTS

ARLANDA (Stockholm)
ATATURK (Istanbul)
BARAJAS (Madrid)
CHARLES DE GAULLE (Paris)
CHANGI (Singapore)
CHIANG KAI-SHEK (Taipei)
COINTRIN (Geneva)
DALLAS-FORT WORTH
  (Dallas)

DORVAL (Montreal)
DOUGLAS (Charlotte)
DULLES (Washington)
ECHTERDINGEN (Stuttgart)
FINDEL (Luxembourg)
FORNEBU (Oslo)
GATWICK (London)
HARTSFIELD (Atlanta)
HEATHROW (London)

HELSINKI-VANTAA (Helsinki)
HONGQIAO (Shanghai)
HOPKINS (Cleveland)
JOHN F. KENNEDY (New York)
(BENITO) JUAREZ (Mexico
  City)
KIMPO (Seoul)
KING KHALED (Riyadh)
KINGSFORD SMITH (Sydney)

251

AIRLINE FLIGHT CODES

LA GUARDIA (New York)
LEONARDO DA VINCI
  (FIUMICINO) Rome
LINATE (Milan)
LINDBERGH FIELD (San
  Diego)
LOGAN (Boston)
LUIS MUÑOZ MARIN (San
  Juan)

MCCARRAN (Las Vegas)
MIRABEL (Montreal)
NARITA (Tokyo)
NINOY AQUINO (Manila)
O'HARE (Chicago)
OKECIE (Warsaw)
ORLY (Paris)
PEARSON (Toronto)
ST PAUL (Minneapolis)

SCHIPHOL (Amsterdam)
SHEREMETYEVO (Moscow)
SKY HARBOR (Phoenix)
SOEKARNO HATTA (Jakarta)
STANSTED (London)
SUBANG (Kuala Lumpur)
TEGEL (Berlin)
TULLAMARINE (Melbourne)
WAYNE COUNTY (Detroit)

AIRLINE FLIGHT CODES

CODE	AIRLINE				
		BBB	Balair	EXX	Air Exel UK
		BBC	Bangladesh Biman	FDE	Federal Express
AAF	Aigle Azur	BCS	European A/T	FIN	Finnair
AAG	Air Atlantique	BEA	Brymon European	FOB	Ford
AAL	American A/L	BEE	Busy Bee	FOF	Fred Olsen
AAN	Oasis	BER	Air Berlin	FUA	Futura
ABB	Air Belgium	BIH	British Intl Heli	FXY	Flexair
ABR	Hunting	BMA	British Midland	GBL	GB Airways
ACA	Air Canada	BRA	Braathens	GEC	German Cargo
ACF	Air Charter Intl	BWA	BWIA	GFA	Gulf Air
ADR	Adria A/W	BZH	Brit Air	GFG	Germania
AEA	Air Europa	CCA	CAAC	GHA	Ghana A/W
AEF	Aero Lloyd	CDN	Canadian A/L Intl	GIA	Garuda
AFL	Aeroflot	CFE	City Flyer	GIL	Gill Air
AFM	Affretair	CFG	Condor	GNT	Business Air
AFR	Air France	CIC	Celtic Air	GRN	Greenair
AGX	Aviogenex	CKT	Caledonian	HAL	Hawaiian Air
AHK	Air Hong Kong	CLH	Lufthansa CityLine	HAS	Hamburg A/L
AIA	Air Atlantis	CLX	Cargolux	HLA	HeavyLift
AIC	Air-India	CMM	Canada 3000 A/L	HLF	Hapag-Lloyd
AIH	Airtours	CNB	Air Columbus	IAW	Iraqi A/W
ALK	Air Lanka	COA	Continental A/L	IBE	Iberia
AMC	Air Malta	CPA	Cathay Pacific	ICE	Icelandair
AMM	Air 2000	CRL	Corse Air	IEA	Inter European
AMT	American Trans Air	CRX	Crossair	INS	Instone A/L
ANA	All Nippon A/W	CSA	Czech A/L	IRA	Iran Air
ANZ	Air New Zealand	CTA	CTA	IST	Istanbul A/L
AOM	Air Outre Mer	CTN	Croatia A/L	ITF	Air Inter
APW	Arrow Air	CYP	Cyprus A/W	JAL	Japan A/L
ARG	Argentine A/W	DAH	Air Algerie	JAT	JAT
ATI	ATI	DAL	Delta A/L	JAV	Janes Aviation
ATT	Aer Turas	DAT	Delta Air Transport	JEA	Jersey European A/W
AUA	Austrian A/L	DLH	Lufthansa	KAC	Kuwait A/W
AUR	Aurigny A/S	DMA	Maersk Air	KAL	Korean Air
AVA	Avianca	DQI	Cimber Air	KAR	Kar-Air
AWC	Titan A/W	DYA	Alyemda	KIS	Contactair
AYC	Aviaco	EGY	Egypt Air	KLM	KLM
AZA	Alitalia	EIA	Evergreen Intl	KQA	Kenya A/W
AZI	Air Zimbabwe	EIN	Aer Lingus	LAA	Libyan Arab A/L
AZR	Air Zaire	ELY	El Al	LAZ	Bulgarian A/L
BAC	BAC Leasing	ETH	Ethiopian A/L	LDA	Lauda Air
BAF	British Air Ferries	EUI	Euralair	LEI	Air UK Leisure
BAL	Britannia A/L	EWW	Emery	LGL	Luxair
BAW	British Airways	EXS	Channel Express	LIB	Air Liberte

LIN	Linjeflyg	RBA	Royal Brunei	TMA	Trans Mediterranean
LIT	Air Littoral	RIA	Rich Intl	TOW	Tower Air
LKA	Alkair	RJA	Royal Jordanian	TRA	Transavia
LOG	Loganair	RNA	Royal Nepal A/L	TSC	Air Transat
LOT	Polish A/L (LOT)	ROT	Tarom	TSW	TEA Basle
LTE	LTE	RWD	Air Rwanda	TWA	TWA
LTS	LTU Sud	RYR	Ryanair	TWE	Transwede
LTU	LTU	SAA	South African A/W	TYR	Tyrolean
MAH	Malev	SAB	Sabena	UAE	Emirates A/L
MAS	Malaysian A/L	SAS	SAS	UAL	United A/L
MAU	Air Mauritius	SAW	Sterling A/W	UGA	Uganda A/L
MDN	Meridiana	SAY	Suckling A/W	UKA	Air UK
MEA	Middle East A/L	SDI	Saudi	UKR	Air Ukraine
MNX	Manx A/L	SEY	Air Seychelles	ULE	Air UK Leisure
MON	Monarch A/L	SIA	Singapore A/L	UPA	Air Foyle
MOR	Morefly	SJM	Southern AT	UPS	United Parcels
MPH	Martinair	SLA	Sobelair	USA	USAir
NAD	Nobleair	SPP	Spanair	UTA	UTA
NAW	Newair	STR	Stellair	UYC	Cameroon A/L
NEX	Northern Executive	SUD	Sudan A/W	VIA	Viasa
NGA	Nigeria A/W	SUT	Sultan Air	VIR	Virgin Atlantic
NSA	Nile Safaris	SWE	Swedair	VIV	Viva Air
NWA	Northwest A/L	SWR	Swissair	VKG	Scanair
NXA	Nationair	SXS	Sun Express	VRG	Varig
OAL	Olympic A/L	SYR	Syrian Arab	WDL	WDL
OYC	Conair	TAP	Air Portugal	WOA	World A/W
PAL	Philippine A/L	TAR	Tunis Air	ZAC	Zambia A/W
PGA	Portugalia	TAT	TAT	ZAS	ZAS A/L of Egypt
PGT	Pegasus	TCT	TUR European		
PIA	Pakistan Intl	THA	Thai A/W Intl	A/W = Airways
QFA	Qantas	THG	Thurston	A/L = Airlines
QSC	African Safaris	THY	Turkish A/L	A/T = Air Transport
RAM	Royal Air Maroc	TLE	Air Toulouse	A/S = Aero Service

MOTORING TERMS

2	5–continued	5–continued	7–continued	8–continued
C.C.	TYRE	GASKET	GEARBOX	MOUNTING
		HEATER	OIL SEAL	RADIATOR
3	5	HUB CAP		ROTOR ARM
BHP	BRAKE	IDLING	8	SELECTOR
CAM	CHOKE	PISTON	ADHESION	SILENCER
FAN	SERVO	REBORE	BRAKE PAD	SMALL END
HUB	SHAFT	STROKE	BULKHEAD	STEERING
JET	VALVE	TAPPET	CALLIPER	THROTTLE
REV	WHEEL	TORQUE	CAMSHAFT	TRACK ROD
ROD		TUNING	CROSS-PLY	
	6		CYLINDER	9
4	BIG END	7	DIPSTICK	BRAKESHOE
AXLE	BONNET	BATTERY	FLYWHEEL	CONDENSER
BOOT	CAMBER	BEARING	FUEL PUMP	DISC BRAKE
BUSH	CLUTCH	BRACKET	IGNITION	DRUM BRAKE
COIL	DAMPER	CHASSIS	KICK-DOWN	GEAR STICK
GEAR	DECOKE	DYNAMIC	KNOCKING	GENERATOR
HORN	DYNAMO	EXHAUST	LIVE AXLE	HALF-SHAFT
LOCK	ENGINE	FAN BELT	MANIFOLD	HANDBRAKE
SUMP	FILTER			

INTERNATIONAL CAR REGISTRATIONS

9–continued
INDUCTION
MISFIRING
OVERDRIVE
OVERSTEER
PROP SHAFT
RADIAL-PLY
SIDE VALVE
SPARK PLUG
TWO-STROKE
UNDERSEAL
WHEELBASE

10
AIR CLEANER
ALTERNATOR
BRAKE FLUID
CRANKSHAFT
DETONATION
DRIVE SHAFT
FOUR-STROKE
GUDGEON PIN
HORSEPOWER

10–continued
PISTON RING
REV COUNTER
SUSPENSION
TACHOMETER
THERMOSTAT
UNDERSTEER
WINDSCREEN

11
ANTI-ROLL BAR
CARBURETTER
CARBURETTOR
COMPRESSION
CROSSMEMBER
DISTRIBUTOR
SERVO SYSTEM
SYNCHROMESH

12
ACCELERATION
CYLINDER HEAD
DIESEL ENGINE

12–continued
DIFFERENTIAL
SPARKING PLUG
SUPERCHARGER
TRANSMISSION
TURBOCHARGER
VISCOUS DRIVE

13
COOLING SYSTEM
DECARBONIZING
FUEL INJECTION
OVERHEAD VALVE
POWER STEERING
RACK-AND-PINION
SHOCK ABSORBER
SLAVE CYLINDER
SPARK IGNITION

14
FOUR-WHEEL DRIVE
PROPELLER SHAFT
UNIVERSAL JOINT

15
FRONT-WHEEL
  DRIVE
HYDRAULIC SYSTEM
PETROL INJECTION

17
INDUCTION
  MANIFOLD
REVOLUTION
  COUNTER

19
CROWN WHEEL AND
  PINION

20+
AUTOMATIC
  TRANSMISSION
INDEPENDENT
  SUSPENSION
POWER ASSISTED
  STEERING

INTERNATIONAL CAR REGISTRATIONS

REGISTRATION LETTER
  Country

A	Austria	GH	Ghana	NIG	Niger	RU	Burundi
AL	Albania	GR	Greece	NL	Netherlands	RWA	Rwanda
AUS	Australia	H	Hungary	NZ	New Zealand	S	Sweden
B	Belgium	HK	Hong Kong	P	Portugal	SD	Swaziland
BDS	Barbados	HKJ	Jordan	PA	Panama	SF	Finland
BG	Bulgaria	I	Italy	PAK	Pakistan	SGP	Singapore
BR	Brazil	IL	Israel	PE	Peru	SME	Surinam
BRG	Guyana	IND	India	PI	Philippines	SN	Senegal
BRN	Bahrain	IR	Iran	PL	Poland	SYR	Syria
BS	Bahamas	IRL	Ireland	PY	Paraguay	T	Thailand
C	Cuba	IRQ	Iraq	R	Romania	TG	Togo
CDN	Canada	IS	Iceland	RA	Argentina	TN	Tunisia
CH	Switzerland	J	Japan	RB	Botswana	TR	Turkey
CI	Côte d'Ivoire	JA	Jamaica	RC	China	TT	Trinidad and
CO	Colombia	KWT	Kuwait	RCA	Central African		Tobago
CR	Costa Rica	L	Luxembourg		Republic	U	Uruguay
CY	Cyprus	LAO	Laos	RCB	Congo	USA	United States
D	Germany	LB	Liberia	RCH	Chile		of America
D	Denmark	LS	Lesotho	RH	Haiti	VN	Vietnam
DZ	Algeria	M	Malta	RI	Indonesia	WAL	Sierra Leone
E	Spain	MA	Morocco	RIM	Mauritania	WAN	Nigeria
EC	Ecuador	MAL	Malaysia	RL	Lebanon	WS	Western
F	France	MEX	Mexico	RM	Malagasy		Samoa
FL	Liechtenstein	MS	Mauritius		Republic	YV	Venezuela
GB	Great Britain	MW	Malawi	RMM	Mali	Z	Zambia
GCA	Guatemala	N	Norway	ROK	South Korea	ZA	South Africa

NAUTICAL TERMS

3
AFT
BOW
FID
LEE

4
ALEE
BEAM
BITT
BOOM
FORE
HOLD
HULL
KEEL
KNOT
LIST
MATE
POOP
PORT
PROW
STAY
STEM
WAKE
WARP

5
ABAFT
ABEAM
ABOUT
ALOFT
AVAST
BELAY
BELLS
BILGE
BOSUN
CABLE

5—continued
CAULK
CLEAT
DAVIT
HATCH
HAWSE
STERN
TRICK
TRUCK
WAIST
WEIGH
WINCH

6
BRIDGE
BUNKER
FATHOM
FENDER
FLUKES
FO'C'SLE
GALLEY
HAWSER
JETSAM
LEAGUE
LEEWAY
OFFING
PURSER
SHROUD
YAWING

7
ADMIRAL
BALLAST
BOLLARD
BULWARK
CAPSTAN
CATWALK

7—continued
COAMING
DRAUGHT
FLOTSAM
GANGWAY
GRAPNEL
GUNWALE
INBOARD
LANYARD
MOORING
QUARTER
RIGGING
SEA MILE
TONNAGE
TOPSIDE
WATCHES

8
BINNACLE
BOWSPRIT
BULKHEAD
COXSWAIN
DOG WATCH
HALYARDS
HATCHWAY
LARBOARD
PITCHING
RATLINES
SCUPPERS
SPLICING
TAFFRAIL
WINDLASS
WINDWARD

9
AMIDSHIPS
COMPANION

9—continued
CROW'S NEST
FREEBOARD
SHIP'S BELL
STARBOARD
WATER-LINE

10
BATTEN DOWN
DEADLIGHTS
DEADWEIGHT
FIRST WATCH
FORE-AND-AFT
FORECASTLE
NIGHT WATCH

11
MIDDLE WATCH
QUARTER-DECK
WEATHER SIDE

12
DISPLACEMENT
JACOB'S LADDER
MARLINE SPIKE
NAUTICAL MILE
PLIMSOLL LINE

13
QUARTERMASTER

14
SUPERSTRUCTURE

15
COMPANION-
   LADDER
DAVY JONES'
   LOCKER

SHIPPING AREAS NAMED IN WEATHER FORECASTS

BAILEY
BISCAY
CROMARTY
DOGGER
DOVER
FAEROES
FAIR ISLE
FASTNET
FINISTERRE
FISHER

FORTH
FORTIES
GERMAN BIGHT
HEBRIDES
HUMBER
IRISH SEA
LUNDY
MALIN
PLYMOUTH
PORTLAND

ROCKALL
SHANNON
SOLE
SOUTH-EAST ICELAND
THAMES
TYNE
VIKING
WIGHT

CLOTHES AND MATERIALS

CLOTHES

3
ABA
ALB
BAL
BAS
BAT
BIB
BRA
COP
FEZ
HAT
LEI
OBI
TAM

4
ABBA
AGAL
ALBA
APEX
BAJU
BARB
BECK
BELT
BENN
BOTA
BUSK
CACK
CAPE
CLOG
COAT
COPE
COTE
COWL
DAPS
DIDO
DISK
GARB
GETA
GOWN
HAIK
HOOD
HOSE
IZAR
JAMA
KEPI
KILT

4–continued
MASK
MAXI
MIDI
MINI
MITT
MUFF
MULE
PUMP
ROBE
RUFF
SARI
SASH
SAYA
SHOE
SLIP
SLOP
SOCK
SPAT
SUIT
TABI
TOGA
TOGS
TOPI
TUTU
VAMP
VEIL
VEST
WRAP

5
ABNET
ACTON
AEGIS
AMICE
AMPYX
APRON
ARCAN
ARMET
ARMOR
ASCOT
BARBE
BARRY
BENJY
BERET
BLAKE
BLUEY

5–continued
BOINA
BOOTS
BURKA
BUSBY
CABAS
CADET
CAPPA
CHALE
CHAPS
CHOGA
CHOLI
CLOAK
CORDY
COTTA
COTTE
CREST
CROWN
CURCH
CYLAS
CYMAR
DERBY
DHOTI
EPHOD
FICHU
FROCK
GANSY
GILET
GIPPO
GLOVE
HABIT
HULLS
IHRAM
JABOT
JAMAH
JEANS
JELAB
JUPON
LAMMY
LODEN
LUNGI
MIDDY
MUFTI
NUBIA
PAGNE
PAGRI
PALLA

5–continued
PANTS
PARKA
PILCH
PIRNY
PUMPS
SABOT
SAREE
SCARF
SHAKO
SHAWL
SHIFT
SHIRT
SKIRT
SMOCK
SNOOD
STOCK
STOLA
STOLE
TAILS
TEDDY
TIARA
TONGS
TOPEE
TOQUE
TREWS
TUNIC
VISOR
VIZOR
WEEDS

6
ABOLLA
ALMUCE
ANADEM
ANALAV
ANKLET
ANORAK
ARCTIC
ARTOIS
BALKAN
BANYAN
BARRET
BARVEL
BASQUE
BAUTTA
BEANIE

6–continued
BEAVER
BÉQUIN
BERTHA
BICORN
BIETLE
BIGGIN
BIKINI
BIRRUS
BISHOP
BLAZER
BLIAUD
BLOUSE
BOATER
BODICE
BOLERO
BONNET
BOOTEE
BOWLER
BOXERS
BRACAE
BRACES
BRAGAS
BRAIES
BRETON
BRIEFS
BROGAN
BROGUE
BUSKIN
BYRNIE
BYRRUS
CABAAN
CADDIE
CAFTAN
CALASH
CALCEI
CALIGA
CALPAC
CAMAIL
CAMISA
CAMISE
CAPOTE
CAPUCE
CAPUTI
CARACO
CASQUE
CASTOR

6–continued

CAUSIA
CESTUS
CHADAR
CHITON
CHOKER
CILICE
CIMIER
CLAQUE
CLOCHE
COBCAB
COCKET
CORNET
CORONA
CORSET
COTHUM
COVERT
CRAVAT
DIADEM
DICKEY
DIRNDL
DOLMAN
DOMINO
DUSTER
EARCAP
FEDORA
FILLET
GAITER
GANSEY
GARTER
GAUCHO
GILLIE
GUIMPE
HALTER
HENNIN
HUIPIL
JACKET
JERKIN
JERSEY
JUBBAH
JUMPER
KABAYA
KIMONO
KIRTLE
KITTEL
LAMMIE
LOAFER
LUNGEE
MAGYAR
MANTEE
MANTLE
MANTUA
MITTEN
MOBCAP
MOGGAN
OUTFIT
PEG-TOP
PEPLOS
PEPLUM
PILEUS
PINNER
PIRNIE

6–continued

PONCHO
PUGREE
PUTTEE
RAGLAN
REEFER
RUFFLE
SANDAL
SARONG
SERAPE
SHIMMY
SHORTS
SHROUD
SLACKS
SONTAG
STEP-IN
SUN HAT
TABARD
TAMISE
TIGHTS
TIPPET
TOP HAT
TOPPER
TRILBY
TRUNKS
T-SHIRT
TUCKER
TURBAN
TUXEDO
TWEEDS
ULSTER
UNDIES
UPLIFT
VAMPAY
VESTEE
WIMPLE
WOOLLY
ZOUAVE

7

AMICTUS
APPAREL
ARISARD
ARM BAND
BABOOSH
BALDRIC
BALTEUS
BANDEAU
BANDORE
BARBUTE
BAROQUE
BASHLYK
BASINET
BAVETTE
BAVOLET
BEDIZEN
BELCHER
BERDASH
BERETTA
BETSIES
BIRETTA
BOTTINE

7–continued

BOX CAPE
BOX COAT
BRIMMER
BROIGNE
BURNOUS
BUSSKIN
CALEÇON
CALOTTE
CAMOURO
CANEZOU
CAPE HAT
CAPUCHE
CAPULET
CASAQUE
CASSOCK
CATSKIN
CAUBEEN
CEREVIS
CHAINSE
CHALWAR
CHAPLET
CHEMISE
CHEVRON
CHIMERE
CHIP HAT
CHLAMYS
CHOPINE
CHOU HAT
CHRISOM
CHUDDAR
CHUDDER
COMMODE
CORONEL
CORONET
COSSACK
COXCOMB
CREPIDA
CRISPIN
CUCULLA
CUIRASS
CULOTTE
CURCHEF
CUTAWAY
DOPATTA
DOUBLET
DRAWERS
DULBAND
DUL HOSE
EARMUFF
ETON CAP
EVERETT
FANCHON
FASHION
FILIBEG
FLATCAP
GARMENT
GHILLIE
G STRING
GUM BOOT
GUM SHOE
GYM SHOE

7–continued

HANDBAG
HIGH-LOW
HOMBURG
HOSIERY
JODHPUR
KLOMPEN
LAYETTE
LEOTARD
MAILLOT
MANTEAU
MONTERA
MONTERO
MUFFLER
OLIVERS
OVERALL
OXFORDS
PANTIES
PARASOL
PATTERN
PELISSE
PETASOS
PIERROT
PILLBOX
PLUVIAL
PUGGREE
PYJAMAS
RAIMENT
REGALIA
ROMPERS
RUBBERS
SARAFAN
SCOGGER
SHALWAR
SILK HAT
SINGLET
SKI BOOT
SLIPPER
SLYDERS
SMICKET
SNEAKER
SOUTANE
SPENCER
SPORRAN
SULTANE
SUN SUIT
SURCOAT
SURTOUT
SWEATER
TANK TOP
TEA GOWN
TOP BOOT
TOP COAT
TRAHEEN
TRICORN
TUNICLE
TWIN SET
UNIFORM
VEILING
WATTEAU
WEDGIES
WING TIE

7–continued

WOOLLEN
WRAPPER
YASHMAK
Y-FRONTS
ZIMARRA

8

ABBÉ CAPE
ALL-IN-ONE
ANALABOS
ANTELOPE
BABUSHKA
BALADRAN
BALMORAL
BANDANNA
BARBETTE
BASQUINE
BATH ROBE
BEARSKIN
BED SOCKS
BENJAMIN
BIGGONET
BINNOGUE
BLOOMERS
BODY COAT
BOMBARDS
BOOT-HOSE
BOTTEKIN
BREECHES
BURGONET
BURNOOSE
BYCOCKET
CABASSET
CAMISOLE
CANOTIER
CAPE COAT
CAPELINE
CAPRIOLE
CAPUCINE
CAPUTIUM
CARCANET
CARDIGAN
CARDINAL
CAROLINE
CASAQUIN
CATERCAP
CHANDAIL
CHAPERON
CHAQUETA
CHASUBLE
CHAUSSES
CHONGSAM
COLOBIUM
COPATAIN
CORSELET
COUCH HAT
COVERALL
CRUSH HAT
CUCULLUS
DANCE SET
DANDY HAT

8–continued

DJELLABA
DOM PEDRO
DORMEUSE
DUCK-BILL
DUNCE CAP
DUST COAT
DUTCH CAP
FALDETTA
FLANNELS
FLIMSIES
FOOTWEAR
GAMASHES
GAUNTLET
GUERNSEY
HALF-HOSE
HALF SLIP
HEADGEAR
JACK BOOT
JUDO COAT
JUMP SUIT
KERCHIEF
KNICKERS
KNITWEAR
LARRIGAN
LAVA-LAVA
LEGGINGS
LINGERIE
LIRIPIPE
MANTELET
MANTILLA
MOCCASIN
NECKLACE
NIGHTCAP
OPERA HAT
OVERALLS
OVERCOAT
OVERSHOE
PARAMENT
PEASECOD
PEIGNOIR
PHILIBEG
PILEOLUS
PINAFORE
PLASTRON
PLATINUM
PLIMSOLL
PULLOVER
SABOTINE
SKULL-CAP
SLIP-OVER
SNOWSHOE
SOMBRERO
STOCKING
SURPLICE
SWIM SUIT
TAIL COAT
TAILLEUR
TARBOOSH
TOQUETTE
TRAINERS
TRENCHER

8–continued

TRICORNE
TROUSERS
TWO-PIECE
WOOLLENS
WOOLLIES
ZOOT SUIT

9

AFTERWELT
ALPARGATA
ALPINE HAT
ANKLE BOOT
APON DRESS
ARMILAUSA
BABY SKIRT
BALAYEUSE
BALL DRESS
BALMACAAN
BAMBIN HAT
BANDOLEER
BARCELONA
BEAVERTOP
BED JACKET
BEEGUM HAT
BELL SKIRT
BILLICOCK
BILLYCOCK
BLOUSETTE
BODY LINEN
BOURRELET
BRASSIÈRE
BROADBRIM
BRODEQUIN
BRUNSWICK
BYZANTINE
CABRIOLET
CAPE DRESS
CAPE STOLE
CARTWHEEL
CASENTINO
CASQUETTE
CASSIMERE
CHEMILOON
CHIN-CLOTH
CHIVARRAS
CHOLO COAT
COAT DRESS
COAT SHIRT
COCKED HAT
COOLIE HAT
COPINTANK
CORNERCAP
COVERSLUT
COWBOY HAT
CREEDMORE
CRINOLINE
DOG COLLAR
DOMINICAL
DRESS COAT
DRESS SHOE
DRESS SUIT

9–continued

DUNGAREES
DUNSTABLE
ESCOFFIAN
FORAGE CAP
FROCK COAT
FULL DRESS
GABARDINE
GABERDINE
GARIBALDI
GLENGARRY
GREATCOAT
HEADDRESS
HEADPIECE
HELMET CAP
HOURI-COAT
HOUSE-COAT
HULA SKIRT
INVERNESS
JOCKEY CAP
JULIET CAP
LOINCLOTH
MILLINERY
NECKCLOTH
NIGHTGOWN
OUTERWEAR
OVERDRESS
OVERSHIRT
OVERSKIRT
PANAMA HAT
PANTALETS
PANTOFFLE
PANTY HOSE
PEA JACKET
PETTICOAT
PILOT COAT
PLUS FOURS
POLONAISE
QUAKER HAT
REDINGOTE
SANBENITO
SHAKSHEER
SHINTIYAN
SHOVEL HAT
SLOPPY JOE
SLOUCH HAT
SNEAKERS
SOU'WESTER
STOMACHER
STRING TIE
SUNBONNET
SURCINGLE
TENT DRESS
THIGH BOOT
TROUSSEAU
TRUNK-HOSE
UNDERCOAT
UNDERGOWN
UNDERVEST
UNDERWEAR
VESTMENTS
VICTORINE

9–continued

WAISTCOAT
WATCH COAT
WIDE-AWAKE
WITCH'S HAT
WYLIECOAT

10

ANGELUS CAP
APRON TUNIC
BABY BONNET
BASIC DRESS
BATHING CAP
BEER JACKET
BELLBOY CAP
BERRETTINO
BIBI BONNET
BICYCLE BAL
BLOUSE COAT
BOBBY SOCKS
BOSOM SHIRT
BOUDOIR CAP
BRIGANDINE
BRUNCH COAT
BUCKET TOPS
BUMPER BRIM
BUSH JACKET
BUSK JACKET
CALZONERAS
CANVAS SHOE
CAPE COLLAR
CAPPA MAGNA
CARMAGNOLE
CERVELIÈRE
CHARTREUSE
CHATELAINE
CHEMISETTE
CHIGNON CAP
CHOUQUETTE
CLOCK-MUTCH
COOLIE COAT
COQUELUCHE
CORPS PIQUÉ
COSSACK CAP
COTE-HARDIE
COUVRE-CHEF
COVERCHIEF
COVERT COAT
CROSSCLOTH
CUMMERBUND
DANCE DRESS
DESHABILLE
DINNER SUIT
DIPLOIDIAN
DOUILLETTE
DRESS PLAID
DRESS SHIRT
DUFFEL COAT
ECLIPSE TIE
ESPADRILLE
ETON JACKET
EUGÉNIE HAT

10–continued

FANCY DRESS
FASCINATOR
FLYING SUIT
FORE-AND-AFT
FUSTANELLA
GARMENTURE
GRASS SKIRT
HAREM SKIRT
HUG-ME-TIGHT
JIGGER COAT
LIRIPIPIUM
LOUNGE SUIT
LUMBERJACK
MESS JACKET
NIGHTDRESS
NIGHTSHIRT
OPERA CLOAK
OVERBLOUSE
OVERGAITER
OXFORD BAGS
OXFORD GOWN
PANTALOONS
PICTURE HAT
PITH HELMET
POKE BONNET
PORK PIE HAT
RIDING-HOOD
SERVICE CAP
SHIRTWAIST
SPORTS COAT
SPORT SHIRT
SPORTSWEAR
STICHARION
STRING VEST
SUNDAY BEST
SUSPENDERS
SWEAT SHIRT
THREE-PIECE
TRENCH COAT
UNDERDRESS
UNDERLINEN
UNDERPANTS
UNDERSHIRT
UNDERSKIRT
VELDSCHOEN
WINDSOR TIE
WING COLLAR

11

ALSATIAN BOW
BATHING SUIT
BIB-AND-BRACE
BOILED SHIRT
BOXER SHORTS
BRACONNIÈRE
BREECHCLOTH
BRITISH WARM
CANCAN DRESS
CAVALIER HAT
CHAPEAU BRAS
CHAPEL DE FER

11–continued

CIRCASSIENE
COMBINATION
CORSET COVER
COWBOY BOOTS
DANCING CLOG
DEERSTALKER
DINNER DRESS
EMPIRE SKIRT
ESPADRILLES
EVENING GOWN
EVENING SLIP
FORMAL DRESS
FORTUNY GOWN
GALLIGASKIN
HOBBLE SKIRT
HOSTESS GOWN
HOUPPELANDE
HUNTING BOOT
MIDDY BLOUSE
NECKERCHIEF
OVERGARMENT
PANTY GIRDLE
RIDING HABIT
RUBBER APRON
RUNNING SHOE
RUSSIAN BOOT
SEWING APRON
SNAP-BRIM HAT
SOUP-AND-FISH
SOUTHWESTER
SPATTERDASH
STOCKING CAP
STRING GLOVE
SWAGGER COAT
TAM-O'SHANTER
TYROLEAN HAT
UNDERGIRDLE
UNDERTHINGS
WALKING SHOE
WEDDING GOWN
WEDDING VEIL
WELLINGTONS
WINDBREAKER
WINDCHEATER

12

AMISH COSTUME
BALKAN BLOUSE
BALLOON SKIRT
BASEBALL BOOT
BATTLE JACKET
BELLY DOUBLET
BLOOMER DRESS
BUSINESS SUIT
CAMICIA ROSSA
CAVALIER BOOT
CHEMISE DRESS
CHEMISE FROCK
CHESTERFIELD
CHUKKER SHIRT
CIGARETTE MIT

12–continued

CORSET BODICE
COTTAGE CLOAK
CRUSADER HOOD
DINNER JACKET
DIVIDED SKIRT
DORIC CHILTON
DRESS CLOTHES
DRESSING GOWN
EASTER BONNET
ENGLISH DRAPE
EVENING DRESS
EVENING SHOES
EVENING SKIRT
HANDKERCHIEF
HEADKERCHIEF
HELMET BONNET
KNEE BREECHES
LOUNGING ROBE
MANDARIN COAT
MONKEY JACKET
MORNING DRESS
MOTORING VEIL
PEDAL PUSHERS
PENITENTIALS
QUAKER BONNET
ROLL-ON GIRDLE
SCOTCH BONNET
SHIRTWAISTER
SLEEPING COAT
SLEEPING SUIT
SMALLCLOTHES
STOVEPIPE HAT
SUGAR-LOAF HAT
TAILORED SUIT
TEN-GALLON HAT
TROUSERETTES
UNDERCLOTHES
UNDERGARMENT
WIDE-AWAKE HAT
ZOUAVE JACKET

13

ACROBATIC SHOE
AFTER-SKI SOCKS
BACK-STRAP SHOE
BEEFEATER'S HAT
BELLBOY JACKET
BUNGALOW APRON
COACHMAN'S COAT
COMBING JACKET
COTTAGE BONNET
DRESSING SAQUE
ELEVATOR SHOES
HAWAIIAN SKIRT
MOTHER HUBBARD
MOURNING DRESS
NORFOLK JACKET
PEEK-A-BOO WAIST
PRINCESS DRESS
SAM BROWNE BELT
SMOKING JACKET

13–continued

SPORTS CLOTHES
SUSPENDER-BELT
TEDDYBEAR COAT
TRUNK-BREECHES
UNDERCLOTHING

14

AFTERNOON DRESS
BATHING COSTUME
BICYCLE CLIP HAT
CACHE-POUSSIÈRE
CAMOUFLAGE SUIT
CARDIGAN BODICE
CONGRESS GAITOR
CONTINENTAL HAT
DRESSING JACKET
DRESSMAKER SUIT
EGYPTIAN SANDAL
EVENING SWEATER
KNICKERBOCKERS
SHOOTING JACKET

15

CARDIGAN SWEATER
CHAPEAU FRANÇAIS
CHEMISE À LA REINE
CHEVALIER BONNET
ENVELOPE CHEMISE
FAIR ISLE SWEATER
MONTGOMERY
  BERET

16

BUTCHER BOY
  BLOUSE
CALMEL'S HAIR
  SHAWL
CHICKEN SKIN
  GLOVE
EISENHOWER
  JACKET
GOING-AWAY
  COSTUME
SWADDLING
  CLOTHES

17

CHEMISE À
  L'ANGLAISE
COAL SCUTTLE
  BONNET
CONFIRMATION
  DRESS
FOUNDATION
  GARMENT
SWALLOW-TAILED
  COAT

18

BETHLEHEM
  HEADDRESS
CHARLOTTE
  CORDAY CAP

MATERIALS

3	5–continued	6–continued	6–continued	7–continued
ABB	LAPIN	CANGAN	SHODDY	ETAMINE
BAN	LINEN	CANVAS	SISSOL	FAKE FUR
FUR	LINON	CASTOR	SKIVER	FISHNET
NET	LISLE	CATGUT	SOUPLE	FITCHEW
REP	LUREX	CHILLO	TARTAN	FLANNEL
	MOIRE	CHINTZ	TINSEL	FOULARD
4	NINON	CHROME	TISSUE	FUR FELT
ACCA	NYLON	CHUNAN	TRICOT	FUSTIAN
ALMA	ORLON	COBURG	TUSSAH	GALATEA
BAKU	PEKIN	CONTRO	TUSSEH	GINGHAM
BRIN	PIQUÉ	COSSAS	VELURE	GOBELIN
BURE	PLUSH	CÔTELÉ	VELVET	GROGRAM
CALF	PRINT	CREPON	VICUNA	GUANACO
CORD	RAYON	CROISE	WINCEY	GUIPURE
CREA	SATIN	CUBICA	WITNEY	HESSIAN
FELT	SCRIM	DAMASK		HOLLAND
FUJI	SERGE	DIAPER	**7**	JACONET
GROS	SISAL	DIMITY	ACRILON	JAP SILK
HEMP	SISOL	DJERSA	ACRYLIC	KASHMIR
HIDE	STRAW	DOMETT	ALAMODE	KIDSKIN
JEAN	STUFF	DOWLAS	ART SILK	LEATHER
LACE	SUEDE	DUCAPE	BAGGING	LEGHORN
LAMÉ	SURAH	ÉPONGE	BATISTE	LIBERTY
LAWN	TAMMY	ERMINE	BATTING	MINIVER
MULL	TISSU	FABRIC	BEMBERG	MOROCCO
PELT	TOILE	FAILLE	BRABANT	NANKEEN
ROAN	TULLE	FISHER	BUNTING	NETTING
SILK	TWEED	FORFAR	BUSTIAN	OILSKIN
SKIN	TWILL	FRIEZE	CAMBAYE	ORGANDY
VAIR	UNION	GALYAC	CAMBRIC	ORGANZA
WOOL	VOILE	GALYAK	CANTOON	OTTOMAN
		GRENAI	CAPENET	PAISLEY
5	**6**	GURRAH	CARACAL	PARAGON
ABACA	ALACHA	KERSEY	CARACUL	PERCALE
ACELE	ALASKA	LAMPAS	CATALIN	PIGSKIN
ACETA	ALPACA	LASTEX	CHALLIS	RACCOON
ARDIL	ANGORA	LINENE	CHAMOIS	RAWHIDE
BAIZE	ARALAC	MADRAS	CHARVET	RAW SILK
BASCO	ARIDEX	MELTON	CHEKMAK	ROMAINE
CADIS	ARMURE	MERINO	CHEVIOT	SACKING
CAFFA	BALINE	MILIUM	CHEYNEY	SAFFIAN
CASHA	BARÈGE	MOHAIR	CHIFFON	SATINET
CLOTH	BENGAL	MOUTON	COOTHAY	SUITING
CRAPE	BERBER	MULMUL	COWHIDE	TAFFETA
CRASH	BIRETZ	MUSLIN	DAMMASÉ	TEXTILE
CRISP	BLATTA	NAPERY	DELAINE	TICKING
CROWN	BOTANY	OXFORD	DOESKIN	TIE SILK
DENIM	BUREAU	PAILLE	DORNICK	TIFFANY
DORIA	BURLAP	PONGEE	DRABBET	TUSSORE
FITCH	BURNET	POPLIN	DRUGGET	VALENCE
GAUZE	BURRAH	RIBBON	DUCHESS	VELOURS
GENET	BYSSUS	RUBBER	DURANCE	VISCOSE
GUNNY	CAFFOY	SAMITE	DUVETYN	VIYELLA
HONAN	CALICO	SATEEN	EARL GLO	WEBBING
JUPON	CAMACA	SAXONY	ÉPINGLÉ	WOOLLEN
KAPOK	CAMLET	SENNIT	ESPARTO	WORSTED
LAINE				

8

AGA BANEE
ALOE LACE
ARMOZEEN
ARMOZINE
ART LINEN
BAGHEERA
BARATHEA
BARRACAN
BAUDEKIN
BEUTANOL
BLANCARD
BOBBINET
BOMBAZET
BOX CLOTH
BUCKSKIN
BUFFSKIN
CALFSKIN
CAPESKIN
CASHMERE
CELANESE
CELENESE
CHAMBRAY
CHARMEEN
CHENILLE
CHIRIMEN
CHIVERET
CORDUROY
COTELINE
CRETONNE
DIAPHANE
DRAP D'ÉTÉ
DUCHESSE
ÉCRU SILK
EOLIENNE
ESTAMENE
EVERFAST
FARADINE
FLORENCE
GOATSKIN
GOSSAMER
HOMESPUN
INDIENNE
KOLINSKY
LAMBSKIN
LUSTRINE
LUSTRING
MARABOUT
MARCELLA
MAROCAIN
MATERIAL
MILANESE
MOGADORE
MOLESKIN
MOQUETTE
MUSLINET
MUSQUASH
NAINSOOK
OILCLOTH
ORGANDIE
PURE SILK
SARCENET

8–continued

SARSENET
SEALSKIN
SHAGREEN
SHANTUNG
SHIRTING
SHOT SILK
TAPESTRY
TARLATAN
TARLETAN
TOILINET
VALENCIA
WAX CLOTH
WHIPCORD
WILD SILK
ZIBELINE

9

ADA CANVAS
AGRA GAUZE
ASBESTALL
ASTRAKHAN
BARK CLOTH
BARK CREPE
BENGALINE
BOMBAZINE
BOMBYCINE
BOOK CLOTH
BOOK LINEN
BROCATELL
BYRD CLOTH
CALAMANCO
CANNEQUIN
CATALOWNE
CHARMEUSE
CHINA SILK
COTTONADE
COTTON REP
CREPELINE
CRINOLINE
CUT VELVET
DACCA SILK
ÉCRU CLOTH
ÉLASTIQUE
FLANNELET
FUR FABRIC
GABARDINE
GEORGETTE
GRENADINE
GROSGRAIN
HAIRCLOTH
HORSEHAIR
HUCKABACK
LONGCLOTH
MARCELINE
MESSALINE
MOSS CREPE
ORGANZINE
PATCHWORK
PETERSHAM
SACKCLOTH
SAIL CLOTH

9–continued

SATINETTE
SHARKSKIN
SHEEPSKIN
SNAKESKIN
STOCKINET
SWANSDOWN
TARPAULIN
TOWELLING
TRICOTINE
VELVETEEN
WORCESTER

10

ABBOT CLOTH
AIDA CANVAS
ANGOLA YARN
AUSTINIZED
BALBRIGGAN
BARLEYCORN
BAUM MARTEN
BEAVERETTE
BEAVERTEEN
BOOK MUSLIN
BOUCLÉ YARN
BROADCLOTH
BROAD GOODS
CADET CLOTH
CAMBRESINE
CHINO CLOTH
CIRCASSIAN
CONGO CLOTH
CREPE LISSE
DRESS LINEN
GRASS CLOTH
HOP SACKING
HORSECLOTH
IRISH LINEN
MARSEILLES
MOUSSELINE
PEAU DE SOIE
PIECE GOODS
PILOT CLOTH
SEERSUCKER
SUEDE CLOTH
TERRY CLOTH
TOILINETTE
WINCEYETTE

11

ABRADED YARN
AERATED YARN
ALBERT CREPE
ARABIAN LACE
ARMURE-LAINE
BABY FLANNEL
BAG SHEETING
BANDLE LINEN
BASKET CLOTH
BATH COATING
BEDFORD CORD
BOMBER CLOTH
BRUSHED WOOL

11–continued

CANTON CREPE
CANTON LINEN
CHAMOISETTE
CHEESECLOTH
CHESS CANVAS
CHINA COTTON
CLAY WORSTED
COTTON CREPE
DACCA MUSLIN
DIAPER CLOTH
DOTTED SWISS
DRAP DE BERRY
DREADNOUGHT
DRUID'S CLOTH
DU PONT RAYON
ESKIMO CLOTH
EVERLASTING
FLANNELETTE
HARRIS TWEED
IRISH POPLIN
LEATHERETTE
MARQUISETTE
NAPA LEATHER
NUN'S VEILING
OVERCOATING
PANNE VELVET
POODLE CLOTH
POULT-DE-SOIE
SCOTCH PLAID
SPONGE CLOTH
TOILE DE JOUY
WAFFLE CLOTH

12

ACETATE RAYON
BALLOON CLOTH
BERLIN CANVAS
BOLIVIA CLOTH
BOLTING CLOTH
BRILLIANTINE
BROWN HOLLAND
BRUSHED RAYON
BUTCHER LINEN
CARACUL CLOTH
CAVALRY TWILL
CONVENT CLOTH
COTTON VELVET
CRINKLE CLOTH
CROISÉ VELVET
DENMARK SATIN
DOUBLE DAMASK
DRESS FLANNEL
ELEMENT CLOTH
EMPRESS CLOTH
GLAZED CHINTZ
MUTATION MINK
SHETLAND WOOL
SLIPPER SATIN
SUMMER ERMINE
VISCOSE RAYON
WELSH FLANNEL

13
AIRPLANE CLOTH
AMERICAN CLOTH
ARMURE-SATINÉE
BRITTANY CLOTH
CANTON FLANNEL
CARDINAL CLOTH
CASEMENT CLOTH
CLOISTER CLOTH
COSTUME VELVET
COTTON FLANNEL
COTTON SUITING
COTTON WORSTED
CRUSHED VELVET
DIAGONAL CLOTH
DIAPER FLANNEL
EGYPTIAN CLOTH

13—continued
END-TO-END CLOTH
LINSEY-WOOLSEY
PATENT LEATHER
RUSSIA LEATHER

14
ALGERIAN STRIPE
AMERICAN COTTON
ARGENTINE CLOTH
BANDOLIER CLOTH
BARONETTE SATIN
BROADTAIL CLOTH
CORKSCREW TWILL
EGYPTIAN COTTON
ELECTORAL CLOTH
FRUIT OF THE LOOM

14—continued
HONEYCOMB CLOTH
JACQUARD FABRIC
SHEPHERD'S PLAID

15
ABSORBENT
  COTTON
ADMIRALITY CLOTH
CACHEMIRE DE SOIE
CAMEL'S HAIR
  CLOTH
EMBROIDERY LINEN
OSTRICH FEATHERS
PARACHUTE FABRIC
SEA-ISLAND COTTON
SHIRTING FLANNEL

15—continued
TATTERSALL CHECK
TATTERSALL PLAID
TROPICAL SUITING

16
CANDLEWICK
  FABRIC
CONSTITUTION
  CORD
MERCERIZED
  COTTON
TURKISH
  TOWELLING

17
CROSS-STITCH
  CANVAS

FOOD AND DRINK

COOKERY TERMS

4
BARD
BEAT
BLEU (AU)
BOIL
BONE
CHOP
COAT
HANG
HASH
LARD
PIPE
RARE
TOSS

5
BASTE
BERNY
BLANC (À)
BLANC (AU)
BROIL
BROWN
BRULÉ
CARVE
CHILL
CROWN
DAUBE
DRAIN
DRESS
GLAZE
GRILL
KNEAD
MELBA
PLUCK
POACH
POINT (À)
PROVE
PURÉE

5–continued
REINE (À LA)
ROAST
RUB IN
SAUTÉ
SCALD
STEAM
SWEAT
TRUSS

6
AURORE
BRAISE
CONFIT
CRÉOLE (À LA)
DECANT
DESALT
DIABLE (À LA)
FILLET
FONDUE
GRATIN
GREASE
MAISON
MIGNON
NATURE
REDUCE
SIMMER
ZEPHYR

7
AL DENTE
ARRÊTER
BLANCHE
BLONDIR
CHEMISE (EN)
COLBERT
CROUTON
DEGLAZE

7–continued
EMINCER
FLAMBER
GRECQUE (À LA)
MARENGO
MÉDICIS
NIÇOISE (À LA)
REFRESH
SUPRÊME
TARTARE (À LA)

8
ALLONGER
ANGLAISE (À L')
APPAREIL
ASSATION
BARBECUE
BELLEVUE (EN)
BRETONNE (À LA)
CATALANE (À LA)
CHAMBORD
CHASSEUR
CHEMISER
CRUDITÉS
DAUPHINE (À LA)
DEVILLED
DUCHESSE (À LA)
EMULSION
ESCALOPE
FLAMANDE (À LA)
INFUSION
JULIENNE
MACERATE
MARINATE
MEUNIÈRE (À LA)
PISTACHE
POT-ROAST
SURPRISE (EN)

9
ACIDULATE
BAKE BLIND
CANELLING
DETAILLER
DIEPPOISE (À LA)
ESPAGNOLE (À L')
FRICASSÉE
KNOCK BACK
LIÉGEOISE (À LA)
LYONNAISE (À LA)
MARINIÈRE (À LA)
MEDALLION
MILANAISE (À LA)

10
ANTILLAISE (À L')
BALLOTTINE
BLANQUETTE
BONNE FEMME
BORDELAISE (À LA)
BOULANGÈRE (À LA)
CHAUD-FROID
DIJONNAISE (À LA)
FLORENTINE (À LA)
PROVENÇALE (À LA)

11
BELLE-HÉLÈNE
BOURGUIGNON
CHARCUTERIE
DAUPHINOISE (À LA)
HOLLANDAISE (À LA)

13
BOURGUIGNONNE
 (À LA)
CLARIFICATION
DEEP-FAT FRYING

KITCHEN UTENSILS AND TABLEWARE

3
CUP
HOB
JAR
JUG
LID

3–continued
MUG
PAN
POT
TIN
WOK

4
BOWL
DISH
EWER
FORK

4–continued
MILL
RACK
SPIT
TRAY

5
BAHUT
BASIN
BOARD
CHOPE
CHURN
FLUTE
GRILL
KNIFE
LADLE
MIXER
MOULD
PELLE
PLATE
PRESS
RUSSE
SIEVE
SPOON
STEEL
STRAW
TONGS
WHISK

6
BASKET
BUCKET
CARAFE
CLOCHE
COOLER
CRIBLE
DIABLE
EGG CUP
FUNNEL
GOBLET
GRADIN
GRATER
KETTLE
MINCER
MORTAR
MUSLIN
PESTLE
PICHET
PITTER
POÊLON
SAUCER
SHAKER
SHEARS
SIPHON
SKEWER

6—continued
STRING
TAJINE
TOUPIN
TUREEN

7
ALEMBIC
ATTELET
BLENDER
BROILER
CAISSES
CHINOIS
CHIP PAN
CHOPPER
COCOTTE
DRAINER
DREDGER
ÉCUELLE
GRINDER
MARMITE
PITCHER
RAMEKIN
RONDEAU
SALT BOX
SAMOVAR
SKILLET
SKIMMER
SPATULA
SYRINGE
TÂTE-VIN
TOASTER

8
CAQUELON
CAULDRON
COLANDER
CRÊPE PAN
CROCKERY
DAUBIÈRE
EGG TIMER
FLAN RING
HOTPLATE
MAZAGRAN
MOUVETTE
SAUCEPAN
SAUTÉ PAN
SCISSORS
STOCKPOT

8—continued
STRAINER
TART RING
TASTE-VIN
TRENCHER

9
ALCARRAZA
AUTOCLAVE
BAIN-MARIE
BAKING TIN
CAFETIÈRE
CASSEROLE
COMPOTIER
CORKSCREW
CRUMB TRAY
DÉCOUPOIR
FISH SLICE
FRYING-PAN
KILNER JAR
MANDOLINE
MIJOTEUSE
PASTRY BAG
PIPING BAG
RING MOULD
SALAD BOWL
SAUCEBOAT
SHARPENER
STEAK BATT
TISANIÈRE
TOURTIÈRE

10
APPLE-CORER
CAISSETTES
CASSOLETTE
CHOPSTICKS
CRUET STAND
DIPPING PIN
FISH KETTLE
LIQUIDISER
MUSTARD POT
PERCOLATOR
ROLLING PIN
ROTISSERIE
SALAMANDER
SALT CELLAR
SALTING TUB
SLOW COOKER

10—continued
STERILIZER
WAFFLE IRON

11
BAKING SHEET
BRAISING PAN
CANDISSOIRE
CHAFING DISH
CHEESECLOTH
COFFEE MAKER
DOUGH TROUGH
DRIPPING PAN
FRUIT STONER
GARGOULETTE
JAMBONNIÈRE
NUTCRACKERS
PASTRY BRUSH
PASTRY WHEEL
SERVING DISH
THERMOMETER
YOGURT-MAKER

12
CARVING KNIFE
DEEP-FAT FRYER
MEASURING JUG
PALETTE KNIFE
PASTRY CUTTER
TURBOT KETTLE

13
BUTCHER'S BLOCK
FOOD PROCESSOR
ICE-CREAM MAKER
KITCHEN SCALES
LARDING NEEDLE
PRESERVING JAR
SACCHAROMETER
VEGETABLE DISH

14
JUICE EXTRACTOR
KNEADING TROUGH
KNIFE SHARPENER
PRESSURE COOKER
TRUSSING NEEDLE

16
MEAT-CARVING
  TONGS

BAKING

3
BAP
BUN
COB
FAR
PIE

4
BABA
CHOU
FLAN
PAVÉ
RUSK

4—continued
TART

5
BAGEL
BÂTON
BREAD

5—continued
CRÊPE
FLÛTE
ICING
PLAIT
SABLÉ

5–continued
SCONE
STICK
TOAST

6
COOKIE
CORNET
ÉCLAIR
LEAVEN
MUFFIN
OUBLIE
ROCHER
TOURTE
WAFFLE

7
BAKLAVA
BANNOCK
BISCUIT
BLOOMER
BRIOCHE
CHAPATI
COTTAGE

7–continued
CRACKER
CRUMPET
FICELLE
FRITTER
GALETTE
PALMIER
PANCAKE
PRALINE
PRETZEL
STOLLEN
STRUDEL
TARTINE
TARTLET

8
AMANDINE
BAGUETTE
BARM CAKE
BÂTONNET
BISCOTTE
DOUGHNUT
DUCHESSE

8–continued
DUMPLING
EMPANADA
FROSTING
GRISSINI
SANDWICH
SPLIT TIN
TORTILLA
TURNOVER

9
ALLUMETTE
BARQUETTE
CROISSANT
FEUILLETÉ
FRIANDISE
KUGELHOPF
PETIT FOUR
VOL-AU-VENT

10
CRISPBREAD
FRANGIPANE
PÂTISSERIE

10–continued
PUFF PASTRY
RELIGIEUSE
SHORTBREAD
SPONGE CAKE

11
CHOUX PASTRY
LINZERTORTE
PETIT-BEURRE
PROFITEROLE

12
LANGUE-DE-CHAT
PUMPERNICKEL
SPONGE FINGER

13
GENOESE SPONGE

14
PAIN AU CHOCOLAT

15
SAVOY SPONGE
  CAKE

CEREALS

3
RYE

4
BRAN
CORN
OATS
RICE

5
MAIZE
SPELT
WHEAT

6
BARLEY
BULGUR

6–continued
MÉTEIL
MILLET

7
BURGHUL
FROMENT
SORGHUM

9
BUCKWHEAT

12
CRACKED WHEAT

CHEESES

4
BRIE (France)
CURD (CHEESE)
EDAM (Netherlands)
FETA (Greece)
TOME (France)

5
BANON (France)
BRICK (US)
CABOC (Scotland)
COMTÉ (France)
DANBO (Denmark)

5–continued
DERBY (England)
FETTA (Greece)
GOUDA (Netherlands)
HERVE (Belgium)
LEIGH (England)
MOLBO (Denmark)
MUROL (France)
NIOLO (Corsica)
TAMIÉ (France)

6
ASIAGO (Italy)

6–continued
BAGNES (Switzerland)
BRESSE (France)
CACHAT (France)
CANTAL (France)
CENDRÉ (France)
DUNLOP (Scotland)
FOURME (France)
GAPRON (France)
GÉROMÉ (France)
HALUMI (Greece)
HRAMSA (Scotland)

6–continued
LEIDEN (Netherlands)
MORVEN (Scotland)
OLIVET (France)
POURLY (France)
ROLLOT (France)
SALERS (France)
SAMSOË (Denmark)
SBRINZ (Switzerland)
SURATI (India)
TILSIT (Switzerland)
VENACO (Corsica)

7
BONDARD (France)
BRINZEN (Hungary)
BROCCIO (Corsica)
BROCCIU (Corsica)
BROUSSE (France)
BRUCCIU (Corsica)
BRYNDZA (Hungary)
CABÉCOU (France)
CHEDDAR (England)
CROWDIE (Scotland)
DAUPHIN (France)
DEMI-SEL (France)
FONTINA (Italy)
GAPERON (France)
GJETÖST (Norway)
GRUYÈRE (France; Switzerland)
JONCHÉE (France)
LANGRES (France)
LEVROUX (France)
LIMBURG (Belgium)
LIVAROT (France)
MACQUÉE (France)
MONT-D'OR (France)
MORBIER (France)
MÜNSTER (France)
NANTAIS (France)
PICODON (France)
QUARGEL (Austria)
RICOTTA (Italy)
SAPSAGO (Switzerland)
STILTON (England)
VENDÔME (France)

8
AUVERGNE (France)
AYRSHIRE (Scotland)
BEAUFORT (France)
BEL PAESE (Italy)
BERGKÄSE (Austria)
BOULETTE (France)
CHAOURCE (France)
CHESHIRE (England)
EDELPILZ (Germany)
EMMENTAL (Switzerland)
EPOISSES (France)
MANCHEGO (Spain)

8—continued
PARMESAN (Italy)
PECORINO (Italy)
PÉLARDON (France)
REMOUDOU (Belgium)
SCAMORZE (Italy)
TALEGGIO (Italy)
VACHERIN (Switzerland)
VALENÇAY (France)

9
APPENZELL (Switzerland)
BROODKAAS (Netherlands)
CAITHNESS (Scotland)
CAMBOZOLA (Italy; Germany)
CAMEMBERT (France)
CHABICHOU (France)
CHEVRETON (France)
EMMENTHAL (Switzerland)
EXCELSIOR (France)
GAMMELÖST (Norway)
LA BOUILLE (France)
LEICESTER (England)
LIMBURGER (Belgium)
MAROILLES (France)
MIMOLETTE (France)
PAVÉ D'AUGE (France)
PORT-SALUT (France)
PROVOLONE (Italy)
REBLOCHON (France)
ROQUEFORT (France)

10
CAERPHILLY (Wales)
DANISH BLUE (Denmark)
DOLCELATTE (Italy)
GLOUCESTER (England)
GORGONZOLA (Italy)
LANCASHIRE (England)
MOZZARELLA (Italy)
NEUFCHÂTEL (Switzerland)
PITHIVIERS (France)
RED WINDSOR (England)
SAINGORLON (France)
STRACCHINO (Italy)

11
CARRÉ DE L'EST (France)

11—continued
COEUR DE BRAY (France)
COULOMMIERS (France)
KATSHKAWALJ (Bulgaria)
PETIT-SUISSE (France)
PONT-L'ÉVÊQUE (France)
SAINTE-MAURE (France)
SAINT-PAULIN (France)
SCHABZIEGER (Switzerland)
TÊTE-DE-MOINE (Switzerland)
WEISSLACKER (Germany)
WENSLEYDALE (England)

12
CACIOCAVALLO (Italy)
RED LEICESTER (England)
SOUMAINTRAIN (France)

13
SAINT-NECTAIRE (France)
SELLES-SUR-CHER (France)

14
BRILLAT-SAVARIN (France)
FEUILLE DE DREUX (France)
LAGUIOLE-AUBRAC (France)
SAINT-FLORENTIN (France)
SAINT-MARCELLIN (France)
TRAPPISTENKÄSE (Germany)

15
BOUTON-DE-CULOTTE
  (France)

16
DOUBLE GLOUCESTER
  (England)

17
RIGOTTE DE PELUSSIN
  (France)

18
CHEVROTIN DES ARAVIS
  (France)
CROTTIN DE CHAVIGNOL
  (France)

19
POULIGNY-SAINT-PIERRE
  (France)

HERBS AND SPICES

3
BAY
RUE

4
BALM
DILL
MINT
SAGE

5
ANISE
BASIL
CHIVE
CLOVE
CUMIN
TANSY
THYME

6
BETONY
BORAGE
BURNET
CICELY
FENNEL
GARLIC
GINGER
LOVAGE

6—continued
PEPPER
SAVORY
SESAME
SORREL

7
BONESET
CARAWAY

7—continued
CHERVIL
COMFREY
DITTANY
MUSTARD
OREGANO
PAPRIKA
PARSLEY
PERILLA
PIMENTO
SAFFRON
SALSIFY

7—continued
TABASCO
VANILLA

8
ALLSPICE
ANGELICA
CAMOMILE
CARDAMOM
CARDAMON
CINNAMON
DROPWORT
FEVERFEW

8—continued
MARJORAM
ROSEMARY
TARRAGON
TURMERIC

9
CHAMOMILE
CORIANDER
FENUGREEK
SPEARMINT

10+
ASAFOETIDA
BLACK-EYED SUSAN
HERB OF GRACE
HORSERADISH
HOTTENTOT FIG
OYSTER PLANT
PEPPERMINT
POT MARIGOLD
VEGETABLE OYSTER

JOINTS OF MEAT

BEEF
BRISKET
CHUCK
FILLET STEAK
FLANK
FORE RIB
LEG
NECK
RIB
ROLLED RIBS

RUMP
SHIN
SILVERSIDE
SIRLOIN
T-BONE
TOPSIDE
UNDERCUT STEAK

PORK
BELLY

BLADE
HAND
HOCK
LEG
LEG FILLET
LOIN
SHOULDER
SPARE RIB
TENDERLOIN
TROTTER

LAMB
BEST END OF NECK
BREAST
CHUMP
CHUMP CHOPS
LEG
LOIN
SCRAG-END
SHOULDER

TYPES OF PASTA

4
PIPE

5
PENNE

6
BIGOLI
DITALI
RISONI
ROTINI

7
CAPELLI
FUSILLI
LASAGNE
LUMACHE

7—continued
NOODLES
RAVIOLI
ROTELLE

8
BUCATINI
DITALINI
DITALONI
FARFALLE
FETTUCCE
FIDELINI
GRAMIGNA
LINGUINE
MACARONI
RIGATONI

8—continued
STELLINE
TAGLIONI
TRENETTE

9
AGNOLOTTI
ANNELLINI
MANICOTTI
SPAGHETTI
TUFFOLONI

10
CANNELLONI
CONCHIGLIE
CRAVATTINE
FARFALLINE

10—continued
FETTUCCINE
TAGLIOLINI
TORTELLINI
TORTELLONI
VERMICELLI

11
CAPPELLETTI
ORECCHIETTE
PAPPARDELLE
SPAGHETTINI
SPAGHETTONE
TAGLIATELLE
TORTIGLIONI

12
PAGLIA E FIENO

DRINKS

WINES AND APERITIFS

4
FINO
HOCK
PORT

5
BYRRH
CRÉPY
FITOU
MÉDOC
MOSEL
RIOJA
TAVEL
TOKAY

6
ALSACE
BANDOL
BAROLO
BARSAC
BEAUNE
CAHORS
CASSIS
CHINON
CLARET
FRANGY
GRAVES
MÁLAGA
SAUMUR
SHERRY
VOLNAY

7
ALIGOTÉ
CAMPARI
CHABLIS
CHIANTI
CLAIRET
CRÉMANT
FALERNO

7–continued
GAILLAC
MADEIRA
MARGAUX
MARSALA
MARTINI
MOSELLE
ORVIETO
POMMARD
RETSINA
VOUVRAY

8
BORDEAUX
BROUILLY
DUBONNET
GIGONDAS
MERCUREY
MONTAGNY
MONTILLA
MUSCADET
PAUILLAC
RIESLING
ROSÉ WINE
SANCERRE
SANTENAY
VALENÇAY
VERMOUTH
VIN JAUNE

9
BOURGUEIL
CHAMPAGNE
CLAIRETTE
CÔTE-RÔTIE
HERMITAGE
LAMBRUSCO
MEURSAULT
MONTLOUIS

9–continued
SAUTERNES

10
BARBARESCO
BEAUJOLAIS
BULL'S BLOOD
MANZANILLA
MONTRACHET
RICHEBOURG
RIVESALTES
VINHO VERDE

11
ALOXE-CORTON
AMONTILLADO
MONBAZILLAC
POUILLY-FUMÉ
SAINT JULIEN
VIN DE PAILLE

12
CÔTES-DU-RHÔNE
ROMANÉE-CONTI
SAINT-EMILION
SAINT ESTEPHE
VALPOLICELLA
VOSNE-ROMANÉE

13
CHÂTEAU D'YQUEM
CHÂTEAU LAFITE
CHÂTEAU LATOUR
ENTRE-DEUX-MERS
POUILLY-FUISSÉ

14
CHÂTEAU MARGAUX
CÔTES-DU-
  VENTOUX
GEWÜRZTRAMINER

14–continued
LACRIMA CHRISTI

15
CÔTES-DE-
  PROVENCE
CÔTES-DU-VIVARAIS
CROZES-
  HERMITAGE
MOREY-SAINT-DENIS

16
CHAMBOLLE-
  MUSIGNY
CHÂTEAU
  HAUT-BRION
GEVREY-
  CHAMBERTIN
SAVIGNY-
  LÈS-BEAUNE

17
CORTON-
  CHARLEMAGNE
CÔTES-DU-
  ROUSSILLON
NUITS-SAINT-
  GEORGES

18
BLANQUETTE DE
  LIMOUX

19
CHASSAGNE-
  MONTRACHET

20+
CHÂTEAU MOUTON-
  ROTHSCHILD

COCKTAILS AND MIXED DRINKS

3
FIX
KIR
NOG

4
FIZZ
FLIP
GROG
RAKI
SOUR

5
JULEP
NEGUS
PUNCH
TODDY

6
BEADLE
BISHOP
GIMLET
POSSET

7
MARTINI
SANGRIA
SIDECAR
WALDORF

8
APPLE CAR
DAIQUIRI
GIN AND IT
GIN SLING
HIGHBALL

8–continued
NIGHTCAP
PINK LADY
WHIZ BANG

9
ALEXANDER
APPLEJACK
BEE'S KNEES
BUCK JONES
BUCKS FIZZ
COMMODORE

9–continued
MANHATTAN
MINT JULEP
MOONLIGHT
MOONSHINE
MULLED ALE
WHITE LADY

10
ANGEL'S KISS
ARCHBISHOP
BLACK MARIA
BLOODY MARY

10–continued
HORSE'S NECK
MERRY WIDOW
MULLED WINE
PINA COLADA
RUM COLLINS
TOM COLLINS

11
BEACHCOMBER
BLACK VELVET
FALLEN ANGEL
JOHN COLLINS

11–continued
WASSAIL BOWL

12
CHURCHWARDEN
ELEPHANT'S EAR
FINE AND DANDY
OLD-FASHIONED
WHITE GIN SOUR

13
CHAMPAGNE BUCK
CORPSE REVIVER

13–continued
KNICKERBOCKER
MAIDEN'S PRAYER
PLANTER'S PUNCH
PRAIRIE OYSTER

16
BETWEEN THE
  SHEETS
HARVEY
  WALLBANGER

BEERS AND BEVERAGES

3
ALE

4
MEAD
MILD

5
CIDER
KVASS
LAGER
PERRY
STOUT

6
BITTER
LAMBIC
SHANDY

8
GUINNESS
HYDROMEL

10
BARLEY BEER
BARLEY WINE

SPIRITS

3
GIN
RUM

4
ARAK
MARC
OUZO

5
CHOUM
VODKA

6
BOUKHA
BRANDY
CHICHA
COGNAC
GRAPPA
KIRSCH
MESCAL
METAXA
PASTIS
PERNOD
PULQUE
WHISKY

7
AKVAVIT
AQUAVIT
BACARDI
BOUKHRA
BOURBON
SCHNAPS
TEQUILA
WHISKEY

8
ARMAGNAC
CALVADOS

8–continued
FALERNUM
SCHNAPPS

9
SLIVOVITZ

10
RYE WHISKEY

11
AGUARDIENTE

LIQUEURS

4
SAKÉ
SAKI

5
ANISE
ANRAM

6
CASSIS
KÜMMEL
MÊLISS
QETSCH
SCUBAC
STREGA

7
ALCAMAS
ALLASCH
BAILEYS
CURAÇAO
ESCUBAC
RATAFIA
SAMBUCA

8
ABSINTHE
ADVOCAAT
ANISETTE
DRAMBUIE
PERSICOT
PRUNELLE

9
ARQUEBUSE
COINTREAU
FRAMBOISE
GUIGNOLET
MIRABELLE
TRIPLE SEC

10
BROU DE NOIX
CHARTREUSE
MARASCHINO

11
BENEDICTINE
TRAPPISTINE

12
CHERRY BRANDY
CRÈME DE CACAO
GRAND MARNIER

13
CRÈME DE MENTHE

15
SOUTHERN
  COMFORT

17
AMARETTO DI
  SARANNO

DRINKS

NON-ALCOHOLIC DRINKS

3
CHA (TEA)
TEA

4
CHAR (TEA)
COLA
MATÉ
SODA

5
LASSI
WATER

6
COFFEE
ORGEAT
TISANE

7
BEEF TEA

7–continued
DIABOLO
SELTZER

8
LEMONADE

9
GRENADINE
MILKSHAKE
ORANGEADE

10
GINGER BEER
TONIC WATER

12
MINERAL WATER

SPORT AND RECREATION

SPORTS

4
GOLF
JUDO
PATO
POLO

5
BOWLS
FIVES
KENDO
RALLY
RODEO

6
AIKIDO
BOULES
BOXING
HOCKEY
KARATE
KUNG FU
PELOTA
ROWING
SHINTY
SKIING
TENNIS

7
ANGLING
ARCHERY
BOWLING
CRICKET
CROQUET
CURLING
FENCING
HURLING
JUJITSU
KABADDI
KARTING

7–continued
NETBALL
RACKETS
SHOT PUT

8
BASEBALL
BIATHLON
CANOEING
COURSING
DRESSAGE
FALCONRY
GYMKHANA
HANDBALL
HURDLING
LACROSSE
LONG JUMP
MARATHON
PETANQUE
PING-PONG
ROUNDERS
SHOOTING
SPEEDWAY
SWIMMING
TUG OF WAR

9
ATHLETICS
BADMINTON
DECATHLON
ICE HOCKEY
MOTO-CROSS
POLE VAULT
SKYDIVING
TAE KWON-DO
WATER POLO
WRESTLING

10
BASKETBALL
DRAG RACING
FLAT RACING
FOXHUNTING
GYMNASTICS
ICE SKATING
REAL TENNIS
RUGBY UNION
TRIPLE JUMP
VOLLEYBALL

11
BEARBAITING
BLOOD SPORTS
BOBSLEDDING
BULLBAITING
DISCUS THROW
HAMMER THROW
HANG-GLIDING
HORSE RACING
HORSE TRAILS
MARTIAL ARTS
MOTOR RACING
PARACHUTING
PENTHATHLON
RUGBY LEAGUE
SEPAK TAKRAW
TABLE TENNIS
TOBOGGANING
WATER SKIING

12
BULLFIGHTING
CABER TOSSING
COCKFIGHTING
ETON WALL GAME

12–continued
JAVELIN THROW
ORIENTEERING
PIGEON RACING
POINT-TO-POINT
STEEPLECHASE

13
EQUESTRIANISM
HARNESS RACING
SKATEBOARDING
SQUASH RACKETS
WEIGHT LIFTING

14
FOOTBALL LEAGUE
MOUNTAINEERING
STOCK-CAR RACING

15
GREYHOUND
  RACING

16
AMERICAN
  FOOTBALL
MOTORCYCLE
  RACING

18
CLAY-PIGEON
  SHOOTING
FREESTYLE
  WRESTLING

19
ASSOCIATION
  FOOTBALL

GAMES

2
GO

4
BRAG
POOL
SNAP

5
BINGO
CAVES
CHESS
CRAPS
DARTS

5–continued
FIVES
POKER
RUMMY
SHOGI
SPOOF

5–continued
WHIST

6
CLUEDO
PAC-MAN
QUOITS

6–continued
TIPCAT

7
BEZIQUE
CANASTA
DOBBERS
MAHJONG
MARBLES
MATADOR
OLD MAID
PACHISI
PONTOON
SNOOKER
YAHTZEE

8
BACCARAT

8–continued
BIRD CAGE
CRIBBAGE
DADDLUMS
DOMINOES
DRAUGHTS
LIAR DICE
MONOPOLY
PATIENCE
ROULETTE
SCRABBLE
SKITTLES

9
AUNT SALLY
BILLIARDS
BLACKJACK

9–continued
POKER DICE
SNAKE-EYES
VINGT-ET-UN

10
BACKGAMMON
BAT AND TRAP
CASABLANCA
RUNNING OUT

11
CHEMIN DE FER
TIDDLYWINKS

12
BAR BILLIARDS
KNUR AND SPELL

12–continued
SHOVE HA'PENNY

13
HAPPY FAMILIES
SPACE INVADERS

14
CONTRACT BRIDGE
TRIVIAL PURSUIT

16
SNAKES AND
  LADDERS

20
DEVIL AMONG THE
  TAILORS

CARD GAMES

3
LOO
PAN
RUM

4
BRAG
JASS
KLOB
SNAP
SPIT
VINT

5
BINGO
BOURE
CINCH
COMET
DARDA
OMBRE
PEDRO
PITCH
POKER
POQUE
RUMMY
SAMBA
WHIST
YUKON

6
BOO-RAY
BOSTON
BRIDGE
CASINO
CHEMMY
ÉCARTÉ
EIGHTS
EUCHRE

6–continued
FAN-TAN
GAIGEL
GO FISH
JULEPE
MAU-MAU
PIQUET
POCHEN
POKINO
QUINZE
RED DOG
SEVENS
SMUDGE
TRUMPS
YABLON

7
AUTHORS
BELOTTE
BEZIQUE
BOLIVIA
CANASTA
COLONEL
COONCAN
OLD MAID
PONTOON
PRIMERA
PRIMERO
PRIMERO
SET-BACK
SEVEN-UP
SNOOKER
SOLOMON
SPINADO
TRIUMPH

8
ACE-DEUCE
CANFIELD
CONQUIAN
CRIBBAGE
GIN RUMMY
IMPERIAL
IRISH LOO
KLONDIKE
LAST CARD
LOW PITCH
NAPOLEON
OKLAHOMA
PATIENCE
PINOCHLE
ROCKAWAY
ROLLOVER
SIXTY SIX
SLAPJACK

9
BLACKJACK
DRAW POKER
FORTY FIVE
IN-BETWEEN
OPEN POKER
SOLITAIRE
SOLO WHIST
SPOIL FIVE
STUD POKER
THIRTY ONE
WILD JACKS

10
DRAW CASINO
JOKER PITCH
PANGUINGUE

10–continued
PISHE PASHA
PUT AND TAKE
TABLANETTE
THIRTY FIVE
WELLINGTON

11
BOSTON WHIST
BRIDGE WHIST
CATCH THE TEN
CHEMIN DE FER
CLOSED POKER
CRAZY EIGHTS
DOUBLE RUMMY
FIVE CARD LOO
FIVE HUNDRED
GERMAN WHIST
HUMBUG WHIST
KLABBERJASS
RACING DEMON
ROYAL CASINO
RUSSIAN BANK
SCOTCH WHIST
SLIPPERY SAM
SPADE CASINO

12
AUCTION PITCH
DOMINO FAN-TAN
JACK CHANGE IT
SWEDISH RUMMY

13
AUCTION BRIDGE
CONCENTRATION
OLD MAN'S BUNDLE
SIX SPOT RED DOG

13–continued
STRAIGHT POKER

14
BACCARET BANQUE
CHINESE BEZIQUE
CONTRACT BRIDGE
FRENCH PINOCHLE
FROGS IN THE
  POND
RACEHORSE PITCH
RUBICON BEZIQUE

14–continued
SIX DECK BEZIQUE
SPITE AND MALICE

15
AROUND THE
  CORNER
AUCTION PINOCHLE
BANKER AND
  BROKER
HOLLYWOOD
  EIGHTS

16
CONTINENTAL
  RUMMY
DOUBLE DUMMY
  WHIST
EIGHT DECK
  BEZIQUE
TRENTE ET
  QUARANTE
TRUMP HUMBUG
  WHIST

17+
BEAT YOUR
  NEIGHBOUR
BEGGAR-MY-
  NEIGHBOUR
BEGGAR-YOUR-
  NEIGHBOUR
FIVE HUNDRED
  BEZIQUE
ROUND THE
  CORNER RUMMY

BRIDGE TERMS

3
BID
FIT

4
ACOL
CALL
DEAL
GAME
LEAD
RUFF
VOID

5
ALERT
DUMMY
ENTRY
GUARD
REBID
TABLE

6
DOUBLE
GERBER
HONOUR
LENGTH
MISFIT
REVOKE
RUBBER
SYSTEM
TENACE
TIMING

7
AUCTION

7–continued
CONTROL
CUE BIDS
DISCARD
FINESSE
JUMP BID
PARTNER
SIGNALS
STAYMAN
STOPPER

8
CONTRACT
DECLARER
DIRECTOR
LIMIT BID
MCKENNEY
OVERCALL
OVER RUFF
REDOUBLE
RESPONSE
SIDE SUIT

9
BLACKWOOD
DOUBLETON
GRAND SLAM
LAVINTHAL
MAJOR SUIT
MINOR SUIT
OVER TRICK
PART SCORE
SACRIFICE
SINGLETON

9–continued
SMALL SLAM
SOLID SUIT

10
CONVENTION
FORCING BID
LINE OF PLAY
REVERSE BID
SYSTEM CARD
UNBALANCED
UNDER TRICK
VULNERABLE

11
DOUBLE DUMMY
MATCH POINTS
OPENING LEAD
PARTNERSHIP
THIRD IN HAND

12
BALANCED HAND
BIDDABLE SUIT
BIDDING SPACE
DISTRIBUTION
FOURTH IN HAND
INTERVENTION
JUMP OVERCALL
PLAYING TRICK
SEMI-BALANCED

13
COMMUNICATION
NOT VULNERABLE

13–continued
PRE-EMPTIVE BID
TAKE OUT DOUBLE
TOUCHING SUITS
TWO-SUITED HAND

14
COMPETITIVE BID
DESTRUCTIVE BID
GRAND SLAM
  FORCE
REBIDDABLE SUIT

15
CONSTRUCTIVE BID
DUPLICATE BRIDGE
INVITATIONAL BID
PLAYING STRENGTH
THREE-SUITED
  HAND

16+
CONTESTED
  AUCTION
MIRROR
  DISTRIBUTION
NEGATIVE
  RESPONSE
PHANTOM
  SACRIFICE
POSITIVE
  RESPONSE
SINGLE SUITED
  HAND

POKER HANDS

ROYAL FLUSH	FULL HOUSE	THREE OF A KIND
STRAIGHT FLUSH	FLUSH	TWO PAIRS
FOUR OF A KIND	STRAIGHT	ONE PAIR

DANCES

3	5–continued	7–continued	8	9–continued
DOG	SIBYL	ARNAOUT	ALEGRIAS	PASO DOBLE
GIG	STOMP	BABORÁK	Ā MOLESON	PASSEPIED
JIG	TANGO	BALL PLA	AURRESKU	POLONAISE
OLE	TRATA	BAMBUCO	BALZTANZ	QUADRILLE
	TWIST	BANJARA	BULL-FOOT	QUICKSTEP
4	VELAL	BATUQUE	CACHUCHA	RENNINGEN
AHIR	WALTZ	BHARANG	CAKEWALK	ROCK 'N' ROLL
BUMP		BOURRÉE	CANACUAS	SARABANDE
CANA	**6**	CANARIE	CANDIOTE	SATECKOVA
HAKA	ABUANG	CANARIO	CHARRADA	TAMBORITO
HORA	AMENER	CINQ PAS	COURANTE	TROYANATS
JIVE	ATINGA	CSARDAS	FANDANGO	
JOTA	BATUTA	FORLANA	GALLIARD	**10**
POGO	BOLERO	FOX-TROT	GYMNASKA	ATNUMOKITA
SHAG	BOOGIE	FURIANT	HABANERA	BANDLTANTZ
VIRA	CALATA	FURLANA	HAND JIVE	BATON DANCE
	CANARY	GAVOTTE	HORNPIPE	BERGERETTA
5	CAN-CAN	GERANOS	HUAPANGO	CHANIOTIKO
BARIS	CAROLE	GLOCSEN	HUELGAS	CHARLESTON
BULBA	CEBELL	GOMBEYS	MAILEHEN	ESPRINGALE
CAROL	CHA CHA	GONDHAL	MOHOBELO	FACKELTANZ
CONGA	DJOGED	GOSHIKI	MOONWALK	FARANDOULO
CUECA	EIXIDA	HIMINAU	MUTCHICO	FURRY DANCE
DANSA	GANGAR	JABADAO	OXDANSEN	GAY GORDONS
DEBKA	GIENYS	LAMENTO	PERICOTE	HOKEY-COKEY
GAVOT	HUSTLE	LANCERS	RIGAUDON	KYNDELDANS
GIGUE	JACARA	LANDLER	RUTUBURI	LAUTERBACH
GOPAK	JARABE	LLORONA	TSAMIKOS	LOCOMOTION
HALOA	JARANA	MADISON		RUNNING SET
HOPAK	KAGURA	MAYPOLE	**9**	STRATHSPEY
KUMMI	KALELA	MAZURKA	BAGUETTES	STRIP TEASE
L'AG-YA	MINUET	MEASURE	BAILECITO	SURUVAKARY
LIMBO	PAVANE	MILONGA	BARN DANCE	TARANTELLA
LOURE	PESSAH	MUNEIRA	BOULANGER	TRENCHMORE
MAMBO	POLSKA	PASILLO	CARDADORA	TURKEY TROT
NAZUN	SHIMMY	PERICON	CLOG DANCE	
NUMBA	TIRANA	PLANXTY	COTILLION	**11**
OKINA	VALETA	PURPURI	ECOSSAISE	BABORASCHKA
POLKA	VELETA	SARDANA	FARANDOLE	BLACKBOTTOM
RUEDA	YUMARI	SATACEK	GALLEGADA	DANSURINGUR
RUMBA		SIKINIK	HAJDUTÂNC	DITHYRAMBOS
SALSA	**7**	TANDAVA	HORN DANCE	FLORAL DANCE
SAMBA	ABRASAX	TANTARA	JITTERBUG	GHARBA
SARBA	ABRAXAS	TRAIPSE	KOLOMEJKA	DANCE
SHAKE	AHIDOUS	WAKAMBA	MISTLETOE	LAMBETH WALK
SIBEL	APARIMA		MOKOROTLO	LINE DANCING

11—continued
MORRIS DANCE
PALAIS GLIDE
PAMPERRUQUE
ROCK AND ROLL
SCHOTTISCHE
SQUARE DANCE
TEWRDANNCKH

12
BREAKDANCING

12—continued
CREUX DE VERVI
DAMHSA NAM BOC
DANSE MACABRE
FUNKY CHICKEN
GREEN GARTERS
REEL O'TULLOCH

13
EIGHTSOME REEL
GHILLIE CALLUM

13—continued
HIGHLAND FLING

14
BABBITY BOWSTER
COUNTRY BUMPKIN
MILKMAIDS' DANCE
STRIP THE WILLOW

15
MILITARY TWO-STEP

15—continued
SELLINGER'S
  ROUND

17
HASTE TO THE
  WEDDING

18
SIR ROGER DE
  COVERLEY

HOBBIES AND CRAFTS

3
DIY

5
BATIK
BINGO

6
BONSAI
SEWING

7
COLLAGE
COOKERY
CROCHET
KEEP FIT
MACRAMÉ
MOSAICS
ORIGAMI
POTTERY
READING
TATTING
TOPIARY
WEAVING

8
AEROBICS
APPLIQUÉ
BASKETRY
CANEWORK

8—continued
FRETWORK
KNITTING
LAPIDARY
PAINTING
QUILTING
SPINNING
TAPESTRY
WOODWORK

9
ASTROLOGY
ASTRONOMY
DÉCOUPAGE
GARDENING
GENEALOGY
MARQUETRY
PALMISTRY
PATCHWORK
PHILATELY
RUG MAKING

10
BEE-KEEPING
BEER MAKING
CROSSWORDS
EMBROIDERY
ENAMELLING
KITE FLYING

10—continued
LACE MAKING
UPHOLSTERY
WINE MAKING

11
ARCHAEOLOGY
BARK RUBBING
BOOK BINDING
CALLIGRAPHY
DRESS MAKING
HANG GLIDING
LEPIDOPTERY
MODEL MAKING
PHOTOGRAPHY
STENCILLING
VINTAGE CARS

12
BEACH COMBING
BIRD WATCHING
BRASS RUBBING
CANDLE-MAKING
FLOWER DRYING
TROPICAL FISH

13
FOSSIL HUNTING
JIG-SAW PUZZLES
MODEL RAILWAYS

13—continued
TRAIN SPOTTING

14
BADGER WATCHING
CAKE DECORATING
COIN COLLECTING
FLOWER PRESSING
GLASS ENGRAVING
PIGEON FANCYING

15
FLOWER
  ARRANGING
LAMPSHADE
  MAKING
SHELL COLLECTING
STAMP COLLECTING

16
AMATEUR
  DRAMATICS
AUTOGRAPH
  HUNTING

19
BUTTERFLY
  COLLECTING

GAMES POSITIONS

3
END

4
POST
SLIP
WING

5
GUARD
GULLY
MID-ON
PIVOT

6
ATTACK

6—continued
BATTER
BOWLER
CENTER
CENTRE
LONG ON
MID-OFF

6—continued
SAFETY
TACKLE

7
BATSMAN
CATCHER
DEFENCE

7—continued
DEFENSE
FIELDER
FORWARD
LEG SLIP
LONG LEG
LONG OFF

7—continued
OFFENSE
PITCHER
STRIKER
SWEEPER

8
FULLBACK
HALFBACK
LEFT BACK
LEFT HALF
LEFT WING
MIDFIELD
SPLIT END
TAILBACK
THIRD MAN
TIGHT END
WINGBACK

9
INFIELDER
MID WICKET
NOSE GUARD
NUMBER ONE
NUMBER TWO

9—continued
RIGHT BACK
RIGHT HALF
RIGHT WING
SCRUM HALF
SHORTSTOP
SQUARE LEG

10
CENTRE BACK
CENTRE HALF
CORNERBACK
COVER POINT
EXTRA COVER
GOAL ATTACK
GOALKEEPER
INSIDE LEFT
LINEBACKER
NUMBER FOUR
OUTFIELDER
SILLY MID-ON
WING ATTACK

11
DEEP FINE LEG

11—continued
FLANKER BACK
GOAL DEFENCE
GOAL SHOOTER
INSIDE RIGHT
LEFT FIELDER
LEFT FORWARD
NUMBER THREE
OUTSIDE LEFT
QUARTERBACK
RUNNING BACK
SILLY MID-OFF
WING DEFENCE
WING FORWARD

12
FIRST BASEMAN
OUTSIDE RIGHT
LEFT-WING BACK
RIGHT FIELDER
RIGHT FORWARD
SHORT FINE LEG
STAND OFF HALF
THIRD BASEMAN
THREE-QUARTER

12—continued
WICKETKEEPER
WIDE RECEIVER

13
CENTRE FIELDER
CENTRE FORWARD
POPPING CREASE
RIGHT-WING BACK
SECOND BASEMAN

14
LEFT-CENTRE BACK
LEFT DEFENSEMAN
SHORT SQUARE LEG

15+
FORWARD SHORT
 LEG
LEFT-WING
 FORWARD
RIGHT-CENTRE
 BACK
RIGHT
 DEFENSEMAN
RIGHT-WING
 FORWARD

STADIUMS AND VENUES

AINTREE (horse racing)
ANAHEIM STADIUM, CALIFORNIA (baseball)
ASCOT (horse racing)
AZTECA STADIUM, MEXICO CITY (olympics, football)
BELFRY, THE (golf)
BELMONT PARK, LONG ISLAND (horse racing)
BERNABAU STADIUM, MADRID (football)
BIG FOUR CURLING RINK (curling)
BRANDS HATCH (motor racing)
BROOKLANDS (motor racing)
CAESAR'S PALACE, LAS VEGAS (boxing)
CARDIFF ARMS PARK (rugby union)
CENTRAL STADIUM, KIEV (football)
CLEVELAND MUNICIPAL STADIUM (baseball)
CORPORATION STADIUM, CALICUR (cricket)
CROKE PARK, DUBLIN (Gaelic football, hurling)
CRUCIBAL, SHEFFIELD (snooker)
CRYSTAL PALACE (athletics)
DAYTONA INTERNATIONAL SPEEDWAY (motor racing, motor cycling)
EDEN GARDENS, CALCUTTA (cricket)
EDGBASTON (cricket)
EPSOM DOWNS (horse racing)
FORUM, THE (gymnastics)
FRANCORCHAMPS, BELGIUM (motor racing)
HAMPDEN PARK, GLASGOW (football)
HEADINGLEY (cricket)
HEYSEL STADIUM, BRUSSELS (football)

LAHORE (cricket)
LANDSDOWNE ROAD, BELFAST (rugby union)
LENIN STADIUM, MOSCOW (football)
LORDS CRICKET GROUND (cricket)
LOUISIANA SUPERDOME (most sports)
MARACANA STADIUM, BRAZIL (football)
MEADOWBANK (athletics)
MEMORIAL COLISEUM, LOS ANGELES (most sports)
MOOR PARK, RICKMANSWORTH (golf)
MUNICH OLYMPIC STADIUM (athletics, football)
MURRAYFIELD (rugby union)
NEWMARKET (horse racing)
NOU CAMP, BARCELONA (football)
ODSAL STADIUM, BRADFORD (rugby league)
OLD TRAFFORD (cricket)
OVAL, THE (cricket)
ST ANDREWS (golf)
SENAYAN MAIN STADIUM, JAKARTA (cricket)
SHANGHAI STADIUM (gymnastics)
SILVERSTONE (motor racing)
STAHOV STADIUM, PRAGUE (gymnastics)
TEXAS STADIUM (most sports)
TWICKENHAM (rugby union)
WEMBLEY CONFERENCE CENTRE (darts)
WEMBLEY STADIUM (football, rugby)
WHITE CITY (greyhound racing)
WIMBLEDON (tennis)
WINDSOR PARK, BELFAST (football)

TROPHIES, EVENTS, AND AWARDS

ADMIRAL'S CUP (sailing)
AFRICAN NATIONS CUP (football)
AIR CANADA SILVER BROOM (curling)
ALL-IRELAND CHAMPIONSHIP (Gaelic football)
ALL-IRELAND CHAMPIONSHIPS (hurling)
ALPINE CHAMPIONSHIPS (skiing)
AMERICA'S CUP (sailing)
ASHES (cricket)
BADMINTON THREE DAY EVENT (equestrian)
BBC SPORTS PERSONALITY OF THE YEAR (all-round)
BENSON & HEDGES CUP (cricket)
BOAT RACE (rowing)
BRITISH OPEN CHAMPIONSHIP (golf)
BRONZE MEDAL (most sports)
CAMANACHD ASSOCIATION CHALLENGE CUP (shinty)
CHELTENHAM GOLD CUP (horse racing)
CLASSICS (horse racing)
COMMONWEALTH GAMES (athletics)
CORNHILL TEST (cricket)
DAVIS CUP (tennis)
DAYTONA 500 (motor racing)
DECATHLON (athletics)
DERBY (horse racing)
EMBASSY WORLD INDOOR BOWLS CROWN (bowls)
EMBASSY WORLD PROFESSIONAL SNOOKER CHAMPIONSHIP (snooker)
ENGLISH GREYHOUND DERBY (greyhound racing)
EUROPEAN CHAMPION CLUBS CUP (football)
EUROPEAN CHAMPIONS CUP (basketball)
EUROPEAN CHAMPIONSHIPS (football)
EUROPEAN CUP WINNERS' CUP (football)
EUROPEAN FOOTBALLER OF THE YEAR (football)
EUROPEAN SUPER CUP (football)
FEDERATION CUP (tennis)
FOOTBALL ASSOCIATION CHALLENGE CUP (football)

FOOTBALL ASSOCIATION CHARITY SHIELD (football)
FOOTBALL LEAGUE CHAMPIONSHIP (football)
FOOTBALL LEAGUE CUP (football)
FULL CAP (football, rugby)
FWA FOOTBALLER OF THE YEAR (football)
GILLETTE CUP (cricket)
GOLDEN BOOT AWARD (football)
GOLD MEDAL (most sports)
GORDEN INTERNATIONAL MEDAL (curling)
GRAND NATIONAL (greyhound racing)
GRAND NATIONAL STEEPLECHASE (horse racing)
GRAND PRIX (motor racing)
GUINNESS TROPHY (tiddlywinks)
HARMSWORTH TROPHY (power boat racing)
HENLEY REGATTA (rowing)
HENRI DELANEY TROPHY (football)
HIGHLAND GAMES
ICY SMITH CUP (ice hockey)
INDIANAPOLIS 500 (motor racing)
INTERNATIONAL CHAMPIONSHIP (bowls)
INTERNATIONAL CROSS-COUNTRY CHAMPIONSHIP (athletics)
INTERNATIONAL INTER-CITY INDUSTRIAL FAIRS CUP (football)
IROQUOIS CUP (lacrosse)
ISLE OF MAN TT (motorcycle racing)
JOHN PLAYER CUP (rugby league)
JOHN PLAYER LEAGUE (cricket)
JULES RIMET TROPHY (football)
KING GEORGE V GOLD CUP (equestrian)
KINNAIRD CUP (fives)
LE MANS 24 HOUR (motor racing)
LITTLEWOODS CHALLENGE CUP (football)
LOMBARD RALLY (motor racing)
LONSDALE BELT (boxing)

MACROBERTSON INTERNATIONAL SHIELD (croquet)
MAN OF THE MATCH (football)
MARATHON (athletics)
MIDDLESEX SEVENS (rugby union)
MILK CUP (football)
MILK RACE (cycling)
MONTE CARLO RALLY (motor racing)
MOST VALUABLE PLAYER (American football)
NATIONAL ANGLING CHAMPIONSHIP (horse racing)
NATIONAL HUNT JOCKEY CHAMPIONSHIP (horse racing)
NATIONAL WESTMINSTER BANK TROPHY (cricket)
NORDIC CHAMPIONSHIPS (skiing)
OAKS (horse racing)
OLYMPIC GAMES (most sports)
ONE THOUSAND GUINEAS (horse racing)
OPEN CROQUET CHAMPIONSHIP (croquet)
OXFORD BLUE (most sports)
PALIO
PENTATHLON
PFA FOOTBALLER OF THE YEAR (football)
PRUDENTIAL WORLD CUP (cricket)
PYONGYANG
QUEEN ELIZABETH II CUP (equestrian)
RAC TOURIST TROPHY (motor racing)
ROSE BOWL (American football)
ROYAL HUNT CUP (horse racing)
RUGBY LEAGUE CHALLENGE CUP (rugby league)
RUNNERS-UP MEDAL (most sports)
RYDER CUP (golf)
SCOTTISH FOOTBALL ASSOCIATION CUP (football)
SILVER MEDAL (most sports)
SIMOD CUP (football)
SKOL CUP (football)
SOUTH AMERICAN CHAMPIONSHIP (football)
STANLEY CUP (ice hockey)
ST LEGER (horse racing)

277

FIRST-CLASS CRICKETING COUNTIES

STRATHCONA CUP (curling)
SUPER BOWL (American football)
SUPER CUP (handball)
SWAYTHLING CUP (table tennis)
THOMAS CUP (badminton)
TOUR DE FRANCE (cycling)
TRIPLE CROWN (rugby union)
TWO THOUSAND GUINEAS (horse racing)

UBER CUP (badminton)
U.E.F.A. CUP (Union of European Football Associations) (football)
UNIROYAL WORLD JUNIOR CHAMPIONSHIPS (curling)
WALKER CUP (golf)
WIGHTMAN CUP (sailing)
WIMBLEDON (tennis)
WINGFIELD SKULLS (rowing)

WINNERS MEDAL (most sports)
WOODEN SPOON! (most sports)
WORLD CLUB CHAMPION-SHIP (football)
WORLD MASTERS CHAMPIONSHIPS (darts)
WORLD SERIES (baseball)
YELLOW JERSEY (cycling)

FIRST-CLASS CRICKETING COUNTIES

DERBYSHIRE
DURHAM
ESSEX
GLAMORGAN
GLOUCESTERSHIRE

HAMPSHIRE
KENT
LANCASHIRE
LEICESTERSHIRE
MIDDLESEX

NORTHAMPTON-SHIRE
NOTTINGHAMSHIRE
SOMERSET
SURREY

SUSSEX
WARWICKSHIRE
WORCESTERSHIRE
YORKSHIRE

CRICKETING TERMS AND EXPRESSIONS

3
BAT
BYE
CUT
L.B.W.
RUN
TON

4
BAIL
DUCK
HOOK
OVER
WIDE

5
BOSIE
COVER
GULLY
MID-ON
POINT
SWEEP

6
BEAMER
BOWLED
BOWLER
CAUGHT
CREASE
GOOGLY
HOWZAT!

6–continued
LEG BYE
LONG ON
MAIDEN
MID-OFF
NO-BALL
RUN OUT
SCORER
SEAMER
UMPIRE
WICKET
YORKER

7
BATSMAN
BOUNCER
CENTURY
COW-SHOT
FIELDER
FINE LEG
FLIPPER
INNINGS
LATE CUT
LEG SLIP
LEG SPIN
LONG HOP
LONG LEG
LONG OFF
OFF SPIN
SHOOTER

7–continued
STRIKER
STUMPED

8
BOUNDARY
CHINAMAN
HAT-TRICK
HOW'S THAT!
LONGSTOP
SHORT LEG
THE SLIPS
THIRD MAN

9
BATSWOMAN
HIT WICKET
IN-SWINGER
LEG GLANCE
MID-WICKET
OVERTHROW
SQUARE CUT
SQUARE LEG
STICKY DOG
TEST MATCH
THE COVERS

10
ALL-ROUNDER
GOLDEN DUCK
NON-STRIKER

10–continued
OUT-SWINGER
SIGHT-SCREEN
SILLY MID-OFF
SILLY MID-ON
SILLY POINT
TOP-SPINNER
TWELFTH MAN

11
DAISY-CUTTER

12
RETURN CREASE
REVERSE SWEEP
STICKY WICKET
STONEWALLING
WICKETKEEPER

13
BATTING CREASE
DEEP SQUARE LEG
POPPING CREASE

14+
BODY-LINE BOWLING
LEG BEFORE WICKET
LEG-SIDE FIELDER
LEG-THEORY BOWLING
OFFSIDE FIELDER

GRAND PRIX CIRCUITS

GRAND PRIX	Circuit		
AUSTRALIAN	Melbourne	GERMAN	Hockenheim
AUSTRIAN	Spielberg	HUNGARIAN	Hungaroring
BELGIAN	Spa-Francorchamps	ITALIAN	Monza
BRAZILIAN	São Paulo	JAPANESE	Suzuka
BRITISH	Silverstone	MALAYSIAN	Kuala Lumpur
CANADIAN	Montreal	MONACO	Monte Carlo
EUROPEAN	Nürburgring, Germany	SAN MARINO	Imola, Italy
FRENCH	Magny-Cours	SPANISH	Barcelona
		UNITED STATES	Indianapolis

MAJOR RUGBY UNION CLUBS

3
GHK

4
BATH
GALA
SALE

5
FLYDE
LEEDS
NEATH
ORREL
OTLEY
RUGBY
WASPS

6
CURRIE
EXETER
HAVANT
HAWICK
MORLEY

7
BEDFORD

7—continued
BRISTOL
CARDIFF
CLIFTON
MELROSE
MOSELEY
NEWPORT
READING
REDRUTH
SHANNON
SWANSEA
WALSALL

8
ABERAVON
ASPATRIA
BRIDGEND
COVENTRY
EBBW VALE
LLANELLI
RICHMOND
SARACENS
TREORCHY
WATERLOO

9
BALLYMENA
GARRYOWEN
HARROGATE
HERIOT'S FP
JEDFOREST
LANDSDOWE
LEICESTER
NEWBRIDGE
NEWCASTLE
OLD WESLEY
ROTHERHAM
WAKEFIELD

10
BLACKHEATH
GLOUCESTER
HARLEQUINS
INSTONIANS
NOTTINGHAM
PONTYPRIDD
WATSONIANS

11
ABERTILLERY

11—continued
BOROUGHMUIR
LONDON IRISH
LONDON WELSH
NORTHAMPTON
ROSSLYN PARK

12
OLD BELVEDERE
YOUNG MUNSTER

14
LONDON SCOTTISH
STIRLING COUNTY
WEST HARTLEPOOL

16+
BLACKROCK
 COLLEGE
CORK
 CONSTABULARY
EDINBURGH
 ACADEMICALS
LIVERPOOL ST
 HELENS

RUGBY LEAGUE CLUBS

4
HULL
YORK

5
LEEDS
WIGAN

6
BATLEY
WIDNES

7
BRAMLEY
HALIFAX

7—continued
SWINTON

8
CARLISLE
DEWSBURY
ST HELENS

9
HIGHFIELD

10
CASTLEFORD
WARRINGTON
WHITEHAVEN

11
OLDHAM BEARS
SALFORD REDS

12
BARROW
 BRAVES

12—continued	14	15+—continued	15+—continued
HUDDERSFIELD	WORKINGTON TOWN	FEATHERSTONE	LEIGH CENTURIONS
HUNSLET HAWKS		ROVERS	PARIS SAINT
	15+	HULL KINGSTON	GERMAIN
13	CHORLEY	ROVERS	ROCHDALE
	CHIEFTAINS		HORNETS
BRADFORD BULLS	DONCASTER	KEIGHLEY	SHEFFIELD EAGLES
LONDON BRONCOS	DRAGONS	COUGARS	WAKEFIELD TRINITY

BRITISH FOOTBALL TEAMS

TEAM	GROUND	NICKNAME
ABERDEEN	PITTODRIE STADIUM	DONS
AIRDRIEONIANS	BROOMFIELD PARK	DIAMONDS; WAYSIDERS
ALBION ROVERS	CLIFTON HALL	WEE ROVERS
ALDERSHOT	RECREATION GROUND	SHOTS
ALLOA	RECREATION PARK	WASPS
ARBROATH	GAYFIELD PARK	RED LICHTIES
ARSENAL	HIGHBURY	GUNNERS
ASTON VILLA	VILLA PARK	VILLANS
AYR UNITED	SOMERSET PARK	HONEST MEN
BARNSLEY	OAKWELL GROUND	TYKES; REDS; COLLIERS
BERWICK RANGERS	SHIELFIELD PARK	BORDERERS
BIRMINGHAM CITY	ST ANDREWS	BLUES
BLACKBURN ROVERS	EWOOD PARK	BLUE & WHITES; ROVERS
BLACKPOOL	BLOMMFIELD ROAD	SEASIDERS
BOLTON WANDERERS	BURNDEN PARK	TROTTERS
BOURNEMOUTH	DEAN COURT	CHERRIES
BRADFORD CITY	VALLEY PARADE	BANTAMS
BRECHIN CITY	GLEBE PARK	CITY
BRENTFORD	GRIFFIN PARK	BEES
BRIGHTON & HOVE ALBION	GOLDSTONE GROUND	SEAGULLS
BRISTOL CITY	ASHTON GATE	ROBINS
BRISTOL ROVERS	TWERTON PARK	PIRATES
BURNLEY	TURF MOOR	CLARETS
BURY	GIGG LANE	SHAKERS
CAMBRIDGE UNITED	ABBEY STADIUM	UNITED
CARDIFF CITY	NINIAN PARK	BLUEBIRDS
CARLISLE UNITED	BRUNTON PARK	CUMBRIANS; BLUES
CELTIC	CELTIC PARK	BHOYS
CHARLTON ATHLETIC	SELHURST PARK	HADDICKS; ROBINS; VALIANTS
CHELSEA	STAMFORD BRIDGE	BLUES
CHESTER CITY	SEALAND ROAD	BLUES
CHESTERFIELD	RECREATION GROUND	BLUES; SPIREITES
CLYDEBANK	KILBOWIE PARK	BANKIES
CLYDE	FIRHILL PARK	BULLY WEE
COLCHESTER UNITED	LAYER ROAD	U'S
COVENTRY CITY	HIGHFIELD ROAD	SKY BLUES
COWDENBEATH	CENTRAL PARK	COWDEN
CREWE ALEXANDRA	GRESTY ROAD	RAILWAYMEN
CRYSTAL PALACE	SELHURST PARK	EAGLES
DARLINGTON	FEETHAMS GROUND	QUAKERS
DERBY COUNTY	BASEBALL GROUND	RAMS
DONCASTER ROVERS	BELLE VUE GROUND	ROVERS
DUMBARTON	BOGHEAD PARK	SONS

DUNDEE	DENS PARK	DARK BLUES; DEE
DUNDEE UNITED	TANNADICE PARK	TERRORS
DUNFERMLINE ATHLETIC	EAST END PARK	PARS
EAST FIFE	BAYVIEW PARK	FIFERS
EAST STIRLINGSHIRE	FIRS PARK	SHIRE
EVERTON	GOODISON PARK	TOFFEES
EXETER CITY	ST JAMES PARK	GRECIANS
FALKIRK	BROCKVILLE PARK	BAIRNS
FORFAR ATHLETIC	STATION PARK	SKY BLUES
FULHAM	CRAVEN COTTAGE	COTTAGERS
GILLINGHAM	PRIESTFIELD STADIUM	GILLS
GRIMSBY TOWN	BLUNDELL PARK	MARINERS
HALIFAX TOWN	SHAY GROUND	SHAYMEN
HAMILTON ACADEMICAL	DOUGLAS PARK	ACCES
HARTLEPOOL UNITED	VICTORIA GROUND	POOL
HEART OF MIDLOTHIAN	TYNECASTLE PARK	HEARTS
HEREFORD UNITED	EDGAR STREET	UNITED
HIBERNIAN	EASTER ROAD	HIBEES
HUDDERSFIELD TOWN	LEEDS ROAD	TERRIERS
HULL CITY	BOOTHFERRY PARK	TIGERS
IPSWICH TOWN	PORTMAN ROAD	BLUES; TOWN
KILMARNOCK	RUGBY PARK	KILLIE
LEEDS UNITED	ELLAND ROAD	UNITED
LEICESTER CITY	FILBERT STREET	FILBERTS; FOXES
LEYTON ORIENT	BRISBANE ROAD	O'S
LINCOLN CITY	SINCIL BANK	RED IMPS
LIVERPOOL	ANFIELD	REDS; POOL
LUTON TOWN	KENILWORTH ROAD	HATTERS
MANCHESTER CITY	MAINE ROAD	BLUES
MANCHESTER UNITED	OLD TRAFFORD	RED DEVILS
MANSFIELD TOWN	FIELD MILL GROUND	STAGS
MEADOWBANK THISTLE	MEADOWBANK STADIUM	THISTLE; WEE JAGS
MIDDLESBROUGH	AYRESOME PARK	BORO
MILLWALL	THE DEN	LIONS
MONTROSE	LINKS PARK	GABLE ENDERS
MORTON	CAPPIELOW PARK	TON
MOTHERWELL	FIR PARK	WELL
NEWCASTLE UNITED	ST JAMES PARK	MAGPIES
NORTHAMPTON TOWN	COUNTY GROUND	COBBLERS
NORWICH CITY	CARROW ROAD	CANARIES
NOTTINGHAM FOREST	CITY GROUND	REDS; FOREST
NOTTS COUNTY	MEADOW LANE	MAGPIES
OLDHAM ATHLETIC	BOUNDARY PARK	LATICS
OXFORD UNITED	MANOR GROUND	U'S
PARTICK THISTLE	FIRHILL PARK	JAGS
PETERBOROUGH UNITED	LONDON ROAD	POSH
PLYMOUTH ARGYLE	HOME PARK	PILGRIMS
PORTSMOUTH	FRATTON PARK	POMPEY
PORT VALE	VALE PARK	VALIANTS
PRESTON NORTH END	DEEPDALE	LILYWHITES; NORTH END
QUEEN OF THE SOUTH	PALMERSTON PARK	DOONHAMERS
QUEEN'S PARK	HAMPDEN PARK	SPIDERS
QUEEN'S PARK RANGERS	LOFTUS ROAD	RANGERS; R'S
RAITH ROVERS	STARK'S PARK	ROVERS
RANGERS	IBROX STADIUM	GERS
READING	ELM PARK	ROYALS
ROCHDALE	SPOTLAND	DALE
ROTHERHAM UNITED	MILLMOOR GROUND	MERRY MILLERS
SCARBOROUGH	SEAMER ROAD	BORO
SCUNTHORPE UNITED	GLANFORD PARK	IRON
SHEFFIELD UNITED	BRAMALL LANE	BLADES
SHEFFIELD WEDNESDAY	HILLSBOROUGH	OWLS

SHREWSBURY TOWN	GAY MEADOW	SHREWS; TOWN
SOUTHAMPTON	DELL	SAINTS
SOUTHEND UNITED	ROOTS HALL	SHRIMPERS
STENHOUSEMUIR	OCHILVIEW PARK	WARRIORS
STIRLING ALBION	ANNFIELD PARK	ALBION
ST JOHNSTONE	MUIRTON PARK	SAINTS
ST MIRREN	LOVE STREET	BUDDIES; PAISLEY SAINTS
STOCKPORT COUNTY	EDGELEY PARK	COUNTY; HATTERS
STOKE CITY	VICTORIA GROUND	POTTERS
STRANRAER	STAIR PARK	BLUES
SUNDERLAND	ROKER PARK	ROKERITES
SWANSEA CITY	VETCH FIELD	SWANS
SWINDON TOWN	COUNTY GROUND	ROBINS
TORQUAY UNITED	PLAINMOOR GROUND	GULLS
TOTTENHAM HOTSPUR	WHITE HART LANE	SPURS
TRANMERE ROVERS	PRENTON PARK	ROVERS
WALSALL	FELLOWS PARK	SADDLERS
WATFORD	VICARAGE ROAD	HORNETS
WEST BROMWICH ALBION	HAWTHORNS	THROSTLES; BAGGIES; ALBION
WEST HAM UNITED	UPTON PARK	HAMMERS
WIGAN ATHLETIC	SPRINGFIED PARK	LATICS
WIMBLEDON	PLOUGH LANE	DONS
WOLVERHAMPTON WANDERERS	MOLINEUX	WOLVES
WREXHAM	RACECOURSE GROUND	ROBINS
YORK CITY	BOOTHAM CRESCENT	MINSTERMEN

EUROPEAN FOOTBALL CLUBS

AUSTRIA

RAPID VIENNA
SALZBURG

BELGIUM

ANDERLECHT
EKEREN
FC BRUGES
ROYAL ANTWERP
STANDARD LIEGE

CROATIA

HAJOUK SPLIT

CZECH REPUBLIC

SLAVIA PRAGUE
SPARTA PRAGUE

DENMARK

BRONDBY

FRANCE

AUXERRE
BASTIA
BORDEAUX
LE HAVRE
LILLE
LYONS
MARSEILLES
METZ
MONACO
MONTPELLIER
NANTES
NICE
PARIS SAINT
  GERMAIN
STRASBOURG

GERMANY

BAYER
  LEVERKUSEN
BAYERN MUNICH
BORUSSIA
  MÖNCHENGLAD-
  BACH
BRANN BERGEN
COLOGNE
DUISBURG
HANSA ROSTOCK
KARLSRUHE
MUNICH
WERDER BREMEN
VFB STUTTGART

GREECE

AEK ATHENS
GALATASARAY
OLYMPIAKOS
PANATHINAIKOS

ITALY

AC MILAN
AS ROMA
ATALANTA
BOLOGNA
CAGLIARI
FIORENTINA
INTER MILAN
INTERNAZIONALE
JUVENTUS
LAZIO
NAPOLI
PARMA
PERUGIA
PIACENZA
SAMPDORIA
VERONA
VICENZA

NETHERLANDS

AJAX
FC VOLENDAM
FEYENOORD
FORTUNA SITTARD
JC KERKRADE
PSV EINDHOVEN
RKC WAALWIJK
TILBURG
UTRECHT
VITESSE ARNHEM

PORTUGAL

AMADORA
BENFICA
BOAVISTA
BRAGA
FARENSE
FC PORTO
SETUBAL
SPORTING LISBON

SPAIN

ATLÉTICO DE
  BILBAO
ATLÉTICO DE
  MADRID

BARCELONA
ESPAÑOL
RACING SANTANDER
REAL MADRID
REAL SOCIEDAO
REAL ZARAGOZA
SEVILLA
SPORTING GIJÓN

VALLENCIA

POLAND
LEGIA WARSAW

ROMANIA
STEAVA
  BUCHAREST

RUSSIA
CSKA MOSCOW
SPARTAK MOSCO

SWEDEN
AIK STOCKHOLM
IFK GOTHENBURG

UKRAINE
DYNAMO KIEV

AMERICAN FOOTBALL TEAMS

ATLANTA FALCONS
BUFFALO BILLS
CHICAGO BEARS
CLEVELAND BROWNS
DALLAS COWBOYS
DENVER BRONCOS
DETROIT LIONS
GREEN BAY PACKERS
HOUSTON OILERS

INDIANAPOLIS COLTS
KANSAS CITY CHIEFS
LOS ANGELES RAIDERS
LOS ANGELES RAMS
MIAMI DOLPHINS
MINNESOTA VIKINGS
NEW ENGLAND PATRIOTS
NEW ORLEANS SAINTS
NEW YORK GIANTS

NEW YORK JETS
PHILADELPHIA EAGLES
PHOENIX CARDINALS
PITTSBURGH STEELERS
SAN DIEGO CHARGERS
SAN FRANCISCO 49ERS
SEATTLE SEAHAWKS
TAMPA BAY BUCCANEERS
WASHINGTON REDSKINS

AMERICAN BASEBALL TEAMS

ATLANTA BRAVES
BALTIMORE ORIOLES
BOSTON RED SOX
BROOKLYN DODGERS
CALIFORNIA ANGELS
CHICAGO WHITE SOX
CINCINNATI REDS
CLEVELAND INDIANS
DETROIT TIGERS

KANSAS CITY ROYALS
LOS ANGELES DODGERS
MILWAUKEE BRAVES
MINNESOTA TWINS
NEW YORK GIANTS
NEW YORK METS
NEW YORK YANKEES
OAKLAND ATHLETICS
PHILADELPHIA PHILLIES

PITTSBURGH PIRATES
ST LOUIS BROWNS
ST LOUIS CARDINALS
SAN FRANCISCO GIANTS
TEXAS RANGERS
TORONTO BLUE JAYS
WASHINGTON SENATORS

GARDENING

GARDENING TERMS

2	4	4 –continued	5 –continued	5 –continued
PH	BOLE	SNAG	CROSS	MULCH
	BULB	SPIT	CROWN	PRUNE
3	LIME		FORCE	SHRUB
	LOAM	5	GENUS	SPORT
BUD	NODE	BLIND	GRAFT	STAKE
POT	PEAT	BLOOM	HARDY	TILTH

5 –continued
TRUSS
TUBER

6
ALPINE
ANNUAL
CLOCHE
CORDON
DIBBER
FLORET
HYBRID
MANURE
RUNNER
STRAIN
SUCKER

7
COMPOST
CUTTING
FRIABLE
LATERAL
NEUTRAL
PERGOLA
RHIZOME

8
ACID SOIL
AERATION
BIENNIAL
DEAD-HEAD
PINCH OUT
PRICK OUT
SEEDLING

8 –continued
STANDARD

9
BLANCHING
CHLOROSIS
DECIDUOUS
EVERGREEN
FUNGICIDE
HALF HARDY
HEELING-IN
PERENNIAL
ROOTSTOCK
SIDE SHOOT

10
BASAL SHOOT

10 –continued
CALCAREOUS
FERTILIZER
HERBACEOUS
VARIEGATED

11
GERMINATION
INSECTICIDE
POLLINATION
PROPAGATION

12+
ALKALINE SOIL
BASTARD
 TRENCHING
BEDDING PLANT
HARDENING OFF

GARDEN FLOWERS

4
FLAX
GEUM
IRIS
SAGE

5
AJUGA
ASTER
ASTER
AVENS
BUGLE
DAISY
HOSTA
INULA
LINUM
LUPIN
PANSY
PEONY
PHLOX
PINKS
POPPY
SEDUM
VIOLA

6
BELLIS
BORAGE
CALTHA
CLEOME
COBAEA
COSMEA
COSMOS
DAHLIA
ECHIUM
IBERIS
MALOPE
NEPETA
PAEONY
RESEDA
SALVIA
SPURGE

6 –continued
STOCKS
VIOLET
YARROW
ZINNIA

7
ALKANET
ALTHAEA
ALYSSUM
ANCHUSA
ANEMONE
ARUNCUS
ASTILBE
BEGONIA
BUGBANE
CAMPION
CATMINT
CELOSIA
CLARKIA
DAY LILY
GAZANIA
GODETIA
HONESTY
IPOMOEA
KINGCUP
LIATRIS
LINARIA
LIRIOPE
LOBELIA
LUNARIA
LYCHNIS
LYTHRUM
MILFOIL
MIMULUS
MONARDA
MULLEIN
NEMESIA
NIGELLA
PAPAVER
PETUNIA
PRIMULA

7 –continued
STACHYS
STATICE
TAGETES
URSINIA
VERBENA

8
ACANTHUS
ACHILLEA
ACONITUM
AGERATUM
ARCTOTIS
BARTONIA
BERGAMOT
BERGENIA
BRUNNERA
CLEMATIS
DIANTHUS
DICENTRA
DROPWORT
ECHINOPS
EREMURUS
ERIGERON
ERYNGIUM
FEVERFEW
FLEABANE
FOXGLOVE
GERANIUM
HELENIUM
HEUCHERA
HIBISCUS
KNAPWEED
KNOTWEED
LARKSPUR
LATHYRUS
LAUATERA
LILY TURF
LIMONIUM
LUNGWORT
MACLEAYA
MYOSOTIS

8 –continued
PHACELIA
PHYSALIS
PRIMROSE
PRUNELLA
SCABIOSA
SCABIOUS
SEA HOLLY
SELF-HEAL
SIDALCEA
SOAPWORT
SOLIDAGO
STOKESIA
SUN PLANT
SWEET PEA
TIARELLA
TICKSEED
TOADFLAX
TROLLIUS
VENIDIUM
VERONICA
VISCARIA

9
ANAPHALIS
AQUILEGIA
ASTRANTIA
BIG BETONY
BUTTERCUP
CALENDULA
CAMPANULA
CANDYTUFT
CARNATION
CENTAUREA
COLUMBINE
COREOPSIS
DICTAMNUS
DIGITALIS
DORONICUM
ECHINACEA
EPIMEDIUM
EUPHORBIA

9 –continued
GOLDEN ROD
HELIOPSIS
HOLLYHOCK
IMPATIENS
KNIPHOFIA
LAMB'S EARS
LIGULARIA
MALCOLMIA
MATTHIOLA
MEADOW RUE
MOLUCELLA
MONKSHOOD
NAVELWORT
NEMOPHILA
NICOTIANA
OENOTHERA
PENSTEMON
POLYGONUM
PORTULACA
PYRETHRUM
RODGERSIA
RUDBECKIA
SAPONARIA
SAXIFRAGE
SNAKEROOT
SPEEDWELL
STONECROP
SUNFLOWER
VERBASCUM

10
ACROLINIUM
AGAPANTHUS
AGROSTEMMA
ALCHEMILLA
AMARANTHUS
BARRENWORT
BELLFLOWER
BISHOP'S HAT
BUSY LIZZIE
CATANANCHE

10 –continued
CHINA ASTER
CIMICIFUGA
CINQUEFOIL
CONEFLOWER
CORN COCKLE
CORNFLOWER
CORTADERIA
CUPID'S DART
DELPHINIUM
FOAM FLOWER
GAILLARDIA
GAYFEATHER
GOAT'S BEARD
GYPSOPHILA
HELIANTHUS
HELIOTROPE
HELLEBORUS
INDIAN PINK
KAFFIR LILY
LENTEN ROSE
LIMNANTHES
LYSIMACHIA
MASTERWORT
MATRICARIA
MECONOPSIS
MIGNONETTE
NASTURTIUM
OMPHALODES
PLATYCODON
PLUME POPPY
POLEMONIUM
POTENTILLA
PULMONARIA
RANUNCULUS
SNAPDRAGON
SNEEZEWORT
SPIDERWORT
THALICTRUM
THUNBERGIA
TROPAEOLUM
WALLFLOWER

11
AFRICAN LILY
ANTIRRHINUM
BABY'S BREATH
BEARD TONGUE
BLAZING STAR
BOUNCING BET
BURNING BUSH
CALCEOLARIA
CENTRANTHUS
CHEIRANTHUS
CONVOLVULUS
CORAL FLOWER
CRANE'S-BILL
FILIPENDULA
FLOSS FLOWER
FORGET-ME-NOT
FOXTAIL LILY
GLOBE FLOWER
HELICHRYSUM
INCARVILLEA
LADY'S MANTLE
LOOSESTRIFE
LOVE-IN-A-MIST
PAMPAS GRASS
PHYSOSTEGIA
POLYGONATUM
POT MARIGOLD
RED HOT POKER
RED VALERIAN
SCHIZANTHUS
SEA LAVENDER
SHASTA DAISY
STOKES' ASTER
STRAW FLOWER
XERANTHEMUM

12
AFRICAN DAISY
ALSTROEMERIA
ANNUAL MALLOW
BABY BLUE EYES
BLUE-EYED MARY
CALLISTEPHUS

12 –continued
ESCHSCHOLZIA
GLOBE THISTLE
HELIOTROPIUM
HEMEROCALLIS
JACOB'S LADDER
LEOPARD'S BANE
MONKEY FLOWER
MORNING GLORY
PERUVIAN LILY
PLANTAIN LILY
SALPIGLOSSIS
SCHIZOSTYLIS
SOLOMON'S SEAL
SPIDER FLOWER
SWEET ALYSSUM
SWEET WILLIAM
TOBACCO PLANT
TRADESCANTIA

13
BALLOON FLOWER
BEAR'S BREECHES
BLANKET FLOWER
BLEEDING HEART
CATHEDRAL BELL
CHRISTMAS ROSE
CHRYSANTHEMUM
DIMORPHOTHECA
MARSH MARIGOLD
OBEDIENT PLANT
PAINTED TONGUE
PRAIRIE MALLOW
SLIPPER FLOWER
VIRGINIA STOCK

14
BELLS OF IRELAND
BLACK-EYED SUSAN
CANTERBURY BELL
CHINESE LANTERN
FLOWER OF AN
  HOUR
FRENCH MARIGOLD

14 –continued
POOR MAN'S
  ORCHID
STAR OF THE VELDT
YOUTH AND OLD
  AGE

15
AFRICAN MARIGOLD
EVENING PRIMROSE
JAPANESE
  ANEMONE
MICHAELMAS DAISY

16
BACHELOR'S
  BUTTONS
CALIFORNIAN
  POPPY
COMMON
  IMMORTELLE
LIVINGSTONE DAISY
MESEMBRYAN-
  THEMUM
PEARL
  EVERLASTING
POACHED EGG
  FLOWER
PURPLE CONE-
  FLOWER

17+
CHINESE BELL-
  FLOWER
CHINESE TRUMPET
  FLOWER
EVERLASTING
  FLOWER
LOVE-LIES-BLEED-
  ING
MONARCH OF THE
  VELDT
PURPLE
  LOOSESTRIFE

ROCKERY PLANTS

4
GEUM

5
ASTER
DRABA
DRYAS
MAZUS
PHLOX
SEDUM

6
ACAENA
ARABIS
ERINUS
IBERIS

6 –continued
ONOSMA
OXALIS
SILENE
THRIFT

7
ALYSSUM
ARMERIA
ASTILBE
CAT'S EAR
GENTIAN
LEWISIA
LINNAEA
LYCHNIS

7 –continued
MIMULUS
MORISIA
PIGROOT
PLEIONE
RAMONDA
RAOULIA
SEA PINK
SHORTIA

8
ACHILLEA
ARENARIA
AUBRIETA
DIANTHUS

8 –continued
ERIGERON
ERYSIMUM
FLEABANE
GENTIANA
GERANIUM
GROMWELL
HABERLEA
HEPATICA
ORIGANUM
ROCK ROSE
SANDWORT
SNOWBELL
UVULARIA

9
ANACYCLUS
ANDROSACE
AUBRIETIA
BLOODROOT
CAMPANULA
CANDYTUFT
CERASTIUM
EDELWEISS
HOUSELEEK
HYPERICUM
PENSTEMON
POLYGONUM
ROCK CRESS
SAPONARIA

GARDENING

9 –continued
SAXIFRAGA
SAXIFRAGE
STONECROP
VERBASCUM

10
AETHIONEMA
ALPINE GEUM
ANTENNARIA
BELLFLOWER
CYANANTHUS
LYSIMACHIA
PULSATILLA
SOLDANELLA
THROATWORT

10 –continued
TWIN FLOWER

11
DODECATHEON
DONKEY PLANT
HELICHRYSUM
MOSS CAMPION
ROCKERY PINK
ROCK JASMINE
ROCK MULLEIN
SANGUINARIA
SEMPERVIVUM
VANCOUVERIA
WALDSTEINIA

12
ALPINE YARROW
HELIANTHEMUM
LEONTOPODIUM
LITHOSPERMUM
MONKEY FLOWER
PASQUE FLOWER
ROCK SOAPWORT
SHOOTING STAR
SISYRINCHIUM
ST JOHN'S WORT
WHITLOW GRASS

13+
ALPINE
  WALLFLOWER

13+ –continued
CREEPING JENNY
EVERLASTING
  FLOWER
INSIDE-OUT
  FLOWER
MOUNTAIN AVENS
MOUNT ATLAS
  DAISY
NEW ZEALAND
  BURR
ROCK CINQUEFOIL
SNOW-IN-SUMMER
SUMMER
  STARWORT
WHITE ROCK CRESS

BULBS

4
IRIS
IXIA
LILY

5
CANNA
TULIP

6
ALLIUM
CRINUM
CROCUS
LILIUM
NERINE
OXALIS
SCILLA
SORREL
TULIPA

7
ANEMONE
BEGONIA
FREESIA
IPHEION
MUSCARI
QUAMASH

8
BLUEBELL
BRODIAEA
CAMASSIA
CORN LILY
CYCLAMEN
DAFFODIL
ERANTHIS
GALTONIA
HYACINTH
LEUCOJUM
SNOWDROP
SPARAXIS
TIGRIDIA
TRILLIUM
TRITONIA

9
AMARYLLIS
COLCHICUM
CROCOSMIA
GALANTHUS
GLADIOLUS
NARCISSUS
SNOWFLAKE
SWORD LILY
WAKE ROBIN

10
ACIDATHERA
CHIONODOXA
FRITILLARY
HYACINTHUS
INDIAN SHOT
MONTBRETIA
PUSCHKINIA
RANUNCULUS
WINDFLOWER

11
BLAZING STAR
CONVALLARIA
ERYTHRONIUM
FRITILLARIA
STERNBERGIA
TIGER FLOWER

12
AUTUMN CROCUS
CARDIOCRINUM
ORNITHOGALUM

13
GRAPE HYACINTH
STRIPED SQUILL
WINTER ACONITE

14
BELLADONNA LILY
GLORY OF THE
  SNOW
SUMMER HYACINTH

15
DOG'S-TOOTH
  VIOLET
FLOWERING GARLIC
HARLEQUIN
  FLOWER
LILY OF THE VALLEY
STAR OF
  BETHLEHEM
TURBAN
  BUTTERCUP

16+
GIANT HIMALAYAN
  LILY
SPRING
  STARFLOWER
YELLOW STAR
  FLOWER

WATER-GARDEN PLANTS

4
GEUM
IRIS
RUSH

5
CALLA
CAREX
CHARA
HOSTA
LEMNA
RHEUM

5 –continued
SEDGE
TRAPA
TYPHA

6
ACORUS
ALISMA
AZOLLA
CALTHA
COTULA
ELODEA

6 –continued
JUNCUS
MENTHA
NUPHAR
PISTIA

7
ARUNCUS
ASTILBE
BOG ARUM
BOG BEAN
BONESET

7 –continued
BULRUSH
BUR-REED
BUTOMUS
CYPERUS
DAY LILY
GUNNERA
LOBELIA
LYCHNIS
LYTHRUM
MIMULUS
ONOCLEA

7 –continued
OSMUNDA
PRIMULA
SCIRPUS
TILLAEA

8
DROPWORT
DUCKWEED
FROG-BIT
GLYCERIA
HORNWORT

8 –continued
HOTTONIA
KNOTWEED
MYOSOTIS
NYMPHAEA
ORONTIUM
POND LILY
PONDWEED
REEDMACE
SAURURUS
TROLLIUS
VERONICA

9
ARROW ARUM
ARROWHEAD
BROOKLIME
CARDAMINE
EICHORNIA
FAIRY MOSS
HAIRGRASS
HYPERICUM
LIGULARIA
PELTANDRA
POLYGONUM
RODGERSIA
ROYAL FERN
STONEWORT
SWEET FLAG
WATER LILY
WATER MINT

10
APONOGETON
ELEOCHARIS
ERIOPHORUM
EUPATORIUM
FONTINALIS
GOAT'S BEARD
GOLDEN CLUB
GOLDEN RAYS
HOUTTUYNIA
KAFFIR LILY
LYSICHITON
LYSIMACHIA
MATTEUCCIA
MENYANTHES
NYMPHOIDES
PONTEDERIA
RANUNCULUS
SAGITTARIA
SPARGANIUM
STRATIOTES
WATER AVENS
WATER GRASS
WILLOW MOSS

11
BLADDERWORT
CALLITRICHE
COTTON GRASS
FILIPENDULA
GLOBE FLOWER

11 –continued
HYDROCHARIS
LOOSESTRIFE
POTAMOGETON
RAGGED ROBIN
UTRICULARIA
WATER FRINGE
WATER VIOLET

12
CUCKOO FLOWER
GOLDFISH WEED
HEMEROCALLIS
LAGAROSIPHON
LIZARD'S TAIL
MONKEY FLOWER
MYRIOPHYLLUM
PELTIPHYLLUM
PICKEREL WEED
PLANTAIN LILY
SCHIZOSTYLIS
SKUNK CABBAGE
WATER LETTUCE
WATER MILFOIL
WATER SOLDIER
ZANTEDESCHIA

13
CERATOPHYLLUM
FLOWERING RUSH
GOLDEN BUTTONS
MARSH MARIGOLD

13 –continued
SENSITIVE FERN
UMBRELLA GRASS
UMBRELLA PLANT
WATER CHESTNUT
WATER HAWTHORN
WATER HYACINTH
WATER PLANTAIN
WATER STARWORT
WHITE ARUM LILY

14
PARROT'S FEATHER
PRICKLY RHUBARB
SWAMP
  STONECROP
WATER BUTTERCUP

15+
CANADIAN
  PONDWEED
MARSH ST JOHN'S
  WORT
ORNAMENTAL
  RHUBARB
OSTRICH FEATHER
  FERN
PURPLE LOOSE-
  STRIFE
WATER FORGET-ME-
  NOT

ANGLING TERMS

3
DUN
FLY
NET
PEG
RIB
ROD
TAG
TIP

4
BAIT
BARB
CAST
GAFF
HEMP
HOOK
LEAD
LINE
LURE
PLUG
POLE

4 –continued
REEL
SHOT
TAIL
WORM

5
BLANK
CREEL
FLOAT
FLOSS
JOKER
LEGER
PASTE
QUILL
SPOON
WHISK

6
CASTER
DRY FLY
HACKLE
MAGGOT

6 –continued
MARKER
PALMER
PINKIE
PRIEST
SLIDER
SPIGOT
SQUATT
STRIKE
SWIVEL
WET FLY
ZOOMER

7
ANTENNA
BALE ARM
BRISTLE
DAPPING
DUBBING
KEEP NET
MISSILE
PLUMMET

7 –continued
ROD REST
ROD RING
SPINNER
WAGGLER

8
BACK SHOT
DEAD BAIT
FREELINE
LEGERING
LINE BITE
SPECIMEN
STOP KNOT
SWINGTIP

9
BITE ALARM
BLOODWORM
BLUED HOOK
CLOUD BAIT
DISGORGER
GORGE BAIT

9 –continued
MICRO SHOT
MIDGE HOOK
QUIVERTIP
ROACH POLE
TYING SILK
WAGGY LURE
WIRE TRACE

10
BREAD FLAKE
BREAD PUNCH
CADDIS HOOK
COFFIN LEAD
DOUBLE HOOK
FLYBODY FUR
GROUND BAIT
GROUND BAIT

10 –continued
HAIR-AND-FUR
LANDING NET
SNAP TACKLE
STICK FLOAT
SWIM FEEDER

11
ARLESEY BOMB
BAIT DROPPER
BUBBLE FLOAT
DEVON MINNOW
DOUGH-BOBBIN
FOUL-HOOKED
GALLOWS TOOL
LOADED FLOAT
PATERNOSTER
SPARKLE BODY

11 –continued
WHIP-FINISH
WING-CUTTER

12
BARBLESS HOOK
DETACHED BODY
DRY-FLY HACKLE
PARACHUTE FLY
SLIDING FLOAT

13
BUTT INDICATOR
CENTRE-PIN REEL
FLEXI-TAIL LURE

14
BLOCKEND FEEDER
BREAKING STRAIN

14 –continued
GRUB-SHRIMP
  HOOK
MULTIPLIER REEL

15+
DANISH DRY FLY
  HOOK
DETACHED-BODY
  HOOK
FLAT-BODIED
  NYMPH HOOK
PARACHUTE-FLY
  HOOK
SWEDISH DRY FLY
  HOOK
YORKSHIRE SEDGE
  HOOK

MISCELLANEOUS

COLOURS

3
AAL
ABA
DUN
JET
RED
TAN

4
BLEU
BLUE
BOIS
BURE
CUIR
DRAB
EBON
ÉCRU
GOLD
GREY
GRIS
HOPI
IRIS
JADE
LAKE
LARK
NAVY
NOIR
ONYX
OPAL
PIED
PINK
PLUM
PUCE
ROSE
RUBY
SAND
SHOT
VERT

5
AMBER
BEIGE
BLACK
BROWN
CAMEL
CAPRI
CHAIR
COCOA
CORAL

5—continued
CREAM
CYMAR
DELFT
FLESH
GREEN
GRÈGE
HAZEL
HENNA
IVORY
JASPÉ
JAUNE
JEWEL
KHAKI
LODEN
MAIZE
MAUVE
OCHRE
OLIVE
OMBRÉ
PEACH
PEARL
PÊCHE
PRUNE
ROUGE
SEPIA
SHADE
TAUPE
TOPAZ
UMBER
WHITE

6
ACAJOU
ALESAN
ARGENT
AUBURN
BASANÉ
BISTRE
BLONDE
BRONZE
BURNET
CASTOR
CENDRÉ
CERISE
CHERRY
CHROMA
CITRON

6—continued
CLARET
COPPER
DORADO
FLAXEN
GARNET
GOLDEN
INDIGO
JASPER
MADDER
MAROON
MATARA
MOTLEY
ORANGE
ORCHID
OYSTER
PASTEL
PEARLY
PIRNED
PURPLE
RACHEL
RAISIN
RESEDA
RUSSET
SALMON
SHRIMP
SILVER
TITIAN
VIOLET
YELLOW
ZIRCON

7
ANAMITE
APRICOT
ARDOISE
AUREATE
BISCUIT
CALDRON
CARAMEL
CARMINE
CHAMOIS
CORBEAU
CRIMSON
EMERALD
FILBERT
FUCHSIA
GRIZZLE

7—continued
HEATHER
INGÉNUE
JACINTH
JONQUIL
LACQUER
LAVANDE
MAGENTA
MOTTLED
MUSTARD
NACARAT
NATURAL
NEUTRAL
OLD ROSE
PEARLED
PLATINA
SAFFRON
SCARLET
SEA BLUE
SKY BLUE
TEA ROSE
THISTLE
TILE RED
TILLEUL
TUSSORE
VIOLINE

8
ABSINTHE
ALIZARIN
AMARANTH
AURULENT
BABY BLUE
BABY PINK
BORDEAUX
BURGUNDY
CAPUCINE
CHALDERA
CHÂTAINE
CHESTNUT
CIEL BLUE
CINNAMON
CREVETTE
CYCLAMEN
EAU DE NIL
ÉCARLATE
EGGPLANT
EGGSHELL

8–continued
GRIZZLED
GUN METAL
HAZEL NUT
HYACINTH
LARKSPUR
LAVENDER
MAHOGANY
MOLE GREY
MULBERRY
NAVY BLUE
PEA GREEN
PISTACHE
POPPY RED
PRIMROSE
SAPPHIRE
SEA GREEN
SHAGREEN
SPECTRUM
VIRIDIAN

9
ALICE BLUE
AUBERGINE
AZURE BLUE
BLUE-GREEN
CADET BLUE
CADET GREY
CARNATION
CARNELIAN
CHAMPAGNE
CHOCOLATE
COCHINEAL
DELPH BLUE
DUTCH BLUE

9–continued
FLESH PINK
GREEN-BLUE
HARLEQUIN
LEAF GREEN
LIME GREEN
MOONSTONE
MOSS GREEN
NILE GREEN
OLIVE DRAB
PARCHMENT
PEARL GREY
RASPBERRY
ROYAL BLUE
TANGERINE
TOMATO RED
TURKEY RED
VERDIGRIS
VERMILION
WALLY BLUE

10
AQUAMARINE
AURICOMOUS
BOIS DE ROSE
CAFÉ AU LAIT
CASTOR GREY
COBALT BLUE
CONGO BROWN
ENSIGN BLUE
LIVER BROWN
MARINA BLUE
MARINE BLUE
OXFORD BLUE
PETROL BLUE

10–continued
POLYCHROME
POWDER BLUE
TERRACOTTA
ZENITH BLUE

11
BOTTLE GREEN
BURNT ALMOND
CARDINAL RED
CLAIR DE LUNE
FOREST GREEN
GOBELIN BLUE
HORIZON BLUE
HUNTER'S PINK
LAPIS LAZULI
LEMON YELLOW
LIPSTICK RED
PARROT GREEN
PEACOCK BLUE
POMEGRANATE
SMOKED PEARL
SOLID COLOUR
ULTRAMARINE
VERSICOLOUR
WALNUT BROWN
YELLOW OCHRE

12
BALL PARK BLUE
CANARY YELLOW
CARROT COLOUR
CASTILIAN RED
CELADON GREEN
HUNTER'S GREEN

12–continued
HYACINTH BLUE
LOGWOOD BROWN
MIDNIGHT BLUE
OVERSEAS BLUE
SAPPHIRE BLUE
SOLFERINO RED
TYRIAN PURPLE
VERDANT GREEN

13
BISHOP'S PURPLE
BISHOP'S VIOLET
CAMBRIDGE BLUE
MOTHER-OF-PEARL
MULTICOLOURED
PARTI-COLOURED
PEPPER-AND-SALT
PRIMARY COLOUR
TORTOISE SHELL
TURQUOISE BLUE

14
HEATHER MIXTURE
PERIWINKLE BLUE
PISTACHIO GREEN
TURQUOISE GREEN

15
CALEDONIAN
  BROWN
CHARTREUSE
  GREEN

16
CHARTREUSE
  YELLOW

THE SIGNS OF THE ZODIAC

SIGN (Symbol; Dates)

ARIES (Ram; 21 Mar–19 Apr)
TAURUS (Bull; 20 Apr–20 May)
GEMINI (Twins; 21 May–21 June)
CANCER (Crab; 22 June–22 July)
LEO (Lion; 23 July–22 Aug)
VIRGO (Virgin; 23 Aug–22 Sept)

SIGN (Symbol; Dates)

LIBRA (Scales; 23 Sept–23 Oct)
SCORPIO (Scorpion; 24 Oct–21 Nov)
SAGITTARIUS (Archer; 22 Nov–21 Dec)
CAPRICORN (Goat; 22 Dec–19 Jan)
AQUARIUS (Water-carrier; 20 Jan–18 Feb)
PISCES (Fish; 19 Feb–20 Mar)

THE TWELVE SIGNS OF THE CHINESE ZODIAC

RAT
OX
TIGER
RABBIT

DRAGON
SNAKE
HORSE
SHEEP

MONKEY
ROOSTER
DOG
BOAR

CALENDARS

GREGORIAN

JANUARY
FEBRUARY
MARCH
APRIL
MAY
JUNE
JULY
AUGUST
SEPTEMBER
OCTOBER
NOVEMBER
DECEMBER

FRENCH REVOLUTIONARY

VENDÉMIAIRE – Vintage (Sept)
BRUMAIRE – Fog (Oct)
FRIMAIRE – Sleet (Nov)
NIVÔSE – Snow (Dec)
PLUVIÔSE – Rain (Jan)
VENTÔSE – Wind (Feb)
GERMINAL – Seed (Mar)
FLORÉAL – Blossom (Apr)
PRAIRIAL – Pasture (May)
MESSIDOR – Harvest (June)
THERMIDOR – Heat (July)
FRUCTIDOR – Fruit (Aug)

HEBREW

SHEVAT (Jan/Feb)
ADAR (Feb/Mar)
NISAN (Mar/Apr)
IYAR (Apr/May)
SIVAN (May/June)
TAMMUZ (June/July)
AV (July/Aug)
ELUL (Aug/Sept)
TISHRI (Sept/Oct)
HESHVAN (Oct/Nov)
KISLEV (Nov/Dec)
TEVET (Dec/Jan)

ISLAMIC

MUHARRAM (Jan)
SAFAR (Feb)
RABIA I (Mar)
RABIA II (Apr)
JUMĀDĀ I (May)
JUMĀDĀ II (June)
RAJAB (July)
SHA'BAN (Aug)
RAMADĀN (Sept)
SHAWWĀL (Oct)
DHŪAL-QA'DAH (Nov)
DHŪAL-HIJJAH (Dec)

CHINESE

XIAO HAN (Jan)
DA HAN (Jan/Feb)
LI CHUN (Feb)
YU SHUI (Feb/Mar)
JING ZHE (Mar)
CHUN FEN (Mar/Apr)
QING MING (Apr)
GU YU (Apr/May)
LI XIA (May)
XIAO MAN (May/June)
MANG ZHONG (June)
XIA ZHI (June/July)
XIAO SHU (July)
DA SHU (July/Aug)
LI QUI (Aug)
CHU SHU (Aug/Sept)
BAI LU (Sept)
QUI FEN (Sept/Oct)
HAN LU (Oct)
SHUANG JIANG (Oct/Nov)
LI DONG (Nov)
XIAO XUE (Nov/Dec)
DA XUE (Dec)
DONG ZHI (Dec/Jan)

BIRTHSTONES

January – GARNET
February – AMETHYST
March – BLOODSTONE/AQUAMARINE
April – DIAMOND
May – EMERALD
June – PEARL

July – RUBY
August – SARDONYX/PERIDOT
September – SAPPHIRE
October – OPAL
November – TOPAZ
December – TURQUOISE

WEDDING ANNIVERSARIES

1st – PAPER
2nd – COTTON
3rd – LEATHER
4th – FRUIT/FLOWERS
5th – WOOD
6th – IRON
7th – WOOL/COPPER
8th – BRONZE/POTTERY

9th – POTTERY/WILLOW
10th – TIN/ALUMINIUM
11th – STEEL
12th – SILK/LINEN
13th – LACE
14th – IVORY
15th – CRYSTAL
20th – CHINA

25th – SILVER
30th – PEARL
35th – CORAL
40th – RUBY
45th – SAPPHIRE
50th – GOLD
55th – EMERALD
60th – DIAMOND

PEERAGE

DUKE	DUCHESS	MARQUIS	MARCHIONESS
EARL	BARONESS	MARQUESS	VISCOUNTESS
BARON	COUNTESS	VISCOUNT	

HERALDIC TERMS

DIVISIONS OF FIELDS

PER PALE
PER FESS
PER CROSS
PER BEND
PER SALTIRE
PER CHEVRON

DESCRIPTIONS OF FIELDS

PARTY
BARRY
BURELY
BENDY
QUARTERLY
ENTY
FRETTY
GIRONNY
BEZANTY

PARTS OF THE ESCUTCHEON

DEXTER (right)
SINISTER (left)
MIDDLE
CHIEF (top)
FLANK (side)
BASE
NOMBRIL POINT
FESS POINT
HONOUR POINT
TRESSURE (border)

TINCTURES

OR (gold)
ARGENT (silver)
ERMINE
VAIR
POTENT
AZURE (blue)
GULES (red)

SABLE (black)
VERT (green)
PURPURE (purple)

CROSSES

FORMY
PATY
FLORY
MOLINE
BOTONNY
CROSLETTED
FITCHY
SALTIRE

LINES

ENGRAILED
EMBATTLED
INDENTED
INVECTED
WAVY, UNDY
NEBULY

DANCETTY
RAGULY
POTENTÉ
DOVETAILED
URDY

OTHER OBJECTS AND DECORATIONS

LOZENGE
ROUNDEL (circle)
ANNULET (ring)
FOUNTAIN (wavy line on a circle)
BILLET (upright object)
MOLET (star)
RAMPANT (rearing up)
COUCHANT (sleeping or sitting)
PASSANT (standing)
BAR

SEVEN DEADLY SINS

PRIDE	LUST	GLUTTONY	SLOTH
COVETOUSNESS	ENVY	ANGER	

SEVEN WONDERS OF THE WORLD

THE PYRAMIDS OF EGYPT	THE STATUE OF ZEUS AT OLYMPIA
THE COLOSSUS OF RHODES	THE TEMPLE OF ARTEMIS AT EPHESUS
THE HANGING GARDENS OF BABYLON	THE PHAROS OF ALEXANDRIA
THE MAUSOLEUM OF HALICARNASSUS	

SEVEN VIRTUES

FAITH	HOPE	LOVE (CHARITY)	TEMPERANCE
FORTITUDE	JUSTICE	PRUDENCE	

MONEY

1&2	4–continued	5–continued	7
AS	PICE	SEMIS	ANGELOT
D	PONY	SOLDO	CAROLUS
L	QUID	STICA	CENTAVA
P	REAL	STYCA	DENARII
S	RYAL	SYCEE	DRACHMA
3	TAEL	TICAL	GUILDER
BIT	UNIK	TICCY	JACOBUS
BOB		TOMAN	MILREIS
COB	**5**	UNCIA	MOIDORE
DAM	ANGEL	UNITE	NGUSANG
ECU	ASPER		PISTOLE
FAR	BELGA	**6**	QUARTER
KIP	BETSO	AMANIA	SEXTANS
LAT	BROAD	AUREUS	STOOTER
MIL	CONTO	BAWBEE	TESTOON
MNA	COPEC	BEZART	UNICORN
PIE	CROWN	CONDOR	
REE	DARIC	COPANG	**8**
REI	DINAR	COPPER	AMBROSIN
SHO	DUCAT	DÉCIME	DENARIUS
SOL	EAGLE	DOBLON	DIDRACHM
SOU	FRANC	DOLLAR	DOUBLOON
YEN	GROAT	ESCUDO	DUCATOON
	LIARD	FLORIN	FARTHING
4	LIBRA	FUORTE	FLORENCE
ANNA	LITAS	GUINEA	JOHANNES
BEKA	LIVRE	GULDEN	KREUTZER
BIGA	LOCHO	KOPECK	LOUIS D'OR
BUCK	LOUIS	MONKEY	MARAVEDI
CASH	MEDIO	NICKEL	NAPOLEON
CENT	MOHAR	PAGODE	PICAYUNE
DAUM	MOHUR	PESETA	QUETZALE
DIME	NOBLE	ROUBLE	SESTERCE
DOIT	OBANG	SCEATT	SHILLING
JOEY	PAOLO	SEQUIN	SIXPENCE
KRAN	PENCE	STATER	
LIRA	PENGO	STIVER	**9**
MAIL	PENNY	TALARI	BOLIVIANO
MARK	PLACK	TALENT	CUARTILLO
MERK	POUND	TANNER	DIDRACHMA
MITE	QURSH	TESTER	DUPONDIUS
OBOL	RUBLE	TESTON	GOLD BROAD
PEAG	SCEAT	THALER	GOLD NOBLE
PESO	SCUDI	TOMAUN	GOLD PENNY
	SCUDO	ZECHIN	HALFPENNY

COLLECTIVE NAMES

COLLECTIVE NAMES

ACROBATS – troupe
APES – shrewdness
ASSES – pace
BABOONS – troop
BAKERS – tabernacle
BARBERS – babble
BARMEN – promise
BAYONETS – grove
BEES – erst, swarm
BELLS – change
BISHOPS – bench, psalter
BISON – herd
BREWERS – feast
BUFFALOES – obstinacy
BULLFINCHES – bellowing
BULLOCKS – drove
BUTCHERS – goring
BUTLERS – sneer
CANONS – chapter, dignity
CATERPILLARS – army
CATTLE – herd
CHOUGHS – chattering
COBBLERS – cutting
CROCODILES – bask
CROWS – murder
DEANS – decanter, decorum
DONS – obscuration
DUCKS – paddling, safe
ELEPHANTS – herd, parade

FERRETS – busyness
FLIES – swarm
GAMBLERS – talent
GEESE – gaggle
GOLDFINCHES – charm
GOVERNESSES – galaxy
GRAMMARIANS – conjunction
HARES – down
HARPISTS – melody
HERONS – serge
HIPPOPOTAMI – bloat
HUNTERS – blast
JELLYFISH – fluther, smack
JUGGLERS – neverthriving
KITTENS – litter
LAPWING – desert
LARKS – exaltation
LEOPARDS – leap, lepe
LIONS – pride, sawt, sowse
LOCUSTS – swarm
MAGPIES – tittering
MERCHANTS – faith
MESSENGERS – diligence
MOLES – labour
MULES – span
NIGHTINGALES – watch
ORCHIDS – coterie
OWLS – parliament, stare
PAINTERS – curse, illusion

PARROTS – pandemonium
PEKINGESE – pomp
PENGUINS – parcel
PIGS – litter
PIPERS – skirl
PORPOISES – turmoil
PREACHERS – converting
RABBITS – bury
RHINOCEROS – crash
ROBBERS – band
SHEEP – flock
SHERIFFS – posse
SHIPS – fleet, armada
SHOEMAKERS – blackening
STARLINGS – murmuration
SWALLOWS – gulp
SWINE – doylt
TAILORS – disguising
TAVERNERS – closing
TROUT – hover
TURKEY – rafter
TURTLES – turn
UNDERTAKERS – unction
WIDOWS – ambush
WILDCATS – destruction, dout
WOODPECKERS – descent
WRITERS – worship
ZEBRAS – zeal

TYPEFACES

3	5	5—continued	6
DOW	ASTER	IONIC	AACHEN
	BEMBO	KABEL	ADROIT
4	BLOCK	LOTUS	AURIGA
BELL	DORIC	MITRA	BECKET
CITY	ERBAR	SABON	BODONI
GILL	FOLIO	SWIFT	BULMER
ZAPF	GOUDY	TIMES	CASLON

6–continued
COCHIN
COOPER
CORONA
FENICE
FUTURA
GLYPHA
GOTHIC
HORLEY
ITALIA
JANSON
LUCIAN
MELIOR
MODERN
OLIVER
ONDINE
OPTIMA
ROMANA

7
ANTIQUE
BASILIA
BAUHAUS
BERNARD
BOOKMAN
BRAMLEY

7–continued
CANDIDA
CENTURY
CORONET
CUSHING
ELECTRA
FLOREAL
IMPRINT
IRIDIUM
KORINNA
LUBALIN
MADISON
MEMPHIS
NEUZEIT
PLANTIN
RALEIGH
SPARTAN
STEMPEL
TIFFANY
UNIVERS
WEXFORD
WINDSOR

8
BENGUIAT
BERKELEY

8–continued
BREUGHEL
CLOISTER
CONCORDE
EGYPTIAN
EHRHARDT
FOURNIER
FRANKLIN
FRUTIGER
GALLIARD
GARAMOND
KENNERLY
NOVARESE
OLYMPIAN
PALATINO
PERPETUA
ROCKWELL
SOUVENIR

9
AMERICANA
ATHENAEUM
BARCELONA
BRITANNIC
CALEDONIA
CLARENDON

9–continued
CLEARFACE
CRITERION
DOMINANTE
EUROSTILE
EXCELSIOR
FAIRFIELD
GROTESQUE
HELVETICA
WORCESTER

10
AVANT GARDE
CHELTENHAM
CHURCHWARD
DEVANAGARI
EGYPTIENNE
LEAMINGTON

11
BASKERVILLE
COPPERPLATE

14
TRUMP MEDIAEVAL

AMERICAN INDIANS

3
FOX
OTO
UTE

4
CREE
CROW
HOPI
HUPA
IOWA
SAUK
TUPI

5
AZTEC
CADDO
CREEK
HAIDA
HURON
KASKA
KIOWA
OMAHA
OSAGE
SIOUX
SLAVE
TETON

5–continued
WAPPO
YUROK

6
ABNAKI
APACHE
ATSINA
CAYUGA
DAKOTA
DOGRIB
MANDAN
MICMAC
MIXTEC
MOHAWK
NAVAJO
NOOTKA
OJIBWA
ONEIDA
OTTAWA
PAIUTE
PAWNEE
QUAPAW
SALISH
SANTEE
SENECA

6–continued
TANANA
TOLTEC
YAKIMA

7
ARIKARA
BEOTHUK
CATAWBA
CHINOOK
CHOKTAW
HIDATSA
INGALIK
KUTCHIN
NATCHEZ
SHAWNEE
SHUSWAP
TLINGIT
WICHITA
WYANDOT

8
CHEROKEE
CHEYENNE
COMANCHE
DELAWARE
ILLINOIS

8–continued
IROQUOIS
KICKAPOO
NEZ PERCÉ
OKANOGAN
ONONDAGA
SHOSHONI
TUTCHONE

9
ALGONQUIN
BLACKFOOT
CHICKASAW
CHIPEWYAN
CHIPPEWAY
MENOMINEE
PENOBSCOT
TAHAGMIUT
TILLAMOOK
TSIMSHIAN
TUSCARORA
WINNEBAGO

10+
KAVIAGMIUT
PASAMAQUODDY
POTAWATOMI

CARTOON CHARACTERS

4
DINO
HUEY

5
BLUTO
DEWEY
GOOFY
HE-MAN
LEWEY
PLUTO
SHE-RA
SNOWY

6
BAM-BAM
BOO-BOO
DROOPY
POPEYE
SHAGGY
SNOOPY
TINTIN
TOP CAT

7
ATOM ANT
BATFINK
MR JINKS
MR MAGOO
MUTTLEY
NIBBLES
PEBBLES
RAPHAEL

8
GARFIELD
GODZILLA
LEONARDO
OLIVE OYL
PORKY PIG
SUPERTED
YOGI BEAR

9
BETTY BOOP
BUGS BUNNY
CHIP 'N' DALE
DAFFY DUCK
DAISY DUCK
DOGTANIAN
DONATELLO
ELMER FUDD
PEPE LE PEW
SCOOBY DOO
SPIDERMAN
SYLVESTER

10
ANTHILL MOB
BARNEY BEAR
DEPUTY DAWG
DONALD DUCK
PEGLEG PETE
ROAD RUNNER
SCRAPPY DOO
TWEETIE PIE

10—continued
WILY COYOTE

11
BART SIMPSON
BETTY RUBBLE
FELIX THE CAT
LISA SIMPSON
MICKEY MOUSE
MIGHTY MOUSE
MINNIE MOUSE
PETE HOTHEAD
PINK PANTHER
ROGER RABBIT
SNAGGLEPUSS
TOM AND JERRY
YOSEMITE SAM

12
BARNEY RUBBLE
HOMER SIMPSON
MARGE SIMPSON
MICHELANGELO
PETER PERFECT

13
DICK DASTARDLY
MAGGIE SIMPSON

14
CAPTAIN CAVEMAN
CAPTAIN HADDOCK
CAPTAIN PUGWASH

14—continued
FOGHORN
  LEGHORN
FRED FLINTSTONE
HONG KONG
  PHOOEY
MAGILLA GORILLA
SECRET SQUIRREL
SPEEDY GONZALES
TASMANIAN DEVIL

15
HECKLE AND
  JECKLE
PENELOPE PITSTOP
WILMA FLINTSTONE
WOODY
  WOODPECKER

16
HUCKLEBERRY
  HOUND
QUICK DRAW
  MACGRAW

17+
GERALD MCBOING
  BOING
GERTIE THE
  DINOSAUR
TEENAGE MUTANT
  NINJA TURTLES

LANGUAGE

LANGUAGES OF THE WORLD

2
WU

3
MIN

4
URDU

5
DUTCH
GREEK
HINDI
IRISH
MALAY
ORIYA
TAMIL
WELSH

6
ARABIC

6–continued
BIHARI
BRETON
DANISH
FRENCH
GAELIC
GERMAN
KOREAN
PAHARI
POLISH
ROMANY
SINDHI
SLOVAK
TELUGU

7
BENGALI
CATALAN
ENGLISH

7–continued
FRISIAN
ITALIAN
LATVIAN
MARATHI
PUNJABI
RUSSIAN
SLOVENE
SORBIAN
SPANISH
SWEDISH
TURKISH

8
ASSAMESE
GUJARATI
JAPANESE
JAVANESE

8–continued
KASHMIRI
MANDARIN
ROMANSCH
RUMANIAN
UKRANIAN

9
AFRIKAANS
BULGARIAN
CANTONESE
ICELANDIC
NORWEGIAN
SINHALESE

10
LITHUANIAN
PORTUGUESE
RAJASTHANI
SERBO-CROAT

THE GREEK ALPHABET

ALPHA
BETA
GAMMA
DELTA
EPSILON
ZETA

ETA
THETA
IOTA
KAPPA
LAMBDA
MU

NU
XI
OMICRON
PI
RHO
SIGMA

TAU
UPSILON
PHI
CHI
PSI
OMEGA

THE HEBREW ALPHABET

ALEPH
BETH
GIMEL
DALETH
HE
VAV

ZAYIN
CHETH
TETH
YOD
KAPH
LAMED

MEM
NUN
SAMEKH
AYIN
PE
SADI

KOPH
RESH
SHIN
SIN
TAV

FOREIGN WORDS

AND
Fr.	ET
Ger.	UND
It.	E, ED
Sp.	E
Lat.	ET

BUT
Fr.	MAIS
Ger.	ABER
It.	MA
Sp.	PERO
Lat.	SED

FOR
Fr.	POUR
Ger.	FÜR
It.	PER
Sp.	PARA, POR
Lat.	PER

TO
Fr.	À
Ger.	AUF, NACH
It.	A
Sp.	A
Lat.	AD

WITH
Fr.	AVEC
Ger.	MIT
It.	CON
Sp.	CON
Lat.	CUM

MISTER, MR
Fr.	MONSIEUR, M.
Ger.	HERR, HR., HRN.
It.	SIGNOR, SIG.
Sp.	SEÑOR, SR.
Lat.	DOMINUS

MADAME, MRS
Fr.	MADAME, MME.
Ger.	FRAU, FR.
It.	SIGNORA, SIG.A., SIG.RA.
Sp.	SEÑORA, SRA.
Lat.	DOMINA

MISS, MS
Fr.	MADEMOISELLE, MLLE
Ger.	FRÄULEIN, FRL.
It.	SIGNORINA, SIG.NA
Sp.	SEÑORITA, SRTA.

FROM
Fr.	DE
Ger.	AUS, VON
It.	DA
Sp.	DE
Lat.	AB

OF
Fr.	DE
Ger.	VON
It.	DI
Sp.	DE
Lat.	DE

GIRL
Fr.	FILLE
Ger.	MÄDCHEN
It.	RAGAZZA
Sp.	CHICA, NIÑA
Lat.	PUELLA

BOY
Fr.	GARÇON
Ger.	JUNGE
It.	RAGAZZO
Sp.	CHICO, NIÑO
Lat.	PUER

BIG
Fr.	GRAND
Ger.	GROSS
It.	GRANDE
Sp.	GRANDE
Lat.	MAGNUS

LITTLE
Fr.	PETIT
Ger.	KLEIN
It.	PICCOLO
Sp.	PEQUENO, CHICO, POCO
Lat.	PAUCUS

VERY
Fr.	TRÈS
Ger.	SEHR
It.	MOLTO
Sp.	MUCHO

FASHIONABLE
Fr.	À LA MODE
Ger.	MODISCH
It.	DI MODA
Sp.	DE MODA

GENTLEMAN
Fr.	MONSIEUR
Ger.	HERR
It.	SIGNORE
Sp.	CABALLERO
Lat.	DOMINUS

LADY
Fr.	DAME
Ger.	DAME
It.	SIGNORA
Sp.	SEÑORA
Lat.	DOMINA

MAN
Fr.	HOMME
Ger.	MANN
It.	UOMO
Sp.	HOMBRE
Lat.	HOMO

WOMAN
Fr.	FEMME
Ger.	FRAU
It.	DONNA
Sp.	DOÑA
Lat.	MULIER

WHO
Fr.	QUI
Ger.	WER
It.	CHI
Sp.	QUIÉN, QUE
Lat.	QUIS

I
Fr.	JE
Ger.	ICH
It.	IO
Sp.	YO
Lat.	EGO

YOU
Fr.	TU, VOUS
Ger.	DU, SIE, IHR
It.	TU, VOI, LEI
Sp.	TU, VOSOTROS VOSOTRAS
Lat.	TU, VOS

WHAT
Fr.	QUOI, QUEL
Ger.	WAS
It.	CHE COSA
Sp.	QUE
Lat.	QUOD

HE
Fr.	IL
Ger.	ER
It.	EGLI
Sp.	EL
Lat.	IS

SHE
Fr.	ELLE
Ger.	SIE
It.	ELLA
Sp.	ELLA
Lat.	EA

WE
Fr.	NOUS
Ger.	WIR
It.	NOI
Sp.	NOSOTROS/AS
Lat.	NOS

THEY
Fr.	ILS, ELLES
Ger.	SIE
It.	ESSI/E, LORO
Sp.	ELLOS, ELLAS
Lat.	EI, EAE

AT HOME
Fr.	CHEZ NOUS *OR* À LA MAISON
Ger.	ZU HAUSE
It.	A CASA
Sp.	EN CASA
Lat.	DOMO

HOUSE
Fr.	MAISON
Ger.	HAUS
It.	CASA
Sp.	CASA
Lat.	VILLA, DOMUS

STREET
Fr.	RUE
Ger.	STRASSE
It.	STRADA
Sp.	CALLE
Lat.	VIA

ROAD
Fr.	ROUTE
Ger.	WEG
It.	VIA
Sp.	CAMINO
Lat.	VIA

BY
Fr.	PAR
Ger.	BEI
It.	PER
Sp.	POR
Lat.	PER

BEFORE
Fr.	AVANT
Ger.	VOR
It.	PRIMA
Sp.	(DEL) ANTE
Lat.	ANTE

AFTER
Fr.	APRÈS
Ger.	NACH
It.	DOPO
Sp.	DESPUES
Lat.	POST

UNDER
Fr.	SOUS
Ger.	UNTER
It.	SOTTO
Sp.	(DE)BAJO
Lat.	SUB

OVER
Fr.	SUR
Ger.	OBER
It.	SOPRA, SU
Sp.	SOBRE
Lat.	SUPER

NEAR
Fr.	PRÈS DE
Ger.	NAHE, BEI
It.	VICINO
Sp.	CERCA
Lat.	PROPE

OUT
Fr.	DEHORS
Ger.	AUS
It.	VIA, FUORI
Sp.	FUERA
Lat.	EX

IN
Fr.	DANS
Ger.	IN
It.	IN
Sp.	EN
Lat.	IN

HOW
Fr.	COMMENT
Ger.	WIE
It.	COME
Sp.	COMO
Lat.	QUO MODO

WHY
Fr.	POURQUOI
Ger.	WARUM
It.	PERCHE
Sp.	POR QUÉ
Lat.	CUR

THE
Fr.	LE, LA, LES
Ger.	DER, DIE, DAS
It.	IL, LO, LA, I, GLI, LE
Sp.	EL, LA, LO, LOS, LAS
Lat.	ILLE

A
Fr.	UN, UNE
Ger.	EIN, EINE
It.	UN, UNO, UNA
Sp.	UN, UNA
Lat.	UNUS

RED
Fr.	ROUGE
Ger.	ROT
It.	ROSSO
Sp.	ROJO
Lat.	RUBER

BLUE
Fr.	BLEU
Ger.	BLAU
It.	AZZURRO
Sp.	AZUL
Lat.	CAERULEUS

YELLOW
Fr.	JAUNE
Ger.	GELB
It.	GIALLO
Sp.	AMARILLO
Lat.	FULVUS

GREEN
Fr.	VERT
Ger.	GRÜN
It.	VERDE
Sp.	VERDE
Lat.	VIRIDIS

BLACK
Fr.	NOIR
Ger.	SCHWARZ
It.	NERO
Sp.	NEGRO
Lat.	NIGER

WHITE
Fr.	BLANC *OR* BLANCHE
Ger.	WEISS
It.	BIANCO
Sp.	BLANCO
Lat.	ALBUS

NUMBERS

	ROMAN NUMERALS	FRENCH	GERMAN	ITALIAN	SPANISH
1	I	UN	EIN	UNO	UNO
2	II	DEUX	ZWEI	DUE	DOS
3	III	TROIS	DREI	TRE	TRES
4	IV	QUATRE	VIER	QUATTRO	CUATRO
5	V	CINQ	FÜNF	CINQUE	CINCO
6	VI	SIX	SECHS	SEI	SEIS
7	VII	SEPT	SIEBEN	SETTE	SIETE
8	VIII	HUIT	ACHT	OTTO	OCHO
9	IX	NEUF	NEUN	NOVE	NUEVE
10	X	DIX	ZEHN	DIECI	DIEZ
20	XX	VINGT	ZWANZIG	VENTI	VEINTE
30	XXX	TRENTE	DREISSIG	TRENTA	TREINTA
40	XL	QUARANTE	VIERZIG	QUARANTA	CUARENTA
50	L	CINQUANTE	FÜNFZIG	CINQUANTA	CINCUENTA
60	LX	SOIXANTE	SECHZIG	SESSANTA	SESENTA
70	LXX	SOIXANTE-DIX	SIEBZIG	SETTANTA	SETENTA
80	LXXX	QUATRE-VINGT	ACHTZIG	OTTANTA	OCHENTA
90	XC	QUATRE-VINGT-DIX	NEUNZIG	NOVANTA	NOVENTA
100	C	CENT	HUNDERT	CENTO	CIEN (CIENTO)
500	D	CINQ CENTS	FÜNFHUNDERT	CINQUECENTO	QUINIENTOS
1000	M	MILLE	TAUSEND	MILLE	MIL

FRENCH PHRASES

5
MÊLÉE – brawl
ON DIT – piece of gossip, rumour

6
DE TROP – unwelcome

7
À LA MODE – fashionable
À PROPOS – to the point
CAP-À-PIE – from head to foot
DE RÈGLE – customary
EN MASSE – all together
EN ROUTE – on the way

8
BÊTE NOIR – person or thing particularly disliked
IDÉE FIXE – obsession
MAL DE MER – seasickness
MOT JUSTE – the appropriate word

9
DE RIGUEUR – required by custom
EN PASSANT – by the way
EN RAPPORT – in harmony
ENTRE NOUS – between you and me

10
À BON MARCHÉ – cheap
BILLET DOUX – love letter
DERNIER CRI – latest fashion, the last word
NOM DE PLUME – writer's assumed name
PENSE À BIEN – think for the best

11
AMOUR PROPRE – self-esteem
GARDEZ LA FOI – keep the faith

11–continued
LÈSE MAJESTÉ – treason
NOM DE GUERRE – assumed name
RAISON D'ÊTRE – justification for existence
SAVOIR FAIRE – address, tact
TOUR DE FORCE – feat or accomplishment of great strength

12
FORCE MAJEURE – irresistible force or compulsion
HORS DE COMBAT – out of the fight, disabled
SANS DIEU RIEN – nothing without God
VENTRE À TERRE – at great speed

14
DOUBLE ENTENDRE – double meaning
ENFANT TERRIBLE – child who causes embarrassment
NOBLESSE OBLIGE – privilege entails responsibility
PREUX CHEVALIER – gallant knight
VÉRITÉ SANS PEUR – truth without fear

15
AMENDE HONORABLE – reparation

15–continued
CHERCHEZ LA FEMME – look for the woman
17
PIÈCE DE RÉSISTANCE – most outstanding item; main dish at a meal
20+
AUTRE TEMPS, AUTRES MOEURS – other times, other manners

LATIN PHRASES

4
FIAT – let it be done or made
IN RE – concerning
STET – let it stand

5
AD HOC – for this special purpose
AD LIB – to speak off the cuff, without notes
AD REM – to the point
CIRCA – about
FECIT – he did it

6
AD USUM – as customary
IN SITU – in its original situation
IN TOTO – entirely
IN VIVO – in life, describing biological occurrences within living bodies
PRO TEM – temporary, for the time being

7
AD FINEM – to the end
A PRIORI – by deduction
CUI BONO? – whom does it benefit?
DE FACTO – in fact
FIAT LUX – let there be light
IN VITRO – in glass, describing biological experiments outside a body
PECCAVI – a confession of guilt (I have sinned)
PER DIEM – by the day
SINE DIE – without a day being appointed
SUB ROSA – confidential
UNA VOCE – with one voice, unanimously

8
ALTER EGO – another self
BONA FIDE – in good faith
EMERITUS – one retired from active official duties
MEA CULPA – an acknowledgement of guilt (I am to blame)
NOTA BENE – observe or note well
PRO FORMA – for the sake of form

9
AD INTERIM – meanwhile
AD LITERAM – to the letter
AD NAUSEAM – to a disgusting, sickening degree
DEI GRATIA – by the grace of God
ET TU, BRUTE – and you, Brutus
EXCELSIOR – still higher
EX OFFICIO – by right of position or office
HIC ET NUNC – here and now
INTER ALIA – among other things
PRO PATRIA – for one's country
STATUS QUO – the existing situation or state of affairs
SUB JUDICE – under consideration
VICE VERSA – the terms being exchanged, the other way round
VOX POPULI – popular opinion

10
ANNO DOMINI – in the year of our Lord
DEO GRATIAS – thanks be to God
EX CATHEDRA – with authority
IN EXTREMIS – in dire straits, at the the point of death
IN MEMORIAM – to the memory of
LOCO CITATO – in the place quoted
POST MORTEM – after death
PRIMA FACIE – at first sight
SINE QUA NON – something indispensable
TERRA FIRMA – solid ground

11
AD INFINITUM – endlessly, to infinity
ANIMO ET FIDE – by courage and faith
DE DIE IN DIEM – from day to day
DE PROFUNDIS – from the depths of misery
EX POST FACTO – after the event
GLORIA PATRI – glory to the Father
LOCUS STANDI – the right to be heard (in a law case)
NON SEQUITUR – an unwarranted conclusion

11–continued

PAX VOBISCUM – peace be with you
TEMPUS FUGIT – time flies

12

ANTE MERIDIEM – before noon
CAVEAT EMPTOR – let the buyer beware
COMPOS MENTIS – of sane mind
FESTINA LENTE – hasten slowly, be quick without impetuosity
JACTA EST ALEA – the die is cast
PERSEVERANDO – by perseverance
POST MERIDIEM – after noon
SERVABO FIDEM – I will keep faith
VENI, VIDI, VICI – I came, I saw, I conquered
VOLO NON VALEO – I am willing but unable

13

CORPUS DELICTI – body of facts that constitute an offence
DUM SPIRO, SPERO – while I breathe, I hope
IN VINO VERITAS – there is truth in wine, that is, the truth comes out
MODUS OPERANDI – a method of operating
NE FRONTI CREDE – trust not to appearances
VINCIT VERITAS – truth conquers
VIRTUTIS AMORE – by love of virtue

14

CETERIS PARIBUS – other things being equal
EDITIO PRINCEPS – the original edition
IN LOCO PARENTIS – in place of a parent
NIL DESPERANDUM – never despair
PRO BONO PUBLICO – for the public good

15

ANIMO NON ASTUTIA – by courage not by craft
FORTITER ET RECTE – courageously and honourably
FORTUNA SEQUATUR – let fortune follow
INFRA DIGNITATEM – beneath one's dignity
NON COMPOS MENTIS – mentally unsound
OMNIA VINCIT AMOR – love conquers all things
PERSONA NON GRATA – an unacceptable person

16

GLORIA IN EXCELSIS – glory to God in the highest

17

LABOR IPSE VOLUPTAS – labour itself is pleasure
NUNQUAM NON PARATUS – always ready
PROBUM NON PAENITET – honesty repents not
VER NON SEMPER VIRET – Spring does not always flourish

18

NEC TEMERE NEC TIMIDE – neither rashly nor timidly
PRO REGE, LEGE, ET GREGE – for the king, the law, and the people
REDUCTIO AD ABSURDUM – reducing to absurdity

19

CANDIDE ET CONSTANTER – fairly and firmly
SOLA NOBILITAS VIRTUS – virtue alone is true nobility
VIRTUTI NON ARMIS FIDO – I trust to virtue and not to arms

20+

DE MORTUIS NIL NISI BONUM – speak only good of the dead
DULCE ET DECORUM EST PRO PATRIA MORI – it is sweet and seemly to die for one's country
FORTUNA FAVET FORTIBUS – fortune favours the brave
PATRIA CARA CARIOR LIBERTAS – my country is dear, but liberty is dearer
QUOD ERAT DEMONSTRANDUM – which was to be demonstrated
SIC TRANSIT GLORIA MUNDI – thus passes the glory of the world
TIMEO DANAOS ET DONA FERENTIS – I fear the Greeks, even when bearing gifts
VIVIT POST FUNERA VIRTUS – virtue survives the grave

COMMON SAYINGS

PROVERBS

A bad penny always turns up.
A bad workman always blames his tools.
A bird in the hand is worth two in the bush.
Absence makes the heart grow fonder.
A cat has nine lives.
A cat may look at a king.
Accidents will happen in the best regulated families.
A chain is no stronger than its weakest link.
Actions speak louder than words.
A drowning man will clutch at a straw.
A fool and his money are soon parted.
A fool at forty is a fool indeed.
A friend in need is a friend indeed.
All cats are grey in the dark.
All good things must come to an end.
All is fair in love and war.
All roads lead to Rome.
All's grist that comes to the mill.
All's well that ends well.
All that glitters is not gold.
All the world loves a lover.
All work and no play makes Jack a dull boy.
A miss is as good as a mile.
An apple a day keeps the doctor away.
An Englishman's home is his castle.
An Englishman's word is his bond.
A nod is as good as a wink to a blind horse.
Any port in a storm.
Any publicity is good publicity.
A trouble shared is a trouble halved.

Attack is the best form of defence.
A watched pot never boils.
A woman's work is never done.
A young physician fattens the churchyard.
Bad news travels fast.
Beauty is in the eye of the beholder.
Beauty is only skin-deep.
Beggars can't be choosers.
Better be an old man's darling than a young man's slave.
Better be safe than sorry.
Better late than never.
Birds of a feather flock together.
Blood is thicker than water.
Books and friends should be few but good.
Caesar's wife must be above suspicion.
Charity begins at home.
Christmas comes but once a year.
Civility costs nothing.
Cold hands, warm heart.
Constant dripping wears away the stone.
Curiosity killed the cat.
Cut your coat according to your cloth.
Dead men tell no tales.
Death is the great leveller.
Divide and rule.
Do as I say, not as I do.
Do as you would be done by.
Dog does not eat dog.
Don't count your chickens before they are hatched.
Don't cross the bridge till you get to it.
Don't cut off your nose to spite your face.
Don't meet troubles half-way.
Don't put all your eggs in one basket.

Don't spoil the ship for a ha'porth of tar.
Don't teach your grandmother to suck eggs.
Don't throw the baby out with the bathwater.
Don't wash your dirty linen in public.
Early to bed and early to rise, makes a man healthy, wealthy and wise.
Easier said than done.
East, west, home's best.
Easy come, easy go.
Empty vessels make the greatest sound.
Even a worm will turn.
Every cloud has a silver lining.
Every dog has his day.
Every dog is allowed one bite.
Every man for himself, and the devil take the hindmost.
Everything comes to him who waits.
Experience is the best teacher.
Faith will move mountains.
Familiarity breeds contempt.
Fight fire with fire.
Fine feathers make fine birds.
Fine words butter no parsnips.
Fish and guests smell in three days.
Forewarned is forearmed.
Forgive and forget.
For want of a nail the shoe was lost; for want of a shoe the horse was lost; for want of a horse the rider was lost.
From clogs to clogs in only three generations.
Give a dog a bad name and hang him.
Give him an inch and he'll take a yard.
Great minds think alike.
Great oaks from little acorns grow.

PROVERBS

Handsome is as handsome does.

He that fights and runs away, may live to fight another day.

He travels fastest who travels alone.

He who hesitates is lost.

He who lives by the sword dies by the sword.

He who pays the piper calls the tune.

He who sups with the devil should have a long spoon.

History repeats itself.

Honesty is the best policy.

If a job's worth doing, it's worth doing well.

If at first you don't succeed, try, try, try again.

If the mountain will not come to Mahomet, Mahomet must go to the mountain.

If you don't like the heat, get out of the kitchen.

Imitation is the sincerest form of flattery.

In for a penny, in for a pound.

In the country of the blind, the one-eyed man is king.

It is no use crying over spilt milk.

It never rains but it pours.

It's an ill wind that blows nobody any good.

It's too late to shut the stable door after the horse has bolted.

It will all come right in the wash.

It will be all the same in a hundred years.

Jack of all trades, master of none.

Keep something for a rainy day.

Kill not the goose that lays the golden egg.

Least said soonest mended.

Let bygones be bygones.

Let sleeping dogs lie.

Let the cobbler stick to his last.

Life begins at forty.

Life is just a bowl of cherries.

Life is not all beer and skittles.

Look before you leap.

Love is blind.

Love laughs at locksmiths.

Lucky at cards, unlucky in love.

Many a true word is spoken in jest.

Many hands make light work.

March comes in like a lion and goes out like a lamb.

March winds and April showers bring forth May flowers.

Marry in haste, and repent at leisure.

More haste, less speed.

Necessity is the mother of invention.

Needs must when the devil drives.

Ne'er cast a clout till May be out.

Never look a gift horse in the mouth.

No time like the present.

Old habits die hard.

Old sins cast long shadows.

One for sorrow, two for joy; three for a girl, four for a boy; five for silver, six for gold; seven for a secret, not to be told; eight for heaven, nine for hell; and ten for the devil's own sel.

One good turn deserves another.

One man's meat is another man's poison.

One swallow does not make a summer.

Out of sight, out of mind.

Patience is a virtue.

Penny wise, pound foolish.

Prevention is better than cure.

Red sky at night, shepherd's delight; red sky in the morning, shepherd's warning.

Revenge is a dish that tastes better cold.

Revenge is sweet.

See a pin and pick it up, all the day you'll have good luck; see a pin and let it lie, you'll want a pin before you die.

Seeing is believing.

See Naples and die.

Silence is golden.

Spare the rod and spoil the child.

Sticks and stones may break my bones, but words will never hurt me.

Still waters run deep.

St. Swithin's Day, if thou dost rain, for forty days it will remain; St. Swithin's Day, if thou be fair, for forty days 'twill rain no more.

Take a hair of the dog that bit you.

The darkest hour is just before the dawn.

The devil finds work for idle hands to do.

The devil looks after his own.

The early bird catches the worm.

The end justifies the means.

The exception proves the rule.

The hand that rocks the cradle rules the world.

Time is a great healer.

There is honour among thieves.

There is more than one way to skin a cat.

There is no accounting for tastes.

There is safety in numbers.

There's many a good tune played on an old fiddle.

There's many a slip' twixt the cup and the lip.

There's no place like home.

There's no smoke without fire.

The road to hell is paved with good intentions.

Time and tide wait for no man.

Time is a great healer.

Too many cooks spoil the broth.

Truth is stranger than fiction.

Two heads are better than one.

Two wrongs do not make a right.

United we stand, divided we fall.

Waste not, want not.

We must learn to walk before we can run.

What you lose on the swings you gain on the roundabouts.

When poverty comes in at the door, love flies out of the window.

When the cat's away, the mice will play.

When the wine is in, the wit is out.

Where there's a will there's a way.

Why keep a dog and bark yourself?

You can lead a horse to the water, but you can't make him drink.

You cannot run with the hare and hunt with the hounds.

You can't make an omelette without breaking eggs.

You can't teach an old dog new tricks.

You can't tell a book by its cover.

SIMILES

as bald as a coot
as black as pitch
as black as the ace of spades
as blind as a bat
as blind as a mole
as bold as brass
as bright as a button
as busy as a bee
as calm as a millpond
as cheap as dirt
as chirpy as a cricket
as clean as a whistle
as clear as a bell
as clear as crystal
as clear as mud
as cold as charity
as common as muck
as cool as a cucumber
as cross as two sticks
as daft as a brush
as dead as a dodo
as dead as a doornail
as dead as mutton
as deaf as a post
as different as chalk and
   cheese
as drunk as a lord
as dry as a bone
as dry as dust
as dull as dishwater
as easy as falling off a log
as easy as pie
as fit as a flea
as flat as a pancake
as free as a bird
as free as air

as free as the wind
as fresh as a daisy
as good as gold
as green as grass
as happy as a lark
as happy as a sandboy
as happy as Larry
as happy as the day is long
as hard as nails
as keen as mustard
as large as life
as light as a feather
as like as two peas in a pod
as lively as a cricket
as mad as a hatter
as mad as a March hare
as meek as a lamb
as merry as a cricket
as neat as a new pin
as nutty as a fruitcake
as obstinate as a mule
as old as the hills
as pale as death
as plain as a pikestaff
as plain as the nose on your
   face
as pleased as Punch
as poor as a church mouse
as poor as Lazarus
as pretty as a picture
as proud as a peacock
as pure as the driven snow
as quick as a flash
as quick as lightning
as quick as thought
as quiet as a mouse

as quiet as the grave
as red as a beetroot
as regular as clockwork
as rich as Croesus
as right as rain
as safe as houses
as sharp as a needle
as sick as a dog
as simple as falling off a log
as slippery as an eel
as snug as a bug in a rug
as sound as a bell
as steady as a rock
as stiff as a board
as stiff as a poker
as stiff as a ramrod
as straight as a die
as straight as an arrow
as stubborn as a mule
as sure as eggs is eggs
as sure as hell
as thick as thieves
as thick as two short planks
as thin as a lath
as thin as a rake
as thin as a stick
as tough as nails
as tough as old boots
as ugly as sin
as warm as toast
as weak as a kitten
as weak as dishwater
as welcome as the flowers in
   May
as white as a sheet

NURSERY RHYMES

A frog he would a-wooing go,
Heigh ho! says Rowley,
A frog he would a-wooing go,
Whether his mother would let him or no.
With a rowley, powley, gammon and spinach,
Heigh ho! says Anthony Rowley.

As I was going to St Ives,
I met a man with seven wives.
Each wife had seven sacks
Each sack had seven cats,
Each cat had seven kits,
How many were going to St Ives?

Baa, baa, black sheep,
Have you any wool?
Yes, sir, yes, sir,
Three bags full;
One for the master,
And one for the dame,
And one for the little boy
Who lives down the lane.

Bobby Shafto's gone to sea,
Silver buckles on his knee;
He'll come back and marry me,
Bonny Bobby Shafto!

Come, let's to bed
Says Sleepy-head;
Tarry a while, says Slow;
Put on the pan;
Says Greedy Nan,
Let's sup before we go.

Ding dong, bell,
Pussy's in the well.
Who put her in?
Little Johnny Green.
Who pulled her out?
Little Tommy Stout.

Doctor Foster went to Gloucester
In a shower of rain:
He stepped in a puddle,
Right up to his middle,
And never went there again.

Georgie Porgie, pudding and pie,
Kissed the girls and made them cry;
When the boys came out to play,
Georgie Porgie ran away.

Goosey, goosey gander,
Whither shall I wander?
Upstairs and downstairs
And in my lady's chamber.

Hey diddle diddle,
The cat and the fiddle,
The cow jumped over the moon;
The little dog laughed
To see such sport,
And the dish ran away with the spoon.

Hickory, dickory, dock,
The mouse ran up the clock.
The clock struck one,
The mouse ran down,
Hickory, dickory, dock.

How many miles to Babylon?
Three score miles and ten.
Can I get there by candle-light?
Yes, and back again.
If your heels are nimble and light,
You may get there by candle-light.

Humpty Dumpty sat on a wall,
Humpty Dumpty had a great fall.
All the king's horses and
All the king's men,
Couldn't put Humpty together again.

Jack and Jill went up the hill
To fetch a pail of water;
Jack fell down and broke his crown,
And Jill came tumbling after.

Jack Sprat could eat no fat,
His wife could eat no lean,
And so between them both you see,
They licked the platter clean.

Little Bo-peep has lost her sheep,
And can't tell where to find them;
Leave them alone, and they'll come home,
Bringing their tails behind them.

Little Boy Blue,
Come blow your horn,
The sheep's in the meadow,
The cow's in the corn.

Little Jack Horner
Sat in the corner,
Eating a Christmas pie;
He put in his thumb,
And pulled out a plum,
And said, What a good boy am I!

Little Miss Muffet
Sat on a tuffet,
Eating her curds and whey;
There came a big spider,
Who sat down beside her
And frightened Miss Muffet away.

Little Tommy Tucker,
Sings for his supper:
What shall we give him?
White bread and butter
How shall he cut it
Without a knife?
How will he be married
Without a wife?

Mary, Mary, quite contrary,
How does your garden grow?
With silver bells and cockle shells,
And pretty maids all in a row.

Monday's child is fair of face,
Tuesday's child is full of grace,
Wednesday's child is full of woe,
Thursday's child has far to go,
Friday's child is loving and giving,
Saturday's child works hard for his living,
And the child that is born on the Sabbath day
Is bonny and blithe, and good and gay.

Oh! the grand old Duke of York
He had ten thousand men;
He marched them up to the top of the hill,
And he marched them down again.
And when they were up they were up,
And when they were down they were down,
And when they were only half way up,
They were neither up nor down.

Old King Cole
Was a merry old soul,
And a merry old soul was he;
He called for his pipe,
And he called for his bowl,
And he called for his fiddlers three.

Old Mother Hubbard
Went to the cupboard,
To fetch her poor dog a bone;
But when she got there
The cupboard was bare
And so the poor dog had none.

One, two, Buckle my shoe;
Three, four, Knock at the door.
Five, six, Pick up sticks;
Seven, eight, Close the gate.
Nine, ten, Big fat hen;
Eleven, twelve, Dig and delve.
Thirteen, fourteen, Maids a'courting;
Fifteen, sixteen, Maids in the kitchen.
Seventeen, eighteen, Maids a'waiting;
Nineteen, twenty, My plate's empty.

Oranges and lemons,
Say the bells of St Clement's.
You owe me five farthings,
Say the bells of St Martin's.
When will you pay me?
Say the bells of Old Bailey.
When I grow rich,
Say the bells of Shoreditch.
When will that be?
Say the bells of Stepney.
I'm sure I don't know,
Says the great bell at Bow.
Here comes a candle to light you to bed,
Here comes a chopper to chop off your head.

Peter Piper picked a peck of pickled pepper;
A peck of pickled pepper Peter Piper picked;
If Peter Piper picked a peck of pickled pepper,
Where's the peck of pickled pepper Peter Piper
  picked?

Polly put the kettle on,
Polly put the kettle on,
Polly put the kettle on,
We'll all have tea.
Sukey take it off again,
Sukey take it off again,
Sukey take it off again,
They've all gone away.

Pussy cat, pussy cat, where have you been?
I've been to London to look at the queen.
Pussy cat, pussy cat, what did you there?
I frightened a little mouse under her chair.

Ride a cock-horse to Banbury Cross,
To see a fine lady upon a white horse;
Rings on her fingers and bells on her toes,
And she shall have music wherever she goes.

Ring-a-ring o'roses,
A pocket full of posies,
A-tishoo! A-tishoo!
We all fall down.

Rub-a-dub-dub,
Three men in a tub,
And who do you think they be?
The butcher, the baker,
The candlestick-maker,
And they all sailed out to sea.

See-saw, Margery Daw,
Jacky shall have a new master;
Jacky shall have but a penny a day,
Because he can't work any faster.

Simple Simon met a pieman,
Going to the fair;
Says Simple Simon to the pieman,
Let me taste your ware.
Says the pieman to Simple Simon,
Show me first your penny;
Says Simple Simon to the pieman,
Indeed I have not any.

Sing a song of sixpence,
A pocket full of rye;
Four and twenty blackbirds,
Baked in a pie.
When the pie was opened,
The birds began to sing;
Was not that a dainty dish,
To set before the king?

The king was in his counting-house,
Counting out his money;
The queen was in the parlour,
Eating bread and honey.
The maid was in the garden,
Hanging out the clothes,
When down came a blackbird,
And pecked off her nose.

Solomon Grundy,
Born on a Monday,
Christened on Tuesday,
Married on Wednesday,
Took ill on Thursday,
Worse on Friday,
Died on Saturday,
Buried on Sunday.
This is the end
Of Solomon Grundy.

The lion and the unicorn
Were fighting for the crown;
The lion beat the unicorn
All round about the town.

There was a crooked man, and he walked a
  crooked mile,
He found a crooked sixpence against a crooked
  stile:
He bought a crooked cat, which caught a crooked
  mouse,
And they all lived together in a little crooked
  house.

There was an old woman who lived in a shoe,
She had so many children she didn't know what
  to do;
She gave them some broth without any bread;
She whipped them all soundly and put them to
  bed.

The twelfth day of Christmas,
My true love sent to me
Twelve lords a-leaping,
Eleven ladies dancing,
Ten pipers piping,
Nine drummers drumming,
Eight maids a-milking,
Seven swans a-swimming,
Six geese a-laying,
Five gold rings,
Four colly birds,
Three French hens,
Two turtle doves, and
A partridge in a pear tree.

This little piggy went to market,
This little piggy stayed at home,
This little piggy had roast beef,
This little piggy had none,
And this little piggy cried, Wee-wee-wee-wee-
  wee,
I can't find my way home.

Three blind mice, see how they run!
They all run after the farmer's wife,
Who cut off their tails with a carving knife,
Did you ever see such a thing in your life,
As three blind mice?

Tinker, Tailor,
Soldier, Sailor,
Rich man, Poor man,
Beggarman, Thief.

Tom, Tom, the piper's son,
Stole a pig and away he run;
The pig was eat
And Tom was beat,
And Tom went howling down the street.

Two little dicky birds,
Sitting on a wall;
One named Peter,
The other named Paul,
Fly away, Peter!
Fly away, Paul!
Come back, Peter!
Come back, Paul!

Wee Willie Winkie runs through the town
Upstairs and downstairs and in his nightgown,
Rapping at the window, crying through the lock,
Are the children all in bed? It's past eight o'clock.

What are little boys made of?
Frogs and snails
And puppy-dogs' tails,
That's what little boys are made of.

What are little girls made of?
Sugar and spice
And all that's nice,
That's what little girls are made of.

Who killed Cock Robin?
I, said the Sparrow,
With my bow and arrow,
I killed Cock Robin.
Who saw him die?
I, said the Fly,
With my little eye,
I saw him die.

COMMON QUOTATIONS

ARNOLD, Matthew (1822–88) British poet

The sea is calm to-night,
The tide is full, the moon lies fair
Upon the Straits.
Dover Beach

A wanderer is man from his birth.
He was born in a ship
On the breast of the river of Time.
The Future

Go, for they call you, Shepherd, from the hill.
The Scholar Gipsy

Tired of knocking at Preferment's door.
The Scholar Gipsy

Before this strange disease of modern life,
With its sick hurry, its divided aims.
The Scholar Gipsy

Truth sits upon the lips of dying men.
Sohrab and Rustum

And see all sights from pole to pole,
And glance, and nod, and bustle by;
And never once possess our soul
Before we die.
A Southern Night

AUDEN, W H (1907–73) British poet

Look, stranger, at this island now
The leaping light for your delight discovers.
Look, Stranger

To the man-in-the-street, who, I'm sorry to say
Is a keen observer of life,
The word Intellectual suggests straight away
A man who's untrue to his wife.
Note on Intellectuals

When it comes, will it come without warning
Just as I'm picking my nose?
Will it knock on my door in the morning,
Or tread in the bus on my toes?
Will it come like a change in the weather?
Will its greeting be courteous or rough?
Will it alter my life altogether?
O tell me the truth about love.
Twelve Songs, XII

AUSTEN, Jane (1775–1817) British novelist
Nobody is healthy in London, nobody can be.
Emma, Ch. 12

Business, you know, may bring money, but
friendship hardly ever does.
Emma, Ch. 34

Let other pens dwell on guilt and misery.
Mansfield Park, Ch. 48

A woman, especially if she have the misfortune of
knowing anything, should conceal it as well as
she can.
Northanger Abbey, Ch. 14

It is a truth universally acknowledged, that a
single man in possession of a good fortune must
be in want of a wife.
Pride and Prejudice, Ch. 1

Happiness in marriage is entirely a matter of
chance.
Pride and Prejudice, Ch. 6

Next to being married, a girl likes to be crossed in
love a little now and then.
Pride and Prejudice, Ch. 24

One cannot be always laughing at a man without
now and then stumbling on something witty.
Pride and Prejudice, Ch. 40

For what do we live, but to make sport for our
neighbours, and laugh at them in our turn?
Pride and Prejudice, Ch. 57

BETJEMAN, John (1906–84) British poet
You ask me what it is I do. Well actually, you know,
I'm partly a liaison man and partly P.R.O.
Essentially I integrate the current export drive
And basically I'm viable from ten o'clock till five.
Executive

I have a vision of the future, chum.
The workers' flats in fields of soya beans
Tower up like silver pencils.
The Planster's Vision

Come, friendly bombs, and fall on Slough
It isn't fit for humans now.
There isn't grass to graze a cow
Swarm over. Death!
Slough

THE BIBLE
And now abideth faith, hope, charity, these three;
but the greatest of these is charity.
I Corinthians, 13: 13

O death, where is thy sting? O grave, where is
thy victory?
I Corinthians, 15: 55

Vanity of vanities, saith the Preacher, vanity of
vanities; all is vanity.
Ecclesiastes, 1: 2

To every thing there is a season, and a time to
every purpose under the heaven:
A time to be born, and a time to die; a time to
plant, and a time to pluck up that which is
planted;
A time to kill, and a time to heal; a time to break
down, and a time to build up;
A time to weep, and a time to laugh; a time to
mourn, and a time to dance;
...
A time to love, and a time to hate; a time of war,
and a time of peace.
Ecclesiastes, 3: 1–8

I returned, and saw under the sun, that the race
is not to the swift, nor the battle to the strong,
neither yet bread to the wise, nor yet riches to
men of understanding, nor yet favour to men of
skill; but time and chance happeneth to them all.
Ecclesiastes, 9: 11

Cast thy bread upon the waters: for thou shalt
find it after many days.
Ecclesiastes, 11: 1

I am the Lord thy God, which have brought thee
out of the land of Egypt, out of the house of
bondage.
Thou shalt have no other gods before me.
Thou shalt not make unto thee any graven image,
or any likeness of any thing that is in heaven
above, or that is in the earth beneath, or that is in
the water under the earth:
Thou shalt not bow down thyself to them, nor
serve them: for Lord thy God am a jealous God,
visiting the iniquity of the fathers upon the
children unto the third and fourth generation of
them that hate me;
And shewing mercy unto thousands of them that
love me, and keep my commandments.
Thou shalt not take the name of the Lord thy God
in vain; for the Lord will not hold him guiltless that
taketh his name in vain.
Remember the sabbath day, to keep it holy.
Six days shalt thou labour, and do all thy work:
But the seventh day is the sabbath of the Lord thy
God: in it thou shalt not do any work, thou, nor
thy son, nor thy daughter, thy manservant, nor thy
maidservant, nor thy cattle, nor thy stranger that
is within thy gates:
For in six days the Lord made heaven and earth,
the sea, and all that in them is, and rested the

309

seventh day: wherefore the Lord blessed the sabbath day, and hallowed it.

Honour thy father and thy mother: that thy days may be long upon the land which the Lord thy God giveth thee.

Thou shalt not kill.

Thou shalt not commit adultery.

Thou shalt not steal.

Thou shalt not bear false witness against thy neighbour.

Thou shalt not covet thy neighbour's house, thou shalt not covet thy neighbour's wife, nor his manservant, nor his maidservant, nor his ox, nor his ass, nor any thing that is thy neighbour's.
Exodus, 20: 2–17

Eye for eye, tooth for tooth, hand for hand, foot for foot
Exodus, 21: 24

Thou shalt not suffer a witch to live.
Exodus, 22: 18

In the beginning God created the heaven and the earth.

And the earth was without form, and void; and darkness was upon the face of the deep. And the Spirit of God moved upon the face of the waters. And God said, Let there be light: and there was light.
Genesis, 1: 1–3

And God said, Let us make man in our image, after our likeness: and let them have dominion over the fish of the sea, and over the fowl of the air, and over the cattle, and over all the earth, and over every creeping thing that creepeth upon the earth.
Genesis, 1: 26

And on the seventh day God ended his work which he had made; and he rested on the seventh day from all his work which he had made.
Genesis, 2: 2

But of the tree of the knowledge of good and evil, thou shalt not eat of it: for in the day that thou eatest thereof thou shalt surely die.
Genesis, 2: 17

And the rib, which the Lord God had taken from man, made he a woman, and brought her unto the man.
Genesis, 2: 22

And the Lord said unto Cain, Where is Abel thy brother? And he said, I know not: Am I my brother's keeper?
Genesis, 4: 9

And the Lord said unto him, Therefore whosoever slayeth Cain, vengeance shall be taken on him sevenfold. And the Lord set a mark upon Cain, lest any finding him should kill him.
Genesis, 4: 15

But his wife looked back from behind him, and she became a pillar of salt.
Genesis, 19: 26

And Jacob said to Rebekah his mother, Behold, Esau my brother is a hairy man, and I am a smooth man.
Genesis, 27: 11

Therefore the Lord himself shall give you a sign; Behold, a virgin shall conceive, and bear a son, and shall call his name Immanuel.
Isaiah, 7: 14

Can the Ethiopian change his skin, or the leopard his spots? Then may ye also do good, that are accustomed to do evil.
Jeremiah, 13: 23

The next day John seeth Jesus coming unto him, and saith, Behold the Lamb of God, which taketh away the sin of the world.
John, 1: 29

So when they continued asking him, he lifted up himself, and said unto them, He that is without sin among you, let him first cast a stone at her.
John, 8: 7

And ye shall know the truth, and the truth shall make you free.
John, 8: 32

In my Father's house are many mansions: if it were not so, I would have told you. I go to prepare a place for you.
John, 14: 2

Greater love hath no man than this, that a man lay down his life for his friends.
John, 15: 13

Now the Lord had prepared a great fish to swallow up Jonah. And Jonah was in the belly of the fish three days and three nights.
Jonah, 1: 17

And it came to pass, as they still went on, and talked, that, behold, there appeared a chariot of fire, and horses of fire, and parted them both asunder; and Elijah went up by a whirlwind into heaven.
II Kings, 2: 11

And it came to pass in those days, that there went out a decree from Caesar Augustus, that all the world should be taxed.
Luke, 2: 1

And she brought forth her firstborn son, and wrapped him in swaddling clothes, and laid him in a manger; because there was no room for them in the inn.
Luke, 2: 7

Then said Jesus, Father, forgive them; for they know not what they do. And they parted his raiment, and cast lots.
Luke, 23: 34

And he asked him, What is thy name? And he answered, saying. My name is Legion: for we are many.
Mark, 5: 9

For what shall it profit a man, if he shall gain the

whole world, and lose his own soul? Or what shall a man give in exchange for his soul?
Mark, 8: 36–37

But he answered and said, It is written, Man shall not live by bread alone, but by every word that proceedeth out of the mouth of God.
Matthew, 4: 4

And he saith unto them, Follow me, and I will make you fishers of men.
Matthew, 4: 19

And if thy right eye offend thee, pluck it out, and cast it from thee: for it is profitable for thee that one of thy members should perish, and not that thy whole body should be cast into hell.
Matthew, 5: 29

Lay not up for yourselves treasures upon earth, where moth and rust doth corrupt, and where thieves break through and steal:
Matthew, 6: 19

Take therefore no thought for the morrow: for the morrow shall take thought for the things of itself. Sufficient unto the day is the evil thereof.
Matthew, 6: 33

Judge not, that ye be not judged.
Matthew, 7: 1

And why beholdest thou the mote that is in thy brother's eye, but considerest not the beam that is in thine own eye?
Matthew, 7: 3

Give not that which is holy unto the dogs, neither cast ye your pearls before swine, lest they trample them under their feet, and turn again and rend you.
Matthew, 7: 6

Because strait is the gate, and narrow is the way, which leadeth unto life, and few there be that find it.
Matthew, 7: 14

And they were offended in him. But Jesus said unto them, A prophet is not without honour, save in his own country, and in his own house.
Matthew, 13: 57

And again I say unto you, It is easier for a camel to go through the eye of a needle, than for a rich man to enter into the kingdom of God.
Matthew, 19: 24

But many that are first shall be last; and the last shall be first.
Matthew, 19: 30

Jesus said unto him, Verily I say unto thee, That this night, before the cock crow, thou shalt deny me thrice.
Matthew, 26: 34

Watch and pray, that ye enter not into temptation: the spirit indeed is willing, but the flesh is weak.
Matthew, 26: 41

Then said Jesus unto him, Put up again thy

sword into his place: for all they that take the sword shall perish with the sword.
Matthew, 26: 52

For the lips of a strange woman drop as an honeycomb, and her mouth is smoother than oil: But her end is bitter as wormwood, sharp as a two-edged sword.
Proverbs, 5: 3–4

Stolen waters are sweet, and bread eaten in secret is pleasant.
Proverbs, 9: 17

He that spareth his rod hateth his son: but he that loveth him chasteneth him betimes.
Proverbs, 13: 24

Pride goeth before destruction, and an haughty spirit before a fall.
Proverbs, 16: 18

For thou shalt heap coals of fire upon his head, and the Lord shall reward thee.
Proverbs, 25: 22

Who can find a virtuous woman? for her price is far above rubies.
Proverbs, 31: 10

And the name of the star is called Wormwood: and the third part of the waters became wormwood; and many men died of the waters, because they were made bitter.
Revelations, 8: 11

Here is wisdom. Let him that hath understanding count the number of the beast: for it is the number of a man; and his number is Six hundred threescore and six.
Revelations, 13: 18

Drink no longer water, but use a little wine for thy stomach's sake and thine often infirmities.
I Timothy, 5: 23

For the love of money is the root of all evil: which while some coveted after, they have erred from the faith, and pierced themselves through with many sorrows.
I Timothy, 6: 10

BLAKE, William (1757–1827) British poet and engraver

To see a World in a grain of sand,
And a Heaven in a wild flower,
Hold Infinity in the palm of your hand,
And Eternity in an hour.
Auguries of Innocence

And did those feet in ancient time
Walk upon England's mountains green?
And was the holy lamb of God
On England's pleasant pastures seen?
Milton, Preface (known as the hymn 'Jerusalem')

I will not cease from mental fight,
Nor shall my sword sleep in my hand,
Till we have built Jerusalem
In England's green and pleasant land.
Milton, Preface (known as the hymn 'Jerusalem')

Love seeketh not itself to please,
Nor for itself hath any care,
But for another gives its ease,
And builds a Heaven in Hell's despair.
Songs of Experience, 'The Clod and the Pebble'

Tiger! Tiger! burning bright
In the forests of the night,
What immortal hand or eye
Could frame thy fearful symmetry?
Songs of Experience, 'The Tiger'

Little Lamb, who made thee?
Dost thou know who made thee?
Songs of Innocence, 'The Lamb'

BRONTË, Charlotte (1816–55) British novelist

Reader, I married him.
Jane Eyre, Ch. 38

BROWNING, Elizabeth Barrett (1806–61)
British poet

'Yes,' I answered you last night;
'No,' this morning, sir, I say.
Colours seen by candle-light
Will not look the same by day.
The Lady's Yes

How do I love thee? Let me count the ways.
Sonnets from the Portuguese, XLIII

I love thee with the breath,
Smiles, tears, of all my life! – and, if God choose,
I shall but love thee better after death.
Sonnets from the Portuguese, XLIII

BROWNING, Robert (1812–89) British poet

Oh, to be in England
Now that April's there,
And whoever wakes in England,
Sees, some morning, unaware,
That the lowest boughs and the brushwood sheaf
Round the elm-tree bole are in tiny leaf,
While the chaffinch sings on the orchard bough
In England—now!
Home Thoughts from Abroad

Rats!
They fought the dogs and killed the cats,
And bit the babies in the cradles.
The Pied Piper of Hamelin

The year's at the spring,
And day's at the morn;
Morning's at seven;
The hill-side's dew-pearled;
The lark's on the wing;
The snail's on the thorn;
God's in His heaven –
All's right with the world.
Pippa Passes, Pt. I

BURNS, Robert (1759–96) Scottish poet

Should auld acquaintance be forgot,
And never brought to min'?
Auld Lang Syne

We'll tak a cup o' kindness yet,
For auld lang syne.
Auld Lang Syne

My love is like a red red rose
That's newly sprung in June:
My love is like the melodie
That's sweetly play'd in tune.
A Red, Red Rose

Wee, sleekit, cow'rin', tim'rous beastie,
O what a panic's in thy breastie!
To a Mouse

The best laid schemes o' mice an' men
Gang aft a-gley,
An' lea'e us nought but grief an' pain
For promis'd joy.
To a Mouse

BYRON, Lord (1788–1824) British poet

While stands the Coliseum, Rome shall stand;
When falls the Coliseum, Rome shall fall;
And when Rome falls – the World.
Childe Harold's Pilgrimage, IV

Man's love is of man's life a thing apart,
'Tis woman's whole existence.
Don Juan, I

'Tis strange – but true; for truth is always strange;
Stranger than fiction: if it could be told,
How much would novels gain by the exchange!
Don Juan, XIV

She walks in beauty, like the night
Of cloudless climes and starry skies;
And all that's best of dark and bright
Meet in her aspect and her eyes.
She Walks in Beauty

Though the night was made for loving,
And the day returns too soon,
Yet we'll go no more a roving
By the light of the moon.
So, we'll go no more a roving

CARROLL, Lewis (Charles Lutwidge Dodgson;
1832–98) British author

'What is the use of a book,' thought Alice, 'without
pictures or conversation?'
Alice's Adventures in Wonderland, Ch. 1

'Curiouser and curiouser!' cried Alice.
Alice's Adventures in Wonderland, Ch. 2

'You are old, Father William,' the young man said,
'And your hair has become very white;
And yet you incessantly stand on your head –
Do you think at your age, it is right?'
Alice's Adventures in Wonderland, Ch. 5

Twinkle, twinkle, little bat!
How I wonder what you're at!
Up above the world you fly!
Like a teatray in the sky.
Alice's Adventures in Wonderland, Ch. 7

'Off with his head!'
Alice's Adventures in Wonderland, Ch. 8

'Will you walk a little faster?' said a whiting to a snail,
'There's a porpoise close behind us, and he's treading on my tail.'
Alice's Adventures in Wonderland, Ch. 10

'Twas brillig, and the slithy toves
Did gyre and gimble in the wabe;
All mimsy were the borogoves,
And the mome raths outgrabe.
Through the Looking-Glass, Ch. 1

Tweedledum and Tweedledee
Agreed to have a battle;
For Tweedledum said Tweedledee
Had spoiled his nice new rattle.
Through the Looking-Glass, Ch. 4

'The time has come,' the Walrus said,
'To talk of many things:
Of shoes – and ships – and sealing-wax –
Of cabbages – and kings –
And why the sea is boiling hot –
And whether pigs have wings.'
Through the Looking-Glass, Ch. 4

The rule is, jam tomorrow and jam yesterday – but never jam today.
Through the Looking-Glass, Ch. 5

'You look a little shy; let me introduce you to that leg of mutton,' said the Red Queen. 'Alice – Mutton; Mutton – Alice.'
Through the Looking-Glass, Ch. 9

CERVANTES, Miguel de (1547–1616) Spanish novelist

Take care, your worship, those things over there are not giants but windmills.
Don Quixote, Pt. I, Ch. 8

Didn't I tell you, Don Quixote, sir, to turn back, for they were not armies you were going to attack, but flocks of sheep?
Don Quixote, Pt. I, Ch. 18

The best sauce in the world is hunger.
Don Quixote, Pt. II, Ch. 5

Well, now, there's a remedy for everything except death.
Don Quixote, Pt. II, Ch. 10

There are only two families in the world, my old grandmother used to say, The *Haves* and the *Have-Nots*.
Don Quixote, Pt. II, Ch. 20

A private sin is not so prejudicial in the world as a public indecency.
Don Quixote, Pt. II, Ch. 22

CHURCHILL, Sir Winston (1874–1965) British statesman and writer

We shall not flag or fail. We shall fight in France, we shall fight on the seas and oceans, we shall fight with growing confidence and growing strength in the air, we shall defend our island, whatever the cost may be, we shall fight on the beaches, we shall fight on the landing grounds, we shall fight in the fields and in the streets, we shall fight in the hills; we shall never surrender.
Speech, House of Commons, 4 June 1940

This was their finest hour.
Speech, House of Commons, 18 June 1940
(Referring to the Dunkirk evacuation)

The battle of Britain is about to begin.
Speech, House of Commons, 1 July 1940

Never in the field of human conflict was so much owed by so many to so few.
Speech, House of Commons, 20 Aug 1940
(Referring to the Battle of Britain pilots)

COLERIDGE, Samuel Taylor (1772–1834) British poet

The frost performs its secret ministry,
Unhelped by any wind.
Frost at Midnight

In Xanadu did Kubla Khan
A stately pleasure-dome decree:
Where Alph, the sacred river, ran
Through caverns measureless to man
Down to a sunless sea.
Kubla Khan

And all should cry, Beware! Beware!
His flashing eyes, his floating hair!
Weave a circle round him thrice,
And close your eyes with holy dread,
For he on honey-dew hath fed,
And drunk the milk of Paradise.
Kubla Khan

It is an ancient Mariner,
And he stoppeth one of three.
'By thy long grey beard and glittering eye,
Now wherefore stopp'st thou me?'
The Rime of the Ancient Mariner, I

He holds him with his glittering eye—
The Wedding-Guest stood still,
And listens like a three years' child:
The Mariner hath his will.
The Rime of the Ancient Mariner, I

With my cross-bow
I shot the albatross.
The Rime of the Ancient Mariner, I

As idle as a painted ship
Upon a painted ocean.
The Rime of the Ancient Mariner, II

Water, water, every where,
Nor any drop to drink.
The Rime of the Ancient Mariner, II

Oh sleep! it is a gentle thing,
Beloved from pole to pole!
The Rime of the Ancient Mariner, V

He prayeth best, who loveth best
All things both great and small;
For the dear God who loveth us,
He made and loveth all.
The Rime of the Ancient Mariner, VII

COWARD, Sir Noël (1899–1973) British actor, dramatist, and songwriter

Don't put your daughter on the stage, Mrs Worthington.
Song title

Mad dogs and Englishmen go out in the mid-day sun.
Song title

The Stately Homes of England
How beautiful they stand,
To prove the upper classes
Have still the upper hand.
Operette, 'The Stately Homes of England'

Strange how potent cheap music is.
Private Lives

COWPER, William (1731–1800) British poet

John Gilpin was a citizen
Of credit and renown,
A train-band captain eke was he
Of famous London town.
John Gilpin

God moves in a mysterious way
His wonders to perform;
He plants his footsteps in the sea,
And rides upon the storm.
Olney Hymns, 35

I am monarch of all I survey,
My right there is none to dispute;
From the centre all round to the sea
I am lord of the foul and the brute.
Verses supposed to be written by Alexander Selkirk

DICKENS, Charles (1812–70) British novelist

This is a London particular...A fog, miss.
Bleak House, Ch. 3

'God bless us every one!' said Tiny Tim, the last of all.
A Christmas Carol

Barkis is willin'.
David Copperfield, Ch. 5

Annual income twenty pounds, annual expenditure nineteen nineteen six, result happiness. Annual income twenty pounds, annual expenditure twenty pounds ought and six, result misery.
David Copperfield, Ch. 12

I am well aware that I am the 'umblest person going.
David Copperfield, Ch. 16

Accidents will occur in the best-regulated families.
David Copperfield, Ch. 28

As she frequently remarked when she made any such mistake, it would be all the same a hundred years hence.
Martin Chuzzlewit, Ch. 9

All is gas and gaiters.
Nicholas Nickleby, Ch. 49

Oliver Twist has asked for more.
Oliver Twist, Ch. 2

Known by the *sobriquet* of 'The artful Dodger.'
Oliver Twist, Ch. 8

Take example by your father, my boy, and be very careful o' vidders all your life.
Pickwick Papers, Ch. 13

Poverty and oysters always seem to go together.
Pickwick Papers, Ch. 22

It was the best of times, it was the worst of times, it was the age of wisdom, it was the age of foolishness, it was the epoch of belief, it was the epoch of incredulity, it was the season of Light, it was the season of Darkness, it was the spring of hope, it was the winter of despair, we had everything before us, we had nothing before us, we were all going direct to Heaven, we were all going direct the other way.
A Tale of Two Cities, Bk. I, Ch. 1

It is a far, far, better thing that I do, than I have ever done; it is a far, far, better rest that I go to, than I have ever known.
A Tale of Two Cities, Bk. II, Ch. 15

DICKINSON, Emily (1830–86) US poet

Because I could not stop for Death,
He kindly stopped for me;
The carriage held but just ourselves
And Immortality.
The Chariot 'Because I could not stop for Death'

Parting is all we know of heaven,
And all we need of hell.
My Life Closed Twice Before its Close

DONNE, John (1572–1631) English poet

Come live with me, and be my love,
And we will some new pleasures prove
Of golden sands, and crystal brooks,
With silken lines, and silver hooks.
The Bait

No man is an Island, entire of itself; every man is a piece of the Continent, a part of the main.
Devotions, 17

Any man's death diminishes me, because I am involved in Mankind; And therefore never send to know for whom the bell tolls; it tolls for thee.
Devotions, 17

Go, and catch a falling star,
Get with child a mandrake root,
Tell me, where all past years are,
Or who cleft the Devil's foot.
Go and Catch a Falling Star

I am two fools, I know,
For loving, and for saying so
In whining Poetry.
The Triple Fool

DOYLE, Sir Arthur Conan (1859–1930) British writer

It is an old maxim of mine that when you have ex-

cluded the impossible, whatever remains, how-
ever improbable, must be the truth.
The Beryl Coronet

You know my method. It is founded upon the observance of trifles.
The Boscombe Valley Mystery

'Excellent!' I cried. 'Elementary,' said he.
The Crooked Man

It is quite a three-pipe problem.
The Red-Headed League

'Is there any other point to which you would wish
to draw my attention?'
'To the curious incident of the dog in the night-time.'
'The dog did nothing in the night-time.'
'That was the curious incident,' remarked Sher-
lock Holmes.
The Silver Blaze

Mediocrity knows nothing higher than itself, but
talent instantly recognizes genius.
The Valley of Fear

DRYDEN, John (1631–1700) British poet and
dramatist

But far more numerous was the Herd of such,
Who think too little, and who talk too much.
Absalom and Achitophel, I

None but the Brave deserves the Fair.
Alexander's Feast

Errors, like Straws, upon the surface flow;
He who would search for Pearls must dive below.
All for Love, Prologue

By viewing Nature, Nature's handmaid, art,
Makes mighty things from small beginnings grow.
Annus Mirabilis

ELIOT, T S (1888–1965) US-born British poet
and dramatist

Time present and time past
Are both perhaps present in time future,
And time future contained in time past.
Four Quartets, 'Burnt Norton'

We are the hollow men
We are the stuffed men
Leaning together
Headpiece filled with straw. Alas!
The Hollow Men

This is the way the world ends
Not with a bang but a whimper.
The Hollow Men

I have measured out my life with coffee spoons.
The Love Song of J. Alfred Prufrock

Macavity, Macavity, there's no one like Macavity,
There never was a Cat of such deceitfulness and
suavity.
He always has an alibi, and one or two to spare:
At whatever time the deed took place – MACAVITY
WASN'T THERE!
Old Possum's Book of Practical Cats, Macavity:
The Mystery Cat

FITZGERALD, Edward (1809–83) British poet
and translator

Here with a Loaf of Bread beneath the Bough,
A Flask of Wine, a Book of Verse – and Thou
Beside me singing in the Wilderness –
And Wilderness is Paradise enow.
The Rubáiyát of Omar Khayyám (1st edn.), XI

Ah, my Belovéd, fill the Cup that clears
TO-DAY of past Regrets and Future Fears:
To-morrow! – Why, To-morrow I may be
Myself with Yesterday's Sev'n thousand Years.
The Rubáiyát of Omar Khayyám (1st edn.), XX

Ah, fill the Cup: – what boots it to repeat
How Time is slipping underneath our Feet:
Unborn TOMORROW, and dead YESTERDAY,
Why fret about them if TODAY be sweet!
The Rubáiyát of Omar Khayyám (1st edn.),
XXXVII

The Moving Finger writes; and, having writ,
Moves on: nor all thy Piety nor Wit
Shall lure it back to cancel half a Line,
Nor all thy Tears wash out a Word of it.
The Rubáiyát of Omar Khayyám (1st edn.), LI

FROST, Robert Lee (1875–1963) US poet

My apple trees will never get across
And eat the cones under his pines, I tell him.
He only says, 'Good fences make good
neighbours.'
North of Boston, 'Mending Wall'

Two roads diverged in a wood, and I –
I took the one less traveled by,
And that has made all the difference.
The Road Not Taken

The woods are lovely, dark, and deep,
But I have promises to keep,
And miles to go before I sleep,
And miles to go before I sleep.
Stopping by Woods on a Snowy Evening

GILBERT, Sir William Schwenk (1836–1911)
British dramatist and comic writer

I'm called Little Buttercup – dear Little Buttercup,
Though I could never tell why.
HMS Pinafore, I

Stick close to your desks and never go to sea,
And you all may be Rulers of the Queen's Navee!
HMS Pinafore, I

I often think it's comical
How Nature always does contrive
That every boy and every gal
That's born into the world alive
Is either a little Liberal
Or else a little Conservative!
Iolanthe, II

As some day it may happen that a victim must be
found
I've got a little list – I've got a little list
Of society offenders who might well be
underground,

And who never would be missed – who never
would be missed!
The Mikado, I

Three little maids from school are we,
Pert as a school-girl well can be,
Filled to the brim with girlish glee.
The Mikado, I

My object all sublime
I shall achieve in time –
To let the punishment fit the crime –
The punishment fit the crime.
The Mikado, II

When constabulary duty's to be done –
A policeman's lot is not a happy one.
The Pirates of Penzance, II

GOLDSMITH, Oliver (1730–74) Irish-born British
writer

This is Liberty-Hall, gentlemen.
She Stoops to Conquer, II

Laws grind the poor, and rich men rule the law.
The Traveller

When lovely woman stoops to folly,
And finds too late that men betray,
What charm can soothe her melancholy,
What art can wash her guilt away?
The Vicar of Wakefield, Ch. 9

Conscience is a coward, and those faults it has
not strength enough to prevent it seldom has
justice enough to accuse.
The Vicar of Wakefield, Ch. 13

GRAY, Thomas (1716–71) British poet

The boast of heraldry, the pomp of pow'r,
And all that beauty, all that wealth e'er gave,
Awaits alike th' inevitable hour,
The paths of glory lead but to the grave.
Elegy Written in a Country Churchyard

Some village-Hampden, that with dauntless breast
The little Tyrant of his fields withstood;
Some mute inglorious Milton here may rest,
Some Cromwell guiltless of his country's blood.
Elegy Written in a Country Churchyard

Far from the madding crowd's ignoble strife,
Their sober wishes never learn'd to stray;
Along the cool sequester'd vale of life
They kept the noiseless tenor of their way.
Elegy Written in a Country Churchyard

Alas, regardless of their doom,
The little victims play!
Ode on a Distant Prospect of Eton College

Yet ah! why should they know their fate?
Since sorrow never comes too late,
And happiness too swiftly flies.
Thought would destroy their paradise.
No more; where ignorance is bliss,
'Tis folly to be wise.
Ode on a Distant Prospect of Eton College

Not all that tempts your wand'ring eyes

And heedless hearts, is lawful prize;
Nor all, that glisters, gold.
Ode on the Death of a Favourite Cat

HOUSMAN, A(lfred) E(dward) (1859–1936)
British poet

Loveliest of trees, the cherry now
Is hung with bloom along the bough,
And stands about the woodland ride
Wearing white for Eastertide.
A Shropshire Lad, '1887'

On Wenlock Edge the wood's in trouble;
His forest fleece the Wrekin heaves;
The wind, it plies the saplings double,
And thick on Severn snow the leaves.
A Shropshire Lad, 'The Welsh Marches'

East and west on fields forgotten
Bleach the bones of comrades slain,
Lovely lads and dead and rotten;
None that go return again.
A Shropshire Lad, 'The Welsh Marches'

Malt does more than Milton can
To justify God's ways to man.
A Shropshire Lad, 'The Welsh Marches'

JOHNSON, Samuel (1709–84) British
lexicographer and writer

When two Englishmen meet, their first talk is of
the weather.
The Idler

Marriage has many pains, but celibacy has no
pleasures.
Rasselas, Ch. 26

It is very strange, and very melancholy, that the
paucity of human pleasures should persuade us
ever to call hunting one of them.
Johnsonian Miscellanies (ed. G. B. Hill), Vol. I

A tavern chair is the throne of human felicity.
Johnsonian Miscellanies (ed. G. B. Hill), Vol. II

Love is the wisdom of the fool and the folly of the
wise.
Johnsonian Miscellanies (ed. G. B. Hill), Vol. II

There are few ways in which a man can be more
innocently employed than in getting money.
Life of Johnson (J. Boswell), Vol. II

A man will turn over half a library to make one
book.
Life of Johnson (J. Boswell), Vol. II

Patriotism is the last refuge of a scoundrel.
Life of Johnson (J. Boswell), Vol. II

There is nothing which has yet been contrived by
man, by which so much happiness is produced
as by a good tavern or inn.
Life of Johnson (J. Boswell), Vol. II

When a man is tired of London, he is tired of life;
for there is in London all that life can afford.
Life of Johnson (J. Boswell), Vol. III

He who praises everybody praises nobody.
Life of Johnson (J. Boswell), Vol. III

No man is a hypocrite in his pleasures.
Life of Johnson (J. Boswell), Vol. IV

KEATS, John (1795–1821) British poet
A thing of beauty is a joy for ever:
Its loveliness increases; it will never
Pass into nothingness; but still will keep
A bower quiet for us, and a sleep
Full of sweet dreams, and health, and quiet
  breathing.
Endymion, I

St Agnes' Eve – Ah, bitter chill it was!
The owl, for all his feathers, was a-cold;
The hare limp'd trembling through the frozen grass,
And silent was the flock in woolly fold.
The Eve of Saint Agnes, I

And they are gone: aye, ages long ago
These lovers fled away into the storm.
The Eve of Saint Agnes, XLII

Oh what can ail thee, knight at arms
Alone and palely loitering;
The sedge has wither'd from the lake,
And no birds sing.
La Belle Dame Sans Merci

'Beauty is truth, truth beauty,' – that is all
Ye know on earth, and all ye need to know.
Ode on a Grecian Urn

No, no, go not to Lethe, neither twist
Wolf's-bane, tight-rooted, for its poisonous wine.
Ode on Melancholy

My heart aches, and a drowsy numbness pains
My sense.
Ode to a Nightingale

O for a beaker full of the warm South,
Full of the true, the blushful Hippocrene,
With beaded bubbles winking at the brim,
And purple-stained mouth.
Ode to a Nightingale

Thou wast not born for death, immortal Bird!
No hungry generations tread thee down;
The voice I hear this passing night was heard
In ancient days by emperor and clown:
Ode to a Nightingale

Darkling I listen; and, for many a time
I have been half in love with easeful Death,
Call'd him soft names in many a musèd rhyme,
To take into the air my quiet breath;
Now more than ever seems it rich to die,
To cease upon the midnight with no pain,
While thou art pouring forth thy soul abroad
In such an ecstasy!
Ode to a Nightingale

Much have I travell'd in the realms of gold,
And many goodly states and kingdoms seen.
On first looking into Chapman's Homer

Season of mists and mellow fruitfulness,
Close bosom-friend of the maturing sun;
Conspiring with him how to load and bless

With fruit the vines that round the thatch-eaves
  run.
To Autumn

KIPLING, Rudyard (1865–1936) British writer
and poet
For the female of the species is more deadly than
  the male.
The Female of the Species

If you can talk with crowds and keep your virtue,
Or walk with Kings – nor lose the common touch,
If neither foes nor loving friends can hurt you,
If all men count with you, but none too much;
If you can fill the unforgiving minute
With sixty seconds' worth of distance run,
Yours is the Earth and everything that's in it,
And – which is more – you'll be a Man my son!
If

Ship me somewheres east of Suez, where the
  best is like the worst,
Where there aren't no Ten Commandments, an' a
  man can raise a thirst:
The Road to Mandalay

It's Tommy this, an' Tommy that, an' 'Chuck him
  out, the brute!'
But it's 'Saviour of 'is country' when the guns
  begin to shoot.
Tommy

They shut the road through the woods
Seventy years ago.
Weather and rain have undone it again,
And now you would never know
There was once a road through the woods.
The Way Through the Woods

LEAR, Edward (1812–88) British artist and writer
Far and few, far and few,
Are the lands where the Jumblies live;
Their heads are green, and their hands are blue,
And they went to sea in a sieve.
The Jumblies

The Owl and the Pussy-Cat went to sea
In a beautiful pea-green boat,
They took some honey, and plenty of money,
Wrapped up in a five-pound note.
The Owl and the Pussy-Cat

They dined on mince, and slices of quince,
Which they ate with a runcible spoon;
And hand in hand, on the edge of the sand,
They danced by the light of the moon.
The Owl and the Pussy-Cat

LONGFELLOW, Henry Wadsworth (1807–82)
US poet
The shades of night were falling fast,
As through an Alpine village passed
A youth, who bore, 'mid snow and ice,
A banner with the strange device,
Excelsior!
Excelsior

By the shore of Gitche Gumee,

By the shining Big-Sea-Water,
Stood the wigwam of Nokomis,
Daughter of the Moon, Nokomis,
The Song of Hiawatha, 'Hiawatha's Childhood'

From the waterfall he named her,
Minnehaha, Laughing Water.
The Song of Hiawatha, 'Hiawatha and
  Mudjekeewis'

He is dead, the sweet musician!
He is the sweetest of all singers!
He has gone from us for ever,
He has moved a little nearer
To the Master of all music,
To the Master of all singing!
O my brother, Chibiabos!
The Song of Hiawatha, 'Hiawatha's Lamentation'

Ships that pass in the night, and speak each
  other in passing;
Only a signal shown and a distant voice in the
  darkness;
So on the ocean of life we pass and speak one
  another,
Only a look and a voice; then darkness again and
  a silence.
Tales of a Wayside Inn, 'The Theologian's Tale.
  Elizabeth'

Under a spreading chestnut tree
The village smithy stands;
The smith, a mighty man is he,
With large and sinewy hands;
And the muscles of his brawny arms
Are strong as iron bands.
The Village Blacksmith

MARVELL, Andrew (1621–78) English poet

I have a garden of my own,
But so with roses overgrown,
And lilies, that you would it guess
To be a little wilderness.
*The Nymph Complaining for the Death of her
  Fawn*

Had we but world enough, and time,
This coyness, lady, were no crime.
To His Coy Mistress

But at my back I always hear
Time's winged chariot hurrying near;
And yonder all before us lie
Deserts of vast eternity.
To His Coy Mistress

The grave's a fine and private place,
But none, I think, do there embrace.
To His Coy Mistress

MASEFIELD, John (1878–1967) British poet

Quinquireme of Nineveh from distant Ophir
Rowing home to haven in sunny Palestine,
With a cargo of ivory,
And apes and peacocks,
Sandalwood, cedarwood, and sweet white wine.
Cargoes

Dirty British coaster with a salt-caked smoke
  stack,
Butting through the Channel in the mad March
  days,
With a cargo of Tyne coal,
Road-rail, pig-lead,
Firewood, iron-ware, and cheap tin trays.
Cargoes

I must down to the seas again, to the lonely sea
  and the sky,
And all I ask is a tall ship and a star to steer her
  by,
And the wheel's kick and the wind's song and the
  white sail's shaking,
And a grey mist on the sea's face and a grey
  dawn breaking.
Sea Fever

MILTON, John (1608–74) English poet

To sport with Amaryllis in the shade,
Or with the tangles of Neaera's hair.
Lycidas

Fame is the spur that the clear spirit doth raise
(That last infirmity of noble mind)
To scorn delights, and live laborious days.
Lycidas

Of Man's first disobedience, and the fruit
Of that forbidden tree, whose mortal taste
Brought death into the World, and all our woe…
Paradise Lost, Bk. I

What in me is dark
Illumine, what is low raise and support;
That, to the height of this great argument,
I may assert Eternal Providence,
And justify the ways of God to men.
Paradise Lost, Bk. I

To reign is worth ambition, though in Hell:
Better to reign in Hell than serve in Heaven.
Paradise Lost, Bk. I

High on a throne of royal state, which far
Outshone the wealth of Ormuz and of Ind,
Or where the gorgeous East with richest hand
Showers on her kings barbaric pearl and gold,
Satan exalted sat, by merit raised
To that bad eminence.
Paradise Lost, Bk. II

For neither man nor angel can discern
Hypocrisy, the only evil that walks
Invisible, except to God alone.
Paradise Lost, Bk. III

Ask for this great deliverer now, and find him
Eyeless in Gaza at the mill with slaves.
Samson Agonistes

When I consider how my light is spent
Ere half my days in this dark world and wide,
And that one talent which is death to hide
Lodged with me useless.
Sonnet. 'On his Blindness'

NEWBOLT, Sir Henry John (1862–1938) British poet

The sand of the desert is sodden red, –
Red with the wreck of a square that broke; –
The gatling's jammed and the colonel dead,
And the regiment blind with the dust and smoke.
The river of death has brimmed its banks
And England's far and honour a name.
But the voice of a schoolboy rallies the ranks:
'Play up! play up! and play the game!'
Vitaï Lampada

ORWELL, George (Eric Blair; 1903–50) British novelist

Man is the only creature that consumes without producing.
Animal Farm, Ch. 1

Four legs good, two legs bad.
Animal Farm, Ch. 3

All animals are equal but some animals are more equal than others.
Animal Farm, Ch. 10

Who controls the past controls the future. Who controls the present controls the past.
Nineteen Eighty-Four

If you want a picture of the future, imagine a boot stamping on a human face – for ever.
Nineteen Eighty-Four

Big Brother is watching you.
Nineteen Eighty-Four

War is Peace, Freedom is Slavery, Ignorance is Strength.
Nineteen Eighty-Four

Doublethink means the power of holding two contradictory beliefs in one's mind simultaneously, and accepting both of them.
Nineteen Eighty-Four

PARKER, Dorothy (1893–1967) US writer

He lies below, correct in cypress wood,
And entertains the most exclusive worms.
Epitaph for a Very Rich Man

Why is it no one ever sent me yet
One perfect limousine, do you suppose?
Ah no, it's always just my luck to get
One perfect rose.
One Perfect Rose

By the time you say you're his,
Shivering and sighing,
And he vows his passion is
Infinite, undying –
Lady, make a note of this:
One of you is lying.
Unfortunate Coincidence

POPE, Alexander (1688–1744) British poet

The right divine of kings to govern wrong.
The Dunciad, IV

Do good by stealth, and blush to find it fame.
Epilogue to the Satires, Dialogue I

Damn with faint praise, assent with civil leer,
And, without sneering, teach the rest to sneer.
Epistle to Dr. Arbuthnot

Of all the causes which conspire to blind
Man's erring judgment, and misguide the mind,

What the weak head with strongest bias rules,
Is Pride, the never-failing vice of fools.
An Essay on Criticism

A little learning is a dangerous thing;
Drink deep, or taste not the Pierian spring:
There shallow draughts intoxicate the brain,
And drinking largely sobers us again.
An Essay on Criticism

To err is human, to forgive, divine.
An Essay on Criticism

For fools rush in where angels fear to tread.
An Essay on Criticism

Hope springs eternal in the human breast;
Man never is, but always to be blest.
An Essay on Man, I

Know then thyself, presume not God to scan,
The proper study of Mankind is Man.
An Essay on Man, II

Where'er you walk, cool gales shall fan the glade,
Trees, where you sit, shall crowd into a shade:
Where'er you tread, the blushing flow'rs shall rise,
And all things flourish where you turn your eyes.
Pastorals, 'Summer'

SASSOON, Siegfried (1886–1967) British poet and writer

And when the war is done and youth stone dead
I'd toddle safely home and die – in bed.
Base Details

'Good morning; good morning!' the general said
When we met him last week on our way to the line.
Now the soldiers he smiled at are most of 'em dead,
And we're cursing his staff for incompetent swine.
The General

SCOTT, Sir Walter (1771–1832) Scottish writer

O Caledonia! stern and wild,
Meet nurse for a poetic child!
Land of brown heath and shaggy wood,
Land of the mountain and the flood,
Land of my sires! what mortal hand
Can e'er untie the filial band
That knits me to thy rugged strand!
The Lay of the Last Minstrel, VI

To that dark inn, the grave!
The Lord of the Isles, VI

O, young Lochinvar is come out of the west,
Through all the wide Border his steed was the best.
Marmion, V

SHAKESPEARE, William (1564–1616) English dramatist and poet

Our remedies oft in ourselves do lie,
Which we ascribe to heaven.
All's Well that Ends Well, I: 1

Where's my serpent of old Nile?
Antony and Cleopatra, I: 5

My salad days,
When I was green in judgment, cold in blood,

To say as I said then!
Antony and Cleopatra, I: 5

The barge she sat in, like a burnish'd throne,
Burn'd on the water. The poop was beaten gold;
Purple the sails, and so perfumed that
The winds were love-sick with them; the oars
  were silver,
Which to the tune of flutes kept stroke and made
The water which they beat to follow faster,
As amorous of their strokes. For her own person,
It beggar'd all description.
Antony and Cleopatra, II: 2

Age cannot wither her, nor custom stale
Her infinite variety. Other women cloy
The appetites they feed, but she makes hungry
Where most she satisfies.
Antony and Cleopatra, II: 2

She shall be buried by her Antony!
No grave upon the earth shall clip in it
A pair so famous.
Antony and Cleopatra, V: 2

Well said; that was laid on with a trowel.
As You Like It, I: 2

And this our life, exempt from public haunt,
Finds tongues in trees, books in the running
  brooks,
Sermons in stones and good in everything.
As You Like It, II: 1

All the world's a stage,
And all the men and women merely players;
They have their exits and their entrances;
And one man in his time plays many parts,
His acts being seven ages.
As You Like It, II: 7

Last scene of all,
That ends this strange eventful history,
Is second childishness and mere oblivion;
Sans teeth, sans eyes, sans taste, sans every
  thing.
As You Like It, II: 7

Men have died from time to time, and worms
have eaten them, but not for love.
As You Like It, IV: 1

Fear no more the heat o' th' sun
Nor the furious winter's rages;
Thou thy worldly task hast done,
Home art gone, and ta'en thy wages.
Golden lads and girls all must,
As chimney-sweepers, come to dust.
Cymbeline, IV: 2

But I have that within which passes show –

these but the trappings and the suits of woe.
Hamlet, I: 2

O! that this too too solid flesh would melt,
Thaw, and resolve itself into a dew.
Or that the Everlasting had not fix'd
His canon 'gainst self-slaughter! O God! O God!
How weary, stale, flat, and unprofitable,
Seem to me all the uses of this world!
Hamlet, I: 2

Frailty, thy name is woman!
Hamlet, I: 2

Foul deeds will rise,
Though all the earth o'erwhelm them, to men's
  eyes.
Hamlet, I: 2

Costly thy habit as thy purse can buy,
But not express'd in fancy; rich, not gaudy;
For the apparel oft proclaims the man.
Hamlet, I: 3

Neither a borrower nor a lender be;
For loan oft loses both itself and friend,
And borrowing dulls the edge of husbandry.
This above all: to thine own self be true,
And it must follow, as the night the day,
Thou canst not then be false to any man.
Hamlet, I: 3

Something is rotten in the state of Denmark.
Hamlet, I: 4

Murder most foul, as in the best it is;
But this most foul, strange, and unnatural.
Hamlet, I: 5

There are more things in heaven and earth,
  Horatio,
Than are dreamt of in your philosophy.
Hamlet, I: 5

Though this be madness, yet there is method in't.
Hamlet, II: 2

There is nothing either good or bad, but thinking
makes it so.
Hamlet, II: 2

What a piece of work is a man! How noble in
reason! how infinite in faculties! in form and moving, how express and admirable! in action, how
like an angel! in apprehension, how like a god!
the beauty of the world! the paragon of animals!
Hamlet, II: 2

I am but mad north-north-west; when the wind is
southerly, I know a hawk from a handsaw.
Hamlet, II: 2

The play, I remember, pleas'd not the million;
'twas caviare to the general.
Hamlet, II: 2

To be, or not to be – that is the question;
Whether 'tis nobler in the mind to suffer
The slings and arrows of outrageous fortune,
Or to take arms against a sea of troubles,
And by opposing end them? To die, to sleep –
No more; and by a sleep to say we end

The heart-ache and the thousand natural shocks
That flesh is heir to, 'tis a consummation
Devoutly to be wish'd. To die, to sleep;
To sleep, perchance to dream. Ay, there's the rub;
For in that sleep of death what dreams may
come,
When we have shuffled off this mortal coil,
Must give us pause.
Hamlet, III: 1

The dread of something after death –
The undiscover'd country, from whose bourn
No traveller returns.
Hamlet, III: 1

Thus conscience does make cowards of us all;
Hamlet, III: 1

Madness in great ones must not unwatch'd go.
Hamlet, III: 1

How all occasions do inform against me,
And spur my dull revenge! What is a man,
If his chief good and market of his time
Be but to sleep and feed? a beast, no more.
Hamlet, IV: 4

When sorrows come, they come not single spies,
But in battalions!
Hamlet, IV: 5

There's rosemary, that's for remembrance; pray,
love, remember: and there is pansies, that's for
thoughts.
Hamlet, IV: 5

Alas, poor Yorick! I knew him, Horatio: a fellow of
infinite jest, of most excellent fancy.
Hamlet, V: 1

There's a divinity that shapes our ends,
Rough-hew them how we will.
Hamlet, V: 2

Out of this nettle, danger, we pluck this flower,
safety.
Henry IV, Part One, II: 3

The better part of valour is discretion; in the
which better part I have saved my life.
Henry IV, Part One, V: 4

Uneasy lies the head that wears a crown.
Henry IV, Part Two, III: 1

Once more unto the breach, dear friends, once
more;
Or close the wall up with our English dead.
Henry V, III: 1

And gentlemen in England, now a-bed
Shall think themselves accurs'd they were not
here,
And hold their manhoods cheap whiles any
speaks
That fought with us upon Saint Crispin's day.
Henry V, IV: 3

Men at some time are masters of their fates:
The fault, dear Brutus, is not in our stars,
But in ourselves, that we are underlings.
Julius Caesar, I: 2

Cry 'Havoc!' and let slip the dogs of war.
Julius Caesar, III: 1

Friends, Romans, countrymen, lend me your ears
I come to bury Caesar, not to praise him.
The evil that men do lives after them;
The good is oft interred with their bones.
Julius Caesar, III: 2

If you have tears, prepare to shed them now.
Julius Caesar, III: 2

There is a tide in the affairs of men
Which, taken at the flood, leads on to fortune;
Julius Caesar, IV: 3

How sharper than a serpent's tooth it is
To have a thankless child!
King Lear, I: 4

I am a man
More sinn'd against than sinning.
King Lear, III: 2

The worst is not
So long as we can say 'This is the worst'.
King Lear, IV: 1

As flies to wanton boys are we to th' gods –
They kill us for their sport.
King Lear, IV: 1

When shall we three meet again
In thunder, lightning, or in rain?
Macbeth, I: 1

I have no spur
To prick the sides of my intent, but only
Vaulting ambition, which o'er-leaps itself,
And falls on th' other.
Macbeth, I: 7

Is this a dagger which I see before me,
The handle toward my hand? Come, let me
clutch thee:
I have thee not, and yet I see thee still.
Macbeth, II: 1

Methought I heard a voice cry, 'Sleep no more!'
Macbeth doth murder sleep,' the innocent sleep,
Sleep that knits up the ravell'd sleave of care,
The death of each day's life, sore labour's bath,
Balm of hurt minds, great nature's second course,
Chief nourisher in life's feast.
Macbeth, II: 2

Eye of newt, and toe of frog,
Wool of bat, and tongue of dog,
Adder's fork, and blind-worm's sting,
Lizard's leg, and howlet's wing,
For a charm of powerful trouble,
Like a hell-broth boil and bubble.
Macbeth, IV: 1

Be bloody bold, and resolute, laugh to scorn
The power of man, for none of woman born
Shall harm Macbeth.
Macbeth, IV: 1

Here's the smell of the blood still. All the perfumes of Arabia will not sweeten this little hand.
Macbeth, V: 1

Tomorrow, and tomorrow, and tomorrow,
Creeps in this petty pace from day to day
To the last syllable of recorded time,
And all our yesterdays have lighted fools
The way to dusty death. Out, out, brief candle!
Life's but a walking shadow, a poor player,
That struts and frets his hour upon the stage,
And then is heard no more; it is a tale
Told by an idiot, full of sound and fury,
Signifying nothing.
Macbeth, V: 5

The devil can cite Scripture for his purpose.
The Merchant of Venice, I: 3

You call me misbeliever, cut-throat dog,
And spit upon my Jewish gaberdine,
And all for use of that which is mine own.
The Merchant of Venice, I: 3

It is a wise father that knows his own child.
The Merchant of Venice, II: 2

Hath not a Jew eyes? Hath not a Jew hands,
organs, dimensions, senses, affections, passions,
fed with the same food, hurt with the same
weapons, subject to the same diseases, healed
by the same means, warmed and cooled by the
same winter and summer, as a Christian is? If
you prick us, do we not bleed? If you tickle us, do
we not laugh? If you poison us, do we not die?
And if you wrong us, shall we not revenge?
The Merchant of Venice, III: 1

The quality of mercy is not strain'd;
It droppeth as the gentle rain from heaven
Upon the place beneath. It is twice blest;
It blesseth him that gives and him that takes.
The Merchant of Venice, IV: 1

How far that little candle throws his beams!
So shines a good deed in a naughty world.
The Merchant of Venice, V: 1

Why, then the world's mine oyster,
Which I with sword will open.
The Merry Wives of Windsor, II: 2

For aught that I could ever read,
Could ever hear by tale or history,
The course of true love never did run smooth.
A Midsummer Night's Dream, I: 1

Ill met by moonlight, proud Titania.
A Midsummer Night's Dream, II: 1

The lunatic, the lover, and the poet,
Are of imagination all compact.
A Midsummer Night's Dream, V: 1

Doth not the appetite alter? A man loves the meat
in his youth that he cannot endure in his age.
Much Ado About Nothing, II: 3

Comparisons are odorous.
Much Ado About Nothing, III: 5

Reputation, reputation, reputation! O, I have lost
my reputation! I have lost the immortal part of
myself, and what remains is bestial.
Othello, II: 3

But he that filches from me my good name
Robs me of that which not enriches him
And makes me poor indeed.
Othello, III: 3

O, beware, my lord, of jealousy;
It is the green-ey'd monster which doth mock
The meat it feeds on.
Othello, III: 3

Then must you speak
Of one that lov'd not wisely, but too well;
Of one not easily jealous, but, being wrought,
Perplexed in the extreme; of one whose hand,
Like the base Indian, threw a pearl away
Richer than all his tribe.
Othello, V: 2

Teach thy necessity to reason thus:
There is no virtue like necessity.
Richard II, I: 3

This royal throne of kings, this sceptred isle,
This earth of majesty, this seat of Mars,
This other Eden, demi-paradise,
This fortress built by Nature for herself
Against infection and the hand of war,
This happy breed of men, this little world,
This precious stone set in the silver sea,
Which serves it in the office of a wall,
Or as a moat defensive to a house,
Against the envy of less happier lands;
This blessed plot, this earth, this realm, this
    England,
This nurse, this teeming womb of royal kings,
Fear'd by their breed, and famous by their birth.
Richard II, II: 1

Now is the winter of our discontent
Made glorious summer by this sun of York.
Richard III, I: 1

A horse! a horse! my kingdom for a horse.
Richard III, V: 4

From forth the fatal loins of these two foes
A pair of star-cross'd lovers take their life.
Romeo and Juliet, Prologue

O! she doth teach the torches to burn bright
It seems she hangs upon the cheek of night
Like a rich jewel in an Ethiop's ear;
Beauty too rich for use, for earth too dear.
Romeo and Juliet, I: 5

My only love sprung from my only hate!
Too early seen unknown, and known too late!
Romeo and Juliet, I: 5

What's in a name? That which we call a rose
By any other name would smell as sweet.
Romeo and Juliet, II: 2

Good night, good night! Parting is such sweet
    sorrow
That I shall say good night till it be morrow.
Romeo and Juliet, II: 2

A plague o' both your houses!
They have made worms' meat of me.
Romeo and Juliet, III: 1

How beauteous mankind is! O brave new world
That has such people in't!
The Tempest, V: 1

If music be the food of love, play on,
Give me excess of it, that, surfeiting,
The appetite may sicken and so die.
Twelfth Night, I: 1

Then come kiss me, sweet and twenty;
Youth's a stuff will not endure.
Twelfth Night, II: 3

Dost thou think, because thou art virtuous, there
shall be no more cakes and ale?
Twelfth Night, II: 3

Some are born great, some achieve greatness,
and some have greatness thrust upon 'em.
Twelfth Night, II: 5

Crabbed age and youth cannot live together:
Youth is full of pleasure, age is full of care;
Youth like summer morn, age like winter
  weather;
Youth like summer brave, age like winter bare.
The Passionate Pilgrim, XII

Shall I compare thee to a summer's day?
Thou art more lovely and more temperate.
Rough winds do shake the darling buds of May,
And summer's lease hath all too short a date.
Sonnet 18

Let me not to the marriage of true minds
Admit impediments. Love is not love
Which alters when it alteration finds,
Or bends with the remover to remove.
O, no! it is an ever-fixed mark,
That looks on tempests and is never shaken.
Sonnet 116

SHAW, George Bernard (1856–1950) Irish
dramatist

When a stupid man is doing something he is
ashamed of, he always declares that it is his duty.
Caesar and Cleopatra, III

He knows nothing; and he thinks he knows
everything. That points clearly to a political
career.
Major Barbara, III

He who can, does. He who cannot, teaches.
Man and Superman, 'Maxims for Revolutionists'

Gin was mother's milk to her.
Pygmalion, III

SHELLEY, Percy Bysshe (1792–1822) British
poet

Let there be light! said Liberty,
And like sunrise from the sea,
Athens arose!
Hellas, I

O Wild West Wind, thou breath of Autumn's being,
Thou, from whose unseen presence the leaves
  dead
Are driven, like ghosts from an enchanter
  fleeing,

Yellow, and black, and pale, and hectic red,
Pestilence-stricken multitudes.
Ode to the West Wind

I met a traveller from an antique land
Who said: Two vast and trunkless legs of stone
Stand in the desert.
Ozymandias

Hail to thee, blithe Spirit!
Bird thou never wert,
That from Heaven, or near it,
Pourest thy full heart
In profuse strains of unpremeditated art.
To a Skylark

STEVENSON, Robert Louis (1850–94) Scottish
writer

Fifteen men on the dead man's chest
Yo-ho-ho, and a bottle of rum!
Drink and the devil had done for the rest –
Yo-ho-ho, and a bottle of rum!
Treasure Island, Ch. 1

Under the wide and starry sky
Dig the grave and let me lie.
Glad did I live and gladly die,
 – And I laid me down with a will.
This is the verse you grave for me:
'Here he lies where he longed to be;
Home is the sailor, home from sea,
And the hunter home from the hill.'
Underwoods, Bk. I, 'Requiem'

TENNYSON, Alfred, Baron (1809–92) British
poet

'Forward the Light Brigade!'
Was there a man dismay'd?
Not tho' the soldier knew
Some one had blunder'd:
Their's not to make reply,
Their's not to reason why,
Their's but to do and die:
Into the valley of Death
Rode the six hundred.
The Charge of the Light Brigade

An arm
Rose up from out the bosom of the lake,
Clothed in white samite, mystic, wonderful.
Idylls of the King, 'The Passing of Arthur'

And slowly answer'd Arthur from the barge:
'The old order changeth, yielding place to new,
And God fulfils himself in many ways.'
Idylls of the King, 'The Passing of Arthur'

I hold it true, whate'er befall;
I feel it, when I sorrow most;
'Tis better to have loved and lost
Than never to have loved at all.
In Memoriam A.H.H., XXVII

I dreamed there would be Spring no more,
That Nature's ancient power was lost.
In Memoriam A.H.H., LXIX

Kind hearts are more than coronets,
And simple faith than Norman blood.
Lady Clara Vere de Vere, VI

On either side the river lie
Long fields of barley and of rye,
That clothe the wold and meet the sky;
And thro' the field the road runs by
To many-tower'd Camelot.
The Lady of Shalott, Pt. I

'The curse is come upon me,' cried
The Lady of Shalott.
The Lady of Shalott, Pt. III

Dear as remembered kisses after death,
And sweet as those by hopeless fancy feign'd
On lips that are for others: deep as love,
Deep as first love, and wild with all regret;
O Death in Life, the days that are no more.
The Princess, IV

THOMAS, Dylan (1914–53) Welsh poet

Though they go mad they shall be sane,
Though they sink through the sea they shall rise
again.
Though lovers be lost love shall not;
And death shall have no dominion.
And death shall have no dominion

Do not go gentle into that good night,
Old age should burn and rave at close of day;
Rage, rage, against the dying of the light.
Do not go gentle into that good night

Now as I was young and easy under the apple
boughs
About the lilting house and happy as the grass
was green.
Fern Hill

Time held me green and dying
Though I sang in my chains like the sea.
Fern Hill

The hands of the clock have stayed still at half
past eleven for fifty years. It is always opening
time in the Sailors Arms.
Under Milk Wood

It is a winter's tale
That the snow blind twilight ferries over the lakes
And floating fields from the farm in the cup of the
vales.
A Winter's Tale

TWAIN, Mark (Samuel Langhorne Clemens;
1835–1910) US writer

There are three kinds of lies: lies, damned lies,
and statistics.
Autobiography

The radical invents the views. When he has worn
them out, the conservative adopts them.
Notebooks

Adam was but human – this explains it all. He did
not want the apple for the apple's sake, he
wanted it only because it was forbidden.
Pudd'nhead Wilson's, Ch. 2

WILDE, Oscar Fingal O'Flahertie Wills
(1856–1900) Irish-born British poet and dramatist

I never saw a man who looked
With such a wistful eye
Upon that little tent of blue
Which prisoners call the sky.
The Ballad of Reading Gaol, I:3

Yet each man kills the thing he loves,
By each let this be heard,
Some do it with a bitter look,
Some with a flattering word.
The coward does it with a kiss,
The brave man with a sword!
The Ballad of Reading Gaol, I:7

To love oneself is the beginning of a lifelong
romance.
An Ideal Husband, III

Other people are quite dreadful. The only
possible society is oneself.
An Ideal Husband, III

I have invented an invaluable permanent invalid
called Bunbury, in order that I may be able to go
down into the country whenever I choose.
The Importance of Being Earnest, I

All women become like their mothers. That is
their tragedy. No man does. That's his.
The Importance of Being Earnest, I

To lose one parent, Mr Worthing, may be
regarded as a misfortune; to lose both looks like
carelessness.
The Importance of Being Earnest, I

I never travel without my diary. One should
always have something sensational to read in the
train.
The Importance of Being Earnest, II

No woman should ever be quite accurate about
her age. It looks so calculating.
The Importance of Being Earnest, III

I can resist everything except temptation.
Lady Windermere's Fan, I

It is absurd to divide people into good and bad.
People are either charming or tedious.
Lady Windermere's Fan, I

We are all in the gutter, but some of us are
looking at the stars.
Lady Windermere's Fan, III

A cigarette is the perfect type of a perfect
pleasure. It is exquisite, and it leaves one unsat-
isfied. What more can one want?
The Picture of Dorian Gray, Ch. 6

Twenty years of romance makes a woman look
like a ruin; but twenty years of marriage make her
something like a public building.
A Woman of No Importance, I

The English country gentleman galloping after a
fox – the unspeakable in full pursuit of the
uneatable.
A Woman of No Importance, I

WORDSWORTH, William (1770–1850) British poet

I travelled among unknown men
In lands beyond the sea;
Nor, England! did I know till then
What love I bore to thee.
I Travelled among Unknown Men

I wandered lonely as a cloud
That floats on high o'er vales and hills,
When all at once I saw a crowd,
A host, of golden daffodils.
I Wandered Lonely as a Cloud

For oft, when on my couch I lie
In vacant or in pensive mood,
They flash upon that inward eye
Which is the bliss of solitude.
I Wandered Lonely as a Cloud

I have learned
To look on nature, not as in the hour
Of thoughtless youth; but hearing often-times
The still, sad music of humanity.
Lines composed a few miles above Tintern Abbey

My heart leaps up when I behold
A rainbow in the sky:
So was it when my life began;
So is it now I am a man;
So be it when I shall grow old,
Or let me die!
The Child is Father of the Man;
And I could wish my days to be
Bound each to each by natural piety.
My Heart Leaps Up

Whither is fled the visionary gleam?
Where is it now, the glory and the dream?
Ode. Intimations of Immortality, IV

Fair seed-time had my soul, and I grew up
Fostered alike by beauty and by fear.
The Prelude, I

Bliss was it in that dawn to be alive,
But to be young was very heaven!
The Prelude, XI

YEATS, W(illiam) B(utler) (1865–1939) Irish poet and dramatist

O chestnut tree, great rooted blossomer,
Are you the leaf, the blossom or the bole?
O body swayed to music; O brightening glance,
How can we know the dancer from the dance?
Among School Children

Wine comes in at the mouth
And love comes in at the eye;
That's all we shall know for truth
Before we grow old and die.
A Drinking Song

For the good are always the merry,
Save by an evil chance,
And the merry love the fiddle,
And the merry love to dance
The Fiddler of Dooney

I will arise and go now, and go to Innisfree,
And a small cabin build there, of clay and wattles made;
Nine bean rows will I have there, a hive for the honey bee,
And live alone in the bee-loud glade.
The Lake Isle of Innisfree

Under bare Ben Bulben's head
In Drumcliff churchyard Yeats is laid...
On limestone quarried near the spot
By his command these words are cut:
    Cast a cold eye
    On life, on death.
    Horseman, pass by!
Under Ben Bulben, VI

When you are old and gray and full of sleep,
And nodding by the fire, take down this book,
And slowly read, and dream of the soft look
Your eyes had once, and of their shadows deep.
When you are Old

Love fled
And paced upon the mountains overhead
And hid his face amid a crowd of stars.
When you are Old

But I, being poor, have only my dreams;
I have spread my dreams under your feet;
Tread softly because you tread on my dreams.
He Wishes for the Cloths of Heaven

MOTTOES

A DEO ET REGE – By God and the King (Earl of Chesterfield)
AD MAJOREM DEI GLORIAM – to the greater glory of God (The Jesuits)
A MARI USQUE AD MARE – from sea to sea (Canada)
APRES NOUS LE DELUGE – after us the deluge (617 Squadron, 'The Dam Busters', RAF)
ARS LONGA, VITA BREVIS – art is long, life is short (Millais)
AUDI, VIDE, TACE – hear, see, keep silence (United Grand Lodge of Freemasons)
AUSPICIUM MELIORIS AEVI – the sign of a better age (Duke of St Albans, Order of St Michael and St George)

BE PREPARED – Scout Association, 1908
CAVENDO TUTUS – safe by being cautious (Duke of Devonshire)
CHE SERA SERA – what will be will be (Duke of Bedford)
DARE QUAM ACCIPERE – to give rather than to receive (Guy's Hospital)
DE PRAESCIENTIA DEI – from the foreknowledge of God (Barbers' Company, 1461)
DICTUM MEUM PACTUM – my word is my bond (Stock Exchange)
DIEU ET MON DROIT – God and my right (British Sovereigns)
DILIGENT AND SECRET (College of Arms, 1484)
DOMINE DIRIGE NOS – Lord, guide us (City of London)
DOMINUS ILLUMINATIO MEA – the Lord is my light (Oxford University)
DONORUM DEI DISPENSATIO FIDELIS – faithful dispensation of the gifts of God (Harrow School)
ENTALENTÉ À PARLER D'ARMES – equipped to speak of arms (The Heraldry Society, 1957)
ESPÉRANCE EN DIEU – hope in God (Duke of Northumberland)
FIDES ATQUE INTEGRITAS – faith and integrity (Society of Incorporated Accountants and Auditors)
FLOREAT ETONA – may Eton flourish (Eton College)
FOR COUNTRY NOT FOR SELF (226 Squadron, RAF)
GARDEZ BIEN – watch well (Montgomery)
HEAVEN'S LIGHT OUR GUIDE (Order of the Star of India)
HELP (Foundling Hospital, London)
HINC LUCEM ET POCULA SACRA – hence light and sacred cups (Cambridge University)
HONI SOIT QUI MAL Y PENSE – evil be to him who evil thinks (Order of the Garter)
HONNEUR ET PATRIE – honour and country (Order of the Legion of Honour)
ICH DIEN – I serve (Prince of Wales)
IMPERATRICUS AUSPICIIS – imperial in its auspices (Order of the Indian Empire)
IN ACTION FAITHFUL AND IN HONOUR CLEAR (Order of the Companions of Honour, 1917)
IN FIDE SALUS – safety in faith (Star of India)
IN SOMNO SECURITAS – security in sleep (Association of Anaesthetists of Great Britain and Ireland)
JUSTITA VIRTUTUM REGINA – justice is queen of the virtues (Goldsmiths' Company)
LABORARE EST ORARE – to labour is to pray (Benedictine Order)
LABOR VIRIS CONVENIT – labour becomes men (Richard I)
LIFE IN OUR HANDS (Institute of Hospital Engineers)
MIHI ET MEA – to me and mine (Anne Boleyn)
NATION SHALL SPEAK PEACE UNTO NATION (British Broadcasting Corporation)
NEC ASPERA TERRENT – difficulties do not daunt (3rd Foot, 'The Buffs', East Kent Regiment)
NEC CUPIAS NEC METUAS – neither desire nor fear (Earl of Hardwicke)
NEMO ME IMPUNE LACESSIT – no one injures me with impunity (Order of the Thistle)
NOLI ME TANGERE – touch me not (Graeme of Garvock, 103 Squadron, RAF)
NON EST VIVERE SED VALERE VITA – life is not living, but health is life (Royal Society of Medicine)
NON SIBI, SED PATRIAE – not for himself, but for his country (Earl of Romney)
NULLIUS IN VERBA – in no man's words (Royal Society)
PAX IN BELLO – peace in war (Godolphin, Duke of Leeds)
PEACE THROUGH UNDERSTANDING (President Eisenhower)
PER ARDUA AD ASTRA – through endeavour to the stars (RAF motto)
PER CAELUM VIA NOSTRA – our way through heaven (Guild of Air Pilots and Navigators)
PISCATORES HOMINUM – fishers of men (National Society)
POWER IN TRUST (Central Electricity Generating Board)
QUIS SEPARABIT? – who shall separate? (Order of St Patrick)
QUOD PETIS HIC EST – here is what you seek (Institute of British Engineers)
RATIONE ET CONCILIO – by reason and counsel (Magistrates Association)
RERUM COGNOSCERE CAUSAS – to know the causes of things (Institute of Brewing)
SEMPER FIDELIS – always faithful (Devonshire regiment, East Devon Militia)
SEMPER PARATUS – always prepared (207 Squadron, RAF)
SOLA VIRTUS INVICTA – virtue alone is invincible (Duke of Norfolk)
TOUCH NOT THE CAT BOT A GLOVE (Macpherson Clan)
TRIA JUNCTA IN UNO – three joined in one (Order of the Bath)
UNITATE FORTIOR – stronger by union (Building Societies Association; Army and Navy Club)
VER NON SEMPER VIRET – the spring does not always flourish
VERNON SEMPER VIRET – *Vernon* always flourishes (Lord Lyveden)
WHO DARES WINS (Special Air Service)

WORDS

PALINDROMES

3
AHA
BIB
BOB
DAD
DID
DUD
ERE
EVE
EWE
EYE
GAG
GIG
HAH
HEH
HUH
MAM
MOM
MUM

3–continued
NUN
OHO
PAP
PEP
PIP
POP
PUP
SIS
SOS
TAT
TIT
TNT
TOT
TUT
WOW

4
BOOB

4–continued
DEED
KOOK
MA'AM
NOON
PEEP
POOP
SEES
TOOT

5
CIVIC
KAYAK
LEVEL
MADAM
MINIM
RADAR
REFER
ROTOR

5–continued
SAGAS
SEXES
SHAHS
SOLOS
TENET

6
DENNED
HALLAH
HANNAH
REDDER
TERRET
TUT-TUT

9
MALAYALAM
ROTAVATOR

BACK WORDS

2
AH – HA
AM – MA
AT – TA
EH – HE
HA – AH
HE – EH
HO – OH
IT – TI
MA – AM
MP – PM
NO – ON
OH – HO
ON – NO
PM – MP
TA – AT
TI – IT

3
AND – DNA

3–continued
BAD – DAB
BAG – GAB
BAN – NAB
BAT – TAB
BIN – NIB
BOG – GOB
BOY – YOB
BUD – DUB
BUN – NUB
BUS – SUB
BUT – TUB
DAB – BAD
DAM – MAD
DEW – WED
DIM – MID
DNA – AND
DOG – GOD
DOH – HOD

3–continued
DON – NOD
DOT – TOD
DUB – BUD
EEL – LEE
GAB – BAG
GAL – LAG
GAS – SAG
GEL – LEG
GOB – BOG
GOD – DOG
GOT – TOG
GUM – MUG
GUT – TUG
HOD – DOH
JAR – RAJ
LAG – GAL
LAP – PAL
LEE – EEL

3–continued
LEG – GEL
MAD – DAM
MAR – RAM
MAY – YAM
MID – DIM
MUG – GUM
NAB – BAN
NAP – PAN
NET – TEN
NIB – BIN
NIP – PIN
NIT – TIN
NOD – DON
NOT – TON
NOW – WON
NUB – BUN
PAL – LAP
PAN – NAP

3—continued

PAR – RAP
PAT – TAP
PAY – YAP
PER – REP
PIN – NIP
PIT – TIP
POT – TOP
PUS – SUP
RAJ – JAR
RAM – MAR
RAP – PAR
RAT – TAR
RAW – WAR
REP – PER
ROT – TOR
SAG – GAS
SUB – BUS
SUP – PUS
TAB – BAT
TAP – PAT
TAR – RAT
TEN – NET
TIN – NIT
TIP – PIT
TOD – DOT
TOG – GOT
TON – NOT
TOP – POT
TOR – ROT
TUB – BUT
TUG – GUT
WAR – RAW
WAY – YAW
WED – DEW
WON – NOW
YAM – MAY
YAP – PAY
YAW – WAY
YOB – BOY

4

ABLE – ELBA
ABUT – TUBA
BARD – DRAB
BATS – STAB
BRAG – GARB
BUNS – SNUB
BUTS – STUB
DEER – REED
DIAL – LAID
DOOM – MOOD
DOOR – ROOD
DRAB – BARD
DRAW – WARD
DRAY – YARD
DUAL – LAUD
EDAM – MADE
EDIT – TIDE
ELBA – ABLE
EMIR – RIME
EMIT – TIME

4—continued

ERGO – OGRE
ET AL – LATE
EVIL – LIVE
FLOG – GOLF
FLOW – WOLF
GALS – SLAG
GARB – BRAG
GNAT – TANG
GOLF – FLOG
GULP – PLUG
GUMS – SMUG
GUNS – SNUG
HOOP – POOH
KEEL – LEEK
KEEP – PEEK
LAID – DIAL
LAIR – RIAL
LATE – ET AL
LAUD – DUAL
LEEK – KEEL
LEER – REEL
LIAR – RAIL
LIVE – EVIL
LOOP – POOL
LOOT – TOOL
MACS – SCAM
MADE – EDAM
MAPS – SPAM
MAWS – SWAM
MEET – TEEM
MOOD – DOOM
MOOR – ROOM
NAPS – SPAN
NIPS – SPIN
NUTS – STUN
OGRE – ERGO
PALS – SLAP
PANS – SNAP
PART – TRAP
PAWS – SWAP
PEEK – KEEP
PETS – STEP
PINS – SNIP
PLUG – GULP
POOH – HOOP
POOL – LOOP
POTS – STOP
RAIL – LIAR
RAPS – SPAR
RATS – STAR
REED – DEER
REEL – LEER
RIAL – LAIR
RIME – EMIR
ROOD – DOOR
ROOM – MOOR
SCAM – MACS
SLAG – GALS
SLAP – PALS
SMUG – GUMS
SNAP – PANS

4—continued

SNIP – PINS
SNOT – TONS
SNUB – BUNS
SNUG – GUNS
SPAM – MAPS
SPAN – NAPS
SPAR – RAPS
SPAT – TAPS
SPAY – YAPS
SPIN – NIPS
SPIT – TIPS
SPOT – TOPS
STAB – BATS
STAR – RATS
STEP – PETS
STEW – WETS
STOP – POTS
STUB – BUTS
STUN – NUTS
SWAM – MAWS
SWAP – PAWS
SWAY – YAWS
SWOT – TOWS
TANG – GNAT
TAPS – SPAT
TEEM – MEET
TIDE – EDIT
TIME – EMIT
TIPS – SPIT
TONS – SNOT
TOOL – LOOT
TOPS – SPOT
TORT – TROT
TOWS – SWOT
TRAP – PART
TROT – TORT
TUBA – ABUT
WARD – DRAW
WETS – STEW
WOLF – FLOW
YAPS – SPAY
YARD – DRAY
YAWS – SWAY

5

ANNAM – MANNA
ATLAS – SALTA
CARES – SERAC
DARAF – FARAD
DECAL – LACED
DENIM – MINED
DEVIL – LIVED
FARAD – DARAF
FIRES – SERIF
KEELS – SLEEK
LACED – DECAL
LAGER – REGAL
LEPER – REPEL
LEVER – REVEL
LIVED – DEVIL
LOOPS – SPOOL

5—continued

MANNA – ANNAM
MINED – DENIM
PACER – RECAP
PARTS – STRAP
POOLS – SLOOP
PORTS – STROP
REBUT – TUBER
RECAP – PACER
REGAL – LAGER
REMIT – TIMER
REPEL – LEPER
REVEL – LEVER
SALTA – ATLAS
SERAC – CARES
SERIF – FIRES
SLEEK – KEELS
SLOOP – POOLS
SMART – TRAMS
SNIPS – SPINS
SPINS – SNIPS
SPOOL – LOOPS
SPOTS – STOPS
STOPS – SPOTS
STRAP – PARTS
STRAW – WARTS
STROP – PORTS
TIMER – REMIT
TRAMS – SMART
TUBER – REBUT
WARTS – STRAW

6

ANIMAL – LAMINA
DELIAN – NAILED
DENIER – REINED
DIAPER – REPAID
DRAWER – REWARD
HARRIS – SIRRAH
LAMINA – ANIMAL
LOOTER – RETOOL
NAILED – DELIAN
PUPILS – SLIP-UP
RECAPS – SPACER
REINED – DENIER
RENNET – TENNER
REPAID – DIAPER
RETOOL – LOOTER
REWARD – DRAWER
SERVES – SEVRES
SEVRES – SERVES
SIRRAH – HARRIS
SLIP-UP – PUPILS
SNOOPS – SPOONS
SPACER – RECAPS
SPOONS – SNOOPS
TENNER – RENNET

8

DESSERTS –
  STRESSED
STRESSED –
  DESSERTS

HOMOPHONES

ACCESSARY – ACCESSORY
ACCESSORY – ACCESSARY
AERIAL – ARIEL
AERIE – AIRY
AIL – ALE
AIR – AIRE, E'ER, ERE, EYRE, HEIR
AIRE – AIR, E'ER, ERE, EYRE, HEIR
AIRSHIP – HEIRSHIP
AIRY – AERIE
AISLE – I'LL, ISLE
AIT – EIGHT, ATE
ALE – AIL
ALL – AWL, ORLE
ALMS – ARMS
ALTAR – ALTER
ALTER – ALTAR
AMAH – ARMOUR
ANTE – ANTI
ANTI – ANTE
ARC – ARK
AREN'T – AUNT
ARES – ARIES
ARIEL – AERIAL
ARIES – ARES
ARK – ARC
ARMOUR – AMAH
ARMS – ALMS
ASCENT – ASSENT
ASSENT – ASCENT
ATE – AIT, EIGHT
AUK – ORC
AUNT – AREN'T
AURAL – ORAL
AUSTERE – OSTIA
AWAY – AWEIGH
AWE – OAR, O'ER, ORE
AWEIGH – AWAY
AWL – ALL, ORLE
AXEL – AXLE
AXLE – AXEL
AY – AYE, EYE, I
AYAH – IRE
AYE – AY, EYE, I
AYES – EYES
BAA – BAH, BAR
BAAL – BASLE
BAH – BAA, BAR
BAIL – BALE
BALE – BAIL
BALL – BAWL
BALM – BARM
BALMY – BARMY
BAR – BAA, BAH
BARE – BEAR
BARM – BALM

BARMY – BALMY
BARON – BARREN
BARREN – BARON
BASE – BASS
BASLE – BAAL
BASS – BASE
BAUD – BAWD, BOARD
BAWD – BAUD, BOARD
BAWL – BALL
BAY – BEY
BEACH – BEECH
BEAN – BEEN
BEAR – BARE
BEAT – BEET
BEATER – BETA
BEAU – BOH, BOW
BEECH – BEACH
BEEN – BEAN
BEER – BIER
BEET – BEAT
BEL – BELL, BELLE
BELL – BEL, BELLE
BELLE – BEL, BELL
BERRY – BURY
BERTH – BIRTH
BETA – BEATER
BEY – BAY
BHAI – BI, BUY, BY, BYE
BI – BHAI, BUY, BY, BYE
BIER – BEER
BIGHT – BITE, BYTE
BIRTH – BERTH
BITE – BIGHT, BYTE
BLEW – BLUE
BLUE – BLEW
BOAR – BOER, BOOR, BORE
BOARD – BAUD, BAWD
BOARDER – BORDER
BOART – BOUGHT
BOER – BOAR, BOOR, BORE
BOH – BEAU, BOW
BOLE – BOWL
BOLT – BOULT
BOOR – BOAR, BOER, BORE
BOOTIE – BOOTY
BOOTY – BOOTIE
BORDER – BOARDER
BORE – BOAR, BOER, BOOR
BORN – BORNE
BORNE – BORN
BOUGH – BOW
BOUGHT – BOART
BOULT – BOLT
BOW – BEAU, BOH
BOW – BOUGH
BOWL – BOLE
BOY – BUOY

BRAKE – BREAK
BREAD – BRED
BREAK – BRAKE
BRED – BREAD
BREDE – BREED, BREID
BREED – BREDE, BREID
BREID – BREDE, BREED
BRIDAL – BRIDLE
BRIDLE – BRIDAL
BROACH – BROOCH
BROOCH – BROACH
BUNION – BUNYAN
BUNYAN – BUNION
BUOY – BOY
BURGER – BURGHER
BURGHER – BURGER
BURY – BERRY
BUS – BUSS
BUSS – BUS
BUY – BHAI, BI, BY, BYE
BUYER – BYRE
BY – BHAI, BI, BUY, BYE
BYE – BHAI, BI, BUY, BY
BYRE – BUYER
BYTE – BIGHT, BITE
CACHE – CASH
CACHOU – CASHEW
CAIN – CANE, KAIN
CALL – CAUL
CALLAS – CALLOUS, CALLUS
CALLOUS – CALLAS, CALLUS
CALLUS – CALLAS, CALLOUS
CANAPÉ – CANOPY
CANE – CAIN, KAIN
CANOPY – CANAPÉ
CARAT – CARROT, KARAT
CARROT – CARAT, KARAT
CART – CARTE, KART
CARTE – CART, KART
CASH – CACHE
CASHEW – CACHOU
CASHMERE – KASHMIR
CAST – CASTE, KARST
CASTE – CAST, KARST
CAUGHT – COURT
CAUL – CALL
CAW – COR, CORE, CORPS
CEDAR – SEEDER
CEDE – SEED
CEIL – SEEL, SEAL
CELL – SELL, SZELL
CELLAR – SELLER
CENSER – CENSOR, SENSOR
CENSOR – CENSER, SENSOR
CENT – SCENT, SENT

CERE – SEAR, SEER
CEREAL – SERIAL
CESSION – SESSION
CHAW – CHORE
CHEAP – CHEEP
CHECK – CZECH
CHEEP – CHEAP
CHOIR – QUIRE
CHOLER – COLLAR
CHORD – CORD
CHORE – CHAW
CHOTT – SHOT, SHOTT
CHOU – SHOE, SHOO
CHOUGH – CHUFF
CHUFF – CHOUGH
CHUTE – SHOOT, SHUTE
CITE – SIGHT, SITE
CLACK – CLAQUE
CLAQUE – CLACK
CLIMB – CLIME
CLIME – CLIMB
COAL – COLE, KOHL
COARSE – CORSE, COURSE
COLE – COAL, KOHL
COLLAR – CHOLER
COLONEL – KERNEL
COLOUR – CULLER
COME – CUM
COMPLEMENTARY –
  COMPLIMENTARY
COMPLIMENTARY –
  COMPLEMENTARY
COO – COUP
COOP – COUPE
COR – CAW, CORE, CORPS
CORD – CHORD
CORE – CAW, COR, CORPS
CORNFLOUR –
  CORNFLOWER
CORNFLOWER –
  CORNFLOUR
CORPS – CAW, COR, CORE
CORSE – COARSE, COURSE
COUNCIL – COUNSEL
COUNSEL – COUNCIL
COUP – COO
COUPE – COOP
COURSE – COARSE, CORSE
COURT – CAUGHT
CREAK – CREEK
CREEK – CREAK
CULLER – COLOUR
CUM – COME
CURB – KERB
CURRANT – CURRENT
CURRENT – CURRANT
CYGNET – SIGNET
CYMBAL – SYMBOL
CZECH – CHECK
DAM – DAMN
DAMN – DAM
DAW – DOOR, DOR

DAYS – DAZE
DAZE – DAYS
DEAR – DEER
DEER – DEAR
DESCENT – DISSENT
DESERT – DESSERT
DESSERT – DESERT
DEW – DUE
DINAH – DINER
DINE – DYNE
DINER – DINAH
DISSENT – DESCENT
DOE – DOH, DOUGH
DOH – DOE, DOUGH
DONE – DONNE, DUN
DONNE – DONE, DUN
DOOR – DAW, DOR
DOR – DAW, DOOR
DOST – DUST
DOUGH – DOE, DOH
DRAFT – DRAUGHT
DRAUGHT – DRAFT
DROOP – DRUPE
DRUPE – DROOP
DUAL – DUEL
DUCKS – DUX
DUE – DEW
DUEL – DUAL
DUN – DONE, DONNE
DUST – DOST
DUX – DUCKS
DYEING – DYING
DYING – DYEING
DYNE – DINE
EARN – URN
EATEN – ETON
E'ER – AIR, AIRE, ERE, EYRE,
  HEIR
EERIE – EYRIE
EIDER – IDA
EIGHT – AIT, ATE
EIRE – EYRA
ELATION – ILLATION
ELICIT – ILLICIT
ELUDE – ILLUDE
ELUSORY – ILLUSORY
EMERGE – IMMERGE
EMERSED – IMMERSED
EMERSION – IMMERSION
ERE – AIR, AIRE, E'ER, EYRE,
  HEIR
ERK – IRK
ERR – UR
ESTER – ESTHER
ESTHER – ESTER
ETON – EATEN
EWE – YEW, YOU
EYE – AY, AYE, I
EYED – I'D, IDE
EYELET – ISLET
EYES – AYES
EYRA – EIRE

EYRE – AIR, AIRE, E'ER, ERE,
  HEIR
EYRIE – EERIE
FA – FAR
FAIN – FANE, FEIGN
FAINT – FEIGNT
FAIR – FARE
FANE – FAIN, FEIGN
FAR – FA
FARE – FAIR
FARO – PHARAOH
FARTHER – FATHER
FATE – FÊTE
FATHER – FARTHER
FAUGH – FOR, FOUR, FORE
FAUN – FAWN
FAWN – FAUN
FAZE – PHASE
FEAT – FEET
FEET – FEAT
FEIGN – FAIN, FANE
FEIGNT – FAINT
FELLOE – FELLOW
FELLOW – FELLOE
FELT – VELD, VELDT
FETA – FETTER
FÊTE – FATE
FETTER – FETA
FEU – FEW, PHEW
FEW – FEU, PHEW
FIR – FUR
FISHER – FISSURE
FISSURE – FISHER
FIZZ – PHIZ
FLAIR – FLARE
FLARE – FLAIR
FLAW – FLOOR
FLEA – FLEE
FLEE – FLEA
FLEW – FLU, FLUE
FLOE – FLOW
FLOOR – FLAW
FLOUR – FLOWER
FLOW – FLOE
FLOWER – FLOUR
FLU – FLEW, FLUE
FLUE – FLEW, FLU
FOR – FAUGH, FOUR, FORE
FORE – FAUGH, FOR, FOUR
FORT – FOUGHT
FORTE – FORTY
FORTH – FOURTH
FORTY – FORTE
FOUGHT – FORT
FOUL – FOWL
FOUR – FAUGH, FOR, FORE
FOURTH – FORTH
FOWL – FOUL
FRIAR – FRIER
FRIER – FRIAR
FUR – FIR
GAIL – GALE

GAIT – GATE
GALE – GAIL
GALLOP – GALLUP
GALLUP – GALLOP
GAMBLE – GAMBOL
GAMBOL – GAMBLE
GATE – GAIT
GAWKY – GORKY
GENE – JEAN
GIN – JINN
GLADDEN – GLADDON
GLADDON – GLADDEN
GNASH – NASH
GNAT – NAT
GNAW – NOR
GORKY – GAWKY
GRATER – GREATER
GREATER – GRATER
GROAN – GROWN
GROWN – GROAN
HAE – HAY, HEH, HEY
HAIL – HALE
HAIR – HARE
HALE – HAIL
HALL – HAUL
HANDEL – HANDLE
HANDLE – HANDEL
HANGAR – HANGER
HANGER – HANGAR
HARE – HAIR
HART – HEART
HAUD – HOARD, HORDE
HAUL – HALL
HAW – HOARE, WHORE
HAY – HAE, HEH, HEY
HEAR – HERE
HEART – HART
HEH – HAE, HAY, HEY
HEIR – AIR, AIRE, E'ER, ERE, EYRE
HEIRSHIP – AIRSHIP
HERE – HEAR
HEROIN – HEROINE
HEROINE – HEROIN
HEW – HUE
HEY – HAE, HAY, HEH
HIE – HIGH
HIGH – HIE
HIGHER – HIRE
HIM – HYMN
HIRE – HIGHER
HO – HOE
HOAR – HAW, WHORE
HOARD – HAUD, HORDE
HOARSE – HORSE
HOE – HO
HOLE – WHOLE
HOO – WHO
HORDE – HAUD, HOARD
HORSE – HOARSE
HOUR – OUR
HOURS – OURS

HUE – HEW
HYMN – HIM
I – AY, AYE, EYE
I'D – EYED, IDE
IDA – EIDER
IDE – EYED, I'D
IDLE – IDOL
IDOL – IDLE
I'LL – AISLE, ISLE
ILLATION – ELATION
ILLICIT – ELICIT
ILLUDE – ELUDE
ILLUSORY – ELUSORY
IMMERGE – EMERGE
IMMERSED – EMERSED
IMMERSION – EMERSION
IN – INN
INCITE – INSIGHT
INDICT – INDITE
INDITE – INDICT
INN – IN
INSIGHT – INCITE
INSOLE – INSOUL
INSOUL – INSOLE
ION – IRON
IRE – AYAH
IRK – ERK
IRON – ION
ISLE – AISLE, I'LL
ISLET – EYELET
JAM – JAMB, JAMBE
JAMB – JAM, JAMBE
JAMBE – JAM, JAMB
JEAN – GENE
JINKS – JINX
JINN – GIN
JINX – JINKS
KAIN – CAIN, CANE
KARAT – CARAT, CARROT
KARST – CAST, CASTE
KART – CART, CARTE
KASHMIR – CASHMERE
KERB – CURB
KERNEL – COLONEL
KEW – KYU, QUEUE
KEY – QUAY
KNAVE – NAVE
KNEAD – NEED
KNEW – NEW, NU
KNIGHT – NIGHT
KNIGHTLY – NIGHTLY
KNIT – NIT
KNOW – NOH, NO
KNOWS – NOES, NOSE
KOHL – COAL, COLE
KYU – KEW, QUEUE
LACKER – LACQUER
LACQUER – LACKER
LAIN – LANE
LANCE – LAUNCE
LANE – LAIN
LAUD – LORD

LAUNCE – LANCE
LAW – LORE
LAY – LEI, LEY
LAYS – LAZE
LAZE – LAYS
LEAD – LED
LEAF – LIEF
LEAH – LEAR, LEER, LEHR
LEAK – LEEK
LEANT – LENT
LEAR – LEAH, LEER, LEHR
LED – LEAD
LEEK – LEAK
LEER – LEAH, LEAR, LEHR
LEHR – LEAH, LEAR, LEER
LEI – LAY, LEY
LEMAN – LEMON
LEMON – LEMAN
LENT – LEANT
LESSEN – LESSON
LESSON – LESSEN
LEY – LAY, LEI
LIAR – LYRE
LIEF – LEAF
LINCS – LINKS, LYNX
LINKS – LINCS, LYNX
LOAD – LODE
LOAN – LONE
LODE – LOAD
LONE – LOAN
LORD – LAUD
LORE – LAW
LUMBAR – LUMBER
LUMBER – LUMBAR
LYNX – LINCS, LINKS
LYRE – LIAR
MA – MAAR, MAR
MAAR – MA, MAR
MADE – MAID
MAID – MADE
MAIL – MALE
MAIN – MAINE, MANE
MAINE – MAIN, MANE
MAIZE – MAZE
MALE – MAIL
MALL – MAUL
MANE – MAIN, MAINE
MANNA – MANNER, MANOR
MANNER – MANNA, MANOR
MANOR – MANNA, MANNER
MAQUIS – MARQUEE
MAR – MA, MAAR
MARC – MARK, MARQUE
MARE – MAYOR
MARK – MARC, MARQUE
MARQUE – MARC, MARK
MARQUEE – MAQUIS
MAUL – MALL
MAW – MOR, MORE, MOOR
MAYOR – MARE
MAZE – MAIZE
MEAN – MESNE, MIEN

MEAT – MEET, METE
MEDAL – MEDDLE
MEDDLE – MEDAL
MEET – MEAT, METE
MESNE – MIEN, MEAN
METAL – METTLE
METE – MEAT, MEET
METTLE – METAL
MEWS – MUSE
MIEN – MESNE, MEAN
MIGHT – MITE
MINER – MINOR
MINOR – MINER
MITE – MIGHT
MOAN – MOWN
MOAT – MOTE
MOCHA – MOCKER
MOCKER – MOCHA
MOOR – MAW, MOR, MORE
MOOSE – MOUSSE
MOR – MAW, MORE, MOOR
MORE – MAW, MOR, MOOR
MORN – MOURN
MORNING – MOURNING
MOTE – MOAT
MOURN – MORN
MOURNING – MORNING
MOUSSE – MOOSE
MOWN – MOAN
MUSCLE – MUSSEL
MUSE – MEWS
MUSSEL – MUSCLE
NAE – NAY, NEAGH, NEIGH,
  NEY
NASH – GNASH
NAT – GNAT
NAUGHT – NOUGHT
NAVAL – NAVEL
NAVE – KNAVE
NAVEL – NAVAL
NAY – NAE, NEAGH, NEIGH,
  NEY
NEAGH – NAE, NAY, NEIGH,
  NEY
NEED – KNEAD
NEIGH – NAE, NAY, NEAGH,
  NEY
NEUK – NUKE
NEW – KNEW, NU
NEY – NAE, NAY, NEAGH,
  NEIGH
NIGH – NYE
NIGHT – KNIGHT
NIGHTLY – KNIGHTLY
NIT – KNIT
NO – KNOW, NOH
NOES – KNOWS, NOSE
NOH – KNOW, NO
NONE – NUN
NOR – GNAW
NOSE – KNOWS, NOES
NOUGHT – NAUGHT

NU – KNEW, NEW
NUKE – NEUK
NUN – NONE
NYE – NIGH
OAR – AWE, O'ER, ORE
O'ER – AWE, OAR, ORE
OFFA – OFFER
OFFER – OFFA
OH – OWE
ORAL – AURAL
ORC – AUK
ORE – AWE, OAR, O'ER
ORLE – ALL, AWL
OSTIA – AUSTERE
OUR – HOUR
OURS – HOURS
OUT – OWT
OVA – OVER
OVER – OVA
OWE – OH
OWT – OUT
PA – PAH, PAR, PARR, PAS
PACKED – PACT
PACT – PACKED
PAH – PA, PAR, PARR, PAS
PAIL – PALE
PAIR – PARE, PEAR
PALATE – PALETTE, PALLET
PALE – PAIL
PALETTE – PALATE, PALLET
PALLET – PALATE, PALETTE
PANDA – PANDER
PANDER – PANDA
PAR – PA, PAH, PARR, PAS
PARE – PEAR, PAIR
PARR – PA, PAH, PAR, PAS
PAS – PA, PAH, PAR, PARR
PAW – POOR, PORE, POUR
PAWKY – PORKY
PAWN – PORN
PEA – PEE
PEACE – PIECE
PEAK – PIQUE, PEAKE,
  PEEK, PEKE
PEAL – PEEL
PEAR – PARE, PAIR
PEARL – PURL
PEARLER – PURLER
PEDAL – PEDDLE
PEDDLE – PEDAL
PEE – PEA
PEEK – PEAK, PEAKE, PEKE,
  PIQUE
PEEL – PEAL
PEKE – PEAK, PEAKE, PEEK,
  PIQUE
PER – PURR
PETREL – PETROL
PETROL – PETREL
PHARAOH – FARO
PHASE – FAZE
PHEW – FEU, FEW

PHIZ – FIZZ
PI – PIE, PYE
PIE – PI, PYE
PIECE – PEACE
PILATE – PILOT
PILOT – PILATE
PIQUE – PEAK, PEAKE,
  PEEK, PEKE
PLACE – PLAICE
PLAICE – PLACE
PLAIN – PLANE
PLANE – PLAIN
POLE – POLL
POLL – POLE
POMACE – PUMICE
POMMEL – PUMMEL
POOR – PAW, PORE, POUR
POPULACE – POPULOUS
POPULOUS – POPULACE
PORE – PAW, POOR, POUR
PORKY – PAWKY
PORN – PAWN
POUR – PAW, POOR, PORE
PRAY – PREY
PREY – PRAY
PRINCIPAL – PRINCIPLE
PRINCIPLE – PRINCIPAL
PROFIT – PROPHET
PROPHET – PROFIT
PSALTER – SALTER
PUCKA – PUCKER
PUCKER – PUCKA
PUMICE – POMACE
PUMMEL – POMMEL
PURL – PEARL
PURLER – PEARLER
PURR – PER
PYE – PI, PIE
QUAY – KEY
QUEUE – KEW, KYU
QUIRE – CHOIR
RACK – WRACK
RACKET – RACQUET
RACQUET – RACKET
RAIN – REIGN, REIN
RAINS – REINS
RAISE – RASE
RAP – WRAP
RAPT – WRAPPED
RASE – RAISE
RAW – ROAR
READ – REDE, REED
RECK – WRECK
REDE – READ, REED
REED – READ, REDE
REEK – WREAK
REIGN – RAIN, REIN
REIN – RAIN, REIGN
REINS – RAINS
RENNES – WREN
RETCH – WRETCH
REVERE – REVERS

REVERS – REVERE
RHEUM – ROOM
RHEUMY – ROOMY
RHO – ROW, ROE
RHÔNE – ROAN, RONE
RIGHT – RITE, WRIGHT,
  WRITE
RING – WRING
RINGER – WRINGER
RITE – RIGHT, WRIGHT,
  WRITE
ROAM – ROME
ROAN – RHÔNE, RONE
ROAR – RAW
ROE – RHO, ROW
ROLE – ROLL
ROLL – ROLE
ROME – ROAM
RONE – RHÔNE, ROAN
ROOD – RUDE
ROOM – RHEUM
ROOMY – RHEUMY
ROOSE – RUSE
ROOT – ROUTE
RORT – WROUGHT
ROTE – WROTE
ROUGH – RUFF
ROUTE – ROOT
ROW – RHO, ROE
RUDE – ROOD
RUFF – ROUGH
RUNG – WRUNG
RUSE – ROOSE
RYE – WRY
SAIL – SALE
SAIN – SANE, SEINE
SALE – SAIL
SALTER – PSALTER
SANE – SAIN, SEINE
SAUCE – SOURCE
SAUT – SORT, SOUGHT
SAW – SOAR, SORE
SAWN – SORN
SCENE – SEEN
SCENT – CENT, SENT
SCULL – SKULL
SEAL – CEIL, SEEL
SEAM – SEEM
SEAR – CERE, SEER
SEED – CEDE
SEEDER – CEDAR
SEEK – SEIK, SIKH
SEEL – CEIL, SEAL
SEEM – SEAM
SEEN – SCENE
SEER – CERE, SEAR
SEIK – SEEK, SIKH
SEINE – SAIN, SANE
SELL – CELL, SZELL
SELLER – CELLAR
SENSOR – CENSER,
  CENSOR

SENT – CENT, SCENT
SERF – SURF
SERGE – SURGE
SERIAL – CEREAL
SESSION – CESSION
SEW – SO, SOH, SOW
SEWN – SONE, SOWN
SHAKE – SHEIK
SHEIK – SHAKE
SHIER – SHYER, SHIRE
SHIRE – SHIER, SHYER
SHOE – CHOU, SHOO
SHOO – CHOU, SHOE
SHOOT – SHUTE, CHUTE
SHOT – SHOTT, CHOTT
SHOTT – SHOT, CHOTT
SHUTE – SHOOT, CHUTE
SHYER – SHIER, SHIRE
SIGHT – CITE, SITE
SIGN – SYN
SIGNET – CYGNET
SIKH – SEEK, SEIK
SIOUX – SOU
SITE – CITE, SIGHT
SKULL – SCULL
SKY – SKYE
SKYE – SKY
SLAY – SLEIGH
SLEAVE – SLEEVE
SLEEVE – SLEAVE
SLEIGH – SLAY
SLOE – SLOW
SLOW – SLOE
SO – SEW, SOH, SOW
SOAR – SAW, SORE
SOH – SEW, SO, SOW
SOLE – SOUL
SOME – SUM
SON – SUN, SUNN
SONE – SEWN, SOWN
SONNY – SUNNI, SUNNY
SORE – SAW, SOAR
SORN – SAWN
SORT – SAUT, SOUGHT
SOU – SIOUX
SOUGHT – SAUT, SORT
SOUL – SOLE
SOURCE – SAUCE
SOW – SEW, SO, SOH
SOWN – SEWN, SONE
STAIR – STARE
STAKE – STEAK
STALK – STORK
STARE – STAIR
STEAK – STAKE
STEAL – STEEL
STEEL – STEAL
STOREY – STORY
STORK – STALK
STORY – STOREY
SUITE – SWEET
SUM – SOME

SUN – SON, SUNN
SUNDAE – SUNDAY
SUNDAY – SUNDAE
SUNN – SON, SUN
SUNNI – SONNY, SUNNY
SUNNY – SONNY, SUNNI
SURF – SERF
SURGE – SERGE
SWAT – SWOT
SWEET – SUITE
SWOT – SWAT
SYMBOL – CYMBAL
SYN – SIGN
SZELL – CELL, SELL
TACIT – TASSET
TAI – TAILLE, THAI, TIE
TAIL – TALE
TAILLE – TAI, THAI, TIE
TALE – TAIL
TALK – TORC, TORQUE
TARE – TEAR
TASSET – TACIT
TAUGHT – TAUT, TORT,
  TORTE
TAUT – TAUGHT, TORT,
  TORTE
TEA – TEE, TI
TEAM – TEEM
TEAR – TARE
TEE – TEA, TI
TEEM – TEAM
TENNER – TENOR
TENOR – TENNER
TERNE – TURN
THAI – TAI, TAILLE, TIE
THAW – THOR
THEIR – THERE, THEY'RE
THERE – THEIR, THEY'RE
THEY'RE – THEIR, THERE
THOR – THAW
THREW – THROUGH, THRU
THROE – THROW
THRONE – THROWN
THROUGH – THREW, THRU
THROW – THROE
THROWN – THRONE
THRU – THREW, THROUGH
THYME – TIME
TI – TEA, TEE
TIC – TICK
TICK – TIC
TIDE – TIED
TIE – TAI, TAILLE, THAI
TIED – TIDE
TIER – TIRE, TYRE
TIGHTEN – TITAN
TIMBER – TIMBRE
TIMBRE – TIMBER
TIME – THYME
TIRE – TIER, TYRE
TITAN – TIGHTEN
TO – TOO, TWO

333

TWO-WORD PHRASES

TOAD – TOED, TOWED
TOE – TOW
TOED – TOAD, TOWED
TOO – TO, TWO
TOR – TORE
TORC – TALK, TORQUE
TORE – TOR
TORQUE – TALK, TORC
TORT – TAUGHT, TAUT, TORTE
TORTE – TAUGHT, TAUT, TORT
TOW – TOE
TOWED – TOAD, TOED
TROOP – TROUPE
TROUPE – TROOP
TUNA – TUNER
TUNER – TUNA
TURN – TERNE
TWO – TO, TOO
TYRE – TIER, TIRE
UR – ERR
URN – EARN
VAIL – VALE, VEIL
VAIN – VANE, VEIN
VALE – VAIL, VEIL
VANE – VAIN, VEIN
VEIL – VAIL, VALE
VEIN – VAIN, VANE
VELD – FELT, VELDT
VELDT – FELT, VELD
WAE – WAY, WHEY
WAIL – WHALE
WAIN – WANE, WAYNE
WAIST – WASTE
WAIT – WEIGHT
WAIVE – WAVE
WANE – WAIN, WAYNE
WAR – WAUGH, WAW, WORE
WARE – WEAR, WHERE

WARN – WORN
WASTE – WAIST
WATT – WHAT, WOT
WAUGH – WAR, WAW, WORE
WAVE – WAIVE
WAW – WAR, WAUGH, WORE
WAY – WAE, WHEY
WAYNE – WAIN, WANE
WEAK – WEEK
WEAKLY – WEEKLY
WEAR – WARE, WHERE
WEAVE – WE'VE
WE'D – WEED
WEED – WE'D
WEEK – WEAK
WEEKLY – WEAKLY
WEEL – WE'LL, WHEAL, WHEEL
WEIGHT – WAIT
WE'LL – WEEL, WHEAL, WHEEL
WEN – WHEN
WERE – WHIRR
WE'VE – WEAVE
WHALE – WAIL
WHAT – WATT, WOT
WHEAL – WEEL, WE'LL, WHEEL
WHEEL – WEEL, WE'LL, WHEAL
WHEN – WEN
WHERE – WARE, WEAR
WHEY – WAE, WAY
WHICH – WITCH
WHINE – WINE
WHIRR – WERE
WHITE – WIGHT, WITE
WHITHER – WITHER
WHO – HOO
WHOA – WO, WOE

WHOLE – HOLE
WHORE – HAW, HOAR
WIGHT – WHITE, WITE
WINE – WHINE
WITCH – WHICH
WITE – WHITE, WIGHT
WITHER – WHITHER
WO – WHOA, WOE
WOE – WHOA, WO
WORE – WAR, WAUGH, WAW
WORN – WARN
WOT – WATT, WHAT
WRACK – RACK
WRAP – RAP
WRAPPED – RAPT
WREAK – REEK
WRECK – RECK
WREN – RENNES
WRETCH – RETCH
WRIGHT – RIGHT, RITE, WRITE
WRING – RING
WRINGER – RINGER
WRITE – RIGHT, RITE, WRIGHT
WROTE – ROTE
WROUGHT – RORT
WRUNG – RUNG
WRY – RYE
YAW – YORE, YOUR
YAWS – YOURS
YEW – EWE, YOU
YOKE – YOLK
YOLK – YOKE
YORE – YAW, YOUR
YOU – EWE, YEW
YOU'LL – YULE
YOUR – YAW, YORE
YOURS – YAWS
YULE – YOU'LL

TWO-WORD PHRASES

FIRST WORD

ABERDEEN – ANGUS, TERRIER
ABLE – BODIED, RATING, SEAMAN
ABSOLUTE – ALCOHOL, HUMIDITY, JUDGMENT, MAGNITUDE, MAJORITY, MONARCHY, MUSIC, PITCH, TEMPERATURE, THRESHOLD, UNIT, VALUE, ZERO
ABSTRACT – EXPRESSIONISM, NOUN
ACCESS – ROAD, TIME
ACCOMMODATION – ADDRESS, BILL, LADDER, PLATFORM
ACHILLES – HEEL, TENDON
ACID – DROP, RAIN, ROCK, SOIL, TEST, VALUE

ACT – AS, FOR, ON, OUT, UP
ACTION – COMMITTEE, GROUP, PAINTING, POTENTIAL, REPLAY, STATIONS
ACTIVE – CENTRE, LIST, SERVICE, TRANSPORT, VOCABULARY, VOLCANO
ADMIRALTY – BOARD, HOUSE, ISLANDS, MILE, RANGE
ADVANCE – BOOKING, COPY, GUARD, MAN, NOTICE, POLL, RATIO
AEOLIAN – DEPOSITS, HARP, ISLANDS, MODE
AFRICAN – LILY, MAHOGANY, TIME, VIOLET
AGONY – AUNT, COLUMN
AIR – ALERT, BAG, BED, BLADDER, BRAKE, BRIDGE, COMMODORE, CONDITIONING, CORRIDOR, COVER,

CURTAIN, CUSHION, CYLINDER, DAM, EMBOLISM, FORCE, GAS, GUN, HARDENING, HOLE, HOSTESS, JACKET, LETTER, MAIL, MARSHAL, MASS, MILE, OFFICER, PLANT, POCKET, POWER, PUMP, RAID, RIFLE, SAC, SCOOP, SCOUT, SHAFT, SHOT, SOCK, SPRAY, SPRING, STATION, TERMINAL, TRAFFIC, TURBINE, VALVE, VICE-MARSHAL

ALL — BLACK, CLEAR, FOURS, HAIL, IN, ONE, OUT, RIGHT, SQUARE, THERE, TOLD

ALPHA — CENTAURI, HELIX, IRON, PARTICLE, PRIVATIVE, RAY, RHYTHM

ALTAR — BOY, CLOTH, -PIECE

AMERICAN — ALOE, CHAMELEON, CHEESE, CLOTH, EAGLE, FOOTBALL, INDIAN, PLAN, REVOLUTION, SAMOA, WAKE

ANCHOR — MAN, PLATE, RING

ANCIENT — GREEK, HISTORY, LIGHTS, MONUMENT

ANGEL — CAKE, DUST, FALLS, FOOD, SHARK

ANGLE — BRACKET, DOZER, IRON, PLATE

ANIMAL — HUSBANDRY, KINGDOM, MAGNETISM, RIGHTS, SPIRITS, STARCH

ANT — BEAR, BIRD, COW, EATER, HEAP, HILL

APPLE — BLIGHT, BOX, BRANDY, BUTTER, GREEN, ISLE, JACK, MAGGOT, POLISHER, SAUCE

ARCTIC — CHAR, CIRCLE, FOX, HARE, OCEAN, TERN, WILLOW

ART — DECO, FORM, NOUVEAU, PAPER

ARTIFICIAL — INSEMINATION, INTELLIGENCE, RESPIRATION

ASH — BLOND, CAN, WEDNESDAY

ATOMIC — AGE, CLOCK, COCKTAIL, ENERGY, HEAT, MASS, NUMBER, PILE, POWER, STRUCTURE, THEORY, VOLUME, WEIGHT

AUTOMATIC — CAMERA, PILOT, REPEAT, TRANSMISSION, TYPESETTING

BABY — BOOM, BUGGY, CARRIAGE, GRAND, SNATCHER, TALK, TOOTH

BACK — BOILER, BURNER, COUNTRY, DOOR, DOWN, END, LIGHT, LIST, MARKER, MATTER, OUT, PASSAGE, PAY, REST, ROOM, SEAT, STRAIGHT, UP, YARD

BAD — BLOOD, FAITH, LANDS, NEWS

BALL — BEARING, BOY, COCK, GAME, VALVE

BANANA — OIL, REPUBLIC, SKIN, SPLIT

BANK — ACCEPTANCE, ACCOUNT, ANNUITIES, BILL, CARD, CLERK, DISCOUNT, HOLIDAY, MANAGER, ON, RATE, STATEMENT

BAR — BILLIARDS, CHART, CODE, DIAGRAM, FLY, GIRL, GRAPH, LINE, MITZVAH, SINISTER

BARLEY — SUGAR, WATER, WINE

BARN — DANCE, DOOR, OWL, SWALLOW

BASE — LOAD, METAL, RATE

BASKET — CASE, CHAIR, HILT, MAKER, WEAVE

BATH — BUN, CHAIR, CHAP, CUBE, OLIVER, SALTS, STONE

BATTLE — CRUISER, CRY, FATIGUE, ROYAL

BAY — LEAF, LYNX, RUM, STREET, TREE, WINDOW

BEACH — BALL, BOYS, BUGGY, FLEA, PLUM

BEAR — DOWN, GARDEN, HUG, OFF, OUT, UP, WITH

BEAUTY — QUEEN, SALON, SLEEP, SPOT

BED — JACKET, LINEN

BELL — BRONZE, BUOY, GLASS, HEATHER, JAR, MAG-PIE, METAL, MOTH, PULL, PUNCH, PUSH, SHEEP, TENT

BELLY — DANCE, FLOP, LANDING, LAUGH

BERMUDA — GRASS, RIG, SHORTS, TRIANGLE

BEST — BOY, END, GIRL, MAN, SELLER

BICYCLE — CHAIN, CLIP, PUMP

BIG — APPLE, BAND, BANG, BEN, BERTHA, BROTHER, BUSINESS, CHEESE, CHIEF, DEAL, DIPPER, END, SCREEN, SHOT, STICK, TIME, TOP, WHEEL

BINARY — CODE, DIGIT, FISSION, FORM, NOTATION, NUMBER, STAR, WEAPON

BIRD — CALL, CHERRY, DOG, PEPPER, SPIDER, STRIKE, TABLE

BIRTH — CERTIFICATE, CONTROL, RATE

BIRTHDAY — HONOURS, SUIT

BIT — PART, RATE, SLICE

BITTER — APPLE, END, LAKES, ORANGE, PRINCIPLE

BLACK — ART, BEAN, BEAR, BEETLE, BELT, BILE, BODY, BOOK, BOTTOM, BOX, COUNTRY, DEATH, DIAMOND, ECONOMY, EYE, FLY, FOREST, FRIAR, FROST, HILLS, HOLE, ICE, MAGIC, MARIA, MARK, MARKET, MASS, MONK, MOUNTAINS, PANTHER, PEPPER, PRINCE, PUDDING, ROD, ROT, SEA, SHEEP, SPOT, SWAN, TIE, TREACLE, VELVET, WATCH, WIDOW

BLANK — CARTRIDGE, CHEQUE, ENDORSEMENT, VERSE

BLANKET — BATH, FINISH, STITCH

BLIND — ALLEY, DATE, FREDDIE, GUT, SNAKE, SPOT, STAGGERS, STAMPING

BLISTER — BEETLE, COPPER, PACK, RUST

BLOCK — DIAGRAM, IN, LETTER, OUT, PRINTING, RELEASE, SAMPLING, TIN, VOTE

BLOOD — BANK, BATH, BROTHER, CELL, COUNT, DONOR, FEUD, FLUKE, GROUP, HEAT, MONEY, ORANGE, POISONING, PRESSURE, PUDDING, RED, RELATION, SPORT, TEST, TYPE, VESSEL

BLUE — BABY, BAG, BILLY, BLOOD, CHEESE, CHIP, DEVILS, ENSIGN, FUNK, GUM, JAY, MOON, MOUNTAINS, MURDER, NILE, PENCIL, PETER, RIBAND, RIBBON, VEIN

BOARDING — HOUSE, OUT, SCHOOL

BOAT — DECK, DRILL, NECK, PEOPLE, RACE, TRAIN

BOBBY — CALF, PIN, SOCKS

BODY — BLOW, BUILDING, CAVITY, CORPORATE, IMAGE, LANGUAGE, POPPING, SHOP, SNATCHER, STOCKING, WARMER

BOG — ASPHODEL, COTTON, DEAL, DOWN, IN, MOSS, MYRTLE, OAK, ORCHID, RUSH, STANDARD

BON — MOT, TON, VIVANT, VOYAGE

BONE — ASH, CHINA, IDLE, MEAL, OIL, UP

BOOBY — HATCH, PRIZE, TRAP

BOOK — CLUB, END, IN, INTO, OUT, SCORPION, TOKEN, UP

BOTTLE — GOURD, GREEN, OUT, PARTY, TREE, UP

BOTTOM — DRAWER, END, HOUSE, LINE, OUT

BOW — LEGS, OUT, TIE, WINDOW

BOWLING — ALLEY, CREASE, GREEN

BOX — CAMERA, COAT, ELDER, GIRDER, JELLYFISH, NUMBER, OFFICE, PLEAT, SEAT, SPANNER, SPRING

BRAIN — CORAL, DEATH, DRAIN, FEVER, STEM, WAVE

BRAKE — BAND, DRUM, FLUID, HORSEPOWER, LIGHT, LINING, PARACHUTE, SHOE, VAN

BRAND — IMAGE, LEADER, NAME

BRANDY — BOTTLE, BUTTER, SNAP

335

BRASS – BAND, FARTHING, HAT, NECK, RUBBING, TACKS

BREAK – DANCE, DOWN, EVEN, IN, INTO, OFF, OUT, THROUGH, UP, WITH

BRING – ABOUT, DOWN, FORWARD, IN, OFF, ON, OUT, OVER, ROUND, TO, UP

BRISTOL – BOARD, CHANNEL, FASHION

BROAD – ARROW, BEAN, CHURCH, GAUGE, JUMP, SEAL

BROWN – BEAR, BOMBER, FAT, OWL, PAPER, RICE, SHIRT, SNAKE, STUDY, SUGAR

BRUSSELS – CARPET, LACE, SPROUT

BUBBLE – BATH, CAR, CHAMBER, FLOAT, GUM, MEMORY, PACK

BUCK – FEVER, RABBIT, UP

BUILDING – BLOCK, LINE, PAPER, SOCIETY

BULL – MASTIFF, NOSE, RUN, SESSION, SNAKE, TERRIER, TONGUE, TROUT

BURNT – ALMOND, OFFERING, SHALE, SIENNA, UMBER

BUS – BOY, LANE, SHELTER, STOP

BUTTER – BEAN, MUSLIN, UP

BUZZ – BOMB, OFF, SAW, WORD

CABBAGE – BUG, LETTUCE, MOTH, PALM, PALMETTO, ROSE, TREE, WHITE

CABIN – BOY, CLASS, CRUISER, FEVER

CABLE – CAR, RAILWAY, RELEASE, STITCH, TELEVISION

CALL – ALARM, BOX, DOWN, FORTH, GIRL, IN, LOAN, MONEY, NUMBER, OFF, OUT, RATE, SIGN, SLIP, UP

CAMP – DAVID, FOLLOWER, MEETING, OVEN, SITE

CANARY – CREEPER, GRASS, ISLANDS, SEED, YELLOW

CANTERBURY – BELL, LAMB, PILGRIMS

CAPE – BUFFALO, CART, COD, COLONY, COLOURED, DOCTOR, DUTCH, FLATS, GOOSEBERRY, HORN, JASMINE, PENINSULA, PIGEON, PRIMROSE, PROVINCE, SPARROW, TOWN, VERDE, YORK

CAPITAL – ACCOUNT, ALLOWANCE, ASSETS, EXPENDITURE, GAIN, GOODS, LEVY, MARKET, PUNISHMENT, SHIP, STOCK, SURPLUS

CARD – FILE, INDEX, PUNCH, READER, VOTE

CARDINAL – BEETLE, FLOWER, NUMBER, POINTS, SPIDER, VIRTUES

CARPET – BEETLE, KNIGHT, MOTH, PLOT, SHARK, SLIPPER, SNAKE, TILES

CARRIAGE – BOLT, CLOCK, DOG, LINE, TRADE

CARRIER – BAG, PIGEON, WAVE

CARRY – AWAY, BACK, FORWARD, OFF, ON, OUT, OVER, THROUGH

CARTRIDGE – BELT, CLIP, PAPER, PEN

CASH – CROP, DESK, DISCOUNT, DISPENSER, FLOW, IN, LIMIT, RATIO, REGISTER, UP

CAST – ABOUT, BACK, DOWN, IRON, ON, OUT, STEEL, UP

CAT – BURGLAR, DOOR, HOLE, LITTER, RIG, SCANNER

CATCH – BASIN, CROP, ON, OUT, PHRASE, PIT, POINTS, UP

CAULIFLOWER – CHEESE, EAR

CENTRE – BIT, FORWARD, HALF, PUNCH, SPREAD, THREE-QUARTER

CHAIN – DRIVE, GANG, GRATE, LETTER, LIGHTNING, MAIL, PRINTER, REACTION, RULE, SAW, SHOT, STITCH, STORE

CHAMBER – COUNSEL, MUSIC, ORCHESTRA, ORGAN, POT

CHARGE – ACCOUNT, DENSITY, HAND, NURSE, SHEET

CHEESE – CUTTER, MITE, SKIPPER, STRAW

CHICKEN – BREAST, FEED, LOUSE, OUT, WIRE

CHILD – ABUSE, BENEFIT, CARE, GUIDANCE, LABOUR, MINDER

CHIMNEY – BREAST, CORNER, STACK, SWALLOW, SWEEP, SWIFT

CHINA – ASTER, BARK, CLAY, INK, ROSE, SEA, TREE

CHINESE – BLOCK, CABBAGE, CHEQUERS, CHIPPENDALE, EMPIRE, GOOSEBERRY, INK, LANTERN, LEAVES, PUZZLE, WALL, WAX, WHITE, WINDLASS

CHIP – BASKET, HEATER, IN, LOG, PAN, SHOT

CHRISTMAS – BEETLE, BOX, CACTUS, CARD, DIS-EASE, EVE, ISLAND, PUDDING, ROSE, STOCKING, TREE

CIGARETTE – CARD, END, HOLDER, LIGHTER, PAPER

CIRCUIT – BINDING, BOARD, BREAKER, JUDGE, RIDER, TRAINING

CITY – BLUES, COMPANY, DESK, EDITOR, FATHER, HALL, MANAGER, PLANNING, SLICKER

CIVIL – DEFENCE, DISOBEDIENCE, ENGINEER, LAW, LIBERTY, LIST, MARRIAGE, RIGHTS, SERVANT, SERVICE, WAR

CLAW – BACK, HAMMER, HATCHET, OFF, SETTING

CLOCK – GOLF, OFF, ON, UP

CLOSE – CALL, COMPANY, DOWN, HARMONY, IN, OUT, PUNCTUATION, QUARTERS, SEASON, SHAVE, WITH

CLOSED – BOOK, CHAIN, CIRCUIT, CORPORATION, GAME, PRIMARY, SCHOLARSHIP, SENTENCE, SET, SHOP

CLOTHES – MOTH, PEG, POLE, PROP

CLUB – FOOT, HAND, MOSS, ROOT, SANDWICH

COAL – GAS, HEAVER, HOLE, MEASURES, OIL, POT, SACK, SCUTTLE, TAR, TIT

COCONUT – BUTTER, ICE, MATTING, OIL, PALM, SHY

COFFEE – BAG, BAR, CUP, HOUSE, MILL, MORNING, NUT, SHOP, TABLE, TREE

COLD – CALL, CHISEL, CREAM, CUTS, DUCK, FEET, FRAME, FRONT, SHOULDER, SNAP, SORE, STORAGE, SWEAT, TURKEY, WAR, WARRIOR, WAVE, WORK

COLLECTIVE – AGREEMENT, BARGAINING, FARM, FRUIT, NOUN, OWNERSHIP, SECURITY, UNCONSCIOUS

COLORADO – BEETLE, DESERT, SPRINGS

COLOUR – BAR, CODE, CONTRAST, FILTER, GUARD, INDEX, LINE, PHASE, SCHEME, SERGEANT, SUP-PLEMENT, TEMPERATURE

COME – ABOUT, ACROSS, ALONG, AT, AWAY, BETWEEN, BY, FORWARD, IN, INTO, OF, OFF, OUT, OVER, ROUND, THROUGH, TO, UP, UPON

COMIC – OPERA, STRIP

COMMAND – GUIDANCE, MODULE, PAPER, PERFORMANCE, POST

COMMERCIAL – ART, BANK, COLLEGE, PAPER, TRAVELLER, VEHICLE

COMMON – COLD, DENOMINATOR, ENTRANCE, ERA, FACTOR, FEE, FRACTION, GOOD, GROUND, KNOWLEDGE, LAW, MARKET, NOUN, ROOM, SENSE, STOCK, TIME

COMMUNITY – CARE, CENTRE, CHEST, SERVICE, SINGING

COMPOUND – EYE, FLOWER, FRACTION, FRACTURE, INTEREST, LEAF, NUMBER, SENTENCE, TIME

CON – AMORE, BRIO, DOLORE, ESPRESSIONE, FUOCO, MAN, MOTO, ROD, SORDINO, SPIRITO, TRICK

CONTINENTAL – BREAKFAST, CLIMATE, DIVIDE, DRIFT, QUILT, SHELF, SYSTEM

CORAL – FERN, REEF, SEA, SNAKE, TREE

CORN – BORER, BREAD, BUNTING, DOLLY, EXCHANGE, FACTOR, LAWS, LILY, MARIGOLD, MEAL, OIL, PONE, POPPY, ROSE, ROW, SALAD, SHOCK, SHUCK, SILK, WHISKY

CORONA – AUSTRALIS, BOREALIS, DISCHARGE

COTTAGE – CHEESE, FLAT, HOSPITAL, INDUSTRY, LOAF, PIANO, PIE

COTTON – BELT, BUSH, CAKE, CANDY, FLANNEL, GRASS, ON, PICKER, SEDGE, STAINER, TO, WASTE, WOOL

COUGH – DROP, MIXTURE, UP

COUNTRY – CLUB, CODE, COUSIN, DANCE, HOUSE, MUSIC, SEAT

COURT – CARD, CIRCULAR, DRESS, MARTIAL, ROLL, SHOE

COVER – CROP, GIRL, NOTE, POINT, VERSION

CRASH – BARRIER, DIVE, HELMET, OUT, PAD

CREAM – CHEESE, CRACKER, PUFF, SAUCE, SODA, TEA

CREDIT – ACCOUNT, CARD, LINE, RATING, SQUEEZE, STANDING

CROCODILE – BIRD, CLIP, RIVER, TEARS

CRYSTAL – BALL, GAZING, MICROPHONE, PALACE, PICK-UP, SET, VIOLET

CUCKOO – BEE, CLOCK, SHRIKE, SPIT

CURTAIN – CALL, LECTURE, SPEECH, WALL

CUSTARD – APPLE, PIE, POWDER

CUT – ACROSS, ALONG, DOWN, GLASS, IN, OFF, OUT, STRING, UP

CUTTY – GRASS, SARK, STOOL

DANISH – BLUE, LOAF, PASTRY

DARK – AGES, CONTINENT, GLASSES, HORSE, LANTERN, REACTION, STAR

DAVY – JONES, LAMP

DAY – BED, LILY, NAME, NURSERY, RELEASE, RETURN, ROOM, SCHOOL, SHIFT, TRIP

DE – FACTO, FIDE, LUXE, PROFUNDIS, RIGUEUR, TROP

DEAD – BEAT, CENTRE, DUCK, END, FINISH, HAND, HEART, HEAT, LETTER, LOSS, MARCH, SEA, SET, WEIGHT

DEATH – ADDER, CAP, CELL, CERTIFICATE, DUTY, GRANT, KNELL, MASK, PENALTY, RATE, RATTLE, RAY, ROW, SEAT, VALLEY, WARRANT, WISH

DECIMAL – CLASSIFICATION, CURRENCY, FRACTION, PLACE, POINT, SYSTEM

DECK – CHAIR, HAND, OVER, TENNIS

DENTAL – CLINIC, FLOSS, HYGIENE, HYGIENIST, NURSE, PLAQUE, SURGEON

DESERT – BOOTS, COOLER, ISLAND, LYNX, OAK, PEA, RAT, SOIL

DIAMOND – ANNIVERSARY, BIRD, JUBILEE, POINT, SNAKE, WEDDING, WILLOW

DINNER – JACKET, LADY, SERVICE

DIPLOMATIC – BAG, CORPS, IMMUNITY, SERVICE

DIRECT – ACCESS, ACTION, EVIDENCE, LABOUR, METHOD, OBJECT, QUESTION, SPEECH

DISC – BRAKE, FLOWER, HARROW, JOCKEY, PLOUGH, WHEEL

DISPATCH – BOX, CASE, RIDER

DOG – BISCUIT, BOX, COLLAR, DAYS, FENNEL, HANDLER, LATIN, PADDLE, ROSE, STAR, TAG, VIOLET

DONKEY – DERBY, ENGINE, JACKET, VOTE

DOUBLE – AGENT, BACK, BAR, BASS, BASSOON, BILL, BOND, CHIN, CREAM, CROSS, DUTCH, ENTENDRE, ENTRY, EXPOSURE, FAULT, FIRST, GLAZING, GLOUCESTER, KNIT, KNITTING, NEGATION, NEGATIVE, PNEUMONIA, STANDARD, TAKE, TALK, TIME, UP

DOWN – PAYMENT, TIME, UNDER

DRAWING – BOARD, CARD, PIN, ROOM

DRESS – CIRCLE, COAT, DOWN, PARADE, REHEARSAL, SHIELD, SHIRT, SUIT, UNIFORM, UP

DRESSING – CASE, GOWN, ROOM, STATION, TABLE

DROP – AWAY, CANNON, CURTAIN, FORGE, GOAL, HAMMER, KICK, LEAF, OFF, SCONE, SHOT, TANK

DRUM – BRAKE, MAJOR, MAJORETTE, OUT, UP

DRY – BATTERY, CELL, DISTILLATION, DOCK, ICE, MARTINI, MEASURE, NURSE, OUT, ROT, RUN, UP

DUST – BOWL, COAT, COVER, DEVIL, DOWN, JACKET, SHOT, STORM

DUTCH – AUCTION, BARN, CAP, CHEESE, COURAGE, DOLL, DOOR, ELM, MEDICINE, OVEN, TREAT, UNCLE

EAR – LOBE, PIERCING, SHELL, TRUMPET

EARLY – BIRD, CLOSING, WARNING

EARTH – CLOSET, MOTHER, PILLAR, RETURN, SCIENCE, UP, WAX

EASTER – CACTUS, EGG, ISLAND, LILY

EASY – CHAIR, GAME, MEAT, MONEY, STREET

EGG – CUP, ROLL, SLICE, SPOON, TIMER, TOOTH, WHITE

ELECTRIC – BLANKET, BLUE, CHAIR, CHARGE, CONSTANT, CURRENT, EEL, EYE, FIELD, FIRE, FURNACE, GUITAR, HARE, NEEDLE, ORGAN, POTENTIAL, RAY, SHOCK, STORM

ELEPHANT – BIRD, GRASS, SEAL, SHREW

EVENING – CLASS, DRESS, PRIMROSE, STAR

EX – CATHEDRA, DIVIDEND, GRATIA, LIBRIS, OFFICIO

EYE – CONTACT, DOG, RHYME, SHADOW, SOCKET, SPLICE

FACE – CLOTH, OUT, PACK, POWDER, VALUE

FAIR – COPY, GAME, ISLE, PLAY, RENT, SEX

FAIRY – CYCLE, GODMOTHER, LIGHTS, PENGUIN, RING, SHRIMP, SWALLOW, TALE

FALL – ABOUT, AMONG, AWAY, BACK, BEHIND, DOWN, FOR, GUY, IN, OFF, ON, OVER, THROUGH, TO

FALSE – ALARM, COLOURS, DAWN, IMPRISONMENT, PRETENCES, STEP, TEETH

FAMILY – ALLOWANCE, BENEFIT, BIBLE, CIRCLE, DOCTOR, MAN, NAME, PLANNING, SKELETON, TREE

FAN – BELT, DANCE, HEATER, MAIL, VAULTING

FANCY – DRESS, GOODS, MAN, WOMAN

FAST – FOOD, LANE, MOTION, TALK

FATHER – CHRISTMAS, CONFESSOR, TIME

FIELD – ARMY, ARTILLERY, BATTERY, CENTRE, DAY, EMISSION, EVENT, GLASSES, HOSPITAL, MARSHAL, OFFICER, SPORTS, STUDY, TRIP, WORK

FIGURE – ON, OUT, SKATING

FILM – LIBRARY, PACK, SET, STAR, STRIP

FILTER – BED, OUT, PAPER, PRESS, PUMP, TIP

FINGER – BOWL, PAINTING, POST, WAVE

FIRE – ALARM, ANT, AWAY, BRIGADE, CLAY, CONTROL, DEPARTMENT, DOOR, DRILL, ENGINE, ESCAPE, HYDRANT, INSURANCE, IRONS, RAISER, SCREEN, SHIP, STATION, WALKING, WALL, WATCHER

FIRING – LINE, ORDER, PARTY, PIN, SQUAD

FIRST – AID, BASE, CLASS, FLOOR, FRUITS, LADY, LANGUAGE, LIEUTENANT, LIGHT, MATE, NAME, NIGHT, OFFENDER, OFFICER, PERSON, POST, PRINCIPLE, READING, REFUSAL, SCHOOL, WATER

FIVE – HUNDRED, KS, NATIONS, STONES, TOWNS

FLAKE – OUT, WHITE

FLASH – BURN, CARD, ELIMINATOR, FLOOD, GUN, PHOTOGRAPHY, PHOTOLYSIS, POINT, SET, SMELTING

FLAT – CAP, KNOT, RACING, SPIN, TUNING

FLIGHT – ARROW, DECK, ENGINEER, FEATHER, FORMATION, LIEUTENANT, LINE, PATH, PLAN, RECORDER, SERGEANT, SIMULATOR, STRIP, SURGEON

FLYING – BOAT, BOMB, BRIDGE, BUTTRESS, CIRCUS, COLOURS, DOCTOR, DUTCHMAN, FISH, FOX, FROG, JIB, LEMUR, LIZARD, MARE, OFFICER, PICKET, SAUCER, SQUAD, SQUIRREL, START, WING

FOLK – DANCE, MEDICINE, MEMORY, MUSIC, SINGER, SONG, TALE, WEAVE

FOOD – ADDITIVE, CHAIN, POISONING, PROCESSOR

FOOT – BRAKE, FAULT, ROT, RULE, SOLDIER

FOREIGN – AFFAIRS, AID, BILL, CORRESPONDENT, EXCHANGE, LEGION, MINISTER, MISSION, OFFICE, SERVICE

FOUL – PLAY, SHOT, UP

FOURTH – DIMENSION, ESTATE, INTERNATIONAL, REPUBLIC, WORLD

FREE – AGENT, ASSOCIATION, CHURCH, ELECTRON, ENERGY, ENTERPRISE, FALL, FLIGHT, FORM, GIFT, HAND, HOUSE, KICK, LOVE, SPACE, SPEECH, STATE, THOUGHT, THROW, TRADE, VERSE, WILL, ZONE

FRENCH – ACADEMY, BEAN, BREAD, CHALK, CRICKET, CUFF, CURVE, DOORS, DRESSING, HORN, KISS, KNICKERS, KNOT, LEAVE, LETTER, MUSTARD, PLEAT, POLISH, SEAM, STICK, TOAST, WINDOWS

FRONT – BENCH, DOOR, LINE, MAN, MATTER

FRUIT – BAT, BODY, COCKTAIL, CUP, FLY, KNIFE, MACHINE, SALAD, SUGAR, TREE

FULL – BLOOD, BOARD, DRESS, HOUSE, MOON, NELSON, PITCH, STOP, TIME, TOSS

GALLEY – PROOF, SLAVE

GALLOWS – BIRD, HUMOUR, TREE

GAME – BIRD, CHIPS, FISH, FOWL, LAWS, PARK, POINT, THEORY, WARDEN

GARDEN – CENTRE, CITY, CRESS, FLAT, FRAME, PARTY, SNAIL, SUBURB, WARBLER

GAS – BURNER, CHAMBER, CONSTANT, ENGINE, EQUATION, FIXTURE, GANGRENE, LAWS, LIGHTER, MAIN, MANTLE, MASK, METER, OIL, OVEN, POKER, RING, STATION, TURBINE

GENERAL – ANAESTHETIC, ASSEMBLY, DELIVERY, ELECTION, HOSPITAL, PRACTITIONER, STAFF, STRIKE, SYNOD, WILL

GIN – PALACE, RUMMY, SLING

GINGER – ALE, BEER, GROUP, SNAP, UP, WINE

GIRL – FRIDAY, GUIDE, SCOUT

GIVE – AWAY, IN, OFF, ONTO, OUT, OVER, UP

GLAD – EYE, HAND, RAGS

GLOVE – BOX, COMPARTMENT, PUPPET

GOLD – BASIS, BEETLE, BRICK, CERTIFICATE, COAST, DUST, FOIL, LEAF, MEDAL, MINE, NOTE, PLATE, POINT, RECORD, RESERVE, RUSH, STANDARD, STICK

GOLDEN – AGE, ASTER, CALF, CHAIN, DELICIOUS, EAGLE, FLEECE, GATE, GOOSE, HANDSHAKE, NUMBER, OLDIE, RETRIEVER, RULE, SECTION, SYRUP

GOLF – BALL, CLUB, COURSE, LINKS

GOOD – AFTERNOON, DAY, EVENING, FRIDAY, MORNING, NIGHT, SAMARITAN, SORT, TURN

GOOSE – BARNACLE, FLESH, STEP

GRAND – CANARY, CANYON, DUCHESS, DUCHY, DUKE, FINAL, GUIGNOL, JURY, LARCENY, MAL, MARNIER, MASTER, NATIONAL, OPERA, PIANO, PRIX, SEIGNEUR, SIÈCLE, SLAM, TOUR

GRANNY – BOND, FLAT, KNOT, SMITH

GRASS – BOX, CLOTH, COURT, HOCKEY, MOTH, ROOTS, SNAKE, TREE, WIDOW

GRAVY – BOAT, TRAIN

GREASE – CUP, GUN, MONKEY

GREAT – AUK, BEAR, BRITAIN, DANE, DIVIDE, LAKES, OUSE, PLAINS, SEAL, TIT, TREK, WAR,

GREEN – BEAN, BELT, BERET, CARD, DRAGON, FINGERS, LIGHT, MONKEY, MOULD, PAPER, PEPPER, PLOVER, THUMB, TURTLE, WOODPECKER

GREGORIAN – CALENDAR, CHANT, TELESCOPE, TONE

GREY – AREA, EMINENCE, FOX, FRIAR, MARKET, MATTER, SQUIRREL, WARBLER, WHALE, WOLF

GROUND – CONTROL, COVER, ENGINEER, FLOOR, GLASS, ICE, IVY, PLAN, PLATE, PROVISIONS, RENT, RULE, SWELL

GROW – BAG, INTO, ON, UP

GUIDE – DOG, ROPE

HAIR – DRYER, FOLLICLE, GEL, LACQUER, RESTORER, SHIRT, SLIDE, SPRAY, TRIGGER

HAPPY – EVENT, HOUR, MEDIUM, RELEASE

HARD – CASH, CHEESE, COPY, CORE, COURT, DISK, FEELING, HAT, HITTER, LABOUR, LINES, ROCK, SELL, SHOULDER, STANDING

HARVEST – HOME, MITE, MOON, MOUSE

HAT – STAND, TRICK

HATCHET – JOB, MAN

HEALTH – CENTRE, FOOD, SALTS, VISITOR

HEN – HARRIER, PARTY, RUN

HIGH – ALTAR, CHURCH, COMEDY, COMMAND, COMMISSIONER, COUNTRY, COURT, DAY, EXPLOSIVE, FASHION, FIDELITY, GERMAN, HAT, HOLIDAYS, JINKS, JUMP, POINT, PRIEST, SCHOOL, SEAS, SEASON, SOCIETY, SPOT, STREET, TABLE, TEA, TECH, TECHNOLOGY, TIDE, TIME, TREASON, WATER, WIRE, WYCOMBE

HIGHLAND – CATTLE, DRESS, FLING, REGION

HIP – BATH, FLASK, JOINT, POCKET

HIT – LIST, MAN, OFF, ON, OUT, PARADE

HOLD – BACK, DOWN, FORTH, IN, OFF, ON, OUT, OVER, TOGETHER, WITH

HOLY – BIBLE, CITY, COMMUNION, DAY, FATHER, GHOST, GRAIL, ISLAND, JOE, LAND, MARY, OFFICE, ORDERS, PLACE, ROLLER, ROOD, SCRIPTURE, SEE, SEPULCHRE, SPIRIT, WAR, WATER, WEEK, WRIT

HOME – AID, COUNTIES, ECONOMICS, FARM, GROUND,

GUARD, HELP, LOAN, OFFICE, PLATE, RANGE, RULE, RUN, SECRETARY, STRAIGHT, TEACHER, TRUTH, UNIT

HORSE – AROUND, BEAN, BRASS, CHESTNUT, GUARDS, LAUGH, MACKEREL, MARINE, MUSHROOM, NETTLE, OPERA, PISTOL, SENSE, TRADING

HOT – AIR, DOG, LINE, METAL, MONEY, PEPPER, POTATO, ROD, SEAT, SPOT, SPRING, STUFF, UP, ZONE

HOUSE – ARREST, GUEST, LIGHTS, MARTIN, MOTH, ORGAN, PARTY, PHYSICIAN, PLANT, SPARROW, SPIDER

HUMAN – BEING, CAPITAL, INTEREST, NATURE, RESOURCES, RIGHTS

HURRICANE – DECK, LAMP

ICE – AGE, AXE, BAG, BLOCK, CREAM, FISH, HOCKEY, HOUSE, LOLLY, MACHINE, MAN, PACK, PICK, PLANT, POINT, SHEET, SHELF, SHOW, SKATE, STATION, WATER, YACHT

ILL – FEELING, HUMOUR, TEMPER, WILL

IN – ABSENTIA, AETERNUM, CAMERA, ESSE, EXTENSO, EXTREMIS, MEMORIAM, NOMINE, PERPETUUM, PERSONAM, RE, REM, SITU, TOTO, UTERO, VACUO, VITRO, VIVO

INDIA – PAPER, PRINT, RUBBER

INDIAN – CLUB, EMPIRE, FILE, HEMP, INK, MALLOW, MILLET, MUTINY, OCEAN, RED, RESERVE, ROPE-TRICK, SUMMER

INNER – CITY, EAR, HEBRIDES, LIGHT, MAN, MONGOLIA, TUBE

INSIDE – FORWARD, JOB, LANE, TRACK

IRISH – COFFEE, MOSS, POTATO, REPUBLIC, SEA, SETTER, STEW, TERRIER, WHISKEY, WOLFHOUND

IRON – AGE, CHANCELLOR, CROSS, CURTAIN, FILINGS, GUARD, HAND, HORSE, LUNG, MAIDEN, MAN, OUT, PYRITES, RATIONS

JACK – FROST, IN, PLANE, RABBIT, ROBINSON, RUSSELL, TAR, UP

KICK – ABOUT, IN, OFF, OUT, PLEAT, TURN, UP, UPSTAIRS

KIDNEY – BEAN, MACHINE, STONE, VETCH

KNIFE – EDGE, GRINDER, PLEAT, SWITCH

LADY – BOUNTIFUL, CHAPEL, DAY, FERN, MAYORESS, MUCK, ORCHID

LAND – AGENT, BANK, BRIDGE, CRAB, FORCES, GIRL, GRANT, LINE, MINE, OFFICE, RAIL, REFORM, TAX, UP, WITH

LAST – JUDGMENT, NAME, OUT, POST, QUARTER, RITES, STRAW, SUPPER, THING

LATIN – AMERICA, CROSS, QUARTER, SQUARE

LAY – ASIDE, AWAY, BROTHER, DAYS, DOWN, FIGURE, IN, INTO, OFF, ON, OUT, OVER, READER, TO, UP

LEADING – AIRCRAFTMAN, ARTICLE, DOG, EDGE, LIGHT, MAN, NOTE, QUESTION, REINS

LEAVE – BEHIND, OFF, OUT

LEFT – BANK, WING

LEMON – BALM, CHEESE, DROP, FISH, GERANIUM, GRASS, SOLE, SQUASH, SQUEEZER, VERBENA

LETTER – BOMB, BOX, CARD

LIBERTY – BODICE, CAP, HALL, HORSE, ISLAND, SHIP

LIE – DETECTOR, DOWN, IN, TO

LIFE – ASSURANCE, BELT, BUOY, CYCLE, EXPECTANCY, FORM, GUARDS, HISTORY, INSURANCE, INTEREST, JACKET, PEER, PRESERVER, RAFT, SCIENCE, SPAN, STYLE

LIGHT – BULB, FACE, FLYWEIGHT, HEAVYWEIGHT, HORSE, INTO, METER, MIDDLEWEIGHT, MUSIC, OPERA, OUT, SHOW, UP, WELTERWEIGHT, YEAR

LIVER – FLUKE, SALTS, SAUSAGE

LIVING – DEATH, FOSSIL, PICTURE, ROOM, WAGE

LOBSTER – MOTH, NEWBURG, POT, THERMIDOR

LOCAL – ANAESTHETIC, AUTHORITY, COLOUR, GOVERNMENT, TIME

LONE – HAND, WOLF

LONG – ARM, BEACH, FACE, HAUL, HOP, ISLAND, JENNY, JOHNS, JUMP, PARLIAMENT, SHOT, SUIT, TOM, VACATION, WEEKEND

LOOK – AFTER, BACK, DOWN, ON, OVER, THROUGH, UP

LOOSE – CHANGE, COVER, END

LORD – ADVOCATE, CHAMBERLAIN, CHANCELLOR, LIEUTENANT, MAYOR, MUCK, PROTECTOR, PROVOST

LOUNGE – LIZARD, SUIT

LOVE – AFFAIR, APPLE, CHILD, FEAST, GAME, KNOT, LETTER, LIFE, MATCH, NEST, POTION, SEAT, SET

LOW – CHURCH, COMEDY, COUNTRIES, FREQUENCY, PROFILE, TECH, TECHNOLOGY, TIDE

LUNAR – CAUSTIC, ECLIPSE, MODULE, MONTH, YEAR

LUNCHEON – CLUB, MEAT, VOUCHER

MACHINE – BOLT, GUN, HEAD, SHOP, TOOL

MACKEREL – BREEZE, SHARK, SKY

MAGIC – CARPET, EYE, LANTERN, MUSHROOM, NUMBER, SQUARE

MAGNETIC – CIRCUIT, COMPASS, CONSTANT, DISK, EQUATOR, FIELD, FLUX, INDUCTION, INK, LENS, MOMENT, NEEDLE, NORTH, PICK-UP, POLE, STORM, TAPE

MAIDEN – NAME, OVER, VOYAGE

MAIL – DROP, ORDER

MAKE – AFTER, AWAY, BELIEVE, FOR, OF, OFF, OUT, OVER, WITH

MALT – EXTRACT, LIQUOR, WHISKY

MANDARIN – CHINESE, COLLAR, DUCK

MARCH – BROWN, HARE, PAST

MARKET – GARDEN, GARDENING, ORDER, PRICE, RENT, RESEARCH, SHARE, TOWN, VALUE

MARRIAGE – BUREAU, GUIDANCE

MARSH – ELDER, FERN, FEVER, GAS, HARRIER, HAWK, HEN, MALLOW, MARIGOLD, ORCHID, TIT

MASTER – BUILDER, CYLINDER, KEY, RACE, SERGEANT

MATINÉE – COAT, IDOL

MAUNDY – MONEY, THURSDAY

MAY – APPLE, BEETLE, BLOBS, BLOSSOM, DAY, QUEEN, TREE

MECHANICAL – ADVANTAGE, DRAWING, ENGINEERING, INSTRUMENT

MEDICAL – CERTIFICATE, EXAMINATION, EXAMINER, JURISPRUDENCE

MEDICINE – BALL, CHEST, LODGE, MAN

MELBA – SAUCE, TOAST

MEMORY – BANK, MAPPING, SPAN, TRACE

MENTAL – AGE, BLOCK, CRUELTY, DISORDER, HANDICAP

MERCHANT – BANK, NAVY, PRINCE

MERCY – FLIGHT, KILLING, SEAT

MESS – ABOUT, HALL, JACKET, KIT

MICHAELMAS – DAISY, TERM

TWO-WORD PHRASES

MICKEY – FINN, MOUSE
MIDDLE – AGE, AGES, C, CLASS, EAR, EAST,
MANAGEMENT, NAME, SCHOOL, TEMPLE
MIDNIGHT – BLUE, SUN
MIDSUMMER – DAY, MADNESS
MILITARY – ACADEMY, HONOURS, LAW, ORCHID, PACE,
POLICE
MILK – BAR, CHOCOLATE, FEVER, FLOAT, LEG, PUD-
DING, PUNCH, ROUND, RUN, SHAKE, STOUT, TOOTH
MINT – BUSH, JULEP, SAUCE
MINUTE – GUN, HAND, MARK, STEAK
MIRROR – CANON, CARP, FINISH, IMAGE, LENS,
SYMMETRY, WRITING
MITRE – BLOCK, BOX, GEAR, JOINT, SQUARE
MIXED – BAG, BLESSING, DOUBLES, ECONOMY,
FARMING, GRILL, MARRIAGE, METAPHOR
MONEY – MARKET, ORDER, SPIDER, SUPPLY
MONKEY – BREAD, BUSINESS, CLIMB, FLOWER,
JACKET, NUT, ORCHID, PUZZLE, SUIT, TRICKS, WRENCH
MORNING – COAT, DRESS, SICKNESS, STAR, TEA,
WATCH
MOSQUITO – BOAT, HAWK, NET
MOSS – AGATE, LAYER, PINK, ROSE, STITCH
MOTHER – COUNTRY, GOOSE, HUBBARD, LODE, SHIP,
SHIPTON, SUPERIOR, TONGUE, WIT
MOTOR – CARAVAN, DRIVE, GENERATOR, SCOOTER,
VEHICLE, VESSEL
MOUNTAIN – ASH, CAT, CHAIN, DEVIL, GOAT, LAUREL,
LION, RANGE, SHEEP, SICKNESS
MUD – BATH, DAUBER, FLAT, HEN, MAP, PIE, PUPPY,
TURTLE
MUSTARD – GAS, OIL, PLASTER
MYSTERY – PLAY, TOUR
NANSEN – BOTTLE, PASSPORT
NARROW – BOAT, GAUGE, SEAS
NATIONAL – ACCOUNTING, AGREEMENT, ANTHEM,
ASSEMBLY, ASSISTANCE, DEBT, FRONT, GALLERY, GRID,
SERVICE, TRUST
NERVE – CELL, CENTRE, FIBRE, GAS, IMPULSE
NEW – BROOM, FOREST, GUINEA, LOOK, MATHS,
MOON, PENNY, TESTAMENT, TOWN, WAVE, WORLD,
YEAR, YORK, ZEALAND
NEWS – AGENCY, CONFERENCE, VENDOR
NIGHT – BLINDNESS, DANCER, FIGHTER, NURSE, OWL,
ROBE, SAFE, SCHOOL, SHIFT, WATCH, WATCHMAN
NINETEENTH – HOLE, MAN
NOBLE – ART, GAS, SAVAGE
NORFOLK – ISLAND, JACKET, TERRIER
NOSE – CONE, DIVE, OUT, RAG, RING
NUCLEAR – BOMB, ENERGY, FAMILY, FISSION, FUEL,
FUSION, ISOMER, PHYSICS, POWER, REACTION,
REACTOR, THRESHOLD, WINTER
NURSERY – RHYME, SCHOOL, SLOPES, STAKES
OFF – CHANCE, COLOUR, KEY, LIMITS, LINE, SEASON
OIL – BEETLE, CAKE, DRUM, HARDENING, PAINT,
PAINTING, PALM, RIG, RIVERS, SHALE, SLICK, VARNISH,
WELL
OLD – BAILEY, BILL, BIRD, BOY, CONTEMPTIBLES,
COUNTRY, GIRL, GOLD, GUARD, HAND, HAT, LADY,
MAID, MAN, MOON, NICK, PRETENDER, SCHOOL,
STYLE, TESTAMENT, WORLD
OLIVE – BRANCH, BROWN, CROWN, DRAB, GREEN, OIL

ON – DIT, KEY, LINE
OPEN – AIR, BOOK, CHAIN, CIRCUIT, COURT, DAY,
DOOR, HOUSE, LETTER, MARKET, PRISON, PUNCTUA-
TION, SANDWICH, SESAME, UNIVERSITY, UP, VERDICT
OPERA – BUFFA, CLOAK, GLASSES, HAT, HOUSE,
SERIA
OPIUM – DEN, POPPY, WARS
ORANGE – BLOSSOM, PEEL, PEKOE, STICK
ORDINARY – LEVEL, RATING, RAY, SEAMAN, SHARES
OXFORD – ACCENT, BAGS, BLUE, ENGLISH, FRAME,
GROUP, MOVEMENT
OYSTER – BED, CRAB, PINK, PLANT, WHITE
PACK – ANIMAL, DRILL, ICE, IN, RAT, UP
PALM – BEACH, CIVET, OFF, OIL, SUGAR, SUNDAY,
VAULTING, WINE
PANAMA – CANAL, CITY, HAT
PANIC – BOLT, BUTTON, BUYING, GRASS, STATIONS
PAPER – CHASE, FILIGREE, MONEY, MULBERRY,
NAUTILUS, OVER, TAPE, TIGER
PAR – AVION, EXCELLENCE, VALUE
PARISH – CLERK, COUNCIL, PUMP, REGISTER
PARTY – LINE, MAN, POLITICS, WALL
PASSING – BELL, NOTE, SHOT
PASSION – FRUIT, PLAY, SUNDAY, WEEK
PATCH – BOARD, POCKET, QUILT, TEST
PAY – BACK, BED, DIRT, DOWN, FOR, IN, OFF, OUT,
TELEVISION, UP
PEACE – CORPS, OFFERING, PIPE, RIVER, SIGN
PEG – CLIMBING, DOWN, LEG, OUT, TOP
PEN – FRIEND, NAME, PAL
PENNY – ARCADE, BLACK, WHISTLE
PER – ANNUM, CAPITA, CENT, CONTRA, DIEM, MENSEM,
MILL, PRO, SE
PERSIAN – BLINDS, CARPET, CAT, EMPIRE,
GREYHOUND, GULF, LAMB, MELON
PETIT – BOURGEOIS, FOUR, JURY, LARCENY, MAL,
POINT
PETROL – BOMB, PUMP, STATION
PETTY – CASH, JURY, LARCENY, OFFICER, SESSIONS
PICTURE – CARD, HAT, HOUSE, MOULDING, PALACE,
WINDOW, WRITING
PIECE – GOODS, OUT, RATE
PILLOW – BLOCK, FIGHT, LACE, LAVA, SHAM, TALK
PILOT – BALLOON, BIRD, BISCUIT, CLOTH, ENGINE,
FILM, FISH, HOUSE, LAMP, LIGHT, OFFICER, PLANT,
STUDY, WHALE
PIN – CURL, DOWN, JOINT, MONEY, RAIL, TUCK,
WRENCH
PINE – CONE, END, MARTEN, NEEDLE, TAR
PINK – ELEPHANTS, GIN, NOISE, SALMON, SLIP
PIPE – CLEANER, DOWN, DREAM, MAJOR, ORGAN,
ROLL, UP
PLACE – CARD, KICK, NAME, SETTING
PLAIN – CHOCOLATE, CLOTHES, FLOUR, SAILING, TEXT
PLAY – ALONG, DOWN, OFF, ON, OUT, UP, WITH
PLYMOUTH – BRETHREN, COLONY, ROCK
POCKET – BATTLESHIP, BILLIARDS, BOROUGH,
GOPHER, MONEY, MOUSE
POETIC – JUSTICE, LICENCE
PONY – EXPRESS, TREKKING
POOR – BOX, LAW, MOUTH, RELATION, WHITE
POP – ART, OFF, SHOP

POST – CHAISE, HOC, HORN, HOUSE, MERIDIEM, OFFICE, ROAD, TOWN

POT – CHEESE, LIQUOR, MARIGOLD, ON, PLANT, ROAST, SHOT, STILL

POTATO – BEETLE, BLIGHT, CHIP, CRISP

POWDER – BLUE, BURN, COMPACT, FLASK, HORN, KEG, MONKEY, PUFF, ROOM

POWER – CUT, DIVE, DRILL, FACTOR, LINE, PACK, PLANT, POINT, POLITICS, STATION, STEERING, STRUCTURE

PRAIRIE – DOG, OYSTER, PROVINCES, SCHOONER, SOIL, TURNIP, WOLF

PRAYER – BEADS, BOOK, MEETING, RUG, SHAWL, WHEEL

PRESS – AGENCY, AGENT, BOX, CONFERENCE, GALLERY, GANG, RELEASE, STUD

PRESSURE – CABIN, COOKER, DRAG, GAUGE, GRADIENT, GROUP, HEAD, POINT, SUIT

PRICE – COMMISSION, CONTROL, DISCRIMINATION, RING, SUPPORT, TAG, WAR

PRICKLY – ASH, HEAT, PEAR, POPPY

PRIME – COST, MERIDIAN, MINISTER, MOVER, NUMBER, RATE, TIME, VERTICAL

PRIVATE – BAR, BILL, COMPANY, DETECTIVE, ENTERPRISE, EYE, HOTEL, INCOME, LANGUAGE, LIFE, MEMBER, PARTS, PATIENT, PRACTICE, PRESS, PROPERTY, SCHOOL, SECRETARY, SECTOR

PRIVY – CHAMBER, COUNCIL, PURSE, SEAL

PRIZE – COURT, MONEY, RING

PRO – FORMA, PATRIA, RATA, TEMPORE

PUBLIC – BAR, BILL, COMPANY, CONVENIENCE, CORPORATION, DEBT, DEFENDER, ENEMY, ENTERPRISE, EXPENDITURE, FOOTPATH, GALLERY, HOLIDAY, HOUSE, LAW, NUISANCE, OPINION, OWNERSHIP, PROSECUTOR, RELATIONS, SCHOOL, SECTOR, SERVANT, SERVICE, SPEAKING, SPENDING, TRANSPORT

PUFF – ADDER, PASTRY

PULL – ABOUT, BACK, DOWN, IN, OFF, ON, OUT, THROUGH, TOGETHER, UP

PURPLE – EMPEROR, GALLINULE, HEART, MEDIC, PATCH

PUSH – ABOUT, ALONG, BUTTON, IN, OFF, ON, THROUGH

PUT – ABOUT, ACROSS, ASIDE, AWAY, BACK, BY, DOWN, FORTH, FORWARD, IN, OFF, ON, OUT, OVER, THROUGH, UP, UPON

QUANTUM – LEAP, MECHANICS, NUMBER, STATE, STATISTICS, THEORY

QUARTER – CRACK, DAY, GRAIN, HORSE, NOTE, PLATE, ROUND, SECTION, SESSIONS, TONE

QUEEN – BEE, CONSORT, DOWAGER, MAB, MOTHER, OLIVE, POST, REGENT, REGNANT, SUBSTANCE

QUEER – FISH, STREET

QUESTION – MARK, MASTER, TIME

RAIN – CHECK, GAUGE, SHADOW, TREE

REAL – ALE, ESTATE, LIFE, NUMBER, PART, PRESENCE, PROPERTY, TENNIS, WAGES

RED – ADMIRAL, ALGAE, BAG, BARK, BEDS, BIDDY, CARPET, CEDAR, CROSS, DUSTER, DWARF, ENSIGN, FLAG, HAT, HEAT, HERRING, INDIAN, MEAT, MULLET, PEPPER, RAG, RIVER, ROSE, SALMON, SEA, SETTER, SHANK, SHIFT, SNAPPER, SPIDER, SQUIRREL, TAPE

RES – ADJUDICATA, GESTAE, JUDICATA, PUBLICA

RIGHT – ABOUT, ANGLE, ASCENSION, AWAY, HONOURABLE, OFF, ON, REVEREND, WING

ROCK – BOTTOM, CAKE, CLIMBING, GARDEN, PLANT, SALT, STEADY

ROLLER – BEARING, CAPTION, COASTER, DERBY, SKATE, TOWEL

ROMAN – ARCH, CALENDAR, CANDLE, CATHOLIC, CATHOLICISM, COLLAR, EMPIRE, HOLIDAY, LAW, MILE, NOSE, NUMERALS

ROOF – GARDEN, RACK

ROOM – SERVICE, TEMPERATURE

ROOT – BEER, CANAL, CROP, NODULE, OUT, POSITION, UP

ROTARY – CLOTHESLINE, CLUB, ENGINE, PLOUGH, PRESS, PUMP

ROUGH – COLLIE, DIAMOND, OUT, PASSAGE, SPIN, STUFF, UP

ROUND – ANGLE, CLAM, DANCE, DOWN, HAND, OFF, ON, OUT, ROBIN, TABLE, TOP, TRIP, UP

ROYAL – ACADEMY, ASSENT, BLUE, BURGH, COMMISSION, DUKE, ENGINEERS, FLUSH, HIGHNESS, ICING, JELLY, MARINES, NAVY, PURPLE, ROAD, STANDARD, TENNIS, WARRANT, WORCESTER

RUBBER – BAND, BRIDGE, CEMENT, CHEQUE, GOODS, PLANT, STAMP, TREE

RUN – ACROSS, AFTER, ALONG, AROUND, AWAY, DOWN, IN, INTO, OFF, ON, OUT, OVER, THROUGH, TO, UP

RUNNING – BOARD, COMMENTARY, HEAD, LIGHT, MATE, REPAIRS, RIGGING, STITCH

RUSSIAN – DRESSING, EMPIRE, REVOLUTION, ROULETTE, SALAD, WOLFHOUND

SAFETY – BELT, CATCH, CHAIN, CURTAIN, FACTOR, FILM, FUSE, GLASS, LAMP, MATCH, NET, PIN, RAZOR, VALVE

SALAD – DAYS, DRESSING

SALLY – ARMY, LUNN

SALT – AWAY, BATH, CAKE, DOME, FLAT, LAKE, LICK, MARSH, OUT, PORK

SAND – BAR, CASTLE, EEL, FLEA, HOPPER, LANCE, LEEK, LIZARD, MARTIN, PAINTING, SHRIMP, TABLE, TRAP, VIPER, WASP, WEDGE, YACHT

SANDWICH – BOARD, CAKE, COURSE, ISLANDS, MAN

SAUSAGE – DOG, ROLL

SCARLET – FEVER, HAT, LETTER, PIMPERNEL, RUNNER, WOMAN

SCATTER – DIAGRAM, PIN, RUG

SCOTCH – BROTH, EGG, MIST, PANCAKE, SNAP, TAPE, TERRIER

SCRAPE – IN, THROUGH, TOGETHER

SCRATCH – PAD, SHEET, TEST, TOGETHER, VIDEO

SECOND – CHILDHOOD, CLASS, COMING, COUSIN, FIDDLE, FLOOR, GENERATION, GROWTH, HAND, LANGUAGE, LIEUTENANT, MATE, NAME, NATURE, READING, SIGHT, STRING, THOUGHT, WIND

SECONDARY – COLOUR, EMISSION, PICKET, PROCESSES, QUALITIES, SCHOOL, STRESS

SECRET – AGENT, POLICE, SERVICE, SOCIETY

SEE – ABOUT, INTO, OF, OFF, OUT, OVER, THROUGH

SENIOR – AIRCRAFTMAN, CITIZEN, MANAGEMENT, SERVICE

SERVICE – AREA, CHARGE, INDUSTRY, MODULE, ROAD, STATION

SET – ABOUT, AGAINST, ASIDE, BACK, DOWN, FORTH, IN, OFF, ON, OUT, PIECE, POINT, SQUARE, THEORY, TO, UP, UPON

SETTLE – DOWN, FOR, IN, WITH

SHAKE – DOWN, OFF, UP

SHEET – ANCHOR, BEND, DOWN, LIGHTNING, METAL, MUSIC

SHOP – AROUND, ASSISTANT, FLOOR, STEWARD

SHORE – BIRD, LEAVE, PATROL

SHORT – CIRCUIT, CUT, FUSE, HEAD, LIST, ODDS, SHRIFT, STORY, STRAW, TIME, WAVE

SHOW – BILL, BUSINESS, CARD, COPY, OFF, STOPPER, TRIAL, UP

SIAMESE – CAT, TWINS

SICK – LEAVE, LIST, NOTE, PAY

SIGN – AWAY, IN, LANGUAGE, MANUAL, OFF, ON, OUT, UP

SINGLE – BOND, CREAM, DENSITY, ENTRY, FILE, TAX, THREAD, TICKET

SIT – BACK, DOWN, ON, OUT, OVER, UNDER, UP

SITTING – BULL, ROOM, TARGET, TENANT

SKI – JUMP, LIFT, PANTS, RUN, STICK, TOW

SKIN – DIVING, EFFECT, FLICK, FOOD, FRICTION, GAME, GRAFT, TEST

SLAVE – ANT, COAST, CYLINDER, DRIVER, SHIP, STATE, TRADE

SLIDE – FASTENER, GUITAR, OVER, REST, RULE, TROMBONE, VALVE

SLIP – GAUGE, RAIL, RING, ROAD, STEP, STITCH, UP

SLOW – BURN, HANDCLAP, MARCH, MOTION, TIME

SMALL – ARMS, BEER, CHANGE, FRY, HOURS, INTESTINE, SLAM, TALK

SMART – ALECK, CARD, MONEY, SET

SMOKE – BOMB, OUT, SCREEN, TREE

SNEAK – PREVIEW, THIEF

SOB – SISTER, STORY, STUFF

SOCIAL – CLIMBER, SCIENCE, SECRETARY, SECURITY, SERVICES, STUDIES, WELFARE, WORK

SODA – ASH, BISCUIT, BREAD, FOUNTAIN, JERK, LIME, NITRE, POP, SIPHON, WATER

SOFT – DRINK, FRUIT, FURNISHINGS, GOODS, LANDING, LINE, OPTION, PORN, SELL, SOAP, SPOT, TOP, TOUCH

SOLAR – ECLIPSE, FLARE, FURNACE, HEATING, MONTH, MYTH, PANEL, PLEXUS, POWER, SYSTEM, WIND, YEAR

SOUND – BARRIER, BOW, CHECK, EFFECT, HEAD, HOLE, MIXER, OFF, OUT, WAVE

SOUR – CHERRY, CREAM, GOURD, GRAPES, GUM, MASH

SPACE – AGE, BLANKET, CADET, CAPSULE, CHARACTER, HEATER, INVADERS, OPERA, PLATFORM, PROBE, SHUTTLE, STATION

SPAGHETTI – JUNCTION, WESTERN

SPARK – CHAMBER, COIL, EROSION, GAP, OFF, PLUG, TRANSMITTER

SPEAK – FOR, OUT, TO, UP

SPECIAL – ASSESSMENT, BRANCH, CASE, CONSTABLE, DELIVERY, EFFECTS, JURY, LICENCE, PLEADING, PRIVILEGE, SCHOOL, SORT

SPEED – LIMIT, TRAP, UP

SPINNING – JENNY, MULE, TOP, WHEEL

SPIRIT – GUM, LAMP, LEVEL, VARNISH

SPLIT – CANE, DECISION, INFINITIVE, PEA, PERSONALITY, SECOND, SHIFT, TIN, UP

SPONGE – BAG, BATH, CAKE, CLOTH, DOWN

SPORTS – CAR, COAT, JACKET, SHIRT

SPRING – BALANCE, CHICKEN, FEVER, LOCK, MATTRESS, ONION, ROLL, TIDE

SPUN – SILK, SUGAR, YARN

SQUARE – AWAY, BRACKET, DANCE, LEG, MEAL, NUMBER, OFF, ROOT, UP

STABLE – DOOR, FLY, LAD

STAFF – ASSOCIATION, COLLEGE, CORPORAL, NURSE, OFFICER, SERGEANT

STAG – BEETLE, PARTY

STAGE – DIRECTION, DOOR, EFFECT, FRIGHT, LEFT, MANAGER, RIGHT, WHISPER

STAMP – ACT, COLLECTING, DUTY, MILL, OUT

STAND – BY, DOWN, FOR, IN, OIL, ON, OUT, OVER, PAT, TO, UP

STAR – CHAMBER, CONNECTION, GRASS, SAPPHIRE, SHELL, STREAM, SYSTEM, THISTLE, WARS

STATUS – QUO, SYMBOL

STEEL – BAND, BLUE, GREY, GUITAR, WOOL

STICK – AROUND, AT, BY, DOWN, INSECT, OUT, TO, TOGETHER, WITH

STICKY – END, WICKET

STIRRUP – BONE, CUP, PUMP

STOCK – CAR, CERTIFICATE, COMPANY, EXCHANGE, FARM, MARKET

STOCKING – CAP, FILLER, FRAME, MASK, STITCH

STORAGE – BATTERY, CAPACITY, DEVICE, HEATER

STORM – BELT, CENTRE, CLOUD, COLLAR, CONE, DOOR, GLASS, LANTERN, PETREL, WARNING, WINDOW

STRAIGHT – BAT, FACE, FIGHT, FLUSH, MAN, OFF, UP

STRAWBERRY – BLONDE, BUSH, MARK, TOMATO, TREE

STREET – ARAB, CREDIBILITY, CRY, DOOR, PIANO, THEATRE, VALUE

STRIKE – DOWN, FAULT, NOTE, OFF, OUT, PAY, THROUGH, UP

STRING – ALONG, BAND, BASS, BEAN, COURSE, LINE, ORCHESTRA, QUARTET, TIE, VARIABLE

STRIP – CARTOON, CLUB, CROPPING, LIGHTING, MILL, MINING, OUT, POKER

SUGAR – BEET, CANDY, CANE, CORN, DADDY, DIABETES, LOAF, MAPLE

SUMMER – HOLIDAY, PUDDING, SCHOOL, SOLSTICE, TIME

SUN – BATH, BEAR, BITTERN, BLIND, BLOCK, DANCE, DECK, DISC, KING, LAMP, LOUNGE

SUPREME – BEING, COMMANDER, COURT, SACRIFICE

SURFACE – MAIL, NOISE, PLATE, STRUCTURE, TENSION

SWAN – DIVE, MAIDEN, NECK, SONG

SWEAT – GLAND, OFF, OUT, SHIRT, SUIT

SWEET – BASIL, BAY, CHERRY, CHESTNUT, CICELY, CIDER, CLOVER, CORN, FERN, FLAG, GALE, GUM, MARJORAM, MARTEN, OIL, PEA, PEPPER, POTATO, SHOP, TOOTH, WILLIAM, WOODRUFF

SWISS – CHARD, CHEESE, GUARD, MUSLIN, ROLL, TOURNAMENT

TABLE – BAY, D'HOTE, LICENCE, MONEY, MOUNTAIN, NAPKIN, SALT, TALK, TENNIS, WINE

TAIL – COAT, COVERT, END, FAN, GATE, OFF, OUT

TAKE – ABACK, AFTER, APART, AWAY, BACK, DOWN, FOR, IN, OFF, ON, OUT, OVER, TO, UP

TALK – ABOUT, AT, BACK, DOWN, INTO, OUT, ROUND, SHOW

TANK – ENGINE, FARMING, TOP, TRAP, UP, WAGON

TAX – AVOIDANCE, DISC, EVASION, EXILE, HAVEN, RATE, RETURN, SHELTER

TEA – BAG, BISCUIT, CLOTH, COSY, GARDEN, GOWN, LEAF, PARTY, ROSE, SERVICE, TOWEL, TROLLEY

TEAR – AWAY, DOWN, DUCT, GAS, INTO, OFF, SHEET

TELEPHONE – BOX, DIRECTORY, NUMBER

TERRA – ALBA, COTTA, FIRMA, INCOGNITA, SIGILLATA

TEST – ACT, BAN, CASE, MARKETING, MATCH, PAPER, PILOT, TUBE

THIRD – CLASS, DEGREE, DIMENSION, ESTATE, EYELID, MAN, PARTY, PERSON, READING, REICH, WORLD

THROW – ABOUT, IN, OFF, OUT, OVER, TOGETHER, UP, WEIGHT

TIME – BOMB, CAPSULE, CLOCK, IMMEMORIAL, MACHINE, SERIES, SHARING, SHEET, SIGNATURE, SWITCH, TRIAL, ZONE

TIN – CAN, GOD, HAT, LIZZIE, PLATE, SOLDIER, WHISTLE

TITLE – DEED, PAGE, ROLE

TOILET – PAPER, SET, SOAP, TRAINING, WATER

TONE – CLUSTER, COLOUR, CONTROL, DOWN, LANGUAGE, POEM, ROW, UP

TOP – BOOT, BRASS, DOG, DRAWER, END, GEAR, HAT, MANAGEMENT, OFF, OUT, UP

TORQUE – CONVERTER, METER, SPANNER, WRENCH

TOUCH – FOOTBALL, JUDGE, OFF, UP

TOWN – CLERK, CRIER, GAS, HALL, HOUSE, MEETING, PLANNING

TRACK – DOWN, EVENT, MEET, RECORD, ROD, SHOE

TRADE – ACCEPTANCE, CYCLE, DISCOUNT, GAP, JOURNAL, NAME, ON, PLATE, SCHOOL, SECRET, UNION, WIND

TRAFFIC – COP, COURT, ISLAND, JAM, LIGHT, OFFICER, PATTERN, WARDEN

TREASURY – BENCH, BILL, BOND, CERTIFICATE, NOTE, TAG

TRENCH – COAT, FEVER, FOOT, KNIFE, MORTAR, MOUTH, WARFARE

TRIPLE – ALLIANCE, BOND, ENTENTE, JUMP, POINT, TIME

TURKISH – BATH, COFFEE, DELIGHT, EMPIRE, TOBACCO, TOWEL

TURN – AGAINST, AWAY, BRIDGE, DOWN, IN, OFF, ON, OUT, OVER, TO, UP

TWELFTH – DAY, MAN, NIGHT

TWIN – BED, BILL, TOWN

UMBRELLA – BIRD, PINE, PLANT, STAND, TREE

UNION – CARD, JACK

UNIT – COST, FACTOR, PRICE, TRUST

UNITED – KINGDOM, NATIONS, PARTY, PROVINCES

VACUUM – CLEANER, FLASK

VALUE – ADDED, DATE, JUDGMENT

VENETIAN – BLIND, GLASS, RED

VENTURE – CAPITAL, SCOUT

VICAR – APOSTOLIC, FORANE, GENERAL

VICE – ADMIRAL, CHANCELLOR, PRESIDENT, SQUAD, VERSA

VIDEO – CASSETTE, GAME, NASTY, TAPE

VIRGIN – BIRTH, ISLANDS, MARY, WOOL

VIRGINIA – BEACH, CREEPER, DEER, REEL, STOCK

VOX – ANGELICA, HUMANA, POP, POPULI

VULGAR – FRACTION, LATIN

WALK – AWAY, INTO, OFF, OUT

WAR – BABY, BONNET, BRIDE, CHEST, CORRESPONDENT, CRIME, CRY, DANCE, GAME, MEMORIAL, OFFICE, PAINT, WHOOP

WASHING – MACHINE, POWDER, SODA

WATCH – CAP, CHAIN, COMMITTEE, FIRE, NIGHT, OUT

WEATHER – EYE, HOUSE, MAP, STATION, STRIP, VANE, WINDOW

WEDDING – BREAKFAST, CAKE, RING

WEIGH – DOWN, IN, UP

WELSH – CORGI, DRESSER, HARP, MOUNTAIN, POPPY, RABBIT, TERRIER

WET – BLANKET, CELL, DREAM, FISH, FLY, LOOK, NURSE, PACK, ROT, STEAM, SUIT

WHITE – ADMIRAL, AREA, BEAR, BIRCH, ELEPHANT, ENSIGN, FEATHER, FISH, FLAG, GOLD, HEAT, HORSE, HOUSE, KNIGHT, LADY, LEAD, LIE, LIGHT, MEAT, OUT, PAPER, PEPPER, SLAVE, SPIRIT, STICK, TIE, WHALE

WINDOW – BOX, ENVELOPE, SASH, SEAT, TAX

WINE – BAR, BOX, CELLAR, COOLER, TASTING

WING – CHAIR, COLLAR, COMMANDER, COVERT, LOADING, NUT, SHOT, TIP

WITCH – DOCTOR, HAZEL

WOLF – CUB, SPIDER, WHISTLE

WORD – ASSOCIATION, BLINDNESS, ORDER, PICTURE, PROCESSING, PROCESSOR, SQUARE

WORK – BACK, CAMP, ETHIC, FUNCTION, IN, OFF, ON, OUT, OVER, SHEET, STATION, THROUGH, UP

WORKING – BEE, CAPITAL, CLASS, DAY, DOG, DRAWING, PAPERS, PARTY, SUBSTANCE, WEEK

WRITE – DOWN, IN, OFF, OUT, UP

YELLOW – BELLY, CARD, FEVER, JACKET, PAGES, PERIL, RIVER, STREAK

YORKSHIRE – DALES, FOG, PUDDING, TERRIER

YOUNG – BLOOD, FOGEY, LADY, MAN, PRETENDER, TURK

YOUTH – CLUB, CUSTODY, HOSTEL

SECOND WORD

ABOUT – BRING, CAST, COME, FALL, HANG, KICK, KNOCK, MESS, MUCK, PUSH, PUT, RIGHT, SET, TALK, THROW

ABSOLUTE – ABLATIVE, DECREE

ACADEMY – FRENCH, MILITARY, ROYAL

ACCESS – DIRECT, RANDOM, SEQUENTIAL

ACCOUNT – BANK, BUDGET, CAPITAL, CHARGE, CONTROL, CREDIT, CURRENT, DEPOSIT, DRAWING, EXPENSE, JOINT, SAVINGS, SHORT, SUSPENSE, TRUST

ACCOUNTANT – CHARTERED, TURF

ACROSS – COME, CUT, GET, PUT, RUN

TWO-WORD PHRASES

ACT — ENABLING, HOMESTEAD, JURISTIC, LOCUTIONARY, RIOT, SPEECH, STAMP, TEST

ADMIRAL — FLEET, REAR, RED, VICE, WHITE

ADVOCATE — DEVIL'S, JUDGE, LORD

AGAINST — COUNT, GO, SET, STACK, TURN

AGENCY — ADVERTISING, EMPLOYMENT, MERCANTILE, NEWS, PRESS, TRAVEL

AGENT — CROWN, DISCLOSING, DOUBLE, ESTATE, FORWARDING, FREE, HOUSE, LAND, LAW, OXIDIZING, PRESS, REDUCING, SECRET, SHIPPING, WETTING

AGREEMENT — COLLECTIVE, GENTLEMEN'S, NATIONAL, PROCEDURAL, STANDSTILL, TECHNOLOGY

AID — ARTIFICIAL, FIRST, FOREIGN, HEARING, HOME, LEGAL, TEACHING

ALARM — CALL, FALSE, FIRE

ALCOHOL — ABSOLUTE, ALLYL, AMYL, BUTYL, ETHYL, GRAIN, LAURYL, METHYL, RUBBING, WOOD

ALE — GINGER, REAL

ALLEY — BLIND, BOWLING

ALLIANCE — DUAL, HOLY, TRIPLE

ALONG — COME, CUT, GET, GO, MUDDLE, PLAY, PUSH, RUB, RUN, SING, STRING

ANGEL — DESTROYING, HELL'S, RECORDING

ANGLE — CENTRAL, COMPLEMENTARY, CRITICAL, EXTERIOR, FACIAL, HOUR, INTERIOR, OBLIQUE, PLANE, RIGHT, STRAIGHT

ANT — AMAZON, ARMY, BULLDOG, DRIVER, FIRE, LEAFCUTTER, LEGIONARY, PHARAOH, SLAVE, VELVET, WHITE, WOOD

APPLE — ADAM'S, BALSAM, BIG, BITTER, CRAB, CUSTARD, LOVE, MAY, OAK, ROSE, SUGAR, THORN

ARCADE — AMUSEMENT, PENNY

ARCH — ACUTE, FALLEN, GOTHIC, HORSESHOE, KEEL, LANCET, NORMAN, OGEE, POINTED, ROMAN, SKEW, TRIUMPHAL, ZYGOMATIC

AREA — CATCHMENT, DEVELOPMENT, GOAL, GREY, MUSH, NO-GO, PENALTY, SERVICE

ARMS — CANTING, ORDER, SIDE, SMALL

ARMY — CHURCH, FIELD, SALLY, SALVATION, STANDING, TERRITORIAL

AROUND — BAT, GET, GO, HORSE, RUN, SHOP, SLEEP, SLOP, STICK

ART — BLACK, COMMERCIAL, FINE, NOBLE, OP, PERFORMANCE, POP

ARTS — GRAPHIC, LIBERAL, PERFORMING, VISUAL

ASH — BONE, FLY, MOUNTAIN, PEARL, PRICKLY, SODA

ASIDE — BRUSH, LAY, PUT, SET

ASSEMBLY — GENERAL, LEGISLATIVE, NATIONAL, UNLAWFUL

ATTORNEY — CROWN, DISTRICT, PROSECUTING

AWAY — BLOW, BOIL, CARRY, CLEAR, COME, EXPLAIN, FALL, FIRE, GET, GIVE, GO, KEEP, LAUGH, LAY, MAKE, PUT, RIGHT, RUN, SALT, SIGN, SOCK, SQUARE, TAKE, TEAR, TRAIL, TUCK, TURN, WALK, WHILE

BABY — BLUE, JELLY, PLUNKET, RHESUS, TEST-TUBE, WAR

BACK — ANSWER, BITE, BOUNCE, CARRY, CAST, CHOKE, CLAW, DOUBLE, FALL, FIGHT, GET, GO, HANG, HARK, HOLD, KEEP, KNOCK, LADDER, LOOK, PAY, PLOUGH, PULL, PUT, RING, SET, SIT, TAKE, TALK

BAG — AIR, BLUE, BODY, CARRIER, COFFEE, COOL, DIPLOMATIC, DOGGY, DUFFEL, GLADSTONE, GROW, ICE, JELLY, JIFFY, LAVENDER, MIXED, SAG, SLEEPING, SPONGE, TEA, TOTE

BALLOON — BARRAGE, HOT-AIR, PILOT, TRIAL

BAND — BIG, BRAKE, BRASS, CITIZENS', CONDUCTION, ELASTIC, ENERGY, FREQUENCY, RUBBER, STEEL

BANK — BLOOD, CENTRAL, CLEARING, COMMERCIAL, COOPERATIVE, DATA, DOGGER, FOG, JODRELL, LAND, LEFT, MEMORY, MERCHANT, NATIONAL, PIGGY, RESERVE, SAVINGS, SOIL, SPERM

BAR — CAPSTAN, COFFEE, COLOUR, DOUBLE, HEEL, HORIZONTAL, INNER, MILK, OUTER, PINCH, PRIVATE, PUBLIC, SAND, SINGLES, SNACK, TORSION, WINE

BARRIER — CRASH, CRUSH, HEAT, SONIC, SOUND, THERMAL, TRANSONIC

BASE — AIR, DATA, FIRST, LEWIS, PRISONER'S, PYRIMIDINE

BASKET — CHIP, MOSES, POLLEN, WASTEPAPER

BASS — BLACK, DOUBLE, FIGURED, GROUND, LARGEMOUTH, ROCK, SEA, SMALLMOUTH, STONE, STRING, THOROUGH, WALKING

BAT — FRUIT, HORSESHOE, INSECTIVOROUS, STRAIGHT, VAMPIRE

BATH — BLANKET, BLOOD, BUBBLE, HIP, MUD, SALT, SPONGE, STEAM, SUN, SWIMMING, TURKISH

BEACON — BELISHA, LANDING, RADAR, RADIO

BEAN — ADSUKI, ADZUKI, BLACK, BROAD, BUTTER, CALABAR, CASTOR, COCOA, DWARF, FRENCH, GREEN, HORSE, JACK, JUMPING, KIDNEY, LIMA, MUNG, PINTO, RUNNER, SHELL, SNAP, SOYA, STRING, TONKA, WAX

BEAR — ANT, BLACK, BROWN, CINNAMON, GREAT, GRIZZLY, HONEY, KOALA, KODIAK, LITTLE, NATIVE, POLAR, SLOTH, SUN, TEDDY, WATER, WHITE, WOOLLY

BEAT — DEAD, MERSEY, WING

BEAUTY — BATHING, CAMBERWELL, SPRING

BED — AIR, APPLE-PIE, BUNK, FEATHER, OYSTER, PAY, SOFA, TRUCKLE, TRUNDLE, TWIN, WATER

BEE — CARPENTER, CUCKOO, HIVE, LEAFCUTTER, MASON, MINING, QUEEN, SPELLING, WORKING

BEER — BOCK, GINGER, KAFFIR, ROOT, SMALL, SPRUCE

BELL — CANTERBURY, DIVING, LUTINE, PASSING, SACRING, SANCTUS, SHARK, SILVER

BELT — BIBLE, BLACK, CARTRIDGE, CHASTITY, CONVEYOR, COPPER, COTTON, FAN, GREEN, LIFE, LONSDALE, SAFETY, SEAT, SHELTER, STOCKBROKER, STORM, SUSPENDER, SWORD

BENCH — FRONT, KING'S, OPTICAL, TREASURY

BENEFIT — CHILD, DISABLEMENT, FAMILY, FRINGE, HOUSING, INJURY, INVALIDITY, MATERNITY, SICKNESS, SUPPLEMENTARY, UNEMPLOYMENT, WIDOW'S

BILL — ACCOMMODATION, BUFFALO, DEMAND, DOUBLE, FINANCE, FOREIGN, OLD, PRIVATE, PUBLIC, REFORM, TREASURY, TRUE, TWIN

BIRD — ADJUTANT, ANT, BRAIN-FEVER, CROCODILE, DIAMOND, EARLY, ELEPHANT, GALLOWS, GAME, PARSON, WATER

BISCUIT — BOURBON, CAPTAIN'S, DIGESTIVE, DOG, PILOT, SEA, SHIP'S, SODA, TARARUA, TEA, WATER

BLACK — ALL, CARBON, GAS, IVORY, JET, LARGE, PENNY, PLATINUM

BLOCK — BREEZE, BUILDING, CAVITY, CYLINDER,

HEART, ICE, MENTAL, OFFICE, PSYCHOLOGICAL, SADDLE, STARTING, STUMBLING, SUN, WOOD

BLOOD — BAD, BLUE, BULL'S, DRAGON'S, FULL, WHOLE, YOUNG

BOARD — ABOVE, ADMIRALTY, BULLETIN, CATCHMENT, CIRCUIT, CRIBBAGE, DIVING, DRAFT, DRAINING, DRAW-ING, EMERY, FULL, HALF, IDIOT, IRONING, NOTICE, PATCH, RUNNING, SANDWICH, SCHOOL, SKIRTING, SOUNDING, WOBBLE

BOAT — CANAL, FLYING, GRAVY, JOLLY, MOSQUITO, NARROW, ROWING, SAILING, SAUCE, SWAMP, TORPEDO

BOMB — ATOM, BORER, BUZZ, CLUSTER, COBALT, FISSION, FLYING, FUSION, HYDROGEN, LETTER, MILLS, NEUTRON, NUCLEAR, PETROL, SMOKE, STINK, TIME, VOLCANIC

BOND — BAIL, CHEMICAL, COORDINATE, COVALENT, DATIVE, DOUBLE, ELECTROVALENT, ENGLISH, FLEMISH, GRANNY, HERRINGBONE, HYDROGEN, INCOME, IONIC, METALLIC, PAIR, PEPTIDE, SINGLE, TREASURY, TRIPLE

BONE — CANNON, CARTILAGE, COFFIN, CRAZY, FET-TER, FRONTAL, FUNNY, HAUNCH, HEEL, INNOMINATE, MEMBRANE, OCCIPITAL, PARIETAL, SPHENOID, SPLINT, STIRRUP, TEMPORAL, TYMPANIC, ZYGOMATIC

BOOK — BLACK, CLOSED, COMMONPLACE, COOKERY, DOMESDAY, DOOMSDAY, HYMN, OPEN, PHRASE, PRAYER, REFERENCE, STATUTE, TALKING

BOTTLE — BRANDY, FEEDING, HOT-WATER, KLEIN, NANSEN, WATER

BOWL — BEGGING, DUST, FINGER, GOLDFISH, RICE

BOX — APPLE, BALLOT, BLACK, CHRISTMAS, COIN, DEED, DISPATCH, FUSE, FUZZ, GLOVE, JUNCTION, JURY, LETTER, MUSIC, PENALTY, PILLAR, POOR, PRESS, SENTRY, SHOOTING, SIGNAL, TELEPHONE, VOICE, WINDOW, WINE, WITNESS

BOY — ALTAR, BALL, BARROW, BEST, BEVIN, BLUE-EYED, CABIN, ERRAND, OFFICE, OLD, PRINCIPAL, RENT, TAR, TEDDY, WHIPPING

BRAKE — AIR, CENTRIFUGAL, DISC, DRUM, FOOT, HYDRAULIC, SHOOTING

BRETHREN — BOHEMIAN, ELDER, EXCLUSIVE, OPEN, PLYMOUTH, TRINITY

BRIDGE — AIR, AUCTION, BAILEY, BALANCE, BOARD, CABLE-STAYED, CANTILEVER, CLAPPER, CONTRACT, COUNTERPOISE, DUPLICATE, FLYING, FOUR-DEAL, LAND, PIVOT, RAINBOW, RUBBER, SNOW, SUSPENSION, SWING, TRANSPORTER, TRUSS, TURN, WHEATSTONE

BRIGADE — BOYS', FIRE, FUR, INTERNATIONAL

BROTHER — BIG, BLOOD, LAY

BUG — ASSASSIN, CABBAGE, CHINCH, CROTON, DAMSEL, DEBRIS, FLOWER, GROUND, HARLEQUIN, JUNE, KISSING, LACE, LIGHTNING, MAORI, MEALY, PILL, RHODODENDRON, SHIELD, SOW, SQUASH, WATER, WHEEL

BUGGY — BABY, BEACH, SWAMP

BUOY — BELL, BREECHES, CAN, LIFE, NUN, SPAR

BURNER — BACK, BUNSEN, GAS, LIME, WELSBACH

BUSH — BURNING, BUTTERFLY, CALICO, COTTON, CRANBERRY, CREOSOTE, DAISY, EMU, GOOSEBERRY, MINT, NATIVE, NEEDLE, ORCHARD, STRAWBERRY, SUGAR

BUSINESS — BIG, MONKEY, SHOW

BY — COME, DO, GET, GO, PASS, PUT, STAND, STICK

CAKE — ANGEL, BANBURY, BARM, COTTON, DUNDEE, ECCLES, FISH, GENOA, JOHNNY, LARDY, LAYER, MADEIRA, MARBLE, OIL, PONTEFRACT, POUND, ROCK, SALT, SANDWICH, SIMNEL, SPONGE, TIPSY, UPSIDE-DOWN, WEDDING

CALL — BIRD, CLOSE, COLD, CURTAIN, LINE, PHOTO, ROLL, TOLL, TRUNK

CAMERA — AUTOMATIC, BOX, CANDID, CINE, COMPACT, GAMMA, IN, MINIATURE, MOVIE, PINHOLE, REFLEX

CAMP — CONCENTRATION, HEALTH, HIGH, HOLIDAY, LABOUR, LOW, MOTOR, TRANSIT, WORK

CANAL — ALIMENTARY, ANAL, CALEDONIAN, ERIE, GRAND, HAVERSIAN, MITTELLAND, PANAMA, ROOT, SEMICIRCULAR, SPINAL, SUEZ, WELLAND

CAP — BATHING, CLOTH, CROWN, DEATH, DUNCE, DUTCH, FILLER, FLAT, FOOL'S, FUNNEL, JOCKEY, JULIET, LEGAL, LIBERTY, MILK, PERCUSSION, ROOT, SHAGGY, STOCKING, WATCH, WAX

CAPITAL — BLOCK, HUMAN, RISK, SMALL, VENTURE, WORKING

CAPSULE — SEED, SPACE, TIME

CARD — BANK, BANKER'S, CALLING, CHEQUE, CHRISTMAS, CIGARETTE, COURT, CREDIT, DONOR, DRAWING, FLASH, GREEN, ID, LASER, LETTER, PICTURE, PLACE, PLAYING, POSTAL, PUNCHED, SHOW, SMART, UNION, VISITING, YELLOW

CASE — ATTACHÉ, BASKET, COT, DISPATCH, DRESSING, LOWER, SPECIAL, SPORE, STATED, TEST, UPPER, WARDIAN, WORST, WRITING

CELL — BLOOD, CADMIUM, CLARK, COLLAR, CONDEMNED, DANIELL, DEATH, DRY, ELECTROLYTIC, FLAME, FUEL, GERM, GRAVITY, GUARD, LYMPH, MAST, NERVE, PADDED, PARIETAL, PHOTOELECTRIC, PRIMARY, SECONDARY, SELENIUM, SOLAR, SOMATIC, STANDARD, STEM, SWARM, UNIT, VOLTAIC, WET

CENTRE — ACTIVE, ATTENDANCE, CIVIC, COMMUNITY, COST, DAYCARE, DEAD, DETENTION, GARDEN, HEALTH, MUSIC, NERVE, REMAND, SHOPPING, STORM

CHAIN — BICYCLE, BRANCHED, CLOSED, DAISY, FOOD, GOLDEN, GRAND, GUNTER'S, LEARNER'S, MARKOV, MOUNTAIN, OPEN, SAFETY, SIDE, SNIGGING, STRAIGHT, SURVEYOR'S, WATCH

CHAIR — BATH, BOATSWAIN'S, DECK, EASY, ELECTRIC, ROCKING, SEDAN, STRAIGHT, SWIVEL, WINDSOR, WING

CHAMBER — BUBBLE, CLOUD, COMBUSTION, DECOMPRESSION, ECHO, FLOAT, GAS, INSPECTION, IONIZATION, LOWER, MAGMA, PRESENCE, PRIVY, SECOND, SPARK, STAR, UPPER

CHART — BAR, BREAKEVEN, CONTROL, FLOW, ORGANIZATION, PIE, PLANE

CHASE — PAPER, WILD-GOOSE

CHEST — COMMUNITY, HOPE, MEDICINE, SEA, SLOP, WAR, WIND

CHILD — FOSTER, LATCHKEY, LOVE, MOON

CHINA — BONE, COCHIN, COMMUNIST, DRESDEN, NATIONALIST, RED, WORCESTER

CHIP — BLUE, LOG, POTATO, SILICON

CIRCLE — ANTARCTIC, ARCTIC, DIP, DRESS, EQUINOCTIAL, FAMILY, GREAT, HOUR, HUT, MERIDIAN, PARQUET, PITCH, POLAR, TURNING, VERTICAL, VICIOUS

CLASS — CABIN, CRYSTAL, EVENING, FIRST, LOWER,

MIDDLE, SECOND, THIRD, UNIVERSAL, UPPER, WORKING

CLAY – BOULDER, CHINA, FIRE, PORCELAIN

CLEF – ALTO, BASS, C, F, G, SOPRANO, TENOR, TREBLE, VIOLA

CLERK – ARTICLED, BANK, DESK, FILING, PARISH, SHIPPING, TALLY, TOWN

CLIP – BICYCLE, BULLDOG, CARTRIDGE, CROCODILE, WOOL

CLOCK – ALARM, ANALOGUE, ATOMIC, BIOLOGICAL, CAESIUM, CARRIAGE, CUCKOO, DIGITAL, GRAND-FATHER, GRANDMOTHER, LONGCASE, QUARTZ, SETTLER'S, SPEAKING, TIME, TOWNHALL, WATER

CLOTH – AEROPLANE, AIRCRAFT, ALTAR, BARK, COVERT, FACE, GRASS, MONK'S, NUN'S, SPONGE, TEA, WIRE

CLUB – BOOK, CHARTERED, COUNTRY, GLEE, GOLF, INDIAN, JOCKEY, LIONS, LUNCHEON, MONDAY, PROVIDENT, PUDDING, ROTARY, STRIP, SUPPER, TRAMPING, YOUTH

COAL – BITUMINOUS, BROWN, CANNEL, GAS, HARD, SOFT, STEAM, WHITE, WOOD

COCKTAIL – ATOMIC, FRUIT, MOLOTOV

CODE – AREA, BAR, BINARY, CHARACTER, CLARENDON, COLOUR, COUNTRY, DIALLING, GENETIC, GRAY, HIGHWAY, JUSTINIAN, MORSE, NAPOLEONIC, NATIONAL, PENAL, STD, TIME, ZIP

COLLAR – CLERICAL, DOG, ETON, HEAD, MANDARIN, ROMAN, SHAWL, STORM, VANDYKE, WING

COLOUR – ACHROMATIC, CHROMATIC, COMPLEMENTARY, CROSS, LOCAL, OFF, PRIMARY, SECONDARY, TONE

COLUMN – AGONY, CORRESPONDENCE, FIFTH, PERSONAL, SPINAL, STEERING, VERTEBRAL

COMPANY – CLOSE, FINANCE, FIRE, FREE, HOLDING, JOINT-STOCK, LIMITED, PARENT, PRIVATE, PUBLIC, REPERTORY, STOCK

COMPLEX – ELECTRA, INFERIORITY, LAUNCH, OEDIPUS, PERSECUTION, SUPERIORITY

CONE – ICE-CREAM, NOSE, PINE, STORM, WIND

CORD – COMMUNICATION, SASH, SPERMATIC, SPINAL, UMBILICAL

COUNTER – CRYSTAL, GEIGER, PROPORTIONAL, REV, SCINTILLATION

COURSE – ASSAULT, BARGE, GOLF, MAGNETIC, MAIN, REFRESHER, SANDWICH

COURT – CLAY, COUNTY, CROWN, DISTRICT, DOMES-TIC, GRASS, HARD, HIGH, INFERIOR, JUSTICE, JUVE-NILE, KANGAROO, MAGISTRATES', MOOT, OPEN, PO-LICE, PRIZE, PROVOST, SHERIFF, SUPERIOR, SUPREME, TERRITORIAL, TOUT, TRAFFIC, TRIAL, WORLD

COVER – AIR, DUST, EXTRA, FIRST-DAY, GROUND, LOOSE

CREAM – BARRIER, BAVARIAN, CLOTTED, COLD, DEVONSHIRE, DOUBLE, GLACIER, ICE, PASTRY, SINGLE, SOUR, VANISHING, WHIPPING

CROP – CASH, CATCH, COVER, ETON, RIDING, ROOT

CROSS – CALVARY, CELTIC, CHARING, DOUBLE, FIERY, GEORGE, GREEK, IRON, JERUSALEM, LATIN, LORRAINE, MALTESE, NORTHERN, PAPAL, PATRIARCHAL, RED, SOUTHERN, TAU, VICTORIA

CROSSING – LEVEL, PEDESTRIAN, PELICAN, ZEBRA

CROW – CARRION, HOODED, JIM

CUP – AMERICA'S, CLARET, COFFEE, DAVIS, EGG, FA, FRUIT, GRACE, GREASE, LOVING, MOUSTACHE, STIRRUP, WORLD

CURRENCY – DECIMAL, FRACTIONAL, MANAGED, RESERVE

CURRENT – ALTERNATING, CROMWELL, DARK, DIRECT, EDDY, ELECTRIC, FOUCAULT, HUMBOLDT, JAPAN, LABRADOR, PERU, THERMIONIC, TURBIDITY

CURTAIN – AIR, BAMBOO, DROP, IRON, SAFETY

CUT – BASTARD, CREW, CULEBRA, GAILLARD, NAVY, OPEN, POWER, SHORT

DASH – EM, EN, PEBBLE, SWUNG

DAYS – DOG, EMBER, HUNDRED, JURIDICAL, LAY, ROGATION, SALAD

DEATH – BLACK, BRAIN, CIVIL, COT, CRIB, HEAT, LIVING, SUDDEN

DECK – 'TWEEN, BOAT, FLIGHT, HURRICANE, LOWER, MAIN, POOP, PROMENADE, SUN, TAPE

DELIVERY – BREECH, FORWARD, GENERAL, JAIL, RECORDED, RURAL, SPECIAL

DERBY – CROWN, DONKEY, KENTUCKY, ROLLER, SAGE

DESK – CASH, CITY, COPY, ROLL-TOP, WRITING

DEVIL – DUST, MOUNTAIN, PRINTER'S, SNOW, TASMANIAN

DIAGRAM – BAR, BLOCK, INDICATOR, RUSSELL, SCATTER, VENN

DIVE – CRASH, NOSE, POWER, SWALLOW, SWAN

DOCTOR – ANGELIC, BAREFOOT, CAPE, FAMILY, FLYING, SAW, WITCH

DOG – BACKING, BIRD, CARRIAGE, COACH, ESKIMO, EYE, GREAT, GUIDE, GUN, HEADING, HOT, KANGAROO, LEADING, LITTLE, NATIVE, PARIAH, PIG, POLICE, PRAIRIE, RACCOON, SAUSAGE, SEA, SHEPHERD, SLED, SNIFFER, SPOTTED, TOP, TRACKER, WORKING

DOOR – BACK, BARN, CAT, DUTCH, FIRE, FOLDING, FRONT, NEXT, OPEN, OVERHEAD, REVOLVING, STABLE, STAGE, STORM, STREET, SWING, TRAP

DOWN – BACK, BEAR, BEAT, BOG, BOIL, BREAK, BRING, BUCKET, BUCKLE, CALL, CAST, CHANGE, CLAMP, CLIMB, CLOSE, CRACK, CRY, CUT, DIE, DO, DRAG, DRESS, DUST, FALL, GET, GO, HAND, HOLD, HUNT, KEEP, KNOCK, LAY, LET, LIE, LIVE, LOOK, MOW, NAIL, PAY, PEG, PIN, PIPE, PLAY, PULL, PUT, RIDE, ROUND, RUB, RUN, SEND, SET, SETTLE, SHAKE, SHOOT, SHOUT, SIMMER, SIT, SLAP, SPONGE, STAND, STEP, STICK, STOP, STRIKE, TAKE, TALK, TEAR, TONE, TRACK, TURN, UPSIDE, VOTE, WASH, WEAR, WEIGH, WIND, WRITE

DRESS – ACADEMIC, COAT, COURT, EVENING, FANCY, FULL, HIGHLAND, MORNING, PINAFORE, TENT

DRESSING – FRENCH, ORE, RUSSIAN, SALAD, TOP, WELL

DRILL – BOAT, FIRE, HAMMER, KERB, PACK, POWER, TWIST

DRIVE – BEETLE, CHAIN, DISK, FLUID, FOUR-WHEEL, MOTOR, WHIST

DROP – ACID, COUGH, DELAYED, DOLLY, KNEE, LEMON, MAIL

DUCK – BLUE, BOMBAY, COLD, DEAD, HARLEQUIN, LAME, MANDARIN, MUSCOVY, MUSK, PARADISE, RUDDY, SEA, TUFTED, WOOD

DUST – ANGEL, BULL, COSMIC, GOLD

DUTY – DEATH, ESTATE, POINT, STAMP

EDGE – DECKLE, KNIFE, LEADING, TRAILING

EGG – CURATE'S, DARNING, EASTER, NEST, SCOTCH

END – BACK, BEST, BIG, BITTER, BOOK, BOTTOM, BUSINESS, CIGARETTE, COD, DEAD, EAST, FAG, GABLE, LAND'S, LOOSE, ROPE'S, STICKY, TAG, TAIL, TOP, WEST

ENGINE – AERO, BEAM, BYPASS, COMPOUND, DIESEL, DONKEY, EXTERNAL-COMBUSTION, FIRE, GAS, HEAT, INTERNAL-COMBUSTION, ION, JET, LIGHT, OVERHEAD-VALVE, PILOT, PLASMA, RADIAL, REACTION, RECIPROCATING, ROCKET, ROTARY, SIDE-VALVE, STATIONARY, STIRLING, TANK, TRACTION, TURBOJET, V-TYPE, VALVE-IN-HEAD, WANKEL

ENSIGN – BLUE, RED, WHITE

EVENT – FIELD, HAPPY, MEDIA, THREE-DAY, TRACK

EVIDENCE – CIRCUMSTANTIAL, CUMULATIVE, DIRECT, HEARSAY, KING'S, PRIMA-FACIE, QUEEN'S, STATE'S

EXCHANGE – CORN, EMPLOYMENT, FOREIGN, ION, LABOUR, PART, POST, STOCK

EYE – BEADY, BLACK, COMPOUND, ELECTRIC, EVIL, GLAD, MAGIC, MIND'S, PHEASANT'S, PINEAL, POPE'S, PRIVATE, RED, SCREW, WEATHER

FACE – BOLD, EN, LIGHT, LONG, OLD, POKER, STRAIGHT

FACTOR – COMMON, CORN, GROWTH, HOUSE, LOAD, POWER, QUALITY, RH, RHESUS, SAFETY, UNIT

FEATHER – COCK, CONTOUR, FLIGHT, SHAFT, SICKLE, WHITE

FILE – CARD, CROSSCUT, INDIAN, SINGLE

FINGER – INDEX, LADY'S, RING

FINISH – BLANKET, DEAD, MIRROR, PHOTO

FIRE – BRUSH, ELECTRIC, GREEK, LIQUID, QUICK, RAPID, RED, WATCH

FLAT – ADOBE, ALKALI, COTTAGE, DOUBLE, GARDEN, GRANNY, MUD, SALT, STUDIO

FOOD – CONVENIENCE, FAST, HEALTH, JUNK, SKIN, SOUL

FORTH – CALL, GO, HOLD, PUT, SET

FORWARD – BRING, CARRY, CENTRE, COME, INSIDE, PUT

FRACTION – COMMON, COMPLEX, COMPOUND, CONTINUED, DECIMAL, IMPROPER, PACKING, PARTIAL, PROPER, SIMPLE, VULGAR

FRACTURE – COLLES', COMMINUTED, COMPOUND, GREENSTICK, POTT'S, SIMPLE

FRAME – CLIMBING, COLD, GARDEN, HALF, OXFORD, PORTAL, SAMPLING, STILL, STOCKING

FRIDAY – GIRL, GOOD, MAN

FRONT – COLD, EYES, NATIONAL, OCCLUDED, PEOPLE'S, POLAR, POPULAR, RHODESIAN, WARM, WAVE

FROST – BLACK, JACK, SILVER, WHITE

FRUIT – ACCESSORY, COLLECTIVE, FALSE, FORBIDDEN, KEY, KIWI, MULTIPLE, PASSION, SIMPLE, SOFT, STONE, WALL

GALLERY – LADIES', NATIONAL, PRESS, PUBLIC, ROGUES', SHOOTING, STRANGER'S, TATE, WHISPERING, WINNING

GAP – CREDIBILITY, DEFLATIONARY, ENERGY, GENERA-TION, INFLATIONARY, SPARK, TRADE, WATER, WIND

GARDEN – BEAR, BOTANICAL, COVENT, KITCHEN,

KNOT, MARKET, PEBBLE, ROCK, ROOF, TEA, WINTER, ZOOLOGICAL

GAS – AIR, BOTTLED, CALOR, COAL, CS, ELECTROLYTIC, IDEAL, INERT, LAUGHING, MARSH, MUSTARD, NATURAL, NERVE, NOBLE, NORTH-SEA, PERFECT, POISON, PRODUCER, RARE, SEWAGE, TEAR, TOWN, WATER

GATE – GOLDEN, HEAD, IRON, KISSING, LICH, LYCH, MORAVIAN, STARTING, TAIL, TARANAKI, WATER

GIRL – BACHELOR, BAR, BEST, CALL, CAREER, CHORUS, CONTINUITY, COVER, DANCING, FLOWER, GIBSON, LAND, MARCHING, OLD, SWEATER

GLASS – BELL, BURNING, CHEVAL, CROWN, CUPPING, CUT, FAVRILE, FIELD, FLINT, FLOAT, GREEN, GROUND, HAND, LEAD, LIQUID, LOOKING, MAGNIFYING, MILK, MURRHINE, OBJECT, OPTICAL, PIER, PLATE, QUARTZ, REDUCING, RUBY, SAFETY, SILICA, SOLUBLE, STAINED, STORM, TIFFANY, VENETIAN, VOLCANIC, WATER, WIRE

GLASSES – DARK, FIELD, OPERA

GOAT – ANGORA, BILLY, KASHMIR, MOUNTAIN, NANNY

GOLD – FILLED, FOOL'S, FREE, MOSAIC, OLD, ROLLED, WHITE

GREEN – APPLE, BACK, BOTTLE, BOWLING, CHROME, CROWN, GRETNA, JADE, KENDAL, LIME, LINCOLN, NILE, OLIVE, PARIS, PEA, PUTTING, RIFLE, SEA

GROUND – BURIAL, CAMPING, COMMON, HOME, HUNTING, MIDDLE, PROVING, RECREATION, STAMPING, VANTAGE

GUARD – ADVANCE, COLOUR, HOME, IRON, NATIONAL, OLD, PRAETORIAN, PROVOST, RED, SECURITY, SWISS

GUIDE – BROWNIE, GIRL, HONEY, QUEEN'S

GUM – ACAROID, BLUE, BUBBLE, CHEWING, COW, FLOODED, GHOST, KAURI, RED, SNOW, SOUR, SPIRIT, SUGAR, SWEET, WATER, WHITE

HALF – BETTER, CENTRE, FLY, SCRUM

HALL – CARNEGIE, CITY, FESTIVAL, LIBERTY, MESS, MUSIC, TAMMANY, TOWN

HAND – CHARGE, CLUB, COURT, DAB, DEAD, DECK, FARM, FREE, GLAD, HELPING, HOUR, IRON, LONE, MINUTE, OLD, ROUND, SECOND, SHED, SWEEP, UPPER, WHIP

HAT – BRASS, COCKED, COSSACK, HARD, HIGH, OLD, OPERA, PANAMA, PICTURE, PORKPIE, RED, SAILOR, SCARLET, SHOVEL, SILK, SLOUCH, TEN-GALLON, TIN, TOP

HEART – BLEEDING, BULLOCK'S, DEAD, FLOATING, PURPLE, SACRED

HEAT – ATOMIC, BLACK, BLOOD, DEAD, LATENT, PRICKLY, RADIANT, RED, TOTAL, WHITE

HISTORY – ANCIENT, CASE, LIFE, NATURAL, ORAL

HITCH – BLACKWALL, CLOVE, HARNESS, MAGNUS, ROLLING, TIMBER, WEAVER'S

HOLE – AIR, BEAM, BLACK, BOLT, COAL, FUNK, GLORY, KETTLE, LUBBER'S, NINETEENTH, SOUND, SPIDER, SWALLOW, WATER, WATERING

HOLIDAY – BANK, BUSMAN'S, HALF, LEGAL, PUBLIC, ROMAN

HOME – EVENTIDE, HARVEST, MOBILE, NURSING, REMAND, STATELY, VILLA

HORSE – CHARLEY, DARK, IRON, LIBERTY, LIGHT, NIGHT, POLE, POST, QUARTER, RIVER, ROCKING,

SADDLE, SEA, SHIRE, TROJAN, WHEEL, WHITE, WILLING, WOODEN

HOUR — ELEVENTH, HAPPY, LUNCH, RUSH, SIDEREAL, WITCHING, ZERO

HOUSE — ACCEPTING, ADMIRALTY, BOARDING, BROILER, BUSH, CHARNEL, CHATTEL, CLEARING, COACH, COFFEE, COUNTING, COUNTRY, CUSTOM, DISCOUNT, DISORDERLY, DOWER, FASHION, FORCING, FREE, FULL, HALFWAY, ICE, ISSUING, LODGING, MANOR, MANSION, MEETING, OPEN, OPERA, PICTURE, POST, PUBLIC, ROOMING, SAFE, SOFTWARE, SPORTING, STATE, STATION, STOREY, TERRACED, THIRD, TOWN, TRINITY, UPPER, WASH, WENDY, WHITE

HUMOUR — AQUEOUS, GALLOWS, ILL, VITREOUS

HUNT — DRAG, FOX, SCAVENGER, STILL, TREASURE

ICE — BLACK, CAMPHOR, COCONUT, DRIFT, DRY, GLAZE, GROUND, PACK, PANCAKE, SHELF, SLOB, WATER

IN — ALL, BLOCK, BLOW, BOOK, BREAK, BRING, BUILD, BURN, BUY, CALL, CASH, CAVE, CHECK, CHIP, CLOSE, COME, DIG, DO, DRAG, DRAW, FALL, FILL, FIT, GET, GIVE, GO, HAND, HANG, HOLD, HORN, INK, JACK, KEEP, KEY, KICK, LAY, LET, LIE, LISTEN, LIVE, LOG, MOVE, MUCK, PACK, PAY, PHASE, PITCH, PLUG, PULL, PUSH, PUT, RAKE, REIN, RING, ROLL, ROPE, RUB, RUN, SCRAPE, SET, SETTLE, SIGN, SINK, SLEEP, STAND, START, STEP, SUCK, SWEAR, TAKE, THROW, TIE, TUCK, TUNE, TURN, WEIGH, WELL, WHIP, WORK, WRITE, ZERO, ZOOM

INTEREST — COMPOUND, CONTROLLING, HUMAN, LIFE, SIMPLE, VESTED

IRON — ALPHA, ANGLE, BETA, CAST, CHANNEL, CORRUGATED, DELTA, GAMMA, GEM, GRAPPLING, GROZING, INGOT, LILY, MALLEABLE, PIG, PUMP, SHOOTING, SMOOTHING, SOLDERING, STEAM, TOGGLE, WROUGHT

IVY — BOSTON, GRAPE, GROUND, JAPANESE, POISON, WEEPING

JACK — JUMPING, MAN, SCREW, UNION, YELLOW

JACKET — AIR, BED, BOMBER, BUSH, DINNER, DONKEY, DUST, ETON, FLAK, HACKING, LIFE, MESS, MONKEY, NORFOLK, PEA, REEFING, SAFARI, SHELL, SMOKING, SPORTS, STEAM, WATER, YELLOW

JELLY — CALF'S-FOOT, COMB, MINERAL, PETROLEUM, ROYAL

JOE — GI, HOLY, SLOPPY

JUDGMENT — ABSOLUTE, COMPARATIVE, LAST, VALUE

JUMP — BROAD, HIGH, LONG, SKI, TRIPLE, WATER

KEY — ALLEN, CHROMA, CHURCH, CONTROL, DEAD, FUNCTION, IGNITION, MASTER, MINOR, NUT, OFF, ON, PRONG, SHIFT, SKELETON, TUNING

KICK — DROP, FLUTTER, FREE, FROG, GOAL, PENALTY, PLACE, SCISSORS, STAB

KNIFE — BOWIE, CARVING, CASE, CLASP, FLICK, FRUIT, HUNTING, PALLET, SHEATH, TRENCH

KNOT — BLACK, FISHERMAN'S, FLAT, FRENCH, GORDIAN, GRANNY, LOOP, LOVE, OVERHAND, REEF, SQUARE, STEVEDORE'S, SURGEON'S, SWORD, THUMB, TRUELOVE, WALL, WINDSOR

LACE — ALENÇON, BOBBIN, BRUSSELS, CHANTILLY, CLUNY, MECHLIN, PILLOW, POINT, SEA, TORCHON

LADY — BAG, DINNER, FIRST, NAKED, OLD, OUR, PAINTED, WHITE, YOUNG

LAMP — ALDIS, DAVY, FLUORESCENT, GLOW, HURRICANE, INCANDESCENT, NEON, PILOT, SAFETY, SPIRIT, SUN, TUNGSTEN

LANGUAGE — BODY, COMPUTER, FIRST, FORMAL, MACHINE, NATURAL, PROGRAMMING, SECOND, SIGN

LANTERN — CHINESE, DARK, FRIAR'S, JAPANESE, MAGIC, STORM

LEAVE — FRENCH, MASS, MATERNITY, SHORE, SICK

LETTER — AIR, BEGGING, BLACK, CHAIN, COVERING, DEAD, DOMINICAL, FORM, FRENCH, LOVE, OPEN, POISON-PEN, SCARLET

LIBRARY — CIRCULATING, FILM, LENDING, MOBILE, SUBSCRIPTION

LICENCE — DRIVING, OCCASIONAL, POETIC, SPECIAL, TABLE

LIFE — FUTURE, LOVE, MEAN, PRIVATE, REAL, SHELF, STILL

LIGHT — ARC, BACK, BACK-UP, BENGAL, BRAKE, COURTESY, FIRST, GREEN, INNER, KLIEG, LEADING, PILOT, REAR, RED, REVERSING, RUSH, TRAFFIC, WHITE

LIGHTING — INDIRECT, STRIP, STROBE

LIGHTNING — CHAIN, FORKED, HEAT, SHEET

LIGHTS — ANCIENT, BRIGHT, FAIRY, HOUSE, NORTHERN, POLAR, SOUTHERN

LINE — ASSEMBLY, BAR, BOTTOM, BRANCH, CLEW, CONTOUR, DATE, FALL, FIRING, FLIGHT, FRONT, GOAL, HARD, HINDENBURG, HOT, LAND, LEAD, LEDGER, MAGINOT, MAIN, MASON-DIXON, NUMBER, ODER-NEISSE, OFF, ON, PARTY, PICKET, PLIMSOLL, PLUMB, POWER, PRODUCTION, PUNCH, SIEGFRIED, SNOW, STORY, TIMBER, WATER

LINK — CUFF, DRAG, MISSING

LION — MOUNTAIN, NEMEAN, SEA

LIST — BACK, CHECK, CIVIL, CLASS, HIT, HONOURS, MAILING, RESERVED, SHORT, SICK, TRANSFER, WAITING

LOCK — COMBINATION, FERMENTATION, MAN, MORTISE, PERCUSSION, SCALP, SPRING, STOCK, VAPOUR, WHEEL, YALE

LOVE — CALF, COURTLY, CUPBOARD, FREE, PUPPY

MACHINE — ADDING, ANSWERING, BATHING, FRUIT, KIDNEY, SEWING, SLOT, TIME, VENDING, WASHING

MAIL — AIR, CHAIN, ELECTRONIC, FAN, SURFACE

MAIN — RING, SPANISH, WATER

MAN — ADVANCE, ANCHOR, BEST, COMPANY, CON, CONFIDENCE, ENLISTED, FAMILY, FANCY, FRONT, HATCHET, HIT, ICE, INNER, IRON, LADIES', LEADING, MEDICINE, MUFFIN, NEANDERTHAL, PALAEOLITHIC, PARTY, PILTDOWN, RAG-AND-BONE, SANDWICH, STRAIGHT, TWELFTH, YES

MARCH — DEAD, FORCED, HUNGER, LONG, QUICK, SLOW

MARIA — AVE, BLACK, HENRIETTA, SANTA, TIA

MARK — BENCH, BLACK, EXCLAMATION, KITE, PUNCTUATION, QUESTION, QUOTATION

MARKET — BLACK, BUYERS', CAPITAL, CAPTIVE, COMMON, FLEA, KERB, MONEY, OPEN, SELLERS', SPOT, STOCK

MARRIAGE — CIVIL, COMMON-LAW, GROUP, MIXED

MASK — DEATH, GAS, LIFE, LOO, OXYGEN, SHADOW, STOCKING

MASTER — CAREERS, GRAND, HARBOUR, INTERNATIONAL, OLD, PAST, QUESTION

MATCH – FRICTION, LOVE, SAFETY, SHIELD, SLANGING, SLOW, TEST

MATE – FIRST, FOOL'S, RUNNING, SCHOLAR'S, SECOND, SOUL

MATTER – BACK, END, FRONT, GREY, SUBJECT, WHITE

MEDICINE – ALTERNATIVE, COMPLEMENTARY, DUTCH, FOLK, FORENSIC, PATENT

MILE – ADMIRALTY, AIR, GEOGRAPHICAL, NAUTICAL, ROMAN, SEA, STATUTE, SWEDISH

MILL – COFFEE, PEPPER, ROLLING, SMOCK, STAMP, STRIP, WATER

MITE – BULB, CHEESE, FLOUR, FOWL, GALL, HARVEST, ITCH, SPIDER, WIDOW'S

MONEY – BIG, BLOOD, CALL, CAUTION, COB, CONSCIENCE, DANGER, EASY, FOLDING, GATE, HEAD, HOT, HUSH, KEY, MAUNDY, NEAR, PAPER, PIN, PLASTIC, POCKET, PRIZE, READY, SEED, SHIP

MOON – BLUE, FULL, HARVEST, HUNTER'S, MOCK, NEW, OLD

MOTHER – EARTH, FOSTER, NURSING, QUEEN, REVEREND, SOLO

MOTION – FAST, HARMONIC, LINK, PERPETUAL, PROPER, SLOW

NAME – BRAND, CHRISTIAN, DAY, FAMILY, FIRST, GIVEN, HOUSEHOLD, LAST, MAIDEN, MIDDLE, PEN, PLACE, PROPRIETARY, SECOND, TRADE

NECK – BOAT, BRASS, CREW, SCOOP, SWAN, V

NEEDLE – CLEOPATRA'S, DARNING, DIP, ELECTRIC, ICE, MAGNETIC, PINE, SHEPHERD'S

NET – DRIFT, GILL, LANDING, MOSQUITO, POUND, SAFETY, SHARK

NIGHT – FIRST, GOOD, TWELFTH, WALPURGIS, WATCH

NOTE – ADVICE, AUXILIARY, BLUE, COVER, CURRENCY, DEMAND, EIGHTH, GOLD, GRACE, LEADING, PASSING, POSTAL, PROMISSORY, QUARTER, SICK, TREASURY, WHOLE

NUMBER – ACCESSION, ALGEBRAIC, ATOMIC, BACK, BINARY, BOX, CALL, CARDINAL, COMPLEX, COMPOSITE, COMPOUND, CONCRETE, E, GOLDEN, INDEX, MACH, MAGIC, OPPOSITE, ORDINAL, PERFECT, PRIME, REAL, REGISTRATION, SERIAL, SQUARE, TELEPHONE, WHOLE, WRONG

OFFERING – BURNT, PEACE

OFFICE – BOX, CROWN, DIVINE, ELECTRONIC, EMPLOYMENT, FOREIGN, HOLY, HOME, LAND, LEFT-LUGGAGE, PATENT, POST, REGISTER, WAR

OIL – CAMPHORATED, CASTOR, COCONUT, COD-LIVER, CORN, CRUDE, DIESEL, ESSENTIAL, FATTY, GAS, LINSEED, MACASSAR, MINERAL, MUSTARD, NUT, OLIVE, PALM, PEANUT, RAPE, SASSAFRAS, SHALE, SPERM, VEGETABLE, WHALE

OPERA – BALLAD, COMIC, GRAND, HORSE, LIGHT, SOAP, SPACE

ORANGE – AGENT, BITTER, BLOOD, MOCK, NAVEL, OSAGE, SEVILLE

ORDER – AFFILIATION, APPLE-PIE, ATTIC, BANKER'S, COMMUNITY-SERVICE, COMPENSATION, ENCLOSED, FIRING, LOOSE, MAIL, MARKET, MONEY, PECKING, POSSESSION, POSTAL, RECEIVING, SHORT, STANDING, SUPERVISION, TEUTONIC, THIRD, WORD

ORDERS – HOLY, MAJOR, MARCHING, MINOR, SEALED

ORGAN – BARREL, ELECTRIC, ELECTRONIC, END, GREAT, HAMMOND, HAND, HOUSE, MOUTH, PIPE, PORTATIVE, REED, SENSE, STEAM

OVER – BIND, BLOW, BOIL, BOWL, BRING, CARRY, CHEW, DO, FALL, GET, GIVE, GLOSS, GO, HAND, HOLD, KEEL, LAY, LOOK, MAIDEN, MAKE, PAPER, PASS, PUT, ROLL, RUN, SEE, SKATE, SLIDE, SMOOTH, SPILL, STAND, TAKE, THINK, THROW, TICK, TIDE, TURN, WARM, WORK

OYSTER – BUSH, PEARL, PRAIRIE, SEED, VEGETABLE

PACK – BLISTER, BUBBLE, COLD, FACE, FILM, ICE, POWER, WET

PAD – CRASH, HARD, LAUNCHING, LILY, SCRATCH, SHOULDER

PAINT – GLOSS, OIL, POSTER, WAR

PALACE – BUCKINGHAM, CRYSTAL, GIN, PICTURE

PAPER – ART, BALLOT, BLOTTING, BOND, BROMIDE, BROWN, BUILDING, CARBON, CARTRIDGE, CIGARETTE, COMMERCIAL, CREPE, FILTER, FLOCK, GRAPH, GREEN, INDIA, LAVATORY, LINEN, MANILA, MERCANTILE, MUSIC, ORDER, RICE, TISSUE, TOILET, TRACING, WAX, WRITING

PARK – AMUSEMENT, CAR, COUNTRY, FOREST, GAME, HYDE, NATIONAL, SAFARI, SCIENCE, THEME

PARTY – BOTTLE, COMMUNIST, CONSERVATIVE, FIRING, GARDEN, HEN, HOUSE, LABOUR, LIBERAL, NATIONAL, NATIONALIST, PEOPLE'S, REPUBLICAN, SEARCH, STAG, TEA, THIRD, WORKING

PASSAGE – BACK, BRIDGE, DRAKE, MIDDLE, MONA, NORTHEAST, NORTHWEST, ROUGH, WINDWARD

PATH – BRIDLE, FLARE, FLIGHT, GLIDE, PRIMROSE, TOWING

PAY – BACK, EQUAL, SEVERANCE, SICK, STRIKE, TAKE-HOME

PEA – BLACK-EYED, DESERT, PIGEON, SPLIT, SUGAR, SWEET

PEAR – ALLIGATOR, ANCHOVY, CONFERENCE, PRICKLY, WILLIAMS

PEN – CARTRIDGE, CATCHING, DATA, FELT-TIP, FOUNTAIN, QUILL, SEA

PENSION – EN, OCCUPATIONAL, RETIREMENT

PIANO – COTTAGE, GRAND, PLAYER, PREPARED, SQUARE, STREET, UPRIGHT

PIE – COTTAGE, CUSTARD, HUMBLE, MINCE, MUD, PORK, SHEPHERD'S

PIN – BOBBY, COTTER, DRAWING, END, FIRING, GUDGEON, PANEL, ROLLING, SAFETY, SCATTER, SHEAR, STICK, SWIVEL, TAPER, WREST, WRIST

PIPE – CORNCOB, ESCAPE, FLUE, INDIAN, JET, PEACE, PITCH, RAINWATER, REED, SOIL, WASTE

PITCH – ABSOLUTE, CONCERT, FEVER, PERFECT, WOOD

PLACE – DECIMAL, HIGH, HOLY, RESTING, WATERING

PLASTER – COURT, MUSTARD, STICKING

PLATE – ANGLE, ARMOUR, BATTEN, BUTT, ECHO, FASHION, FUTTOCK, GLACIS, GOLD, GROUND, HOME, LICENSE, NICKEL, QUARTER, REGISTRATION, SCREW, SILVER, SOUP, SURFACE, SWASH, TIN, TRADE, WALL, WOBBLE

PLAY – CHILD'S, DOUBLE, FAIR, FOUL, MATCH, MIRA-CLE, MORALITY, MYSTERY, PASSION, SHADOW, STROKE

PLEAT – BOX, FRENCH, INVERTED, KICK, KNIFE

POCKET – AIR, HIP, PATCH, SLASH, SLIT

TWO-WORD PHRASES

POINT – BOILING, BREAKING, BROWNIE, CHANGE, CLOVIS, COVER, CRITICAL, CURIE, DEAD, DECIMAL, DEW, DIAMOND, DRY, END, EQUINOCTIAL, FESSE, FIXED, FLASH, FOCAL, FREEZING, GALLINAS, GAME, GOLD, HIGH, ICE, LIMIT, MATCH, MELTING, OBJECTIVE, PETIT, POWER, PRESSURE, SAMPLE, SATURATION, SET, SPECIE, STEAM, STRONG, SUSPENSION, TRANSITION, TRIG, TRIPLE, TURNING, VANISHING, VANTAGE, WEST, YIELD

POLE – BARBER'S, CELESTIAL, MAGNETIC, NORTH, SOUTH, TOTEM

POLL – ADVANCE, DEED, GALLUP, OPINION, RED, STRAW

POST – COMMAND, FINGER, FIRST, GOAL, GRADED, GRADIENT, HITCHING, LAST, LISTENING, NEWEL, OBSERVATION, REGISTERED, STAGING, TOOL, TRADING, WINNING

POT – CHAMBER, COAL, LOBSTER, MELTING, PEPPER, WATERING

POTATO – HOT, IRISH, SEED, SWEET, WHITE

POWDER – BAKING, BLACK, BLEACHING, CHILLI, CURRY, CUSTARD, FACE, GIANT, TALCUM, TOOTH, WASHING

PRESS – DRILL, FILTER, FLY, FOLDING, GUTTER, HYDRAULIC, PRINTING, PRIVATE, RACKET, STOP

PRESSURE – ATMOSPHERIC, BAROMETRIC, BLOOD, CRITICAL, FLUID, OSMOTIC, PARTIAL, VAPOUR

PRICE – ASKING, BID, BRIDE, INTERVENTION, LIST, MARKET, OFFER, RESERVE, STARTING, UNIT

PROFESSOR – ASSISTANT, ASSOCIATE, FULL, REGIUS, VISITING

PUDDING – BLACK, BLOOD, CABINET, CHRISTMAS, COLLEGE, EVE'S, HASTY, MILK, PEASE, PLUM, SUET, SUMMER, WHITE, YORKSHIRE

PUMP – AIR, BICYCLE, CENTRIFUGAL, ELECTROMAG-NETIC, FILTER, FORCE, HEAT, LIFT, PARISH, PETROL, ROTARY, STIRRUP, STOMACH, SUCTION, VACUUM

PUNCH – BELL, CARD, CENTRE, KEY, MILK, PLANTER'S, RABBIT, SUFFOLK, SUNDAY

PURSE – LONG, MERMAID'S, PRIVY, SEA

PUZZLE – CHINESE, CROSSWORD, JIGSAW, MONKEY

QUARTER – EMPTY, FIRST, LAST, LATIN

QUESTION – DIRECT, INDIRECT, LEADING, RHETORICAL

RABBIT – ANGORA, BUCK, JACK, ROCK, WELSH

RACE – ARMS, BOAT, BUMPING, CLAIMING, DRAG, EGG-AND-SPOON, MASTER, OBSTACLE, RAT, RELAY, SACK, THREE-LEGGED

RACK – CLOUD, ROOF, TOAST

RATE – BANK, BASE, BASIC, BIRTH, BIT, DEATH, EXCHANGE, LAPSE, MORTALITY, MORTGAGE, PIECE, POOR, PRIME, TAX

RECORDER – FLIGHT, INCREMENTAL, TAPE, WIRE

RED – BLOOD, BRICK, CHINESE, CHROME, CONGO, INDIAN, TURKEY, VENETIAN

RELATIONS – COMMUNITY, INDUSTRIAL, LABOUR, PUBLIC, RACE

RELIEF – HIGH, LOW, OUTDOOR, PHOTO

RENT – COST, ECONOMIC, FAIR, GROUND, MARKET, PEPPERCORN

RESERVE – CENTRAL, GOLD, INDIAN, NATURE, SCENIC

REVOLUTION – AMERICAN, BLOODLESS, CHINESE, CULTURAL, FEBRUARY, FRENCH, GLORIOUS, GREEN, INDUSTRIAL, OCTOBER, PALACE, RUSSIAN

RING – ANCHOR, ANNUAL, BENZENE, ENGAGEMENT, ETERNITY, EXTENSION, FAIRY, GAS, GROWTH, GUARD, KEEPER, NOSE, PISTON, PRICE, PRIZE, RETAINING, SEAL, SIGNET, SLIP, SNAP, TEETHING, TREE, VORTEX, WEDDING

ROAD – ACCESS, CLAY, CONCESSION, DIRT, ESCAPE, POST, RING, SERVICE, SLIP, TRUNK

ROD – AARON'S, BLACK, BLUE, CON, CONNECTING, CONTROL, DIVINING, DOWSING, DRAIN, FISHING, FLY, HOT, PISTON, STAIR, TIE, TRACK, WELDING

ROLL – BARREL, BRIDGE, COURT, DANDY, EGG, FORWARD, MUSIC, MUSTER, PIANO, PIPE, SAUSAGE, SNAP, SPRING, SWISS, VICTORY, WESTERN

ROOM – BACK, COMBINATION, COMMON, COMPOSING, CONSULTING, DAY, DINING, DRAWING, DRESSING, ENGINE, GUN, LIVING, MEN'S, OPERATIONS, ORDERLY, POWDER, PUMP, RECEPTION, RECREATION, REST, ROBING, RUMPUS, SITTING, SMOKING, STILL, TIRING, UTILITY, WAITING, WITHDRAWING

ROOT – BUTTRESS, CLUB, CUBE, CULVER'S, MALLEE, PLEURISY, PROP, SQUARE

ROT – BLACK, BROWN, DRY, FOOT, SOFT, WET

ROUND – BRING, CHANGE, COME, MILK, RALLY, SCRUB, TALK

ROW – CORN, DEATH, NOTE, SKID, TONE

ROYAL – ANNAPOLIS, BATTLE, PAIR, PORT, PRINCE, PRINCESS, RHYME

RUBBER – COLD, CREPE, HARD, INDIA, PARÁ, SMOKED, SORBO, SYNTHETIC, WILD

RULE – CHAIN, FOOT, GLOBAL, GOLDEN, GROUND, HOME, PARALLELOGRAM, PHASE, PLUMB, SETTING, SLIDE

RUN – BOMBING, BULL, DRY, DUMMY, GROUND, HEN, HOME, MILK, MOLE, SKI, TRIAL

SALAD – CORN, FRUIT, RUSSIAN, WALDORF

SALE – BOOT, BRING-AND-BUY, CAR-BOOT, JUMBLE, RUMMAGE, WHITE

SALTS – BATH, EPSOM, HEALTH, LIVER, SMELLING

SAUCE – APPLE, BÉCHAMEL, BREAD, CHILLI, CREAM, HARD, HOLLANDAISE, MELBA, MINT, MOUSSELINE, SOY, TARTAR, WHITE, WORCESTER

SAW – BACK, BAND, BUZZ, CHAIN, CIRCULAR, COMPASS, COPING, CROSSCUT, CROWN, FLOORING, FRET, GANG, PANEL, SCROLL, STONE, TENON

SCHOOL – APPROVED, BOARD, BOARDING, CHOIR, COMPREHENSIVE, CORRESPONDENCE, DAME, DAY, DIRECT-GRANT, ELEMENTARY, FINISHING, FIRST, GRAM-MAR, HIGH, INDEPENDENT, INFANT, JUNIOR, LOWER, MIDDLE, NIGHT, NURSERY, PREP, PREPARATORY, PRIMARY, PRIVATE, PUBLIC, RESIDENTIAL, SECONDARY, SPECIAL, STATE, SUMMER, SUNDAY, UPPER

SCIENCE – BEHAVIOURAL, CHRISTIAN, COGNITIVE, DOMESTIC, EARTH, HARD, INFORMATION, LIFE, NATURAL, PHYSICAL, POLICY, POLITICAL, RURAL, SOCIAL, VETERINARY

SCOUT – AIR, BOY, CUB, GIRL, KING'S, QUEEN'S, SEA, TALENT, VENTURE

SCREEN – BIG, FIRE, ORGAN, ROOD, SILVER, SMALL, SMOKE

SCREW – ARCHIMEDES', CAP, COACH, GRUB, ICE, INTERRUPTED, LAG, LEAD, LEVELLING, LUG, MACHINE, MICROMETER, PHILLIPS

SEASON – CLOSE, HIGH, OFF, SILLY

SEAT – BACK, BOX, BUCKET, COUNTRY, COUNTY, DEATH, EJECTION, HOT, JUMP, LOVE, MERCY, RUMBLE, SAFE, SLIDING, WINDOW

SECRETARY – COMPANY, HOME, PARLIAMENTARY, PRIVATE, SOCIAL

SERVICE – ACTIVE, CIVIL, COMMUNITY, DINNER, DIPLOMATIC, DIVINE, FOREIGN, LIP, NATIONAL, PUBLIC, ROOM, SECRET, SENIOR, SILVER, TEA

SET – CLOSED, COMPANION, CRYSTAL, DATA, DEAD, FILM, FLASH, JET, LOVE, NAIL, OPEN, ORDERED, PERMANENT, POWER, SAW, SMART, SOLUTION, TOILET, TRUTH

SHAFT – AIR, BUTT, DRIVE, ESCAPE, PROPELLER

SHEET – BALANCE, CHARGE, CRIME, DOPE, FLOW, FLY, ICE, SCRATCH, SWINDLE, TEAR, THUNDER, TIME, WINDING, WORK

SHIFT – BACK, BLUE, DAY, EINSTEIN, FUNCTION, NIGHT, RED, SOUND, SPLIT, SWING

SHIRT – BOILED, BROWN, DRESS, HAIR, SPORTS, STUFFED, SWEAT, TEE

SHOE – BLOCKED, BRAKE, COURT, GYM, HOT, LAUNCHING, PILE, TENNIS, TRACK

SHOP – BETTING, BODY, BUCKET, CLOSED, COFFEE, DUTY-FREE, FISH-AND-CHIP, JUNK, MACHINE, OPEN, PRINT, SEX, SWAP, SWEET, TALKING, TUCK, UNION

SHOT – APPROACH, BIG, BOOSTER, DIRECT-MAIL, DROP, FOUL, JUMP, LONG, PARTHIAN, PASSING, POT

SHOW – CHAT, DUMB, FLOOR, ICE, LIGHT, MINSTREL, RAREE, ROAD, TALK

SICKNESS – ALTITUDE, BUSH, DECOMPRESSION, FALLING, MILK, MORNING, MOTION, MOUNTAIN, RADIATION, SERUM, SLEEPING, SWEATING

SIDE – DISTAFF, FLIP, PROMPT, SPEAR, SUNNY

SLEEVE – BALLOON, BATWING, BISHOP, DOLMAN

SOAP – CASTILE, GREEN, JOE, METALLIC, SADDLE, SOFT, SUGAR, TOILET

SODA – CAUSTIC, CREAM, ICE-CREAM, WASHING

SOLDIER – FOOT, GALLANT, OLD, RETURNED, TIN, UNKNOWN, WAGON, WATER

SONG – FOLK, PART, PATTER, PRICK, SWAN, THEME, TORCH

SPEECH – CURTAIN, DIRECT, FREE, INDIRECT, KING'S, QUEEN'S, REPORTED

SPIRIT – HOLY, PROOF, SURGICAL, TEAM, WHITE, WOOD

SPOT – BEAUTY, BLACK, BLIND, HIGH, HOT, LEAF, SOFT, TROUBLE

SQUAD – FIRING, FLYING, FRAUD, SNATCH, VICE

SQUARE – ALL, BEVEL, LATIN, MAGIC, MITRE, SET, TIMES, WORD

STAMP – DATE, POSTAGE, RUBBER, TRADING

STAND – HALL, HAT, MUSIC, ONE-NIGHT, UMBRELLA

STANDARD – DOUBLE, GOLD, LAMP, ROYAL, SILVER

STAR – BINARY, BLAZING, DARK, DOG, DOUBLE, DWARF, EVENING, EXPLODING, FALLING, FEATHER, FILM, FIXED, FLARE, GIANT, MORNING, MULTIPLE, NEUTRON, NORTH, POLE, PULSATING, RADIO, SHOOTING

START – BUMP, FLYING, HEAD

STEAK – MINUTE, T-BONE, TARTAR

STICK – BIG, CANCER, COCKTAIL, CONTROL, FRENCH, JOSS, POGO, SHOOTING, SKI, SWAGGER, SWIZZLE, WALKING, WHITE

STITCH – BLANKET, BUTTONHOLE, CABLE, CHAIN, GARTER, LOCK, MOSS, RUNNING, SATIN, SLIP, STOCKING, TENT

STOCK – CAPITAL, COMMON, DEAD, JOINT, LAUGHING, PREFERRED, ROLLING, VIRGINIA

STONE – BATH, BLARNEY, CINNAMON, COPING, FOUNDATION, IMPOSING, KIDNEY, MOCHA, OAMARU, PAVING, PHILOSOPHER'S, PRECIOUS, ROSETTA, STEPPING

STOOL – CUCKING, CUTTY, DUCKING, MILKING, PIANO

STRAW – CHEESE, LAST, SHORT

STRIKE – BIRD, GENERAL, HUNGER, OFFICIAL, SIT-DOWN, SYMPATHY, TOKEN, WILDCAT

STUDY – BROWN, CASE, FEASIBILITY, FIELD, MOTION, NATURE, PILOT, TIME

STUFF – HOT, KIDS', ROUGH, SMALL, SOB

SUGAR – BARLEY, BEET, BROWN, CANE, CASTER, CONFECTIONERS', FRUIT, GRANULATED, GRAPE, ICING, INVERT, LOAF, MAPLE, MILK, PALM, SPUN, WOOD

SUIT – BATHING, BIRTHDAY, BOILER, DIVING, DRESS, JUMP, LONG, LOUNGE, MAJOR, MAO, MINOR, MONKEY, PATERNITY, PRESSURE, SAFARI, SAILOR, SLACK, TROUSER, WET, ZOOT

TABLE – BIRD, COFFEE, DRESSING, GATE-LEG, GLACIER, HIGH, LEAGUE, LIFE, MULTIPLICATION, OCCASIONAL, OPERATING, PEMBROKE, PERIODIC, POOL, REFECTORY, ROUND, SAND, TIDE, WATER, WOOL, WRITING

TALK – BABY, DOUBLE, PEP, PILLOW, SALES, SMALL

TAPE – CHROME, FRICTION, GAFFER, GRIP, IDIOT, INSULATING, MAGNETIC, MASKING, PAPER, PERFORATED, PUNCHED, RED, SCOTCH, TICKER, VIDEO

TAR – COAL, JACK, MINERAL, PINE, WOOD

TENNIS – COURT, DECK, LAWN, REAL, ROYAL, TABLE

TERM – HALF, HILARY, INKHORN, LAW, LENT, MICHAELMAS, TRINITY

THROUGH – BREAK, CARRY, COME, FOLLOW, MUDDLE, PULL, PUSH, PUT, ROMP, RUN, SCRAPE, SEE, WALK, WORK

TICKET – MEAL, ONE-WAY, PARKING, PAWN, PLATFORM, RETURN, ROUND-TRIP, SEASON, SINGLE

TIDE – HIGH, LOW, NEAP, RED, SPRING

TIE – BLACK, BOW, CUP, ENGLISHMAN'S, STRING, WHITE, WINDSOR

TIME – BIG, BORROWED, CLOSING, COMMON, COMPOUND, CORE, DAYLIGHT-SAVING, DOUBLE, DOWN, DRINKING-UP, EXTRA, FATHER, FOUR-FOUR, FULL, HIGH, IDLE, INJURY, LIGHTING-UP, LOCAL, MEAN, OPENING, PRIME, QUADRUPLE, QUESTION, QUICK, RESPONSE, SHORT, SIX-EIGHT, SLOW, STANDARD, SUMMER, THREE-FOUR, TRIPLE, TWO-FOUR, UNIVERSAL

TO – BRING, COME, FALL, GO, HEAVE, KEEP, RISE, RUN, SET, SPEAK, STAND, STICK, TAKE, TUMBLE, TURN

TOGETHER – GO, HANG, HOLD, LIVE, PULL, SCRAPE, SCRATCH, STICK, THROW

TOM – LONG, PEEPING, UNCLE

TOOTH – BABY, EGG, MILK, SWEET, WISDOM

TOP – BIG, DOUBLE, FIGHTING, HUMMING, PEG, ROUND, SCREW, SOFT, SPINNING, TANK

ABBREVIATIONS

TOWN – BOOM, CAPE, COUNTY, GEORGE, GHOST, MARKET, NEW, POST, TWIN

TRADE – CARRIAGE, FREE, RAG, SLAVE

TRAIN – BOAT, DOG, GRAVY, WAGON, WAVE

TRAP – BOOBY, LIVE, POVERTY, RADAR, SAND, SPEED, STEAM, STENCH, STINK, TANK

TRIANGLE – BERMUDA, CIRCULAR, ETERNAL, PASCAL'S, RIGHT, RIGHT-ANGLED, SPHERICAL

TRICK – CON, CONFIDENCE, DIRTY, HAT, THREE-CARD

TRIP – DAY, EGO, FIELD, ROUND

TROT – JOG, RISING, SITTING, TURKEY

TUBE – CAPILLARY, CATHODE-RAY, DRIFT, ELECTRON, EUSTACHIAN, FALLOPIAN, GEISSLER, INNER, NIXIE, PICTURE, PITOT, POLLEN, SHOCK, SIEVE, SPEAKING, STATIC, TELEVISION, TEST, VACUUM

TURN – ABOUT, GOOD, KICK, LODGING, PARALLEL, STEM, THREE-POINT

UNDER – DOWN, GO, KEEP, KNUCKLE, SIT

WALL – ANTONINE, CAVITY, CELL, CHINESE, CLIMBING, CURTAIN, FIRE, HADRIAN'S, HANGING, PARTY, RETAINING, SEA, WAILING, WESTERN

WATCH – BLACK, MIDDLE, MORNING, NIGHT

WAVE – BRAIN, ELECTROMAGNETIC, FINGER, GROUND, HEAT, LONG, LONGITUDINAL, MEDIUM, NEW, PERMANENT, RADIO, SEISMIC, SHOCK, SHORT, SKY, SOUND, STANDING, STATIONARY, TIDAL

WAX – CHINESE, COBBLER'S, EARTH, JAPAN, MINERAL, MONTAN, PARAFFIN, SEALING, VEGETABLE

WAY – APPIAN, EACH, FLAMINIAN, FLY, FOSSE, MILKY, PENNINE, PERMANENT, UNDER

WHEEL – BALANCE, BIG, BUFFING, CATHERINE, CROWN, DISC, DRIVING, EMERY, ESCAPE, FERRIS, GRINDING, PADDLE, POTTER'S, PRAYER, SPINNING, STEERING, STITCH, TAIL, WATER, WIRE

WHISKEY – IRISH, CORN, MALT

WHISTLE – PENNY, STEAM, TIN, WOLF

WINDOW – BAY, BOW, COMPASS, GABLE, JESSE, LANCET, LAUNCH, PICTURE, RADIO, ROSE, SASH, STORM, WEATHER, WHEEL

WIRE – BARBED, CHICKEN, FENCING, HIGH, LIVE, RAZOR

WITH – BEAR, BREAK, CLOSE, DEAL, GO, LIVE, PLAY, SETTLE, SLEEP, STICK

WOMAN – FANCY, LITTLE, OLD, PAINTED, SCARLET, WIDOW

WORK – FIELD, NUMBER, OUTSIDE, SOCIAL

YARD – BACK, MAIN, SCOTLAND

YEAR – ASTRONOMICAL, CALENDAR, CIVIL, EQUINOCTIAL, FINANCIAL, FISCAL, GREAT, HOLY, LEAP, LIGHT, LUNAR, NEW, SABBATICAL, SCHOOL, SIDEREAL, SOLAR, TROPICAL

ZONE – ECONOMIC, ENTERPRISE, FREE, FRIGID, HOT, NUCLEAR-FREE, SKIP, SMOKELESS, TEMPERATE, TIME, TORRID, TWILIGHT

ABBREVIATIONS

AA (Alcoholics Anonymous; Automobile Association)

AAA (Amateur Athletic Association)

AB (able seaman)

ABA (Amateur Boxing Association)

ABP (archbishop)

ABTA (Association of British Travel Agents)

AC (alternating current; account)

ACA (Associate of the Institute of Chartered Accountants)

ACAS (Advisory Conciliation and Arbitration Service)

ACIS (Associate of the Chartered Institute of Secretaries)

AD (anno domini)

ADC (aide-de-camp;

amateur dramatic club)

ADJ (adjective)

ADM (Admiral)

ADV (adverb)

AD VAL (ad valorem)

AFA (Amateur Football Association)

AFC (Air Force Cross)

AFM (Air Force Medal)

AGM (annual general meeting)

AI (artificial insemination; artificial intelligence)

AIB (Associate of the Institute of Bankers)

AIDS (Acquired Immune Deficiency Syndrome)

ALA (Alabama)

AM (ante meridiem)

AMU (atomic mass unit)

ANON (anonymous)

AOB (any other business)

AOC (Air Officer Commanding)

APEX (Association of Professional, Executive, Clerical, and Computer Staff)

APOCR (Apocrypha)

APPROX (approximate)

APT (Advanced Passenger Train)

ARA (Associate of the Royal Academy)

ARAM (Associate of the Royal Academy of Music)

ARCM (Associate of the Royal College of Music)

ARCS (Associate of the Royal College of Science)

ARIBA (Associate of

the Royal Institute of British Architects)

ARIZ (Arizona)

ARK (Arkansas)

ASA (Advertising Standards Authority)

ASAP (as soon as possible)

ASH (Action on Smoking and Health)

ASLEF (Associated Society of Loco-motive Engineers and Firemen)

AT (atomic)

ATC (air traffic control; Air Training Corps)

ATS (Auxiliary Territorial Service)

ATTN (for the attention of)

ATTRIB (attributive)

AT WT (atomic weight)

AU (Ångstrom unit; astronomical unit)

AUEW (Amalgamated Union of Engineering Workers)

AUG (August)

AV (ad valorem; Authorized Version)

AVDP (avoirdupois)

AVE (avenue)

AWOL (absent without leave)

BA (Bachelor of Arts; British Academy; British Airways; British Association)

BAA (British Airports Authority)

BAFTA (British Academy of Film and Television Arts)

B ARCH (Bachelor of Architecture)

BART (baronet)

BBC (British Broadcasting Corporation)

BC (before Christ)

BCH (Bachelor of Surgery)

BCL (Bachelor of Civil Law)

BCOM (Bachelor of Commerce)

BD (Bachelor of Divinity)

BDA (British Dental Association)

BDS (Bachelor of Dental Surgery)

BE (bill of exchange)

B ED (Bachelor of Education)

B ENG (Bachelor of Engineering)

BHP (brake horsepower)

BIM (British Institute of Management)

B LITT (Bachelor of Letters)

BMA (British Medical Association)

BMC (British Medical Council)

BMJ (British Medical Journal)

BMUS (Bachelor of Music)

BN (billion)

BOC (British Oxygen Company)

BP (bishop)

BPAS (British

Pregnancy Advisory Service)

BPHARM (Bachelor of Pharmacy)

BPHIL (Bachelor of Philosophy)

BR (British Rail)

BRCS (British Red Cross Society)

BROS (brothers)

BSC (Bachelor of Science)

BSI (British Standards Institution)

BST (British Standard Time; British Summer Time)

BT (Baronet)

BTA (British Tourist Authority)

BVA (British Veterinary Association)

C (centigrade; circa)

CA (chartered accountant)

CAA (Civil Aviation Authority)

CAD (computer-aided design)

CADCAM (computer-aided design and manufacture)

CAL (California; calorie)

CAM (computer-aided manufacture)

CAMRA (Campaign for Real Ale)

C AND G (City and Guilds)

C AND W (country and western)

CANT (canticles)

CANTAB (of Cambridge – used with academic awards)

CAP (capital)

CAPT (captain)

CARD (Cardinal)

CB (Citizens' Band; Companion of the Bath)

CBE (Commander of the British Empire)

CBI (Confederation of British Industry)

CC (County Council; Cricket Club; cubic centimetre)

CDR (Commander)

CDRE (Commodore)

CE (Church of England; civil engineer)

CEGB (Central Electricity Generating Board)

C ENG (Chartered Engineer)

CENTO (Central Treaty Organization)

CERT (certificate; certified; certify)

CET (Central European Time)

CF (compare)

CFE (College of Further Education)

CFI (cost, freight, and insurance)

CGM (Conspicuous Gallantry Medal)

CH (chapter; church; Companion of Honour)

CHAS (Charles)

CI (curie; Order of the Crown of India)

CIA (Central Intelligence Agency)

CID (Criminal Investigation Department)

CIE (Companion of the Indian Empire)

CIF (cost, insurance, and freight)

CII (Chartered Insurance Institute)

C IN C (Commander in Chief)

CIS (Chartered Institute of Secretaries)

CL (centilitre)

CLLR (councillor)

CM (centimetre)

CMG (Companion of St Michael and St George)

CNAA (Council for National Academic Awards)

CND (Campaign for Nuclear Disarmament)

CO (commanding officer; company; county)

COD (cash on delivery)

C OF E (Church of England)

C OF S (Church of Scotland)

COHSE

(Confederation of Health Service Employees)

COL (colonel; Colorado; Colossians)

CONN (Connecticut)

CONT (continued)

COR (Corinthians)

COS (cosine)

CR (credit)

CRO (cathode ray oscilloscope; Criminal Records Office)

CSE (Certificate of Secondary Education)

CSI (Companion of the Star of India)

CSM (Company Sergeant Major)

CU (cubic)

CV (curriculum vitae)

CVO (Commander of the Victorian Order)

CWT (hundredweight)

D (daughter; died; penny)

DA (District Attorney)

DAK (Dakota)

DAN (Daniel)

DBE (Dame Commander of the British Empire)

DC (Detective Constable; direct current; from the beginning)

DCB (Dame Commander of the Bath)

DCL (Doctor of Civil Law)

DCM (Distinguished Conduct Medal)

DCMG (Dame Commander of St Michael and St George)

DCVO (Dame Commander of the Victorian Order)

DD (direct debit; Doctor of Divinity)

DDS (Doctor of Dental Surgery)

DEL (Delaware)

DEPT (department)

DES (Department of Education and Science)

DEUT (Deuteronomy)

DF (Defender of the Faith)

DFC (Distinguished Flying Cross)

DFM (Distinguished Flying Medal)

DG (by the grace of God)

DHSS (Department of Health and Social Security)

DI (Detective Inspector)

DIAL (dialect)

DIP (Diploma)

DIP ED (Diploma in Education)

DIY (do-it-yourself)

D LITT (Doctor of Literature)

DM (Doctor of Medicine)

D MUS (Doctor of Music)

DNB (Dictionary of National Biography)

DO (ditto)

DOA (dead on arrival)

DOB (date of birth)

DOE (Department of the Environment)

DOM (to God, the best and greatest)

DOZ (dozen)

DPHIL (Doctor of Philosophy)

DPP (Director of Public Prosecutions)

DR (debtor; doctor; drive)

DSC (Distinguished Service Cross; Doctor of Science)

DSM (Distinguished Service Medal)

DSO (Distinguished Service Order)

DT (delirium tremens)

DV (God willing)

DVLC (Driver and Vehicle Licensing Centre)

E (East; Easterly; Eastern)

EA (each)

EC (East Central – London postal district)

ECCLES (Ecclesiastes)

ECCLUS (Ecclesiasticus)

ECG (electrocardiogram)

ECS (European Communication Satellite)

EE (Early English)

EEC (European Economic Community)

EEG (electroencephalogram)

EFTA (European Free Trade Association)

EG (for example)

EMA (European Monetary Agreement)

EMF (electromotive force)

ENC (enclosed; enclosure)

ENE (east-northeast)

ENSA (Entertainments National Service Association)

ENT (ear, nose and throat)

EOC (Equal Opportunities Commission)

EOF (end of file)

EP (electroplate; epistle)

EPH (Ephesians)

EPNS (electroplated nickel silver)

EPROM (erasable programmable read only memory)

ER (Edward Rex; Elizabeth Regina)

ESE (east-southeast)

ESN (educationally subnormal)

ESQ (esquire)

ESTH (Esther)

ETA (estimated time of arrival)

ETC (etcetera)

ETD (estimated time of departure)

ET SEQ (and the following one)

EX DIV (without dividend)

EX LIB (from the books)

EXOD (Exodus)

EZEK (Ezekiel)

F (Fahrenheit; franc)

FA (Football Association)

FANY (First Aid Nursing Yeomanry)

FAS (free alongside ship)

FBA (Fellow of the British Academy)

FBI (Federal Bureau of Investigation)

FC (Football Club)

FCA (Fellow of the Institute of Chartered Accountants)

FCII (Fellow of the Chartered Insurance Institute)

FCIS (Fellow of the Chartered Institute of Secretaries)

FCO (Foreign and Commonwealth Office)

FIFA (International Football Federation)

FL (flourished)

FLA (Florida)

FO (Field Officer; Flying Officer; Foreign Office)

FOB (free on board)

FOC (Father of the Chapel; free of charge)

FPA (Family Planning Association)

FRAM (Fellow of the Royal Academy of Music)

FRAS (Fellow of the Royal Astronomical Society)

FRCM (Fellow of the Royal College of Music)

FRCO (Fellow of the Royal College of Organists)

FRCOG (Fellow of the Royal College of Obstetricians and Gynaecologists)

FRCP (Fellow of the Royal College of Physicians)

FRCS (Fellow of the Royal College of Surgeons)

FRCVS (Fellow of the Royal College of Veterinary Surgeons)

FRGS (Fellow of the Royal Geographical Society)

FRIBA (Fellow of the Royal Institute of British Architects)

FRIC (Fellow of the Royal Institute of Chemistry)

FRICS (Fellow of the Royal Institution of

Chartered Surveyors)

FRPS (Fellow of the Royal Photographic Society)

FRS (Fellow of the Royal Society)

FRSA (Fellow of the Royal Society of Arts)

FSA (Fellow of the Society of Antiquaries)

FZS (Fellow of the Zoological Society)

G (gram)

GA (Georgia)

GAL (Galatians)

GATT (General Agreement on Tariffs and Trade)

GB (Great Britain)

GBE (Knight/Dame Grand Cross of the British Empire)

GBH (grievous bodily harm)

GC (George Cross)

GCB (Knight/Dame Grand Cross of the Bath)

GCE (General Certificate of Education)

GCHQ (Government Communications Headquarters)

GCIE (Grand Commander of the Indian Empire)

GCMG (Knight/Dame Grand Cross of St Michael and St George)

GCSE (General Certificate of Secondary Education)

GCVO (Knight/Dame Grand Cross of the Victorian Order)

GDP (gross domestic product)

GDR (German Democratic Republic)

GEO (George)

GER (German)

GHQ (general headquarters)

GIB (Gibraltar)

GLC (Greater London Council)

GM (George Medal; gram)

GMT (Greenwich Mean Time)

GNP (gross national product)

GOM (grand old man)

GP (general practitioner)

GPO (general post office)

H (hour)

HCF (highest common factor)

HEB (Hebrews)

HF (high frequency)

HGV (heavy goods vehicle)

HIH (His/Her Imperial Highness)

HIM (His/Her Imperial Majesty)

HM (headmaster; headmistress; His/Her Majesty)

HMI (His/Her Majesty's Inspector)

HMS (His/Her Majesty's Ship)

HMSO (His/Her Majesty's Stationery Office)

HNC (Higher National Certificate)

HND (Higher National Diploma)

HO (Home Office; house)

HON (honorary; honour; honourable)

HONS (honours)

HON SEC (Honorary Secretary)

HOS (Hosea)

HP (hire purchase; horsepower)

HQ (headquarters)

HR (holiday route; hour)

HRH (His/Her Royal Highness)

HSH (His/Her Serene Highness)

HT (height)

HV (high velocity; high-voltage)

IA (Institute of Actuaries; Iowa)

IAAF (International Amateur Athletic Federation)

IABA (International Amateur Boxing Association)

IATA (International Air Transport Association)

IB (ibidem; Institute of Bankers)

IBA (Independent Broadcasting Authority)

IBID (ibidem)

IC (in charge; integrated circuit)

ICE (Institution of Civil Engineers)

ICHEME (Institute of Chemical Engineers)

ID (idem; identification)

IE (that is)

IEE (Institution of Electrical Engineers)

IHS (Jesus)

ILL (Illinois)

I MECH E (Institution of Mechanical Engineers)

IMF (International Monetary Fund)

INC (incorporated)

INCL (included; including; inclusive)

IND (Indiana)

INST (instant)

IOM (Isle of Man)

IOW (Isle of Wight)

IPA (International Phonetic Alphabet)

IQ (intelligence quotient)

IR (Inland Revenue)

IRA (Irish Republican Army)

IS (Isaiah)

ISO (Imperial Service Order)

ITA (initial teaching alphabet)

ITAL (italic; italicized)

ITV (Independent Television)

JAM (James)

JC (Jesus Christ; Julius Caesar)

JER (Jeremiah)

JP (Justice of the Peace)

JR (junior)

KAN (Kansas)

KB (King's Bench)

KBE (Knight Commander of the British Empire)

KC (King's Counsel)

KCB (Knight Commander of the Bath)

KCIE (Knight Commander of the Indian Empire)

KCMG (Knight Commander of St Michael and St George)

KCSI (Knight Commander of the Star of India)

KCVO (Knight Commander of the Victorian Order)

KG (kilogram; Knight of the Garter)

KGB (Soviet State Security Committee)

KKK (Ku Klux Klan)

KM (kilometre)

KO (knock-out)

KP (Knight of St Patrick)

KSTJ (Knight of St John)

KT (Knight of the Thistle)

KY (Kentucky)

L (Latin; learner; pound)

LA (Louisiana)

LAT (latitude)

LB (pound)

LBW (leg before wicket)

LCD (liquid crystal display; lowest common denominator)

LCJ (Lord Chief Justice)

LEA (Local Education Authority)

LEV (Leviticus)

LF (low frequency)

LIEUT (Lieutenant)

LITT D (Doctor of Letters; Doctor of Literature)

LJ (Lord Justice)

LJJ (Lords Justices)

LLB (Bachelor of Laws)

LLD (Doctor of Laws)

LLM (Master of Laws)

LOC CIT (in the place cited)

LOQ (he/she speaks)

LPG (liquefied petroleum gas)

LPO (London Philharmonic Orchestra)

LPS (Lord Privy Seal)

LRAM (Licentiate of the Royal Academy of Music)

LS (locus sigilli)

LSD (pounds, shillings, and pence)

LSE (London School of Economics)

LSO (London Symphony Orchestra)

LTD (limited)

LW (long wave)

M (male; married; motorway; thousand)

MA (Master of Arts)

MACC (Maccabees)

MAJ (Major)

MAL (Malachi)

MASH (mobile army surgical hospital)

MASS (Massachusetts)

MATT (Matthew)

MB (Bachelor of Medicine)

MBE (Member of the British Empire)

MC (Master of Ceremonies)

MCC (Marylebone Cricket Club)

MCP (male chauvinist pig)

MD (Doctor of Medicine; Managing Director; Maryland)

ME (Maine)

MEP (Member of the European Parliament)

MET (meteorological; meteorology; metropolitan)

MF (medium frequency)

MG (milligram)

MIC (Micah)

MICH (Michigan)

MINN (Minnesota)

MISS (Mississippi)

ML (millilitre)

M LITT (Master of Letters)

MLR (minimum lending rate)

MM (millimetre)

MO (Medical Officer; Missouri)

MOD (Ministry of Defence)

MOH (Medical Officer of Health)

MONT (Montana)

MP (Member of Parliament; Metropolitan Police; Military Police)

MPG (miles per gallon)

MPH (miles per hour)

MPHIL (Master of Philosophy)

MR (Master of the Rolls)

MRCOG (Member of the Royal College of Obstetricians and Gynaecologists)

MRCP (Member of the Royal College of Physicians)

MRCS (Member of the Royal College of Surgeons)

MRCVS (Member of the Royal College of Veterinary Surgeons)

MS (manuscript; multiple sclerosis)

MSC (Master of Science)

MSM (Meritorious Service Medal)

MSS (manuscripts)

MT (Mount)

MVO (Member of the Victorian Order)

N (North)

NA (North America; not applicable)

NAAFI (Navy, Army, and Air Force Institutes)

NALGO (National and Local Government Officers Association)

NASA (National Aeronautics and Space Administration)

NAT (Nathaniel)

NATO (North Atlantic Treaty Organization)

NATSOPA (National Society of Operative Printers, Graphical and Media Personnel)

NB (note well)

NCB (National Coal Board)

NCO (non-commissioned officer)

NCP (National Car Parks)

NCT (National Childbirth Trust)

NCV (no commercial value)

NDAK (North Dakota)

NE (Northeast)

NEB (Nebraska)

NEC (National Executive Committee)

NEH (Nehemiah)

NEV (Nevada)

NFU (National Farmers' Union)

NGA (National Graphical Association)

NHS (National Health Service)

NI (National Insurance; Northern Ireland)

NNE (north-northeast)

NNW (north-northwest)

NO (not out; number)

NORM (normal)

NOS (numbers)

NP (new paragraph)

NR (near; Northern Region)

NSB (National Savings Bank)

NSPCC (National Society for the Prevention of Cruelty to Children)

NT (National Trust; New Testament)

NUBE (National Union of Bank Employees)

NUGMW (National Union of General and Municipal Workers)

NUJ (National Union of Journalists)

NUM (National Union of Mineworkers)

NUPE (National Union of Public Employees)

NUR (National Union of Railwaymen)

NUS (National Union of Seamen; National Union of Students)

NUT (National Union of Teachers)

NW (Northwest)

NY (New York)

O (Ohio)

OAP (old-age pensioner)

OB (outside broadcast)

OBAD (Obadiah)

OBE (Officer of the British Empire)

OCTU (Officer Cadets Training Unit)

OFM (Order of Friars Minor)

OHMS (On His/Her Majesty's Service)

OKLA (Oklahoma)

OM (Order of Merit)

ONC (Ordinary National Certificate)

OND (Ordinary National Diploma)

ONO (or near offer)

OP (opus)

OP CIT (in the work cited)

OPEC (Organization of Petroleum Exporting Countries)

OPS (operations)

OREG (Oregon)

OS (ordinary seaman; Ordnance Survey)

OSA (Order of St Augustine)

OSB (Order of St Benedict)

OSF (Order of St Francis)

OT (occupational therapy; Old Testament)

OTC (Officers' Training Corps)

OU (Open University)

OUDS (Oxford University Dramatic Society)

OXFAM (Oxford Committee for Famine Relief)

OZ (ounce)

P (page; penny; purl)

PA (Pennsylvania; per annum; personal assistant; public address system)

PAYE (pay as you earn)

PC (per cent; personal computer; police constable)

PD (paid)

PDSA (People's Dispensary for Sick Animals)

PE (physical education)

PEI (Prince Edward Island)

PER PRO (by the agency of)

PG (paying guest; postgraduate)

PHD (Doctor of Philosophy)

PHIL (Philippians)

PL (place; plural)

PLC (public limited company)

PLO (Palestine Liberation Organization)

PM (post meridiem; Prime Minister)

PO (Petty Officer; Pilot Officer; postal order; Post Office)

POW (prisoner of war)

PP (pages; per pro)

PPS (further post-script; Parliamentary Private Secretary)

PR (public relations)

PRAM (programmable random access memory)

PRO (Public Records Office; public relations officer)

PROM (programmable read-only memory)

PROV (Proverbs)

PS (postscript; Private Secretary)

PT (physical training)

PTA (Parent-Teacher Association)

PTO (please turn over)

PVA (polyvinyl acetate)

PVC (polyvinyl chloride)

QB (Queen's Bench)

QC (Queen's Counsel)

QED (which was to be demonstrated)

QM (quartermaster)

QR (quarter; quire)

QT (quart)

QV (which see)

R (king; queen; right; river)

RA (Royal Academy; Royal Artillery)

RAC (Royal Automobile Club)

RADA (Royal Academy of Dramatic Art)

RAF (Royal Air Force)

RAM (random access memory; Royal Academy of Music)

RAMC (Royal Army Medical Corps)

R AND D (research and development)

RBA (Royal Society of British Artists)

RBS (Royal Society of British Sculptors)

RC (Roman Catholic)

RCA (Royal College of Art)

RCM (Royal College of Music)

RCN (Royal College of Nursing)

RCP (Royal College of Physicians)

RCS (Royal College of Surgeons)

RCVS (Royal College of Veterinary Surgeons)

RD (road)

RE (religious education; Royal Engineers)

REME (Royal Electrical and Mechanical Engineers)

REV (Reverend)

RFC (Royal Flying Corps)

RH (Royal Highness; right hand)

RHA (Royal Horse Artillery)

RI (religous instruction)

RIBA (Royal Institute of British Architects)

RIC (Royal Institute of Chemistry)

RICS (Royal Institution of Chartered Surveyors)

RIP (may he rest in peace)

RK (religious knowledge)

RM (Resident Magistrate; Royal Mail; Royal Marines)

RMA (Royal Military Academy)

RN (Royal Navy)

RNIB (Royal National Institute for the Blind)

RNLI (Royal National Lifeboat Institution)

ROM (read only memory)

ROSPA (Royal Society for the Prevention of Accidents)

RPM (revolutions per minute)

RS (Royal Society)

RSA (Royal Society of Arts)

RSC (Royal Shake-speare Company)

RSM (Regimental Sergeant Major; Royal Society of Medicine)

RSPB (Royal Society for the Protection of Birds)

RSPCA (Royal Society for the Prevention of Cruelty to Animals)

RSVP (please answer)

RT HON (Right Honourable)

RT REV (Right Reverend)

RU (Rugby Union)

RUC (Royal Ulster Constabulary)

S (second; shilling; South)

SA (Salvation Army; sex appeal)

SAE (stamped addressed envelope)

SALT (Strategic Arms Limitation Talks)

SAS (Special Air Service)

SATB (soprano, alto, tenor, bass)

SAYE (save-as-you-earn)

SCD (Doctor of Science)

SE (southeast)

SEC (second; secretary)

SEN (senior; State Enrolled Nurse)

SEQ (the following)

SF (science fiction)

SGT (Sergeant)

SHAPE (Supreme Headquarters Allied Powers Europe)

SI (International System of Units)

SIN (sine)

SLADE (Society of Lithographic Artists, Designers, and Etchers)

SLR (single lens reflex)

SNCF (French National Railways)

SNP (Scottish National Party)

SNR (senior)

SOGAT (Society of Graphical and Allied Trades)

SOP (soprano)

SQ (square)

SRN (State Registered Nurse)

SSE (south-southeast)

SSW (south-southwest)

ST (saint; street)

STD (subscriber trunk dialling)

SW (southwest)

TA (Territorial Army)

TAN (tangent)

TASS (official news agency of the former Soviet Union)

TB (tubercle bacillus)

TCCB (Test and County Cricket Board)

TEFL (teaching English as a foreign language)

TENN (Tennessee)

TEX (Texas)

TGWU (Transport and General Workers' Union)

THESS (Thessalonians)

THOS (Thomas)

TM (trademark; transcendental meditation)

TOPS (Training Opportunities Scheme)

TSB (Trustee Savings Bank)

TT (teetotal; teetotaller)

TU (trade union)

TUC (Trades Union Congress)

TV (television)

UC (upper case)

UCATT (Union of Construction, Allied Trades, and Technicians)

UCCA (Universities Central Council on Admissions)

UCL (University College, London)

UDI (unilateral declaration of independence)

UEFA (Union of European Football Associations)

UHF (ultrahigh frequency)

UHT (ultrahigh temperature)

UK (United Kingdom)

ULT (ultimo)

UN (United Nations)

UNCTAD (United Nations Commission for Trade and Development)

UNESCO (United Nations Educational, Scientific, and Cultural Organization)

UNO (United Nations Organization)

UPOW (Union of Post Office Workers)

US (United States)

USA (United States of America)

USDAW (Union of Shop, Distributive, and Allied Workers)

USSR (Union of Soviet Socialist Republics)

V (verse; versus; volt)

VA (Order of Victoria and Albert; Virginia)

VAT (value-added tax)

VB (verb)

VC (Vice Chancellor; Victoria Cross)

VD (venereal disease)

VDU (visual display unit)

VE (Victory in Europe)

VG (very good)

VHF (very high frequency)

VIP (very important person)

VIZ (namely)

VLF (very low frequency)

VR (Victoria Regina; Volunteer Reserve)

VS (verse)

ABBREVIATIONS

VSO (Voluntary Service Overseas)
VT (Vermont)
W (west)
WAAC (Women's Army Auxiliary Corps)
WAAF (Women's Auxiliary Air Force)
WC (water closet; West Central)
WI (West Indies; Women's Institute)

WIS (Wisconsin)
WK (week)
WM (William)
WNW (west-northwest)
WO (Warrant Officer)
WP (word processor)
WPC (Woman Police Constable)
WPM (words per minute)
WRAC (Women's Royal Army Corps)

WRAF (Women's Royal Air Force)
WRNS (Women's Royal Naval Service)
WRVS (Women's Royal Voluntary Service)
WSW (west-southwest)
WT (weight)
WW (Word War)
WWF (World Wildlife Fund)

WYO (Wyoming)
XL (extra large)
YHA (Youth Hostels Association)
YMCA (Young Men's Christian Association)
YR (year)
YWCA (Young Women's Christian Association)
ZECH (Zechariah)
ZEPH (Zephania)

FIRST NAMES

GIRLS' NAMES

2	3–continued	4–continued	4–continued	4–continued
DI	LYN	BEAT	GALE	LILY
EM	MAE	BELL	GAYE	LINA
JO	MAY	BESS	GERT	LISA
VI	MEG	BETA	GILL	LISE
	MEL	BETH	GINA	LITA
3	MIA	BINA	GLAD	LIZA
ADA	NAN	CARA	GWEN	LOIS
AMY	NAT	CARY	GWYN	LOLA
ANN	ONA	CASS	HEBE	LORA
AUD	PAM	CATH	HEDY	LORI
AVA	PAT	CERI	HOPE	LORN
BAB	PEG	CISS	ILMA	LUCE
BEA	PEN	CLEM	ILSE	LUCY
BEE	PIA	CLEO	IMMY	LULU
BEL	PRU	CORA	INEZ	LYNN
CIS	RAE	DAFF	IOLA	LYRA
DEB	RIA	DALE	IONA	MAIR
DEE	ROS	DANA	IRIS	MARA
DOT	SAL	DAPH	IRMA	MARY
EDA	SAM	DAWN	ISLA	MAUD
ENA	SIB	DOLL	IVAH	META
ETH	SUE	DORA	JADE	MIMA
EVA	UNA	EDEN	JAEL	MIMI
EVE	VAL	EDIE	JANE	MINA
FAN	VIV	EDNA	JEAN	MIRA
FAY	WIN	EILY	JESS	MOLL
FLO	ZOË	EIRA	JILL	MONA
GAY		ELLA	JOAN	MYRA
GUS	**4**	ELMA	JODI	NADA
IDA	ABBY	ELSA	JODY	NELL
INA	ADAH	EMMA	JOSS	NEST
ISA	ADDY	ENID	JUDI	NEVA
ITA	AINE	ERIN	JUDY	NINA
IVY	ALDA	ERYL	JUNE	NITA
JAN	ALEX	ESME	KARA	NOLA
JAY	ALIX	ETTA	KATE	NONA
JEN	ALLY	ETTY	KATH	NORA
JOY	ALMA	EVIE	KATY	NOVA
KAY	ALVA	FAYE	KERI	OLGA
KIM	ALYS	FERN	KYLE	OONA
KIT	ANIS	FIFI	LANA	OPAL
LEE	ANNA	FLOY	LELA	OZZY
LES	ANNE	FRAN	LENA	PETA
LIL	ANYA	GABI	LETA	PHIL
LIZ	AVIS	GABY	LILA	POLL
LOU	BABS	GAIL	LILI	PRUE

359

4–continued	5–continued	5–continued	5–continued	5–continued
RENA	AMATA	DIANE	HETTY	LUCIE
RENE	AMBER	DILYS	HILDA	LUCKY
RHEA	AMICE	DINAH	HOLLY	LYDIA
RICA	ANGEL	DIONE	HORRY	LYNDA
RIKA	ANGIE	DODIE	HULDA	LYNNE
RINA	ANITA	DOLLY	HYLDA	MABEL
RITA	ANNIE	DONNA	ILONA	MABLE
ROMA	ANNIS	DORIA	IRENE	MADDY
RONA	ANONA	DORIS	ISMAY	MADGE
ROSA	ANWEN	DREDA	JACKY	MAEVE
ROSE	APHRA	DULCE	JANET	MAGDA
ROXY	APRIL	EDITH	JANEY	MAIRE
RUBY	ASTRA	EFFIE	JANIE	MAMIE
RUTH	AUDRA	ELAIN	JANIS	MANDY
SARA	AUREA	ELENA	JAYNE	MARAH
SIAN	AVICE	ELISE	JEMMA	MARCY
SÍLE	AVRIL	ELIZA	JENNA	MARGE
SÍNE	BEATA	ELLEN	JENNY	MARGO
SUZY	BECKY	ELLIE	JEWEL	MARIA
TACY	BELLA	ELROY	JINNY	MARIE
TARA	BELLE	ELSIE	JODIE	MARLA
TESS	BERNY	ELVIE	JOSIE	MARNI
THEA	BERRY	EMILY	JOYCE	MARTA
TINA	BERTA	EMMIE	JUDOC	MARTI
TONI	BERYL	EPPIE	JULIA	MARTY
TRIS	BESSY	ERICA	JULIE	MATTY
TRIX	BETSY	ERIKA	KAREN	MAUDE
TYRA	BETTE	ESMEE	KARIN	MAURA
VERA	BETTY	ESSIE	KATHY	MAVIS
VIDA	BIDDY	ETHEL	KATIE	MEAVE
VINA	BONNY	ETHNE	KELDA	MEGAN
VITA	BRIDE	ETTIE	KELLY	MEGGY
VIVA	BRITA	EVITA	KEREN	MELBA
WYNN	BRITT	FAITH	KERRI	MELVA
ZANA	CANDY	FANNY	KERRY	MERCY
ZARA	CAREY	FARON	KEZIA	MERLE
ZENA	CARLA	FIONA	KIRBY	MERRY
ZITA	CARLY	FLEUR	KITTY	MERYL
ZOLA	CAROL	FLORA	KYLIE	MILLY
ZORA	CARYL	FLOSS	LAURA	MINNA
	CARYS	FREDA	LAURI	MINTY
5	CASEY	FREYA	LEIGH	MITZI
ABBEY	CATHY	GABBY	LEILA	MOIRA
ABBIE	CELIA	GAYLE	LENNY	MOLLY
ADDIE	CERYS	GEMMA	LEONA	MORAG
ADELA	CHLOE	GERDA	LETTY	MORNA
ADELE	CHRIS	GERRY	LIANA	MOYNA
ADLAI	CILLA	GILDA	LIBBY	MOYRA
AGGIE	CINDY	GINNY	LIDDY	MYRNA
AGNES	CISSY	GRACE	LIESL	MYSIE
AILIE	CLARA	GRETA	LILAC	NADIA
AILIS	CLARE	GUSTA	LILLA	NAHUM
AILSA	CORAL	HAGAR	LINDA	NANCE
AIMEE	DAISY	HATTY	LINDY	NANCY
ALANA	DARCY	HAZEL	LIZZY	NANNY
ALEXA	DEBRA	HEDDA	LOLLY	NAOMI
ALICE	DELIA	HEIDI	LOREN	NELLY
ALINA	DELLA	HELEN	LORNA	NERYS
ALINE	DELMA	HELGA	LORNE	NESSA
ALLIE	DERYN	HENNY	LOTTY	NESTA
ALVIE	DIANA	HEPSY	LUCIA	NETTA

5—continued	5—continued	6—continued	6—continued	6—continued
NICKY	SONYA	AILEEN	BOBBIE	EILWEN
NIKKI	SOPHY	AILITH	BONITA	EIRIAN
NOELE	STACY	AITHNE	BONNIE	EITHNE
NORAH	SUKEY	ALANNA	BRENDA	ELAINE
NORMA	SUSAN	ALBINA	BRIDIE	ELINED
NUALA	SUSIE	ALDITH	BRIGID	ELINOR
NYREE	SYBIL	ALEXIA	BRIGIT	ELISHA
ODILE	TACEY	ALEXIS	BRIONY	ELISSA
OLIFF	TAMAR	ALICIA	BRYONY	ELOISA
OLIVE	TAMMY	ALISON	CANICE	ELOISE
OLLIE	TANIA	ALTHEA	CARINA	ELSPIE
OLWEN	TANSY	ALVINA	CARITA	ELUNED
OLWYN	TANYA	AMABEL	CARMEL	ELVINA
ORIEL	TEGAN	AMALIA	CARMEN	ELVIRA
OWENA	TERRI	AMALIE	CAROLA	EMELYN
PANSY	TERRY	AMANDA	CAROLE	EMILIA
PATSY	TESSA	AMELIA	CARRIE	ESTHER
PATTI	TETTY	AMICIA	CASSIE	EUNICE
PATTY	THORA	AMINTA	CATRIN	EVADNE
PAULA	THYRA	ANDREA	CECILE	EVELYN
PEACE	TIBBY	ANDRÉE	CECILY	EVONNE
PEARL	TILDA	ANEIRA	CELINA	FARRAN
PEGGY	TILLY	ANGELA	CELINE	FARREN
PENNY	TISHA	ANNICE	CHARIS	FEDORA
PETRA	TONIA	ANNIKA	CHERIE	FELICE
PHEBE	TONYA	ANNORA	CHERRY	FINOLA
PIPPA	TOPSY	ANSTEY	CHERYL	FLAVIA
POLLY	TOTTY	ANTHEA	CICELY	FLOWER
POPPY	TRACY	ARIANE	CISSIE	FOSTER
RAINA	TRINA	ARLEEN	CLAIRE	FRANCA
RAINE	TRUDI	ARLENE	COLINA	FRANNY
REINE	TRUDY	ARLINE	CONNIE	FRIEDA
RENÉE	UNITY	ARMINA	DAGMAR	GABBIE
RENIE	VALDA	ARMINE	DANITA	GAENOR
RHIAN	VANDA	ASHLEY	DANUTA	GARNET
RHODA	VELDA	ASTRID	DAPHNE	GAYNOR
RHONA	VELMA	ATHENE	DAVIDA	GERTIE
ROBYN	VENUS	AUDREY	DAVINA	GINGER
RONNA	VERNA	AURIEL	DEANNA	GISELA
ROSIE	VICKI	AURIOL	DEANNE	GLADYS
ROWAN	VICKY	AURORA	DEBBIE	GLENDA
SADIE	VIKKI	AURORE	DECIMA	GLENIS
SALLY	VILMA	AVERIL	DELWEN	GLENNA
SAMMY	VINNY	BARBIE	DELWYN	GLENYS
SANDY	VIOLA	BARBRA	DELYTH	GLINYS
SARAH	VIVIA	BAUBIE	DENISE	GLORIA
SARAI	WANDA	BEATTY	DENNIE	GLYNIS
SARRA	WENDA	BENITA	DIANNE	GOLDIE
SELMA	WENDY	BERNIE	DIONNE	GRACIE
SENGA	WILLA	BERTHA	DORCAS	GRANIA
SHANI	WILMA	BESSIE	DOREEN	GRETEL
SHARI	WYNNE	BETHAN	DORICE	GRIZEL
SHEBA	XENIA	BETHIA	DORITA	GUSSIE
SHENA	ZELDA	BEULAH	DORRIE	GWENDA
SHIRL	ZELMA	BIANCA	DOTTIE	HAIDEE
SHONA	ZORAH	BILLIE	DULCIE	HANNAH
SIBBY		BIRDIE	DYMPNA	HATTIE
SIBYL	**6**	BIRGIT	EARTHA	HAYLEY
SISSY	AGACIA	BLANCH	EASTER	HEDWIG
SONIA	AGATHA	BLODYN	EDWINA	HELENA
SONJA	AGNETA	BLYTHE	EILEEN	HELENE

6–continued	6–continued	6–continued	6–continued	7–continued
HENNIE	LILIAS	NOREEN	SOPHIE	ALETHEA
HEPSEY	LILITH	ODETTE	SORCHA	ALFREDA
HEPSIE	LILLAH	ODILIA	STACEY	ALLEGRA
HERMIA	LILLIE	OLIVET	STELLA	ALLISON
HESTER	LINNET	OLIVIA	STEVIE	ALOISIA
HILARY	LIZZIE	OONAGH	SYLVIA	ALOYSIA
HONORA	LLINOS	ORIANA	SYLVIE	ANNABEL
HOWARD	LOLITA	PAMELA	TAMARA	ANNAPLE
HULDAH	LOREEN	PATTIE	TAMSIN	ANNETTE
IANTHE	LOTTIE	PEPITA	TANITH	ANOUSKA
IDONEA	LOUISA	PETULA	TEGWEN	ANSELMA
IMOGEN	LOUISE	PHEMIE	TERESA	ANSTICE
INGRID	LUCINA	PHOEBE	TESSIE	ANTOINE
ISABEL	LUELLA	PORTIA	THECLA	ANTONIA
ISEULT	MADDIE	PRISCA	THEKLA	ARIADNE
ISHBEL	MAGGIE	PRISSY	THELMA	ARIANNA
ISOBEL	MAHALA	QUEENA	THIRSA	ARLETTA
ISOLDA	MAIDIE	QUEENY	THIRZA	ARLETTE
ISOLDE	MAIRIN	RACHEL	TIRZAH	ASPASIA
JACKIE	MAISIE	RAMONA	TRACEY	AUGUSTA
JACOBA	MARCIA	REGINA	TRICIA	AURELIA
JACQUI	MARCIE	RENATA	TRISHA	AUREOLA
JANICE	MARGIE	RHONDA	TRIXIE	AUREOLE
JANINE	MARGOT	ROBINA	TRUDIE	AVELINE
JANSIS	MARIAM	ROISIN	ULRICA	BABETTE
JEANIE	MARIAN	ROSINA	URSULA	BARBARA
JEANNE	MARIEL	ROSITA	VASHTI	BARBARY
JEHANE	MARINA	ROSLYN	VERENA	BASILIA
JEMIMA	MARION	ROWENA	VERITY	BASILIE
JENNIE	MARISA	ROXANA	VERONA	BASILLA
JESSIE	MARITA	ROXANE	VICKIE	BEATRIX
JOANNA	MARLIN	RUBINA	VINNIE	BEATTIE
JOANNE	MARLYN	RUTHIE	VIOLET	BEDELIA
JOLEEN	MARNIE	SABINA	VIVIAN	BELINDA
JOLENE	MARSHA	SALENA	VIVIEN	BERNICE
JUDITH	MARTHA	SALINA	VYVYAN	BETHANY
JULIET	MARTIE	SALOME	WALLIS	BETTINA
KARINA	MATTIE	SANDIE	WINNIE	BETTRYS
KEELEY	MAUDIE	SANDRA	XANTHE	BEVERLY
KELLIE	MAXINE	SARINA	YASMIN	BLANCHE
KENDRA	MEGGIE	SARITA	YVETTE	BLODWEN
KERRIE	MEGHAN	SELENA	YVONNE	BLOSSOM
KEZIAH	MEHALA	SELINA	ZANDRA	BRANWEN
KIRSTY	MELODY	SERENA	ZILLAH	BRIDGET
LALAGE	MERCIA	SHARON	ZINNIA	BRIGHID
LAUREL	MERIEL	SHAUNA		BRONWEN
LAUREN	MIGNON	SHEENA	7	BRONWYN
LAURIE	MILLIE	SHEILA	ABIGAIL	CAITLIN
LAVENA	MINNIE	SHELLY	ADAMINA	CAMILLA
LAVINA	MIRIAM	SHERRI	ADELINA	CAMILLE
LEANNE	MONICA	SHERRY	ADELINE	CANDACE
LEILAH	MURIEL	SHERYL	ADRIANA	CANDICE
LENNIE	MYRTLE	SIBBIE	AINSLEY	CANDIDA
LENORE	NADINE	SIDONY	AINSLIE	CARLEEN
LEONIE	NELLIE	SILVIA	AISLING	CARLENE
LESLEY	NERINA	SIMONA	AISLINN	CARMELA
LESLIE	NESSIE	SIMONE	ALBERTA	CAROLYN
LETTIE	NETTIE	SINEAD	ALBINIA	CECILIA
LIANNE	NICOLA	SISLEY	ALBREDA	CECILIE
LIESEL	NICOLE	SISSIE	ALDREDA	CEINWEN
LILIAN	NOELLE	SOPHIA	ALEDWEN	CELESTE

7–continued	7–continued	7–continued	7–continued	7–continued
CHARITY	FRANNIE	LILLIAS	NICHOLA	SILVANA
CHARLEY	GENEVRA	LINDSAY	NINETTE	SIOBHAN
CHARLIE	GEORGIA	LINDSEY	NOELEEN	SUSANNA
CHATTIE	GEORGIE	LINETTE	NOELINE	SUSANNE
CHRISSY	GILLIAN	LISBETH	OCTAVIA	SUZANNA
CHRISTY	GINETTE	LISETTE	OLYMPIA	SUZANNE
CLARICE	GINEVRA	LIZANNE	OPHELIA	SUZETTE
CLARRIE	GISELLE	LIZBETH	OTTILIA	SYBELLA
CLAUDIA	GRAINNE	LORAINE	OTTILIE	SYBILLA
CLODAGH	GRIZZEL	LORETTA	PAMELIA	TABITHA
COLETTE	GWLADYS	LORETTE	PANDORA	TALITHA
COLLEEN	GWYNEDD	LORINDA	PASCALE	TATIANA
CORALIE	GWYNETH	LOUELLA	PAULINE	THERESA
CORINNA	HALCYON	LOVEDAY	PEARLIE	THÉRÈSE
CORINNE	HARRIET	LUCASTA	PERDITA	TIFFANY
CRYSTAL	HEATHER	LUCETTA	PERONEL	TRISSIE
CYNTHIA	HÉLOÏSE	LUCETTE	PETRINA	VALERIA
DAMARIS	HEULWEN	LUCIANA	PHILLIS	VALERIE
DANETTE	HILLARY	LUCILLA	PHYLLIS	VANESSA
DARLENE	HONORIA	LUCILLE	QUEENIE	VENETIA
DAVINIA	HORATIA	LUCINDA	RACHAEL	VIVIANA
DEBORAH	HYPATIA	LUCRECE	RAELENE	YOLANDA
DEIRDRE	ISADORA	LYNETTE	RAFAELA	YOLANDE
DELILAH	ISIDORA	MABELLA	REBECCA	ZENOBIA
DEMELZA	JACINTA	MABELLE	REBEKAH	ZULEIKA
DESIREE	JACINTH	MAHALAH	RHONWEN	
DIAMOND	JANETTA	MAHALIA	RICARDA	8
DOLORES	JANETTE	MALVINA	RICHMAL	ADELAIDE
DONALDA	JASMINE	MANUELA	ROBERTA	ADELHEID
DORETTE	JEANNIE	MARILYN	ROMAINE	ADRIANNE
DORINDA	JENIFER	MARISSA	RONALDA	ADRIENNE
DOROTHY	JESSICA	MARLENE	ROSABEL	ANGELICA
DYMPHNA	JILLIAN	MARTINA	ROSALIA	ANGELINA
EILUNED	JOCASTA	MARTINE	ROSALIE	ANGELINE
ELDREDA	JOCELYN	MATILDA	ROSALYN	ANGHARAD
ELEANOR	JOHANNA	MAUREEN	ROSANNA	ANNALISA
ELFREDA	JONQUIL	MEHALAH	ROSANNE	ANTONINA
ELFRIDA	JOSEPHA	MEHALIA	ROSEANN	ANTONNIA
ELSPETH	JOSETTE	MEIRION	ROSELYN	APPOLINA
EMELINE	JUANITA	MELANIA	ROSETTA	APPOLINE
EMERALD	JULIANA	MELANIE	ROSSLYN	ARABELLA
ESTELLA	JULITTA	MELINDA	ROXANNA	ARAMINTA
ESTELLE	JUSTINA	MELIORA	ROXANNE	BEATRICE
EUGENIA	JUSTINE	MELISSA	RUPERTA	BERENICE
EUGENIE	KATHRYN	MELODIE	SABRINA	BEVERLEY
EULALIA	KATRINA	MELVINA	SAFFRON	BIRGITTA
EULALIE	KATRINE	MERILYN	SANCHIA	BRIGITTA
EVELEEN	KETURAH	MERRION	SARANNA	BRIGITTE
EVELINA	KIRSTEN	MICHELE	SCARLET	BRITTANY
EVELINE	KRISTEN	MILDRED	SEPTIMA	BRUNETTA
FABIANA	KRISTIN	MINERVA	SHANNON	CARLOTTA
FELICIA	LARAINE	MIRABEL	SHARRON	CAROLINA
FENELLA	LARISSA	MIRANDA	SHEILAH	CAROLINE
FEODORA	LAUREEN	MODESTY	SHELAGH	CATHLEEN
FIDELIA	LAURINA	MONIQUE	SHELLEY	CATRIONA
FLORRIE	LAVERNE	MYFANWY	SHIRLEY	CERIDWEN
FLOSSIE	LAVINIA	NANETTE	SIBELLA	CHARISSA
FORTUNE	LEONORA	NATALIA	SIBILLA	CHARLENE
FRANCES	LETITIA	NATALIE	SIBYLLA	CHARMIAN
FRANCIE	LETTICE	NATASHA	SIDONIA	CHRISSIE
FRANKIE	LILLIAN	NERISSA	SIDONIE	CHRISTIE

8—continued	8—continued	8—continued	9—continued
CLARIBEL	JOSCELIN	ROSALIND	CELESTINA
CLARINDA	JULIANNE	ROSALINE	CELESTINE
CLARISSA	JULIENNE	ROSAMOND	CHARLOTTE
CLAUDINE	JULIETTE	ROSAMUND	CHARMAINE
CLEMENCE	KATHLEEN	ROSEANNA	CHRISTIAN
CLEMENCY	KIMBERLY	ROSEANNE	CHRISTINA
CLOTILDA	KRISTINA	ROSELINE	CHRISTINE
CONCEPTA	KRISTINE	ROSEMARY	CHRISTMAS
CONCETTA	LAETITIA	SAMANTHA	CLAUDETTE
CORDELIA	LARRAINE	SAPPHIRA	CLEMENTIA
CORNELIA	LAURAINE	SAPPHIRE	CLEOPATRA
COURTNEY	LAURETTA	SCARLETT	COLUMBINA
CRESSIDA	LAURETTE	SHEELAGH	COLUMBINE
CYTHEREA	LAURINDA	SHUSHANA	CONSTANCE
DANIELLA	LORRAINE	STEFANIE	CONSTANCY
DANIELLE	LUCIENNE	SUSANNAH	COURTENAY
DELPHINE	LUCRETIA	TALLULAH	DESDEMONA
DIONYSIA	LUCREZIA	TAMASINE	DOMINIQUE
DOMINICA	LYNNETTE	THEODORA	DONALDINA
DOROTHEA	MADELINA	THERESIA	ELISABETH
DOWSABEL	MADELINE	THOMASIN	ELIZABETH
DRUSILLA	MAGDALEN	TIMOTHEA	EMMANUELA
ELEANORA	MAGNOLIA	TRYPHENA	ERNESTINE
ELEONORA	MARCELLA	VERONICA	ESMERALDA
EMANUELA	MARCELLE	VICTORIA	ETHELINDA
EMMELINE	MARGARET	VIOLETTA	FIONNUALA
EUPHEMIA	MARIAMNE	VIOLETTE	FRANCESCA
EUSTACIA	MARIANNE	VIRGINIA	FRANCISCA
FAUSTINA	MARIETTA	VIVIENNE	FREDERICA
FELICITY	MARIETTE	WALBURGA	FREDERIKA
FLORENCE	MARIGOLD	WILFREDA	GABRIELLA
FLORETTA	MARJORIE	WILFRIDA	GABRIELLE
FLORETTE	MELICENT	WINEFRED	GENEVIEVE
FLORINDA	MELISENT	WINIFRED	GEORGETTE
FRANCINE	MELLONEY		GEORGIANA
FREDRICA	MERCEDES	**9**	GERALDINE
FREDRIKA	MEREDITH	ALBERTINA	GHISLAINE
GEORGINA	MERRILYN	ALBERTINE	GUENDOLEN
GERMAINE	MICHAELA	ALEXANDRA	GUINEVERE
GERTRUDE	MICHELLE	AMARYLLIS	GWENDOLEN
GILBERTA	MORWENNA	AMBROSINA	GWENDOLYN
GRETCHEN	MYRTILLA	AMBROSINE	GWENLLIAN
GRISELDA	PATIENCE	ANASTASIA	HARRIETTE
GULIELMA	PATRICIA	ANGELIQUE	HENRIETTA
GWYNNETH	PAULETTE	ANNABELLA	HENRIETTE
HADASSAH	PENELOPE	ANNABELLE	HEPHZIBAH
HELEWISE	PERPETUA	ANNELIESE	HILDEGARD
HEPZIBAH	PHILIPPA	APOLLONIA	HIPPOLYTA
HERMIONE	PHILLIDA	ARTEMISIA	HORTENSIA
HORTENSE	PHILLIPA	ARTHURINA	HYACINTHA
HYACINTH	PHYLLIDA	ARTHURINE	JACQUELYN
INGEBORG	PRIMROSE	AUGUSTINA	JACQUETTA
IOLANTHE	PRUDENCE	BATHSHEBA	JEANNETTE
ISABELLA	PRUNELLA	BENEDICTA	JESSAMINE
ISABELLE	RAPHAELA	BERNADINA	JOSEPHINE
JACOBINA	RAYMONDE	BERNADINE	KATHARINE
JAMESINA	RHIANNON	BRITANNIA	KATHERINE
JEANETTE	RICHENDA	CARMELITA	KIMBERLEY
JEANNINE	ROCHELLE	CASSANDRA	LAURENCIA
JENNIFER	RONNETTE	CATHARINE	LAURENTIA
JESSAMYN	ROSALEEN	CATHERINE	MADELEINE

9–continued
MAGDALENA
MAGDALENE
MARGARETA
MARGARITA
MEHETABEL
MEHITABEL
MÉLISANDE
MILLICENT
MIRABELLA
MIRABELLE
NICOLETTE
PARTHENIA
PHILLIPPA
PHILOMENA
PLEASANCE
POLLYANNA
PRISCILLA
ROSABELLA
ROSABELLE
ROSALINDA
ROSEMARIE

9–continued
SERAPHINA
SHUSHANNA
SOPHRONIA
STEPHANIE
THEODOSIA
THEOPHILA
THOMASINA
THOMASINE
VALENTINA
VALENTINE
VÉRONIQUE
VICTORINE
VINCENTIA
WINNIFRED

10
ALEXANDRIA
ALPHONSINE
ANTOINETTE
ARTHURETTA
BERENGARIA

10–continued
BERNADETTE
BERNARDINA
BERNARDINE
CHRISTABEL
CHRISTIANA
CINDERELLA
CLEMENTINA
CLEMENTINE
CONSTANTIA
DULCIBELLA
ERMINTRUDE
ERMYNTRUDE
ETHELDREDA
EVANGELINA
EVANGELINE
GILBERTINE
GWENDOLINE
HILDEGARDE
JACQUELINE
KINBOROUGH
MARGARETTA

10–continued
MARGUERITA
MARGUERITE
MARIABELLA
MILBOROUGH
PETRONELLA
PETRONILLA
TEMPERANCE
THEOPHANIA
WILHELMINA
WILLIAMINA

11
ALEXANDRINA
CHRISTIANIA
FIONNGHUALA

12
KERENHAPPUCH
PHILADELPHIA

BOYS' NAMES

2
AL
CY
ED
TY

3
ABE
ALF
ART
ASA
BAS
BAT
BAZ
BEN
BOB
BUD
CAI
DAI
DAN
DEE
DEL
DES
DON
DUD
ELI
ERN
GIB
GIL
GUS
GUY

3–continued
HAL
HAM
HEW
HOB
HUW
IAN
IKE
IRA
IVO
JAN
JAY
JED
JEM
JIM
JOB
JOE
JON
KAY
KEN
KIM
KIT
LEE
LEN
LEO
LES
LEW
LEX
LOU
LYN
MAT

3–continued
MAX
MEL
NAT
NED
NYE
ODO
PAT
PIP
RAB
RAY
REG
REX
ROB
ROD
RON
ROY
SAM
SEB
SID
SIM
STU
SYD
TAM
TED
TEL
TEX
TIM
TOM
VIC
VIN

3–continued
WAL
WAT
WIN
ZAK

4
ABEL
ADAM
ALAN
ALDO
ALEC
ALED
ALEX
ALGY
ALUN
ALVA
AMOS
ANDY
ARTY
AXEL
BART
BEAU
BERT
BILL
BING
BOAZ
BOYD
BRAD
BRAM
BRET

4–continued
BRYN
BURT
CARL
CARY
CERI
CHAD
CHAS
CHAY
CLEM
COLM
CONN
CURT
DALE
DANA
DAVE
DAVY
DEAN
DEWI
DICK
DION
DIRK
DOUG
DREW
DUKE
EARL
EBEN
EDDY
EDEN
EDOM
EMIL

4—continued	4—continued	4—continued	5—continued	5—continued
ENOS	LUKE	WILF	BLAIR	DONNY
ERIC	LYLE	WILL	BLAKE	DORAN
ERIK	MARC	WYNN	BLANE	DROGO
ERLE	MARK	YVES	BLASE	DUANE
ESAU	MATT	ZACK	BOBBY	DYLAN
ESME	MERV	ZANE	BONAR	EAMON
EVAN	MICK	ZEKE	BORIS	EDDIE
EWAN	MIKE		BOYCE	EDGAR
EWEN	MILO	**5**	BRENT	EDWIN
EZRA	MORT	AARON	BRETT	EDWYN
FRED	MOSS	ABNER	BRIAN	ELDON
GARY	MUIR	ABRAM	BRICE	ELIAS
GENE	NEAL	ADAIR	BROCK	ELIHU
GLEN	NEIL	ADOLF	BRUCE	ELIOT
GLYN	NICK	AIDAN	BRUNO	ELLIS
GREG	NOAH	ALAIN	BRYAN	ELMER
GWYN	NOEL	ALBAN	BRYCE	ELTON
HAMO	NORM	ALBIN	BYRON	ELVIN
HANK	OLAF	ALDEN	CADEL	ELVIS
HANS	OLAV	ALDIS	CAIUS	ELWYN
HERB	OMAR	ALDUS	CALEB	EMERY
HUEY	OSSY	ALFIE	CALUM	EMILE
HUGH	OTHO	ALGAR	CAREY	EMLYN
HUGO	OTIS	ALGER	CARLO	EMRYS
IAGO	OTTO	ALGIE	CAROL	ENOCH
IAIN	OWEN	ALICK	CASEY	EPPIE
IFOR	PAUL	ALLAN	CECIL	ERNIE
IGOR	PETE	ALLEN	CHRIS	ERROL
IOLO	PHIL	ALVAH	CHUCK	ETHAN
IVAN	RAFE	ALVAR	CLARK	FARON
IVES	RENÉ	ALVIE	CLAUD	FELIX
IVOR	RHYS	ALVIN	CLIFF	FIDEL
JACK	RICH	ALVIS	CLINT	FLOYD
JAGO	RICK	ALWYN	CLIVE	FRANK
JAKE	ROLF	AMIAS	CLYDE	GAIUS
JEFF	ROLY	AMYAS	COLIN	GARRY
JOCK	RORY	ANCEL	COLUM	GARTH
JOEL	ROSS	ANDRÉ	CONAN	GAVIN
JOEY	RUDI	ANGEL	CONOR	GEOFF
JOHN	RUDY	ANGUS	COSMO	GERRY
JOSÉ	RUSS	ANSEL	CRAIG	GILES
JOSH	RYAN	ANTON	CUDDY	GLENN
JUAN	SAUL	ARCHY	CYRIL	GRANT
JUDD	SEAN	ARMIN	CYRUS	GREGG
JUDE	SETH	ARTIE	DAMON	GUIDO
KANE	SHAW	ASHER	DANNY	GYLES
KARL	SHEM	ATHOL	DANTE	HAMON
KEIR	STAN	AULAY	DARBY	HARDY
KENT	STEW	AVERY	DARCY	HARRY
KING	THEO	BARON	DARYL	HAYDN
KIRK	THOM	BARRY	DAVID	HEATH
KRIS	TOBY	BASIE	DENIS	HEBER
KURT	TODD	BASIL	DENNY	HENRI
KYLE	TONY	BENET	DENYS	HENRY
LARS	TREV	BENJY	DERBY	HERVÉ
LEON	TROY	BENNY	DEREK	HIRAM
LEVI	VERE	BERNY	DERRY	HOMER
LIAM	VICK	BERRY	DERYK	HONOR
LORI	WADE	BEVIS	DICKY	HORRY
LORN	WALT	BILLY	DIGBY	HOWEL
LUDO	WARD	BJORN	DONAL	HUMPH

5–continued	5–continued	5–continued	6–continued	6–continued
HYMAN	MORTY	SHANE	AUSTEN	DOUGIE
HYMIE	MOSES	SHAUN	AUSTIN	DUDLEY
HYWEL	MOSHE	SHAWN	AYLMER	DUGALD
IDRIS	MUNGO	SILAS	AYLWIN	DUGGIE
INIGO	MYLES	SIMON	BALDIE	DUNCAN
IRVIN	MYRON	SOLLY	BARNET	DURAND
IRWIN	NEDDY	STEVE	BARNEY	DUSTIN
ISAAC	NEILL	TAFFY	BARRIE	DWAYNE
ITHEL	NEVIL	TEDDY	BARRON	DWIGHT
IZAAK	NIALL	TERRI	BARTLE	EAMONN
JABEZ	NICKY	TERRY	BENITO	EASTER
JACKY	NICOL	TIMMY	BENNET	EDMOND
JACOB	NIGEL	TITUS	BERNIE	EDMUND
JAMES	NIKKI	TOLLY	BERTIE	EDWARD
JAMIE	NOLAN	TOMMY	BETHEL	EGBERT
JARED	OGDEN	TUDOR	BILLIE	ELDRED
JASON	OLAVE	ULRIC	BLAINE	ELIJAH
JEMMY	OLLIE	UPTON	BLAISE	ELLERY
JERRY	ORSON	URBAN	BOBBIE	ELLIOT
JESSE	ORVAL	URIAH	BONAMY	EOGHAN
JESUS	OSCAR	VINCE	BOTOLF	ERNEST
JIMMY	OSSIE	VITUS	BOTULF	ESMOND
JONAH	OSWIN	WALDO	BUSTER	EUGENE
JONAS	OWAIN	WALLY	CADELL	EVELYN
JUDAH	OZZIE	WAYNE	CAESAR	FABIAN
JUDAS	PABLO	WILLY	CALLUM	FARRAN
JULES	PADDY	WYATT	CALVIN	FARREN
KAROL	PAOLO	WYNNE	CARLOS	FERGIE
KEITH	PARRY		CAROLE	FERGUS
KENNY	PEDRO	**6**	CARTER	FINLAY
KEVIN	PERCE	ADOLPH	CASPAR	FLURRY
KIRBY	PERCY	ADRIAN	CEDRIC	FRANCO
LABAN	PERRY	AENEAS	CERDIC	FRASER
LANCE	PETER	ALARIC	CLAUDE	FRAZER
LANTY	PIERS	ALBANY	COLLEY	FREDDY
LARRY	PIRAN	ALBERT	CONNOR	GARETH
LAURI	QUINN	ALDOUS	CONRAD	GARNET
LEIGH	RALPH	ALDRED	CORMAC	GARRET
LEROY	RAMON	ALDWIN	CORNEY	GASPAR
LEWIS	RANDY	ALDWYN	COSIMO	GAWAIN
LLOYD	RAOUL	ALEXIS	CUDDIE	GEORGE
LOREN	RICKI	ALFRED	CURTIS	GERALD
LORIN	RICKY	ALONSO	DAFYDD	GERARD
LORNE	RIKKI	ALONZO	DAMIAN	GERWYN
LOUIE	ROALD	ALURED	DAMIEN	GETHIN
LOUIS	ROBIN	ANDREW	DANIEL	GIDEON
LUCAS	RODDY	ANGELO	DARREL	GILROY
LYULF	RODGE	ANSELL	DARREN	GODWIN
MADOC	ROGER	ANSELM	DARRYL	GORDON
MANNY	ROLLO	ANTONY	DECLAN	GRAEME
MANUS	ROLLY	AQUILA	DENNIS	GRAHAM
MARCO	ROLPH	ARCHER	DENZIL	GREGOR
MARIO	ROWAN	ARCHIE	DERMOT	GROVER
MARTY	ROYAL	ARMAND	DERYCK	GUNTER
MICAH	RUFUS	ARNAUD	DEXTER	GUSSIE
MICKY	SACHA	ARNOLD	DICKIE	GUSTAF
MILES	SAMMY	ARTHUR	DICKON	GUSTAV
MITCH	SAXON	ASHLEY	DILLON	GWILYM
MONTE	SCOTT	AUBERT	DONALD	GWYLIM
MONTY	SELBY	AUBREY	DORIAN	HAMISH
MORAY	SERGE	AUGUST	DOUGAL	HAMLET

6–continued	6–continued	6–continued	6–continued	7–continued
HAMLYN	LESTER	PRINCE	WARREN	CHAUNCY
HAMNET	LIONEL	QUINCY	WESLEY	CHESTER
HARLEY	LONNIE	RABBIE	WILBUR	CHRISTY
HAROLD	LOVELL	RAFAEL	WILLIE	CLAYTON
HARVEY	LOWELL	RAINER	WILLIS	CLEDWYN
HAYDEN	LUCIAN	RAMSAY	WILMER	CLEMENT
HAYDON	LUCIEN	RAMSEY	WILMOT	CLIFTON
HECTOR	LUCIUS	RANALD	WINNIE	CLINTON
HEDLEY	LUTHER	RANDAL	WYBERT	COLUMBA
HERBIE	LYNDON	RAYNER	WYSTAN	CRISPIN
HERMAN	LYULPH	RAYNOR	XAVIER	CRYSTAL
HERVEY	MAGNUS	REGGIE	YEHUDI	CYPRIAN
HILARY	MALISE	REUBEN		DARRELL
HOBART	MALORY	RICHIE	**7**	DECIMUS
HOLDEN	MALVIN	ROBBIE	ABRAHAM	DENHOLM
HONOUR	MANLEY	ROBERT	ABSALOM	DERRICK
HORACE	MANSEL	RODGER	ABSOLON	DESMOND
HOWARD	MANUEL	RODNEY	ADAMNAN	DIGGORY
HOWELL	MARCEL	ROLAND	ADOLPHE	DOMINIC
HUBERT	MARCUS	RONALD	AINSLEY	DONOVAN
HUGHIE	MARIUS	RONNIE	AINSLIE	DOUGLAS
INGRAM	MARTIN	RUDOLF	ALBERIC	DUNSTAN
IRVINE	MARTYN	RUPERT	ALDHELM	EARNEST
IRVING	MARVIN	RUSSEL	ALFONSO	ELEAZAR
ISAIAH	MARVYN	RUSSEL	AMBROSE	ELKANAH
ISRAEL	MELVIN	SAMSON	ANDREAS	ELLIOTT
JACKIE	MELVYN	SAMUEL	ANEIRIN	EMANUEL
JACQUI	MERLIN	SEAMUS	ANEURIN	EPHRAIM
JARRED	MERTON	SEFTON	ANTHONY	ERASMUS
JARROD	MERVIN	SELWYN	ANTONIO	EUSTACE
JARVIS	MERVYN	SERGEI	ARTEMAS	EVERARD
JASPER	MICKEY	SERGIO	ARTEMUS	EZEKIEL
JEREMY	MILTON	SEUMAS	AUBERON	FEARGUS
JEROME	MORGAN	SEWARD	AZARIAH	FITZROY
JETHRO	MORRIS	SEXTUS	BALDWIN	FLORIAN
JOHNNY	MURRAY	SHAMUS	BARCLAY	FRANCIS
JOLYON	NATHAN	SHELLY	BARNABY	FRANKIE
JORDAN	NEDDIE	SHOLTO	BARNARD	FREDDIE
JOSEPH	NELSON	SIDNEY	BARRETT	FREDRIC
JOSHUA	NEWTON	SIMEON	BARTLET	FULBERT
JOSIAH	NINIAN	STEVEN	BASTIAN	GABRIEL
JOSIAS	NORMAN	STEVIE	BEDFORD	GARRETT
JOTHAM	NORRIS	ST JOHN	BENNETT	GARRICK
JULIAN	NORTON	STUART	BENTLEY	GAYLORD
JULIUS	NOWELL	SYDNEY	BERNARD	GEORDIE
JUNIOR	OBERON	TALBOT	BERTRAM	GEORGIE
JUSTIN	OLIVER	TAYLOR	BETHELL	GERAINT
KELVIN	ORRELL	TEDDIE	BOTOLPH	GERRARD
KENDAL	OSBERT	THOMAS	BRADLEY	GERSHOM
KENELM	OSBORN	TOBIAS	BRANDAN	GERVAIS
KENTON	OSMOND	TRAVIS	BRANDON	GERVASE
KESTER	OSMUND	TREFOR	BRENDAN	GILBERT
KIERAN	OSWALD	TREVOR	CAMERON	GILLEAN
LAUNCE	PALMER	TYBALT	CARADOC	GILLIAN
LAUREN	PARKER	TYRONE	CARADOG	GODFREY
LAURIE	PASCAL	VAUGHN	CARLTON	GOLDWIN
LAWRIE	PASCOE	VERNON	CAROLUS	GOLDWYN
LAYTON	PELHAM	VICTOR	CEDRYCH	GRAHAME
LEMUEL	PHILIP	VIRGIL	CHARLES	GREGORY
LENNOX	PIERRE	WALLIS	CHARLEY	GUNTHER
LESLIE	POLDIE	WALTER	CHARLIE	GUSTAVE

7–continued	7–continued	8	8–continued
GWYNFOR	PATRICK	ADOLPHUS	HARRISON
HADRIAN	PHILLIP	ALASDAIR	HERCULES
HAMMOND	PHINEAS	ALASTAIR	HEREWARD
HARTLEY	PRESTON	ALGERNON	HEZEKIAH
HERBERT	QUENTIN	ALISTAIR	HUMPHREY
HERMANN	QUINTIN	ALOYSIUS	IGNATIUS
HILLARY	RANDALL	ALPHONSE	IORWERTH
HORATIO	RAPHAEL	ALPHONSO	JEDIDIAH
HUMBERT	RAYMOND	AUGUSTIN	JEPHTHAH
ICHABOD	REDVERS	AUGUSTUS	JEREMIAH
ISIDORE	REYNARD	AURELIAN	JEREMIAS
JACQUES	REYNOLD	BARDOLPH	JERMAINE
JAPHETH	RICARDO	BARNABAS	JOHANNES
JEFFERY	RICHARD	BARTLETT	JONATHAN
JEFFREY	RODOLPH	BENEDICK	JOSCELIN
JILLIAN	RODRIGO	BENEDICT	KIMBERLY
JOACHIM	ROWLAND	BENJAMIN	KINGSLEY
JOCELYN	ROYSTON	BERENGER	LANCELOT
JOHNNIE	RUDOLPH	BERKELEY	LAURENCE
KENDALL	RUSSELL	BERNHARD	LAWRENCE
KENNETH	SALAMON	BERTHOLD	LEIGHTON
KENRICK	SAMPSON	BERTRAND	LLEWELYN
KIMBALL	SERGIUS	BEVERLEY	MANASSEH
LACHLAN	SEYMOUR	BONIFACE	MANASSES
LAMBERT	SHANNON	CAMILLUS	MARSHALL
LAZARUS	SHELDON	CAMPBELL	MATTHIAS
LEANDER	SHELLEY	CARLETON	MELVILLE
LEOFRIC	SIGMUND	CARTHACH	MEREDITH
LEOLINE	SOLOMON	CHARLTON	MITCHELL
LEONARD	SPENCER	CHAUNCEY	MONTAGUE
LEOPOLD	STANLEY	CHRISTIE	MORDECAI
LINCOLN	STEPHEN	CHRYSTAL	MORTIMER
LINDSAY	STEWART	CLARENCE	NAPOLEON
LORENZO	SWITHIN	CLAUDIUS	NEHEMIAH
LUDOVIC	TANCRED	CLIFFORD	NICHOLAS
MALACHI	TERENCE	CONSTANT	OCTAVIAN
MALACHY	TERTIUS	COURTNEY	OCTAVIUS
MALCOLM	THORLEY	CRISPIAN	PERCEVAL
MALLORY	TIMOTHY	CUTHBERT	PERCIVAL
MANFRED	TORQUIL	DIARMAIT	PHILEMON
MANSELL	TRAVERS	DIARMUID	PHINEHAS
MATTHEW	TRISTAN	DOMINICK	RADCLIFF
MAURICE	ULYSSES	EBENEZER	RANDOLPH
MAXWELL	VAUGHAN	EMMANUEL	REGINALD
MAYNARD	VINCENT	ETHELRED	RODERICK
MEIRION	WALLACE	FARQUHAR	SALVADOR
MERRION	WARWICK	FERNANDO	SEPTIMUS
MICHAEL	WENDELL	FLETCHER	SHERIDAN
MILBURN	WILBERT	FLORENCE	SILVANUS
MONTAGU	WILFRED	FLUELLEN	SINCLAIR
MURDOCH	WILFRID	FRANKLIN	STAFFORD
MURTAGH	WILLARD	FREDERIC	STANFORD
NEVILLE	WILLIAM	FREDRICK	STIRLING
NICOLAS	WINDSOR	GAMALIEL	SYLVANUS
NORBERT	WINFRED	GARFIELD	TALIESIN
OBADIAH	WINFRID	GEOFFREY	TERRENCE
OLIVIER	WINSTON	GRAYBURN	THADDEUS
ORLANDO	WOODROW	GRIFFITH	THEOBALD
ORVILLE	WYNDHAM	GUSTAVUS	THEODORE
OSBORNE	WYNFORD	HAMILTON	THORNTON
PADRAIG	ZACHARY	HANNIBAL	THURSTAN

8–continued
THURSTON
TRISTRAM
TURLOUGH
WINTHROP
ZEDEKIAH

9
ALEXANDER
ALPHONSUS
AMBROSIUS
ARCHELAUS
ARCHIBALD
ATHELSTAN
AUGUSTINE
BALTHASAR
BALTHAZAR
BRODERICK
CADWALADR
CHRISTIAN
CHRISTMAS
CORNELIUS

9–continued
COURTENAY
DIONYSIUS
ENDEAVOUR
ETHELBERT
FERDINAND
FRANCESCO
FRANCISCO
FREDERICK
GERONTIUS
GRANVILLE
GRENVILLE
JEFFERSON
KENTIGERN
KIMBERLEY
LAUNCELOT
LLEWELLYN
MARCELLUS
MARMADUKE
NATHANAEL
NATHANIEL

9–continued
NICODEMUS
ONUPHRIUS
PEREGRINE
PHILIBERT
RADCLIFFE
SALVATORE
SEBASTIAN
SIEGFRIED
SIGISMUND
SILVESTER
STANISLAS
SYLVESTER
THEODORIC
VALENTINE
ZACCHAEUS
ZACHARIAH
ZACHARIAS
ZECHARIAH
ZEPHANIAH

10
BARRINGTON
CARACTACUS
FORTUNATUS
HIERONYMUS
HILDEBRAND
HIPPOLYTUS
MAXIMILIAN
MONTGOMERY
STANISLAUS
THEOPHILUS
WASHINGTON
WILLOUGHBY

11
BARTHOLOMEW
CADWALLADER
CHRISTOPHER
CONSTANTINE
SACHEVERELL

INDEX

Entries in bold face type (e.g. **COUNTRIES OF THE WORLD** 1) refer to tables or lists in the text, with their page numbers. Other index entries suggest tables that might be useful (e.g. SHELLS *see* SEASHELLS, or INSTRUMENT *try* MUSICAL INSTRUMENTS; TOOLS. We have also included a selection of cue words for cryptic clues (e.g. the word ZERO often indicates the letter O).